Webster's Students Thesaurus

A Merriam-Webster®

G. & C. Merriam Company, *Publishers*
Springfield, Massachusetts, U.S.A.

Library of Congress Cataloging in Publication Data
Main entry under title:

Webster's students thesaurus.

   SUMMARY: Includes more than 43,000 synonyms, antonyms,
and related and contrasted words.

   1. English language—synonyms and antonyms. [1. English
language—synonyms and antonyms]

PE1591.W44   423′.1   78-585
ISBN 0-87779-078-7

Made in the United States of America

   12345RRD807978

Preface

Webster's Students Thesaurus is especially designed for young people who want to enlarge their vocabulary and acquaint themselves with the rich variety of the English language. It is a product of years of study and planning directed toward developing a thesaurus that is both easy to use and sufficiently inclusive to provide real help in vocabulary building and word selection. Webster's Students Thesaurus is offered as a reference book that is close to being an adult tool. In order to provide the student with as large a selection of words as possible, the pages are not filled with cartoons or half-tone illustrations. Nor is the print-size inflated to make the book appear to hold more than it does. The primary purpose of this book, to afford the reader access to a usable thesaurus, has been the main consideration throughout the editing process.

What does the user look for in a thesaurus? It is generally agreed that he is seeking a term more appropriate than the one he has in mind. This very broad concept is remote from the typical thesaurus presentation of "synonyms" and sometimes "antonyms". As a matter of fact, the user may want a synonym, a stronger or weaker word, one of slightly different meaning, an idiomatic phrase that conveys the same idea, or a word that to a greater or less degree contrasts with the word the user has in mind. This variety of uses cannot possibly be covered by the simple ideas of "synonym" and "antonym". Webster's Students Thesaurus is designed to present a wide range of material in an accessible form that minimizes the user's need to grope and guess.

In earlier Merriam-Webster publications the pattern of supplementing synonym lists with lists of related and contrasted words, words that are relevant to the group under study yet not quite synonyms or antonyms respectively, was extensively tested and favorably received. It offered not only more exact limitation of synonyms and antonyms but gave the user much additional pertinent assistance. The same plan of supplementing synonyms and antonyms with relevant additional material has been made a feature of this new thesaurus.

Additional features of Webster's Students Thesaurus designed to make it easy to use are main entries which have a brief statement showing exactly in which meaning a group of words are to be understood as synonyms, a strictly alphabetical ordering of synonyms within the list, and the entry at its own alphabetical place of each word that is a synonym at a main entry. Thus, Webster's Students Thesaurus is designed to make search for the appropriate term as easy as possible. We sincerely hope that these devices will encourage young people to use it freely in word-seeking and that they will find it really helpful in adding to their vocabulary and in encouraging their interest in the English language.

The student and teacher alike will find in the Introduction to this book an informative discussion on just what makes a word a synonym or an antonym, a related word or a contrasted one, for the purposes of Webster's Students Thesaurus. A careful reading of the Introduction will add to the understanding of how words are used especially in relation to one another.

The Explanatory Notes which follow the Introduction are even more important to study. They contain an explanation of the way Webster's Students Thesaurus is organized and discuss the kinds of information which may be found at each entry in the book. Anyone who wishes to use this book effectively is urged to read them carefully.

The material in Webster's Students Thesaurus is based primarily on Webster's Third New International, the Merriam-Webster unabridged dictionary containing more than 460,000 entries. The editors have not restricted themselves, however, to this one source, but have freely consulted existent thesauruses and Webster's New Collegiate Dictionary, and have not hesitated to use the resources of the more than 12,000,000 citations of the Merriam-Webster file of English usage to settle doubtful points. Entries of words having more than one sense ordinarily follow the sequence of senses in, though not necessarily the identical numbering of, Webster's Third New International Dictionary.

Various members of the Merriam-Webster editorial staff have worked on the assembling and correlation of word lists. The editor, however, takes full responsibility for adapting the original lists to fit the needs and interests of school students. She cannot, however, close this preface without expressing appreciation for the advice and aid of E. Ward Gilman, senior editor.

Kathleen M. Doherty
Assistant Editor

Introduction

The book in your hands is a thesaurus. Historically, a thesaurus was a storehouse and this book can be a real storehouse of useful words waiting to give precision and sparkle to the vocabulary of those who are willing to use it. Anyone who has been in a large storehouse or warehouse knows how elaborately cataloged the contents are and how hard it is to find things without understanding the catalog. This Introduction and the following Explanatory Notes are in a very real way a catalog of what your thesaurus contains, planned to make it perfectly understandable and easy to use. Let us now consider the elements that make up our catalog.

The Synonym

As all of you know, English is a very complex language. With its intricate interweaving of strands of Celtic, earlier Roman and later churchly Latin, northern and western Germanic tongues, and, through Norman-French, the whole body of Romance languages, it is not surprising that it is a language peculiarly rich in synonyms.

Synonyms lend character and flexibility to writing and speech. They relieve monotony and enhance expressiveness. But just what are synonyms? To the earlier writers the meaning was clear; they viewed synonyms as words meaning the same thing. Unfortunately, during the last century or so this simple, clearcut meaning has become blurred. To many synonymists the term has come to mean little more than words that are somewhat similar in meaning. We feel this loose definition to be unsuitable for the selection of terms for a thesaurus since it deprives you of the guidance you have a right to expect.

As a result we looked for a new approach and were soon convinced that to identify synonyms we had to isolate a segment of denotation that two or more words had in common. In order to analyze each word carefully, then, we had to think of synonymy not just as a relationship between words, nor even between dictionary senses of words. We had to look for separate objective denotations not marked by such peripheral aspects of meaning as connotations, implications, or quirks of idiomatic usage. Only by taking apart senses could we reach the word's ultimate meaning, which for the sake of simplicity we call an *elementary meaning*. Perhaps if we explain this approach by using an example, it will be clearer to you. In Webster's Third New International Dictionary, a sense of the noun *input* reads:

> : power or energy put into a machine or system for storage (as into a storage battery) or for conversion in kind (as into a mechanically driven electric generator or a radio receiver) or conversion of characteristics (as into a transformer or electric amplifier) usu. with the intent of sizable recovery in the form of output

Much of this definition contains peripheral matter, and from the dictionary point of view it is necessary to include it because it helps guide and orient you in knowing how and when to use the word. However, the fundamental meaning of this sense, its denotation, may be restated as

> power or energy put into a machine or system for storage
> or for conversion in kind
> or conversion of characteristics

When we express this graphically

power		machine		storage
energy	put into a	system	for	conversion in kind
				conversion of characteristics

you can see that there are twelve simple statements of denotation or individual elementary meanings associated in this single sense of *input*. Of these twelve only one, "energy put into a system for storage," can reasonably be considered a synonym of *charge* as applied to a storage battery. If we were compiling a list of synonyms for *charge* as applied to a storage battery, we would consider *input* a synonym because of this shared elementary meaning. For the purposes of Webster's Students Thesaurus, then, we consider a word to be a synonym only if it or one of its senses shares with another word or a sense of another word one or more such elementary meanings.

When we look at the synonymous relationship of words in terms of elementary meanings, the process of choosing synonyms is simpler and more exact. For example, it is easy to see that no term more restricted in definition than the pertinent meaning of the headword can be its synonym, i.e., *station wagon* cannot be a synonym of *automobile* and *biceps* cannot be a synonym of *muscle*. Even though a very definite relationship exists between the members of each pair, *station wagon* is a type of automobile and *biceps* is a type of muscle, and so are narrower in their range of application. On the other hand, a word more broadly defined than another word in the dictionary may be considered a synonym of the other word so long as the two words share one or more elementary meanings. In order to pin down the area of shared meaning for you, each main entry in Webster's Students Thesaurus contains before its synonym list a *meaning core* (see p. 9a) which states the elementary meaning or meanings that are shared by all the words in that particular synonym group.

The Antonym

Like *synonym*, *antonym* has been used by some writers with a great deal of vagueness and often applied loosely to words which show no real oppositeness when compared one to another. We feel that a reappraisal of the antonym concept is long overdue. As in the case of synonyms, the relation needs to be seen as one between segments of meaning which can be isolated, rather than between words or dictionary senses of words. For the purpose of this book, we consider a word to be an antonym when one or more of its elementary meanings precisely opposes or negates the same area of meaning of another word. This definition excludes from consideration as antonyms several classes of words that are sometimes treated as antonyms but that actually contain words which neither directly oppose or directly negate the words with which they are said to be antonymous. Three such groups seem worth a little attention.

1. *Relative terms* have such a relationship to each other that one can scarcely be used without suggesting the other (as *husband* and *wife, father* and *son, buyer* and *seller*), yet there is no real opposition or real negation between such pairs. Their relation is reciprocal or correlative rather than antonymous.

2. *Complementary terms* in a similar way are usually paired and have a reciprocal relationship to the point that one seems incomplete without the other (as in such pairs as *question* and *answer, seek* and *find*). This relation which involves no negation is better seen as sequential than antonymous.

3. *Contrastive terms* differ sharply from their "opposites" only in some parts of their meaning. They neither oppose nor negate fully, since they are significantly different in range of meaning and applicability, in emphasis, and in the suggestions they convey. For example, *destitute* (a strong word carrying suggestions of misery and distress) is contrastive rather than antonymous with respect to *rich* (a rather neutral and matter-of-fact term), while *poor* (another neutral and matter-of-fact term) is the appropriate antonym of *rich*. Basically, contrastive words are only opposed incidentally; they do not meet head on.

In Webster's Students Thesaurus such words, where appropriate, appear as contrasted words.

What then do we consider antonyms? In Webster's Students Thesaurus three classes of words have been accepted as truly antonymous and as sources from which antonyms may reasonably be drawn. These are

1. *Opposites without intermediates*. These are words that are so opposed that they are mutually exclusive and leave no middle ground between them. Each denies, point by point and item by item, whatever its opposite affirms. Thus, what is *perfect* can be in no way *imperfect* and what is *imperfect* to however slight a degree cannot be viewed as *perfect;* you cannot at the same time *accept* and *reject* or *agree* and *disagree*.

2. *Opposites with intermediates*. Such words make up the extremes in a range of difference and are so completely opposed that the language allows no wider difference. Thus, a scale of excellence might include *superiority, adequacy, mediocrity,* and *inferiority,* but only *superiority* and *inferiority* are so totally opposed that each exactly negates what its opposite affirms.

3. *Reverse opposites*. These are words that are opposed in such a way that each means the undoing or nullification of what the other affirms. Such reverse opposites exactly oppose and fully negate the special features of their opposites. Thus, *disprove* and its synonym *refute* so perfectly oppose and so clearly negate the implications of *prove* that they fit the concept of antonyms as well as does *unkind* with respect to *kind,* or *come* with respect to *go*.

Related and Contrasted Words

What if you are not looking for an exact synonym or antonym, but are looking for a word somewhat similar or somewhat opposed to a known word? To meet such needs, Webster's Students Thesaurus includes lists of related and contrasted words wherever these seem appropriate and likely to be helpful. We can thus offer a wider range of material for use in word finding and vocabulary building without doing violence to our rather strict interpretation of the synonym and antonym. Related words (near-synonyms) and contrasted words (near-antonyms) are so closely related to, or so clearly contrastable with, the members of a synonym group that you have a right to expect them under the appropriate headings.

Phrases and Idiomatic Equivalents

In the search for longer synonym lists synonymists increasingly have included phrases among their synonyms. These phrases fall into three classes:

1. *Word equivalents.* These are phrases that act as if they were single words. More often than not they are combinations of noun and attributive noun (as *county agent*) or noun and adjective (as *hard sell*) or of verb and adverb (as *make up*). However, such phrases may be made up of any kinds of word elements and may act as any part-of-speech (as *in passing,* adverb; *except for,* preposition; ‖*half-seas over,* adjective; *as long as,* conjunction). These fixed combinations that act as if they were single words cannot be entirely excluded from word lists. Webster's Students Thesaurus includes such combinations when they are so firmly fixed in usage that they are entered in major modern dictionaries with part-of-speech labels.

2. *Glosses.* These are phrases that say the meaning of a word in another way. Essentially, they are brief definitions. There is no definition of synonym that reasonably can be used to justify including these restatements or definitions in synonym lists. Thus "do heavy menial service" is a gloss rather than a synonym of *drudge,* "have an opinion" is a gloss of *opine,* and "in a state of inferiority to" is a gloss of *under.* Such glosses are excluded from Webster's Students Thesaurus since they add nothing useful to the vocabulary of the user of a thesaurus.

3. *Idioms.* These are phrases that have a meaning different from the overall meaning of the words that make them up. For example, there are no literal meanings of *compare* and *note* that allow the phrase "compare notes" to mean "to exchange observations and views"; yet, this is what it does mean. There are no literal meanings of the words that allow the phrase "come a long way" to mean "make progress, succeed"; yet, it does mean this. When idiomatic phrases mean the same thing as particular words it is difficult not to include them in relevant synonym lists. Such phrases, however, do not have the qualities that allow word equivalents to be included in synonym lists — they do not function as words but, rather, as different ways of conveying the same meaning as particular words do. As in the case of glosses there is no definition of synonym that justifies including idioms in a synonym list. Still, we think that such idiomatic equivalents can be helpful to you since they can add force and variety to your expression. Webster's Students Thesaurus has arrived at a compromise and included selected idiomatic equivalents of synonym groups or of particular words in synonym lists in separate lists that follow the relevant lists of synonyms or related words.

Explanatory Notes

How to use Webster's Students Thesaurus

If you expect to make effective use of this thesaurus, you should read and study these Explanatory Notes. In the paragraphs that follow you will find brief explanations of the order of entries, the kinds of entries, and how each entry is put together. The explanations are illustrated with the actual examples taken from the book. In addition you will find a keyline at the foot of every other page of the main vocabulary to serve as a reminder of the information contained in these Explanatory Notes.

A thesaurus consists mostly of lists of words. It is often difficult for the user to be sure what meaning of a word the editor intended when including it in a list. Webster's Students Thesaurus has been edited with features — such as the meaning cores and verbal illustrations — which will help keep you aware of the meaning intended. But because the English language has so many different ways of combining words and so many subtle shades of meaning, you should always use Webster's Students Thesaurus along with an adequate dictionary. Most of the time you will find that a good desk-size dictionary, such as Webster's New Collegiate Dictionary or Webster's New Students Dictionary, will be extremely helpful.

Scope of Webster's Students Thesaurus

This thesaurus is concerned with the general vocabulary of English. Most obsolete and archaic words and highly technical terms have been left out. Since the vocabulary of Webster's Students Thesaurus is based on Webster's Third New International Dictionary, its editors feel that enough unusual words have been retained to satisfy the student in search of a sprinkling of out-of-the-ordinary terms to use. Some of these words will not be found in a desk-size dictionary and it then may be necessary for you to use an unabridged dictionary to check the suitability of a particular term. If you do not have ready access to an unabridged dictionary, you may not be able to be sure about some of the rarer words. You should use rare or unusual terms, therefore, with caution. Most of you will find that the words entered in a good desk-size dictionary will provide adequate stimulus for the growth of your vocabulary.

Entry Order

The body of the book consists of main entries and secondary entries. These entries are arranged in alphabetical order. Each main and secondary entry is introduced by a boldface headword, as seen in the following examples:

raid *vb* **1** to make a raid on < Indians *raided* the settlers frequently >
   syn foray, harass, harry, maraud
   rel despoil, devastate, ravage, sack, spoliate, waste; loot, plunder, rifle, rob
   2 *syn* see INVADE 1

raider *n syn* see MARAUDER

rail *n syn* see RAILING

In the above examples, *raid, raider,* and *rail* are the headwords introducing either a main entry, as *raid vb* **1** does, or a secondary entry, as **raider** *n* or **rail** *n* do.

Homograph headwords, that is, words which are spelled alike, are entered in historical order. The one first used in English is entered first, as

   till *prep*
   till *conj*
   till *vb*

Verbs used frequently with one or two prepositions or adverbs may be headwords introducing main entries or secondary entries. If they are used as headwords, they are entered with the verb part in boldface type followed by the preposition or adverb in parentheses in lightface type. Such combinations immediately follow the base verb in alphabetical order. In the following example, you can see that the base verb **put** comes first and is followed in alphabetical order by the entries with preposition or adverb in parentheses, **put** (back), **put** (on), and **put** (on *or* upon):

8a

```
put vb ├─────────────────────────── base-verb homograph
put (back) vb ┐
put (on) vb ├──────────────── verb combinations
put (on or upon) vb ┘
put n ├─────────────────────────── noun homograph
```

All of these verb entries are then followed by the noun **put.** Two-word verbs (verbs regularly followed by an adverb) that are commonly entered in dictionaries have been entered in boldface at their own alphabetical places in this book. However, they follow in alphabetical order all of those entries showing a verb with a preposition or adverb in parentheses. You can see this in the following example:

```
take vb ├─────────────────────────── base verb
take (from) vb ┐
take (to) vb ├──────────────── verb combinations
take away vb ┐
take back vb │
take down vb ├──────────────── two-word verbs
take in vb │
take off vb ┘
```

Headwords are entered according to normal dictionary practices. This means that nouns appear in the singular and verbs in the infinitive form. Special situations such as those showing plural usage or variant spellings are signaled by showing them in boldface subheads, as at the following entries

crossroad *n, usu* **crossroads** *pl but sing or pl in constr syn* see JUNCTURE 2
woe *n* . . . **3** *usu* **woes** *pl syn* see DISASTER
catercorner (*or* **catty-corner** *or* **kitty-corner**) *adv syn* see DIAGONALLY

In the above, **crossroads** and **woes** are subheads indicating plural usage of the headwords. **Catty-corner** and **kitty-corner** are subheads showing variant spellings of the headword.

The Main Entry and Its Elements

Each main entry is made up of a boldface headword followed by a part-of-speech label, a sense number when needed, a meaning core with a short verbal illustration, and a list of synonyms. Nearly all the time, the main entry also has lists of related words, idiomatic equivalents, contrasted words, and antonyms. A typical main entry is

calm *adj* **1** free from storm or rough activity < the wind died and the sea became *calm* >
  syn halcyon, hushed, placid, quiet, still, stilly, untroubled
  rel inactive, quiescent, reposing, resting; pacific, smooth, tranquil, unruffled
  idiom calm as a millpond, still as death
  con agitated, disturbed, perturbed, restless, turbulent, uneasy
  ant stormy

The headword **calm** is followed by the italic part-of-speech label *adj* which indicates that this word is an adjective. Other part-of-speech labels used in the book are *adv* (adverb), *conj* (conjunction), *interj* (interjection), *n* (noun), *prep* (preposition), *pron* (pronoun), and *vb* (verb).
Individual senses of entries such as **calm** *adj* with more than one sense are introduced by a boldface sense number.

The meaning core indicates the area of meaning in which a group of words are synonymous. At **calm 1**, for example, this reads "free from storm or rough activity". This is the meaning in which the words *calm, halcyon, hushed, placid, quiet, still, stilly,* and *untroubled* can be viewed as synonyms. In other words, the meaning core pinpoints the exact relationship between the main-entry headword and its synonyms.

Material showing a typical or occasionally a single object of reference is enclosed in parentheses, as in the meaning core of **express** *vb* **2**

to give expression to (as a thought, an opinion, or an emotion)

The parenthesized material is included to alert you to the fact that when this sense of **express** is used, it is usually in connection with "a thought, an opinion, or an emotion".

A meaning core also may have a usage note introduced by a lightface dash. This is used when more information or comments on usage are needed, as in the following example:

yet *adv* **1** beyond this — used as an intensive to stress the comparative degree

Some interjections express feelings but cannot be translated into a simple meaning; in such cases, the meaning core itself may be replaced by a usage note which describes the function of the interjection:

good-bye *interj* — used as a conventional expression of good wishes at parting

Each meaning core is followed by a verbal illustration enclosed by angle brackets, as

< the wind died and the sea became *calm* >

Here, the verbal illustration shows a typical use of the headword *calm* in the sense expressed by the meaning core.

The verbal illustration has another use. You can use it as a frame in which to test the suitability of a synonym or a related term in this particular context. At **calm 1,** for instance, you might want to see if the synonym *hushed* can be used exactly the same way *calm* can be. If you substitute *hushed* for *calm* in the verbal illustration, you will get

< the wind died and the sea became *hushed* >

You will probably notice at once that this sounds a bit odd. Apparently *hushed* cannot always be used where *calm* can be used. English is full of similar slight differences in meaning and it is for this reason that you are urged to consult the more specific definitions in a good dictionary for any case that seems doubtful to you.

The boldface italic abbreviation **syn** introduces a synonym list that appears at each main entry on a line below the meaning core and the verbal illustration. In the Introduction on page 4a, you read about the aspects which governed the choosing of synonyms. The **syn** list may have only one synonym, as at the entry **hitherto** *adv* **2,** where *here* is the only synonym, or the list may have many synonyms, as *halcyon, hushed, placid, quiet, still, stilly,* and *untroubled* which are shown at **calm** *adj* **1.** Each synonym in a main-entry list is entered in boldface at its own alphabetical place.

A compare cross-reference may appear at the end of a main-entry *syn* list. This cross-reference is introduced by the italic word *compare.* You will find it when two or more groups of synonyms are very closely related and the editors felt that the user looking at one list should know of the existence of the other list. Examples of compare cross-references are found at the entries **assassin** and **murderer:**

assassin *n* a person hired or hirable to commit murder < found out who paid the *assassin* >
   syn bravo, cutthroat, gun, gunman, ‖gunsel, gunslinger, hatchet man, hit man, torpedo,
   triggerman; *compare* MURDERER

murderer *n* one who kills a human being < a *murderer* who wouldn't hesitate to kill
   in cold blood >
   syn homicide, killer, manslayer, slayer; *compare* ASSASSIN

You will notice that although the headwords are related, there are differences between **assassin** and **murderer** and their respective synonyms. It will help you, then, to find exactly the word you are looking for if you check out these compare cross-references when you see them.

The compare cross-reference is also used when closely related entries such as **ration** and **share** 1 both include some of the same words as synonyms. This results from the way language tends to change, sometimes narrowing, sometimes broadening or even subdividing meanings. When this has happened the compare cross-reference warns you of words that, though appropriate to more than one synonym list, may in some contexts blur fine distinctions that you would like to make. A comparison of the main entries of **ration** *n* and **share** *n* **1** will point this up:

ration *n* an amount allotted or made available especially from a limited supply < saved
   up their gasoline *ration* for a vacation trip >
   syn allotment, allowance, apportionment, measure, need, part, portion, quantum, quota,
   share; *compare* SHARE 1

share *n* **1** something belonging to, assumed by, or falling to one (as in division or
   apportionment) < wanted his *share* of the prize money >
   syn allotment, allowance, bite, cut, lot, part, partage, portion, quota, slice; *compare* RATION

You will see that the synonyms *allotment, allowance, part, portion, quota,* and *share* are found in both lists. By taking these synonyms and substituting them in the verbal illustrations, you will find that they sound right, and can be interchanged. If, on the other hand, you take a synonym found in one list, but not in the other, for instance *cut* from the list at **share,** and substitute it in the verbal illustration at **ration,** you will find that the differences between the meaning cores become more obvious. If you say < wanted his *cut* of the prize money >, you are choosing a word which fits the context. If you try using *cut* in the verbal illustration at *ration,* < saved up their gasoline *cut* for a vacation trip > you will find that *cut* doesn't sound right. So, even though some of the same synonyms appear in both lists, you must be careful to distinguish among all the synonyms in every list. Don't forget to keep a good dictionary on hand to help you do this.

Many main entries include lists of related words, idiomatic equivalents, contrasted words, and antonyms. If an entry has all of these lists, they are shown in the order mentioned above. The boldface abbreviation *rel* introduces a list of related words. The related words are ones that are almost but not quite synonymous with the headword. These come immediately after the *syn* list. For example, at the main entry:

> **splendid** *adj* ... **2** extraordinary or transcendently impressive < a *splendid* new city >
> **syn** glorious, gorgeous, magnificent, proud, resplendent, splendiferous, splendorous,
> sublime, superb
> **rel** eminent, illustrious; grand, impressive, lavish, luxurious, royal, sumptuous; divine,
> exquisite, lovely; incomparable, matchless, peerless, superlative, supreme, unparalleled,
> unsurpassed; surpassing, transcendent ...

the *rel* list is made up of twenty words separated by semicolons into five subgroups. Each of these subgroups shares a common relation to the headword and its synonyms. Related words are not entered in boldface at their own alphabetical places unless they are synonyms in other lists or head their own main entries.

The boldface italic abbreviation *idiom* introduces a list of idiomatic phrases that are essentially the same in meaning as the words of a synonym group. For a more detailed discussion of these phrases, you might look again at pages 5a & 6a in the Introduction. An *idiom* list at a main entry includes phrases that are generally pertinent to the entire *syn* list and the headword, as the ones at:

> **speak** *vb* **1** to articulate words in order to express thoughts < always *speak* clearly >
> **syn** talk, utter, verbalize, vocalize, voice
> **rel** ...
> **idiom** break silence, give voice (*or* tongue *or* utterance) to, let fall, make public (*or* known),
> open one's mouth (*or* lips), put in (*or* into) words, say one's say, speak one's piece ...

Some idiomatic expressions may be used in more than one form. Such variation is shown in this thesaurus by including the variant word in parentheses. At **slavery** *n* **2**

> **idiom** the yoke (*or* chains) of slavery

gives you the choice of using either *yoke* or *chains* in the phrase.

Idiomatic phrases, including those fixed verb plus preposition combinations that act as idioms rather than as literal meanings of the verb are not entered in boldface at their own alphabetical places in this book.

The boldface italic abbreviation *con* introduces a list of contrasted words. This category contains terms that may be strongly contrasted with the headword, but are not quite antonyms of the headword. An example of a *con* list is:

> **watchful** *adj* paying close attention usually with a view to anticipating approaching danger or
> opportunity < adopted a policy of *watchful* waiting >
> **syn** alert, open-eyed, unsleeping, vigilant, wakeful, wide-awake
> **rel** ...
> **idiom** ...
> **con** careless, heedless, thoughless; inadvertent; absentminded, abstracted, faraway
> **ant** ...

At this main entry, the *con* list is made up of seven words separated by semicolons into three subgroups. Each of these words may be contrasted with the headword *watchful* and with the words in its *syn* list. Contrasted words are not entered in boldface at their own alphabetical places unless they are synonyms in other lists or head their own main entries.

The boldface italic abbreviation *ant* introduces the last possible part of an entry. This is an antonym, as at the entry:

> **perfect** *adj* ... **2** ...
> **ant** imperfect

Where *imperfect* is the antonym of **perfect 2,** or a list of antonyms as at the entry

> **quiet** *adj* ... **4** not showy or obtrusive
> **ant** gaudy, loud

In the Introducton to this book on page 5a, you learned about the different classes of opposites to which antonyms belong. When antonyms come from different classes of opposites, they are separated by a semicolon, as at

> **assistance** *n syn* see HELP 1
> **rel** backing, supporting, upholding; advantage, avail, profit, use; appropriation, grant, subsidy, subvention
> **con** checking, hampering, hindering, hindrance; balking, foiling, frustrating, thwarting
> **ant** impediment, impeding; obstructing, obstruction

In the above, *impediment* and *impeding* belong to the class of antonyms that are opposites with intermediates. If you study the **rel** and **con** lists at **assistance** you will see that the first sets of each group form a continuous series

> backing, supporting, upholding checking, hampering, hindering, hindrance

of which *assistance* forms one extreme and *impeding* (or *impediment*) forms the other. The second pair of antonyms are separated from the first by a semicolon because they belong to a different class — that of antonyms that are reverse opposites. The difference should be plain; *obstruction* (or *obstructing*) amouns to the undoing of whatever is implied by *assistance*.

You may find material in parentheses following antonyms, as at **abrogate** *vb* 2:

> **ant** establish, fix (*as a right, a quality, or a custom*)

In such cases an antonym or group of antonyms is associated with a particular object or objects of reference. This information will help orient you in choosing the best word possible. Like related and contrasted words, antonyms are not entered in boldface at their own alphabetical places unless they are synonyms in other lists or head their own main entries.

The Secondary Entry

A secondary entry consists of a boldface headword followed by a part-of-speech label, a boldface sense number when needed, and most importantly, a *syn* see cross-reference in small capital letters directing you to the appropriate main entry in whose *syn* list the secondary entry appears. If this main entry has more than one sense, a lightface number follows the see cross-reference to tell you the sense to look for at the main entry.

Like the main entry, the secondary entry may also have lists of related words, idiomatic phrases, contrasted words, and antonyms. If it does, as at:

> **short** *adj* ... **7** *syn* see CONCISE
> **rel** compact; pointed
> **idiom** to the point
> **con** extended, protracted, spun-out
> **ant** lengthy, long-drawn-out

the term in the lists apply only to the boldface headword and not necessarily to all of the synonyms at the main entry to which there is a cross-reference. Normally, only a few related words, idiomatic phrases, contrasted words, and antonyms found at the main entry are repeated at the secondary entry. For this reason you should check the main entry for the most complete collection of terms.

Main and Secondary Entries: the One Arbitrary Rule

There is one rule in particular which the editors have followed in working with both main and secondary entries : *no word may appear in more than one list at any single sense of a main or a secondary entry.* For example, *nice* is a synonym at **pleasant** *adj* 1, which has the meaning core "highly acceptable to the mind or senses". You might reasonably consider other senses of *nice* to qualify it as a related word at **pleasant** *adj* 1, in addition to its entry as a synonym. This could be the sense meaning "mild", in < the *nice* weather of late spring > or that meaning "suitable", as in < the *nice* clothes she wears >. Further, there is even a sense of *nice* which means "unpleasant", as in < got into a *nice* fix > which could qualify it as a contrasted word or even as an antonym. You can see how confusing the entry would have looked with *nice* shown at three or four places. In order to be as clear as possible, then, each entry shows a word in only one list at any one sense.

Labels

As we mentioned earlier, the part-of-speech label found at each entry is one of the following: *adj* (adjective), *adv* (adverb), *conj* (conjunction), *interj* (interjection), *n* (noun), *prep* (preposition), *pron* (pronoun), and *vb* (verb).

Words that are labeled *cap* or *usu*[ally] *cap* in Webster's Third New International Dictionary are capitalized in this book:

> **Gehenna** *n syn* see HELL

If only one entered sense of a word is capitalized, an italic *cap* label followed by the boldface capitalized form is shown at the appropriate sense:

pandemonium *n* **1** *cap* **Pandemonium** *syn* see HELL
   2 *syn* see SINK 1
   3 *syn* see DEN 1

Pandemonium should be capitalized when it is used as a synonym of *hell*. When *pandemonium* is used as a synonym of *sink* 1 or *din* 1, it is not capitalized. In addition to the part-of-speech label, an italic label *pl* may be present to indicate that a word or a sense of a word is used in the plural.

Some words are always used in the plural. A typical example is:

years *n pl syn* see OLD AGE

The *pl* label shows that the headword **years** is plural in form and takes a plural verb when used to mean *old age.*

Some words are often used in the plural and are so labeled:

road *n* **1** *often* **roads** *pl syn* see HARBOR 3
   2 *syn* see WAY 1
   3 *syn* see WAY 2

This label means that about half the time the word is used in the plural and about half the time it is used in the singular. In the above example, only sense 1 of the headword is often used in the plural.

Some words are usually used in the plural and are so labeled. This means that more often than not, the word will be found in the plural:

minutia *n, usu* **minutiae** *pl* **1** *syn* see INS AND OUTS
   2 *syn* see TRIVIA

The placing of the label before both senses indicates that the headword **minutia** is usually but not always used in the plural in both senses.

There are words which are plural in form, but which may sometimes take a singular verb in construction. An example is:

trivia *n pl but sometimes sing in constr* . . .

Other words are plural in form but are as likely to take a plural verb as a singular one. The first entered sense of **common** is such a case:

common *n* **1** **commons** *pl but sing or pl in constr*
   syn see COMMONALTY

The label shows that in this use *common* occurs only in plural form but may take either a plural or a singular verb.

Finally, there are nouns which are plural in form and always take a singular verb:

outdoors *n pl but sing in constr* the space where air is unconfined < every night he let the dog run in the *outdoors* >

One other label which you will see used a few times in Webster's Students Thesaurus is an italic subject guide phrase. The subject guide phrase precedes the meaning core and indicates that the meaning core is limited in application. At **set** *vb*

set *vb* . . . **11** *of a fowl* to incubate eggs by crouching upon them . . .

the phrase *of a fowl* indicates that in this sense **set** is used of a fowl (and not, for instance, of people or crocodiles).

Symbol

One warning symbol is used in this book: double bars ‖. This is placed before a word to alert you that its usage is in some way restricted. Whenever this symbol appears you should check the word in a good dictionary if you are unfamiliar with it. A double-barred word might be slang, as ‖*fat cat* at the entry **notable** *n.* A word may be used by only one segment of the English-speaking population, as ‖*nipper* at **kid** *n* which is chiefly British, or ‖*swarf* at **faint** *vb* which is Scottish. The word might also be an American regional term, such as the Western word ‖*Rocky Mountain Canary* which is a synonym of **donkey n,** or the Southern word ‖*glade* which is a related word at **swamp n.** These words have been included in Webster's Students Thesaurus to introduce you to the extensive range of the English language and to help you stretch your vocabulary. In order to know exactly which restriction the double bars for each term carries, you are urged to consult a good dictionary.

All double-barred words in Webster's Students Thesaurus follow the labels shown in Webster's Third New International Dictionary.

A

aback *adv syn* see UNAWARES

abaft *adv* toward or at the stern (of a vessel) < headed *abaft* for a smoke >
syn aft, astern
rel after, back, behind
ant forward

abaft *prep* to the rear of < huddled in a nook *abaft* the chimney >
syn back of, behind

abalienate *vb syn* see TRANSFER 4

abandon *vb* **1** to give up without intent to return or re-claim < *abandoned* his family >
syn chuck, desert, forsake, quit, renounce, throw over
rel cast (off), discard, disuse, drop, junk, scrap; reject, repudiate
idiom have done with, leave flat, quit cold, run out on, turn one's back on (*or* upon), walk out on
con hold, keep, possess, retain; redeem, rescue, save; acquire, gain, get, procure, win; cherish, foster
ant re-claim
2 *syn* see RELINQUISH
ant retain

abandon *n* **1** *syn* see UNCONSTRAINT
2 carefree disregard for consequences < behave with *abandon* >
syn impulsiveness, uninhibitedness, unrestraint; *compare* UNCONSTRAINT
rel freedom, liberty, license; exuberance, heedlessness, laxity, laxness, looseness, unruliness, wildness; incontinence, licentiousness, wantonness; fun, games, play, sport
con constraint, inhibitedness, inhibition, restraint; repression, suppression
ant self-restraint

abandoned *adj* **1** *syn* see DERELICT 1
2 free from moral restraint < led a thoroughly *abandoned* life >
syn dissolute, licentious, profligate, reprobate, self-abandoned, unprincipled
rel debased, debauched, depraved, perverted, riotous; incorrigible; lascivious, lecherous, lewd, wanton; corrupt, degenerate
idiom dead to honor, gone to the bad, lost to shame, rotten (*or* at) the core
con ethical, high-principled, moral, reputable, virtuous; correct, decent, decorous, proper, seemly
ant scrupulous, upright

abase *vb syn* see HUMBLE
rel demote, diminish, downgrade, reduce; fawn, grovel, toady; cower, cringe, truckle
con elevate, lift, raise
ant exalt; extol

abash *vb syn* see EMBARRASS 1
rel abase, demean, humble, humiliate
idiom make one eat humble pie
ant embolden, reassure

abashment *n syn* see EMBARRASSMENT

abate *vb* **1** *syn* see ABOLISH 1
2 *syn* see ANNIHILATE 2
3 *syn* see DECREASE
4 to lessen in force or intensity < the storm *abated* slowly >
syn ||bate, die (down *or* away), ease off, ebb, fall, let up, lull, moderate, relent, slacken, subside, wane
rel decrease, diminish, dwindle, lessen, weaken
idiom run its course

con augment, expand, extend, increase; mount, rage, soar, surge
ant revive; rise

abatement *n syn* see DEDUCTION 1
con enlargement, increase
ant addition

abbreviate *vb syn* see SHORTEN
rel attenuate, extenuate
con enlarge, increase; amplify, dilate, expand
ant lengthen; extend

ABC *n* **1** *usu* **ABC's** *pl syn* see ALPHABET 1
2 *often* **ABC's** *pl syn* see ALPHABET 2

abdicate *vb* **1** to part formally or definitely with a position of honor or power < the king *abdicated* the throne in order to marry a commoner >
syn demit, renounce, resign; *compare* RELINQUISH
rel abandon, leave, relinquish, surrender; drop; withdraw
con appropriate, arrogate, confiscate; grab, seize, take over, wrest
ant assume, usurp
2 *syn* see DISCARD
con keep, retain, treasure

abdomen *n* the part of the body between the chest and the pelvis < intense pain in the lower *abdomen* >
syn belly, ||gut, paunch, stomach, tummy, venter
rel bay window, ||breadbasket, corporation, pod, pot, potbelly; middle, midriff, midsection

abduct *vb syn* see KIDNAP
rel grab, seize

abecedarian *n syn* see AMATEUR 2

aberrant *adj* **1** *syn* see ABNORMAL 1
rel different, disparate, divergent; eccentric, odd, peculiar, strange; exceptional, unusual
con natural, normal, regular, typical; customary, usual, wonted
ant true (*to a type*)
2 *syn* see ERRANT 2

aberration *n* **1** *syn* see DEVIATION 1
rel abnormality; mistake, slip; curiosity, oddity, prodigy, rarity
con average, mean, norm; normality
ant conformity; regularity
2 *syn* see INSANITY 1
ant soundness (*of mind*)

abet *vb* **1** *syn* see INCITE
rel egg, exhort, goad, prod, spur, urge; advocate, countenance, encourage, endorse
con forbid, prevent, prohibit; debar, deter, discourage
2 *syn* see HELP 1

abettor *n syn* see CONFEDERATE

abeyance *n* a state of temporary inactivity < the warm dry weather kept his asthma in *abeyance* >
syn abeyancy, cold storage, doldrums, dormancy, intermission, interruption, latency, quiescence, quiescency, suspension
rel break, interval, pause, respite
con activeness, activity, stir
ant continuance

abeyancy *n syn* see ABEYANCE

---

syn synonym(s)　　　　　　　　　　**rel** related word(s)
ant antonym(s)　　　　　　　　　　**con** contrasted word(s)
idiom idiomatic equivalent(s)
|| use limited; if in doubt, see a dictionary

ant continuancy

abeyant *adj syn* see LATENT
   rel deferred, intermitted, postponed, stayed, suppressed; repressed
   con refreshed, renewed, restored
   ant active, operative; revived

abhor *vb* **1** *syn* see HATE
   2 *syn* see DESPISE
   con dote (on *or* upon), like, love
   ant admire

abhorrence *n syn* see ABOMINATION 2
   rel distaste, repellency; dismay, horror
   con affection, attachment, love
   ant admiration; enjoyment

abhorrent *adj* **1** *syn* see HATEFUL 2
   ant admirable
   2 *syn* see REPUGNANT 1
   rel antipathetic; uncongenial, unsympathetic
   con alluring, attractive, captivating; enticing, seductive, tempting
   ant congenial

abide *vb* **1** *syn* see STAY 2
   rel adhere, cleave, cling, stick; dwell, live, reside
   con go, leave, quit; move, remove, shift
   ant depart
   2 *syn* see CONTINUE 1
   rel linger; exist, subsist
   con avoid, elude, escape, evade
   ant pass
   3 *syn* see BEAR 10
   rel accept, receive; accede, consent
   idiom put up with
   4 *syn* see RESIDE 1

abiding *adj syn* see SURE 2
   rel durable, lasting, perdurable, persistent
   con ephemeral, impermanent, short-lived, transient, transitory

ability *n* **1** physical, mental, or legal power to perform <he has the *ability* to accomplish whatever he sets his mind to>
   syn adequacy, capability, capacity, competence, might, qualification, qualifiedness
   rel address, adroitness, cleverness, dexterity; aptitude, aptness, facility, knack
   idiom what it takes
   con impotence, inadequacy, incapability, incompetence
   ant inability
   2 natural or acquired proficiency especially in a particular activity <he has unusual *ability* in planning and designing>
   syn command, expertise, expertism, expertness, knack, knowhow, mastership, mastery, skill
   rel adroitness, deftness, efficiency, handiness, proficiency; ingenuity, resourcefulness; talent
   con inadequacy, incompetence, ineffectualness, unfitness; fatuity, futility, inanity

abject *adj syn* see DOWNTRODDEN

abjure *vb* to give up (something formerly adhered to) irrevocably and usually solemnly or formally <an immigrant solemnly *abjuring* allegiance to his former country>
   syn forswear, palinode, recall, recant, retract, take back, unsay, withdraw
   rel disavow, disown, renounce, repudiate; abandon, desert, forsake; cede, relinquish, surrender
   idiom eat one's words

ablaze *adj* **1** *syn* see BURNING 1
   2 *syn* see ALIGHT 2

able *adj* possessed of or marked by a high level of efficiency and ability <an *able* student always near the head of his class>
   syn au fait, capable, competent, good, proper, qualified, wicked
   rel effective, effectual, efficient; expert, proficient, skilled, skillful; alert, clever, keen, sharp; brainy, brilliant, intelligent, smart; enterprising, go-ahead, up-and-coming
   con ineffective, ineffectual, inefficient; incapable, incompetent, unqualified; fair, indifferent, mediocre; lackluster, maladroit
   ant inept; unable

abnegation *n syn* see RENUNCIATION

abnormal *adj* **1** departing significantly from the normal or a norm <the *abnormal* rains caused flooding>
   syn aberrant, anomalous, atypical, deviant, deviative, heteroclite, preternatural, unrepresentative, untypical

   rel divergent, offtype; irregular, unnatural; uncustomary, unusual, unwonted; heteromorphic; paratypic
   con common, familiar, natural, ordinary, regular, typical; customary, usual, wonted
   ant normal
   2 *syn* see IRREGULAR 1

abode *n syn* see HABITATION 2

abolish *vb* **1** to bring to an end often by formal or concerted action <*abolish* a tax>
   syn abate, abrogate, annihilate, annul, circumduct, invalidate, negate, nullify, quash, undo, vitiate
   rel cancel, disallow, disannul, repeal, rescind, revoke, vacate
   idiom bring to naught, make void, set aside
   con conserve, preserve, save; keep, retain
   2 *syn* see ANNIHILATE 2
   con found, institute
   ant establish

abominable *adj syn* see HATEFUL 2
   rel accursed, cursed; loathsome, offensive, repugnant, revolting
   con applaudable, commendable
   ant laudable (*as practices, customs*); delightful, enjoyable

abominate *vb syn* see HATE
   rel curse, damn, objurgate
   idiom hold in abomination, take an aversion to
   con admire, regard
   ant enjoy; esteem

abomination *n* **1** one that is a source of utter disgust or intense dislike <found the new tax form an *abomination* of confused complexity>
   syn anathema, bête noire, black beast, bugbear, detestation, hate
   rel annoyance, pest, plague, trial; bogey, bugaboo, incubus
   con delectation, delight, joy, pleasure; treasure
   2 a feeling of extreme disgust and dislike <they hold every indulgence in *abomination*>
   syn abhorrence, aversion, detestation, hate, hatred, horror, loathing, repugnance, repugnancy, repulsion, revulsion
   rel contempt, despite, disdain, scorn; disfavor, dislike, disrelish, distaste
   con admiration, regard, respect; fondness, liking, relish, taste; approbation, approval, countenance, favor; acceptance, tolerance
   ant esteem; enjoyment

aboriginal *adj syn* see NATIVE 2
   rel primeval, primitive, primordial, pristine; barbarian, barbaric, barbarous, savage
   con advanced, progressive; civilized, cultured; sequent, successive

abortion *n syn* see FREAK 2

abortive *adj syn* see FUTILE
   rel unformed; immature, unmatured, unripe
   con accomplished, completed, concluded, finished
   ant consummated

abound *vb syn* see TEEM

abounding *adj syn* see ALIVE 5
   rel full, jammed, packed, stuffed

about *adv* **1** in every direction <looked carefully *about*>
   syn around, round, round about
   2 in a circuitous way or course <took the long way *about*>
   syn circuitously, round about
   3 *syn* see NEARLY
   4 here or there without plan or order <left his tools lying *about*>
   syn anyhow, any which way, anywise, around, at random, haphazard, haphazardly, helter-skelter, random, randomly
   rel back and forth, hither and thither, to and fro; aimlessly, carelessly, casually
   5 in the vicinity <talked to the people standing *about*>
   syn near, near-at-hand, nearby
   idiom close by
   6 in the opposite direction <he turned *about* and saw her>
   syn again, around, back, backward, in reverse, round, round about
   idiom in one's course

about *prep* **1** in the vicinity of <*about* five miles to go>
   syn around, circa, close on, near, nearby, nigh
   idiom hard by, not far from
   2 *syn* see APROPOS
   idiom in point of, with regard to

3 syn see OVER 3
4 here and there upon or within < traveled *about* the country >
  syn round, through, throughout
  idiom all over
about–face *n syn* see REVERSAL 1
above *adv* **1 syn** see OVER 4
  ant below
  2 higher on the same page or on a preceding page < earlier examples appear *above* >
  syn supra
  ant below, infra
above *prep* **1 syn** see OVER 1
  ant below
  2 syn see BEYOND 2
aboveboard *adj syn* see STRAIGHTFORWARD 2
  rel open, scrupulous; artless, ingenuous, unsophisticated
  con clandestine, covert, furtive, secret, surreptitious; deceitful; crooked, devious, oblique
  ant underhand, underhanded
abracadabra *n syn* see GIBBERISH 3
  rel mystification; argot, cant, jargon
abrade *vb* **1** to injure or flaw by frictional action < wind-driven sand *abraded* the glass >
  syn chafe, corrade, erode, gall, graze, rub, ruffle, wear
  rel corrode, eat away, fret; grate, rasp, scrape
  2 syn see CHAFE 3
  rel burn
  3 syn see ANNOY 1
  rel disorganize, disturb, flurry, rattle; confuse, distract, perturb
  con calm, relieve, soothe
Abraham's bosom *n syn* see HEAVEN 2
abreast *adj* **1 syn** see UP-TO-DATE
  2 syn see FAMILIAR 3
abridge *vb* **1** to make less by in some manner restricting < laws that *abridge* freedom of speech >
  syn curtail, diminish, lessen, minify
  rel limit, narrow, reduce, restrict; minimize
  con augment, broaden, enlarge, extend
  ant amplify
  2 syn see SHORTEN
  con amplify, augment, enlarge, increase
  ant expand, extend
abridgment *n* a shortened version of a larger work or treatment produced by condensing and omitting without basic alteration of intent and language < an *abridgment* of a dictionary >
  syn abstract, boildown, breviary, breviate, brief, condensation, conspectus, epitome, synopsis
  rel aperçu, compendium, digest, outline, précis, sketch, syllabus; capsule, summary; sum, summation, summing-up
  con elaboration; paraphrase
  ant expansion
abroad *adv syn* see OVERSEAS
abrogate *vb* **1 syn** see ANNUL 4
  rel abate, extinguish
  con establish, found; confirm, ratify
  ant institute (*as by enacting or decreeing*)
  2 syn see ABOLISH 1
  rel extinguish; blot out, cancel, obliterate; ruin, wreck
  con support, uphold
  ant establish, fix (*as a right, a quality, or a custom*)
abrupt *adj* **1 syn** see PRECIPITATE 1
  rel hastened; casual, informal, unceremonious; quick, speedy
  con dilatory, laggard; easy, relaxed
  ant deliberate, leisurely
  2 syn see BLUFF
  rel brisk, crisp, sharp; impetuous, quick, ready
  con calm, easy, relaxed
  3 syn see STEEP 1
  rel perpendicular, plumb, vertical
  con inclined, slanting; flat, level, plane, smooth
  ant sloping
abruptly *adv syn* see SHORT 1
abscess *n* a localized swollen area of infection containing pus < had an *abscess* on his leg >
  syn boil, carbuncle, furuncle, pimple, pustule
  rel lesion, sore, trauma; botch, ulcer
abscond *vb syn* see ESCAPE 1
  rel go, leave, quit, withdraw

  idiom do the disappearing act, skip out, take French leave
  con render, surrender, yield
  ant give (oneself) up
absence *n* the state of being absent or missing < the *absence* of news was disturbing >
  syn dearth, default, defect, lack, ‖miss, privation, want; *compare* FAILURE 3
  rel deficiency, drought, inadequacy, insufficiency; exigency, necessity, need; vacuum, void; nonappearance, nonattendance
  con abundance, copiousness, plenty
  ant presence
absent *adj* **1** not now present < all missed their *absent* friend >
  syn away, gone, lacking, missing, omitted, wanting
  ant present
  2 syn see ABSTRACTED
  rel absorbed; forgetful, heedless
  con attending, hearkening, listening; considerate, thoughtful
  ant attentive
absentminded *adj syn* see ABSTRACTED
  rel unnoticing, unobserving, unperceiving, unseeing; heedless, inattentive
  idiom lost in thought
  con alert; awake
  ant wide-awake
absolute *adj* **1 syn** see PERFECT 2
  rel pure, sheer, simple
  con circumscribed, limited, partial, restricted
  2 syn see PURE 2
  rel abstract, ideal; real, true
  con imperfect, incomplete
  ant mixed, qualified
  3 syn see UTTER
  4 exercising power or authority without external restraint < an *absolute* monarch >
  syn arbitrary, autarchic, autocratic, despotic, monocratic, tyrannical, tyrannous; *compare* TOTALITARIAN 1
  rel dictatorial, magisterial; authoritarian, totalitarian; domineering, imperious, masterful; plenipotential, plenipotentiary, unlimited
  con circumscribed, limited, restrained, restricted; constitutional, lawful
  5 syn see ACTUAL 2
  6 syn see ULTIMATE 3
  rel ideal, transcendent, transcendental; autonomous, free, independent, sovereign; boundless, eternal, infinite
  con circumscribed, limited, restricted; conditional, contingent, dependent
absolutely *adv syn* see EASILY 2
absolution *n syn* see PARDON
  rel condonation
  con censure, reprehension, reprobation
  ant condemnation
absolve *vb* **1 syn** see EXEMPT
  2 syn see EXCULPATE
  rel discharge, free, release
  con condemn, doom, sentence; chasten, discipline, punish
  ant charge (with), hold (to)
absorb *vb* **1** to take in and make a part of one's being < *absorb* knowledge from reading >
  syn assimilate, imbibe, incorporate, inhaust, insorb
  rel embody, imbue, impregnate, infuse, permeate
  con disgorge, eject, expel, vomit; discharge, eliminate, emit, give off, pass
  ant exude, give out
  2 syn see MONOPOLIZE
  rel concern, engage, immerse, involve, preoccupy
  con diffuse, disperse, scatter
  ant dissipate (*as time, attention*)
absorbed *adj syn* see INTENT
  rel involved
  idiom caught up in, up to the elbows (*or* ears) in
  con apathetic, disinterested, indifferent, unconcerned; uninterested; absent, abstracted

---

syn synonym(s)   **rel** related word(s)
ant antonym(s)   **con** contrasted word(s)
idiom idiomatic equivalent(s)
‖ use limited; if in doubt, see a dictionary

ant distracted

absorbing *adj syn* see ENGROSSING
   ant irksome

abstain *vb* **1** *syn* see DENY 3
   rel abnegate, eschew, forgo; decline, refuse, reject, spurn
   idiom dispense with, do without, let alone
   con pamper; gratify, regale; sate, satiate, surfeit
   ant indulge
   2 *syn* see REFRAIN 1

abstemious *adj* marked by restraint in satisfying desires (as for food, drink, or pleasure) <an *abstemious* man, little given to self-indulgence>
   syn abstentious, abstinent, continent, self-restraining, sober, temperate; *compare* SOBER 3
   rel self-abnegating, self-denying; ascetic, austere; sparing
   con greedy, rapacious, voracious; epicurean, sybaritic, voluptuous
   ant gluttonous

abstentious *adj syn* see ABSTEMIOUS
   ant gluttonous

abstinence *n syn* see TEMPERANCE 2
   rel renunciation
   con gorging, sating, surfeiting; immoderateness, overdoing, unrestraint; crapulence, excess, extravagance
   ant self-indulgence

abstinent *adj syn* see ABSTEMIOUS
   ant gluttonous

abstract *adj* **1** having conceptual rather than concrete existence <the *abstract* perfect society>
   syn hypothetical, ideal, theoretical, transcendent, transcendental
   rel academic, impractical, utopian, visionary; speculative, undemonstrable; conceptual, notional; inconcrete
   con corporeal, material, objective, phenomenal, physical; actual, factual, real
   ant concrete
   2 *syn* see NEUTRAL

abstract *n syn* see ABRIDGMENT
   con enlargement, expansion
   ant amplification

abstract *vb* **1** *syn* see DETACH
   rel divide, part, separate
   con insinuate, interpolate, interpose
   ant insert, introduce
   2 *syn* see STEAL 1

abstracted *adj* withdrawn in mind and inattentive to external matters <seemed *abstracted* and remote>
   syn absent, absentminded, bemused, distrait, faraway, inconscient, lost, preoccupied
   rel engrossed, intent, rapt; oblivious, unmindful, unminding; heedless, inattentive
   idiom in a brown study, lost in thought, lost to the world
   con attentive, vigilant, watchful, wide-awake; noticing, noting, observant, seeing
   ant alert

abstruse *adj syn* see RECONDITE
   rel complex, complicated, intricate, knotty; abstract, hypothetical, ideal
   con clear, evident, manifest, palpable; clear, lucid, perspicuous; easy, facile, simple
   ant obvious, plain

absurd *adj syn* see FOOLISH 2
   rel comic, droll, funny; asinine, fatuous, simple; irrational, unreasonable
   con logical, ratiocinative, subtle
   ant rational, sensible

absurdity *n syn* see FOOLISHNESS

abundance *n syn* see PROSPERITY 2
   rel adequacy, competence, enough, plenty, sufficiency; lavishness, prodigality
   idiom enough and to spare
   con deficiency, inadequacy, insufficiency, lack, paucity

abundant *adj syn* see PLENTIFUL
   rel lavish, lush, luxuriant, profuse; crammed, crowded, thick; common
   idiom in good supply
   con infrequent, rare, uncommon; inadequate, scanty
   ant scarce

abuse *vb* **1** *syn* see DECRY 2

ant praise
   2 to put to a bad or improper use <*abuse* the prerogatives of office>
   syn misapply, misemploy, mishandle, misimprove, misuse, pervert, prostitute
   rel mar, spoil; corrupt, debase, desecrate, profane
   idiom make ill use of
   con esteem, honor, respect
   3 *syn* see EXPLOIT 2
   4 to treat without compassion and usually in a hurtful manner <parents who *abuse* children>
   syn ill-treat, ill-use, maltreat, mistreat, misuse, outrage
   rel damage, harm, hurt, impair, injure; oppress, persecute, wrong; manhandle, mess (up)
   idiom do one dirt, do violence to
   con cherish, prize, treasure; esteem, revere, reverence, venerate
   ant honor, respect

abuse *n* vehemently and usually coarsely expressed condemnation or disapproval <had an unequaled vocabulary of *abuse*>
   syn billingsgate, contumely, invective, obloquy, scurrility, vituperation
   rel calumny, defamation, malignment, mud, vilification; cursing, profanity, swearing; berating, railing, rating, reviling
   con acclaim, laudation, praise; applause, commendation, compliment
   ant adulation

abusive *adj* coarse, insulting, and contemptuous in character or utterance <an *abusive* denunciation>
   syn contumelious, invective, opprobrious, scurrile, scurrilous, truculent, vituperative, vituperatory, vituperous
   rel affronting, insulting, offending, outraging; dirty, odious, offensive; aspersing, maligning, vilifying
   con acclaiming, extolling, lauding, praising; eulogistic, panegyrical; flattering
   ant complimentary; respectful

abut *vb syn* see ADJOIN

abutting *adj syn* see ADJACENT 3
   rel connecting, joining; impinging
   con detached, disengaged; disassociated, disconnected, disjoined, parted, separated

abysm *n syn* see GULF 2

abysmal *adj* **1** *syn* see BOTTOMLESS 2
   2 *syn* see DEEP 1
   rel illimitable, infinite

abyss *n* **1** *syn* see HELL
   2 *syn* see GULF 2
   3 *syn* see DEPTH 2

academic *adj* **1** *syn* see PEDANTIC
   con ignorant, illiterate, unlettered; down-to-earth, everyday, practical, realistic, straightforward
   2 *syn* see THEORETICAL 1
   rel impractical, utopian, visionary; chimerical, imaginary

accede *vb syn* see ASSENT
   rel concur, cooperate; allow, let, permit
   con decline; balk, shy, stick; expostulate, kick, object, protest; fight, oppose, resist, withstand
   ant demur

accelerate *vb syn* see SPEED 3
   rel drive, impel
   idiom get going, make up for lost time
   con clog, hamper; delay, detain, slow
   ant decelerate; retard

accent *n* **1** *syn* see INFLECTION
   2 *syn* see EMPHASIS
   rel cadence, meter, rhythm; beat, pulsation, pulse, throb

accentuation *n syn* see EMPHASIS
   con evenness, sameness, steadiness, uniformity
   ant inaccentuation

accept *vb* **1** *syn* see APPROVE 1
   rel fancy, like, relish; admire, esteem
   con discountenance, disesteem, dislike, disrelish
   ant reject
   2 to take or sustain without protest or repining <a losing candidate must *accept* the decision of the electorate>
   syn bear (with), endure, pocket, swallow, tolerate, tough (out); *compare* BEAR 10
   rel acquiesce (in), agree (to *or* with), assent (to), subscribe (to); respect; bow, capitulate, yield

idiom put up with
con disavow, disown; brush (aside), deny, reject, repudiate
3 *syn* see BELIEVE 1
4 *syn* see APPREHEND 1
acceptable *adj syn* see DECENT 4
rel average, commonplace, ordinary; bearable, endurable, supportable
con insupportable, intolerable, unbearable, unendurable
ant unacceptable
acceptably *adv syn* see WELL 4
acceptant *adj syn* see RECEPTIVE 1
acceptation *n syn* see MEANING 1
accepted *adj* **1** *syn* see USUAL 1
rel conventional, established, recognized; correct, orthodox, proper, right
idiom according to custom (*or* use)
con irregular, questionable, unacceptable, unconventional; incongruent, unconformable, unorthodox
2 *syn* see ORTHODOX 1
acceptive *adj syn* see RECEPTIVE 1
access *n* **1** *syn* see ATTACK 3
rel onset; taking; pang, stitch, twinge
2 *syn* see OUTBURST 1
3 *syn* see DOOR 2
rel passage, route
con departure, retreat, withdrawal
ant egress; outlet
accessible *adj* **1** *syn* see OPEN 4
rel approachable
con limited, restricted; remote
2 *syn* see OPEN 5
ant inaccessible
accession *n syn* see ADDITION
ant discard
accessory *n* **1** *syn* see APPENDAGE
rel accompaniment, concomitant; accretion, addition, increment
2 *syn* see CONFEDERATE
ant principal
accessory *adj syn* see AUXILIARY
rel secondary, subordinate, tributary; coincident, concomitant, concurrent; adventitious, incidental
con constitutional, ingrained, inherent, intrinsic; cardinal, fundamental, vital; essential, indispensable, necessary
ant constituent, integral
accident *n* **1** absence of positive plan or intent < we stopped there by *accident* >
syn chance, fortuity, hap, luck
rel fluke, fortune, hazard
con design, premeditation
ant intent
2 a chance event bringing injury, loss, or distress < the school was closed by an *accident* to the heating system >
syn casualty, misadventure, mischance, mishap
rel calamity, catastrophe, disaster, tragedy; misfortune; chance, destiny, fate, kismet
con foreordination, predestination
accidental *adj* resulting from chance < an *accidental* meeting >
syn casual, chance, contingent, fluky, fortuitous, incidental, odd; *compare* RANDOM, UNINTENTIONAL
rel conditional, dependent; coincident, coincidental; inadvertent, undesigned, unintended, unintentional, unmeant, unplanned, unpurposed, unwitting
con designed, intended, purposed; constitutional, inherent, intrinsic; innate
ant planned; essential
accidentally *adv syn* see INCIDENTALLY 1
acclaim *vb syn* see COMMEND 2
rel cheer, root (for); exalt, magnify; glorify, honor
con berate, rate, revile; damn, execrate, objurgate; censure, denounce
ant vituperate
acclaim *n syn* see APPLAUSE
rel homage, honor, reverence; éclat, glory
con abuse, invective, obloquy; censure, condemnation, denunciation, reprobation
ant vituperation
acclamation *n syn* see APPLAUSE
acclimate *vb syn* see HARDEN 2

acclimatize *vb syn* see HARDEN 2
accolade *n syn* see HONOR 1
accommodate *vb* **1** *syn* see ADAPT
rel bow, defer, submit, yield; alter, change, modify, vary
con alienate, estrange
ant constrain
2 *syn* see HARMONIZE 3
3 *syn* see OBLIGE 2
rel cater (to), humor, indulge
con annoy, harass, harry; irk, vex, worry
ant incommode
4 *syn* see CONTAIN 2
rel encase, enclose
5 *syn* see HARBOR 2
accommodations *n pl* shelter, food, and services (as at a hotel) < searched for *accommodations* as night drew near >
syn lodging, lodgment, room and board
rel bed, room; keep; housing, shelter
idiom bed and breakfast
accompaniment *n* **1** something added to a principal thing usually to increase its impact or effectiveness < her song had a soft orchestral *accompaniment* >
syn augmentation, complement, enhancement, enrichment
rel accessory, addition, supplement; aid, assistance, help
2 an accompanying individual, situation, or occurrence < smog is an inevitable *accompaniment* of excessive numbers of automobiles >
syn associate, companion, concomitant, consort, fellow, mate
rel attendant, colleague, comrade, partner; corollary, equivalent
accompany *vb* to go or be together with < *accompanied* his wife to the theater >
syn attend, bear, ǁbring, ǁcarry, chaperon, companion, company, conduct, consort (with), convoy, escort
rel associate, combine, join, link; defend, guard, protect, safeguard, shield; guide, lead, pilot, steer
idiom bear one company, go along with, go hand in hand with
con leave, quit, withdraw; abandon, forsake
accompanying *adj syn* see CONCOMITANT
accomplice *n syn* see CONFEDERATE
rel aider, assistant, helper; flunky, stooge
accomplish *vb syn* see GAIN 1
accomplished *adj syn* see CONSUMMATE 1
rel adept, expert, masterly, proficient; all-around, many-sided, versatile
accomplishment *n* **1** *syn* see ACQUIREMENT
rel art, craft, skill; adeptness, expertise, expertness, proficiency
2 *syn* see ACTION 1
accord *vb* **1** *syn* see AGREE 4
rel coincide, concur; blend, coalesce, fuse, merge
con differ, disagree; compare, contrast
ant conflict
2 *syn* see GRANT 1
rel allot
con deny, gainsay; refuse; detain, hold, reserve
ant withhold
3 *syn* see GIVE 2
accord *n* **1** *syn* see HARMONY 2
rel affinity, attraction, empathy, sympathy; solidarity, union
idiom community of interest(s)
con conflict, contention, difference; animosity, antipathy, hostility
ant dissension, strife; antagonism
2 *syn* see AGREEMENT 2
3 *syn* see HARMONY 1
accordant *adj syn* see HARMONIOUS 2
accordingly *adv syn* see THEREFORE
idiom by reason of that (*or* this), for that (*or* this) reason
according to *prep syn* see BY 5
accost *vb* **1** *syn* see ADDRESS 7
rel buttonhole
con ignore, overlook, slight; avoid, elude, evade, shun
2 to approach boldly or in a challenging or sometimes a defensive manner < *accosted* by a beggar who demanded money >

---

syn synonym(s)   *rel* related word(s)
ant antonym(s)   *con* contrasted word(s)
idiom idiomatic equivalent(s)
ǁ use limited; if in doubt, see a dictionary

syn confront, face, front

rel affront, insult, offend, outrage; annoy, bother; challenge, dare, outface

idiom come face to face with, meet face to face

3 *syn* see ADDRESS 4

rel call (to), hail, halloo; buttonhole; dog, hound, pester, worry

accouchement *n syn* see CONFINEMENT 2

account *n* **1** *syn* see BILL 1

2 *syn* see USE 3

con immateriality, inconsequence, insignificance, unimportance; bootlessness, fruitlessness, futility

3 *syn* see WORTH 1

4 *syn* see REGARD 4

rel consequence, dignity, distinction, note; reputation, repute

5 *syn* see EXPLANATION 2

6 *syn* see SCORE 4

7 a statement of real or purported events, occurrences, or conditions < wrote an *account* of his travels >

syn chronicle, history, narrative, report, story, version; *compare* STORY 2

account *vb* **1** *syn* see CONSIDER 3

rel appraise, assess, estimate, evaluate, rate; esteem

con underestimate, underrate, undervalue

2 *syn* see EXPLAIN 3

rel answer, elucidate, expound, interpret

accountable *adj syn* see RESPONSIBLE

con absolute, arbitrary, autocratic; imperious, magisterial, masterful

ant unaccountable

accouter *vb syn* see FURNISH 1

rel attire, dress; adorn, deck, decorate, embellish; fix (up), prepare, ready

accouterment *n, usu* **accouterments** *pl syn* see EQUIPMENT

rel appointment(s); furnishing(s); bravery, regalia, trappings

accredit *vb* **1** *syn* see APPROVE 2

rel commend, recommend; attest, certify, vouch (for)

con belittle, deprecate, depreciate, disapprove; reject, repudiate

2 *syn* see ASCRIBE

3 *syn* see AUTHORIZE 1

rel introduce, present

accretion *n syn* see ADDITION

rel enlargement; attachment, joining, uniting; adjunct, appendage

accroach *vb* **1** *syn* see ARROGATE 1

2 *syn* see APPROPRIATE 1

accumulate *vb* to bring together and form a store of < *accumulate* knowledge >

syn amass, cumulate, garner, hive, lay up, roll up, stockpile, store (up), uplay; *compare* HOARD

rel assemble, collect, gather, lay by, lay down, lay in; heap, mass, pile, stock; fund, hoard, treasure

idiom squirrel away

con decrease, diminish, lessen; deal, dispense, distribute, dole (out); dispel, disperse, scatter; consume, expend, spend, use, use up

ant dissipate

accumulation *n* a mass, quantity, or number that has accumulated < an *accumulation* of rubbish >

syn agglomeration, aggregation, amassment, collection, colluvies, conglomeration, cumulation, hoard, trove

rel bank, heap, mass, pile; cumulus, reserve, stock, store

con dispersal, dispersion, scattering

accumulative *adj syn* see CUMULATIVE

rel aggregative, conglomerative; augmentative, multiplicative

con contractile, contractive, reducing, reductive; dispelling, dispersing, dispersive, dissipative, scattering

accuracy *n syn* see PRECISION

accurate *adj* **1** *syn* see CORRECT 2

con slipshod, slovenly; careless, heedless, lax

ant inaccurate

2 *syn* see CERTAIN 3

accurately *adv syn* see JUST 1

accursed *adj syn* see EXECRABLE 1

rel abhorrent, abominable, detestable, hateful, odious; offensive, repugnant, revolting

con admirable, estimable; honorable; divine, holy, sacred

ant blessed

accuse *vb* to declare one guilty of a fault or offense < *accused* her daughter of neglecting her children >

syn arraign, charge, criminate, impeach, incriminate, inculpate, indict, tax

rel blame, censure, criticize, denounce, reprobate; complain

idiom bring charges (against), point the finger at, prefer charges (against)

con absolve, acquit, exonerate, vindicate; accept, approve, endorse, sanction

ant exculpate

accustom *vb* to make something familiar or acceptable through use or experience < *accustom* oneself to city life >

syn familiarize, habituate, inure, use, wont

rel accommodate, adapt, adjust; acclimatize, harden, season

con alienate, estrange, wean; abjure, reject, repudiate; rebuff, repel, repulse, scorn

ant disaccustom

accustomed *adj* **1** *syn* see HABITUAL 2

2 *syn* see USUAL 1

rel commonplace, everyday; conventional, regulation, standard

con infrequent, occasional, uncommon; erratic, odd, peculiar, queer, singular

ant unaccustomed

ace *n* **1** *syn* see HAIR

2 *syn* see PARTICLE

acedia *n syn* see SLOTH 2

acerb *adj* **1** *syn* see SOUR 1

2 *syn* see SARCASTIC

acerbate *vb syn* see EXACERBATE

acerbic *adj* **1** *syn* see SOUR 1

2 *syn* see SARCASTIC

acerbity *n* **1** *syn* see ACRIMONY

rel acidity, sourness, tartness; crabbedness, dourness, saturninity, surliness; acridity, bitterness; harshness, roughness

con blandness, gentleness, mildness, smoothness; amiability, complaisance, good nature

ant mellowness

2 *syn* see SARCASM

acetose *adj syn* see SOUR 1

ache *vb* **1** *syn* see HURT 4

2 *syn* see COMPASSIONATE

rel deplore; sorrow (over); comfort, console, solace

3 *syn* see LONG

ache *n syn* see PAIN 1

rel injury; rack

con alleviation, assuagement, mitigation, relief; comfort, ease

acheronian *adj syn* see GLOOMY 3

acherontic *adj syn* see GLOOMY 3

achieve *vb* **1** *syn* see PERFORM 2

rel complete, conclude, finish; conquer, overcome, surmount

idiom bring to a happy issue, bring to pass

con begin, commence, start

ant fail (in or to do)

2 *syn* see GAIN 1

rel acquire, get, obtain, secure; actualize; arrive, come

idiom gain one's end

con depart, deviate, swerve; avoid, elude, escape, shun

ant miss

achievement *n* **1** *syn* see FEAT 2

con omission, slighting

ant failure

2 *syn* see ACQUIREMENT

Achilles' heel *n syn* see SOFT SPOT 2

aching *adj syn* see PAINFUL 1

rel achy

acicular *adj syn* see POINTED 1

aciculate *adj syn* see POINTED 1

acid *adj syn* see SOUR 1

con bland, mild, neutral

ant sweet; alkaline, basic

acidulous *adj syn* see SOUR 1

rel biting, cutting, sharp; piquant, pungent

con bland, mild, neutral; mellow, smooth, suave

ant saccharine

acknowledge *vb* **1** to show often grudgingly by word or deed that one knows of and agrees to or with something < *acknowledge* the justice of a complaint >

syn admit, allow, avow, concede, confess, fess (up), grant, let on, own, own up

rel disclose, divulge, reveal, tell; announce, declare, proclaim, publish

con disallow, disavow, disown, ‖nix, reject; contradict, gainsay, impugn, negate, negative
ant deny
2 to take notice of and accept as being as stated <he is generally *acknowledged* to be the leader in his profession>
syn admit, agree, recognize
rel accept, receive; concede, consider, deem, hold, view
con disregard, neglect, slight; reject, repudiate, spurn
ant ignore

acknowledgment *n* *syn* see CREDIT 4

acme *n* *syn* see APEX 2

acoustic *adj* *syn* see AUDITORY

acquaint *vb* **1** *syn* see INTRODUCE 4
idiom make acquainted
2 *syn* see INFORM 2
rel disclose, divulge, reveal; accustom, habituate
con hold, hold back, reserve, withhold; conceal, hide

acquaintance *n* **1** knowledge of something based on personal exposure <had a considerable *acquaintance* with modern poetry>
syn experience, familiarity, intimacy, inwardness
rel apprehension, grasp, ken; appreciation, awareness, consciousness
con inexperience, unfamiliarity; greenness, verdancy
2 *syn* see FRIEND
rel associate, companion, comrade, crony
con outsider, stranger

acquainted *adj* *syn* see FAMILIAR 3

acquiesce *vb* *syn* see ASSENT
rel accommodate, adapt, adjust, reconcile; bow, coincide, concur
con balk, demur, shy (away); kick, protest, remonstrate; differ, dissent
ant object

acquiescence *n* weak or passive agreement to what is asked or demanded <his childish *acquiescence* to all claims on his time>
syn compliance, conformity, resignation
rel complaisance; submissiveness; deference
con contumaciousness, insubordination; independence, self-assurance
ant rebellion, rebelliousness

acquiescent *adj* *syn* see PASSIVE 2

acquire *vb* **1** *syn* see GET 1
rel achieve, reach; add
con alienate, convey, transfer; abandon, relinquish, surrender, yield
ant forfeit
2 *syn* see EARN 1
rel accumulate, amass, collect, cumulate, garner
3 *syn* see DEVELOP 4

acquirement *n* a power or skill that results from persistent endeavor and cultivation <proud of his scholastic *acquirements*>
syn accomplishment, achievement, acquisition, attainment, finish
rel accretion, addition; advance, advancement; education, erudition, knowledge
con dearth, defect, lack, privation, want

acquisition *n* *syn* see ACQUIREMENT
rel accession, increment; assets, belongings, means, possessions

acquisitive *adj* *syn* see COVETOUS
rel demanding, exacting, exigent
con eschewing, forbearing, forgoing; sacrificing
ant abnegating, self-denying

acquit *vb* **1** *syn* see EXCULPATE
rel discharge, free, liberate, release; justify
con condemn, damn, doom, proscribe, sentence
ant convict
2 *syn* see BEHAVE 1

acres *n pl* *syn* see ESTATE 3

acrid *adj* having or being a noticeable, persistent, and usually unpleasant flavor or sometimes odor <the tonic had an *acrid* aftertaste>
syn amaroidal, astringent, austere, bitter, harsh, sharp
rel biting, caustic, cutting; piquant, pungent; cloying, oversweet, saccharine
con palatable, sapid, tasty, toothsome; delectable, delicious, luscious
ant savory

acrimonious *adj* *syn* see ANGRY
rel cranky, cross, irascible, splenetic, testy; belligerent, contentious, quarrelsome
con benign, benignant, kind, kindly
ant irenic, peaceable

acrimony *n* sharpness or rancor manifested in words, manner, or disposition <the dispute was renewed with increasing *acrimony*>
syn acerbity, asperity, mordancy
rel bitterness, ill will, malevolence, malice, malignity, spite, spleen; animosity, animus, antipathy, rancor
con civility, courtesy, graciousness, politeness; diplomacy, urbanity
ant suavity

acroamatic *adj* *syn* see RECONDITE

across *adv* **1** so as to intersect the length of something <cut the board *across*>
syn athwart, crossways, crosswise
2 *syn* see OVER 1

across *prep* from one side to the other <drew the curtain *across* the window>
syn athwart, cross, over

act *vb* **1** to present a role or performance on or as if on the stage <*acted* the part of Hamlet's father>
syn discourse, do, enact, impersonate, perform, personate, play, playact
rel characterize, portray, represent; masquerade; counterfeit, feign, sham, simulate
2 *syn* see ASSUME 4
idiom act a part, put on an act (of)
3 *syn* see BEHAVE 1
rel perform
4 to perform the duties or function of <he *acted* as president for over a year>
syn function, officiate, serve
idiom do duty (as), discharge the office (of), serve in the office (or capacity) of
5 to perform especially in an indicated way <the laxative *acted* quickly>
syn behave, function, operate, perform, react, take, work
idiom take effect
6 *syn* see FUNCTION 3

act *n* *syn* see ACTION 1
rel exploit, feat

actify *vb* *syn* see VITALIZE

acting *adj* *syn* see TEMPORARY

action *n* **1** something done or effected <a kindly *action*>
syn accomplishment, act, deed, doing, thing
rel discharge, effectuation, execution, fulfillment, performance; activity, behavior, operation, reaction, work; procedure, proceeding, process
2 *syn* see BATTLE
rel affray, combat, conflict, fray
3 *syn* see SERVICE 1
4 *syn* see SUIT 1

activate *vb* *syn* see VITALIZE
rel arouse, awaken, rally, rouse, stir, wake, waken
ant arrest

active *adj* **1** being at work or in effective operation <marginal mines that are *active* only when prices are high>
syn alive, dynamic, functioning, live, operative, running, working
rel assiduous, busy, diligent, industrious; energetic, strenuous, vigorous; alert, wide-awake; rushing
con dormant, latent, quiescent; idle, inert, passive, supine; dead, dull, slow
ant inactive; abeyant
2 *syn* see AGILE
rel animated, spirited, vivacious; flexible, graceful, supple
con inert, lumpish, torpid
ant inactive
3 *syn* see ENERGETIC 2
rel expeditious, prompt, ready

---

syn synonym(s)   **rel** related word(s)
ant antonym(s)   **con** contrasted word(s)
idiom idiomatic equivalent(s)
‖ use limited; if in doubt, see a dictionary

con disinterested, indifferent, unconcerned

actively *adv syn* see SERIOUSLY 1

activity *n syn* see EXERCISE 2

activize *vb syn* see VITALIZE

actor *n* **1** one who takes part in an exhibition simulating happenings in real life <had been an *actor* on the stage and in television>
syn impersonator, mime, mimic, mummer, performer, playactor, player, thespian, trouper
2 *syn* see PARTICIPANT
rel mainstay, supporter, sustainer, upholder
con abettor, backer, patron, promoter

actual *adj* **1** existing in act <our *actual* intentions>
syn existent, extant
ant possible, potential
2 existing in or based on fact <problems of *actual* life>
syn absolute, factual, genuine, hard, positive, sure-enough
rel commonplace, everyday, ordinary, routine, usual; concrete, real, tangible
con conjectural, hypothetical, theoretical; putative, reputed, supposititious
ant apparent, nominal
3 *syn* see REAL 3
rel material, objective, phenomenal, physical; authentic, bona fide, legitimate
con abstract, transcendent, transcendental; academic, speculative, theoretical; fabulous, fictitious, mythical
ant ideal; imaginary

actuality *n* **1** *syn* see EXISTENCE 1
rel actualization, externalization, incarnation, materialization; achievement, attainment
con abstraction, ideality, transcendence
ant possibility, potentiality
2 something that has existence <the *actualities* of daily life>
syn materiality, reality
rel basis, essence, substance; embodiment, incarnation
3 *syn* see FACT 1

actually *n syn* see VERY 2

actuate *vb* **1** *syn* see MOVE 5
2 *syn* see MOBILIZE 1
rel excite, galvanize, provoke; arouse, rouse, stir; vitalize

act up *vb syn* see CUT UP 2

acumen *n syn* see WIT 3
rel acuteness, sharpness
con denseness, density, slowness
ant obtuseness, obtusity

acuminate *adj syn* see POINTED 1

acuminous *adj syn* see POINTED 1

acute *adj* **1** *syn* see POINTED 1
rel barbed, prickly, spiky, spined, spiny
ant blunt
2 *syn* see SHARP 4
rel cutting, incisive, trenchant; piercing
con crass, dense, dull, slow, stupid
ant obtuse
3 perceiving clearly and sensitively <an *acute* ear>
syn keen, perceptive, sensitive, sharp
rel observant, penetrating, probing; accurate, meticulous, precise
con imperceptive, insensitive; imprecise, inaccurate; inexact, uncritical
ant dull
4 elevated in pitch <an *acute* note>
syn argute, high, piercing, piping, sharp, shrill, thin, treble
rel penetrating; reedy, screechy, shrieky, shrilly, squeaky; tinny
con bass, deep, low
ant grave
5 *syn* see SHARP 8
6 serious to the point of approaching a crisis <an *acute* housing shortage>
syn climacteric, critical, crucial, desperate, dire
rel afflictive, grave, serious; aggravated, intensified; dangerous, hazardous, menacing, perilous, precarious, threatening; exigent, urgent

adage *n syn* see SAYING

adamant *adj syn* see INFLEXIBLE 2
rel immobile, immovable; unsubmitting
con placable, relenting, submitting; complaisant, obliging; subdued, submissive

ant yielding

adamantine *adj syn* see INFLEXIBLE 2
rel immobile, immovable; unsubmitting
con placable, relenting, submitting; complaisant, obliging; subdued, submissive
ant yielding

adapt *vb* to bring into correspondence or make suitable <*adapted* himself easily to the company he found himself with>
syn accommodate, adjust, conform, fit, quadrate, reconcile, square, suit, tailor, tailor-make
rel qualify, temper; acclimate, acclimatize
ant unfit

adaptable *adj* **1** *syn* see VERSATILE
2 *syn* see PLASTIC
con intractable, irreconcilable, nonconforming, refractory, unaccommodating
ant inadaptable, unadaptable

adapted *adj syn* see ASSORTED 2

add *vb* **1** to bring in or join on something more so as to form a larger or more inclusive whole <*added* music to his accomplishments>
syn annex, append, subjoin, superadd, take on
rel affix, attach, fasten, superimpose, tack (on); augment, enlarge, increase; burden, clutter, cumber, encumber, saddle
con abstract, detach; curtail, decrease, diminish, lessen, reduce
ant deduct, subtract
2 to combine numbers or quantities into one sum <*add* up a column of figures>
syn cast, figure, foot, sum, summate, tot, total, totalize, tote
rel calculate, compute, estimate, reckon; score, tally

added *adj syn* see ADDITIONAL

addendum *n, sometimes* **addenda** *pl but sing or pl in constr syn* see APPENDIX 1

addict *vb syn* see HABITUATE 2
rel bias, dispose, incline, predispose; address, apply, direct
con alienate, estrange; detach, disengage, disincline, indispose
ant wean

addict *n* a person who by habit or strong inclination indulges in something <a science fiction *addict*>
syn aficionado, buff, devotee, fan, habitué, hound, lover, votary
rel enthusiast, fanatic, zealot; hobbyist, putterer, tinkerer

addition *n* something that tends to increase something else (as in size, number, or content) <there are several new *additions* to our staff>
syn accession, accretion, augmentation, increase, increment, raise, rise
rel accessory, adjunct, appanage, appurtenance, supplement; continuation, extension, rider; accrual, accruement, accumulation
con deduction, lessening, reduction

additional *adj* being or coming by way of addition <gave *additional* reasons to justify his position>
syn added, another, else, farther, fresh, further, more, new, other
rel accessory, adscititious, collateral, extra, supplemental, supplementary

additionally *adv* **1** *syn* see ALSO 2
2 *syn* see AGAIN 4

additive *adj syn* see CUMULATIVE
rel component, constituent, elemental

additory *adj syn* see CUMULATIVE

addle *vb syn* see CONFUSE 2
rel confound, dumbfound, nonplus; amaze, astound, flabbergast
idiom addle one's wits
con animate, enliven, quicken, vivify
ant refresh (*mentally*)

address *vb* **1** *syn* see DIRECT 2
2 *syn* see SEND 1
3 to occupy (oneself or one's attention or efforts) with something <*addressed* himself to the job and soon finished it>
syn apply, bend, buckle (down), devote, direct, give, throw, turn
rel associate, connect, couple, link, relate; aim, level, point
idiom bring (oneself) into relation with something, tax (one's energies) with something
con disregard, ignore, overlook
4 to communicate directly to or with <*addressed* the governor with his petition>
syn accost, apply (to), approach, bespeak, memorialize

rel speak (to), talk (with); appeal (to); apostrophize; petition
con ignore, overlook, pass up, slight; avoid, cut, disregard
5 *syn* see TALK 7
6 to affix directions for delivery <*address* a letter>
syn direct, superscribe
7 to seek the attention of usually orally and in order to gain recognition <*address* a stranger to ask directions>
syn accost, call (to), greet, hail, salute
rel converse, speak, talk
idiom attract one's attention
8 to direct one's attention to in the role of a suitor <ready to marry the first man that *addressed* her>
syn court, make up (to), pursue, spark, sue, sweetheart, woo
rel attend, escort, squire; neck, pet, romance, rush, smooch, spoon
idiom make a play for, pay (one's) addresses to, run after
address *n* **1** the quality or state of being ready or skillful <to bring off such a coup requires *address*>
syn adroitness, deftness, dexterity, dexterousness, prowess, readiness, skill, sleight; *compare* TACT
rel competence, efficiency, expertise, know-how, proficiency; craft, finesse; ingeniousness, ingenuity, resourcefulness
con inadequacy, ineptitude, ineptness, unskillfulness; awkwardness, clumsiness, gawkiness, lubberliness, stupidity
2 *syn* see TACT
rel dexterity, ease, facility; cleverness, readiness; affability, graciousness
con awkwardness, clumsiness, gaucheness; boorishness, churlishness
ant maladroitness
3 *syn* see BEARING 1
4 *syn* see SPEECH 2
adduce *vb* to bring forward for consideration <*adduce* evidence in support of a hypothesis>
syn advance, allege, cite, lay, offer, present
rel animadvert, comment, commentate, remark; document, exemplify, illustrate; prefer, proffer, propose, submit, suggest, tender
add up *vb syn* see AMOUNT 1
add up (to) *vb syn* see MEAN 2
adept *n syn* see EXPERT
ant bungler, incompetent
adept *adj syn* see PROFICIENT
rel clever; adroit, deft, dexterous
con amateurish, dabbling, dilettantish; awkward, clumsy, maladroit
ant bungling, inapt, inept
adequacy *n* **1** *syn* see ABILITY 1
rel equality, satisfactoriness, sufficiency
idiom enough on the ball
ant inadequacy, inadequateness
2 *syn* see ENOUGH
adequate *adj* **1** *syn* see SUFFICIENT 1
con meager, scanty, sparse
ant inadequate, unadequate
2 *syn* see DECENT 4
adequately *adv* **1** *syn* see ENOUGH 1
2 *syn* see WELL 4
adequation *n syn* see EQUIVALENCE
adhere *vb syn* see STICK 2
rel combine, join, link, unite
con disjoin, disunite
adherence *n* **1** a physical adhering <the close *adherence* of scales to a plant bud>
syn adhesion, bond, cling, clinging, coherence, cohesion, stickage, sticking
rel agglutination, cementation, concretion, conglutination; congelation, set, setting, solidification
con detachment, disjunction, parting, separation
2 *syn* see ATTACHMENT 1
con fickleness, inconstancy
adherent *n syn* see FOLLOWER
rel backer, champion, upholder
con apostate, recreant; deserter, forsaker; adversary, antagonist, opponent
ant renegade
adhesion *n* **1** *syn* see ADHERENCE 1
ant nonadhesion

2 *syn* see ATTACHMENT 1
con fickleness, inconstancy
adhesive *adj syn* see STICKY 1
adieu *interj syn* see GOOD-BYE
adieu *n syn* see PARTING
ad interim *adj syn* see TEMPORARY
ant permanent
adipose *adj syn* see FATTY 1
adiposity *n syn* see OBESITY
adit *n syn* see DOOR 2
adjacent *adj* **1** *syn* see NEIGHBORING
ant remote
2 *syn* see CONVENIENT 2
3 having a common border <the brothers built on *adjacent* lots>
syn abutting, adjoining, approximal, bordering, conterminous, contiguous, juxtaposed, touching
rel closest, nearest, next; consecutive, successive; attached, connected, joined, linked
con distant, far, remote, removed; parted, separated
ant nonadjacent
adjoin *vb* to be contiguous or adjacent to <the new suburb *adjoins* farmland>
syn abut, border, butt (on *or* against), communicate, join, line, march, neighbor, touch, verge
rel meet, run (into); end
adjoining *adj syn* see ADJACENT 3
ant detached
adjourn *vb* **1** *syn* see DEFER
rel curb, hold back, restrain
con advance, expedite, further, promote
2 to bring to a formal close <*adjourn* the legislature>
syn dissolve, prorogate, prorogue, recess, rise, terminate
rel break up, close, disband, discontinue, disperse; stay, suspend
con open; mobilize, muster, rally
ant convene, convoke
adjudge *vb syn* see JUDGE 1
rel accord, allot, assign, award, grant
adjudicate *vb syn* see JUDGE 1
adjunct *n syn* see APPENDAGE
rel accretion, addition; appanage; affix, attachment, fixture
adjust *vb* **1** *syn* see ADAPT
rel accord, correspond; attune, harmonize
2 to alter so as to make efficient or more efficient <*adjust* a carburetor>
syn fix, regulate, tune (up)
rel correct, rectify, right; balance, stabilize, steady, trim, true; arrange, order, rig
idiom make right, put (*or* set) in order, put right (*or* to rights), set right (*or* to rights)
con disarrange, disorder, disturb, upset
ant derange
3 *syn* see HABITUATE 2
adjuvant *adj syn* see AUXILIARY
rel synergistic
con antagonistic, negating, negativing, neutralizing; hindering, impeding, obstructing
ant counteractive
ad-lib *vb syn* see IMPROVISE
admeasure *vb syn* see ALLOT
admeasurement *n syn* see SIZE 1
adminicular *adj syn* see CORROBORATIVE
administer *vb* **1** to supervise the affairs or the provision, use, or conduct of especially in the capacity of an agent or steward <*administer* justice>
syn administrate, carry out, execute, govern, render
rel conduct, direct, manage, run, supervise
2 to provide in appropriate amount <*administer* a laxative>
syn apportion, deal (out), dispense, dole (out), mete (out), portion (out), share out
rel distribute, give, give out, issue; allot, assign, consign; allocate, ration

---

syn synonym(s)   *rel* related word(s)
ant antonym(s)   *con* contrasted word(s)
idiom idiomatic equivalent(s)
|| use limited; if in doubt, see a dictionary

3 syn see GIVE 10

administrate *vb syn* see ADMINISTER 1

administrator *n syn* see EXECUTIVE

admirable *adj syn* see WORTHY 1

admiration *n* **1 syn** see WONDER 2
rel surprise; ecstasy, rapture, transport
con aloofness, indifference, unconcern
2 syn see REGARD 4
rel appreciation; adoration, reverence, veneration, worship
con detestation, hate, hatred, loathing; dislike, disrelish, distaste
ant abhorrence

admire *vb* **1** to view with an elevated feeling of pleasure < *admired* the scene that spread out before them >
syn appreciate, cherish, delight (in), relish; *compare* APPRECIATE 1
rel adore, revere, reverence, venerate, worship
idiom go into raptures over, take delight in
con disesteem, disfavor, dislike, disrelish, mislike
ant disdain
2 to hold in high esteem < *admired* his ability to get things done >
syn consider, esteem, regard, respect
rel appreciate, cherish, prize, treasure, value
idiom have (or hold) a high opinion of, rate highly, set (great) store by, think much (or highly) of
con abominate, detest, hate, loathe; contemn, despise, disdain, scorn
ant abhor

admirer *n syn* see AMATEUR 1

admissible *adj syn* see PERMISSIBLE

admission *n syn* see DOOR 2

admit *vb* **1 syn** see TAKE 10
rel allow, permit, suffer; entertain, harbor, house, lodge, shelter
con debar, exclude, shut out; bar, block, hinder, obstruct
ant eject, expel
2 syn see ACKNOWLEDGE 1
rel acquiesce, agree, assent, subscribe
ant gainsay
3 syn see ENTER 2
rel induct, initiate, install; insert, interject, interpose
con debar, shut out; eject, expel, oust
ant exclude
4 syn see ACKNOWLEDGE 2

admittance *n syn* see DOOR 2

admix *vb syn* see MIX 1

admixture *n* **1** an added ingredient that alters the character of something < her love had a marring *admixture* of selfishness >
syn adulterant, alloy, denaturant
rel doctor, fortification, taint; accretion, addition; bit, dash, shade, smack, spice, tinge
2 syn see MIXTURE

admonish *vb syn* see REPROVE
rel caution, forewarn, warn
idiom have a word with
con applaud, approve, compliment
ant commend

admonishing *adj syn* see MONITORY

admonishment *n syn* see REBUKE

admonition *n* **1 syn** see REBUKE
2 syn see WARNING

admonitory *adj syn* see MONITORY

ado *n syn* see STIR 1
rel effort, exertion, pains, trouble; confusion, hurly-burly, turmoil, uproar
con calm, peace, serenity, tranquillity; quiet, silence, stillness

adolescence *n syn* see YOUTH 1
ant senescence

adopt *vb* to make one's own what in some fashion one owes to another < *adopt* a new style >
syn embrace, espouse, take on, take up
rel affect, assume; appropriate, arrogate, take, usurp; domesticate, naturalize
idiom adapt to one's own ends, go in for
con reject, spurn; abjure, forswear, renounce
ant discard; repudiate

adoption *n syn* see ESPOUSAL 4

adorable *adj* **1 syn** see LOVABLE
2 syn see DELIGHTFUL

adoration *n* deep, ardent, and often excessive attachment or love < the *adoration* given popular heroes >
syn idolatry, idolization, worship
rel affection, attachment, devotion, love; crush, infatuation, passion, weakness
con antipathy, aversion; disfavor, dislike, distaste
ant detestation

adore *vb* **1 syn** see REVERE
rel extol, laud, praise
con curse, execrate
2 syn see LOVE 2
3 to love, admire, or enjoy excessively < she *adores* and spoils her grandchildren >
syn dote (on *or* upon), idolize, worship
rel admire, esteem, love; coddle, indulge, pamper, spoil
idiom be silly over
con abhor, abominate, hate, loathe; contemn, despise, disdain, scorn
ant detest
4 syn see LOVE 1

adorn *vb* to add something nonessential to enhance the appearance or beauty of < a hat *adorned* with feathers >
syn beautify, bedeck, deck, decorate, dress (up), embellish, garnish, ornament, prank, trim
rel enrich, furbish, smarten, spruce (up); bedizen, dandify, fancy up; enhance, heighten, intensify
con clear, divest, expose, strip, uncover; deface, mar, scar, spoil
ant disfigure

ad rem *adj syn* see RELEVANT

adroit *adj* **1 syn** see DEXTEROUS 1
ant maladroit
2 syn see SKILLFUL 2
3 syn see CLEVER 4
rel astute, perspicacious, shrewd; intelligent, quick-witted, smart; artful, subtle
con dense, dull, stupid; apathetic, heavy, impassive, phlegmatic, stodgy
ant stolid

adroitness *n* **1 syn** see ADDRESS 1
2 syn see ART 1

adscititious *adj syn* see ADVENTITIOUS

adulation *n syn* see FLATTERY
rel acclaim, applause
ant abuse

adult *adj syn* see MATURE 1
rel aged
con adolescent, pubescent
ant juvenile, puerile

adulterant *n syn* see ADMIXTURE 1

adulterate *vb* to alter fraudulently usually for profit < sausage *adulterated* with cereal products >
syn debase, doctor, dope (up), load, sophisticate, weight
rel cut, dilute; denaturalize, denature, manipulate, tamper (with); defile, impurify, pollute, taint; deacon
con better, improve; augment, fortify, supplement
ant refine

adumbrate *vb* **1** to give a hint or indication of something to come < social unrest that *adumbrated* the revolt >
syn foreshadow, hint, prefigurate, prefigure, shadow (forth); *compare* SUGGEST 5
rel augur, bode, forebode, foretell, portend, presage; lower, menace, threaten; symbolize, typify
idiom cast its shadow before
2 syn see FORETELL
rel argue, bespeak, betoken, indicate
3 syn see SKETCH
4 syn see SUGGEST 5
rel denote, mean, signify
5 syn see OBSCURE

adumbration *n syn* see SHADE 1
rel hint, intimation, suggestion; sign, symptom, token; emblem, symbol, type
con disclosure, discovery, divulgence
ant revelation

advance *vb* **1** to cause to proceed or progress toward a goal < warm rains *advanced* the crops >
syn encourage, forward, foster, further, promote, serve
rel aid, assist, help; accelerate, quicken, speed

con hinder, impede; delay, slow; curb, restrain
ant retard; check
2 to raise in rank or position <was *advanced* to the presidency>
syn elevate, prefer, promote, upgrade
rel aggrandize, exalt, raise, uplift; glorify, immortalize, magnify
ant hold back; reduce (*in rank*)
3 syn see LEND
4 syn see ADDUCE
rel air, broach, expose
5 to go forward in space or time or toward an objective <prices *advanced* sharply>
syn get along, get on, march, move, proceed, progress
rel heighten, increase, intensify; develop, mature
idiom forge ahead, gain ground, get ahead, make headway (*or* progress), make one's way, make rapid strides
con retire, retreat, retrograde, withdraw
ant recede

advance *n* **1 syn** see PROGRESS 2
2 forward movement especially on a course of action or development <the recent *advance* of technology>
syn advancement, anabasis, headway, march, ongoing, proficiency, progress
rel betterment, furtherance, improvement; development, evolution; breakthrough
con retreat, retrogression; ebbing, retiring, withdrawal
ant recession
3 syn see OVERTURE 1
rel offer, proffer

advanced *adj* **1 syn** see PRECOCIOUS
con retrograde, retrogressive
ant backward
2 syn see LIBERAL 3
rel adventurous, daring, venturesome
ant conservative

advancement *n* **1** the act of raising or the status of being raised in grade, rank, or dignity <his *advancement* in his profession was rapid>
syn elevation, preference, preferment, prelation, promotion, upgrading
rel aggrandizement, dignification, magnification, raising, uplifting
con demotion, downgrading, reduction
ant degradation
2 syn see ADVANCE 2

advantage *n* **1 syn** see BETTER 2
2 syn see WELFARE
3 something giving one person or side a position of superiority (as in a contest) <he had the *advantage* of greater height>
syn allowance, bulge, ‖deadwood, draw, edge, handicap, head start, odds, ‖overhand, start, vantage; *compare* BETTER 2
rel drop, jump, lead, running start; ascendancy, domination, leadership; mastery, superiority, upper hand, whip hand
idiom ace in the hole, inside track
con embarrassment, hamper, hindrance, impediment, inconvenience
ant disadvantage
4 syn see USE 3
rel betterment, improvement; enhancement; heightening
con damage, harm, hurt, injury
ant detriment
5 syn see GOOD 1

advantage *vb* **syn** see BENEFIT

advantageous *adj* **1** yielding a profit <sold on very *advantageous* terms>
syn gainful, good, lucrative, moneymaking, paying, profitable, remunerative, well-paying, worthwhile
rel acceptable, agreeable, desirable, pleasing, satisfactory, satisfying
idiom in the black, paying its (own) way
con disadvantageous, unfavorable, unprofitable; damaging, hurtful
2 syn see GOOD 1
rel remedial, salutary; conducive, contributory, implemental, instrumental; advisable, expedient
con unfavorable; inconvenient; deleterious, detrimental
ant disadvantageous

advenient *adj* **syn** see ADVENTITIOUS

advent *n* **syn** see ARRIVAL 1
rel approach, nearing
ant exit

advential *adj* **syn** see ADVENTITIOUS

adventitious *adj* coming from without and not participating in the fundamental nature of something <*adventitious* notions that have corrupted the primitive doctrine>
syn adscititious, advenient, advential, supervenient
rel accidental, casual, contingent, fortuitous, incidental
con constitutional, essential, intrinsic; inborn, inbred, innate
ant inherent

adventure *n* an undertaking or experience that involves hazard and requires boldness <recounted the *adventures* of his solitary voyage>
syn emprise, enterprise, exploit, feat, gest, venture
rel hazard, peril, risk; quest; achievement

adventure *vb* **syn** see VENTURE 1

adventuresome *adj* **syn** see ADVENTUROUS
ant unadventurous; cautious

adventurous *adj* courting danger or exposing oneself to danger beyond the call of duty or courage <*adventurous* boys scrambled over the cliff face>
syn adventuresome, audacious, daredevil, daring, foolhardy, rash, reckless, temerarious, venturesome, venturous
rel bold, doughty, intrepid; brash, harebrained, hotheaded, impetuous, imprudent, madcap, overconfident
con shrinking, timid, timorous; afraid, alarmed, fearful, scared; apprehensive, uneasy
ant unadventurous; cautious

adversary *n* **syn** see OPPONENT
rel assaulter, attacker
con backer, supporter, upholder
ant ally

adverse *adj* **1** acting against or in a contrary direction <hindered by *adverse* forces>
syn antagonistic, anti, antipathetic, opposed, opposing, oppugnant
rel contrary, counter, counteractive; hindering, impeding, obstructive; hostile, unfriendly
con coactive, collaborative, cooperative; adjuvant, synergistic; favorable, propitious
2 being opposed to one's interests <an *adverse* balance of trade>
syn detrimental, negative, unfavorable
rel deleterious, harmful, hurtful, injurious; disadvantageous, prejudicial, unpropitious, unsatisfactory
con advantageous, favorable, positive, propitious, satisfactory

adversity *n* **syn** see MISFORTUNE
rel distress, misery, suffering; deprivation, destitution, indigence, poverty
con bliss, felicity, happiness; comfort, ease
ant prosperity

advert *vb* **syn** see REFER 3
rel animadvert, note, notice, observe, remark
con disregard, ignore, neglect, overlook

advertent *adj* **syn** see ATTENTIVE 1

advertise *vb* **1 syn** see DECLARE 1
rel recount, relate, report; communicate, impart; ballyhoo, promote, propagandize, publicize
con conceal, repress, suppress; bury, hide, obscure
2 syn see PUBLICIZE
3 syn see PROMOTE 3

advertisement *n* **syn** see DECLARATION
rel ballyhoo, promotion, propaganda, publicity

advertising *n* **syn** see PUBLICITY

advice *n* **1** recommendation regarding a decision or course of conduct <benefited from his *advice* on study habits>
syn advisement, counsel
rel direction, guidance, instruction, teaching; admonition; caution, cautioning, forewarning, warning
2 syn see NEWS

advisable *adj* **syn** see EXPEDIENT
rel commendable, desirable; becoming, seemly, suitable; sensible

---

syn synonym(s)   **rel** related word(s)
ant antonym(s)   **con** contrasted word(s)
idiom idiomatic equivalent(s)
‖ use limited; if in doubt, see a dictionary

ant inadvisable

advise *vb* **1** *syn* see COUNSEL
  rel caution, forewarn, warn; coax, induce, persuade, win (over)
  con bedazzle, misadvise, mislead
  2 *syn* see CONFER 2
  rel deliberate
  3 *syn* see INFORM 2
  rel disclose, let out, reveal; communicate, impart

advised *adj syn* see DELIBERATE 1
  rel intended, intentional, meant; knowing, purposeful, willful

advisement *n syn* see ADVICE 1

advocate *n syn* see EXPONENT

advocate *vb* **1** *syn* see ENCOURAGE 2
  2 *syn* see SUPPORT 2
  rel justify, vindicate; advance, forward, promote
  idiom hold a brief for
  con assail, attack; combat, fight, oppose
  ant impugn

aegis *n* **1** *syn* see DEFENSE 1
  2 *syn* see BACKING

aeneous *adj syn* see BRAZEN 4

aeon *n syn* see AGE 2

aerial *adj* **1** *syn* see AIRY 1
  2 *syn* see LOFTY 6
  3 *syn* see AIRY 3
  rel immaterial, incorporeal; impalpable, imperceptible, imponderable

aesthete *n syn* see CONNOISSEUR
  rel perfectionist, stickler; fussbudget, old maid
  con barbarian; clod, lout, oaf

affable *adj* **1** *syn* see GRACIOUS 1
  rel courteous, polite; suave, urbane; loquacious, talkative
  con crabbed, glum, surly; reticent, withdrawn; silent, taciturn, uncommunicative
  ant reserved
  2 *syn* see GENTLE 2

affair *n* **1** something done or dealt with < trying to get at the truth of the *affair* >
  syn business, concern, matter, shooting match, thing
  rel care, lookout, responsibility; pie, proceeding
  idiom cup of tea
  2 *s. n* see BUSINESS 8
  3 *syn* see LOVE AFFAIR
  4 *syn* see AMOUR 2

affect *vb* **1** *syn* see ASSUME 4
  2 *syn* see FREQUENT

affect *vb* to produce a usually mental or emotional effect on one capable of reaction < much *affected* by the touching scene >
  syn carry, get, impress, influence, inspire, move, strike, sway, touch
  rel actuate, draw, drive, impel; penetrate, pierce
  idiom work on

affectation *n syn* see POSE 2
  rel ostentation, pretentiousness
  con ingenuousness, naiveté, naturalness, simplicity, unsophistication
  ant artlessness

affected *adj* **1** *syn* see INTERESTED
  2 *syn* see SELF-CONSCIOUS
  3 *syn* see GENTEEL 3
  4 *syn* see PRECIOUS 4
  5 *syn* see ARTIFICIAL 3

affecting *adj syn* see MOVING 2
  rel piteous, pitiable, pitiful; distressful, distressing, disturbing, troubling

affection *n* **1** *syn* see FEELING 3
  rel leaning, penchant, propensity; bias, predilection; bent, faculty, turn
  con aversion, hate, hatred; dislike, distaste
  ant antipathy
  2 *syn* see LOVE 1
  rel sympathy, tenderness, warmth; attention, concern, interest; doting, enjoying
  con coolness, frigidity
  ant coldness

affection *vb syn* see LOVE 2

affection *n* **1** *syn* see DISEASE 1
  rel access, attack, paroxysm, spell; derangement, disordering, disturbance

2 *syn* see QUALITY 1

affectionate *adj syn* see LOVING
  rel sympathetic, tender, warm
  con apathetic, impassive, stolid; remote, uninterested, withdrawn
  ant cold; undemonstrative

affective *adj syn* see EMOTIONAL 2

affectivity *n syn* see FEELING 3

affianced *adj syn* see ENGAGED 2

affianced *n syn* see BETROTHED

affiche *n syn* see POSTER

affiliated *adj syn* see RELATED
  con autonomous, free, independent
  ant unaffiliated

affiliation *n syn* see ASSOCIATION 1

affinity *n* **1** *syn* see ATTRACTION 2
  con antipathy, aversion; dislike, distaste; repugnance, repellency, repulsion
  2 *syn* see LIKENESS
  rel accord

affirm *vb syn* see ASSERT 1
  rel attest, certify, guarantee, vouch, witness; say, state
  con debate

affirmative *adj syn* see POSITIVE 6

affix *vb syn* see FASTEN 1
  rel add, annex, append, subjoin
  con disengage, disjoin
  ant detach

afflation *n syn* see INSPIRATION

afflatus *n syn* see INSPIRATION

afflict *vb* to inflict upon one something hard to endure < he was *afflicted* with boils >
  syn agonize, crucify, excruciate, harrow, martyr, martyrize, rack, smite, strike, torment, torture, try, wring
  rel annoy, harass, harry, pester, plague, press, worry; bother, irk, vex; lacerate, wound
  con console, delight, gladden, please, rejoice; ease, relieve, solace
  ant comfort

afflicted *adj syn* see WOEFUL 1

affliction *n* **1** *syn* see TRIAL 1
  rel mischance, mishap
  con alleviation, assuagement, easement, relief
  ant consolation, solace
  2 *syn* see SORROW
  3 *syn* see SICKNESS 1

afflictive *adj* **1** *syn* see PAINFUL 1
  2 *syn* see DEPLORABLE
  3 *syn* see BITTER 2

affluent *adj syn* see RICH 1
  rel acquisitive, grasping
  con poor; bankrupt, impoverished
  ant impecunious; straitened

affranchise *vb syn* see ENFRANCHISE

affray *n* **1** *syn* see BRAWL 2
  2 *syn* see CLASH 2

affright *vb syn* see FRIGHTEN
  rel bewilder, confound
  con animate, fire, inspire
  ant embolden, nerve

affront *vb* **1** *syn* see OFFEND 3
  rel criticize, dispraise
  con compliment; laud, praise; dignify, honor
  2 *syn* see CONFRONT 1

affront *n* a speech or an action designed to impugn the honor or worth of someone or something < her costume was an *affront* to the solemnity of the occasion >
  syn contumely, despite, indignity, insult, slap
  rel dishonor, flouting, offense, outrage, slight; aspersion, barb, defamation, dig
  idiom slap in the face
  con deference, homage, honor; adulation, compliment, flattery

aficionado *n syn* see ADDICT

afield *adj syn* see AMISS 2

afire *adj* **1** *syn* see BURNING 1
  2 *syn* see ALIGHT 2

aflame *adj* **1** *syn* see BURNING 1
  2 *syn* see ALIGHT 2

aflicker *adj syn* ALIGHT 2, ablaze, afire, aflame, aglow
à fond *adv syn* see WELL 3
aforementioned *adj syn* see SUCH 1
aforesaid *adj syn* see SUCH 1
aforethought *adj syn* see DELIBERATE 1
afraid *adj* **1** suffering the effects of apprehension, fear, or terror
 <too *afraid* to even cry for help>
   syn aghast, anxious, ‖ascared, fearful, frightened, scared, scary,
   terrified; *compare* FEARFUL 2
   rel shrinking, shy, timid, timorous; cautious, chary, wary;
   jumpy, skittish
   idiom frightened out of one's wits, in a (blue) funk, scared to
   death, terror stricken
   con confident, dauntless, fearless; assured, collected, poised,
   self-possessed
   ant unafraid
 2 *syn* see FEARFUL 2
   idiom all of a twitter (or flutter)
   ant unafraid; sanguine
 3 *syn* see DISINCLINED
afresh *adv* **1** *syn* see OVER 7
 2 *syn* see NEW
‖**African dominoes** *n pl syn* see DICE
aft *adv syn* see ABAFT
   rel hind, posterior
   con ahead, before, forward
   ant fore
after *adv* so as to follow in time or space <*after*, we turned
   toward home>
   syn afterward, afterwhile, behind, by and by, infra, later, latterly, next, subsequently
   rel abaft, aft, astern
   idiom after a time (or while), in the wake of
   con ahead, forward
   ant before
after *prep* **1** so as to resemble or follow in some respect <named
   after his father>
   syn for, from
 2 later in time or lower in place or rank <*after* our discus-
   sion>
   syn behind, below, following, next, since, subsequent to
   con ante, ere, in advance of, preceding, prior to
   ant before
 3 *syn* see BEYOND 1
after *adj* **1** *syn* see SUBSEQUENT 1
 2 *syn* see POSTERIOR 2
   con antecedent, preceding, prior
after all *adv syn* see HOWEVER
aftereffect *n syn* see EFFECT 1
   rel remainder, residual, residuum
afterlife *n* **1** *syn* see ETERNITY 2
 2 *syn* see HEREAFTER 2
afterlight *n syn* see REVIEW 5
aftermath *n syn* see EFFECT 1
   rel remainder, residual, residuum
aftertime *n syn* see FUTURE
afterward *adv syn* see AFTER
afterward *n syn* see FUTURE
afterwhile *adv syn* see AFTER
afterword *n syn* see EPILOGUE 1
afterworld *n syn* see HEREAFTER 2
again *adv* **1** *syn* see ABOUT 6
 2 *syn* see OVER 7
 3 *syn* see THEN 1
 4 as another point, fact, or instance <*again*, consider taxes>
   syn additionally, also, besides, further, in addition, then; *compare* ALSO 2
   idiom by the same token, into the bargain, on top of that
 5 as an alternative and especially a converse <he may win and
   again he may not>
   syn contra, contrariwise, contrary, contrawise, conversely, oppositely, vice versa; *compare* HOWEVER
   idiom at the same time, be that as it may, just the same, on the
   other hand
again and again *adv syn* see OFTEN
against *prep* **1** directly opposite <stood *against* the crowd and
   shouted for order>
   syn contra, facing, fronting, over against, toward, vis-à-vis

   idiom counter to, face to face with
 2 so as to touch <vines trained *against* the wall>
   syn to, touching
   idiom in contact with, next to
 3 *syn* see VERSUS 1
 4 without being prevented or obstructed by <succeeded *against*
   grave handicaps>
   syn despite, in spite of, notwithstanding, regardless of
   idiom in the face of
 5 *syn* see FROM 2
 6 *syn* see APROPOS
agape *adj syn* see AGHAST 2
age *n* **1** *syn* see OLD AGE
   ant youth
 2 *often* **ages** *pl* a long or seemingly long period of time <ha-
   ven't seen her for *ages*>
   syn aeon, blue moon, coon's age, dog's age, donkey's years,
   eternity, long
   idiom month of Sundays, ‖right smart spell
   con flash, instant, minute, moment, second, split second, trice
 3 *syn* see PERIOD 2
age *vb syn* see MATURE
aged *adj* **1** being in the declining phase of life <*aged* pensioners>
   syn ancient, elderly, old, olden
   rel pensioned (off), retired, superannuated; senior; hoary, patriarchal, venerable; doddering, senescent, senile, tottery
   idiom along in years, getting on, getting on (or along) in years,
   gray with age, on one's last legs, stricken with years
   con juvenile, puerile
   ant youthful
 2 *syn* see ANCIENT 1
 3 *syn* see RIPE 3
ageless *adj syn* see ETERNAL 4
agency *n syn* see MEAN 2
   rel antecedent, cause, determinant; gear
agenda *n syn* see PROGRAM 1
agent *n* **1** *syn* see MEAN 2
   rel doer, executive, executor, performer; actor, worker; activator, energizer
 2 one who acts for another <diplomatic *agents* serving
   abroad>
   syn assignee, attorney, deputy, factor, proxy; *compare* DELEGATE
   rel go-between, middleman; instrument, minister, tool; commis-
   sioner, institor, proctor, procurator, representative, steward;
   buyer, commissionaire
   ant principal
 3 *syn* see SPY
age-old *adj syn* see ANCIENT 1
agglomerate *n syn* see AGGREGATE 1
   rel heap, mass, pile
agglomeration *n* **1** *syn* see ACCUMULATION
   rel association, combination
 2 *syn* see AGGREGATE 1
aggrandize *vb* **1** *syn* see INCREASE 1
   rel amplify, build up
 2 *syn* see EXALT 1
   ant belittle
aggrandizement *n syn* see APOTHEOSIS 2
aggravate *vb* **1** *syn* see INTENSIFY
   rel augment, enlarge, increase, multiply; aggrandize
   con extenuate, palliate
   ant alleviate
 2 *syn* see IRRITATE
   rel disturb, perturb, upset; annoy, bedevil
   con calm, tranquilize
   ant appease
aggravation *n syn* see ANNOYANCE 2
aggregate *vb syn* see AMOUNT 1
aggregate *n* **1** a mass or body formed of particles or parts that
   retain their individuality <an *aggregate* of ill-planned ar-
   guments>
   syn agglomerate, agglomeration, aggregation, conglomerate,
   conglomeration; *compare* ACCUMULATION

---

syn synonym(s)   *rel* related word(s)
ant antonym(s)   *con* contrasted word(s)
idiom idiomatic equivalent(s)
‖ use limited; if in doubt, see a dictionary

ant constituent, element
2 syn see BODY 5
ant individual, unit; particular
3 syn see WHOLE 1
aggregation *n* **1 syn** see AGGREGATE 1
ant constituent, element
2 syn see ACCUMULATION
rel backlog, reserve, stockpile
3 syn see GATHERING 2
aggress *vb* **syn** see ATTACK 1
aggression *n* **1 syn** see ATTACK 1
2 syn see ATTACK 2
rel incursion, inroad, invasion, raid; irruption
ant resistance
aggressive *adj* marked by bold determination and readiness for conflict < an *aggressive* fighter >
syn assertive, assertory, militant, pushful, pushing, pushy, self-assertive
rel belligerent, combative, contentious, scrappy; domineering, imperious, masterful, tough; energetic, hard-hitting, strenuous, vigorous
con passive, unassertive; meek, submissive, yielding
aggressiveness *n* **syn** see ATTACK 2
aggrieve *vb* **1 syn** see DISTRESS 2
rel abuse, misuse, outrage; pain
con delight, gladden, please
2 syn see WRONG
rel afflict, torment, try; annoy, harass, harry, plague, worry
con benefit, profit
aghast *adj* **1 syn** see AFRAID 1
rel appalled, horrified, horror-struck; undone, unmanned
idiom scared stiff (*or* white)
2 struck by an intense emotional reaction (as surprise, disgust, or bewilderment) < *aghast* at the lack of discipline >
syn agape, confounded, dismayed, dumbfounded, overwhelmed, shocked, thunderstruck
rel agog, amazed, startled; awed, awestricken; astonished, flabbergasted, surprised
idiom struck all of a heap, taken aback, unable to believe one's eyes (*or* senses)
con acceptant, acquiescent, tolerant
agile *adj* acting or moving with easy alacrity < an *agile* mind >
syn active, brisk, brisky, catty, lively, nimble, sprightly, spry, volant, yare, zippy
rel adroit, deft, dexterous; fleet, quick, speedy; limber, lissome, lithe, supple; light-footed, tripping
con inactive, inert, passive; heavy, lethargic, logy; dull, slow, sluggish
ant torpid
agitable *adj* **syn** see EXCITABLE
agitate *vb* **1 syn** see SHAKE 4
rel bounce, joggle, jounce; actuate, drive, impel, move
con lull, quiet, still
2 syn see DISCOMPOSE 1
rel exasperate, irritate, peeve, provoke, rile, ruffle
ant calm, tranquilize
3 syn see DISCUSS 1
rel air, broach, ventilate; consider; assail, attack
agitation *n* **syn** see COMMOTION 2
rel ado, bustle, disturbance, stir
ant tranquillity
agitator *n* **syn** see INSTIGATOR
aglow *adj* **syn** see ALIGHT 2
rel gleaming, glowing, shining; lucent, luminous, radiant
agnate *adj* **1 syn** see RELATED
2 syn see LIKE
agog *adj* **syn** see EAGER
rel aroused, roused, stirred; excited, galvanized, stimulated; restive; zestful
ant aloof
agonize *vb* **1 syn** see AFFLICT
rel distress, trouble; chafe, fret, gall
2 syn see WRITHE 1
rel bear, endure, suffer
agonizing *adj* **syn** see EXCRUCIATING
rel exquisite, fierce, intense, vehement, violent
agony *n* **syn** see DISTRESS
con repose, rest

agrarian *adj* **syn** see WILD 1
agree *vb* **1 syn** see ACKNOWLEDGE 2
rel allow, concede, grant, own
con except, exclude
ant deny
2 syn see ASSENT
rel allow, concede, grant; receive; acknowledge, admit
con expostulate, kick, object, remonstrate; balk, demur, jib; oppose, resist, withstand
ant protest (against); differ (with)
3 to achieve harmony (as of opinion, feeling, or purpose) < they *agreed* finally on all major issues >
syn coincide, concert, concord, concur, harmonize
rel coact, cooperate, unite
idiom fall in with, hit it off with
con bicker, quarrel, squabble, wrangle; argue, debate, dispute, hassle
ant differ; disagree
4 to exist or go together without conflict or incongruity < his conclusion *agrees* with the evidence >
syn accord, check, check out, cohere, comport, conform, consist, consort, correspond, dovetail, fit (in), ‖gee, go, harmonize, jibe, march, quadrate, rhyme, square, suit, tally
rel approach, equal, match, rival, touch; complete, fulfill, round out, supplement
idiom go hand in hand
con negate, negative, nullify; clash, conflict, jar
ant differ (from)
agree (with) *vb* **syn** see SUIT 4
agreeability *n* **syn** see AMENITY 1
agreeable *adj* **1 syn** see PLEASANT 1
rel delectable, delightful
ant disagreeable
2 syn see CONSONANT 1
con conflicting, inharmonious, jarring, uncongenial
agreeableness *n* **syn** see AMENITY 1
agreed *adv* **syn** see YES 1
agreement *n* **1 syn** see HARMONY 2
ant disagreement
2 a settlement reached by parties to a dispute or negotiation < the company has reached an *agreement* with the striking workers >
syn accord, deal, understanding; *compare* CONTRACT
rel cartel, concordat, convention, entente, pact; compact, contract, covenant, treaty; engagement
3 syn see TREATY
4 syn see CONTRACT
agrestal *adj* **syn** see WILD 1
agrestic *adj* **syn** see RURAL
agriculture *n* the science or business of raising useful plants and animals < opening the country for *agriculture* >
syn farming, husbandry
aground *adj* being or becoming forced onto the ground or shore < the boat is *aground* and breaking up >
syn beached, grounded, stranded
idiom high and dry, on the rocks
ant afloat
ahead *adv* **1 syn** see BEFORE 1
con after
ant behind
2 further on in the direction in question < the road stretched *ahead* toward the west >
syn alee, forth, forward, onward
ahead of *prep* **syn** see BEFORE 1
aid *vb* **syn** see HELP 1
rel alleviate, lighten, mitigate, relieve
ant impede
aid *n* **1 syn** see HELP 1
2 syn see HELP 2
rel alleviation, assuagement, mitigation; backing, support
idiom a leg up
con check, curb, restraint; bar, obstacle, obstruction
ant impediment
3 syn see HELPER
4 syn see ASSISTANT 2
rel aider, befriender, benefactor, ministrant, succorer; striker
aidant *adj* **syn** see HELPFUL 1
aide *n* **syn** see ASSISTANT 2

aide–de–camp *n syn* see ASSISTANT 2
aiding *adj syn* see HELPFUL 1
ail *vb syn* see TROUBLE 1
   rel afflict, try
   idiom be the matter (with), give one trouble
   con alleviate, ease, relieve; comfort, console, solace
ailing *adj syn* see UNWELL
   rel debilitated, enfeebled, gone, strengthless, weak; droopy, limp, sapless, spiritless
   con hale, lusty, robust, rugged, vigorous
ailment *n* **1** *syn* see DISEASE
   2 *syn* see UNREST
aim *vb* **1** *syn* see DIRECT 2
   rel concentrate, fix, focus
   idiom draw a bead on, take aim
   2 to have as a controlling desire something that transcends one's present capacity for attainment <from a boy he had *aimed* at high office>
   syn aspire, pant
   rel attempt, endeavor, essay, strive, try; design, intend, propose, purpose; covet, crave, yearn (for)
   idiom have an eye to, reach for the stars, set one's eyes upon
   3 *syn* see INTEND 2
   rel choose, desire, want, wish; expect
   idiom have (*or* keep) in view, promise oneself (to)
   4 *syn* see SLANT 2
aim *n syn* see AMBITION 2
   rel desideratum, desire, idol, urge
   idiom end in view
aimless *adj syn* see RANDOM
air *n* **1** *syn* see BEARING 1
   rel manner, style
   2 *usu* **airs** *pl syn* see POSE 2
   rel loftiness, ostentation, pretentiousness, show; complacency, self-importance, vainglory, vanity
   3 a pervading influence that colors outward appearance or apparent character <the village had an *air* of decay>
   syn atmosphere, aura, feel, feeling, mood, semblance
   rel character, property, quality
   con basis, essence, reality
   4 *syn* see MELODY
air *vb syn* see EXPRESS 2
   rel discover, divulge, reveal; broadcast, declare, proclaim, publish
   idiom make public, noise (*or* sound) abroad, spread far and wide
airless *adj syn* see STUFFY 1
airman *n syn* see PILOT 2
airy *adj* **1** of or relating to air <clouds drifting on *airy* currents>
   syn aerial, atmospheric, pneumatic
   rel gaseous, vaporous
   2 *syn* see LOFTY 6
   rel exposed, windswept; supernal
   3 resembling or suggesting air especially in lightness or lack of substance <*airy* persiflage>
   syn aerial, ethereal, vaporous, vapory
   rel frivolous, light, volatile; rare, rarefied, tenuous, thin; dainty, delicate, diaphanous, exquisite, spirituel
   con corporeal, material, physical; bulky, massive, massy
   ant substantial
   4 *syn* see ELASTIC 2
   rel animated, high-spirited, spirited
   5 *syn* see WINDY 1
akin *adj* **1** *syn* see RELATED
   2 *syn* see LIKE
   rel kindred; according, agreeing, conforming, harmonizing
   con extraneous, foreign
   ant alien
alacrity *n* promptness in responding or acting <accepted the invitation with *alacrity*>
   syn dispatch, expedition, goodwill, promptitude, readiness
   rel briskness, eagerness; enthusiasm, fervor, heartiness, zeal; promptness, quickness
   con hesitation, procrastination, temporization, vacillation; apathy, indifference, lethargy, phlegm, sluggishness
   ant dilatoriness
a la mode *adj syn* see STYLISH
alarm *n* **1** a signal that warns or calls to action <the door's squeak gave the *alarm*>

   syn alert, SOS, tocsin
   rel caution, forewarning, prenotice, warning
   2 *syn* see FEAR 1
   rel upset; strain, stress, tension
   con calm, calmness, serenity, tranquillity; equanimity, sangfroid
   ant assurance; composure
alarm *vb syn* see FRIGHTEN
   rel amaze, astonish, surprise
   idiom give one a turn
   con comfort, console, solace
   ant assure, relieve
alarmable *adj syn* see EXCITABLE
albeit *conj syn* see THOUGH
album *n syn* see ANTHOLOGY
alcohol *n syn* see LIQUOR 2
alcoholic *adj syn* see SPIRITUOUS
alcoholized *adj syn* see INTOXICATED 1
alcove *n syn* see SUMMERHOUSE
alee *adv syn* see AHEAD 2
alehouse *n* an establishment serving primarily beer and ale <warm country *alehouses*>
   syn beer garden, beer hall, ‖beerhouse, bierstube, mughouse, stube; *compare* BAR 4
   rel barrelhouse, bistro, bottle club, brasserie, cabaret, café, honky-tonk, nightclub, rathskeller, roadhouse, wineshop
alembicated *adj syn* see PRECIOUS 4
alert *adj* **1** *syn* see WATCHFUL
   rel attentive, heedful, mindful; careful
   idiom all eyes and ears, on (one's) guard, on the alert
   con inattentive, unmindful; aloof, detached, indifferent, unconcerned
   2 *syn* see INTELLIGENT 2
   rel apt, prompt, quick, ready
   con lackadaisical, languid, listless
   3 *syn* see LIVELY 1
   rel frisky; mercurial
   idiom full of life
   con inactive, indolent
   ant inert
alert *n syn* see ALARM 1
alfresco *adj syn* see OUTDOOR
algetic *adj syn* see PAINFUL 1
alias *n syn* see PSEUDONYM
alibi *n syn* see EXCUSE 1
alien *adj syn* see EXTRINSIC
   rel exotic, outlandish, strange; incompatible, incongrous, inconsonant
   con cognate, kindred, related; compatible, congenial, congruous, consonant; germane, material, pertinent, relevant
   ant akin; assimilable
alien *n syn* see STRANGER
   con national, subject
   ant citizen
alien *vb* **1** *syn* see ESTRANGE
   rel alter, change, convert
   con accommodate, adjust, conform, reconcile
   ant unite; reunite
   2 *syn* see TRANSFER 4
   rel give up, hand over, relinquish
alienate *vb* **1** *syn* see TRANSFER 4
   rel give up, hand over, relinquish
   2 *syn* see ESTRANGE
   rel alter, change, convert
   con accommodate, adjust, conform, reconcile
   ant unite; reunite
alienation *n* **1** *syn* see ESTRANGEMENT
   2 *syn* see INSANITY 1
alight *vb* to come to rest after or as if after a flight, a descent, or a fall <snowflakes *alighting* on the bare trees>
   syn land, light, perch, roost, set down, settle, sit down, touch down
   rel drop, fall, tumble
   con arise, ascend, rise, soar

---

syn synonym(s)	*rel* related word(s)
ant antonym(s)	*con* contrasted word(s)
idiom idiomatic equivalent(s)	
‖ use limited; if in doubt, see a dictionary	

alight *adj* **1** *syn* see BURNING 1
 2 made bright by or as if by fire < her face *alight* with joy >
 syn ablaze, afire, aflame, aflicker, aglow
 rel bright, effulgent, fulgent, refulgent; blazing, flaming, flaring, glowing
 con dark, dusky, gloomy, heavy, lowery, shadowed, shadowy

align *vb* *syn* see LINE 1
 rel adjust, fix, regulate
 con unsettle

alike *adj* *syn* see LIKE
 con separate
 ant unlike; different

alikeness *n* *syn* see LIKENESS

aliment *n* *syn* see FOOD 2

alimentary *adj* *syn* see NUTRITIVE 1

alimentation *n* *syn* see LIVING

alimentative *adj* *syn* see NUTRITIVE 1

alimony *n* *syn* see LIVING

alive *adj* **1** *syn* see LIVING 1
 con inactive, inert
 ant dead, defunct
 2 *syn* see EXTANT 1
 3 *syn* see ACTIVE 1
 rel fresh, green, verdant
 con dormant, inactive, quiescent
 ant dead, extinct
 4 *syn* see AWARE
 rel vigilant, watchful, wide-awake; intelligent, quick, quick-witted
 con heedless, inattentive, oblivious, unmindful; careless, neglectful, negligent
 ant blind (to)
 5 full of vigorous life, animation, or activity < the streets were *alive* with shoppers >
 syn abounding, overflowing, replete, rife, swarming, teeming, thronged
 rel crowded, populous, thick; filled, flush, full
 con barren, empty, vacant, void; unoccupied, unpopulated, untenanted

all *adj* **1** *syn* see WHOLE 4
 rel full, plenary
 2 each member or individual of < *all* my friends came with me >
 syn each, every
 ant no

all *adv* **1** without exception < the money was *all* spent >
 syn all in all, altogether, exactly, in toto, just, purely, quite, stick, totally, utterly, wholly
 idiom in its entirety
 2 *syn* see APIECE

all *pron* **1** *syn* see EVERYTHING
 2 *syn* see EVERYBODY

all *n* *syn* see WHOLE 1

all–around *adj* **1** *syn* see VERSATILE
 rel complete, consummate
 2 not narrowly particularized < taking an *all-around* view of the problem >
 syn comprehensive, general, global, inclusive, overall, sweeping
 rel broad, extensive, panoramic, wide; all-inclusive, unexcluding, unexclusive, wide-ranging; synoptic
 con express, particular, specific; narrow, precise, restricted; individual, singular

allay *vb* **1** *syn* see RELIEVE 1
 con arouse, rouse, stir; excite, provoke, stimulate; aggravate, enhance
 ant intensify
 2 *syn* see CALM
 rel ease, soften, subdue; deaden, dull, temper; disburden, disembarrass, disencumber; deliver, free, release
 con aggravate, enhance, heighten, magnify, worsen
 ant intensify

all but *adv* **1** *syn* see NEARLY
 2 *syn* see ALMOST 2

allege *vb* *syn* see ADDUCE
 rel affirm, assert, avouch, avow, declare, profess; recite, recount, rehearse, state
 con contradict, deny, gainsay, impugn, negate, negative; controvert, disprove, rebut, refute

ant contravene

alleged *adj* of questionable truth or genuineness < had doubts of the *alleged* miracle >
 syn ostensible, pretended, professed, purported, so-called, supposed; *compare* SUPPOSED 1
 rel credible, plausible, specious; doubtful, dubious, questionable; self-styled, soi-disant, would-be
 idiom in name only
 con authentic, bona fide, genuine, veritable; actual, real, true; delusory, erroneous, fallacious, false, illusory, imaginary, unreal

allegiance *n* *syn* see FIDELITY 1
 rel firmness; consecration, dedication; deference, homage, honor
 con alienation, disaffection; disloyalty, treason

allegiant *adj* *syn* see FAITHFUL 1

allegory *n* **1** a method of indirect representation (as in literature or art) of ideas or truths < by *allegory* such abstractions as love and fear can be depicted >
 syn figuration, symbolism, symbolization, typification
 2 a literary form that tells a story to present a truth or enforce a moral < Orwell's *Animal Farm* is a well-known English *allegory* >
 syn apologue, fable, myth, parable; *compare* MYTH 1

allergy *n* *syn* see ANTIPATHY 2
 rel rejection, repulsion, revulsion
 con affinity, attraction, sympathy

alleviate *vb* *syn* see RELIEVE 1
 rel cure, remedy
 idiom temper the wind to the shorn lamb
 con augment, heighten, intensify
 ant aggravate

alleviation *n* *syn* see EASE 3

all–fired *adj* *syn* see UTTER

alliance *n* **1** *syn* see ASSOCIATION 1
 2 an association (as of nations) for a common object < a world *alliance* in support of peace >
 syn anschluss, coalition, confederacy, confederation, federation, league, union; *compare* UNIFICATION
 rel association, club, order, society

allied *adj* *syn* see RELATED
 rel linked, united; parallel, similar
 con alien, extraneous, foreign; discrete, separate, several
 ant unallied

all in *adj* *syn* see EFFETE 2
 idiom at last gasp

all in all *adv* **1** *syn* see ALL 1
 2 *syn* see ALTOGETHER 3

allineate *vb* *syn* see LINE 1

allness *n* *syn* see ENTIRETY 1

allocate *vb* **1** *syn* see ALLOT
 con reserve, sequester, stockpile
 2 *syn* see DESIGNATE 3

allocution *n* *syn* see SPEECH 2

allot *vb* to give as one's share, portion, role, or place < *allotted* himself a daily hour for exercise >
 syn admeasure, allocate, allow, apportion, assign, give, lot, mete (out)
 rel deal (out), dispense, distribute, dole (out); equip, fit out, furnish; accord, grant, vouchsafe; appoint, ordain, prescribe
 con detain, hold, hold back, keep, retain, withhold; appropriate, arrogate, confiscate

allotment *n* **1** *syn* see SHARE 1
 2 *syn* see RATION

all–out *adj* *syn* see TOTAL 5

all over *adv* *syn* see EVERYWHERE 1

allover *adj* *syn* see OMNIPRESENT

‖**all–overs** *n pl* *syn* see JITTERS

allow *vb* **1** *syn* see ALLOT
 rel bestow, confer
 con refuse
 2 *syn* see ACKNOWLEDGE 1
 rel accede, acquiesce, assent
 con confute, refute, reject
 ant disallow
 3 *syn* see LET 2
 rel brook, endure, stand, tolerate; defer, submit, yield
 con avert, prevent, ward (off)
 ant inhibit

allowable *adj* *syn* see PERMISSIBLE

allowance *n* **1** *syn* see RATION
rel assignment; appropriation, grant, subsidy
2 *syn* see SHARE 1
3 *syn* see ADVANTAGE 3
rel aid, assistance, help; bounty, grant, subsidy
4 *syn* see PERMISSION
rel countenance, favor; indulgence, toleration
con refusal, rejection; contradiction, contravention, negation
5 a taking into account of extenuating circumstances or of contingencies <we must make *allowance* for the inexperience of youth>
syn concession
rel accommodation, adaptation, adjustment; extenuation, mitigation, palliation
alloy *n* **1** *syn* see ADMIXTURE 1
2 *syn* see MIXTURE
all–powerful *adj syn* see OMNIPOTENT
all right *adv syn* see YES 1
all right *adj syn* see DECENT 4
all round (or **all around**) *adv syn* see EVERYWHERE 1
all there *adj syn* see SANE 2
all told *adv syn* see ALTOGETHER 3
allude *vb syn* see REFER 3
rel hint, imply, intimate, suggest
allure *vb* **1** *syn* see ATTRACT 1
rel delude; woo
con avoid, elude, eschew, shun; alienate, disaffect, estrange, wean
2 *syn* see LURE
allure *n syn* see CHARM 3
allurement *n* **1** *syn* see ATTRACTION 1
2 *syn* see LURE 2
alluring *adj syn* see ATTRACTIVE 1
rel appetizing; beguiling, delusive
con repellent; disagreeable, displeasing, uninviting, unlikable, unpleasant
ant repulsive
almighty *adj syn* see OMNIPOTENT
almost *adv* **1** *syn* see NEARLY
2 not actually but in effect <he paid *almost* nothing for it>
syn all but, as good as, as much as, essentially, practically, well-nigh; *compare* VIRTUALLY
idiom for all practical purposes, in effect, just about, to all intents and purposes
alms *n pl syn* see DONATION
aloft *adv syn* see OVER 4
rel high; skyward, upward
idiom in the clouds
alone *adj* **1** separated from others <the house was *alone* on a windy ridge>
syn apart, detached, isolate, isolated, removed, unaccompanied
rel out-of-the-way, private, remote, retired, secluded, withdrawn
idiom off the beaten track
con adjacent, close-by, near-at-hand, nearly, neighboring, nigh
2 *syn* see LONE 1
3 having no equal or rival and being single in kind or excellence <a drug *alone* in its curative powers>
syn matchless, only, peerless, unequaled, unique, unmatched, unparalleled, unrivaled; *compare* SUPREME
rel inimitable; incomparable, unexcelled, unsurpassed; excellent, good, superior
idiom second to none
con common, commonplace, everyday, ordinary, usual; accustomed, conventional, customary, regular
4 *syn* see ONLY 2
alone *adv syn* see ONLY 1
aloneness *n syn* see SOLITUDE
along *adv* **1** so as to make forward progress <hurrying *along* toward town>
syn forth, forward, on, onward; *compare* AHEAD 2
2 *syn* see ALSO 2
alongside *prep syn* see BESIDE 1
aloof *adj* **1** *syn* see INDIFFERENT 2
rel arrogant, disdainful, haughty, proud; chilly, cold, cool, frigid; constrained, reserved, restrained, reticent, standoffish
con affable, companionable, gregarious, sociable, social; friendly, neighborly
ant familiar; outgoing

2 *syn* see UNSOCIABLE
alp *n syn* see MOUNTAIN 1
alpha *n syn* see BEGINNING
ant omega
alphabet *n* **1** a set of characters in which a language can be written <the Greek *alphabet*>
syn ABC(s), christcross-row, letters
2 the simplest fundamental part or level <learning the *alphabet* of science>
syn ABC's, elements, fundamentals, grammar, principles, rudiments
rel beginning, commencement, start; outset
idiom first steps
con entirety, total, whole; details, minutiae, trivia
already *adv* **1** *syn* see BEFORE 2
2 *syn* see EVEN 2
also *adv* **1** in the same manner <those *also* serve who support the workers>
syn correspondingly, likewise, similarly, so
idiom in like manner
2 in addition to that <he was stern but *also* just>
syn additionally, along, as well, besides, futhermore, item, likewise, more, moreover, still, too, withal, yea, yet
idiom into the bargain, on top of that, to boot
3 *syn* see AGAIN 4
alter *vb* **1** *syn* see CHANGE 1
rel accommodate, adapt, adjust, moderate, modulate, temper; doctor
idiom work a change (in)
con conserve, keep, preserve, retain
ant fix
2 *syn* see STERILIZE
alteration *n* **1** *syn* see CHANGE 1
rel accommodation, adaptation, adjustment; conversion, metamorphosis, transformation; fluctuation, shilly-shally, vacillation, wavering
con perdurability, permanence, stability; continuance, endurance, persistence
ant fixation, fixity
2 *syn* see TRANSITION
3 *syn* see CONVERSION 2
altercate *vb syn* see QUARREL
rel agitate, argue, debate, dispute
con accord, get along; accommodate, adapt, adjust, conform
ant concur
altercation *n syn* see QUARREL
rel argument; combat, contest
con agreement, concord, consonance, harmony; empathy, likemindedness, sympathy, understanding
ant accord; concurrence
alterity *n syn* see DISSIMILARITY
alternate *adj* **1** *syn* see INTERMITTENT
rel alternant, alternating, rotating; complementary, corresponding, reciprocal
con sequent, successive
ant consecutive
2 *syn* see SUBSTITUTE 1
rel equivalent, proxy, replacing; exchangeable, interchangeable; makeshift, provisional, tentative
alternate *vb syn* see ROTATE 2
rel fluctuate, oscillate, sway, waver; recur, return, revert
con follow, succeed
alternate *n syn* see SUBSTITUTE
alternately *adv syn* see INSTEAD
alternation *n syn* see SUCCESSION 2
rel recurrence, return, reversion; reappearance, repetition
alternative *adj syn* see SUBSTITUTE 1
rel equivalent, proxy, replacing; exchangeable, interchangeable; makeshift, provisional, tentative
alternative *n syn* see CHOICE 1
rel attainable, contingency, possibility
alternatively *adv syn* see INSTEAD
although *conj syn* see THOUGH

---

syn synonym(s)   *rel* related word(s)
ant antonym(s)   *con* contrasted word(s)
idiom idiomatic equivalent(s)
‖ use limited; if in doubt, see a dictionary

altitude *n syn* see HEIGHT
  rel apex, eminence, peak, summit
  con depth
altitudinous *adj syn* see HIGH 1
altogether *adv* **1** *syn* see WELL 3
  2 *syn* see ALL 1
  3 as a total <*altogether* it cost over a thousand dollars>
  syn all told, in all, quite
  idiom taken together
  4 with minor exceptions or flaws <*altogether* the party was a success>
  syn all in all, by and large, en masse, generally, on the whole
  idiom all things considered, as a whole, for the most part, generally speaking, in the main
altruistic *adj syn* see CHARITABLE 1
  rel considerate, kind, unselfish; bounteous, bountiful, generous, liberal, open-handed; bighearted, magnanimous, noble-minded
  con egotistic, self-centered, selfish, self-seeking; illiberal, mean, niggardly, stingy, ungenerous
  ant egoistic
always *adv* **1** on every relevant occasion <*always* made the same mistake>
  syn constantly, continuously, ever, invariably, perpetually
  rel frequently, often, regularly, usually
  idiom in every case (*or* instance), without exception
  con rarely, seldom
  ant never
  2 *syn* see EVER 2
‖**amah** *n syn* see NURSEMAID
amalgam *n syn* see MIXTURE
amalgamate *vb syn* see MIX 1
  rel compact, consolidate, unify
  con crumble, decompose, disintegrate; disperse, dissipate, scatter
amalgamation *n* **1** *syn* see MIXTURE
  2 *syn* see CONSOLIDATION 2
amaranthine *adj syn* see EVERLASTING 1
amaroidal *adj syn* see ACRID
amass *vb syn* see ACCUMULATE
  ant distribute
amassment *n syn* see ACCUMULATION
amateur *n* **1** one having a marked and usually informed taste or liking for something <an *amateur* of fine fabrics>
  syn admirer, devotee, fan, fancier, votary
  rel crank, enthusiast, faddist, infatuate, ‖nut, zealot; aesthete, cognoscente, connoisseur, dilettante; illuminato, illuminist
  con abecedarian, dabbler, tyro; adept, expert
  2 one who follows a pursuit without attaining mastery or professional status <a nation handicapped by *amateurs* in high office>
  syn abecedarian, dabbler, dilettante, nonprofessional, smatterer, tyro, uninitiate
  rel beginner, greenhorn, neophyte; apprentice, novice, probationer; potterer, putterer, tinker
  con adept, virtuoso, wizard
  ant expert, master; professional
amateurish *adj* lacking or marked by lack of expert skill or finish <an *amateurish* actor>
  syn dabbling, dilettante, dilettantish, dilettantist, jackleg, unaccomplished, unfinished, ungifted, unskilled
  rel clumsy, crude, green, raw, untutored; defective, deficient, faulty, flawed
  con accomplished, expert, gifted, skilled
  ant professional
amative *adj syn* see EROTIC
amatory *adj syn* see EROTIC
  rel admiring, attracted, yearning
amaze *vb syn* see SURPRISE 2
  rel affect, impress, move, strike, touch
amaze *n syn* see WONDER 2
  rel confoundment; surprise
amazement *n syn* see WONDER 2
  rel confoundment; surprise
amazing *adj syn* see MARVELOUS 1
amazon *n syn* see VIRAGO
ambidextrous *adj* **1** *syn* see TWO-HANDED 2
  2 *syn* see VERSATILE
  3 *syn* see INSINCERE

ambience *n syn* see ENVIRONMENT
ambient *n syn* see ENVIRONMENT
ambiguity *n* expression or an expression obscure because subject to more than one interpretation <a speech full of *ambiguities*>
  syn amphibology, double entendre, double meaning, equivocality, equivocation, equivoque, tergiversation
  rel dodge, evasion, hedge, quibble, shift, subterfuge; cavil, haggling, hair-splitting, quibbling; obscurity, uncertainty, vagueness
  con definiteness, expressness, specificity; clearness, exactness, precision
  ant explicitness; lucidity
ambiguous *adj* **1** *syn* see OBSCURE 3
  rel doubtful, dubious, questionable
  con clear, lucid, perspicuous; categorical, express, specific
  ant explicit
  2 *syn* see DOUBTFUL 1
ambit *n* **1** *syn* see CIRCUMFERENCE
  2 *syn* see RANGE 2
ambition *n* **1** strong desire for advancement <a life ruled by *ambition*>
  syn ambitiousness, aspiration, pretension
  rel drive, go-ahead, push; anxiety, avidity, eagerness, keenness; energy, enterprise, spirit; goad, incentive, motive, spur
  con contentment, satisfaction; faineance, indolence, lethargy, sloth
  2 an object of desire or intent <his *ambition* was to have enough to live on without working>
  syn aim, goal, mark, objective, quaesitum, target; *compare* INTENTION
  rel design, intent, purpose; desire, fancy, hope, wish; dream, ideal, nirvana
  3 *syn* see ENTERPRISE 4
ambitious *adj* **1** marked by intense desire for advancement (as in power, fame, or wealth) <a ruthlessly *ambitious* politician>
  syn aspiring, emulous, vaulting
  rel aggressive, enterprising, go-ahead, pushing, up-and-doing; energetic, hard-working, indefatigable; anxious, avid, eager, keen
  con apathetic, phlegmatic, stolid; faineant, indolent, lazy, slothful
  2 of a kind to try or exceed one's powers of performance <an *ambitious* scheme to recover gold from seawater>
  syn grandiose, lofty, pretentious, utopian, visionary
  rel audacious, bold, daring; chimerical, extravagant, high-flown, impractical, unrealistic
  con easy, plain, straightforward; feasible, practicable, realistic; unpretentious
  ant modest
ambitiousness *n syn* see AMBITION 1
ambivalent *adj syn* see EQUIVOCAL 2
amble *vb syn* see SAUNTER
  rel dally, dawdle, dillydally, loiter
ambrosial *adj* **1** *syn* see DELIGHTFUL
  2 *syn* see SWEET 2
ambulant *adj syn* see ITINERANT
  ant bedfast, bedridden
ambulate *vb syn* see WALK 1
ambulatory *adj syn* see ITINERANT
ambuscade *n syn* see AMBUSH
ambush *vb syn* see SURPRISE 1
  rel assail, assault, attack; ensnare, entrap, snare, trap
ambush *n* a device to entrap an enemy by lying in hiding until a surprise attack is feasible <planned an *ambush* on the cliff above the trail>
  syn ambuscade, ambushment
  rel lure, snare, trap; blind, cover, hideout, retreat
ambushment *n syn* see AMBUSH
ameliorate *vb* **1** *syn* see IMPROVE 1
  rel alleviate, lighten, mitigate, relieve
  con damage, harm, hurt, impair, injure, mar, spoil; aggravate, intensify
  ant worsen; deteriorate
  2 *syn* see IMPROVE 3
amenable *adj* **1** *syn* see RESPONSIBLE
  rel open, subject; dependent, subordinate
  con autarchic, free
  ant independent (of); autonomous
  2 *syn* see OBEDIENT
  rel subdued, tame; receptive, responsive, willing; adaptable, impressionable, malleable, plastic, pliable, pliant

con fierce, mulish, obstinate, stubborn, truculent
ant recalcitrant, refractory
amend *vb* **1** *syn* see CORRECT 1
rel repair; elevate, lift, raise
con corrupt, debauch, deprave, pervert, vitiate
ant debase
2 *syn* see IMPROVE 1
rel advance, forward, promote
ant worsen; impair
amends *n pl syn* see REPARATION
amenity *n* **1** the quality of being pleasant or agreeable < a discussion conducted in perfect *amenity* > < the *amenity* of the climate >
syn agreeability, agreeableness, amiability, cordiality, enjoyableness, geniality, gratefulness, pleasance, pleasantness, sweetness and light
rel attractiveness, charm, delightfulness; fascination, pleasingness
con disagreeableness, distastefulness, unattractiveness, unpleasantness
2 a feature that makes for pleasantness or ease < among the *amenities* of the house is central air-conditioning >
syn comfort, convenience, facility
rel betterment, enhancement, enrichment, improvement; excellence, merit, quality, virtue
con difficulty, hardship, trial, vicissitude
3 *pl* **amenities** *syn* see MANNER 5
4 *syn* see LUXURY
5 *syn* see COURTESY 1
rel civility, courteousness, politeness; affability, cordiality, geniality, graciousness, sociability
con discourtesy, impoliteness, incivility; affront, indignity, insult; acrimony
ant rudeness
ament *n syn* see FOOL 4
amerce *vb syn* see PENALIZE
amercement *n syn* see FINE
amiability *n syn* see AMENITY 1
amiable *adj* **1** of a generally agreeable nature especially in social interaction < the meeting ended on an *amiable* note >
syn complaisant, easy, good-humored, good-natured, good-tempered, lenient, mild, obliging
rel affable, cordial, genial, gracious; courteous, mannerly; benign, benignant, kind, kindly; responsive, warm, warmhearted
idiom easy to get along with
con discourteous, ill-mannered, ill-natured, impolite, rude; crabbed, dour, unsociable
ant unamiable; surly
2 *syn* see GENTLE 2
amicable *adj* **1** characterized by peaceableness and goodwill < the negotiators joined in *amicable* discussion >
syn friendly, neighborly
rel empathic, like-minded, sympathetic, understanding; accordant, agreeing, concordant, frictionless, harmonious; pacific, peaceable, peaceful
con bellicose, belligerent, combative, contentious, pugnacious, quarrelsome; antipathetic, hostile, suspicious, uncooperative
2 *syn* see HARMONIOUS 3
amical *adj syn* see HARMONIOUS 3
amid *prep* **1** in or into the central part of < the bomb burst *amid* the crowd >
syn among, mid, midst
idiom in (or into) the middle of, in (or into) the midst of, in (or into) the thick of
2 *syn* see AMONG 1
3 *syn* see DURING
amigo *n syn* see FRIEND
amiss *adv* **1** in a mistaken, inappropriate, or reprehensible way < I feel you judge him *amiss* >
syn faultily, incorrectly, wrongly
rel inaccurately; indiscreetly, unwisely
con accurately, correctly, properly, rightly; cleverly, wisely
ant right
2 out of the proper course < our planning had gone *amiss* >
syn afield, astray, awry, badly, unfavorably, wrong; *compare* HARD 5
idiom beside (or off) the mark
con auspiciously, famously, favorably, promisingly, propitiously, well

ant aright
amiss *adj* **1** *syn* see BAD 1
2 *syn* see FAULTY
3 *syn* see BLAMEWORTHY
amity *n syn* see GOODWILL 1
rel accord, agreement, concord, harmony; amicableness, neighborliness
con animosity, antagonism, antipathy, hostility; conflict, contention, discord, dissension, strife
ant enmity
amnesty *n syn* see PARDON
among *prep* **1** surrounded by < the valley nestled *among* high mountains >
syn amid, mid, midst
2 *syn* see AMID 1
3 *syn* see BETWEEN
amorist *n syn* see GALLANT 2
amorous *adj syn* see EROTIC
rel enamored, infatuated; lustful
con aloof, detached, indifferent; cold, cool; apathetic, impassive, unconcerned
ant frigid
amorousness *n syn* see LOVE 2
amorphous *adj syn* see FORMLESS
amount *vb* **1** to make up as a total < their expenses *amounted* to just a hundred dollars >
syn add up, aggregate, come, number, run (to *or* into), sum (to *or* into), total
rel comprehend, comprise, embody, include, incorporate, reach, subsume
2 to be essentially equivalent < that utter terror that *amounts* to madness >
syn approach, correspond (to), equal, match, partake (of), rival, touch
rel hint, imply, intimate, smack (of), suggest
idiom be near to, come to the same thing as, have all the earmarks (or features) of
amount *n* **1** *syn* see BODY 5
2 *syn* see SUBSTANCE 2
amour *n* **1** *syn* see LOVE AFFAIR
2 an illicit or informal sexual relation < memoirs devoted to accounts of his *amours* >
syn affair, intrigue, liaison
rel entanglement, intimacy, relationship; love affair, romance
3 *syn* see LOVE 2
amour propre *n* **1** *syn* see PRIDE 2
2 *syn* see CONCEIT 2
rel complacency, self-complacency, self-satisfaction, smugness; pride
amphibological *adj syn* see OBSCURE 3
amphibology *n syn* see AMBIGUITY
ample *adj* **1** *syn* see SPACIOUS
rel distended, expanded, inflated, swollen
con scant, skimpy, spare; cramped, exiguous, narrow, strait
ant meager; circumscribed
2 *syn* see PLENTIFUL
rel lavish, prodigal, profuse; handsome
idiom enough and to spare
con scrimpy, spare, sparse; beggarly, miserable, niggardly
ant meager, scant
amplify *vb* **1** *syn* see EXPAND 4
rel augment, extend, increase; unfold
con abbreviate, shorten
ant abridge, condense
2 *syn* see EXPAND 3
amplitude *n* **1** *syn* see SIZE 2
2 *syn* see BREADTH 2
con closeness, limitation, restriction, straitness
ant narrowness
3 *syn* see EXPANSE
rel bigness, greatness, largeness; capaciousness, commodiousness, roominess, spaciousness
con circumscription, restriction

---

syn synonym(s)   **rel** related word(s)
ant antonym(s)   **con** contrasted word(s)
idiom idiomatic equivalent(s)
‖ use limited; if in doubt, see a dictionary

ant straitness; limitation
amply *adv syn* see WELL 4
amulet *n syn* see CHARM 2
rel lucky piece, rabbit-foot
amuse *vb* to pass or cause to pass time in pleasant or agreeable activity < simple toys to *amuse* children on long trips >
syn divert, entertain, recreate
rel absorb, distract, engross; animate, enliven, fleet, quicken; beguile, charm, delight, enchant, fascinate, wile; while
con fatigue, irk, jade, pall (on), tire, wear (on), weary; bore, ennui
amusement *n syn* see ENTERTAINMENT
ana *n syn* see ANTHOLOGY
anabasis *n syn* see ADVANCE 2
anachronism *n* **1** a chronological error < *anachronisms* of several centuries mar some earlier chronicles >
syn misdate, misdating, mistiming, parachronism
rel antedate, anticipation, prochronism, prolepsis; ‖metachronism, postdate
2 one that is inappropriately situated especially in time < born centuries too late, he was an *anachronism* in modern urban society >
syn solecism
rel bevue, faux pas, gaffe; defect, flaw, mistake, slip
anadem *n syn* see WREATH
anagogic *adj syn* see MYSTICAL 1
rel esoteric, occult, recondite; allegorical, symbolical
analects *n pl syn* see ANTHOLOGY
analgesic *n syn* see ANODYNE 1
ant irritant
analogous *adj syn* see LIKE
rel convertible, corresponding, interchangeable; kindred
analogue *n syn* see PARALLEL
rel cognate, congener
analogy *n* **1** *syn* see LIKENESS
2 expression or an expression involving explicit or implied comparison of things basically unlike but with some striking similarities < God can be described only by *analogy* >
syn metaphor, simile, similitude
rel ambiguity, equivocation, equivoque, tergiversation
con demonstration, description, formulation
analphabet *n syn* see ILLITERATE
analysis *n* **1** separation of a whole into its fundamental elements or constituent parts < *analysis* of a problem >
syn breakdown, breakup, dissection, resolution
rel division, separation; decomposition, disintegration
con combination, union; concatenation, integration, unification
ant synthesis
2 *syn* see EXAMINATION
analytic *adj syn* see LOGICAL 2
rel deep, profound; acute, keen, sharp; penetrating, piercing
con constructive, creative, inventive
analytical *adj syn* see LOGICAL 2
analyze *vb* to divide a complex whole into its constituent parts or elements < *analyze* the plot of a novel >
syn anatomize, break down, decompose, decompound, dissect, resolve
rel divide, part, separate; assort, classify, pigeonhole; examine, inspect, investigate, scrutinize
con articulate, concatenate, integrate
ant compose, compound; construct
anamnesis *n syn* see MEMORY 2
Ananias *n syn* see LIAR
anarch *n syn* see REBEL
anarchism *n* **1** a political theory opposed to all forms of government and advocating voluntary cooperation and interaction of individuals and groups in satisfying their common needs < the doubtful premises of *anarchism* about human nature >
syn anarchy
rel utopianism; communism, Marxism, syndicalism
con absolutism, authoritarianism, dictatorship; elitism
2 *syn* see DISORDER 2
anarchist *n syn* see REBEL
anarchy *n* **1** absence of effective government or the resulting social disorder < complete *anarchy* followed the breakdown of communications >
syn chaos, lawlessness, mobocracy, ochlocracy
rel confusion, disorder, disorganization

idiom mob rule (*or* law), reign of terror
2 *syn* see ANARCHISM
3 *syn* see DISORDER 2
anastomose *vb syn* see INTERJOIN
anathema *n* **1** *syn* see CURSE 1
rel censure, condemnation, denunciation, reprehension, reprobation, reproof
con eulogy, laudation, praise
2 *syn* see ABOMINATION 1
rel leper, pariah, outcast, untouchable
anathematize *vb syn* see EXECRATE 1
rel impugn, reproach
con approbate, approve, countenance, endorse, favor
anatomize *vb syn* see ANALYZE
ancestor *n* **1** a person from whom one is descended < proud of his pioneer *ancestors* >
syn antecedent (used in pl.), ascendant, forebear, forefather, primogenitor, progenitor
ant descendant
2 *syn* see FORERUNNER 2
ancestry *n* one's progenitors or their character or quality as a whole < a man of noble *ancestry* >
syn blood, descent, extraction, lineage, origin, pedigree
rel family, kindred, line, race, stock; derivation, source; breed, breeding
ant descendants; posterity
anchor *vb syn* see FASTEN 2
rel imbed, plant
idiom make fast (*or* secure)
anchorage *n syn* see HARBOR 3
ancient *adj* **1** persisting from the distant past < an *ancient* monument >
syn aged, age-old, antediluvian, antique, hoary, Noachian, old, timeworn, venerable; *compare* OBSOLETE
rel primal, primeval, primordial, pristine; forgotten, immemorial, remote, traditional; ageless, dateless
idiom old as time, older than God (*or* the hills), out of the dim past
con current, fresh, new, novel, prevailing, up-to-date
ant modern
2 *syn* see AGED 1
rel doddering, doting, fading, sinking, waning, wasting
idiom old as Methuselah (*or* the hills)
ancient *n syn* see OLDSTER
ancilla *n syn* see HELPER
ancillary *adj* **1** *syn* see AUXILIARY
2 *syn* see CONCOMITANT
androgynous *adj syn* see BISEXUAL
android *n syn* see ROBOT 1
anecdote *n syn* see STORY 2
rel recital, relation; episode, event, incident
anemic *adj syn* see PALE 2
anent *prep syn* see APROPOS
anesthetic *adj syn* see INSENSIBLE 5
rel impenetrable, impermeable, impervious; obtuse
con responsive, sensitive
anesthetic *n syn* see ANODYNE 1
ant stimulant
anesthetized *adj syn* see NUMB 1
anew *adv* **1** *syn* see OVER 7
2 *syn* see NEW
anfractuous *adj syn* see WINDING
angel *n syn* see SPONSOR
rel ‖butter-and-egg man
angelic *adj syn* see SAINTLY
anger *n* emotional excitement induced by intense displeasure < a man easily aroused to *anger* >
syn fury, indignation, ire, mad, rage, wrath
rel ‖dander, dudgeon, ‖Dutch, huff, ‖monkey, pet, pique, temper; annoyance, exasperation, infuriation, irritation
ant forbearance
anger *vb* **1** to make angry < their constant heedless interruptions *angered* her >
syn enrage, incense, infuriate, ire, mad, madden, steam up, umbrage
rel annoy, irk, vex; aggravate, exasperate, irritate, nettle, provoke, rile; affront, offend, outrage
idiom burn one up, make one hot under the collar, put (*or* get) one's dander up, set one by the ears

con appease, conciliate, mollify, placate, propitiate, soothe
ant gratify; pacify
2 to be or become angry <he *angers* easily>
syn blow up, boil, boil over, bristle, burn, flare (up), fume, rage, seethe
rel chafe, fret, stew; rant, rave, storm
idiom breathe fire, fly into a rage, get hot under the collar, get one's blood (or dander) up, hit the ceiling, lose one's temper, see red
ant calm (down)
angle *vb syn* see HINT 4
angle *n* **1** *syn* see VIEWPOINT 2
2 *syn* see PHASE
rel detail, item, particular
3 *syn* see TURN 4
angle *vb* **1** *syn* see SLANT 2
2 *syn* see SLANT 3
angry *adj* feeling or showing strong displeasure or bad temper <*angry* at the children's lack of consideration>
syn acrimonious, choleric, heated, indignant, irate, ireful, mad, shirty, waxy, wrathful, wrathy, wroth, wrothful, wrothy
rel aggravated, exasperated, perturbed, put out, riley, upset, uptight, worked up, wrought (up); angered, enraged, incensed, infuriate, infuriated, maddened, sore, vexed; orey-eyed, red-faced, wild-eyed
idiom foaming at the mouth, hot under the collar, in a taking, in a temper (or rage), mad as a hornet (or wet hen)
con calm, placid, tolerant; content, pleased, satisfied
anguish *n syn* see SORROW
rel anxiety, worry; ache, pain, pang, throe; torment, torture
con comfort, consolation, solace; alleviation, assuagement, mitigation
ant relief
angular *adj* **1** *syn* see RUDE 1
2 *syn* see LEAN
rel lathy, ribby, weedy
con chubby, chuffy
ant rotund
anima *n syn* see SOUL 1
animadversion *n* a remark or statement that constitutes an adverse and usually uncharitable criticism <her spiteful *animadversions* on her neighbors' children>
syn aspersion, obloquy, reflection, slam, slur, stricture
rel censure, criticism, reprehension; accusation, imputation, insinuation; captiousness, carping, caviling, faultfinding
con acclaim, extolling, laudation, praise; approbation, approval
ant commendation
animadvert *vb syn* see REMARK 2
rel declare, say, state, tell, utter; descant, dilate, expatiate, perorate; adduce, offer, present
con disregard, ignore, overlook
animal *n syn* see BEAST
animal *adj* **1** *syn* see BRUTISH
2 *syn* see CARNAL 2
rel bestial, brutal, brutish
con intellectual, mental, psychic; reasoning, thinking; nonphysical, spiritual
ant rational
animalism *n syn* see ANIMALITY
rel lasciviousness, lecherousness, lechery, licentiousness, lustfulness, unchastity; sensualism, sensuality, voluptuousness
animality *n* the animal aspect or quality of human beings or human nature <his violent reaction was sheer *animality*>
syn animalism, carnality, fleshliness
rel maleness, masculinity, virility; sensuality; brutishness, coarseness, grossness
ant spirituality
animalize *vb syn* see DEBASE 1
animate *adj* **1** *syn* see LIVING 1
rel breathing, viable
ant inanimate
2 *syn* see LIVELY 1
rel active, dynamic, live; activated, energized, vitalized
con dead, inanimate, lifeless; passive
ant inert
animate *vb* **1** *syn* see ENCOURAGE 1
rel invigorate, refresh, renew; fortify, reinforce, strengthen
idiom give a lift (to), put on (or upon) one's mettle, raise the spirits of

2 *syn* see QUICKEN 1
3 *syn* see FIRE 2
rel activate, actuate, motivate; drive, impel, move
con check, curb, restrain; frustrate, thwart
ant inhibit
animated *adj* **1** *syn* see LIVING 1
rel activated, energized, vitalized
con passive
ant inert
2 *syn* see LIVELY 1
rel exuberant, high-spirited, zestful
con enervated, spiritless; comatose
ant dejected, depressed
animating *adj syn* see INVIGORATING
animation *n syn* see SPIRIT 5
animosity *n syn* see ENMITY
con amity; esteem
ant goodwill
animus *n* **1** *syn* see INTENTION
2 *syn* see SOUL 1
3 *syn* see ENMITY
rel grudge; bias, discrimination, prejudice
con partiality, predilection; sympathy
ant favor
annals *n pl syn* see HISTORY 2
annex *vb* **1** *syn* see ADD 1
rel associate, connect, join, link, unite
con disengage; divorce, part, separate
2 *syn* see GET 1
3 *syn* see APPROPRIATE 1
4 *syn* see STEAL 1
annex *n* a subsidiary structure associated with a main building <built an *annex* to the museum to hold a new collection>
syn arm, block, ell, extension, wing
rel addition, continuation
annihilate *vb* **1** *syn* see ABOLISH 1
2 to destroy utterly <matter cannot be *annihilated*>
syn abate, abolish, blot out, eradicate, exterminate, extinguish, extirpate, murder, root out, uncreate, uproot, wipe (out)
rel cancel, efface, erase, expunge, obliterate
con renew, restore; create, discover, invent; fashion, forge, form, make, shape
3 *syn* see DESTROY 1
4 *syn* see SLAUGHTER 3
rel rout
5 *syn* see CRUSH 5
annihilative *adj syn* see DESTRUCTIVE
annotate *vb* to add or append comment <*annotate* a volume of poems>
syn gloss
rel construe, elucidate, explain, expound; comment, commentate, remark
announce *vb* **1** *syn* see DECLARE 1
rel communicate, impart
con hush (up), smother, stifle, suppress
2 to point to as a future occurrence or development <the shortening days *announce* the coming of winter>
syn forerun, foreshow, harbinger, herald, preindicate, presage
rel augur, forebode, forecast, foretell, predict
3 *syn* see INDICATE 2
rel present, set forth, show (forth)
announcement *n syn* see DECLARATION
rel affirmation, assertion, averment, statement
annoy *vb* **1** to disturb and upset nervously <her persistent prying soon *annoyed* her hostess>
syn abrade, bother, ‖bug, chafe, exercise, fret, gall, irk, provoke, ruffle, vex; *compare* IRRITATE
rel agitate, disturb, perturb, upset
idiom get in one's hair
con comfort, console, solace; content, gratify, please, satisfy
ant soothe
2 *syn* see WORRY 1
rel badger, bait, chivy, heckle, hector; chafe, distress, gall, rub

---

syn synonym(s)   *rel* related word(s)
ant antonym(s)   *con* contrasted word(s)
idiom idiomatic equivalent(s)
‖ use limited; if in doubt, see a dictionary

idiom get (*or* grate) on one's nerves, rub one the wrong way
con disregard, ignore, overlook; appease, calm, dulcify, mollify; cool, lull, subdue

annoyance *n* **1** the act of annoying <devoted himself to the *annoyance* of his patient wife>
syn bothering, harassment, irking, provocation, provoking, vexation, vexing
rel pestering, teasing
2 the state or feeling of being annoyed <her *annoyance* increased as he continued to pester her>
syn aggravation, bother, botheration, exasperation, pother
rel anger, indignation, ire, wrath; aversion, repugnance, repulsion, revulsion; disgust, dislike, distaste
con appreciation, enjoyment, liking, pleasure
3 something that causes an annoyed state or feeling <his constant baiting was an *annoyance* to her>
syn besetment, bother, botheration, botherment, exasperation, irritant, nuisance, pest, pester, ‖pesterment, plague
rel affliction, aggravation, distress, provocation, trial; riding

annual *n syn* see YEARBOOK
annuary *n syn* see YEARBOOK
annul *vb* **1** *syn* see ERASE
rel abstract, dispose (of), eliminate, remove
2 *syn* see NEUTRALIZE
rel outweigh, overbalance
3 *syn* see ABOLISH 1
rel counteract, negative, neutralize; blot out, cancel, efface, obliterate; extinguish
idiom make void, set aside
con enact, ordain, pass
4 to deprive of legal validity, force, or authority <*annul* a marriage>
syn abrogate, discharge, dissolve, quash, vacate, void
rel abolish, cancel, countermand, invalidate, nullify, undo
idiom make void

annunciate *vb syn* see DECLARE 1
rel affirm, assert, asseverate, aver; profess, protest; pronounce, state

anodyne *n* **1** something used to relieve or prevent pain <opium and its derivatives are still our most potent *anodynes*>
syn analgesic, anesthetic, pain-killer
rel calmative, depressant, sedative, tranquilizer; hypnotic, somnifacient, soporific, stupefacient
2 something that soothes or, often, dulls or deadens the senses or sensibilities <the kind of religion that is no more than an *anodyne*>
syn narcotic, nepenthe, opiate
ant energizer, stimulant; irritant

anomalous *adj* **1** *syn* see IRREGULAR 1
rel monstrous, prodigious
2 *syn* see ABNORMAL 1
rel foreign, peculiar, singular, strange; monstrous, prodigious
con accustomed, customary, usual, wonted

anon *adv* **1** *syn* see PRESENTLY 1
2 *syn* see THEN 1
anonym *n syn* see PSEUDONYM
anonymous *adj* not identified by name <saved by an *anonymous* hero>
syn innominate, nameless, undesignated, unnamed
rel incognito, unidentified, unknown, unrecognized, unspecified
ant named, onymous

another *adj* **1** *syn* see THAT 1
2 *syn* see ADDITIONAL
rel second

anschauung *n syn* see INTUITION
anschluss *n syn* see ALLIANCE 2
answer *n* **1** something spoken or written by way of return to a question or demand <a sullen *answer*>
syn antiphon, rejoinder, reply, respond, response, retort, return
rel comment, observation, remark; defense, justification; rebuttal, refutation; replication
con inquiry, interrogation, query, question, quiz
2 something attained by mental effort and especially by computation <got the *answer* by trial-and-error methods>
syn result, solution
answer *vb* **1** to say, write, or do something in response (as to a question) <*answered* his critics with documented facts>
syn come in, rejoin, reply, respond, retort, return

rel acknowledge, recognize; disprove, rebut, refute; countercharge, recriminate
idiom come back (at), make reply (to)
con ask, inquire, interrogate, query, question, quiz
2 *syn* see SATISFY 5

answerable *adj syn* see RESPONSIBLE
rel bound, compelled, constrained, duty-bound, obligated, obliged

Antaean *adj syn* see HUGE
antagonism *n* **1** *syn* see ENMITY
rel opposition, oppugnancy, resistance, withstanding; clashing, conflict, difference, disagreement, discord, friction
con concord, consonance, harmony; agreement, understanding
ant comity
2 an opposing state, action, or position <the natural *antagonism* of predators and prey>
syn antithesis, con, contradistinction, contraposition, contrariety, opposition, opposure
rel disagreement, discrepancy, disparity, incongruity; annulling, negation, nullification; counteraction
con agreement, congruity; alliance, association, rapport; empathy, sympathy

antagonist *n syn* see OPPONENT
con adherent, henchman, partisan
ant supporter

antagonistic *adj* **1** *syn* see BITTER 3
2 *syn* see ADVERSE 1
rel discordant, incompatible, inconsonant; averse, disinclined, indisposed, unwilling; conflicting, hostile
con advantageous, beneficial; auspicious, benign, propitious
ant favorable
3 *syn* see ANTIPATHETIC 1
rel adverse, counter, counteractive, reactive; discordant; antonymous, opposing, oppugnant

ante *adv syn* see BEFORE 1
ante *prep syn* see BEFORE 1
ante *n syn* see BET
antecede *vb syn* see PRECEDE 2
antecedence *n syn* see PRIORITY
antecedent *n* **1** *syn* see CAUSE 1
rel forebear, forerunner, precursor; agency, instrumentality, means
con sequel; upshot
ant consequence
2 *syn* see FORERUNNER 2
3 — used in pl. *syn* see ANCESTOR 1
antecedent *adj syn* see PRECEDING
ant consequent; subsequent
antecedently *adv syn* see BEFORE 1
antecessor *n syn* see FORERUNNER 2
antedate *vb syn* see PRECEDE 2
antediluvian *adj syn* see ANCIENT 1
antediluvian *n syn* see FOGY
anterior *adj syn* see PRECEDING
con after, back, hind, hinder, rear
ant posterior

anthology *n* a collection of selected artistic and especially literary pieces or passages <an *anthology* of sacred music>
syn album, ana, analects, florilegium, garland, miscellany, omnibus, posy
rel collection, compilation; delectus, treasure-house, treasury

anthropoid *adj* resembling man <*anthropoid* apes>
syn anthropomorphic, anthropomorphous, humanoid, manlike
anthropomorphic *adj syn* see ANTHROPOID
anthropomorphous *adj syn* see ANTHROPOID
anti *n syn* see OPPONENT
anti *adj syn* see ADVERSE 1
ant pro

antic *n syn* see PRANK
rel artifice, wile; romp
antic *adj* **1** *syn* see FANTASTIC 2
rel foolish; comic, comical, farcical, laughable, ludicrous
con prudent, sensible, wise; conventional, formal; grave, sedate, serious, solemn, somber
2 characterized by a light gay quality <a briskly *antic* and delightful tale>
syn frolicsome, playful, rollicking, sprightly
rel gay, lively, spirited; light, whimsical; casual, easy, suave

con constrained, controlled, curbed, guarded, inhibited, restrained
3 syn see PLAYFUL 1
anticipant *adj syn* see EXPECTANT 1
anticipate *vb* **1 syn** see PREVENT 1
rel forecast, foretell, presage
idiom be one step ahead of
con disregard, ignore, neglect, overlook, slight
2 syn see FORESEE
rel await, contemplate, expect; foretaste
idiom be on the lookout (*or* watch) for, look forward to, look (*or* watch) out for
anticipation *n syn* see EXPECTANCY 1
anticipative *adj syn* see EXPECTANT 1
anticipatory *adj syn* see EXPECTANT 1
antidote *n syn* see REMEDY 2
rel negator, neutralizer, nullifier, offset; backfire
antipasto *n syn* see APPETIZER
antipathetic *adj* **1** having a natural or inherent opposition <national needs *antipathetic* to peace>
syn antagonistic, clashing, conflicting, contrariant, contrary, discordant
rel antipodal, antithetical, antonymous, contradictory, opposite
idiom at cross purposes, at daggers drawn, at war with one another
con agreeing, consonant, correspondent, harmonious; coactive, collaborative, cooperative
ant concordant
2 arousing marked aversion or dislike <found his sister's husband in every way *antipathetic*>
syn aversive, kindless, repellent, repugnant, uncongenial, ungenial, unsympathetic
rel abhorrent, obnoxious; disgustful, disgusting, distasteful, loathsome, repulsive
con compatible, consonant, sympathetic; alluring, attractive, charming; agreeable, pleasant, pleasing, satisfying, soothing
ant congenial
3 syn see ADVERSE 1
antipathy *n* **1 syn** see ENMITY
rel disrelish, distaste, repellency, repugnance; avoidance, escape, eschewal, evasion
con liking, partiality, predilection, prepossession; attachment, love; attraction, taste (for)
ant affection (for)
2 the state of mind induced by what is antipathetic <a strong *antipathy* to modern art>
syn allergy, aversion, dyspathy
rel abhorrence, dislike, disrelish, distaste, repellency, repugnance; avoidance, escape, eschewal, evasion
con liking, partiality, predilection, prepossession; affection, attachment, love; attraction
ant taste (for)
antiphon *n syn* see ANSWER 1
antipodal *adj syn* see OPPOSITE
antipode *n syn* see OPPOSITE
antipodean *adj syn* see OPPOSITE
antipole *n syn* see OPPOSITE
antiquate *vb syn* see OUTDATE
antiquated *adj syn* see OLD-FASHIONED
con modern, new, novel
ant modernistic
antique *adj* **1 syn** see ANCIENT 1
rel ancestral, dateless, immemorial, legendary, time-honored, traditional
con advanced, current, recent
2 syn see OLD-FASHIONED
antisocial *adj* averse to the society of others <a pure scholar, remote and *antisocial*>
syn eremitic, misanthropic, reclusive, reserved, solitary, standoffish
rel ascetic, austere, cold, remote; cynical, introverted, withdrawn
con affable, friendly, gregarious; communicative, outgoing, sociable
ant social
antithesis *n* **1 syn** see ANTAGONISM 2
2 syn see OPPOSITE
antithetical *adj syn* see OPPOSITE

anxiety *n syn* see CARE 2
rel doubt, mistrust, uncertainty; distress, misery, suffering; dread; panic
con composure, equanimity, sangfroid; aplomb, confidence, self=possession; certainty, certitude, faith, trust
ant security
anxious *adj* **1 syn** see AFRAID 1
rel agitated, apprehensive, jittery, perturbed, upset, worried; alarmed, bothered, disquieted, troubled, uneasy
idiom ill at ease
con calm, collected, cool, easy, imperturbable, unruffled; assured, confident, sanguine, sure
2 syn see EAGER
rel importunate, pressing, urgent
idiom all agog, bursting to
con averse, disinclined, hesitant, indisposed, reluctant
ant loath
anyhow *adv syn* see ABOUT 4
anytime *adv syn* see EVER 4
anyway *adv syn* see EVER 5
any which way *adv syn* see ABOUT 4
anywise *adv* **1 syn** see ABOUT 4
2 syn see EVER 5
A1 *adj syn* see EXCELLENT
apace *adv syn* see FAST 2
apart *adv* **1** as a discrete item <taken *apart*, his view seemed sound enough>
syn independently, individually, one by one, separately, severally, singly
idiom one at a time
2 excluded from consideration <these slips *apart*, he had done very well>
syn aside
idiom to one side
3 in or into parts <tore the sheets *apart*>
syn asunder, sky-high
idiom all to pieces, to bits (*or* flinders)
apart *adj syn* see ALONE 1
apart from *prep syn* see EXCEPT
apartheid *n syn* see SEGREGATION
apartment *n* **1** a set of rooms (as in a private house or a block) rented or leased for use as a dwelling place <had a tiny top=floor *apartment*>
syn ‖chambers, flat, lodging(s), rental, rooms, suite, tenement
2 syn see ROOM 1
apathetic *adj syn* see IMPASSIVE 1
rel dull, inert, languid, sluggish, torpid; anesthetic, impassible, insensible, insensitive; callous, unmoved, untouched; limp, spiritless
con aroused, awake, aware, conscious, impressionable, perceptive, receptive; vigilant, watchful, wide-awake
ant alert
apathy *n* **1** lack of emotional responsiveness <hid her sorrow behind a dull brooding *apathy*>
syn impassivity, insensibility, phlegm, stoicism, stolidity, unresponsiveness
rel inertness, passivity, supineness; aloofness, detachment, indifference, unconcern; lethargy, torpidity, torpor; listlessness, numbness, stupefaction, stupor
con ardor, fervor, passion, responsiveness, warmth; alertness, awareness, concern, solicitude
ant zeal; enthusiasm
2 lack of interest or concern <public *apathy* toward the school crisis>
syn disinterest, disregard, heedlessness, indifference, insouciance, lassitude, lethargy, listlessness, unconcern, unmindfulness
rel callousness, hardness, insensitivity, obduracy, unawareness; coldness, halfheartedness, lukewarmness; calmness, dispassion, dispassionateness
con attentiveness, concern, heedfulness, interest; awareness, mindfulness, sensitivity, solicitude; ardency, fervency, passion, warmth, zeal
ape *vb syn* see MIMIC

syn synonym(s)   **rel** related word(s)
ant antonym(s)   **con** contrasted word(s)
idiom idiomatic equivalent(s)
‖ use limited; if in doubt, see a dictionary

rel caricature; emulate, rival
idiom make like

aperçu *n syn* see COMPENDIUM 1

aperitive *adj syn* see PALATABLE

aperture *n* a discontinuity allowing passage < the mouse squeezed through a narrow *aperture* in the wall >
syn hole, opening, orifice, outlet, vent
rel discontinuity, gap, hiatus, interstice; bore, perforation, pinhole, prick, puncture; chasm, cleft, cut, gash, slash, slit; breach, break, rupture

apery *n syn* see MIMICRY

apex *n* **1** *syn* see TOP 1
rel extremity, limit, spire
ant nadir
2 the culminating point < the *apex* of his career >
syn acme, apogee, capsheaf, capstone, climax, comble, crescendo, crest, crown, culmen, culmination, meridian, ne plus ultra, noon, noontide, peak, pinnacle, sublimity, summit, zenith
rel last word, prime, quintescence, ultimate; achievement, attainment, consummation, realization
ant nadir
3 *syn* see POINT 9
rel cap, crest, peak, prominence, spire

aphorism *n syn* see MAXIM

aphrodisia *n syn* see LUST 2

aphrodisiac *adj syn* see EROTIC
ant anaphrodisiac

apiarist *n syn* see BEEKEEPER

apical *adj syn* see TOP 1

apiculturist *n syn* see BEEKEEPER

apiece *adv* by, for, or to each one < gave the boys a dollar *apiece* >
syn all, aside, each, ‖per, per capita, per caput
rel individually, one by one, respectively, severally, singly, successively

apish *adj syn* see SLAVISH 3

aplomb *n syn* see CONFIDENCE 2
rel poise, savoir faire; coolness, imperturbability, levelheadedness, nonchalance; composure, ease, easiness, equanimity, sangfroid
idiom presence of mind
con bewilderment, distraction, perplexity; befuddlement, confusion, fluster, fuddlement; discomfiture, embarrassment, perturbation
ant shyness

apocalypse *n syn* see REVELATION
rel envisioning, foresight, precognition, prevision

apocalyptic *adj* **1** *syn* see PROPHETIC
2 *syn* see OMINOUS

apocryphal *adj syn* see SPURIOUS 3
rel false, erroneous, inaccurate, incorrect, untrue, wrong; doubtful, dubious, questionable
idiom open to question
con accurate, correct, established, factual, true, truthful, veracious; authentic

apogee *n syn* see APEX 2

Apollyon *n syn* see DEVIL 1

apologetic *adj syn* see REMORSEFUL

apologetic *n syn* see APOLOGY 1

apologia *n syn* see APOLOGY 1
rel clarification, elucidation, explanation, interpretation

apologue *n syn* see ALLEGORY 2

apology *n* **1** a presentation intended to justify or defend something < the white paper is essentially an *apology* for recent foreign policy >
syn apologetic, apologia, defense, justification; *compare* EXCUSE 1
rel excuse, extenuation, mitigation, palliation; advocating, advocation, championing, espousal, espousing, support
idiom pleading one's cause, putting in a good word for, speaking up for
con blame, censure, condemnation, decrial, reprehension, reprobation
2 an acknowledgment expressing regret for a wrong, improper, or discommoding act < murmured a brief *apology* for her lateness >
syn excuse, regrets; *compare* EXCUSE 1
rel amends, atonement; acknowledgment, admission, concession, confession, mea culpa; reparation, redress, satisfaction

3 *syn* see EXCUSE 3

aporetic *adj syn* see INCREDULOUS

apostasy *n syn* see DEFECTION
rel perfidy, treacherousness

apostate *n syn* see RENEGADE
rel bolter; dissenter, nonconformist, recusant
con adherent, follower, partisan; convert, proselyte

apostatize *vb syn* see DEFECT

a posteriori *adj syn* see INDUCTIVE

apostle *n syn* see MISSIONARY

apothecary *n syn* see DRUGGIST

apothegm *n syn* see MAXIM

apotheosis *n* **1** the consummate form, example, or instance (as of a quality) < the *apotheosis* of vulgarity >
syn epitome, last word, quintessence, ultimate; *compare* EMBODIMENT
rel acme, culmination, height, peak, summit
idiom ‖the living end
2 a raising to a state of eminent triumph or glory < the *apotheosis* of a folk hero >
syn aggrandizement, deification, dignification, exaltation, glorification
rel elevation, ennoblement, enshrinement, idolization, immortalization, lionization
con debasement, defamation, degradation, denigration, sullying

appall *vb syn* see DISMAY 1
rel awe, faze, overawe
con brace (up), buck up, cheer (up); assure, hearten, inspire, inspirit
ant embolden, nerve

appalling *adj syn* see FEARFUL 3
rel daunting, dismaying, horrifying; bewildering, confounding, dumbfounding
con assuring, heartening, inspiriting
ant reassuring

appanage *n syn* see RIGHT 2

apparatus *n syn* see EQUIPMENT
rel implement, instrument, tool, utensil; furnishings, provisions, supplies

apparel *vb syn* see CLOTHE
rel appoint
con bare, denude
ant divest

apparel *n syn* see CLOTHES

apparent *adj* **1** *syn* see CLEAR 5
rel ponderable; noticeable, prominent; discernible, observable, perceivable
idiom plain as day, plain to be seen
con ambiguous, hidden, obscure
ant inapparent
2 being other than seems to be the case < her *apparent* goodwill masked an inner loathing >
syn Barmecidal, illusive, illusory, ostensible, seeming, semblant
rel deceptive, delusive, delusory, misleading; credible, plausible, specious; factitious, fake, false, pseudo, sham, supposititious, suppositious
con genuine, true, valid; basic, essential, fundamental, inherent, intrinsic
ant actual, real

apparently *adv syn* see OSTENSIBLY

apparition *n* a visible appearance of something not present and especially of a dead person < illusions that the superstitious see as *apparitions* >
syn bogey, eidolon, ghost, ‖haunt, phantasm, phantom, revenant, shade, shadow, specter, spectrum, spirit, ‖spook, umbra, wraith
rel delusion, hallucination, illusion; corposant, foxfire, ignis fatuus, jack-o'-lantern, marshfire, Saint Elmo's fire, will-o'-the-wisp

appeal *n* **1** *syn* see PRAYER
rel asking, requesting, solicitation
con claim, demand, exaction; kick, objection, protest
2 *syn* see ATTRACTION 1
3 *syn* see CHARM 3
rel draw; pleasantness
con disagreeableness, unpleasantness

appeal *vb* **1** *syn* see BEG
2 *syn* see PETITION

3 syn see INTEREST

appealing *adj syn* see ATTRACTIVE 1

appear *vb* **1** to become visible <the sun *appeared* from behind a cloud>
syn emerge, loom, show
rel arrive, come; arise, emanate, issue, materialize, outcrop, rise, spring
idiom come in sight, come into view, meet (*or* strike) the eye, show one's face
con go, leave; depart, retire, withdraw
ant disappear, vanish
2 syn see SEEM
idiom give an appearance of, strike one as

appearance *n* **1** the state or form in which one appears <his disheveled *appearance* surprised his guests>
syn aspect, look, mien, seeming
rel air, bearing, countenance, demeanor, manner
2 *usu* **appearances** *pl* outward and often deceptive indication or look <to all *appearances* he was guilty>
syn face, guise, seeming, semblance, show, showing, simulacrum; *compare* MASK
rel fiction, make-believe, pretense, pretension; disguise, facade, front, masquerade, outside, pose
idiom outward show
con fact, reality, truth

appease *vb* **1 syn** see PACIFY
rel calm (down), ease, soothe; extenuate, gloss (over), palliate, whitewash
con annoy, bother, irk, vex; anger, enrage, incense, infuriate; discompose, disturb, perturb, upset
ant exasperate
2 syn see SATISFY 3
rel ease, relieve; cater (to), coddle, pamper, spoil
ant aggravate

appellation *n syn* see NAME 1

appellative *n syn* see NAME 1

append *vb syn* see ADD 1

appendage *n* something accompanying or attached to another thing to which it is usually subordinate or nonessential <people to whom culture is a mere *appendage* to life>
syn accessory, adjunct, appendix, appurtenance
rel auxiliary, incidental, subsidiary, supplement; collateral, extra, nonessential

appendix *n* **1** additional material subjoined to a writing and especially a book <a dictionary with an *appendix* of new words>
syn addendum, codicil, rider, supplement
2 rel APPENDAGE, accessory, adjunct, appurtenance

apperception *n syn* see RECOGNITION 1
rel apprehension, grasp, perception; comprehension, understanding

appertain *vb* **1 syn** see BELONG 2
2 syn see BEAR (on *or* upon)

appetence *n syn* see APPETITE 1

appetent *adj syn* see EAGER
rel craving, desirous, lusting, yearning
idiom consumed with desire

appetite *n* **1** a natural enjoyment of food <all fell to with a hearty *appetite*>
syn appetence, stomach, taste
rel gluttony, greed, hunger, voracity; epicurism, gourmandise
2 syn see DESIRE 1
rel cupidity, greed, urgency
con abnegation, asceticism, renunciation, self-denial; distaste, revulsion
3 an attraction toward something <had a great *appetite* for gossip>
syn fondness, inclination, liking, soft spot, taste, weakness
rel bent, bias, flair, leaning, penchant, proclivity, propensity
con disinclination, dislike, distaste; disinterest, unconcern

appetition *n syn* see DESIRE 1

appetizer *n* food or drink served before a meal to stimulate appetite <*appetizers* such as cocktails, and canapés>
syn antipasto, hors d'oeuvre, whet, zakuska
rel dainty, delicacy, goody, tidbit; savory

appetizing *adj syn* see PALATABLE
ant disgusting, nauseating

applaud *vb* **1 syn** see COMMEND 2
rel boost, plug

ant censure; admonish
2 to express enthusiastic approval <*applauded* wildly when his team won a point>
syn cheer, rise (to), root
rel acclaim, extol, laud, praise; eulogize, glorify, magnify, panegyrize
con deride, mock, ridicule, taunt; contemn, disdain, scorn, scout
ant boo, hiss

applause *n* public expression of approbation <her appearance was greeted with *applause*>
syn acclaim, acclamation, plaudit(s)
rel cheers, hand, ovation, round; cheering, clapping, rooting
con derision, mockery, ridicule, taunting; Bronx cheer, raspberry
ant booing, hissing

‖**apple knocker** *n syn* see RUSTIC

apple-polish *vb syn* see FAWN

apple-polisher *n syn* see SYCOPHANT

‖**applesauce** *n syn* see NONSENSE 2

appliance *n syn* see USE 1

applicability *n syn* see USE 3
con irrelevance, unsuitability
ant inapplicability

applicable *adj* **1 syn** see RELEVANT
rel alliable, associable, compatible, congenial, connective
con incompatible, uncongenial; inappropriate, unfit, unsuitable
ant inapplicable
2 syn see FIT 1
rel correct, good, seemly
idiom as it ought to be, as it should be
con improper, incorrect

applicant *n syn* see CANDIDATE

application *n* **1 syn** see ATTENTION 1
rel busyness, zeal; energy, indefatigability
con bemusement, wool-gathering; faineance, laziness, sloth
ant indolence
2 syn see USE 1
3 syn see EXERCISE 1
4 syn see PRAYER

applicative *adj syn* see RELEVANT

applicatory *adj syn* see RELEVANT

apply *vb* **1 syn** see ADDRESS 3
rel set about, take on, undertake; drudge, grind, toil
idiom burn the midnight oil, keep one's nose to the grindstone, work like a horse (*or* dog); concern (oneself) with something, set (one's hand) to something
con let slide, neglect, pass over, slight
2 syn see BEAR (on *or* upon)
idiom come into relation with
3 syn see RESORT 2
rel appeal, petition; beg, beseech, entreat, implore, supplicate; importune, press, urge
idiom make application to
4 syn see USE 2

apply (to) *vb syn* see ADDRESS 4

appoint *vb* **1 syn** see DESIGNATE 2
rel accredit, authorize, commission
con cashier, discharge, dismiss; debar, exclude, reject
2 syn see FURNISH 1
rel embellish, enrich, furbish, garnish; dress up, set off, spruce (up)
con denude, dismantle, divest, strip

appointment *n* **1 syn** see JOB 2
2 syn see ENGAGEMENT 3

apportion *vb* **1 syn** see ALLOT
rel divide, partition, share
con assemble, collect, gather
2 to separate something into shares with care and accuracy and distribute it among a number <Christ *apportioned* the loaves and fishes>
syn divide, ‖divvy, parcel, portion, prorate, quota, ration, share, ‖shift

---

syn synonym(s)   **rel** related word(s)
ant antonym(s)   **con** contrasted word(s)
idiom idiomatic equivalent(s)
‖ use limited; if in doubt, see a dictionary

rel accord, award, bestow, distribute; give, grant, present; part, separate, split

3 *syn* see ADMINISTER 2

rel dish out, serve

apportionment *n syn* see RATION

apposite *adj syn* see RELEVANT

rel felicitous, happy; opportune, pat, seasonable, timely

idiom to the point (*or* purpose)

con awkward, inept; casual, haphazard, hit-or-miss, random

ant inapposite, inapt

appositeness *n syn* see ORDER 11

appraisal *n* **1** *syn* see ESTIMATE 1

2 *syn* see ESTIMATION 1

appraise *vb syn* see ESTIMATE 1

rel adjudge, deem, esteem, judge; audit, examine, inspect, scrutinize

idiom set (*or* place) a value on, take the measure of

appraisement *n* **1** *syn* see ESTIMATE 1

2 *syn* see ESTIMATION 1

appreciable *adj syn* see PERCEPTIBLE

rel noticeable; apparent, clear, evident, manifest, obvious, plain; concrete, material, real, substantial

con impalpable, imperceptible, imponderable, insensible, intangible

ant inappreciable

appreciate *vb* **1** to hold in high estimation <*appreciate* the kindness of a friend>

syn apprize, cherish, esteem, prize, treasure, value; *compare* ADMIRE 1

rel admire, regard, respect; adore, ‖eat up, enjoy, like, love, relish

idiom rate highly, set great store by, think much (*or* well) of

con contemn, disapprove, disdain, scorn; decry, depreciate, disparage

ant despise

2 *syn* see ADMIRE 1

rel enjoy, like, savor

con contemn, disdain, scorn

3 *syn* see KNOW 1

rel catch, seize, take in

appreciation *n syn* see TESTIMONIAL 3

apprehend *vb* **1** to recognize the existence or meaning of <as a child learns to *apprehend* the relation between naughtiness and punishment>

syn accept, catch, compass, comprehend, conceive, cotton (to *or* on to), ‖dig, follow, grasp, make out, see, take, take in, tumble (to), twig, understand

rel realize, recognize, sense; absorb, digest, seize; catch on, wise (up); penetrate

idiom catch (*or* get) the drift of, get the idea, get through one's head, make head or tail of

ant misapprehend

2 *syn* see ARREST 2

3 *syn* see FORESEE

rel dread, fear

idiom be on pins and needles, have one's heart in one's mouth, wait with bated breath

4 *syn* see KNOW 1

idiom be acquainted with, be cognizant of

apprehensible *adj syn* see UNDERSTANDABLE

apprehension *n* **1** *syn* see IDEA

2 *syn* see ARREST

3 fear that something is going or will go wrong <had the strongest *apprehension* about her sister's health>

syn apprehensiveness, foreboding, misgiving, premonition, prenotion, presage, presentiment

rel agitation, angst, anxiety, care, concern, disquiet, disquietude, solicitude, unease, uneasiness, worry; alarm, dread, fear, panic

idiom the anxious seat

con assurance, composure, equanimity, sangfroid, self-possession; faith, reliance, trust

ant confidence

apprehensive *adj* **1** *syn* see AWARE

2 *syn* see FEARFUL 2

ant confident

apprehensiveness *n syn* see APPREHENSION 3

apprentice *n syn* see NOVICE

rel starter; amateur

con adept, expert, specialist

apprenticed *adj syn* see BOUND 2

apprise *vb syn* see INFORM 2

rel announce, communicate, declare, proclaim, publish; disclose, discover, divulge, reveal, tell

idiom make known to, serve (one) notice

apprize *vb syn* see APPRECIATE 1

approach *vb* **1** to come or go near or nearer <as a boy *approaches* manhood>

syn approximate, near, nigh

rel achieve, arrive (at), attain, gain, hit, make, reach; draw on

idiom come to close quarters with

con recede, retire, retreat, withdraw; depart, go, leave

2 *syn* see ADDRESS 4

rel advise, confer, consult, counsel, negotiate, parley; beg, beseech, entreat, implore, plead, supplicate

3 *syn* see REACH 3

4 *syn* see AMOUNT 2

con depart, deviate, digress; differ, disaccord, disharmonize, vary

5 *syn* see BORDER 3

approach *n syn* see OVERTURE 1

rel attempt, endeavor, essay, try; call, invitation

ant withdrawal

approaching *adj syn* see FORTHCOMING

approbate *vb syn* see APPROVE 1

approbation *n* warmly commending acceptance or agreement <expressed *approbation* of their progress>

syn approval, benediction, blessing, favor, OK (*or* okay)

rel commendation, countenance, goodwill, sanction; admiration, esteem, liking, regard, respect; pleasure, satisfaction

con censure, condemnation, criticism, disapproval, disfavor, reprehension; annoyance, disgust, irritation; distress, regret, sorrow

ant disapprobation

approbative *adj syn* see FAVORABLE 1

approbatory *adj syn* see FAVORABLE 1

appropinquity *n syn* see PROXIMITY

appropriate *vb* **1** to take over as if by preeminent right <limitations on the right of the state to *appropriate* private property>

syn accroach, annex, arrogate, commandeer, confiscate, expropriate, preempt, seize, sequester, take; *compare* ARROGATE 1

rel grab, grasp, snatch; claim, exact, extort, wrench; conscript, draft, press

idiom help oneself to, lay hold of, make free with, take possession of

2 *syn* see STEAL 1

rel despoil, spoil; forage, raid

3 *syn* see ARROGATE 1

appropriate *adj* **1** *syn* see FIT 1

rel apposite, germane, pertinent, relevant; opportune, pat, seasonable, timely

con incompatible, incongruous, inconsonant

ant inappropriate

2 *syn* see GOOD 2

rel agreeable, desirable, enjoyable, pleasant; acceptable, admissible, eligible, entitled, right, worthy

con disagreeable undesirable, unpleasant; inadmissible, ineligible, unworthy, wrong

ant inappropriate

3 *syn* see JUST 3

con unfair, unjustified, unmerited, unreasonable; unsuitable

ant inappropriate

4 *syn* see TRUE 7

ant inappropriate

appropriately *adv syn* see WELL 4

appropriateness *n* **1** *syn* see USE 3

2 *syn* see ORDER 11

appropriation *n* property (as money) set apart or given by official or formal action for a predetermined use by others <an increased *appropriation* for public housing>

syn grant, subsidy, subvention

rel allotment, allowance, stipend; aid, assistance, grant-in-aid, help

approval *n syn* see APPROBATION

rel applause, commendation, compliment; acceptance, endorsement, sanction, suffrage

con depreciation, derogation, disparagement

ant disapproval

approve *vb* **1** to find acceptable < they were unable to *approve* his behavior >
syn accept, approbate, countenance, favor, go (for), hold (with)
rel back (up), stand by, support, sustain, uphold; bear, endure, put up (with), tolerate
idiom be in favor of, pat on the back, take kindly to, think well (or highly) of, view with approval (or favor)
con deprecate, disfavor, dislike, frown (on or upon); object (to), oppose
ant disapprove
2 to give an often formal expression of approval and support < the committee *approved* the plans for the new clubhouse >
syn accredit, certify, endorse, OK (or okay), sanction
rel applaud, commend, compliment; confirm, initial, ratify; clear
con refuse, reject, repudiate, spurn; censure, condemn, criticize, reprehend, reprobate
ant disapprove

approving *adj syn* see FAVORABLE 1
approximal *adj syn* see ADJACENT 3
approximate *adj* **1** *syn* see COMPARATIVE
2 *syn* see RUDE 3
approximate *vb* **1** *syn* see APPROACH 1
idiom be in the neighborhood of
2 *syn* see ESTIMATE 3
approximately *adv syn* see NEARLY
idiom in round numbers, right about
ant exactly, precisely
appulse *n syn* see IMPACT
appurtenance *n syn* see APPENDAGE
rel appointment (usu appointments pl), equipment, furnishings, furniture
appurtenant *adj syn* see AUXILIARY
a priori *adj syn* see DEDUCTIVE
apriorism *n syn* see ASSUMPTION 2
apropos *adj syn* see RELEVANT
rel meet, proper
con clumsy, gauche, inappropriate, inept
ant malapropos
apropos *prep* in reference to < it is impossible to reach a decision *apropos* this matter at present >
syn about, against, anent, as for, as regards, as respects, as to, concerning, in re, in respect to, re, regarding, respecting, touching, toward, with respect to
apt *adj* **1** having a tendency or inclination < it is *apt* to be cool late in the evening >
syn given, inclined, liable, likely, prone
rel disposed, minded, predisposed
con averse, disinclined, indisposed, loath; doubtful, improbable, unlikely
2 *syn* see FIT 1
rel apposite, apropos, pertinent, relevant; compelling, convincing, telling; exact, nice, precise
con awkward, clumsy, maladroit
ant inapt, inept
3 *syn* see QUICK 2
rel alert, brainy, bright; gifted, talented
con laggard
aptness *n* **1** *syn* see ORDER 11
rel helpfulness, propitiousness
2 *syn* see GIFT 2
‖**apurpose** *adv syn* see INTENTIONALLY
apyrous *adj syn* see NONCOMBUSTIBLE
aquake *adj syn* see TREMULOUS
aqua vitae *n syn* see LIQUOR 2
aqueduct *n syn* see CHANNEL 1
aquiculture *n syn* see HYDROPONICS
aquiver *adj syn* see TREMULOUS
arab *n* **1** *syn* see VAGABOND
‖**2** *syn* see PEDDLER
arable *adj* suitable for tilling and for growing crops < used their *arable* land intensively >
syn cultivable, cultivatable, tillable
rel fat, fertile, fruitful, productive
con barren, sterile, unfertile, unfruitful, unproductive
arbiter *n syn* see JUDGE 1
rel moderator

arbitrary *adj* **1** characterized by or given to willful and often unwise or irrational choices and demands < a proud fitful *arbitrary* nature >
syn capricious, erratic, freakish, vagarious, wayward, whimsical, whimsied
rel undisciplined, unruly, wild, willful; arrogant, unconstrained, unreasonable; careless, heedless, impetuous, indiscreet, precipitate, rash; kooky, screwball, zany
con circumspect, discreet, heedful, judicious, politic, reflective; calculating, discriminative, judicial, prudent, well-advised
2 *syn* see ABSOLUTE 4
rel authoritarian, dictatorial, magisterial, oracular
con lawful, legal, licit, rightful
ant legitimate
arbitrate *vb syn* see JUDGE 1
rel intermediate, intervene, mediate; appease, placate, soothe
arbitrator *n* **1** *syn* see MODERATOR
2 *syn* see JUDGE 1
arbor *n* a shelter (as in a garden) formed of vines or branches or of latticework covered with climbing shrubs or vines < the children picnicked under the *arbor* >
syn bower, pergola
rel belvedere, casino, gazebo, summerhouse
arc *n syn* see CURVE
arcadia *n syn* see UTOPIA
arcane *adj syn* see MYSTERIOUS
rel eerie, uncanny, weird; anagogic, mystical
arced *adj syn* see CURVED
arch *n syn* see CURVE
arch *adj* **1** *syn* see FIRST 3
rel conspicuous, notable, noteworthy; extraordinary, extreme
2 *syn* see SAUCY 1
rel impish, mischievous, playful, roguish, waggish; bold, cheeky, cocky, flippant, fresh; derisive, mocking, twitting
con modest, quiet, respectful, submissive
3 *syn* see COY 2
archaic *adj* **1** *syn* see OLD-FASHIONED
idiom behind the times, of the old school
con fresh, modern, new, novel; fashionable
ant up-to-date
2 *syn* see PRIMITIVE 3
arched *adj syn* see CURVED
archetypal *adj syn* see TYPICAL 1
archetype *n* **1** *syn* see ORIGINAL 1
2 *syn* see MODEL 2
archfiend *n syn* see DEVIL 2
archilochian *adj syn* see SARCASTIC
archimage *n syn* see MAGICIAN 1
architect *n syn* see FATHER 2
architecture *n syn* see MAKEUP 1
archive *n, usu* **archives** *pl* **1** *syn* see LIBRARY
2 *syn* see DOCUMENT
rel papers, parchments, scrolls, writings; clippings, cuttings, excerpts, extracts, fragments, gleanings, remains
arciform *adj syn* see CURVED
arctic *adj syn* see COLD 1
rel bitter, boreal, hyperborean; numbing, rigorous; hibernal, hiemal
idiom cold as charity, cold enough to freeze a brass monkey
ant torrid
ardent *adj* **1** *syn* see IMPASSIONED
rel enthusiastic, urgent; avid, desirous, eager, keen
con calm, composed, imperturbable, nonchalant; apathetic, impassive, phlegmatic; disinterested, dispassionate, impartial, uninterested
ant cool
2 very deep or moving < had an *ardent* longing for knowledge >
syn extreme, intense
rel crying, importunate, insistent, urgent; great, mighty, powerful, strong
con feeble, minimal, slight, trivial
3 *syn* see EAGER

---

syn synonym(s)   *rel* related word(s)
ant antonym(s)   *con* contrasted word(s)
idiom idiomatic equivalent(s)
‖ use limited; if in doubt, see a dictionary

rel hasty, impetuous, impulsive, precipitate; fervid, fiery, hectic, hot; uncontrolled, ungoverned; earnest, intent, urgent, vehement
con dull, heavy, inert, leaden, lumpish; languid, lethargic, listless; apathetic, impassive, phlegmatic
ant easygoing
4 *syn* see FAITHFUL 1
5 *syn* see HOT 1
6 *syn* see SPIRITUOUS
ardor *n* **1** *syn* see PASSION 6
rel avidity; gusto, spirit, verve, zest; excitement, galvanization, quickening, stimulation
con aloofness, detachment, disinterest, unconcern; apathy, lackadaisy, languor, listlessness
ant coolness; indifference
2 *syn* see EAGERNESS
rel ardency, fervor, warmth
3 *syn* see FIDELITY 1
rel adoration, love, worship
arduous *adj* **1** *syn* see HARD 6
2 *syn* see STEEP 1
3 *syn* see TIGHT 4
arduously *adv* *syn* see HARD 8
con easily, facilely
ant effortlessly
area *n* **1** a distinguishable extent of surface and especially of the earth's surface < a large wooded *area* >
syn belt, region, territory, tract, zone
rel expanse, stretch; district, locality, place; lot, plot, section; terrain; circuit
2 *syn* see LOCALITY 1
arena *n* *syn* see SCENE 4
arete *n* *syn* see EXCELLENCE
argent *adj* *syn* see SILVERY
argentate *adj* *syn* see SILVERY
argenteous *adj* *syn* see SILVERY
argentine *adj* *syn* see SILVERY
argot *n* *syn* see DIALECT 2
arguable *adj* *syn* see MOOT
argue *vb* **1** *syn* see DISCUSS 1
rel analyze, investigate, review, sift, study, ventilate; expostulate, object, protest, remonstrate
2 to contend in words < *arguing* about who should answer the phone >
syn argufy, bicker, dispute, hassle, quibble, squabble, wrangle; *compare* QUARREL
rel differ, disaccord, disagree, dissent; balk, demur, jib; clash, conflict
idiom bandy words, have it out, join (*or* take) issue
con accord, agree, concur
3 *syn* see INDICATE 2
4 *syn* see MAINTAIN 2
argue (into) *vb* *syn* see INDUCE 1
argufy *vb* *syn* see ARGUE 2
argument *n* **1** *syn* see REASON 3
rel basis, foundation; position, posture, stance, standpoint
2 a vigorous often heated discussion of a moot question < their continuing *argument* over household expenses >
syn contention, controversy, dispute, hurrah, rumpus
rel argumentation, debate, disputation, polemic; disagreement, dissension, squabbling; embroilment, fuss, hassle, wrangle
3 *syn* see SUBJECT 2
rel position, proposition, statement, thesis
argumentation *n* the act or art or an exercise of one's powers of argument < noted for his skill in *argumentation* >
syn debate, dialectic, disputation, forensic, mooting
rel argument, controversy, dispute; declamation, elocution, eloquence, oratory, rhetoric
argumentative *adj* *syn* see CONTENTIOUS 2
argute *adj* **1** *syn* see SHREWD
2 *syn* see ACUTE 4
aria *n* *syn* see SONG 2
arid *adj* **1** *syn* see DRY 1
rel barren, infertile, sterile, unfruitful
con fecund, fertile, fruitful
2 lacking in interest or liveliness < some of the most *arid* prose ever written >
syn bromidic, dry, dryasdust, dull, dusty, insipid, tedious, uninteresting, wearyful, wearisome; *compare* TEPID 2, UNORIGINAL

rel drab, dreary, flat, heavy, lackluster, leaden, unanimated, unlively; academic, bookish, pedantic; boring, humdrum, monotonous, unimaginative, uninspired
con appealing, bright, lively, sparkling, stimulating, vigorous, vivid
aright *adv* *syn* see WELL 1
arise *vb* **1** *syn* see RISE 4
ant recline; slump
2 *syn* see ROLL OUT
3 *syn* see SPRING 1
rel ensue, follow, succeed
4 *syn* see BEGIN 2
aristarch *n* *syn* see CRITIC
aristo *n* *syn* see GENTLEMAN
aristocracy *n* the highest stratum of a society < the self-centered attitude of some *aristocracies* >
syn aristoi, blue blood, carriage trade, crème de la crème, elite, flower, gentility, gentry, haut monde, optimacy, patriciate, quality, society, upper class, upper crust, who's who
rel nobility, noblesse, patricians; county; beau monde, bon ton, jet set, smart set
con canaille, mob, rabble, riffraff; commoners, commons, masses, people, plebeians
aristocrat *n* *syn* see GENTLEMAN
ant commoner
aristoi *n* *syn* see ARISTOCRACY
arithmetic *n* *syn* see COMPUTATION
arm *n* **1** *syn* see INLET
2 *syn* see ANNEX
3 *syn* see POWER 4
arm *vb* *syn* see FURNISH 1
rel prepare, ready
idiom put in (*or* into) shape
ant disarm
armament *n* *syn* see DEFENSE 1
armamentarium *n* *syn* see SUPPLY
armed forces *n pl* *syn* see TROOP 2
armistice *n* *syn* see TRUCE
armor *n* *syn* see DEFENSE 1
rel cloak, mantle, shroud, veil; buckler, cover, screen, shelter
armory *n* a place where military arms and supplies are stored < the problem of weapon theft from *armories* >
syn arsenal, depot, dump, magazine
army *n* *syn* see MULTITUDE 1
rel crush, horde, mob, press, throng
aroma *n* **1** *syn* see FRAGRANCE
2 *syn* see SMELL 1
rel fetor, mephitis, reek, stench, stink
aromal *adj* *syn* see SWEET 2
rel penetrating, piquant, pungent
ant acrid
aromatic *adj* *syn* see SWEET 2
ant acrid
aromatize *vb* *syn* see SCENT 2
around *adv* **1** *syn* see ABOUT 1
2 *syn* see THROUGH 1
3 *syn* see ABOUT 4
4 *syn* see ABOUT 6
around *prep* *syn* see ABOUT 1
around *adj* *syn* see EXTANT 1
around–the–clock *adj* *syn* see CONTINUAL
arouse *vb* *syn* see STIR 1
rel alert, excite, work up; electrify, thrill; fire, inflame
idiom fan the fire (*or* flame), raise to fever heat, set on fire, stir one's blood (*or* feelings)
con allay, alleviate, assuage, ease, mitigate, relieve; mollify, pacify, placate
ant calm, quiet
arraign *vb* *syn* see ACCUSE
rel cite, summon; test, try
idiom bring to book, call to account
con absolve, acquit, exculpate, exonerate, vindicate; defend, justify
arrange *vb* **1** *syn* see ORDER 1
rel assort, categorize, pigeonhole, sort
con disorder, disorganize, disturb, unsettle; confuse, jumble, muddle, tumble; disperse, scatter
ant derange, disarrange

2 *syn* see DESIGN 3
3 *syn* see PLAN 2
4 *syn* see NEGOTIATE 1
rel design, plan, project, scheme
5 *syn* see HARMONIZE 4
arrangement *n syn* see ORDER 3
rel layout, lineup, setup; method, system
ant disarrangement
arrant *adj* **1** *syn* see UTTER
rel plain, pure, regular, sheer
2 *syn* see SHAMELESS
array *vb* **1** *syn* see ORDER 1
ant disarray
2 *syn* see CLOTHE
array *n* **1** *syn* see GROUP 3
2 *syn* see DISPLAY 2
rel exhibition, exposing, showing; arranging, marshaling, ordering
arrear *n, usu* **arrears** *pl syn* see DEBT 3
arrearage *n* **1** *syn* see DEBT 3
2 *syn* see INDEBTEDNESS 1
arrect *adj* **1** *syn* see ERECT
2 *syn* see ATTENTIVE 1
arrest *vb* **1** to bring to a halt <science cannot yet *arrest* the process of aging>
syn check, halt, interrupt, stall, stay; *compare* STOP 3
rel balk, frustrate, thwart; choke, obstruct, stop (up); delay, detain, hamper, hinder, restrain, retard; interfere, interpose, intervene; contain, stem, withstand
idiom bring to a halt (*or* stand *or* standstill), bring up short, check in full career, cut short
con advance, forward, further, promote; expedite, hasten, quicken, speed
2 to take and hold in custody under authority of the law <*arrested* for murder>
syn apprehend, ‖bust, detain, nab, pick up, pinch, pull in, run in; *compare* CATCH 1
rel immure, imprison, incarcerate, jail, lock (up), ‖slough; attach
idiom lay by the heels, lay hands on
con discharge, free, liberate, release
arrest *n* the taking and holding of a person in custody under authority of the law <unwilling to submit to *arrest*>
syn apprehension, arrestation, arrestment, detention, ‖nab, pickup, pinch
rel capture, catch, collar, seizure, taking
con discharge, freeing, liberation, release
arrestation *n syn* see ARREST
arresting *adj syn* see NOTICEABLE
rel attractive, enchanting, fascinating; affective, appealing, impressive, moving, touching
idiom enough to make one stop and take notice
con common, familiar, ordinary, run-of-the-mill; hackneyed, stereotyped, trite
arrestive *adj syn* see NOTICEABLE
arrestment *n syn* see ARREST
arride *vb syn* see PLEASE 2
rel beguile, divert, entertain, recreate
idiom tickle one's fancy
con bore, ennui, jade, weary
arrival *n* **1** the reaching of a destination <the train was late in its *arrival*>
syn advent, coming
rel appearance, emergence, entrance, issuance, manifestation
con disappearance, going, leaving, withdrawal; recession, retirement, retreat
ant departure
2 *syn* see SUCCESS
arrive *vb* **1** *syn* see COME 1
con get away, go, retire
ant depart
2 *syn* see SUCCEED 3
arriviste *n syn* see UPSTART
arrogance *n syn* see PRIDE 3
ant humility
arrogant *adj* **1** *syn* see PROUD 1
rel domineering, imperative, peremptory; affected, artificial, highfalutin, mannered, showy

idiom too big for one's britches
con humble; deferential, submissive; abject, obsequious, subservient, truckling
ant meek
2 *syn* see POMPOUS 1
arrogate *vb* **1** to claim or take over in a high-handed manner <*arrogated* to himself the right to make all decisions>
syn accroach, appropriate, assume, commandeer, preempt, usurp; *compare* APPROPRIATE 1
rel annex, preempt, preoccupy, sequester; grab, seize, take, take over
idiom help oneself to, make free with, take into one's own hands
con cede, relinquish, resign, surrender, yield
ant renounce
2 *syn* see APPROPRIATE 1
arrondi *adj syn* see CURVED
arroyo *n syn* see RAVINE
arsenal *n* **1** *syn* see ARMORY
2 *syn* see DEPOT 2
arsonist *n syn* see INCENDIARY
arsy–varsy *adj syn* see UPSIDE-DOWN 2
art *n* **1** a usually acquired proficiency in doing or performing <there's an *art* to competent public speaking>
syn adroitness, craft, cunning, dexterity, expertise, know-how, skill
rel capability, competence, handiness, proficiency; address, finesse, ‖savvy
con clumsiness, maladroitness
2 *syn* see CUNNING 2
rel acuteness, astuteness
con candor, frankness, sincerity; directness, straightforwardness, bluffness, bluntness
3 *syn* see TRADE 1
artery *n syn* see WAY 1
artful *adj syn* see SLY 2
rel diplomatic, oily, politic, smooth, suave; facile, specious, superficial; adroit, dexterous
ant artless
artfulness *n syn* see CUNNING 2
article *n* **1** *syn* see POINT 1
rel division, section, segment
2 *syn* see ESSAY 2
rel critique, manifesto, report, statement, study, survey
3 *syn* see THING 3
rel detail, particular
articled *adj syn* see BOUND 2
articulate *adj* **1** *syn* see VOCAL 1
rel clear, distinct, intelligible
ant inarticulate; dumb
2 *syn* see VOCAL 3
rel meaningful, significant; garrulous, prolix, talkative; uttering, venting
ant inarticulate
articulate *vb* **1** *syn* see INTEGRATE 3
rel connect, join, relate; methodize, order, organize, systematize; adjust, coordinate, harmonize, regulate; assemble, collect, gather; unify
con dissect, resolve; divide, part, separate
2 to form speech sounds <regional differences in *articulating* the letter *r*>
syn enunciate, phonate, pronounce, say
rel sound, utter
articulation *n syn* see VOCALIZATION
artifice *n* **1** *syn* see CUNNING 2
rel ingenuity, inventiveness, originality; adroitness, cleverness, keenness, quickness, shrewdness; adeptness, proficiency
2 *syn* see TRICK 1
rel chicane, chicanery, trickery; knavery, rascality, skulduggery; deceit, dissimulation, duplicity, guile
artificial *adj* **1** *syn* see SYNTHETIC
rel fabricated, fashioned, made
con native

---

syn synonym(s)
ant antonym(s)
idiom idiomatic equivalent(s)
‖ use limited; if in doubt, see a dictionary

rel related word(s)
con contrasted word(s)

ant natural

2 taking the place of something else and especially of something finer or more costly < *artificial* diamonds >
  syn dummy, ersatz, false, imitation, mock, sham, simulated, spurious, substitute; *compare* FICTITIOUS 2, SPURIOUS 3
  rel fake, papier-mâché, ‖pretend, unreal; hollow, painted
  con authentic, bona fide, genuine, real, sure-enough, true, veritable

3 lacking in spontaneity and genuineness < exchanged *artificial* smiles >
  syn affected, assumed, feigned, put-on, spurious
  rel histrionic, insincere, overdone, quaint, stagy, theatrical, unnatural; cute, cutesy, goody-goody, mincing, overrefined, simpering; contrived, forced, labored
  con genuine, sincere, spontaneous, unaffected

artist *n syn* see EXPERT
  rel ace, crackerjack, first-rater, shark, topnotcher; genius, prodigy, wonder

artiste *n syn* see EXPERT

artless *adj syn* see NATURAL 5
  rel free, relaxed; aboveboard, forthright, straightforward; childlike, trusting, unsuspicious; untouched, virginal
  con cunning, insidious, sly, wily; calculating, designing, intriguing, scheming; artificial, insincere
  ant artful; affected

arty *adj syn* see PRETENTIOUS 3

arty–crafty *adj syn* see PRETENTIOUS 3

as *conj syn* see BECAUSE

as a rule *adv syn* see USUALLY 2

‖**ascared** *adj syn* see AFRAID 1

ascend *vb* **1** to move upward to or toward a summit < *ascend* a mountain >
  syn climb, escalade, escalate, mount, scale, upclimb, upgo
  rel clamber, get up, scramble, shin; crest, surmount, top
  idiom scale the heights, work one's way up
  ant descend

2 *syn* see RISE 4

ascendancy *n syn* see SUPREMACY

ascendant *n* **1** *syn* see SUPREMACY

2 *syn* see ANCESTOR 1
  rel forerunner, precursor, predecessor
  ant descendant

ascendant *adj syn* see DOMINANT 1

ascension *n syn* see ASCENT

ascent *n* a moving upward or an upward movement < the slow *ascent* of the creaky old elevator >
  syn ascension, rise, rising
  rel elevation, raising, uplifting
  ant descent

ascertain *vb syn* see DISCOVER 3
  rel ask, inquire, interrogate, query, question; appraise, inspect, observe, survey, view; consider, contemplate, study, weigh
  con assume, presume; conjecture, guess, surmise

ascetic *adj syn* see SEVERE 1
  rel abstemious, abstinent, forbearing; self-abasing self-abnegating, self-denying, self-forgetful, selfless; disciplined, restrained, schooled, trained
  con epicurean, sensual, sensuous, sybaritic; abandoned, dissolute, licentious, self-indulgent
  ant luxurious, voluptuous

ascribe *vb* to refer especially to a supposed cause, source, or author < a manuscript commonly *ascribed* to Saint Augustine >
  syn accredit, assign, attribute, charge, credit, impute, lay, refer
  rel attach (to), connect (with), fix (on *or* upon), pin (on), saddle (on *or* upon *or* with); affix, fasten; conjecture, guess, surmise; adduce, advance, allege, cite

aseptic *adj syn* see UNDEMONSTRATIVE

as for *prep syn* see APROPOS

as good as *adv* **1** *syn* see NEARLY

2 *syn* see ALMOST 2

ash *n* the residue left when material is consumed by fire < cold whitened *ash* on the hearth >
  syn ashes, cinders, clinkers
  rel dross, scoria, slag; charcoal, coal(s), coke, ember(s); fumes, smoke, soot

ashake *adj syn* see TREMULOUS

ashamed *adj* humiliated or disconcerted usually by feelings of guilt, disgrace, or impropriety < *ashamed* of her brother's noisy boasting >

syn chagrined, mortified, shamed
  rel abashed, discomfited, embarrassed; abased, humbled, humiliated; abject, hangdog, mean; contrite, penitent, repentant
  idiom unable to show one's face
  con arrogant, assured, overbearing, self-assured; vain, vainglorious
  ant proud

ashen *adj syn* see PALE 1
  rel corpselike, ghostly, macabre; blanched, bleached, decolorized, faded

ashes *n pl syn* see ASH

ashiver *adj syn* see TREMULOUS

ashy *adj syn* see PALE 1

aside *adv* **1** in a slanting or sloping direction < his head hung *aside* as if he lacked the strength to hold it up >
  syn aslant, aslope, obliquely, sideways, sidewise, slant, slantingly, slantingways, slantly, slantways, slantwise, ‖slaunchways, slopeways; *compare* SIDEWAYS 1
  rel askance, askant, askew, awry; downgrade, downhill
  con erectly, uprightly, vertically

2 *syn* see APART 2

3 *syn* see APIECE

‖**aside** *prep syn* see NEAR 2

aside *n syn* see DIGRESSION

aside from *prep syn* see EXCEPT

asinine *adj syn* see SIMPLE 3
  rel puerile; absurd, irrational, unreasonable
  con prudent, sage, sane, sapient, wise; clever, intelligent, knowing, smart; rational, reasonable
  ant judicious, sensible

ask *vb* **1** to call upon for an answer or information < *asked* him to explain his behavior >
  syn catechize, examine, inquire, interrogate, query, question, quiz
  rel argue, canvass, debate, deliberate, discuss, review, talk (over)
  con answer, rejoin, reply, respond, retort

2 to seek to obtain by making one's needs or desires known < *asked* for time to consider the problem >
  syn bespeak, desire, request, solicit
  rel claim, demand, exact, require; beg, beseech, entreat, implore, importune
  idiom put in for

3 *syn* see DEMAND 2

4 *syn* see INVITE
  rel canvass, request, seek

askance *adv* **1** *syn* see AWRY 1
  ant directly

2 with absence of approval or trust < a proceeding one must view more than a little *askance* >
  syn distrustfully, doubtfully, mistrustfully, skeptically, suspiciously
  rel captiously, critically, cynically, doubtingly; deprecatingly, depreciatively, disparagingly
  con approvingly, favorably

askant *adv syn* see AWRY 1
  ant directly

asker *n syn* see SUPPLIANT

askew *adv syn* see AWRY 1
  ant straight

aslant *adv syn* see ASIDE 1

asleep *adj* **1** *syn* see DEAD 1

2 *syn* see NUMB 1

3 *syn* see INACTIVE

as long as *conj syn* see BECAUSE

aslope *adv syn* see ASIDE 1

as much as *adv syn* see ALMOST 2

asomatous *adj syn* see IMMATERIAL 1

aspect *n* **1** *syn* see APPEARANCE 1
  rel countenance, face, visage; air, bearing, port, presence

2 *syn* see PHASE
  rel point of view, slant, standpoint

asperity *n* **1** *syn* see DIFFICULTY 1
  rel austerity, bitterness, grimness, harshness, inclemency, severity, stringency
  con blandness, gentleness, mildness, softness

2 *syn* see INEQUALITY 1

3 *syn* see ACRIMONY

rel harshness, keenness, roughness, sharpness; irritability, snappishness, tartness, waspishness
con blandness, smoothness, suavity, urbanity; courtesy, gallantry
ant amenity

asperous *adj syn* see ROUGH 1

asperse *vb* **1** *syn* see MALIGN
rel deride, mock, taunt; affront, insult, offend
con applaud, commend, compliment
2 *syn* see BAPTIZE

aspersion *n syn* see ANIMADVERSION
rel abuse, invective, muck, vituperation; backbiting, calumny, detraction, scandal, slander; lampoon, libel, pasquinade, skit, squib
con eulogy, extolling, laudation, praise; acclaim, acclamation, applause, plaudits; commendation, compliment

asphyxiate *vb syn* see SUFFOCATE

aspirant *n syn* see CANDIDATE

aspiration *n syn* see AMBITION 1
rel aim, direction, goal, objective; desire, lust, passion, urge

aspire *vb* **1** *syn* see AIM 2
rel hunger, long, pine, thirst; bid (for), strain (for *or* after), struggle (for), try (for)
idiom cry for the moon, have at heart, have one's heart set on, reach for (*or* keep one's eyes on) the stars
con condescend, deign, look down (on); grovel, stoop, wallow
2 *syn* see RISE 4

aspiring *adj syn* see AMBITIOUS 1
rel desirous, impassioned, urgent; wanting, wishful, yearning

as regards *prep syn* see APROPOS

as respects *prep syn* see APROPOS

ass *n* **1** *syn* see DONKEY 1
2 *syn* see FOOL 1

assail *vb syn* see ATTACK 1
rel beat, belabor, buffet, pound, pummel
idiom round on

assailment *n syn* see ATTACK 1

assassin *n* a person hired or hirable to commit murder <found out who paid the *assassin*>
syn bravo, cutthroat, gun, gunman, ‖gunsel, gunslinger, hatchet man, hit man, torpedo, triggerman; *compare* MURDERER
rel apache, desperado, goon, ‖gorilla, highbinder, strong arm, thug

assassinate *vb syn* see MURDER 1

assault *n syn* see ATTACK 1
rel brush, clash, invasion, melee, skirmish; brawl, contest, fracas, set-to

assault *vb syn* see ATTACK 1
rel battle, fight, war; clash, collide, encounter, engage; skirmish

assay *vb* **1** *syn* see TRY 5
rel venture
idiom make an effort to
2 *syn* see ESTIMATE 1
rel demonstrate, prove, test, try; analyze, resolve; calculate, compute, reckon

assemblage *n syn* see GATHERING 1

assemble *vb* **1** *syn* see CONVOKE
2 *syn* see GATHER 6
rel associate, combine, unite; convene, convoke
con dispel, dissipate, scatter; leave, part, quit, separate
ant disperse
3 *syn* see GROUP 1
rel accumulate, aggregate, amass, garner; bunch, clump; bank, heap, mound, pile, stack
con dispel, dissipate, scatter; leave, part, quit, separate; break up, disband
ant disperse
4 *syn* see MAKE 3

assembly *n* **1** *syn* see GATHERING 2
rel association, band, conclave, party, troupe
2 *syn* see GROUP 1
rel crowd, push; faction, interest, sect, wing; brotherhood, fellowship, fraternity
con masses, multitude; canaille, rabble, riffraff, ruck, trash

assent *vb* to give or express one's consent or concurrence <*assented* grudgingly to her plans for the evening>
syn accede, acquiesce, agree, consent, subscribe, yes

rel adopt, embrace, espouse; accept; abide, bear (with), endure, stand, suffer, tolerate; down, stomach, swallow, take; defer, relent, submit, yield
idiom be at one with, cast one's vote for, give the nod of approval, go along with, see eye to eye with
con rebuff, refuse, reject, scorn, scout, spurn; deny, gainsay
ant dissent

assert *vb* **1** to state firmly, positively, or assuredly <he continued to *assert* his innocence>
syn affirm, aver, avouch, avow, constate, declare, depose, predicate, profess, protest
rel adduce, advance, allege, cite, claim, pretend; announce, broadcast, disseminate, proclaim, promulgate, publish, spread
idiom have it
con contradict, contravene, dispute, gainsay, negate, negative, traverse; confute, disprove, rebut, refute
ant deny; controvert
2 *syn* see MAINTAIN 2
rel declare, express, utter, voice; advance, state, stipulate, submit

assertive *adj* **1** *syn* see EMPHATIC
2 *syn* see AGGRESSIVE
rel affirmative; arbitrary, dogmatic, peremptory, positive; assured, certain, cocksure, opinionated, opinionative, self-assured, sure; confident, presumptuous, sanguine, self-confident
con bashful, diffident, modest, shy; amenable, biddable, docile, submissive
ant retiring; acquiescent

assertory *adj syn* see AGGRESSIVE

assess *vb* **1** *syn* see LEVY
2 *syn* see ESTIMATE 1
rel calculate, compute; account, consider, deem, reckon, weigh

assessment *n* **1** *syn* see ESTIMATION 1
2 *syn* see ESTIMATE 1
3 *syn* see TAX 1

asset *n* **1** assets *pl syn* see MEAN 3
rel bankroll, money; equity; principal
ant liabilities
2 *syn* see CREDIT 3
rel distinction, glory, honor, ornament
con detriment, disadvantage, discredit, liability
ant handicap

asshead *n syn* see FOOL 1

assiduous *adj* marked by careful attention or persistent application <learned to speak French fluently by *assiduous* practice>
syn diligent, industrious, operose, sedulous; *compare* BUSY 1
rel hardworking, laborious, moiling; indefatigable, tireless, untiring, unwearied, zealous
idiom hard at it
con casual, haphazard, happy-go-lucky, hit-or-miss, intermittent, random; careless, lax, remiss, slack, sloppy, slovenly; indolent, lazy, slothful
ant desultory

assiduously *adv syn* see HARD 3

assign *vb* **1** *syn* see TRANSFER 4
2 *syn* see ALLOT
rel establish, fix, set, settle
3 *syn* see ASCRIBE
rel associate, link, relate; classify, pigeonhole
4 *syn* see PRESCRIBE 2
rel decide, determine; commit, consign, entrust, relegate

assignation *n syn* see ENGAGEMENT 3
rel agreement, arrangement, understanding; get-together

assignee *n syn* see AGENT 2

assignment *n syn* see TASK 1
rel incumbency, liability, obligation, responsibility

assimilate *vb* **1** *syn* see ABSORB 1
rel imbue, infuse, ingrain, inoculate, leaven, suffuse; adopt, embrace, espouse; corner, engross, monopolize
2 *syn* see EQUATE 2

assimilation *n syn* see RECOGNITION 1
rel awareness, consciousness, mindfulness

assist *vb syn* see HELP 1

---

syn synonym(s)   *rel* related word(s)
ant antonym(s)   *con* contrasted word(s)
idiom idiomatic equivalent(s)
‖ use limited; if in doubt, see a dictionary

rel accompany, attend, escort; concur, cooperate
con clog, fetter, trammel; forestall, prevent; burden, encumber, handicap, tax, weigh down
ant hamper; impede

assist *n syn* see HELP 1

assistance *n syn* see HELP 1
rel backing, supporting, upholding; advantage, avail, profit, use; appropriation, grant, subsidy, subvention
con checking, hampering, hindering, hindrance; balking, foiling, frustration, thwarting
ant impediment, impeding; obstructing, obstruction

assistant *n* **1** *syn* see HELPER
2 a person who takes over part of the duties of a superior < started as *assistant* to the secretary >
syn aid, aide, aide-de-camp, coadjutant, coadjutor, lieutenant
rel acolyte, attendant, second; flunky, henchman, minion, stooge; girl Friday, right-hand man; agent, attorney, deputy, factor, proxy; fall guy, patsy; co-worker, workfellow, yokemate

assistive *adj syn* see HELPFUL 1

assize *n* **1** *syn* see LAW 1
2 *syn* see STANDARD 4

associate *vb syn* see JOIN 1
rel amalgamate, blend, coalesce, merge, mingle, mix; ally, confederate, federate, league
con alienate, estrange; divide, divorce, part

associate *n* **1** *syn* see PARTNER
rel affiliate, ally, confederate, leaguer; abettor, accomplice, collaborator
2 *syn* see COLLEAGUE
3 a person regularly frequenting the company of another < a man is judged by the *associates* he keeps >
syn buddy, chum, comate, companion, comrade, crony, ‖cully, pal, running mate; *compare* FRIEND
rel acquaintance, friend, sympathizer; confidant, familiar, intimate; brother-in-arms, comrade-in-arms
4 *syn* see ACCOMPANIMENT 2
rel complement, correlate, correlative, counterpart, match; correspondent
con competitor, rival; adversary, antagonist, opponent

association *n* **1** the quality or state of being associated < worked in close *association* with the courts >
syn affiliation, alliance, cahoots, combination, conjointment, conjunction, connection, hookup, partnership, tie-up, togetherness
rel coaction, collaboration, concert, cooperation, teamwork; conviviality, gaiety, joviality, sociability
con aloofness, apartness, disjunction, disunion, isolation, separation
ant disassociation, dissociation
2 an organization of persons sharing a common interest or purpose < a buyers' *association* >
syn brotherhood, club, congress, fellowship, fraternity, guild, league, order, society, sodality, union
rel alliance, axis, bloc, coalition, federation, organization; faction, interest, sect, wing; combine, gang, machine, ring
3 *syn* see LEAGUE 4
4 something (as a feeling or recollection) associated in the mind with a particular person or thing < the thought of her childhood home always carried an *association* of loving warmth >
syn connotation, hint, implication, overtone, suggestion, undertone
rel image, picture, vision; appearance, fantasy, illusion, mirage

assort *vb* to arrange systematically < *assort* yarn by color >
syn categorize, class, classify, group, pigeonhole
rel arrange, methodize, order, systematize; distribute, divide, separate; screen, sift; stratify
con derange, disarrange, disorder, disorganize; commingle, jumble, mingle, mix, scramble

assorted *adj* **1** *syn* see MISCELLANEOUS
con chosen, picked, preferred, selected
2 corresponding in such manner or degree as to be appropriately associated < they made a well-*assorted* pair >
syn adapted, conformable, fitted, matched, suited
rel chosen, picked, preferred, selected; associated, bracketed, coupled, linked
con confused, disordered, fouled-up, haywire, jumbled, muddled, scrambled

assortment *n* **1** *syn* see VARIETY 2

2 *syn* see MISCELLANY 1

assuage *vb* **1** *syn* see RELIEVE 1
rel placate
con augment, increase, recruit, reinforce; enhance, exaggerate, heighten, intensify, magnify, strengthen
ant exacerbate
2 *syn* see PACIFY
rel calm, ease, relax, slack, slacken, soothe
con annoy, inflame, nettle, provoke, ruffle, vex

as such *adv syn* see PER SE

assumably *adv syn* see PRESUMABLY

assume *vb* **1** *syn* see DON 2
2 *syn* see DON 1
3 *syn* see ARROGATE 1
rel grab, seize, snatch, take
idiom take over the helm, take possession (*or* command)
4 to take on or present a false or deceptive appearance < their gaiety was *assumed* >
syn act, affect, bluff, counterfeit, fake, feign, pretend, put on, sham, simulate
rel camouflage, cloak, conceal, disguise, dissemble, hide, mask
idiom make believe
5 *syn* see PRESUPPOSE
rel affirm, assert, aver, predicate, profess; allow, concede, grant
6 *syn* see UNDERSTAND 3

assumed *adj syn* see ARTIFICIAL 3
rel factitious, synthetic; deceptive, delusory, illusory, insubstantial, unreal
con authentic, bona fide, genuine, veritable; real, true

assumption *n* **1** *syn* see PRESUPPOSITION
2 something that is taken for granted or advanced as fact < decisions based on *assumptions* about the nature of society >
syn apriorism, posit, postulate, postulation, premise, presumption, presupposition, supposition, thesis
rel conjecture, guess, surmise; hypothesis, theory; axiom, fundamental, law, principle, theorem

asssurance *n* **1** *syn* see WORD 8
rel parole, promise, troth; plight; agreement, compact, covenant, pact, understanding
2 *syn* see CERTAINTY
rel credit; dependence, reliance, trust
con suspicion, uncertainty; disbelief, incredulity, unbelief
ant mistrust; dubiousness
3 *syn* see SAFETY
4 *syn* see CONFIDENCE 2
rel composure, equanimity, sangfroid
con agitation, disquiet, jumpiness, nervousness, shakiness, skittishness; anxiety, doubt, foreboding, funk, perturbation, trepidation
ant alarm
5 *syn* see TEMERITY
rel brazenness, cockiness, presumption; conceit, self-conceit, self-importance, vanity
con diffidence, modesty, shyness, timidity; self-depreciation, self-effacement, unassumingness, unpretentiousness

assure *vb* **1** *syn* see ENSURE
con abash, discomfit, embarrass; buffalo, bulldoze, cow, daunt, intimidate, shake; demoralize, disquiet, unman, unnerve
ant alarm
2 to make one sure or certain of something < pinched his arm to *assure* himself he was awake >
syn convince, persuade, satisfy
idiom bring (*or* drive) home to, lead one to believe, sell one on something

assured *adj* **1** *syn* see CONFIDENT 1
rel collected, composed, cool, imperturbable, unflappable, unruffled; game, plucky, resolute, spunky
con abashed, discomfited, disconcerted, embarrassed, rattled; hesitant, insecure, reluctant, uncertain; apprehensive, timorous
2 *syn* see DECIDED 1
rel certain, fixed, set
con ambiguous, uncertain; enigmatic, mysterious, obscure

assuredness *n syn* see CERTAINTY

astern *adv syn* see ABAFT
rel rear
con ahead, before, forward

as to *prep* **1** *syn* see APROPOS
2 *syn* see BY 5

astonish *vb syn* see SURPRISE 2
　rel overwhelm; affright, alarm, terrify
astonishing *adj syn* see MARVELOUS 1
astound *vb syn* see SURPRISE 2
astounding *adj syn* see MARVELOUS 1
astral *adj* 1 *syn* see STELLAR 1
　2 *syn* see DREAMY 1
　3 *syn* see EXALTED 1
astray *adv syn* see AMISS 2
astricted *adj syn* see CONSTIPATED
astringent *adj* 1 *syn* see ACRID
　rel puckery
　con bland, mellow, mild
　2 *syn* see SEVERE 1
　rel biting, cutting, incisive, penetrating, piercing, stabbing; brisk, caustic, keen, sharp
　con lax, loose, relaxed, slack, weak; unexacting
　3 *syn* see TONIC 1
astucious *adj syn* see SHREWD
　rel discreet, foresighted, prudent; cunning, sly, wily
　con ingenuous, naive, simple, unsophisticated; dull, heavy, obtuse, slow; arid, barren, staid, stuffy, uninspired
　ant gullible
astucity *n syn* see WIT 3
astute *adj* 1 *syn* see SHREWD
　rel discreet, foresighted, prudent; cunning, sly, wily
　con ingenuous, naive, simple, unsophisticated; dull, heavy, obtuse, slow; arid, barren, staid, stuffy, uninspired
　ant gullible
　2 *syn* see SLY 2
　rel subtile, subtle; keen, knowing, sharp
　idiom slippery as an eel, too clever by half
　con aboveboard, forthright, straightforward; ingenuous, naive, simple, unsophisticated
astuteness *n syn* see WIT 3
asudden *adv syn* see SHORT 1
asunder *adv syn* see APART 3
　idiom all to pieces, one part from the other, to shreds
as usual *adv syn* see USUALLY 1
asweat *adj syn* see SWEATY
as well *adv* 1 *syn* see ALSO 2
　idiom over and above
　2 *syn* see EVEN 1
as well as *prep syn* see BESIDES 1
as yet *adv syn* see HITHERTO 1
asylum *n* 1 *syn* see SHELTER 1
　2 *syn* see REFUGE 1
　rel inviolability; security
　3 an institution for the care of the insane <demand for improved *asylums* >
　syn booby hatch, ‖bughouse, crazy house, loony bin, madhouse, ‖nuthouse
　rel farm, home, institution, sanatorium
　idiom ‖funny farm, insane (*or* lunatic) asylum, mental hospital (*or* institution), state hospital
asymmetric *adj syn* see LOPSIDED
at all *adv* 1 *syn* see EVER 5
　2 *syn* see EVER 4
ataraxy *n syn* see EQUANIMITY
atavism *n syn* see REVERSION 1
ataxia *n syn* see CONFUSION 3
at close hand *adv syn* see CLOSE
atelier *n syn* see STUDIO
athenaeum *n syn* see LIBRARY
athirst *adj* 1 *syn* see THIRSTY 1
　rel dehydrated, desiccated, dried up
　2 *syn* see EAGER
　con lackadaisical, languid, listless; autistic, withdrawn
athletic *adj syn* see MUSCULAR 2
　rel active, energetic, strenuous, vigorous
　con delicate; decadent, effete, flabby, soft
athletics *n pl* physical activities engaged in for exercise or pleasure <went in heavily for *athletics* >
　syn games, sports
　rel calisthenics, exercise, gymnastics; drill, practice, workout; amusement, diversion, entertainment, pastime, recreation
athwart *adv* 1 *syn* see ACROSS 1
　2 *syn* see OVER 1

athwart *prep syn* see ACROSS
atiptoe *adj syn* see EXPECTANT 1
atmosphere *n* 1 *syn* see AIR 3
　rel character, flavor, property, quality; characteristic, individuality, peculiarity; impression, suggestion
　2 *syn* see ENVIRONMENT
atmospheric *adj syn* see AIRY 1
atom *n syn* see PARTICLE
　rel dash, touch, trace; shade, smack, spice, soupçon, suggestion, suspicion, tincture, tinge
atomize *vb syn* see DESTROY 1
at once *adv* 1 *syn* see TOGETHER 1
　2 *syn* see AWAY 3
atone *vb syn* see EXPIATE
　rel compensate, pay, recompense, satisfy; appease, conciliate, propitiate
　idiom set one's house in order
atone (for) *vb syn* see COMPENSATE 1
atramentous *adj syn* see BLACK 1
at random *adv syn* see ABOUT 4
atrocious *adj* 1 *syn* see OUTRAGEOUS 2
　rel flagitious, infamous, iniquitous, vicious; barbarous, savage; glaring, rank; abominable, contemptible, despicable, execrable, odious, vile
　con fine, righteous, upright, virtuous; benign, gentle, kindly
　ant humane
　2 *syn* see OFFENSIVE
　rel displeasing, distasteful
　con alluring, magnetic
atrociousness *n syn* see ENORMITY 1
atrocity *n syn* see ENORMITY 1
atrophy *n syn* see DETERIORATION 1
attach *vb syn* see FASTEN 1
　rel associate; add, annex, append; bind, tie
　con disassociate, dissociate; disembarrass, disencumber, disengage, disentangle
　ant detach
attachment *n* 1 the state of being firmly attached to someone or something (as by affection, sympathy, or self-interest) <his *attachment* to an outworn code>
　syn adherence, adhesion, constancy, faithfulness, fidelity, loyalty
　rel firmness, staunchness, steadfastness; allegiance, devotion, fealty
　con disloyalty, faithlessness, infidelity, unfaithfulness; aloofness, distance, remoteness; disinterest, disregard, unconcern, unmindfulness
　ant detachment
　2 *syn* see LOVE 1
　rel piety; devotedness
　con antipathy, disinclination, dislike; alienation, disaffection, estrangement
　ant aversion
attack *vb* 1 to act in violent opposition <cavalry *attacked* the Indian camp>
　syn aggress, assail, assault, beset, fall (on *or* upon), storm, strike
　rel invade, irrupt; charge, raid, rush; besiege, blockade, encompass, invest; beleaguer, beset, harass, harry, press; turn (on)
　idiom gang up on, light into, sail into, set upon, take the offensive
　con defend, guard, protect, shield; combat, oppose, resist, withstand
　2 to begin to work vigorously (as at a task) <*attack* a problem>
　syn bang away (at), tackle
　rel buckle (to *or* down *or* down to), fall to, pitch in, wade (in *or* into)
　idiom address (*or* apply *or* devote) oneself to, give oneself up to
　con dawdle, lag, poke, putter
attack *n* 1 an act of attacking especially in the form of an attempt to injure, destroy, or defame <insecticides that are essential for successful *attack* on insect pests>

---

syn synonym(s)　　　　　　　　　*rel* related word(s)
ant antonym(s)　　　　　　　　　*con* contrasted word(s)
idiom idiomatic equivalent(s)
‖ use limited; if in doubt, see a dictionary

syn aggression, assailment, assault, offense, offensive, onfall, onset, onslaught

rel charge, descent, drive, foray, push, raid, sally, sortie; blitz, incursion, inroad, surprise; action, battle

con championing, justification, protection, support, vindication; opposition, resistance; defending, guarding, protecting, sheltering

ant defense

2 action or an attitude in a struggle that calls for or is opposed by defense < his policy had always been one of *attack* >

syn aggression, aggressiveness, belligerence, combativeness, fight, pugnacity

rel bellicosity, chauvinism, jingoism, warmongering; activation, militarization, mobilization, muster

con submissiveness, yielding

3 an episode of bodily or mental disorder < a sudden *attack* of dizziness >

syn access, fit, seizure, spell, throe, turn; *compare* SIEGE

rel outbreak, paroxysm, spasm; affection, ailment, complaint, disease, disorder

attain *vb syn* see GAIN 1

idiom gain one's end, make good

attainable *adj syn* see AVAILABLE 1

attainment *n syn* see ACQUIREMENT

attempt *vb syn* see TRY 5

rel begin, commence, inaugurate, initiate, start; venture

idiom give (something) a try, take a crack (*or* whack) at

con accomplish, achieve, effect, execute, fulfill, perform; attain, compass, gain, reach

ant succeed

attempt *n* an effort made to do or accomplish something < made a determined *attempt* to improve her writing >

syn endeavor, essay, hassle, striving, struggle, trial, try, undertaking

rel care, effort, pains, trouble; beginning, commencement, initiation, offer, shy, start

con accomplishment, achievement, attainment, finish, fulfillment

attend *vb* **1** *syn* see LISTEN

idiom be attentive (to), give heed (to)

2 *syn* see TEND 2

rel govern, oversee, supervise; direct, handle, manage, regulate, run; aid, assist, help

3 *syn* see ACCOMPANY

rel associate, fraternize, join, mingle, mix

attendant *adj syn* see CONCOMITANT

attendant *n syn* see HELPER

attending *adj syn* see CONCOMITANT

attention *n* **1** a focusing of the mind on something < gave the problem careful *attention* >

syn application, concentration, consideration, debate, deliberation, heed, study

rel assiduity, diligence, industry, sedulity, sedulousness; notice, observation, regard, remark; absorption, engrossment, immersion, intentness

con absence, absentmindedness, abstraction, detachment, remoteness, withdrawal; disinterest, indifference, unconcern, unmindfulness

ant inattention

2 *syn* see NOTICE 1

rel awareness, consciousness, mindfulness, sensibility

con disregard, heedlessness, insensibility, unawareness, unconsciousness

3 *syn* see COURTESY 1

rel deference, homage, honor, reverence; benignity; considerateness, consideration, kindliness, solicitude

con neglect, negligence; aloofness, indifference, unconcern; discourtesy

attentive *adj* **1** concentrating one's attention on something < listeners *attentive* to the speaker's appeal >

syn advertent, arrect, heedful, intentive, observant, regardful

rel alert, aware, mindful; agog, eager, interested, keen; concentrating, earnest, intent; open-eared, open-eyed

idiom all ears (*or* eyes), on the ball, paying attention

con absorbed, abstracted, bemused, preoccupied; absentminded, daydreaming, faraway, oblivious, wandering, woolgathering

ant absent; inattentive

2 *syn* see THOUGHTFUL 3

con aloof, indifferent

ant inattentive; neglectful

attenuate *vb* **1** *syn* see THIN 1

rel lessen; sap; dissipate; constrict, contract, deflate, shrink

con amplify, dilate, distend, expand, inflate, swell; augment, enlarge, increase; enrich

2 *syn* see WEAKEN 1

3 *syn* see THIN 2

attenuate *adj* **1** *syn* see THIN 1

2 *syn* see THIN 2

attenuated *adj syn* see THIN 2

attest *vb* **1** *syn* see CERTIFY 1

rel confirm, corroborate, substantiate, verify; support, sustain, uphold, warrant; affirm, asseverate, depone, swear, testify

con confute, controvert, disprove, refute; contradict, deny, gainsay

2 *syn* see INDICATE 2

rel authenticate, confirm, substantiate

con falsify, misrepresent; distort, garble, pervert, twist, warp

ant belie

3 *syn* see TESTIFY 1

attestation *n syn* see TESTIMONY

at times *adv syn* see SOMETIMES

attire *vb syn* see CLOTHE

rel accouter, appoint, arm, equip, outfit

con bare, denude, dismantle, strip

ant divest

attire *n syn* see CLOTHES

attirement *n syn* see CLOTHES

attitude *n* **1** *syn* see POSTURE 1

rel air, demeanor, port, presence

2 *syn* see POSITION 1

rel point of view; bias, predilection, prejudice, prepossession

attitudinize *vb syn* see POSE 4

attorney *n* **1** *syn* see AGENT 2

rel alternate, locum tenens, stand-in, substitute, supply

2 *syn* see LAWYER

attorney-at-law *n syn* see LAWYER

attract *vb* **1** to exert an irresistible or compelling influence on < her beauty *attracted* all eyes >

syn allure, bewitch, captivate, charm, draw, enchant, fascinate, magnetize, take, wile

rel entice, lure, seduce, tempt; beguile, draw (in), intrigue, inveigle, suck (in); enrapture, entrance; court, invite, solicit

con fend (off), hold (off *or* away), rebuff, repulse; disgust, offend, revolt

ant repel

2 *syn* see INTEREST

attracting *adj syn* see ATTRACTIVE 1

attraction *n* **1** a quality that elicits admiration or pleased responsiveness < yielding to the *attraction* of the balmy afternoon >

syn allurement, appeal, attractiveness, call, draw, drawing power, lure, pull, seduction

rel charm, glamour, interest; delight, pleasure; bait, hook, snare

con offensiveness, repulsiveness, ugliness

2 a relationship characteristic of individuals that are drawn together naturally or involuntarily and exert a degree of influence on one another < the *attraction* between iron and the magnet >

syn affinity, sympathy

rel accord, concord, harmony

idiom drawing together

con conflict, discord, friction, tension

attractive *adj* **1** having the power to attract < an area *attractive* to wildlife >

syn alluring, appealing, attracting, bewitching, captivating, charming, drawing, enchanting, engaging, fascinating, glamorous, magnetic, mesmeric, prepossessing, seductive, siren

rel beautiful, bonny, comely, fair, lovely, pretty; Circean, enticing, fetching, luring, tempting; interesting, taking, winning; beckoning, come-hither, inviting, provocative, tantalizing, teasing; likable, simpatico

con abhorrent, distasteful, obnoxious, repugnant; loathsome, offensive, repulsive, revolting; antipathetic, unsympathetic

ant repellent, repelling; forbidding

2 *syn* see BEAUTIFUL

rel agreeable, goodly, ‖likely, pleasing, sightly

con homely, ill-favored, plain, uncomely, unprepossessing

ant unattractive

attractiveness *n syn* see ATTRACTION 1

attribute *n* **1** *syn* see QUALITY 1

rel particularity, singularity, specialty; brand, earmark, impress, stamp

2 *syn* see SYMBOL 1

attribute *vb syn* see ASCRIBE
rel calendar, chronologize, date, place

attrition *n syn* see PENITENCE

attritional *adj syn* see REMORSEFUL

attune *vb syn* see HARMONIZE 3
rel balance, compensate, counterbalance; accord, agree; fix, rectify, regulate
idiom put in tune, set to rights (*or* in order)
con divide, separate, wean

‖**atween** *prep syn* see BETWEEN 2

‖**atwixt** *prep syn* see BETWEEN 2

atypical *adj syn* see ABNORMAL 1
rel irregular, unnatural; different, divergent; exceptional, odd, peculiar, queer, strange
con customary, usual
ant typical; representative

auberge *n syn* see HOTEL

au courant *adj* **1** *syn* see AWARE
2 *syn* see UP-TO-DATE
3 *syn* see FAMILIAR 3

audacious *adj* **1** *syn* see BRAVE 1
rel adventurous, daredevil, daring, foolhardy, rash, reckless, venturesome; brash, brazen, shameless
con calculating, cautious, chary, wary; judicious, prudent, sane, wise; careful, circumspect, discreet
2 *syn* see ADVENTUROUS
rel fearless, valiant, valorous
con careful, circumspect, discreet; calculating, cautious, chary, wary
3 *syn* see INSOLENT 2
4 free from constraint and formality <found life an *audacious* ever-changing adventure>
syn uncurbed, ungoverned, unhampered, uninhibited, unrestrained, untrammeled
rel emancipated, free, independent; easy, relaxed; careless, heedless, thoughtless; self-absorbed, self-centered, selfish
con checked, curbed, governed, hampered, inhibited, restrained, trammeled; careful, cautious, heedful, mindful, thoughtful; considerate, generous, self-abnegating, self-effacing; drab, dull, pedestrian

audacity *n syn* see TEMERITY
rel cheek, effrontery, face, gall; brass, brazenness, cockiness; forwardness, impudence, resolution; courage, mettle, spirit
con calculation, caution, wariness; shyness, timidity, timorousness; agitation, disquiet, nervousness, perturbation, trepidation
ant circumspection

audible *adj syn* see AURAL 1
ant inaudible

audience *n* **1** *syn* see HEARING 2
rel attention, consideration, ear
2 *syn* see FOLLOWING 2
rel admirers, devotees, fanciers, fans, votaries

audile *adj syn* see AUDITORY

audit *n syn* see EXAMINATION
rel investigation, probe; check, control, corrective

audition *n syn* see HEARING 2

auditory *adj* of, relating to, or experienced through the sense of hearing <*auditory* disorders>
syn acoustic, audile, aural; *compare* AURAL 1

au fait *adj* **1** *syn* see ABLE
2 *syn* see FAMILIAR 3
3 *syn* see DECOROUS 1

au fond *adv syn* see ESSENTIALLY 1

Augean stable *n syn* see SINK 1

aught (*or* **ought**) *n syn* see ZERO 1

augment *vb* **1** *syn* see INCREASE 1
2 *syn* see INCREASE 2

augment *n syn* see INCREASE 1
rel exalt, hike, raise
con attenuate, decrease, dwindle; abridge; alleviate, assuage, relieve
ant abate

augmentation *n* **1** *syn* see ACCOMPANIMENT 1
rel adjunct, annex, attachment, fixture, reinforcement; bonus, boot, extra, plus

2 *syn* see ADDITION
con subtraction

augur *n syn* see PROPHET

augur *vb* **1** *syn* see FORETELL
rel argue, bespeak, indicate
2 to indicate or suggest a future probability <their enthusiasm *augurs* well for the success of the enterprise>
syn betoken, bode, forebode, foreshadow, foreshow, foretoken, omen, portend, presage, promise
rel hint, imply, intimate, suggest; prefigure, shadow (forth)
idiom bid fair to, give promise (*or* fair promise) of, hold out hope of, lead one to believe (*or* expect)

augury *n syn* see FORETOKEN
rel anticipation, premonition, presentiment
con accomplishment, effecting, effectuation, fulfillment; actualization, materialization, realization; appearance, emergence, forthcoming, issuance

august *adj syn* see GRAND 1
rel splendid, sublime, superb; impressive, moving, striking; awe-inspiring, awful, fearful, overwhelming

au naturel *adj syn* see NUDE 2

aura *n syn* see AIR 3
rel appearance, aspect, suggestion; aureole, radiance

aural *adj* **1** heard or perceived with the ear <responded to *aural* stimuli>
syn audible, auricular; *compare* AUDITORY
2 *syn* see AUDITORY

aureate *adj syn* see RHETORICAL
rel baroque, rococo
con moderate, quiet, restrained, sober, temperate
ant austere

auricular *n syn* see AURAL 1

aurora *n syn* see DAWN 1

auslander *n syn* see STRANGER

auspex *n syn* see PROPHET

auspices *n pl syn* see BACKING

auspicious *adj* **1** *syn* see FAVORABLE 5
rel hopeful; golden, halcyon, roseate, rosy
con ominous, portentous, unpropitious; adverse, antagonistic
ant inauspicious; ill-omened
2 *syn* see TIMELY 1

austere *adj* **1** *syn* see SEVERE 1
rel bald, bare, simple, unadorned, undecorated, unembellished, unornamented; earnest, grave, serious, sober, somber
con complicated, elaborate, fancy, flamboyant, fussy, ornate; frivolous, light, light-minded, shallow, superficial
2 *syn* see ACRID
rel biting, keen, rough
con bland, mellow, smooth, soft
3 *syn* see GRIM 2

autarchic *adj* **1** *syn* see ABSOLUTE 4
rel commanding, dogmatic, imperious; nonconstitutional, undemocratic
2 *syn* see FREE 1
rel self-dependent, self-reliant, self-sufficient

autarkic *adj syn* see FREE 1
rel self-dependent, self-reliant, self-sufficient

authentic *adj* **1** worthy of acceptance because of accuracy <an *authentic* portrayal of ancient customs>
syn convincing, credible, faithful, trustworthy, trusty
rel accurate, dependable, factual, reliable, sure; solid, sound, straight, valid; authoritative, cathedral, official, standard
idiom all wool and a yard wide; to be depended (*or* relied) on
con incredible, unconvincing, untrustworthy; equivocal, obscure, uncertain, vague; hypothetical, purported, putative, supposed, supposititious; debatable, doubtful, questionable; nonstandard
ant inauthentic
2 being exactly as appears or is claimed <an *authentic* masterpiece>
syn blown-in-the-bottle, bona fide, genuine, indubitable, pukka, questionless, real, right, simon-pure, sure-enough, true, undoubted, undubitable, unquestionable, veritable, very

---

syn synonym(s)	*rel* related word(s)
ant antonym(s)	*con* contrasted word(s)
idiom idiomatic equivalent(s)	
‖ use limited; if in doubt, see a dictionary	

rel cognizable, identifiable, knowable, recognizable; honest, pure, unadulterated, unalloyed
con deceptive, delusive, delusory, false, misleading, wrong; unidentifiable, unrecognizable
ant spurious
3 syn see CERTAIN 3

authenticate *vb* **1 syn** see CONFIRM 2
rel accredit, approve, endorse; demonstrate, prove, test, try; avouch, vouch (for)
con reject, repudiate, spurn; contradict, deny, negate
ant impugn

author *n syn* see FATHER 2
rel origin, source; ancestor, parent, procreator

authoritarian *adj* **1 syn** see DICTATORIAL
rel heavy-handed, high-handed, oppressive, strict, stringent
ant libertarian; anarchistic
2 syn see TOTALITARIAN 1
rel fascistic, nazi; patriarchal
ant democratic

authoritative *adj* **1 syn** see OFFICIAL
2 syn see TRUE 9
rel attested, authenticated, circumstantiated, confirmed, proven, validated, verified; convincing, indisputable, irrefutable, sure, unrefutable; cathedral, cathedratic
con contestable, controversial, debatable, disputable, refutable; dubious, questionable, suspect, unreliable
3 syn see DICTATORIAL
4 syn see ORTHODOX 1

authority *n* **1 syn** see EXPERT
2 syn see POWER 1
rel governance, government, rule
3 syn see INFLUENCE 1
rel example, exemplar, ideal, model, pattern, standard; force, power, pressure

authorization *n syn* see PERMISSION

authorize *vb* **1** to invest with power or the right to act < I did not *authorize* him to speak for me >
syn accredit, commission, empower, enable, license
rel approve, countenance, endorse; aid, assist, help, support, subserve; advance, facilitate, forward, further, promote
con bar, disallow, enjoin, forbid, interdict, prohibit
2 syn see ENTITLE 2
rel allow, let, permit; approve, countenance, endorse
idiom give one the right to
3 syn see INVEST 2

auto *n syn* see CAR
auto *vb* **1 syn** see DRIVE 5
2 syn see RIDE 1

autobiographer *n syn* see BIOGRAPHER
autobiographist *n syn* see BIOGRAPHER
autobiography *n syn* see BIOGRAPHY
rel diary, journal, letters

autocar *n syn* see CAR

autochthonous *adj syn* see NATIVE 2
con alien, extraneous, extrinsic, foreign; imported, introduced
ant naturalized

autocracy *n syn* see TYRANNY

autocratic *adj syn* see ABSOLUTE 4
rel arrogant, haughty, overbearing, overweening
con deferential, submissive, yielding; forbearing, indulgent, lenient, tolerant

autodidactic *adj syn* see SELF-TAUGHT
autograph *vb syn* see SIGN 1
autognosis *n syn* see SELF-KNOWLEDGE
autoist *n syn* see MOTORIST
automatic *adj* **1 syn** see SPONTANEOUS
rel prompt, quick, ready; accustomed, confirmed, habitual, habituated
2 syn see PERFUNCTORY

automaton *n* **1 syn** see ROBOT 1
2 syn see ROBOT 2

automobile *n syn* see CAR
automobilist *n syn* see MOTORIST
autonomous *adj syn* see FREE 1
rel self-governed; unconstrained, uncontrolled, unsubordinated
con controlled, subordinated; governed, ruled; affiliated, allied

autopsy *n* examination of the body after death usually to determine the cause of death < the *autopsy* of a murder victim >

syn necropsy, ‖post, postmortem, postmortem examination

autoschediasm *n syn* see IMPROVISATION
autoschediastic *adj syn* see EXTEMPORANEOUS

auxiliary *adj* capable of supplying or intended to supply aid or support < an *auxiliary* police unit >
syn accessory, adjuvant, ancillary, appurtenant, collateral, contributory, subservient, subsidiary
rel complementary, supplementary; peripheral, secondary, subordinate, tributary; backing, supporting, upholding; aiding, assisting, helping
con chief, leading, main, principal; sole, solitary, unique

avail *vb syn* see BENEFIT
rel answer, fill, fulfill, meet, satisfy
con damage, harm, hurt, injure

avail *n syn* see USE 3
rel interest; appositeness, suitability
con inappropriateness, unsuitableness

available *adj* **1** that is accessible or may be obtained < the best pen *available* at the present time >
syn attainable, disponible, gettable, obtainable, procurable, securable
rel accessible, convenient, handy
idiom to be had
con unattainable, unobtainable; absent, deficient, lacking, missing
ant unavailable
2 syn see PURCHASABLE 1

avarice *n syn* see CUPIDITY
rel frugality, parsimony, thrift; miserliness, niggardliness, parsimoniousness, stinginess; acquisitiveness, covetousness, graspingness, piggishness
con extravagance; bountifulness, bounty, generosity, liberality, munificence, openhandedness
ant prodigality

avariciousness *n syn* see CUPIDITY

avenge *vb* to inflict punishment by way of repayment for < *avenge* an insult >
syn redress, revenge, venge, vindicate
rel compensate, pay (back), pay out, recompense, repay, requite, retaliate, retribute; chasten, chastise, punish; correct, right
idiom get an eye for an eye, get even with, settle accounts, wreak one's vengeance
con condone, disregard, ignore, overlook; absolve, amnesty, forgive, pardon, remit; bear, endure, stand, suffer, tolerate

avengement *n syn* see RETALIATION
avenging *n syn* see RETALIATION
avenue *n* **1 syn** see WAY 1
‖**2 syn** see DRIVEWAY

aver *vb syn* see ASSERT 1
rel defend, hold, justify, maintain
con deny

average *n* something (as a number, quantity, or condition) that represents a middle point between extremes < somewhat sweeter than *average* >
syn mean, median, norm, par
ant maximum; minimum

average *adj syn* see MEDIUM
rel common, familiar, ordinary; customary, usual
idiom common or garden variety
con choice, excellent, exceptional, prime, superior; conspicuous, noticeable, outstanding, prominent; bad, inferior, low-grade, poor, punk

averagely *adv syn* see ENOUGH 2
avernal *adj syn* see INFERNAL 2
averse *adj syn* see DISINCLINED
rel balky, contrary, perverse; flinching, quailing, recoiling, resistant, shrinking; uncongenial, unsympathetic
ant avid (of *or* for)

aversion *n* **1 syn** see DISLIKE
rel antagonism, antipathy, hostility; dread, fear, horror
con bias, partiality; leaning, propensity, taste
ant predilection
2 syn see ANTIPATHY 2
rel abhorrence, distaste, repellency, repugnance, repulsion, revulsion; disgust, dread, loathing
con bias, partiality, penchant; flair, inclination, leaning, taste
ant attachment; predilection
3 syn see ABOMINATION 2

ant delight

aversive *adj syn* see ANTIPATHETIC 2

avert *vb* **1** *syn* see TURN 6
rel remove, transfer
2 *syn* see PREVENT 2
rel anticipate; balk, foil, frustrate, thwart; check, halt, stay, stop
con advance, further, promote

aviary *n* a house, enclosure, or large cage for confining live birds < the zoo's *aviary* >
syn birdhouse
rel dovecote, dovehouse; columbary, pigeon house

aviator *n syn* see PILOT 2

avid *adj syn* see EAGER
rel covetous, craving, desirous, wanting, wishful; importunate, insistent, pressing, urgent; gluttonous, omnivorous
con aloof, disinterested, uninterested; disinclined, indisposed, loath
ant indifferent; averse

avidity *n syn* see CUPIDITY

avoid *vb syn* see ESCAPE 2
rel avert, deflect, divert, obviate, prevent, ward (off); debar, exclude, preclude; forbid, prohibit
idiom give a miss (*or* a wide berth), have no truck with, set one's face against, steer clear of, turn one's back on
con court, invite, solicit
ant face; meet

avoidance *n syn* see ESCAPE 2

avouch *vb syn* see ASSERT 1
rel confirm, corroborate; acknowledge, admit, confess, own
con deny, impugn

avow *vb* **1** *syn* see ASSERT 1
rel defend, maintain, vindicate; asseverate, swear, testify
2 *syn* see ACKNOWLEDGE 1
con repudiate, withdraw

avowry *n syn* see PATRON SAINT

await *vb syn* see EXPECT 1
rel abide, stay, wait
idiom bide one's time, sweat (*or* tough) it out

awake *vb syn* see WAKE 1

awake *adj syn* see AWARE
rel vigilant, watchful; aroused, awakened, roused, stirred up; excited
con drowsy, sleepy, slumberous, somnolent; inactive, inert, supine

awaken *vb* **1** *syn* see WAKE 1
2 *syn* see STIR 1
rel fire, inflame; alert
idiom stir the feelings (*or* blood) of
con arrest, check, retard, subdue; calm, compose, restrain

awanting *prep syn* see WITHOUT 2

award *vb* **1** *syn* see GRANT 1
rel allocate, allot, apportion, assign; dower, endow, endue
2 *syn* see GIVE 2

award *n syn* see HONOR 2

aware *adj* marked by realization, perception, or knowledge often of something not generally realized, perceived, or known < *aware* of her own inner weakness >
syn alive, apprehensive, au courant, awake, cognizant, conscious, conversant, knowing, mindful, sensible, sentient, ware, witting

rel acquainted, apprised, informed; alert, heedful; impressionable, perceptive, receptive
con anesthetic, impassible, insensible, insensitive; ignorant, unknowing
ant unaware

awash *adj syn* see FULL 1

away *adv* **1** from this or that place < come *away* at once >
syn hence, thence
rel forth, out, therefrom
2 at some distance from a place expressed or implied < he lived several blocks *away* >
syn off, over
rel afar, far; apart, aside
3 without hesitation or delay < fire *away* when you see the target >
syn at once, directly, first off, forthwith, immediately, instanter, instantly, now, PDQ, right, right away, right off, straight, straight away, straight off, straightway
rel momentarily, promptly, ‖pronto, punctually; expeditiously, quickly, speedily, swiftly

away *adj syn* see ABSENT 1

awe *n syn* see REVERENCE 2
rel esteem, regard, respect, veneration, worship; admiration, amazement, wonder, wonderment
con despite, scorn; arrogance, insolence, superciliousness

awe *vb syn* see FRIGHTEN

aweless *adj syn* see BRAVE 1

awful *adj syn* see FEARFUL 3
rel impressive, moving; august, imposing, majestic; splendid, superb; grave, serious, solemn; ominous, portentous

‖**awful** *adv syn* see VERY 1

awfully *adv syn* see VERY 1

awkward *adj* **1** *syn* see CLUMSY 1
rel blundering, bumbling, bungling; clownish, lubberly, oafish; cumbrous, hulking, ponderous
idiom all thumbs
2 marked by a lack of grace, ease, skill, or fitness (as in action or speech) < his *awkward* approach to the problem >
syn bumbling, clumsy, gauche, halting, ham-handed, heavy-handed, inept, lumbering, maladroit, unhandy, unhappy, wooden; compare CLUMSY 1
rel rigid, stiff; discomfited, disconcerted, embarrassed; bunglesome, bungling, inefficient, inexpert, unskillful
con adept, adroit, dexterous, expert, finished, polished, proficient, skilled, skillful, smooth; easy, effortless, facile, simple
ant deft; graceful
3 *syn* see INCONVENIENT
4 *syn* see INFELICITOUS

awry *adv* (*or adj*) **1** deviating from a straight line or direction < the coverlet was pulled *awry* >
syn askance, askant, askew, ‖cam, cock-a-hoop, cockeyed, crookedly
rel aside, aslant, obliquely, slantways
con even, straight, true; directly, undeviatingly
2 *syn* see AMISS 2
rel erroneously, faultily, untruly; aside

ax *vb syn* see DISMISS 3

axiom *n* **1** *syn* see PRINCIPLE 1
2 *syn* see MAXIM

‖**ayah** *n syn* see NURSEMAID

aye *adv syn* see YES 1

B

Babbitt *n syn* see PHILISTINE

babblative *adj syn* see TALKATIVE

babble *vb* **1** *syn* see GIBBER

  2 to talk nonsensically < silly people *babbling* on about trivia >
  syn blabber, blather, drivel, drool, gabble, prate, prattle, twaddle, ‖waffle
  rel clack, jaw, rattle, run on, yak, yammer, yap
  idiom run off at the mouth
  3 *syn* see CHAT 1

babble *n* **1** *syn* see CHATTER
  2 *syn* see GIBBERISH 1

babe *n syn* see BABY 1

babel *n syn* see DIN
  con hush, noiselessness; peace, quiet, silence

babushka *n syn* see KERCHIEF 1

baby *n* **1** a very young child especially in the first year of life < the love of a mother for her *baby* >
  syn babe, bantling, infant, neonate, newborn
  rel bambino, little one, toddler, tot; nursling, suckling, weanling; bratling
  idiom babe in arms
  2 *syn* see WEAKLING
  ‖**3** *syn* see GIRL FRIEND 2

baby *vb* to treat with special, excessive, or fond care < *baby* a sick husband >
  syn cater (to), cocker, coddle, cosset, cotton, humor, indulge, mollycoddle, pamper, spoil
  rel dry-nurse, wet-nurse; dote (on *or* upon), favor; gratify, please, satisfy
  con control, discipline, restrain; abuse, ill-treat, ill-use, mistreat, oppress; neglect, overlook, slight

baby buggy *n syn* see BABY CARRIAGE

baby carriage *n* a four-wheeled push carriage with a folding top for a baby < used the *baby carriage* to wheel home firewood >
  syn baby buggy, bassinet, ‖perambulator, ‖pram

babyhood *n syn* see INFANCY 1

babyish *adj syn* see CHILDISH

bacchanal *n syn* see ORGY 2

bacchanalia *n syn* see ORGY 2

back *n* **1** the surface or part most remote from the front < the *back* of his neck >
  syn posterior, rear, rearward
  rel extremity, tail; reverse
  con anterior
  ant front
  2 *syn* see SPINE

back *adv syn* see ABOUT 6

back *adj* **1** distant from settled areas < *back* regions in the hill country >
  syn frontier, outlandish, remote, unsettled
  rel uncultivated, uninhabited, unoccupied, unpopulated, wild
  con built-up, settled, urban
  2 *syn* see POSTERIOR 2
  ant front

back *vb* **1** *syn* see SUPPORT 2
  rel aid, assist, help; abet
  2 *syn* see CAPITALIZE
  3 *syn* see MOUNT 5
  4 *syn* see RECEDE 1
  con advance, progress

back answer *n syn* see RETORT 2

backbiting *n syn* see DETRACTION
  rel animadversion, reflection, stricture; abuse, invective, obloquy, vituperation
  con accolade, commendation, encomium, eulogy, laudation, paean, panegyric, praise, tribute; adulation, blarney, compliment, flattery, soft soap

backbiting *adj syn* see LIBELOUS

backbone *n* **1** *syn* see SPINE
  2 *syn* see FORTITUDE
  rel hardihood; heart
  con irresoluteness, irresolution

  ant backbonelessness, spinelessness
  3 *syn* see MAINSTAY

backchat *n syn* see BANTER

backcountry *n syn* see FRONTIER 2

‖**backdoor trots** *n pl but sing or pl in constr syn* see DIARRHEA

back down *vb* to withdraw from a previous agreement or stand < a politician *backing down* on an earlier promise >
  syn back off, back out, backpedal, backwater, crawfish (out), cry off, declare off, renege, resile, welsh
  rel disavow, recall, recant, retract, take back, withdraw; backtrack; beg off, weasel (out); balk, demur, hold back, stickle
  idiom get out of, go back on

backer *n syn* see SPONSOR
  rel ally, protagonist; bankroller, ‖grubstaker, ‖meal ticket, promoter

backer–up *n syn* see SPONSOR

backfire *vb* to have the reverse of the desired effect < the new policy *backfired* disastrously >
  syn backlash, boomerang, bounce (back), kick back
  rel fall (through), fizzle, miscarry, miss, ricochet
  idiom come to grief, go on the rocks, ‖lay an egg
  con come off, succeed, work out

backhouse *n syn* see PRIVY 1

backing *n* aid or support given to an undertaking < the project had the *backing* of the city fathers >
  syn aegis, auspices, patronage, sponsorship
  rel championship, cooperation, fosterage; guidance, tutelage; encouragement; assistance, help, support

backland *n syn* see FRONTIER 2

backlash *vb syn* see BACKFIRE

backlog *n syn* see RESERVE

back of *prep syn* see ABAFT

back off *vb syn* see BACK DOWN

back out *vb syn* see BACK DOWN

backpack *n* a carrying case (as of canvas or nylon) held on the back by shoulder straps < carried his supplies in a *backpack* >
  syn haversack, knapsack, pack, packsack, rucksack

backpedal *vb syn* see BACK DOWN
  rel dodge, duck, elude, evade, get around, shirk, sidestep

backset *n syn* see SETBACK

backside *n syn* see BUTTOCKS

backslide *vb syn* see LAPSE
  rel regress, retrovert, return, revert; defect, desert, tergiversate, turn
  idiom fall away, fall (*or* sink *or* slide *or* slip) back into, give in to

backsliding *n syn* see LAPSE 2

backstabbing *n syn* see DETRACTION

backstage *adj or adv* off or away from the part of the stage visible to the audience < *backstage* sounds that gave the impression of a storm >
  syn offstage
  idiom behind the scenes
  ant onstage

backstop *vb syn* see SUPPORT 2

back talk *n* impudent and insolent talk < do as you're told and no *back talk* >
  syn guff, ‖jaw, ‖lip, mouth, sass, sauce
  rel cheek, impudence, insolence

‖**backveld** *n syn* see FRONTIER 2

backward *adv syn* see ABOUT 6

backward *adj* **1** directed, turned, or executed backward < the *backward* swimming of the crayfish >
  syn retral, retrograde
  rel inverted, reversed
  ant advance, forward
  2 *syn* see DISINCLINED
  rel bashful, diffident
  3 *syn* see SHY 1
  4 *syn* see RETARDED
  5 holding to outworn or traditional views, ideas, or principles < had a *backward* attitude toward social inferiors >

syn benighted, ignorant, unenlightened, unprogressive
rel conservative, reactionary; obtuse, stupid, thickheaded; bigoted, hidebound, narrow; blind; unenlightened, uninformed
con advanced, aware, enlightened, forward-looking, progressive, unbenighted
6 not developing or progressing especially in economic and social areas <*backward* nations using primitive farming methods>
syn behindhand, underdeveloped, undeveloped, unprogressive
rel poor, struggling; medieval; benighted, retarded, uncultivated, uncultured
idiom behind the times
con forward-looking, progressive; civilized, cultivated, cultured; modern
ant advanced
backwash *n syn* see FRONTIER 2
backwater *n syn* see FRONTIER 2
backwater *vb syn* see BACK DOWN
rel dodge, duck, elude, evade, get around, shirk, sidestep
backwoods *n pl but sing or pl in constr syn* see FRONTIER 2
‖**backwoodser** *n syn* see RUSTIC
backwoodsman *n syn* see RUSTIC
bad *adj* **1** falling short of a standard of what is satisfactory <a *bad* repair job>
syn amiss, ‖bum, ‖crappy, dissatisfactory, poor, ‖punk, rotten, unsatisfactory, up, wrong
rel deficient, inadequate, inferior; careless, slipshod; defective, disordered, off, unsound; execrable, ‖lousy, miserable, wretched; inadmissible, objectionable, unacceptable; insufferable, intolerable
idiom below par, not up to snuff (*or* scratch)
con excellent, fine, meritorious; acceptable, adequate, sound
2 *syn* see WRONG 1
rel arrant, peccant; graceless, improper, indecorous, untoward; disorderly, misbehaving, naughty, rowdy, ruffianly, unruly; froward, perverse
ant good
3 *syn* see EVIL 5
4 *syn* see EVIL 6
5 having undergone decay <one *bad* apple can spoil the barrel>
syn decayed, putrid, rotten, spoiled
rel fusty, stale; mildewed, moldered, moldy, moth-eaten, musty, rancid, worm-eaten, decomposed, putrefied, putrifacted; tainted, turned
con crisp, dewy, fresh, sweet, unspoiled; choice, picked, prime
ant good
6 *syn* see NAUGHTY 1
7 *syn* see TOUGH 8
8 arousing discomfort or distaste <a *bad* smell>
syn ‖chiselly, disagreeable, displeasing, rotten, sour, unhappy, unpleasant
rel disgusting, foul, nauseating, noisome, noxious, offensive, repulsive, sickening; abhorrent, hateful, loathsome, obnoxious; uneasy; thankless, ungrateful; distasteful, distressing, sticky; ungracious, unhandsome
con agreeable, pleasant, pleasing, refreshing, soothing; unoffensive
9 *syn* see HARMFUL
10 *syn* see DOWNCAST
11 *syn* see NULL
bad actor *n syn* see TROUBLEMAKER
bad books *n pl syn* see DISLIKE
badge *n* **1** *syn* see INSIGNIA
2 *syn* see HONOR 2
badger *vb syn* see BAIT 2
rel plague, tease, worry
badinage *n syn* see BANTER
rel chaffing, guying, japery, joshing, kidding, sport
badland *n syn* see WASTE 1
‖**bad lot** *n syn* see WASTREL 1
badly *adv* **1** *syn* see HARD 5
2 *syn* see AMISS 2
ant well
badman *n syn* see OUTLAW
rel criminal, villain; hood, hoodlum, hooligan, thug; blackguard, devil, knave, rascal, rapscallion, rascallion, rogue, scoundrel

bad–tempered *adj syn* see ILL-TEMPERED
rel cantankerous, cranky, crusty, temperamental, touchy
con forbearing, long-suffering, patient
ant good-tempered
Baedeker *n syn* see HANDBOOK
baffle *vb syn* see FRUSTRATE 1
rel confound, dumbfound, flummox, mystify, nonplus, puzzle; addle, ball up, befuddle, confuse, fog, mix up, muddle; discomfit, disconcert, embarrass, faze, rattle
con enlighten, illuminate
bag *n* **1** a container made of a flexible material and open or opening at the top <a grocery *bag*>
syn ‖poke, pouch, sack
‖**2** *syn* see HAG 2
bag *vb syn* see CATCH 1
rel clench, ‖cop, ‖glom, hook, land, nab, net, sack, scoop
idiom lay by the heels
baggage *n syn* see WANTON
‖**bagged** *adj syn* see INTOXICATED 1
bagnio *n syn* see BROTHEL
bail *n syn* see GUARANTEE 1
bail *vb syn* see DIP 2
bailiwick *n syn* see FIELD
rel district, jurisdiction, neighborhood, place, quarter, realm; beat, circuit, round, walk
bait *vb* **1** *syn* see MOLEST
2 to persist in tormenting or harassing another <*baiting* him with gibes about his humble origin>
syn badger, bullyrag, chivy, heckle, hector, hound, ride
rel annoy, bother, bedevil, devil, rag, worry; harass, harry, haze, vex; ‖bug, nag, pester, push around
3 *syn* see LURE
bait *n* **1** *syn* see LURE 2
‖**2** *syn* see SNACK
bake *vb* **1** *syn* see BURN 3
2 *syn* see FIRE 6
baking *adj syn* see HOT 1
balance *n* **1** the stability resulting from the equalization of opposing forces <keeping his emotional *balance* when under stress>
syn counterpoise, equilibrium, equipoise, equiponderation, poise, stasis
rel collectedness, composure, cool, coolness, coolth, equanimity, repose, sangfroid; aplomb, assurance, self-assurance, self-possession; control, self-control, stability, steadiness; stagnancy, stagnation
con imbalance, unbalance; instability, nervousness, shakiness, uncontrol, unsteadiness
2 *syn* see SYMMETRY
rel congruity, consistency, correspondence, sameness
con disbalance, disharmony, disproportion, incongruity, inconsistency, irregularity, overbalance, unbalance
ant imbalance
3 *syn* see REMAINDER
balance *vb syn* see COMPENSATE 1
rel adjust, attune, harmonize, tune; accord, agree, correspond; even, level, square
idiom strike a balance
bald *adj* **1** *syn* see HAIRLESS
rel bobbed, clipped, cropped, polled, shaven, sheared
con bushy, hairy, hirsute, shaggy; unshaven, unshorn; fleecy, furry, woolly; downy, fuzzy, pilose, pubescent
2 *syn* see BARE 1
rel austere, severe; plain, unadorned, undecorated, unembellished, ungarnished, unornamented; colorless, lackluster, lifeless, lusterless, uncolored
balderdash *n syn* see NONSENSE 2
baldhead *n* one who has a bald head
syn baldpate, ‖baldy, ‖skinhead
baldpate *n syn* see BALDHEAD
‖**baldy** *n syn* see BALDHEAD
balefire *n syn* see BEACON 1
baleful *adj syn* see SINISTER

---

syn synonym(s)   *rel* related word(s)
ant antonym(s)   *con* contrasted word(s)
idiom idiomatic equivalent(s)

‖ use limited; if in doubt, see a dictionary

rel deadly, evil, harmful, pernicious; bodeful, foreboding; unfavorable, unpromising
con auspicious, benign, favorable, promising, propitious; advantageous, beneficial
ant beneficent
2 syn see OMINOUS

balk *n syn* see TIMBER 2

balk *vb* **1 syn** see FRUSTRATE 1
idiom stand in the way of
con back, support, uphold; aid, assist, help
ant forward
2 syn see DEMUR
rel decline, refuse, turn down; flinch, hang back, quail, recoil, shrink
con capitulate, give in

balky *adj syn* see CONTRARY 3
rel immovable, inflexible, unbending, unmanageable; averse, disinclined, hesitant, indisposed, loath, reluctant
con subdued, submissive, tame

ball *n* a more or less spherical body or mass <a *ball* of string>
syn globe, orb, rondure, round, sphere
rel egg, oval, ovoid

ball *vb* to form into a more or less spherical body or mass <*balled* the cookie dough with her hands>
syn conglobate, conglobe, ensphere, round, sphere
rel bead, pill; clot, wad

balladmonger *n syn* see POETASTER

ball and chain *n* **1 syn** see RESTRICTION 1
‖**2 syn** see WIFE

ballast *vb syn* see STABILIZE

ballerina *n syn* see DANCER

ballet girl *n syn* see DANCER

ballot *n* **1** a piece of paper used to cast a vote in an election <deliberately spoiled his *ballot*>
syn ticket, vote
rel Australian ballot, Indiana ballot, Massachusetts ballot, office-block ballot, office-group ballot, party-column ballot, secret ballot
2 syn see SUFFRAGE

ballot *vb syn* see ELECT 2

‖**ballup** *n syn* see CONFUSION 3

ball up *vb syn* see CONFUSE 2

ballyhoo *vb syn* see TOUT

balm *n* **1 syn** see OINTMENT
2 syn see FRAGRANCE

balm *vb syn* see CALM

balmy *adj* **1 syn** see SWEET 2
rel musky; refreshing, rejuvenating, restorative; pleasant, pleasing
2 syn see GENTLE 1
rel agreeable, delightful, gratifying, pleasant, pleasing; allaying, assuaging, balsamic, easing, lightening, relieving, soothing
con annoying, bothering, bothersome, irking, irksome, vexing
‖**3 syn** see FOOLISH 2

‖**baloney** *n syn* see NONSENSE 2

balustrade *n syn* see RAILING

bamboozle *vb syn* see DUPE
rel bilk, diddle, swindle

ban *vb syn* see FORBID
rel illegalize, outlaw
con approve, authorize; suffer, tolerate

ban *n syn* see TABOO

banal *adj syn* see INSIPID 3
rel hackneyed, pedestrian, trite, warmed-over; bromidic, commonplace, corny, platitudinous, stock; bewhiskered, hoary, old; asinine, fatuous, silly, simple
con fresh, new, novel; different, uncommon, unusual; stimulating, zesty; choice, rare, recherché
ant original

banality *n syn* see COMMONPLACE

banausic *adj* **1 syn** see DULL 9
2 syn see MATERIALISTIC

band *n syn* see STRIP 1
rel belt, border, edge, line; tape; fascia, taenia; streak, vein

band *vb* **1 syn** see BELT 1
2 syn see UNITE 2
rel amalgamate, unionize; consociate; club, team (up)
con disintegrate, disperse, dissolve, separate

ant break up, disband

band *n* **1 syn** see COMPANY 4
rel assembly, bevy, body, bunch, covey, group; detachment, detail
2 syn see GROUP 1
3 syn see ORCHESTRA

bandage *vb* to cover with a bandage <*bandage* wounds>
syn bind, dress

bandanna *n syn* see KERCHIEF 1

bandar-log *n syn* see CHATTERBOX

bandbox *adj syn* see DAPPER

bandeau *n syn* see STRIP 1

banderole *n syn* see FLAG

‖**bandido** *n syn* see OUTLAW
rel brigand, footpad, highwayman, holdup man; bravo, cutthroat, gunman, villain; gangster, mobster, racketeer

banding *n syn* see STRIP 1

bandit *n* **1 syn** see OUTLAW
rel brigand, footpad, highwayman, holdup man; bravo, cutthroat, villain; gangster, mobster, racketeer; jayhawker
2 syn see MARAUDER

bandwagon *n syn* see FASHION 3

bandy *vb syn* see EXCHANGE 3
rel chuck, flip, pitch, throw, toss; banter; answer, repay, retort
idiom bat (or beat) back and forth

bandy *adj syn* see BOWLEGGED

bandy-legged *adj syn* see BOWLEGGED

bane *n* **1 syn** see POISON
2 syn see DOWNFALL 2

baneful *adj* **1 syn** see PERNICIOUS
rel injurious; insalubrious, noisome, unhealthy, unwholesome
con benign, favorable, propitious; advantageous, helpful, profitable; healthful, salubrious, salutary, wholesome
ant beneficial
2 syn see OMINOUS

‖**bang** *vb syn* see SURPASS 1

bang *n* **1 syn** see BLOW 1
2 a loud percussive or explosive noise <slammed the book shut with a *bang*>
syn blast, boom, burst, clap, crack, crash, slam, smash, wham
rel noise, report, sound; discharge, explosion, pop, shot; howl, roar, roll, rumble, thunder
3 syn see THRILL
4 syn see SMASH 6
5 syn see VIGOR 2

bang *adv syn* see JUST 1

bang away (at) *vb syn* see ATTACK 2

bang-up *adj syn* see EXCELLENT

banish *vb* to eject by force or authority from a country, state, or sovereignty <*banish* an enemy of the king>
syn cast out, deport, displace, exile, expatriate, expel, expulse, ‖lag, ostracize, oust, relegate, run out, transport; *compare* EJECT 1
rel disfellowship, excommunicate, rusticate; debar, exclude, shut out; drive out, eject, evict, turn out; bump, can, cashier, discharge, dismiss, fire, put out, sack; blackball, blacklist, boycott

banishment *n syn* see EXILE 1

banister *n syn* see RAILING

bank *n* **1 syn** see PILE 1
rel snowbank, snowdrift; cloudage, fogbank
2 syn see SHORE
rel bankside, levee, riverfront, streamside; lakefront, lakeshore, lakeside, margin; oceanfront, seabank, seabeach, seaboard, seafront, sea frontage, sea line, sea sands, shingle
idiom water's edge

bank *vb syn* see HEAP 1
rel compact, concentrate

bank *vb* to place money in a bank <*banks* half his paycheck every week>
syn deposit
rel invest, lay aside, lay away, salt away, salt down, save, set aside, sock away; cache, coffer, hoard, squirrel (away), stash
con draw out, take out, withdraw; disburse, expend, fork (over *or* out), lay out, pay (out), spend

bank (on *or* upon) *vb syn* see RELY (on *or* upon)
rel intend, plan; bet (on), gamble (on), stake, venture, wager
idiom bank the rent on, bet one's bottom dollar on, go bail on, lay money on

bankroll *vb syn* see CAPITALIZE

bankrupt *vb* **1** *syn* see DEPLETE
  rel break, impair, incapacitate
  con rebuild, repair, restore, revive; augment, bolster, fortify, strengthen
  2 *syn* see STRIP 2
  3 *syn* see RUIN 3
  4 *syn* see RUIN 2
banned *adj* **1** *syn* see FORBIDDEN
  2 *syn* see CONTRABAND
banner *n* *syn* see FLAG
  rel banneret
banner *adj* *syn* see EXCELLENT
bannerol *n* *syn* see FLAG
banquet *n* *syn* see DINNER
  rel bridale, feed, ‖gaudy, harvest home, repast, ‖tuck, ‖tuck-in, ‖tuck-out
bantam *adj* **1** *syn* see SMALL 1
  2 *syn* see SAUCY 1
banter *vb* **1** to make fun of good-naturedly < the students resented their teacher's *bantering* them about mistakes >
  syn chaff, fool, fun, jest, ‖jive, joke, jolly, josh, kid, rag, razz, rib
  rel deride, guy, mock, quiz, rally, ridicule, satirize, taunt, tease, twit
  idiom make fun of, make merry with, poke fun at
  ‖**2** *syn* see FACE 3
  ‖**3** *syn* see COAX
banter *n* animated back-and-forth exchange of remarks < entertained the group with their jolly *banter* >
  syn backchat, badinage, ‖cross talk, persiflage, repartee, snip=snap
  rel chitchat, gossip, gossipry, small talk; rallying, teasing; exchange, give-and-take
  con debate, deliberation, discussion
bantling *n* *syn* see BABY 1
baptismal name *n* *syn* see GIVEN NAME
baptize *vb* **1** to administer the rite of baptism < a child *baptized* in the Catholic Church >
  syn asperse, christen, immerse, sprinkle
  rel cleanse, purify, regenerate
  2 *syn* see NAME 1
bar *n* **1** a solid piece of material usually rectangular and considerably longer than it is wide < a *bar* of gold >
  syn billet, ingot, rod, slab, stick, strip
  2 something that stands in the way of some objective < his religion was a *bar* to membership in that exclusive club >
  syn barricade, barrier, blank wall, block, blockade, fence, roadblock, stop, wall
  rel clog, encumbrance, hamper, hindrance, impediment; hurdle, obstacle, obstruction, stumbling block; check, checkrein, control, curb; bamboo curtain, iron curtain; difficulty, hardship, vicissitude
  3 *syn* see OBSTACLE
  rel check, checkrein, control, curb
  con accommodation, convenience, facility, service
  ant advantage
  4 *syn* see COURT 2
  5 a room or public establishment where alcoholic beverages are served < nightly discussions in the *bar* >
  syn barroom, ‖boozer, ‖bucket shop, buvette, cantina, cocktail lounge, drinkery, drunkery, ‖gin mill, ‖groggery, ‖grogshop, lounge, pothouse, pub, ‖public house, ‖rum-hole, rummery, ‖rum-mill, rumshop, saloon, tap, taproom, tavern, watering hole, watering place; compare ALEHOUSE
  rel barrelhouse, bistro, bottle club, cabaret, café, dive, honky=tonk, nightclub, rathskeller, roadhouse, wineshop
bar *vb* **1** *syn* see LIMIT 2
  2 *syn* see EXCLUDE
  rel block, hinder; leave out, omit, pass over; banish, deport, exile, ostracize
  con accept, receive, welcome; allow, let, permit
  ant admit, include
  3 *syn* see HINDER
  rel halt, stop
  con back, support, uphold
bar *prep* *syn* see EXCEPT
barathrum *n* *syn* see HELL
barb *n* *syn* see SHAFT 2

barbarian *adj* **1** of, relating to, or characteristic of people that are not fully civilized < the *barbarian* tribes that sacked Rome >
  syn barbaric, barbarous, Gothic, Hunnic, Hunnish, rude, savage, uncivil, uncivilized, uncultivated, wild
  rel heathenish, vandal, vandalic; backward, coarse, crude, ill=mannered, primitive, rough; untamed; uncouth, uncultured; beastish, bloodthirsty, brutal, cruel, ferocious, inhuman
  con gentle, peaceful, subdued, submissive, tame; cultured, enlightened, humane, sophisticated; genteel, refined, well-bred, well-mannered
  ant civilized
  2 *syn* see BARBARIC 1
barbaric *adj* **1** marked by a lack of restraint, cultivated taste, and refinement < the *barbaric* use of color and ornament >
  syn barbarian, barbarous, graceless, outlandish, tasteless, vulgar, wild
  rel coarse, crude, rough, rude, uncouth; flamboyant, florid, ornate, ostentatious, showy; blatant, flashy, garish, gaudy, loud, tawdry; cacophonous, harsh, raucous; aggressive
  con quiet, restrained, soft, subdued; concinnous, cultivated, elegant, polished, refined; smooth, sophisticated, urbane
  2 *syn* see BARBARIAN 1
barbarism *n* a word or expression which in form or use offends against contemporary standards of correctness or purity in a language < many writers consider *irregardless* a *barbarism* >
  syn corruption, impropriety, slangism, solecism, vernacularism, vulgarism
  rel neologism; colloquialism, foreignism; shibboleth; Goldwynism, Irish bull, malaprop, malapropism, spoonerism, caconym; error, lapse, misuse, slip
barbarous *adj* **1** *syn* see BARBARIAN 1
  2 *syn* see OUTRAGEOUS 1
  3 *syn* see BARBARIC 1
  rel backward, benighted, cretinous, ignorant, illiterate, lowbrow, philistine, uneducated, unlettered, unread, unschooled, untaught, untutored
  con aware, informed, sophisticated, with-it; finished, polished, rounded; well-bred, well-mannered; educated, intelligent, learned, schooled; erudite, well-read
  4 *syn* see FIERCE 1
  rel heartless, uncompassionate, unmerciful; atrocious, monstrous, outrageous; bloody, butcherly, sanguinary; fiendish, sadistic
  con forbearing, lenient, merciful, tolerant; compassionate, sympathetic, tender; benevolent, humane, humanitarian
  ant clement
barbate *adj* *syn* see BEARDED
barber *n* one whose occupation is primarily cutting hair
  syn haircutter
  rel coiffeur, coiffeuse, friseur, hairdresser, hair stylist; beautician, cosmetologist; clipper, cropper, shaver
bard *n* **1** a poet-singer who sang or recited verse to the accompaniment of a stringed instrument (as a harp) < *bards* were the theater of olden times >
  syn jongleur, minstrel, troubadour
  rel meistersinger, minnesinger, rhapsodist; gleeman; skald; conteur
  2 *syn* see POET
bardlet *n* *syn* see POETASTER
bardling *n* *syn* see POETASTER
bare *adj* **1** lacking a natural or usual cover or finish < the room looked *bare* without curtains and pictures >
  syn bald, naked, nude
  rel denuded, dismantled, divested, peeled, stripped, uncovered; baldish, depilated, hairless; unattired, unclad, unclothed, undressed, unrobed; arid, bleak, desert, desolate
  con attired, clad, clothed, dressed, garbed; furry, hairy; green, leafy, luxuriant, verdant; complete, consummate, finished, perfect
  ant covered
  2 *syn* see OPEN 2
  3 *syn* see EMPTY 1

---

syn synonym(s)   *rel* related word(s)
ant antonym(s)   *con* contrasted word(s)
idiom idiomatic equivalent(s)
‖ use limited; if in doubt, see a dictionary

rel barren, depleted, destitute, dried-up, emptied, exhausted; unfilled, unstocked, unsupplied

con bountiful, bursting, chock-full, complete, crammed, laden, overflowing, overfull, replete, stuffed; full, stocked, supplied

4 *syn* see VERY 4

bare *vb syn* see STRIP 2

rel disclose, exhibit, expose, reveal, show, unveil

con camouflage, cloak, disguise, dissemble, mask; apparel, attire, dress, garb, invest, robe

ant cover

barefaced *adj syn* see SHAMELESS

rel blunt, candid, frank, open, plain, temerarious; indecent, indecorous, unseemly

con covert, secret, secretive, stealthy; cautious, circumspect, discreet, tactful

ant furtive

barefisted *adj or adv syn* see BARE-HANDED

barefoot *adj* **1** wearing no shoes or stockings < always went *barefoot* in the summer >

syn shoeless, unsandaled, unshod

con socked, stockinged; sockless; booted, sandaled, shod

2 *syn* see DISCALCED

bare–handed *adj or adv* without covering on the hands < box *bare-handed* >

syn barefisted, bareknuckle

ant gloved

bareknuckle *adj or adv syn* see BARE-HANDED

barely *adv syn* see JUST 2

con amply; adequately, enough, sufficiently

barf *vb syn* see VOMIT

bargain *n* **1** an advantageous purchase < at that price the car is a *bargain* >

syn buy, closeout, pennyworth, steal

rel deal; giveaway

con cheat, flimflam, gouge, sticking, sting

2 *syn* see CONTRACT

bargain *vb* **1** *syn* see HAGGLE 2

rel arrange, confer, negotiate; compromise

2 *syn* see TRADE 1

barge *vb syn* see LUMBER

bark *vb syn* see SNAP 1

barkeeper *n* **1** *syn* see SALOONKEEPER

2 *syn* see BARTENDER

‖**barmaid** *n syn* see BARTENDER

barman *n syn* see BARTENDER

Barmecidal *adj syn* see APPARENT 2

barnacle *n syn* see PARASITE

‖**barney** *n syn* see QUARREL

barnyard *adj syn* see OBSCENE 2

baron *n syn* see MAGNATE

baronial *adj syn* see GRAND 1

baroque *adj syn* see ORNATE

rel embellished, gilt, ornamented, scrolled

con austere, gray

barrage *n* a vigorous expulsion or projection of many things at once < the announcement was met with a *barrage* of protests >

syn bombardment, broadside, burst, cannonade, drumfire, fusillade, hail, salvo, shower, storm, volley

rel burst, eruption, flare, outburst, stream, surge, tornado

barrel *n* **1** *syn* see CASK

2 *syn* see MUCH

barrel *vb syn* see HURRY 2

barrelhouse *n syn* see DIVE

barrelhouse *vb syn* see HURRY 2

barren *adj* **1** *syn* see STERILE 1

rel childless, fallow, heirless, issueless

con pregnant; fertile

ant fecund

2 deficient in production of vegetation and especially crops < *barren* deserts and wastelands >

syn hardscrabble, infertile, unbearing, unfertile, unproductive

rel fallow; irreclaimable, uncultivable, unhusbanded, untillable, wild; bleak, depleted, improverished, poor, worn-out; vegetationless, verdureless; arid, desert, dry, parched

con arable, fruitful, productive; fat, rich; lush, luxuriant; green, verdant, verdurous

ant fertile

barren *n syn* see WASTE 1

barricade *n syn* see BAR 2

barrier *n syn* see BAR 2

barring *prep syn* see EXCEPT

barroom *n syn* see BAR 5

bar sinister *n syn* see STIGMA

bartender *n* one who serves alcoholic beverages at a bar < worked for some years as a *bartender* >

syn barkeeper, ‖barmaid, barman, mixologist, tapster; *compare* SALOONKEEPER

barter *vb syn* see TRADE 1

basal *adj* **1** *syn* see FUNDAMENTAL 1

rel pedimental; bottommost, lowermost, lowest, nethermost, undermost

con highest, uppermost

2 *syn* see ELEMENTARY 1

base *n* **1** something on which another thing is reared or built or by which it is supported or fixed in place < the *base* of a lamp >

syn basement, basis, bed, bedrock, bottom, footing, foundation, ground, groundwork, hardpan, infrastructure, rest, seat, seating, substratum, substruction, substructure, underpinning, understructure; *compare* BASIS 1

rel bolster, buttress, framework, prop, stand, stay, support; foot

2 *syn* see BASIS 1

3 *syn* see BOTTOM 3

base *vb* to supply or to serve as a basis < *based* his accusation on sound evidence >

syn bottom, establish, found, ground, predicate, rest, stay

rel build, construct, fix, plant, seat, set up

base *adj* **1** *syn* see IGNOBLE 1

2 *syn* see CHEAP 2

3 contemptible because beneath minimal standards of human decency < a *base* lying cheat >

syn despicable, ignoble, low, low-down, servile, sordid, squalid, ugly, vile, wretched; *compare* CONTEMPTIBLE

rel beggarly, lousy, sorry; abominable, disgraceful, loathsome; bad, evil, wicked; base-minded, low-minded, meanspirited; caitiff, cowardly, dastardly, recreant; unworthy; dirty, filthy; degrading, humiliating, ignominious

con honest, honorable, upright; virtuous; ethical, moral, righteous; fair, forbearing, open-minded, patient, reasonable, tolerant, understanding

ant noble

baseborn *adj* **1** *syn* see IGNOBLE 1

2 *syn* see ILLEGITIMATE 1

baseless *adj* being without cause or occasion < anxious old ladies with their *baseless* fears >

syn bottomless, foundationless, gratuitous, groundless, uncalled-for, unfounded, ungrounded, unwarranted

rel false, wrong; indefensible, reasonless, unjustifiable, unsolid, unsupported, unsustained, untenable; empty, idle, vain; needless, pointless, senseless, unnecessary, unneeded

con actual, real, reasonable, true; authentic, bona fide, genuine, valid

basement *n syn* see BASE 1

bash *n* **1** *syn* see BLOW 1

2 *syn* see SHINDIG 1

bashful *adj syn* see SHY 1

rel timorous; recoiling, shrinking; mousy; abashed, embarrassed; blushful

con assured, bold, intrepid; arrogant, barefaced, brazen, impudent, shameless; loquacious, talkative

ant brash, forward

basic *adj* **1** *syn* see FUNDAMENTAL 1

rel capital, chief, main, principal

2 *syn* see ELEMENTAL 1

basic *n syn* see ESSENTIAL 1

basically *adv syn* see ESSENTIALLY 1

basin *n syn* see DEPRESSION 2

basis *n* **1** something that supports or sustains anything immaterial < his argument rested on a *basis* of conjecture >

syn base, bedrock, footing, foundation, ground, groundwork, infrastructure, root, substratum, underpinning; *compare* BASE 1

rel axiom, fundamental, law, principle, theorem; assumption, postulate, premise, presumption, presupposition; essence, heart

2 *syn* see BASE 1

3 something serving as a reason or justification for an action or opinion < resented such a challenge without *basis* or reason >

syn foundation, warrant
rel call, justification, right; ground(s), reason

bask *vb* **1** *syn* see SUN
  2 *syn* see WALLOW 3
bassinet *n syn* see BABY CARRIAGE
bastard *n* **1** one born out of wedlock < bore a *bastard* before she was fifteen >
  syn by-blow, catch colt, chance child, come-by-chance, filius nullius, filius populi, illegitimate, love child, natural child, whoreson, woods colt
  2 *syn* see HYBRID
bastard *adj* **1** *syn* see ILLEGITIMATE 1
  2 *syn* see SPURIOUS 3
bastardize *vb syn* see DEBASE 1
bastardy *n syn* see ILLEGITIMACY 1
baste *vb* **1** *syn* see BEAT 1
  rel clobber, ‖larrup, mill, whip
  2 *syn* see SCOLD 1
bastille *n syn* see JAIL
bastille *vb syn* see IMPRISON
bastinado *n syn* see BLOW 1
bastion *n syn* see BULWARK
bat *n* **1** *syn* see BLOW 1
  2 *syn* see CUDGEL
  ‖**3** *syn* see SPEED 2
  4 *syn* see BINGE 1
‖**bat** *n syn* see HAG 2
bat *vb syn* see WANDER 1
bat *vb syn* see WINK
batch *n syn* see GROUP 3
bate *vb* ‖**1** *syn* see ABATE 4
  ‖**2** *syn* see DECREASE
  3 *syn* see EXCLUDE
bath *n, usu* **baths** *pl syn* see SPA 1
‖**bath** *vb syn* see BATHE 1
bathe *vb* **1** to clean oneself with a bath < *bathed* only on Saturday nights >
  syn ‖bath, shower, tub, wash
  rel soap; douse, soak
  2 to flow or splash against < waves *bathed* the rocky shore >
  syn lap, lave, lip, wash
  rel drench, soak, sop, souse; flush
bathetic *adj* **1** *syn* see TRITE
  2 *syn* see SENTIMENTAL
bathtub gin *n syn* see MOONSHINE 2
bating *prep syn* see EXCEPT
baton *n syn* see CUDGEL
batter *vb* **1** to affect (as by repeated blows) so severely as to disfigure or damage < so *battered* in the fight he couldn't even crawl away > < a boat *battered* to pieces by stormy seas >
  syn ‖bung up, mangle, maul
  rel disable, disfigure; maim, mutilate; cripple, lame; bruise, contuse, lacerate; baste, clobber, pummel; shatter, wreck
  idiom beat black and blue, beat to pieces (*or* shreds), beat within an inch of one's life
  2 *syn* see BEAT 1
battery *n syn* see GROUP 3
battle *n* a hostile meeting between opposing military forces < the *battle* continued until nightfall >
  syn action, engagement
  rel brush, clash, encounter, pitched battle, scrimmage, skirmish; assault, attack, onset, onslaught, sortie; combat, conflict, contest, fight; hostilities
battle *vb syn* see CONTEND 1
  rel clash, scrimmage; assail, assault, attack, bombard
battle cry *n* a word or phrase used as a slogan by a faction < "death to the invader" was the *battle cry* >
  syn cry, motto, rallying cry, war cry; *compare* CATCHWORD
battlesome *adj syn* see QUARRELSOME 2
‖**batty** *adj syn* see INSANE 1
bauble *n syn* see KNICKKNACK
bavardage *n syn* see SMALL TALK
bawd *n syn* see PROSTITUTE
bawdy house *n syn* see BROTHEL
bawl *vb* **1** *syn* see ROAR
  rel holler, scream, screech, shout, shriek, squall, yammer, yell
  2 to cry and weep loudly or lustily especially from distress < the baby *bawled* and kicked when its bottle was taken away >

syn howl, squall, wail, yowl; *compare* CRY 2, ROAR
  rel blubber, boohoo, cry, sob, weep
bawl out *vb syn* see SCOLD 1
  rel condemn, denounce
  idiom read a lecture (*or* lesson)
bay *n, usu* **bays** *pl syn* see HONOR 2
bay *vb syn* see HOWL 1
bay *n syn* see INLET
baygall *n syn* see SWAMP
bayou *n syn* see INLET
bay window *n syn* see POTBELLY
bazoo *n* ‖**1** *syn* see MOUTH 1
  2 *syn* see RASPBERRY
be *vb* to have actuality or reality < I think, therefore I *am* >
  syn breathe, exist, live, move, subsist
  rel hold, obtain, stand; abide, continue, endure, go on, persist, prevail, remain; come
beach *n syn* see SHORE
  rel oceanfront; lakeshore, lakeside
beach *vb syn* see SHIPWRECK 1
beached *adj syn* see AGROUND
beacon *n* **1** a signal fire usually on an elevated place < a *beacon* on the hill to warn of danger >
  syn balefire, watchfire
  rel flare; bonfire
  2 *syn* see LIGHTHOUSE
beak *n* **1** *syn* see BILL 1
  2 *syn* see NOSE 1
  3 *syn* see PROMONTORY
  ‖**4** *syn* see JUDGE 2
beak *vb syn* see PECK 1
be-all and end-all *n* **1** *syn* see ESSENCE 2
  2 *syn* see WHOLE 1
beam *n* **1** *syn* see TIMBER 2
  2 *syn* see RAY 1
  3 *syn* see BUTTOCKS
beam *vb* **1** *syn* see SHINE 1
  2 *syn* see SMILE
beaming *adj syn* see BRIGHT 1
‖**bean** *n syn* see HEAD 1
beanery *n syn* see EATING HOUSE
beany *adj syn* see SPIRITED 2
bear *vb* **1** *syn* see CARRY 1
  rel shoulder
  2 *syn* see BEHAVE 1
  3 to have attached to one < the bottle *bears* the label "poisonous" >
  syn carry, have, possess
  rel display, exhibit, show
  con lack, need, want
  4 *syn* see ACCOMPANY
  5 to give birth to offspring < she has *borne* several children >
  syn ‖birth, ‖born, bring forth, deliver
  idiom bring abed, bring to bed, bring to birth, give birth to, have a baby
  con abort, miscarry
  6 *syn* see PRESS 8
  7 *syn* see PRESS 1
  8 *syn* see PROCREATE 1
  9 to bring forth a product < the apple trees *bear* every year >
  syn produce, turn out, yield
  rel breed, engender, generate, propagate, reproduce; fructify, fruit; fabricate, fashion, form, make, shape; create, invent
  10 to put up with something trying or difficult < can't *bear* the tension of the work >
  syn abide, brook, digest, endure, go, lump, stand, ‖stick, stick out, stomach, suffer, support, sustain, swallow, sweat out, take, tolerate; *compare* ACCEPT 2
  rel afflict, torment, torture, try; allow, condone, countenance, permit; acquiesce, bow, defer, submit, yield
  idiom make do, put up with, take lying down
  con decline, refuse, reject, spurn; avoid, bypass, elude, evade, shun

---

syn synonym(s)   *rel* related word(s)
ant antonym(s)   *con* contrasted word(s)
idiom idiomatic equivalent(s)
‖ use limited; if in doubt, see a dictionary

11 syn see HEAD 3

bear (on *or* upon) *vb* to have a connection especially logically <this situation *bears* directly upon the question under discussion>
  syn appertain, apply, pertain, relate
  rel refer; affect, concern, involve, touch; correspond, parallel
  idiom have to do with, tie in with

bear (with) *vb syn* see ACCEPT 2

bearable *adj* capable of being borne <his outrageous behavior is hardly *bearable*>
  syn endurable, livable, sufferable, supportable, sustainable, tolerable
  rel acceptable, admissible, allowable, satisfactory
  con insufferable, insupportable, intolerable, unendurable, unsupportable
  ant unbearable

beard *n* the natural growth of hair on a man's face <some men look better with *beards*>
  syn beaver, whiskers; *compare* SIDE-WHISKERS
  rel charley, galways, goatee, imperial, spade beard, Vandyke; fuzz

beard *vb syn* see FACE 3
  idiom beard the lion in his den

bearded *adj* having a beard <an old *bearded* philosopher>
  syn barbate, bewhiskered, whiskered
  rel beardy; goateed; hairy; stubbed, stubbly, unshaven
  con barefaced, clean-faced, clean-shaven, shaven, smooth-faced, whiskerless
  ant beardless

bear down *vb syn* see CONQUER 1

bearer *n* **1 syn** see MESSENGER
  2 a man who carries baggage and supplies for travelers <native *bearers* serving the safari>
  syn carrier, drogher, porter
  rel boy, cargador, coolie; redcap, skycap

bearing *n* **1** the way in which or the quality by which a person outwardly manifests his personality <a dowager with a regal *bearing*>
  syn address, air, comportment, demeanor, deportment, mien, port, presence, set
  rel aspect, brow, look; attitude, carriage, pose, posture, stand; poise; display, front; behavior, conduct
  2 syn see BIRTH 1

bearish *adj syn* see CANTANKEROUS

bear out *vb syn* see CONFIRM 2

bear up *vb syn* see SUPPORT 4

beast *n* a lower animal as distinguished from man <*beasts* of the field>
  syn animal, brute, creature, ‖critter
  rel beastie, varmint; quadruped

beastly *adj syn* see BRUTISH

beat *vb* **1** to strike repeatedly <robbed and *beaten* by thugs>
  syn baste, batter, belabor, buffet, drub, ‖dump, hammer, lam, lambaste, paste, pelt, pound, pummel, thrash, tromp, wallop, whop
  rel bastinado, baton, bludgeon, cudgel, fustigate, pistol-whip; flog, lace, lash, tan, whip; lay on, maul, muss up, rough (up)
  idiom give one beans, rain blows on
  2 syn see WHIP 2
  3 syn see SCOUR 2
  4 syn see WHIP 3
  5 syn see WAG
  6 syn see HAMMER 1
  7 syn see SURPASS 1
  idiom beat (all) hollow
  8 syn see NONPLUS 1
  9 syn see CHEAT
  10 syn see FRUSTRATE 1
  11 syn see SCOOP 3
  12 syn see PULSATE
  13 syn see WIN 1

beat *n* **1 syn** see RHYTHM
  2 syn see SCOOP

beat down *vb syn* see CONQUER 1

beating *n syn* see DEFEAT 1
  rel lump(s)

beatitude *n syn* see HAPPINESS
  rel ecstasy, rapture, transport

con affliction, trial, tribulation; anguish, grief, sorrow, woe; agony, suffering
  ant despair, dolor

beau *n* **1 syn** see BOYFRIEND 1
  2 syn see BOYFRIEND 2

Beau Brummel *n syn* see FOP

beau ideal *n syn* see MODEL 2
  idiom shining example

‖**beaut** *n syn* see BEAUTY

beauteous *adj syn* see BEAUTIFUL

beautiful *adj* very pleasing or delightful to look at <the most *beautiful* woman in the world>
  syn attractive, beauteous, ‖bonny, comely, fair, good-looking, handsome, lovely, pretty, pulchritudinous, stunning, well-favored
  rel choice, elegant, exquisite; glorious, resplendent, splendid, sublime, superb; eye-appealing, eye-filling, ‖proper; personable, pleasing
  con offensive, repugnant, repulsive, revolting; homely, plain, ordinary, unattractive, unbeauteous, uncomely, unhandsome, unlovely, unpretty
  ant ugly, unbeautiful

beautiful people *n pl syn* see SMART SET

beautify *vb syn* see ADORN
  rel glamorize, prettify
  con deface, disfigure; damage, mar, spoil
  ant uglify

beauty *n* a physically attractive woman <a charming woman and a *beauty* to boot>
  syn ‖beaut, eyeful, knockout, looker, lovely, stunner
  rel charmer, dazzler, dream, eye-opener, good-looker, peach; belle, toast
  idiom raving beauty
  con dog, gorgon, hag, slattern, witch

beaver *n syn* see BEARD

becalm *vb syn* see CALM

because *conj* for the reason that <I left *because* I was bored>
  syn as, as long as, ‖being, 'cause, considering, for, inasmuch as, now, seeing, since, whereas
  idiom in view of the fact

because of *prep syn* see OVER 6

becloud *vb* **1 syn** see OBSCURE
  rel befuddle, confuse, perplex, puzzle
  con illuminate
  2 syn see CONFUSE 4

become *vb* **1** to commence to be <*became* sick yesterday>
  syn come, ‖come over, get, go, grow, run, turn, wax
  rel arise, mount, rise, soar
  idiom get to be, turn out to be
  2 syn see SUIT 4
  3 syn see FLATTER

becoming *adj syn* see DECOROUS 1
  rel attractive, flattering; tasteful
  con unattractive, unflattering; distasteful; inappropriate, unfitting, unrespectable, unsuitable
  ant unbecoming

becomingly *adv syn* see WELL 4

becrush *vb syn* see CRUSH 2

bed *n syn* see BASE 1

bed *vb* **1** to put to bed <getting the children *bedded*>
  syn tuck (in)
  rel cradle
  2 syn see RETIRE 4

bedamn *vb syn* see SWEAR 3

bedaub *vb syn* see SMEAR 1

bedaze *vb syn* see DAZE 2

bedazzle *vb syn* see DAZE 1

bedcover *n syn* see BEDSPREAD

bedeck *vb syn* see ADORN
  rel bedaub, bedizen

bedevil *vb syn* see WORRY 1

bedfast *adj syn* see BEDRIDDEN

bedim *vb syn* see OBSCURE
  con highlight, illuminate

bedlamite *n syn* see LUNATIC 1

bedlamite *adj syn* see INSANE 1

bedog *vb syn* see TAIL

bedraggled *adj syn* see SHABBY 1

bedridden *adj* confined to one's bed by illness or injury <a *bedridden* invalid>
  syn bedfast
  rel confined, incapacitated, laid up; feeble, infirm, sickly, weak
  idiom flat on one's back
  con healed, well; hale, healthy, whole
  ant ambulant, ambulatory
bedrock *n* **1** *syn* see BASE 1
  2 *syn* see BASIS 1
bedspread *n* an often ornamental outer covering for a bed <an appliquéd *bedspread*>
  syn bedcover, counterpane, coverlet, ‖coverlid, spread
bee *n* *syn* see CAPRICE
  rel idea; impulse
beef *n* **1** *syn* see MUSCLE 1
  2 *syn* see POWER 4
  3 *syn* see QUARREL
‖**beef** *vb* *syn* see GRIPE
beef (up) *vb* *syn* see INCREASE 1
beefheaded *adj* *syn* see STUPID 1
beef–witted *adj* *syn* see STUPID 1
beefy *adj* *syn* see HUSKY 1
beekeeper *n* one who engages in the production of and caring for bees and honey <special masks and gloves for *beekeepers*>
  syn apiarist, apiculturist, beeman, beemaster
beeline *vb* *syn* see HURRY 2
Beelzebub *n* *syn* see DEVIL 1
beeman *n* *syn* see BEEKEEPER
beemaster *n* *syn* see BEEKEEPER
beer garden *n* *syn* see ALEHOUSE
beer hall *n* *syn* see ALEHOUSE
‖**beerhouse** *n* *syn* see ALEHOUSE
beetle *vb* **1** *syn* see HANG 4
  2 *syn* see BULGE
beetlehead *n* *syn* see DUNCE
beetleheaded *adj* *syn* see STUPID 1
‖**beezer** *n* *syn* see NOSE 1
befall *vb* *syn* see HAPPEN 1
befit *vb* *syn* see SUIT 4
befitting *adj* **1** *syn* see FIT 1
  ant unbefitting
  2 *syn* see DECOROUS 1
befittingly *adv* *syn* see WELL 1
befog *vb* **1** *syn* see OBSCURE
  2 *syn* see CONFUSE 4
  3 *syn* see PUZZLE
befool *vb* *syn* see DUPE
before *adv* **1** so as to precede something in order or time <racing on *before* to give warning>
  syn ahead, ante, antecedently, beforehand, fore, forward, in advance, precedently, previous
  con behind; abaft, aft, astern
  ant after
  2 in time past <had heard that joke *before*>
  syn already, earlier, erstwhile, formerly, heretofore, once, previously; *compare* THEN 1
  ant after
  3 until now or then <you'll get it tomorrow and not *before*>
  syn beforehand, earlier, sooner
before *prep* **1** coming before in space or time <be home *before* dark>
  syn ahead of, ante, ere, in advance of, preceding, prior to, to; *compare* UNTIL
  con since, subsequent to
  ant after
  2 in the presence of <stood *before* the court>
  syn confronting, facing
  idiom face to face with
  3 *syn* see UNTIL
beforehand *adv* **1** *syn* see BEFORE 1
  2 *syn* see BEFORE 3
befoul *vb* **1** *syn* see CONTAMINATE 2
  2 *syn* see MALIGN
befuddle *vb* *syn* see CONFUSE 2
  rel daze
befuddlement *n* *syn* see HAZE 2
  rel confusion, mix-up
  con clearheadedness, lucidity

beg *vb* to ask for or ask one for something urgently <*beg* one's life from an attacker> <*beg* a stranger for help>
  syn appeal, beseech, brace, conjure, crave, entreat, implore, importune, invoke, plead, pray, supplicate
  rel ask, call (on), request, solicit; petition, sue; besiege, demand, press; nag, worry
  idiom throw oneself at the feet of (*or* on the mercy of)
  con hint, intimate, suggest
‖**begats** *n pl* **1** *syn* see GENEALOGY
  2 *syn* see OFFSPRING
begem *vb* *syn* see BEJEWEL
beget *vb* **1** *syn* see FATHER
  2 *syn* see PROCREATE 1
beggar *n* **1** one who begs especially habitually or as a livelihood <*beggars* crying out to tourists>
  syn bummer, cadger, moocher, panhandler, ‖schnorrer
  rel deadbeat, freeloader, sponge, sponger; ‖bindle stiff, hobo, tramp
  2 *syn* see SUPPLIANT
  3 *syn* see PAUPER
beggared *adj* *syn* see POOR 1
beggarly *adj* *syn* see CONTEMPTIBLE
  rel wretched; ‖cheesy, trashy; measly, paltry
beggary *n* **1** *syn* see POVERTY 1
  2 *syn* see MENDICANCY
begin *vb* **1** to carry out the first act or step of an action or operation <*began* his lecture with a joke>
  syn commence, embark (on *or* upon), enter, get off, inaugurate, initiate, jump (off), kick off, launch, lead off, open, set to, start, take up, tee off
  rel establish, found, institute; introduce, usher in; broach; attack, tackle; prepare; break in; dig in
  idiom get the show on the road, get to work, get underway
  con cease, desist, discontinue, quit, stop; close, complete, conclude, finish, terminate; abandon, forsake, leave, quit; back out, renege, withdraw
  ant end
  2 to come into existence <not since civilization *began* has there been such distress>
  syn arise, commence, originate, start; *compare* SPRING 1
  rel spring; open
  idiom raise its head
  con end, finish, terminate
beginner *n* *syn* see NOVICE
beginning *n* the first part or stage of a process or development <the first few chapters at the *beginning* of the novel>
  syn alpha, birth, commencement, dawn, dawning, day spring, genesis, onset, opening, opening gun, outset, outstart, setout, start
  rel creation, inception, origin, origination, root, source, spring; anlage, rudiment, sprout; prologue; appearance, emergence, rise; incipiency, infancy
  idiom the word go
  con consummation, termination; closing, completion, conclusion; omega
  ant end, ending
beginning *adj* **1** *syn* see INITIAL 1
  2 *syn* see ELEMENTARY 1
begird *vb* **1** *syn* see BELT 1
  2 *syn* see SURROUND 1
begirdle *vb* *syn* see BELT 1
begone *vb* *syn* see GET OUT 1
begrime *vb* *syn* see SOIL 2
begrudge *vb* *syn* see ENVY
beguile *vb* **1** *syn* see MANIPULATE 2
  2 *syn* see DECEIVE
  rel entice, lure, seduce
  3 *syn* see WHILE
beguiling *adj* *syn* see MISLEADING
béguin *n* *syn* see INFATUATION
behave *vb* **1** to act in a specified way <*behave* as people of good breeding should>

---

syn synonym(s)   *rel* related word(s)
ant antonym(s)   *con* contrasted word(s)
idiom idiomatic equivalent(s)
‖ use limited; if in doubt, see a dictionary

syn acquit, act, bear, carry, comport, conduct, demean, deport, disport, do, go on, move, quit

rel control, direct, manage

idiom make as if (*or* as though); be on one's best behavior, mind one's p's and q's

ant misbehave, misconduct

2 *syn* see ACT 5

behavior *n* one's actions in general or on a particular occasion < his flustered *behavior* before women >

syn comportment, conduct, deportment, tenue

rel bearing, demeanor, mien; action, manner, way

con misbehavior, misconduct

behead *vb* to sever the head < nobles *beheaded* for treason >

syn decapitate, decollate, guillotine, head, neck

idiom bring to the block

behemoth *n syn* see GIANT

behemothic *adj syn* see HUGE

behest *n syn* see COMMAND 1

rel demand; prompting, request, solicitation

behind *adv syn* see AFTER

behind *prep* 1 *syn* see ABAFT

2 *syn* see AFTER 2

behind *n syn* see BUTTOCKS

behindhand *adj* 1 *syn* see NEGLIGENT

2 *syn* see BACKWARD 6

3 *syn* see TARDY

ant beforehand

behold *vb syn* see SEE 1

beholden *adj syn* see INDEBTED

beholder *n syn* see SPECTATOR

being *n* 1 *syn* see EXISTENCE 1

rel character, individuality, personality

ant nonbeing

2 *syn* see THING 4

3 *syn* see ENTITY 1

4 *syn* see ESSENCE 1

5 *syn* see HUMAN

‖**being** *conj syn* see BECAUSE

bejewel *vb* to ornament with or as if with jewels < a *bejeweled* headdress > < cobwebs all *bejeweled* with glittering morning dew >

syn begem, beset, enjewel, gem, jewel

rel bespangle, spangle; diamond; encrust

belabor *vb syn* see BEAT 1

belated *adj* 1 *syn* see TARDY

2 *syn* see OLD-FASHIONED

belch *vb* 1 to expel gas suddenly from the stomach through the mouth < ate and ate until he *belched* >

syn burp, eruct, eructate

2 *syn* see ERUPT 1

beldam *n* 1 a woman of advanced years < a crotchety *beldam* hunched over the fire >

syn dame, gammer, grandam; *compare* GAFFER, OLDSTER

rel grandmother, granny; grand dame; matron; matriarch

idiom old girl

con damsel, lass, maid, miss

2 *syn* see HAG 2

beleaguer *vb* 1 *syn* see BESIEGE

rel siege, storm

idiom set upon from all sides

2 *syn* see WORRY 1

belfry *n* 1 *syn* see BELL TOWER

‖2 *syn* see HEAD 1

belie *vb syn* see MISREPRESENT

rel contradict, contravene, negative; controvert, disprove; conceal, disguise, hide

con bespeak, betoken, indicate; disclose, discover, reveal

ant attest

belief *n* 1 the act of assenting intellectually to something proposed as true or the state of mind of one who so assents < offered ready *belief* to anyone he trusted >

syn credence, credit, faith

rel assurance, certainty, certitude, conviction, sureness; acquiescence, assent; trust; credibility, trustworthiness

con distrust, doubt, mistrust, uncertainty; incredulity; question

ant disbelief, unbelief

2 *syn* see OPINION

rel doctrine, dogma, fundamental, law, precept, principle; concept, idea

believable *adj* worthy of belief < the author's bizarre characterizations are hardly *believable* >

syn colorable, credible, creditable, plausible

rel likely, possible, probable, tenable; conceivable, rational, reasonable; presumable, supposable; unquestionable; convincing, impressive, persuasive, satisfying; meaningful, solid, substantial

con improbable, unlikely; doubtable, doubtful, dubious, fishy, questionable, specious; implausible, incredible; inconceivable, untenable; fabulous, mythological

ant unbelievable

believe *vb* 1 to have a firm conviction in the reality of something < *believes* in ghosts >

syn accept, ‖buy, swallow

rel accredit, credit, trust; admit

idiom have no doubts about, hold the belief that, take (*or* accept) as gospel, take at one's word, take one's word for

con discredit, distrust, doubt, mistrust, question, suspect; challenge, dispute; reject, turn down

ant disbelieve, misbelieve

2 *syn* see FEEL 3

3 *syn* see UNDERSTAND 3

belittle *vb syn* see DECRY 2

rel criticize, discredit; underestimate, underrate, undervalue

con intensify; boast, crow

ant aggrandize; magnify

belittlement *n syn* see DETRACTION

bell *vb syn* see RING

‖**bell cow** *n syn* see LEADER 1

bellicose *adj syn* see BELLIGERENT

rel aggressive, assertive; factious, fighting, rebellious

idiom full of fight

con gentle, moderate, temperate

ant amicable; pacific

bellicerence *n syn* see ATTACK 2

belligerent *adj* having or taking an aggressive or fighting attitude < a *belligerent* reply to a diplomatic note >

syn bellicose, combative, contentious, gladiatorial, militant, pugnacious, quarrelsome, ‖ructious, scrappy, truculent, warlike; *compare* QUARRELSOME 2

rel battling, fighting, warring; attacking, invading; aggressive, antagonistic, fierce, hostile; ardent, hot, hot-tempered

con neutral; pacific, pacifist, peaceable, peaceful; conciliatory; amicable

ant friendly

‖**belling** *n syn* see SHIVAREE

bellow *vb syn* see ROAR

rel bark, bay, yelp; cry, wail; low, moo

bell ringer *n syn* see SMASH 6

bell tower *n* a tower that supports or shelters a bell or group of bells < a *bell tower* stood free from the church >

syn belfry, campanile, carillon

bellwether *n syn* see LEADER 1

belly *n syn* see ABDOMEN

bellyache *n syn* see STOMACHACHE

‖**bellyache** *vb syn* see GRIPE

‖**bellyacher** *n syn* see GROUCH

belong *vb* 1 to be suitable, appropriate, or advantageous or to be in a proper or fitting place or situation < the boxes *belong* in the attic >

syn fit, go, set

rel become, befit, suit; accord, agree, chime, harmonize; correspond, match, tally

idiom have one's place

2 to be the property of (a person or thing) < the books *belong* to the library >

syn appertain, pertain, vest

3 to be an attribute, part, adjunct, or function (of a person or thing) < good humor and wit *belong* to his personality >

syn indwell, inhere

idiom run in one's blood (*or* family)

belongings *n pl syn* see POSSESSION 2

beloved *adj syn* see FAVORITE 1

beloved *n* 1 *syn* see SWEETHEART 1

2 *syn* see GIRL FRIEND 2

3 *syn* see BOYFRIEND 2

below *adv* 1 in or at a lower position than something expressed or implied < several business establishments were situated *below* >

syn beneath, under, underneath

ant above

2 lower on the same page or on a following page <for additional examples see *below* >
syn infra
ant above, supra

below *prep* **1** in a lower position relative to some other object or place <lives just *below* me>
syn beneath, under, underneath
con over
ant above

2 *syn* see AFTER 2

belt *n* **1** a strip of flexible material worn around the waist <a leather *belt* >
syn ceinture, cincture, girdle, sash, waistband
rel baldric, cummerbund; band

2 *syn* see AREA 1
rel stretch, strip

belt *vb* **1** to bind about or around with or as if with a belt <gold lamé *belting* the gown>
syn band, begird, begirdle, cincture, encincture, engird, engirdle, gird, girdle
rel tie (up); loop; sash; circle, encircle, ring

2 *syn* see SLAM 1

belt *n* *syn* see BLOW 1

belvedere *n* *syn* see SUMMERHOUSE

bemean *vb* *syn* see HUMBLE

bemedaled *adj* having or wearing decorations especially as awarded by the military <the general's *bemedaled* uniform>
syn beribboned, decorated

bemired *adj* *syn* see MUDDY 1

bemoan *vb* *syn* see DEPLORE 1
rel regret; complain
con applaud, cheer, huzzah; delight, jubilate, rejoice
ant exult

bemuse *vb* *syn* see DAZE 2
rel addle; perplex, puzzle
con enlighten, illuminate

bemused *adj* *syn* see ABSTRACTED

benchmark *n* *syn* see STANDARD 3

bend *vb* **1** *syn* see CURVE
rel arch, curl, double, hook
ant straighten

2 *syn* see GIVE 12
3 *syn* see INCLINE 3
4 *syn* see ADDRESS 3

bend (over) *vb* *syn* see HANG 4

bend *n* **1** *syn* see TURN 2
2 *syn* see TURN 4
3 *syn* see CURVE

bender *n* *syn* see BINGE 1

bending *adj* *syn* see CROOKED 1

beneath *adv* *syn* see BELOW 1

beneath *prep* *syn* see BELOW 1
ant above, over

benediction *n* **1** *syn* see BLESSING 1
2 *syn* see GRACE 1
3 *syn* see APPROBATION
4 *syn* see GOOD 1

benefact *vb* *syn* see HELP 1

benefaction *n* *syn* see DONATION

benefic *adj* *syn* see GOOD 1
rel desirable, pleasing, satisfying
con damaging, harmful, injurious
ant malefic

beneficence *n* *syn* see DONATION

beneficial *adj* *syn* see GOOD 1
rel salutary, wholesome
con baneful, deleterious, noxious, pernicious
ant detrimental, harmful

benefit *n* **1** *syn* see GOOD 1
2 *syn* see WELFARE
rel account, behalf, sake; gain, profit
con catastrophe, disaster, misfortune; detriment
ant harm, ill

benefit *vb* to be useful or profitable to <medicines that *benefit* mankind>
syn advantage, avail, profit, serve, work (for)
rel advance, ameliorate, better, contribute (to), favor, improve; relieve, succor; build, further, promote; aid, assist, help

idiom do a world of good
con hinder, impede; damage, impair, injure; distress, upset; afflict, anguish; oppose
ant harm, hurt

benet *vb* *syn* see CATCH 3

benevolence *n* **1** *syn* see GOODWILL 1
con animosity, bitterness, ill will; antagonism, hostility; inimicality, unkindliness; stinginess
2 *syn* see GIFT 1

benevolent *adj* **1** *syn* see GENEROUS 1
rel beneficent; charitable; humane; compassionate, tenderhearted
con cruel, inhuman, malicious, spiteful
ant malevolent

2 *syn* see CHARITABLE 1
rel bighearted, freehearted, generous, greathearted, largehearted, liberal, openhanded; public-spirited; do-good
con niggardly, stingy; callous, indifferent, insensitive, unconcerned, unfeeling

benighted *adj* **1** *syn* see IGNORANT 1
rel backward, unenlightened; uninformed
idiom in the dark
con informed, intelligent
2 *syn* see BACKWARD 5

benightedness *n* *syn* see IGNORANCE 1

benign *adj* **1** *syn* see KIND
rel gracious
con malevolent, malicious, malignant, spiteful; acrid, caustic, mordant
ant malign

2 *syn* see FAVORABLE 5
rel gentle, mild; benevolent, charitable, humane; clement, forbearing, merciful
con menacing, threatening
ant malign

benignant *adj* *syn* see KIND
rel mild; gracious
con malevolent, malicious, spiteful; relentless
ant malignant

benison *n* *syn* see BLESSING 1

bent *n* **1** *syn* see LEANING 2
2 *syn* see GIFT 2
con antipathy, aversion; inability, incapacity

bent *adj* **1** *syn* see CURVED
2 *syn* see DECIDED 2

benumb *vb* **1** *syn* see DEADEN 1
2 *syn* see DAZE 2

benumbed *adj* *syn* see NUMB 1

bequeath *vb* **1** *syn* see WILL
con disinherit, exheridate
2 *syn* see HAND DOWN

bequest *n* *syn* see LEGACY 1

berate *vb* *syn* see SCOLD 1
con acclaim, praise; applaud; commend, compliment

berceuse *n* *syn* see LULLABY

bereave *vb* *syn* see DEPRIVE 2

bereaved *adj* suffering the death of a loved one <the *bereaved* family>
syn bereft
rel distressed, sorrowing

bereft *adj* *syn* see BEREAVED

beribboned *adj* *syn* see BEMEDALED

berth *n* **1** *syn* see WHARF
2 *syn* see JOB 2

beseech *vb* *syn* see BEG

beset *vb* **1** *syn* see BEJEWEL
2 *syn* see ATTACK 1
3 *syn* see BESIEGE
4 *syn* see INFEST 1
5 *syn* see SURROUND 1
idiom come at from all directions (*or* sides)

besetment *n* *syn* see ANNOYANCE 3

beside *prep* **1** at or by the side of <left the car *beside* the road>

---

syn synonym(s)   *rel* related word(s)
ant antonym(s)   *con* contrasted word(s)
idiom idiomatic equivalent(s)
|| use limited; if in doubt, see a dictionary

syn alongside, by, ||fornent, next to
rel near, opposite
2 *syn* see NEAR 2
3 *syn* see BESIDES 1
4 *syn* see EXCEPT

besides *adv* **1** *syn* see ALSO 2
idiom at that
2 *syn* see AGAIN 4

besides *prep* **1** in addition to < *besides* being tall, he's thin >
syn as well as, beside, beyond, over and above
idiom along with, together with
2 *syn* see EXCEPT

besides *adj syn* see ADDITIONAL

besiege *vb* to surround an enemy in a fortified or strong position so as to prevent ingress and egress < Troy was *besieged* by Greeks for ten years >
syn beleaguer, beset, blockade, invest
rel encircle, encompass, hem (in), surround; trap; assail, assault, attack

besmear *vb* **1** *syn* see SMEAR 1
2 *syn* see TAINT 1

besmirch *vb syn* see TAINT 1

besoil *vb syn* see SOIL 2

besotted *adj syn* see INFATUATED

bespangle *vb syn* see SPANGLE 1

bespatter *vb* **1** *syn* see SPOT 1
2 *syn* see MALIGN

bespeak *vb* **1** *syn* see RESERVE 2
2 *syn* see ADDRESS 4
3 *syn* see ASK 2
idiom put in for
4 *syn* see INDICATE 2

bespeckle *vb syn* see SPECKLE 1

bespectacled *adj* having or wearing glasses < *bespectacled* thesaurists >
syn spectacled

bespot *vb syn* see SPOT 1

besprinkle *vb syn* see SPRINKLE 1

best *adj* much more than half < passed the *best* part of a month at the shore >
syn better, ||bettermost, greater, largest, most

best *vb* **1** *syn* see CONQUER 2
2 *syn* see SURPASS 1
3 *syn* see DEFEAT 2

best *n* the choicest one or part < always gave the *best* that she had >
syn choice, cream, elite, fat, flower, pick, pride, prime, primrose, prize, top
rel gem; nonesuch, nonpareil; exemplar, model, paragon, pattern
idiom cock of the walk, flower of the flock, one in a thousand (or million)
ant worst

bestain *vb syn* see STAIN 1

best bib and tucker *n syn* see FINERY

best girl *n syn* see GIRL FRIEND 1

bestial *adj syn* see BRUTISH

bestialize *vb syn* see DEBASE 1

bestir *vb syn* see STIR 1

bestow *vb* **1** *syn* see USE 2
2 *syn* see STOW
3 *syn* see HARBOR 2
4 *syn* see GIVE 1

bestower *n syn* see DONOR

bestrew *vb syn* see STREW 1

bestride *vb* **1** *syn* see MOUNT 5
2 to sit with one leg on each side < boys *bestriding* a fallen log >
syn straddle, ||striddle, stride

bet *n* something of value (as money) staked on a winner-take-all basis on the outcome of an uncertainty < laid a *bet* at three to one on the champion >
syn ante, pot, stake, wager

bet *vb syn* see GAMBLE 1

bête noire *n syn* see ABOMINATION 1

bethink *vb syn* see REMEMBER

betide *vb syn* see HAPPEN 1

betimes *adv* **1** *syn* see EARLY 1

2 *syn* see EARLY 2
||**3** *syn* see SOMETIMES

betoken *vb* **1** *syn* see INDICATE 2
2 *syn* see AUGUR 2

betray *vb* **1** *syn* see DECEIVE
rel ensnare, entrap, snare, trap
2 to prove faithless or treacherous < *betrayed* his own people by going over to the enemy >
syn cross, double-cross, sell, sell out, ||split
rel desert, renegade; give away, inform, turn in; collaborate; apostatize
idiom act (or play) the traitor, break faith, round on, sell down the river
3 *syn* see REVEAL 1
rel demonstrate, evidence, evince, manifest, show; betoken, indicate
con defend, guard, protect, safeguard, shield

betrayer *n syn* see INFORMER

betrothal *n syn* see ENGAGEMENT 2

betrothed *n* either member of a couple engaged to be married
syn affianced, intended
rel fiancé, husband-to-be; bride-to-be, fiancée, wife-to-be

betrothed *adj syn* see ENGAGED 2

betrothing *n syn* see ENGAGEMENT 2

betrothment *n syn* see ENGAGEMENT 2

better *adj* **1** *syn* see BEST
2 more worthy or pleasing than an alternative < it is *better* to lose gracefully than to win arrogantly >
syn ||bettermost, preferable, superior; *compare* GOOD
rel exceeding, exceptional, surpassing; choice, desirable, excellent
idiom more than a match for
ant worse

better *adv syn* see MORE 2
ant worse

better *n* **1** *syn* see SUPERIOR
2 a superior or winning position < had the *better* of the argument >
syn advantage, superiority, upper hand, victory, whip hand; *compare* ADVANTAGE 3
rel success, triumph, win
con collapse, defeat, disadvantage, loss; beating, drubbing, licking
ant worse

better *vb* **1** *syn* see IMPROVE 1
ant worsen
2 *syn* see SURPASS 1

||**bettermost** *adj* **1** *syn* see BETTER 2
2 *syn* see BEST

between *prep* **1** in common to (as in position, in a distribution, or in participation) < a treaty *between* three powers >
syn among
2 in the time, space, or interval that separates < *between* the ages 12 and 20 >
syn ||atween, ||atwixt, ||betwixt, in between, tween, twixt

||**betwixt** *prep syn* see BETWEEN 2

bevel *adj syn* see DIAGONAL

beveled *adj syn* see DIAGONAL

||**bever** *n syn* see SNACK

beverage *n syn* see DRINK 1

bevy *n syn* see GROUP 1

bewail *vb syn* see DEPLORE 1
ant rejoice

beware *vb* to be cautious < *beware* of the dog >
syn look out, mind, watch out
rel attend, heed, notice, watch
idiom be on one's guard, be on the lookout (or watch), keep at a safe distance, take care (or heed)
con disregard, ignore, neglect

bewhiskered *adj syn* see BEARDED

bewilder *vb* **1** *syn* see PUZZLE
rel baffle, fuddle, muddle
2 *syn* see CONFUSE 2

bewitch *vb* **1** to practice witchcraft on < medicine men who *bewitch* ignorant tribesmen >
syn charm, enchant, ensorcell, hex, spell, voodoo, witch
rel bedevil, demonize, overlook, possess, sorcerize; beglamour, dazzle, trick

idiom cast a spell on (*or* over), give (*or* cast) the evil eye, put a curse on
2 syn see ATTRACT 1
rel beglamour, ‖snow
bewitched *adj syn* see ENAMORED 3
bewitching *adj syn* see ATTRACTIVE 1
con forbidding, grim
bewitchment *n syn* see MAGIC 1
beyond *adv* **1** on or to the farther side < a house with mountains *beyond* >
syn farther, further, ‖yon, yonder
2 syn see OVER 1
beyond *prep* **1** on or to the farther side of < the store is just *beyond* the next house >
syn after, outside, past, without
2 out of the reach, sphere, or comprehension of < it's *beyond* me how he did it >
syn above, past
idiom beyond one's depth (*or* power), over (*or* above) one's head, too deep (*or* much) for
3 syn see BESIDES 1
beyond *adj syn* see ADDITIONAL
beyond *n syn* see HEREAFTER 2
‖**b'hoy** *n syn* see TOUGH
bias *n* **1 syn** see LEANING 2
2 syn see PREJUDICE
rel inclination, predisposition; slant, standpoint, viewpoint
con dispassionateness; fairness, justness
bias *adj syn* see DIAGONAL
bias *vb* **1 syn** see SLANT 3
2 syn see INCLINE 3
3 syn see PREJUDICE 2
biased *adj* **1 syn** see DIAGONAL
2 exhibiting or characterized by a highly personal and unreasoned distortion of judgment < a *biased* estimate of the book's worth >
syn colored, jaundiced, one-sided, partial, partisan, prejudiced, prepossessed, tendentious, unindifferent, unneutral, warped
rel bent, disposed, inclined, predisposed; influenced, interested, swayed; opinionated
con detached, dispassionate, impartial, neutral, open-minded; fair, honest, just
ant unbiased
bibber *n syn* see DRUNKARD
bibble–babble *n syn* see CHATTER
bibelot *n syn* see KNICKKNACK
Bible *n* the sacred volume of Christians < students of the *Bible* >
syn Book, Holy Writ, Sacred Writ, Scripture
idiom Book of Books, Good Book, Word of God
bibliopole *n syn* see BOOKDEALER
bicker *vb* **1 syn** see ARGUE 2
rel battle, contend, fight, war
2 syn see QUARREL
3 syn see RATTLE 1
bickering *n syn* see QUARREL
bicycle *n* a pedal-propelled vehicle with two wheels tandem, a steering handle, and a saddle seat < ten-speed *bicycles* >
syn bike, cycle, two-wheeler, velocipede
bid *vb* **1 syn** see COMMAND
rel summon
con interdict, prohibit
ant forbid
2 syn see INVITE
rel request
biddable *adj syn* see OBEDIENT
rel amiable, good-natured, obliging
con mulish, obstinate, stiff-necked, stubborn
ant recalcitrant
bidding *n syn* see COMMAND 1
rel call, summoning
biddy *n* **1 syn** see MAID 2
2 syn see HAG 2
bide *vb* **1 syn** see STAY 2
rel continue
2 syn see RESIDE 1
bierstube *n syn* see ALEHOUSE
biff *n syn* see BLOW 1
‖**biff** *vb syn* see STRIKE 2

‖**biffy** *n syn* see PRIVY 1
bifold *adj syn* see TWOFOLD 1
big *adj* **1** of significant size or scope < a *big* expanse of mud > < *big* plans >
syn considerable, extensive, hefty, large, large-scale, major, sizable
rel bumper, hulking, whacking, whopping; clumsy, unwieldy; ample, biggish, capacious, commodious, comprehensive, copious, roomy, spacious, voluminous; distended, inflated, swollen
con paltry, piddling, trivial; slight, small; insignificant; minute, tiny, wee
ant little
2 syn see LARGE 1
3 syn see PREGNANT 1
4 syn see FULL 1
rel flushed, overflowing; cloyed, glutted, sated, satiated, satisfied
idiom full to bursting (*or* overflowing), full to the ears, stuffed to the gills
con empty
5 syn see IMPORTANT 1
6 syn see PRETENTIOUS 3
7 syn see GENEROUS 1
‖**big** *adv syn* see VERY 1
big *n syn* see NOTABLE 1
big boy *n syn* see NOTABLE 1
‖**big bug** *n syn* see NOTABLE 1
‖**big cheese** *n syn* see NOTABLE 1
‖**big chief** *n syn* see NOTABLE 1
‖**biggety** *adj syn* see WISE 5
‖**biggie** *n syn* see NOTABLE 1
big gun *n syn* see NOTABLE 1
‖**big house** *n syn* see JAIL
bight *n syn* see INLET
big name *n syn* see CELEBRITY 2
bigness *n syn* see SIZE 2
‖**big noise** *n syn* see NOTABLE 1
bigot *n syn* see ENTHUSIAST
rel approver, liker, relisher; mumpsimus, racist, segregationist
con depreciator, disparager, knocker; disliker, disrelisher, hater, loather, misliker
bigoted *adj syn* see ILLIBERAL
rel lily-white; conservative
big shot *n syn* see NOTABLE 1
big-timer *n syn* see NOTABLE 1
‖**big wheel** *n syn* see NOTABLE 1
bigwig *n syn* see NOTABLE 1
bike *n syn* see BICYCLE
bilge *n syn* see NONSENSE 2
bilk *vb* **1 syn** see FRUSTRATE 1
con fulfill
2 syn see CHEAT
3 syn see ESCAPE 2
rel dodge, shake
bill *n* **1** the jaws of a bird with their projecting horny covering < the huge *bill* of the toucan >
syn beak, neb, nib, pecker
2 syn see PROMONTORY
3 syn see VISOR 1
bill *n* **1** a statement of the amount due a creditor < *bills* from the grocer and doctor >
syn account, invoice, reckoning, score, statement, tab
rel charges, damage
idiom statement of account
2 syn see CHECK 2
3 syn see POSTER
4 syn see DOLLAR
billet *n syn* see JOB 2
billet *vb* **1** to assign quarters to soldiers < the troops were *billeted* in private homes >
syn canton, quarter
rel bed, house, lodge, put up; bestow
2 syn see HARBOR 2

---

syn synonym(s)   *rel* related word(s)
ant antonym(s)   *con* contrasted word(s)
idiom idiomatic equivalent(s)
‖ use limited; if in doubt, see a dictionary

billet *n syn* see BAR 1
billet–doux *n syn* see LOVE LETTER
billingsgate *n syn* see ABUSE
billy *n syn* see CUDGEL
billy club *n syn* see CUDGEL
‖**bim** *n syn* see WANTON
bimanal *adj syn* see TWO-HANDED 2
bimanual *adj syn* see TWO-HANDED 1
‖**bimbo** *n syn* see WANTON
binary *adj syn* see TWOFOLD 1
bind *vb* 1 *syn* see TIE 1
  con release
  ant unloose
  2 *syn* see BANDAGE
‖**bindle stiff** *n syn* see VAGABOND
‖**bing** *n syn* see PILE 1
binge *n* 1 a drunken revel < hung over after a weekend *binge* >
  syn bat, bender, blowoff, booze, brannigan, bum; bust, ca-rousal, carouse, compotation, drunk, jag, orgy, ran-tan, rowdy-dow, soak, souse, spree, tear, ‖time, toot, wassail
  rel bacchanal, bacchanalia, debauch; blast, ‖blowout; ‖bun
  2 *syn* see SPREE 1
bio *n syn* see BIOGRAPHY
biocide *n syn* see PESTICIDE
biographer *n* one who writes a biography < irresponsible *biogra-phers* whose work is more fiction than fact >
  syn autobiographer, autobiographist, Boswell, memoirist
biography *n* a more or less detailed account of the events and cir-cumstances of a person's life < wrote a *biography* of his grandfa-ther >
  syn autobiography, bio, confessions, life, memoir
  rel diary, journal, letters; adventures, history, story; profile; obit, obituary
biologic *n syn* see DRUG 1
bird *n syn* see RASPBERRY
birdbrain *n syn* see SCATTERBRAIN
birdhouse *n syn* see AVIARY
birdman *n syn* see PILOT 2
bird–witted *adj syn* see GIDDY 1
birr *n syn* see ENERGY 2
birth *n* 1 the act or process of bringing forth young from the womb < had a very hard *birth* after a prolonged labor >
  syn bearing, ‖birthing, childbearing, childbirth, delivery, partu-rition
  rel abortion, miscarriage, slip
  2 *syn* see BEGINNING
birth *vb* ‖1 *syn* see BEAR 5
  2 *syn* see SPRING 1
birth control *n* control of the number of children born especially by preventing or lessening the frequency of conception < cul-tural and religious aspects of *birth control* >
  syn contraception
  rel rhythm method; planned parenthood; vasectomy; (the) pill
‖**birthing** *n syn* see BIRTH 1
birthmark *n* 1 a congenital pigmented area on the skin < *birth-marks* often appear on the neck >
  syn mole, nevus
  2 *syn* see CHARACTERISTIC 1
birth pang *n, usu* **birth pangs** *pl syn* see LABOR 2
birthright *n* 1 *syn* see RIGHT 2
  2 *syn* see HERITAGE 1
bisexual *adj* being structurally and functionally both male and female < many lower animals are *bisexual* >
  syn androgynous, hermaphrodite, hermaphroditic
bistered *adj syn* see DARK 3
bistro *n syn* see NIGHTCLUB
bit *n* 1 *syn* see MORSEL 1
  2 *syn* see PARTICLE
  3 *syn* see END 4
  4 *syn* see WHILE 1
bit *vb syn* see RESTRAIN 1
bit by bit *adv syn* see GRADUALLY
bite *vb* 1 to seize with the teeth so that they enter < *bite* into a pear >
  syn champ, chomp
  rel gnaw, nibble, tooth; ‖chaw, chew, crunch, masticate, munch, scrunch; eat
  idiom sink one's teeth into

  2 *syn* see EAT 3
  3 *syn* see SMART
bite *n* 1 *syn* see MORSEL 1
  2 *syn* see SNACK
  3 *syn* see SHARE 1
biting *adj syn* see INCISIVE
‖**bitsy** *adj syn* see TINY
bitter *adj* 1 *syn* see ACRID
  rel acerb, acid, bitterish
  con delicious; bland, flat, insipid
  2 difficult to accept mentally < the *bitter* truth >
  syn afflictive, distasteful, galling, grievous, painful, unpalatable
  rel annoying, distressing, disturbing, woeful; bad, disagreeable, displeasing, offensive, unpleasant; galling, provoking, vexatious
  con agreeable, gratifying, satisfying
  3 marked by intense animosity < *bitter* contempt >
  syn antagonistic, hostile, rancorous, virulent, vitriolic
  rel alienated, divided, estranged; irreconcilable
  4 *syn* see SEVERE 3
  con mild, springlike, summery
bitter–ender *n syn* see DIEHARD 1
bitterly *adv syn* see HARD 6
bivouac *vb syn* see CAMP
‖**bivvy** *vb syn* see CAMP
bizarre *adj* 1 *syn* see STRANGE 4
  2 *syn* see FANTASTIC 2
  con normal, ordinary, regular
blab *n syn* see CHATTER
blab *vb syn* see GOSSIP
blab (out) *vb syn* see REVEAL 1
blabber *vb syn* see BABBLE 2
blabber *n syn* see CHATTER
blabber *n syn* see CHATTERBOX
blabbermouth *n syn* see CHATTERBOX
blabmouth *n syn* see CHATTERBOX
black *adj* 1 having the color of soot or coal < a *black* hearse >
  syn atramentous, ebon, ebony, inky, jet, jetty, onyx, pitch=black, pitch-dark, pitchy, raven, sable
  rel blackish; charcoal, slate; piceous; dusky, swart, swarthy; brunet
  idiom black as a crow (*or* a shoe *or* the ace of spades), black as hell (*or* night)
  ant white
  2 *syn* see DIRTY 1
  3 *syn* see GLOOMY 3
  4 *syn* see UTTER
black *vb syn* see BRUISE 1
black (out) *vb syn* see ERASE
black and white *n syn* see PRINT 2
black–a–vised *adj syn* see DARK 3
black beast *n syn* see ABOMINATION 1
‖**blackcoat** *n syn* see CLERGYMAN
black dog *n syn* see SADNESS
blacken *vb syn* see MALIGN
  idiom blacken one's good name, give one a black eye, throw mud at
black eye *n* 1 a bruise about the eye < got a *black eye* in a fight >
  syn mouse, shiner
  rel contusion
  2 *syn* see STIGMA
blackguard *n syn* see VILLAIN 1
black out *vb syn* see FAINT
blackout *n syn* see FAINT
blague *n syn* see NONSENSE 2
blah *n syn* see NONSENSE 2
blah *adj syn* see DULL 9
blamable *adj syn* see BLAMEWORTHY
blame *vb syn* see CRITICIZE
  rel accuse, charge; impute
  idiom lay at one's door (*or* doorstep), lay (*or* put) the blame on
  con exculpate, vindicate; praise
blame *n* responsibility for misdeed or delinquency < accepted the *blame* for his foolish act >
  syn culpability, fault, guilt, onus
  rel accountability, answerability, liability; accusation, charge, imputation; censure, condemnation, denunciation, reprehension
  idiom burden of guilt

con commendation, compliment; acclaim, applause, praise

blamed *adj* **1** *syn* see DAMNED 2
  2 *syn* see UTTER

blameful *adj* *syn* see BLAMEWORTHY

blameless *adj* **1** *syn* see INNOCENT 2
  2 *syn* see GOOD 11
  rel unimpeachable
  ant blameworthy

blameworthy *adj* deserving reproach and punishment < though not criminal, his behavior was certainly *blameworthy* >
  syn amiss, blamable, blameful, censurable, culpable, demeritorious, guilty, reprehensible, sinful, unholy
  rel illaudable, uncommendable, unpraiseworthy, unpretty; delinquent, faultful; punishable; foolish, irresponsible, reckless
  idiom at fault, to blame
  con faultless, flawless, impeccable, irreproachable, unimpeachable; guiltless, innocent, sinless; creditable, high-principled, upright
  ant blameless; unblamable

blanch *vb* *syn* see WHITEN 1

blanch (over) *vb* *syn* see PALLIATE

blanch *vb* *syn* see RECOIL

blanched *adj* *syn* see PALE 1

bland *adj* **1** *syn* see SUAVE
  rel good-natured, ingratiating
  con bluff, crusty, gruff
  ant brusque
  2 *syn* see GENTLE 1
  3 *syn* see INSIPID 3
  con pungent, savory, spicy, zestful

blandish *vb* *syn* see COAX
  rel flatter; beguile, charm
  con threaten

blandishment *n* *syn* see FLATTERY

blank *adj* **1** *syn* see EXPRESSIONLESS
  2 *syn* see UTTER

blank *n* *syn* see OMISSION

blank check *n* *syn* see CARTE BLANCHE

blanket *vb* *syn* see COVER 3

blankety–blank *adj* **1** *syn* see DAMNED 2
  2 *syn* see UTTER

blankness *n* *syn* see VACUITY 2

blank wall *n* *syn* see BAR 2

blare *vb* **1** *syn* see BLAZE
  2 *syn* see SCREAM 4

blaring *adj* *syn* see LOUD 1

blarney *vb* *syn* see COAX

blarney *n* *syn* see FLATTERY

blasé *adj* *syn* see SOPHISTICATED 2
  con awed, wide-eyed; artless, naive, natural, unsophisticated

blasphemous *adj* *syn* see SACRILEGIOUS

blasphemy *n* **1** impious or irreverent language < cursing God is *blasphemy* >
  syn cursing, cussing, execration, imprecation, profanity, swearing
  rel affront, indignity, insult; abuse, billingsgate, scurrility, vituperation
  con reverence, veneration, worship
  ant adoration
  2 *syn* see PROFANATION
  rel abuse, befouling, shaming

blast *n* *syn* see BANG 2

blast *vb* **1** to ruin or to injure severely, suddenly, or surprisingly < we'll have no peaches; frost *blasted* the blossoms this year >
  syn blight, dash, nip
  rel destroy, ruin, wreck; damage, injure, spoil; shrivel, stunt, wither
  2 *syn* see SLAM 1
  3 *syn* see WHIP 2

blasted *adj* **1** *syn* see DAMNED 2
  2 *syn* see UTTER

blat *vb* *syn* see EXCLAIM

blatant *adj* **1** *syn* see VOCIFEROUS
  rel screaming; obtrusive
  con modest, soft-spoken
  2 *syn* see GAUDY
  3 *syn* see SHAMELESS

blather *vb* *syn* see BABBLE 2

blather *n* *syn* see NONSENSE 2

blatherskite *n* *syn* see NONSENSE 2

‖**blatter** *n* *syn* see CHATTER

blaze *vb* to burn or appear to burn brightly < the hot sun *blazed* down >
  syn blare, flame, flare, glare, glow
  rel illuminate, illumine, light; radiate, shine; coruscate, fulgurate, scintillate, sparkle; incandesce

blaze (abroad) *vb* *syn* see DECLARE 1

blazes *n pl* *syn* see HELL

blazing *adj* **1** *syn* see BURNING 1
  2 *syn* see IMPASSIONED

blazon *vb* *syn* see DECLARE 1

bleach *vb* *syn* see WHITEN 1

bleak *adj* **1** *syn* see GRIM 2
  2 *syn* see GLOOMY 3

blear *vb* *syn* see DULL 4

blear *adj* *syn* see FAINT 2

blear–eyed *adj* *syn* see STUPID 1

blear–witted *adj* *syn* see STUPID 1

bleary *adj* **1** *syn* see FAINT 2
  2 *syn* see EFFETE 2

bleat *vb* *syn* see GRIPE

bleed *vb* **1** *syn* see EXUDE
  2 *syn* see FLEECE 1

bleeding *adj* **1** *syn* see DAMNED 2
  2 *syn* see UTTER

blemish *vb* *syn* see INJURE 1

blemish *n* an imperfection (as a spot or crack) < a *blemish* on the face >
  syn defect, flaw, vice
  rel fault, scar; blister, blotch, disfigurement, pockmark, wart; catch, snag, tear

blench *vb* *syn* see RECOIL

blench *vb* *syn* see WHITEN 1

blend *vb* **1** *syn* see MIX 1
  rel combine, integrate
  con resolve, separate
  2 *syn* see HARMONIZE 4

blend *n* *syn* see MIXTURE

blending *adj* *syn* see HARMONIOUS 1

bless *vb* **1** to make holy by religious rite or word < the priest *blessed* the water and wine >
  syn consecrate, hallow, sanctify
  rel dedicate
  con defile, desecrate, profane
  2 *syn* see PRAISE 2

blessed *adj* **1** *syn* see HOLY 1
  2 *syn* see DAMNED 2
  3 *syn* see UTTER

blessedness *n* *syn* see HAPPINESS
  con agony, suffering
  ant misery

blessing *n* **1** an expression or utterance of good wishes < on departing, he received his father's *blessing* >
  syn benediction, benison
  rel Godspeed, valediction
  2 *syn* see APPROBATION
  3 *syn* see GOOD 1
  4 *syn* see GRACE 1

‖**bless out** *vb* *syn* see SCOLD 1

blight *vb* *syn* see BLAST 1

blighted *adj* **1** *syn* see DAMNED 2
  2 *syn* see UTTER

‖**blighter** *n* *syn* see WRETCH 1

blimp *n* **1** *syn* see FATTY
  2 *syn* see REACTIONARY
  3 *cap* *syn* see STUFFED SHIRT

blind *adj* **1** lacking the power to see < kittens are *blind* at birth >
  syn ‖dark, eyeless, sightless, stone-blind, visionless
  rel dim-sighted, purblind, short-sighted; blindish; blindfolded; unseeing
  idiom blind as a bat

---

syn synonym(s)   *rel* related word(s)
ant antonym(s)   *con* contrasted word(s)
idiom idiomatic equivalent(s)
‖ use limited; if in doubt, see a dictionary

con seeing, sighted; keen, sharp
2 *syn* see INTOXICATED 1
3 *syn* see DULL 7
blind *vb syn* see DAZE 1
blind *n* 1 *syn* see FRONT 3
2 *syn* see DECOY 2
blind alley *n syn* see DEAD END
blinding *adj* 1 *syn* see DAMNED 2
2 *syn* see UTTER
blink *vb* 1 *syn* see WINK
2 to shine intermittently <we'll signal by *blinking* the headlights>
syn flash, flicker, twinkle
rel glimmer, scintillate, shimmer
blink (at) *vb syn* see CONNIVE 1
blink (at *or* away) *vb syn* see NEGLECT
‖**blinking** *adj* 1 *syn* see DAMNED 2
2 *syn* see UTTER
blip *vb* 1 *syn* see SLAP 1
2 *syn* see CENSOR
bliss *n* 1 *syn* see HAPPINESS
con dolor, misery, woe
ant anguish
2 *syn* see HEAVEN 2
blissfulness *n syn* see HAPPINESS
rel ecstasy, euphoria, exaltation; heaven, paradise
blister *vb syn* see LAMBASTE 3
blistering *adj* 1 *syn* see HOT 1
‖2 *syn* see DAMNED 2
blithe *adj* 1 *syn* see CHEERFUL 1
2 *syn* see MERRY
ant atrabilious, morose
blithering *adj syn* see UTTER
blithesome *adj syn* see MERRY
blitz *vb syn* see BOMBARD
‖**bloat** *n syn* see DRUNKARD
bloated *adj syn* see POMPOUS 1
bloc *n syn* see COMBINATION 2
block *n* 1 *syn* see BAR 2
2 *syn* see ANNEX
block *vb* 1 *syn* see HINDER
2 *syn* see INTERCEPT
3 *syn* see FILL 1
block (out) *vb syn* see SKETCH
blockade *n* 1 *syn* see BAR 2
‖2 *syn* see MOONSHINE 2
blockade *vb syn* see BESIEGE
block and block *adj syn* see FULL 1
blockhead *n syn* see DUNCE
blockheaded *adj syn* see STUPID 1
blockish *adj syn* see STUPID 1
block out *vb syn* see SCREEN 3
‖**bloke** *n syn* see MAN 3
blond *adj* 1 of a pale soft yellow color <*blond* hair>
syn flaxen, golden, straw
rel blondish; platinum; champagne, towheaded
con dark; brunet
2 *syn* see FAIR 3
blood *n* 1 the fluid that circulates in the heart, arteries, capillaries, and veins of a vertebrate animal <*blood* covered the battlefield>
syn ‖claret, gore
rel ichor; humor
2 *syn* see ANCESTRY
3 *syn* see MURDER
4 *syn* see FOP
blood–and–guts *adj syn* see INTENSIVE
bloodbath *n syn* see MASSACRE
bloodless *adj* 1 *syn* see PALE 2
rel colorless; lifeless
con alive; vigorous; florid
ant plethoric; sanguine
2 *syn* see INSENSIBLE 5
bloodshed *n syn* see MASSACRE
bloodstained *adj syn* see BLOODY 1
bloodsucker *n syn* see PARASITE
bloodthirsty *adj syn* see MURDEROUS

bloody *adj* 1 affected by or involving the shedding of blood <a *bloody* knife> <when will this long and *bloody* conflict cease?>
syn bloodstained, ensanguined, gory, imbrued, sanguinary, sanguine, sanguineous
rel bloodthirsty, grim, murderous, slaughterous; cutthroat, red=handed
2 *syn* see MURDEROUS
bloom *n* 1 *syn* see FLOWER 1
2 a state or time of beauty, freshness, and vigor <the *bloom* of youth>
syn blossom, flush
rel glow
3 a rosy appearance of the cheeks <recovered all her health and *bloom*>
syn blossom, blush, flush, glow
bloom *vb syn* see BLOSSOM
‖**blooming** *adj* 1 *syn* see DAMNED 2
2 *syn* see UTTER
blooper *n* 1 *syn* see ERROR 2
2 *syn* see FAUX PAS
blossom *n* 1 *syn* see FLOWER 1
rel capitulum, corymb, cyme, inflorescence, panicle, raceme, spike, umbel
2 *syn* see BLOOM 2
3 *syn* see BLOOM 3
blossom *vb* to produce flowers or be in flower <lilacs *blossom* in the spring>
syn bloom, blow, burgeon, effloresce, flower, outbloom
rel bud; leaf; shoot; open, unfold
idiom burst into bloom, come into flower, put forth blossoms (*or* flowers *or* bloom)
con fade, fall, wither
blot *n syn* see STIGMA
rel blemish, flaw, defect
blot *vb syn* see STAIN 1
blotch *vb syn* see SPLOTCH
blot out *vb* 1 *syn* see ERASE
2 *syn* see ANNIHILATE 2
‖**blotter** *n syn* see DRUNKARD
‖**blotto** *adj syn* see INTOXICATED 1
bloviate *vb syn* see ORATE
blow *vb* 1 to produce a current of air on <let the wind *blow* your hair dry>
syn fan, ruffle, wind, winnow
2 *syn* see BOAST
3 *syn* see PANT 1
4 *syn* see WASTE 2
5 *syn* see TREAT 3
‖6 *syn* see BOTCH
‖7 *syn* see GO 2
blow *n syn* see BREAK 4
blow *vb syn* see BLOSSOM
blow *n* 1 a forceful sharp stroke (as with the fist or an instrument) <struck him a sudden *blow*>
syn bang, bash, bastinado, bat, belt, biff, bop, crack, ‖ding, ‖douse, pound, slam, slosh, smack, smash, sock, ‖swap, thwack, wallop, ‖welt, whack, whop; *compare* CUFF, HIT 1
rel recumbentibus, slug, ‖souse; clip, pelt, plug, punch, swat
2 *syn* see IMPACT
blow–by–blow *adj syn* see CIRCUMSTANTIAL
blowen *n syn* see HARLOT 1
blower *n syn* see BRAGGART
blowhard *n syn* see BRAGGART
‖**blow in** *vb syn* see COME 1
blown–in–the–bottle *adj syn* see AUTHENTIC 2
‖**blow off** *vb syn* see GRIPE
blowoff *n syn* see BINGE 1
‖**blowout** *n syn* see SHINDIG 1
blowsy *adj syn* see SLATTERNLY
ant spruce
blow up *vb* 1 *syn* see EXPLODE 1
2 *syn* see DISCREDIT 2
3 *syn* see ANGER 2
blowy *adj syn* see WINDY 1
blub *vb syn* see CRY 2
blubber *vb syn* see CRY 2
bludgeon *n syn* see CUDGEL

bludgeon *vb syn* see INTIMIDATE
blue *adj* **1** *syn* see DOWNCAST
  2 *syn* see RISQUÉ
  3 *syn* see UTTER
blue *n syn* see OCEAN
blue blood *n* **1** *syn* see GENTLEMAN
  2 *syn* see ARISTOCRACY
‖**bluebottle** *n syn* see POLICEMAN
bluecoat *n syn* see POLICEMAN
blue–eyed *adj syn* see FAVORITE 1
blue moon *n syn* see AGE 2
bluenose *n syn* see PRUDE
bluenosed *adj syn* see PRIM 1
blueprint *n syn* see PLAN 1
  rel outline, sketch
blueprint *vb syn* see PLAN 2
blue–ribbon *adj syn* see EXCELLENT
blues *n pl but sometimes sing in constr syn* see SADNESS
bluff *adj* direct and unceremonious in speech or manner <*bluff* aggressive questions>
  syn abrupt, blunt, breviloquent, brief, brusque, crusty, curt, gruff, rough, short, short-spoken, snippety, snippy
  rel hearty, honest, sincere; barefaced, candid, direct, forthright, frank, no-nonsense, outspoken, plainspoken, straightforward; bearish, rude, tactless; sharp, tart; laconic, terse
  idiom to the point
  con civil, courteous, courtly, gallant, polite; diplomatic, urbane
  ant smooth, suave
bluff *vb* **1** *syn* see DECEIVE
  rel fool, joke, trick
  2 *syn* see ASSUME 4
blunder *vb* **1** *syn* see STUMBLE 3
  2 *syn* see WALLOW 2
  3 *syn* see BOTCH
blunder (away) *vb syn* see WASTE 2
blunder *n syn* see ERROR 2
blunderbuss *n syn* see STUMBLEBUM
blunderer *n syn* see STUMBLEBUM
blunt *adj* **1** *syn* see DULL 6
  rel unpointed, unsharp; insensitive
  con acuminate, acute
  ant keen, sharp
  2 *syn* see BLUFF
  con politic, smooth, suave
  ant subtle; tactful
blunt *vb* **1** *syn* see DULL 3
  2 *syn* see DEADEN 1
  3 *syn* see DULL 5
  4 *syn* see WEAKEN 1
‖**blunt** *n syn* see MONEY
blur *n syn* see STIGMA
blur *vb* **1** *syn* see TAINT 1
  2 *syn* see CONFUSE 4
  3 *syn* see DULL 4
blurb *n syn* see PUFF 3
blurt (out) *vb syn* see EXCLAIM
blush *vb* to turn or glow red in the face <*blushed* from embarrassment>
  syn color, crimson, flush, glow, mantle, pink, pinken, redden, rose, rouge
blush *n syn* see BLOOM 3
bluster *vb* **1** *syn* see ROAR
  rel blast, storm, rage
  2 *syn* see INTIMIDATE
blustering *adj syn* see WILD 6
blustery *adj syn* see WILD 6
board *vb* **1** to get aboard of <*boarded* the wrong bus>
  syn embark
  rel embus, emplane, entrain
  idiom get on
  con debus, deplane, detrain; land
  ant debark, disembark, get off
  2 *syn* see HARBOR 2
  rel care (for), cherish, nurture, tend
board *n* **1 boards** *pl syn* see DRAMA
  2 *syn* see TABLE 1
boast *vb* to express pride in oneself or one's accomplishments <*boasting* about all the girl friends he had>

  syn blow, brag, cock-a-doodle-doo, crow, gasconade, mouth, prate, puff, rodomontade, vaunt
  rel pique, plume, preen, pride, quack; gush, vapor; aggrandize, exalt, glory, triumph; bluster, ‖bounce, bully, ruffle, swash, swashbuckle, swagger; flaunt, parade, show off
  idiom blow one's horn, congratulate oneself, hug oneself, pat oneself on the back
  con belittle, decry, degrade, disparage, knock, minimize, run down
  ant depreciate
boaster *n syn* see BRAGGART
boastful *adj* given to or characterized by boasting <a *boastful* old windbag>
  syn braggadocian, braggart, braggy, rodomontade, self-glorifying, vaunting
  rel arrogant, pretentious; cock-a-hoop, exultant; big-headed, conceited, swelled-headed; self-aggrandizing, self-applauding, self-flattering, vainglorious
  idiom having a high opinion of oneself, seeing oneself larger than life
  con self-depreciating, self-effacing, unassuming; bashful, demure, sheepish, shy, timid; quiet, reserved, restrained, retiring
  ant modest
bob *vb syn* see TAP 1
bobbery *n syn* see BRAWL 2
bobble *vb syn* see BOTCH
‖**bobby** *n syn* see POLICEMAN
‖**bodacious** *adj syn* see NOTEWORTHY
bode *vb syn* see AUGUR 2
bodement *n syn* see FORETOKEN
bodiless *adj syn* see IMMATERIAL 1
bodily *adj* of or relating to the human body <*bodily* pain>
  syn carnal, corporal, corporeal, fleshly, physical, somatic
  rel animal, sensual
  con intellectual, mental, psychic, psychological; spiritual, unworldly
boding *n syn* see FORETOKEN
body *n* **1** *syn* see HUMAN
  2 *syn* see CORPSE
  3 the main, central, or essential part <the *body* of the discussion dealt with ways to ensure equal opportunities for all>
  syn bulk, core, corpus, mass, staple, substance; *compare* ESSENCE 2, SUBSTANCE 2, TENOR 1
  rel majority; sum, total, whole; basis, crux, fundamental, gravamen; gist, pith
  con angle, aspect, facet, feature, side; accessory, extension, offshoot, side issue
  4 a discrete portion of matter <unknown *bodies* in space>
  syn bulk, mass, object, volume
  5 a determinable or measurable whole <collected a large *body* of evidence>
  syn aggregate, amount, budget, bulk, quantity, quantum, total
  rel extent, range; number, stock, sum, whole
  6 *syn* see GROUP 3
  7 *syn* see SUBSTANCE 2
body (forth) *vb syn* see REPRESENT 2
boeotian *n syn* see PHILISTINE
bog *n syn* see SWAMP
bog (down) *vb syn* see DELAY 1
bogey *n syn* see APPARITION
boggle *vb* **1** *syn* see DEMUR
  2 *syn* see BOTCH
  3 *syn* see STAGGER 5
bogus *adj syn* see COUNTERFEIT
  rel forged; imitation
  con bona fide, good
  ant authentic, genuine, real
Bohemian *n* a person (as an artist) who has an unconventional life-style that often reflects protest against or indifference to convention <a gathering place for radicals and *Bohemians*>
  syn maverick, nonconformist
  rel beat, beatnik, dropout, hippie; iconoclast; eccentric, original; recusant

---

syn synonym(s)   *rel* related word(s)
ant antonym(s)   *con* contrasted word(s)
idiom idiomatic equivalent(s)
‖ use limited; if in doubt, see a dictionary

con conformer, conventionalist, formalist, pedant

bohunk *n syn* see OAF 2

boil *n syn* see ABSCESS

boil *vb* **1** *syn* see SEETHE 4

2 to prepare (as food) in a liquid heated to the point that it begins to give off steam < *boil* eggs >
syn parboil, seethe, simmer, stew
rel coddle, poach; decoct; steam

3 *syn* see ANGER 2

4 *syn* see RUSH 1

boil down *vb syn* see SIMPLIFY

boildown *n syn* see ABRIDGMENT

‖**boiled** *adj syn* see INTOXICATED 1

boiling *adj syn* see HOT 1

boil over *vb syn* see ANGER 2

boisterous *adj* **1** *syn* see TURBULENT 1

2 *syn* see VOCIFEROUS
rel brawling, noisy, riotous, rollicking, rowdy
con sedate, sober, staid; noiseless

‖**boko** *n syn* see NOSE 1

bold *adj* **1** *syn* see BRAVE 1
con pusillanimous, shrinking, timid, timorous
ant cowardly

2 *syn* see WISE 5
rel audacious; bluff
con mousy, quiet, shy

3 *syn* see INSOLENT 2

‖**boldacious** *adj syn* see INSOLENT 2

bold–faced *adj syn* see WISE 5

boldhearted *adj syn* see BRAVE 1

boldness *n syn* see INSOLENCE

bollix *vb syn* see BOTCH

Bolshevik *n syn* see COMMUNIST

‖**Bolshie** *n syn* see COMMUNIST

bolster *vb* **1** *syn* see SUPPORT 4
rel reinforce, strengthen

2 *syn* see SUPPORT 5

bolt *n syn* see THUNDERBOLT

bolt *vb* **1** *syn* see START 1

2 *syn* see RUSH 1

3 *syn* see RUN 2

4 *syn* see EXCLAIM

5 *syn* see GULP

bomb *n* **1** *syn* see FAILURE 5

‖**2** *syn* see FORTUNE 4

bomb *vb syn* see BOMBARD

bombard *vb* to assault with bombs or shells < cities *bombarded* by planes and artillery >
syn blitz, bomb, cannonade, shell
rel barrage, strafe, strike
idiom open up on, pour a broadside into

bombardment *n syn* see BARRAGE

bombast *n* pretentious inflated speech or writing < adolescent *bombast* about Youth and Destiny >
syn fustian, highfalutin, lexiphanicism, rant, rhapsody, rhetoric, rodomontade
rel grandiloquence, magniloquence; flatulence, orotundity, tumidity, turgidity; heroics, pyrotechnics, sesquipedality; Johnsonese; spread-eagleism; nonsense
idiom purple prose

bombastic *adj syn* see RHETORICAL
rel flatulent
con unimpassioned; unaffected

‖**bombed** *adj syn* see INTOXICATED 1

bombinate *vb syn* see HUM

bona fide *adj syn* see AUTHENTIC 2

bona fides *n syn* see GOOD FAITH

bonanza *n* a place of great abundance or a source of great wealth or opportunity < the town proved to be a *bonanza* for entrepreneurs >
syn eldorado, Golconda, gold mine, mine, treasure-house, treasure trove, treasury

bond *n* **1** *usu* **bonds** *pl syn* see SHACKLE

2 *syn* see CONTRACT

3 a uniting or binding element or force < the *bonds* of friendship >
syn knot, ligament, ligature, link, nexus, tie, vinculum, yoke
rel bridge, connection, connective, liaison; interrelationship, relationship

4 *syn* see ADHERENCE 1

5 *syn* see GUARANTEE 1

bondage *n* the state of subjection to an owner or master < prisoners sold into *bondage* >
syn enslavement, helotry, peonage, serfage, serfdom, servility, servitude, slavery, thrall, thralldom, villenage, yoke
rel subjection, subjugation
con freedom, independence, liberty

bondman *n syn* see SLAVE 1

bondslave *n syn* see SLAVE 1

bondsman *n syn* see SLAVE 1

bone *n* **1** **bones** *pl syn* see DICE

‖**2** *syn* see DOLLAR

bone (up) *vb syn* see CRAM 4

bone–dry *adj* **1** *syn* see DRY 1

2 *syn* see DRY 3

bonehead *n syn* see DUNCE

boneless *adj syn* see WEAK 4

boner *n* **1** *syn* see ERROR 2

2 *syn* see FAUX PAS

‖**boneyard** *n syn* see CEMETERY

bong *vb syn* see RING

boniface *n syn* see SALOONKEEPER

‖**bonkers** *adj syn* see INSANE 1

bonne bouche *n syn* see DELICACY

‖**bonnet** *n syn* see DECOY 2

‖**bonny** *adj syn* see BEAUTIFUL

bon vivant *n syn* see EPICURE
rel bon viveur, boulevardier, high liver, man-about-town, sport

bony *adj syn* see LEAN

boo *n syn* see RASPBERRY

boo *n syn* see MARIJUANA

boob *n* **1** *syn* see DUNCE

2 *syn* see PHILISTINE

‖**boo–boo** *n syn* see FAUX PAS

booby *n syn* see DUNCE

booby hatch *n syn* see ASYLUM 3

booby trap *n syn* see PITFALL

boodle *n* **1** *syn* see FORTUNE 4

2 *syn* see SPOIL

boodle *vb syn* see CHEAT

boohoo *vb syn* see CRY 2

book *n* **1** a collection of folded, cut, bound, and usually printed sheets < a *book* of poems >
syn tome, volume
rel publication, work, writing; scroll; booklet, brochure, folder, leaflet, magazine, pamphlet; compendium, handbook, manual, monograph, textbook, tract, treatise; codex; novel

2 *cap* **Book** *syn* see BIBLE

book *vb* **1** *syn* see LIST 3

2 *syn* see TIME 1

3 *syn* see RESERVE 2

bookdealer *n* one who deals in books < sold his library to a *bookdealer* >
syn bibliopole, bookman, bookseller
rel bouquiniste

bookie *n syn* see BOOKMAKER

bookish *adj syn* see PEDANTIC
rel booksy, highbrow

book–learned *adj syn* see PEDANTIC

bookmaker *n* one who determines odds and receives and pays off bets < *bookmakers* who welsh on paying off winners >
syn bookie, layer
rel pricemaker; runner

bookman *n syn* see BOOKDEALER

bookseller *n syn* see BOOKDEALER

booky *adj syn* see PEDANTIC

boom *n* **1** *syn* see BANG 2

2 *syn* see PROSPERITY 4

boomerang *vb syn* see BACKFIRE

booming *adj syn* see FLOURISHING

boon *n* **1** *syn* see GIFT 1

2 *syn* see GOOD 1

boon *adj syn* see MERRY

‖**boondocks** *n pl syn* see FRONTIER 2

‖**boonies** *n pl syn* see FRONTIER 2

boor *n* an uncouth ungainly fellow < an ill-mannered *boor* >
syn ‖bosthoon, chuff, churl, clodhopper, clown, grobian, mucker

rel barbarian, vulgarian; looby, lubber; farmer, loon, rustic, swain; ‖carl; bohunk; boob, buffoon, oaf
con slicker, smoothy; gentleman; cosmopolitan, cosmopolite, sophisticate
boorish *adj* uncouth in manner or appearance <a *boorish* fellow lacking all grace>
syn churlish, cloddish, clodhopping, clownish, ill-bred, loutish, lowbred, lubberly, lumpish, robustious, rugged, swainish, uncivilized, uncultured, unpolished, unrefined; *compare* COARSE 3
rel barbarian, barbaric, outlandish, tasteless, vulgar; bucolic, countrified, inurbane, provincial, rustic, yokelish; ill-mannered, impolite, rude, uncivil, ungracious; graceless, unpoised
con cultivated, cultured, refined; suave, urbane; courteous, courtly, genteel, polite, well-bred; graceful, gracious, poised
boost *vb* **1 syn** see RAISE 9
  2 syn see INCREASE 1
  3 syn see PROMOTE 3
  ‖**4 syn** see SHOPLIFT
boost *n syn* see RISE 3
‖**booster** *n syn* see DECOY 2
boot *n* **1 syn** see THRILL
  2 syn see NOVICE
boot (out) *vb* **1 syn** see EJECT 1
  2 syn see DISMISS 3
‖**boot hill** *n syn* see CEMETERY
bootleg *n syn* see MOONSHINE 2
bootleg *vb syn* see SMUGGLE
bootless *adj syn* see FUTILE
  rel frustrating; profitless, worthless
bootlick *vb syn* see FAWN
bootlick *n syn* see SYCOPHANT
bootlicker *n syn* see SYCOPHANT
bootlicking *adj syn* see FAWNING
booty *n syn* see SPOIL
booze *vb syn* see DRINK 3
booze *n* **1 syn** see LIQUOR 2
  2 syn see BINGE 1
‖**boozed** *adj syn* see INTOXICATED 1
boozehound *n syn* see DRUNKARD
boozer *n* **1 syn** see DRUNKARD
  ‖**2 syn** see BAR 5
‖**boozy** *adj syn* see INTOXICATED 1
bop *n syn* see BLOW 1
borasca *n syn* see POVERTY 1
bordello *n syn* see BROTHEL
border *n* **1** a line or relatively narrow space that marks the outermost bound of something <the *border* of the rug>
syn brim, brink, edge, fringe, hem, margin, perimeter, periphery, rim, selvage, skirt, verge; *compare* CIRCUMFERENCE
rel butts and bounds, lines, metes and bounds; bound, circumference, confine, end, extremity, limit, termination; boundary, frontier, march, pale; beginning, door, entrance, threshold; sideline; lip
con inside, interior; recesses; center; body, bulk, mass, whole
  2 syn see FRONTIER 1
border *vb* **1** to form a border to <hedges *border* the park>
syn bound, define, edge, fringe, hem, margin, outline, rim, skirt, surround, verge
rel circumscribe, encircle, enclose, frame; contour, delineate, mark (off), outline, set off; flank, line, side; trim
  2 syn see ADJOIN
  3 to come to be closely similiar to a specified thing <ideas that *border* on the absurd>
syn approach, trench, verge
rel approximate, compare, near
idiom come close (*or* near) to
bordering *adj syn* see ADJACENT 3
borderland *n syn* see FRONTIER 1
borderline *adj syn* see DOUBTFUL 1
bore *vb* **1 syn** see PERFORATE
  2 syn see GAZE 1
bore *vb* to induce a state of boredom in <*bored* to death by his endless sermon>
syn ennui, pall, tire, weary
rel jade; fatigue, wear; annoy, irk, irritate; afflict, bother, discomfort
idiom put one to sleep

con amuse, entertain; excite, fascinate, intrigue; absorb, beguile, engross, enthrall, grip; enliven, freshen, invigorate, quicken, stimulate
ant interest
boreal *adj syn* see COLD 1
boredom *n syn* see TEDIUM
rel fatigue, weariness; disgust, distaste
con amusement, diversion, entertainment; excitement, fascination; engrossment, enthrallment
boresome *adj syn* see IRKSOME
rel deadly, dreary, dull, humdrum, monotonous
con amusing, entertaining; exciting, fascinating, intriguing; absorbing, engrossing, enthralling, gripping, stimulating
ant interesting
boring *adj syn* see IRKSOME
born *adj syn* see INHERENT
‖**born** *vb syn* see BEAR 5
borné *adj syn* see LITTLE 2
bosh *n syn* see NONSENSE 2
bosom *n syn* see HEART 1
bosomy *adj syn* see BUXOM
boss *n syn* see LEADER 2
‖**boss** *adj syn* see EXCELLENT
boss *vb syn* see SUPERVISE
bossy *adj syn* see MASTERFUL 1
‖**bosthoon** *n syn* see BOOR
Boswell *n syn* see BIOGRAPHER
botch *vb* to do or proceed ineffectively or badly through clumsiness, stupidity, or lack of ability <a complete incompetent —*botches* everything he puts his hand to>
syn ‖blow, blunder, bobble, boggle, bollix, bugger up, bumble, bungle, cobble, dub, flub, fluff, foozle, fumble, goof (up), gum (up), louse up, mess, ‖muck, mucker, muff, ‖screw (up)
rel butcher, mangle, murder, mutilate; mar, ruin, spoil; destroy, wreck; hash; tinker; misconduct, mishandle, mismanage; confuse, disorder
idiom play (*or* wreak) havoc with, play hell with
botch *n syn* see MESS 3
botchery *n syn* see MESS 3
botchy *adj syn* see SLIPSHOD 3
bother *vb* **1 syn** see DISCOMPOSE 1
  2 syn see ANNOY 1
bother *n* **1 syn** see ANNOYANCE 2
  2 syn see ANNOYANCE 3
  3 syn see INCONVENIENCE
botheration *n* **1 syn** see ANNOYANCE 2
  2 syn see ANNOYANCE 3
bothering *n syn* see ANNOYANCE 1
botherment *n syn* see ANNOYANCE 3
bothersomeness *n syn* see INCONVENIENCE
bottega *n syn* see STUDIO
bottle (up) *vb* **1 syn** see RESTRAIN
  2 syn see CORNER
bottom *n* **1** the under surface as opposed to the top surface <gum was stuck to the *bottom* of her shoe>
syn sole, underneath, underside, undersurface
rel belly, underbelly, underbody; base, floor, foot, ground
con acme, apex, cap, crest, crown, tip, upper
ant top
  2 syn see BUTTOCKS
  3 the lower or lowest point <the *bottom* of the page>
syn base, foot, nadir
rel basement, floor, ground; end; low
con acme, apex, pinnacle, zenith
ant top
  4 syn see BASE 1
  5 syn see ESSENCE 2
bottom *vb syn* see BASE
bottom *adj* **1 syn** see BOTTOMMOST
  2 syn see FUNDAMENTAL 1
bottom dog *n syn* see VICTIM 2
bottomless *adj* **1 syn** see BASELESS
rel reasonless, unjustifiable, unsupportable

---

2 extremely deep < the *bottomless* sea>
syn abysmal, fathomless, plumbless, plummetless, soundless, unfathomable; *compare* DEEP 1
rel endless, infinite
bottommost *adj* that is at the very bottom < the ladder's *bottommost* rung>
syn bottom, lowermost, lowest, nethermost, rock-bottom, undermost
con top, upper, uppermost
ant topmost
bough *n syn* see LIMB
bought *adj syn* see READY-MADE
‖**boughten** *adj syn* see READY-MADE
boulevard *n syn* see WAY 1
bounce *vb* **1** *syn* see JUMP 1
2 *syn* see DISMISS 3
‖**3** *syn* see INTIMIDATE
bounce (back) *vb* **1** *syn* see RECOVER 3
2 *syn* see BACKFIRE
bouncer *n* ‖**1** *syn* see LIE
rel exaggeration, hyperbole, overstatement
idiom tall tale
2 a person employed to restrain or eject disorderly persons (as at a bar) < tossed out by the *bouncer* >
syn chucker, ‖chucker-out, houseman
rel goon, muscleman, strong arm
bouncy *adj syn* see ELASTIC 2
bound *n* **1** *usu* **bounds** *pl syn* see ENVIRONS 1
2 *syn* see LIMIT 1
bound *vb* **1** *syn* see DEMARCATE 1
2 *syn* see BORDER 1
bound *adj* **1** *syn* see FINITE
2 obliged to serve a master or in a clearly defined capacity for a certain length of time by the terms of a contract or mutual agreement < brought to the American colonies as a *bound* servant>
syn apprenticed, articled, indentured
rel contracted; enslaved
con free, freed
3 *syn* see CONSTIPATED
bound *vb syn* see JUMP 1
boundary *n syn* see ENVIRONS 1
bounded *adj syn* see FINITE
ant unbounded
bounder *n syn* see CAD
boundless *adj syn* see LIMITLESS
bounteous *adj* **1** *syn* see LIBERAL 1
con cheap, illiberal, scant
ant niggardly
2 *syn* see PLENTIFUL
con insufficient, scant, sparse
bountiful *adj* **1** *syn* see LIBERAL 1
2 *syn* see PLENTIFUL
bouquet *n* **1** cut flowers arranged for wear or display < a *bouquet* of spring flowers>
syn nosegay, posy
rel arrangement; boutonniere, corsage; spray; wreath; garland, festoon; lei
2 *syn* see COMPLIMENT 1
3 *syn* see FRAGRANCE
Bourbon *n syn* see REACTIONARY
bout *n* **1** *syn* see SPELL 1
2 *syn* see SIEGE
boutade *n syn* see CAPRICE
bow *vb syn* see YIELD 2
bow *n* **1** *syn* see CURVE
2 *syn* see TURN 4
bow *vb syn* see CURVE
bowdlerize *vb syn* see CENSOR
bowed *adj* **1** *syn* see CURVED
2 *syn* see BOWLEGGED
bowel *vb syn* see EVISCERATE
bower *n syn* see ARBOR
bowery *n syn* see SKID ROW
bowl *n syn* see STADIUM
‖**bowl** (down *or* out) *vb syn* see WHIP 2
bowl (down *or* over) *vb syn* see FELL 1
bowlegged *adj* having legs bent outward < a *bowlegged* cowboy>

syn bandy, bandy-legged, bowed
rel bent, crooked, curved, misshapen
bowwow *n syn* see DOG 1
‖**box** *n* **1** *syn* see HUT
2 *syn* see PREDICAMENT
box *n syn* see CUFF
box *vb syn* see SLAP 1
boxing *n* the art of attack and defense with the fists practiced as a sport < he liked *boxing* —at least as a spectator sport>
syn fisticuffs, prizefighting, pugilism, ring
boy *n* **1** a male person not fully matured < a *boy* of nine>
syn lad, laddie, shaveling, son, stripling, tad
rel gamin, ragamuffin, street arab, urchin; hobbledehoy, whippersnapper; schoolboy
idiom little shaver, small fry
2 *syn* see MAN 3
boyfriend *n* **1** a man who is a woman's usual or preferred escort or companion < went to the movies with her *boyfriend*>
syn beau, gentleman friend, swain, young man
rel admirer
2 a man who shares with a woman a strong and usually sexually oriented mutual attraction < this was the *boyfriend* she hoped to marry>
syn beau, beloved, flame, inamorato, lover, steady, sweetheart, truelove
rel crush, heartthrob; fiancé
3 *syn* see LOVER 1
brabble *vb syn* see QUARREL
brabble *n* **1** *syn* see QUARREL
2 *syn* see CHATTER
brace *n* **1** *syn* see COUPLE
2 *syn* see SUPPORT 3
3 braces *pl syn* see SUSPENDERS
brace *vb* **1** *syn* see GIRD 3
2 *syn* see SUPPORT 4
3 *syn* see BEG
bracing *adj syn* see INVIGORATING
bracket *vb* **1** *syn* see JOIN 1
2 *syn* see COMPARE 2
brag *vb syn* see BOAST
con apologize, deprecate
braggadocian *adj syn* see BOASTFUL
braggadocio *n syn* see BRAGGART
braggart *n* one who boasts < too much of a *braggart* about his strength>
syn blower, blowhard, boaster, braggadocio, bragger, ‖gasbag, puckfist, rodomont, rodomontade, vaunter
rel bluffer, blusterer, loudmouth, miles gloriosus, ranter, raver, windbag
con Milquetoast
braggart *adj syn* see BOASTFUL
bragger *n syn* see BRAGGART
braggy *adj syn* see BOASTFUL
Brahmin *n syn* see INTELLECTUAL 2
brain *n* **1** *syn* see MIND 1
2 *syn* see INTELLECT 2
3 *often* **brains** *pl syn* see INTELLIGENCE 1
brainchild *n syn* see INVENTION
brainless *adj syn* see SIMPLE 3
brainpower *n syn* see INTELLIGENCE 1
brainsick *adj syn* see INSANE 1
brainwork *n syn* see THOUGHT 1
brainy *adj syn* see INTELLIGENT 2
brake *vb syn* see HINDER
rel slow, stop
branch *n* **1** *syn* see LIMB
rel branchlet
2 *syn* see CREEK 2
brand *n* **1** *syn* see MARK 7
2 *syn* see STIGMA
brandish *vb syn* see SHOW 4
brand–new *adj* conspicuously new and unused < a *brand-new* car right out of the showroom>
syn fire-new, mint, spang-new, spanking-new, span-new, spick=and-span
rel untouched, unused; clean, fresh, pristine
con hand-me-down, secondhand, used; outworn, shabby, worn, worn-out

ant old

brannigan *n* **1** *syn* see BINGE 1
  2 *syn* see QUARREL
brash *adj* **1** *syn* see RASH 1
  2 *syn* see EXUBERANT 1
  3 *syn* see TACTLESS
  4 *syn* see PRESUMPTUOUS
  rel bold, brazen; rash, reckless; headlong, impetuous; cocksure
brashness *n* **1** *syn* see TEMERITY
  2 *syn* see EFFRONTERY
brass *n* ‖**1** *syn* see MONEY
  2 *syn* see EFFRONTERY
brassbound *adj* **1** *syn* see ILLIBERAL
  2 *syn* see INFLEXIBLE 2
  3 *syn* see PRESUMPTUOUS
brass hat *n* *syn* see SUPERIOR
brassy *adj* **1** *syn* see SHAMELESS
  2 *syn* see BRAZEN 4
brave *adj* **1** having or showing no fear when faced with something dangerous, difficult, or unknown <made a *brave* attempt to save the burning house>
  syn audacious, aweless, bold, boldhearted, bravehearted, chin-up, courageous, dauntless, doughty, fearless, gallant, game, greathearted, ‖gutsy, heroic, intrepid, lionhearted, manful, manly, ‖plucked, plucky, soldierly, spunky, stalwart, stout, stouthearted, unafraid, unblenched, unblenching, undauntable, undaunted, unfearful, unfearing, valiant, valorous
  rel daring, defiant, gritty, hardy, mettlesome, resolute, spirited, steadfast, unapprehensive, undismayed, unflinching, unfrightened, unquailing, unshrinking, unswerving, unwincing, unyielding, venturesome; chivalrous, noble, preux; confident
  con cringing, flinching, frightened, pusillanimous, scared, shrinking, timid; chickenhearted, fainthearted, lily-livered, nerveless, soft, spineless, unmanly, weakhearted, weak-kneed, yellow
  ant cowardly, craven
  2 *syn* see COLORFUL
  3 *syn* see GOOD 1
brave *vb* *syn* see FACE 3
  con avoid
bravehearted *adj* *syn* see BRAVE 1
bravery *n* *syn* see FINERY
bravo *n* *syn* see ASSASSIN
brawl *vb* *syn* see QUARREL
brawl *n* **1** *syn* see QUARREL
  2 a rough, noisy, and often prolonged hand-to-hand fight usually involving several people <windows and furniture were broken in the barroom *brawl*>
  syn affray, bobbery, broil, dogfight, donnybrook, fight, fracas, fray, free-for-all, knock-down-and-drag-out, maul, melee, mellay, ‖muss, rough-and-tumble, row, rowdydow, ruction, scrap, scrimmage, scuffle, set-to; *compare* QUARREL
  rel fistfight, fisticuffs, slugfest; struggle, tussle; conflict, contention, contest, riot; altercation, embroilment, imbroglio, quarrel, wrangle; commotion, disturbance, eruption, hubbub, pandemonium, ruckus, rumpus, turn-to, ‖turnup, upheaval, uproar; incident, ‖rumble
  idiom a coming to blows, exchange of blows
brawling *adj* *syn* see QUARRELSOME 2
brawlsome *adj* *syn* see QUARRELSOME 2
brawly *adj* *syn* see QUARRELSOME 2
brawn *n* *syn* see MUSCLE 1
brawny *adj* *syn* see MUSCULAR 2
  rel lusty, red-blooded, vigorous, vital; tough
  con lanky, lean, rawboned, skinny, thin
  ant scrawny
bray *vb* *syn* see PULVERIZE 1
brazen *adj* **1** *syn* see INSOLENT 2
  2 *syn* see SHAMELESS
  3 *syn* see GAUDY
  4 of the color of polished brass <a *brazen* sky at sunset>
  syn aeneous, brassy
  rel bronze
brazenfaced *adj* *syn* see SHAMELESS
breach *n* **1** the act or offense of failing to keep the law or to do what law, duty, or obligation requires <sued for *breach* of contract> <his behavior was a gross *breach* of good manners>
  syn contravention, infraction, infringement, transgression, trespass, violation

rel disregard, nonobservance; delinquency, dereliction, neglect
  con conformance, conformity, observance
  ant observance
  2 *syn* see GAP 1
  3 an interruption of accustomed friendly relations <a trivial misunderstanding caused a *breach* between the brothers>
  syn break, fissure, fracture, rent, rift, rupture, schism, split; *compare* SCHISM 3
  rel division, separation, severance; alienation, estrangement; difference, discord, disharmony, dissension, disunity, strife, variance; secession, withdrawal; falling-out, quarrel
  idiom parting of ways
  con integrity, solidarity, union, unity; communion, community; accord, concord, harmony
  4 *syn* see GAP 2
breach *vb* **1** *syn* see OPEN 3
  rel bore, penetrate
  2 *syn* see VIOLATE 1
bread *n* **1** *syn* see FOOD 1
  2 *syn* see LIVING
  ‖**3** *syn* see MONEY
bread and butter *n* *syn* see LIVING
breadth *n* **1** *syn* see EXPANSE
  2 spaciousness of extent <the *breadth* of his knowledge on the subject is awesome>
  syn amplitude, comprehensiveness, fullness, scope, wideness
  rel compass, gamut, orbit, range, reach, sweep; expanse, spread, stretch
  con limitation, restriction
  ant narrowness
breadthen *vb* *syn* see BROADEN
break *vb* **1** *syn* see GIVE 12
  2 *syn* see PLOW
  3 *syn* see VIOLATE 1
  ant observe
  4 *syn* see ESCAPE 1
  5 *syn* see FAIL 5
  idiom go broke
  6 *syn* see RUIN 3
  7 *syn* see DEGRADE 1
  8 *syn* see DISPROVE 1
  9 *syn* see COMMUNICATE 1
  10 *syn* see SOLVE 2
  11 *syn* see DECODE
  12 *syn* see HAPPEN 1
  13 *syn* see GET OUT 2
  ‖**14** *syn* see CLEAR 9
break *n* **1** *syn* see GAP 1
  2 *syn* see GAP 3
  3 *syn* see INTERLUDE
  4 a usually short rest period <took a *break* for coffee>
  syn blow, breath, breather, breathing space (or spell), respite, ten; *compare* PAUSE
  5 *syn* see BREACH 3
  6 *syn* see FAUX PAS
  7 *syn* see OPPORTUNITY
breakable *adj* *syn* see FRAGILE 1
break down *vb* **1** *syn* see ANALYZE
  2 *syn* see DECAY
  3 *syn* see COLLAPSE 2
breakdown *n* **1** *syn* see NERVOUS BREAKDOWN
  2 *syn* see COLLAPSE 2
  3 *syn* see ANALYSIS 1
break in *vb* **1** *syn* see HOUSEBREAK
  idiom break and enter
  2 *syn* see INTERRUPT 2
breakneck *adj* *syn* see FAST 3
break out *vb* *syn* see ERUPT 2
breakout *n* *syn* see ESCAPE 1
breakthrough *n* *syn* see RISE 3
break up *vb* **1** *syn* see SEPARATE 1
  2 *syn* see DISBAND
breakup *n* *syn* see ANALYSIS 1

---

syn synonym(s)   *rel* related word(s)
ant antonym(s)   *con* contrasted word(s)
idiom idiomatic equivalent(s)
‖ use limited; if in doubt, see a dictionary

breast *n syn* see HEART 1
breast–feed *vb syn* see NURSE 1
breastwork *n syn* see BULWARK
breath *n* **1** *syn* see HINT 2
  2 *syn* see BREAK 4
breathe *vb* **1** *syn* see BE
  2 *syn* see REST 3
  3 to draw (as air) into and expel from the lungs < *breathe* clean air >
  syn respire
  rel exhale, inhale
  4 *syn* see CONFIDE 1
breathe (in) *vb syn* see INHALE
breathe (out) *vb syn* see EXHALE
breather *n syn* see BREAK 4
breathing *n syn* see INSTANT 1
breathing space (or spell) *n syn* see BREAK 4
breathless *adj* **1** *syn* see EAGER
  2 *syn* see STUFFY 1
bred–in–the–bone *adj syn* see INVETERATE 1
breech *n syn* see BUTTOCKS
breed *vb* **1** *syn* see PROCREATE 1
  2 *syn* see FATHER 1
  3 *syn* see GENERATE 3
  4 *syn* see GROW 1
breed *n syn* see TYPE
breeding *n syn* see CULTURE
  rel civility, courtesy, gentility, grace
  con barbarism, boorishness; coarseness, grossness; discourtesy, rudeness
  ant vulgarity
breeding ground *n* a place or environment which favors growth < the slum was a *breeding ground* for crime >
  syn forcing bed, forcing house, hotbed, hothouse
breeze *n syn* see SNAP 1
breeze *vb* to proceed quickly and easily < *breezed* through customs >
  syn waltz, zip
  rel skim, slide, slip
  con drag, falter, flag, lag, trail
breezy *adj* **1** *syn* see WINDY 1
  2 *syn* see EASYGOING 3
breviary *n syn* see ABRIDGMENT
breviate *n syn* see ABRIDGMENT
breviloquent *adj* **1** *syn* see CONCISE
  2 *syn* see BLUFF
brew *vb syn* see LOOM 2
brew *n syn* see MISCELLANY 1
bribable *adj syn* see VENAL 1
bribe *vb* to give or promise money or favor to a person in a position of trust to influence his judgment or conduct < *bribed* a building inspector >
  syn buy, buy off, fix, have, ‖lubricate, sop, square, tamper (with)
  rel approach; corrupt, instigate, suborn; soften (up), sweeten
  idiom grease the palm (or hand), oil the palm (or hand), tickle the palm
bridal *n syn* see WEDDING
bridewell *n syn* see JAIL
bridle *vb syn* see RESTRAIN 1
  rel repress, suppress; control, manage; govern, rule
  con air, express, utter, ventilate, voice
  ant vent
brief *adj* **1** *syn* see SHORT 1
  rel fleeting, momentary, passing, transient
  ant long
  2 *syn* see CONCISE
  3 *syn* see BLUFF
brief *n syn* see ABRIDGMENT
briefly *adv* in a few words < he answered *briefly* and to the point >
  syn concisely, in brief, in short, laconically, shortly, succinctly, tersely
  rel accurately, crisply, exactly, precisely
  idiom in a capsule, in a nutshell, in a word, to make a long story short
  con diffusely, long-windedly, profusely, prolixly, protractedly, verbosely, wordily; at length, comprehensively, fully

‖**brig** *n syn* see JAIL
brigand *n syn* see MARAUDER
bright *adj* **1** shining or glowing with light < the *bright* sun >
  syn beaming, brilliant, effulgent, fulgent, incandescent, lambent, lucent, lucid, luminous, lustrous, radiant, refulgent
  rel clear, light, undimmed; illuminated, lighted; coruscating, flashing, gleaming, glistening, glittering, scintillating, shimmering, sparkling; blazing, flaming, glowing; burnished, polished, shiny; sunshiny
  con dark, dusky, gloomy, murky, tenebrous; colorless, drab, dreary, lackluster, leaden; somber; cloudy, gray, overcast, shadowy; moonless, starless, sunless; faint, pale, weak
  ant dim; dull
  2 *syn* see COLORFUL
  3 *syn* see GLAD 2
  4 *syn* see FAVORABLE 5
  5 *syn* see INTELLIGENT 2
  rel advanced, precocious
  con retarded
  ant dense, dull
  6 *syn* see LIVELY 1
brilliant *adj* **1** *syn* see BRIGHT 1
  ant subdued
  2 *syn* see INTELLIGENT 2
  rel erudite, learned; sage, wise
brim *n syn* see BORDER 1
brimful *adj* **1** *syn* see FULL 1
  2 *syn* see BIG 3
brimming *adj* **1** *syn* see FULL 1
  2 *syn* see BIG 3
brine *n syn* see OCEAN
bring *vb* **1** *syn* see CONVERT 1
  ‖**2** *syn* see ACCOMPANY
  3 *syn* see SELL 4
bring about *vb syn* see EFFECT 1
bring around *vb syn* see INDUCE 1
bring down *vb syn* see FELL 1
bring forth *vb syn* see BEAR 5
bring in *vb* **1** *syn* see YIELD 5
  2 *syn* see SELL 4
  3 *syn* see EARN 1
bring off *vb syn* see EFFECT 2
bring out *vb syn* see SAY 1
bring up *vb* **1** to give a child a parent's fostering care < the orphan was *brought up* by his aunt >
  syn ‖fetch up, raise, rear
  rel breed, cultivate, foster, nurture; feed, nourish, provide (for); discipline, educate, train
  con abuse, ill-use, maltreat; neglect
  2 *syn* see STOP 4
  3 *syn* see REFER 3
  4 *syn* see BROACH
  5 *syn* see VOMIT
brink *n* **1** *syn* see BORDER 1
  2 *syn* see VERGE 2
‖**briny** *n syn* see OCEAN
brio *n syn* see SPIRIT 5
brisk *adj syn* see AGILE
  rel adroit; quick
  con inactive, torpid
  ant sluggish
brisky *adj syn* see AGILE
bristle *vb syn* see ANGER 2
brittle *adj syn* see SHORT 6
broach *n syn* see BROOCH
broach *vb* to open up (a subject) for discussion < would be awkward to *broach* the matter now >
  syn bring up, introduce, moot, ventilate
  rel interject, interpose; mention, speak (about); propose, suggest
  con hush (up), quash, stifle, suppress; black out, censor
broad *adj* **1** *syn* see LIBERAL 3
  2 *syn* see EXTENSIVE 1
  3 *syn* see RISQUÉ
broadcast *n syn* see DECLARATION
broadcast *vb* **1** *syn* see STREW 1
  2 *syn* see DECLARE 1
  rel communicate, radio, televise, transmit
  idiom spread a report, spread far and wide

broaden *vb* to grow or become broad or broader <the street *broadens* into an avenue>
  syn breadthen, widen
  rel expand; spread (out); open
  con contract, shrink; slim, thin
  ant narrow
broad–minded *adj syn* see LIBERAL 3
broadside *n syn* see BARRAGE
Brobdingnagian *adj syn* see HUGE
brocard *n syn* see MAXIM
||**brogue** *vb syn* see IDLE
broil *vb syn* see BURN 3
broil *n syn* see BRAWL 2
broiling *adj syn* see HOT 1
broke *adj syn* see POOR 1
broken–down *adj syn* see SHABBY 1
broker *n syn* see GO-BETWEEN 2
bromide *n syn* see COMMONPLACE
bromidic *adj syn* see ARID 2
||**Bronx cheer** *n syn* see RASPBERRY
brooch *n* an ornament with a pin or clasp now worn usually by women <a diamond *brooch*>
  syn broach, clip, pin
brood *n syn* see OFFSPRING
brood *vb* 1 *syn* see SET 11
  2 syn see MOPE 1
brook *vb syn* see BEAR 10
brook *n syn* see CREEK 2
brothel *n* an establishment where prostitutes ply their trade <madam of the local *brothel*>
  syn bagnio, bawdy house, bordello, call house, cathouse, crib, disorderly house, fancy house, ||hookshop, ||joyhouse, lupanar, parlor house, seraglio, sporting house, stew, whorehouse
  idiom house of ill fame (*or* repute), house of prostitution
brotherhood *n syn* see ASSOCIATION 2
brouhaha *n* 1 *syn* see DIN
  2 syn see COMMOTION 3
brow *n syn* see FOREHEAD
browbeat *vb syn* see INTIMIDATE
browbeater *n syn* see BULLY 1
brownie *n syn* see FAIRY
||**brownnose** *vb syn* see FAWN
||**brownnose** *n syn* see SYCOPHANT
||**brownnoser** *n syn* see SYCOPHANT
brown study *n syn* see REVERIE
browse *vb* to read through, study, or examine cursorily <*browsed* through the book looking for illustrations>
  syn dip (into), flip (through), glance (at *or* over), leaf (through), riff (through), riffle (through), run (through *or* over), scan, skim (through), thumb (through)
  rel go (through *or* over), look (over), peruse, skip (through)
  idiom give the once over, run the eye over
  con examine, study; delve (into), dig (into)
  ant pore (over)
bruise *n* an injury involving rupture of small blood vessels and discoloration without break in the overlying skin <got an ugly *bruise* when he fell>
  syn contusion; *compare* BLACK EYE
  rel ||boo-boo; abrasion, scrape, scratch
  idiom black-and-blue spot (*or* mark)
bruise *vb* **1** to inflict a bruise on <fell down and *bruised* his hip>
  syn black, contuse
  rel batter, ||bung up
  2 syn see CRUSH 2
bruit (about) *vb syn* see DECLARE 1
  rel hint, intimate, rumor, suggest
bruja *n syn* see WITCH 1
brume *n syn* see HAZE 1
brummagem *adj syn* see COUNTERFEIT
brunet *adj syn* see DARK 3
brush *vb* to touch or strike lightly (as in passing) <they *brushed* fenders but no real damage was done>
  syn glance, graze, kiss, shave, skim
  rel bump, clash, collide, sideswipe; clip, contact, scrape, touch
brush *n* 1 *syn* see ENCOUNTER
  rel clash, engagement
  2 syn see CLASH 2

brush up *vb syn* see TOUCH UP
brusque *adj syn* see BLUFF
brutal *adj* **1** *syn* see BRUTISH
  2 syn see SEVERE 3
brutalize *vb syn* see DEBASE 1
brute *adj syn* see BRUTISH
brute *n syn* see BEAST
brutish *adj* marked by animal traits and by a lack of man's dignity or refinement <a graceless *brutish* hulk of a man>
  syn animal, beastly, bestial, brutal, brute, feral, ferine, swinish
  rel animalistic; coarse, crude; base, low, mean, scurvy, vile
bubble *vb* **1** *syn* see SLOSH 1
  2 syn see SEETHE 4
bubble *n syn* see PIPE DREAM
buccaneer *n syn* see PIRATE
buck *n* **1** *syn* see MAN 3
  2 syn see FOP
  ||**3 syn** see DOLLAR
  4 syn see SAWHORSE
buck *vb* **1** *syn* see RESIST
  2 syn see CARRY 1
  3 syn see PASS 9
buck (off) *vb syn* see THROW 2
buck *vb syn* see PULVERIZE 1
||**bucket** *n syn* see JAIL
bucket *vb syn* see HURRY 2
||**bucket shop** *n syn* see BAR 5
buckle (down) *vb* **1** *syn* see ADDRESS 3
  2 syn see PITCH IN 1
buckle (under) *vb syn* see YIELD 2
buckram *adj syn* see STIFF 4
buck up *vb syn* see COMFORT
bucolic *adj syn* see RURAL
  ant urbane
bucolic *n syn* see RUSTIC
bud *n* **1** *syn* see CHILD 1
  2 syn see SEED 2
buddy *n syn* see ASSOCIATE 3
||**buddy–buddy** *adj syn* see INTIMATE 4
||**budge** *n syn* see LIQUOR 2
budget *n syn* see BODY 5
budtime *n syn* see SPRING 5
buff *n syn* see ADDICT
buff *vb syn* see POLISH 1
buffalo *vb* **1** *syn* see FRUSTRATE 1
  2 syn see NONPLUS 1
buff–bare *adj syn* see NUDE 2
buffet *n syn* see CUFF
buffet *vb* **1** *syn* see SLAP 1
  2 syn see BEAT 1
||**buffet** *n syn* see EATING HOUSE
||**bufflehead** *n syn* see DUNCE
||**buffle–headed** *adj syn* see SIMPLE 3
buffoon *n syn* see CLOWN 3
||**buffy** *adj syn* see INTOXICATED 1
bug *n syn* see ENTHUSIAST
||**bug** *vb syn* see ANNOY 1
bugbear *n syn* see ABOMINATION 1
||**bugger** *n syn* see SNOT 1
||**bugger** *vb syn* see EXHAUST 4
bugger up *vb syn* see BOTCH
||**buggy** *adj* **1** *syn* see ENTHUSIASTIC
  2 syn see INSANE 1
||**buggy** *n syn* see CAR
||**bughouse** *n syn* see ASYLUM 3
||**bughouse** *adj syn* see INSANE 1
||**bugs** *adj* **1** *syn* see INSANE 1
  2 syn see ENTHUSIASTIC
build *vb* **1** to form or fashion a structure <will *build* either a garage or carport>
  syn construct, erect, put up, raise, rear, uprear; *compare* ERECT 3, MAKE 3

---

syn synonym(s)   *rel* related word(s)
ant antonym(s)   *con* contrasted word(s)
idiom idiomatic equivalent(s)
|| use limited; if in doubt, see a dictionary

rel fabricate, fashion, frame, manufacture; run up, throw up; prefabricate
con demolish, destroy, dismantle, level, pull down, raze, take down, tear down, wreck
2 syn see MAKE 3
3 syn see INCREASE 1
4 syn see INCREASE 2
build (on) *vb syn* see RELY (on *or* upon)
build *n syn* see PHYSIQUE
rel conformation
building *n* a usually roofed and walled structure built for permanent use <a *building* with four apartments>
syn fabric, structure; *compare* EDIFICE, HUT
build up *vb* **1 syn** see ERECT 5
2 syn see PUBLICIZE
buildup *n syn* see PUBLICITY
‖**built** *adj syn* see CURVACEOUS
built–in *adj syn* see INHERENT
bulge *vb* to extend outward beyond the usual or normal line <the box was so full that the sides *bulged*>
syn beetle, jut, overhang, poke, pouch, pout, project, protrude, protuberate, stand out, stick out
rel bag, belly, dilate, distend, expand, swell
bulge *n* **1 syn** see PROJECTION 1
rel bump, lump, swelling
con depression, hollow, pit
2 syn see ADVANTAGE 3
bulk *n* **1** a body of usually material substance that constitutes a thing or unit <his industry was proven by the *bulk* of his accomplishment> <a great dark *bulk* blocked the alley>
syn mass, volume
rel bigness, greatness, largeness, magnitude, quantity, totality
2 syn see BODY 4
3 syn see BODY 5
4 syn see BODY 3
bulk *vb syn* see LOOM 3
bull *n* **1 syn** see ERROR 2
‖**2 syn** see NONSENSE 2
‖**3 syn** see POLICEMAN
bull *adj syn* see LARGE 1
‖**bull band** *n syn* see SHIVAREE
bulldoze *vb* **1 syn** see INTIMIDATE
rel menace, threaten; harass, harry
2 syn see PUSH 2
bulldozer *n syn* see BULLY 1
bullet *vb syn* see HURRY 2
bullfighter *n* one who fights bulls <moved with the grace of an experienced *bullfighter*>
syn matador, toreador, torero
rel banderillero; cuadrillero, picador; cuadrilla
bullheaded *adj syn* see OBSTINATE
bullwork *n syn* see WORK 2
bully *n* **1** an insolent, overbearing person who persists in tormenting another <a big *bully* who picked on little kids>
syn browbeater, bulldozer, harasser, harrier, hector, intimidator; *compare* TOUGH
rel annoyer, antagonizer, heckler, persecutor, pest, tease, tormenter
2 syn see PIMP 1
bully *adj syn* see EXCELLENT
bully *vb syn* see INTIMIDATE
rel torment, torture; menace, threaten
ant coax
bullyboy *n syn* see TOUGH
bullyrag *vb* **1 syn** see INTIMIDATE
2 syn see BAIT 2
bulwark *n* an aboveground defensive structure that forms part of a fortification <the *bulwarks* were woefully undermanned>
syn bastion, breastwork, parapet, rampart
rel citadel, fort, fortress, stronghold
con bunker, dugout
bulwark *vb syn* see DEFEND 1
‖**bum** *vb syn* see HUM
bum *vb syn* see IDLE
bum *n* **1 syn** see VAGABOND
2 syn see SLUGGARD
‖**bum** *adj syn* see BAD 1
bum *n syn* see BINGE 1

bumble *vb syn* see HUM
bumble *vb* **1 syn** see BOTCH
2 syn see STUMBLE 3
bumbling *adj syn* see AWKWARD 2
‖**bumfuzzle** *vb syn* see CONFUSE 2
bummel *vb syn* see SAUNTER
bummer *n* **1 syn** see BEGGAR 1
2 syn see MARAUDER
bumming *n syn* see MENDICANCY
bump *vb* **1** to meet with or come up against forcibly <the two cars *bumped* with a great crumpling of fenders>
syn clash, collide, ‖prang
rel bang, carom, crash, hit, knock, slam, strike; impinge; jar, jolt
idiom whang together
2 syn see HAPPEN 2
3 syn see DEGRADE 1
bump *n* **1 syn** see IMPACT
2 a swelling of tissue usually resulting from a blow <fell and got a *bump* on his head>
syn bunch, knot, lump, ‖pumpknot
rel protuberance, swelling
3 a marked unevenness in a road surface likely to jolt a passing vehicle
syn ‖cahot, thank-you-ma'am
rel chuckhole, mudhole, pothole, rut
4 syn see GIFT 2
bumpkin *n syn* see RUSTIC
bump off *vb syn* see MURDER 1
‖**bump–off** *n syn* see MURDER
bunch *n* **1 syn** see BUMP 2
2 syn see GROUP 3
3 syn see SET 5
4 syn see GROUP 1
bunco steerer *n syn* see SWINDLER
bundle *n* **1 syn** see GROUP 3
2 syn see FORTUNE 4
bundle up *vb* to dress warmly <*bundle up*, it's cold outside>
syn ‖hap, muffle, wrap (up)
rel envelop, mummify, swaddle, swathe
‖**bung** *vb syn* see THROW 1
bung–full *adj syn* see FULL 1
bungle *vb syn* see BOTCH
bungle *n syn* see ERROR 2
bungler *n syn* see STUMBLEBUM
‖**bung up** *vb syn* see BATTER 1
bunk *vb syn* see HARBOR 2
‖**bunk** *vb syn* see ESCAPE 1
‖**bunk** *n syn* see NONSENSE 2
‖**bunk** *vb syn* see DECEIVE
bunkum *n syn* see NONSENSE 2
‖**bunkum** *adj* **1 syn** see EXCELLENT
2 syn see HEALTHY 1
Bunyanesque *adj syn* see HUGE
buoy (up) *vb syn* see SUPPORT 5
buoyancy *n syn* see EBULLIENCE
buoyant *adj syn* see ELASTIC 2
burble *vb* **1 syn** see SLOSH 1
2 syn see CHAT 1
burden *n* **1 syn** see LOAD 1
2 syn see LOAD 3
burden *vb* to lay a heavy load on or to lie like a heavy load on a person or thing <*burdened* his men with needless heavy work> <I won't *burden* you with this lengthy story>
syn charge, clog, cumber, encumber, lade, load, lumber, saddle, task, tax, weigh, weight
rel overburden, overload, overweigh; handicap; afflict, oppress
idiom bear down on (*or* upon)
con alleviate, ease, lighten, relieve, unload; disburden, disencumber
ant unburden
burden *n syn* see SUBSTANCE 2
burdensome *adj syn* see ONEROUS
burdensomely *adv syn* see HARD 8
bureaucrat *n* a member of a bureaucracy <*bureaucrats* were blamed for the error>
syn mandarin
rel civil servant, functionary, official

burg *n* a small, insignificant, remote town < the *burg* had only two stores and one gas station >
 syn hick town, jerkwater town, mudhole, one-horse town, Podunk, tank town, whistle-stop
 rel cowtown; crossroads; jumping-off place; hamlet, village
 con city, metropolis
burgee *n syn* see FLAG
burgeon *vb* **1** *syn* see INCREASE 2
 2 *syn* see BLOSSOM
burghal *adj syn* see URBAN
burgher *n syn* see TOWNSMAN
burglarize *vb* to commit an act of breaking open and entering with a felonious purpose the dwelling house of another by night < that night several homes were *burglarized* >
 syn burgle; *compare* HOUSEBREAK, ROB 1
 rel knock over, rob; ransack, rifle; screw
burgle *vb syn* see BURGLARIZE
burial *n* **1** *syn* see GRAVE
 2 the act or ceremony of burying < his *burial* took place yesterday >
 syn entombment, inhumation, interment, sepulture
 rel burying, exequies, funeral, obsequies; deposition; deep six
 con disinterment, exhumation
burial ground *n syn* see CEMETERY
buried *adj syn* see ULTERIOR
burke *vb* **1** *syn* see SUPPRESS 3
 2 *syn* see SKIRT 3
burlesque *n* **1** *syn* see MOCKERY 2
 2 *syn* see CARICATURE 2
burlesque *vb syn* see MIMIC
burly *adj syn* see HUSKY 1
‖**burn** *n syn* see CREEK 2
burn *vb* **1** *syn* see SHINE 1
 2 to undergo combustion < the wood is too green to *burn* >
 syn combust
 rel fire, flame, ignite, kindle, light; consume, use; smolder, sputter
 3 to be hot as if on fire < sand *burning* in the blazing sun >
 syn bake, broil, cook, melt, roast, scorch, swelter
 rel parch, toast, warm; char
 con chill, cool, freeze
 4 *syn* see ANGER 2
 5 *syn* see SMART
 6 *syn* see FIRE 6
 ‖**7** *syn* see CHEAT
burn (up) *vb syn* see IRRITATE
burnable *adj syn* see COMBUSTIBLE 1
burning *adj* **1** on fire < the *burning* house >
 syn ablaze, afire, aflame, alight, blazing, conflagrant, fiery, flaming, flaring, ignited, lighted
 rel aglow, glowing, incandescent
 idiom in flames
 con burned-out, cold
 2 *syn* see HOT 1
 ant icy
 3 *syn* see FEVERISH 2
 4 *syn* see IMPASSIONED
 5 *syn* see PRESSING
burnish *vb syn* see POLISH 1
burnished *adj syn* see LUSTROUS 1
burn off *vb syn* see CLEAR 9
burnsides *n pl syn* see SIDE-WHISKERS
burp *vb syn* see BELCH 1
burro *n syn* see DONKEY 1
burrow *n* **1** *syn* see LAIR 1
 2 *syn* see HOVEL
burrow *vb syn* see SNUGGLE
burst *vb* **1** *syn* see EXPLODE 1
 2 *syn* see SHATTER 1
 3 *syn* see PLUNGE 2
burst (forth) *vb syn* see ERUPT 2
burst *n* **1** *syn* see OUTBREAK 1
 2 *syn* see OUTBURST 1
 3 *syn* see BANG 2
 4 *syn* see BARRAGE
bury *vb* **1** to deposit (a corpse) in or as if in the earth < the pharaohs were *buried* in pyramids > < *buried* at sea >
 syn entomb, inhume, inter, lay away, plant, put away, sepulcher, sepulture, tomb; *compare* ENTOMB 1

 rel inurn; coffin
 idiom consign to the grave, lay to rest, put six feet under
 con dig (up), disentomb, disinter, exhume, untomb; burn, cremate
 2 *syn* see HIDE
burying ground *n syn* see CEMETERY
‖**bus** *n syn* see CAR
bush *n syn* see FRONTIER 2
‖**bush up** *vb syn* see HIDE
bushwa *n syn* see NONSENSE 2
business *n* **1** *syn* see FUNCTION 1
 2 *syn* see PATRONAGE 2
 3 *syn* see WORK 1
 4 activity concerned with the supplying and distribution of commodities < the lumber *business* depends heavily on the housing *business* >
 syn commerce, industry, trade, traffic
 5 *syn* see ENTERPRISE 3
 6 *syn* see AFFAIR 1
 7 *syn* see DOODAD
 8 something personal to oneself < that is none of your *business* >
 syn affair, concern, lookout, occasions, palaver
businessman *n syn* see MERCHANT
buss *vb syn* see KISS 1
bust *vb* **1** *syn* see RUIN 3
 2 *syn* see DEGRADE 1
 ant promote
 3 *syn* see FAIL 5
 ‖**4** *syn* see ARREST 2
bust *n* ‖**1** *syn* see CUFF
 2 *syn* see FAILURE 5
 3 *syn* see BINGE 1
 4 *syn* see RAID 2
‖**busthead** *n syn* see MOONSHINE 2
bustle *vb syn* see HURRY 2
bustle *n* **1** *syn* see STIR 1
 2 *syn* see COMMOTION 4
bustling *adj* full of activity < a *bustling* frontier town >
 syn busy, fussy, hopping, humming, hustling, lively, popping
 rel active, brisk, energetic
 idiom on its way, on the go (*or* move), up and doing
busty *adj syn* see BUXOM
busy *adj* **1** engaged in activity < I can't stop to talk. I'm *busy* >
 syn employed, engaged, occupied, working; *compare* ASSIDUOUS
 idiom at work, on the fly
 con idle, inactive
 ant free
 2 *syn* see BUSTLING
 3 *syn* see IMPERTINENT 2
busy *vb syn* see ENGAGE 4
busybody *n* one who concerns himself with affairs not his own < a meddlesome *busybody* who saw all and tattled all she saw >
 syn butt-in, ‖buttinsky, intermeddler, kibitzer, meddler, Meddlesome Mattie, nose, nosey Parker, Paul Pry, polypragmatist, pragmatic, pragmatist, prier (*or* pryer), quidnunc, rubber, rubberneck, snoop, ‖sticky-beak; *compare* GOSSIP 1, INFORMER
 rel gossip, gossipmonger, newsmonger, rumormonger, scandalmonger, tabby, talebearer, telltale
 idiom curiosity shop, question box
busybody *vb* **1** *syn* see SNOOP
 2 *syn* see MEDDLE
but *conj* **1** *syn* see ONLY
 2 *syn* see EXCEPT 1
but *prep syn* see EXCEPT
but *adv* **1** *syn* see ONLY 1
 2 *syn* see JUST 3
butcher *vb* **1** *syn* see SLAUGHTER 1
 2 *syn* see SLAUGHTER 2
butchery *n syn* see MASSACRE
butt *n* **1** *syn* see TARGET 1
 2 *syn* see LAUGHINGSTOCK
 3 *syn* see FOOL 3

---

syn synonym(s)   *rel* related word(s)
ant antonym(s)   *con* contrasted word(s)
idiom idiomatic equivalent(s)
‖ use limited; if in doubt, see a dictionary

butt (on *or* against) *vb syn* see ADJOIN
‖**butt** *n* **1** *syn* see BUTTOCKS
  2 *syn* see CIGARETTE
butt *n syn* see CASK
butterball *n syn* see FATTY
butt in *vb* **1** *syn* see INTRUDE 1
  con abstain, forbear, restrain
  2 *syn* see MEDDLE
butt–in *n syn* see BUSYBODY
‖**buttinsky** *n syn* see BUSYBODY
buttocks *n pl* the part of the back on which a person sits < gave the boy a whack across the *buttocks* >
  syn backside, beam, behind, bottom, breech, ‖butt, ‖can, cheeks, derriere, ‖duff, fanny, fundament, hams, haunches, heinie (*or* hiney), hind end, ‖hinder, hunkers, ‖keister, nates, podex, posterior, rear, rear end, rump, seat, ‖stern, tail, tail end, ‖tokus
  idiom seat of one's pants
button–down *adj syn* see CONVENTIONAL 1
buttress *n syn* see SUPPORT 3
buttress *vb syn* see SUPPORT 4
buvette *n syn* see BAR 4
buxom *adj* having an amply developed bosom < a *buxom* young woman >
  syn bosomy, busty, chesty, full-bosomed; *compare* CURVACEOUS
  rel ‖stacked; full-figured, Junoesque, shapely, well-developed, well-proportioned
buy *vb* **1** to acquire something for money or the equivalent < *bought* a new car >
  syn purchase, take
  rel acquire, get, obtain, procure
  ant sell
  2 *syn* see RANSOM
  3 *syn* see BRIBE
  ‖**4** *syn* see BELIEVE 1
buy *n syn* see BARGAIN 1
buyable *adj syn* see VENAL 1
buyer *n syn* see PURCHASER
buy off *vb syn* see BRIBE
buzz *vb* **1** *syn* see HUM
  2 *syn* see HISS
  ‖**3** *syn* see TELEPHONE
buzz *n syn* see REPORT 1
‖**buzzed** *adj syn* see INTOXICATED 1

by *prep* **1** *syn* see BESIDE 1
  2 *syn* see NEAR 2
  3 *syn* see VIA 1
  4 *syn* see VIA 2
  5 with reference to < sorted *by* color >
  syn according to, as to
by *adv syn* see OVER 5
by *interj syn* see GOOD-BYE
by all odds *adv syn* see FAR AND AWAY
by a long shot *adv syn* see FAR AND AWAY
by and by *adv* **1** *syn* see AFTER
  2 *syn* see PRESENTLY 1
by–and–by *n syn* see FUTURE
by and large *adv syn* see ALTOGETHER 3
by–blow *n syn* see BASTARD 1
by dint of *prep syn* see VIA 2
bye–bye *interj syn* see GOOD-BYE
by far *adv syn* see FAR AND AWAY
bygone *adj* **1** *syn* see FORMER 2
  2 *syn* see OLD-FASHIONED
  3 *syn* see EXTINCT 2
by long odds *adv syn* see FAR AND AWAY
by means of *prep syn* see VIA 2
byname *n syn* see NICKNAME
by odds *adv syn* see FAR AND AWAY
by ordinary *adv syn* see USUALLY 2
bypass *vb* **1** *syn* see SKIRT 2
  2 *syn* see SKIRT 3
byplace *n syn* see NOOK
by–product *n syn* see OUTGROWTH 2
by–sitter *n syn* see SPECTATOR
bystander *n syn* see SPECTATOR
by stealth *adv syn* see SECRETLY
by–talk *n syn* see SMALL TALK
by the bye *adv syn* see INCIDENTALLY 2
by the way *adv syn* see INCIDENTALLY 2
by–the–way *adj syn* see INDIFFERENT 2
by virtue of *prep syn* see VIA 2
by way of *prep* **1** *syn* see VIA 1
  2 *syn* see VIA 2
byword *n* **1** *syn* see SAYING
  2 *syn* see CATCHWORD
  3 *syn* see NICKNAME
Byzantine *adj syn* see COMPLEX 2

cab *n syn* see TAXICAB
‖**cab** *n syn* see CRUD
cabal *n* **1** *syn* see CLIQUE
  2 *syn* see PLOT 2
cabalistic *adj syn* see MYSTERIOUS
cabaret *n syn* see NIGHTCLUB
‖**cabbage** *n syn* see MONEY
cabbage *vb syn* see STEAL 1
cabbagehead *n syn* see DUNCE
cabin *n syn* see HUT
‖**caboose** *n syn* see HUT
‖**caboose** *n syn* see JAIL
‖**ca' canny** *n syn* see SLOWDOWN 2
cache *vb syn* see HIDE
  con discover, unearth
cachet *n syn* see STATUS 2
‖**cack** *vb syn* see VOMIT
cackle *vb syn* see CHAT 1
cackle *n syn* see CHATTER
cacophonic *adj syn* see DISSONANT 1
cacophonous *adj syn* see DISSONANT 1
cad *n* a person without gentlemanly instincts < gloated over his rival's distress like the *cad* that he was >
  syn bounder, cur, rotter, yellow dog

  rel boor, churl, clown, lout; guttersnipe, mucker, vulgarian; ‖creep; bastard, heel, louse, rat, stinker
  idiom Jack Nasty
  ant gentleman
cadaver *n syn* see CORPSE
cadaverous *adj* **1** *syn* see GHASTLY 2
  2 *syn* see EMACIATED
  rel careworn, haggard, pinched, worn
cadence *n syn* see RHYTHM
  rel accent, accentuation, emphasis, stress; pulsation, pulse, throb
cadency *n syn* see RHYTHM
cadet *n syn* see PIMP 1
cadger *n syn* see BEGGAR 1
cadging *n syn* see MENDICANCY
caducity *n syn* see OLD AGE
  rel childishness, dotardy, dotingness
café *n* **1** *syn* see EATING HOUSE
  2 *syn* see NIGHTCLUB
cage *vb syn* see ENCLOSE 1
  rel imprison, incarcerate, jail
cagey *adj syn* see SHREWD
cageyness *n syn* see CUNNING 2
cahoots *n pl syn* see ASSOCIATION 1
‖**cahot** *n syn* see BUMP 3

cajole *vb syn* see COAX
   rel beguile, deceive, delude; tantalize; crowd, push
cake *vb* **1** to cover with a surface layer <the floor was *caked* with filth >
   syn crust, encrust (*or* incrust), incrustate, rime
   rel besmear, coat, smear, spread; cover, daub
   2 *syn* see HARDEN 1
   rel compress, condense, contract, shrink
cakewalk *n syn* see RUNAWAY
‖**calaboose** *n syn* see JAIL
calamitous *adj* **1** *syn* see FATAL 2
   2 *syn* see DEPLORABLE
calamity *n syn* see DISASTER
   rel collapse, ruin, wreck; affliction, cross, trial, tribulation, visitation
   con fortune, luck; benefaction; favor, gift
   ant boon
calamity howler *n syn* see PESSIMIST
calculate *vb* to determine or approximate a mathematical value (as speed, cost, or quantity) <*calculate* the cost of a new car>
   syn cipher, compute, estimate, figure, reckon
   rel consider, study, weigh; ascertain, determine, discover; appraise, evaluate, price, value; assess, prize, rate
   con conjecture, guess, surmise
calculate (on *or* upon) *vb syn* see RELY (on *or* upon)
calculating *adj syn* see CAUTIOUS
   rel artful, crafty, cunning, guileful, sly, wily
   con improvident, imprudent, indiscreet
   ant rash, reckless
calculation *n syn* see COMPUTATION
calembour *n syn* see PUN
calendar *n syn* see PROGRAM 1
calenture *n syn* see PASSION 6
caliber *n* **1** *syn* see QUALITY 1
   rel ability, capability, capacity; force, power
   2 *syn* see QUALITY 3
caliginous *adj syn* see DARK 1
call *vb* **1** to speak or utter in a loud distinct carrying voice <*call* for help>
   syn cry, hallo, holler, hollo, shout, vociferate, yell; *compare* SHOUT 1
   rel bawl, bellow, hoot, howl, roar, scream, screech, shriek, shrill, whoop, yowl
   con murmur, whisper
   2 *syn* see DEMAND 1
   3 *syn* see SUMMON 2
   rel assemble, collect, gather, round up; bid, invite
   4 *syn* see CONVOKE
   5 *syn* see TELEPHONE
   6 *syn* see NAME 1
   7 *syn* see PREDICT 2
   8 *syn* see ESTIMATE 3
   9 *syn* see FORETELL
   10 *syn* see VISIT 2
call (for) *vb syn* see DEMAND 2
call (to) *vb syn* see ADDRESS 7
call *n* **1** the natural vocal sound of an animal and especially a bird <the clear *call* of a bellbird>
   syn cry, note, song
   rel cheep, chirp, peep, twitter, warble
   2 *syn* see ATTRACTION 1
   3 *syn* see OCCASION 3
   4 *syn* see VISIT 1
call down *vb syn* see REPROVE
caller *n syn* see VISITOR 1
‖**callet** *n syn* see PROSTITUTE
call girl *n syn* see PROSTITUTE
call house *n syn* see BROTHEL
calligraphy *n syn* see HANDWRITING
call in *vb syn* see SUMMON 2
calling *n* **1** *syn* see MISSION
   2 *syn* see TRADE 1
   3 *syn* see WORK 1
‖**callithump** *n syn* see SHIVAREE
call off *vb syn* see CANCEL 2
callous *adj syn* see UNFEELING 2
   rel indurated, set
callow *adj* **1** *syn* see YOUNG 1

   2 *syn* see INEXPERIENCED
callowness *n syn* see INEXPERIENCE
call up *vb* to summon for active military duty <*called up* the army reserves>
   syn order up; *compare* DRAFT 1
   rel mobilize
   idiom call to the colors
   ant discharge, muster out
calm *n syn* see QUIET 1
calm *adj* **1** free from storm or rough activity <the wind died and the sea became *calm*>
   syn halcyon, hushed, placid, quiet, still, stilly, untroubled
   rel inactive, quiescent, reposing, resting; pacific, smooth, tranquil, unruffled
   idiom calm as a millpond, still as death
   con agitated, disturbed, perturbed, restless, turbulent, uneasy
   ant stormy
   2 free from mental or emotional distress or agitation <a man who remained *calm* under stress>
   syn collected, composed, easy, easygoing, placid, poised, possessed, self-composed, self-possessed, serene, tranquil
   rel cool, imperturbable, nonchalant, unflappable, unruffled; even-tempered, impassive, phlegmatic, steady; firm, stable, staunch
   con discomposed, disturbed, perturbed, upset; anxious, bothered, confused, nervous; fidgety, jittery, jumpy, shaky, tense
   ant agitated
calm *vb* to relieve from or bring to an end whatever distresses, agitates, or disturbs <that inner faith that *calms* the troubled spirit>
   syn allay, balm, becalm, compose, lull, quiet, ‖quieten, settle, soothe, ‖soother, still, tranquilize
   rel alleviate, assuage, mitigate, relieve; appease, mollify, pacify, placate; relax, steady
   con bother, discompose, disquiet, disturb, flurry, perturb, stir up, upset
   ant agitate; arouse
calmant *n syn* see SEDATIVE
calmative *n syn* see SEDATIVE
calmness *n syn* see EQUANIMITY
calumniate *vb syn* see MALIGN
   ant eulogize; vindicate
calumnious *adj syn* see LIBELOUS
calumny *n syn* see DETRACTION
   rel animadversion, reflection, stricture
   con encomium, panegyric, tribute; adulation, compliment, flattery
   ant eulogy; vindication
calvary *n syn* see TRIAL 1
‖**cam** *adv syn* see AWRY 1
camaraderie *n* a spirit of friendly goodwill typical of comrades <the easy *camaraderie* of a cozy neighborhood bar>
   syn comradery, good-fellowship
   rel affability, friendliness, gregariousness, sociability; cheer, conviviality, jollity
   con aloofness, coldness, frigidity, inaccessibility, reclusiveness, remoteness, self-containment; exclusiveness, self-sufficiency, unsociability
camarilla *n syn* see CLIQUE
cameraman *n syn* see PHOTOGRAPHER
camerist *n syn* see PHOTOGRAPHER
camouflage *vb syn* see DISGUISE
   rel becloud, befog, dim
camp *n* **1** a place where a number of people (as vacationers or soldiers) live temporarily together in usually more or less casual housing <planned to summer at a fishing *camp* in Maine>
   syn campground, encampment
   2 *syn* see CLIQUE
   3 *syn* see HUT
camp *vb* to live temporarily in a camp or the outdoors <*camped* under the trees for the night>
   syn bivouac, ‖bivvy, encamp, ‖laager, ‖maroon, tent
   idiom rough it

---

syn synonym(s)   *rel* related word(s)
ant antonym(s)   *con* contrasted word(s)
idiom idiomatic equivalent(s)
‖ use limited; if in doubt, see a dictionary

con decamp

campanile *n syn* see BELL TOWER

campestral *adj syn* see RURAL

camp follower *n syn* see PROSTITUTE

campground *n syn* see CAMP 1

‖**cample** *vb syn* see SCOLD 1

‖**can** *n* **1** *syn* see JAIL

2 *syn* see TOILET

3 *syn* see BUTTOCKS

‖**can** *vb syn* see DISMISS 3

Canaan *n syn* see HEAVEN 2

canaille *n syn* see RABBLE 2

canal *n syn* see CHANNEL 1

canard *n syn* see LIE

rel hoax, humbug, mare's-nest, sell, spoof; artifice, dodge, trick

‖**canary** *n syn* see INFORMER

cancel *vb* **1** *syn* see ERASE

2 to give up something previously arranged or agreed on < decided to *cancel* his appointment with the dentist >

syn call off, drop, scrub

rel end, terminate; annul, invalidate, rescind, revoke; give up, relinquish, surrender

cancel (out) *vb syn* see NEUTRALIZE

candid *adj* **1** *syn* see FAIR 4

rel aboveboard, forthright, straightforward; honest, scrupulous, upright

2 *syn* see FRANK

ant evasive

candidate *n* one who seeks an office, honor, position, or award < examining *candidates* for editorial positions >

syn applicant, aspirant, hopeful, seeker

rel nominee; dark horse; also-ran, has-been; campaigner, electioneerer, stumper, whistle-stopper

candy *vb syn* see SUGARCOAT 1

canine *n syn* see DOG 1

canker *vb syn* see DEBASE 1

cankered *adj syn* see CANTANKEROUS

cannabis *n syn* see MARIJUANA

canned *adj* **1** *syn* see CONDENSED

‖**2** *syn* see INTOXICATED 1

cannibalic *adj syn* see FIERCE 1

canniness *n* **1** *syn* see PRUDENCE 1

2 *syn* see CUNNING 2

‖**cannon** *n syn* see PICKPOCKET

cannonade *n syn* see BARRAGE

cannonade *vb syn* see BOMBARD

canny *adj* **1** *syn* see CLEVER 4

2 *syn* see SPARING

3 *syn* see WISE 4

canon *n* **1** *syn* see LAW 1

2 *syn* see DOCTRINE

canonical *adj syn* see ORTHODOX 1

‖**cant** *adj syn* see LIVELY 1

cant *vb syn* see SLANT 1

cant *n* **1** *syn* see DIALECT 2

rel diction, language, phraseology, vocabulary; idiom, speech

2 *syn* see TERMINOLOGY

3 *syn* see HYPOCRISY

cantankerous *adj* habitually ill-humored, irritable, and disagreeable < one of our more *cantankerous* fellow workers >

syn bearish, cankered, cranky, cross-grained, crotchety, ornery, rantankerous, vinegarish, vinegary, waspish, waspy; *compare* IRASCIBLE, IRRITABLE

rel dour, morose, sour; crabbed, cross, crusty, huffy, petulant, prickly, snappish; dyspeptic, ill-conditioned, ill-natured; liverish

idiom like a bear with a sore paw

con benign, kindly, mellow, mild; amiable, congenial, friendly, pleasant, well-disposed; benevolent, gracious, kind

canter *n syn* see VAGABOND

cantina *n syn* see BAR 5

canting *adj syn* see HYPOCRITICAL

canton *vb syn* see BILLET 1

‖**canty** *adj syn* see LIVELY 1

canvass *vb* **1** *syn* see SCRUTINIZE 1

2 *syn* see DISCUSS 1

3 *syn* see SOLICIT 1

cap *vb* **1** *syn* see SURMOUNT 3

‖**2** *syn* see PUZZLE

3 *syn* see COVER 3

4 *syn* see SURPASS 1

5 *syn* see CLIMAX

capability *n* **1** *syn* see ABILITY 1

rel art, craft, cunning, skill

con inability, disability

ant incapability, incompetence

2 *syn* see EFFICACY 1

capable *adj syn* see ABLE

ant incapable

capacious *adj syn* see SPACIOUS

rel dilatable, distensible, expandable, expansive, extensile; abundant, copious, plentiful

ant exiguous

capacity *n* **1** *syn* see ABILITY 1

rel bent, faculty, gift, knack, talent, twin; caliber, stature

con impotence, ineffectiveness, powerlessness

ant incapacity

2 *syn* see STATUS 1

cape *n syn* see PROMONTORY

caper *vb syn* see GAMBOL

idiom cut capers

caper *n* **1** *syn* see ESCAPADE

2 *syn* see PRANK

rel devilment, impishness, mischief, roguery, waggishness

‖**capernoited** *adj syn* see INTOXICATED 1

capital *adj* **1** *syn* see EGREGIOUS

2 *syn* see CHIEF 2

rel cardinal, essential, vital; basic, fundamental, underlying

3 *syn* see EXCELLENT

capital *n syn* see MEAN 3

capitalize *vb* to supply capital for or to < agreed to *capitalize* the venture >

syn back, bankroll, finance, grubstake, stake

rel aid, assist, help, subsidize, support; fund; promote, sponsor

capitulate *vb syn* see YIELD 2

capitulation *n syn* see SURRENDER

capper *n syn* see DECOY 2

caprice *n* an arbitrary, impulsive, and often illogical notion or change of mind < given to sudden *caprices* and random fancies >

syn bee, boutade, conceit, crank, crotchet, fancy, freak, humor, maggot, megrim, notion, vagary, whigmaleerie, whim, whimsy

rel mood, temper, vein; contrariety, inconsistency, perversity; characteristic, foible, habit, mannerism, peculiarity, trait, trick

capricious *adj* **1** *syn* see ARBITRARY 1

2 *syn* see INCONSTANT 1

rel humorsome, moody; effervescent

con constant, steady

ant steadfast

3 *syn* see UNCERTAIN 1

capsheaf *n syn* see APEX 2

capstone *n syn* see APEX 2

capsule *adj syn* see CONDENSED

caption *n* an explanatory or identifying comment accompanying a pictorial illustration < the *captions* were under the wrong figures >

syn legend, underline

captious *adj syn* see CRITICAL 1

rel demanding, exacting, finicky; contrary, perverse; irritable, peevish, petulant, snappish, snappy, testy

con judicious, sensible, wise; rational, reasonable; knowing, knowledgeable

ant appreciative

captivate *vb syn* see ATTRACT 1

rel delight, gratify, please; entterall, grip, hold, mesmerize, spellbind

ant repulse

captivated *adj syn* see ENAMORED 3

captivating *adj syn* see ATTRACTIVE 1

capture *vb syn* see CATCH 1

Capuan *adj syn* see LUXURIOUS 3

car *n* a usually private passenger-carrying automotive vehicle < drove a shabby old *car* >

syn auto, autocar, automobile, buggy, ‖bus, machine, motor, motorcar

rel coach, convertible, coupe, hardtop, limousine, phaeton, roadster, runabout, sedan, station wagon, touring car; ‖clunker, ‖crate, ‖heap, ‖jalopy, junker, ‖wreck

caravansary *n syn* see HOTEL
carbon *n syn* see REPRODUCTION
carbon copy *n syn* see REPRODUCTION
carbuncle *n syn* see ABSCESS
carcass *n syn* see CORPSE
‖**carcel** *n syn* see JAIL
card *n* **1** *syn* see WAG 1
 2 *syn* see PROGRAM 1
 3 *syn* see MENU
card *vb syn* see SCHEDULE 1
cardboard *adj syn* see STIFF 4
 rel unlifelike, unreal, unrealistic
cardinal *adj* **1** *syn* see ESSENTIAL 2
 2 *syn* see CENTRAL 1
care *n* **1** *syn* see SORROW
 rel strain, stress, tension
 2 a burdened or disquieted state of mind < a mind full of *care* and sadness >
 syn anxiety, concern, concernment, disquiet, disquietude, solicitude, unease, uneasiness, worry
 rel apprehension, foreboding, misgiving, suspense; agitation, disturbance, perturbation; alarm, consternation, dismay, fear
 con calm, ease, peace, quietude; assurance, comfort, easiness
 3 *syn* see TRIAL 2
 4 serious and heedful attentiveness < attended his words with *care* >
 syn carefulness, concern, consciousness, heed, heedfulness, regard; *compare* ATTENTION 1
 rel curiosity; enthusiasm, interest; consideration, solicitude, thoughtfulness; effort, exertion, pains, trouble; alertness, vigilance, watchfulness
 con carelessness, disregard, heedlessness, unconcern; boredom, disinterest, ennui
 5 *syn* see OVERSIGHT 1
 6 *syn* see CUSTODY
care (for) *vb* **1** *syn* see TEND 2
 2 *syn* see MINISTER (to)
 idiom take care of
careen *vb syn* see LURCH 2
career *vb syn* see COURSE
carefree *adj* **1** *syn* see HAPPY-GO-LUCKY
 2 *syn* see IRRESPONSIBLE
careful *adj* **1** *syn* see CAUTIOUS
 rel attentive, heedful, observant
 2 closely attentive to details or showing such attention < *careful* workmanship >
 syn conscientious, conscionable, exact, fussy, heedful, meticulous, painstaking, punctilious, punctual, scrupulous
 rel accurate, nice, precise; deliberate, studied; foresighted, provident, prudent; critical, discriminating, finical, finicky; observant, particular, religious; duteous, dutiful, intent
 con disorderly, lax, negligent, slack, slipshod, slovenly; heedless, neglectful, remiss
 ant careless
carefulness *n syn* see CARE 4
careless *adj* **1** lacking in or showing lack of care and attention < *careless* of the harm his neglect might do to others > < unwilling to accept such *careless* shoddy work >
 syn feckless, heedless, inadvertent, irreflective, thoughtless, uncaring, unheeding, unrecking, unreflective, unthinking; *compare* INCAUTIOUS, RASH 1
 rel forgetful, inattentive, oblivious, unmindful; lax, neglectful, negligent, slack, unconcerned, uninterested; inadequate, incapable, unfit, unqualified
 con careful, heedful, thoughtful; concerned, considerate, punctilious, scrupulous
 ant careful
 2 *syn* see IRRESPONSIBLE
 3 *syn* see NEGLIGENT
 4 *syn* see SLIPSHOD 3
 5 *syn* see SLOVENLY 1
caress *vb* to express interest, affection, or love by touching or handling < *caress* a frightened child >
 syn cosset, cuddle, dandle, fondle, love, pet
 rel cocker, coddle, indulge, pamper; coquet, dally, flirt, toy, trifle; nuzzle, pat, stroke
careworn *adj syn* see HAGGARD
 rel distressed, troubled; exhausted, fagged, jaded, tuckered

 ant carefree
cargo *n syn* see LOAD 1
caricature *n* **1** *syn* see MOCKERY 2
 2 a grotesque or bizarre imitation < a doting attentiveness that was a sickly *caricature* of motherhood >
 syn burlesque, parody, takeoff, travesty
 rel lampoon, libel, pasquinade; laughingstock, mockery; cheat, fake, imitation, phony, sham; bosh, bunk, gammon, hokum, moonshine; clinquant, pinchbeck, shoddy, tinsel
carillon *n syn* see BELL TOWER
caritas *n syn* see MERCY
cark *vb* **1** *syn* see TROUBLE 1
 2 *syn* see WORRY 3
carnage *n syn* see MASSACRE
carnal *adj* **1** *syn* see BODILY
 rel material, substantial; earthly, earthy
 2 characterized by physical rather than intellectual or spiritual day-to-day < giving too much heed to the *carnal* aspects of day=to-day life >
 syn animal, fleshly, sensual; *compare* SENSUOUS
 rel bodily, corporal, corporeal, physical; coarse, gross, obscene, vulgar; earthly, earthy, mundane, temporal, worldly; lascivious, lewd, lustful, wanton; Pandemic, sensuous
 con ethical, moral, noble, righteous, virtuous; aerial, ethereal, otherworldly, supernal; chaste, decent, modest, pure
 ant spiritual; intellectual
carnality *n syn* see ANIMALITY
carom *vb syn* see GLANCE 1
carousal *n syn* see BINGE 1
carouse *n syn* see BINGE 1
carouse *vb syn* see REVEL 1
carp (at) *vb syn* see NAG
carper *n syn* see CRITIC
‖**carpet** *vb syn* see SCOLD 1
 idiom call on the carpet, take to task
carpet knight *n syn* see HEDONIST
carping *adj syn* see CRITICAL 1
 rel blaming, criticizing, reprehending, reprobating; jawing, railing, upbraiding; blameful, condemnatory, damnatory, objurgatory, reproachful, reprobatory
 con applauding, commendatory, complimentary; approving, endorsing; extolling, laudatory, praiseful
 ant fulsome
carriage *n* **1** *syn* see TRANSPORTATION 1
 2 *syn* see POSTURE 1
carriageable *adj syn* see PORTABLE
carriage trade *n syn* see ARISTOCRACY
carrier *n* **1** *syn* see BEARER 2
 2 *syn* see MESSENGER
 3 *syn* see VECTOR
carrot *n syn* see REWARD
carry *vb* **1** to be the agent or means by which someone or something is shifted from one place to another < *carried* the child on his shoulder >
 syn bear, buck, convey, ferry, ‖hump, ‖jag, lug, pack, tote, transport
 rel bring, fetch, take; move, remove, shift, transfer; send, transmit
 ‖**2** *syn* see ACCOMPANY
 3 *syn* see AFFECT
 4 *syn* see BEAR 3
 5 *syn* see CONDUCT 4
 6 *syn* see BEHAVE 1
 7 *syn* see SUPPORT 4
 8 *syn* see STOCK
carrying *n syn* see TRANSPORTATION 1
carry off *vb syn* see KILL 1
carry on *vb* **1** *syn* see CONDUCT 3
 2 *syn* see CUT UP 2
 3 *syn* see PERSEVERE
carry out *vb* **1** *syn* see ADMINISTER 1
 rel complete, finalize; discharge, effect, effectuate, fulfill; prosecute, transact

---

syn synonym(s)   *rel* related word(s)
ant antonym(s)   *con* contrasted word(s)
idiom idiomatic equivalent(s)
‖ use limited; if in doubt, see a dictionary

idiom put in force (*or* into effect); sign, seal, and deliver
2 syn see EFFECT 2
carrytale *n syn* see GOSSIP 1
carry through *vb* **1 syn** see EFFECT 2
2 syn see CONTINUE 1
carte blanche *n* full discretionary power < was given *carte blanche* to build, landscape, and furnish the house >
syn blank check, free hand
rel license, prerogative, right; authority, power; say, say-so
idiom power of attorney
carte d'entrée *n syn* see TICKET 2
carte du jour *n syn* see MENU
cartel *n* **1 syn** see DEFIANCE 1
rel gage, gauntlet, glove; blow, slap
2 syn see SYNDICATE
rel corporation; multinational; consortium, merger
carve *vb* **1 syn** see CUT 5
2 syn see SCULPTURE
Casanova *n* **1 syn** see GALLANT 2
2 syn see WOLF
cascade *n syn* see WATERFALL
‖**cascade** *vb syn* see VOMIT
case *n* **1 syn** see EVENT 4
2 syn see ORDER 9
3 syn see SUIT 1
4 syn see INSTANCE
rel circumstance, episode, event, incident, occurrence; condition, situation, state
5 syn see ECCENTRIC
case *n syn* see HULL
‖**case** *vb syn* see SCRUTINIZE 1
case history *n syn* see INSTANCE
cash *n syn* see MONEY
cashier *vb* **1 syn** see DISMISS 3
rel eject, expel, oust; bar, eliminate, exclude; pass over, shelve
con appoint, designate, elect, name; employ, engage, hire
2 syn see DISCARD
cash in *vb syn* see DIE 1
cask *n* a vessel made of staves, headings, and hoops < a *cask* of cider >
syn barrel, butt, hogshead, keg, pipe, tun
Cassandra *n syn* see PESSIMIST
cassock *n syn* see CLERGYMAN
cast *vb* **1 syn** see THROW 1
rel broadcast, disperse, distribute, scatter
2 syn see DIRECT 2
3 syn see DISCARD
rel abandon, leave, relinquish, surrender, yield; dismiss, drop
‖**4 syn** see VOMIT
5 syn see ADD 2
6 syn see PLAN 2
cast *n* **1 syn** see LOOK 2
2 syn see PREDICTION
3 syn see COLOR 1
4 syn see HINT 2
5 syn see TYPE
6 syn see FORM 1
cast about *vb syn* see SEEK 1
cast away *vb* **1 syn** see WASTE 2
2 syn see SHIPWRECK 1
castaway *n syn* see OUTCAST
cast down *vb syn* see HUMBLE
cast down *adj syn* see DOWNCAST
castigate *vb* **1 syn** see PUNISH 1
rel baste, beat, belabor, drub, pummel, thrash; berate, rail, rate, tongue-lash, upbraid, wig; penalize
2 syn see LAMBASTE 3
castigation *n syn* see PUNISHMENT
castigatory *adj syn* see PUNITIVE
castle *n syn* see MANSION
castle-builder *n syn* see DREAMER
cast out *vb* **1 syn** see BANISH
‖**2 syn** see QUARREL
castrate *vb* **1 syn** see STERILIZE
2 syn see UNNERVE
rel bleed, drain, empty, exhaust
casual *adj* **1 syn** see ACCIDENTAL
rel unplanned, unpremeditated; extemporaneous, extempore, impromptu, improvised, offhand; impulsive, spontaneous

con advised, considered, deliberate, intentional, planned, premeditated, studied
ant deliberate
2 syn see INDIFFERENT 2
3 syn see EASYGOING 3
con ceremonial, conventional, formal
4 syn see LITTLE 3
casually *adv syn* see INCIDENTALLY 1
casualty *n* **1 syn** see ACCIDENT 2
2 syn see FATALITY 2
3 syn see VICTIM 2
casuistry *n syn* see FALLACY 2
‖**cat** *n syn* see MAN 3
‖**cat** *vb syn* see VOMIT
cataclysm *n* **1 syn** see FLOOD 2
2 syn see DISASTER
cataclysmic *adj syn* see FATAL 2
catacomb *n syn* see CRYPT
catalog *n syn* see LIST
rel program, prospectus, syllabus
catalog *vb* **1 syn** see INVENTORY
2 syn see LIST 3
rel admit, enter, introduce; count, enumerate, number
catalyst *n syn* see STIMULUS
cataplasm *n syn* see POULTICE
cataract *n* **1 syn** see WATERFALL
2 syn see FLOOD 2
catastrophe *n syn* see DISASTER
catastrophic *adj syn* see FATAL 2
catcall *n syn* see RASPBERRY
catch *vb* **1** to obtain physical mastery and possession of < the cat *caught* a mouse >
syn bag, capture, collar, ‖cotch, get, nail, prehend, secure, take; *compare* ARREST 2, SEIZE 2
rel clutch, grab, snatch; clasp, grasp, grip; ensnare, entangle, entrap, snare, tangle, trap
con free, release
ant miss
2 syn see SEIZE 2
3 to put at a disadvantage or bring under control by or as if by enmeshing in a net < *caught* in the fallacy of his own argument >
syn benet, catch up, ensnare, entangle, entrap, snare, tangle, trap; *compare* ENTANGLE 3
rel baffle, confound, nonplus, perplex, stick, stump; abash, disturb, embarrass, put out; confuse, flurry, fluster, rattle
4 syn see DUPE
5 syn see FIND 1
6 syn see MARRY 1
7 to come up with often unexpectedly < the storm *caught* them unawares >
syn ‖cotch, overhaul, overtake, take
rel reach
idiom come upon
8 syn see SEIZE 3
9 syn see INTERCEPT
10 syn see CONTRACT 1
idiom fall ill (of *or* with), fall victim to
11 syn see FASTEN 2
12 syn see STRIKE 2
13 syn see APPREHEND 1
catch colt *n syn* see BASTARD
catching *adj* **1 syn** see INFECTIOUS 2
2 syn see INFECTIOUS 3
catch on *vb syn* see DISCOVER 3
catchphrase *n syn* see CATCHWORD
catchpole *n syn* see DELEGATE
catch up *vb* **1 syn** see CATCH 3
2 syn see ENTHRALL 2
catchword *n* a word or phrase that catches the eye or ear and is repeated so often that it becomes representative of a political party, school of thought, or point of view < "new deal" became the *catchword* of supporters and critics of Franklin Roosevelt >
syn byword, catchphrase, phrase, shibboleth, slogan, watchword; *compare* BATTLE CRY
rel household word; maxim, motto
catchy *adj syn* see FITFUL
catechize *vb syn* see ASK 1

categorical *adj* **1** *syn* see ULTIMATE 3
  con conjectural, hypothetical, supposititious; conditional, contingent, dependent, relative
  2 *syn* see EXPLICIT
  rel certain, positive, sure; direct, downright, forthright
  con ambiguous; doubtful, dubious, problematic, questionable
  3 *syn* see POSITIVE 1
categorically *adv* *syn* see EXPRESSLY 1
categorize *vb* *syn* see ASSORT
  rel identify, nail down, peg, put down
category *n* *syn* see CLASS 1
cater (to) *vb* **1** *syn* see BABY
  idiom make much of
  2 *syn* see INDULGE 1
cateran *n* *syn* see MARAUDER
catercorner (*or* **catty-corner** *or* **kitty≠ corner**) *adv* *syn* see DIAGONALLY
cater–cousin *n* *syn* see FRIEND
caterwaul *vb* *syn* see QUARREL
catharsis *n* *syn* see PURIFICATION
catholic *adj* **1** *syn* see UNIVERSAL 2
  rel comprehensive, inclusive; general, generic, indeterminate; extensive, large-scale
  ant parochial; provincial
  2 *syn* see ECLECTIC 2
catholicon *n* *syn* see PANACEA
cathouse *n* *syn* see BROTHEL
catlike *adj* *syn* see STEALTHY 2
catnap *n* *syn* see NAP
catnap *vb* *syn* see NAP
‖**catouse** *n* *syn* see COMMOTION 3
cat's–paw *n* *syn* see TOOL 2
catty *adj* **1** *syn* see STEALTHY 2
  2 *syn* see AGILE
  3 *syn* see MALICIOUS
‖**caulk** (off) *vb* *syn* see NAP
‖**caulker** *n* *syn* see DRAM
causatum *n* *syn* see EFFECT 1
cause *n* **1** that (as a person, fact, or condition) which is responsible for an effect < the storm was the *cause* of all our difficulties >
  syn antecedent, determinant, occasion, reason
  rel goad, impulse, incentive, inducement, motive, spring; origin, prime mover, root, source; author, creator, generator, originator
  con consequence, effect, issue, outcome, result
  2 *syn* see MOTIVE 1
  3 *syn* see OCCASION 3
  4 *syn* see SUIT 1
cause *vb* **1** *syn* see GENERATE 3
  2 *syn* see EFFECT 1
  rel elicit, evoke, provoke
  idiom be at the root of, give origin to, set on foot
'cause *conj* *syn* see BECAUSE
causerie *n* *syn* see CHAT 2
caustic *adj* **1** marked by sharp and often witty incisiveness < a *caustic* critic >
  syn mordacious, mordant, salty, scathing, trenchant; *compare* SARCASTIC
  rel biting, cutting, incisive; acrid, bitter, pungent, tart; acute, keen, sharp; ironic, sarcastic, satiric, stinging; harsh, rough, severe, stringent; crisp, pithy, succinct, terse
  con gentle, mild; cordial, gracious; bland, diplomatic, suave, urbane
  ant genial
  2 *syn* see SARCASTIC
causticity *n* *syn* see SARCASM
caution *n* **1** *syn* see WARNING
  2 *syn* see PRUDENCE 1
caution *vb* *syn* see WARN 1
cautionary *adj* *syn* see MONITORY
cautioning *adj* *syn* see MONITORY
cautious *adj* marked by careful prudence especially in reducing or avoiding risk or danger < a *cautious* approach to marriage >
  syn calculating, careful, chary, circumspect, considerate, discreet, gingerly, guarded, safe, wary
  rel alert, vigilant, watchful; cagey, canny, cozy, foresighted, precautious, shrewd; forethoughtful, prethoughtful, provident, prudent; calculating, scheming, shrewd; expedient, judicious, politic

  idiom on one's guard, on the safe side, playing it safe
  con daring, rash, reckless, venturesome; headlong, impetuous, precipitate
  ant adventurous, temerarious
cavalier *adj* *syn* see PROUD 1
cave *n* a usually natural underground chamber < the limestone *caves* of Kentucky >
  syn cavern, grotto, subterrane, subterranean
cave *vb* **1** *syn* see GIVE 12
  2 *syn* see YIELD 2
cave (in) *vb* *syn* see COLLAPSE 2
caveat *n* *syn* see WARNING
cavern *n* *syn* see CAVE
cavernous *adj* **1** suggestive of a cave < a *cavernous* fireplace that gulped in wood >
  syn chasmal, gaping, yawning
  rel commodious, vast
  2 *syn* see HOLLOW 1
cavil *vb* *syn* see QUIBBLE 1
caviler *n* *syn* see CRITIC
caviling *adj* *syn* see CRITICAL 1
  rel contrary, perverse; demanding, exacting; finicky, fussy, picky; mean, petty, small; hairsplitting, niggling, nitpicking
  con amiable, complaisant, good-natured, tolerant; accommodating, easy, obliging
cavillous *adj* *syn* see CRITICAL 1
cavity *n* *syn* see HOLE 3
cavort *vb* *syn* see GAMBOL
  rel carry on, cut up, horse (around), horseplay, roughhouse
caw *vb* *syn* see SQUALL 1
cease *vb* *syn* see STOP 3
  rel close, conclude, end, finish, terminate; intermit
  con continue, persist; extend, prolong, protract; arise, originate, rise, spring
cease *n* *syn* see END 2
cease-fire *n* *syn* see TRUCE
ceaseless *adj* **1** *syn* see CONTINUAL
  2 *syn* see EVERLASTING 1
cede *vb* **1** *syn* see RELINQUISH
  rel accord, concede, grant, vouchsafe
  con hold, hold back, keep back, retain, withhold
  2 *syn* see TRANSFER 4
ceinture *n* *syn* see BELT 1
‖**celeb** *n* *syn* see CELEBRITY 2
celebrate *vb* **1** *syn* see KEEP 2
  2 *syn* see PRAISE 2
celebrated *adj* *syn* see FAMOUS 2
celebrious *adj* *syn* see FAMOUS 2
celebrity *n* **1** *syn* see FAME 2
  ant obscurity
  2 a widely known and popularly esteemed person < youngsters making a great to-do over sports *celebrities* >
  syn big name, ‖celeb, luminary, name, notability, notable, somebody
  rel hero, immortal, mahatma, star, superstar; lion; personage, worthy; cynosure
  idiom center of attraction, person of note (*or* mark)
  con back number; nobody
celerity *n* **1** *syn* see HASTE 1
  rel alacrity, briskness, legerity
  2 *syn* see SPEED 2
celestial *adj* of, relating to, or befitting heaven or the heavens < *celestial* music from an angelic choir >
  syn empyreal, empyrean, heavenly
  rel ethereal, supernal, transcendental; otherworldly, unearthly, transmundane; beatific, blessed, elysian, Olympian
  con earthly, earthy, mundane, sublunary, worldly; chthonian, hellish, infernal
  ant terrestrial, uncelestial
cemetery *n* a piece of land used for burying the dead < the quiet peace of a country *cemetery* >

---

syn synonym(s)	*rel* related word(s)
ant antonym(s)	*con* contrasted word(s)
idiom idiomatic equivalent(s)	
‖ use limited; if in doubt, see a dictionary	

syn ‖boneyard, ‖boot hill, burial ground, burying ground, God's acre, graveyard, memorial park, necropolis, polyandrium, potter's field
rel churchyard; catacomb
idiom city of the dead

censor *vb* to remove matter considered objectionable by expurgation or alteration <*censor* a movie>
syn blip, bowdlerize, expurgate, screen
rel cut out, excise, exscind; blue-pencil, delete, edit, red-pencil; bleach, clean (up), purge, purify; narrow, restrain, restrict

censorious *adj syn* see CRITICAL 1
rel chiding, reproachful, reproaching; condemnatory, condemning, denouncing, denunciatory, reprehending; accusatory, culpatory
con acclaiming, acclamatory, extolling, laudatory, lauding, praising; adulatory, complimentary, flattering
ant eulogistic

censurable *adj syn* see BLAMEWORTHY
rel improper, incorrect, objectionable, wrong, wrongful; discreditable, doubtful, questionable; inadmissible, unacceptable
con correct, proper, right; acceptable, admissible; creditable
ant uncensurable

censure *vb syn* see CRITICIZE
rel rebuke, reprimand, reproach, reprove; contemn, disdain, scorn, scout, strafe; disallow, disapprove, oppose, reject, stigmatize
con applaud, compliment, recommend; allow, approve, support
ant commend

center *n* **1** a point or part in a surface or solid more or less equidistant from the periphery <the *center* of the earth>
syn core, middle, midpoint, midst
rel inside, interior
con circumference, compass, perimeter, periphery; bounds, confines, limits
2 one eminent in or central to a particular activity, condition, or interest <a *center* of international trade>
syn focal point, focus, heart, hub, nerve center, polestar, seat; *compare* ESSENCE 2
3 a source or point of origin (as of an influence, pressure, or effect) <the group proved a *center* of discontent>
syn core, heart, pith, quick, root
rel activator, dynamo, energizer, stimulant

center *adj* **1** *syn* see MIDDLE 1
2 *syn* see MIDDLE 2

centermost *adj syn* see MIDDLE 1

central *adj* **1** occupying a dominant or supremely important position <the *central* theme of American foreign policy>
syn cardinal, overriding, overruling, pivotal, ruling
rel dominant, paramount, predominant, preponderant; important, significant; outstanding, salient, signal; chief, essential, foremost, leading, main; all-absorbing, controlling, master; focal, key; basic, fundamental, primary, radical
con insignificant, minor, trivial, unimportant; borderline, marginal
ant peripheral
2 *syn* see MIDDLE 2

centralizing *adj syn* see INTEGRATIVE

centripetal *adj syn* see INTEGRATIVE

‖**cep** *prep syn* see EXCEPT

cerate *n syn* see OINTMENT

cerberus *n syn* see CUSTODIAN

cerebral *adj* **1** *syn* see MENTAL 1
2 *syn* see INTELLECTUAL 2

cerebrate *vb syn* see THINK 5

cerebration *n syn* see THOUGHT 1

ceremonial *adj* stressing or concerned with careful attention to form and detail <his *ceremonial* approach to everyday life>
syn ceremonious, conventional, formal, solemn, stately
rel mannered, studied, stylized; liturgical, ritual, ritualistic; august, courtly, imposing, lofty; fixed, rigid, set, starchy, stiff
con casual, easy, informal, relaxed; artless, ingenuous, open, sincere

ceremonial *n* **1** *syn* see FORM 2
2 *syn* see RITE 2

ceremonious *adj syn* see CEREMONIAL
rel decorous, proper, seemly; impressive, moving, striking; grandiose, imposing, majestic
ant unceremonious

ceremony *n* **1** *syn* see FORM 2
2 *syn* see RITE 2

certain *adj* **1** *syn* see FIRM 4
rel assured, certified, guaranteed, warranted; ensured, insured, sure
2 constituting an indeterminate and otherwise unidentified part of a group or whole <*certain* students dispute this finding>
syn some, various
rel a, an, one; many, numerous; divers, several, sundry
con no; all
3 being such beyond a doubt <no *certain* likeness of this saint survives>
syn accurate, authentic, dependable, reliable
rel credible, plausible, well-grounded
con counterfeit, false, spurious; controversial, doubtful, dubious, questionable
ant uncertain
4 *syn* see INFALLIBLE 2
5 *syn* see POSITIVE 3
rel confirmable, demonstrable, establishable, provable, verifiable; doubtless, trustworthy, unerring
con controversial, iffy
ant uncertain
6 *syn* see INEVITABLE
rel indefeasible, irrevocable, unalterable, written; fated, predestinated, predetermined
ant uncertain
7 *syn* see SURE 5
rel assured, confident, sanguine
con hesitant, indecisive, vague, wavering; doubtful, dubious, questionable
ant uncertain

certainty *n* a state of mind in which one is free from doubt <answered with complete *certainty*>
syn assurance, assuredness, certitude, confidence, conviction, sureness, surety
rel belief, credence, faith; absoluteness, definiteness, dogmatism, positiveness, positivism; firmness, staunchness, steadiness
con doubt, mistrust, skepticism, unsureness; fluctuation, irresolution, shifting, trimming, vacillation, wavering; obscurity, vagueness
ant uncertainty

certify *vb* **1** to testify usually formally and in writing to the truth or genuineness of something <*certify* a student's college transcript>
syn attest, vouch, witness
rel assert, aver, avouch, avow, profess
2 *syn* see WARRANT 2
3 *syn* see APPROVE 2
rel authorize, commission, license
con antagonize, counter, oppose

certitude *n syn* see CERTAINTY
rel cocksureness
con uncertainty
ant doubt

‖**cess** *n syn* see TAX 1

cessation *n syn* see END 2

cesspit *n syn* see SINK 1

cesspool *n syn* see SINK 1

‖**chack** *n syn* see SNACK

chafe *vb* **1** *syn* see ANNOY 1
2 *syn* see ABRADE 1
3 to make sore or raw through friction <the high stiff collar *chafed* his neck>
syn abrade, excoriate, fret, gall, rub
rel damage, hurt, impair, injure; flay, peel, skin; inflame, irritate; graze, scrape, scratch
con ease, relieve, soothe

chaff *vb syn* see BANTER 1
idiom make merry over

chaffer *vb syn* see HAGGLE 2
rel beg, coax, plead

chafing *adj syn* see IMPATIENT 1

chagrined *adj syn* see ASHAMED
rel crushed, disconcerted; discomposed, perturbed, upset
idiom put out of countenance

chain *n* **1** chains *pl syn* see SHACKLE
2 *syn* see SUCCESSION 2

3 syn see SYNDICATE
chain *adj* **1 syn** see CUMULATIVE
2 syn see TRITE
chair *vb* **syn** see PRESIDE
chair car *n* **syn** see PARLOR CAR
chalk (out) *vb* **syn** see SKETCH
chalk up *vb* **syn** see GET 1
challenge *vb* **1 syn** see DEMAND 1
2 syn see QUESTION 2
3 syn see FACE 3
rel question; dispute; strive, struggle, try
idiom throw down the (*or* one's) gage
con by-pass, evade
4 syn see STIR 1
challenge *n* **1 syn** see DEMUR 2
2 syn see DEFIANCE 1
rel calling, claiming, demanding, exacting; importuning, insistence
chamber *n* **1 syn** see ROOM 1
‖**2 chambers** *pl* **syn** see APARTMENT 1
chamber *vb* **syn** see HARBOR 1
champ *vb* **1 syn** see CHEW 1
rel crush, macerate, mash, smash
2 syn see BITE 1
rel nibble, nip; gum, mouth, mumble; peck, pick
champaign *n* **syn** see FIELD
champion *n* **syn** see EXPONENT
champion *vb* **syn** see SUPPORT 2
rel battle, contend, fight (for)
idiom put in a good word for, stand behind (*or* back of), stand up for
con resist, withstand; denounce, condemn
ant combat
champion *adj* **1 syn** see EXCELLENT
rel distinguished, illustrious, outstanding, splendid
2 syn see FIRST 3
chance *n* **1 syn** see ACCIDENT 1
con certainty, inevitability, necessity; destiny, fate, foreordination, predestination
ant law
2 an unpurposed, unpredictable, and uncontrollable master force <the folly of depending on *chance* for success in life>
syn fortune, hazard, luck
rel advantage, break, fluke; fate, lot; contingency
3 syn see OPPORTUNITY
rel likelihood, possibility, probability; outlook, prospect
chance *vb* **1 syn** see HAPPEN 1
2 syn see HAPPEN 2
3 syn see GAMBLE 2
4 syn see VENTURE 1
idiom put at (*or* in) hazard
con cherish, protect, safeguard, secure
chance *adj* **syn** see ACCIDENTAL
rel careless, heedless, offhand
chance child *n* **syn** see BASTARD 1
chancy *adj* **1 syn** see UNCERTAIN 1
rel hazardous, risky, speculative, unsound; precarious, ticklish, touchy, tricky
idiom hanging by a thread, on thin ice (*or* slippery ground)
con safe, secure, sound, stable
2 syn see DANGEROUS 1
change *vb* **1** to make or become different <*changed* her will again and again> <our needs *change* as we grow older>
syn alter, modify, mutate, refashion, turn, vary; *compare* TRANSFORM
rel convert, metamorphose, transform, transmute; diversify, variegate; exchange, interchange
idiom go (*or* pass through) a change
con establish, fix, set
2 syn see TRANSFORM
3 syn see REVERSE 1
4 syn see STERILIZE
5 to make substitution for or among <it's time to *change* the subject>
syn replace, shift
rel exchange, swap, trade; substitute
6 syn see EXCHANGE 2
change *n* **1** a making different <saw a gradual *change* of attitude in the community>

syn alteration, modification, mutation, turn, variation
rel aberration, deviation, divergence; diversification; shift; innovation
ant uniformity
2 a result of such change <amazed at the *changes* in the town>
syn innovation, mutation, novelty, permutation, sport, vicissitude
rel conversion, metamorphosis, transformation, transmutation; shift, substitute, surrogate; avatar
changeable *adj* **1** alterable or changing under slight provocation <*changeable* April weather>
syn changeful, fluid, mobile, mutable, protean, unsettled, unstable, unsteady, variable, weathery; *compare* INCONSTANT 1, MUTABLE 2
rel adaptable, impressionable, plastic, pliant; ever-changing, kaleidoscopic; restless, unfixed; inconstant, uncertain, vicissitudinous
con constant, invariable, permanent; certain, fixed, immutable, unalterable, unmodifiable; abiding, enduring, persistent
ant unchangeable; unchanging
2 syn see MUTABLE 2
3 syn see INCONSTANT 1
changeabout *n* **syn** see REVERSAL 1
changeful *adj* **syn** see CHANGEABLE 1
rel active, dynamic, live; lively, vigorous
con durable, lasting, perdurable, stable; steady, uniform
ant changeless, unchanging
changeover *n* **syn** see CONVERSION 2
channel *n* **1** passage through which a fluid (as water) flows or is led <the river cut a new *channel* to the sea>
syn aqueduct, canal, conduit, course, duct, watercourse
rel pass, passage, way
2 syn see MEAN 2
3 syn see PIPELINE
channel *vb* **syn** see CONDUCT 4
chant *vb* **syn** see SING 1
chaos *n* **1 syn** see CONFUSION 3
2 syn see ANARCHY 1
rel misrule, unruliness
chap *n* **syn** see MAN 3
chaperon *vb* **1 syn** see ACCOMPANY
rel guide, overlook, oversee, supervise
2 syn see SUPERVISE
chapfallen *adj* **syn** see DOWNCAST
chaplet *n* **syn** see WREATH
character *n* **1** an arbitrary or conventional device used in writing or printing <an inscription in runic *characters*>
syn mark, sign, symbol
rel cipher, device, monogram; letter
2 syn see CHARACTERISTIC 1
3 syn see QUALITY 1
rel distinction, uniqueness, uniquity
4 syn see TYPE
5 syn see DISPOSITION 3
rel soul, spirit; courage, mettle, resolution; intellect, intelligence, mind
6 syn see ROLE 1
7 syn see STATUS 1
8 syn see CREDENTIALS
9 syn see NOTABLE 1
10 syn see ECCENTRIC
‖**11 syn** see HUMAN
12 syn see REPUTATION 2
character assassination *n* **syn** see DETRACTION
characteristic *adj* being or revealing a quality specific or identifying to an individual or group <her *characteristic* down-to-earth approach to a problem>
syn diacritic, diagnostic, distinctive, idiosyncratic, individual, peculiar, proper
rel especial, particular, special, specific; natural, normal, regular, typical
con general, generic, universal

---

syn synonym(s)   **rel** related word(s)
ant antonym(s)   **con** contrasted word(s)
idiom idiomatic equivalent(s)
‖ use limited; if in doubt, see a dictionary

ant uncharacteristic

characteristic *n* **1** something that marks or sets apart < *characteristics* that distinguish man from lower primates >
syn birthmark, character, feature, point, trait; *compare* QUALITY 1
rel badge, mark, sign, token; flavor, odor, savor, smack, tang; differentia; singularity
2 *syn* see QUALITY 1

characterize *vb* **1** *syn* see SKETCH
2 to be a peculiar or significant quality or feature of something < a man *characterized* by quiet dignity >
syn distinguish, individualize, individuate, mark, qualify, signalize, singularize
rel define, describe, differentiate, identify; peculiarize, personalize
idiom be a feature of

characterless *adj* lacking in character or solid qualities < a drab *characterless* little man that no one ever seemed to notice >
syn namby-pamby, pantywaist, wishy-washy
rel childish, infantile; sissified, sissy, unmanly; futile, weak; impotent, powerless
con manly, strong, vigorous, virile

charade *n syn* see PRETENSE 2

chare *n syn* see TASK 1

charge *vb* **1** *syn* see BURDEN
2 *syn* see LOAD 3
3 *syn* see PERMEATE
4 *syn* see ENTRUST 1
5 *syn* see COMMAND
rel ask, request, solicit; adjure
6 *syn* see ACCUSE
rel impugn, reprehend, reproach
idiom bring (*or* prefer) charges
con excuse, forgive, pardon, remit; acquit
ant absolve
7 *syn* see ASCRIBE
8 *syn* see RUSH 1

charge *n* **1** *syn* see LOAD 3
rel business, devoir, place
2 *syn* see OBLIGATION 2
3 *syn* see OVERSIGHT 1
4 *syn* see COMMAND 1
5 *syn* see PRICE 1

chargeless *adj syn* see FREE 5

charger *n syn* see COURSER

charioteer *vb syn* see DRIVE 5

charisma *n syn* see CHARM 3

charitable *adj* **1** having or showing interest in or concern for the welfare of others < spent generously for *charitable* aid to the needy >
syn altruistic, benevolent, eleemosynary, good, humane, humanitarian, philanthropic
rel accommodating, helpful, obliging; benign, kindhearted, kindly, sympathetic
2 *syn* see FORBEARING
rel benevolent, considerate, kindly, thoughtful
con cold, harsh, heartless, unfeeling
ant uncharitable

charity *n* **1** *syn* see MERCY
rel affection, attachment, love; altruism, benevolence, humaneness; kindliness; amity, friendliness, goodwill
con malevolence, malignancy, malignity, spite, spleen
ant ill will, malice
2 *syn* see DONATION

charivari *n syn* see SHIVAREE

charlatan *n* one who pretends unscrupulously to knowledge or skill < the professions overrun with *charlatans* and rogues >
syn mountebank, quack, quacksalver, quackster, saltimbanque; *compare* IMPOSTER
rel bluff, four-flusher, sham

Charlie McCarthy *n syn* see STOOGE 1

charm *n* **1** *syn* see SPELL
2 an object worn or cherished to ward off evil or attract good fortune < the Indian medicine bag is essentially a *charm* >
syn amulet, fetish, juju, luck, mascot, periapt, phylactery, talisman, zemi
3 a quality or combination of qualities that is wholly attractive and irresistible < the *charm* of her smile >
syn allure, appeal, charisma, fascination, glamour, magnetism, witchcraft, witchery
rel allurement, attraction, attractiveness, lure; agreeableness, delightfulness, gratefulness
con hatefulness, obnoxiousness, odiousness, repulsiveness; distastefulness, unpleasantness

charm *vb* **1** *syn* see ATTRACT 1
2 *syn* see BEWITCH 1

charmed *adj syn* see ENAMORED 3

charmer *n syn* see MAGICIAN 1

charming *adj syn* see ATTRACTIVE 1
ant charmless

chart *n* **1** a stylized or symbolic depiction of something incapable of direct verbal or pictorial representation (as because of complexity or abstractness) < a *chart* of anticipated economic progress >
syn graph, map
rel plan, plat, plot, scheme
2 *syn* see TABLE 2

chart *vb syn* see PLAN 2

charter *n syn* see DEED 3

charter *vb syn* see HIRE 1

chary *adj* **1** *syn* see CAUTIOUS
rel disinclined, hesitant, loath, reluctant; economical, frugal, sparing, thrifty; constrained, inhibited, restrained
2 *syn* see SPARING

chase *vb* **1** *syn* see FOLLOW 2
con flee, fly
2 *syn* see HUNT 1
3 *syn* see EJECT 1
4 *syn* see RUSH 1
5 *syn* see COURSE

chase *n* **1** *syn* see HUNTING
2 *syn* see GAME 3

chaser *n syn* see WOLF

chasm *n* **1** *syn* see GULF 2
2 *syn* see RAVINE
3 *syn* see OMISSION
4 *syn* see SCHISM 3

chasmal *adj syn* see CAVERNOUS 1

chaste *adj* free from every trace of the lewd or salacious < was as *chaste* in language as in conduct >
syn clean, decent, immaculate, modest, pure, spotless, stainless, unblemished, undefiled, unsullied
rel ethical, moral, righteous, virtuous; maidenly, virgin, virginal; becoming, decorous, proper, seemly; abstinent, continent
con coarse, gross, obscene, ribald, vulgar; lascivious, lecherous, licentious, lustful; gluttonous, incontinent, self-indulgent
ant unchaste

chasten *vb syn* see PUNISH 1
rel abase, humble, humiliate; afflict, try
con baby, humor, indulge, spoil
ant pamper

chastise *vb syn* see PUNISH 1
rel baste, beat, belabor, pummel, thrash

chastisement *n syn* see PUNISHMENT

chat *vb* **1** to emit a ready flow of inconsequential talk < *chats* on the phone for hours >
syn babble, burble, cackle, chatter, chin-chin, clack, clatter, ‖dish, dither, gab, gabble, ‖gas, jaw, ‖natter, patter, prate, prattle, rattle, run-on, smatter, talk, tinkle, twaddle, twitter, yak, yakety-yak, yammer, yatter; *compare* CONVERSE
rel yap; blab, gossip; gush, lallygag; confabulate
idiom beat one's gums, ‖chew the fat (*or* rag), ‖shoot (*or* bat) the breeze, ‖shoot (*or* sling) the bull
con discourse, expound; declaim, harangue, hold forth, orate, preach
2 *syn* see CONVERSE

chat *n* **1** *syn* see CHATTER
2 an informal conversation < had a satisfactory little *chat* with the new assistant >
syn causerie, chin, prose, rap, talk, yarn; *compare* CONVERSATION 2
rel gossip, tête-à-tête
idiom bull session, rap session
con debate, deliberation, discussion
3 *syn* see CONVERSATION 1

chateau *n syn* see MANSION

chattel *n* **1 chattels** *pl syn* see POSSESSION 2
  2 *syn* see SLAVE 1
chatter *vb* **1** *syn* see GIBBER
  2 *syn* see CHAT 1
chatter *n* idle and often loud and incessant talk < schoolgirl *chatter* >
  syn babble, bibble-babble, blab, blabber, ‖blatter, brabble, cackle, chat, chin-chin, ‖chin music, chitchat, chitter-chatter, clack, gab, gabble, gibble-gabble, jabber, palaver, prate, prattle, stultiloquence, talkee-talkee, tittle-tattle, yak, yakety-yak, yak-yak, yatter
  rel ‖bull, gossip, small talk
  idiom tongue wagging
chatterbox *n* one who engages in chatter < that old *chatterbox* will talk your arm off >
  syn bandar-log, blabber, blabbermouth, blabmouth, chatterer, chewet, gabber, jabberer, magpie, prater, prattler
  rel busybody, gossip, newsmonger, quidnunc, scandalmonger, tabby, tattletale
chatterer *n syn* see CHATTERBOX
chatty *adj syn* see TALKATIVE
‖**chaw** *vb* **1** *syn* see CHEW 1
  2 *syn* see PONDER 2
chawbacon *n syn* see RUSTIC
cheap *adj* **1** costing little < produce is usually *cheaper* in summer >
  syn inexpensive, low, low-cost, low-priced, popular, reasonable, uncostly, undear
  rel bargain-basement, bargain-counter, cut-rate, reduced; dirt-cheap
  con dear, high, high-priced
  ant costly, expensive
  2 of inferior quality < *cheap* furniture is never a bargain >
  syn base, cheesy, common, mean, ‖ornery, paltry, poor, rubbishing, rubbishly, rubbishy, shoddy, sleazy, tatty, trashy, trumpery; compare INFERIOR 2
  rel cheap-jack, valueless, worthless; flashy, garish, meretricious, tawdry; brummagem, fake, phony, sham; bad, rotten, terrible
  con capital, excellent, fine, good; first-class, first-rate, high-class, high-grade, superior, tip-top, top-notch
  ant precious
  3 *syn* see CONTEMPTIBLE
  rel wrong; base, low, vile; measly, paltry, petty, trifling
  ant noble
cheapen *vb syn* see DEPRECIATE 1
cheap-jack (*or* **cheap-john**) *n syn* see PEDDLER
cheapskate *n syn* see MISER
cheat *n* **1** *syn* see DECEPTION 1
  2 *syn* see IMPOSTURE
  rel bamboozlement, cozening, hoaxing; chicane, chicanery, trickery
  3 *syn* see SWINDLER
cheat *vb* to obtain something (as money) from or an advantage over by dishonesty and trickery < *cheated* out of his inheritance by a grasping lawyer >
  syn beat, bilk, boodle, ‖burn, chisel, chouse, cozen, ‖crook, defraud, diddle, do, ‖doodle, ‖dry-shave, ‖duff, flimflam, gyp, ‖mace, ‖mump, overreach, ream, ‖screw, sucker, swindle, take; compare EXTORT 1, FLEECE 1
  rel befool, dupe, fool, gull, slick; bunco, con, fudge, short; beguile, deceive, delude, double-cross, mislead
cheater *n syn* see SWINDLER
check *vb* **1** *syn* see ARREST 1
  rel cease, desist, discontinue, stop; repress, suppress; circumvent, foil, frustrate, thwart
  ant expedite
  2 *syn* see RESTRAIN 1
  rel baffle, balk; obviate, preclude, prevent
  ant accelerate (*of speed*); advance (*as of hopes, plans*); release (*of feelings, energies*)
  3 *syn* see TRY 1
  4 *syn* see AGREE 4
check *n* **1** *syn* see SETBACK
  2 a statement of charges for food and drink consumed (as at a restaurant) < shocked at the size of the *check* >
  syn bill, tab
  rel damage, score
check out *vb* ‖**1** *syn* see DIE 1

  2 *syn* see AGREE 4
check over *vb syn* see SCRUTINIZE 1
check-over *n syn* see EXAMINATION
check up *vb syn* see SCRUTINIZE 1
checkup *n syn* see EXAMINATION
cheek *n* **1 cheeks** *pl syn* see BUTTOCKS
  2 *syn* see EFFRONTERY
cheeky *adj syn* see WISE 5
cheep *vb syn* see CHIRP
cheer *vb* **1** *syn* see COMFORT
  2 *syn* see ENCOURAGE 1
  3 *syn* see APPLAUD 2
cheerful *adj* **1** marked by or suggestive of lighthearted ease of mind and spirit < a *cheerful* smile >
  syn blithe, cheery, ‖chirk, chirpy, chirrupy, lightsome, sunbeamy, sunny; compare LIVELY 1
  rel airy, carefree, debonair, jaunty; animated, gay, lighthearted, lively, vivacious; buoyant, corky
  idiom in good (*or* high) spirits, of good cheer
  con blue, dejected, depressed, melancholy; dispirited, heavy-hearted; joyless, mournful, sorrowful, woeful; dour, morose, saturnine, sullen; doleful, lugubrious; austere, forbidding, grim, stern
  ant gloomy, glum
  2 *syn* see GLAD 2
  ant cheerless
‖**cheerio** *interj syn* see GOOD-BYE
cheerless *adj syn* see GLOOMY 3
  rel dejecting
  ant cheerful
cheery *adj* **1** *syn* see GLAD 2
  2 *syn* see CHEERFUL 1
cheeseparer *n syn* see MISER
cheeseparing *adj syn* see STINGY
  rel cheap, grudging, mean, shabby; illiberal
cheesy *adj syn* see CHEAP 2
chef d'oeuvre *n* **1** *syn* see MASTERPIECE 1
  2 *syn* see SHOWPIECE
‖**chemist** *n syn* see DRUGGIST
cherish *vb* **1** *syn* see NURSE 2
  rel conserve, preserve, save; entertain, harbor, keep, shelter; defend, guard, safeguard, shield
  con reject, repudiate, scorn
  ant abandon
  2 *syn* see APPRECIATE 1
  rel revere, reverence, venerate
  idiom hold in high esteem
  con disregard, forget, ignore, overlook, slight
  ant neglect
  3 *syn* see ADMIRE 1
chest *n syn* see TREASURY 2
chesty *adj syn* see BUXOM
chew *vb* **1** to crush or grind with the teeth < *chew* your food well >
  syn champ, ‖chaw, chomp, ‖chonk, chumble, chump, crunch, masticate, munch, ruminate, scrunch
  rel bite; gnaw, nibble; consume, devour, eat; gum, mumble
  ‖**2** *syn* see SCOLD 1
chewet *n syn* see CHATTERBOX
‖**chew out** *vb syn* see SCOLD 1
chiaus *n syn* see SWINDLER
chic *n syn* see FASHION 3
chic *adj syn* see STYLISH
chicane *vb* **1** *syn* see QUIBBLE 1
  2 *syn* see DUPE
chicane *n syn* see DECEPTION 1
  rel artifice, feint, gambit, maneuver, ploy, ruse, stratagem, trick, wile; furtiveness, surreptitiousness, underhandedness
  con forthrightness, straightforwardness
chicanery *n syn* see DECEPTION 1
  rel intrigue, machination, plot; furtiveness, surreptitiousness, underhandedness

---

syn synonym(s)   *rel* related word(s)
ant antonym(s)   *con* contrasted word(s)
idiom idiomatic equivalent(s)
‖ use limited; if in doubt, see a dictionary

con forthrightness, straightforwardness; honesty, honor, integrity, probity

chichi *adj* **1** *syn* see SHOWY
  2 *syn* see PRECIOUS 4

chick *n* **1** *syn* see CHILD 1
  ||**2** *syn* see GIRL FRIEND 1

chickabiddy *n* *syn* see CHILD 1

chicken *n* *syn* see COWARD

||**chicken** *adj* *syn* see COWARDLY

chide *vb* *syn* see REPROVE
  rel berate, rate, scold, upbraid
  con applaud, compliment; approve, endorse, sanction
  ant commend

chiding *n* *syn* see REBUKE

chief *n* **1** *syn* see LEADER 2
  rel dictator, duce, führer
  2 *syn* see NOTABLE 1

chief *adj* **1** *syn* see FIRST 3
  2 standing apart by reason of superior importance, significance, or influence < his *chief* claim to consideration is his unquestionable uprightness >
  syn capital, ||cock, dominant, main, major, number one, outstanding, predominant, preeminent, principal, star, stellar
  rel primal, primary, prime; important, prominent, significant; consequential, momentous, weighty; effective, potent, telling; controlling, master, ruling
  con inconsequential, minor, trivial, unimportant; collateral, contingent, secondary

chiefly *adv* *syn* see GENERALLY 1

chieftain *n* *syn* see LEADER 2

chiffer *n* *syn* see NUMBER

child *n* **1** a young person < a movie for both *children* and adults >
  syn bud, chick, chickabiddy, chit, juvenile, kid, moppet, ||nipper, puss, youngling, young one, youngster, youth
  rel minor; adolescent, teenager, teener, teenybopper; brat, bratling, dickens, runabout; cherub, innocent, lamb, sweetling
  idiom a slip of a boy (*or* girl), small fry, young hopeful
  ant adult, grown-up
  2 children *pl* *syn* see OFFSPRING

childbearing *n* **1** *syn* see BIRTH 1
  2 *syn* see LABOR 2

childbed *n* *syn* see CONFINEMENT 2

childbirth *n* **1** *syn* see BIRTH 1
  2 *syn* see LABOR 2

childing *adj* **1** *syn* see PREGNANT 1
  2 *syn* see FERTILE

childish *adj* significantly deficient in maturity < a *childish* and spiteful attitude >
  syn babyish, immature, infantile, infantine, prekindergarten, puerile
  rel asinine, fatuous, foolish, silly, simple; naive, unsophisticated; arrested, backward, moronic, retarded, slow, ||wanting
  ant adult

child's play *n* *syn* see SNAP 1

chill *vb* *syn* see DISCOURAGE 1

chill *adj* **1** *syn* see COLD 1
  2 *syn* see COLD 2
  rel distant, formal, reserved, solitary, standoffish, uncompanionable, withdrawn; abstracted, disinterested, uninterested
  con easy, gregarious, informal; sociable

chiller *n* *syn* see THRILLER

chillsome *adj* *syn* see COLD 1

chilly *adj* *syn* see COLD 1

chime *n* *syn* see HARMONY 2

chime *vb* *syn* see RING

chime in *vb* **1** *syn* see INTERRUPT 2
  2 *syn* see SAY 1

chimera *n* *syn* see PIPE DREAM

chimerical *adj* *syn* see FICTITIOUS 1
  rel ambitious, pretentious, utopian; deceptive, delusive, delusory; fabulous, mythical; absurd, preposterous
  con believable, plausible, rational, reasonable; possible, practicable
  ant feasible

chiming *adj* *syn* see HARMONIOUS 1

chin *n* *syn* see CHAT 2

chin *vb* *syn* see CONVERSE

chin–chin *vb* *syn* see CHAT 1

chin–chin *n* *syn* see CHATTER

||**chinchy** *adj* *syn* see STINGY

chine *n* *syn* see RIDGE 1

Chinese puzzle *n* *syn* see MYSTERY

Chinese wall *n* *syn* see OBSTACLE

chink *n* *syn* see CRACK 3
  rel interruption

chink *vb* *syn* see JINGLE

||**chink** *n* *syn* see MONEY

chinkle *vb* *syn* see JINGLE

||**chin music** *n* *syn* see CHATTER

chintzy *adj* *syn* see GAUDY

chin–up *adj* *syn* see BRAVE 1

chip *vb* *syn* see CHIRP

chip in *vb* **1** *syn* see CONTRIBUTE 1
  2 *syn* see INTERRUPT 2

chipper *vb* *syn* see CHIRP

chipper *adj* **1** *syn* see LIVELY 1
  2 *syn* see NEAT 2

||**chippy** *n* *syn* see DOXY 1

||**chips** *n* *pl* *syn* see MONEY

||**chirk** *adj* **1** *syn* see LIVELY 1
  2 *syn* see CHEERFUL 1

chirk (up) *vb* *syn* see ENCOURAGE 1

||**chirm** *n* *syn* see DIN

||**chirm** *vb* *syn* see CHIRP

chirography *n* *syn* see HANDWRITING

chirp *vb* to make a short, sharp, and usually repetitive sound < sparrows *chirping* on the lawn >
  syn cheep, chip, chipper, ||chirm, chirrup, clutter, peep, tweedle, tweet, twitter

chirpy *adj* *syn* see CHEERFUL

chirrup *vb* *syn* see CHIRP

chirrupy *adj* *syn* see CHEERFUL 1

chisel *vb* **1** *syn* see SCULPTURE
  2 *syn* see CHEAT

chisel (in) *vb* *syn* see INTRUDE 1

||**chiselly** *adj* *syn* see BAD 8

chit *n* *syn* see CHILD 1

chit *n* *syn* see NOTE 2

chitchat *n* **1** *syn* see CHATTER
  2 *syn* see SMALL TALK

chitter *vb* *syn* see CHIRP

chitter–chatter *n* **1** *syn* see CHATTER
  2 *syn* see SMALL TALK

chivalrous *adj* *syn* see GENEROUS 1
  rel knightly, manly, noble
  con churlish common, low

chivy *vb* **1** *syn* see FOLLOW 2
  2 *syn* see BAIT 2
  rel afflict, torment, try; chase, pursue, trail

choate *adj* *syn* see WHOLE 3

chockablock *adj* *syn* see FULL 1

chock–full *adj* *syn* see FULL 1

choice *n* **1** the act, right, opportunity, or faculty of choosing or deciding < the *choice* lies with the electorate >
  syn alternative, ||druthers, election, option, preference, selection
  rel decision, determination, finding, judgment, verdict; appraisal, evaluation, rating
  2 *syn* see BEST

choice *adj* having qualities that appeal to a fine or highly refined taste < a few *choice* spirits gathered nightly to discuss the day's events >
  syn dainty, delicate, elegant, exquisite, rare, recherché, select, superior
  rel incomparable, peerless, preeminent, prime, superlative, supreme, surpassing, transcendent, unsurpassed; chosen, culled, picked, selected
  con common, ordinary; average, fair, mediocre, medium, middling, run-of-the-mill, second-rate; drab, dull, lackluster, lusterless
  ant indifferent

||**choicy** *adj* *syn* see NICE 1

choke *vb* **1** to check normal breathing especially by compressing or obstructing the windpipe < *choked* by a bone in the throat >
  syn strangle, throttle; *compare* SUFFOCATE
  2 *syn* see SUFFOCATE

3 syn see FILL 1
4 syn see LOAD 3
choke (off) *vb syn* see SILENCE
‖**chokey** *n syn* see JAIL
choking *n syn* see REPRESSION 1
choleric *adj* **1 syn** see IRASCIBLE
  rel acrimonious, angry, fiery, indignant, irate, mad, spunky, wrathful, wroth; captious, carping, faultfinding
  con calm, serene, tranquil; composed, cool, nonchalant
  ant placid
  2 syn see ANGRY
chomp *vb* **1 syn** see CHEW 1
  2 syn see BITE 1
‖**chonk** *vb syn* see CHEW 1
choose *vb* **1** to fix upon one among alternatives as the one to be taken, accepted, or adopted <*chose* the largest apple but found it sour>
  syn cull, elect, mark, opt (for), optate, pick, pick out, prefer, select, single (out), take
  rel adopt, embrace, espouse; crave, desire, love, want, wish
  con decline, refuse, repudiate, spurn; abnegate, forbear, forgo
  ant reject; eschew
  2 syn see WILL
  rel favor, prefer
  ‖**3 syn** see DESIRE 1
choosy *adj syn* see NICE 1
chop *vb* **1 syn** see FELL 2
  2 to cut into fragments by repeated strokes <*chop* meat and onions for hash>
  syn hash, mince
  rel cut up, dice, fragment
  idiom cut to bits, make mincemeat of
chop *n syn* see CUFF
chop–chop *adv syn* see FAST 2
chore *n* **1 syn** see TASK 1
  2 syn see TASK 2
  rel trial, tribulation
chortle *vb syn* see LAUGH
chorus *n syn* see HARMONY 1
chosen *adj syn* see SELECT 1
chouse *n syn* see TRICK 1
chouse *vb syn* see CHEAT
‖**chow** *n* **1 syn** see FOOD 1
  2 syn see MEAL
chowchow *adj syn* see MISCELLANEOUS
chowchow *n syn* see MISCELLANY 1
chowderhead *n syn* see DUNCE
chrism *n syn* see OINTMENT
christcross–row *n syn* see ALPHABET 1
christen *vb* **1 syn** see BAPTIZE
  2 syn see NAME 1
Christian *adj syn* see DECOROUS 1
Christian name *n syn* see GIVEN NAME
Christmas *n* a festival or holiday commemorating the birth of Christ <gave presents on *Christmas*>
  syn Nativity, noel, Xmas, yule, yuletide
chronic *adj* **1 syn** see HABITUAL 2
  2 syn see USUAL 1
chronicle *n* **1 syn** see HISTORY 2
  2 syn see ACCOUNT 7
  rel narration, recital, recountal
chthonian *adj syn* see INFERNAL 1
chthonic *adj syn* see INFERNAL 1
chubby *adj syn* see ROTUND 2
  ant slim
chuck *vb* **1 syn** see DISCARD
  2 syn see EJECT 1
  3 syn see ABANDON 1
‖**chuck** *n syn* see HARBOR 3
chucker *n syn* see BOUNCER 2
‖**chucker–out** *n syn* see BOUNCER 2
chuckhole *n syn* see POTHOLE
chuckle *vb syn* see LAUGH
chucklehead *n syn* see DUNCE
chuckleheaded *adj syn* see STUPID 1
chuff *n* **1 syn** see BOOR
  2 syn see MISER
‖**chuff** *adj syn* see SULLEN

‖**chuffy** *adj syn* see STOCKY
‖**chuffy** *adj syn* see SULLEN
chum *n syn* see ASSOCIATE 3
chumble *vb syn* see CHEW 1
chummy *adj* **1 syn** see FAMILIAR 1
  2 syn see INTIMATE 4
chump *n* ‖**1 syn** see HEAD 1
  2 syn see DUNCE
  3 syn see FOOL 3
chump *vb syn* see CHEW 1
‖**chumpy** *adj syn* see STOCKY
chunk *n syn* see LUMP 1
chunky *adj syn* see STOCKY
  rel chubby, rotund
‖**chunter** *vb syn* see MUMBLE
church *n* **1 syn** see HOUSE OF WORSHIP
  2 syn see RELIGION 2
church *adj syn* see ECCLESIASTICAL
churchly *adj syn* see ECCLESIASTICAL
churchman *n syn* see CLERGYMAN
churchmanly *adj syn* see ECCLESIASTICAL
churl *n syn* see BOOR
  ant aristocrat, gentleman
churlish *adj syn* see BOORISH
  rel crude, discourteous; blunt, brusque, crusty, curt, gruff; dour, surly; naive, unschooled
  con bland, politic, smooth; polished, sophisticated
  ant courtly
churn *vb syn* see SEETHE 4
chute *n syn* see WATERFALL
cicatrix *n syn* see SCAR
cicatrize *vb syn* see SCAR
‖**cig** *n syn* see CIGARETTE
cigarette *n* a paper-wrapped tube of finely cut smoking tobacco <dependence on *cigarettes*>
  syn ‖butt, ‖cig, ‖coffin nail, fag, ‖gasper, ‖pill, ‖skag, smoke
cimmerian *adj syn* see INFERNAL 2
cinch *n syn* see SNAP 1
cinch *vb syn* see ENSURE
cincture *n syn* see BELT 1
cincture *vb syn* see BELT 1
cinders *n pl syn* see ASH
cine *n syn* see MOVIE
‖**cinema** *n syn* see MOVIE
cipher *n* **1 syn** see ZERO 1
  2 syn see NUMBER
  3 syn see MONOGRAM
  4 syn see NONENTITY
cipher *vb* **1 syn** see CALCULATE
  ‖**2 syn** see SOLVE 2
ciphering *n syn* see COMPUTATION
circa *prep syn* see ABOUT 1
Circean *adj syn* see ENTICING
circle *n* **1 syn** see RANGE 2
  2 syn see CYCLE 1
  3 syn see SET 5
  rel acquaintance; cronies, friends, intimates; associates, companions, comrades
  4 syn see CLIQUE
circle *vb* **1 syn** see SURROUND 1
  2 syn see TURN 1
circuit *n* **1 syn** see CIRCUMFERENCE
  rel course, route, way; journey, tour, travels, trip
  2 syn see REVOLUTION 1
  3 syn see TOUR 2
  4 syn see LEAGUE 4
circuitous *adj syn* see INDIRECT 1
  ant straight
circuitously *adv syn* see ABOUT 2
circular *adj* **1 syn** see ROUND 1
  2 syn see INDIRECT 1
circulate *vb* **1 syn** see SPREAD 1
  rel exchange, interchange; flow; revolve, rotate

---

syn synonym(s)   *rel* related word(s)
ant antonym(s)   *con* contrasted word(s)
idiom idiomatic equivalent(s)
‖ use limited; if in doubt, see a dictionary

2 syn see MOBILIZE 1
circulation n syn see REVOLUTION 1
circulator n syn see GOSSIP 1
circumambages n pl syn see VERBIAGE 1
circumambulate vb syn see WANDER 1
circumbendibus n syn see VERBIAGE 1
circumduct vb 1 syn see TURN 1
2 syn see ABOLISH 1
circumference n a continuous line or course about an area <strolled along the *circumference* of the reservoir>
syn ambit, circuit, compass, perimeter, periphery; *compare* BORDER 1
rel boundary, bounds, confines, limits; border, margin, rim
circumlocution n syn see VERBIAGE 1
con conciseness, concision, pithiness, succinctness, terseness; compactness
circumnavigate vb syn see SKIRT 2
circumscribe vb syn see LIMIT 2
rel fetter, hamper, trammel
con amplify, distend, inflate, swell; enlarge
ant dilate, expand
circumscribed adj syn see DEFINITE 1
rel bound, bounded, finite; confined, cramped, strait
circumscription n 1 syn see RESTRICTION 1
2 syn see RESTRICTION 2
circumspect adj syn see CAUTIOUS
rel meticulous, punctilious, scrupulous
con adventurous, daredevil, foolhardy; careless, heedless; bold
ant audacious
circumstance n 1 syn see OCCURRENCE
rel detail, item, particular; component, constituent, element, factor
2 syn see FATE
circumstantial adj marked by careful attention to relevant details <gave a *circumstantial* account of his adventure>
syn blow-by-blow, clocklike, detailed, full, itemized, minute, particular, particularized, thorough
rel accurate, exact, nice, precise; complete, replete; close, strict
con compendious, concise, laconic, pithy, short, succinct, terse; abbreviated, curtailed, cut, pruned, shortened, trimmed
ant abridged; summary
circumvent vb 1 syn see FRUSTRATE 1
rel befool, dupe, hoodwink, trick; avoid, elude, escape, evade
ant conform (*to laws, orders*); cooperate (*with persons*)
2 syn see SKIRT 2
3 syn see SKIRT 3
circumvolution n syn see REVOLUTION 1
cit n syn see TOWNSMAN
citadel n syn see FORT
citation n syn see ENCOMIUM
rel award, guerdon, reward
cite vb 1 syn see REMEMBER
2 syn see MENTION
3 syn see ADDUCE
rel count, enumerate, number, tell
citizen n 1 syn see TOWNSMAN
2 a person regarded as a member of a sovereign state, entitled to its protection, and subject to its laws <the subtle bond between the *citizen* and the nation>
syn national, subject
con foreigner, stranger
ant alien
city adj syn see URBAN
civic adj syn see PUBLIC 1
civil adj 1 syn see PUBLIC 1
2 adequate in courtesy <made a *civil* inquiry about their health>
syn courteous, genteel, mannerly, polite, well-mannered; *compare* COURTLY
rel cultivated, refined, well-bred; accommodating, affable, cordial, obliging; bland, diplomatic, gracious, politic, suave, urbane
con boorish, churlish, loutish, uncouth; discourteous, ill-mannered, impolite, ungracious
ant uncivil; rude
civilities n pl syn see MANNER 5
civilized adj 1 syn see DECOROUS 1
2 syn see SUAVE
Civitas Dei n syn see HEAVEN 2

||**clabber** vb syn see CURDLE
clack vb 1 syn see CHAT 1
2 syn see RATTLE 1
clack n 1 syn see CHATTER
2 syn see GOSSIP 1
clad vb 1 syn see CLOTHE
2 syn see SHEATHE
||**claggy** adj 1 syn see STICKY 1
2 syn see MUDDY 1
claim vb 1 syn see DEMAND 1
rel adduce, advance, allege; assert, defend, justify, maintain, vindicate
con abnegate, forgo; refuse, reject, repudiate; disavow, disown
ant disclaim; renounce
2 syn see MAINTAIN 2
claim n 1 a real or assumed right to demand something as one's own or one's due <his genial wit was his greatest *claim* to fame>
syn ||dibs, pretense, pretension, title
rel birthright, prerogative, privilege, right; affirmation, assertion, declaration, protestation
2 syn see INTEREST 1
clamant adj syn see PRESSING
clamber vb syn see SCRAMBLE 1
clamor n 1 syn see COMMOTION 4
2 syn see DIN
3 syn see COMMOTION 1
clamor vb syn see ROAR
rel claim, demand; agitate, debate, dispute
idiom make the welkin ring, raise the roof
clamorous adj 1 syn see VOCIFEROUS
rel articulate, eloquent, vocal, voluble; adjuring, begging, imploring, importunate
ant taciturn
2 syn see PRESSING
clamp n syn see HOLD
clampdown n syn see REPRESSION 2
clan n 1 syn see FAMILY 1
2 syn see CLIQUE
clandestine adj syn see SECRET 1
rel illegitimate, illicit; artful, foxy, sly
con aboveboard, forthright, straightforward
ant open
clandestinely adv syn see SECRETLY
clangorous adj syn see NOISY
clap n syn see BANG 2
claptrap n syn see NONSENSE 2
||**claret** n syn see BLOOD 1
clarify vb 1 syn see PURIFY 1
2 to make clear and understandable <felt a need to *clarify* his position on the question>
syn clear, clear up, elucidate, explain, illuminate, illustrate; *compare* EXPLAIN 1
rel settle, straighten out; define, delineate, formulate; analyze, break down, simplify
idiom make plain
con befog, cloud, obfuscate, obscure; confuse, foul up, muddle, ||snafu
clarion adj syn see FAIR 2
clarity n notable precision of thought or expression <*clarity* of expression depends on use of exactly the right words in precisely the right way>
syn clearness, limpidity, lucidity, perspicuity, plainness
rel articulateness, articulation; care, exactitude, fussiness, meticulousness, nicety, precision; accuracy, correctitude, propriety
con haziness, imprecision, indefiniteness, unclearness, vagueness; inexactness, laxity, looseness, sloppiness, slovenliness
ant obscurity
||**clarty** adj 1 syn see MUDDY 1
2 syn see STICKY 1
clash vb 1 syn see BUMP 1
2 to be markedly out of harmony <garish colors that *clashed* almost painfully>
syn conflict, disaccord, discord, disharmonize, jangle, jar, mismatch
rel fret, gall, grate, try
idiom swear at one another
con accord, blend, conform, correspond; fit, meet, suit

ant harmonize

clash *n* **1** *syn* see IMPACT

2 a sharp and usually brief conflict especially between military units < recurrent border *clashes* >
syn affray, brush, fray, melee, mellay, scrimmage, skirmish
rel brawl, broil, fracas, riot, row, rumpus, scrap, set-to; action, battle, conflict, engagement; embroilment, encounter
idiom clash of arms, passage at (*or* of) arms

clashing *adj syn* see ANTIPATHETIC 1

clasp *n syn* see HOLD

clasp *vb* **1** *syn* see EMBRACE 1

2 *syn* see TAKE 4

class *n* **1** a unit or a subunit of a larger whole made up of members sharing one or more characteristics < miniaturization of circuitry made possible a whole new *class* of small computers and calculators >
syn category, grade, group, grouping, league, pigeonhole, tier
rel brand, color, description, feather, genre, grain, ilk, kidney, kind, nature, order, sort, stamp, style, type; bracket, branch, denomination, division, head, section; genus, species

2 *syn* see QUALITY 3

3 *syn* see TYPE

class *vb* **1** *syn* see ASSORT

2 to put into an appropriate class < he is generally *classed* among our leading theoretical physicists >
syn classify, evaluate, grade, rank, rate
rel appraise, gauge, judge; divide, part, separate; allot, assign; account, assess, consider, hold, reckon, regard; mark, score

classic *adj* **1** *syn* see EXCELLENT

2 *syn* see VINTAGE 1

3 *syn* see TYPICAL 1

classic *n syn* see MASTERPIECE 1

classical *adj* **1** *syn* see EXCELLENT

2 *syn* see VINTAGE 1

3 *syn* see TYPICAL 1

classify *vb* **1** *syn* see ASSORT

2 *syn* see CLASS 2

‖**classy** *adj syn* see STYLISH

clatter *vb* **1** *syn* see RATTLE 1

2 *syn* see CHAT 1

clatter *n syn* see COMMOTION 4

clattery *adj syn* see NOISY

claviger *n syn* see CUSTODIAN

‖**clawback** *n syn* see SYCOPHANT

clean *adj* **1** free from dirt < kept a *clean* house in a dirty neighborhood >
syn cleanly, immaculate, spotless, taintless, unsoiled, unsullied
rel bright, shining, sparkling; fresh, pure, untainted, wholesome
idiom clean as a whistle (*or* new penny)
con dingy, grimy, grubby, messy, mussy, slovenly; filthy, foul, noisome
ant dirty, unclean

2 *syn* see INNOCENT 2

3 *syn* see CHASTE
ant unclean

4 *syn* see FAIR 5

clean *vb* **1** *syn* see PURIFY 1

2 to make clean < *cleaned* his car every week >
syn cleanse, clean up
rel do, neaten, order, police, spruce, straighten (up), tidy, trim; brighten, freshen, furbish, recondition; renew, renovate
idiom make spick-and-span
con begrime, daub, dirty, sully; besmirch, defile, foul, pollute
ant soil

3 *syn* see DRESS 3

clean–cut *adj syn* see EXPLICIT

clean–limbed *adj syn* see SHAPELY

cleanly *adj syn* see CLEAN 1
rel neat, orderly, spick-and-span, tidy, trim; dainty, fastidious, fussy, nice
con disheveled, disorderly, slipshod, sloppy, slovenly, unkempt
ant uncleanly

cleanse *vb* **1** *syn* see CLEAN 2
rel disinfect, sanitize, sterilize

2 *syn* see PURIFY 1

3 *syn* see PURIFY 2

cleansing *n syn* see PURIFICATION

clean up *vb* **1** *syn* see CLEAR 6

2 *syn* see CLEAN 2

3 *syn* see SETTLE 7

‖**clean up** (on) *vb* *syn* see WHIP 2

clear *adj* **1** *syn* see FAIR 2

2 *syn* see TRANSPARENT 1

3 *syn* see TRANSLUCENT 3
rel milky, opalescent

4 free from obscurity or ambiguity < his account of the accident was perfectly *clear* >
syn clear-cut, crystal, lucent, lucid, luculent, luminous, pellucid, perspicuous, translucent, transparent, transpicuous, unambiguous, unblurred; *compare* UNDERSTANDABLE
rel apprehensible, comprehensible, graspable, knowable, understandable; plain, simple, straightforward, uncomplicated, unperplexed; defined, definite
idiom clear as day (*or* crystal), plain as the nose on one's face
con clouded, dark, mysterious, unclear; hazy, ill-defined, vague
ant obscure

5 readily perceived or apprehended < a *clear* case of embezzlement >
syn apparent, conspicuous, distinct, evident, manifest, obvious, open-and-shut, openhanded, palpable, patent, plain, straightforward, unambiguous, unequivocal, univocal, unmistakable; *compare* SELF-EXPLANATORY, UNDERSTANDABLE
rel appreciable, perceptible, recognizable, sensible, tangible; overt, public, published, unhidden, unobscured; exact, precise
con dim, dusky, gloomy, murky; cryptic, dark, enigmatic, equivocal, indistinct, vague; arcane, esoteric, mysterious, occult
ant obscure

6 *syn* see EMPTY 1

clear *adv syn* see WELL 3

clear *vb* **1** *syn* see EXCULPATE

2 *syn* see CLARIFY 2

3 *syn* see VACATE 2

4 *syn* see RID
rel eliminate, rule out; clean, cleanse

5 to make right by presenting what is due < *clear* one's accounts >
syn clear off, discharge, liquidate, pay, pay up, quit, satisfy, settle, square
rel close, pay off, repay, sink, solve

6 to obtain as a profit or return < he *cleared* several thousand on the deal >
syn clean up, gain, make, net
rel acquire, get, obtain, secure; earn, win; accumulate, gather, glean, pick up

7 *syn* see EXTRICATE 2

8 to pass over or by < *cleared* the hurdle with perfect form >
syn hurdle, leap, negotiate, over, overleap, surmount, vault

9 to become fair < the weather *cleared* later in the day >
syn ‖break, burn off
rel ameliorate, better, improve, meliorate; settle, stabilize

10 *syn* see VANISH

clear away *vb* **1** *syn* see REMOVE 4

2 *syn* see EXTRICATE 2

clear–cut *adj* **1** *syn* see CLEAR 4

2 *syn* see EXPLICIT

3 *syn* see INCISIVE
rel clear, distinct, manifest, plain; definite, explicit, express; exact, nice, precise
con fogged, hazy, misty; confused, muddled; obscured, overcast

4 *syn* see DECIDED 1
rel indubitable, undisputed, undoubted, unquestioned
idiom beyond a shade (*or* shadow) of doubt, past dispute

clearness *n syn* see CLARITY

clear off *vb syn* see CLEAR 5

clear out *vb syn* see GET OUT 1

clear–sightedness *n syn* see WIT 3

clear up *vb* **1** *syn* see CLARIFY 2

2 *syn* see SOLVE 2

cleavage *n syn* see SCHISM 3

cleave *vb syn* see STICK 2
rel associate, combine, conjoin, join, link, unite

---

syn synonym(s)   *rel* related word(s)
ant antonym(s)   *con* contrasted word(s)
idiom idiomatic equivalent(s)
‖ use limited; if in doubt, see a dictionary

con alienate, disaffect, disunite, estrange, separate

cleave *vb* **1** *syn* see CUT 5
  2 *syn* see TEAR 1
    rel divide, divorce, separate; chop, hew
    con join, link, unite; attach, fasten

cleft *n* **1** *syn* see CRACK 3
  2 *syn* see RAVINE
  3 *syn* see SCHISM 3

clemency *n* **1** *syn* see MERCY
    rel gentleness, mildness; equitableness, fairness, justness
    con austerity, severity, sternness; rigidity, rigorousness, strictness; inexorableness, inflexibility, obduracy
    ant harshness
  2 *syn* see FORBEARANCE 2
    rel endurance, sufferance
    con firmness, hardness, inflexibility, obdurateness, relentlessness, rigidity
    ant harshness

clement *adj* *syn* see FORBEARING
    rel compassionate, sympathetic, tender; benign, benignant, kind, kindly; benevolent, charitable, humane
    con austere, severe, stern; rigid, rigorous, strict, stringent
    ant harsh; barbarous

clench *n* *syn* see HOLD

clergyman *n* one duly ordained to the service of God in the Christian church <the responsibility of the *clergyman* to the whole community>
    syn ‖blackcoat, cassock, churchman, cleric, clerical, clerk, ‖devil-dodger, divine, ‖dominie, ecclesiast, ecclesiastic, ‖Holy Joe, minister, parson, preacher, pulpitarian, pulpiteer, pulpiter, reverend, sermonizer, sky pilot
    rel evangelist, missionary; chaplain, curate, pastor, vicar; father, priest, shepherd; predicant
    idiom man of God, man of the cloth

cleric *n* *syn* see CLERGYMAN
clerical *n* *syn* see CLERGYMAN
clerisy *n* *syn* see INTELLIGENTSIA
clerk *n* *syn* see CLERGYMAN
clerkish *adj* *syn* see NICE 1

clever *adj* **1** *syn* see SKILLFUL 2
  2 *syn* see DEXTEROUS 1
  3 *syn* see INTELLIGENT 2
    rel apt, prompt, quick, ready; able, capable, competent; all-around, many-sided, versatile
    idiom quick as a flash, sharp (*or* smart) as a whip
    con asinine, fatuous, foolish, simple
    ant dull
  4 highly skilled in devising or contriving <very *clever* about getting her own way>
    syn adroit, canny, ‖coony, cunning, dexterous, ingenious, ‖sleighty, slim, sly; *compare* SKILLFUL 2
    rel able, adept, expert, handy, masterly, proficient, skilled, skillful; capable, competent, qualified; crafty, deceitful, slick, tricky
    con awkward, clumsy, gauche, inept, maladroit; dilatory, laggard, slow, sluggish; incapable, incompetent, inept, unqualified
  5 pleasing because of aptness, sparkle, and usually wit <delighted her audience with a series of *clever* comparisons>
    syn good, scintillating, smart, sprightly
    rel bright, brilliant, coruscating, dazzling, sparkling; piquant, racy, salty; fanciful, whimsical; amusing, entertaining, pleasing; facetious, funny, humorous, witty; laughable, risible
    con drab, dull, humdrum, monotonous, stodgy; barren, empty, inane; fatuous, pointless; absurd, foolish, nonsensical, ridiculous
    ant stupid

‖**cleverly** *adv* *syn* see WELL 3
cliché *n* *syn* see COMMONPLACE
cliché *adj* *syn* see TRITE
clichéd *adj* *syn* see TRITE
click *vb* *syn* see SUCCEED 2
client *n* *syn* see CUSTOMER
clientage *n* *syn* see FOLLOWING 2
clientele *n* *syn* see FOLLOWING 2
climacteric *adj* *syn* see ACUTE 6
climate *n* *syn* see ENVIRONMENT
climatize *vb* *syn* see HARDEN 2
climax *n* *syn* see APEX 2
climax *vb* to bring to or come to a satisfying termination <the feast was *climaxed* by a glorious plum pudding>

syn cap, crown, culminate, finish off, round off, top off
    rel content, please, satisfy; conclude, end, finish, terminate

climb *vb* *syn* see ASCEND 1
‖**clinch** *vb* *syn* see EMBRACE 1
clinch *n* *syn* see HOLD
clincher *n* *syn* see TRUMP CARD
cling *vb* *syn* see STICK 2
cling *n* *syn* see ADHERENCE 1
clinging *n* *syn* see ADHERENCE 1
clink *vb* *syn* see JINGLE
‖**clink** *n* *syn* see JAIL
clinkers *n pl* *syn* see ASH
‖**clip** *vb* *syn* see EMBRACE 1
clip *n* *syn* see BROOCH
clip *vb* **1** *syn* see CUT 6
  2 *syn* see MOW
  3 *syn* see REDUCE 2
  4 *syn* see OVERCHARGE 1

clique *n* a narrowly exclusive group of people usually held together by a common often selfish interest or purpose <there was a politically minded *clique* on the campus>
    syn cabal, camarilla, camp, circle, clan, coterie, in-group, mob, ring; *compare* SET 5

clitter *vb* *syn* see RATTLE 1
cloak *n* *syn* see MASK 2
cloak *vb* *syn* see DISGUISE
    rel blanket, curtain, screen, shroud, veil
    ant uncloak

clobber *vb* ‖**1** *syn* see WHIP 2
  2 *syn* see SLAM 1
clochard *n* *syn* see VAGABOND
clock *vb* *syn* see TIME 2
‖**clock** *vb* *syn* see SET 11
clocklike *adj* *syn* see CIRCUMSTANTIAL
clockwise *adj* *syn* see RIGHT-HANDED
clod *n* **1** *syn* see LUMP 1
  2 *syn* see DUNCE
cloddish *adj* *syn* see BOORISH
clodhopper *n* **1** *syn* see RUSTIC
  2 *syn* see BOOR
clodhopping *adj* *syn* see BOORISH
clodpate *n* *syn* see DUNCE
clodpoll *n* *syn* see DUNCE
clog *n* *syn* see ENCUMBRANCE
clog *vb* **1** *syn* see BURDEN
  2 *syn* see HAMPER
  3 *syn* see FILL 1
cloggy *adj* *syn* see STICKY 1
cloister *vb* *syn* see SECLUDE
cloistered *adj* *syn* see SECLUDED
clonk *vb* *syn* see THUD
‖**Cloot** *n, usu* **Cloots** *pl* *syn* see DEVIL 1
‖**Clootie** *n* *syn* see DEVIL 1
close *vb* **1** to fill an opening with an appropriate closure <be sure to *close* the gate>
    syn ‖put to, shut
    rel bang, clap, slam; block, choke, clog, obstruct, occlude, stop; debar, exclude
    ant open
  2 *syn* see SCREEN 3
  3 to bring or come to a limit or to a natural or appropriate stopping point <*closed* the meeting as soon as the discussion was over>
    syn complete, conclude, consummate, determine, do, end, finish, halt, terminate, ultimate, wind up, wrap up
    rel cease, desist, quit, stop; finalize, write off
    idiom call it a day, set a period to
    con begin, commence, enter (on *or* upon), inaugurate, initiate, start
  4 *syn* see FILL 1
  5 *syn* see DECREASE
  6 *syn* see MEET 6
close *n* **1** *syn* see END 2
  2 *syn* see FINALE
    ant opening
‖**close** *n* *syn* see COURT 1
close *adj* **1** *syn* see SILENT 3
    idiom close as a clam

con candid, frank, plain
ant open
2 syn see STUFFY 1
rel humid, muggy, sticky
3 syn see STINGY
ant liberal
4 having the constituent parts massed closely together < a paper of fine *close* texture >
syn compact, crowded, dense, thick, tight
rel compacted, compressed, condensed, consolidated, constricted, contracted; firm, solid, substantial; impenetrable, impermeable; close-grained
con lax, loose, slack; unconsolidated
5 syn see TIGHT 3
6 not far removed (as in space, time, or relationship) from something stipulated or understood < true and veritable are *close* synonyms > < the park is very *close* to the river > < it is *close* to closing time >
syn immediate, near, near-at-hand, nearly, nigh, proximate; *compare* NEIGHBORING
rel abutting, adjacent, adjoining, contiguous; convenient, handy; nearest, nearmost, next
idiom at hand, at one's fingers' ends (*or* fingertips), under one's nose
con distant, far, faraway, far-off, removed
ant remote
7 syn see FAMILIAR 1
con cool, remote, withdrawn
ant aloof
close *adv* into proximity with respect to space, time, or approach < hoping to come *closer* to the truth of the matter >
syn at close hand, hard, near, nearby, nigh
rel almost, nearabout, nearly
idiom as near as no matter (*or* never mind), in hailing (*or* spitting) distance, within an inch (*or* an ace) of, within a stone's throw
con afar, distantly, far
ant remotely
close–at–hand *adj* **1 syn** see NEIGHBORING
2 syn see CONVENIENT 2
close–by *adj* **1 syn** see NEIGHBORING
2 syn see CONVENIENT 2
closed *adj syn* see SELF-SUFFICIENT
closed book *n syn* see MYSTERY
closed–minded *adj syn* see OBSTINATE
closefisted *adj syn* see STINGY
rel clinging, clutching, grasping, keeping, tenacious
close in *vb syn* see ENCLOSE 1
close–lipped *adj syn* see SILENT 3
closely *adv syn* see HARD 4
rel carefully, heedfully, mindfully, thoughtfully; meticulously, minutely, punctiliously, scrupulously
con carelessly, heedlessly, thoughtlessly
closemouthed *adj syn* see SILENT 3
close off *vb syn* see ISOLATE
close on *prep syn* see ABOUT 1
close out *vb syn* see SELL OUT 1
closeout *n syn* see BARGAIN 1
‖**closet** *n syn* see PRIVY 1
closet *adj* **1 syn** see PRIVATE 2
2 syn see THEORETICAL 1
close–tongued *adj syn* see SILENT 3
closing *n syn* see END 2
closing *adj syn* see LAST
closure *n syn* see END 2
clot *n syn* see GROUP 3
clot *vb syn* see COAGULATE
clothe *vb* to cover with or as if with garments < forests *clothe* the rocky slopes >
syn apparel, array, attire, clad, dress, enclothe, garb, garment, raiment
rel costume, do up, dress up, tog (up *or* out); cloak, mantle, robe; accouter, equip, outfit, rig (out); bedrape, drape, swathe; endue, invest
con dismantle, divest, strip
ant unclothe
clothes *n pl* a person's garments as a whole < dressed in new *clothes* from the skin out >

syn apparel, attire, attirement, clothing, dress, duds, habiliment(s), rags, raiment, rigging, things, togs
rel array, garb, toggery, vestments, vesture; costume, getup, outfit, rig
clothing *n* **1 syn** see CLOTHES
2 syn see ROLE 1
cloud *n syn* see MULTITUDE 1
cloud *vb* **1 syn** see OBSCURE
rel addle, befuddle, confuse, muddle; distract, perplex, puzzle
2 syn see CONFUSE 4
3 syn see TAINT 1
clouded *adj syn* see DOUBTFUL 1
cloudless *adj syn* see FAIR 2
cloudy *adj* **1 syn** see OVERCAST
2 syn see HAZY
3 syn see MURKY 3
clough *n syn* see RAVINE
clout *n* **1 syn** see CUFF
2 syn see PULL 2
clout *vb* **1 syn** see STRIKE 2
‖**2 syn** see STEAL 1
clove *n syn* see RAVINE
clown *n* **1 syn** see RUSTIC
2 syn see BOOR
3 a performer (as in a circus) who entertains by grotesque appearance and actions < children delighted by the antics of the *clowns* >
syn buffoon, harlequin, merry-andrew, zany
rel comedian; fool, jester, mountebank; mime, mummer
4 syn see ZANY 2
clownish *adj syn* see BOORISH
rel awkward, clumsy, gauche; green, raw, rough, rude, uncouth
ant urbane
cloy *vb syn* see SATIATE
con excite, pique, provoke, stimulate
ant whet
club *n* **1 syn** see CUDGEL
2 syn see ASSOCIATION 2
club car *n syn* see PARLOR CAR
‖**cluck** *n syn* see DUNCE
clue *n syn* see HINT 1
clue (*or* **clew**) *vb syn* see INFORM 2
clump *n* **1 syn** see GROUP 3
rel clutter, hodgepodge, jumble, omnium-gatherum
2 syn see LUMP 1
clump *vb syn* see LUMBER
clumsy *adj* **1** lacking in physical ease and grace usually because of coarse cumbersome build or poor coordination < a *clumsy* boy constantly stumbling over his own feet > < the *clumsy* gait of a young puppy >
syn awkward, gawky, lumbering, lumpish, splathering, splay, ungainly; *compare* AWKWARD 2
rel butterfingered, heavy-handed, left-handed, unhandy; graceless, inelegant, uncouth; bulky, hulking, unwieldy
idiom all thumbs, fingers all thumbs
con comely, shapely, well-formed, well-proportioned; apt, deft, handy, quick, ready
2 syn see AWKWARD 2
clunk *vb syn* see THUD
clunker *n syn* see JALOPY
cluster *n* **1 syn** see GROUP 3
2 syn see GROUP 1
cluster *vb syn* see GROUP 1
rel accumulate, aggregate, associate, cumulate; bundle, package, parcel
clutch *vb syn* see SEIZE 2
rel clench, clinch, gripe; cherish, harbor, hold, keep
clutch *n syn* see HOLD
clutch *n syn* see GROUP 3
clutter *n* **1 syn** see CONFUSION 3
2 a disordered nondescript mass or group < a *clutter* of ornaments on the mantel >

---

syn synonym(s)   **rel** related word(s)
ant antonym(s)   **con** contrasted word(s)
idiom idiomatic equivalent(s)
‖ use limited; if in doubt, see a dictionary

syn hash, hugger-mugger, jumble, jungle, litter, mash, mishmash, muddle, rummage, scramble, shuffle, tumble

rel hodgepodge, macédoine, medley, mélange; disarray, mess, muss, ruck

con arrangement, array, order; grouping, ordering, pigeonholing, ranking, sorting

‖**cly** *vb syn* see STEAL 1

coact *vb syn* see INTERACT

coacting *adj syn* see COOPERATIVE

coactive *adj syn* see COOPERATIVE

coadjutant *n syn* see ASSISTANT 2

coadjute *vb syn* see UNITE 2

coadjutor *n syn* see ASSISTANT 2

coadunate *vb syn* see JOIN 1

coadunation *n syn* see UNIFICATION

coagment *vb syn* see JOIN 1

coagulate *vb* to alter by chemical reaction from a liquid to a more or less firm jelly <the blood *coagulated* and closed the wound>

syn clot, congeal, gel, gelate, gelatinize, jell, jellify, jelly, set

rel concrete, harden, solidify; curdle, inspissate; compact, concentrate, consolidate; coalesce; freeze; dehydrate, dry; condense, thicken

con deliquesce, fluidify, liquefy, liquesce; flux, fuse, melt, run

coalesce *vb syn* see JOIN 1

rel adhere, cleave, cling, stick; blend, fuse, merge, mingle, mix

coalition *n* 1 *syn* see UNIFICATION

2 *syn* see COMBINATION 2

3 *syn* see ALLIANCE 2

coarct *vb syn* see RESTRAIN 1

coarse *adj* 1 made up of relatively large particles <*coarse* sand>

syn grainy, granular

rel caked, cakey, lumpy, particulate

2 *syn* see CRUDE 5

3 deficient in refinement of manner and delicacy of feeling <a *coarse* practical man lacking all social graces>

syn crass, crude, gross, incult, inelegant, low, raw, rough, rude, uncouth, uncultivated, uncultured, unrefined, vulgar; *compare* BOORISH

rel raffish, roughneck, rowdy, vulgarian; common, tacky

con considerate, courtly, gracious; cultivated, polished, refined

4 *syn* see OBSCENE 2

‖5 *syn* see WILD 6

coast *n syn* see SHORE

coast *vb syn* see SLIDE 6

coax *vb* to influence or persuade by artful ingratiation <*coaxed* her friend to help her with her work>

syn ‖barter, blandish, blarney, cajole, con, soft-soap, sweet-talk, wheedle

rel pester, plague, tease; importune, press, urge; get, induce, persuade, prevail; entice, inveigle, lure, tempt; butter (up)

con coerce, compel, constrain, force, oblige; browbeat, bulldoze, cow, intimidate

ant bully

cob *vb syn* see SURPASS 1

cobble *vb syn* see BOTCH

rel confuse, foul up, snafu, snarl (up)

cobweb *n syn* see WEB 2

cock *n* 1 *syn* see FAUCET

2 *syn* see LEADER 2

‖3 *syn* see NONSENSE 2

‖**cock** *adj syn* see CHIEF 2

cock *vb syn* see LORD

cock *n syn* see PILE 1

cock *vb syn* see HEAP 1

cock–a–doodle–doo *vb syn* see BOAST

cock–a–hoop *adj* 1 *syn* see EXULTANT

2 *syn* see AWRY 1

Cockaigne *n syn* see UTOPIA

cock–and–bull story *n syn* see LIE

cock–a–whoop *adj syn* see EXULTANT

cockcrow *n syn* see DAWN 1

cockcrowing *n syn* see DAWN 1

cocker *vb syn* see BABY

‖**cocket** *adj syn* see SAUCY 1

cockeyed *adj* 1 *syn* see AWRY 1

2 *syn* see INTOXICATED 1

cockle *vb syn* see RIPPLE

cocksure *adj syn* see SURE 5

cocktail lounge *n syn* see BAR 5

‖**coco** *n syn* see HEAD 1

coconspirator *n syn* see CONFEDERATE

‖**coconut** *n syn* see HEAD 1

cocotte *n syn* see PROSTITUTE

coddle *vb syn* see BABY

codicil *n syn* see APPENDIX 1

coefficient *adj syn* see COOPERATIVE

coerce *vb syn* see FORCE 2

rel beset, push, urge; browbeat, bulldoze, bully, cow, intimidate; menace, terrorize, threaten

coercion *n syn* see FORCE 4

rel menace, menacing, threat, threatening

coetaneous *adj syn* see CONTEMPORARY 1

coeval *adj syn* see CONTEMPORARY 1

coexistent *adj syn* see CONTEMPORARY 1

coexisting *adj syn* see CONTEMPORARY 1

coffee shop *n syn* see EATING HOUSE

coffer *n syn* see TREASURY 2

‖**coffin nail** *n syn* see CIGARETTE

cogency *n syn* see POINT 3

rel pertinence, relevance; bearing, concern, connection

cogent *adj* 1 *syn* see VALID

rel compelling, constraining, forceful, forcible, potent, powerful, puissant; inducing, persuasive; justified, well-founded, well-grounded

con ineffective, ineffectual, inefficacious; feeble, forceless, impotent, powerless, weak

2 *syn* see WELL-FOUNDED

rel consequential, influential, momentous, weighty; meaningful, significant

cogitable *adj syn* see THINKABLE 1

cogitate *vb* 1 *syn* see THINK 5

rel conceive, envisage, envision, imagine

2 *syn* see PLOT

cogitation *n syn* see THOUGHT 1

cogitative *adj syn* see THOUGHTFUL 1

cognate *adj syn* see RELATED

rel common, general, generic, universal

con different, disparate, divergent, diverse, various

cognizance *n syn* see NOTICE 1

cognizant *adj syn* see AWARE

con forgetful, oblivious, unmindful; heedless, ignoring, neglectful, slighting, unmindful

ant ignorant

cognize *vb syn* see KNOW 1

cognomen *n syn* see NAME 1

cognoscente *n syn* see CONNOISSEUR

rel ‖dab, proficient, specialist; authority, critic, judge

cohere *vb* 1 *syn* see STICK 2

rel blend, coalesce, fuse, merge; associate, combine, connect, join, unite

con disembarrass, disentangle, untangle

2 *syn* see AGREE 4

coherence *n* 1 *syn* see ADHERENCE 1

rel integrity, solidarity, union, unity

ant incoherence

2 *syn* see CONSISTENCY

cohesion *n* 1 *syn* see ADHERENCE 1

ant incohesion

2 *syn* see SOLIDARITY

cohort *n* 1 *syn* see PARTNER

2 *syn* see FOLLOWER

coil *n syn* see COMMOTION 3

coil *vb syn* see WIND 2

rel revolve, rotate, turn

‖**coin** *n syn* see MONEY

idiom coin of the realm

coinage *n syn* see INVENTION

coincide *vb syn* see AGREE 3

rel accord, correspond, jibe, tally; equal, match

con deviate, divagate, divaricate, diverge; bias, skew, twist, warp

ant differ

coincident *adj syn* see CONCOMITANT

coincidentally *adv syn* see TOGETHER 1

coincidently *adv syn* see TOGETHER 1

coinstantaneously *adv syn* see TOGETHER 1
cold *adj* 1 marked by a deficiency of warmth <a *cold* day>
   syn arctic, chill, chillsome, chilly, cool, freezing, frigid, frore, frosty, gelid, glacial, icy, nippy, shivery
   rel biting, bleak, chilling, cutting, nipping, polar, raw, sharp; frozen, iced, wintry; bracing, brisk, crisp, snappy
   con calid, genial, mild
   ant warm
   2 lacking cordiality or emotional warmth <a *cold* greeting>
   syn chill, emotionless, frigid, glacial, icy, indifferent, unemotional
   rel unenthusiastic, unresponsive, unsympathetic
   con cordial, friendly, genial, hearty, warm; empathic, sympathetic
   3 *syn* see MATTER-OF-FACT 3
   4 *syn* see FRIGID 3
   ant hot
   5 *syn* see GLOOMY 3
   6 *syn* see DEAD 1
   7 *syn* see INSENSIBLE 2
cold-blooded *adj* 1 *syn* see UNFEELING 2
   2 *syn* see MATTER-OF-FACT 3
cold feet *n syn* see FEAR 1
coldhearted *adj syn* see UNFEELING 2
   ant warmhearted
‖**cold meat** *n syn* see CORPSE
cold-shoulder *vb syn* see CUT 7
cold storage *n syn* see ABEYANCE
colic *n syn* see STOMACHACHE
coliseum *n syn* see STADIUM
‖**coll** *vb syn* see EMBRACE 1
collapse *vb* 1 *syn* see GIVE 12
   rel break up, disintegrate, shatter
   idiom fall to pieces
   2 to lose energy, stamina, or control under stress <exhausted to the point of *collapsing* helplessly on the bed>
   syn break down, cave (in), drop, ‖flake out, give out, peg out, succumb, wilt
   rel droop, fail, languish, weaken; exhaust, fag, flag, play out, tire, weary
   con enliven, invigorate, stimulate
collapse *n* 1 *syn* see NERVOUS BREAKDOWN
   2 a sudden and grave failure <the *collapse* of an overextended market>
   syn breakdown, crack-up, crash, debacle, smash, smashup, wreck
   rel breakup, disorganization, disruption, undoing; cataclysm, catastrophe; destruction, ruination, ruining; failure
collar *vb* 1 *syn* see CORNER
   2 *syn* see CATCH 1
   3 *syn* see STEAL 1
collate *vb syn* see COMPARE 2
collateral *adj* 1 *syn* see CONCOMITANT
   2 *syn* see INDIRECT 1
   3 *syn* see CORROBORATIVE
   4 *syn* see SUBORDINATE
   rel allied, cognate, kindred, related; complementary, corresponding, reciprocal
   con major, prominent
   5 *syn* see AUXILIARY
‖**collateral** *n syn* see REFUSE
colleague *n* one affiliated with another usually through a common office or profession <he claims to speak for his *colleagues* in the Senate>
   syn associate, compatriot, compeer, confrere
   rel consociate, copartner, fellow, partner; co-worker, workfellow; buddy, chum, companion, crony, pal; aide, assistant, helper
collect *vb* 1 *syn* see GATHER 6
   con assort, sort; sever, sunder; deal, dispense, divide, dole
   ant disperse; distribute
   2 *syn* see INFER
   3 *syn* see COMPOSE 4
   4 *syn* see GROUP 1
   rel align, array, dispose, marshal, order, rank
   con broadcast, disperse, distribute, scatter
collected *adj* 1 *syn* see CALM 2
   rel peaceful, quiet, still
   ant distraught

2 *syn* see COOL 2
   rel assured, confident, sanguine, sure; complacent, self-satisfied, smug
   con disordered, troubled
collection *n* 1 *syn* see GATHERING 2
   rel band, crew, outfit, party
   2 *syn* see ACCUMULATION
   rel assortment, medley, miscellany, variety; bunch, clump, cluster, group; armamentarium; boiling, caboodle, kit, lot
‖**college** *n syn* see JAIL
collide *vb syn* see BUMP 1
   rel atomize, fragment, pulverize, shatter, smash, splinter; break up, crunch, scrap
collimate *vb syn* see PARALLEL 2
collision *n syn* see IMPACT
   rel dilapidation, ruin, wreck; demolishment, destruction
collocate *vb syn* see PARALLEL 2
collogue *vb* ‖1 *syn* see PLOT
   2 *syn* see CONFER 2
colloque *vb syn* see CONVERSE
colloquial *adj syn* see VERNACULAR
colloquial *n syn* see VERNACULAR 3
colloquium *n syn* see CONFERENCE 2
colloquy *n* 1 *syn* see CONVERSATION 1
   2 *syn* see CONVERSATION 2
   3 *syn* see CONFERENCE 2
collude *vb syn* see PLOT
collusion *n syn* see COMPLICITY
colluvies *n* 1 *syn* see ACCUMULATION
   2 *syn* see MISCELLANY 1
collywobbles *n pl but sing or pl in constr syn* see STOMACHACHE
Colonel Blimp *n syn* see STUFFED SHIRT
color *n* 1 a property of a visible thing recognizable only when rays of light fall upon it and serving to distinguish things otherwise visually identical (as in size, shape, or texture) <the green *color* of foliage turns rainbow-hued in autumn>
   syn cast, hue, shade, tinge, tint, tone
   2 *syn* see MASK 2
   3 *syn* see VERISIMILITUDE
   4 *syn* see POSITION 1
   5 *syn* see FLAG
   6 something used to impart visible color to something <dyed her curtains with one of the new easy-to-use *colors*>
   syn colorant, dye, dyestuff, pigment, stain, tincture
color *vb* 1 *syn* see EMBROIDER
   rel disguise, distort, fake, misrepresent
   con constrain, minimize, reduce, soften, temper; blue-pencil, censor, edit
   2 *syn* see MISREPRESENT
   3 *syn* see BLUSH
colorable *adj syn* see BELIEVABLE
   rel cogent, compelling, convincing, sound, telling, valid
colorant *n syn* see COLOR 6
colored *adj syn* see BIASED 2
colorful *adj* making a fine display of usually showy color <a *colorful* bed of asters>
   syn brave, bright, colory, gay, vivid
   rel blatant, florid, garish, gaudy, loud; flashy, showy, splashy
   con blanched, bleached, pallid, wan; dim, dull, faint, pale, weak
   ant colorless
coloring *n* 1 *syn* see MASK 2
   2 *syn* see EXAGGERATION
colorless *adj* 1 *syn* see PALE 1
   2 lacking in sparkle and vitality <an accurate but *colorless* recital of facts>
   syn drab, dull, flat, lackluster, lifeless, lusterless, prosaic, prosy
   rel blurry, hazy, obscure, vague; feeble, insipid, milk-and-water, namby-pamby, weak, wishy-washy; unimaginative, uninspired
   con clear, concise, exact, precise; exciting, provocative, rousing, stimulating, stirring
   ant colorful
   3 *syn* see NEUTRAL
   rel aloof, remote, withdrawn

---

syn synonym(s)   *rel* related word(s)
ant antonym(s)   *con* contrasted word(s)
idiom idiomatic equivalent(s)
‖ use limited; if in doubt, see a dictionary

colory *adj syn* see COLORFUL
colossal *adj syn* see HUGE
colporteur *n syn* see MISSIONARY
colt *n syn* see NOVICE
coltish *adj syn* see PLAYFUL 1
columbary *n syn* see DOVECOTE
column *n* 1 *syn* see PILLAR 1
  2 *syn* see SUPPORT 3
coma *n* 1 *syn* see FAINT
  2 *syn* see LETHARGY 1
comate *n syn* see ASSOCIATE 3
comatose *adj* 1 *syn* see INSENSIBLE 2
  2 *syn* see LETHARGIC
  rel anesthetic, impassible, insensitive
  ant awake
comb *vb* 1 *syn* see SORT 2
  2 *syn* see SCOUR 2
  rel examine, inspect, scrutinize; investigate, probe, sift
combat *vb syn* see RESIST
  rel battle, contend, war
combat *n syn* see SERVICE 1
combative *adj syn* see BELLIGERENT
  rel energetic, strenuous, vigorous; manful, manly, virile
  ant pacifistic
combativeness *n syn* see ATTACK 2
‖**combe** *n syn* see VALLEY
combination *n* 1 *syn* see UNIFICATION
  2 individuals or organized interests banded together to further a common end <a *combination* of citizens devoted to holding down taxes>
  syn bloc, coalition, combine, faction, party, ring
  rel cartel, pool, syndicate, trust; cabal, circle, clique, coterie, set
  3 *syn* see ASSOCIATION 1
combine *vb* 1 *syn* see JOIN 1
  rel amalgamate, blend, commingle, fuse, mingle, mix; consolidate, unify
  con divide, divorce, part
  ant separate
  2 *syn* see EMBODY 2
  3 *syn* see UNITE 2
  rel agree, coincide; merge, pool
combine *n* 1 *syn* see COMBINATION 2
  2 *syn* see SYNDICATE
comble *n syn* see APEX 2
combust *vb syn* see BURN 2
combustible *adj* 1 capable of catching or being set on fire <*combustible* materials should be stored away from open fire>
  syn burnable, flammable, ignitable, inflammable
  rel comburent, combustive; burning, firing, igniting, kindling
  con fireproof; flameproof, nonflammable; fire-resistant, fire-resistive, fire-retardant
  ant incombustible, noncombustible
  2 *syn* see EXCITABLE
come *vb* 1 to attain to a destination <when will they *come*>
  syn arrive, ‖blow in, get, get in, reach, show, show up, turn up
  rel approach, near, nigh
  con depart, leave, quit, retreat, withdraw
  ant go
  2 *syn* see AMOUNT 1
  3 *syn* see HAPPEN 1
  4 *syn* see BECOME 1
come (from) *vb* 1 *syn* see SPRING
  2 *syn* see ORIGINATE 5
come (in) *vb syn* see ENTER 1
comeback *n syn* see RETORT 2
come by *vb syn* see VISIT 2
come–by–chance *n syn* see BASTARD 1
comedian *n* 1 *syn* see HUMORIST 2
  2 *syn* see WAG 1
come down (with) *vb syn* see CONTRACT 1
comedown *n* a loss of status <bitter over their *comedown* in the world>
  syn descent, discomfiture, down; *compare* SETBACK
  rel collapse, crash, downfall, fall, ruin, smash, undoing, wreck
  con advance, headway, progress
  ant rise
comedy *n syn* see HUMOR 4
come in *vb syn* see ANSWER 1

comely *adj* 1 *syn* see BEAUTIFUL
  ant homely
  2 *syn* see DECOROUS 1
come off *vb* 1 *syn* see SUCCEED 2
  2 *syn* see HAPPEN 1
come–off *n syn* see ESCAPE 2
come–on *n* 1 *syn* see LURE 2
  ‖2 *syn* see FOOL 3
  3 *syn* see SWINDLER
come out *vb* 1 *syn* see GET OUT 2
  2 *syn* see DEBUT
come out (with) *vb syn* see SAY 1
come over *vb* 1 *syn* see VISIT 2
  2 *syn* see BECOME 1
come round *vb syn* see RECOVER 2
comestible *adj syn* see EDIBLE
comestibles *n pl syn* see FOOD 1
come through *vb* 1 *syn* see SURVIVE 2
  2 *syn* see CONTRIBUTE 1
comeuppance *n syn* see DUE 1
comfort *n* 1 *syn* see HELP 1
  2 *syn* see AMENITY 2
comfort *vb* to make or try to make brighter a person overcome by grief or misery <*comforting* her widowed sister with words of hope>
  syn buck up, cheer, console, solace, upraise
  rel brighten, gladden, lighten; allay, alleviate, assuage, mitigate, relieve; refresh, renew, restore; reassure; commiserate, condole, sympathize
  idiom give a lift to
  con torment, torture, try; distress, trouble, worry; annoy, irk, vex
  ant afflict; bother
comfortable *adj* 1 *syn* see SUFFICIENT 1
  2 enjoying or providing conditions that make for comfort and security <lived in a *comfortable* home on a quiet street>
  syn comfy, cozy, cushy, easeful, easy, snug, soft
  rel agreeable, grateful, gratifying, welcome; pleasant, pleasing; restful; comforting, consoling, solacing; content, pleased, satisfied
  con distressing, perturbing, troubling; annoying, bothering, irking, vexing; inferior, miserable, poor, substandard, wretched
  ant uncomfortable
  3 *syn* see PROSPEROUS 3
  idiom in comfortable circumstances
‖**comfortable** *n syn* see QUILT
comforter *n syn* see QUILT
comfortless *adj syn* see UNCOMFORTABLE
comfy *adj syn* see COMFORTABLE 2
comic *adj syn* see LAUGHABLE
  rel antic, fantastic, grotesque; mocking, ridiculing
  ant tragic
comic *n syn* see HUMORIST 2
comical *adj syn* see LAUGHABLE
  rel absurd, foolish, silly; impish, roguish, sportive, waggish
  con doleful, dolorous, lugubrious, melancholy
  ant pathetic
comicality *n syn* see HUMOR 4
comicalness *n syn* see HUMOR 4
coming *n syn* see ARRIVAL 1
coming *adj* 1 *syn* see FORTHCOMING
  2 *syn* see NEXT
coming in *n, usu* comings in *pl syn* see REVENUE
comingle *vb syn* see MIX 1
comity *n syn* see GOODWILL 1
  rel accord, concord, harmony; camaraderie, companionship, comradeship, good-fellowship
comma *n syn* see PAUSE
command *vb* to issue orders or an order to <the general *commanded* the troops to advance>
  syn bid, charge, direct, enjoin, instruct, order, tell, warn
  rel demand, exact, require; coerce, compel, constrain, force, oblige; conduct, control, manage; ask, call (on), request, say
  ant comply, obey
command *n* 1 a direction that must or should be obeyed <failure to obey a direct *command* subjects the soldier to grave penalties>
  syn behest, bidding, charge, dictate, injunction, mandate, order, word

rel direction, directive, instruction; canon, law, ordinance, precept, rule, statute; devoir, duty, obligation, responsibility
2 *syn* see POWER 1
rel rule
3 *syn* see ABILITY 2
rel aplomb, assurance, confidence, poise
con incertitude, insecurity, uncertainty, unsureness; indecisiveness, vagueness
commandeer *vb* **1** *syn* see APPROPRIATE 1
2 *syn* see ARROGATE 1
comme il faut *adj syn* see DECOROUS 1
commemorate *vb* **1** *syn* see KEEP 2
2 *syn* see MEMORIALIZE 2
commemorative *adj syn* see MEMORIAL
commemoratory *adj syn* see MEMORIAL
commence *vb* **1** *syn* see BEGIN 1
2 *syn* see BEGIN 2
idiom come into being (*or* existence)
commencement *n syn* see BEGINNING
commend *vb* **1** *syn* see COMMIT 1
rel resign, yield; proffer, tender
2 to indicate one's warm approval <the teacher *commended* her pupils' studious attitude>
syn acclaim, applaud, compliment, hail, kudize, praise, recommend, ‖roose
rel eulogize, extol; approve, countenance, endorse, support
con blame, criticize, reprehend, reprobate; chide, rebuke, reprimand, reproach, reprove
ant censure; admonish
commendable *adj syn* see WORTHY 1
commensurable *adj syn* see PROPORTIONAL
commensurate *adj syn* see PROPORTIONAL
comment *n* **1** *syn* see REMARK 2
2 *syn* see CRITICISM
comment *vb syn* see REMARK 2
rel construe, elucidate, explain, explicate, expound; annotate, gloss
commentary *n syn* see REMARK 2
commentate *vb syn* see REMARK 2
commerce *n* **1** *syn* see CONTACT 2
2 a situation characterized by mutual exchange (as of ideas) <those who feel that art should have no *commerce* with morality>
syn communion, dealings, intercourse, traffic, truck
rel communication, congress, contact, exchange, interchange, intercommunication; basis, common ground, takeoff
3 *syn* see BUSINESS 4
commie *n syn* see COMMUNIST
commination *n syn* see CURSE 1
commingle *vb syn* see MIX 1
rel integrate, unify
comminute *vb syn* see PULVERIZE 1
commiserable *adj syn* see PITIFUL 1
commiserate *vb syn* see COMPASSIONATE
commiseration *n syn* see PITY
commission *vb* **1** *syn* see AUTHORIZE 1
rel appoint, designate, name, nominate; bid, charge, command, enjoin, instruct, order
2 *syn* see DELEGATE
commit *vb* **1** to assign (as to a person) especially for use or safekeeping <it is unwise to *commit* all power and authority to one man> <sainted beings who *commit* their spirits to God>
syn commend, confide, consign, entrust, hand over, relegate, turn over
rel allocate, allot, assign, destine, ordain; move, remove, shift, transfer; deliver, give, offer, submit; delegate, deputize
idiom give into the charge (*or* hands) of
2 to be responsible for or guilty of (an offense or wrongdoing) <*commit* a crime>
syn perpetuate, pull
rel accomplish, achieve, do, effectuate, execute, perform, pull off; contravene, transgress, trespass, violate; offend, scandalize, sin
commitment *n syn* see OBLIGATION 2
committal *n syn* see OBLIGATION 2
commix *vb syn* see MIX 1
commixture *n syn* see MIXTURE
commodious *adj syn* see SPACIOUS

con cramped, narrow, strait
ant incommodious
commodities *n pl syn* see MERCHANDISE
rel articles, items, things
common *adj* **1** generally shared in or participated in by members of a community <our *common* civic responsibilities>
syn communal, conjoint, conjunct, intermutual, joint, mutual, public, shared
rel general, generic, universal; like, reciprocal, similar; corporate
con personal, private, restricted
ant individual
2 *syn* see GENERAL 2
rel popular, public
3 *syn* see IMPURE 3
4 taking place often <a *common* occurrence>
syn customary, everyday, familiar, frequent
rel repetitious, routine, usual
con infrequent, occasional, unfrequent; casual, chance, incidental
ant rare, uncommon
5 *syn* see GENERAL
6 conforming to a type without noteworthy excellences or faults <just a *common* everyday sort trying to get by in life>
syn commonplace, ordinary, prosaic, uneventful, unexceptional, unnoteworthy
rel down-to-earth, matter-of-fact, prosy, unexciting; dull, flat, trite, stale, uninteresting
con exceptional, noteworthy, remarkable; excellent, marvelous, prodigious, wonderful; aberrant, divergent, eccentric
ant extraordinary
7 *syn* see DECENT 4
8 *syn* see CHEAP 2
9 *syn* see INFERIOR 2
‖**10** *syn* see EASYGOING 3
common *n* **1** **commons** *pl but sing or pl in constr syn* see COMMONALTY
2 an often improved and ornamentally planted open space for public use in a built-up area <in summer a band played on the village *common* >
syn green, plaza, square
rel garden, park, pleasance, pleasure ground
commonage *n syn* see COMMONALTY
commonalty *n* persons without rank or authority or the political estate made up of these <laws that both the gentles and the *commonalty* recognized as just>
syn commonage, commoners, common men, commune, people, plebeians, plebes, plebs, populace, rank and file, third estate
rel masses, mob, multitude, proletariat, public
con aristocracy, elite, gentility, nobility; classes, gentry, nobs
commoners *n pl syn* see COMMONALTY
commonition *n syn* see WARNING
commonly *adv syn* see USUALLY 2
idiom more often than not
common men *n pl syn* see COMMONALTY
commonplace *n* an idea or expression deficient in originality or freshness <lazily exchanging *commonplaces* over their beer>
syn banality, bromide, cliché, platitude, prosaicism, prosaism, rubber stamp, shibboleth, tag, truism
rel chestnut, corn, prose, stereotype; inanity, shallowness, wishy-washiness; threadbareness, triteness
ant profundity
commonplace *adj* **1** *syn* see COMMON 6
2 *syn* see GENERAL 1
3 *syn* see PROSAIC 3
4 *syn* see TRITE
idiom a dime a dozen, as everyday as breakfast
common sense *n syn* see SENSE 6
commorancy *n syn* see HABITATION 2
commotion *n* **1** a state of often disorderly civic unrest <the whole city was in *commotion* over the new restrictions>
syn clamor, convulsion, ferment, outcry, tumult, upheaval, upturn

---

syn synonym(s)	*rel* related word(s)
ant antonym(s)	*con* contrasted word(s)
idiom idiomatic equivalent(s)	
‖ use limited; if in doubt, see a dictionary	

rel insurgence, insurrection, mutiny, rebellion, revolt, riot, uprising

2 a state of usually mental or emotional excitement <this challenge threw him into great *commotion* of mind>
syn agitation, confusion, dither, flap, lather, pother, stew, tumult, turbulence, turmoil
rel discompose, disquiet, flurry, fluster, perturbation, upset; annoyance, bother, irritation, vexation; strain, tension
con calm, placidity, quietude, relaxation, serenity

3 a noisy and often unruly disturbance <the children created a *commotion* over missing the circus>
syn brouhaha, ‖catouse, coil, foofaraw, furore, fuss, hurrah, ruckus, rumpus, shindig, shindy, to-do, uproar
rel din, hubbub, hullabaloo, pandemonium, racket; fracas, ruction, row

4 a state of noisy confusion <never saw such *commotion* as the time the old sow got out and knocked the preacher into the midden>
syn bustle, clamor, clatter, hassle, hubbub, hurly-burly, lather, moil, pother, rowdydow, ruction, storm, to-do, tow-row, tumult, turmoil, uproar, whirl, whoopla; *compare* DIN, STIR 1
con calmness, order, peace, quiet

commove *vb syn* see ELATE
communal *adj syn* see COMMON 1
commune *n syn* see COMMONALTY
communicable *adj* **1** *syn* see INFECTIOUS 2
2 *syn* see COMMUNICATIVE
communicate *vb* **1** to make known <*communicated* the whole story under a pledge of secrecy>
syn break, convey, impart, pass on, transmit
rel betray, disclose, discover, divulge, ‖let out, reveal, tell; hint, imply, let on, suggest; broadcast, disseminate, publicize
con conceal, hide, obscure, screen, veil; dissemble; distort, garble, twist, warp; camouflage, disguise
2 *syn* see ADJOIN
communication *n* **1** *syn* see MESSAGE 1
2 *syn* see CONTACT 2
3 interchange of thoughts or opinions through shared symbols <the difficulties of *communication* between people of different cultural backgrounds>
syn communion, converse, intercommunication, intercourse
rel exchange, interchange; conversing, discussing, talking; conversation, discussion, talk; advice, intelligence, news, tidings
communicative *adj* inclined to talk freely and sometimes indiscreetly <too *communicative* to be trusted with a secret>
syn communicable, expansive; *compare* FRANK
rel garrulous, loquacious, talkative, voluble; conversational; demonstrative, effusive, gushing
con constrained, guarded, inhibited, restrained; bridled, controlled, curbed
communion *n* **1** *syn* see COMMERCE 2
2 *syn* see COMMUNICATION 3
3 *syn* see CONTACT 2
4 *syn* see RELIGION 2
Communist *n* a member of the Russian Communist party <restructuring of Russia by the *Communists*>
syn Bolshevik, ‖Bolshie, commie, comrade, Red
rel fellow traveler, pink, pinko; Leninist, Marxist, Stalinist, Trotskyist; apparatchik
community *n syn* see SOCIETY 3
commutable *adj syn* see INTERCHANGEABLE
commute *vb syn* see TRANSFORM
compact *adj* **1** *syn* see PITHY
2 *syn* see CLOSE 4
rel hard; appressed, bunched, packed
con loose, slack, unconstrained; rare, tenuous, thin
compact *vb syn* see UNIFY 1
rel compress, condense, contract; combine, unite; set, solidify
con disperse, dissipate; fluff, loosen
compact *n syn* see CONTRACT
compacting *adj syn* see INTEGRATIVE
companion *n* **1** *syn* see ASSOCIATE 3
rel colleague, fellow, partner; chaperon, escort
2 *syn* see MATE 5
3 *syn* see ACCOMPANIMENT 2
companion *vb syn* see ACCOMPANY
companionable *adj syn* see SOCIAL 1
rel amiable, complacent, good-natured

con uncongenial, unsympathetic; reserved, taciturn, uncommunicative
companionship *n syn* see COMPANY 1
company *n* **1** association between individuals especially on pleasant or intimate terms <we always enjoyed his *company*>
syn companionship, fellowship, society
rel camaraderie, comradeship, consociation
2 persons visiting especially in one's house <invited *company* for dinner>
syn guests, visitors; *compare* VISITOR 1
3 *syn* see GATHERING 2
4 a group of persons associated in a joint effort or for a common purpose <a *company* of thieves lay in wait by the highway>
syn band, corps, outfit, party, troop, troupe
rel crew, gang, pack, team; circle, clique, coterie, set; association, club, order, society; crowd, horde, mob, throng; group
5 *syn* see ENTERPRISE 3
company *vb syn* see ACCOMPANY
comparable *adj syn* see LIKE
ant disparate
comparative *adj* being such in comparison with an expressed or implied standard or absolute <living in *comparative* poverty>
syn approximate, near, relative
rel equivalent, like, similar
con genuine, real, true
ant absolute
compare *vb* **1** *syn* see EQUATE 2
2 to examine side by side or point by point in order to establish likenesses and differences <*compare* the effects of two diets on weight loss>
syn bracket, collate, contrast
rel approach, equal, match, rival, touch; examine, inspect, observe, scan, scrutinize, size (up); consider, contemplate, ponder, study, weigh
comparison *n syn* see LIKENESS
compass *vb* **1** *syn* see SURROUND 1
2 *syn* see GET 1
3 *syn* see APPREHEND 1
compass *n* **1** *syn* see CIRCUMFERENCE
rel domain, field, sphere; enclosure
2 *syn* see ENVIRONS 1
3 *syn* see RANGE 2
rel bounds, limits; circumscription, limitation, restriction
compassion *n* **1** *syn* see SYMPATHY 2
rel charity, clemency, grace, lenity, mercy; benevolence, humaneness, humanity
con aloofness, indifference, unconcern; cruelty, harshness, mercilessness; implacability, relentlessness
2 *syn* see PITY
compassionate *adj syn* see TENDER
rel clement, forbearing; piteous, pitiful
con grim, implacable, merciless, relentless, unrelenting; adamant, inexorable, inflexible, obdurate
compassionate *vb* to feel or express compassion for <a kindly man who *compassionated* all human misery>
syn ache, commiserate, feel (for), pity, sympathize (with)
rel grieve (over), regret, repine; lament, mourn, sorrow (for *or* over); deplore
con accept, endure, tolerate; disregard, ignore, overlook, pass over
compassionless *adj syn* see UNFEELING 2
compatible *syn* see CONSONANT 1
rel appropriate, fit, fitting, meet, proper, suitable
ant incompatible
compatriot *n syn* see COLLEAGUE
compeer *n syn* see COLLEAGUE
compel *vb syn* see FORCE 2
compellation *n syn* see NAME 1
compendiary *adj syn* see CONCISE
compendious *adj syn* see CONCISE
rel close, compact
con amplified, elaborated, expanded, inflated; complete, full
compendium *n* **1** a condensed treatment of a subject <prepared a *compendium* of the state laws dealing with education>
syn aperçu, digest, pandect, précis, sketch, survey, syllabus, sylloge
rel abridgment, abstract, brief, conspectus, epitome; overview

con elaboration, expansion
2 syn see HANDBOOK

compenetrate *vb syn* see PERMEATE

compensate *vb* **1** to make good the defects of < her kind heart *compensated* for her nosy ways >
syn atone (for), balance, counterbalance, counterpoise, countervail, make up, offset, outweigh, redeem, set off
rel abrogate, annul, invalidate, negate, nullify; counteract, negative, neutralize; better, fix (up), improve, repair; redress
idiom make amends (*or* reparations), make matters right
2 syn see PAY 1
3 to make proper payment to (as for injury, loss, or damage) < *compensated* a worker injured on the job >
syn indemnify, pay, recompense, reimburse, remunerate, repay, requite
rel recoup, refund
idiom make restitution (*or* reparation)

compensation *n syn* see REPARATION

compete *vb* **1** to strive to gain mastery or obtain a prize < students *competing* for a scholarship >
syn contend, contest, rival, vie
rel dispute; battle, fight, strive, struggle; attempt, essay, try
2 syn see RIVAL 2
rel approach, equal, match, touch

competence *n* **1** *syn* see ENOUGH
2 syn see ABILITY 1
rel appropriateness, fitness, suitability
ant incompetence

competent *adj* **1** *syn* see ABLE
rel adept, finished, masterly, polished
ant incompetent
2 syn see SUFFICIENT 1

competition *n* **1** *syn* see CONTEST 1
2 syn see CONTEST 2
3 syn see RIVAL

competitor *n syn* see RIVAL

complacence *n syn* see CONCEIT 2

complacency *n syn* see CONCEIT 2

complacent *adj* feeling or showing an often excessive or unjustified satisfaction and pleasure in one's status, possessions, or attainments < had the *complacent* air of superiority that often mars an ignorant self-made man >
syn priggish, self-complacent, self-contented, self-pleased, self-satisfied, smug
rel assured, confident, self-assured, self-confident, self-possessed; conceited, egoistic, egotistic
con humble, modest; diffident, shy

complain *vb* to express discontent, resentment, or regret usually peaceably and as if seeking sympathy < a nice girl but given to *complaining* over trifles >
syn fuss, kick, murmur, repine, wail, whine; *compare* GRIPE 2, GRUMBLE 1
rel fret, worry; nag, pester
idiom air a grievance, find fault, register a complaint, sing (*or* cry) the blues
con accept, condone, countenance, tolerate

complainer *n syn* see GROUCH

complaint *n syn* see DISEASE 1

complaisant *adj syn* see AMIABLE 1
rel accommodating, agreeable, generous, indulgent; submissive
con harsh, rigorous, stern; determined, firm, masterful

complement *n* **1** something that makes up a deficiency in another thing < bought the farm with its *complement* of equipment and livestock >
syn supplement
rel correlate, counterpart; makeweight
2 syn see ACCOMPANIMENT 1
3 syn see COUNTERPART 1

complete *adj* **1** *syn* see WHOLE 3
2 syn see UNABRIDGED
3 syn see WHOLE 4
4 brought to completion < each *complete* revolution of the earth >
syn completed, concluded, done, down, ended, finished, terminated, through
rel accomplished, achieved, effected, executed, realized; attained, compassed
idiom all over, done with, set at rest

ant incomplete
5 syn see EXHAUSTIVE
ant incomplete
6 syn see UTTER

complete *vb* **1 syn** see CLOSE 3
rel accomplish, achieve, discharge, effect, execute, fulfill, perform
idiom carry through, go through with
2 syn see FULFILL 1

completed *adj syn* see COMPLETE 4

completely *adv* **1** *syn* see DOWN 2
idiom down to the ground
2 syn see THOROUGHLY 2
3 syn see WELL 3

completeness *n* **1** *syn* see ENTIRETY 1
2 syn see INTEGRITY 2

complex *adj* **1** made up of two or more separable or identifiable elements < the *complex* vascular system of higher plants >
syn composite, compound
rel blended, compounded, mingled, mixed; heterogeneous, varied; elaborate, intricate, involved; complicated, confused, mixed-up
con homogeneous, uniform
ant simple
2 difficult to comprehend because of a multiplicity of interrelated elements < a *complex* plot to undermine the government by discrediting its leaders >
syn Byzantine, complicated, daedal, elaborate, gordian, intricate, involved, knotty, labyrinthine, sophisticated
rel bewildering, confusing, distracting, disturbing; baffling, confounding, mysterious, mystifying, perplexing, puzzling, equivocal, obscure, vague; involute, involuted, reticular
con clear, defined, definite, distinct, plain, recognizable, uncomplicated, uninvolved; comprehensible, explicable, intelligible, knowable
ant simple

complex *n syn* see SYSTEM 1
con constituent, element, factor; member, part, piece, portion; detail, item, particular
ant component

complexion *n syn* see DISPOSITION 3
rel kind, sort, style, type

complexion *vb syn* see TINT

complexionless *adj syn* see PALE 1

compliance *n syn* see ACQUIESCENCE
rel amenability, docility, obedience, tractability; deference, submission, submissiveness
con contumacy, obstinacy, stubbornness
ant frowardness

complicate *vb* to make complex, involved, or difficult < a disagreement *complicated* by intense personal animosities >
syn entangle, ‖muck, muddle, perplex, ravel, snarl, tangle
rel jumble, ‖snafu; derange, disarrange, disorder, mix up, upset
con arrange, order; disentangle, straighten (out), untangle
ant simplify

complicated *adj* **1** *syn* see ELABORATE 2
2 syn see COMPLEX 2
rel arduous, difficult, hard; abstruse, recondite
con easy, facile, light; clear-cut, precise, straightforward
ant simple

complicity *n* association with an improper or unlawful activity < failed to prove his *complicity* in the cover-up >
syn collusion, connivance
rel implication, involvement; engineering, machination, manipulation, wire-pulling

compliment *n* **1** an expression of regard or praise < a man meriting the *compliments* and homage of his fellows >
syn bouquet, kudo, orchid(s)
rel trade-last; laud, laudation, praise; accolade, commendation, honor; blessing(s), congratulation(s), felicitation(s); encomium, eulogy, tribute
con dig, gibe, jeer, slam
ant taunt

---

syn synonym(s)	*rel* related word(s)
ant antonym(s)	*con* contrasted word(s)
idiom idiomatic equivalent(s)	
‖ use limited; if in doubt, see a dictionary	

‖**2** *syn* see GIFT 1
compliment *vb syn* see COMMEND 2
  idiom take off one's hat to
  con belittle, decry, denigrate, depreciate, disparage, run down
complimentary *adj syn* see FREE 5
comply *vb syn* see OBEY
component *n syn* see ELEMENT 2
  con admixture, amalgam, blend, compound, mixture
  ant composite; complex
comport *vb* **1** *syn* see AGREE 4
  2 *syn* see BEHAVE 1
comportment *n* **1** *syn* see BEARING 1
  2 *syn* see BEHAVIOR
compose *vb* **1** *syn* see CONSTITUTE 1
  rel consist (of)
  2 to bring into being by mental and especially artistic effort < *compose* a ballad or a history of England >
  syn create
  rel devise, invent, make up, originate; dream up
  3 *syn* see CALM
  rel ease, lessen, soften; comfort, console, solace
  con agitate, embroil, trouble, unsettle
  ant discompose
  4 to bring oneself or one's emotions under control < *composed* himself and turned to face the new attack >
  syn collect, contain, control, cool, re-collect, rein, repress, restrain, simmer down, smother, suppress
  rel down, mitigate, moderate, modulate, pocket, temper, tune down; bottle (up), check, hold in; ease (off *or* up), let up, relax, slacken
  idiom calm down, control one's feelings (*or* emotions), get hold of oneself, master one's feelings, pull oneself together
composed *adj* **1** *syn* see CALM 2
  2 *syn* see COOL 2
  rel quiet, still; sedate, serious, staid; repressed, suppressed
  con concerned, worried
  ant discomposed, ruffled
composite *adj syn* see COMPLEX 1
composite *n syn* see MIXTURE
  rel combination, union
composition *n* **1** *syn* see MAKEUP 1
  2 *syn* see COMPROMISE
  3 *syn* see ESSAY 2
compos mentis *adj syn* see SANE 2
compost *n syn* see MIXTURE
composure *n syn* see EQUANIMITY
  ant discomposure, perturbation
compotation *n syn* see BINGE 1
compound *vb* **1** *syn* see JOIN 1
  2 *syn* see MIX 1
  3 *syn* see INCREASE 1
compound *adj syn* see COMPLEX 1
compound *n syn* see MIXTURE
comprehend *vb* **1** *syn* see APPREHEND 1
  2 *syn* see KNOW 1
  rel envisage, envision, see
  3 *syn* see INCLUDE
comprehendible *adj syn* see UNDERSTANDABLE
  ant incomprehensible
comprehensible *adj syn* see UNDERSTANDABLE
  ant incomprehensible
comprehensive *adj* **1** *syn* see ENCYCLOPEDIC
  2 *syn* see ALL-AROUND 2
  idiom in depth
comprehensiveness *n syn* see BREADTH 2
compress *vb* **1** *syn* see CONTRACT 3
  rel compact, consolidate; cram, crowd, press, squeeze
  con disperse, dissipate, scatter
  ant stretch; spread
  2 *syn* see PRESS 1
comprise *vb syn* see CONSTITUTE 1
compromise *n* a settlement reached by mutual concession < the company and the union agreed to a *compromise* on fringe benefits >
  syn composition
  rel golden mean, mean, middle ground, middle way; agreement, compact, contract, pact; arrangement, bargain, understanding
  idiom happy medium

compromise *vb syn* see ENDANGER
  rel blast, blight, mar, queer, ruin, spoil
  idiom cook one's goose; play havoc (*or* hob) with, settle one's hash
compulsatory *adj syn* see MANDATORY
compulsion *n syn* see FORCE 4
  rel driving, impelling, pressing; exigency, necessity, need; pressure, stress
  con coaxing, inducing, persuasion; choice, election, option, preference
compulsory *adj syn* see MANDATORY
compunction *n* **1** *syn* see PENITENCE
  rel conscience, conscientiousness, punctiliousness, scrupulosity, scrupulousness
  con brazenness, callousness, hardness, insensitivity; disinterest, indifference, unconcern; obduracy, recalcitrance
  2 *syn* see QUALM
  rel disinclination; hesitancy, hesitation
compunctious *adj syn* see REMORSEFUL
computation *n* the act or action of calculating mathematically < by his *computation* they could not possibly afford a new car >
  syn arithmetic, calculation, ciphering, estimation, figuring, reckoning
compute *vb syn* see CALCULATE
comrade *n* **1** *syn* see ASSOCIATE 3
  rel consort, fellow, mate; adjunct, ally, auxiliary
  2 *syn* see COMMUNIST
comradery *n syn* see CAMARADERIE
comstock *n syn* see PRUDE
con *vb* **1** *syn* see SCRUTINIZE 1
  2 *syn* see MEMORIZE
con *n* **1** *syn* see OPPONENT
  ant pro
  2 *syn* see ANTAGONISM 2
con *vb* **1** *syn* see DUPE
  2 *syn* see COAX
‖**con** *n syn* see CONVICT
concatenate *vb syn* see INTEGRATE 3
concavity *n syn* see DEPRESSION 2
conceal *vb syn* see HIDE
  rel camouflage, disguise, dissemble
  idiom keep (something) dark
  con betray, divulge; evidence, evince, manifest
  ant reveal
concealed *adj syn* see ULTERIOR
concede *vb* **1** *syn* see ACKNOWLEDGE 1
  rel cede, relinquish, waive
  con agitate, argue, debate, discuss; answer, confute, refute; controvert
  ant dispute
  2 *syn* see GRANT 1
  con refuse, reject
  ant deny
conceit *n* **1** *syn* see IDEA
  2 an attitude of regarding oneself with favor < his constant boasting was an indication of *conceit* >
  syn amour propre, complacence, complacency, conceitedness, consequence, egoism, egotism, narcissism, outrecuidance, pride, self-admiration, self-complacency, self-conceit, self-consequence, self-esteem, self-exaltation, self-glory, self-importance, self-love, self-opinion, self-pride, swelled head, swellheadedness, vainglory, vainness, vanity
  rel assurance, pomposity, self-partiality, smugness, stuffiness
  con humbleness, humility, self-depreciation, unpretentiousness
  ant modesty
  3 *syn* see CAPRICE
‖**conceit** *vb syn* see UNDERSTAND 3
conceited *adj syn* see VAIN 3
conceitedness *n syn* see CONCEIT 2
‖**conceity** *adj syn* see VAIN 3
conceivable *adj* **1** *syn* see THINKABLE 2
  2 *syn* see PROBABLE
conceive *vb* **1** *syn* see THINK 1
  rel excogitate; cogitate, speculate; meditate, ponder, ruminate
  2 *syn* see APPREHEND 1
  rel heed, mark, note, notice, observe, remark
  3 *syn* see UNDERSTAND 3
  rel judge; deem, feel

concenter *vb* 1 *syn* see FASTEN 3
  2 *syn* see CONVERGE
concentrate *vb* 1 *syn* see FASTEN 3
  rel establish, set, settle
  2 *syn* see UNIFY 1
  rel assemble, collect, gather; heap, mass, pile
  con dispel, disperse; attenuate, dilute, extenuate, rarefy, thin; dispense, distribute
  ant dissipate
  3 *syn* see CONTRACT 3
  4 *syn* see CONVERGE
concentrated *adj* 1 *syn* see STRONG 3
  2 *syn* see WHOLE 5
  rel complete, entire, total
  3 *syn* see INTENSE 1
concentrating *adj* *syn* see INTEGRATIVE
concentration *n* *syn* see ATTENTION 1
  rel enthrallment, raptness
  ant distraction
concept *n* *syn* see IDEA
  con percept, sensation, sense-datum, sensum
conception *n* *syn* see IDEA
conceptual *adj* existing or dealing with what exists only in the mind <*conceptual* analysis of a problem>
  syn ideal, ideational, notional
  rel abstract, transcendent, transcendental; absolute, categorical, ultimate; obscure, remote; fanciful, imaginary, visionary
  con practical, pragmatic, realistic; concrete, material, substantial, tangible
concern *n* 1 *syn* see INTEREST 3
  2 *syn* see AFFAIR 1
  3 *syn* see BUSINESS 8
  4 *syn* see CARE 4
  5 *syn* see CONSIDERATION 3
  6 *syn* see UNCERTAINTY
  rel faltering, irresolution; apprehension, misgiving; inquietude, suspense
  7 *syn* see CARE 2
  rel attention, consideration, thoughtfulness
  con aloofness, incuriousness, indifference
  ant unconcern
  8 *syn* see ENTERPRISE 3
  9 *syn* see GADGET 1
concerned *adj* *syn* see INTERESTED
concerning *prep* *syn* see APROPOS
concernment *n* *syn* see CARE 2
concert *vb* 1 *syn* see NEGOTIATE 1
  rel argue, debate, discuss; concur, cooperate, unite
  2 *syn* see AGREE 3
concert *n* *syn* see HARMONY 1
concession *n* *syn* see ALLOWANCE 5
conciliate *vb* *syn* see PACIFY
  rel intervene, mediate; persuade, prevail; calm, quiet, soothe, tranquilize
  con alienate, disaffect, estrange; foment, incite; excite, pique, provoke, stimulate
  ant antagonize
concise *adj* presented with or given to brevity of expression <a *concise* statement of the problem> <a very *concise* thinker>
  syn breviloquent, brief, compendiary, compendious, curt, laconic, short, short and sweet, succinct, summary, terse; *compare* PITHY
  rel abridged, compressed, condensed; marrowy, meaty, pithy; lean
  con diffuse, long-winded, prolix, rambling, voluble, wordy
  ant redundant; verbose
concisely *adv* *syn* see BRIEFLY
conclude *vb* 1 *syn* see DECIDE
  2 *syn* see CLOSE 3
  idiom ring down the curtain
  ant open
  3 *syn* see INFER
concluded *adj* *syn* see COMPLETE 4
concluding *adj* *syn* see LAST
  ant opening
conclusion *n* 1 *syn* see INFERENCE 2
  2 *syn* see FINALE
  3 *syn* see END 2

  4 *syn* see DECISION 1
conclusive *adj* putting an end to debate or question usually by reason of irrefutability <the evidence was *conclusive* and no defense was possible>
  syn definitive
  rel cogent, compelling, convincing, telling; incontrovertible, irrefragable, irrefrangible, irrefutable, unanswerable; deciding, decisive, determinant, determinate, determinative; clear, precise, unambiguous
  con doubtful, dubious, problematic, questionable; credible, plausible, specious; ambiguous, cryptic, enigmatic, obscure
  ant inconclusive
concoct *vb* *syn* see CONTRIVE 2
  rel conceive, envisage, envision; create, discover, originate
concomitant *adj* occurring in company with <good manners are likely to be *concomitant* with good behavior>
  syn accompanying, ancillary, attendant, attending, coincident, collateral, incident, satellite
  rel accessory, adjuvant, supplementary; correlative, corresponding
concomitant *n* *syn* see ACCOMPANIMENT 2
concord *n* 1 *syn* see HARMONY 2
  rel amity, comity, friendship, goodwill; calmness, peace, placidity, serenity, tranquillity
  con conflict, contention, difference, dissension, strife, variance
  ant discord
  2 *syn* see HARMONY 3
  3 *syn* see HARMONY 1
  4 *syn* see TREATY
concord *vb* *syn* see AGREE 3
concordance *n* *syn* see HARMONY 2
concordant *adj* *syn* see HARMONIOUS 2
concours *n* *syn* see CONTEST 2
concourse *n* a coming, flocking, or flowing together <they doubt the universe originated in a chance *concourse* of atoms>
  syn concursion, confluence, gathering, junction, meeting
  rel association, joining, linkage
  con disassociation, parting, separation
concrete *vb* 1 *syn* see HARDEN 1
  2 *syn* see JOIN 1
concupiscence *n* *syn* see LUST 2
concupiscent *adj* *syn* see LUSTFUL 2
concur *vb* 1 *syn* see UNITE 2
  rel accord, agree, harmonize, jibe
  2 *syn* see AGREE 3
  rel accede, acquiesce, assent, consent
  ant contend; altercate
concurrent *adj* *syn* see CONTEMPORARY 1
concurrently *adv* *syn* see TOGETHER 1
concursion *n* *syn* see CONCOURSE
concuss *vb* 1 *syn* see SHAKE 4
  2 *syn* see FORCE 2
concussion *n* *syn* see IMPACT
  rel beating, buffeting, jarring, jolting, pounding, shaking; blow, clip, clout
condemn *vb* 1 *syn* see CRITICIZE
  rel belittle, decry, depreciate, disparage; deprecate, disapprove
  idiom damn with faint praise, find fault with
  con applaud, commend, compliment; acclaim, eulogize, extol, laud, praise; condone, excuse, forgive, pardon
  2 *syn* see SENTENCE
  con deliver, redeem, rescue, save
condemned *adj* *syn* see DAMNED 1
  rel fallen, fated
condensation *n* *syn* see ABRIDGMENT
condense *vb* 1 *syn* see CONTRACT 3
  rel compact, consolidate; curtail, minimize
  con amplify
  2 *syn* see EPITOMIZE 1
  con broaden, expand, extend, widen
  ant amplify
condensed *adj* made shorter and typically simpler <a *condensed* biography>

---

syn synonym(s)
ant antonym(s)
idiom idiomatic equivalent(s)
‖ use limited; if in doubt, see a dictionary

rel related word(s)
con contrasted word(s)

syn canned, capsule, epitomized, pocket, potted
rel abbreviated, abridged, bobbed, bobtail, bobtailed, curtailed, shortened
con elaborated, polished, refined; amplified, enlarged, expanded
condescend *vb syn* see STOOP 1
condign *adj syn* see JUST 3
rel grim, rigorous, stern, strict, stringent; atrocious, awful, dreadful, horrible
condition *n* **1** something that limits or qualifies an agreement or offer < included the *condition* that any heir contesting the will would be automatically disinherited >
syn provision, proviso, reservation, stipulation, strings, terms
rel prerequisite, requirement, requisite; exception, exemption, limitation, modification, qualification, restriction, saving clause
2 *syn* see ESSENTIAL 2
3 *syn* see STATE 1
4 *syn* see ORDER 9
5 *syn* see ORDER 10
6 *syn* see DISEASE 1
conditional *adj* **1** containing or dependent on a condition < our agreement is *conditional* on your raising the needed funds >
syn provisional, provisionary, provisory, tentative
rel iffy, obscure, uncertain; limited, modified, qualified, restricted
con fixed, set, sure
ant unconditional
2 *syn* see DEPENDENT 1
rel provisional, tentative; problematic, questionable; fortuitous, incidental
ant unconditional
condonable *adj syn* see JUSTIFIABLE
rel acceptable, tolerable
condone *vb syn* see EXCUSE 1
rel disregard, forget, ignore, overlook
con deplore, deprecate, disapprove; impugn, reproach
conduce *vb syn* see CONTRIBUTE 2
conduct *n* **1** *syn* see OVERSIGHT 1
2 *syn* see BEHAVIOR
rel bearing, demeanor, mien, posture, stance
conduct *vb* **1** *syn* see GUIDE
2 *syn* see ACCOMPANY
rel convey, transmit
3 to have the direction of and responsibility for < he had *conducted* a small market for many years >
syn carry on, direct, keep, manage, operate, ordain, run
rel administer, handle, head, oversee, supervise; arrange, control, keep up, order, regulate, rule; engineer, lead, pilot, steer
4 to act as a conduit for < shady transactions that *conducted* profits away from the stockholders >
syn carry, channel, convey, funnel, pipe, siphon, traject, transmit
rel remove, separate, take away, withdraw
5 *syn* see BEHAVE 1
conduit *n* **1** *syn* see CHANNEL 1
2 *syn* see PIPELINE
confab *vb syn* see CONFER 2
confabulate *vb syn* see CONFER 2
confabulation *n* **1** *syn* see CONVERSATION 1
2 *syn* see CONVERSATION 2
3 *syn* see CONFERENCE 1
confederacy *n syn* see ALLIANCE 2
confederate *n* one associated with another or others in a wrong or unlawful act < conspiring with his *confederates* to overthrow the government >
syn abettor, accessory, accomplice, coconspirator, conspirator
rel collaborator, fellow traveler; associate, colleague, fellow, partner
confederation *n syn* see ALLIANCE 2
confer *vb* **1** *syn* see GIVE 2
rel allot, provide; vouchsafe
2 to carry on a conversation or discussion usually directed toward reaching a decision or settlement < the President *conferred* with his cabinet about the scandal >
syn advise, collogue, confab, confabulate, consult, huddle, parley, powwow, treat
rel bargain, chaffer, deal, negotiate; argue, debate, discuss; converse, speak, talk
idiom put one's head together with

conference *n* **1** an interchanging of views < took several hours of *conference* to find a solution to the problem >
syn confabulation, deliberation, discussion, rap, ventilation
2 a meeting for the purpose of serious discussion and interchange of views < the association held a *conference* on the problems of aging >
syn colloquium, colloquy, palaver, rap session, seminar
rel round robin, round table
3 *syn* see TALK 4
4 *syn* see LEAGUE 4
conferrer *n syn* see DONOR
confess *vb syn* see ACKNOWLEDGE 1
idiom make a clean breast, open one's heart
confessions *n pl syn* see BIOGRAPHY
confidant *n syn* see FRIEND
confide *vb* **1** to tell confidentially < shyly *confided* her secret >
syn breathe, whisper
rel hint, insinuate, intimate, suggest
con advertise, broadcast, proclaim, publish
2 *syn* see COMMIT 1
rel bestow, present
confidence *n* **1** *syn* see TRUST 1
con distrust, mistrust; despair, hopelessness
ant doubt; apprehension
2 a feeling or showing of adequacy and reliance on oneself and one's powers < had serene *confidence* in his own ability to win through >
syn aplomb, assurance, self-assurance, self-assuredness, self-confidence, self-trust; *compare* EQUANIMITY
rel courage, mettle, resolution, spirit, tenacity; brashness, impudence, presumption
con apprehension, incertitude, misgiving, self-depreciation, self-doubt, uncertitude
ant diffidence
3 *syn* see CERTAINTY
4 *syn* see EFFRONTERY
confidence man *n syn* see SWINDLER
confident *adj* **1** marked by a strong, fearless, and bold belief in oneself and one's capacities < faced his accusers with a *confident* air >
syn assured, sanguine, secure, self-assured, self-confident, undoubtful
rel certain, cocksure, cocky, perky, positive, sure; self-possessed, self-reliant; bold, brave, courageous, dauntless, fearless, intrepid, unafraid, undaunted, valiant
con jittery, nervous, uneasy; afraid, daunted, fearful; doubtful, dubious
ant apprehensive
2 *syn* see SURE 5
3 *syn* see PRESUMPTUOUS
confidential *adj* **1** *syn* see PRIVATE 2
2 *syn* see FAMILIAR 1
rel secret; tried, trustworthy, trusty
configuration *n syn* see FORM 1
confine *vb* **1** *syn* see LIMIT 2
2 *syn* see IMPRISON
confine *n, usu* **confines** *pl* **1** *syn* see ENVIRONS 1
2 *syn* see LIMIT 1
rel circumference, compass, periphery
3 *syn* see RANGE 2
confined *adj syn* see CRAMPED
confinement *n* **1** *syn* see RESTRICTION 2
2 the state attending and consequent to childbirth < had a long difficult *confinement* >
syn accouchement, childbed, lying-in
rel parturition; labor, travail
confirm *vb* **1** *syn* see RATIFY
rel accede, acquiesce, assent, consent, subscribe; validate
idiom make good
con decline, refuse, reject
2 to attest to the truth, genuineness, accuracy, or validity of something < a surprise witness *confirmed* his account of the incident >
syn authenticate, bear out, corroborate, justify, substantiate, validate, verify
rel attest, certify, vouch, witness; back, support, underpin, uphold, warrant; check, check out
con confute, controvert, disprove, refute; contravene, gainsay, impugn, negative, traverse

ant deny; contradict
confirm (in) *vb syn* see HABITUATE 2
confirmation *n syn* see TESTIMONY
confirmative *adj syn* see CORROBORATIVE
confirmatory *adj syn* see CORROBORATIVE
confirmed *adj* **1** *syn* see HABITUAL 2
  2 *syn* see INVETERATE 1
confiscate *vb syn* see APPROPRIATE 1
confiture *n syn* see JAM
conflagrant *adj syn* see BURNING 1
conflagration *n syn* see FIRE 1
conflict *n* **1** *syn* see CONTEST 1
  rel argument, controversy, dispute
  2 *syn* see CONTEST 2
  3 *syn* see DISCORD
conflict *vb syn* see CLASH 2
  rel differ, disagree, vary; disturb, interfere
  idiom run against the tide
conflicting *adj* **1** *syn* see ANTIPATHETIC 1
  2 *syn* see INCONSONANT 1
confluence *n syn* see CONCOURSE
conform *vb* **1** *syn* see ADAPT
  rel attune, harmonize, tune
  2 *syn* see AGREE 4
  con conflict, differ, disagree
  ant diverge
  3 *syn* see HARMONIZE 3
  4 *syn* see OBEY
  idiom toe the line
conformable *adj syn* see ASSORTED 2
  rel appropriate, fitting, suitable; applicable, usable
conformation *n syn* see FORM 1
conforming *adj syn* see DECOROUS 1
conformity *n* **1** *syn* see CONSISTENCY
  2 *syn* see ACQUIESCENCE
confound *vb* **1** *syn* see PUZZLE
  idiom take aback
  2 *syn* see MISTAKE 1
  ant discriminate, distinguish
  3 *syn* see EMBARRASS
  4 *syn* see DISPROVE 1
confounded *adj* **1** *syn* see AGHAST 2
  2 *syn* see DAMNED 2
  3 *syn* see UTTER
confoundedly *adv syn* see EVER 6
confrere *n* **1** *syn* see COLLEAGUE
  2 *syn* see PARTNER
confront *vb* **1** to stand over against in the role of an adversary or enemy < he *confronted* his accusers with perfect aplomb >
  syn affront, encounter, face, meet; *compare* MEET 6
  rel beard, brave, challenge, defy; flout, scorn, scout; oppose, resist, withstand
  idiom come to close quarters with, come up against
  con avoid, elude, evade
  2 *syn* see ACCOST 2
confronting *prep syn* see BEFORE 2
confuse *vb* **1** *syn* see EMBARRASS
  2 to make unclear in mind or purpose < found the city hustle and noise very *confusing* >
  syn addle, ball up, befuddle, bewilder, ‖bumfuzzle, discombobulate, distract, dizzy, fluster, fuddle, mix up, ‖mizzle, ‖momble, muddle, mull, throw off, throw out
  rel misguide, mislead; agitate, bother, discompose, disquiet, flurry, perturb, upset
  3 *syn* see PUZZLE
  4 to make indistinct the elements or true character of (as a discussion) < *confuse* an issue in a debate >
  syn becloud, befog, blur, cloud, fog, muddy
  rel complicate, confound, involve, mix up
  idiom lose in a fog
  con clarify, elucidate; simplify
  5 to throw into disorder < surging waves *confused* the waters > < her accounts were totally *confused* >
  syn foul up, jumble, mix up, muddle, ‖snafu, snarl up, tumble; *compare* DISORDER 1
  rel derange, disarrange, disorder, disorganize, disturb, mess (up), unsettle
  idiom put in a flutter, throw into confusion

6 *syn* see MISREPRESENT
7 *syn* see MISTAKE 1
  ant differentiate
confusion *n* **1** *syn* see RUIN 3
  2 *syn* see EMBARRASSMENT
  3 a condition in which things are out of their normal or proper places or relationships < the room was in complete *confusion* >
  syn ataxia, ‖ballup, chaos, clutter, disarray, disorder, huddle, misorder, muddle, ‖mullock, pell-mell, snarl, topsy-turviness
  rel derangement, disarrangement, disturbance; foul-up, mess, mix-up, muck, ‖mux, ‖snafu; babel, din, hullabaloo, pandemonium
  con methodization, ordering, organization, systematization; method, order, system
  4 *syn* see COMMOTION 2
  rel disorder, disorganization, disturbance; discomfiture, embarrassment
confute *vb syn* see DISPROVE 1
congé *n syn* see PARTING
congeal *vb* **1** *syn* see HARDEN 1
  rel chill, cool, freeze
  2 *syn* see COAGULATE
congenial *adj* **1** *syn* see HARMONIOUS 3
  ant uncongenial
  2 *syn* see CONSONANT 1
  rel companionable, cooperative, social; affable, cordial, genial, gracious, sociable; pleasant, pleasing
  ant uncongenial; antipathetic (*of persons*); abhorrent (*of tasks, responsibilities*)
  3 *syn* see PLEASANT 1
  4 *syn* see GRACIOUS 1
congenital *adj* **1** *syn* see INNATE 1
  2 *syn* see INHERENT
congeries *n syn* see GATHERING 2
congest *vb syn* see FILL 1
conglobate *vb syn* see BALL
conglobe *vb syn* see BALL
conglomerate *adj syn* see MISCELLANEOUS
conglomerate *n* **1** *syn* see AGGREGATE 1
  2 *syn* see SYNDICATE
conglomeration *n* **1** *syn* see ACCUMULATION
  2 *syn* see AGGREGATE 1
congratulate *vb* to express to another one's pleasure in his good fortune or success < *congratulate* a friend when he wins a race >
  syn felicitate
  rel applaud, laud, praise; bless, compliment
  idiom pat one on the back, tender (*or* offer) congratulation, wish one joy, wish one well
  con belittle, depreciate, disparage, knock, run down, slur
congregate *vb syn* see GATHER 6
  rel swarm, teem
  ant disperse
congregation *n syn* see GATHERING 2
  rel audience, disciples, following, public
congress *n syn* see ASSOCIATION 2
congress *vb syn* see GATHER 6
congruity *n syn* see CONSISTENCY
congruous *adj* **1** *syn* see CONSONANT 1
  rel appropriate, fit, fitting, meet; proper, seemly
  ant incongruous
  2 *syn* see HARMONIOUS 2
conjectural *adj syn* see SUPPOSED 1
  con demonstrated; unquestionable
conjecture *n syn* see THEORY 2
  ant fact
conjecture *vb* to draw an inference from slight or inadequate evidence < when he failed to arrive on time she *conjectured* that he was drinking again >
  syn guess, presume, pretend, suppose, surmise, think; *compare* INFER, UNDERSTAND 3
  rel assume, expect, suspect; believe, deem, feel; conceive, fancy, imagine; conclude, estimate, gather, glean, infer, judge
  idiom hazard a conjecture, take for granted

---

syn synonym(s)   **rel** related word(s)
ant antonym(s)   **con** contrasted word(s)
idiom idiomatic equivalent(s)
‖ use limited; if in doubt, see a dictionary

con demonstrate, prove, test, try; ascertain, determine, discover, learn

conjoin *vb* **1** *syn* see JOIN 1
2 *syn* see UNITE 2

conjoint *adj* **1** *syn* see COMMON 1
2 *syn* see COOPERATIVE

conjointly *adv* *syn* see TOGETHER 3

conjointment *n* *syn* see ASSOCIATION 1

conjugal *adj* *syn* see MATRIMONIAL

conjugality *n* *syn* see MARRIAGE 1

conjugate *vb* *syn* see JOIN 1

conjunct *adj* *syn* see COMMON 1

conjunction *n* *syn* see ASSOCIATION 1

conjuration *n* *syn* see SPELL

conjure *vb* *syn* see BEG

conjurer *n* **1** *syn* see MAGICIAN 1
2 *syn* see MAGICIAN 2

conjuring *n* **1** *syn* see MAGIC 1
2 *syn* see MAGIC 2

conjury *n* *syn* see MAGIC 1

‖**conk** *n* **1** *syn* see NOSE 1
2 *syn* see HEAD 1

‖**conk** *n* *syn* see HIT 1

conk *vb* *syn* see DIE 1

con man *n* *syn* see SWINDLER
rel shill
con mark, sucker, victim; greenhorn

connate *adj* **1** *syn* see INNATE 1
2 *syn* see INHERENT
3 *syn* see RELATED

connatural *adj* **1** *syn* see INNATE 1
2 *syn* see RELATED

connect *vb* *syn* see JOIN 1
ant disconnect

connection *n* **1** *syn* see ASSOCIATION 1
2 *syn* see JOINT 1
3 *syn* see JOB 2
4 *syn* see RELIGION 2

connivance *n* *syn* see COMPLICITY

connive *vb* **1** to secretly favor or sympathize with something improper or illicit < *connive* at treason >
syn blink (at), wink (at)
rel condone, disregard, ignore, overlook, tolerate
idiom close (or shut) one's eyes to, let go by (or get by) one's eye, regard with indulgence
con disapprove, disfavor, frown (at *or* upon); disallow, reject, repudiate; disdain, scorn, scout, spurn
2 *syn* see PLOT

connoisseur *n* a person who enjoys with discrimination and appreciation of subtleties and details especially in matters of culture or art < a *connoisseur* of fine wines >
syn aesthete, cognoscente, dilettante
rel bon vivant, epicure, gourmet; adept, authority, critic, expert
con abecedarian, amateur, dabbler, tyro

connotation *n* *syn* see ASSOCIATION 4

connote *vb* **1** *syn* see MEAN 2
2 *syn* see SUGGEST 1

connubial *adj* *syn* see MATRIMONIAL

connubiality *n* *syn* see MARRIAGE 1

conquer *vb* **1** to overcome or gain dominion over by force of arms < leaders who have tried and failed to *conquer* the world >
syn bear down, beat down, crush, defeat, overpower, reduce, subdue, subjugate, vanquish; *compare* DEFEAT 2, OVERTHROW 2, WHIP 2, WIN 1
rel baffle, balk, circumvent, foil, frustrate, outwit, override, thwart; bend, control, master, overmaster, subject, worst
idiom bring one to one's knees, trample in the dust, trample underfoot
con bow, cave, give up, succumb, yield; capitulate, submit, surrender
2 to gain mastery over something by getting the better of obstacles and difficulties < trials faced by the men who *conquered* Mount Everest >
syn best, master, overcome, prevail, triumph; *compare* OVERCOME 1
3 *syn* see OVERCOME 1

conqueror *n* *syn* see VICTOR 1

conquest *n* *syn* see VICTORY 1

rel defeating, overthrow, rout, routing, subdual

consanguine *adj* *syn* see RELATED

‖**consarned** *adj* **1** *syn* see DAMNED 2
2 *syn* see UTTER

conscience *n* *syn* see QUALM

conscienceless *adj* *syn* see UNSCRUPULOUS
rel devious, shifty, tricky, unfair
ant conscientious

conscientious *adj* **1** *syn* see UPRIGHT 2
ant conscienceless
2 *syn* see CAREFUL 2

conscionable *adj* *syn* see CAREFUL 2

conscious *adj* **1** *syn* see AWARE
rel noticing, noting, observing, perceiving, remarking; vigilant, watchful
con forgetful, oblivious, unmindful; disregarding, ignoring, overlooking
ant unconscious
2 *syn* see SELF-CONSCIOUS

consciousness *n* *syn* see CARE 4

conscribe *vb* *syn* see DRAFT 1

conscript *vb* *syn* see DRAFT 1

consecrate *vb* **1** *syn* see DEVOTE 1
con desecrate, profane; defile, pollute
2 *syn* see BLESS 1

consecrated *adj* *syn* see HOLY 1

consecution *n* **1** *syn* see ORDER 5
2 *syn* see SUCCESSION 2

consecutive *adj* following one after another in orderly fashion < it rained for five *consecutive* days >
syn sequent, sequential, serial, subsequent, subsequential, succedent, succeeding, successional, successive; *compare* NEXT
rel after, ensuing, following, later; enlarging, increasing, progressive
con antecedent, preceding, prior

consecutively *adv* *syn* see TOGETHER 2

consent *vb* *syn* see ASSENT
rel allow, let, permit; approve, sanction; concur
con decline; balk, demur, stick, stickle

consent *n* **1** *syn* see PERMISSION
2 *syn* see AGREEMENT 2

consentaneous *adj* *syn* see UNANIMOUS

consentient *adj* *syn* see UNANIMOUS

consequence *n* **1** *syn* see EFFECT 1
con origin, root, source
ant antecedent
2 *syn* see IMPORTANCE
rel exigency, need; fame, honor, renown, reputation, repute
3 *syn* see STATUS 2
4 *syn* see CONCEIT 2

consequent *adj* *syn* see RATIONAL

consequential *adj* *syn* see IMPORTANT 1

consequently *adv* *syn* see THEREFORE

conservancy *n* *syn* see CONSERVATION 1

conservation *n* **1** a deliberate planned guarding and protecting of something felt as precious < *conservation* of our natural resources >
syn conservancy, husbanding, preserval, preservation, salvation, saving
rel attention, care, cherishing, protection; control, directing, governing, management, managing, supervising, supervision
con neglect, squandering, waste
2 *syn* see PRESERVATION 1

conservative *adj* **1** tending to resist or oppose change < took a very *conservative* stance politically >
syn die-hard, fogyish, old-line, orthodox, reactionary, right, tory, traditionalistic
con modern, progressive, radical
ant advanced
2 kept or keeping within bounds < equally *conservative* in speech and action >
syn controlled, discreet, moderate, reasonable, restrained, temperate, unexcessive, unextreme
rel cautious, chary, wary; circumspect, politic, proper, prudent
con expansive, unconstrained; excessive, freewheeling, uncontrolled, unrestrained

conservative *n* *syn* see DIEHARD 1

conservatory *n* *syn* see GREENHOUSE

conserve *vb syn* see SAVE 3
  rel keep up, maintain, support, sustain
  con dissipate, fritter, squander, waste
conserve *n syn* see JAM
consider *vb* **1** to give serious thought to <*consider* the risk you would be taking>
  syn contemplate, excogitate, mind, perpend, ponder, study, think (out *or* over), weigh
  rel meditate, muse, ruminate; cogitate, reason, reflect, speculate, think; examine, inspect, look (at), scan, scrutinize, see
  idiom bestow thought to, chew the cud over, revolve (*or* turn over) in one's mind
  con disregard, ignore, neglect, overlook, slight
  2 *syn* see EYE 1
  rel envisage, envision
  3 to come to view, judge, or classify <he *considered* thrift essential to success>
  syn account, deem, reckon, regard, view; *compare* FEEL 3
  rel conceive, fancy, imagine, think; conclude, gather, infer, judge, rule
  4 *syn* see ADMIRE 2
  5 *syn* see FEEL 3
considerable *adj* **1** *syn* see IMPORTANT 1
  2 tending more to the large than the small <buckled down with his ax and made a *considerable* impression on the woodpile>
  syn good, respectable, ‖right smart, sensible, sizable, ‖smart
  rel able, capable, competent; active, effective, efficacious; important, notable, significant; goodly, pretty, substantial, tidy
  con insignificant, meager, slight, trivial; big, grand, great, huge
  3 *syn* see BIG 1
considerably *adv syn* see WELL 8
considerate *adj* **1** *syn* see CAUTIOUS
  2 *syn* see THOUGHTFUL 3
  rel kind, kindly; compassionate, sympathetic, tender, warmhearted; amiable, complaisant, obliging
  ant inconsiderate
  3 *syn* see GENEROUS 1
considerately *adv syn* see WELL 2
  rel solicitously, tenderly; altruistically, benevolently, charitably
  con austerely, harshly, severely, strictly
considerateness *n syn* see CONSIDERATION 3
consideration *n* **1** *syn* see ATTENTION 1
  2 *syn* see MOTIVE 1
  3 thoughtful and sympathetic attention <showed great *consideration* to the needs of others>
  syn concern, considerateness, regard, solicitude
  rel awareness, heed, heedfulness, mindfulness; forbearance, mercy, quarter
  con disregard, heedlessness, unconcern, unmindfulness; inconsiderateness; contempt, despite, disdain, disinterest, scorn
  4 *syn* see REGARD 4
considered *adj syn* see DELIBERATE 1
  rel intentional, voluntary, willful
  con impulsive, instinctive, spontaneous; headlong, impetuous, precipitate
  ant unconsidered
considering *conj syn* see BECAUSE
consign *vb* **1** *syn* see COMMIT 1
  rel resign, surrender, yield
  2 *syn* see SEND 1
consist *vb* **1** to have existence or a place <our national strength *consists* not solely in military readiness>
  syn dwell, exist, inhere, lie, reside
  rel be, subsist; abide, repose, rest
  idiom have one's (*or* a) place
  2 *syn* see AGREE 4
consistency *n* agreement or harmony of parts, traits, or features <his adversary had to admit the *consistency* of his position>
  syn coherence, conformity, congruity, correspondence; *compare* HARMONY 2
  rel agreement, concord, consonance; likeness, similarity; apposition, aptness, felicity, fitness, suitability
  con incoherence, incongruity; impropriety, inappropriateness, unsuitability
  ant inconsistency
consistent *adj* **1** *syn* see SAME 3
  2 *syn* see CONSONANT 1

consistently *adv syn* see USUALLY 1
consociate *n syn* see PARTNER
console *vb syn* see COMFORT
  rel calm, relieve, tranquilize; animate, hearten, inspirit
  idiom lift the spirits of
  con agitate, discompose, disquiet, disturb, perturb, upset
consolidate *vb syn* see UNIFY 1
  rel amalgamate, blend, fuse, merge; set, solidify
  con part, sever, sunder; liquefy, melt
consolidating *adj syn* see INTEGRATIVE
consolidation *n* **1** *syn* see UNIFICATION
  2 a union of two or more businesses <*consolidation* is often accompanied by a new corporate name>
  syn amalgamation, merger
  ant dissolution
consonance *n* **1** *syn* see HARMONY 2
  con discrepancy, incompatibility, incongruousness
  ant discord
  2 *syn* see HARMONY 1
  ant dissonance
consonant *adj* **1** conforming (as to a pattern, a standard, or a relationship) without discord or difficulty <his performance was seldom *consonant* with his very real abilities>
  syn agreeable, compatible, congenial, congruous, consistent, sympathetic; *compare* HARMONIOUS 2
  rel accordant, conformable, harmonious; coincident, concurrent; en rapport
  con discordant, discrepant; incompatible, incongruous, inconsistent
  ant inconsonant
  2 *syn* see HARMONIOUS 1
  ant dissonant
  3 *syn* see LIKE
  4 *syn* see RESONANT
consort *n* **1** *syn* see ACCOMPANIMENT 2
  2 *syn* see SPOUSE
consort *vb syn* see AGREE 4
consort (with) *vb syn* see ACCOMPANY
consortium *n syn* see ASSOCIATION 2
conspectus *n syn* see ABRIDGMENT
conspicuous *adj* **1** *syn* see CLEAR 5
  2 *syn* see NOTICEABLE
  rel celebrated, eminent, illustrious; showy
  con common, everyday, ordinary; covert, secret; concealed, hidden
  ant inconspicuous
conspiracy *n syn* see PLOT 2
  rel sedition, treason; disloyalty, faithlessness, falsity, perfidiousness, perfidy, treacherousness, treachery
  con faith, faithfulness, fealty, loyalty
conspirator *n syn* see CONFEDERATE
conspire *vb syn* see PLOT
‖**constable** *n syn* see POLICEMAN
constancy *n syn* see ATTACHMENT 1
constant *adj* **1** *syn* see FAITHFUL 1
  rel abiding, clinging, enduring, lasting, persistent, persisting
  con capricious, mercurial
  ant fickle, inconstant
  2 *syn* see INFLEXIBLE 3
  con fluctuant, fluctuating, fluctuational, unstable
  ant inconstant, variable
  3 *syn* see SAME 3
  4 *syn* see STEADY 2
  5 *syn* see CONTINUAL
  rel chronic, confirmed, inveterate; dogged, obstinate, pertinacious; persevering
  con alternate, intermittent, recurrent; infrequent, occasional, sporadic
  ant fitful
constantly *adv syn* see ALWAYS 1
  idiom day after day, day in, day out
  ant occasionally
constate *vb syn* see ASSERT 1

---

syn synonym(s)   *rel* related word(s)
ant antonym(s)   *con* contrasted word(s)
idiom idiomatic equivalent(s)
‖ use limited; if in doubt, see a dictionary

consternate *vb syn* see DISMAY 1
consternation *n syn* see FEAR 1
  rel confusion, muddle, muddlement; bewilderment, distraction, perplexity
  con composure, equanimity, phlegm, sangfroid; aplomb, poise, self-command, self-possession
constipate *vb syn* see STULTIFY
constipated *adj* being unable to defecate regularly and without difficulty <complained that she was constantly *constipated* >
  syn astricted, bound, costive, obstipated
constituent *n syn* see ELEMENT 2
  rel division, fraction, part, portion
  con complex, economy, organism, system; amalgam, blend, composite, compound
  ant aggregate, whole
constitute *vb* 1 to be all or a fundamental part of the substance of <water *constitutes* the greater part of the human body>
  syn compose, comprise, form, make, make up
  rel embody, incorporate, integrate; complement, complete, fill out, flesh (out)
  2 *syn* see ENACT 1
  3 *syn* see FOUND 2
constitution *n* 1 *syn* see PHYSIQUE
  2 *syn* see MAKEUP 1
constitutional *adj syn* see INHERENT
  con anomalous, irregular, unnatural
  ant advenient
constitutional *n syn* see WALK 1
  rel ambulation, footwork, legwork, perambulation
constitutive *adj syn* see ESSENTIAL 2
constrain *vb* 1 *syn* see FORCE 2
  2 *syn* see RESTRAIN 1
  3 *syn* see DENY 3
  rel abridge, curtail, deprive; ban, bar, disallow, enjoin
  4 *syn* see IMPRISON
  5 *syn* see PRESS 1
  6 *syn* see DISTRESS 2
constrained *adj syn* see RESERVED 1
constrainment *n syn* see RESTRICTION 2
constraint *n* 1 *syn* see FORCE 4
  rel repression, suppression; driving, impelling, impulsion; goad, motive, spring, spur
  2 *syn* see RESTRICTION 2
constrict *vb* 1 *syn* see CONTRACT 3
  rel curb, restrain; circumscribe, confine, limit, restrict
  con enlarge, expand, increase, maximize
  2 to make narrow or narrower <the muscles that *constrict* the sphincter>
  syn constringe, narrow
  rel gather, plait, pucker; compress, constrain, squeeze; astringe
  con broaden, dilate, distend, widen
  ant expand
constringe *vb syn* see CONSTRICT 2
construal *n syn* see EXPLANATION 1
construct *vb* 1 *syn* see MAKE 3
  2 *syn* see BUILD 1
  3 *syn* see ERECT 5
construction *n* 1 *syn* see MAKEUP 1
  2 *syn* see EXPLANATION 1
constructive *adj syn* see IMPLICIT 2
  rel inferential, ratiocinative; construable, interpretable, renderable
  con clear, evident, obvious, patent
  ant manifest
construe *vb syn* see EXPLAIN 1
consuetude *n syn* see HABIT 1
consult *vb syn* see CONFER 2
  rel cogitate, counsel, deliberate; consider, examine, review
consume *vb* 1 to bring to an end by or as if by the action of a destroying force <the village was *consumed* by fire>
  syn devour, eat, eat up, exhaust, use up
  rel destroy, raze, ruin, wreck; annihilate, extinguish; crush, overwhelm, suppress
  con bolster, brace, buttress, hold up, prop, stay, support, sustain; build, construct, create, make, produce; renew, restore
  2 *syn* see WASTE 2
  3 *syn* see GO 4
  4 *syn* see EAT 1

5 to eat or drink usually gluttonously or without measure <*consumed* dozens of burgers and a case of beer>
  syn polish off, punish, put away, put down, shift, swill; *compare* EAT 1
  rel absorb, ingest; devour, gobble (up), gorge, wolf; down, gulp, guzzle, inhale, swallow
  idiom dispose of
  6 *syn* see MONOPOLIZE
consumedly *adv syn* see EVER 6
consuming *adj syn* see ENGROSSING
consummate *adj* 1 brought to the highest possible point of perfection <the difficult allegro passages displayed her *consummate* skill>
  syn accomplished, finished, perfected, ripe, virtuosic; *compare* PERFECT 2
  rel faultless, flawless, impeccable, perfect; practiced, skilled, trained; able, gifted, talented; inimitable, peerless, superb, superlative, supreme, transcendent, unsurpassable
  con callow, crude, green, raw, rough, uncouth; defective, deficient, inadequate
  2 *syn* see UTTER
consummate *vb syn* see CLOSE 3
consumption *n syn* see TUBERCULOSIS
contact *n* 1 the state of being in or coming into close association or connection <shuddered at the *contact* of his icy hand>
  syn contingence, touch
  rel closeness, contiguity, nearness, propinquity, proximity; impingement, taction, touching; association, connection, relation; oneness, union, unity
  con breach, break, rift, rupture, split; insularity, isolation, seclusion, segregation, separation; distance, farness, remoteness
  2 a situation permitting exchange of ideas and opinions <tried for several days to get in *contact* with her brother>
  syn commerce, communication, communion, intercommunication, intercourse
  rel association, companionship, fellowship; oneness, union, unity; accord, concord, harmony, rapport; empathy, sympathy, understanding
contact *vb syn* see REACH 4
contagion *n syn* see POISON
  rel contamination, corruption, pollution, taint; miasma
contagious *adj* 1 *syn* see INFECTIOUS 2
  2 *syn* see INFECTIOUS 3
contain *vb* 1 *syn* see COMPOSE 4
  2 to have or be capable of having within <the box *contained* family papers> <a mug that will *contain* a quart of ale>
  syn accommodate, hold
  rel harbor, house, lodge, shelter; admit, receive, take, take in
  3 *syn* see INCLUDE
contaminate *vb* 1 to debase by making impure or unclean <feared her child's morals would be *contaminated* by others>
  syn defile, pollute, soil, taint; *compare* TAINT 1
  rel corrupt, debase, debauch, deprave, pervert, vitiate; harm, injure, spoil
  con better, elevate, improve
  ant purify
  2 to render unfit for use by the introduction of unwholesome or undesirable elements <water *contaminated* by sewage>
  syn befoul, foul, pollute
  rel infect; poison; dirty, soil
  ant purify
contemn *vb syn* see DESPISE
contemplate *vb* 1 *syn* see EYE 1
  rel ponder, reflect, study; examine, inspect, scan, scrutinize
  2 *syn* see CONSIDER 1
  rel drift, roam
  3 *syn* see INTEND 2
  idiom have in view
contemplative *adj syn* see THOUGHTFUL 1
  rel musing, weighing; reasoning
  idiom in a brown study
contemporaneous *adj syn* see CONTEMPORARY 1
contemporary *adj* 1 existing or occurring at the same time <the story has come down from several *contemporary* sources>
  syn coetaneous, coeval, coexistent, coexisting, concurrent, contemporaneous, simultaneous, synchronal, synchronic, synchronous

rel accompanying, attendant, attending, coincident, concomitant; current, existing, present; associated, connected, linked, related
con antecedent, foregoing, preceding, previous, prior; ensuing, following, succeeding
2 syn see PRESENT
3 syn see UP-TO-DATE

contempt *n* **1 syn** see DESPITE 1
rel antipathy, aversion; distaste, repugnance
con awe, fear, reverence
ant regard
2 syn see DISGRACE
3 syn see DEFIANCE 2

contemptible *adj* arousing or meriting scorn or disdain <a *contemptible* attempt to blame his wife for his failure>
syn beggarly, cheap, despicable, despisable, mean, pitiable, pitiful, scummy, scurvy, shabby, sorry; *compare* BASE 3
rel abhorrent, abominable, detestable, hateful, odious; abject, ignoble, sordid; bad, inferior, poor, sad; disgusting, scrimy, shameful; outcast
con creditable, estimable, honorable, noble; high-minded, high-principled, principled, true, upright; honest, square, straight
ant admirable

contend *vb* **1** to strive in opposition to someone or something <*contending* against the temptation to look behind him>
syn battle, fight, oppugn, tug, war
rel combat, oppose, resist, withstand; contest, cope (with), vie
2 syn see MAINTAIN 2
rel report, say, tell; charge, enjoin, urge; dictate, prescribe
3 syn see COMPETE 1
rel combat, oppose, resist, withstand; confront, encounter, face, meet, stand

content *vb* **syn** see SATISFY 3
rel delight, thrill, tickle; bewitch, captivate, charm, enrapture
con disappoint, dishearten, displease
ant discontent

contention *n* **1 syn** see DISCORD
rel altercation, quarrel, squabble, wrangle; argument, controversy, dispute
con agreement, coincidence, concurrence
2 syn see ARGUMENT 2
3 syn see THESIS 1

contentious *adj* **1 syn** see BELLIGERENT
rel contrary, froward, perverse; captious, carping, caviling, faultfinding
con calm, serene, tranquil; amiable, complaisant, good-natured, obliging
ant peaceable
2 prone to wordy contention <a *contentious* old chap, always ready for an argument>
syn argumentative, controversial, disputatious, litigious, polemical
rel fiery, hasty, hotheaded, impetuous, peppery; belligerent, bellicose, scrappy
con amiable, complaisant, good-natured, obliging; agreeable, cooperative, understanding

conterminous *adj* **syn** see ADJACENT 3

contest *vb* **1 syn** see COMPETE 1
rel endeavor
2 syn see RESIST

contest *n* **1** earnest struggle for superiority or victory <the rival factions continued in *contest* for several years>
syn competition, conflict, emulation, rivalry, strife, striving, tug-of-war, warfare
rel brush, encounter, skirmish; action, battle, engagement
2 a competitive encounter between groups or individuals <there were *contests* of skill and of wit>
syn competition, concours, conflict, meet, meeting, rencontre
rel proving, testing, trial, trying

contestation *n* **syn** see THESIS 1

contiguity *n* **syn** see PROXIMITY

contiguous *adj* **1 syn** see ADJACENT 3
rel close, near, nearby, nigh
con apart, separate; distant, remote
2 syn see NEIGHBORING

contiguously *adv* **syn** see IMMEDIATELY 1

contiguousness *n* **syn** see PROXIMITY

continence *n* **syn** see TEMPERANCE 2

rel self-restraint; moderation, temperateness; chasteness, chastity, purity
con self-indulgence; excessiveness, inordinateness; lasciviousness, lecherousness, lewdness, licentiousness, wantonness
ant incontinence

continent *adj* **syn** see ABSTEMIOUS
rel bridled, curbed, inhibited, restrained; chaste, pure
con self-indulgent, spoiled
ant incontinent

contingence *n* **syn** see CONTACT 1

contingency *n* **syn** see JUNCTURE 2
rel break, chance, occasion, opportunity

contingent *adj* **1 syn** see ACCIDENTAL
rel unanticipated, unforeseeable, unforeseen; likely, possible, probable
con certain, inevitable, necessary
2 syn see DEPENDENT 1

continual *adj* continuing without intermission and seemingly without end <they were tired of her *continual* nagging>
syn around-the-clock, ceaseless, constant, continuous, endless, everlasting, incessant, interminable, minutely, perpetual, timeless, unceasing, unending, unintermitted, unintermittent, uninterrupted, unremitting
rel abiding, enduring, persistent, persisting, staying; unvarying; unchanging, unfailing, unflagging, unwaning; relentless, running, steady
con ephemeral, evanescent, impermanent, short-lived, temporary, transient, transitory

continually *adv* **syn** see TOGETHER 2

continuance *n* **syn** see RUN 2
rel constancy, longevity, permanence; survival

continuation *n* **1** uninterrupted existence or succession <the *continuation* of political disorder in Northern Ireland>
syn continuity, duration, endurance, persistence
rel extension, prolongation, protraction
ant termination
2 syn see RUN 2
ant cessation

continue *vb* **1** to remain indefinitely in existence or in a particular state or course <many traditional beliefs still *continue*> <do you expect to *continue* in school for the rest of your life?>
syn abide, carry through, endure, last, perdure, persist
rel carry on, carry over, ride, run on; outlast, outlive, survive; remain, stay
con cease, desist, discontinue, quit; arrest, check, interrupt; defer, intermit, postpone, stay, suspend
ant discontinue
2 syn see RESUME 2

continuing *adj* **syn** see OLD 2

continuity *n* **syn** see CONTINUATION 1

continuous *adj* **syn** see CONTINUAL
ant discontinuous

continuously *adv* **1 syn** see TOGETHER 2
2 syn see ALWAYS 1

contort *vb* **syn** see DEFORM
rel bend, curve, twist

contour *n* **syn** see OUTLINE

contra *prep* **syn** see AGAINST 1

contra *adv* **syn** see AGAIN 5

contra *n* **syn** see OPPOSITE

contraband *adj* prohibited or excluded by law or treaty <fur or feathers from endangered species are *contraband* in advanced nations>
syn banned, hot
rel disapproved, proscribed, taboo; forbidden, prohibited; excluded, shut out

contraband *vb* **syn** see SMUGGLE

contraception *n* **syn** see BIRTH CONTROL

contract *n* a usually legally enforceable arrangement between two or more parties <a *contract* for a new roof>
syn agreement, bargain, bond, compact, convention, covenant, pact, transaction; *compare* AGREEMENT 2, TREATY

---

syn synonym(s)	*rel* related word(s)
ant antonym(s)	*con* contrasted word(s)
idiom idiomatic equivalent(s)	
‖ use limited; if in doubt, see a dictionary	

contract *vb* **1** to become affected by a disease or disorder <*contracted* a severe cold that later turned into pneumonia>
syn catch, come down (with), get, sicken (with *or* of), take
rel acquire, obtain; decline, fail, sink, weaken; afflict, derange, disorder, indispose, upset; bring on, cause, induce; succumb (to)
idiom be laid by the heels by, fall (a) victim to
2 *syn* see INCUR
3 to make or become smaller in bulk or volume <*contract* a muscle>
syn compress, concentrate, condense, constrict, shrink
rel decrease, diminish, dwindle, lessen, reduce
con dilate, distend, inflate, swell
ant expand
contracted *adj syn* see ENGAGED 2
contradict *vb syn* see DENY 4
rel dispute; belie, falsify, garble
con authenticate, substantiate, verify
ant corroborate; confirm
contradiction *n syn* see DENIAL 2
contradictory *n syn* see OPPOSITE
contradictory *adj syn* see OPPOSITE
rel negating, nullifying; adverse, antagonistic, counteractive
con agreeing, jibing, squaring, tallying
ant corroboratory; confirmatory
contradistinction *n syn* see ANTAGONISM 2
contraposition *n syn* see ANTAGONISM 2
contraption *n syn* see DEVICE 2
contrariant *n syn* see ANTIPATHETIC 1
contrariety *n syn* see ANTAGONISM 2
contrariwise *adv syn* see AGAIN 5
idiom on (*or* to) the contrary
contrary *n syn* see OPPOSITE
contrary *adj* **1** *syn* see OPPOSITE
2 *syn* see ANTIPATHETIC 1
3 obstinately self-willed in refusing to concur, conform, or submit <why be *contrary* about something that you cannot change>
syn balky, cross-grained, froward, ornery, perverse, restive, wayward, wrongheaded
rel headstrong, intractable, recalcitrant, refractory, unruly; contumacious, insubordinate, rebellious; dissentient, dissident, nonconforming, nonconformist, recusant; obstinate, stubborn
con amenable, biddable, docile, obedient, tractable; amiable, obliging; acquiescent, compliant; forbearing, long-suffering, tolerant
ant complaisant
contrary *adv syn* see AGAIN 5
contrast *vb syn* see COMPARE 2
contravene *vb* **1** *syn* see VIOLATE 1
rel encroach, intrude, overstep, trespass
2 *syn* see DENY 4
rel combat, fight, oppose, resist; abjure, disclaim, disown, exclude, reject, repudiate, spurn
con accept, agree, subscribe (to); admit, allow, own
ant uphold (*as a principle*); allege (*as a right or claim*)
contravention *n syn* see BREACH 1
rel crime, offense, sin, vice
contrawise *adv syn* see AGAIN 5
contretemps *n syn* see MISFORTUNE
contribute *vb* **1** to give in common with others <*contribute* to a fund for handicapped children>
syn chip in, come through, kick in, pitch in, subscribe; *compare* GIVE 1
idiom put something in the pot, sweeten the kitty
2 to have a share in something (as an act or effect) <careful planning *contributed* greatly to the success of the project>
syn conduce, redound, tend
rel aid, help, assist; add (to), augment, supplement; fortify, recruit, reinforce, strengthen
idiom do one's bit, have a hand in
con detract, minus, subtract, take away
contribution *n syn* see DONATION
contributory *adj syn* see AUXILIARY
contrite *adj syn* see REMORSEFUL
contriteness *n syn* see PENITENCE
contrition *n syn* see PENITENCE
contriturate *vb syn* see PULVERIZE 1
contrivance *n* **1** *syn* see DEVICE 2

2 *syn* see INVENTION
contrive *vb* **1** *syn* see PLOT
rel develop, elaborate, work out
2 to use ingenuity in making or doing or achieving an end <*contrived* a useful camp stove from a few bricks and a piece of screen>
syn concoct, cook (up), devise, dream up, formulate, frame, hatch (up), invent, make up, vamp (up)
rel plan, plot, project, scheme; fabricate, fashion, make, manufacture; handle, manipulate, move; rig
control *vb* **1** *syn* see COMPOSE 4
rel adjust, regulate; curb, master, quell, subdue
2 *syn* see GOVERN 3
rel regulate, supervise; discipline
idiom put through the mill (*or* a course of sprouts), take in hand
control *n syn* see POWER 1
controlled *adj syn* see CONSERVATIVE 2
controversial *adj syn* see CONTENTIOUS 2
controversy *n* **1** *syn* see ARGUMENT 2
2 *syn* see QUARREL
controvert *vb syn* see DISPROVE 1
rel challenge, oppugn, question
contumacious *adj syn* see INSUBORDINATE
rel contrary, froward, perverse; alienated, disaffected, estranged, irreconcilable
con acquiescent, compliant, resigned
ant obedient
contumacy *n syn* see DEFIANCE 2
contumelious *adj* **1** *syn* see ABUSIVE
2 *syn* see INSOLENT 2
ant obsequious
contumely *n* **1** *syn* see ABUSE
rel animadversion, aspersion, reflection, stricture
idiom hard (*or* bitter) words
2 *syn* see AFFRONT
contuse *vb syn* see BRUISE 1
contusion *n syn* see BRUISE
conundrum *n syn* see MYSTERY
convalesce *vb syn* see IMPROVE 3
convenance *n syn* see FORM 3
convene *vb* **1** to begin a session (as of a legislature or conference) <the council *convened* at 10 o'clock>
syn meet, open, sit
idiom hold a meeting (*or* session)
2 *syn* see SUMMON 2
rel convoke, muster
3 *syn* see CONVOKE
convenience *n* **1** *syn* see AMENITY 2
2 *syn* see TOILET
convenience *vb syn* see OBLIGE 2
convenient *adj* **1** *syn* see GOOD 2
2 situated within easy reach <left his glasses *convenient* to his book>
syn adjacent, close-at-hand, close-by, handy, near-at-hand, nearby
rel close, near, nigh; immediate, next
idiom at one's beck and call, at one's fingertips, in one's immediate neighborhood, under one's nose
ant inconvenient
convention *n* **1** *syn* see TREATY
2 *syn* see CONTRACT
rel accord, understanding
3 *syn* see FORM 3
rel canon, law, precept, rule; custom, practice
conventional *adj* **1** according with or based on generally accepted and well-established usage <took a very *conventional* view of his duty>
syn button-down, orthodox, square, straight; *compare* TRADITIONAL 1
rel moderate, sober, temperate; constrained, restrained; dependable, reliable, responsible; conscientious, fastidious, nice, punctilious, scrupulous; conservative, traditionalistic
ant unconventional
2 *syn* see TRADITIONAL 1
3 *syn* see CEREMONIAL
rel decent, decorous, proper, seemly; correct, precise, right
con lax, negligent, remiss, slack; artless, ingenuous, naive, natural, simple, unsophisticated

ant unconventional

converge *vb* to come to or trend toward a common point < the main streets *converge* on a central square >
  syn concenter, concentrate, focus, meet
  idiom come to a center, come (*or* run) together

conversant *adj* **1 syn** see AWARE
  ant ignorant
  2 syn see FAMILIAR 3
  rel sensible; up-to-date; apprehending, comprehending, perceptive, percipient
  con unfamiliar; nescient
  ant unconversant

conversation *n* **1** oral exchange of information or ideas < leaned against the fence in casual *conversation* >
  syn chat, colloquy, confabulation, converse, dialogue, parley
  rel discussion; discourse, speech, talk
  2 an instance of conversational exchange < had a long *conversation* about family problems >
  syn colloquy, confabulation, dialogue, talk; *compare* CHAT 2
  rel debate, deliberation, discussion, ventilation; comment, observation, remark; cross talk, repartee

conversation piece *n syn* see CURIOSITY 2

converse *vb* to engage in conversation < they *conversed* quietly while waiting for their friend >
  syn chat, chin, colloque, talk, visit, yarn; *compare* CHAT 1

converse (in) *vb syn* see SPEAK 3

converse *n* **1 syn** see CONVERSATION 1
  2 syn see COMMUNICATION 3

converse *adj syn* see OPPOSITE

converse *n syn* see OPPOSITE

conversely *adv syn* see AGAIN 5

conversion *n* **1** fundamental alteration in one's system of beliefs < Judaism does not encourage *conversion* of gentiles >
  syn metanoia, rebirth
  rel about-face, reversal, turning; reclamation, regeneration
  idiom change of heart
  2 change of one thing to another usually by substitution < *conversion* of locomotives from steam to diesel power >
  syn alteration, changeover, shift, transformation
  rel change, modification, qualification; metamorphosis, mutation, permutation, transmutation; innovation, novelty

convert *vb* **1** to induce (another or others) to accept the validity of something (as a belief, course of action, or point of view) < Chinese missionaries *converted* many Japanese to Buddhism >
  syn bring, lead, move, persuade
  rel redeem, reform, save; bend, bias, incline, sway; actuate, budge, impel; proselyte, proselytize
  2 syn see TRANSFORM
  rel fabricate, forge, make, manufacture; apply, employ, use, utilize

convey *vb* **1 syn** see CARRY 1
  2 syn see COMMUNICATE 1
  rel project, put across
  3 syn see TRANSFER 4
  rel commit, consign, relegate
  4 syn see CONDUCT 4

conveyance *n* **1 syn** see TRANSPORTATION 1
  2 syn see DEED 3
  3 syn see VEHICLE 3

convict *n* a person serving time in prison after conviction as a criminal < mixing hardened *convicts* with juvenile offenders >
  syn ‖con, jailbird, ‖lag, loser, prison bird
  rel long-termer, longtimer; ‖stir bug; recidivist, repeater

conviction *n* **1 syn** see CERTAINTY
  con dubiety, dubiosity, uncertainty; disbelief, incredulity, unbelief
  2 syn see OPINION
  rel doctrine, dogma, tenet

convince *vb* **1 syn** see ASSURE 2
  2 syn see INDUCE 1

convincing *adj* **1 syn** see AUTHENTIC 1
  2 syn see VALID

convivial *adj syn* see SOCIAL 1
  rel lively, vivacious; jocund, jolly, merry
  con grave, sedate, serious, sober, solemn, somber; reserved, reticent, silent
  ant taciturn; stolid

convoke *vb* to bring together by or as if by summons < the ruler *convoked* his council >

syn assemble, call, convene, summon; *compare* SUMMON 2
  rel collect, congregate, gather; ask, bid, invite, request; meet, sit
  con adjourn, close, dissolve, prorogue, recess, suspend; disperse, scatter

convoluted *adj syn* see WINDING

convoy *vb syn* see ACCOMPANY
  rel defend, guard, protect, safeguard, shield

convulse *vb syn* see SHAKE 4

convulsion *n syn* see COMMOTION 1
  rel cataclysm, disaster; quaking, rocking, shaking, tottering, trembling

cook *vb* **1** to make ready or fit for eating by the use of heat < liked everything well-*cooked* >
  syn do
  2 syn see BURN 3

cook (up) *vb syn* see CONTRIVE 2

cookshop *n syn* see EATING HOUSE

cool *adj* **1 syn** see COLD 1
  ant warm
  2 freed or giving the impression of freedom from all agitation or excitement < they looked *cool* and very formidable >
  syn collected, composed, disimpassioned, imperturbable, nonchalant, unflappable, unruffled; *compare* HAPPY-GO-LUCKY
  rel calm, placid, serene, tranquil; aloof, detached, indifferent; impassive, phlegmatic, stolid; assured, confident, self-possessed
  con fervent, fervid, impassioned, passionate, perfervid; discomposed, disturbed, flurried, flustered, perturbed, upset
  ant ardent; agitated
  3 syn see UNSOCIABLE
  ‖**4 syn** see MARVELOUS 2

cool *vb* **1 syn** see COMPOSE 4
  2 syn see MURDER 1

cooler *n syn* see JAIL

coolness *n syn* see EQUANIMITY

‖**coon** *vb syn* see STEAL 1

coon's age *n syn* see AGE 2

‖**coony** *adj syn* see CLEVER 4

coop *n syn* see JAIL

coop *vb syn* see ENCLOSE 1
  rel bar, block, hinder, impede, obstruct

cooperate *vb syn* see UNITE 2
  rel agree, coincide
  con annul, negate, nullify; negative, neutralize
  ant counteract

cooperative *adj* involving joint action in producing a result < the need of *cooperative* efforts to effect lasting social change >
  syn coacting, coactive, coefficient, conjoint, synergetic, synergic
  rel collaborative, concerted; noncompetitive, uncompetitive
  con competitive, emulous, rivaling, vying; antagonistic, conflicting, oppugnant
  ant counteractive

coordinate *vb syn* see HARMONIZE 3

coordinate *n* **1 syn** see OPPOSITE NUMBER
  2 syn see MATE 5

‖**cop** *vb syn* see STEAL 1

cop *n syn* see POLICEMAN

copartner *n syn* see PARTNER

copious *adj syn* see PLENTIFUL
  rel exuberant, lush, luxuriant
  con exiguous, scant, scanty, scrimpy, spare, sparse; slender, slight, slim, tenuous, thin
  ant meager

‖**cop out** *vb syn* see DIE 1

‖**copper** *n syn* see POLICEMAN

copy *n* **1 syn** see IMITATION
  2 syn see REPRODUCTION
  rel counterpart, parallel; impress, impression, imprint, print; effigy, image, likeness
  ant original

copy *vb* to make a copy of < had her more valuable jewelry *copied* >
  syn duplicate, imitate, reduplicate, replicate, reproduce

---

rel ditto, repeat; counterfeit, fake, sham, simulate; ape, burlesque, mock, parody, take off, travesty
ant originate

coquet *vb syn* see TRIFLE 1

coquette *n syn* see FLIRT

coquettish *adj syn* see COY 2

cordial *adj syn* see GRACIOUS 1
rel responsive, sympathetic, tender, warm, warmhearted; heartfelt, hearty, sincere, wholehearted
con cold, cool, frigid, frosty; aloof, detached, disinterested, indifferent; reserved, silent, taciturn

cordiality *n syn* see AMENITY 1
rel responsiveness, sympathy, understanding, warmth; mutuality, reciprocity; approbation, approval, favor
con cross-purposes, difference, disagreement, misunderstanding, odds, variance; disapprobation, disapproval, disfavor

core *n* 1 *syn* see CENTER 1
2 *syn* see BODY 3
3 *syn* see SUBSTANCE 2
rel consequence, import, importance, significance
4 *syn* see CENTER 3
rel base, basis, foundation; beginning, commencement, origin, start

‖**corker** *n syn* ‖DILLY, crackerjack, ‖daisy, dandy, humdinger, jimdandy, knockout, ‖lalapalooza, ‖lulu, nifty

corkscrew *vb syn* see WIND 2

corner *n* 1 *syn* see PREDICAMENT
2 *syn* see MONOPOLY

corner *vb* to get into one's control or a position from which escape is difficult < *cornered* him at a party and tried to borrow a hundred dollars >
syn bottle (up), collar, tree
rel bother, disturb, put out, trouble; capture, catch, nab, seize, trap
idiom chase up a tree, drive (or run) into a corner, get (or have) on the ropes

cornerwise *adv syn* see DIAGONALLY

corny *adj syn* see TRITE

corollary *n syn* see EFFECT 1

coronal *n syn* see WREATH

coronet *n syn* see WREATH

corporal *adj syn* see BODILY 1

corporation *n syn* see POTBELLY

corporeal *adj* 1 *syn* see BODILY 1
2 *syn* see MATERIAL 1

corps *n syn* see COMPANY 4

corpse *n* a dead body especially of a human being < concealed the *corpse* under some rubbish >
syn body, cadaver, carcass, ‖cold meat, ‖deader, mort, remains, stiff
rel carrion; bones

corpselike *adj* 1 *syn* see DEATHLY 1
2 *syn* see GHASTLY 2

corpsy *adj syn* see DEATHLY 1

corpulence *n syn* see OBESITY

corpulent *adj syn* see FAT 2

corpus *n* 1 *syn* see BODY 3
2 *syn* see OEUVRE

corrade *vb syn* see ABRADE 1

corral *vb syn* see ENCLOSE 1

correct *vb* 1 to set right something that is wrong < *correct* a misstatement >
syn amend, emend, mend, rectify, right
rel ameliorate, better, improve; redress, remedy, revise; make over, reform; adjust, fix, regulate
con damage, harm, hurt, impair, injure, mar, spoil
2 *syn* see PUNISH 1
con baby, coddle, cosset, humor, indulge, pamper, spoil

correct *adj* 1 *syn* see DECOROUS 1
rel careful, meticulous, punctilious, scrupulous
2 conforming to or agreeing with fact < the *correct* solution to the problem >
syn accurate, exact, nice, precise, proper, right, rigorous
rel faithful, true, undistorted, veracious, veridical; faultless, flawless, impeccable, perfect
con fallacious, false, wrong; defective, faulty, flawed, imperfect
ant incorrect

correction *n syn* see PUNISHMENT

correctitude *n syn* see ORDER 7

corrective *n syn* see REMEDY 2

correctly *adv syn* see WELL 1

correctness *n* 1 *syn* see ORDER 7
2 *syn* see PRECISION

correlate *n* 1 *syn* see COUNTERPART 1
2 *syn* see PARALLEL

correspond *vb syn* see AGREE 4

correspond (to) *vb syn* see AMOUNT 2

correspondence *n syn* see CONSISTENCY
ant divergence

correspondent *n syn* see PARALLEL

corresponding *adj syn* see LIKE

correspondingly *adv syn* see ALSO 1

corridor *n syn* see PASSAGE 4

corrival *n syn* see RIVAL

corroborate *vb syn* see CONFIRM 2
con invalidate, negate, nullify
ant contradict

corroborative *adj* serving or tending to corroborate < *corroborative* evidence >
syn adminicular, collateral, confirmative, confirmatory, corroboratory, verificatory
rel ancillary, auxiliary, supplementary, supportive; assisting, helping
con confutative, refutative, refutatory; contradictory, negatory

corroboratory *adj syn* see CORROBORATIVE

corrode *vb syn* see EAT 3

corrosive *adj syn* see SARCASTIC

corrosiveness *n syn* see SARCASM

corrugation *n syn* see WRINKLE

corrupt *vb* 1 *syn* see DEBASE 1
rel abase, degrade; ruin, wreck
con amend, correct, reform
2 *syn* see DECAY
rel befoul, defile, foul; smirch, tarnish

corrupt *adj* 1 *syn* see VICIOUS 2
rel crooked, devious, oblique; baneful, deleterious, detrimental, noxious, pernicious; abased, degraded, low
2 seeking sordid advantage with little regard to moral or legal bars < a *corrupt* politician >
syn mercenary, praetorian, unethical, unprincipled, unscrupulous, venal; *compare* CROOKED 2, VENAL 1
rel undependable, unreliable, untrustworthy; faithless, inconstant, unfaithful; double-dealing, perfidious, treacherous, two-faced; bribable, corruptible; blackguardly, knavish, reprobate
con ethical, principled, scrupulous, upright; dependable, reliable, trustworthy, trusty
3 *syn* see CROOKED 2

corrupted *adj syn* see DEBASED

corruptible *adj syn* see VENAL 1

corruption *n* 1 *syn* see VICE 1
2 *syn* see BARBARISM

corsair *n syn* see PIRATE

coruscate *vb syn* see FLASH 1

coruscation *n syn* see FLASH 1

corybantic *adj syn* see FURIOUS 2

coryphée *n syn* see DANCER

cosmic *adj syn* see UNIVERSAL 2

cosmopolitan *adj* 1 exhibiting or characterized by a sophistication and savoir faire arising from cultured urban life and wide travel < had a thoroughly *cosmopolitan* outlook on life >
syn metropolitan, urbane; *compare* SOPHISTICATED 2
rel civilized, polished, smooth; sophisticated, worldly-wise; cultivated, cultured
con boorish, cloddish, rude, rustic; insular, parochial, provincial
2 *syn* see UNIVERSAL 2

cosmos (or **kosmos**) *n syn* see UNIVERSE

cosset *vb* 1 *syn* see CARESS
2 *syn* see BABY

cost *n* 1 *syn* see PRICE 1
2 *syn* see EXPENSE 1
3 *syn* see EXPENSE 2

costive *adj* 1 *syn* see CONSTIPATED
2 *syn* see STINGY

costless *adj syn* see FREE 5

costly *adj* 1 commanding or being a large price < the scarcer an item becomes the more *costly* it is >

syn dear, expensive, high; *compare* PRECIOUS 1
rel excessive, exorbitant, extravagant, inordinate, steep, stiff; fancy, premium, top
con inexpensive, low, low-priced, reasonable
ant cheap
2 syn see PRECIOUS 1
costume *n* style of clothing and adornment < her *costume* was always suitable to the occasion >
syn dress, getup, guise, outfit, rig, setout, turnout
rel fashion, mode, style
cot *n syn* see HUT
‖**cotch** *vb* **1 syn** see SEIZE 2
2 syn see CATCH 1
3 syn see CATCH 7
coterie *n syn* see CLIQUE
cottage *n syn* see HUT
cotton *vb* **1 syn** see BABY
2 syn see FAWN
cotton (to *or* on to) *vb syn* see APPREHEND 1
cottony *adj syn* see SOFT 3
couch *vb* **1 syn** see WORD
2 syn see LOWER 3
couch *n syn* see LAIR 1
couleur de rose *adj syn* see HOPEFUL 2
couloir *n syn* see PASSAGE 4
counsel *n syn* see ADVICE 1
counsel *vb* to give advice to or about < *counseled* him to wait for a more propitious occasion >
syn advise, recommend
rel admonish, reprehend, warn; direct, order, prescribe; charge, enjoin, prompt, urge; advocate, suggest
count *vb* **1** to ascertain the total of units in a collection by noting one after another < *counted* the sheep in the pasture >
syn enumerate, number, numerate, tale, tally, tell
rel add, cast, figure, foot, sum, tot, total; calculate, compute, estimate, reckon; tell off
2 syn see MATTER
3 syn see WEIGH 3
count (on) *vb syn* see RELY (on *or* upon)
count (on *or* upon) *vb syn* see EXPECT 1
countenance *n* **1 syn** see LOOK 2
idiom (the) cut of one's jib
2 syn see FACE 1
countenance *vb* **1 syn** see ENCOURAGE 2
rel applaud, commend; back, champion, support, uphold
con deride, ridicule; criticize, reprehend, reprobate; reproach, reprove
ant discountenance
2 syn see APPROVE 1
counter *vb syn* see OPPOSE 1
counter *n syn* see OPPOSITE
counter *adj syn* see OPPOSITE
rel hostile, inimical; adverse, antagonistic, anti, oppugnant; hindering, impeding, obstructive
counteract *vb syn* see NEUTRALIZE
rel correct, fix, rectify, right
con cooperate, coordinate, synergize; back, reinforce, support
counteractant *n syn* see REMEDY 2
counteractive *n syn* see REMEDY 2
counteragent *n syn* see REMEDY 2
counterbalance *vb syn* see COMPENSATE 1
rel amend, correct, rectify
con overbalance, unbalance
counterblow *n syn* see RETALIATION
countercheck *vb syn* see NEUTRALIZE
counterfactual *adj syn* see FALSE 1
counterfeit *vb syn* see ASSUME 4
rel ape, copy, imitate, mimic
counterfeit *adj* being an imitation intended to mislead or deceive < *counterfeit* money > < *counterfeit* sympathy >
syn bogus, brummagem, fake, false, phony, pinchbeck, pseudo, sham, snide, spurious; *compare* SPURIOUS 3
rel feigned, pretended, simulated; deceptive, delusive, delusory, misleading; fraudulent
con authentic, veritable; actual, real, true; unquestionable, valid
ant bona fide, genuine
counterfeit *n syn* see IMPOSTURE
rel copy, facsimile, reproduction; dummy, simulacrum

countermeasure *n syn* see REMEDY 2
counterpane *n syn* see BEDSPREAD
counterpart *n* **1** something that completes or complements < export controls as a *counterpart* of domestic distribution controls >
syn complement, correlate, pendant; *compare* PARALLEL
rel analogue, correlate, correspondent; equal, equivalent, like, match
con counterpoint, opposite
2 syn see PARALLEL
3 syn see EQUAL
4 syn see OPPOSITE NUMBER
counterpoise *n syn* see BALANCE 1
counterpoise *vb syn* see COMPENSATE 1
rel ballast, poise, stabilize, steady, trim
con capsize, overturn, upset
counterpole *n syn* see OPPOSITE
countersign *n syn* see PASSWORD 1
counterstep *n syn* see REMEDY 2
countertype *n syn* see PARALLEL
countervail *vb syn* see COMPENSATE 1
rel amend, correct, rectify; foil, frustrate, thwart; overcome, surmount
countless *adj syn* see INNUMERABLE
count out *vb syn* see EXCLUDE
countrified *adj syn* see RURAL
country *n* the nation-state to which one belongs or from which one originated < returned to his own *country* after years of exile >
syn fatherland, home, homeland, land, mother country, motherland, soil
country *adj syn* see RURAL
country jake *n syn* see RUSTIC
countryman *n syn* see RUSTIC
couple *vb* **1 syn** see JOIN 1
2 syn see HITCH 2
rel hook up, ‖inspan
couple *n* two individuals of the same or a similar kind that occur, function, or are considered together < a *couple* of ideas for improving the book > < the happiest *couple* I know >
syn brace, doublet, duo, dyad, pair, twosome
rel span, team, yoke
coupling *n syn* see JOINT 1
courage *n* a quality of mind or temperament that enables one to stand fast in the face of opposition, hardship, or danger < had the kind of *courage* that could appreciate a danger yet steadfastly face it >
syn dauntlessness, guts, heart, mettle, ‖moxie, pluck, resolution, spirit, spunk; *compare* FORTITUDE
rel audacity, boldness, bravery, doughtiness, fearlessness, intrepidity; gallantry, heroism, valor; backbone, fortitude, grit, sand; assurance, determination, firmness, persistence, tenacity
con chickenheartedness, faintheartedness, unmanliness, yellowness; baseness, cravenness, poltroonery, pusillanimity; timidity, timorousness
ant cowardice
courageous *adj syn* see BRAVE 1
rel fiery, high-spirited; strong, tenacious
con afraid, apprehensive, fearful
ant pusillanimous
courier *n syn* see MESSENGER
course *n* **1 syn** see WAY 2
rel circuit, orbit, range, scope
2 syn see CHANNEL 1
3 way of acting or proceeding < hard to decide on the best *course* to follow >
syn line, policy, polity, procedure, program
rel design, pattern, plan, platform, scheme; manner, system, way
idiom course of action
4 syn see PROGRESS 2
5 syn see SUCCESSION 2

---

syn synonym(s)   *rel* related word(s)
ant antonym(s)   *con* contrasted word(s)
idiom idiomatic equivalent(s)
‖ use limited; if in doubt, see a dictionary

course *vb* to proceed with great celerity (as in pursuing or competing) <the fox *coursed* after the hare>
syn career, chase, race, rush, speed, tear; *compare* RUSH 1
rel hasten, hurry, hustle; dart, dash, scamper, scoot, scurry; run, sprint
idiom step on the gas, stir one's stumps

courser *n* a strong vigorous horse formerly used in mounted combat <heroes mounted on great fiery *coursers*>
syn charger, war-horse

court *n* 1 an open space wholly or partly enclosed (as by buildings or walls) <the window looked on the *court*>
syn ‖close, courtyard, curtilage, enclosure, quad, quadrangle, yard
2 a place or the persons assembled for the administration of justice <the *court* was called to order>
syn bar, lawcourt, tribunal
3 *syn* see JUDGE 2

court *vb syn* see ADDRESS 8
rel allure, attract, captivate, charm

courteous *adj syn* see CIVIL 2
rel attentive, considerate, thoughtful
con blunt, brusque, curt, gruff; insolent, overbearing, supercilious
ant discourteous

courtesan *n syn* see HARLOT 1

courtesy *n* 1 courteous behavior or a courteous act <noted for her *courtesy* and graciousness> <such little *courtesies* take little time but often brighten lonely lives>
syn amenity, attention, gallantry
rel affability, cordiality, geniality, graciousness; comity, complaisance; chivalry, civility, courteousness, courtliness; attentiveness, considerateness, consideration, thoughtfulness
con boorishness, churlishness; impoliteness, incivility, rudeness, ungraciousness
ant discourtesy
2 *syn* see FAVOR 4

courtly *adj* marked by elaborate and often ceremonious courtesy <this was indeed a *courtly* gentleman of the old school>
syn gallant, gracious, preux, stately; *compare* CIVIL 2
rel august, dignified, imposing, lofty; prim, starchy, stiff, stilted, studied; ceremonious, conventional, formal; civilized
con discourteous, ill-mannered, impolite, rude, uncivil, ungracious; boorish, coarse, gross, loutish, uncouth, vulgar
ant churlish

courtyard *n syn* see COURT 1

cousinage *n syn* see KIN 2

cousinhood *n syn* see KIN 2

cove *n syn* see INLET

covenant *n syn* see CONTRACT

covenant *vb syn* see VOW
rel agree, concur

cover *vb* 1 *syn* see DEFEND 1
2 *syn* see HIDE
3 to spread over or put something over <a smile *covered* her face> <*cover* the garden with manure>
syn blanket, cap, crown, overcast, overlay, overspread
rel conceal, hide, screen; defend, protect, shield; enclose, enfold, envelop, shroud, wrap; overspread, superimpose, superpose
con display, exhibit, expose
ant bare, uncover
4 *syn* see TRAVEL 2
5 *syn* see SET 11

cover *n* 1 *syn* see SHELTER 1
rel concealment, hiding, screen; safety, security
ant exposure
2 *syn* see MASK 2

coverlet *n syn* see BEDSPREAD

‖**coverlid** *n syn* see BEDSPREAD

covert *adj* 1 *syn* see SECRET 1
rel camouflaged, cloaked, disguised, dissembled, masked
con candid, frank, open
ant overt
2 *syn* see ULTERIOR
con direct, forthright; honest, square, straight

covert *n syn* see SHELTER 1

covertly *adv syn* see SECRETLY

covet *vb syn* see DESIRE 1
con abjure, forswear

ant renounce

covetous *adj* having or marked by an urgent and often unscrupulous desire for possessions <the *covetous* eye of an avid collector>
syn acquisitive, desirous, grabby, grasping, greedy, itchy, prehensile
rel esurient, gluttonous, rapacious, ravenous, voracious; hoggish, lickerish, piggish, swinish; avid, eager, keen; envious, jealous; grudging, selfish
con generous, liberal, munificent; ungrudging, unselfish; abstemious, abstinent, ascetic, austere; moderate, restrained, temperate

covey *n syn* see GROUP 1

covin *n syn* see PLOT 2

cow *vb syn* see INTIMIDATE
rel appall, daunt, dismay; abash, discomfit, disconcert, embarrass, faze, rattle
con cower, cringe, fawn, toady, truckle

coward *n* one who shows or yields to ignoble fear <a treacherous *coward* who betrayed his friends to save his own skin>
syn chicken, craven, dastard, funk, funker, poltroon, quitter, yellowbelly
rel baby, fraidycat, invertebrate, jellyfish, milksop, scaredy-cat; caitiff, recreant
con gallant, hero, palladin, stalwart; ideal, model, pattern, standard

coward *adj syn* see COWARDLY

cowardly *adj* marked by or arising from a base lack of courage <a *cowardly* desertion>
syn ‖chicken, coward, cowhearted, craven, gutless, lily-livered, milk-livered, poltroon, poltroonish, poor-spirited, pusillanimous, spunkless, unmanly, white-livered, yellow
rel afraid, chickenhearted, fainthearted, fearful, timid, timorous; funky, panicky; caitiff, dastardly, recreant, vile, worthless
con courageous, fearless, intrepid, valiant; daring, reckless, temerarious
ant brave

cower *vb syn* see FAWN
rel blench, flinch, quail, recoil, shrink, wince
con browbeat, bulldoze, bully, cow, intimidate; bristle, strut, swagger

cowering *adj syn* see FAWNING

cowhearted *adj syn* see COWARDLY

coxcomb *n syn* see FOP

coy *adj* 1 *syn* see SHY 1
rel decent, decorous, nice, proper, seemly
con brash, brazen, impudent
2 marked by a light playful artlessness <glanced up with a *coy* twinkle in her eye>
syn arch, coquettish, roguish
rel capricious, kittenish, lively, mischievous, playful, skittish
con serious, sober, thoughtful

cozen *vb* 1 *syn* see CHEAT
2 *syn* see DECEIVE

cozy *adj* 1 *syn* see COMFORTABLE 2
rel safe, secure
2 *syn* see INTIMATE 4

crab *vb syn* see GRIPE
idiom fret and fume

crab *n syn* see GROUCH

crabbed *adj syn* see SULLEN
rel blunt, brusque, crusty, gruff; choleric, cranky, splenetic, testy; huffy, irascible, irritable, snappish
con amiable, complaisant, good-natured, obliging; benign, benignant, kind, kindly; agreeable, pleasing; affable, genial, gracious

crabber *n syn* see GROUCH

crabby *adj syn* see SULLEN

crabwise *adv syn* see SIDEWAYS 1

crack *vb syn* see DECODE
rel puzzle out

crack *n* 1 *syn* see BANG 2
rel splintering, splitting; percussion
2 *syn* see JOKE 1
rel dig, fling, potshot
idiom flash of wit
3 a usually narrow opening, break, or discontinuity made by splitting and rupture <a *crack* in the ice>

syn chink, cleft, fissure, rift, rima, rimation, rime, split
rel rent; discontinuity, interstice, interval; cranny, niche; crevasse, crevice
4 syn see INSTANT 1
idiom flash of lightning
5 syn see BLOW 1
6 syn see FLING 1
crack *adj syn* see PROFICIENT
rel excellent, superior
crackbrain *n syn* see CRACKPOT
idiom cracked wit
crackbrained *adj syn* see INSANE 1
crackdown *n syn* see REPRESSION 2
rel quashing
idiom lowering the boom
cracked *adj syn* see INSANE 1
idiom ‖off in the upper story
crackerjack *n syn* see ‖DILLY
crackerjack *adj syn* see PROFICIENT
‖crackers *adj syn* see INSANE 1
cracking *adj syn* see MONSTROUS 1
crackpot *n* one given to extremely eccentric or lunatic ideas or actions <a *crackpot* who wrote threatening letters to public figures>
syn crackbrain, crank, cuckoo, ding-a-ling, harebrain, kook, lunatic, nut, screwball
rel case, character, ‖dingbat, eccentric, oddball, oddity, ‖wack; loon, loony, madman, maniac
crack–up *n* **1 syn** see NERVOUS BREAKDOWN
2 syn see CRASH 3
3 syn see COLLAPSE 2
rel decline, deterioration
‖cracky *adj syn* see INSANE 1
cradlesong *n syn* see LULLABY
craft *n* **1 syn** see ART 1
2 syn see TRADE 1
rel job
3 syn see CUNNING 2
craftiness *n syn* see CUNNING 2
crafty *adj syn* see SLY 2
rel adroit, clever, tidy; acute, keen, sharp; deceitful, fawning, ‖sleekit, ‖sleeky
cragged *adj syn* see ROUGH 1
craggy *adj syn* see ROUGH 1
cram *vb* **1** to fill (a limited space) forcibly with more than is practicable or fitting <*crammed* the suitcase chock-full and had to sit on it to close it>
syn jam, jam-pack, ‖pang, ram, stuff, tamp; *compare* LOAD 3, PRESS 7
rel pack, stive; fill, heap; chock, choke; press, shove, thrust; drive, force; squeeze, wedge
2 syn see PRESS 7
3 syn see GULP
rel overeat
idiom pack it in
4 to study intensively or under pressure <had to *cram* all night before the exam>
syn bone (up), ‖mug (up)
rel study; review
idiom burn the midnight oil
cram–full *adj syn* see FULL 1
crammed *adj syn* see FULL 1
idiom crammed full, crammed to the bursting point, fit (*or* ready) to burst
ant emptied
cramp *n* **1 syn** see RESTRICTION 1
rel shackle
2 syn see RESTRICTION 2
rel constipation, stultification
cramp *adj syn* see CRAMPED
cramped *adj* having insufficient size or capacity <a *cramped* cubbyhole of an office>
syn confined, cramp, incommodious, squeezy, ‖tucked up
rel close, narrow, tight, two-by-four; little, minute, small, tiny
con commodious, unconfined
ant spacious
crank *n* **1 syn** see CAPRICE
2 syn see CRACKPOT

rel freak
3 syn see GROUCH
cranky *adj* **1 syn** see INSANE 1
2 syn see CANTANKEROUS
rel contrary, difficult, froward, perverse
3 syn see IRASCIBLE
rel bad-humored, ill-humored; disagreeable; ugly
idiom out of sorts
cranny *n syn* see NOOK
‖crap *n syn* see NONSENSE 2
‖crap out *vb syn* see FAINT
‖crappy *adj syn* see BAD 1
crash *vb syn* see FAIL 5
ant skyrocket
crash *n* **1 syn** see BANG 2
2 syn see IMPACT
3 a wrecking or smashing especially of a vehicle <an air *crash*>
syn crack-up, pileup, ‖prang, smash, smashup, ‖stramash, wreck
rel accident; collision
4 syn see COLLAPSE 2
crashing *adj syn* see UTTER
crass *adj syn* see COARSE 3
rel churlish, loutish
ant refined
crate *n syn* see JALOPY
crave *vb* **1 syn** see BEG
2 syn see DESIRE 1
con contemn, despise, disdain, scorn
ant spurn
3 syn see LONG
idiom have a craving for
4 syn see DEMAND 2
craven *adj syn* see COWARDLY
craven *n syn* see COWARD
craving *n syn* see DESIRE 1
crawfish (out) *vb syn* see BACK DOWN
crawl *vb* **1 syn** see CREEP 1
rel grovel; worm
2 syn see TEEM
‖3 syn see LAMBASTE 3
craze *vb syn* see MADDEN 1
craze *n syn* see FASHION 3
rel enthusiasm, fever
crazed *adj syn* see INSANE 1
craziness *n syn* see FOOLISHNESS
crazy *adj* **1 syn** see INSANE 1
rel doting, gaga, moonstruck; beheaded, silly; erratic, possessed
idiom as crazy as a loon, having a screw loose, having bats in one's belfry, not having all one's marbles (*or* buttons)
ant sane
2 syn see FOOLISH 2
rel goofy, senseless
idiom beyond the realm of reason, out of all reason
con practical, reasonable, reasoned, sensible
ant sane
‖crazy *adv syn* see VERY 1
crazy house *n syn* see ASYLUM 3
cream *n* **1 syn** see OINTMENT
2 syn see BEST
idiom (the) top cream
‖cream *vb syn* see WHIP 2
crease *n syn* see WRINKLE
create *vb* **1 syn** see GENERATE 1
idiom call into being
2 syn see FOUND 2
3 syn see COMPOSE 2
rel conceive, formulate; imagine
creation *n syn* see UNIVERSE
creative *adj syn* see INVENTIVE
rel causal, institutive, occasional; Promethean
ant uncreative

---

syn synonym(s)   **rel** related word(s)
ant antonym(s)   **con** contrasted word(s)
idiom idiomatic equivalent(s)
‖ use limited; if in doubt, see a dictionary

creator *n syn* see FATHER 2
 rel brain(s), brainpower, mastermind
creature *n* **1** *syn* see BEAST
 2 *syn* see HUMAN
 3 *syn* see SYCOPHANT
credence *n syn* see BELIEF 1
 rel acceptance, accepting, admission, admitting; confidence, reliance, trust
 con skepticism; distrust, mistrust; disbelief, incredulity, unbelief
credentials *n pl* something presented or held by one as proof that he is what or who he claims to be < her academic *credentials* were excellent >
 syn character, recommendation, reference, testimonial
 rel document(s), documentation, paper(s), voucher; accreditation, certification, endorsement, sanction
credible *adj* **1** *syn* see BELIEVABLE
 rel satisfactory, satisfying; solid, sound, straight, valid
 idiom to be believed
 con unsatisfactory; preposterous, ridiculous
 ant incredible
 2 *syn* see AUTHENTIC 1
 rel likely, probable; rational, reasonable; conclusive, determinative
 ant incredible
credit *n* **1** *syn* see BELIEF 1
 rel confidence, reliance, trust
 2 *syn* see INFLUENCE 1
 rel fame, renown, reputation, repute
 con disrepute, ignominy, obloquy, opprobrium
 ant discredit
 3 one that enhances another < he is a *credit* to his family >
 syn asset
 rel honor
 4 favorable notice or attention resulting from an action or achievement < took all the *credit* for the idea >
 syn acknowledgment, recognition
 rel attention, notice; distinction, fame, honor; glory, kudos
credit *vb* **1** *syn* see FEEL 3
 con disbelieve, pooh-pooh
 ant discredit
 2 *syn* see ASCRIBE
creditable *adj* **1** *syn* see BELIEVABLE
 ant discreditable
 2 *syn* see RESPECTABLE 1
 rel satisfactory; suitable
 ant discreditable
credo *n syn* see IDEOLOGY
credulous *adj* ready or inclined to believe especially on slight or insufficient evidence < deceiving the *credulous* young girls >
 syn unsuspecting, unsuspicious, unwary
 rel believing; accepting, unquestioning; trustful, trusting; green, inexperienced; naive, simple, unsophisticated; dupable, gullible
 con mistrustful, suspecting, suspicious; careful, wary; doubtful, doubting, questioning
 ant incredulous, skeptical
creed *n* **1** *syn* see RELIGION 1
 2 *syn* see RELIGION 2
 3 *syn* see IDEOLOGY
creek *n* ||**1** *syn* see INLET
 rel ria
 2 a natural stream of water normally smaller than and often tributary to a river < went wading in the *creek* >
 syn ||branch, brook, ||burn, ||crick, gill, race, ||rindle, ||rithe, rivulet, ||run, runnel, stream
 rel ||beck, brooklet, ||rigolet, rill, rillet, runlet; streamlet; freshet; ditch, watercourse; wadi
creep *vb* **1** to move along a surface in a prone or crouching position < a cat *creeping* through the grass >
 syn crawl, slide, snake
 rel glide, slither; sneak, steal, tiptoe; edge, inch; sniggle, wriggle
 2 *syn* see STEAL 3
 3 *syn* see SNEAK
crème de la crème *n syn* see ARISTOCRACY
crepehanger *n syn* see PESSIMIST
crescendo *n syn* see APEX 2
crest *n* **1** *syn* see TOP 1
 rel cap
 2 *syn* see RIDGE 1

 3 *syn* see APEX 2
crest *vb syn* see SURMOUNT 3
crestfallen *adj syn* see DOWNCAST
 idiom ||in a funk
 ant elated
cretin *n syn* see FOOL 4
 rel zombie
crew *n syn* see GROUP 1
 rel aggregation, collection, congregation; gang, retinue, set
crib *n* **1** *syn* see BROTHEL
 2 *syn* see PONY
 rel plagiarism
||**crib** *vb syn* see GRIPE
||**crick** *n syn* see CREEK 2
crime *n* **1** a serious breach of the public law < armed robbery is a *crime* >
 syn misdeed, offense
 rel criminality, illegality, lawlessness; delict, delictum; breach, break, infringement, transgression, violation; wrong, wrongdoing; felony
 2 *syn* see EVIL 3
crimeless *adj syn* see INNOCENT 2
criminal *adj syn* see UNLAWFUL
criminal *n* one who has committed a usually serious offense < car thieves and other *criminals* >
 syn felon, lawbreaker, malefactor, offender
 rel scofflaw; transgressor, trespasser, wrongdoer; crook, ||twicer; gangster, hood, mobster, racketeer, thug; fugitive, outlaw; convict, jailbird
criminate *vb syn* see ACCUSE
 ant exonerate
crimp *vb* **1** *syn* see CRUMPLE 1
 2 *syn* see RESTRAIN 1
crimp *n syn* see OBSTACLE
crimple *vb syn* see CRUMPLE 1
crimson *vb syn* see BLUSH
 ant blanch
cringe *vb syn* see FAWN
 rel blench, flinch, quail, recoil, wince; ||croodle, crouch, shrink
 idiom bow and scrape, eat dirt
cringing *adj syn* see FAWNING
 rel obeisant, prostrate
 idiom bowing and scraping, eating dirt, eating humble pie, on one's hands and knees
crinkle *vb syn* see CRUMPLE 1
crinkle *n syn* see WRINKLE
 rel crimp
cripple *vb* **1** *syn* see MAIM
 rel lame
 2 *syn* see PARALYZE 1
 3 *syn* see WEAKEN 1
crisis *n syn* see JUNCTURE 2
crisp *adj* **1** *syn* see SHORT 6
 con flabby, flaccid, limp
 2 *syn* see INCISIVE
 rel piquing, provoking, stimulating
crisscross *vb syn* see INTERSECT
criterion *n syn* see STANDARD 3
 rel adjudgment, judgment
critic *n* one given to harsh or captious judgment < chronic *critics* of the administration >
 syn aristarch, carper, caviler, criticizer, faultfinder, knocker, momus, smellfungus, Zoilus
 rel Monday morning quarterback; nitpicker, quibbler; belittler, disparager; complainer; censurer; muckraker, mudslinger
 con backer, supporter; partisan; advocate, champion, protagonist
critic *adj syn* see CRITICAL 1
critical *adj* **1** exhibiting the spirit of one who looks for and points out faults and defects < constant *critical* comments about her attire >
 syn captious, carping, caviling, cavillous, censorious, critic, faultfinding, hypercritical, overcritical
 rel discerning, discriminating, penetrating; finicky, fussy, particular; belittling, demeaning, disparaging, humbling, lowering
 con cursory, shallow, superficial; encouraging, flattering, praising
 ant uncritical

2 syn see ACUTE 6
rel conclusive, decisive, determinative; consequential, important, momentous, significant, weighty
criticism *n* a discourse that evaluates or analyzes something (as a work of art or literature) <read every *criticism* of the new play>
syn comment, critique, notice, review, reviewal
rel analysis, examination, study; commentary, observation; opinion; appraisal, assessment, estimate, rating
criticize *vb* to make adverse comments about (someone or something) openly, often publicly, and with varying severity <*criticized* his opponent's liberal views>
syn blame, censure, condemn, cut up, denounce, denunciate, knock, pan, rap, reprehend, reprobate, skin; *compare* LAMBASTE 3, REPROVE, SCOLD 1
rel blast, castigate, fulminate (against), fustigate, roast, scathe
idiom find fault with, pull (*or* pick *or* tear) to pieces, take to task
con approve, countenance, endorse, OK (*or* okay)
ant praise
criticizer *n syn* CRITIC, aristarch, carper, caviler, faultfinder, knocker, momus, smellfungus, Zoilus
critique *n syn* see CRITICISM
‖**critter** *n syn* see BEAST
croak *vb* **1 syn** see GRUMBLE 1
rel complain, quarrel
‖**2 syn** see DIE 1
‖**croaker** *n syn* see PHYSICIAN
croaking *adj syn* see HOARSE 1
croaky *adj syn* see HOARSE 1
‖**crocked** *adj syn* see INTOXICATED 1
crone *n syn* see HAG 2
rel frump, slattern, sloven
crony *n syn* see ASSOCIATE 3
idiom bosom buddy
‖**crooch** *vb syn* see CROUCH
‖**croodle** *vb syn* see SNUGGLE
crook *vb* **1 syn** see CURVE
‖**2 syn** see STEAL 1
‖**3 syn** see CHEAT
crooked *adj* **1** departing from a straight line or course <a *crooked* road>
syn bending, curving, devious, twisting; *compare* CURVED, WINDING
rel oblique; circuitous, indirect, roundabout; errant, meandering, rambling, serpentine, snaky, tortuous, winding; zigzag
con direct, undeviating
ant straight
2 deviating from rectitude <*crooked* police officers on the take>
syn corrupt, dishonest, snide; *compare* CORRUPT 2, VENAL 1
rel devious, indirect, shifty, underhand; double-dealing, fraudulent; deceitful, lying, untruthful; ruthless, unscrupulous
con aboveboard, forthright, straightforward; conscientious, honorable, just, proper, righteous, scrupulous, upright
ant honest, straight
crookedly *adv syn* see AWRY 1
ant straight
crop *n syn* see HARVEST 2
crop *vb* **1 syn** see TOP 1
rel chop, hew, slash; detach, disengage
2 syn see MOW
3 syn see CUT 6
rel snip
cropping *n syn* see HARVEST 1
cross *n* **1 syn** see TRIAL 1
idiom a cross to bear
2 syn see HYBRID
cross *vb* **1 syn** see DENY 4
2 syn see BETRAY 2
idiom bite the hand that feeds one, stab in the back
3 syn see TRAVERSE 4
4 to cause (an animal or plant) to breed with one of a different kind <*crossing* a horse with an ass results in a mule>
syn crossbreed, cross-mate, hybridize, interbreed, intercross
rel mongrelize
5 syn see INTERSECT
idiom lie (*or* be) athwart

cross *adj syn* see IRASCIBLE
rel captious, carping, caviling, faultfinding
idiom cross as a bear
cross *prep syn* see ACROSS
crossbred *n syn* see HYBRID
crossbreed *vb syn* see CROSS 4
crossbreed *n syn* see HYBRID
crosscut *vb syn* see INTERSECT
cross–examination *n* a thorough, typically formal questioning for full information <*cross-examination* of a hostile witness>
syn grill, grilling, interrogation, third degree
rel debriefing; questioning
cross–grained *adj* **1 syn** see CANTANKEROUS
2 syn see CONTRARY 3
rel difficult
crossing *adj syn* see TRANSVERSE
cross–mate *vb syn* see CROSS 4
crosspatch *n syn* see GROUCH
crossroad *n*, *usu* **crossroads** *pl but sing or pl in constr* **syn** see JUNCTURE 2
‖**cross talk** *n syn* see BANTER
crossways *adv syn* see ACROSS 1
rel transversely; askew, awry, crisscross
con lengthwise
ant longways
crosswise *adv syn* see ACROSS 1
con longwise
ant lengthwise
crosswise *adj syn* see TRANSVERSE
ant lengthwise
crotchet *n syn* see CAPRICE
rel eccentricity, kink, kinkiness, quirk, twist
idiom bee in one's bonnet (*or* brain), flea in one's nose, kink in one's horn, maggot in one's brain
crotchety *adj syn* see CANTANKEROUS
crouch *vb* to stoop low with the limbs close to the body <*crouched* behind a rock and watched>
syn ‖crooch, huddle, hunch, scrooch (down); *compare* SQUAT
rel bend, bow, dip, duck; hunker (down), ‖quat, squat, stoop, ‖swat; cower, cringe, flinch, quail, wince; grovel
crow *vb syn* see BOAST
rel cry, exult, jubilate
crowd *vb* **1 syn** see PRESS 1
rel ram, shove
2 syn see PRESS 7
rel bunch, cluster
crowd *n* **1** a usually large group of people <a *crowd* gathered before the palace>
syn crush, drove, horde, multitude, press, push, squash, throng; *compare* MULTITUDE 1
rel army, host, legion; flock, gaggle, herd, swarm; mob, rabble, rout
2 syn see GATHERING 2
rel huddle, parley; troop; herd; rally
3 syn see MULTITUDE 1
4 syn see SET 5
crowded *adj* **1 syn** see FULL 1
rel overcharged, overloaded
ant uncrowded
2 syn see CLOSE 4
ant uncrowded
crown *n* **1 syn** see TOP 1
2 syn see WREATH
rel diadem, tiara
3 syn see APEX 2
crown *vb* **1 syn** see SURMOUNT 3
2 syn see COVER 3
3 syn see CLIMAX
crown (with) *vb syn* see ENDOW 1
crucial *adj syn* see ACUTE 6
rel deciding, decisive, important; necessary, vital; clamorous, compelling, crying, imperative, insistent, pressing
crucible *n syn* see TRIAL 1

---

syn synonym(s)   *rel* related word(s)
ant antonym(s)   *con* contrasted word(s)
idiom idiomatic equivalent(s)
‖ use limited; if in doubt, see a dictionary

crucify *vb syn* see AFFLICT
  rel bedevil, bother, browbeat
  idiom kill by inches, nail to the cross, put on the rack
crud *n* a deposit or incrustation of something filthy, greasy, or sticky <machinery all covered with *crud*>
  syn ‖cab, goo, gook, gunk; *compare* GOO 1
  rel filth, muck, slime, sludge; debris, junk, rubbish, trash
‖**cruddle** *vb syn* see CURDLE
crude *adj* 1 *syn* see UNREFINED 3
  2 *syn* see COARSE 3
  rel backward, ignorant, unenlightened; boorish, cloddish, clodhopping, ill-bred, loutish, lowbred; savage; insensible
  3 *syn* see RUDE 1
  rel immature, unmatured; coarse, graceless
  con cultivated, cultured, refined; developed, matured, ripened
  ant consummate, finished
  4 *syn* see OBSCENE 2
  rel blue, risqué
  idiom rated X
  5 rough in plan or execution <*crude* imitations, completely lacking in the original artistry>
  syn coarse, inexpert, prentice; *compare* RUDE 1
  rel amateurish, unproficient, unskilled, untaught, untrained; raw, rough, rude, unfinished, unpolished; inadequate, ineffective, inferior, poor
  con finished, perfected, polished
  ant expert
cruel *adj syn* see FIERCE 1
  rel atrocious, heinous, monstrous, outrageous; bestial, bloodthirsty, brutish; heartless, implacable, relentless; impiteous, unpitying
  con compassionate, sympathetic, tender; clement, forbearing, lenient, merciful; humane, kindly
‖**cruise** *vb syn* see GO 1
cruise *n syn* see VOYAGE
  rel sail
‖**cruiser** *n syn* see PROSTITUTE
crumb *n syn* see PARTICLE
crumble *vb syn* see DECAY
  rel mush, squash
crumbly *adj syn* see SHORT 6
  rel rubbery
‖**crump** *adj syn* see SHORT 6
crumple *vb* 1 to press or twist into folds or wrinkles <*crumple* a piece of paper>
  syn crimp, crimple, crinkle, ‖crunkle, rimple, ruck (up), ‖ruckle, rumple, screw, scrunch, wrinkle
  rel crease, fold; buckle, cockle; wad
  ant smooth
  2 *syn* see GIVE 12
crunch *vb syn* see CHEW 1
crunchy *adj syn* see SHORT 6
‖**crunkle** *vb syn* see CRUMPLE 1
crusading *adj syn* see EVANGELICAL
crush *vb* 1 *syn* see PRESS 3
  rel ‖scruze, squeeze
  2 to reduce or be reduced to a pulpy or broken mass <*crushed* rose petals>
  syn becrush, bruise, mash, ‖mush (up), pulp, squash
  rel press, squeeze; contuse; batter, maim; beat, pound; dash, quash, ‖quat, smash; comminute, powder, pulverize, triturate
  3 *syn* see PULVERIZE 1
  4 *syn* see PRESS 1
  5 to bring to an end by destroying or defeating <the police *crushed* the rebellion>
  syn annihilate, extinguish, put down, quash, quell, quench, squash, suppress; *compare* SUPPRESS 2
  rel ‖quelch, repress, squelch, strangle; beat down, conquer, defeat, subdue, subjugate; ruin, wreck; abolish, demolish, destroy; blot out, obliterate
  idiom crush (or grind) under one's heel, ride down into the dust, roll (or trample) in the dust
  6 *syn* see CONQUER 1
  idiom bring one to his knees
  7 *syn* see PRESS 7
crush *n* 1 *syn* see CROWD 1
  2 *syn* see INFATUATION
  rel calf love, puppy love

‖**crust** *n syn* see EFFRONTERY
crust *vb syn* see CAKE 1
crusty *adj* 1 *syn* see BLUFF
  rel irritable, snappish, waspish; choleric, cranky, irascible, splenetic, testy; crabbed, dour, saturnine, surly
  2 *syn* see OBSCENE 2
crux *n syn* see SUBSTANCE 2
cry *vb* 1 *syn* see CALL 1
  rel bleat
  2 to show distress, grief, or pain by tears and usually incoherent utterances <the little girl *cried* when she fell down>
  syn blub, blubber, boohoo, ‖pipe, sob, wail, weep; *compare* BAWL 2, WHIMPER
  rel sniff, snivel, whimper, whine; break down, choke up; groan, moan, sigh; bemoan, bewail, keen, lament, mourn, sorrow; bawl, howl, squall, yowl
  idiom cry one's eyes (or heart) out, ‖pipe one's eye, shed tears
  3 *syn* see SHOUT 1
  4 *syn* see PUBLICIZE
cry *n* 1 *syn* see BATTLE CRY
  rel slogan
  2 *syn* see REPORT 1
  3 *syn* see FASHION 3
  4 *syn* see CALL 1
  rel screech, squawk; squeak; caw
cry down *vb syn* see DECRY 2
  ant cry up
crying *adj* 1 *syn* see PRESSING
  rel necessary, needed
  2 *syn* see OUTRAGEOUS 2
cry off *vb syn* see BACK DOWN
cry out *vb syn* see EXCLAIM
crypt *n* a subterranean chamber <a burial *crypt*>
  syn catacomb, undercroft, vault
  rel cell; chamber, compartment, room; cave, cavern, grotto
cryptanalyze *vb syn* see DECODE
cryptic *adj* being intentionally obscure and mysterious <the senator made some *cryptic* statements about intelligence operations>
  syn dark, Delphian, enigmatic, mystifying; *compare* OBSCURE 3
  rel equivocal, murky, obscure, opaque, tenebrous, unclear, uninformative, vague; incomprehensible, inexplicable, strange, unfathomable; abstruse, mysterious; evasive, secretive
crystal *adj syn* see CLEAR 4
  idiom clear as crystal, crystal clear
cry up *vb syn* see PRAISE 2
  idiom beat the drum for, praise to the skies
  ant cry down
cubby *n syn* see CUBBYHOLE
cubbyhole *n* an excessively small room or place <a cramped *cubbyhole* of an office>
  syn cubby, mousehole, pigeonhole
  rel recess; niche; cubicle
  idiom hole in the wall
‖**cubes** *n pl syn* see DICE
cuckoo *n syn* see CRACKPOT
cuckoo *adj syn* see INSANE 1
cuddle *vb* 1 *syn* see CARESS
  rel embrace, enfold, hold
  2 *syn* see SNUGGLE
cudgel *n* a short solid stick used as a weapon or an instrument of punishment <beat the prisoner with a *cudgel*>
  syn bat, baton, billy, billy club, bludgeon, club, knobkerrie, mace, nightstick, ‖shillelagh, spontoon, truncheon, war club
  rel birch, cane, ferule, hickory, paddle, rattan, rod, switch; blackjack; quarterstaff; bastinado
cue *n syn* see HINT 1
cuff *vb syn* see SLAP 1
cuff *n* a sharp blow typically delivered with the hand <gave him a good *cuff* in the face>
  syn box, buffet, ‖bust, chop, clout, haymaker, ‖paste, poke, punch, slap, smack, sock, spank, ‖spat, ‖swack; *compare* BLOW 1, HIT 1
  rel bat, blow, clip, wallop
cul–de–sac *n syn* see DEAD END
  rel stalemate
cull *vb* 1 *syn* see GLEAN
  rel accumulate, amass, collect, round up

2 *syn* see CHOOSE 1
rel discriminate
idiom separate the sheep from the goats, separate the wheat from the chaff
‖**cull** *n syn* see FOOL 3
‖**cully** *n syn* see ASSOCIATE 3
culmen *n syn* see APEX 2
culminate *vb syn* see CLIMAX
culmination *n syn* see APEX 2
rel extremity, limit, maximum
culpability *n syn* see BLAME
con blamelessness, innocence
ant inculpability
culpable *adj syn* see BLAMEWORTHY
rel impeachable, indictable
ant inculpable
cult *n* **1** *syn* see RELIGION 1
2 *syn* see RELIGION 2
cultivable *adj syn* see ARABLE
ant uncultivable
cultivatable *adj syn* see ARABLE
ant uncultivatable
cultivate *vb* **1** *syn* see TILL
rel crop, farm, manage
2 *syn* see NURSE 2
rel raise, rear; educate, instruct, teach, train; ameliorate, better, improve
con disregard, ignore, neglect, slight
3 *syn* see GROW 1
rel develop, mature, ripen
cultivated *adj syn* see GENTEEL 1
rel courteous, polite
ant uncultivated
cultivation *n syn* see CULTURE
culture *n* enlightenment and excellence of taste acquired by intellectual and aesthetic training <a man of *culture* is known by his reading>
syn breeding, cultivation, polish, refinement
rel education, enlightenment, erudition, learning; gentility, manners; discrimination, taste; savoir-faire, sophistication, urbanity; class, elegance
con greenness, ignorance, inexperience, verdancy; crudeness, vulgarity
cultured *adj syn* see GENTEEL 1
rel educated, enlightened, erudite, learned, literate; civilized
ant uncultured
culverhouse *n syn* see DOVECOTE
cumber *vb syn* see BURDEN
cumbersome *adj syn* see UNWIELDY
rel irksome, tiresome, wearisome
cumbrance *n syn* see ENCUMBRANCE
rel burden, charge, pressure
cumbrous *adj syn* see UNWIELDY
rel clogging, hampering, hindering, impeding
cumshaw *n syn* see GRATUITY
cumulate *vb syn* see ACCUMULATE
rel obtain, secure
ant dissipate
cumulation *n syn* see ACCUMULATION
rel stockpile, snowball
cumulative *adj* increasing or produced by addition of like or similar things <the *cumulative* effect of several drugs>
syn accumulative, additive, additory, chain, summative
rel accumulated, amassed; augmenting, increasing, multiplying; advancing, heightening, intensifying, magnifying, snowballing
con dispersed, dissipated, scattered
cunning *adj* **1** *syn* see CLEVER 4
rel well-devised, well-laid, well-planned; crackerjack, masterful
idiom too clever by half
2 *syn* see SLY 2
rel acute, keen, sharp; knowing, smart; wary
idiom not to be caught with chaff
con artless, naive, unsophisticated
cunning *n* **1** *syn* see ART 1
rel deftness, dexterousness; adeptness, expertness; cleverness, ingeniousness, ingenuity
2 skill in devising or using indirect or subtle methods <a woman able to maneuver people with great *cunning*>

syn art, artfulness, artifice, cageyness, canniness, craft, craftiness, foxiness, slyness, wiliness
rel savvy, sharpness, shrewdness; cleverness, ingeniousness, ingenuity; agility, facility, finesse, slickness; subtlety; insidiousness, shiftiness, trickiness
3 *syn* see DECEIT 1
idiom satanic cunning, the cunning of the serpent
cupidity *n* intense desire for possessions and wealth <the sight of so much money aroused his *cupidity*>
syn avarice, avariciousness, avidity, greed, rapacity
rel acquisitiveness, greediness, possessiveness, rapaciousness; eagerness, voracity; craving, desire; lust; infatuation, passion
cur *n* **1** *syn* see SNOT 1
rel riffraff
2 *syn* see CAD
curative *adj* restoring or tending to restore to a state of normalcy or health <a *curative* drug>
syn curing, healing, remedial, remedying, restorative, sanative, sanatory, vulnerary, wholesome
rel medicable, medicative, medicinal; corrective, therapeutic; invigorating, tonic; beneficial, helpful, salutary, wholesome
curb *vb* **1** *syn* see HAMPER
2 *syn* see DENY 3
rel repress, suppress
ant goad
3 *syn* see RESTRAIN 1
rel fetter, hamper, hog-tie, manacle, shackle
idiom hold in leash, keep a tight rein on
con unbridle, unleash
ant spur
curd *vb syn* see CURDLE
curdle *vb* to cause to become coagulated or thickened and often sour <hot weather will *curdle* milk>
syn ‖clabber, ‖cruddle, curd, ‖lopper, turn
rel clot, coagulate, condense, thicken; ferment; go off, sour, spoil
cure *n* **1** *syn* see REMEDY 1
2 *syn* see REMEDY 2
cure *vb* to rectify an unhealthy or undesirable condition <aspirin *cured* his headache>
syn heal, remedy
rel doctor, medicate; restore; ameliorate, better, improve
cure–all *n syn* see PANACEA
cureless *adj syn* see HOPELESS 2
curing *adj syn* see CURATIVE
curio *n syn* see KNICKKNACK
curiosity *n* **1** *syn* see INTEREST 3
rel inquisitiveness, questioning
ant disinterest
2 something that arouses interest especially because of uncommon or exotic characteristics <an architectural *curiosity*>
syn conversation piece, oddity
rel exception, nonesuch, rarity; marvel, prodigy, wonder; anomaly; freak, monstrosity
idiom something to write home about
curious *adj* **1** *syn* see INQUISITIVE 1
rel searching; analytical; prurient
ant incurious
2 interested in what is not one's personal or proper concern <a *curious* old woman prying into her neighbors' affairs>
syn inquisitive, inquisitorial, inquisitory, ‖nibby, nosy, peery, prying, snoopy
rel interfering, intermeddling, meddling, tampering; examining, inspecting, scrutinizing; impertinent, intrusive, meddlesome
idiom consumed (or burning or eaten up) with curiosity, curious as a cat (or monkey)
con aloof, detached, disinterested, indifferent, unconcerned, uninterested; apathetic, impassive, phlegmatic, stolid
ant incurious
3 *syn* see STRANGE 4
curl *vb syn* see WIND 2
rel crook; roll; ringlet; kink
con straighten, unkink, unwind

---

syn synonym(s)   *rel* related word(s)
ant antonym(s)   *con* contrasted word(s)
idiom idiomatic equivalent(s)
‖ use limited; if in doubt, see a dictionary

ant uncurl

currency *n syn* see MONEY

current *adj* **1** *syn* see PRESENT
  rel topical, up-to-date
  con antiquated, antique, obsolete
  2 *syn* see PREVAILING
  rel accustomed, customary; a la mode, fashionable, modern, popular
  ant antique

current *n* **1** *syn* see FLOW
  2 *syn* see TENDENCY 1

curry *vb syn* see WHIP 2

curse *n* **1** a denunciation that conveys a wish or threat of evil <the dying man's *curse* against his family>
  syn anathema, commination, imprecation, malediction, malison
  rel execration, objurgation; damning, denunciation; blasphemy, profanation, profanity, sacrilege
  ant blessing
  2 *syn* see SWEARWORD
  3 *syn* see PLAGUE 1

curse *vb* **1** *syn* see EXECRATE 1
  rel blaspheme; blight; doom
  idiom call down curses on the head of, call down evil on
  ant bless
  2 *syn* see SWEAR 3
  idiom ‖curse up a storm

cursed *adj* **1** *syn* see DAMNED 2
  rel hateful
  2 *syn* see EXECRABLE 1
  rel disgusting; odious
  ant blessed

cursing *n syn* see BLASPHEMY 1

cursive *adj syn* see EASY 9

cursory *adj syn* see SUPERFICIAL 2
  rel fast, hasty, hurried, quick, rapid, speedy, swift; brief, short; casual, desultory, haphazard, random
  con careful, meticulous, scrupulous
  ant painstaking

curt *adj* **1** *syn* see CONCISE
  2 *syn* see BLUFF
  rel imperious, peremptory
  ant voluble

curtail *vb* **1** *syn* see SHORTEN
  ant prolong, protract
  2 *syn* see ABRIDGE 1
  ant extend

curtains *n pl but sing in constr syn* see DEATH 1

curtilage *n syn* see COURT 1

curvaceous *adj* having a shapely figure marked by pronounced curves <*curvaceous* bikini-clad girls swarmed over the beach>
  syn ‖built, curvesome, curvilinear, curvy, Junoesque, rounded, ‖stacked, well-developed; *compare* BUXOM, SHAPELY
  rel shapeful, shapely, statuesque, well-proportioned; attractive, charming, pleasing

curvation *n syn* see CURVE

curvature *n syn* see CURVE

curve *vb* to swerve or cause to swerve from a straight line or course <the road *curves* to the right>
  syn bend, bow, crook, round; *compare* WIND 2
  rel deflect, divert, turn; deviate, swerve, veer; coil, curl, spiral, twist, wind; incurve
  ant straighten

curve *n* something (as a line or surface) that curves or is curved <a slight *curve* to her eyebrows>
  syn arc, arch, bend, bow, curvation, curvature, round
  rel incurvation, incurvature; inflection; rondure; circuit, circumference, compass

curved *adj* having or characterized by a curve or curves <a *curved* vault>
  syn arced, arched, arciform, arrondi, bent, bowed, curvilinear, round, rounded; *compare* CROOKED 1
  rel declinate; embowed, incurvate, incurved; excurved; bending, twisted, twisting
  ant straight

curvesome *adj syn* see CURVACEOUS

curvilinear *adj* **1** *syn* see CURVED
  2 *syn* see CURVACEOUS

curving *adj syn* see CROOKED 1

curvy *adj syn* see CURVACEOUS

cushy *adj syn* see COMFORTABLE 2

cusp *n syn* see POINT 9

cuspidate *adj syn* see POINTED 1

cuss *n* **1** *syn* see SWEARWORD
  2 *syn* see MAN 3

cuss *vb syn* see SWEAR 3
  idiom ‖cuss up a blue streak

cussed *adj syn* see DAMNED 2

cussing *adj syn* see BLASPHEMY 1

cussword *n syn* see SWEARWORD

custodian *n* one that guards, protects, or maintains (as property or records) <was the *custodian* of the manor for many years>
  syn cerberus, claviger, ‖custodier, custos, guardian, keeper, warden, watchdog
  rel curator, steward; castellan, governor; overseer, supervisor

‖custodier *n syn* see CUSTODIAN

custody *n* the act or duty of guarding and preserving <the government has *custody* of all state gifts>
  syn care, guardianship, keeping, safekeeping, trust, ward
  rel caretaking; charge, management, supervision; protection

custom *n* **1** *syn* see HABIT 1
  rel precedent; ritual; mold; fixture, institution; prescription, rubric; canon, law, precept, rule
  idiom matter of course
  con departure, deviation, shift; exception; irregularity
  2 *syn* see PATRONAGE 2

custom *adj syn* see CUSTOM-MADE

customarily *adv syn* see USUALLY 1
  rel conventionally, traditionally; normally, ordinarily; routinely
  idiom as a matter of course
  con rarely; never
  ant occasionally

customary *adj* **1** *syn* see USUAL 1
  rel acknowledged, recognized, understood; standard; conventional, orthodox, traditional; prescriptive, regulation, stipulated
  idiom being the customary (*or* usual) thing
  con occasional; infrequent, inhabitual, sporadic, uncommon; irregular
  ant uncustomary
  2 *syn* see COMMON 4
  rel household, popular; general, universal
  ant uncustomary

custom–built *adj syn* see CUSTOM-MADE

customer *n* one that patronizes or uses the services of something (as a store or restaurant) <many *customers* in the shop>
  syn client, patron
  rel buyer, consumer, purchaser, shopper

customized *adj syn* see CUSTOM-MADE

custom–made *adj* made according to personal order and individual specifications <he always wore a *custom-made* suit>
  syn custom, custom-built, customized, custom-tailored, made-to-order, tailor-made
  ant mass-produced

custom–tailored *adj syn* see CUSTOM-MADE

custos *n syn* see CUSTODIAN

cut *vb* **1** to penetrate with or as if with a sharp edge <*cut* his hand on a broken bottle>
  syn gash, incise, pierce, slash, slice, slit
  rel cleave, dissever, sever, sunder; rend, rip, rive, tear; lacerate, wound
  2 *syn* see SHORTEN
  3 *syn* see REDUCE 2
  4 *syn* see MOW
  5 to penetrate and divide with an edged tool or instrument <*cut* the melon into slices>
  syn carve, cleave, dissect, dissever, sever, slice, split, sunder
  rel divide, part, separate; chop, dice, hash, mince, mow
  idiom lay open
  6 to reduce by severing parts <the barber *cut* his hair too short>
  syn clip, crop, pare, prune, shave, shear, skive, trim
  rel cut back, dock, lop, poll, pollard, shrub; amputate; curtail
  7 to refuse social recognition especially by way of rebuke <his friends *cut* him after the scandal broke>
  syn cold-shoulder, ostracize, snob, snub
  rel disdain, ignore, rebuff, reject, slight, turn away; affront, insult, offend

idiom give the cold shoulder (to), show one his place, slam the door in one's face, slam the door on, slap one in the face, turn aside (*or* away) from, turn one's back (on *or* upon)
8 syn see DILUTE
9 syn see FELL 2
10 syn see OPERATE 2
cut *n* **1 syn** see PART 1
2 syn see SHARE 1
3 syn see TRENCH
4 syn see TYPE
cut *adj* **syn** see INTOXICATED 1
cut back *vb* **1 syn** see SHORTEN
2 syn see REDUCE 2
cut down *vb* **syn** see REDUCE 2
cut in *vb* **syn** see INTRUDE 1
cut off *vb* **1 syn** see KILL 1
2 syn see INTERCEPT
3 syn see ISOLATE
4 syn see DISINHERIT 1
cutoff *n* **syn** see SHORTCUT
cut out *vb* **1 syn** see EXCISE
2 syn see SUPPLANT 1
cutpurse *n* **syn** see PICKPOCKET
cutthroat *n* **syn** see ASSASSIN

cutting *adj* **syn** see INCISIVE
rel piercing, probing
cut up *vb* **1 syn** see CRITICIZE
2 to behave in a boisterously comic or unruly manner <children *cutting up* in front of company>
syn act up, carry on, horse, horseplay
rel caper, cavort, romp; clown; show off; roughhouse; misbehave
idiom cut a dido (*or* shine), cut up rough, ‖kick up a shindy, raise Cain (*or* Ned), whoop it up
cutup *n* **syn** see ZANY 2
cycle *n* **1** a complete course of recurrent operations or events <a 24-hour *cycle* of medication>
syn circle, round, wheel; *compare* SUCCESSION 2
rel chain, sequel, sequence, series; course, run; circuit, loop, ring
2 syn see BICYCLE
cyclone *n* **syn** see TORNADO
cyclopean *adj* **syn** see HUGE
ant lilliputian
cynical *adj* **syn** see SARDONIC
cyprian *n* **syn** see WANTON
czar *n* **syn** see MAGNATE

D

dab *vb* **syn** see SMEAR 1
‖dab *n* **syn** see EXPERT
dabbler *n* **syn** see AMATEUR 2
con adept, artist, connoisseur; expert, master, professional
dabbling *adj* **syn** see AMATEURISH
rel sciolistic, shallow, sophomoric, superficial
con adept, capable, competent
‖dabster *n* **syn** see EXPERT
dad *n* **syn** see FATHER 1
dada *n* **syn** see FATHER 1
dad–blamed *adj* **1 syn** see DAMNED 2
2 syn see UTTER
dad–blasted *adj* **1 syn** see DAMNED 2
2 syn see UTTER
dad–burned *adj* **1 syn** see DAMNED 2
2 syn see UTTER
daddy *n* **syn** see FATHER 1
daedal *adj* **syn** see COMPLEX 2
daffy *adj* **syn** see INSANE 1
daft *adj* **syn** see INSANE 1
daily *adj* of each or every day <*daily* prayers for the dead>
syn diurnal, quotidian
con nocturnal; alternate, intermittent, periodic, recurrent, spasmodic; erratic, fitful, fluctuating, infrequent, irregular; occasional, sporadic
ant nightly
dainty *n* **syn** see DELICACY
dainty *adj* **1 syn** see CHOICE
rel beautiful, bonny, fair, lovely, pretty; delectable, delicious, delightful; airy, diaphanous, ethereal, light
con coarse, vulgar
ant gross
2 syn see NICE 1
rel acute, penetrative, perceptive
con careless, neglectful, negligent, thoughtless
‖daisy *n* **syn** ‖DILLY, ‖corker, crackerjack, dandy, humdinger, jim=dandy, knockout, ‖lalapalooza, ‖lulu, nifty
dale *n* **syn** see VALLEY
dally *vb* **1 syn** see TRIFLE 1
rel frolic, gambol, play, rollick, romp, sport; caress, cosset, cuddle, dandle, fondle, pet
2 syn see DELAY 2
con fleet, rush, scurry, skedaddle
ant hasten

dam *vb* **syn** see HINDER
rel repress, suppress
con air, express, utter, vent
damage *n* **syn** see INJURY 1
rel impairment, marring; deterioration, dilapidation, disrepair, ruining, wrecking; deleteriousness, disadvantage, drawback
con amelioration, betterment, improvement; benefit, profit; advantage, service, use
ant repair
damage *vb* **syn** see INJURE 1
rel demolish, destroy, raze, ruin, wreck; deteriorate, dilapidate; abuse, ill-treat, maltreat, mistreat, misuse, outrage
con ameliorate, amend, better, improve; mend
ant repair
damaged *adj* having been injured <*damaged* merchandise>
syn flawed, impaired, marred, spoiled
rel blemished, broken, imperfect, injured, unsound
con flawless, good, intact, unbroken, unhurt, unimpaired, uninjured, unmarred, whole; corrected, improved, rectified, repaired
ant undamaged
damaging *adj* **syn** see HARMFUL
dame *n* **1 syn** see MATRIARCH
2 syn see BELDAM 1
damn *vb* **1 syn** see SENTENCE
rel castigate, discipline, penalize, punish; banish, cast out, expel
con deliver, ransom, redeem, rescue; reward
ant save
2 syn see EXECRATE 1
rel abominate; vituperate
3 syn see SWEAR 3
damn *n* **syn** see PARTICLE
damnable *adj* **1 syn** see EXECRABLE 1
rel abhorrent, abominable, detestable, hateful, odious; damned
con admirable, commendable, estimable; laudable, praiseworthy
2 syn see DAMNED 2
3 syn see UTTER
damned *adj* **1** being doomed to eternal punishment <a *damned* soul>
syn condemned, doomed, lost
rel anathematized, cursed, reprobate; done for

---

syn synonym(s)	**rel** related word(s)
ant antonym(s)	**con** contrasted word(s)
idiom idiomatic equivalent(s)	
‖ use limited; if in doubt, see a dictionary	

idiom gone to blazes, hell bound
con delivered, ransomed, redeemed
ant saved
2 deserving censure or strong disapproval —often used as a generalized expression of annoyance < this *damned* door won't open >
syn blamed, blankety-blank, blasted, bleeding, blessed, blighted, blinding, ‖blinking, ‖blistering, ‖blooming, confounded, ‖consarned, cursed, cussed, dad-blamed, dad-blasted, dad-burned, damnable, dang, darn (*or* durn), dashed, doggone, dratted, execrable, goldarn, infernal, perishing, so-and-so
3 *syn* see UTTER
damned *adv syn* see VERY 1
damp *adj* slightly or relatively wet < her dress was still *damp* >
syn dampish, dank, moist, moisty, wettish
rel drenched, saturated, soaked, soaking; soggy, water-logged
con arid, dry
dampen *vb syn* see MUFFLE 2
dampish *adj syn* see DAMP
damsel *n syn* see GIRL 1
dance *vb* **1** to perform a rhythmic and patterned succession of steps usually to music < the band was good enough to *dance* to >
syn foot (it), hoof (it), prance, step, tread
rel shuffle, trip, truck
idiom ‖cut a rug, trip the light fantastic
2 *syn* see FLIT 2
rel quaver, quiver, shake, tremble, wobble
dancer *n* a professional performer of dances < *dancers* performing a ballet >
syn ballerina, ballet girl, coryphée, dancing girl, danseur, danseuse, figurant, figurante, hoofer
rel chorine, chorus boy, chorus girl, chorus man; danseur noble, premier danseur, premiere danseuse, prima ballerina
dancing girl *n syn* see DANCER
dandle *vb syn* see CARESS
rel disport, play, sport
dandy *n* **1** *syn* see FOP
con clod, lout, lump, oaf, slob, slouch
ant sloven
2 *syn* ‖DILLY, ‖corker, crackerjack, ‖daisy, humdinger, jim=dandy, ‖lalapalooza, ‖lulu, nifty, peach
‖**dandy** *adj* **1** *syn* see MARVELOUS 2
2 *syn* see EXCELLENT
rel grand, hunky-dory, keen, nifty, swell
idiom fine and dandy
con ‖bum, ‖crummy, grim, ‖lousy, ‖putrid, rotten
ant blah
dang *adj* **1** *syn* see DAMNED 2
2 *syn* see UTTER
danger *n* the state of being exposed to injury, pain, or loss < they are seeking a place where children can play without *danger* >
syn hazard, jeopardy, peril, risk
rel menace, precariousness, threat; emergency, exigency, pass; precipice
idiom dangerous ground, thin ice
con safety; exemption, immunity; defense, guard, protection, safeguard, shield
ant security
dangerous *adj* **1** attended by or involving the possibility of injury, pain, or loss < a *dangerous* crossing >
syn chancy, ‖dangersome, hairy, hazardous, jeopardous, parlous, perilous, risky, treacherous, unhealthy, unsound, wicked; *compare* GRAVE 3
rel insecure, precarious, uncertain, unsafe; chance, haphazard, hit-or-miss, random; critical, menacing, serious, threatening
idiom beset (*or* fraught) with danger, on a collision course
con certain, reliable; harmless, innocent
ant safe, secure
2 *syn* see GRAVE 3
‖**dangersome** *adj syn* see DANGEROUS 1
dangle *vb syn* see HANG 1
dank *adj syn* see DAMP
danseur *n syn* see DANCER
danseuse *n syn* see DANCER
dap *vb syn* see GLANCE 1
dapper *adj* trimly neat and tidy < a *dapper* dresser, always neat as a pin >

syn bandbox, doggish, doggy, natty, sassy, sparkish, spiffy, spruce, sprucy, well-groomed; *compare* NEAT 2, STYLISH
rel chichi; jaunty, rakish; showy
con dowdy, drab, unstylish; disheveled, disordered, slipshod, sloppy, slovenly, unkempt, untidy; blowsy, dowdy, frowsy, shabby, slatternly
dappled *adj syn* see VARIEGATED
con pure, smooth, spotless, unbroken, uniform
dare *vb syn* see FACE 3
rel change, hazard, risk
idiom take the bull by the horns
con avoid, evade; flee, run
dare *n syn* see DEFIANCE 1
daredevil *adj syn* see ADVENTUROUS
con timid, timorous; cautious, chary, circumspect, wary; discreet, judicious, prudent, sane, sensible
daring *adj syn* see ADVENTUROUS
dark *adj* **1** deficient in light < a *dark* room >
syn caliginous, dim, dun, dusk, dusky, gloomy, lightless, murky, obscure, somber, tenebrous, unilluminated
rel cloudy, dull, shadowy, shady; pitch-black, pitch-dark
con bright, brilliant, luminous, radiant; enlightened, illuminated, illumined, lighted
ant light
2 *syn* see CRYPTIC
rel abstruse, esoteric, hidden, occult, recondite; anagogic, cabalistic, darkling, mystic, mystical; complicated, intricate, knotty
con clear, perspicuous; easy, facile, light, simple
ant lucid
3 of dark complexion < her *dark* good looks >
syn bistered, black-a-vised, brunet, dark-skinned, dusky, swart, swarth, swarthy
con blond, fair, light; ruddy, tawny
‖**4** *syn* see BLIND 1
darken *vb syn* see OBSCURE
ant illuminate
dark–skinned *adj syn* see DARK 3
darling *n syn* see SWEETHEART 1
darling *adj* **1** *syn* see FAVORITE 1
2 *syn* see DELIGHTFUL
darn (*or* durn) *adj* **1** *syn* see DAMNED 2
2 *syn* see UTTER
dart *n syn* see SHAFT 2
dart *vb syn* see FLY 1
rel hasten, hurry, precipitate, speed; run, scamper, scoot, scurry, sprint, spurt
con dally, dawdle, delay, linger, tarry; lumber, plod, slog, trudge
dash *vb* **1** *syn* see RUSH 1
rel run, scamper, scoot, scurry, sprint
con dally, dawdle, delay, linger, tarry; lumber, plod, slog, trudge
2 *syn* see RUN 1
3 *syn* see BLAST 1
4 *syn* see FRUSTRATE 1
dash *n* **1** *syn* see SPIRIT 5
rel energy, force, might, power, strength; intensity, vehemence; impressiveness
con apathy, dullness, languor, lethargy, listlessness, sluggishness, stagnation, torpor
2 *syn* see HINT 2
rel impress, impression, stamp
dashed *adj* **1** *syn* see DAMNED 2
2 *syn* see UTTER
dashing *adj* **1** *syn* see LIVELY 1
2 *syn* see STYLISH
rel flashy, flaunting; dapper, jaunty, spiffy, spruce
idiom cutting a fine figure
con unfashionable, unstylish; modest, unostentatious, unpretentious
ant drab
dastard *n syn* see COWARD
date *vb* to go or take on a date < he *dated* her several times that winter >
syn see, take out
rel accompany, escort; court, woo
idiom go out with
date *n* **1** *syn* see ENGAGEMENT 3

2 syn see ESCORT 1
dated *adj syn* see OLD-FASHIONED
  ant up-to-the-minute
dateless *adj syn* see ETERNAL 4
  ant ephemeral
daub *vb syn* see SMEAR 1
  rel spatter, speckle, spot; dapple, fleck, variegate
daunt *vb syn* see DISMAY 1
  rel browbeat, bully, cow, intimidate; baffle, foil, frustrate, thwart
  con arouse, awaken, rally, rouse, stir, waken; actuate, drive, impel, move; activate, energize, vitalize
  ant enhearten
dauntless *adj syn* see BRAVE 1
  rel indomitable, invincible, unconquerable
  con hesitant, reluctant
  ant poltroon
dauntlessness *n syn* see COURAGE
  ant poltroonery
dawdle *vb* 1 *syn* see IDLE
  2 syn see DELAY 2
  rel amble, saunter, stroll; stay, wait; toy, trifle; fritter, waste
  idiom fritter away time
  con arouse, rally, rouse, stir; hasten, hurry, speed
dawdler *n syn* see LAGGARD
dawn *n* 1 the first appearance of light in the morning < birds which sing at *dawn* >
  syn aurora, cockcrow, cockcrowing, dawning, daybreak, daylight, light, morn, morning, sunrise, sunup
  rel prime
  idiom break of day, crack of dawn, first blush (*or* flush) of day, first light, peep of day, the wee small hours
  2 syn see BEGINNING
  ant sunset
dawning *n* 1 *syn* see DAWN 1
  2 syn see BEGINNING
  ant sunset
day *n* 1 the time of light between one night and the next < waiting for *day* to dawn >
  syn daylight, daytime
  rel light, sunlight, sunshine
  con dark, nighttime
  ant night
  2 usu days *pl syn* see PERIOD 2
daybreak *n syn* see DAWN 1
daydream *n syn* see FANCY 4
  rel conceiving, fancying, imagination, imagining
  con substantiality, tangibility; authenticity, truth, verity
daydreaming *adj syn* see DREAMY 1
daydreamy *adj syn* see DREAMY 1
daylight *n* 1 *syn* see DAWN 1
  syn see DAY 1
dayspring *n syn* see BEGINNING
daystar *n syn* see SUN 1
daytime *n syn* see DAY 1
daze *vb* 1 to confuse with light < the bright sunlight *dazed* him >
  syn bedazzle, blind, dazzle
  rel overcome, overpower, overwhelm; dizzy
  2 to dull or deaden the powers of the mind through some disturbing experience or influence < *dazed* by the news of the accident >
  syn bedaze, bemuse, benumb, paralyze, petrify, stun, stupefy
  rel bewilder, confound, disorder, distract, dumbfound, mystify; befuddle, confuse, fuddle, muddle; dazzle, dizzy; rock
  con enhance, expand, heighten, sharpen; alert, arouse, waken
daze *n syn* see HAZE 2
dazzle *vb syn* see DAZE 1
dead *adj* 1 devoid of life < a *dead* person >
  syn asleep, cold, deceased, defunct, departed, exanimate, extinct, inanimate, late, lifeless, spiritless, unanimated
  rel bloodless, breathless; gone, reposing; inactive, inert; belowground, buried
  idiom dead as a doornail, gone the way of all flesh, out of one's misery, pushing up daisies
  con animate, animated, living, vital; being, existing; active, live
  ant alive
  2 syn see DEATHLY 1
  rel insensible, insentient, numb, unfeeling, unresponsive; inanimate, unconscious

con feeling, responsive, sensitive, sentient; animate, animated, living, spirited, vivacious
  ant alive
  3 syn see NUMB 1
  4 syn see OBSOLETE
  ant living; viable
  5 syn see EXTINCT 2
  6 syn see DULL 7
  rel bleak, dismal
  con glorious, resplendent
  7 syn see UTTER
dead *adv syn* see DIRECTLY 1
deaden *vb* 1 to impair in vigor, force, activity, or sensation < the news *deadened* his distress >
  syn benumb, blunt, desensitize, dull, mull, numb
  rel anesthetize, paralyze, unnerve; stun, stupefy
  con animate, vivify; energize, invigorate; activate, vitalize
  ant enliven
  2 syn see MUFFLE 2
dead end *n* a course which leads to nothing further < had reached a *dead end* in negotiations >
  syn blind alley, cul-de-sac, impasse, pocket
  rel corner, hole; deadlock, halt, standstill; bottleneck
deadened *adj* 1 *syn* see DEATHLY 1
  2 syn see NUMB 1
‖**deader** *n syn* see CORPSE
deadfall *n syn* see PITFALL
deadliness *n syn* see FATALITY 1
deadlock *n syn* see DRAW 4
  rel condition, posture, situation, state; dilemma, plight, predicament, quandary
  con decision, determination, resolution, solution
deadly *adj* 1 causing or causative of death < a *deadly* disease >
  syn deathly, fatal, lethal, mortal, mortiferous, pestilent, pestilential; *compare* PERNICIOUS
  rel destroying, destructive; killing, slaying; internecine; baneful, noxious, pernicious; poisonous, toxic, virulent
  con healthful, healthy, wholesome; advantageous, beneficial, restorative, sanative
  2 syn see PERNICIOUS
  con harmless, innocuous, inoffensive, unoffending
  3 syn see DEATHLY 1
deadpan *adj syn* see EXPRESSIONLESS
dead to rights *adv syn* see RED-HANDED
deadweight *n syn* see LOAD 3
‖**deadwood** *n syn* see ADVANTAGE 3
deaf *adj syn* see OBSTINATE
deal *vb* 1 *syn* see DISTRIBUTE 1
  rel partake, participate, share
  con receive, take; detain, hold, hold back, keep, retain, withhold; appropriate, arrogate, confiscate
  2 syn see GIVE 10
  rel impart, mete, render
  con annul, cancel, remove, rescind, revoke
deal (out) *vb syn* see ADMINISTER 2
  rel dish, dish out, help, serve; offer, present, proffer, tender
  con hold, hold back, keep, retain, withhold
deal (with) *vb syn* see TREAT 2
  rel control, direct; clear, rid, unburden
  con misconduct, misdirect, mishandle, mismanage; disregard, ignore, neglect; burden, cumber, encumber
deal *n* 1 *syn* see AGREEMENT 2
  2 treatment received in a transaction from another < a fair *deal* >
  syn shake
dealer *n syn* see MERCHANT
dealings *n pl syn* see COMMERCE 1
  rel affairs, business, concerns, doings, matters, things; proceedings
deambulatory *adj syn* see ITINERANT
dean *n syn* see LEADER 1
dear *adj* 1 *syn* see FAVORITE 1
  2 syn see LOVING

---

syn synonym(s)   *rel* related word(s)
ant antonym(s)   *con* contrasted word(s)
idiom idiomatic equivalent(s)
‖ use limited; if in doubt, see a dictionary

3 *syn* see COSTLY 1
  con inexpensive, low, moderate, modest, nominal
  ant cheap

dear *n syn* see SWEETHEART 1

dearth *n syn* see ABSENCE
  rel infrequency, rareness, scarcity, uncommonness; exiguousness, meagerness, scantiness, scantness; paucity, insufficiency
  con superfluity, surplus; lavishness, prodigality, profusion
  ant excess

death *n* **1** the end or the ending of life < *death* of a man > < *death* of an enterprise >
  syn curtains, decease, defunction, demise, dissolution, grim reaper, (the) Pale Horse, passing, quietus, silence, sleep
  rel annihilation, ending, expiration, extinction, grave, termination
  idiom crossing the bar
  ant life
  2 *syn* see FATALITY 2

deathful *adj syn* see DEATHLY 1

deathless *adj syn* see IMMORTAL 1
  rel eternal; abiding, lasting, persisting

deathlike *adj* **1** *syn* see DEATHLY 1
  2 *syn* see GHASTLY 2

deathly *adj* **1** suggesting death (as in inertness or appearance) < fell in a *deathly* faint >
  syn corpselike, corpsy, dead, deadened, deadly, deathful, deathlike
  rel cadaverous, haggard, wasted; ghastly, grisly, gruesome, macabre; appalling, dreadful, horrible
  con healthy, hearty, robust; stout, sturdy; energetic, strenuous, vigorous
  2 *syn* see DEADLY 1

debacle *n* **1** *syn* see DEFEAT 1
  2 *syn* see COLLAPSE 2

debar *vb syn* see EXCLUDE
  rel forbid, interdict; block, hinder, impede, obstruct
  con accept, receive; allow, let, permit
  ant admit

debark *vb syn* see DISEMBARK

debase *vb* **1** to cause to become impaired in quality or character < vulgarly outrageous movies that *debase* the taste of the people >
  syn animalize, bastardize, bestialize, brutalize, canker, corrupt, debauch, demoralize, deprave, pervert, poison, rot, stain, vitiate, warp; *compare* ADULTERATE
  rel damage, harm, impair, injure, mar, spoil; contaminate, defile, dishonor, pollute, taint; commercialize
  con enhance, heighten; lift, raise; ameliorate, better, improve
  ant elevate; amend
  2 *syn* see HUMBLE
  rel cripple, debilitate, disable, enfeeble, sap, undermine, weaken
  con acclaim, laud, praise; refresh, rejuvenate, renew, restore
  3 *syn* see ADULTERATE
  rel damage, impair, worsen; corrupt, defile, spoil
  idiom play the devil (*or* the mischief) with
  con amend, upgrade

debased *adj* being lowered in quality or character < became *debased* in his greed for money >
  syn corrupted, debauched, depraved, perverted, vitiate, vitiated
  rel decadent, degenerate, degenerated, deteriorated; abandoned, dissolute, profligate, reprobate
  con ameliorated, bettered, improved; elevated, lifted, raised
  ant elevated

debatable *adj syn* see MOOT
  ant undebatable

debate *n* **1** *syn* see ARGUMENTATION
  rel controverting, rebutting, refuting
  2 *syn* see ATTENTION 1

debate *vb syn* see DISCUSS 1
  rel altercate, quarrel, wrangle; confute, controvert, disprove, rebut, refute; demonstrate, prove; contend, contest
  con agree, coincide, concur; affirm, aver, maintain, profess

debauch *vb* **1** *syn* see DEBASE 1
  rel decoy, inveigle, lure, seduce, tempt
  con amend, remedy; clean, cleanse, purge, purify; preserve, reclaim, save
  2 *syn* see SEDUCE 2

debauch *n syn* see ORGY 2

debauched *adj syn* see DEBASED
  rel lascivious, lecherous, lewd, libertine, libidinous, licentious, wanton
  con delivered, reclaimed, redeemed, rescued, saved; chaste, decent, pure; moral, virtuous; continent, temperate

debilitate *vb syn* see WEAKEN 1
  rel devitalize; attenuate, extenuate; harm, hurt, mar, spoil
  con energize, vitalize; fortify, reinforce, strengthen; refresh, rejuvenate, renew, restore; rally, rouse, stir
  ant invigorate

debility *n syn* see INFIRMITY 1

debris *n syn* see REFUSE
  rel dregs, dross, rubble

debt *n* **1** *syn* see EVIL 1
  2 *syn* see INDEBTEDNESS 1
  3 something (as money) that is owed < struggling to keep ahead of his *debts* >
  syn arrear(s), arrearage, due, indebtedness, liability; *compare* INDEBTEDNESS 1
  rel default, deficit, delinquency, nonpayment, outstandings; debit, demurrage
  con asset, credit; compensation, refund, reimbursement, remuneration

debunk *vb syn* see EXPOSE 4

debut *vb* to make one's formal entrance into society < she *debuted* on her 20th birthday >
  syn come out
  idiom make one's bow

decadence *n syn* see DETERIORATION 1
  rel regress, regression, regressiveness, retrogradation, retrograding, retrogression, retrogressiveness; debasement, degradation
  con advance, progress, progression; amelioration, bettering, betterment, improvement
  ant rise; flourishing

decadent *adj syn* see EFFETE 3

decamp *vb* **1** *syn* see GET OUT 1
  2 *syn* see ESCAPE 1
  rel exit, go, leave, quit, retire, withdraw; avoid, elude, evade, shun
  con arrive, come

decapitate *vb* **1** *syn* see BEHEAD
  2 *syn* see DESTROY 1

decay *vb* to undergo or to cause to undergo destructive changes < apples *decaying* in the basket >
  syn break down, corrupt, crumble, decompose, disintegrate, molder, ‖perish, putrefy, putresce, rot, spoil, taint, turn
  rel deteriorate, debilitate, enfeeble, sap, undermine, weaken; contaminate, defile, pollute, dilapidate, ruin, wreck; curdle, ferment, sour, work; dry-rot
  idiom go bad, go to pot, go to seed, go to wrack and ruin
  con mature, ripen; refresh, renew, restore; activate, energize, vitalize; cleanse, purify; galvanize, quicken, stimulate, strengthen

decayed *adj* **1** *syn* see EFFETE 3
  2 *syn* see BAD 5

decease *n syn* see DEATH 1

decease *vb syn* see DIE 1

deceased *adj syn* see DEAD 1

deceit *n* **1** the act or practice of imposing upon the credulity of others by dishonesty, fraud, or trickery < he was full of *deceit* in his business dealings >
  syn cunning, dissemblance, dissimulation, duplicity, guile
  rel chicane, chicanery, deception, double-dealing, fraud, trickery; artifice, craft; cheating, cozening, defrauding, entrapping, overreaching, trapping
  con honesty, scrupulosity, scrupulousness, uprightness; candidness, candor, frankness, openness; forthrightness, straightforwardness
  2 *syn* see IMPOSTURE

deceitful *adj syn* see DISHONEST 1
  rel artful, crafty, cunning, foxy, guileful, insidious, sly, tricky, wily; clandestine, furtive, stealthy, underhand, underhanded; deceptive, delusive, delusory, misleading
  con assuring, convincing, reassuring
  ant trustworthy

deceive *vb* to lead astray or frustrate by underhandedness < advertising that *deceives* the public >
  syn beguile, betray, bluff, ‖bunk, cozen, delude, double-cross, four-flush, humbug, illude, juggle, mislead, mock, sell out, suck in, take in, two-time

rel cheat, defraud, do, overreach; circumvent, outwit; bamboozle, befool, dupe, gull, hoax, hoodwink, spoof, trick, victimize; throw off

idiom pull one's leg, pull the wool over one's eyes, put something over (or across), take for a ride, take into camp, throw off the scent (or track)

con correct, disabuse, rectify, unblind; acquaint, advise, apprise, inform

ant undeceive; enlighten

deceiving adj syn see MISLEADING
ant undeceiving; enlightening

decelerate vb syn see DELAY 1
ant accelerate

decency n syn see DECORUM 1
rel appropriateness, fittingness, fitness, suitability; ceremoniousness, conventionality, formality
con impropriety, indecorousness, unseemliness; inappropriateness, unfitness, unsuitability; discourteousness, impoliteness, rudeness
ant indecency

decent adj 1 syn see DECOROUS 1
con awkward, clumsy, gauche, inept, maladroit; discomfiting, disconcerting, embarrassing; crude, rough, rude, uncouth
2 syn see CHASTE
rel noble; good, right; rigid, strict; ascetic, austere, severe
con lewd; libertine, wanton; abandoned, dissolute, profligate, reprobate
ant indecent; obscene
3 syn see RESPECTABLE 5
4 better than mediocre but less than excellent < the accommodations were *decent* >
syn acceptable, adequate, all right, common, good, respectable, right, satisfactory, sufficient, tolerable, unexceptionable, unexceptional, unimpeachable, unobjectionable; *compare* RESPECTABLE 5, SUFFICIENT 1
rel average, fair, mediocre, middling
con imperfect, inadequate, unacceptable, unsatisfactory; excellent, fine, superior
5 syn see SUFFICIENT 1

decently adv syn see WELL 1

deception n 1 the act of deliberately deceiving < resort to falsehood and *deception* in avoiding the tax >
syn cheat, chicane, chicanery, dipsy-doodle, dirt, dishonesty, double-dealing, dupery, fourberie, fraud, hanky-panky, highbinding, indirection, sharp practice, subterfuge, ‖suck-in, trickery
rel cunning, deceit, dissimulation, duplicity, guile; cheating, cozening, defrauding, overreaching; bamboozling, befooling, duping, gulling, hoaxing, hoodwinking; manipulation; ride, ‖snow job
con candidness, frankness, openness; honesty, integrity, probity; artlessness, ingenuousness, naiveté
2 syn see IMPOSTURE
rel delusion, hallucination, illusion, mirage
3 syn see FALLACY 2

deceptive adj syn see MISLEADING
rel colorable, plausible, specious; apparent, illusory, ostensible, seeming
con authentic, bona fide, genuine, veritable; actual, real, true; dependable, reliable, trustworthy

deceptiveness n syn see FALLACY 2

decide vb to come or to cause to come to a conclusion < he *decided* how to solve the problem >
syn conclude, determine, figure, resolve, rule, settle
rel gather; adjudge, adjudicate, judge; conjecture, guess, surmise; establish, fix, set
idiom cast the die, make up one's mind, settle in one's mind
con falter, hesitate, vacillate, waver; fluctuate, oscillate; balk, demur, scruple, shy

decided adj 1 beyond any doubt or ambiguity < a *decided* advantage over her opponent >
syn assured, clear-cut, definite, pronounced
rel determined, resolved; certain, positive, sure; categorical, explicit, express, unequivocal; clear, obvious, unmistakable, runaway
con doubtful, dubious, problematic, uncertain; equivocal, obscure, vague
ant questionable
2 free from doubt or wavering < he had a *decided* manner >

syn bent, decisive, determined, intent, resolute, resolved, set, settled
rel certain, cocksure, positive, sure; iron-jawed; established, fixed; earnest, purposeful, serious; unfaltering, unhesitating, unwavering
con doubtful, dubious, irresolute, uncertain; faltering, hesitant, vacillating, wavering; undetermined, unresolved, unsettled, unsure
ant undecided
3 syn see POSITIVE 1

decidedness n syn see DECISION 2

decimate vb 1 syn see DESTROY 1
2 syn see SLAUGHTER 3

decipher vb 1 syn see DECODE
ant cipher, encipher
2 syn see SOLVE 2
rel paraphrase, translate; analyze, break down
idiom find the key of
con misconstrue, misinterpret, misunderstand; confuse, muddle; bewilder, confound, mystify, puzzle; jumble, mix, scramble

decision n 1 a position arrived at after consideration < the *decision* of the committee remains firm >
syn conclusion, determination, resolution, settlement
rel accord, agreement, understanding; accommodation, adjustment, arrangement; compromise, reconciliation; choice, preference, selection
con deadlock, draw, stalemate, standoff, tie
2 freedom from doubt or wavering < a man of unusual *decision* >
syn decidedness, determination, firmness, purposefulness, purposiveness, resoluteness, resolution, resolve
rel doggedness, obstinacy, obstinance, perseverance, persistence, stubbornness; earnestness, seriousness; backbone, fortitude, grit, pluck
con changeableness, indetermination, irresolution; uncertainty, unsureness; faltering, fluctuation, hesitation, vacillation, wavering
ant indecision

decisive adj syn see DECIDED 2
rel imperative, imperious, masterful, peremptory; assured, self-assured, self-confident; steadfast, unswerving, unwavering
con fluctuating, oscillating; hesitant, reluctant; doubtful, dubious, irresolute, uncertain, undecided
ant indecisive

deck vb syn see ADORN
rel apparel, array, attire, clothe, dress; accouter, appoint, furnish
con deface, disfigure; impair, mar, spoil; contort, deform, distort; dismantle, divest, strip

deck (out) vb syn see DRESS UP 1

declaim vb syn see ORATE

declamatory adj syn see RHETORICAL

declaration n the act of declaring, proclaiming, or publicly announcing < a *declaration* of war >
syn advertisement, announcement, broadcast, proclamation, promulgation, pronouncement, pronunciamento, publication
rel information, notice, notification; communication; disclosure, revelation; report, statement; acknowledgment, avowal
con concealment, hiding; denial, disaffirmation; recall, recantation, retraction, revocation

declare vb 1 to make known openly or publicly < *declared* his intention to run for the senate >
syn advertise, announce, annunciate, blaze (abroad), blazon, broadcast, bruit (about), disseminate, proclaim, promulgate, publish, sound, toot, vend
rel acquaint, advise, apprise, inform, notify; communicate, impart; pronounce; disclose, discover, divulge, reveal; report
idiom declare oneself, make public (or known)
con hold, hold back, keep back, reserve, withhold; recall, recant, retract, revoke
2 syn see ASSERT 1
rel air, broach, express, utter, vent, ventilate, voice; acknowledge, admit, own

---

syn synonym(s)   **rel** related word(s)
ant antonym(s)   **con** contrasted word(s)
idiom idiomatic equivalent(s)
‖ use limited; if in doubt, see a dictionary

idiom have one's say
con controvert; deny; repress, suppress; conceal, hide
3 *syn* see SAY 1
rel broach, express, voice
idiom speak one's piece
declare off *vb syn* see BACK DOWN
declass *vb syn* see DEGRADE 1
rel disbar, exclude, rule out; abash, discomfit, disconcert
con aggrandize, exalt, magnify
déclassé *adj syn* see INFERIOR 2
declension *n syn* see DETERIORATION 1
rel regression, regressiveness, retrogression, retrogressiveness; dilapidation, ruination
con ascension, ascent; rise, rising; advance, progress, progression; development, maturation
declination *n* **1 *syn*** see DETERIORATION 1
2 *syn* see FAILURE 4
decline *vb* **1 *syn*** see SET 12
ant ascend
2 *syn* see FAIL 1
rel backslide, lapse, relapse; slide; return, revert; recede, retrograde; abate, ebb, subside, wane
idiom go downhill, take a turn for the worse
con advance, progress; develop, mature; gain, recover
3 *syn* see DETERIORATE 1
4 to turn away by not accepting, receiving, or considering < he *declined* the invitation >
syn disapprove, dismiss, refuse, reject, reprobate, repudiate, spurn, turn down
rel balk, boggle, demur, jib, scruple, shy, stick, stickle; abstain, forbear, refrain; deny, gainsay; abjure, renounce; bypass
idiom send regrets
con receive, take; accede, acquiesce, assent, consent; choose, select; adopt, embrace, espouse
ant accept
decline *n* **1 *syn*** see FAILURE 4
rel devitalization, weakening
con advancement, progress; recovery; development, maturation
2 *syn* see DETERIORATION 1
rel comedown, descent, drop, fall, falling off, slump; ebb, wane; backsliding, lapse, relapse
con development, evolution
3 a downward movement (as in price or value) < stocks suffered a *decline* in the market >
syn dip, downslide, downswing, downtrend, downturn, drop, falloff, sag, slide, slip, slump
rel lapse, loss, lowering; depression; decrease, drop-off, sell-off
con upswing, uptrend, upturn
4 *syn* see DESCENT 4
declivate *adj syn* see INCLINED 3
declivitous *adj syn* see INCLINED 3
declivity *n syn* see DESCENT 4
ant acclivity
decode *vb* to convert code into ordinary language < *decode* a message >
syn break, crack, cryptanalyze, decipher, decrypt
rel anagram; render, translate; ‖dope out, figure out, make out; resolve, solve, unfold, unravel, unriddle, work, work out; elucidate, explain, interpret
con cipher, codify, encipher; anagrammatize
ant code, encode, encrypt
decollate *vb syn* see BEHEAD
decolor *vb syn* see WHITEN 1
rel wash out; achromatize, fume, peroxide
con blacken; dye, imbue, stain, tinge, tint; paint, shade
ant color
decolorize *vb syn* see WHITEN 1
ant color
decompose *vb* **1 *syn*** see ANALYZE
con combine, join, link, write; synthesize, unify; amalgamate, merge, mix
ant compound
2 *syn* see DECAY
rel deliquesce, liquefy, melt; break up, dissolve
decompound *vb syn* see ANALYZE
ant compound
decorate *vb syn* see ADORN
rel accouter, appoint, equip, furnish, outfit

con impair, injure, mar, spoil; blot, blotch, foul, mutilate, scar, uglify; dismantle, divest, strip
decorated *adj syn* see BEMEDALED
decoration *n syn* see HONOR 2
decorous *adj* **1** conforming to an accepted standard of propriety or good form < *decorous* behavior seems regrettably out of fashion >
syn au fait, becoming, befitting, Christian, civilized, comely, conforming, correct, decent, de rigueur, done, nice, proper, respectable, right, seemly
rel ceremonial, ceremonious, conventional, formal; dignified, elegant; appropriate, fit, fitting, meet, seasonable, suitable; prim, punctilious, rigid, stiff, stuffy
con blatant, clamorous, obstreperous, strident; aggressive, assertive, pushing, pushy; coarse, gross, vulgar; easy, fast, loose; improper, incorrect, unbecoming
ant indecorous
2 *syn* see GOOD 13
decorously *adv syn* see WELL 1
decorousness *n syn* see ORDER 7
rel ceremoniousness, conventionality, formality, solemnity; convenance, convention, form, usage
con inappropriateness, incorrectness; unfitness, unsuitability, unsuitableness; disorder, misbehavior, misconduct, misdeed, misdemeanor
ant indecorousness
decorticate *vb syn* see SKIN 2
rel bark; scalp; denude, divest
decorum *n* **1** socially acceptable behavior or accepted standards of this < they found his conduct quite lacking in *decorum* >
syn decency, dignity, etiquette, propriety, seemliness
rel convenance, convention, form, usage
con laxity, laxness, license, slackness; carelessness, heedlessness, inconsiderateness, mannerlessness; inappropriateness, incorrectness
ant indecorum
2 *syn* see ORDER 7
rel ceremoniousness, conventionality, formality, solemnity; convenance, convention, form, usage
con inappropriateness, incorrectness; unfitness, unsuitability, unsuitableness; disorder, misbehavior, misconduct, misdeed, misdemeanor
ant indecorum; license
3 *usu* **decorums** *syn* see MANNER 3
decoy *n* **1 *syn*** see LURE 2
rel chicane, chicanery, deception, trickery; drawing card
con rebuff, repellence, repellency, repellent, repugnance, repulse, repulsion
2 a person used as a lure < used the detective as a *decoy* to catch the pushers >
syn blind, ‖bonnet, ‖booster, capper, shill, shillaber, stick
rel lugger, roper, steerer; come-on, front, plant, stall
decoy *vb syn* see LURE
rel deceive, delude, mislead; ensorcell, wile
con disgust, repel, sicken; offend, repulse, revolt
decrease *vb* to grow less especially gradually < his influence *decreased* as a new generation grew up >
syn abate, bate, close, diminish, drain (away), dwindle, lessen, peak (out), peter (out), rebate, recede, reduce, taper, taper off
rel abbreviate, abridge, clip, curtail, retrench, shorten, trim; contract, shrink; allay, alleviate, ease, lighten, mitigate; ebb, subside; cut, cut back, cut down, lower; deduct, subtract
con augment, enlarge, multiply; elongate, extend, lengthen, prolong, protract; amplify, dilate, distend, expand, swell; accumulate, amass
ant increase
decree *n* **1 *syn*** see EDICT 1
2 *syn* see LAW 1
rel behest, bidding, injunction, order; charge, charging, direction, instruction; announcement, declaration, proclamation, promulgation, pronouncement
decree *vb syn* see DICTATE
rel compel, constrain, force, oblige; demand, require
decrepit *adj* **1 *syn*** see WEAK 1
rel haggard, wasted, worn; aged, old, superannuated; creaky, quavering, shaking, tottering
con strong; lusty; hale, healthy, hearty, robust, sound, well
ant sturdy

2 syn see SHABBY 1

rel damaged, impaired, injured, marred, spoiled; cast-off, ragged, used; slipshod, sloppy, unkempt

decrepitude *n syn* see INFIRMITY 1

ant vigor

decretum *n syn* see LAW 1

decry *vb* **1 syn** see DEPRECIATE 1

2 to indicate one's low opinion of something <*decrying* his opponent's character>

syn abuse, belittle, cry down, depreciate, derogate, detract (from), diminish, discount, disparage, dispraise, downcry, ‖lowrate, minimize, opprobriate, run down, take (from), take away, write off

rel deprecate, disapprove; censure, condemn, criticize, denounce, reprehend, reprobate; asperse, calumniate, defame, malign, traduce, vilify; discredit, disgrace

idiom bring into discredit, cast a slur upon, cast blame upon, throw stones at

con acclaim, eulogize, laud, praise; aggrandize, exalt, magnify; applaud, commend, compliment, recommend; endorse, sanction; approve, countenance, favor

ant extol, puff

decrypt *vb syn* see DECODE

decumbent *adj syn* see PRONE 4

decussate *vb syn* see INTERSECT

dedicate *vb syn* see DEVOTE 1

rel address, apply, direct, give, surrender; commit, confide, consign, entrust; allot, appropriate, assign, set (aside)

idiom give over to

dedition *n syn* see SURRENDER

deduce *vb syn* see INFER

rel cogitate; consider, deem, regard; conceive, fancy, imagine; assume, presume, presuppose; read (into)

idiom take to mean

deducible *adj syn* see DEDUCTIVE

deduct *vb* **1** to take away one quantity from another <*deduct* the cost from his bill>

syn discount, draw back, knock off, substract, subtract, take, take away, take off, take out

rel decrease, diminish, lessen, reduce; roll back

con cast, figure, sum, tot, total

ant add

2 syn see INFER

deduction *n* **1** an amount subtracted from a sum <*deductions* from gross income>

syn abatement, discount, rebate, reduction, subtraction

rel allowance, credit, cut; decrease, decrement, depreciation, diminution; charge-off, offtake, takeoff, write-off; dockage

con accession, accretion, augmentation, increase, increment, raise, rise; appreciation

ant addition

2 syn see INFERENCE 1

3 syn see INFERENCE 2

rel cogitation, deliberation, reasoning, reflection, speculation, thinking; consideration, contemplation; meditation, mulling, musing, pondering, rumination

deductive *adj* that can be deduced or developed from premises <*deductive* laws >

syn a priori, deducible, derivable, dogmatic, reasoned

rel illative, inferential, ratiocinative; conjectural, hypothetical, purported, putative, supposed, suppositious; academic, speculative, theoretical

con categorical, definite, explicit, express; instinctive, intuitive

deed *n* **1 syn** see ACTION 1

2 syn see FEAT 2

rel gaining, securing, winning; adventure, enterprise, quest; cause, crusade

idiom bold stroke

3 a written, signed, and usually sealed instrument that spells out some bargain, transfer, or contract <the *deed* to the property>

syn charter, conveyance

rel bargain, compact, contract, covenant, pact

deed *vb syn* see TRANSFER 4

deem *vb* **1 syn** see CONSIDER 3

rel conjecture, guess, surmise, suspect, ‖suspicion, understand; ‖allow, assume, believe, ‖calculate, daresay, divine, expect, presume, suppose

idiom hold to be true

2 syn see FEEL 3

idiom take for granted

de—emphasize *vb syn* see SOFT-PEDAL

deep *adj* **1** having great extension downward or inward <a *deep* well > <a *deep* closet>

syn abysmal, profound; *compare* BOTTOMLESS 2

con depthless, shallow, superficial, unprofound; flat, level, plain, plane

ant shallow

2 syn see INTENSIVE

3 syn see RECONDITE

rel complex, complicated, intricate; arcane, mysterious; concealed, hidden

con easy, facile, simple; apparent, clear, distinct, evident, manifest, obvious; lucid, perspicuous; depthless, shallow, superficial, unprofound

4 syn see SLY 2

rel shrewd; acute, keen, knowing, sharp; contriving, intriguing, plotting

con ingenuous, naive, simple, unsophisticated; aboveboard, forthright, straightforward

5 syn see INTENT

rel abstracted, concentrated; centered, fixed, focused, set

con distracted, diverted; detached, disinterested, indifferent, unconcerned, uninterested

deep *n syn* see OCEAN

deep—dyed *adj syn* see INVETERATE 1

deepen *vb syn* see INTENSIFY

deepness *n* **1 syn** see DEPTH 1

ant shallowness

2 syn see DEPTH 2

deep—rooted *adj syn* see INVETERATE 1

deep—seated *adj* **1 syn** see INHERENT

2 syn see INVETERATE 1

rel constitutional, immanent, indwelling, ingrained, inherent, intrinsic; deep, profound; inner, internal, inward; implanted; infixed

con peripheral, shallow, superficial, surface; adventitious, casual, chance, incidental

ant skin-deep

‖deep—six *vb syn* see DISCARD

deep water *n syn* see PREDICAMENT

deface *vb* to mar the appearance of <*deface* the wall with graffiti>

syn disfashion, disfeature, disfigure

rel blemish, damage, harm, impair, injure, mar, spoil; contort, deform, distort, misshape; batter, mangle, mutilate; demolish, destroy; dilapidate, ruin, wreck

con mend, patch, repair; freshen, improve, refurbish, renew, restore; adorn, beautify, deck, decorate, embellish, ornament

defacer *n syn* see VANDAL

de facto *adv syn* see VERY 2

defalcation *n syn* see FAILURE 3

rel laxness, negligence, remissness, slackness; failing, fault

con discharge, effectuation, execution, fulfillment; completion, conclusion

defamation *n syn* see DETRACTION

ant puffery

defamatory *adj syn* see LIBELOUS

defame *vb syn* see MALIGN

rel belie, misrepresent

idiom cast a slur on, throw mud at

con applaud, commend, compliment; exalt, magnify; back, champion, support, uphold

ant laud; puff

default *n* **1 syn** see FAILURE 1

rel deficiency, fault, imperfection, shortcoming; lapse, weakness; disregard, omission, overlooking, slight

2 syn see ABSENCE

defeasance *n syn* see DEFEAT 1

defeat *vb* **1 syn** see CONQUER 1

rel bar, block, hinder, impede, obstruct; repress, suppress

---

syn synonym(s)   *rel* related word(s)

ant antonym(s)   *con* contrasted word(s)

idiom idiomatic equivalent(s)

‖ use limited; if in doubt, see a dictionary

idiom beat all hollow, get the better of, grind into the dust
con capitulate, defer, give in, submit; back down, withdraw
2 to win a victory over < *defeated* his opponent in the race >
syn best, down, outdo, ‖pip, worst; *compare* CONQUER 1, WHIP 2
rel outfight, outgame; nose out
idiom get the better of

defeat *n* **1** an overthrow especially of an army in battle < the brigade suffered a *defeat* >
syn beating, debacle, defeasance, discomfiture, downcast, downthrow, drubbing, ‖dusting, licking, overthrow, rout, shellacking, thrashing, trouncing, vanquishment, warming
rel bafflement, check, foil, frustration; rebuff, repulse, reversal, reverse, setback; ‖cleaning, ‖cleanup, clobbering, lambasting
con conquest, triumph; gaining, securing, winning; ascendancy, supremacy
ant victory
2 *syn* see FAILURE 2

defeater *n syn* see VICTOR 1
ant defeated

defect *n* **1** *syn* see BLEMISH
rel failing, fault, foible, frailty; infirmity, weakness; deficiency, imperfection, shortcoming
con excellence, faultlessness, impeccability; merit, perfection, virtue
2 *syn* see ABSENCE
rel scantiness, scarceness, scarcity, shortage
con overage, overplus, superfluity, surplus, surplusage
ant excess

defect *vb* to desert a cause or party often in order to espouse another < he *defected* from the Communist party >
syn apostatize, desert, rat, renounce, repudiate, tergiversate, tergiverse, turn
rel abandon, forsake; back out, renege, withdraw; depart, go, leave, quit; reject, spurn
idiom change sides, go back on, go over, turn one's coat, walk (*or* run) out on
con adhere (to), cling (to), hang on, stick (to *or* with); cherish, cultivate, foster

defection *n* conscious abandonment of allegiance or duty < *defection* from family responsibilities in times of trouble >
syn apostasy, desertion, falseness, recreancy, tergiversation
rel alienation, disaffection, estrangement; disloyalty, faithlessness; abandonment, forsaking; divorce, parting, runout, separation, sundering; disownment, rejection, repudiation
idiom running out on, ‖taking a runout powder
con constancy, faithfulness, loyalty, resoluteness, staunchness, steadfastness; allegiance, fealty, fidelity; dependability, reliability, trustworthiness

defective *adj* **1** *syn* see FAULTY
rel broken, damaged, impaired, injured
con faultless, flawless, impeccable, unblemished, undamaged
ant defectless
2 *syn* see DEFICIENT 1
rel corrupted, debased, vitiated; deranged, disordered, disturbed, unsettled; unhealthy, unsound
con entire, perfect, whole; complete, full, plenary; healthy, sound
ant intact; defectless

defector *n syn* see RENEGADE

defend *vb* **1** to keep safe (as from danger or against attack) < *defend* the country from aggression >
syn bulwark, cover, fend, guard, protect, safeguard, screen, secure, shield
rel avert, prevent, ward; oppose, resist, withstand; battle, contend, fight, war; conserve, preserve, save
idiom stand on the defensive, stave off from
con aggress, assail, assault, fall (on *or* upon); bombard, storm; beset, besiege, overrun; capitulate, cave, submit, yield
ant attack
2 *syn* see MAINTAIN 2
rel air, express, utter, vent, voice; account, explain, justify, rationalize; back, champion, support, uphold
idiom speak (*or* stand *or* stick) up for
con contradict, deny, gainsay, traverse; confute, controvert, disprove, rebut, refute

defendable *adj syn* see TENABLE 1
ant undefendable

defense *n* **1** means or method of defending < the skunk's powerful *defense* against attackers >

syn aegis, armament, armor, guard, protection, safeguard, security, shield, ward
rel arms, munitions, weaponry, weapons; fastness, fort, fortress, stronghold
con aggression, offense, offensive
ant attack
2 *syn* see APOLOGY 1
rel answer, rejoinder, reply, response, retort, return; exculpation, excuse, explanation, rationalization
con censure, condemnation, criticism, decrial, reprehension, reprobation, reproof; assault, attack, onset, onslaught

defenseless *adj syn* see HELPLESS 1

defensible *adj* **1** *syn* see TENABLE 1
ant indefensible
2 *syn* see JUSTIFIABLE
ant indefensible

defer *vb* to delay an action or proceeding < decided to *defer* voting until the next meeting >
syn adjourn, delay, hold off, hold over, hold up, intermit, lay over, postpone, prorogue, put off, put over, remit, shelve, stand over, stay, suspend, waive
rel detain, retard, slow; block, hinder, impede, obstruct; stall; extend, lengthen, prolong, protract
idiom hold up on, lay to one side, put on ice, set aside
con accelerate, hasten, hurry, speed; expedite, further, promote
ant advance

defer *vb syn* see YIELD 2
rel accede, acquiesce, agree, assent; accommodate, adapt, adjust, conform; cringe, fawn, truckle
con combat, fight, oppose, resist; object, remonstrate; balk, demur, stickle, strain
ant withstand

deference *n syn* see HONOR 1
rel acquiescence, compliance; submission, submissiveness
con insolence, irreverence; disesteem, disfavor; discourtesy, incivility, rudeness
ant disrespect

deferential *adj* **1** *syn* see RESPECTFUL
2 *syn* see INGRATIATING

defi *n syn* see DEFIANCE 1

defiance *n* **1** the act or an instance of defying < presented a *defiance* to his rival >
syn cartel, challenge, dare, defi, defy, stump
rel call, muster, summons; command, enjoinder, order
con capitulation, submission, surrender
2 disposition to resist or unwillingness to brook opposition < exhibited *defiance* toward his teacher >
syn contempt, contumacy, despite, recalcitrance, stubbornness
rel factiousness, insubordination, insurgency, rebelliousness; headstrongness, intractableness, unruliness; boldness, bravado, brazenness, impudence, insolence; audacity, effrontery, hardihood, temerity; contrariness, perversity
con acquiescence, compliance; amenableness, docility, obedience, tractableness; submissiveness

deficiency *n* **1** *syn* see FAILURE 3
rel absence, default, defect, want
con copiousness, plenty; great deal, heap, lot, much
2 *syn* see IMPERFECTION
rel dearth, defect, lack, privation, want; default, dereliction, miscarriage, neglect
ant excess

deficient *adj* **1** showing lack of something necessary < *deficient* in judgment >
syn defective, inadequate, incomplete, insufficient, lacking, uncomplete, wanting
rel faulty, flawed, imperfect, unsound; damaged, impaired, injured, marred; amiss, bad, unsatisfactory
idiom in want of
con complete, entire, intact, whole; acceptable, adequate, sufficient
2 *syn* see SHORT 3
rel infrequent, rare, uncommon
idiom found wanting
con excessive, extravagant, immoderate, inordinate; enough, satisfactory, sufficing
ant adequate, sufficient

deficit *n syn* see FAILURE 3
con copiousness, plenty; excess, surplus, surplusage

defile *vb* **1** *syn* see CONTAMINATE 1
  rel desecrate, profane; befoul, dirty, foul, sully, tarnish
  con consecrate, hallow
  ant cleanse; purify
  2 *syn* see RAPE
  rel dishonor, shame, soil, sully
  3 *syn* see TAINT 1
defiled *adj syn* see IMPURE
define *vb* **1** *syn* see PRESCRIBE 2
  rel circumscribe, limit, mark (off), mark (out); designate; delineate, describe
  con confound, confuse, mistake
  2 *syn* see BORDER 1
  3 *syn* see ETCH 2
  rel explain, expound, interpret
definite *adj* **1** having distinct or certain limits <*definite* dimensions>
  syn circumscribed, determinate, fixed, limited, narrow, precise, restricted
  rel assigned, defined, prescribed; established, set; decided, determined, settled
  con ambiguous, obscure, vague; unconditional, unlimited, unqualified, unrestricted; indeterminate, uncircumscribed; imprecise, loose, undefined
  ant indefinite
  2 *syn* see EXPLICIT
  rel complete, full; downright, forthright; incisive
  con doubtful, dubious, questionable; ambiguous
  ant indefinite; equivocal
  3 *syn* see POSITIVE 1
  4 *syn* see DECIDED 1
  ant uncertain
definitely *adv* **1** *syn* see EXPRESSLY 1
  2 *syn* see EASILY 2
definiteness *n syn* see PRECISION
  ant indefiniteness
definitive *adj* **1** *syn* see CONCLUSIVE
  rel determining, settling; concluding, final, last, terminal, ultimate; closing, completing, ending, finishing, terminating; absolute, categorical
  con inconclusive, indecisive; temporary, transitory
  ant provisional, tentative
  2 *syn* see EXPLICIT
  rel actual, real
  con doubtful, dubious, questionable; ambiguous
  ant indefinitive
definitiveness *n syn* see PRECISION
  ant indefinitiveness, indefinitude
definitude *n syn* see PRECISION
  ant indefinitiveness, indefinitude
deflect *vb* **1** *syn* see TURN 6
  rel disperse, swerve; hook, skew
  2 *syn* see WARD 1
  rel hold off, keep off
deflection *n* **1** *syn* see DEVIATION 1
  rel bending, curving, twisting; departing, swerve, swerving, veer, veering
  2 *syn* see TURN 2
deflorate *vb syn* see RAPE
deflower *vb* **1** *syn* see RAPE
  2 *syn* see RAVAGE
deform *vb* to mar or spoil by or as if by twisting <a face *deformed* by bitterness>
  syn contort, distort, misshape, torture, warp, wind
  rel batter, cripple, maim, mangle, mutilate; deface, disfigure; damage, impair, injure, mar, spoil; blemish, flaw; screw (up), squinch
deformity *n* a physical blemish or disfigurement <the dwarf's humpback *deformity*>
  syn distortion, malconformation, malformation, misshape
  rel defacement, deformation, disfigurement; damage, impairment, injury; aberration, abnormality; irregularity, unnaturalness
defraud *vb syn* see CHEAT
  rel bamboozle, hoax, trick; circumvent, foil, outwit; fleece, milk, stick; take in
  idiom do out of, put over a fast one, take to the cleaner's
defrauder *n syn* see SWINDLER
deft *adj syn* see DEXTEROUS 1

  rel agile, brisk, fleet; apt, prompt, quick, ready; adept, crack, crackerjack; ingenious, neat
  con heavy-handed, unskillful; blundering, bungling, butterfingered; rigid, stiff, wooden
  ant awkward, unhandy
deftness *n syn* see ADDRESS 1
  rel agility, fleetness, nimbleness; assuredness, confidence
  con incompetence, inefficiency; clumsiness, heavy-handedness, maladroitness
  ant awkwardness
defunct *adj* **1** *syn* see DEAD 1
  rel inactive, inert
  ant alive; live
  2 *syn* see EXTINCT 2
  ant surviving
defunction *n syn* see DEATH 1
defy *vb syn* see FACE 3
  rel deride, mock, ridicule; gibe, flout; scorn, scout, spurn; disregard, ignore
  idiom fling (or throw) down the gauntlet, hurl defiance at
  con blench, flinch, quail, shrink
  ant recoil
defy *n syn* see DEFIANCE 1
dégagé *adj syn* see EASYGOING 3
  ant mannered
degeneracy *n syn* see DETERIORATION 1
degenerate *adj* **1** *syn* see EFFETE 3
  rel deteriorating, retrograde, retrogressive, worsening; failing, sinking
  2 *syn* see VICIOUS 2
  rel degraded, demeaned
  con ethical, moral, virtuous; honorable, just, upright
  ant regenerate
degenerate *vb syn* see DETERIORATE 1
  rel corrupt, deprave, vitiate; backslide, lapse; return, revert
  con improve, upgrade; lift, uplift
degeneration *n syn* see DETERIORATION 1
  rel regression, regressiveness, retrogression, retrogressiveness; depreciation; corruption, depravation, depravedness, depravity, perversion
  con regeneracy, regenerateness; progress, progression
  ant regeneration
degradation *n syn* see DEMOTION
  ant advancement; elevation
degrade *vb* **1** to lower in station, rank, or grade <*degraded* in rank for misconduct>
  syn break, bump, bust, declass, demerit, demote, disgrade, disrate, downgrade, put down, reduce
  rel abase, debase, humble, humiliate, lower; disbar, rule out
  con advance, further; boost, lift, raise; enhance, heighten
  ant elevate
  2 *syn* see HUMBLE
  rel belittle, decry, derogate, detract, disparage; diminish, lessen, reduce
  con elevate, raise; acclaim, extol, laud, praise
  ant uplift
degree *n* **1** a unitary component of a process, course, or order of classification <advanced by *degrees*>
  syn grade, notch, rung, stage, step
  2 relative size or character of the parts or components in a complex whole compared with other like things <the *degree* of difference between the two jobs> <his work demands a high *degree* of intelligence>
  syn proportion, rate, ratio, scale
  rel dimension; extent, magnitude, measure, size
dégringolade *n syn* see DETERIORATION 1
dehydrate *vb syn* see DRY 1
  ant hydrate; rehydrate
deific *adj* **1** *syn* see DIVINE 1
  2 *syn* see DIVINE 2
deification *n syn* see APOTHEOSIS 2
deign *vb syn* see STOOP 1
deject *vb syn* see DISCOURAGE 1

---

syn synonym(s)   *rel* related word(s)
ant antonym(s)   *con* contrasted word(s)
idiom idiomatic equivalent(s)
‖ use limited; if in doubt, see a dictionary

ant exhilarate; cheer

dejected *adj syn* see DOWNCAST
idiom down in the dumps (*or* mouth), in the dumps
ant animated

dejection *n syn* see SADNESS
rel despair, desperation
ant exhilaration

‖**dekko** *vb syn* see SEE 2

delay *vb* **1** to cause to be late or behind in movement or progress
< was *delayed* by traffic >
syn bog (down), decelerate, detain, embog, hang up, mire, retard, set back, slacken, slow (up *or* down)
rel block, hinder, impede, obstruct; defer, hold over, hold up,
intermit, postpone, put off, stay, suspend; arrest, check, interrupt
idiom hang fire
con accelerate, hasten, hurry, precipitate, quicken, speed; advance, forward, further, promote
ant expedite
2 to move or act slowly so that progress or work is retarded
< their landlord kept *delaying* in making repairs >
syn dally, dawdle, dilly, dillydally, drag, lag, linger, loiter,
mull, poke, procrastinate, put off, tarry, trail
rel hang back, idle, wait; drone; falter, hesitate, vacillate, waver
idiom take one's own sweet (*or* good) time
ant hasten, hurry
3 *syn* see DEFER

delectable *adj syn* see DELIGHTFUL
rel choice, dainty, delicate, exquisite, rare; palatable, sapid, savory, tasty, toothsome
con loathsome, offensive, repulsive, revolting
ant distasteful

delectate *vb syn* see PLEASE 2

delectation *n* **1** *syn* see PLEASURE 2
rel gratification, gratifying, regalement, regaling; enjoyment,
relish
ant distaste
2 *syn* see ENJOYMENT 1

‖**deleerit** *adj syn* see INTOXICATED 1

delegate *n* a person standing in the place of another or others
< was a *delegate* to the convention >
syn catchpole, deputy, representant, representative; *compare*
AGENT 2
rel agent, factor, proxy; alternate, replacement, stand-in, substitute, surrogate; mouthpiece, spokesman; emissary, envoy

delegate *vb* to appoint as one's representative < *delegated* her to
watch the children >
syn commission, depute, deputize
rel ascribe, assign, charge; appoint, designate, name; choose,
pick, select

delete *vb syn* see ERASE
rel eliminate, exclude, rule out; omit

deleterious *adj syn* see HARMFUL
rel destroying, destructive; ruining, ruinous
con advantageous, profitable; healthful, healthy, salubrious,
wholesome
ant salutary

deliberate *adj* **1** arrived at after due thought < a *deliberate* judgment >
syn advised, aforethought, considered, designed, premeditated,
prepense, studied, studious, thought-out
rel planned, projected, schemed; calculated; careful, meticulous,
scrupulous; foresighted, forethoughtful, provident, prudent
con chance, chancy, desultory, haphazard, happy-go-lucky, hit=
or-miss, random; aimless, designless, purposeless; hasty, hurried;
abrupt, impetuous, sudden; automatic, instinctive, spontaneous
ant casual
2 *syn* see VOLUNTARY
rel intended, meant, meditated, purposed; determined, purposeful; aware, cognizant, conscious
con careless, heedless, inadvertent, thoughtless; unintended, unpurposed
ant impulsive
3 *syn* see SLOW 2
rel calculating, cautious, chary, circumspect, wary; careful,
heedful; collected, composed, cool, imperturbable
con hasty, headlong, impetuous, sudden
ant abrupt, precipitate

deliberate *vb* **1** *syn* see PONDER 2
2 *syn* see THINK 5
rel excogitate, study, weigh; argue, debate, discuss, talk over

deliberately *adv syn* see INTENTIONALLY

deliberation *n* **1** *syn* see ATTENTION 1
2 *syn* see THOUGHT 1
3 *syn* see CONFERENCE 1

delicacy *n* something special and delicious to eat < fresh fruit in
the winter was once an uncommon *delicacy* >
syn bonne bouche, dainty, goody, kickshaw, morsel, tidbit (*or*
titbit), treat
rel banquet, feast, regale; cosseting, indulgence, luxury
idiom choice bit, dish fit for a king

delicate *adj* **1** *syn* see CHOICE
rel delectable, delicious, delightful; balmy, gentle, lenient, mild,
soft; aerial, airy, ethereal
con coarse, crude, vulgar
ant gross
2 *syn* see FINE 1
3 *syn* see NICE 1
rel perceptive, sensitive
con insensitive, undiscriminating, unperceptive
4 *syn* see FRAGILE 1
5 lacking in strength or substance < a *delicate* constitution >
syn flimsy, slight
rel feeble, fragile, frail, weak; sickly, unhealthy; decrepit, infirm
con stalwart, stout, strong, sturdy, tenacious, tough; hale,
healthy, robust, sound, well, wholesome
6 *syn* see TACTFUL
rel adept, expert, masterly, proficient; discreet, foresighted, prudent; careful, heedful; cautious, wary
con impolitic; imprudent, indiscreet; awkward, clumsy, gauche,
inept, maladroit; unskillful
7 marked by or requiring tact < a *delicate* situation >
syn precarious, sensitive, ticklish, touchy, tricky
rel uncertain, unpredictable; hair-trigger, volatile; sticky

delicatesse *n syn* see TACT
ant indelicacy

delicious *adj syn* see DELIGHTFUL
rel appetizing, palatable, sapid, savory, toothsome; choice,
dainty, delicate, exquisite, rare
con banal, flat, inane, insipid, jejune, wishy-washy

delight *vb* **1** *syn* see EXULT
2 *syn* see PLEASE 2
rel amuse, divert, entertain; allure, attract, charm, enchant, fascinate; enrapture, entrance, transport
con aggrieve, distress, pain, trouble; afflict, try; grieve; bother,
irk; bore

delight (in) *vb* **1** *syn* see ADMIRE 1
rel enjoy, like, savor; eat up, luxuriate (in)
con abhor, abominate, hate, loathe
2 *syn* see LOVE 1

delight *n syn* see PLEASURE 2
rel glee, hilarity, jollity, mirth; ecstasy, rapture, transport; contentment, satisfaction; relish
con abhorrence, detestation, hate, hatred; dislike, distaste; discontent, dissatisfaction
ant aversion; disappointment

delightful *adj* highly pleasing to the senses or to aesthetic taste
< a *delightful* view >
syn adorable, ambrosial, darling, delectable, delicious, heavenly,
luscious, lush, scrumptious, yummy
rel charming, enchanting, fascinating; alluring, attractive; beautiful, fair, lovely; ineffable; agreeable, gratifying, pleasant, pleasing; satisfying
con miserable, wretched; distasteful, obnoxious, repellent, repugnant; abhorrent, detestable, hateful, odious; boring, irksome,
tedious; distressing, troubling
ant abominable, horrid

delimit *vb* **1** *syn* see DEMARCATE 1
rel decide
2 *syn* see LIMIT 2

delimitate *vb* **1** *syn* see DEMARCATE 1
2 *syn* see LIMIT 2

delineate *vb* **1** *syn* see REPRESENT 1
rel design, plan; evoke, paint
2 *syn* see ETCH 2

delineation *n* **1** *syn* see REPRESENTATION

rel design, plan; evocation, painting; account, story, version
2 syn see OUTLINE

delinquency *n syn* see FAILURE 1
rel nonobservance; nonfulfillment; lapse, weakness

delinquent *adj syn* see NEGLIGENT

deliquesce *vb syn* see LIQUEFY
rel decay, decompose, disintegrate
con cake, harden, indurate, set, solidify

delirious *adj* 1 disordered in mind especially temporarily < *delirious* from the fever >
syn raving, wandering
rel deranged, disarranged, disordered, disturbed, unsettled; bewildered, confused, distracted; rambling; irrational, unreasonable; crazed, crazy, demented, insane, lunatic, mad, maniac
idiom out of one's head (*or* mind)
con rational, reasonable; sane, sensible; comatose, unconscious
2 syn see FURIOUS 2
rel overexcited, overwrought; ecstatic, rapturous, transported; delighted, enthused, thrilled
idiom all agog, beside oneself
con collected, composed, easy, relaxed; unexcited, unmoved, unstimulated

delirium *n* frenzied excitement or wild enthusiasm < in a *delirium* of patriotic feeling >
syn frenzy, furor
rel ardor, enthusiasm, fervor, passion, zeal; ecstasy, rapture, transport
con nonchalance, sangfroid; indifference, unconcern
ant apathy

deliver *vb* 1 *syn* see RESCUE
con immure, imprison, incarcerate, intern, jail; capture, catch, ensnare, entrap, snare, trap; condemn, damn, doom
2 syn see GIVE 3
rel relinquish, resign, surrender, yield
con keep, retain
3 syn see BEAR 5
4 syn see SAY 1
rel broach, express, vent, voice; communicate, impart
5 syn see GIVE 10
rel dispatch, send, transmit; fling, hurl, pitch, throw

delivery *n syn* see BIRTH 1

Delphian *adj* 1 *syn* see PROPHETIC
2 syn see CRYPTIC

delude *vb syn* see DECEIVE
idiom play tricks (*or* a trick) on
con enlighten, illume, illuminate, illustrate, light, lighten; elucidate, explain

deluding *adj syn* see MISLEADING

deluge *n syn* see FLOOD 2
rel flux; overrunning

deluge *vb* 1 to flow over so as to submerge or enclose < the lowlands were completely *deluged* >
syn drown, engulf, flood, inundate, overflow, overwhelm, submerge, swamp, whelm
rel overrun; flush, gush, pour, sluice, stream
2 syn see WET
con dehydrate, desiccate, dry, parch
3 to affect overwhelmingly as if by a deluge of water < he was *deluged* by telephone calls >
syn flood, overwhelm, swamp, whelm
rel overcome; oversupply; abound, teem

delusion *n* 1 something accepted as true that is actually false or unreal < people who suffer from *delusions* of persecution >
syn hallucination, ignis fatuus, illusion, mirage, phantasm
rel chicane, chicanery, deception, trickery; cheat, counterfeit, deceit, fake, fraud, humbug, imposture, sham; daydream, dream, fancy, fantasy, figment, vision; apparition, eidolon, ghost, phantom, shade
ant reality
2 syn see FALLACY 2
ant verity

delusive *adj syn* see MISLEADING
rel chimerical, fanciful, fantastic, imaginary, quixotic, visionary; apparent, illusory, ostensible, seeming
con authentic, bona fide, genuine, veritable; actual, real, true

delusory *adj syn* see MISLEADING

deluxe *adj syn* see LUXURIOUS 3
rel choice, dainty, delicate, elegant, exquisite, rare, recherché

con coarse, common, ordinary; inelegant

delve *vb* ‖1 *syn* see DIG 1
rel gouge (out), hollow (out), quarry (out), scoop (out); burrow, tunnel; comb, ferret out, search, seek
2 syn see MINE

delve (into) *vb syn* see EXPLORE

delve *n syn* see HOLE 1

delving *n syn* see INQUIRY 1

demagogue *n* a leader who makes use of popular prejudices and false claims especially for political advantage < *demagogues* who endanger the orderly processes of democratic government >
syn rabble-rouser
rel fomenter, inciter, instigator; agitator, firebrand, hothead, incendiary, inflamer; troublemaker

demand *n* 1 *syn* see REQUIREMENT 1
2 syn see NEED 3

demand *vb* 1 to ask for something as or as if one's right or due < the physician *demanded* payment of his bill >
syn call, challenge, claim, exact, postulate, require, requisition, solicit
rel ask, request; bid, charge, command, direct, enjoin, order; cite, summon, summons; coerce, compel, constrain, force, oblige; necessitate
con cede, relinquish, resign, waive; allow, concede, grant; give, offer, tender
2 to have as a need or requirement < it *demands* considerable practice to master the piano >
syn ask, call (for), crave, necessitate, require, take
rel fail, lack, need, want
idiom need (*or* want), doing, stand in need of

demanding *adj syn* see ONEROUS
rel rigid, rigorous, severe, stern, strict, stringent; crying, imperative, importunate, instant, pressing, urgent
ant undemanding

demarcate *vb* 1 to mark the limits of < *demarcate* the boundary between two countries >
syn bound, delimit, delimitate, determine, limit, mark (out), measure
rel establish, fix, set; assign, define, prescribe; circumscribe, confine, restrict
2 syn see DISTINGUISH
rel insulate, isolate, seclude, segregate, sequester

demean *vb syn* see BEHAVE 1

demean *vb syn* see HUMBLE
rel belittle, decry, derogate, detract, disparage; contemn, despise, scorn
con elevate, enhance, heighten

demeanor *n syn* see BEARING 1
rel behavior, conduct

dement *n syn* see LUNATIC 1

demented *adj syn* see INSANE 1
rel delirious, frenzied, hysterical

demerit *n syn* see IMPERFECTION

demerit *vb syn* see DEGRADE 1

demeritorious *adj syn* see BLAMEWORTHY
ant meritorious

demesne *n syn* see FIELD

demigod *n syn* see SUPERMAN

demimondaine *n syn* see HARLOT 1

demimonde *n syn* see HARLOT 1

demirep *n syn* see HARLOT 1

demise *vb syn* see DIE 1

demise *n syn* see DEATH 1
rel annihilation, ending, expiration, extinction

demit *vb syn* see ABDICATE 1

demit *vb syn* see LOWER 3

demiurgic *adj syn* see INVENTIVE

‖**demob** *vb syn* see DISCHARGE 7
ant mobilize

demobilize *vb syn* see DISCHARGE 7
rel break up, disband, dispel, disperse, scatter; retire, withdraw
ant mobilize

---

syn synonym(s)   *rel* related word(s)
ant antonym(s)   *con* contrasted word(s)
idiom idiomatic equivalent(s)
‖ use limited; if in doubt, see a dictionary

democratic *adj* of or relating to a political system in which the supreme power is held and exercised by the people <a *democratic* government>
  syn popular, self-governing, self-ruling
  rel representative; libertarian
  con totalitarian; absolute, arbitrary, autocratic, despotic; tyrannical, tyrannous; fascistic, nazi, patriarchal
  ant authoritarian; undemocratic

démodé *adj syn* see OLD-FASHIONED
  ant a la mode

demoded *adj syn* see OLD-FASHIONED
  ant a la mode

demolish *vb* 1 *syn* see DESTROY 1
  rel dilapidate; crush, smash; break, burst, crack
  con build, erect, frame, raise, rear
  ant construct; rebuild
  2 *syn* see TOTAL 3

demon *n syn* see DEVIL 2

demoniac *adj syn* see FIENDISH
  rel crazed, crazy, insane, maniac; fired, inspired
  con celestial, heavenly
  ant angelic

demonian *adj syn* see FIENDISH
  rel crazed, crazy, insane, maniac; fired, inspired
  con celestial, heavenly
  ant angelic

demonic *adj syn* see FIENDISH
  rel crazed, crazy, insane, maniac; fired, inspired
  con celestial, heavenly
  ant angelic

demonstrate *vb* 1 *syn* see SHOW 2
  rel display, exhibit, expose, flaunt, parade; explain, set forth
  idiom go to show
  con conceal, hide, secrete; camouflage, cloak, disguise, dissemble, mask
  2 *syn* see PROVE 1
  rel authenticate, validate
  3 *syn* see ESTABLISH 6

demonstration *n syn* see EXHIBITION 1

demonstrative *adj* marked by display of feeling <was *demonstrative* in his welcome>
  syn expansive, outgoing, unconstrained, unreserved, unrestrained
  rel affectionate, loving; effusive, outpouring, profuse; candid, frank, open, outspoken, plain
  con constrained, reserved, restrained, reticent, taciturn; bashful, shy; retiring, shrinking, introverted; aloof, detached, indifferent, unconcerned; chilly, cold, frigid, glacial, icy
  ant undemonstrative

demoralize *vb* 1 *syn* see DEBASE 1
  rel debilitate, undermine, weaken; damp, dampen
  2 *syn* see DISCOURAGE 1
  rel agitate, disturb, upset; disarrange, disorder, disorganize, unsettle; confuse, jumble, muddle, snarl; debilitate, undermine, weaken; unman, unnerve
  con arrange, order, organize; energize, fortify, invigorate, strengthen

demote *vb syn* see DEGRADE 1
  rel demean, lower
  ant promote

demotion *n* the action or an instance of demoting <received a *demotion* from sergeant to corporal>
  syn degradation, downgrading, reduction
  rel debasement, humbling, humiliation; blackballing, disbarment, exclusion, suspension
  con advancement, preferment, upgrading; aggrandizement; boost, elevation, lift, raise
  ant promotion

demur *vb* to object or have scruples <he *demurred* at any horseplay>
  syn balk, boggle, gag, jib, scruple, shy, stick, stickle, strain, stumble
  rel falter, hesitate, vacillate, waver; combat, fight, oppose, resist; expostulate, object, protest, remonstrate; deprecate, disapprove
  con accept, admit, receive, take; acquiesce, agree, assent, consent, subscribe, yes; concur; defer, relent, succumb, submit, yield
  ant accede

demur *n* 1 *syn* see QUALM
  rel faltering, hesitancy, hesitation; aversion, disinclination, loathness; expostulation, protest
  con promptness, quickness, readiness
  2 the act of objecting or taking exception <accepted without *demur*>
  syn challenge, demurral, demurrer, difficulty, objection, protest, question, remonstrance, remonstration
  rel reluctance, unwillingness; faltering, hesitancy, hesitation; deprecation, disapproval; protestation; difference, disagreement, dissent, variance
  con acquiescence, agreement, assent, consent; concurrence; submission

demure *adj syn* see SHY 1
  rel decent, decorous, nice, proper, seemly; prim; earnest, serious, solemn; close, reserved, reticent, silent
  con impertinent, intrusive, meddlesome, obtrusive, officious; brash, forward, unbashful, unretiring

demurral *n syn* see DEMUR 2

demurrer *n syn* see DEMUR 2

den *n* 1 *syn* see LAIR 1
  2 *syn* see HIDEOUT
  3 *syn* see SINK 1

denaturant *n syn* see ADMIXTURE 1

denial *n* 1 refusal to satisfy a request or desire <*denial* of his visiting privileges>
  syn disallowance, refusal, rejection
  rel declination, nonacceptance
  con allowing, conceding, grant, letting; leave, permission, sufferance
  2 refusal to admit the truth <his *denial* that he took the money>
  syn contradiction, gainsaying, negation
  rel controversion, disproof, rebuttal, refutal, refutation; refusal, rejection, repudiation
  con acknowledgment, avowal, confession; affirmation, assertion, confirmation
  ant admission
  3 *syn* see RENUNCIATION
  rel abstaining, refraining
  con indulgence, self-indulgence; overdoing, overindulgence

denigrate *vb syn* see MALIGN

denizen *n* 1 *syn* see INHABITANT
  rel citizen, national, subject
  2 *syn* see HABITUÉ 1

denominate *vb syn* see NAME 1

denomination *n* 1 *syn* see NAME 1
  2 *syn* see RELIGION 2

denotative *adj syn* see INDICATIVE

denote *vb syn* see MEAN 2
  rel insinuate; announce, argue, bespeak, prove

denotive *adj syn* see INDICATIVE

denounce *vb syn* see CRITICIZE
  rel accuse, arraign, charge, impeach, incriminate, indict, tax; revile, vituperate; delate, inform
  idiom cry harrow (*or* haro)
  con panegyrize, praise
  ant eulogize

de novo *adv syn* see OVER 7

dense *adj* 1 *syn* see CLOSE 4
  rel heaped, massed, piled; crammed, crowded, jam-packed
  con dispersed, dissipated, scattered; rare, thin; exiguous, meager, scant, scanty, spare
  ant sparse; tenuous
  2 *syn* see STUPID 1
  rel obtuse; impassive, phlegmatic, stolid; lethargic, sluggish, torpid
  ant subtle; bright

denticulate *adj syn* see SERRATE

denudate *vb syn* see STRIP 2

denude *vb* 1 *syn* see STRIP 1
  2 *syn* see STRIP 2

denuded *adj syn* see OPEN 2

denunciate *vb syn* see CRITICIZE
  rel delate, inform; menace, threaten
  ant eulogize

deny *vb* 1 *syn* see DISCLAIM
  rel abandon, desert, forsake

con adopt, embrace, espouse; recognize
ant acknowledge; admit
2 to refuse to grant < he was unwilling to *deny* the child's request >
syn disallow, keep back, refuse, withhold
idiom say no to, turn thumbs down on
con allow, concede, let, permit; afford, give
ant grant
3 to restrain (as oneself) from or forgo what is pleasant or satisfying < decided to *deny* himself a second piece of pie >
syn abstain, constrain, curb, hold back, refrain
rel eschew, forbear, forgo, sacrifice; inhibit, restrain; avoid, shun
con overdo, overindulge
ant indulge
4 to refuse to accept as true, valid, or worthy of consideration < *denying* the existence of witches >
syn contradict, contravene, cross, disaffirm, gainsay, impugn, negate, negative, traverse
rel decline, refuse, reject, repudiate; confute, controvert, disprove, rebut, refute; downface
con affirm, assert, aver; allow, grant; authenticate, corroborate, substantiate, validate, verify; avow, confess; claim, submit
ant concede; confirm
depart *vb* **1** *syn* see GO 2
rel set out, start, strike out, toddle
con linger, stay, tarry, wait; come; approach, near
ant arrive; abide, remain
2 *syn* see DIE 1
con exist, live, survive
3 *syn* see SWERVE 2
rel abandon, desert, forsake; reject, repudiate; cast, discard; differ, disagree, dissent, vary
4 *syn* see DIGRESS 2
departed *adj* **1** *syn* see DEAD 1
idiom called home, gone to a better land
2 *syn* see EXTINCT 2
departing *adj* *syn* see PARTING
departure *n* **1** the act of going, coming out, or leaving a place < the hasty *departure* of the refugees >
syn egress, egression, exit, exiting, exodus, offgoing, setting-out, withdrawal
rel going, leaving, quitting, retreat; decampment, flight; farewell, leave-taking
con coming, entering, ingress
ant arrival
2 *syn* see DEVIATION 1
rel rambling, straying, wandering
depend *vb* *syn* see HANG 1
depend (on *or* upon) *vb* **1** to rest or to be contingent upon something uncertain, variable, or indeterminable < our trip *depends* upon the weather >
syn hang (on *or* upon), hinge (on *or* upon), ‖pend, stand (on *or* upon), turn (on *or* upon)
rel base, bottom, found, ground, rest, stay
idiom hang in the balance
2 *syn* see RELY (on *or* upon)
rel incline, lean
dependable *adj* **1** *syn* see RELIABLE 1
rel assured, confident, sure; responsible; constant, faithful, loyal, staunch, steadfast, steady
idiom as good as one's word, to be counted on
con capricious, fickle, inconstant, mercurial, unstable; dishonest, lying, mendacious, untruthful
ant independable, undependable
2 *syn* see TRUE 9
3 *syn* see CERTAIN 3
dependence *n* *syn* see TRUST 1
dependent *adj* **1** determined or conditioned by another < a conclusion that is *dependent* on a premise >
syn conditional, contingent, relative, reliant
rel exposed, liable, open, subject, susceptible; iffy, provisional, provisory; uncertain; circumscribed, limited, restricted
con categorical, ultimate; boundless, eternal, illimitable, uncircumscribed; basal, basic, fundamental, primary, underived
ant absolute; infinite; original
2 *syn* see SUBORDINATE
rel counting, depending, reckoning, relying, trusting; accessory, ancillary, appurtenant; abased, debased, humbled

con principal; paramount, predominant, preponderant, preponderating, sovereign
ant independent
depict *vb* *syn* see REPRESENT 1
rel narrate, recite, recount, rehearse, relate, report, state; outline, sketch
depiction *n* *syn* see REPRESENTATION
deplete *vb* to bring to a low estate by depriving of something essential < an epidemic which *depletes* an army of manpower >
syn bankrupt, drain, draw, draw down, exhaust, impoverish, use up
rel cripple, debilitate, disable, enfeeble, sap, undermine, weaken; decrease, diminish, lessen, reduce; bleed, draw off, dry up, empty, milk; consume, expend, finish, spend, wash up
idiom dig into
con augment, enlarge, increase; bolster, fortify, strengthen; rebuild, repair, restore, revive
ant renew, replace
depleted *adj* *syn* see EFFETE 2
rel sapped, weakened
con augmented, enlarged, increased
deplorable *adj* of a kind to cause great distress < a *deplorable* loss of life >
syn afflictive, calamitous, dire, distressing, dolorous, grievous, heartbreaking, heartrending, lamentable, mournful, regrettable, unfortunate, woeful
rel awful, dreadful, terrible; horrifying, intolerable, overwhelming, sickening, unbearable; miserable, wretched; disastrous
idiom as bad as bad can be, as bad as can be
con beneficial, helpful, salutary; advantageous, favorable, propitious
deplore *vb* **1** to manifest grief or sorrow for something < *deplore* the death of a close friend >
syn bemoan, bewail, grieve, lament, moan, weep
rel deprecate, disapprove; mourn, sorrow; cry, keen, wail
con boast, brag, crow, vaunt; rejoice
2 *syn* see REGRET
depone *vb* *syn* see TESTIFY 2
deport *vb* **1** *syn* see BEHAVE 1
2 *syn* see BANISH
deportation *n* *syn* see EXILE 1
deportment *n* **1** *syn* see BEHAVIOR
2 *syn* see BEARING 1
depose *vb* **1** to remove from a throne or other high position < trying to *depose* the king in favor of his brother > < *deposed* industrial leaders >
syn dethrone, discrown, disenthrone, displace, disthrone, uncrown, unmake
rel overthrow, subvert, upset; chuck, dismiss, eject, oust, throw out
con inaugurate, induct, install, instate, invest; crown, enthrone, throne
2 *syn* see ASSERT 1
3 *syn* see TESTIFY 2
deposit *vb* *syn* see BANK
rel put by, store, stow
deposit *n* *syn* see SEDIMENT
depository *n* *syn* see DEPOT 2
depot *n* **1** *syn* see ARMORY
2 a place where something is deposited or stored < a gasoline *depot* >
syn arsenal, depository, magazine, repository, store, storehouse
rel storeroom, warehouse
3 *syn* see RAILROAD STATION
rel terminal, terminus
deprave *vb* *syn* see DEBASE 1
con elevate, ennoble, exalt, raise, uplift
depraved *adj* **1** *syn* see DEBASED
rel degenerate, infamous, vicious, villainous; degraded; twisted, warped
con scrupulous, upright
2 *syn* see VICIOUS 2
depravity *n* *syn* see VICE 1

---

syn synonym(s)　　　　　　　　　　**rel** related word(s)
ant antonym(s)　　　　　　　　　　**con** contrasted word(s)
idiom idiomatic equivalent(s)
‖ use limited; if in doubt, see a dictionary

deprecate *vb syn* see DISAPPROVE 1
  rel bemoan, bewail, deplore, lament; derogate, detract
  ant endorse
depreciate *vb* **1** to reduce the value of <*depreciate* the dollar>
  syn cheapen, decry, devalorize, devaluate, devalue, downgrade, lower, mark down, soften, underprize, underrate, undervalue, write down, write off
  rel depress; abate, decrease, diminish, dwindle, lessen, reduce; erode
  con augment, increase; bloat, blow up, expand, inflate; amplify, magnify
  ant appreciate
  2 *syn* see DECRY 2
  rel underestimate, underrate, undervalue; discountenance, disfavor, disesteem
  con cherish, prize, treasure, value; comprehend, understand
  ant appreciate
depreciation *n syn* see DETRACTION
depreciative *adj syn* see DEROGATORY
  rel underestimating, underrating, undervaluing
  ant appreciative
depreciatory *adj syn* see DEROGATORY
  rel underestimating, underrating, undervaluing
  ant appreciative
depredate *vb syn* see RAVAGE
depredator *n syn* see MARAUDER
depress *vb* **1** *syn* see LOWER 3
  2 to lower in spirit or mood <the thought of all his debts *depressed* him>
  syn oppress, press, sadden, weigh down
  rel ail, distress, trouble; afflict, torment, try; contrist, deject, discourage, dishearten, dispirit; bother, disturb, perturb, upset
  con delight, gladden, gratify, please, rejoice; excite, inspire, stimulate; brighten, cheer up, encourage; buoy, elevate
  ant elate, exhilarate; cheer
depressant *adj syn* see GLOOMY 3
depressed *adj* **1** *syn* see DOWNCAST
  rel lugubrious, melancholy
  ant exhilarated; animated
  2 *syn* see UNDERPRIVILEGED
depressing *adj* **1** *syn* see GLOOMY 3
  con cheering, elevating, uplifting; exciting, inspiring
  ant exhilarating
  2 *syn* see SAD 2
depression *n* **1** *syn* see SADNESS
  rel boredom, doldrums, ennui, tedium
  con glee, hilarity, mirth
  ant buoyancy; elation
  2 a low spot <a *depression* in the land>
  syn basin, concavity, dip, hollow, sag, sink, sinkage, sinkhole; *compare* NOTCH 1
  rel cavity, hole, pocket, vacuity, vacuum, void; crater, pit; scoop
  3 a period of lowered economic activity and extensive unemployment <indicators that warn of a coming *depression*>
  syn recession, slump, stagnation
  rel crash, decline, dislocation, drop; sag; paralysis; ‖stagflation
  con expansion; booming, development, growth; advancement, progress
  ant boom
depressive *adj syn* see GLOOMY 3
deprivation *n syn* see PRIVATION 2
deprive *vb* **1** *syn* see STRIP 2
  2 to prevent one from possessing <to *deprive* a person of his civil rights>
  syn bereave, disinherit, dispossess, divest, lose, oust, rob; *compare* STRIP 2
  rel dock; bare, denude, dismantle, strip
  con furnish, give, supply; clothe, endow, equip, fit (out), invest, outfit
  ant provide
deprived *adj syn* see UNDERPRIVILEGED
deprivement *n syn* see PRIVATION 2
depth *n* **1** the perpendicular extent or measurement downward from a surface <measured the *depth* of the river>
  syn deepness, drop
  rel profoundness, profundity; lowness; sounding; draft
  con shallowness; altitude, elevation

2 the quality of being profound (as in insight) or full (as of knowledge) <her answer showed she had great *depth* in that subject>
  syn abyss, deepness, profoundness, profundity
  rel sense, wisdom, wiseness; brain, intellect, intelligence; keenness, sharpness
  con shallowness, superficiality, unprofoundness; sciolism, smatter, smattering
depthless *adj syn* see SUPERFICIAL 2
depurate *vb syn* see PURIFY 1
depute *vb syn* see DELEGATE
deputize *vb syn* see DELEGATE
deputy *n* **1** *syn* see AGENT 1
  rel substitute, surrogate; replacement
  2 *syn* see DELEGATE
derange *vb* **1** *syn* see DISORDER 1
  rel perturb; discommode, incommode, inconvenience
  con compose, settle
  ant arrange; adjust
  2 *syn* see UPSET 5
  3 *syn* see MADDEN 1
deranged *adj syn* see INSANE 1
  rel disarranged, disordered, disturbed
derangement *n syn* see INSANITY 1
  rel disarrangement, disorder; confusion; disturbance; unsoundness
derelict *adj* **1** given up especially by the owner or occupant <a *derelict* old home>
  syn abandoned, deserted, desolate, forsaken, lorn, solitary, uncouth
  rel dilapidated, dingy, faded, run-down, seedy, shabby, threadbare
  con cherished, prized, treasured; attended, kept up, maintained
  2 *syn* see NEGLIGENT
  rel irresponsible, undependable, unreliable, untrustworthy
  con dependable, reliable, responsible, trustworthy; careful, heedful, thoughtful
  ant faithful
derelict *n* **1** *syn* see OUTCAST
  2 *syn* see VAGABOND
dereliction *n syn* see FAILURE 1
  rel abuse, misuse, outrage
  ant faithfulness
deride *vb syn* see RIDICULE
  rel banter, chaff, jolly, kid, rag, rib
de rigueur *adj syn* see DECOROUS 1
derision *n syn* see LAUGHINGSTOCK
derivable *adj syn* see DEDUCTIVE
derivate *adj syn* see SECONDARY 2
derivation *n syn* see SOURCE
derivational *adj syn* see SECONDARY 2
derivative *adj syn* see SECONDARY 2
  ant underivative
derivative *n syn* see OUTGROWTH 2
derive *vb* **1** to reach (as a conclusion) as an end point of reasoning and observation <evidence from which he *derived* a startling new set of axioms>
  syn educe, evolve, excogitate
  rel conclude, deduce, gather, infer, judge; arrive (at), elicit, extract, reach; develop, elaborate, formulate, put (together), work out
  2 *syn* see INFER
  3 *syn* see TAKE 14
derive (from) *vb syn* see SPRING 1
derived *adj syn* see SECONDARY 2
dernier cri *n syn* see FASHION 3
dernier ressort *n syn* see RESOURCE 3
derogate *vb syn* see DECRY 2
  rel decrease, lessen, reduce; discredit, disgrace
  con enhance, heighten, intensify
derogatory *adj* designed or tending to belittle <*derogatory* comments about the actor's performance>
  syn depreciative, depreciatory, detracting, disadvantageous, disparaging, dyslogistic, pejorative, slighting, uncomplimentary
  rel belittling, decrying, minimizing; aspersing, calumnious, defamatory, maligning, vilifying; degrading, demeaning, humiliating; despiteful, malevolent, malicious, spiteful; contumelious, disdainful, scornful

con admiring, esteeming; acclaiming, laudatory, praising; appreciative
ant complimentary
derout *vb syn* see ROUT 1
derriere *n syn* see BUTTOCKS
descant *n* 1 *syn* see MELODY
2 *syn* see SONG 2
descant *vb syn* see DISCOURSE 1
descend *vb* 1 *syn* see FALL 1
ant rise
2 *syn* see STOOP 2
3 *syn* see DETERIORATE 1
descendant *n* 1 descendants *pl syn* see OFFSPRING
ant ascendants, ancestors
2 *syn* see OUTGROWTH 2
descent *n* 1 the act or process of passing from a higher to a lower level or state <a parachute *descent* > <his slow *descent* to the gutter>
syn drop, fall
rel plummeting, plunging, sinking
con rise, upswing, upturn; advance, headway, progress, progression; betterment, improvement
ant ascent
2 *syn* see COMEDOWN
3 *syn* see ANCESTRY
4 an inclination downward <the steep *descent* of the mountain>
syn decline, declivity, dip, drop, fall
rel downgrade, grade, gradient, incline, slope; drop, drop-off
con acclivity, upgrade, uphill
ant ascent, rise
describe *vb* 1 *syn* see RELATE 1
rel communicate, impart; transmit; construe, elucidate, explain, explicate, expound; exemplify, illustrate; characterize, distinguish
2 *syn* see REPRESENT 1
description *n* 1 *syn* see REPRESENTATION
2 a descriptive statement <a fascinating *description* of his adventures>
syn narration, recital, recountal, recounting
rel anecdote, narrative, story, tale, yarn; account, chronicle, version; report, statement
3 *syn* see TYPE
descry *vb* 1 *syn* see SEE 1
2 *syn* see FIND 1
rel appreciate, comprehend, understand; realize
desecrate *vb syn* see RAVAGE
desecrated *adj syn* see IMPURE 3
desecration *n syn* see PROFANATION
ant consecration
desensitize *vb syn* see DEADEN 1
ant sensitize
desert *n syn* see WASTE 1
desert *n usu* deserts *pl syn* see DUE 1
rel chastening, chastisement, discipline, disciplining, punishment
idiom just deserts
desert *vb* 1 *syn* see ABANDON 1
rel depart, go, leave
con adhere, cohere
ant cleave (to), stick (to)
2 *syn* see DEFECT
rel abscond, decamp, escape, flee, fly
idiom go over the hill
con abide, remain, stay
deserted *adj syn* see DERELICT 1
rel empty, vacant; uninhabited, unoccupied; bare, barren
desertion *n syn* see DEFECTION
rel perfidiousness, perfidy, treacherousness, treachery
deserve *vb syn* see EARN 2
rel gain, get, win; demand
idiom have it coming
deserved *adj syn* see JUST 3
ant undeserved
deserving *n syn* see DUE 1
deserving *adj syn* see WORTHY 1
ant undeserving
desexualize *vb syn* see STERILIZE
desiccate *vb* 1 *syn* see DRY 1
2 to drain or be drained of emotional or intellectual vitality <this book is *desiccated* by undue concentration on statistics>

syn devitalize, dry up
rel deplete, drain, exhaust; divest; decay, fade, shrivel, wither, wizen
con brighten, enliven
desiderate *vb syn* see DESIRE 1
desight *n syn* see EYESORE
design *vb* 1 *syn* see INTEND 2
2 *syn* see PLAN 2
rel delineate, diagram; create, invent; construct, fashion, form, frame, produce; contrive
con accomplish, achieve, effect, execute, fulfill, perform
3 to work out the arrangement of the parts of <*design* an urban center>
syn arrange, lay out, map (out), plan, set out; *compare* PLAN 2
rel delineate, diagram, draft, outline, sketch
design *n* 1 *syn* see PLAN 1
rel delineation, diagram, draft, outline, sketch, tracing; creation, invention
con accomplishment, achievement, execution, fulfillment, performance
2 *syn* see INTENTION
rel conation, volition, will; deliberation, reflection, thinking, thought; intrigue, machination, plot
con accident, chance, fortuity, hap; impulse
3 *syn* see FIGURE 3
4 *syn* see MAKEUP 1
designate *vb* 1 *syn* see NAME 1
2 to declare a person one's choice <*designated* him to fill the position>
syn appoint, finger, make, name, nominate, tap
rel choose, elect, opt, pick, select, single; assign, delegate, depute; dictate
con disapprove, disfavor, object (to), oppose; disallow, reject, turn down
3 to set aside (as funds) for a specific use <*designated* the income to be used for charity>
syn allocate, earmark
rel specify; appropriate, reserve; stipulate; allot, apportion, mete (out)
designation *n syn* see NAME 1
rel identification, recognition; classification, pigeonhole, pigeonholing
designative *adj syn* see INDICATIVE
designed *adj syn* see DELIBERATE 1
rel decided, determined, resolved
con casual, chance, contingent, fluky, fortuitous, incidental; impulsive, spontaneous; natural, normal, regular, typical
ant accidental
designedly *adv syn* see INTENTIONALLY
designless *adj syn* see RANDOM
desire *n* 1 a longing for something that promises enjoyment or satisfaction <he had a strong *desire* for fame and fortune>
syn appetite, appetition, craving, itch, lust, passion, urge
rel hankering, hunger, hungering, longing, pining, thirst, thirsting, yearning; desideratum, desiderium; avarice, cupidity, greed, rapacity; concupiscence, eros
con abhorrence, repellency, repugnance, repulsion; aversion, disfavor, dislike
ant distaste
2 *syn* see LUST 2
desire *vb* 1 to have a longing for something <men who *desire* success>
syn ‖choose, covet, crave, desiderate, want, wish
rel hanker, hunger, long, pine, thirst, yearn; enjoy, fancy, like; aim, aspire, pant
idiom set one's eyes (*or* heart) upon
con abhor, abominate, detest, hate, loath; decline, refuse, reject, repudiate, spurn
2 *syn* see ASK 2
desired *adj syn* see TRUE 7
desirous *adj syn* see COVETOUS
desist *vb syn* see STOP 3
rel abstain, forbear; abandon, relinquish, resign, yield

---

syn synonym(s)   **rel** related word(s)
ant antonym(s)   **con** contrasted word(s)
idiom idiomatic equivalent(s)
‖ use limited; if in doubt, see a dictionary

idiom have done with
con continue; persevere
ant persist
desistance *n syn* see END 2
desk *n* a table, frame, or case with a sloping or horizontal surface especially for writing < sat meditating at her *desk* >
syn escritoire, secretaire, secretary, writing desk
rel lectern, reading desk
desolate *adj* **1** *syn* see DERELICT 1
rel empty, vacant; uninhabited, unoccupied
2 syn see INCONSOLABLE
3 syn see GLOOMY 3
rel bare, barren; destitute, poor, poverty-stricken; dark, murky
desolate *vb syn* see RAVAGE
despair *vb* to lose all hope or confidence < *despaired* of winning >
syn despond, give up
rel abandon, drop, relinquish, renounce, resign, surrender, yield
idiom lose heart (*or* courage *or* faith *or* hope)
con await, count (on), depend (on), hope, look (for); trust (in *or* to)
ant expect
despairing *adj syn* see DESPONDENT
rel atrabilious, melancholic, melancholy; cynical, misanthropic, pessimistic; depressed, oppressed, weighed down
con optimistic, roseate, rose-colored; assured, confident, sanguine, sure
ant hopeful
desperado *n syn* see OUTLAW
rel convict, criminal, lawbreaker
desperate *adj* **1** *syn* see DESPONDENT
rel foolhardy, rash, reckless, venturesome; headlong, precipitate; baffled, balked, circumvented, foiled, frustrated, outwitted, thwarted
con collected, composed, cool, nonchalant; assured, confident, sanguine, sure
2 syn see ACUTE 6
3 syn see INTENSE 1
4 syn see OUTRAGEOUS 2
despicable *adj* **1** *syn* see CONTEMPTIBLE
rel disgraceful, disreputable, ignominious, infamous, loathsome
con applaudable, commendable
ant laudable, praiseworthy
2 syn see BASE 3
despisable *adj syn* see CONTEMPTIBLE
despisal *n syn* see DESPITE 1
despise *vb* to regard as beneath one's notice and unworthy of consideration or interest < he had always *despised* the weak >
syn abhor, contemn, disdain, look down, scorn, scout
rel abominate, detest, execrate, hate, loathe; reject, repudiate, spurn; avoid, eschew, renounce, shun; disregard, ignore, overlook, slight, snub
idiom have no use for, look down one's nose at
con apprize, cherish, prize, treasure, value; admire, regard, respect
ant appreciate, esteem
despisement *n syn* see DESPITE 1
despite *n* **1** the feeling or attitude of despising < felt *despite* toward the lowly >
syn contempt, despisal, despisement, disdain, disparagement, scorn
rel disdainfulness, insolence, superciliousness; abhorrence, abomination, detestation, hate, hatred, loathing; rejection, repudiation, spurning; aversion, disfavor, dislike, distaste; cold shoulder, rebuff, slight, snub; disgust, loathing
con admiration, esteem, honor, regard, respect; attraction, liking
2 syn see MALICE
rel contempt, disdain, scorn; abhorrence, abomination, detestation, hate, hatred, loathing
con admiration, esteem, respect; awe, fear, reverence
ant appreciation
3 syn see DEFIANCE 2
rel harm, hurt, injury
4 syn see AFFRONT
rel cut, discourtesy, incivility; rebuff, slight, snub
despite *prep syn* see AGAINST 4
despiteful *adj syn* see MALICIOUS
despitefulness *n syn* see MALICE

despoil *vb syn* see RAVAGE
despoiler *n* **1** *syn* see MARAUDER
2 syn see VANDAL
despond *vb* **1** *syn* see DESPAIR
rel droop, sag; languish
idiom reach the depths
con expect, hope, look
2 syn see MOPE 1
despondent *adj* having lost all or nearly all hope < *despondent* about his health >
syn despairing, desperate, desponding, forlorn, hopeless
rel grieving, mourning, sorrowful; dejected, depressed, melancholy, sad; disconsolate, dispirited, downcast, woebegone; discouraged, disheartened
con cheerful, glad, happy, joyful, joyous; buoyant, elastic, resilient, volatile; hopeful, optimistic
ant lighthearted
desponding *adj syn* see DESPONDENT
despot *n syn* see TYRANT
despotic *adj syn* see ABSOLUTE 4
despotism *n syn* see TYRANNY
despotize *vb syn* see TYRANNIZE
desquamate *vb syn* see SCALE 2
destine *vb syn* see PREDESTINE 1
destiny *n syn* see FATE
rel design, goal, intent, intention, objective
destitute *adj* **1** *syn* see DEVOID
rel deficient; bankrupt, bankrupted, depleted, drained, exhausted; divested, stripped
con complete, full, replete
2 syn see POOR 1
rel depleted, drained, exhausted
idiom on one's uppers, on the rocks
con comfortable, prosperous, well-fixed, well-off, well-to-do
ant opulent
destituteness *n syn* see POVERTY 1
rel absence, dearth, lack; adversity, misfortune
con competence, sufficiency
ant opulence
destitution *n syn* see POVERTY 1
rel absence, dearth, lack, privation, want; adversity, misfortune
con competence, sufficiency
ant opulence
destroy *vb* **1** to bring to ruin < the army *destroyed* the enemy village > < his health was finally *destroyed* by drink >
syn annihilate, atomize, decapitate, decimate, demolish, destruct, discreate, dismantle, dissolve, dynamite, pull down, pulverize, quench, raze, rub out, ruin, ‖ruinate, shatter, shoot, smash, tear down, unbuild, undo, unframe, unmake, wrack, wreck; *compare* TOTAL 3
rel abolish, extinguish; devastate, pillage, ravage, sack, waste; eradicate, exterminate, extirpate, wipe; mangle, mutilate; rubble; doom
idiom blow to bits, bring to an end, dispose of, tear to shreds
con establish, found, institute, organize; fabricate, fashion, forge, form, make, manufacture, shape; conserve, preserve, protect, save
2 syn see KILL 1
destroyer *n* **1** *syn* see VANDAL
2 syn see DOWNFALL 2
destruct *vb syn* see DESTROY 1
destruction *n* **1** *syn* see DOWNFALL 2
2 syn see RUIN 3
destructive *adj* having the capability, property, or effect of destroying < a *destructive* windstorm > < his brother was a *destructive* influence in his life >
syn annihilative, ruinous, shattering, wrackful, wreckful
rel calamitous, disastrous, deadly, fatal, lethal, mortal; consumptive; internecine; baneful, deleterious, detrimental
con creative, formative; harmless, innocuous, inoffensive; helpful, improving
ant constructive
desuetude *n* **1** *syn* see END 2
2 syn see DISUSE
desultory *adj* **1** *syn* see FITFUL
rel erratic; shifting, vagrant, wavering
con constant, invariable, unchanging, unfailing
ant steady

2 syn see RANDOM
  rel fitful, spasmodic; disorderly, unmethodical, unsystematic; capricious, fickle, inconstant, mercurial
  con orderly, systematic
  ant assiduous; methodical
detach *vb* to remove one thing from another with which it is in union or association <*detach* sheets from a loose-leaf book>
  syn abstract, disassociate, disconnect, disengage, dissociate, uncouple, unfix
  rel cut off, divorce, part, separate, sever, sunder; disjoin, disunite; disassemble, dismantle, dismember, dismount; disaffiliate
  idiom take apart
  con fasten, fix; bind, tie; combine, conjoin, unite
  ant affix, attach
detached *adj* **1 syn** see ALONE 1
  rel separate, unconnected
  con abutting, adjacent; connected, joined, linked
  ant adjoining; attached
  2 syn see INDIFFERENT 2
  con anxious, concerned, solicitous; self-centered, selfish
  ant interested
  3 syn see NEUTRAL
  rel distant, remote, removed
detachment *n syn* see SEPARATION 1
detail *n syn* see POINT 1
  con anatomy, framework, skeleton, structure; bulk, mass; design, plan
detail *vb syn* see SPECIFY 3
detailed *adj syn* see CIRCUMSTANTIAL
  rel abundant, copious; exhausting, exhaustive, thoroughgoing
detailedly *adv syn* see THOROUGHLY 2
detain *vb* **1 syn** see ARREST 2
  rel buttonhole, hold, restrain
  2 syn see KEEP 5
  3 syn see DELAY 1
  rel check, curb, inhibit, restrain
detect *vb syn* see FIND 1
detectable *adj syn* see PERCEPTIBLE
detection *n syn* see DISCOVERY
detective *n* one employed or engaged in detecting lawbreakers or in getting information that is not readily or publicly accessible <used *detectives* to locate the missing witness>
  syn dick, ‖eye, gumshoe, hawkshaw, investigator, plainclothesman, Sherlock, Sherlock Holmes, sleuth, ‖tec; *compare* INFORMER, PRIVATE DETECTIVE
  rel G-man; roper; shoofly
detention *n syn* see ARREST
  rel imprisonment, incarceration, internment
deter *vb* **1 syn** see DISSUADE
  rel prevent; block, hinder, impede, obstruct; debar, shut out; frighten, scare; inhibit, restrain
  con abet, incite, instigate; excite, provoke, stimulate; actuate, motivate
  2 syn see PREVENT 2
deteriorate *vb* **1** to pass from a higher to a lower type or condition <the road quickly *deteriorated* into a bumpy path>
  syn decline, degenerate, descend, disimprove, disintegrate, retrograde, rot, sink, worsen
  rel crumble, decay, decompose; impair, mar, spoil; debilitate, undermine, weaken; depreciate, lessen
  idiom be the worse for wear, go downhill, go to pot (*or* the dogs)
  con better, improve; advance, progress; enhance, heighten
  ant ameliorate
  2 syn see FAIL 1
deterioration *n* **1** a falling from a higher to a lower level (as of quality or character) <the *deterioration* of business during the depression>
  syn atrophy, decadence, declension, declination, decline, degeneracy, degeneration, dégringolade, devaluation, devolution, downfall, downgrade, ruin
  rel impairment, spoiling; crumbling, decay, decaying, decomposition, disintegration, dissolution, dry rot, rotting; debasement, degradation, depreciation, lessening; dislocation, disruption
  con betterment, help; enhancement, heightening, improvement
  ant amelioration
  2 syn see FAILURE 4
  con convalescence, recovering, recuperation

  ant improvement
determinable *adj syn* see TERMINABLE
determinant *n syn* see CAUSE 1
  rel factor; authority, influence, weight
determinate *adj* **1 syn** see INFLEXIBLE 3
  2 syn see DEFINITE 1
  ant indeterminate
determinate *vb syn* see IDENTIFY
determination *n* **1 syn** see DECISION 1
  2 syn see DECISION 2
  ant indetermination
determine *vb* **1 syn** see ESTABLISH 6
  rel fix, set; settle
  2 syn see PREDESTINE 1
  3 syn see DEMARCATE 1
  4 syn see DECIDE
  rel bias, dispose, incline, predispose; actuate, drive, impel, move; induce, persuade
  5 syn see CLOSE 3
  6 syn see DISCOVER 3
determined *adj syn* see DECIDED 2
  rel earnest, purposeful, serious; unfaltering, unhesitating, unwavering
  con unresolved, unsettled; hesitating, hesitant, wavering
  ant undetermined
detest *vb syn* see HATE
  rel reject, repudiate, spurn
  con love; appreciate, treasure, value
  ant adore
detestable *adj syn* see HATEFUL 2
  rel sorry; atrocious, heinous, monstrous, outrageous
  ant adorable
detestation *n* **1 syn** see ABOMINATION 2
  rel antipathy, disgust
  con affection, attachment, love; forbearance, indulgence, tolerance
  ant adoration
  2 syn see ABOMINATION 1
  ant adoration
dethrone *vb syn* see DEPOSE 1
  ant enthrone, throne
detonate *vb syn* see EXPLODE 1
detour *n* an indirect course often temporarily replacing part of a usual route <a *detour* around road construction> <took a *detour* to show him the lake>
  syn roundabout, runaround
  rel bypass
detour *vb syn* see SKIRT 2
detract (from) *vb syn* see DECRY 2
  rel libel, slander; decrease, lessen, reduce
  con enhance, heighten, intensify
detracting *adj* **1 syn** see DEROGATORY
  2 syn see LIBELOUS
detraction *n* the expression of damaging or malicious opinions <his persistent *detraction* of his rival's motives was wholly unfair>
  syn backbiting, backstabbing, belittlement, calumny, character assassination, defamation, depreciation, disparagement, scandal, slander, sycophancy, tale
  rel damage, harm, hurt, injury; injustice, wrong; aspersion, calumniation, libel, libeling, maligning, slandering, traducing, vilification
  con enhancement, heightening, laudation, praise; approbation, approval
  ant commendation
detractive *adj syn* see LIBELOUS
detractory *adj syn* see LIBELOUS
detriment *n syn* see DISADVANTAGE
  rel damage, harm, hurt, injury, mischief; impairment, marring, spoiling
  ant advantage, benefit
detrimental *adj syn* see HARMFUL
  con aiding, helpful, helping; harmless

---

syn synonym(s)   *rel* related word(s)
ant antonym(s)   *con* contrasted word(s)
idiom idiomatic equivalent(s)
‖ use limited; if in doubt, see a dictionary

ant beneficial
2 *syn* see ADVERSE 2
de trop *adj syn* see SUPERFLUOUS
detruncate *vb syn* see TOP 1
deuced *adj syn* see UTTER
‖**deval** *vb syn* see STOP 3
devalorize *vb syn* see DEPRECIATE 1
devaluate *vb syn* see DEPRECIATE 1
devaluation *n syn* see DETERIORATION 1
devalue *vb syn* see DEPRECIATE 1
devast *vb syn* see RAVAGE
devastate *vb syn* see RAVAGE
devastation *n syn* see RUIN 3
‖**devel** *vb syn* see STRIKE 2
develop *vb* **1 *syn*** see EXPAND 4
2 *syn* see UNFOLD 3
rel actualize, materialize, realize
3 *syn* see MATURE
rel dilate, expand; enroot, establish; flourish, prosper, thrive
con shrivel, wither, wizen
4 to come to have usually gradually < *develop* a taste for dry wine >
syn acquire, form
rel gain, get, obtain; achieve, attain, reach
5 *syn* see HAPPEN 1
development *n* progressive advance from a lower or simpler to a higher or more complex form < *development* of a seed into a plant > < *development* of an industry >
syn evolution, evolvement, flowering, growth, progress, progression, unfolding, upgrowth
rel advance, advancement, ongoing
con decadence, declension, degeneration, deterioration, devolution
ant decline
deviant *adj* **1 *syn*** see ABNORMAL 1
con normal; natural
2 *syn* see IRREGULAR 1
deviate *vb* **1 *syn*** see SWERVE 2
2 *syn* see ERR
idiom deviate from the path of virtue
deviation *n* **1** departure from a course or procedure or from a norm or standard < no *deviation* from traditional methods was permitted >
syn aberration, deflection, departure, divergence, diversion, turning
rel alteration, change, modification, variation; breach, transgression, violation; anomaly, failing, fault; blunder, error, lapse
con accordance, agreement, conformance, conformity, correspondence
2 *syn* see TURN 2
deviative *adj syn* see ABNORMAL 1
device *n* **1 *syn*** see TRICK 1
2 something (as a mechanical device) that performs a function or effects a desired end < invented many handy household *devices* >
syn contraption, contrivance; *compare* GADGET 1
rel appliance, implement, instrument, tool, utensil; apparatus, machine, mechanism; expedient, makeshift, resort, resource, shift; creation, invention; dingus, doohickey, hickey, thingumbob
3 *syn* see FIGURE 3
rel attribute, emblem, symbol, type; insignia, motto
deviceful *adj syn* see INVENTIVE
devil *n* **1** *often cap* the personal supreme spirit of evil and unrighteousness in Jewish and Christian theology
syn Apollyon, Beelzebub, ‖Cloot(s), ‖Clootie, diablo, fiend, Lucifer, Old Gooseberry, Old Nick, Old Scratch, Satan, serpent
rel cacodemon; dybbuk
idiom Prince of Darkness
2 an extremely and malignantly wicked person < he was a *devil* who would stop at nothing to get what he wanted >
syn Archfiend, demon, fiend, Satan, Succubus; *compare* SCAMP, VILLAIN 1
rel blackguard, caitiff, knave; scoundrel, villain; beast, brute
3 *syn* see SCAMP
‖**devil–devil** *n syn* see SPELL
‖**devil–dodger** *n syn* see CLERGYMAN
deviling *n syn* see IMP 1
devilish *adj* **1 *syn*** see FIENDISH

rel iniquitous, nefarious, villainous; accursed, cursed, damnable, execrable; bad, evil, wicked
ant angelic
2 *syn* see SATANIC 1
devilkin *n syn* see IMP 1
devil–may–care *adj syn* see WILD 7
rel rash, reckless
con careful, heedful, responsible, thoughtful
devilment *n syn* see MISCHIEVOUSNESS
devilry *n syn* see MISCHIEVOUSNESS
‖**devil's–bones** *n pl syn* see DICE
deviltry *n syn* see MISCHIEVOUSNESS
devious *adj* **1 *syn*** see OBSCURE 2
2 *syn* see CROOKED 1
rel deviating, digressing, diverting
ant straightforward
3 *syn* see ERRATIC 1
4 *syn* see ERRANT 2
rel artful, crafty, cunning, foxy, insidious, sly, tricky
5 *syn* see UNDERHAND
ant straightforward
devise *n syn* see LEGACY 1
devise *vb* **1 *syn*** see PLAN 2
2 *syn* see CONTRIVE 2
rel create, discover; forge, form, shape; design
3 *syn* see PLOT
4 *syn* see WILL
devitalize *vb syn* see DESICCATE 2
rel deprive; eviscerate, weaken
ant vitalize
devoid *adj* showing a want or lack < a poem *devoid* of worth >
syn destitute, empty, innocent, void
rel bare, barren; lacking, wanting; deficient
con filled, full; furnished, provided, supplied
ant replete
devoir *n* **1 *syn*** see OBLIGATION 2
2 *syn* see TASK 1
devolution *n syn* see DETERIORATION 1
rel regression, regressiveness, retrogression, retrogressiveness; receding, recession, retrogradation, retrograding
con development; progress, progression
ant evolution
devote *vb* **1** to set apart for a particular and often a better or higher use or end < a woman who *devotes* her life to helping others >
syn consecrate, dedicate, hallow
rel sanctify, vow; commit, confide, consign, entrust
idiom set apart
2 *syn* see GIVE 1
3 *syn* see ADDRESS 3
rel attempt, endeavor, strive, struggle, try; employ, use, utilize
devote (to) *vb syn* see HABITUATE 2
rel attach, wrap (up)
devoted *adj syn* see LOVING
rel constant, faithful, loyal, true; thoughtful; fervid, zealous
devotee *n* **1 *syn*** see ADDICT
2 *syn* see AMATEUR 1
devotion *n* **1 *syn*** see FIDELITY 1
rel enthusiasm, fervor, passion, zeal; affection, attachment, love; consecration, dedication, devotement
2 *syn* see LOVE 1
devour *vb* **1 *syn*** see EAT 1
2 *syn* see EAT UP 1
idiom eat like a horse, eat one's head off
3 *syn* see CONSUME 1
4 *syn* see RAVAGE
rel demolish, destroy; ruin, wreck; dissipate, squander
5 to exhibit avid interest in or enjoyment of < the crowd *devoured* the lurid scene >
syn ‖eat up
rel delight (in), enjoy, rejoice (in), relish, revel (in); feast (on), gloat (over *or* on)
con avoid, eschew, shun
devout *adj* showing fervor in the practice of religion < a *devout* churchgoer >
syn godly, holy, pietistic, pious, prayerful, religious
rel ardent, fervent, fervid, zealous; adoring, revering, venerating, worshiping

con impious, irreligious, ungodly, unholy; irreverent; apostate, backsliding
ant undevout

dexter *adj syn* see FAVORABLE 5
ant sinister

dexterity *n* **1** *syn* see ADDRESS 1
rel adeptness, skillfulness; effortlessness, smoothness
con awkwardness, maladroitness
ant clumsiness
2 *syn* see ART 1

dexterous *adj* **1** ready and skilled in physical movements <a *dexterous* worker>
syn adroit, clever, deft, handy, neat-handed, nimble
rel agile; adept, expert, masterly, proficient, skilled, skillful; easy, effortless, facile, smooth
con awkward, gauche, inept, maladroit
ant clumsy
2 *syn* see CLEVER 4

dexterousness *n syn* see ADDRESS 1
ant clumsiness

dextrorotatory *adj syn* see RIGHT-HANDED
ant levorotatory

diablerie *n* **1** *syn* see MISCHIEVOUSNESS
2 *syn* see EVIL 3

diablo *n syn* see DEVIL 1

diabolic *adj* **1** *syn* see SATANIC 1
2 *syn* see FIENDISH
rel evil, ill, wicked
ant angelic

diabolism *n syn* see SATANISM

diabolonian *adj syn* see FIENDISH

diacritic *adj syn* see CHARACTERISTIC

diagnose *vb syn* see IDENTIFY

diagnostic *adj syn* see CHARACTERISTIC

diagnosticate *vb syn* see IDENTIFY

diagonal *adj* between horizontal and vertical in direction <cloth with a *diagonal* stripe>
syn bevel, beveled, bias, biased, slanted, slanting; *compare* INCLINED 3

diagonally *adv* in a line running across from corner to corner <decided to place the couch *diagonally* at the end of the room>
syn catercorner (*or* catty-corner *or* kitty-corner), cornerwise, slantingways, slantways, slantwise, ‖slaunchways
idiom on the bias
con parallelly, square, straight

‖**dial** *n syn* see FACE 1
dial *vb syn* see TUNE 3

dialect *n* **1** *syn* see LANGUAGE 1
2 a form of language that is not recognized as standard <the Doric *dialect* of ancient Greece>
syn argot, cant, jargon, lingo, patois, patter, slang, vernacular; *compare* TERMINOLOGY, VERNACULAR 3
rel localism, provincialism, regionalism

dialectic *n syn* see ARGUMENTATION

dialogue *n* **1** *syn* see CONVERSATION 1
2 *syn* see CONVERSATION 2

diametric *adj syn* see OPPOSITE

diapason *n syn* see MELODY

diaphanous *adj syn* see FILMY

diarrhea *n* abnormally frequent intestinal evacuations with more or less fluid stools <they were taken with severe *diarrhea*>
syn ‖backdoor trots, dysentery, flux, ‖runs, scour(s), ‖squirts
idiom Montezuma's revenge, summer complaint

diatribe *n syn* see TIRADE

‖**dibs** *n pl* **1** *syn* see MONEY
2 *syn* see CLAIM 1

dice *n pl, sing* **die** a pair or set of small cubes marked on each face with from one to six spots and used in various games and in gambling by being shaken and thrown to come to rest at random <staked everything on a cast of the *dice*>
syn ‖African dominoes, bones, ‖cubes, ‖devil's-bones, ‖ivory, ‖tats

dice *vb syn* see DISCARD

dichotomize *vb syn* see SEPARATE 1

dick *n* **1** *syn* see DETECTIVE

dicker *vb syn* see HAGGLE 2

dickey *adj syn* see WEAK 2

dictate *vb* to promulgate expressly something to be followed, observed, obeyed, or accepted <the commission *dictated* the policies to be followed>
syn decree, impose, lay down, ordain, prescribe, set
rel control, direct, manage; guide, lead; govern, rule; say, tell, utter; bid, charge, command, enjoin, instruct, order

dictate *n syn* see COMMAND 1

dictative *adj syn* see DICTATORIAL

dictator *n syn* see TYRANT

dictatorial *adj* imposing one's will or opinions on others <the chief was inclined to be *dictatorial* with his subordinates>
syn authoritarian, authoritative, dictative, doctrinaire, dogmatic, magisterial; *compare* TOTALITARIAN 1
rel bossy, domineering, imperative, imperious, masterful, peremptory; absolute, arbitrary, autocratic, despotic, tyrannical; arrogant, haughty, overbearing, proud; firm, stern
con amenable, biddable, docile, obedient, tractable; menial, obsequious, servile, slavish, subservient

dictatorship *n syn* see TYRANNY

diction *n syn* see WORDING

dictionary *n syn* see TERMINOLOGY

dictum *n syn* see MAXIM

‖**dicty** *adj syn* see SNOBBISH

didactic *adj* overburdened with instruction and the proprieties <his speech to the new freshmen was painfully *didactic*>
syn moral, moralizing, preachy, schoolmasterish, sermonic, sermonizing, teachy
rel advisory, exhortative, hortative; preceptive
ant undidactic

‖**didder** *vb syn* see SHAKE 1

diddle *vb* **1** *syn* see IDLE
2 *syn* see CHEAT

diddle–daddle *vb syn* see IDLE

diddler *n syn* see SWINDLER

dido *n* **1** *usu* **didoes** *pl syn* see PRANK
2 *syn* see KNICKKNACK

die *vb* **1** to pass from physical life <he *died* at an advanced age>
syn cash in, ‖check out, conk, ‖cop out, ‖croak, decease, demise, depart, drop, expire, go, ‖kick in, ‖kick off, pass, pass away, pass out, peg out, perish, pip, pop off, ‖snuff (out), succumb, ‖swelt
idiom be gathered to one's fathers, bite the dust (*or* ground), breathe one's last, cash in one's checks (*or* chips), give up the ghost, ‖kick the bucket, ‖kick up one's heels, meet one's end, shuffle off this mortal coil, ‖snuff it, turn up one's toes (to the daisies)
con be, exist, subsist; flourish, thrive
ant live
2 *syn* see PERISH 2

die (down *or* away) *vb syn* see ABATE 4
rel recede; disappear
con ascend, mount, rise
ant come up

die *n* **1** *see* DICE
‖**2** *syn* see TOY 2

die–away *adj syn* see LANGUID

diehard *n* **1** an irreconcilable opponent of change <party *diehards* who would make no concessions>
syn bitter-ender, conservative, fundamentalist, old liner, praetorian, pullback, right, rightist, right wing, right-winger, standpat, standpatter, tory; *compare* REACTIONARY
rel mossback, old fogy, stick-in-the-mud; intransigent; true blue; right-center
con liberal, progressive, radical
2 *syn* see REACTIONARY

die–hard *adj syn* see CONSERVATIVE 1

differ *vb* **1** to be unlike or distinct in nature, form, or characteristics <the houses *differ* only in a few minor details>
syn disagree, vary
rel depart, deviate, diverge
con accord, conform, correspond
ant agree

---

syn synonym(s)   **rel** related word(s)
ant antonym(s)   **con** contrasted word(s)
idiom idiomatic equivalent(s)
‖ use limited; if in doubt, see a dictionary

2 to be of unlike or opposite opinion < men who *differ* on religious matters >
syn disaccord, disagree, discord, dissent, divide, vary
rel clash, conflict, jar; bicker, quarrel, squabble; argue, debate, dispute; oppose, protest (against)
idiom differ in opinion, hold opposite views
con coincide, concert, concur, harmonize; accord, conform, correspond
ant agree

difference *n* **1** *syn* see DISSIMILARITY
rel modification, variation
con equivalence, equivalency, sameness
ant resemblance
2 *syn* see DISCORD
rel clash, conflict
3 *syn* see VARIANCE 1

difference *vb* *syn* see KNOW 4

different *adj* **1** unlike in kind or character < could hardly be more *different* >
syn disparate, dissimilar, distant, divergent, diverse, other, otherwise, unalike, unequal, unlike, unsimilar, various
rel particular, single; distinctive, individual, peculiar; divers, sundry
con akin, analogous, comparable, like, parallel, similar, uniform; equal, equivalent, self-same
ant alike, identical, same
2 *syn* see DISTINCT 1

differential *adj* *syn* see DISCRIMINATORY

differentiate *vb* *syn* see KNOW 4
rel comprehend, understand
con confound, mistake
ant confuse

differently *adv* *syn* see OTHERWISE 1

difficile *adj* *syn* see HARD 6

difficult *adj* *syn* see HARD 6
rel problem, problematic
idiom easier said than done, no picnic, tough sledding
ant simple

difficultly *adv* *syn* see HARD 8

difficulty *n* **1** something obstructing one's course and demanding effort and endurance if one's end is to be attained < he encountered great *difficulties* on his way to success >
syn asperity, hardness, hardship, rigor, vicissitude
rel impediment, obstacle, obstruction, snag; dilemma, fix, jam, pickle, plight, predicament, quandary, scrape; emergency, exigency, pass, pinch, strait; bother, inconvenience, problem, trouble
idiom hard nut to crack, hard row to hoe, heavy sledding
2 *syn* see DEMUR 2
3 *syn* see QUARREL

diffident *adj* *syn* see SHY 1
rel blenching, flinching, shrinking; hesitant, reluctant
con assured, presumptuous, sanguine, sure; self-assured, self-confident, self-possessed, self-reliant; brazen, impudent, shameless
ant confident

difform *adj* *syn* see LOPSIDED

diffuse *adj* *syn* see WORDY
rel exuberant, lavish, profuse; casual, desultory, random; lax, loose, slack; lengthy, long
con concentrated; condensed
ant succinct

diffuse *vb* **1** *syn* see SPREAD 1
rel extend; expand
con compact, consolidate; center, centralize, focus
ant concentrate
2 *syn* see INTERFUSE 2

dig *vb* **1** to loosen and turn over or remove (as soil) with or as if with a spade < *dig* for potatoes > < *dug* through her drawer looking for the scarf >
syn ‖delve, excavate, grub, shovel, spade
rel quarry; enter, penetrate, pierce, probe; dig up, root, rootle, root out
2 to form by digging < *dig* a trench >
syn dig out, excavate, scoop, shovel, spade
3 *syn* see THRUST 2
‖**4** *syn* see RESIDE 1
5 *syn* see POKE 1

‖**6** *syn* see APPREHEND 1
7 *syn* see ENJOY 1

dig (into) *vb* *syn* see EXPLORE

dig *n* **1** *syn* see POKE 1
2 *syn* see SITE 3

digest *n* *syn* see COMPENDIUM 1
rel abridgment, synopsis

digest *vb* **1** *syn* see BEAR 10
2 *syn* see EPITOMIZE 1

digit *n* *syn* see NUMBER

dignification *n* *syn* see APOTHEOSIS 2

dignify *vb* *syn* see EXALT 1
con abase, debase
ant demean

dignitary *n* *syn* see NOTABLE 1

dignity *n* **1** *syn* see STATUS 2
2 *syn* see DECORUM 1
rel excellence, merit, perfection, virtue; ethicalness, ethics, morality, nobleness, nobility
con impropriety, indecency, indecorum, unseemliness
3 *syn* see ELEGANCE
rel augustness, grandeur, grandness, magnificence, majesty, nobleness, nobility; address, poise

dig out *vb* **1** *syn* see DIG 2
2 *syn* see RUMMAGE 3

digress *vb* **1** *syn* see SWERVE 2
2 to turn aside from the main subject of attention or course of argument < he *digressed* into too many side issues >
syn depart, divagate, diverge, excurse, ramble, stray, wander
rel drift, roam
idiom get off the subject, go off on a tangent
con advance, proceed, progress

digression *n* a departure from a subject or theme < a *digression* from the main point of the speech >
syn aside, discursion, divagation, excursion, excursus, parenthesis
rel episode, excurse, incident, underaction; deflection, deviation, divergence; departure; drifting, rambling, straying, wandering

‖**dike** (out *or* up) *vb* *syn* see DRESS UP 1

dilapidate *vb* *syn* see RUIN 2
rel crumble, decay, decompose, disintegrate; disregard, forget, ignore, neglect, overlook, slight
con mend, rebuild, repair; rejuvenate, renew, renovate, restore

dilapidated *adj* *syn* see SHABBY 1
rel damaged, impaired, injured, marred; crumbled, decayed

dilate *vb* *syn* see EXPAND 3
rel augment, enlarge, increase; extend, lengthen, prolong, protract; broaden, widen
con compress, condense, contract, shrink; attenuate
ant circumscribe; constrict

dilate (on *or* upon) *vb* *syn* see DISCOURSE 1
rel describe, narrate, recite, recount, rehearse, relate
con abbreviate, abridge, curtail, shorten

dilatory *adj* *syn* see SLOW 2
rel lax, neglectful, negligent, remiss, slack
con assiduous, busy, industrious, sedulous; prompt, quick, ready; hasty, impetuous, precipitate
ant diligent

dilemma *n* *syn* see PREDICAMENT
rel bewilderment, mystification, perplexity
idiom horns of a dilemma

dilettante *n* **1** *syn* see CONNOISSEUR
2 *syn* see AMATEUR 2

dilettante *adj* *syn* see AMATEURISH

dilettantish *adj* *syn* see AMATEURISH

dilettantist *adj* *syn* see AMATEURISH

diligent *adj* *syn* see ASSIDUOUS
rel persevering, persistent, persisting; unflagging
con deliberate, laggard, leisurely, slow; desultory
ant dilatory

‖**dilly** *adj* *syn* see FOOLISH 2

‖**dilly** *n* one that is remarkable or extraordinary of its kind < came up with a *dilly* of an idea to sell the product >
syn ‖corker, crackerjack, ‖daisy, dandy, ‖dinger, ‖doozer, humdinger, jim-dandy, knockout, ‖lalapalooza, ‖lulu, nifty, peach, ‖pip, pippin, ripper, ripsnorter, rouser

dilly *vb* *syn* see DELAY 2

dillydally *vb* *syn* see DELAY 2

dilute *vb* to make less strong or concentrated < *dilute* acid >
 syn cut, thin, weaken
 rel moderate, qualify, temper; deliquesce, liquefy; alter, modify
 con enrich, fortify, richen, upgrade; condense, densify, evaporate, thicken
 ant concentrate
dilute *adj* of relatively low strength or concentration < *dilute* acid >
 syn diluted, thin, washy, watered-down, waterish, watery, weak
 rel reduced; adulterated, sophisticated; impaired, impoverished, weakened
 con condensed, densified, thickened
 ant concentrated
diluted *adj syn* see DILUTE
 ant concentrated
dim *adj* **1** *syn* see DARK 1
 ant bright
 2 *syn* see DULL 7
 ‖**3** *syn* see DULL 9
 4 *syn* see FAINT 2
 con manifest, plain
 ant distinct
dim *vb* **1** *syn* see OBSCURE
 2 *syn* see DULL 1
 3 *syn* see DULL 4
dime novel *n* a usually paperback melodramatic novel < read mostly *dime novels* >
 syn dreadful, penny dreadful, shilling shocker, shocker, yellowback
 rel bloodcurdler, chiller, ‖killer-diller; thriller; pulp
dimension *n* **1** *usu* **dimensions** *pl syn* see SIZE 1
 2 *usu* **dimensions** *pl syn* see RANGE 2
dimensionality *n syn* see SIZE 1
diminish *vb* **1** *syn* see ABRIDGE 1
 2 *syn* see DECREASE
 rel ebb, subside, wane; moderate, temper; attenuate, extenuate
 con aggravate, enhance, heighten, intensify
 3 *syn* see DECRY 2
diminutive *adj syn* see TINY
‖**dimmet** *n syn* see EVENING 1
dimple *vb syn* see RIPPLE
‖**dimps** *n syn* see EVENING 1
dim-sighted *adj syn* see PURBLIND
‖**dimpsy** *n syn* see EVENING 1
dimwit *n syn* see DUNCE
dim-witted *adj syn* see RETARDED
 con alert, keen
din *n* a welter of discordant sounds < the *din* of a machine shop >
 syn babel, brouhaha, ‖chirm, clamor, hubbub, hullabaloo, jangle, music, pandemonium, racket, racketry, tintamarre, tumult, uproar; *compare* COMMOTION 4
 rel blatancy, boisterousness, clamorousness, stridency; bedlam; clangor, clatter, rattle; clash, percussion; ‖row; noise, sound
 con calm, lull, quietude, stillness; concord, consonance, harmony; melody, musicality, tunefulness
diner *n syn* see EATING HOUSE
‖**dinero** *n syn* see MONEY
ding *vb* **1** *syn* see STRIKE 2
 2 *syn* see SURPASS 1
‖**ding** *n syn* see BLOW 1
ding-a-ling *n syn* see CRACKPOT
dingdong *adv syn* see HARD 3
dinge *n syn* see SADNESS
‖**dinger** *n syn* ‖DILLY, ‖corker, crackerjack, ‖daisy, dandy, humdinger, jim-dandy, knockout, ‖lalapalooza, ‖lulu
dingus *n syn* see DOODAD
dingy *adj syn* see SHABBY 1
 rel grimed, smirched, soiled, sullied, tarnished; dull; dusky, gloomy, murky
 con bright, brilliant, luminous, shining; clean, cleanly
dining table *n syn* see TABLE 1
dinky *adj syn* see MINOR 2
‖**dinky-di** *adj syn* see FAITHFUL 1
dinner *n* a usually elaborate meal served to guests or a group often to mark an occasion or honor an individual < the annual club *dinner* >
 syn banquet, feast, regale, spread

 rel ‖blowout, festival, fete, junket; breakfast, collation, luncheon
dinner table *n syn* see TABLE 1
dinosauric *adj syn* see HUGE
‖**dinsome** *adj syn* see VOCIFEROUS
dint *n syn* see POWER 4
dip *vb* **1** to plunge or thrust momentarily or partially under the surface of a liquid < *dip* a dress in cleansing fluid >
 syn douse, duck, dunk, immerse, souse, submerge, submerse
 rel pitch, plunge
 2 to lift a portion of by reaching below the surface with something shaped to hold liquid < *dip* drinking water from a spring >
 syn bail, lade, ladle, scoop
 rel dish, spoon; bucket (up *or* out), draw
 ‖**3** *syn* see PAWN
 4 *syn* see DUCK 2
 5 *syn* see PLUMMET
 6 *syn* see SET 12
 7 *syn* see SWERVE 1
dip (into) *vb syn* see BROWSE
dip *n* **1** *syn* see DESCENT 4
 2 *syn* see DECLINE 3
 3 *syn* see DEPRESSION 2
 ‖**4** *syn* see PICKPOCKET
diplomacy *n syn* see TACT
diplomatic *adj syn* see TACTFUL
 rel bland, smooth; courteous, polite; astute, shrewd; artful, crafty, guileful, wily
 ant undiplomatic
‖**dippy** *adj syn* see FOOLISH 2
‖**dipsy-doodle** *n syn* see DECEPTION 1
dire *adj* **1** *syn* see FEARFUL 3
 2 *syn* see DEPLORABLE
 rel depressing, oppressing
 3 *syn* see OMINOUS
 4 *syn* see PRESSING
 5 *syn* see ACUTE 6
direct *vb* **1** *syn* see ADDRESS 6
 2 to turn something toward its appointed or intended mark or goal < *directed* his eyes to the door >
 syn address, aim, cast, head, incline, lay, level, point, present, set, train, turn, zero (in)
 rel beam; divert; fasten, focus
 3 *syn* see ADDRESS 3
 rel fix, set, settle
 con deflect, divert; deviate, digress, diverge, swerve
 4 *syn* see GUIDE
 ant misdirect
 5 *syn* see GOVERN 3
 6 *syn* see CONDUCT 3
 7 *syn* see COMMAND
 rel assign, define, prescribe
direct *adj* **1** being or passing in a straight line of descent from parent to offspring < *direct* ancestors >
 syn lineal
 2 admitting free or continuous passage < a *direct* route to the beach >
 syn straight, straightforward, through, uninterrupted
 rel linear; continuous, unbroken, undeviating, unswerving
 con circuitous, roundabout
 ant indirect
 3 *syn* see FRANK
 ant devious
 4 marked by absence of an intervening agency, instrumentality, or influence < he had no *direct* knowledge of the crime >
 syn firsthand, immediate, primary
 rel contiguous, next, proximate
 ant indirect
direct *adv* **1** *syn* see DIRECTLY 1
 2 *syn* see VERBATIM
direction *n* **1** *syn* see VIEWPOINT 2
directive *n* **1** *syn* see EDICT 1
 2 *syn* see MEMORANDUM 2

---

syn synonym(s)   *rel* related word(s)
ant antonym(s)   *con* contrasted word(s)
idiom idiomatic equivalent(s)
‖ use limited; if in doubt, see a dictionary

3 syn see MESSAGE 1

directly *adv* **1** without deviation of course <the turnpike runs *directly* east and west>
syn dead, direct, due, right, straight, straightly, undeviatingly
idiom as the crow flies, in a beeline
con circuitously, deviously, round about; discursively, ramblingly
ant indirectly
2 syn see VERBATIM
3 syn see IMMEDIATELY 1
4 syn see AWAY 3
5 syn see PRESENTLY 1

direful *adj* **1 syn** see FEARFUL 3
2 syn see OMINOUS

dirt *n* **1 syn** see EARTH 2
2 syn see DECEPTION 1

dirt poor *adj syn* see POOR 1

dirty *adj* **1** soiled or begrimed with dirt <wash those *dirty* hands>
syn black, dungy, filthy, foul, grubby, impure, mucky, murky, nasty, soily, sordid, squalid, unclean, uncleanly
rel contaminated, defiled, polluted, tainted; dreggy; draggled, draggletailed, draggly
idiom dirty as a pig
con immaculate, spotless; unsoiled, unspotted, unsullied
ant clean
2 syn see IMPURE 1
ant clean
3 syn see OBSCENE 2
4 syn see WILD 6

dirty *vb* **1 syn** see SOIL 2
ant clean
2 syn see TAINT 1
idiom dirty one's hands

disability *n syn* see DISADVANTAGE

disable *vb* **1 syn** see DISQUALIFY
2 syn see PARALYZE 1
3 syn see WEAKEN 1
rel harm, hurt, mar, spoil; batter, maim, mangle, mutilate; ruin, wreck
con restore, resuscitate, revive, revivify
ant rehabilitate

disabuse *vb* to set free from mistakes (as in reasoning or judgment) <he was *disabused* of his belief when the facts were presented>
syn purge, undeceive, undelude
rel amend, correct, emend, rectify, redress; disillude, disillusion, unblind; enlighten, illuminate; free, liberate, release
idiom open one's eyes, prick the (*or* one's) bubble, puncture one's balloon, set (*or* put) right (*or* straight)
con deceive, delude, mislead; dupe, gull

disaccord *vb* **1 syn** see CLASH 2
2 syn see DIFFER 2
ant accord

disaccord *n syn* see DISCORD
ant accord

disacknowledge *vb syn* see DISCLAIM

disadvantage *n* an unfavorable or prejudicial quality or circumstance <the machine has two serious *disadvantages*>
syn detriment, disability, drawback, handicap
rel bar, impediment, obstacle, obstruction; blocking, hamper, hindrance, imposition
con aid, assistance, help; service, usefulness, utility, value, worth
ant advantage

disadvantaged *adj syn* see UNDERPRIVILEGED
ant advantaged

disadvantageous *adj syn* see DEROGATORY

disadvise *vb syn* see DISSUADE

disaffect *vb syn* see ESTRANGE
rel agitate, discompose, disquiet, disturb, upset
ant win (over)

disaffection *n syn* see ESTRANGEMENT

disaffirm *vb syn* see DENY 4

disagree *vb* **1 syn** see DIFFER 1
ant agree
2 syn see DIFFER 2
ant agree

disagreeable *adj* **1 syn** see BAD 8
rel annoying, distressing, disturbing, woeful
ant agreeable
2 syn see IRRITABLE
ant agreeable

disallow *vb* **1 syn** see DENY 2
con accede, acquiesce, assent
ant allow
2 syn see DISCLAIM
rel debar, exclude, shut out
ant allow

disallowance *n syn* see DENIAL 1

disappear *vb syn* see VANISH
rel go, leave
ant appear

disappoint *vb syn* see FRUSTRATE 1

disapprove *vb* **1** to feel or express an objection <*disapprove* of his actions>
syn deprecate, discommend, discountenance, disesteem, disfavor, frown, object
rel blame, censure, condemn, criticize, denounce, reprehend, reprobate; decry, depreciate, detract, disparage, dispraise; expostulate, remonstrate
idiom look askance at, make a wry face at, not go for, take a dim view of, take exception to
con applaud, commend, compliment, recommend; accredit, certify, endorse, sanction; approbate, countenance, favor
ant approve
2 syn see DECLINE 4

disarm *vb* **1 syn** see PARALYZE 1
2 to influence favorably by persuasive words or acts <*disarmed* by her smile>
syn unarm, unsteel, win (over)
rel allure, attract, bewitch, captivate, charm, enchant, fascinate
con alert, caution, tip (off), warn
ant arm

disarming *adj syn* ingratiating, deferential, ingratiatory, insinuating, insinuative, saccharine, silken, silky

disarrange *vb syn* see DISORDER 1
rel mislay, misplace; displace, replace; overturn
ant arrange

disarray *n syn* see CONFUSION 3
con arrangement, marshaling

disarray *vb syn* see DISORDER 1
ant array

disassemble *vb syn* see DISMOUNT

disassociate *vb syn* see DETACH

disaster *n* a sudden calamitous event bringing great damage, loss, or destruction <a flood *disaster* struck the valley>
syn calamity, cataclysm, catastrophe, misadventure, tragedy, woe(s)
rel accident, casualty, fatality, mishap; adversity, distress, misadventure, mischance, misfortune; rock(s)

disastrous *adj syn* see FATAL 2
rel hapless, luckless, unfortunate; destructive
con fortunate, happy, lucky, providential

disavow *vb syn* see DISCLAIM
rel impugn, negate, negative
con allow, concede, grant; assert, justify, maintain
ant avow

disband *vb* to cease to exist as a unit <the dance group *disbanded* after a farewell concert>
syn break up, disperse, dissolve
rel dispel, dissipate, scatter; dichotomize, disjoin, disjoint, dissect, dissever, disunite, divide, divorce, part, separate, sever, sunder
idiom go their several ways, part company
con combine, concur, conjoin, cooperate, unite; assemble, collect, congregate, gather; call up, summon
ant band

disbelief *n syn* see UNBELIEF
rel atheism, deism; rejection, repudiation, spurning
con credence, credit, faith
ant belief

disbelieve *vb* to hold not to be true or real <*disbelieved* his professions of sincerity>
syn discredit, unbelieve
rel distrust, doubt, mistrust, question, suspect; eschew, reject, scorn, scout

con accept, ‖buy, swallow
ant believe
disbelieving *adj syn* see INCREDULOUS
disbodied *adj syn* see IMMATERIAL 1
disburden *vb syn* see UNLOAD
disburse *vb* **1** *syn* see SPEND 1
　2 *syn* see DISTRIBUTE 1
disbursement *n syn* see EXPENSE 1
discalceate *adj syn* see DISCALCED
discalced *adj* wearing only sandals on the feet < *discalced*
　monks >
　syn barefoot, discalceate
　con calced, shod
discard *vb* to get rid of < *discard* old clothes > < people who *dis-*
　card traditional values >
　syn abdicate, cashier, cast, chuck, ‖deep-six, ‖dice, ditch, dump,
　jettison, junk, lay aside, reject, scrap, shed, ‖shoot, shuck (off),
　slough, throw away, throw out, wash out
　rel abandon, desert, forsake; repudiate, spurn; dismiss, eject,
　oust
　idiom do away with, let go by the board
　con adopt, embrace, espouse, take on, take up; employ, use,
　utilize; hold, hold back, keep, retain; cherish, esteem, nurture
discarding *n syn* see DISPOSAL 2
discarnate *adj syn* see IMMATERIAL 1
　ant carnate, incarnate
discept *vb syn* see DISCUSS 1
discern *vb* **1** *syn* see SEE 1
　rel ascertain, discover; anticipate, apprehend, divine, foresee
　2 *syn* see KNOW 4
discernible *adj syn* see PERCEPTIBLE
　ant indiscernible
discerning *adj syn* see WISE 1
　ant undiscerning
discernment *n syn* see WIT 3
　rel intuition, reason; sagaciousness, sagacity
　con crassness, density, slowness; blindness
discharge *vb* **1** *syn* see UNLOAD
　2 *syn* see EXEMPT
　3 *syn* see SHOOT 1
　4 *syn* see FREE
　rel dismiss, eject, expel, oust; eliminate, exclude
　5 to give outlet to < the river *discharges* its waters into the
　bay >
　syn disembogue, emit, flow, give off, pour, void
　rel eject, exude, release
　6 *syn* see DISMISS 3
　rel displace, replace, supersede, supplant
　con hire; contract
　ant engage
　7 to release from service with the armed forces < *discharged*
　from the army with the rank of sergeant >
　syn ‖demob, demobilize, muster out, separate
　rel disenroll; deactivate, inactivate; bounce, cashier, dismiss,
　drop, fire, sack
　8 *syn* see CLEAR 5
　9 *syn* see ANNUL 4
discinct *adj syn* see NEGLIGENT
disciple *n syn* see FOLLOWER
　rel enthusiast, fanatic, zealot
disciplinary *adj syn* see PUNITIVE
discipline *n* **1** *syn* see PUNISHMENT
　2 *syn* see WILL 3
discipline *vb* **1** *syn* see PUNISH 1
　rel overcome, reduce, subdue, subjugate; bridle, check, curb,
　inhibit, restrain
　2 *syn* see TEACH
　rel guide, lead; conduct, control, direct, manage
disclaim *vb* to refuse to admit, accept, or approve < the senator
　disclaimed the comment attributed to him > < *disclaim* respon-
　sibility for a subordinate's mistake >
　syn deny, disacknowledge, disallow, disavow, disown, repudiate
　rel contradict, contravene, gainsay, traverse; refuse, reject,
　spurn; deprecate; belittle, disparage, minimize; abjure, forswear,
　recant, renounce, retract; challenge, criticize
　idiom turn one's back on, wash one's hands of
　con acknowledge, avow, own; accept, admit, receive, take
　ant claim

disclose *vb* **1** *syn* see OPEN 2
　2 *syn* see REVEAL 1
　rel acknowledge, admit, avow, confess, own
　idiom make public
　con conceal, hide; camouflage, cloak, disguise, dissemble, mask
discolor *vb* **1** *syn* see TAINT 1
　2 *syn* see STAIN 1
discolor *adj syn* see VARIEGATED
discombobulate *vb* **1** *syn* see DISCOMPOSE 1
　2 *syn* see CONFUSE 2
discomfit *vb syn* see EMBARRASS
　rel annoy, bother, irk, vex; disturb, perturb, upset
discomfiture *n* **1** *syn* see DEFEAT 1
　2 *syn* see COMEDOWN
　3 *syn* see EMBARRASSMENT
　rel agitation, disquiet, perturbation, upset; commotion; prickles
discomforting *adj syn* see UNCOMFORTABLE
　ant comforting
discommend *vb syn* see DISAPPROVE 1
　rel admonish; criticize, reprehend; censure
　con approve, endorse, sanction
　ant commend; recommend
discommode *vb syn* see INCONVENIENCE
　rel flurry, fluster, perturb, upset; bother, irk, vex
discommoding *adj syn* see INCONVENIENT
discommodious *adj syn* see INCONVENIENT
discompose *vb* **1** to destroy or impair one's capacity for collected
　thought or decisive action < *discomposed* by the rudeness of his
　friend >
　syn agitate, bother, discombobulate, dismay, disquiet, disturb,
　flurry, fluster, perturb, unhinge, unsettle, untune, upset; *compare*
　EMBARRASS
　rel disagree; annoy, irk, vex; harass, harry, pester, plague,
　worry
　con calm, quiet, settle, soothe, tranquilize; allay, alleviate, as-
　suage; appease, conciliate, mollify, pacify, placate, propitiate
　ant compose
　2 *syn* see DISORDER 1
　ant compose
discomposure *n syn* see EMBARRASSMENT
　ant composure
disconcert *vb syn* see EMBARRASS
　rel bewilder, nonplus, perplex, puzzle
disconcertion *n syn* see EMBARRASSMENT
disconcertment *n syn* see EMBARRASSMENT
disconfirm *vb syn* see DISPROVE 1
disconnect *vb syn* see DETACH
　ant connect
disconnected *adj syn* see INCOHERENT 2
　ant connected
disconsolate *adj* **1** *syn* see DOWNCAST
　rel comfortless, inconsolable; sorrowful, woeful; doleful, melan-
　choly; unhappy
　ant cheerful
　2 *syn* see INCONSOLABLE
　3 *syn* see GLOOMY 3
　ant cheerful, cheery
disconsonant *adj syn* see INCONSONANT 1
discontent *adj syn* see DISCONTENTED
　ant content
discontented *adj* showing or expressing a sense of grievance or
　thwarted aspirations or desires < *discontented* with his posi-
　tion >
　syn discontent, disgruntled, dissatisfied, malcontent, malcon-
　tented, uncontent, uncontented, ungratified
　rel disquieted, disturbed, perturbed, restless, upset; displeased;
　unhappy
　con satisfied; gratified, pleased; happy; elated, exultant, jubi-
　lant, triumphant
　ant contented
discontinuance *n syn* see END 2
　ant continuance, continuation
discontinuation *n syn* see END 2

---

syn synonym(s)　　　　　　　　　　　**rel** related word(s)
ant antonym(s)　　　　　　　　　　　　**con** contrasted word(s)
idiom idiomatic equivalent(s)
‖ use limited; if in doubt, see a dictionary

ant continuance, continuation

discontinue *vb syn* see STOP 3
ant continue

discontinuity *n syn* see GAP 1
ant continuity

discontinuous *adj syn* see INCOHERENT 2
ant continuous

‖**disconvenience** *n syn* see INCONVENIENCE
ant convenience

‖**disconvenience** *vb syn* see INCONVENIENCE
ant convenience

discord *n* the state of those who disagree and lack harmony < a household full of turmoil and *discord* >
syn conflict, contention, difference, disaccord, disharmony, dispeace, dissension, dissent, dissidence, dissonance, disunion, disunity, division, inharmony, mischief, strife, unpeace, variance
rel discrepancy, incompatibility, incongruity, inconsistency, inconsonance, uncongeniality; animosity, antagonism, antipathy, enmity, hostility, rancor; polarization; collision
con accord, consonance; agreement, concordance, concurrence
ant concord, harmony

discord *vb 1 syn* see CLASH 2
ant concord, harmonize
2 syn see DIFFER 2
ant accord

discordant *adj 1 syn* see INHARMONIOUS 2
2 syn see INCONSONANT 1
con according, agreeing, congenial, harmonious, harmonizing
ant concordant
3 syn see ANTIPATHETIC 1
ant concordant
4 syn see DISSONANT 1

discotheque *n syn* see NIGHTCLUB

discount *n syn* see DEDUCTION 1

discount *vb 1 syn* see DEDUCT 1
con boost, hike, increase, mark up, raise
2 syn see NEGLECT
3 syn see DECRY 2

discountenance *vb 1 syn* see EMBARRASS
idiom put out of countenance
2 syn see DISAPPROVE 1
rel reproach, reprove
con encourage, favor
ant countenance

discourage *vb 1* to weaken the stamina, interest, or zeal of < the long winter and lack of fuel *discouraged* the settlers >
syn chill, deject, demoralize, dishearten, disparage, dispirit
rel depress, weigh; afflict, try; damp, dampen, droop; distress, trouble; bother, irk, vex
idiom take the heart out of
con cheer, embolden, hearten, inspirit, nerve, steel
ant encourage
2 syn see DISSUADE
rel check, inhibit, restrain; prevent; frighten, scare
idiom lay a wet blanket on, throw cold water on
con advocate, countenance, favor; approve, back, endorse
ant encourage

discouraging *adj syn* see GLOOMY 3
rel deterring; hindering
ant encouraging

discourse *n 1 syn* see SPEECH 1
2 a systematic, serious, and often learned exposition of a subject or topic < his *discourses* during the seminar were long remembered >
syn disquisition, dissertation, memoir, monograph, monography, thesis, tractate, treatise
rel article, essay, paper; lecture, sermon; rhetoric, speech, talk

discourse *vb 1* to express oneself especially formally and at length < *discourses* knowledgeably about the laws of nature >
syn descant, dilate (on *or* upon), discuss, dissert, dissertate, expatiate, sermonize
rel converse, speak, talk, voice; argue, dispute; harangue, lecture, orate, perorate; amplify, develop, elaborate, enlarge, expand; explain, expound; comment, commentate, remark
2 syn see ACT 1

discourteous *adj syn* see RUDE 6
con chivalrous, civil, courtly, gallant
ant courteous

discover *vb 1 syn* see EXPOSE 4
2 syn see REVEAL 1
rel advertise, proclaim, publish
con repress, suppress
3 to become or be made aware of something not previously known < *discover* a secret >
syn ascertain, catch on, determine, find out, hear, learn, see, tumble, unearth
rel descry, detect, encounter, espy, hit (on *or* upon), meet (with), spot; discern, note, observe, perceive
idiom get wise to
con miss, overlook; disregard, ignore

discovery *n* the gaining knowledge of or ascertaining the existence of something previously unknown or unrecognized < the *discovery* of a new chemical element >
syn detection, espial, find, strike, unearthing
rel disclosure, exposition, exposure, revelation, uncovering

discreate *vb syn* see DESTROY 1

discredit *vb 1 syn* see DISBELIEVE
ant credit
2 to deprive of credibility < he *discredited* the rumor immediately >
syn blow up, disprove, explode, puncture, shoot
rel expose, show up; destroy, ruin
idiom bring to naught, knock the bottom out of, not leave a leg to stand on
con accept, believe, credit

discredit *n syn* see DISGRACE
ant credit

discreditable *adj syn* see DISREPUTABLE 1

discreet *adj 1 syn* see CAUTIOUS
con foolhardy
ant indiscreet
2 syn see PLAIN 1
3 syn see CONSERVATIVE 2

discreetness *n syn* see PRUDENCE 1
ant indiscreetness

discrepancy *n syn* see DISSIMILARITY

discrepant *adj syn* see INCONSONANT 1
rel different, disparate, divergent, diverse; disagreeing, varying
con agreeing, conforming, corresponding, jibing, squaring, tallying; alike, identical, like, parallel, similar, uniform

discrepate *vb syn* see KNOW 4

discrete *adj syn* see DISTINCT 1
con blended, fused, merged, mingled
ant indiscrete

discretion *n syn* see PRUDENCE 1
rel moderation, restraint; gumption, judgment, sense, wisdom
con asininity, fatuousness, foolishness, simplicity; foolhardiness, rashness, recklessness
ant indiscretion

discretionary *adj syn* see OPTIONAL

discriminate *vb syn* see KNOW 4
rel note, perceive, remark; collate, compare, contrast
ant confound

discriminating *adj syn* see ECLECTIC 1
rel careful; judicious, prudent, wise
ant undiscriminating

discrimination *n syn* see WIT 3
rel judgment, sense
con crassness, density, slowness

discriminative *adj syn* see DISCRIMINATORY
ant undiscriminative

discriminatory *adj* applying or favoring discrimination in treatment < *discriminatory* employment practices against women >
syn discriminative
rel biased, inequitable, partial, partisan, prejudiced, prepossessed, unfair, unjust
con dispassionate, equal, equitable, fair, impartial, just, objective, unbiased, uncolored, unprejudiced
ant nondiscriminatory

discrown *vb syn* see DEPOSE 1

disculpate *vb syn* see EXCULPATE
ant inculpate

discumber *vb syn* see EXTRICATE 2

discursion *n syn* see DIGRESSION

discuss *vb 1* to exchange views about something in order to arrive at the truth or to convince others < met to *discuss* community needs >

syn agitate, argue, canvass, debate, discept, dispute, ‖kick around, moot, pro and con, thrash out, toss (around)
rel deliberate, hash over, reason (out), talk over; consider, weigh
idiom consider pro and con, go into, reason the point
2 syn see DISCOURSE 1
rel elucidate, explicate, interpret

discussion *n syn* see CONFERENCE 1

disdain *n* **1 syn** see DESPITE 1
rel antipathy, aversion; arrogance, haughtiness, insolence, superciliousness
con awe, fear, reverence
2 syn see PRIDE 3

disdain *vb syn* see DESPISE
con accept, receive, take; acknowledge, admit, own; esteem, respect
ant admire

disdainful *adj syn* see PROUD 1
rel rejecting, repudiating, spurning; contemning, despising, scorning, scouting; antipathetic, averse, unsympathetic
ant admiring; respectful

disdainfulness *n syn* see PRIDE 3

disease *n* **1** a kind or instance of impairment of a living being that interferes with normal bodily function <tuberculosis has become a controllable *disease* >
syn affection, ailment, complaint, condition, disorder, ill, infirmity, malady, sickness, syndrome; *compare* INFIRMITY 1, SICKNESS 1
rel bug, ‖epizootic, ‖misery, virus
2 syn see INFIRMITY 1
ant health

diseasedness *n syn* see SICKNESS 1

disedge *vb syn* see DULL 3

disembark *vb* to go ashore out of a ship <*disembark* at the next port>
syn debark, land
rel put in
con board, get on
ant embark

disembarrass *vb syn* see EXTRICATE 2
rel clear, rid, unburden
ant embarrass

disembodied *adj syn* see IMMATERIAL 1

disembogue *vb syn* see DISCHARGE 5

disembowel *vb syn* see EVISCERATE

disembroil *vb syn* see EXTRICATE 2
ant embroil

disemploy *vb syn* see DISMISS 3

disenable *vb syn* see DISQUALIFY

disenchanted *adj syn* see SOPHISTICATED 2

disencumber *vb syn* see EXTRICATE 2
rel alleviate, lighten, relieve
con depress, oppress, weigh
ant encumber

disenfranchise *vb syn* see DISFRANCHISE

disengage *vb* **1 syn** see DETACH
rel free, liberate, release
con associate, connect, join, link, unite
ant engage
2 syn see LOOSE 3

disentangle *vb syn* see EXTRICATE 2
rel detach, disengage; part, separate, sever, sunder
con enmesh, involve
ant entangle, tangle

disenthrall *vb syn* see FREE

disenthrone *vb syn* see DEPOSE 1

disentranced *adj syn* see SOPHISTICATED 2

disentwine *vb syn* see EXTRICATE 2

disesteem *vb syn* see DISAPPROVE 1

disesteem *n syn* see DISGRACE
ant esteem

disfashion *vb syn* see DEFACE

disfavor *n* **1 syn** see DISLIKE
rel distrust, mistrust
con approbation, approval; admiration, esteem, liking, regard, respect
ant favor
2 syn see DISGRACE

disfavor *vb syn* see DISAPPROVE 1
con approve, accept, approbate, countenance, go (for), hold (with)
ant favor

disfeature *vb syn* see DEFACE

disfigure *vb syn* see DEFACE
ant adorn

disfranchise *vb* to deprive of a legal right and especially of the right to vote <people subtly *disfranchised* by community apathy>
syn disenfranchise
rel deprive, take away
ant affranchise, enfranchise, franchise

disgorge *vb* **1 syn** see VOMIT
2 syn see ERUPT 1

disgrace *n* the state of one who has lost esteem and good repute <retired in *disgrace* after the scandal became public>
syn contempt, discredit, disesteem, disfavor, dishonor, disrepute, ignominy, infamy, obloquy, odium, opprobrium, shame
rel abasement, debasement, debasing, degradation, humbling, humiliation; black eye, blot, brand, spot, stain, stigma
con admiration, regard; awe, fear, reverence; fame, glory, honor, renown, repute
ant esteem, respect

disgraceful *adj syn* see DISREPUTABLE 1
ant respectable; respectworthy

disgracious *adj syn* see RUDE 6
ant gracious

disgrade *vb syn* see DEGRADE 1

disgruntled *adj syn* see DISCONTENTED

disguise *vb* to alter so as to hide the true appearance or character of <*disguised* herself with a wig> <*disguised* his anger behind a false geniality>
syn camouflage, cloak, dissemble, dissimulate, dress up, mask
rel conceal, hide; obfuscate, obscure; belie, falsify, garble, misrepresent; affect, assume, counterfeit, feign, pretend, sham, simulate
con display, exhibit, expose, flaunt, parade, show; betray, disclose, discover, reveal

disguise *n* **1 syn** see MASK 2
rel deception, delusion; speciousness
2 syn see PRETENSE 2

disguised *adj syn* see INTOXICATED 1

disguisement *n syn* see MASK 2

disgust *vb* to be offensive to the taste or sensibilities of <the sight of filth *disgusted* him>
syn nauseate, reluct, repel, repulse, revolt, sicken
rel offend, outrage
idiom make one sick, stick in one's craw (*or* crop *or* gizzard), turn one's stomach
con charm, entice, tempt; delight, gratify, please, rejoice, tickle

disgusted *adj syn* see FED UP

disgusting *adj syn* see OFFENSIVE

‖dish *vb syn* see CHAT 1

disharmonic *adj syn* see DISSONANT 1
ant harmonic, harmonious

disharmonious *adj syn* see DISSONANT 1
ant harmonic, harmonious

disharmonize *vb syn* see CLASH 2
ant harmonize

disharmony *n syn* see DISCORD
ant harmony

dishearten *vb syn* see DISCOURAGE 1
ant hearten

disheartening *adj syn* see GLOOMY 3
rel despondent, pessimistic
con encouraging, optimistic
ant heartening

disheveled *adj syn* see SLOVENLY 1

dishonest *adj* **1** unworthy of trust or belief <made a *dishonest* report on their progress>
syn deceitful, knavish, lying, mendacious, roguish, shifty, unhonest, untruthful

---

syn synonym(s)   **rel** related word(s)
ant antonym(s)   **con** contrasted word(s)
idiom idiomatic equivalent(s)
‖ use limited; if in doubt, see a dictionary

rel crooked, devious, furtive, oblique; faithless, false, perfidious, untrustworthy; cheating, cozening, ‖cronk, defrauding, double= dealing, fraudulent, swindling, two-faced; insidious, tricky
con conscientious, honorable, just, scrupulous, upright; above- board, forthright, straightforward; candid, fair, frank, open, plain; dependable, reliable, sure, trustworthy, trusty
ant honest
2 syn see CROOKED 2
dishonesty *n syn* see DECEPTION 1
dishonor *n syn* see DISGRACE
con reverence, veneration; authority, credit, influence, prestige, weight
ant honor
dishonorable *adj syn* see DISREPUTABLE 1
ant honorable
dish out *vb syn* see GIVE 3
disillusioned *adj syn* see SOPHISTICATED 2
con beguiled, deceived, deluded, misled
disimpassioned *adj syn* see COOL 2
ant heated, impassioned
disimprison *vb syn* see FREE
ant imprison
disimprove *vb syn* see DETERIORATE 1
ant improve
disinclination *n syn* see DISLIKE
ant inclination
disinclined *adj* lacking the will or desire to do something <*disin- clined* to accept his story>
syn afraid, averse, backward, hesitant, indisposed, loath, reluc- tant, shy, uneager, unwilling, unwishful
rel antipathetic, unsympathetic; doubtful, dubious; opposing, resisting; balking, boggling, shying, sticking, stickling; objecting, protesting
con anxious, avid, eager, keen; disposed, predisposed, ready, willing
ant inclined
disingenuous *adj* lacking in candor and often giving a false ap- pearance of simple frankness <had a *disingenuous* way of ask- ing for advice when he really wanted help>
syn uncandid, unfrank
rel false, feigned, insincere, left-handed; artful, crafty, cunning, foxy, guileful, insidious, sly, tricky, wily; devious, indirect, oblique
con artless, naive, natural, simple, unsophisticated; candid, frank, open, plain; sincere, unfeigned; aboveboard, direct, straightforward
ant ingenuous
disinherit *vb* **1** to deprive (an heir apparent) of the right to inherit <the father *disinherited* his wayward son in his will>
syn cut off
rel disown, repudiate; dispossess
idiom cut off without a cent
2 syn see DEPRIVE 2
disinhume *vb syn* see EXHUME
ant inhume
disintegrate *vb* **1 syn** see DECAY
rel deliquesce; disperse, dissipate, scatter
con articulate, concatenate; blend, coalesce, fuse, merge; associ- ate, combine, conjoin, connect, join, link, unite
2 syn see DETERIORATE 1
disinter *vb syn* see EXHUME
ant inter
disinterest *n syn* see APATHY 2
ant interest
disinterested *adj* **1 syn** see INDIFFERENT 2
rel negative, neutral
con concerned, curious; fervent, impassioned, passionate
ant interested
2 syn see NEUTRAL
rel fair, just, impartial, unbiased
con biased, prejudiced; involved
ant concerned
disject *vb syn* see STREW 1
disjoin *vb syn* see SEPARATE 1
disjoint *vb* **1 syn** see SEPARATE 1
2 syn see DISORDER 1
disjointed *adj syn* see INCOHERENT 2

dislike *n* a state of mind or feeling marked by an inner avoidance of something usually felt as unpleasant or repugnant <a pro- nounced *dislike* for mathematics>
syn aversion, bad books, disfavor, disinclination, disliking, dis- pleasure, disrelish, dissatisfaction, distaste, indisposition
rel detestation, hate, hatred; deprecation, disapproval; preju- dice, scunner
idiom ‖a derry on
con affection, attachment, love; partiality, predilection, prefer- ence
ant liking
disliking *n syn* see DISLIKE
ant liking
dislimb *vb syn* see MAIM
dislimn *vb syn* see OBSCURE
dislocate *vb* **1 syn** see DISORDER 1
2 syn see MOVE 4
disloyal *adj syn* see FAITHLESS
rel alienated, disaffected, estranged
ant loyal
disloyalty *n* **1 syn** see INFIDELITY
ant loyalty
2 syn see TREACHERY
ant loyalty
dismal *adj syn* see GLOOMY 3
con animated, gay, lively; cheerful
dismals *n pl, used with* the *syn* see SADNESS
dismantle *vb* **1 syn** see STRIP 2
con appoint, equip, outfit
2 syn see DESTROY 1
3 syn see REVOKE 2
4 syn see DISMOUNT
dismay *n syn* see FEAR 1
con aplomb, assurance, confidence, self-possession; mettle, reso- lution, spirit
dismay *vb* **1** to unnerve and check by arousing fear, apprehension, or aversion <*dismayed* by the task that lay ahead>
syn appall, consternate, daunt, horrify, shake
rel bewilder, confound, dumbfound, mystify, nonplus, perplex, puzzle; abash, discomfit, disconcert, embarrass, faze, rattle; dis- courage, dishearten; affright, alarm, frighten, scare, terrify
idiom set one back on one's heels, take aback
con assure, ensure, secure; excite, galvanize, pique, provoke, quicken, stimulate
2 syn see DISCOMPOSE 1
dismayed *adj syn* see AGHAST 2
rel discomfited, disconcerted, fazed, rattled
ant undismayed
dismember *vb* **1 syn** see MAIM
rel part, separate, sever, sunder
2 syn see DISMOUNT
dismiss *vb* **1 syn** see DIVORCE 2
2 syn see DECLINE 4
3 to let go from one's employ or service <during the recession thousands of employees were *dismissed*>
syn ax, boot (out), bounce, ‖can, cashier, discharge, disemploy, drop, fire, kick out, let out, sack, terminate, turn off
rel depose, displace, furlough, lay off, remove, retire, suspend, unseat; reject, turn away; riff
idiom give one the gate (*or* one's walking papers), let go; give the ax (*or* the can) to
con hire; contract, engage; get, obtain, procure, secure
ant employ
4 syn see EJECT 1
rel cast, discard, shed, slough
idiom send one to Coventry
5 to refuse to consider seriously <*dismisses* the other performers as mere amateurs>
syn kiss off, pooh-pooh
rel deride, mock, rally, ridicule, taunt, twit; flout, gibe, gird, jeer, scoff; contemn, despise, disdain, scorn, scout; reject
dismissive *adj syn* see PROUD 1
dismount *vb* to take down or apart from an assembled position <*dismount* a revolver for cleaning>
syn disassemble, dismantle, dismember, take down
rel detach, disengage; disconnect, disjoin, disunite, separate
idiom take apart, take to pieces
con assemble, construct, put together; combine, unite

disobedient *adj* refusing or neglecting to obey < the *disobedient* child refused to come in >
  syn naughty, obstreperous, unruly; *compare* CONTRARY 3, NAUGHTY 1
  rel headstrong, recalcitrant, willful; contumacious, insubordinate, rebellious
  con amenable, biddable, docile, tractable; decorous, good, well-behaved
  ant obedient

disoblige *vb syn* see INCONVENIENCE
  con accommodate, convenience, favor
  ant oblige

disorder *n* 1 *syn* see CONFUSION 3
  con orderliness; pattern, plan
  ant order
  2 breach of public order < the overthrow of the government caused *disorder* in the country >
  syn anarchism, anarchy, distemper, misrule, riot
  rel anomie; agitation, commotion, convulsion, tumult, turbulence, turmoil, upheaval
  ant order
  3 *syn* see DISEASE 1
  4 *syn* see SICKNESS 1

disorder *vb* 1 to undo the fixed or proper order of something < *disorder* the carefully arranged contents of a drawer >
  syn derange, disarrange, disarray, discompose, disjoint, dislocate, disorganize, disrupt, distemper, disturb, jumble, ‖mammock, mess (up), mix up, muddle, muss (up), ‖mux, rummage, shuffle, tumble, unsettle, upset; *compare* CONFUSE 5
  rel ball up, embroil; dishevel, rumple
  idiom make hay of
  con arrange, marshal, methodize, organize, systematize; align, array, line, line up, range; adjust, fix, regulate
  ant order
  2 *syn* see UPSET 5

disordered *adj* 1 *syn* see INCOHERENT 2
  2 *syn* see INSANE 1

disorderly *adj syn* see TURBULENT 1

disorderly house *n syn* see BROTHEL

disorganize *vb syn* see DISORDER 1
  ant organize

disown *vb syn* see DISCLAIM
  ant own

disparage *vb* 1 *syn* see DECRY 2
  ant applaud
  2 *syn* see DISCOURAGE 1

disparagement *n* 1 *syn* see DETRACTION
  rel animadversion, aspersion, reflection, stricture
  2 *syn* see DESPITE 1

disparaging *adj syn* see DEROGATORY
  rel underestimating, underrating, undervaluing
  con acclaiming, extolling, praising; exalting, magnifying

disparate *adj syn* see DIFFERENT 1
  rel discordant, discrepant, incompatible, inconsistent, inconsonant; distinct, separate
  ant analogous, comparable

disparity *n* the state of being different (as in degree, rank, excellence, or number) < the *disparity* between the rich and the poor > < their stories showed significant *disparity* >
  syn disproportion, imparity, inequality, unevenness
  rel alterity, difference, dissemblance, dissimilarity, dissimilitude, distinction, divergence, divergency, otherness, unlikeness
  con adequation, equality, equatability, equivalence, equivalency, sameness; correlation, correspondence, likeness; evenness
  ant parity

dispassionate *adj* 1 *syn* see NEUTRAL
  rel imperturbable, unflappable, unruffled
  con fervent, vehement; intemperate
  2 *syn* see FAIR 4
  rel aloof, indifferent; frank, open; aboveboard, straightforward

dispatch *vb* 1 *syn* see SEND 1
  rel hasten, quicken, speed
  2 *syn* see KILL 1
  3 *syn* see EAT UP 1

dispatch *n* 1 *syn* see HASTE 1
  con dawdling, loitering, procrastination
  ant delay
  2 *syn* see ALACRITY

  rel diligence, industriousness

dispeace *n syn* see DISCORD

dispel *vb syn* see SCATTER 1
  rel dismiss, eject, expel, oust; crumble, disintegrate

dispensable *adj* capable of being dispensed with < many household gadgets are readily *dispensable* >
  syn nonessential, unessential, unrequired
  rel needless, unnecessary, unneeded; minor, trivial, unimportant
  con essential, imperative, necessary, necessitous, required; vital
  ant indispensable

dispensation *n syn* see FAVOR 4

dispense *vb* 1 *syn* see DISTRIBUTE 1
  2 *syn* see GIVE 3
  rel portion, prorate
  3 *syn* see ADMINISTER 2
  4 *syn* see HANDLE 2
  5 *syn* see EXEMPT

disperse *vb* 1 *syn* see SCATTER 1
  rel discharge, dismiss
  con call, cite, convene, convoke, summon
  ant assemble, congregate; collect
  2 *syn* see DISTRIBUTE 1
  3 *syn* see SPREAD 1
  4 *syn* see DISBAND

dispirit *vb syn* see DISCOURAGE 1
  idiom dampen (*or* lower) one's spirits
  ant inspirit

dispirited *adj syn* see DOWNCAST
  rel melancholy, sad
  ant high-spirited, inspirited

dispiriting *adj syn* see GLOOMY 3
  rel dejecting, distressing; oppressing
  ant inspiriting

displace *vb* 1 *syn* see BANISH
  2 *syn* see DEPOSE 1
  3 *syn* see SUPPLANT 1

displaced person *n syn* see REFUGEE

displacement *n syn* see EXILE 1

display *vb* 1 *syn* see OPEN 2
  rel demonstrate, evidence, evince, lay out, manifest, show
  con camouflage, cloak, disguise, dissemble, mask; conceal, hide, secrete
  2 *syn* see SHOW 4
  3 *syn* see SHOW 1

display *n* 1 *syn* see EXHIBITION 1
  2 a striking or spectacular exhibition < a parvenu's *display* of wealth >
  syn array, fanfare, panoply, parade, pomp, shine, show
  rel ostentation, ostentatiousness, pretension, pretentiousness, showiness; setout

displeasing *adj syn* see BAD 8
  rel annoying, bothersome, irksome, vexing
  con agreeable, gratifying, pleasant
  ant pleasing

displeasure *n syn* see DISLIKE
  rel anger; vexation
  con delight, enjoyment
  ant pleasure

disponible *adj syn* see AVAILABLE 1

disport *n syn* see PLAY 1
  rel jollity, merriment

disport *vb* 1 *syn* see SHOW 4
  2 *syn* see BEHAVE 1
  3 *syn* see PLAY 1

disposal *n* 1 *syn* see ORDER 3
  2 the act of ridding oneself of something < incinerators used for the *disposal* of trash >
  syn discarding, disposition, dumping, jettison, junking, relegation, riddance, scrapping, throwing away
  rel chucking, clearance; demolishing, demolition, destroying, destruction
  con acquirement, acquisition; accumulation, collection, cumulation, deposit, hoard, trove

---

dispose *vb* **1** *syn* see INCLINE 3
  ant indispose
  2 *syn* see ORDER 1
disposed *adj syn* see WILLING 1
  ant indisposed
disposition *n* **1** *syn* see DISPOSAL 2
  rel control, controlling, direction, management
  2 *syn* see ORDER 3
  3 the complex of especially mental and emotional qualities that
  distinguish an individual < a man of irritable *disposition* >
  syn character, complexion, humor, individualism, individuality,
  makeup, nature, personality, temper, temperament
  rel mood, tone, vein; cast, stamp, tenor, type; being; identity
  idiom frame of mind
  4 *syn* see LEANING 2
dispossess *vb syn* see DEPRIVE 2
  con provide, supply
dispossession *n syn* see PRIVATION 2
dispraise *vb syn* see DECRY 2
  ant praise
disproportion *n syn* see DISPARITY
disproportional *adj syn* see LOPSIDED
disproportionate *adj syn* see LOPSIDED
  ant proportionate
disprove *vb* **1** to show by presenting evidence that something is
  not true < the defendant's claims were *disproved* by the testimony >
  syn break, confound, confute, controvert, disconfirm, evert, rebut, refute
  rel contravene, impugn, negative, traverse; overthrow, overturn
  con evidence, show; demonstrate, display, illustrate, manifest;
  argue, bespeak, tell
  ant prove
  2 *syn* see DISCREDIT 2
disputable *adj syn* see MOOT
disputation *n syn* see ARGUMENTATION
disputatious *adj syn* see CONTENTIOUS 2
dispute *vb* **1** *syn* see ARGUE 2
  con give in, surrender
  2 *syn* see DISCUSS 1
  rel confute, controvert, disprove, rebut, refute
  con allow, grant
  ant concede
  3 *syn* see QUESTION 2
  4 *syn* see RESIST
dispute *n* **1** *syn* see ARGUMENT 2
  rel conflict, discord, dissension, strife
  2 *syn* see QUARREL
disqualified *adj syn* see UNFIT 2
  ant qualified
disqualify *vb* to deprive of a power, right, or privilege < a conviction of perjury *disqualified* him from being a witness >
  syn disable, disenable, incapacitate
  rel bar, bate, debar, eliminate, except, exclude, rule out, suspend
  con empower, enable
  ant qualify
disquiet *vb syn* see DISCOMPOSE 1
  rel distress, trouble
  con calm, compose, lull, still
  ant quiet, soothe, tranquilize
disquiet *n* **1** *syn* see CARE 2
  ant quiet
  2 *syn* see UNREST
  ant quiet
disquietude *n* **1** *syn* see CARE 2
  2 *syn* see UNREST
  ant quietness, quietude
disquisition *n syn* see DISCOURSE 2
  rel inquiry, investigation; argumentation, debate, disputation
disquisitive *adj syn* see INQUISITIVE 1
disrate *vb syn* see DEGRADE 1
disregard *vb syn* see NEGLECT
  con attend, mind, tend, watch; note, notice, observe, remark
  ant regard
disregard *n syn* see APATHY 2
  rel forgetting, ignoring, neglecting, omission, omitting, overlooking, slighting

  con consideration, thoughtfulness
disregardful *adj syn* see NEGLIGENT
  ant regardful
disrelish *n syn* see DISLIKE
  ant relish
disremember *vb syn* see FORGET 1
disreputable *adj* **1** not reputable or decent < was punished for his
  disreputable conduct >
  syn discreditable, disgraceful, dishonorable, ignominious, inglorious, shabby, shady, shameful, shoddy, unrespectable
  rel abject, mean, sordid; beggarly, cheap, contemptible, despicable, pitiable, scurvy, sorry
  con admirable, creditable, estimable, honorable, respectable
  ant reputable
  2 *syn* see SHABBY 1
disrepute *n syn* see DISGRACE
  ant repute
disrespect *n syn* see INSOLENCE
  ant respect
disrespectful *adj syn* see RUDE 6
  ant respectful
disrobe *vb* **1** *syn* see STRIP 1
  2 *syn* see STRIP 2
disrupt *vb* **1** *syn* see OPEN 3
  2 *syn* see DISORDER 1
dissatisfaction *n syn* see DISLIKE
  ant satisfaction
dissatisfactory *adj syn* see BAD 1
  ant satisfactory
dissatisfied *adj syn* see DISCONTENTED
  rel annoyed, bothered, irked, vexed
  con content, contented, gratified
  ant satisfied
dissect *vb* **1** *syn* see SEPARATE 1
  2 *syn* see CUT 5
  rel penetrate, pierce, probe
  3 *syn* see ANALYZE
dissection *n syn* see ANALYSIS 1
  rel examination, inspection, review, scrutiny; criticism, critique
dissemblance *n syn* see DISSIMILARITY
  ant resemblance, semblance
dissemblance *n syn* see DECEIT 1
dissemble *vb syn* see DISGUISE
  con demonstrate, evidence, evince, manifest, show
dissembler *n syn* see HYPOCRITE
disseminate *vb* **1** *syn* see SPREAD 1
  2 *syn* see DECLARE 1
  3 *syn* see STREW 1
dissension *n syn* see DISCORD
  rel altercation, bickering, quarrel, wrangle; argument, controversy, dispute
  con amity, friendship, goodwill
  ant accord; comity
dissent *vb syn* see DIFFER 2
  rel balk, boggle, demur, shy, stickle
  con accede, acquiesce, agree, subscribe
  ant assent; concur
dissent *n* **1** *syn* see DISCORD
  2 *syn* see HERESY
  rel disagreement, nonagreement, nonconcurrence
dissenter *n syn* see HERETIC
dissert *vb syn* see DISCOURSE 1
dissertate *vb syn* see DISCOURSE 1
dissertation *n syn* see DISCOURSE 2
  rel exposition; argumentation, disputation
dissever *vb* **1** *syn* see SEPARATE 1
  2 *syn* see CUT 5
dissidence *n* **1** *syn* see DISCORD
  2 *syn* see HERESY
dissident *adj syn* see HERETICAL
dissident *n syn* see HERETIC
dissimilar *adj syn* see DIFFERENT 1
  rel antithetical, antonymous, contradictory, contrary, opposite
  ant similar
dissimilarity *n* lack of agreement or correspondence or an instance
  of this < the *dissimilarities* in the cultures of the two countries >
  syn alterity, difference, discrepancy, dissemblance, dissimilitude,
  distance, distinction, divarication, divergence, divergency, otherness, unlikeness

rel disparity, diversity; discordance, incongruity, inconsistency, inconsonance; discord, variance; severance; offset; margin
con affinity, analogy, likeness, resemblance, similitude; accordance, congruity, consistency, consonance; agreement, conformity, correspondence
ant similarity

dissimilitude *n syn* see DISSIMILARITY
ant similitude

dissimulate *vb syn* see DISGUISE

dissimulation *n syn* see DECEIT 1
rel camouflaging, cloaking, disguising, dissembling, masking; concealing, hiding, secreting; feigning, pretending, pretense, shamming; hypocrisy, pharisaism, sanctimony

dissimulator *n syn* see HYPOCRITE

dissipate *vb* **1** *syn* see SCATTER 1
rel crumble, disintegrate
ant accumulate; concentrate (*as efforts, thoughts*)
2 *syn* see WASTE 2
rel disappear, evanesce, evaporate, vanish
ant absorb (*as time, attention*)

dissipation *n syn* see ENTERTAINMENT

dissociate *vb syn* see DETACH
rel alienate, estrange
ant associate

dissolute *adj syn* see ABANDONED 2
rel lax, light, loose, slack, wanton, wayward; fast, raffish, rakish, wild

dissolution *n* **1** *syn* see SEPARATION 1
2 *syn* see DEATH 1

dissolve *vb* **1** *syn* see DESTROY 1
2 *syn* see ADJOURN 2
3 *syn* see ANNUL 4
4 *syn* see LIQUEFY
5 *syn* see SOLVE 2
6 *syn* see DISBAND

dissonance *n syn* see DISCORD

dissonant *adj* **1** marked by a mingling of discordant sounds < the two bands playing different pieces at the same time sounded *dissonant* >
syn cacophonic, cacophonous, discordant, disharmonic, disharmonious, immusical, inharmonic, inharmonious, rude, unharmonious, unmusical
rel grating, harsh, hoarse, jarring, raucous, rugged, strident
con blending, chiming, concerted, harmonic, symphonious; euphonious, harmonious, mellifluous, mellow, melodious, musical; agreeable, pleasing
ant consonant
2 *syn* see INCONSONANT 1

dissuade *vb* to turn one aside from a purpose, a project, or a plan < they tried to *dissuade* a friend from making a mistake >
syn deter, disadvise, discourage, divert
rel derail, throw off; advise, counsel; exhort, prick, urge
idiom talk out of
con get, induce, prevail; affect, influence, touch
ant persuade

distance *n* **1** an extent of areal or linear measure < he did not know the *distance* he had walked >
syn length, stretch
rel area, extent; ambit, compass, extension, orbit, purview, radius, range, reach, scope, sweep
2 the length of a literal or figurative course traversed or to be traversed < he had come a long *distance* from his pitiful beginnings >
syn way, ways
rel extent, size; piece, spell
3 *syn* see EXPANSE
4 *syn* see DISSIMILARITY

distance *vb syn* see OUTSTRIP 1

distant *adj* **1** not close in space, time, or relationship < traveling to a more *distant* place > < the *distant* days of the Pilgrim fathers > < a *distant* cousin >
syn far, faraway, far-flung, far-off, off-lying, outlying, remote, removed
rel apart, isolated, obscure, out-of-the-way, retired, secret; secluded, sequestered
idiom at a distance
con close, near, nearby, next, nigh; adjacent, adjoining, contiguous

2 *syn* see DIFFERENT 1
3 *syn* see UNSOCIABLE
rel arrogant, haughty, proud; modest, retiring, shy
con forward, presuming, ‖pushy, self-assertive

distaste *n syn* see DISLIKE
rel abhorrence, repugnance, repulsion, revulsion; antipathy, hostility
con relish, zest; appetite, desire; enjoyment
ant taste

distasteful *adj* **1** *syn* see UNPALATABLE 1
ant tasteful, tasty
2 *syn* see BITTER 2
rel obnoxious, repellent, repugnant, repulsive; abominable, detestable, hateful, odious
con agreeable, grateful, gratifying, pleasant, pleasing, welcome

distemper *vb syn* see DISORDER 1

distemper *n syn* see DISORDER 2

distend *vb syn* see EXPAND 3
rel augment, enlarge, increase; extend, lengthen
ant constrict

disthrone *vb syn* see DEPOSE 1

distill *vb syn* see DRIP

distinct *adj* **1** capable of being distinguished as differing < the novel has two related, but nevertheless *distinct*, plots >
syn different, discrete, diverse, separate, several, various
rel distinctive, individual, peculiar; particular, single, sole; especial, individual, special, specific; disparate, dissimilar, divergent
con identical, same, selfsame; corresponding, equivalent, like, similar
ant indistinguishable
2 *syn* see CLEAR 5
rel defined, prescribed; categorical, definite, explicit, express, specific; lucid, perspicuous; clear-cut, incisive, trenchant
con faint, obscure
ant indistinct; nebulous

distinction *n* **1** *syn* see DISSIMILARITY
con affinity, analogy, likeness, similarity, similitude
ant indistinction, resemblance
2 *syn* see EMINENCE 1
3 *syn* see HONOR 2

distinctive *adj syn* see CHARACTERISTIC
rel separate, single, unique; discrete, distinct, several
con common, familiar, ordinary, popular, vulgar; alike, analogous, comparable, identical, like, parallel; equal, equivalent, same

distinctively *adv syn* see ESPECIALLY 1

distinctiveness *n syn* see INDIVIDUALITY 3

distingué *adj syn* see GENTEEL 1

distinguish *vb* **1** *syn* see KNOW 4
rel divide, part; detach, disengage; demarcate, set off
con confuse, mistake
ant confound
2 *syn* see EXALT 1
3 *syn* see CHARACTERIZE 2
idiom set apart
4 *syn* see SEE 1
5 *syn* see IDENTIFY

distinguished *adj syn* see FAMOUS 2
rel courtly, dignified, grand, imposing, stately
ant undistinguished

distort *vb* **1** *syn* see MISREPRESENT
rel misconstrue, misinterpret; alter, change
2 *syn* see DEFORM
rel bend, curve, twist

distortion *n syn* see DEFORMITY

distract *vb* **1** *syn* see CONFUSE 2
2 *syn* see MADDEN 1

distracted *adj syn* see DISTRAUGHT

distraction *n* **1** *syn* see INSANITY 1
2 *syn* see ENTERTAINMENT

distrait *adj* **1** *syn* see ABSTRACTED
2 *syn* see DISTRAUGHT

---

syn synonym(s)   **rel** related word(s)
ant antonym(s)   **con** contrasted word(s)
idiom idiomatic equivalent(s)
‖ use limited; if in doubt, see a dictionary

distraught *adj* **1** agitated with doubt or mental conflict < *distraught* over the health of her child >
syn distracted, distrait, distressed, harassed, tormented, troubled, worried
rel agitated, concerned, discomposed, flustered, perturbed, upset; addled, confused, muddled; bewildered, nonplussed
idiom beside oneself
con composed, cool, imperturbable, nonchalant, unflappable, unruffled; calm, tranquil; unconcerned, undisturbed, unworried
ant collected
2 syn see INSANE 1

distress *n* the state of being in serious trouble or in mental or physical anguish < in great *distress* over the decision he had to make >
syn agony, dolor, misery, passion, suffering
rel affliction, cross, trial, tribulation, visitation; anguish, grief, heartbreak, sorrow, woe; exigency, pass, pinch, strait; difficulty, hardship, rigor, vicissitude; ache, pain, pang, throe, twinge
con comfort, comforting, consolation, solace, solacing; allaying, alleviation, assuagement, ease, relief, relieving; ease, peace, security

distress *vb* **1 syn** see TRY 2
rel afflict, rack, torment, torture
con allay, alleviate, assuage, lighten, mitigate, relieve
2 to cause pain or suffering to < the death of his longtime friend *distressed* him deeply >
syn aggrieve, constrain, grieve, hurt, injure, pain
rel harass, strain, stress, try, trouble; depress, oppress, weigh
con comfort, console, solace; aid, assist, help
3 syn see TROUBLE 1
rel annoy, harry, pester, plague

distressed *adj syn* see DISTRAUGHT
distressing *adj syn* see DEPLORABLE

distribute *vb* **1** to give out, usually in shares, to each member of a group < *distributed* his possessions among his heirs >
syn deal, disburse, dispense, disperse, divide, ‖divvy, dole (out), lot (out), measure (out), partition
rel allocate, allot, apportion, assign, mete (out); parcel, portion, prorate, ration; administer; dribble; bestow, donate, give, present
con assemble, gather; accumulate, hoard
ant amass; collect
2 syn see SPREAD 1

distribution *n syn* see ORDER 3
district *n* **1 syn** see QUARTER 2
2 syn see LOCALITY 1
rel division, parcel

distrust *vb* to have no trust or confidence in < he *distrusted* most politicians >
syn doubt, misdoubt, mistrust, suspect, ‖suspicion
rel disbelieve, discredit, unbelieve
con bank, count, depend, reckon, rely; commit, confide, consign, entrust
ant trust

distrustful *adj syn* see SUSPICIOUS 2
distrustfully *adv syn* see ASKANCE 2
disturb *vb* **1 syn** see MOVE 4
2 syn see DISCOMPOSE 1
rel alarm, frighten, scare, terrify; bewilder, distract, perplex, puzzle; discommode, incommode, inconvenience, trouble
3 syn see DISORDER 1
rel displace, replace; move, remove, shift; interfere, intermeddle, meddle, tamper
con establish, fix, set, settle; adjust, regulate

disunify *vb syn* see ESTRANGE
disunion *n* **1 syn** see SEPARATION 1
2 syn see DISCORD
disunite *vb* **1 syn** see SEPARATE 1
2 syn see ESTRANGE
disunity *n syn* see DISCORD
disusage *n syn* see DISUSE
disuse *n* cessation of use, practice, or exercise < to keep the mind from falling into *disuse*, one must exercise one's reading abilities > < his muscles became atrophied from *disuse* >
syn desuetude, disusage
con appliance, application, employment, operation, play, usance; exercise
ant use

disused *adj syn* see OBSOLETE
ditch *n syn* see TRENCH
ditch *vb* **1 syn** see DISCARD
‖**2 syn** see HIDE
‖**dite** *n syn* see PARTICLE
dither *vb* **1 syn** see SHAKE 1
2 syn see HESITATE
3 syn see CHAT 1
dither *n* **1 syn** see JITTERS
2 syn see COMMOTION 2
dithyrambic *adj syn* see IMPASSIONED
ditto *n syn* see REPRODUCTION
ditty *n syn* see SONG 2
diurnal *adj syn* see DAILY
ant nocturnal
diuturnal *adj syn* see LASTING
divagate *vb syn* see DIGRESS 2
divagation *n syn* see DIGRESSION
divarication *n syn* see DISSIMILARITY
dive *vb syn* see PLUNGE 2
rel bound, jump, leap, spring; impel, move
dive *n* a shabby or disreputable place for drinking or entertainment < got a schooner of beer at the *dive* down the street >
syn barrelhouse, hangout, honky-tonk, joint
rel dump, hole; bar, barroom, lounge, pothouse, pub, saloon, taproom, tavern
‖**diver** *n syn* see PICKPOCKET
diverge *vb* **1 syn** see SWERVE 2
rel differ, disagree, vary; divide, part, separate
ant converge; conform
2 syn see DIGRESS 2
divergence *n* **1 syn** see DISSIMILARITY
rel diversity, variety
con accord, concord, consonance, harmony
ant conformity, correspondence
2 syn see DEVIATION 1
rel division, parting, separation; differing, disagreeing, varying
con agreement, coincidence, concurrence
ant convergence
divergency *n syn* see DISSIMILARITY
divergent *adj* **1 syn** see DIFFERENT 1
rel antithetical, contradictory, contrary, opposite; aberrant, abnormal, atypical
con alike, identical, parallel, same
ant convergent
2 syn see IRREGULAR 1
divers *adj syn* see SEVERAL 3
divers *pron, pl in constr syn* see SUNDRY
diverse *adj* **1 syn** see DIFFERENT 1
rel contrasted, contrasting, contrastive; contradictory, contrary, opposite
con equal, equivalent, same
ant identical, selfsame
2 syn see DISTINCT 1
idiom of every description
3 syn see MANIFOLD
diversely *adv syn* see OTHERWISE 1
diverseness *n syn* see VARIETY 1
diversiform *adj syn* see MANIFOLD
diversion *n* **1 syn** see DEVIATION 1
2 syn see PLAY 1
3 syn see ENTERTAINMENT
rel frivolity, levity
4 syn see ENJOYMENT 1
diversity *n syn* see VARIETY 1
rel difference, dissimilarity, distinction, divergence, divergency, unlikeness
ant uniformity; identity
divert *vb* **1 syn** see TURN 6
rel swerve; alter, change, modify
con fix, set, settle
2 syn see DISSUADE
rel abstract, detach, disengage
3 syn see AMUSE
rel delight, gladden, please, regale, tickle
divertissement *n syn* see ENTERTAINMENT
divest *vb* **1 syn** see STRIP 2
ant invest, vest; apparel, attire, clothe

2 syn see DEPRIVE 2
  rel despoil, plunder, spoil
  ant invest, vest
divestiture *n syn* see PRIVATION 2
divide *vb* **1 syn** see SEPARATE 1
  rel carve, chop, cut
  ant unite
  2 syn see DISTRIBUTE 1
  3 syn see APPORTION 2
  rel allocate, allot, assign
  4 syn see DIFFER 2
  rel part, separate
  con combine, concur, conjoin, cooperate
  ant unite
dividend *n syn* see REWARD
divine *n syn* see CLERGYMAN
divine *vb syn* see FORESEE
divine *adj* **1** of or relating to God or a god < the *divine* will >
  syn deific, godly
  rel chthonian
  2 like or like that of God or a god < men who aspire to *divine* honors >
  syn deific, godlike
  rel extramundane, superhuman, superphysical, transmundane
  3 syn see MARVELOUS 2
division *n* **1 syn** see PART 1
  2 syn see SEPARATION 1
  3 syn see DISCORD
divorce *n syn* see SEPARATION 1
divorce *vb* **1 syn** see SEPARATE 1
  rel disaffect, wean
  2 to end a marriage by legal action < unable to agree, they decided to *divorce* > < *divorced* his wife >
  syn dismiss, put away, unmarry
  rel break up, separate, split; annul, cancel
divorcement *n syn* see SEPARATION 1
divulge *vb syn* see REVEAL 1
  rel proclaim; gossip, tattle
||**divvy** *vb* **1 syn** see DISTRIBUTE 1
  2 syn see APPORTION 2
||**dizzard** *n syn* see DUNCE
dizzy *adj* **1 syn** see GIDDY 1
  rel asinine, fatuous, foolish; inane
  2 affected by a sensation of being whirled about or around < the speed with which she dispatched her tasks made the onlookers *dizzy* >
  syn giddy, light, light-headed, swimming, swimmy, vertiginous
  rel reeling, whirling; bewildered, confounded, distracted, puzzled; addled, befuddled, confused, dazed, dazzled, fuddled, muddled
  idiom with spots before one's eyes
  3 syn see EXCESSIVE 1
dizzy *vb syn* see CONFUSE 2
do *vb* **1 syn** see PERFORM 2
  2 syn see CLOSE 3
  3 syn see ACT 1
  4 syn see CHEAT
  idiom do out of, sell one a bill of goods
  5 syn see COOK 1
  6 syn see BEHAVE 1
  7 syn see SHIFT 5
  8 syn see HAPPEN 1
  9 syn see TRAVEL 2
  10 syn see SERVE 3
  11 syn see SERVE 5
||**do** *n syn* see SUCCESS
doable *adj syn* see POSSIBLE 1
doc *n syn* see PHYSICIAN
docile *adj syn* see OBEDIENT
  rel adaptable, pliable, pliant
  con obstinate, self-willed, stubborn, willful
  ant indocile; ungovernable, unruly
||**docious** *adj syn* see OBEDIENT
dock *n syn* see WHARF
docket *n syn* see PROGRAM 1
doctor *n syn* see PHYSICIAN
doctor *vb* **1 syn** see TREAT 4
  2 syn see MEND 2

3 syn see ADULTERATE
doctrinaire *adj syn* see DICTATORIAL
  rel bullheaded, dogged, mulish, obstinate, pertinacious, pigheaded, stiff-necked, stubborn
  ant undoctrinaire
doctrine *n* a principle accepted as valid and authoritative < the *doctrine* of evolution >
  syn canon, dogma, tenet
  rel instruction, teaching; axiom, basic, fundamental, principle
  idiom article of belief (*or* faith)
document *n* something preserved and serving as evidence (as of an event, a situation, or the culture of a period) < ceramic and flint artifacts provide our only *document* of this ancient people >
  syn archive(s), monument, record
  rel evidence, testimony
doddering *adj syn* see SENILE
doddery *adj syn* see SENILE
dodge *vb* **1** to avoid or evade by some maneuver or shift < *dodging* in and out among the crowd > < *dodged* his pursuer with ease >
  syn duck, fence, parry, shirk, sidestep
  rel malinger; avoid, elude, escape, evade, skirt; slide, slip; short-circuit
  idiom fight shy of
  con ||banter, beard, brave, challenge, dare, defy, front, venture; confront, encounter, meet
  ant face
  2 syn see EQUIVOCATE 2
dodo *n syn* see DUNCE
||**dods** *n pl syn* see SULK
||**dodunk** *n syn* see DUNCE
doff *vb syn* see REMOVE 3
do for *vb syn* see HELP 1
dofunny *n syn* see DOODAD
dog *n* **1** a highly variable carnivorous domesticated mammal < many households have *dogs* as pets >
  syn bowwow, canine, hound, ||pooch, tyke
  rel pup, puppy; cur, ||feist, mongrel, mutt
  2 syn see SNOT 1
  3 syn see FRANKFURTER
  4 syn see JALOPY
dog *vb syn* see TAIL
Dogberry *n syn* see POLICEMAN
dogfall *n syn* see DRAW 4
dogfight *n syn* see BRAWL 2
dogged *adj* **1 syn** see INFLEXIBLE 2
  2 syn see PERSISTENT 1
doggery *n syn* see RABBLE 2
doggish *adj syn* see DAPPER
doggone *adj* **1 syn** see DAMNED 2
  2 syn see UTTER
doggy *adj syn* see DAPPER
dogma *n syn* see DOCTRINE
  rel belief, conviction, persuasion, view
dogmatic *adj* **1 syn** see DICTATORIAL
  2 syn see DEDUCTIVE
dog nap *n syn* see NAP
dog's age *n syn* see AGE 2
do in *vb* **1 syn** see RUIN 2
  2 syn see MURDER 1
  3 syn see EXHAUST 4
doing *n syn* see ACTION 1
doit *n syn* see PARTICLE
doldrums *n pl* **1 syn** see TEDIUM
  rel blues, dejection, depression, dumps, gloom; apathy, disinterest, indifference, listlessness
  con high spirits, spirits
  2 syn see ABEYANCE
  rel depression, retardation, slump, stagnation; inactivity
dole (out) *vb* **1 syn** see ADMINISTER 2
  2 syn see DISTRIBUTE 1
||**dole** *n* **1 syn** see SORROW
  2 syn see MISFORTUNE

---

syn synonym(s)   *rel* related word(s)
ant antonym(s)   *con* contrasted word(s)
idiom idiomatic equivalent(s)
|| use limited; if in doubt, see a dictionary

doleful *adj* **1** *syn* see DOWNCAST
  2 *syn* see WOEFUL 1
  3 *syn* see MELANCHOLY 2
  rel grieving, mourning, sorrowing; piteous, pitiful
  con blithe, blithesome, radiant, sparkling, sunny
  ant cheerful, cheery
dolefuls *n pl, used with the* *syn* see SADNESS
dolent *adj* *syn* see WOEFUL 1
dolesome *adj* *syn* see MELANCHOLY 2
dolittle *n* *syn* see SLUGGARD
dollar *n* a currency bill representing one hundred cents < had a single *dollar* left >
  syn bill, ‖bone, ‖buck, ‖fish, ‖frogskin, ‖ironman, oner, rock, ‖skin, ‖smacker, ‖smackeroo
dollop *n* *syn* see DRAM 1
doll out *vb* *syn* see DRESS UP 1
doll up *vb* *syn* see DRESS UP 1
dolor *n* *syn* see DISTRESS
  con blessedness, bliss, felicity, happiness
  ant beatitude
dolorous *adj* **1** *syn* see DEPLORABLE
  2 *syn* see WOEFUL 1
  3 *syn* see MELANCHOLY 2
dolt *n* *syn* see DUNCE
dolthead *n* *syn* see DUNCE
doltish *adj* *syn* see STUPID 1
domain *n* *syn* see FIELD
‖**dome** *n* *syn* see HEAD 1
domestic *adj* **1** of or relating to the household or family < *domestic* chores required to maintain a home >
  syn family, home, household
  con civic, public; personal, private; business, occupational, professional
  2 of, relating to, or carried on within an indicated or implied country < charts of *domestic* as well as foreign waters >
  syn home, ‖inland, internal, intestine, municipal, national, native
  ant foreign
  3 *syn* see TAME
domesticate *vb* to adapt (an animal or plant) to life in intimate association with and to the advantage of man < the man who *domesticated* the first dog >
  syn domesticize, domiciliate, master, tame
  rel gentle, subdue; housebreak; break, bust, train
domesticated *adj* *syn* see TAME
domesticize *vb* *syn* see DOMESTICATE
domicile *n* *syn* see HABITATION 2
domicile *vb* *syn* see HARBOR 2
domiciliate *vb* **1** *syn* see HARBOR 2
  2 *syn* see DOMESTICATE
dominance *n* *syn* see SUPREMACY
dominant *adj* **1** superior to all others in power, influence, or importance < the Sumerians were a *dominant* race of ancient times >
  syn ascendant, master, outweighing, overbalancing, overbearing, overweighing, paramount, predominant, predominate, preponderant, prevalent, regnant, sovereign
  rel prevailing; preeminent, supreme, surpassing, transcendent; chief, first, foremost, leading, main, principal; governing, ruling
  con collateral, dependent, secondary, subject, tributary; unimportant
  ant subordinate
  2 *syn* see CHIEF 2
dominate *vb* **1** *syn* see GOVERN 3
  2 *syn* see RULE 2
  3 *syn* see OVERLOOK 2
domination *n* **1** *syn* see SUPREMACY
  2 *syn* see POWER 1
dominator *n* *syn* see LEADER 2
domineer *vb* *syn* see RULE 2
domineering *adj* *syn* see MASTERFUL 1
  rel arrogant, insolent, lordly
  con obsequious, servile, slavish; bootlicking, groveling, sycophantic, toadying
  ant subservient; fawning
‖**dominie** *n* *syn* see CLERGYMAN
dominion *n* **1** *syn* see SUPREMACY
  2 *syn* see FIELD

  3 *syn* see OWNERSHIP
domino *n* *syn* see MASK 1
domitae naturae *adj* *syn* see TAME
don *vb* **1** to place on one's person (an article of clothing) < *donned* a raincoat for his trip >
  syn assume, draw on, get on, huddle (on), put on, slip (on), throw
  rel apparel, array, attire, clad, clothe, dress, enclothe, garb, garment, raiment
  con cast, pull (off), remove, take off, throw off; unclothe, undress; disrobe
  ant doff
  2 to clothe or envelop oneself in < able to *don* a new personality at will >
  syn assume, pull, put on, strike, take on
  rel camouflage, color, disguise; belie, falsify, garble, misrepresent
donate *vb* *syn* see GIVE 1
donation *n* a gift of money or its equivalent to a charity, humanitarian cause, or public institution < sought *donations* for victims of the flood >
  syn alms, benefaction, beneficence, charity, contribution, offering
  rel aid, assistance, help, relief; philanthropy; bequest, endowment; appropriation, grant, subsidy, subvention; allowance, dole, pittance, ration
donator *n* *syn* see DONOR
done *adj* **1** *syn* see DECOROUS 1
  2 *syn* see COMPLETE 4
  3 *syn* see EFFETE 2
  4 *syn* see THROUGH 4
done for *adj* *syn* see THROUGH 3
done in *adj* *syn* see EFFETE 2
‖**doney** *n* *syn* see GIRL FRIEND 1
‖**donicker** *n* *syn* see TOILET
Don Juan *n* **1** *syn* see GALLANT 2
  2 *syn* see WOLF
donk *n* *syn* see DONKEY 1
donkey *n* **1** the domestic ass < the *donkey*, a typical pack animal >
  syn ass, burro, donk, jackass, ‖moke, ‖neddy, ‖Rocky Mountain canary
  rel ‖dickey, jack; hinny, mule; jennet, jenny, jenny ass
  2 *syn* see FOOL 1
donkeyish *adj* *syn* see FOOLISH 2
donkey's years *n pl* *syn* see AGE 2
donkeywork *n* *syn* see WORK 2
donnybrook *n* *syn* see BRAWL 2
donor *n* one that gives something to another < a *donor* of funds to research foundations >
  syn bestower, conferrer, donator, giver, presenter
  rel contributor, subscriber
do–nothing *n* *syn* see SLUGGARD
‖**donsie** *adj* *syn* see UNWELL
doodad *n* something trivial which is hard to classify or whose name is unknown < wondered what the little round *doodad* was for >
  syn business, dingus, dofunny, doohickey, gadget, gizmo, ‖hootenanny, jigger, rigamajig, thingum, thingumajig, thingumbob, thingummy; *compare* GADGET 1, WHAT-DO-YOU-CALL-IT
doodle *n* *syn* see FOOL 1
‖**doodle** *vb* *syn* see CHEAT
doodle *vb* *syn* see FIDDLE 2
doohickey *n* *syn* see DOODAD
doom *n* *syn* see FATE
  rel calamity, cataclysm, catastrophe, disaster, tragedy
doom *vb* *syn* see SENTENCE
doom (to) *vb* *syn* see PREDESTINE 1
doomed *adj* *syn* see DAMNED 1
doomful *adj* *syn* see OMINOUS
door *n* **1** an opening by which one can enter or leave a structure and especially a building < looked through the front *door* >
  syn doorway, entrance, entranceway, entry, entryway, portal
  2 a means or right of entering, approaching, or participating < viewed education as the *door* to success >
  syn access, adit, admission, admittance, entrance, entrée, entry, ingress, way
doormat *n* *syn* see WEAKLING

doorway *n syn* see DOOR 1

‖**doozer** *n syn* ‖DILLY, ‖corker, ‖daisy, dandy, ‖dinger, humdinger, jim-dandy, ‖lalapalooza, ‖lulu, peach

dope *n* **1** *syn* see DRUG 2
  2 *syn* see DUNCE

dope (up) *vb syn* see ADULTERATE

doped *adj syn* see DRUGGED

‖**dope out** *vb* **1** *syn* see SOLVE 2
  2 *syn* see INFER
  3 *syn* see PLAN 2

dopey *adj syn* see LETHARGIC

‖**do–re–mi** *n syn* see MONEY

‖**dorm** *vb syn* see DOZE

dormancy *n syn* see ABEYANCE

dormant *adj syn* see LATENT
  ant active

‖**dort** *vb syn* see SULK

‖**dorts** *n pl syn* see SULK

‖**dorty** *adj syn* see SULLEN

‖**doss** *n syn* see SLEEP 1

‖**doss** *vb syn* see SLEEP

dot *n syn* see POINT 11

dot *vb* **1** *syn* see SPECKLE 1
  2 *syn* see SPOT 2

dot *n syn* see DOWRY

dotage *n* advanced age accompanied by a decline of mental poise and alertness <a doddering eighty-year-old entering his *dotage*>
  syn second childhood, senility; *compare* OLD AGE
  rel decrepitude, feebleness, infirmity; age, elderliness, senectitude
  con adolescence, youth; maturity

dote (on *or* **upon)** *vb syn* see ADORE 3
  rel enjoy, fancy, like
  idiom be sweet on
  ant loathe

‖**doted** *adj syn* see SENILE

doting *adj* **1** *syn* see SENILE
  2 *syn* see LOVING
  rel asinine, fatuous, foolish, silly, simple

dottiness *n syn* see FOOLISHNESS

dotty *adj* **1** *syn* see INFATUATED
  2 *syn* see FOOLISH 2

double *adj* **1** *syn* see TWOFOLD 1
  2 *syn* see TWIN
  3 *syn* see TWOFOLD 2
  4 *syn* see INSINCERE

double *n* **1** *syn* see MATE 5
  2 *syn* see IMAGE 1
  3 *syn* see TURN 2
  rel departure, digression, divergence, swerving, veering

double *vb* **1** to make twice as great or as many <*doubled* the amount of his salary>
  syn dualize, dupe, duplicate
  rel replicate; amplify, augment, enlarge, increase, magnify; supplement
  con decrease, lessen, minimize
  ant halve
  2 to make of two thicknesses by turning or bending usually in the middle <he *doubled* the towel for better absorbency>
  syn fold
  rel pleat, plicate, turn over
  3 *syn* see ESCAPE 2
  4 *syn* see DUB

double–barreled *adj* **1** *syn* see TWOFOLD 2
  2 *syn* see TWOFOLD 1

double–cross *vb* **1** *syn* see DECEIVE
  2 *syn* see BETRAY 2

double–dealer *n syn* see SWINDLER

double–dealing *n syn* see DECEPTION 1

double–dealing *adj syn* see INSINCERE

double–distilled *adj syn* see UTTER

‖**double–dog dare** *vb syn* see FACE 3

double–dome *n syn* see INTELLECTUAL 2

double–dyed *adj syn* see UTTER

double–edged *adj syn* see OBSCURE 3

double entendre *n syn* see AMBIGUITY

double–faced *adj* **1** *syn* see OBSCURE 3

  2 *syn* see INSINCERE

doublehearted *adj syn* see INSINCERE

double meaning *n syn* see AMBIGUITY

double–minded *adj* **1** *syn* see VACILLATING 2
  idiom of two minds
  2 *syn* see INSINCERE

doublet *n syn* see COUPLE

double–talk *n* **1** *syn* see NONSENSE 2
  2 *syn* see GOBBLEDYGOOK

double–tongued *adj syn* see INSINCERE

doubt *vb* **1** *syn* see QUESTION 2
  2 *syn* see DISTRUST
  con accredit, credit, trust; accept, believe, ‖buy, swallow

doubt *n syn* see UNCERTAINTY
  rel dubiousness, questionableness; disbelief, incredulity, unbelief
  con dependence, faith, reliance, trust
  ant certitude; confidence

doubtable *adj syn* see DOUBTFUL 1
  ant undoubtable

doubter *n syn* see SKEPTIC

doubtful *adj* **1** not having or affording assurance of the certainty or soundness of something or someone <their chance of success is *doubtful*>
  syn ambiguous, borderline, clouded, doubtable, dubious, dubitable, equivocal, fishy, impugnable, indecisive, open, precarious, problematic, queasy, shady, shaky, suspect, suspicious, uncertain, unclear, undecided, uneasy, unsettled, unstable, unsure; *compare* MOOT
  rel question-begging; touch-and-go; chancy, insecure, questionable, speculative; hazy, obscure; unlikely; contingent, iffy
  idiom at issue, in dispute, in doubt, in question
  con decisive, open-and-shut, positive, sure; inarguable, incontestable, unarguable, undeniable, undoubted, unquestionable
  ant indubitable
  2 *syn* see MOOT
  3 *syn* see IMPROBABLE 1

doubtfully *adv syn* see ASKANCE 2

doubtfulness *n syn* see UNCERTAINTY

doubting Thomas *n syn* see SKEPTIC

doubtless *adv* **1** *syn* see EASILY 2
  2 *syn* see PRESUMABLY

doubtlessly *adv* **1** *syn* see WELL 7
  ant doubtfully
  2 *syn* see EASILY 2

dough *n syn* see MONEY

doughface *n syn* see MASK 1

‖**doughhead** *n syn* see DUNCE

doughty *adj syn* see BRAVE 1

doughy *adj syn* see PALE 1

do up *vb syn* see MEND 2

dour *adj* **1** *syn* see GRIM 2
  rel rigid, rigorous, strict; implacable
  2 *syn* see SULLEN

‖**douse** *n syn* see BLOW 1

douse *vb syn* see REMOVE 3

douse *vb* **1** *syn* see DIP 1
  2 *syn* see WET
  con bake, dehydrate, desiccate, dry, parch
  3 *syn* see SPLASH
  4 *syn* see EXTINGUISH 1

‖**dout** *vb syn* see EXTINGUISH 1

dove *n syn* see PACIFIST
  ant hawk

dovecote *n* a small compartmented raised house or box for domestic pigeons <old countryseats with elaborate stone *dovecotes*>
  syn columbary, culverhouse, dovehouse, pigeon house, pigeonry
  rel aviary, birdhouse; perch, roost

dovehouse *n syn* see DOVECOTE

‖**dover** *n syn* see NAP

dovetail *vb syn* see AGREE 4

dowager *n syn* see MATRIARCH

dowd *n syn* see SLATTERN 1

---

syn synonym(s)	*rel* related word(s)
ant antonym(s)	*con* contrasted word(s)
idiom idiomatic equivalent(s)	
‖ use limited; if in doubt, see a dictionary	

dowdy *n syn* see SLATTERN 1
dowdy *adj* **1** *syn* see SLATTERNLY
  con chic, fashionable, modish, stylish; flashy, garish, gaudy
  ant smart
  2 *syn* see TACKY 2
  ant smart
  3 *syn* see OLD-FASHIONED
dower *n syn* see DOWRY
dower *vb syn* see ENDOW 1
  rel accouter, appoint, equip, furnish, outfit
‖**dowly** *adj syn* see OVERCAST
down *adv* **1** from a higher to a lower level < the land sloped *down* toward the sea >
  syn downward, downwardly, downwards, netherwards
  rel below, earthward, groundward; downgrade, downhill, downslope
  con aloft, upward, upwardly, upwards
  ant up
  2 to completion < wash *down* the car >
  syn completely, fully, through-and-through
  idiom from top to bottom
  3 *syn* see SERIOUSLY 1
down *adj* **1** *syn* see SLOW 3
  2 *syn* see DOWNCAST
  ant up
  3 *syn* see SICK 1
  4 *syn* see LOWER
  ant up
  5 *syn* see COMPLETE 4
down *n syn* see COMEDOWN
down *vb* **1** *syn* see SWALLOW 1
  2 *syn* see DEFEAT 2
  3 *syn* see FELL 1
  4 *syn* see KILL 1
  5 *syn* see OVERCOME 1
down *n* a soft fluffy material or covering < the *down* on a peach >
  syn floss, flue, fluff, fur, fuzz, lint, pile
down–and–out *n syn* see PAUPER
down–at–heel *adj syn* see SHABBY 1
downcast *n syn* see DEFEAT 1
downcast *adj* low in spirits < felt *downcast* by the rejection >
  syn bad, blue, cast down, chapfallen, crestfallen, dejected, depressed, disconsolate, dispirited, doleful, down, downhearted, down-in-the-mouth, downthrown, droopy, dull, heartsick, heartsore, hipped, low, low-spirited, mopey, soul-sick, spiritless, sunk, woebegone; *compare* SAD 1
  rel discouraged, disheartened; oppressed, weighed down; distressed, troubled; despondent, forlorn; listless; broody, moody; gloomy, glum, morose
  idiom in the depths
  con cheerful, happy, joyous, lighthearted; excited, exhilarated, intoxicated; buoyed up, gladdened; encouraged, heartened; animated, gay, lively, sprightly, vivacious; delighted, pleased
  ant elated
downcry *vb syn* see DECRY 2
downfall *n* **1** *syn* see DETERIORATION 1
  rel comedown, descent, discomfiture, down
  2 something that causes a downfall < drink was his *downfall* >
  syn bane, destroyer, destruction, ruin, ruination, undoing
  rel headache, problem, trouble
  idiom road to ruin
  con aid, help, support
downgrade *n syn* see DETERIORATION 1
  ant upgrade
downgrade *vb* **1** *syn* see DEPRECIATE 1
  ant upgrade
  2 *syn* see DEGRADE 1
  ant upgrade
downgrading *n syn* see DEMOTION
  ant upgrading
downhearted *adj syn* see DOWNCAST
down-in-the-mouth *adj syn* see DOWNCAST
downright *adj* **1** *syn* see UTTER
  2 being what is stated beyond any possibility of doubt < a *downright* lie >
  syn flat, indubitable, unquestionable, up-and-down; *compare* POSITIVE 3
  rel out-and-out, sure-enough; absolute, positive; certain, clear

downside–up *adj syn* see UPSIDE-DOWN 2
downslide *n syn* see DECLINE 3
downswing *n syn* see DECLINE 3
downthrow *n syn* see DEFEAT 1
downthrown *adj syn* see DOWNCAST
down-to-date *adj syn* see UP-TO-DATE
down-to-earth *adj syn* see REALISTIC
downtrend *n syn* see DECLINE 3
downtrodden *adj* oppressed by superior power < the *downtrodden* peasants >
  syn abject, underfoot
  rel oppressed, persecuted; abused, maltreated, mistreated
downturn *n syn* see DECLINE 3
downward *adv syn* see DOWN 1
  ant upward
downwardly *adv syn* see DOWN 1
  ant upwardly
downwards *adv syn* see DOWN 1
  ant upwards
‖**downy** *adj syn* see SLY 2
dowry *n* the money, goods, or estate that a woman brings to her husband in marriage < from a poor family, she came to her marriage with no *dowry* >
  syn dot, dower, marriage portion
  con bride-price, bridewealth; settlement
doxy *n* **1** a usually young woman who is sexually promiscuous < a *doxy* who frequented singles bars >
  syn ‖chippy, floozy, grisette, light-o'-love, nymph, nymphet, party girl, tart, ‖tootsie
  idiom woman of easy virtue
  ‖**2** *syn* see MISTRESS
doyen *n* **1** *syn* see LEADER 1
  2 *syn* see EXPERT
doze *vb* to sleep lightly < he was inclined to *doze* at his desk >
  syn ‖dorm, drowse, ‖sloom, slumber, ‖snoozle, ‖sog; *compare* NAP, SLEEP
doze (off) *vb* to fall into a light sleep < *dozed* off while sitting before the fire >
  syn drop off, drowse (off)
  idiom drift off
doze *n* a light sleep < was caught in a *doze* at his desk >
  syn drowse, ‖sloom, slumber; *compare* NAP, SLEEP 1
dozy *adj syn* see SLEEPY 1
DP *n syn* see REFUGEE
drab *n* **1** *syn* see HAG 2
  2 *syn* see SLATTERN 1
  3 *syn* see PROSTITUTE
drab *adj* **1** *syn* see DULL 8
  2 *syn* see COLORLESS 2
  rel bleak, desolate, dismal, dispiriting, dreary; dingy, faded
  con bright, brilliant, luminous
draconian *adj syn* see RIGID 3
draffy *adj syn* see WORTHLESS 1
draft *n* DRINK 3, drag, drain, drench, ‖peg, swig, swill
draft *vb* **1** to enroll in the armed forces by compulsion < *drafted* when he was barely eighteen >
  syn conscribe, conscript; *compare* CALL UP
  rel induct; enlist, enroll, muster (in *or* out); impress, press
  2 *syn* see SKETCH
  3 to formulate and produce < *drafting* plans to meet an emergency >
  syn draw up, formulate, frame, make, prepare
  rel concoct, contrive, devise, invent; fabricate, fashion, forge, form, manufacture, shape; plan, project; outline, sketch
  4 *syn* see DRAIN 1
drag *n* **1** *syn* see DRAW 1
  2 *syn* see DRINK 3
  ‖**3** *syn* see PULL 2
  ‖**4** *syn* see WAY 1
drag *vb* **1** *syn* see PULL 2
  con propel, push, shove, thrust; drive, impel, move
  2 *syn* see DELAY 2
  idiom drag one's feet (*or* heels)
  con hasten, hurry
  3 to hang down and be drawn behind < her dress *dragged* in the dust >
  syn draggle, trail, traipse
  rel droop, hang, sag

‖**drag down** *vb syn* see EARN 1
dragging *adj syn* see LONG 2
draggle *vb syn* see DRAG 3
draggle–tail *n syn* see SLATTERN 1
draggletailed *adj syn* see SLATTERNLY
dragoon *vb syn* see INTIMIDATE
drain *vb* **1** to draw off (liquid) by degrees <*drain* the water from the swimming pool>
  syn draft, draw, draw off, pump, siphon, tap
  rel milk; bleed; suck; empty, exhaust
  2 *syn* see TIRE 1
  3 *syn* see DEPLETE
  idiom bleed white
drain (away) *vb syn* see DECREASE
drain *n syn* see DRINK 3
drained *adj syn* see EFFETE 2
dram *n* **1** a small quantity of something (as alcoholic liquor) to drink <a *dram* of brandy helped to break his chill>
  syn ‖caulker, dollop, drop, jolt, nip, shot, slug, snifter, snort, snorter, spot, toothful, tot, ‖wet
  rel draft, drink, ‖peg, potation, pull, swig, swill; finger; jigger; dash; ‖splash; snack; quick one
  2 *syn* see PARTICLE
drama *n* dramatic art, literature, or affairs <was interested in *drama* during his college years>
  syn boards, footlights, (the) stage, theater
  rel show business
dramatic *adj* **1** of or relating to drama <made no objections to his son's *dramatic* ambitions>
  syn dramaturgic, histrionic, theatral, theatric, theatrical, thespian
  2 *syn* see THEATRICAL 2
  ant undramatic
dramatist *n syn* see PLAYWRIGHT
dramatizer *n syn* see PLAYWRIGHT
dramaturge *n syn* see PLAYWRIGHT
dramaturgic *adj syn* see DRAMATIC 1
drape *vb* **1** *syn* see SWATHE
  2 *syn* see SPRAWL 1
dratted *adj syn* see DAMNED 2
draw *vb* **1** *syn* see PULL 2
  rel bring, fetch; educe, elicit, evoke, extract
  con propel, push, shove, thrust; drive, impel, move
  2 *syn* see DRAIN 1
  3 *syn* see ATTRACT 1
  4 *syn* see INDUCE 1
  5 *syn* see TAKE 14
  6 *syn* see INFER
  7 *syn* see EXTEND 3
  8 *syn* see DEPLETE
  9 *syn* see EVISCERATE
draw *n* **1** a sucking pull on something (as a sipping straw or cigarette) <took a long *draw* on his pipe before answering>
  syn drag, puff, pull
  rel smoke; inhale
  2 *syn* see ADVANTAGE 3
  3 *syn* see ATTRACTION 1
  4 an indecisive ending to a contest or competition <the prizefight ended in a *draw*>
  syn deadlock, dogfall, stalemate, standoff, tie
  rel dead heat, photo finish; standstill
  con loss; win
draw back *vb syn* see DEDUCT 1
drawback *n syn* see DISADVANTAGE
  rel evil, ill; inconvenience, trouble
  con advantage, edge
draw down *vb* **1** *syn* see EARN 1
  2 *syn* see DEPLETE
draw in *vb syn* see INDUCE 1
drawing *adj syn* see ATTRACTIVE 1
drawing power *n syn* see ATTRACTION 1
drawing room *n syn* see SALON 1
drawn *adj syn* see HAGGARD
  con hale, robust
drawn–out *adj syn* see LONG 2
draw off *vb syn* see DRAIN 1
  rel abstract; withdraw; move, remove, shift, transfer
draw on *vb* **1** *syn* see EFFECT 1

  2 *syn* see INDUCE 1
  3 *syn* see DON 1
draw out *vb syn* see EXTEND 3
draw up *vb* **1** *syn* see DRAFT 3
  2 *syn* see STOP 4
dray horse *n syn* see SLAVE 2
dread *n syn* see FEAR 1
dreadful *adj syn* see FEARFUL 3
‖**dreadful** *adv syn* see VERY 1
dreadful *n syn* see DIME NOVEL
dreadfully *adv syn* see VERY 1
dream *n* **1** *syn* see FANCY 4
  2 *syn* see PIPE DREAM
dream *vb syn* see LONG
dreamer *n* one whose conduct is guided more by ideals than practicalities <a *dreamer* proposing glorious plans impossible to make work>
  syn castle-builder, idealist, ideologue, utopian, visionary
  rel daydreamer, illusionist, lotus-eater, wishful thinker; Don Quixote; theorist
  con pragmatist, realist; Babbitt, Philistine; pedant
dream up *vb syn* see CONTRIVE 2
dreamy *adj* **1** given to dreaming, reverie, or fancy <a *dreamy* and most impractical person>
  syn astral, daydreaming, daydreamy, otherworldly, unworldly, visionary
  rel fanciful, idealistic, romantic, whimsical
  con down-to-earth, practical, pragmatic, realistic; actual, factual
  2 *syn* see MARVELOUS 2
drear *adj syn* see GLOOMY 3
dreary *adj* **1** *syn* see GLOOMY 3
  2 *syn* see DULL 9
dreck *n syn* see REFUSE
dreg *n, usu* **dregs** *pl* **1** *syn* see SEDIMENT
  2 *syn* see RABBLE 2
‖**dreich** *adj syn* see LONG 2
drench *n syn* see DRINK 3
drench *vb* **1** *syn* see WET
  rel dip, duck, dunk, immerse, submerge
  2 *syn* see SOAK 1
  3 *syn* see POUR 3
drenched *adj syn* see WET 1
dress *vb* **1** *syn* see CLOTHE
  ant undress
  2 *syn* see BANDAGE
  3 to remove the entrails from <*dress* fish, fowl, or game>
  syn clean, gut
  rel butcher, slaughter
  4 *syn* see TILL
  rel fertilize, topdress
dress (up) *vb syn* see ADORN
dress *n* **1** *syn* see CLOTHES
  2 *syn* see COSTUME
dress down *vb syn* see SCOLD 1
dress up *vb* **1** to attire in best or formal clothes <*dressed up* to go to the theater>
  syn deck (out), ‖dike (out *or* up), doll out, doll up, ‖dude up, fix up, gussy up, prank, ‖prick (up), primp, prink (up), slick, smarten (up), smug, spiff, spruce (up), tog (out *or* up), ‖toggle, trick (off, out, *or* up)
  rel prettify, pretty (up); apparel, array, attire, clad, clothe, dress, enclothe, garb, garment, raiment; overdress; preen; prim (up)
  idiom dress fit to kill, dress to the nines, put on the dog
  2 *syn* see DISGUISE
drib *vb syn* see DRIP
drib *n syn* see DROP 1
dribble *vb* **1** *syn* see DRIP
  2 *syn* see DROOL 2
dribble (away) *vb syn* see WASTE 2
dribble *n syn* see PITTANCE
driblet *n* **1** *syn* see PITTANCE
  2 *syn* see DROP 1

---

syn synonym(s)   *rel* related word(s)
ant antonym(s)   *con* contrasted word(s)
idiom idiomatic equivalent(s)
‖ use limited; if in doubt, see a dictionary

drift *n* **1** *syn* see FLOW
   2 *syn* see PILE 1
   rel array, batch, bunch, bundle, clump, cluster, clutch, group, lot, parcel, set
   ‖**3** *syn* see DROVE 2
   4 *syn* see TENDENCY 1
   rel motion, movement, progress, progression; aim, intent, intention, purpose
   5 *syn* see LEANING 2
   6 *syn* see TENOR 1
   rel direction, line, set
drift *vb* **1** to become carried or floated along < cakes of ice *drifting* along the stream >
   syn float, ride, wash
   rel dart, fly, sail, scud, shoot, skim; dance, flicker, flit, flitter, flutter, hover
   2 *syn* see SAUNTER
   3 *syn* see WANDER 1
   4 *syn* see SLIDE 6
   5 *syn* see HEAP 1
drifter *n* **1** *syn* see ROVER
   2 *syn* see VAGABOND
driftwood *n* vagrant impoverished people < the *driftwood* of skid row >
   syn flotsam, jetsam, wreckage
drill *vb* **1** *syn* see PERFORATE
   2 *syn* see EXERCISE 3
   rel accustom, habituate
drill *n* *syn* see EXERCISE 3
drilling *n* *syn* see EXERCISE 3
drink *vb* **1** to take in (potable liquid) < the boys *drank* all the soda >
   syn imbibe, quaff, sip, sup (off *or* up), swallow, toss
   rel drain, gulp, guzzle, slosh, slurp, swig, swill; wash down
   idiom wet one's whistle
   2 to salute and wish honor and health to (a person) by raising and then drinking from a vessel < *drink* to the bride and groom >
   syn pledge, toast
   rel honor, salute; wet
   3 to partake of alcoholic liquors especially habitually or to excess < he *drinks* but does not smoke >
   syn booze, guzzle, imbibe, liquor (up), ‖lush (up), nip, soak, swig, swill, swizzle, tank up, tipple, tope
   idiom bend the elbow, cheer the inner man, drink like a fish, go on a binge, hit the bottle, take a nip
drink *n* **1** liquid suitable for swallowing < able to make palatable *drink* from seawater >
   syn beverage, drinkable, liquor, potable
   rel liquid; brew; potion
   2 *syn* see LIQUOR 2
   3 a portion of potable liquid < took a *drink* from the cup >
   syn draft, drag, drain, drench, ‖peg, swig, swill
   rel draw, pull; finger, jigger; libation
   4 *syn* see OCEAN
drinkable *adj* *syn* see POTABLE
drinkable *n* *syn* see DRINK 1
drinkery *n* *syn* see BAR 5
drip *vb* to let fall drops of moisture or liquid < trees *dripping* after the rain >
   syn distill, drib, dribble, drop, trickle, trill, weep
   rel spatter, sprinkle, spurtle; gush, pour, sluice, stream
‖**drip** *n* **1** *syn* see NONSENSE 2
   2 *syn* see DUNCE
dripping *adj* *syn* see WET 1
drippy *adj* *syn* see SENTIMENTAL
drive *vb* **1** *syn* see MOVE 5
   rel coerce, compel, force; incite, instigate
   con check, curb, inhibit, restrain; guide, lead, pilot, steer
   2 *syn* see PUSH 1
   3 to urge along (as cattle) < cowboys *driving* the great herds north >
   syn ‖drove, herd, run
   rel shepherd; wrangle; egg, exhort, goad, prick, prod, punch, sic, spur, urge
   4 *syn* see THRUST 2
   5 to operate and steer (a motor vehicle) < *drive* a car >
   syn auto, charioteer, motor, pilot, tool, wheel

rel operate, run, work; guide, steer; roll; chauffeur
   6 *syn* see IMPRESS 3
   7 *syn* see PLUNGE 2
   8 *syn* see LABOR 1
drive *n* **1** a short trip in a vehicle < took a *drive* around town >
   syn ride, spin, turn; *compare* TRIP 1
   rel whirl; joyride; excursion, outing
   2 *syn* see DRIVEWAY
   3 *syn* see ENTERPRISE 4
   4 *syn* see VIGOR 2
   rel impetus, momentum, speed, velocity
drivel *vb* **1** *syn* see DROOL 2
   2 *syn* see BABBLE 2
   3 *syn* see WASTE 2
drivel *n* **1** *syn* see NONSENSE 2
   2 *syn* see GIBBERISH 1
driveling *adj* *syn* see INSIPID 3
driver *n* *syn* see MOTORIST
driveway *n* a private road giving access from a public way < the *driveway* to a house >
   syn ‖avenue, drive
   rel court, place, row, street
driving *adj* *syn* see ENERGETIC 2
drizzle *vb* *syn* see SPRINKLE 5
drogher *n* *syn* see BEARER 2
drôlerie *n* *syn* see JOKE 1
droll *adj* *syn* see LAUGHABLE
   rel absurd, preposterous
droll *n* *syn* see HUMORIST 2
drollery *n* **1** *syn* see JOKE 1
   2 *syn* see HUMOR 4
drollness *n* *syn* see HUMOR 4
drone *vb* **1** *syn* see HUM
   2 *syn* see IDLE
drony *adj* *syn* see LAZY
drool *vb* **1** to secrete or become filled with saliva usually in anticipation of food < mouths *drooled* as we waited for dinner >
   syn water
   idiom water at the mouth
   2 to let saliva or some other substance flow from the mouth < babies often *drool* uncontrollably >
   syn dribble, drivel, salivate, slabber, slaver, slobber
   3 *syn* see ENTHUSE 2
   4 *syn* see BABBLE 2
drool *n* *syn* see NONSENSE 2
droop *vb* **1** *syn* see SLOUCH
   2 *syn* see LOWER 3
   3 to become literally or figuratively limp through loss of vigor or freshness < he walked along, his shoulders *drooping* from exhaustion >
   syn flag, sag, swag, wilt
   rel drop, fall, sink, slump, subside; dangle, hang, loll, lop, sling, suspend; decline, deteriorate, ‖dwine, fade, fail, languish, weaken
droopy *adj* *syn* see DOWNCAST
drop *n* **1** the quantity of fluid that falls in one spherical mass < a *drop* of rain >
   syn drib, driblet, droplet, globule, gobbet
   rel dribble, drip, trickle
   2 *syn* see PARTICLE
   3 *syn* see DRAM
   4 *syn* see DESCENT 4
   5 *syn* see DESCENT 1
   6 *syn* see DECLINE 3
   7 *syn* see DEPTH 1
drop *vb* **1** *syn* see FALL 2
   2 *syn* see FALL 1
   ant mount
   3 *syn* see PLUMMET
   rel slide, slip
   con rally, rebound; ascend, climb; soar
   ant mount
   4 *syn* see COLLAPSE 2
   rel backslide, lapse, relapse
   5 *syn* see DIE 1
   6 *syn* see DRIP
   7 *syn* see FELL 1
   8 *syn* see QUIT 6
   9 *syn* see CANCEL 2

10 *syn* see DISMISS 3
11 *syn* see LOSE 2
12 *syn* see LOSE 1
drop (in *or* by) *vb syn* see VISIT 2
drop (off) *vb syn* see SLIP 6
droplet *n syn* see DROP 1
drop off *vb syn* see DOZE (off)
dropsical *adj syn* see INFLATED
dropsied *adj syn* see INFLATED
drossy *adj syn* see WORTHLESS 1
droughty *adj syn* see DRY 1
‖**drouk** *vb syn* see SOAK 1
drove *n* **1** *syn* see CROWD 1
2 a group of domestic animals reared or handled as a unit < a *drove* of cattle >
  syn ‖drift, flock, herd
  rel drive; pack; school
‖**drove** *vb syn* see DRIVE 3
drown *vb* **1** *syn* see OVERWHELM 4
2 *syn* see DELUGE 1
3 *syn* see WET
drowse *vb syn* see DOZE
drowse (off) *vb syn* see DOZE (off)
drowse *n syn* see DOZE
drowsy *adj syn* see SLEEPY 1
  rel lackadaisical, languid, languorous
  con alert, vigilant, watchful; active, dynamic, live; animated, lively, vivacious
drub *vb* **1** *syn* see BEAT 1
2 *syn* see LAMBASTE 3
3 *syn* see WHIP 2
drubbing *n syn* see DEFEAT 1
drudge *vb* to perform hard, menial, or monotonous work < *drudged* all day washing floors >
  syn grind, grub, ‖muck, plod, slave, slog, toil
  rel hammer, peg (away *or* at *or* on), plow, plug, pound (away); perform, work
  idiom keep one's nose to the grindstone
  con idle, laze, loaf, lounge; dally, dawdle, potter, putter; cheat, chisel
drudge *n* **1** *syn* see SLAVE 2
2 *syn* see WORK 2
3 *syn* see HACK 2
drudgery *n syn* see WORK 2
drudging *adj syn* see IRKSOME
drug *n* **1** a substance used by itself or in a mixture in the treatment or diagnosis of disease < a life-sustaining *drug* >
  syn biologic, medicinal, pharmaceutic, pharmaceutical
  rel cure, medicament, medication, medicine, physic, remedy, specific; simple
2 a narcotic substance or preparation < depended on *drugs* to make life bearable >
  syn dope, ‖hop, narcotic, opiate
drugged *adj* being under the influence of a drug taken for nonmedical purposes < was *drugged* on LSD >
  syn doped, high, hopped-up, spaced-out, stoned, tripped out, turned on, ‖wiped out, zonked
  idiom on a trip
  ant straight
druggist *n* one who deals in medicinal drugs
  syn apothecary, ‖chemist, pharmacist
  rel pharmacologist
drum *vb syn* see SOLICIT 1
drumfire *n syn* see BARRAGE
drumhead *adj syn* see SUMMARY 2
drum up *vb syn* see SOLICIT 1
drunk *adj syn* see INTOXICATED 1
  rel drinking, drinky
  idiom roaring drunk
  con bone-dry, dry
  ant sober
drunk *n* **1** *syn* see BINGE 1
2 *syn* see DRUNKARD
drunkard *n* one who drinks alcoholic liquors to excess < *drunkards* lurching homeward when the bar finally closes >
  syn bibber, ‖bloat, ‖blotter, boozehound, boozer, drunk, fuddler, guzzler, inebriate, lush, ‖lusher, rumdum, rummy, ‖rumpot, ‖shicker, soak, soaker, sot, sponge, stiff, swillbowl, swiller, tippler, toper, tosspot

  rel alcoholic, dipsomaniac; wino; drammer
  idiom elbow bender (*or* crooker)
  ant teetotaler
drunken *adj syn* see INTOXICATED 1
drunkery *n syn* see BAR 5
‖**druthers** *n syn* see CHOICE 1
dry *adj* **1** devoid of or deficient in moisture < preferred a *dry* climate >
  syn arid, bone-dry, droughty, moistureless, sere, thirsty, unwatered, waterless
  rel baked, dehydrated, desiccated, parched; bald, bare, barren; depleted, drained, exhausted, impoverished; juiceless, sapless, sapped
  con drenched, dripping, saturated, soaked, soaking, sodden, sopping, soppy, soused, wringing-wet; damp, dank, humid, moist; exuberant, lush, luxuriant, prodigal, profuse
  ant wet
2 *syn* see THIRSTY 1
3 marked by the absence of or abstention from alcoholic beverages < a *dry* party >
  syn bone-dry, teetotal
  ant wet
4 *syn* see IMPASSIVE 1
5 *syn* see ARID 2
6 *syn* see PLAIN 1
7 *syn* see SOUR 1
  ant sweet
8 *syn* see HARSH 3
dry *vb* **1** to treat or affect so as to deprive of moisture < clothes *dried* in the wind >
  syn dehydrate, desiccate, exsiccate, parch, sear
  rel evaporate; anhydrate; deplete, drain, exhaust; shrivel, wither, wizen
  con deluge, douse, drench, soak, sop, souse; damp, dampen, moisten
  ant wet
2 *syn* see HARDEN 1
dryasdust *adj syn* see ARID 2
dry land *n syn* see EARTH 2
‖**dry–shave** *vb syn* see CHEAT
dry up *vb* **1** *syn* see DESICCATE 2
2 *syn* see WITHER
3 *syn* see SHUT UP 2
dual *adj* **1** *syn* see TWOFOLD 1
2 *syn* see TWIN
dualistic *adj syn* see TWOFOLD 1
dualize *vb syn* see DOUBLE 1
dub *vb* **1** *syn* see NAME 1
2 *syn* see BOTCH
dub *vb* to provide (a motion-picture film) with a new sound track (as for substituting dialogue in a foreign language) < *dubbed* the Italian movie into English >
  syn double
dubiety *n syn* see UNCERTAINTY
  rel hesitancy; faltering, vacillation, wavering
  con decidedness, decisiveness
  ant decision
dubiosity *n syn* see UNCERTAINTY
  rel addlement, confusion, muddlement; faltering, vacillation, wavering
  con cocksureness, positiveness
  ant decidedness
dubious *adj* **1** *syn* see MOOT
2 *syn* see DOUBTFUL 1
  rel skeptical; mistrustful; disinclined, hesitant, reluctant
  con dependable, tried, trustworthy, trusty; certain, positive, sure
  ant cocksure; reliable
3 *syn* see IMPROBABLE 1
4 *syn* see UNRELIABLE 1
  ant trustworthy
dubitable *adj syn* see DOUBTFUL 1
  ant indubitable
dubitancy *n syn* see UNCERTAINTY

---

syn synonym(s)	*rel* related word(s)
ant antonym(s)	*con* contrasted word(s)
idiom idiomatic equivalent(s)	
‖ use limited; if in doubt, see a dictionary	

duce *n syn* see TYRANT
||**duck** *n syn* see ECCENTRIC
duck *vb* **1** *syn* see DIP 1
  2 to lower (as the head or body) quickly <had to *duck* his head to get through the door>
  syn dip, stoop
  rel bend; bow
  3 *syn* see DODGE 1
  rel avert, prevent, ward
  4 *syn* see ESCAPE 2
duck soup *n syn* see SNAP 1
duct *n syn* see CHANNEL 1
ductile *adj syn* see PLASTIC
  rel responsive; submitting; fluid, liquid
  con intractable, refractory; adamant, obdurate
ductus *n syn* see HANDWRITING
dud *n syn* see FAILURE 5
dude *n syn* see FOP
||**dude up** *vb syn* see DRESS UP 1
dudgeon *n syn* see OFFENSE 2
  rel fury, ire, rage, wrath; humor, mood, temper
duds *n pl* **1** *syn* see CLOTHES
  ||**2** *syn* see RAGS 1
due *adj* **1** *syn* see JUST 3
  rel good, right; equitable, fair, just; coming, earned
  con excessive, exorbitant, extravagant, immoderate, inordinate; deficient
  ant undue
  2 having reached the date at which payment is required <a note that would become *due* after eighteen months>
  syn mature, payable
  3 *syn* see UNPAID 2
due *n* **1** what one fairly has coming <the artist has finally been accorded his *due*>
  syn comeuppance, desert(s), deserving, lumps, merit, right(s)
  rel deservedness, dueness, entitlement; compensation, payment, recompense, recompensing, repayment, satisfaction; reprisal, retaliation, retribution, revenge, vengeance; guerdon, need, reward
  idiom what is coming to one
  2 *syn* see DEBT 3
due *adv syn* see DIRECTLY 1
duel *vb syn* see RESIST
due to *prep syn* see OVER 6
||**duff** *vb syn* see CHEAT
||**duff** *n syn* see BUTTOCKS
duffer *n* ||**1** *syn* see PEDDLER
  2 *syn* see DUNCE
dulcet *adj* **1** *syn* see MELODIOUS 1
  con grinding, rasping, scraping, scratching
  ant grating
  2 *syn* see SWEET 1
dull *adj* **1** *syn* see STUPID 1
  ant sharp
  2 *syn* see RETARDED
  con advanced, precocious
  3 *syn* see INSENSIBLE 5
  4 *syn* see DOWNCAST
  5 *syn* see COLORLESS 2
  ant bright
  6 lacking sharpness of edge or point <a knife with a *dull* blade>
  syn blunt, obtuse
  rel blunted, dulled, unsharpened
  con honed, keen, razor-sharp, unblunted, whetted
  ant sharp
  7 lacking warmth, luster, or brilliance <a smooth *dull* finish>
  syn blind, dead, dim, flat, lackluster, lusterless, mat, muted
  rel cold, dingy, drab, dun, leaden, somber; deadened, lifeless
  con beaming, bright, brilliant, effulgent, fulgent, incandescent, lambent, lucent, lucid, luminous, lustrous, radiant, refulgent; burnished, polished, shiny
  ant clear; rich
  8 cloudy in color <a *dull* brown>
  syn drab, muddy, murky, subfusc
  rel blurry, cloudy, hazy; flat, lackluster, lifeless, lusterless; mousy
  ant clear; rich
  9 being so unvaried or uninteresting as to provoke boredom or tedium <any routine constantly repeated can become *dull*>

syn banausic, blah, ||dim, dreary, humdrum, monotone, monotonous, pedestrian, plodding, poky, stodgy
  rel boring, irksome, tedious, tiring, wearisome; brainless; exhausting, fagging, fatiguing
  con animating, exciting, stimulating; gay, spritely
  ant lively
  10 *syn* see OVERCAST
  11 *syn* see ARID 2
  rel matter-of-fact, prosaic, prosy; bloodless
  idiom dull as ditchwater
  con exciting, stimulating
  ant lively
dull *vb* **1** to make less clear, distinct, or bright <colors *dulled* by the sun>
  syn dim, fade, muddy, pale, tarnish
  rel discolor, wash out; blur
  con brighten, freshen, intensify
  2 *syn* see DEADEN 1
  ant sharpen
  3 to deprive of sharpness (as of edge or point) <*dull* a spade>
  syn blunt, disedge, obtund, turn
  idiom take the edge off
  con edge, hone
  ant sharpen
  4 to impair one or more of the senses <age had *dulled* his hearing>
  syn blear, blur, dim
  rel debilitate, enfeeble, weaken; darken; retard, slow
  ant sharpen
  5 to make slow or obtuse <his mind had been *dulled* by drink>
  syn blunt, hebetate, stupefy
  rel becloud, befog, cloud, darken, dim; benumb, deaden, numb; retard, slow
  con quicken, stimulate, whet
  ant sharpen
dullard *n syn* see DUNCE
dullhead *n syn* see DUNCE
dullness *n syn* see LETHARGY 1
  rel denseness, stupidity
  con edge, incisiveness, keenness
  ant sharpness
dumb *adj* **1** lacking the power to speak <deaf and *dumb* from birth>
  syn inarticulate, mute, silent, speechless, unarticulate, voiceless; *compare* SILENT 2
  ant articulate
  2 *syn* see SILENT 2
  rel incoherent, indistinct, maundering, tongue-tied
  3 *syn* see SILENT 3
  con speaking, talking; talkative, verbose
  4 *syn* see STUPID 1
  idiom dumb as an ox
dumb (up) *vb syn* see SHUT UP 2
dumbbell *n syn* see DUNCE
||**dumb bunny** *n syn* see DUNCE
||**dumb cluck** *n syn* see DUNCE
dumbfound *vb* **1** *syn* see SURPRISE 2
  2 *syn* see STAGGER 5
dumbfounded *adj syn* see AGHAST 2
||**dumbhead** *n syn* see DUNCE
||**dummkopf** *n syn* see DUNCE
dummy *n* **1** *syn* see DUNCE
  2 *syn* see STOOGE 1
dummy *adj syn* see ARTIFICIAL 2
||**dummy (up)** *vb syn* see SHUT UP 2
dump *vb* **1** *syn* see DISCARD
  ||**2** *syn* see BEAT 1
dump *n* **1** *syn* see ARMORY
  2 *syn* see STY 1
dumping *n syn* see DISPOSAL 2
dumpling *n syn* see FATTY
dumps *n pl syn* see SADNESS
  idiom low spirits
dumpy *adj syn* see STOCKY
  rel formless, shapeless, unformed
dun *adj syn* see DARK 1
dun *vb syn* see WORRY 1

dunce *n* a dull-witted person <the traditional *dunce* in pointed cap>
  syn beetlehead, blockhead, bonehead, boob, booby, ‖bufflehead, cabbagehead, chowderhead, chucklehead, chump, clod, clodpate, clodpoll, ‖cluck, dimwit, ‖dizzard, dodo, ‖dodunk, dolt, dolt-head, dope, ‖doughhead, ‖drip, duffer, dullard, dullhead, dumb-bell, ‖dumb bunny, ‖dumb cluck, ‖dumbhead, ‖dummkopf, dummy, dunderhead, dunderpate, fathead, featherweight, goof, ‖goon, hammerhead, idiot, ignoramus, ironhead, knothead, knucklehead, lackwit, lame-brain, lunk, lunkhead, ‖moonraker, moron, muddlehead, mug, muggins, mutt, muttonhead, nitwit, noddy, noodle, numskull, oaf, pinhead, poke, prune, pumpkin head, put, ‖schnook, simp, simpleton, ‖spoon, squarehead, ‖stunpoll, ‖stupe, stupid, thickhead, thickskull, turnip, wantwit, woodenhead, zombie
  rel lightweight; ass, donkey, fool, imbecile, jackass, jerk, nincompoop, ninny, ‖schmo, ‖schmuck; birdbrain, featherbrain, scatterbrain
  idiom dumb ox, Simple Simon
  con brain, highbrow, intellectual, thinker, wit; pundit, sage, savant, scholar, wise man; prodigy, wizard; genius, mastermind
duncical *adj syn* see STUPID 1
dunderhead *n syn* see DUNCE
dunderpate *n syn* see DUNCE
dundrearies *n pl syn* see SIDE-WHISKERS
dungeon *n* a close dark prison or vault commonly underground <the prisoners were kept in lightless *dungeons*>
  syn oubliette
  rel vault; black hole; cell; jail, prison
dungy *adj syn* see DIRTY 1
dunk *vb syn* see DIP 1
  rel saturate, soak, sop
duo *n syn* see COUPLE
dupe *n syn* see FOOL 3
dupe *vb* to delude by underhand methods <the public is easily *duped* by extravagant claims in advertising>
  syn bamboozle, befool, catch, chicane, con, dust, flimflam, fool, gull, hoax, hoodwink, hornswoggle, job, kid, pigeon, ‖rig, spoof, trick, victimize
  rel beguile, betray, deceive, delude, double-cross, mislead; cheat, cozen, defraud, overreach; baffle, circumvent, outwit
  idiom pull one's leg, put something over (*or* across)
  con enlighten, inform, wise (up)
dupe *vb syn* see DOUBLE 1
dupery *n syn* see DECEPTION 1
duple *adj syn* see TWOFOLD 1
duplex *adj syn* see TWOFOLD 1
duplicate *adj syn* see SAME 2
duplicate *n* **1** *syn* see REPRODUCTION
  rel analogue, counterpart, parallel
  2 *syn* see MATE 5
duplicate *vb* **1** *syn* see DOUBLE 1
  2 *syn* see COPY
duplicitous *adj syn* see UNDERHAND
duplicity *n syn* see DECEIT 1
  rel faithlessness, perfidiousness, perfidy, treacherousness, treachery
durable *adj syn* see LASTING
  rel stout, strong, tenacious
  con feeble, fragile, frail, weak
duration *n* **1** *syn* see CONTINUATION 1
  2 *syn* see RUN 2
  3 *syn* see TERM 2
duress *n syn* see FORCE 4
during *prep* in the course of <*during* the disorder some men kept their heads>
  syn amid, mid, midst, over, throughout
dusk *adj syn* see DARK 1

dusk *n syn* see EVENING 1
‖dusk dark *n syn* see EVENING 1
dusky *adj* **1** *syn* see DARK 3
  2 *syn* see DARK 1
  3 *syn* see GLOOMY 3
  4 *syn* see OBSCURE 3
dust *n* **1** *syn* see DUSTING
  2 *syn* see QUARREL
  ‖3 *syn* see REFUSE
dust *vb* **1** *syn* see SPRINKLE 1
  2 *syn* see WHIP 2
  3 *syn* see DUPE
  idiom throw dust in one's eyes
  ‖4 *syn* see HURRY 2
dusting *n* **1** a small quantity lightly applied to or sprinkled on <a *dusting* of sugar on the cake>
  syn dust, powdering, sprinkling
  ‖2 *syn* see DEFEAT 1
‖dust off *vb syn* see MURDER 1
dustup *n syn* see QUARREL
dusty *adj syn* see ARID 2
Dutch *n syn* see TROUBLE 3
duteous *adj syn* see RESPECTFUL
dutiful *adj syn* see RESPECTFUL
duty *n* **1** *syn* see OBLIGATION 2
  rel accountability, amenability, answerability, liability
  2 *syn* see FUNCTION 1
  3 *syn* see LOAD 3
  4 *syn* see TAX 1
  5 *syn* see TASK 1
  6 *syn* see USE 4
dwarf *n* a very small person <she was a tiny little thing, almost a *dwarf*>
  syn homunculus, hop-o'-my-thumb, Lilliputian, manikin, midge, midget, peewee, pygmy, runt, Tom Thumb
  rel ‖ribe, ‖shrimp, wart; dwarfling; minimus
  ant giant
dwarf *vb syn* see STUNT
dwarf *adj syn* see TINY
dwarfish *adj syn* see TINY
dwell *vb* **1** *syn* see RESIDE 1
  2 *syn* see CONSIST 1
dweller *n syn* see INHABITANT
dwelling *n syn* see HABITATION 2
dwindle *vb* **1** *syn* see DECREASE
  rel ebb, subside, wane; attenuate, extenuate, thin; moderate; disappear
  2 *syn* see FAIL 3
‖dwine *vb syn* see FAIL 1
dyad *n syn* see COUPLE
dye *n syn* see COLOR 6
dyed-in-the-wool *adj syn* see INVETERATE 1
dyestuff *n syn* see COLOR 6
dying *adj syn* see MORIBUND
dynamic *adj* **1** *syn* see ACTIVE 1
  rel activating, energizing, vitalizing
  ant static
  2 *syn* see VIGOROUS
  rel forceful, forcible; intense, vehement, violent
  con idle, inactive, passive
  ant inert
dynamite *vb syn* see DESTROY 1
dynamo *n syn* see HUSTLER 1
dysentery *n syn* see DIARRHEA
dyslogistic *adj syn* see DEROGATORY
  ant eulogistic
dyspathy *n syn* see ANTIPATHY 2
dyspeptic *adj syn* see ILL-TEMPERED
dysphoria *n syn* see SADNESS

---

syn synonym(s)   *rel* related word(s)
ant antonym(s)   *con* contrasted word(s)
idiom idiomatic equivalent(s)
‖ use limited; if in doubt, see a dictionary

each *adj syn* see ALL 2
  rel any, several, various; particular, respective, specific
each *adv syn* see APIECE
  idiom a shot, a throw, a whack
eager *adj* moved by a strong and urgent desire or interest
  < young executives *eager* to succeed >
  syn agog, anxious, appetent, ardent, athirst, avid, breathless,
  impatient, keen, raring, solicitous, thirsty
  rel enthusiastic, gung ho, heated, hot; ambitious, intent; acquisitive, covetous, craving, desirous, hankering, ‖honing, hungry,
  longing, pining, wishful, yearning; impatient, restive, restless
  idiom champing at the bit, ready and willing
  con aloof, disinterested, incurious, indifferent, unconcerned, uninterested; apathetic, detached, impassive, stolid
  ant listless
eagerness *n* a strong and urgent desire or interest < an *eagerness*
  to learn >
  syn ardor, enthusiasm, zing
  rel alacrity, avidity, keenness, quickness; ambition; gusto, ‖mus-
  tard, zest
  con lackadaisicality, languor, lethargy; aloofness, disinterest;
  apathy, deliberation, detachment, impassivity, stolidity
  ant listlessness
eagle eye *n syn* see EYE 3
eagle–eyed *adj syn* see SHARP-EYED
ear *n syn* see NOTICE 1
earlier *adv* 1 *syn* see BEFORE 2
  2 *syn* see HITHERTO 1
  3 *syn* see BEFORE 3
earliest *adj syn* see FIRST 2
  con final, terminal, ultimate
  ant latest
early *adv* 1 at or nearly at the beginning of a period, course, process, or series < it is much too *early* to guess the outcome >
  syn betimes, seasonably, soon, timely
  rel first
  2 in advance of the expected or usual time < these apples bear
  early and heavy >
  syn betimes, oversoon, prematurely
  rel beforehand
  idiom ahead of time, bright and early
early *adj* 1 of, relating to, or occurring near the beginning of a
  period of time, a development, or a series < *early* Renaissance >
  < *early* art forms >
  syn primitive, primordial
  rel original, pristine; ancient, antediluvian, antiquated, primal,
  primeval; antecedent, preceding, prevenient, prior
  con conclusive, final, last, terminal, ultimate; eventual; intermediate, middle, midmost
  ant late
  2 occurring before the expected or usual time < an *early*
  death > < an *early* peach >
  syn overearly, oversoon, premature, previous, ‖soon, untimely;
  compare PRECOCIOUS
  rel anticipative, anticipatory, precipitant, precocious; unanticipated, unexpected
  con slow, tardy; anticipated, expected
  ant late
earmark *vb syn* see DESIGNATE 3
earn *vb* 1 to receive as return for effort < *earn* a living wage >
  syn acquire, bring in, ‖drag down, draw down, gain, get, knock
  down, make, win
  rel attain, effect, obtain, procure, realize, receive, secure
  2 to be or make worthy of < his devotion to duty *earned* him a
  promotion >
  syn deserve, merit, rate
  rel bag, come by, harvest, net, reap, score
earnest *n syn* see EARNESTNESS
  rel attention, interest; enthusiasm, warmth, zeal
  ant jest, play
earnest *adj syn* see SERIOUS 1

  rel ardent, enthusiastic, passionate, pressing, warm, zealous;
  assiduous, busy, diligent, industrious, perseverant, sedulous; sincere, wholehearted, whole-souled
  con buoyant, effervescent, elastic, flippant, light
  ant frivolous
earnest *n syn* see PLEDGE 1
earnestly *adv* 1 *syn* see HARD 3
  rel seriously, soberly, solemnly, thoughtfully; zealously
  2 *syn* see SERIOUSLY 1
earnestness *n* a state of freedom from all jesting or trifling < he
  studied with great *earnestness* >
  syn earnest, intentness, serious-mindedness, seriousness
  rel doggedness, perseverance, persistence; decision, determination, firmness, purposefulness, resolve; absorption, attentiveness,
  concentration, engrossment; deliberation; gravity, sobriety
  con levity, lightness; shallowness, superficiality; carelessness,
  slackness
  ant frivolity
earnings *n pl syn* see PROFIT
earshot *n* the range within which something (as a voice) may be
  heard < the gossips were still within *earshot* of her >
  syn hearing, sound
  idiom carrying (*or* hearing) distance
earsplitting *adj syn* see LOUD 1
  rel penetrating, shrill
earth *n* 1 the entire area in which man lives and acts < expect the
  destruction of the *earth* >
  syn globe, (the) planet, world
  rel orb, sphere; cosmos, creation, macrocosm, universe, vale
  2 areas of land as distinguished from sea and air < clayey *earth*,
  difficult to drain >
  syn dirt, dry land, ground, land, soil, terra firma
  rel clay, gravel, humus, loam, mud, sand; fill, subsoil; terrain,
  turf; clod
earthlike *adj syn* see EARTHY 1
earthly *adj* 1 of, relating to, or characteristic of this earth or
  man's life on earth < *earthly* pursuits >
  syn earthy, mundane, sublunary, tellurian, telluric, terrene, terrestrial, uncelestial, worldly
  rel carnal, corporeal, earthbound, physical; material, temporal;
  unspiritual
  con celestial, empyreal, empyrean, heavenly; ideal, utopian; divine, spiritual
  2 *syn* see PROBABLE
  rel imaginable, potential
earthquake *n* a shaking or trembling of the earth that is volcanic
  or tectonic in origin < homes destroyed by *earthquakes* >
  syn quake, ‖quaker, shake, shock, temblor (*or* tremblor), tremor
earthy *adj* 1 consisting of, resembling, or suggesting earth < a
  stale *earthy* smell >
  syn earthlike, terrene, terrestrial
  rel clayey, dusty, muddy, sandy
  2 *syn* see EARTHLY 1
  3 *syn* see MATERIALISTIC
  4 *syn* see REALISTIC
  ant impractical
ease *n* 1 *syn* see REST 1
  rel idleness, inactivity, inertia, inertness, passivity, supinity;
  calmness, security
  con labor, toil, travail; adversity, difficulty; burden, care, worry
  2 *syn* see UNCONSTRAINT
  3 freedom from or mitigation of pain < medication brought him
  instant *ease* >
  syn alleviation, easement, mitigation, relief
  rel decrease, diminishment, moderation, reduction; calming,
  soothing
  con discomfort, unrest; agony, pain
  4 *syn* see READINESS 3
  rel adroitness, artfulness, cleverness, deftness, effortlessness, expertise, expertness, fluency, knack, poise, skillfulness, smoothness; efficiency, dispatch

con awkwardness, clumsiness, maladroitness, stiffness, woodenness; constraint; inconvenience, pains; exertion
ant effort
5 syn see PROSPERITY 2
ease *vb* **1 syn** see RELIEVE 1
rel deaden, dull; ameliorate, help
con afflict, torment
2 see LOOSE 5
rel disengage, free, release
con bind, restrain, tighten
3 to make less difficult <new laws that will *ease* voting requirements>
syn facilitate
rel aid, assist, better, help, improve; forward, further, promote, speed
idiom clear (*or* prepare) the way (for), grease the wheels, open the door (to *or* for)
con hinder, impede, retard
easeful *adj syn* see COMFORTABLE 2
easement *n syn* see EASE 3
rel allayment, appeasement, assuagement, mollification
ease off *vb* **1 syn** see LOOSE 5
2 syn see ABATE 4
3 syn see RELAX 2
easily *adv* **1** without discomfort, difficulty, or reluctance <*easily* translated the document>
syn effortlessly, facilely, freely, lightly, readily, smoothly, well
rel competently, dexterously, efficiently, fluently, handily, simply
idiom hands down, slick as a whistle
con awkwardly, clumsily, ineptly, stiffly; arduously, wearily
ant laboriously
2 without question <this is *easily* the best course of action>
syn absolutely, definitely, doubtless, doubtlessly, positively, unequivocally, unquestionably
rel actually, assuredly, certainly, clearly, decidedly, indeed, really, truly, undoubtedly
idiom no doubt
con apparently, perhaps, probably, seemingly; doubtfully, equivocally, questionably
3 syn see WELL 7
easy *adj* **1** causing or involving little or no difficulty <an *easy* solution>
syn effortless, facile, light, royal, simple, smooth, untroublesome
rel apparent, clear, distinct, evident, manifest, obvious, plain; clear-cut, straightforward, uncomplicated, uncompounded, uninvolved
idiom easy as falling off a log, easy as pie, nothing to it
con arduous, difficult, troublesome; abstruse, complex, complicated, intricate, knotty
ant hard
2 syn see FORBEARING
rel compassionate, condoning, excusing, forgiving, pardoning, sympathetic; benign, kindly; lax, moderate, soft; humoring, mollycoddling, pampering, spoiling
con austere, exacting, rigid, severe, stern, strict, stringent
3 easily taken advantage of or imposed upon <he was *easy* prey to her wiles>
syn fleeceable, gullible, naive, susceptible
rel credulous, trusting, unmistrusting, unsuspicious; deceivable, deludable, dupable, exploitable; artless, dewy-eyed, green, simple, unsophisticated
con critical, cynical, disbelieving, mistrustful, scoffing, skeptical, suspicious, unbelieving
4 syn see FAST 7
5 syn see COMFORTABLE 2
rel secure
con discontented, dissatisfied; miserable
ant uncomfortable
6 syn see AMIABLE 1
rel familiar, gregarious, informal; courtly, diplomatic, pleasant, polite, sociable; smooth, suave, urbane
con brusque, curt, unfriendly, unpleasant; constrained, embarrassed, formal, restrained; discourteous, impolite, undiplomatic, ungracious; stiff, unsocial, withdrawn, wooden
ant ill at ease
7 syn see CALM 2

rel relaxed; lethargic, unambitious
con agitated, tense, troubled, uptight
8 syn see PROSPEROUS 3
rel successful, thriving
idiom in easy circumstances, on easy street
con straitened
9 marked by ready facility (as of expression) <an *easy* style of writing>
syn cursive, effortless, flowing, fluent, running, smooth
rel facile; graceful
con effortful, labored
ant difficult
easygoing *adj* **1 syn** see CALM 2
con agitated, flurried, flustered, harassed; anxious, concerned, upset, worried
ant uptight
2 syn see LAZY
rel apathetic, careless, indifferent, unconcerned; unambitious
con active, ambitious, diligent, dynamic, energetic, industrious, live, vigorous
3 not constrained or bound by rigid standards <enjoyed the *easygoing* morality of a commune>
syn breezy, casual, ‖common, dégagé, informal, low-pressure, relaxed, ‖sonsy, unconstrained, unfussy, unreserved
rel affable, folksy; flexible, lax, moderate, offhand, off-handed, unaffected; carefree, devil-may-care, happy-go-lucky; outgiving; uninhibited
idiom free and easy
con ceremonious, decorous, formal, proper, stuffy; constrained, inflexible, inhibited, restrained, rigid, starchy, stiff
easy mark *n* **1 syn** see FOOL 3
2 syn see SOFT TOUCH 1
‖easy rider *n* **1 syn** see SYCOPHANT
2 syn see PIMP 1
easy street *n syn* see PROSPERITY 2
eat *vb* **1** to take in as food <they quickly *ate* a hearty breakfast>
syn consume, devour, feed (on), ingest, meal, partake (of), take; *compare* CONSUME 5
rel banquet, feast, gormandize; eat up, gobble (up *or* down), gorge (on), ‖mop (up), polish off, scoff; breakfast, dine, lunch, snack, sup; mouth, ‖muckamuck; nibble, pick
idiom break bread, get away with, have (*or* take) a bite, take nourishment, ‖put on the feed bag
2 syn see CONSUME 1
3 to consume gradually <the acid *ate* the surface of the copper>
syn bite, corrode, eat away, erode, gnaw, scour, wear (away)
rel nibble (away); consume, decompose, disintegrate, dissolve
eatable *adj syn* see EDIBLE
eat away *vb syn* see EAT 3
eating house *n* a cheap often small restaurant <grabbed a quick sandwich at a local *eating house*>
syn beanery, ‖buffet, café, coffee shop, cookshop, diner, ‖greasy spoon, ‖hashery, ‖hash house, lunch counter (*or* bar), luncheonette, lunchroom, lunch wagon (*or* cart), quick-lunch, sandwich shop, snack bar (*or* counter)
rel cafeteria, eatery, tearoom; trattoria
‖eats *n pl syn* see FOOD 1
eat up *vb* **1** to eat completely and without delay <*eat up* your dinner before it gets cold>
syn devour, dispatch, polish off
rel down, eat; bolt, gobble (up *or* down), gorge (on), ‖mop (up), wolf
2 syn see CONSUME 1
‖3 syn see DEVOUR 5
rel luxuriate (in), riot (in), wallow (in)
idiom be beside oneself over, be thrilled to death by, smack one's lips over, take delight in
‖4 syn see LOVE 1
ebb *vb syn* see ABATE 4
rel decline, peter (out); recede, retreat, retrograde
con ascend, increase, mount, rise; advance, progress
ant flow

---

syn synonym(s)	*rel* related word(s)
ant antonym(s)	*con* contrasted word(s)
idiom idiomatic equivalent(s)	
‖ use limited; if in doubt, see a dictionary	

ebbing *n syn* see FAILURE 4
rel declining, sinking

ebon *adj syn* see BLACK 1

ebony *adj syn* see BLACK 1

ebullience *n* lively or enthusiastic expression of thoughts or feelings < her bubbling *ebullience* was infectious >
syn buoyancy, effervescence, exuberance, exuberancy
rel animation, enthusiasm, gaiety, high-spiritedness, liveliness, vitality, vivaciousness, vivacity; agitation, excitement, exhilaration, ferment
con apathy, impassivity, languor, lethargy, listlessness, passivity, sluggishness, stolidity, torpidity, torpor; enervation, inactivity, inertia, lifelessness; disinterest, unconcern, uninterest

ebullient *adj syn* see EXUBERANT 1

eccentric *adj* **1** not having the same center < *eccentric* spheres >
syn off-center
rel uncentered; off-balance, unbalanced
con centered; balanced
ant concentric
2 *syn* see STRANGE 4
rel anomalous, irregular, unnatural; exceptionable, exceptional, quirky, quizzical; beheaded, ‖dippy, wacky; fantastic, grotesque
con customary, habitual; natural, normal, regular, typical

eccentric *n* one who deviates from established patterns especially in odd or whimsical ways < an *eccentric* who filled his house with statues of himself >
syn case, character, ‖duck, oddball, oddity, original, quiz, ‖spook, ‖wack, zombie
rel bohemian, maverick, nonconformist, unconformist; dissenter, heretic; caution, coot, ‖geezer; crackpot, crank, freak, kook, screwball
idiom queer duck (*or* potato)
con conformer, conformist, conventionalist, traditionalist; bore, bromide, dullard

ecclesiast *n syn* see CLERGYMAN

ecclesiastic *n syn* see CLERGYMAN

ecclesiastical *adj* of, relating to, or belonging to a church especially as an established institution < *ecclesiastical* law >
syn church, churchly, churchmanly, spiritual
rel apostolic, canonical, episcopal, episcopalian, evangelistic, theological; clerical, ministerial, papal, pastoral, patriarchal, pontifical, prelatial, priestly, rabbinical, sacerdotal; cathedralesque, churchlike, pantheonic, synagogal, synagogical, tabernacular, templelike
con lay, secular

ecdysiast *n syn* see STRIPTEASER

echelon *n syn* see LINE 5

echoic *adj syn* see ONOMATOPOEIC

éclat *n syn* see FAME 2
rel bang, brilliance, brilliancy, display, luster, noticeableness, prominence, remarkableness; distinction, standing; kudos
con oblivion, obscurity; contempt, derision, scorn

eclectic *adj* **1** selecting what appears to be the best from various doctrines, methods, or styles < an *eclectic* taste in music >
syn discriminating, select, selective
rel elective, selecting; choosing, choosy, discerning, fastidious, finicky, fussy, particular, picky
2 composed of elements drawn from various sources < an *eclectic* art incorporating romanticism and impressionism >
syn catholic
rel broad, comprehensive, inclusive; assorted, mingled, mixed; diverse, diversified, heterogeneous, multifarious, multiform, varied; derived, unoriginal
con distinctive, narrow; new, original

eclipse *vb syn* see OBSCURE

economical *adj syn* see SPARING
rel careful, forehanded, prudent; economizing, penny-wise; cheeseparing, close, mean, miserly, niggardly, penny-pinching, penurious, scrimping, skimping, spare, stingy
con generous, lavish, wasteful
ant extravagant

economic poison *n syn* see PESTICIDE

economize *vb* to avoid unnecessary waste or expense < *economize* on food by using leftovers >
syn save
rel conserve; scrimp, skimp
con dissipate, scatter, waste
ant squander, throw away

economy *n* careful management of material resources < retired people often must learn to practice *economy* >
syn forehandedness, frugality, husbandry, providence, prudence, thrift, thriftiness
rel meanness, miserliness, niggardliness, parcity, parsimony, scrimping, skimping, stinginess; carefulness, discretion
con improvidence, lavishness, prodigality, squandering, thriftlessness, wastefulness
ant extravagance

ecstasy *n* intense exaltation of mind and feelings < was in *ecstasy* over flying >
syn heaven, rapture, rhapsody, seventh heaven, transport; *compare* EXHILARATION
rel beatitude, blessedness, bliss, blissfulness, felicity, gladness, happiness; delectation, delight, elation, joy, joyfulness, overjoyfulness, pleasure; enchantment, euphoria, intoxication, madness; exaltation, inspiration; paradise; afflatus, frenzy, fury
idiom cloud nine
con dejection, downheartedness, lowness, lowspiritedness, oppression; blues, dumps, melancholy
ant depression

ecumenical *adj syn* see UNIVERSAL 2
rel heaven-wide; all-comprehending, all-comprehensive, all-covering, all-including, all-pervading; comprehensive, general, inclusive
con diocesan, local, parochial, provincial; circumscribed, insular, limited, narrow, restricted

edacious *adj syn* see VORACIOUS

eddy *n* a swirling mass especially of water < dark *eddies* in the flooded stream >
syn maelstrom, vortex, whirl, whirlpool
rel gurge, surge, swirl, twirl, whirl; back current, back stream, countercurrent, counterflow, counterflux; backwash, backwater

eddy *vb syn* see SWIRL

edge *n* **1** *syn* see BORDER 1
rel end, extremity; ledge, side
con area, surface
2 a cutting quality < there was an *edge* to his voice as he answered >
syn incisiveness, keenness, sharpness
rel bite, cut, sting; knife-edge, razor-edge; acerbity, acidity, acridity, causticity; astringency, stringency; acuteness, penetration, shrillness, thinness
3 *syn* see VERGE 2
4 *syn* see ADVANTAGE 3
con bar, encumbrance, obstacle; disadvantage

edge *vb* **1** *syn* see SHARPEN
2 *syn* see BORDER 1
3 *syn* see SIDLE

edge in *vb syn* see INSINUATE 3

edgy *adj* **1** *syn* see TENSE 2
rel skittish; excitable, excited, high-strung, overstrung; irritable, touchy; impatient, restless
idiom on edge
con detached; peaceful, placid; patient
2 *syn* see EXCITABLE

edible *adj* suitable for use as food < *edible* plant products >
syn comestible, eatable, esculent
rel digestible; nourishing, nutritious, nutritive; palatable, savory, succulent, tasty, toothsome
ant inedible

edibles *n pl syn* see FOOD 1

edict *n* **1** a publicly proclaimed order or rule of conduct by a competent authority < a government *edict* regarding curfew enforcement >
syn decree, directive, ruling, ukase
rel instrument; order; manifesto, proclamation, pronouncement, pronunciamento; bull
2 *syn* see LAW 1

edifice *n* a large, magnificent, or massive building < a marble *edifice* now used as a museum >
syn erection, pile, structure; *compare* BUILDING, HUT

edify *vb syn* see ILLUMINATE 2
rel better, enhance; elucidate; educate, instruct, teach
con debase, deprave

edition *n* the total number of copies of the same work printed during a stretch of time < the initial *edition* of 50,000 copies was exhausted in a month >

syn impression, printing, reissue, reprinting

educate *vb syn* see TEACH
  rel cultivate, nurture; brief, explain, inform

education *n* **1** the act or process of educating <devoted himself to the *education* of illiterate adults>
  syn instruction, schooling, teaching, training, tuition, tutelage
  rel coaching, pedagogy, tutorage, tutoring, tutorship; direction, guidance
  2 the product or result of being educated <obtained his *education* in local schools and in college>
  syn erudition, knowledge, learning, scholarship, science
  rel culture, edification, enlightenment, learnedness, literacy
  con ignorance, illiteracy

educational *adj syn* see INFORMATIVE

educative *adj syn* see INFORMATIVE

educe *vb* **1** to draw out something hidden, latent, or reserved <*educed* important information from the witness>
  syn elicit, evince, evoke, extort, extract, milk
  rel drag, draw, draw out, pull, wrest, wring; gain, get, obtain, procure, secure; distill
  con miss, overlook, pass over
  2 *syn* see DERIVE 1
  rel reason (out), think (out)

eerie *adj syn* see WEIRD 1
  rel bizarre, fantastic, grotesque; arcane; crawly

efface *vb syn* see ERASE
  rel eradicate, extirpate; eliminate, exclude, rule out

effect *n* **1** a condition or occurrence traceable to a cause <the *effect* of the medicine was dizziness>
  syn aftereffect, aftermath, causatum, consequence, corollary, end product, event, eventuality, issue, outcome, precipitate, result, sequel, sequence, upshot
  rel pursuance; development, fruit, outgrowth, ramification; denouement, repercussion; conclusion, end; side effect
  con antecedent, determinant, occasion, reason; base, basis, foundation, ground, groundwork
  ant cause
  2 effects *pl syn* see POSSESSION 2

effect *vb* **1** to induce to come into being <specific genes *effect* specific bodily characters>
  syn bring about, cause, draw on, make, produce, secure
  rel conceive, create, generate; bring on, induce; enact, render, turn out, yield
  con impede, limit, restrict; repress, suppress
  2 to carry to a successful conclusion <found a pass that allowed them to *effect* passage through the mountains>
  syn bring off, carry out, carry through, effectuate; *compare* FULFILL 1, PERFORM 2
  rel actualize, realize; achieve, procure
  con fail, fall down
  3 *syn* see ENFORCE

effective *adj* producing or capable of producing a result <an *effective* rebuke>
  syn effectual, efficacious, efficient, virtuous
  rel adequate, capable, competent; cogent, compelling, convincing, sound, telling, valid; able, active, dynamic; operative, useful; direct
  con abortive, bootless, fruitless, futile, vain; empty, hollow, idle, nugatory, otiose, pointless; inoperative, useless, worthless
  ant ineffective

effectiveness *n* **1** *syn* see POINT 3
  rel forcefulness, potency, power, strength, verve, vigor
  con impotence, weakness
  ant ineffectiveness
  2 *syn* see EFFICIENCY 1
  3 *syn* see EFFICACY 1

effectual *adj syn* see EFFECTIVE
  rel accomplishing, achieving, effecting, fulfilling; practicable, sound, useful, valid, workable; conclusive, decisive, determinative, influential; authoritative, potent, powerful, strong, toothy
  con impotent, weak
  ant ineffectual

effectuate *vb syn* see EFFECT 2

effeminate *adj* lacking manly strength and purpose <an *effeminate* preoccupation with trifles>
  syn epicene, Miss-Nancyish, pansified, prissy, sissified, sissy, unmanly
  rel chichi, old-maidish, overnice, precious; foppish, sappy, silken

ant manly, masculine

effervescence *n syn* see EBULLIENCE
  rel bubbling, ebullition, fizzing, foaming
  con deadness, flatness, staleness

effervescent *adj* **1** *syn* see EXUBERANT 1
  2 *syn* see ELASTIC 2
  rel animated, boiling, bubbly, excited, gay, lively, sparkling, sprightly, vivacious; gleeful, hilarious, jolly, mirthful
  con lifeless, listless, subdued; earnest, sedate, serious, solemn

effete *adj* **1** *syn* see STERILE 1
  2 having lost energy or drive <*effete*, weary, burned-out revolutionaries>
  syn all in, bleary, depleted, done, done in, drained, exhausted, far-gone, spent, used up, washed-out, worn-out
  rel consumed; debilitated, enfeebled, fatigued
  idiom on one's last legs, out on one's feet
  con alive, lively, vigorous, vital
  3 having lost character <a soft, *effete* society>
  syn decadent, decayed, degenerate, overripe
  rel decaying, declining; soft, weak; dissolute, immoral

efficacious *adj syn* see EFFECTIVE
  rel active, operative, productive; influential, potent, powerful, puissant, strong
  con abortive; impotent, powerless, useless, vain, weak
  ant inefficacious

efficacy *n* **1** the power to produce an effect <*efficacy* of the drug>
  syn capability, effectiveness, efficiency, potency
  rel capableness, productiveness, use; adequacy, capacity, sufficiency
  con ineffectiveness, inefficiency; uselessness, worthlessness
  ant inefficacy
  2 *syn* see EFFICIENCY 1

efficiency *n* **1** the capacity to produce desired results with a minimum expenditure of energy, time, or resources <demands a high degree of *efficiency* on the job>
  syn effectiveness, efficacy, performance
  rel ability, address, adeptness, competence, expertise, know-how, proficiency, prowess, skill; capability, resourcefulness; productivity
  con inadequacy, incompetence, ineffectiveness; unproductiveness
  ant inefficiency
  2 *syn* see EFFICACY 1

efficient *adj syn* see EFFECTIVE
  rel able, capable, competent, fitted, qualified; adept, expert, masterly, proficient, skilled, skillful
  con incapable, incompetent, inexpert, unadept, unproficient, unqualified, unsuitable; unproductive; ineffectual
  ant inefficient

effloresce *vb syn* see BLOSSOM

effort *n* **1** the active use of energy in producing a result <thought the job wasn't worth the *effort*>
  syn elbow grease, exertion, pains, trouble, while
  rel labor, toil, travail, work; energy, force, might, power, puissance; attempt, endeavor, essay
  idiom sweat of one's brow
  con adroitness, facility, smoothness; do-nothingness, inaction, indolence, inertia, lackadaisicalness, languor, laziness
  ant ease
  2 *syn* see TASK 2

effortful *adj syn* see HARD 6

effortless *adj* **1** *syn* see EASY 1
  rel adept, expert, masterly, proficient, ready, skilled, skillful
  con laborious, toilsome, trying
  ant painstaking
  2 *syn* see EASY 9

effortlessly *adv syn* see EASILY 1
  rel adeptly, adroitly, efficiently, expertly, proficiently, skillfully
  con painstakingly
  ant arduously, laboriously

effrontery *n* flagrant disregard of courtesy or propriety and an arrogant assumption of privilege <had the *effrontery* to insult her father>

---

syn synonym(s)   **rel** related word(s)
ant antonym(s)   **con** contrasted word(s)
idiom idiomatic equivalent(s)
|| use limited; if in doubt, see a dictionary

syn brashness, brass, cheek, confidence, ‖crust, face, gall, nerve, presumption; *compare* INSOLENCE

rel audacity, hardihood, temerity; assurance, self-assurance, self=confidence; brazenness, impudence; impertinence, insolence

con courtesy, grace, propriety

effulgent *adj syn* see BRIGHT 1

rel vivid; glorious, resplendent, splendid

con dark, dusky, gloomy, murky

effusive *adj* unduly demonstrative < *effusive* assurances of undying love >

syn gushing, gushy, slobbering, slobbery, sloppy

rel expansive, fulsome, outpouring, profuse; demonstrative, unconstrained, unreserved, unrestrained; cloying, slushy; smarmy

con close, restrained, reticent, taciturn; bashful, modest, shy

ant reserved

egg (on) *vb syn* see URGE

rel agitate, excite, pique, stimulate; instigate; arouse, drive, rally, stir up, whip (on *or* up)

con arrest, bridle

egghead *n syn* see INTELLECTUAL 2

egocentric *adj* **1** concerned with the individual person rather than society < an *egocentric* approach to world problems >

syn individualist, individualistic

rel self-centered, selfish

2 concerned only with one's own activities or needs and usually tending to self-assertion or self-satisfaction < an *egocentric* man, lacking feeling for others >

syn egoistic, egomaniacal, egotistic, self-absorbed, self-centered, self-concerned, self-interested, self-involved, selfish, self-seeking, self-serving; *compare* POMPOUS 1

rel conceited, narcissistic, self-affected, self-applauding, self-conceited, self-concentered, self-indulgent, self-loving, stuck-up, vainglorious; megalomaniac

idiom wrapped up in oneself

egoism *n* **1** *syn* see EGOTISM 1

rel self-assurance, self-confidence, self-possession

ant altruism

2 *syn* see CONCEIT 2

rel self-satisfaction

con meekness, modesty

ant humility

egoistic *adj syn* see EGOCENTRIC 2

rel individualistic; self-satisfied, swellheaded

con humble, modest

ant altruistic

egomaniacal *adj syn* see EGOCENTRIC 2

rel self-exalting, self-glorifying, vainglorious

egotism *n* **1** an exaggerated sense of one's own importance < in believing that he was indispensable, he exhibited consummate *egotism* >

syn egoism, self-importance

rel conceit, conceitedness, narcissism, self-esteem, self-love, vainness; boastfulness, boasting, bragging, gasconade, gasconism, megalomania, vaunting

con humility, lowliness; bashfulness, diffidence, shyness; modesty

ant altruism

2 *syn* see CONCEIT 2

rel arrogance, superiority; contempt

con humbleness, self-effacement

ant humility

egotistic *adj syn* see EGOCENTRIC 2

rel boastful, cocky, inflated, pretentious, proud, puffed up, self=satisfied; conceited, stuck-up

idiom in love with oneself, stuck on oneself

con humble, modest; self-effacing, shy

egregious *adj* conspicuously bad or objectionable < an *egregious* mistake >

syn capital, flagrant, glaring, gross, rank

rel arrant, outright, stark; infamous, nefarious, notorious; atrocious, deplorable, heinous, monstrous, outrageous, preposterous

con measly, minor, petty, piddling, slender, slight, trifling, trivial

egress *n* **1** *syn* see DEPARTURE 1

rel emergence, emerging

con coming, entering; arrival

ant ingress

2 a place or means of going out < a gate providing *egress* from the pasture >

syn exit, outlet

rel opening, passage; escape

idiom way out

con entrance, entry, entryway

ant access, ingress

egression *n syn* see DEPARTURE 1

con entrance, entering

ant ingression

eidolon *n syn* see APPARITION

ejaculate *vb syn* see EXCLAIM

rel call (out), shout, vociferate, yell

eject *vb* **1** to drive or force (somebody) out < *eject* an intruder from one's home >

syn boot (out), chase, chuck, dismiss, evict, extrude, kick out, out, throw out; *compare* BANISH

rel displace, dispossess; drive off, rout, run off; debar, disbar, eliminate, exclude, rule out, shut out; bump, cashier, discharge, fire, sack; discard, shed; reject, repudiate, spurn

idiom give one his walking papers, send packing, show one the door

con accept, admit, install, receive; entertain, harbor, house, lodge, shelter

2 *syn* see ERUPT 1

elaborate *adj* **1** *syn* see COMPLEX 2

2 marked by complexity of detail or ornament < an *elaborate* coiffure >

syn complicated, fancy, intricate

rel detailed, highly-wrought; decorated, dressy, embellished, ornate; elegant; busy, overdone, overworked, overwrought

con common, ordinary, plain, unpolished; inartificial, inornate, natural

ant simple

elaborate *vb* **1** *syn* see EXPAND 4

rel comment, discuss, dwell (upon); clarify, explain, expound, interpret

2 *syn* see UNFOLD 3

élan *n syn* see SPIRIT 5

rel impetus

élan vital *n syn* see SOUL 1

elapse *vb syn* see PASS 3

rel flow, glide, pass (by), slide, slip (by); lapse, run out

elastic *adj* **1** able to withstand strain without being permanently affected or injured < a rubber band is *elastic* >

syn flexible, resilient, springy, stretch, stretchy, supple, whippy

rel ductile, malleable, pliable, pliant, plastic, rubberlike, rubbery; adaptable, moldable, stretchable, yielding; bouncy, limber, lithe

con brittle; inflexible, stiff, tense

ant rigid

2 able to recover quickly from depression and maintain high spirits < had an *elastic* optimistic nature >

syn airy, bouncy, buoyant, effervescent, expansive, resilient, volatile

rel animated, gay, lively, sprightly, vivacious; ebullient, high=spirited, mettlesome, soaring, spirited; adaptable, recuperative

con blue, dejected, depressed, gloomy, melancholy, sad; flaccid, limp

elate *vb* to elevate the spirits of < the phenomenal sales record *elated* him >

syn commove, excite, exhilarate, inspire, set up, spirit (up), stimulate

rel brighten, cheer, cheer up, encourage; delight, gladden, gratify, overjoy; buoy, elevate, exalt, uplift

con distress; oppress, weigh; weary

ant depress

elated *adj syn* see INTOXICATED 2

rel enchanted, enraptured, exalted, transported; delighted, ecstatic, euphoric, exultant, jubilant, overjoyed

idiom in heaven, in seventh heaven, on cloud nine

con blue, deflated, unhappy

elation *n* **1** the quality or state of being elated < felt great *elation* when he won the presidential nomination >

syn euphoria, exaltation, exhilaration

rel buoyancy; happiness, joy; excitement; rapture, transport

idiom stars in one's eyes

con blues, depression; distress, misery, sadness, unhappiness

ant deflation

2 *syn* see EUPHORIA 2

ant depression

elbow *vb syn* see PUSH 2

elbowroom *n syn* see ROOM 3
  rel space

elder *n* **1** *syn* see SENIOR 2
  2 *syn* see OLDSTER
  3 *syn* see SUPERIOR

elderliness *n syn* see OLD AGE

elderly *adj syn* see AGED 1
  rel aging, declining
  con juvenile, young
  ant youthful

eldorado *n syn* see BONANZA

elect *adj syn* see SELECT 1
  rel choice, rare; hand-picked, singled out; designated, destined, ordained; delivered, redeemed, saved
  con refused, rejected, repudiated, spurned; disdained, scorned; damned, doomed, reprobate

elect *vb* **1** *syn* see CHOOSE 1
  rel decide, determine, resolve, settle; conclude, judge; accept, admit, receive
  con reject; dismiss, eject, expel, oust
  ant abjure
  2 to select by or as if by ballot <the board of directors *elected* a new chairman>
  syn ballot, vote (in)
  rel choose, designate, name, opt, pick, select, single; nominate; appoint
  3 *syn* see WILL

election *n syn* see CHOICE 1

elective *adj syn* see OPTIONAL

electrify *vb syn* see THRILL
  rel provoke; jar, stagger, stun

eleemosynary *adj syn* see CHARITABLE 1
  rel beneficent, generous, liberal, munificent, openhanded
  con close, parsimonious, tight

elegance *n* impressive beauty of form, appearance, or behavior <the sumptuous *elegance* of the furnishings>
  syn dignity, grace
  rel beauty, charm; cultivation, culture, polish, refinement, sophistication, style, taste, tastefulness; lushness, magnificence, ornateness, poshness, richness, splendor, sumptuousness
  con grotesqueness, ugliness; clumsiness, crudeness, roughness, rudeness; austerity, bareness, inornateness, severity

elegant *adj syn* see CHOICE
  rel august, grand, majestic, noble, stately; beautiful, graceful, handsome, lovely; cultivated, cultured, finished, polished, refined, tasteful; luxurious, opulent, sumptuous
  con crude, rough, rude, uncouth; grotesque

element *n* **1** *syn* see ESSENTIAL 1
  2 one of the parts, substances, or principles that make up a compound or complex whole <analyzed the various *elements* of the problem>
  syn component, constituent, factor, ingredient; *compare* POINT 1
  rel fundamental, principle; item, member, part, particle, piece, portion; detail, particular; aspect, facet, feature, view
  con bulk, mass, volume; entirety, whole; sum, total, totality
  ant composite, compound
  3 **elements** *pl syn* see ALPHABET 2
  rel basics, basis, foundations, groundwork; outlines
  4 *syn* see POINT 1
  rel division, member, section, sector, segment

elemental *adj* **1** of, relating to, or being an ultimate and irreducible element <such *elemental* aspects of life as sex and nutrition>
  syn basic, elementary, essential, fundamental, primitive, substratal, underlying
  rel primary, prime, primordial; inherent, intrinsic, radical
  con secondary, subordinate; casual, incidental, trivial, unimportant
  2 *syn* see ELEMENTARY 1
  3 *syn* see INHERENT

elementary *adj* **1** of, relating to, or dealing with the simplest principles of something <can't handle the most *elementary* decision-making>
  syn basal, beginning, elemental, rudimental, rudimentary, simplest
  rel introductory, prefatory, preliminary; easy, simple; rude, unsubtle

con complex, complicated, elaborate, intricate, labyrinthine; sophisticated
  ant advanced
  2 *syn* see ELEMENTAL 1

elephantine *adj* **1** *syn* see HUGE
  con slender, slight, slim, thin; dainty
  2 *syn* see PONDEROUS 2
  rel awkward, clumsy, graceless, maladroit, ungraceful
  con graceful, nimble, quick

elevate *vb* **1** *syn* see LIFT 1
  rel ensky, erect
  con cut (down), deflate, depress, scale (down)
  ant lower
  2 *syn* see ADVANCE 2
  rel boost; enhance, glorify, heighten
  con demote, downgrade, lower, reduce; abase, debase, degrade

elevated *adj* **1** being positioned above a surface <an *elevated* monorail>
  syn lifted, raised, upheaved, uplifted, upraised, uprisen
  rel high; aerial
  con ground-level, low, lowered, low-lying, unelevated
  ant sunken
  2 being on a high moral or intellectual plane <*elevated* ideas>
  syn high-minded, moral, noble
  rel ethical, honorable, righteous, upright, upstanding, virtuous
  con base, ignoble, mean; immoral, low, unethical; intolerable, unacceptable
  3 *syn* see GRAND 3
  4 being exceedingly dignified in form, tone, or style <an *elevated* prose style>
  syn eloquent, high, lofty
  rel dignified, formal; grand, grandiloquent, grandiose, high=flown, majestic, stately, towering
  con informal; lowly, unassuming

elevation *n* **1** *syn* see HEIGHT
  rel acclivity, ascent, rise
  con depression, descent; flatness, levelness
  2 *syn* see ADVANCEMENT 1
  rel advance, boost, raise; ennoblement, exaltation, glorification, lionization; apotheosis, deification, immortalization, magnification
  con downgrading; depreciation, detraction, disparagement
  ant degradation

elf *n syn* see FAIRY

elicit *vb syn* see EDUCE 1
  rel bring, fetch
  con eschew, forego; abandon

elide *vb syn* see NEGLECT

eligible *adj* qualified to be or worthy of being chosen <an *eligible* bachelor>
  syn fit, suitable
  rel acceptable, desirable, likely, preferable, seemly; capable, fitted, qualified, suited, worthy; marriageable, nubile; visitable
  con undesirable; disqualified, unfit, unqualified, unsuitable, unworthy
  ant ineligible

eliminate *vb* **1** *syn* see EXCLUDE
  rel freeze out, shut out; dismiss, ‖dump, eject, evict, expel, oust; delete, erase, expunge
  con accept, receive
  2 *syn* see REMOVE 4
  3 *syn* see PURGE 3

elite *n* **1** *syn* see BEST
  rel elect, pink, select; ‖hoi polloi
  idiom cream of the crop, crème de la crème, pick of the bunch
  2 *syn* see ARISTOCRACY
  rel drawing rooms; Four Hundred; beautiful people, jet set, smart set
  idiom high society, horsey set
  con hoi polloi, (the) masses, mob, peasantry, people, proletariat, rabble

elixir *n syn* see PANACEA
  rel balm, cure, therapy, therapeutic

---

syn synonym(s)   **rel** related word(s)
ant antonym(s)   **con** contrasted word(s)
idiom idiomatic equivalent(s)

‖ use limited; if in doubt, see a dictionary

ell *n syn* see ANNEX

elocution *n syn* see ORATORY

elongate *vb syn* see EXTEND 3
  rel drag (out); string
  con contract, draw in; compress; curtail, retrench; shrink
  ant abbreviate, shorten

elongate *adj syn* see LONG 1
  rel lengthened
  ant abbreviated, shortened

elongated *adj syn* see LONG 1
  rel drawn (out), lengthened, prolongated, prolonged, protracted, stretched
  con contracted, drawn (in), shrunken
  ant shortened

elongation *n syn* see EXTENSION 1

elope *vb* to go away secretly usually with the intention of marrying <decided to *elope* rather than endure a big wedding>
  syn run away
  idiom go to Gretna Green

eloquence *n* discourse marked by force and persuasiveness suggesting strong feeling <read the poem with *eloquence*>
  syn expression, expressiveness, expressivity, facundity
  rel meaningfulness, persuasiveness; fervor, force, forcefulness, passion, power, spirit, vigor

eloquent *adj* 1 *syn* see VOCAL 3
  rel forceful, potent, powerful; ardent, fervent, fervid, impassioned, passionate; glib, silver-tongued, voluble
  con inarticulate, ineffective, weak
  2 *syn* see EXPRESSIVE
  rel graphic, indicative, revealing, suggestive, telling; affecting, impressive, moving, poignant, touching
  3 *syn* see ELEVATED 4

else *adv syn* see OTHERWISE 2

else *adj syn* see ADDITIONAL

||**elseways** *adv syn* see OTHERWISE 2

elsewise *adv syn* see OTHERWISE 2

elucidate *vb syn* see CLARIFY 2
  rel exemplify; demonstrate, prove; annotate, spell out; enlighten
  con confuse; darken

elude *vb syn* see ESCAPE 2
  rel baffle, circumvent, foil, frustrate, outwit, thwart; flee, fly
  idiom give the slip
  con accost, face; chase, follow, pursue, tag, tail, trail

elusion *n syn* see ESCAPE 2

elusive *adj* not easily perceived, grasped, comprehended, pinned down, or isolated <inspiration need not be forever *elusive*> <they finally isolated the *elusive* virus that caused the disease>
  syn elusory, evasive, intangible
  rel evanescent, fleeting, fugitive; baffling, imponderable, incomprehensible, mysterious; insubstantial, phantom

elusory *adj syn* see ELUSIVE
  rel nebulous, vague

elvish *adj syn* see PLAYFUL 1

elysium *n syn* see HEAVEN 2

emaciated *adj* being very lean through loss of flesh (as from hunger or disease) <*emaciated* bony hands clutched at him>
  syn cadaverous, gaunt, skeletal, wasted
  rel bony, lean, scrawny, skinny, wizened; starved, underfed, undernourished
  idiom all skin and bones, thin as a rail
  con fit, husky, solid, well-fed, well-nourished; chubby, plump, portly, rotund, stocky, stout; corpulent, obese
  ant fleshy

emanate *vb syn* see SPRING 1
  rel initiate; emit, exude, radiate

emancipate *vb syn* see FREE
  ant enslave

emasculate *vb syn* see UNNERVE
  rel debilitate, devitalize
  con energize, vitalize

emasculate *adj syn* see WEAK 4

embark *vb syn* see BOARD 1

embark (on *or* upon) *vb syn* see BEGIN 1

embarrass *vb* to throw into a state of self-conscious distress <bawdy stories *embarrassed* her>
  syn abash, confound, confuse, discomfit, disconcert, discountenance, faze, rattle; *compare* DISCOMPOSE 1

  rel agitate, bother, discompose, flurry, fluster, perturb; nonplus; chagrin, distress, vex; queer
  idiom put on the spot, put to the blush
  con calm, relieve, soothe

embarrassing *adj syn* see INCONVENIENT

embarrassment *n* the quality, state, or condition of being embarrassed <felt great *embarrassment* when she fell down>
  syn abashment, confusion, discomfiture, discomposure, disconcertion, disconcertment, unease, uneasiness
  rel constraint, strain; agitation, discombobulation, perturbation; chagrin, distress, vexation; humiliation, mortification; difficulty, Queer Street
  con assurance, calm, imperturbability, savoir faire

embed *vb syn* see ENTRENCH 1

embellish *vb* 1 *syn* see ADORN
  rel apparel, array, ||doll up, dress up, emblaze, embroider, enrich, furbish
  con bare, denude, divest, strip
  2 *syn* see EMBROIDER

embellishment *n syn* see EXAGGERATION
  rel floridity, ostentation

embezzle *vb* to appropriate dishonestly and fraudulently to one's own use <*embezzled* a trust fund>
  syn misappropriate, peculate
  rel loot, pilfer, steal, thieve

embitter *vb syn* see EXACERBATE
  rel bitter, sour

emblem *n* 1 *syn* see SYMBOL 1
  2 *syn* see INSIGNIA

emblematize *vb syn* see REPRESENT 2

embodiment *n* a concrete or actual entity in which something (as an idea, principle, or type) is embodied <he is the *embodiment* of all our hopes>
  syn incarnation, personification; *compare* APOTHEOSIS 1
  rel manifestation; prosopopoeia; archetype; apotheosis, epitome, quintessence

embody *vb* 1 to make an abstraction concrete or perceptible often by representation in human or animal form <Dickens *embodied* hypocrisy in his Uriah Heep>
  syn exteriorize, externalize, incarnate, manifest, materialize, objectify, personalize, personify, personize, substantiate; *compare* REPRESENT 2
  rel actualize, hypostatize, realize, reify, symbolize, typify; demonstrate, evince, exemplify, exhibit, illustrate, show (forth)
  ant disembody
  2 to cause to become a body or part of another body <*embodied* a revenue provision in the new law>
  syn combine, incorporate, integrate
  rel absorb, amalgamate, assimilate, blend, consolidate, fuse, merge, unify
  3 *syn* see INCLUDE
  rel compose, consist (of), constitute
  4 *syn* see REPRESENT 2

embog *vb syn* see DELAY 1

embolden *vb syn* see ENCOURAGE 1
  rel impel; inspire; chance, hazard, venture
  con deter, discourage
  ant abash

embouchement *n syn* see MOUTH 5

embouchure *n syn* see MOUTH 5

embowel *vb syn* see EVISCERATE

embrace *vb* 1 to gather into one's arms usually as a gesture of affection <*embraced* his wife>
  syn clasp, ||clinch, ||clip, ||coll, enfold, hug, press, squeeze
  rel cling, grip, hold; encircle, entwine, envelop, enwind, fold, lock, twine, wrap; cuddle, fondle, nuzzle, snuggle; cradle, hold
  idiom ||go into a clinch
  2 *syn* see ADOPT
  rel accept, accommodate, admit, incorporate, receive, take (over), take in; seize (upon), welcome
  con reject; abjure, deny, forswear, renounce
  ant spurn
  3 *syn* see INCLUDE
  rel compose, cover, enclose, hold

embracement *n syn* see ESPOUSAL 4

embracing *n syn* see ESPOUSAL 4

embrangle *vb syn* see ENTANGLE 3

embroider *vb* to give an elaborate account of, often with florid language and fictitious details <*embroidered* the story of his adventures in the army>
syn color, embellish, exaggerate, fudge, magnify, overcharge, overdraw, overpaint, overstate, pad, stretch
rel aggrandize, amplify, build up, distend, elaborate, enhance, enlarge (upon), expand; dramatize, hyperbolize, overdo, overelaborate, overembellish, overemphasize, overestimate
idiom lay it on thick, stretch (*or* strain) the truth
con deemphasize, minimize, play (down), underestimate, understate
embroidering *n syn* see EXAGGERATION
embroil *vb syn* see INVOLVE 1
embroilment *n* 1 *syn* see QUARREL
   2 *syn* see ENTANGLEMENT 1
embryo *n syn* see SEED 2
emend *vb syn* see CORRECT 1
rel alter, edit, emendate; polish, retouch
emerge *vb syn* see APPEAR 1
rel derive, originate, spring, stem; arise, materialize, rise; come (forth), come out, emanate, flow, issue (forth); proceed
idiom appear on the horizon, come on the scene, come out in the open, come to light, make its appearance
con disappear, fade, fade (out); evaporate; dissolve
emergency *n syn* see JUNCTURE 2
rel difficulty, extremity; clutch, fix, hole, pinch, push, squeeze, vicissitude; climax
idiom turn of events
emigrant *n* one that leaves one place to settle in another <a city teeming with *emigrants* from many lands>
syn immigrant, migrant
rel alien, displaced person, DP, émigré, evacuee, exile, expatriate, fugitive, refugee; migrator, migratory
con aborigine, native
emigrate *vb syn* see MIGRATE
émigré *n* 1 a person forced to immigrate usually for political reasons <a city filled with White Russian *émigrés*>
syn exile, expatriate, expellee
rel emigrant, immigrant; alien, displaced person, DP, evacuee, fugitive, refugee
   2 *syn* see REFUGEE
eminence *n* 1 a condition, position, or state of great importance or superiority <the *eminence* of the presidency>
syn distinction, illustriousness, kudos, preeminence, prestige, prominence, prominency, renown
rel greatness, loftiness, prepotency, significance, superiority; authority, credit, dignity, importance, influence, power, weight; fame, famousness, glory, honor, reputation, repute
con insignificance, unimportance; obscurity
   2 *syn* see NOTABLE 1
   3 a natural elevation <the house stood on an *eminence* overlooking the river>
syn projection, prominence
rel peak, raise, rise, uprise; altitude, elevation, height; highness, loftiness
con cavity, depression, dip
eminency *n syn* see FORTE
eminent *adj syn* see FAMOUS 2
rel well-known; august, dominant, exalted, important, lofty, noble, preeminent; big league, big-name, big-time
con uncelebrated, unremarkable, unrenowned; common, lowly
eminently *adv syn* see VERY 1
emissary *n syn* see MESSENGER
emit *vb* 1 *syn* see DISCHARGE 5
   2 to discharge something such as moisture, vapor, or fumes <a smokestack *emitting* effluents>
syn give off, give out, issue, release, throw off, vent
rel discharge, evacuate, expel; let out, loose, pass (off); pour (out), reek; drip, emanate, excrete, extrude, exude, ooze, secrete; exhale, expire
emolument *n syn* see WAGE
rel guerdon
emote *vb* to give expression to emotion especially on or as if on the stage <she *emotes*, postures, and harangues at the slightest provocation>
syn emotionalize
rel gush, sentimentalize; carry on, rage, rant, storm, take on
emotion *n syn* see FEELING 3

rel excitability, responsiveness, sensibility, sensitiveness, sensitivity, susceptibilities; sensation
con coldness, detachment, reserve, unfeelingness
emotionable *adj syn* see EMOTIONAL 1
emotional *adj* 1 dominated by, prone to, or moved by emotion <an irritable *emotional* woman who was easily upset by trivialities>
syn emotionable, feeling, sensitive, sentient
rel responsive, susceptible, susceptive; softhearted, sympathetic; ardent, fervent, passionate; rhapsodic, rhapsodical
con cold, detached, insensitive, reserved, taciturn, unfeeling
ant emotionless, unemotional
   2 appealing to or arousing emotion <an *emotional* sermon>
syn affective, emotive, moving; *compare* MOVING 2
rel affecting, stirring, touching
emotionalize *vb syn* see EMOTE
emotionless *adj* 1 *syn* see COLD 2
rel nonemotional, undemonstrative; cool, dispassionate, distant, immovable, impassive, remote, reserved; heartless, unfeeling
con responsive, softhearted, sympathetic; ardent, fervent, passionate
ant emotional
   2 *syn* see MATTER-OF-FACT 3
emotive *adj syn* see EMOTIONAL 2
empathy *n syn* see SYMPATHY 2
rel accord, affinity, communion, compatibility, concord, congeniality, fellow feeling, rapport, responsiveness, warmth; appreciation, comprehension, understanding
idiom community of interests
con animosity, animus, antagonism, antipathy, enmity
emphasis *n* force brought to bear on something to bring out what is important <the school's *emphasis* on discipline>
syn accent, accentuation, stress
rel attention; force, insistence; weight
emphasize *vb* to give emphasis to especially by displaying more or less prominently <the papers *emphasized* crime stories>
syn feature, italicize, play (up), stress, underline, underscore
rel accent, accentuate, charge, highlight, mark, pinpoint, point (up), punctuate, spotlight; assert, press
idiom bear down on (*or* upon)
con depreciate, minimize, play (down), shrug off, underrate, understate
ant de-emphasize
emphatic *adj* marked by, uttered with, or made prominent by stress or emphasis <made his point in an *emphatic* argument>
syn assertive, forceful, insistent, resounding
rel aggressive, energetic, insistive, vigorous; accented, accentuated, assertative, decided, emphasized, marked, pointed, stressed, underlined
con insipid, milk-and-water, unaggressive, unassertive, weak, wishy-washy; de-emphasized, played (down), understated
ant unemphatic
empirical *adj* originating in, relying on, or based on factual information, observation, or direct sense experience <an *empirical* basis for an ethical theory>
syn experient, experiential, experimental
rel observational; factual
con conjectural, speculative, unproved, unsubstantiated; ideal, imagined
ant theoretical
employ *vb* 1 *syn* see USE 2
rel avail, exert, practice, work; devote, engross, monopolize
   2 to provide with a job that pays wages <*employed* a new draftsman>
syn engage, hire, put on, take on
rel add, contract (for), obtain, procure, retain, secure, sign (on *or* up)
employable *adj syn* see OPEN 5
employed *adj syn* see BUSY 1
employment *n* 1 *syn* see USE 1
rel purpose; disposition, exercise, exploitation, handling, utilization
   2 *syn* see EXERCISE 1

---

syn synonym(s)   **rel** related word(s)
ant antonym(s)   **con** contrasted word(s)
idiom idiomatic equivalent(s)
‖ use limited; if in doubt, see a dictionary

3 syn see WORK 1
rel assignment, mission; office, position, post, situation; function
4 the act of employing for wages < handled the *employment* of new workers >
syn engagement, engaging, hiring
rel enlistment, enrollment, recruitment, signing on
empower *vb* **1 syn** see INVEST 2
2 syn see AUTHORIZE 1
3 syn see ENABLE 2
rel endow, invest; authorize, charge, commission, entitle, entrust, license, privilege, sanction
con debar, disallow, disbar, exclude, rule out, shut out
emprise *n syn* see ADVENTURE
emptiness *n syn* see VACUITY 2
emptor *n syn* see PURCHASER
empty *adj* **1** lacking contents that could or should be present < an *empty* apartment > < the whole book is *empty* of meaning >
syn bare, clear, stark, vacant, vacuous, void
rel barren, blank; abandoned, deserted, emptied, forsaken, godforsaken, unfilled, unfurnished uninhabited, untenanted, vacated; destitute, devoid; depleted, drained, exhausted
con complete, replete; filled, occupied, packed, teeming
ant full
2 syn see VAIN 1
rel paltry, petty, trifling, trivial; banal, flat, inane, ineffectual, insipid, jejune, vapid; dumb, fatuous, foolish, ignorant, silly, simple
con meaningful, pregnant, significant; authentic, bona fide, genuine, veritable
3 syn see EXPRESSIONLESS
4 syn see DEVOID
empty *vb syn* see VACATE 2
empty–headed *adj* **1 syn** see GIDDY 1
rel brainless, rattleheaded; ignorant, simple
2 syn see VACUOUS 2
3 syn see IGNORANT 1
empyreal *adj syn* see CELESTIAL
rel aerial, airy; extraterrestrial; divine, holy, spiritual, sublime
ant terrestrial
empyrean *adj syn* see CELESTIAL
empyrean *n* **1 syn** see HEAVEN 2
2 syn see SKY
emulate *vb syn* see RIVAL 2
rel challenge, outvie
emulation *n syn* see CONTEST 1
emulative *adj syn* see SLAVISH 3
emulous *adj syn* see AMBITIOUS 1
rel aiming, striving; agog, athirst; competitive, vying
con unambitious, unaspiring; detached, disinterested, uninterested
enable *vb* **1 syn** see AUTHORIZE 1
rel allow, let, permit, sanction
2 to render able often by giving power, strength, or competence to < his education *enabled* him to find an excellent job >
syn empower
rel allow, let, permit; condition, fit, prepare, qualify, ready
con inhibit, preclude, prevent; disallow, enjoin, forbid, prohibit
enact *vb* **1** to cause to be by legal and authoritative act < *enact* a law >
syn constitute, establish, make
rel bring about, institute; authorize, decree, proclaim; accomplish, carry (through), effect, effectuate, execute, legislate, pass, put (through), ratify
con abolish, abrogate, annul, cancel, invalidate, nullify, rescind, revoke; overturn
ant repeal
2 syn see ACT 1
rel depict, portray, represent
enamored *adj* **1** moved by intense sexual attraction < became more desperately *enamored* of the man every day >
syn mashed, smitten, soft (on), spoony (over or on)
rel infatuated; crazy (over or about), mad (about), nuts (about), silly (over or about), wild (about); amorous, devoted, loving
idiom head over heels in love, stuck on, sweet on
2 syn see INFATUATED
3 taking great pleasure in something < found herself *enamored* of those huge English teas >

syn bewitched, captivated, charmed, enchanted, entranced, fascinated
rel fond
encamp *vb syn* see CAMP
encampment *n syn* see CAMP 1
enceinte *adj syn* see PREGNANT 1
enchant *vb* **1 syn** see BEWITCH 1
2 syn see ATTRACT 1
rel delight, enthrall, please, send, thrill; mesmerize
idiom carry away, knock dead
con disillusion, dissatisfy, let down
ant disenchant
enchanted *adj syn* see ENAMORED 3
rel delighted, pleased; pixilated
ant disenchanted
enchanter *n syn* see MAGICIAN 1
enchanting *adj syn* see ATTRACTIVE 1
rel attractive, pleasing; delectable, delightful; beguiling, enthralling, entrancing, intriguing, witching; exciting, sirenic
con repellent
enchantment *n syn* see MAGIC 1
enchantress *n syn* see WITCH 1
enchiridion *n syn* see HANDBOOK
rel book, text
encincture *vb syn* see BELT 1
encircle *vb syn* see SURROUND 1
rel band, cincture, circuit, enring; halo, wreathe
enclose *vb* **1** to shut up or confine by or as if by barriers < a valley *enclosed* by mountains >
syn cage, close in, coop, corral, envelop, fence, hedge, hem, immure, mew, mure, pen, shut in, wall
rel bound, circumscribe, confine, contain, limit, restrict; circle, compass, encircle, encompass, surround; environ; enlock
2 syn see ENFOLD 1
enclosure *n syn* see COURT 1
enclothe *vb syn* see CLOTHE
encomiastic *adj syn* see EULOGISTIC
encomium *n* a formal expression of praise < an unstinted *encomium* of a national hero >
syn citation, eulogy, panegyric, salutation, tribute
rel approval, kudos, laud, laudation, magnification, praise; acclaim, acclamation, applause, plaudits; accolade, commendation, compliment
con abuse, invective, obloquy, vituperation; criticism, critique, faultfinding
encompass *vb* **1 syn** see SURROUND 1
rel bound, delimit
2 syn see INCLUDE
encounter *vb* **1 syn** see CONFRONT 1
rel clash, collide, conflict
2 syn see ENGAGE 5
3 syn see MEET 6
rel ||bump (into), come (across), run (across), run (into)
idiom cross the path of, fall in with, meet up with
con miss, pass (by)
4 syn see FIND 1
encounter *n* a sudden, hostile, and usually brief confrontation or dispute between factions or persons < a sharp courtroom *encounter* between opposing lawyers >
syn brush, run-in, set-to, skirmish, velitation
rel conflict, contest; scrap; fray, fight; battle; argument, contention, quarrel
encourage *vb* **1** to fill with courage or strength of purpose especially in preparation for a hard task < the teacher's praise *encouraged* the student to try harder >
syn animate, cheer, chirk (up), embolden, enhearten, hearten, inspirit, nerve, ||pearten (up), steel, strengthen; *compare* SUPPORT 5
rel assure, reassure; boost, excite, galvanize, pique, provoke, quicken, stimulate; buck up, buoy (up), energize, fortify, invigorate; rally, stir
idiom give a shot in the arm
con deject, depress, discourage, dishearten, dispirit; affright, caution, frighten
ant discourage
2 to give the support of one's approval to < the government openly *encouraged* East-West détente >
syn advocate, countenance, favor

rel approve, back, endorse, go (for), sanction, subscribe (to); abet, assist, reinforce, support, sustain; incite, instigate; induce, prevail

idiom lend one's countenance to, lend one's favor (*or* support) to, smile upon

con deter, dissuade, divert, hinder; inhibit, restrain; disapprove

ant discourage

3 *syn* see ADVANCE 1

rel patronize, push, support; develop, improve, subsidize

con weaken; check, retard, slow

ant discourage

encouraging *adj syn* see HOPEFUL 2

encroach *vb syn* see TRESPASS 2

rel barge (in), ‖bust (in), butt (in), chisel (in), horn (in), muscle (in), worm (in); interfere, interpose, intervene, meddle; overstep

idiom foist oneself upon, stick one's nose in (*or* into)

con ignore, let (alone), pass over; avoid

encrust (*or* **incrust**) *vb syn* see CAKE 1

encumber *vb syn* see BURDEN

rel freight; discommode, incommode, inconvenience; fetter, hamper, handicap; block, impede, obstruct; oppress, overburden

encumbrance *n* something that impedes and makes action difficult < told his story simply without the *encumbrance* of unnecessary details >

syn clog, cumbrance, hindrance, impedance, impediment

rel disadvantage, handicap, load; difficulty, hardship, inconvenience

con aid; catalyst, impetus, stimulus

ant assist, assistance

encyclopedic *adj* embracing, comprehensively treating, or informed in a wide range of subjects < an *encyclopedic* article on world history >

syn comprehensive, inclusive

rel all-comprehensive, all-embracing, all-inclusive, complete; extensive, general; discursive

end *n* **1** *syn* see LIMIT 1

rel borderline, tip; extreme, extremity

con center, hub, middle

2 ceasing of a course (as of action or activity) or the point at which something ceases < the *end* of the war >

syn cease, cessation, close, closing, closure, conclusion, desistance, desuetude, discontinuance, discontinuation, ending, finish, period, stop, termination, terminus; *compare* FINALE

rel consummation, culmination; expiration; coda, curtains, finale, finality, finis, terminal, windup

idiom cutoff point, end of the line, stopping point

con genesis, inception

ant beginning

3 *syn* see FINALE

4 something residual < melted down candle *ends* >

syn bit, fragment, scrap

rel butt end, fag end, leaving, remainder, remnant, residue; part, particle, piece

end *vb syn* see CLOSE 3

ant begin

endable *adj syn* see TERMINABLE

endanger *vb* to bring into peril (as of harm or disaster) < conspirators who were *endangering* the cause of freedom >

syn compromise, hazard, imperil, jeopard, jeopardize, jeopardy, menace, peril, risk

rel expose, lay (open); chance, venture

con guard, protect, shelter, shield; preserve, save

endeavor *vb syn* see TRY 5

rel determine, intend, purpose; address, apply, bid (for), drive (at), go (for); strain

endeavor *n syn* see ATTEMPT

rel exertion, push; labor, toil, travail, work

ended *adj syn* see COMPLETE 4

endemic *adj syn* see NATIVE 2

rel home-bred, native-born

con pandemic; extraneous, extrinsic

ant exotic

ending *n* **1** *syn* see END 2

ant beginning

2 *syn* see FINALE

endless *adj* **1** *syn* see LIMITLESS

2 *syn* see EVERLASTING 1

rel constant, continuous; deathless, immortal, undying; boundless, limitless, unbounded, unlimited; self-perpetuating

3 *syn* see CONTINUAL

rel overlong

endorse *vb syn* see APPROVE 2

rel attest, authenticate, pass (on *or* upon), vouch, witness; command, recommend; advocate, back (up), champion, stand by, support, uphold

con deprecate, disapprove; anathematize, denounce

endorsement *n syn* see SANCTION

endow *vb* **1** to furnish or provide with a gift, talent, or good quality < poets *endowed* with genius >

syn crown (with), dower, endue

rel bestow, confer; accord, award, grant; empower, enable; enhance, enrich, heighten

con bare, denude, divest, strip; despoil, ravage, spoliate; deplete, drain, exhaust

2 to furnish, (as an institution) with a store of capital < *endowed* a hospital >

syn finance, fund, subsidize

rel found, organize; bequeath, contribute, donate, subscribe, support; award, grant; back, promote, sponsor; provide, supply

con beggar, impoverish, pauperize; drain, draw (on)

end product *n syn* see EFFECT 1

endue *vb syn* see ENDOW 1

rel clothe, invest, vest; accouter, equip, furnish, outfit

endurable *adj syn* see BEARABLE

endurance *n* **1** *syn* see CONTINUATION 1

2 *syn* see TOLERANCE 1

endure *vb* **1** *syn* see CONTINUE 1

rel bide, linger

con crumble, decay, disintegrate; collapse, fall

ant perish

2 *syn* see ACCEPT 2

rel stand, submit (to), suffer, sustain; undergo

con break, collapse, give in, resign

3 *syn* see BEAR 10

enduring *adj* **1** *syn* see LASTING

ant fleeting

2 *syn* see OLD 2

3 *syn* see SURE 2

rel durable, resolute, solid, sound, stable, staunch, sturdy, substantial

con capricious, changeable, fickle, inconstant, mercurial, unstable, variable

endways *adv syn* see LENGTHWISE

endwise *adv syn* see LENGTHWISE

enemy *n* an individual or group that is hostile toward another < the senator was blackmailed by a political *enemy* >

syn foe

rel adversary, antagonist, opponent; assailant, attacker, combatant, invader; competitor, contender, emulator, rival

con benefactor, friend, supporter; ally, collaborator, colleague, confederate, friendly; adherent, follower, partisan, upholder

energetic *adj* **1** *syn* see VIGOROUS

rel aggressive, emphatic, vibrant; indefatigable

con easygoing; faineant, idle, languorous, lethargic

2 disposed to or having a capacity for action < an *energetic* campaign worker >

syn active, driving, enterprising, lively

rel animated, breezy, brisk, fresh, kinetic, peppy, spirited, sprightly, spry, vivacious, zippy

idiom full of go (*or* life *or* pep *or* zip)

con apathetic, inert; lethargic, limp, listless, passive, phlegmatic, spiritless, spunkless

ant inactive

energetically *adv syn* see HARD 1

rel firmly, strenuously; busily, industriously, zealously

idiom at full tilt

con idly, lazily, lethargically, listlessly; slowly

ant unenergetically

energize *vb* **1** *syn* see VITALIZE

idiom put pep (*or* zip) into

con emasculate, enervate; debilitate, enfeeble

2 *syn* see STRENGTHEN 2

---

syn synonym(s)   *rel* related word(s)
ant antonym(s)   *con* contrasted word(s)
idiom idiomatic equivalent(s)
‖ use limited; if in doubt, see a dictionary

rel arm, empower, enable; build (up), sustain
con daunt

energy *n* **1** *syn* see POWER 4
rel activity, operativeness; forcefulness, mightiness, powerfulness
con impotence; decrepitude, feebleness, weakness; powerlessness
ant inertia
2 vigorous and effectual application and operation of power < work with *energy* >
syn birr, go, hardihood, ‖moxie, pep, potency, tuck, vigor; *compare* VIGOR 2
rel application, effectiveness, efficacy; effort, operativeness; toughness
con kef, languor, lethargy, listlessness, sluggishness; ergophobia

enervate *vb syn* see UNNERVE
rel debilitate, devitalize, disable; exhaust, fatigue, jade, tire, weary
con activate, energize, vitalize; galvanize, quicken, stimulate

enervated *adj syn* see LANGUID
rel debilitated, devitalized, enfeebled, undermined, weakened; exhausted, fatigued, run-down, tired, weary; decadent, degenerate, degenerated, deteriorated
con active, animated, energetic, lusty, strenuous, vigorous, vital; strong, sturdy, tenacious, tough

enfant terrible *n syn* see SCAMP

enfeeble *vb syn* see WEAKEN 1
rel devitalize, exhaust
con galvanize; harden, strengthen
ant fortify

enfold *vb* **1** to surround or cover closely < a heavy fog *enfolded* the ships >
syn enclose, enshroud, envelop, enwrap, invest, shroud, veil, wrap; *compare* SWATHE
rel cover, drape; encase, ensheathe; encircle, encompass, environ, gird, girdle, surround
2 *syn* see EMBRACE 1

enforce *vb* to put something into effect or operation < *enforce* a law >
syn effect, implement, invoke
rel accomplish, administer, carry (out *or* through), discharge, execute, fulfill, perform; compel, force, oblige
con disregard, forget, ignore, neglect; relax

enfranchise *vb* to admit to full political rights as a freeman or citizen < slaves were emancipated in 1863 but were not *enfranchised* until the fifteenth amendment went into effect in 1870 >
syn affranchise, franchise
rel emancipate, free, liberate, release; deliver, extricate, rescue
con enslave, oppress, subject
ant disenfranchise, disfranchise

engage *vb* **1** to come into contact and interlock with < the teeth of one gear wheel *engaging* those of another >
syn intermesh, mesh
rel interact, interlace, interlock, interplay
con free, release
ant disengage
2 *syn* see PROMISE 1
rel commit; bind, tie; affiance, betroth, troth
3 *syn* see EMPLOY 2
con dismiss, eject, fire
ant discharge
4 to hold the attention of < the puzzle *engaged* him all evening >
syn busy, engross, immerse, occupy, soak
rel absorb, imbue, involve; arrest, captivate, enthrall, fascinate, grip; monopolize, preengage, preoccupy
5 to enter into contest or conflict with < ordered to seek out and *engage* the enemy fleet >
syn encounter, face, meet, take on
rel assault, attack, strike; battle, fight
idiom do battle with, join battle with
con elude, escape, evade

engaged *adj* **1** *syn* see BUSY 1
ant unengaged
2 pledged in marriage < the *engaged* couple made a charming pair >
syn affianced, betrothed, contracted, intended, plighted, ‖promised
rel committed, pledged
con free, uncommitted, unpledged

ant unengaged
3 *syn* see INTENT

engagement *n* **1** *syn* see PROMISE
2 the act or state of being engaged to be married < the couple recently announced their *engagement* >
syn betrothal, betrothing, betrothment, espousal, troth
rel pledge, plight, promise
ant disengagement
3 a promise to be in an agreed place at a specified time, usually for a particular purpose < had an *engagement* with him for nine that evening >
syn appointment, assignation, date, rendezvous, tryst
rel arrangement, invitation; interview, get-together, meeting, visit
4 *syn* see EMPLOYMENT 4
5 *syn* see BATTLE

engaging *adj* **1** *syn* see ATTRACTIVE 1
2 *syn* see SWEET 1
rel alluring, appealing, attractive, captivating, charming, enchanting, entrancing, fetching; fascinating, interesting, intriguing
con repellent, repelling, repulsive; unappealing, unattractive, uninteresting
ant loathsome

engaging *n syn* see EMPLOYMENT 4

engender *vb syn* see GENERATE 3
rel develop; excite, stimulate; arouse, quicken, rouse, stir

engineer *vb* to contrive or plan out usually with subtle skill or craft < *engineered* an agreement between the two rival governments >
syn finagle, machinate, maneuver, wangle; *compare* MANIPULATE 2
rel arrange, contrive, devise, mastermind, plan (out), set up; intrigue, plot, scheme; manage, manipulate, negotiate; put (over), put (through), swing
idiom pull strings (*or* wires)

engird *vb syn* see BELT 1

engirdle *vb syn* see BELT 1

englut *vb syn* see GULP

engrave *vb* **1** to cut into a surface usually with a graving tool in order to form an inscription or a pictorial illustration < *engraved* a banknote design on the copper plate >
syn etch, grave, incise
rel chase, enchase; carve; inscribe
2 to impress deeply < the incident was *engraved* in his memory >
syn etch, impress, imprint, inscribe
rel carve; fix; instill; print; embed, entrench, infix, ingrain, root

engross *vb* **1** *syn* see WRITE
rel enscroll, scroll; superscribe
2 *syn* see MONOPOLIZE
rel apply, fill, occupy, preoccupy; assimilate, take up; arrest, engage, grip, ‖hog, hold, immerse, involve; attract, captivate, enthrall
con bewilder, distract; disperse, dissipate, scatter
3 *syn* see ENGAGE 4

engrossed *adj syn* see INTENT
rel consumed, monopolized, occupied; submerged; assiduous, busy, diligent, industrious, sedulous
idiom caught up in, lost in, taken up with
con detached, disinterested, indifferent, unconcerned, uninterested

engrossing *adj* gripping the attention completely so as to exclude everything else < the *engrossing* nature of his task made the time pass quickly >
syn absorbing, consuming, monopolizing
rel all-consuming, controlling, gripping; interesting, intriguing; exciting, provoking, stimulating; obsessing, preoccupying
con boring, drab, dull, monotonous; unentertaining, unexciting, uninteresting

engulf *vb syn* see DELUGE 1

enhance *vb* **1** *syn* see INTENSIFY
rel elevate, lift, raise; enlarge (upon), exaggerate, strengthen; augment, build (up), increase; adorn, beautify, embellish, embroider
con belittle, deprecate, detract, minimize
2 *syn* see FLATTER

enhancement *n syn* see ACCOMPANIMENT 1
rel improvement, intensification

enhearten *vb syn* see ENCOURAGE 1

enigma *n syn* see MYSTERY
rel crux, knot, puzzler, sticker; bewilderment, perplexity, question, question mark
idiom hard nut to crack

enigmatic *adj syn* see CRYPTIC

enisle *vb syn* see ISOLATE

enjewel *vb syn* see BEJEWEL

enjoin *vb* **1** *syn* see COMMAND
rel decree, dictate, impose, prescribe, rule; adjure, advise, counsel; admonish, caution, forewarn
con acquiesce, agree, comply, conform, obey, submit, yield
2 *syn* see FORBID
rel deny, disallow

enjoy *vb* **1** to take pleasure in or receive satisfaction from < *enjoyed* the meal >
syn ∥dig, go, like, ∥mind, relish
rel cotton (to); take (to); appreciate, dote (on *or* upon), fancy, love; delight (in), drink (in), eat up, luxuriate (in), savor
con abhor, abominate, detest, hate, loathe; condemn, despise, scorn
2 *syn* see HAVE 1
rel fill, occupy, maintain; boast, command

enjoyableness *n syn* see AMENITY 1
rel attractiveness, pleasingness, pleasurableness; niceness

enjoyment *n* **1** an attitude, circumstance, or favorable response to a stimulus that tends to make one gratified or happy < gave himself up to vigorous *enjoyment* of his pipe >
syn delectation, diversion, pleasure, relish; *compare* PLEASURE 2
rel delight, joy; amusement, entertainment; indulgence, savor; recreation, relaxation; gratification, satisfaction
con abhorrence, antipathy, aversion; repugnance, repulsion
2 *syn* see PLEASURE 2

enkindle *vb syn* see LIGHT 1

enlarge *vb* **1** *syn* see INCREASE 1
rel add (to), embroider, exaggerate; grow, stretch, widen
con attenuate; abridge; compress
2 *syn* see EXPAND 4
3 *syn* see INCREASE 2

enlargement *n syn* see EXPANSION 2

enlighten *vb syn* see ILLUMINATE 2
rel direct, educate, guide, inform, instruct, school, teach, train; acquaint, advise, apprise, inform
con bewilder, confuse, mystify, perplex, puzzle; addle, fuddle, muddle

enlightening *adj* tending to dissipate ignorance or increase knowledge and awareness < an *enlightening* glimpse of government in action >
syn illuminant, illuminating, illuminative, illumining
rel broadening, edifying, educational, instructive; clarifying, elucidative, explanatory
con unedifying, uninstructive; confusing, obfuscatory, obscuring

enlist *vb syn* see ENTER 3

enliven *vb syn* see QUICKEN 1
rel refresh, rejuvenate, renew, restore; excite, galvanize, invigorate, jazz (up), pep (up), provoke, stimulate; amuse, cheer, divert, entertain, recreate; exhilarate, fire, inspire
idiom give (new) life to
con depress, oppress, weigh
ant subdue

en masse *adv syn* see ALTOGETHER 3

enmesh *vb syn* see ENTANGLE 3
rel drag (into), draw (in), hook, tangle; embarrass, implicate
idiom make party to
con disembarrass, disentangle
ant extricate

enmeshment *n syn* see ENTANGLEMENT 1

enmity *n* deep-seated dislike or ill will or a manifestation of such feeling < the country had experienced generations of racial *enmity* >
syn animosity, animus, antagonism, antipathy, hostility, rancor
rel uncordiality, unfriendliness; alienation, dead set, disaffection, estrangement; abhorrence, detestation, dislike, hate, hatred, loathing; aversion; bad blood, bitterness, daggers, gall, ill will, malevolence, malice, malignancy, malignity, spite, spleen
con amicability, cordiality, friendliness, neighborliness; comity, empathy, friendship, goodwill, sympathy, understanding
ant amity

ennoble *vb syn* see EXALT 1

ennui *n syn* see TEDIUM
rel blues, dejection, depression, dumps, melancholy, sadness; boredom; fatigue, languidness, languor, listlessness, spiritlessness, tiredness, weariness; satiety, surfeit

ennui *vb syn* see BORE
con enliven, stimulate, vitalize

enormity *n* **1** the quality or state of being abnormally, monstrously, or outrageously evil < the utter *enormity* of the crime >
syn atrociousness, atrocity, heinousness, monstrousness
rel grossness, outrage, outrageousness, rankness; depravity; flagrancy
con excusableness, remissibility, veniality; bearableness, tolerability
2 the quality or state of being huge < the *enormity* of the task confounded him >
syn enormousness, hugeness, immensity, magnitude, tremendousness, vastness
rel bigness, greatness, massiveness; graveness, seriousness, weightiness
con diminutiveness, minuteness, smallness, tininess; triviality, unimportance

enormous *adj syn* see HUGE
rel stupendous
ant tiny

enormousness *n syn* see ENORMITY 2
rel monstrousness, prodigiousness, stupendousness

enough *adj syn* see SUFFICIENT 1

enough *adv* **1** in or to a degree or quantity that satisfies some condition < unstable *enough* to react with water >
syn adequately, sufficiently
rel abundantly, amply; acceptably, admissibly, satisfactorily; commensurately, proportionately
2 in a tolerable degree < she sang well *enough* >
syn averagely, fairly, moderately, passably, rather, so-so, tolerably
rel acceptably, decently, satisfactorily

enough *n* as much as is needed or wanted < we have *enough* for all of our needs >
syn adequacy, competence, sufficiency, sufficient
rel abundance, ampleness, plenty
con inadequateness; deficiency, deficit, lack, shortage, want; outage, ullage, wantage
ant inadequacy, insufficiency

enounce *vb syn* see ENUNCIATE 1

enrage *vb syn* see ANGER 1
idiom make one's blood boil, work up into a passion
ant placate

enrapture *vb syn* see TRANSPORT 2
rel elate, gladden, gratify, please, rejoice; allure, attract, captivate, charm, enchant, enthrall, fascinate

enravish *vb syn* see TRANSPORT 2

enrich *vb* to make financially rich or richer < *enriched* himself through speculation >
syn richen

enrichment *n syn* see ACCOMPANIMENT 1

enroll *vb* **1** to take in (as a person) by entering identification in a list, catalog, or roll < the school *enrolls* about 800 students >
syn list, register
rel enter, insert; catalog, inscribe, record; enlist, line (up), recruit, sign (up); join, matriculate
con discard, omit, reject
2 *syn* see LIST 3
3 *syn* see ENTER 3

ensample *n* **1** *syn* see MODEL 2
2 *syn* see EXAMPLE 3

ensanguined *adj syn* see BLOODY 1

ensconce *vb* **1** *syn* see HIDE
2 to establish or place firmly, comfortably, or snugly < was happily *ensconced* on the sofa before the fire >
syn install, settle
rel establish, fix, locate, place, plant, seat, set, situate, station

---

syn synonym(s)   *rel* related word(s)
ant antonym(s)   *con* contrasted word(s)
idiom idiomatic equivalent(s)
∥ use limited; if in doubt, see a dictionary

ensepulcher *vb syn* see ENTOMB 1

enshroud *vb syn* see ENFOLD 1
rel cloak, conceal, curtain, hide
con disclose, display, illustrate, open (up), reveal, show, uncover, unveil

ensign *n syn* see FLAG

enslave *vb* to reduce to and hold in a state of servitude <free peasants reduced to serfdom or *enslaved*>
syn enthrall, subjugate
rel disenfranchise, disfranchise; subject; oppress, shackle, yoke
con affranchise, enfranchise; free, liberate
ant emancipate

enslavement *n syn* see BONDAGE

ensnare *vb syn* see CATCH 3
rel decoy, entice, inveigle, lure; hook, net, snag; bag, capture

ensnarl *vb* 1 *syn* see ENTANGLE 1
2 *syn* see ENTANGLE 3

ensorcell *vb syn* see BEWITCH 1

ensorcellment *n syn* see MAGIC 1

ensphere *vb syn* see BALL

ensue *vb syn* see FOLLOW 1
rel derive, emanate, issue, proceed, stem; attend, result
idiom be subsequent (to), come next
con antecede, forerun, preface

ensuing *adj* 1 *syn* see SUBSEQUENT 1
2 *syn* see NEXT

ensure *vb* to make something certain or sure <provisions *ensuring* that the rank and file have a voice in union policy-making>
syn assure, cinch, insure, secure
rel certify, guarantee, warrant; arrange, establish, provide, set out

enswathe *vb syn* see SWATHE

entangle *vb* 1 to twist or interweave so as to make separation difficult <*entangled* the yarn>
syn ensnarl, intertangle, perplex, snarl, tangle
rel intertwine, interweave, ‖snirl, twist; ball up
2 *syn* see COMPLICATE
3 to catch or hold as if in a net from which escape is difficult <a firm hopelessly *entangled* in financial difficulties>
syn embrangle, enmesh, ensnarl, trammel; *compare* CATCH 3, INVOLVE 1
rel burden, clog, fetter, hamper, impede; bag, capture, catch, ensnare, entrap, snare, trap; discomfit, embarrass, embroil
con extricate, untangle; detach, disengage; clear, free; disburden, unfetter
ant disentangle
4 *syn* see CATCH 3

entanglement *n* 1 the condition of being deeply involved or closely linked often in an embarrassing or compromising way <*entanglements* with underworld figures tarnished his reputation>
syn embroilment, enmeshment, involvement; *compare* WEB 2
rel ensnarement; affair, intrigue, liaison; association, contact
2 *syn* see WEB 2

enter *vb* 1 to come or go into some place or thing <he *entered* the room>
syn come (in), go in, ingress, penetrate
rel pierce, probe
idiom set foot in
con egress, exit, go out, leave; come out, emerge, sally; escape, flee
ant issue
2 to cause or permit to go in or into <*enter* synonyms in a thesaurus>
syn admit, introduce
rel inject, insert, intercalate, interpolate, put (in), set down; docket, inscribe, list, post, record, register; enroll
3 to make or become a member of <decided to *enter* the army>
syn enlist, enroll, join (up), muster, sign on, sign up
rel come (into), go (into)
idiom get oneself into, take up (*or* out) membership (in)
4 *syn* see BEGIN 1

enterprise *n* 1 *syn* see ADVENTURE
rel attempt, effort, endeavor, striving, struggle; campaign, cause, project, pursuit, task, undertaking; deed
2 *syn* see PROJECT 2
rel speculation

3 a unit of economic or business organization or activity <an economy encouraging the expansion of small, privately owned *enterprises*>
syn business, company, concern, establishment, firm, house, outfit
rel interest; organization; corporation; industry
4 readiness to attempt or engage in what requires energy or daring <complained about his brother's lack of *enterprise*>
syn ambition, drive, get-up-and-go, initiative, push; *compare* VIGOR 2
rel ambitiousness, eagerness, energy, enthusiasm, ‖hustle, vigor; boldness, courage, daring, venturesomeness; inventiveness, self=reliance
con languor, lethargy; indolence, laziness, sloth; apathy, inertia

enterprising *adj* 1 *syn* see ENERGETIC 2
rel aggressive, ambitious, busy, eager, hustling, pushing, up=and-coming; adventurous, venturesome
2 showing initiative, resolution, and determined effort (as in pursuing a course or a career) <an *enterprising* young man likely to go far>
syn go-ahead, gumptious, up-and-coming
rel aggressive, pushing; diligent, hardworking, industrious, zealous; ambitious, aspiring, craving, hungry, itching, lusting, yearning; audacious, daring, dashing, venturesome
idiom on one's toes
ant unenterprising

entertain *vb* 1 *syn* see HARBOR 2
rel invite; admit, receive; cherish, cultivate, foster; feed, nourish
con banish, eject, throw out; ignore, neglect
2 *syn* see AMUSE
rel delight, enliven, gladden, gratify, please, regale, rejoice

entertainment *n* something diverting, amusing, or entertaining <staged a floor show as *entertainment* for her guests>
syn amusement, dissipation, distraction, diversion, divertissement, recreation
rel disport, play, sport; enjoyment, gaiety, pleasure; relaxation, relief

enthrall *vb* 1 *syn* see ENSLAVE
rel master, subdue
con emancipate
2 to hold spellbound <told mystery stories that *enthralled* his playmates>
syn catch up, fascinate, grip, hold, mesmerize, spellbind
rel absorb, engage, preoccupy; charm, enchant, engross, intrigue
con bore, ennui, weary

enthuse *vb* 1 *syn* see THRILL
2 to show great enthusiasm <tourists *enthusing* over the medieval towns>
syn drool, rave, rhapsodize, rhapsody
con censure, criticize; belittle, depreciate, disparage, dispraise, knock, undervalue

enthusiasm *n* 1 *syn* see PASSION 6
rel craze, fascination, infatuation, mania
con impassivity, phlegm, stolidity; aloofness, detachment, indifference, unconcern
ant apathy
2 *syn* see EAGERNESS
rel earnest, interest; ebullience, élan

enthusiast *n* a person who manifests extreme and often uncritical ardor, fervor, or devotion in an attachment <an increasing number of ecology *enthusiasts*>
syn bigot, bug, fanatic, fiend, freak, maniac, nut, zealot
rel addict, aficionado, buff, bum, devotee, fan, habitué, lover, votary; partisan, supporter; bear, extremist
con depreciator, detractor, disparager, knocker

enthusiastic *adj* filled with or marked by enthusiasm <was *enthusiastic* about golf>
syn ‖buggy, ‖bugs, gung ho, keen, nutty, warm, zealous
rel ardent, devoted, eager, fervent, hearty, spirited; gaga, ‖gone (on), hopped-up; hipped, obsessed; passionate, vascular; rabid
con apathetic, detached, indifferent, reluctant, uninterested
ant unenthusiastic

entice *vb syn* see LURE
con alarm, fright, frighten (off), terrify
ant scare (off)

enticement *n syn* see LURE 2

enticing *adj* being extremely and often dangerously attractive <she looked at him with an *enticing* smile>

syn Circean, fetching, luring, tempting
rel attractive, beguiling, bewitching, enchanting, fascinating, intriguing, inviting, siren, witching; captivating; likable, pleasant, pleasing

entify *vb syn* see MATERIALIZE 2

entire *adj* **1** *syn* see WHOLE 3
rel all, gross; plenary
con incomplete, unfinished; limited, qualified
ant partial
2 *syn* see WHOLE 1
rel concatenated, integrated; compacted, consolidated, unified
con broken (up); faulty
ant impaired
3 *syn* see WHOLE 4

entirely *adv* **1** *syn* see WELL 3
2 *syn* see ONLY 1

entireness *n* **1** *syn* see ENTIRETY 1
con incompleteness
2 *syn* see INTEGRITY 2

entirety *n* **1** the state of being complete <the striking *entirety* and self-sufficiency of the feudal community>
syn allness, completeness, entireness, oneness, totality, wholeness
rel collectiveness, unity; integrity, plenitude; comprehensiveness, omneity, universality
con disunity, division, separateness; fragmentation, incompleteness
2 *syn* see WHOLE 1
rel collectivity, complex, everything
con component, detail, element, item, part
ant particular

entitle *vb* **1** *syn* see NAME 1
2 to furnish with proper authority or grounds for seeking or claiming something <this ticket *entitles* the bearer to free admission>
syn authorize, qualify
rel empower, license; allow, enable, let, permit

entity *n* **1** one that has real and independent existence <each *entity* of the series requires separate study>
syn being, existence, existent, individual, something, thing
rel body, object
2 *syn* see THING 4
3 *syn* see WHOLE 2

entomb *vb* **1** to deposit in or as if in a tomb <relics *entombed* in pyramids>
syn ensepulcher, sepulcher, sepulture, tomb; *compare* BURY 1
rel bury, inhume, inter, ‖plant; inurn; enshrine, shrine
con dig (up), disinhume, disinter, exhume, unbury
ant disentomb
2 *syn* see BURY 1

entombment *n* *syn* see BURIAL 2

entourage *n* one's attendants or subordinates <the queen's *entourage*>
syn following, retinue, suite, train
rel associates, attendants, courtiers, followers, retainers; hangers-on, sycophants, toadies

entrails *n pl* the internal organs of the body <some of the *entrails* are valued as food>
syn gut(s), innards, insides, internals, inwards, ‖pudding(s), stuffing, tripes, viscera
rel bowels, intestines; vitals; giblets, pluck, purtenance

entrammel *vb syn* see HAMPER
con assist, expedite, facilitate; extricate

entrance *n* **1** the act or fact of going in or coming in <awaited the *entrance* of the army into the city>
syn entry, ingress, ingression
rel arrival, coming, incoming, ingoing; penetration
con departure, egress, emergence, emerging, emigration, exit
ant egression, exiting
2 *syn* see DOOR 1
rel access, aperture, opening, threshold
ant exit
3 *syn* see DOOR 2
rel open door

entrance *vb syn* see TRANSPORT 2
rel gladden, please, rejoice; attract, bewitch, captivate, charm, enchant, fascinate; enthrall, hypnotize, spellbind
con disappoint, disgust, repel, repulse; bore

entranced *adj syn* see ENAMORED 3

entranceway *n syn* see DOOR 1

entrap *vb* **1** *syn* see CATCH 3
2 *syn* see LURE

entreat *vb syn* see BEG
rel blandish, coax, wheedle; pester, plague, press, urge

entreaty *n syn* see PRAYER

entrée *n syn* see DOOR 2
rel introduction; open door

entrench *vb* **1** to establish so solidly or strongly as to make dislodgment or change extremely difficult <prejudices *entrenched* for generations>
syn embed, fix, infix, ingrain, lodge, root
rel found, ground; implant; confirm, define, establish, settle, strengthen
con eliminate, eradicate, root out, uproot; banish, cast out, eject, expel; remove
ant dislodge
2 *syn* see TRESPASS 2
rel interfere, intervene
idiom break in upon, stick one's nose into

entrenched *adj syn* see INVETERATE 1

entrepreneur *n* **1** one who owns, launches, manages, and assumes the risks of an economic venture <theatrical *entrepreneurs* making fortunes from successful shows>
syn undertaker
rel organizer; backer, impresario; contractor; administrator, manager; producer; promoter
2 *syn* see GO-BETWEEN 2

entrust *vb* **1** to confer a trust upon <*entrusted* him with responsibility for completing the work>
syn charge, trust
rel confer, impose; delegate, relegate; allocate, allot, assign
2 *syn* see COMMIT 1
rel deliver, deposit, leave, trust; bank, count, depend, reckon, rely
idiom give in trust

entry *n* **1** *syn* see ENTRANCE 1
2 *syn* see DOOR 1
rel access, opening, threshold
con egress
ant exit
3 *syn* see DOOR 2

entryway *n syn* see DOOR 1
rel threshold
con egress
ant exit

entwine *vb syn* see WIND 2
rel entangle, entwist, interlace, interplait, intertwine, interweave; enmesh
con uncoil, undo, unravel, untwine, untwist, unwind, unwrap; straighten (out)

enumerate *vb* **1** *syn* see COUNT 1
2 to specify one after the other <*enumerated* the advantages of his position>
syn list, numerate, tick off
rel run (over), tell off; identify, mention, recite, recount, relate, specify
3 *syn* see ITEMIZE 1

enunciate *vb* **1** to make a definite or systematic statement of <was the first to *enunciate* the modern principle of inertia>
syn enounce, state
rel develop, formulate, outline, postulate; advance, lay down, submit; announce, declare, proclaim; affirm; show
idiom set forth
2 *syn* see ARTICULATE 2
rel express, intone, modulate, vocalize, voice

envelop *vb* **1** *syn* see ENFOLD 1
rel cloak, hide, mask
2 *syn* see SWATHE
3 *syn* see ENCLOSE 1
rel guard, protect, shield

envenom *vb syn* see EXACERBATE

---

syn synonym(s)
ant antonym(s)
idiom idiomatic equivalent(s)
rel related word(s)
con contrasted word(s)
‖ use limited; if in doubt, see a dictionary

envious *adj* maliciously grudging another's advantages < *envious* of her rival's charm >
   syn envying, green-eyed, invidious, jealous
   rel coveting, covetous, grasping, greedy; begrudging, grudging; appetent, desirous, longing, yearning; resentful, umbrageous
   idiom green with envy
   con benign, benignant; generous, kind; tolerant; unconcerned, uninterested

enviousness *n syn* see ENVY

environ *vb syn* see SURROUND 1
   rel enclose, fence, go (around)

environment *n* surrounding or associated matters that influence or modify a course of development < the socioeconomic *environment* in Germany that produced Hitler >
   syn ambience, ambient, atmosphere, climate, medium, milieu, mise-en-scène, surroundings
   rel habitat; backdrop, background, context, setting; situation, status

environs *n pl* 1 an enclosing line or margin < several thousand businesses located within the *environs* of the city >
   syn bound(s), boundary, compass, confine(s), limits, precinct(s), purlieus; *compare* LIMIT 1
   rel fringes
   2 the suburban areas or districts around a city or heavily populated area < a new system of parks for the national capital and its *environs* >
   syn outskirt(s), purlieus, suburbs
   rel locality, neighborhood, vicinity; surroundings

envisage *vb syn* see THINK 1
   rel behold, grasp, look (upon), picture, regard, survey, view; externalize, materialize, objectify; foresee
   idiom form a mental picture of, have a picture of, picture to oneself, view in the mind's eye

envision *vb syn* see THINK 1
   rel call up, conjure up, summon up; picture, view; foresee
   idiom have a mental picture of, picture to oneself, view in the mind's eye

envoy *n* 1 a representative with a rank between an ambassador and a minister resident who is accredited to a foreign government < the President received the *envoy* from Spain >
   syn envoy extraordinary, minister plenipotentiary
   rel ambassador, attaché, chargé d'affaires, consul, councillor, internuncio, legate, minister, nuncio; diplomat
   2 *syn* see MESSENGER

envoy extraordinary *n syn* see ENVOY 1

envy *n* spiteful malice and resentment over another's advantage < his lavish life-style provoked *envy* among his colleagues >
   syn enviousness, invidiousness, jealousy
   rel covetousness; grudging; resentment

envy *vb* to experience envy < while she outwardly criticized her sister's looks, she secretly *envied* them >
   syn begrudge, grudge
   rel covet, crave, desire, hanker, long, want, yearn
   idiom be green with envy

envying *adj syn* see ENVIOUS

enwrap *vb* 1 *syn* see SWATHE
   2 *syn* see ENFOLD 1
   rel enswathe, swaddle, swathe; sheathe

ephemeral *adj syn* see TRANSIENT
   rel brief, short, temporary, unenduring; episodic
   idiom here today and gone tomorrow
   con endless, enduring, eternal, everlasting, lasting
   ant perpetual

epicene *adj syn* see EFFEMINATE

epicure *n* one who takes great and fastidious pleasure in eating and drinking < was a real *epicure*, and his dinners were excellent >
   syn bon vivant, gastronome, gastronomer, gastronomist, gourmand, gourmet
   rel amateur, connoisseur, epicurean; glutton, ravener; high liver

epicurean *adj syn* see SENSUOUS

epidemic *n* the sudden widespread occurrence of something felt to resemble an epidemic disease < an *epidemic* of art forgeries >
   syn outbreak, plague, rash; *compare* OUTBREAK 1

epigrammatic *adj syn* see PITHY

epilogue *n* 1 the final part that rounds out or completes the design of a nondramatic literary work < the author wrote an *epilogue* to his book explaining that some of his earlier impressions were wrong >
   syn afterword
   rel postlude; conclusion, ending
   con prelude; foreword, introduction, preface
   ant prologue
   2 something that resembles an epilogue in rounding out or giving point to something else < an incident that can be regarded as an *epilogue* to the history of Roman Britain >
   syn sequel
   rel follow-up, postscript
   ant prologue

episode *n syn* see OCCURRENCE

epistle *n syn* see LETTER 2
   rel communication

epitaph *n* an inscription on a tombstone in memory of the one buried there
   syn hic jacet

epitome *n* 1 *syn* see ABRIDGMENT
   2 *syn* see SUMMARY
   3 *syn* see APOTHEOSIS 1

epitomize *vb* 1 to make or give an epitome of < a report which *epitomizes* one of the most complex theories of all time >
   syn condense, digest, inventory, nutshell, sum, summarize, summate, sum up, synopsize
   rel boil down, capsulize; outline, tabulate
   con elaborate, enlarge (on), expand
   2 to serve as the typical representation or ideal expression of < he *epitomized* safe, dull conservatism >
   syn exemplify, typify
   rel embody, incarnate, incorporate, personify, represent, symbolize
   3 *syn* see REPRESENT 2

epitomized *adj syn* see CONDENSED

epoch *n syn* see PERIOD 2
   rel interval, term

epochal *adj* uniquely or highly significant < had to make an *epochal* decision: whether or not to declare war >
   syn momentous
   rel consequential, far-reaching, important; unmatched, unparalleled
   con inconsequential, minor, petty, small-time, trivial, unimportant

equable *adj syn* see STEADY 2
   rel methodical, orderly, regular, systematic; immutable, invariable, unchangeable; equal, equivalent, same
   con variable; fitful, spasmodic
   ant inequable, unequable

equal *adj* 1 *syn* see SAME 2
   rel equable, even, uniform; alike, like; commensurate, corresponding, proportionate
   idiom one and the same
   con different, disparate, divergent, diverse, varied; unalike, unequable, uneven; irregular
   ant unequal
   2 *syn* see FAIR 4
   idiom without distinction
   con discriminating, discriminative, unfair
   ant inequitable
   3 *syn* see EVEN 3
   4 *syn* see EVEN 4
   5 *syn* see PROPORTIONAL

equal *n* one that is equal to another in status, achievement, value, meaning, or effect < he has no *equal* in common sense and honesty >
   syn counterpart, equivalent, like, match; *compare* OPPOSITE NUMBER, PARALLEL
   rel companion, fellow, mate, peer; alter ego, double, twin; competitor, rival; similar

equal *vb* 1 *syn* see AMOUNT 2
   rel compare, parallel; accord, agree, square, tally; reach
   idiom amount to the same thing
   2 *syn* see EVEN 2
   3 to make or produce something equal to (as in quality or value) < *equal* that if you can >
   syn match, measure up, meet, rival, tie, touch
   rel beat, top

equality *n syn* see EQUIVALENCE

equalize *vb* 1 to make equal in amount, degree, or status < *equalize* educational opportunities >

syn equate, even
rel balance, level, square
2 *syn* see EVEN 2
equally *adv* **1** *syn* see EVENLY 1
2 *syn* see EVENLY 2
equanimity *n* the characteristic quality of one who is self-possessed and not easily disturbed or perturbed < faced disaster with bland *equanimity* >
syn ataraxy, calmness, composure, coolness, imperturbability, phlegm, sangfroid, self-possession; *compare* CONFIDENCE 2
rel balance, equilibrium, equipoise, poise; aplomb, assurance, confidence, self-assurance; detachment; placidity, serenity, tranquillity
con alarm, anxiety, apprehension; excitability, nervousness; agitation, discomposure, disquiet, disturbance, perturbation
equatability *n* *syn* see EQUIVALENCE
equate *vb* **1** *syn* see EQUALIZE 1
2 to treat, represent, or regard as equal, equivalent, or comparable < *equated* retreat with cowardice >
syn assimilate, compare, liken, match, paragon, parallel
rel associate, relate, similize; consider, hold, regard, represent, treat
equidistant *adj* *syn* see MIDDLE 1
equilibrium *n* *syn* see BALANCE 1
rel stabilization, steadiness, steadying; counterbalance, counterpoise
con top-heaviness
equip *vb* *syn* see FURNISH 1
rel provide, supply; fit (out), rig (up *or* out), turn (out); gear, prepare, qualify
equipment *n* items needed for the performance of a task or useful in effecting an end < the *equipment* for the polar expedition included ships, instruments, sleds, dogs, and supplies >
syn accouterment(s), apparatus, gear, habiliments, machinery, material(s), matériel, outfit, paraphernalia, tackle, tackling
rel accessories, appurtenances, attachments, fittings, trappings; baggage, belonging(s), impedimenta, rig, things, traps; equipage, provisioning, provisions
equipoise *n* *syn* see BALANCE 1
rel counterbalance, counterpoise, counterweight
equiponderation *n* *syn* see BALANCE 1
equitable *adj* **1** *syn* see FAIR 4
rel level, stable; equivalent, identical, same
idiom fair and square
con discriminatory
ant inequitable, unfair
2 *syn* see EVEN 3
equity *n* *syn* see JUSTICE 1
rel equitableness, justness
con bias, discrimination, partiality, unfairness
ant inequity
equivalence *n* the state or property of being equivalent or the result of making equivalent < the *equivalence* of paper money and coins >
syn adequation, equality, equatability, equivalency, par, parity, sameness
rel likeness; compatibility, correlation, correspondence; exchangeability, interchangeability
con discrepancy, disparity, divergence, incompatibility, inequality, unlikeness
ant difference
equivalency *n* *syn* see EQUIVALENCE
equivalent *adj* **1** *syn* see SAME 2
rel commensurate, proportionate; convertible, correlative, corresponding, parallel, reciprocal, substitute
con disparate, divergent, diverse, various; discordant, discrepant, incompatible, inconsonant
ant different
2 *syn* see LIKE
equivalent *n* *syn* see EQUAL
rel obverse, reciprocal, substitute; parallel
equivocal *adj* **1** *syn* see OBSCURE 3
rel hazy, indistinct; doubtful, dubious, questionable; indeterminate, multivocal
idiom clear as mud
con clear, distinct, understandable; categorical, explicit, unambiguous, univocal; certain, conclusive
ant unequivocal

2 characterized by a mixture of opposing feelings < an *equivocal* attitude toward the expensive proposal >
syn ambivalent
rel uncertain, undecided
idiom having mixed (*or* divided) feelings
con assured, certain, decided, sure
3 *syn* see DOUBTFUL 1
rel disreputable
idiom open to question
con credible
equivocality *n* *syn* see AMBIGUITY
equivocate *vb* **1** *syn* see LIE
rel elude, escape, evade
2 to avoid committing oneself by speaking evasively < he'd rather be brutally frank with them than *equivocate* on that issue >
syn dodge, evade, hedge, pussyfoot, shuffle, sidestep, tergiversate, tergiverse, weasel; *compare* SKIRT 3
rel cavil, prevaricate, quibble; fence, parry; avoid, elude, eschew
idiom beat around (*or* about) the bush, beg the question, mince words
equivocating *adj* *syn* see EVASIVE 1
rel deceptive, delusive, misleading
equivocation *n* **1** *syn* see AMBIGUITY
rel hedging; coloring, distortion, misrepresentation; deceit, dissimulation, duplicity
ant explicitness
2 *syn* see FALLACY 2
rel haggling, quibbling; fib, fibbing, lie, lying
equivoque *n* *syn* see AMBIGUITY
era *n* *syn* see PERIOD 2
rel term; stage
eradicate *vb* *syn* see ANNIHILATE 2
rel demolish, destroy, raze; liquidate, purge
con establish, fix, set; implant, inculcate, instill; breed, engender, generate, propagate
erase *vb* to eliminate or neutralize with or as if with a stroke of the pen < time has *erased* their sad memories > < *erase* an error >
syn annul, black (out), blot out, cancel, delete, efface, expunge, obliterate, wipe (out), x (out)
rel disannul, negate, nullify; abolish, blank (out), cross (off *or* out), cut out, dele, eliminate, excise, extirpate, rub out, scrape, sponge (out), strike (out); neutralize; remove, take out, withdraw
con impress, imprint, print, stamp; insert; reinstate, renew, restore
ere *prep* *syn* see BEFORE 1
erect *adj* standing up straight < the dog's *erect* ears pricked forward >
syn arrect, raised, stand-up, straight-up, upright, upstanding
rel erectile; elevated, lifted, upraised; perpendicular, standing, vertical
con decumbent, flat, prostrate, recumbent; drooping, hanging, pendent
erect *vb* **1** *syn* see BUILD 1
2 *syn* see MAKE 3
rel compose, create; make up, run up
con demolish, destroy, tear up, unbuild, wreck
3 to fix in an upright position < *erected* a flagpole >
syn put up, raise, rear, set up; *compare* BUILD 1
rel elevate, heighten, hoist, lift, upraise, uprear; upend
4 *syn* see EXALT 1
idiom put on a pedestal
ant abase
5 to bring into existence as if by raising a building < *erect* social barriers along religious lines >
syn build up, construct, establish, hammer (out), set up
rel fabricate, fashion, forge, form, shape; bring about, effect
con break down, tear down; liquidate, purge; dispose (of), eliminate, remove
erection *n* *syn* see EDIFICE
eremitic *adj* *syn* see ANTISOCIAL

---

syn synonym(s)   *rel* related word(s)
ant antonym(s)   *con* contrasted word(s)
idiom idiomatic equivalent(s)
‖ use limited; if in doubt, see a dictionary

ergo *adv syn* see THEREFORE
erode *vb* **1** *syn* see EAT 3
  rel crumble, decay, deteriorate, disintegrate; consume
  2 *syn* see ABRADE 1
  rel grate, rub (off *or* away), scrape (off *or* away)
erotic *adj* of, devoted to, affected by, or tending to arouse sexual love or desire < *erotic* art >
  syn amative, amatory, amorous, aphrodisiac
  rel ardent, fervent, fervid, impassioned, lovesome, passionate; earthy; carnal, epicurean, fleshly, voluptuous; bawdy, sexy, spicy; concupiscent, lecherous; lascivious, lewd, lickerish, prurient, salacious, sensual
eroticism *n syn* see LUST 2
err *vb* to depart from a standard (as of wisdom or morality) < the human tendency to *err* >
  syn deviate, stray, wander
  rel miscalculate; lapse, slip (up), stumble, trip; transgress, trespass; offend; sin
  idiom go astray (*or* amiss *or* wrong), leave the straight and narrow
errable *adj syn* see FALLIBLE
errant *adj* **1** *syn* see ERRATIC 1
  rel drifting, itinerant, meandering, rambling, ranging, roaming, roving, shifting, straying
  con static, unmoving
  2 deviating from an accepted pattern or standard < a parent scolding his *errant* child >
  syn aberrant, devious, erring
  rel deviating, straying, wandering; misbehaving, mischievous, naughty
  idiom off the straight and narrow
  3 *syn* see FALLIBLE
  rel aberrant, erring; unreliable
  con perfect, trustworthy
  ant inerrant
erratic *adj* **1** moving about aimlessly or irregularly without a fixed course < an *erratic* breeze barely stirred the leaves of the tree >
  syn devious, errant, stray, wandering
  rel curving, meandering, roundabout, winding; shifting, undirected
  con fixed, stable, unmoving; active, animated, brisk, lively, sprightly
  ant static
  2 *syn* see UNCERTAIN 1
  rel doubtful, dubious
  ant stable
  3 *syn* see ARBITRARY 1
  rel changeable, inconsistent, inconstant, unpredictable, variable; mercurial, unstable, volatile
  con consistent, conventional, predictable, stable
  4 *syn* see STRANGE 4
  rel anomalous, irregular, unnatural
  con natural, normal, regular, typical; customary, usual
erring *adj syn* see ERRANT 2
erroneous *adj* **1** *syn* see FALSE 1
  rel amiss, askew, awry, off; defective; mistaken
  idiom all off, all wrong, way off the mark
  con right, true
  ant accurate, correct
  2 *syn* see MISTAKEN
erroneousness *n syn* see FALLACY 1
  rel inaccurateness, mistakenness
  con accuracy, accurateness, rightness
  ant correctness
error *n* **1** an often unintentional deviation from truth or accuracy < made an *error* in adding the figures >
  syn mistake, x
  rel inaccuracy; miscalculation, miscomputation; oversight, slip
  2 something (as an act, statement, or belief) that departs from what is or is generally held to be acceptable < spying on the opposing party proved to be a grave *error* >
  syn blooper, blunder, boner, bull, bungle, fluff, lapse, miscue, misstep, mistake, rock, slip, slipup, trip; *compare* FAUX PAS
  rel bevue, fault, misdoing, misjudgment, stumble; ‖boo-boo, botch, fumble, muff; howler, screamer; impropriety, indecorum
  3 *syn* see FALLACY 1
  rel misreading, misunderstanding; delusion, illusion
errorless *adj syn* see IMPECCABLE 1

con imprecise, inaccurate, incorrect, unexact, wrong
ersatz *adj syn* see ARTIFICIAL 2
  rel factitious, synthetic; fake
ersatz *n syn* see IMITATION
erstwhile *adv syn* see BEFORE 2
erstwhile *adj syn* see FORMER 2
eruct *vb* **1** *syn* see BELCH 1
  idiom bring up gas
  2 *syn* see ERUPT 1
eructate *vb syn* see BELCH 1
erudite *adj syn* see LEARNED
  rel lettered, well-read; studious
  ant illiterate
eruditeness *n syn* see ERUDITION 2
erudition *n* **1** *syn* see EDUCATION 2
  2 the quality or state of being erudite < a scholar of great cultivation and *erudition* >
  syn eruditeness, learnedness, scholarliness, scholarship
  rel cultivation, culture, education, intellectuality, literacy; bookishness, pedantry, studiousness
  ant illiteracy
erupt *vb* **1** to give off or release (as something pent up) forcefully < the volcano *erupted* gouts of lava >
  syn belch, disgorge, eject, eruct, expel, irrupt, spew
  rel cast (out *or* up), hurl, throw off; boil, discharge, emit; jet, spout, spurt; extravasate
  2 to break away or burst from limits or restraint < riots *erupted* in the ghetto >
  syn break out, burst (forth), explode
  rel detonate, touch off; go off
eruption *n* **1** *syn* see OUTBURST 1
  2 *syn* see OUTBREAK 1
escalade *vb syn* see ASCEND 1
  con clamber (down), climb (down); go (down)
escalate *vb* **1** *syn* see ASCEND 1
  2 to increase in extent, volume, amount, number, intensity, or scope < a little war threatens to *escalate* into a huge, ugly one >
  syn expand, grow
  rel broaden, enlarge, heighten, increase, intensify, spread, widen
  con decrease, limit, minimize; constrict, contract, narrow; collapse, shrink, shrivel
  ant de-escalate
escapade *n* a usually adventurous action that runs counter to approved or conventional conduct < childish *escapades* on Halloween >
  syn caper, lark, rollick; *compare* PRANK
  rel antic, frolic, vagary; prank; fling, spree; mischief, roguery
escape *vb* **1** to run away especially from something that limits one's freedom and threatens one's well-being < trying to *escape* from prison >
  syn abscond, break, ‖bunk, decamp, flee, fly, scape
  rel get away, make off, mosey, run away; bail out, ‖ditch, double, duck out, flit, jump, skip; depart; disappear, vanish
  idiom cut and run, cut loose, fly the coop, take it on the lam
  con come back, return; abide, remain, stay; chase, follow, pursue, tag, trail
  2 to get away or keep away from what one does not wish to incur, endure, or encounter < made every effort to *escape* suspicion >
  syn avoid, bilk, double, duck, elude, eschew, evade, shun, shy; *compare* SHAKE 5, SKIRT 3
  rel burke, bypass, circumvent; dodge, shake, shun, skit; miss
  idiom fight shy of, give the slip
  con catch, contract, incur; abide, bear, brook, endure, stand, suffer, tolerate; dare, face, meet
escape *n* **1** the act or fact of escaping or having escaped physically < succeeded in making his *escape* from the prison >
  syn breakout, escapement, escaping, flight, getaway, lam, ‖scape, slip
  rel departure; deliverance, liberation, release
  con return; grasp, grip, hold, retention; imprisonment, incarceration
  2 the act or fact of escaping or having escaped what one does not wish to incur, encounter, or endure < sought *escape* from responsibility >
  syn avoidance, come-off, elusion, escaping, eschewal, evasion, runaround, shunning
  rel bypassing, circumvention, dodging, ducking, sidestepping; elusiveness, evasiveness

con abidance, abiding, bearing, endurance, enduring, submission, submitting, toleration; facing

escapement *n syn* see ESCAPE 1

escaping *n* **1** *syn* see ESCAPE 1
  2 *syn* see ESCAPE 2

eschew *vb* **1** *syn* see ESCAPE 2
  idiom shy away from, steer clear of
  con adopt, embrace, espouse
  ant choose
  2 *syn* see FORGO
  rel abstain, refrain
  idiom let well enough alone

eschewal *n syn* see ESCAPE 2
  rel shirking; shying

escort *n* **1** a boy or man who goes on a date with a girl or woman <had her pick of *escorts* to the dance>
  syn date
  rel beau, boyfriend, fellow; cavalier, gallant, squire, vis-à-vis
  2 a person who leads or directs another or others in a way or course (as through difficult terrain) <served as our *escort* when we drove through the desert>
  syn guide
  rel attendant, companion, guard

escort *vb* **1** *syn* see ACCOMPANY
  2 *syn* see GUIDE
  rel bring; squire

escritoire *n syn* see DESK

esculent *adj syn* see EDIBLE

esoteric *adj syn* see RECONDITE

especial *adj* **1** *syn* see SPECIAL 1
  rel preeminent, supreme, surpassing; dominant, paramount, predominant, preponderant; exceptional, notable, singular, unusual
  con unexceptional, usual
  ant general
  2 *syn* see EXPRESS 2

especially *adv* **1** in a special way <was *especially* good at math>
  syn distinctively, particularly, special, specially, specifically
  rel remarkably, unusually; exceptionally, markedly, peculiarly, singularly, uniquely; eminently, notably, preeminently, supremely
  idiom before all else
  2 *syn* see EXPRESSLY 2

espial *n syn* see DISCOVERY

espionage *n* systematic secret observation in order to accumulate information <agents engaged in industrial *espionage* >
  syn spying
  rel observation, reconnaissance, sleuthing, surveillance, watching

espousal *n* **1** *syn* see ENGAGEMENT 2
  2 *often* **espousals** *pl syn* see WEDDING
  3 *syn* see MARRIAGE
  rel mating; union
  idiom getting hitched, taking on the ball and chain, tying the knot
  con estrangement, separation
  4 ready acceptance of or the taking up of a cause or belief <his wholehearted *espousal* of left-wing philosophies worried his family>
  syn adoption, embracement, embracing
  rel acceptance, approval; advocacy; aid, promotion, support
  con denial, rejection; disapproval, dislike, distaste; antipathy, aversion, intolerance
  ant repudiation

espouse *vb* **1** *syn* see MARRY 1
  2 *syn* see ADOPT
  rel accept, approve; advocate, back, champion, support, uphold
  con abandon, desert, forsake; deny, reject; disapprove, dislike
  ant repudiate

esprit *n* **1** *syn* see SPIRIT 5
  rel acumen, acuteness, brains, brightness, cleverness, intelligence, mind, quick-wittedness, sharpness, wit; courage, mettle, tenacity; fervor, passion
  2 *syn* see MORALE
  rel camaraderie, fellowship; devotion, loyalty; enthusiasm, fervor, passion
  3 *syn* see WIT 5

esprit de corps *n syn* see MORALE
  rel camaraderie, comradeship, fellowship; partisanism, partisanship; devotion, loyalty; enthusiasm, spirit

espy *vb* **1** *syn* see SEE 1
  rel recognize, take in; sight, spot, spy; witness
  idiom catch sight of, get a load of
  2 *syn* see FIND 1
  rel spy; make out; notice

essay *vb syn* see TRY 5
  rel venture; labor, toil, travail, work
  idiom give it a try (*or* fling *or* go), have at it, make a stab at, take a crack (*or* whack) at

essay *n* **1** *syn* see ATTEMPT
  rel exertion; labor, toil, travail, work; go, venture
  2 a relatively brief discourse written for others' reading or consideration <an *essay* on free will>
  syn article, composition, paper, theme
  rel discourse, discussion, explication, exposition, study; piece; tract, treatise; dissertation, thesis

essence *n* **1** a basic underlying or constituting entity, substance, or form <succeeds in conveying completely the cruel *essence* of loneliness>
  syn being, essentia, essentiality, nature, texture
  rel entity, form, substance
  2 the most basic, significant, and indispensable element, attribute, quality, property, or aspect of a thing <the very *essence* of Machiavellianism is the belief that in politics there is neither good nor evil>
  syn be-all and end-all, bottom, essentiality, marrow, pith, quintessence, quintessential, rock bottom, root, soul, stuff, substance, virtuality; *compare* BODY 3, CENTER 2, SUBSTANCE 2
  rel timber; element, fiber, property; aspect, attribute, quality, spirit; inwardness, significance; crux, gist, kernel, nub, nubbin; distillate, distillation

essentia *n syn* see ESSENCE 1

essential *adj* **1** *syn* see INHERENT
  con conditional, contingent, dependent
  ant accidental
  2 so important to the nature and essence of a thing as to be indispensable <the *essential* ingredient in this medicine is a new drug>
  syn cardinal, constitutive, fundamental, vital
  rel basal, basic, underlying; capital, chief, foremost, leading, main, principal; primal, primary, prime
  con dependent, secondary, subordinate; accessory, auxiliary, contributory, subsidiary
  3 *syn* see ELEMENTAL 1
  4 urgently required <raw materials *essential* to industry>
  syn imperative, indispensable, necessary, necessitous, prerequisite
  rel needed, needful; required, requisite, wanted; right-hand; vital
  con dispensable, unnecessary, unneeded, unrequired, unwanted
  ant nonessential

essential *n* **1** something that forms part of the minimal body, character, or structure of a thing <prosperity is an *essential* of the good life>
  syn basic, element, fundamental, part and parcel, rudiment
  rel essence, stuff, substance; must, necessary, prerequisite, sine qua non
  2 something necessary, required, or unavoidable <work was an *essential* to survival>
  syn condition, must, necessity, precondition, prerequisite, requirement, requisite, sine qua non
  idiom name of the game

essentiality *n* **1** *syn* see ESSENCE 1
  2 *syn* see ESSENCE 2

essentially *adv* **1** in regard to the essential points <*essentially* the problem is this: he is unreliable>
  syn au fond, basically, fundamentally, in essence
  rel actually, really
  idiom at bottom
  2 *syn* see ALMOST 2
  rel substantially, virtually
  idiom in the main

establish *vb* **1** *syn* see SET 1

---

syn synonym(s)   *rel* related word(s)
ant antonym(s)   *con* contrasted word(s)
idiom idiomatic equivalent(s)
‖ use limited; if in doubt, see a dictionary

rel enroot, entrench, implant, inculcate, infix, instill, root; set down, set up; moor, rivet, secure; found, ground
con eradicate, exterminate, extirpate, uproot, wipe (out)
ant abrogate
2 syn see BASE
idiom lay the foundation for (*or* of)
3 syn see ENACT 1
rel formulate; authorize, decree, legislate, prescribe
ant repeal
4 syn see FOUND 2
rel endow, provide; originate; build
con disestablish; demolish, tear down
ant abolish
5 syn see ERECT 5
6 to make clear beyond a reasonable doubt < *established* an alibi for the time of the crime >
syn demonstrate, determine, make out, prove, show
rel authenticate, confirm, corroborate, document, substantiate, verify; attest; clarify
idiom afford (*or* offer) proof of
con discredit, expose, show up; confute, invalidate, parry, rebut, refute
ant disprove
established *adj syn* see FIRM 3
establishment *n* **1 syn** see ENTERPRISE 3
rel workplace; institute, institution; foundation
2 *often cap* a group of influential leaders who represent an established order of society < the literary *establishment* >
syn Old Guard
rel conservative(s), diehard(s)
con liberal(s)
estate *n* **1 syn** see ORDER 9
rel form, state
2 a class of people in a community distinguishable by social or political duties or privileges < a party platform appealing to people of every *estate* >
syn grade, rank
rel bracket, category; footing, level, order, standing; place, position, station; caste, class
3 an extensive landed property < spent the weekend at his country *estate* >
syn acres, land, manor, quinta
rel farm, ranch; plantation; villa
esteem *n syn* see REGARD 4
rel approval, liking; appreciation, valuation
ant abomination
esteem *vb* **1 syn** see APPRECIATE 1
rel idolize, revere, worship
idiom hold dear, think the world of
ant despise
2 syn see ADMIRE 2
rel revere, venerate
idiom hold in esteem (*or* high regard)
con abhor
ant abominate
estimable *adj* **1 syn** see WORTHY 1
2 syn see RESPECTABLE 1
rel admired, esteemed, respected
con disreputable, unworthy; bad
3 syn see HONORABLE 1
estimate *vb* **1** to judge something with respect to its worth < *estimated* the value of the jewels >
syn appraise, assay, assess, evaluate, rate, set (at), survey, valuate, value
rel adjudge, adjudicate, judge; ascertain, determine, discover; price, prize; decide, settle
2 syn see CALCULATE
rel cast, sum; count, enumerate
3 to fix some value (as size, distance, or composition) more or less accurately < *estimated* the rainfall at over six inches >
syn approximate, call, judge, place, put, reckon
rel round, round off; conjecture, guess, suppose, surmise; fancy, imagine; deduce, infer
con calculate, compute; measure
estimate *n* **1** the act of appraising or valuing the nature, character, quality, status, or worth of something < his influence as President is beyond *estimate* >
syn appraisal, appraisement, assessment, estimation, evaluation, valuation

rel calculation, measurement, reckoning; sizing up; projection
2 syn see ESTIMATION 1
idiom point of view
estimation *n* **1** the result of evaluating something < his *estimation* of the man's ability proved incorrect >
syn appraisal, appraisement, assessment, estimate, evaluation, judgment, stock
rel impression; opinion
2 syn see COMPUTATION
3 syn see ESTIMATE 1
4 syn see REGARD 4
estrange *vb* to cause one to break a bond or tie of affection or loyalty < her arrogance *estranged* her children and friends >
syn alien, alienate, disaffect, disunify, disunite, wean
rel break up, divide, divorce, part, separate, sever, split, sunder
idiom set at odds
con appease, conciliate, pacify, propitiate; associate, espouse, join, link, unite
ant reconcile
estrangement *n* the act of estranging or the condition of being estranged < a petty dispute resulted in total *estrangement* >
syn alienation, disaffection
rel division, divorce, schism; withdrawal
con appeasement, conciliation, propitiation
ant reconciliation
etceteras *n pl syn* see SUNDRIES
etch *vb* **1 syn** see ENGRAVE 1
2 to set forth in a sharp, clear-cut manner with minute attention to detail < the most sharply *etched* character in the novel >
syn define, delineate
rel outline, set forth; depict, describe, picture, portray, represent
3 syn see ENGRAVE 2
eternal *adj* **1 syn** see INFINITE 1
rel endless, interminable, unceasing, unending; lasting, permanent, perpetual; deathless, immortal, undying
con ephemeral, evanescent, momentary, passing, short-lived, temporary, transient
ant mortal
2 syn see EVERLASTING 1
rel deathless, undying
3 syn see CONTINUAL
con interrupted, sporadic
4 valid or existing unaltered at all times < right and wrong are *eternal* verities that cannot be changed >
syn ageless, dateless, intemporal, timeless
rel immemorial, lasting, perdurable, permanent, perpetual; immutable, inalterable, unalterable, unchangeable, unchanging
con alterable, changeable, changing, fluctuating, varying; debatable, questionable, suspect
eternalize *vb syn* see PERPETUATE
eternally *adv syn* see EVER 2
eternity *n* **1** a totality of infinite time < in *eternity* there is no change or passing away >
syn infinity, sempiternity
rel endlessness, infiniteness, infinitude, perpetuity, timelessness
con ephemerality, impermanence, transience; limitedness, restrictedness
ant finiteness
2 unending existence after death < belief in the *eternity* of our spiritual nature >
syn afterlife, everlastingness, eviternity, immortality, world-without-end
3 syn see AGE 2
idiom forever and a day, forever and ever
eternize *vb syn* see PERPETUATE
ethereal *adj syn* see AIRY 3
rel celestial, empyreal, empyrean, heavenly; vaporish, vaporlike, unsubstantial; filmy, gossamer; delicate, fragile, light
con heavy, thick
ant substantial
ethic *n* **1 ethics** *pl but usu sing in constr* the discipline dealing with what is good and bad and with moral duty and obligation < *ethics* has been called the science of the ideal of human character >
syn morals
2 a group of moral principles or set of values < the Christian *ethic* >

syn morality, morals, mores

3 ethics *pl* the code of conduct or behavior governing an individual or a group (as the members of a profession) < medical *ethics* >
syn principles
rel moralities, morals, mores; criteria, standards
4 the complex of ideals, beliefs, or standards that characterizes or pervades a group, community, or people < the American work *ethic* >
syn ethos
rel belief, ideal, standard, value

ethical *adj syn* see MORAL 1
rel high-principled; elevated; upright, upstanding
con flagitious, iniquitous, nefarious; improper, indecent, indecorous, unbecoming, unseemly; immoral, low

ethnic *adj* **1** *syn* see HEATHEN
rel non-Christian, unchristian
2 of, relating to, or originating from the traits shared by members of a group as a product of their common heredity and cultural tradition < only a person thoroughly familiar with Yiddish can recognize the *ethnic* quality of the pun > < *ethnic* cookery >
syn racial
rel national; tribal

ethos *n syn* see ETHIC 4

etiquette *n* **1** *syn* see MANNER 5
2 *syn* see DECORUM 1
rel behavior, conduct, deportment, manners; amenities, civilities, formalities; convention, form, protocol
idiom social graces

eulogistic *adj* of, relating to, characterized by, or bestowing praise < the speaker made *eulogistic* remarks on the group's accomplishment >
syn encomiastic, laudative, laudatory, panegyrical, praiseful
rel approbatory, approving, commendatory, complimentary
con uncomplimentary; critical, disapproving, disparaging; abusive
ant dyslogistic

eulogize *vb syn* see PRAISE 2
rel applaud; belaud, bepraise
idiom praise to the skies, sing the praises of
ant vilify

eulogy *n syn* see ENCOMIUM
rel adulation, glorification
con calumny, slander
ant vilification

euphemism *n* an agreeable or inoffensive expression that is substituted for one that might offend or suggest unpleasantness < vandalism that goes under the *euphemism* of souvenir hunting >
syn nice Nelly, nice-nellyism
ant dysphemism

euphonic *adj syn* see MELODIOUS 1
euphonious *adj syn* see MELODIOUS 1
euphoria *n* **1** *syn* see ELATION 1
ant deflation, dysphoria
2 an often groundless or excessive feeling of well-being and happiness < drug-induced *euphoria* >
syn elation, exaltation, intoxication
rel ecstasy, frenzy; madness; glee
con anxiety, unease, uneasiness
ant depression

euphuistic *adj syn* see RHETORICAL
rel elaborate; colorful; verbose; elevated
con concise, simple, straightforward; lean

evacuee *n syn* see REFUGEE

evade *vb* **1** *syn* see ESCAPE 2
rel flee, fly, slip (away); foil, outwit, thwart
idiom keep (*or* know) one's distance
con accost, confront, dare, face
2 *syn* see EQUIVOCATE 2
rel bypass, circumvent, duck; parry, turn (aside)
idiom give (someone) the runaround
con confront, face; elucidate, explain

evaluate *vb* **1** *syn* see ESTIMATE 1
rel appreciate; class, gauge, rank; criticize
2 *syn* see CLASS 2

evaluation *n* **1** *syn* see ESTIMATE 1
rel interpreting; judging, rating

2 *syn* see ESTIMATION 1
rel appreciation; interpretation; decision

evanesce *vb syn* see VANISH
rel disintegrate, dispel, disperse, dissipate, dissolve, scatter
idiom go up in smoke, vanish into thin air
con appear; coalesce
ant materialize

evanescent *adj syn* see TRANSIENT
rel temporary; flying; dissolving, fading, melting; disappearing, vanishing

evangelical *adj* characterized by or reflecting a missionary, reforming, or redeeming impulse or purpose < a mood of *evangelical* nationalism >
syn crusading, evangelistic
rel ardent, fervid, impassioned, militant, zealous; missionary, propagandizing, proselytizing

evangelist *n syn* see MISSIONARY

evangelistic *adj syn* see EVANGELICAL
rel missionary, reforming

evangelize *vb syn* see PREACH 1

evanish *vb syn* see VANISH
idiom pass out of the picture

evaporate *vb syn* see VANISH
rel escape, pass (away *or* off); weaken; vaporize
idiom go pouf

evasion *n syn* see ESCAPE 2
rel dodging, equivocating, equivocation, evading, excuse, subterfuge; haggling, quibbling; escapism
con confrontation, confronting; daring
ant facing

evasive *adj* **1** tending to evade or avoid confrontation < his answers were ambiguous and *evasive* >
syn equivocating, prevaricative, prevaricatory, shifty, shuffling
rel ambiguous, equivocal, unclear, vague; sliding, slippery, sly
con categorical, definite, explicit, unambiguous, univocal; candid, forthright
ant direct
2 *syn* see ELUSIVE

even *adj* **1** *syn* see LEVEL
con bent, crooked, curved, twisted
ant uneven
2 *syn* see STEADY 2
rel equal, identical, same; consistent, continual, continuous, undeviating, unvaried
3 giving no advantage to either side < an *even* exchange >
syn equal, equitable, fair
rel balanced, fair and square, square; honest, straightforward, unprejudiced
con inequitable, unequal, unfair
ant uneven
4 being nicely in balance < his chances for success or failure are *even* >
syn equal, even-up, fifty-fifty
rel balanced, comparable, proportionate
con disproportionate, unbalanced
ant uneven
5 being neither more nor less than the named or understood amount, extent, or number < an *even* mile >
syn exact, square
con approximate, imprecise, inaccurate

even *adv* **1** in a like manner < they can learn *even* as others do >
syn as well, exactly, expressly, just, precisely
2 at the very time < perhaps *even* now the moment has come to consider a retreat >
syn already
3 not this merely but also — used as an intensive to emphasize the identity or character of something < a huge, *even* monstrous animal >
syn indeed, nay, truly, verily, yea
rel absolutely, positively; quite, really
4 — used as an intensive to indicate an extreme, hypothetical, or unlikely case or instance < refused *even* to look at her > < *even* if this were so, it should not change our plans >

---

syn synonym(s)   **rel** related word(s)
ant antonym(s)   **con** contrasted word(s)
idiom idiomatic equivalent(s)
‖ use limited; if in doubt, see a dictionary

syn so much as
idiom even so much as
5 syn see YET 1

even *vb* **1** to make (as a surface) smooth, even, level, or flat <*even* the soil with a spade>
syn flatten, flush, lay, level, plane, smooth, smoothen
rel grade, roll; align; symmetrize; uniform; pancake
con rough, roughen
2 to make even or balanced in advantage <hoped to *even* the odds by training>
syn equal, equalize
rel balance, square
con unbalance, unequalize, upset; derange, disarrange
3 syn see EQUALIZE 1

evening *n* **1** the closing part of day and the early part of night <the last light of *evening* >
syn ‖dimmet, ‖dimps, ‖dimpsy, dusk, ‖dusk dark, eventide, gloaming, nightfall, owl-light, twilight
rel afternoon; sundown, sunset; duskiness, duskness
con sunrise; dawn
ant morning
2 a latter portion or a period of decline <in the *evening* of life>
syn sunset, twilight
3 a party taking place in the evening <their *evenings* were notable affairs>
syn soiree
rel reception; salon; party

evenly *adv* **1** in equal parts <a career divided *evenly* between stage and screen>
syn equally, fifty-fifty, squarely
rel commensurably, proportionately
con disproportionately, unequally
ant unevenly
2 in a just or fair manner <she was *evenly* polite to everyone>
syn equally, impartially
rel fairly, justly
con unfairly, unjustly
3 without variation or fluctuation <spread the paint *evenly* >
syn flatly, smooth, smoothly, uniformly
con irregularly, roughly
ant unevenly

event *n* **1 syn** see OCCURRENCE
rel act, action, deed; achievement, exploit, feat; accident, chance, fortune
2 a matter worthy of remark <the trip was an *event* in their dull routine>
syn milepost, milestone, occasion
rel affair, landmark; delight, treat
idiom historic event
con insignificancy, trifle, triviality
3 syn see EFFECT 1
rel offshoot, outgrowth; product, resultant, sequent
idiom end result
4 a postulated outcome, condition, or contingency <in the *event* of rain, we will not meet>
syn case, eventuality
rel chance, fortuity, hap, happenstance
5 any of the contests in a sports program <track-and-field *events*>
syn match, meet
rel competition, contest
6 syn see FACT 2

eventide *n* **syn** see EVENING 1

eventual *adj* **syn** see LAST
rel consequent, ensuing, inevitable, succeeding; ending, endmost
con antecedent, beginning, inceptive, initial, original

eventuality *n* **1 syn** see EVENT 4
rel contingency, possibility
2 syn see EFFECT 1
con antecedent, beginning, root

eventually *adv* **syn** see YET 2
idiom in the long run

even–up *adj* **syn** see EVEN 4

ever *adv* **1 syn** see ALWAYS 1
2 through all or an indefinite time <a name that will *ever* be respected>
syn always, eternally, evermore, forever, forevermore, in perpetuum

3 in each and every case <war and suffering have *ever* gone hand in hand>
syn invariably
rel consistently, regularly, usually
4 at any time or on any occasion <he is seldom if *ever* absent>
syn anytime, at all
5 in any way <nor was it *ever* important>
syn anyway, anywise, at all, once
6 — used as an intensive after an inverted verb-subject construction <is he *ever* proud of himself>
syn confoundedly, consumedly, excessively, extremely, immensely, inordinately, over, overfull, overly, overmuch, super, too, unduly
rel annoyingly, plaguey; grievously, mortally; consummately

ever and again *adv* **syn** see SOMETIMES

ever and anon *adv* **syn** see SOMETIMES

everlasting *adj* **1** lasting or enduring through all time <*everlasting* laws governing the physical universe>
syn amaranthine, ceaseless, endless, eternal, immortal, never-ending, unending, world-without-end; *compare* IMMORTAL 1
rel lasting, perdurable, permanent, perpetual; boundless, infinite, limitless, termless
con ephemeral, evanescent, momentary, short-lived, transitory
2 syn see CONTINUAL
con interrupted, off-and-on, periodic, sporadic

everlastingness *n* **syn** see ETERNITY 2

evermore *adv* **syn** see EVER 2

evert *vb* **syn** see DISPROVE 1

every *adj* **syn** see ALL 2

everybody *pron* every person <*everybody* must do what his conscience dictates>
syn all, everyman, everyone
idiom all and sundry
ant nobody

everyday *adj* **1 syn** see COMMON 4
con distinctive, singular, unique; uncommon, unusual
ant exceptional
2 syn see PROSAIC 3
3 syn see ORDINARY 1

everyman *pron* **syn** see EVERYBODY
idiom the man in the street

everyone *pron* **syn** see EVERYBODY
ant no one

everyplace *adv* **syn** see EVERYWHERE 1
idiom all over the place

everything *pron* the whole amount <lost *everything* in the fire>
syn all
idiom all in all, the lot, the whole bit (*or* shebang), the whole kit and kaboodle, the works

everywhere *adv* **1** in every place or in all places <poverty anywhere is a danger to peace and prosperity *everywhere* >
syn all over, all round (*or* all around), everyplace, far and near, far and wide, high and low, overall, throughout
idiom in all quarters, in every quarter
2 syn see WHEREVER

evict *vb* **syn** see EJECT 1
rel dislodge, dispossess, force (out), put out, shut out, turn out
idiom turn (*or* put) out bag and baggage, turn out of doors, turn out of house and home
con harbor, house, lodge, shelter

evidence *n* **1 syn** see INDICATION 3
2 syn see TESTIMONY

evidence *vb* **syn** see SHOW 2
rel display, expose; attest, bespeak, betoken, confirm, indicate, prove, testify

evident *adj* **syn** see CLEAR 5
rel noticeable, prominent, pronounced
idiom as plain as the nose on one's face, plain as day
con inconspicuous; ambiguous, unapparent, unrecognizable; concealed, hidden
ant inevident

evidently *adv* **syn** see OSTENSIBLY

evil *n* **1** whatever is harmful, distressing, or disastrous <attempts to grasp the nature of *evil* >
syn ill
rel bad, badness, devilry, diablerie, diabolism, evilness, satanism, satanity, wickedness, wrong

con goodness, virtue
ant good
2 whatever is morally unacceptable < return good for *evil* >
syn debt, sin, wickedness, wrong
rel evildoing, misconduct, sinfulness, wrongdoing
con rectitude, righteousness, virtue
ant good
3 a particular thing (as an act) that is evil < choose the lesser of two *evils* >
syn crime, diablerie, iniquity, sin, tort, wrong, wrongdoing
rel badness, evilness, maleficence, vice, wickedness; misdeed, offense

evil *adj* **1** *syn* see WRONG 1
rel base, low, vile; flagitious, nefarious; baneful, pernicious; black, damnable, execrable
con high, noble; exemplary, salutary
ant good
2 *syn* see OFFENSIVE
rel distasteful, repellent; fetid, putrid, stinking
3 *syn* see MALICIOUS
rel angry, disagreeable, ugly, unpleasant, wrathful; harmful, hurtful, injurious, mischievous; destructive
4 *syn* see HARMFUL
rel calamitous, destructive, disastrous
con harmless, noninjurious
ant innocuous
5 reporting or predicting harm or misfortune < messengers bearing *evil* tidings >
syn bad, ill, unfavorable; *compare* OMINOUS
rel baleful, baneful, inauspicious; ill-boding, ill-omened, ominous
con auspicious, favorable
ant good
6 marked by misfortune or calamity < the family fell upon *evil* times >
syn bad, inauspicious
rel unfavorable, unfortunate, unlucky; difficult, hard, trying; calamitous, disastrous
con favorable; lucky; easy, prosperous; auspicious, halcyon, happy
ant good

evince *vb* **1** *syn* see SHOW 2
rel argue, attest, bespeak, betoken, confirm, indicate, prove; display, exhibit, expose, illustrate, signify
con repress, suppress; conceal, hide
2 *syn* see EDUCE 1
rel bring (about), cause; provoke, stimulate

eviscerate *vb* to take out the entrails of < *eviscerate* a turkey >
syn bowel, disembowel, draw, embowel, exenterate, gut, paunch

eviternity *n* *syn* see ETERNITY 2

evocative *adj* serving or tending to call something (as a mood) forth < conduct *evocative* of the utmost contempt >
syn evocatory, suggestive
rel meaningful, pregnant, weighty; arousing, moving, stimulating, stirring; causing, effecting, inducing, producing

evocatory *adj* *syn* see EVOCATIVE

evoke *vb* *syn* see EDUCE 1
rel excite, provoke, stimulate; arouse, awaken, rally, rouse, stir, waken; call forth, call up, conjure (up), raise, summon (forth *or* up)

evolution *n* *syn* see DEVELOPMENT
rel change, transformation

evolve *vb* **1** *syn* see DERIVE 1
rel get (at), obtain; advance
2 *syn* see UNFOLD 3
rel advance, progress; mature, open (up), ripen

evolvement *n* *syn* see DEVELOPMENT
rel metamorphosis, transformation

evulse *vb* *syn* see EXTRACT 1

exacerbate *vb* to cause to become increasingly bitter or severe < foolish words that only *exacerbated* the quarrel >
syn acerbate, embitter, envenom
rel annoy, exasperate, irritate, provoke; aggravate, heighten, intensify; inflame
idiom add fuel to the flame, fan the flames, feed the fire, pour oil on the fire
con appease, mollify, pacify, placate, quell; lessen, moderate
ant assuage

exact *vb* **1** *syn* see EXTORT 1
2 *syn* see LEVY
3 *syn* see DEMAND 1
rel coerce, compel, constrain, force, oblige; extort, extract, squeeze, wrest, wring

exact *adj* **1** *syn* see CORRECT 2
2 *syn* see EVEN 5
ant imprecise, inexact
3 *syn* see SAME 1
4 *syn* see CAREFUL 2
5 *syn* see PRECISE 4

exacting *adj* *syn* see ONEROUS
rel rigid, rigorous, severe, stern, strict, stringent; finicky, fussy, particular; critical, hypercritical
con laissez-faire, lenient
ant unexacting

exactitude *n* *syn* see PRECISION

exactly *adv* **1** *syn* see JUST 1
rel ‖plumb, plunk; specifically
idiom on the dot (*or* nose), right on the nail
con about, around, more or less, roughly
ant approximately
2 *syn* see ALL 1
rel absolutely, expressly, positively; completely
3 as you say or state — used to express agreement or concurrence < "You are accusing me of lying?" he asked. "*Exactly*," she replied. >
syn precisely, yes
idiom quite so, (that's) for sure (*or* certain)
4 *syn* see EVEN 1

exactness *n* *syn* see PRECISION

exaggerate *vb* *syn* see EMBROIDER
rel hyperbolize, overcolor, romance, romanticize
idiom blow up out of (all) proportion, draw the long bow, make the eagle scream
ant understate

exaggeration *n* an overstepping of the bounds of truth < the passage shows the author's penchant for grotesque *exaggeration* >
syn coloring, embellishment, embroidering, hyperbole, overstatement
rel aggrandizement, amplification, enlargement; overcoloring, overdrawing, romance, stretching
idiom flight of fancy, tall talk
con minimizing, underestimation
ant understatement

exalt *vb* **1** to enhance the status of < propaganda that *exalts* nationalism to the level of religion >
syn aggrandize, dignify, distinguish, ennoble, erect, glorify, honor, magnify, pedestal, stellify, sublime, uprear
rel boost, build up, elevate, lift, promote, raise, upgrade, uplift; enhance, heighten, intensify; acclaim, enhalo, extol, laud, praise; apotheosize
con debase, degrade, demean, humble, humiliate; belittle, decry, depreciate, derogate, detract, disparage, downgrade, minimize
ant abase
2 *syn* see FIRE 2
rel pique, stimulate, quicken; deepen, enhance, sharpen; encourage, inspirit, spirit (up), uplift

exaltation *n* **1** *syn* see APOTHEOSIS 2
rel upgrading, uplifting; extolment, laudation, praise
con debasement, degradation, demeanment, humiliation; belittlement, depreciation, derogation, disparagement, downgrading
ant abasement
2 *syn* see ELATION 1
rel delectation, delight; bliss, joy, rapture
ant deflation
3 *syn* see EUPHORIA 2
ant depression

exalted *adj* **1** raised to or having high rank < moved in *exalted* circles > < Alexander was *exalted* to the papal throne in 1492 >
syn astral, highest, highest-ranking, top-drawer, top-ranking
rel august, noble; eminent, illustrious, prominent; high, high-ranking; foremost, number one; first, leading, outstanding

---

syn synonym(s)   *rel* related word(s)
ant antonym(s)   *con* contrasted word(s)
idiom idiomatic equivalent(s)
‖ use limited; if in doubt, see a dictionary

con low, lowly, low-ranking, unimportant; minor; humble, plebeian
ant abject
2 syn see GRAND 3
ant abject

examination *n* a careful, detailed, and often formal study designed to uncover pertinent information < the doctor gave him a physical *examination* >
syn analysis, audit, check-over, checkup, inspection, perlustration, review, scan, scrutiny, survey, view
rel assay, breakdown, diagnosis, dissection; sifting, winnowing; canvass, catechization, inquiry, questioning, quizzing, testing

examine *vb* **1 syn** see SCRUTINIZE 1
rel check (out), go (over), investigate, look (into); contemplate, look (at *or* over), observe
idiom give a going over, give the once-over, go over with a fine-toothed comb
2 syn see TRY 1
3 syn see ASK 1
rel cross-examine; grill; pump
idiom give the third degree to, put to the question

example *n* **1 syn** see INSTANCE
2 syn see MODEL 2
idiom shining example
3 an instance that illustrates a rule or provides practice in its application < worked out his arithmetic *examples* >
syn ensample, illustration, problem
idiom case in point

exanimate *adj* *syn* see DEAD 1

exasperate *vb* *syn* see IRRITATE
rel agitate, work up
idiom try one's temper (*or* patience)
ant appease; mollify

exasperation *n* **1 syn** see ANNOYANCE 2
rel irritation, vexation; displeasure; resentment
2 syn see ANNOYANCE 3

ex cathedra *adj* *syn* see OFFICIAL

excavate *vb* **1 syn** see DIG 1
rel gouge (out), hollow (out), scoop (out), scrape (out), quarry (out)
2 syn see DIG 2

exceed *vb* **1** to go or be beyond a natural or set limit < the policeman *exceeded* his authority > < this task *exceeds* my powers >
syn outstep, overrun, overstep, surpass
rel outreach, overreach; dare, presume, venture
2 syn see SURPASS 1

exceedingly *adv* *syn* see VERY 1

excel *vb* *syn* see SURPASS 1

excellence *n* something that gives especial worth or value < the particular *excellence* of this cake is its lightness >
syn arete, excellency, merit, perfection, quality, virtue
rel value, worth; distinction, fineness, superiority; goodness, niceness, superbness; class
con blemish, defect, flaw; failing, foible, frailty, vice
ant fault

excellency *n* *syn* see EXCELLENCE

excellent *adj* meritoriously near the standard or model and eminently good of its kind < an *excellent* restaurant specializing in French cuisine >
syn A1, bang-up, banner, blue-ribbon, ‖boss, bully, ‖bunkum, capital, champion, classic, classical, ‖dandy, famous, fine, first-class, first-rate, first-string, five-star, front-rank, Grade A, number one, par excellence, prime, quality, royal, skookum, ‖slap-up, sovereign, stunning, superior, ‖swingeing, top, top-notch, whiz-bang; *compare* MARVELOUS 2, SUPREME
rel high-class, high-grade, proper; ‖rum; distinguished, exceptional, premium; brag, incomparable, magnificent, nobby, sensational, smart, superb, superlative, terrific, tip-top, unsurpassed
idiom all wool and a yard wide, beyond compare, out of this world
con mediocre; bad, inadequate, inferior, low, low-grade, low-quality, substandard; fourth-rate, second-class, second-rate; poor, shoddy, sorry, unsatisfactory, wretched; commonplace, mediocre, ordinary
ant execrable

except *vb* **1 syn** see EXCLUDE
rel omit, pass over; exempt; reject

con incorporate, receive, work in
ant admit
2 syn see OBJECT 1

except *prep* with the exclusion or exception of < *except* Christmas, we had no long holiday >
syn apart from, aside from, bar, barring, bating, beside, besides, but, ‖cep, except for, excluding, exclusive of, outside, outside of, save, saving

except *conj* **1** on any other condition than that < wouldn't go near that woman *except* I had to >
syn but, save, saving, unless, ‖without
2 syn see ONLY

except for *prep* *syn* see EXCEPT

exceptionable *adj* *syn* see OBJECTIONABLE
con unimpeachable; exemplary
ant unexceptionable

exceptional *adj* **1** being out of the ordinary < an *exceptional* opportunity >
syn extraordinary, phenomenal, rare, remarkable, singular, uncommon, uncustomary, unimaginable, unique, unordinary, unthinkable, unusual, unwonted; *compare* STRANGE 4
rel infrequent, scarce; distinct, exceptional, notable, noteworthy
con frequent; common, commonplace, familiar, ordinary, usual
ant unexceptional
2 syn see SUPERIOR 4
rel good; excellent, marvelous, outstanding, phenomenal, wonderful; extraordinary, singular, special
con common, ordinary, run-of-the-mill
ant average

exceptionally *adv* *syn* see VERY 1
rel especially, particularly; extraordinarily, unusually; marvelously, phenomenally, stupendously, wonderfully

excerpt *vb* to select (passages or details) as typical of a larger store < quotations *excerpted* from many authors >
syn extract
rel cull, glean; choose, pick, pick out, select, single; cite, quote

excess *n* **1** whatever exceeds a limit, measure, bound, or accustomed degree < the proper balance between sufficiency and *excess* >
syn fat, overabundance, overflow, overkill, overmuch, overplus, plethora, superfluity, surfeit, surplus, surplusage
rel overbalance, overspill; oversupply; profusion; superabundance
idiom enough and then some, enough and to spare, too much of a good thing
con insufficiency, lack, scarcity
ant deficiency; dearth
2 the amount or degree by which a thing or number exceeds another < an *excess* of 10 bushels over what was needed >
syn overage, overstock, oversupply, plus, surplus, surplusage
rel overproduction; overmeasure
ant deficit, shortfall
3 *often* **excesses** *pl* undue or immoderate personal indulgence especially in eating and drinking < *excess* at table is seldom healthful > < his *excesses* led to his failure in business >
syn immoderation, inordinateness, intemperance, overindulgence
rel extravagance, overdoing; indulgence, self-indulgence; immoderacy, immoderateness; dissipation, prodigality, Saturnalia
con moderation; sobriety, temperateness; restraint, self-discipline, self-restraint
ant temperance

excess *adj* *syn* see SUPERFLUOUS
rel redundant; unessential

excessive *adj* **1** going beyond a normal or acceptable limit < spend an *excessive* amount on clothes >
syn dizzy, exorbitant, extravagant, extreme, immoderate, inordinate, sky-high, steep, stiff, stratospheric, supernatural, towering, unconscionable, undue, unmeasurable
rel boundless, limitless, unbounded; over, overboard, overmuch, overweening; super
idiom out of bounds
con exiguous, meager, narrow, scant, scanty, skimpy, sparse, tight
ant deficient
2 given to personal excesses < an *excessive* drinker, often drunk and never quite sober >
syn immoderate, inordinate, intemperate, overindulgent, unrestrained, untempered

rel extravagant; indulgent, self-indulgent; dissipated, prodigal
con conservative, moderate, sober, temperate
ant restrained

excessively *adv syn* see EVER 6
exchange *vb* **1** *syn* see TRADE 1
2 to give up, taking in return something else < *exchanged* his uniform for civilian clothes >
syn change, substitute, swap, switch, trade; *compare* TRADE 1
rel displace, replace
3 to give and receive reciprocally < *exchanged* a few words with his neighbor >
syn bandy, interchange
rel pay back, reciprocate
idiom give as much as one takes, give tit for tat, return the compliment

exchangeable *adj syn* see INTERCHANGEABLE
exchequer *n syn* see TREASURY 2
excise *vb* to remove by or as if by dissecting < *excise* a tumor > < *excised* some wordy passages >
syn cut out, exsect, extirpate, resect
rel amputate, cut off; elide, remove, strike out; eradicate, root out; delete, expurgate, exscind, slash

excitable *adj* easily excited < an *excitable* child who needs a firm hand >
syn agitable, alarmable, combustible, edgy, skittery, skittish, startlish, volatile
rel high-strung, mercurial, temperamental, unstable; touchy
idiom like a bundle of nerves, likely to go off at half cock, on edge, on the ragged edge
con calm, collected, cool, easy, easygoing, phlegmatic, placid, quiet
ant unexcitable

excite *vb* **1** *syn* see PROVOKE 4
rel agitate, discompose, disquiet, disturb, perturb, stir up; impassion; charge (up), energize, touch off, turn on
idiom set astir, set on fire, stir the blood
con allay, placate, soothe
ant quiet
2 *syn* see ELATE
rel move; fire
con depress, dishearten
3 *syn* see INTEREST

excited *adj syn* see INTOXICATED 2
rel animated, atwitter; agitated, charged (up), inflamed, pink; delighted, enthusiastic
idiom all fired up, all of a twitter, beside oneself
con apathetic, unmoved; deflated
ant unexcited

exciting *adj* absorbingly interesting < the most *exciting* day of her life > < an *exciting* personality >
syn exhilarant, exhilarating, exhilarative, eye-popping, inspiring, intoxicating, rousing, stimulating, stirring
rel arresting, interesting, intriguing; moving, provocative; heady, thrilling
con blah, dull, uninteresting, unintriguing; humdrum, monotonous, tedious
ant unexciting

exclaim *vb* to speak or utter suddenly and usually sharply, vehemently, or passionately < *exclaimed* in delight at the sight of the toy >
syn blat, blurt (out), bolt, cry out, ejaculate
rel burst (out); roar, snort

exclude *vb* to prevent the participation, consideration, or inclusion of < *excluded* that subject from discussion >
syn bar, bate, count out, debar, eliminate, except, rule out, suspend
rel ban; close out, estop, obviate, preclude, prevent, prohibit, ward (off); blackball, blacklist, ostracize; block; disbar; lock out, put out, shut out
idiom close (or shut) the door on
con comprehend, involve; embrace, take in
ant admit; include

excluding *prep syn* see EXCEPT
exclusionary *adj syn* see EXCLUSIVE 1
exclusive *adj* **1** having or exercising the power to limit or exclude < a tangle of *exclusive* laws >
syn exclusionary, exclusory
rel barring, debarring, excluding; limitative, limiting, restrictive; preclusive, prohibitive

con free, unlimited, unrestricted, unrestrictive
ant admissive
2 *syn* see SELECT 1
rel aristocratic, elite, preferred, privileged, tony; aloof, clannish, cliquish, cliquy; high-hat, snobbish, standoffish
con catholic, cosmopolitan, universal; common, familiar, ordinary, popular, vulgar
ant inclusive
3 *syn* see STYLISH
con tasteless; frumpy, unfashionable
4 *syn* see SOLE 4
rel individual, lone, only
con common, general, public
5 *syn* see WHOLE 5
con divided, partial

exclusive *n syn* see SCOOP
exclusively *adv syn* see ONLY 1
rel completely, wholly; particularly
exclusive of *prep syn* see EXCEPT
exclusory *adj syn* see EXCLUSIVE 1
excogitate *vb* **1** *syn* see CONSIDER 1
2 *syn* see DERIVE 1
rel contrive, invent, think (up); develop, think (out)
excoriate *vb* **1** *syn* see CHAFE 3
2 *syn* see LAMBASTE 3
idiom tear into
excorticate *vb syn* see SKIN 2
excrescence *n syn* see OUTGROWTH 1
excrescency *n syn* see OUTGROWTH 1
excruciate *vb syn* see AFFLICT
rel inflame, irritate; hurt, pain, wound; convulse
idiom prolong the agony

excruciating *adj* intensely or unbearably painful < his suffering was *excruciating* >
syn agonizing, harrowing, racking, tearing, tormenting, torturing, torturous
rel acute, extreme; piercing, sharp, shooting, stabbing; consuming, rending

exculpate *vb* to free from alleged fault or guilt < the court *exculpated* him after a thorough investigation >
syn absolve, acquit, clear, disculpate, exonerate, vindicate
rel explain, justify, rationalize; condone, excuse, forgive, pardon, remit; amnesty, free, let off
idiom clear the (or one's) record, wipe the slate clean
con blame, censure, denounce, reprehend, reprobate; incriminate; accuse, charge; arraign, indict; impeach; convict
ant inculpate

excurse *vb syn* see DIGRESS 2
excursion *n* **1** a trip not involving a prolonged or definite separation from one's usual abode or way of life < an afternoon *excursion* to the city >
syn jaunt, junket, outing, roundabout, sally
rel expedition, journey, trek, trip, safari; circuit, tour; one-way trip, pleasure trip, round trip; ||pasear, paseo, walk, ||walkabout
2 *syn* see DIGRESSION

excursus *n syn* see DIGRESSION
excusable *adj* **1** *syn* see VENIAL
2 *syn* see JUSTIFIABLE
excuse *vb* **1** to exact neither punishment nor redress for or from < she was much too ready to *excuse* her children's faults >
syn condone, forgive, pardon, remit
rel alibi, apologize (for), explain, justify, pretext, rationalize; absolve, acquit, clear, exculpate, exonerate, vindicate; extenuate, gloss (over), gloze, overlook, palliate, pass over, shrug off, whitewash, wink (at)
con blame, censure, criticize, reprehend, reprobate; castigate, chasten, chastise, correct, discipline; admonish, chide, rebuke, reprimand
ant punish
2 *syn* see EXEMPT

excuse *n* **1** a justifying explanation of a fault or defect < what's your *excuse* for being late >
syn alibi, plea, pretext, ||right; *compare* APOLOGY 1, 2

---

syn synonym(s)　　　　　　　　　*rel* related word(s)
ant antonym(s)　　　　　　　　　*con* contrasted word(s)
idiom idiomatic equivalent(s)
|| use limited; if in doubt, see a dictionary

rel defense; explanation, justification, rationalization; reason

2 *syn* see APOLOGY 2

3 an inferior example of a specified kind < this heap is a sorry *excuse* for a car >

syn apology

rel makeshift, shift, stopgap, substitute

idiom a sorry specimen

con nonpareil, paragon; gem, jewel, treasure

exec *n syn* see EXECUTIVE

execrable *adj* **1** so odious as to be utterly detestable < an *execrable* crime >

syn accursed, cursed, damnable

rel atrocious, heinous, horrific, horrifying, monstrous; base, despicable, foul, low, vile; detestable, loathsome, nauseating, repulsive, revolting

idiom beneath (*or* below) contempt, not to be put up with (*or* endured)

2 *syn* see DAMNED 2

execrate *vb* **1** to denounce violently < *execrated* those responsible for the concentration camps >

syn anathematize, curse, damn, objurgate

rel censure, condemn, denounce, reprehend, reprobate, reprove; ban; revile; accurse, imprecate

con applaud, commend, compliment; acclaim, extol, laud, praise; admire

ant eulogize

2 *syn* see HATE

3 *syn* see SWEAR 3

execration *n syn* see BLASPHEMY 1

execute *vb* **1** *syn* see PERFORM 2

rel act; bring about, cause; carry out, complete, discharge, transact

2 *syn* see ADMINISTER 1

rel discharge, dispatch, transact; conduct, handle

3 *syn* see FULFILL 1

rel put through

4 *syn* see MURDER 1

rel eliminate, purge

idiom put to death

executive *n* one who holds an administrative or managerial position < a senior sales *executive* >

syn administrator, exec, manager, officer, official

rel businessman, businesswoman; entrepreneur; higher-up; director, leader, supervisor

exegesis *n syn* see EXPLANATION 1

exegetic *adj syn* see EXPLANATORY

exemplar *n syn* see MODEL 2

rel soul; exponent, illustration; prototype

exemplary *adj* **1** *syn* see GOOD 11

rel ideal, model; admirable, commendable, praiseworthy, worthy

con evil, corrupt; unworthy

2 *syn* see TYPICAL 1

exemplify *vb* **1** to use examples in order to clarify < a good teacher *exemplifies* each complex point >

syn illustrate, instance

rel clarify, clear up, spell out; cite, quote; enlighten, illuminate

2 *syn* see EPITOMIZE 2

rel demonstrate; illustrate

3 *syn* see REPRESENT 2

exempt *vb* to free from a liability or requirement < *exempt* a man from military service >

syn absolve, discharge, dispense, excuse, let off, privilege (from), relieve, spare

rel except; free

idiom give (one) exemption

exemption *n* freeing or the state of being free or freed from a charge or obligation to which others are subject < received a tax *exemption* >

syn immunity, impunity

rel exception; discharge, freedom, release

exenterate *vb syn* see EVISCERATE

exercise *n* **1** the act of bringing into play or realizing in action < one can usually avoid accidents by the *exercise* of foresight >

syn application, employment, exercising, exertion, operation, use; *compare* USE 1

con dereliction, disregard, neglect; carelessness, heedlessness, inattention, laxity

2 regular or repeated appropriate use of a faculty, power, or bodily organ < muscular atrophy from lack of *exercise* >

syn activity, exercising, exertion

rel action, movement; practice, use, workout

con inactiveness, inactivity; idleness, unemployment

3 something practiced or performed in order to develop, improve, or display a specific power or skill < spelling *exercises* >

syn drill, drilling, practice

4 a performance having a strongly marked secondary or ulterior aspect < his writing is an *exercise* in confusion >

syn lesson, study

exercise *vb* **1** *syn* see USE 2

idiom put into practice

2 *syn* see EXERT

3 to use repeatedly in order to master or strengthen < beginning swimmers *exercising* their new skill > < games that *exercise* the muscles >

syn drill, practice, rehearse

rel break in, condition, groom, prepare, train; cultivate, develop, foster, improve; fix, set

4 *syn* see ANNOY 1

exercising *n* **1** *syn* see EXERCISE 1

2 *syn* see EXERCISE 2

exert *vb* to bring to bear especially with sustained effort or lasting effect < *exerted* tremendous influence over his son's development >

syn exercise, ply, put out, throw, wield

rel apply, employ, use

idiom put forth

exertion *n* **1** *syn* see EXERCISE 1

2 *syn* see EFFORT 1

rel strain, striving, struggle

idiom hard (*or* long) pull

con ease, leisure, relaxation, repose, rest; inactivity, idleness

ant inertia

3 *syn* see EXERCISE 2

exfoliate *vb syn* see SCALE 2

exhale *vb* to let or force out of the lungs < *exhaled* a cloud of cigarette smoke >

syn breathe (out), expire, outbreathe

rel emit, let (out); blow

ant inhale, inspire

exhaust *vb* **1** *syn* see DEPLETE

rel dispel, disperse, dissipate, scatter; run out

idiom suck dry

con conserve, preserve, save; renew, restore

2 *syn* see CONSUME 1

3 *syn* see GO 4

4 to tire utterly < the 14-hour flight *exhausted* everyone >

syn see ‖BUGGER; *compare* TIRE 1

rel overdo, overdrive, overexert, overextend, overply, overwork; debilitate, enfeeble, weaken

idiom run one ragged, tire to death

con relax, rest, unlax

exhausted *adj syn* see EFFETE 2

rel run-down, weak, weakened; ‖beat, dog-tired, tired, ‖tucked up; limp; dead

idiom all done in (*or* for)

exhaustion *n syn* see FATIGUE

rel collapse, prostration

exhaustive *adj* testing all possibilities or considering all the elements of < an *exhaustive* investigation was soon under way >

syn complete, full-dress, thorough, thoroughgoing, whole-hog

rel all-encompassing, all-out, comprehensive, full-blown, full-scale, out-and-out, profound, total; intensive, radical, sweeping

con cursory, shallow; incomplete, partial; slipshod, unthorough

ant superficial

exhaustively *adv* **1** *syn* see HARD 3

con cursorily, superficially; incompletely, partially

2 *syn* see THOROUGHLY 2

exhibit *vb* **1** *syn* see SHOW 2

2 *syn* see LOOK 4

3 *syn* see SHOW 4

idiom parade one's wares, strut one's stuff

exhibit *n syn* see EXHIBITION 2

exhibition *n* **1** an act or instance of showing, evincing, or showing off < she gave an incredible *exhibition* of bad manners >

syn demonstration, display, show, spectacle

rel manifestation, sight
2 a public display of objects of interest < a trade *exhibition* >
syn exhibit, exposition, fair, show
rel demonstration, display, offering, presentation, showing
exhibitive *adj syn* see INDICATIVE
exhilarant *adj syn* see EXCITING
exhilarate *vb syn* see ELATE
rel animate, enliven, invigorate, vitalize; boost, buoy, exhalt, inspirit, lift, pep (up), uplift; cheer, delight, gladden, ‖send, thrill
idiom send into ecstasies
con deject, dishearten, dispirit, weigh down
ant depress
exhilarated *adj syn* see INTOXICATED 2
rel buoyed up, exalted, gladdened, pepped up, uplifted
idiom in ecstasies, on cloud nine
con blue, dispirited, down, low, unhappy, weighed down
ant depressed
exhilarating *adj* **1** *syn* see EXCITING
rel animating, animative, enlivening, inspiriting, invigorating, quickening; cheering, elevating, uplifting; breathtaking, electric
con deflating, disheartening, dispiriting
ant depressing
2 *syn* see INVIGORATING
exhilaration *n syn* see ELATION 1 *compare* ECSTASY
rel animation, enlivement, firing, invigoration, quickening, stimulation, vitalization, vivification; electrification, excitation, excitement, galvanization; elevation, inspiration, uplift
ant dejection
exhilarative *adj* **1** *syn* see EXCITING
2 *syn* see INVIGORATING
exhort *vb syn* see URGE
rel admonish, plead; call upon, insist; stimulate
con block, deter, discourage, impede
exhumate *vb syn* see EXHUME
exhume *vb* to take out of a place of burial < the body was *exhumed* and burned >
syn disinhume, disinter, exhumate, unbury, uncharnel
rel dig up, disentomb, unearth; disembalm
con bury, entomb, inter, ‖plant
ant inhume
exigency *n* **1** *syn* see JUNCTURE 2
rel difficulty, hardship, rigor, vicissitude; dilemma, fix, jam, pickle, scrape; pressure, urgency
2 *syn* see NEED 4
rel demand, imperativeness, insistence, requirement; coercion, compulsion, constraint; duress, pressure, urgency
idiom matter of life and death
exigent *adj* **1** *syn* see PRESSING
rel acute; necessary; menacing, threatening
2 *syn* see ONEROUS
exiguous *adj syn* see MEAGER 2
rel diminutive, little, small, tiny; slender, slight, tenuous, thin; confined, limited, narrow, restricted, straitened
ant ample
exile *n* **1** forced removal from one's native country < a deposed king living in *exile* in Rome >
syn banishment, deportation, displacement, expulsion, ostracism, relegation
rel exclusion; extradition; expatriation; diaspora, dispersion, migration, scattering
con recall, restoration
2 *syn* see ÉMIGRÉ
rel nonperson, outcast, unperson
idiom man without a country
exile *vb syn* see BANISH
rel dispossess; evacuate; extradite; drive out
idiom turn out of house and home
con recall, restore
exist *vb* **1** *syn* see BE
2 *syn* see CONSIST 1
existence *n* **1** the state or fact of having independent reality < customs that have recently come into *existence* >
syn actuality, being
rel life; presence; reality; perseity
ant nonexistence
2 *syn* see ENTITY 1
rel essence; individuality
existent *adj* **1** *syn* see ACTUAL 1

rel existing; present
2 *syn* see EXTANT 1
3 *syn* see PRESENT
existent *n syn* see ENTITY 1
existing *adj syn* see EXTANT 1
exit *n* **1** *syn* see DEPARTURE 1
ant entry
2 *syn* see EGRESS 2
ant entrance, entry
exit *vb syn* see GO 2
idiom make an (*or* one's) exit
con arrive, come
ant enter
exiting *n syn* see DEPARTURE 1
ant entering
exodus *n syn* see DEPARTURE 1
rel emigration, migration; flight
con immigration; ingress
ant influx
ex officio *adj syn* see OFFICIAL
exonerate *vb syn* see EXCULPATE
rel disburden, free
ant incriminate
exorbitant *adj syn* see EXCESSIVE 1
rel overboard, overmuch; unwarranted; outrageous, preposterous; exacting, extortionate
idiom out of sight
con equitable, fair, just; rational, reasonable
exordium *n syn* see INTRODUCTION
rel preliminary
con afterword, conclusion, epilogue, postscript
exotic *adj* **1** not native to the place where found < *exotic* fish >
syn foreign
rel imported, introduced, naturalized; alien, extrinsic, strange
con aboriginal, autochthonous, endemic, native; domestic, local
ant indigenous
2 excitingly or enticingly different or unusual < he was moved by her *exotic* beauty >
syn romanesque, romantic, strange
rel different, unusual; alluring, enticing, fascinating, glamorous, mysterious
expand *vb* **1** *syn* see OPEN 4
2 *syn* see INCREASE 1
3 to increase or become increased in bulk, volume, or size < water *expands* when heated >
syn amplify, dilate, distend, inflate, swell
rel grow; bulk (up), enlarge, fill (out); bolster; mushroom, ‖plim, puff (up)
con condense, decrease, deflate, shrink, shrivel; dwindle, lessen
ant contract
4 to express more fully and in greater detail < *expanded* his notes into an essay >
syn amplify, develop, elaborate, enlarge
rel detail, explicate; augment; discourse, expatiate
con compress, condense, contract
ant abridge
5 *syn* see INCREASE 2
6 *syn* see ESCALATE 2
rel prolong, protract
con de-escalate; circumscribe
ant limit, restrict
expanse *n* a significantly large area or range < a trackless *expanse* of moor >
syn amplitude, breadth, distance, expansion, space, spread, stretch
rel compass, extent, orbit, range, reach, scope, sweep; area, domain, field, sphere, territory; immensity, magnitude
expansion *n* **1** *syn* see EXPANSE
2 the act or process of increasing in some way < the recent *expansion* of science >
syn enlargement, extension, spread
con contraction, decrease, shrinking
expansive *adj* **1** *syn* see ELASTIC 2

---

syn synonym(s)   *rel* related word(s)
ant antonym(s)   *con* contrasted word(s)
idiom idiomatic equivalent(s)
‖ use limited; if in doubt, see a dictionary

rel communicative, demonstrative, extroverted, gregarious, unconstrained, unreserved, unrestrained; effusive, gushy, lavish; generous, liberal, openhanded
con austere, severe, stern; reserved, reticent, silent, taciturn
2 syn see DEMONSTRATIVE
ant withdrawn
3 syn see COMMUNICATIVE
4 syn see EXTENSIVE 1
rel ample, large; big, great
ant limited

expatiate *vb syn* see DISCOURSE 1
rel narrate, recite, recount, rehearse, relate; ramble

expatriate *vb syn* see BANISH
ant repatriate

expatriate *n syn* see ÉMIGRÉ
ant repatriate

expect *vb* **1** to anticipate in the mind <did not *expect* him for dinner>
syn await, count (on *or* upon), hope, look
rel anticipate, apprehend, divine, foreknow, foresee
idiom bargain on (*or* for), look for
ant despair (of)
2 syn see UNDERSTAND 3
rel feel, sense; presume, presuppose

expectancy *n* **1** the state of one who looks forward to something <had an air of wistful *expectancy*>
syn anticipation, expectation
rel presensation, presentiment
2 syn see EXPECTATION 2

expectant *adj* **1** characterized by expectation <an *expectant* crowd>
syn anticipant, anticipative, anticipatory, atiptoe, expecting
rel open-eyed, openmouthed; hopeful; eager; alert, watchful
con apathetic, indifferent, uninterested; unconcerned, unimpressed, unmoved
2 syn see PREGNANT 1
idiom anticipating a blessed event, waiting for the stork

expectation *n* **1 syn** see EXPECTANCY 1
2 something that is expected <each had his own dreams and *expectations*>
syn expectancy
rel design, hope, intention, motive, notion; prospect

expecting *adj* **1 syn** see EXPECTANT 1
2 syn see PREGNANT 1

expediency *n* **1 syn** see ORDER 11
rel propitiousness; convenience
2 syn see RESOURCE 3
rel design, strategy, tactic; measure, step
idiom card up one's sleeve, means to an end

expedient *adj* dictated by practical or prudential motives <decided it was not *expedient* to interfere yet>
syn advisable, politic, prudent, tactical, wise
rel advantageous, beneficial, convenient, practical, profitable, useful, utilitarian; opportune, seasonable, timely, well-timed; feasible, possible, practicable; appropriate, fit, fitting, suitable; judicious
con deleterious, detrimental; harmful, hurtful, injurious; fruitless, futile, vain; inappropriate, uncalled-for, unfitting, unsuitable; impolite, imprudent, inadvisable, injudicious, unwise
ant inexpedient

expedient *n syn* see RESOURCE 3
rel agency, instrument, instrumentality, means, medium

expedition *n* **1 syn** see JOURNEY
rel campaign; entrada, exploration
2 syn see HASTE 1
rel alacrity, promptitude
con delay, retardation, slackening, slowing
ant procrastination
3 syn see ALACRITY
rel expeditiousness, speediness, swiftness; punctuality
con dawdling, delaying, faltering, hesitation

expeditious *adj syn* see FAST 3
rel effective, effectual, efficacious, efficient; prompt, ready
con ineffective, ineffectual, inefficacious, inefficient; dilatory, laggard, leisurely, slow
ant sluggish

expeditiously *adv syn* see FAST 2
rel effectively, efficaciously; punctually

con ineffectively; deliberately, dilatorily, leisurely, slowly
ant sluggishly

expeditiousness *n syn* see HASTE 1

expeditive *adj syn* see FAST 3

expel *vb* **1 syn** see ERUPT 1
rel blow off, blow out, ejaculate, exhaust
2 syn see BANISH
rel drum out, read out; eliminate, turn out; ‖bounce
idiom give (one) the boot, give the bum's rush, give the old heave-ho, send to Coventry, throw out on one's ear
ant admit

expellee *n syn* see ÉMIGRÉ

expend *vb* **1 syn** see SPEND 1
rel dispense, distribute; blow, exhaust, use up
idiom loose (*or* untie) the purse strings, open one's purse
con hoard, lay up, save
2 syn see GO 4

expenditure *n syn* see EXPENSE 1

expense *n* **1** something expended to secure a benefit or bring about a result <spared no *expense* in furnishing their home>
syn cost, disbursement, expenditure, outlay
2 a loss incurred in the course of gaining something <won the war at the *expense* of many lives>
syn cost, price, toll
rel decrement, forfeit, forfeiture, sacrifice; deprivation, loss

expensive *adj syn* see COSTLY 1
rel immoderate, uneconomical; big-ticket, high-priced
con economical, moderate; bargain, low-cost, low-priced, thrifty; cheap
ant inexpensive

experience *n syn* see ACQUAINTANCE 1
rel background; observation; know-how, practice, skill; savoir faire, sophistication; wisdom
ant inexperience

experience *vb* **1** to meet with directly (as through participation or observation) <*experience* pain> <trying to *experience* the problems of a different culture>
syn have, know, see, suffer, sustain, undergo
rel encounter, meet; accept, receive
2 syn see FEEL 2
rel behold, see, survey, view

experienced *adj* made skillful or wise through practice <an *experienced* sales executive>
syn old, old-time, practical, practiced, seasoned, skilled, versed, vet, veteran; *compare* PROFICIENT
rel broken in; accomplished, skillful; expert, qualified; old-line, wise
idiom having been around, knowing the score (*or* the ropes)
con apprentice, beginning, freshman, green, new, novice, raw, untested, untried
ant experienceless, inexperienced

experient *adj syn* see EMPIRICAL

experiential *adj syn* see EMPIRICAL

experiment *n* an operation or process carried out to resolve an uncertainty <*experiments* that added much to our understanding of nutritional needs>
syn experimentation, test, trial, trial and error, trial run
rel probe, research, search; examination, investigation; analysis, study

experiment *vb* to engage in experimentation <*experimenting* with regional solutions to urban problems>
syn experimentalize, experimentize, test (out), try (out), try on
rel investigate, probe, research, search; analyze, scrutinize, study, weigh
idiom play around with

experimental *adj* **1 syn** see EMPIRICAL
2 of, relating to, or having the characteristics of experiment <*experimental* missile flights>
syn experimentative, test, trial
rel preliminary, preparatory; developmental; provisional, temporary, tentative
con tested, tried; permanent, proved; accepted, established, standard

experimentalize *vb syn* see EXPERIMENT

experimentation *n syn* see EXPERIMENT

experimentative *adj syn* see EXPERIMENTAL 2

experimentize *vb syn* see EXPERIMENT

expert *adj syn* see PROFICIENT

rel schooled, trained; adroit, deft, dexterous; pro, professional
con unpracticed; unschooled
ant amateur, inexpert

expert *n* one who has acquired special skill in or knowledge and mastery of something < a fingerprint *expert* >
syn adept, artist, artiste, authority, ‖dab, ‖dabster, doyen, master, master-hand, maven, passed master, past master, pro, professional, proficient, swell, virtuoso, whiz, wiz, wizard
rel ‖darb; specialist
con dabbler, dilettante, tyro; apprentice, novice, probationer
ant amateur

expertise *n* **1** *syn* see ABILITY 2
rel readiness; competence; skillfulness
2 *syn* see ART 1
rel quickness; cleverness, ingeniousness; finesse; savvy

expertism *n* *syn* see ABILITY 2

expertness *n* *syn* see ABILITY 2
rel prowess; facility

expiate *vb* to make amends or give satisfaction for wrong done < *expiated* his crime with his life >
syn atone
rel amend, compensate (for), correct, rectify, redress, remedy
idiom make up for, put right

expiative *adj* *syn* see PURGATIVE

expiatory *adj* *syn* see PURGATIVE

expire *vb* **1** *syn* see DIE 1
idiom draw one's last breath; give up the breath of life
con live, thrive
2 *syn* see PASS 3
3 *syn* see EXHALE
ant inspire

explain *vb* **1** to make something comprehensible or more comprehensible < a commentary that *explains* the allegory >
syn construe, explicate, expound, interpret, spell out; *compare* CLARIFY 2
rel decipher, disentangle, undo, unravel, unriddle, unscramble, untangle; analyze, break down; clear up, resolve, solve
idiom put into plain English
con confound, confuse, puzzle
ant obfuscate
2 *syn* see CLARIFY 2
3 to give the reason for or cause of < unable to *explain* his strange conduct >
syn account, explain away, justify, rationalize
rel condone, excuse; absolve, acquit, exculpate, exonerate, vindicate

explain away *vb* *syn* see EXPLAIN 3

explanation *n* **1** something that makes clear what is obscure < sought some *explanation* of the difficult passage >
syn construal, construction, exegesis, explication, exposé, exposition, interpretation
rel disentanglement, unscrambling; enlightenment, illumination; definition, meaning; resolution, solution; demonstration, example, exemplification, illustration
2 a statement of causes, grounds, or motives < refused an *explanation* for his act >
syn account, justification, rationale, rationalization, reason
rel grounds; motive

explanative *adj* *syn* see EXPLANATORY

explanatory *adj* serving to explain < *explanatory* notes in a book >
syn exegetic, explanative, explicative, explicatory, expositional, expositive, expository, interpretive
rel enlightening, illuminating; discursive; demonstrative, illustrative
con baffling, bewildering, confusing, misleading, mystifying, puzzling
ant obfuscatory

expletive *n* *syn* see SWEARWORD

explicate *vb* *syn* see EXPLAIN 1
rel amplify, develop, dilate, enlarge (upon), expand, expatiate; demonstrate
idiom dot the *i*'s (and cross the *t*'s)

explication *n* *syn* see EXPLANATION 1
rel amplification, development, enlargement, expansion, expatiation

explicative *adj* *syn* see EXPLANATORY
rel annotative, exemplificative, scholiastic

explicatory *adj* *syn* see EXPLANATORY

explicit *adj* characterized by full precise expression < gave the guard *explicit* orders about whom to admit >
syn categorical, clean-cut, clear-cut, definite, definitive, express, specific, unambiguous
rel certain, clear, distinct, lucid, perspicuous, plain, sure, understandable, unequivocal; accurate, correct, exact, precise
con cryptic, dark, enigmatic, equivocal, obscure, unclear, vague; implicit, implied, inferred; imprecise, inaccurate, incorrect, inexact
ant ambiguous

explicitly *adv* *syn* see EXPRESSLY 1

explode *vb* **1** to burst violently and noisily usually due to pressure within < the bomb *exploded* >
syn blow up, burst, detonate, go off, mushroom
rel blast, discharge
idiom blow sky-high, blow to kingdom come
con fail, fizzle, peter (out)
2 *syn* see ERUPT 2
rel flame (up), flare (up)
idiom blow a fuse (*or* gasket)
3 *syn* see DISCREDIT 2
rel invalidate; deflate
idiom shoot full of holes

exploit *n* **1** *syn* see ADVENTURE
rel effort, job; maneuver
2 *syn* see FEAT 2
rel do, performance, stunt; blow, coup, stroke
idiom bold stroke

exploit *vb* **1** *syn* see USE 2
rel cultivate, work
2 to take unfair advantage of < *exploits* his friend's good nature >
syn abuse, impose (on *or* upon), use
rel manipulate; bleed, fleece, skin, soak, stick
3 *syn* see MANIPULATE 2

explore *vb* to search through or into < *explored* the possibilities of reaching an agreement >
syn delve (into), dig (into), go (into), inquire (into), investigate, look (into), probe, prospect, sift
rel burrow, mouse (out); quarry, search; examine, test, try; inquisite, question
idiom nose around

explosion *n* *syn* see OUTBURST 1

exponent *n* one who actively promotes or backs something < an *exponent* of arbitration in labor disputes >
syn advocate, champion, expounder, proponent, supporter
rel backer, booster, partisan, promoter, protagonist; defender, upholder
con antagonist, enemy; opposition
ant opponent

expose *vb* **1** to make accessible to something detrimental or dangerous < he needlessly *exposed* his troops to enemy fire >
syn lay (open), subject, uncover
rel endanger, hazard, imperil, jeopard, jeopardize, jeopardy, peril, risk
idiom put (*or* leave) in harm's way
con cover, shelter; guard, protect
ant shield
2 *syn* see OPEN 2
rel unfold, unshroud
3 *syn* see SHOW 4
rel advertise, air, broadcast, publish
4 to reveal the faults, frailties, unsoundness, or pretensions of < the monograph *exposed* the theory as being pure myth >
syn debunk, discover, show up, uncloak, undress, unmask, unshroud
rel disclose, reveal, uncover
idiom lay bare

exposé *n* *syn* see EXPLANATION 1

exposed *adj* **1** *syn* see OPEN 2
rel apparent, evident, manifest; unconcealed, unhidden; revealed; visible

---

syn synonym(s)   *rel* related word(s)
ant antonym(s)   *con* contrasted word(s)
idiom idiomatic equivalent(s)
‖ use limited; if in doubt, see a dictionary

idiom laid bare
con covered, enveloped, sheathed
2 syn see LIABLE 2
rel likely; menaced, threatened
con defended, guarded, protected, safeguarded, shielded
exposition *n* **1 syn** see EXPLANATION 1
rel presentation; discourse, discussion, disquisition, expounding; statement; delineation, enunciation
2 syn see EXHIBITION 2
rel display, production
expositional *adj syn* see EXPLANATORY
expositive *adj syn* see EXPLANATORY
rel depictive, descriptive, graphic; illuminative; delineative
expository *adj syn* see EXPLANATORY
rel disquisitional; critical
expostulate *vb syn* see OBJECT 1
rel combat, fight, oppose, resist; argue, debate, discuss, dispute
idiom raise one's voice against
exposure *n* the condition of being exposed to something detrimental < *exposure* to attack >
syn liability, openness, vulnerability, vulnerableness
rel susceptibility, susceptiveness, susceptivity; defenselessness, helplessness, unprotection; danger, jeopardy, peril, risk
con bulwark, cover, protection, safeguard, shelter, shield, shielding
expound *vb syn* see EXPLAIN 1
rel express, present, state; comment, discourse; clarify, delineate, describe, exemplify, illustrate
expounder *n syn* see EXPONENT
rel explainer, expositor
express *adj* **1 syn** see EXPLICIT
rel expressed, uttered, voiced; out-and-out, unmistakable; unconditional, unqualified
con unexpressed, unsaid, unstated; ambiguous, equivocal; conditional, qualified
2 of a particular or exact sort < came for the *express* purpose of buying a car >
syn especial, set, special, specific
rel individual; definite, particular; explicit; intended, intentional, premeditated
ant vague
express *vb* **1 syn** see WORD
2 to give expression to (as a thought, an opinion, or an emotion) < *expressed* his views freely >
syn air, give, put, state, vent, ventilate; *compare* SAY 1, WORD
rel broach, circulate, put about; disclose, tell; frame; enunciate, phrase; announce, declare, proclaim, pronounce; discharge, drain
con hint, insinuate, intimate, suggest
ant imply
3 syn see MEAN 2
rel communicate, convey, impart
4 syn see PRESS 3
expression *n* **1** an act, process, or instance of expressing in words < his anger found *expression* in a string of oaths >
syn statement, utterance, vent, voice
rel issue; manifestation, representation; observation, reflection
con hint, insinuation, intimation, suggestion
2 syn see PHRASE 2
rel word; verbalism; idiom; clause
3 one thing that calls to mind another often symbolically < sent flowers as an *expression* of sympathy >
syn gesture, indication, reminder, sign, token
rel embodiment, manifestation, representation, symbol; demonstration, show
4 syn see ELOQUENCE
rel graphicness, vividness
5 syn see LOOK 2
expressionless *adj* lacking expression < cold *expressionless* eyes >
syn blank, deadpan, empty, inexpressive, unexpressive, vacant
rel dull, lackluster, lusterless, vacuous; impassive, inscrutable, stolid, wooden; dead
con lustrous; responsive; alive, vital
ant expressive
expressive *adj* clearly conveying or manifesting something < a forceful and *expressive* word >
syn eloquent, facund, meaningful, pregnant, rich, sententious, significant
rel revealing, revelatory, suggestive; graphic, pictorial, vivid; alive, demonstrative, lively, responsive, senseful, spirited

con banal, commonplace, drab, dull, flat, jejune, inane, insipid, vacuous, vapid; impassive, indifferent; austere, severe, stern, stiff, wooden; blank, deadpan, empty, expressionless, vacant; dead
ant inexpressive, unexpressive
expressiveness *n syn* see ELOQUENCE
ant inexpressiveness
expressivity *n syn* see ELOQUENCE
expressly *adv* **1** in direct and unmistakable terms < his beliefs *expressly* repudiate the church's teachings >
syn categorically, definitely, explicitly, specifically
rel directly; unmistakably
con ambiguously, equivocally; conditionally; likely, possibly, probably
2 for the express purpose < programs designed *expressly* to serve immediate political objectives >
syn especially, in specie, specially, specifically
3 syn see EVEN 1
expropriate *vb syn* see APPROPRIATE 1
rel dispossess; take (away)
expulse *vb syn* see BANISH
rel ‖bounce; eject
con admit, receive
expulsion *n syn* see EXILE 1
rel driving out, forcing out; ejection, ousting; removal
idiom the boot, the old heave-ho
expunge *vb syn* see ERASE
rel discard, drop, exclude, omit; annihilate, eradicate
expurgate *vb* **1 syn** see PURIFY 2
2 syn see CENSOR
expurgation *n syn* see PURIFICATION
expurgatorial *adj syn* see PURGATIVE
expurgatory *adj syn* see PURGATIVE
exquisite *adj* **1 syn** see CHOICE
rel consummate, finished; faultless, flawless, impeccable
2 syn see IMPECCABLE 1
rel superb, superlative
con faulty, flawed, imperfect
3 syn see INTENSE 1
rel acute, extreme; consummate, transcending
exquisite *n syn* see FOP
exsect *vb syn* see EXCISE
exsiccate *vb syn* see DRY 1
extant *adj* **1** that is in existence < the most talented writer *extant* >
syn alive, around, existent, existing, living
con dead, defunct, destroyed, exterminated, extinct; departed, gone, lost
ant nonextant
2 syn see ACTUAL 1
rel current, immediate, present
con possible, potential
3 syn see PRESENT
extemporaneous *adj* composed, devised, or done at the moment rather than beforehand < made an *extemporaneous* speech after the dinner >
syn autoschediastic, extemporary, extempore, impromptu, improvised, offhand, spur-of-the-moment, unrehearsed, unstudied; *compare* UNINTENTIONAL
rel casual, informal; unprepared, unthought-out; impulsive, snap, spontaneous
idiom off the cuff, on the spur of the moment
con designed, planned, prepared, projected, schemed, thought-out; considered, deliberated, premeditated, studied
extemporary *adj syn* see EXTEMPORANEOUS
extempore *adj syn* see EXTEMPORANEOUS
extemporization *n syn* see IMPROVISATION
extemporize *vb syn* see IMPROVISE
rel dash off, knock off, toss off
idiom do offhand, play (it) by ear
con cook up, plan, prepare, think out
extend *vb* **1 syn** see OPEN 4
con close, fold
2 syn see OFFER 1
rel allocate, allot; accord, advance, award, bestow, confer, grant; donate
idiom place at one's disposal
3 to make or become longer < *extended* his visit by a week >

syn draw, draw out, elongate, lengthen, prolong, prolongate, protract, spin (out), stretch
rel amplify, enlarge, expand, increase
con abridge; curtail
ant shorten
4 *syn* see INCREASE 1
5 *syn* see RUN 8
rel advance, proceed; continue
6 *syn* see RANGE 3
7 to reach a certain point <his education doesn't *extend* beyond elementary school>
syn go
rel reach, run; advance; attain
extended *adj* **1 *syn*** see LONG 1
rel prolonged, protracted, spread out, stretched out (*or* forth)
ant contracted
2 *syn* see EXTENSIVE 1
rel far-flung, widespread
con narrow; inextensive
ant unextended
extension *n* **1** the act or state of extending or being extended <a one-month *extension* of the price freeze seems likely>
syn elongation, lengthening, production, prolongation, prolongment, protraction
rel continuation, continuing; drawing out, stretch, stretch-out
con abridgment, shortening; contraction, curtailment, shrinking
2 *syn* see EXPANSION 2
rel augmentation, increase; spreading out
con abridgment, curtailment; reduction
ant contraction
3 *syn* see RANGE 2
rel magnitude, size, spread; comprehensiveness
4 *syn* see ANNEX
extensity *n syn* see RANGE 2
extensive *adj* **1** widely ranging in scope or application <*extensive* privileges>
syn broad, expansive, extended, scopic, scopious, wide
rel comprehensive, general, inclusive; far-reaching, far-spreading, spacious, wide-ranging; all-encompassing, all-inclusive, blanket, boundless, indiscriminate, unrestricted, wholesale
con circumscribed, constricted, limited, narrow, restricted; unextended
2 *syn* see BIG 1
con little, small
extent *n* **1 *syn*** see RANGE 2
rel domain, field, province, sphere
2 *syn* see SIZE 1
rel compass, extension, orbit, radius, reach, scope, sweep
3 *syn* see ORDER 4
extenuate *vb* **1 *syn*** see THIN 1
rel mitigate; moderate, qualify, temper
con aggravate, enhance, heighten
2 *syn* see PALLIATE
rel explain, justify, rationalize; apologize
idiom put a gloss on (*or* upon *or* over), put a good face upon
exterior *adj syn* see OUTER
rel outermost, outmost
con inner, ingrained, inherent, intrinsic
ant interior
exteriorize *vb syn* see EMBODY 1
ant interiorize
exterminate *vb* **1 *syn*** see ANNIHILATE 2
rel finish off; execute; kill (off)
idiom do away with, put an end to, put out of the way
2 *syn* see SLAUGHTER 3
idiom wipe off the face of the earth, wipe off the map
external *adj syn* see OUTER
rel out, outermost, outmost, peripheral
con ingrained, inherent, intrinsic
ant internal
externalize *vb syn* see EMBODY 1
ant internalize
extinct *adj* **1 *syn*** see DEAD 1
2 that has died out altogether <an *extinct* civilization>
syn bygone, dead, defunct, departed, gone, lost, vanished
rel nonexistent; collapsed, fallen, overthrown; disappeared
idiom gone from the face of the earth
con existent, existing, living, active; contemporary, current

ant extant
3 *syn* see OBSOLETE
rel antiquated, archaic, old-fashioned
con modern; contemporary
ant current
extinguish *vb* **1** to cause to cease burning <firemen *extinguishing* the blaze>
syn douse, ‖dout, out, put out, quench, ‖squench
rel blow out, snuff out; smother
con fire, kindle, start; torch
ant ignite
2 *syn* see ANNIHILATE 2
rel erase, expunge, obliterate
3 *syn* see CRUSH 5
rel check; smother, stifle; snuff (out); choke (out), trample (down)
idiom put the lid (*or* the kibosh) on
con encourage, fire (up)
ant inflame
extinguishment *n syn* see REPRESSION 1
extirpate *vb* **1 *syn*** see ANNIHILATE 2
rel efface, erase, expunge, demolish, destroy, raze; kill off
con breed, engender, generate, propagate
2 *syn* see EXCISE
extol *vb syn* see PRAISE 2
idiom beat the drum for, make much of
ant decry
extort *vb* **1** to obtain something by pressure or intimidation <racketeers *extorting* protection money>
syn exact, gouge, pinch, screw, shake down, squeeze, wrench, wrest, wring; *compare* CHEAT, FLEECE 1
rel demand; coerce, force; extract, get, obtain, secure; bleed, fleece, skin
idiom bleed one white, make one pay through the nose, put the screws to
2 *syn* see EDUCE 1
extra *adj syn* see SUPERFLUOUS
rel added, additional, supplemental, supplementary
extra *adv* to a degree or extent beyond the usual <she was *extra* smart>
syn extremely, rarely, ‖uncommon, uncommonly, unusually
rel especially; particularly; considerably, markedly, noticeably
con barely, scarcely
extract *vb* **1** to draw out forcibly or with effort <*extract* a confession> <*extract* a tooth>
syn evulse, pull, tear, yank
rel pry; avulse
2 *syn* see EKE OUT 3
3 *syn* see GLEAN
4 *syn* see EDUCE 1
5 *syn* see EXCERPT
rel abridge, condense, shorten
extraction *n syn* see ANCESTRY
extraneous *adj* **1 *syn*** see EXTRINSIC
rel accidental, adventitious, incidental
con constitutional, ingrained, inherent; germane, material, pertinent
2 *syn* see IRRELEVANT
rel incidental; unessential; unrelated; pointless; inappropriate
idiom beside the point
ant relevant
extraordinary *adj syn* see EXCEPTIONAL 1
rel amazing; stupendous, terrific, wonderful
idiom out of the ordinary
con customary, normal, regular, usual
ant ordinary
extravagance *n* **1 *syn*** see LUXURY
2 the quality, state, fact, or an instance of being extravagant <by living simply and avoiding *extravagance* they saved enough for the trip>
syn extravagancy, lavishness, overdoing, prodigality, squander, unthrift, waste, wastefulness

---

syn synonym(s)
ant antonym(s)
idiom idiomatic equivalent(s)
‖ use limited; if in doubt, see a dictionary

rel related word(s)
con contrasted word(s)

rel improvidence, spendthriftness; excess, indulgence, overindulgence

con moderation, temperateness; care, forehandedness, frugality; austerity

ant economy

extravagancy *n syn* see EXTRAVAGANCE 2

extravagant *adj* **1** grossly exaggerated < *extravagant* accusations>
syn fantastic, preposterous, wild
rel unbalanced, unrestrained; absurd, foolish, ludicrous, nonsensical, ridiculous, silly; bizarre, crazy; exaggerated, implausible
con plausible, sensible; restrained
ant reasonable
2 *syn* see EXCESSIVE 1
rel exuberant, lavish, profuse; prodigal, profligate, wasteful
con economical, frugal, sparing
ant restrained

extreme *adj* **1** very great < the project demanded *extreme* secrecy>
syn utmost, uttermost
2 *syn* see ARDENT 2
rel deep, moving
3 departing sharply from the traditional or usual < *extreme* political views>
syn extremist, fanatic, rabid, radical, revolutionary, revolutionary, revolutionist, ultra, ultraist; *compare* OUTLANDISH 3
rel excessive, immoderate; desperate, drastic; extravagant, unreasonable; violent, wild
con conservative, moderate, restrained; reasonable, sensible
4 *syn* see EXCESSIVE 1
rel intolerable, unwarranted
5 most distant from a center < the *extreme* edge of the city>
syn farthest, furthermost, furthest, outermost, outmost, remotest, utmost, uttermost

extreme *n* **1** an extreme state or condition < an *extreme* of poverty>
syn extremity
rel excess, inordinancy
2 something situated at or marking one end or the other of a range < *extremes* of heat and cold>
syn extremity, limit
rel climax, consummation, culmination; ceiling, crest, crown, height; peak, pinnacle, summit, top; maximum, utmost, uttermost

extremely *adv* **1** *syn* see EVER 6
2 *syn* see VERY 1
3 *syn* see EXTRA

extremist *n syn* see RADICAL

extremist *adj syn* see EXTREME 3

extremity *n* **1** *syn* see EXTREME 2
rel acme, apex, apogee, vertex, zenith
2 *syn* see EXTREME 1

extricate *vb* **1** *syn* see KNOW 4
2 to free from an undesirable situation or condition < *extricate* himself from financial difficulties>
syn clear, clear away, discumber, disembarrass, disembroil, disencumber, disentangle, disentwine, unentangle, unscramble, untangle, untie, untwine
rel unravel; abstract, detach, disengage; disburden, disemburden; deliver, disinvolve, free, liberate, release, rescue; resolve
con embroil, entangle, tangle; clog, fetter, hog-tie, manacle, shackle, trammel; block, hamper, hinder, impede, obstruct

extrinsic *adj* not properly part of a thing < a point *extrinsic* to his basic thesis>
syn alien, extraneous, foreign
rel acquired, gained; exterior, external, outer, outside, outward
con native; inner, inside, interior, internal, inward; individual, personal
ant intrinsic

extrude *vb syn* see EJECT 1

exuberance *n syn* see EBULLIENCE
rel gayness; friskiness, life, liveliness, sprightliness, zest, zestfulness; abandon, ardor

exuberancy *n syn* see EBULLIENCE

exuberant *adj* **1** joyously unrestrained and enthusiastic < his warm *exuberant* personality>
syn brash, ebullient, effervescent, high-spirited, vivacious
rel gay, lively, spirited, sprightly, zestful; frolicsome; ardent, passionate
con constrained, inhibited, repressed, restrained, subdued; calm, impassive, quiet
ant austere
2 *syn* see PROFUSE
rel fecund, fertile, fruitful, prolific; rampant, rank; diffuse
con scant, scanty, spare

exude *vb* to flow slowly out < a sticky resin *exuded* from the bark>
syn bleed, ooze, percolate, ‖screeve, seep, ‖sew, ‖sicker, strain, sweat, transude, weep
rel emanate; discharge, emit; trickle

exult *vb* to rejoice especially with feelings or display of triumph or self-satisfaction < the team were *exulting* in their victory>
syn delight, glory, jubilate, triumph
rel rejoice; celebrate; boast, brag, crow, show off
con lament, mourn
ant bemoan

exultance *n syn* see EXULTATION

exultant *adj* manifesting proud elation < *exultant* over his successes>
syn cock-a-hoop, cock-a-whoop, exulting, jubilant, triumphal, triumphant
rel happy, joyous, overjoyed; delighting, rejoicing; elated, flushed
idiom in high feather
con depressed, mournful, unhappy

exultation *n* the act of exulting or the state of being exultant < the *exultation* of victory and the thrill of power>
syn exultance, jubilance, jubilation, triumph
rel delight, elation, satisfaction; celebration, rejoicing; gloating

exulting *adj syn* see EXULTANT

exuviate *vb syn* see SHED 2

eye *n* **1** an organ of sight < turned his *eyes* to the view>
syn lamp, ocular, oculus, ‖ogle, orb, peeper, winker
2 the faculty of seeing with or as if with the eyes < had a keen *eye* for details>
syn eyesight, seeing, sight, vision
3 very close watching or observation < kept an *eye* on him>
syn eagle eye, scrutiny, surveillance, tab, watch
4 *often* **eyes** *pl* a way of looking at something < in the *eyes* of the law, a man is innocent until proven guilty>
syn view, viewpoint; *compare* VIEWPOINT 2
rel attitude, position, thinking; conception, grasp; conclusion, judgment
5 *syn* see OPINION
6 *syn* see LOOP 1
7 *syn* see LOOP 2
‖8 *syn* see DETECTIVE

eye *vb* **1** to fix the eyes on < the child *eyed* the presents with delight>
syn consider, contemplate, gaze (upon), look (at *or* upon), view; *compare* LOOK 7
rel regard; stare (at)
2 to keep a close watch on < the detective *eyed* the suspect>
syn eyeball, scrutinize, watch; *compare* TAIL
rel stare (at); size up
idiom keep a close (*or* an eagle) eye on
3 *syn* see LOOK 7

eyeball *vb syn* see EYE 2

eye-catching *adj syn* see NOTICEABLE

eyeful *n syn* see BEAUTY

eyeless *adj syn* see BLIND 1

eye-popping *adj syn* see EXCITING

eyesight *n syn* see EYE 2

eyesore *n* something offensive to the sight < the old abandoned house was a neighborhood *eyesore*>
syn desight, fright, mess, monstrosity, sight

eyewash *n syn* see NONSENSE 2

eyewitness *n syn* see SPECTATOR

fable *n* **1** *syn* see FICTION
2 *syn* see ALLEGORY 2
fabric *n* **1** *syn* see BUILDING
2 *syn* see TEXTURE 2
fabricate *vb syn* see MAKE 3
rel turn out; create, formulate, invent; concoct, contrive, devise
fabrication *n syn* see FICTION
rel creation; deceit, fib; artifact, opus, product, production, work
fabulous *adj syn* see MYTHICAL
rel amazing, astonishing, astounding, incredible, marvelous, unbelievable, wonderful; exorbitant, extravagant, inordinate, outrageous, preposterous; monstrous, prodigious, stupendous
con believable, colorable, credible
facade *n syn* see MASK 2
face *n* **1** the front part of the head including the eyes, nose, mouth, cheeks, chin, and usually forehead <hid his *face* from the camera>
syn countenance, ‖dial, features, ‖kisser, ‖map, mug, ‖mush, muzzle, ‖pan, phiz, ‖puss, visage
rel lineaments, physiognomy
2 *syn* see LOOK 2
3 *syn* see APPEARANCE 2
4 *syn* see MASK 2
5 *syn* see EFFRONTERY
6 a distortion of the face usually as an expression of contempt or distaste <the old man made a *face* at the flat beer>
syn grimace, moue, mouth, mouthing, mow, mug
rel frown, glower, lower, pout, scowl
idiom wry face, wry mouth
con grin, simper, smile, smirk
7 *syn* see MAKEUP 3
8 *syn* see TOP 2
face *vb* **1** to have the face or front in a specified direction <the house *faces* toward the river>
syn front, look
rel border, meet
ant back
2 *syn* see MEET 6
rel watch; gaze, glare, stare; await, expect, look (for)
3 to confront with courage or boldness <ready to *face* his accusers>
syn ‖banter, beard, brave, challenge, dare, defy, ‖double-dog dare, front, outdare, outface, venture
rel confront, encounter, meet; oppose, resist, withstand; contend, fight
idiom brazen it out, face the music, face up to, take the bull by the horns
con elude, escape, eschew, evade, shun
ant avoid
4 *syn* see CONFRONT 1
5 *syn* see ACCOST 2
rel beard, brave, challenge, dare, defy
idiom stand up to
6 *syn* see ENGAGE 5
7 *syn* see SHEATHE
facet *n syn* see PHASE
rel face, front
facetious *adj syn* see WITTY
rel jesting, joking, quipping, wisecracking; blithe, jocund, jolly, jovial, merry; comic, comical, droll, funny, laughable, ludicrous
con grave, serious, sober, solemn, somber
ant lugubrious
facile *adj syn* see EASY 1
rel adroit, deft, dexterous; fluent, glib, voluble; cursory, shallow, superficial, uncritical
con awkward, clumsy, constrained, cumbersome, labored, maladroit; tongue-tied; deep, profound, thorough
ant arduous
facilely *adv syn* see EASILY 1
ant arduously
facilitate *vb syn* see EASE 3

facility *n* **1** *syn* see READINESS 3
rel skill, wit; aptitude, bent, leaning, propensity, turn; abandon, spontaneity, unconstraint; address, poise, tact; effortlessness, lightness, smoothness
con awkwardness, clumsiness, ineptness, maladroitness; rigidity, stiffness, woodenness; effort, exertion, pains
2 *syn* see AMENITY 2
rel accommodation, advantage, aid, fitting
con difficulty, hardship, inconvenience
facing *prep* **1** *syn* see AGAINST 1
con side by side
2 *syn* see BEFORE 2
facsimile *n syn* see REPRODUCTION
con archetype, model, original, pattern, prototype, standard
fact *n* **1** the quality of being actual <the realm of *fact* is distinct from fancy>
syn actuality, reality
rel authenticity, genuineness, truth
con fancy, fantasy, fiction
2 something that has actual existence <stubborn *facts* that cannot be confuted>
syn event, phenomenon
rel circumstance, detail, episode, particular; happening, incident, occurrence; observable
con contingency, eventuality, hope, possibility, potentiality, probability
ant illusion
faction *n syn* see COMBINATION 2
rel camp, offshoot, wing
idiom splinter group
factious *adj syn* see INSUBORDINATE
rel contending, fighting, warring; belligerent, contentious, quarrelsome; alienated, disaffected, estranged
con companionable, gregarious, social; acquiescent, compliant; faithful, loyal, true
ant cooperative
factitious *adj syn* see SYNTHETIC
rel affected, assumed, counterfeited, false, feigned, forced, pretended, sham, shammed, simulated
con authentic, bona fide, genuine, veritable; artless, naive, simple, spontaneous
ant natural
factor *n* **1** *syn* see ELEMENT 2
rel antecedent, cause, determinant; agency, agent, instrument, instrumentality, means
2 *syn* see AGENT 2
rel bailiff, majordomo, seneschal, steward; adjutant, aid, assistant, coadjutor, helper
factory *n* an establishment for the manufacturing of goods <a shoe *factory*>
syn manufactory, mill, plant, works
factual *adj syn* see ACTUAL 2
rel certain, undoubted, veritable; authentic, legitimate, unquestionable, valid
con erroneous, false, questionable, wrong
ant illusory
facultative *adj syn* see OPTIONAL
faculty *n* **1** *syn* see GIFT 2
rel instinct; property, quality; leaning, penchant, proclivity, propensity; predilection
con inability, incapability, incapacity, ineptness
2 *syn* see POWER 3
facund *adj syn* see EXPRESSIVE
facundity *n syn* see ELOQUENCE
fad *n syn* see FASHION 3
rel caprice, conceit, fancy, vagary, whim, whimsy

---

syn synonym(s)	*rel* related word(s)
ant antonym(s)	*con* contrasted word(s)
idiom idiomatic equivalent(s)	
‖ use limited; if in doubt, see a dictionary	

con custom, habit, practice, usage

fade *vb* **1** *syn* see FAIL 1

2 *syn* see DULL 1

3 *syn* see VANISH

rel deliquesce, dissolve, melt; abate, diminish, dwindle, ebb, lessen, moderate, wane; attenuate, rarefy, thin

idiom fade like a shadow

con intensify; eternalize, immortalize, perpetuate

faded *adj* *syn* see SHABBY 1

rel haggard, washed-out, wasted, worn; dim, murky; achromatic, colorless; ashen, pale, pallid, wan

con energetic, lusty, vigorous; colorful; vivid

fag *n* *syn* see CIGARETTE

fag *vb* *syn* see EXHAUST 4

con refresh, relax, rest, restore

fag *n* *syn* see HOMOSEXUAL

faggot *n* *syn* see HOMOSEXUAL

fail *vb* **1** to lose strength, power, vitality, or intensity <his health *failed* and he retired early >

syn decline, deteriorate, ‖dwine, fade, flag, languish, weaken

rel jade, sink, slip, waste (away), worsen

idiom go downhill, hit the skids

con better, improve, strengthen

2 to become used up <food *failed* before they got back to civilization >

syn give out, run out

rel dwindle, shrink, wane

3 to be or become inadequate or deficient <the spring gradually *failed* as the drought persisted >

syn dwindle, shrink, wane, waste (away), weaken

rel decrease, diminish, lessen; give out, run out; short

idiom be found wanting

con appreciate, gain, grow, increase, wax

4 to be less than adequate or successful <the attack *failed* >

syn ‖flop, flummox, wash out

rel bankrupt, bomb, deplete, drain, exhaust, impoverish; bust out, flunk, ‖spin

idiom come to grief, fall flat (*or* short), go on the rocks, ‖lay an egg, ‖take the count

ant succeed

5 to be unable to meet financial engagements <the bank *failed* >

syn break, bust, crash, fold

rel gazette; close, end, finish, terminate

idiom be ruined, go bankrupt, go broke, go on the rocks, go to the wall, go under

con boom, prosper

6 *syn* see NEGLECT

idiom be found wanting, come (*or* fall) short of

failing *n* *syn* see FAULT 2

rel imperfection, shortcoming

idiom weak point

failing *adj* *syn* see SHORT 3

failure *n* **1** omission of performance of an action or task <the mechanic's *failure* to adjust the brakes >

syn default, delinquency, dereliction, neglect, oversight

rel laxity, negligence, remissness, slackness; indifference, unconcern

con accomplishment, achievement, discharge, effectuation, fulfillment

2 lack of satisfactory performance or effect <the *failure* of the candidate in the election >

syn defeat, insuccess, nonsuccess, unsuccess, unsuccessfulness

rel failing, fault, imperfection, shortcoming

idiom no go

ant success

3 the fact or state of being inadequate <the crop *failure* brought on a near famine >

syn defalcation, deficiency, deficit, inadequacy, insufficience, insufficiency, lack, scantiness, shortage, underage; *compare* ABSENCE, SCARCITY

rel inferiority, meagerness, poorness, skimpiness; dearth, paucity

con abundance, adequacy, sufficiency

4 a marked weakening <felt a warning *failure* of physical strength >

syn declination, decline, deterioration, ebbing, waning

rel debilitation, enfeeblement, exhaustion, flagging, weakness

con improvement; invigoration, revitalization, strengthening

5 one that has failed <he is a *failure* in school because of inattention >

syn bomb, bust, dud, flop, lemon, loser

rel botch, fiasco, fizzle, hash, muddle, washout; might-have-been

ant success

fain *adj* *syn* see WILLING 1

faineant *n* *syn* see SLUGGARD

faineant *adj* *syn* see LAZY

rel apathetic, impassive, phlegmatic

con active, energetic, vigorous; busy, industrious

faint *adj* **1** *syn* see GENTLE 1

2 scarcely or imperfectly perceptible <he had only a *faint* idea of how he could help >

syn blear, bleary, dim, fuzzy, ill-defined, indistinct, obscure, shadowy, unclear, undefined, undetermined, undistinct, vague; *compare* OBSCURE 3

rel blurred, dusty, pale, wan, weak; hushed, inaudible, low, muffled, small, soft, stifled, thin

con bright, distinct, evident, obvious, patent, unmistakable; certain, sure

ant clear

faint *n* the act or condition of losing consciousness <was so frightened she fell into a *faint* >

syn blackout, coma, swoon, syncope

rel grayout, swim; dizziness, vertigo

idiom a dead faint

faint *vb* to lose consciousness <*fainted* at the sight of blood >

syn black out, ‖crap out, pass out, ‖swarf, ‖swelt, swoon

rel gray out

idiom faint dead away, fall in a faint, go out like a light, pass out cold

faintly *adv* *syn* see SOTTO VOCE

fair *adj* **1** *syn* see BEAUTIFUL

rel dainty, delicate, exquisite; charming, enchanting; chaste, pure

con ill-favored, ugly

ant foul

2 not stormy <a *fair* day >

syn clarion, clear, cloudless, fine, pleasant, rainless, sunny, sunshine, sunshining, sunshiny, unclouded, undarkened

rel calm, placid, tranquil, unthreatening; balmy, clement, mild, pretty

con overcast, stormy, threatening

3 of light complexion <*fair* people often sunburn badly >

syn blond, light

rel ruddy, tawny

con brunet, dark, swarthy

4 characterized by honesty, justice, and freedom from improper influence <a *fair* decision by the judge >

syn candid, dispassionate, equal, equitable, impartial, impersonal, indifferent, just, nondiscriminatory, nonpartisan, objective, square, unbiased, uncolored, undistinctive, unprejudiced, unprepossessed

rel detached, disinterested; balanced, rational, reasonable, sane; open-minded, straight

con biased, inequitable, partial, partisan, prejudiced, prepossessed, unjust

ant unfair

5 observing the rules <a *fair* fight >

syn clean, sportsmanlike, sportsmanly

rel decent, honest, lawful

con dirty, dishonest, fixed

ant unfair

6 *syn* see EVEN 3

7 *syn* see MEDIUM

rel common, ordinary

con choice, good, prime, right; bad, poor, wrong

fair *n* *syn* see EXHIBITION 2

rel carnival, festival

fair–haired *adj* *syn* see FAVORITE 1

fairish *adj* *syn* see MEDIUM

fairly *adv* **1** *syn* see ENOUGH 2

2 *syn* see SOMEWHAT 2

fairy *n* a benevolent mythical being <children who believe in *fairies* >

syn brownie, elf, fay, nisse, pixie, sprite

rel gremlin, imp, leprechaun, puck; dwarf, gnome, goblin, kobold
con ogre, troll
fairyland *n syn* see UTOPIA
faith *n* 1 *syn* see BELIEF 1
con dubiety, dubiosity, skepticism, uncertainty
2 *syn* see TRUST 1
con disbelief, incredulity, unbelief; apprehension, misgiving
3 *syn* see RELIGION 1
4 *syn* see RELIGION 2
rel doctrines, dogmas, tenets
faithful *adj* 1 firm in adherence to whatever one is bound to by duty or promise <a *faithful* public official, conscientious and above reproach>
syn allegiant, ardent, constant, ‖dinky-di, fast, liege, loyal, resolute, staunch, steadfast, steady, ‖true
rel dependable, reliable, tried, trustworthy; affectionate, devoted, loving; dyed-in-the-wool
con disloyal, false, perfidious, traitorous, treacherous; fickle, inconstant, unstable
ant faithless
2 *syn* see TRUE 3
idiom at one with, on all fours with
3 *syn* see AUTHENTIC 1
faithfulness *n* 1 *syn* see ATTACHMENT 1
2 *syn* see FIDELITY 1
faithless *adj* not true to allegiance or duty <a *faithless* husband>
syn disloyal, false, perfidious, recreant, traitorous, treacherous, unfaithful, unloyal, untrue
rel capricious, fickle, inconstant, unstable; fluctuating, wavering; changeable, changeful
con constant, loyal, resolute, staunch, steadfast, true
ant faithful
faithlessness *n* 1 *syn* see TREACHERY
2 *syn* see INFIDELITY
fake *vb syn* see ASSUME 4
fake *n* 1 *syn* see IMPOSTURE
2 *syn* see IMPOSTOR
fake *adj* 1 *syn* see COUNTERFEIT
rel fabricated, forged; concocted, framed, invented
con bona fide, genuine
2 *syn* see FICTITIOUS 2
faker *n syn* see IMPOSTOR
rel cheat, cheater, cozener, defrauder, swindler
fall *vb* 1 to pass downward <fruit *falling* off a tree> <the temperature *fell* sharply>
syn descend, drop, lower
rel decline, dip, plummet, sink; decrease, diminish, lessen; dangle, drag, droop, trail
ant rise
2 to come down suddenly and involuntarily <*fell* on the ice>
syn drop, go down, keel (over), pitch, plunge, slump, topple, tumble
rel slip, sprawl, stumble, trip
idiom come a cropper, take a header, take a spill
con ascend, climb
3 to suffer ruin, defeat, or failure <the city *fell* after a long siege>
syn go down, go under, submit, succumb, surrender
rel give up, yield
con endure, prevail, resist; conquer, triumph, vanquish, win
4 *syn* see ABATE 4
ant rise
5 *syn* see PLUMMET
fall (off *or* away) *vb syn* see SLIP 6
fall (on *or* upon) *vb syn* see ATTACK 1
fall *n* 1 *syn* see DESCENT 1
2 *syn* see DESCENT 4
3 *usu* **falls** *pl but sing or pl in constr syn* see WATERFALL
fallacious *adj* 1 *syn* see ILLOGICAL
ant valid, sound
2 *syn* see MISLEADING
ant veritable
fallaciousness *n syn* see FALLACY 1
rel ambiguity, equivocation; deception, deluding, misleading; faultiness, illogicality, unreasonableness
ant soundness, validity
fallacy *n* 1 a false or erroneous idea <his argument is based on a *fallacy*>

syn erroneousness, error, fallaciousness, falsehood, falseness, falsity, untruth
rel misconception, misconstrual, misinterpretation, misunderstanding
con comprehension, grasp, understanding; correctitude, correctness, truth
ant verity
2 unsound and misleading reasoning <the *fallacy* of his theory is clearly evident>
syn casuistry, deception, deceptiveness, delusion, equivocation, sophism, sophistry, speciousness, spuriousness
rel elusion, evasion, inconsistency, quibble, quibbling
fall back *vb* 1 *syn* see RETREAT 2
2 *syn* see RECEDE 1
fall flat *vb syn* see FAIL 4
fall guy *n* 1 *syn* see SCAPEGOAT
2 *syn* see FOOL 3
fallible *adj* liable or inclined to error <a *fallible* rule>
syn errable, errant
rel careless, faulty, heedless
con careful, heedful; inerrable, inerrant, unerring; exact, perfect, precise
ant infallible
falling-out *n syn* see QUARREL
falloff *n syn* see DECLINE 3
fall out *vb* 1 *syn* see HAPPEN 1
2 *syn* see QUARREL
fall to *vb syn* see PITCH IN 1
false *adj* 1 not in conformity with what is true <the information turned out to be *false*>
syn counterfactual, erroneous, inaccurate, incorrect, specious, unsound, untrue, wrong; *compare* ILLOGICAL
rel deceptive, delusive, delusory, distorted, fallacious, misleading; deceitful, dishonest, fraudulent, lying, mendacious, untruthful
idiom contrary to fact, off the mark
con accurate, correct, established, factual, truthful, veracious, veridical
ant true
2 *syn* see MISLEADING
3 *syn* see FAITHLESS
rel apostate, backsliding, renegade; crooked, devious; hollow
ant true
4 *syn* see COUNTERFEIT
rel apparent, ostensible, seeming
con bona fide, genuine
ant real
5 *syn* see ARTIFICIAL 2
false face *n syn* see MASK 1
false front *n syn* see MASK 2
falsehood *n* 1 *syn* see FALLACY 1
2 *syn* see LIE
rel fakery, feigning, pretense, sham; deceit, dissimulation, fraud
ant truth
3 *syn* see MENDACITY
falseness *n* 1 *syn* see FALLACY 1
2 *syn* see INFIDELITY
3 *syn* see DEFECTION
falsifier *n syn* see LIAR
falsify *vb* 1 *syn* see LIE
2 *syn* see MISREPRESENT
rel alter, change; cook, doctor; contort; contradict, contravene, deny, traverse
falsity *n* 1 *syn* see LIE
2 *syn* see FALLACY 1
rel bluff, fabrication, fake, sham; disingenuousness, hypocrisy, insincerity, uncandidness
ant verity
3 *syn* see INFIDELITY
falter *vb* 1 *syn* see TEETER
2 *syn* see HESITATE
rel blench, flinch, quail, recoil, shrink; quake, quaver, shake, shudder, tremble; tick over

syn synonym(s) *rel* related word(s)
ant antonym(s) *con* contrasted word(s)
idiom idiomatic equivalent(s)
‖ use limited; if in doubt, see a dictionary

con persevere, persist; decide, determine, resolve

faltering *adj syn* see VACILLATING 2

fame *n* **1** *syn* see REPUTATION 2
2 the state of being widely known for one's deeds < his *fame* was short-lived >
syn celebrity, éclat, notoriety, renown, ‖rep, reputation, repute
rel acclaim, acclamation, applause; acknowledgment, recognition; conspicuousness, prominence; distinction, eminence, glory, greatness, honor, illustriousness, note, preeminence
con disgrace, dishonor, disrepute, ignominy, obloquy, odium, opprobrium, shame
ant obscurity; infamy

famed *adj syn* see FAMOUS 2
ant obscure; ill-famed

familiar *n syn* see FRIEND

familiar *adj* **1** closely associated < time and interests have made them *familiar* >
syn chummy, close, confidential, intimate, thick
rel amicable, friendly, neighborly; affable, boon, cordial, genial, gracious, sociable; comfortable, cozy, easy, snug; forward, fresh, impertinent, intrusive, obtrusive, officious
con detached, disinterested, incurious, indifferent, remote, unconcerned; ceremonial, ceremonious, conventional, formal
ant aloof
2 *syn* see COMMON 4
rel accustomed, habitual, wonted; commonplace, prosaic
con new, newfangled, new-fashioned, novel; rare, strange, uncommon; chimerical, fantastic
ant unfamiliar
3 well-informed especially through study or experience < *familiar* with what is being taught in the schools >
syn abreast, acquainted, au courant, au fait, conversant, informed, up, versant, versed
rel aware, cognizant, conscious, mindful
con unacquainted, unconversant, uninformed, unversed; insensible, unaware, unconscious, unmindful; ignorant, unenlightened, unknowing
ant unfamiliar

familiarity *n syn* see ACQUAINTANCE 1
rel awareness, cognition, comprehension, knowledge, understanding
ant unfamiliarity

familiarize *vb syn* see ACCUSTOM
rel acquaint, adapt, adjust, condition, naturalize, season

family *n* **1** a group of persons of or regarded as of common ancestry < traditionally all men belong to the *family* of Noah >
syn clan, folk, house, kindred, lineage, race, stock, tribe
rel brood, dynasty, line, stirp, strain; issue, offspring, progeny
idiom kith and kin, one's own flesh and blood
2 a group of usually related persons living in one house and under one head < was the only child in her *family* >
syn folks, house, household, ménage

family *adj syn* see DOMESTIC 1

family tree *n syn* see GENEALOGY

famished *adj syn* see HUNGRY

famous *adj* **1** *syn* see WELL-KNOWN
2 widely known and honored for achievement < a *famous* physician >
syn celebrated, celebrious, distinguished, eminent, famed, great, illustrious, notable, prestigious, prominent, redoubtable, renowned; *compare* WELL-KNOWN
rel estimable, honorable, reputable, respectable, well-thought-of
idiom held in esteem
con humble, inconspicuous, undistinguished, unimportant, unknown
ant obscure; infamous
3 *syn* see EXCELLENT
ant wretched

fan *n* **1** *syn* see ADDICT
2 *syn* see AMATEUR 1

fan *vb* **1** *syn* see BLOW 1
‖**2** *syn* see SEARCH 2

fan (out) *vb syn* see OPEN 4

fanatic *adj syn* see EXTREME 3

fanatic *n syn* see ENTHUSIAST

fancied *adj syn* see IMAGINARY 1

fancier *n syn* see AMATEUR 1

fanciful *adj* **1** *syn* see IMAGINARY 1

rel apocryphal, fabulous, fictitious, legendary, mythical; bizarre, fantastic, grotesque; absurd, preposterous; false, wrong
con matter-of-fact, prosaic; truthful, veracious
ant realistic
2 *syn* see FICTITIOUS 1
ant veridical

fancy *n* **1** *syn* see WILL 1
2 *syn* see CAPRICE
rel idea; irrationality, unreasonableness; contrariness, perverseness
3 *syn* see IMAGINATION
rel envisagement, envisioning, objectification
idiom flight of fancy
con awareness, experience, perception
4 an idea or image present in the mind but having no concrete or objective reality < unable to tell fact from *fancy* >
syn daydream, dream, fantasy (*or* phantasy), nightmare, phantasm, vision
rel fable, fabrication, fiction, figment, invention; concept, conception, idea, notion; chimera, delusion, illusion; fata morgana, hallucination, mirage
idiom figment of the imagination
con actuality, fact, reality

fancy *vb* **1** *syn* see LIKE
rel approve, endorse, sanction
idiom have a fancy (*or* hankering) for; have one's heart set on
con deprecate, disapprove; abhor, abominate, detest, dislike, hate, loathe
2 *syn* see THINK 1
con demonstrate, prove, test, try

fancy *adj syn* see ELABORATE 2

fancy–free *adj syn* see FREE 6

fancy house *n syn* see BROTHEL

fancy man *n* **1** *syn* see LOVER 1
2 *syn* see PIMP 1

fancy woman *n syn* see HARLOT 1

fanfare *n syn* see DISPLAY 2

fanny *n syn* see BUTTOCKS

fantastic *adj* **1** *syn* see FICTITIOUS 1
rel implausible, incredible, unbelievable; absurd, preposterous; irrational, unreasonable; deceptive, delusive, delusory, misleading
con common, commonplace, everyday, familiar, ordinary; customary, prevailing, universal, usual
2 conceived or made without reference to reality < their explanation was *fantastic* >
syn antic, bizarre, grotesque
rel adroit, clever, ingenious; eccentric, erratic, odd, queer, singular, strange; absurd, nonsensical, preposterous, ridiculous
con factual, solid, sound, valid, well-grounded; plausible, reasonable
3 *syn* see FOOLISH 2
4 *syn* see MONSTROUS 1
5 *syn* see EXTRAVAGANT 1

fantasy (*or* phantasy) *n* **1** *syn* see IMAGINATION
rel conceiving, envisioning, fancying, imagining; externalizing, objectifying
2 *syn* see FANCY 4
rel caprice, freak, vagary, whim, whimsy; bizarrerie, grotesquerie
con actuality, fact, reality
3 *syn* see PIPE DREAM

far *adv syn* see WELL 8

far *adj syn* see DISTANT 1
idiom a long day's journey
ant near

far and away *adv* by a considerable margin < he was *far and away* the best man for the job >
syn by all odds, by a long shot, by far, by long odds, by odds, out and away
rel decidedly, definitely; doubtless, unconditionally, undoubtedly, unequivocally, unquestionably; absolutely, positively; just, quite, very
con barely; slightly; possibly

far and near *adv syn* see EVERYWHERE 1

far and wide *adv syn* see EVERYWHERE 1

faraway *adj* **1** *syn* see DISTANT 1
ant near-at-hand

2 syn see ABSTRACTED
rel disregardful, heedless, oblivious, stargazing, unheeding, unmindful
idiom off one's guard
farce *n syn* see MOCKERY 2
farceur *n syn* see ZANY 2
farcical *adj syn* see LAUGHABLE
rel absurd, extravagant, nonsensical, outrageous, preposterous
fare *vb* **1 syn** see GO 1
rel advance, progress
idiom make headway
con stay, stop
2 syn see SHIFT 5
farewell *interj syn* see GOOD-BYE
farewell *n syn* see PARTING
farewell *adj syn* see PARTING
farfetched *adj syn* see FORCED
rel bizarre, fantastic, grotesque; eccentric, erratic, queer, strange
con accustomed, usual, wonted
far–flung *adj syn* see DISTANT 1
far–gone *adj syn* see EFFETE 2
farming *n syn* see AGRICULTURE
rel cultivation, tillage; agronomy, geoponics, hydroponics
far–off *adj syn* see DISTANT 1
idiom behind the farthest range
ant nearby
far–out *adj syn* see OUTLANDISH 3
farther *adv syn* see BEYOND 1
farther *adj syn* see ADDITIONAL
farthest *adj syn* see EXTREME 5
ant nearest
fascinate *vb* **1 syn** see ENTHRALL 2
2 syn see ATTRACT 1
rel affect, impress, influence, strike, sway, touch; delight, gladden, please, rejoice; absorb, engage, engross, occupy, preoccupy
con disgust, horrify, repel; affront, insult, offend, outrage, shame
3 syn see INTEREST
fascinated *adj syn* see ENAMORED 3
fascinating *adj syn* see ATTRACTIVE 1
rel delectable, delightful; seducing
fascination *n syn* see CHARM 3
fashion *n* **1 syn** see METHOD 1
rel custom, habit, practice, usage, wont
2 syn see VEIN 1
3 the prevailing or accepted custom <follow the *fashion*>
syn bandwagon, chic, craze, cry, dernier cri, fad, furore, mode, rage, style, ton, trend, ‖twig, vogue
rel drift, tendency; convention, form, usage
idiom the in thing, the last word, the latest thing
fashion *vb syn* see MAKE 3
rel contrive, devise; design, plan, plot; turn out
fashionable *adj syn* see STYLISH
rel current, popular, prevalent, up-to-the-minute
idiom all the rage
ant unfashionable
fast *adj* **1 syn** see SURE 1
rel fixed, held, inextricable, stuck, wedged
con insecure, loose, shaky, unstable
2 syn see FAITHFUL 1
3 moving, proceeding, or acting with great celerity <a *fast* horse>
syn breakneck, expeditious, expeditive, fleet, harefooted, hasty, posthaste, quick, raking, rapid, snappy, speedy, swift
rel active, alert, brisk, keen, lively
idiom quick as lightning, quick as thought, swift as an arrow
con lethargic, logy, poky, sluggish, tardy, torpid; languid, languorous; deliberate, gradual
ant slow
4 persistent in adhering to something <a *fast* grip>
syn firm, fixed, secure, set, tenacious, tight; *compare* STABLE 4, SURE 1
idiom stuck fast
con insecure, loose, relaxed, unfirm, weak; free, unattached, unfixed
5 syn see WILD 7
6 syn see LICENTIOUS 2
7 sexually promiscuous—usually used of a woman <she's said to be *fast*>

syn easy, light, loose, ‖riggish, unchaste, wanton, whorish
rel careless, heedless, lax, slack; bawdy, indecent; lascivious, lecherous, lewd, libertine, licentious, lickerish, riotous
idiom no better than one should be, of easy virtue
con chaste, decent, decorous, modest, moral, pure, virtuous
fast *adv* **1 syn** see HARD 7
2 in a rapid manner <run up the hill as *fast* as you know how>
syn apace, chop-chop, expeditiously, flat-out, fleetly, full tilt, hastily, lickety-split, posthaste, presto, promptly, pronto, quick, quickly, rapidly, soon, speedily, swift, swiftly
idiom by leaps and bounds, in a flash, in a twinkling, in nothing flat, in short order, like a bat out of hell, like a blue streak, like a flash, like a house afire, like a shot, like a streak, like greased lightning, like wildfire
con deliberately, leisurely; apathetically, lethargically, sluggishly
ant slow, slowly
fasten *vb* **1** to cause one thing to hold to another <*fasten* a feather to a hat>
syn affix, attach, fix, rivet
rel connect, join, link, unite; adhere, cleave, cling, cohere, stick
con divide, divorce, part, separate, sever, sunder; loose, loosen
ant unfasten
2 to fix in place or in a desired position <*fasten* the door>
syn anchor, catch, fix, moor, secure
rel bed, implant, infix, lodge, set, settle; embed, join, wedge; establish; bar, hitch, hook
idiom make fast (*or* secure *or* sure)
con loose, undo, unloose, unloosen
ant unfasten
3 to direct (as attention or hope) directly and steadily <*fastened* his whole mind on the problem>
syn concenter, concentrate, fix, fixate, focus, put, rivet
rel address, apply, devote, direct, train, turn
con falter, vacillate, waver
fastidious *adj syn* see NICE 1
rel demanding, exacting; captious, critical, hypercritical
con cursory, uncritical
fastigium *n syn* see TOP 1
fastness *n syn* see FORT
rel retreat, shelter; defense, guard, protection; adytum, sanctum
fat *adj* **1 syn** see FATTY 1
2 having excess adipose tissue <a *fat* woman overflowing her chair>
syn corpulent, fleshy, gross, heavy, obese, overblown, overweight, porcine, portly, pursy, stout, upholstered, weighty; *compare* ROTUND 2
rel beefy, bulky, chunky, dumpy, full-bodied, heavyset, squat, stocky, stubby, thick, thickset; paunchy, potbellied; brawny, burly, husky
idiom broad in the beam, fat as a pig
con angular, gaunt, lank, lanky, rawboned, scrawny, skinny, spare; slender, slight, slim, thin
ant lean
3 syn see LARGE 1
rel broad, deep, wide
con narrow, skinny
4 syn see RESONANT
‖**5 syn** see REMOTE 4
fat *n* **1 syn** see BEST
2 syn see EXCESS 1
fatal *adj* **1 syn** see DEADLY 1
2 bringing on an adverse fate <to accept his word was a *fatal* mistake>
syn calamitous, cataclysmic, catastrophic, disastrous, fateful, ruinous
rel baneful, pernicious; baleful, malefic, maleficent, malign, sinister; ill-fated, ill-starred, unlucky
con advantageous, beneficial, profitable; auspicious, benign, favorable, propitious
fatal *n syn* see FATALITY 2
fatality *n* **1** the condition of causing death <the tuberculosis *fatality* remains high>

---

syn synonym(s)
ant antonym(s)
idiom idiomatic equivalent(s)
‖ use limited; if in doubt, see a dictionary
rel related word(s)
con contrasted word(s)

syn deadliness, lethality, mortality

rel malignancy, noxiousness, perniciousness, poisonousness, virulence

2 an instance of dying especially as the result of accident or disaster <two *fatalities* over the weekend>

syn casualty, death, fatal

‖**fat cat** *n syn* see NOTABLE 1

fate *n* whatever is destined or inevitably decreed for one <the *fate* of the bill has not been decided>

syn circumstance, destiny, doom, kismet, lot, moira, portion, weird

rel consequence, effect, issue, outcome, result, upshot; end, ending, termination; ineluctability, inescapableness, inevitability, inevitableness, unavoidability

con accident, chance, fortune, hazard, luck

fate *vb syn* see PREDESTINE 1

fateful *adj* **1** *syn* see OMINOUS

rel important, momentous, significant; conclusive, decisive, determinative; acute, critical, crucial

con inconclusive, insignificant, trivial, unimportant

2 *syn* see FATAL 2

fathead *n syn* see DUNCE

fatheaded *adj syn* see STUPID 1

father *n* **1** a male human parent <scarcely knew his *father*>

syn dad, dada, daddy, ‖governor, ‖old man, pa, ‖pap, papa, ‖pappy, ‖pater, pop, poppa; *compare* MOTHER 1

2 one that originates or institutes <the *father* of radiotelegraphy>

syn architect, author, creator, founder, generator, inventor, maker, originator, patriarch, sire

rel builder, encourager, motor, mover, organizer, prime mover, producer, promoter, promulgator, supporter; inaugurator, initiator, introducer

con disciple, follower

father *vb* **1** to be the male parent in reproduction <didn't know who *fathered* the child>

syn beget, breed, get, procreate, progenerate, sire

rel engender, generate, ingenerate; spawn

2 *syn* see GENERATE 1

fatherland *n syn* see COUNTRY

fatherless *adj syn* see ILLEGITIMATE 1

fathom *vb* **1** *syn* see SOUND

2 *syn* see KNOW 1

rel penetrate, pierce, probe; perceive, recognize; ‖dig, savvy

fathomable *adj syn* see UNDERSTANDABLE

fathomless *adj syn* see BOTTOMLESS 2

fatidic *adj syn* see PROPHETIC

fatigue *n* complete depletion of strength <suffering from *fatigue*>

syn exhaustion, lassitude, tiredness, weariness

rel enervation, ennui, languor, listlessness; debilitation, faintness, feebleness, weakness

con briskness, energy, liveliness, vigor, vitality; endurance, strength

fatigue *vb syn* see TIRE 1

rel deplete; exhaust, fag, tucker, wear out; debilitate, disable, weaken; annoy, bother, irk, vex

con refresh, rejuvenate, renew, restore; assuage, relieve

fatigued *adj syn* see TIRED 1

fatness *n syn* see OBESITY

‖**fatso** *n syn* see FATTY

fatty *adj* **1** containing fat especially in unusual amounts <a rather *fatty* steak>

syn adipose, fat

rel blubbery, lardy, suety

ant lean

2 having the qualities of fat <the constant frying left a *fatty* deposit on the kitchen woodwork>

syn greasy, oily, oleaginous, unctuous

fatty *n* a fat person <*fatties* trying to diet>

syn blimp, butterball, dumpling, ‖fatso, ‖tub

rel overweight; pudge, roly-poly, strapper; potbelly

idiom tons of fun

ant skinny

fatuous *adj syn* see SIMPLE 3

rel idiotic, imbecile, moronic; besotted, fond, infatuated, insensate; absurd, dumb, silly, stupid

con judicious, prudent, sage, sane, sapient, wise

ant sensible

faucet *n* a fixture for controlling the passage of fluid <turn off the *faucet*>

syn cock, gate, hydrant, petcock, spigot, stopcock, tap, valve

rel bung, spile

fault *n* **1** *syn* see IMPERFECTION

rel infirmity, weakness

con faultlessness, impeccability; meticulousness, preciseness, precision

2 an imperfection in character or an ingrained moral weakness <he has few *faults*>

syn failing, foible, frailty, vice

rel infirmity, weakness; blemish, defect, flaw

con excellence, perfection, virtue; desirability, goodness, rightness

ant merit

3 *syn* see BLAME

rel accountability, answerability, liability, responsibility; crime, error, offense, sin, transgression

faultfinder *n* **1** *syn* see CRITIC

2 *syn* see GROUCH

faultfinding *adj syn* see CRITICAL 1

rel particular, pernickety; ultracritical

con appreciative, cherishing, prizing, valuing

faultily *adv syn* see AMISS 1

rel erroneously, fallaciously, inaccurately, mistakenly, unfairly

con correctly, right

faultless *adj* **1** *syn* see IMPECCABLE 1

rel entire, intact, perfect, whole; blameless

con defective, deficient, imprecise, inaccurate, inexact, uncorrect

ant faulty

2 *syn* see INNOCENT 2

faulty *adj* marked by a fault or defect <a *faulty* mechanism>

syn amiss, defective, flawed, imperfect, sick

rel imprecise, inaccurate, inexact, uncorrect; deficient, inadequate, incomplete; erroneous, fallacious, fallible, specious, wrong; blemished, damaged, defaced, disfigured, marred

con accurate, correct, exact, nice, precise, right; complete, entire, intact, perfect, whole; excellent, good; unflawed, unimpaired

ant faultless

faux pas *n* a breach of etiquette or of social convention <hustled him out of the room before he could commit another *faux pas*>

syn blooper, boner, ‖boo-boo, break, gaffe, impropriety, indecorum, solecism; *compare* ERROR 2

rel bungle, misstep, stumble; howler, screamer; indiscretion, misjudgment, oversight, pratfall

favor *n* **1** *syn* see REGARD 4

ant disfavor

2 *syn* see APPROBATION 1

con depreciation, derogation, disparagement

ant disfavor

3 *syn* see GIFT 1

rel aid, assistance, backing, encouragement, help, support

4 a special privilege <willing to grant a *favor* to a good friend>

syn courtesy, dispensation, indulgence, kindness, service

rel aid, assistance, cooperation, help

favor *vb* **1** *syn* see APPROVE 1

rel endorse, OK (*or* okay), sanction; appreciate, prize, value

idiom set great store by

con decry, depreciate, disparage

ant disfavor

2 *syn* see OBLIGE 2

rel humor, indulge, pamper

idiom do one a favor (*or* service), do right by

con baffle, circumvent, foil, frustrate, thwart

3 *syn* see ENCOURAGE 2

4 *syn* see RESEMBLE

con contradict, differ

favorable *adj* **1** expressing approval <a *favorable* recommendation>

syn approbative, approbatory, approving

rel benignant, kind, kindly; recommendatory, well-disposed; commendatory, complimentary, laudatory, praiseful

idiom in one's favor

con depreciative, disapprobatory, disapproving, disparaging, uncomplimentary; censorious, condemnatory, critical, faultfinding *ant* unfavorable

2 *syn* see PLEASANT 1

3 *syn* see GOOD 1

rel healthful, salutary, wholesome

con disadvantageous, unpropitious; damaging, hampering

ant unfavorable

4 *syn* see TIMELY 1

5 indicative of a successful outcome <*favorable* conditions for opening a new business>

syn auspicious, benign, bright, dexter, fortunate, propitious, white

rel advantageous, beneficial, profitable; happy, lucky, promising, providential; cheering, encouraging, reassuring

idiom full of promise

con calamitous, cataclysmic, catastrophic, disastrous, fatal, fateful, ruinous; baleful, malefic, maleficent, malign, sinister; ill-fated, ill-starred, unlucky; inauspicious, unpromising, unpropitious

ant unfavorable

favorably *adv syn* see WELL 5

favored *adj syn* see FAVORITE 2

favoring *adj syn* see GOOD 1

favorite *adj* **1** accorded special treatment or attention <a *favorite* daughter>

syn beloved, blue-eyed, darling, dear, fair-haired, loved, pet, precious, white-haired, white-headed

rel admired, adored, esteemed, revered; cherished, prized, treasured

idiom dear as the apple of one's eye, dear to one's heart, held dear

con contemned, despised, disdained; abhorrent, detested, hated

2 constituting a favorite <*favorite* melodies>

syn favored, popular, preferred, well-liked

rel laudable, pleasant, praiseworthy; cherished, prized, treasured

con despised, detested, disliked, hated, unpopular; eschewed, rejected

fawn *vb* to act or behave with abjectness in the presence of a superior <*fawn* on the master>

syn apple-polish, bootlick, ‖brownnose, cotton, cower, cringe, grovel, honey (up), kowtow, slaver, toady, truckle

rel blandish, cajole, coax, wheedle; butter (up), flatter, make up (to); cater (to), pander (to); crawl; abase, debase, demean; bow, cave, defer, submit, yield; court, invite, woo

idiom be at one's beck and call, curry favor, dance attendance, kiss one's feet, lick one's shoes (or boots), make a doormat of oneself

con contemn, despise, disdain, scorn, scout; reject, repudiate, spurn; flout, gibe, jeer, scoff; deride, mock, ridicule, taunt

ant domineer

fawning *adj* characteristic of one that fawns <sent *fawning* greetings>

syn bootlicking, cowering, cringing, groveling, kowtowing, parasitic, sycophant, sycophantic, sycophantical, sycophantish, toadying, toadyish, truckling

rel flunkyish, obsequious, servile, slavish, subservient; compliant, deferential, humble, submissive, yielding; ingratiating; adulatory, flattering, mealy-mouthed; crawling, spineless; abject, ignoble, mean

con arrogant, disdainful, haughty, insolent, lordly, overbearing, proud, supercilious; contemptuous, insulting, scathing, scornful; authoritative, imperious, magisterial, masterful

ant domineering

fay *n syn* see FAIRY

faze *vb syn* see EMBARRASS

rel confound, dumbfound, mystify, nonplus, perplex, puzzle; confuse, muddle; appall, daunt, dismay, horrify; annoy, bother, irritate, vex

con calm, compose, quiet, relax, soothe; ease, relieve

fealty *n syn* see FIDELITY 1

rel faith, trueness, truth; dependability, reliability, trustworthiness; devotedness, support

con disloyalty, traitorousness, treacherousness

ant perfidy

fear *n* **1** agitation or dismay in the anticipation of or in the presence of danger <living in *fear* of what the future might hold>

syn alarm, cold feet, consternation, dismay, dread, fright, horror, panic, terror, trepidation, trepidity

rel apprehension, foreboding, misgiving, presentiment; angst, anxiety, concern, worry; agitation, discomposure, disquietude,

perturbation; chickenheartedness, cowardice, cowardliness, faintheartedness, timidity, timorousness; funk, scare

idiom cold sweat

con boldness, bravery, courage, courageousness, dauntlessness, fortitude, gallantry, intrepidity, prowess, valiancy, valor

ant fearlessness

2 *syn* see REVERENCE 2

rel esteem, respect

con contempt, scorn

fearful *adj* **1** *syn* see AFRAID 1

rel agitated, alarmed, discomposed, disquieted, disturbed, perturbed

con audacious, bold, brave, courageous, dauntless, unafraid, valiant

ant fearless

2 inspired or moved by fear <*fearful* of loud noises>

syn afraid, apprehensive; *compare* AFRAID 1

rel alarmed, disquieted, disturbed; aflutter, agitated, jittery, nervous, perturbed, uneasy; anxious, concerned, solicitous, worried

con assured, confident, sanguine, sure; collected, composed, cool, imperturbable, nonchalant, unflappable, unperturbed

ant unafraid

3 causing fear <a *fearful* sight>

syn appalling, awful, dire, direful, dreadful, formidable, frightful, horrible, horrific, redoubtable, shocking, terrible, terrific, tremendous

rel alarming, frightening, terrifying; ghastly, grim, grisly, gruesome, lurid, macabre; baleful, malign, sinister; overwhelming, sublime

con attractive, charming, delightful, enchanting, pleasant, pleasing

ant reassuring

fearless *adj syn* see BRAVE 1

rel assured, confident, sanguine, sure

con afraid, frightened, scared, terrified

ant fearful

feasible *adj syn* see POSSIBLE 1

rel practical; advantageous, beneficial, profitable; appropriate, fit, fitting, suitable

con impossible, impracticable, unachievable, unattainable, unworkable; ambitious, pretentious, utopian

ant infeasible, unfeasible

feast *n syn* see DINNER

rel entertainment, festivity; refreshment, repast; meal

feat *n* **1** *syn* see ADVENTURE

idiom bold stroke, deed of derring-do

2 a remarkable act or performance <Washington's *feat* of tossing a dollar across the river>

syn achievement, deed, exploit, tour de force

rel act, action; accomplishment, consummation, execution, performance; conquest, triumph, victory

3 *syn* see TRICK 3

feather *n syn* see TYPE

featherbrain *n syn* see SCATTERBRAIN

featherbrained *adj syn* see GIDDY 1

rel capricious, fickle, impulsive, whimsical; shallow, superficial, unprofound

featherhead *n syn* see SCATTERBRAIN

featherlight *adj syn* see LIGHT 1

featherweight *n syn* see DUNCE

featherweight *adj syn* see LIGHT 1

feature *n* **1** *syn* see QUALITY 1

2 *syn* see CHARACTERISTIC 1

rel article, detail, item, particular; component, constituent, element, factor, ingredient; individuality, particularity, peculiarity, speciality, specialty; attribute, property, quality

3 features *pl syn* see FACE 1

feature *vb* ‖**1** *syn* see RESEMBLE

2 *syn* see THINK 1

3 *syn* see EMPHASIZE

febrile *adj syn* see FEVERISH 1

feckless *adj* **1** having no real worth or purpose <after years of *feckless* negotiations>

---

syn synonym(s)   *rel* related word(s)

ant antonym(s)   *con* contrasted word(s)

idiom idiomatic equivalent(s)

‖ use limited; if in doubt, see a dictionary

syn fustian, good-for-nothing, meaningless, purposeless, unpurposed, useless, worthless

rel bootless, fruitless, futile, unavailing, vain; ineffective, ineffectual, inefficacious

con meaningful, purposeful, worthwhile; fruitful; effective, effectual, efficacious; consequential, important, momentous, significant, weighty

ant efficient, ‖feckful

2 syn see CARELESS 1

rel carefree, easygoing, happy-go-lucky, lackadaisical, nonchalant; remiss; irresponsible, undependable, unreliable, untrustworthy

con attentive, considerate, thoughtful; meticulous, punctilious, punctual, scrupulous; dependable, reliable, responsible, trustworthy

3 syn see IRRESPONSIBLE

ant ‖feckful

fecund *adj syn* see FERTILE

rel breeding, generating, propagating, reproducing

con infertile, sterile

ant barren

fecundity *n* **1 syn** see FERTILITY

rel productiveness, productivity; exuberance, lavishness, lushness, luxuriance, prodigality, profuseness, profusion

con infertility, sterility, unproductiveness

ant barrenness, infecundity

2 syn see ELOQUENCE

federation *n syn* see ALLIANCE 2

fed up *adj* disgusted and completely out of patience <*fed up* with her bad behavior>

syn disgusted, sick, tired, weary

rel bored; glutted, sated, satiated, surfeited

idiom fed to the gills (*or* teeth), full up to here with, sick and tired of, sick (*or* tired) to death

con enchanted, enraptured, enthralled; delighted, excited, exhilarated, pleased, thrilled

fee *n syn* see WAGE

rel consideration; charge, cost, expense, price

‖**feeb** *n syn* see FOOL 4

feeble *adj* **1 syn** see WEAK 1

rel emasculated, enervated, unmanned, unnerved; helpless; aged, doddering, senile; ailing, sapless

con hale, healthy, sound; lusty, strenuous; strong

ant robust

2 syn see TENUOUS 3

feebleminded *adj syn* see RETARDED

ant strong-minded

feebleness *n syn* see INFIRMITY 1

feed *vb syn* see GIVE 3

feed (on) *vb syn* see EAT 1

idiom have (*or* take) a bite, ‖put on the feed bag (*or* nose bag)

feed *n* **1 syn** see MEAL

2 syn see FOOD 1

rel banquet, feast, meal, repast

feel *vb* **1 syn** see TOUCH 1

rel manipulate, ply, wield; explore, sound; fumble, grope

2 to have as an emotional response <*felt* pleasure in her company>

syn experience, know, savor, taste

rel apprehend; notice, observe, perceive; encounter, meet; endure, suffer, undergo

idiom be aware (*or* conscious) of, be sensible of

con disregard, ignore

3 to view as right or true <we *feel* that he should retire soon>

syn believe, consider, credit, deem, hold, sense, think; *compare* CONSIDER 3

rel assume, presume, suppose, suspect; conclude, deduce, gather, infer, judge; conjecture, guess, surmise; esteem; repute

idiom take (it) into one's head

con challenge, distrust, doubt, misdoubt, mistrust, question

4 syn see GROPE

feel (for) *vb syn* see COMPASSIONATE

feel *n* **1 syn** see TOUCH 3

2 syn see TOUCH 4

3 syn see AIR 3

con basis, essence, reality

feeler *n* an attempt to ascertain opinion <the letter was a *feeler* to see how they would react>

syn trial balloon

rel query, question; inquiry, probe, test; leader, leading question; sounding board; intimation, representation; prospectus; kiteflying

feeling *n* **1 syn** see SENSATION 1

rel action, behavior, reaction; responsiveness; palpability, palpableness, perceptivity, perceptibleness, tangibility, tangibleness

con apathy, indifference, insensibility, numbness

2 syn see TOUCH 4

3 subjective response or reaction (as to a person or situation) <a *feeling* of sadness>

syn affection, affectivity, emotion, passion, sentiment

rel humor, mood, temper, vein; attitude, outlook; belief, opinion, view; concept, idea, impression, notion, thought

4 syn see OPINION

5 syn see AIR 3

rel impress, impression, imprint

feeling *adj syn* see EMOTIONAL 1

con numb, unmoved, unresponsive

ant unfeeling

feel out *vb syn* see PROBE 2

feign *vb syn* see ASSUME 4

feigned *adj syn* see ARTIFICIAL 3

rel counterfeit, false, sham

con heartfelt, hearty, sincere, wholehearted, whole-souled

feint *n syn* see TRICK 1

rel make-believe, pretense, pretension; befooling, hoax, hoodwinking; cheat, counterfeit, deceit, fake, humbug, imposture, sham; expedient, resort, shift

felicitate *vb syn* see CONGRATULATE

rel commend, compliment, recommend; salute

con comfort, console, solace; commiserate, condole (with), pity; gibe, jeer, scoff; deride, mock, ridicule, taunt; contemn

felicitous *adj syn* see FIT 1

rel convincing, telling; opportune, pat, seasonable, timely, well-timed; apposite, apropos, germane, pertinent, relevant

con awkward, clumsy, gauche, inept, maladroit; unfortunate, unhappy, unlucky

ant infelicitous

feline *adj syn* see STEALTHY 2

fell *vb* **1** to force an opponent off his feet <*felled* the heckler with a single blow>

syn bowl (down *or* over), bring down, down, drop, flatten, floor, ground, knock down, knock over, lay low, level, mow (down), prostrate, throw down, tumble

rel shoot, shoot down

idiom lay level with the ground

con pick up, raise

2 to bring down by cutting <*felled* the great oak by the driveway>

syn chop, cut, hew

rel flatten, level, raze; cleave, rive, split; sever, sunder; gash, hack, mangle, slash

fell *adj* **1 syn** see FIERCE 1

rel baleful, malefic, maleficent, malign, sinister; implacable, relentless, unrelenting; fearful, horrible, horrific, terrific

con compassionate, sympathetic, tender; clement, forbearing, lenient, merciful; humane

2 syn see GRAVE 3

fell *n syn* see HIDE

fellow *n* **1 syn** see PARTNER

2 syn see ACCOMPANIMENT 2

3 syn see MATE 5

4 syn see MAN 3

fellow feeling *n syn* see SYMPATHY 2

fellowship *n* **1 syn** see COMPANY 1

2 syn see ASSOCIATION 2

felo–de–se *n syn* see SUICIDE

felon *n syn* see CRIMINAL

femme fatale *n syn* see SIREN

fen *n syn* see SWAMP

fence *n syn* see BAR 2

fence *vb* **1 syn** see ENCLOSE 1

2 syn see DODGE 1

rel feint, maneuver; baffle, foil, outwit

fend *vb* **1 syn** see DEFEND 1

2 syn see WARD 1

fend (off) *vb* to give a sharp check to <tried to *fend* off his attentions>

syn hold off, keep off, rebuff, rebut, repel, repulse, stave off, ward (off)

rel refuse, reject; snub, spurn; avert, avoid

idiom hold (*or* keep) at bay, keep at a distance, keep at arm's length

con allure, attract, captivate, charm, enchant, fascinate; embolden, hearten

feral *adj* **1** *syn* see BRUTISH

rel barbaric, barbarous, ferocious, fierce, inhuman, savage, vicious

con gentle, mild, tame

2 *syn* see SAVAGE 1

ferine *adj syn* see BRUTISH

ferment *vb syn* see SEETHE 4

ferment *n* **1** *syn* see UNREST

2 *syn* see COMMOTION 1

ferocious *adj* **1** *syn* see FIERCE 1

rel rapacious, ravening, ravenous, voracious; implacable, relentless

ant tender

2 *syn* see SAVAGE

ferret out *vb syn* see SEEK 1

rel elicit, extract; nose out, pry (out); penetrate, pierce, probe; chase, follow, pursue, trail; ascertain, determine, discover, learn

con conceal, hide, screen, secrete; camouflage, disguise; cover (up), hush (up), suppress

ant squirrel (away)

ferry *vb syn* see CARRY 1

fertile *adj* marked by abundant productivity < *fertile* soil > <a *fertile* mind >

syn childing, fecund, fruitful, productive, proliferant, prolific, rich, spawning

rel bearing, producing, yielding; abundant, bountiful, copious, exuberant, generous, lush, luxuriant, plenteous, plentiful, teeming; creative, ingenious, inventive, pregnant, resourceful; exciting, galvanizing, provoking, quickening, stimulating

con barren, impotent, unfruitful; dull, imitative, stupid, unproductive

ant infertile, sterile

fertility *n* the quality or state of being fertile < insure the *fertility* of the soil >

syn fecundity, fruitfulness, prolificacy

rel abundance, copiousness, plentifulness; creativity, ingenuity, inventiveness, resourcefulness

con barrenness, impotence, unfruitfulness

ant infertility, sterility

fervent *adj syn* see IMPASSIONED

rel devout, pious, religious; responsive, tender, warm, warmhearted; heartfelt, hearty, sincere, unfeigned, wholehearted, whole-souled; earnest, serious; eager, enthusiastic

con apathetic, impassive, phlegmatic; aloof, detached, indifferent, unconcerned

fervid *adj* **1** *syn* see IMPASSIONED

con collected, composed, cool, imperturbable, nonchalant

ant gelid

2 *syn* see FEVERISH 2

fervor *n syn* see PASSION 6

rel devoutness, piety, piousness; earnestness, seriousness, solemnity; heartiness, sincerity, wholeheartedness; empressement, warmth

con apathy, impassiveness, impassivity; aloofness, detachment, indifference, unconcern; languor, lethargy, torpor

fescennine *adj syn* see OBSCENE 2

fess (up) *vb syn* see ACKNOWLEDGE 1

fester *vb syn* see RANKLE

festive *adj syn* see MERRY

festivity *n syn* see MERRYMAKING

fetch *vb syn* see SELL 4

fetching *adj syn* see ENTICING

fetch up *vb* ‖**1** *syn* see BRING UP 1

2 *syn* see STOP 4

fetid *adj syn* see MALODOROUS 1

rel loathsome, repugnant, repulsive, revolting

con aromatic, balmy, odorous, redolent

ant fragrant

fetish *n* **1** *syn* see CHARM 2

2 irrational reverence or attachment < had a *fetish* for red hair >

syn fixation, mania, obsession, thing

rel preoccupation, prepossession; bias, partiality, predilection, prejudice; leaning, penchant, proclivity, propensity

con antipathy, aversion, repugnance, repulsion; dislike, disrelish, distaste

fetter *n,* usu **fetters** *pl syn* see SHACKLE

fetter *vb syn* see HAMPER

con disembarrass, disencumber, disentangle, extricate, untangle; detach, disengage

fettle *n syn* see ORDER 10

feud *n* **1** *syn* see VENDETTA

2 *syn* see QUARREL

rel argument; combat, contest

fevered *adj* **1** *syn* see FEVERISH 1

ant afebrile

2 *syn* see FEVERISH 2

feverish *adj* **1** abnormally heated by fever < the child's forehead felt *feverish* >

syn febrile, fevered, fiery

rel burning, flushed, hectic, hot, inflamed, pyretic

ant afebrile

2 marked by intense emotion or activity <a *feverish* imagination >

syn burning, fervid, fevered, heated, hectic

rel excited, high-strung, nervous, overwrought; frenzied, furious, passionate

idiom keyed up

con calm, composed, cool, serene, tranquil; apathetic, languid, lethargic, listless, phlegmatic

few *adj syn* see INFREQUENT

few *n* a small quantity or number < sold a *few* of the books >

syn handful, scattering, smatch, smatter, smattering, spatter, spattering, sprinkling

con abundance, many, multitude, numbers

fiat *n syn* see SANCTION

fib *n syn* see LIE

rel equivocation, evasiveness; mendacity, untruthfulness

idiom tall tale

fib *vb syn* see LIE

rel concoct, fabricate, make up, trump up

idiom draw the long bow, stretch the truth

fibber *n syn* see LIAR

fibbery *n syn* see MENDACITY

fiber *n syn* see TEXTURE 2

fibrous *adj syn* see MUSCULAR 1

fibster *n syn* see LIAR

fickle *adj syn* see INCONSTANT 1

rel unfaithful; undependable, unreliable

con stable, unchanging

ant constant, true

fiction *n* a story, account, explanation, or conception which is an invention of the human mind < his belief was based on a *fiction* >

syn fable, fabrication, figment

rel concoction, fantasy, invention; falsehood, lie, misrepresentation, untruth; anecdote, narrative, story, tale, yarn; fish story

con actuality, reality

ant fact

fictional *adj syn* see FICTITIOUS 1

fictitious *adj* **1** suggestive of fiction especially in lacking a sound factual basis < *fictitious* values in logic >

syn chimerical, fanciful, fantastic, fictional, fictive, illusory, imaginary, suppositious, supposititious, unreal

rel concocted, created, invented, made; fabricated, fashioned; cooked-up, false, made-up, trumped-up, untrue; romantic

con actual, real, true; authentic, genuine; factual, veritable; truthful, veracious, verisimilar

2 not genuine < the gigolo wooed the heiress with *fictitious* ardor >

syn fake, mock, sham, simulated; *compare* ARTIFICIAL 2

rel deceptive, delusive, delusory, misleading; dishonest, unreal, untrue; artificial, ersatz, factitious, synthetic

con authentic, bona fide, veritable; actual, honest, real, true

---

syn synonym(s)   *rel* related word(s)

ant antonym(s)   *con* contrasted word(s)

idiom idiomatic equivalent(s)

‖ use limited; if in doubt, see a dictionary

ant genuine

fictive *adj syn* see FICTITIOUS 1

fiddle *vb* **1** to handle something nervously or absently <always *fiddling* with his tie>
syn fidget, play, trifle, twiddle
rel feel, handle, touch
2 to work aimlessly, fruitlessly, or pointlessly <*fiddled* around with the engine for hours>
syn doodle, mess, mess around, potter, puddle, putter, tinker
rel dabble, fool, monkey

fiddle–faddle *n syn* see NONSENSE 2

fiddlesticks *n pl syn* see NONSENSE 2

fidelity *n* **1** constancy to something to which one is bound by a pledge or duty <we must practice *fidelity* to our word>
syn allegiance, ardor, devotion, faithfulness, fealty, loyalty, piety
rel constancy, staunchness, steadfastness; dependability, reliability, trustworthiness
con disloyalty, falseness, falsity, perfidiousness, traitorousness, treacherousness, treachery; undependableness, unreliability, untrustworthiness
ant perfidy; faithlessness
2 *syn* see ATTACHMENT 1
ant infidelity

fidget *vb syn* see FIDDLE 1

fidgety *adj syn* see NERVOUS

field *n* a limited area of knowledge or endeavor to which pursuits, activities, and interests are confined <a lawyer eminent in his *field*>
syn bailiwick, champaign, demesne, domain, dominion, precinct, province, region, sphere, terrain, territory, walk
rel bounds, confines, limits; area, department; compass, orbit, purview, range, reach, scope, sweep
con terra incognita

fiend *n syn* see DEVIL 1
2 *syn* see DEVIL 2
3 *syn* see ENTHUSIAST

fiendish *adj* having or manifesting qualities associated with devils, demons, and fiends <inflicted *fiendish* tortures on his captive>
syn demoniac, demonian, demonic, devilish, diabolic, diabolonian, satanic, serpentine, unhallowed
rel hellish, infernal; baleful, malefic, maleficent, malign, sinister; malevolent, malicious, malignant; atrocious, heinous, monstrous, outrageous; barbarous, cruel, ferocious, inhuman, savage, vicious
con benign, benignant, kind, kindly; gentle, mild; compassionate, sympathetic, tender

fierce *adj* **1** displaying fury or malignity in looks or actions <*fierce* native tribes>
syn barbarous, cannibalic, cruel, fell, ferocious, grim, inhuman, inhumane, savage, truculent, wolfish
rel menacing, threatening; enraged, infuriated, maddened; aggressive, bellicose, belligerent, pugnacious; brutal, merciless, pitiless, ruthless, vicious, wild
con benign, benignant, gentle, kind, kindly; peaceful; subdued, submissive, tame
ant mild
2 *syn* see INTENSE 1
rel excessive, extreme, inordinate; penetrating, piercing; superlative, supreme, transcendent
con gentle, mild, subdued

fiercely *adv syn* see HARD 2

fiery *adj* **1** *syn* see BURNING 1
2 *syn* see HOT 1
ant frigid, icy
3 *syn* see FEVERISH 1
4 *syn* see SPIRITED 2
rel headlong, hotheaded, impetuous, madcap, precipitate; fervid, impassioned, perfervid; fierce, intense, vehement, violent; enthusiastic, excitable, impulsive, unrestrained; irascible, irritable
con deliberate, leisurely, slow; apathetic, dull, impassive, lethargic, phlegmatic, sluggish; enervated, listless, spiritless
5 *syn* see IMPASSIONED
ant icy

fifty–fifty *adv syn* see EVENLY 1

fifty–fifty *adj syn* see EVEN 4

fight *vb* **1** *syn* see CONTEND 1
rel strive, struggle; rowdy, scuffle, tussle; debate, dispute; altercate, bicker, quarrel, scrap, spat, squabble, tiff, wrangle

idiom ‖mix it, mix it up, put up a fight
con bow, capitulate, submit, succumb, yield
2 *syn* see RESIST
con abide, bear, endure, suffer; advocate, back, champion, support, uphold; defend, guard, protect, shield

fight *n* **1** *syn* see BRAWL 2
2 *syn* see QUARREL
3 *syn* see ATTACK 2

fighter *n syn* see SOLDIER

fighting man *n syn* see SOLDIER

figment *n syn* see FICTION
rel daydream, dream, fancy, nightmare; bubble, chimera, illusion; creation

figurant *n syn* see DANCER

figurante *n syn* see DANCER

figuration *n* **1** *syn* see OUTLINE
2 *syn* see ALLEGORY 1

figure *n* **1** *syn* see NUMBER
rel character, symbol
2 *syn* see FORM 1
rel delineation; appearance, build, frame, physique
3 a unit in a decorative composition (as in a fabric) <a rug with geometrical *figures* in blue and red>
syn design, device, motif, motive, pattern
rel decoration, embellishment, ornamentation

figure *vb* **1** *syn* see CALCULATE
2 *syn* see ADD 2
rel count, enumerate, number
3 *syn* see DECIDE

figure out *vb syn* see SOLVE 2
rel disentangle, unscramble, untangle; crack, decode
con obfuscate, obscure; conceal, hide, screen

figuring *n syn* see COMPUTATION

filch *vb syn* see STEAL 1

filcher *n syn* see THIEF

file *n syn* see LINE 5

filius nullius *n syn* see BASTARD 1

filius populi *n syn* see BASTARD 1

fill *vb* **1** to make full in a way or to a degree that prevents further entry or passage <*fill* a cavity in a tooth>
syn block, choke, clog, close, congest, obstruct, occlude, plug, stop, stopper
rel bar, dam, jam; ‖bung, pug
con clear, free
2 *syn* see LOAD 3
3 *syn* see SATISFY 5
4 *syn* see SATIATE
rel overfeed, overfill, overstuff

fille de joie *n syn* see PROSTITUTE

fillet *n syn* see STRIP 1

fill in *vb* **1** *syn* see INTRODUCE 6
2 *syn* see INFORM 2

fill–in *n syn* see SUBSTITUTE

film *n* **1** *syn* see HAZE 1
2 *syn* see MOVIE

filmy *adj* characterized by fineness and delicacy of texture <*filmy* curtains>
syn diaphanous, flimsy, gauzy, gossamer, sheer, tiffany, transparent
rel dainty, delicate, fine
con coarse, heavy, opaque, rough

filthy *adj* **1** *syn* see DIRTY 1
rel disheveled, slipshod, sloppy, slovenly, unkempt; loathsome, offensive, repulsive, revolting, verminous; coarse, gross, obscene, ribald, vulgar
con cleaned, cleansed; clean, cleanly; neat, shipshape, tidy, trig, trim
ant immaculate, spick-and-span
2 *syn* see OBSCENE 2

filthy lucre *n syn* see MONEY

finagle *vb syn* see ENGINEER

final *adj syn* see LAST
rel crowning, ending, finishing; conclusive, decisive, definitive, determinative; irrefutable, unanswerable, unappealable
con earliest, maiden, original, primary; beginning, incipient, introductory; inaugural
ant initial

finale *n* a final part or element (as of a sequence, series, or action) <the solution of the mystery forms the *finale* of the play>

syn close, conclusion, end, ending, finish, windup; *compare* END 2

rel climax, consummation, culmination; denouement, payoff; cessation, termination

con beginning, genesis, initiation, rise, start; inception, origin, root, source

ant prologue

finally *adv syn* see YET 2
  idiom at last, at length, at long last, in the long run, when all is said and done

finance *vb* **1** *syn* see CAPITALIZE
  idiom put up the money, raise the dough
  2 *syn* see ENDOW 2
  rel back, bank, bankroll, grubstake, stake, underwrite; patronize, promote, sponsor, support

financial *adj* of or relating to finance < the *financial* interests of the country >
  syn fiscal, monetary, pecuniary, pocket
  rel business, commercial, economic

find *vb* **1** to come upon < they soon *found* what they needed >
  syn catch, descry, detect, encounter, espy, hit (on *or* upon), meet (with), spot, turn up
  rel discern, discover, note, sight; distinguish, identify, recognize; dig up, scare up
  idiom bring to light, come up with, fall in with, lay one's finger (on *or* upon), lay one's hand (on *or* upon)
  con miss, overlook, pass (over)
  ant lose
  2 *syn* see GIVE 3

find *n* **1** one of unexpected worth or merit obtained or encountered more or less by chance < the young understudy proved to be a remarkable *find* >
  syn treasure, treasure trove
  rel boast, gem, jewel, pride
  idiom one in a thousand (*or* million)
  2 *syn* see DISCOVERY

find out *vb syn* see DISCOVER 3

fine *n* a pecuniary penalty exacted by an authority < paid a *fine* of ten dollars >
  syn amercement, forfeit, mulct, penalty
  rel damages, reparation; punishment; assessment

fine *vb syn* see PENALIZE
  rel distrain, exact, levy, tax; confiscate, sequestrate

fine *adj* **1** marked by subtlety of perception or discrimination < I cannot follow these *fine* distinctions >
  syn delicate, finespun, hairline, hairsplitting, nice, refined, subtle
  rel abstruse, esoteric, recondite; cryptic, enigmatic, obscure; minute, petty, trifling
  con definite, explicit, express, specific; clear, lucid, perspicuous; broad, extensive, general, generic, indefinite, wide
  2 consisting of small particles < *fine* sand >
  syn impalpable, powdery, pulverized
  rel light, loose, porous
  ant coarse
  3 *syn* see EXCELLENT
  rel beautiful, splendid; enjoyable, pleasant
  idiom fine and dandy
  con miserable, wretched; atrocious, awful, objectionable, unpleasant
  4 *syn* see FAIR 2

finecomb *vb syn* see SCOUR 2

finery *n* dressy clothing < decked out in all her *finery* >
  syn ‖best bib and tucker, bravery, frippery, full dress, ‖glad rags, regalia, Sunday best, war paint
  rel apparel, clothes; foofaraw, frill, gewgaw, ornament, trimming
  con rags, tatters

finespun *adj syn* see FINE 1

finesse *vb syn* see MANIPULATE 2

fine–tooth–comb *vb syn* see SCOUR 2

finger *vb* **1** *syn* see TOUCH 1
  2 *syn* see DESIGNATE 2
  3 *syn* see IDENTIFY

finical *adj syn* see NICE 1
  con slipshod, sloppy, slovenly; blowsy, dowdy, frowzy, slatternly

finicking *adj syn* see NICE 1

finicky *adj syn* see NICE 1

finish *vb* **1** *syn* see CLOSE 3
  rel accomplish, achieve, effect, fulfill
  idiom have done with
  2 *syn* see GO 4
  3 *syn* see KILL 1
  4 *syn* see MURDER 1

finish *n* **1** *syn* see END 2
  2 *syn* see FINALE
  3 *syn* see ACQUIREMENT
  rel correctness, discrimination, propriety, refinement; elegance, grace, polish; cultivation, taste

finished *adj* **1** *syn* see COMPLETE 4
  2 *syn* see THROUGH 3
  3 *syn* see CONSUMMATE 1
  rel cultivated, cultured, refined; smooth, suave, urbane; elegant, exquisite; all-around, many-sided, versatile
  con imperfect, incomplete
  ant crude; unfinished

finish off *vb syn* see CLIMAX

finite *adj* having definite or definable limits or boundaries < a *finite* thickness >
  syn bound, bounded, limited
  rel confined, restricted; definable, defined, definite, determinate, fixed, terminable; exact, precise, specific
  con boundless, unbounded, unlimited; absolute, complete, total
  ant infinite

‖**fink** *n syn* see INFORMER

fire *n* **1** a destructive burning < the house was destroyed by *fire* >
  syn conflagration, holocaust, inferno
  rel blaze, flame, flare, glare; burning, charring, scorching, searing
  idiom sea of flames, sheet of fire
  2 *syn* see PASSION 6
  rel animation, exhilaration, liveliness; dash, drive, energy, ginger, gusto, heartiness, pep, punch, snap, spirit, starch, verve, vigor, vim, zest, zing, zip
  con languor, lassitude, lethargy, listlessness, stupor, torpidity, torpor; apathy, impassivity, phlegm

fire *vb* **1** *syn* see LIGHT 1
  idiom set fire to, set on fire
  con extinguish, quench, smother
  2 to stimulate (as mental powers) to higher or more intense activity < a painting that *fired* the viewer's imagination >
  syn animate, exalt, inform, inspire; *compare* PROVOKE 4
  rel arouse, enliven, rouse, stir; electrify, excite; heighten, intensify; enthuse, thrill
  con appall, dismay; alarm, frighten, terrify
  ant daunt
  3 *syn* see DISMISS 3
  rel eject, expel, oust
  idiom give the pink slip, give the sack, strike off the rolls
  con engage; appoint, designate, elect, name
  ant hire
  4 *syn* see SHOOT 1
  5 *syn* see THROW 1
  6 to dry or harden by subjecting to heat < *fire* bricks >
  syn bake, burn, kiln

firebug *n syn* see INCENDIARY

fire–new *adj syn* see BRAND-NEW

firewater *n syn* see LIQUOR 2

firm *adj* **1** *syn* see FAST 4
  2 *syn* see STABLE 4
  3 having a texture or consistency that resists deformation by external force < *firm* flesh >
  syn hard, solid
  rel close, compact, dense, thick; inelastic, inflexible, rigid, stiff, unyielding; sturdy, substantial, tough
  con flaccid, flimsy, floppy, limp, loose, slack, sleazy, soft, squishy
  ant flabby
  4 that has been established and is not usually subject to change < a *firm* price >

---

syn synonym(s)   *rel* related word(s)
ant antonym(s)   *con* contrasted word(s)
idiom idiomatic equivalent(s)
‖ use limited; if in doubt, see a dictionary

syn certain, fixed, set, settled, stated, stipulated
rel established, going, prevailing; consistent, stable, steady, un-wavering; definite, exact, explicit, specific, undeviating; flat
con changeable, fluctuating, shaky, shifting, unsteady, variable
5 *syn* see SURE 1
6 *syn* see SURE 2
firm *adv syn* see HARD 7
firm *n syn* see ENTERPRISE 3
firmament *n syn* see SKY
firmly *adv* **1** *syn* see HARD 7
2 *syn* see HARD 9
firmness *n* **1** *syn* see STABILITY
2 *syn* see DECISION 2
first *adj* **1** being number one in a series <the *first* day of the week>
syn foremost, headmost, inaugural, initial, leading
con final, terminal, ultimate; interjacent, intermediary, interme-diate, intervenient, intervening
ant last
2 preceding all others <succeeded at his *first* try>
syn earliest, initial, maiden, original, pioneer, primary, prime
rel early, pristine; primal, primogenial, primordial
con derivative, imitative, secondary
ant final
3 exceeding all others <he was the *first* statesman of his era>
syn arch, champion, chief, foremost, head, leading, premier, principal
rel eminent, highest, preeminent, primary, prime, supreme; dominant, paramount, predominant, sovereign; main, outstand-ing
con ancillary, auxiliary, secondary, subsidiary
ant subordinate
4 most rudimentary <had not the *first* chance of success>
syn least, slightest, smallest
rel measly, slight, slim, trifling, trivial
con considerable, goodly, significant, substantial, tolerable, worthwhile
first *adv syn* see FIRSTLY
first–class *adj syn* see EXCELLENT
idiom in a class by itself
con fair, indifferent, middling; unexceptional, unnoteworthy, unremarkable
firsthand *adj syn* see DIRECT 4
firstly *adv* as the first thing to be mentioned <*firstly*, we wish to consider the economic problem>
syn first, initially
rel incipiently, originally, primarily
idiom before all (or anything) else, first of all, first off, to begin with
con ultimately
ant finally, lastly
first off *adv syn* see AWAY 3
first–rate *adj syn* see EXCELLENT
con fair, indifferent, middling, poor; unexceptional, un-noteworthy, unremarkable
first–string *adj syn* see EXCELLENT
firth *n syn* see INLET
fiscal *adj syn* see FINANCIAL
fish *n* **1** *syn* see FOOL 3
‖**2** *syn* see DOLLAR
fish *vb syn* see HINT 4
fishwife *n syn* see VIRAGO
fishy *adj syn* see DOUBTFUL 1
fissure *n* **1** *syn* see CRACK 3
rel abyss, chasm, gorge, ravine; breach, rent, rupture; gash, hole, opening
2 *syn* see BREACH 3
fist *n syn* see HANDWRITING
fisticuffs *n pl syn* see BOXING
fit *n syn* see ATTACK 3
fit *adj* **1** adapted to an end or use by nature or art <food *fit* for a king>
syn applicable, appropriate, apt, befitting, felicitous, fitting, happy, just, meet, proper, right, rightful, suitable; *compare* JUST 3
rel adapted, adjusted; congruous, consonant; decent, decorous; acceptable, adequate, tolerable
con improper, inadequate, inappropriate, unsuitable; false, wrong

ant unfit
2 *syn* see ELIGIBLE
rel able, competent
3 *syn* see GOOD 2
4 *syn* see HEALTHY 1
idiom fit as a fiddle
ant unfit
fit *vb* **1** *syn* see SUIT 4
2 *syn* see BELONG 1
3 *syn* see PREPARE 1
4 *syn* see ADAPT
fit (in) *vb syn* see AGREE 4
fitful *adj* lacking steadiness or regularity in course, movement, or succession <a *fitful* breeze>
syn catchy, desultory, on-again-off-again, spasmodic, sporadic, spotty
rel intermittent, interrupted, irregular, periodic, recurrent; hap-hazard, hit-or-miss, random; changeable, variable; capricious, inconstant, unstable
con equable, even, steady, uniform; methodical, orderly, regu-lar, systematic
ant constant
fitly *adv syn* see WELL 1
fitness *n* **1** *syn* see ORDER 10
2 *syn* see ORDER 11
rel decency, decorum, harmony
ant unfitness
3 *syn* see USE 3
fit out *vb syn* see FURNISH 1
fitted *adj syn* see ASSORTED 2
fitting *adj* **1** *syn* see FIT 1
rel apposite, apropos, germane, pertinent, relevant, seemly; ac-cordant, concordant, harmonious
2 *syn* see TRUE 7
fittingly *adv* **1** *syn* see WELL 1
2 *syn* see WELL 4
fivefold *adj syn* see QUINTUPLE
five–star *adj syn* see EXCELLENT
fix *vb* **1** *syn* see SET 1
rel stabilize, steady; decide, determine, rule; specify
con change, modify, vary
ant alter; abrogate
2 *syn* see ENTRENCH 1
rel inculcate, instill
con overthrow, overturn, subvert, upset
3 *syn* see FASTEN 1
4 *syn* see FASTEN 2
con dislodge, displace
5 *syn* see FASTEN 3
6 *syn* see PREPARE 1
7 *syn* see MEND 2
8 *syn* see ADJUST 2
rel mend, patch, rebuild, repair; amend, emend, revise
con disorganize, unsettle
9 *syn* see SOLVE 1
10 *syn* see STERILIZE
11 *syn* see BRIBE
fix *n syn* see PREDICAMENT
fixate *vb syn* see FASTEN 3
fixation *n syn* see FETISH 2
rel craze, fascination, infatuation
idiom bee in one's bonnet
fixed *adj* **1** *syn* see FAST 4
2 *syn* see IMMOVABLE 1
3 *syn* see DEFINITE 1
4 *syn* see INFLEXIBLE 3
5 *syn* see FIRM 4
con changing, variable, varying
6 *syn* see SURE 2
7 *syn* see WHOLE 5
con distracted, erratic, wandering
fixedly *adv syn* see HARD 7
rel stubbornly, tenaciously
fixture *n syn* see INSTITUTION
fix up *vb syn* see DRESS UP 1
fizz *vb syn* see HISS
fizzle *vb syn* see HISS
flabbergast *vb syn* see SURPRISE 2

rel overwhelm, shock

flabby *adj syn* see LIMP 1
  rel soft, yielding; impotent, powerless; enervated, languid, listless, spiritless
  con taut, tense, tight; strong, sturdy, tenacious, tough; gritty, plucky
  ant firm

flaccid *adj syn* see LIMP 1
  rel emasculated, enervated, unnerved; debilitated, enfeebled, sapped, weakened
  con elastic, flexible, springy, supple; limber, lithe; energetic, lusty, nervous, vigorous
  ant resilient

flag *n* a piece of fabric that is used as a symbol (as of a nation) or as a signaling device <we respect the *flag* of our fathers>
  syn banderole, banner, bannerol, burgee, color, ensign, gonfalon, gonfanon, jack, oriflamme, pendant, pennant, pennon, standard, streamer

flag *vb syn* see SIGNAL

flag *vb* 1 *syn* see FAIL 1
  2 *syn* see DROOP 3
  rel abate, ebb, wane

flagellate *vb syn* see WHIP 1

flagitious *adj syn* see VICIOUS 2
  rel criminal, scandalous, sinful, wicked; disgraceful, shameful; flagrant, glaring, gross
  con good, upstanding, virtuous

flagrant *adj syn* see EGREGIOUS
  rel bold, conspicuous, obvious, striking; heinous; flagitious, wicked; disgraceful, scandalous, shameful, shocking
  con hidden, inconspicuous, obscure; excusable, unimportant

flagrante delicto *adv syn* see RED-HANDED

flag-waver *n syn* see PATRIOTEER

flair *n syn* see GIFT 2

flake (off) *vb syn* see SCALE 2

‖flake out *vb syn* see COLLAPSE 2

flam *n syn* see IMPOSTURE

flamboyant *adj* 1 *syn* see ORNATE
  2 *syn* see SHOWY

flame *n* 1 *syn* see SWEETHEART 1
  2 *syn* see GIRL FRIEND 2
  3 *syn* see BOYFRIEND 2

flame *vb syn* see BLAZE
  rel coruscate, glint; fire, ignite, kindle, light

flaming *adj* 1 *syn* see BURNING 1
  2 *syn* see IMPASSIONED

flammable *adj syn* see COMBUSTIBLE 1
  ant incombustible, nonflammable

flap *n syn* see COMMOTION 2

flapdoodle *n syn* see NONSENSE 2

flare *vb syn* see BLAZE
  rel dart, shoot; flicker, flutter
  idiom burst into flame
  ant gutter out

flare (up) *vb syn* see ANGER 2
  idiom ‖blow one's stack (*or* top *or* lid), fly into a passion, fly off the handle
  con calm (down), cool (off *or* down), simmer down

flare *n syn* see OUTBREAK 1

flare-up *n syn* see OUTBURST 1

flaring *adj syn* see BURNING 1

flash *vb* 1 to shoot forth light (as in rays or sparks) <lightning *flashed* in the sky>
  syn coruscate, glance, gleam, glimmer, glint, glisten, glitter, scintillate, shimmer, spangle, sparkle, twinkle
  rel dart, shoot; blare, blaze, burn, flame, flare, glare, glow, incandesce; blink, flicker, spark; dazzle; beam, radiate, shine
  2 *syn* see BLINK 2
  3 *syn* see SHOW 4

flash *n* 1 a sudden brief light <saw a *flash* sweep across the sky>
  syn coruscation, glance, gleam, glimmer, glint, glisten, glitter, quiver, scintillation, shimmer, sparkle, twinkle
  rel blare, blaze, flame, flare, glare, glow; flicker; beam, ray
  2 *syn* see INSTANT 1
  idiom half a second (*or* shake), twinkling of an eye

flashy *adj syn* see GAUDY
  rel flamboyant, florid, ornate; flashing, glittering, sparkling

con dowdy, slatternly; natural, simple, unaffected; chic, modish, smart

flat *adj* 1 *syn* see LEVEL
  idiom flat as a billiard table (*or* pancake)
  con rugged, scabrous, uneven; hilly, mountainous
  2 *syn* see PRONE 4
  3 *syn* see DOWNRIGHT 2
  4 *syn* see COLORLESS 2
  5 *syn* see INSIPID 3
  rel dull, lifeless; flavorless, stale, tasteless
  6 *syn* see UNPALATABLE 1
  7 *syn* see POOR 1
  8 *syn* see DULL 7

flat *n syn* see APARTMENT 1

‖flatfoot *n syn* see POLICEMAN

flatly *adv syn* see EVENLY 3

flat-out *adj syn* see UTTER

flat-out *adv syn* see FAST 2

flatten *vb* 1 *syn* see EVEN 1
  2 *syn* see FELL 1

flatter *vb* to be becoming to <a neckline designed to *flatter* the stylishly stout>
  syn become, enhance, suit
  rel adorn, beautify, decorate, embellish, ornament; finish, perfect
  idiom put in the best light
  con deface, disfigure; distort; mar, spoil

flattery *n* flattering speech or attentions <*flattery* will get you nowhere>
  syn adulation, blandishment, blarney, incense, oil, soft soap
  rel compliments; laud, laudation, praise; cajolery, coaxing, wheedling; fulsomeness, unctuousness; bootlicking, fawning, ingratiation, obsequiousness, sycophancy, toadying, truckling
  idiom honeyed words
  con censure, condemnation, criticism, reprehension, reprobation; castigation, excoriation; aspersion, insult; contempt, disdain, scorn; belittling, depreciation, derogation, detraction, disparagement

flatulent *adj syn* see INFLATED
  rel empty, hollow, vain; shallow, superficial
  con weighty; cogent, compelling, convincing, telling; forceful, forcible, potent

flaunt *vb syn* see SHOW 4
  rel boast, brag, gasconade, vaunt; disclose, discover, divulge, reveal; advertise, broadcast, declare, proclaim, publish; flourish, wave
  idiom dangle before the (*or* one's) eyes
  con camouflage, cloak, disguise, dissemble, mask; bury, conceal, hide, screen, secrete

flavor *n syn* see TASTE 3

flavorless *adj syn* see UNPALATABLE 1
  ant flavorsome

flavorsome *adj syn* see PALATABLE
  con flat, insipid, vapid, wishy-washy; bland, mild; displeasing, tasteless, unflavored, unpalatable, unpleasant, unsavory
  ant flavorless

flaw *n syn* see BLEMISH
  rel cleavage, rent, rip, riving, split, tear

flawed *adj* 1 *syn* see DAMAGED
  ant flawless
  2 *syn* see FAULTY
  ant flawless

flawless *adj* 1 *syn* see WHOLE 1
  ant flawed
  2 *syn* see PERFECT 2
  3 *syn* see IMPECCABLE 1
  con defective, faulty, flawed, imperfect, unsound
  4 *syn* see IDEAL 3

flaxen *adj syn* see BLOND 1

flay *vb syn* see LAMBASTE 3
  rel assail, attack, berate, tongue-lash

fleckless *adj syn* see PERFECT 2

flection *n syn* see TURN 4

---

syn synonym(s)   *rel* related word(s)
ant antonym(s)   *con* contrasted word(s)
idiom idiomatic equivalent(s)
‖ use limited; if in doubt, see a dictionary

fledgling *n syn* see NOVICE
flee *vb* **1** *syn* see ESCAPE 1
  rel avoid, elude, evade, shun
  idiom take a (runout) powder
  2 *syn* see RUN 2
  con stand, stay
fleece *vb* **1** to obtain something valuable from by improper means
  < a corrupt mayor who *fleeced* the town treasury >
  syn bleed, milk, mulct, rook, stick, sweat; *compare* CHEAT, EX-
  TORT 1
  rel cheat, cozen, defraud, do, hustle, ‖rope (in), swindle, take;
  pluck
  idiom sell one a bill of goods, take for a sucker, take to the
  cleaner's
  2 *syn* see OVERCHARGE 1
fleeceable *adj syn* see EASY 3
fleecy *adj syn* see HAIRY 1
fleer *vb* **1** *syn* see SNEER 1
  2 *syn* see SCOFF
  rel grin, smile, smirk
  idiom cast in one's teeth, curl one's lip at, laugh one out of
  court
fleet *vb* **1** *syn* see WHILE
  rel dally, fritter, idle, potter, squander, waste
  2 *syn* see FLY 4
  idiom go like the wind (*or* lightning), make (good) time
  3 *syn* see HURRY 2
fleet *adj syn* see FAST 3
  rel agile, brisk, nimble, spry; alert, animated, lively, spirited,
  sprightly, vivacious
fleeting *adj syn* see TRANSIENT
  con abiding, enduring, persistent
  ant lasting
fleetly *adv syn* see FAST 2
flesh *n syn* see MANKIND
fleshiness *n syn* see OBESITY
fleshliness *n syn* see ANIMALITY
fleshly *adj* **1** *syn* see BODILY
  2 *syn* see CARNAL 2
  rel epicurean, luxurious, sensuous, sybaritic, voluptuous; lay,
  profane, secular, temporal
  con divine, religious, spiritual; intellectual, mental, psychic
fleshy *adj syn* see FAT 2
  ant emaciated
flexible *adj syn* see ELASTIC 1
  rel amenable, docile, manageable, tractable; acquiescent, compliant
  con brittle, crisp, fragile, frangible; firm, hard, rigid, stiff, unyielding, wooden; intractable, recalcitrant, refractory, ungovernable; callous, hardened, indurated
  ant inflexible
flexuous *adj syn* see WINDING
flexure *n syn* see TURN 4
flibbertigibbet *n syn* see SCATTERBRAIN
flick *n syn* see MOVIE
flicker *vb* **1** *syn* see FLIT 2
  2 *syn* see BLINK 2
  rel fluctuate, oscillate, swing, vibrate, waver; blaze, flame, flare,
  glare; coruscate, glance, gleam, glint, glitter, sparkle; quaver,
  quiver, tremble
flier *n syn* see PILOT 2
flight *n syn* see ESCAPE 1
flightiness *n syn* see LIGHTNESS
  rel capriciousness, fickleness, inconstancy, instability, mercurialness
  con constancy, equableness, steadfastness
  ant steadiness
flighty *adj syn* see GIDDY 1
  rel changeable, inconstant, mercurial, unstable; buoyant, effervescent, volatile; gay, lively, sprightly; irresponsible
  con constant, dependable, reliable, responsible, trustworthy; stable; sedate
  ant steady
flimflam *n* **1** *syn* see IMPOSTURE
  2 *syn* see NONSENSE 2
flimflam *vb* **1** *syn* see DUPE
  2 *syn* see CHEAT
flimflammer *n syn* see SWINDLER

flimsy *adj* **1** *syn* see FILMY
  2 *syn* see IMPLAUSIBLE
  ant substantial
  3 *syn* see DELICATE 5
  4 *syn* see WEAK 1
  ant sturdy
  5 *syn* see LIMP 1
flinch *vb syn* see RECOIL
  rel avoid, elude, escape, eschew, evade, shun; retire, withdraw;
  recede, retreat
fling *vb* **1** *syn* see RUSH 1
  2 *syn* see THROW 1
  con catch, grab, receive
fling *n* **1** a casual attempt < I'm willing to take a *fling* at almost
  any job >
  syn crack, go, pop, shot, slap, stab, ‖stagger, try, whack, whirl
  rel attempt, effort, essay, trial
  con best, limit, maximum
  ant utmost
  2 *syn* see SPREE 1
flip (through) *vb syn* see BROWSE
flippancy *n syn* see LIGHTNESS
  rel archness, pertness, sauciness; impishness, mischievousness,
  playfulness, roguishness, waggishness; cheekiness, cockiness,
  freshness
  con earnestness, gravity, soberness, solemnity
  ant seriousness
flirt *vb syn* see TRIFLE 1
  rel disport, play, sport; caress, fondle, pet
flirt *n* a woman who trifles amorously < a charming girl but an
  outrageous *flirt* >
  syn coquette, vamp
flit *vb* **1** *syn* see HURRY 2
  2 to move briskly, irregularly, and usually intermittently < the
  hummingbird *flitted* from flower to flower >
  syn dance, flicker, flitter, flutter, hover
  rel dart, float, fly, scud, skim
  3 *syn* see FLY 4
flitter *vb syn* see FLIT 2
  rel quaver, quiver, teeter
float *vb* **1** *syn* see DRIFT 1
  2 *syn* see HANG 3
  3 *syn* see FLY 1
  rel drift, waft
floater *n syn* see VAGABOND
flock *n* **1** *syn* see MULTITUDE 1
  2 *syn* see DROVE 2
flog *vb syn* see WHIP 1
flood *n* **1** *syn* see FLOW
  2 a great or overwhelming flow of or as if of water < a *flood* of
  messages >
  syn cataclysm, cataract, deluge, flooding, inundation, niagara,
  overflow, pour, spate, torrent
  rel current, flow, stream, tide; excess, superfluity, surplus; out-
  gushing, outpouring
  con dribble, drip, dropping
  ant trickle
flood *vb* **1** *syn* see DELUGE 1
  2 *syn* see DELUGE 3
flooding *n syn* see FLOOD 2
floor *vb syn* see FELL 1
floozy *n syn* see DOXY 1
‖flop *vb* **1** *syn* see RETIRE 4
  2 *syn* see FAIL 4
  con come off, go over, succeed
flop *n syn* see FAILURE 5
floppy *adj syn* see LIMP 1
florid *adj* **1** *syn* see RHETORICAL
  2 *syn* see ORNATE
  rel ostentatious, pretentious, showy
  con bald, bare, barren; austere, unadorned
  3 *syn* see RUDDY
  ant pallid
florilegium *n syn* see ANTHOLOGY
floss *n syn* see DOWN
flotsam *n syn* see DRIFTWOOD
flounce *vb syn* see SASHAY
flounder *vb syn* see WALLOW 2

rel strive, struggle; labor, toil, travail

flourish *vb syn* see SUCCEED 3
   rel bloom, blossom, flower; augment, increase, multiply; amplify, expand; develop, grow, wax
   con shrivel, wither; contract, shrink; abate, ebb, subside, wane
   ant languish

flourishing *adj* enjoying a vigorous growth <a *flourishing* economy>
   syn booming, prospering, prosperous, roaring, robust, thrifty, thriving; *compare* SUCCESSFUL
   rel vigorous; rampant, rank; exuberant, lush, luxuriant, profuse
   idiom going strong, in full swing
   con decadent, declining, deteriorating; failing; decreasing, dwindling
   ant languishing

flout *vb syn* see SCOFF
   rel disregard, slight; repudiate, spurn; insult; defy
   idiom thumb one's nose at
   con admire, esteem, regard, respect
   ant revere

flow *vb* 1 *syn* see POUR 2
   rel cascade, jet, spout, spurt; well; course, ripple, run
   2 *syn* see SPRING 1
   3 *syn* see TEEM
   4 *syn* see DISCHARGE 5

flow *n* something suggestive of running water <she expressed herself in a *flow* of words>
   syn current, drift, flood, flux, rush, spate, stream, tide
   rel progression, sequence, series, succession; continuance, continuation, continuity

flower *n* 1 the often showy part of a seed plant that bears reproductive organs <children picking *flowers* in the meadow>
   syn bloom, blossom, posy
   rel bud, floret; shoot, spray
   2 *syn* see BEST
   3 *syn* see ARISTOCRACY

flower *vb syn* see BLOSSOM

flowering *n syn* see DEVELOPMENT
   ant fading

flowery *adj syn* see RHETORICAL
   rel diffuse, prolix, redundant, verbose, wordy
   con compendious, concise, laconic, pithy, succinct, summary, terse

flowing *adj syn* see EASY 9

flub *vb syn* see BOTCH

fluctuant *adj* 1 *syn* see WEAK 2
   2 *syn* see UNCERTAIN 1

flue *n syn* see DOWN

fluent *adj* 1 *syn* see VOCAL 3
   rel loquacious, talkative; easy, effortless, facile, smooth; apt, prompt, quick, ready
   con stammering, stuttering; tongue-tied; dumb; fettered, hampered, trammeled
   2 *syn* see EASY 9

fluff *n* 1 *syn* see DOWN
   2 *syn* see ERROR 2

fluff *vb syn* see BOTCH

fluid *adj syn* see CHANGEABLE 1

fluky *adj syn* see ACCIDENTAL

flummadiddle *n syn* see NONSENSE 2

flummox *vb syn* see FAIL 4

flurry *n syn* see STIR 1
   rel confusion, excitement, turbulence, turmoil; haste, hurry

flurry *vb syn* see DISCOMPOSE 1
   rel bewilder, distract, perplex; excite, galvanize, provoke, quicken, stimulate

flush *n* 1 *syn* see BLOOM 3
   2 *syn* see BLOOM 2

flush *vb* 1 *syn* see BLUSH
   2 *syn* see EVEN 1

flush *adj* 1 *syn* see RICH 1
   2 *syn* see RUDDY
   3 *syn* see LEVEL

flushed *adj syn* see RUDDY

fluster *vb* 1 *syn* see DISCOMPOSE 1
   rel bewilder, confound, distract, mystify, nonplus, perplex, puzzle; addle, confuse, fuddle, muddle
   ant steady

   2 *syn* see CONFUSE 2

flutter *vb syn* see FLIT 2
   rel quaver, quiver, shake, tremble, wobble; beat, palpitate, pulsate, throb; fluctuate, oscillate, swing, vibrate; flap

flux *n* 1 *syn* see DIARRHEA
   2 *syn* see FLOW

flux *vb syn* see LIQUEFY

fly *vb* 1 to pass lightly or quickly over or above a surface <clouds *flying* across the sky>
   syn dart, float, sail, scud, shoot, skim, skirr
   rel dance, flicker, flit, flitter, flutter, hover; arise, ascend, mount, rise, soar; glide, slide, slip
   2 *syn* see RUN 2
   rel hide; retreat, withdraw
   3 *syn* see ESCAPE 1
   4 to pass swiftly as if on wings <how time *flies* when we are happy>
   syn fleet, flit, sail, sweep, wing
   rel soar; hasten, hurry, speed; barrel, skim, whisk, whiz, zip; breeze, dart, dash, rush, tear
   idiom go like the wind (*or* lightning), outstrip the wind
   con dally, dawdle, dillydally, drift; lag, linger, loiter, trail; crawl, creep, poke
   ant drag
   5 *syn* see HURRY 2

fly–boy *n syn* see PILOT 2

fly–by–night *adj syn* see UNRELIABLE 1

flying colors *n pl syn* see SUCCESS

flyspeck *n syn* see POINT 11

foam *n* a mass of bubbles gathering in or on the surface of a liquid or something as insubstantial as such a mass <a *foam* of delicate lace at her throat>
   syn froth, lather, spume, suds, yeast

fob off *vb syn* see FOIST 3

focal point *n syn* see CENTER 2

focus *n syn* see CENTER 2
   idiom center of attraction (*or* interest), focus of attention

focus *vb* 1 *syn* see FASTEN 3
   2 *syn* see CONVERGE
   idiom come to a focus

foe *n syn* see ENEMY
   con associate, companion, comrade
   ant friend

fog *n syn* see HAZE 2

fog *vb* 1 *syn* see OBSCURE
   rel bewilder, distract, mystify, perplex, puzzle
   2 *syn* see CONFUSE 4
   rel addle, muddle

foggy *adj syn* see HAZY
   idiom in a fog

fogram *n syn* see FOGY

fogy *n* a person who is behind the times or overconservative <his father is an old *fogy*>
   syn antediluvian, fogram, fossil, fuddy-duddy, mid-Victorian, mossback, square, stick-in-the-mud
   rel conservative, diehard; back number
   idiom regular old fogy
   ant modern

fogyish *adj syn* see CONSERVATIVE 1
   ant up-to-the-minute

foible *n syn* see FAULT 2
   rel imperfection, shortcoming

foil *vb syn* see FRUSTRATE 1
   rel discomfit, disconcert, embarrass, faze, rattle; curb, restrain

foist *vb* 1 *syn* see INSINUATE 3
   2 *syn* see IMPOSE 4
   3 to pass or offer (something spurious) as genuine or worthy <his theory was far more reasonable than many *foisted* on the public>
   syn fob off, palm (on *or* upon), palm off, pass off, work off; *compare* IMPOSE 4

---

syn synonym(s)   *rel* related word(s)
ant antonym(s)   *con* contrasted word(s)
idiom idiomatic equivalent(s)
|| use limited; if in doubt, see a dictionary

rel beguile, deceive, delude, mislead; bamboozle, dupe, gull, hoax, hoodwink, trick; cheat, defraud, overreach, swindle; impose, inflict, wish

fold *n syn* see WRINKLE

fold *vb* **1** *syn* see DOUBLE 2
    2 *syn* see FAIL 5

fold up *vb* **1** *syn* see GIVE 12
    2 *syn* see RUIN 3

foliage *n* the leaves of plants < a tree with handsome *foliage* >
    syn leafage, umbrage, verdure
    rel greenness, herbage; growth, vegetation

folk *n* **1** *syn* see FAMILY 1
    2 folks *pl syn* see FAMILY 2

folklore *n syn* see LORE 2

follow *vb* **1** to come after in time < a juggling act *followed* the singer >
    syn ensue, succeed, supervene
    rel displace, replace, supersede, supplant; postdate
    con herald, lead, preface, usher (in); antedate, predate
    ant precede
    2 to go after or on the track of < *followed* the boys to their hiding place >
    syn chase, chivy, pursue, trail; *compare* TAIL
    rel trace, track; hunt, search, seek; dog, hound, tag; accompany, attend, convoy; ape, copy, imitate; exercise, practice
    con guide, lead, pilot, steer; elude, escape, evade; abandon, desert
    ant precede; forsake
    3 *syn* see OBEY
    4 *syn* see APPREHEND 1

follower *n* one who attaches himself to another < he is a born *follower* >
    syn adherent, cohort, disciple, henchman, partisan, satellite, sectary, sectator, supporter
    rel addict, devotee, freak, habitué, votary; admirer, fan, fancier; advocate; bootlicker, hanger-on, lickspittle, parasite, sycophant, toady
    ant leader

following *adj syn* see NEXT

following *n* **1** *syn* see ENTOURAGE
    2 the body of persons who attach themselves to another especially as disciples, patrons, or admirers < he has a strong *following* in this country >
    syn audience, clientage, clientele, public

following *prep syn* see AFTER 2

folly *n syn* see FOOLISHNESS
    rel fatuity, stupidity
    ant wisdom

foment *vb syn* see INCITE
    rel goad, spur; cultivate, foster, nurse, nurture
    con repress, suppress
    ant quell

fomenter *n syn* see INSTIGATOR

fond *adj* **1** *syn* see OPTIMISTIC
    2 *syn* see LOVING
    rel responsive, romantic, sentimental, sympathetic, tender, warm; indulgent
    idiom silly over

fondle *vb syn* see CARESS
    rel clasp, embrace, hug; nestle, snuggle

fondness *n* **1** *syn* see LOVE 1
    2 *syn* see APPETITE 3
    rel partiality, predilection; relish
    con disgust; hate

font name *n syn* see GIVEN NAME

food *n* **1** things that are edible < conserve a nation's supply of *food* >
    syn bread, ‖chow, comestibles, ‖eats, edibles, feed, foodstuff, grub, meat, ‖muckamuck, nurture, provender, provisions, scoff, ‖tuck, viands, victuals, vivres
    2 material which feeds and supports the mind or spirit < *food* for thought >
    syn aliment, nourishment, nutriment, pabulum, pap, sustenance

foodstuff *n syn* see FOOD 1

foofaraw *n syn* see COMMOTION 3

fool *n* **1** a person lacking in judgment or prudence < stop acting like a *fool* >

syn ass, asshead, donkey, doodle, idiot, imbecile, jackass, jerk, madman, mooncalf, nincom, nincompoop, ninny, ninnyhammer, poop, ‖schmo, ‖schmuck, tomfool
    rel blockhead, dimwit, dope, dumbbell, dummy, nitwit, numskull, pinhead; birdbrain, featherbrain, featherhead, rattlebrain, scatterbrain; goose, silly
    2 a retainer formerly kept to provide casual entertainment < a king's *fool* >
    syn idiot, jester, motley
    rel buffoon, clown, comedian, comic, merry-andrew
    3 one who is victimized or made to appear foolish < he's nobody's *fool* >
    syn butt, chump, ‖come-on, ‖cull, dupe, easy mark, fall guy, fish, gudgeon, gull, mark, monkey, ‖mug, patsy, pigeon, sap, saphead, ‖schlemiel, simple, sucker, victim
    rel pushover; laughingstock; loser; instrument, tool
    4 one who is mentally deficient < a badly retarded child, little more than a *fool* >
    syn ament, cretin, ‖feeb, half-wit, idiot, imbecile, moron, natural, simpleton, softhead, underwit, zany

fool *vb* **1** *syn* see TRIFLE 1
    2 *syn* see MEDDLE
    3 *syn* see BANTER
    4 *syn* see DUPE

fool (around) *vb syn* see PHILANDER

fool (away) *vb syn* see WASTE 2

foolhardy *adj syn* see ADVENTUROUS
    rel headlong, impetuous, precipitate
    con calculating, cautious, circumspect; careful, prudent
    ant wary

fooling *n syn* see HORSEPLAY

foolish *adj* **1** *syn* see SIMPLE 3
    rel idiotic, imbecilic, moronic; daft, feebleminded, half-witted; half-cocked; irrational
    con bright, clever, intelligent, quick-witted
    ant smart
    2 felt to be ridiculous because not exhibiting good or conventional sense < a *foolish* investment >
    syn absurd, ‖balmy, crazy, ‖dilly, ‖dippy, donkeyish, dotty, fantastic, harebrained, idleheaded, insane, loony, loopy, lunatic, mad, ‖potty, preposterous, sappy, silly, tomfool, unearthly, wacky
    rel laughable, ludicrous, ridiculous; half-baked, headless, jerky, nonsensical; offbeat, unacceptable, unconventional, unorthodox
    con judicious, sage, sapient; discreet, foresighted, prudent; canny, shrewd, slick
    ant sensible; wise

foolishness *n* the quality or state of being foolish < the *foolishness* of so many of her schemes >
    syn absurdity, craziness, dottiness, folly, inanity, insanity, lunacy, preposterousness, senselessness, silliness, witlessness
    rel imprudence, indiscretion, injudiciousness, insensibility, unwiseness; irrationality, unreasonableness; impracticality; absurdness, ludicrousness, ridiculousness; bull, bunk, nonsense
    con discretion, judiciousness, prudence, sensibility, wiseness; rationality, reasonableness; practicality; soundness; canniness, shrewdness
    ant sense, wisdom

foot *n syn* see BOTTOM 3

foot *vb syn* see ADD 2

foot (it) *vb* **1** *syn* see DANCE 1
    2 *syn* see WALK 1

footing *n* **1** *syn* see BASIS 1
    2 *syn* see STATUS 1
    3 *syn* see BASE 1
    4 *syn* see TERM 5

footlicker *n syn* see SYCOPHANT

footlights *n pl syn* see DRAMA

footprint *n* the mark or impression made by a foot < *footprints* in the sand >
    syn footstep, spoor, step, track, tract, vestige
    rel sign, trace; pug, pugmark

footslog *vb syn* see PLOD 1

footstep *n syn* see FOOTPRINT

footstone *n syn* see TOMBSTONE

foozle *vb syn* see BOTCH

fop *n* a man who is conspicuously fashionable or elegant in dress or appearance < felt contempt for the mincing overdressed *fop* >

syn Beau Brummel, blood, buck, coxcomb, dandy, dude, exquisite, gallant, lounge lizard, macaroni, petit-maître, popinjay
rel fashion plate, silk stocking; blade, cavalier, man-about-town, spark, sport, swell; ladies' man, lady-killer, masher
idiom man of the world
for *prep* **1** *syn* see TO 5
2 on the side of <I'm *for* Smith all the way>
syn in favor of, pro, with
con anti, contra
ant against
3 *syn* see AFTER 1
for *conj* *syn* see BECAUSE
forage *vb* *syn* see SCOUR 2
forager *n* *syn* see MARAUDER
foray *vb* **1** *syn* see INVADE 1
2 *syn* see RAID 1
foray *n* *syn* see INVASION
forbear *vb* **1** *syn* see FORGO
rel bridle, curb, inhibit, restrain; avoid, escape, evade, shun; cease, desist
2 *syn* see REFRAIN 1
rel bear, endure, suffer, tolerate
forbearance *n* **1** *syn* see PATIENCE
rel restraint, temperance; endurance
2 the quality of being forbearing <she is known for her *forbearance* with children>
syn clemency, indulgence, lenience, leniency, mercifulness, tolerance, toleration; *compare* MERCY
rel longanimity, long-suffering, patience; charity, grace, lenity, mercy
con firmness, inflexibility, rigidity, sternness, strictness; austerity, harshness, inexorability
ant vindictiveness
forbearing *adj* disinclined to be severe or rigorous <*forbearing* toward her husband's weaknesses>
syn charitable, clement, easy, indulgent, lenient, merciful, tolerant
rel gentle, mild; longanimous, long-suffering, patient; considerate, thoughtful
con grim, implacable, merciless, relentless; impatient, nervous, restive; firm, inflexible, rigid, stern, strict; austere, harsh
ant unrelenting
forbid *vb* to debar one from using, doing, or entering or something from being used, done, or entered <smoking is *forbidden* here> <security regulations *forbid* the entry of unauthorized persons>
syn ban, enjoin, inhibit, interdict, outlaw, prohibit, taboo
rel debar, exclude, rule out, shut out; estop, obviate, preclude, prevent; forestall; proscribe, veto; check, curb, halt, restrain, stop; bar, block, hinder, impede, obstruct
con allow, let, suffer; authorize, license; approve, endorse, sanction; command, order; abide, bear, endure, tolerate
ant permit; bid
forbiddance *n* *syn* see TABOO
forbidden *adj* not permitted or allowed <accepting bribes is *forbidden*>
syn banned, prohibited, verboten
ant permitted
force *n* **1** *syn* see POWER 4
rel pressure, strain, stress, tension; headway, impetus, momentum, speed, velocity; vigor
2 *syn* see POINT 3
3 *forces* *pl* *syn* see TROOP 2
4 the exercise of power in order to impose one's will on a person or to have one's will with a thing <move a huge boulder by main *force*>
syn coercion, compulsion, constraint, duress, violence
rel fierceness, intensity, vehemence; effort, exertions, pains, trouble
con compliance, submission, yielding; impotence, powerlessness, weakness
ant forcelessness
force *vb* **1** *syn* see RAPE
2 to cause a person or thing to yield to pressure <hunger *forced* him to steal the food>
syn coerce, compel, concuss, constrain, make, oblige, shotgun
rel drive, impel, move; command, enjoin, order; demand, exact, require; press, pressure, sandbag; cause, occasion

con blandish, cajole, coax, wheedle; get, induce, persuade, prevail; entice, inveigle, lure, seduce, tempt
force (on *or* upon) *vb* *syn* see INFLICT 2
‖**force** *n* *syn* see WATERFALL
forced *adj* produced or kept up through effort <a *forced* laugh>
syn farfetched, labored, strained
rel coerced, compelled, constrained; artificial, factitious; unnatural; inflexible, rigid, stiff, wooden; exhausting, fatiguing
con easy, effortless, smooth; impulsive, instinctive, spontaneous; artless, natural, normal, unaffected, unsophisticated
ant unforced
forceful *adj* **1** *syn* see POWERFUL 2
rel compelling, constraining; manful, virile; cogent, telling
con decrepit, frail, infirm
ant feeble
2 *syn* see EMPHATIC
forcefully *adv* *syn* see HARD 1
forceless *adj* *syn* see WEAK 4
forcible *adj* *syn* see POWERFUL 2
rel intense, vehement, violent; aggressive, assertive, militant, self-assertive; coercive
forcibly *adv* *syn* see HARD 1
forcing bed *n* *syn* see BREEDING GROUND
forcing house *n* *syn* see BREEDING GROUND
fore *adv* *syn* see BEFORE 1
forebear *n* *syn* see ANCESTOR 1
forebode *vb* *syn* see AUGUR 2
foreboding *n* *syn* see APPREHENSION 3
rel augury, foretoken, omen, portent, prognostic; forewarning, warning
forecast *vb* *syn* see FORETELL
rel conjecture, guess, surmise; conclude, gather, infer
forecast *n* *syn* see PREDICTION
forecaster *n* *syn* see PROPHET
foredestine *vb* *syn* see PREDESTINE 2
forefather *n* *syn* see ANCESTOR 1
forefeel *vb* *syn* see FORESEE
foregoer *n* *syn* see FORERUNNER 2
foregoing *adj* *syn* see PRECEDING
ant following
forehandedness *n* *syn* see ECONOMY
forehead *n* the part of the face above the eyes <his broad noble *forehead*>
syn brow, frons, front
foreign *adj* **1** *syn* see EXOTIC 1
ant native
2 *syn* see EXTRINSIC
rel incompatible, incongruous, inconsistent, inconsonant; distasteful, obnoxious, repellent, repugnant; accidental, adventitious
con applicable, apposite, apropos, material, pertinent, relevant; akin, alike, uniform
ant germane
3 *syn* see IRRELEVANT
foreigner *n* *syn* see STRANGER
foreknow *vb* *syn* see FORESEE
rel conclude, gather, infer
foreland *n* *syn* see PROMONTORY
foremost *adj* **1** *syn* see FIRST 1
2 *syn* see FIRST 3
forename *n* *syn* see GIVEN NAME
forenoon *n* *syn* see MORNING 2
forensic *n* *syn* see ARGUMENTATION
foreordain *vb* **1** *syn* see PREDESTINE 1
2 *syn* see PREDESTINE 2
forerun *vb* **1** *syn* see PRECEDE 2
2 *syn* see ANNOUNCE 2
forerunner *n* **1** one that goes before and in some way announces the coming of another <a coma is often a *forerunner* of death>
syn harbinger, herald, outrider, precursor
rel anticipator; advertiser, announcer; advertisement, announcement, augury, foretoken, omen, portent, presage, prognostic; forewarning, warning; mark, sign, symptom, token; foreshadow

---

syn synonym(s)   *rel* related word(s)
ant antonym(s)   *con* contrasted word(s)
idiom idiomatic equivalent(s)
‖ use limited; if in doubt, see a dictionary

2 one belonging to an early developmental period of something contemporary or fully developed < the water-driven dynamo that was a *forerunner* of present-day giant atomic power plants >
syn ancestor, antecedent, antecessor, foregoer, precursor, predecessor, prototype
rel example, exemplar, model, pattern; pioneer; author, initiator, originator
con consequence, result; effect, event, issue, outgrowth; conclusion, consummation, culmination
ant end product

foresee *vb* to know or expect in advance that something will happen or come into existence or be made manifest < he had not *foreseen* his present problems >
syn anticipate, apprehend, divine, forefeel, foreknow, preknow, previse, prevision, see, visualize
rel forebode, forecast, foretell, predict, presage, prognosticate, prophesy; descry, discern, espy, perceive
idiom look for, look forward to

foreseer *n syn* see PROPHET
foreshadow *vb* **1** *syn* see ADUMBRATE 1
　2 *syn* see AUGUR 2
foreshow *vb* **1** *syn* see AUGUR 2
　2 *syn* see ANNOUNCE 2
foresight *n syn* see PRUDENCE
rel clairvoyance, discernment, perception
ant hindsight

forest *n* a heavily wooded area
syn timber, timberland, weald, wood(s), woodland
rel coppice, copse, grove, thicket; wildwood, woodlot
con field, meadow, plain, prairie

forestall *vb* **1** *syn* see PREVENT 2
con court, invite, woo; advance, forward, further, promote
　2 *syn* see PREVENT 1

foretell *vb* to tell something before it happens through or as if through special knowledge or occult power < the prophet *foretold* the fall of the city >
syn adumbrate, augur, call, forecast, portend, predict, presage, prognosticate, prophesy, soothsay, vaticinate
rel anticipate, apprehend, divine, foreknow, foresee; announce, declare, proclaim; disclose, divulge, reveal; forewarn, warn; bode, forebode, foreshadow, foreshow, foretoken, promise; prefigure

foreteller *n syn* see PROPHET
foretelling *n syn* see PREDICTION
forethink *vb syn* see PREMEDITATE
forethought *n syn* see PRUDENCE 1
rel deliberation, premeditation; gumption, judgment, sense
ant rashness; impetuosity

foretime *n syn* see PAST
foretoken *n* something that serves as a sign of future happenings < they felt that his new job was a *foretoken* of good fortune >
syn augury, bodement, boding, omen, portent, presage, prognostic
rel badge, indication, mark, note, sign, symptom, token; forerunner, harbinger, herald, precursor; forewarning, shadow, warning; intimation, promise; ostent; hint, inkling, suggestion

foretoken *vb syn* see AUGUR 2
forever *adv syn* see EVER 2
forevermore *adv syn* see EVER 2
forewarn *vb syn* see WARN 1
forewarning *n syn* see WARNING
foreword *n syn* see INTRODUCTION
forfeit *n syn* see FINE
forfeit *vb syn* see LOSE 1
forfend *vb syn* see PREVENT 2
forgather *vb syn* see GATHER 6
forge *vb syn* see MAKE 3
rel beat, pound, turn out; copy, imitate

forget *vb* **1** to lose the remembrance of < I soon *forgot* his name >
syn disremember, ‖misremember, unknow
rel misrecollect; blow up, fluff; unlearn
idiom clean forget, draw a blank
con recall, recollect
ant remember
　2 *syn* see NEGLECT
con bethink, mind, recall, recollect
ant remember

forgetful *adj* tending to lose or let go from one's mind something once known or learned < she is growing *forgetful* >
syn oblivious, unmindful, unwitting
rel lax, neglectful, negligent, remiss, slack; careless, heedless, thoughtless; absent, absentminded, abstracted, bemused
con alert, alive, awake, aware, cognizant, conscious, sensible; attentive, considerate, thoughtful

forgetfulness *n syn* see OBLIVION
forgivable *adj syn* see VENIAL
forgive *vb syn* see EXCUSE 1
idiom forgive and forget

forgo *vb* to deny oneself something for the sake of an end < he vowed to *forgo* all luxuries until the debt was paid >
syn eschew, forbear, sacrifice
rel abandon, relinquish, surrender, waive; abdicate, renounce, resign; forsake, give up

fork (out) *vb syn* see SPEND 1
forlorn *adj* **1** dejected and saddened especially by reason of being alone < a *forlorn* lost child >
syn lonely, lonesome, lorn
rel abandoned, deserted, desolate, forgotten, forsaken; miserable, wretched; friendless, homeless; defenseless, helpless; depressed, oppressed, weighed down; alone, solitary
　2 *syn* see DESPONDENT
rel cynical, pessimistic; fruitless, futile, vain
con hopeful, optimistic, roseate, rose-colored

form *n* **1** outward appearance of something as distinguished from the substance of which it is made < the carefully graded *form* of the curves >
syn cast, configuration, conformation, figure, shape
rel contour, outline, profile, silhouette; anatomy, framework, skeleton, structure; economy, organism, scheme, system
2 conduct regulated by an external control (as custom or a formal protocol of procedure) < observing the *forms* of polite society >
syn ceremonial, ceremony, formality, liturgy, rite, ritual
rel procedure, proceeding, process; custom, habit, practice, usage; canon, law, precept, regulation, rule; method, mode; decorum, etiquette, propriety
3 a fixed or accepted way of doing or sometimes of expressing something < good *form* in swimming >
syn convenance, convention, usage
rel fashion, manner, mode, style, way

form *vb* **1** *syn* see MAKE 3
rel devise; create, invent; turn out; design, plan, plot, project, scheme; establish, found, organize
con demolish, destroy, ruin, wreck
　2 *syn* see DEVELOP 4
　3 *syn* see CONSTITUTE 1

formal *adj* **1** *syn* see CEREMONIAL
rel methodical, orderly, regular, systematic; decorous, proper, seemly; prim, unbending; distant, reserved
ant informal
　2 *syn* see NOMINAL

formality *n* **1** *syn* see FORM 2
rel convenance, convention
ant informality
　2 *syn* see RITE 2

formation *n syn* see MAKEUP 1
former *adj* **1** *syn* see PRECEDING
con following, succeeding, supervening
ant latter
　2 having been such at some previous time < *former* friends >
syn bygone, erstwhile, late, old, once, onetime, past, quondam, sometime, whilom
con current, present; future, prospective

formerly *adv syn* see BEFORE 2
formidable *adj* **1** *syn* see FEARFUL 3
ant comforting
　2 *syn* see HARD 6
ant simple

formless *adj* having no definite or recognizable form < a *formless* fear >
syn amorphous, inchoate, shapeless, unformed, unshaped
rel chaotic, orderless, unordered, unorganized; indistinct, obscure, unclear, vague; indefinite, indeterminate, undefined; crude, raw, rough, rude
con distinct, formed; definite, explicit, express, specific; ordered, organized

formulate *vb* **1** *syn* see WORD
  2 *syn* see CONTRIVE 2
  3 *syn* see DRAFT 3
‖**fornent** *prep* *syn* see BESIDE 1
for real *adv* *syn* see SERIOUSLY 1
forsake *vb* *syn* see ABANDON 1
  rel spurn; leave; abdicate, resign
  ant return (to), revert (to)
forsaken *adj* *syn* see DERELICT 1
forswear *vb* **1** *syn* see ABJURE
  2 *syn* see PERJURE
fort *n* a structure or place offering resistance to a hostile force
  < settlers fled to the *fort* >
  syn citadel, fastness, fortress, redoubt, stronghold
forte *n* that in which one excels < cooking is her strongest *forte* >
  syn eminency, long suit, medium, métier, oyster, strong suit
  rel ableness, effectiveness, efficiency; ability, competence; bag, thing
  idiom cup of tea, dish of tea, strong point
  con inadequacy, incapability, incompetence, inefficiency; greenness, rawness
forth *adv* **1** *syn* see AHEAD 2
  2 *syn* see ALONG 1
forthcome *vb* *syn* see LOOM 2
forthcoming *adj* being soon to appear or take place < the *forthcoming* holidays >
  syn approaching, coming, nearing, oncoming, upcoming
  rel future; imminent, impending, pending; anticipated, awaited, expected
  con distant, far-off, remote; bygone, former, gone, gone-by, past
forthright *adj* **1** *syn* see STRAIGHTFORWARD 2
  con covert, secret, stealthy, surreptitious, underhand; deceitful, mendacious, untruthful
  ant furtive
  2 *syn* see FRANK
forthwith *adv* **1** *syn* see AWAY 3
  2 *syn* see SHORT 1
fortify *vb* **1** *syn* see STRENGTHEN 2
  rel arouse, rally, rouse, stir; refresh, renew, restore
  con dilute, thin
  ant enfeeble
  2 *syn* see GIRD 3
fortitude *n* a quality of character combining courage and staying power < she bore up under all her problems with admirable *fortitude* >
  syn backbone, grit, guts, intestinal fortitude, ‖moxie, nerve, sand, spunk; *compare* COURAGE
  rel courage, mettle, pith, resoluteness, resolution, spirit, stick-to-itiveness, tenacity; boldness, bravery, courageousness, dauntlessness, fearlessness, intrepidity, valiancy, valor, valorousness; endurance, stamina, strength; constancy, determination, perseverance; bottom
  con cowardliness, fearfulness, timidity, timorousness; faintheartedness, milksoppiness, weakness; cowardice, yellowness
  ant pusillanimity
fortress *n* *syn* see FORT
fortuitous *adj* *syn* see ACCIDENTAL
  con activated, actuated, motivated; projected, schemed
  ant deliberate
fortuitously *adv* *syn* see INCIDENTALLY 1
  ant deliberately
fortuity *n* *syn* see ACCIDENT 1
  ant deliberation
fortunate *adj* **1** *syn* see FAVORABLE 5
  ant disastrous
  2 *syn* see LUCKY
  ant unfortunate
fortunately *adv* *syn* see WELL 5
fortunateness *n* *syn* see LUCK 3
  ant unfortunateness
fortune *n* **1** *syn* see CHANCE 2
  rel destiny, doom, portion
  con design, intent, intention
  2 *syn* see LUCK 3
  ant misfortune
  3 *syn* see WEALTH 2
  4 a very large amount of money < those furs must have cost a *fortune* >

  syn ‖bomb, boodle, bundle, mint, packet, pile, pot, ‖roll, wad
  idiom king's ransom, pretty penny, tidy sum
fortuneless *adj* *syn* see POOR 1
forty winks *n pl but sing or pl in constr* *syn* see NAP
forward *adj* **1** *syn* see PRESUMPTUOUS
  2 *syn* see WISE 5
  ant bashful
  3 *syn* see PRECOCIOUS
  con regressive, retrograde, retrogressive
  ant backward
forward *adv* **1** *syn* see BEFORE 1
  2 *syn* see AHEAD 2
  ant backward
  3 *syn* see ALONG 1
forward *vb* **1** *syn* see ADVANCE 1
  rel back, champion, support, uphold
  con baffle, circumvent, foil, frustrate, outwit, thwart
  ant balk
  2 *syn* see SEND 1
fossil *n* *syn* see FOGY
foster *vb* **1** *syn* see NURSE 2
  rel back, champion, support, uphold; entertain, harbor, house, lodge, shelter; accommodate, assist, favor, help, oblige
  con combat, fight, oppose, resist, withstand; curb, inhibit, restrain; ban, forbid, interdict, prohibit; abuse, disregard, neglect
  2 *syn* see ADVANCE 1
foul *adj* **1** *syn* see OFFENSIVE
  2 *syn* see DIRTY 1
  rel fetid, malodorous, noisome, putrid, stinking; loathsome, offensive, repulsive, revolting
  ant fair; undefiled
  3 *syn* see OBSCENE 2
foul *vb* **1** *syn* see SOIL 2
  rel contaminate, defile, pollute; desecrate, profane
  2 *syn* see CONTAMINATE 2
foul play *n* *syn* see MURDER
foul up *vb* *syn* see CONFUSE 5
found *vb* **1** *syn* see BASE
  rel support, sustain; erect, raise, rear
  2 to set going or to bring into existence < *founded* a new school for graduate studies >
  syn constitute, create, establish, institute, organize, set up, start
  rel begin, commence, inaugurate, initiate; fashion, form
  con close, conclude, end, finish, terminate; arrest, check, halt, stay, stop
foundation *n* **1** *syn* see BASIS 1
  2 *syn* see BASIS 3
  3 *syn* see BASE 1
foundational *adj* *syn* see FUNDAMENTAL 1
foundationless *adj* *syn* see BASELESS
founder *n* *syn* see FATHER 2
founder *vb* *syn* see SINK 1
fount *n* *syn* see SOURCE
fountain *n* *syn* see SOURCE
fountainhead *n* *syn* see SOURCE
four *n* *syn* see QUARTET
fourberie *n* *syn* see DECEPTION 1
four–flush *vb* *syn* see DECEIVE
foursome *n* *syn* see QUARTET
foursquare *adj* *syn* see SQUARE 1
fourth *n* *syn* see QUARTER 1
foxiness *n* *syn* see CUNNING 2
foxy *adj* *syn* see SLY 2
  rel deceitful, dishonest
  con aboveboard, forthright, straightforward
foyer *n* *syn* see VESTIBULE
fracas *n* **1** *syn* see QUARREL
  2 *syn* see BRAWL 2
fractional *adj* *syn* see INCOMPLETE 1
fractious *adj* **1** *syn* see UNRULY 1
  ant orderly
  2 *syn* see IRRITABLE
  ant peaceable

---

syn synonym(s)   *rel* related word(s)
ant antonym(s)   *con* contrasted word(s)
idiom idiomatic equivalent(s)
‖ use limited; if in doubt, see a dictionary

fracturable *adj syn* see FRAGILE 1

fracture *n syn* see BREACH 3

fragile *adj* **1** easily broken <a *fragile* dish of the finest porcelain>
syn breakable, delicate, fracturable, frail, frangible, shatterable, shattery
rel brittle, crisp, crumbly, crunchy, friable, short
con infrangible, unbreakable; elastic, flexible, resilient; stout, strong, sturdy, tenacious
ant tough
2 *syn* see WEAK 1
ant durable

fragment *n* **1** *syn* see PARTICLE
2 *syn* see END 4

fragment *vb syn* see SHATTER 1

fragmentary *adj syn* see INCOMPLETE 1

fragrance *n* a sweet or pleasant odor <the *fragrance* of flowers>
syn aroma, balm, bouquet, incense, perfume, redolence, scent, spice
rel odor, smell
con fetidness, fetor, malodor, noisomeness, rancidness, rankness
ant stench, stink

fragrant *adj syn* see SWEET 2
rel delectable, delicious, delightful
ant fetid

frail *adj* **1** *syn* see WEAK 1
rel slender, slight, slim, tenuous, thin; petty, puny
con hale, healthy, sound
ant robust
2 *syn* see FRAGILE 1
con solid, substantial

frailty *n syn* see FAULT 2

frame *vb* **1** *syn* see CONTRIVE 2
2 *syn* see DRAFT 3
3 *syn* see MAKE 3

framework *n syn* see STRUCTURE 3

franchise *n syn* see SUFFRAGE

franchise *vb syn* see ENFRANCHISE

frangible *adj syn* see FRAGILE 1

frank *adj* marked by free, forthright, and sincere expression <a *frank* answer>
syn candid, direct, forthright, man-to-man, open, openhearted, plain, plainspoken, single, single-eyed, single-hearted, single-minded, straightforward, unconcealed, undisguised, undissembled, undissembling, unmannered, unreserved, unvarnished; *compare* COMMUNICATIVE, STRAIGHTFORWARD 2
rel ingenuous, naive, natural, simple, unsophisticated; bluff, blunt; heart-to-heart, sincere; honest, scrupulous, upright; dispassionate, fair, impartial, just, unbiased; barefaced, brazen, outspoken, uninhibited
con reserved, reticent, secretive, silent, taciturn, uncommunicative; covert, furtive, secret, sneaking, underhand; deceitful, deceptive, dishonest, evasive, false, lying, mendacious, tricky, untruthful; insincere
ant reticent

frank *n syn* see FRANKFURTER

frankfurter *n* a seasoned beef or beef and pork sausage
syn dog, frank, hot dog, wiener, wienerwurst, ‖wienie

frantic *adj syn* see FURIOUS 2

frantically *adv syn* see HARD 2

fraternity *n syn* see ASSOCIATION 2

fraud *n* **1** *syn* see DECEPTION 1
2 *syn* see IMPOSTURE
rel bamboozlement, bamboozling, dupery, duping, hoodwinking
3 *syn* see IMPOSTOR

fray *n* **1** *syn* see BRAWL 2
rel contention, discord, dissension, strife
2 *syn* see CLASH 2

frayed *adj syn* see RAGGED

frazzle *vb syn* see EXHAUST 4

frazzled *adj syn* see RAGGED

freak *n* **1** *syn* see CAPRICE
2 one that is physically abnormal <pitiful *freaks* displayed in sideshows>
syn abortion, lusus, miscreation, monster, monstrosity
rel aberration, chimera, malconformation, malformation, misshape, mosaic, mutation, sport; abnormality, anomaly, curiosity, oddity; rara avis, rarity; androgyne, hermaphrodite

idiom freak of nature
3 *syn* see ENTHUSIAST

freakish *adj syn* see ARBITRARY 1

freckle *vb syn* see SPECKLE 1

free *adj* **1** not subject to the rule or control of another <a *free* country>
syn autarchic, autarkic, autonomous, independent, separate, sovereign
rel free-born, unenslaved; delivered, emancipated, enfranchised, freed, liberated, released; democratic, self-directing, self-governing, self-ruling; sui juris; individualistic, unregimented
con coerced, compelled, constrained, forced, obliged; dependent, restricted, subject; inferior, subordinate, subservient; captive, enslaved, enthralled, subjugated
ant bond
2 not bound, confined, or detained by force <the prisoner was now *free*>
syn loose, unconfined, unrestrained
rel unbound, unchained, unfettered, unshackled, untied; clear, loose, scot-free; emancipated, freed, liberated; independent
idiom at liberty, free as a bird, free as air, free to come and go
con confined, restrained; impounded, imprisoned, incarcerated, interned, jailed; bound, chained, fettered, shackled, tied
3 *syn* see LIBERAL 1
ant close
4 *syn* see OUTSPOKEN
5 not costing or charging anything <a *free* public school>
syn chargeless, complimentary, costless, gratis, gratuitous
rel unpaid, unrecompensed, unremunerated
idiom for free, for love, for nothing, on the cuff, on the house
con charged, paid; costly, dear, expensive, high, high priced
6 not having the affections fixed on a particular object <she was happy to be *free* and in no hurry to fall in love again>
syn fancy-free, heart-whole

free *vb* to relieve from constraint or restraint <*free* an oppressed people>
syn discharge, disenthrall, disimprison, emancipate, liberate, loose, loosen, manumit, redeem, release, ‖spring, unbind, unchain, unshackle
rel clear, detach, disencumber, disengage, disentangle, extricate; deliver, ransom, redeem, rescue; affranchise, enfranchise
idiom cut loose
con fetter, hamper, hog-tie, manacle, shackle, trammel; immure, imprison, incarcerate, intern, jail; circumscribe, confine, limit, restrict; curb, inhibit, restrain; enslave, enthrall, subjugate

freebooter *n* **1** *syn* see MARAUDER
2 *syn* see PIRATE

freedom *n* the power or condition of acting without compulsion <*freedom* of the press>
syn liberty, license
rel exemption, immunity; prerogative, privilege, right; compass, latitude, scope, sweep
con coercion, compulsion, constraint; restraint
ant necessity

free-for-all *n syn* see BRAWL 2

free hand *n syn* see CARTE BLANCHE

freehanded *adj syn* see LIBERAL 1

freeloader *n syn* see PARASITE

freely *adv* EASILY 1, effortlessly, facilely, lightly, readily, smoothly, well

free-minded *adj syn* see HAPPY-GO-LUCKY

free-spoken *adj syn* see OUTSPOKEN

freezer *n syn* see JAIL

freezing *adj syn* see COLD 1
ant scorching

freight *n syn* see LOAD 1

frenetic *adj syn* see FURIOUS 2

frenzied *adj syn* see FURIOUS 2

frenziedly *adv syn* see HARD 2

frenzy *n syn* see DELIRIUM

frenzy *vb syn* see MADDEN 1

frequent *adj syn* see COMMON 4
ant infrequent, rare

frequent *vb* to go to or be in often <he *frequents* the bar down the street>
syn affect, hang around, hang out, haunt, resort
rel attend, go (to); visit; infest, overrun
con avoid, miss, sidestep

ant shun

frequenter *n syn* see HABITUÉ 1

frequently *adv* 1 *syn* see OFTEN
ant infrequently
2 *syn* see USUALLY 2

fresh *adj* 1 *syn* see NEW 1
rel gleaming, glistening, sparkling; striking, vital, vivid; virginal, youthful; crude, green, raw, uncouth; artless, naive, natural, unsophisticated
con hackneyed, shopworn, stereotyped, threadbare, trite
ant stale
2 *syn* see ADDITIONAL
3 *syn* see INEXPERIENCED
4 *syn* see WISE 5

freshman *n syn* see NOVICE

freshness *n syn* see INEXPERIENCE

fret *vb* 1 *syn* see WORRY 3
rel chafe, fume; brood, mope
idiom eat one's heart out
2 *syn* see ANNOY 1
3 *syn* see CHAFE 3
4 *syn* see RIPPLE

fretful *adj* 1 *syn* see IRRITABLE
rel captious, carping, caviling, critical, faultfinding; contrary, perverse
con forbearing, long-suffering, patient, resigned; subdued, submissive, tame
2 *syn* see IMPATIENT 1

friable *adj syn* see SHORT 6

fribble *adj syn* see GIDDY 1

fribbling *adj syn* see GIDDY 1

fried *adj syn* see INTOXICATED 1

friend *n* a person with whom one is on good and, usually, familiar terms < he is one of my closest *friends* >
syn acquaintance, amigo, cater-cousin, confidant, familiar, intimate, mate; *compare* ASSOCIATE 3
rel alter ego, best friend, bosom friend; ally, colleague, partner; nodding acquaintance
con enemy; adversary, antagonist, opponent; competitor, rival
ant foe

friendliness *n syn* see GOODWILL 1
rel affability, amiability, congeniality, cordiality, neighborliness, sociability
ant unfriendliness

friendly *adj* 1 *syn* see AMICABLE 1
rel close, familiar, intimate; affectionate, devoted, loving
ant unfriendly; belligerent
2 *syn* see HARMONIOUS 3
3 *syn* see SYMPATHETIC 2
ant unfriendly

friendship *n syn* see GOODWILL 1
rel affinity, attraction; empathy; accord, concord, consonance, harmony; alliance, coalition, federation, fusion, league
con antagonism, antipathy, hostility, rancor; hate
ant animosity

fright *n* 1 *syn* see FEAR 1
2 *syn* see EYESORE

fright *vb syn* see FRIGHTEN

frighten *vb* to strike or to fill with fear or dread < the puppy was *frightened* by the unfamiliar noises >
syn affright, alarm, awe, fright, scare, ‖spook, startle, terrify, terrorize
rel appall, astound, daunt, disconcert, dismay, faze, horrify, shock; demoralize, unman, unnerve; browbeat, bulldoze, cow, intimidate; agitate, discompose, disquiet, perturb, upset
idiom curdle the blood, curl the hair, frighten one out of one's wits, freeze the blood, give one a scare, give one a turn, make one's blood run cold, make one's flesh creep, make one's hair stand on end, make one's teeth chatter, make one tremble, put one's heart in one's mouth, scare hell out of, scare one spitless, scare one stiff, scare the life out of, scare the pants off of, scare to death, strike terror into, take one's breath away
con embolden, encourage, hearten, reassure

frightened *adj syn* see AFRAID 1
idiom in a fright
ant unfrightened

frightful *adj syn* see FEARFUL 3

frigid *adj* 1 *syn* see COLD 1

2 *syn* see COLD 2
3 free from or deficient in passion < claimed his wife was a *frigid* woman >
syn cold, inhibited, passionless, undersexed, unresponsive
idiom as cold as an iceberg
con affectionate, demanding, loving
ant ardent; amorous

frill *n syn* see LUXURY

fringe *n syn* see BORDER 1

fringe *vb syn* see BORDER 1

frippery *n syn* see FINERY

frisk *vb* 1 *syn* see GAMBOL
2 *syn* see SEARCH 2

frisky *adj syn* see PLAYFUL 1

fritter *vb syn* see WASTE 2

frivol away *vb syn* see WASTE 2

frivolity *n syn* see LIGHTNESS
rel coquetting, dallying, flirting, toying, trifling; fun, game, jest, play, sport
ant seriousness; staidness

frivolous *adj syn* see GIDDY 1
rel shallow, superficial, unprofound; gay, light, playful
ant serious

‖**frogskin** *n syn* see DOLLAR

frolic *vb* 1 *syn* see REVEL 1
2 *syn* see GAMBOL

frolic *n syn* see PRANK

frolicsome *adj* 1 *syn* see ANTIC 2
2 *syn* see PLAYFUL 1

from *prep* 1 *syn* see AFTER 1
2 in the face of < protect them *from* exploitation >
syn against

frondeur *n syn* see REBEL

frons *n syn* see FOREHEAD

front *n* 1 *syn* see FOREHEAD
2 *syn* see MASK 2
3 a person, group, or thing used to mask the identity or true character of a controlling agent < the export company was a *front* for illegal activities >
syn blind
rel disguise, facade, mask

front *vb* 1 *syn* see FACE 1
2 *syn* see FACE 3
3 *syn* see MEET 6
4 *syn* see ACCOST 2

frontier *n* 1 a region between two countries < lived on the *frontier* between Mexico and the U.S. >
syn border, borderland, march, marchland
2 a rural region that forms the margin of settled or developed territory < settlers found living on the *frontier* was a hard life >
syn backcountry, backland, ‖backveld, backwash, backwater, backwoods, ‖boondocks, ‖boonies, bush, hinterland, ‖outback, sticks, up-country
idiom the back of beyond

frontier *adj syn* see BACK 1

fronting *prep syn* see AGAINST 1

front-rank *adj syn* see EXCELLENT

frore *adj syn* see COLD 1

frosty *adj syn* see COLD 1

froth *n syn* see FOAM
rel flippancy, frivolity, levity, lightness

froward *adj syn* see CONTRARY 3

frown *vb* 1 to put on a dark or malignant countenance or aspect < he *frowned* at the naughty child >
syn gloom, glower, lower, scowl
rel glare; grimace; pout, sulk
idiom look black, look daggers
con grin, laugh
ant smile
2 *syn* see DISAPPROVE 1

frowsy *adj* 1 *syn* see SLATTERNLY
rel lax, neglectful, negligent, remiss, slack
ant trim; smart

---

syn synonym(s)   *rel* related word(s)
ant antonym(s)   *con* contrasted word(s)
idiom idiomatic equivalent(s)
‖ use limited; if in doubt, see a dictionary

2 *syn* see MALODOROUS 1
frugal *adj syn* see SPARING
  rel careful, meticulous; discreet, prudent; conserving, preserving; cheeseparing, penny-pinching, scrimping, stinting
  ant wasteful
frugality *n syn* see ECONOMY
‖**fruit** *n syn* see HOMOSEXUAL
fruitage *n syn* see HARVEST 2
fruitful *adj syn* see FERTILE
  rel breeding, propagating, reproducing; abounding
  con abortive, bootless, futile, vain
  ant unfruitful; fruitless
fruitfulness *n syn* see FERTILITY
fruition *n syn* see PLEASURE 2
  rel actualization, materialization, realization; accomplishment, fulfillment; achievement, attainment
fruitless *adj syn* see FUTILE
  rel barren, infertile, sterile, unfruitful; foiled, frustrated, thwarted; infructuous, unprofitable
  con fecund, fertile, prolific
  ant fruitful
‖**fruity** *adj syn* see INSANE 1
frumpish *adj syn* see TACKY 2
frumpy *adj syn* see TACKY 2
frustrate *vb* **1** to come between a person and his aim or desire or to defeat another's plan <my efforts are *frustrated* at every turn>
  syn baffle, balk, beat, bilk, buffalo, circumvent, dash, disappoint, foil, ruin, thwart; *compare* OUTWIT
  rel annul, cancel, counteract, negative, neutralize, nullify; anticipate, forestall; conquer, defeat, lick, overcome; forbid, inhibit, prohibit; obviate, preclude, prevent; bar, block, hinder, impede, obstruct; arrest, check, halt, interrupt
  idiom cut the ground from under one, dash one's hope, defeat expectation, throw a monkey wrench into the works, upset one's applecart
  con accomplish, achieve, bring about, effect, perform; advance, forward, further, promote; abet, foment, incite, instigate
  ant fulfill
  2 *syn* see NEUTRALIZE
frying pan *n* a pan with a handle used for frying food <some still prefer the sturdy cast-iron *frying pan* >
  syn skillet, spider
fuddle *vb syn* see CONFUSE 2
  ant clarify, clear
fuddler *n syn* see DRUNKARD
fuddy–duddy *n* **1** *syn* see FOGY
  2 *syn* see STUFFED SHIRT
  3 *syn* see FUSSBUDGET
fudge *vb syn* see EMBROIDER
fudge *n syn* see NONSENSE 2
fugacious *adj syn* see TRANSIENT
fugitive *adj syn* see TRANSIENT
fugitive *n syn* see REFUGEE
fulfill *vb* **1** to do what is required by the terms of so as to make effective <found themselves unable to *fulfill* their contract>
  syn complete, execute, implement, perform; *compare* EFFECT 2
  rel effect, effectuate; discharge
  2 *syn* see SATISFY 5
fulgent *adj syn* see BRIGHT 1
full *adj* **1** containing as much as is possible <the hamper is *full* >
  syn awash, big, block and block, brimful, brimming, bung-full, chockablock, chock-full, cram-full, crammed, crowded, jam-full, jammed, jam-packed, loaded, packed, ‖packed out, replete, stuffed, ‖trig
  rel abounding, teeming
  idiom full to bursting (*or* overflowing), ready to burst
  con blank, vacant, void; bare, barren
  ant empty
  2 *syn* see CIRCUMSTANTIAL
  ant incomplete
  3 *syn* see WHOLE 2
  con denuded, dismantled, divested, stripped
  4 *syn* see SATIATED
full–blooded *adj* **1** *syn* see PUREBRED
  2 *syn* see RUDDY
full–blown *adj* **1** *syn* see MATURE 1

2 *syn* see TOTAL 5
full–bosomed *adj syn* see BUXOM
full–bodied *adj syn* see STRONG 3
full dress *n syn* see FINERY
full–dress *adj syn* see EXHAUSTIVE
full–fledged *adj syn* see MATURE 1
full–grown *adj syn* see MATURE 1
full–mouthed *adj syn* see LOUD 1
fullness *n syn* see BREADTH 2
full–out *adj syn* see TOTAL 5
full–scale *adj syn* see TOTAL 5
full tilt *adv syn* see FAST 2
fully *adv* **1** *syn* see DOWN 2
  2 *syn* see WELL 3
fulsome *adj* too obviously extravagant or ingratiating to be accepted as genuine or sincere <offering sickeningly *fulsome* praise >
  syn oily, oleaginous, slick, smarmy, soapy, unctious, unctuous
  rel canting, holier-than-thou, hypocritical, pecksniffian, pharisaical, sanctimonious; bland, glib, honey-mouthed, honey=tongued, ingratiating, mealy-mouthed, oily-tongued, smooth, smooth-tongued, suave; buttery, flattering, wheedling; excessive, extravagant, exuberant, lavish, profuse; cloying, satiating, sating; bombastic, grandiloquent, magniloquent
  con earnest, genuine, heartfelt, hearty, sincere, true, truthful, unfeigned, wholehearted, whole-souled
fumble *vb* **1** *syn* see GROPE
  2 *syn* see BOTCH
  rel flounder, stumble
  3 *syn* see MUMBLE
fume *n syn* see SNIT
fume *vb syn* see ANGER 2
fun *vb syn* see BANTER
fun *n* **1** action or speech intended to amuse or arouse laughter <you know he only said it in *fun* >
  syn game, jest, joke, play, sport
  rel amusement, diversion, entertainment, recreation; blitheness; jocundity, joviality, merriment; glee, hilarity, jollity, mirth; mischief, teasing
  con soberness, thoughtfulness
  ant earnestness, seriousness
  2 *syn* see PLAY 1
function *n* **1** the acts or operations expected of a person or thing <fulfill one's *function* as a mother>
  syn business, duty, office, province, role
  rel affair, concern; job, task, work
  2 *syn* see USE 4
  3 *syn* see POWER 3
  rel action, behavior, operation
function *vb* **1** *syn* see ACT 4
  2 *syn* see ACT 5
  3 to operate in the proper or expected manner <finally succeeded in getting the motor to *function* >
  syn act, go, run, work
  rel do, operate, perform
functional *adj syn* see PRACTICAL 2
functioning *adj syn* see ACTIVE 1
fund *n syn* see SUPPLY
fund *vb syn* see ENDOW 2
fundament *n syn* see BUTTOCKS
fundamental *adj* **1** forming or affecting the groundwork, roots, or lowest part of something <the *fundamental* rules of poetry >
  syn basal, basic, bottom, foundational, primary, radical, underlying
  rel primal, prime, primordial; elemental, elementary
  con incidental
  2 *syn* see ELEMENTAL 1
  3 *syn* see ESSENTIAL 2
  rel indispensable, necessary, needful, requisite; dominant, paramount
fundamental *n* **1** *syn* see PRINCIPLE 1
  rel component, constituent, factor, element
  2 *syn* see ESSENTIAL 1
  3 *usu* fundamentals *pl syn* see ALPHABET 2
fundamentalist *n syn* see DIEHARD 1
fundamentally *adv syn* see ESSENTIALLY 1
  ant superficially
funeral director *n syn* see MORTICIAN

funereal *adj syn* see GLOOMY 3
  rel grave, solemn
  con animated, gay, lively, sprightly, vivacious; blithe, jocund, jolly, jovial, merry
  ant festive
fungible *adj syn* see INTERCHANGEABLE
funk *vb syn* see SMELL 3
funk *n syn* see COWARD
funker *n syn* see COWARD
funky *adj syn* see MALODOROUS 1
funnel *vb syn* see CONDUCT 4
funniness *n syn* see HUMOR 4
funny *adj syn* see LAUGHABLE
  rel antic, bizarre, fantastic, grotesque
  idiom too funny for words
  con doleful, dolorous, lugubrious, melancholy, plaintive
  ant unfunny
funnyman *n syn* see HUMORIST 2
fur *n* **1** *syn* see HIDE
  2 *syn* see DOWN
furbish *vb syn* see POLISH 1
furious *adj* **1** *syn* see WILD 6
  2 marked by uncontrollable excitement often under the stress of a powerful emotion <in a state of *furious* activity>
  syn corybantic, delirious, frantic, frenetic, frenzied, mad, rabid, wild
  rel excited, provoked, stimulated; enthusiastic, fanatic; desperate, feverish, hasty, impetuous; fierce, intense, vehement, violent; excessive, extravagant, extreme, inordinate; enraged, incensed, infuriated, maddened; hysterical, irrational, unreasonable; bewildered, distracted, upset; crazed, demented, insane, mad, maniac
  con calm, composed, peaceful, placid, quiet, serene, subdued, tranquil; apathetic, impassive, imperturbable, inexcitable
  3 *syn* see INTENSE 1
furiously *adv syn* see HARD 2
furl *vb syn* see ROLL 3
furnish *vb* **1** to supply one with what is needed (as for daily living or a particular activity) <*furnished* him the papers for his application>
  syn accouter, appoint, arm, equip, fit out, gear, outfit, rig, turn out
  rel dower, endow, endue; apparel, array, clothe; mount; give, provide, supply
  con denude, dismantle, divest, strip; despoil, spoliate; relieve (of), take away
  2 *syn* see GIVE 3
furor *n syn* see DELIRIUM
furore *n* **1** *syn* see STIR 1
  2 *syn* see FASHION 3
  3 *syn* see COMMOTION 3
furrow *n syn* see WRINKLE
  rel channel, groove, rut
further *adv* **1** *syn* see BEYOND 1
  2 *syn* see AGAIN 4
further *adj syn* see ADDITIONAL
further *vb syn* see ADVANCE 1
  rel engender, generate, propagate
  con bar, block, impede, obstruct; forestall, prevent
  ant hinder; retard
furthermore *adv syn* see ALSO 2
furthermost *adj syn* see EXTREME 5
furthest *adj syn* see EXTREME 5

furtive *adj* **1** *syn* see SECRET 1
  rel artful, crafty, cunning, foxy, guileful, insidious, scheming, shifty, sly, sneaky, tricky, wily; calculating, cautious, circumspect, wary; cloaked, disguised, masked
  con brash, impudent, presumptuous
  ant forthright; barefaced, brazen
  2 *syn* see STEALTHY 2
  ant open
furtively *adv syn* see SECRETLY
  ant openly
furuncle *n syn* see ABSCESS
fury *n syn* see ANGER
  rel passion; furor; acerbity, acrimony, asperity
fuse *vb* **1** *syn* see LIQUEFY
  2 *syn* see MIX 1
  rel compact, consolidate, unify
fusillade *n syn* see BARRAGE
fusion *n syn* see MIXTURE
fuss *n* **1** *syn* see STIR 1
  rel fluster, perturbation; bother, flap, stew; racket, rumpus; haste, hurry, speed
  2 *syn* see COMMOTION 3
  3 *syn* see QUARREL
fuss *vb* **1** *syn* see WORRY 3
  idiom fret and fume
  2 *syn* see COMPLAIN
  3 *syn* see GRIPE
  4 *syn* see NAG
fussbudget *n* one who becomes upset over trifles <he is the biggest *fussbudget* I know, always going into a tizzy over nothing>
  syn fuddy-duddy, fusser, fusspot, granny, old lady, old maid
  rel perfectionist, precisionist, stickler
fusser *n syn* see FUSSBUDGET
fusspot *n syn* see FUSSBUDGET
fussy *adj* **1** *syn* see BUSTLING
  2 *syn* see CAREFUL 2
  3 *syn* see NICE 1
  rel fretful, irritable, querulous
fustian *n syn* see BOMBAST
fustian *adj syn* see FECKLESS 1
fusty *adj* **1** *syn* see MALODOROUS 1
  rel close, moldy; dirty, filthy, squalid; disheveled, slipshod, sloppy, slovenly, unkempt
  2 *syn* see OLD-FASHIONED
futile *adj* barren of results <efforts to convince him were *futile*>
  syn abortive, bootless, fruitless, ineffective, ineffectual, unavailable, unavailing, unprevailing, unproductive, useless, vain
  rel empty, hollow, idle, nugatory, otiose; inadequate, inefficacious, inefficient, insufficient; unsatisfactory, unsuccessful
  idiom in vain, no dice, of no avail, to no effect
  con effectual, efficacious, fruitful; advantageous, beneficial, profitable
  ant effective
future *n* time that is to come <you must try to do better in the *future*>
  syn aftertime, afterward, by-and-by, hereafter, offing, to-be; *compare* PRESENT
  idiom time to come
  ant past
fuzz *n* **1** *syn* see DOWN
  ‖**2** *syn* see POLICEMAN
fuzzy *adj syn* see FAINT 2

---

syn synonym(s)   *rel* related word(s)
ant antonym(s)   *con* contrasted word(s)
idiom idiomatic equivalent(s)
‖ use limited; if in doubt, see a dictionary

gab *vb syn* see CHAT 1
gab *n syn* see CHATTER
gabber *n syn* see CHATTERBOX
gabble *vb* **1** *syn* see GIBBER
  2 *syn* see BABBLE 2
  3 *syn* see CHAT 1
gabble *n syn* see CHATTER
gabby *adj syn* see TALKATIVE
gad *vb syn* see WANDER 1
gadget *n* **1** a usually small and often novel mechanical or electronic device or contrivance <a new kitchen *gadget* for separating egg whites>
  syn concern, gimmick, gizmo, jigger, widget; *compare* DEVICE 2, DOODAD, WHAT-DO-YOU-CALL-IT
  rel apparatus, appliance, contraption, tool, utensil
  2 *syn* see DOODAD
gaffe *n syn* see FAUX PAS
gaffer *n* a man of advanced years <doddering *gaffers* on the park benches>
  syn graybeard, patriarch; *compare* BELDAM 1, OLDSTER
  rel duffer, geezer, grandfather, old boy, veteran
gag *vb* **1** *syn* see RETCH
  2 *syn* see DEMUR
gag *n syn* see JOKE 1
  rel ruse, trick, wile
gaiety *n* **1** *syn* see MERRYMAKING
  2 *syn* see MIRTH
  rel cheerfulness, gladness, happiness; geniality, pleasantness, winsomeness; animation, conviviality, entertainment, exhilaration, liveliness, merrymaking, radiance, spiritedness, vivacity
  con blues, cheerlessness, dismalness, dreariness, gloom, grief, infelicity, joylessness, misery, moodiness, moroseness, pensiveness, solemnity, somberness, sorrow, sullenness, uncheerfulness, wistfulness, woe
gain *n syn* see PROFIT
  rel cut, rake-off, share, take, winnings
  ant loss
gain *vb* **1** to arrive at a goal, point, or end <*gained* success in the theater>
  syn accomplish, achieve, attain, rack up, reach, realize, score, win
  rel complete, consummate, fulfill, perfect, produce; succeed
  con falter, flop, flounder, flunk, lose
  2 *syn* see IMPROVE 3
  rel invigorate, renew, strengthen; cure, heal, remedy
  3 *syn* see EARN 1
  4 *syn* see GET 1
  ant lose
  5 *syn* see CLEAR 6
  ant lose
gainful *adj syn* see ADVANTAGEOUS 1
  rel fat, fruitful, generous, lush, productive, rich; satisfying, substantial
gainsay *vb syn* see DENY 4
  rel combat, fight, oppose, resist, withstand
  ant admit
gainsaying *n syn* see DENIAL 2
  ant admission; admitting
gait *n syn* see SPEED 2
gal *n* **1** *syn* see GIRL 1
  2 *syn* see GIRL FRIEND 1
gall *n syn* see EFFRONTERY
  rel arrogance, conceit, haughtiness, loftiness, lordliness, overbearance, pomposity, pride, priggishness, self-importance, smugness
  con bashfulness, humbleness, humility, lowliness, modesty, shyness
  ant meekness
gall *vb* **1** *syn* see ABRADE 1
  rel bark, burn, file, fray, frazzle, grate, graze, scrape, scratch, scuff, skin
  2 *syn* see CHAFE 3

  rel distress, pain; cut, score, wound
  3 *syn* see ANNOY 1
  4 *syn* see IRRITATE
  rel chide, disturb, harass, harry, torment, worry; bedevil, needle, trouble
gallant *n* **1** *syn* see FOP
  2 an individual who is amorously attracted to the opposite sex <his fiancee accused him of being a trifling *gallant*>
  syn amorist, Casanova, Don Juan, lothario, paramour, Romeo
  rel dirty old man, lecher, libertine, rake, satyr; admirer, adorer, beau, date, escort, lover, sparker, suitor, swain, wooer
  idiom gay blade
gallant *adj* **1** *syn* see COURTLY
  rel urbane, suave; attentive, considerate, thoughtful
  con heedless, inattentive, indifferent, thoughtless, unconcerned
  ant ungallant
  2 *syn* see BRAVE 1
  ant dastardly
gallantry *n* **1** *syn* see COURTESY 1
  rel deference, duty, homage, honor; reverence, suavity, urbanity; address, poise, savoir faire, tact
  con boorishness, churlishness, clownishness, loutishness; discourteousness
  ant discourtesy
  2 *syn* see HEROISM
  rel bravery, dauntlessness; mettle, resolution, spirit
  ant dastardliness
gallery *n syn* see MUSEUM
galley slave *n syn* see SLAVE 2
gallimaufry *n syn* see MISCELLANY 1
galling *adj syn* see BITTER 2
gallivant *vb syn* see WANDER 1
gallows *n pl syn* see SUSPENDERS
galluptious *adj syn* see MARVELOUS 2
galluses *n pl syn* see SUSPENDERS
galoot *n syn* see MAN 3
galumph *vb syn* see LUMBER
galvanize *vb syn* see PROVOKE 4
  rel activate, energize, vitalize
gambit *n syn* see TRICK 1
  rel design, plan, plot
gamble *vb* **1** to engage in a game of chance for something of value <swore he would never *gamble* for high stakes again>
  syn bet, game, lay, play, put (on), set, stake, wager
  rel chance, hazard, lot, risk, speculate, venture
  idiom buck the odds, take a flyer (on), try one's luck
  2 to take a chance on something <*gambled* on the train being late>
  syn chance, hazard, risk, venture; *compare* VENTURE 1
  rel brave, challenge, dare, defy, face; endanger, imperil, jeopardize
  idiom go it blind, take a chance (*or* one's chances), tempt fortune, trust to luck
gambol *vb* to leap or tumble about playfully <young lambs *gamboling* in the meadow>
  syn caper, cavort, frisk, frolic, rollick, romp
  rel lark, revel, roister; bound, leap, spring
  idiom kick up one's heels, let off steam
game *n* **1** *syn* see FUN 1
  con business, duty, labor, study, toil
  2 games *pl syn* see ATHLETICS
  3 animals under pursuit <hunting big *game* is a risky and expensive sport>
  syn chase, prey, quarry
  rel kill, ravin, victim
game *vb syn* see GAMBLE 1
game *adj syn* see BRAVE 1
game plan *n syn* see PLAN 1
gamesome *adj syn* see PLAYFUL 1
gamin *n syn* see URCHIN
gamine *n syn* see TOMBOY
gammer *n syn* see BELDAM 1

gamy *adj syn* see MALODOROUS 1
‖**gander** *n syn* see PEEP
gangling *adj* being tall, thin, and usually loose-jointed <a *gangling* high-school boy>
  syn gangly, lanky, rangy, spindling, spindly
  rel bony, gaunt, lank, lean, scrawny, skinny, spare, tall, thin
  con low, low-set, low-statured, short, squat, stocky, sturdy, thickset
gangly *adj syn* see GANGLING
‖**gangrel** *n syn* see VAGABOND
gap *n* **1** an open space in a barrier <the sheep got through a *gap* in the fence>
  syn breach, break, discontinuity, hole, opening
  rel fracture, rupture; chink, cleavage, cleft, crack, crevice, fissure, slit, slot; division, interspace, interval, separation; aperture, cranny, orifice
  2 *syn* see RAVINE
  3 a period of discontinuity <a *gap* of an hour between speakers>
  syn breach, break, hiatus, interim, interruption, interval, lacuna; *compare* PAUSE
  rel caesura, intermission, lull, pause, respite, rest
gape *vb* **1** *syn* see GAZE 1
  2 *syn* see LOOK 7
  3 *syn* see YAWN
gaping *adj syn* see CAVERNOUS 1
garb *vb syn* see CLOTHE
garbage *n syn* see REFUSE
  rel dregs, rubble; filth, sewage, slop
garble *vb syn* see MISREPRESENT
  rel becloud, conceal, hide, obfuscate, obscure
garden house *n syn* see SUMMERHOUSE
gargantuan *adj syn* see HUGE
  ant lilliputian
garish *adj syn* see GAUDY
  rel overdone, overwrought
  con dark, dim, dreary, dull, dusky, murky; quiet, unpretentious
  ant somber
garland *n* **1** *syn* see WREATH
  2 *syn* see ANTHOLOGY
garment *vb syn* see CLOTHE
garner *vb* **1** *syn* see REAP
  2 *syn* see GLEAN
  3 *syn* see ACCUMULATE
  rel gather, glean, harvest, reap; hoard, store
  con disseminate, spread
garnish *vb syn* see ADORN
garrulous *adj syn* see TALKATIVE
  rel blabbing, prattling, prolix, verbose, windy, wordy
  con concise; terse; blunt, brusque, curt
  ant taciturn
‖**gas** *n syn* see NONSENSE 2
‖**gas** *vb syn* see CHAT 1
‖**gasbag** *n syn* see BRAGGART
gasconade *vb syn* see BOAST
gash *vb syn* see CUT 1
  rel carve, split; injure, wound; furrow, mark, notch; lance, nip
gasp *vb syn* see PANT 1
‖**gasper** *n syn* see CIGARETTE
gastronome *n syn* see EPICURE
  rel aesthete, connoisseur, dilettante
gastronomer *n syn* see EPICURE
gastronomist *n syn* see EPICURE
gate *n syn* see FAUCET
gather *vb* **1** *syn* see GROUP 1
  rel choose, cull, pick, select; accumulate, amass
  idiom separate the wheat from the chaff (*or* the sheep from the goats)
  con dispel, disperse, dissipate
  ant scatter
  2 *syn* see REAP
  rel cull, pick, pluck; heap, mass, pile, stack
  3 *syn* see GLEAN
  4 *syn* see INFER
  rel catch, fathom, follow, grasp, take in
  idiom put two and two together
  5 *syn* see UNDERSTAND 3
  6 to bring or come together <a crowd *gathered* to watch the fight>

syn assemble, collect, congregate, congress, forgather, muster, raise, rendezvous; *compare* GROUP 1
  rel aggregate, troop; affiliate, ally, associate, league; encounter, meet
  con break up, disband, disperse, part, separate; disintegrate, disorganize, dissolve
  ant scatter
  7 *syn* see LOOM 2
gathering *n* **1** *syn* see CONCOURSE
  2 a number of individuals come or brought together <a *gathering* in the town park>
  syn aggregation, assemblage, assembly, collection, company, congeries, congregation, crowd, group, muster, ruck; *compare* GROUP 1
  rel bunch, crew, crush, flock, gang, horde, mass, press, rout, swarm, turnout
  3 *syn* see HARVEST 1
gauche *adj syn* see AWKWARD 2
  rel crude, green, unpolished
  con bland, smooth, suave, urbane
  ant adroit
gaudy *adj* cheaply or vulgarly showy <*gaudy* sideshow posters>
  syn blatant, brazen, chintzy, flashy, garish, glaring, loud, meretricious, tawdry, tinsel
  rel obtrusive, ostentatious, pretentious, showy, tasteless; coarse, crude, gross, vulgar; brummagem, fake, phony, sham
  con restrained, tasteful, unobtrusive; factual, illuminating, informative
  ant quiet
gauge *n syn* see STANDARD 3
  rel check, mark, model, norm, pattern, rule, type
gauge *vb syn* see MEASURE 2
‖**gaum** *n syn* see OAF 2
gaunt *adj* **1** *syn* see LEAN
  2 *syn* see EMACIATED
  ant bloated
‖**gaup** (*or* **gawp**) *vb* **1** *syn* see LOOK 7
  2 *syn* see GAZE 1
gauzy *adj syn* see FILMY
gawk *vb syn* see GAZE 1
gawk *n syn* see OAF 2
gawky *adj syn* see CLUMSY 1
gay *adj* **1** *syn* see MERRY
  2 *syn* see LIVELY 1
  rel frolicsome, playful, sportive
  con earnest, sedate, serious, solemn, somber, staid; quiet, silent, still
  ant grave, sober
  3 *syn* see COLORFUL
  4 *syn* see WILD 7
  5 *syn* see HOMOSEXUAL
  6 *syn* see PRESUMPTUOUS
gaze *vb* **1** to look long and usually attentively <*gazed* out the window>
  syn bore, gape, ‖gaup (*or* gawp), gawk, glare, gloat, goggle, peer, stare; *compare* LOOK 7
  rel look, see, watch; peek, peep; contemplate, inspect, observe, scrutinize, survey; admire, ogle, regard
  con glance, skim, skip
  2 *syn* see LOOK 7
gaze (upon) *vb syn* see EYE 1
gazebo *n syn* see SUMMERHOUSE
gear *n syn* see EQUIPMENT
  rel accessories, adjuncts, appendages, appurtenances; belongings, effects, means, possessions
gear *vb syn* see FURNISH 1
‖**gee** *n syn* see MAN 3
‖**gee** *vb syn* see AGREE 4
Gehenna *n syn* see HELL
gel *vb syn* see COAGULATE
gelastic *adj syn* see LAUGHABLE
gelate *vb syn* see COAGULATE
gelatinize *vb syn* see COAGULATE

---

syn synonym(s)   *rel* related word(s)
ant antonym(s)   *con* contrasted word(s)
idiom idiomatic equivalent(s)
‖ use limited; if in doubt, see a dictionary

geld *vb syn* see STERILIZE

gelid *adj syn* see COLD 1
  con ardent, burning, fervent, scorching, sweltering, torrid
  ant fervid

‖**gelt** *n syn* see MONEY

gem *vb syn* see BEJEWEL

‖**gendarme** *n syn* see POLICEMAN

genealogy *n* an account often in chart form recording a line of ancestors <decided to prepare a *genealogy* of his family>
  syn ‖begats, family tree, pedigree, stemma

general *adj* **1** conforming to what is expected in the ordinary course of events <the *general* problems of everyday life>
  syn common, commonplace, matter-of-course, natural, normal, prevalent, regular, run-of-the-mill, typic, typical, usual
  rel everyday, popular; familiar, universal; habitual, humdrum, routine, uneventful
  con abnormal, extraordinary, irregular, novel, strange, unexpected, unforeseeable, unusual
  2 belonging or relating to the whole <a *general* change in the weather>
  syn common, generic, universal
  rel natural, normal, regular, typical; broad, inclusive, wide
  con individual, particular, special; characteristic, distinctive, peculiar
  3 *syn* see ALL-AROUND 2
  4 *syn* see PUBLIC 4

generally *adv* **1** in a reasonably inclusive manner <the forest was *generally* coniferous>
  syn chiefly, largely, mainly, mostly, overall, predominantly, primarily, principally
  rel about, approximately, practically, roughly, roundly
  con altogether, totally, wholly
  2 *syn* see ALTOGETHER 3
  3 *syn* see USUALLY 2

generate *vb* **1** to bring into existence <*generate* new business>
  syn create, father, hatch, make, originate, parent, procreate, produce, sire, spawn
  rel bring about, effect, impose, occasion; introduce; cause; found, inaugurate, institute, set up; develop, induce, whip (up)
  idiom bring to pass, give birth to, give rise to
  con demolish, destroy, extinguish, ruin; degenerate, deteriorate, impair, worsen
  2 *syn* see PROCREATE 1
  3 to be the cause or source of something immaterial <actions that *generated* a good deal of suspicion>
  syn breed, cause, engender, get up, hatch, induce, muster (up), occasion, produce, provoke, work up
  rel accomplish, achieve, perform
  idiom give birth to, give rise to

generator *n syn* see FATHER 2

generic *adj syn* see GENERAL 2
  ant specific

generous *adj* **1** marked by a noble or forbearing spirit <*generous* toward the weakness of others>
  syn benevolent, big, chivalrous, considerate, greathearted, lofty, magnanimous
  rel altruistic, charitable, kindhearted, kindly, thoughtful, ungrudging, unselfish; fair, honest; long-suffering, tolerant; helpful, willing
  con base, ignoble, mean, self-centered, selfish; grim, hard, harsh, intolerant
  ant ungenerous
  2 *syn* see LIBERAL 1
  ant stingy
  3 *syn* see PLENTIFUL
  rel lavish; luxuriant; affluent, wealthy
  con scant, scanty, sparse

generously *adv syn* see WELL 2

genesis *n syn* see BEGINNING
  rel provenance, provenience
  con cessation, conclusion, culmination, end, finish, termination

genial *adj* **1** *syn* see GRACIOUS 1
  rel amicable, friendly, neighborly; blithe, cheerful, jocund, jolly, jovial, merry
  con discourteous, rude, uncivil, ungracious; crabbed, morose, sullen; ironic, sarcastic, sardonic, satiric
  ant caustic (*remarks, comments*); saturnine (*manner, disposition, aspect*)

2 *syn* see GENTLE 2

geniality *n syn* see AMENITY 1

genitalia *n pl* the external components of the reproductive system <the gradual adolescent differentiation of the *genitalia*>
  syn genitals, parts, private parts, privates, privities, privy parts, pudendum (*usu* pudenda *pl*), secrets

genitals *n pl syn* see GENITALIA

genius *n syn* see GIFT 2
  rel creativity, ingenuity, inventiveness, originality; astuteness, brains, grasp, intellect, intelligence, understanding

gent *n syn* see MAN 3

genteel *adj* **1** having characteristics or qualities befitting the upper classes <in those days croquet was a very *genteel* sport> <his manner was perfectly *genteel*>
  syn cultivated, cultured, distingué, polished, refined, urbane, well-bred
  rel elegant, fashionable, graceful, stylish; chivalrous, gentlemanly, knightly, ladylike, noble; mannerly, well-mannered
  con coarse, common, crude, ill-bred, rough, rude, uncouth, uncultured, unpolished, vulgar
  ant ungenteel
  2 *syn* see CIVIL 2
  rel well-behaved; aristocratic, cultured
  con crude, discourteous, inconsiderate, rough, rude
  3 involving or excessively preoccupied with the airs and forms of middle-class or upper-class proprieties <a shy *genteel* girl terrified of blundering socially>
  syn affected, la-di-da, ‖lardy-dardy, mincing, pretentious, stilted, too-too; *compare* PRECIOUS 4, PRIM 1
  rel artificial, formal, high-falutin
  con cultured, genuine, honest, refined; gracious, polished; gentlemanly, ladylike
  4 *syn* see PRIM 1
  rel narrow; intolerant, uncharitable; confined, insular, parochial, provincial
  idiom nasty nice
  con charitable, tolerant, understanding; broad-minded, easy, relaxed

gentile *adj syn* see HEATHEN

gentility *n syn* see ARISTOCRACY

gentle *adj* **1** free from all harshness, roughness, or intensity <a *gentle* summer breeze>
  syn balmy, bland, faint, lenient, mild, smooth, soft
  rel delicate, mellow, tender; hushed, low, soothing; calm, halcyon, peaceful, placid, quiet, serene, tranquil
  con coarse, harsh, rough; exquisite, fierce, intense, savage, vehement, violent; forceful, forcible, powerful
  2 having a pleasant easygoing nature <a *gentle* person in everything she does>
  syn affable, amiable, genial
  rel kind, pleasant, pleasing, tender; agreeable, benign, mild; compassionate, kindly, softhearted, sympathetic, warmhearted
  con belligerent, cantankerous, contentious, ill-natured, petty, quarrelsome; aggressive, demanding, overbearing
  ant harsh, stern

gentleman *n* **1** a person of good or noble birth <the contributions of the country *gentleman* to social stability>
  syn aristo, aristocrat, blue blood, patrician
  rel Brahmin; chevalier; nob, swell
  con churl, clown, lout
  ant boor
  2 *syn* see MAN 3

gentleman friend *n syn* see BOYFRIEND 1

gentry *n syn* see ARISTOCRACY

genuine *adj* **1** *syn* see AUTHENTIC 2
  con artificial, ersatz, factitious; counterfeited, sham, simulated; sophisticated
  ant fraudulent
  2 *syn* see ACTUAL 2
  con uncommon, unordinary, unusual; alleged, apocryphal, apparent, fabulous, fictitious, mythical
  3 free from hypocrisy or pretense <a *genuine* love for his fellowman>
  syn heart-whole, honest, real, sincere, true, undesigning, undissembled, unfeigned; *compare* NATURAL 5, SINCERE 1
  rel reliable, trustworthy, unaffected, unimpeachable, veritable
  con affected, hypocritical
  ant insincere

genuinely *adv syn* see VERY 2

germ *n syn* see SEED 2

germane *adj syn* see RELEVANT
  con incompatible, incongruous, inconsonant
  ant foreign

gest *n syn* see ADVENTURE

gestapo *adj syn* see TERRORISTIC

gestation *n syn* see PREGNANCY

gesture *n syn* see EXPRESSION 3

gesture *vb syn* see SIGNAL

get *vb* **1** to come into possession of < hoped to *get* a fortune from his invention >
  syn acquire, annex, chalk up, compass, gain, have, land, obtain, pick up, procure, pull, secure, win
  rel educe, elicit, evoke, extort, extract, ‖promote; accept, receive; clutch, grab, grasp, take; accomplish, achieve, effect; capture, carry; draw
  idiom come by
  con abnegate, eschew, forbear, forgo, give up, sacrifice; abandon, forsake, renounce
  2 *syn* see EARN 1
  3 *syn* see BECOME 1
  rel achieve, attain, effect, realize
  idiom get to be, turn out to be
  4 *syn* see CONTRACT 1
  5 *syn* see FATHER 1
  6 *syn* see PREPARE 1
  rel arrange, order, right; adjust, coordinate, organize
  7 *syn* see CATCH 1
  8 *syn* see AFFECT
  rel bend, bias, dispose, predispose, prompt
  con benumb, deaden, numb; blunt, dull, harden
  9 *syn* see NONPLUS 1
  rel bother, distress, disturb, perturb, upset; discomfit, disconcert, embarrass
  10 *syn* see IRRITATE
  idiom try one's temper
  con calm, compose, cool, lull, soothe, subdue
  11 *syn* see LEARN 1
  idiom get into one's head
  12 *syn* see MEMORIZE
  13 *syn* see INDUCE 1
  rel provoke; beg, coax, press, pressure, urge
  14 *syn* see REACH 4
  15 *syn* see COME 1

get along *vb* **1** *syn* see ADVANCE 5
  rel depart, go
  con recede, regress, retreat, retrogress, reverse, revert
  2 *syn* see SHIFT 5
  rel flourish, prosper, succeed, thrive

get away *vb syn* see GO 2

getaway *n syn* see ESCAPE 1

get back *vb syn* see RECOVER 1

get by *vb syn* see SHIFT 5

get in *vb syn* see COME 1

get off *vb* **1** *syn* see GO 2
  rel advance, progress
  2 *syn* see BEGIN 1

get on *vb* **1** *syn* see DON 1
  2 *syn* see ADVANCE 5
  3 *syn* see SHIFT 5

get out *vb* **1** to go away quickly, immediately, and often secretly < had to *get out* before the police arrived >
  syn begone, clear out, decamp, hightail, kite, scram, skedaddle, skiddoo, take off, ‖vamoose
  rel depart, duck (out), egress, exit, go, leave, split
  idiom beat it, be off, make tracks, take a powder, take a runout powder
  con abide, remain, reside, stay
  2 to become known < we can't let this story *get out* >
  syn break, come out, leak, out, transpire
  3 *syn* see PUBLISH 2

gettable *adj syn* see AVAILABLE 1

get up *vb* **1** *syn* see ROLL OUT
  2 *syn* see RISE 1
  3 *syn* see GENERATE 3

getup *n* **1** *syn* see COSTUME
  2 *syn* see VIGOR 2

get–up–and–go *n* **1** *syn* see VIGOR 2
  2 *syn* see ENTERPRISE 4

gewgaw *n syn* see KNICKKNACK

ghastly *adj* **1** disturbingly frightening or repellent in appearance or aspect < the *ghastly* sight of burned and rotting bodies >
  syn grim, grisly, gruesome, hideous, horrible, horrid, horrifying, lurid, macabre, terrible, terrifying
  rel appalling, awful, dreadful, frightening, frightful, shocking; disgustful, disgusting, nauseant, nauseating, sickening
  con appealing, attractive, charming, pleasant, touching; acceptable, bearable; trivial, unimportant
  2 resembling or suggestive of a ghost < a *ghastly* form slightly visible through the fog >
  syn cadaverous, corpselike, deathlike, ghostlike, ghostly, shadowy, spectral
  rel ashen, livid, lurid, pale; uncanny, weird; gruesome, haggard, macabre; dim, faint, weak; charnel, mortuary, sepulchral

ghost *n syn* see APPARITION
  rel demon, devil

ghost *vb syn* see GHOSTWRITE

ghostlike *adj syn* see GHASTLY 2

ghostly *adj syn* see GHASTLY 2

ghostwrite *vb* to write for and in the name of another < a *ghost-written* autobiography >
  syn ghost, ‖spook

GI *n syn* see SOLDIER

giant *n* something of monstrous size, appearance, or power < a *giant* of a tractor >
  syn behemoth, leviathan, mammoth, monster, whale
  rel cyclops, polypheme

giant *adj syn* see HUGE
  rel gross, hulking
  con paltry, petty, puny, trifling, trivial
  ant dwarf

gibber *vb* to utter or speak rapidly, inarticulately, and usually unintelligibly < a *gibbering* idiot >
  syn babble, chatter, gabble, jabber
  rel blather, drivel, prate, prattle, yammer; stammer, stutter; mumble, mutter; mow
  idiom run off at the mouth
  con articulate, enunciate, pronounce

gibberish *n* **1** unintelligible or meaningless talk < the *gibberish* of an imbecile >
  syn babble, drivel, Greek, jabber, jabberwocky, nonsense, skimble-skamble; *compare* GIBBERISH 3
  rel blather, bunkum, claptrap, twaddle; blabber, gabble, palaver, prattle
  2 *syn* see GOBBLEDYGOOK
  3 speech or actions that are esoteric in nature and suggest the magical, strange, or unknown < the shaman's strange *gibberish* >
  syn abracadabra, hocus-pocus, mumbo jumbo, mummery
  rel magic, sorcery, thaumaturgy

gibbet *vb syn* see HANG 2

gibble–gabble *n syn* see CHATTER

gibe *vb syn* see SCOFF
  rel rail, rally, revile, scold, twit

giddy *adj* **1** having a lightheartedly silly nature < tried to teach a bunch of *giddy* Girl Scouts how to make a fire >
  syn bird-witted, dizzy, empty-headed, featherbrained, flighty, fribble, fribbling, frivolous, harebrained, hoity-toity, light, light-headed, rattlebrained, scatterbrained, silly, skittish, volage, yeasty
  rel capricious, fickle, impulsive, whimsical; brainless, exuberant, thoughtless, witless
  idiom giddy as a goose
  con earnest, pensive, sedate, serious, sober, solemn, staid, thoughtful
  2 *syn* see DIZZY 2
  rel bemused, flustered
  idiom going around in circles, like a chicken with its head cut off, seeing double

---

syn synonym(s)   *rel* related word(s)
ant antonym(s)   *con* contrasted word(s)
idiom idiomatic equivalent(s)
‖ use limited; if in doubt, see a dictionary

gift *n* **1** something freely given by one person to another for his benefit or pleasure < the watch was a graduation *gift* >
syn benevolence, boon, ‖compliment, favor, largess, present
rel alms, benefaction, contribution, donation; award, bestowal, grant, presentation; legacy; offering, reward, tip; remembrance, souvenir, token
2 a natural or special facility or capableness < has a *gift* for electronics >
syn aptness, bent, bump, faculty, flair, genius, head, knack, nose, set, talent, turn; *compare* LEANING 2
rel ability, aptitude, capability; accomplishment, acquirement, attainment; instinct, numen, power; forte, leaning, propensity, specialty
con awkwardness, clumsiness, maladroitness
gigantean *adj syn* see HUGE
gigantesque *adj syn* see HUGE
gigantic *adj syn* see HUGE
rel hulking, stupendous
con paltry, petty, puny, trifling, trivial
giggle *vb syn* see LAUGH
gill *n syn* see CREEK 2
gimcrack *n syn* see KNICKKNACK
gimmick *n* **1** *syn* see GADGET 1
2 *syn* see TRICK 1
rel cheat, counterfeit, deceit, dodge, fake, humbug, imposture; fun, game, jest, method, sport
gimp *n syn* see SPIRIT 5
gingerly *adj syn* see CAUTIOUS
gingery *adj syn* see SPIRITED 2
con lethargic, listless, poky, slow; dead, dull, flat, insipid, stuffy; dreary; blasé, lackadaisical, nonchalant
‖gin mill *n syn* see BAR 5
gird *vb* **1** *syn* see BELT 1
ant ungird
2 *syn* see SURROUND 1
rel wrap, wreathe
3 to prepare oneself for action < *girded* himself for the coming trial >
syn brace, fortify, prepare, ready, steel, strengthen
rel bolster, buttress, support, sustain; harden, reinforce, shore (up); invigorate; dispose, forearm, prepare
idiom gird one's loins, whet the knife
gird *vb syn* see SCOFF
girdle *n syn* see BELT 1
girdle *vb* **1** *syn* see BELT
2 *syn* see SURROUND 1
girl *n* **1** a young unmarried female person < hired a *girl* to baby-sit >
syn damsel, gal, lass, lassie, maid, maiden, miss, missy, ‖quail, ‖quiff, wench
rel hoyden, tomboy; deb, debutante, subdeb, subdebutante; bobby-soxer; schoolgirl; gamine
2 *syn* see MAID 2
3 *syn* see GIRL FRIEND 1
girl Friday *n syn* see RIGHT-HAND MAN
girl friend *n* **1** a woman who is a man's usual or preferred companion < took his *girl friend* out every weekend >
syn best girl, ‖chick, ‖doney, gal, girl, lady friend, lass, mouse, popsy
2 a woman who shares with a man a strong and usually sexually oriented mutual attraction < his wife caught him with his *girl friend* >
syn ‖baby, beloved, flame, honey, inamorata, ladylove, steady, sweetheart, sweetie, truelove
3 *syn* see MISTRESS
gist *n syn* see SUBSTANCE 2
rel sap, soul, spirit; subject, theme, topic; bearing, drift, tenor
give *vb* **1** to provide gratuitously < *gave* their labor to rebuild the burned church >
syn bestow, devote, donate, give away, hand out, present; *compare* CONTRIBUTE 1
rel accord, award, confer, grant, hand; afford, contribute, furnish, provide; aid, assist, benefact, help
con keep, retain, withhold; lease, sell
2 to provide by or as if by formal action < he was *given* a diploma >
syn accord, award, confer, grant; *compare* GRANT 1
rel bestow, hand over, present; allocate, appropriate, assign

con decline, refuse; hold back, withhold
3 to put into the possession of another usually for use or consumption < *gave* the dog a drink of water >
syn deliver, dish out, dispense, feed, find, furnish, hand, hand over, provide, supply, transfer, turn over
rel administer, commit, offer; deal, disburse, disperse, distribute, divide, dole (out), lot (out); afford, lend
con have, hold, hold back, keep, keep back, reserve, retain, withhold
4 *syn* see OFFER 1
rel bestow, confer, render; administer, dispense, issue
5 *syn* see EXPRESS 2
6 *syn* see ALLOT
7 to furnish as a result or product < 6 +6 *gives* 12 >
syn produce, yield
rel be, equal, make; afford, furnish, offer, supply
8 *syn* see SPEND 1
9 *syn* see SELL 2
10 to bestow or dispense by some action < *gave* him a punch in the nose >
syn administer, deal, deliver, inflict, strike
rel bestow, dispense; fetch
11 *syn* see ADDRESS 3
12 to fail in response to physical stress < the bridge *gave* under the heavy load >
syn bend, break, cave, collapse, crumple, fold up, go, yield
rel fail, relax, relent, slacken, weaken
idiom cave in, give way
13 *syn* see HAPPEN 1
give away *vb* **1** *syn* see GIVE 1
2 *syn* see REVEAL 1
give back *vb* **1** *syn* see RETREAT 2
rel back out, backtrack, backwater; crumble, fail, falter, weaken
2 *syn* see RESTORE 5
given *adj syn* see APT 1
given name *n* the name that precedes one's surname < arguing over the baby's *given name* >
syn baptismal name, Christian name, font name, forename, personal name, prename
rel first name, middle name; appellation, appellative, compellation, denomination, style; praenomen; epithet, label, tag
give off *vb* **1** *syn* see EMIT 2
2 *syn* see DISCHARGE 5
give out *vb* **1** *syn* see EMIT 2
2 *syn* see COLLAPSE 2
3 *syn* see FAIL 2
give over *vb syn* see STOP 3
giver *n syn* see DONOR
give up *vb* **1** *syn* see RELINQUISH
2 *syn* see DESPAIR
gizmo *n* **1** *syn* see DOODAD
2 *syn* see GADGET
glabrous *adj syn* see HAIRLESS
rel beardless, shaven, smooth-shaven
con bristled, bristly, hairy, hirsute, stubbled, stubbly
glacial *adj* **1** *syn* see COLD 1
2 *syn* see COLD 2
rel aloof, distant, remote, reserved, standoffish, withdrawn; exclusive, inaccessible, seclusive, unapproachable
con affable, gregarious, sociable
glad *adj* **1** characterized by or expressing the mood of one who is pleased or delighted < he was *glad* to be on vacation >
syn happy, joyful, joyous, lighthearted
rel delighted, gratified, pleased, rejoiced, tickled; blithe, exhilarated, jocund, jolly, jovial, merry; gleeful, hilarious, mirthful
idiom filled with (*or* full of) delight
con blue, dejected, depressed, downcast, melancholy; despondent, dispirited, heavyhearted, sadhearted, unhappy; forlorn, joyless, sorrowful, woeful
ant sad
2 full of brightness and cheerfulness < a *glad* spring morning >
syn bright, cheerful, cheery, radiant
rel beaming, sparkling; beautiful; genial, pleasant
con dark, dim, dull, gloomy, somber
gladden *vb syn* see PLEASE 2
rel comfort, console, solace; animate, enliven, exhilarate, invigorate, liven, quicken, vivify
con depress, oppress, weigh; discourage, dishearten, dispirit; damp, dampen; bother, irk

ant sadden

gladiatorial *adj syn* see BELLIGERENT

‖**glad rags** *n pl syn* see FINERY

glamorous *adj syn* see ATTRACTIVE 1

glamour *n syn* see CHARM 3

glance *vb* **1** to strike a surface obliquely so as to go off at an angle <the bullet *glanced* off the stone wall>
  syn carom, dap, graze, ricochet, skim, skip
  rel brush, kiss, scrape, shave, slant; contact, hit, strike, touch; bounce, careen, rebound
  con center, focus
  2 *syn* see BRUSH
  3 *syn* see FLASH 1

glance (at *or* over) *vb syn* see BROWSE

glance *n* **1** *syn* see FLASH 1
  2 *syn* see PEEP

glance *vb syn* see POLISH 1

glare *vb* **1** *syn* see BLAZE
  rel dazzle, flash, gleam, glisten, glitter
  2 *syn* see GAZE 1
  rel frown, glower, lower, scowl

glaring *adj* **1** *syn* see EGREGIOUS
  rel conspicuous, noticeable, outstanding; excessive, extreme, inordinate; obtrusive
  ant unnoticeable
  2 *syn* see GAUDY
  rel cheap, coarse, crude, gross
  con elegant, tasteful

glass *n syn* see MIRROR 1

glass *vb syn* see REFLECT 1

‖**glasshouse** *n syn* see GREENHOUSE

glassy *adj syn* see SLEEK

glaze *vb syn* see POLISH 1

glaze *n syn* see LUSTER

gleam *n syn* see FLASH 1

gleam *vb* **1** *syn* see SHINE 1
  2 *syn* see FLASH 1
  rel burn

gleaming *adj syn* see LUSTROUS 1

glean *vb* to gather by effort and usually bit by bit <evidence *gleaned* from various testimonies>
  syn cull, extract, garner, gather, pick up
  rel sift, winnow; ascertain, conclude, deduce, learn
  con amass, heap, pile

glee *n syn* see MIRTH
  rel delectation, delight, enjoyment, joy, pleasure; blitheness; joyousness
  ant gloom

gleeful *adj syn* see MERRY

glen *n syn* see VALLEY

glib *adj* characterized by very fluent often superficial address toward others <*glib* chatter>
  syn silver-tongued, vocative, voluble, well-hung; *compare* TALKATIVE
  rel articulate, eloquent, facile, fluent, vocal
  con inarticulate, unfluent

glide *vb* **1** *syn* see SLIDE 1
  rel float, fly, sail, scud, shoot, skim
  2 *syn* see STEAL 1
  3 *syn* see SNEAK

glimmer *vb syn* see FLASH 1

glimmer *n syn* see FLASH 1

glimpse *n syn* see PEEP

glint *vb syn* see FLASH 1

glint *n* **1** *syn* see FLASH 1
  2 *syn* see LUSTER

glissade *vb syn* see SLIDE 1
  rel float, fly, sail, scud, shoot, skim

glisten *vb syn* see FLASH 1

glisten *n syn* see FLASH 1

glistening *adj syn* see LUSTROUS 1

glitter *vb* **1** *syn* see FLASH 1
  2 *syn* see SPANGLE 1

glitter *n syn* see FLASH 1

gloaming *n syn* see EVENING 1

gloat *vb syn* see GAZE 1
  con begrudge, covet, envy, grudge

global *adj* **1** *syn* see UNIVERSAL 2

ant parochial
  2 *syn* see ALL-ROUND 2
  rel all-inclusive, blanket, catholic, grand, universal

globe *n* **1** *syn* see BALL
  2 *syn* see EARTH 1

globule *n syn* see DROP 1

gloom *vb* **1** *syn* see FROWN 1
  rel brood, mope
  con smile; bubble, effervesce, enthuse, sparkle
  2 *syn* see OBSCURE

gloom *n syn* see SADNESS
  con hilarity, jollity, mirth; gaiety, gladness
  ant glee

gloomy *adj* **1** *syn* see DARK 1
  rel bleak, dismal, dreary
  ant brilliant
  2 *syn* see SULLEN
  rel cheerless, dejected, depressed, downcast, joyless, melancholy, oppressed, solemn, unhappy, weary
  con glad, happy, joyful, joyous, lighthearted; blithe, jocund, jovial, merry
  ant cheerful
  3 causing or marked by gloom <the *gloomy* atmosphere of the dungeon>
  syn acheronian, acherontic, black, bleak, cheerless, cold, depressant, depressing, depressive, desolate, disconsolate, discouraging, disheartening, dismal, dispiriting, drear, dreary, dusky, funereal, joyless, lugubrious, morne, oppressive, somber, tenebrific, unhappy, woebegone
  rel despondent, mirthless, pessimistic; melancholy, mournful, sad; drab, dull, muzzy
  con bright, cheerful, happy; cheering, emboldening, encouraging, heartening, optimistic
  ant gloomless

glorification *n syn* see APOTHEOSIS 2

glorify *vb* **1** *syn* see PRAISE 2
  2 *syn* see EXALT 1

glorious *adj* **1** *syn* see SPLENDID 2
  rel brilliant, effulgent, lustrous, radiant; imposing, impressive; majestic, noble; ravishing, stunning; beautiful
  ant inglorious
  2 *syn* see MARVELOUS 2

glory *vb syn* see EXULT

gloss *n syn* see LUSTER
  rel glossiness, silkiness, sleekness, slickness; burnish

gloss *vb syn* see POLISH 1

gloss (over) *vb syn* see PALLIATE
  rel account, explain, justify, rationalize; belie, falsify, miscolor, misrepresent

gloss *vb syn* see ANNOTATE

glossy *adj* **1** *syn* see LUSTROUS 1
  2 *syn* see SLEEK

glow *vb* **1** *syn* see BLAZE
  rel burn; ignite, kindle, light
  2 *syn* see BLUSH

glow *n syn* see BLOOM 3

glower *vb syn* see FROWN 1
  rel stare; look, watch

glowing *adj* **1** *syn* see RUDDY
  2 *syn* see IMPASSIONED
  rel enthusiastic; avid, desirous, eager, fierce, keen; burning, heated

gloze (over) *vb syn* see PALLIATE
  rel account, explain, justify, rationalize; belie, falsify, miscolor, misrepresent

gluey *adj syn* see STICKY 1

glum *adj syn* see SULLEN
  rel close-lipped, silent, taciturn, tight-lipped; depressed, oppressed, weighed down
  con glad, happy, joyful, joyous, lighthearted
  ant cheerful

glut *vb syn* see SATIATE
  rel cram, feast, stuff

---

syn synonym(s)	***rel*** related word(s)
ant antonym(s)	***con*** contrasted word(s)
idiom idiomatic equivalent(s)	
‖ use limited; if in doubt, see a dictionary	

idiom make a pig of (oneself)
con scant, skimp
ant stint
glutted *adj syn* see SATIATED
gluttonous *adj syn* see VORACIOUS
  rel hoggish, piggish; indulgent, intemperate
  con sober, temperate; ascetic, austere; sparing
  ant abstemious
gnaw *vb* **1** *syn* see WORRY 1
  rel haunt, irritate, rankle
  2 *syn* see EAT 3
  rel abrade, fret; consume, crumble
gnome *n syn* see MAXIM
gnostic *adj syn* see WISE 1
go *vb* **1** to move on a course <they were glad to be *going* toward home>
  syn ‖cruise, fare, hie, journey, pass, proceed, ‖process, push on, repair, travel, wend
  rel advance; approach, near
  idiom gain ground, get over the ground, make one's way
  ant stay; stop
  2 to move out of and away from where one is <it's time to *go* now>
  syn ‖blow, depart, exit, get away, get off, leave, ‖mog, move, pop off, pull out, push off, quit, retire, run along, shove off, take off, withdraw
  rel abscond, decamp, escape, flee, fly, hightail
  idiom take a powder
  con abide, remain, stay; arrive
  ant come
  3 *syn* see RUN 8
  4 to be brought to or toward an end <his money will soon be *gone*>
  syn consume, exhaust, expend, finish, run through, spend, use up, wash up
  rel deplete, devour, dissipate, fritter (away), overspend, squander, waste
  con conserve, preserve, save
  5 *syn* see DIE 1
  6 *syn* see PASS 3
  7 *syn* see GIVE 12
  8 *syn* see HAPPEN 1
  9 *syn* see BECOME 1
  10 *syn* see RANGE 3
  11 *syn* see SUCCEED 3
  12 *syn* see SUCCEED 2
  13 *syn* see RESORT 2
  14 *syn* see FUNCTION 3
  15 *syn* see EXTEND 7
  16 *syn* see AGREE 4
  17 *syn* see BELONG 1
  18 *syn* see BEAR 10
  19 *syn* see ENJOY 1
go (for) *vb syn* see APPROVE 1
go (into) *vb syn* see EXPLORE
go (together *or* **with)** *vb syn* see SUIT 4
go *n* **1** *syn* see OCCURRENCE
  2 *syn* see VIGOR 2
  3 *syn* see ENERGY 2
  4 *syn* see FLING 1
  5 *syn* see SPELL 1
  6 *syn* see SIEGE
  7 *syn* see SUCCESS
goad *n syn* see STIMULUS
  rel compulsion, drive, impulsion; desire, lust, passion, urge, zeal
  ant curb
goad *vb syn* see URGE
  rel impel, move; coerce, compel, force; instigate
go–ahead *adj syn* see ENTERPRISING 2
goal *n* **1** *syn* see AMBITION 2
  2 *syn* see USE 4
goat *n syn* see SCAPEGOAT
goatish *adj syn* see LUSTFUL 2
gob *n* **1** *syn* see LUMP 1
  2 *usu* **gobs** *pl syn* see SCAD
gob *n syn* see MOUTH 1
gobbet *n syn* see DROP 1
gobble *vb syn* see GULP

gobbledygook *n* wordy unintelligible language <*gobbledygook* of bureaucrats>
  syn double-talk, gibberish
  rel double Dutch, Greek, jabberwocky; ‖bull, bunkum, claptrap, drivel, garbage, malarkey, nonsense, poppycock, twaddle
go–between *n* **1** *syn* see MARRIAGE BROKER
  2 an intermediate agent between individuals or groups <served as *go-between* in the labor dispute>
  syn broker, entrepreneur, interagent, interceder, intercessor, intermediary, intermediate, intermediator, mediator, middleman
  rel agent, attorney, deputy, factor, proxy; emissary, envoy, messenger; delegate, representative; arbitrator, negotiator
godless *adj syn* see IRRELIGIOUS
  rel agnostic, atheistic, infidel
  ant godly
godlike *adj syn* see DIVINE 2
godly *adj* **1** *syn* see DIVINE 1
  2 *syn* see SAINTLY
  3 *syn* see DEVOUT
  ant godless
go down *vb* **1** *syn* see FALL 2
  rel droop, sag, sink; cave (in), collapse, crumple, fold
  2 *syn* see SET 12
  3 *syn* see SINK 1
  4 *syn* see FALL 3
God's acre *n syn* see CEMETERY
godsend *n syn* see GOOD 1
go–getter *n syn* see HUSTLER 1
goggle *vb* **1** *syn* see LOOK 7
  2 *syn* see GAZE 1
go in *vb syn* see ENTER 1
Golconda *n syn* see BONANZA
goldarn *adj* **1** *syn* see DAMNED 2
  2 *syn* see UTTER
goldbrick *n syn* see SLACKER
goldbrick *vb syn* see IDLE
golden *adj* **1** *syn* see BLOND 1
  2 *syn* see MELLIFLUOUS
golden–ager *n syn* see OLDSTER
gold mine *n syn* see BONANZA
golem *n syn* see ROBOT 2
gone *adj* **1** *syn* see EXTINCT 2
  2 *syn* see ABSENT 1
  3 *syn* see LOST 2
  4 *syn* see PREGNANT 1
gonfalon *n syn* see FLAG
gonfanon *n syn* see FLAG
goo *n* **1** a sticky substance <slipped on a patch of greasy *goo* on the walk>
  syn gook, goop, gumbo, gunk, muck; *compare* CRUD
  rel dope
  2 *syn* see CRUD
good *adj* **1** having a helpful or auspicious character <a *good* wind>
  syn advantageous, benefic, beneficial, brave, favorable, favoring, helpful, propitious, toward, useful
  rel convenient, suitable; desirable, needed; appropriate, proper, right
  con disadvantageous, unfavorable; damaging, hampering, harmful; unwanted
  ant ill
  2 adapted to the end in view <they doubted that the fruit was *good* to eat>
  syn appropriate, convenient, fit, meet, proper, suitable, useful
  rel all right, apt, becoming, conformable, congruous, fitting, seemly
  con inadequate, inappropriate, undesirable, unfit, unsuitable, useless
  3 *syn* see WHOLE 1
  con blemished, damaged, defective, flawed, impaired, imperfect, unsound
  ant bad
  4 *syn* see ADVANTAGEOUS 1
  5 *syn* see PLEASANT 1
  6 *syn* see HEALTHFUL
  7 *syn* see CLEVER 5
  8 *syn* see CONSIDERABLE 2
  9 *syn* see WELL-FOUNDED

10 *syn* see DECENT 4

11 conforming to a high standard of morality or virtue < if you can't be *good*, be careful >

syn blameless, exemplary, guiltless, inculpable, innocent, irreprehensible, irreproachable, lily-white, pure, righteous, unblamable, virtuous

rel incorrupt, sound, uncorrupted, untainted

con blameworthy, impure, unrighteous; evil, iniquitous, reprobate, sinful

ant bad

12 *syn* see CHARITABLE 1

13 behaving in an acceptable or desirable manner < a *good* child >

syn decorous, well-behaved

rel polite, proper; considerate, kindly, thoughtful

con ill-behaved, indecorous, naughty; careless, heedless, inconsiderate, mischievous, thoughtless

ant bad

14 *syn* see SKILLFUL 2

ant bad

15 *syn* see ABLE

good *n* **1** something that is desirable or beneficial < it's an ill wind that blows no *good* >

syn advantage, benediction, benefit, blessing, boon, godsend

con bane, harm, misfortune; detriment, jinx

ant evil, ill

2 *syn* see RIGHT 1

3 *syn* see WELFARE

4 goods *pl syn* see POSSESSION 2

5 goods *pl syn* see MERCHANDISE

good–bye *interj* — used as a conventional expression of good wishes at parting < the party was over; the time had come to say *good-bye* >

syn adieu, by, bye-bye, ‖cheerio, farewell, so long, ‖toodle-oo

rel good day, good evening, good morning, good night

idiom be good, be seeing you, fare you well, keep in touch, see you (later)

con hello, how do, howdy, hullo

good–bye *n syn* see PARTING

good–bye *adj syn* see PARTING

good faith *n* a state of mind characterizing one free from fraud, deceit, or misconduct < determined to act in *good faith* >

syn bona fides, sincereness, sincerity, uberrima fides

rel decency, decorum, propriety, seemliness; ethicality, morality, virtuousness

good–fellowship *n syn* see CAMARADERIE

good–for–nothing *n syn* see WASTREL 1

good–for–nothing *adj* **1** *syn* see FECKLESS 1

2 *syn* see WORTHLESS 1

ant precious

good–hearted *adj syn* see KIND

good–humored *adj syn* see AMIABLE 1

rel buoyant, cheerful, cheery, genial, smiling

ant ill-humored

good–looking *adj syn* see BEAUTIFUL

ant ill-looking

good–natured *adj syn* see AMIABLE 1

rel altruistic, benevolent, charitable; acquiescent, compliant

con choleric, cranky, cross, irascible, splenetic, touchy; crabbed, gloomy, glum, morose, splenetic

ant contrary; ill-natured

goodness *n* the quality or state of being morally excellent < that eternal *goodness* that burns away evil >

syn morality, probity, rectitude, righteousness, rightness, uprightness, virtue

rel honesty, honor, integrity; grace, merit, quality, superiority

ant badness, evil

good sense *n syn* see SENSE 6

good–tasting *adj syn* see PALATABLE

good–tempered *adj syn* see AMIABLE 1

con crabbed, surly; snappish, touchy; irascible

ant bad-tempered, ill-tempered

goodwill *n* **1** benevolent interest or concern < trying to promote interracial *goodwill* >

syn amity, benevolence, comity, friendliness, friendship, kindliness

rel altruism, charity, favor, generosity, helpfulness, kindness, rapport, sympathy, tolerance

con animus, disfavor, enmity, hatred, intolerance, malevolence

ant animosity, ill will

2 *syn* see ALACRITY

goody *n syn* see DELICACY

goody–goody *n syn* see PRUDE

gooey *adj* **1** *syn* see STICKY 1

2 *syn* see SENTIMENTAL

goof *n syn* see DUNCE

‖**goof** (off) *vb syn* see IDLE

goof (up) *vb syn* see BOTCH

go off *vb syn* see EXPLODE 1

gook *n* **1** *syn* see GOO

2 *syn* see CRUD

3 *syn* see NONSENSE 2

go on *vb* **1** *syn* see PERSEVERE

2 *syn* see BEHAVE 1

‖**goon** *n syn* see DUNCE

goop *n syn* see GOO 1

goose egg *n syn* see ZERO 1

goosey *adj* **1** *syn* see STUPID 1

2 *syn* see NERVOUS

go over *vb syn* see SUCCEED 2

gordian *adj syn* see COMPLEX 2

gore *n syn* see BLOOD 1

gorge *n syn* see RAVINE

gorge *vb syn* see SATIATE

rel bolt, devour, gobble, guzzle, raven, wolf; overeat, overindulge, stuff

idiom eat like a horse, eat one out of house and home

gorged *adj syn* see SATIATED

gorgeous *adj* **1** *syn* see SPLENDID 2

rel elegant, luxurious, opulent, plush, sumptuous; flamboyant, garish, gaudy, ostentatious, pretentious, showy; beautiful, colorful

2 *syn* see GRAND 2

‖**gorilla** *n syn* see THUG 1

gory *adj syn* see BLOODY 1

gospel *n syn* see VERACITY 2

gossamer *adj syn* see FILMY

gossip *n* **1** a person who habitually retails private, scandalous, or sensational and often inaccurate information < her life ruined by a vicious old *gossip* >

syn carrytale, circulator, clack, gossiper, gossipmonger, ‖long tongue, mumblenews, newsmonger, quidnunc, rumorer, rumormonger, scandalizer, scandalmonger, sieve, tabby, talebearer, telltale; *compare* BUSYBODY, INFORMER

2 *syn* see REPORT 1

rel account, chronicle, conversation, story, tale; babble, banter, chatter, prate

gossip *vb* to disclose something, often of questionable veracity, that is better kept to oneself < *gossiped* about his neighbor's business >

syn blab, noise (about *or* abroad), rumor, talk, tattle

rel babble, chat, chatter, prate, prattle; hint, imply, insinuate, intimate, suggest

idiom dish the dirt, spill the beans, tell idle tales, tell tales out of school

gossiper *n syn* see GOSSIP 1

gossipmonger *n syn* see GOSSIP 1

Gothic *adj syn* see BARBARIAN 1

rel brutal, coarse, crude

gouge *vb syn* see EXTORT 1

rel cheat, con, swindle; overcharge

go under *vb* **1** *syn* see FALL 3

2 *syn* see SINK 1

gourmand *n syn* see EPICURE

gourmet *n syn* see EPICURE

govern *vb* **1** to exercise sovereign authority < a dictator may *govern* in a thoroughly enlightened manner >

syn overrule, reign, rule, sway

rel captain, command, head; administer, conduct, control, direct, manage, master; regulate, supervise

2 *syn* see ADMINISTER 1

---

syn synonym(s)　　　　　　　　　*rel* related word(s)

ant antonym(s)　　　　　　　　　*con* contrasted word(s)

idiom idiomatic equivalent(s)

‖ use limited; if in doubt, see a dictionary

3 to exercise a decisive role in influencing the actions and conduct of < parents who *govern* their children wisely >
syn control, direct, dominate, handle, manage
rel directionalize, guide, lead, shepherd, steer; boss, oversee, supervise
idiom be at the helm (*or* wheel), be in the driver's seat, hold the reins
‖**governor** *n syn* see FATHER 1
grab *vb syn* see SEIZE 2
grabble *vb syn* see GROPE
grabby *adj syn* see COVETOUS
grace *n* **1** a short prayer either asking a blessing before or giving thanks after a meal < taught each child a *grace* of his own >
syn benediction, blessing, thanks, thanksgiving
rel invocation, petition
2 *syn* see MERCY
rel compassionateness, responsiveness, tenderness; forbearance, indulgence, leniency; goodness
3 *syn* see ELEGANCE
graceless *adj* **1** *syn* see BARBARIC 1
2 *syn* see INFELICITOUS
ant graceful
gracious *adj* **1** marked by kindly courtesy < her *gracious* attitude toward those around her >
syn affable, congenial, cordial, genial, sociable, ‖sonsy
rel amiable, complaisant, easy, obliging; benign, benignant, kind, kindly; chivalrous, courteous, courtly; approachable, bonhomous, clubby, forthcoming, forthgoing, outgoing
con boorish, churlish; blunt, brusque, crabbed, crusty, curt, gruff, short, sullen, surly
ant ungracious
2 *syn* see COURTLY
rel mannered, starchy
gradation *n* the difference or variation between two things that are nearly alike < the *gradations* were too small to be seen with the unaided eye >
syn nuance, shade
rel difference, distinction, divergence; change, modification, variation
grade *n* **1** *syn* see DEGREE 1
2 *syn* see ESTATE 2
3 *syn* see CLASS 1
4 *syn* see QUALITY 3
5 *syn* see SLOPE
grade *vb syn* see CLASS 2
rel arrange, order; assort, sort
Grade A *adj syn* see EXCELLENT
gradient *n syn* see SLOPE
gradual *adj* proceeding slowly usually by minute or imperceptible steps or degrees < his health showed *gradual* improvement >
syn piecemeal, step-by-step
rel deliberate, dilatory, lagging, poky, sluggish
con acute, sharp, sudden
ant abrupt
gradually *adv* by small degrees or amounts < *gradually* he learned the new job >
syn bit by bit, little by little, piecemeal
idiom a little at a time, by degrees
con quickly, rapidly, speedily; at once, immediately, suddenly
grain *n syn* see PARTICLE
grainy *adj syn* see COARSE 1
grammar *n syn* see ALPHABET 2
grand *adj* **1** large and impressive in size, scope, extent, or conception < the platform provided a *grand* view of the canyon >
syn august, baronial, grandiose, imposing, lordly, magnific, magnificent, majestic, noble, princely, royal, stately; *compare* HUGE
rel monumental, prodigious, stupendous, tremendous; towering; gorgeous, splendid, sublime, superb
con measly, paltry, petty, puny, trifling, trivial
2 marked by great magnificence, display, and usually ceremony or formality < delighted to attend the *grand* presidential fete >
syn gorgeous, impressive, lavish, luxurious, splendid, sumptuous
rel magnificent, majestic; flashy, garish, gaudy, ornate, ostentatious, showy
con crude, meretricious, obtrusive, vulgar; flimsy, tawdry
3 noble in character or spirit < a *grand* outlook on life >
syn elevated, exalted, lofty, sublime, superb

rel magnificent, splendid
con average, common, commonplace, ordinary; base, lowly, mean, poor
grandam *n syn* see BELDAM 1
grande dame *n syn* see MATRIARCH
grandiloquent *adj syn* see RHETORICAL
grandiose *adj* **1** *syn* see GRAND 1
rel ostentatious, pretentious, showy; cosmic, overwhelming, unfathomable, vast
2 *syn* see AMBITIOUS 2
granny *n syn* see FUSSBUDGET
grant *vb* **1** to give as a favor or right < *granted* him an extension of payments >
syn accord, award, concede, vouchsafe
rel bestow, confer, donate, give, present; allow, permit; cede, relinquish, yield
con decline, refuse, turn down
2 *syn* see ACKNOWLEDGE 1
con differ, disagree, dissent; challenge, dispute, object, protest
3 *syn* see GIVE 2
grant *n syn* see APPROPRIATION
rel gift; assistance, benefaction, contribution, donation; alms, charity, dole, handout
granular *adj syn* see COARSE 1
grapevine *n syn* see REPORT 1
graph *n syn* see CHART 1
rel diagram, outline, sketch
graphic *adj* **1** giving a clear visual impression especially in words < gave a *graphic* description of the whole incident >
syn photographic, pictorial, picturesque, vivid
rel clear, lucid, perspicuous; clear-cut, incisive; cogent, compelling, convincing, telling; definite, explicit, precise, realistic, striking, visual
con confused, hazy, indistinct, obscure
2 *syn* see PICTORIAL 1
grapple *n syn* see HOLD
grapple *vb* **1** *syn* see SEIZE 2
2 *syn* see WRESTLE
grasp *vb* **1** *syn* see TAKE 4
2 *syn* see APPREHEND 1
rel envisage, fathom, perceive
3 *syn* see KNOW 1
grasp *n syn* see HOLD
graspable *adj syn* see UNDERSTANDABLE
ant ungraspable
grasping *adj syn* see COVETOUS
rel extorting, extortionate
grass *n syn* see MARIJUANA
grate *vb* **1** *syn* see SCRAPE 1
rel abrade, bark, chafe, fray, gall, scuff, skin
2 *syn* see IRRITATE
grateful *adj* **1** feeling or expressing gratitude < was *grateful* for the gift >
syn obliged, thankful
rel appreciative, beholden; gratified, pleased
idiom filled with gratitude
ant ungrateful
2 *syn* see PLEASANT 1
rel comforting, consoling, solacing; refreshing, rejuvenating, renewing, restorative, restoring; delectable, delicious, delightful
ant obnoxious
gratefulness *n syn* see AMENITY 1
gratify *vb* **1** *syn* see PLEASE 2
rel appease, baby, cater (to), coddle, favor, humor, indulge, oblige, pamper
con bother, irk; aggravate, exasperate, irritate, nettle, rile; agitate, disturb, perturb, upset
2 *syn* see SATISFY 3
3 *syn* see INDULGE 1
idiom do one proud
gratifying *adj syn* see PLEASANT 1
rel contenting, satisfying; delighting, gladdening, regaling, rejoicing
con invidious, obnoxious; offensive, revolting
grating *adj syn* see HARSH 3
gratis *adj syn* see FREE 5
gratuitous *adj* **1** *syn* see FREE 5
rel voluntary, willing

2 *syn* see SUPEREROGATORY

3 *syn* see BASELESS

rel indefensible, reasonless, unsupportable

gratuity *n* something given over and above what is due, generally in return for or expectation of good service < he found that an occasional *gratuity* smoothed his path >

syn cumshaw, lagniappe, largess, ‖palm grease, ‖palm oil, ‖perk(s), perquisite, pourboire, tip

rel alms, benefaction, contribution, donation; offering, reward

grave *vb* **1** *syn* see ENGRAVE 1

2 *syn* see IMPRESS 3

grave *n* a place of interment < his *grave* is in the church burial ground >

syn burial, ‖pit, sepulcher, sepulture, tomb

rel catacomb, crypt, vault; mausoleum; ossuary; cinerarium

idiom final resting place

grave *adj* **1** *syn* see SERIOUS 2

2 *syn* see SERIOUS 1

rel heavy, ponderous; grim, sad, saturnine; awful, dreadful, horrible, terrible

con flippant, light, light-minded

ant gay

3 involving marked risk of impairment or destruction < a *grave* illness >

syn dangerous, fell, grievous, major, serious, ugly; compare DANGEROUS 1

rel deadly, destructive, dire, fatal, killing, murderous; frightening, ghastly, terrible; afflictive, severe

con paltry, petty, trivial; harmless, innocuous; temporary, transitory

gravely *adv* *syn* see SERIOUSLY 2

grave marker *n* *syn* see TOMBSTONE

gravestone *n* *syn* see TOMBSTONE

graveyard *n* *syn* see CEMETERY

gravid *adj* *syn* see PREGNANT 1

gravidity *n* *syn* see PREGNANCY

graybeard *n* *syn* see GAFFER

gray matter *n* *syn* see MIND 1

graze *vb* **1** *syn* see BRUSH

2 *syn* see GLANCE 1

3 *syn* see ABRADE 1

rel harm, hurt, injure; bruise, contuse, wound

greasy *adj* **1** *syn* see FATTY 2

2 *syn* see SLICK 1

‖greasy spoon *n* *syn* see EATING HOUSE

great *adj* **1** *syn* see LARGE 1

con measly, paltry, petty, puny, trifling, trivial

ant little

2 *syn* see FAMOUS 2

rel superlative, supreme, surpassing, transcendent

great deal *n* *syn* see MUCH

greater *adj* **1** *syn* see BEST

2 *syn* see SUPERIOR 1

great gun *n* *syn* see NOTABLE 1

greathearted *adj* **1** *syn* see BRAVE 1

2 *syn* see GENEROUS 1

greatly *adv* *syn* see VERY 1

greatness *n* *syn* see SIZE 2

greed *n* *syn* see CUPIDITY

rel gluttonousness, gluttony, rapaciousness, ravenousness, voraciousness

greedy *adj* *syn* see COVETOUS

con bounteous, bountiful, generous, liberal, munificent, open-handed; exuberant, lavish, prodigal, profuse

Greek *n* *syn* see GIBBERISH 1

green *adj* **1** *syn* see YOUNG 1

2 *syn* see INEXPERIENCED

con grown-up, ripe, mature, matured; educated, instructed, trained; proficient, skilled, skillful

ant experienced

green *n* *syn* see COMMON 2

‖greenbacks *n pl* *syn* see MONEY

green–eyed *adj* *syn* see ENVIOUS

greenhorn *n* *syn* see RUSTIC

greenhouse *n* a glass-enclosed structure for the cultivation and protection of tender plants < a small window *greenhouse* full of bloom >

syn conservatory, ‖glasshouse

rel coolhouse, hotbed, hothouse

greenness *n* **1** *syn* see YOUTH 1

2 *syn* see INEXPERIENCE

greet *vb* *syn* see ADDRESS 7

greeting *n* the ceremonial words or acts of one who meets, welcomes, or formally addresses another < after the *greeting* the chairman called the roll >

syn salutation, salute

rel address, hail, hello, welcome

con farewell, good-bye

ant valediction

gregarious *adj* *syn* see SOCIAL 2

grief *n* *syn* see SORROW

rel bemoaning, bewailing, deploring, lamenting

con comfort, comforting, consolation, solace, solacing

ant joy

grievance *n* *syn* see INJUSTICE 2

rel hardship, rigor; affliction, cross, trial, tribulation

grieve *vb* **1** *syn* see DISTRESS 2

2 to feel or express deep distress < *grieved* at the loss of so many lives >

syn mourn, sorrow

rel bear, endure, suffer; bemoan, bewail, deplore, lament; cry, keen, wail, weep

ant rejoice

3 *syn* see DEPLORE 1

grievous *adj* **1** *syn* see ONEROUS

2 *syn* see BITTER 2

3 *syn* see GRAVE 3

4 *syn* see DEPLORABLE

‖grifter *n* *syn* see SWINDLER

grill *n* *syn* see CROSS-EXAMINATION

grilling *n* *syn* see CROSS-EXAMINATION

grim *adj* **1** *syn* see FIERCE 1

rel foreboding, ominous

2 forbidding in action or appearance < had a *grim* and determined expression on his face >

syn austere, bleak, dour, hard, harsh, severe, stringent

rel cold, forbidding, ‖off-putting; fixed, rigid, set; determined, firm, stern

con calm, mellow, mild, soft, warm; attractive, beautiful, pleasing

ant pleasant

3 being extremely obdurate or firm in action or purpose < fought with *grim* determination >

syn implacable, ironfisted, merciless, mortal, relentless, ruthless, unappeasable, unflinching, unrelenting, unyielding

rel adamant, inexorable, inflexible, obdurate, resolute, stubborn, unforgiving, vindictive; certain, inevitable; determined, dogged

con considerate, gentle, mild; clement, forbearing, indulgent

ant lenient

4 *syn* see GHASTLY 1

rel loathsome, offensive, repugnant, repulsive, revolting

grimace *n* *syn* see FACE 6

grimace *vb* to distort one's face by way of expressing a feeling < *grimaced* with pain >

syn mop, mouth, mow, mug, ‖mump

rel contort, deform, distort, misshape

idiom make a face (*or* mouth), make a wry face (*or* mouth), pull a face, screw up one's face

grime *vb* *syn* see SOIL 2

grim reaper *n* *syn* see DEATH 1

grin *vb* *syn* see SMILE

con frown, gloom

ant grimace

grind *vb* *syn* see DRUDGE

grind *n* **1** *syn* see WORK 2

2 *syn* see ROUTINE

grip *vb* **1** *syn* see TAKE 4

2 *syn* see ENTHRALL 2

grip *n* *syn* see HOLD

rel coercion, constraint, duress, restraint

---

syn synonym(s)   *rel* related word(s)

ant antonym(s)   *con* contrasted word(s)

idiom idiomatic equivalent(s)

‖ use limited; if in doubt, see a dictionary

gripe *vb* to complain emphatically and often petulantly < students *griping* about the cafeteria food >
  syn ‖beef, ‖bellyache, bleat, ‖blow off, crab, ‖crib, fuss, squawk, yammer, yawp (*or* yaup); *compare* COMPLAIN
  rel brawl, kick, take on; croak, grouch, grouse, grumble, murmur, mutter
  con applaud, approve, cheer; rejoice; accept, bear, endure, tolerate

gripe *n* **1** *syn* see HOLD
  2 *usu* **gripes** *pl syn* stomachache, bellyache, colic, collywobbles

griper *n syn* see GROUCH

grisette *n syn* see DOXY 1

grisly *adj syn* see GHASTLY 1
  rel eerie, uncanny, weird

grit *n syn* see FORTITUDE
  con faltering, hesitation, vacillation, wavering
  ant faintheartedness

grobian *n syn* see BOOR 2

grog *n syn* see LIQUOR 2

‖**groggery** *n syn* see BAR 5

‖**grogshop** *n syn* see BAR 5

groove *n syn* see ROUTINE

groovy *adj syn* see MARVELOUS 2

grope *vb* to reach out or about blindly (as in testing or searching) < *groped* along the wall in search of a door >
  syn feel, fumble, grabble
  rel poke, pry, root; examine, explore, search

gross *adj* **1** *syn* see EGREGIOUS
  rel excessive, exorbitant, extreme, immoderate, inordinate
  con paltry, trifling, trivial
  ant petty
  2 *syn* see UTTER
  3 *syn* see FAT 2
  4 *syn* see WHOLE 4
  ant net
  5 *syn* see MATERIAL 1
  6 *syn* see COARSE 3
  7 *syn* see OBSCENE 2
  rel animal, carnal, fleshy, sensual; loathsome, offensive, repulsive, revolting; improper, unrefined
  con decent, decorous, proper, refined

gross *n syn* see WHOLE 1

grotesque *adj syn* see FANTASTIC 2
  rel baroque, flamboyant, rococo; eerie, uncanny, weird; extravagant, extreme; comic, comical, droll, ludicrous

grotto *n syn* see CAVE

grouch *n* an habitually irritable or complaining person < it's hard to live with a *grouch* >
  syn ‖bellyacher, complainer, crab, crabber, crank, crosspatch, faultfinder, griper, grouser, growler, grumbler, grump, kicker, malcontent, sorehead, sourpuss
  con optimist, Pollyanna

grouch *vb syn* see GRUMBLE 1

ground *n* **1** *syn* see BASIS 1
  2 *syn* see BASE 1
  3 *syn* see REASON 3
  rel evidence, testimony; antecedent, cause, determinant; demonstration, test, trial
  4 **grounds** *pl syn* see SEDIMENT
  5 *syn* see EARTH 2

ground *vb* **1** *syn* see FELL 1
  2 *syn* see BASE
  rel buttress, support, sustain

grounded *adj syn* see AGROUND

groundless *adj syn* see BASELESS
  ant well-founded, well-grounded

groundwork *n* **1** *syn* see BASIS 1
  2 *syn* see BASE 1

group *n* **1** a usually comparatively small assemblage of individuals < people gathered in *groups* about the hall >
  syn assembly, band, bevy, bunch, cluster, covey, crew, party; *compare* COMPANY 1, GATHERING
  rel circle, clique, cotery, set
  con crowd, crush, horde, mob, press, rout, throng
  2 *syn* see GATHERING 2
  3 an assemblage of things constituting a unit < a *group* of houses behind the church >
  syn array, batch, battery, body, bunch, bundle, clot, clump, cluster, clutch, lot, parcel, passel, platoon, set, sort, suite

  rel assemblage, collection, mess, shooting match
  4 *syn* see SET 5
  5 *syn* see SYNDICATE
  6 *syn* see CLASS 1

group *vb* **1** to make into or bring together in a group < *grouped* the children according to age >
  syn assemble, cluster, collect, gather, round up; *compare* GATHER 6
  rel adjust, arrange, harmonize, organize, systematize; allocate, dispose, distribute, place; bunch, crowd, huddle
  idiom bring together, get together
  con disband, disperse, scatter, separate
  2 *syn* see ASSORT

grouping *n syn* see CLASS 1

grouse *vb syn* see GRUMBLE 1

grouser *n syn* see GROUCH

grovel *vb syn* see FAWN
  idiom lick the dust (*or* one's boots)

groveler *n syn* see SYCOPHANT

groveling *adj syn* see FAWNING

grow *vb* **1** to cause (something living) to exist or flourish < *grew* a crop of wheat >
  syn breed, cultivate, produce, propagate, raise
  rel care (for), foster, nurse, nurture, rear, tend
  2 *syn* see MATURE
  3 *syn* see ESCALATE 2
  4 *syn* see BECOME 1

growl *vb syn* see RUMBLE

growler *n syn* see GROUCH

grown *adj* **1** *syn* see MATURE 1
  2 *syn* see OVERGROWN

grown–up *adj syn* see MATURE 1
  ant childish; callow

growth *n syn* see DEVELOPMENT

grow up *vb syn* see MATURE

grub *vb* **1** *syn* see DIG 1
  rel burrow, poke, root
  2 *syn* see SCOUR 2
  3 *syn* see DRUDGE

grub *n* **1** *syn* see HACK 2
  2 *syn* see FOOD 1

grubber *n syn* see HACK 2

grubby *adj syn* see DIRTY 1
  ant immaculate

grubstake *vb syn* see CAPITALIZE

grudge *vb syn* see ENVY
  rel deny; refuse

grudge *n syn* see MALICE
  rel grievance, injury, injustice

gruesome *adj syn* see GHASTLY 1
  rel appalling, daunting; horrendous, horrific; baleful, sinister

gruff *adj* **1** *syn* see BLUFF
  rel crabbed, dour, morose, saturnine, sullen, surly; boorish, churlish; fierce, truculent
  con bland, smooth, suave, urbane; fulsome, oily, slick, soapy, unctuous
  2 *syn* see HOARSE 1

grumble *vb* **1** to complain in a low harsh voice and often in a surly manner < workers *grumbling* about the low wages >
  syn croak, grouch, grouse, ‖grunt, murmur, mutter, scold; *compare* COMPLAIN
  rel ‖beef, ‖bellyache, brawl, crab, fuss, gripe, holler, squawk, whine; groan, moan; complain, kick
  con applaud, cheer; rejoice
  2 *syn* see RUMBLE

grumbler *n syn* see GROUCH

grump *n* **1** **grumps** *pl syn* see SULK
  2 *syn* see GROUCH

grump *vb syn* see SULK

Grundy *n syn* see PRUDE

‖**grunt** *vb syn* see GRUMBLE 1

guarantee *n* **1** an assurance for the fulfillment of a condition < gave him a *guarantee* that the work would be done according to specifications >
  syn bail, bond, guaranty, security, surety, warranty; *compare* PLEDGE 1
  rel earnest, pledge, promise, token, undertaking, word; oath, vow

2 *syn* see WORD 8
guarantee *vb syn* see WARRANT 2
guarantor *n syn* see SPONSOR
guaranty *n syn* see GUARANTEE 1
  rel bargain, contract
guaranty *vb syn* see WARRANT 2
guard *n* **1** *syn* see DEFENSE 1
  2 a person or group on sentinel duty <posted six *guards* around the diamond necklace> <turned out the *guard*>
  syn lookout, picket, sentinel, sentry, ward, watch, watchman
  rel guardian, jailer, keeper, turnkey, warden, warder; patrolman; outguard, patrol
guard *vb syn* see DEFEND 1
  rel attend, mind, tend, watch; accompany, chaperon, conduct, convoy, escort
guarded *adj* **1** *syn* see ULTERIOR
  2 *syn* see CAUTIOUS
  ant unguarded
guardian *n syn* see CUSTODIAN
guardianship *n syn* see CUSTODY
guardroom *n syn* see JAIL
gudgeon *n syn* see FOOL 3
guerdon *n syn* see REWARD
guerdon *vb syn* see PAY 1
guerrilla *n syn* see PARTISAN 2
guess *vb* **1** *syn* see CONJECTURE
  rel reason, speculate; deduce; estimate, reckon
  idiom venture a guess
  2 *syn* see PREDICT 2
guest *n* **1** *syn* see VISITOR 1
  2 guests *pl syn* see COMPANY 2
guff *n* **1** *syn* see NONSENSE 2
  2 *syn* see BACK TALK
guffaw *vb syn* see LAUGH
guide *vb* to put or lead on a course or into the way to be followed <*guided* them safely through the minefields>
  syn conduct, direct, escort, lead, pilot, route, see, shepherd, show, steer
  rel accompany, chaperon, convoy; control, manage; contrive, engineer, maneuver
  idiom set one on one's way
  con bewilder, distract, mystify, perplex, puzzle; beguile, deceive, delude, mislead
  ant misguide
guide *n* **1** *syn* see LEADER 1
  2 *syn* see ESCORT 2
  rel conductor, director, leader, pilot
  3 *syn* see HANDBOOK
guidebook *n syn* see HANDBOOK
guild *n syn* see ASSOCIATION 2
guile *n syn* see DECEIT 1
  ant ingenuousness; candor
guileful *adj* **1** *syn* see SLY 2
  ant guileless
  2 *syn* see UNDERHAND
guileless *adj syn* see NATURAL 5
  ant guileful
guillotine *vb syn* see BEHEAD
guilt *n syn* see BLAME
  rel crime, offense, sin; responsibility
  ant innocence; guiltlessness
guiltless *adj* **1** *syn* see GOOD 11
  2 *syn* see INNOCENT 2
  ant guilty
guilty *adj syn* see BLAMEWORTHY
  rel accountable, answerable, responsible; impeached, incriminated, indicted
  ant innocent; guiltless
guise *n* **1** *syn* see COSTUME
  2 *syn* see APPEARANCE 2
  3 *syn* see MASK 2

gulch *n syn* see RAVINE
gulf *n* **1** *syn* see INLET
  2 a hollow place of vast width and depth <a *gulf* extending deep into the earth>
  syn abysm, abyss, chasm
  rel cave, cavity, hollow; crevasse, gulch, ravine; pit, shaft, well
gull *vb syn* see DUPE
gull *n syn* see FOOL 3
gullible *adj syn* see EASY 3
  ant astute
gulp *vb* to swallow hurriedly or greedily or in one swallow <*gulped* his lunch and ran off>
  syn bolt, cram, englut, gobble, guzzle, ingurgitate, slop, slosh, wolf
  rel devour, glut, stuff
  con nibble, pick
gum (up) *vb syn* see BOTCH
gumbo *n syn* see GOO 1
gummy *adj syn* see STICKY 1
gumption *n syn* see SENSE 6
  rel astuteness, perspicaciousness, perspicacity, sagaciousness, sagacity, shrewdness
gumptious *adj syn* see ENTERPRISING 2
gumshoe *n* **1** *syn* see DETECTIVE
  2 *syn* see POLICEMAN
gumshoe *vb syn* see SNEAK
gun *n syn* see ASSASSIN
gung ho *adj syn* see ENTHUSIASTIC
gunk *n* **1** *syn* see GOO 1
  2 *syn* see CRUD
gunman *n syn* see ASSASSIN
‖**gunsel** *n syn* see ASSASSIN
gunslinger *n syn* see ASSASSIN
gurge *vb syn* see SWIRL
gurgle *vb syn* see SLOSH 1
gush *vb syn* see POUR 2
  rel flood, flush; emanate, issue, spring
gushing *adj syn* see EFFUSIVE
gushy *adj syn* see EFFUSIVE
gussy up *vb syn* see DRESS UP 1
gust *n syn* see OUTBURST 1
gusto *n syn* see TASTE 4
  rel delectation, delight, enjoyment, pleasure; ardor, enthusiasm, fervor, passion, zeal
gusty *adj syn* see WINDY 1
‖**gusty** *adj syn* see PALATABLE
gut *n* **1** *usu* **guts** *pl syn* see ENTRAILS
  ‖**2** *syn* see ABDOMEN
  3 guts *pl syn* see COURAGE
  4 guts *pl syn* see FORTITUDE
gut *vb* **1** *syn* see EVISCERATE
  2 *syn* see DRESS 3
gut *adj syn* see INNER 2
gutless *adj syn* see COWARDLY
  ant ‖gutsy
‖**gutsy** *adj syn* see BRAVE 1
guy *n syn* see MAN 3
guzzle *vb* **1** *syn* see DRINK 3
  2 *syn* see GULP
guzzler *n syn* see DRUNKARD
gyp *n* **1** *syn* see SWINDLER
  2 *syn* see IMPOSTURE
gyp *vb syn* see CHEAT
gypper *n syn* see SWINDLER
gyrate *vb* **1** *syn* see TURN 1
  2 *syn* see SPIN 1
gyration *n syn* see REVOLUTION 1
gyre *vb* **1** *syn* see TURN 1
  2 *syn* see SPIN 1
gyre *n syn* see REVOLUTION 1
gyve *n, usu* **gyves** *pl syn* see SHACKLE

---

syn synonym(s)
ant antonym(s)
idiom idiomatic equivalent(s)
‖ use limited; if in doubt, see a dictionary

rel related word(s)
con contrasted word(s)

habiliment *n* **1 habiliments** *pl syn* see EQUIPMENT
2 *usu* **habiliments** *pl syn* see CLOTHES

habit *n* **1** a mode of behaving or doing fixed by constant repetition <it was his *habit* to rise early>
syn consuetude, custom, habitude, manner, practice, praxis, trick, usage, use, way, wont
rel bent, disposition, inclination, proclivity, tendency, turn; convention, fashion, form, mode, pattern, style; addiction; groove, rote, routine, rut, set
2 *syn* see PHYSIQUE
rel carcass; framework; contour, outline

habitable *adj syn* see LIVABLE 1
ant unhabitable, uninhabitable

habitant *n syn* see INHABITANT

habitat *n* the physical environment natural to a kind of being <the watery *habitat* of the eel>
syn haunt, home, locality, range, site, stamping ground
rel environment, locale, surroundings, territory

habitation *n* **1** the act of inhabiting or the state of being inhabited <places suitable for *habitation*>
syn inhabitancy, inhabitation, occupancy, occupation, residence, settlement
rel colonization, domiciliation, peopling; sojourning
2 the place where one lives <*habitations* unfit for human occupancy>
syn abode, commorancy, domicile, dwelling, home, house, residence, residency
rel apartment, flat, tenement; housing, lodging, lodgment, quarters; haunt, haven, homeplace, homestead, place, seat; ‖digs, nest, nook, ‖pad, ‖roost; astre, fireside, hearth, hearthside, hearthstone, roof, rooftree
idiom roof over one's head, where one hangs one's hat

habitual *adj* **1** *syn* see USUAL 1
rel constant, established, ingrained, inveterate, persistent, steady
con infrequent, irregular, sporadic, uncommon
ant occasional
2 acting by force of habit <*habitual* smokers who blue the air>
syn accustomed, chronic, confirmed, habituated
rel continual, inveterate, persistent, regular, steady; automatic, instinctive, involuntary; addicted; customary, wonted
con conscious, deliberate, premeditative, purposive, witting

habitually *adv syn* see USUALLY 1
ant occasionally

habituate *vb* **1** *syn* see ACCUSTOM
2 to make acceptable or desirable (as to oneself) through use <*habituate* oneself to poverty>
syn addict, adjust, confirm (in), devote (to), take (to)
rel bear, endure, inure, support, tolerate; condition, familiarize, season
con balk (at), object (to), resist

habituated *adj syn* see HABITUAL 2

habitude *n syn* see HABIT 1
rel attitude, position, stand; condition, situation, state
con humor, mood, temper; caprice, freak, vagary, whim

habitué *n* **1** one who frequents a place <an *habitué* of libraries>
syn denizen, frequenter, haunter
rel customer, devotee, patron, sojourner; employer, user
2 *syn* see ADDICT

habitus *n syn* see PHYSIQUE

hack *vb* to cut with repeated crude or ruthless blows <*hack* a path through the jungle>
syn hackle, haggle, slash
rel gash, mangle; chop, cut, fell, hew

hack *n* **1** *syn* see TAXICAB
2 one who surrenders intellectual or personal integrity for an assured reward (as a regular income) <party *hacks* and hangers-on>
syn drudge, grub, grubber, hireling, mercenary, slavey
rel grind, lackey, servant, slave; machine, plodder; potboiler

hack *adj* **1** *syn* see INFERIOR 2

rel commonplace, dull, ordinary, trite, usual; inconsequential, petty, trivial
con individual, original, uncommon, unusual
2 *syn* see TRITE
rel antiquated, old, outmoded, outworn
con lively; unfamiliar

hackle *vb syn* see HACK

hackneyed *adj syn* see TRITE
rel antediluvian, antiquated, archaic, obsolete, outmoded, out-of-date; conventional, everyday, quotidian, stock; moth-eaten
ant unhackneyed

Hadean *adj syn* see INFERNAL 1
rel gloomy, murky, stygian

hades *n syn* see HELL

hag *n* **1** *syn* see WITCH 1
2 an ugly or evil-looking old woman <a pitiful homeless *hag*>
syn ‖bag, ‖bat, beldam, biddy, crone, drab, trot, witch
rel gammer, grandam; ‖battle-ax, fishwife, gorgon, harpy, harridan, shrew, slattern, virago, vixen

haggard *adj* thin and contracted by or as if by fatigue or inner distress <*haggard* from their long vigil>
syn careworn, drawn, pinched, worn
rel angular, gaunt, lank, lean, scraggy, scrawny, skinny, spare; ashen, faded, pale, pallid, wan; exhausted, fagged, fatigued, tired, wearied, worn-down
con energetic, lusty, strenuous, vigorous; easy, relaxed

haggle *vb* **1** *syn* see HACK
2 to argue as to terms <*haggle* over prices>
syn bargain, chaffer, dicker, higgle, huckster, palter
rel barter, deal, horse-trade, trade; bicker, cavil, dispute, quibble, squabble, stickle, wrangle

hagridden *adj syn* see OBSESSED

hagride *vb syn* see WORRY 1

hail *n syn* see BARRAGE

hail *vb* **1** *syn* see ADDRESS 7
rel hallo, hallow, holler, shout
2 *syn* see COMMEND 2
con belittle, depreciate, disparage, downgrade; berate, censure, condemn, libel, rap; dismiss, reject

hail (from) *vb syn* see ORIGINATE 5

hair *n* a minute distance, degree, or margin <won the election by a *hair*>
syn ace, hairbreadth, whisker; *compare* HINT 2
rel bit, fraction, jot, mite, particle, trace, trifle

hairbreadth *n syn* see HAIR

haircutter *n syn* see BARBER

hairless *adj* lacking hair <he had a shining *hairless* head>
syn bald, glabrous, smooth
rel baldish; shaved, shaven, shorn, tonsured
ant hairy

hairline *adj syn* see FINE 1

hairsplitting *adj syn* see FINE 1

hair-trigger *adj syn* see INSTANTANEOUS

hairy *adj* **1** covered with or as if with hair <wore a *hairy* overcoat>
syn fleecy, hirsute, pileous, pilose, whiskered, woolly
rel bristly, bushy, downy, fluffy, fuzzy, lanate, nappy, pubescent, rough, shaggy, tomentose, tufted, unshorn, villous
con bald, barefaced, beardless, glabrous, shaved, shaven, shorn, smooth
ant hairless
2 *syn* see DANGEROUS 1
3 *syn* see ROUGH 1

halcyon *adj syn* see CALM 1
con blustery, fevered, foul, raging, rough, stormy, tempestuous, troubled, tumultuous, wild

hale *adj syn* see HEALTHY 1
rel husky, stout, strapping
idiom hale and hearty
ant infirm

haleness *n syn* see HEALTH

half-blind *adj syn* see PURBLIND

half blood *n syn* see HYBRID
  ant full blood
half–breed *n syn* see HYBRID
  ant full blood
halfhearted *adj syn* see TEPID 2
||**half–seas over** *adj syn* see INTOXICATED 1
halfway *adj syn* see MIDDLE 1
half–wit *n syn* see FOOL 4
half–witted *adj syn* see RETARDED
hall *n syn* see PASSAGE 4
hallo *vb syn* see CALL 1
hallow *vb* **1** *syn* see BLESS 1
  2 *syn* see DEVOTE 1
  con defile, desecrate, pollute, profane
hallowed *adj syn* see HOLY 1
hallucination *n syn* see DELUSION 1
  rel apparition, fata morgana, phantom, wraith
hallway *n syn* see PASSAGE 4
halt *vb syn* see LIMP 1
halt *vb* **1** *syn* see STOP 4
  ant proceed
  2 *syn* see STOP 3
  3 *syn* see ARREST 1
  4 *syn* see HESITATE
  5 *syn* see CLOSE 2
halting *adj* **1** *syn* see AWKWARD 2
  2 *syn* see VACILLATING 2
ham–handed *adj syn* see AWKWARD 2
hammer *vb* **1** to strike or shape with or as if with a hammer < brass *hammered* into bowls and trays >
  syn beat, malleate, pound
  rel elaborate, fashion, form, shape
  2 *syn* see BEAT 1
  3 *syn* see IMPRESS 3
  ||**4** *syn* see STAMMER 1
hammer (out) *vb syn* see ERECT 5
hammerhead *n syn* see DUNCE
hammerheaded *adj syn* see STUPID 1
hamper *vb* to impede in moving, progressing, or acting freely < the long dress *hampered* her escape >
  syn clog, curb, entrammel, fetter, hobble, hog-tie, leash, shackle, tie, tie up, trammel; *compare* HINDER, RESTRAIN 1
  rel cumber, encumber, handicap, hinder, impede, lumber, obstruct; baffle, balk, bar, block, foil, frustrate, thwart; restrain, restrict, retard; discomfit, embarrass; check, inconvenience, inhibit
  idiom tie one's hands
  con free, liberate, loose, release, unfetter, unleash, unshackle
  ant aid, facilitate
hamper *n syn* see OBSTACLE 1
hams *n pl syn* see BUTTOCKS
hand *n* **1** *syn* see SIDE 1
  2 *syn* see PHASE
  3 *syn* see HANDWRITING
  4 *syn* see HELP 1
  5 *syn* see WORKER
  6 *syn* see TOUCH 6
hand *vb* **1** *syn* see GIVE 3
  2 *syn* see PASS 9
handbill *n syn* see POSTER
handbook *n* a concise reference book < a *handbook* of wild flowers >
  syn Baedeker, compendium, enchiridion, guide, guidebook, manual, vade mecum
  con cyclopedia, encyclopedia
hand down *vb* to convey in succession < a skill *handed down* from father to son >
  syn bequeath, hand on, pass (on), transmit
  con get, obtain, receive
handful *n syn* see FEW
handicap *n* **1** *syn* see DISADVANTAGE
  rel burden, encumbrance, load; embarrassment
  ant asset
  2 *syn* see ADVANTAGE 3
handicraft *n syn* see TRADE 1
hand in *vb syn* see SUBMIT 2
handkerchief *n* a small usually square piece of cloth used especially for blowing the nose < carry a pocket *handkerchief* >

syn hankie, kerchief, ||wipe, ||wiper
||**handle** *n* **1** *syn* see NAME 1
  2 *syn* see NICKNAME
handle *vb* **1** *syn* see TOUCH 1
  rel test, try; manipulate
  2 to deal with or manage usually with dexterity or efficiency < *handles* his tools with great skill >
  syn dispense, maneuver, manipulate, ply, swing, wield
  rel direct, guide, manage, operate, run, work; brandish, flourish, shake, wave; aim, lay, level, point
  3 *syn* see OPERATE 3
  4 *syn* see TREAT 2
  rel conduct, control, direct, manage
  5 *syn* see GOVERN 3
  6 *syn* see USE 2
handling *n syn* see OVERSIGHT 1
handmaid *n syn* see MAID 2
hand on *vb syn* see HAND DOWN
hand out *vb syn* see GIVE 1
hand over *vb* **1** *syn* see RELINQUISH
  2 *syn* see GIVE 3
  3 *syn* see COMMIT 1
hand running *adv syn* see TOGETHER 2
handsome *adj* **1** *syn* see LIBERAL 1
  con economical, frugal, sparing; scrimpy, skimpy
  2 *syn* see BEAUTIFUL
  rel august, majestic, noble, stately; chic, dashing, fashionable, modish, smart, stylish
  con inelegant, unsightly
  ant unhandsome
handwriting *n* writing in which the letters are formed by a hand-guided implement (as a pen) < legible *handwriting* >
  syn calligraphy, chirography, ductus, fist, hand, penmanship, script
  rel longhand
handy *adj* **1** *syn* see CONVENIENT 2
  idiom at one's hand (*or* elbow), ready to hand
  ant unhandy
  2 *syn* see PRACTICAL 2
  rel adaptable, advantageous, beneficial, wieldy
  con clumsy, cumbersome, cumbrous, unwieldy
  ant unhandy
  3 *syn* see DEXTEROUS 1
hang *vb* **1** to place or be placed so as to be supported at one point or side usually at the top < *hang* the washing on the line >
  syn dangle, depend, sling, suspend
  rel attach, hook; fix, pin, tack (up); adhere, cling, stick
  2 to put to death by suspending by the neck < was *hanged* for stealing a sheep >
  syn gibbet, noose, scrag, string (up), turn off
  rel execute, lynch
  idiom bring to the gallows, hang by the neck, make dance on air (*or* nothing)
  3 to remain poised or stationary as if suspended in midair < clouds *hanging* in the west >
  syn float, hover, poise
  4 to project outward or incline downward < children *hanging* out the windows to watch a parade >
  syn beetle, bend (over), jut, lean (over), overhang
  rel drape, droop, loll, lop, sag, trail
hang (on *or* upon) *vb syn* see DEPEND (on *or* upon) 1
hang *n* the special method of doing, using, or dealing with something < can't get the *hang* of this gadget >
  syn knack, swing, trick
  rel art, craft, skill
hang around *vb syn* see FREQUENT
hanger–on *n syn* see PARASITE
  rel bystander, follower, spectator, sycophant
hanging *adj syn* see SUSPENDED
hang on *vb syn* see PERSEVERE
hang out *vb* **1** *syn* see RESIDE 1
  2 *syn* see FREQUENT

---

syn synonym(s)   *rel* related word(s)
ant antonym(s)   *con* contrasted word(s)
idiom idiomatic equivalent(s)
|| use limited; if in doubt, see a dictionary

hangout *n* **1** *syn* see RESORT 2
  2 *syn* see DIVE
hang up *vb syn* see DELAY 1
hanker *vb syn* see LONG
  rel covet, desire, wish
hankie *n syn* see HANDKERCHIEF
hanky–panky *n syn* see DECEPTION 1
hap *n syn* see ACCIDENT 1
  rel destiny, fate, lot, portion
hap *vb syn* see HAPPEN 1
‖**hap** *vb syn* see BUNDLE UP
haphazard *adj syn* see RANDOM
  rel accidental; careless, helter-skelter, slipshod; unorganized, unsystematic
  con deliberate, designed, intentional, voluntary, willful
  ant planned
haphazard *adv syn* see ABOUT 4
  rel accidentally, aimlessly, carelessly, casually, promiscuously
haphazardly *adv syn* see ABOUT 4
  rel accidentally, aimlessly, carelessly, casually, promiscuously
hapless *adj syn* see UNLUCKY
  rel infelicitous; miserable, woeful, wretched
happen *vb* **1** to take place or come about <the incident *happened* at midnight>
  syn befall, betide, break, chance, come, come off, develop, do, fall out, give, go, hap, occur, pass, rise, transpire
  rel go off, turn out
  idiom come to pass
  2 to come by chance <he unexpectedly *happened* on a new method>
  syn bump, chance, hit, light, luck, meet, stumble, tumble
  rel befall
happening *n syn* see OCCURRENCE
happify *vb syn* see PLEASE 2
happily *adv syn* see WELL 5
happiness *n* a state of well-being or pleasurable satisfaction <felt *happiness* at her husband's success>
  syn beatitude, blessedness, bliss, blissfulness
  rel content, contentedness, satisfaction; cheer, cheerfulness, felicity, gladness; gaiety, jollity, joy; delectation, delight, enjoyment, pleasure
  con discontent, dissatisfaction, vexation; cheerlessness, despair, desperation, despondency, hopelessness; distress, misery, wretchedness
  ant unhappiness
happy *adj* **1** *syn* see LUCKY
  rel accidental, casual, fortuitous, incidental; opportune, seasonable, timely
  ant unhappy
  2 *syn* see FIT 1
  rel effective, effectual, efficacious, efficient; cogent, convincing, telling; pat, seasonable, well-timed; correct, nice, right
  ant unhappy
  3 *syn* see GLAD 1
  rel content, contented, satisfied
  ant unhappy; disconsolate
happy–go–lucky *adj* disposed to accept cheerfully whatever happens <enjoyed a *happy-go-lucky* existence without needlessly worrying>
  syn carefree, free-minded, insouciant, lighthearted, lightsome; *compare* COOL 2
  rel casual, easy, easygoing; blithe, careless, cheerful, feckless, heedless, lackadaisical; debonair, nonchalant, unconcerned; devil-may-care, reckless
  con careful, cautious, circumspect, discreet, guarded, prudent
happy hunting ground *n syn* see HEAVEN 2
hara–kiri *n syn* see SUICIDE
harangue *n syn* see TIRADE
harangue *vb syn* see ORATE
harass *vb* **1** *syn* see RAID 1
  2 *syn* see WORRY 1
  rel badger, bait, bullyrag, chivy, devil, heckle, hector, hound, ride
  idiom give a bad (*or* hard) time
  3 *syn* see TRY 2
harassed *adj syn* see DISTRAUGHT
harasser *n syn* see BULLY 1
harassment *n syn* see ANNOYANCE 1

  rel aggravation, disturbance, exasperation, irritation, perturbation
harbinger *n syn* see FORERUNNER 1
harbinger *vb syn* see ANNOUNCE 2
harbor *n* **1** *syn* see SHELTER 1
  2 *syn* see INLET
  3 a place where seacraft may ride secure <a yacht *harbor*>
  syn anchorage, ‖chuck, harborage, haven, port, riding, road(s), roadstead
harbor *vb* **1** to provide with shelter or a refuge <*harbored* the refugees in our homes>
  syn chamber, haven, house, roof, shelter, shield
  rel cherish, foster, nurse, nurture; conceal, hide, secrete; guard, protect, safeguard, screen
  idiom give shelter (*or* asylum) to
  con eject, evict, expel, oust; banish, deport, exile; eliminate, exclude, shut out
  2 to provide with a usually temporary place to live <the miners were *harbored* in camps>
  syn accommodate, bestow, billet, board, bunk, domicile, domiciliate, entertain, house, hut, lodge, put up, quarter, room, roost
  rel cabin, camp, encamp
harborage *n syn* see SHELTER 1
  2 *syn* see REFUGE 1
  3 *syn* see HARBOR 3
hard *adj* **1** *syn* see FIRM 2
  rel compacted, compressed, concentrated, consolidated, packed; callous, hardened, indurate, indurated, set; adamantine, flinty, granitic, iron, ironhard
  con fluid, liquid; flabby, limp; ductile, malleable, pliable, pliant, plastic; elastic, flexible, limber, resilient, supple
  ant soft
  2 *syn* see SPIRITUOUS
  ant soft
  3 *syn* see REALISTIC
  4 *syn* see INSENSIBLE 5
  5 *syn* see INTENSIVE
  6 demanding great toil and effort <a *hard* but rewarding task>
  syn arduous, difficile, difficult, effortful, formidable, heavy, knotty, labored, laborious, operose, rough, rugged, serious, severe, slavish, sticky, strenuous, terrible, toilful, toilsome, tough, uphill
  rel burdensome, exacting, onerous; complex, complicated, intricate, involved, scabrous; backbreaking, distressing, exhausting, fatiguing, grinding, tiring, wearing, wearisome, wearying; bothersome, demanding, irksome, rocky, straining, troublesome, trying; merciless, unsparing
  con effortless, facile, light, simple, smooth
  ant easy
  7 *syn* see ACTUAL 2
  8 *syn* see GRIM 2
  9 *syn* see SEVERE 3
hard *adv* **1** with great or utmost force <hit the nail *hard*>
  syn energetically, forcefully, forcibly, hardly, might and main, mightily, powerfully, strongly, vigorously
  rel actively, animatedly, briskly, snappily, spiritedly, sprightly, vivaciously; earnestly, intensely, keenly, seriously, urgently, wholeheartedly
  idiom with all one's might
  con faintly, feebly, nervelessly, softly, strengthlessly, unenergetically, weakly
  ant easily, easy
  2 in a violent manner <the wind blew *hard* all the next day>
  syn fiercely, frantically, frenziedly, furiously, hardly, madly, stormily, tumultuously, turbulently, violently, wildly
  rel boisterously, exuberantly, rowdily, uproariously; angrily, brutally, ferociously, savagely, viciously
  idiom like a house afire, like fury, like mad
  con gently, mildly, softly
  3 with intentness and determination <made up his mind to study *hard*>
  syn assiduously, dingdong, earnestly, exhaustively, intensely, intensively, painstakingly, thoroughly, unremittingly
  rel conscientiously, meticulously, punctiliously
  con carelessly, casually, desultorily, fitfully, haphazardly
  4 in a fixed and intensive manner <stared *hard* at the offender>

syn closely, intently, searchingly, sharply
con casually, cursorily, idly, offhand
5 in such manner as to cause hardship, difficulty, or defeat < things will go *hard* with him if he doesn't reform >
syn badly, hardly, harshly, painfully, rigorously, roughly, severely; *compare* AMISS 2
rel cruelly; relentlessly; meanly, shabbily, unfairly
con comfortably, pleasantly, smoothly; acceptably, satisfactorily, satisfyingly
ant easily, easy
6 with great or excessive resentment or grief < don't take your setback so *hard* >
syn bitterly, hardly, keenly, rancorously, resentfully, sorely
con casually, lightly, nonchalantly, offhandedly
7 in a firm manner < hold on *hard* >
syn fast, firm, firmly, fixedly, solidly, steadfastly, tight, tightly
con easily, easy, loose, loosely, slackly
8 with difficulty < breathing *hard* after the climb >
syn arduously, burdensomely, difficultly, hardly, laboriously, onerously, toilsomely
rel exhaustingly, gruelingly, painfully, tiredly; awkwardly, cumbersomely, cumbrously, inconveniently, ponderously, unhandily, unwieldily
con effortlessly, evenly, handily, readily, smoothly
ant easily, easy
9 to the point of hardness < the pond is frozen *hard* >
syn firmly, hardly, solid, solidly
10 *syn* see CLOSE
hard–boiled *adj* **1** *syn* see UNFEELING 2
rel coarse, crude, rough; seasoned, sophisticated, worldly-wise
idiom not born yesterday
con artless, guileless, naive, simple-hearted, unsophisticated; kindly, mild, soft
2 *syn* see REALISTIC
harden *vb* **1** to make or become physically hard or solid < this substance *hardens* immediately on exposure to air >
syn cake, concrete, congeal, dry, indurate, set, solidify
rel compact, consolidate, densify, firm, stiffen; anneal, case-harden, temper; calcify, fossilize, lithify, ossify, petrify
con deliquesce, dissolve, fuse, liquefy, melt
ant soften
2 to make proof against hardship, strain, or exposure < frontier life *hardened* most men quickly to rough conditions >
syn acclimate, acclimatize, climatize, season, toughen
rel accustom, habituate, indurate, inure; accommodate, adapt, adjust, conform
con emasculate, enervate; debilitate, devitalize, enfeeble, sap, undermine, weaken
ant soften
hardened *adj syn* see UNFEELING 2
hardfisted *adj syn* see STINGY
ant openhanded
hardhanded *adj syn* see STINGY
ant openhanded
hardheaded *adj* **1** *syn* see OBSTINATE
2 *syn* see REALISTIC
hardhearted *adj syn* see UNFEELING 2
hardihood *n* **1** *syn* see TEMERITY
rel boldness, intrepidity; brazenness, cockiness; fortitude, grit, guts, pluck, sand
ant cowardice; timidity
2 *syn* see INSOLENCE
3 *syn* see ENERGY 2
hardiness *n syn* see TEMERITY
ant cowardice; timidity
hard–line *adj syn* see TOUGH 3
hardly *adv* **1** *syn* see HARD 1
2 *syn* see HARD 2
3 *syn* see HARD 5
4 *syn* see HARD 6
5 *syn* see HARD 8
6 *syn* see JUST 2
7 *syn* see HARD 9
hardly ever *adv syn* see SELDOM
hardness *n syn* see DIFFICULTY 1
ant easiness
hardpan *n syn* see BASE 1
hardscrabble *adj syn* see BARREN 2

hard–shell *adj syn* see INVETERATE 1
hardship *n syn* see DIFFICULTY 1
rel adversity, mischance, misfortune; danger, hazard, peril; affliction, trial, tribulation; drudgery, toil, travail; discomfort, distress
con comfort, ease
hardy *adj syn* see TOUGH 4
ant tender
harebrain *n* **1** *syn* see SCATTERBRAIN
2 *syn* see CRACKPOT
harebrained *adj* **1** *syn* see GIDDY 1
2 *syn* see FOOLISH 2
harefooted *adj syn* see FAST 3
hark *vb syn* see LISTEN
rel mark, mind, note, notice, remark
idiom be all ears, not miss a trick
harlequin *n syn* see CLOWN 3
harlot *n* **1** a woman who engages in unlawful or socially unacceptable sexual intercourse often for material gain < ply the trade of a *harlot* >
syn blowen, courtesan, demimondaine, demimonde, demirep, fancy woman, hetaera, kept woman, paphian, whore
2 *syn* see PROSTITUTE
harlotry *n syn* see PROSTITUTION
harm *n syn* see INJURY 1
rel deleteriousness; banefulness, noxiousness, perniciousness; mischance, misfortune, misuse; impairment, marring
con aid, help; accommodation, benefaction; charity, favor, service
ant benefit
harm *vb syn* see INJURE 1
rel abuse, ill-use, maltreat, mistreat, misuse, molest; dilapidate, ruin; discommode, incommode, inconvenience; sabotage, sap, undermine
idiom do violence to
con ameliorate, better, improve; avail, profit
ant benefit
harmful *adj* inflicting or capable of inflicting injury < a *harmful* drug >
syn bad, damaging, deleterious, detrimental, evil, hurtful, ill, injurious, mischievous, nocent, nocuous, prejudicial, prejudicious
rel baleful, baneful, malefic, malign, malignant, noisome, noxious, pernicious, toxic; insalubrious, unhealthful, unhealthy, unwholesome; dangerous, hazardous, risky, unsafe
con innocuous, inoffensive, nontoxic; beneficent, beneficial, benign, benignant, favorable, helpful, salutary, useful; safe, unhazardous
ant harmless
harmless *adj* not having hurtful or injurious qualities < *harmless* pastimes >
syn innocent, innocuous, innoxious, inobnoxious, inoffensive, unoffending, unoffensive; *compare* SAFE 3
rel guiltless; nontoxic, painless, safe
con baneful, dangerous, malignant, noxious, pernicious, toxic, virulent; damaging, detrimental, destructive, hurtful, injurious; deadly, fell, ruinous; improper, unsuitable, wrong
ant harmful
harmonic *adj syn* see HARMONIOUS 1
harmonious *adj* **1** musically concordant < a *harmonious* morning chorus of birds >
syn blending, chiming, consonant, harmonic, musical, symphonic, symphonious
rel canorous, dulcet, euphonious, melodious, mellifluous, mellisonant, musical, silvery, sonorous, sweet, tuneful; chordal, contrapuntal, counterpointed, polyphonic
idiom in concert, in tune
con clashing, discordant, dissonant, grating, harsh, jangling, jarring, raucous, shrill, strident, tuneless, unmusical, untuneful; atonal
ant disharmonious, inharmonious, unharmonious
2 having the parts agreeably related < a building with *harmonious* proportions >
syn accordant, concordant, congruous; *compare* CONSONANT 1

---

syn synonym(s)   *rel* related word(s)
ant antonym(s)   *con* contrasted word(s)
idiom idiomatic equivalent(s)
|| use limited; if in doubt, see a dictionary

rel agreeable, pleasing, satisfying; concinnate, symmetrical
con clashing, incongruous, unsymmetrical; askew, distorted, skewed
ant inharmonious, unharmonious
3 marked by accord in sentiment or action < a *harmonious* effort to reach a practicable agreement >
syn amicable, amical, congenial, friendly
rel coactive, collaborative, cooperative; empathetic, empathic, simpatico, sympathetic; calm, irenic, pacific, peaceful
idiom of one accord
con incompatible, uncongenial, uncooperative, unfriendly, unsympathetic; belligerent, contentious, pugnacious
ant inharmonious, unharmonious
harmonize *vb 1 syn* see AGREE 3
rel cooperate, match, unite
con differ, disagree
ant clash; conflict
2 *syn* see AGREE 4
ant differ (from)
3 to bring into consonance or accord < *harmonize* the factions of a political party >
syn accommodate, attune, conform, coordinate, integrate, proportion, reconcile, reconciliate, tune
rel adapt, adjust, correlate; coapt, relate
con alienate, disrupt, estrange
ant disharmonize
4 to combine or adapt so as to achieve a desired effect < *harmonize* the elements of a story >
syn arrange, blend, integrate, orchestrate, symphonize, synthesize, unify
rel coordinate, correlate
harmonizing *n syn* see RECONCILIATION
harmony *n* 1 musical agreement of sounds < singing in *harmony* >
syn accord, chorus, concert, concord, consonance, tune
rel mellifluousness, melodiousness, melody, musicality, sonority, tunefulness; diapason, polyphony
con cacophony, discord, discordance, discordancy, dissonance, harshness, inharmoniousness, jangle, stridency, tunelessness, unharmoniousness, unmusicalness, untunefulness; atonality
ant disharmony, inharmony
2 the effect produced when different things come together without clashing or disagreement < goals that are in *harmony* with our capabilities >
syn accord, agreement, chime, concord, concordance, consonance, tune; *compare* CONSISTENCY
rel conformance, conformity, correspondence; articulation, coaptation, compatibility, congruity; concatenation, concurrence, integration, oneness, togetherness, unity
con disagreement, discord, disparity, dissidence, disunity, variance
ant conflict
3 the state of persons who are in full and perfect agreement < friends who live in *harmony* >
syn concord, rapport, unity
rel affinity, empathy, fellow-feeling, kinship; peace, tranquillity
idiom meeting of minds
con contention, dissension, strife
ant discord
4 *syn* see SYMMETRY
rel concinnity, consonance; dignity, elegance, grace; integrity, unity
con asymmetry, discordance, discordancy, imbalance
ant inharmony
harness *vb syn* see HITCH 2
‖**harness bull (or cop)** *n syn* see POLICEMAN
harpy *n syn* see VIRAGO
harrier *n syn* see BULLY 1
harrow *vb syn* see AFFLICT
rel fret, irritate, pester; badger, bait, bedevil, devil, heckle, hector, needle, tantalize, tease
harrowing *adj syn* see EXCRUCIATING
harry *vb* 1 *syn* see RAVAGE
2 *syn* see RAID 1
3 *syn* see WORRY 1
rel disturb, irk, perturb, upset; badger, irritate
harsh *adj* 1 *syn* see ROUGH 1
rel coarse, granular, loose; bristly, scraggly, scratchy, shaggy, stubbly

con glossy, satiny, silken, silky, sleek, slick, velvety
2 *syn* see ACRID
rel acerb, acerbic, biting, burning, mordant; pungent, tangy; dry, sour, tart
con mild, smooth, sweet, velvety
3 disagreeable to the ear < many birds have *harsh* cries >
syn dry, grating, hoarse, jarring, rasping, raucous, rough, rugged, rusty, squawky, strident, stridulous
rel discordant, dissonant, immelodious, ineuphonious, inharmonious, unmelodious, unmusical; grinding, jangling, scraping; blaring, brassy; ear-piercing, piercing, shrill, squeaky
con euphonious, harmonious, mellow, melodic, melodious, musical, sonorous, sweet; low, soft; agreeable, pleasing
4 *syn* see UNCOMFORTABLE
5 *syn* see GRIM 2
6 *syn* see SEVERE 3
ant mild
harshly *adv syn* see HARD 5
con considerately; gently, lightly, well; famously
ant smoothly
haruspex *n syn* see PROPHET
harvest *n* 1 the act, process, or occasion of gathering a crop < the time of *harvest* >
syn cropping, gathering, harvesting, ingathering, reaping
rel garnering, storing
con planting, seedtime, sowing
2 the gathered produce of land < a bountiful *harvest* saved the settlers >
syn crop, fruitage
rel yield; bearing, vintage
harvest *vb syn* see REAP
rel assemble, collect; accumulate, amass, bin, store (up), stow (away); cache, hide, hoard, squirrel, stash
harvesting *n syn* see HARVEST 1
hash *vb syn* see CHOP 2
hash *n* 1 *syn* see MISCELLANY 1
2 *syn* see CLUTTER 2
3 *syn* see MESS 3
‖**hashery** *n syn* see EATING HOUSE
‖**hash house** *n syn* see EATING HOUSE
hassle *n* 1 *syn* see QUARREL
2 *syn* see COMMOTION 4
3 *syn* see ATTEMPT
hassle *vb syn* see ARGUE 2
rel cavil; brawl, fight, spar, struggle
haste *n* 1 rapidity of motion or action < we finished our job with great *haste* >
syn celerity, dispatch, expedition, expeditiousness, hurry, hustle, rustle, speed, speediness, swiftness
rel fastness, fleetness, quickness, rapidity; pace, velocity; dash, drive
con languidness, languor, leisureliness, reluctance, slowness; lethargy, sluggishness, torpor
ant deliberateness, deliberation
2 rash or headlong action < oversights due to *haste* >
syn hastiness, hurriedness, precipitance, precipitancy, precipitateness, precipitation, rush
rel impetuosity, impetuousness, impulsiveness
con care, carefulness, circumspection, hastelessness, unhurriedness
ant deliberateness, deliberation
haste *vb syn* see HURRY 2
hasten *vb syn* see SPEED 3
2 *syn* see HURRY 2
hastily *adv syn* see FAST 2
rel agilely, nimbly; impetuously, impulsively, unpremeditatedly; carelessly, recklessly, thoughtlessly; precipitately, prematurely, suddenly
con carefully, designedly, studiedly, thoughtfully; gradually, leisurely, slowly, sluggishly
ant deliberately
hastiness *n syn* see WASTE 2
hasty *adj* 1 *syn* see FAST 3
rel agile, brisk, nimble; hurried, quickened
con dilatory, laggard, leisured, leisurely
2 *syn* see PRECIPITATE 1
ant deliberate
3 *syn* see RASH 1

rel devil-may-care, slambang, slapdash

hatch *vb* **1** *syn* see GENERATE 3

  2 *syn* see GENERATE 1

hatch (up) *vb* *syn* see CONTRIVE 2

hatchet man *n* *syn* see ASSASSIN

hate *n* **1** *syn* see ABOMINATION 2

  rel animosity, animus, antipathy, hostility, ill will, rancor; disgust, scorn, spite

  con affection; toleration; adoration, veneration

  ant love

  2 *syn* see ABOMINATION 1

  rel bother, grievance, gripe, irritant, nuisance, ‖pain, trouble

  ant delight

hate *vb* to feel extreme enmity or dislike <Cain *hated* his brother> <*hate* to meet strangers>

  syn abhor, abominate, detest, execrate, loathe

  rel contemn, despise, disdain, dislike, scorn; deprecate, disapprove; resent

  con cherish, enjoy, fancy, like, relish; favor, prefer, prize; esteem, respect, revere; dote; idolize, worship

  ant love

hateable *adj* *syn* see HATEFUL 2

  ant lovable

hateful *adj* **1** *syn* see MALICIOUS

  rel acrimonious, ill-natured; bitter, resentful; mean

  con benevolent, charitable, cordial, genial, good-humored, good-natured, kind, kindly, pleasant

  2 deserving of or arousing hate <found himself in a *hateful* situation>

  syn abhorrent, abominable, detestable, hateable, horrid, odious

  rel distasteful, distressing, obnoxious, repellent, repulsive; contemptible, despicable, execrable, opprobrious, reprehensible, scurvy; foul, infamous, vile; accursed, blasphemous, damnable, unspeakable

  con compatible, congenial, consonant; alluring, appealing, attractive, charming, enchanting; agreeable, delectable, delightful, likable, pleasant, pleasing

  ant lovable; sympathetic

hatred *n* *syn* see ABOMINATION 2

  rel antipathy, dislike; animosity, enmity, hostility, rancor

  con affability, benevolence, benignity, charitableness, cordiality

  ant love; admiration

haughtiness *n* *syn* see PRIDE 3

  ant lowliness

haughty *adj* *syn* see PROUD 1

  rel aloof, detached, distant, indifferent, reserved; egotistic; contemptuous, scornful

  con humble; obsequious, servile, subservient

  ant lowly

haul *vb* *syn* see PULL 2

  rel move, remove, shift; boost, elevate, hoist, lift, raise

haul *n* *syn* see LOAD 1

haul up *vb* *syn* see STOP 4

haunches *n pl* *syn* see BUTTOCKS

haunt *vb* *syn* see FREQUENT

haunt *n* **1** *syn* see RESORT 2

  2 *syn* see HABITAT

  3 *syn* see APPARITION

haunter *n* *syn* see HABITUÉ 1

hauteur *n* *syn* see PRIDE 3

  ant lowliness

haut monde *n* *syn* see ARISTOCRACY

have *vb* **1** to keep, control, or experience as one's own <can't *have* your cake and eat it too>

  syn enjoy, hold, own, possess, retain

  idiom to be possessed of, have in hand

  con lack, need, want

  2 *syn* see INCLUDE

  rel admit, compose, comprise

  3 *syn* see BEAR 3

  4 *syn* see GET 1

  5 *syn* see EXPERIENCE 1

  6 *syn* see LET 2

  7 *syn* see KNOW 1

  8 *syn* see OUTWIT

  9 *syn* see BRIBE

  10 *syn* see MUST 2

haven *n* **1** *syn* see HARBOR 3

  2 *syn* see SHELTER 1

haven *vb* *syn* see HARBOR 1

haversack *n* *syn* see BACKPACK

havoc *n* *syn* see RUIN 3

  rel calamity, cataclysm, catastrophe; despoiling, pillaging, ravaging; vandalism

havoc *vb* *syn* see RAVAGE

hawk *vb* *syn* see PEDDLE 2

hawker *n* *syn* see PEDDLER

hawk-eyed *adj* *syn* see SHARP-EYED

hawkshaw *n* *syn* see DETECTIVE

haymaker *n* *syn* see CUFF

hayseed *n* *syn* see RUSTIC

  ant city slicker, slicker

hazard *n* **1** *syn* see CHANCE 2

  2 *syn* see DANGER

hazard *vb* **1** *syn* see VENTURE 1

  2 *syn* see GAMBLE 2

  3 *syn* see ENDANGER

hazardous *adj* *syn* see DANGEROUS 1

  ant safe; unhazardous

haze *vb* *syn* see OBSCURE

haze *n* **1** an atmospheric condition that is characterized by the presence of fine particulate material in the air and that deprives the air of its transparency <*haze* obscured the distant hills>

  syn brume, film, mist, smaze

  rel cloud, ‖drisk, fog, murk, ‖smeech, smog, smoke, vapor; cloudiness, mistiness, murkiness, smokiness

  2 a state of mental vagueness or obtuseness <lived in a *haze* of pleasant memories>

  syn befuddlement, daze, fog, ‖maze, muddledness, muddleheadedness, muddlement

  rel dream, reverie, stupor, trance; absentmindedness, abstraction, bemusement, preoccupation, woolgathering

  con alertness, attentiveness, awareness

hazy *adj* obscured or made dim by or as if by haze <had only a *hazy* idea of where they were>

  syn cloudy, foggy, misty, mushy, vague, vaporous, vapory

  rel blurred, clouded, dim, indefinite, indistinct, murky, nebulous, obscure; bemused, dreamy, tranced, stuporous; dazed, ‖mazed, muzzy

he *n* *syn* see MAN 3

head *n* **1** the upper division of the body that contains the brain, the chief sense organs, and the mouth <put your hat on your *head*>

  syn ‖bean, ‖belfry, ‖chump, ‖coco, ‖coconut, ‖conk, ‖dome, headpiece, noddle, noggin, noodle, ‖nut, ‖pallet, pate, poll, sconce

  rel brainpan, cranium, crown, scalp

  2 *syn* see MIND 1

  3 *syn* see GIFT 2

  4 *syn* see LEADER 2

  con subordinate; aide, assistant, helper

  5 *syn* see PROMONTORY

  6 *syn* see TOILET

  7 *syn* see HEADLINE

  8 *syn* see SUBJECT 2

head *adj* *syn* see FIRST 3

head *vb* **1** *syn* see BEHEAD

  2 *syn* see DIRECT 2

  3 to commence to go in an indicated direction <the cowboys *headed* for town>

  syn bear, light out, make, set out, strike out, take off

  rel go, proceed, start

  idiom make a beeline for

  4 *syn* see SPRING 1

heading *n* *syn* see HEADLINE

headland *n* *syn* see PROMONTORY

headline *n* a word or group of words usually in large type introducing and summarizing a newspaper story <*headlines* that screamed the news of the president's death>

  syn head, heading

---

syn synonym(s)　　　　　　*rel* related word(s)

ant antonym(s)　　　　　　*con* contrasted word(s)

idiom idiomatic equivalent(s)

‖ use limited; if in doubt, see a dictionary

rel banner, banner head, bannerline, scarehead, screamer, spreadhead

headlong *adj syn* see PRECIPITATE 1
  rel daredevil, daring, foolhardy, rash, reckless

headman *n syn* see LEADER 2

headmost *adj syn* see FIRST 1

headpiece *n syn* see HEAD 1

headshaker *n syn* see SKEPTIC

head start *n syn* see ADVANTAGE 3

headstone *n syn* see TOMBSTONE

headstrong *adj syn* see OBSTINATE
  con subdued, tame; amenable, biddable, docile, meek, obedient, tractable

headway *n* 1 *syn* see ADVANCE 2

heady *adj syn* see SHREWD

heal *vb syn* see CURE

healing *adj syn* see CURATIVE

health *n* the state of being sound in body or mind <the patient was nursed back to *health* >
  syn haleness, healthiness, soundness, wholeness
  rel stamina, vitality, well-being; euphoria
  con debility, decrepitude, feebleness; ill health, illness, sickliness
  ant disease, infirmity

healthful *adj* conducive or beneficial to the health or soundness of body or mind <regular exercise is a *healthful* practice>
  syn good, healthy, hygienic, salubrious, salutary, salutiferous, wholesome
  rel advantageous, beneficial, profitable, useful; corrective, curative, remedial; aiding, alleviative, helpful, mitigative, restorative, sanative
  con insalubrious, unhealthy, unhygienic, unwholesome; damaging, deleterious, detrimental, harmful, injurious, mischievous, pernicious
  ant unhealthful

healthiness *n syn* see HEALTH
  ant unhealthiness

healthy *adj* 1 enjoying or manifesting health <a *healthy* baby>
  syn ||bunkum, fit, hale, right, sane, sound, well, well-conditioned, well-liking, whole, wholesome
  rel hearty, iron, lusty, robust, thriving, vigorous; rugged, stalwart, strong, sturdy, tough; agile, chipper, spry; blooming, rosy, thriving
  idiom fit as a fiddle, in (top) condition, in fine fettle, in shape, in trim, sound as a dollar, up to snuff
  con decrepit, delicate, feeble, fragile, frail, weak; infirm, ||poorly, sickly
  ant unhealthy
  2 *syn* see HEALTHFUL
  ant unhealthful
  3 *syn* see SAFE 3

heap *n* 1 *syn* see PILE 1
  rel congeries, gathering
  2 *syn* see MUCH
  3 *syn* see SCAD
  4 *syn* see JALOPY

heap *vb* 1 to throw or collect in a pile <*heap* up leaves for a bonfire>
  syn bank, cock, drift, hill, mound, pile, stack
  rel cord, ||dess, rick, shock; bunch, clump, lumber, lump, mass; deposit, dump; accumulate, amass, assemble, collect, gather, group
  con broadcast, disperse, distribute, scatter, separate, spread, strew
  2 *syn* see LOAD 3

hear *vb* 1 *syn* see LISTEN
  idiom get wind of
  2 *syn* see DISCOVER 3

hearing *n* 1 *syn* see EARSHOT
  2 an opportunity to be heard <they finally obtained a *hearing* on their complaints>
  syn audience, audition
  rel conference, interview, meeting, parley; test, tryout; discussion, negotiation

hearken *vb syn* see LISTEN

hearsay *n syn* see REPORT 1

heart *n* 1 the seat or center of secret thoughts and emotions <in his *heart* he knew he was seriously in the wrong>
  syn bosom, breast, soul

  idiom bottom of the heart, cockles of the heart
  2 *syn* see COURAGE
  3 *syn* see TASTE 4
  4 *syn* see CENTER 2
  5 *syn* see CENTER 3

heartache *n syn* see SORROW
  idiom aching heart, heavy heart

heartbreak *n* 1 *syn* see SORROW
  rel agony, bale, torment
  idiom bleeding heart

heartbreaking *adj syn* see DEPLORABLE

hearten *vb syn* see ENCOURAGE 1
  rel energize, enliven; arouse, rally, rouse, stir
  con damp, dampen; weigh
  ant dishearten

heartfelt *adj syn* see SINCERE 1
  rel bona fide, genuine, honest, true, unfeigned; deep, profound
  con hypocritical, insincere; false, pretended

heartless *adj syn* see UNFEELING 2

heartrending *adj syn* see DEPLORABLE

heart–searching *n syn* see INTROSPECTION

heartsick *adj syn* see DOWNCAST

heartsore *adj syn* see DOWNCAST

heartthrob *n syn* see SWEETHEART 1

heart–whole *adj* 1 *syn* see FREE 6
  2 *syn* see GENUINE 3

hearty *adj syn* see SINCERE 1
  rel responsive, warm, warmhearted; deep, profound; exuberant, profuse
  con cold, dispassionate, emotionless
  ant hollow

||**heat** *n syn* see POLICEMAN

heated *adj* 1 *syn* see HOT 1
  ant chilled
  2 *syn* see FEVERISH 2
  3 *syn* see ANGRY

heathen *adj* of or relating to people who do not acknowledge the God of the Bible <ancient *heathen* sacrificial rites>
  syn ethnic, gentile, infidel, infidelic, pagan, profane
  rel heathenish, paganish

heave *vb* 1 *syn* see THROW 1
  2 *syn* see TOSS 2
  3 *syn* see PANT 1
  4 *syn* see RETCH
  ||5 *syn* see VOMIT

heaven *n* 1 *usu* **heavens** *pl syn* see SKY
  2 an abode of blissful spiritual life after death <the religious conceptions of *heaven* and hell>
  syn Abraham's bosom, bliss, Canaan, Civitas Dei, elysium, empyrean, happy hunting ground, kingdom come, New Jerusalem, nirvana, paradise, Zion
  rel afterworld, eternity, glory, hereafter, promised land; everlastingness, immortality
  idiom Beulah Land (*or* Land of Beulah), City of God, Kingdom of God, Kingdom of Heaven
  con earth, world; Gehenna, hades, inferno, netherworld, perdition, pit, Sheol, Tartarus, Tophet, underworld
  ant hell
  3 *syn* see UTOPIA
  4 *syn* see ECSTASY

heavenly *adj* 1 *syn* see CELESTIAL
  con hadean, Tartarean
  ant hellish
  2 *syn* see DELIGHTFUL

heavy *adj* 1 having great or relatively great weight <a *heavy* load>
  syn hefty, massive, ponderous, weighty; *compare* UNWIELDY
  rel awkward, bulky, clumsy, lumbering, lumbersome; unhandy, unmanageable, unwieldy; cumbersome, cumbrous
  con airy, buoyant, weightless; handy, manageable, wieldy
  ant light
  2 *syn* see FAT 2
  3 *syn* see SERIOUS 2
  4 *syn* see RECONDITE
  5 *syn* see PREGNANT 1
  6 *syn* see LETHARGIC
  7 *syn* see OVERCAST
  8 *syn* see HARD 6

9 *syn* see RICH 3

heavy–footed *adj syn* see PONDEROUS 2

heavy–handed *adj* **1** *syn* see AWKWARD 2
2 *syn* see PONDEROUS 2

heavyhearted *adj syn* see SAD 1
ant lighthearted

heavyheartedness *n syn* see SADNESS
ant lightheartedness

heavyset *adj syn* see STOCKY

heavyweight *n syn* see NOTABLE 1
con lightweight

hebetate *vb syn* see DULL 5

hebetude *n syn* see LETHARGY 1

hebetudinous *adj syn* see LETHARGIC

heckle *vb* **1** *syn* see BAIT 2
rel plague, worry; discomfit, disconcert, embarrass, faze, rattle; tease, torment
2 *syn* see MOLEST

hectic *adj syn* see FEVERISH 2

hector *n syn* see BULLY 1

hector *vb* **1** *syn* see INTIMIDATE
2 *syn* see BAIT 2

hedge *vb* **1** *syn* see EQUIVOCATE 2
2 *syn* see ENCLOSE 1

hedonist *n* one given to the zealous pursuit of pleasure < lead the life of a *hedonist* >
syn carpet knight, pleasuremonger, sybarite
rel bon vivant, man-about-town; epicure, epicurean, gourmand, gourmet; debauchee, libertine, rake; sensualist, voluptuary; pleasure-seeker
ant ascetic

hedonistic *adj syn* see SYBARITIC
con austere, self-denying, self-disciplined, self-restricted
ant ascetic

heebie–jeebies *n pl syn* see JITTERS

heed *vb syn* see LISTEN
rel mark, mind, note; observe, see, watch
idiom give (*or* pay) heed to

heed *n* **1** *syn* see NOTICE 1
rel awareness, interest, mindfulness; audience, hearing
2 *syn* see ATTENTION 1
rel concern, interest
con inattention, unconcern
3 *syn* see CARE 4

heedful *adj* **1** *syn* see ATTENTIVE 1
ant heedless, unheeding
2 *syn* see MINDFUL 2
ant heedless, unheeding
3 *syn* see CAREFUL 2

heedfully *adv syn* see WELL 2
ant heedlessly, unheeding

heedfulness *n syn* see CARE 4
ant heedlessness

heedless *adj syn* see CARELESS 1
ant heedful, heeding

heedlessness *n syn* see APATHY 2
ant heedfulness

hee–haw *vb syn* see LAUGH

heel *n* **1** *syn* see REMAINDER
2 *syn* see VILLAIN 1

heel *vb syn* see SLANT 1

hefty *adj* **1** *syn* see HEAVY 1
2 *syn* see HUSKY 1
3 *syn* see BIG 1

height *n* the distance a thing rises above the level on which it stands < the *height* of a building >
syn altitude, elevation
rel highness, loftiness, rise, tallness, stature
con lowness, profundity
ant depth

heighten *vb* **1** *syn* see INCREASE 1
2 *syn* see INCREASE 2
rel elevate, lift, raise; better, improve; enlarge, increase
con diminish, lessen, shrink
3 *syn* see INTENSIFY

heinie (*or* **hiney**) *n syn* see BUTTOCKS

heinous *adj syn* see OUTRAGEOUS 2
con paltry, petty, trifling, trivial

ant venial

heinousness *n syn* see ENORMITY 1

heir *n* one who inherits < died without *heirs* >
syn heritor, inheritor

‖**heist** *vb syn* see STEAL 1

hell *n* a place or state of the dead or of the damned < went to *hell* for his sins >
syn abyss, barathrum, blazes, Gehenna, hades, inferno, netherworld, Pandemonium, perdition, pit, Sheol, Tophet
rel limbo, Styx, Tartarus
idiom the hot place, infernal regions, place of torment
ant heaven

hell *vb syn* see REVEL 1

hell–fired *adj syn* see UTTER

hellish *adj syn* see INFERNAL 2

helotry *n syn* see BONDAGE

help *n* **1** an act or instance of giving what will benefit or assist < the stranded travelers received *help* from passersby >
syn aid, assist, assistance, comfort, hand, lift, relief, secours, succor, support
rel benefit, cooperation, service
ant hindrance
2 something that is beneficial < the rain was a real *help* to late crops >
syn aid, support
rel benefit, use
3 *syn* see HELPER

help *vb* **1** to give assistance or support < *help* the children with their lessons >
syn abet, aid, assist, benefact, do for, help out, stead
rel back, bolster, boost, champion, second, support, uphold; avail, benefit, profit; advance, facilitate, forward, further, promote, serve; befriend, succor
idiom give a lift, lend a hand (*or* a helping hand), stand back of (*or* behind)
con bar, block, impede, obstruct, oppose; baffle, balk, foil, frustrate, thwart; discomfit, embarrass; damage, harm, hurt, injure
ant hinder
2 *syn* see IMPROVE 1
rel alleviate, mitigate, palliate, relieve
con harm, impair, worsen

helper *n* one that helps < was made boss and assigned a dozen *helpers* >
syn aid, ancilla, assistant, attendant, help, striker
rel helpmate, helpmeet; auxiliary, deputy, subordinate; associate, follower; employee, laborer, servant, worker
idiom helping hand, right-hand man

helpful *adj* **1** of service or assistance < *helpful* suggestions >
syn aidant, aiding, assistive, serviceable
rel beneficial, effective, profitable, salutary, usable; constructive, practical, useful
con timeserving, uncooperative, unreliable; impractical, ineffectual
ant unhelpful
2 *syn* see GOOD 1

helpless *adj* **1** lacking protection or support < *helpless* nestlings >
syn defenseless, unprotected
rel abandoned, desolate, forlorn, forsaken, friendless; feeble, weak
2 *syn* see POWERLESS

helplessly *adv syn* see WILLY-NILLY

help out *vb syn* see HELP 1

helter–skelter *adv* **1** *syn* see PELL-MELL
2 *syn* see ABOUT 4

hem *n syn* see BORDER 1

hem *vb* **1** *syn* see BORDER
2 *syn* see ENCLOSE 1
3 *syn* see SURROUND 1

hence *adv* **1** *syn* see AWAY 1
2 *syn* see THEREFORE

henceforth *adv* from this time forward < made up his mind to keep out of trouble *henceforth* >
syn henceforward, hereafter; *compare* THENCEFORTH

---

syn synonym(s)   *rel* related word(s)
ant antonym(s)   *con* contrasted word(s)
idiom idiomatic equivalent(s)
‖ use limited; if in doubt, see a dictionary

idiom from now on
henceforward *adv syn* see HENCEFORTH
henchman *n syn* see FOLLOWER
  rel attendant; lackey, minion, stooge
henpeck *vb syn* see NAG
hep *adj syn* see WISE 4
herald *n syn* see FORERUNNER 1
  rel courier, crier, messenger
herald *vb* **1** *syn* see ANNOUNCE 2
  2 *syn* see TOUT
Herculean *adj syn* see HUGE
herd *n syn* see DROVE 2
herd *vb syn* see DRIVE 3
here *adv syn* see HITHERTO 2
hereafter *adv syn* see HENCEFORTH
hereafter *n* **1** *syn* see FUTURE
  2 an existence or place of existence after this life < buried pots
  and tools with the dead for use in the *hereafter* >
  syn afterlife, afterworld, beyond, otherworld
  idiom great beyond (*or* hereafter), life after death, next world
  (*or* life), world beyond the grave, world to come
  con here and now
here and there *adv syn* see SOMETIMES
heresy *n* defection from a dominant belief or ideology < the *heresy* of the flat-earth theory >
  syn dissent, dissidence, heterodoxy, misbelief, nonconformism,
  nonconformity, schism, unorthodoxy
  rel impiety, infidelity; apostasy, defection, revisionism; error,
  fallacy
heretic *n* one who is not orthodox in his beliefs < a *heretic* in religion >
  syn dissenter, dissident, misbeliever, nonconformist, schismatic,
  schismatist, sectary, separatist
  rel apostate, defector, iconoclast, recreant, recusant, renegade;
  infidel, unbeliever; deviationist, revisionist
  ant orthodox
heretical *adj* of, relating to, or characterized by heresy < *heretical*
  beliefs >
  syn dissident, heterodox, nonconformist, schismatic, sectarian,
  unorthodox
  rel apostate, infidel, miscreant, revisionist; differing, disagreeing,
  dissentient, dissenting, dissentive, misbelieving, unbelieving
  con conventional, established; agreeing, conforming, conformist
  ant orthodox
heretofore *adv syn* see BEFORE 2
heritage *n* **1** something that one receives or is entitled to receive
  by succession (as from a parent) < the *heritage* of freedom >
  syn birthright, heritance, inheritance, legacy, patrimony
  2 *syn* see TRADITION 1
heritance *n syn* see HERITAGE 1
heritor *n syn* see HEIR
hermaphrodite *adj syn* see BISEXUAL
hermaphroditic *adj syn* see BISEXUAL
hermetic *adj* **1** *syn* see RECONDITE
  2 *syn* see SECLUDED
hermit *n syn* see RECLUSE
heroic *adj* **1** *syn* see BRAVE 1
  ant pusillanimous
  2 *syn* see HUGE
heroism *n* conspicuous courage or bravery < received an award
  for *heroism* >
  syn gallantry, prowess, valiance, valiancy, valor, valorousness
  rel boldness, bravery, courage, doughtiness, fearlessness, intrepidity, spirit; chivalry, nobility
  con cowardice, spiritlessness, timidity, timorousness, weakness
  ant pusillanimity
hesitancy *n syn* see HESITATION
hesitant *adj* **1** *syn* see DISINCLINED
  con resolute, staunch, steadfast
  2 *syn* see VACILLATING 2
hesitate *vb* to show irresolution or uncertainty < *hesitate* to buy a
  new car just now >
  syn dither, falter, halt, shilly-shally, stagger, vacillate, waver,
  whiffle, wiggle-waggle
  rel balk, boggle, demur, scruple, stick, stickle; fluctuate, oscillate, swing; dawdle, delay, dillydally, hang back, procrastinate,
  stall, temporize; pause
hesitating *adj syn* see VACILLATING 2

hesitation *n* the act or action of hesitating < several persons vol-
  unteered without *hesitation* >
  syn hesitancy, indecision, indecisiveness, irresolution, shilly=
  shally, to-and-fro, vacillation, wavering
  rel doubt, dubiety, dubiosity, mistrust, uncertainty; dawdling,
  delay, procrastination; averseness, indisposition, reluctance
  con alacrity, eagerness; courage, mettle, resolution, spirit, tenacity; aplomb, assurance, confidence
hetaera *n syn* see HARLOT 1
heteroclite *adj syn* see ABNORMAL 1
heterodox *adj syn* see HERETICAL
  ant orthodox
heterodoxy *n syn* see HERESY
  ant orthodoxy
heterogeneous *adj syn* see MISCELLANEOUS
  ant homogeneous
hew *vb syn* see FELL 2
hex *vb syn* see BEWITCH 1
hex *n* **1** *syn* see JINX
  2 *syn* see WITCH 1
hiatus *n syn* see GAP 3
hic jacet *n syn* see EPITAPH
hick *n syn* see RUSTIC
hick town *n syn* see BURG
hidden *adj syn* see ULTERIOR
  ant open
hide *vb* to withdraw or withhold from sight or observation < they
  hid their loot in a cave >
  syn bury, ‖bush up, cache, conceal, cover, ‖ditch, ensconce, occult, plant, screen, secrete, stash
  rel mantle, mask, obscure, shade, shield; entomb, inter; cloak,
  curtain, shroud, veil; harbor, lodge, seclude, shelter
  con bare, disclose, discover, display, exhibit, expose, reveal,
  show; uncover, unmask, unveil, unwrap; flaunt, parade, show off
hide *n* an animal skin < tanned *hides* for shoe leather >
  syn fell, fur, jacket, pelt, skin
hide *vb syn* see WHIP 1
hideaway *n syn* see HIDEOUT
hidebound *adj syn* see ILLIBERAL
hideous *adj* **1** *syn* see UGLY 2
  ant lovely
  2 *syn* see OFFENSIVE
  3 *syn* see GHASTLY 1
hideout *n* a place of retreat or concealment < a gangsters' *hideout* >
  syn den, hideaway, lair
  rel covert, haven, hermitage, refuge, retreat, sanctuary, shelter;
  robbers' roost
hie *vb syn* see GO 1
hierarch *n syn* see LEADER 2
hieratic *adj syn* see SACERDOTAL
higgle *vb syn* see HAGGLE 2
higgler *n syn* see PEDDLER
high *adj* **1** having a relatively great upward extension < a *high*
  building >
  syn altitudinous, tall; *compare* LOFTY 6
  rel aerial, eminent, lofty, soaring, towering; big, gigantic, grand,
  large, prominent
  idiom tall (*or* high) as a steeple
  con little, short, squat
  ant low
  2 *syn* see COSTLY 1
  ant low
  3 *syn* see MALODOROUS 1
  4 *syn* see ELEVATED 4
  5 *syn* see ACUTE 4
  6 *syn* see DRUGGED
high and low *adv syn* see EVERYWHERE 1
high-and-mighty *adj syn* see PROUD 1
highball *vb syn* see HURRY 2
highbinding *n syn* see DECEPTION 1
highbrow *n syn* see INTELLECTUAL 2
highbrow *adj syn* see INTELLECTUAL 2
highbrowed *adj syn* see INTELLECTUAL 2
  ant lowbrow, low-browed
higher *adj syn* see SUPERIOR 1
higher-up *n syn* see SUPERIOR
highest *adj* **1** *syn* see TOP 1

ant lowest
2 *syn* see EXALTED 1
highest–ranking *adj syn* see EXALTED 1
highfalutin *adj syn* see RHETORICAL
  con down-to-earth, matter-of-fact
highfalutin *n syn* see BOMBAST
high–flown *adj syn* see RHETORICAL
high–handed *adj syn* see MASTERFUL 1
high hat *n syn* see SNOB
high–hat *adj syn* see SNOBBISH
high–hearted *adj syn* see SPIRITED 2
high jinks *n pl* **1 *syn*** see HORSEPLAY
  2 *syn* see REVELRY 2
highly *adv syn* see VERY 1
high–minded *adj syn* see ELEVATED 2
  ant low-minded
high–muck–a–muck *n syn* see NOTABLE 1
high–principled *adj syn* see HONORABLE 1
high roller *n syn* see SPENDTHRIFT
high sign *n* **1 *syn*** see SIGN 1
  2 a private usually covert signal, warning, or cue <I gave him the *high sign* when I saw the police approaching>
  syn ‖office
  rel tip, tip-off, wink; nod; alarm, SOS, warning
high–sounding *adj syn* see PRETENTIOUS 3
high–spirited *adj* **1 *syn*** see SPIRITED 2
  rel jolly, lighthearted, merry, mirthful
  ant low-spirited
  2 *syn* see EXUBERANT 1
high–strung *adj* **1 *syn*** see TENSE 3
  2 *syn* see NERVOUS
hightail *vb syn* see GET OUT 1
highway *n syn* see WAY 1
high yellow *n syn* see MULATTO
hike *vb* **1 *syn*** see RAISE 9
  2 to travel about or through on foot <*hiked* through the woods>
  syn tramp, tromp
  rel footslog; stroll, walk; ramble, rove, wander; explore
hike *n* **1 *syn*** see TRAMP 3
  2 *syn* see RISE 3
hilarity *n syn* see MIRTH
hill *n syn* see PILE 1
hill *vb syn* see HEAP 1
hillbilly *n syn* see RUSTIC
hillman *n syn* see RUSTIC
hind *adj syn* see POSTERIOR 2
hind end *n syn* see BUTTOCKS
hinder *vb* to put obstacles in the way of <their cause was *hindered* by the excesses of overzealous supporters>
  syn bar, block, brake, dam, impede, obstruct, overslaugh; *compare* HAMPER
  rel arrest, check, interrupt, retard; clog, entrammel, fetter, hamper, hog-tie, manacle, shackle, trammel; curb, deter, hamstring, inhibit, restrain, tie (down); embog, mire; burden, handicap, lumber; baffle, balk, frustrate, thwart
  idiom bog down
  con abet, advance, aid, assist, ease, encourage, facilitate, forward, promote; accelerate, hasten, quicken, speed
  ant further, help
hinder *adj syn* see POSTERIOR 2
  ant fore, front
‖**hinder** *n syn* see BUTTOCKS
hindmost *adj* **1 *syn*** see POSTERIOR 2
  con foremost, headmost
  2 *syn* see LAST
hindrance *n syn* see ENCUMBRANCE
  ant help
hinge (on *or* upon) *vb syn* see DEPEND (on *or* upon) 1
hint *n* **1** a slight or indirect pointing out of something and especially of the way to an end <give me a *hint* on how you would deal with the matter>
  syn clue, cue, indication, inkling, intimation, notion, suggestion, telltale, wind
  rel innuendo, insinuation; inspiration, prompting; aiming, direction, pointing; key, pointer, tip; advice, assistance
  con command, directive, instruction, order
  2 a very small amount or admixture <add a *hint* of garlic to the salad>

syn breath, cast, dash, intimation, lick, shade, shadow, smack, smatch, smell, soupçon, spice, sprinkling, strain, streak, suggestion, suspicion, taste, tincture, tinge, touch, trace, trifle, twang, vein, whiff, whisper, wink; *compare* HAIR
  rel adumbration, taint, vestige; particle, scintilla
  con abundance, heap, lot
  ant oodles
  3 *syn* see ASSOCIATION 4
hint *vb* **1 *syn*** see SUGGEST 1
  2 *syn* see POINT 2
  3 *syn* see ADUMBRATE 1
  4 to seek to obtain by sly or indirect means <kept *hinting* for an invitation to the party>
  syn angle, fish
  rel beg, coax, plead; importune, press; seek, solicit
  con ask (for), demand, insist (on *or* upon)
hinterland *n syn* see FRONTIER 2
hipped *adj* **1 *syn*** see DOWNCAST
  2 *syn* see OBSESSED
hire *n syn* see WAGE
hire *vb* **1** to take or engage something or grant the use of something for a stipulated price or rate <*hire* a conveyance>
  syn charter, lease, let, rent
  rel contract (for), engage; sublease, sublet, subrent
  2 *syn* see EMPLOY 2
  ant fire
hired girl *n syn* see MAID 2
hireling *n syn* see HACK 2
hiring *n syn* see EMPLOYMENT 4
hirsute *adj syn* see HAIRY 1
  ant hairless
hiss *vb* to make a sibilant sound <he thought he heard a snake *hiss*>
  syn buzz, fizz, fizzle, sibilate, sizz, sizzle, swish, wheeze, whish, whisper, whiz, whoosh
hiss *n syn* see RASPBERRY
history *n* **1 *syn*** see ACCOUNT 7
  2 a chronological record of events <a *history* of the American Revolution>
  syn annals, chronicle
  rel account, recital, relation, report; diary, journal, memoir; epic, saga, tale
histrionic *adj syn* see DRAMATIC 1
hit *vb* **1 *syn*** see STRIKE 2
  rel buffet, pound, stroke
  idiom give one a clip
  2 *syn* see OCCUR 2
  3 *syn* see HAPPEN 2
hit (on *or* upon) *vb syn* see FIND 1
hit *n* **1** a stroke delivered with a part of the body or an instrument <gave the disobedient boy a *hit* on the head with her ruler>
  syn ‖conk, knock, lick, rap, swat, swipe, wipe; *compare* BLOW 1, CUFF
  2 *syn* see SMASH 6
hitch *vb* **1 *syn*** see LIMP 1
  2 to attach as a means of motive power <*hitched* the team to a wagon>
  syn couple, harness, yoke
  idiom make fast
  con free, release, unfasten; uncouple, unharness, unyoke
  ant unhitch
  ‖**3 *syn*** see MARRY 2
  4 *syn* see HITCHHIKE
hitchhike *vb* to travel by securing free rides <*hitchhiked* to California>
  syn hitch, thumb
  idiom bum (*or* hook) a ride
hitherto *adv* **1** up to this particular point or time <imposed order upon what was *hitherto* haphazard>
  syn as yet, earlier, so far, thus far, yet
  rel before, formerly, heretofore, once, previously
  idiom up to now (*or* then)

---

syn synonym(s)   ***rel*** related word(s)
ant antonym(s)   ***con*** contrasted word(s)
idiom idiomatic equivalent(s)
‖ use limited; if in doubt, see a dictionary

2 to this place < the appointed delegate shall come *hither-to* >
 syn here
hit man *n syn* see ASSASSIN
hit–or–miss *adj syn* see RANDOM
hive *vb syn* see ACCUMULATE
hoard *n* **1** *syn* see ACCUMULATION
 2 *syn* see RESERVE
hoard *vb* to store up beyond one's present or reasonable need < *hoarding* sugar during war >
 syn squirrel, stash; *compare* ACCUMULATE, SAVE 4
 rel ‖sock away; garner, lay by, lay up
 idiom take all one can lay one's hands on
hoarse *adj* **1** rough or dry in sound < developed a *hoarse* cough >
 syn croaking, croaky, gruff, husky
 rel coarse, dry, guttural, thick
 2 *syn* see HARSH 3
 con honeyed, mellifluent, mellifluous, smooth
hoary *adj syn* see ANCIENT 1
hoax *vb syn* see DUPE
hoax *n syn* see IMPOSTURE
hobble *vb* **1** *syn* see LIMP 1
 2 *syn* see HAMPER
hobo *n syn* see VAGABOND
hoboism *n syn* see VAGRANCY
hock *vb syn* see PAWN
hocus–pocus *n syn* see GIBBERISH 3
‖hodge *n syn* see RUSTIC
hodgepodge *n syn* see MISCELLANY 1
hogback *n syn* see RIDGE 1
hogshead *n syn* see CASK
hog–tie *vb syn* see HAMPER
hogwash *n syn* see NONSENSE 2
hoi polloi *n syn* see RABBLE 2
hoist *vb syn* see LIFT 1
hoity–toity *adj syn* see GIDDY 1
hokum *n syn* see NONSENSE 2
hold *vb* **1** *syn* see KEEP 5
 2 *syn* see ENTHRALL 2
 3 *syn* see HAVE 1
 4 *syn* see CONTAIN 2
 5 *syn* see FEEL 3
hold (with) *vb syn* see APPROVE 1
hold *n* the act or manner of grasping or holding < lost his *hold* on the side of the boat >
 syn clamp, clasp, clench, clinch, clutch, grapple, grasp, grip, gripe, tenure
 rel handclasp, handhold; purchase
hold back *vb* **1** *syn* see RESTRAIN 1
 2 *syn* see KEEP 5
 3 *syn* see DENY 3
hold down *vb syn* see RESTRAIN 1
holder *n syn* see OWNER
hold in *vb syn* see RESTRAIN 1
hold off *vb* **1** *syn* see FEND (off)
 2 *syn* see DEFER
hold out *vb syn* see OFFER 1
hold over *vb syn* see DEFER
hold up *vb syn* see DEFER
hole *n* **1** *syn* see APERTURE
 2 *syn* see GAP 1
 3 a space within the substance of a body or mass < buried their trash in a *hole* in the ground >
 syn cavity, hollow, vacuity, void
 rel gap, hiatus, lacuna; cranny, interstice, niche; fissure, rent, rift; vacancy, vacuum
 4 *syn* see HOVEL
 5 *syn* see PREDICAMENT
hole *vb syn* see OPEN 3
hole–and–corner *adj syn* see SECRET 1
holiday *n syn* see VACATION
holiness *n* a state of spiritual soundness and unimpaired virtue < the *holiness* of the saints >
 syn saintliness, sanctity
 rel blessedness, divineness, divinity, sacredness; consecration, devotion, devoutness, piety, piousness, spirituality
holler *vb syn* see CALL 1
hollo *vb syn* see CALL 1

hollow *adj* **1** having a muffled or reverberating quality < had a deep *hollow* gloomy voice >
 syn cavernous, reverberant, sepulchral
 rel echoing, resonant, resounding, reverberating, sounding
 con dead, dull, flat, toneless
 2 *syn* see VAIN 1
hollow *n* **1** *syn* see DEPRESSION 2
 2 *syn* see HOLE 3
holocaust *n syn* see FIRE 1
holy *adj* **1** dedicated to the service of or set apart by religion < pilgrimages to *holy* places >
 syn blessed, consecrated, hallowed, sacred, sanctified, unprofane; *compare* SACRED 2
 rel adored, glorified, revered, reverenced, venerated, worshiped; divine, religious, spiritual
 2 *syn* see SAINTLY
 ant unholy
 3 *syn* see DEVOUT
‖Holy Joe *n syn* see CLERGYMAN
holy place *n syn* see SHRINE
Holy Writ *n syn* see BIBLE
homage *n syn* see HONOR 1
home *n* **1** *syn* see HABITATION 2
 2 *syn* see HABITAT
 3 *syn* see COUNTRY
home *adj* **1** *syn* see DOMESTIC 1
 2 *syn* see DOMESTIC 2
homeland *n syn* see COUNTRY
homely *adj* **1** *syn* see PLAIN 1
 rel commonplace, familiar, intimate
 2 *syn* see PLAIN 5
 idiom homely as a mud (*or* hedge) fence, homely enough to sour milk
 ant comely
homicidal *adj syn* see MURDEROUS
homicide *n* **1** *syn* see MURDERER
 2 *syn* see MURDER
homilize *vb syn* see PREACH 1
hominine *adj syn* see HUMAN
hominoid *n syn* see ANTHROPOID
homo *n syn* see HOMOSEXUAL
homoerotic *adj syn* see HOMOSEXUAL
homophile *adj syn* see HOMOSEXUAL
Homo sapiens *n syn* see MANKIND
homosexual *adj* relating to or exhibiting sexual desire toward a member of one's own sex < *homosexual* acts between consenting adults >
 syn gay, homoerotic, homophile, inverted, queer, uranian
 rel androgynous, bisexual, epicene; transvestite; lesbian, sapphic; effeminate, swishy
homosexual *n* one who is inclined to or practices homosexuality < a bar frequented by *homosexuals* >
 syn fag, faggot, ‖fruit, homo, invert, queer, uranian, uranist
 rel transvestite; fairy, nance, nancy, pansy, queen, ‖swish; lesbian, sapphist
homunculus *n syn* see DWARF
honcho *n syn* see LEADER 2
hone *vb syn* see SHARPEN
honed *adj syn* see SHARP 1
honest *adj* **1** *syn* see GENUINE 3
 rel reliable, unaffected, unimpeachable
 2 *syn* see UPRIGHT 2
 rel candid, forthright, frank, open, plain; dispassionate, objective; truthful, veracious
 ant dishonest
honestness *n syn* see HONESTY
 ant dishonesty
honesty *n* uprightness as evidenced in character and actions < he was generally known as a person of scrupulous *honesty* >
 syn honestness, honor, honorableness, incorruption, integrity
 rel conscientiousness, justness, probity, scrupulousness; uprightness; dependability, reliability, trustworthiness; goodness, morality, rectitude, virtue
 con deceitfulness, mendaciousness, mendacity, untruthfulness; deceit, duplicity, guile
 ant dishonesty
honey *n* **1** *syn* see SWEETHEART 1
 2 *syn* see GIRL FRIEND 2

honey *vb syn* see SUGARCOAT 1
honey (up) *vb syn* see FAWN
honeybunch *n syn* see SWEETHEART 1
honeyed *adj syn* see MELLIFLUOUS
honky–tonk *n syn* see DIVE
honor *n* **1** respect or esteem shown one as his due or claimed by one as a right < received the *honor* due his rank >
syn deference, homage, obeisance, reverence
rel admiration, esteem; adoration, adulation, devotion, veneration, worship; acknowledgment, compliment, recognition, regard, respect
con contempt, despite, disdain, scorn; disregard, neglect, slighting
ant dishonor
2 an evidence or symbol of distinction < received many *honors* for his devoted public service >
syn accolade, award, badge, bays, decoration, distinction, kudos, laurels
rel deference, esteem, respect; admiration, approval
3 *syn* see HONESTY
con disgrace, ignominy, shame
ant dishonor, dishonorableness
honor *vb syn* see EXALT 1
ant dishonor
honorable *adj* **1** deserving of or entitled to honor (as because of rank, achievements, or service) < medicine is an *honorable* profession >
syn estimable, high-principled, noble, sterling, worthy; *compare* VENERABLE 1
rel august, illustrious, reverend, venerable, worshipful
ant dishonorable
2 *syn* see UPRIGHT 2
ant dishonorable
honorableness *n syn* see HONESTY
ant dishonor, dishonorableness
‖**hooch** *n* **1** *syn* see LIQUOR 2
2 *syn* see MOONSHINE 2
‖**hood** *n syn* see THUG 1
hoodlum *n syn* see THUG 1
hoodoo *n syn* see JINX
hoodwink *vb syn* see DUPE
hooey *n syn* see NONSENSE 2
hoof *vb syn* see WALK 1
hoof (it) *vb syn* see DANCE 1
hoofer *n syn* see DANCER
hook *vb syn* see STEAL 1
‖**hooker** *n syn* see PROSTITUTE
‖**hookshop** *n syn* see BROTHEL
hookup *n syn* see ASSOCIATION 1
hooligan *n syn* see THUG 1
‖**hoosegow** *n syn* see JAIL
hoosier *n syn* see RUSTIC
hoot *n* **1** *syn* see RASPBERRY
2 *syn* see PARTICLE
‖**hootenanny** *n syn* see DOODAD
hop *vb* **1** *syn* see SKIP 1
2 *syn* see JUMP 1
‖**hop** *n syn* see DRUG 2
hope *vb syn* see EXPECT 1
hope *n syn* see TRUST 1
hopeful *adj* **1** full of hope or inclined to hope < the candidate was *hopeful* of winning >
syn hoping; *compare* CONFIDENT 1, EXPECTANT 1, OPTIMISTIC
rel anticipative, assured, satisfied, secure; cheerful, content, easy, undisturbed; fond, optimistic, Pollyannaish, rose-colored, sanguine, upbeat
con doubtful, insecure, pessimistic, uncertain; discouraged, disheartened, gloomy, glum
ant hopeless
2 exhibiting qualities that inspire hope < a *hopeful* prospect for improvement >
syn couleur de rose, encouraging, likely, promiseful, promising, roseate, rose-colored, rosy
rel advantageous, auspicious, propitious; bright, cheering, cheery, golden, halcyon, happy, sunny; budding, up-and-coming
con discouraging, disheartening, dismal, dreary, gloomy, pessimistic
ant hopeless

hopeful *n syn* see CANDIDATE
hopeless *adj* **1** *syn* see DESPONDENT
rel gloomy, glum, morose
con cheerful; assured, confident, optimistic, sanguine, sure
ant hopeful
2 offering no prospect of change for the better < his case was *hopeless* and beyond all human aid >
syn cureless, immedicable, impossible, incurable, insanable, irremediable, irreparable, uncorrectable, uncurable, unrecoverable
rel insoluble; incorrigible, irredeemable
idiom beyond hope (*or* remedy *or* repair), beyond human aid
con correctable, curable, medicable, remediable, reparable
ant hopeful
hoper *n syn* see OPTIMIST
hoping *adj syn* see HOPEFUL 1
hop–o'–my–thumb *n syn* see DWARF
hopped–up *adj syn* see DRUGGED
hopping *adj syn* see BUSTLING
horde *n syn* see CROWD 1
horizon *n syn* see KEN
horn in *vb* **1** *syn* see MEDDLE
2 *syn* see INTRUDE 1
‖**horning** *n syn* see SHIVAREE
hornswoggle *vb syn* see DUPE
horrible *adj* **1** *syn* see GHASTLY 1
rel abhorrent, abominable, detestable, hateful; loathsome, obnoxious, offensive, repulsive, revolting
con gratifying, pleasing, soothing
2 *syn* see FEARFUL 3
3 *syn* see OFFENSIVE
horrid *adj* **1** *syn* see GHASTLY 1
2 *syn* see HATEFUL 2
3 *syn* see OFFENSIVE
horrific *adj syn* see FEARFUL 3
horrify *vb syn* see DISMAY 1
horrifying *adj syn* see GHASTLY 1
horror *n* **1** *syn* see FEAR 1
rel distress, pain, shock, throe, wrench
2 *syn* see ABOMINATION 2
hors d'oeuvre *n syn* see APPETIZER
horse *n syn* see SAWHORSE
horse *vb syn* see CUT UP 2
‖**horsefeathers** *n pl syn* see NONSENSE 2
horse opera *n syn* see WESTERN
horseplay *n* rough or boisterous play < their friendly *horseplay* almost ended in tragedy >
syn fooling, high jinks, roughhouse, roughhousing, rowdiness, skylarking
rel buffoonery, clowning
horseplay *vb syn* see CUT UP 2
horse sense *n syn* see SENSE 6
hospice *n syn* see HOTEL
hospitable *adj syn* see SOCIAL
ant inhospitable
host *n syn* see MULTITUDE 1
hostage *n syn* see PLEDGE
rel guaranty, security, surety
hostel *n syn* see HOTEL
hostelry *n syn* see HOTEL
hostile *adj* **1** marked by lack of friendliness or by opposition < takes a *hostile* view of a tax increase > < *hostile* tribes >
syn ill, inimicable, inimical, unfriendly
rel argumentative, competitive, contrary, dim, disaffected, disapproving, opposed, opposite, unfavorable; dour, sour; bellicose, belligerent, contentious, pugnacious; militant, warlike
con amicable, benign, friendly
ant unhostile
2 *syn* see BITTER 3
hostility *n syn* see ENMITY
hot *adj* **1** marked by a notable amount of heat < a *hot* day >
syn ardent, baking, blistering, boiling, broiling, burning, fiery, heated, red-hot, scalding, scorching, sizzling, sultry, sweltering, sweltry, torrid, white-hot

---

syn synonym(s)   *rel* related word(s)
ant antonym(s)   *con* contrasted word(s)
idiom idiomatic equivalent(s)
‖ use limited; if in doubt, see a dictionary

rel febrile, fevered, feverish, feverous, hectic; summery, tropic, tropical; mild, warm
idiom hot as a firecracker (*or* furnace), hot as an oven, hot as hell
con chilly, cool, frigid, icy
ant cold
2 *syn* see LUSTFUL 2
3 *syn* see MARVELOUS 2
4 *syn* see CONTRABAND
hot air *n syn* see NONSENSE 2
hotbed *n syn* see BREEDING GROUND
hot–blooded *adj syn* see IMPASSIONED
con callous, hard, unfeeling
ant cold-blooded
hotchpotch *n syn* see MISCELLANY 1
hot dog *n syn* see FRANKFURTER
hotel *n* an establishment for the lodging and entertainment especially of transients <spent their vacation at a resort *hotel*>
syn auberge, caravansary, hospice, hostel, hostelry, inn, lodge, public house, roadhouse, tavern
rel boardinghouse, lodging house, pension, rooming house, spa; boatel, motel, motor inn; ‖fleabag, ‖flophouse
hotfoot *adv syn* see PELL-MELL
hotfoot *vb syn* see HURRY 2
hotheaded *adj syn* see RASH 1
ant cool
hothouse *n syn* see BREEDING GROUND
hot spot *n syn* see NIGHTCLUB
hot–tempered *adj* **1** *syn* see ILL-TEMPERED
2 *syn* see IRASCIBLE
hot water *n* **1** *syn* see PREDICAMENT
2 *syn* see TROUBLE 3
hound *n* **1** *syn* see DOG 1
2 *syn* see ADDICT
hound *vb syn* see BAIT 2
house *n* **1** *syn* see HABITATION 2
2 *syn* see FAMILY 2
3 *syn* see FAMILY 1
4 *syn* see ENTERPRISE 3
house *vb* **1** *syn* see HARBOR 1
2 *syn* see HARBOR 2
housebreak *vb* to commit an act of breaking open and entering with a felonious purpose the dwelling of another by day or night <was arrested again in September for *housebreaking*>
syn break in; *compare* BURGLARIZE, ROB 1
rel knock over, rob; ransack, rifle
idiom break and enter
household *n syn* see FAMILY 2
household *adj syn* see DOMESTIC 1
housemaid *n syn* see MAID 2
houseman *n syn* see BOUNCER 2
house of God *syn* see HOUSE OF WORSHIP
house of prayer *syn* see HOUSE OF WORSHIP
house of worship a building for religious exercises <there are many *houses of worship* in this city>
syn church, house of God, house of prayer, tabernacle, temple
rel abbey, basilica, bethel, cathedral, chantry, chapel, conventicle, ‖fane, ‖kirk, masjid, meetinghouse, minster, mosque, oratory, pagoda, sanctuary, shrine, stupa, synagogue
idiom the Lord's house
housing *n syn* see SHELTER 2
hovel *n* a small wretched dwelling place <migrants forced to live in *hovels*>
syn burrow, hole; *compare* HUT
rel hut, hutch, shack, shanty; pigpen, pigsty, sty
hover *vb* **1** *syn* see FLIT 2
2 *syn* see HANG 3
howbeit *adv syn* see HOWEVER
howbeit *conj syn* see THOUGH
however *conj syn* see ONLY
however *adv* in spite of that <I accept your decision; I cannot, *however*, approve of it>
syn after all, howbeit, nevertheless, nonetheless, notwithstanding, per contra, still, still and all, though, withal, yet
idiom all the same, be that as it may, for all that, on the other hand
howl *vb* **1** to utter or emit a loud sustained doleful sound or outcry <the dogs *howled* through the night>

syn bay, quest, ululate, wail
rel bark, growl, yelp; blubber, cry, keen, weep, whimper; bawl, squall, yowl
2 *syn* see YELL 2
3 *syn* see BAWL 2
howl *n syn* see RIOT 2
hoyden *n syn* see TOMBOY
hub *n syn* see CENTER 2
hubbub *n* **1** *syn* see DIN
2 *syn* see COMMOTION 4
‖hubby *n syn* see HUSBAND
hubristic *adj syn* see PROUD 1
huckster *n syn* see PEDDLER
huckster *vb* **1** *syn* see HAGGLE 2
2 *syn* see PEDDLE 2
huddle *vb* **1** *syn* see CROUCH
2 *syn* see CONFER 2
huddle (on) *vb syn* see DON 1
huddle *n syn* see CONFUSION 3
hue *n syn* see COLOR 1
huff *vb* **1** *syn* see PANT 1
2 *syn* see IRRITATE
huff *n syn* see OFFENSE 2
huffy *adj* **1** *syn* see PROUD 1
2 *syn* see IRRITABLE
hug *vb syn* see EMBRACE 1
huge *adj* exceedingly or excessively large <*huge* corporations> <ate a *huge* dinner>
syn Antaean, behemothic, Brobdingnagian, Bunyanesque, colossal, cyclopean, dinosauric, elephantine, enormous, gargantuan, giant, gigantean, gigantesque, gigantic, Herculean, heroic, immense, jumbo, leviathan, lusty, mammoth, massive, massy, mastodonic, mighty, monster, monstrous, monumental, mountainous, planetary, prodigious, pythonic, ‖swapping, Titan, titanic, tremendous, unfathomed, untold, vast, walloping, whacking, whaling, whopping; *compare* GRAND 1
rel bulky, extensive, great, immeasurable, magnificent, towering; outsize, oversize
con diminutive, little, miniature, minute, petite, small, teeny, tiny, wee, weeny
hugely *adv syn* see VERY 1
hugeness *n syn* see ENORMITY 2
hugger–mugger *n* **1** *syn* see SECRECY
2 *syn* see CLUTTER 2
hugger–mugger *adv syn* see SECRETLY
hugger–mugger *adj syn* see SECRET 1
hugger–muggery *n syn* see SECRECY
hull *n* an outer covering of a fruit or seed <peanut *hulls*>
syn case, husk, pod, shell, shuck, skin, ‖slough
rel chaff; bark, peel, rind
hull *vb syn* see SHUCK
hullabaloo *n syn* see DIN
hum *vb* to make a low prolonged sound <the wind *hummed* in the chimney>
syn bombinate, ‖bum, bumble, buzz, drone, ‖sowf, strum, thrum
rel moan, murmur, purr, vibrate, whisper
con howl, roar, shriek
human *adj* of, relating to, or characteristic of mankind <problems of *human* relationships>
syn hominine, mortal
rel anthropological, ethnologic, ethological; anthropoid, hominid, hominoid
con angelic, divine, superhuman; animal, brute, subhuman
human *n* a member of the human race <every *human* has a right to live>
syn being, body, ‖character, creature, individual, life, man, mortal, party, person, personage, soul, wight; *compare* MAN 3, MANKIND
humane *adj syn* see CHARITABLE 1
rel chickenhearted, compassionate, kindhearted, soft-hearted; benevolent, gentle, kind, kindly, mild
ant inhuman, inhumane
humanitarian *adj syn* see CHARITABLE 1
humanity *n syn* see MANKIND
humankind *n syn* see MANKIND
humanoid *adj syn* see ANTHROPOID
humble *adj* **1** lacking all signs of pride, aggressiveness, or self-assertiveness <accepted his success with *humble* appreciation>

syn lowly, meek, modest, unassuming
rel simple, unobtrusive, unostentatious, unpretentious; acquiescent, compliant, resigned; quiet, subdued, submissive
con ostentatious, pretentious, showy; vain, vainglorious; arrogant, disdainful, haughty, lordly, overbearing, proud, toplofty
ant conceited
2 syn see IGNOBLE 1
humble *vb* to make lower in status, prestige, or esteem < his devotion to duty *humbled* his critics >
syn abase, bemean, cast down, debase, degrade, demean, humiliate, lower, sink
rel chagrin, mortify; abash, discomfit, embarrass
idiom bring low, take down a peg or two
con aggrandize, exalt, magnify
humbug *n* **1 syn** see IMPOSTURE
2 syn see IMPOSTOR
3 syn see NONSENSE 2
humbug *vb syn* see DECEIVE
humdinger *n syn* ‖DILLY, ‖corker, crackerjack, ‖daisy, dandy, jim≠dandy, ‖lulu, nifty, peach, ‖pip
humdrum *adj syn* see DULL 9
humdrum *n syn* see MONOTONY
humid *adj* containing or characterized by an uncomfortable amount of atmospheric warmth and moisture < a *humid* climate >
syn mucky, muggy, soggy, sticky, sultry; *compare* STIFLING 1, STUFFY 1
rel clammy, dank, sodden; close, oppressive, stuffy; sweltering
con arid, dry; cool, crisp, fresh
humiliate *vb syn* see HUMBLE
humming *adj syn* see BUSTLING
humor *n* **1 syn** see DISPOSITION 3
2 syn see MOOD 1
3 syn see CAPRICE
4 that quality or element which appeals to a sense of the ludicrous or incongruous < see the *humor* in a situation >
syn comedy, comicality, comicalness, drollery, drollness, funniness, humorousness, wittiness
rel jocosity, jocularity, jocundity, jocundness; flippancy, levity, lightness; banter, chaffing, jesting, joking, kidding
con earnestness, seriousness, solemnity; depth, profundity
5 something that is or is designed to be humorous < his heavy *humor* fell flat >
syn wit
rel banter, chitchat, pleasantry, repartee
6 syn see WIT 5
ant humorlessness
humor *vb* **1 syn** see INDULGE 1
2 syn see BABY
humorist *n* **1 syn** see WAG 1
2 a person noted for or specializing in humor < a writer best known as a *humorist* >
syn comedian, comic, droll, funnyman, jester, joker, jokester, quipster, wag, wit
rel buffoon, card, clown, cutup, gagman, gagster, jokesmith, merry-andrew, prankster, punster, zany; banterer, kidder
humorous *adj syn* see WITTY
humorousness *n syn* see HUMOR 4
humorsome *adj syn* see MOODY
‖**hump** *vb syn* see CARRY 1
hunch *vb syn* see CROUCH
hunch *n syn* see LUMP 1
hunger *vb syn* see LONG
hungry *adj* feeling distressed from lack of food < a group of *hungry* children >
syn famished, ‖peckish, ravenous, starved, starving
rel rapacious, voracious
con full, glutted, gorged, sated, satiated
ant surfeited
hunk *n syn* see LUMP 1
hunker (down) *vb syn* see SQUAT
hunkers *n pl syn* see BUTTOCKS
hunks *n pl but sing or pl in constr syn* see MISER
hunky-dory *adj syn* see MARVELOUS 2
Hunnic *adj syn* see BARBARIAN 1
Hunnish *adj syn* see BARBARIAN 1
hunt *vb* **1** to search for or pursue (game or prey) for the purpose of capturing or killing < *hunted* deer in bow-and-arrow season only >

syn chase, run
rel dog, ferret, hawk, hound; course, drive, stalk, start, still≠hunt, track; capture, kill, snare; gun, shoot
idiom go hunting
2 syn see SEEK 1
hunt (down *or* out *or* up) *vb syn* see RUMMAGE 3
hunting *n* the act or practice of seeking and taking wild and especially game animals < lived by *hunting* and fishing >
syn chase, venery
rel angling, coursing, falconry, fishing, gunning, hawking, shooting
hurdle *n syn* see OBSTACLE
hurdle *vb* **1 syn** see CLEAR 8
2 syn see JUMP 1
3 syn see OVERCOME 1
hurl *vb syn* see THROW 1
hurly-burly *n syn* see COMMOTION 4
hurrah *n* **1 syn** see PASSION 6
2 syn see COMMOTION 3
3 syn see ARGUMENT 2
hurricane *n* a violent rotating storm or system of winds originating in the tropics and often moving into temperate latitudes < the *hurricane* struck the coast early today >
syn tropical cyclone, tropical storm, typhoon, ‖willy-willy; *compare* TORNADO, WHIRLWIND 1
rel williwaw
hurried *adj syn* see PRECIPITATE 1
ant unhurried
hurriedness *n syn* see HASTE 2
hurry *vb* **1 syn** see SPEED 3
2 to proceed or move with dispatch < *hurry* home after school >
syn barrel, barrelhouse, beeline, bucket, bullet, bustle, ‖dust, fleet, flit, fly, haste, hasten, highball, hotfoot, hustle, ‖nip, pelt, rock, rocket, run, rush, scoot, scour, ‖skeet, skin, smoke, speed, stave, ‖tatter, whirl, whish, whisk, whiz, zip; *compare* RUSH 1
rel jog, peg, skelp, trot; bowl (along), breeze; dig in; post
idiom get a move on, go (*or* move) like lightning, make tracks, step on it, step on the gas
con creep, dally, dawdle, drag, lag, linger, loiter, poke, saunter, stroll
hurry *n syn* see HASTE 1
hurry-scurry *adv syn* see PELL-MELL
hurt *vb* **1 syn** see INJURE 1
rel abuse, afflict, mistreat, misuse
ant benefit
2 syn see INJURE 3
3 syn see DISTRESS 2
4 to experience or be the seat of sharp physical distress < my arm still *hurts* >
syn ache, pain, ‖suffer; *compare* SMART
hurt *n syn* see INJURY 1
hurtful *adj* **1 syn** see HARMFUL
con harmless, innocuous
2 syn see PAINFUL 1
hurting *adj syn* see PAINFUL 1
husband *n* the male partner in a marriage < neglected his responsibilities as a *husband* >
syn ‖hubby, lord, man, ‖master, mister, Mr., ‖old man
rel consort, helpmate, helpmeet, mate, other half, spouse; benedict, bridegroom
husbanding *n syn* see CONSERVATION 1
ant squandering
husbandry *n* **1 syn** see ECONOMY
2 syn see AGRICULTURE
hush *vb syn* see SILENCE
hush (up) *vb syn* see SUPPRESS 3
hush *adj syn* see STILL 3
hush *n* **1 syn** see QUIET 1
2 syn see SECRECY
hushed *adj* **1 syn** see CALM 1
2 syn see PRIVATE 2
hushful *adj syn* see STILL 3

---

syn synonym(s)   **rel** related word(s)
ant antonym(s)   **con** contrasted word(s)
idiom idiomatic equivalent(s)
‖ use limited; if in doubt, see a dictionary

hush–hush *adj syn* see SECRET 1
hush–hush *n syn* see SECRECY
husk *n syn* see HULL
husk *vb syn* see SHUCK
husky *adj syn* see HOARSE 1
husky *adj* **1** big and muscular <a *husky* man carried in the trunks>
   syn beefy, burly, hefty
   rel brawny, muscular, well-built; stalwart, stout, strapping, strong, sturdy; Herculean, mighty, powerful; Bunyanesque, gigantic
   con delicate, fragile, frail; puny, scrawny, slight; elfin; mousey
   2 *syn* see LARGE 1
hussy *n* **1** *syn* see WANTON
   2 *syn* see MINX
hustle *vb* **1** *syn* see PUSH 2
   2 *syn* see HURRY 2
hustle *n syn* see HASTE 1
hustler *n* **1** an alert enterprising individual <he's a *hustler*, eager to get ahead in the world>
   syn dynamo, go-getter, live wire, peeler, rustler, self-starter
   rel humdinger, hummer; new broom; doer, powerhouse
   idiom busy bee
   con dawdler, idler; slow coach, slowpoke, stick-in-the-mud
   2 *syn* see PROSTITUTE
hustling *adj syn* see BUSTLING
hut *n* a small, simply constructed dwelling often for temporary or intermittent occupancy <the shepherds lived in *huts* in the summer>
   syn ‖box, cabin ‖caboose, camp, cot, cottage, lodge, shack, shanty; *compare* BUILDING, EDIFICE, HOVEL
   rel cabana, chalet, crib, dacha, hovel, hutch, lean-to, shed, summer house
hut *vb syn* see HARBOR 2
Hyblaean *adj syn* see MELLIFLUOUS
hybrid *n* an offspring produced by parents of different strains, breeds, varieties, species, or genera <the mule is a *hybrid* of the ass and the horse>
   syn bastard, cross, crossbred, crossbreed, half blood, half-breed, mongrel, mule
   rel incross, incrossbred, outcross; combination, composite, mixture
   con pureblood, purebred, thoroughbred
hybridize *vb syn* see CROSS 4
hydrant *n syn* see FAUCET
‖**hydro** *n syn* see SPA 1
hydroponics *n* the growing of plants in nutrient solution and without soil <tomatoes grown by *hydroponics*>
   syn aquiculture, nutriculture
   idiom soilless agriculture

hygienic *adj syn* see HEALTHFUL
   ant unhygienic
hymeneal *adj syn* see MATRIMONIAL
hymn *n syn* see SONG 2
hymn *vb* **1** *syn* see PRAISE 2
   2 *syn* see SING
hypaethral *adj syn* see OUTDOOR
hyperbole *n syn* see EXAGGERATION
   con depreciation, minimization, understatement
   ant litotes
hypercritical *adj syn* see CRITICAL 1
hypercriticize *vb syn* see QUIBBLE 1
hypnotic *adj syn* see SOPORIFIC 1
hypocorism *n syn* see NICKNAME
hypocrisy *n* the pretense or affectation of having virtues, principles, or beliefs that one does not actually have <political *hypocrisy*>
   syn cant, hypocriticalness, pecksniffery, pharisaicalness, pharisaism, sanctimoniousness, sanctimony, sham, Tartuffery, Tartuffism
   rel pietism, religiosity; casuistry, glibness, insincerity, self-righteousness, unctuousness; charlatanry, humbug, quackery
   con candidness, fairness, openness; honesty, probity, truthfulness
   ant sincerity
hypocrite *n* one who affects virtues, qualities, or attitudes he does not have <don't be a *hypocrite* — if you don't approve, say so>
   syn dissembler, dissimulator, lip server, pharisee, Tartuffe, whited sepulcher
   rel pietist; actor, attitudinizer, bluffer, charlatan, faker, four=flusher, fraud, humbug, impostor, masquerader, phony, poser, poseur, pretender, quack, sham
hypocritical *adj* **1** characterized by hypocrisy <*hypocritical* compliments>
   syn canting, pecksniffian, pharisaic, pharisaical, sanctimonious, self-righteous
   rel goody-goody, holier-than-thou, moralistic, pietistic, religiose; casuistic; affected, insincere; bland, glib, mealymouthed, oily, smooth, smooth-spoken, smooth-tongued, unctuous
   con honest, open, straightforward
   ant sincere
   2 *syn* see INSINCERE
hypocriticalness *n syn* see HYPOCRISY
   ant sincerity
hypostatize *vb syn* see MATERIALIZE 2
hypothesis *n syn* see THEORY 1
hypothetical *adj* **1** *syn* see SUPPOSED 1
   rel doubtful, problematic
   2 *syn* see ABSTRACT 1

I

icky *adj syn* see OFFENSIVE
iconographic *adj syn* see PICTORIAL 1
icy *adj* **1** *syn* see COLD 1
   ant fiery
   2 *syn* see COLD 2
   ant fiery
idea *n* what exists in the mind as a representation (as of something comprehended) or as a formulation (as of a plan) <that's not my *idea* of a good time>
   syn apprehension, conceit, concept, conception, image, impression, intellection, notion, perception, thought
   rel assumption, belief, conclusion, conviction, estimation, feeling, inclination, judgment, opinion, persuasion, presumption, reaction, reflection, sentiment, view; conjecture, guess, hypothesis, speculation, supposition, surmise, suspicion, theory; caprice, fancy, fantasy, vagary, whim, whimsy; brainstorm, inspiration
ideal *adj* **1** *syn* see ABSTRACT 1
   ant actual
   2 *syn* see CONCEPTUAL

3 constituting a standard (as of perfection or excellence) <the *ideal* man of letters>
   syn flawless, indefectible, model
   rel archetypal, archetypical, prototypal, prototypical
   con average, normal, representative, typical
   4 *syn* see PERFECT 3
   5 *syn* see TYPICAL 1
ideal *n* **1** *syn* see MODEL 2
   2 *syn* see PARAGON
idealist *n syn* see DREAMER
idealist *adj syn* see IDEALISTIC
idealistic *adj* characterized by idealism <made an *idealistic* speech on human rights>
   syn idealist, utopian, visionary
   rel impractical, poetical, quixotic, romantic, starry, starry-eyed, unrealistic
   con empirical, matter-of-fact, practical, pragmatic, rational, realistic

ant unidealistic
ideational *adj syn* see CONCEPTUAL
identic *adj syn* see SAME 2
   ant nonidentical
identical *adj* **1** *syn* see SAME 1
   2 *syn* see SAME 2
   ant nonidentical
identicalness *n syn* see IDENTITY 1
identification *n syn* see RECOGNITION 1
identify *vb* to establish the identity of < the culprit was *identified* by his fingerprints >
   syn determinate, diagnose, diagnosticate, distinguish, finger, pinpoint, place, recognize, spot
   rel find; determine, establish, make out, pick out, select, separate (out)
identity *n* **1** the quality of being the same in all that constitutes the objective reality of separate things < the *identity* of the two texts is exact >
   syn identicalness, oneness, sameness, selfsameness
   rel agreement, likeness, resemblance, semblance, similarity, similitude; correspondence, equality, equivalence; uniformity
   con dissimilarity, dissimilitude, unlikeness, unsimilarity
   ant nonidentity
   2 *syn* see INDIVIDUALITY 4
ideologue *n syn* see DREAMER
ideology *n* an overall view of or attitude toward life < an *ideology* based on tolerance >
   syn credo, creed, weltanschauung
   rel outlook, philosophy, view
idiom *n syn* see LANGUAGE 1
idiosyncratic *adj* **1** *syn* see CHARACTERISTIC
   2 *syn* see STRANGE 4
idiot *n* **1** *syn* see FOOL 1
   2 *syn* see FOOL 2
   3 *syn* see FOOL 4
   4 *syn* see DUNCE
idle *adj* **1** *syn* see VAIN 1
   2 *syn* see VACANT 4
   3 *syn* see INACTIVE
   ant busy
idle *vb* to spend time in idleness < people *idling* in the park >
   syn ‖brogue, bum, dawdle, diddle, diddle-daddle, drone, goldbrick, ‖goof (off), ‖lallygag, laze, lazy, loaf, loiter, loll, lounge
   rel relax, repose, rest; amble, linger, mooch, mosey, saunter, stroll, tarry; hang around, sit around, sit back, sit by
   idiom dog it, kill time, lie around, mark time
idleheaded *adj syn* see FOOLISH 2
idleness *n syn* see SLOTH 1
idler *n syn* see SLUGGARD
idolatry *n syn* see ADORATION
idolization *n syn* see ADORATION
idolize *vb syn* see ADORE 3
   idiom worship the ground one walks on
iffy *adj syn* see UNCERTAIN 1
ignis fatuus *n syn* see DELUSION 1
ignitable *adj syn* see COMBUSTIBLE 1
ignite *vb syn* see LIGHT 1
ignited *adj syn* see BURNING 1
ignoble *adj* **1** belonging to or characteristic of socially or economically inferior classes < a person of *ignoble* antecedents >
   syn base, baseborn, humble, low, lowborn, lowly, mean, plebeian, unennobled, unwashed
   rel coarse, common, homely, inferior, inglorious, modest, ordinary, peasant, plain, poor, popular, simple, vulgar
   con highborn, highbred, wellborn, well-bred; eminent, high, lofty, proud, superior
   ant noble
   2 *syn* see BASE 3
   ant noble
ignominious *adj syn* see DISREPUTABLE 1
ignominy *n syn* see DISGRACE
   rel contempt, despite, disdain, scorn; chagrin, mortification
   con glory, honor; esteem, respect
ignoramus *n syn* see DUNCE
ignorance *n* **1** the state of being unlearned < the blight of *ignorance* >
   syn benightedness, illiteracy
   rel callowness, greenness, inexperience, naiveté, rawness, simpleness, simplicity, uncouthness, uncultivation, unsophistication;

empty-headedness, unintelligence, witlessness; know-nothingism, philistinism
   con education, enlightenment, erudition, learning, literacy
   2 the state of being unaware or uninformed < *ignorance* of the law >
   syn innocence, inscience, nescience, unacquaintance, unacquaintedness, unawareness, unfamiliarity, unknowingness
   con acquaintance, acquaintanceship, experience; awareness, familiarity, knowledgeableness
ignorant *adj* **1** lacking knowledge or education < an *ignorant* boy with no taste for school >
   syn benighted, empty-headed, illiterate, know-nothing, rude, uneducated, uninstructed, unlettered, unschooled, untaught, untutored
   rel lowbrow, uncultured, unintellectual; callow, green, inexperienced; crude, gross, raw, uncouth; ingenuous, naive, simple, unsophisticated
   con educated, erudite, learned, literate
   2 lacking information on or awareness of something < was *ignorant* of the circumstances surrounding the affair >
   syn incognizant, inconversant, oblivious, unacquainted, unaware, unfamiliar, uninformed, uninstructed, unknowing, unwitting
   idiom in the dark
   con aware, conscious, conversant, informed, knowing, knowledgeable
   3 *syn* see BACKWARD 5
ignore *vb syn* see NEGLECT
   rel avoid, evade
ilk *n syn* see TYPE
ill *adj* **1** *syn* see EVIL 5
   ant good
   2 *syn* see HARMFUL
   3 *syn* see SICK 1
   4 *syn* see RUDE 6
   5 *syn* see HOSTILE 1
ill *n* **1** *syn* see EVIL 1
   ant benefit
   2 *syn* see DISEASE 1
ill-adapted *adj syn* see UNFIT 1
ill-advised *adj* **1** *syn* see RASH 1
   2 *syn* see INADVISABLE
   ant well-advised
   3 *syn* see UNWISE
   ant well-advised
illation *n* **1** *syn* see INFERENCE 1
   2 *syn* see INFERENCE 2
ill-behaved *adj syn* see NAUGHTY 1
ill-boding *adj syn* see OMINOUS
ill-bred *adj* **1** *syn* see BOORISH
   ant well-bred
   2 *syn* see RUDE 6
   ant well-bred, well-mannered
ill-chosen *adj syn* see INFELICITOUS
ill-defined *adj syn* see FAINT 2
   ant well-defined
illegal *adj syn* see UNLAWFUL
   rel banned, forbidden, interdicted, prohibited, proscribed, outlawed, unauthorized, unlicensed, unwarranted; felonious; contraband, hot; actionable, irregular
   con authorized, lawful, licensed, licit, permitted, regular, right
   ant legal
illegality *n* the quality or state of being illegal < the *illegality* of an act >
   syn illegitimacy, illicitness, unlawfulness
   rel badness, impropriety, wrongness
   con lawfulness, legitimacy, licitness; propriety
   ant legality
illegible *adj* incapable of being read or deciphered < an *illegible* signature >
   syn indecipherable, undecipherable, unreadable
   rel faint, indistinct, obscure, unclear
   ant legible, readable

---

syn synonym(s)   *rel* related word(s)
ant antonym(s)   *con* contrasted word(s)
idiom idiomatic equivalent(s)
‖ use limited; if in doubt, see a dictionary

illegitimacy *n* **1** the state or condition of being born out of wedlock <he accepted the fact of his *illegitimacy* >
syn bastardy, illegitimateness, supposititiousness
rel bar sinister
ant legitimacy, legitimateness
2 *syn* see ILLEGALITY
ant legitimacy, legitimateness

illegitimate *adj* **1** not recognized by law as lawful offspring <an *illegitimate* child>
syn baseborn, bastard, fatherless, misbegotten, natural, spurious, supposititious, unfathered
rel birthless; adulterine
ant legitimate
2 *syn* see UNLAWFUL
ant legitimate

illegitimate *n syn* see BASTARD 1
ant legitimate

illegitimateness *n syn* see ILLEGITIMACY 1
ant legitimacy, legitimateness

ill–famed *adj syn* see INFAMOUS 1

ill–fated *adj syn* see UNLUCKY

ill–favored *adj* **1** *syn* see UGLY 2
ant well-favored
2 *syn* see OBJECTIONABLE

ill–flavored *adj syn* see UNPALATABLE 1

ill–humored *adj syn* see ILL-TEMPERED
ant good-humored, good-natured

illiberal *adj* unwilling or unable to grasp the point of view of others <had the *illiberal* outlook of an old-time schoolmaster>
syn bigoted, brassbound, hidebound, intolerant, narrow, narrow-minded, small-minded, unenlarged
rel biased, jaundiced, one-sided, opinionated, partial, partisan, prejudiced; grudging, little, mean, paltry, petty, small, uncharitable, ungenerous; insular, parochial, provincial; rigid, rigorous, stringent
con broad-minded, open-minded, tolerant, unbigoted; advanced, progressive, radical
ant liberal

illicit *adj syn* see UNLAWFUL
ant licit

illicitness *n syn* see ILLEGALITY

illimitable *adj syn* see INFINITE 1
rel endless, interminable
ant limitable; limited

illiteracy *n syn* see IGNORANCE 1

illiterate *adj syn* see IGNORANT 1
ant literate; erudite

illiterate *n* one who cannot read or write <the training of adult *illiterates* >
syn analphabet
rel functional illiterate, semiliterate, subliterate
ant literate

ill–judged *adj syn* see UNWISE

ill–kempt *adj syn* see SLOVENLY 1

ill–looking *adj syn* see UGLY 2
ant good-looking, ‖well-looked

ill–mannered *adj syn* see RUDE 6
ant well-bred, well-mannered

ill–natured *adj syn* see ILL-TEMPERED
ant good-humored, good-natured

illness *n syn* see SICKNESS 1
ant health

illogical *adj* contrary to or devoid of logic <came to an *illogical* conclusion from the facts presented>
syn fallacious, invalid, irrational, mad, nonrational, reasonless, sophistic, unreasonable, unreasoned; *compare* FALSE 1
rel inconsistent; plausible, specious; unscientific, unsound; absurd, meaningless, senseless
idiom without rhyme or reason
con rational, reasonable, sensible; sane, sound, valid
ant logical

ill–omened *adj syn* see OMINOUS
ant auspicious

ill–seasoned *adj syn* see UNSEASONABLE 1
ant seasonable

ill–starred *adj syn* see UNLUCKY
rel bodeful, fateful, foreboding, ominous, portentous; baleful, malefic, malign, sinister; unfavorable, unpromising, unpropitious

ill–suited *adj syn* see UNFIT 1

ill–tempered *adj* having a bad temper <an *ill-tempered* old man>
syn bad-tempered, dyspeptic, hot-tempered, ill-humored, ill-natured, ‖rusty, tempersome
rel crabbed, surly; fractious, huffy, irritable, peevish, petulant, querulous, snappish, sour, waspish; shrewish, vixenish
con calm, easy, placid, serene, tranquil; amiable, complaisant, considerate, good-natured, kindly, obliging, tolerant
ant good-tempered, sweet-tempered, well-tempered

ill–timed *adj* **1** *syn* see UNSEASONABLE 1
ant seasonable
2 *syn* see IMPROPER 1

ill–treat *vb syn* see ABUSE 4
rel aggrieve, harass, harry, molest
con befriend, relieve, succor; countenance, encourage, favor, patronize

illude *vb syn* see DECEIVE

illume *vb* **1** *syn* see ILLUMINATE 1
2 *syn* see ILLUMINATE 2

illuminant *adj syn* see ENLIGHTENING

illuminate *vb* **1** to supply with physical light <a room dimly *illuminated* by firelight>
syn illume, illumine, light, lighten
rel brighten; irradiate; floodlight, highlight, spotlight; fire, ignite, kindle
con blur, cloud, darken, dim, dull, obscure, pale
2 to supply with spiritual or intellectual light <the worth of a truly *illuminating* book>
syn edify, enlighten, illume, illumine, improve, irradiate, uplift
rel better, improve; ennoble, exalt, refine; finish, mature, perfect, polish
con becloud, cloud, darken, obfuscate, obscure, overshadow, shadow
3 *syn* see CLARIFY 2
rel construe, define, dramatize, expound, express, gloss, interpret
idiom shed light on (*or* upon)
con baffle, confound, confuse, mystify, pose, puzzle, stump

illuminati *n pl syn* see INTELLIGENTSIA

illuminating *adj syn* see ENLIGHTENING

illuminative *adj syn* see ENLIGHTENING

illumine *vb* **1** *syn* see ILLUMINATE 1
2 *syn* see ILLUMINATE 2

illumining *adj syn* see ENLIGHTENING

ill–use *vb syn* see ABUSE 4
con befriend, relieve, succor; countenance, encourage, favor, patronize

illusion *n* **1** *syn* see DELUSION 1
rel invention; bubble, chimera, dream, will-o'-the-wisp; appearance, seeming, semblance
2 *syn* see PIPE DREAM

illusionist *n syn* see MAGICIAN 2

illusive *adj syn* see APPARENT 2

illusory *adj* **1** *syn* see FICTITIOUS 1
ant factual
2 *syn* see APPARENT 2
rel chimerical, fanciful, fantastic, imaginary, unreal, visionary; deceptive, delusive, delusory, misleading
con actual, real, veritable; authentic, true, valid
ant factual

illustrate *vb* **1** *syn* see CLARIFY 2
rel display, exhibit, expose, show; disclose, discover, reveal
con cloak, conceal, enshroud, mask, screen, shroud, veil
2 *syn* see EXEMPLIFY 1
rel elucidate, explain, expound, interpret; demonstrate, manifest, show; enliven, vivify
3 *syn* see REPRESENT 2
4 *syn* see SHOW 2

illustration *n* **1** *syn* see EXAMPLE 3
2 *syn* see INSTANCE

illustrational *adj syn* see PICTORIAL 1

illustrative *adj syn* see PICTORIAL 1

illustratory *adj syn* see PICTORIAL 1

illustrious *adj syn* see FAMOUS 2
rel glorious, resplendent, splendid, sublime; conspicuous, lofty, outstanding, signal, striking
con abject, inglorious, mean; disgraceful, dishonorable, ignoble, ignominious, shameful

ant infamous

illustriousness *n syn* see EMINENCE 1
   ant infamy

ill will *n syn* see MALICE
   rel hostility, rancor, venom
   ant goodwill

image *n* 1 one strikingly like another especially in appearance or manner <she was the *image* of her mother>
   syn double, picture, portrait, ringer, simulacrum, spit, spitting image
   rel counterpart, equal, equivalent, match
   idiom chip off the old block, dead ringer, speaking likeness, spit and image
   2 *syn* see IDEA

image *vb* 1 *syn* see REPRESENT 1
   2 *syn* see THINK 1
   3 *syn* see REFLECT 1

imaginable *adj syn* see THINKABLE 2
   ant unimaginable

imaginary *adj* 1 having no real existence but existing in imagination <elves are *imaginary* beings>
   syn fancied, fanciful, imagined, notional, shadowy
   rel imaginative; abstract, hypothetical, ideal, visionary; apparitional, chimerical, fantastic, figmental, hallucinatory, illusory, phantasmal, phantasmic, quixotic, spectral; unreal, unsubstantial
   con genuine, true, valid
   ant actual, real
   2 *syn* see FICTITIOUS 1
   ant actual, real

imagination *n* the power or function of the mind by which mental images are formed or the exercise of that power <children have great *imagination*>
   syn fancy, fantasy (*or* phantasy), imaginativeness
   rel creativity, inspiration, invention, inventiveness, visualization
   con literalness, matter-of-factness, prosaism, unimaginativeness

imaginativeness *n syn* see IMAGINATION
   ant unimaginativeness

imagine *vb* 1 *syn* see THINK 1
   2 *syn* see UNDERSTAND 3

imagined *adj syn* see IMAGINARY 1
   con known, recognized, seen

imbecile *adj syn* see RETARDED

imbecile *n* 1 *syn* see FOOL 4
   2 *syn* see FOOL 1

imbibe *vb* 1 *syn* see ABSORB 1
   2 *syn* see DRINK 1
   3 *syn* see DRINK 3

imbricate *vb syn* see OVERLAP

imbroglio *n syn* see QUARREL

imbrued *adj syn* see BLOODY 1

imbue *vb syn* see INFUSE 1

imitate *vb* 1 *syn* see COPY
   2 *syn* see MIMIC

imitation *adj syn* see ARTIFICIAL 2
   ant real

imitation *n* something made or produced as an often inferior likeness of something else <usually wore *imitations* of her costly jewels>
   syn copy, ersatz, simulacrum
   rel counterfeit, fake, forgery, phony, sham, simulation; counterpart, duplicate, replica, reproduction; likeness, semblance
   ant original

imitative *adj* 1 *syn* see ONOMATOPOEIC
   2 *syn* see SLAVISH 3

immaculate *adj* 1 *syn* see CHASTE
   ant maculate
   2 *syn* see IMPECCABLE 1
   3 *syn* see CLEAN 1

immalleable *adj syn* see STIFF 1
   ant malleable

immaterial *adj* 1 not composed of matter <*immaterial* forces>
   syn asomatous, bodiless, disbodied, discarnate, disembodied, incorporeal, insubstantial, metaphysical, nonmaterial, nonphysical, spiritual, unbodied, ||uncorporal, unembodied, unfleshly, unmaterial, unphysical, unsubstantial
   rel impalpable, imponderable; psychic, subjective; aerial, airy, ethereal; insensible, unearthly, unworldly; supernatural; celestial, heavenly; apparitional, ghostly, shadowy

con bodily, corporeal, fleshly, incarnate; material, objective, palpable, physical, substantial; mundane, terrestrial, worldly
   ant material
   2 *syn* see IRRELEVANT
   ant material

immature *adj* 1 *syn* see YOUNG 1
   rel precocious, premature
   ant mature
   2 *syn* see CHILDISH
   ant mature

immeasurable *adj* 1 *syn* see INCALCULABLE 1
   2 *syn* see LIMITLESS

immediacy *n syn* see PROXIMITY

immediate *adj* 1 *syn* see DIRECT 4
   ant distant (*of relatives*)
   2 *syn* see INSTANTANEOUS
   3 *syn* see CLOSE 6

immediately *adv* 1 in direct connection without intermediary <*immediately* in front of the viewers>
   syn contiguously, directly
   2 *syn* see AWAY 3
   rel anon, shortly, soon
   idiom right now

immedicable *adj syn* see HOPELESS 2
   ant medicable

immense *adj syn* see HUGE

immensely *adv syn* see EVER 6

immensity *n syn* see ENORMITY 2

immerse *vb* 1 *syn* see DIP 1
   rel saturate, soak
   2 *syn* see BAPTIZE
   3 *syn* see ENGAGE 4

immersed *adj syn* see INTENT

immigrant *n syn* see EMIGRANT

imminent *adj* 1 about to take place <their departure is *imminent*>
   syn impending, proximate
   rel approaching, coming, nearing, upcoming; brewing, gathering; pending; likely, possible, probable; ineluctable, inescapable, inevasible, inevitable, unavoidable, unescapable
   idiom in prospect, in store, in the cards, in the offing, in the wind, in view
   con distant, far-off, remote
   2 menacingly near <a thunderstorm was *imminent*>
   syn lowering (*or* louring), lowery (*or* loury), menacing, overhanging, threatening
   rel alarming, ominous, sinister; brewing, gathering; minatory

immingle *vb syn* see MIX 1

immix *vb syn* see MIX 1

immixture *n syn* see MIXTURE

immobile *adj* 1 *syn* see IMMOVABLE 1
   ant mobile, movable
   2 *syn* see STATIC

immobilize *vb syn* see PARALYZE 1

immoderate *adj* 1 *syn* see EXCESSIVE 1
   ant moderate
   2 *syn* see EXCESSIVE 2
   ant moderate

immoderation *n syn* see EXCESS 3
   ant moderation

immolate *vb syn* see SACRIFICE 1

immoral *adj* 1 *syn* see IMPURE 1
   ant moral
   2 *syn* see WRONG 1
   ant moral

immorality *n syn* see VICE 1
   ant morality

immortal *adj* 1 not subject to death <the *immortal* gods>
   syn deathless, undying; *compare* EVERLASTING 1
   rel endless, enduring, imperishable, indestructible, perpetual, sempiternal, timeless
   con ephemeral, evanescent, fleeting, fugitive, passing, short-lived, transient, transitory

---

syn synonym(s)   **rel** related word(s)
ant antonym(s)   **con** contrasted word(s)
idiom idiomatic equivalent(s)
|| use limited; if in doubt, see a dictionary

ant mortal
2 syn see EVERLASTING 1
immortality *n syn* see ETERNITY 2
ant mortality
immortalize *vb syn* see PERPETUATE
immotile *adj syn* see IMMOVABLE 1
ant motile
immotive *adj syn* see IMMOVABLE 1
immovable *adj* 1 incapable of moving or being moved <an *immovable* rock>
syn fixed, immobile, immotile, immotive, irremovable, ‖sitfast, steadfast, unmovable
rel adamant, fast, rooted, stable, stationary, stuck, unmoving, unyielding
con portable, removable, transferable, transportable
ant movable
2 syn see INFLEXIBLE 3
immunity *n syn* see EXEMPTION
ant susceptibility
immure *vb* 1 *syn* see ENCLOSE 1
2 syn see IMPRISON
immusical *adj syn* see DISSONANT 1
ant musical
immutable *adj syn* see INFLEXIBLE 3
ant mutable
imp *n* 1 a small demon, devil, or wicked spirit <the *imps* of hell>
syn deviling, devilkin
rel elf, gnome, goblin, gremlin, ‖hob, hobgoblin, kobold, ouph, pixie, puck, sprite, troll
2 syn see URCHIN
impact *n* a forcible or enforced contact between two or more things <a crater formed by the *impact* of a meteorite>
syn appulse, blow, bump, clash, collision, concussion, crash, impingement, jar, jolt, jounce, percussion, shock, smash, wallop
rel brunt; buffet, hit, pound, punch, rap, slap, smiting, strike, stroke; bounce, quake, quiver, rock, shake, tremble, tremor; encounter, meeting
impair *vb syn* see INJURE 1
rel sap, undermine, weaken
con ameliorate, better
ant improve; repair
impaired *adj syn* see DAMAGED
impale *vb* to pierce or fix with or as if with something pointed <an insect *impaled* on a pin>
syn lance, skewer, skiver, spear, spike, spit, transfix, transpierce
rel perforate, pierce, prick, punch, puncture, stab
impalpable *adj* 1 *syn* see IMPERCEPTIBLE
ant palpable
2 syn see FINE 2
imparity *n syn* see DISPARITY
ant parity
impart *vb syn* see COMMUNICATE 1
impartial *adj syn* see FAIR 4
ant partial
impartially *adv syn* see EVENLY 2
impassable *adj* 1 not allowing passage <an *impassable* barrier>
syn impenetrable, impermeable, imperviable, impervious, unpierceable
con penetrable, permeable, pervious
ant passable
2 syn see INSUPERABLE
impasse *n* 1 *syn* see DEAD END
2 syn see PREDICAMENT
impassible *adj syn* see INSENSIBLE 5
rel cold, emotionless, passionless, unemotional, unfeeling; inert, unresponsive
ant passible
impassioned *adj* actuated by or showing intense feeling <*impassioned* oratory>
syn ardent, blazing, burning, dithyrambic, fervent, fervid, fiery, flaming, glowing, hot-blooded, overheated, passionate, perfervid, red-hot, torrid, white-hot
rel feverish, fierce, furious, intense, vehement, violent; deep, profound, warm, zealous; gushing, gushy, maudlin, melodramatic, mushy, overemotional, romantic, sentimental
con cold, cool, dispassionate, frigid, icy, unemotional; objective
ant unimpassioned

impassive *adj* 1 unresponsive to what might normally excite interest or emotion <*impassive* endurance of pain>
syn apathetic, dry, matter-of-fact, phlegmatic, stoic, stolid
rel calm, cold, cool; collected, composed, dispassionate, emotionless, imperturbable, inexcitable, unexcitable, unflappable; inexpressive, reserved, reticent, taciturn, unemotional, unexpressive; bovine, placid, passionless, spiritless, unconcerned, wooden; callous, hardened, indurated, insensible; cold-blooded, cold-hearted, heartless
con compassionate, sympathetic, tender, warm, warmhearted
ant responsive
2 syn see INSUSCEPTIBLE
impassivity *n syn* see APATHY 1
impatient *adj* 1 lacking power to endure hardship, distress, or opposition <married to an *impatient* self-centered man>
syn chafing, fretful, unpatient
rel abrupt, hasty, headlong, impetuous; anxious, edgy, itchy, nervous; irascible, irritable
idiom all of a stew
con enduring, forbearing, tolerant; self-controlled, Spartan, stoic
ant patient
2 syn see INTOLERANT 1
rel demanding, harsh
3 syn see EAGER
ant patient
impeach *vb syn* see ACCUSE
impeccable *adj* 1 absolutely correct and beyond criticism <*impeccable* manners>
syn errorless, exquisite, faultless, flawless, immaculate, irreproachable
rel accurate, clean, correct, exact, nice, perfect, precise, right; infallible, unerring
con defective, deficient, faulty; blameworthy, censurable, criticizable, culpable; cursory, shallow, superficial, uncritical
ant peccant
2 syn see PERFECT 2
impecunious *adj syn* see POOR 1
ant affluent; flush
impecuniousness *n syn* see POVERTY 1
ant affluence; flushness
impedance *n syn* see ENCUMBRANCE
impede *vb syn* see HINDER
rel discomfit, disconcert, embarrass, faze, rattle
ant aid, assist
impediment *n* 1 *syn* see ENCUMBRANCE
ant aid, assistance
2 syn see OBSTACLE
impel *vb syn* see MOVE 5
rel compel, constrain, force; foment, incite, instigate; goad, spur; inspire, motivate
con check, curb, inhibit
ant restrain
impend *vb syn* see LOOM 2
impending *adj syn* see IMMINENT 1
impenetrable *adj* 1 *syn* see IMPASSABLE 1
rel firm, solid, substantial
ant penetrable
2 syn see INCOMPREHENSIBLE 1
ant penetrable
3 syn see MYSTERIOUS
impenetrate *vb syn* see PERMEATE
impenitent *adj syn* see REMORSELESS
ant penitent
imperative *adj* 1 *syn* see MASTERFUL 1
rel bidding, commanding, ordering; harsh, stern
con begging, entreating, imploring; lenient, mild, soft
2 syn see PRESSING
rel acute, critical, crucial
3 syn see ESSENTIAL 4
rel basic, fundamental; claimed, demanded, exacted
4 syn see MANDATORY
imperceptible *adj* incapable of being apprehended by the senses or intellect <*imperceptible* changes in temperature>
syn impalpable, imponderable, inappreciable, indiscernible, insensible, intangible, invisible, unapparent, unappreciable, undiscernible, unobservable, unperceivable
rel faint, inconspicuous, indistinct, indistinguishable, insignificant, obscure, undistinguishable, unnoticeable, vague; ephemeral, evanescent, fugitive, momentary; slight, trivial

con apparent, appreciable, discernible, observable, palpable, ponderable, sensible, visible
ant perceptible, perceivable

imperceptive *adj* lacking perception or insight < *imperceptive* criticism >
syn impercipient, unperceiving, unperceptive
rel unappreciative, undiscerning, unobservant; cursory, shallow, slapdash, superficial
con astute, discerning, discriminating, judicious, perspicacious; delicate, nice, refined, sensitive, subtle
ant perceiving, perceptive, percipient

impercipient *adj syn* see IMPERCEPTIVE
ant perceiving, perceptive, percipient

imperfect *adj syn* see FAULTY
ant perfect

imperfection *n* an instance of failure to reach a standard of excellence or perfection < watch for *imperfections* in the cloth >
syn deficiency, demerit, fault, shortcoming, sin
rel blemish, defect, flaw; failing, foible, frailty
ant perfection

imperial *adj syn* see MASTERFUL 1

imperil *vb syn* see ENDANGER

imperious *adj* **1** *syn* see MASTERFUL 1
rel heavy-handed, oppressive, strict, stringent; absolute, arbitrary
con considerate, easy, gentle, kindly
2 *syn* see MANDATORY

imperishable *adj syn* see INDESTRUCTIBLE

impermanent *adj syn* see TRANSIENT
ant permanent

impermeable *adj syn* see IMPASSABLE 1
ant permeable

impersonal *adj* **1** *syn* see NEUTRAL
2 *syn* see FAIR 4
3 *syn* see MATTER-OF-FACT 3

impersonate *vb syn* see ACT 1

impersonator *n syn* see ACTOR 1

impertinence *n syn* see INSOLENCE

impertinent *adj* **1** *syn* see IRRELEVANT
ant pertinent
2 going beyond what is proper or acceptable in thrusting oneself into the affairs of others < *impertinent* interference with her sister's family >
syn busy, intrusive, meddlesome, ‖nebby, obtrusive, officious, polypragmatic
rel arrogant, bold, brash, brazen, fresh, impudent, pert, presumptuous, saucy; inquisitive, interfering, meddling, nosy, prying; offensive, rude
con decent, decorous, proper, seemly; reserved, reticent, silent; apposite, germane, pertinent, relevant
3 *syn* see RUDE 6
4 *syn* see INSOLENT 2

imperturbability *n syn* see EQUANIMITY

imperturbable *adj syn* see COOL 2
rel complacent, self-satisfied, smug; unaffected, unmoved, untouched
con discomfited, disconcerted, fazed, rattled; irascible, splenetic, testy
ant choleric; touchy

imperviable *adj syn* see IMPASSABLE 1

impervious *adj syn* see IMPASSABLE 1
ant pervious

impetuous *adj syn* see PRECIPITATE 1
rel spontaneous; restive; ardent, fervid, impassioned, passionate
con equable, even, steady; advised, considered, deliberate, planned, premeditated

impetuously *adv syn* see PELL-MELL

impetus *n syn* see STIMULUS

impignorate *vb syn* see PAWN

impingement *n syn* see IMPACT

impious *adj* **1** lacking reverence for holy or sacred matters < made *impious* remarks about the church >
syn irreverent, irreverential, profane, ungodly, unhallowed, unholy
rel godless, iconoclastic, irreligious, sacrilegious, scandalous, undevout
con devout, godly, religious, spiritual
ant pious

2 lacking due respect (as toward one's parents) < an *impious* son >
syn unduteous, undutiful
rel disobedient, froward, unfaithful, wayward; contrary, perverse, wrongheaded
con duteous, dutiful

impish *adj syn* see PLAYFUL 1
rel arch, pert, saucy; flippant, fresh, giddy; casual, devil-may-care, free and easy, offhand

impishness *n syn* see MISCHIEVOUSNESS

implacable *adj syn* see GRIM 3
con peaceable, tractable; kindly, tolerant
ant placable

implant *vb* to introduce into the mind < *implanted* worthy ideals in their children >
syn inculcate, infix, inseminate, instill
rel imbue, infuse, ingrain, inoculate, leaven, root; impenetrate, impregnate, penetrate, permeate, pervade, saturate; inspire

implausible *adj* not plausible or readily believable < an *implausible* explanation >
syn flimsy, improbable, inconceivable, incredible, thick, thin, unbelievable, unconceivable, unconvincing, unsubstantial, weak; *compare* TENUOUS 3
rel doubtful, dubious, fishy; problematic, puzzling, suspect
idiom a bit thick
con meaty, pithy; solid, sound, substantial; believable, conceivable, credible; likely, probable
ant plausible

implement *n* a usually relatively simple device for performing a mechanical or manual operation < spades, hoes, and other gardener's *implements* >
syn instrument, tool, utensil
rel apparatus, appliance; contrivance, device; contraption, gadget

implement *vb* **1** *syn* see FULFILL 1
2 *syn* see ENFORCE
rel actualize, materialize, realize

implemental *adj syn* see INSTRUMENTAL

impliable *adj syn* see STIFF 1
ant pliable

implicate *vb syn* see INVOLVE 1
rel affect, concern; incriminate
con absolve, acquit, exculpate, exonerate

implicated *adj syn* see INTERESTED

implication *n syn* see ASSOCIATION 4

implicit *adj* **1** *syn* see TACIT 1
idiom taken for granted
ant explicit
2 being such in essential character < our *implicit* freedom is better than your nominal liberty >
syn constructive, practical, virtual
rel absolute, complete, unqualified, wholehearted; genuine, real
ant spelled out

implied *adj syn* see TACIT 1

imploration *n syn* see PRAYER

implore *vb syn* see BEG

imply *vb* **1** *syn* see POINT 2
2 *syn* see SUGGEST 1
con state; express; affirm, assert, declare

impolite *adj syn* see RUDE 6
ant polite

impolitic *adj* **1** *syn* see UNWISE
ant politic
2 *syn* see INADVISABLE
ant politic
3 *syn* see TACTLESS

imponderable *adj syn* see IMPERCEPTIBLE
ant appreciable, ponderable

imponderous *adj syn* see LIGHT 1
ant ponderous

import *vb* **1** *syn* see MEAN 2
2 *syn* see MATTER

import *n* **1** *syn* see MEANING 1

---

syn synonym(s)
ant antonym(s)
idiom idiomatic equivalent(s)
‖ use limited; if in doubt, see a dictionary

rel related word(s)
con contrasted word(s)

rel construction, interpretation
2 syn see IMPORTANCE
rel value, worth; design, intent, object, objective, purpose; emphasis, stress
importance *n* the quality or state of being of notable worth or influence < persons of national and worldwide *importance* >
syn consequence, import, magnitude, moment, momentousness, pith, significance, ‖signification, weight, weightiness
rel conspicuousness; distinction, eminence, mark, prominence, salience; notability, note, noteworthiness, reputation, standing; substance, value, worth, worthiness; gravity, seriousness
con inconsequence, insignificance, paltriness, pettiness, triviality
ant unimportance
important *adj* **1** marked by or indicative of notable worth or consequence < an *important* discovery > < his manner was grave and *important* >
syn big, consequential, considerable, material, meaningful, momentous, significant, substantial, weighty
rel conspicuous, distinctive, exceptional, impressive, marked, memorable, notable, noteworthy, noticeable, outstanding, prominent, remarkable, salient, unusual; essential; valuable, worthwhile; worthy; effective, potent, powerful, telling; big-time, first-class, first-rate, front-page, top-notch; distinguished, eminent, famous, noted
con inconsiderable, little, minor, paltry, petty, slight, trivial
ant unimportant
2 syn see POMPOUS 1
importunate *adj syn* see PRESSING
rel persevering, persistent; dogged, pertinacious
importune *vb syn* see BEG
impose *vb* **1 syn** see DICTATE
rel charge, command, enjoin, order; demand, exact, require; compel, constrain, oblige
2 syn see LEVY
3 syn see INFLICT 2
4 to force another to accept < *imposed* all the dirty jobs on her sister >
syn foist, wish; *compare* FOIST 3, INFLICT 2
rel burden, lade, saddle; fob, fob off, palm off
idiom take advantage of
5 to take usually unwarranted advantage < did not wish to *impose* by turning up unannounced >
syn infringe, intrude, obtrude, presume
rel encroach, trespass
idiom make free, take liberties
impose (on *or* upon) *vb syn* see EXPLOIT 2
imposing *adj* **1 syn** see GRAND 1
rel impressive, moving; imperial, regal
ant unimposing
2 syn see PRETENTIOUS 3
impossible *adj* **1** not capable of being realized or attained < *impossible* goals >
syn impracticable, impractical, infeasible, irrealizable, unattainable, unfeasible, unrealizable, unworkable
rel absurd, inexecutable, unobtainable, unreasonable, unthinkable
idiom out of the question
con attainable, feasible, realizable; practicable, practical, rational, reasonable
ant possible
2 syn see HOPELESS 2
impost *n syn* see TAX 1
impostor *n* one who passes himself off as something or someone he is not < the presumed heir was discovered to be an *impostor* >
syn fake, faker, fraud, humbug, phony, pretender; *compare* CHARLATAN
rel imitator, mimic; beguiler, deceiver, misleader; cheat, pettifogger, shyster, trickster; hypocrite; charlatan, mountebank, quack; bluffer, dissembler, four-flusher, shammer
idiom wolf in sheep's clothing
imposture *n* the act, practice, or an instance of imposing on another by use of an assumed character or name < his claims were based on *imposture* >
syn cheat, counterfeit, deceit, deception, fake, flam, flimflam, fraud, gyp, hoax, humbug, mare's nest, phony, put-on, ‖rig, sell, sham, spoof, swindle

rel copy, imitation; fabrication, forgery; artifice, feint, gambit, maneuver, ploy, ruse, sleight, stratagem, trick, wile; make-believe, pretense, pretension
impotent *adj* **1 syn** see POWERLESS
rel crippled, disabled, enfeebled
con able, capable, competent
ant potent
2 syn see WEAK 4
con forceful, powerful, puissant, strenuous, vigorous
ant potent
3 syn see STERILE 1
impoverish *vb* **1 syn** see DEPLETE
ant enrich
2 syn see RUIN 3
impoverished *adj syn* see POOR 1
impoverishment *n syn* see POVERTY 1
impracticable *adj* **1 syn** see IMPOSSIBLE 1
ant feasible, practicable
2 incapable of being successfully used or turned to account < a route through the mountains that is *impracticable* in winter >
syn impractical, nonfunctional, unfunctional, unserviceable, unusable, unworkable, useless
rel disadvantageous, unacceptable, undesirable, unsatisfactory; awkward, inconvenient, troublesome
con functional, practical, serviceable, usable, useful, workable
ant practicable
impractical *adj* **1** incapable of dealing prudently with practical matters < a very *impractical* person whose checkbook never balanced >
syn ivory-tower, ivory-towered, ivory-towerish, nonrealistic, unpractical, unrealistic, viewy
rel idealistic, otherworldly, quixotic, romantic, starry-eyed, visionary
con commonsensible, commonsensical, realistic, sensible, worldly-wise
ant practical
2 syn see IMPRACTICABLE 2
ant practical
3 syn see IMPOSSIBLE 1
imprecate *vb syn* see SWEAR 3
imprecation *n* **1 syn** see BLASPHEMY 1
2 syn see PRAYER
3 syn see CURSE 1
con blessing
impregnable *adj syn* see INVINCIBLE 1
rel safe, secure; defended, guarded, protected, safeguarded, shielded
con exposed, open, susceptible
impregnate *vb* **1 syn** see PERMEATE
rel inoculate, leaven
2 syn see SOAK 1
impress *vb* **1 syn** see ENGRAVE 2
2 syn see AFFECT
rel enthuse, electrify, thrill; excite, galvanize, pique, provoke, stimulate
idiom make (*or* leave) one's mark
3 to fix in the mind or memory by emphasis or repetition < the speaker *impressed* his principal thesis upon his audience >
syn drive, grave, hammer, pound, stamp
rel establish, fix, set
idiom drive home to one, fix in one's mind, get into one's head
impress *n syn* see IMPRESSION 1
impressible *adj syn* see SENTIENT 3
impression *n* **1** the perceptible trace or traces left by pressure < the *impression* made by a die >
syn impress, imprint, indentation, print, stamp
rel dent, dint, hollow; trace, track, vestige; mark, sign
2 syn see IDEA
3 syn see EDITION
impressionable *adj syn* see SENTIENT 3
rel affectable, influenceable
impressive *adj* **1 syn** see MOVING 2
rel august, grand, imposing, majestic, noble; splendid, superb; arresting, notable, striking
ant unimpressive
2 syn see GRAND 2
imprint *vb syn* see ENGRAVE 2
imprint *n syn* see IMPRESSION 1

imprison *vb* to shut up closely so that escape is impossible or unlikely < the offender was quickly sentenced and *imprisoned* >
syn bastille, confine, constrain, immure, incarcerate, intern, jail, jug, ||prison, ||quod
rel circumscribe, limit, restrict; check, curb, restrain
idiom put under lock and key
con free, liberate, release

improbable *adj* **1** not likely to be true or to occur < the immediate success of their plan is *improbable* >
syn doubtful, dubious, questionable, unlikely
ant probable
2 *syn* see IMPLAUSIBLE

impromptu *n syn* see IMPROVISATION

impromptu *adj syn* see EXTEMPORANEOUS
rel prompt, quick

improper *adj* **1** unsuited to the circumstances or the occasion < wore quite *improper* dress for such a formal reception >
syn ill-timed, inadmissible, inappropriate, inapt, inept, intempestive, malapropos, unapt, unbecoming, unbefitting, uncomely, undue, unfitting, unseasonable, unseemly, unsuitable, untimely
rel infelicitous, unhappy; inapplicable, inapposite; fresh, impertinent, sassy; crude, gauche, tactless
idiom out of place, out of season
con apposite, appropriate, apropos, apt, becoming, befitting, felicitous, fitting, germane, happy, opportune, pat, pertinent, seasonable, suitable, timely, well-timed
ant proper
2 *syn* see INDECOROUS
rel informal, unceremonious, unconventional
con correct, right
ant proper

impropriety *n* **1** the quality or state of being improper (as in social behavior) < was shocked by the *impropriety* of their actions >
syn incorrectness, indecorousness, indecorum, inelegance, unbecomingness, unmeetness, unseemliness, untowardness
rel inadmissibility, objectionableness, unacceptableness
con becomingness, decency, decorousness, decorum, meetness
ant propriety, seemliness
2 *syn* see FAUX PAS *compare* ERROR 2
3 *syn* see BARBARISM

improve *vb* **1** to make more acceptable or bring nearer to some standard < studied hard to *improve* his chances of success >
syn ameliorate, amend, better, help, meliorate
rel cultivate, develop, perfect; correct, emend, rectify, reform, remedy; edit, revise; enhance, enrich, refine, rub up, upgrade
con diminish, downgrade, lessen, lower
2 *syn* see ILLUMINATE 2
3 to grow or become better (as in health or well-being) < the invalid is steadily *improving* >
syn ameliorate, convalesce, gain, look up, mend, perk (up), recuperate
rel advance, better, progress; recover; rally, revive, strengthen
idiom gain ground, make progress
con decline, deteriorate, fail, flag, languish, run down, sink, weaken

improvident *adj* not foreseeing or providing for the future < an *improvident* way of life >
syn thriftless, unthrift, unthrifty
rel careless, heedless, imprudent; extravagant, prodigal, profligate, spendthrift; lavish, profuse, reckless; uneconomical, wasteful
con careful, economical, frugal, parsimonious, prudent, saving, sparing
ant provident, thrifty

improvisate *vb syn* see IMPROVISE

improvisation *n* something that is improvised < the pianist played several clever *improvisations* >
syn autoschediasm, extemporization, impromptu

improvise *vb* to perform or provide on the spur of the moment < *improvise* an excuse for being late >
syn ad-lib, extemporize, improvisate
rel concoct, contrive, devise, invent

improvised *adj syn* see EXTEMPORANEOUS

imprudent *adj* **1** *syn* see UNWISE
ant prudent
2 *syn* see INADVISABLE

ant prudent

impudence *n syn* see INSOLENCE

impudent *adj* **1** *syn* see WISE 5
2 *syn* see INSOLENT 2
3 *syn* see SHAMELESS

impugn *vb syn* see DENY 4
rel assail, attack
idiom call in (or into) question (or doubt), throw doubt on
con back, support, uphold
ant advocate; authenticate

impugnable *adj syn* see DOUBTFUL 1

impulse *n syn* see STIMULUS
rel excitant; lust, passion, urge; actuation, drive, impulsion

impulsive *adj syn* see SPONTANEOUS
rel abrupt, hasty, headlong, impetuous, precipitate, sudden
con considered, designed, premeditated; calculating, cautious, circumspect
ant deliberate

impulsiveness *n syn* see ABANDON 2

impunity *n syn* see EXEMPTION

impure *adj* **1** morally or mentally unclean < *impure* thoughts >
syn dirty, immoral, unchaste, unclean, uncleanly
rel belowstairs, carnal, immodest, indecent, indecorous, lascivious, lewd, lustful, prurient, scarlet, sensual; filthy, vile
con chaste, clean, cleanly, decent, decorous, immaculate, modest, virtuous; moral
ant pure
2 *syn* see DIRTY 1
3 made unfit for ceremonial purposes < altars overturned and sacred vessels made *impure* by the touch of profane hands >
syn common, defiled, desecrated, polluted, profaned, unclean
rel unhallowed, unholy
con clean, consecrated, undefiled
ant pure
4 *syn* see UNREFINED 3

impute *vb syn* see ASCRIBE
rel accuse, indict; adduce; hint, insinuate, intimate

in *adj syn* see STYLISH

in *n syn* see PULL 2

inability *n* lack of sufficient power, resources, or capacity to perform < suffered from an *inability* to make quick decisions >
syn inadequacy, incapability, incapacity, incompetence, ineffectiveness, ineffectualness, inefficacy
rel inadeptness, inaptitude, inaptness, inefficiency, ineptitude, ineptness
con adequacy, capability, capacity; competence, efficiency
ant ability

inaccessible *adj* not capable of being achieved < an *inaccessible* goal >
syn inapproachable, unapproachable, unattainable, un-come-at-able, ungetatable, unobtainable, unreachable
rel distant, far, faraway, far-off, out-of-the-way, remote
ant accessible

inaccurate *adj syn* see FALSE 1
con right, true
ant accurate

inaction *n* lack of action or activity < the delay was due to the committee's *inaction* >
syn inactiveness, inactivity
rel drift, idleness, indolence, inertness, lethargy, quiescence, slackness, slothfulness, torpidity
con activeness, activity

inactive *adj* not characterized by or engaged in usual or normal activity < forced by illness to lead an *inactive* life >
syn asleep, idle, inert, passive, quiet, sleepy
rel abeyant, dormant, inoperative, latent, quiescent; do-nothing, indolent, lethargic, lymphatic, slack, slothful, sluggish, torpid; motionless, sedentary, static; disengaged, jobless, unemployed, unoccupied, unworking; ossified
con busy, employed, engaged, occupied; energetic, strenuous, vigorous; animated, brisk, lively
ant active

inactiveness *n syn* see INACTION

---

syn synonym(s)   *rel* related word(s)
ant antonym(s)   *con* contrasted word(s)
idiom idiomatic equivalent(s)
|| use limited; if in doubt, see a dictionary

inactivity *n syn* see INACTION
  ant activity
in addition *adv syn* see AGAIN 4
inadept *adj syn* see UNSKILLFUL 1
  ant adept
inadequacy *n* **1** *syn* see INABILITY
  2 *syn* see FAILURE 3
  ant adequacy
inadequate *adj* **1** *syn* see DEFICIENT 1
  ant adequate
  2 *syn* see SHORT 3
  ant adequate
  3 *syn* see MEAGER
  ant adequate
  4 *syn* see WEAK 4
  ant adequate
inadmissible *adj* **1** *syn* see IMPROPER 1
  2 *syn* see OBJECTIONABLE
  ant admissible
in advance *adv syn* see BEFORE 1
in advance of *prep* **1** *syn* see BEFORE 1
  2 *syn* see UNTIL
inadvertent *adj* **1** *syn* see CARELESS 1
  ant advertent
  2 *syn* see UNINTENTIONAL
inadvisable *adj* not likely to have a satisfactory outcome <it seemed *inadvisable* to go any farther because of threatening weather>
  syn ill-advised, impolitic, imprudent, inexpedient, unadvisable, unexpedient
  rel careless, inappropriate, incautious, rash, undesirable, unsensible; foolish, indiscreet, pointless, unwise; foolhardy, harebrained
  con expedient, judicious, politic, prudent, sensible, wise
  ant advisable
in all *adv syn* see ALTOGETHER 2
in all probability *adv syn* see PRESUMABLY
inalterable *adj syn* see INFLEXIBLE 3
  ant alterable
inamorata *n* **1** *syn* see GIRL FRIEND 2
  2 *syn* see MISTRESS
inamorato *n syn* see BOYFRIEND 2
in and out *adv syn* see THOROUGHLY 2
inane *adj syn* see INSIPID 3
  rel asinine, fatuous, foolish, silly; idle, vain; blank, empty, hollow
  con expressive, meaningful, pregnant, significant, weighty
  ant deep, profound
inanimate *adj* **1** *syn* see INSENSATE 1
  ant animate
  2 *syn* see DEAD 1
  ant animate; living
inanity *n syn* see FOOLISHNESS
inapplicable *adj syn* see IRRELEVANT
  ant applicable
inapposite *adj syn* see IRRELEVANT
  ant apposite
inappreciable *adj* **1** *syn* see IMPERCEPTIBLE
  ant appreciable
  2 *syn* see MEAGER
inapproachable *adj syn* see INACCESSIBLE
  ant approachable
inappropriate *adj* **1** *syn* see UNFIT 1
  rel indecorous, unseemly; inconsonant
  con felicitous, fitting, happy, meet, proper; fit, suitable
  ant appropriate
  2 *syn* see IMPROPER 1
inapt *adj* **1** *syn* see UNFIT 1
  rel awkward, clumsy, gauche, maladroit; banal, flat, insipid, jejune
  con apposite, germane, pertinent, relevant
  ant apt
  2 *syn* see IMPROPER 1
  ant apt
  3 *syn* see UNSKILLFUL 1
  ant adept
inarguable *adj syn* see POSITIVE 3
  ant arguable

inarticulate *adj* **1** *syn* see DUMB 1
  ant articulate
  2 *syn* see TACIT 1
  3 failing to give or incapable of giving clear or effective verbal expression to one's ideas or feelings <made some *inarticulate* explanation for being late> <was completely *inarticulate* when it came to expressing affection>
  syn incoherent, maundering, tongue-tied, unvocal
  rel faltering, halting, hesitating, mumbling, stammered, stammering; blurred, indistinct
  con facile, glib, smooth
  ant articulate
inartificial *adj syn* see NATURAL 5
  ant artificial
inasmuch as *conj syn* see BECAUSE
inattentive *adj* not paying proper attention <an *inattentive* pupil dozing at his desk>
  syn inobservant, unheeding, unnoticing, unobservant, unobserving, unperceiving, unwatchful
  rel distracted, distrait, distraught; careless, heedless, thoughtless, undiscerning, unmindful, unthinking; bored, ennuyé
  ant attentive; observant
inaugural *adj syn* see FIRST 1
inaugural *n syn* see INITIATION
inaugurate *vb* **1** *syn* see INITIATE 3
  2 *syn* see BEGIN 1
  3 *syn* see INTRODUCE 3
inauguration *n syn* see INITIATION
inauspicious *adj* **1** *syn* see OMINOUS
  ant auspicious
  2 *syn* see EVIL 6
in between *prep syn* see BETWEEN 2
inborn *adj* **1** *syn* see INNATE 1
  ant acquired
  2 *syn* see INHERENT
inbred *adj syn* see INHERENT
in brief *adv syn* see BRIEFLY
incalculable *adj* **1** being great beyond calculation <*incalculable* damage>
  syn immeasurable, inestimable, measureless, uncountable, unmeasurable, unmeasured, unreckonable
  rel countless, innumerable, unnumbered, untold; boundless, enormous, infinite, limitless, vast
  con minimal, slight, trivial
  ant infinitesimal
  2 *syn* see UNCERTAIN 1
  ant calculable
in camera *adv syn* see SECRETLY
incandescent *adj syn* see BRIGHT 1
incantation *n* **1** *syn* see SPELL
  2 *syn* see MAGIC 1
incapability *n syn* see INABILITY
  ant capability
incapable *adj* **1** *syn* see UNFIT 2
  ant capable
  2 *syn* see INEFFICIENT 2
  ant capable
incapacitate *vb* **1** *syn* see PARALYZE 1
  2 *syn* see DISQUALIFY
  ant capacitate
incapacity *n syn* see INABILITY
  ant capacity
incarcerate *vb syn* see IMPRISON
incarnadine *vb syn* see REDDEN 1
incarnate *vb syn* see EMBODY 1
incarnation *n syn* see EMBODIMENT
incautious *adj* **1** lacking in caution <made an *incautious* prediction>
  syn unalert, unguarded, unvigilant, unwary, unwatchful; *compare* CARELESS 1
  rel imprudent, indiscreet, injudicious; bold, brash, impetuous, rash, reckless; neglectful, negligent, regardless, thoughtless, unmindful; hasty
  idiom caught napping, off one's guard
  con careful, circumspect, judicious, wary, watchful; discreet, judicious, prudent; sensible, thoughtful, wise
  ant cautious
  2 *syn* see RASH 1

ant cautious
3 *syn* see IRRESPONSIBLE
incendiary *n* a person who deliberately and unlawfully sets fire to a building or other property < a fire set by an *incendiary* >
syn arsonist, firebug, torch
rel pyromaniac
incendiary *adj syn* see INFLAMMATORY
incense *n* **1** *syn* see FRAGRANCE
2 *syn* see FLATTERY
incense *vb syn* see ANGER 1
ant placate
incentive *n syn* see STIMULUS
inception *n syn* see SOURCE
con closing, completion, conclusion
ant termination
inceptive *adj syn* see INITIAL 1
ant terminal
incertitude *n syn* see UNCERTAINTY
ant certitude
incessant *adj syn* see CONTINUAL
ant intermittent
inchoate *adj* **1** *syn* see FORMLESS
2 *syn* see INCOHERENT 2
incident *n syn* see OCCURRENCE
incident *adj* **1** *syn* see CONCOMITANT
ant essential, fundamental
2 *syn* see RELATED
incidental *adj syn* see ACCIDENTAL
ant essential
incidentally *adv* **1** by chance < in this discussion grave questions were brought up *incidentally* >
syn accidentally, casually, fortuitously
ant deliberately
2 by way of interjection or digression < another leading industry, *incidentally*, has quadrupled its business in four years >
syn by the bye, by the way, in passing, obiter, parenthetically
idiom in the bygoing
incipient *adj syn* see INITIAL 1
incise *vb* **1** *syn* see CUT 1
2 *syn* see ENGRAVE 1
incisive *adj* having, manifesting, or suggesting a keen alertness of mind < a man well known for his *incisive* wit >
syn biting, clear-cut, crisp, cutting, ingoing, penetrating, trenchant
rel acute, drilling, keen, sharp; acerb, acerbic, caustic, mordant, scathing, slashing, tart; concise, laconic, succinct, terse
con diffuse, prolix, verbose, wordy; feeble, limp, pithless, sapless
ant unincisive
incisiveness *n syn* see EDGE 2
incitation *n syn* see STIMULUS
incite *vb* to aid or promote the activity or development of < incite a riot >
syn abet, foment, instigate, provoke, raise, set, set on, stir (up), whip (up)
rel forward, further, promote, stimulate; set off, trigger; agitate, solicit; encourage, motivate, motive; excite, inflame, rouse
con check, curb, discourage, inhibit, restrain; calm, quiet, subdue
incitement *n syn* see STIMULUS
ant restraint; inhibition
inciter *n syn* see INSTIGATOR
incivil *adj syn* see RUDE 6
ant civil
inclement *adj syn* see SEVERE 3
ant clement
inclination *n* **1** *syn* see LEANING 2
ant disinclination
2 *syn* see WILL 1
ant disinclination
3 *syn* see APPETITE 3
ant disinclination
4 *syn* see SLOPE
incline *vb* **1** *syn* see TEND 1
2 *syn* see SLANT 1
rel deflect, turn
3 to have an attitude toward or to influence one to take an attitude < *inclined* to believe the story > < his argument *inclined* me to share his view >

syn bend, bias, dispose, predispose; *compare* PREJUDICE 2, TEND 1
rel affect, influence, prompt, sway; drive, impel, induce, move, persuade
ant disincline, indispose
4 *syn* see DIRECT 2
incline *n syn* see SLOPE
inclined *adj* **1** *syn* see WILLING 1
ant disinclined
2 *syn* see APT 1
ant disinclined
3 sloping from the horizontal or perpendicular < cars running on an *inclined* track >
syn declivate, declivitous, inclining, leaning, oblique, pitched, pitching, sloped, sloping, tilted, tilting, tipped; *compare* DIAGONAL
rel dipping, graded, raked
inclining *n syn* see LEANING 2
inclining *adj syn* see INCLINED 3
include *vb* to possess as an integral part of a whole < the park *includes* a zoo and a botanical garden >
syn comprehend, contain, embody, embrace, encompass, have, involve, subsume, take in
rel comprise, cover, encircle, enclose, hold; number; admit, receive
con leave out, omit; preclude, reject; debar; eliminate, rule out
ant exclude
inclusive *adj* **1** *syn* see ALL-AROUND 2
2 *syn* see ENCYCLOPEDIC
incogitable *adj syn* see INCREDIBLE 1
ant cogitable
incogitant *adj syn* see RASH 1
incognizable *adj syn* see INCOMPREHENSIBLE 1
ant cognizable
incognizant *adj syn* see IGNORANT 2
ant cognizant
incoherent *adj* **1** *syn* see LOOSE 3
2 lacking cohesion or continuity < an *incoherent* presentation >
syn disconnected, discontinuous, disjointed, disordered, inchoate, incohesive, muddled, unconnected, uncontinuous, unorganized
rel discordant, incompatible, incongruous, inconsistent, inconsonant, inharmonious
con ordered, orderly; connected; organized, planned, plotted
ant coherent
3 *syn* see INARTICULATE 3
incohesive *adj syn* see INCOHERENT 2
ant cohesive
incombustible *adj syn* see NONCOMBUSTIBLE
ant combustible
income *n syn* see REVENUE
incommode *vb syn* see INCONVENIENCE
rel block, hinder, impede, obstruct; annoy, bother, irk, vex
con favor, oblige; humor, indulge; gratify, please
ant accommodate
incommodious *adj* **1** *syn* see INCONVENIENT
ant commodious
2 *syn* see CRAMPED
ant commodious
incommunicable *adj* **1** *syn* see UNUTTERABLE
ant communicable
2 *syn* see RESERVED 1
ant communicable, communicative
incomparable *adj syn* see SUPREME
rel matchless
con common, commonplace, ordinary; indifferent, mediocre, medium, middling
ant average
incompatible *adj syn* see INCONSONANT 1
rel adverse, antagonistic, counter; antipathetic; antipodal, antipodean, antithetical, contradictory, contrary, opposite; irreconcilable, unadaptable, unconformable
ant compatible
2 *syn* see IRRECONCILABLE

---

syn synonym(s)   *rel* related word(s)
ant antonym(s)   *con* contrasted word(s)
idiom idiomatic equivalent(s)
‖ use limited; if in doubt, see a dictionary

ant compatible

incompetence *n syn* see INABILITY

incompetent *adj* **1** *syn* see UNFIT 2
ant competent
2 *syn* see INEFFICIENT 2
ant competent

incomplete *adj* **1** lacking a part or parts < an *incomplete* text of a speech >
syn fractional, fragmentary, part, partial
rel broken, deficient, incoherent, lacking, short, wanting; bitty, composite, scrappy
con intact, undamaged, whole
ant complete
2 *syn* see DEFICIENT 1
ant complete

incompliant *adj* **1** *syn* see OBSTINATE
ant compliant
2 *syn* see STIFF 1

incomprehensible *adj* **1** lying above or beyond the reach of the human mind < the *incomprehensible* universe >
syn impenetrable, incognizable, uncomprehensible, unfathomable, ungraspable, unintelligible, unknowable
rel inscrutable, mysterious, mystifying, unsearchable; cryptic, enigmatic, obscure, unclear; imperceptible, indistinguishable
con cognizable, fathomable, graspable, intelligible, knowable; clear, lucid, plain, simple, straightforward; rational, reasonable
ant comprehensible, understandable
2 *syn* see INCONCEIVABLE 1
ant comprehensible, graspable

inconceivable *adj* **1** impossible to comprehend in the absence of actual experience or knowledge < color is *inconceivable* to those born blind >
syn incomprehensible, unimaginable, unknowable, ununderstandable
idiom beyond one's grasp
con comprehensible, imaginable, knowable, understandable
ant conceivable
2 *syn* see INCREDIBLE 1
ant conceivable
3 *syn* see IMPLAUSIBLE
con believable, convincing, credible, plausible
ant conceivable

inconclusive *adj* leading to no conclusion or definite result < the report was *inconclusive* >
syn indecisive
rel open, uncertain, undecided, unsettled; incomplete, unfinished
con clarifying, illuminating; decisive
ant conclusive

incondite *adj syn* see RUDE 6

inconformable *adj syn* see IRRECONCILABLE
ant conformable

incongruent *adj syn* see INCONSONANT 1
ant congruent, congruous

incongruous *adj syn* see INCONSONANT 1
rel alien, extraneous, foreign; bizarre, fantastic, grotesque
idiom out of place
con appropriate, fit, fitting, meet, seemly, suitable
ant congruent, congruous

inconnu *n syn* see STRANGER

inconquerable *adj* **1** *syn* see INVINCIBLE 1
2 *syn* see INSUPERABLE

inconscient *adj syn* see ABSTRACTED
ant conscient, conscious

inconscious *adj syn* see INSENSIBLE 2
ant conscious

inconsequent *adj syn* see PETTY 2

inconsequential *adj syn* see PETTY 2
ant consequential

inconsiderable *adj* **1** *syn* see LITTLE 3
ant considerable
2 *syn* see MEAGER
ant considerable
3 *syn* see PETTY 2
ant considerable

inconsiderate *adj* **1** *syn* see RASH 1
ant considerate
2 *syn* see SHORT 5

ant considerate

inconsistent *adj* **1** *syn* see INCONSTANT 1
ant consistent
2 *syn* see INCONSONANT 1
ant consistent
3 *syn* see IRRECONCILABLE
ant consistent

inconsolable *adj* incapable of being consoled < she was *inconsolable* over the loss of her child >
syn desolate, disconsolate, unconsolable
rel comfortless, dejected, forlorn, heartsick
ant consolable

inconsonant *adj* **1** not in agreement with one another or not agreeable one to the other < his actions are *inconsonant* with his words >
syn conflicting, disconsonant, discordant, discrepant, dissonant, incompatible, incongruent, incongruous, inconsistent, unmixable
rel ill-matched, ill-suited, mismated, uncongenial; inappropriate, unsuitable
con accordant, compatible, congenial, congruous, consistent
ant consonant
2 *syn* see INHARMONIOUS 2
ant consonant

inconspicuous *adj* not readily noticeable < occupied an *inconspicuous* position >
syn obscure, unconspicuous, unemphatic, unnoticeable
rel indistinct, insignificant, unnoticeable, unobtrusive, vague
con eye-catching, showy, striking; distinct, noticeable
ant conspicuous, prominent

inconstant *adj* **1** lacking firmness or steadiness (as in purpose or devotion) < depended too much on an *inconstant* friend >
syn capricious, changeable, fickle, inconsistent, lubricious, mercurial, temperamental, ticklish, uncertain, unstable, variable, volatile; *compare* CHANGEABLE 1, MUTABLE 2, UNCERTAIN 1
rel changeful, mutable, protean, unsettled, unsteady; elusive, erratic, vacillating, vagrant, wavering, wayward; irresolute, shifty, shilly-shally; undependable, unreliable; disloyal, faithless, false, perfidious, traitorous, treacherous, untrue; frivolous, light, light-minded
con dependable, reliable, trustworthy, trusty; faithful, loyal, resolute, staunch, steadfast, true
ant constant
2 *syn* see MUTABLE 2
ant constant

incontestable *adj syn* see POSITIVE 3
ant contestable

incontinent *adj syn* see LICENTIOUS 2
ant continent

incontinently *adv syn* see PELL-MELL

incontrovertible *adj syn* see POSITIVE 3
ant controvertible

inconvenience *n* the quality or state of being inconvenient < he hated the *inconvenience* of not having a telephone >
syn bother, bothersomeness, ‖disconvenience, troublesomeness
rel annoyance, aggravation, exasperation, trial; fuss, pother, stew
ant convenience

inconvenience *vb* to subject to disturbance or discomfort < was not seriously *inconvenienced* by the bad weather >
syn discommode, ‖disconvenience, disoblige, incommode, put about, put out, trouble
rel discompose, disturb; interfere, intermeddle, meddle; aggravate, exasperate, try
idiom put to trouble
ant convenience

inconvenient *adj* not conducive to physical, mental, or social ease and comfort < he came at an *inconvenient* time >
syn awkward, discommoding, discommodious, embarrassing, incommodious
rel bothersome, pestiferous, troublesome; inexpedient; detrimental, disadvantageous, prejudicial
con appropriate, becoming, fitting, suitable; acceptable, bearable, tolerable; advantageous, desirable, helpful
ant convenient

inconversable *adj syn* see SILENT 3
ant conversable

inconversant *adj syn* see IGNORANT 2

ant conversant

incorporate *vb* 1 *syn* see ABSORB 1
2 *syn* see EMBODY 2

incorporeal *adj syn* see IMMATERIAL 1
ant corporeal

incorrect *adj syn* see FALSE 1
ant correct

incorrectly *adv syn* see AMISS 1
ant correctly

incorrectness *n syn* see IMPROPRIETY 1
ant correctitude, correctness

incorruptible *adj syn* see INDESTRUCTIBLE
ant corruptible

incorruption *n syn* see HONESTY
ant corruption

increase *vb* 1 to make greater or more numerous <*increase* crops by good cultural practices>
syn aggrandize, augment, beef (up), boost, build, compound, enlarge, expand, extend, heighten, magnify, manifold, multiply, plus, push
rel aggravate, enhance, intensify; amplify, dilate, distend, inflate, swell; elongate, lengthen, prolong, protract; reinforce, strengthen
con abate, abbreviate, condense, contract; depreciate, diminish, lessen, lower, reduce; curtail, shorten, shrink; minimize
ant decrease
2 to become greater or more numerous <his wealth *increased* over the years>
syn augment, build, burgeon, enlarge, expand, heighten, mount, multiply, rise, run up, snowball, upsurge, wax
rel dilate, distend, inflate, intensify; lengthen, strengthen, swell; pullulate, swarm, teem
con abate, condense, contract, diminish, lessen, lower, reduce, shorten, shrink; die off, die (out), end, terminate
ant decrease
3 *syn* see RAISE 9

increase *n* 1 *syn* see ADDITION
ant decrease
2 *syn* see RISE 3

increate *adj syn* see SELF-EXISTENT
ant created

incredible *adj* 1 too extraordinary or improbable to admit of belief <an *incredible* story of privations overcome>
syn incogitable, inconceivable, insupposable, unbelievable, unimaginable, unthinkable
rel absurd, outlandish, preposterous, ridiculous; impossible, untenable
idiom beyond belief, out of the question
con acceptable, believable, conceivable, likely, plausible, reasonable
ant credible
2 *syn* see IMPLAUSIBLE
ant credible

incredulity *n syn* see UNBELIEF
con gullibility, naiveté
ant credulity, credulousness

incredulous *adj* unwilling to admit or accept what is offered as true <his explanation met an *incredulous* response from his listeners>
syn aporetic, disbelieving, questioning, quizzical, show-me, skeptical, unbelieving
rel hesitant, suspicious, uncertain, wary; distrustful, distrusting, mistrustful; doubting, dubious, unconvinced, unsatisfied
con trustful, trusting; unsuspecting, unsuspicious, unwary; gullible, naive
ant credulous

increment *n syn* see ADDITION

incriminate *vb syn* see ACCUSE
rel implicate, involve
ant exonerate

incrustate *vb syn* see CAKE 1

inculcate *vb syn* see IMPLANT
rel educate, instruct, teach; communicate, impart

inculpable *adj* 1 *syn* see GOOD
ant culpable
2 *syn* see INNOCENT 2
ant culpable

inculpate *vb syn* see ACCUSE

ant exculpate

incult *adj syn* see COARSE 3

incur *vb* to bring (something usually unpleasant) upon oneself <he foolishly *incurred* debts beyond his ability to pay>
syn contract
rel acquire, get; bring on, induce
idiom bring down on (*or* upon)
con avoid, elude, escape, eschew, evade, shun; discharge, pay, settle

incurable *adj syn* see HOPELESS 2
ant curable

incurious *adj syn* see INDIFFERENT 2
rel absent, absentminded, abstracted, distraught, preoccupied
con nosy, prying, snoopy; impertinent, intrusive, meddlesome; observant, observing
ant curious, inquisitive

incursion *n syn* see INVASION

indebted *adj* owing gratitude or recognition (as for a favor or service rendered) <was *indebted* to the book for most of his information>
syn beholden, obligated, obliged
rel duty-bound, honor-bound

indebtedness *n* 1 a state of owing something <unable to escape from *indebtedness*>
syn arrearage, debt, liability, obligation; *compare* DEBT 3
rel delinquency, nonpayment; bankruptcy, failure, insolvency
con discharge, liquidation, satisfaction; exoneration, freeing, release
2 *syn* see DEBT 3

indecent *adj* 1 *syn* see INDECOROUS
ant decent
2 *syn* see OBSCENE 2
ant decent

indecipherable *adj syn* see ILLEGIBLE
ant decipherable

indecision *n syn* see HESITATION
ant decision, decisiveness

indecisive *adj* 1 *syn* see INCONCLUSIVE
ant decisive
2 *syn* see DOUBTFUL 1
con certain, incontrovertible, undebatable, unequivocal
ant decisive
3 *syn* see VACILLATING 2
rel undecided, unsettled
idiom of two minds
con decided, determined, firm, positive, resolved, settled, unfaltering, unhesitant, unhesitating, unwavering
ant decisive

indecisiveness *n syn* see HESITATION
ant indecision, indecisiveness

indecorous *adj* not conforming with accepted standards of propriety or good taste <they regarded argument in public as *indecorous*>
syn improper, indecent, indelicate, malodorous, ridiculous, rough, unbecoming, undecorous, ungodly, unseemly, untoward
rel inappropriate, incorrect, unbefitting, unfit, unfitting; immodest, inelegant, undignified; coarse, gross, loose, offensive, shameful, tasteless, vulgar; discourteous, ill-mannered, impolite, rude, uncivil; irregular, unlawful
idiom in bad form
con becoming, courteous, decent, nice, proper, seemly; conventional, formal
ant decorous

indecorousness *n syn* see IMPROPRIETY 1
ant decorousness

indecorum *n* 1 *syn* see FAUX PAS
2 *syn* see IMPROPRIETY 1
ant decorum

indeed *adv* 1 *syn* see WELL 7
2 *syn* see EVEN 3

indefatigable *adj* capable of prolonged and arduous effort <a teacher who has *indefatigable* patience with slow learners>

syn inexhaustible, tireless, unflagging, untiring, unweariable, unwearying, weariless

rel assiduous, diligent, painstaking, sedulous; determined, dogged, patient, persevering, persistent, pertinacious, relentless, steadfast, stubborn, tenacious, unfaltering, unflinching, unrelenting, unwavering; energetic, strenuous, vigorous

con dawdling, dilatory, laggard, lagging, procrastinating; faineant, indolent, lackadaisical, lazy, slothful, sluggish

ant fatigable

indefectible *adj* 1 *syn* see PERFECT 2
2 *syn* see IDEAL 3

indefensible *adj syn* see INEXCUSABLE
ant defensible

indefinable *adj syn* see UNUTTERABLE
ant definable

indefinite *adj* 1 having no exact limits <a region with *indefinite* boundaries>
syn indeterminate, indistinct, inexact, undeterminable
rel unclear, undefined, unfixed, unspecific; broad, loose, wide; general, obscure, vague
con exact, measured; known
ant definite
2 *syn* see LIMITLESS
ant definite

indelible *adj* that cannot be removed or erased <made an *indelible* impression on his hearers>
syn ineffaceable, ineradicable, inerasable, inexpungible, inextirpable, uneradicable, unerasable
rel indestructible, undestroyable; enduring, permanent
con eradicable, effaceable, erasable, removable; ephemeral, evanescent, passing, temporary, transitory
ant delible

indelicate *adj syn* see INDECOROUS
rel callow, crude, rude, uncouth; lewd, wanton
con chaste, modest, pure
ant delicate

indemnification *n syn* see REPARATION
indemnify *vb syn* see COMPENSATE 3
indemnity *n syn* see REPARATION
indentation *n* 1 *syn* see NOTCH 1
2 *syn* see IMPRESSION 1
indenture *n syn* see NOTCH 1
indentured *adj syn* see BOUND 2
independent *adj* 1 *syn* see FREE 1
2 *syn* see SELF-SUFFICIENT
ant dependent
independently *adv syn* see APART 1
idiom on one's own
indescribable *adj syn* see UNUTTERABLE
ant describable
indestructible *adj* incapable of being destroyed <*indestructible* idealism>
syn imperishable, incorruptible, inexterminable, inextinguishable, inextirpable, irrefragable, irrefrangible, quenchless, undestroyable, unperishable
rel changeless, immutable, unalterable, unchangeable; deathless, immortal, perpetual, undying; durable, enduring, lasting, permanent; indelible, ineradicable; unextinguishable, unquenchable
con alterable, changeable, corruptible, impermanent, temporary, transient, unlasting; mortal, temporal; evanescent
ant destroyable, destructible, perishable
indeterminate *adj syn* see INDEFINITE 1
ant determinate
index *n syn* see INDICATION 3
Indian sign *n syn* see JINX
indicate *vb* 1 *syn* see POINT 2
2 to give evidence of or serve as ground for a valid or reasonable inference <several polls *indicate* a landslide for the incumbent>
syn announce, argue, attest, bespeak, betoken, testify, witness
rel denote, import, mean, signify; demonstrate, prove; evidence, evince, manifest, show; display, exhibit, express, illustrate; connote, hint, imply, suggest
3 *syn* see SHOW 5
indication *n* 1 *syn* see HINT 1
2 *syn* see EXPRESSION 3
3 something that is an outward manifestation of something else <such *indications* of prosperity as second cars and color TVs>

syn evidence, index, indicia, mark, sign, significant, symptom, token; *compare* SYMBOL 1, TESTIMONY
rel expression, manifestation; hint, suggestion; proof; prefiguration, type

indicative *adj* serving to indicate <the roar of the crowd was *indicative* of its approval>
syn denotative, denotive, designative, exhibitive, indicatory, indicial, significative
rel characteristic, demonstrative, evidential, evincive, expressive, suggestive, symbolic, symptomatic, testatory

indicatory *adj syn* see INDICATIVE
indicia *n pl syn* see INDICATION 3
indicial *adj syn* see INDICATIVE
indict *vb syn* see ACCUSE
indifference *n syn* see APATHY 2
indifferent *adj* 1 *syn* see FAIR 4
2 marked by a lack of interest or concern <was *indifferent* to suffering and poverty>
syn aloof, by-the-way, casual, detached, disinterested, incurious, numb, pococurante, remote, unconcerned, uncurious, uninterested, withdrawn; *compare* UNSOCIABLE
rel apathetic, impassive, insensible; dispassionate; careless, heedless, negligent, regardless, uncaring, unmindful; inattentive, unobserving
con attentive, considerate, heedful, interested, mindful, regardful, sympathetic
ant concerned
3 *syn* see COLD 2
4 *syn* see MEDIUM

indigence *n syn* see POVERTY 1
ant affluence, opulence
indigency *n syn* see POVERTY 1
ant affluence, opulence
indigenous *adj* 1 *syn* see NATIVE 2
con alien, extraneous, foreign
ant exotic; naturalized
2 *syn* see INNATE 1
indigent *adj syn* see POOR 1
ant affluent, opulent
indignant *adj syn* see ANGRY
ant gratified
indignation *n syn* see ANGER
ant gratification
indignity *n syn* see AFFRONT
rel grievance, injury, injustice, wrong
indirect *adj* 1 deviating from a direct line or straightforward course <made *indirect* inquiries about the new neighbor>
syn circuitous, circular, collateral, oblique, roundabout
rel circumlocutory, crooked, devious; meandering, serpentine, sinuous, tortuous, twisting, winding; errant, vagrant, wandering
ant direct; forthright, straightforward
2 *syn* see UNDERHAND
ant straight
indirection *n syn* see DECEPTION 1
indiscernible *adj syn* see IMPERCEPTIBLE
ant discernible, distinguishable
indiscreet *adj syn* see UNWISE
ant discreet
indiscriminate *adj* 1 including all or nearly all within the range of choice, operation, or effectiveness <her charity was *indiscriminate* but generous>
syn indiscriminating, indiscriminative, sweeping, undiscriminated, undiscriminating, undistinguishing, wholesale
rel assorted, heterogeneous, miscellaneous, promiscuous; shallow, superficial, uncritical; broad, extensive, wide
con discretionary, discriminative; choosy, picky; critical, perfectionist
ant selective; discriminate, discriminated
2 *syn* see RANDOM
3 *syn* see MISCELLANEOUS
indiscriminating *adj syn* see INDISCRIMINATE 1
ant discriminating
indiscriminative *adj syn* see INDISCRIMINATE 1
ant discriminative
indispensable *adj syn* see ESSENTIAL 4
rel cardinal, fundamental
ant dispensable
indisposed *adj* 1 *syn* see UNWELL

2 syn see DISINCLINED
rel antagonistic, antipathetic, hostile, inimical
con amicable, neighborly; responsive, sympathetic
ant disposed
indisposition *n* **1 syn** see DISLIKE
  2 syn see SICKNESS 1
indisputable *adj* **1 syn** see POSITIVE 3
  ant disputable
  2 syn see REAL 3
indistinct *adj* **1 syn** see INDEFINITE 1
  ant distinct
  2 syn see FAINT 2
  ant distinct
indistinguishable *adj* **syn** see SAME 2
  ant distinguishable
indite *vb* **syn** see WRITE
individual *adj* **1 syn** see PERSONAL 1
  ant common, popular
  2 syn see SPECIAL 1
  rel separate, single, sole
  con generic, universal
  ant general
  3 syn see CHARACTERISTIC
  ant common
  4 syn see SEVERAL 1
individual *n* **1 syn** see ENTITY 1
  2 syn see THING 4
  3 syn see HUMAN
individualism *n* **1 syn** see DISPOSITION 3
  2 syn see INDIVIDUALITY 3
individualist *adj* **syn** see EGOCENTRIC 1
individualistic *adj* **syn** see EGOCENTRIC 1
individuality *n* **1 syn** see DISPOSITION 3
  2 syn see UNITY 1
  3 distinctive character < a person of marked *individuality* >
  syn distinctiveness, individualism, particularity, singularity
  rel character, personality
  4 individual identity < a teacher who respects children's *individualities* >
  syn identity, ipseity, personality, seity, selfdom, selfhood, selfness, singularity
  rel independence, separateness, uniqueness; difference, dissimilarity, unlikeness
  con likeness, resemblance, similarity
individualize *vb* **syn** see CHARACTERIZE 2
individually *adv* **syn** see APART 1
individuate *vb* **syn** see CHARACTERIZE 2
indocile *adj* **syn** see UNRULY 1
  ant docile
indolence *n* **syn** see SLOTH 1
  ant industry
indolent *adj* **syn** see LAZY
  con active, diligent, energetic, vigorous
  ant industrious
indomitable *adj* **1 syn** see INVINCIBLE 1
  ant domitable
  2 syn see INSUPERABLE
  rel dogged, pertinacious, stubborn; resolute, staunch, steadfast
  ant domitable
  3 syn see UNRULY 1
indoors *adv* in or into a building < stayed *indoors* during the storm >
  syn inside, within, withindoors, withinside
  con outdoors, outside, without, withoutdoors
  ant outdoors
indubitable *adj* **1 syn** see POSITIVE 3
  ant dubitable, questionable
  2 syn see AUTHENTIC 2
  ant doubtful, dubious
  3 syn see DOWNRIGHT 2
induce *vb* **1** to move another to do or agree to something < *induced* him to give up smoking for the sake of his health >
  syn argue (into), bring around, convince, draw, draw in, draw on, get, oversway, persuade, prevail (on *or* upon), procure, prompt, talk (into), win (over)
  rel influence, sway; abet, incite, lead; actuate, impel, move; activate, motivate
  con check, curb, hold back, restrain

  2 syn see GENERATE 3
inducible *adj* **syn** see INDUCTIVE
induct *vb* **syn** see INITIATE 3
induction *n* **syn** see INITIATION
inductive *adj* **1** derived or derivable by reasoning from a part to a whole, from particulars to generals, or from the individual to the universal < used an *inductive* approach to the problem >
  syn a posteriori, inducible
  rel Baconian, epagogic
  2 syn see PRELIMINARY
indulge *vb* **1** to give free rein to (as curiosity or a desire) < *indulged* their taste for gourmet foods >
  syn cater (to), gratify, humor
  rel favor, oblige, satisfy; delight, please, regale
  idiom give rein to
  con bridle, check, constrain, curb, restrain
  2 syn see BABY
  3 syn see WALLOW 3
indulgence *n* **1 syn** see FORBEARANCE 2
  rel benignancy, benignity, benignness, kindliness, kindness; gentleness, mildness
  con rigor, severity, sternness; rigidity, rigorousness; harshness
  ant strictness
  2 syn see FAVOR 4
indulgent *adj* **syn** see FORBEARING
  rel cosseting, pampering, permissive; condoning, excusing, forgiving, pardoning; benign, benignant, kind, kindly
  con severe, stern; harsh, rigorous, stringent
  ant strict
indurate *vb* **syn** see HARDEN 1
industrious *adj* **syn** see ASSIDUOUS
  rel active, busy, live, dynamic; persevering, persistent
  con idle, inactive; lethargic, sluggish
  ant indolent, slothful; unindustrious
industry *n* **syn** see BUSINESS 4
indwell *vb* **syn** see BELONG 3
indweller *n* **syn** see INHABITANT
indwelling *adj* **syn** see INHERENT
inebriant *n* **syn** see LIQUOR 2
inebriate *n* **syn** see DRUNKARD
inebriated *adj* **syn** see INTOXICATED 1
inebrious *adj* **syn** see INTOXICATED 1
inedible *adj* not fit for food < an *inedible* plant >
  syn inesculent, uneatable
  rel indigestible, unwholesome; insipid, unappetizing; baneful, noxious, poisonous
  con eatable, esculent; digestible, wholesome; appetizing, savory, tasty; harmless, innocuous, innoxious, nonpoisonous
  ant edible
ineffable *adj* **syn** see UNUTTERABLE
  rel celestial, empyreal, empyrean, heavenly; ethereal; divine, holy, sacred, spiritual; abstract, ideal, transcendent, transcendental
  con expressible; utterable
ineffaceable *adj* **syn** see INDELIBLE
ineffective *adj* **1 syn** see FUTILE
  ant effective
  2 syn see WEAK 4
  3 not producing or not capable of producing a required result < *ineffective* remedies >
  syn ineffectual, inefficacious, inefficient
  rel inadequate, incompetent, inferior; useless, worthless
  con active, effectual, efficacious; esteemed, valuable
  ant effective
ineffectiveness *n* **syn** see INABILITY
  ant effectiveness
ineffectual *adj* **1 syn** see FUTILE
  ant effectual
  2 syn see INEFFECTIVE 3
  ant effectual
  3 syn see WEAK 4
  4 syn see LITTLE 2
ineffectualness *n* **syn** see INABILITY

---

syn synonym(s)   *rel* related word(s)
ant antonym(s)   *con* contrasted word(s)
idiom idiomatic equivalent(s)
|| use limited; if in doubt, see a dictionary

ant effectualness

inefficacious *adj syn* see INEFFECTIVE 3
ant efficacious

inefficacy *n syn* see INABILITY
ant efficacy

inefficient *adj* 1 *syn* see INEFFECTIVE 3
ant efficient
2 incapable of the proper performance of duties <*inefficient* workmen>
syn incapable, incompetent, inept, inexpert, unexpert, unskilled, unskillful, unworkmanlike
rel careless, slipshod, slovenly; unfitted, unprepared, unqualified, untrained; unskilled, unskillful
con able, adept, capable, competent, expert, proficient, qualified, skilled, skillful, workmanlike
ant efficient

inelaborate *adj syn* see PLAIN 1
ant elaborate

inelastic *adj syn* see STIFF 1
ant elastic

inelegance *n syn* see IMPROPRIETY 1
ant elegance

inelegant *adj syn* see COARSE 3

ineligible *adj syn* see UNFIT 2
ant eligible

ineluctable *adj syn* see INEVITABLE
con doubtful, dubious, questionable; likely, possible, probable

ineludible *adj syn* see INEVITABLE

inenarrable *adj syn* see UNUTTERABLE

inept *adj* 1 *syn* see IMPROPER 1
ant apt
2 *syn* see INFELICITOUS
ant apropos, apt
3 *syn* see AWKWARD 2
ant apt; adept
4 *syn* see UNSKILLFUL 1
ant able
5 *syn* see INEFFICIENT 2
ant competent, efficient

inequable *adj syn* see INEQUITABLE
ant equable

inequality *n* 1 the quality of being uneven <hampered by the *inequality* of the ground>
syn asperity, irregularity, roughness, unevenness
rel cragginess, jaggedness, ruggedness, rugosity
con equality, evenness, levelness, smoothness
2 *syn* see DISPARITY
ant equality

inequitable *adj* not fair or just <an *inequitable* tax burden>
syn inequable, unequitable, unfair, unjust, unrighteous
rel undeserved, undue, unmerited; bad, wrong, wrongful; arbitrary, high-handed, oppressive
con fair, just
ant equitable

inequitableness *n syn* see INJUSTICE 1
ant equitableness

inequity *n syn* see INJUSTICE 1
ant equity

ineradicable *adj syn* see INDELIBLE
ant eradicable

inerasable *adj syn* see INDELIBLE
ant erasable

inerrable *adj syn* see INFALLIBLE 1
ant errable

inerrant *adj syn* see INFALLIBLE 1
rel accurate, correct, exact, precise; dependable, reliable, trustworthy
ant errant

inert *adj syn* see INACTIVE
rel impotent, powerless; apathetic, impassive, phlegmatic, stolid; dead, inanimate, lifeless
con animated, awake; alert, vigilant, watchful; live, operative
ant animated; dynamic

inerudite *adj syn* see UNSCHOLARLY
ant erudite, learned

inescapable *adj syn* see INEVITABLE
ant escapable

inescapably *adv syn* see WILLY-NILLY

inesculent *adj syn* see INEDIBLE
ant esculent

in essence *adv* 1 *syn* see ESSENTIALLY 1
2 *syn* see VIRTUALLY

inessential *adj syn* see UNNECESSARY
ant crucial, essential

inestimable *adj* 1 *syn* see INCALCULABLE 1
2 *syn* see PRECIOUS 1

inevasible *adj syn* see INEVITABLE

inevitable *adj* incapable of being avoided or escaped <the effect of the scandal on the election was *inevitable*>
syn certain, ineluctable, ineludible, inescapable, inevasible, necessary, returnless, unavoidable, unescapable, unevadable
rel ineliminable, sure, unpreventable; decided, settled; destined, foreordained; inexorable, inflexible
idiom as sure to follow as night follows day, in the cards
con eludible, escapable, evadable
ant avoidable, evitable

inevitably *adv syn* see WILLY-NILLY

inexact *adj syn* see INDEFINITE 1
ant exact

inexcusable *adj* being without excuse or justification <an *inexcusable* blunder>
syn indefensible, inexpiable, unforgivable, unjustifiable, unpardonable, untenable
rel blamable, blameworthy, censurable, criticizable; impermissible, unallowable, unpermissible; intolerable, reprehensible
con allowable, blameless, defensible, forgivable, justifiable, pardonable, venial
ant excusable

inexhaustible *adj syn* see INDEFATIGABLE

inexorable *adj syn* see INFLEXIBLE 2
rel resolute; immobile, immovable
con compassionate, responsive, sympathetic, tender; clement, forbearing, indulgent, lenient

inexpedient *adj syn* see INADVISABLE
ant expedient

inexpensive *adj syn* see CHEAP 1
ant expensive

inexperience *n* lack or serious deficiency of practical wisdom <his failure was due to his *inexperience*>
syn callowness, freshness, greenness, rawness
rel ignorance, naiveté; amateurishness; unfamiliarity; unsophistication, verdancy
con grasp, understanding; polish, sophistication; skill, training
ant experience

inexperienced *adj* lacking knowledge, skill, or practice based on direct observation and participation <hired *inexperienced* help>
syn callow, fresh, green, inexpert, raw, rude, unconversant, unexperienced, unfleshed, unpracticed, unseasoned, untried, unversed, young
rel ignorant, immature, inept, naive; prentice, unacquainted, unfamiliar, unskilled, untrained
con expert, old, practiced, seasoned, skilled, versed, veteran
ant experienced

inexpert *adj* 1 *syn* see INEXPERIENCED
ant expert
2 *syn* see UNSKILLFUL 1
ant expert
3 *syn* see INEFFICIENT 2
ant expert
4 *syn* see CRUDE 5

inexpiable *adj syn* see INEXCUSABLE
ant expiable

inexplainable *adj syn* see INEXPLICABLE
ant explainable, explicable

inexplicable *adj* not capable of being explained or accounted for <an *inexplicable* discrepancy in the accounts>
syn inexplainable, unaccountable, unexplainable; *compare* MYSTERIOUS
rel indecipherable, indescribable, inscrutable, undefinable, unfathomable, unsolvable; mysterious, odd, peculiar, strange
con clear, obvious, plain; comprehensible, graspable, intelligible
ant explainable, explicable

inexpressible *adj syn* see UNUTTERABLE
ant expressible

inexpressive *adj syn* see EXPRESSIONLESS

ant expressive

inexpugnable *adj syn* see INVINCIBLE 1
 rel irresistible, unopposable
 con assailable, attackable
 ant expugnable
inexpungible *adj syn* see INDELIBLE
inexterminable *adj syn* see INDESTRUCTIBLE
inextinguishable *adj syn* see INDESTRUCTIBLE
 ant extinguishable
inextirpable *adj* **1** *syn* see INDESTRUCTIBLE
 2 *syn* see INDELIBLE
inextricable *adj syn* see INSOLUBLE
 ant extricable
infallible *adj* **1** incapable of being in error <an *infallible* ear for pitch in music>
 syn inerrable, inerrant, sure, unerring
 rel faultless, flawless, impeccable, undeceivable; correct, exact, perfect
 con deceivable, faulty, unsure; doubtful, dubious, questionable
 ant fallible
 2 not liable to mislead, deceive, or disappoint <an *infallible* remedy>
 syn certain, sure, surefire, unfailing
 rel effective, efficacious, efficient; handy, helpful, useful; acceptable, agreeable, satisfying; satisfactory
 con doubtful, questionable, uncertain, unsure; useless, worthless; unacceptable, unsatisfying; unsatisfactory
 ant fallible
infamous *adj* **1** having an extremely and deservedly bad reputation <one of the most *infamous* of the dictator's henchmen>
 syn ill-famed, notorious, opprobrious
 rel abominable, atrocious, evil, hateful, heinous, iniquitous, odious, scandalous, vile, villainous; contemptible, despicable, scurvy, sorry
 con distinguished, eminent, esteemed, honored, illustrious, notable, prestigious, reputable
 2 *syn* see VICIOUS 2
 rel disgraceful, disreputable, ignominious, shameful
 con glorious, splendid, sublime
 ant illustrious
infamy *n syn* see DISGRACE
 rel notoriety, notoriousness
infancy *n* **1** early childhood <the helplessness of *infancy*>
 syn babyhood, infanthood
 rel childhood, immaturity, juvenility, nonage
 con adulthood, maturity, old age, senescence
 2 the state or period of being under the age established by law for the attainment of full civil rights <his heirs were still in *infancy*>
 syn minority, nonage
 rel immaturity, juniority, juvenility
 con adulthood, adultness, maturity, seniority
 ant majority
infant *n syn* see BABY 1
infant *adj syn* see YOUNG 1
infanthood *n syn* see INFANCY 1
infantile *adj syn* see CHILDISH
 ant adult
infantine *adj syn* see CHILDISH
 ant adult
infatuate *adj syn* see INFATUATED
infatuated *adj* possessed with or marked by a strong attachment or foolish or unreasoning love or desire <*infatuated* with a woman he can't have>
 syn besotted, dotty, enamored, infatuate
 rel bewitched, captivated, enraptured, obsessed; foolish, silly
 con detached, dispassionate, objective, undazzled, unprepossessed
infatuation *n* a strong and unreasoning but transitory attachment <went through a series of *infatuations* before he settled down>
 syn béguin, crush, ‖pash, passion
 rel ardor, craze, devotion, fascination, obsession, rage
in favor of *prep syn* see FOR 1
infeasible *adj syn* see IMPOSSIBLE 1
 ant feasible
infectious *adj* **1** capable of causing infection <viruses and other *infectious* agents>
 syn infective

 rel mephitic, miasmic, noxious, pestilent, pestilential, poisonous, toxic, virulent
 con healthful, hygienic, salutary, wholesome
 2 transmissible by infection <*infectious* diseases>
 syn catching, communicable, contagious
 3 easily communicated or diffused <her enthusiasm was *infectious*>
 syn catching, contagious, taking
 rel irresistible, sympathetic
infective *adj syn* see INFECTIOUS 1
infecund *adj syn* see STERILE 1
 ant fecund
infelicitous *adj* marked by a lack of appropriateness and grace of expression <made a very *infelicitous* remark>
 syn awkward, graceless, ill-chosen, inept, unfortunate, unhappy
 rel inappropriate, inapropos, inapt, malapropos, unapt; deplorable, gauche, regrettable
 con fortunate, graceful, happy
 ant felicitous
infer *vb* to arrive at by reasoning from evidence or from premises <we *inferred* from his questions that he was a stranger in the vicinity>
 syn collect, conclude, deduce, deduct, derive, ‖dope out, draw, gather, judge, make, make out; *compare* CONJECTURE
 rel induce; conjecture, glean, guess, reckon, speculate, surmise, think; ascertain, construe, interpret, reason, understand
 idiom come to (or draw or reach) a conclusion; read between the lines
inference *n* **1** the deriving of a conclusion by reasoning <the answer was obtainable by *inference*>
 syn deduction, illation, judgment, ratiocination
 rel conjecture, guessing, reckoning, supposition, surmise
 2 a determination arrived at by reasoning <a wrong *inference* based on incomplete evidence>
 syn conclusion, deduction, illation, judgment, ratiocination, sequitur
 rel assumption, conjecture, guess, presumption, reckoning, supposition, surmise
inferior *adj* **1** being or regarded as being below the level of another thing <the *inferior* latitudes of the northern hemisphere>
 syn lesser, low, lower, nether, subjacent, under
 rel junior, minor, secondary, subaltern, subordinate
 con greater, higher, over, overlying
 ant superior
 2 of little or less importance, value, or merit <sold *inferior* goods at high prices>
 syn common, déclassé, hack, low-grade, mean, poor, second-class, second-drawer, second-rate; *compare* CHEAP 2
 rel average, fair, indifferent, mediocre, middling, ordinary; bad, base, paltry, punk, shoddy, sleazy, sorry, tawdry, tin-pot, wretched; good-for-nothing, lousy, ‖no-account, no-good, unworthy, valueless, worthless
 con choice, excellent, first-class, first-rate, high-grade, prime
 ant superior
inferior *n* one lower than another (as in station or worth) <a man inclined to be disdainful of his social *inferiors*>
 syn poor relation, scrub, secondary, subaltern, subordinate, underling, understrapper
 rel attendant, auxiliary, deputy; retainer, satrap, subject, vassal; hanger-on, heeler, henchman, hireling, minion, satellite, sycophant; adherent, disciple, follower
 con chief, head, leader, master, principal
 ant superior
infernal *adj* **1** of or relating to a nether world of the dead <the *infernal* regions>
 syn chthonian, chthonic, Hadean, plutonian, plutonic, sulphurous, Tartarean
 con celestial, elysian, Hesperidean, paradisaic, paradisal, paradisiacal
 ant supernal
 2 resembling or appropriate to hell or its inhabitants <an *infernal* glow in the sky>

---

syn synonym(s)   *rel* related word(s)
ant antonym(s)   *con* contrasted word(s)
idiom idiomatic equivalent(s)
‖ use limited; if in doubt, see a dictionary

syn avernal, cimmerian, hellish, pandemoniac, plutonian, plutonic, stygian
rel demoniac, devilish, diabolic, fiendish; sulphurous
ant celestial, heavenly
3 syn see DAMNED 2
4 syn see UTTER
inferno *n* **1 syn** see HELL
2 syn see FIRE 1
inferred *adj syn* see TACIT 1
infertile *adj* **1 syn** see STERILE 1
rel depleted, drained, exhausted, impoverished
con breeding, generating, propagating, reproducing
ant fertile
2 syn see BARREN 2
ant fertile
infest *vb* **1** to spread or swarm over in a troublesome manner < lawns *infested* with weeds >
syn beset, overrun, overspread, overswarm
rel abound, crawl, swarm, teem; annoy, harass, harry, pester, plague, worry
2 to live in or on as a parasite < a dog *infested* by fleas >
syn parasite, parasitize
infidel *adj syn* see HEATHEN
infidelic *adj syn* see HEATHEN
infidelity *n* betrayal of a moral obligation < a leader guilty of *infidelity* to the responsibilities he had accepted >
syn disloyalty, faithlessness, falseness, falsity, perfidiousness, perfidy, unfaithfulness; *compare* TREACHERY
rel fickleness, inconstancy; treacherousness, treachery, treason
idiom bad faith
con devotion, faithfulness, fealty; constancy, loyalty, steadfastness
ant fidelity
infiltrate *vb syn* see INSINUATE 3
infinite *adj* **1** being without known limits < the idea of an *infinite* universe >
syn eternal, illimitable, perdurable, sempiternal, supertemporal
rel everlasting, perpetual
con bounded, circumscribed, limited, restricted
ant finite
2 syn see LIMITLESS
ant finite
infinity *n syn* see ETERNITY 1
infirm *adj syn* see WEAK 1
ant hale
infirmity *n* **1** the quality or state of being enfeebled and weakened in health < suffering from old age and attendant physical *infirmity* >
syn debility, decrepitude, disease, feebleness, infirmness, malaise, sickliness, unhealthiness; *compare* DISEASE 1, SICKNESS 1
rel debilitation, decay, enfeeblement, failing, frailty, weakening, weakness; diseasedness, unwellness; illness, indisposition, sickness, unhealth
ant haleness
2 syn see DISEASE 1
3 syn see SICKNESS 1
infirmness *n syn* see INFIRMITY 1
infix *vb* **1 syn** see ENTRENCH 1
2 syn see IMPLANT
inflame *vb* **1 syn** see LIGHT 1
ant extinguish
2 syn see IRRITATE
inflammable *adj syn* see COMBUSTIBLE 1
ant nonflammable, noninflammable
inflammatory *adj* exciting or tending to excite anger, animosity, or disorder < *inflammatory* speeches designed to spark rebellion >
syn incendiary
rel exciting, incitive, instigative, provocative; revolutionary, seditionary, seditious
con calming, moderating, soothing, temperate
inflate *vb syn* see EXPAND 3
ant deflate
inflated *adj* swollen with or as if with something insubstantial < had an *inflated* idea of his own importance >
syn dropsical, dropsied, flatulent, overblown, tumescent, tumid, turgid, windy
rel aureate, bombastic, flowery, grandiloquent, magniloquent, rhetorical; ostentatious, pretentious, showy; fustian, ranting, rhapsodical; diffuse, prolix, verbose, wordy

con compendious, concise, laconic, pithy, succinct, summary, terse
inflatus *n syn* see INSPIRATION
inflection *n* a particular manner of employing the sounds of the voice in speech < questions end on a rising *inflection* >
syn accent, intonation, tone
rel articulation, enunciation, pronunciation; timbre, tonality
idiom tone of voice
inflexible *adj* **1 syn** see STIFF 1
rel immobile, immovable
con elastic, resilient, springy, supple; ductile, malleable, plastic, pliable, pliant; fluid, liquid
ant flexible
2 rigidly firm in will or purpose < a person of *inflexible* resolution >
syn adamant, adamantine, brassbound, dogged, inexorable, iron, obdurate, relentless, rigid, rockbound, rock-ribbed, single=minded, steadfast, stubborn, unbendable, unbending, uncompliant, uncompromising, unswayable, unyielding; *compare* STIFF 1
rel intractable, obstinate; indomitable, invincible, unconquerable; grim, hard, implacable, unrelenting; dyed-in-the-wool, fixed, set, ‖sot
con agreeable, amenable, compliant, docile, pliant, responsive, swayable, yielding; mild, open
ant flexible
3 incapable of changing or being changed < *inflexible* rules >
syn constant, determinate, fixed, immovable, immutable, inalterable, invariable, ironclad, unalterable, unchangeable, unmodifiable, unmovable
rel strict; rigorous; established, set, settled; changeless, unchanging
con adaptable, adjustable, alterable, changeable, mutable, variable
ant flexible
4 syn see TOUGH 3
inflict *vb* **1 syn** see GIVE 10
2 to cause one to endure (something damaging or painful) < *inflict* retribution >
syn force (on *or* upon), impose, visit, wreak, wreck; *compare* IMPOSE 4
rel expose, subject
idiom lay open to, put on the spot
con guard, protect, shelter, shield
inflow *n syn* see INFLUX
ant outflow, outflux
influence *n* **1** power exerted over the minds or behavior of others < a person of great *influence* in national politics >
syn authority, credit, prestige, weight; *compare* PULL 2
rel command, domination, dominion, mastery; ascendancy, dominance, eminence, predominance; consequence, importance, moment; ‖drag, in, pull
2 syn see PULL 2
influence *vb* **1 syn** see AFFECT
2 syn see PREJUDICE 2
influenceable *adj syn* see RECEPTIVE 1
influx *n* a flowing in < anticipated an *influx* of immigrants >
syn inflow, influxion, inpour, inpouring, inrush
rel accession, augmentation, increase; illapse
con outpour, outpouring, outrush; efflux, effluxion, exodus
ant outflow, outflux
influxion *n syn* see INFLUX
ant effluxion
inform *vb* **1 syn** see FIRE 2
rel imbue, infuse, leaven, permeate; enlighten, illuminate; endow, endue
2 to make aware or cognizant of something < was kept *informed* of developments >
syn acquaint, advise, apprise, clue (*or* clew), fill in, notify, post, tell, warn, wise (up)
rel educate, enlighten, instruct, teach; familiarize; caution, forewarn
idiom keep posted
3 to give information about someone especially as an informer < his suspicions aroused, he *informed* on his neighbor to the police >
syn ‖nark, peach, ‖pimp, rat, ‖sing, snitch, squeak, squeal, ‖stool; *compare* TALK 6
rel blab, tattle, tell; betray, give away, turn in

informal *adj* **1** conducted or carried out without rigidly prescribed procedure <carried on an *informal* investigation>
syn irregular, unceremonious, unofficial
rel casual, spontaneous; unauthorized; unconventional; private, special
con authorized, ceremonious, conventional, official, regular
ant formal
2 *syn* see EASYGOING 3
rel familiar, natural, simple
con affected, mannered, prim, rigid, stiff, stilted
ant formal

information *n* **1** *syn* see KNOWLEDGE 2
2 *syn* see NEWS

informational *adj syn* see INFORMATIVE

informative *adj* imparting information <gave an *informative* talk>
syn educational, educative, informational, informatory, instructional, instructive
rel edifying, elucidative, enlightening, explanatory, illuminating
ant uninformative

informatory *adj syn* see INFORMATIVE

informed *adj syn* see FAMILIAR 3
ant uninformed

informer *n* one who informs against another <his arrest was brought about by an *informer*>
syn betrayer, ||canary, ||fink, ||nark, ||pimp, snitch, squawker, ||squeaker, squealer, stool, stoolie, stool pigeon, talebearer, tattler, tattletale, tipster; *compare* BUSYBODY, DETECTIVE, GOSSIP 1, SPY

infra *adv* **1** *syn* see BELOW 2
ant above, supra
2 *syn* see AFTER

infract *vb syn* see VIOLATE 1

infraction *n syn* see BREACH 1
rel crime, offense, sin; error, faux pas, lapse, slip

infrastructure *n* **1** *syn* see BASE 1
ant superstructure
2 *syn* see BASIS 1

infrequent *adj* appearing, happening, or met with so seldom as to attract attention <held only *infrequent* press conferences>
syn few, occasional, rare, scarce, seldom, semioccasional, sporadic, uncommon, unfrequent
rel isolated, scattered; meager, scant, scanty, sparse; exceptional, limited, unusual; odd, spasmodic, stray
idiom few and far between
con abundant, common, numerous, regular; ordinary, routine
ant frequent

infrequently *adv* **1** *syn* see SELDOM
ant frequently
2 *syn* see OCCASIONALLY
ant frequently

infringe *vb* **1** *syn* see TRESPASS 2
2 *syn* see VIOLATE 1
3 *syn* see IMPOSE 5

infringement *n syn* see BREACH 1

infuriate *vb syn* see ANGER 1

infuse *vb* **1** to introduce one thing into another so as to change or affect it <a teacher who *infused* her pupils with the desire to learn>
syn imbue, ingrain, inoculate, invest, leaven, steep, suffuse
rel animate, fire, inform, inspire; implant, inculcate, instill; impregnate, permeate, pervade, saturate; indoctrinate
2 *syn* see INTERFUSE 2

ingather *vb syn* see REAP

ingathering *n syn* see HARVEST 1

ingeminate *vb syn* see REPEAT

ingenerate *adj syn* see INHERENT

ingenious *adj* **1** *syn* see INVENTIVE
2 *syn* see CLEVER 4

ingenuous *adj syn* see NATURAL 5
con covert, furtive, stealthy, surreptitious, underhand; artful, crafty, foxy, guileful, insidious, sly, tricky, wily
ant disingenuous

ingest *vb syn* see EAT 1

inglorious *adj syn* see DISREPUTABLE 1
ant glorious

ingoing *adj syn* see INCISIVE

ingot *n syn* see BAR 1

ingrain *vb* **1** *syn* see ENTRENCH 1

rel engrave, etch, grave, incise
2 *syn* see INFUSE 1

ingrained *adj syn* see INHERENT
rel chronic, confirmed, deep-rooted, inveterate
con exterior, external, outer, outside, outward

ingratiating *adj* intended or designed to gain favor <an *ingratiating* smile>
syn deferential, disarming, ingratiatory, insinuating, insinuative, saccharine, silken, silky
rel adulatory; fawning, sycophantic

ingratiatory *adj syn* see INGRATIATING

ingredient *n syn* see ELEMENT 2

ingress *n* **1** *syn* see ENTRANCE 1
ant egress
2 *syn* see DOOR 2
ant egress

ingress *vb syn* see ENTER 1
ant egress

ingression *n syn* see ENTRANCE 1
ant egression

ingroup *n syn* see CLIQUE
ant outgroup

ingurgitate *vb syn* see GULP

inhabit *vb* to dwell in as a place of settled residence <islands *inhabited* by Polynesians>
syn occupy, people, populate, tenant
rel settle; abide, dwell, live

inhabitable *adj syn* see LIVABLE 1
ant uninhabitable

inhabitancy *n syn* see HABITATION 1

inhabitant *n* one that occupies a particular place regularly <*inhabitants* of large cities>
syn denizen, dweller, habitant, indweller, liver, occupant, resident, ||residenter, resider
rel aborigine, autochthon, indigene, native

inhabitation *n syn* see HABITATION 1

inhale *vb* to draw (as air) into the lungs <*inhaling* smoke>
syn breathe (in), inspire
ant exhale, expire

inharmonic *adj syn* see DISSONANT 1
ant harmonic

inharmonious *adj* **1** *syn* see DISSONANT 1
ant harmonious
2 lacking harmony especially in sentiment <the committee meeting was singularly *inharmonious*>
syn discordant, inconsonant, uncongenial, unharmonious
rel antagonistic, cat-and-dog, conflicting, conflictive, differing, disagreeing, incompatible, incongruous, quarrelsome
con concordant, congenial, consonant; amiable, compatible; collaborative
ant harmonious

inharmony *n syn* see DISCORD
ant harmony

inhaust *vb syn* see ABSORB 1

inhere *vb* **1** *syn* see CONSIST 1
2 *syn* see BELONG 3

inherent *adj* being a part, element, or quality of a thing's inmost being <*inherent* rights of every citizen>
syn born, built-in, congenital, connate, constitutional, deep≠seated, elemental, essential, inborn, inbred, indwelling, ingenerate, ingrained, innate, intimate, intrinsic
rel inner, internal, inward, resident; basic, elementary, fundamental, immanent, integral; characteristic, distinctive, individual, peculiar; natural, normal, regular, typical; bred-in-the-bone
con shallow, superficial; accidental, fortuitous, incidental; alien, extraneous, extrinsic, foreign
ant adventitious

inheritance *n* **1** *syn* see HERITAGE 1
2 *syn* see LEGACY 1

inherited *adj syn* see INNATE 1

inheritor *n syn* see HEIR

inhibit *vb* **1** *syn* see FORBID
rel avert, ward

---

syn synonym(s)   *rel* related word(s)
ant antonym(s)   *con* contrasted word(s)
idiom idiomatic equivalent(s)
|| use limited; if in doubt, see a dictionary

ant allow
2 *syn* see RESTRAIN 1
ant activate; animate
inhibited *adj syn* see FRIGID 3
ant uninhibited
inhuman *adj syn* see FIERCE 1
rel malicious, malign, malignant; implacable, relentless, unrelenting; devilish, diabolical, fiendish
con altruistic, benevolent, charitable, eleemosynary, humanitarian, philanthropic; compassionate, tender
ant humane
inhumane *adj syn* see FIERCE 1
ant humane
inhumation *n syn* see BURIAL 2
ant exhumation
inhume *vb syn* see BURY 1
ant disinhume, exhume
inimicable *adj syn* see HOSTILE 1
inimical *adj syn* see HOSTILE 1
iniquitous *adj syn* see WRONG 1
iniquity *n syn* see EVIL 3
initial *adj* **1** marking a commencement or constituting a start < *initial* symptoms of the disease >
syn beginning, inceptive, incipient, initiative, initiatory, introductory, nascent
rel basic, elementary, first, fundamental; embryonic, germinal; early, infant; antecedent; earliest, introductory, primary
con closing; concluding, conclusive; terminal, terminative; last, ultimate
ant final
2 *syn* see FIRST 2
3 *syn* see FIRST 1
ant final
initially *adv* **1** in the beginning < *initially* we were confused but soon enough we fully understood >
syn originally, primarily, primitively
rel first, firstly, incipiently
idiom at first, at the first go-off, from the word go
con lastly, ultimately
ant finally
2 *syn* see FIRSTLY
initiate *vb* **1** *syn* see BEGIN 1
ant terminate
2 *syn* see INTRODUCE 3
3 to put through the formalities for becoming a member or official < the club *initiated* four new members >
syn inaugurate, induct, install, instate, invest
rel institute; admit, enter, introduce, take in
initiation *n* the process or an instance of being formally introduced into an office or made a member of an organization < a fraternity *initiation* >
syn inaugural, inauguration, induction, installation, investiture
rel baptism; institution, introduction
initiative *adj syn* see INITIAL 1
initiative *n syn* see ENTERPRISE 4
initiatory *adj syn* see INITIAL 1
injudicious *adj syn* see UNWISE
ant judicious
injunction *n syn* see COMMAND 1
injure *vb* **1** to deplete the soundness, strength, effectiveness, or perfection of something < *injured* his prestige by making rash statements >
syn blemish, damage, harm, hurt, impair, mar, prejudice, spoil, tarnish, vitiate
rel disserve; disadvantage; endamage, weaken; blight, queer; foul up, louse up; contort, deface, deform, disfigure, distort; bespatter, foul, smirch; disable, incapacitate
con assist, help, succor; better, enhance, improve; benefit; strengthen
ant aid
2 *syn* see DISTRESS 2
idiom do dirt to
3 to inflict bodily hurt on < was *injured* in an auto accident >
syn hurt, wound
rel damage, harm; afflict, torment, torture; batter, cripple, maim, mangle, mutilate
idiom draw blood
injurious *adj syn* see HARMFUL

injury *n* **1** an act or the result of inflicting something that causes loss or pain < we cannot forgive his *injury* of the painting > < his falsehood caused grave *injury* to his brother's reputation >
syn damage, harm, hurt, mischief, outrage, ruin
rel agony, discomfiture, distress, misery, suffering; pain, pang; detriment, disservice, loss; bad, evil, ill
2 *syn* see INJUSTICE 2
injustice *n* **1** absence of justice < preached against *injustice* >
syn inequitableness, inequity, unfairness, unjustness, wrong
rel crime, malfeasance, malpractice, villainy, wrongdoing; favoritism, inequality, partiality, partisanship
con equity, fairness, right
ant justice, justness
2 an act or instance of unjustness < pointed out various *injustices* in the law > < you do him an *injustice* when you call him lazy >
syn grievance, injury, wrong
rel damage, harm, hurt, mischief, outrage, ruin; breach, infraction, infringement, tort, transgression, trespass, violation
ink *vb syn* see SIGN 1
inkling *n syn* see HINT 1
inky *adj syn* see BLACK 1
||**inland** *adj syn* see DOMESTIC 2
ant foreign
inlet *n* a recess in the shores of a body of water < *inlets* of lakes and rivers >
syn arm, bay, bayou, bight, cove, ||creek, firth, gulf, harbor, ||loch, ||lough, slough
inn *n syn* see HOTEL
innards *n pl syn* see ENTRAILS
innate *adj* **1** existing in or belonging to an individual inherently < *innate* vigor >
syn congenital, connate, connatural, inborn, indigenous, inherited, native, natural, unacquired
rel constitutional, deep-seated, essential, ingrained, inherent, intrinsic; hereditary; normal, regular, standard, typical
con accidental, adventitious, fortuitous, incidental; affected, assumed, feigned, simulated; cultivated, fostered, nurtured
ant acquired
2 *syn* see INHERENT
inner *adj* **1** situated further in < the *inner* layers were less worn >
syn ||innermore, inside, interior, internal, intestine, inward
rel central, focal, middle, nuclear; close, familiar, intimate; constitutional, essential, inherent, intrinsic
con exterior, external, outside, outward
ant outer
2 arising from one's inmost self < *inner* thoughts and feelings >
syn gut, interior, internal, intimate, visceral, viscerous
rel individual, personal, private; concealed, hidden, secret
con exterior, outer; open, public
||**innermore** *adj syn* see INNER 1
innervate *vb syn* see PROVOKE 4
innerve *vb syn* see PROVOKE 4
innholder *n syn* see SALOONKEEPER
innkeeper *n syn* see SALOONKEEPER
innocence *n syn* see IGNORANCE 2
innocent *adj* **1** *syn* see GOOD 11
rel unstained, unsullied, white, white-handed
2 free from legal guilt or fault < the defendant was found *innocent* >
syn blameless, clean, crimeless, faultless, guiltless, inculpable, unguilty
idiom in the clear
ant guilty
3 *syn* see LAWFUL
4 *syn* see DEVOID
5 *syn* see NATURAL 5
6 *syn* see HARMLESS
con harmful, injurious, mischievous
innocuous *adj* **1** *syn* see HARMLESS
con harmful, injurious; evil; troublesome
ant pernicious
2 *syn* see INSIPID 3
innominate *adj syn* see ANONYMOUS
innovation *n syn* see CHANGE 2
rel deviation, introduction, wrinkle
innovational *adj syn* see INVENTIVE

innovative *adj syn* see INVENTIVE

innovator *n* one who introduces something new <an *innovator* of bold ideas in the field of computers>
syn introducer, inventor, original, originator
rel author, creator, maker, producer; architect, builder, developer

innovatory *adj syn* see INVENTIVE

innoxious *adj syn* see HARMLESS
ant noxious

innuendo *n syn* see INSINUATION

innumerable *adj* too many to be counted <received *innumerable* requests for help>
syn countless, innumerous, numberless, uncountable, uncounted, unnumberable, unnumbered, untold
ant numberable, numerable

innumerous *adj syn* see INNUMERABLE

inobnoxious *adj syn* see HARMLESS
ant obnoxious

inobservant *adj syn* see INATTENTIVE
ant observant

inobtrusive *adj syn* see QUIET 4
ant obtrusive

inoculate *vb syn* see INFUSE 1
rel admit, enter, introduce

inodorous *adj syn* see ODORLESS
ant odorous; smelly

inoffensive *adj syn* see HARMLESS
con loathsome, repulsive, revolting; distasteful, obnoxious, repellent, repugnant
ant offensive

inopportune *adj syn* see UNSEASONABLE 1
ant opportune

inordinate *adj* 1 *syn* see EXCESSIVE 1
rel irrational, unreasonable; gratuitous, supererogatory, uncalled-for, wanton; extra, superfluous, surplus
con moderate, temperate; checked, curbed, inhibited, restrained
2 *syn* see EXCESSIVE 2

inordinately *adv syn* see EVER 6

inordinateness *n syn* see EXCESS 3

in passing *adv syn* see INCIDENTALLY 2

in perpetuum *adv syn* see EVER 2

inpour *n syn* see INFLUX
ant outpour, outpouring

inpouring *n syn* see INFLUX
ant outpour, outpouring

inquest *n syn* see INQUIRY 1

inquietude *n syn* see UNREST
rel anxiety, uneasiness
ant quiet, quietness, quietude

inquire *vb syn* see ASK 1
rel investigate, probe, search; scrutinize, study

inquire (into) *vb syn* see EXPLORE

inquiring *adj syn* see INQUISITIVE 1

inquiry *n* 1 the act or an instance of seeking truth, information, or knowledge about something <an exhaustive *inquiry* revealed no evidence of a conspiracy>
syn delving, inquest, inquisition, investigation, probe, probing, quest, research
rel catechizing, interrogation, questioning; audit, check, examination, inspection, scrutiny; hearing; inquirendo
2 a request for information <addressed his *inquiry* to the personnel director>
syn interrogation, interrogatory, query, question, questioning

inquisition *n syn* see INQUIRY 1

inquisitive *adj* 1 given to examination or investigation <an *inquisitive* child who was interested in everything around him>
syn curious, disquisitive, inquiring, investigative, questioning
rel nosy, prying, snoopy
con indifferent, unconcerned, uninquisitive, uninterested
ant incurious
2 *syn* see CURIOUS 2
ant incurious, uninquiring

inquisitorial *adj syn* see CURIOUS 2

inquisitory *adj syn* see CURIOUS 2

in re *prep syn* see APROPOS

in respect to *prep syn* see APROPOS

in reverse *adv syn* see ABOUT 6

inroad *n syn* see INVASION

inroad *vb syn* see INVADE 1

inrush *n syn* see INFLUX
ant outrush

insalubrious *adj syn* see UNWHOLESOME 1
ant salubrious, salutary

insalutary *adj syn* see UNWHOLESOME 1
ant salubrious, salutary

insanable *adj syn* see HOPELESS 2

ins and outs *n pl* characteristic peculiarities or technicalities <soon learned the *ins and outs* of his job>
syn minutiae, ropes
rel details, incidentals, particulars; ramifications; oddities, peculiarities, quirks

insane *adj* 1 being afflicted by or manifesting unsoundness of mind or an inability to control one's rational processes <adjudged *insane* after a period of observation>
syn ‖batty, bedlamite, ‖bonkers, brainsick, ‖buggy, ‖bughouse, ‖bugs, crackbrained, cracked, ‖crackers, ‖cracky, ‖cranky, crazed, crazy, cuckoo, daffy, daft, demented, deranged, disordered, distraught, ‖fruity, ‖loco, lunatic, mad, maniac, ‖mental, mindless, non compos mentis, nuts, nutsy, nutty, reasonless, screwy, teched, unbalanced, unsane, unsound, wacky, witless, wrong
rel irrational, unreasonable; bewildered, distracted; dotty, eccentric, off, rocky, strange, touched; ‖dippy
idiom around the bend, crazy as a coot, not all there, not right in one's head, ‖off one's dot, off one's nut (or rocker), ‖off one's onion, out of (or off) one's head, out of one's mind, touched in the head
con judicious, sapient, sensible, wise; rational, reasonable; balanced; logical, subtle; healthy, sound; clear, lucid
ant sane
2 *syn* see FOOLISH 2
rel fanciful, fantastic, imaginary, visionary; impractical, unrealistic
con feasible, possible, practicable, usable; rational, reasonable, sane, sensible; practical, realistic

insaneness *n syn* see INSANITY 1
ant saneness, sanity

insanity *n* 1 grave disorder of mind that impairs one's capacity to function safely or normally in society <his *insanity* required confinement in a mental institution>
syn aberration, alienation, derangement, distraction, insaneness, lunacy, madness, psychopathy, unbalance
rel acromania; delirium, frenzy, hysteria; delusion, hallucination, illusion; irrationality, unreasonableness; dotage
con judiciousness, sageness, sensibility, wiseness; rationality, reasonableness; healthiness, soundness, wholesomeness
ant saneness, sanity
2 *syn* see FOOLISHNESS
rel asininity, fatuousness, stupidity; impracticality

insatiable *adj* incapable of being satisfied or appeased <an *insatiable* lust for glory>
syn insatiate, quenchless, unappeasable, unquenchable, unsatiate, unsatisfiable
rel unsatiated, unsatisfied; demanding, exigent, importunate, insistent, urgent; clamorous, crying, pressing, yearning
con appeasable, quenchable, satisfiable; satiate, satiated, satisfied; controlled, curbed, restrained
ant satiable

insatiably *adv syn* see VERY 1

insatiate *adj syn* see INSATIABLE
ant satiate, satiated

inscience *n syn* see IGNORANCE 2

inscribe *vb* 1 *syn* see WRITE
rel engrave, enscroll
2 *syn* see LIST 3
3 *syn* see ENGRAVE 2

inscrutable *adj syn* see MYSTERIOUS

insecure *adj* 1 not confident or sure <feels very *insecure* about his future>
syn unassured, unconfident, unsure
rel hesitant, questioning, uncertain

---

syn synonym(s)
ant antonym(s)
idiom idiomatic equivalent(s)
‖ use limited; if in doubt, see a dictionary

rel related word(s)
con contrasted word(s)

idiom in suspense, up in the air
con assured, confident, self-assured, self-confident, sure
ant secure
2 *syn* see WEAK 2
ant secure
inseminate *vb syn* see IMPLANT
insensate *adj* **1** lacking animate awareness or sensation <would often talk to stones and other *insensate* objects>
syn inanimate, insensible, insentient, senseless, unfeeling
rel exanimate, unanimated; anesthetic, insensitive
con aware, cognizant, conscious; feeling, sensible, sensient
ant sensate
2 *syn* see SIMPLE 3
3 *syn* see INSENSIBLE 5
insensibility *n syn* see APATHY 1
ant sensibility
insensible *adj* **1** *syn* see INSENSATE 1
ant sensible
2 deprived of consciousness <knocked *insensible* by a sudden punch>
syn cold, comatose, inconscious, senseless, unconscious
idiom out cold
3 *syn* see NUMB 1
4 *syn* see IMPERCEPTIBLE
ant sensible
5 devoid or insusceptible of emotion or passion <*insensible* to love or compassion>
syn anesthetic, bloodless, dull, hard, impassible, insensate, insensitive, rocky
rel blunt, obtuse; apathetic, impassive, phlegmatic, stoic, stolid; callous, hardened, indurated, pachydermatous, thick-skinned; absorbed, engrossed, intent, rapt
con alert, alive, awake, aware, cognizant, conscious; affected, impressed, influenced, touched
ant sensible
insensitive *adj* **1** *syn* see INSENSIBLE 5
rel aloof, incurious, indifferent, unconcerned
con compassionate, responsive, tender
ant sensitive
2 *syn* see NUMB 1
ant sensitive
3 *syn* see INSUSCEPTIBLE
ant sensitive
insentient *adj* **1** *syn* see INSENSATE 1
ant sentient
2 *syn* see INSUSCEPTIBLE
insert *vb syn* see INTRODUCE 6
rel interlope, intrude, obtrude; implant, inculcate, instill; admit, enter
con detach, disengage
ant abstract, extract
in short *adv syn* see BRIEFLY
inside *n* **1** *syn* see INTERIOR
ant outside
2 insides *pl syn* see ENTRAILS
inside *adj* **1** *syn* see INNER 1
ant outside
2 *syn* see PRIVATE 2
inside *adv syn* see INDOORS
ant outside
inside out *adv syn* see THOROUGHLY 2
insidious *adj syn* see SLY 2
rel perfidious, treacherous; dangerous, perilous; gradual, subtle
insight *n* **1** *syn* see SAGACITY
2 *syn* see INTUITION
insighted *adj syn* see WISE 1
insightful *adj syn* see WISE 1
rel discriminating, penetrating; inseeing
insignia *n* a distinguishing mark of authority, office, or honor <wore a coronet with the strawberry leaf *insignia* of his ducal rank>
syn badge, emblem
rel decoration; regalia
insignificancy *n syn* see NONENTITY
insignificant *adj* **1** *syn* see SENSELESS 5
ant significant
2 *syn* see MINOR 2
3 *syn* see LITTLE 3

ant significant
insincere *adj* not being or expressing what one appears to be or express <an *insincere* person who could not be trusted>
syn ambidextrous, double, double-dealing, double-faced, doublehearted, double-minded, double-tongued, hypocritical, left=handed, mala fide
rel deceitful, dishonest, lying, mendacious, untruthful; shifty, slippery, tricky
con candid, frank, open, plain; direct, forthright, straight, straightforward
ant sincere
insinuate *vb* **1** *syn* see INTRODUCE 6
2 *syn* see SUGGEST 1
rel ascribe, impute
con affirm, assert, aver, avouch, avow, declare, profess; air, broach, express, state, voice
3 to introduce (as oneself) by stealthy, smooth, or artful means <*insinuated* himself into the confidence of others>
syn edge in, foist, infiltrate, work in, worm
rel insert, intercalate, interject, interpolate, interpose, introduce
insinuating *adj syn* see INGRATIATING
insinuation *n* a stealthy or indirect hinting or suggestion <*insinuations* about his opponent's probity>
syn innuendo, insinuendo
rel hint, hinting, implication, implying, intimation, suggestion; animadversion, aspersion, reflection; ascription, imputation
insinuative *adj syn* see INGRATIATING
insinuendo *n syn* see INSINUATION
insipid *adj* **1** *syn* see UNPALATABLE 1
rel bland, mild
con appetizing, flavorable, tasty
ant sapid, savory
2 *syn* see ARID 2
rel commonplace, ordinary, plain; mundane, prosaic, unimaginative
3 devoid of qualities that make for spirit and character <an *insipid* little story of teenage puppy love>
syn banal, bland, driveling, flat, inane, innocuous, jejune, milk=and-water, namby-pamby, sapless, swashy, vapid, waterish, watery, wishy-washy
rel slight, tenuous, thin; feeble, weak; subdued, tame; mild, soft; pointless
con piquant, poignant, pungent, racy, spicy; fiery, gingery, high-spirited, mettlesome, peppery, spirited, spunky; exciting, piquing, provocative, provoking
ant sapid
insistent *adj* **1** *syn* see PERSISTENT 1
2 *syn* see EMPHATIC
rel persevering, persistent, pressing; obtrusive
3 *syn* see PRESSING
insociable *adj syn* see UNSOCIABLE
ant sociable
insolate *vb syn* see SUN
insolence *n* the quality, state, or an instance of being insulting or grossly lacking in respect <court-martialed because of *insolence* to an officer>
syn boldness, disrespect, hardihood, impertinence, impudence, insolency, insolentness; *compare* EFFRONTERY
rel brazenness; presumption; arrogance; rudeness; contempt
con deference; correctness, decency, decorum, decorousness, properness, seemliness
ant respect, respectfulness
insolency *n syn* see INSOLENCE
ant respect, respectfulness
insolent *adj* **1** *syn* see PROUD 1
rel imperative, peremptory; dictatorial, magisterial
ant deferential
2 exhibiting boldness or effrontery <an *insolent* child with no respect or regard for anyone>
syn audacious, bold, ||boldacious, brazen, contumelious, impertinent, impudent, procacious, saucy
rel arrogant, disdainful, overbearing; discourteous, impolite, rude, uncivil, ungracious
con humble, lowly, meek, modest, unassertive; civil, courteous, polite
ant deferential
insolentness *n syn* see INSOLENCE
ant respect, respectfulness

insoluble *adj* admitting of no solution <seemingly *insoluble* problems faced the city council>
  syn inextricable, insolvable, irresoluble, irresolvable, unsoluble, unsolvable
  rel inexplicable, unexplainable; inconceivable, unaccountable; mysterious
  con answerable, explicable, understandable; resolvable; clear, plain, straightforward
  ant soluble, solvable
insolvable *adj syn* see INSOLUBLE
  ant soluble, solvable
insomnia *n* prolonged inability to obtain adequate sleep <sleeping pills failed to relieve his *insomnia*>
  syn insomnolence, sleeplessness
  rel restlessness, wakefulness; stress, tension
insomnolence *n syn* see INSOMNIA
insorb *vb syn* see ABSORB 1
insouciance *n syn* see APATHY 2
insouciant *adj syn* see HAPPY-GO-LUCKY
inspect *vb syn* see SCRUTINIZE 1
  rel notice, observe; catechize, inquire, interrogate, question; review
inspection *n syn* see EXAMINATION
  rel inquest, inquiry, inquisition, investigation, probe, research; oversight, supervision, surveillance
inspiration *n* a divine or seemingly divine imparting of knowledge or power <*inspiration* is the only plausible explanation for his exquisite work>
  syn afflation, afflatus, inflatus
  rel animus, genius, muse, vision; enlightenment, illumination; brainstorm, brain wave
inspire *vb* 1 *syn* see INHALE
  ant expire
  2 *syn* see FIRE 2
  rel quicken, stimulate; infect, infuse; endow, endue
  3 *syn* see ELATE
  4 *syn* see AFFECT
inspiring *adj syn* see EXCITING
  ant uninspiring
inspirit *vb syn* see ENCOURAGE 1
  rel exalt, fire, inform, inspire
  ant dispirit
in spite of *prep syn* see AGAINST 4
instability *n* the state or quality of not being firm or fixed <the *instability* of the economy>
  syn precariousness, shakiness, unfixedness, unsettledness, unstability, unstableness, unsteadfastness, unsteadiness
  rel undependability, unreliability; inconstancy, insecurity
  con firmness, soundness, stoutness, sturdiness; fixity, solidity
  ant stability, stableness
install *vb* 1 *syn* see INITIATE 3
  2 *syn* see ENSCONCE 2
installation *n syn* see INITIATION
instance *n* an individual that clearly belongs to an indicated class <their rescue was an *instance* of great courage>
  syn case, case history, example, illustration, representative, sample, sampling, specimen
  rel ground, proof, reason; detail, item, particular; exponent
instance *vb* 1 *syn* see EXEMPLIFY 1
  2 *syn* see MENTION
  rel exemplify, illustrate
instant *n* 1 an infinitesimal space of time <came not an *instant* too soon>
  syn breathing, crack, flash, ‖jiff, jiffy, minute, moment, second, shake, split second, ‖tick, trice, twinkle, twinkling, wink
  2 *syn* see POINT 7
  3 *syn* see OCCASION 5
instant *adj* 1 *syn* see PRESSING
  2 *syn* see PRESENT
  3 *syn* see INSTANTANEOUS
instantaneous *adj* done, occurring, or acting without any perceptible duration of time <*instantaneous* answers to tough questions>
  syn hair-trigger, immediate, instant; *compare* QUICK 2
  rel spontaneous; fast, quick, rapid; momentary, transitory
  con late, tardy; slow, sluggish
instanter *adv syn* see AWAY 3
instantly *adv syn* see AWAY 3

idiom in a flash, on a dime, on the spot
instate *vb syn* see INITIATE 3
instead *adv* as an alternative to something expressed or implied <longed *instead* for a quiet country life>
  syn alternately, alternatively, in lieu, rather
insteep *vb syn* see SOAK 1
instigate *vb syn* see INCITE
  rel activate, actuate; hint, insinuate, suggest; plan, plot, scheme; goad, urge; fire, inflame
instigation *n syn* see STIMULUS
instigator *n* one that goads or urges forward <the *instigator* of the riot>
  syn agitator, fomenter, inciter, mover
  rel firebrand, incendiary, inflamer, rabble-rouser
instill *vb syn* see IMPLANT
instinctive *adj* 1 prompted by natural instinct or propensity <was quite unable to control her *instinctive* fear of snakes>
  syn instinctual, intuitive, visceral
  rel congenital, inborn, innate; ingrained, inherent, intrinsic; natural
  ant reasoned
  2 *syn* see SPONTANEOUS
  rel natural, normal, regular, typical
  ant intentional
instinctual *adj syn* see INSTINCTIVE 1
institute *vb* 1 *syn* see FOUND 2
  ant abrogate
  2 *syn* see INTRODUCE 3
institute *n syn* see LAW 1
institution *n* something or someone well established in a customary relationship <he's been in the office so long that he has become an *institution*>
  syn fixture
  rel custom, habit; establishment, rite
instruct *vb* 1 *syn* see TEACH
  rel acquaint, apprise, inform; engineer, guide, lead, pilot, steer
  2 *syn* see COMMAND
  rel assign, define, prescribe
instruction *n syn* see EDUCATION 1
instructional *adj syn* see INFORMATIVE
instructive *adj syn* see INFORMATIVE
  rel didactic, moralistic, moralizing
instrument *n* 1 *syn* see MEAN 2
  2 *syn* see IMPLEMENT
  rel equipment, gear, machinery, paraphernalia, tackle
instrumental *adj* serving as a means, agent, or tool <was *instrumental* in organizing the strike>
  syn implemental, ministerial
  rel conducive, helpful; serviceable, useful
instrumentality *n syn* see MEAN 2
  rel energy, force, might, power
instrumentation *n syn* see MEAN 2
insubordinate *adj* unwilling to submit to authority <*insubordinate* soldiers are court-martialed>
  syn contumacious, factious, insurgent, mutinous, rebellious, seditious
  rel intractable, recalcitrant, refractory, ungovernable, unruly; indocile, uncompliant, uncomplying; disaffected, dissentious
  con amenable, biddable, docile, obedient, tractable; subdued, submissive, tame
  ant subordinate
insubstantial *adj* 1 *syn* see IMMATERIAL 1
  ant substantial
  2 *syn* see WEAK 1
  ant substantial
  3 *syn* see TENUOUS 3
  ant substantial
insuccess *n syn* see FAILURE 2
  ant success, successfulness
insufferable *adj* incapable of being endured <that man is an *insufferable* bore>
  syn insupportable, intolerable, unbearable, unbrookable, unendurable, unsufferable, unsupportable

---

syn synonym(s)   *rel* related word(s)
ant antonym(s)   *con* contrasted word(s)
idiom idiomatic equivalent(s)
‖ use limited; if in doubt, see a dictionary

rel distressing, painful; unacceptable
ant sufferable
insufficience *n* **1** *syn* see FAILURE 3
ant sufficiency
2 *syn* see SCARCITY
ant sufficiency
insufficiency *n* **1** *syn* see FAILURE 3
ant sufficiency
2 *syn* see SCARCITY
ant sufficiency
insufficient *adj* **1** *syn* see DEFICIENT 1
ant sufficient
2 *syn* see SHORT 3
ant sufficient
insular *adj* having the narrow and limited outlook characteristic of geographic isolation < the *insular* thinking of peasant communities >
syn local, ‖parish-pump, parochial, provincial, sectarian, small≠town
rel regional, sectional; insulated, isolated, secluded; circumscribed, confined, limited, restricted; illiberal, narrow, narrow≠minded
con broad-minded, liberal; cosmopolitan, metropolitan, urban
insulate *vb* *syn* see ISOLATE
insult *vb* *syn* see OFFEND 3
rel abase, debase, degrade, humble, humiliate; fleer, flout, gibe, gird, jeer, scoff, sneer; deride, mock, ridicule, taunt; rump
con admire, esteem, respect
ant honor
insult *n* *syn* see AFFRONT
rel abuse, invective, obloquy, vituperation; disgrace, ignominy, opprobrium, shame; disdainfulness, insolence, superciliousness; contempt, disdain, scorn; unpleasantry
con deference, homage, honor, obeisance, reverence
insuperable *adj* incapable of being surmounted, overcome, or passed over < they met with *insuperable* difficulties >
syn impassable, inconquerable, indomitable, insurmountable, invincible, unconquerable, unsurmountable
rel unachievable, unattainable; unsurpassable; impregnable, impenetrable, invulnerable
con surmountable; achievable, negotiable
ant superable
insupportable *adj* *syn* see INSUFFERABLE
ant bearable, supportable
insupposable *adj* *syn* see INCREDIBLE 1
ant supposable
insuppressible *adj* *syn* see IRREPRESSIBLE
ant suppressible
insuppressive *adj* *syn* see IRREPRESSIBLE
insure *vb* *syn* see ENSURE
rel guard, protect, safeguard, shield
insurgent *n* *syn* see REBEL
insurgent *adj* *syn* see INSUBORDINATE
insurmountable *adj* *syn* see INSUPERABLE
ant surmountable
insurrect *vb* *syn* see REVOLT 1
insurrectionist *n* *syn* see REBEL
insusceptible *adj* incapable of being moved, affected, or impressed < *insusceptible* to flattery >
syn impassive, insensitive, insentient, unimpressible, unimpressionable, unresponsive, unsusceptible
con impressible, impressionable, responsive, sensitive, sentient
ant susceptible
intact *adj* **1** *syn* see WHOLE 1
ant defective
2 *syn* see VIRGIN 1
ant deflowered
intangible *adj* **1** *syn* see IMPERCEPTIBLE
rel rare, tenuous, thin; slender, slight; aerial, aeriform, airy, ethereal; eluding, elusive, evading, evasive; touchless
ant tangible
2 *syn* see ELUSIVE
integer *n* *syn* see NUMBER
integral *adj* *syn* see WHOLE 3
integral *n* *syn* see WHOLE 2
integrate *n* *syn* see WHOLE 2
integrate *vb* **1** *syn* see HARMONIZE 4
2 *syn* see HARMONIZE 3

3 to join together systematically < an economic system that successfully *integrates* private gain with public responsibility >
syn articulate, concatenate
rel combine, conjoin, link, unite; compact, concentrate, consolidate, unify; blend, coalesce, fuse, merge; organize, systematize
con disperse, dissipate, scatter; analyze, break down, resolve
ant disintegrate
4 *syn* see UNIFY 1
5 *syn* see EMBODY 2
integrative *adj* tending to integrate < *integrative* forces in a fragmented society >
syn centralizing, centripetal, compacting, concentrating, consolidating, unifying
ant disintegrative
integrity *n* **1** *syn* see HONESTY
rel forthrightness, straightforwardness
2 the quality or state of being complete or undivided < trying to maintain the *integrity* of the empire >
syn completeness, entireness, perfection, wholeness
rel soundness, stability; absoluteness, purity, simplicity
intellect *n* **1** *syn* see REASON 5
rel comprehension; intuition
2 a person with great intellectual powers < one of the great *intellects* of his time >
syn brain, intellectual, intelligence
rel genius; egghead, pundit; thinker
intellection *n* *syn* see IDEA
intellective *adj* *syn* see MENTAL 1
intellectual *adj* **1** *syn* see MENTAL 1
con animal, fleshly, sensual
ant carnal
2 devoted to or engaged in the creative use of the intellect < the play appealed to the *intellectual* members of the audience >
syn cerebral, highbrow, highbrowed, intellectualistic
intellectual *n* **1** *syn* see INTELLECT 2
2 a person who possesses or has pretensions of strong intellectual interest or superiority < accused of being an *intellectual* and a snob >
syn Brahmin, double-dome, egghead, highbrow
3 intellectuals *pl* *syn* see INTELLIGENTSIA
intellectualistic *adj* *syn* see INTELLECTUAL 2
intelligence *n* **1** the ability to learn and to cope < what he lacked in education, he made up in *intelligence* >
syn brain(s), brainpower, mentality, mother wit, sense, wit
rel acumen, discernment, insight, judgment; perspicacity, sagacity, wisdom
2 *syn* see INTELLECT 2
3 *syn* see NEWS
intelligent *adj* **1** *syn* see RATIONAL
con irrational, unreasonable
ant unintelligent
2 mentally keen or quick < quite *intelligent* for his age >
syn alert, brainy, bright, brilliant, clever, knowing, knowledgeable, quick-witted, ready-witted, sharp, smart; *compare* WISE 4
rel astute, perspicacious, sagacious, shrewd; acute, keen; adroit, cunning, ingenious
con foolish, idiotic, imbecilic, moronic; crass, dense, dull, dumb, slow, stupid
ant unintelligent
intelligentsia *n* a class of articulate persons devoted to intellectual, cultural, and social matters < the *intelligentsia* posed a threat to the new regime >
syn clerisy, illuminati, intellectuals, literati
rel avant-garde, vanguard
intelligible *adj* *syn* see UNDERSTANDABLE
ant unintelligible
intemperance *n* *syn* see EXCESS 3
rel drunkenness, insobriety; debauchery
ant temperance
intemperate *adj* **1** *syn* see EXCESSIVE 2
rel bibacious, bibulous, crapulous, drunken; gluttonous
ant temperate, tempered
2 *syn* see SEVERE 3
ant temperate
intempestive *adj* *syn* see IMPROPER 1
intemporal *adj* *syn* see ETERNAL 4
ant temporal
intend *vb* **1** *syn* see MEAN 2

2 to have in mind as a purpose < *intended* to read the book >
syn aim, contemplate, design, mean, ‖mind, plan, propose, purpose
rel attempt, endeavor, essay, strive, try; plot, scheme; assign, designate, destine
idiom figure on, have in mind to, look forward to

intendance *n syn* see OVERSIGHT 1

intended *adj syn* see ENGAGED 2

intended *n syn* see BETROTHED

intendment *n* **1** *syn* see INTENTION
2 *syn* see MEANING 1

intensate *vb syn* see INTENSIFY

intense *adj* **1** extreme in degree, power, or effect < *intense* hatred >
syn concentrated, desperate, exquisite, fierce, furious, terrible, vehement, vicious, violent
rel aggravated, enhanced, heightened, intensified; accentuated, emphasized, stressed
ant subdued
2 *syn* see INTENSIVE
3 *syn* see ARDENT 2
ant slight

intensely *adv* **1** *syn* see HARD 3
rel fiercely, furiously, vehemently, viciously, violently
2 *syn* see SERIOUSLY 2

intensify *vb* to increase markedly in measure or degree < both companies *intensified* their efforts to win the contract > < the pain *intensified* sharply >
syn aggravate, deepen, enhance, heighten, intensate, magnify, mount, redouble, rise, rouse
rel accent, accentuate, emphasize, stress; aggrandize, exalt; sharpen
con moderate, qualify; alleviate, ease, lighten, relieve; decrease, diminish, lessen, reduce
ant abate; allay, mitigate; temper

intensive *adj* highly concentrated < an *intensive* study of the causes of the war >
syn blood-and-guts, deep, hard, intense, profound
con casual, shallow, superficial

intensively *adv syn* see HARD 3

intent *n* **1** *syn* see INTENTION
rel conation, volition, will
con chance, fortune, hap, hazard, luck
ant accident
2 *syn* see MEANING 1

intent *adj* **1** having one's mind or attention deeply fixed < the student was too *intent* on his work to hear the phone >
syn absorbed, deep, engaged, engrossed, immersed, preoccupied, rapt, wrapped, wrapped up
rel attending, attentive, minding, watching; concentrated, riveted
con absent, absent-minded, abstracted, bemused, faraway, preoccupied; daydreaming, napping, oblivious
ant distracted
2 *syn* see DECIDED 2

intention *n* what one purposes to accomplish or do < his *intention* was to finish by noon >
syn animus, design, intendment, intent, meaning, plan, purpose; *compare* AMBITION 2
rel project, scheme; desire, hope, wish

intentional *adj syn* see VOLUNTARY
rel intended, meant, proposed, purposed; advised, considered, designed, designful, premeditated, studied
con accidental, casual, fortuitous; careless, heedless, inadvertent, thoughtless
ant unintentional

intentionally *adv* with intention < hurt her *intentionally* >
syn ‖apurpose, deliberately, designedly, on purpose, prepensely, purposedly, purposely, purposively
ant unintentionally

intentive *adj syn* see ATTENTIVE 1

intently *adv syn* see HARD 4

intentness *n syn* see EARNESTNESS

inter *vb syn* see BURY 1
ant disinter

interact *vb* to act upon one another < humor and pathos *interacted* to make a moving drama >
syn coact, interplay, interreact

rel collaborate, cooperate; combine, join, merge, unite

interagent *n syn* see GO-BETWEEN 2

interblend *vb syn* see MIX 1

interbreed *vb syn* see CROSS 4

intercalate *vb syn* see INTRODUCE 6

intercede *vb syn* see INTERPOSE 2

interceder *n syn* see GO-BETWEEN 2

intercept *vb* to stop, seize, or interrupt in progress or course < *intercept* a forward pass >
syn block, catch, cut off
rel grab, seize, take; check, curb
con fumble, miss; loose, release

intercessor *n syn* see GO-BETWEEN 2

interchange *vb syn* see EXCHANGE 3
rel reverse, transpose

interchangeable *adj* permitting mutual substitution < *interchangeable* parts >
syn commutable, exchangeable, fungible, interconvertible, substitutable
rel changeable, convertible; reciprocal, reciprocative

interchurch *adj syn* see NONSECTARIAN

intercommunication *n* **1** *syn* see COMMUNICATION 3
2 *syn* see CONTACT 2

intercomparable *adj syn* see LIKE

interconnect *vb syn* see INTERJOIN

interconvertible *adj syn* see INTERCHANGEABLE

intercourse *n* **1** *syn* see COMMERCE 2
2 *syn* see COMMUNICATION 3
3 *syn* see CONTACT 2

intercreedal *adj syn* see NONSECTARIAN

intercross *vb* **1** *syn* see INTERSECT
2 *syn* see CROSS 4

interdenominational *adj syn* see NONSECTARIAN

interdict *vb syn* see FORBID
ant sanction

interdiction *n syn* see TABOO
ant sanction

interest *n* **1** participation in advantage, profit, and responsibility < he owned a half *interest* in a furniture store >
syn claim, share, stake
2 *syn* see WELFARE
3 readiness to be concerned with or moved by something < had an *interest* in art >
syn concern, curiosity, interestedness, regard
rel enthusiasm, excitement, passion; attention, care, concernment; absorption, engrossment
con apathy, indifference, unconcern
ant disinterest

interest *vb* to engage the attention and interest of < his appeal failed to *interest* his listeners >
syn appeal, attract, excite, fascinate, intrigue
rel arouse, tantalize, titillate; lure, pull, snare, tempt; pique
ant bore

interested *adj* having a share or concern in some affair < all *interested* parties met for the reading of the will >
syn affected, concerned, implicated, involved
rel biased, partial, partisan, prejudiced
con aloof, incurious, indifferent, unconcerned; apathetic, bored, ennuyé
ant detached, disinterested

interestedness *n syn* see INTEREST 3

interfere *vb* **1** *syn* see INTERPOSE 2
rel bar, block, hinder, impede, obstruct
2 *syn* see MEDDLE
rel discommode, incommode, inconvenience, trouble; baffle, balk, foil, frustrate, thwart

interflow *vb syn* see MIX 1

interfuse *vb* **1** *syn* see MIX 1
2 to cause to pass into or through < *interfused* illuminating anecdotes with the informative text >
syn diffuse, infuse, interlard, intersow, intersperse, intersprinkle
rel impenetrate, impregnate, interpenetrate, penetrate, pervade, saturate

---

syn synonym(s)   **rel** related word(s)
ant antonym(s)   **con** contrasted word(s)
idiom idiomatic equivalent(s)
‖ use limited; if in doubt, see a dictionary

3 syn see PERMEATE

interfusion *n syn* see MIXTURE

interim *n syn* see GAP 3

interim *adj syn* see TEMPORARY

interior *adj* 1 *syn* see INNER 1
  con extraneous, extrinsic, foreign
  ant exterior
  2 syn see INNER 2

interior *n* the internal or inner part < the *interior* of the house >
  syn inside, inward(s), within
  rel center, heart; belly, bosom; innards, internals
  ant exterior, outside

interject *vb syn* see INTRODUCE 6

interjoin *vb* to join mutually < *interjoined* several stations into a new system >
  syn anastomose, interconnect, interlink, intertie
  rel interdigitate, interlace, interlock, interrelate
  con disunite, part, separate, sunder
  ant disjoin

interknit *vb syn* see INTERWEAVE

interlace *vb syn* see INTERWEAVE

interlard *vb syn* see INTERFUSE 2

interlink *vb syn* see INTERJOIN

interlope *vb* 1 *syn* see INTRUDE
  2 syn see MEDDLE

interlude *n* an intervening or interruptive period or space < an *interlude* of happiness in a tragic story > < woodland broken by *interludes* of meadow >
  syn break, intermission, interregnum, interval, parenthesis
  rel breather, lull, pause, respite, rest; episode, idyll; meantime, meanwhile, spell; entr'acte

intermeddle *vb syn* see MEDDLE
  rel encroach, entrench, invade, trespass

intermeddler *n syn* see BUSYBODY

intermediary *adj syn* see MIDDLE 2

intermediary *n* 1 *syn* see GO-BETWEEN 2
  2 syn see MEAN 2

intermediate *vb syn* see INTERPOSE 2

intermediate *adj* 1 *syn* see MIDDLE 2
  2 syn see MEDIUM

intermediate *n syn* see GO-BETWEEN 2

intermediator *n syn* see GO-BETWEEN 2

interment *n syn* see BURIAL 2
  ant disinterment

intermesh *vb syn* see ENGAGE 1

interminable *adj syn* see CONTINUAL
  rel eternal, infinite; lasting, permanent
  con intermittent, periodic; discontinued, stopped; closed, completed, ended, finished, terminated

intermingle *vb* see MIX 1

intermission *n* 1 *syn* see ABEYANCE
  2 syn see INTERLUDE

intermit *vb syn* see DEFER
  rel arrest, check, interrupt
  con continue, persist; iterate, reiterate, repeat

intermittent *adj* occurring or appearing in interrupted sequence < they predict *intermittent* rain throughout the day >
  syn alternate, isochronal, isochronous, periodic, periodical, recurrent, recurring
  rel cyclic, cyclical, iterant, iterative, metrical, rhythmic, rhythmical, seasonal, serial; arrested, checked, interrupted; fitful, spasmodic; infrequent, occasional, sporadic; discontinuing, discontinuous
  con constant, perpetual; everlasting, interminable
  ant continual, continuous; incessant, unceasing

intermix *vb syn* see MIX 1

intermixture *n syn* see MIXTURE

intermutual *adj syn* see COMMON 1

intern *vb syn* see IMPRISON

internal *adj* 1 *syn* see INNER 1
  ant external
  2 syn see INNER 2
  3 syn see DOMESTIC 2
  ant external

internals *n pl syn* see ENTRAILS

internuncio *n syn* see MESSENGER

interpenetrate *vb syn* see PERMEATE

interplay *vb syn* see INTERACT

interpolate *vb syn* see INTRODUCE 6
  rel admit, enter; interlope, intrude; add, annex, append, superadd
  con cancel, delete, erase, expunge

interpose *vb* 1 *syn* see INTRODUCE 6
  rel cast, throw, toss; push, shove, thrust
  2 to come between disagreeing elements < forced to *interpose* when the argument grew heated >
  syn intercede, interfere, intermediate, intervene, mediate, step in
  rel butt in, interlope, intrude, obtrude; intermeddle, meddle; arbitrate, moderate, negotiate

interpret *vb* 1 *syn* see EXPLAIN 1
  rel exemplify, illustrate; annotate, gloss; comment, commentate
  con contort, deform, distort; garble, misrepresent; misconstrue, misunderstand
  2 syn see REPRESENT 1

interpretation *n* 1 *syn* see EXPLANATION 1
  2 manner of artistic presentation in performance or adaptation or an instance of this < *interpretation* involves a re-creative effort by the performer >
  syn reading, rendering, rendition, version

interpretive *adj syn* see EXPLANATORY

interreact *vb syn* see INTERACT

interregnum *n syn* see INTERLUDE

interrogate *vb syn* see ASK 1

interrogation *n* 1 *syn* see CROSS-EXAMINATION
  2 syn see INQUIRY 2

interrogatory *n syn* see INQUIRY 2

interrupt *vb* 1 *syn* see ARREST 1
  rel defer, intermit, postpone, suspend
  2 to ask questions or make remarks while another is speaking < a chatterbox who habitually *interrupts* everyone >
  syn break in, chime in, chip in
  rel cut in, put in
  idiom break in on (or upon)

interruption *n* 1 *syn* see GAP 3
  rel rent, rift, rupture, split
  2 syn see ABEYANCE

intersect *vb* to divide by passing through or across < parallel lines can never *intersect* >
  syn crisscross, cross, crosscut, decussate, intercross
  rel traverse; bisect

intersow *vb syn* see INTERFUSE 2

intersperse *vb syn* see INTERFUSE 2

intersprinkle *vb syn* see INTERFUSE 2

intertangle *vb syn* see ENTANGLE 1

intertie *vb syn* see INTERJOIN

intertrude *vb syn* see INTRUDE 1

intertwine *vb syn* see INTERWEAVE

intertwist *vb syn* see INTERWEAVE

interval *n* 1 *syn* see PAUSE
  2 syn see INTERLUDE
  3 syn see GAP 3

intervene *vb syn* see INTERPOSE 2
  rel divide, part, separate, sever

intervolve *vb syn* see INTERWEAVE

interweave *vb* to blend or unite intimately < joy and melancholy are often closely *interwoven* >
  syn interknit, interlace, intertwine, intertwist, intervolve, interwind, interwork, interwreathe, inweave
  rel associate, join, link; blend, fuse, mix

interwind *vb syn* see INTERWEAVE

interwork *vb syn* see INTERWEAVE

interwreathe *vb syn* see INTERWEAVE

intestinal fortitude *n syn* see FORTITUDE

intestine *adj* 1 *syn* see DOMESTIC 2
  2 syn see INNER 1

intimacy *n syn* see ACQUAINTANCE 1

intimate *vb syn* see SUGGEST 1
  rel attest, bespeak, betoken, indicate
  con air, express, utter, vent, voice; affirm, assert, aver, avouch, declare, profess

intimate *adj* 1 *syn* see INHERENT
  2 syn see INNER 2
  3 syn see FAMILIAR 1
  rel nearest, next; affectionate, devoted, fond, loving; privy, secret
  con distant, remote

4 having or marked by a warm personal relation <*intimate* friends for many years> <an *intimate* friendship>
syn ‖buddy-buddy, chummy, cozy, pally, ‖palsy-walsy
idiom thick as thieves
intimate *n syn* see FRIEND
rel associate, companion, comrade, crony
con outsider, stranger
intimation *n* **1** *syn* see HINT 1
2 *syn* see HINT 2
intimidate *vb* to frighten or coerce into submission or obedience <refused to be *intimidated* by the manager>
syn bludgeon, bluster, ‖bounce, browbeat, bulldoze, bully, bullyrag, cow, dragoon, hector, ‖ruffle, strong-arm, terrorize
rel alarm, disquiet, frighten, scare, terrify; badger, bait, chivy, hound, ride; coerce, compel, constrain, force, oblige; ‖ruffianize
con blandish, cajole, coax, wheedle; induce, persuade, prevail
intimidator *n syn* see BULLY 1
into *prep syn* see TO 1
intolerable *adj syn* see INSUFFERABLE
ant tolerable
intolerant *adj* **1** unwilling or unable to endure with composure <he was inclined to be very *intolerant* of interruption>
syn impatient, unforbearing, unindulgent
rel contemptuous, disdainful; fractious, irritable, snappish, waspish; indignant, irate, outraged, stuffy, upset, worked up
con forbearing, indulgent, long-suffering, patient; resigned, uncomplaining
ant tolerant
2 *syn* see ILLIBERAL
rel inflexible, obdurate; antipathetic, averse, unsympathetic
con forbearing, indulgent, lenient
ant tolerant
intonation *n syn* see INFLECTION
in toto *adv syn* see ALL 1
intoxicant *n syn* see LIQUOR 2
intoxicated *adj* **1** significantly under the influence of alcoholic liquor <some people become *intoxicated* more easily than others>
syn alcoholized, ‖bagged, blind, ‖blotto, ‖boiled, ‖bombed, ‖boozed, ‖boozy, ‖buffy, ‖buzzed, ‖canned, ‖capernoited, cock-eyed, ‖crocked, cut, ‖deleerit, disguised, drunk, drunken, fried, ‖half-seas over, inebriated, inebrious, ‖jagged, ‖juiced, ‖lit, ‖lit up, ‖loaded, looped, ‖lushed, muddled, ‖oiled, ‖organized, ‖pickled, ‖pie-eyed, ‖pipped, pixilated, ‖plastered, polluted, ‖potted, rum-dum, ‖screwy, ‖shick, ‖shicker, ‖shot, slewed, slopped, sloppy, ‖smashed, soshed, sozzled, ‖spiflicated, squiffed, ‖stewed, stiff, ‖stinking, ‖stinko, stoned, ‖swacked, tanked, ‖tiddly, tight, unsober, wet, zonked
rel befuddled, bemused, besotted, dazed, dopey, fuddled, loopy, maudlin, sodden, soppy, sotted, tipsy
idiom disguised with drink, full as a tick, in drink (*or* liquor), in one's cups, in the bag, stewed to the gills, the worse for drink, three sheets in (*or* to) the wind, under the table, under the weather, with drink taken
con abstemious, abstinent, moderate, temperate
ant sober
2 profoundly and usually pleasantly moved <*intoxicated* with the beauty of the scene>
syn elated, excited, exhilarated, turned-on
rel affected, concerned, interested, moved; galvanized, piqued, quickened, stimulated
con disinterested, unconcerned; depressed, disheartened, distressed, saddened
intoxicating *adj syn* see EXCITING
intoxication *n syn* see EUPHORIA 2
intractable *adj* **1** *syn* see UNRULY 1
ant tractable
2 *syn* see OBSTINATE
ant tractable
intransigent *adj syn* see OBSTINATE
intrepid *adj syn* see BRAVE 1
ant craven
intricate *adj* **1** *syn* see COMPLEX 2
rel arduous, difficult, hard
2 *syn* see ELABORATE 2
intrigue *vb* **1** *syn* see INTEREST
2 *syn* see PLOT
intrigue *n* **1** *syn* see PLOT 2

2 *syn* see AMOUR 2
intrinsic *adj syn* see INHERENT
con added, annexed, appended, superadded
ant extrinsic
intrinsically *adv syn* see PER SE
introduce *vb* **1** *syn* see ENTER 2
rel inaugurate, induct, install; bring forward
2 *syn* see BROACH
3 to bring into practice or use <*introduce* reforms in the welfare system>
syn inaugurate, initiate, institute, launch, originate, set up, usher in
rel establish, found, organize; innovate, invent; unveil; pioneer
4 to cause to know each other personally <planned to *introduce* her to his mother>
syn acquaint, present, ‖quaint
5 *syn* see PRECEDE 3
6 to put among or between others <*introduced* several new lines of dialogue>
syn fill in, insert, insinuate, intercalate, interject, interpolate, interpose, throw in
rel inlay, inlet, inset; inject, instill; work in
con eject, evict, oust; eliminate, exclude
ant abstract; withdraw
introducer *n syn* see INNOVATOR
introduction *n* something that serves as a preliminary or antecedent <the crisis could be the *introduction* to a general war>
syn exordium, foreword, overture, preamble, preface, prelude, prelusion, proem, prolegomenon, prologue
introductory *adj* **1** *syn* see PRELIMINARY
ant closing, concluding
2 *syn* see INITIAL 1
introspection *n* the examination of one's own thought and feeling <a man much given to *introspection*>
syn heart-searching, self-contemplation, self-examination, self=observation, self-questioning, self-reflection, self-scrutiny, self=searching, soul-searching
rel contemplation, meditation, reflection; self-analysis
ant extrospection
intrude *vb* **1** to thrust or force in without permission, welcome, or fitness <constantly *intruded* himself into his sister's affairs>
syn butt in, chisel (in), cut in, horn in, intertrude, obtrude
rel encroach, entrench, infringe, invade, muscle, trespass; insinuate, intercalate, interject, interpolate, interpose, introduce; interfere, intervene; intermeddle, meddle; bother, disturb, pester
con retire, stand off, withdraw
2 *syn* see IMPOSE 5
intrusive *adj syn* see IMPERTINENT 2
rel butting in, intruding, obtruding
con bashful, coy, diffident, modest, retiring, shy
ant unintrusive
intuition *n* immediate apprehension or cognition <skeptical of the traditional woman's *intuition*>
syn anschauung, insight, intuitiveness
rel second sight, sixth sense
ant ratiocination
intuitive *adj syn* see INSTINCTIVE 1
rel direct, immediate, presentative
ant ratiocinative
intuitiveness *n syn* see INTUITION
inumbrate *vb syn* see SHADE
inundate *vb syn* see DELUGE 1
inundation *n syn* see FLOOD 2
inurbane *adj syn* see RUDE 6
ant urbane
inure *vb syn* see ACCUSTOM
rel discipline, train
inutile *adj syn* see WORTHLESS 1
ant utile
invade *vb* **1** to enter for conquest or plunder <the Danes *invaded* England>
syn foray, inroad, overrun, overswarm, raid
rel loot, pillage, plunder, ravage

---

syn synonym(s)	**rel** related word(s)
ant antonym(s)	**con** contrasted word(s)
idiom idiomatic equivalent(s)	
‖ use limited; if in doubt, see a dictionary	

2 *syn* see TRESPASS 2
 rel impenetrate, interpenetrate, permeate, pervade
invalid *adj* **1** *syn* see ILLOGICAL
 ant valid
 2 *syn* see NULL
invalidate *vb* *syn* see ABOLISH 1
 rel counteract, counterbalance, negative, neutralize, offset; discredit
 ant validate
invaluable *adj* *syn* see PRECIOUS 1
 ant worthless
invariable *adj* **1** *syn* see INFLEXIBLE 3
 ant variable
 2 *syn* see SAME 3
 ant variable, varying
invariably *adv* **1** *syn* see ALWAYS 1
 2 *syn* see EVER 3
invasion *n* a hostile entrance into the territory of another < Hitler's *invasion* of Poland >
 syn foray, incursion, inroad, irruption, raid
 rel aggression, attack, offense, offensive; breach, infraction, infringement, transgression, trespass, violation; encroachment, entrenchment
invective *adj* *syn* see ABUSIVE
 rel censorious, condemnatory, damnatory, denunciatory, reproachful
invective *n* *syn* see ABUSE
 rel diatribe, jeremiad, philippic, tirade
inveigh (against) *vb* *syn* see OBJECT 1
inveigle *vb* *syn* see LURE
inveiglement *n* *syn* see LURE 2
invent *vb* *syn* see CONTRIVE 2
 rel conceive, envision, imagine; create, mint, produce, turn out; inaugurate, initiate
invention *n* a product of creative imagination < his most famous *invention* is the electric light bulb >
 syn brainchild, coinage, contrivance
 rel concoction, contraption, innovation, novelty; creation, opus, original
inventive *adj* adept or prolific at producing new things and ideas < had a very *inventive* turn of mind > < he was an *inventive* genius >
 syn creative, demiurgic, deviceful, ingenious, innovational, innovative, innovatory, original, originative
 rel fertile, fruitful, productive, teeming; causative, constructive, formative
 con sterile, uncreative, unproductive
 ant uninventive
inventor *n* **1** *syn* see INNOVATOR
 2 *syn* see FATHER 2
inventory *n* **1** *syn* see SUPPLY
 2 *syn* see RESERVE
inventory *vb* **1** to make an itemized report or record of < will *inventory* all office supplies >
 syn catalog, itemize, tally
 rel list, record, register; enumerate, tabulate
 idiom take account (*or* stock) of
 2 *syn* see ITEMIZE 1
 3 *syn* see EPITOMIZE 1
inveracity *n* *syn* see LIE
 ant veracity
inverse *vb* *syn* see REVERSE 1
inversion *n* *syn* see REVERSAL 1
invert *vb* *syn* see REVERSE 1
 rel flip, turn down, turn over
invert *n* *syn* see HOMOSEXUAL
invertebrate *n* *syn* see WEAKLING
invertebrate *adj* *syn* see WEAK 4
 rel disorganized, structureless
inverted *adj* **1** *syn* see UPSIDE-DOWN 1
 2 *syn* see HOMOSEXUAL
invest *vb* **1** *syn* see INITIATE 3
 rel endow, endue; consecrate, honor
 ant divest, strip
 2 to make a formal grant of power or authority < the Constitution *invests* the Congress with taxation powers >
 syn authorize, empower, vest
 rel bequeath, endow

con hold back, keep back, reserve, withhold
 ant divest
 3 *syn* see ENFOLD 1
 4 *syn* see BESIEGE
 5 *syn* see INFUSE 1
investigate *vb* *syn* see EXPLORE
 rel muckrake, poke, pry
investigation *n* *syn* see INQUIRY 1
 rel observation, observing; sounding, survey, surveying
investigative *adj* *syn* see INQUISITIVE 1
investigator *n* *syn* see DETECTIVE
investiture *n* *syn* see INITIATION
inveterate *adj* **1** firmly established or having something firmly established < the *inveterate* tendency to overlook the obvious >
 syn bred-in-the-bone, confirmed, deep-dyed, deep-rooted, deep-seated, dyed-in-the-wool, entrenched, hard-shell, irradicable, settled, sworn
 rel accustomed, addicted, chronic, habituated; customary, habitual, usual; hardened, indurated; established, fixed, set; inbred, innate; abiding, enduring, persistent, persisting
 2 *syn* see OLD 2
invidious *adj* **1** *syn* see LIBELOUS
 2 *syn* see ENVIOUS
 rel bitter; hateful
 3 *syn* see REPUGNANT 1
 rel abominable, detestable, hateful, odious
 con agreeable, grateful, gratifying, pleasant, pleasing
invidiousness *n* *syn* see ENVY
invigorate *vb* *syn* see STRENGTHEN 2
 rel refresh, rejuvenate, renew, restore; rally, rouse, stir; activate, animate, stimulate, vitalize, vitaminize
 ant debilitate
invigorating *adj* having an enlivening effect < an *invigorating* discussion >
 syn animating, bracing, exhilarating, exhilarative, quickening, stimulating, stimulative, tonic, vitalizing
 rel brisk, lively; fascinating, interesting
 con anesthetic, numbing, somniferous
 ant deadening
invincible *adj* **1** incapable of being conquered < the team proved to be *invincible* >
 syn impregnable, inconquerable, indomitable, inexpugnable, invulnerable, unassailable, unbeatable, unconquerable, undefeatable
 rel inviolable, untouchable; unattackable
 con conquerable, subduable, surmountable, vanquishable
 ant vincible
 2 *syn* see INSUPERABLE
 ant vincible
inviolable *adj* *syn* see SACRED 3
 rel consecrated, hallowed; blessed, divine, holy; chaste, pure
 ant violable
inviolate *adj* *syn* see SACRED 3
 rel intact, perfect; faultless, flawless
 con desecrated, profaned; defiled, polluted
invisible *adj* *syn* see IMPERCEPTIBLE
 rel hidden, unseeable
 ant visible
invitation *n* *syn* see PROPOSAL
invite *vb* to request the presence or participation of < *invited* guests to dinner > < *invited* the major nations to confer >
 syn ask, bid
 rel call, call in, summon; court, solicit, woo; entice, inveigle, lure, tempt
invoice *n* *syn* see BILL 1
invoke *vb* **1** *syn* see BEG
 2 *syn* see ENFORCE
involuntary *adj* *syn* see SPONTANEOUS
 rel unintended, unintentional, unwitting
 ant voluntary
involve *vb* **1** to bring a person or thing into circumstances or a situation from which extrication is difficult < nations *involved* in war >
 syn embroil, implicate, mire, tangle; *compare* ENTANGLE 3
 rel catch up; draw (into)
 2 *syn* see INCLUDE
involved *adj* **1** *syn* see COMPLEX 2
 rel confused, muddled

con easy, facile, simple
2 syn see INTERESTED
rel enmeshed, entangled
ant uninvolved
involvement *n syn* see ENTANGLEMENT 1
invulnerable *adj syn* see INVINCIBLE 1
ant vulnerable
inward *adj syn* see INNER 1
con alien, extraneous, extrinsic, foreign
ant outward
inward *n* **1** *often* **inwards** *pl syn* see INTERIOR
2 inwards *pl syn* see ENTRAILS
inwardness *n syn* see ACQUAINTANCE 1
inweave *vb syn* see INTERWEAVE
iota *n syn* see PARTICLE
ipseity *n syn* see INDIVIDUALITY 4
irascible *adj* easily aroused to anger <an *irascible* fellow and hard to get along with>
syn choleric, cranky, cross, hot-tempered, ireful, passionate, peppery, quick-tempered, ratty, ‖stomachy, temperish, testy, tetchy, touchy; *compare* CANTANKEROUS, IRRITABLE
rel fractious, huffy, irritable, peevish, petulant, querulous, snappish, waspish; impatient, jittery, jumpy, nervous, restive; bristly, crabbed, surly
con amiable, complaisant, good-natured, obliging; calm, quiet, relaxed; long-suffering, patient, tolerant
irate *adj syn* see ANGRY
ire *n syn* see ANGER
ire *vb syn* see ANGER 1
ireful *adj* **1** *syn* see ANGRY
2 syn see IRASCIBLE
irenic *adj syn* see PACIFIC
ant acrimonious
irk *vb* **1** *syn* see ANNOY 1
rel discommode, incommode, inconvenience, trouble
2 syn see TRY 2
irking *n syn* see ANNOYANCE 1
irksome *adj* tending to cause boredom or tedium <an *irksome* task>
syn boresome, boring, drudging, tedious, tiresome, tiring
rel dull, stupid; exhausting, fagging, fatiguing, wearisome
con exciting, inspiring, provocative, stimulative, stirring
ant absorbing, engrossing
iron *n, usu* **irons** *pl syn* see SHACKLE
iron *adj syn* see INFLEXIBLE 2
ironbound *adj syn* see ROUGH 1
ironclad *adj syn* see INFLEXIBLE 3
ironfisted *adj* **1** *syn* see STINGY
2 syn see GRIM 3
ironhanded *adj syn* see RIGID 3
ironhead *n syn* see DUNCE
ironhearted *adj syn* see UNFEELING 2
ant softhearted
ironic *adj syn* see SARDONIC
rel biting, cutting, incisive, trenchant; caustic, mordant, scathing
‖**ironman** *n syn* see DOLLAR
irradiate *vb syn* see ILLUMINATE 2
irradicable *adj syn* see INVETERATE 1
irrational *adj syn* see ILLOGICAL
rel crazy, demented, insane
con logical, reasonable, sensible
ant rational
irrealizable *adj syn* see IMPOSSIBLE 1
ant realizable
irrebuttable *adj syn* see POSITIVE 3
ant rebuttable
irreclaimable *adj syn* see IRRECOVERABLE
ant reclaimable
irreconcilable *adj* incapable of being made consistent <the two versions of the story are completely *irreconcilable*>
syn incompatible, inconformable, inconsistent
rel discordant, discrepant, dissonant, inaccordant, incongruent, incongruous, inharmonious
ant reconcilable
irrecoverable *adj* not capable of being recovered, regained, remedied, or rectified <suffered an *irrecoverable* loss in the fire>
syn irreclaimable, irredeemable, irremediable, irreparable, irretrievable

ant recoverable
irredeemable *adj syn* see IRRECOVERABLE
ant redeemable
irreflective *adj syn* see CARELESS 1
ant reflective
irrefragable *adj syn* see INDESTRUCTIBLE
irrefrangible *adj syn* see INDESTRUCTIBLE
irrefutable *adj syn* see POSITIVE 3
ant refutable
irregular *adj* **1** not according with or explainable by law, rule, or custom <unusual problems require *irregular* solutions>
syn abnormal, anomalous, deviant, divergent, off-key, unnatural, unregular
rel aberrant, atypical; exceptional, odd, peculiar, queer, singular, strange, unique
con natural, normal, typical; accustomed, customary, habitual, usual, wonted
ant regular
2 syn see INFORMAL 1
3 syn see LOPSIDED
ant regular
4 syn see RANDOM
rel occasional, sporadic; erratic, fitful, spasmodic; inconstant, uneven, unsteady
5 syn see SPOTTY 1
irregular *n syn* see PARTISAN 2
irregularity *n syn* see INEQUALITY 1
ant regularity
irregularly *adv syn* see OCCASIONALLY
ant regularly
irrelative *adj syn* see IRRELEVANT
ant relative
irrelevant *adj* not applicable or pertinent <age should be *irrelevant* to employability>
syn extraneous, foreign, immaterial, impertinent, inapplicable, inapposite, irrelative
rel inconsequential, insignificant, unimportant
idiom beside the point, neither here nor there, out of the question
con applicable, appurtenant, germane, material, pertinent, significant
ant relevant
irreligious *adj* lacking religious emotions, doctrines, or practices <an *irreligious* person but not openly hostile to organized religion>
syn godless, nonreligious, unreligious
rel indevout, undevout; ungodly, unholy, unsanctimonious; blasphemous, impious, profane, sacrilegious; amoral, unmoral
con devout, pious
ant religious
irremediable *adj* **1** *syn* see IRRECOVERABLE
ant remediable
2 syn see HOPELESS 2
irremovable *adj syn* see IMMOVABLE 1
ant removable
irreparable *adj* **1** *syn* see IRRECOVERABLE
ant reparable
2 syn see HOPELESS 2
irreprehensible *adj syn* see GOOD 11
ant reprehensible
irrepressible *adj* impossible to repress, restrain, or control <an *irrepressible* joy over his brother's good fortune>
syn insuppressible, insuppressive, irrestrainable, uncontainable, uncontrollable, unrestrainable
rel bubbling over, effervescent, enthusiastic, rhapsodical
ant repressible
irreproachable *adj* **1** *syn* see GOOD 11
2 syn see IMPECCABLE 1
irresoluble *adj syn* see INSOLUBLE
ant resoluble
irresolute *adj syn* see VACILLATING 2
ant resolute
irresolution *n syn* see HESITATION

---

syn synonym(s)   *rel* related word(s)
ant antonym(s)   *con* contrasted word(s)
idiom idiomatic equivalent(s)
‖ use limited; if in doubt, see a dictionary

ant resolution

irresolvable *adj syn* see INSOLUBLE
ant resolvable

irresponsible *adj* lacking in responsibility <*irresponsible* behavior>
syn carefree, careless, feckless, incautious, reckless, uncareful, wild
rel undependable, unreliable, untrustworthy; unaccountable, unanswerable
con careful, cautious, discreet, heedful; dependable, reliable, trustworthy
ant responsible

irrestrainable *adj syn* see IRREPRESSIBLE
ant restrainable

irretrievable *adj syn* see IRRECOVERABLE
ant retrievable

irreverent *adj syn* see IMPIOUS 1
ant reverent

irreverential *adj syn* see IMPIOUS 1
ant reverential

irreversible *adj syn* see IRREVOCABLE
ant reversible

irrevocable *adj* incapable of being recalled or revoked <an *irrevocable* decision of the Supreme Court>
syn irreversible, nonreversible, unrepealable
rel constant, established, fixed; immutable, unchangeable, unmodifiable
con repealable, reversible; alterable, changeable, modifiable
ant revocable

irritable *adj* easily exasperated <the miserable weather made us all *irritable*>
syn disagreeable, fractious, fretful, huffy, peevish, pettish, petulant, ‖pindling, prickish, prickly, querulent, querulential, querulous, raspish, raspy, snappish, snappy, twitty, waspish, waspy, whiny; *compare* CANTANKEROUS, IRASCIBLE
rel cranky, cross, testy, touchy; choleric, irascible, splenetic
con amiable, complaisant, good-natured, obliging; affable, cordial, genial, gracious, sociable
ant easygoing

irritant *n syn* see ANNOYANCE 3

irritate *vb* to excite to angry annoyance <his rude interruptions really *irritated* her>
syn aggravate, burn (up), exasperate, gall, get, grate, huff, inflame, nettle, peeve, pique, provoke, put out, rile, roil; *compare* ANNOY 1
rel abrade, bother, ‖bug, chafe, exercise, fret, irk, ruffle, try, vex; anger, enrage, incense, infuriate, madden; affront, offend
con appease, conciliate, mollify, pacify, placate, propitiate; delight, gladden, gratify, please

irrupt *vb syn* see ERUPT 1

irruption *n syn* see INVASION

Ishmael *n syn* see OUTCAST

Ishmaelite *n syn* see OUTCAST

island *vb syn* see ISOLATE

isochronal *adj syn* see INTERMITTENT

isochronous *adj syn* see INTERMITTENT

isolate *vb* to set apart from others <the jury was *isolated* for several days>
syn close off, cut off, enisle, insulate, island, segregate, separate, sequester
rel quarantine; block (off); abstract, detach, disengage, remove; divide, part, sever, sunder
con associate, connect, join, link, unite

isolate *adj syn* see ALONE 1

isolated *adj syn* see ALONE 1
rel retired, secluded, withdrawn; abandoned, deserted, forsaken, stranded

isolation *n syn* see SOLITUDE

issue *n* **1** *syn* see OFFSPRING
2 *syn* see EFFECT 1
3 *syn* see PROBLEM 2
rel matter; subject, topic

issue *vb* **1** *syn* see SPRING 1
2 *syn* see EMIT 2
3 *syn* see PUBLISH 2

italicize *vb syn* see EMPHASIZE

itch *n* **1** *syn* see DESIRE 1
2 *syn* see LUST 2

itch *vb syn* see LONG

itchy *adj syn* see COVETOUS

item *adv syn* see ALSO 2

item *n syn* see POINT 1
rel component, piece; incidental, minutia

itemize *vb* **1** to set down in detail or by particulars <*itemize* deductions on a tax form>
syn enumerate, inventory, list, particularize, specialize, specify; *compare* SPECIFY 3
rel circumstantiate, document; count, number; cite, instance, mention; spell out
ant summarize
2 *syn* see INVENTORY

itemized *adj syn* see CIRCUMSTANTIAL
ant summarized

iterate *vb syn* see REPEAT

itinerant *adj* traveling from place to place <*itinerant* preachers>
syn ambulant, ambulatory, deambulatory, itinerate, nomadic, perambulant, perambulatory, peripatetic, roving, vagabond, vagrant, wandering, wayfaring
rel rambling, ranging, roaming; moving, shifting

itinerate *adj syn* see ITINERANT

itsy-bitsy *adj syn* see TINY

itty-bitty *adj syn* see TINY

‖**ivory** *n often* **ivories** *pl syn* see DICE

ivory-tower *adj syn* see IMPRACTICAL 1
ant down-to-earth

ivory-towered *adj syn* see IMPRACTICAL 1

ivory-towerish *adj syn* see IMPRACTICAL 1

J

jab *vb syn* see POKE 1

jab *n* **1** *syn* see POKE 1
2 *syn* see PRICK

jabber *vb syn* see GIBBER

jabber *n* **1** *syn* see GIBBERISH 1
2 *syn* see CHATTER

jabberer *n syn* see CHATTERBOX

jabberwocky *n syn* see GIBBERISH 1

jack *n* **1** *syn* see MARINER
2 *syn* see FLAG
‖**3** *syn* see MONEY

jack (up) *vb syn* see RAISE 9

jackass *n* **1** *syn* see DONKEY 1
2 *syn* see FOOL 1

jacket *n syn* see HIDE

jackleg *adj syn* see AMATEURISH

jackleg lawyer *n syn* see PETTIFOGGER

jackpot *n syn* see POT 3

jack-tar *n syn* see MARINER

jade *n* **1** *syn* see WANTON
2 *syn* see MINX

jade *vb* **1** *syn* see TIRE 1
rel cloy, pall, sate, satiate, surfeit; emasculate, enervate, unman, unnerve; depress, oppress, weigh
con rejuvenate, renew, restore
ant refresh
2 *syn* see SATIATE

jaded *adj* **1** *syn* see TIRED 1
ant refreshed

2 syn see SATIATED

‖**jag** *n syn* see PRICK

jag *n syn* see BINGE 1

‖**jag** *vb syn* see CARRY 1

jagged *adj syn* see ROUGH 1

‖**jagged** *adj syn* see INTOXICATED 1

jail *n* a building or institution for the confinement of persons held in lawful custody < sent to *jail* for perjury >
  syn bastille, ‖big house, bridewell, ‖brig, ‖bucket, ‖caboose, ‖calaboose, ‖can, ‖carcel, ‖chokey, ‖clink, ‖college, cooler, coop, freezer, guardroom, ‖hoosegow, jug, keep, lockup, pen, penitentiary, ‖pokey, prison, reformatory, rock pile, skookum-house, slammer, ‖stir, stockade
  idiom house of correction

jail *vb syn* see IMPRISON
  ant release

jailbird *n syn* see CONVICT

jake *n syn* see RUSTIC

jakes *n pl but sing or pl in constr syn* see PRIVY 1

jalopy *n* a dilapidated old automobile < bought a *jalopy* for $50 >
  syn clunker, crate, dog, heap, junker, wreck

jam *vb* **1** *syn* see PRESS 1
  rel tamp, wad
  2 syn see CRAM 1
  3 syn see PRESS 7

jam *n syn* see PREDICAMENT

jam *n* a rich spread prepared by boiling fruit and sugar until the mixture thickens < enjoyed his mother's tasty berry *jams* >
  syn confiture, conserve, preserve
  rel jelly, marmalade

jam-full *adj syn* see FULL 1

jammed *adj syn* see FULL 1

jam-pack *vb syn* see CRAM 1

jam-packed *adj syn* see FULL 1

jangle *vb syn* see CLASH 2

jangle *n syn* see DIN

jape *n syn* see JOKE 1

jar *vb* **1** *syn* see CLASH 2
  2 syn see SHAKE 2

jar *n syn* see IMPACT
  rel fluctuation, sway, vibration; agitation, disturbance, upset

jargon *n* **1** *syn* see TERMINOLOGY
  2 syn see DIALECT 2
  rel idiom, speech; abracadabra, gibberish

jarring *adj syn* see HARSH 3
  ant soothing

jaundiced *adj syn* see BIASED 2

jaunt *n syn* see EXCURSION 1

‖**jaw** *n syn* see BACK TALK

jaw *vb* **1** *syn* see SCOLD 1
  2 syn see CHAT 1

jay *n syn* see RUSTIC

jazz *n syn* see NONSENSE 2

jealous *adj* **1** intolerant of rivalry or unfaithfulness < her husband was *jealous* of her flirting with other men >
  syn possessive, possessory
  rel covetous, demanding; grasping, grudging; envious, green-eyed, invidious; mistrustful, suspicious; doubting, questioning
  con tolerant, trusting, understanding
  2 syn see ENVIOUS
  3 syn see SUSPICIOUS 2

jealousy *n syn* see ENVY

jeer *vb syn* see SCOFF
  con fawn, toady, truckle; approve, endorse, OK, sanction

jejune *adj syn* see INSIPID 3
  rel slight, slim, tenuous, thin; arid, dry

jell *vb syn* see COAGULATE
  rel stiffen, thicken; cohere, stick

jellify *vb syn* see COAGULATE

jelly *vb syn* see COAGULATE

jellyfish *n syn* see WEAKLING

jeopard *vb syn* see ENDANGER

jeopardize *vb syn* see ENDANGER

jeopardous *adj syn* see DANGEROUS 1

jeopardy *n syn* see DANGER
  rel exposure; liability, openness, susceptibility; accident, chance, hap
  ant safety

jeopardy *vb syn* see ENDANGER

jeremiad *n syn* see TIRADE

jerk *vb* to act on with or make a sudden sharp quick movement < *jerked* to one side > < *jerk* a root from the ground >
  syn lug, lurch, snap, twitch, vellicate, yank
  rel drag, pull; fling, sling, throw, toss; wrench, wrest, wring

jerk *n syn* see FOOL 1

jerkwater town *n syn* see BURG

jerry-build *vb syn* see THROW UP 1

jest *n* **1** *syn* see JOKE 1
  rel banter, chaff, jolly; derision, ridicule, twit
  2 syn see FUN 1
  con gravity, seriousness, soberness
  ant earnest
  3 syn see LAUGHINGSTOCK

jest *vb* **1** *syn* see SCOFF
  2 syn see BANTER

jestee *n syn* see LAUGHINGSTOCK

jester *n* **1** *syn* see FOOL 2
  2 syn see HUMORIST 2

jet *adj syn* see BLACK 1

jet *vb syn* see SQUIRT

jetsam *n syn* see DRIFTWOOD

jet set *n syn* see SMART SET

jettison *n syn* see DISPOSAL 2

jettison *vb syn* see DISCARD
  ant salvage

jetty *n syn* see WHARF

jetty *adj syn* see BLACK 1

jewel *n syn* see PARAGON

jewel *vb syn* see BEJEWEL

jezebel *n syn* see WANTON

jib *vb syn* see DEMUR

jibe *vb syn* see AGREE 4

‖**jiff** *n syn* see INSTANT 1

jiffy *n syn* see INSTANT 1

jig *n syn* see TRICK 1

jigger *n* **1** *syn* see DOODAD
  2 syn see GADGET 1

‖**jiggery-pokery** *n syn* see NONSENSE 2

jiggle *vb syn* see SHAKE 3

jillion *n syn* see SCAD

jim-dandy *n syn* see ‖DILLY

‖**jimjams** *n syn* see JITTERS

‖**jimmies** *n syn* see JITTERS

jimmy *vb syn* see PRY

jingle *vb* to make a repeated sharp light ringing sound < the coins *jingled* in his pocket >
  syn chink, chinkle, clink, tingle, tinkle
  rel clack, clatter, rattle

jinx *n* something that is felt or meant to bring bad luck < his continual bad luck seemed due to a *jinx* >
  syn hex, hoodoo, Indian sign, voodoo, whammy
  rel charm, enchantment, spell; curse, evil eye

jitters *n pl* a sense of panic or extreme nervousness < got the *jitters* whenever he thought of the money he had lost >
  syn all-overs, dither, heebie-jeebies, ‖jimjams, ‖jimmies, jumps, shakes, shivers, willies

jittery *adj syn* see NERVOUS

‖**jive** *vb syn* see BANTER

job *n* **1** *syn* see TASK 1
  rel affair, concern, matter, thing
  2 a regular remunerative employment < held two *jobs* to make ends meet >
  syn appointment, berth, billet, connection, office, place, position, post, situation, spot; *compare* WORK 1
  rel assignment, engagement, posting; calling, employment, occupation, pursuit; profession, trade, vocation; niche, opening, slot
  3 syn see WORK 1
  4 syn see TASK 2

job *vb syn* see DUPE

jobless *adj syn* see UNEMPLOYED

---

syn synonym(s)   **rel** related word(s)
ant antonym(s)   **con** contrasted word(s)
idiom idiomatic equivalent(s)
‖ use limited; if in doubt, see a dictionary

jockey *vb syn* see MANIPULATE 2
jocose *adj syn* see WITTY
  rel playful, roguish, sportive, waggish, whimsical; comic, comical, droll, laughable, ludicrous; blithe, jocund, jolly, jovial
  con demure, earnest, grave, sedate, serious, sober, solemn, staid
  ant lugubrious
jocular *adj syn* see WITTY
  rel jolly, jovial, merry; playful, sportive; comic, comical, droll, laughable, ludicrous
  con earnest, grave, serious, sober, solemn
jocularity *n syn* see MIRTH
jocund *adj syn* see MERRY
  rel mischievous, playful, sportive
  con dour, gloomy, glum, morose, saturnine, sullen; grave, sedate, serious, solemn, somber, staid
jocundity *n syn* see MIRTH
jog *vb syn* see POKE 1
  rel agitate, shake
joggle *vb syn* see SHAKE 3
john *n syn* see TOILET
John Law *n syn* see POLICEMAN
johnny *n syn* see TOILET
join *vb* 1 to bring or come together into some manner of union <the couple were *joined* in marriage soon thereafter>
  syn associate, bracket, coadunate, coagment, coalesce, combine, compound, concrete, conjoin, conjugate, connect, couple, link, marry, one, relate, unite, wed, yoke
  rel agree, concur, cooperate; articulate, concatenate, integrate; affix, attach, fasten; knit, weave; bind, tie, tie up
  con separate, sever, sunder; detach, disengage; disembarrass, disentangle, untangle
  ant disjoin, part
  2 *syn* see ADJOIN
join (up) *vb syn* see ENTER 3
joining *n syn* see JOINT 1
joint *n* 1 a place where two or more things are united <the leak was found at a *joint* in the pipeline>
  syn connection, coupling, joining, junction, juncture, seam, union
  rel crux, link, tie; interconnection; abutment, articulation, suture; concourse, confluence, meeting
  2 *syn* see DIVE
joint *adj syn* see COMMON 1
jointly *adv syn* see TOGETHER 3
joke *n* 1 a remark, story, or action intended to evoke laughter <had a good memory for *jokes*>
  syn crack, drôlerie, drollery, gag, jape, jest, quip, sally, waggery, wisecrack, witticism, ‖yak
  rel antic, caper, dido, monkeyshine, prank; bijouterie, bon mot; burlesque, caricature, parody, quiz, rib; badinage, persiflage, raillery; facetiousness, humorousness, jocoseness, jocularity, wittiness; humor, repartee, sarcasm, wit
  2 *syn* see FUN 1
  3 *syn* see LAUGHINGSTOCK
joke *vb syn* see BANTER
joker *n* 1 *syn* see WAG 1
  2 *syn* see HUMORIST 2
  3 *syn* see ZANY 2
jokester *n* 1 *syn* see HUMORIST 2
  2 *syn* see ZANY 2
jollity *n* 1 *syn* see MIRTH
  rel blitheness; disport, frolic, gambol, play, rollick, romp, sport
  con earnestness, gravity, sedateness, seriousness, solemnity, staidness
  ant somberness
  2 *syn* see MERRYMAKING
jolly *adj syn* see MERRY
  rel frolicsome, mischievous, playful, roguish, sportive, waggish
  con earnest, grave, sedate, serious, solemn, staid; doleful, dolorous, lugubrious, rueful
  ant somber
jolly *vb syn* see BANTER
  rel blandish, cajole
jolt *vb syn* see SHOCK 2
jolt *n* 1 *syn* see IMPACT
  2 *syn* see DRAM
jongleur *n syn* see BARD 1
josh *vb syn* see BANTER

joskin *n syn* see RUSTIC
jostle *vb syn* see PUSH 2
jot *n syn* see PARTICLE
jounce *n syn* see IMPACT
journal *n* a publication that appears at regular intervals <a monthly scientific *journal*>
  syn magazine, newspaper, organ, periodical, review
journey *n* passing or a passage from one place to another <at that time it was a four day *journey* from Boston to New York> <she was tired though their *journey* was barely begun>
  syn expedition, peregrination(s), travel(s), trek, trip; *compare* TRIP 1
  rel excursion, jaunt, junket, sally, tour; cruise, voyage; pilgrimage, progress, safari
journey *vb syn* see GO 1
jovial *adj syn* see MERRY
  rel facetious, humorous, jocose, jocular; affable, genial, sociable; amiable, good-natured; bantering, chaffing, jollying, joshing
  con dour, gloomy, glum, morose, saturnine, sullen; grave, sedate, serious, solemn, staid
joviality *n syn* see MIRTH
joy *n syn* see PLEASURE 2
  rel ecstasy, rapture, transport
  ant sorrow; misery
joyance *n syn* see PLEASURE 2
joyful *adj syn* see GLAD 1
  rel buoyant, effervescent, expansive
  con despairing, desperate, despondent, forlorn, hopeless; depressed, oppressed, weighed down
  ant joyless
‖joy girl *n syn* see PROSTITUTE
‖joyhouse *n syn* see BROTHEL
‖joy–juice *n syn* see LIQUOR 2
joyless *adj* 1 *syn* see SAD 2
  2 *syn* see GLOOMY 3
joyous *adj syn* see GLAD 1
  rel ecstatic, rapturous, transported
  con doleful, dolorous, melancholy; miserable, wretched
  ant lugubrious
jubilance *n syn* see EXULTATION
jubilant *adj syn* see EXULTANT
jubilate *vb syn* see EXULT
jubilation *n syn* see EXULTATION
judge *n* 1 a person who impartially decides unsettled questions or controversial issues <the *judge* declared the ruling invalid>
  syn arbiter, arbitrator, referee, umpire
  rel intermediary, mediator, negotiator; conciliator, peacemaker, reconciler
  2 an official entrusted with administration of laws <the *judge* gave the defendant a suspended sentence>
  syn beak, court, justice, magistrate
judge *vb* 1 to decide something in dispute or controversy upon its merits and upon evidence <the committee will *judge* the truth of the testimony>
  syn adjudge, adjudicate, arbitrate, referee, umpire
  rel decide, determine, rule, settle
  2 *syn* see INFER
  rel demonstrate, prove, show; check, test, try
  3 *syn* see ESTIMATE 3
judgmatic *adj syn* see WISE 2
judgment *n* 1 *syn* see INFERENCE 1
  rel decision, determination, ruling; belief, conviction, opinion, persuasion, view
  2 *syn* see INFERENCE 2
  3 *syn* see ESTIMATION 1
  4 *syn* see SENSE 6
  rel astuteness, perspicacity, sagacity, shrewdness; acumen, discernment, insight, penetration
judicious *adj syn* see WISE 2
  rel rational, reasonable; dispassionate, equitable, fair, objective
  con irrational, thoughtless, unreasonable; ill-considered
  ant injudicious; asinine
jug *n syn* see JAIL
jug *vb syn* see IMPRISON
juggle *vb syn* see DECEIVE
‖juice *n syn* see LIQUOR 2
‖juiced *adj syn* see INTOXICATED 1
juicy *adj syn* see SUCCULENT

juju *n syn* see CHARM 2
jumble *vb* **1** *syn* see CONFUSE 5
  2 *syn* see DISORDER 1
jumble *n* **1** *syn* see CLUTTER 2
  2 *syn* see MISCELLANY 1
jumbo *adj syn* see HUGE
jump *vb* **1** to move suddenly through space by or as if by muscular action <*jumped* across the open trench>
  syn bounce, bound, hop, hurdle, leap, lop, saltate, spring, vault
  2 *syn* see START 1
  3 *syn* see RAISE 9
jump (in *or* into) *vb syn* see PITCH IN 1
jump (off) *vb syn* see BEGIN 1
jumps *n pl syn* see JITTERS
jumpy *adj syn* see NERVOUS
  idiom on pins and needles
junction *n* **1** *syn* see CONCOURSE
  2 *syn* see JOINT 1
juncture *n* **1** *syn* see JOINT 1
  2 a critical or crucial time or state of affairs <was at a *juncture* where he had to make a decision>
  syn contingency, crisis, crossroad(s), emergency, exigency, pass, pinch, strait, turning point, zero hour
  rel condition, posture, situation, state, status; plight, predicament, quandary
  3 *syn* see POINT 7
jungle *n* **1** *syn* see CLUTTER 2
  2 *syn* see MAZE 1
junk *n syn* see REFUSE
junk *vb syn* see DISCARD
junker *n syn* see JALOPY
junket *n syn* see EXCURSION 1
junking *n syn* see DISPOSAL 2
Junoesque *adj syn* see CURVACEOUS
jurisdiction *n syn* see POWER 1
  rel bounds, confines, limits; compass, range, reach, scope; bailiwick, domain, field, province, sphere, territory
just *adj* **1** *syn* see WELL-FOUNDED
  2 *syn* see TRUE 3
  3 being what is called for by circumstances or accepted standards <punishments once considered fair and *just* are now held to be cruel, excessive, and unreasonable>
  syn appropriate, condign, deserved, due, merited, requisite, rhadamanthine, right, rightful, suitable; *compare* FIT 1
  rel fit, fitting, meet, proper
  con farfetched, irrelevant, remote, unconnected; improper, inapplicable, inapposite, inappropriate; abusive, cruel, harsh
  ant unjust
  4 *syn* see UPRIGHT 2
  rel rigid, strict; dependable, reliable, tried, trustworthy
  5 *syn* see FAIR 4
  rel aloof; condign, due, rightful
  ant unjust
  6 *syn* see FIT 1
just *adv* **1** as stated or indicated without deviation <*just* six inches long>

syn accurately, bang, exactly, precisely, right, sharp, ‖smack⸗ dab, spang, square, squarely
rel definitely, directly, expressly, unmistakably
con almost, nearly; approximately, imprecisely, inaccurately, inexactly, loosely
  2 by a very small margin <*just* enough food for one meal>
syn barely, hardly, scarce, scarcely
rel almost, approximately, nearly
con copiously, fully, generously, lavishly, unstintedly, unstintingly
  3 no more than <*just* a note to remind you>
syn but, merely, only, simply
idiom nothing but
  4 *syn* see ALL 1
  5 *syn* see EVEN 1
just about *adv syn* see NEARLY
justice *n* **1** the action, practice, or obligation of awarding each his just due <his *justice* was stern but absolutely fair>
syn equity
rel evenness, fairness, impartiality
con foul play, inequity, unjustness; bias, leaning, one-sidedness, partiality
ant injustice
  2 *syn* see JUDGE 2
justifiable *adj* capable of being justified <thought her absence was not *justifiable*>
syn condonable, defensible, excusable, tenable, vindicable, warrantable
rel admissible, allowable, legitimate, reasonable; forgivable, pardonable, remissible
ant unjustifiable
justification *n* **1** *syn* see EXPLANATION 2
  2 *syn* see APOLOGY 1
justified *adj syn* see WELL-FOUNDED
ant unjustified
justify *vb* **1** *syn* see MAINTAIN 2
rel demonstrate, prove; back, support, uphold
con confute, disprove, refute
  2 *syn* see CONFIRM 2
  3 *syn* see EXPLAIN 3
rel extenuate, gloss, gloze, palliate, whitewash
con accuse, arraign, incriminate, indict; blame, condemn, denounce
  4 to constitute sufficient grounds <thought the storm warning *justified* his leaving early>
syn warrant
rel allow, permit; approve, authorize, sanction
justly *adv syn* see WELL 1
jut *vb* **1** *syn* see BULGE
rel elongate, extend, lengthen
  2 *syn* see HANG 4
jut *n syn* see PROJECTION 1
juvenile *adj syn* see YOUNG 1
ant adult
juvenile *n syn* see CHILD 1
juvenility *n syn* see YOUTH 1
juxtaposed *adj syn* see ADJACENT 3

---

syn synonym(s)   *rel* related word(s)
ant antonym(s)   *con* contrasted word(s)
idiom idiomatic equivalent(s)
‖ use limited; if in doubt, see a dictionary

‖kale *n syn* see MONEY
keck *vb syn* see RETCH
keel (over) *vb syn* see FALL 2
keen *adj* **1** *syn* see SHARP 1
2 *syn* see ENTHUSIASTIC
3 *syn* see EAGER
rel fervent, fervid, perfervid; fierce, intense, vehement; fired
con apathetic, impassive, phlegmatic, stolid; languid, listless
4 *syn* see SHARP 4
5 *syn* see ACUTE 3
con dull, obtuse
6 *syn* see LIVELY 1
‖7 *syn* see MARVELOUS 2
keenly *adv syn* see HARD 6
keenness *n* **1** *syn* see EDGE 2
2 *syn* see WIT 3
keep *vb* **1** *syn* see OBEY
ant neglect
2 to notice or honor a day, occasion, or deed <remember the Sabbath and *keep* it rightly>
syn celebrate, commemorate, observe, solemnize
rel regard, respect; bless, consecrate, sanctify; honor, laud, praise
idiom keep the faith
con disregard, forget, ignore, neglect, omit, overlook, slight; contravene, infringe, transgress, violate
ant break
3 *syn* see STOCK
4 *syn* see RESTRAIN 1
ant release
5 to hold in one's possession or under one's control <*kept* all the money for himself>
syn detain, hold, hold back, keep back, keep out, reserve, retain, withhold
rel conserve, preserve, save; enjoy, have, own, possess; conduct, control, direct, manage
con cast, discard, junk; refuse, reject, repudiate, spurn; abandon, resign, surrender, yield
ant relinquish
6 *syn* see REFRAIN 1
7 *syn* see CONDUCT 3
keep *n* **1** *syn* see LIVING
2 *syn* see JAIL
keep back *vb* **1** *syn* see KEEP 5
2 *syn* see DENY 2
keeper *n syn* see CUSTODIAN
keeping *n* **1** *syn* see CUSTODY
2 *syn* see PRESERVATION 1
keep off *vb syn* see FEND (off)
keep out *vb syn* see KEEP 5
keepsake *n syn* see REMEMBRANCE 3
keep up *vb syn* see MAINTAIN 1
keg *n syn* see CASK
‖keister *n syn* see BUTTOCKS
kelter *n syn* see REFUSE
ken *n* the extent of one's recognition, comprehension, perception, understanding, or knowledge <abstractions that are beyond the *ken* of small children>
syn horizon, purview, range, reach
rel comprehension, grasp, perception, understanding
kept woman *n syn* see HARLOT 1
kerchief *n* **1** a square of cloth used as a head covering or scarf <wore a *kerchief* around his neck>
syn babushka, bandanna
2 *syn* see HANDKERCHIEF
kernel *n syn* see SUBSTANCE 2
key *n syn* see PASSPORT
kibitzer *n syn* see BUSYBODY
kick *vb* **1** *syn* see OBJECT 1
rel combat, fight, oppose, resist, withstand; anathematize, condemn, curse, damn, execrate
idiom put up a fight (against)

2 *syn* see COMPLAIN
kick *n syn* see THRILL
‖kick around *vb syn* see DISCUSS 1
kick back *vb syn* see BACKFIRE
kicker *n syn* see GROUCH
‖kick in *vb* **1** *syn* see CONTRIBUTE 1
2 *syn* see DIE 1
kick off *vb* **1** *syn* see BEGIN 1
‖2 *syn* see DIE 1
kick out *vb* **1** *syn* see DISMISS 3
2 *syn* see EJECT 1
kickshaw *n syn* see DELICACY
kid *n syn* see CHILD 1
kid *vb* **1** *syn* see DUPE
2 *syn* see BANTER
kidnap *vb* to carry off a person surreptitiously for an illegal purpose <an ex-convict *kidnapped* the child for ransom>
syn abduct, ‖snatch, spirit (away)
rel shanghai, waylay; coax, decoy, entice, inveigle, lure, seduce
idiom make off with
con deliver, ransom, redeem, rescue; bring (back), give back, restore, return
kidney *n syn* see TYPE
kid stuff *n syn* see SNAP 1
kill *vb* **1** to deprive of life <found it hard to *kill* animals>
syn carry off, cut off, destroy, dispatch, down, finish, lay low, put away, scrag, slay, take off; *compare* MURDER 1
rel butcher, choke, drown, massacre, poison, shoot, slaughter, suffocate; knife, sacrifice, stifle; annihilate, exterminate, ruin
idiom do (or make) away with, do for, put out of the way, put (or do) to death, put to sleep, take one's life
2 *syn* see VETO
killer *n syn* see MURDERER
killing *n syn* see MURDER
kiln *vb syn* see FIRE 6
kilter *n syn* see ORDER 10
kin *n* **1** *syn* see FAMILY
2 the members of one's immediate or extended family <all our *kin* gathered to celebrate great grandma's birthday>
syn cousinage, cousinhood, kinfolk, kinsmen
3 *syn* see RELATIVE
kind *n syn* see TYPE
kind *adj* showing or having a gentle considerate nature <mother was a *kind* person, always willing to help others>
syn benign, benignant, good-hearted, kindly
rel altruistic, benevolent, charitable, eleemosynary, humane, humanitarian, openhearted, philanthropic, propitious; compassionate, kindhearted, responsive, sympathetic, tender, warm, warmhearted; clement, forbearing, indulgent, lenient, merciful, tolerant; affable, amiable, cordial, genial, good-humored, good-natured, good-tempered, sweet-tempered; complaisant, obliging; gentle, good
con cruel, fell, fierce, inhuman, savage; hard, harsh, rough; grim, implacable, merciless, unrelenting
ant unkind
kindhearted *adj syn* see TENDER
kindle *vb* **1** *syn* see LIGHT 1
rel blaze, flame, flare, glow; excite, provoke, stimulate; arouse, foment, incite, instigate, rouse, stir
ant smother
2 *syn* see STIR 1
ant stifle
kindless *adj syn* see ANTIPATHETIC 2
kindliness *n syn* see GOODWILL 1
ant unkindliness
kindly *adj syn* see KIND
rel gracious, sociable; friendly, neighborly; attentive, considerate, thoughtful
con malevolent, malicious, malign, spiteful
ant unkindly; acrid (*of temper, attitudes, comments*)
kindly *adv syn* see WELL 2
kindness *n syn* see FAVOR 4

kind of *adv syn* see SOMEWHAT 2
kindred *n syn* see FAMILY 1
kindred *adj syn* see RELATED
  ant alien
kinfolk *n pl syn* see KIN 2
king *n syn* see MAGNATE
kingdom come *n syn* see HEAVEN 2
kinglike *adj syn* see KINGLY
kingly *adj* of, relating to, or befitting a king <a *kingly* entourage>
  syn kinglike, majestic, monarchal, monarchial, monarchical, regal, royal, sovereign
  rel imperious, lordly, masterful, powerful, puissant; imperial, princely, queenly
kinky *adj syn* see OUTLANDISH 3
kinsman *n* **1** *syn* see RELATIVE
  2 kinsmen *pl syn* see KIN 2
kinswoman *n syn* see RELATIVE
kismet *n syn* see FATE
kiss *vb* **1** to touch with the lips especially as a sign of affection <*kissed* his mother good night>
  syn buss, lip, osculate, peck, smack, smooch, ‖smoodge, ‖smouch
  2 *syn* see BRUSH
‖**kisser** *n syn* see FACE 1
kiss off *vb syn* see DISMISS 5
kite *vb syn* see GET OUT 1
kittenish *adj syn* see PLAYFUL 1
kitty *n syn* see POT 3
klutz *n syn* see OAF 2
knack *n* **1** *syn* see GIFT 2
  rel quickness, readiness
  ant ineptitude
  2 *syn* see ABILITY 2
  3 *syn* see HANG
knapsack *n syn* see BACKPACK
knave *n syn* see VILLIAN 1
knavish *adj syn* see DISHONEST
knell *vb syn* see RING
knickknack *n* a small or trivial ornamental article <a collection of pretty *knickknacks* was displayed on the mantel>
  syn bauble, bibelot, curio, dido, gewgaw, gimcrack, novelty, objet d'art, pretty-pretty, rattletrap(s), toy, trifle, trinket, whatnot, whigmaleerie
  rel souvenir; bric-a-brac, virtu; miniature; kickshaw, notion; trumpery
knifelike *adj syn* see SHARP 8
  ant dull
knobkerrie *n syn* see CUDGEL
knock *vb* **1** *syn* see TAP 1
  2 *syn* see CRITICIZE
  ant boost
knock *n syn* see HIT 1
knock about *vb syn* see MANHANDLE
knock down *vb* **1** *syn* see FELL 1
  2 *syn* see EARN 1
knock–down–and–drag–out *n* **1** *syn* see BRAWL
  2 *syn* see QUARREL
knocker *n syn* see CRITIC
knock off *vb* **1** *syn* see STOP 3
  2 *syn* see DEDUCT 1

  3 *syn* see MURDER 1
  ‖**4** *syn* see ROB 1
knock out *vb syn* see EXHAUST 4
knockout *n* **1** *syn* see ‖DILLY
  2 *syn* see BEAUTY
knock over *vb* **1** *syn* see FELL 1
  2 *syn* see OVERTURN 1
  3 *syn* see OVERWHELM 4
  4 *syn* see ROB 1
knot *n* **1** *syn* see BOND 3
  2 *syn* see BUMP 2
  3 *syn* see MAZE 1
knothead *n syn* see DUNCE
knotty *adj* **1** *syn* see COMPLEX 2
  2 *syn* see HARD 6
know *vb* **1** to possess an intellectual hold of <*knows* several languages>
  syn appreciate, apprehend, cognize, comprehend, fathom, grasp, have, understand
  rel apperceive; differentiate, discern, discriminate, distinguish, realize
  idiom have at one's fingertips, see through
  2 *syn* see EXPERIENCE 1
  3 *syn* see FEEL 2
  4 to recognize the differences between <*know* right from wrong>
  syn difference, differentiate, discern, discrepate, discriminate, distinguish, extricate, separate, sever, severalize
  con confound, mingle, mix
  ant confuse, mix up
  5 *syn* see RECOGNIZE 1
knowable *adj syn* see UNDERSTANDABLE
  ant unknowable
know-how *n* **1** *syn* see ABILITY 2
  2 *syn* see ART 1
knowing *adj* **1** *syn* see INTELLIGENT 2
  rel vigilant, watchful; discerning, observant, perceptive
  con blunt, obtuse
  2 *syn* see WISE 1
  3 *syn* see WISE 4
  4 *syn* see AWARE
  5 *syn* see SOPHISTICATED 2
know-it-all *n syn* see SMART ALECK
knowledge *n* **1** *syn* see EDUCATION 2
  ant ignorance
  2 the body of things known about or in science <made major contributions to scientific *knowledge*>
  syn information, lore, science, wisdom
  rel advice, intelligence, news; data, evidence, facts
knowledgeable *adj* **1** *syn* see INTELLIGENT 2
  2 *syn* see WISE 1
know-nothing *adj syn* see IGNORANT 1
know-nothing *n syn* see DUNCE
knuckle *vb syn* see YIELD 2
knucklehead *n syn* see DUNCE
knuckle under *vb syn* see YIELD 2
kook *n syn* see CRACKPOT
kowtow *vb syn* see FAWN
kowtowing *adj syn* see FAWNING
kudize *vb syn* see COMMEND 2
kudo *n syn* see COMPLIMENT 1
kudos *n* **1** *syn* see EMINENCE 1
  2 *syn* see HONOR 2

---

syn synonym(s)   *rel* related word(s)
ant antonym(s)   *con* contrasted word(s)
idiom idiomatic equivalent(s)
‖ use limited; if in doubt, see a dictionary

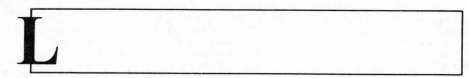

laager *vb syn* see CAMP
label *n syn* see TICKET 1
  rel mark, marker
labor *n* **1** *syn* see WORK 2
  rel endeavor, struggle
  con ease, leisure, relaxation, repose, rest; amusement, diversion, entertainment, recreation; idleness, inactivity, inertia, inertness, passiveness
  2 the physical activities involved in parturition <first *labors* are sometimes difficult>
  syn birth pang(s), childbearing, childbirth, travail
labor *vb* **1** to exert one's powers of mind or body especially with painful or strenuous effort <*labored* all day to make a living>
  syn drive, moil, strain, strive, toil, tug, work
  idiom break one's neck
  con idle, laze, loaf, lounge; goof (off), shirk; dawdle, poke, putter
  ‖**2** *syn* see TILL
labored *adj* **1** *syn* see HARD 6
  2 *syn* see FORCED
  rel heavy, ponderous, weighty; awkward, clumsy, inept, maladroit
laborer *n syn* see WORKER
laborious *adj syn* see HARD 6
  ant easy, effortless
laboriously *adv syn* see HARD 8
  ant easily, effortlessly
labyrinth *n syn* see MAZE 1
labyrinthine *adj syn* see COMPLEX 2
lacerated *adj* having jagged cuts or breaks <the *lacerated* area was badly swollen>
  syn mangled, rent, torn
  rel gashed, mutilated, ripped, slashed; jagged, ragged, saw-toothed, scalloped, scored; serrated
lachrymose *adj syn* see TEARFUL
lack *vb* to be without something and especially something essential or greatly needed <the building *lacks* a fire escape>
  syn need, require, want
  con enjoy, have, hold, own, possess
lack *n* **1** *syn* see ABSENCE
  2 *syn* see FAILURE 3
lackadaisical *adj syn* see LANGUID
  rel incurious, indifferent, unconcerned; faineant, indolent, lazy, slothful; idle, passive; emasculated; romantic, sentimental
  con energetic, lusty, strenuous, vigorous; active, dynamic, live
lacking *adj* **1** *syn* see ABSENT 1
  2 *syn* see DEFICIENT 1
lacking *prep syn* see WITHOUT 2
lackluster *adj* **1** *syn* see DULL 7
  2 *syn* see COLORLESS 2
  rel dead, leaden, rusty, tarnished
  con lustrous
lackwit *n syn* see DUNCE
laconic *adj syn* see CONCISE
  rel brusque
  con garrulous, glib, loquacious, talkative
  ant verbose, wordy
laconically *adv syn* see BRIEFLY
lacuna *n syn* see GAP 3
lad *n syn* see BOY 1
laddie *n syn* see BOY 1
lade *vb* **1** *syn* see BURDEN
  2 *syn* see DIP 2
la–di–da *adj* **1** *syn* see PRECIOUS 4
  2 *syn* see GENTEEL 3
ladies' man *n syn* see WOLF
lading *n syn* see LOAD 1
ladle *vb syn* see DIP 2
lady *n syn* see WIFE
lady friend *n syn* see GIRL FRIEND 1
lady–killer *n syn* see WOLF
ladylove *n syn* see GIRL FRIEND 2

lag *vb syn* see DELAY 2
  rel retard, slacken, slow; stay
lag *adj syn* see LAST
‖**lag** *vb syn* see BANISH
‖**lag** *n syn* see CONVICT
laggard *adj syn* see SLOW 2
  rel dawdling, delaying, loitering, procrastinating; comatose, lethargic, sluggish; apathetic, impassive, phlegmatic
  con alert, vigilant, watchful, wide-awake; expeditious, fast, fleet, speedy
  ant prompt, quick
laggard *n* one that delays unnecessarily or falls behind <no room for *laggards* on the expedition>
  syn dawdler, lingerer, loiterer, slow coach, slowpoke, straggler
  rel lazybones, loafer
  con dynamo, go-ahead, go-getter, hustler, live wire, rustler; eager beaver
lagniappe *n syn* see GRATUITY
lair *n* **1** a resting or living place of a wild animal <photographed the wolf at the entrance to his *lair*>
  syn burrow, couch, den, lodge
  2 *syn* see HIDEOUT
‖**lalapalooza** *n syn* ‖DILLY, ‖corker, crackerjack, ‖daisy, dandy, humdinger, jim-dandy, ‖lulu, peach, ‖pip
‖**lallygag** *vb syn* see IDLE
lam *vb syn* see BEAT 1
lam *n syn* see ESCAPE 1
lambaste *vb* **1** *syn* see BEAT 1
  2 *syn* see WHIP 2
  3 to assail with withering oral or written denunciation <the senator has been publicly *lambasted* for taking bribes>
  syn blister, castigate, ‖crawl, drub, excoriate, flay, lash (into), roast, scarify, scathe, scorch, score, scourge, slam, slap, slash, ‖slate; *compare* CRITICIZE, REPROVE, SCOLD 1
  rel censure, criticize, denounce, pan; berate, scold, tongue-lash; assail, attack, squabash
  idiom burn one's ears, ‖crawl all over, give (one) a roasting, pin one's ears back, rake (one) over the coals, read the riot act, rip into
  con applaud, extol, praise; approve, countenance, endorse
lambent *adj syn* see BRIGHT 1
lame–brain *n syn* see DUNCE
lament *vb syn* see DEPLORE 1
  ant exult; rejoice
lamentable *adj* **1** *syn* see DEPLORABLE
  2 *syn* see MELANCHOLY 2
lamia *n syn* see WITCH 1
lamp *n syn* see EYE 1
lampoonery *n syn* see SATIRE
lampooning *adj syn* see SATIRIC
lance *vb syn* see IMPALE
land *n* **1** *syn* see EARTH 2
  2 *syn* see COUNTRY
  3 *syn* see ESTATE 3
land *vb* **1** *syn* see DISEMBARK
  2 *syn* see ALIGHT
  3 *syn* see GET 1
‖**lang syne** *n syn* see PAST
language *n* **1** a body or system of words and phrases used by a large community or by a people, a nation, or a group of nations <the English and French *languages*>
  syn dialect, idiom, speech, tongue, vernacular
  rel argot, cant, jargon, lingo, patois, slang
  2 *syn* see TERMINOLOGY
languid *adj* lacking in vim or energy <doing the job in a slow and *languid* manner>
  syn die-away, enervated, lackadaisical, languishing, languorous, limp, listless, spiritless
  rel comatose, lethargic, sluggish, torpid; apathetic, impassive, phlegmatic; inactive, inert, supine
  con alert, awake, ‖fly, keen, lively, wide-awake
  ant vivacious; chipper

languish *vb syn* see FAIL 1
 ant flourish
languishing *adj syn* see LANGUID
 rel debilitated, enfeebled, weakened; faineant, indolent; longing, pining, yearning
 con hale, healthy, robust, sound; energetic, lusty, vigorous
 ant flourishing, thriving; unaffected
languor *n syn* see LETHARGY 1
 rel exhaustion, fatigue, weariness; blues, depression, dumps; doldrums, ennui, tedium
 con celerity, legerity; gusto, zest
 ant alacrity
languorous *adj syn* see LANGUID
 rel dilatory, laggard, leisurely, slow; faineant, indolent, slothful; passive; lax, loose, relaxed, slack; indulged, pampered
 ant vigorous; strenuous (*of times, seasons*)
lank *adj syn* see LEAN
 rel attenuated, extenuated
 con chubby
 ant burly
lanky *adj* 1 *syn* see GANGLING
 2 *syn* see LEAN
lap *vb syn* see OVERLAP
lap *vb* 1 *syn* see SLOSH 1
 2 *syn* see BATHE 2
lapse *n* 1 *syn* see ERROR 2
 rel crime, offense, sin, vice; failing, foible, frailty; breach, transgression, trespass, violation
 2 a temporary deviation or fall especially from a higher to a lower state < a *lapse* into nonproductiveness > < ashamed of his *lapse* from grace >
 syn backsliding, relapse
 rel decadence, declension, decline, degeneration, deterioration, devolution; recession, retrogradation; regression, retrogression
 con advance, progress; development, maturation; amendment; betterment, improvement
lapse *vb* to fall from a better or higher state into a lower or poorer one < *lapsed* into his old vulgar ways >
 syn backslide, recidivate, relapse
 rel return, revert; slide, slip; decline, degenerate, deteriorate; subside; descend; recede, retrograde; apostatize
 con advance, progress; develop, mature; amend, mend; better, improve
larcener *n syn* see THIEF
larcenist *n syn* see THIEF
larcenous *adj* prone to committing larceny < *larcenous* employees were robbing the company blind >
 syn sticky-fingered, thieving, thievish
 rel burglarious; light-fingered
larceny *n syn* see THEFT
‖**lardy–dardy** *adj syn* see GENTEEL 3
lares and penates *n pl syn* see POSSESSION 2
large *adj* 1 above the average of its kind in magnitude < a *large* increase in the tax rate >
 syn big, bull, fat, great, husky, oversize
 rel colossal, enormous, gigantic, huge, immense, mammoth, vast, voluminous; monstrous, monumental, prodigious, stupendous, tremendous; excessive, exorbitant, extravagant, extreme, immoderate, inordinate
 con diminutive, little, minute, tiny, wee; slender, slight, slim, thin
 ant small
 2 *syn* see BIG 1
largely *adv syn* see GENERALLY 1
largeness *n syn* see SIZE 2
large–scale *adj syn* see BIG 1
largess *n* 1 *syn* see GIFT 1
 2 *syn* see GRATUITY
largest *adj syn* see BEST
lark *n* 1 *syn* see ESCAPADE
 2 *syn* see PRANK
larkish *adj syn* see PLAYFUL 1
‖**larrup** *vb* 1 *syn* see WHIP 1
 2 *syn* see WHIP 2
‖**larruping** *adv syn* see VERY 1
lascivious *adj* 1 *syn* see LICENTIOUS 2
 rel coarse, gross, obscene
 2 *syn* see LUSTFUL 2

lash *vb* 1 *syn* see RUSH 1
 2 *syn* see POUR 3
 3 *syn* see WHIP 1
 4 *syn* see WAG
 5 *syn* see SCOLD 1
lash (into) *vb syn* see LAMBASTE 3
lashings *n pl syn* see MUCH
lass *n* 1 *syn* see GIRL 1
 2 *syn* see GIRL FRIEND 1
lassie *n syn* see GIRL 1
lassitude *n* 1 *syn* see FATIGUE
 2 *syn* see APATHY 2
 3 *syn* see LETHARGY 1
 rel doldrums, ennui, tedium; blues, depression, dumps; impotence, powerlessness
 con energy, force, might, power, strength
 ant vigor
last *vb syn* see CONTINUE 1
last *adj* following all relevant others (as in time, order, or importance) < he was the *last* one in line >
 syn closing, concluding, eventual, final, hindmost, lag, latest, latter, rearmost, terminal, terminating, ultimate
 rel bottommost, end, extreme, furthest, outermost, remotest, utmost, uttermost
 con beginning, inaugural, initial, introductory, original, primary, prime
 ant first
lasting *adj* existing or continuing for so long a time as to seem fixed or established < his reading made a *lasting* impression on him >
 syn diuturnal, durable, enduring, perdurable, perduring, permanent, stable; *compare* OLD 2
 rel abiding, continuing, persisting; endless, everlasting, unceasing; continual, continuous, incessant, perennial, unremitting; eternal, sempiternal; indelible, indissoluble, inexhaustible, inexpugnable, inexpungible
 con ephemeral, evanescent, fugitive, momentary, passing, short‐lived, transient, transitory
 ant fleeting
last word *n syn* see APOTHEOSIS 1
late *adj* 1 *syn* see TARDY
 con opportune, seasonable, well-timed
 ant early; prompt, punctual
 2 *syn* see DEAD 1
 3 *syn* see FORMER 2
 4 *syn* see MODERN 1
lated *adj syn* see TARDY
lately *adv syn* see NEW
latency *n syn* see ABEYANCE
latent *adj* not now manifest or showing signs of existence or activity < a *latent* infection >
 syn abeyant, dormant, lurking, potential, prepatent, quiescent
 rel concealed, hidden; idle, inactive, inert; immature, unmatured, unripe
 con active, dynamic, live, operative; activated, energized, vitalized
 ant patent
later *adj syn* see SUBSEQUENT 1
later *adv syn* see AFTER
 ant earlier
laterally *adv syn* see SIDEWAYS 1
latest *adj syn* see LAST
 ant earliest
lather *n* 1 *syn* see FOAM
 2 *syn* see COMMOTION 4
 3 *syn* see COMMOTION 2
lather *vb syn* see WHIP 1
latitude *n syn* see ROOM 3
latrine *n syn* see TOILET
latter *adj syn* see LAST
 ant former
latterly *adv syn* see AFTER
laud *vb syn* see PRAISE 2

---

syn synonym(s)   *rel* related word(s)
ant antonym(s)   *con* contrasted word(s)
idiom idiomatic equivalent(s)
‖ use limited; if in doubt, see a dictionary

rel adore, revere, reverence, venerate, worship; admire; flatter
con blame, condemn; anathematize, curse, damn, execrate, objurgate
ant revile

laudable *adj syn* see WORTHY 1
  ant illaudable

laudative *adj syn* see EULOGISTIC

laudatory *adj syn* see EULOGISTIC

laugh *vb* to show mirth, joy, or scorn with a smile and a usually explosive sound < *laughed* at all the funny things that happened >
  syn chortle, chuckle, giggle, guffaw, hee-haw, snicker, ||sniggle, tehee, titter
  rel cachinnate, cackle, crow, roar, whoop; beam, grin, simper, smile, smirk

laughable *adj* provoking laughter or mirth < the *laughable* antics of the clowns >
  syn comic, comical, droll, farcical, funny, gelastic, ludicrous, ridiculous, risible
  rel amusing, diverting, entertaining, rich; facetious, humorous, jocose, jocular, witty; derisive, derisory, mocking
  con grave, serious, solemn; boring, irksome, tedious, tiresome, wearisome; affecting, impressive, moving, pathetic, poignant, touching

laughingstock *n* an object of ridicule < totally unaware that he was the *laughingstock* of the entire office >
  syn butt, derision, jest, jestee, joke, mock, mockery, pilgarlic, sport
  rel gazingstock; mark, target

launch *vb* **1** *syn* see THROW 1
  2 *syn* see BEGIN 1
  3 *syn* see INTRODUCE 3

laurels *n pl syn* see HONOR 2

lavatory *n syn* see TOILET

lave *vb syn* see BATHE 2

lavish *adj* **1** *syn* see PROFUSE
  con scant, scanty; economical, frugal, thrifty; discreet, provident, prudent; miserly, niggardly, parsimonious, penurious, stingy
  ant sparing
  2 *syn* see GRAND 2

lavishness *n syn* see EXTRAVAGANCE 2
  ant sparingness

law *n* **1** a principle governing conduct, action, or procedure < found it hard to live by outdated *laws* >
  syn assize, canon, decree, decretum, edict, institute, ordinance, precept, prescript, prescription, regulation, rule, statute
  rel command, dictate, mandate
  2 *syn* see PRINCIPLE 1
  rel exigency, necessity
  ant chance

lawbreaker *n syn* see CRIMINAL

lawcourt *n syn* see COURT 2

lawful *adj* being in accordance with law < obtained *lawful* custody of the child >
  syn innocent, legal, legitimate, licit
  rel condign, due, rightful; allowable, permissible; justifiable, warrantable; bona fide
  idiom of right
  con flagitious, iniquitous, nefarious; improper, unjustifiable, wrong; criminal, guilty, peccant; illegitimate, illicit
  ant lawless, unlawful

lawless *adj syn* see UNLAWFUL
  ant lawful

lawlessness *n syn* see ANARCHY 1
  rel conflict, contention, difference, discord, dissension, strife, variance

lawsuit *n syn* see SUIT 1

lawyer *n* a person authorized to practice law in the courts or to serve clients in the capacity of legal agent or adviser < took the problem to his family *lawyer* >
  syn attorney, attorney-at-law; *compare* PETTIFOGGER
  rel advocate, ||barrister, counsel, counselor, ||mouthpiece, pleader, ||solicitor; jurisconsult, jurisprudent, jurist; legist

lax *vb syn* see LOOSE 5

lax *adj* **1** *syn* see LOOSE 1
  con firm, hard, solid; elastic, resilient, springy
  ant rigid

  2 *syn* see NEGLIGENT
  rel forgetful, oblivious, unmindful
  con austere, severe, stern; rigid, rigorous; conscientious, honest, upright, scrupulous
  ant strict, stringent

lay *vb* **1** *syn* see SET 1
  2 *syn* see GAMBLE 1
  3 *syn* see EVEN 1
  4 *syn* see ASCRIBE
  5 *syn* see DIRECT 2
  6 *syn* see SET 5
  7 *syn* see ADDUCE

lay (for) *vb syn* see SURPRISE 1

lay (open) *vb syn* see EXPOSE 1

lay *n* **1** *syn* see MELODY
  2 *syn* see SONG 2

lay *adj syn* see PROFANE 1
  con professional

lay aside *vb* **1** *syn* see DISCARD
  2 *syn* see SAVE 4

lay away *vb* **1** *syn* see SAVE 4
  2 *syn* see BURY 1

lay by *vb syn* see SAVE 4

lay down *vb* **1** *syn* see RELINQUISH
  2 *syn* see PRESCRIBE 2
  3 *syn* see DICTATE

layer *n syn* see BOOKMAKER

lay in *vb syn* see SAVE 4

lay low *vb* **1** *syn* see FELL 1
  2 *syn* see KILL 1

lay off *vb syn* see REST 3

lay out *vb* **1** *syn* see DESIGN 3
  2 *syn* see SPEND 1

lay over *vb syn* see DEFER

lay up *vb* **1** *syn* see ACCUMULATE
  2 *syn* see SAVE 4

laze *vb syn* see IDLE
  con drudge, grind, labor, toil, travail, work

laze *n syn* see SLOTH 1

laziness *n syn* see SLOTH 1
  ant industriousness

lazy *adj* not easily aroused to action or activity < the hot humid weather made them *lazy* >
  syn drony, easygoing, faineant, indolent, slothful, slowgoing, work-shy
  rel idle, inactive, inert, passive, supine, trifling; comatose, lethargic, sluggish, torpid; lackadaisical, languid, languorous, listless, unenergetic, unindustrious; lax, neglectful, negligent, remiss, shiftless, slack
  con diligent, hardworking; brisk, chipper, energetic, vigorous; active, animated, lively, spry, vivacious; prompt, quick, ready
  ant industrious

lazy *vb syn* see IDLE

lazybones *n syn* see SLUGGARD

lead *vb* **1** *syn* see GUIDE
  rel get, induce, persuade, prevail
  con drive, impel; coerce, compel, constrain, force, oblige
  ant follow
  2 *syn* see PRECEDE 3
  3 *syn* see CONVERT 1

lead *n syn* see LEADER 1

leader *n* **1** one that takes the lead or initiative < each group selected its own *leader* for the tour >
  syn ||bell cow, bellwether, dean, doyen, guide, lead, pilot
  rel pacemaker, pacesetter; forerunner, harbinger, herald, precursor; conductor, director, rector
  con adherent, dependent, hanger-on, henchman, satellite
  ant follower
  2 a person in whom resides authority or ruling power < the company had only one *leader* >
  syn boss, chief, chieftain, cock, dominator, head, headman, hierarch, honcho, master
  rel captain, commander, general; director, principal, superintendent, superior; foreman, manager, straw boss
  con inferior, subaltern, subordinate, underling, understrapper
  3 *syn* see NOTABLE 1

leading *adj* **1** *syn* see FIRST 1
  2 *syn* see FIRST 3

ant subordinate
3 syn see WELL-KNOWN
lead off *vb syn* see BEGIN 1
lead on *vb* **1 syn** see LURE
  2 syn see TRIFLE 1
leaf (through) *vb syn* see BROWSE
leafage *n syn* see FOLIAGE
league *n* **1 syn** see ALLIANCE 2
  2 syn see ASSOCIATION 2
  3 syn see CLASS 1
  4 a group of sports clubs or teams that play one another competitively <the new baseball *league*>
  syn association, circuit, conference, loop, wheel
  rel division
league *vb syn* see UNITE 2
leak *vb syn* see GET OUT 2
lean *vb* **1 syn** see SLANT 1
  rel bend, curve; deflect, divert, sheer, turn
  2 syn see TEND 1
lean (over) *vb syn* see HANG 4
lean *n syn* see SLOPE
lean *adj* thin because of absence of superfluous flesh <a *lean* strong horse>
  syn angular, bony, gaunt, lank, lanky, meager, rawboned, scraggy, scrawny, skinny, spare; *compare* THIN 1
  rel slender, slight, slim, spare-set, stringy, thin; cadaverous, haggard, pinched, wasted, worn; wizened
  con brawny, burly, husky, muscular, sinewy; stalwart, stout, strong, sturdy; corpulent, fat, fatty, flabby, obese, plump, portly, rotund
  ant fleshy
leaning *n* **1 syn** see SLOPE
  2 an attraction to a particular activity, thing, or end <a strong *leaning* toward liberal views>
  syn bent, bias, disposition, drift, inclination, inclining, lurch, partiality, penchant, predilection, predisposition, proclivity, propensity, sentiment, tendency; *compare* GIFT 2, PREJUDICE
  rel favor, favoritism, odds
  con avoidance, evasion, shunning; disdaining, scorning, scouting, spurning; disinterest, dislike, distaste
leaning *adj syn* see INCLINED 3
leap *vb* **1 syn** see JUMP 1
  rel arise, ascend, mount, rise, soar
  con drop, fall, sink, slump
  2 syn see CLEAR 8
learn *vb* **1** to acquire knowledge of or skill in by study and experience <*learn* a trade>
  syn get, master, pick up
  rel con, peruse, study
  idiom make oneself master of
  2 syn see MEMORIZE
  3 syn see DISCOVER 3
learned *adj* possessing or manifesting unusually wide and deep knowledge <a most *learned* scholar in his field>
  syn erudite, scholarly, scholastic
  rel cultivated, cultured; academic, bookish, pedantic, professorial; abstruse, esoteric, polymath, recondite
  con ignorant, illiterate, uneducated, unlearned, unlettered, untutored
learnedness *n syn* see ERUDITION 2
learning *n syn* see EDUCATION 2
lease *vb syn* see HIRE 1
leash *vb syn* see HAMPER
least *adj syn* see FIRST 4
leave *vb* **1 syn** see WILL
  rel commit, confide, consign, entrust; allot, apportion, assign
  2 syn see LET 2
  3 syn see GO 2
  4 syn see QUIT 6
  5 syn see RELINQUISH
leave *n* **1 syn** see PERMISSION
  rel assent
  con refusal, rejection; forbiddance, interdiction, prohibition
  2 syn see VACATION
leaven *vb syn* see INFUSE 1
  rel moderate, qualify, temper; enliven, quicken, vivify
leave off *vb syn* see STOP 3
leave-taking *n syn* see PARTING

leaving *n,* usu **leavings** *pl syn* see REMAINDER
  rel fragments, pieces, portions; discards, junk, scrap
lecherous *adj syn* see LICENTIOUS 2
lecture *n syn* see SPEECH 2
lecture *vb syn* see TALK 7
ledger *n syn* see TOMBSTONE
leech *n syn* see PARASITE
leer *vb syn* see SNEER 1
lees *n pl syn* see SEDIMENT
leeway *n syn* see ROOM 3
left-handed *adj syn* see INSINCERE
legacy *n* **1** a gift by will especially of money or personal property <received a *legacy* of $5,000 from her late uncle>
  syn bequest, devise, inheritance
  2 syn see HERITAGE 1
legal *adj syn* see LAWFUL
  ant illegal
legal tender *n syn* see MONEY
legate *vb syn* see WILL
legend *n* **1 syn** see MYTH 1
  2 syn see CAPTION
  3 syn see LORE 2
legendary *adj syn* see MYTHICAL
legerdemain *n syn* see MAGIC 2
legion *n syn* see MULTITUDE 1
legion *adj syn* see MANY
legitimate *adj* **1 syn** see LAWFUL
  rel cogent, sound, valid; acknowledged, recognized; customary, usual; natural, normal, regular, typical
  ant illegitimate
  2 syn see TRUE 8
  ant arbitrary
leisure *n syn* see REST 1
  con drudgery, grind, labor
  ant toil
leisurely *adj syn* see SLOW 2
  rel lax, relaxed, slack; delayed, retarded, slackened; comfortable, easy, restful
  con fast, hasty, quick, rapid, speedy; headlong, impetuous, precipitate
  ant hurried; abrupt
leitmotiv *n* a dominant recurring thematic element or feature (as in a work of art) <the *leitmotiv* of man against nature often appears in his paintings>
  syn motif
  rel motive, theme
lemon *n syn* see FAILURE 5
lend *vb* to give into another's keeping for temporary use on condition that the borrower return the same or its equivalent <I do not have another copy of the book to give, but I can *lend* you mine>
  syn advance, loan
  rel lease-lend, lend-lease; allow, furnish, give; accommodate, oblige
length *n* **1 syn** see DISTANCE 1
  2 syn see RANGE 2
lengthen *vb syn* see EXTEND 3
  ant shorten; abbreviate
lengthening *n syn* see EXTENSION 1
  ant shortening
lengthways *adv syn* see LENGTHWISE
  ant widthways, widthwise
lengthwise *adv* in the direction of the length <the students folded their papers *lengthwise*>
  syn endways, endwise, lengthways, longitudinally, longways, longwise
  con latitudinally, widthways; broadside, broadway, broadwise
  ant widthways, widthwise
lengthy *adj* **1 syn** see LONG 2
  ant short
  2 syn see LONG 1
lenience *n syn* see FORBEARANCE 2
leniency *n syn* see FORBEARANCE 2

---

syn synonym(s)   *rel* related word(s)
ant antonym(s)   *con* contrasted word(s)
idiom idiomatic equivalent(s)
|| use limited; if in doubt, see a dictionary

lenient *adj* **1** *syn* see GENTLE 1
ant caustic
2 *syn* see FORBEARING
rel condoning, excusing, forgiving, pardoning; benign, benignant, kindly; compassionate, tender; humoring, indulging, pampering, mollycoddling, spoiling
con rigid, rigorous, stringent; austere, severe
ant stern; exacting
3 *syn* see AMIABLE 1

lenity *n* *syn* see MERCY
rel tenderness; benevolence, charitableness, humaneness
con rigidity, rigorousness, strictness, stringency; austerity, sternness
ant severity

leper *n* *syn* see OUTCAST

lessen *vb* **1** *syn* see ABRIDGE 1
rel amputate, clip, crop, truncate
2 *syn* see DECREASE
rel attenuate, dilute, thin, weaken

lesser *adj* **1** *syn* see INFERIOR 1
2 *syn* see MINOR 2

lesson *n* *syn* see EXERCISE 4

lesson *vb* *syn* see REPROVE

let *vb* **1** *syn* see HIRE 1
2 to neither forbid nor prevent < *let* the boy go to the movies >
syn allow, have, leave, permit, suffer
rel accredit, approve, certify, endorse, sanction; authorize, commission, license; concede, grant
con ban, enjoin, forbid, inhibit, interdict, prohibit; bar, block, hinder, impede, obstruct; circumvent, foil, frustrate, thwart

let down *vb* *syn* see LOWER 3

lethal *adj* *syn* see DEADLY 1
con renewing, restorative, restoring

lethality *n* *syn* see FATALITY 1

lethargic *adj* deficient in alertness or activity < became *lethargic* after taking the drug >
syn comatose, dopey, heavy, hebetudinous, sluggish, slumberous, stupid, torpid
rel dormant, idle, inactive, inert, passive, supine; apathetic, impassive, phlegmatic, spiritless, stolid; lackadaisical, languid, languorous, listless; dilatory, laggard, slow
con alert, aware, responsive; apt, prompt, quick, ready; brisk, gingery, peppery, spirited
ant energetic

lethargy *n* **1** physical and mental inertness < disgusted, he sank into a state of *lethargy* >
syn coma, dullness, hebetude, languor, lassitude, sleep, slumber, stupor, torpidity, torpidness, torpor
rel comatoseness, sluggishness; indolence, laziness, sloth, slothfulness; idleness, inactivity, inertia, inertness, passiveness, supineness; apathy, impassivity, inanition, phlegm
con aptness, promptness, quickness, readiness; alertness, quick-wittedness
ant vigor
2 *syn* see APATHY 2

lethe *n* *syn* see OBLIVION

let off *vb* *syn* see EXEMPT

let on *vb* **1** *syn* see ACKNOWLEDGE 1
2 *syn* see REVEAL 1

let out *vb* ‖**1** *syn* see REVEAL 1
2 *syn* see DISMISS 3

letter *n* **1** letters *pl* *syn* see ALPHABET 1
2 a direct or personal written or printed message addressed to a person or organization < wrote several *letters* to his friends >
syn epistle, missive, note
rel dispatch, memorandum, message, report

‖**lettuce** *n* *syn* see MONEY

let up *vb* *syn* see ABATE 4

levee *n* **1** *syn* see WHARF
2 *syn* see RED-LIGHT DISTRICT

level *vb* **1** *syn* see EVEN 1
2 *syn* see DIRECT 2
3 *syn* see FELL 1

level *adj* having a surface without bends, curves, or irregularities < looked for a *level* spot to land the plane >
syn even, flat, flush, planate, plane, smooth
rel akin, alike, identical, like, parallel, similar, uniform; aligned; regular; equal, equivalent, same

con bumpy, irregular, lumpy, uneven; unaligned, unparallel; changing, varying; fluctuating, rolling, swaying, undulating; coarse, rough

lever *vb* *syn* see PRY

leviathan *n* *syn* see GIANT

leviathan *adj* *syn* see HUGE

levity *n* *syn* see LIGHTNESS
rel absurdity, folly, foolishness, silliness
con collection, quietude, sobriety
ant gravity

levy *n* *syn* see TAX 1

levy *vb* to determine and require satisfaction of (as a tax or obligation) < several broad-based taxes were *levied* >
syn assess, exact, impose, put (on *or* upon)
rel extort, wrest, wring; charge, lay (on *or* upon), place, set
con remit; abate, diminish, lessen

lewd *adj* *syn* see LICENTIOUS 2
rel coarse, gross, obscene; improper, indecent, indelicate
con modest, proper, self-restrained; temperate
ant chaste

lexicon *n* **1** *syn* see VOCABULARY 1
2 *syn* see TERMINOLOGY

lexiphanicism *n* *syn* see BOMBAST

liability *n* **1** *syn* see DEBT 3
ant asset
2 *syn* see INDEBTEDNESS 1
3 *syn* see EXPOSURE

liable *adj* **1** *syn* see RESPONSIBLE
rel bound, tied
con exempt, immune; free, independent
2 being likely to be affected by some usually adverse contingency or action < without the heat shield he was *liable* to be burned >
syn exposed, obnoxious, open, prone, sensitive, subject, susceptible
rel assailable, penetrable, vulnerable; attackable, beatable, conquerable, vincible
ant unliable
3 *syn* see APT 1
ant unliable

liaison *n* *syn* see AMOUR 2

liar *n* one that tells lies < he is a compulsive *liar* >
syn Ananias, falsifier, fibber, fibster, perjurer, prevaricator, storyteller

libel *vb* *syn* see MALIGN
rel burlesque, caricature, travesty

libelous *adj* injurious to reputation < the campaign degenerated into an exchange of *libelous* statements >
syn backbiting, calumnious, defamatory, detracting, detractive, detractory, invidious, maligning, scandalous, slanderous, traducing, vilifying
rel depreciative, depreciatory, derogative, disparaging, pejorative; contumelious, debasing, malevolent, vituperative
con adulating, adulatory, applauding, commendatory, eulogistic, eulogizing, laudatory, praising

liberal *adj* **1** marked by generosity and openhandedness < a *liberal* allowance for his son >
syn bounteous, bountiful, free, freehanded, generous, handsome, munificent, openhanded, unsparing
rel exuberant, lavish, prodigal, profuse; benevolent, charitable, eleemosynary, philanthropic
con closefisted, miserly, niggardly, parsimonious, penurious, stingy, tight, tightfisted; meager, scanty
ant close
2 *syn* see PLENTIFUL
3 not bound by authoritarianism, orthodoxy, or traditional forms < modern young people usually have a *liberal* attitude toward sex >
syn advanced, broad, broad-minded, progressive, radical, tolerant, wide
rel forbearing, indulgent, lenient
con rigid, rigorous, strict, stringent; dictatorial, doctrinaire, dogmatic, oracular; conservative, reactionary
ant authoritarian

liberate *vb* *syn* see FREE
rel detach, unhook; untangle; disembarrass
con bind, tie; ensnare, entrap, snare, trap; constrain, restrain, restrict

libertine *adj syn* see LICENTIOUS 2
  con ethical; continent, sober, temperate
  ant straitlaced
liberty *n syn* see FREEDOM
  rel autonomy, independence; delivery, emancipation, enfranchisement, liberation
  con circumscription, confinement, limitation, restriction
  ant restraint
libidinous *adj* **1** *syn* see LICENTIOUS 2
  rel coarse, gross, obscene
  2 *syn* see LUSTFUL 2
library *n* a place in which literary, musical, artistic, or reference materials (as books or films) are kept for use but not for sale < planned to study all evening in the *library* >
  syn archive(s), athenaeum
  rel reading room
license *n syn* see FREEDOM
  rel laxity, looseness, relaxation, slackness
  con duty, obligation; decency, propriety; continence, sobriety, temperance
  ant decorum
license *vb syn* see AUTHORIZE 1
  rel allow, let, permit, suffer; certify, sanction
  con check, curb, restrain
  ant ban
licentious *adj* **1** *syn* see ABANDONED 2
  2 disregarding sexual restraints < a coarse *licentious* man >
  syn fast, incontinent, lascivious, lecherous, lewd, libertine, libidinous, lustful, randy, salacious, satyric
  rel animal, carnal, fleshly, oversexed, sensual; abandoned, dissolute, profligate, reprobate; corrupt, debauched, depraved, scabrous; amoral, immoral, unmoral; lax, loose, relaxed
  con chaste, decent, pure; moral, virtuous; rigid, strict; ascetic, austere, severe
  ant continent
licit *adj syn* see LAWFUL
  rel approved, sanctioned; authorized, licensed
  con banned, forbidden, inhibited, interdicted, prohibited
  ant illicit
lick *vb* **1** *syn* see WHIP 2
  2 *syn* see OVERCOME 1
lick *n* **1** *syn* see HINT 2
  2 *syn* see HIT 1
lickerish *adj syn* see LUSTFUL 2
lickerishness *n syn* see LUST 2
lickety–split *adv syn* see FAST 2
licking *n syn* see DEFEAT 1
lickspit *n syn* see SYCOPHANT
lickspittle *n syn* see SYCOPHANT
lie *vb* **1** *syn* see REST 1
  2 *syn* see CONSIST 1
lie *vb* to be untruthful directly or indirectly < *lying* under oath is a crime >
  syn equivocate, falsify, fib, palter, prevaricate
  rel beguile, deceive, delude, misguide, misinform, misinstruct, mislead; distort, exaggerate, misstate
lie *n* a statement or declaration that is not true < was sued for printing *lies* about the candidate >
  syn ‖bouncer, canard, cock-and-bull story, falsehood, falsity, fib, inveracity, misrepresentation, misstatement, prevarication, ‖rapper, story, tale, taradiddle, untruism, untruth
  rel deceitfulness, dishonesty, distortion, fraudulence, inaccuracy, mendacity; fable, flam, myth; falsification, forgery, libel, perjury; fish story, song and dance
  con veracity, verisimilitude, verity
  ant truth
lie by *vb syn* see REST 3
lied *n syn* see SONG 2
lie down *vb syn* see REST 1
liege *adj syn* see FAITHFUL 1
lieutenant *n syn* see ASSISTANT 2
life *n* **1** *syn* see BIOGRAPHY
  2 *syn* see HUMAN
  3 *syn* see SPIRIT 5
lifeless *adj* **1** *syn* see DEAD 1
  ant living
  2 *syn* see COLORLESS 2
  ant lifeful

lifelong *adj syn* see OLD 2
lifework *n syn* see MISSION
lift *vb* **1** to remove from a lower to a higher place or position < *lifted* the sack to his shoulder >
  syn elevate, hoist, pick up, raise, rear, take up, uphold, uplift, upraise, uprear
  rel arise, ascend, levitate, mount, rise, rocket, soar, surge, tower; aggrandize, exalt, magnify
  con decrease, diminish, lessen, reduce; abase, debase, degrade, demean, humble, humiliate; depress, oppress, weigh
  ant lower
  2 *syn* see REVOKE 2
  ant invoke
  3 *syn* see STEAL 1
  4 *syn* see RISE 4
lift *n* **1** *syn* see THEFT
  2 *syn* see HELP 1
lifted *adj syn* see ELEVATED 1
ligament *n syn* see BOND 3
ligature *n syn* see BOND 3
light *n syn* see DAWN 1
light *adj syn* see FAIR 3
light *vb* **1** to cause something to start burning < *lighted* the fuse on the dynamite >
  syn enkindle, fire, ignite, inflame, kindle
  con douse, ‖dout, put out, quench, snuff; damp (down), smother, stamp (out)
  ant extinguish
  2 *syn* see ILLUMINATE 1
light *adj* **1** having little weight < the package was *light* >
  syn featherlight, featherweight, imponderous, lightweight, unheavy, weightless
  rel inconsequential, trifling, trivial; little, petty, small; flimsy, meager, slender, slight
  idiom light as a feather
  con bulky, burdensome, cumbersome, huge, massive, overweight, ponderous, portly, unwieldy, weighty
  ant heavy
  2 *syn* see EASY 1
  ant arduous
  3 *syn* see FAST 7
  4 *syn* see GIDDY 1
  5 *syn* see LITTLE 3
  6 *syn* see DIZZY 2
light *vb* **1** *syn* see ALIGHT
  2 *syn* see HAPPEN 2
lighted *adj syn* see BURNING 1
  ant unlighted, unlit
lighten *vb syn* see ILLUMINATE 1
  ant darken
lighten *vb syn* see RELIEVE 1
  rel attenuate, dilute, extenuate, thin
  con depress, oppress, weigh
light–headed *adj* **1** *syn* see GIDDY 1
  2 *syn* see DIZZY 2
lighthearted *adj* **1** *syn* see HAPPY-GO-LUCKY
  ant heavyhearted
  2 *syn* see GLAD 1
  rel buoyant, effervescent, expansive, resilient, volatile; high-spirited, spirited; gay, lively, sprightly, vivacious
  con gloomy, glum, morose, sullen
  ant despondent
  3 *syn* see MERRY
  ant heavyhearted
lighthouse *n* a building equipped to guide sea navigators by means of a powerful light < rowed out to the *lighthouse* >
  syn beacon, pharos
  rel direction, guidance
lightless *adj syn* see DARK 1
  ant bright, ‖lightful
lightly *adv syn* see EASILY 1
light–mindedness *n syn* see LIGHTNESS

---

syn synonym(s)   *rel* related word(s)
ant antonym(s)   *con* contrasted word(s)
idiom idiomatic equivalent(s)
‖ use limited; if in doubt, see a dictionary

lightness *n* gaiety or indifference where seriousness and attention are called for < a crisis that allowed no room for *lightness* >
   syn flightiness, flippancy, frivolity, levity, light-mindedness, volatility
   rel buoyancy, effervescence, elasticity, expansiveness, resiliency; gaiety, liveliness, vivacity; cheerfulness, lightheartedness
   con earnestness, gravity, sedateness, soberness, somberness, staidness
   ant seriousness

light–o'–love *n syn* see DOXY 1

light out *vb syn* see HEAD 3

lightsome *adj* **1** *syn* see CHEERFUL 1
   2 *syn* see HAPPY-GO-LUCKY

lightweight *adj syn* see LIGHT 1

like *vb* **1** *syn* see ENJOY 1
   rel choose, elect, prefer, select; admire, esteem, regard, respect; approve, endorse; appreciate, comprehend, understand
   ant dislike
   2 *syn* see WILL

like *adj* being so similar as to appear to be the same or nearly the same (as in appearance, character, or quantity) < shirts of *like* design >
   syn agnate, akin, alike, analogous, comparable, consonant, corresponding, equivalent, intercomparable, parallel, similar, such, suchlike, undifferenced, undifferentiated, uniform; *compare* SAME 2
   rel equal, equivalent, identical, same, selfsame; allied, cognate, close, related, resembling; coextensive, commensurate
   idiom of that ilk, on the order of
   con different, disparate, divergent, diverse, various; dissimilar, distinct; discordant, discrepant, inconsistent, inconsonant
   ant unlike

like *n syn* see EQUAL

likely *adj* **1** *syn* see PROBABLE
   con problematic; certain, inevitable, necessary
   ant unlikely
   2 *syn* see APT 1
   ant unlikely
   3 *syn* see HOPEFUL 2

likely *adv syn* see PRESUMABLY

liken *vb syn* see EQUATE 2

likeness *n* agreement or correspondence in details (as of appearance, structure, or quality) < the remarkable *likeness* of the two cousins >
   syn affinity, alikeness, analogy, comparison, resemblance, semblance, similarity, simile, similitude
   rel equality, equivalence, identicalness, identity, sameness; agreement, conformity, correspondence; analogousness, comparableness, parallelism, uniformity
   con difference, dissimilarity, distinction, divergence, divergency; disaffinity, opposition
   ant unlikeness

likewise *adv* **1** *syn* see ALSO 1
   2 *syn* see ALSO 2

liking *n* **1** *syn* see APPETITE 3
   ant disliking
   2 *syn* see WILL 1

lilliputian *adj syn* TINY, diminutive, minute, teensy, teensy-weensy, teenty, teeny, teeny-weeny, wee, weeny
   ant Brobdingnagian

lilliputian *n syn* see DWARF

lily–livered *adj syn* see COWARDLY

lily–white *adj syn* see GOOD 11

limb *n* **1** a member of a woody plant that is an outgrowth from a main stem or from one of its divisions < hung the swing from a tree's *limb* >
   syn bough, branch
   rel shoot, spray, sprig, switch, twig; arm
   2 *syn* see SCAMP

limber *adj syn* see SUPPLE 3
   rel plastic, pliable, pliant; elastic, flexible, resilient, springy
   con inflexible, rigid, stark, stiff, tense, wooden

limit *n* **1** a material or immaterial point beyond which something does not or cannot extend < there seemed no *limit* to the problems they faced >
   syn bound, confine(s), end, limitation, term; *compare* ENVIRONS 1
   rel circumscription, confinement, restriction, termination; border, brim, brink, edge, margin, rim, verge

   2 limits *pl syn* see ENVIRONS 1
   3 *syn* see EXTREME 2

limit *vb* **1** *syn* see DEMARCATE 1
   2 to prescribe or serve as a restricting boundary < *limited* the naughty child to the house for three days > < ignorance that *limits* spiritual growth >
   syn bar, circumscribe, confine, delimit, delimitate, prelimit, restrict
   rel constrict, contract, lessen, narrow, pinch; check, curb, hinder, inhibit, restrain; appoint, assign, define, prescribe, set
   con enlarge, expand, extend, increase, widen; develop, grow
   ant broaden

limitation *n* **1** *syn* see LIMIT 1
   2 *syn* see RESTRICTION 1

limited *adj* **1** *syn* see DEFINITE 1
   rel inexhaustive, inextensive
   con boundless, infinite
   ant unlimited
   2 *syn* see FINITE
   3 *syn* see QUALIFIED 2
   4 *syn* see LITTLE 2

limitless *adj* having no limits < the *limitless* black of deep space >
   syn boundless, endless, immeasurable, indefinite, infinite, measureless, unbounded, unlimited, unmeasured
   rel bottomless, countless, incalculable, incomprehensible, inexhaustible, innumerable, undrainable, unfathomable, vast, wasteless
   con bound, bounded, finite, fixed, limited, measurable; comprehensible, fathomable; confined, restricted
   ant limited

limn *vb syn* see REPRESENT 1

limp *vb* **1** to walk lamely < *limped* across the floor after his fall >
   syn halt, hitch, hobble
   rel toddle, totter, waddle; falter, stagger, stumble, wobble
   2 *syn* see STUMBLE 6

limp *adj* **1** deficient in firmness of texture, substance, or structure < plants going *limp* from lack of water >
   syn flabby, flaccid, flimsy, floppy, sleazy
   rel lax, loose, relaxed, slack; limber, supple
   con inflexible, rigid, stark, stiff, tense, wooden; firm, hard, solid; brittle, crisp
   2 *syn* see LANGUID

limpid *adj syn* see TRANSPARENT 1

limpidity *n syn* see CLARITY

line *n* **1** *syn* see WAY 2
   2 *syn* see COURSE 3
   3 *syn* see WORK 1
   ‖**4** *syn* see SPIEL
   5 a series of things arranged in continuous or uniform order < a *line* of cars waiting at the light >
   syn echelon, file, queue, rank, row, string, tier
   rel column, progression, succession, train; sequence, series
   6 *syn* see OUTLINE
   7 *syn* see MERCHANDISE

line *vb* **1** to arrange in a line or lines < *lined* the bottles along the shelf >
   syn align, allineate, line up, range
   rel arrange, array, marshal, order, ordinate
   con derange, disarrange, disorder, disturb; disperse, dissipate, scatter
   2 *syn* see ADJOIN

lineage *n* **1** *syn* see ANCESTRY
   2 *syn* see FAMILY 1

lineal *adj syn* see DIRECT 1

lineament *n syn* see OUTLINE

lineation *n syn* see OUTLINE

line up *vb syn* see LINE 1

linger *vb* **1** *syn* see STAY 2
   2 *syn* see DELAY 2
   3 *syn* see SAUNTER

lingerer *n syn* see LAGGARD

lingo *n syn* see DIALECT 2

link *n syn* see BOND 3

link *vb syn* see JOIN 1

lint *n syn* see DOWN

lion *n syn* see NOTABLE 1

lionhearted *adj syn* see BRAVE 1

‖**lip** *n syn* see BACK TALK

lip *vb* **1** *syn* see KISS 1
 2 *syn* see BATHE 2
lip server *n syn* see HYPOCRITE
liquefy *vb* to convert or to become converted to a liquid state < *liquefy* a block of ice by heating >
 syn deliquesce, dissolve, flux, fuse, liquesce, melt, run, thaw
 rel soften; thin
 con clot, coagulate, congeal; harden, set; gel, jellify, jelly; condense, inspissate, thicken
 ant solidify
liquesce *vb syn* see LIQUEFY
liquid *adj syn* see MELLIFLUOUS
liquidate *vb* **1** *syn* see CLEAR 5
 2 *syn* see PURGE 3
 3 *syn* see MURDER 1
liquor *n* **1** *syn* see DRINK 1
 2 an intoxicating beverage usually distilled after being fermented < belted down a slug of *liquor* >
 syn alcohol, aqua vitae, booze, ‖budge, drink, firewater, grog, ‖hooch, inebriant, intoxicant, ‖joy-juice, ‖juice, ‖lush, ‖sauce, spirit(s), ‖strunt, tipple
 idiom Demon Rum, the bottle
liquor (up) *vb syn* see DRINK 3
lissome *adj syn* see SUPPLE 3
list *n* a series of items (as names) written down or printed especially as a memorandum or record < all the people on the *list* were present >
 syn catalog, register, roll, roll call, roster, schedule
 rel checklist, handlist; index; inventory
list *vb* **1** *syn* see ENUMERATE 2
 2 *syn* see ITEMIZE 1
 3 to enter in a list < his name was not *listed* in the telephone book >
 syn book, catalog, enroll, inscribe
 rel file, index, note, post, schedule, tabulate; record, register, roster
 4 *syn* see ENROLL 1
list *vb syn* see SLANT 1
listen *vb* to perceive by ear usually with careful or responsive attention < now hear me; *listen* to my words >
 syn attend, hark, hear, hearken, heed
 idiom give a hearing to, give ear to, hang upon the lips (*or* words) of, keep one's ears open, lend one's (*or* an) ear, prick up one's ears, strain one's ears
listless *adj syn* see LANGUID
 rel careless, heedless, thoughtless
 con agog, anxious, avid, keen; alert, vigilant, watchful; energetic, lusty, vigorous; prompt, quick, ready
 ant eager
listlessness *n syn* see APATHY 2
‖lit *adj syn* see INTOXICATED 1
literal *adj syn* see VERBATIM
literally *adv syn* see VERBATIM
literati *n pl syn* see INTELLIGENTSIA
literatim *adv syn* see VERBATIM
lithe *adj syn* see SUPPLE 3
 rel slender, slight, slim, thin; lean, spare
 con awkward, clumsy, gauche, inept, maladroit; inflexible, stiff, tense, wooden
lithesome *adj syn* see SUPPLE 3
litigious *adj syn* see CONTENTIOUS 2
litter *n* **1** *syn* see REFUSE
 2 *syn* see CLUTTER 2
little *adj* **1** *syn* see SMALL 1
 ant big
 2 contemptibly limited < men with *little* minds picking at flaws in a great leader >
 syn borné, ineffectual, limited, mean, narrow, paltry, set, small
 rel bigoted, hidebound, illiberal, narrow-minded, provincial; contemptible; niggard, niggardly, self-centered, selfish
 ant great
 3 lacking importance < the nagging *little* details of a job >
 syn casual, inconsiderable, insignificant, light, minor, minute, petty, ‖potty, shoestring, small, small-beer, trivial, unimportant; *compare* PETTY 2
 rel fortuitous; incidental; collateral, secondary, subordinate, subsidiary
 con consequential, meaningful, significant, substantial, weighty; basal, basic, essential, foundational, fundamental

 ant important
little *adv syn* see SELDOM
 ant much
little by little *adv syn* see GRADUALLY
‖little woman *n syn* see WIFE
‖lit up *adj syn* see INTOXICATED 1
liturgy *n* **1** *syn* see FORM 2
 2 *syn* see RITE 2
livable *adj* **1** suitable for living < a very *livable* apartment >
 syn habitable, inhabitable, lodgeable, occupiable, tenantable
 rel cozy, homelike, homey, snug; acceptable, bearable, tolerable
 ant unlivable
 2 *syn* see BEARABLE
live *vb* **1** *syn* see BE
 2 *syn* see RESIDE 1
live *adj syn* see ACTIVE 1
 rel effective, effectual, efficacious, efficient
 ant inactive, inert; dormant (*as a volcano*); defunct (*as an institution, journal*)
livelihood *n syn* see LIVING
 rel art, craft, handicraft, profession, trade; emolument, fee, pay, salary, stipend, wage
lively *adj* **1** keenly alive and brisk < always thought of as a *lively* teacher >
 syn alert, animate, animated, bright, ‖cant, ‖canty, chipper, ‖chirk, dashing, gay, keen, ‖peart, peppy, pert, rousing, spirited, ‖spirity, sprightful, sprightly, unpedantic, vivacious; *compare* CHEERFUL 1
 rel agile, brisk, nimble, spry; buoyant, effervescent, elastic, expansive, resilient, volatile; blithe, cock-a-hoop, jocund, jolly, merry; gleeful, hilarious, mirthful; chirping, chirpy, chirrupy
 con lethargic, sluggish, torpid; lackadaisical, languid, languorous, listless; apathetic, impassive, phlegmatic, stolid; boring, irksome, tedious
 ant dull, unlively
 2 *syn* see AGILE
 idiom full of pep
 3 *syn* see ENERGETIC 2
 4 *syn* see BUSTLING
 ant unanimated
liven *vb syn* see QUICKEN 1
liver *n syn* see INHABITANT
live wire *n syn* see HUSTLER 1
livid *adj* **1** *syn* see PALE 1
 rel grisly; dusky, gloomy, murky
 con bright, brilliant, effulgent, lucent, luminous, lustrous, radiant
 2 *syn* see SENSATIONAL 2
living *adj* **1** having or showing life < the *living* things of a locality >
 syn alive, animate, animated, vital, zoetic
 rel being, existing, subsisting; active, dynamic, live, operative
 con dead, deceased, defunct, demised, departed, gone, inanimate
 ant lifeless
 2 *syn* see EXTANT 1
living *n* supplies or resources needed to live < kept trying to earn a *living* the honest way >
 syn alimentation, alimony, bread, bread and butter, keep, livelihood, maintenance, salt, subsistence, support, sustenance
 rel sustainment, sustentation
load *n* **1** something which is carried, conveyed, or transported from one place to another < a *load* of grain just arrived >
 syn burden, cargo, freight, haul, lading, payload
 rel bale, pack, parcel, shipment
 2 something heavy < could not lift the *load* >
 syn weight
 3 a burdensome or laborious responsibility < considered taking care of the children a heavy *load* >
 syn burden, charge, deadweight, duty, millstone, onus, task, tax, weight
 rel care, liability, obligation, responsibility; drag, drain, pressure
 idiom millstone around one's neck

---

syn synonym(s)   *rel* related word(s)
ant antonym(s)   *con* contrasted word(s)
idiom idiomatic equivalent(s)
‖ use limited; if in doubt, see a dictionary

con breeze, child's play, cinch, duck soup, picnic, ‖pipe, push-over, snap
  ant sinecure
  4 *usu* **loads** *pl syn* see SCAD
load *vb* **1** *syn* see BURDEN
  rel bear, carry, convey, transport
  ant unload
  2 *syn* see ADULTERATE
  3 to make full or overfull <a basket *loaded* with fresh fruit>
  syn charge, choke, fill, heap, pack, pile; *compare* CRAM 1
  rel glut, gorge, surfeit; flood, oversupply, swamp
loaded *adj* **1** *syn* see FULL 1
  ‖**2** *syn* see INTOXICATED 1
loaf *vb* *syn* see IDLE
  con labor, toil, travail, work
loafer *n* *syn* see SLUGGARD
loan *vb* *syn* see LEND
loan shark *n* one who lends money to individuals at exorbitant rates of interest <got involved with *loan sharks*>
  syn Shylock, usurer
  rel lender, loaner, moneylender; shark
loath *adj* *syn* see DISINCLINED
  ant anxious
loathe *vb* *syn* see HATE
  rel decline, refuse, reject, repudiate, spurn
  con covet, crave, desire, want, wish
  ant tolerate
loathing *n* *syn* see ABOMINATION 2
  ant tolerance
loathsome *adj* *syn* see OFFENSIVE
  rel hateful, invidious, obnoxious
  con bearable, endurable, sufferable, supportable; engaging, inviting; alluring, bewitching, charming, enchanting, fascinating
  ant tolerable
lobby *n* *syn* see VESTIBULE
lobster *n* *syn* see OAF 2
local *adj* *syn* see INSULAR
  ant cosmopolitan
locale *n* *syn* see SCENE 3
  rel area, district, neighborhood, vicinage, vicinity
locality *n* **1** a more or less definitely circumscribed place or region <searched for the child in the *locality* of the waterfront>
  syn area, district, neighborhood, vicinage, vicinity
  rel belt, region, tract, zone; section, sector; bailiwick, domain, field, province, sphere, territory
  idiom neck of the woods
  2 *syn* see HABITAT
located *adj* *syn* see SITUATED
location *n* *syn* see PLACE 1
‖**loch** *n* *syn* see INLET
lockup *n* *syn* see JAIL
‖**loco** *adj* *syn* see INSANE 1
locum tenens *n* *syn* see SUBSTITUTE
locus *n* *syn* see PLACE 1
locution *n* *syn* see PHRASE 2
lodge *vb* **1** *syn* see HARBOR 2
  rel accept, admit, receive, take; accommodate, contain, hold
  2 *syn* see ENTRENCH 1
lodge *n* **1** *syn* see HUT
  2 *syn* see HOTEL
  3 *syn* see LAIR 1
lodgeable *adj* *syn* see LIVABLE 1
lodging *n* **1** *syn* see ACCOMMODATIONS
  2 *usu* **lodgings** *pl syn* see APARTMENT 1
lodgment *n* *syn* see ACCOMMODATIONS
loftiest *adj* *syn* see TOP 1
loftiness *n* *syn* see PRIDE 3
lofty *adj* **1** *syn* see PROUD 1
  2 *syn* see AMBITIOUS 2
  3 *syn* see GRAND 3
  4 *syn* see GENEROUS 1
  5 *syn* see ELEVATED 4
  6 extending or rising high in the air so as to have great or imposing height <a *lofty* monument to human aspiration>
  syn aerial, airy, skyscraping, soaring, spiring, topless, towering, towery; *compare* HIGH 1
  rel elevated, lifted, raised; aggrandized, exalted, magnified; august, imposing, majestic, stately

con humble, low, modest
logical *adj* **1** *syn* see RATIONAL
  ant illogical
  2 having or showing skill in thinking or reasoning <a *logical* argument>
  syn analytic, analytical, ratiocinative, subtle
  rel cogent, compelling, convincing, sound, telling, valid; clear, lucid, perspicuous; rational, reasonable; discriminating
  con instinctive, intuitive; irrational, unreasonable; casuistical, sophistical
  ant illogical
logo *n* *syn* see MARK 7
logotype *n* *syn* see MARK 7
loiter *vb* **1** *syn* see DELAY 2
  2 *syn* see IDLE
loiterer *n* *syn* see LAGGARD
loll *vb* **1** *syn* see SLOUCH
  2 *syn* see IDLE
‖**lollop** *vb* *syn* see SLOUCH
lone *adj* **1** having no company <a *lone* figure walking through the snow>
  syn alone, lonely, lonesome, solitary
  rel single, sole, unique; abandoned, deserted, forsaken; isolated, secluded
  con attended, chaperoned, companioned, convoyed, escorted
  ant accompanied
  2 *syn* see ONLY 2
  3 *syn* see SINGLE 2
lonely *adj* **1** *syn* see LONE 1
  2 *syn* see FORLORN 1
loneness *n* *syn* see SOLITUDE
lonesome *adj* **1** *syn* see LONE 1
  2 *syn* see FORLORN 1
  3 *syn* see OBSCURE 2
long *adj* **1** having considerable extension in space or time <a *long* road> <it has been a *long* time since we have seen you>
  syn elongate, elongated, extended, lengthy
  rel extensive, longish, outstretched
  con brief, curtailed
  ant short
  2 unduly extended <went through many *long* days of misery>
  syn dragging, drawn-out, ‖dreich, lengthy, long-drawn-out, longsome, overlong, prolonged, protracted
  rel diffuse, diffusive, long-winded, prolix; flatulent, verbose, wordy
  con ephemeral, evanescent, fleeting, fugacious, fugitive, impermanent, passing, short-lived, transient, transitory; abbreviated, abridged, curtailed, shortened
  ant brief
long *n* *syn* see AGE 2
long *vb* to desire urgently <*long* for peace>
  syn ache, crave, dream, hanker, hunger, itch, lust, pine, sigh, suspire, thirst, yearn, yen
  rel aim, aspire, want; miss
  idiom have an appetite (or a longing) for
  con abhor, detest, dread, fear, loathe
longanimity *n* *syn* see PATIENCE
long-drawn-out *adj* *syn* see LONG 2
  ant short; curtailed
‖**long green** *n* *syn* see MONEY
longitudinally *adv* *syn* see LENGTHWISE
  ant horizontally
long-lasting *adj* *syn* see OLD 2
  ant ephemeral
long-lived *adj* *syn* see OLD 2
  ant short-lived
longsome *adj* *syn* see LONG 2
long–suffering *n* *syn* see PATIENCE
  rel subduedness; humility, lowliness, meekness
  con impatience, uneasiness; irksomeness, tediousness, wearisomeness; boredom, ennui, tedium
long suit *n* *syn* see FORTE
  rel specialism, specialization, specialty
longtimer *n* *syn* see VETERAN
  con apprentice, neophyte, novice; newcomer, rookie, tenderfoot
‖**long tongue** *n* *syn* see GOSSIP 1
longways *adv* *syn* see LENGTHWISE
long–winded *adj* *syn* see WORDY

rel extended, lasting, lengthy, long, long-drawn-out, prolonged, protracted
con brief, close, compact
longwise *adv syn* see LENGTHWISE
‖**loo** *n syn* see TOILET
looby *n syn* see OAF 2
look *vb* **1** to make sure or take care (that something is or is not done) < *look* that you accuse no one unjustly >
syn mind, see, watch
rel attend, heed, tend; note, notice, observe; beware
2 *syn* see SEE 2
rel note, notice, observe, spot
idiom get a load of, take a gander at
3 *syn* see EXPECT 1
rel divine, forecast, foretell
ant despair (of)
4 to make apparent by the expression of the eyes or countenance < *looked* her annoyance at this interruption >
syn exhibit, show; *compare* SHOW 2
rel display, express, indicate, manifest
5 *syn* see SEEM
idiom strike one as
6 *syn* see FACE 1
7 to gaze in wonder or surprise < you should have seen them *look* >
syn eye, gape, ‖gaup (*or* gawp), gaze, goggle, ogle, rubberneck, stare; *compare* GAZE 1
rel gawk; glare, gloat, glower; peer
8 *syn* see TEND 1
look (at *or* upon) *vb syn* see EYE 1
look (into) *vb syn* see EXPLORE
look *n* **1** the directing of one's eyes in order to see < he wanted one last *look* before departing >
syn sight, view
rel glance, glimpse, peek, peep, squint; cast, slant; eye, ‖gander, ‖look-see, regard; eyeful, gaze, stare, survey
2 facial aspect especially as indicative of mood or feeling < you should have seen the *look* on her face >
syn cast, countenance, expression, face, visage
rel mug, physiognomy, ‖puss
3 *syn* see APPEARANCE 1
look down *vb* **1** *syn* see OVERLOOK 2
2 *syn* see DESPISE
3 *syn* see STARE DOWN
looker *n syn* see BEAUTY
looker–on *n syn* see SPECTATOR
look in *vb syn* see VISIT 2
look–in *n syn* see OPPORTUNITY
looking glass *n syn* see MIRROR 1
look out *vb syn* see BEWARE
lookout *n* **1** *syn* see GUARD 2
2 an elevated place affording a wide view for observation < guards posted at a *lookout* to watch for enemy troops entering the valley >
syn observatory, outlook, overlook
rel watchtower; crow's nest; cupola, widow's walk; firetower
3 a careful looking or watching < kept a constant *lookout* for new developments >
syn surveillance, tout, vigil, vigilance, watch, watch and ward
rel observance, observation
4 *syn* see VISTA
5 *syn* see BUSINESS 8
look up *vb* **1** *syn* see IMPROVE 3
2 *syn* see VISIT 2
loom *vb* **1** *syn* see APPEAR 1
2 to take shape as an impending occurrence < an international economic crisis *looms* ahead >
syn brew, forthcome, gather, impend
rel approach, come on, make up, near
con disappear, fade, pass, vanish; die (down *or* away), diminish, dwindle, wane; recede, retreat, withdraw
3 to appear in an impressively great or exaggerated form < the power of the enemy *loomed* in the soldiers' imagination >
syn bulk, stand out
rel lower, rear, threaten, tower
con die (down *or* away), diminish, dwindle, wane
loon *n syn* see LUNATIC 1
loony *adj syn* see FOOLISH 2

loony *n syn* see LUNATIC 1
loony bin *n syn* see ASYLUM 3
loop *n* **1** a curving or doubling of a line so as to form a closed or partly open curve < the transit makes a *loop* around town >
syn eye, ring
rel circlet, circuit, circumference, hoop, wreath; curve
2 a circular or curved piece used often to form a fastening or a handle < one of his belt *loops* is broken >
syn eye, ring, staple
rel hook
3 *syn* see LEAGUE 4
loop *vb syn* see SURROUND 1
rel arc, arch, bend, coil, curve
looped *adj syn* see INTOXICATED 1
loopy *adj syn* see FOOLISH 2
loose *adj* **1** not tightly bound, held, restrained, or stretched < *loose* rope >
syn lax, relaxed, slack
rel detached, free; flabby, flaccid, limp; desultory, negligent, remiss
con rigid, rigorous, stringent, taut, tense; exact, precise; bound, checked, curbed, inhibited, restrained, tied
ant strict; tight
2 *syn* see FREE 2
rel clear; disconnected, unattached, unconnected, undone, unfastened
con fast
3 not dense, close, or compact in structure < *loose* soil >
syn incoherent, nonadhesive
rel disconnected, disjointed, separate, unconnected
con compressed, condensed, contracted; concentrated, crammed, crowded, localized; close, compact, dense, thick
4 *syn* see FAST 7
rel capricious, extravagant, free, inconstant, reckless, unrestrained
loose *vb* **1** *syn* see FREE
2 *syn* see TAKE OUT (on)
3 to set free from a fastened or fixed condition < *loose* a knot >
syn disengage, unbind, undo, unfasten, unfix, unloose, unloosen
rel unbandage, unbar, unbolt, unbuckle, unbutton, unchain, unclasp, unglue, unhitch, unhook, unlace, unlash, unlatch, unlock, unpin, unscrew, unsnap, unstick, unstrap, untie
con bind, engage, fasten, fix, secure
4 *syn* see SHOOT 1
5 to make less rigid or tight < exercise *loosed* his muscles >
syn ease, ease off, lax, loosen, relax, slack, slacken, untighten
rel abate, alleviate, bate, lessen, let up, mitigate
con anchor, cement, clamp, clinch, fasten, knit, secure, set, tauten
ant tighten
loose–lipped *adj syn* see TALKATIVE
ant closemouthed
loosen *vb* **1** *syn* see LOOSE 5
ant tighten
2 *syn* see FREE
loosen up *vb syn* see RELAX 2
ant tighten (up)
loose–tongued *adj syn* see TALKATIVE
ant closemouthed
loot *n* **1** *syn* see SPOIL
rel lift, pillage, seizure
2 *syn* see MONEY
loot *vb syn* see ROB 1
looter *n syn* see MARAUDER
lop *vb* **1** *syn* see SLOUCH
2 *syn* see JUMP 1
lope *vb syn* see SKIP 1
rel run, sprint; romp, trip
‖**lopper** *vb syn* see CURDLE
lopsided *adj* lacking in balance, symmetry, or proportion < the arrangement of the furniture was *lopsided* >
syn asymmetric, difform, disproportional, disproportionate, irregular, nonsymmetrical, off-balance, overbalanced, proportion-

---

syn synonym(s)   *rel* related word(s)
ant antonym(s)   *con* contrasted word(s)
idiom idiomatic equivalent(s)
‖ use limited; if in doubt, see a dictionary

less, unbalanced, unequal, uneven, unproportionate, unsymmetrical

rel cockeyed, crooked, top-heavy, unsteady

con balanced, even, regular, symmetrical

loquacious *adj syn* see TALKATIVE

rel jabbering, overtalkative; prolix, verbose, wordy

con breviloquent, concise, succinct, taciturn, terse; abrupt, brusque, curt

lord *n syn* see HUSBAND

lord *vb* to affect an air of superiority and authority <nouveau riche love to *lord* it>

syn cock, peacock, pontificate, swagger, swank, swell

rel affect, pretend, put on; boss, order (about *or* around), overawe, overbear; tyrannize

idiom put on airs

lordly *adj* **1** *syn* see GRAND 1

2 *syn* see PROUD 1

rel egotistic, puffed; affected, snobbish, swollen; authoritarian, dictatorial, magisterial

con humble; abject, mean; subdued, submissive

lore *n* **1** *syn* see KNOWLEDGE 2

2 a body of traditions relating to a person, institution, or place <the Scottish highlands are rich in local *lore*>

syn folklore, legend, myth, mythology, mythos, tradition

rel custom, folkway, traditionalism; fable, old wives' tale, saga, superstition, tale

Lorelei *n syn* see SIREN

lorn *adj* **1** *syn* see DERELICT 1

2 *syn* see FORLORN 1

lose *vb* **1** to suffer deprivation of <*lost* all his savings in a poor investment>

syn drop, forfeit, sacrifice

rel mislay, misplace, miss; give up, relinquish, surrender, yield

con cash in, profit; clear, make, realize, take in; obtain, win

ant gain

2 to fail to win, gain, or obtain <*lost* every contest she entered>

syn drop, lose out

rel decline, fall, succumb, yield

ant win

3 *syn* see DEPRIVE 2

4 *syn* see SHAKE 5

5 *syn* see RID

lose out *vb syn* see LOSE 2

loser *n* **1** *syn* see FAILURE 5

rel also-ran, underdog

ant winner

2 *syn* see CONVICT

losing *n syn* see LOSS 1

loss *n* **1** the action of having something go out of one's control or possession <took precautions against *loss* or theft of his property>

syn losing, mislaying, misplacement, misplacing; *compare* PRIVATION 2

rel forfeit, forfeiture, sacrifice; bereavement, deprivation, deprivement, dispossession, divestiture, divestment, privation

2 *syn* see PRIVATION 2

3 *syn* see RUIN 3

lost *adj* **1** *syn* see DAMNED 1

rel incorrigible, irreclaimable, irredeemable, irreformable, unconverted, unregenerate; graceless

2 no longer possessed <earned his *lost* reputation by his outrageous behavior>

syn gone, missing

rel absent, lacking; passed; irrecoverable, irretrievable, irrevocable

con cherished, protected, treasured

3 *syn* see EXTINCT 2

4 *syn* see ABSTRACTED

rel absorbed; daydreamy, musing, unconscious

lot *n* **1** *syn* see SHARE 1

2 *syn* see FATE

rel decree, fortune; foreordination, predestination, predetermination

3 a measured portion of land having fixed boundaries <building *lots*>

syn parcel, plat, plot, tract

rel clearing, field, patch; part, plottage; block, frontage, real estate

4 *syn* see GROUP 3

rel aggregate, aggregation, conglomerate, conglomeration

5 *syn* see SET 5

6 *syn* see TYPE

7 *syn* see MUCH

lot *vb syn* see ALLOT

‖**lot** (on *or* upon) *vb syn* see RELY (on *or* upon)

lot (out) *vb syn* see DISTRIBUTE 1

lothario *n syn* see GALLANT 2

loud *adj* **1** marked by intensity or volume of sound <a *loud* blast on a trumpet>

syn blaring, earsplitting, full-mouthed, piercing, roaring, stentorian, stentorious, stentorophonic

rel booming, deafening, ear-piercing, fulminating, pealing, ringing, thunderous; resonant, resounding, sonorous; harsh, hoarse, raucous, stertorous, strident

con dulcet, gentle, mellifluous, mellow, quiet, smooth

ant low, soft

2 *syn* see GAUDY

rel brassy, vulgar; obnoxious, offensive; obtrusive

loudmouthed *adj syn* see VOCIFEROUS

‖**lough** *n syn* see INLET

lounge *vb syn* see IDLE

rel drift, vegetate; dally, slack; lie, lie down, recline

lounge *n syn* see BAR 5

lounge car *n syn* see PARLOR CAR

lounge lizard *n* **1** *syn* see FOP

2 *syn* see PARASITE

louse *n syn* see SNOT 1

louse up *vb syn* see BOTCH

lout *n syn* see OAF 2

rel boor, bumpkin, churl, clodhopper, hayseed, hick, peasant, rube, rustic, yokel; dolt

lout *vb syn* see RIDICULE

loutish *adj syn* see BOORISH

rel awkward, bungling, clumsy, inept, maladroit, rusty; callow, crude, gauche, raw, rough, uncouth

lovable *adj* gifted with traits and qualities that attract affection <a *lovable* child>

syn adorable, lovesome

rel admirable, agreeable, attractive, desirable, genial, likable, pleasing, winning, winsome; alluring, appealing, bewitching, captivating, charming, enchanting, engaging, enthralling, entrancing, fetching, ravishing, seductive

con dislikable, displeasing, distasteful, unattractive, unlikable, unpleasing; odious, offensive; abhorrent, abominable, obnoxious, repellent; contemptible, despicable, detestable

ant hateful; unlovable

love *n* **1** the feeling which animates a person who is genuinely fond of someone or something <a mother's *love* for her child>

syn affection, attachment, devotion, fondness

rel like(s), liking, regard; adoration, idolatry, piety, worship; allegiance, fealty, fidelity, loyalty; emotion, sentiment; crush, infatuation, passion, yearning; ardency, ardor, enthusiasm, fervor, zeal

con antipathy, aversion; animosity, animus, enmity, hostility, rancor; abhorrence, detestation, hatred

ant hate

2 the affection and tenderness felt by lovers <the ability to distinguish between *love* and lust was the mark of her maturity>

syn amorousness, amour, passion

rel crush, infatuation; desire, lust, yearning; ardency, ardor, fervor

idiom (the) tender passion

3 *syn* see LOVE AFFAIR

4 *syn* see SWEETHEART 1

love *vb* **1** to like or desire actively <she *loves* her material possessions all too dearly>

syn adore, delight (in), ‖eat up

rel appreciate, cherish, prize, treasure, value; dote (on *or* upon), fancy

idiom hold dear

con abjure, give up, reject, relinquish

2 to feel a lover's passion, devotion, or tenderness for <in spite of all their misfortunes, they continued to *love* each other devotedly>

syn adore, affection, worship

rel deify, exalt, idolize, revere, venerate; cherish, dote (on *or* upon); admire, fancy, like

con avoid, disregard, ignore, neglect, overlook, shun, slight
3 *syn* see CARESS

love affair *n* a romantic attachment or episode between lovers
< saddened by the end of a summer *love affair* >
syn affair, amour, love, romance
rel flirtation, intrigue; triangle, ménage à trois

love child *n syn* see BASTARD 1

loved *adj syn* see FAVORITE 1

love letter *n* a letter expressing a lover's affection < she had never
received a *love letter* >
syn billet-doux, mash note
rel valentine

loveling *n syn* see SWEETHEART 1

lovely *adj syn* see BEAUTIFUL
rel alluring, bewitching, captivating, charming, enchanting, engaging, entrancing, lovesome; delectable, delightful; dainty, delicate, exquisite, rare; graceful
ant hideous; unlovely

lovely *n syn* see BEAUTY

lover *n* **1** a man who is a woman's regular partner in nonmarital
sexual activity
syn boyfriend, fancy man, man, master, paramour
rel cavalier servente, sugar daddy
2 *syn* see BOYFRIEND 2
3 *syn* see ADDICT
4 *syn* see MISTRESS

lovesome *adj* **1** *syn* see LOVABLE
2 *syn* see LOVING

lovey-dovey *adj syn* see SENTIMENTAL

loving *adj* feeling or expressing love < his *loving* son unfailingly
waited upon him during his last years >
syn affectionate, dear, devoted, doting, fond, lovesome
rel adoring, attached, benevolent, cordial, kind, tender, warmhearted; attentive, caring, considerate, solicitous; amatory, amorous, erotic; enamored, infatuated; ardent, fervent, impassioned,
passionate; faithful; bound up
con aloof, detached, indifferent, unconcerned; chilly, cold, frigid
ant unloving

low *adj* ||**1** *syn* see SHORT 2
rel squatty; unelevated
2 *syn* see INFERIOR 1
3 *syn* see POOR 1
4 *syn* see IGNOBLE 1
rel lowbred, rude
5 *syn* see BASE 3
rel scrubby, scruffy; miserable, woebegone, woeful
con decent, decorous, proper, seemly; ethical, moral, noble;
high, lofty
6 *syn* see COARSE 3
7 *syn* see UNWELL
rel declining, weak; dizzy, faint, feverish
8 *syn* see DOWNCAST
9 of lesser degree, size, or amount than average or ordinary
< the energy crisis resulted in *lower* speed limits for all vehi-
cles >
syn subaverage, subnormal
rel fallen, reduced; brief, short; mediocre, moderate; atypical
10 *syn* see CHEAP 1
rel economical; moderate, nominal; cut, cut-rate, marked down,
slashed
con elevated, enhanced, increased, raised

lowborn *adj syn* see IGNOBLE 1
ant highborn

lowbred *adj syn* see BOORISH
ant highbred

low-cost *adj syn* see CHEAP 1

low-down *adj syn* see BASE 3

lower *vb syn* see FROWN 1
rel peer, stare; intimidate, menace, threaten

lower *adj syn* see INFERIOR 1
ant higher

lower *vb* **1** *syn* see FALL 1
ant rise
2 *syn* see DEPRECIATE 1
rel demote; de-escalate, deflate
con raise
3 to cause or allow to descend < *lowered* the landing gear of the
aircraft >

syn couch, demit, depress, droop, let down, sink
rel detrude, submerge; debase, reduce
con elevate, hoist, lift, pull up, raise
4 *syn* see REDUCE 2
ant raise
5 *syn* see HUMBLE
ant elevate

lowering (*or* **louring**) *adj* **1** *syn* see IMMINENT 2
rel frowning, gloomy, sullen; black, dark; foreboding, impending, portentous
2 *syn* see OVERCAST

lowermost *adj syn* see BOTTOMMOST
ant uppermost

lowery (*or* **loury**) *adj syn* see IMMINENT 2

lowest *adj syn* see BOTTOMMOST
ant highest

low-grade *adj syn* see INFERIOR 2

low-key *adj syn* see SUBDUED 2

low-keyed *adj syn* see SUBDUED 2

lowlife *n* **1** *syn* see WRETCH 1
2 *syn* see VILLAIN 1

lowly *adj* **1** *syn* see HUMBLE 1
rel retiring, withdrawing; deferential, obeisant, reverential; obsequious, servile
ant haughty
2 *syn* see IGNOBLE 1
3 *syn* see PROSAIC 3

low-pressure *adj syn* see EASYGOING 3
ant high-pressure

low-priced *adj syn* see CHEAP 1

||**low-rate** *vb syn* see DECRY 2

low-set *adj syn* see SHORT 2

low-spirited *adj syn* see DOWNCAST
ant high-spirited

low-statured *adj syn* see SHORT 2

loyal *adj syn* see FAITHFUL 1
con faithless; alienated, disaffected, estranged; contumacious,
factious, insubordinate, mutinous, rebellious, seditious
ant disloyal

loyalist *n syn* see PATRIOT 1

loyalty *n* **1** *syn* see FIDELITY 1
rel trueness, truth
ant disloyalty
2 *syn* see ATTACHMENT 1

lubber *n syn* see OAF 2

lubberland *n syn* see UTOPIA

lubberly *adj syn* see BOORISH

||**lubricate** *vb syn* see BRIBE

lubricious *adj* **1** *syn* see INCONSTANT 1
2 *syn* see SLICK 1

lucent *adj* **1** *syn* see BRIGHT 1
2 *syn* see CLEAR 4

lucid *adj* **1** *syn* see BRIGHT 1
2 *syn* see SANE 2
3 *syn* see UNDERSTANDABLE
4 *syn* see CLEAR 4
con dusky, gloomy, murky; muddy, turbid

lucidity *n* **1** *syn* see CLARITY
rel comprehensibility, intelligibility, understandability; distinct-
ness, explicitness
ant ambiguity
2 *syn* see WIT 2

Lucifer *n syn* see DEVIL 1

luck *n* **1** *syn* see CHANCE 2
rel break, occasion, opportunity
2 *syn* see ACCIDENT 1
3 success dependent on chance < he had all the *luck* in the
world and was greatly envied by every one of his associates >
syn fortunateness, fortune, luckiness
rel advantage, break, fluke, godsend, opportunity, windfall;
weal; hap, kismet
ant ill-fortune
4 *syn* see CHARM 2

syn synonym(s)   *rel* related word(s)
ant antonym(s)   *con* contrasted word(s)
idiom idiomatic equivalent(s)
|| use limited; if in doubt, see a dictionary

luck *vb syn* see HAPPEN 2
luckiness *n syn* see LUCK 3
luckless *adj syn* see UNLUCKY
   rel miserable, wretched
   ant lucky
lucky *adj* having a favorable outcome or an unforeseen or unpredictable success < he can only be described as *lucky*, as his success and fame are unearned >
   syn fortunate, happy, providential, ‖sonsy, well
   rel auspicious, benign, favorable, propitious; advantageous, beneficial, profitable; felicitous
   idiom in luck
   con baleful, malefic, maleficent, malign, sinister
   ant luckless, unlucky
lucrative *adj syn* see ADVANTAGEOUS 1
lucre *n* 1 *syn* see PROFIT
   2 *syn* see MONEY
luculent *adj syn* see CLEAR 4
ludicrous *adj syn* see LAUGHABLE
   rel absurd, foolish, preposterous, silly; antic, bizarre, fantastic, grotesque
   con doleful, dolorous, lugubrious, melancholy
lug *vb* 1 *syn* see PULL 2
   2 *syn* see CARRY 1
   3 *syn* see JERK
‖**lug** *n syn* see OAF 2
‖**lugs** *n pl syn* see POSE 2
lugubrious *adj* 1 *syn* see MELANCHOLY 2
   rel depressing, oppressing, oppressive; dour, glum, morose, saturnine, sullen
   con blithe, jocund, jolly, jovial, merry; cheerful, glad, joyful
   ant facetious
   2 *syn* see GLOOMY 3
lukewarm *adj* 1 *syn* see TEPID 1
   2 *syn* see TEPID 2
   rel irresolute, irresolved, uncommitted, unresolved; hesitant, indecisive, uncertain, undecided; cool; wishy-washy
   ant icy; boiling
lull *vb* 1 *syn* see CALM
   rel moderate, qualify, temper
   ant agitate
   2 *syn* see ABATE 4
lull *n* 1 *syn* see QUIET 1
   2 *syn* see PAUSE
   rel abeyance, quiescence
lullaby *n* a song to quiet children or lull them to sleep < sang a *lullaby* to the baby every night >
   syn berceuse, cradlesong
‖**lulu** *n syn* see ‖DILLY
lumber *vb* to tread heavily or clumsily < the tired old man slowly *lumbered* home >
   syn barge, clump, galumph, stumble, stump
   rel plod, trudge; shamble, slog
lumber *vb syn* see BURDEN
lumbering *adj* 1 *syn* see CLUMSY 1
   rel cumbersome, cumbrous, ponderous; hulking, hulky
   2 *syn* see AWKWARD 2
luminary *n* 1 *syn* see CELEBRITY 2
   rel leading light
   2 *syn* see NOTABLE 1
luminous *adj* 1 *syn* see BRIGHT 1
   2 *syn* see CLEAR 4
   3 *syn* see UNDERSTANDABLE
lummox *n syn* see OAF 2
lump *n* 1 a compact mass of indefinite size and shape < dropped a large *lump* of butter into the steaming chowder >
   syn chunk, clod, clump, gob, hunch, hunk, nugget, wad
   rel particle, piece, portion; batch, bunch, ‖swad; bit, chip, crumb, morsel, scrap; wedge; block, bulk
   2 *syn* see MUCH
   3 *syn* see BUMP 2
   rel bulge, protuberance, swelling
   4 *syn* see OAF 2
   5 **lumps** *pl syn* see DUE 1
lump *vb syn* see BEAR 10
lumpish *adj* 1 *syn* see BOORISH
   2 *syn* see CLUMSY 1
lumpkin *n syn* see OAF 2

lumpy *adj syn* see RUDE 1
lunacy *n* 1 *syn* see INSANITY 1
   rel absurdity, folly, foolery, foolishness; asininity, fatuity, inanity, ineptitude, stupidity
   2 *syn* see FOOLISHNESS
lunatic *adj* 1 *syn* see INSANE 1
   2 *syn* see FOOLISH 2
lunatic *n* 1 a person who is insane or of unsound mind < Bedlam was a famous old English asylum for *lunatics* >
   syn bedlamite, dement, loon, loony, madling, madman, maniac, non compos, nut, Tom o' Bedlam
   rel demoniac, energumen; raver; neuropath, neurotic, paranoid, psycho, psychoneurotic
   2 *syn* see CRACKPOT
lunch counter (*or* **bar**) *n syn* see EATING HOUSE
luncheonette *n syn* see EATING HOUSE
lunchroom *n syn* see EATING HOUSE
lunch wagon (*or* **cart**) *n syn* see EATING HOUSE
lunge *vb syn* see PLUNGE 2
lunk *n syn* see DUNCE
lunkhead *n syn* see DUNCE
lupanar *n syn* see BROTHEL
lurch *n syn* see LEANING 2
lurch *vb* 1 *syn* see SEESAW
   2 to move forward unsteadily while swaying from side to side < the sodden drunk *lurched* uncertainly toward the door >
   syn careen, stagger, ‖stoit, ‖stoiter, ‖stot, sway, swing, weave, wobble; *compare* TEETER
   rel reel, rock, roll, swag, toss, totter, whirl; bob; wave, waver
   con march, stride
   3 *syn* see TEETER
   rel pitch, plunge
   4 *syn* see JERK
   5 *syn* see WALLOW 2
   6 *syn* see STUMBLE 3
lure *n* 1 *syn* see ATTRACTION 1
   2 something that leads an individual into a place or situation from which escape is difficult < used her charm as a *lure* to trap the unsuspecting youth >
   syn allurement, bait, come-on, decoy, enticement, inveiglement, seducement, siren song, snare, ‖stale, temptation, trap
   rel appeal, attraction, incentive, inducement; con game, gimmick, suck-in, trick; ambush, blind, camouflage, delusion, fake, illusion
   con caution, caveat, warning
lure *vb* to draw from a usual, desirable, or proper course or situation into one felt as unusual, undesirable, or wrong < the promise of money *lured* him away from his steady job >
   syn allure, bait, decoy, entice, entrap, inveigle, lead on, seduce, tempt, toll, train
   rel bag, capture, catch, draw in, ensnare, rope, snare, suck in; attract, beguile, bewitch, captivate, charm, enchant, fascinate, invite; draw, draw on; blandish, cajole, wheedle
   idiom bait the hook, give the come-on
   con drive (away *or* off), rebuff, repulse
   ant repel
lurid *adj* 1 *syn* see PALE 1
   2 *syn* see GHASTLY 1
   rel ashen, ashy, livid, pale, pallid, wan; baleful, malefic, maleficent, malign, sinister
   3 *syn* see SENSATIONAL 2
luring *adj syn* see ENTICING
   ant repellent, repelling
lurk *vb syn* see SNEAK
lurking *adj syn* see LATENT
luscious *adj* 1 *syn* see DELIGHTFUL
   rel appetizing, flavorsome, nectarious, palatable, piquant; choice, distinctive, exquisite, rare, rich
   ant austere
   2 *syn* see LUXURIOUS 3
   3 *syn* see SENSUOUS
   4 *syn* see ORNATE
lush *adj* 1 *syn* see PROFUSE
   rel luxurious, sumptuous
   2 *syn* see DELIGHTFUL
   3 *syn* see SENSUOUS
   4 *syn* see LUXURIOUS 3
lush *n* ‖1 *syn* see LIQUOR 2

2 syn see DRUNKARD
lush (up) *vb syn* see DRINK 3
∥lushed *adj syn* see INTOXICATED 1
∥lusher *n syn* see DRUNKARD
lust *n* **1 syn** see DESIRE 1
  rel coveting, yearning, yen
  2 sexual appetency < they mistakenly thought that *lust* was lasting love>
  syn aphrodisia, concupiscence, desire, eroticism, itch, lickerishness, lustfulness, passion, prurience, pruriency
  rel nymphomania, priapism, satyriasis, satyrism; excitement, heat, hunger, libido, rut; fervor; carnality, lasciviousness, lecherousness, lechery, lubricity, salacity
lust *vb syn* see LONG
  rel desire, wish
luster *n* the quality or condition of shining by reflected light < the satiny *luster* of fine pearls>
  syn glaze, glint, gloss, polish, sheen, shine
  rel iridescence, opalescence; brilliance, brilliancy, effulgence, luminosity, radiance, refulgence; afterglow, gleam, glow; candescence, incandescence
lusterless *adj* **1 syn** see DULL 7
  ant lustrous
  2 syn see COLORLESS 2
lustful *adj* **1 syn** see LICENTIOUS 2
  2 sexually excited < *lustful* old man>
  syn concupiscent, goatish, hot, lascivious, libidinous, lickerish, passionate, prurient, ruttish, rutty, satyric
  rel burning, hot-blooded, itching; lecherous, salacious
lustfulness *n syn* see LUST 2
lustral *adj syn* see PURGATIVE
lustrate *vb syn* see PURIFY 2
lustration *n syn* see PURIFICATION
lustratory *adj syn* see PURGATIVE
lustrous *adj* **1** having a high gloss or shine < a *lustrous* star sapphire>
  syn burnished, gleaming, glistening, glossy, polished, sheeny, shining, shiny
  rel gleamy, glimmering, glinting, sparkling; radiant
  con dull, flat, lackluster, mat
  ant lusterless

2 syn see BRIGHT 1
  rel glorious, resplendent, splendid
lusty *adj* **1 syn** see VIGOROUS
  rel hale, healthy
  ant effete
  2 syn see STRONG 3
  3 syn see HUGE
lusus *n syn* see FREAK 2
luxuriant *adj* **1 syn** see PROFUSE
  rel fecund, fertile, fruitful, prolific; rampant, rank
  con barren, infertile, sterile, unfruitful
  2 syn see LUXURIOUS 3
luxuriate *vb syn* see WALLOW 3
  rel overindulge, overdo; eat up, enjoy, feast, love, riot
luxurious *adj* **1 syn** see SENSUOUS
  rel self-indulging, self-pampering; languishing, languorous
  con self-abnegating, self-denying; austere, severe, stern
  ant ascetic
  2 syn see GRAND 2
  rel imposing, majestic, stately
  3 ostentatiously rich or magnificent < the robber barons built *luxurious* homes which rivaled the palaces of Europe>
  syn Capuan, deluxe, luscious, lush, luxuriant, opulent, palace, palatial, plush, plushy, sumptuous, upholstered
  rel extravagant, grandiose, ostentatious, posh, pretentious, showy; awful, grand, imposing, magnificent, majestic, stately; Lucullan; elaborate, fancy; costly, expensive, precious
  con economical, frugal, sparing, thrifty; exiguous, meager, scant, scanty, scrimpy, skimpy, spare
luxury *n* something adding to pleasure but not absolutely necessary < the poor cannot even afford the essentials, let alone occasional *luxuries*>
  syn amenity, extravagance, frill, luxus, superfluity
  rel comfort; embellishment, redundancy, self-indulgence; dainty, delicacy
  con basics, essential(s), fundamental(s)
luxus *n syn* see LUXURY
lying *adj syn* see DISHONEST
  rel false, wrong; deceptive, delusive, delusory, misleading
lying–in *n syn* see CONFINEMENT 2
lyncean *adj syn* see SHARP-EYED
lynx–eyed *adj syn* see SHARP-EYED

ma *n syn* see MOTHER 1
macabre *adj syn* see GHASTLY 1
  rel deadly, deathlike, deathly; ghostlike, ghostly
macaroni *n syn* see FOP
mace *n syn* see CUDGEL
∥mace *n syn* see SWINDLER
∥mace *vb syn* see CHEAT
machinate *vb* **1 syn** see ENGINEER
  2 syn see PLOT
machination *n syn* see PLOT 2
machine *n* **1 syn** see CAR
  2 syn see ROBOT 2
machinery *n syn* see EQUIPMENT
  rel agency, agent, channel, instrument, instrumentality, means, medium, organ, vehicle; contraption, contrivance, device, gadget; appliance, implement, instrument, tool, utensil
∥mack *n syn* see PIMP 1
macquereau *n syn* see PIMP 1
macrocosm *n syn* see UNIVERSE
  ant microcosm
macrocosmos *n syn* see UNIVERSE
  ant microcosm
mad *adj* **1 syn** see INSANE 1
  rel delirious, frantic, frenetic, furious, rabid, wild
  2 syn see FOOLISH 2
  3 syn see ILLOGICAL

4 syn see ANGRY
  rel sore, worked up; affronted, offended, outraged
  5 syn see FURIOUS 2
mad *vb syn* see ANGER 1
mad *n syn* see ANGER
mad–brained *adj syn* see RASH 1
madcap *adj syn* see RASH 1
madden *vb* **1** to make insane < prolonged solitary confinement had *maddened* the prisoners>
  syn craze, derange, distract, frenzy, unbalance, unhinge
  rel shatter; possess
  idiom drive insane (*or* mad *or* crazy)
  2 syn see ANGER 1
  con allay, assuage, mitigate, relieve
made–to–order *adj syn* see CUSTOM-MADE
madhouse *n syn* see ASYLUM 3
madid *adj syn* see WET 1
madling *n syn* see LUNATIC 1
madly *adv syn* see HARD 2
  rel foolishly, insanely, irrationally; hastily, rashly
madman *n* **1 syn** see LUNATIC 1
  2 syn see FOOL 1

---

syn synonym(s)   *rel* related word(s)
ant antonym(s)   *con* contrasted word(s)
idiom idiomatic equivalent(s)
∥ use limited; if in doubt, see a dictionary

madness *n syn* see INSANITY 1
maelstrom *n syn* see EDDY
rel commotion, confusion, fury, storm, turmoil
magazine *n* **1** *syn* see DEPOT 2
rel cache, lumber room
2 *syn* see ARMORY
3 *syn* see JOURNAL
rel publication; digest, gazette; annual, bimonthly, biweekly, daily, monthy, quarterly, semiweekly, weekly
mage *n syn* see MAGICIAN 1
maggot *n syn* see CAPRICE
magian *n syn* see MAGICIAN 1
magian *adj syn* see MAGIC
magic *n* **1** the use of means (as charms or spells) believed to have supernatural power over natural forces < the practice of *magic* >
syn bewitchment, conjuring, conjury, enchantment, ensorcellment, incantation, magicking, necromancy, sorcery, thaumaturgy, witchcraft, witchery, witching, wizardry
rel abracadabra, alchemy, augury, charm, divining, exorcism, fortune-telling, mumbo jumbo, occultism, soothsaying, sortilege, voodooism; devilry, deviltry, diablerie, diabolism, satanism; wicca
2 the art of producing mysterious effects by illusion and sleight of hand < the club presented a program of clever *magic* to raise funds >
syn conjuring, legerdemain
idiom sleight of hand
magic *adj* having seemingly supernatural qualities or powers < modern medicine has developed a host of *magic* drugs >
syn magian, magical, mystic, necromantic, sorcerous, thaumaturgic, witchy, wizardly
rel extraordinary, marvelous, prodigious, remarkable, stupendous, unbelievable, unprecedented
magical *adj syn* see MAGIC
magician *n* **1** one who practices magical arts < a *magician* cast a spell over the child >
syn archimage, charmer, conjurer, enchanter, mage, magian, magus, necromancer, sorcerer, voodoo, voodooist, warlock, wizard; *compare* WITCH 1
rel augurer, brujo, diviner, exorciser, exorcist, invocator, thaumaturge, thaumaturgist; medicine man, shaman; prophet, seer, soothsayer; fortune-teller, medium; diabolist, satanist
2 one who practices tricks of illusion and sleight of hand < a *magician* performed tricks for the children at the party >
syn conjurer, illusionist, trickster
magicking *n syn* see MAGIC 1
magisterial *adj* **1** *syn* see DICTATORIAL
rel disdainful, insolent, lordly, supercilious
2 *syn* see MASTERFUL 1
3 *syn* see POMPOUS 1
magistrate *n syn* see JUDGE 2
magnanimous *adj syn* see GENEROUS 1
rel altruistic, liberal, unselfish; great, highminded, knightly, noble, nobleminded, princely
con measly, paltry, petty, picayunish, picayune
magnate *n* a businessman of exceptional wealth, influence, or power < the oil and steel *magnates* who controlled whole nations >
syn baron, czar, king, merchant prince, mogul, prince, tycoon
rel figure, name, personage; ‖biggie, big gun, big-timer, ‖big wheel, fat cat, lion, nabob; plutocrat
idiom captain of industry
magnetic *adj syn* see ATTRACTIVE 1
rel arresting, irresistible; charismatic
con repellent, repugnant, repulsive
magnetism *n syn* see CHARM 3
magnetize *vb syn* see ATTRACT 1
magnific *adj syn* see GRAND 1
magnificent *adj* **1** *syn* see GRAND 1
rel glorious, resplendent, splendid, sublime, superb; luxurious, opulent, sumptuous
con abject, ignoble, mean, sordid; humble, lowly, meek; paltry
ant modest
2 *syn* see SPLENDID 2
3 *syn* see SUPERB 3
magnify *vb* **1** *syn* see PRAISE 2
2 *syn* see EXALT 1

rel augment, enlarge, increase; amplify, dilate, distend, expand, inflate, swell
ant belittle, minimize
3 *syn* see INCREASE 1
ant minify
4 *syn* see INTENSIFY
5 *syn* see OVERPLAY 2
6 *syn* see EMBROIDER
magniloquent *adj syn* see RHETORICAL
magnitude *n* **1** *syn* see ENORMITY 2
2 *syn* see SIZE 1
3 *syn* see SIZE 2
4 *syn* see ORDER 4
5 *syn* see IMPORTANCE
magnum opus *n syn* see MASTERPIECE 1
magpie *n syn* see CHATTERBOX
magus *n syn* see MAGICIAN 1
mahogany *n syn* see TABLE 1
maid *n* **1** *syn* see GIRL 1
2 a woman hired to do housework < in addition to her other duties the *maid* was expected to care for the baby >
syn biddy, girl, handmaid, hired girl, housemaid, maidservant
rel au pair girl; chambermaid, nursemaid, parlormaid; handmaiden; domestic, factotum, ‖muchacha, servant
idiom maid of all work
maiden *n syn* see GIRL 1
maiden *adj* **1** *syn* see VIRGIN 1
rel husbandless; old-maidish, spinsterish, spinsterly
2 *syn* see FIRST 2
maidenhead *n syn* see VIRGINITY
maidenhood *n syn* see VIRGINITY
maiden lady *n syn* see SPINSTER
maidservant *n syn* see MAID 2
maim *vb* to wound so severely as to deprive of the use of or to cause loss of a limb or member < an arm hanging useless, *maimed* in an auto accident >
syn cripple, dislimb, dismember, mayhem, mutilate; *compare* PARALYZE 1
rel disable, disfigure, hamstring; batter, break, ‖bung up, mangle, massacre, maul
con rehabilitate, restore, salvage; cure, fix, heal, mend, remedy, repair
main *n syn* see OCEAN
main *adj syn* see CHIEF 2
rel foremost, head, leading, paramount; cardinal, controlling, essential, fundamental, vital; prevailing
‖**main** *adv syn* see VERY 1
‖**mainline** *vb syn* see SHOOT UP 2
mainly *adv syn* see GENERALLY 1
mainstay *n* a chief reliance < the *mainstay* of the organization held things together >
syn backbone, pillar, sinew(s)
rel brace, buttress, crutch, maintainer, prop, staff, standby, stay, support, supporter, sustainer, upholder
maintain *vb* **1** to keep in a state of repair, efficiency, or validity < he followed a careful regimen to *maintain* his good health >
syn keep up, preserve, save, sustain; *compare* SAVE 3
rel husband, manage; care (for), cultivate; guard, protect
con disregard, ignore, neglect, omit, overlook, slight
2 to uphold as true, right, proper, or acceptable often in the face of challenge or indifference < I *maintain* that his actions were justified by the circumstances >
syn argue, assert, claim, contend, defend, justify, vindicate, warrant
rel affirm, aver, avouch, avow, declare, profess, protest; emphasize, insist, persist, stress; correct, rectify, right
con contradict, deny, gainsay, traverse; challenge, query, question
3 *syn* see SUPPORT 3
maintenance *n syn* see LIVING
majestic *adj* **1** *syn* see GRAND 1
rel courtly, dignified; ceremonious; imperial
2 *syn* see KINGLY
major *adj* **1** *syn* see CHIEF 2
rel better, greater, higher, superior
2 *syn* see BIG 1
3 *syn* see GRAVE 3
make *vb* **1** *syn* see EFFECT 1

rel initiate, originate, start
2 *syn* see GENERATE 1
rel brew
3 to bring something into being by forming, shaping, combining, or altering materials <*made* a dress from odd bits of material>
syn assemble, build, construct, erect, fabricate, fashion, forge, form, frame, manufacture, mold, produce, put together, shape; *compare* BUILD 1
4 *syn* see DRAFT 3
5 *syn* see CONSTITUTE 1
6 *syn* see PREPARE 1
7 *syn* see DESIGNATE 2
8 *syn* see ENACT 1
9 *syn* see INFER
10 *syn* see EARN 1
rel harvest, reap
11 *syn* see CLEAR 6
12 *syn* see FORCE 2
13 *syn* see HEAD 3
rel break (for)
‖**14** *syn* see MEDDLE
15 *syn* see RUN 8
make–believe *n syn* see PRETENSE 2
make off *vb syn* see RUN 2
rel depart, go, leave, quit, retire, withdraw; abscond, decamp, escape
make out *vb* **1** *syn* see APPREHEND 1
2 *syn* see ESTABLISH 6
3 *syn* see INFER
‖**4** *syn* see SHIFT 5
5 *syn* see SUCCEED 3
make over *vb syn* see TRANSFER 4
make–peace *n syn* see PEACEMAKER
maker *n syn* see FATHER 2
rel executor, operator; manufacturer
makeshift *n syn* see RESOURCE 3
makeshift *adj* serving as a temporary expedient <forced to make *makeshift* plans>
syn provisional, rough-and-ready, rough-and-tumble, stopgap
make up *vb* **1** *syn* see CONTRIVE 2
2 *syn* see MIX 1
3 *syn* see PREPARE 1
4 *syn* see CONSTITUTE 1
5 *syn* see COMPENSATE 1
make up (to) *vb syn* see ADDRESS 8
makeup *n* **1** the way in which parts or constituents are related in an organized whole <the complex *makeup* of the eye>
syn architecture, composition, constitution, construction, design, formation
rel arrangement, ordering, organization, plan, setup; form, shape, style
2 *syn* see DISPOSITION 3
rel cast, fiber, grain, mold, stamp, stripe, vein; constitution, frame
3 cosmetics used to color and beautify the face or body <with *makeup* on, she didn't look bad>
syn face, maquillage, paint, war paint
rel powder; blackface, grease paint
maladroit *adj* **1** *syn* see AWKWARD 2
rel blundering, floundering, stumbling, ungraceful; left-handed, unskilled
con deft, dexterous, handy; clever, cunning, ingenious
ant adroit
2 *syn* see TACTLESS
malady *n syn* see DISEASE 1
mala fide *adj syn* see INSINCERE
ant bona fide
malaise *n syn* see INFIRMITY 1
malapert *adj syn* see SAUCY 1
malapert *n syn* see MINX
malapropos *adj* **1** *syn* see IMPROPER 1
ant apropos
2 *syn* see UNSEASONABLE 1
malarkey *n syn* see NONSENSE 2
malconformation *n syn* see DEFORMITY
malcontent *n* **1** *syn* see GROUCH
2 *syn* see REBEL

malcontent *adj syn* see DISCONTENTED
rel alienated, disaffected, estranged; disobedient, ungovernable, unruly; restless; contumacious, factious, insubordinate, mutinous, rebellious, seditious
malcontented *adj syn* see DISCONTENTED
male *adj syn* see VIRILE
malediction *n syn* see CURSE 1
ant benediction
malefactor *n syn* see CRIMINAL
rel blackguard, knave, miscreant, rascal, rogue, scoundrel; evildoer, sinner, wrongdoer
malefic *adj syn* see SINISTER
ant benefic
maleficent *adj syn* see SINISTER
ant beneficent
malevolence *n syn* see MALICE
rel antagonism, hostility; abhorrence, abomination, detestation
ant benevolence
malevolent *adj syn* see MALICIOUS
rel baleful, malefic, maleficent, sinister
con benign, benignant, kind, kindly
ant benevolent
malformation *n syn* see DEFORMITY
malice *n* a desiring or wishing pain, injury, or distress to another <they sought to ruin his reputation out of pure *malice*>
syn despite, despitefulness, grudge, ill will, malevolence, maliciousness, malignancy, malignity, spite, spitefulness, spleen
rel bane, poison, venom; bile; animosity, animus, antipathy, down, enmity; hate, hatefulness, hatred, invidiousness, meanness; bitterness, resentment, unbrage
con benevolence, benignancy, benignity, charity, kindliness, kindness
malicious *adj* having, showing, or indicative of intense often vicious ill will <the helpless victim of *malicious* rumors>
syn catty, despiteful, evil, hateful, malevolent, malign, malignant, nasty, rancorous, spiteful, spitish, vicious, wicked
rel poisonous, poison-pen, venomous, virulent; baneful, deleterious, detrimental, noxious, pernicious; envious, green, green=eyed, jealous; mean, petty
con benevolent, charitable, friendly, kind, kindly; considerate, thoughtful
maliciousness *n syn* see MALICE
malign *adj* **1** *syn* see SINISTER
rel baneful, deleterious, detrimental, injurious, noxious, pernicious
con auspicious, favorable, propitious; fortunate, happy, lucky, providential
ant benign
2 *syn* see MALICIOUS
rel antagonistic, antipathetic, hostile, inimical
con benignant, kind, kindly
ant benign
malign *vb* to speak evil of for the purpose of injuring and without regard for the truth <the candidates increasingly *maligned* each other as the campaign degenerated>
syn asperse, befoul, bespatter, blacken, calumniate, defame, denigrate, libel, ‖scandal, scandalize, slander, slur, smear, spatter, tear down, traduce, vilify, villainize
rel decry, depreciate, derogate, detract, disparage; opprobriate, revile, vituperate; backbite, besmirch, defile, pollute, smirch, soil, stain, sully, taint, tarnish
idiom blow upon, cast aspersion(s) on (*or* upon)
con acclaim, applaud, eulogize, extol, laud, praise; defend, justify, maintain, vindicate
malignancy *n syn* see MALICE
malignant *adj syn* see MALICIOUS
rel devilish, diabolical, fiendish
con altruistic, benevolent, charitable, humane
ant benignant
maligning *adj syn* see LIBELOUS
malignity *n syn* see MALICE
rel revengefulness, vengefulness, vindictiveness
ant benignity

---

syn synonym(s)   *rel* related word(s)
ant antonym(s)   *con* contrasted word(s)
idiom idiomatic equivalent(s)
‖ use limited; if in doubt, see a dictionary

malison *n syn* see CURSE 1
   ant benison
‖**malkin** *n syn* see SLATTERN 1
malleable *adj syn* see PLASTIC
   rel governable, manageable; transformable
   con intractable, recalcitrant, ungovernable, unmanageable, unruly
   ant refractory
malleate *vb syn* see HAMMER 1
malodorous *adj* 1 having an unpleasant smell < *malodorous* cheeses >
   syn fetid, frowsy, funky, fusty, gamy, high, mephitic, musty, nidorous, noisome, olid, putrid, rancid, rank, reeking, reeky, ‖smellful, smelly, stale, stenchful, stenchy, stinking, stinky, strong, whiffy; *compare* ODOROUS
   rel bad, foul, offensive, nauseating, vile; decayed, decomposed, fuggy, off, rotten, spoiled, tainted; nasty, noxious, pestilential, poisonous, polluted
   con clean, deodorized, fresh
   ant fragrant, sweet
   2 *syn* see INDECOROUS
maltreat *vb syn* see ABUSE 4
‖**mam** *n syn* see MOTHER 1
mama (or **mamma**) *n syn* see MOTHER 1
‖**mammock** *vb syn* see DISORDER 1
mammoth *n syn* see GIANT
mammoth *adj syn* see HUGE
mammy *n syn* see MOTHER 1
man *n* 1 *syn* see HUMAN
   2 *syn* see MANKIND
   3 a male human being < just an average *man* trying to get by >
   syn ‖bloke, boy, buck, ‖cat, chap, cuss, fellow, galoot, ‖gee, gent, gentleman, guy, he, ‖mun, skate, snap, ‖stirra; *compare* HUMAN
   4 *syn* see HUSBAND
   5 *syn* see LOVER 1
   6 *syn* see POLICEMAN
manage *vb* 1 *syn* see CONDUCT 3
   rel superintend; guide
   2 *syn* see GOVERN 3
   3 *syn* see SHIFT 5
   rel bring about, carry out, contrive, effect, execute; accomplish, achieve, succeed
   idiom sink or swim on one's own
   con collapse, fail, fall down; give up, poop (out)
management *n syn* see OVERSIGHT 1
manager *n syn* see EXECUTIVE
   rel handler, impresario, producer
man-at-arms *n syn* see SOLDIER
mancipium *n syn* see SLAVE 1
mandarin *n syn* see BUREAUCRAT
mandate *n syn* see COMMAND 1
   rel decree, fiat, imperative; authority, authorization
mandatory *adj* containing or constituting a command < *mandatory* entrance examinations >
   syn compulsatory, compulsory, imperative, imperious, obligatory, required
   rel essential, indispensable, irremissible, necessary, needful, requisite; binding, commanding, compelling, de rigueur; forced, involuntary
   con discretionary, elective, voluntary
   ant optional
maneuver *n* 1 *syn* see MEASURE 7
   2 *syn* see TRICK 1
   rel contrivance, device; intrigue, machination, manipulation, plot; demarche, movement, plan; finesse, subterfuge
maneuver *vb* 1 *syn* see ENGINEER
   rel navigate; finesse; design
   2 *syn* see HANDLE 2
   rel navigate
   3 *syn* see MANIPULATE 2
man Friday *n syn* see RIGHT-HAND MAN
manful *adj syn* see BRAVE 1
mangle *vb syn* see BATTER 1
   rel damage, impair, injure, mar; deface, disfigure; contort, deform, distort; butcher, hack
mangled *adj syn* see LACERATED
mangy *adj syn* see SHABBY 1

manhandle *vb* to treat roughly < riot police *manhandled* innocent bystanders >
   syn knock about, mishandle, rough (up), roughhouse, slap around
   rel abuse, maltreat, mistreat; batter, ‖bung up, mangle, maul
mania *n syn* see FETISH 2
   rel craze, enthusiasm, fancy, fascination, infatuation, passion; compulsion, fixed idea, hangup, idée fixe
maniac *adj syn* see INSANE 1
   rel berserk, delirious, frantic, frenetic, frenzied, furious, rabid, raging, ranting, violent, wild
maniac *n* 1 *syn* see LUNATIC 1
   2 *syn* see ENTHUSIAST
manifest *adj syn* see CLEAR 5
   rel disclosed, divulged, revealed, told; evidenced, evinced, shown; noticeable, prominent
   con implicit; obscure
manifest *vb* 1 *syn* see EMBODY 1
   2 *syn* see SHOW 2
   rel display, expose; express, utter, vent, voice
   con adumbrate, shadow
   ant suggest
manifold *adj* comprehending or uniting various features < a *manifold* operation >
   syn diverse, diversiform, multifarious, multifold, multiform, multiplex, multivarious
   rel multiphase, polymorphic, polymorphous
   con homogeneous, pure, uniform; plain, simple, straightforward, uncomplex, uncomplicated
manifold *vb syn* see INCREASE 1
manikin *n syn* see DWARF
manipulate *vb* 1 *syn* see HANDLE 2
   2 to control or play upon by artful, unfair, or insidious means < the sycophant cleverly *manipulated* his master >
   syn beguile, exploit, finesse, jockey, maneuver, play; *compare* ENGINEER
   rel machinate, use; conduct, control, direct, engineer, manage
mankind *n* the human race < all *mankind* will benefit from this new discovery >
   syn flesh, Homo sapiens, humanity, humankind, man, mortality; *compare* HUMAN
manlike *adj* 1 *syn* see ANTHROPOID
   2 *syn* see VIRILE
manly *adj* 1 *syn* see VIRILE
   2 *syn* see BRAVE 1
man-made *adj syn* see SYNTHETIC
manner *n* 1 *syn* see HABIT 1
   2 *syn* see METHOD 1
   rel custom, habit, habitude, practice, usage, use, wont; form, style
   3 *syn* see STYLE 4
   4 *syn* see VEIN 1
   rel form, turn; affectation, affectedness, mannerism; idiosyncrasy, peculiarity
   5 **manners** *pl* habitual conduct or deportment in social intercourse evaluated according to some conventional standard of politeness or civility < a person with impeccable *manners* >
   syn amenities, civilities, decorum(s), etiquette, mores, proprieties
   rel formalities, protocol; elegancies; bearing, behavior, demeanor, deportment, mien, p's and q's; mannerliness
   idiom conduct becoming a gentleman
   con mannerlessness, unmannerliness
mannered *adj syn* see SELF-CONSCIOUS
mannerism *n syn* see POSE 2
   rel eccentricity, idiosyncrasy; oddness, peculiarity, queerness, singularity
mannerless *adj syn* see RUDE 6
   ant mannerly
mannerly *adj syn* see CIVIL 2
   ant mannerless, unmannerly
manor *n* 1 *syn* see MANSION
   2 *syn* see ESTATE 3
mansion *n* a large imposing residence < the governor's *mansion* >
   syn castle, chateau, manor, villa
   rel estate, hall, house
manslaughter *n syn* see MURDER
manslayer *n syn* see MURDERER

mantic *adj syn* see PROPHETIC
mantle *vb syn* see BLUSH
man–to–man *adj syn* see FRANK
manual *n syn* see HANDBOOK
  rel abecedarium, hornbook, primer; text, textbook
manufactory *n syn* see FACTORY
manufacture *vb syn* see MAKE 3
manumit *vb syn* see FREE
  ant enslave
many *adj* consisting of a goodly but indefinite number < *many* lives were lost in the flood >
  syn legion, multifarious, multitudinal, multitudinous, numerous, populous, ‖several, sundry, various, voluminous
  rel divers, manifold, multiple, multiplicate, multiplied, myriad; abounding, abundant, bounteous, bountiful, copious, plentiful
  con meager, scant, scanty, sparse; only, sole
  ant few
many *pron syn* see SUNDRY
many–sided *adj* **1** *syn* see MULTILATERAL
  2 *syn* see VERSATILE
map *n* **1** *syn* see CHART 1
  rel picture, portrayal; delineation, design, diagram, draft, outline, sketch, tracing
  ‖**2** *syn* see FACE 1
map (out) *vb syn* see DESIGN 3
maquillage *n syn* see MAKEUP 3
mar *vb syn* see INJURE 1
  rel bruise, scar, scratch, warp; ruin, wreck
  con adorn, beautify, decorate, embellish; mend, patch, repair; amend, correct, emend, rectify, reform, revise
maraud *vb syn* see RAID 1
marauder *n* one who raids in search of plunder < *marauders* sacked village after village >
  syn bandit, brigand, bummer, cateran, depredator, despoiler, forager, freebooter, looter, pillager, plunderer, raider, ravager, ravisher, sacker, spoiler, spoliator
  rel buccaneer, desperado, pirate; wrecker
marblehearted *adj syn* see UNFEELING 2
  ant softhearted
marbles *n pl syn* see WIT 2
march *n syn* see FRONTIER 1
  rel boundary, periphery; territory; outlands, provinces
march *vb syn* see ADJOIN
  rel fringe, hem, rim, skirt; extend; parallel
march *vb* **1** *syn* see AGREE 4
  2 *syn* see STRIDE 1
  3 *syn* see ADVANCE 5
march *n syn* see ADVANCE 2
marchland *n syn* see FRONTIER 1
mare's nest *n syn* see IMPOSTURE
  rel babel, clamor, din, hubbub, hullabaloo, racket, uproar
margin *n* **1** *syn* see BORDER 1
  rel frame, trimming; shore; side
  2 *syn* see ROOM 3
  3 *syn* see MINIMUM
margin *vb syn* see BORDER 1
  rel abut, connect, join, line, neighbor, touch
marijuana *n* the dried leaves and flowering tops of the pistillate hemp plant sometimes smoked for their intoxicating effect < *marijuana* was smoked by several students at the party >
  syn boo, cannabis, grass, ‖Mary Jane, moocah, pot, ‖tea, weed
  rel joint, reefer; hash, hashish
marine *adj* **1** of or relating to the sea < *marine* biology >
  syn maritime, oceanic, thalassic
  rel hydrographic oceanographic; abyssal, bathyal, bathybic, bathysmal, benthic, dipsey, neritic, pelagic; aquatic, fluvial, fluviatile, lacustrine
  2 of or relating to the navigation of the sea < *marine* charts and maps >
  syn maritime, nautical, navigational
  rel naval; seamanlike, seamanly; deep-sea, ocean-going, seafaring, seagoing
mariner *n* one engaged in sailing or handling a ship < the tanker crew was made up mostly of experienced *mariners* >
  syn jack, jack-tar, sailor, sailorman, salt, seaman, tar, tarpaulin
  rel bluejacket, gob, rating, ‖swab, ‖swabbie; ‖lascar, ‖limey; old salt, sea dog, shellback
marital *adj syn* see MATRIMONIAL

maritime *adj* **1** *syn* see MARINE 2
  2 *syn* see MARINE 1
mark *n* **1** *syn* see AMBITION 2
  2 *syn* see TARGET 1
  3 *syn* see USE 4
  4 *syn* see FOOL 3
  5 *syn* see INDICATION 3
  rel attribute, emblem, symbol, type; character, property, quality
  6 *syn* see QUALITY 1
  7 a device (as a word) pointing distinctly to the origin or ownership of merchandise to which it is applied and legally reserved to the exclusive use of the owner < the company was brought to court for illegally using the *mark* of its rival >
  syn brand, logo, logotype, trademark
  rel label, stamp
  idiom brand name
  8 *syn* see CHARACTER 1
  9 *syn* see NOTICE 1
mark *vb* **1** *syn* see CHOOSE 1
  2 *syn* see SHOW 5
  3 *syn* see SHOW 2
  4 *syn* see CHARACTERIZE 2
  rel bespeak, betoken, denote, signify
  idiom set apart
  5 *syn* see SEE 1
  rel record, register; attend, heed, regard
mark (out) *vb syn* see DEMARCATE 1
  rel lay off, mark off; chart, lay out, map
mark down *vb* **1** *syn* see REDUCE 2
  ant mark up
  2 *syn* see DEPRECIATE 1
marked *adj syn* see NOTICEABLE
  rel distinguished, noted; considerable
market *n syn* see STORE 4
market *vb* **1** *syn* see SELL 3
  rel wholesale
  2 *syn* see SELL 2
marketable *adj* capable of being sold < *marketable* commodities >
  syn merchandisable, merchantable, salable, sellable, trafficable, vendible
  rel commercial; profitable, selling; fit, good, sound, wholesome
  con unmerchantable, unsalable
  ant unmarketable
‖maroon *vb syn* see CAMP
marred *adj syn* see DAMAGED
  rel banged-up, battered, bruised, mutilated; ruined, wrecked
  ant unmarred
marriage *n* **1** the state of being united to a person of the opposite sex as husband or wife < *marriage* was not in the plans of this couple >
  syn conjugality, connubiality, matrimony, wedlock
  rel match, union
  2 *syn* see WEDDING
marriage broker *n* one who arranges marriages < the old widow served as the town's *marriage broker* >
  syn go-between, matchmaker
  rel shadchan
marriage portion *n syn* see DOWRY
married *adj syn* see MATRIMONIAL
marrow *n syn* see ESSENCE 2
  rel core, heart, kernel, meat
marrowy *adj syn* see PITHY
marry *vb* **1** to take as spouse < he *married* her for her money >
  syn catch, espouse, wed
  rel wive
  idiom get hitched, get married, tie the knot
  con annul, divorce, separate
  2 to join in wedlock < the minister *married* all three daughters in one ceremony >
  syn ‖hitch, mate, splice, tie, wed
  idiom tie the knot, unite in marriage
  3 *syn* see JOIN 1
marsh *n syn* see SWAMP

---

syn synonym(s)   *rel* related word(s)
ant antonym(s)   *con* contrasted word(s)
idiom idiomatic equivalent(s)
‖ use limited; if in doubt, see a dictionary

marshal *vb* **1** *syn* see ORDER 1
rel distribute, space; escort, guide, shepherd, usher
2 *syn* see MOBILIZE 3
marshland *n* *syn* see SWAMP
martial *adj* belonging to, engaged in, or appropriate to the affairs of war <the reviewing officer saw the company standing in *martial* array>
syn military, warlike
rel bellicose, belligerent, combative, pugnacious; aggressive, militant; high-spirited, mettlesome, spirited
con civil, civilian; irenic, pacific, peaceable, peaceful
ant unmartial
martyr *vb* *syn* see AFFLICT
martyrize *vb* *syn* see AFFLICT
marvel *n* *syn* see WONDER 1
marveling *n* *syn* see WONDER 2
rel surprise
marvelous *adj* **1** causing or exciting wonder <the way in which he could bring together opposing forces was truly *marvelous*>
syn amazing, astonishing, astounding, miraculous, prodigious, spectacular, staggering, strange, stupendous, surprising, wonderful, wondrous
rel awe-inspiring, awesome, awful, awing; incomprehensible, inconceivable, incredible, unimaginable; fabulous, phenomenal, supernatural; exceptional, extraordinary; bewildering, confounding, striking, stunning
con commonplace, ordinary, routine; blah, unexciting, uninteresting
2 superior or outstanding of its kind <had a *marvelous* weekend>
syn ‖cool, ‖dandy, divine, dreamy, ‖galluptious, glorious, groovy, hot, hunky-dory, ‖keen, ‖neat, nifty, peachy, ripping, sensational, super, swell, terrific, wonderful; *compare* EXCELLENT, SUPERIOR 4, SUPREME
rel agreeable, enjoyable, pleasant, pleasurable; rewarding, satisfying
con dreary, dull, humdrum, monotonous, tedious; inferior, low=grade, mean, poor, punk
‖**Mary Jane** *n* *syn* see MARIJUANA
mascot *n* *syn* see CHARM 2
masculine *adj* *syn* see VIRILE
ant effeminate, unmasculine
mash *n* *syn* see CLUTTER 2
mash *vb* **1** *syn* see CRUSH 2
‖**2** *syn* see PRESS 1
mashed *adj* *syn* see ENAMORED 1
masher *n* *syn* see WOLF
mash note *n* *syn* see LOVE LETTER
mask *n* **1** a cover or partial cover for the face that has openings for the eyes and is used especially for disguise <on Halloween he wore a pirate's *mask*>
syn domino, doughface, false face, visor, vizard
rel disguise, masquerade; veil
2 an outward appearance that seeks to obscure an underlying true character <he was able to maintain a *mask* of dignity and tranquillity in his time of anxiety>
syn cloak, color, coloring, cover, disguise, disguisement, facade, face, false front, front, guise, masquerade, muffler, pretense, pretext, put-on, semblance, show, veil, veneer, window dressing; *compare* APPEARANCE 2
rel affectation, air, pose, posture; fakery, sham; dissembling, dissimulation, seeming, simulation; appearance, aspect
mask *vb* *syn* see DISGUISE
rel screen, secrete, veil; blur; defend, guard, protect, safeguard, shield
masquerade *n* *syn* see MASK 2
masquerade *vb* *syn* see POSE 4
mass *n* **1** *syn* see BODY 4
2 *syn* see PILE 1
3 *syn* see BULK 1
rel aggregate, aggregation, conglomerate, conglomeration; sum, whole
4 *syn* see BODY 3
5 *syn* see MUCH
6 *usu* **masses** *pl* *syn* see RABBLE 2
massacre *vb* *syn* see SLAUGHTER 3
massacre *n* the act or an instance of killing a considerable number of human beings under circumstances of atrocity or cruelty <the *massacre* of the Indians by the soldiers and settlers>

syn bloodbath, bloodshed, butchery, carnage, slaughter
rel blood purge, decimation, genocide, pogrom; internecion; assassination, killing, murder, slaying
massive *adj* **1** *syn* see HEAVY 1
rel hulking, hulky, massy
2 *syn* see HUGE
3 *syn* see MONSTROUS 1
massy *adj* *syn* see HUGE
master *n* **1** *syn* see EXPERT
rel maestro, savant; genius, mastermind; guru, swami
2 *syn* see LEADER 2
rel overlord, overman, overseer
3 *syn* see VICTOR 1
‖**4** *syn* see HUSBAND
5 *syn* see LOVER 1
master *vb* **1** *syn* see OVERCOME 1
2 *syn* see DOMESTICATE
rel dominate, govern, predominate, rule
3 *syn* see CONQUER 2
4 *syn* see LEARN 1
master *adj* **1** *syn* see DOMINANT 1
2 *syn* see PROFICIENT
masterdom *n* *syn* see SUPREMACY
masterful *adj* **1** disposed to exercise or flaunt dictatorial authority in a way to override any protestation <the royal favorite was pompous and *masterful* when dealing with subordinates>
syn bossy, domineering, high-handed, imperative, imperial, imperious, magisterial, overbearing, peremptory
rel absolute, arbitrary, authoritarian, authoritative, dictative, dictatorial, doctrinaire, dogmatic; autocratic, despotic, tyrannical; high-and-mighty, self-willed
con humble, modest, unpretentious; indecisive, irresolute; submissive, yielding; feeble, weak
2 *syn* see PROFICIENT
rel adroit, deft, dexterous; preeminent, superlative, supreme, transcendent
master–hand *n* *syn* see EXPERT
masterly *adj* *syn* see PROFICIENT
rel preeminent, superlative, supreme, transcendent
masterpiece *n* **1** something done or made with extraordinary skill or brilliance <his latest work is unquestionably a *masterpiece*>
syn chef d'oeuvre, classic, magnum opus, masterwork, tour de force
rel objet d'art, masterstroke
con botch, disaster, fiasco
2 *syn* see SHOWPIECE
mastership *n* *syn* see ABILITY 2
masterwork *n* *syn* see MASTERPIECE 1
mastery *n* **1** *syn* see POWER 1
2 *syn* see ABILITY 2
masticate *vb* *syn* see CHEW 1
rel bruise, crush, macerate, mash, pulp, pulpify, smash, squash
mastodonic *adj* *syn* see HUGE
mat *adj* *syn* see DULL 7
matador *n* *syn* see BULLFIGHTER
match *n* **1** *syn* see OPPONENT
2 *syn* see EQUAL
rel analogue, parallel
3 *syn* see MATE 5
4 *syn* see PARALLEL
5 *syn* see EVENT 5
rel bout, engagement, game
match *vb* **1** *syn* see OPPOSE 1
2 *syn* see EQUATE 2
3 *syn* see AMOUNT 2
rel complement, supplement
4 *syn* see EQUAL 3
rel compare, stack up
idiom hold a candle to
matched *adj* *syn* see ASSORTED 2
rel balanced, equated, evened, similar; coordinated, harmonized; coupled, joined, mated, paired, yoked
ant unmatched
matchless *adj* *syn* see ALONE 3
ant matchable
matchmaker *n* *syn* see MARRIAGE BROKER
mate *n* **1** *syn* see PARTNER
2 *syn* see ACCOMPANIMENT 2

3 *syn* see FRIEND
rel bedmate, classmate, co-mate, helpmate, playmate, roommate, schoolmate, teammate
4 *syn* see SPOUSE
rel match, parti
5 one of a pair matched in one or more qualities < the *mate* of a shoe >
syn companion, coordinate, double, duplicate, fellow, match, riciprocal, twin
rel alter ego, complement, sosie; compeer, equal, equivalent, peer
mate *vb syn* see MARRY 2
rel breed, crossbreed, pair; generate, procreate
‖**mater** *n syn* see MOTHER 1
material *adj* **1** of or belonging to actuality < for him the *material* world is the only world >
syn corporeal, gross, objective, phenomenal, physical, sensible, substantial, tangible
rel actual, real, true; appreciable, palpable, perceptible; earthly, worldly; animal, carnal, fleshly, sensual
con impalpable, imperceptible, intangible, unsubstantial; spiritual
ant immaterial, nonmaterial
2 *syn* see IMPORTANT 1
ant immaterial
3 *syn* see RELEVANT
rel consequential, important, momentous, significant; cardinal, essential, fundamental, vital
ant immaterial
material *n* **1** *syn* see THING 4
rel component, constituent, element, ingredient; apparatus, equipment, machinery
2 *usu* **materials** *pl syn* see EQUIPMENT
materialistic *adj* of or relating to a preoccupation with or stress upon material rather than intellectual or spiritual things < *materialistic* values characterize the modern age >
syn banausic, earthy, mundane, sensual, temporal, worldly
rel carnal, profane; earthly, terrestrial; secular, unspiritual
con intellectual, mental; spiritual, unfleshly, unworldly; heavenly
materiality *n syn* see ACTUALITY 2
materialize *vb* **1** *syn* see EMBODY 1
rel appear, emerge, loom, show; issue, rise, spring
2 to convert mentally into something concrete < with the help of graphs and figures abstract ideas can be *materialized* >
syn entify, hypostatize, reify
rel actualize, pragmatize, realize; corporealize; symbolize, typify
matériel *n syn* see EQUIPMENT
matriarch *n* a dignified, usually elderly woman of some rank or authority < the local *matriarchs* controlled the town's social functions >
syn dame, dowager, grande dame, matron
rel materfamilias, mother
matrimonial *adj* of, relating to, or characteristic of marriage < the *matrimonial* bond between husband and wife >
syn conjugal, connubial, hymeneal, marital, married, nuptial, spousal, wedded
rel bridal, epithalamic
matrimony *n syn* see MARRIAGE 1
matron *n syn* see MATRIARCH
matter *n* **1** *syn* see SUBJECT 2
2 *syn* see AFFAIR 1
rel complication, grievance, to-do, worry; circumstance, predicament
3 *syn* see SUBSTANCE 2
4 *syn* see THING 4
5 *syn* see ORDER 4
matter *vb* to be of importance < being your own self is what really *matters* >
syn count, import, mean, signify, weigh
idiom carry weight
matter–of–course *adj syn* see GENERAL 1
matter–of–fact *adj* **1** *syn* see REALISTIC
rel objective, sound
2 *syn* see PROSAIC 1
3 involving no display of emotion < the *matter-of-fact* reading of the judge masked his inner anguish >
syn cold, cold-blooded, emotionless, impersonal, unimpassioned

rel unaffected, unsentimental; prosaic
con emotional, impassioned, personal
4 *syn* see IMPASSIVE 1
maturate *vb syn* see MATURE
mature *adj* **1** having attained the normal peak of natural growth and development < *mature* plants ready to bear fruit >
syn adult, full-blown, full-fledged, full-grown, grown, grown-up, matured, ripe, ripened
rel developed, ready
idiom of age
con childish, childlike; boyish, green, juvenile, maiden, puerile, youthful
ant immature
2 *syn* see DUE 2
3 *syn* see UNPAID 2
mature *vb* to become fully developed or ripe < she *matured* as an actress after several years of summer stock >
syn age, develop, grow, grow up, maturate, mellow, ‖ripe, ripen
rel blossom, flower; advance, progress, round; season; decline, deteriorate, olden, wane
idiom come of age
matured *adj* **1** *syn* see MATURE 1
rel completed, finished; advised, considered, deliberate, designed, premeditated, studied
con callow, crude, green, raw, rough, rude, uncouth
ant premature, unmatured
2 *syn* see RIPE 3
maudlin *adj syn* see SENTIMENTAL
rel addled, befuddled, confused, fuddled, muddled; silly
maul *n syn* see BRAWL 2
maul *vb syn* see BATTER 1
rel flagellate, flail, lash, whip; bang, bash, buffet, pound; abuse, maltreat, manhandle, molest, rough (up)
maunder *vb syn* see WANDER 1
maundering *adj syn* see INARTICULATE 3
maven *n syn* see EXPERT
maverick *n syn* see BOHEMIAN
mawkish *adj syn* see SENTIMENTAL
rel banal, flat; cloying, nauseating, sickening
maxim *n* a general truth or fundamental principle usually expressed sententiously < Francis Bacon is noted for his fondness for *maxims* >
syn aphorism, apothegm, axiom, brocard, dictum, gnome, moral, rule, truism
rel commonplace, motto, platitude; law, precept, prescript; theorem; proverb
idiom rule of thumb
maximal *adj syn* see MAXIMUM
ant minimal
maximize *vb syn* see OVERPLAY 2
ant minimize
maximum *adj* greatest in quantity or highest in degree attainable or attained < apply *maximum* pressure above the point of injury >
syn maximal, outside, top, topmost, utmost; *compare* SUPREME
rel greatest, highest, largest
con least, lowest, slightest, smallest
ant minimum
maybe *adv syn* see PERHAPS
mayhem *vb syn* see MAIM
maze *n* **1** something intricately or confusingly elaborate or complicated < the landscape soon became a *maze* of superhighways >
syn jungle, knot, labyrinth, mesh, mizmaze, morass, skein, snarl, tangle, web
rel fog, haze; gordian knot; conglomeration, hodgepodge, miscellany, mishmash
‖**2** *syn* see HAZE 2
‖**mazuma** *n syn* see MONEY
MD *n syn* see PHYSICIAN
meager *adj* **1** *syn* see LEAN
2 being smaller than what is normal, necessary, or desirable < the remains of dinner provided only a *meager* meal that evening >

---

syn synonym(s)　　　　　　　*rel* related word(s)
ant antonym(s)　　　　　　　*con* contrasted word(s)
idiom idiomatic equivalent(s)
‖ use limited; if in doubt, see a dictionary

syn exiguous, poor, scant, scanty, scrimp, scrimpy, skimp, skimpy, spare, sparse; *compare* SHORT 3

rel deficient, inadequate, insufficient; inappreciable, inconsiderable, slight; bare, mere, minimum; miserable, shabby

con adequate, enough, sufficient; appreciable, considerable; copious, plentiful

ant ample

meal *n* the portion of food taken at one time to satisfy appetite <the noonday dinner was the big *meal* of the day in those times>

syn ‖chow, feed, refection, repast

rel feast, spread; refreshment, regalement; collation, snack; fare, grub, meat, mess, victuals; board, table

meal *vb syn* see EAT 1

mean *adj* **1** *syn* see IGNOBLE 1

ant wellborn

2 *syn* see INFERIOR 2

3 *syn* see LITTLE 2

4 *syn* see CONTEMPTIBLE

5 *syn* see CHEAP 2

6 *syn* see STINGY

7 *syn* see TROUBLESOME

rel difficult, formidable, rough, rugged, tough

8 *syn* see UNWELL

mean *vb* **1** *syn* see INTEND 2

rel desire, want, wish

2 to convey (as an idea) to the mind <your answer *means* nothing to me>

syn add up (to), connote, denote, express, import, intend, signify, spell

rel designate, name; attest, betoken, indicate; hint, imply, intimate, suggest

3 *syn* see MATTER

mean *n* **1** *syn* see AVERAGE

2 *usu* **means** *sing or pl in constr* one by which work is accomplished or an end effected <careful planning is a major *means* of improving output> <use any *means* to secure peace>

syn agency, agent, channel, instrument, instrumentality, instrumentation, intermediary, medium, ministry, organ, vehicle

rel fashion, manner, method, mode, system, way; apparatus, equipment, machinery, paraphernalia

3 means *pl* one's total property including real property and intangibles <people of moderate *means* are feeling the effects of inflation worse>

syn assets, capital, resources, wealth

rel finances, fortune, funds, moneybags, pocket, purse; ‖bundle, nest egg, pile, reserves, savings; estate, holdings, possessions; intangibles

mean *adj* **1** *syn* see MIDDLE 2

2 *syn* see MEDIUM

meander *vb syn* see WANDER 1

rel snake, turn, twist, wind

meanderer *n syn* see ROVER

meandering *adj syn* see WINDING

meandrous *adj syn* see WINDING

meaning *n* **1** the idea that something conveys to the mind <critics have endlessly debated the *meaning* of the poem>

syn acceptation, import, intendment, intent, message, purport, sense, significance, significancy, signification, sum and substance, understanding; *compare* SUBSTANCE 2, TENOR 1

rel drift, effect, essence, tenor; force, point, value; hint, implication, intimation, suggestion; connotation, denotation, definition

2 *syn* see INTENTION

meaningful *adj* **1** *syn* see EXPRESSIVE

ant meaningless

2 *syn* see IMPORTANT 1

meaningless *adj* **1** *syn* see SENSELESS 5

rel blank, empty, vacant

ant meaningful

2 *syn* see FECKLESS 1

measly *adj syn* see PETTY 2

measure *n* **1** *syn* see RATION

2 *syn* see TEMPERANCE 1

3 *syn* see SIZE 1

4 *syn* see MELODY

5 *syn* see RHYTHM

6 *syn* see STANDARD 3

7 an action planned or taken toward the accomplishment of a purpose <developed a new set of safety *measures*>

syn maneuver, move, procedure, proceeding, step

rel effort, project, proposal, proposition; expedient, makeshift, resort, resource, shift, stopgap

measure *vb* **1** *syn* see DEMARCATE 1

2 to ascertain the quantity, mass, extent, or degree of in terms of a standard unit or fixed amount <*measure* the depth of the water>

syn gauge, scale

rel size, size up; calculate, compute, estimate, figure, reckon

measure (out) *vb syn* see DISTRIBUTE 1

measureless *adj* **1** *syn* see INCALCULABLE 1

ant measurable

2 *syn* see LIMITLESS

ant measurable

measure up *vb syn* see EQUAL 3

meat *n* **1** *syn* see FOOD 1

2 *syn* see SUBSTANCE 2

meathead *n syn* see OAF 2

meaty *adj syn* see PITHY

mechanical *adj syn* see PERFUNCTORY

meddle *vb* to concern oneself with officiously, impertinently, or indiscreetly <continually *meddling* in other people's affairs>

syn busybody, butt in, fool, horn in, interfere, interlope, intermeddle, ‖make, mess around, monkey (with), tamper (with)

rel intervene, intrude, invade, obtrude; pry, snoop, trespass

idiom put (*or* shove *or* stick) one's oar in, stick one's nose into

con disregard, ignore, neglect, omit, overlook, slight; avoid, eschew, shun

meddler *n syn* see BUSYBODY

meddlesome *adj syn* see IMPERTINENT 2

Meddlesome Mattie *n syn* see BUSYBODY

medial *adj* **1** *syn* see MIDDLE 1

2 *syn* see MIDDLE 2

3 *syn* see MEDIUM

median *n syn* see AVERAGE

rel center, middle

median *adj* **1** *syn* see MIDDLE 1

2 *syn* see MIDDLE 2

mediate *vb syn* see INTERPOSE 2

mediator *n* **1** *syn* see GO-BETWEEN 2

rel arbitrator, judge; conciliator, peacemaker; negotiator, troubleshooter

2 *syn* see MODERATOR

medical *n syn* see PHYSICIAN

medicament *n syn* see REMEDY 1

medicant *n syn* see REMEDY 1

medication *n syn* see REMEDY 1

medicinal *n syn* see DRUG 1

medicine *n syn* see REMEDY 1

mediciner *n syn* see PHYSICIAN

medico *n syn* see PHYSICIAN

mediocre *adj syn* see MEDIUM

rel bad, inferior, poor; common, commonplace, ordinary, unexceptional

idiom no great shakes, nothing to write home about

meditate *vb syn* see PONDER 2

meditative *adj* **1** *syn* see THOUGHTFUL 1

rel musing, ruminant; wistful

2 *syn* see PENSIVE 2

medium *adj* midway between the extremes of a scale, measurement, or evaluation <bought a suit of *medium* quality>

syn average, fair, fairish, indifferent, intermediate, mean, medial, mediocre, middle, middle-rate, middling, moderate, run-of-mine, run-of-the-mill, so-so

rel median, par; passable, tolerable; neutral; popular, vulgar; normal, standard

idiom fair to middling

con inferior, low-grade, poor; excellent, first-class, high-grade, prime, superior

medium *n* **1** *syn* see MEAN 2

rel intermediate, intermedium

2 *syn* see ENVIRONMENT

3 *syn* see FORTE

medley *n syn* see MISCELLANY 1

‖meech *vb syn* see SNEAK

meed *n* **1** *syn* see REWARD

rel recompensing, satisfaction

2 *syn* see RATION

rel desert, due, merit

meek *adj syn* see HUMBLE 1
  rel gentle, mild; tame; forbearing, lenient, tolerant; long-suffering, patient
  con high-spirited, mettlesome, spirited, spunky; contumacious, insubordinate, rebellious
  ant arrogant

meet *vb* **1** *syn* see HAPPEN 2
  2 *syn* see CONFRONT 1
  3 *syn* see ENGAGE 5
  rel brave, oppose
  4 *syn* see EQUAL 3
  5 *syn* see SATISFY 5
  rel approach, equal, match, rival, tie, touch
  6 to come together face-to-face or as if face-to-face < the two leaders agreed to *meet* in a series of summit talks >
  syn close, encounter, face, front; *compare* CONFRONT 1
  rel accost, greet, salute; bump, clash, collide, cross; grapple, tussle, wrestle; experience, suffer, sustain, undergo
  con elude, escape, evade, shun
  ant avoid
  7 *syn* see CONVERGE
  8 *syn* see CONVENE 1

meet (with) *vb syn* see FIND 1

meet *n* **1** *syn* see EVENT 5
  2 *syn* see CONTEST 2

meet *adj* **1** *syn* see FIT 1
  rel accommodated, conformed, reconciled; good, right; equitable, fair, just
  ant unmeet
  2 *syn* see GOOD 2
  ant unmeet

meeting *n* **1** *syn* see CONTEST 2
  2 *syn* see CONCOURSE
  3 *syn* see TALK 4
  rel congress, moot

meetness *n syn* see ORDER 11
  ant unmeetness

megacosm *n syn* see UNIVERSE
  ant microcosm

megrim *n syn* see CAPRICE
  rel impulse, urge

melancholic *adj syn* see SAD 2

melancholy *n syn* see SADNESS
  rel miserableness, misery, wretchedness; despair, desperation; boredom, ennui, tedium
  con hopefulness, optimism
  ant exhilaration

melancholy *adj* **1** *syn* see SAD 1
  2 expressing or suggesting sorrow or mourning < the gloomy day led him to a *melancholy* train of thought >
  syn doleful, dolesome, dolorous, lamentable, lugubrious, moanful, mournful, plaintive, rueful, sighful, sorrowful, wailful, woeful; *compare* SAD 1, SAD 2
  rel pensive, reflective, thoughtful; discomposing, disquieting, disturbing, perturbing; dismal, dreary, funereal, gloomy, lachrymose, somber, sombrous
  con cheerful, glad, happy, joyful, joyous, lighthearted; gay, lively, vivacious
  3 *syn* see SAD 2

mélange *n syn* see MISCELLANY 1

meld *vb syn* see MIX 1

melding *n syn* see UNIFICATION

melee *n* **1** *syn* see CLASH 2
  rel dogfight, scuffle
  2 *syn* see BRAWL 2
  3 *syn* see MISCELLANY 1

meliorate *vb syn* see IMPROVE 1

melisma *n syn* see MELODY

mellay *n* **1** *syn* see BRAWL 2
  2 *syn* see CLASH 2

mellifluent *adj syn* see MELLIFLUOUS

mellifluous *adj* having a smooth rich flow < his *mellifluous* voice held his audience in a trance >
  syn golden, honeyed, Hyblaean, liquid, mellifluent, mellow; *compare* MELODIOUS 1
  rel accordant, canorous, euphonic, euphonious, harmonious, mellisonant, silvery; golden-tongued, silver-tongued; dulcet, sweet; resonant, sonorous

  con blatant, boisterous, clamorous, obstreperous, strident, vociferous; discordant, grating, harsh

mellisonant *adj syn* see MELODIOUS 1

mellow *adj* **1** *syn* see RIPE 3
  2 *syn* see MELLIFLUOUS

mellow *vb syn* see MATURE

melodia *n syn* see MELODY

melodic *adj* **1** *syn* see MELODIOUS 2
  2 *syn* see MELODIOUS 1

melodious *adj* **1** pleasing to the ear < *melodious* sounds of the forest >
  syn dulcet, euphonic, euphonious, mellisonant, melodic, sweet, tuneful; *compare* MELLIFLUOUS
  rel canorous, harmonious
  con discordant, grating, harsh
  ant unmelodious
  2 containing, constituting, or characterized by melody < his voice shows marked improvement and a new richly *melodious* quality >
  syn melodic, musical, songful, tuned, tuneful
  rel cantabile, lyric, melic

melody *n* a rhythmic succession of single tones organized as an aesthetic whole < took out his flute and played a simple *melody* >
  syn air, descant, diapason, lay, measure, melisma, melodia, strain, tune, warble; *compare* SONG 2
  rel song; bel canto, canto, vocalise; lyrics

melt *vb* **1** *syn* see LIQUEFY
  rel heat, warm
  con coagulate, harden, set
  ant freeze; solidify
  2 *syn* see BURN 3
  rel perspire, sweat

member *n syn* see PART 1

memento *n* **1** *syn* see REMEMBRANCE 3
  2 *syn* see VESTIGE 1

memo *n* **1** *syn* see NOTE 2
  2 *syn* see MEMORANDUM 2

memoir *n* **1** *syn* see BIOGRAPHY
  rel anecdote; memory, recollection, remembrance, reminiscence
  2 *syn* see DISCOURSE 2

memoirist *n syn* see BIOGRAPHER

memorable *adj syn* see NOTEWORTHY
  rel momentous, rememberable; deathless, unfadable, unforgettable
  ant unmemorable

memorandum *n* **1** *syn* see NOTE 2
  2 a communication that contains directive, advisory, or informative matter < the *memorandum* announced the holiday schedule >
  syn directive, memo, notice
  rel announcement, dispatch, minute; epistle, letter, missive, note; reminder, tickler; message; diary

memorial *adj* serving to preserve remembrance < a *memorial* plaque >
  syn commemorative, commemoratory
  rel celebrative, consecrative, dedicatory, enshrining

memorial *n* **1** *syn* see REMEMBRANCE 3
  2 *syn* see MONUMENT 2

memorialize *vb* **1** *syn* see ADDRESS 4
  2 to record or honor the memory of by or as if by a monument < the new library *memorializes* the late President >
  syn commemorate, monument, monumentalize
  rel etch, grave, impress, imprint; jog, nudge, remind
  idiom bring to mind, fix in the (*or* one's) mind (*or* memory), impress on one's mind, treasure in one's heart
  con forget, neglect, overlook

memorial park *n syn* see CEMETERY

memorize *vb* to commit to memory < the actors hadn't even *memorized* their lines >
  syn con, get, learn
  rel study
  idiom get (*or* learn) by heart, get (*or* learn) word for word

---

syn synonym(s)   *rel* related word(s)
ant antonym(s)   *con* contrasted word(s)
idiom idiomatic equivalent(s)
‖ use limited; if in doubt, see a dictionary

con forget

memory *n* **1** the power or process of reproducing or recalling what has been learned < blessed with a good *memory* >
syn recollection, remembrance, reminiscence
rel reflection, retrospection; retention, retentiveness; mind, recall; mind's eye; awareness, cognizance, consciousness
con forgetfulness, obliviousness, unmindfulness; lethe, oblivion
2 a particular act of recalling < her *memory* of her wedding day remains vivid >
syn anamnesis, recall, recollection, remembrance, reminiscence
rel memento, souvenir

menace *vb* **1** *syn* see THREATEN
rel alarm, frighten, scare; endanger, torment; loom, lower
2 *syn* see ENDANGER

menacing *adj syn* see IMMINENT 2

ménage *n syn* see FAMILY 2
rel ménage à trois

mend *vb* **1** *syn* see CORRECT 1
2 to put into good shape or working order again < *mends* garments in her spare time >
syn doctor, do up, fix, overhaul, patch, rebuild, recondition, reconstruct, repair, revamp, ‖right, ‖rightle, vamp
rel condition, ready, service; refurbish, rejuvenate, renew, renovate, restore; correct, emend, rectify, redress, reform; heal
3 *syn* see IMPROVE 3

mendacious *adj syn* see DISHONEST
rel false, wrong; erroneous, fallacious, spurious; equivocating, fibbing, paltering, prevaricating
ant veracious

mendaciousness *n syn* see MENDACITY
ant veraciousness, veracity

mendacity *n* the practice or an instance of lying < he was ultimately caught by his own outrageous *mendacity* >
syn falsehood, fibbery, mendaciousness, truthlessness, untruthfulness, unveracity
rel boggling, caviling, dodging, equivocation, hedging, quibbling, shifting, sidestepping
ant veraciousness, veracity

mendicancy *n* the practice or act of begging < the city passed an ordinance against *mendicancy* >
syn beggary, bumming, cadging, mendicity, mooching, panhandling
rel sponging

mendicity *n syn* see MENDICANCY

menial *adj syn* see SUBSERVIENT 2

mental *adj* **1** of or relating to the mind < the *mental* aspects of the problem >
syn cerebral, intellective, intellectual, psychic, psychical, psychological
rel immaterial, inner, spiritual; telepathic; intelligent, rational, reasoning, thinking; ideological
con bodily, corporal, corporeal, physical, somatic; perceptive; sensual, sensuous
‖**2** *syn* see INSANE 1

mentality *n syn* see INTELLIGENCE 1

mention *vb* to refer to someone or something in a clear unmistakable manner < several donors were *mentioned* in the article >
syn cite, instance, name, specify
rel denominate, designate; detail; advert, allude, refer; quote
idiom make mention of
con disregard, ignore, neglect, overlook, pass by, pass over, slight

menu *n* a list of the dishes that may be ordered (as at a restaurant) or that are to be served (as at a banquet) < hoped to find something tasty on the *menu* > < he saved the elaborate *menu* as a souvenir of the awards banquet >
syn card, carte du jour
idiom bill of fare

Mephistophelian *adj syn* see SATANIC 1

mephitic *adj* **1** *syn* see MALODOROUS 1
2 *syn* see POISONOUS

mercenary *n syn* see HACK 2

mercenary *adj syn* see CORRUPT 2
ant unmercenary

merchandisable *adj syn* see MARKETABLE
ant unmerchantable, unsalable

merchandise *n* the products that are bought and sold in business < *merchandise* of inferior quality >

syn commodities, goods, line, vendible(s), wares
rel effects; job lot, stock; staples

merchandise *vb syn* see SELL 3
rel advertise, publicize

merchandiser *n syn* see MERCHANT

merchant *n* a buyer and seller of commodities for profit < a *merchant* of dry goods >
syn businessman, dealer, merchandiser, trader, tradesman, trafficker
rel jobber, retailer, wholesaler

merchantable *adj syn* see MARKETABLE
ant unmerchantable, unsalable

merchant prince *n syn* see MAGNATE

merciful *adj syn* see FORBEARING
rel compassionate, pitiful, softhearted; benign, kind, kindly; condoning, forgiving, pardoning
ant merciless, unmerciful

mercifulness *n syn* see FORBEARANCE 2
rel commiseration, pity, ruth
con severeness, severity, sternness
ant mercilessness, unmercifulness

merciless *adj* **1** *syn* see PITILESS
ant merciful
2 *syn* see GRIM 3
rel compassionless, cutthroat, pitiless; gratuitous, uncalled-for, wanton
con charitable, lenient, tolerant; easy, easygoing
ant merciful

mercurial *adj syn* see INCONSTANT 1
rel buoyant, effervescent, elastic, expansive, resilient; mobile, movable; adroit, clever, cunning, ingenious
ant saturnine

mercy *n* a show of or a disposition to show kindness or compassion < the *mercy* of the Lord knows all seasons >
syn caritas, charity, clemency, grace, lenity; *compare* FORBEARANCE 2
rel commiseration, compassion, pity, ruth; benevolence, benignancy, benignity, kindliness, kindness; generosity, goodwill
con reprisal, retaliation, retribution, revenge, vengeance; castigation, chastening, chastisement, punishment

mere *adj syn* see VERY 4

merely *adv syn* see JUST 3

meretricious *adj syn* see GAUDY
rel deceptive, delusive, delusory, misleading, spurious; insincere

meretrix *n syn* see PROSTITUTE

merge *vb syn* see MIX 1

mergence *n syn* see UNIFICATION

merger *n* **1** *syn* see CONSOLIDATION 2
2 *syn* see UNIFICATION

merging *n syn* see UNIFICATION

meridian *n syn* see APEX 2

merit *n* **1** *syn* see EXCELLENCE
ant fault
2 *syn* see QUALITY 2
3 *syn* see DUE 1
rel gaining(s), winning(s)

merit *vb syn* see EARN 2
rel award, reward; recompense, repay, requite; entitle, justify, warrant

meritable *adj syn* see WORTHY 1
ant meritless

merited *adj syn* see JUST 3
rel entitled, justified, warranted
ant unmerited

meritorious *adj syn* see WORTHY 1

merriment *n* **1** *syn* see MIRTH
2 *syn* see MERRYMAKING

merry *adj* indicative of or marked by high spirits or lightheartedness < the *merry* life of the town folk was a joy to see >
syn blithe, blithesome, boon, festive, gay, gleeful, jocund, jolly, jovial, lighthearted, mirthful, riant
rel animated, lively, sprightly, vivacious; cheerful, glad, happy, joyful, joyous; hilarious, mad, unconstrained, wild
con gloomy, glum, melancholy; grave, sober, somber; earnest, sedate, serious, staid

merry–andrew *n syn* see CLOWN 3

merrymaking *n* gay or festive activity < a night of *merrymaking* >

syn festivity, gaiety, jollity, merriment, revel, reveling, revelment, revelry, whoopee
rel enjoyment, indulgence, pleasure, self-indulgence

mesh *n* **1** *usu* **meshes** *pl syn see* WEB 2
2 *syn see* MAZE 1
rel net, network

mesh *vb syn see* ENGAGE 1

meshuggaas *n syn see* NONSENSE 2

mesmeric *adj syn see* ATTRACTIVE 1

mesmerize *vb syn see* ENTHRALL 2
rel entrance, hypnotize

mess *n* ‖**1** *syn see* MUCH
2 *syn see* EYESORE
3 a confused or disordered state, condition, or situation < upon becoming president, he proceeded to make a *mess* of the government >
syn botch, botchery, hash, mess-up, mix-up, muddle, mull, muss, shambles; *compare* MISCELLANY 1
rel confusion, disorder; wreck, wreckage
idiom kettle of fish

mess *vb* **1** *syn see* BOTCH
rel confuse, disorder, jumble
idiom make a mess of
2 *syn see* FIDDLE 2

mess (up) *vb syn see* DISORDER 1
rel damage, mar, ruin, spoil; ‖muck, mucker, muff

message *n* **1** something (as information) conveyed by writing, speech, or signals < left a *message* before he went out >
syn communication, directive, word
rel communiqué, dispatch, report; memo, memorandum; epistle, letter, missive, note
2 *syn see* MEANING 1

mess around *vb* **1** *syn see* FIDDLE 2
2 *syn see* MEDDLE
3 *syn see* PHILANDER

messenger *n* one who bears a message or does an errand < blamed the *messenger* for the bad news he brought >
syn bearer, carrier, courier, emissary, envoy, internuncio
rel herald; go-between, intermediary, mediator; dispatcher, post

mess–up *n syn see* MESS 3

messy *adj* **1** *syn see* SLOVENLY 1
rel dirty, grimy, grubby
con clean
ant neat
2 *syn see* SLIPSHOD 3

metagrobolize *vb syn see* PUZZLE

metamorphize *vb syn see* TRANSFORM

metamorphose *vb syn see* TRANSFORM
rel age, develop, mature, ripen

metanoia *n syn see* CONVERSION 1

metaphor *n syn see* ANALOGY 2
rel comparison, trope; allegory, personification
idiom figure of speech

metaphysical *adj* **1** *syn see* IMMATERIAL 1
rel supernatural, transcendent, transcendental
2 *syn see* SUPERNATURAL 1

mete (out) *vb* **1** *syn see* ADMINISTER 2
rel measure
2 *syn see* ALLOT

meter *n syn see* RHYTHM

method *n* **1** the means or procedures used in attaining an end < he claimed that his ends justified his *methods* >
syn fashion, manner, mode, modus, system, technique, way, wise
rel design, plan, schema, scheme; form, style; course, line; modus operandi, practice, procedure, process, routine; wrinkle
2 *syn see* ORDER 8

methodic *adj syn see* ORDERLY 1
ant desultory, unmethodical

methodical *adj syn see* ORDERLY 1
rel methodized, organized, systematized; analytical, logical; careful, meticulous, scrupulous
con casual, hit-or-miss, random; confused, jumbled
ant desultory, unmethodical

methodize *vb syn see* ORDER 1
rel establish, fix, set, settle

meticulous *adj syn see* CAREFUL 2
rel fastidious, pernickety, picky; cautious, strict, thorough; microscopic

métier *n* **1** *syn see* TRADE 1
2 *syn see* FORTE

metropolitan *adj syn see* COSMOPOLITAN 1

mettle *n syn see* COURAGE

mettlesome *adj syn see* SPIRITED 2
rel edgy, excitable, high-strung, skittish, startlish

mew *vb syn see* ENCLOSE 1

Mickey Mouse *adj syn see* PETTY 2

mid *adj* **1** *syn see* MIDDLE 2
2 *syn see* MIDDLE 1

mid *prep* **1** *syn see* AMID 1
2 *syn see* AMONG 1
3 *syn see* DURING

middle *adj* **1** equally distant from the extremes < the *middle* finger >
syn center, centermost, equidistant, halfway, medial, median, mid, middlemost, midmost
2 being at neither extreme < paid a *middle* price for it >
syn center, central, intermediary, intermediate, mean, medial, median, mid

middle *n syn see* CENTER 1

middlebrow *n syn see* PHILISTINE

middleman *n syn see* GO-BETWEEN 2

middlemost *adj syn see* MIDDLE 1

middle–of–the–road *adj syn see* MODERATE 4

middle–rate *adj syn see* MEDIUM

middle–road *adj syn see* MODERATE 4

middling *adj syn see* MEDIUM
rel inferior, poor, second-rate

midge *n syn see* DWARF

midget *n syn see* DWARF

midget *adj syn see* TINY

midmost *adj syn see* MIDDLE 1

midpoint *n syn see* CENTER 1

midst *n syn see* CENTER 1

midst *prep* **1** *syn see* AMID 1
2 *syn see* AMONG 1
3 *syn see* DURING

mid–Victorian *n syn see* FOGY
rel bluenose, goody-goody, Mrs. Grundy, prig, prude, puritan; Victorian

mien *n* **1** *syn see* BEARING 1
rel expression, manner, mannerism
2 *syn see* APPEARANCE 1

miff *n* **1** *syn see* OFFENSE 2
rel conniption, fit
2 *syn see* QUARREL

might *n* **1** *syn see* POWER 1
2 *syn see* POWER 4
rel energeticness, lustiness, strenuousness, vigor, vigorousness; forcefulness, forcibleness, powerfulness
3 *syn see* ABILITY 1
4 *syn see* MUSCLE 1

might and main *adv syn see* HARD 1

mightily *adv* **1** *syn see* HARD 1
rel arduously, laboriously, strenuously, toilsomely
2 *syn see* VERY 1

mighty *adj* **1** *syn see* POWERFUL 2
2 *syn see* STRONG 1
3 *syn see* HUGE
rel eminent, illustrious, renowned; august, grand, imposing, impressive, moving

mighty *adv syn see* VERY 1

migrant *adj syn see* MIGRATORY

migrant *n syn see* EMIGRANT
rel in-migrant, out-migrant; drifter, mover, nomad, traveler, wanderer

migrate *vb* to move from one country, place, or locality to another < his father had *migrated* to the Far West years before >
syn emigrate, transmigrate
rel immigrate, in-migrate, out-migrate, remigrate; drift, trek; nomadize, range, roam, rove, wander

---

syn synonym(s)   **rel** related word(s)
ant antonym(s)   **con** contrasted word(s)
idiom idiomatic equivalent(s)
‖ use limited; if in doubt, see a dictionary

migrative *adj syn* see MIGRATORY
 ant nonmigratory
migratorial *adj syn* see MIGRATORY
 ant nonmigratory
migratory *adj* moving habitually or occasionally from one region or climate to another < the study of *migratory* birds >
 syn migrant, migrative, migratorial, mobile, transmigratory
 rel errant, nomad, nomadic, ranging, roving, wandering
 ant nonmigratory
mild *adj* **1** *syn* see GENTLE 1
 rel choice, dainty, delicate, exquisite; moderate, temperate; benign, benignant
 con intense, severe, sharp, vehement
 ant fierce, harsh
 2 *syn* see AMIABLE 1
 rel docile, meek; subdued, submissive; deferential, obeisant, subservient
milepost *n syn* see EVENT 2
milestone *n syn* see EVENT 2
milieu *n syn* see ENVIRONMENT
militant *adj* **1** *syn* see BELLIGERENT
 rel martial, military
 2 *syn* see AGGRESSIVE
military *adj syn* see MARTIAL
 rel chauvinistic, jingoistic, militaristic, warmongering; soldierlike, soldierly
 ant unmilitary
military *n syn* see TROOP 2
militate *vb syn* see WEIGH 3
milk *vb* **1** *syn* see FLEECE 1
 rel exact, exploit, extort; drain, empty, exhaust, pump, suck, wring
 2 *syn* see EDUCE 1
milk–and–water *adj syn* see INSIPID 3
milk–livered *adj syn* see COWARDLY
milksop *n syn* see WEAKLING
 rel effeminate; coward
milk–warm *adj syn* see TEPID 1
mill *n syn* see FACTORY
million *n syn* see SCAD
millstone *n syn* see LOAD 3
Milquetoast *n syn* see WEAKLING
mime *n syn* see ACTOR 1
mimic *n syn* see ACTOR 1
mimic *vb* to copy or exaggerate (as manner or gestures) often by way of mockery < *mimicked* her halting speech >
 syn ape, burlesque, imitate, mock, parody, take off, travesty
 rel hit off, mime, mum; act, do, enact, impersonate, perform, personate, play; copycat; pantomime
mimicry *n* the art or practice of closely imitating another in speech, gestures, or manners < engaged in *mimicry* of café society >
 syn apery
 rel imitation, mimesis, mimetism; mock, mockery; caricature, parody
miminy–piminy *adj syn* see NICE 1
mince *vb* **1** *syn* see CHOP 2
 2 *syn* see SASHAY
mincing *adj syn* see GENTEEL 3
 rel dainty, delicate, fastidious, finical, finicking, finicky, fussy, nice, particular, pernickety, persnickety, squeamish
‖**mincy** *adj syn* see NICE 1
mind *n* **1** the element or complex of elements in an individual that feels, perceives, thinks, wills, and especially reasons < sad to see such a *mind* dulled by drink and drugs >
 syn brain, gray matter, head, ‖upper story, ‖upperworks, wit
 rel brainpower, intellect, intelligence; consciousness, mentality; faculty, function, power
 2 *syn* see WILL 1
 rel disposition, temper, temperament
 con aversion, disinclination, indisposition
 3 *syn* see WIT 2
 4 *syn* see OPINION
 5 *syn* see MOOD 1
 ‖**6** *syn* see NOTICE 1
mind *vb* ‖**1** *syn* see REMEMBER
 ‖**2** *syn* see ENJOY 1
 3 *syn* see SEE 1

‖**4** *syn* see INTEND 2
 5 *syn* see OBEY
 6 *syn* see LOOK 1
 7 *syn* see BEWARE
 8 *syn* see TEND 2
 rel oversee, superintend, supervise; discipline, govern
 con forget, slight
 9 *syn* see CONSIDER 1
minded *adj syn* see WILLING 1
 rel contemplating, intending, planning, purposing
mindful *adj* **1** *syn* see AWARE
 ant unmindful
 2 inclined to be aware < *mindful* of the ever-changing social scene >
 syn heedful, observant, observative, observing, regardful, thoughtful
 rel attentive, conscientious; aware, cognizant, conscious, conversant, sensible; alert, vigilant, watchful
 con heedless, inattentive
 ant mindless, unmindful
mindless *adj* **1** *syn* see SIMPLE 3
 2 *syn* see INSANE 1
mine *n syn* see BONANZA
 rel lode, quarry, vein; spring, well, wellspring
mine *vb* to dig into for the purpose of obtaining items of use or value < *mined* manuscripts looking for undiscovered masterpieces >
 syn delve, quarry
 rel burrow, drill, excavate, sap, scoop; work
mingle *vb* **1** *syn* see MIX 1
 2 *syn* see SOCIALIZE
mingle–mangle *n syn* see MISCELLANY 1
mingy *adj syn* see STINGY
miniature *n syn* see MODEL 1
miniature *adj syn* see TINY
 rel small-scale, subminiature
 con large-scale
minify *vb syn* see ABRIDGE 1
 rel dwarf, miniaturize, shrink
minikin *adj syn* see TINY
minim *n syn* see PARTICLE
minimal *adj* constituting the least possible < *minimal* differences of opinion >
 syn minimum
 rel littlest, lowest, slightest, smallest; basal, basic, essential, fundamental
 con maximum, topmost, utmost; greatest, highest, largest, most
 ant maximal
minimize *vb syn* see DECRY 2
 rel dwarf, reduce
 ant magnify, maximize
minimum *n* the least quantity assignable, admissible, or possible < testing the use of a *minimum* of security at the prison >
 syn margin
 rel dab, hair, iota, jot, modicum, particle, pittance, smidgen, speck, whit
 con abundance, bushel(s), gob(s), ‖lashings, load(s), lot(s), mass(es), much, oodles, profusion, scads, slather(s), ton(s), world(s)
 ant maximum
minimum *adj syn* see MINIMAL
 ant maximum
minion *n syn* see SYCOPHANT
minister *n syn* see CLERGYMAN
minister (to) *vb* to attend to the wants and comforts of someone < *minister* to the sick and dying >
 syn care (for), mother, nurse, serve, wait (on)
 rel cure, heal, remedy; doctor, treat; pander
ministerial *adj syn* see INSTRUMENTAL
minister plenipotentiary *n syn* see ENVOY 1
ministry *n syn* see MEAN 2
minor *adj* **1** *syn* see LITTLE 3
 rel dependent; inferior, piddling, trifling; junior, lower
 con meaningful, significant
 ant major
 2 lower in standing or reputation than others of the same class < a *minor* poet of the late eighteenth century >
 syn dinky, insignificant, lesser, minor-league, secondary, small, small-fry, small-time

rel average, fair, indifferent, mediocre, medium, middling, second-rate, undistinguished, unnoticeable; trivial, unimportant
con chief, foremost, leading, principal
ant major

minor *n syn* see INFANT 2

minority *n syn* see INFANCY 2
ant majority

minor–league *adj syn* see MINOR 2

minstrel *n syn* see BARD 1
rel balladist, singer, wait

mint *n syn* see FORTUNE 4

mint *adj syn* see BRAND-NEW
rel intact, original, perfect, unmarred

minus *prep syn* see WITHOUT 2
ant plus

minute *n syn* see INSTANT 1

minute *adj* **1** *syn* see TINY
2 *syn* see LITTLE 3
3 *syn* see CIRCUMSTANTIAL
rel careful, meticulous, punctilious, scrupulous
con abstract; general, universal; comprehending, comprehensive, embracing, embracive, including, inclusive

minutely *adj syn* see CONTINUAL

minutia *n, usu* **minutiae** *pl* **1** *syn* see INS AND OUTS
2 *syn* see TRIVIA

minx *n* a pert girl < her rivals called her a brazen *minx* >
syn hussy, jade, malapert, saucebox, slut, snip
rel broad, brat, upstart; baggage, chippy, drab, floozy, strumpet, tart, trollop, trull

miracle *n syn* see WONDER 1

miraculous *adj* **1** *syn* see SUPERNATURAL 1
2 *syn* see MARVELOUS 1
con natural, normal

mirage *n syn* see DELUSION 1

mire *n syn* see SWAMP
rel muck

mire *vb* **1** *syn* see DELAY 1
rel bemire, sink; adhere, cleave, cling, cohere, stick; enmesh, ensnare, entangle, entrap, involve, snare, trap
2 *syn* see INVOLVE 1

mirror *n* **1** a polished or smooth surface (as of glass) that forms images by reflection < spent hours looking at herself in the *mirror* >
syn glass, looking glass, ‖seeing glass
rel cheval glass, pier glass, reflector, speculum
2 *syn* see MODEL 2

mirror *vb* **1** *syn* see REFLECT 1
2 *syn* see REPRESENT 2

mirth *n* a mood or temper characterized by joy and high spirits and usually manifested in laughter and merrymaking < a man of contentment, but seldom of *mirth* >
syn glee, hilarity, jocularity, jocundity, jollity, joviality, merriment
rel cheer, cheerfulness, joyfulness, lightheartedness; gladness, happiness; frivolity, levity
con blues, dejection, depression, dumps, gloom, sadness; boredom, ennui, tedium; anguish, misery, woe; infelicity, wretchedness
ant melancholy

mirthful *adj syn* see MERRY
ant mirthless

miry *adj syn* see MUDDY 1

misadventure *n* **1** *syn* see DISASTER
2 *syn* see ACCIDENT 2
rel blunder, boner, bull, error, faux pas, howler, lapse, slip

misanthropic *adj syn* see ANTISOCIAL
rel misogynic
con altruistic, benevolent, charitable, humane, humanitarian
ant philanthropic

misapply *vb syn* see ABUSE 2
rel misappropriate, misdirect, mismanage

misapprehend *vb* **1** *syn* see MISUNDERSTAND 1
ant apprehend
2 *syn* see MISUNDERSTAND 2
ant apprehend

misappropriate *vb syn* see EMBEZZLE
misbegotten *adj syn* see ILLEGITIMATE 1
misbehaving *adj syn* see NAUGHTY 1

ant well-behaved

misbehavior *n syn* see MISCONDUCT
misbelief *n syn* see HERESY
misbeliever *n syn* see HERETIC

miscalculate *vb* to calculate wrongly < *miscalculate* the distance > < he seriously *miscalculated* the effect of his remark >
syn misestimate, misjudge, misreckon
rel discount, disregard, overlook; misconstrue, misinterpret, misunderstand; overestimate, overprize, overrate, overvalue; underestimate, underprize, underrate, undervalue

miscarry *vb* to go wrong or amiss < his plans *miscarried* almost from the start >
syn misfire, miss
rel abort; fail, flop
idiom fall through, miss fire, miss the mark
con come off, prevail, succeed

miscellaneous *adj* consisting of diverse things or members < gathered together a *miscellaneous* lot of books for sale >
syn assorted, chowchow, conglomerate, heterogeneous, indiscriminate, mixed, motley, multifarious, promiscuous, unassorted, unsorted, varied
rel different, disparate, divergent, diverse, various; divers, many, sundry; odd; commingled, jumbled, mingled, scrambled
con akin, alike, identical, like, parallel, similar, uniform

miscellany *n* **1** an unorganized mixture of various dissimilar items or elements < sold a *miscellany* of old household effects >
syn assortment, brew, chowchow, colluvies, gallimaufry, hash, hodgepodge, hotchpotch, jumble, medley, mélange, melee, mingle-mangle, mishmash, mixed bag, motley, odds and ends, olio, olla podrida, omnium-gatherum, pasticcio, pastiche, patchwork, porridge, potpourri, rumble-bumble, salad, salmagundi, smorgasbord, stew
rel mess, muddle; accumulation, aggregation, congeries, conglomeration, cumulation; combination, mix, mixture
2 *syn* see ANTHOLOGY

mischance *n* **1** *syn* see MISFORTUNE
2 *syn* see ACCIDENT 2

mischief *n* **1** *syn* see INJURY 1
rel difficulty, hardship, trouble
2 *syn* see SCAMP
3 *syn* see MISCHIEVOUSNESS
4 *syn* see DISCORD

‖mischiefful *adj syn* see PLAYFUL 1
mischief–maker *n syn* see TROUBLEMAKER

mischievous *adj* **1** *syn* see HARMFUL
rel dangerous, hazardous, perilous, precarious, risky
2 *syn* see NAUGHTY 1
rel annoying, bothering, bothersome, irking, irksome, vexatious, vexing
3 *syn* see PLAYFUL 1
rel artful, foxy, insidious, sly, tricky

mischievousness *n* action or conduct that annoys or irritates without causing or meaning serious harm < a wag who was forever engaging in *mischievousness* >
syn devilment, devilry, deviltry, diablerie, impishness, mischief, roguery, roguishness, sportiveness, waggery, waggishness
rel doggery, odiousness, offensiveness; evil, harm, hurt, injury; annoying, pestering, teasing

miscolor *vb syn* see MISREPRESENT
miscomprehend *vb syn* see MISUNDERSTAND 1
misconceive *vb syn* see MISUNDERSTAND 2

misconduct *n* improper behavior < was charged with *misconduct* >
syn misbehavior, misdoing, wrongdoing
rel impropriety; malfeasance, malversation, misfeasance

misconstrue *vb syn* see MISUNDERSTAND 2
miscreant *adj syn* see VICIOUS 2
miscreant *n syn* see VILLAIN 1
miscreation *n syn* see FREAK 2
rel deformation, deformity
miscue *n syn* see ERROR 2
misdate *n syn* see ANACHRONISM 1
misdating *n syn* see ANACHRONISM 1

---

syn synonym(s)
ant antonym(s)
idiom idiomatic equivalent(s)
‖ use limited; if in doubt, see a dictionary
rel related word(s)
con contrasted word(s)

misdeed *n syn* see CRIME 1

misdeem *vb* 1 *syn* see MISJUDGE 2
    2 *syn* see MISTAKE 1

misdoing *n syn* see MISCONDUCT

misdoubt *vb syn* see DISTRUST
    rel apprehend, dread, fear

mise–en–scène *n* 1 *syn* see SCENE 1
    2 *syn* see SCENE 3
    3 *syn* see ENVIRONMENT

misemploy *vb syn* see ABUSE 2

miser *n* a mean grasping person <an old *miser* who loved only his bank account>
    syn cheapskate, cheeseparer, chuff, hunks, moneygrubber, muckworm, nabal, niggard, ‖nipcheese, penny pincher, piker, scrooge, skin, skinflint, stiff, tightwad
    rel glutton, hog, pig

miserable *adj syn* see WOEFUL 1
    rel despairing, despondent, forlorn, hopeless; piteous, pitiable, pitiful; melancholy
    con cheerful, glad, happy, joyful, joyous, lighthearted

miserly *adj syn* see STINGY
    rel avaricious, covetous, grasping, greedy; abject, ignoble, sordid
    con bountious, generous; altruistic, benevolent, charitable

misery *n* 1 a state of suffering and want that is the result of poverty or conditions beyond one's control <the poor learn to live with *misery*> <the utter *misery* in which the flood victims survived>
    syn unhappiness, woe, wretchedness
    rel agony, anguish; despondency, grief, sorrow; desolation, squalor
    con beatitude, blessedness, bliss, felicity, happiness; content, ease, satisfaction
    2 *syn* see DISTRESS
    rel adversity, misfortune; dejection, depression, melancholy, sadness
    ant blessedness
    ‖3 *syn* see PAIN 1

misesteem *vb syn* see MISJUDGE 2

misestimate *vb syn* see MISCALCULATE

misfire *vb syn* see MISCARRY

misfortunate *adj syn* see UNLUCKY
    ant fortunate

misfortune *n* adverse fortune or an instance of this <his hopes and dreams soon ended in *misfortune*> <unable to grasp why he had been struck by such a *misfortune*>
    syn adversity, contretemps, ‖dole, mischance, mishap, tragedy, ‖unluck
    rel calamity, cataclysm, catastrophe, disaster; accident, casualty; affliction, cross, trial, tribulation, visitation
    con break, chance, luck, opportunity
    ant fortune

misgiving *n syn* see APPREHENSION 3
    rel doubt, fear, qualm, suspicion; distrust, mistrust

misguided *adj syn* see MISTAKEN

mishandle *vb* 1 *syn* see MANHANDLE
    2 *syn* see ABUSE 2

mishap *n* 1 *syn* see MISFORTUNE
    2 *syn* see ACCIDENT 2

mishmash *n* 1 *syn* see MISCELLANY 1
    2 *syn* see CLUTTER 2

misidentify *vb syn* see MISTAKE 1

misimprove *vb syn* see ABUSE 2

misinterpret *vb syn* see MISUNDERSTAND 2

misjudge *vb* 1 *syn* see MISCALCULATE
    2 to have a mistaken opinion of <her first impression led her to *misjudge* the girl>
    syn misdeem, misesteem, mistake
    rel misapprehend, miscomprehend, misconceive, misconstrue, misinterpret, misunderstand
    con catch on (to), penetrate, tumble (to), wise (up)

misknow *vb syn* see MISUNDERSTAND 1

mislaying *n syn* see LOSS 1

mislead *vb syn* see DECEIVE
    rel lie, misguide, misinform; entice, inveigle, lure, seduce, tempt

misleading *adj* having an appearance or character that leads one astray or into error <the president made several *misleading* statements to the people>

syn beguiling, deceiving, deceptive, deluding, delusive, delusory, fallacious, false
    rel casuistical, sophistical, specious; wrong; bewildering, confounding, distracting, perplexing, puzzling; deceitful, inaccurate
    con clarifying, elucidative, explanatory, illuminating

‖**mismannered** *adj syn* see RUDE 6

mismatch *vb syn* see CLASH 2

misorder *n syn* see CONFUSION 3

misplacement *n syn* see LOSS 1

misplacing *n syn* see LOSS 1

misread *vb syn* see MISUNDERSTAND 2

misreckon *vb syn* see MISCALCULATE

‖**misremember** *vb syn* see FORGET 1

misrepresent *vb* to give a false, imperfect, or misleading representation of <the summary totally *misrepresents* the facts of the case>
    syn belie, color, confuse, distort, falsify, garble, miscolor, misstate, pervert, twist, warp, wrench, wrest
    rel dress, embellish, embroider, gild, gloss, varnish; camouflage, cloak, disguise, dissemble, mask; counterfeit, feign, simulate; equivocate, lie, palter, prevaricate, weasel
    idiom give a false coloring, put a false construction (*or* appearance) on

misrepresentation *n syn* see LIE

misrule *n syn* see DISORDER 2

miss *vb* 1 *syn* see NEGLECT
    2 *syn* see MISUNDERSTAND 1
    3 *syn* see MISCARRY

‖**miss** *n syn* see ABSENCE

miss *n syn* see GIRL 1

misshape *vb syn* see DEFORM

misshape *n syn* see DEFORMITY

missing *adj* 1 *syn* see ABSENT 1
    2 *syn* see LOST 2

mission *n* a continuing task or responsibility that one is destined or fitted to do or specially called upon to undertake <his *mission* in life was to serve humanity>
    syn calling, lifework, vocation
    rel goal, purpose; business, profession, trade

missionary *n* one who attempts to convert others to a specific way of life, set of ideas, or course of action <served as a *missionary* for the feminist cause>
    syn apostle, colporteur, evangelist, missioner, propagandist
    rel revivalist; promoter

missioner *n syn* see MISSIONARY

missish *adj syn* see PRIM 1

missive *n syn* see LETTER 2

Miss–Nancyish *adj syn* see EFFEMINATE

misstate *vb syn* see MISREPRESENT

misstatement *n syn* see LIE

misstep *n syn* see ERROR 2

‖**missus** *n syn* see WIFE

missy *n syn* see GIRL 1

mist *n syn* see HAZE 1

mist *vb syn* see OBSCURE

mistake *vb* 1 to take one thing to be another <he *mistakes* sarcasm for wit>
    syn confound, confuse, misdeem, misidentify, mix, mix up
    rel misconceive, misknow; addle, jumble, muddle, tumble
    con discern, distinguish, grasp, perceive; differentiate, separate
    ant recognize
    2 *syn* see MISUNDERSTAND 2
    3 *syn* see MISJUDGE 2

mistake *n* 1 *syn* see ERROR 2
    rel confounding, confusion, mistaking; inadvertence; disregarding, neglect, neglecting, omission, omitting, slight, slighting
    2 *syn* see ERROR 1

mistaken *adj* acting, thinking, or judging in a manner at variance with truth or the facts <he is *mistaken* in his evaluation of the crisis>
    syn erroneous, misguided, wrong
    rel confounded, confused; deceived, deluded, misinformed
    idiom all wet, off base, off the track
    con accurate, correct, right, unerring; exact, precise

mister *n syn* see HUSBAND

mistimed *adj syn* see UNSEASONABLE 1
    ant well-timed

mistiming *n syn* see ANACHRONISM 1

mistreat *vb syn* see ABUSE 4
mistress *n* a woman who is a man's regular partner in nonmarital sexual activity <gave up his *mistress* when he married>
 syn ‖doxy, girl friend, inamorata, lover, paramour, woman
 rel bedmate; concubine; kept woman; dulcinea
mistrust *n syn* see UNCERTAINTY
 rel apprehension, foreboding, misgiving, presentiment
 con dependence, faith, reliance
 ant assurance, trust
mistrust *vb* **1** *syn* see DISTRUST
 rel anticipate, apprehend, foresee; alarm, frighten, scare; appall, dismay
 ant trust
 2 *syn* see QUESTION 2
mistrustful *adj syn* see SUSPICIOUS 2
 ant trustful, trusting
mistrustfully *adv syn* see ASKANCE 2
 ant trustfully, trustingly
misty *adj syn* see HAZY
misunderstand *vb* **1** to fail to understand <he *misunderstood* the full meaning of the novel>
 syn misapprehend, miscomprehend, misknow, miss
 rel misconceive, misconstrue, misinterpret, misread, mistake
 con apprehend, conceive, know, realize; fathom, follow, grasp, seize, take in
 ant comprehend, understand
 2 to interpret incorrectly <*misunderstood* the instructions>
 syn misapprehend, misconceive, misconstrue, misinterpret, misread, mistake
 rel misexplain, mistranslate; miscomprehend, misknow
 con fathom, follow, take in
 ant understand
misuse *vb* **1** *syn* see ABUSE 2
 2 *syn* see ABUSE 4
mite *n syn* see PARTICLE
mitigate *vb syn* see RELIEVE 1
 rel extenuate, palliate
 con aggravate, enhance, heighten; augment, increase
 ant intensify
mitigation *n syn* see EASE 3
mix *vb* **1** to combine or be combined into a more or less uniform whole <*mixed* the ingredients to make a thick sauce>
 syn admix, amalgamate, blend, comingle, commingle, commix, compound, fuse, immingle, immix, interblend, interflow, interfuse, intermingle, intermix, make up, meld, merge, mingle
 rel associate, combine, conjoin, inosculate, join, link, unite; braid, lump, work in; coalesce; blunge
 con divide, part, separate, sever, sunder
 2 *syn* see MISTAKE 1
mix *n syn* see MIXTURE
mixed *adj syn* see MISCELLANEOUS
 rel amalgamated, blended, fused, merged, mingled
mixed bag *n syn* see MISCELLANY 1
mixologist *n syn* see BARTENDER
mixture *n* a product formed by the combination of two or more things <the tea is actually a *mixture* of several varieties>
 syn admixture, alloy, amalgam, amalgamation, blend, commixture, composite, compost, compound, fusion, immixture, interfusion, intermixture, mix, mix-up
 rel brew, concoction, confection, mélange
mix up *vb* **1** *syn* see CONFUSE 2
 ant straighten (out)
 2 *syn* see CONFUSE 5
 3 *syn* see MISTAKE 1
 4 *syn* see DISORDER 1
 ant straighten (out *or* up)
mix-up *n* **1** *syn* see MESS 3
 2 *syn* see MIXTURE
mizmaze *n syn* see MAZE 1
‖mizzle *vb syn* see SPRINKLE 5
‖mizzle *vb syn* see CONFUSE 2
moan *vb syn* see DEPLORE 1
moanful *adj syn* see MELANCHOLY 2
mob *n* **1** *syn* see RABBLE
 2 a large disorderly crowd of people usually bent on riotous or destructive action <the *mob* screamed for a lynching>
 syn rabble, rout
 rel posse; crowd, crush, horde, press, push, throng; herd, swarm

 3 *syn* see CLIQUE
‖mob *vb syn* see SCOLD 1
mobile *adj* **1** *syn* see MOVABLE
 rel fluid, liquid; protean; capricious, fickle, inconstant, mercurial
 con immutable, invariable, unchangeable
 ant immobile
 2 *syn* see CHANGEABLE 1
 ant immobile, stable
 3 *syn* see VERSATILE
 4 *syn* see MIGRATORY
mobilize *vb* **1** to put into movement or circulation <an increase in prices *mobilizes* the whole cycle of inflation>
 syn actuate, circulate, set off
 rel activate; impel, propel
 idiom set in motion
 con inactivate, slow (down *or* up)
 ant immobilize
 2 *syn* see MOVE 5
 3 to assemble (as resources) and make ready for use or action <the president tried to *mobilize* support for the new proposal>
 syn marshal, muster, organize, rally
mobocracy *n syn* see ANARCHY 1
mock *vb* **1** *syn* see RIDICULE
 rel buffoon, burlesque, caricature, parody, travesty
 2 *syn* see DECEIVE
 3 *syn* see MIMIC
 rel affect, assume, counterfeit, feign, simulate
mock *n* **1** *syn* see LAUGHINGSTOCK
 2 *syn* see MOCKERY 2
mock *adj* **1** *syn* see ARTIFICIAL 2
 rel pseudo, quasi, so-called
 2 *syn* see FICTITIOUS 2
 rel bogus, phony
mockery *n* **1** *syn* see LAUGHINGSTOCK
 2 an insincere, contemptible, or impertinent imitation of something worthwhile <arbitrary methods that make a *mockery* of justice>
 syn burlesque, caricature, farce, mock, sham, travesty
 rel derision, ridicule, sport; parody, satire, take-off; joke, laughingstock
mode *n* **1** *syn* see VEIN 1
 2 *syn* see METHOD 1
 3 *syn* see STATE 1
mode *n syn* see FASHION 3
model *n* **1** a miniature representation of something <a *model* of the dam that was accurate down to the last detail>
 syn miniature, pocket edition
 rel copy, mock-up, replica, reproduction; dummy, effigy
 2 something set or held before one for guidance or imitation <Samuel Johnson's literary style is often used as a *model* for writers seeking precision and clarity>
 syn archetype, beau ideal, ensample, example, exemplar, ideal, mirror, paradigm, pattern, standard; *compare* PARAGON
 rel apotheosis, nonesuch, nonpareil, paragon; emblem, symbol, type; embodiment, epitome, quintessence; criterion, gauge, touchstone
model *adj* **1** *syn* see IDEAL 3
 rel commendable, exemplary
 2 *syn* see PERFECT 3
 3 *syn* see TYPICAL 1
moderate *adj* **1** *syn* see SOBER 3
 2 not excessive in degree, amount, or intensity <the new proposals were met with only *moderate* enthusiasm> <the snowfall is expected to be no more than *moderate*>
 syn modest, reasonable, temperate
 rel bland, gentle, mild, soft; inconsequential, inconsiderable, slight, small; paltry, piddling, trifling, trivial
 con excessive, extreme, inordinate, intemperate, radical, unreasonable
 ant immoderate
 3 *syn* see MEDIUM
 rel constant, equable, even, steady

---

syn synonym(s)   *rel* related word(s)
ant antonym(s)   *con* contrasted word(s)
idiom idiomatic equivalent(s)
‖ use limited; if in doubt, see a dictionary

4 avoiding extreme political or social measures < party policy became increasingly *moderate* >
syn middle-of-the-road, middle-road, soft-shell
con conservative, right, tory; left, radical, red; extremist, fanatical, ultra
5 *syn* see CONSERVATIVE 2

moderate *vb* **1** to modify as to avoid an extreme or keep within bounds < actors *moderate* their voices and gestures to fit the size of the theatre >
syn modulate, restrain, temper
rel abate, decrease, diminish, lessen, reduce; alleviate, cushion, lighten, mitigate, mollify, relieve, slacken, slow; constrain, control, qualify; chasten, cool, subdue, tone (down)
con aggravate, enhance, heighten, intensify; augment, increase
2 *syn* see ABATE 4

moderately *adv* **1** *syn* see ENOUGH 2
2 *syn* see SOMEWHAT 2
ant extremely, immoderately

moderateness *n* *syn* see TEMPERANCE 1
ant immoderateness, immoderation

moderation *n* *syn* see TEMPERANCE 1
ant immoderateness, immoderation

moderator *n* one who arbitrates < the labor dispute was finally referred to a *moderator* >
syn arbitrator, mediator
rel arbiter, judge; conciliator, negotiator, peacemaker

modern *adj* **1** having taken place, existed, or developed in times close to the present < *modern* concepts of engineering made the bridge possible >
syn late, recent
rel contemporary, present-day; latter
con antiquated, old-fashioned, old hat, outdated, outmoded, outworn
ant old-time
2 *syn* see NEW 1
rel coincident, concomitant, concurrent, contemporaneous, contemporary; current, prevailing, prevalent
ant ancient, antique

modernistic *adj* *syn* see NEW 1
rel futuristic
ant antiquated

modernize *vb* *syn* see RENEW 1

modest *adj* **1** *syn* see HUMBLE 1
rel moderate, temperate; retiring, withdrawing; unboastful; unpresuming, unpresumptuous, unpretending
con barefaced, brazen, impudent, shameless
ant ambitious
2 *syn* see SHY 1
rel reticent, silent; nice, proper, seemly
3 *syn* see CHASTE
rel priggish, prim, prissy, prudish, puritanical, straitlaced, stuffy
con improper, indecent, indecorous, indelicate, unseemly
ant immodest
4 *syn* see MODERATE 2
5 *syn* see PLAIN 1

modicum *n* *syn* see PARTICLE

modification *n* *syn* see CHANGE 1
rel conversion, metamorphosis, transformation, transmogrification; qualification, tempering

modified *adj* *syn* see QUALIFIED 2

modify *vb* *syn* see CHANGE 1
rel modulate, restrain, temper; qualify

modish *adj* *syn* see STYLISH
rel voguish

modulate *vb* *syn* see MODERATE 1

modus *n* *syn* see METHOD 1

‖**mog** *vb* *syn* see GO 2

mogul *n* *syn* see MAGNATE

moiety *n* *syn* see PART 1

moil *vb* **1** *syn* see LABOR 1
  ‖**2** *syn* see SEETHE 4

moil *n* **1** *syn* see WORK 2
2 *syn* see COMMOTION 4

moira *n* *syn* see FATE

moist *adj* **1** *syn* see DAMP
2 *syn* see SENTIMENTAL

moistureless *adj* *syn* see DRY 1
ant moist

moisty *adj* *syn* see DAMP

‖**moke** *n* *syn* see DONKEY 1

mold *n* *syn* see TYPE

mold *vb* *syn* see MAKE 3

moldable *adj* *syn* see PLASTIC

molder *vb* *syn* see DECAY

moldy *adj* *syn* see OLD-FASHIONED

mole *n* *syn* see BIRTHMARK 1

molecule *n* *syn* see PARTICLE

molest *vb* to annoy or disturb with hostile intent or injurious effect < he was specifically warned by the court not to *molest* his former wife >
syn bait, heckle, persecute, torment
rel annoy, badger, bother, irk, pester; pother, tease; bedevil, beset, devil, trouble; harass, harry, vex

moll *n* *syn* see PROSTITUTE

mollify *vb* **1** *syn* see PACIFY
rel lighten; temper; abate, decrease, lessen, reduce
ant exasperate
2 *syn* see RELIEVE 1

‖**molly** *n* *syn* see WEAKLING

mollycoddle *n* *syn* see WEAKLING
rel ‖mollycot

mollycoddle *vb* *syn* see BABY
ant neglect; abuse

molt *vb* *syn* see SHED 2

mom *n* *syn* see MOTHER 1

‖**momble** *vb* *syn* see CONFUSE 2

moment *n* **1** *syn* see INSTANT 1
ant eternity
2 *syn* see POINT 7
3 *syn* see OCCASION 5
4 *syn* see IMPORTANCE
rel advantage, avail, profit, use

momentaneous *adj* *syn* see TRANSIENT

momentary *adj* *syn* see TRANSIENT
rel brief, quick, short; impulsive
ant agelong

momentous *adj* **1** *syn* see IMPORTANT 1
ant trivial
2 *syn* see EPOCHAL

momentousness *n* *syn* see IMPORTANCE
ant triviality

mommy *n* *syn* see MOTHER 1

momus *n* *syn* see CRITIC

monarchal *adj* *syn* see KINGLY

monarchial *adj* *syn* see KINGLY

monarchical *adj* *syn* see KINGLY

mondaine *adj* *syn* see SOPHISTICATED 2

monetary *adj* *syn* see FINANCIAL
rel numismatic

money *n* something (as pieces of stamped metal or paper certificates) customarily and legally used as a medium of exchange < the only thing that he liked about his job was the *money* >
syn ‖blunt, ‖brass, ‖bread, ‖cabbage, cash, ‖chink, ‖chips, ‖coin, currency, ‖dibs, ‖dinero, ‖do-re-mi, dough, filthy lucre, ‖gelt, ‖greenbacks, ‖jack, ‖kale, legal tender, ‖lettuce, ‖long green, loot, lucre, ‖mazuma, ‖moolah, ‖mopus, needful, ‖ooftish, pelf, rhino, rocks, ‖scratch, ‖shekels, ‖smash, stuff, ‖stumpy, ‖sugar, swag, ‖wampum
rel bankroll, capital, coinage, finances, funds, mammon, resources, riches, treasure, wealth, wherewithal; boodle, hay; ‖stiff

moneyed *adj* *syn* see RICH 1
ant penniless, unmoneyed

moneygrubber *n* *syn* see MISER

moneymaking *adj* *syn* see ADVANTAGEOUS 1

monger *n* *syn* see PEDDLER

monger *vb* *syn* see PEDDLE 2

mongerer *n* *syn* see PEDDLER

mongrel *n* *syn* see HYBRID

‖**moniker** *n* **1** *syn* see NAME 1
  2 *syn* see NICKNAME

monish *vb* *syn* see REPROVE

monition *n* *syn* see WARNING

monitorial *adj* *syn* see MONITORY

monitory *adj* giving a warning < the parents wrote their son a *monitory* letter >
syn admonishing, admonitory, cautionary, cautioning, monitorial, warning

rel advisory, counseling; critical, expostulatory, remonstratory; exhortatory, hortatory; moralistic, moralizing, preachy

monkey *n* **1** *syn* see FOOL 3

2 *syn* see URCHIN

monkey *adj* *syn* see SMALL 1

monkey (with) *vb* *syn* see MEDDLE

monkeyshine *n* *syn* see PRANK

monocratic *adj* *syn* see ABSOLUTE 4

con democratic

monogram *n* a sign of identity usually formed of the combined initials of a name <everything he owned had his *monogram* on it>

syn cipher

rel device, initials; John Hancock, signature

monograph *n* *syn* see DISCOURSE 2

monography *n* *syn* see DISCOURSE 2

monopolize *vb* to take up completely <he would attempt to *monopolize* every conversation>

syn absorb, consume, engross, sew up

rel corner, hog; devour; have, hold, own, possess; employ, use, utilize; control, manage

con contribute, participate, share

monopolizing *adj* *syn* see ENGROSSING

monopoly *n* exclusive possession <neither party has a *monopoly* on morality>

syn corner

rel cartel, consortium, pool, syndicate, trust; copyright; ownership, possessorship, proprietorship

monotone *n* *syn* see MONOTONY

monotone *adj* *syn* see DULL 9

monotonous *adj* *syn* see DULL 9

rel samely, uniform, unvaried; repetitious, jogtrot, singsong

con changing, varying; fresh, new, novel; absorbing, engrossing, interesting

monotonousness *n* *syn* see MONOTONY

monotony *n* a tedious sameness or reiteration <the *monotony* of his job finally got to him>

syn humdrum, monotone, monotonousness

rel boredom, ennui, tedium; dryness, flatness, uniformity

con variability, variation; diversification, diversity, multifariousness, variety

monster *n* **1** *syn* see FREAK 2

rel demon, devil, fiend, hellhound; bandersnatch

2 *syn* see GIANT

monster *adj* *syn* see HUGE

monstrosity *n* **1** *syn* see FREAK 2

2 *syn* see EYESORE

monstrous *adj* **1** extremely impressive <the traditional burial ceremonies turned into a *monstrous* spectacle>

syn cracking, fantastic, massive, monumental, mortal, prodigious, stupendous, towering, tremendous

rel grandiose, impressive, magnificent, showy, splendid, superb; colossal, enormous, huge, immense, mammoth, vast

con mean, petty, picayune, poky, small-time

2 *syn* see HUGE

3 *syn* see OUTRAGEOUS 2

rel glaring, rank; fateful, ominous, portentous; flagitious, infamous

||**monstrous** *adv* *syn* see VERY 1

monstrousness *n* *syn* see ENORMITY 1

monument *n* **1** *syn* see DOCUMENT 2

2 a lasting evidence or reminder of someone or something notable <the whole body of students who learned from him form his *monument*>

syn memorial, testimonial

rel memento, tribute

3 *syn* see TOMBSTONE

monument *vb* *syn* see MEMORIALIZE 2

monumental *adj* **1** *syn* see HUGE

2 *syn* see MONSTROUS 1

3 *syn* see TOWERING 4

monumentalize *vb* *syn* see MEMORIALIZE 2

moocah *n* *syn* see MARIJUANA

mooch *vb* *syn* see WANDER 1

moocher *n* *syn* see BEGGAR 1

mooching *n* *syn* see MENDICANCY

mood *n* **1** a state of mind in which an emotion or set of emotions gains ascendancy <a melancholy *mood* induced by the sight of ancient ruins>

syn humor, mind, strain, temper, tone, vein

rel character, disposition, individuality, personality, temperament; soul, spirit; affection, emotion, feeling, response

2 *syn* see TEMPER 1

3 *syn* see AIR 3

moody *adj* subject to moods <a *moody* person whose behavior was erratic and whose actions were unpredictable>

syn humorsome, temperamental

rel capricious, fickle, inconstant, mercurial, unstable, whimsical; broody

con calm, dispassionate, stable, steady, unexcitable; bovine, impassive, stolid

||**moolah** *n* *syn* see MONEY

mooncalf *n* *syn* see FOOL 1

||**moonraker** *n* *syn* see DUNCE

moonshine *n* **1** *syn* see NONSENSE 2

2 illegally distilled liquor <his death was caused by bad *moonshine*>

syn bathtub gin, ||blockade, bootleg, ||busthead, ||hooch, mountain dew, white lightning

rel homebrew; ||bug juice, grappa, ||jake, smoke, squareface

moor *vb* *syn* see FASTEN 2

moot *vb* **1** *syn* see BROACH

2 *syn* see DISCUSS 1

moot *adj* open to question <it is a *moot* point whether he would have been tried and convicted>

syn arguable, debatable, disputable, doubtful, dubious, mootable, problematic, questionable, uncertain; *compare* DOUBTFUL 1

rel controversial, suspect; unsettled

con confirmed, established, settled; inarguable, indisputable, undebatable, unproblematic, unquestionable; certain, sure

mooting *n* *syn* see ARGUMENTATION

mootable *adj* *syn* see MOOT

mop *vb* *syn* see GRIMACE

mop (up) *vb* *syn* see WHIP 2

mope *vb* **1** to become listless or dejected <*moped* for several days after the divorce>

syn brood, despond

rel ache, grieve, grump, pout, sulk

2 *syn* see SAUNTER

mopes *n pl* *syn* see SADNESS

mopey *adj* *syn* see DOWNCAST

moppet *n* *syn* see CHILD 1

||**mopus** *n* *syn* see MONEY

moral *adj* **1** conforming to a standard of what is right and good <*moral* goodness may be distinguished from intellectual goodness>

syn ethical, moralistic, noble, principled, righteous, right-minded, virtuous

rel good, right; conscientious, honest, honorable, just, scrupulous, upright; chaste, decent, modest, pure

con amoral, nonmoral, unmoral

ant immoral

2 *syn* see DIDACTIC

3 *syn* see ELEVATED 2

moral *n* *syn* see MAXIM

morale *n* a sense of common purpose or a degree of dedication to a common task regarded as characteristic of or dominant in a group <*morale* was high among the troops>

syn esprit, esprit de corps

rel drive, spirit, vigor; assurance, confidence, self-confidence, self-possession

con enervation; aimlessness, purposelessness; egoism, egotism, self-centeredness

moralistic *adj* *syn* see MORAL 1

rel didactic

morality *n* **1** *syn* see GOODNESS

rel godliness, saintliness

2 *syn* see ETHIC 2

moralize *vb* to make moral reflections usually in an officious or tiresome manner <people avoided him as he was always *moralizing*>

syn preach, preachify, sermonize

---

syn synonym(s)   *rel* related word(s)
ant antonym(s)   *con* contrasted word(s)
idiom idiomatic equivalent(s)
|| use limited; if in doubt, see a dictionary

rel lecture, pontificate

moralizing *adj syn* see DIDACTIC

morally *adv syn* see VIRTUALLY

morals *n pl* **1** *syn* see ETHIC 1
  2 *syn* see ETHIC 2
  rel conduct, habits, standards

morass *n* **1** *syn* see SWAMP
  2 *syn* see MAZE 1
  rel dunghill

moratorium *n syn* see SUSPENSION 2

morbid *adj* abnormally susceptible to or characterized by gloomy or unwholesome feelings <his *morbid* poetry is the product of his lifelong frustrations>
  syn morose, sick, sickly
  rel gloomy, melancholic; psychotic; dark, moody, saturnine, sullen
  con healthy, sound, well, wholesome; solid, stable, stolid, sturdy

mordacious *adj syn* see CAUSTIC 1

mordancy *n syn* see ACRIMONY
  rel incisiveness, pungency, trenchancy; acidity, acridity, causticity, mordacity

mordant *adj syn* see CAUSTIC 1

more *adj syn* see ADDITIONAL

more *adv syn* **1** see ALSO 2
  2 to a greater or higher degree <were *more* evenly matched>
  syn better

more or less *adv* **1** *syn* see SOMEWHAT 2
  2 *syn* see NEARLY

moreover *adv syn* see ALSO 2

mores *n pl* **1** *syn* see ETHIC 2
  2 *syn* see MANNER 5

morgue *n syn* see PRIDE 3

moribund *adj* approaching death or a final end <found lying *moribund* in her bed> <fox hunting is a *moribund* sport>
  syn dying
  rel expiring, fading, going; decadent, deteriorating, regressing
  idiom at death's door, on one's last legs, with one foot in the grave
  con booming, flourishing, prospering, thriving; lively, viable

morn *n* **1** *syn* see DAWN 1
  2 *syn* see MORNING 2

morne *adj syn* see GLOOMY 3

morning *n* **1** *syn* see DAWN 1
  con sundown, sunset
  2 the time before noon <it rained most of the *morning*>
  syn forenoon, morn
  con afternoon, evening; day, night

moron *n* **1** *syn* see FOOL 4
  2 *syn* see DUNCE

moronic *adj syn* see RETARDED

morose *adj* **1** *syn* see SULLEN
  rel choleric, cranky, irascible, splenetic, testy; irritable, waspish; brusque, gruff
  con jocund, jolly, jovial, merry
  ant blithe
  2 *syn* see MORBID

morsel *n* **1** a small piece or quantity of food <tossed a *morsel* of meat to the dog>
  syn bit, bite, mouthful
  rel taste; tidbit; crumb, ort, scrap
  2 *syn* see SNACK
  3 *syn* see DELICACY

mort *n syn* see CORPSE

‖**mortacious** *adv syn* see VERY 1

mortal *adj* **1** *syn* see DEADLY 1
  rel implacable, relentless, unrelenting
  2 *syn* see GRIM 3
  3 *syn* see MONSTROUS 1
  4 *syn* see HUMAN
  rel finite, temporal; frail, weak
  5 *syn* see PROBABLE

mortal *n syn* see HUMAN

mortality *n* **1** *syn* see FATALITY 1
  2 *syn* see MANKIND

mortally *adv syn* see VERY 1

mortgage *vb syn* see PAWN

mortician *n* one whose business is to prepare the dead for burial and to arrange and manage funerals <*morticians* must be certified>
  syn funeral director, undertaker
  rel embalmer

mortiferous *adj syn* see DEADLY 1

mortified *adj* **1** *syn* see SEVERE 1
  2 *syn* see ASHAMED
  rel annoyed, harassed, harried, worried

mortuary *adj syn* see SEPULCHRAL 1

mosey *vb syn* see SAUNTER

‖**moss** *n syn* see SWAMP

mossback *n* **1** *syn* see RUSTIC
  2 *syn* see FOGY

most *adj syn* see BEST
  rel greatest, highest, maximum, utmost, uttermost

most *adv syn* see VERY 1

most *adv syn* see NEARLY

mostly *adv syn* see GENERALLY 1
  idiom for the most part

mote *n syn* see POINT 11

moth–eaten *adj* **1** *syn* see SHABBY 1
  2 *syn* see OLD-FASHIONED

mother *n* **1** a female human parent <the *mother* of seven children>
  syn ma, ‖mam, mama (*or* mamma), mammy, ‖mater, mom, mommy, ‖mum, mummy, ‖old lady, ‖old woman; *compare* FATHER 1
  2 *syn* see SOURCE

mother *vb syn* see MINISTER (to)

mother country *n syn* see COUNTRY

motherland *n syn* see COUNTRY

mother–naked *adj syn* see NUDE 2

mother wit *n syn* see INTELLIGENCE 1

motif *n* **1** *syn* see LEITMOTIV
  2 *syn* see SUBJECT 2
  3 *syn* see FIGURE 3

motion *n* **1** the act or an instance of moving <the *motion* of the planets>
  syn move, movement, stir, stirring
  rel agitation, fluctuation, oscillation, sway, swing, wavering; locomotion
  con inertia, inertness, passivity
  2 an impulse or inclination of the mind or will <a *motion* of the will toward what appears good>
  syn movement
  rel goad, impulse, incentive, inducement, motive, spring, spur
  con inertia, stagnation, vegetation

motion *vb syn* see SIGNAL

motionless *adj* being without motion <stood *motionless* so that he would remain undiscovered>
  syn still, stock-still, stone-still
  rel stagnant, static, stationary, unmoving; fixed, immobile, immotile, immotive, immovable, irremovable, ‖sitfast, steadfast, unmovable
  con active, changing, mobile, moving

motion picture *n syn* see MOVIE

motivate *vb syn* see PROVOKE 4

motivation *n syn* see STIMULUS

motive *n* **1** the object influencing a choice or prompting an action <trying to discover what was his *motive* in killing the girl>
  syn cause, consideration, reason, spring; *compare* STIMULUS
  rel antecedent, determinant; emotion, feeling, passion; aim, end, intent, intention, purpose
  2 *syn* see FIGURE 3
  3 *syn* see SUBJECT 2

motley *adj* **1** *syn* see VARIEGATED
  2 *syn* see MISCELLANEOUS
  rel discrepant, incompatible, incongruous, uncongenial

motley *n* **1** *syn* see FOOL 2
  2 *syn* see MISCELLANY 1

motor *n syn* see CAR

motor *vb* **1** *syn* see RIDE 1
  2 *syn* see DRIVE 5

motorcar *n syn* see CAR

motorist *n* a person who travels by automobile <the roads were crowded with *motorists* going to work>
  syn autoist, automobilist, driver, operator

mottle *vb syn* see SPLOTCH
motto *n syn* see BATTLE CRY
rel byword, catchphrase, catchword, shibboleth, slogan, watchword, word
moue *n syn* see FACE 6
mound *vb syn* see HEAP 1
mound *n syn* see PILE 1
mount *n syn* see MOUNTAIN 1
mount *vb* **1** *syn* see INCREASE 2
2 *syn* see ASCEND 1
con descend, fall, lower
ant drop
3 *syn* see RISE 4
ant drop
4 *syn* see INTENSIFY
5 to get on (something) as a means of conveyance <*mount* a horse>
syn back, bestride
rel seat, settle
ant dismount
‖**6** *syn* see TESTIFY 2
7 *syn* see STAGE
mountain *n* **1** a relatively steep and high elevation of land <why are *mountains* in New England considered no more than hills in Colorado>
syn alp, mount, peak
rel butte, mesa; bald, dome; hill; bluff; volcano; sierra
con bottom, bottomland, dale, dell, vale, valley
2 *syn* see PILE 1
3 *syn* see MUCH
4 *syn* see OBSTACLE
mountain dew *n syn* see MOONSHINE 2
mountaineer *n syn* see RUSTIC
mountainous *adj syn* see HUGE
mountebank *n* **1** *syn* see CHARLATAN
2 *syn* see SWINDLER
mourn *vb syn* see GRIEVE 2
con delight, gladden, please, rejoice
mournful *adj* **1** *syn* see SAD 1
2 *syn* see SAD 2
3 *syn* see MELANCHOLY 2
4 *syn* see DEPLORABLE
mournfulness *n syn* see SADNESS
mouse *n* **1** *syn* see GIRL FRIEND 1
2 *syn* see BLACK EYE 1
mouse *vb* **1** *syn* see SNOOP
2 *syn* see STEAL 3
mousehole *n syn* see CUBBYHOLE
mousetrap *n syn* see PITFALL
mouth *n* **1** the opening through which food passes into the body of an animal <the *mouth* in vertebrates is one of the features of the face>
syn ‖bazoo, gob, ‖mush, ‖row, ‖trap, ‖yap
rel mug, muzzle
2 *syn* see FACE 6
3 *syn* see SPOKESMAN
4 *syn* see BACK TALK
5 the place where a tributary enters a larger stream or body of water <the *mouth* of the Mississippi river is in the Gulf of Mexico>
syn embouchement, embouchure
rel estuary; delta
mouth *vb* **1** *syn* see ORATE
2 *syn* see BOAST
3 *syn* see REVEAL 1
4 *syn* see GRIMACE
mouthful *n syn* see MORSEL 1
mouthing *n syn* see FACE 6
mouthpiece *n syn* see SPOKESMAN
mouth–watering *adj syn* see PALATABLE
‖**mouthy** *adj* **1** *syn* see TALKATIVE
2 *syn* see RHETORICAL
movable *adj* capable of moving or of being moved <a device with a *movable* attachment>
syn mobile, moving, unstable, unsteadfast, unsteady
rel remotive, removable; motile; changeable, changeful, mutable, variable; roving
con immobile, immotile, immotive, irremovable, steadfast; established, fixed, set, settled; stagnant, static, unmoving

movables *n pl syn* see POSSESSION 2
move *vb* **1** *syn* see GO 2
2 *syn* see ADVANCE 5
3 *syn* see BE
4 to change or cause to change from one place to another <he *moved* quickly down the staircase> <*move* the chair across the room>
syn dislocate, disturb, remove, shift, ship, transfer
rel displace, replace, supersede, supplant; bear, carry, convey, transmit, transport
5 to set or keep in motion or action <the mechanism that *moves* the locomotive>
syn actuate, drive, impel, mobilize, propel
rel activate, motivate
con bring up, draw up, fetch up, halt, haul up, pull up, stop
6 *syn* see PROVOKE 4
7 *syn* see AFFECT
rel induce, persuade, prevail
8 *syn* see CONVERT 1
9 *syn* see BEHAVE 1
move *n* **1** *syn* see MEASURE 7
2 *syn* see MOTION 1
rel alteration, change, modification, variation
movement *n* **1** *syn* see MOTION 1
rel action, act, deed; activity, dynamism, liveness, operation, operativeness
2 *syn* see MOTION 2
mover *n syn* see INSTIGATOR
movie *n* a representation (as of a story) by means of motion pictures <tired old *movies* that appear on TV>
syn cine, ‖cinema, film, flick, motion picture, moving picture, photoplay, picture, picture show, show
rel cinematics, cinematography
moving *adj* **1** *syn* see MOVABLE
2 having the power to excite deep and usually somber emotion <made a *moving* appeal for help for the orphaned children>
syn affecting, impressive, poignant, touching; *compare* EMOTIONAL 2
rel eloquent, expressive, facund, meaningful, pregnant, sententious, significant; arousing, awakening, rallying, rousing, stirring; exciting, provoking, quickening, stimulating; breathless, gripping
con unaffecting, unimpressive, untouching; casual, cold, formal
ant unmoving
3 *syn* see EMOTIONAL 2
moving picture *n syn* see MOVIE
mow *n syn* see PILE 1
mow *vb* to cut down standing grass or grain with a tool or a machine <*mowed* the lawn every week>
syn clip, crop, cut
rel reap; pare, trim
mow (down) *vb syn* see FELL 1
mow *n syn* see FACE 6
mow *vb syn* see GRIMACE
moxie *n* **1** *syn* see ENERGY 2
2 *syn* see COURAGE
3 *syn* see FORTITUDE
‖**mozo** *n syn* see WORKER
Mr. *n syn* see HUSBAND
Mrs. *n syn* see WIFE
Mrs. Grundy *n syn* see PRUDE
much *adv* **1** *syn* see VERY 1
2 *syn* see OFTEN
3 *syn* see NEARLY
much *n* a great quantity, amount, extent, or degree <learned *much* worth remembering from his experiences in the army>
syn barrel, great deal, heap, lashings, lot, lump, mass, ‖mess, mountain, multiplicity, pack, peck, pile, plenty, ‖power, ‖sight; *compare* MULTITUDE 1, SCAD
rel excess, overage, oversupply, plethora, superfluity
idiom all kinds of
con bit, crumb, modicum, trifle; deficiency, inadequacy, insufficiency, undersupply
ant little

syn synonym(s)	*rel* related word(s)
ant antonym(s)	*con* contrasted word(s)
idiom idiomatic equivalent(s)	
‖ use limited; if in doubt, see a dictionary	

‖**much** *vb syn* see BABY
much as *conj syn* see THOUGH
muck *n* 1 *syn* see SLIME
  2 *syn* see REFUSE
  3 *syn* see GOO 1
muck *vb* 1 *syn* see SOIL 2
  ‖2 *syn* see BOTCH
  ‖3 *syn* see COMPLICATE
  4 *syn* see DRUDGE
  ‖5 *syn* see SAUNTER
‖**muckamuck** *n syn* see FOOD 1
muckamuck *n syn* see NOTABLE 1
mucker *vb syn* see BOTCH
mucker *n* 1 *syn* see BOOR
  2 *syn* see WRETCH 1
  3 *syn* see TOUGH
mucking *adj syn* see DAMNED 2
muckworm *n syn* see MISER
mucky *adj* 1 *syn* see DIRTY 1
  2 *syn* see MURKY 3
  3 *syn* see HUMID
‖**mucky** *vb syn* see SOIL 2
mucronate *adj syn* see POINTED 1
mud *vb syn* see ROIL 1
muddle *vb* 1 *syn* see ROIL 1
  2 *syn* see MUMBLE
  3 *syn* see CONFUSE 2
  4 *syn* see DISORDER 1
  5 *syn* see CONFUSE 5
  6 *syn* see COMPLICATE
  7 *syn* see STUMBLE 6
muddle (away) *vb syn* see WASTE 2
muddle *n* 1 *syn* see CONFUSION 3
  2 *syn* see MESS 3
  3 *syn* see CLUTTER 2
muddled *adj* 1 *syn* see INCOHERENT 2
  2 *syn* see INTOXICATED 1
muddledness *n syn* see HAZE 2
muddlehead *n syn* see DUNCE
muddleheadedness *n syn* see HAZE 2
muddlement *n syn* see HAZE 2
muddle through *vb syn* see SHIFT 5
muddy *adj* 1 having a great deal of mud < playing in the wet field, he got his shoes all *muddy* >
  syn bemired, ‖claggy, ‖clarty, miry, oozy
  rel black, dirty, dungy, filthy, foul, grubby, impure, nasty, soily, sordid, squalid, unclean, uncleanly; bedraggled, draggled
  con clean, cleanly, immaculate, spotless, taintless, unsoiled, unsullied
  ant mudless
  2 *syn* see TURBID
  rel gloomy, murky; addled, confused, muddled
  3 *syn* see DULL 8
muddy *vb* 1 *syn* see SOIL 2
  2 *syn* see ROIL 1
  3 *syn* see DULL 1
  4 *syn* see CONFUSE 4
  rel conceal, hide, screen
  con illuminate, illumine, light, lighten
mudhole *n* 1 *syn* see POTHOLE
  2 *syn* see BURG
muff *vb syn* see BOTCH
muffle *vb* 1 *syn* see BUNDLE UP
  rel cover, envelop, overspread, shroud, veil
  2 to dull the sound of < closed the door to *muffle* the outside noises >
  syn dampen, deaden, mute, stifle
  rel mellow, soften, soft-pedal, subdue, tone (down); smother
  con amplify, enhance, heighten, magnify, reinforce, strengthen
  3 *syn* see SUPPRESS 2
muffler *n syn* see MASK 2
mug *n* 1 *syn* see FACE 1
  2 *syn* see FACE 6
  3 *syn* see DUNCE
  ‖4 *syn* see FOOL 3
  5 *syn* see TOUGH
mug *vb syn* see GRIMACE
‖**mug** (up) *vb syn* see CRAM 4

muggins *n syn* see DUNCE
muggy *adj syn* see HUMID
  rel damp, dampish, moist, moisty, wettish
  con dry
mughouse *n syn* see ALEHOUSE
mug–up *n syn* see SNACK
mugwump *n syn* see NOTABLE 1
mulatto *n* a person of mixed Caucasian and Negro ancestry < the special conflicts faced by *mulattoes* with both whites and blacks >
  syn high yellow
  rel mulatta, mulattress; octoroon, quadroon; sambo, zambo; mustee; half-breed
mulct *n syn* see FINE
mulct *vb* 1 *syn* see PENALIZE
  rel claim, demand, exact, require
  2 *syn* see FLEECE 1
mule *n syn* see HYBRID
muleheaded *adj syn* see OBSTINATE
muley *adj syn* see OBSTINATE
mulish *adj syn* see OBSTINATE
  rel ungovernable, unruly; fixed, set
mull *n syn* see MESS 3
mull *vb* 1 *syn* see DEADEN 1
  2 *syn* see CONFUSE 2
  3 *syn* see DELAY 2
mull (over) *vb syn* see PONDER 2
mulligrubs *n pl syn* see SULK
  rel blues, dejection, depression, (the) dismals, dumps, gloom, heavyheartedness, melancholy, mournfulness, sadness, unhappiness
‖**mullock** *n* 1 *syn* see REFUSE
  2 *syn* see CONFUSION 3
multeity *n syn* see VARIETY 1
multicolor *adj syn* see VARIEGATED
  ant monotone
multicolored *adj syn* see VARIEGATED
  ant monotone
multifarious *adj* 1 *syn* see MANY
  2 *syn* see MANIFOLD
  3 *syn* see MISCELLANEOUS
multifariousness *n syn* see VARIETY 1
multifold *adj syn* see MANIFOLD
multiform *adj syn* see MANIFOLD
  ant uniform
multiformity *n syn* see VARIETY 1
  ant uniformity
multihued *adj syn* see VARIEGATED
  ant monotone
multilateral *adj* having many sides < *multilateral* figures >
  syn many-sided
  ant one-sided, unilateral
multiloquent *adj syn* see TALKATIVE
multiloquious *adj syn* see TALKATIVE
multiplex *adj syn* see MANIFOLD
multiplicity *n* 1 *syn* see VARIETY 1
  ant unity
  2 *syn* see MUCH
multiply *vb* 1 *syn* see INCREASE 1
  2 *syn* see INCREASE 2
  3 *syn* see PROCREATE 1
multitude *n* 1 a very large number of individuals or things < that child always asks a *multitude* of questions >
  syn army, cloud, crowd, flock, host, legion, rout, scores; compare CROWD 1, MUCH, SCAD
  rel numbers, oodles, quantities
  con few, handful, scattering, smatter, smattering, sprinkling
  ant none
  2 *syn* see CROWD 1
multitudinal *adj syn* see MANY
  rel countless, innumerable, innumerous, numberless, uncountable, uncounted, unnumberable, unnumbered, untold
multitudinous *adj syn* see MANY
  rel countless, innumerable, innumerous, numberless, uncountable, uncounted, unnumberable, unnumbered, untold
multivarious *adj syn* see MANIFOLD
multivocal *adj syn* see VOCIFEROUS
mum *adj syn* see SILENT 2

‖**mum** *n syn* see MOTHER 1

mumble *vb* to utter with a low inarticulate voice <embarrassed, he *mumbled* an apology>
  syn ‖chunter, fumble, muddle, ‖mump, murmur, mutter, swallow
  rel maunder; limp, shuffle, stumble; ‖hammer, stammer, ‖stut, stutter; speak, talk, utter, verbalize, vocalize, voice
  idiom speak with mush in one's mouth
  con speak out, speak up; clamor, cry out, shout, vociferate

mumble *n syn* see MURMUR 1

mumblenews *n pl but sing or pl in constr syn* see GOSSIP 1

mumbo jumbo *n syn* see GIBBERISH 3

‖**mumchance** *adj syn* see SILENT 2

mummer *n syn* see ACTOR 1

mummery *n syn* see GIBBERISH 3

mummify *vb syn* see WITHER

mummy *n syn* see MOTHER 1

mummy *vb syn* see WITHER

‖**mump** *vb* **1** *syn* see MUMBLE
  2 *syn* see GRIMACE
  3 *syn* see SULK

‖**mump** *vb syn* see CHEAT

mumpish *adj syn* see SULLEN

mumps *n pl syn* see SULK

‖**mun** *vb syn* see MUST 2

‖**mun** *n syn* see MAN 3

munch *vb syn* see CHEW 1

mundane *adj* **1** *syn* see EARTHLY 1
  rel profane, secular, temporal
  ant eternal
  2 *syn* see MATERIALISTIC
  rel animal, carnal, fleshly
  3 *syn* see PROSAIC 3

municipal *adj* **1** *syn* see DOMESTIC 2
  2 *syn* see URBAN

munificent *adj syn* see LIBERAL 1
  con close, mean, niggard, ungiving

murder *n* the crime of killing a person <a *murder* occurred during a gang shoot-out>
  syn blood, ‖bump-off, foul play, homicide, killing, manslaughter

murder *vb* **1** to kill (a human being) unlawfully and with premeditated malice <planned a safe way to *murder* his rival>
  syn assassinate, ‖bump off, cool, do in, ‖dust off, execute, finish, knock off, liquidate, put away, rub out, scrag, slay; *compare* KILL 1
  rel asphyxiate, behead, decapitate, electrocute, garrote, guillotine, hang, lynch, smother, strangle
  idiom take for a ride
  2 *syn* see ANNIHILATE 2

murderer *n* one who kills a human being <a *murderer* who wouldn't hesitate to kill in cold blood>
  syn homicide, killer, manslayer, slayer; *compare* ASSASSIN
  rel butcher, slaughterer

murdering *adj syn* see MURDEROUS

murderous *adj* characterized by or of a kind to cause murder or bloodshed <made a *murderous* assault on his former friend>
  syn bloodthirsty, bloody, homicidal, murdering, sanguinary, sanguine, sanguineous
  rel deadly; destructive, devastating, ruinous
  con harmless, innocuous, trivial

mure *vb syn* see ENCLOSE 1

murk *vb* **1** *syn* see OBSCURE
  2 *syn* see SOIL 2

murky *adj* **1** *syn* see DARK 1
  rel glooming, glowering, lowering
  con bright, brilliant, effulgent, radiant
  2 *syn* see OBSCURE 3
  3 having visible material in suspension <a *murky* liquid>
  syn cloudy, mucky
  rel muddy, roily, turbid
  con clear, limpid, lucent, translucent, transparent; clean, fresh, pure, unpolluted
  4 *syn* see DULL 8
  5 *syn* see DIRTY 1

murmur *n* **1** a low indistinct but often continuous sound (as of voices) <could hear the *murmur* of the audience throughout the entire performance>
  syn mumble, mutter, rumor, susurration, undertone, whisper

  rel murmuration; buzz, drone, hum, purr; brool
  2 *syn* see REPORT 1

murmur *vb* **1** *syn* see GRUMBLE 1
  2 *syn* see COMPLAIN
  3 *syn* see MUMBLE

muscle *n* **1** muscular strength <loading cargo calls for real *muscle*>
  syn beef, brawn, might, sinew, thew
  rel power, strength
  con impotence
  2 *syn* see POWER 4

muscle–bound *adj syn* see STIFF 4

muscular *adj* **1** marked by good well-developed musculature <his arms were lean but *muscular*>
  syn fibrous, ropy, sinewy, stringy, wiry
  rel flexible, elastic, resilient, springy, supple
  con flabby, flaccid, flimsy, floppy, limp, sleazy; feeble, weak
  2 strong and powerful in build or action <a *muscular* lad who could wield an ax like a man>
  syn athletic, brawny, sinewy; *compare* STRONG 1
  rel stalwart, stout, strong, sturdy; well-built, well-knit, well=set; beefy, burly, husky; Herculean, mighty, powerful
  con faint, fragile, frail; delicate, feeble, weak; ‖pindling, puny, slight

muse *vb syn* see PONDER 2
  rel excogitate, study

muse *n syn* see REVERIE

muse *n syn* see POET

museum *n* a room, building, or locale where a collection of objects is put on exhibition <an art *museum* with a famous collection of jade>
  syn gallery
  rel salon; picture gallery, pinacotheka

‖**mush** *n* **1** *syn* see MOUTH 1
  2 *syn* see FACE 1

‖**mush** (up) *vb syn* see CRUSH 2

mushroom *vb syn* see EXPLODE 1

mushy *adj* **1** *syn* see SOFT 6
  2 *syn* see HAZY
  3 *syn* see SENTIMENTAL

music *n syn* see DIN

musical *adj* **1** *syn* see HARMONIOUS 1
  ant unmusical; musicless
  2 *syn* see MELODIOUS 2
  ant unmusical; musicless

musician *n* one skilled in music <the one playing the sax is a real *musician*>
  syn musicianer, ‖musicker, musico, virtuoso
  rel performer, player

musicianer *n syn* see MUSICIAN

‖**musicker** *n syn* see MUSICIAN

musico *n syn* see MUSICIAN

muskeg *n syn* see SWAMP

muss *n* ‖**1** *syn* see BRAWL 2
  2 *syn* see MESS 3

muss (up) *vb syn* see DISORDER 1
  rel dishevel, rumple, wrinkle

mussy *adj syn* see SLOVENLY 1

must *verbal auxiliary* **1** *syn* see WANT 3
  2 — used to indicate requirement by immediate or future need or purpose <we *must* hurry if we want to catch the bus>
  syn have, ‖mun, need
  rel ought, should want
  idiom have got to, must needs

must *n* **1** *syn* see OBLIGATION 2
  2 *syn* see ESSENTIAL 2

muster *vb* **1** *syn* see ENTER 3
  2 *syn* see MOBILIZE 3
  3 *syn* see GATHER 6

muster (up) *vb syn* see GENERATE 3

muster *n* **1** *syn* see GATHERING 2
  2 *syn* see ROSTER 1

muster out *vb syn* see DISCHARGE 7

---

syn synonym(s)   *rel* related word(s)
ant antonym(s)   *con* contrasted word(s)
idiom idiomatic equivalent(s)
‖ use limited; if in doubt, see a dictionary

ant call up, draft
muster roll *n syn* see ROSTER 1
musty *adj* **1** *syn* see MALODOROUS 1
　rel dirty, filthy, squalid
　2 *syn* see TRITE
mutable *adj* **1** *syn* see CHANGEABLE 1
　rel fluctuating, swaying, swinging, wavering; fickle, inconstant, unstable
　con equable, even, steady, uniform; durable, lasting, permanent, stable
　ant immutable
　2 liable to change or to be changed < a flexible and perhaps too *mutable* policy >
　syn changeable, inconstant, shifty, slippery, uncertain, unstable, unsteady, variable; *compare* CHANGEABLE 1, INCONSTANT 1
　rel changeful, protean, unsettled; capricious, fickle, inconsistent, lubricious, mercurial, temperamental, ticklish, volatile; fluctuating, shilly-shally, vacillating, wavering
　con constant, established, fixed, immovable, inalterable, invariable, set, unalterable, unchangeable, unmodifiable, unmovable
　ant immutable
mutate *vb* **1** *syn* see TRANSFORM
　2 *syn* see CHANGE 1
mutation *n* **1** *syn* see CHANGE 1
　2 *syn* see CHANGE 2
mute *adj* **1** *syn* see DUMB 1
　2 *syn* see SILENT 2
　con articulate, eloquent, fluent, glib, vocal, voluble
mute *vb syn* see MUFFLE 2
muted *adj syn* see DULL 7
mutedly *adv syn* see SOTTO VOCE
mutilate *vb* **1** *syn* see MAIM
　rel damage, hurt, injure, mar, spoil; deface
　2 *syn* see STERILIZE
mutineer *n syn* see REBEL
mutinous *adj syn* see INSUBORDINATE
　rel alienated, disaffected
mutiny *vb syn* see REVOLT 1
mutt *n syn* see DUNCE
mutter *vb* **1** *syn* see MUMBLE
　2 *syn* see GRUMBLE 1
　rel repine, wail
mutter *n syn* see MURMUR 1
muttonchops *n pl syn* see SIDE-WHISKERS
muttonhead *n syn* see DUNCE
mutual *adj syn* see COMMON 1
　rel partaken, participated; associated, connected, related, united
mutually *adv syn* see TOGETHER 3
‖**mux** *vb syn* see DISORDER 1
muzzle *n syn* see FACE 1
myopic *adj* affected by a condition in which the visual images come to a focus in front of the retina of the eye resulting especially in defective vision of distant objects < so *myopic* that he used glasses even to read >
　syn nearsighted, shortsighted
　rel presbyopic; astigmatic
　ant farsighted, hyperopic, longsighted

myriad-minded *adj syn* see VERSATILE
mysterial *adj syn* see MYSTERIOUS
mysterious *adj* being beyond one's powers to discover, understand, or explain < he had a *mysterious* sense of humor, laughing when other people did not >
　syn arcane, cabalistic, impenetrable, inscrutable, mysterial, mystic, numinous, unaccountable, unexaminable, unguessed, unknowable; *compare* INEXPLICABLE, STRANGE 4
　rel impenetrable, incognizable, incomprehensible, uncomprehensible, ungraspable, unintelligible, unknowable; abstruse, esoteric, occult, recondite; ambiguous, cryptic, enigmatic, equivocal, obscure
　con explainable, explicable; apprehensible, comprehendible, comprehensible, fathomable, graspable, intelligible, knowable, lucid, scrutable; candid, frank, honest, straightforward
　ant unmysterious
mystery *n* something which baffles or perplexes < the *mystery* of his disappearance has never been solved >
　syn Chinese puzzle, closed book, conundrum, enigma, mystification, puzzle, puzzlement, riddle, why
　rel poser, problem, stumper; perplexity; brainteaser, brain twister
　con open book
mystic *adj* **1** *syn* see MYSTICAL 1
　rel imaginary, visionary; quixotic
　2 *syn* see MYSTERIOUS
　3 *syn* see MAGIC
mystical *adj* **1** having a spiritual meaning or reality that is neither apparent to the senses nor obvious to the intelligence < the *mystical* food of the sacrament >
　syn anagogic, mystic, telestic
　rel abysmal, deep, profound; absolute, categorical, ultimate; divine, holy, sacred, spiritual; miraculous, supernatural, supranatural
　2 *syn* see SECRET 1
mystification *n syn* see MYSTERY
mystifying *adj syn* see CRYPTIC
myth *n* **1** a traditional story of ostensibly historical content whose origin has been lost < the various Greek *myths* that have come down to us >
　syn legend, mythos, mythus; *compare* ALLEGORY 2
　rel saga; fable, fabrication, fiction, figment; creation, invention
　2 *syn* see ALLEGORY 2
　3 *syn* see LORE 2
mythical *adj* lacking factual basis or historical validity < a *mythical* account attributes the founding of the city to Noah >
　syn fabulous, legendary, mythological
　rel fictional, fictitious, fictive, imaginary, supposititious, unreal; fanciful, fantastic, visionary; created, invented
　con actual, real, true; authentic, genuine, veritable; truthful, veracious, verisimilar
　ant historical
mythological *adj syn* see MYTHICAL
mythology *n syn* see LORE 2
mythos *n* **1** *syn* see MYTH 1
　2 *syn* see LORE 2
mythus *n syn* see MYTH 1

nab *vb* **1** *syn* see ARREST 2
  2 *syn* see SEIZE 2
  3 *syn* see STEAL 1
‖**nab** *n* **1** *syn* see POLICEMAN
  2 *syn* see ARREST
nabal *n syn* see MISER
nabob *n syn* see NOTABLE 1
nada *n syn* see NOTHINGNESS
nadir *n syn* see BOTTOM 3
  con acme, climax, culmination; peak, summit
  ant apex, zenith
nag *vb* to find fault incessantly < stop *nagging* her over nothing >
  syn carp (at), fuss, henpeck, peck (at)
  rel annoy, harass, harry, pester, plague, tease, worry; bother, irk, vex; badger, bait, chivy, heckle, hector, hound, ride; egg, goad, needle, prod, urge
  idiom give a bad (or hard) time, pick at (or on), take it out on
  con commend, compliment, praise; acclaim, applaud, hail
nail *vb* **1** *syn* see CATCH 1
  ‖**2** *syn* see SEIZE 2
  ‖**3** *syn* see STEAL 1
  ‖**4** *syn* see STRIKE 2
naive *adj* **1** *syn* see NATURAL 5
  rel fresh, original
  ant sophisticated
  2 *syn* see EASY 3
naked *adj* **1** *syn* see BARE 1
  2 *syn* see NUDE 2
  3 *syn* see OPEN 2
  rel disclosed, discovered, revealed; evident, manifest, obvious, palpable; colorless, uncolored; pure, sheer, simple
namby–pamby *adj* **1** *syn* see INSIPID 3
  2 *syn* see CHARACTERLESS
namby–pamby *n syn* see WEAKLING
name *n* **1** the word or combination of words by which something is called and by means of which it can be distinguished or identified < the *name* always given to the eldest son > < what is the *name* of that bird? >
  syn appellation, appellative, cognomen, compellation, denomination, designation, ‖handle, ‖moniker, nomen, rubric, style, title
  rel baptismal name, Christian name, font name, forename, personal name, prename; byname, byword, hypocorism, nickname, pet name, sobriquet; epithet, label, tag; alias, incognito, nom de guerre, nom de plume, pen name, pseudonym
  2 *syn* see REPUTATION 2
  3 *syn* see CELEBRITY 2
name *vb* **1** to give a name to < *named* the child for his grandfather >
  syn baptize, call, christen, denominate, designate, dub, entitle, style, term, title
  rel label, tag, ticket; nickname
  idiom give a handle, pin a moniker on
  2 *syn* see DESIGNATE 2
  rel advertise, announce, declare, publish
  3 *syn* see MENTION
  rel identify, recognize
nameable *adj syn* see NOTEWORTHY
nameless *adj* **1** *syn* see OBSCURE 5
  2 *syn* see ANONYMOUS
  ant named
namely *adv* that is to say < understandably his wife disapproves of his bad habits, *namely* gambling and fornication >
  syn scilicet, to wit, videlicet
  rel especially, expressly, particularly, specially, specifically
nana *n syn* see NURSEMAID
‖**nanny** *n syn* see NURSEMAID
nap *n* a short sleep < generally took an hour's *nap* after lunch >
  syn catnap, dog nap, ‖dover, forty winks, siesta, snooze; *compare* DOZE, SLEEP 1
  rel dogsleep; break, interlude, intermission, let up, pause, respite, rest
nap *vb* to sleep briefly < *napped* for an hour after lunch >

  syn catnap, ‖caulk (off), siesta, snooze; *compare* DOZE, SLEEP
  rel drowse; relax, rest, unlax
  idiom catch a wink of sleep, catch forty winks, take a nap (or siesta or snooze)
narcissism *n syn* see CONCEIT 2
narcissistic *adj syn* see VAIN 3
narcotic *n* **1** *syn* see DRUG 2
  2 *syn* see ANODYNE 2
narcotic *adj syn* see SOPORIFIC 1
‖**nark** *n syn* see INFORMER
‖**nark** *vb syn* see INFORM 3
narrate *vb syn* see RELATE 1
  rel descant, dilate, discourse, expatiate
narration *n* **1** *syn* see DESCRIPTION 2
  2 *syn* see STORY 2
narrative *n* **1** *syn* see STORY 2
  2 *syn* see ACCOUNT 7
narrow *adj* **1** *syn* see DEFINITE 1
  2 *syn* see LITTLE 2
  3 *syn* see ILLIBERAL
  rel inexorable, inflexible, obdurate
  con forbearing, indulgent, lenient, tolerant
  ant broad
  ‖**4** *syn* see STINGY
narrow *vb syn* see CONSTRICT 2
narrow–fisted *adj syn* see STINGY
  ant openhanded
narrowhearted *adj syn* see STINGY
  ant openhearted
narrow–minded *adj syn* see ILLIBERAL
  ant broad-minded
nascent *adj syn* see INITIAL 1
nasty *adj* **1** *syn* see DIRTY 1
  rel coarse, gross, obscene, ribald, vulgar; improper, indecent, indecorous, indelicate, unseemly
  2 *syn* see OFFENSIVE
  3 *syn* see OBSCENE 2
  4 *syn* see MALICIOUS
nates *n pl syn* see BUTTOCKS
national *adj* **1** *syn* see PUBLIC 1
  2 *syn* see DOMESTIC 2
national *n syn* see CITIZEN 2
native *adj* **1** *syn* see INNATE 1
  2 belonging to a locality by birth or origin < a *native* tradition > < delighted with the tasty *native* fruits >
  syn aboriginal, autochthonous, endemic, indigenous
  rel domestic, local
  con adopted, introduced, naturalized
  ant alien, foreign, nonnative
  3 *syn* see DOMESTIC 2
  4 *syn* see WILD 1
  5 *syn* see UNREFINED 3
Nativity *n syn* see CHRISTMAS
‖**natter** *vb syn* see CHAT 1
natty *adj syn* see DAPPER
natural *adj* **1** *syn* see ILLEGITIMATE 1
  2 *syn* see INNATE 1
  ant abnormal, unnatural
  3 *syn* see GENERAL 1
  4 *syn* see WILD 1
  5 free from pretension or calculation < he spoke in a perfectly *natural* manner >
  syn artless, guileless, inartificial, ingenuous, innocent, naive, simple, simplehearted, unaffected, unartful, unartificial, unschooled, unsophisticated, unstudied, untutored, unworldly; *compare* GENUINE 3

---

syn synonym(s)   *rel* related word(s)
ant antonym(s)   *con* contrasted word(s)
idiom idiomatic equivalent(s)
‖ use limited; if in doubt, see a dictionary

rel impulsive, instinctive, spontaneous; easy, unlabored; constitutional, ingrained, inherent; folksy, homespun, unpretentious; ignorant, primitive, undesigning; unconstrained, unembarrassed; candid, frank, open, plain; sincere, unfeigned; provincial, rustic
con ceremonial, ceremonious, conventional, formal; ostentatious, pretentious, showy; assumed, contrived, counterfeited, feigned, pretended; artful, sophisticated, studied
ant affected; artificial, unnatural

natural *n syn* see FOOL 4
natural child *n syn* see BASTARD 1
naturalness *n syn* see UNCONSTRAINT
ant unnaturalness
nature *n* 1 *syn* see TYPE
rel anatomy, framework, structure; conformation, figure, shape
2 *syn* see ESSENCE 1
3 *syn* see DISPOSITION 3
4 *syn* see UNIVERSE
naught (*or* **nought**) *n* 1 *syn* see NOTHING 1
2 *syn* see ZERO
naughty *adj* 1 guilty of misbehavior < a *naughty* boy who teased the cat and upset the milk >
syn bad, ill-behaved, misbehaving, mischievous, paw; *compare* DISOBEDIENT
rel contrary, froward, perverse, wayward; headstrong, intractable, recalcitrant, refractory, ungovernable, unruly, willful; disorderly, rowdy, ruffianly; evil, indecorous, wicked
con decorous, good, well-behaved; amenable, docile, obedient, tractable; amiable, complaisant, good-natured, obliging; polite, proper; considerate, kindly, thoughtful
2 *syn* see DISOBEDIENT
nausea *n* a stomach distress with an urge to vomit < overcome with *nausea* as the boat continued to pitch and wallow >
syn qualmishness, queasiness, squeamishness
nauseate *vb syn* see DISGUST
nauseated *adj* affected with nausea < was *nauseated* after taking the drug >
syn nauseous, squeamish; *compare* SQUEAMISH 1
rel choking, gagging; heaving; barfing, upchucking, vomiting
idiom ready (*or* about) to lose one's cookies
nauseating *adj syn* see OFFENSIVE
ant appetizing
nauseous *adj syn* see NAUSEATED
nautical *adj syn* see MARINE 2
navigable *adj syn* see PASSABLE
ant unnavigable
navigational *adj syn* see MARINE 2
nawob *n syn* see NOTABLE 1
nay *adv* 1 *syn* see NO
2 *syn* see EVEN 3
naze *n syn* see PROMONTORY
neanderthal *adj syn* see OLD-FASHIONED
near *adv* 1 *syn* see CLOSE
ant far
2 *syn* see ABOUT 5
near *prep* 1 *syn* see ABOUT 1
2 not far distant from < kept the boy *near* him >
syn ‖aside, beside, by, nearby, nigh, round
idiom close to, hard by, within earshot, within reach, within sight
near *adj* 1 *syn* see CLOSE 6
ant far
2 *syn* see COMPARATIVE
near *vb syn* see APPROACH 1
rel equal, match, rival, touch
con alter, change, modify, vary; differ
‖**nearabout** *adv syn* see NEARLY
near-at-hand *adj* 1 *syn* see NEIGHBORING
2 *syn* see CLOSE 6
3 *syn* see CONVENIENT 2
near-at-hand *adv syn* see ABOUT 5
nearby *adv* 1 *syn* see CLOSE
2 *syn* see ABOUT 5
nearby *prep* 1 *syn* see NEAR 2
2 *syn* see ABOUT 1
nearby *adj* 1 *syn* see CLOSE 6
2 *syn* see NEIGHBORING
3 *syn* see CONVENIENT 2
nearing *adj syn* see FORTHCOMING

nearly *adv* very close to < our work is *nearly* done for today >
syn about, all but, almost, approximately, as good as, just about, more or less, most, much, ‖nearabout, nigh, practically, roughly, round, roundly, rudely, say, some, somewhere, well≈ nigh
rel virtually
idiom as near as never mind(s), in effect, in essence, in substance, in the main, nigh on (*or* onto *or* upon), to all (practical) intents and purposes
nearsighted *adj syn* see MYOPIC
neat *adj* 1 *syn* see STRAIGHT 3
2 manifesting care and orderliness < always kept a *neat* house >
syn chipper, orderly, prim, shipshape, snug, spick-and-span, tidy, trig, trim, uncluttered, well-groomed; *compare* DAPPER
rel clean, immaculate, spotless; dainty, fastidious, finicky, nice; methodical, regular, systematic; accurate, correct, exact, precise
idiom in good order, neat as a pin (*or* bandbox), neat as can be, neat as wax
con disheveled, disordered, slipshod, sloppy, slovenly, unkempt, untidy; dirty, filthy, foul, nasty; lax, negligent, remiss, slack
ant disorderly, messy
‖3 *syn* see MARVELOUS 2
neat-handed *adj syn* see DEXTEROUS 1
neb *n syn* see BILL 1
‖**nebby** *adj syn* see IMPERTINENT 2
‖**necessary** *n syn* see PRIVY 1
necessary *adj* 1 *syn* see ESSENTIAL 4
rel compelling, compulsory, constraining, mandatory, obligatory; important, momentous, significant; cardinal, fundamental
con insignificant, unessential, unimportant
ant unnecessary
2 *syn* see INEVITABLE
rel inerrable, inerrant, infallible, unerring
necessitate *vb syn* see DEMAND 2
necessitous *adj* 1 *syn* see POOR 1
rel depleted, drained, exhausted
2 *syn* see ESSENTIAL 4
necessity *n* 1 *syn* see NEED 4
rel coercion, compulsion, constraint, duress, obligation; indispensableness, needfulness, requisiteness
2 *syn* see OCCASION 3
3 *syn* see ESSENTIAL 2
neck *vb syn* see BEHEAD
necrology *n syn* see OBITUARY
necromancer *n syn* see MAGICIAN 1
necromancy *n syn* see MAGIC 1
necromantic *adj syn* see MAGIC
necropolis *n syn* see CEMETERY
necropsy *n syn* see AUTOPSY
‖**neddy** *n syn* see DONKEY 1
need *n* 1 *syn* see OBLIGATION 2
2 *syn* see REQUIREMENT 1
3 opportunity or requirement to employ < found little *need* for his rifle >
syn demand, occasion, use
rel call, claim, exaction
4 a pressing lack of something essential < he is in *need* of food >
syn exigency, necessity
rel deficiency, deficit, lack, shortage, want
con adequacy, enough, sufficiency
5 *syn* see POVERTY 1
need *vb* 1 *syn* see LACK
rel claim, demand, exact; hanker, hunger, long, pine, thirst, yearn; covet, crave, desire, wish
2 *syn* see MUST 2
needed *adj syn* see NEEDFUL
ant unneeded
needful *adj* necessary for supply or relief < provided them with everything *needful* >
syn needed, required, requisite
rel essential, imperative, indispensable, necessary; lacked, wanted; cardinal, fundamental, vital
con excess, redundant, superfluous; nonessential, unessential; uncalled-for, unnecessary, unneeded
ant needless
needful *n syn* see MONEY
neediness *n syn* see POVERTY 1

needle *vb syn* see WORRY 1
needless *adj syn* see UNNECESSARY
  ant needful
needy *adj syn* see POOR 1
ne'er *adv syn* see NEVER
ne'er–do–well *n syn* see WASTREL 1
nefarious *adj syn* see VICIOUS 2
  rel atrocious, heinous, monstrous, outrageous; flagrant, glaring, gross, rank
  ant exemplary
negate *vb 1 syn* see DENY 4
  ant affirm
  2 *syn* see ABOLISH 1
  3 *syn* see NEUTRALIZE
negation *n syn* see DENIAL 2
  ant affirmation
negative *adj syn* see ADVERSE 2
negative *vb 1 syn* see VETO
  2 *syn* see DENY 4
  ant affirm
  3 *syn* see NEUTRALIZE
  rel abrogate, invalidate, nullify
neglect *vb* to pass over without giving due attention <*neglected* his family for the sake of his mistress>
  syn blink (at *or* away), discount, disregard, elide, fail, forget, ignore, miss, omit, overleap, overlook, overpass, pass, pass by, pass over, pretermit, slight, slough over, slur (over)
  rel brush (off *or* aside), disdain, dismiss, reject, scant, scorn, shrug away, shrug off
  idiom pay no attention to, pay no heed (*or* mind), think little of
  con appreciate, prize, treasure, value; cultivate, foster, nurse, nurture
  ant cherish
neglect *n syn* see FAILURE 1
neglected *adj* not properly or sufficiently attended to or cared for <the whole property had a *neglected* appearance>
  syn run-down, uncared-for, untended
  rel disregarded, ignored, overlooked, slighted, unheeded
  con prized, treasured; fostered, tended; guarded, supervised, watched
  ant cherished
neglectful *adj syn* see NEGLIGENT
  ant attentive
negligent *adj* failing to give proper attention or care <*negligent* in taking care of the children> <a *negligent* man, prone to forgetfulness>
  syn behindhand, careless, delinquent, derelict, discinct, disregardful, lax, neglectful, regardless, remiss, slack
  rel heedless, inadvertent, inattentive, inconsiderate, thoughtless, unheedful, unthinking; incurious, indifferent, unconcerned; slipshod, slovenly
  con rigid, rigorous, strict; attentive, considerate, heedful, thoughtful; careful, exact, fussy, meticulous, punctilious, punctual, scrupulous
  ant attentive
negligible *adj syn* see REMOTE 4
  ant significant
negotiable *adj syn* see PASSABLE
  ant nonnegotiable
negotiate *vb 1* to bring about by mutual agreement <*negotiate* a treaty>
  syn arrange, concert, settle
  rel adjust, compose, transact; agree, bargain, contract, covenant
  con break off, intermit, interrupt, suspend; differ, disagree, dissent
  2 *syn* see CLEAR 8
neigh *vb* to make the cry typical of a horse <the frightened horse *neighed* and stamped>
  syn nicker, whicker, ‖whinner, whinny
neighbor *vb syn* see ADJOIN
neighborhood *n 1 syn* see LOCALITY 1
  2 *syn* see ORDER 4
neighboring *adj* not distant <the need for understanding between *neighboring* countries>
  syn adjacent, close-at-hand, close-by, contiguous, near-at-hand, nearby; *compare* CLOSE 6
  rel abutting, adjoining, bordering, conterminous, touching; close, near

  con distant, far, faraway, far-off, remote, removed; parted, separated
neighborly *adj syn* see AMICABLE
  rel cooperative, gregarious, hospitable, social; cordial, gracious, sociable
  ant unneighborly; ill-disposed
neonate *n syn* see BABY 1
neophyte *n syn* see NOVICE
neoteric *adj syn* see NEW 1
nepenthe *n syn* see ANODYNE 2
ne plus ultra *n syn* see APEX 2
nerve *n 1 syn* see FORTITUDE
  2 *syn* see TEMERITY
  3 *syn* see EFFRONTERY
nerve *vb syn* see ENCOURAGE 1
nerve center *n syn* see CENTER 2
nervous *adj* easily upset or irritated <a *nervous* fretful woman>
  syn fidgety, goosey, high-strung, jittery, jumpy, nervy, spooky, twittery, unrestful
  rel agitated, edgy, excitable, skittish, volatile; fretful, irritable, querulous, snappish, waspish
  con calm, placid, serene, steady, tranquil; collected, composed, cool, imperturbable, inexcitable, poised, unflappable, unruffled
  ant nerveless
nervous breakdown *n* an emotional disorder often characterized by depression, tenseness, irritability, headache, and susceptibility to fatigue <worked and worried himself into a *nervous breakdown*>
  syn breakdown, collapse, crack-up, nervous prostration
  rel neurasthenia; prostration
nervous prostration *n syn* see NERVOUS BREAKDOWN
nervy *adj 1 syn* see WISE 5
  2 *syn* see NERVOUS
  rel excitable, fidgety, jerky, tense, twitchy
  idiom tied up in knots
  con composed, easy, relaxed
  ant phlegmatic
  3 *syn* see TENSE 2
nescience *n syn* see IGNORANCE 2
nest egg *n syn* see RESERVE
nestle *vb syn* see SNUGGLE
net *vb syn* see CLEAR 6
nether *adj syn* see INFERIOR 1
nethermost *adj syn* see BOTTOMMOST
  ant uppermost
netherwards *adv syn* see DOWN 1
  ant upwards
netherworld *n syn* see HELL
nettle *vb syn* see IRRITATE
  rel agitate, discompose, disturb, perturb, upset
nettlesome *adj syn* see THORNY
neuter *vb syn* see STERILIZE
neutral *adj* not experiencing or generating a strong emotional commitment or response <made a *neutral* response to his challenge>
  syn abstract, colorless, detached, disinterested, dispassionate, impersonal, poker-faced, unpassioned
  rel clinical, collected, composed, cool, nonchalant; calm, easy, relaxed; aloof, indifferent
  con intemperate, loaded; fervent, impassioned, passionate, vehement
neutralize *vb* to make inoperative or ineffective usually by means of an opposite force, influence, or effect <attacked by the kind of propaganda that is difficult to *neutralize*>
  syn annul, cancel (out), counteract, countercheck, frustrate, negate, negative, redress
  rel balance, compensate, counterbalance, counterpoise, countervail, offset; abrogate, invalidate, nullify; conquer, defeat, overcome, subdue; override, overrule
  con activate, animate, dynamize, vitalize
never *adv* not at any time <they had *never* seen him before>
  syn ne'er

---

syn synonym(s)   *rel* related word(s)
ant antonym(s)   *con* contrasted word(s)
idiom idiomatic equivalent(s)
‖ use limited; if in doubt, see a dictionary

idiom never in all one's born days, never in one's life, never in the world, never on earth
con constantly, continuously, ever, invariably, perpetually
ant always
never–ending *adj syn* see EVERLASTING 1
ant ended; transitory
never–failing *adj syn* see SURE 2
nevertheless *adv syn* see HOWEVER
nevus *n syn* see BIRTHMARK 1
new *adj* **1** recently come into existence or use or a particular state or relation <*new* styles that flatter stout figures>
syn fresh, modern, modernistic, neoteric, newfangled, new-fashioned, new-sprung, novel, recent
rel first-hand, independent, primary
con dated, outdated, outmoded, out-of-date; shabby, worn; hackneyed, old hat, trite
ant old
2 *syn* see UNFAMILIAR 1
3 *syn* see ADDITIONAL
4 *syn* see REFRESHED
new *adv* within recent time <the scent of *new*-mown grass>
syn afresh, anew, lately, newly, of late, recently
con aforetime, before, earlier, formerly; heretofore, hitherto
ant once
newborn *n syn* see BABY 1
newcomer *n syn* see NOVICE
newfangled *adj syn* see NEW 1
ant oldfangled
new–fashioned *adj syn* see NEW 1
ant old-fashioned
New Jerusalem *n syn* see HEAVEN 2
newly *adv syn* see NEW
news *n pl but sing in constr* a report of events or conditions not previously known <her friend gave her the bad *news*>
syn advice, information, intelligence, speerings, tidings, word
rel announcement, report; dope, lowdown, ‖poop; gossip, rumor, tattle
newsmonger *n syn* see GOSSIP 1
newspaper *n syn* see JOURNAL
new–sprung *adj syn* see NEW 1
next *adj* being the one that comes immediately after another <the *next* day>
syn coming, ensuing, following; *compare* CONSECUTIVE
rel proximate
next *adv syn* see AFTER
next *prep syn* see AFTER 2
next to *prep syn* see BESIDE 1
nexus *n syn* see BOND 3
niagara *n syn* see FLOOD 2
nib *n syn* see BILL 1
‖**nibby** *adj syn* see CURIOUS 2
nice *adj* **1** having or displaying exacting standards <too *nice* about his food to like camp cooking>
syn ‖choicy, choosy, clerkish, dainty, delicate, fastidious, finical, finicking, finicky, fussy, miminy-piminy, ‖mincy, niminy-piminy, old-maidish, old-womanish, particular, pernickety, persnickety, picksome, picky, precious, squeamish, squeamy
rel discerning, discriminating, penetrating; overparticular; queasy; careful, meticulous, punctilious, scrupulous; judicious, sage, sapient, wise
con coarse, gross, vulgar; callow, crude, green, raw, uncouth; lax, neglectful, negligent, remiss, slack; careless, sloppy, slovenly
2 *syn* see FINE 1
3 *syn* see PLEASANT 1
4 *syn* see CORRECT 2
rel rigid, strict, stringent; exquisite, rare
con haphazard, happy-go-lucky, hit-or-miss, random; careless, heedless, inadvertent
5 *syn* see DECOROUS 1
nicely *adv syn* see WELL 1
nice Nelly *n* **1** *syn* see PRUDE
2 *syn* see EUPHEMISM
nice–nellyism *n syn* see EUPHEMISM
niche *n syn* see NOOK
nick *n syn* see NOTCH 1
‖**nick** *vb syn* see STEAL 1
nicker *vb syn* see NEIGH

nickname *n* a descriptive or familiar name that is used instead of or in addition to one's proper name <because he was a redhead his friends gave him the *nickname* "Red">
syn byname, byword, ‖handle, hypocorism, ‖moniker, sobriquet
rel first name, middle name; appellation, appellative, compellation, denomination, style; epithet, label, tag
nictate *vb syn* see WINK
nictitate *vb syn* see WINK
nidorous *adj syn* see MALODOROUS 1
nifty *adj syn* see MARVELOUS 2
nifty *n syn* see ‖DILLY
niggard *n syn* see MISER
niggard *adj syn* see STINGY
niggardly *adj syn* see STINGY
ant bounteous, bountiful
niggling *adj syn* see PETTY 2
nigh *adv* **1** *syn* see CLOSE
2 *syn* see NEARLY
nigh *adj syn* see CLOSE 6
nigh *prep* **1** *syn* see NEAR 2
2 *syn* see ABOUT 1
nigh *vb syn* see APPROACH 1
night *n* the time from dusk to dawn <stayed up all *night*>
syn nighttide, nighttime
con day, daytime
night *adj syn* see NIGHTLY
night and day *adv syn* see TOGETHER 2
nightclub *n* a restaurant serving liquor and providing entertainment <Las Vegas *nightclubs*>
syn bistro, cabaret, café, discotheque, hot spot, nightery, night spot, nitery, supper club, watering hole, watering place
nightery *n syn* see NIGHTCLUB
nightfall *n syn* see EVENING 1
nightly *adj* of, relating to, or associated with the night <*nightly* noises>
syn night, nocturnal
con daily, diurnal; matutinal, morning; evening, twilight, vespertine
nightmare *n syn* see FANCY 4
night spot *n syn* see NIGHTCLUB
nightstick *n syn* see CUDGEL
nighttide *n syn* see NIGHT
nighttime *n syn* see NIGHT
nightwalker *n syn* see PROSTITUTE
nihility *n syn* see NOTHINGNESS
nil *n syn* see NOTHING 1
nim *vb syn* see STEAL 1
nimble *adj* **1** *syn* see AGILE
rel light, lightsome; alert, vigilant, watchful, wide-awake
2 *syn* see DEXTEROUS 1
nimble–witted *adj syn* see WISE 4
ant slow-witted
niminy–piminy *adj syn* see NICE 1
nimmer *n syn* see THIEF
nincom *n syn* see FOOL 1
nincompoop *n syn* see FOOL 1
ninny *n syn* see FOOL 1
ninnyhammer *n syn* see FOOL 1
nip *vb* **1** *syn* see BLAST 1
rel arrest, check; press, squeeze; balk, frustrate, thwart
2 *syn* see STEAL 1
‖**3** *syn* see HURRY 2
nip *n syn* see DRAM
nip *vb syn* see DRINK 3
‖**nipcheese** *n syn* see MISER
‖**nipper** *n syn* see CHILD 1
nipping *adj syn* see COLD 1
nippy *adj syn* see COLD 1
nirvana *n syn* see HEAVEN 2
nisse *n syn* see FAIRY
‖**nit** *adv syn* see NO
nitery *n syn* see NIGHTCLUB
nitwit *n syn* see DUNCE
nitwitted *adj syn* see SIMPLE 3
‖**nix** *n syn* see NOTHING 1
‖**nix** *adv syn* see NO
‖**nix** *vb syn* see VETO
no *adv* — used as a function word to express negation, dissent, denial, or refusal <*no*, you can't come with me>

syn nay, ‖nit, ‖nix, ‖nope
idiom by no manner of means, by no means, in no case, no dice, not at any price, not for love or money, not for the life of me, not for the world, nothing doing, not on your life, on no account, on no condition, under no circumstances
ant yes
‖**no-account** *adj syn* see WORTHLESS 1
Noachian *adj syn* see ANCIENT 1
noble *adj* **1** *syn* see GRAND 1
rel eminent, illustrious
con beggarly, contemptible, despicable, scurvy, sorry
ant cheap, ignoble, unnoble
2 *syn* see ELEVATED 2
ant base
3 *syn* see HONORABLE 1
ant ignoble
4 *syn* see MORAL 1
nobody *pron syn* see NO ONE
ant everybody; somebody
nobody *n syn* see NONENTITY
ant somebody
nocent *adj syn* see HARMFUL
ant innocent
nocturnal *adj syn* see NIGHTLY
con daily, diurnal
nocuous *adj syn* see HARMFUL
ant innocuous
nodding *adj syn* see SLEEPY 1
noddle *n syn* see HEAD 1
noddy *n syn* see DUNCE
noel *n syn* see CHRISTMAS
noggin *n syn* see HEAD 1
no-good *adj syn* see WORTHLESS 1
no-good *n* **1** *syn* see WASTREL 1
2 *syn* see WRETCH 1
noise *n syn* see SOUND 1
rel babel, clamor, din, hubbub, pandemonium, racket, uproar
con quiet, silence, stillness
noise (about *or* abroad) *vb syn* see GOSSIP
noiseful *adj syn* see NOISY
ant noiseless, silent
noiseless *adj syn* see STILL 3
con boisterous, clamorous, strident, vociferous
ant noiseful, noisy
noiselessness *n syn* see SILENCE 1
ant noisiness
noisome *adj* **1** *syn* see UNWHOLESOME 1
ant wholesome
2 *syn* see MALODOROUS 1
rel dirty, filthy, squalid; loathsome, revolting
ant balmy
3 *syn* see OFFENSIVE
noisy *adj* making noise < the *noisiest* car you ever heard >
syn clangorous, clattery, noiseful, rackety, sonorous, uproarious
rel blatant, boisterous, clamorous, obstreperous, strepitous, strident, vociferous; tumultuous, turbulent
con quiet, silent, still, stilly
ant noiseless
nomadic *adj syn* see ITINERANT
no man *pron syn* see NO ONE
ant everybody, everyman
nom de guerre *n syn* see PSEUDONYM
nomen *n syn* see NAME 1
nominal *adj* being something in name or form only < the *nominal* head of his party >
syn formal, so-called, titular
rel apparent, ostensible, seeming; alleged, pretended, professed
idiom in name only
con genuine, real, true
ant actual
nominate *vb syn* see DESIGNATE 2
rel intend, mean, propose, purpose; offer, present, proffer, tender
nonadhesive *adj syn* see LOOSE 3
nonage *n syn* see INFANCY 2
ant age
nonchalant *adj syn* see COOL 2
rel cheerful, glad, lighthearted; easy, effortless, light, smooth

con anxious, careful, concerned, solicitous, worried
noncombustible *adj* incapable of being burned < *noncombustible* material was used whenever possible >
syn apyrous, incombustible, nonflammable, noninflammable, uninflammable
rel fireproof, fire-resistant, fire-resistive, fire-retardant, flameproof
con flammable, inflammable
ant combustible
noncommittal *adj syn* see RESERVED 1
noncompos *n syn* see LUNATIC 1
non compos mentis *adj syn* see INSANE 1
nonconformism *n syn* see HERESY
ant conformism
nonconformist *n* **1** *syn* see HERETIC
ant conformist
2 *syn* see BOHEMIAN
ant conformist
nonconformist *adj syn* see HERETICAL
nonconformity *n syn* see HERESY
ant conformity
noncreative *adj syn* see UNORIGINAL
ant creative
nondiscriminatory *adj syn* see FAIR 4
ant discriminatory
none *pron syn* see NO ONE
nonentity *n* an utterly insignificant person < tired of dealing with subordinates and *nonentities* >
syn cipher, insignificancy, nobody, nothing, nullity, rushlight, whiffet, whippersnapper, whipster, zero, zilch
rel lightweight, obscurity, sad sack, small beer, small fry
idiom blank space in the rear rank, man in the street, no great shakes
nonesuch *n syn* see PARAGON
idiom one in a million
nonessential *adj syn* see DISPENSABLE
ant essential
nonetheless *adv syn* see HOWEVER
nonexistence *n syn* see NOTHINGNESS
ant existence; reality
nonflammable *adj syn* see NONCOMBUSTIBLE
ant flammable, inflammable
nonfunctional *adj syn* see IMPRACTICABLE 2
ant functional
noninflammable *adj syn* see NONCOMBUSTIBLE
ant flammable, inflammable
nonliterate *adj syn* see PRIMITIVE 6
nonmaterial *adj syn* see IMMATERIAL 1
ant material
nonobligatory *adj syn* see OPTIONAL
ant obligatory
no-nonsense *adj syn* see SERIOUS 1
nonpareil *n syn* see PARAGON
nonpartisan *adj syn* see FAIR 4
ant partisan
nonphysical *adj syn* see IMMATERIAL 1
ant physical
non-placet *vb syn* see VETO
nonplus *vb* **1** to cause to be at a total loss as to how to act or decide < was totally *nonplussed* by the economic problems >
syn beat, buffalo, get, stick, stump; *compare* PUZZLE
rel baffle, frustrate, stymie, thwart; confound, perplex; mystify; dumbfound; overcome, throw; paralyze; confuse, flurry, fluster, muddle, rattle
idiom put (*or* drive) to one's wit's end, put up a tree (*or* stump), throw on one's beam end
2 *syn* see STAGGER 5
rel faze, rattle; baffle, balk, frustrate
nonprofessional *n syn* see AMATEUR 2
ant professional
nonrational *adj syn* see ILLOGICAL
ant rational
nonrealistic *adj syn* see IMPRACTICAL 1

---

syn synonym(s)   *rel* related word(s)
ant antonym(s)   *con* contrasted word(s)
idiom idiomatic equivalent(s)
‖ use limited; if in doubt, see a dictionary

ant realistic

nonreligious *adj syn* see IRRELIGIOUS
  rel lay, profane, secular, temporal
  ant religious

nonresistant *adj syn* see PASSIVE 2
  ant resistant, resisting

nonresisting *adj syn* see PASSIVE 2
  ant resistant, resisting

nonreversible *adj syn* see IRREVOCABLE
  ant reversible

nonsectarian *adj* not affiliated with or restricted to a particular religious group < the problems facing *nonsectarian* colleges >
  syn interchurch, intercreedal, interdenominational, undenominational, unsectarian
  con denominational
  ant sectarian

nonsense *n* **1** *syn* see GIBBERISH 1
  2 something uttered or proposed that seems senseless or absurd < his theories are mere *nonsense* >
  syn ‖applesauce, balderdash, ‖baloney, bilge, blague, blah, blather, blatherskite, bosh, ‖bull, ‖bunk, bunkum, bushwa, claptrap, ‖cock, ‖crap, double-talk, ‖drip, drivel, drool, eyewash, fiddle-faddle, fiddlesticks, flapdoodle, flimflam, flummadiddle, fudge, ‖gas, gook, guff, hogwash, hokum, hooey, ‖horsefeathers, hot air, humbug, jazz, ‖jiggery-pokery, malarkey, meshuggaas, moonshine, piffle, pishposh, poppycock, punk, rot, rubbish, slipslop, tomfoolery, tommyrot, tosh, trash, trumpery, twaddle, whangdoodle, windbaggery
  idiom stuff and nonsense

nonsuccess *n syn* see FAILURE 2
  ant success, successfulness

nonsymmetrical *adj syn* see LOPSIDED
  ant symmetrical

nonviolent *adj syn* see PACIFIC
  ant violent

noodle *n* **1** *syn* see DUNCE
  2 *syn* see HEAD 1

nook *n* a secluded or sheltered place < resting in a shady *nook* >
  syn byplace, cranny, niche
  rel alcove, recess; cubbyhole, hole

noon *n syn* see APEX 2

no one *pron* no person < *no one* will be allowed to leave early >
  syn nobody, no man, none
  idiom never a one, nobody on earth, nobody under the sun, not a blessed soul, not a soul
  con all, everyman; many, some
  ant everybody, everyone

noontide *n syn* see APEX 2

noose *vb syn* see HANG 2

‖**nope** *adv syn* see NO
  ant ‖yep, ‖yup

norm *n syn* see AVERAGE

normal *adj* **1** *syn* see SANE 2
  2 *syn* see GENERAL 1

nose *n* **1** the prominent part of the human face that bears the nostrils and covers the nasal passage < had a large *nose* >
  syn beak, ‖beezer, ‖boko, ‖conk, pecker, proboscis, ‖schnozzle, smeller, ‖sneezer, ‖snitch, snoot, snout
  2 *syn* see BUSYBODY
  3 *syn* see GIFT 2

nose *vb* **1** *syn* see SMELL 1
  2 *syn* see SNOOP

nose-dive *vb syn* see PLUMMET

nosegay *n syn* see BOUQUET 1

nosey Parker *n syn* see BUSYBODY

Nostradamus *n syn* see PROPHET

nostrum *n syn* see PANACEA

nosy *adj syn* see CURIOUS 2

notability *n* **1** *syn* see NOTABLE 1
  2 *syn* see CELEBRITY 2

notable *adj* **1** *syn* see NOTEWORTHY
  2 *syn* see FAMOUS 2

notable *n* **1** a person of consequence or prominence < *notables* of Congress and the diplomatic corps >
  syn big, big boy, ‖big bug, ‖big cheese, ‖big chief, ‖biggie, big gun, ‖big noise, big shot, big-timer, ‖big wheel, bigwig, character, chief, dignitary, eminence, ‖fat cat, great gun, heavyweight, high-muck-a-muck, leader, lion, luminary, muckamuck, mug-

wump, nabob, nawob, notability, personage, personality, pooh=bah, pot, somebody, VIP
  rel figure; baron, czar, king, magnate, mogul, prince; light, star; power
  idiom big-time operator, his nibs, Mr. Big
  con cipher, nobody, nonentity; functionary, underling
  2 *syn* see CELEBRITY 2

notably *adv syn* see VERY 1

notandum *n syn* see NOTE 2

notation *n syn* see NOTE 2

notch *n* **1** a usually V-shaped depression in an edge or surface < a *notch* in the table >
  syn indentation, indenture, nick; *compare* DEPRESSION 2
  rel cut, gash, incision, score, scratch; cleft, gap, nock
  2 *syn* see DEGREE 1

note *vb syn* see SEE 1

note *n* **1** *syn* see CALL 1
  2 a written reminder < made a *note* to return the call >
  syn chit, memo, memorandum, notandum, notation
  3 *syn* see REMARK 2
  rel reminder
  4 *syn* see LETTER 2
  5 *syn* see NOTICE 1

noted *adj syn* see WELL-KNOWN
  ant unnoted

note-perfect *adj syn* see PERFECT 2

noteworthy *adj* having a quality that attracts one's attention < a *noteworthy* event >
  syn ‖bodacious, memorable, nameable, notable, observable, red=letter, rubric
  rel conspicuous, noticeable, outstanding, prominent, remarkable; evident, manifest, patent; exceptional, extraordinary
  con blah, common, commonplace, inconsequential, insignificant, ordinary, quotidian, unimportant, unremarkable
  ant unnoteworthy

nothing *n* **1** something that does not exist < his hopes were based on *nothing* >
  syn naught (*or* nought), nil, ‖nix, wind
  idiom nothing at all, nothing whatever
  con something
  2 *syn* see ZERO 1
  3 *syn* see NONENTITY
  idiom (the) little end of nothing whittled down to a point

nothing *adj syn* see WORTHLESS 1

nothingness *n* the quality or state of being nothing < the house was blown into *nothingness* by the force of the explosion >
  syn nada, nihility, nonexistence, nullity, vacuity
  rel emptiness; vacuum, void
  con concreteness, solidity, substantiality; materiality, reality
  ant somethingness

notice *n* **1** a noting of or concerning oneself with something < take *notice* of the gathering clouds >
  syn attention, cognizance, ear, heed, mark, ‖mind, note, observance, observation, regard, remark
  rel care, concern, consideration, thought; apprehension, grasp, understanding
  con disinterest, disregard, indifference, unconcern; carelessness, heedlessness, unmindfulness; insouciance, negligence, recklessness
  2 *syn* see MEMORANDUM 2
  3 *syn* see CRITICISM

notice *vb syn* see SEE 1
  rel acknowledge, recognize; advert, allude, refer
  con disregard, ignore, neglect, overlook, slight

noticeable *adj* attracting or compelling notice or attention < they both showed a *noticeable* aversion to his company >
  syn arresting, arrestive, conspicuous, eye-catching, marked, outstanding, pointed, prominent, remarkable, salient, sensational, signal, striking
  rel notable, noteworthy; evident, manifest, obvious, palpable, patent; spectacular
  con obscure, vague; concealed, hidden, shrouded; insignificant, undistinguished
  ant unnoticeable

notify *vb syn* see INFORM 2
  rel announce, broadcast, declare, proclaim, promulgate, publish; disclose, discover, divulge, reveal

notion *n* **1** *syn* see IDEA

2 *syn* see CAPRICE
3 *syn* see HINT 1
notional *adj* **1** *syn* see CONCEPTUAL
  2 *syn* see IMAGINARY 1
  ant real
notoriety *n syn* see FAME 2
  rel ballyhoo, promotion, propaganda, publicity
notorious *adj* **1** *syn* see WELL-KNOWN
  2 *syn* see INFAMOUS 1
notwithstanding *prep syn* see AGAINST 4
notwithstanding *adv syn* see HOWEVER
nourish *vb* **1** *syn* see NURSE 1
  2 *syn* see NURSE 2
nourishing *adj syn* see NUTRITIOUS
  ant unnourishing
nourishment *n syn* see FOOD 2
  rel keep, living, maintenance, support
nouveau riche *n syn* see UPSTART
novel *adj syn* see NEW 1
  rel different, odd, peculiar, singular, special, strange, uncommon, unfamiliar, unique, unusual
  con customary, habitual, usual; common, familiar, ordinary
novelty *n* **1** *syn* see CHANGE 2
  con old story
  2 *syn* see KNICKKNACK
novice *n* one who is just entering a field in which he has no previous experience < a *novice* in the theater —had never even had a walk-on role >
  syn apprentice, beginner, boot, colt, fledgling, freshman, neophyte, newcomer, novitiate, prentice, punk, recruit, rookie, tenderfoot, tyro
  rel amateur; cub; postulant, probationer; greenhorn, greeny; learner, student, trainee, undergraduate
  con expert, pro, professional
  ant doyen, old hand, old-timer, veteran
novitiate *n syn* see NOVICE
now *adv* **1** *syn* see TODAY
  ant then
  2 *syn* see AWAY 3
now *conj syn* see BECAUSE
now *n syn* see PRESENT
nowadays *adv syn* see TODAY
now and again *adv syn* see SOMETIMES
now and then *adv syn* see SOMETIMES
noxious *adj* **1** *syn* see UNWHOLESOME 1
  ant wholesome; sanitary
  2 *syn* see PERNICIOUS
  rel fetid, putrid, noisome, stinking
  ant innocuous, innoxious
nuance *n syn* see GRADATION
  rel dash, soupçon, suggestion, suspicion, tinge, touch; nicety, refinement, subtlety
nub *n syn* see SUBSTANCE 2
nubbin *n syn* see SUBSTANCE 2
nubilous *adj* **1** *syn* see OVERCAST
  2 *syn* see OBSCURE 3
nucleus *n syn* see SEED 2
nude *adj* **1** *syn* see BARE 1
  con covered
  2 not wearing any clothes < all the boys liked to swim *nude* >
  syn au naturel, buff-bare, mother-naked, naked, raw, stark, stark-naked, stripped, unclad, unclothed, undressed
  rel peeled, uncovered; dishabille, garmentless, unattired, unrobed
  idiom ‖buck naked, in a state of nature, in one's birthday suit, in one's skin, in the altogether, in the buff, in the raw, stripped to the buff, without a stitch on, without a stitch to one's name
  con attired, robed; decent; covered
  ant clad, clothed, dressed
nudge *vb syn* see POKE 1
nudnick *n syn* see PEST 2
nugatory *adj syn* see VAIN 1
nugget *n syn* see LUMP 1
nuisance *n* **1** *syn* see PEST 2
  2 *syn* see ANNOYANCE 3
null *adj* having no legal or binding force or validity < a *null* ballot >
  syn bad, invalid, null and void, void

rel ineffective, ineffectual, inefficacious, useless, worthless
  con acceptable, good, valid
null and void *adj syn* see NULL
nullify *vb syn* see ABOLISH 1
  rel counteract, neutralize; compensate, counterbalance, countervail, offset; confine, limit, restrict
nullity *n* **1** *syn* see NOTHINGNESS
  2 *syn* see NONENTITY
numb *adj* **1** devoid of sensation or feeling < my arm is *numb* >
  syn anesthetized, asleep, benumbed, dead, deadened, insensible, insensitive, numbed, senseless, unfeeling
  rel insensate, insentient, stupefied; comatose, unconscious
  con alert; aware, conscious; sensitive
  2 *syn* see INDIFFERENT 2
numb *vb syn* see DEADEN 1
  rel chill, freeze, frost
numbed *adj syn* see NUMB 1
number *n* a character by which an arithmetical value is designated < you must add the *numbers* of the first column >
  syn chiffer, cipher, digit, figure, integer, numeral, whole number
number *vb* **1** *syn* see COUNT 1
  2 *syn* see AMOUNT 1
numberless *adj syn* see INNUMERABLE
  ant numberable
number one *adj* **1** *syn* see CHIEF 2
  2 *syn* see EXCELLENT
numeral *n syn* see NUMBER
numerate *vb* **1** *syn* see ENUMERATE 2
  2 *syn* see COUNT 1
numerous *adj syn* see MANY
  rel big, great, large
numinous *adj* **1** *syn* see SUPERNATURAL 1
  2 *syn* see SACRED 2
  3 *syn* see SPIRITUAL 4
  4 *syn* see MYSTERIOUS
numskull *n syn* see DUNCE
numskulled *adj syn* see STUPID 1
nuptial *adj syn* see MATRIMONIAL
nuptial *n, usu* **nuptials** *pl syn* see WEDDING
nurse *n syn* see NURSEMAID
nurse *vb* **1** to feed from the breast < decided to *nurse* her baby >
  syn breast-feed, nourish, suckle
  rel bottle-feed
  2 to promote the growth, development, or progress of < *nursed* the flame into a blaze >
  syn cherish, cultivate, foster, nourish, nursle, nurture
  rel feed; advance, forward, further, promote; humor, indulge, pamper
  con check, hold back, retard, slow
  3 *syn* see MINISTER (to)
nursemaid *n* one who is regularly employed to look after children < the *nursemaid* had three children in her charge >
  syn ‖amah, ‖ayah, nana, ‖nanny, nurse, nurserymaid
  rel babysitter, ‖minder, sitter; chaperon; governess
nurserymaid *n syn* see NURSEMAID
nursle *vb syn* see NURSE 2
nurture *n syn* see FOOD 1
nurture *vb syn* see NURSE 2
  rel bring up, raise, rear; discipline, educate, school, train; back, bolster, support, sustain, uphold
  con disregard, ignore, neglect, overlook, pass over, slight
nut *n* **1** *syn* see PROBLEM 2
  ‖**2** *syn* see HEAD 1
  3 *syn* see CRACKPOT
  4 *syn* see LUNATIC 1
  5 *syn* see ENTHUSIAST
‖**nuthouse** *n syn* see ASYLUM 3
nutriculture *n syn* see HYDROPONICS
nutrient *adj syn* see NUTRITIOUS
nutriment *n syn* see FOOD 2
  rel bread, bread and butter, keep, livelihood, living, maintenance, subsistence, support
nutrimental *adj syn* see NUTRITIOUS

---

syn synonym(s)   *rel* related word(s)
ant antonym(s)   *con* contrasted word(s)
idiom idiomatic equivalent(s)
‖ use limited; if in doubt, see a dictionary

nutritional *adj syn* see NUTRITIVE 1
nutritious *adj* promoting growth and repairing natural waste < *nutritious* food >
   syn nourishing, nutrient, nutrimental, nutritive
   rel good, healthful, salubrious, salutary, wholesome; balanced
   con indigestible; bad, insalubrious, unhealthful, unwholesome
   ant innutritious
nutritive *adj* **1** relating to or concerned with nutrition < *nutritive* organs of the body >
   syn alimentary, alimentative, nutritional
   rel digestive, metabolic; constructive, creative, formative, productive
   2 *syn* see NUTRITIOUS
nuts *adj syn* see INSANE 1
nutshell *vb syn* see EPITOMIZE 1
nutsy *adj syn* see INSANE 1
nutty *adj* **1** *syn* see ENTHUSIASTIC
   2 *syn* see INSANE 1
nuzzle *vb syn* see SNUGGLE
nymph *n syn* see DOXY 1
nymphet *n syn* see DOXY 1

oaf *n* **1** *syn* see DUNCE
   2 a big clumsy, usually slow-witted person < an *oaf* who bumped into everything he passed >
   syn bohunk, ‖gaum, gawk, klutz, lobster, looby, lout, lubber, ‖lug, lummox, lump, lumpkin, meathead, palooka, slouch
   rel ‖baboon, beast, bruiser, brute, bull, gorilla, hulk, missing link, ox; clod, clown, dub, galoot, slob; blunderbuss, blunderer, blunderhead
oar *vb syn* see ROW
oater *n syn* see WESTERN
oath *n syn* see SWEARWORD
obdurate *adj* **1** *syn* see UNFEELING 2
   con tender
   2 *syn* see INFLEXIBLE 2
   rel mulish, stiff-necked; immovable
   con relenting, submitting
obedient *adj* submissive to the will, guidance, or control of another < children should always be *obedient* to their parents >
   syn amenable, biddable, docile, ‖docious, tractable
   rel acquiescent, compliant, sheeplike, submissive, yielding; duteous, dutiful, loyal; law-abiding; obeisant, subservient
   con insubordinate, rebellious; contrary, froward, perverse, wayward, willful; headstrong, intractable, recalcitrant, refractory, uncontrollable, ungovernable, unruly
   ant contumacious, disobedient
obeisance *n syn* see HONOR 1
   rel allegiance, fealty, loyalty
obeisant *adj syn* see SUBSERVIENT 2
obese *adj syn* see FAT 2
   ant skinny
obesity *n* a condition characterized by excessive bodily fat < could barely walk because of his *obesity* >
   syn adiposity, corpulence, fatness, fleshiness
   rel chubbiness, chunkiness, embonpoint, grossness, plumpness, portliness, pudginess, rotundity, stockiness, stoutness, tubbiness
   con lankiness, leanness, scrawniness, slenderness, slimness
   ant skinniness
obey *vb* to act or behave in conformity with (as an order) or in duty to (as a parent) < *obey* a superior's order >
   syn comply, conform, follow, keep, mind, observe
   rel bow, defer, submit, yield; accede, acquiesce, agree, assent; fulfill, satisfy; carry out; heed, regard
   idiom abide by
   con break, disregard, transgress, violate; command, order
   ant disobey
obfuscate *vb syn* see OBSCURE
   ant clarify
obit *n syn* see OBITUARY
obiter *adv syn* see INCIDENTALLY 2
obiter dictum *n syn* see REMARK 2
obituary *n* a notice of a person's death usually with a short biographical account < always read the *obituaries* in the paper >
   syn necrology, obit
object *n* **1** *syn* see THING 3
   rel doodad; gadget
   2 *syn* see THING 4
   3 *syn* see BODY 4

   4 *syn* see VIEW 6
   5 *syn* see USE 4
object *vb* **1** to oppose by arguing against < *objecting* because the evidence was unclear >
   syn except, expostulate, inveigh (against), kick, protest, remonstrate
   rel balk, boggle, demur, dissent, jib, stickle; complain; criticize; challenge; spurn; rail, rant, rave, storm
   con accede, agree, assent, consent; accredit, approve, sanction
   ant acquiesce
   2 *syn* see DISAPPROVE 1
objectify *vb syn* see EMBODY 1
objection *n syn* see DEMUR 2
objectionable *adj* arousing or likely to arouse objection < the language in that movie is *objectionable* >
   syn exceptionable, ill-favored, inadmissible, unacceptable, undesirable, unwanted, unwelcome
   rel abhorrent, loathsome, offensive, repellent, repugnant, repulsive, revolting; disagreeable, distasteful, invidious, obnoxious, unpleasant; unfit, unsuitable; censurable, reprehensible
   con acceptable, agreeable, gratifying, pleasant, pleasing, welcome
   ant unobjectionable
objective *adj* **1** *syn* see MATERIAL 1
   rel external, outer, outside, outward
   ant subjective
   2 *syn* see FAIR 4
   ant subjective
objective *n* **1** *syn* see AMBITION 2
   2 *syn* see USE 4
objectless *adj syn* see RANDOM
objet d'art *n syn* see KNICKKNACK
objurgate *vb syn* see EXECRATE 1
   rel castigate, censure
obligated *adj syn* see INDEBTED
obligation *n* **1** *syn* see OCCASION 3
   2 something one is bound to do or forbear < it is our *obligation* to obey the law >
   syn charge, commitment, committal, devoir, duty, must, need, ought, ‖right
   rel compulsion, constraint, restraint; burden, requirement, responsibility; business, part, place
   con choice, discretion, free will, option; decision, determination, pleasure, will
   3 *syn* see INDEBTEDNESS 1
obligatory *adj syn* see MANDATORY
   ant nonobligatory
oblige *vb* **1** *syn* see FORCE 2
   2 to do a service or courtesy < you will *oblige* me greatly if you will get there on time >
   syn accommodate, convenience, favor
   rel gratify, please; avail, benefit, profit; aid, assist, contribute, help
   con bother, discommode, incommode, inconvenience, trouble
   ant disoblige
obliged *adj* **1** *syn* see GRATEFUL 1
   2 *syn* see INDEBTED
obliging *adj syn* see AMIABLE 1

ant disobliging

oblique *adj* **1** *syn* see INCLINED 3
  2 *syn* see INDIRECT 1
  ant straight

obliquely *adv* *syn* see ASIDE 1
  ant straight

obliterate *vb* *syn* see ERASE

oblivion *n* a state of forgetting or the fact of having forgotten
  < the *oblivion* of sleep >
  syn forgetfulness, lethe, obliviousness
  rel nirvana; insensibleness
  con alertness, awareness, consciousness; memory, recall, recalling, recollection, remembrance

oblivious *adj* **1** *syn* see FORGETFUL
  rel absorbed, unaware, unconscious
  idiom turned off
  2 *syn* see IGNORANT 2

obliviousness *n* *syn* see OBLIVION

obloquy *n* **1** *syn* see ABUSE
  2 *syn* see ANIMADVERSION
  3 *syn* see DISGRACE

obnoxious *adj* **1** *syn* see LIABLE 2
  ant unobnoxious
  2 *syn* see REPUGNANT 1
  con congenial, likable, simpatico
  ant grateful; unobnoxious

obscene *adj* **1** *syn* see OFFENSIVE
  2 marked by the use of words regarded as taboo in polite usage
  < knew all the *obscene* expressions for the genitalia >
  syn barnyard, coarse, crude, crusty, dirty, fescennine, filthy, foul, gross, indecent, nasty, paw, profane, rank, raunchy, ‖raw, rocky, scatological, scurrilous, smutty, vulgar; *compare* RISQUÉ
  rel bawdy, ribald, smoking-room; impure, lascivious, lewd, warm; lurid, pornographic, salacious, scabrous, sultry; earthy, rich; unprintable; foulmouthed
  con acceptable, proper, tolerable; appropriate, fit, suitable; clean, decent, decorous, seemly

obscure *adj* **1** *syn* see DARK 1
  rel clouded, cloudy, fuliginous; shadowy, shady, umbrageous
  con clear, lucid; bright, brilliant, luminous
  2 withdrawn from the main centers of human activity < was exiled to an *obscure* Siberian village >
  syn devious, lonesome, out-of-the-way, remote, removed, retired, secret
  rel distant, far, far-off; close, hidden, odd, secluded, sequestered, solitary; blind; inaccessible
  idiom back of beyond, off the beaten track (*or* path), in the boondocks (*or* sticks)
  con central; urban; populous
  3 not readily understood or grasped < an *obscure* textual reference >
  syn ambiguous, amphibological, double-edged, double-faced, dusky, equivocal, murky, nubilous, opaque, sibylline, tenebrous, uncertain, unclear, unexplicit, unintelligible, vague; *compare* CRYPTIC, FAINT 2
  rel difficult, incomprehensible, inexplicable, puzzling, unfathomable; illegible; abstruse, Delphian, enigmatic, esoteric, inscrutable, mysterious, mystic, mystical; inconclusive, indecisive, indefinite
  con definite, explicit, obvious; clear, express, unambiguous, unequivocal
  ant lucid
  4 *syn* see INCONSPICUOUS
  rel humble, lowly, minor, unimportant
  5 lacking the prominence, showiness, or worth by which attention might be attracted < an *obscure* Roman poet >
  syn nameless, uncelebrated, unfamed, unheard-of, unknown, unnoted, unrenowned
  rel inconspicuous; minor, undistinguished, unimportant
  con celebrated, distinguished, named, notable, noted, noteworthy, renowned, well-known
  ant famed, famous
  6 *syn* see FAINT 2
  ant clear

obscure *vb* to make dark, dim, or indistinct < fog *obscured* our view >
  syn adumbrate, becloud, bedim, befog, cloud, darken, dim, dislimn, eclipse, fog, gloom, haze, mist, murk, obfuscate, overcast, overcloud, overshadow, shadow

rel blear, blur, fuzz; blind, conceal, dim out, hide, screen, shade, shroud; bemask, camouflage, cloak, cover, disguise, mask, veil; belie, falsify, misrepresent
  con brighten, light (up), lighten; clarify, enlighten; elucidate, exemplify, explain
  ant illuminate, illumine

obscured *adj* *syn* see ULTERIOR

obsequious *adj* *syn* see SUBSERVIENT 2
  rel deferential; parasitic, sycophantic, toadying
  con self-assertive

observable *adj* **1** *syn* see PERCEPTIBLE
  ant unobservable
  2 *syn* see NOTEWORTHY

observance *n* **1** *syn* see RITE 2
  2 *syn* see NOTICE 1
  ant nonobservance, unobservance

observant *adj* **1** *syn* see ATTENTIVE 1
  rel awake
  ant unobservant
  2 *syn* see MINDFUL 2

observation *n* **1** *syn* see NOTICE 1
  2 *syn* see REMARK 2

observative *adj* *syn* see MINDFUL 2

observatory *n* *syn* see LOOKOUT 2

observe *vb* **1** *syn* see OBEY
  2 *syn* see KEEP 2
  rel revere, reverence, venerate
  ant break, violate
  3 *syn* see SEE 1
  4 *syn* see REMARK 2

observer *n* *syn* see SPECTATOR

observing *adj* *syn* see MINDFUL 2
  ant unobserving

obsessed *adj* preoccupied intensely or abnormally < *obsessed* with cleanliness >
  syn hagridden, hipped, queer
  rel bewitched, dominated, gripped, held, possessed, prepossessed; bedeviled, beset, dogged, harassed, haunted, plagued, troubled; overcome
  idiom have on the brain
  con detached, unconcerned, uninterested; indifferent, neutral; cool, easy-going

obsession *n* *syn* see FETISH 2

obsolesce *vb* *syn* see OUTDATE

obsolete *adj* no longer active or in use < *obsolete* social customs >
  syn dead, disused, extinct, outmoded, outworn, passé, superseded; *compare* ANCIENT 1
  rel old-fashioned, old hat, old-time, old-timey, out-of-date, unfashionable; dusty, fusty, moldy, moth-eaten, musty, stale, time-worn
  idiom behind the times
  con contemporary, modern, new-fashioned, up-to-date, up-to-the-minute; novel, original, unique
  ant current

obsolete *vb* *syn* see OUTDATE

obstacle *n* something that seriously hampers action or progress < lack of education is an *obstacle* to advancement >
  syn bar, Chinese wall, crimp, hamper, hurdle, impediment, mountain, obstruction, rub, snag, stumbling block, traverse
  rel clog, encumbrance, handicap, hindrance; bump, difficulty, hardship, vicissitude; catch, hitch; disincentive
  con aid, assist, assistance, help
  ant advantage

obstinate *adj* unwilling to submit (as to reason or control) < he had an *obstinate* determination to live as he pleased >
  syn bullheaded, closed-minded, deaf, hardheaded, headstrong, incompliant, intractable, intransigent, muleheaded, muley, mulish, pertinacious, perverse, pervicacious, pigheaded, refractory, self-willed, ‖sot, stiff, stiff-necked, stubborn, tough, unpliable, unpliant, unyielding, willful, wrongheaded; *compare* UNRULY 1
  rel resistant, unsubmissive, withstanding; contrary, crabbed, recalcitrant, renitent; inexorable, inflexible, obdurate; opinionated; resolute, staunch, steadfast, unbudging

---

syn synonym(s)   *rel* related word(s)
ant antonym(s)   *con* contrasted word(s)
idiom idiomatic equivalent(s)
‖ use limited; if in doubt, see a dictionary

con acquiescent, complaisant, compliant; submissive, yielding; agreeable, cooperative, willing

ant pliable, pliant

obstipated *adj syn* see CONSTIPATED

obstreperous *adj* **1** *syn* see VOCIFEROUS

2 *syn* see DISOBEDIENT

obstruct *vb* **1** *syn* see FILL 1

2 *syn* see HINDER

3 *syn* see SCREEN 3

obstruction *n syn* see OBSTACLE

obtain *vb syn* see GET 1

obtainable *adj* **1** *syn* see AVAILABLE 1

rel derivable

2 *syn* see PURCHASABLE 1

obtrude *vb* **1** *syn* see IMPOSE 5

2 *syn* see INTRUDE 1

obtrusive *adj syn* see IMPERTINENT 2

ant unobtrusive

obtund *vb syn* see DULL 3

obtuse *adj syn* see DULL 6

obviate *vb syn* see PREVENT 2

rel anticipate; interfere, interpose, intervene

obvious *adj syn* see CLEAR 5

ant abstruse, obscure; unobvious

occasion *n* **1** *syn* see OPPORTUNITY

2 *syn* see CAUSE 1

3 something that provides a reason for something else < there is no *occasion* for alarm >

syn call, cause, necessity, obligation

rel basis, foundation, ground, warrant; justification, right; excuse

4 *syn* see OCCURRENCE

5 a particular point of time at which something takes place < we always spoke, but on that *occasion* we didn't >

syn instant, moment, time, while

idiom point in time

6 *syn* see NEED 3

7 occasions *pl syn* see BUSINESS 8

8 *syn* see EVENT 2

occasion *vb syn* see GENERATE 3

occasional *adj syn* see INFREQUENT

rel incidental; casual, random

con accustomed, habitual, usual; constant, continual, continuous

ant customary

occasionally *adv* on a few occasions < *occasionally* she'll walk instead of drive >

syn infrequently, irregularly, on occasion, sporadically, uncommonly; *compare* SOMETIMES

rel off and on, once or twice

idiom every now and then, from time to time, ∥once in a way, once in a while

con continually, continuously, frequently; commonly, customarily, habitually, often; hardly ever, rarely, scarcely, seldom; never

ant constantly

occlude *vb syn* see FILL 1

occult *vb syn* see HIDE

occult *adj syn* see RECONDITE

rel arcane, mysterious; cabalistic, mystical, supernatural; eerie, unearthly, weird

occupancy *n syn* see HABITATION 1

occupant *n syn* see INHABITANT

occupation *n* **1** *syn* see WORK 1

2 *syn* see HABITATION 1

occupiable *adj syn* see LIVABLE 1

occupied *adj syn* see BUSY 1

ant unoccupied

occupy *vb* **1** *syn* see ENGAGE 4

2 *syn* see INHABIT

occur *vb* **1** *syn* see HAPPEN 1

2 to enter one's mind < it just *occurred* to me: she can't drive >

syn hit, strike

idiom come into one's head, come to mind, cross one's mind, flash across one's mind, go through one's head

occurrence *n* something that happens or takes place < the chance encounter turned out to be a fortunate *occurrence* >

syn circumstance, episode, event, go, happening, incident, occasion, thing

rel contingency, emergency, exigency, juncture, pass; condition, situation, state; adventure, experience

ocean *n* the body of water that covers nearly three-fourths of the earth < pulled the downed pilot from the *ocean* >

syn blue, brine, ∥briny, deep, drink, main, sea

oceanic *adj syn* see MARINE 1

ochlocracy *n syn* see ANARCHY 1

ocular *adj* **1** *syn* see VISUAL 2

2 *syn* see VISUAL 1

ocular *n syn* see EYE 1

oculus *n syn* see EYE 1

odd *adj* **1** being without a corresponding mate < had only an *odd* glove; the other was lost >

syn unmatched, unpaired

rel lone, only, single

con matched, paired

2 *syn* see ACCIDENTAL

3 *syn* see STRANGE 4

oddball *n syn* see ECCENTRIC

oddball *adj syn* see STRANGE 4

oddity *n* **1** *syn* see ECCENTRIC

2 *syn* see CURIOSITY 2

oddments *n pl syn* see SUNDRIES

odds *n pl syn* see ADVANTAGE 3

odds and ends *n pl* **1** *syn* see SUNDRIES

2 *syn* see MISCELLANY 1

odiferous *adj syn* see ODOROUS

odious *adj syn* see HATEFUL 2

odium *n* **1** *syn* see DISGRACE

rel hate, hatred

ant honor

2 *syn* see STIGMA

odor *n syn* see SMELL 1

odoriferous *adj syn* see ODOROUS

odorize *vb syn* see SCENT 2

odorless *adj* having no odor < *odorless* castor oil >

syn inodorous, scentless, smell-less

rel deodorant, deodorizing; unscented

con scented, smelly

ant odorous

odorous *adj* having or emitting an odor < *odorous* chemicals are often malodorous >

syn odiferous, odoriferous, scented; *compare* MALODOROUS 1, SWEET 2

rel redolent, reeking, smelling, smelly; heady, pungent, strong; olfactive, olfactory

ant inodorous, odorless, scentless

o'er *prep syn* see OVER 1

oeuvre *n* a substantial body of work constituting the lifework of a writer, composer, or artist < one of the more popular operas in the Mozart *oeuvre* >

syn corpus, opera omnia

rel output

off *adv syn* see AWAY 2

off *adj* **1** *syn* see REMOTE 4

2 *syn* see SLOW 3

offal *n syn* see REFUSE

off–balance *adj syn* see LOPSIDED

off–center *adj syn* see ECCENTRIC

off–color *adj* **1** *syn* see UNWELL

2 *syn* see RISQUÉ

offend *vb* **1** *syn* see TRESPASS 1

2 *syn* see VIOLATE 1

3 to cause hurt feelings or deep resentment < *offended* her by his cruel remark >

syn affront, insult, outrage

rel aggrieve, hurt, sting, wound; exasperate, gall, irritate, nettle; excite, provoke; appall, horrify, scandalize, shock; disoblige, displease, distress, disturb, miff, pique, upset

idiom hurt one's feelings, ruffle one's feathers, step (*or* tread) on one's toes

con delight, gratify, please, tickle; captivate, charm, enchant; flatter

offender *n syn* see CRIMINAL

offense *n* **1** *syn* see ATTACK 1

2 an emotional response to a slight or indignity < he is so sensitive that he takes *offense* at the slightest criticism >

syn dudgeon, huff, miff, pique, resentment, ∥snuff, umbrage *rel* affront, indignity, insult; anger, indignation; displeasure; cat-fit, conniption, fit, tantrum; pet, tizzy; explosion, flare-up, out-burst, scene

con delight, pleasure

3 *syn* see CRIME 1

offensive *adj* utterly unpleasant or distasteful to the senses or sen-sibilities < the *offensive* odor of stale garbage > < her arrogant assurance was more than a little *offensive* >

syn atrocious, disgusting, evil, foul, hideous, horrible, horrid, icky, loathsome, nasty, nauseating, noisome, obscene, repellent, repugnant, repulsive, revolting, sickening, ungrateful, unwhole-some, vile

rel abhorrent, bad, disagreeable, objectionable, uncongenial, unpleasant; abominable, detestable, fulsome, odious; rank; ap-palling, awful, beastly, dreadful, frightful, ghastly, grim, grisly, gruesome, lurid, shocking, terrible; unappetizing, unpalatable, unsavory

con agreeable, appealing, attractive, pleasant, pleasing; favor-able, unobjectionable, welcome; appetizing, palatable, savory; divine

ant inoffensive, unoffensive

offensive *n* *syn* see ATTACK 1

offer *vb* **1** to put something before another for acceptance or con-sideration < he was soon *offered* another job >

syn extend, give, hold out, pose, present, proffer, tender

rel display, exhibit, show

con accept, receive, take; decline, refuse, reject

2 *syn* see ADDUCE

3 *syn* see TRY 5

4 *syn* see SHOW 1

offering *n* **1** *syn* see VICTIM 1

2 *syn* see DONATION

offgoing *n* *syn* see DEPARTURE 1

offhand *adj* *syn* see EXTEMPORANEOUS

office *n* **1** *syn* see JOB 2

2 *syn* see FUNCTION 1

‖**3** *syn* see PRIVY 1

‖**4** *syn* see HIGH SIGN 2

officer *n* **1** *syn* see POLICEMAN

2 *syn* see EXECUTIVE

official *n* *syn* see EXECUTIVE

official *adj* derived from the proper office, officer, or authority < the mayor's office issued an *official* statement >

syn authoritative, ex cathedra, ex officio

rel approved, authorized, certified, cleared, endorsed, OK'd, sanctioned; canonical, cathedral

ant officious (*in diplomatic use*), unofficial

officially *adv* *syn* see OSTENSIBLY

officiate *vb* *syn* see ACT 4

officious *adj* *syn* see IMPERTINENT 2

offing *n* *syn* see FUTURE

offish *adj* **1** *syn* see UNSOCIABLE

2 *syn* see UNWELL

off–key *adj* *syn* see IRREGULAR 1

off–load *vb* *syn* see UNLOAD

off–lying *adj* *syn* see DISTANT 1

offscouring *n* *syn* see OUTCAST

offset *vb* *syn* see COMPENSATE 1

rel check, stop

offshoot *n* *syn* see OUTGROWTH 2

offspring *n* *pl* those who follow in direct parental line < a mother of numerous *offspring* >

syn ‖begats, brood, children, descendants, issue, posterity, pro-geniture, progeny, scions, seed

rel hatch, swarm; produce, spawn, young

con antecedents, ascendants, forebears, forefathers, progenitors

ant ancestors

offstage *adj or adv* *syn* see BACKSTAGE

ant onstage

of late *adv* *syn* see NEW

oft *adv* *syn* see OFTEN

often *adv* many times < we called *often* but still could not reach you >

syn again and again, frequently, much, oft, oftentimes, ofttimes, over and over, repeatedly, time and again

idiom a number of times, many a time, many times over, time and time again

con infrequently, rarely; now and then, occasionally

ant seldom

oftentimes *adv* *syn* see OFTEN

ofttimes *adv* *syn* see OFTEN

ogle *vb* *syn* see LOOK 7

‖**ogle** *n* *syn* see EYE 1

ogress *n* *syn* see VIRAGO

oil *n* *syn* see FLATTERY

‖**oiled** *adj* *syn* see INTOXICATED 1

oily *adj* **1** *syn* see FATTY 2

2 *syn* see FULSOME

ointment *n* a semisolid medicinal or cosmetic preparation for ap-plication to the skin < put *ointment* on the burned skin >

syn balm, cerate, chrism, cream, salve, unction, unguent

rel embrocation, liniment; demulcent, emollient; lotion; dressing

OK (*or* **okay**) *adv* *syn* see YES 1

OK (*or* **okay**) *vb* *syn* see APPROVE 2

OK (*or* **okay**) *n* *syn* see APPROBATION

‖**okeydoke** *adv* *syn* see YES 1

old *adj* **1** *syn* see ANCIENT 1

con contemporary, current, recent; advanced

ant new

2 of long standing < the ending of such an *old* friendship was tragic >

syn continuing, enduring, inveterate, lifelong, long-lasting, long-lived, perennial; *compare* LASTING

rel constant, perpetual, staying; established, firm, solid, steady

con newfound, recent; brief, short-lived; casual, temporary, transitory, weak

ant new

3 *syn* see OLD-FASHIONED

rel primitive; traditional

con newish

ant modern, new

4 *syn* see AGED 1

idiom along in years, getting on

con juvenile, young

ant youthful

5 *syn* see EXPERIENCED

con young

ant new

6 *syn* see FORMER 2

old age *n* the final stage of the normal life span < spent his *old age* in a nursing home >

syn age, caducity, elderliness, senectitude, senescence, years; *compare* DOTAGE

rel decrepitude, feebleness; infirmity

idiom advanced years, declining years, winter of life

ant youth

olden *adj* **1** *syn* see ANCIENT 1

2 *syn* see AGED 1

oldest profession *n* *syn* see PROSTITUTION

oldfangled *adj* *syn* see OLD-FASHIONED

ant newfangled

old–fashioned *adj* typical of an earlier time and often replaced by something more modern or fashionable < *old-fashioned* high-buttoned shoes >

syn antiquated, antique, archaic, belated, bygone, dated, démodé, demoded, dowdy, fusty, moldy, moth-eaten, neander-thal, old, oldfangled, old hat, old-time, old-timey, outdated, out-moded, out-of-date, passé, rococo, unmodern, vintage

rel aged, ancient; discarded, disused, obsolete; outworn, unfash-ionable; crusty, fogyish, fuddy-duddy, fusty, moss-backed, moss-grown, mossy, stodgy; Victorian; old-line

con modernistic, modish, newfangled, stylish, ‖trendy; current, recent, timely; new-fashioned, up-to-date, up-to-the-minute

ant contemporary; modern

Old Gooseberry *n* *syn* see DEVIL 1

Old Guard *n* *syn* see ESTABLISHMENT 2

old hand *n* *syn* see VETERAN

old hat *adj* **1** *syn* see OLD-FASHIONED

2 *syn* see TRITE

old lady *n* ‖**1** *syn* see WIFE

‖**2** *syn* see MOTHER 1

---

syn synonym(s)   *rel* related word(s)

ant antonym(s)   *con* contrasted word(s)

idiom idiomatic equivalent(s)

‖ use limited; if in doubt, see a dictionary

3 *syn* see FUSSBUDGET

old–line *adj syn* see CONSERVATIVE 1

old liner *n syn* see DIEHARD 1

old maid *n* **1** *syn* see SPINSTER

    2 *syn* see FUSSBUDGET

old–maidish *adj syn* see NICE 1

‖**old man** *n* **1** *syn* see HUSBAND

    2 *syn* see FATHER 1

Old Nick *n syn* see DEVIL 1

Old Scratch *n syn* see DEVIL 1

oldster *n* a person of advanced years < an *oldster* long retired from the business world >

    syn ancient, elder, golden-ager, old-timer, senior, senior citizen; *compare* BELDAM 1, GAFFER

    ant youngster, youth

old–time *adj* **1** *syn* see OLD-FASHIONED

    2 *syn* see EXPERIENCED

old–timer *n* **1** *syn* see VETERAN

    2 *syn* see OLDSTER

old–timey *adj syn* see OLD-FASHIONED

‖**old woman** *n* **1** *syn* see WIFE

    2 *syn* see MOTHER 1

old–womanish *adj syn* see NICE 1

oleaginous *adj* **1** *syn* see FATTY 2

    2 *syn* see FULSOME

olid *adj syn* see MALODOROUS 1

olio *n syn* see MISCELLANY 1

olla podrida *n syn* see MISCELLANY 1

omen *n syn* see FORETOKEN

omen *vb syn* see AUGUR 2

ominous *adj* indicative of future misfortune or calamity < dark *ominous* clouds preceded the storm >

    syn apocalyptic, baleful, baneful, dire, direful, doomful, fateful, ill-boding, ill-omened, inauspicious, threatening, unlucky, unpropitious; *compare* EVIL 5, SINISTER

    rel portentous; malefic, maleficent, malign, sinister; comminatory, forbidding, grim, lowering, menacing; hostile, inhospitable, unfriendly

    con auspicious, benign, favorable, promising, propitious; beneficial

omission *n* something omitted or missing < several *omissions* in the list >

    syn blank, chasm, overlook, oversight, preterition, pretermission, skip

    rel inadvertence, inadvertency, lapse, slip; break, gap, hiatus, lacuna

    con inclusion; accession, addition, augmentation, increase, reinforcement; superaddition

omit *vb syn* see NEGLECT

omitted *adj syn* see ABSENT 1

    ant included

omnibus *n syn* see ANTHOLOGY

omnipotent *adj* having virtually unlimited authority or influence < an *omnipotent* leader >

    syn all-powerful, almighty

    rel divine, godlike; unlimited, unrestricted

    con impotent, powerless; limited, restricted

omnipresent *adj* present at all places at all times < *omnipresent* God >

    syn allover, ubiquitous, universal

    rel boundless, endless, immeasurable, infinite, limitless, unending

    con bounded, finite, limited, restricted; cramped, straitened; narrow, strait

omnium–gatherum *n syn* see MISCELLANY 1

on *prep* **1** *syn* see OVER 4

    2 *syn* see OVER 3

on *adv syn* see ALONG 1

on–again–off–again *adj syn* see FITFUL

onanism *n syn* see SELF-GRATIFICATION

onanistic *adj syn* see SYBARITIC

once *adv* **1** *syn* see EVER 5

    2 *syn* see BEFORE 2

once *adj syn* see FORMER 2

once and again *adv syn* see SOMETIMES

once more *adv syn* see OVER 7

oncoming *adj syn* see FORTHCOMING

on–dit *n syn* see REPORT 1

one *adj syn* see SINGLE 2

one *vb syn* see JOIN 1

one by one *adv syn* see APART 1

one–horse town *n syn* see BURG

oneness *n* **1** *syn* see UNITY 1

    ant multiplicity

    2 *syn* see UNIQUENESS

    3 *syn* see ENTIRETY 1

    4 *syn* see IDENTITY 1

oner *n syn* see DOLLAR

onerous *adj* imposing great hardship or strain < found the care of his old mother an *onerous* burden >

    syn burdensome, demanding, exacting, exigent, grievous, oppressive, superincumbent, taxing, tough, trying, weighty

    rel arduous, difficult, hard, laborious; heavy, hefty, ponderous; cumbersome, unruly, unwieldy; driving, heavy-handed

    con easy, effortless; facile, light, simple, smooth, unexacting, untaxing

onerously *adv syn* see HARD 8

one–sided *adj syn* see BIASED 2

    rel lopsided, weighted

    con many-sided

one–sidedness *n syn* see PREJUDICE

    con manysidedness

onetime *adj syn* see FORMER 2

onfall *n syn* see ATTACK 1

ongoing *n syn* see ADVANCE 2

    rel development, growth

onlooker *n syn* see SPECTATOR

only *adj* **1** *syn* see ALONE 3

    2 being one or more of which there exist no others < the *only* survivors of the wreck >

    syn alone, lone, singular, sole, solitary, solo, unexampled, unique, unrepeatable

    rel incomparable, inimitable, matchless, peerless, transcendent, unequaled, unparalleled, unrivaled; companionless, separate, unaccompanied, unattended, uncompanied, uncompanioned

    con divers, many, multifarious, numerous, sundry, various

    3 *syn* see SINGLE 2

only *adv* **1** to the exclusion of any alternative or competitor < he will confess *only* to you >

    syn alone, but, entirely, exclusively, solely

    2 *syn* see JUST 3

only *conj* in spite of which < it looks delicious, *only* I'm not hungry >

    syn but, except, however, save, yet

on occasion *adv syn* see OCCASIONALLY

on offer *adj syn* see PURCHASABLE 1

onomatopoeic *adj* formed in imitation of a natural sound < *buzz* is an *onomatopoeic* word to describe the sound of bees >

    syn echoic, imitative, onomatopoetic

    rel emulative, simulative; mimetic, mimic, mimical

onomatopoetic *adj syn* see ONOMATOPOEIC

on purpose *adv syn* see INTENTIONALLY

onset *n* **1** *syn* see ATTACK 1

    2 *syn* see BEGINNING

onslaught *n syn* see ATTACK 1

on the whole *adv syn* see ALTOGETHER 3

onus *n* **1** *syn* see LOAD 3

    2 *syn* see BLAME

    3 *syn* see STIGMA

onward *adv* **1** *syn* see AHEAD 2

    2 *syn* see ALONG 1

onyx *adj syn* see BLACK 1

oodles *n pl but sometimes sing in constr syn* see SCAD

‖**ooftish** *n syn* see MONEY

‖**oofy** *adj syn* see RICH 1

ooid *adj syn* see OVAL

oomph *n syn* see SPIRIT 5

ooze *vb syn* see EXUDE

oozy *adj syn* see MUDDY 1

opaque *adj syn* see OBSCURE 3

    ant transparent, transpicuous

ope *vb syn* see OPEN 1

open *adj* **1** not closed or obstructed < escaped through the *open* gate >

    syn patent, unclosed, unobstructed

rel agape, dehiscent, gaping, patulous, ringent, wide, yawning; ajar; unbarred, unbolted, unfastened, unlocked, unsealed; clear, unimpeded

con blocked, obstructed; constricted, cramped, narrow, strait

ant closed, shut

2 lacking a cover or covering <an *open* wound that continued to ooze blood> <his chest *open* to the sun>

syn bare, denuded, exposed, naked, peeled, stripped, uncovered

3 *syn* see LIABLE 2

ant closed

4 not restricted to a particular group or situation <favored *open* enrollment in the schools>

syn accessible, open-door, public, unrestricted

rel attainable, available, obtainable, reachable, securable

idiom to be had, within reach

con limited, restricted; inaccessible, private

ant closed

5 available for use or consideration or decision <there are only two courses *open* to us>

syn accessible, employable, operative, practicable, usable

rel appropriate, fit, proper, suitable; acceptable, agreeable, pleasing

idiom within reach

con inaccessible, inoperative, unusable

ant closed

6 *syn* see DOUBTFUL 1

7 *syn* see FRANK

ant close; clandestine

open *vb* **1** to change from a closed to an open condition <*open* the window>

syn ope, unblock, unclose, undo, unshut, unstop

rel clear, free, release; bare, disclose, expose, reveal

idiom lay open, swing open, throw open

con block, occlude, stop

ant close, shut

2 to make physically or mentally visible <dawn *opened* a surprising scene to his startled eyes>

syn disclose, display, expose, reveal, unclothe, uncover, unveil

rel adumbrate, hint, shadow, suggest

idiom bring to light, bring to (*or* into) view, lay bare, make plain, show forth

con cloak, conceal, hide, screen, secrete, shroud

3 to make an opening in <decided to *open* a can of beans>

syn breach, disrupt, hole, rupture

rel break, broach, tap, undo; cut, gash, slash; perforate, pierce

idiom lay open

con occlude, shut; fasten, secure

ant close

4 to spread out <the falcon slowly *opened* her mighty wings>

syn expand, extend, fan (out), outspread, outstretch, spread, unfold

rel billow, dilate, distend, swell; cover, mantle, overspread

con collect, concentrate, contract, gather (in)

ant close

5 *syn* see BEGIN 1

ant close

6 *syn* see CONVENE 1

open *n syn* see OUTDOORS

open air *n syn* see OUTDOORS

open–air *adj syn* see OUTDOOR

con indoor, inside; enclosed

open–and–shut *adj syn* see CLEAR 5

open–door *adj syn* see OPEN 4

open–eyed *adj syn* see WATCHFUL

openhanded *adj* **1** *syn* see LIBERAL 1

ant closefisted, tightfisted

2 *syn* see CLEAR 5

openhearted *adj syn* see FRANK

opening *n* **1** *syn* see BEGINNING

ant closing

2 *syn* see APERTURE

3 *syn* see GAP 1

4 *syn* see OPPORTUNITY

opening gun *n syn* see BEGINNING

openmouthed *adj syn* see VOCIFEROUS

openness *n syn* see EXPOSURE

open sesame *n syn* see PASSPORT

open up *vb syn* see OPERATE 2

opera omnia *n syn* see OEUVRE

operate *vb* **1** *syn* see ACT 5

2 to perform surgery <*operated* on him to remove a brain tumor>

syn cut, open up

3 to cause to function <knew how to *operate* earth-moving equipment>

syn handle, run, use, work

rel play; manage, maneuver; drive, pilot, steer; ply, wield

idiom make go

4 *syn* see CONDUCT 3

operation *n* **1** *syn* see EXERCISE 1

2 *syn* see USE 1

operative *adj* **1** *syn* see ACTIVE 1

ant inoperative

2 *syn* see OPEN 5

operative *n* **1** *syn* see WORKER

2 *syn* see PRIVATE DETECTIVE

operator *n syn* see MOTORIST

operose *adj* **1** *syn* see HARD 6

2 *syn* see ASSIDUOUS

opiate *adj syn* see SOPORIFIC 1

opiate *n* **1** *syn* see DRUG 2

2 *syn* see ANODYNE 2

opine *vb* to form or express an opinion <he *opined* that the story was true>

syn ‖opinion, opinionate

rel accept, believe, consider, hold, judge, regard, think, view; speculate

con deny, disclaim, disown, reject, repudiate; disbelieve, discredit, doubt

opinion *n* an idea or judgment held as true or valid <seek an expert *opinion* on the authenticity of the painting>

syn belief, conviction, eye, feeling, mind, persuasion, sentiment, view

rel attitude, impression, notion, think, thought; conclusion, estimate, estimation, judgment, reaction; assumption, conjecture, speculation, supposition, theory

idiom point of view

con disbelief, discredit, doubt, unbelief; distrust, mistrust, questioning, skepticism

‖**opinion** *vb syn* see OPINE

opinionate *vb syn* see OPINE

opponent *n* one who expresses or manifests opposition <his *opponent* in the debate>

syn adversary, antagonist, anti, con, match, opposer, oppugnant

rel enemy, foe; competitor, rival; assailant, combatant; counteragent

con ally, colleague, comrade, confederate, partner; advocate, champion

ant exponent, pro, proponent

opportune *adj syn* see TIMELY 1

rel appropriate, felicitous, happy

ant inopportune

opportunity *n* a state of affairs or combination of circumstances favorable to some end <all he asked was an *opportunity* to show what he could do>

syn break, chance, look-in, occasion, opening, shot, show, squeak, time

rel room, space; leisure, liberty; relief, spell, turn; juncture, pass; dog's chance, hope, prayer

oppose *vb* **1** to place over against something to provide resistance or counterbalance <*oppose* one military force to another>

syn counter, match, pit, play (off), vie

rel array, confront, face

idiom set over against

2 *syn* see RESIST

opposed *adj syn* see ADVERSE 1

opposer *n syn* see OPPONENT

opposing *adj syn* see ADVERSE 1

opposite *n* something that is exactly opposed or contrary <virtue and vice are *opposites*>

---

syn synonym(s)   *rel* related word(s)
ant antonym(s)   *con* contrasted word(s)
idiom idiomatic equivalent(s)
‖ use limited; if in doubt, see a dictionary

syn antipode, antipole, antithesis, contra, contradictory, contrary, converse, counter, counterpole, reverse

rel contrast, counterpoint, foil; contrapositive, inverse, obverse; antonym

idiom the other extreme, the other side of the coin

con analogon, analogue, counterpart, like, parallel, similar; equal, equivalent; correlate, correlative; carbon copy, duplicate, replica

ant same

opposite *adj* being so far apart as to be or to seem irreconcilable < held *opposite* views on the solution of the problem >
syn antipodal, antipodean, antithetical, contradictory, contrary, converse, counter, diametric, polar, reverse
rel contrasting; contrapositive, inverse, obverse; antonymous; different, dissimilar, divergent, opposed, unalike, unlike, unsimilar; independent, separate, unconnected, unrelated
con alike, analogous, equivalent, like, parallel, similar; equal; correlative
ant same

opposite *prep syn* see TO 6

oppositely *adv syn* see AGAIN 5

opposite number *n* one holding an equivalent or parallel position < the Secretary of State and his *opposite number*, the Foreign Minister >
syn coordinate, counterpart, vis-à-vis; *compare* EQUAL
rel complement, cousin, equal, equivalent, like, match, tally

opposition *n syn* see ANTAGONISM 2

opposure *n syn* see ANTAGONISM 2

oppress *vb* 1 *syn* see WRONG
rel harass, harry; afflict, torment, torture; conquer, overcome, overthrow, subjugate
2 *syn* see DEPRESS 2
rel burden, distress, trouble

oppressive *adj* 1 *syn* see ONEROUS
ant unoppressive
2 *syn* see GLOOMY 3

oppressor *n syn* see TYRANT

opprobriate *vb syn* see DECRY 2

opprobrious *adj* 1 *syn* see ABUSIVE
2 *syn* see INFAMOUS 1

opprobrium *n syn* see DISGRACE
rel abuse, scurrility, vituperation
con credit, prestige

oppugn *vb syn* see CONTEND 1

oppugnant *adj syn* see ADVERSE 1

oppugnant *n syn* see OPPONENT

opt (for) *vb syn* see CHOOSE 1

optate *vb syn* see CHOOSE 1

optic *adj syn* see VISUAL 1

optical *adj syn* see VISUAL 1

optimacy *n syn* see ARISTOCRACY

optimism *n* an inclination to put the most favorable construction on actions and events or to anticipate the best possible outcome < was a practitioner of *optimism* in his everyday life >
syn Pollyannaism, rose-colored spectacles, sanguineness, sanguinity
rel brightness, buoyancy, happiness; idealism, positivism
con hopelessness; despair, gloom, melancholy; malism; defeatism, fatalism; cynicism
ant pessimism

optimist *n* one given to optimism < was a jaunty *optimist* >
syn hoper, Pollyanna
rel dreamer, idealist, positivist
con defeatist, fatalist; cynic, doubter, skeptic
ant pessimist

optimistic *adj* anticipating only the best to happen and minimizing all other possibilities < was *optimistic* about book sales that year >
syn fond, Pollyannaish, sanguine, upbeat; *compare* HOPEFUL 1
rel bright, cheerful, merry, sunny; hopeful, hoping; assured, confident
idiom feeling on top of the world, looking on the bright side, riding (*or* sitting) on cloud nine
con cynical; doubtful, uncertain
ant pessimistic

option *n syn* see CHOICE 1
rel prerogative, privilege, right

optional *adj* not compulsory < attendance at the meeting is *optional* >

syn discretionary, elective, facultative, nonobligatory
rel free, voluntary; alternative
con demanded, imperative; enforced, involuntary; essential, necessary
ant compulsory, mandatory, obligatory, required

opulent *adj* 1 *syn* see RICH 1
rel lavish, prodigal, profuse; extravagant, ostentatious, pretentious, showy; plush, swank
con modest, simple, unpretentious
2 *syn* see LUXURIOUS 3
3 *syn* see PROFUSE

oracle *n syn* see REVELATION

oracular *adj syn* see PROPHETIC

oral *adj* 1 *syn* see VOCAL 1
2 expressed or transmitted vocally < stories of folk heroes kept alive in *oral* tradition >
syn spoken, traditional, unwritten, verbal, word-of-mouth
rel narrated, recounted, related, told
con chronicled, recorded, written, written down

orate *vb* to talk in a declamatory, grandiloquent, or impassioned manner < *orated* to the crowd about the flag and patriotism >
syn bloviate, declaim, harangue, mouth, perorate, rant, rave, soapbox
rel elocute; bombast, rodomontade, sermonize, speechify; blah=blah

oratorical *adj syn* see RHETORICAL

oratory *n* the art of speaking in public eloquently and effectively < a politician who was a master at *oratory* >
syn elocution, rhetoric, speechcraft

orb *n* 1 *syn* see BALL
2 *syn* see EYE 1

orbit *n syn* see RANGE 2

orchestra *n* a usually large group of musicians who perform together < a string *orchestra* played at the reception >
syn band, philharmonic, symphony
rel combo, ensemble

orchestrate *vb syn* see HARMONIZE 4

orchidaceous *adj syn* see SHOWY

orchids *n pl syn* see COMPLIMENT 1

ordain *vb* 1 *syn* see CONDUCT 3
2 *syn* see DICTATE

ordeal *n syn* see TRIAL 1

order *n* 1 *syn* see ASSOCIATION 2
2 *syn* see TYPE
rel bracket, branch, pigeonhole, set; estate, grade, rank, status
3 sequential occurrence in space or time < changed the *order* of the books on the shelf >
syn arrangement, disposal, disposition, distribution, ordering, sequence
rel array, arrayal, collocation; allocation, allotment, apportionment, arrayment, proration
con disarrangement, disordering; chaos, confusion, disorder, mix-up, muddle
4 general or approximate size or amount < a loss on the *order* of seven million dollars >
syn extent, magnitude, matter, neighborhood, range, tune, vicinity
rel approach, approximation, closeness, nearness, proximity
5 manner of being arranged in space or of occurring in time < tell everything in the *order* in which it happened >
syn consecution, procession, sequence, succession
rel consecutiveness, following, successiveness; chain, progression, series, train
6 *syn* see SUCCESSION 2
7 orderly conduct < about to call the meeting to *order* when the interruption occurred >
syn correctitude, correctness, decorousness, decorum, orderliness, properness, propriety, seemliness
rel goodness, niceness, rightness; fitness, suitability; integrity, probity, rectitude, uprightness
con impropriety, indecorousness, indecorum, unseemliness
ant disorder
8 orderly arrangement or disposition < troubled by the lack of *order* in their daily lives >
syn method, orderliness, pattern, plan, system
con anarchy, chaos, confusion, muddle, ‖snafu
ant disorder
9 state with respect to quality, functioning, or status < the equipment was in very poor *order* >

syn case, condition, estate, repair, shape
rel fettle, fitness, kilter, trim
10 a state of soundness <had his car put in *order* for spring>
syn condition, fettle, fitness, kilter, repair, shape, trim
rel adjustment, amendment, correction, gear, rectification
idiom working order
con disrepair
11 the state of being appropriate to or required by the circumstances <that remark is definitely out of *order* >
syn appositeness, appropriateness, aptness, expediency, fitness, meetness, propriety, rightness, suitability, suitableness
rel opportuneness, seasonableness, timeliness; auspiciousness, favorableness; felicity, grace
con inappropriateness, unfitness, unsuitability, unsuitableness
12 *syn* see COMMAND 1
rel authorization, permission
order *vb* **1** to bring about an orderly disposition of individuals, units, or elements <*ordered* his affairs in preparation for marriage>
syn arrange, array, dispose, marshal, methodize, organize, systematize
rel adjust, fix, regulate, right; align, line, line up, range; classify, codify, hierarchize; regiment, routine, routinize; streamline
idiom put (*or* set) in order, put in shape, put (*or* set) to rights, reduce to order, whip into shape (*or* order)
ant disorder
2 *syn* see COMMAND
ordering *n syn* see ORDER 3
orderliness *n* **1 *syn*** see ORDER 7
ant disorderliness
2 *syn* see ORDER 8
ant disorderliness
orderly *adj* **1** following a set arrangement, design, or pattern <work out an *orderly* procedure and stick to it> <an *orderly* row of houses surrounded the village green>
syn methodic, methodical, regular, systematic
rel accurate, correct, exact, precise; alike, uniform; businesslike; conventional, formal
idiom in apple-pie order
con haphazard, irregular, unmethodical, unsystematic; careless, casual, free and easy
ant chaotic, disorderly
2 *syn* see NEAT 2
rel picked up
ant disordered; disorderly
order up *vb syn* see CALL UP
ordinance *n syn* see LAW 1
ordinarily *adv syn* see USUALLY 2
ordinary *adj* **1** of the customary or common type encountered in the normal course of events <*ordinary* traffic had been stopped to let the marchers pass>
syn everyday, plain, plain Jane, quotidian, routine, unremarkable, usual, workaday
rel commonplace, natural, normal, regular; customary, familiar, frequent
con infrequent, rare, uncommon; accidental, casual, chance, fortuitous
ant extraordinary
2 *syn* see COMMON 6
organ *n* **1 *syn*** see MEAN 2
2 *syn* see JOURNAL
organize *vb* **1 *syn*** see FOUND 2
rel construct, put together
2 *syn* see ORDER 1
rel coordinate, integrate
3 *syn* see MOBILIZE 3
||**organized** *adj syn* see INTOXICATED 1
orgulous *adj syn* see PROUD 1
orgy *n* **1 *syn*** see BINGE 1
2 an act or occasion of excessive indulgence in sex <the house detective investigated an *orgy* in the penthouse suite>
syn bacchanal, bacchanalia, debauch, party, saturnalia
3 *syn* see SPREE 1
orifice *n syn* see APERTURE
oriflamme *n syn* see FLAG
origin *n* **1 *syn*** see ANCESTRY
rel maternity, parentage, paternity
2 *syn* see SOURCE

original *n* **1** a first form from which copies or reproductions can be produced <students copying the da Vinci *original* >
syn archetype, protoplast, prototype
rel forerunner, mother, precursor; model, pattern; precedent
con dummy, imitation, simulacrum; counterfeit, fake, forgery
ant copy, reproduction
2 *syn* see INNOVATOR
3 *syn* see ECCENTRIC
original *adj* **1 *syn*** see FIRST 2
rel archetypal, prototypal
2 *syn* see PRIMARY 5
3 *syn* see INVENTIVE
con banal, trite; derivative, initative
ant unoriginal
originally *adv syn* see INITIALLY 1
originate *vb* **1 *syn*** see GENERATE 1
2 *syn* see INTRODUCE 3
3 *syn* see SPRING 1
4 *syn* see BEGIN 2
5 to have one's origin or home base in <he *originates* from Ohio>
syn come (from), hail (from)
rel derive (from), spring (from), stem (from)
originative *adj syn* see INVENTIVE
ant unoriginative
originator *n* **1 *syn*** see FATHER 2
2 *syn* see INNOVATOR
orison *n syn* see PRAYER
ornament *vb syn* see ADORN
rel enrich; embroider
ornate *adj* elaborately and often pretentiously decorated or designed <a very *ornate* room—all marble, gilt, and brocade>
syn baroque, flamboyant, florid, luscious, rich, rococo
rel elaborate, high-wrought, resplendent; labored, overdone, overelaborated, overembellished, overworked, overwrought; luxuriant, luxurious, opulent, sumptuous; aureate, gilded
con natural, plain, quiet, simple; severe, unembellished, unornamented, unostentatious, unpretentious; restrained, subdued
ant austere; chaste
ornery *adj* ||**1 *syn*** see CHEAP 2
2 *syn* see CANTANKEROUS
3 *syn* see CONTRARY 3
orotund *adj* **1 *syn*** see RESONANT
rel loud, stentorian
2 *syn* see RHETORICAL
orphan *adj* deprived by death of one and usually both parents <seeking homes for the countless *orphan* children from the disaster area>
syn orphaned, parentless, unparented
rel alone, solitary; abandoned, cast-off, forsaken, lost; disregarded, ignored, neglected, slighted
orphaned *adj syn* see ORPHAN
orphic *adj syn* see RECONDITE
orthodox *adj* **1** conforming to doctrines or practices that are held to be right or true by an authority, standard, or tradition <those who still hold an *orthodox* view about evolution>
syn accepted, authoritative, canonical, received, sanctioned, sound
rel acknowledged, admitted, approved; customary, official, recognized, standard, traditional; correct, proper, right
con heretical, heterodox, unauthoritative, uncanonical
ant unorthodox
2 *syn* see CONVENTIONAL 1
3 *syn* see CONSERVATIVE 1
ant unorthodox
oscillate *vb syn* see SWING 2
osculate *vb syn* see KISS 1
ostend *vb syn* see SHOW 2
ostensible *adj* **1 *syn*** see APPARENT 2
2 *syn* see ALLEGED
ostensibly *adv* to all outward appearances <*ostensibly* it was a business trip but actually it was all pleasure>

---

syn apparently, evidently, officially, outwardly, professedly, seemingly
rel externally, superficially; sensibly
idiom on the face of it, on the surface, to the eye
con genuinely, really, truly; au fond, basically

ostentatious *adj syn* see SHOWY
ant unostentatious

ostracism *n syn* see EXILE 1

ostracize *vb* 1 *syn* see BANISH
con accept, entertain, receive, welcome; harbor, haven, refuge, shelter
2 *syn* see CUT 7

other *adj* 1 *syn* see DIFFERENT 1
2 *syn* see ADDITIONAL

‖**othergates** *adv syn* see OTHERWISE 1

other half *n syn* see RABBLE 2

otherness *n syn* see DISSIMILARITY

‖**otherways** *adv syn* see OTHERWISE 2

‖**otherwhile** *adv syn* see SOMETIMES

otherwise *adv* 1 in a different way or manner <he could not act *otherwise* >
syn differently, diversely, ‖othergates, variously
ant likewise
2 under different conditions <might *otherwise* have left >
syn else, ‖elseways, elsewise, ‖otherways

otherwise *adj syn* see DIFFERENT 1

otherworld *n syn* see HEREAFTER 2

otherworldly *adj* 1 of or relating to a world other than the actual world <believed in the existence of *otherworldly* phenomena >
syn transcendental, transmundane
rel exterrestrial, extramundane, extraterrestrial; unearthly, unworldly
2 *syn* see DREAMY 1

otiose *adj syn* see VAIN 1
rel purposeless, useless; inexcusable; superfluous, supernumerary, surplus

oubliette *n syn* see DUNGEON

ought *vb syn* see WANT 3

ought *n syn* see OBLIGATION 2

ounce *n syn* see PARTICLE

oust *vb* 1 *syn* see DEPRIVE 2
2 *syn* see BANISH

out *adv syn* see OUTDOORS

out *vb* 1 *syn* see EJECT 1
2 *syn* see EXTINGUISH 1
3 *syn* see GET OUT 2

out *n syn* see SHOWING 1

out and away *adv syn* see FAR AND AWAY

out–and–out *adj syn* see UTTER

‖**outback** *n syn* see FRONTIER 2

outbalance *vb syn* see OUTWEIGH 1

outbloom *vb syn* see BLOSSOM

outbreak *n* 1 a sudden or violent beginning of activity <an *outbreak* of new housing starts >
syn burst, eruption, flare, outburst; *compare* EPIDEMIC
rel beginning, commencement, dawn, onset, outset
2 *syn* see EPIDEMIC

outbreathe *vb syn* see EXHALE

outburst *n* 1 a violent expression of emotion <an *outburst* of anger >
syn access, burst, eruption, explosion, flare-up, gust, sally
rel scene, storm, tantrum; frenzy, rapture, transport(s)
2 *syn* see OUTBREAK 1

outcast *n* one who is cast out by society <a political *outcast* >
syn castaway, derelict, Ishmael, Ishmaelite, leper, offscouring, pariah, untouchable
rel hobo, tramp, vagabond, vagrant; displaced person; exile, expatriate; reprobate
con big name, bigwig, celebrity, lion, luminary, name, notable, personage, somebody

outcome *n syn* see EFFECT 1

outcomer *n syn* see STRANGER

out–country *adj syn* see RURAL

outcrier *n syn* see PEDDLER

outcry *n syn* see COMMOTION 1

outdare *vb syn* see FACE 3

outdate *vb* to make obsolete or out-of-date <the automobile *outdated* the horse and buggy >

syn antiquate, obsolesce, obsolete, outmode, superannuate
rel age, date, fossilize; replace, supersede

outdated *adj syn* see OLD-FASHIONED
ant up-to-the-minute

outdistance *vb syn* see OUTSTRIP 1

outdo *vb* 1 *syn* see SURPASS 1
idiom out-Herod Herod, steal (*or* get) a march on
2 *syn* see DEFEAT 2

outdoor *adj* taking place, done, or existing in the open air <an *outdoor* restaurant >
syn alfresco, hypaethral, open-air, out-of-door, outside
ant indoor, inside

outdoors *adv* in or into the open air <went *outdoors* for some fresh air >
syn out, out of doors, outside, without, withoutdoors
ant indoors, inside, withindoors

outdoors *n pl but sing in constr* the space where air is unconfined <every night he let the dog run in the *outdoors* >
syn open, open air, out-of-doors, outside, without
idiom God's good (*or* green) earth

outer *adj* being or located outside something <the sheep's thick *outer* coat of wool >
syn exterior, external, outside, outward, over
rel extraneous, extrinsic, superficial, surface; outlying, remote
con inside, interior, internal, inward
ant inner

outermost *adj syn* see EXTREME 5
ant inmost, innermost

outface *vb syn* see FACE 3

outfit *n* 1 *syn* see EQUIPMENT
2 *syn* see COSTUME
3 *syn* see COMPANY 4
4 *syn* see ENTERPRISE 3

outfit *vb syn* see FURNISH 1

outfox *vb syn* see OUTWIT

outgeneral *vb syn* see OUTWIT
rel outfight, outflank, outgame
idiom steal a march

outgo *vb syn* see SURPASS 1

outgoing *adj syn* see DEMONSTRATIVE
ant aloof

outgrowth *n* 1 a projecting part of an organism <a warty *outgrowth* on the skin >
syn excrescence, excrescency, process, processus
rel enlargement, prolongation, swelling; offshoot, shoot
2 something that develops or grows directly out of something else <the new TV series was an *outgrowth* of a popular play >
syn by-product, derivative, descendant, offshoot, spin-off
rel branch, member; child, offspring, product; aftereffect, consequence, effect, issue, outcome, result
con origin, root, source; antecedent, cause, determinant

outhouse *n syn* see PRIVY 1

outing *n syn* see EXCURSION 1

outjockey *vb syn* see OUTWIT

outland *adj syn* see RURAL

outlander *n syn* see STRANGER

outlandish *adj* 1 *syn* see BARBARIC 1
rel foreign, strange
2 *syn* see STRANGE 4
rel monstrous; outré
con commonplace, everyday
3 marked by sharp departure from the traditional or usual <men who wear beads, feathers, and other *outlandish* gear >
syn far-out, kinky, outré, ultra; *compare* EXTREME 3
rel bizarre, extravagant, outrageous, wild; unconventional, unorthodox
con conservative, conventional; compliant, conformable; moderate
4 *syn* see BACK 1

outlast *vb syn* see OUTLIVE

outlaw *n* a criminal of the American western frontier <*outlaws* held up stagecoaches >
syn badman, ‖bandido, bandit, desperado
rel gunman, gunslinger
idiom bad guy

outlaw *vb syn* see FORBID

outlay *vb syn* see SPEND 1

outlay *n syn* see EXPENSE 1

outlet *n* **1** *syn* see APERTURE
 2 *syn* see EGRESS 2
 rel escape; release
 3 *syn* see STORE 4
outline *n* the line that gives form or shape to a body or a figure <saw only a dark *outline* of the house through the gloom>
 syn contour, delineation, figuration, line, lineament, lineation, profile, silhouette
 rel configuration, conformation, figure, form, shape; skyline
 con bulk, hulk, mass
outline *vb* **1** *syn* see BORDER 1
 2 *syn* see SKETCH
outlive *vb* to remain in existence longer than <the committee has *outlived* its usefulness>
 syn outlast, outwear, survive
 rel outstand, outstay
outlook *n* **1** *syn* see LOOKOUT 2
 2 *syn* see VISTA
 3 *syn* see VIEW 4
 4 *syn* see VIEWPOINT 2
outlying *adj* *syn* see DISTANT 1
outmaneuver *vb* *syn* see OUTWIT
 idiom steal a march (on)
outmatch *vb* *syn* see SURPASS 1
outmode *vb* *syn* see OUTDATE
outmoded *adj* **1** *syn* see OLD-FASHIONED
 2 *syn* see OBSOLETE
 3 *syn* see TACKY 2
outmost *adj* *syn* see EXTREME 5
 ant inmost, innermost
out–of–date *adj* **1** *syn* see OLD-FASHIONED
 ant up-to-date
 2 *syn* see TACKY 2
out–of–door *adj* *syn* see OUTDOOR
out–of–doors *n pl but sing in constr* *syn* see OUTDOORS
out of doors *adv* *syn* see OUTDOORS
out–of–the–way *adj* *syn* see OBSCURE 2
outpace *vb* *syn* see OUTSTRIP 1
outplace *vb* *syn* see REPLACE 3
output *n* the amount of something produced <an annual *output* of 3,000,000 units>
 syn outturn, product, production, turnout, yield
 rel gain, get, profit, take; crop, harvest
 con input; raw material
outrage *n* *syn* see INJURY 1
outrage *vb* **1** *syn* see RAPE
 2 *syn* see ABUSE 4
 3 *syn* see WRONG
 4 *syn* see OFFEND 3
outrageous *adj* **1** exceeding the limits of what is normal or tolerable <*outrageous* prices that threaten our way of life>
 syn barbarous, unchristian, uncivilized, unconscionable, ungodly, unholy, wicked
 rel abominable, awful, beastly, dreadful, ghastly, horrible, horrid, impossible, intolerable, terrible, unreasonable; scandalous, shocking
 con normal, reasonable, tolerable; acceptable, bearable, endurable, supportable
 2 enormously or flagrantly bad or horrible <*outrageous* treatment of prisoners>
 syn atrocious, crying, desperate, heinous, monstrous, scandalous, shocking
 rel enormous, flagrant, gross; egregious, nefarious, notorious, villainous
 con condonable, excusable, forgivable, pardonable; defensible, justifiable; legitimate, reasonable; comprehensible, plausible, understandable
outrank *vb* *syn* see PRECEDE 1
outré *adj* *syn* see OUTLANDISH 3
outreach *vb* *syn* see OUTWIT
outrecuidance *n* *syn* see CONCEIT 2
outrider *n* *syn* see FORERUNNER 1
outright *adj* **1** *syn* see UTTER
 2 *syn* see WHOLE 4
outrun *vb* *syn* see OUTSTRIP 1
outset *n* *syn* see BEGINNING
outshine *vb* *syn* see SURPASS 1
outside *n* *syn* see OUTDOORS

outside *adj* **1** *syn* see OUTER
 rel alien, foreign
 ant inside
 2 *syn* see OUTDOOR
 3 *syn* see MAXIMUM
 4 *syn* see REMOTE 4
outside *adv* *syn* see OUTDOORS
outside *prep* **1** *syn* see BEYOND 1
 2 *syn* see EXCEPT
outside of *prep* *syn* see EXCEPT
outsider *n* *syn* see STRANGER
 con insider
outskirt *n usu* **outskirts** *pl* *syn* see ENVIRONS 2
outslick *vb* *syn* see OUTWIT
outsmart *vb* *syn* see OUTWIT
outspeed *vb* *syn* see OUTSTRIP 1
outspoken *adj* speaking without fear or reserve <quite *outspoken* in her views on child rearing>
 syn free, free-spoken, round, vocal
 rel candid, direct, forthright, frank, open, plain, plainspoken, straightforward, unreticent; bluff, blunt; explicit, point-blank, unequivocal; strident
 con reserved, restrained, reticent; private, retiring, shrinking; unassertive
outspread *vb* *syn* see OPEN 4
 ant folded (*of wings or a fan*)
outstanding *adj* **1** *syn* see UNPAID 2
 2 *syn* see NOTICEABLE
 3 *syn* see CHIEF 2
 4 *syn* see SUPERB 3
outstare *vb* *syn* see STARE DOWN
outstart *n* *syn* see BEGINNING
outstep *vb* *syn* see EXCEED 1
outstretch *vb* *syn* see OPEN 4
outstrip *vb* **1** to go faster than <could *outstrip* even the fastest horse>
 syn distance, outdistance, outpace, outrun, outspeed
 rel outfly, outsoar, outwing; outfoot, outrace, outride; outsail; outtravel; lose, shake off
 con follow, trail; drag, hang back, lag
 2 *syn* see SURPASS 1
outsweepings *n pl* *syn* see REFUSE
outthink *vb* *syn* see OUTWIT
outthrust *n* *syn* see PROJECTION 1
outtire *vb* *syn* see EXHAUST 4
outturn *n* *syn* see OUTPUT
outward *adj* *syn* see OUTER
 ant inward
outwardly *adv* *syn* see OSTENSIBLY
 ant inwardly
outwear *vb* **1** *syn* see EXHAUST 4
 2 *syn* see OUTLIVE
 rel endure, hold up
outweigh *vb* **1** to exceed in weight, value, or importance <her brother *outweighed* her by nearly fifty pounds> <the facts *outweigh* his argument>
 syn outbalance, overbalance, overweigh, overweight
 rel overbear
 2 *syn* see COMPENSATE 1
outweighing *adj* *syn* see DOMINANT 1
outwit *vb* to defeat or get the better of by superior cleverness or ingenuity <*outwitted* the enemy by taking a different route>
 syn have, outfox, outgeneral, outjockey, outmaneuver, outreach, outslick, outsmart, outthink, overreach, undo; *compare* FRUSTRATE 1
 rel bamboozle, befool, dupe, gull, hoax, hoodwink, outtrick, outtrump, trick; outdo; outguess
outworn *adj* *syn* see OBSOLETE
oval *adj* having the shape of a longitudinal section of an egg <an *oval* pond>
 syn ooid, ovate, oviform, ovoid
 rel ovaloid; ellipsoidal, elliptic
ovate *adj* *syn* see OVAL

---

syn synonym(s)
ant antonym(s)
idiom idiomatic equivalent(s)
|| use limited; if in doubt, see a dictionary

rel related word(s)
con contrasted word(s)

over *adv* **1** from one point to another across intervening space <sailed *over* to the island>
  syn across, athwart, beyond, transversely
  2 syn see AWAY 2
  3 syn see EVER 6
  4 at a higher point <the plane was directly *over*>
  syn above, aloft, overhead
  idiom on high
  ant under
  5 at or to an end <it's all *over* between them>
  syn by, through
  6 syn see THROUGH 1
  7 yet another time <do the work *over*>
  syn afresh, again, anew, de novo, once more
  idiom over again
over *prep* **1** at a higher level <clouds hung *over* the town>
  syn above, o'er
  ant under
  2 syn see ACROSS
  3 with respect to <children squabbling *over* toys>
  syn about, on, upon, with
  4 so as to make contact with <hit him *over* the head>
  syn on, upon
  5 syn see DURING
  6 as the result of <quarreled *over* money matters>
  syn because of, due to, owing to, through
over *adj* **1 syn** see SUPERIOR 1
  ant under
  2 syn see OUTER
over *vb* **syn** see CLEAR 8
overabounding *adj* **syn** see SUPERABUNDANT
overabundance *n* **syn** see EXCESS 1
overabundant *adj* **syn** see SUPERABUNDANT
overact *vb* to exaggerate in acting especially on the stage or screen <was criticized for *overacting* the part>
  syn overplay
  rel ham, mug; declaim, rant, spout
  idiom chew the scenery
  ant underact, underplay
over against *prep* **1 syn** see AGAINST 1
  2 syn see VERSUS 2
overage *n* **syn** see EXCESS 2
  ant shortage, underage
overall *adv* **1 syn** see EVERYWHERE 1
  2 syn see GENERALLY 1
overall *adj* **syn** see ALL-AROUND 2
over and above *prep* **syn** see BESIDES 1
over and over *adv* **syn** see OFTEN
overbalance *vb* **syn** see OUTWEIGH 1
overbalanced *adj* **syn** see LOPSIDED
overbalancing *adj* **syn** see DOMINANT 1
overbearing *adj* **1 syn** see MASTERFUL 1
  2 syn see DOMINANT 1
  3 syn see PROUD 1
  rel absolute, autocratic, despotic, tyrannical
  con passive, unassertive; acquiescent, compliant, unresisting
  ant subservient
overblown *adj* **1 syn** see FAT 2
  2 syn see INFLATED
  3 syn see RHETORICAL
  4 syn see PRETENTIOUS 3
overbold *adj* **syn** see SHAMELESS
overbrim *vb* **syn** see OVERFLOW 2
overburden *vb* **syn** see OVERLOAD
overcast *vb* **1 syn** see OBSCURE
  2 syn see COVER 3
overcast *adj* clouded over <a gray *overcast* March day>
  syn cloudy, ‖dowly, dull, heavy, lowering (*or* louring), nubilous, overclouded
  rel brooding, dirty, oppressive, sullen
  ant clear, cloudless
overcharge *vb* **1** to charge excessively for service or goods <a clip joint well known for *overcharging* customers>
  syn clip, fleece, skin, soak, stick
  ant undercharge
  2 syn see OVERLOAD
  3 syn see EMBROIDER
overcloud *vb* **syn** see OBSCURE

overclouded *adj* **syn** see OVERCAST
overcome *vb* **1** to get the better of <*overcome* a bad habit>
  syn conquer, down, hurdle, lick, master, surmount, throw; *compare* CONQUER 2
  rel beat, defeat; outlive, prevail
  con adopt, embrace, take up; indulge
  2 syn see CONQUER 2
  3 syn see OVERWHELM 4
  4 syn see WIN 1
overconfident *adj* **syn** see PRESUMPTUOUS
overcritical *adj* **syn** see CRITICAL 1
overdo *vb* to make excessive use or application of <he has *overdone* that joke to the point that it is no longer funny>
  syn overplay, overuse, overwork
  idiom go overboard, go to extremes, run into the ground
overdoing *n* **syn** see EXTRAVAGANCE 2
overdraw *vb* **syn** see EMBROIDER
overdue *adj* **1 syn** see UNPAID 2
  2 syn see TARDY
  ant early
overearly *adj* **syn** see EARLY 2
overemphasize *vb* **syn** see OVERPLAY 2
  ant underemphasize
overesteem *vb* **syn** see OVERVALUE
overestimate *vb* **syn** see OVERVALUE
  ant underestimate
overfill *vb* **syn** see OVERFLOW 2
overflow *vb* **1 syn** see DELUGE 1
  2 to flow over the brim <the river *overflowed* its banks>
  syn overbrim, overfill, overrun, run over, spill, well over
  rel brim, cascade, slop, slosh
  con drop, recede, withdraw
overflow *n* **1 syn** see FLOOD 2
  2 syn see EXCESS 1
overflowing *adj* **1 syn** see ALIVE 5
  2 syn see SUPERABUNDANT
overfull *adv* **syn** see EVER 6
overgrown *adj* covered with growth or herbage <a vacant lot *overgrown* with weeds>
  syn grown, rank
  rel braky, brambly, brushy, copsy, jungly, thicketed, thickety; dense, overrun, thick; lush
‖**overhand** *n* **syn** see ADVANTAGE 3
overhang *vb* **1 syn** see BULGE
  2 syn see HANG 4
overhanging *adj* **syn** see IMMINENT 2
overhaul *vb* **1 syn** see MEND 2
  2 syn see CATCH 7
overhead *adv* **syn** see OVER 4
  ant underfoot
overheated *adj* **syn** see IMPASSIONED
overindulgence *n* **syn** see EXCESS 3
overindulgent *adj* **syn** see EXCESSIVE 2
overkill *n* **syn** see EXCESS 1
overlade *vb* **syn** see OVERLOAD
overlap *vb* to extend over and cover a part of <each course of shingles should *overlap* the preceding course by several inches>
  syn imbricate, lap, overlie, override, ride, shingle
overlay *vb* **syn** see COVER 3
overleap *vb* **1 syn** see CLEAR 8
  2 syn see NEGLECT
overlie *vb* **syn** see OVERLAP
overload *vb* to load to excess <*overload* a ship>
  syn overburden, overcharge, overlade, overtax, overweigh, overweight
  con lighten
overlong *adj* **syn** see LONG 2
overlook *vb* **1 syn** see SURVEY 3
  2 to rise above and afford a view of <the tower *overlooks* the city>
  syn dominate, look down, overtop, tower (above *or* over)
  rel oversee
  3 syn see NEGLECT
  4 syn see SUPERVISE
overlook *n* **1 syn** see OMISSION
  2 syn see LOOKOUT 2
overly *adv* **syn** see EVER 6
overlying *adj* **syn** see SUPERIOR 1

ant underlying
overmuch *n syn* see EXCESS 1
overmuch *adv syn* see EVER 6
overnice *adj syn* see PRECIOUS 4
overpaint *vb syn* see EMBROIDER
overpass *vb syn* see NEGLECT
overpeopled *adj syn* see OVERPOPULATED
 ant underpeopled
overplay *vb* **1** *syn* see OVERACT
 ant underact, underplay
 2 to give undue attention or emphasis to <*overplaying* the ephemeral at the expense of the significant>
 syn magnify, maximize, overemphasize, overstress
 rel accent, accentuate, point up; dramatize, exaggerate, hyperbolize, overdraw, overstate, stretch; overvalue
 idiom lay it on thick
 con downgrade, downplay; minimize
 3 *syn* see OVERDO
overplus *n syn* see EXCESS 1
overpopulated *adj* populated too densely <*overpopulated* cities>
 syn overpeopled
 rel congested, dense, overcrowded
 con empty, vacant, void; unpopulated
 ant underpopulated
overpower *vb* **1** *syn* see CONQUER 1
 2 *syn* see OVERWHELM 4
overpress *vb syn* see PRESSURE
overprize *vb syn* see OVERVALUE
 ant underprize, undervalue
overrate *vb syn* see OVERVALUE
 ant underrate
overreach *vb* **1** *syn* see CHEAT
 2 *syn* see OUTWIT
overreckon *vb syn* see OVERVALUE
overrefined *adj syn* see PRECIOUS 4
override *vb syn* see OVERLAP
overriding *adj syn* see CENTRAL 1
 rel primary, principal
overripe *adj syn* see EFFETE 3
overrule *vb syn* see GOVERN 1
overruling *adj syn* see CENTRAL 1
overrun *vb* **1** *syn* see WHIP 2
 2 *syn* see INVADE 1
 3 *syn* see INFEST 1
 4 *syn* see EXCEED 1
 5 *syn* see OVERFLOW 2
oversea *adj syn* see OVERSEAS
overseas *adv* beyond or across the sea <served *overseas* for two years>
 syn abroad
 con stateside
overseas *adj* situated, originating in, or relating to lands overseas <attempting to tap the potential of *overseas* markets>
 syn oversea, transmarine, ultramarine
 rel alien, exotic, foreign, strange
 con domestic, home; stateside
oversee *vb* **1** *syn* see SURVEY 3
 2 *syn* see SUPERVISE
overset *vb* **1** *syn* see OVERTURN 1
 2 *syn* see OVERTHROW 2
overshadow *vb syn* see OBSCURE
oversight *n* **1** the function or duty of watching or guarding for the sake of proper direction or control <had *oversight* of the children as they played>
 syn care, charge, conduct, handling, intendance, management, running, superintendence, superintendency, supervision
 rel custody, guard, guardianship; keeping, maintenance; surveillance; aegis, tutelage; ciceronage; chaperonage; check, control
 2 *syn* see FAILURE 1
 3 *syn* see OMISSION
oversize *adj syn* see LARGE 1
 ant undersized
overslaugh *vb syn* see HINDER
oversoon *adj syn* see EARLY 2
oversoon *adv syn* see EARLY 2
overspread *vb* **1** *syn* see COVER 3
 2 *syn* see INFEST 1
overstate *vb syn* see EMBROIDER

ant understate
overstatement *n syn* see EXAGGERATION
 ant understatement
overstep *vb syn* see EXCEED 1
 rel infringe, transgress, trespass
overstock *n syn* see EXCESS 2
 ant understock
overstress *vb syn* see OVERPLAY 2
oversupply *n syn* see EXCESS 2
 ant undersupply
overswarm *vb* **1** *syn* see INFEST 1
 2 *syn* see INVADE 1
oversway *vb syn* see INDUCE 1
overtake *vb syn* see CATCH 7
overtax *vb syn* see OVERLOAD
overthrow *vb* **1** *syn* see OVERTURN 1
 2 to cause the downfall of <*overthrow* the government>
 syn overset, overturn, topple, tumble, unhorse; *compare* CONQUER 1
 rel depose, dethrone, oust, remove, unseat; liquidate, purge; conquer, defeat, destroy, ruin
 con create, establish, found, set up
overthrow *n syn* see DEFEAT 1
overtone *n syn* see ASSOCIATION 4
overtop *vb syn* see OVERLOOK 2
overture *n* **1** action intended to attract favorable attention <made friendly *overtures* to the new member of the class>
 syn advance, approach
 rel bid, proposal, proposition, tender
 2 *syn* see INTRODUCTION
overturn *vb* **1** to turn from an upright or level position <the embarrassed boy backed into the table and *overturned* a lamp>
 syn knock over, overset, overthrow, tip (over), topple, turn over, upset
 rel capsize, keel (over *or* up), upend, upturn; prostrate; down; roll (over)
 con erect, right, set up, straighten (up)
 2 *syn* see OVERTHROW 2
overturn *n syn* see SHAKE-UP
overuse *vb syn* see OVERDO
 ant underuse
overvalue *vb* to set too high a value on <inclined to *overvalue* his own charm>
 syn overesteem, overestimate, overprize, overrate, overreckon
 rel cherish, prize, treasure; adore, idolize, worship
 con belittle, depreciate
 ant underprize, undervalue
overweening *adj syn* see PRESUMPTUOUS
overweigh *vb* **1** *syn* see OUTWEIGH 1
 2 *syn* see OVERLOAD
overweighing *adj syn* see DOMINANT 1
overweight *vb* **1** *syn* see OUTWEIGH 1
 2 *syn* see OVERLOAD
overweight *adj syn* see FAT 2
 ant underweight
overwhelm *vb* **1** *syn* see DELUGE 1
 2 *syn* see DELUGE 3
 3 *syn* see WHIP 2
 4 to subject to the grip of something overpowering and usually distressing or damaging <*overwhelmed* by the death of his only child> <human wants that tend to *overwhelm* environmental realities>
 syn drown, knock over, overcome, overpower, prostrate, whelm
 rel demoralize, devastate, dumbfound, shatter; floor, sink; disturb, upset; destroy, ruin, wreck; downgrade, lower, subordinate
overwhelmed *adj syn* see AGHAST 2
overwhelming *adj syn* see TOWERING 4
overwork *vb syn* see OVERDO
oviform *adj syn* see OVAL
ovoid *adj syn* see OVAL
owing *adj syn* see UNPAID 2
owing to *prep syn* see OVER 6
owl–light *n syn* see EVENING 1

---

syn synonym(s) *rel* related word(s)
ant antonym(s) *con* contrasted word(s)
idiom idiomatic equivalent(s)
|| use limited; if in doubt, see a dictionary

own *vb* **1** *syn* see HAVE 1
  2 *syn* see ACKNOWLEDGE 1
  con deny, disclaim
  ant disown, repudiate
owner *n* one that has the legal or rightful title <*owner* of the shop>
  syn holder, possessor, proprietor
  rel lord, master

con lessee, renter, tenant; squatter; interloper, intruder, trespasser
ownership *n* lawful claim or title <would soon have *ownership* of the house>
  syn dominion, possession, possessorship, property, proprietary, proprietorship
  rel hand
own up *vb* *syn* see ACKNOWLEDGE 1
oyster *n* *syn* see FORTE

pa *n* *syn* see FATHER 1
pablum *n* *syn* see PAP 2
pabulum *n* *syn* see FOOD 2
pace *n* **1** *syn* see TEMPO
  2 *syn* see SPEED 2
  3 *syn* see ROUTINE
pace *vb* **1** *syn* see WALK 1
  2 *syn* see PRECEDE 2
pacific *adj* affording or promoting peace <a *pacific* policy>
  syn irenic, nonviolent, pacificatory, pacifist, peaceable, peaceful
  rel appeasing, conciliating, conciliatory, pacifying, propitiating, propitiatory; dovelike, gentle, inoffensive
  con belligerent, combative, contentious, pugnacious, quarrelsome; unpeaceable, unpeaceful; hawkish, violent, warlike
  ant bellicose, unpacific
pacificator *n* *syn* see PEACEMAKER
pacificatory *adj* *syn* see PACIFIC
pacificist *n* *syn* see PACIFIST
  idiom man of peace
pacifist *n* one who opposes war or violence as a means of settling disputes <*pacifists* who fight war with argument and propaganda>
  syn dove, pacificist
  rel satyagrahi; ‖conchie, conscientious objector; peacemonger
  con belligerent, combatant; chauvinist, hawk, jingo, jingoist, warmonger
  ant bellicist
pacifist *adj* *syn* see PACIFIC
  ant combative
pacify *vb* to allay anger or agitation <saw his mounting rage and tried to *pacify* him>
  syn appease, assuage, conciliate, mollify, placate, propitiate, sweeten
  rel dulcify, soften; allay, alleviate, mitigate, relieve; moderate, qualify, smooth (over), temper
  idiom pour balm into, pour oil on (the) troubled waters
  con arouse, stir (up)
  ant anger
pack *n* **1** *syn* see BACKPACK
  2 *syn* see MUCH
pack *vb* **1** *syn* see STOW
  2 *syn* see LOAD 3
  3 *syn* see CARRY 1
packed *adj* *syn* see FULL 1
  idiom packed like sardines (*or* herrings)
‖**packed out** *adj* *syn* see FULL 1
packet *n* *syn* see FORTUNE 4
packman *n* *syn* see PEDDLER
packsack *n* *syn* see BACKPACK
pact *n* **1** *syn* see CONTRACT
  rel settlement
  2 *syn* see TREATY
‖**pad** *n* *syn* see PROTECTION 2
pad *vb* *syn* see EMBROIDER
paddle *vb* *syn* see ROW
‖**paddy** *n* *syn* see POLICEMAN
pagan *adj* *syn* see HEATHEN
pageant *n* *syn* see PRETENSE 2
pagoda *n* *syn* see SUMMERHOUSE

pain *n* **1** a bodily sensation that causes acute discomfort or suffering <suffering from chest *pains*>
  syn ache, ‖misery, pang, stitch, throe, twinge
  rel discomfort, distress, hurt, suffering; agony, torment, torture
  2 pains *pl* *syn* see EFFORT 1
  rel assiduousness, diligence, industry, sedulousness
pain *vb* **1** *syn* see HURT 4
  rel agonize, convulse, crucify, excruciate, harrow, lacerate
  2 *syn* see DISTRESS 2
  rel afflict; distress, upset; wound; anguish
  idiom ‖hit one where one lives
  3 *syn* see TRY 2
painful *adj* **1** causing, marked by, or affected with pain <a *painful* wound>
  syn aching, afflictive, algetic, hurtful, hurting, sore
  rel raw; acute, piercing, sharp, shooting, stabbing, stinging; agonizing, excruciating, harrowing, racking, tormenting, torturous
  ant painless, unpainful
  2 *syn* see BITTER 2
  rel unappetizing, unsavory
  ant painless
painfully *adv* *syn* see HARD 5
  ant painlessly
pain-killer *n* *syn* see ANODYNE 1
painstaking *adj* *syn* see CAREFUL 2
painstakingly *adv* *syn* see HARD 3
  rel carefully, meticulously; lovingly
paint *n* *syn* see MAKEUP 3
pair *n* *syn* see COUPLE
paired *adj* *syn* see TWIN
pal *n* *syn* see ASSOCIATE 3
palace *adj* *syn* see LUXURIOUS 3
palace car *n* *syn* see PARLOR CAR
palatable *adj* agreeable or pleasant especially to the sense of taste <a *palatable* meal>
  syn aperitive, appetizing, flavorsome, good-tasting, ‖gusty, mouth-watering, relishing, sapid, saporous, savorous, savorsome, savory, tasteful, tasty, toothsome, toothy
  rel delectable, delicious, delightful, luscious, scrumptious, yummy; tempting; saporific
  con bad-tasting, disagreeable, distasteful, ill-flavored, unappetizing
  ant unpalatable
palate *n* *syn* see TASTE 4
palatial *adj* *syn* see LUXURIOUS 3
  rel noble, regal; monumental; impressive; rich, splendid
palaver *n* **1** *syn* see CONFERENCE 2
  rel dialogue, discussion; parley
  2 *syn* see CHATTER
  rel gas, guff, hot air
  3 *syn* see TERMINOLOGY
  4 *syn* see BUSINESS 8
palaverous *adj* *syn* see WORDY
pale *adj* **1** deficient in color or in intensity of color <a *pale* face>
  syn ashen, ashy, blanched, colorless, complexionless, doughy, livid, lurid, pallid, paly, wan, waxen
  rel sallow, sick, sickly; gray, pasty, pasty-faced, waxlike; white, whitened; deathlike, ghastly
  con flushed, ruddy; bright, colorful, florid

2 being weak and thin in substance or in vital qualities < a *pale*, inadequate foreign policy >
　syn anemic, bloodless, pallid, waterish, watery
　rel inane, insipid, jejune, wishy-washy; insubstantial, unsubstantial; ineffective, ineffectual; faint, feeble, weak
　con strong, substantial; effective, effectual; bright, colorful
　ant brilliant

pale *vb syn* see DULL 1

Pale Horse *n, used with the syn* see DEATH 1

palinode *vb syn* see ABJURE

pall *vb* **1** *syn* see BORE
　2 *syn* see SATIATE
　rel disgust, weary

‖**pallet** *n syn* see HEAD 1

palliate *vb* to give a speciously fine appearance to what is erroneous, base, or evil < did not try to conceal or *palliate* his errors >
　syn blanch (over), extenuate, gloss (over), gloze (over), prettify, sugarcoat, varnish, veneer, white, whiten, whitewash
　rel alleviate, lighten, mitigate; condone, excuse; moderate, qualify, soften, temper; camouflage, cloak, conceal, cover up, disguise, dissemble, mask; hush (up)
　idiom paper over the cracks, put a good face on (*or* upon)

pallid *adj* **1** *syn* see PALE 1
　2 *syn* see PALE 2

pally *adj syn* see INTIMATE 4

palm (on *or* upon) *vb syn* see FOIST 3

‖**palm grease** *n syn* see GRATUITY

palm off *vb syn* see FOIST 3

‖**palm oil** *n syn* see GRATUITY

palooka *n syn* see OAF 2

palpable *adj* **1** *syn* see TANGIBLE 1
　2 *syn* see PERCEPTIBLE
　rel apparent, ostensible, seeming; believable, colorable, credible, plausible
　3 *syn* see CLEAR 5
　rel certain, positive, sure; arresting, noticeable, remarkable, striking
　con doubtful, dubious, problematic, questionable
　ant impalpable

palpate *vb syn* see TOUCH 1

palpation *n syn* see TOUCH 2

palpitate *vb syn* see PULSATE
　rel pitter-patter

‖**palsy-walsy** *adj syn* see INTIMATE 4

palter *vb* **1** *syn* see LIE
　rel evade, fence
　idiom play false, play fast and loose
　2 *syn* see HAGGLE 2

paltry *adj* **1** *syn* see CHEAP 2
　rel beggarly, shabby; pitiful
　2 *syn* see LITTLE 2
　rel base, low, low-down, vile
　3 *syn* see PETTY 2
　rel insignificant, unimportant

paly *adj syn* see PALE 1

pamper *vb syn* see BABY
　rel regale, tickle; caress, dandle, fondle, pet; overindulge

‖**pan** *n syn* see FACE 1

pan *vb syn* see CRITICIZE

panacea *n* a remedy for all ills or difficulties < bicycles are not a *panacea* for the traffic problem >
　syn catholicon, cure-all, elixir, nostrum
　rel relief; remedy
　idiom universal (*or* sovereign) remedy

pandect *n syn* see COMPENDIUM 1

pandemoniac *adj syn* see INFERNAL 2

pandemonium *n* **1** *cap* **Pandemonium** *syn* see HELL
　2 *syn* see SINK 1
　3 *syn* see DIN

pander *n syn* see PIMP 1

panegyric *n syn* see ENCOMIUM

panegyrical *adj syn* see EULOGISTIC

panegyrize *vb syn* see PRAISE 2

pang *n syn* see PAIN 1
　rel prick, stab, ‖stang

‖**pang** *vb syn* see CRAM 1

panhandler *n syn* see BEGGAR 1

panhandling *n syn* see MENDICANCY

panic *n* **1** *syn* see FEAR 1
　rel frenzy, hysteria; stampede
　con composure, equanimity, sangfroid, self-possession
　‖**2** *syn* see RIOT 1

‖**pank** *vb syn* see PANT 1

panoply *n syn* see DISPLAY 2

panorama *n syn* see RANGE 2

pan out *vb syn* see SUCCEED 2

pansified *adj syn* see EFFEMINATE

pant *vb* **1** to breathe quickly, spasmodically, or in a labored manner < was *panting* after running up the stairs >
　syn blow, gasp, heave, huff, ‖pank, ‖pegh, puff
　rel gulp; wheeze; wind; chuff
　idiom be out of breath
　2 *syn* see AIM 2
　rel hunger, long, pine, thirst; desire, want, wish
　idiom be consumed with desire (for)

pantywaist *n syn* see WEAKLING

pantywaist *adj syn* see CHARACTERLESS

pap *n* **1** *syn* see FOOD 2
　2 something (as reading matter) lacking in solid value or substance < the sentimental *pap* that he offered his readers >
　syn pablum, rubbish, slop
　rel garbage, trash

‖**pap** *n syn* see FATHER 1

papa *n syn* see FATHER 1

paper *n syn* see ESSAY 2

paphian *n syn* see HARLOT 1

pappy *adj syn* see SOFT 6

‖**pappy** *n syn* see FATHER 1

par *n* **1** *syn* see EQUIVALENCE
　2 *syn* see AVERAGE
　rel standard

parable *n syn* see ALLEGORY 2
　rel comparison, similitude

parachronism *n syn* see ANACHRONISM 1

parade *n syn* see DISPLAY 2
　rel exhibition

parade *vb syn* see SHOW 4
　rel disclose, divulge, reveal; advertise, declare, proclaim, publish; boast, brag, gasconade
　idiom parade one's wares
　con camouflage, cloak, disguise, dissemble, mask

paradigm *n syn* see MODEL 2

paradigmatic *adj syn* see TYPICAL 1

paradise *n* **1** *syn* see HEAVEN 2
　idiom the next world (*or* life)
　2 *syn* see UTOPIA

paragon *n* an individual of unequaled excellence often serving as a model < she is a *paragon* of a housewife >
　syn ideal, jewel, nonesuch, nonpareil, phoenix; *compare* MODEL 2
　rel apotheosis, epitome, last word, quintessence, ultimate; archetype, beau ideal, exemplar, pattern; ‖beaut, beauty, crackerjack, gem, love, lovely, peach, trump; champ, champion; cream, pick, tops

paragon *vb syn* see EQUATE 2

parallel *adj syn* see LIKE
　ant nonparallel, unparallel

parallel *n* one that corresponds to or closely resembles another < we seek in vain a *parallel* for this situation >
　syn analogue, correlate, correspondent, counterpart, countertype, match; *compare* COUNTERPART 1, EQUAL
　rel equivalent; double, duplicate, duplication

parallel *vb* **1** *syn* see EQUATE 2
　2 to place (something) so as to be parallel with another < machines that combed and *paralleled* the fibers >
　syn collimate, collocate, parallelize
　rel align, line up

parallelize *vb syn* see PARALLEL 2

paralyze *vb* **1** to render completely powerless, ineffective, or inert < a general strike that *paralyzed* the nation >

---

syn synonym(s)	*rel* related word(s)
ant antonym(s)	*con* contrasted word(s)
idiom idiomatic equivalent(s)	
‖ use limited; if in doubt, see a dictionary	

syn cripple, disable, disarm, immobilize, incapacitate, prostrate; *compare* MAIM, WEAKEN 1

rel deaden, enfeeble, weaken; close, shut (down); freeze; demolish, destroy, knock out

idiom bring to a grinding halt, tie hand and foot

2 *syn* see DAZE 2

rel appall, daunt, dismay, horrify; cripple, disable, enfeeble, weaken; astound, flabbergast, nonplus

con animate, enliven, pep (up), stimulate

ant galvanize

paramount *adj syn* see DOMINANT 1

rel capital, headmost; commanding, controlling; cardinal, crowning

paramour *n* **1** *syn* see GALLANT 2

2 *syn* see LOVER 1

3 *syn* see MISTRESS

parapet *n syn* see BULWARK

paraphernalia *n pl but sometimes sing in constr syn* see EQUIPMENT 1

paraphrase *n syn* see VERSION 1

paraphrase *vb* to express or interpret something (as a text or passage) in other words <*paraphrased* the complicated document>

syn rephrase, restate, reword, translate (into)

rel summarize; transcribe

con quote, reproduce

parasite *n* a person who is supported or seeks support from another without making an adequate return <lived as a *parasite* in his father's house>

syn barnacle, bloodsucker, freeloader, hanger-on, leech, lounge lizard, ‖spiv, sponge, sponger, sucker; *compare* SYCOPHANT

rel dependent; smell-feast; deadbeat, idler, laze

parasite *vb syn* see INFEST 2

parasitic *adj syn* see FAWNING

rel freeloading, leechlike, sponging

parasitize *vb syn* see INFEST 2

parboil *vb syn* see BOIL 2

parcel *n* **1** *syn* see PART 1

2 *syn* see LOT 3

3 *syn* see GROUP 3

parcel *vb syn* see APPORTION 2

rel allocate, allot, assign; deal, disburse, disperse; dole (out), lot (out)

parch *vb syn* see DRY 1

‖**pard** *n syn* see PARTNER

pardon *n* a remission of penalty or punishment <the governor granted the prisoner a *pardon*>

syn absolution, amnesty

rel acquittal, exculpation, exoneration, indemnification, indemnity; forgiveness, remission; justification, vindication

con conviction; condemnation

ant punishment

pardon *vb syn* see EXCUSE 1

rel justify; accept, tolerate; free, liberate, release

idiom let bygones be bygones, wipe the slate clean

con amerce, fine, mulct, penalize

ant punish

pardonable *adj syn* see VENIAL

ant unpardonable

pare *vb* **1** *syn* see CUT 6

rel flay, scalp, skin, strip

2 *syn* see REDUCE 2

parent *vb syn* see GENERATE 1

parenthesis *n* **1** *syn* see DIGRESSION

2 *syn* see INTERLUDE

parenthetically *adv syn* see INCIDENTALLY 2

parentless *adj syn* see ORPHAN

ant parented

par excellence *adj syn* see EXCELLENT

pariah *n syn* see OUTCAST

rel déclassé

‖**parish–pump** *adj syn* see INSULAR

parity *n syn* see EQUIVALENCE

rel analogy, parallelism, similitude; approximation, closeness, nearness

ant disparity, imparity

parlance *n syn* see WORDING

parley *vb* **1** *syn* see SPEAK 3

2 *syn* see CONFER 2

parley *n* **1** *syn* see TALK 4

rel rap session

2 *syn* see CONVERSATION 1

parlor car *n* a railroad passenger car equipped with individual revolving and reclining chairs and providing the services of an attendant

syn chair car, club car, lounge car, palace car, tavern car

parlor house *n syn* see BROTHEL

parlous *adj syn* see DANGEROUS 1

parlous *adv syn* see VERY 1

Parnassian *n syn* see POET

parochial *adj syn* see INSULAR

rel prejudiced; bigoted

con unprejudiced; uncircumscribed, unlimited; cosmic, universal

ant catholic

parody *n syn* see CARICATURE 2

rel spoof, spoofery, rib, ridicule

parody *vb syn* see MIMIC

paronomasia *n syn* see PUN

parous *adj syn* see PREGNANT 1

parry *vb* **1** *syn* see DODGE 1

rel preclude, prevent; anticipate, forestall

2 *syn* see WARD 1

parsimonious *adj syn* see STINGY

idiom penny-wise and pound-foolish

ant prodigal

parson *n syn* see CLERGYMAN

part *n* **1** something less than the whole to which it belongs <a *part* of the road was paved>

syn cut, division, member, moiety, parcel, piece, portion, section, segment

rel component, constituent, element, ingredient; detail, fraction, fragment; bit, chip, scrap

con aggregate, total; combination, complex; entirety, entity, totality, unity

ant whole

2 parts *pl syn* see GENITALIA

3 *syn* see RATION

4 *syn* see SHARE 1

rel chunk

5 *syn* see SIDE 4

part *vb syn* see SEPARATE 1

ant unite

part *adj syn* see INCOMPLETE 1

partage *n syn* see SHARE 1

partake *vb syn* see SHARE 2

rel accept, receive, take

idiom take part in

partake (of) *vb* **1** *syn* see EAT 1

2 *syn* see AMOUNT 2

idiom bear resemblance (to)

partaker *n syn* see PARTICIPANT

part and parcel *n syn* see ESSENTIAL 1

partial *adj* **1** *syn* see BIASED 2

ant impartial

2 *syn* see INCOMPLETE 1

rel halfway

ant whole

partiality *n* **1** *syn* see PREJUDICE

2 *syn* see LEANING 2

participant *n* one that takes part in something <were *participants* in the uprising>

syn actor, partaker, participator, party, sharer

rel aide, assistant, helper; colleague, confrere, fellow, partner

con bystander, looker-on, nonparticipant, observer, onlooker, spectator, watcher

participate *vb syn* see SHARE 2

rel enter (into), join (in)

idiom be a party to, be in on, be (*or* get) in the act, have to do with

con observe, watch; retire, withdraw

participator *n syn* see PARTICIPANT

particle *n* a tiny or insignificant amount, part, or piece <not a *particle* of sense>

syn ace, atom, bit, crumb, damn, ‖dite, doit, dram, drop, fragment, grain, hoot, iota, jot, minim, mite, modicum, molecule, ounce, ray, ‖rissom, scrap, scruple, shred, smidgen, smitch, snap, speck, spot, syllable, tittle, whit, whoop

rel morsel; snip; dribbet, dribble; dot
parti-color *adj syn* see VARIEGATED
parti-colored *adj syn* see VARIEGATED
  ant unicolor, unicolorous
particular *adj* 1 *syn* see SINGLE 2
  ant general
  2 *syn* see CIRCUMSTANTIAL
  rel careful, meticulous, punctilious, scrupulous
  3 *syn* see SPECIAL 1
  rel appropriate; distinct; singular
  ant universal
  4 *syn* see SEVERAL 1
  5 *syn* see NICE 1
particular *n syn* see POINT 1
  rel speciality, specific
  con entirety
  ant universal
particularity *n syn* see INDIVIDUALITY 3
particularize *vb* 1 *syn* see SPECIFY 3
  idiom draw it fine
  2 *syn* see ITEMIZE 1
particularized *adj syn* see CIRCUMSTANTIAL
  ant generalized
particularly *adv syn* see ESPECIALLY 1
parting *n* a mutual separation of two or more persons <saddened by their approaching *parting* >
  syn adieu, congé, farewell, good-bye, leave-taking
  rel separation; departure
  con joining, meeting; return
  ant reunion
parting *adj* given, taken, or performed during leave-taking <remembered his father's *parting* advice >
  syn departing, farewell, good-bye, valedictory
  rel final, last
partisan *n* 1 *syn* see FOLLOWER
  rel backer, champion, upholder; die-hard, stalwart
  con adversary, antagonist, opponent
  2 an irregular soldier who operates behind enemy lines <a train blown up by *partisans* >
  syn guerrilla, irregular, patriot
partisan *adj syn* see BIASED 2
  rel denominational, factional, sectarian; blind, devoted, die-hard, fanatic, unreasoning
  con impartial, indifferent, unbiased, unprejudiced
  ant nonpartisan
partition *n syn* see SEPARATION 1
partition *vb syn* see DISTRIBUTE 1
partner *n* one that is associated in any action with another <*partners* in crime >
  syn associate, cohort, confrere, consociate, copartner, fellow, mate, ‖pard
  rel assistant, helper, sidekick; bedfellow, buddy, chum, companion, comrade, crony, pal
partnership *n syn* see ASSOCIATION 1
  rel consociation, fellowship
parturient *adj syn* see PREGNANT 1
parturition *n syn* see BIRTH 1
party *n* 1 *syn* see COMBINATION 2
  rel alliance, union; side
  2 *syn* see PARTICIPANT
  3 *syn* see HUMAN
  4 *syn* see GROUP 1
  5 *syn* see COMPANY 4
  6 *syn* see ORGY 2
party girl *n* 1 *syn* see DOXY 1
  2 *syn* see PROSTITUTE
parvenu *n syn* see UPSTART
  idiom codfish aristocrat, pig in clover
‖pash *vb syn* see SHATTER 1
‖pash *n syn* see INFATUATION
pass *vb* 1 *syn* see GO 1
  rel jog, ‖mog
  2 *syn* see DIE 1
  idiom pass on to the Great Beyond
  con linger
  3 to move or come to a termination or end <as time *passes*, the pain too will *pass* >
  syn see ELAPSE

rel slip (by); roll (on); fade (away), peter (out); cease, close, discontinue, end, stop, terminate
  con continue; linger
  4 *syn* see HAPPEN 1
  idiom come to pass
  5 *syn* see SURPASS 1
  idiom leave way behind, shoot ahead of
  6 *syn* see SPEND 3
  7 *syn* see NEGLECT
  8 *syn* see PROMISE 1
  9 to transfer by hand from one person to another <*pass* the salt >
  syn buck, hand, reach, ‖shoot
  rel give; fork (over)
pass (as *or* for) *vb syn* see POSE 4
pass (on) *vb syn* see HAND DOWN
pass (over) *vb syn* see TRAVEL 2
pass *n syn* see JUNCTURE 2
passable *adj* capable of being passed, crossed, or traveled <*passable* roads >
  syn navigable, negotiable, travelable
  rel open, unblocked; ‖motorable; accessible, attainable, reachable
  con blocked, closed; unnavigable; inaccessible, unattainable, unreachable
  ant impassable
passably *adv syn* see ENOUGH 2
passage *n* 1 movement or transference from one place or point to another <air *passage* from New York to London > <the *passage* of current through a wire >
  syn transit, travel
  rel traject, trajet, traverse, traversing; transfer, transference, transmission, transmittal, transmittance
  2 *syn* see TRANSITION
  3 *syn* see WAY 2
  4 a typically long narrow way connecting parts of a building <the office building contained endless *passages* >
  syn corridor, couloir, hall, hallway, passageway
  rel areaway
passageway *n syn* see PASSAGE 3
pass away *vb* 1 *syn* see DIE 1
  2 *syn* see PASS 3
pass by *vb syn* see NEGLECT
passé *adj* 1 *syn* see OBSOLETE
  2 *syn* see OLD-FASHIONED
  ant a la mode
passed master *n syn* see EXPERT
passel *n syn* see GROUP 3
passing *n syn* see DEATH 1
passing *adj syn* see TRANSIENT
  con lingering
passion *n* 1 *syn* see DISTRESS
  2 *syn* see DESIRE 1
  rel coveting; aiming, aspiring, panting
  3 *syn* see FEELING 3
  ant dispassion
  4 *syn* see TEMPER 4
  rel outbreak, outburst
  5 *syn* see LOVE 2
  rel heartthrob
  6 intense, high-wrought emotion that compels to action <the *passion* of an evangelist >
  syn ardor, calenture, enthusiasm, fervor, fire, hurrah, zeal
  rel dedication, devotion; eagerness, lust; lyricism; ecstasy, rapture, transport; fury, rage
  7 *syn* see LUST 2
  rel amorousness; sensuality, sensuousness
  8 *syn* see INFATUATION
passionate *adj* 1 *syn* see IRASCIBLE
  2 *syn* see IMPASSIONED
  rel excited, quickened, stimulated; high-powered, high-pressure, steamed up; headlong, impetuous, precipitate
  ant dispassionate

---

syn synonym(s)   *rel* related word(s)
ant antonym(s)   *con* contrasted word(s)
idiom idiomatic equivalent(s)
‖ use limited; if in doubt, see a dictionary

3 *syn* see LUSTFUL 2
rel steamy, sultry
ant passionless
passionless *adj syn* see FRIGID 3
rel detached, impassive, unsusceptible; unaffected, unmoved; apathetic, indifferent, uncaring, unconcerned, unfeeling; cold‑blooded, coldhearted, frozen, heartless
ant passionate, passionful
passive *adj* **1** *syn* see INACTIVE
rel apathetic, impassive, phlegmatic, stolid
ant active
2 receiving or enduring without resistance < a *passive* acceptance of her fate >
syn acquiescent, nonresistant, nonresisting, resigned, submissive, unresistant, unresisting, yielding
rel bearing, enduring, patient; compliant, docile, tractable; nonviolent
con resistant, resisting, unresigned, unsubmissive, unyielding
pass off *vb* **1** *syn* see FOIST 3
2 *syn* see POSE 4
pass on *vb* *syn* see COMMUNICATE 1
pass out *vb* **1** *syn* see FAINT
2 *syn* see DIE 1
pass over *vb* *syn* see NEGLECT
passport *n* a means of entry into a desirable group, society, or condition of life < his skill at sports was a *passport* to fame and fortune >
syn key, open sesame, password, ticket
password *n* **1** a word or phrase that must be spoken by a person before he may pass a guard < give the *password* before entering the fort >
syn countersign, watchword, word
rel tessera
2 *syn* see PASSPORT
3 something (as a short phrase) used as a sign of recognition among members of the same society, class, or group < a fraternity that has secret handshakes and *passwords* >
syn watchword, word
past *adj* **1** *syn* see PRECEDING
2 *syn* see FORMER 2
rel bypast, gone-by; late, previous
ant present
past *prep* **1** *syn* see BEYOND 1
rel by
ant before
2 *syn* see BEYOND 2
past *n* former time < reminisced about the *past* >
syn foretime, ‖lang syne, yesterday, yesteryear, yore; *compare* PRESENT
rel antiquity
idiom bygone days (*or* times), days gone by, the good old days
con here and now; tomorrow
ant present; future
paste *vb* *syn* see BEAT 1
idiom give one a pasting
‖**paste** *n* *syn* see CUFF
pasticcio *n* *syn* see MISCELLANY 1
pastiche *n* *syn* see MISCELLANY 1
past master *n* *syn* see EXPERT
pastoral *adj* *syn* see RURAL
rel agrarian
patch *vb* *syn* see MEND 2
patchwork *n* *syn* see MISCELLANY 1
patchy *adj* *syn* see SPOTTY 1
pate *n* *syn* see HEAD 1
patent *adj* **1** *syn* see OPEN 1
2 *syn* see CLEAR 5
rel prominent; flagrant, glaring, gross, rank
idiom patently obvious
con impalpable, imperceptible, insensible; concealed, hidden, secreted
ant latent
‖**pater** *n* *syn* see FATHER 1
path *n* **1** *syn* see TRAIL
2 *syn* see WAY 1
3 *syn* see WAY 2
pathetic *adj* *syn* see PITIFUL 1
pathos *n* a quality that moves one to pity and sorrow < the *pathos* of the play was rarely offset by moments of comedy >

syn poignance, poignancy
rel bathos
pathway *n* *syn* see TRAIL
patience *n* the power or capacity to endure without complaint something difficult or disagreeable < it took a lot of *patience* to put up with him >
syn forbearance, longanimity, long-suffering, patientness, resignation, uncomplainingness
rel composure, cool, equanimity, imperturbability, self-control; endurance, sufferance, suffering, tolerance, toleration; nonresistance, passiveness, passivity, submission, submissiveness
con fretfulness; restiveness, restlessness; hastiness; rebellion, resistance
ant impatience
patientness *n* *syn* see PATIENCE
patois *n* **1** *syn* see VERNACULAR 3
2 *syn* see DIALECT 2
patriarch *n* **1** *syn* see FATHER 2
2 *syn* see GAFFER
patriarchal *adj* *syn* see VENERABLE 1
patrician *n* *syn* see GENTLEMAN
ant plebeian
patriciate *n* *syn* see ARISTOCRACY
ant plebs
patrimony *n* *syn* see HERITAGE 1
patriot *n* **1** a person who loves his country and supports its interests < *patriots* who asked what they could do for their country >
syn loyalist
rel nationalist
ant traitor
2 *syn* see PATRIOTEER
3 *syn* see PARTISAN 2
patrioteer *n* one who is ostentatiously and chauvinistically patriotic < bloodthirsty *patrioteers* immersed in political witch‑hunts >
syn flag-waver, patriot, superpatriot
rel jingo, jingoist
patrolman *n* *syn* see POLICEMAN
patron *n* **1** *syn* see PATRON SAINT
2 *syn* see SPONSOR
ant client; protégé
3 *syn* see CUSTOMER
patronage *n* **1** *syn* see BACKING
rel benefaction, guardianship, protection; subsidy
2 commercial transactions of customers and patrons < developed a large *patronage* by offering fair prices and courteous service >
syn business, custom, trade, traffic
rel clientage, clientele
3 the power to make appointments to government jobs on a basis other than merit alone < ousted his enemies from office and used *patronage* to support his policies >
syn pork-barreling
rel cronyism
patron saint *n* a saint to whose protection and intercession a person, society, church, or place is dedicated < Saint Christopher is the *patron saint* of travelers >
syn avowry, patron
rel titular; guardian angel
patsy *n* **1** *syn* see SCAPEGOAT
2 *syn* see FOOL 3
patter *vb* *syn* see CHAT 1
patter *n* *syn* see DIALECT 2
pattern *n* **1** *syn* see MODEL 2
rel original
2 *syn* see FIGURE 3
rel patterning
3 *syn* see ORDER 8
rel arrangement, constellation
paucity *n* *syn* see SCARCITY
rel fewness
Paul Pry *n* *syn* see BUSYBODY
paunch *n* **1** *syn* see ABDOMEN
2 *syn* see POTBELLY
paunch *vb* *syn* see EVISCERATE
pauper *n* a person having no financial resources except those derived from charity

syn beggar, down-and-out
rel have-not, indigent; ‖casual; almsman, lazarus
con millionaire, plutocrat
pauper *vb syn* see RUIN 3
pauperism *n syn* see POVERTY 1
pauperize *vb syn* see RUIN 3
pausation *n syn* see PAUSE
pause *n* a temporary cessation of activity or of an activity <a *pause* in the conversation>
syn comma, interval, lull, pausation; *compare* BREAK 4, GAP 3
rel caesura, hush, lapse, letup, suspension; interlude, intermission; recess, respite; wait; break, gap, interruption; cessation, ‖deval
con continuation, progression
paw *vb syn* see TOUCH 1
paw *adj* **1** *syn* see NAUGHTY 1
   2 *syn* see OBSCENE 2
pawn *n syn* see PLEDGE 1
pawn *vb* to give or deposit as security for the payment of a loan or debt or for the fulfillment of an obligation <had to *pawn* all her jewels>
syn ‖dip, hock, impignorate, mortgage, pledge, ‖pop, ‖spout
ant redeem
pawn *n syn* see TOOL 2
pay *vb* **1** to discharge an obligation to usually with money <*paid* the doctor for his services>
syn compensate, guerdon, remunerate
rel indemnify, recompense, satisfy; cough (up), plunk down, pony (up), pungle (up), remit, render, tender; pay off
   2 *syn* see CLEAR 5
   3 *syn* see SPEND 1
   4 *syn* see COMPENSATE 3
   idiom make up for
   5 *syn* see YIELD 5
pay *n syn* see WAGE
payable *adj* **1** *syn* see DUE 2
   ant unpayable
   2 *syn* see UNPAID 2
pay envelope *n syn* see WAGE
paying *adj syn* see ADVANTAGEOUS 1
   rel productive; sound; solvent
payload *n syn* see LOAD 1
pay up *vb syn* see CLEAR 5
PDQ *adv syn* see AWAY 3
peaceable *adj syn* see PACIFIC
   rel amicable, friendly, neighborly; amiable, complaisant
   ant acrimonious; contentious; warlike
peaceful *adj syn* see PACIFIC
   rel collected, composed, cool, unruffled; constant, equable, steady
   con agitated, discomposed, disquieted, disturbed, perturbed, upset
peacemaker *n* one that makes or seeks to make peace <a president who was remembered as a great *peacemaker*>
   syn make-peace, pacificator
   rel arbitrator, mediator, negotiator; placater; appeaser, peacemonger; peacekeeper
   con chauvinist, jingo, jingoist, militarist, war dog, warmonger; peacebreaker
peace officer *n syn* see POLICEMAN
peach *n syn* ‖DILLY, crackerjack, ‖daisy, dandy, humdinger, jim-dandy, ‖lalapalooza, ‖lulu, nifty, ‖pip
   rel pearl
peach *vb syn* see INFORM 3
peachy *adj syn* see MARVELOUS 2
peacock *vb syn* see LORD
peacockish *adj syn* see SHOWY
peacocky *adj syn* see SHOWY
peak *n* **1** *syn* see VISOR 1
   2 *syn* see TOP 1
   3 *syn* see MOUNTAIN 1
   4 *syn* see APEX 2
peak (out) *vb syn* see DECREASE
peaked *adj syn* see POINTED 1
peaked *adj syn* see SICKLY 2
‖**peaking** *adj syn* see SICKLY 2
peaky *adj syn* see POINTED 1
peaky *adj syn* see SICKLY 2

peal *vb syn* see RING
peanut *adj syn* see PETTY 2
‖**peart** *adj syn* see LIVELY 1
‖**pearten** (up) *vb syn* see ENCOURAGE 1
peasant *n syn* see RUSTIC
peck *n syn* see MUCH
peck *vb* **1** to strike at or pick up with the beak <a hen *pecking* the scattered grain from the ground>
   syn beak, pick
   2 *syn* see KISS 1
peck (at) *vb syn* see NAG
pecker *n* **1** *syn* see BILL 1
   2 *syn* see NOSE 1
‖**peckish** *adj syn* see HUNGRY
pecksniffery *n syn* see HYPOCRISY
pecksniffian *adj syn* see HYPOCRITICAL
peculate *vb syn* see EMBEZZLE
peculiar *adj* **1** *syn* see CHARACTERISTIC
   rel unique
   2 *syn* see STRANGE 4
   rel uncustomary
   con normal
peculiarity *n syn* see QUALITY 1
pecuniary *adj syn* see FINANCIAL
pedantic *adj* too narrowly concerned with scholarly matters <intellectual life that was *pedantic* rather than broad and humane>
   syn academic, bookish, book-learned, booky, quodlibetic, scholastic
   rel erudite, learned; didactic, donnish, inkhorn, schoolish, schoolteacherish; arid, dry, dryasdust, dull
   ant unpedantic
peddle *vb* **1** *syn* see PUSH 6
   2 to sell or offer for sale from place to place <*peddled* fish from a pushcart>
   syn hawk, huckster, monger, vend
   rel sell; push
peddler *n* one who travels about with merchandise to sell <*peddlers* were once common in rural areas>
   syn ‖arab, cheap-jack (*or* cheap-john), ‖duffer, hawker, higgler, huckster, monger, mongerer, outcrier, packman, piepoudre, roadman, vendor
   rel colporteur, costermonger; pusher
peddling *adj syn* see PETTY 2
pedestal *vb syn* see EXALT 1
pedestrian *adj syn* see DULL 9
   rel commonplace, platitudinous, truistic; banal, inane, jejune, wishy-washy; heavy
pedigree *n* **1** *syn* see GENEALOGY
   2 *syn* see ANCESTRY
pedigree *adj syn* see PUREBRED
pedigreed *adj syn* see PUREBRED
peek (in *or* out) *vb syn* see PEEP
peek *n syn* see PEEP
peel *vb* **1** *syn* see SKIN 2
   2 *syn* see SCALE 2
peeled *adj syn* see OPEN 2
peeler *n* **1** *syn* see STRIPTEASER
   2 *syn* see HUSTLER
‖**peeler** *n syn* see POLICEMAN
peep *vb syn* see CHIRP
   rel pip
peep *vb* to peer through or as if through a hole or crevice <*peeped* cautiously under the bed>
   syn peek (in *or* out)
   rel glance; look; peer, stare
   idiom take a peep (*or* peek)
peep *n* a brief and sometimes furtive look <take a *peep* at the new neighbors>
   syn ‖gander, glance, glimpse, peek
   rel look-over, look-see; oeillade, ogle; stare
peeper *n* **1** *syn* see PEEPING TOM
   2 *syn* see EYE 1

---

syn synonym(s)	**rel** related word(s)
ant antonym(s)	**con** contrasted word(s)
idiom idiomatic equivalent(s)	
‖ use limited; if in doubt, see a dictionary	

peeping tom *n* a pruriently prying person <a *peeping tom* spying on the couple>
  syn peeper, voyeur
  rel prowler, snoop, snooper
  idiom porch climber, window (*or* transom) peeper
‖**peepy** *adj syn* see SLEEPY 1
peer *vb syn* see GAZE 1
  rel eye, rubberneck; pry, snoop
peerless *adj syn* see ALONE 3
  rel dominant, paramount, predominant, sovereign
peery *adj syn* see CURIOUS 2
peeve *vb syn* see IRRITATE
  rel disturb; miff
  idiom make one hot under the collar
peevish *adj syn* see IRRITABLE
  rel captious, carping, caviling, critical, faultfinding
  idiom being in a peeve
peewee *n syn* see DWARF
peewee *adj syn* see TINY
‖**peg** *n syn* see DRINK 3
‖**pegh** *vb syn* see PANT 1
peg out *vb* 1 *syn* see COLLAPSE 2
  2 *syn* see DIE 1
pejorative *adj syn* see DEROGATORY
  con acclaiming, extolling, lauding, praising; aggrandizing, exalting, magnifying
pelf *n* 1 *syn* see MONEY
  ‖2 *syn* see REFUSE
pell–mell *adv* in or as if in confused haste <barged in *pell-mell* without thinking>
  syn helter-skelter, hotfoot, hurry-scurry, impetuously, incontinently
  rel hurriedly; indiscreetly; carelessly, heedlessly, rashly, thoughtlessly
  idiom on the spur of the moment
pell–mell *n syn* see CONFUSION 3
pell–mell *vb syn* see STAMPEDE 2
pellucid *adj* 1 *syn* see TRANSPARENT 1
  rel sheer
  con muddy, roily, turbid
  2 *syn* see CLEAR 4
pelt *n syn* see HIDE
pelt *vb* 1 *syn* see BEAT 1
  2 *syn* see HURRY 2
pen *vb syn* see ENCLOSE 1
  ant unpen
pen *n syn* see JAIL
penalize *vb* to inflict a penalty on <*penalize* a delinquent taxpayer with a stiff fine>
  syn amerce, fine, mulct
  rel castigate, chasten, chastise, correct, discipline, punish; condemn; judge
penalty *n syn* see FINE
penance *n syn* see PENITENCE
penchant *n syn* see LEANING 2
‖**pend** *vb syn* see DEPEND (on *or* upon) 1
pendant *n* 1 *syn* see FLAG
  2 *syn* see COUNTERPART 1
pendent *adj* 1 *syn* see SUSPENDED
  2 *syn* see PENDING
pending *adj* not yet settled or decided <a claim still *pending*>
  syn pendent, undecided, undetermined, unsettled
  idiom hanging in the balance, in suspense, up in the air
  con decided, determined, settled
  ant closed
pendulant *adj syn* see SUSPENDED
pendulate *vb syn* see SWING 2
pendulous *adj* 1 *syn* see SUSPENDED
  2 *syn* see VACILLATING 2
penetrable *adj syn* see PERMEABLE
  ant impenetrable
penetrate *vb* 1 *syn* see ENTER 1
  rel encroach, invade, trespass
  2 to enter or go through by or as if by overcoming resistance <the icy wind *penetrated* the heavy parka>
  syn pierce
  rel bore, perforate, prick, puncture; jab, knife, stab; drill, drive
  3 *syn* see PERMEATE

  rel insert, insinuate, interpolate, introduce
penetrating *adj* 1 *syn* see INCISIVE
  rel penetrant, penetrative
  2 *syn* see SHARP 4
penetration *n syn* see WIT 3
  rel penetrativeness
penetrative *adj syn* see SHARP 4
penitence *n* regret for sin or wrongdoing <forgiveness following true *penitence*>
  syn attrition, compunction, contriteness, contrition, penance, penitency, remorse, remorsefulness, repentance, rue, ruth
  rel qualm, scruple; self-accusation, self-castigation, self-punishment, self-reproach, self-reproof; anguish, distress, grief, regret, sadness, sorrow; debasement, degradation, humbling, humiliation
  con adamancy, inexorableness, obduracy, obdurateness, stubbornness
penitency *n syn* see PENITENCE
penitent *adj syn* see REMORSEFUL
penitential *adj syn* see REMORSEFUL
penitentiary *n syn* see JAIL
  idiom correctional institution
penmanship *n syn* see HANDWRITING
pennant *n syn* see FLAG
pennilessness *n syn* see POVERTY 1
pennon *n syn* see FLAG
penny dreadful *n syn* see DIME NOVEL
penny pincher *n syn* see MISER
penny–pinching *adj syn* see STINGY
penny–wise *adj syn* see STINGY
pennyworth *n syn* see BARGAIN
pensile *adj syn* see SUSPENDED
pension (off) *vb syn* see RETIRE 2
pensive *adj* 1 *syn* see THOUGHTFUL 1
  rel musing, ruminating
  2 being musingly sad and thoughtful <gazed out the window with a *pensive* expression on her face>
  syn meditative, ‖pensy, wistful
  rel absorbed, abstracted, contemplative, musing, preoccupied, thoughtful, withdrawn; blue, melancholy, sad, saddened
  con alert, aware, interested, outgoing
‖**pensy** *adj* 1 *syn* see PENSIVE 2
  2 *syn* see THOUGHTFUL 1
  3 *syn* see SQUEAMISH 1
penumbra *n syn* see SHADE 1
penurious *adj* 1 *syn* see POOR 1
  2 *syn* see STINGY
penury *n syn* see POVERTY 1
  ant luxury
peon *n syn* see SLAVE 2
peonage *n syn* see BONDAGE
people *n* 1 *syn* see SOCIETY 3
  2 *syn* see COMMONALTY
people *vb syn* see INHABIT
pep *n* 1 *syn* see ENERGY 2
  2 *syn* see VIGOR 2
pepper *vb syn* see SPECKLE 1
peppery *adj* 1 *syn* see PUNGENT
  2 *syn* see IRASCIBLE
  3 *syn* see SPIRITED 2
  rel pepperish; alert, keen, lively, peppy
peppy *adj syn* see LIVELY 1
per *prep syn* see VIA 2
‖**per** *adv syn* see APIECE
perambulant *adj syn* see ITINERANT
perambulate *vb syn* see TRAVERSE 5
‖**perambulator** *n syn* see BABY CARRIAGE
perambulatory *adj syn* see ITINERANT
per capita *adv syn* see APIECE
per caput *adv syn* see APIECE
perceive *vb syn* see SEE 1
  rel divine, identify, realize, recognize; grasp, seize, take; apprehend
perceptible *adj* apprehensible as real or existent <a *perceptible* change in attitude>
  syn appreciable, detectable, discernible, observable, palpable, sensible, tangible; *compare* TANGIBLE 1
  rel distinguishable, recognizable; cognizable, understandable; clear, lucid, perspicuous; conspicuous, noticeable, signal

con impalpable, indiscernible, intangible, invisible, unappreciable, undetectable, undiscernible, unnoticeable, unobservable
ant imperceptible
perception *n syn* see IDEA
perceptive *adj* 1 *syn* see ACUTE 3
rel responsive
ant imperceptive, unperceptive
2 *syn* see WISE 1
rel prehensile, prehensive, prehensorial
ant imperceptive, unperceptive
perch *vb syn* see ALIGHT
perchance *adv syn* see PERHAPS
percipience *n syn* see WIT 3
percolate *vb* 1 *syn* see PERMEATE
2 *syn* see EXUDE
per contra *adv syn* see HOWEVER
percussion *n syn* see IMPACT
rel percussiveness
perdition *n syn* see HELL
perdurable *adj* 1 *syn* see LASTING
ant fleeting
2 *syn* see INFINITE 1
perdure *vb syn* see CONTINUE 1
perduring *adj syn* see LASTING
ant fleeting
peregrination *n, usu* peregrinations *pl syn* see JOURNEY
peremptory *adj syn* see MASTERFUL 1
rel certain, positive; decided, decisive; absolute, fixed, uncompromising; obstinate
perennial *adj syn* see OLD 2
rel durable, perdurable
perfect *adj* 1 *syn* see WHOLE 1
ant imperfect
2 being entirely without flaw and meeting supreme standards of excellence <a ballerina whose technique was *perfect* >
syn absolute, flawless, fleckless, impeccable, indefectible, note-perfect, unflawed; *compare* CONSUMMATE 1
rel excellent; consummate; expert, finished, masterful, masterly
con defective, faulty, flawed; deficient, inadequate, wanting; unfinished, unpolished; unsound
ant imperfect
3 precisely appropriate or right <found the *perfect* gift for him>
syn ideal, model, very
rel needed, required, requisite; appropriate, fit, proper, right, suitable; exact, express, precise
idiom being just the thing
con foolish, inappropriate, undesirable, unsuitable
4 *syn* see PURE 2
5 *syn* see WHOLE 3
rel consummate
6 *syn* see UTTER
perfect *vb syn* see POLISH 2
perfected *adj syn* see CONSUMMATE 1
ant unperfected
perfectibilian *n syn* see PERFECTIONIST
perfectibilist *n syn* see PERFECTIONIST
perfection *n* 1 *syn* see INTEGRITY 2
2 *syn* see EXCELLENCE
ant imperfection
perfectionist *n* one that demands or works to achieve perfection <a *perfectionist* who rehearsed one scene fifty times>
syn perfectibilian, perfectibilist, perfectist
rel precisian, precisionist, stickler
perfectist *n syn* see PERFECTIONIST
perfectly *adv syn* see WELL 3
perfervid *adj syn* see IMPASSIONED
rel enhanced, heightened, intensified
perfidious *adj syn* see FAITHLESS
rel mercenary, venal; alienated, disaffected, estranged; deceitful, dishonest
perfidiousness *n* 1 *syn* see INFIDELITY
2 *syn* see TREACHERY
perfidy *n* 1 *syn* see TREACHERY
rel foul play
idiom Judas' kiss
ant fealty
2 *syn* see INFIDELITY

rel betrayal, sellout
perforate *vb* to pierce through so as to leave a hole <*perforate* a sheet of postage stamps>
syn bore, drill, prick, ‖pritch, punch, puncture
rel pit; probe; drive, penetrate, pierce
perforce *adv syn* see WILLY-NILLY
perform *vb* 1 *syn* see FULFILL 1
2 to carry something (as a process) to a successful conclusion <*perform* a surgical procedure>
syn achieve, do, execute; *compare* EFFECT 2
rel accomplish, bring off; complete, end, finish, wind up
idiom carry to completion (*or* a successful conclusion), do to a turn, do up brown
3 *syn* see ACT 1
4 *syn* see ACT 5
performance *n syn* see EFFICIENCY 1
performer *n syn* see ACTOR 1
perfume *n syn* see FRAGRANCE
perfume *vb syn* see SCENT 2
perfumed *adj syn* see SWEET 2
perfumy *adj syn* see SWEET 2
perfunctory *adj* characterized by routine and often done merely as a duty <gave her his usual *perfunctory* nod>
syn automatic, mechanical
rel cursory, superficial; involuntary, unaware; routine, usual; standard, stock; cool, impersonal, indifferent; wooden; unconcerned, uninterested
con cordial, friendly, genial, hearty, warm
pergola *n syn* see ARBOR
perhaps *adv* conceivably but not certainly so <*perhaps* this is true, but I think it's debatable>
syn maybe, perchance, possibly
rel conceivably, feasibly, imaginably
idiom as it may be, as the case may be, for all one knows
con certainly, definitely, doubtlessly, surely, undoubtedly, unquestionably
perhaps *n syn* see THEORY 2
periapt *n syn* see CHARM 2
peril *n syn* see DANGER
rel exposure, liability, openness, subjection; endangerment
idiom cause for alarm, rocks (*or* breakers) ahead
peril *vb syn* see ENDANGER
perilous *adj syn* see DANGEROUS 1
rel shaky, tottery, unstable, unsteady; delicate, ticklish, touchy
perimeter *n* 1 *syn* see CIRCUMFERENCE
2 *syn* see BORDER 1
period *n* 1 *syn* see END 2
2 an extent of time set off or typified by someone or something <the Victorian *period* > <a *period* of expansion>
syn age, day(s), epoch, era, time
periodic *adj syn* see INTERMITTENT
rel on-again-off-again
periodical *adj syn* see INTERMITTENT
periodical *n syn* see JOURNAL
peripatetic *adj syn* see ITINERANT
periphery *n* 1 *syn* see CIRCUMFERENCE
2 *syn* see BORDER 1
periphrase *n syn* see VERBIAGE 1
periphrasis *n syn* see VERBIAGE 1
perish *vb* 1 *syn* see DIE 1
ant survive
2 to suffer spiritual or moral death <nations *perishing* for lack of true leaders>
syn die
rel decline; collapse, go under; expire, succumb; disappear, vanish; cease, end
con flourish, prosper, thrive
ant endure
‖3 *syn* see DECAY
perishing *adj syn* see DAMNED 2
perjure *vb* to make a false swearer of oneself by violating one's oath to tell the truth <a *perjured* witness>
syn forswear

---

syn synonym(s)   *rel* related word(s)
ant antonym(s)   *con* contrasted word(s)
idiom idiomatic equivalent(s)
‖ use limited; if in doubt, see a dictionary

rel equivocate; deceive, delude, mislead, trick; lie, prevaricate
idiom commit perjury, lie under oath, swear falsely

perjurer *n syn* see LIAR
perk (up) *vb syn* see IMPROVE 3
‖**perk** *n, usu* **perks** *pl syn* see GRATUITY
perlustrate *vb syn* see SCRUTINIZE 1
perlustration *n syn* see EXAMINATION
permanent *adj syn* see LASTING
　rel imperishable, invariable
　ant temporary
permeable *adj* capable of being permeated especially by fluids < a *permeable* membrane >
　syn penetrable, pervious, porose, porous
　rel passable
　con impassable, impenetrable, impervious
　ant impermeable
permeate *vb* to pass or cause to pass through every part of a thing < air *permeated* with cigar smoke >
　syn charge, compenetrate, impenetrate, impregnate, interfuse, interpenetrate, penetrate, percolate, pervade, saturate, transfuse
　rel invade; imbrue, imbue, infiltrate, infuse, ingrain; diffuse, suffuse; drench, soak, steep; fill
permissible *adj* that may be permitted < a *permissible* error >
　syn admissible, allowable
　rel unforbidden, unprohibited; allowed, permitted, tolerated; approved, authorized, endorsed, sanctioned; acceptable, bearable, tolerable
　con banned, forbidden, disallowed, prohibited, unpermitted, verboten; unacceptable, unbearable
　ant impermissible
permission *n* a sanctioning to act or do something that is granted by one in authority < received *permission* to leave work early >
　syn allowance, authorization, consent, leave, permit, sanction, sufferance
　rel acceptance, acquiescence; approbation, approval; endorsement
　ant prohibition
permit *vb syn* see LET 2
　rel tolerate
　idiom give one his head
　ant forbid, prohibit
permit *n syn* see PERMISSION
permutation *n syn* see CHANGE 2
　rel alteration, modification
pernicious *adj* exceedingly harmful or destructive < *pernicious* gossip >
　syn baneful, deadly, noxious, pestiferous, pestilent, pestilential; *compare* DEADLY 1
　rel damaging, deleterious, detrimental, harmful, hurtful; baleful, malefic, maleficent, malign, sinister; miasmatic, miasmic, poisonous, toxic, venomous; malignant, swart, virulent; destructive, devastating, ruinous; fatal, killing, lethal, mortal
　con harmless, uninjurious; nonmalignant, nonpoisonous, nontoxic
　ant innocuous
pernickety *adj syn* see NICE 1
perorate *vb syn* see ORATE
perpend *vb syn* see CONSIDER 1
perpendicular *adj syn* see VERTICAL
　rel stand-up, straight
　ant horizontal
perpendicularity *n syn* see VERTICALITY
　rel erectness, uprightness
　ant horizontality
perpetrate *vb syn* see COMMIT 2
　rel effect; inflict, wreak
　idiom ‖up and do
perpetual *adj syn* see CONTINUAL
　ant ephemeral, transient
perpetually *adv syn* see ALWAYS 1
perpetuate *vb* to make perpetual or cause to last indefinitely < *perpetuate* his memory for future generations >
　syn eternalize, eternize, immortalize
　rel bolster, conserve, keep, maintain, preserve, secure, support, sustain
　con annihilate, blot out, erase, expunge
　ant obliterate
perplex *vb* **1** *syn* see PUZZLE

rel discompose, perturb; balk, thwart; astonish, astound, surprise
　idiom put (*or* drive) to one's wit's end
　2 *syn* see COMPLICATE
　3 *syn* see ENTANGLE 1
perquisite *n* **1** *syn* see GRATUITY
　2 *syn* see RIGHT 2
per se *adv* by, of, or in itself or oneself or themselves < a lover of language *per se* >
　syn as such, intrinsically
　rel alone, independently, solely
persecute *vb* **1** *syn* see WRONG
　rel dragoon, rack, torment, torture
　con back, champion, support, uphold
　2 *syn* see MOLEST
　rel worry; hound, ride
　con humor, indulge, pamper; accommodate, favor, oblige
perseverant *adj syn* see PERSISTENT 1
perseverative *adj syn* see PERSISTENT 1
persevere *vb* to continue in a state, enterprise, or undertaking in spite of counter influences, opposition, or discouragement < *persevered* in his unpopular economic policy >
　syn carry on, go on, hang on, persist
　rel continue, get on, press (on), proceed
　idiom hang in there, keep at it, keep driving, never say die, stick (*or* tough) it out
　con falter, hesitate, vacillate, waver; renounce, surrender, yield
　ant give up
persevering *adj syn* see PERSISTENT 1
persiflage *n syn* see BANTER
persist *vb* **1** *syn* see PERSEVERE
　con cease, discontinue, quit, stop
　ant desist
　2 *syn* see CONTINUE 1
　rel go on; linger; obtain, prevail
　ant desist
persistence *n* **1** *syn* see CONTINUATION 1
　2 *syn* see RUN 2
　rel course
persistent *adj* **1** continuing in a course of action without regard to discouragement, opposition, or previous failure < a *persistent* suitor >
　syn dogged, insistent, perseverant, perseverative, persevering, persisting, persistive
　rel determined, steadfast, tenacious, unshakable; relentless, unremitting
　con malleable, pliant, tractable, yielding; infirm, invertebrate, spineless; vacillating, wavery, wobbling
　2 *syn* see PRIMITIVE 3
persisting *adj syn* see PERSISTENT 1
persistive *adj syn* see PERSISTENT 1
persnickety *adj syn* see NICE 1
person *n syn* see HUMAN
　rel chap, ‖cookie, coot, fellow, galoot, guy, specimen, stick
personage *n* **1** *syn* see NOTABLE 1
　2 *syn* see HUMAN
personal *adj* **1** of, relating to, or affecting a particular person < owed his *personal* allegiance to his wife >
　syn individual
　rel particular, peculiar, special
　con general, universal; common, joint, mutual, shared; commonplace, everyday, ordinary
　2 *syn* see PRIVATE 1
personal effects *n pl* privately owned items (as clothing and toilet articles) normally worn or carried on the person < packed his *personal effects* in a small bag >
　syn ‖plunder, stuff, things, traps, tricks
　rel belongings, goods, possessions
　idiom personal belongings
personality *n* **1** *syn* see INDIVIDUALITY 4
　2 *syn* see DISPOSITION 3
　3 *syn* see NOTABLE 1
personalize *vb* **1** *syn* see EMBODY 1
　rel anthropomorphize
　2 *syn* see REPRESENT 2
personal name *n syn* see GIVEN NAME
personate *vb* **1** *syn* see ACT 1
　2 *syn* see REPRESENT 2

personification *n syn* see EMBODIMENT
personify *vb* **1** *syn* see EMBODY 1
  rel reincarnate
  2 *syn* see REPRESENT 2
personize *vb syn* see EMBODY 1
perspective *n syn* see VISTA
perspicacious *adj syn* see SHREWD
  rel quick-sighted, sharp-sighted, sharp-witted
perspicacity *n syn* see WIT 3
perspicuity *n syn* see CLARITY
  rel intelligibility; explicitness
perspicuous *adj syn* see CLEAR 4
perspiring *adj syn* see SWEATY
perspiry *adj syn* see SWEATY
persuadable *adj syn* see RECEPTIVE 1
  ant unpersuadable
persuade *vb* **1** *syn* see INDUCE 1
  rel affect, impress, touch; reason; convert
  con discourage, hinder, prevent
  ant dissuade
  2 *syn* see CONVERT 1
  3 *syn* see ASSURE 2
  ant dissuade
persuasible *adj syn* see RECEPTIVE 1
  ant unpersuasible
persuasion *n* **1** *syn* see OPINION
  rel bias, partiality, predilection, prejudice, prepossession
  2 *syn* see RELIGION 1
  3 *syn* see RELIGION 2
  rel affiliation; order
  4 *syn* see TYPE
pert *adj* **1** *syn* see SAUCY 1
  rel bold, daring; audacious, brazen
  con shy
  ant coy
  2 *syn* see WISE 5
  rel disrespectful, rude
  3 *syn* see LIVELY 1
pertain *vb* **1** *syn* see BELONG 2
  2 *syn* see BEAR (on *or* upon)
  rel associate, combine, connect, join
  idiom be pertinent (*or* relevant) to
pertinacious *adj syn* see OBSTINATE
  rel fixed, unshakable; dogged, tenacious
pertinent *adj syn* see RELEVANT
  rel pertaining
  ant impertinent
perturb *vb syn* see DISCOMPOSE 1
  rel trouble; unsettle
  ant compose
pervade *vb syn* see PERMEATE
  idiom spread through and through
perverse *adj* **1** *syn* see VICIOUS 2
  2 *syn* see OBSTINATE
  rel cranky, irritable, unreasonable
  3 *syn* see CONTRARY 3
pervert *vb* **1** *syn* see DEBASE 1
  rel abuse, maltreat, mistreat, misuse, outrage; ruin
  2 *syn* see ABUSE 2
  rel ill-treat
  3 *syn* see MISREPRESENT
perverted *adj syn* see DEBASED
  rel defiled, polluted, tainted; contorted, distorted, warped; abused, misused, outraged
pervicacious *adj syn* see OBSTINATE
pervious *adj syn* see PERMEABLE
  ant impervious
pesky *adj syn* see TROUBLESOME
pesky *adv syn* see VERY 1
pessimist *n* one who emphasizes adverse aspects or conditions and expects the worst <*pessimists* predicting another depression>
  syn calamity howler, Cassandra, crepehanger, worrywart
  rel fussbudget; Job's comforter; defeatist; killjoy; cynic, misanthrope
  con positivist; idealist; Pollyanna
  ant optimist
pest *n* **1** *syn* see ANNOYANCE 3
  rel bane, trouble, vexation, worry

  idiom pain in the neck, pea in the shoe, thorn in the flesh
  2 one who pesters or annoys <a little *pest* who constantly asked questions>
  syn nudnick, nuisance, pesterer
  rel badgerer, heckler, tormentor
  idiom pain in the neck
pester *vb syn* see WORRY 1
  rel ride
  idiom drive (one) crazy, drive (one) up the wall, pester to death
pester *n syn* see ANNOYANCE 3
pesterer *n syn* see PEST 2
‖**pesterment** *n syn* see ANNOYANCE 3
pesticide *n* a chemical agent used to destroy pests <the need to control indiscriminate use of *pesticides*>
  syn biocide, economic poison
  rel bactericide, fungicide, germicide, insecticide, microbicide, rodenticide, vermicide
pestiferous *adj syn* see PERNICIOUS
pestilence *n syn* see PLAGUE 1
pestilent *adj* **1** *syn* see DEADLY 1
  2 *syn* see PERNICIOUS
pestilential *adj* **1** *syn* see DEADLY 1
  2 *syn* see PERNICIOUS
pet *adj syn* see FAVORITE 1
pet *vb syn* see CARESS
  rel embrace, hug
pet *vb syn* see SULK
petcock *n syn* see FAUCET
peter (out) *vb syn* see DECREASE
Peter Funk *n syn* see SWINDLER
petite *adj syn* see SMALL 1
  rel diminutive, dwarf, lilliputian, miniature, wee
petition *n syn* see PRAYER
  rel request
petition *vb* to make an earnest, formal, and often written request <*petitioned* for a hearing before the labor board>
  syn appeal, sue (for *or* to)
  rel ask, request; beg, beseech, entreat, implore, plead, pray, supplicate
  con claim, demand, exact, press (for)
petitioner *n syn* see SUPPLIANT
petit–maître *n syn* see FOP
petrify *vb syn* see DAZE 2
  rel alarm, frighten, startle, terrify; appall, dismay, horrify; numb
  idiom turn to stone
pettifogger *n* an unscrupulous lawyer <done out of his rights by a slick *pettifogger*>
  syn jackleg lawyer, shyster; *compare* LAWYER
  rel ambulance chaser, Philadelphia lawyer; ‖bush lawyer
pettifogging *adj syn* see PETTY 2
pettish *adj syn* see IRRITABLE
petty *adj* **1** *syn* see LITTLE 3
  2 being often contemptibly insignificant or unimportant <*petty* quarrels and intrigues>
  syn inconsequent, inconsequential, inconsiderable, measly, Mickey Mouse, niggling, paltry, peanut, peddling, pettifogging, picayune, picayunish, piddling, piffling, pimping, puny, small, trifling, trivial, unconsequential, unconsidered, ungenerous, unvital; *compare* LITTLE 3
  rel negligible, unimportant; hair-drawn, hairsplitting; impertinent, irrelevant
  con consequential, considerable; big, gross; significant, vital
  ant important, momentous
petulant *adj syn* see IRRITABLE
  rel grouchy, sulky
phantasm *n* **1** *syn* see DELUSION 1
  rel fabrication, fiction, invention
  2 *syn* see APPARITION
  3 *syn* see FANCY 4
phantom *n syn* see APPARITION
pharisaic *adj syn* see HYPOCRITICAL
pharisaical *adj syn* see HYPOCRITICAL

---

syn synonym(s)   *rel* related word(s)
ant antonym(s)   *con* contrasted word(s)
idiom idiomatic equivalent(s)
‖ use limited; if in doubt, see a dictionary

pharisaicalness *n syn* see HYPOCRISY
pharisaism *n syn* see HYPOCRISY
pharisee *n syn* see HYPOCRITE
pharmaceutic *n syn* see DRUG 1
pharmaceutical *n syn* see DRUG 1
pharmacist *n syn* see DRUGGIST
pharmacon *n syn* see REMEDY 1
pharos *n syn* see LIGHTHOUSE
phase *n* one of the possible ways of viewing or being presented to view <the moral *phase* of the problem>
  syn angle, aspect, facet, hand, side
  rel condition, situation, state; position, posture, view, viewpoint; appearance, look, semblance; color, complexion
phenomenal *adj* **1** *syn* see MATERIAL 1
  con ontic
  ant noumenal
  2 *syn* see EXCEPTIONAL 1
phenomenon *n* **1** *syn* see FACT 2
  rel experience; actuality, reality
  2 *syn* see WONDER 1
  rel abnormality; anomaly, paradox; peculiarity, singularity, uniqueness, unusualness
philander *n syn* see WOLF
  idiom ‖skirt chaser
philander *vb* to have many love affairs <his reputation for *philandering* with married women>
  syn fool (around), mess around, play (around), wolf, womanize
  rel dally, flirt, trifle; chase, pursue; ‖tomcat (around)
  idiom ‖chase skirts, play Don Juan, play the femmes
philanderer *n syn* see WOLF
philanthropic *adj syn* see CHARITABLE 1
  rel bighearted, freehearted, greathearted, kindhearted, largehearted, openhearted; contributing, donating, freehanded, giving, magnanimous; civic-minded, public-spirited
  ant misanthropic
philharmonic *n syn* see ORCHESTRA
philippic *n syn* see TIRADE
philistine *n* a crass, prosaic, often priggish individual guided by material rather than artistic or intellectual values <*philistines* who opposed everything new and creative in art>
  syn Babbitt, boeotian, boob, middlebrow
  rel bourgeois; capitalist; materialist; boor, clown, lout, vulgarian
  ant aesthete
phiz *n syn* see FACE 1
phlegm *n* **1** *syn* see APATHY 1
  2 *syn* see EQUANIMITY
  rel nonchalance, unconcern
phlegmatic *adj syn* see IMPASSIVE 1
  rel calm, undemonstrative; aloof, incurious, indifferent, unconcerned; lethargic, sluggish
phoebus *n syn* see SUN 1
phoenix *n syn* see PARAGON
phonate *vb syn* see ARTICULATE 2
phone *vb syn* see TELEPHONE
phony *adj syn* see COUNTERFEIT
phony *n* **1** *syn* see IMPOSTURE
  2 *syn* see IMPOSTOR
photo *vb syn* see PHOTOGRAPH
  idiom take a photo (of)
photog *n syn* see PHOTOGRAPHER
photograph *vb* to use a camera to make a picture, image, or likeness of <*photographed* the whole family>
  syn photo, shoot
  rel cinematize, ‖cinematograph, cinemize, film, filmize, picture; kodak, snap, snapshoot, snapshot; mug
  idiom capture on film, take a picture (*or* photograph)
photographer *n* one who takes photographs <a newspaper *photographer*>
  syn cameraman, camerist, photog, photographist, photoist
  rel snapshooter, ‖snapshotter; shutterbug
photographic *adj syn* see GRAPHIC 1
  rel accurate, detailed, exact
photographist *n syn* see PHOTOGRAPHER
photoist *n syn* see PHOTOGRAPHER
photoplay *n syn* see MOVIE
phrase *n* **1** *syn* see WORDING
  rel styling

2 a group of words which, taken together, express a notion and may constitute part of a sentence <an adverbial *phrase*> <a trite *phrase*>
  syn expression, locution
  rel phrasing; idiom; catchword, slogan
  3 *syn* see CATCHWORD
phrase *vb syn* see WORD
phraseology *n syn* see WORDING
  idiom choice of words
phrasing *n syn* see WORDING
phthisis *n syn* see TUBERCULOSIS
phylactery *n syn* see CHARM 2
physic *n syn* see REMEDY 1
physical *adj* **1** *syn* see MATERIAL 1
  rel natural; elemental, elementary
  ant spiritual
  2 *syn* see BODILY
  rel visceral; lusty; brute
  ant mental
physician *n* a doctor of medicine <the shortage of *physicians* in rural areas>
  syn ‖croaker, doc, doctor, MD, medical, mediciner, medico, ‖sawbones
  rel medic; general practitioner, practitioner; surgeon; specialist
  idiom medical doctor, medical man
physique *n* bodily makeup or type <a muscular *physique*>
  syn build, constitution, habit, habitus
  rel anatomy, structure; configuration, shape; body, figure, form, frame
picaroon *n syn* see PIRATE
picayune *adj syn* see PETTY 2
picayunish *adj syn* see PETTY 2
pick *vb* **1** *syn* see CHOOSE 1
  idiom pick and choose
  ant reject
  2 *syn* see PECK 1
pick *n syn* see BEST
pick *adj syn* see SELECT 1
picked *adj syn* see SELECT 1
picket *n syn* see GUARD 2
pickle *n syn* see PREDICAMENT
  idiom pretty pickle, ‖sticky wicket, tight spot
‖pickled *adj syn* see INTOXICATED 1
pick out *vb syn* see CHOOSE 1
pickpocket *n* one who steals from pockets <his wallet was lifted by a *pickpocket*>
  syn ‖cannon, cutpurse, ‖dip, ‖diver, purse cutter, ‖wire
  rel ‖ganef, thief; ‖mobsman, ‖swell-mobsman
  idiom ‖pocket prowler
picksome *adj syn* see NICE 1
pick up *vb* **1** *syn* see LIFT 1
  2 *syn* see GLEAN
  3 *syn* see GET 1
  4 *syn* see LEARN 1
  5 *syn* see ARREST 2
  rel book
  idiom ‖take (someone) downtown
  6 *syn* see RESUME 2
  idiom pick up the thread again
pickup *n syn* see ARREST
  rel booking
picky *adj syn* see NICE 1
picnic *n syn* see SNAP 1
pictorial *adj* **1** consisting of or relating to pictures <a collection of *pictorial* materials>
  syn graphic, iconographic, illustrational, illustrative, illustratory, pictoric
  rel photographic, pictographic
  2 *syn* see GRAPHIC 1
pictoric *adj syn* see PICTORIAL 1
picture *n* **1** *syn* see REPRESENTATION
  2 *syn* see IMAGE 1
  3 *syn* see MOVIE
picture *vb syn* see REPRESENT 1
  rel draw
picture show *n syn* see MOVIE
picturesque *adj syn* see GRAPHIC 1
piddling *adj syn* see PETTY 2

pie *n syn* see SNAP 1
piece *n* **1** *syn* see PART 1
|| **2** *syn* see SNACK
pièce de résistance *n syn* see SHOWPIECE
piecemeal *adv syn* see GRADUALLY
piecemeal *adj syn* see GRADUAL
||**pie–eyed** *adj syn* see INTOXICATED 1
piepoudre *n syn* see PEDDLER
pier *n* **1** *syn* see WHARF
  rel pierage, wharfage
  2 *syn* see PILLAR 1
pierce *vb* **1** *syn* see CUT 1
  rel penetrate, perforate
  2 *syn* see PENETRATE 2
  rel run through
piercing *adj* **1** *syn* see SHARP 8
  2 *syn* see LOUD 1
  3 *syn* see ACUTE 4
pietistic *adj syn* see DEVOUT
  rel reverencing, reverential
piety *n syn* see FIDELITY 1
  rel docility, obedience; enthusiasm, fervor, passion, zeal; holiness, sanctity
piffle *n syn* see NONSENSE 2
piffling *adj syn* see PETTY 2
||**pig** *n* **1** *syn* see WANTON
  2 *syn* see POLICEMAN
pigeon *n syn* see FOOL 3
pigeon *vb syn* see DUPE
pigeonhole *n* **1** *syn* see CUBBYHOLE
  2 *syn* see CLASS 1
  rel niche, slot
pigeonhole *vb syn* see ASSORT
  rel identify, label, name; place, rank, rate; catalog; break down, subdivide
pigeon house *n syn* see DOVECOTE
pigeonry *n syn* see DOVECOTE
pigheaded *adj syn* see OBSTINATE
  idiom not to be moved (*or* budged)
pigment *n syn* see COLOR 6
pigpen *n syn* see STY 1
pigsty *n syn* see STY 1
piked *adj syn* see POINTED 1
piker *n syn* see VAGABOND
piker *n syn* see MISER
pilaster *n syn* see PILLAR 1
pile *n* **1** a quantity of things heaped or stacked together < a *pile* of dirty clothes >
  syn bank, ||bing, cock, drift, heap, hill, mass, mound, mountain, mow, pyramid, rick, ||rickle, ||ruck, shock, stack, stockpile, windrow
  rel barrow, pyre, tumulus; ||dess, haycock, hayrick, haystack; accumulation, aggregate, aggregation, amassment, assemblage, collection, conglomeration, glomeration, hoard, jumble
  2 *syn* see MUCH
  3 *syn* see EDIFICE
  4 *syn* see FORTUNE 4
  idiom a pile of money
pile *vb* **1** *syn* see HEAP 1
  2 *syn* see LOAD 3
pile (in) *vb syn* see RETIRE 4
pile (out) *vb syn* see ROLL OUT
  idiom ||get the lead out, ||shake it out
pile *n syn* see DOWN
pileous *adj syn* see HAIRY 1
  con bare; pileless
pile up *vb syn* see SHIPWRECK 1
pileup *n syn* see CRASH 3
pilfer *vb syn* see STEAL 1
pilferer *n syn* see THIEF
pilgarlic *n syn* see LAUGHINGSTOCK
||**pill** *n syn* see CIGARETTE
pillage *vb* **1** *syn* see RAVAGE
  rel encroach, invade, trespass; appropriate, arrogate, confiscate, usurp
  idiom lay waste
  2 *syn* see STEAL 1
pillager *n syn* see MARAUDER

pillar *n* **1** a firm upright support for a superstructure < stone *pillars* supported the ceiling >
  syn column, pier, pilaster
  rel prop; pedestal; post
  2 *syn* see MAINSTAY
pilose *adj syn* see HAIRY 1
pilot *n* **1** *syn* see LEADER 1
  2 one who flies or is qualified to fly an airplane < jet *pilots* >
  syn airman, aviator, birdman, flier, fly-boy
  rel aerialist
pilot *vb* **1** *syn* see GUIDE
  2 *syn* see DRIVE 5
pimp *n* **1** a man who solicits for a prostitute, lives off her earnings, and often lives with her < after dark, the *pimp* appeared on the street seeking clients for his girls >
  syn bully, cadet, ||easy rider, fancy man, ||mack, macquereau, pander
  rel procurer; white slaver
  ||**2** *syn* see INFORMER
||**pimp** *vb syn* see INFORM 3
pimping *adj syn* see PETTY 2
pimple *n syn* see ABSCESS
  rel ||plouk
pimple *vb syn* see SPOT 2
pin *n syn* see BROOCH
pinch *vb* **1** *syn* see EXTORT 1
  2 *syn* see STEAL 1
  3 *syn* see ARREST 2
  4 *syn* see SCRIMP
pinch *n* **1** *syn* see JUNCTURE 2
  2 *syn* see THEFT
  3 *syn* see ARREST
pinchbeck *adj syn* see COUNTERFEIT
pinched *adj syn* see HAGGARD
  con stalwart, stout, strong, sturdy; healthy, robust
pinching *adj syn* see STINGY
pinch hitter *n syn* see SUBSTITUTE
pinchpenny *adj syn* see STINGY
||**pindling** *adj syn* see IRRITABLE
pine *vb syn* see LONG
  rel brood, fret, mope; grieve, mourn; agonize
pinhead *n syn* see DUNCE
pinhead *adj syn* see STUPID 1
pinheaded *adj syn* see STUPID 1
pink *vb syn* see BLUSH
pinken *vb syn* see BLUSH
Pinkerton *n syn* see PRIVATE DETECTIVE
pin money *n syn* see POCKET MONEY
pinnacle *n syn* see APEX 2
pinpoint *vb syn* see IDENTIFY
pint–size *adj syn* see TINY
pioneer *adj syn* see FIRST 2
  rel pilot
pious *adj syn* see DEVOUT
  rel priestlike, priestly
  ant impious
pip *vb* ||**1** *syn* see DEFEAT 2
  2 *syn* see DIE 1
||**pip** *n syn* see ||DILLY, ||corker, crackerjack, ||daisy, dandy, humdinger, jim-dandy, ||lalapalooza, ||lulu, nifty
pipe *n* **1** *syn* see CASK
  ||**2** *syn* see PIPE DREAM
  ||**3** *syn* see SNAP 1
pipe *vb* ||**1** *syn* see CRY 2
  2 *syn* see CONDUCT 4
pipe down *vb syn* see SHUT UP 2
pipe dream *n* an illusory or fantastic plan or hope < *pipe dreams* of universal peace >
  syn bubble, chimera, dream, fantasy (*or* phantasy), illusion, ||pipe, rainbow
  rel expectation, hope, prospect
pipeline *n* a person through whom information is transmitted < she was his news *pipeline* from the mayor's office >

---

syn synonym(s)   *rel* related word(s)
ant antonym(s)   *con* contrasted word(s)
idiom idiomatic equivalent(s)
|| use limited; if in doubt, see a dictionary

syn channel, conduit

rel grapevine; origin, source, wellspring; supplier; connection, contact

piping *adj syn* see ACUTE 4

‖**pipped** *adj syn* see INTOXICATED 1

pippin *n syn* ‖DILLY, ‖corker, crackerjack, dandy, ‖dinger, ‖doozer, humdinger, jim-dandy, ‖lalapalooza, ‖pip

piquant *adj syn* see PUNGENT

rel high-flavored, well-flavored; appetizing, sparkling

con inane, jejune

ant banal

pique *n syn* see OFFENSE 2

rel annoyance, irk, irking, vexation; exasperation, irritation, provocation

pique *vb* 1 *syn* see IRRITATE

2 *syn* see PROVOKE 4

rel prick, punch; ignite

3 *syn* see PRIDE

pirate *n* a robber on the high seas <little boys dreaming of sailing as *pirates* >

syn buccaneer, corsair, freebooter, picaroon, rover, sea dog, sea robber, sea rover, sea wolf

rel viking; privateer; looter, marauder, pillager, plunderer, raider

‖**pirl** *vb syn* see SPIN 1

‖**piroot** *vb syn* see SNOOP

pirouette *vb syn* see SPIN 1

pishposh *n syn* see NONSENSE 2

pit *n* ‖1 *syn* see GRAVE

2 *syn* see HELL

pit *vb syn* see OPPOSE 1

pitch *vb* 1 *syn* see THROW 1

rel hoist, raise; move

2 *syn* see THROW 2

‖3 *syn* see PLANT 1

4 *syn* see FALL 2

idiom take a pitch

5 *syn* see PLUNGE 2

rel drop, fall, sink

6 *syn* see TOSS 2

7 *syn* see SEESAW

pitch *n syn* see SPIEL

rel persuasion

pitch–black *adj syn* see BLACK 1

pitch–dark *adj syn* see BLACK 1

pitched *adj syn* see INCLINED 3

pitch in *vb* 1 to set about doing something energetically <had a lot to do and decided to *pitch in* >

syn buckle (down), fall to, jump (in *or* into), set to, wade (in *or* into)

rel attack, tackle; launch, tee off; begin, commence, start (off *or* out *or* up)

idiom fall to it, fall to work, get busy (*or* cracking), get down to it, get going, get (*or* have) with it, go to it, hop (*or* jump) to it

con dally, dawdle, procrastinate, stall; vacillate

2 *syn* see CONTRIBUTE 1

pitching *adj syn* see INCLINED 3

pitchy *adj syn* see BLACK 1

piteous *adj syn* see PITIFUL 1

rel beseeching, entreating, imploring, supplicating; doleful, dolorous, melancholy, plaintive; ruined

pitfall *n* a hidden or obscure source of danger, error, or harm <*pitfalls* that trap the unwary investigator >

syn booby trap, deadfall, mousetrap, springe, trapfall

rel danger, hazard, peril, risk; cobweb, entanglement, mesh(es), toil(s), web; bait, lure, snare, trap

pith *n* 1 *syn* see ESSENCE 2

rel center, focus, nucleus; meaning, meaningfulness

2 *syn* see SUBSTANCE 2

idiom the long and (the) short

3 *syn* see CENTER 3

rel fulcrum; hub

4 *syn* see IMPORTANCE

pithy *adj* being rich in meaning and tersely cogent in expression <a *pithy* summary >

syn compact, epigrammatic, marrowy, meaty; *compare* CONCISE

rel brief, concise, lean, short, short and sweet, succinct; crisp, curt, terse; effective, forceful; meaningful, significant, substantial

idiom brief and to the point, down to brass tacks, right to the point

con flatulent, inflated, tumid, turgid; prolix, verbose, wordy

ant diffuse

pitiable *adj* 1 *syn* see PITIFUL 1

2 *syn* see CONTEMPTIBLE

rel miserable, wretched; deplorable, lamentable

pitiful *adj* 1 arousing or deserving pity <*pitiful* refugees driven from their homes >

syn commiserable, pathetic, piteous, pitiable, poor, rueful

rel affecting, moving, touching; miserable, woeful, wretched; heartrending

2 *syn* see CONTEMPTIBLE

pitiless *adj* devoid of or unmoved by pity <a *pitiless* concentration camp guard >

syn merciless, unmerciful, unpitying; *compare* UNFEELING 2

rel coldhearted, hardhearted, heartless, ironhearted, marblehearted, stony, stonyhearted, uncompassionate, unfeeling; barbarous, brutal, cruel, cutthroat, inhumane, savage

idiom lacking bowels of compassion, without an ounce of pity

con compassionate, humane, sympathetic; clement, merciful; tender, warmhearted

ant pitying

pittance *n* a small, often barely sufficient amount or allowance <a *pittance* of an education > <worked for a mere *pittance* >

syn dribble, driblet, ‖scrimption

rel bit, mite, scrap, smidgen, trace; inadequacy, insufficiency

idiom a drop in the bucket, cheeseparings and candle ends, ‖pinchgut money

con abundance, opulence, plenty, wealth

pity *n* sympathetic feeling for one suffering, distressed, or unhappy <felt the deepest *pity* for the prisoners >

syn commiseration, compassion, rue, ruth, sympathy

rel dejection, distress, melancholy, sadness, sorrow; charity, clemency, lenity, mercy

con contempt, disdain, disgust, scorn

pity *vb syn* see COMPASSIONATE

pivot *vb syn* see TURN 6

pivotal *adj syn* see CENTRAL 1

rel essential, vital; momentous; capital, principal

pixie *n* 1 *syn* see FAIRY

2 *syn* see SCAMP

pixie *adj syn* see PLAYFUL 1

pixieish *adj syn* see PLAYFUL 1

pixilated *adj* 1 *syn* see PLAYFUL 1

2 *syn* see INTOXICATED 1

placard *n syn* see POSTER

placard *vb syn* see POST

placate *vb syn* see PACIFY

rel comfort; tranquilize

idiom lay the dust

con anger, incense, infuriate, madden; excite, pique, provoke, stimulate

ant enrage

place *n* 1 the portion of space occupied by or chosen for something <the *place* where we'll meet >

syn location, locus, point, position, site, situation, spot, station, where

rel district, locality, vicinity; area, region, tract, zone; field, province, territory

2 *syn* see STATUS 1

3 *syn* see JOB 2

place *vb* 1 *syn* see SET 1

2 *syn* see ESTIMATE 3

3 *syn* see IDENTIFY

rel know, tell; nail, peg

idiom put one's finger on

placed *adj syn* see SITUATED

ant displaced

placid *adj* 1 *syn* see CALM 1

rel irenic, peaceful, serene, unagitated, unstirring

ant roiled

2 *syn* see CALM 2

rel detached, inexcitable, unmoved

con fidgety, jittery, jumpy, skittery; agitated

ant choleric

plague *n* 1 an epidemic disease causing a high mortality rate <smallpox finally ceased to be a *plague* in those nations >

syn curse, pestilence, scourge
rel infestation, invasion; affliction, disease; epidemic; ravage
2 syn see ANNOYANCE 3
rel bane, curse
3 syn see EPIDEMIC
plague vb syn see WORRY 1
rel chafe, gall; badger, bait, hassle, hector, hound, ride; afflict, torment
plain adj **1** free from all ostentation or superficial embellishment < just give the plain facts >
syn discreet, dry, homely, inelaborate, modest, simple, unadorned, unbeautified, undecorated, unelaborate, unembellished, unembroidered, ungarnished, unornamented, unostentatious, unpretentious
rel muted, restrained; austere, bald, bare, severe, spartan, stark, unluxurious; homespun
con adorned, beautified, elaborate, embellished, embroidered, exaggerated; high-flown, ostentatious, pretentious; flamboyant, rococo
ant rich
2 syn see STRAIGHT 3
3 syn see CLEAR 5
rel broad, unmistakable; legible
ant abstruse
4 syn see FRANK
rel unfeigned; abrupt
idiom plain and open
5 lacking allure without being positively ugly < a plain woman, drably dressed >
syn homely, unalluring, unattractive, unbeauteous, unbeautiful, uncomely, unhandsome, unpretty
rel plain-featured; inelegant; ordinary, plain Jane, unremarkable; ill-favored
idiom not much for looks, not much to look at, short on looks
con alluring, attractive, beautiful, comely, handsome; elegant; striking; knockout, sensational
6 syn see ORDINARY 1
plainclothesman n syn see DETECTIVE
plain dealing adj syn see STRAIGHTFORWARD 2
plain Jane adj syn see ORDINARY 1
plainness n syn see CLARITY
ant abstruseness
plainspoken adj syn see FRANK
plaintive adj syn see MELANCHOLY 2
rel deploring, lamenting, wailing; piteous, pitiful; sad, saddening
plan n **1** a method devised for making or doing something or attaining an end < each company had a plan for increasing profits >
syn blueprint, design, game plan, project, scheme, strategy
rel conception, idea, notion; ground plan, projection, projet; intent, intention, platform, purpose; means, method, way
idiom course (or plan) of action
2 syn see INTENTION
rel policy
3 syn see ORDER 8
plan vb **1 syn** see DESIGN 3
2 to formulate a plan for arranging, realizing, or achieving something < planned next year's program >
syn arrange, blueprint, cast, chart, design, devise, ||dope out, project; compare DESIGN 3
rel contemplate, meditate; cut out, draft, outline, sketch; figure (out), think (out); formulate, work out; organize
3 syn see INTEND 2
idiom be planning (or counting) on, have all intentions of, have every intention of
planate n syn see LEVEL
plane vb syn see EVEN 1
plane adj syn see LEVEL
planet n, used with the syn see EARTH 1
planetary adj **1 syn** see HUGE
2 syn see UNIVERSAL 2
plangent adj syn see RESONANT
plant vb **1** to put or set into the ground for growth < plant corn >
syn ||pitch, put in, seed, sow
rel drill; broadcast, dust, scatter; seed down
con crop, gather, harvest, reap

2 syn see HIDE
3 syn see BURY 1
plant n syn see FACTORY
plash vb syn see SPLASH
plaster vb syn see SMEAR
||plastered adj syn see INTOXICATED 1
plastic adj susceptible of being modified in form or nature < the plastic quality of modeling clay > < the plastic affections of children >
syn adaptable, ductile, malleable, moldable, pliable, pliant, supple
rel elastic, flexible, resilient, supple, workable; impressionable, influenceable, suggestible, susceptible; amenable, bending, giving, tractable, yielding
con inflexible, rigid, stiff; accepted, customary, prevailing, set, standard, wonted
plat n syn see LOT 3
plateau n a usually extensive level land area raised sharply above adjacent land on at least one side < the plateaus of central Bolivia >
syn table, tableland, upland
rel mesa
con dale, glen, vale, valley; bottom, bottomland, lowland
platitude n syn see COMMONPLACE
rel inanity, insipidity, vapidity; mawkishness, sentimentality
platoon n syn see GROUP 3
plaudit n, usu **plaudits** pl syn see APPLAUSE
rel kudos
plausibility n syn see VERISIMILITUDE
plausible adj syn see BELIEVABLE
rel likely, possible, probable; presumable
con impossible, improbable, unlikely
ant implausible
play n **1** activity engaged in for amusement < children need periods of work and play >
syn disport, diversion, fun, recreation, sport
rel amusement, entertainment; frolic, gambol, romp; delectation, delight, enjoyment, pleasure
con business, duty, obligation; labor; drudgery
ant work
2 syn see FUN 1
rel sportiveness
ant earnest
3 syn see TRICK 1
4 syn see USE 1
5 syn see ROOM 3
play vb **1** to engage in an activity for amusement or recreation < played outside for hours >
syn disport, recreate, sport
rel amuse, divert, engage, entertain; frolic, gambol, rollick, romp
con labor, toil, travail; drudge, fag, slave
ant work
2 syn see FIDDLE 1
3 syn see TREAT 2
4 syn see MANIPULATE 2
5 syn see ACT 1
6 syn see GAMBLE 1
play (around) vb syn see PHILANDER
play (down) vb syn see SOFT-PEDAL
rel restrain; mute, soften
ant play (up)
play (off) vb syn see OPPOSE 1
play (up) vb syn see EMPHASIZE
idiom make a (big) production of
ant play (down)
playact vb syn see ACT 1
playactor n syn see ACTOR 1
player n syn see ACTOR 1
playful adj **1** given to or characterized by play, jests, or tricks < in a playful mood >
syn antic, coltish, elvish, frisky, frolicsome, gamesome, impish, kittenish, larkish, ||mischiefful, mischievous, pixie, pixieish, pixi-

lated, prankful, prankish, pranky, puckish, roguish, sportive, waggish, wicked

rel gay, lighthearted, whimsical; dashing, larking, lively, sprightly; blithe, jocund, jolly, jovial, merry; gleeful, hilarious, mirthful

idiom as playful as a kitten (*or* colt), feeling one's oats

con grim, stern, stolid; grave, serious

2 *syn* see ANTIC 2

||**play-pretty** *n syn* see TOY 2

plaything *n syn* see TOY 2

playwright *n* one who writes plays <a famous Broadway *playwright* >

syn dramatist, dramatizer, dramaturge

rel librettist; scenarist

plaza *n syn* see COMMON 2

plea *n* 1 *syn* see EXCUSE 1

rel extenuation, mitigation, palliation; apology; out; vindication

2 *syn* see PRAYER

rel overture; call, cry

idiom solemn entreaty (*or* plea)

plead *vb syn* see BEG

pleasance *n syn* see AMENITY 1

pleasant *adj* 1 highly acceptable to the mind or senses <a *pleasant* personality > <a *pleasant* respite>

syn agreeable, congenial, favorable, good, grateful, gratifying, nice, pleasing, pleasurable, pleasureful, welcome

rel cheerful, cheering, cheery, glad, joyful, joyous; alluring, attractive, charming, pretty; convivial, engaging

con displeasing, distasteful; harsh; obnoxious, repellent, repelling, repugnant, repulsive

ant unpleasant

2 *syn* see FAIR 2

pleasantness *n syn* see AMENITY 1

rel goodness, niceness

ant unpleasantness

please *vb* 1 *syn* see WILL

2 to give or be a source of pleasure to <her work *pleased* him>

syn arride, delectate, delight, gladden, gratify, happify, pleasure

rel content, satisfy, suit; amuse, tickle, titillate; regale, rejoice; overjoy

con vex; annoy; anger

ant displease

3 *syn* see SUIT 6

pleasing *adj syn* see PLEASANT 1

rel satisfactory, suitable; enchanting, winning; adorable, darling, delightful

ant displeasing, repellent

pleasurable *adj syn* see PLEASANT 1

ant unpleasurable

pleasure *n* 1 *syn* see WILL 1

2 the agreeable emotion accompanying the expectation, acquisition, or possession of something good or desirable <the *pleasures* and pains of growing up>

syn delectation, delight, enjoyment, fruition, joy, joyance; *compare* ENJOYMENT 1

rel bliss, felicity, happiness; kick, thrill

con vexation; annoyance; anger; affliction, distress, sorrow, trouble

ant displeasure

3 *syn* see ENJOYMENT 1

ant displeasure

pleasure *vb syn* see PLEASE 2

pleasure dome *n syn* see RESORT 3

pleasureful *adj syn* see PLEASANT 1

pleasuremonger *n syn* see HEDONIST

pleb *n* **plebs** *pl syn* see COMMONALTY

plebeian *adj syn* see IGNOBLE 1

ant patrician

plebeians *n pl syn* see COMMONALTY

ant patricians

plebs *n* **plebes** *pl syn* see COMMONALTY

rel peasantry, peasants

ant patricians, patriciate

pledge *n* 1 something given or held as a sign of another's good faith or intentions <the new school is the *pledge* given by the community to its children>

syn earnest, pawn, security, token, warrant; *compare* GUARANTEE 1, PROMISE

rel bail, bond, guarantee, guaranty, surety, warranty; promise, word; oath, vow

2 *syn* see WORD 8

pledge *vb* 1 *syn* see PAWN

2 *syn* see DRINK 2

3 *syn* see PROMISE 1

rel bind, tie; commit, confide, consign, entrust

idiom give (*or* make) a solemn pledge, pledge one's honor

4 *syn* see VOW

plenteous *adj syn* see PLENTIFUL

rel full, hearty; fruitful, galore, prolific; luxurious, opulent, sumptuous; lavish, prodigal, profuse, profusive, rampant, rife

plentiful *adj* being more than sufficient without being excessive <a *plentiful* harvest>

syn abundant, ample, bounteous, bountiful, copious, generous, liberal, plenteous, plenty

rel enough, sufficient; fulsome, rich, unstinted; excessive, extravagant, overabundant, overflowing, superabundant; abounding, bumper, bursting, swarming, swimming, teeming

con deficient, exiguous, meager, skimpy; inadequate, insufficient

ant scant, scanty

plenty *n syn* see MUCH

rel abundance, cornucopia

plenty *adj syn* see PLENTIFUL

pleonasm *n syn* see VERBIAGE 1

plethora *n syn* see EXCESS 1

rel much, plenty; many; deluge, flood

pliable *adj syn* see PLASTIC

rel manipulable, manipulatable

con unadaptable, unflexible, unmalleable, unpliant

ant unpliable

pliant *adj syn* see PLASTIC

rel spongy

ant unpliant

plica *n syn* see WRINKLE

plight *vb syn* see VOW

idiom plight one's honor

plight *n syn* see PROMISE

plight *n syn* see PREDICAMENT

rel quandary

plighted *adj syn* see ENGAGED 2

plink *vb syn* see TINKLE 1

plod *vb* 1 to walk laboriously and heavily <slowly *plodded* across the sodden field>

syn footslog, ||plodge, plunther, slog, slop, stodge, toil, ||trash, trudge; *compare* TRAMP 1

rel tramp, trample, tromp; stamp, stomp, stump; flounder, wallow

2 *syn* see DRUDGE

idiom plug away at it

plodding *adj syn* see DULL 9

||**plodge** *vb syn* see PLOD 1

plot *n* 1 *syn* see LOT 3

2 a secret plan for accomplishing a usually evil or unlawful end <an assassination *plot* >

syn cabal, conspiracy, covin, intrigue, machination, practice, scheme

rel design, plan; connivance, conniving; collusion, complicity; contraption, contrivance, device; artifice, maneuver, ruse, stratagem, trick

plot *vb* to work out a plan especially for something unlawful or wrong <*plotted* the overthrow of the government>

syn cogitate, ||collogue, collude, connive, conspire, contrive, devise, intrigue, machinate, scheme (out)

rel lay; brew, concoct, cook (up), hatch, set up; finagle, maneuver

plow *vb* to cut into and work the surface of (soil) <*plow* a field>

syn break, plow up, turn, turn over

rel cultivate, till; fallow; ||backset; furrow, list, ridge, trench; harrow, rake

plow up *vb syn* see PLOW

rel plow out

ploy *n syn* see TRICK 1

pluck *n syn* see COURAGE

||**plucked** *adj syn* see BRAVE 1

plucky *adj syn* see BRAVE 1

idiom full of pluck (*or* spunk)

con feeble, weak

ant pluckless

plug *n syn* see PUFF 3

plug *vb* **1** *syn* see FILL 1
  rel pack; cork
  2 *syn* see PROMOTE 3

plugging *n syn* see WORK 2

plug–ugly *n syn* see TOUGH

plum *n syn* see REWARD
  rel catch, find

‖**plumb** *adv syn* see WELL 3

plumb *vb syn* see SOUND

plumb *adj syn* see VERTICAL

plumbless *adj syn* see BOTTOMLESS 2
  con plumbable

plumb–line *vb syn* see SOUND

plumbness *n syn* see VERTICALITY

plume *vb syn* see PRIDE

plummet *vb* to decrease suddenly and sharply in financial value or price <the stock *plummeted* 60 points when the story broke>
  syn dip, drop, fall, nose-dive, plunge, skid, tumble
  rel decline, decrease, descend, sink; dump; precipitate; collapse, crash
  idiom take a sudden downturn (*or* downtrend)
  con increase; rise; shoot up
  ant skyrocket, soar

plummetless *adj syn* see BOTTOMLESS 2

plump *adj syn* see ROTUND 2
  rel fleshy, portly
  idiom plump as a partridge
  ant skinny

plumpish *adj syn* see ROTUND 2
  idiom like a butterball

plumpy *adj syn* see ROTUND 2

plunder *vb syn* see ROB 1

plunder *n* **1** *syn* see SPOIL
  ‖**2** *syn* see PERSONAL EFFECTS

plunderage *n syn* see SPOIL

plunderer *n syn* see MARAUDER

plunge *vb* **1** *syn* see THRUST 2
  2 to thrust or cast oneself or something into or as if into deep water <*plunged* into the crowd>
  syn burst, dive, drive, lunge, pitch, ‖splunge; *compare* RUSH 1
  rel dip, immerse, submerge; plump, plunk; propel, push, shove, thrust; boil, charge, fling, rush, tear
  idiom plunge headlong
  con ease, glide, slide, slip
  3 *syn* see FALL 2
  idiom take a plunge
  4 *syn* see PLUMMET
  idiom drop like a rock, take a downward plunge

plunther *vb syn* see PLOD 1

plus *n syn* see EXCESS 2

plus *vb syn* see INCREASE 1

plush *adj syn* see LUXURIOUS 3
  idiom fit for the gods

plushy *adj syn* see LUXURIOUS 3

plutonian *adj* **1** *syn* see INFERNAL 1
  2 *syn* see INFERNAL 2

plutonic *adj* **1** *syn* see INFERNAL 1
  2 *syn* see INFERNAL 2

ply *vb* **1** *syn* see HANDLE 2
  rel exercise; function
  2 *syn* see EXERT

pneuma *n syn* see SOUL 1

pneumatic *adj syn* see AIRY 1

pocket *n syn* see DEAD END

pocket *vb* **1** *syn* see STEAL 1
  2 *syn* see ACCEPT 2

pocket *adj* **1** *syn* see TINY
  2 *syn* see CONDENSED
  3 *syn* see FINANCIAL

pocket edition *n syn* see MODEL 1

pocket money *n* money for small personal expenses or incidentals <he had spent all his *pocket money* on candy and snacks>
  syn pin money, spending money
  rel petty cash; change, small change
  con fortune, resources; income

pocket–size *adj syn* see TINY

pococurante *adj syn* see INDIFFERENT 2

pod *n* **1** *syn* see HULL
  2 *syn* see POTBELLY

podex *n syn* see BUTTOCKS

podgy *adj syn* see ROTUND 2

Podunk *n syn* see BURG

poem *n* a particular example of metrical writing <recited a *poem* by Robert Frost>
  syn poesy, poetry, rhyme, rune, verse

poesy *n* **1** *syn* see POEM
  2 *syn* see POETRY 1

poet *n* a writer of verse <a *poet* to stir men's souls>
  syn bard, muse, Parnassian
  rel jongleur, rhapsodist, trouvère, trouveur; balladist, elegist, idyllist, lyricist, lyrist, odist, satirist, sonneteer, sonnetist

poetaster *n* a writer of mediocre or inferior verse <*poetasters* who churn out tasteless verse>
  syn balladmonger, bardlet, bardling, poeticule, poetling, rhymer, rhymester, verseman, versemonger, verser, versesmith, versificator, versifier

poeticule *n syn* see POETASTER

poetling *n syn* see POETASTER

poetry *n* **1** metrical language or writing <studied the *poetry* of Milton>
  syn poesy, rhyme, song, verse
  2 *syn* see POEM

poignance *n syn* see PATHOS

poignancy *n syn* see PATHOS

poignant *adj* **1** *syn* see PUNGENT
  ant dull
  2 *syn* see MOVING 2
  rel agitating, disturbing, perturbing

point *n* **1** one unitary part of a whole made up of two or more parts <listened to each *point* of his opponent's argument>
  syn article, detail, element, item, particular, thing; *compare* ELEMENT 2
  rel characteristic, feature, trait; constituent, material, part; circumstantial, circumstantiality
  con aggregate, sum, total, whole
  2 *syn* see CHARACTERISTIC 1
  3 the quality of an utterance that arouses interest and produces an effect <a book that lacks *point*>
  syn cogency, effectiveness, force, punch, validity, validness
  rel appositeness, convincement, significance, suggestiveness; appeal, attraction, charm, fascination, interest
  4 *syn* see SUBJECT 2
  5 *syn* see TIP
  6 *syn* see PLACE 1
  7 a particular limited and often critical interval of time <at that *point* he was interrupted>
  syn instant, juncture, moment
  rel brink, threshold, verge
  8 *syn* see VERGE 2
  9 a sharp or slender and tapering terminal part <the *point* of a sword>
  syn apex, cusp, tip
  rel awn, barb, jag, nib, prong, snag, spike, tag, tine
  10 *syn* see PROMONTORY
  11 a tiny mark or spot <saw a distant *point* of light>
  syn dot, flyspeck, mote, speck
  rel bit, fleck, iota, minim, mite, particle, scrap, tittle, trace

point *vb* **1** *syn* see PUNCTUATE
  2 to tend to show something as probable <all signs *point* to an economic recovery>
  syn hint, imply, indicate, suggest; *compare* SUGGEST 1
  idiom make (*or* give) promise of, lead one to expect, offer a good prospect of
  3 *syn* see DIRECT 2

point (out) *vb syn* see REFER 3

point (to) *vb syn* see TESTIFY 1

pointed *adj* **1** tapering to a thin tip <a *pointed* rock>
  syn acicular, aciculate, acuminate, acuminous, acute, cuspidate, mucronate, peaked, peaky, piked, pointy, sharp

---

syn synonym(s)   *rel* related word(s)
ant antonym(s)   *con* contrasted word(s)
idiom idiomatic equivalent(s)
‖ use limited; if in doubt, see a dictionary

con dull, rounded
ant blunt
2 *syn* see NOTICEABLE
pointer *n syn* see TIP
pointful *adj syn* see RELEVANT
pointless *adj syn* see SENSELESS 5
‖**pointsman** *n syn* see POLICEMAN
pointy *adj syn* see POINTED 1
poise *vb* **1** *syn* see STABILIZE
rel back, support, uphold
con agitate, disturb, upset; overthrow, overturn, subvert
2 *syn* see HANG 3
poise *n* **1** *syn* see BALANCE 1
2 *syn* see TACT
rel aplomb, assurance, confidence, self-possession; calmness, serenity, tranquillity; dignity, elegance, grace
poised *adj syn* see CALM 2
poison *n* something that harms, interferes with, or destroys the activity, progress, or welfare of something else < the publicity was *poison* to them >
syn bane, contagion, venom, virus
rel adulteration, contamination, corruption, sophistication
con catholicon, elixir, panacea
ant antidote
poison *vb syn* see DEBASE 1
poison *adj syn* see POISONOUS
poisonous *adj* having the properties or effect of poison < *poisonous* propaganda >
syn mephitic, poison, toxic, toxicant, venomous, virulent
rel miasmal, miasmatic, miasmic, pestilential; deadly, fatal, lethal, mortal; baneful, deleterious, detrimental, nocuous, noxious, pernicious
con corrective, countervailing, emendatory, healing, remedial
ant antidotal
‖**poke** *n syn* see BAG 1
poke *vb* **1** to thrust something into so as to stir up, urge on, or attract attention < he *poked* the man in front of him to get his attention >
syn dig, jab, jog, nudge, prod, punch
rel push, shove, thrust; arouse, awaken, rouse, stir; excite, galvanize, provoke, quicken, stimulate
2 *syn* see SNOOP
3 *syn* see DELAY 2
4 *syn* see BULGE
poke *n* **1** a quick thrust with or as if with the hand < gave him a *poke* in the ribs with my finger >
syn dig, jab, punch, stab
rel bunt, butt; boost, push, shove
2 *syn* see CUFF
3 *syn* see DUNCE
poker-faced *adj* **1** *syn* see SERIOUS 1
2 *syn* see NEUTRAL
‖**pokey** *n syn* see JAIL
poky *adj syn* see DULL 9
polar *adj syn* see OPPOSITE
polemical *adj syn* see CONTENTIOUS 2
polestar *n syn* see CENTER 2
police *n syn* see POLICEMAN
‖**police constable** *n syn* see POLICEMAN
policeman *n* a member of a police force < ask the *policeman* for directions >
syn ‖bluebottle, bluecoat, ‖bobby, ‖bull, ‖constable, cop, ‖copper, Dogberry, ‖flatfoot, ‖fuzz, ‖gendarme, gumshoe, ‖harness bull (*or* cop), ‖heat, John Law, ‖man, ‖nab, officer, ‖paddy, patrolman, peace officer, ‖peeler, ‖pig, ‖pointsman, police, ‖police constable, police officer, ‖rozzer, ‖trap
police officer *n syn* see POLICEMAN
policy *n syn* see COURSE 3
polish *vb* **1** to make smooth or glossy usually by friction < *polished* the silver >
syn buff, burnish, furbish, glance, glaze, gloss, rub, shine
rel brighten, scour, scrub
con roughen
2 to give an elegant finish to < attended classes to *polish* his manners >
syn perfect, refine, round, sleek, slick, smooth
rel better, improve, mend; brush up, furbish, touch up; mature, perfect

polish *n* **1** *syn* see LUSTER
2 *syn* see CULTURE
polished *adj* **1** *syn* see LUSTROUS 1
2 *syn* see SLEEK
3 *syn* see GENTEEL 1
polish off *vb* **1** *syn* see CONSUME 5
2 *syn* see EAT UP 1
polite *adj syn* see CIVIL 2
rel attentive, considerate, thoughtful
ant impolite
politic *adj* **1** *syn* see EXPEDIENT
rel astute, perspicacious, sagacious, shrewd
2 *syn* see TACTFUL
rel judicious, wise
polity *n syn* see COURSE 3
poll *n syn* see HEAD 1
pollard *vb syn* see TOP 1
polloi *n syn* see RABBLE 2
pollute *vb* **1** *syn* see CONTAMINATE 1
2 *syn* see CONTAMINATE 2
polluted *adj* **1** *syn* see IMPURE 3
2 *syn* see INTOXICATED 1
Pollyanna *n syn* see OPTIMIST
rel daydreamer, wishful thinker
Pollyannaish *adj syn* see OPTIMISTIC
Pollyannaism *n syn* see OPTIMISM
‖**polly-fox** *vb syn* see SKIRT 3
poltroon *n syn* see COWARD
poltroon *adj syn* see COWARDLY
poltroonish *adj syn* see COWARDLY
polyandrium *n syn* see CEMETERY
polychromatic *adj syn* see VARIEGATED
polychrome *adj syn* see VARIEGATED
polypragmatic *adj syn* see IMPERTINENT 2
polypragmatist *n syn* see BUSYBODY
pomp *n syn* see DISPLAY 2
rel ceremonial, ceremony, form, formality, liturgy, ritual
pom-pom girl *n syn* see PROSTITUTE
pompous *adj* **1** characterized by or exhibiting self-importance < a *pompous* old fool >
syn arrogant, bloated, important, magisterial, pontifical, puffy, self-important, stuffy, wiggy; *compare* EGOCENTRIC 2, PROUD 1
rel conceited, narcissistic, self-conceited, stuck-up, vain, vainglorious; affected, highfalutin, hoity-toity, pretentious; presumptuous, self-centered, selfish; flaunting, flossy, ostentatious
con natural, unaffected, unpretentious; humble, meek, plain, simple; modest, unassuming
2 *syn* see RHETORICAL
ponder *vb* **1** *syn* see CONSIDER 1
rel appraise, evaluate
2 to consider or examine attentively or deliberately < *ponder* the best way to do it >
syn ‖chaw, deliberate, meditate, mull (over), muse, revolve, roll, ruminate, turn over
rel cogitate, reason, reflect, speculate, think; brood, debate, dwell
pondering *adj syn* see THOUGHTFUL 1
ponderous *adj* **1** *syn* see HEAVY 1
rel substantial; burdensome, onerous, oppressive
2 lacking all lightness and grace < a *ponderous* prose style >
syn elephantine, heavy-footed, heavy-handed, uninspired
rel dreary, dry, dull, humdrum, lifeless, monotonous, pedestrian, plodding, stodgy, stuffy; arid, barren; flat, insipid, savorless, vapid; buckram, cardboard, muscle-bound, stiff, stilted, wooden
con sparkling, vivid; easy, natural, relaxed, supple, unlabored
3 *syn* see UNWIELDY
pontifical *adj syn* see POMPOUS 1
pontificate *vb syn* see LORD
pony *n* a literal translation of a foreign language text used especially surreptitiously by students in rendering a lesson < had his *pony* hidden in his lap >
syn crib, trot
‖**pooch** *n syn* see DOG 1
pooh *n syn* see RASPBERRY
pooh-bah *n syn* see NOTABLE 1
pooh-pooh *n syn* see RASPBERRY
pooh-pooh *vb syn* see DISMISS 5

pool *n* a small body of standing liquid <saw the *pool* of blood on the floor>
  syn puddle
pool *n* **1** *syn* see POT 3
  2 *syn* see SYNDICATE
poop *n* *syn* see FOOL 1
‖**poop** *vb* *syn* see EXHAUST
poor *adj* **1** lacking money or material possessions <they were so *poor* that the children had no winter coats>
  syn beggared, broke, destitute, dirt poor, flat, fortuneless, impecunious, impoverished, indigent, low, necessitous, needy, penurious, poverty-stricken, stone-broke, stony, strapped, unprosperous
  rel distressed, embarrassed, pinched, reduced, straitened; bankrupt, bankrupted, insolvent; hardscrabble; moneyless, penceless, penniless, unmoneyed; beggarly, down-and-out, pauperized; underprivileged
  idiom down to one's bottom dollar, flat broke, hard up, in need, in penury, in rags, in want, on one's beam-ends, on one's uppers, out at elbows, out of pocket, poor as a church mouse, unable to keep the wolf from the door, unable to make ends meet
  con affluent, comfortable, moneyed, ‖oofy, opulent, pecunious, prosperous, wealthy, well-fixed, well-heeled, well-off, well-to-do
  ant rich
  2 *syn* see MEAGER 2
  3 *syn* see PITIFUL 1
  4 *syn* see CHEAP 2
  5 *syn* see INFERIOR 2
  6 *syn* see BAD 1
poorly *adj* *syn* see UNWELL
poorness *n* *syn* see POVERTY 1
poor relation *n* *syn* see INFERIOR
poor–spirited *adj* *syn* see COWARDLY
pop *vb* **1** *syn* see STRIKE 2
  ‖**2** *syn* see PAWN
pop *n* *syn* see FLING 1
pop *n* *syn* see FATHER 1
pop (in) *vb* *syn* see VISIT 2
popinjay *n* *syn* see FOP
pop off *vb* **1** *syn* see GO 2
  2 *syn* see DIE 1
poppa *n* *syn* see FATHER 1
popping *adj* *syn* see BUSTLING
poppycock *n* *syn* see NONSENSE 2
popsy *n* *syn* see GIRL FRIEND 1
populace *n* *syn* see COMMONALTY
popular *adj* **1** *syn* see PUBLIC 4
  2 *syn* see DEMOCRATIC
  3 *syn* see CHEAP 1
  4 *syn* see PREVAILING
  5 *syn* see FAVORITE 2
  ant unpopular
  6 *syn* see WELL-KNOWN
  ant unpopular
populate *vb* *syn* see INHABIT
populous *adj* *syn* see MANY
porcine *adj* *syn* see FAT 2
pork–barreling *n* *syn* see PATRONAGE 3
porky *adj* *syn* see FATTY 2
porose *adj* *syn* see PERMEABLE
porous *adj* *syn* see PERMEABLE
porridge *n* *syn* see MISCELLANY 1
port *n* **1** *syn* see HARBOR 3
  2 *syn* see SHELTER 1
port *n* *syn* see BEARING 1
portable *adj* capable of being carried or moved about <a *portable* TV>
  syn carriageable, portative, transportable
  rel convenient, handy, manageable, wieldy
  con fixed, stationary
portal *n* *syn* see DOOR 1
portative *adj* *syn* see PORTABLE
portend *vb* **1** *syn* see AUGUR 2
  2 *syn* see FORETELL
portent *n* **1** *syn* see FORETOKEN
  2 *syn* see WONDER 1
porter *n* *syn* see BEARER 2

portion *n* **1** *syn* see SHARE 1
  2 *syn* see FATE
  3 *syn* see PART 1
  4 *syn* see RATION
portion *vb* *syn* see APPORTION 2
portion (out) *vb* *syn* see ADMINISTER 2
portly *adj* *syn* see FAT 2
portrait *n* *syn* see IMAGE 1
portraiture *n* *syn* see REPRESENTATION
portray *vb* *syn* see REPRESENT 1
  rel photograph; copy, duplicate, reproduce
portrayal *n* *syn* see REPRESENTATION
pose *vb* **1** *syn* see OFFER 1
  2 *syn* see PROPOSE 1
  rel ask, query, question; confound, puzzle; baffle
  3 to assume a particular physical posture <they *posed* for a family portrait>
  syn posture, sit
  rel peacock, strut
  4 to assume an artificial or pretended attitude or character usually to deceive or impress <*posed* as a salesman>
  syn attitudinize, masquerade, pass (as *or* for), pass off, posture
  rel fake, feign, pretend, sham; profess, purport; grandstand, show off
pose *n* **1** *syn* see POSTURE 1
  2 an adopted way of speaking or acting <his reticence is just a *pose*>
  syn affectation, air(s), lugs, mannerism, prettyism
  rel dog, prettiness; fake, pretense, pretension
pose *vb* *syn* see OFFER 1
pose *vb* *syn* see PUZZLE
posh *adj* *syn* see STYLISH
posit *vb* *syn* see PRESUPPOSE
posit *n* *syn* see ASSUMPTION 2
position *n* **1** a firmly held point of view or way of regarding something <took a conservative *position* on educational issues>
  syn attitude, color, stance, stand; *compare* SIDE 4
  rel belief, judgment, opinion, view; angle, slant, standpoint, viewpoint
  2 *syn* see PLACE 1
  3 *syn* see STATUS 1
  4 *syn* see STATUS 2
  5 *syn* see JOB 2
positioned *adj* *syn* see SITUATED
positive *adj* **1** expressed clearly and usually peremptorily <her answer was a *positive* no>
  syn categorical, decided, definite, unequivocal
  rel clear, unmistakable; decisive, emphatic, energetic, firm, forceful, forcible; explicit, express, specific, unambiguous
  con irresolute, uncertain, undecided, unsure
  2 *syn* see SURE 5
  ant doubtful
  3 not subject to being disputed or called in question <gave *positive* proof that he had been there>
  syn certain, inarguable, incontestable, incontrovertible, indisputable, indubitable, irrebuttable, irrefutable, sure, uncontestable, uncontrovertible, undeniable, undisputable, undoubtable, unequivocal, unquestionable; *compare* DOWNRIGHT 2
  rel assured, clear, decisive
  con contestable, controvertible, debatable, disputable, doubtful, dubious, inconclusive, questionable, unconvincing
  4 *syn* see UTTER
  5 *syn* see ACTUAL 2
  6 capable of being constructively applied <*positive* proposals for improving the city>
  syn affirmative
  rel practical, reasonable, sound
  con impractical, unsound, unusable
  ant negative
  7 *syn* see RIGHT-HANDED
positively *adv* *syn* see EASILY 2
positure *n* *syn* see POSTURE 1
possess *vb* **1** *syn* see HAVE 1

---

syn synonym(s)	**rel** related word(s)
ant antonym(s)	**con** contrasted word(s)
idiom idiomatic equivalent(s)	
‖ use limited; if in doubt, see a dictionary	

2 *syn* see BEAR 3

possessed *adj syn* see CALM 2

possession *n* **1** *syn* see OWNERSHIP

2 possessions *pl* things one owns usually excluding real property and intangibles <lost all their *possessions* in the fire>
syn belongings, chattels, effects, goods, lares and penates, movables, things,
rel appointments, fixtures, furnishings, furniture; accessories, appurtenances, baggage, ‖duds, duffle, equipment, impedimenta, paraphernalia, trappings, tricks; havings; tangibles

possessive *adj syn* see JEALOUS 1

possessor *n syn* see OWNER

possessorship *n syn* see OWNERSHIP

possessory *adj syn* see JEALOUS 1

possibilities *n pl syn* see POTENTIAL

possible *adj* **1** capable of being realized <a cure is still *possible*>
syn doable, feasible, practicable, viable, workable
rel advisable, expedient; achievable, attainable, available
con futile, hopeless, impracticable
ant impossible
2 *syn* see PROBABLE
rel dormant, latent, potential
3 *syn* see POTENTIAL 1

possibly *adv syn* see PERHAPS

post *vb* to affix to a usual place (as a wall) for public notices <*posted* the notice on the bulletin board>
syn placard, poster

post *vb syn* see INFORM 2

post *n syn* see JOB 2

post *vb syn* see STATION

‖**post** *n syn* see AUTOPSY

poster *n* a notice or announcement for posting in a public place <nailed the *poster* to the side of the building>
syn affiche, bill, handbill, placard
rel advertisement, announcement, banner, broadside, notice, sign; billboard, signboard

poster *vb syn* see POST

posterior *adj* **1** *syn* see SUBSEQUENT 1

2 situated at or toward the back <the *posterior* part of the animal>
syn after, back, hind, hinder, hindmost, rear, retral
con fore, front
ant anterior

posterior *n* **1** *syn* see BACK 1

2 *syn* see BUTTOCKS

posterity *n syn* see OFFSPRING
ant ancestry

posthaste *adv syn* see FAST 2

posthaste *adj syn* see FAST 3

posthumous *adj* occurring after one's death <*posthumous* fame>
syn postmortal, postmortem, post-obit, post-obituary
rel delayed, late, retarded
con opportune, seasonable, timely
ant antemortem

postliminary *adj syn* see SUBSEQUENT 1

postmortal *adj syn* see POSTHUMOUS

postmortem *adj syn* see POSTHUMOUS
ant antemortem

postmortem *n syn* see AUTOPSY

postmortem examination *n syn* see AUTOPSY

post-obit *adj syn* see POSTHUMOUS

post-obituary *adj syn* see POSTHUMOUS

postpone *vb syn* see DEFER

postulate *vb* **1** *syn* see DEMAND 1

2 *syn* see PRESUPPOSE
rel affirm, assert, aver, predicate

postulate *n syn* see ASSUMPTION 2

postulation *n syn* see ASSUMPTION 2

posture *n* **1** the position or bearing of the body <erect *posture*>
syn attitude, carriage, pose, positure, stance
rel bearing, deportment, mien
2 *syn* see STATE 1
rel promptness, quickness, readiness

posture *vb* **1** *syn* see POSE 3

2 *syn* see POSE 4

posy *n* **1** *syn* see FLOWER 1

2 *syn* see BOUQUET 1

3 *syn* see ANTHOLOGY

pot *n* **1** *syn* see FORTUNE 4

2 *syn* see BET

3 the total of the bets at stake at one time <lost track of how much was in the *pot*>
syn jackpot, kitty, pool

4 *syn* see POTSHOT

‖**5** *syn* see POTBELLY

6 *syn* see NOTABLE 1

7 *syn* see MARIJUANA

‖**8** *syn* see TOILET

potable *adj* suitable for drinking <*potable* water>
syn drinkable
rel clean, fresh, pure, uncontaminated, unpolluted
con dirty, foul, impure, polluted, unclean
ant impotable

potable *n syn* see DRINK 1

potbelly *n* an enlarged, swollen, or protruding abdomen <he had the biggest *potbelly* we had ever seen>
syn bay window, corporation, paunch, pod, ‖pot

potency *n* **1** *syn* see POWER 4
ant impotence
2 *syn* see EFFICACY 1
3 *syn* see ENERGY 2
ant impotence

potent *adj* **1** *syn* see POWERFUL 2
ant impotent
2 *syn* see STRONG 3

potential *adj* **1** existing in possibility <a *potential* site for the new factory>
syn possible
rel conceivable, imaginable, likely, plausible, probable, thinkable
idiom within the realm (*or* range) of possibility
con existent, extant; doubtful, impossible, questionable; impracticable, unsuitable
ant actual
2 *syn* see LATENT

potential *n* something that can develop or become actual <industrial *potential*>
syn possibilities, potentiality
ant actuality, reality

potentiality *n syn* see POTENTIAL
ant actuality

pother *n* **1** *syn* see COMMOTION 4

2 *syn* see STIR 1

3 *syn* see ANNOYANCE 2

4 *syn* see COMMOTION 2

pother *vb syn* see WORRY 3

pothole *n* a hole, depression, or rut in a road surface <*potholes* all over that stretch of highway>
syn chuckhole, mudhole

pothouse *n syn* see BAR 5

potpourri *n syn* see MISCELLANY 1

potshot *n* a critical remark made in a random or sporadic manner <took a few *potshots* at his neighbor's argument>
syn pot, shy, sideswipe
rel cut, crack, dig; gibe, jeer; aspersion, criticism, insult

potted *adj* **1** *syn* see CONDENSED

‖**2** *syn* see INTOXICATED 1

potter *vb syn* see FIDDLE 2

potter (away) *vb syn* see WASTE 2

potter's field *n syn* see CEMETERY

potty *adj* ‖**1** *syn* see LITTLE 3

‖**2** *syn* see FOOLISH 2

3 *syn* see SNOBBISH

‖**potty** *n syn* see TOILET

pouch *n syn* see BAG 1

pouch *vb syn* see BULGE

pouf *n syn* see QUILT

poule *n syn* see PROSTITUTE

poultice *n* a soft, usually heated, and sometimes medicated mass spread on cloth and applied to sores or other lesions <slapped a bread *poultice* over the boil>
syn cataplasm
rel plaster; compress; dressing

pound *vb* **1** *syn* see HAMMER 1

2 *syn* see BEAT 1

3 *syn* see IMPRESS 3

pound *n syn* see BLOW 1
pour *vb* **1** *syn* see DISCHARGE 5
2 to send forth or come forth abundantly <medical supplies *poured* into the stricken area>
syn flow, gush, roll, sluice, stream, surge
rel issue, proceed, spring; course, rill, run, rush, swarm; cascade, cataract; deluge, flood, inundate
3 to rain heavily <it *poured* for two solid days>
syn drench, lash, teem
rel beat; deluge, flood, stream
idiom come down in buckets (*or* torrents), rain cats and dogs
pour *n syn* see FLOOD 2
pourboire *n syn* see GRATUITY
pout *vb* **1** *syn* see SULK
2 *syn* see BULGE
pouts *n pl syn* see SULK
poverty *n* **1** the state of one with insufficient resources <repeated crop failures had reduced the farmers to *poverty*>
syn beggary, borasca, destituteness, destitution, impecuniousness, impoverishment, indigence, indigency, need, neediness, pauperism, pennilessness, penury, poorness, privation, unprosperousness, want
rel exigency, necessity; juncture, pass, pinch, strait; difficulty, distress, embarrassment; hardship, suffering; mendicancy
idiom hand-to-mouth existence, straitened circumstances
con affluence, comfort, luxury, opulence, prosperity, richness, wealth
ant riches
2 *syn* see SCARCITY
poverty–stricken *adj syn* see POOR 1
powder *vb* **1** *syn* see SPRINKLE 1
2 *syn* see PULVERIZE 1
powdering *n syn* see DUSTING
powdery *adj syn* see FINE 2
power *n* **1** the right or prerogative of determining, ruling, or governing or the exercise of that right or prerogative <party in *power*>
syn authority, command, control, domination, jurisdiction, mastery, might, strings, sway
rel birthright, prerogative, privilege, right; direction, management; ascendancy, dominance, dominion, masterdom, sovereignty, supremacy; superiority; influence, prestige, weight; force, strength
con forcelessness, impotence, weakness
ant impuissance, powerlessness
‖**2** *syn* see MUCH
3 the ability of a living being to perform in a given way or a capacity for a particular kind of performance <the *power* to think clearly>
syn faculty, function
rel ability, capability, capacity; aptitude, bent, turn; endowment, gift, talent
con inability, incapability, incapacity; inaptness, ineptitude
4 the ability to exert effort for a purpose <raised the productive *power* of the nation>
syn arm, beef, dint, energy, force, might, muscle, potency, puissance, sinew, steam, strength, strong arm, vigor, virtue
rel ability, capability, capacity; effectiveness; dynamism, powder, voltage; dynamis, potentiality; competence, qualification
con inability, incapability, incapacity; ineffectiveness; incompetence
powerful *adj* **1** *syn* see STRONG 1
2 having or manifesting power to effect great or striking results <a *powerful* leader>
syn forceful, forcible, mighty, potent, puissant
rel able, capable, competent; effective, effectual, efficacious, efficient; dynamic, energetic, strenuous, vigorous; convincing, great, invincible; authoritative, dominant, influential, weighty
con faulty, feeble, flawed; impotent, inadequate, incompetent, weak
ant powerless
powerfully *adv syn* see HARD 1
powerless *adj* unable to effect one's purpose, intention, or end <*powerless* to leave>
syn helpless, impotent
rel inactive, inert, passive, supine; decrepit, feeble, infirm, weak; incapable, incompetent, ineffective, unfit
con effective, effectual, efficient; able, capable, competent; potent, puissant

ant powerful
powwow *syn* see TALK 4
powwow *vb syn* see CONFER 2
‖**prabble** *n syn* see QUARREL
practic *adj syn* see REALISTIC
practicable *adj* **1** *syn* see POSSIBLE 1
ant impracticable
2 *syn* see PRACTICAL 2
3 *syn* see OPEN 5
ant impracticable
practical *adj* **1** *syn* see IMPLICIT 2
2 capable of being turned to use or account <had a *practical* rather than a theoretical acquaintance with mechanics>
syn functional, handy, practicable, serviceable, useful, utile
con abstract, academic, theoretical
ant impractical, unpractical
3 *syn* see REALISTIC
ant impractical, unpractical
4 *syn* see EXPERIENCED
practically *adv* **1** *syn* see VIRTUALLY
2 *syn* see ALMOST 2
3 *syn* see NEARLY
practice *vb syn* see EXERCISE 3
rel execute, fulfill, perform; follow, pursue; iterate, repeat
practice *n* **1** *syn* see HABIT 1
rel procedure, proceeding, process; method, mode, system
2 *syn* see PLOT 2
3 *syn* see EXERCISE 3
rel use, usefulness, utility; convenance, convention, form, usage
ant theory; precept
practiced *adj syn* see EXPERIENCED
ant unpracticed
praetorian *adj syn* see CORRUPT 2
praetorian *n syn* see DIEHARD 1
pragmatic *n syn* see BUSYBODY
pragmatic *adj syn* see REALISTIC
pragmatical *adj syn* see REALISTIC
pragmatist *n syn* see BUSYBODY
praisable *adj syn* see WORTHY 1
praise *vb* **1** *syn* see COMMEND 2
ant censure, criticize
2 to glorify and exalt especially in song or writing <*praised* God for all his blessings>
syn bless, celebrate, cry up, eulogize, extol, glorify, hymn, laud, magnify, panegyrize, psalm, psalmody, resound
rel aggrandize, dignify, distinguish, ennoble, erect, exalt, honor, sublime, uprear; enhance, heighten, intensify; apotheosize; proclaim
idiom sing the praises of
con asperse, calumniate, defame, libel, malign, traduce, vilify; belittle, decry, depreciate, derogate, detract (from), discount, disparage, minimize, opprobriate; censure, criticize, denounce, reprehend, reprobate; abuse, reproach, revile
ant dispraise; blame
praiseful *adj syn* see EULOGISTIC
praiseworthy *adj syn* see WORTHY 1
ant despicable
‖**pram** *n syn* see BABY CARRIAGE
prance *vb* **1** *syn* see SASHAY
2 *syn* see DANCE 1
‖**prang** *vb syn* see BUMP 1
‖**prang** *n syn* see CRASH 3
prank *n* a mischievous or roguish act <he was always playing *pranks* on his sister>
syn antic, caper, dido(es), frolic, lark, monkeyshine, ‖rig, shenanigan, shine(s), ‖skite, tomfoolery, trick, wheeze; *compare* ESCAPADE, TRICK 1
rel fooling, high jinks, horseplay, roughhouse, roughhousing, rowdiness, skylarking; gambol, play, rollick, sport; frivolity, levity, lightness; caprice, conceit, fancy, freak, vagary, whim, whimsy
prank *vb* **1** *syn* see ADORN
2 *syn* see DRESS UP 1

---

syn synonym(s)   *rel* related word(s)
ant antonym(s)   *con* contrasted word(s)
idiom idiomatic equivalent(s)
‖ use limited; if in doubt, see a dictionary

prankful *adj syn* see PLAYFUL 1
prankish *adj syn* see PLAYFUL 1
pranky *adj syn* see PLAYFUL 1
‖**prat** *n syn* see TRICK 1
prate *vb* **1** *syn* see CHAT 1
  2 *syn* see BOAST
  3 *syn* see BABBLE 2
prate *n syn* see CHATTER
prater *n syn* see CHATTERBOX
prattle *vb* **1** *syn* see CHAT 1
  2 *syn* see BABBLE 2
prattle *n syn* see CHATTER
prattler *n syn* see CHATTERBOX
praxis *n syn* see HABIT 1
pray *vb syn* see BEG
prayer *n* an earnest and usually a formal request for something
  < the *prayer* in a bill in equity is the part that specifies the kind
  of relief sought >
  syn appeal, application, entreaty, imploration, imprecation, orison, petition, plea, suit, supplication
  rel begging, beseeching, imploring, pleading; adoration, worship
  con claim, demand, exaction
prayer *n syn* see SUPPLIANT
prayerful *adj syn* see DEVOUT
preach *vb* **1** to discourse publicly on a religious subject < *preached*
  at Sunday services >
  syn evangelize, homilize, sermonize
  rel minister, mission, missionary; prophesy; address, lecture,
  speak, talk
  2 *syn* see MORALIZE
preach *n syn* see SERMON
preacher *n syn* see CLERGYMAN
preachify *vb syn* see MORALIZE
preaching *n syn* see SERMON
preachment *n syn* see SERMON
preachy *adj syn* see DIDACTIC
preamble *n syn* see INTRODUCTION
precarious *adj* **1** *syn* see DOUBTFUL 1
  2 *syn* see DELICATE 7
precariousness *n syn* see INSTABILITY
precaution *n syn* see PRUDENCE 1
precede *vb* **1** to go before in rank, dignity, or importance < the
  small countries at the conference were *preceded* by the large
  wealthy ones > < those who still feel that age should *precede*
  beauty >
  syn outrank, rank
  2 to go before in time < all-out war was *preceded* by many
  small raids >
  syn antecede, antedate, forerun, pace, predate
  rel announce, herald, foreshadow, harbinger, presage
  con ensue, supervene
  ant follow, succeed
  3 to cause to be preceded < *preceded* his address with a welcome to the visitors >
  syn introduce, lead, preface, usher
  ant follow
precedence *n syn* see PRIORITY
precedency *n syn* see PRIORITY
precedent *adj syn* see PRECEDING
precedently *adv syn* see BEFORE 1
preceding *adj* being before especially in time or in arrangement
  < the *preceding* day >
  syn antecedent, anterior, foregoing, former, past, precedent,
  previous, prior
  rel other; preexistent; precursive, precursory; erstwhile, heretofore, hitherto
  con coming, ensuing, next, sequent, sequential, subsequent, successive
  ant following, succeeding
preceding *prep syn* see BEFORE 1
precept *n syn* see LAW 1
  rel axiom, fundamental, principle; doctrine, dogma, tenet; behest, bidding, injunction
  ant practice; counsel
précieux *adj syn* see PRECIOUS 4
precinct *n* **1** *syn* see QUARTER 2
  2 *syn* see FIELD
  3 precincts *pl syn* see ENVIRONS 1

precious *adj* **1** of such great value that a suitable price is hard to
  estimate < a *precious* twelfth century painting >
  syn costly, inestimable, invaluable, priceless, valuable; *compare*
  COSTLY 1
  rel choice, exquisite, rare, recherché; treasurable; rich; prizable
  idiom of price
  con base, common, mean, paltry, poor, rubbishy, shabby,
  trashy; contemptible, despicable, miserable; claptrap, gimcrack,
  trumpery
  ant cheap; worthless
  2 *syn* see FAVORITE 1
  3 *syn* see NICE 1
  4 excessively refined < too *precious* to mingle with the common
  people >
  syn affected, alembicated, chichi, la-di-da, overnice, overrefined,
  précieux; *compare* GENTEEL 3
  rel ostentatious, pretentious, showy; artful, sophisticated, studied
  con artless, ingenuous, naive, natural, simple, unaffected, unartful, unschooled, unsophisticated, unstudied, untutored; down-to-
  earth, matter-of-fact, practical, pragmatic, rational
precipitance *n syn* see HASTE 2
precipitancy *n syn* see HASTE 2
precipitant *adj syn* see PRECIPITATE 1
precipitate *n* **1** *syn* see SEDIMENT
  2 *syn* see EFFECT 1
precipitate *adj* **1** characterized by impetuous or unexpected haste
  < beat a *precipitate* retreat >
  syn abrupt, hasty, headlong, hurried, impetuous, precipitant,
  precipitous, rushing, subitaneous, sudden
  rel breakneck, headstrong, hotheaded, impatient, impulsive,
  madcap, refractory, uncontrolled, willful; unanticipated, unexpected, unforeseen, unlooked-for; overhasty
  con leisurely, slow, unhurried
  ant deliberate
  2 *syn* see STEEP 1
precipitateness *n syn* see HASTE 2
precipitation *n* **1** *syn* see HASTE 2
  2 *syn* see SEDIMENT
precipitous *adj* **1** *syn* see PRECIPITATE 1
  2 *syn* see STEEP 1
précis *n syn* see COMPENDIUM 1
precise *adj* **1** *syn* see DEFINITE 1
  2 *syn* see CORRECT 2
  rel rigid, stringent
  con careless, heedless; lax, slack
  ant imprecise; loose
  3 *syn* see PRIM 1
  4 distinguished from every other < arrived just at the *precise*
  moment when he was needed >
  syn exact, very
  rel specific; individual; particular
  con general, inexact, nonspecific
  ant imprecise
precisely *adv* **1** *syn* see JUST 1
  idiom on the button
  ant imprecisely; approximately
  2 *syn* see EVEN 1
  3 *syn* see EXACTLY 3
preciseness *n syn* see PRECISION
  ant impreciseness
precisian *n syn* see PURIST
precision *n* the quality or character of what is precise < the *preci-*
  sion involved in close-tolerance machining >
  syn accuracy, correctness, definiteness, definitiveness, definitude,
  exactitude, exactness, preciseness
  rel care, carefulness; attention, heed
  con inaccuracy, incorrectness, indefiniteness, inexactness; obscurity, unclearness, vagueness; unreliability, untrustworthiness
  ant imprecision
precisionist *n syn* see PURIST
preclude *vb syn* see PREVENT 2
  rel cease, discontinue, quit, stop
precocious *adj* exceptionally early in development < a *precocious*
  child, smart beyond his years >
  syn advanced, forward; *compare* EARLY 2
  rel ahead, early, overearly, oversoon, premature, previous,
  ‖soon; developed, mature

con backward, undeveloped; dull, slow, slow-witted, sluggish
ant retarded
precogitate *vb syn* see PREMEDITATE
preconception *n* an attitude, belief, or impression formed before-hand <had a lot of *preconceptions* about a man she'd never met >
syn prejudgment, prepossession; *compare* PREJUDICE
rel illusion; delusion
idiom preconceived notion (*or* idea *or* opinion)
precondition *n syn* see ESSENTIAL 2
precursor *n* **1** *syn* see FORERUNNER 1
2 *syn* see FORERUNNER 2
predacious *adj syn* see RAPACIOUS 1
predate *vb syn* see PRECEDE 2
predative *adj syn* see RAPACIOUS 1
predatorial *adj syn* see RAPACIOUS 1
predatory *adj syn* see RAPACIOUS 1
predecessor *n syn* see FORERUNNER 2
predestinate *vb syn* see PREDESTINE 2
predestine *vb* **1** to fix the future of in advance <his treasured scribblings were *predestined* to light a kitchen fire>
syn destine, determine, doom (to), fate, foreordain, predetermine, preform, preordain
rel predecide; prejudge; preestablish
2 to determine by or as if by divine decree or eternal purpose <some believe that God *predestines* individuals to eternal life or to eternal death>
syn foredestine, foreordain, predestinate, predetermine, preordain
predetermine *vb* **1** *syn* see PREDESTINE 2
2 *syn* see PREMEDITATE
3 *syn* see PREDESTINE 1
predicament *n* a difficult, perplexing, or trying situation <was in a *predicament*, trying to decide whether or not to take the job>
syn box, corner, deep water, dilemma, fix, hole, hot water, impasse, jam, pickle, plight, quagmire, scrape, soup, spot
rel emergency, exigency, juncture, pass, pinch, strait; asperity, difficulty, hardness, hardship, rigor, vicissitude; Dutch, trouble; condition, posture, situation, state
idiom ‖in a bind
predicate *vb* **1** *syn* see ASSERT 1
2 *syn* see BASE
predict *vb* **1** *syn* see FORETELL
2 to conjecture correctly <*predicted* the turn of the market months in advance>
syn call, guess
rel conjecture, presume, suppose, surmise, think; conclude, gather, infer, judge
idiom hazard a conjecture (*or* guess)
prediction *n* something that is predicted <the *prediction* was for a good outcome>
syn cast, forecast, foretelling, prevision, prognosis, prognostication, prophecy, weird
rel conjecture, guess, surmising
predictor *n syn* see PROPHET
predilection *n syn* see LEANING 2
predispose *vb syn* see INCLINE 3
rel impress, strike, sway
con disaffect, disincline, disinterest, indispose
predisposed *adj syn* see WILLING 1
ant indisposed
predisposition *n syn* see LEANING 2
ant indisposition
predominant *adj* **1** *syn* see DOMINANT 1
ant subordinate
2 *syn* see CHIEF 2
predominantly *adv syn* see GENERALLY 1
predominate *adj syn* see DOMINANT 1
predominate *vb syn* see RULE 2
preeminence *n* **1** *syn* see SUPREMACY
2 *syn* see EMINENCE 1
preeminent *adj* **1** *syn* see SUPREME
2 *syn* see CHIEF 2
preempt *vb* **1** *syn* see APPROPRIATE 1
2 *syn* see ARROGATE 1
preen *vb syn* see PRIDE
preengage *vb* **1** *syn* see RESERVE 2
2 *syn* see PREPOSSESS 1

preface *n syn* see INTRODUCTION
preface *vb syn* see PRECEDE 3
prefatial *adj syn* see PRELIMINARY
prefatorial *adj syn* see PRELIMINARY
prefatory *adj syn* see PRELIMINARY
prefer *vb* **1** *syn* see ADVANCE 2
2 *syn* see CHOOSE 1
3 *syn* see PROPOSE 1
preferable *adj syn* see BETTER 2
preference *n* **1** *syn* see CHOICE 1
rel partiality, predilection, prepossession
2 *syn* see ADVANCEMENT 1
preferment *n syn* see ADVANCEMENT 1
preferred *adj syn* see FAVORITE 2
prefigurate *vb syn* see ADUMBRATE 1
prefigure *vb syn* see ADUMBRATE 1
preform *vb syn* see PREDESTINE 1
pregnance *n syn* see PREGNANCY
pregnancy *n* the condition of containing unborn young within the body <she was in the last trimester of her *pregnancy* >
syn gestation, gravidity, pregnance, situation
pregnant *adj* **1** containing unborn young within the body <she was *pregnant* with her second child>
syn big, childing, enceinte, expectant, expecting, gone, gravid, heavy, parous, parturient
idiom in an interesting condition, in the family way, with child (*or* young)
con barren, infertile; delivered; postpartum
2 *syn* see EXPRESSIVE
rel consequential, important, momentous, significant, weighty
prehend *vb syn* see CATCH 1
prehensile *adj syn* see COVETOUS
preindicate *vb syn* see ANNOUNCE 2
prejudgment *n syn* see PRECONCEPTION
prejudice *n* the inclination to take a stand (as in a conflict) usu-ally without just grounds or sufficient information <could not review his competitor's work without *prejudice*>
syn bias, one-sidedness, partiality; *compare* LEANING 2, PRECON-CEPTION
rel partisanship
idiom jaundiced eye
con detachment, dispassion, impartiality, indifference, neutrality
ant objectivity
prejudice *vb* **1** *syn* see INJURE 1
2 to cause to have opinions formed without due knowledge or examination <*prejudice* a man against his neighbor by innuen-do>
syn bias, influence, prepossess; *compare* INCLINE 3, SLANT 3
rel bend, dispose, incline, predispose; angle, skew, slant; pre-judge
prejudiced *adj syn* see BIASED 2
ant unprejudiced; disinterested
prejudicial *adj* **1** *syn* see HARMFUL
2 *syn* see DISCRIMINATORY
prejudicious *adj syn* see HARMFUL
prekindergarten *adj syn* see CHILDISH
preknow *vb syn* see FORESEE
prelation *n syn* see ADVANCEMENT 1
prelect *vb syn* see TALK 7
‖prelim *adj syn* see PRELIMINARY
preliminary *adj* serving to make ready the way for something that follows <held a *preliminary* discussion to set up the agenda of the conference>
syn inductive, introductory, prefatial, prefatorial, prefatory, ‖prelim, preludial, prelusive, preparative, preparatory, proemial
rel primal, primary; elemental, elementary; basic, fundamental; fitting, preparing, readying
ant postliminary
prelimit *vb syn* see LIMIT 2
preliterate *adj syn* see PRIMITIVE 6
prelude *n syn* see INTRODUCTION
preludial *adj syn* see PRELIMINARY
prelusion *n syn* see INTRODUCTION

---

syn synonym(s)   **rel** related word(s)
ant antonym(s)   **con** contrasted word(s)
idiom idiomatic equivalent(s)
‖ use limited; if in doubt, see a dictionary

prelusive *adj syn* see PRELIMINARY

premature *adj syn* see EARLY 2

prematurely *adv syn* see EARLY 2

premeditate *vb* to think on and revolve in the mind beforehand <carefully *premeditating* each step of his plan of campaign>
syn forethink, precogitate, predetermine
rel prearrange, preplan, set up; predecide; prepare

premeditated *adj syn* see DELIBERATE 1
ant unpremeditated; spontaneous

premier *adj syn* see FIRST 3

premise *n syn* see ASSUMPTION 2

premise *vb syn* see PRESUPPOSE

premium *n syn* see REWARD

premium *adj syn* see SUPERIOR 4

premonition *n syn* see APPREHENSION 3

prename *n syn* see GIVEN NAME

prenotion *n syn* see APPREHENSION 3

prentice *n syn* see NOVICE

prentice *adj syn* see CRUDE 5

preoccupied *adj* **1** *syn* see INTENT
  2 *syn* see ABSTRACTED
rel absorbed; forgetful
ant unpreoccupied

preoccupy *vb syn* see PREPOSSESS 1

preordain *vb* **1** *syn* see PREDESTINE 1
  2 *syn* see PREDESTINE 2

preparative *adj syn* see PRELIMINARY

preparatory *adj syn* see PRELIMINARY

prepare *vb* **1** to make ready in advance usually for a particular use or disposition <*prepared* rooms for the expected guests>
syn fit, fix, get, make, make up, ready
rel furnish, provide, supply; dower, endow, endue; equip, outfit; dispose, incline, predispose; prime
idiom set the stage (for)
ant unprepare
  2 *syn* see DRAFT 3
  3 *syn* see GIRD 3

prepared *adj syn* see READY 1
ant unprepared

prepatent *adj syn* see LATENT

prepense *adj syn* see DELIBERATE 1

prepensely *adv syn* see INTENTIONALLY

preponderance *n syn* see SUPREMACY

preponderancy *n syn* see SUPREMACY

preponderant *adj syn* see DOMINANT 1

preponderate *vb syn* see RULE 2

preponderation *n syn* see SUPREMACY

prepossess *vb* **1** to influence or affect strongly beforehand <was *prepossessed* with the notion of his own superiority>
syn preengage, preoccupy
rel busy, engage, engross, immerse, occupy, soak; absorb, imbue, involve
  2 *syn* see PREJUDICE 2

prepossessed *adj syn* see BIASED 2
ant unprepossessed

prepossessing *adj syn* see ATTRACTIVE 1

prepossession *n syn* see PRECONCEPTION

preposterous *adj* **1** *syn* see FOOLISH 2
rel irrational, unreasonable
  2 *syn* see EXTRAVAGANT 1

preposterousness *n syn* see FOOLISHNESS

prepotence *n syn* see SUPREMACY

prepotency *n syn* see SUPREMACY

prerequisite *n syn* see ESSENTIAL 2

prerequisite *adj syn* see ESSENTIAL 4

prerogative *n syn* see RIGHT 2
rel exemption, immunity

presage *n* **1** *syn* see FORETOKEN
  2 *syn* see APPREHENSION 3

presage *vb* **1** *syn* see AUGUR 2
rel bespeak, indicate
  2 *syn* see ANNOUNCE 2
  3 *syn* see FORETELL

prescribe *vb* **1** *syn* see DICTATE
  2 to fix arbitrarily or authoritatively for the sake of order or of a clear understanding <the Constitution *prescribes* the conditions under which it may be amended>
syn assign, define, lay down

rel establish, fix, set, settle; decide, determine; choose, pick out, select

prescript *n syn* see LAW 1

prescription *n syn* see LAW 1

presence *n syn* see BEARING 1
rel appearance, aspect, look, seeming

present *n syn* see GIFT 1

present *vb* **1** *syn* see INTRODUCE 4
  2 *syn* see GIVE 1
  3 *syn* see OFFER 1
  4 *syn* see ADDUCE
  5 *syn* see DIRECT 2

present *adj* now existing or in progress <the *present* state of the economy seems to be shaky from all reports>
syn contemporary, current, existent, extant, instant, present-day, todayish
rel contemporaneous, modern; newfashioned, up-to-date, up-to-the-minute
con bygone, erstwhile, late, old, once, onetime, quondam, sometime, whilom
ant past

present *n* the present time <the course covers U.S. history from 1900 to the *present*>
syn now, today; *compare* FUTURE, PAST
idiom here and now, this day and age
ant past; future

presentable *adj syn* see RESPECTABLE 5

present–day *adj syn* see PRESENT

presenter *n syn* see DONOR

presentiment *n syn* see APPREHENSION 3
rel discomposing, discomposure, disquietude, disturbance, perturbation

presently *adv* **1** without undue time lapse <the results will be evident *presently*>
syn anon, by and by, directly, shortly, soon
  2 *syn* see TODAY

presentment *n syn* see REPRESENTATION

preserval *n syn* see CONSERVATION 1

preservation *n* **1** the act of preserving or the state of being preserved <the *preservation* of peace in the world>
syn conservation, keeping, safekeeping, salvation, saving, sustentation
rel defense, guard, protection, safeguard, shield; care, guardianship, ward
  2 *syn* see CONSERVATION 1

preserve *vb* **1** *syn* see SAVE 3
  2 *syn* see MAINTAIN 1

preserve *n syn* see JAM

preside *vb* to occupy the place of authority (as in an assembly) <the chief justice *presides* over the supreme court> <the *presiding* elders of the church>
syn chair
rel carry on, conduct, control, direct, keep, manage, operate, ordain, run; administer, handle, head, oversee, supervise

press *n syn* see CROWD 1

press *vb* **1** to act upon through steady pushing or thrusting force exerted in contact <*pressed* his nose against the window>
syn bear, compress, constrain, crowd, crush, jam, ‖mash, push, ‖squab, squash, squeeze, squish, squush
rel propel, shove, thrust; drive, impel, move
  2 *syn* see DEPRESS 2
  3 to squeeze out the juice or contents of <*press* grapes>
syn crush, express
rel compress, squeeze
  4 *syn* see PUSH 2
  5 *syn* see PRESSURE
  6 *syn* see EMBRACE 1
  7 to crowd closely against or around someone or something <hundreds *pressed* around the performer after the show>
syn cram, crowd, crush, jam, squash, squeeze; *compare* CRAM 1
rel pack, ram, stuff, tamp; mass, pile; assemble, collect, congregate, gather
  8 to force or push one's way (as through a crowd or against obstruction) <had to *press* through the traffic to get to the other side of town>
syn bear, squeeze
rel force, push, shove

press–agent *vb syn* see PUBLICIZE

press–agentry *n syn* see PUBLICITY
pressing *adj* demanding or claiming especially immediate attention < he was barely able to pay his most *pressing* debts >
syn burning, clamant, clamorous, crying, dire, exigent, imperative, importunate, insistent, instant, urgent
rel direct, immediate; claiming, demanding, exacting, requiring; compelling, constraining, forcing, obliging; acute, critical, crucial
pressure *n syn* see STRESS 1
pressure *vb* to insist upon unduly < *pressured* him into making the wrong move >
syn overpress, press, push
rel drive, impel; rush
prestige *n* **1** *syn* see STATUS 2
2 *syn* see INFLUENCE 1
rel power, sway
3 *syn* see EMINENCE 1
prestigious *adj syn* see FAMOUS 2
presto *adv syn* see FAST 2
presumably *adv* by reasonable assumption < *presumably* the best qualified for the job should get it >
syn assumably, doubtless, likely, presumptively, probably
con indubitably, surely, undoubtedly, unquestionably
presume *vb* **1** *syn* see CONJECTURE
2 *syn* see PRESUPPOSE
3 *syn* see IMPOSE 5
presuming *adj syn* see PRESUMPTUOUS
ant unassuming, unpresuming
presumption *n* **1** *syn* see EFFRONTERY
2 *syn* see PRESUPPOSITION 1
3 *syn* see ASSUMPTION 2
presumptively *adv syn* see PRESUMABLY
presumptuous *adj* marked by or based on bold and excessive self= confidence < in such company his demand for attention was utterly *presumptuous* >
syn brash, brassbound, confident, forward, gay, overconfident, overweening, presuming, pushful, pushing, ‖pushy, self-asserting, self-assertive, uppish, uppity
rel pretentious, self-assured, self-conceited; lofty, pompous, supercilious; complacent, self-satisfied, smug; inexcusable, outrageous
idiom above one's britches
con deferential, dutiful, respectful, submissive; appropriate, proper
presuppose *vb* to take something for granted or as true or existent especially as a basis for action or reasoning < a lecturer who talks above the heads of his listeners *presupposes* too extensive a knowledge on their part >
syn assume, posit, postulate, premise, presume
rel conjecture, guess, surmise; deduce, infer, judge; believe, expect, gather, imagine, reckon, suppose, suspect, take, think, understand; preconceive
presupposition *n* **1** an act of presupposing < going on his *presupposition* that they would succeed >
syn assumption, presumption
rel conjecture, guess, surmise; deduction, inference, judgment; belief, conviction, opinion, view
2 *syn* see ASSUMPTION 2
pretend *vb* **1** *syn* see ASSUME 4
rel beguile, deceive, delude, mislead; profess, purport
idiom make believe
2 *syn* see CONJECTURE
pretended *adj syn* see ALLEGED
pretender *n syn* see IMPOSTOR
pretense *n* **1** *syn* see CLAIM 1
2 the offering of something false as real or true < there is too much *pretense* in his piety >
syn charade, disguise, make-believe, pageant, pretension, pretentiousness
rel deceit, deception, fake, fraud, humbug, imposture, sham; affectation, air, mannerism, pose
con sincereness; reality, soundness, substantiality, validity; fairness, honesty
ant sincerity
3 *syn* see MASK 2
pretension *n* **1** *syn* see CLAIM 1
2 *syn* see AMBITION 1
3 *syn* see PRETENSE 2
pretentious *adj* **1** *syn* see SHOWY

ant unpretentious
2 *syn* see GENTEEL 3
ant unpretentious
3 flamboyant, turgid, or bombastic in manner or content < a *pretentious* literary style >
syn arty, arty-crafty, big, high-sounding, imposing, overblown
rel affected, feigned, put-on; pompier; aureate, bombastic, euphuistic, flowery, grandiloquent, magniloquent, rhetorical; inflated, tumid, turgid
con heartfelt, hearty, sincere, unfeigned, wholehearted, whole= souled; artless, genuine, natural, simple, unaffected
ant unpretentious
4 *syn* see AMBITIOUS 2
pretentiousness *n syn* see PRETENSE 2
ant unpretentiousness
preterition *n syn* see OMISSION
pretermission *n syn* see OMISSION
pretermit *vb syn* see NEGLECT
preternatural *adj* **1** *syn* see SUPERNATURAL 1
rel anomalous, unnatural; nonnatural
2 *syn* see ABNORMAL 1
ant natural
pretext *n* **1** *syn* see EXCUSE 1
2 *syn* see MASK 2
prettify *vb syn* see PALLIATE
pretty *adj* **1** *syn* see SKILLFUL 2
2 *syn* see BEAUTIFUL
rel darling, ducky; cunning, cute
ant unpretty
pretty *adv syn* see SOMEWHAT 2
idiom pretty much
‖**pretty** *n syn* see TOY 2
prettyism *n syn* see POSE 2
pretty–pretty *n syn* see KNICKKNACK
preux *adj syn* see COURTLY
prevail *vb* **1** *syn* see CONQUER 2
2 *syn* see WIN 1
3 *syn* see RULE 2
prevail (on *or* upon) *vb syn* see INDUCE 1
rel affect, impress
prevailing *adj* general (as in circulation, acceptance, or use) in a given place or at a given time < the *prevailing* point of view among farmers >
syn current, popular, prevalent, rampant, regnant, rife, ruling, widespread
rel dominant, predominant, preponderant; common, familiar, ordinary; general, universal
con exceptional, uncommon, unusual
prevalent *adj* **1** *syn* see DOMINANT 1
2 *syn* see PREVAILING
3 *syn* see GENERAL 1
rel accustomed, customary, wonted
prevaricate *vb syn* see LIE
rel belie, garble, misrepresent
prevarication *n syn* see LIE
prevaricative *adj syn* see EVASIVE 1
prevaricator *n syn* see LIAR
prevaricatory *adj syn* see EVASIVE 1
prevent *vb* **1** to be or get ahead of or to deal with beforehand < many problems are *prevented* easily if one plans wisely >
syn anticipate, forestall
rel baffle, balk, foil, frustrate, thwart; arrest, check, interrupt
2 to stop from advancing or occurring < take steps to *prevent* war > < measures designed to *prevent* the spread of disease >
syn avert, deter, forestall, forfend, obviate, preclude, rule out, stave off, ward
rel bar, block, dam, hinder, impede, obstruct; debar, shut out; forbid, inhibit, interdict, prohibit
con allow, leave, let, suffer
ant permit
previous *adj* **1** *syn* see PRECEDING
ant subsequent; consequent
2 *syn* see EARLY 2

---

syn synonym(s) | *rel* related word(s)
ant antonym(s) | *con* contrasted word(s)
idiom idiomatic equivalent(s)
‖ use limited; if in doubt, see a dictionary

previous *adv syn* see BEFORE 1
previously *adv syn* see BEFORE 2
  ant subsequently; consequently
previousness *n syn* see PRIORITY
previse *vb syn* see FORESEE
prevision *n syn* see PREDICTION
prevision *vb syn* see FORESEE
prey *n* **1** *syn* see GAME 3
  2 *syn* see VICTIM 2
‖**pribble** *n syn* see QUARREL
price *n* **1** the quantity of one thing that is exchanged or demanded in barter or sale for another <what is the *price* of this book>
  syn charge, cost, price tag, rate, tab, tariff
  2 *syn* see EXPENSE 2
priceless *adj syn* see PRECIOUS 1
  rel cherished, prized, treasured, valued
  idiom without price
price tag *n syn* see PRICE 1
prick *n* a mark or shallow hole made by or as if by a pointed tool <a needle *prick* in his arm>
  syn jab, ‖jag, puncture, stab
  rel prickle; hole
prick *vb* **1** *syn* see PERFORATE
  rel enter; cut, slash, slit
  2 *syn* see URGE
  rel excite, pique, stimulate
‖**prick (up)** *vb syn* see DRESS UP 1
prickish *adj syn* see IRRITABLE
prickly *adj* **1** *syn* see THORNY
  rel annoying, bothersome
  2 *syn* see IRRITABLE
pride *n* **1** *syn* see CONCEIT 2
  rel bighead, cockiness, overconfidence, self-assurance
  idiom overweening pride
  ant humility
  2 a reasonable or justifiable sense of one's worth or position <inhumane treatment in prison caused him to lose his *pride*>
  syn amour propre, self-esteem, self-regard, self-respect
  rel dignity, face, pridefulness, self-confidence, self-trust
  con humiliation, mortification; shamefacedness
  ant shame
  3 proud or disdainful behavior or actions <her snobbishness and overbearing *pride* were offensive>
  syn arrogance, disdain, disdainfulness, haughtiness, hauteur, loftiness, morgue, superbity, superciliousness
  rel condescension, snobbishness; contempt, scorn; insolence; smugness; pretentiousness
  idiom haughty airs
  con humbleness, modesty, unpretentiousness
  ant humility
  4 *syn* see BEST
  idiom pride of the herd
pride *vb* to congratulate (oneself) for something one is, has, or has done or achieved <he *prides* himself on his ancestry>
  syn pique, plume, preen
  rel boast, brag, crow, gasconade, vaunt; congratulate, felicitate
  ant efface
‖**pridy** *adj syn* see PROUD 1
prier (*or* **pryer**) *n syn* see BUSYBODY
priestal *adj syn* see SACERDOTAL
priestish *adj syn* see SACERDOTAL
priestlike *adj syn* see SACERDOTAL
priestly *adj syn* see SACERDOTAL
‖**prig** *vb syn* see STEAL 1
prig *n syn* see THIEF
prig *n syn* see PRUDE
prig *adj syn* see PRIM 1
priggish *adj* **1** *syn* see COMPLACENT
  rel self-righteous; self-esteeming, self-loving
  2 *syn* see PRIM 1
prim *adj* **1** excessively concerned with what one regards as proper or right <a *prim* woman, easily shocked by vulgar language>
  syn bluenosed, genteel, missish, precise, prig, priggish, prissy, proper, prudish, puritanical, straitlaced, stuffy, tight-laced, Victorian; *compare* GENTEEL 3
  rel correct, nice, precise; decorous; rigid, stiff, wooden; ceremonial, ceremonious, conventional, formal, straight

  idiom prim and proper
  con lax, loose, slack; easy, easygoing, free
  2 *syn* see NEAT 2
prima facie *adj syn* see SELF-EVIDENT
primarily *adv* **1** *syn* see GENERALLY 1
  2 *syn* see INITIALLY 1
primary *adj* **1** *syn* see FIRST 2
  2 *syn* see PRIMITIVE 4
  3 *syn* see FUNDAMENTAL 1
  4 *syn* see DIRECT 4
  5 not based on or derived from something else <the *primary* studies in nuclear physics>
  syn original, prime, primitive, underivative, underived
  rel first, firsthand; basic, foundational, fundamental, principal, underlying
  con derivate, derivational, derivative, derived; borrowed, secondhand
  ant secondary
prime *n* **1** *syn* see MORNING 1
  2 *syn* see YOUTH 1
  3 *syn* see BEST
prime *adj* **1** *syn* see FIRST 2
  2 *syn* see EXCELLENT
  3 *syn* see PRIMARY 5
prime *vb syn* see PROVOKE 4
primeval *adj syn* see PRIMITIVE 4
primevous *adj syn* see PRIMITIVE 4
primitial *adj syn* see PRIMITIVE 4
primitive *adj* **1** *syn* see PRIMARY 5
  2 *syn* see EARLY 1
  3 closely approximating an early ancestral type <the opossums are *primitive* mammals>
  syn archaic, persistent, undeveloped, unevolved
  ant advanced
  4 of or relating to earlier ages of the world or of human history <archaeology is concerned especially with the study of *primitive* man>
  syn primary, primeval, primevous, primitial
  ant unprimitive
  5 *syn* see ELEMENTAL 1
  6 characterized by a lack of written language, simple technology, and a relatively simple social organization
  syn nonliterate, preliterate
  rel barbarian, uncivilized, uncultivated
  con advanced, civilized, cultivated
primitively *adv syn* see INITIALLY 1
primogenitor *n syn* see ANCESTOR 1
primordial *adj* **1** *syn* see EARLY 1
  2 *syn* see FIRST
primp *vb syn* see DRESS UP 1
primrose *n syn* see BEST
prince *n syn* see MAGNATE
princely *adj syn* see GRAND 1
principal *adj* **1** *syn* see CHIEF 2
  2 *syn* see FIRST 3
principally *adv syn* see GENERALLY 1
principium *n syn* see PRINCIPLE 1
principle *n* **1** a comprehensive and fundamental rule, doctrine, or assumption <the *principle* of free speech>
  syn axiom, fundamental, law, principium, theorem
  rel basis, foundation, ground; canon, precept, rule; convention, form, usage
  2 **principles** *pl syn* see ETHIC 3
  3 **principles** *pl syn* see ALPHABET 2
principled *adj syn* see MORAL 1
  ant unprincipled
‖**prink** *vb syn* see SASHAY
prink (up) *vb syn* see DRESS UP 1
print *n* **1** *syn* see IMPRESSION 1
  2 printed state or form <to see his name in *print*>
  syn black and white, writing
printing *n syn* see EDITION
prior *adj syn* see PRECEDING
  rel ahead, before, forward
  con after, behind
priority *n* the act, the fact, or the right of preceding another <the right to inherit a title is dependent mainly on *priority* of birth>
  syn antecedence, precedence, precedency, previousness

rel arrangement, order, ordering; ascendancy, supremacy; preeminence, transcendence

prior to *prep* **1** *syn* see BEFORE 1
  2 *syn* see UNTIL

prison *n syn* see JAIL

‖**prison** *vb syn* see IMPRISON

prison bird *n syn* see CONVICT

prissy *adj* **1** *syn* see PRIM 1
  rel fastidious, finicky, squeamish
  2 *syn* see EFFEMINATE

‖**pritch** *vb syn* see PERFORATE

private *adj* **1** belonging to or concerning an individual person, company, or interest <*private* property>
  syn personal, privy
  rel intimate
  con common, general, shared
  ant public
  2 known only to a select few <the group had *private* information about the strike>
  syn closet, confidential, hushed, inside
  rel secret; discreet; concealed, hidden
  con common, general, open
  ant public

private detective *n* a person concerned with the maintenance of lawful conduct or the investigation of crime either as a regular employee of a private interest (as a hotel) or as a contractor for fees <obtained a *private detective* to report on his wife's associates>
  syn operative, Pinkerton, ‖private eye, ‖shamus; *compare* DETECTIVE

‖**private eye** *n syn* see PRIVATE DETECTIVE

privately *adv syn* see SECRETLY

private parts *n pl syn* see GENITALIA

privates *n pl syn* see GENITALIA

privation *n* **1** *syn* see ABSENCE
  2 the state of one deprived of something previously or normally possessed <suffered great *privation* during the famine>
  syn deprivation, deprivement, dispossession, divestiture, loss; *compare* LOSS 1
  rel distress, misery, suffering; losing, mislaying, misplacement, misplacing
  3 *syn* see POVERTY 1

privilege *n syn* see RIGHT 2
  rel allowance, concession; boon, favor

privilege (from) *vb syn* see EXEMPT

privities *n pl syn* see GENITALIA

privy *adj* **1** *syn* see PRIVATE 1
  2 *syn* see ULTERIOR

privy *n* **1** an outdoor toilet <in less settled areas, *privies* often take the place of indoor plumbing>
  syn backhouse, ‖biffy, ‖closet, jakes, ‖necessary, ‖office, outhouse
  2 *syn* see TOILET

privy parts *n pl syn* see GENITALIA

prize *n* **1** *syn* see REWARD
  2 *syn* see BEST

prize *vb syn* see APPRECIATE 1

prize *n syn* see SPOIL

prize *vb syn* see PRY

prizefighting *n syn* see BOXING

pro *prep syn* see FOR 2
  ant anti, con

pro *n syn* see EXPERT

pro and con *vb syn* see DISCUSS 1

probable *adj* being such as may become true or actual <seems to be a *probable* candidate>
  syn conceivable, earthly, likely, mortal, possible
  rel believable, colorable, credible, plausible; rational, reasonable; apparent, illusory, ostensible, seeming
  con doubtful, dubious, questionable, unlikely
  ant improbable, unprobable

probably *adv syn* see PRESUMABLY
  ant improbably

probe *n syn* see INQUIRY 1

probe *vb* **1** *syn* see EXPLORE
  2 to try to find out (as by discreet questioning) the views or intentions of <*probed* the neighbors on the subject of political reform>

syn feel out, sound (out)
  rel ask, catechize, examine, inquire, interrogate, query, quiz
  idiom feel the pulse, put out a feeler, see how the land lies, see which way the wind blows
  3 *syn* see SCOUT

probing *n syn* see INQUIRY 1

probity *n syn* see GOODNESS

problem *n* **1** *syn* see EXAMPLE 3
  2 something requiring thought and skill to arrive at a proper conclusion or decision <what to do now is a *problem*>
  syn issue, nut, question
  rel enigma, mystery, puzzle; bugaboo, bugbear; count, point
  idiom a hard nut to crack

problematic *adj* **1** *syn* see DOUBTFUL 1
  ant unproblematic
  2 *syn* see MOOT
  ant unproblematic

proboscis *n syn* see NOSE 1

procacious *adj* **1** *syn* see INSOLENT 2
  2 *syn* see WISE 5

procedure *n* **1** *syn* see COURSE 3
  2 *syn* see MEASURE 7
  3 *syn* see PROCESS 1

proceed *vb* **1** *syn* see SPRING 1
  2 *syn* see GO 1
  3 *syn* see ADVANCE 5
  ant recede

proceeding *n* **1** *syn* see MEASURE 7
  2 *syn* see PROCESS 1

proceeds *n pl syn* see PROFIT

process *n* **1** the series of actions, operations, or motions involved in the accomplishment of an end <the *process* of making sugar from sugarcane>
  syn procedure, proceeding
  rel fashion, manner, method, mode, modus, system, technique, way, wise; routine; operation
  2 *syn* see OUTGROWTH 1

‖**process** *vb syn* see GO 1

procession *n syn* see ORDER 5

processus *n syn* see OUTGROWTH 1

proclaim *vb* **1** *syn* see DECLARE 1
  rel utter, vent, ventilate, voice
  2 *syn* see SHOW 2

proclamation *n syn* see DECLARATION

proclivity *n syn* see LEANING 2

procrastinate *vb syn* see DELAY 2
  rel defer, postpone, stay, suspend; prolong, protract

procreate *vb* **1** to produce offspring <*procreate* children>
  syn bear, beget, breed, generate, multiply, produce, propagate, reproduce
  rel mother; engender; hatch, spawn; proliferate
  idiom give birth to, multiply the earth
  2 *syn* see GENERATE 1
  3 *syn* see FATHER 1

procumbent *adj syn* see PRONE 4

procurable *adj syn* see AVAILABLE 1

procure *vb* **1** *syn* see GET 1
  2 *syn* see INDUCE 1

prod *vb* **1** *syn* see POKE 1
  2 *syn* see URGE
  rel instigate; excite, pique, provoke, stimulate

prodigal *adj syn* see PROFUSE
  ant parsimonious; frugal

prodigal *n syn* see SPENDTHRIFT

prodigality *n syn* see EXTRAVAGANCE 2
  ant parsimoniousness

prodigalize *vb syn* see WASTE 2

prodigious *adj* **1** *syn* see MARVELOUS 1
  2 *syn* see MONSTROUS 1
  3 *syn* see HUGE

prodigy *n syn* see WONDER 1

produce *vb* **1** *syn* see PROCREATE 1
  2 *syn* see STAGE

---

syn synonym(s)   *rel* related word(s)
ant antonym(s)   *con* contrasted word(s)
idiom idiomatic equivalent(s)
‖ use limited; if in doubt, see a dictionary

3 syn see EFFECT 1
4 syn see GENERATE 1
5 syn see GENERATE 3
6 syn see MAKE 3
7 syn see BEAR 9
8 syn see GIVE 7
9 syn see GROW 1
produce n syn see PRODUCT 1
product n **1** something produced by physical labor or intellectual effort <the literary *products* of the Age of Reason>
syn produce, production
rel handiwork; consequence, effect, offshoot, outcome, outgrowth, result; fruit, harvest
2 syn see OUTPUT
production n **1 syn** see PRODUCT 1
2 syn see EXTENSION 1
3 syn see OUTPUT
productive adj syn see FERTILE
ant unproductive
proem n syn see INTRODUCTION
proemial adj syn see PRELIMINARY
profanation n a violation or misuse of something normally held sacred <the *profanation* of a religious ritual>
syn blasphemy, desecration, sacrilege, violation
rel contamination, defilement, pollution; corruption, debasement, perversion, vitiation; transgression, trespass
con glorification, hallowing, sanctification
ant purification; consecration
profane adj **1** not concerned with religion or religious purposes <he was speaking of *profane* history, not the history found in the Bible>
syn lay, secular, temporal, unsacred
rel earthly, mundane, terrestrial, worldly
con consecrated, hallowed, holy, sanctified; divine, religious, spiritual
ant sacred
2 syn see HEATHEN
3 syn see IMPIOUS 1
4 syn see SACRILEGIOUS
5 syn see OBSCENE 2
profaned adj syn see IMPURE 3
ant unprofaned
profanity n syn see BLASPHEMY 1
profess vb syn see ASSERT 1
professed adj syn see ALLEGED
professedly adv syn see OSTENSIBLY
profession n syn see TRADE 1
professional n syn see EXPERT
ant amateur
proffer vb syn see OFFER 1
proffer n syn see PROPOSAL
proficiency n syn see ADVANCE 2
proficient adj having or manifesting the knowledge, skill, and experience needed for sucess in a particular field or endeavor <a *proficient* glider pilot>
syn adept, crack, crackerjack, expert, master, masterful, masterly, skilled, skillful; *compare* EXPERIENCED, SKILLFUL 2
rel checked-out, drilled, exercised, practiced; effective, effectual, efficient; able, capable, competent, qualified; accomplished, consummate, finished
con ignorant, untaught, untrained; inexperienced; unskilled
ant incompetent
proficient n syn see EXPERT
profile n syn see OUTLINE
profit n the excess of returns over expenditure in a transaction or a series of transactions <his *profits* from the business venture were rewarding>
syn earnings, gain, lucre, proceeds, return
rel cleaning, cleanup, killing; receipt(s); output, outturn, product, production, turnout, yield
con cost, expenditure, expense, outgo
ant loss
profit vb syn see BENEFIT
ant lose
profitable adj syn see ADVANTAGEOUS 1
ant profitless, unprofitable
profligate adj syn see ABANDONED 2
profligate n **1 syn** see WASTREL 1

2 syn see SPENDTHRIFT
profound adj **1 syn** see RECONDITE
2 syn see DEEP 1
3 syn see INTENSIVE
profoundness n syn see DEPTH 2
profundity n syn see DEPTH 2
profuse adj proffered in or characterized by great abundance <*profuse* apologies> <a *profuse* flow of blood>
syn exuberant, lavish, lush, luxuriant, opulent, prodigal, profusive, riotous
rel abundant, copious; abounding, swarming, teeming; excessive, extravagant, immoderate; bounteous, bountiful, generous, liberal, munificent, openhanded
con exiguous, meager, scrimpy, skimpy, slight, small, sparse
ant scant, scanty
profusive adj syn see PROFUSE
progenerate vb syn see FATHER 1
progenitor n syn see ANCESTOR 1
progeniture n syn see OFFSPRING
progeny n syn see OFFSPRING
prognosis n syn see PREDICTION
prognostic n syn see FORETOKEN
prognosticate vb syn see FORETELL
prognostication n syn see PREDICTION
prognosticator n syn see PROPHET
program n **1** a formulated plan listing things to be done or to take place especially in their time order <the *program* of a concert>
syn agenda, calendar, card, docket, programma, schedule, sked, timetable
rel bill; slate; plan
idiom order of the day
2 syn see COURSE 3
programma n syn see PROGRAM 1
progress n **1 syn** see ADVANCE 2
ant regression, retrogression
2 a movement onward (as in time or space) <the *progress* of a disease> <they made slow *progress* toward their destination>
syn advance, course, progression
rel passage
3 syn see DEVELOPMENT
progress vb syn see ADVANCE 5
ant retrogress
progression n **1 syn** see PROGRESS 2
2 syn see SUCCESSION 2
3 syn see DEVELOPMENT
ant regression, retrogression
progressive adj syn see LIBERAL 3
ant reactionary
prohibit vb syn see FORBID
ant permit
prohibited adj syn see FORBIDDEN
prohibition n syn see TABOO
ant permission
project n **1 syn** see PLAN 1
2 something (as a business operation) that one engages in or attempts <large-scale *projects* involving large sums of money>
syn enterprise, undertaking
rel affair, business, concern, matter, proposition, thing; adventure, emprise, exploit, feat, gest, venture
project vb **1 syn** see PLAN 2
rel intend, propose, purpose; delineate, diagram
2 syn see THINK 1
‖3 syn see WANDER 1
4 syn see BULGE
rel extend, lengthen, prolong
projection n **1** something which extends beyond a level or a normal outer surface <buttresses are *projections* which serve to support a wall>
syn bulge, jut, outthrust, protrusion, protuberance
rel bump, bunch, swelling; extension, prolongation; hook, knob, point, spine, spur
ant depression
2 syn see EMINENCE 3
prolegomenon n syn see INTRODUCTION
proletariat n syn see RABBLE 2
proliferant adj syn see FERTILE
prolific adj syn see FERTILE

rel abounding, swarming; breeding, generating, propagating, reproducing, reproductive
ant barren, unfruitful
prolificacy *n syn* see FERTILITY
ant barrenness, unfruitfulness
prolix *adj syn* see WORDY
rel irksome, tedious, tiresome, wearisome; prolonged, protracted
prolixity *n syn* see VERBOSITY
prolixness *n syn* see VERBOSITY
prologue *n syn* see INTRODUCTION
ant epilogue
prolong *vb syn* see EXTEND 3
rel continue, endure, last, persist
con abbreviate, retrench, shorten
ant curtail
prolongate *vb syn* see EXTEND 3
prolongation *n syn* see EXTENSION 1
prolonged *adj syn* see LONG 2
ant curtailed
prolongment *n syn* see EXTENSION 1
prominence *n* 1 *syn* see EMINENCE 1
2 *syn* see EMINENCE 3
prominency *n syn* see EMINENCE 1
prominent *adj* 1 *syn* see NOTICEABLE
ant inconspicuous
2 *syn* see FAMOUS 2
3 *syn* see WELL-KNOWN
promiscuous *adj* 1 *syn* see MISCELLANEOUS
2 *syn* see RANDOM
promise *vb* 1 to give one's word to do, bring about, or provide <*promised* to render all possible assistance to the flood victims>
syn engage, pass, pledge, undertake; *compare* VOW
rel accede, agree, assent, consent; bargain, compact, contract; covenant, plight, swear, vow; assure, ensure, insure; guarantee
idiom give (*or* make) a promise, pass one's word
2 *syn* see AUGUR 2
promise *n* a declaration that one will do or refrain from doing something specified <never gave a *promise* that he did not intend to keep>
syn engagement, plight, word; *compare* PLEDGE 1, WORD 8
rel earnest, guarantee, pawn, pledge, security, token; covenant, swear, vow; assurance, warrant
idiom word of honor
‖**promised** *adj syn* see ENGAGED 2
promised land *n syn* see UTOPIA
promiseful *adj syn* see HOPEFUL 2
promising *adj syn* see HOPEFUL 2
ant unpromising
promontory *n* a high point of land or rock projecting into a body of water beyond the line of coast <stood on the *promontory* watching boats come in with the tide>
syn beak, bill, cape, foreland, head, headland, naze, point
promote *vb* 1 *syn* see ADVANCE 2
con break, bust, declass, degrade, demerit, disgrade, disrate, downgrade, reduce
ant bump, demote
2 *syn* see ADVANCE 1
3 to encourage public acceptance of (as a policy or merchandise) through publicity <official attempts to *promote* energy conservation> <television helped *promote* the new smaller cars>
syn advertise, boost, plug, push; *compare* PUBLICIZE
rel ballyhoo, propagandize; build up, cry, press-agent, publicize, puff; communicate, impart
idiom make much of
con belittle, decry, depreciate, discredit, knock, run down
ant disparage
promotion *n* 1 *syn* see ADVANCEMENT 1
ant demotion
2 *syn* see PUBLICITY
rel advertisement
prompt *vb* 1 *syn* see INDUCE 1
2 *syn* see URGE
prompt *adj* 1 *syn* see QUICK 2
rel alert, vigilant, watchful, wide-awake; expeditious, speedy, swift
con lax, remiss, slack; dilatory

2 *syn* see PUNCTUAL 2
promptitude *n syn* see ALACRITY
promptly *adv syn* see FAST 2
promulgate *vb syn* see DECLARE 1
promulgation *n syn* see DECLARATION
prone *adj* 1 *syn* see WILLING 1
2 *syn* see LIABLE 2
3 *syn* see APT 1
4 lying down <lying *prone* on the floor>
syn decumbent, flat, procumbent, prostrate, reclining, recumbent
rel resupine, supine; level
con arrect, raised, stand-up, straight-up, upright, upstanding
ant erect
pronounce *vb syn* see ARTICULATE 2
pronounced *adj syn* see DECIDED 1
pronouncement *n syn* see DECLARATION
‖**pronto** *adv syn* see FAST 2
pronunciamento *n syn* see DECLARATION
proof *n* 1 *syn* see REASON 3
2 *syn* see TESTIMONY
prop *n syn* see SUPPORT 3
prop *vb* 1 *syn* see SUPPORT 4
2 *syn* see SUPPORT 5
propagandist *n syn* see MISSIONARY
propagate *vb* 1 *syn* see PROCREATE 1
2 *syn* see GROW 1
3 *syn* see SPREAD 1
propel *vb* 1 *syn* see PUSH 1
2 *syn* see MOVE 5
3 *syn* see URGE
propellant *n syn* see STIMULUS
propensity *n syn* see LEANING 2
ant antipathy
proper *adj* 1 *syn* see FIT 1
ant improper
2 *syn* see TRUE 7
ant improper
3 *syn* see DECOROUS 1
ant improper
4 *syn* see ABLE
5 *syn* see GOOD 2
ant improper
6 *syn* see CHARACTERISTIC
‖7 *syn* see UTTER
8 *syn* see CORRECT 2
9 *syn* see PRIM 1
properly *adv* 1 *syn* see WELL 4
ant improperly
2 *syn* see WELL 1
idiom by rights
ant improperly
properness *n syn* see ORDER 7
ant improperness
property *n* 1 *syn* see QUALITY 1
2 *syn* see WEALTH 2
3 *syn* see OWNERSHIP
prophecy *n* 1 *syn* see REVELATION
2 *syn* see PREDICTION
prophesier *n syn* see PROPHET
prophesy *vb syn* see FORETELL
prophet *n* one who predicts events or developments <there have been many *prophets* foretelling the end of the world>
syn augur, auspex, forecaster, foreseer, foreteller, haruspex, Nostradamus, predictor, prognosticator, prophesier, seer, soothsayer
prophetic *adj* of, relating to, or characteristic of a prophet or prophecy <the old woman seemed to have *prophetic* powers>
syn apocalyptic, Delphian, fatidic, mantic, oracular, prophetical, sibylline, vatic, vaticinal
rel revelatory; interpretive; mysterious, mystic, strange, unexplainable
ant unprophetic

---

syn synonym(s)   *rel* related word(s)
ant antonym(s)   *con* contrasted word(s)
idiom idiomatic equivalent(s)
‖ use limited; if in doubt, see a dictionary

prophetical *adj syn* see PROPHETIC
propinquity *n syn* see PROXIMITY
propitiate *vb syn* see PACIFY
  rel adapt, adjust, conform, reconcile; content, satisfy; intercede, mediate
propitiatory *adj syn* see PURGATIVE
propitious *adj* 1 *syn* see FAVORABLE 5
  ant unpropitious; adverse
  2 *syn* see TIMELY 1
  ant unpropitious
  3 *syn* see GOOD 1
  ant unpropitious; adverse
‖**propone** *vb syn* see PROPOSE 1
proponent *n syn* see EXPONENT
  ant opponent
proportion *n* 1 *syn* see DEGREE 2
  2 *syn* see SYMMETRY
  ant disproportion
  3 *syn* see SIZE 1
proportion *vb syn* see HARMONIZE 3
proportional *adj* being in proportion < his weight is *proportional* to his size >
  syn commensurable, commensurate, equal, symmetrical
  rel correlative, corresponding, reciprocal; contingent, dependent, relative
  con asymmetrical, disproportionate, irregular, lopsided, nonsymmetrical, off-balance, overbalanced, unbalanced, unequal, uneven, unsymmetrical
  ant disproportional
proportionless *adj syn* see LOPSIDED
proposal *n* something which is proposed to another for consideration < his *proposal* for a new bussing plan >
  syn invitation, proffer, proposition, suggestion
  rel motion; recommendation; idea, plan, project; outline, scheme
propose *vb* 1 to set before the mind for consideration < he *proposed* Mr. Smith for secretary of the club >
  syn pose, prefer, ‖propone, proposition, propound, put, suggest
  rel move (for); offer, present, submit, tender; ask, request, solicit
  idiom put forth (*or* forward)
  ant withdraw
  2 *syn* see INTEND 2
proposition *n syn* see PROPOSAL
proposition *vb syn* see PROPOSE 1
propound *vb syn* see PROPOSE 1
proprietary *n syn* see OWNERSHIP
proprietor *n syn* see OWNER
proprietorship *n syn* see OWNERSHIP
propriety *n* 1 *syn* see ORDER 11
  2 *syn* see DECORUM 1
  ant impropriety
  3 *syn* see ORDER 7
  ant impropriety
  4 **proprieties** *pl syn* see MANNER 5
prorate *vb syn* see APPORTION 2
prorogate *vb syn* see ADJOURN 2
prorogue *vb* 1 *syn* see DEFER
  2 *syn* see ADJOURN 2
prosaic *adj* 1 belonging to or characteristic of prose as distinguished from poetry < his poetry is far more fanciful than his *prosaic* writings >
  syn matter-of-fact, prose, prosing, prosy
  rel actual, factual; literal
  con figurative, metaphorical, symbolic; fanciful, florid, flowery, ornate
  ant poetic
  2 *syn* see COLORLESS 2
  3 belonging to or suitable to the everyday world < the *prosaic* business of day-to-day housekeeping >
  syn commonplace, everyday, lowly, mundane, workaday, workday
  rel practicable, practical; boring, irksome, tedious
  4 *syn* see COMMON 6
prosaicism *n syn* see COMMONPLACE
prosaism *n syn* see COMMONPLACE
proscribe *vb syn* see SENTENCE
proscription *n syn* see TABOO

prose *n syn* see CHAT 2
prose *adj syn* see PROSAIC 1
prosing *adj syn* see PROSAIC 1
prospect *n syn* see VISTA
prospect *vb syn* see EXPLORE
prosper *vb syn* see SUCCEED 3
  rel augment, increase, multiply; bear, produce, turn out, yield
prospering *adj syn* see FLOURISHING
prosperity *n* 1 *syn* see SUCCESS
  2 a state of good fortune and especially of financial success < his wise investments finally brought him a life of *prosperity* >
  syn abundance, ease, easy street, prosperousness, thriving, well=being
  rel affluence, riches, wealth
  idiom bed of roses, comfortable (*or* easy) circumstances, life of ease, the good life
  con misery, suffering; distress, embarrassment, indigence, poverty, straits
  ant adversity
  3 *syn* see WELFARE
  4 a state of high general economic activity marked by relatively full employment < a war economy often generates *prosperity* >
  syn boom, prosperousness
  rel expansion; growth; inflation
  con recession, slump, stagnation; bust
  ant depression
prosperous *adj* 1 *syn* see TIMELY 1
  rel appropriate, convenient, desirable; felicitous, fortunate, happy, lucky
  con ill-seasoned, ill-timed, inauspicious, inopportune, unpropitious, unseasonable, untimely
  ant unprosperous
  2 *syn* see SUCCESSFUL
  3 enjoying or marked by economic well-being < in *prosperous* circumstances >
  syn comfortable, easy, ‖snug, substantial, well, well-fixed, well=heeled, well-off, well-to-do
  rel affluent, opulent, rich, wealthy; halcyon
  idiom comfortably off, comfortably situated, in (the) clover, in good case
  con impecunious, necessitous, needy, poor; failing, unfortunate, unsuccessful
  ant unprosperous
  4 *syn* see FLOURISHING
  rel lusty, strong
  con decrepit, feeble, spindling, weak
prosperously *adv syn* see WELL 5
  ant unprosperously
prosperousness *n* 1 *syn* see PROSPERITY 2
  ant unprosperousness
  2 *syn* see PROSPERITY 4
prostitute *vb syn* see ABUSE 2
  rel corrupt, debase, debauch, deprave, vitiate
prostitute *n* a woman who engages in promiscuous sexual intercourse especially for money < streets haunted by *prostitutes* >
  syn bawd, ‖callet, call girl, camp follower, cocotte, ‖cruiser, drab, fille de joie, harlot, ‖hooker, hustler, ‖joy girl, meretrix, moll, nightwalker, party girl, pom-pom girl, poule, quean, sporting girl, street girl, streetwalker, ‖tomato, whore
  rel bar girl, B-girl, pickup; V-girl, victory girl; cocodette
  idiom lady of pleasure, lady of the evening, woman of the street (*or* streets), woman of the town
prostitution *n* the act or practice of engaging in promiscuous sexual intercourse especially for money < the problem of *prostitution* around military installations >
  syn harlotry, oldest profession, (the) social evil, streetwalking, whoredom
prostrate *adj syn* see PRONE 4
prostrate *vb* 1 *syn* see FELL 1
  2 *syn* see PARALYZE 1
  3 *syn* see OVERWHELM 4
  4 *syn* see EXHAUST 4
prosy *adj* 1 *syn* see PROSAIC 1
  2 *syn* see COLORLESS 2
protean *adj syn* see CHANGEABLE 1
protect *vb syn* see DEFEND 1
  rel conserve, preserve, save; harbor, shelter
protection *n* 1 *syn* see DEFENSE 1

2 money paid under threat of depredation < offered *protection* to keep his store from being vandalized >
syn ‖pad
rel extortion, shakedown, squeeze; graft; bribe

pro tem *adj syn* see TEMPORARY

pro tempore *adj syn* see TEMPORARY

protest *n syn* see DEMUR 2

protest *vb* **1** *syn* see ASSERT 1
2 *syn* see OBJECT 1
rel demonstrate; combat, fight, oppose, resist
ant agree

protoplast *n syn* see ORIGINAL 1

prototypal *adj syn* see TYPICAL 1

prototype *n* **1** *syn* see ORIGINAL 1
2 *syn* see FORERUNNER 2

prototypical *adj syn* see TYPICAL 1

protract *vb syn* see EXTEND 3
ant curtail

protracted *adj syn* see LONG 2
ant curtailed

protraction *n syn* see EXTENSION 1
rel dallying, dawdling, delay, lag; stay, suspension
ant curtailment

protrude *vb syn* see BULGE

protrusion *n syn* see PROJECTION 1

protuberance *n syn* see PROJECTION 1

protuberate *vb syn* see BULGE

proud *adj* **1** showing or feeling superiority toward others < a woman who was too *proud* to do her share of menial tasks >
syn arrogant, cavalier, disdainful, dismissive, haughty, high-and-mighty, hubristic, huffy, insolent, lofty, lordly, orgulous, overbearing, ‖pridy, proudhearted, supercilious, superior, toploftical, toplofty; *compare* POMPOUS 1, VAIN 3
rel contemptuous, scornful; misproud; ostentatious, pretentious; bloated, important, pompous, self-important, stuffy, wiggy; conceited, narcissistic, self-conceited, stuck-up, vain, vainglorious; domineering, high-handed, imperious, masterful
con lowly, meek, modest, unassuming; chagrined, mortified
ant humble
2 *syn* see SPLENDID 2

proudhearted *adj syn* see PROUD 1

prove *vb* **1** to establish a point by appropriate objective means < gathered evidence that *proved* the need for better controls >
syn demonstrate, test, try
rel confirm, corroborate, substantiate, verify; argue, attest, bespeak, betoken, indicate
ant disprove; refute
2 *syn* see TRY 1
3 *syn* see ESTABLISH 6

provenance *n syn* see SOURCE

provender *n syn* see FOOD 1

provenience *n syn* see SOURCE

prove out *vb syn* see SUCCEED 2

proverb *n syn* see SAYING

provide *vb syn* see GIVE 3

provide (for) *vb syn* see SUPPORT 3

providence *n* **1** *syn* see ECONOMY
ant improvidence
2 *syn* see PRUDENCE 1
ant improvidence

provident *adj syn* see SPARING
ant improvident

providential *adj syn* see LUCKY
rel benignant, kind, kindly

province *n* **1** *syn* see FUNCTION 1
rel calling, pursuit, work
2 *syn* see FIELD

provincial *n syn* see RUSTIC

provincial *adj* **1** *syn* see RURAL
2 *syn* see INSULAR
rel bigoted, hidebound
con cosmic, universal; progressive
ant catholic

provision *n syn* see CONDITION 1

provisional *adj* **1** *syn* see CONDITIONAL 1
rel temporary; contingent, dependent
ant definitive
2 *syn* see MAKESHIFT

provisionary *adj syn* see CONDITIONAL 1

provisions *n pl syn* see FOOD 1

proviso *n syn* see CONDITION 1

provisory *adj syn* see CONDITIONAL 1

provocation *n syn* see ANNOYANCE 1

provocative *n syn* see STIMULUS

provoke *vb* **1** *syn* see IRRITATE
rel insult, outrage
ant gratify
2 *syn* see ANNOY 1
rel anger, incense, madden
3 *syn* see INCITE
rel perturb, upset
4 to lead one into doing or feeling or to produce by so leading a person < was *provoked* into finding a solution to the problem > < this foolish answer *provoked* an outburst of rage >
syn excite, galvanize, innervate, innerve, motivate, move, pique, prime, quicken, rouse, ‖roust, stimulate, suscitate; *compare* FIRE 2, STIR 1
rel arouse, awaken, bestir, build up, challenge, kindle, rally, stir, wake, waken, whet; animate, exalt, fire, inform, inspire; electrify, enthuse, thrill; titillate, titivate
idiom bring (one) to one's feet
con calm, relax, soothe
5 *syn* see GENERATE 3

provoking *n syn* see ANNOYANCE 1

prowess *n* **1** *syn* see HEROISM
2 *syn* see ADDRESS 1

proximate *adj* **1** *syn* see CLOSE 6
2 *syn* see IMMINENT 1
3 *syn* see RUDE 3
ant exact

proximity *n* the quality or state of being near < the two houses are in close *proximity* >
syn appropinquity, contiguity, contiguousness, immediacy, propinquity
rel togetherness; closeness, nearness; adjacency, juxtaposition
con farness, remoteness
ant distance

proxy *n syn* see AGENT 2

prude *n* a person who is excessively or priggishly attentive to propriety or decorum < in that narrow atmosphere she hardened into a rigid, inhibited, censorious person—a thorough *prude* >
syn bluenose, comstock, goody-goody, Grundy, Mrs. Grundy, nice Nelly, prig, puritan, ‖wowser
rel spoilsport, stick-in-the-mud, wet blanket; fuddy-duddy, old fogy, stuffed shirt; fussbudget, old maid
con freethinker, latitudinarian, libertarian

prudence *n* **1** a quality in a person that allows him to choose the sensible course < displayed *prudence* in setting up his business >
syn canniness, caution, discreetness, discretion, foresight, forethought, precaution, providence; *compare* WIT 3
rel acumen, astucity, astuteness, clear-sightedness, discrimination, keenness, penetration, percipience, perspicacity, shrewdness, wit; insight, sagaciousness, sagacity, sageness, sapience, wisdom; advisableness, expediency; calculation, circumspection
con indiscretion, unreasonableness, unwiseness
ant imprudence
2 *syn* see ECONOMY

prudent *adj* **1** *syn* see WISE 2
ant imprudent
2 *syn* see EXPEDIENT

prudish *adj syn* see PRIM 1
rel strict; austere, severe, stern

prune *n syn* see DUNCE

prune *vb syn* see CUT 6
rel brash, lop; thin; eliminate, exclude

prurience *n syn* see LUST 2

pruriency *n syn* see LUST 2

prurient *adj syn* see LUSTFUL 2
rel bawdy, erotic, lewd; sensual

pry *vb syn* see SNOOP
idiom nose into

---

syn synonym(s)   *rel* related word(s)
ant antonym(s)   *con* contrasted word(s)
idiom idiomatic equivalent(s)
‖ use limited; if in doubt, see a dictionary

pry *vb* to raise, move, or pull apart with or as if with a pry <*pry* up a floorboard>
syn jimmy, lever, prize
rel elevate, hoist, lift, pick up, raise, rear, take up, uphold, uplift, upraise, uprear; turn, twist; disengage, disjoin, divide, separate
prying *adj syn* see CURIOUS 2
rel obtrusive, officious
psalm *vb syn* see PRAISE 2
psalmody *vb syn* see PRAISE 2
pseudo *adj syn* see COUNTERFEIT
rel wrong
pseudonym *n* a fictitious or assumed name <used a *pseudonym* in many of his adventures>
syn alias, anonym, nom de guerre
rel ananym; nom de plume, pen name; stage name; incognito
psychal *adj syn* see PSYCHIC 1
psyche *n syn* see SOUL 1
psychic *adj* 1 sensitive to nonphysical forces and influences <because he foretold many things correctly, people regarded him as *psychic*>
syn psychal, psychical, supersensible, supersensory
rel telepathic; spiritual; impressible, impressionable, responsive, sensible, sensile, sensitive, sentient, susceptible, susceptive
2 *syn* see MENTAL 1
psychical *adj* 1 *syn* see PSYCHIC 1
2 *syn* see MENTAL 1
psychological *adj syn* see MENTAL 1
psychopathy *n syn* see INSANITY 1
pub *n syn* see BAR 5
puberty *n syn* see YOUTH 1
pubescence *n syn* see YOUTH 1
public *adj* 1 of, relating to, or affecting the people as an organized community <*public* affairs>
syn civic, civil, national
rel government, governmental; community; state; municipal, urban
2 *syn* see OPEN 4
rel common, general, universal
con private
3 *syn* see COMMON 1
con private
4 held by or applicable to the majority of the people <*public* opinion>
syn general, popular, vulgar
rel prevalent, usual, widespread
ant private
public *n* 1 *syn* see SOCIETY 3
2 *syn* see FOLLOWING 2
rel hangers-on, suite
‖**publican** *n syn* see SALOONKEEPER
publication *n syn* see DECLARATION
rel dissemination
public house *n* 1 *syn* see HOTEL
‖2 *syn* see BAR 5
publicity *n* information with news value issued to gain public attention or support <$100,000 was allocated for new-product *publicity*>
syn advertising, buildup, press-agentry, promotion, puffery
rel broadcasting, promulgation, skywriting; réclame; announcement, write-up; blurb, commercial, plug, puff; ballyhoo, hoopla; propaganda; hard sell
publicize *vb* to give publicity to <*publicize* a new book>
syn advertise, build up, cry, press-agent, puff; *compare* PROMOTE 3
rel announce, broadcast, headline, promulgate, skywrite; advance, boost, plug, push; extol; bruit, tout, trumpet; propagandize
idiom bring into the limelight, throw the spotlight on
publish *vb* 1 *syn* see DECLARE 1
rel broach, express, utter, vent, ventilate
idiom bring to public notice, lay before the public, publish (*or* noise *or* spread) abroad, put forth
2 to produce for publication and allow to be distributed and sold <*published* a newspaper>
syn get out, issue, put out
rel produce; bring out; market; distribute
puckfist *n syn* see BRAGGART

puckish *adj syn* see PLAYFUL 1
‖**pudding** *n, usu* **puddings** *pl syn* see ENTRAILS
puddle *n syn* see POOL
puddle *vb syn* see FIDDLE 2
puddy *adj syn* see ROTUND 2
pudendum *n, usu* **pudenda** *pl syn* see GENITALIA
pudgy *adj syn* see ROTUND 2
rel ‖chuffy, ‖chumpy, squab, squdgy, ‖stuggy, stumpy, thick=bodied
puerile *adj syn* see CHILDISH
puff *vb* 1 *syn* see PANT 1
idiom huff and puff, pant and blow
2 *syn* see BOAST
3 *syn* see PUBLICIZE
puff *n* 1 *syn* see DRAW 1
rel inhalation, inhaling
2 *syn* see QUILT
3 a commendatory and often extravagant publicity notice or review <this book fails to deliver what the *puff* promises>
syn blurb, plug, puffing, write-up
rel boost, buildup, push; laudation, praise
puffery *n syn* see PUBLICITY
puffing *n syn* see PUFF 3
puffy *adj syn* see POMPOUS 1
‖**puggy** *adj syn* see SWEATY
pugilism *n syn* see BOXING
pugnacious *adj syn* see BELLIGERENT
rel pushing, pushy, self-assertive; defiant, rebellious; brawling
idiom itching for a fight, itching (*or* ready) to fight, ready to fight at the drop of a hat
con bland, easygoing, mild; calm, peaceful; quiet
ant pacific
pugnacity *n syn* see ATTACK 2
puissance *n syn* see POWER 4
rel clout, influence, sway
con powerlessness, weakness
ant impuissance
puissant *adj syn* see POWERFUL 2
rel influential; commanding, ruling
con ineffectual, inefficacious, powerless
ant impuissant
puke *n syn* see SNOT 1
pukka *adj syn* see AUTHENTIC 2
pulchritudinous *adj syn* see BEAUTIFUL
pule *vb syn* see WHIMPER
pull *vb* 1 *syn* see EXTRACT 1
2 to cause to move toward or after an applied force <*pull* a trunk across the floor>
syn drag, draw, haul, lug, tow, tug
rel strain; heave; jerk, wrench, yank; drive, impel, push, shove
3 *syn* see STRAIN 2
4 *syn* see ROW
idiom pull on the oar (*or* oars)
5 *syn* see COMMIT 2
idiom ‖go and do
6 *syn* see DON 2
7 *syn* see GET 1
pull *n* 1 *syn* see DRAW 1
2 the power or ability to secure special favor or partiality <had lots of *pull* with the government>
syn clout, ‖drag, in, influence; *compare* INFLUENCE 1
rel persuasion; wire-pulling
idiom backstairs influence
3 *syn* see ATTRACTION 3
pullback *n syn* see DIEHARD 1
pull down *vb syn* see DESTROY 1
pull in *vb* 1 *syn* see RESTRAIN 1
2 *syn* see ARREST 2
pull out *vb syn* see GO 2
ant pull in
pull through *vb syn* see SURVIVE 2
pullulate *vb syn* see TEEM
pull up *vb syn* see STOP 4
pulp *vb syn* see CRUSH 2
pulpitarian *n syn* see CLERGYMAN
pulpiteer *n syn* see CLERGYMAN
pulpiter *n syn* see CLERGYMAN
pulpous *adj syn* see SOFT 6

pulpy *adj syn* see SOFT 6

pulsate *vb* to course or move with or as if with rhythmic strokes < blood *pulsating* through his veins >
  syn beat, palpitate, pulse, throb
  rel fluctuate, oscillate, vibrate; pump; drum, pound, roar, thrum

pulse *vb syn* see PULSATE

pulverize *vb* **1** to reduce (as by crushing, beating, or grinding) to minute particles < *pulverized* the ore in a stamp mill >
  syn bray, buck, comminute, contriturate, crush, powder, triturate; *compare* SHATTER 1
  rel break up; abrade, grate, grind; crumble, crunch, mull; levigate; atomize, fragment, fragmentalize, fragmentize, micronize; beat, shatter, smash, smatter, splinter; flour, mill
  2 *syn* see DESTROY 1

pulverized *adj syn* see FINE 2
  rel pulverous, pulverulent; dusty, granular, splintery
  ant unpulverized

pummel *vb syn* see BEAT 1

pump *vb syn* see DRAIN 1

pumpkin head *n syn* see DUNCE

‖**pumpknot** *n syn* see BUMP 2

pun *n* the humorous use of a word so as to suggest different meanings, or of words having the same or similar sound but different meanings < "mourning shall come with approaching day" is a *pun* >
  syn calembour, paronomasia
  rel double entendre
  idiom play on words

punch *vb* **1** *syn* see POKE 1
  rel hit, slap, strike
  2 *syn* see PERFORATE

punch *n* **1** *syn* see CUFF
  2 *syn* see POKE 1
  3 *syn* see POINT 3
  4 *syn* see VIGOR 2

punctilious *adj syn* see CAREFUL 2
  rel conventional, formal, observant; overconscientious, overscrupulous

punctual *adj* **1** *syn* see CAREFUL 2
  ant unpunctual
  2 marked by exact adherence to an appointed time < a *punctual* arrival >
  syn prompt, timely
  rel quick, ready
  idiom on the dot, on time
  con late, tardy
  ant unpunctual

punctuate *vb* to mark or divide (written matter) with punctuation marks < *punctuated* the sentence >
  syn point
  rel divide, separate

puncture *n syn* see PRICK
  rel perforation

puncture *vb* **1** *syn* see PERFORATE
  rel riddle
  2 *syn* see DISCREDIT 2
  idiom shoot full of holes

pungent *adj* sharp and stimulating to the mind or senses < his *pungent* wit >
  syn peppery, piquant, poignant, racy, snappy, spicy, zesty
  rel acute, keen, salt, salty, sharp; biting, bitter, cutting, hot, incisive, trenchant; exciting, provocative, stimulating; rich
  con banal, corny, dull, flat, hackneyed, insipid, old hat, platitudinous, prosaic, prosy, stale, stodgy, tasteless, unimaginative, uninteresting
  ant bland

punish *vb* **1** to inflict a penalty on in requital for a wrongdoing < *punished* the child for misbehaving >
  syn castigate, chasten, chastise, correct, discipline
  rel criticize, reprove; amerce, fine, mulct, penalize; avenge, fix, revenge; lambaste, scourge
  con overlook; absolve, acquit, exculpate, exonerate, vindicate; let off, release
  ant excuse, pardon
  2 *syn* see CONSUME 5

punishing *adj syn* see PUNITIVE

punishment *n* the act or an instance of punishing < a spanking was his *punishment* >
  syn castigation, chastisement, correction, discipline, punition, rod
  rel criticism, reproof; amercement, fine, mulct, penalty; avengement, revenge
  idiom carrot-and-stick treatment, disciplinary action, dose of strap oil, what for
  con overlooking; acquittal, exculpation, exoneration, vindication
  ant excuse, pardon

punition *n syn* see PUNISHMENT
  idiom punitive measures

punitive *adj* inflicting, involving, or constituting punishment < took *punitive* action against him >
  syn castigating, disciplinary, punishing, punitory
  rel correctional, penal

punitory *adj syn* see PUNITIVE

punk *n* **1** *syn* see NONSENSE 2
  2 *syn* see NOVICE
  3 *syn* see TOUGH

‖**punk** *adj syn* see BAD 1

puny *adj* **1** *syn* see PETTY 2
  rel feeble, weak
  2 *syn* see WEAK 1

pup *n syn* see TWERP

puppet *n syn* see TOOL 2
  rel dupe; slave

puppy *n syn* see TWERP

purblind *adj* partly blind < *purblind* with cataracts >
  syn dim-sighted, half-blind
  rel myopic, nearsighted, shortsighted; dim; blind, dark, sightless

purchasable *adj* **1** capable of being bought < *purchasable* goods >
  syn available, obtainable, on offer
  rel marketable, salable
  idiom on (or for) sale, on the market, to be had
  con rare; unavailable, unobtainable
  ant unpurchasable
  2 *syn* see VENAL 1
  rel undependable, unreliable; slippery, tricky; treacherous

purchase *vb syn* see BUY 1
  idiom make a purchase
  ant sell

purchaser *n* one to whom something is sold < instruction booklets for new-car *purchasers* >
  syn buyer, emptor, vendee
  rel marketer, shopper; client, customer, patron; consumer, user
  con seller, vendor

pure *adj* **1** *syn* see STRAIGHT 3
  ant impure
  2 being such and no other < his solution of the problem was *pure* genius >
  syn absolute, perfect, pure and simple, sheer, simple, unadulterated, unalloyed, undiluted, unmitigated, unmixed, unqualified; *compare* UTTER
  rel complete, plenary, total; authentic, genuine; classic; out-and-out, plain, utter
  con mixed, qualified; doubtful, dubious, questionable, uncertain
  3 *syn* see UTTER
  4 *syn* see GOOD 11
  ant impure
  5 *syn* see CHASTE
  rel fresh, inviolate, unblighted, unprofaned
  idiom as pure as the driven snow
  con contaminated, dirty, sullied
  ant immoral, impure

‖**pure** *adv syn* see VERY 1

pure and simple *adj syn* see PURE 2

pureblood *adj syn* see PUREBRED

purebred *adj* being of unmixed ancestry < a *purebred* collie >
  syn full-blooded, pedigree, pedigreed, pureblood, thoroughbred
  rel registered
  con bastard, hybrid, lowbred, mixed
  ant mongrel

‖**puredee** (*or* pure–D) *adj syn* see UTTER

---

syn synonym(s)   *rel* related word(s)
ant antonym(s)   *con* contrasted word(s)
idiom idiomatic equivalent(s)
‖ use limited; if in doubt, see a dictionary

purely *adv syn* see ALL 1
purgation *n syn* see PURIFICATION
purgative *adj* cleansing or purifying especially from sin <confession as a *purgative* ritual>
  syn expiative, expiatory, expurgatorial, expurgatory, lustral, lustratory, propitiatory, purgatorial
purgatorial *adj syn* see PURGATIVE
‖**purgatory** *n syn* see SWAMP
purge *vb* **1** *syn* see DISABUSE
  rel absolve, cleanse; clear, rid
  2 *syn* see PURIFY 2
  3 to get rid of often by exile, imprisonment, or murder <Stalin *purged* all the Party dissidents>
  syn eliminate, liquidate, remove
  rel debar, exclude, shut out; dismiss, eject, expel, oust; erase, expunge, wipe (out); exterminate
  con rehabilitate; reinstate; repatriate; accept, bear (with), tolerate
  ant depurge
purification *n* a freeing from something morally harmful, offensive, or sinful <sought *purification* through repentance>
  syn catharsis, cleansing, expurgation, lustration, purgation
  rel atonement, expiation; absolution, forgiveness; grace, redemption, salvation; rebirth, regeneration; sanctification
  con contamination, defilement
purify *vb* **1** to free from material impurities or noxious matter <*purify* the water for drinking>
  syn clarify, clean, cleanse, depurate
  rel elutriate; filter; refine
  con dirty, foul, soil
  ant contaminate, pollute
  2 to free from guilt or moral blemish (often ceremonially) <*purify* one's heart through confession>
  syn cleanse, expurgate, lustrate, purge
  rel atone, expiate; absolve, remit
  con defile, sully, tarnish
purist *n* one who adheres strictly and often excessively to a tradition <*purists* who believe in prescriptive grammar>
  syn precisian, precisionist, traditionalist
  rel Atticist, classicist; bitter-ender, conservative, diehard, Puritan
  con liberal, radical, young Turk
  ant revisionist
puritan *n syn* see PRUDE
puritanical *adj syn* see PRIM 1
  rel rigorous, strict; bigoted, hidebound, illiberal, intolerant, narrow, narrow-minded
  con liberal, tolerant; modern
purl *vb syn* see SWIRL
‖**purl** *vb syn* see SPIN 1
purlieu *n* **1** *syn* see RESORT 2
  2 purlieus *pl syn* see ENVIRONS 1
  3 purlieus *pl syn* see ENVIRONS 2
purloin *vb syn* see STEAL 1
purloiner *n syn* see THIEF
purloining *n syn* see THEFT
purple *adj* **1** *syn* see RISQUÉ
  2 *syn* see RHETORICAL
purport *n* **1** *syn* see MEANING 1
  2 *syn* see TENOR 1
  rel connotation; implication
  3 *syn* see SUBSTANCE 2
purported *adj syn* see ALLEGED
  rel postulated, presupposed; suppositional, suppositive; academic, speculative, theoretical; reputed, rumored; suspected
purportless *adj syn* see SENSELESS 5
purpose *n* **1** *syn* see INTENTION
  rel destination, direction; aim, goal, mission, objective, point; ambition, aspiration; proposal, proposition
  2 *syn* see USE 4
  rel mission
purpose *vb syn* see INTEND 2
  rel meditate, ponder; consider; conclude, decide, determine, resolve
purposedly *adv syn* see INTENTIONALLY
purposefulness *n syn* see DECISION 2
  rel certainty, confidence, sureness
  con indecision, irresoluteness, irresolution, vacillation, waffling, wavering, weakness; aimlessness, indirection

ant purposelessness
purposeless *adj* **1** *syn* see FECKLESS 1
  rel unhelpful, unprofitable; purportless, senseless; nonsensical
  con helpful, profitable
  ant purposeful
  2 *syn* see RANDOM
  ant purposeful
purposely *adv syn* see INTENTIONALLY
  rel expressly; explicitly
  con unintentionally
  ant accidentally
purposively *adv syn* see INTENTIONALLY
purposiveness *n syn* see DECISION 2
purse cutter *n syn* see PICKPOCKET
pursual *n syn* see PURSUIT 2
pursuance *n syn* see PURSUIT 2
pursue *vb* **1** *syn* see FOLLOW 2
  rel persevere, persist; oppress, persecute; badger, bait, hound, ride
  idiom go in pursuit (of)
  2 *syn* see ADDRESS 8
pursuing *n syn* see PURSUIT 2
pursuit *n* **1** *syn* see WORK 1
  2 a following with a view to reach, accomplish, or obtain <the *pursuit* of happiness>
  syn pursual, pursuance, pursuing, quest, search, seeking
  rel following; reaching; obtaining; accomplishing, accomplishment
  idiom a going all out (after)
pursy *adj syn* see FAT 2
purview *n* **1** *syn* see RANGE 2
  2 *syn* see KEN
push *vb* **1** to use force so as to cause to move ahead or aside <*push* a wheelbarrow across the yard>
  syn drive, propel, shove, thrust
  rel launch; impel, move; force, ram
  con brake, check, stay
  ant pull
  2 to do, effect, or accomplish by forcing aside obstacles or opposition <*pushed* his way through the crowd> <*pushed* the measure through congress>
  syn bulldoze, elbow, hustle, jostle, press, ‖shog, shoulder, shove
  rel dig, nudge; hunch; drive, force, thrust; bump, butt, ram
  con ease, facilitate, slide (by), slip (through); expedite, help (along)
  3 *syn* see INCREASE 1
  4 *syn* see PRESSURE
  5 *syn* see PROMOTE 3
  rel oversell
  6 to engage in the illicit sale of (narcotics) <*pushing* drugs to teenagers>
  syn peddle, shove
  7 *syn* see PRESS 1
push *n* **1** *syn* see ENTERPRISE 4
  2 *syn* see VIGOR 2
  3 *syn* see STIMULUS
  4 *syn* see CROWD 1
  5 *syn* see SET 5
push around *vb syn* see BAIT 2
pushful *adj* **1** *syn* see AGGRESSIVE
  2 *syn* see PRESUMPTUOUS
  rel imposing, intrusive, obtruding, obtrusive, officious; assured, confident, self-confident
pushing *adj* **1** *syn* see AGGRESSIVE
  idiom ‖not backward in going forward
  2 *syn* see PRESUMPTUOUS
push off *vb syn* see GO 2
push on *vb syn* see GO 1
pushover *n syn* see SNAP 1
pushy *adj* **1** *syn* see AGGRESSIVE
  ‖**2** *syn* see PRESUMPTUOUS
pusillanimous *adj syn* see COWARDLY
puss *n syn* see CHILD 1
‖**puss** *n syn* see FACE 1
pussyfoot *vb* **1** *syn* see SNEAK
  2 *syn* see EQUIVOCATE 2
pustule *n syn* see ABSCESS
put *vb* **1** *syn* see SET 1

2 *syn* see FASTEN 3
3 *syn* see PROPOSE 1
4 *syn* see WORD
5 *syn* see TRANSLATE 1
6 *syn* see EXPRESS 2
7 *syn* see ESTIMATE 3

put (back) *vb syn* see RESTORE 5
put (on) *vb syn* see GAMBLE 1
put (on *or* **upon)** *vb syn* see LEVY
put *n syn* see DUNCE
put about *vb syn* see INCONVENIENCE
putative *adj syn* see SUPPOSED 1

put away *vb* **1** *syn* see DIVORCE 2
2 *syn* see CONSUME 5
3 *syn* see MURDER 1
4 *syn* see BURY 1
5 *syn* see KILL 1
put by *vb syn* see SAVE 4

put down *vb* **1** *syn* see CRUSH 5
2 *syn* see DEGRADE 1
3 *syn* see CONSUME 5
put in *vb syn* see PLANT 1

put off *vb* **1** *syn* see DELAY 2
idiom drag one's feet
2 *syn* see DEFER
idiom lay on the table, let the matter stand
3 *syn* see REMOVE 3
ant put on

put on *vb* **1** *syn* see DON 1
ant put off
2 *syn* see DON 2
rel affect, feign, sham, simulate; masquerade, pose
idiom make as if (*or* as though)
3 *syn* see ASSUME 4
idiom put on a (false) front, put on an act
4 *syn* see EMPLOY 2
5 *syn* see STAGE

put–on *adj syn* see ARTIFICIAL 3
rel mannered, posed; faked, sham
put–on *n* **1** *syn* see IMPOSTURE
2 *syn* see MASK 2

put out *vb* **1** *syn* see EXERT
2 *syn* see EXTINGUISH 1
3 *syn* see PUBLISH 2
4 *syn* see IRRITATE
5 *syn* see INCONVENIENCE
rel displease, dissatisfy; annoy, irritate
idiom put out of the way, put to it

put over *vb syn* see DEFER
putrefy *vb syn* see DECAY
putresce *vb syn* see DECAY
putrid *adj* **1** *syn* see BAD 5
2 *syn* see MALODOROUS 1
3 *syn* see VICIOUS 2
putter *vb syn* see FIDDLE 2
rel boondoggle; dawdle
‖**put to** *vb syn* see CLOSE 1
put together *vb syn* see MAKE 3
put up *vb* **1** *syn* see HARBOR 2
2 *syn* see BUILD 1
rel forge, make, put together, shape
3 *syn* see ERECT 3
4 *syn* see RAISE 9
rel elevate, escalate
‖**puxy** *n syn* see SWAMP
puzzle *vb* to baffle and disturb mentally <a persistent fever that *puzzled* her doctor>
syn befog, bewilder, ‖cap, confound, confuse, metagrobolize, perplex, pose, stumble; *compare* NONPLUS 1
rel baffle, foil, frustrate; befuddle, ‖bumfuzzle, fuddle; disconcert, distract, disturb, upset; addle, muddle; mystify; amaze, dumbfound, flabbergast
con enlighten, inform
puzzle *n syn* see MYSTERY
puzzlement *n syn* see MYSTERY
puzzle out *vb syn* see SOLVE 2
idiom find the key to, pick the lock
pygmy *n syn* see DWARF
ant giant
pygmy *adj syn* see TINY
pyramid *n syn* see PILE 1
Pyrrhonian *n syn* see SKEPTIC
Pyrrhonist *n syn* see SKEPTIC
pythonic *adj syn* see HUGE

quack *n syn* see CHARLATAN
rel counterfeiter, pretender, shammer, simulator
‖**quackle** *vb syn* see SUFFOCATE
quacksalver *n syn* see CHARLATAN
quackster *n syn* see CHARLATAN
quad *n syn* see COURT 1
quadrangle *n syn* see COURT 1
quadrate *adj syn* see SQUARE 1
quadrate *vb* **1** *syn* see AGREE 4
2 *syn* see ADAPT
quadratic *adj syn* see SQUARE 1
quadratical *adj syn* see SQUARE 1
quaesitum *n syn* see AMBITION 2
quaff *vb syn* see DRINK 1
quag *n syn* see SWAMP
quaggy *adj syn* see SOFT 6
quagmire *n* **1** *syn* see SWAMP
2 *syn* see PREDICAMENT
quail *n syn* see GIRL 1
quail *vb syn* see RECOIL
rel cower, cringe
quaint *adj syn* see STRANGE 4
rel droll, funny, laughable; antiquated, antique, archaic
‖**quaint** *vb syn* see INTRODUCE 4
quake *vb* **1** *syn* see SHAKE 2
rel fluctuate, waver
2 *syn* see SHAKE 1

quake *n syn* see EARTHQUAKE
‖**quaker** *n syn* see EARTHQUAKE
quaking *adj syn* see TREMULOUS
quaky *adj syn* see TREMULOUS
qualification *n syn* see ABILITY 1
qualified *adj* **1** *syn* see ABLE
rel disciplined, instructed, trained; catechized, examined, quizzed; proved, tested, tried
con incapable, incompetent, unequipped, unfit
ant disqualified, unqualified
2 not unlimited and complete <gave only a *qualified* endorsement to the project>
syn limited, modified, reserved
rel circumscribed, definite, determined, fixed, restricted; partial
con complete, entire, full, total, utter, whole; unlimited, unrestricted
ant absolute, unqualified
qualifiedness *n syn* see ABILITY 1
qualify *vb* **1** *syn* see CHARACTERIZE 2
rel ascribe, assign, attribute, impute; predicate

---

syn synonym(s)   *rel* related word(s)
ant antonym(s)   *con* contrasted word(s)
idiom idiomatic equivalent(s)
‖ use limited; if in doubt, see a dictionary

2 *syn* see ENTITLE 2

quality *n* **1** something inherent and distinctive <learned the special *qualities* of the native herbs>
syn affection, attribute, character, characteristic, feature, mark, peculiarity, property, savor, trait, virtue; *compare* CHARACTERISTIC 1
rel individuality; affirmation, predication; element, factor, parameter
2 a usually high level of merit or superiority <merchandise of *quality*>
syn caliber, merit, stature, value, virtue, worth
rel arete, excellence, excellency, perfection, superbness, superiority
con inferiority, meanness, mediocrity, poorness; inadequacy; deficiency
3 degree of excellence <upgrading the *quality* of incoming students>
syn caliber, class, grade
rel capacity, character, footing, place, position, rank, situation, standing, state, station, status
4 *syn* see STATUS 1
5 *syn* see ARISTOCRACY
6 *syn* see EXCELLENCE
quality *adj syn* see EXCELLENT
qualm *n* a misgiving about what one is going to do <had *qualms* about the secret meeting>
syn compunction, conscience, demur, scruple, squeam
rel apprehension, foreboding, misgiving, presentiment; doubt, mistrust, suspicion, uncertainty; agitation, insecurity, perturbation; objection, remonstrance; reluctance, unwillingness; impatience, nervousness, unease, uneasiness
con aplomb, assurance, confidence, self-assurance, self-confidence, self-possession; certainty, certitude, conviction
qualmish *adj syn* see SQUEAMISH 1
qualmishness *n syn* see NAUSEA
qualmy *adj syn* see SQUEAMISH 1
quantity *n* **1** *syn* see BODY 5
2 quantities *pl syn* see SCAD
quantum *n* **1** *syn* see BODY 5
2 *syn* see RATION
quarrel *n* a usually verbal dispute marked by anger or discord <a *quarrel* over who would drive the car>
syn altercation, ‖barney, beef, bickering, brabble, brannigan, brawl, controversy, difficulty, dispute, dust, dustup, embroilment, falling-out, feud, fight, fracas, fuss, hassle, imbroglio, knock-down-and-drag-out, miff, ‖prabble, ‖pribble, rhubarb, row, ruckus, run-in, set-to, spat, squabble, squall, tiff, to-and-fro, word(s), wrangle; *compare* BRAWL 2
rel battle royal, catfight; affray, bobbery, broil, donnybrook, fray, free-for-all, melee, ruction, rumpus, scrap, scrimmage, scuffle; conflict, contention, difference, discord, dissension, strife, variance; disagreement, misunderstanding
idiom ‖pribbles and prabbles
con accord, concord, harmony; agreement, likemindedness, understanding, unity
quarrel *vb* to contend noisily or captiously <with his belligerent personality he was always *quarreling* with someone>
syn altercate, bicker, brabble, brawl, ‖cast out, caterwaul, fall out, row, scrap, spat, squabble, tiff, wrangle; *compare* ARGUE 2
rel differ, disaccord, dissent, divide, vary; bump, clash, collide, conflict, thwart; battle, contend, fight, war
idiom have words with, pull caps
con agree, coincide, concur
quarrelsome *adj* **1** *syn* see BELLIGERENT
rel adverse, antagonistic, counter; antipathetic, hostile, inimical, rancorous
idiom having a chip on one's shoulder
2 apt or disposed to quarrel <when he's in a bad mood he becomes so *quarrelsome*>
syn battlesome, brawling, brawlsome, brawly, scrappy; *compare* BELLIGERENT
rel argumentative; disputatious; cankered, crabbed, irascible, irritable
con conciliatory, propitiatory
quarry *n syn* see GAME 3
quarry *vb syn* see MINE
quarter *n* **1** one of four equal parts <ate one *quarter* of the pie>
syn fourth, quartern

rel quadrant
2 a division or part of a town or city <the market *quarter* in Paris>
syn district, precinct, section, sector
rel division, part; area; locality; barrio
quarter *vb* **1** *syn* see HARBOR 2
2 *syn* see BILLET 1
quarterage *n syn* see SHELTER 2
quarterback *vb syn* see SUPERVISE
quartern *n syn* see QUARTER 1
quarter–witted *adj syn* see RETARDED
quartet *n* a group consisting of four individuals <a singing *quartet*>
syn four, foursome, quartetto, quaternion, quatuor, tetrad
rel quadruplet
quartetto *n syn* see QUARTET
quash *vb* **1** *syn* see ANNUL 4
2 *syn* see ABOLISH 1
3 *syn* see CRUSH 5
quashing *n syn* see REPRESSION 1
‖**quat** *vb syn* see SQUAT
quaternion *n syn* see QUARTET
quatuor *n syn* see QUARTET
quaver *vb syn* see SHAKE 1
rel falter, hesitate, vacillate, waver
‖**quawk** *vb syn* see SQUALL 1
quay *n syn* see WHARF
‖**queak** *vb syn* see SQUEAK 1
quean *n syn* see PROSTITUTE
queasiness *n syn* see NAUSEA
queasy *adj* **1** *syn* see DOUBTFUL 1
2 *syn* see SQUEAMISH 1
queer *adj* **1** *syn* see STRANGE 4
rel doubtful, dubious, questionable; droll, funny, laughable
2 *syn* see OBSESSED
3 *syn* see HOMOSEXUAL
4 *syn* see SQUEAMISH 1
queer *n syn* see HOMOSEXUAL
‖**quelch** *vb syn* see SUPPRESS 2
quell *vb syn* see CRUSH 5
rel conquer, overcome, subjugate, vanquish
con abet, incite, instigate
ant foment
quench *vb* **1** *syn* see EXTINGUISH 1
2 *syn* see CRUSH 5
rel end, terminate
3 *syn* see DESTROY 1
4 to bring (as thirst) to an end with or as if with a refreshing drink <after being in the hot sun, he found it difficult to *quench* his thirst>
syn slake, ‖squench
rel appease, content, gratify, satisfy; sate, satiate; allay, alleviate, assuage, lighten, mitigate, relieve; decrease, diminish, lessen, reduce
quenching *n syn* see REPRESSION 1
quenchless *adj* **1** *syn* see INSATIABLE
2 *syn* see INDESTRUCTIBLE
querulent *adj syn* see IRRITABLE
querulential *adj syn* see IRRITABLE
querulous *adj syn* see IRRITABLE
rel blubbering, crying, wailing, weeping, whimpering; bemoaning, deploring, lamenting
query *n* **1** *syn* see INQUIRY 2
2 *syn* see UNCERTAINTY
query *vb syn* see ASK 1
quest *n* **1** *syn* see INQUIRY 1
2 *syn* see PURSUIT 2
quest *vb* **1** *syn* see HOWL 1
2 *syn* see SEEK 1
question *n* **1** *syn* see INQUIRY 2
2 *syn* see PROBLEM 2
3 *syn* see DEMUR 2
question *vb* **1** *syn* see ASK 1
2 to express doubt about <*questioned* his decision to take a new job>
syn challenge, dispute, doubt, mistrust
rel suspect, ‖suspicion; hesitate (over), puzzle (over), wonder (about)

questionable *adj* **1** *syn* see IMPROBABLE 1
  ant unquestionable
  2 *syn* see MOOT
  rel refutable; equivocal, obscure, vague
  con dependable, true, trustworthy, trusty; genuine, indubitable, real, undoubted, undubitable, veritable, very
  ant authoritative; unquestionable, unquestioned
  3 *syn* see UNRELIABLE 1
questioning *n* *syn* see INQUIRY 2
questioning *adj* **1** *syn* see INCREDULOUS
  ant questionless, unquestioning
  2 *syn* see INQUISITIVE 1
questionless *adj* *syn* see AUTHENTIC 2
queue *n* *syn* see LINE 5
quibble *vb* **1** to find fault with something usually on minor grounds <was a peevish critic, always ready to *quibble* >
  syn cavil, chicane, hypercriticize
  rel carp, criticize
  idiom split hairs
  con applaud, commend, compliment, recommend; approve, endorse, sanction
  2 *syn* see ARGUE 2
quick *adj* **1** *syn* see FAST 3
  rel agile, brisk, nimble; abrupt, impetuous
  idiom quick on the trigger
  con dilatory, laggard, leisurely, slow, unhasty, unhurried; comatose
  ant sluggish
  2 able to respond without delay or hesitation or indicative of such ability <very *quick* in perception > <his *quick* eye spotted the trouble >
  syn apt, prompt, ready; *compare* INSTANTANEOUS
  rel clever, intelligent, quick-witted, smart; adroit, deft, dexterous; acute, keen, sharp; able, capable, competent, effective, effectual
  con comatose, lethargic, logy, poky, torpid; crass, dense, dull, dumb, stupid
  ant slow; sluggish
  3 *syn* see WISE 4
quick *adv* *syn* see FAST 2
quick *n* *syn* see CENTER 3
quicken *vb* **1** to make alive or lively <warm spring days that *quicken* the earth>
  syn animate, enliven, liven, vivificate, vivify
  rel activate, energize, vitalize; arouse, awaken, rouse, stir, wake
  con blunt, dull; slow (down)
  ant deaden
  2 *syn* see PROVOKE 4
  rel activate, actuate, motivate; goad, induce, spur
  con check, halt, interrupt, stall, stay; curb, inhibit, restrain
  ant arrest
  3 *syn* see SPEED 3
  con bog (down), detain, embog, hang up, mire
  ant slacken
quickening *adj* *syn* see INVIGORATING
quick–lunch *n* *syn* see EATING HOUSE
quickly *adv* *syn* see FAST 2
quickness *n* *syn* see SPEED 2
  ant slowness
quick–sighted *adj* *syn* see SHARP 4
quick–tempered *adj* *syn* see IRASCIBLE
quick–witted *adj* **1** *syn* see SHARP 4
  2 *syn* see INTELLIGENT 2
  rel apt, prompt, quick, ready
  3 *syn* see WISE 4
  rel acute, keen; facetious, humorous, witty
  ant slow-witted
quidnunc *n* **1** *syn* see BUSYBODY
  2 *syn* see GOSSIP 1
quiescence *n* *syn* see ABEYANCE
quiescency *n* *syn* see ABEYANCE
quiescent *adj* *syn* see LATENT
  rel calm, halcyon, hushed, placid, quiet, still, stilly, untroubled
quiet *n* **1** a period of intensified silence <the *quiet* before the storm >
  syn calm, hush, lull
  rel cessation, stop, termination
  con din, hubbub, racket, uproar

  2 *syn* see SILENCE 1
quiet *adj* **1** *syn* see CALM 1
  con harsh, rough; disquieted, disturbed, perturbed, upset
  ant unquiet
  2 *syn* see INACTIVE
  3 *syn* see STILL 3
  con blatant, boisterous, clamorous, strident, vociferous
  4 not showy or obtrusive <always dressed in *quiet* good taste>
  syn inobtrusive, restrained, subdued, tasteful, tasty, unobtrusive
  rel homely, plain, simple, unpretentious
  con blatant, brazen, flashy, garish, glaring, meretricious, tawdry, tinsel; elaborate
  ant gaudy, loud
quiet *vb* **1** *syn* see SILENCE
  rel abate, decrease, lessen
  con excite, provoke, quicken, stimulate; awaken, rally, stir
  2 *syn* see CALM
  con agitate; unhinge, untune
  ant disquiet; excite
‖**quieten** *vb* **1** *syn* see SILENCE
  2 *syn* see CALM
  ant arouse; excite
quietive *adj* *syn* see SEDATIVE
quietness *n* *syn* see SILENCE 1
quietude *n* *syn* see SILENCE 1
quietus *n* *syn* see DEATH 1
‖**quiff** *n* *syn* see GIRL 1
quilt *n* a bed coverlet made of two layers of cloth with a stuffing (as of cotton, wool, or feathers) between <a warm *quilt* is nice on a winter night >
  syn ‖comfortable, comforter, pouf, puff
  rel bedcover, bedspread, counterpane; eiderdown
quinary *adj* *syn* see QUINTUPLE
quinta *n* *syn* see ESTATE 3
quintessence *n* **1** *syn* see ESSENCE 2
  2 *syn* see APOTHEOSIS 1
quintessential *adj* *syn* see TYPICAL 1
quintessential *n* *syn* see ESSENCE 2
quintuple *adj* consisting of five <the problem is viewed as having *quintuple* aspects>
  syn fivefold, quinary
  rel quintuplicate
quip *n* *syn* see JOKE 1
quip (at) *vb* *syn* see SCOFF
quipster *n* *syn* see HUMORIST 2
quit *vb* **1** *syn* see CLEAR 5
  2 *syn* see BEHAVE 1
  3 *syn* see GO 2
  4 *syn* see ABANDON 1
  rel relinquish, resign, surrender
  5 *syn* see STOP 3
  6 to give up (as a habit, activity, or employment) especially with finality <*quit* a job> <determined to *quit* smoking>
  syn drop, leave, resign, terminate
  rel retire, secede, withdraw
  idiom draw one's time, give notice
  con hire on, hire out
quite *adv* **1** *syn* see WELL 3
  2 *syn* see ALTOGETHER 2
  3 *syn* see ALL 1
  4 *syn* see WELL 8
quittance *n* *syn* see REPARATION
quitter *n* *syn* see COWARD
quiver *n* *syn* see FLASH 1
quiver *vb* *syn* see SHAKE 1
  rel beat, palpatate, pulsate, pulse, throb
quivering *adj* *syn* see TREMULOUS
quivery *adj* *syn* see TREMULOUS
quiz *n* *syn* see ECCENTRIC
quiz *vb* **1** *syn* see RIDICULE
  2 *syn* see ASK 1
quizzical *adj* *syn* see INCREDULOUS
  rel curious, inquisitive; probing, searching

---

syn synonym(s)   *rel* related word(s)
ant antonym(s)   *con* contrasted word(s)
idiom idiomatic equivalent(s)
‖ use limited; if in doubt, see a dictionary

‖**quod** *vb syn* see IMPRISON
quodlibetic *adj syn* see PEDANTIC
quondam *adj syn* see FORMER 2
quota *n* **1** *syn* see SHARE 1

2 *syn* see RATION
quota *vb syn* see APPORTION 2
quotidian *adj* **1** *syn* see DAILY
   2 *syn* see ORDINARY 1

rabbity *adj syn* see SHY 1
rabble *n* **1** *syn* see MOB 2
   2 the lowest class of people < the *rabble* of the city >
   syn canaille, doggery, dreg(s), hoi polloi, mass(es), mob, other half, polloi, proletariat, raff, ‖ragabash, ragtag, ragtag and bobtail, riffraff, roughscuff, rout, scum, scurf, tag and rag, tagrag and bobtail, trash, unwashed
   rel bourgeoisie, commonalty, many, people, populace, public, rank and file
   idiom the great unwashed, the scum of the earth, the submerged tenth
   con aristocracy, aristoi, elite, Four Hundred, gentility, nobility, upper class, upper crust, upper ten, upper ten thousand
rabble–rouser *n syn* see DEMAGOGUE
rabid *adj* **1** *syn* see FURIOUS 2
   rel crazed, crazy, demented, deranged, insane
   2 *syn* see EXTREME 3
   rel enthusiastic, keen, obsessed, zealous
race *n syn* see CREEK 2
race *vb* **1** *syn* see RUSH 1
   2 *syn* see COURSE
race *n syn* see FAMILY 1
   rel culture, nation, nationality, people; breed, type, variety
rachis *n syn* see SPINE
rachitic *adj syn* see RICKETY
racial *adj syn* see ETHNIC 2
racialism *n syn* see RACISM
racism *n* racial prejudice or discrimination < an act of overt *racism* >
   syn racialism
   rel discrimination, prejudice; illiberality, unfairness; bias, one≈sidedness, partiality
   con broad-mindedness, liberalness, open-mindedness, tolerance; indifference, neutrality
rack *vb syn* see AFFLICT
   rel distress, pain; oppress, persecute
‖**rack back** *vb syn* see REPROVE
racket *n* **1** *syn* see DIN
   ‖**2** *syn* see WORK 1
racketry *n syn* see DIN
rackety *adj* **1** *syn* see NOISY
   2 *syn* see RICKETY
racking *adj syn* see EXCRUCIATING
   rel barbarous, cruel, ferocious, fierce, inhuman, savage
rack up *vb syn* see GAIN 1
racy *adj* **1** *syn* see PUNGENT
   rel fiery, gingery, mettlesome, spirited
   con banal, inane, jejune
   2 *syn* see RISQUÉ
radiant *adj* **1** *syn* see BRIGHT 1
   2 *syn* see GLAD 2
radiate *vb* **1** *syn* see SHINE 1
   2 *syn* see SPREAD 1
   rel diverge
radical *adj* **1** *syn* see FUNDAMENTAL 1
   rel cardinal, essential, vital; constitutional, inherent, intrinsic
   ant superficial
   2 *syn* see EXTREME 3
   3 *syn* see LIBERAL 3
radical *n* one who favors rapid and sweeping changes < the *radicals* advocated overthrow of the government >
   syn extremist, revolutionary, revolutionist, ultraist; *compare* REACTIONARY
   rel liberal, progressive, reformer; agitator, insurgent, insurrec-

tionist, rebel; anarchist, nihilist, red, subversive; out-and-outer; secessionist, separatist
   con bitter-ender, diehard, fogy, intransigent, mossback, reactionary, rightist, standpatter
   ant conservative
radius *n syn* see RANGE 2
raff *n syn* see RABBLE 2
raffish *adj syn* see WILD 7
rag *vb* **1** *syn* see SCOLD 1
   2 *syn* see BANTER
‖**ragabash** *n syn* see RABBLE 2
ragamuffin *n* a person dressed in ragged clothing < a poor *ragamuffin* found begging >
   syn ragshag, scarecrow, tatterdemalion
   rel hobo, tramp, vagabond, vagrant; bum, loafer, wastrel; orphan, waif
   con buck, coxcomb, dandy, dude, fop
rage *n* **1** *syn* see ANGER
   rel acerbity, acrimony, asperity; frenzy, hysteria, mania; agitation, perturbation, upset
   2 *syn* see FASHION 3
   rel caprice, conceit, crotchet, fancy, freak, vagary, whim
rage *vb syn* see ANGER 2
ragged *adj* torn or worn to tatters < never saw such *ragged* clothes >
   syn frayed, frazzled, shreddy, tattered
   rel rent, torn; battered, patched; dilapidated, dingy, faded, seedy, shabby, threadbare, worn-out
raging *adj syn* see WILD 6
rags *n pl* **1** poor or ragged clothing < a beggar in *rags* >
   syn ‖duds, tatters
   rel odds and ends, ribbons, shreds
   2 *syn* see CLOTHES
ragshag *n syn* see RAGAMUFFIN
ragtag *n syn* see RABBLE 2
ragtag and bobtail *n syn* see RABBLE 2
raid *n* **1** *syn* see INVASION
   rel assault, onset, onslaught
   2 a sudden attack by officers of the law < a *raid* on a gambling joint >
   syn ‖bust
raid *vb* **1** to make a raid on < Indians *raided* the settlers frequently >
   syn foray, harass, harry, maraud
   rel despoil, devastate, ravage, sack, spoliate, waste; loot, plunder, rifle, rob
   2 *syn* see INVADE 1
raider *n syn* see MARAUDER
rail *n syn* see RAILING
rail *vb syn* see SCOLD 1
railing *n* a usually protective barrier consisting essentially of an elongated raised member < a staircase without a *railing* >
   syn balustrade, banister, rail
raillery *n syn* see SATIRE
railroad station *n* a building containing accommodations for railroad passengers or freight < an old *railroad station* fallen into disrepair >
   syn depot, station, station house
raiment *n syn* see CLOTHES
raiment *vb syn* see CLOTHE
rainbow *n syn* see PIPE DREAM
rainless *adj syn* see FAIR 2
   ant rainy
raise *vb* **1** *syn* see LIFT 1

ant lower
2 syn see INCITE
3 syn see RESURRECT 1
4 syn see ERECT 3
5 syn see BUILD 1
6 syn see BRING UP 1
7 syn see GROW 1
8 syn see GATHER 6
9 to make larger in amount *< raised* the rent >
syn boost, hike, increase, jack (up), jump, put up, up
rel inflate
idiom send through the roof
con cut back, decrease, drop, lessen, reduce, roll back; minimize
ant lower
raise *n syn* see ADDITION
raised *adj* **1 syn** see ELEVATED 1
2 syn see ERECT
rake *vb syn* see SCOUR 2
rakehell *adj syn* see WILD 7
raking *adj syn* see FAST 3
rakish *adj syn* see WILD 7
rally *vb* **1 syn** see MOBILIZE 3
2 syn see STIR 1
rel fire; refresh, renew, restore
3 syn see RECOVER 2
rel brace (up), enliven, invigorate, perk (up), pick up
rally *vb syn* see RIDICULE
rel harass, harry, tantalize, tease, worry
rallying cry *n syn* see BATTLE CRY
ram *vb* **1 syn** see THRUST 2
2 syn see CRAM 1
ramble *vb* **1 syn** see WANDER 1
2 syn see DIGRESS 2
3 syn see SPRAWL 2
ramble *n syn* see WALK 1
rambler *n syn* see ROVER
rambunctious *adj syn* see TURBULENT 1
rampage *n syn* see SPREE 1
rel turmoil, uproar
rampant *adj* **1 syn** see RANK 1
rel excessive, immoderate, inordinate
con moderate, temperate; checked, curbed, restrained
2 syn see PREVAILING
rampart *n syn* see BULWARK
rancid *adj syn* see MALODOROUS 1
rel ‖reasty; loathsome, repulsive
ant sweet
rancor *n syn* see ENMITY
rel bitterness, vindictiveness, virulence
rancorous *adj* **1 syn** see MALICIOUS
2 syn see BITTER 3
rancorously *adv syn* see HARD 6
random *adj* lacking a definite plan, purpose, or pattern *< a random* choice >
syn aimless, designless, desultory, haphazard, hit-or-miss, indiscriminate, irregular, objectless, promiscuous, purposeless, slapdash, spot, unaimed, unconsidered, unplanned; *compare* ACCIDENTAL
rel contingent, fluky, fortuitous, incidental, odd
con arranged, organized, planned; methodical, systematic; deliberate, purposeful
ant purposive
random *adv syn* see ABOUT 4
ant orderly
randomly *adv syn* see ABOUT 4
ant orderly
randy *adj syn* see LICENTIOUS 2
range *vb* **1 syn** see LINE 1
rel assort, classify, sort; bias, dispose, incline, predispose
2 syn see WANDER 1
3 to change or differ within limits *< discounts range* from 10% to 40% >
syn extend, go, run, vary
rel differ, fluctuate
range *n* **1 syn** see HABITAT
2 sphere of action, expression, or influence *< a political movement worldwide in its range* and power >

syn ambit, circle, compass, confine(s), dimension(s), extension, extensity, extent, length, orbit, panorama, purview, radius, reach, realm, scope, stretch, sweep, width
rel area, space, span; domain, field, province, sphere, territory; amplitude, expanse, gamut, spread
3 syn see KEN
rel compass
idiom range of comprehension
4 syn see ORDER 4
rangy *adj syn* see GANGLING
ant compact
rank *adj* **1** growing or increasing at an immoderate rate *< rank* weeds >
syn rampant
rel exuberant, lavish, lush, luxuriant, profuse
con scanty, sparse, thin
2 syn see OVERGROWN
3 syn see OBSCENE 2
4 syn see EGREGIOUS
rel conspicuous, noticeable, outstanding
5 syn see UTTER
6 syn see MALODOROUS 1
rel dank, humid; loathsome, repulsive
rank *n* **1 syn** see LINE 5
2 syn see ESTATE 2
3 syn see STATUS 1
4 syn see STATUS 2
rank *vb* **1 syn** see CLASS 2
rel arrange, order; assort, sort
2 syn see PRECEDE 1
rank and file *n syn* see COMMONALTY
rankle *vb* to produce continual or progressive anger, irritation, or bitterness *< this decision has long rankled* as an act of injustice >
syn fester
rel annoy, bother, irk, vex; aggravate, exasperate, irritate; harass, obsess, plague, torment
ransack *vb* **1 syn** see SCOUR 2
2 syn see ROB 1
ransom *vb* to liberate by paying a price *< ransomed* the king >
syn buy, redeem
rel recover, regain, retrieve; emancipate, free, liberate; extricate, release
rant *vb* **1 syn** see ORATE
rel bluster, huff; rage, storm
2 syn see SCOLD 1
rant *n syn* see BOMBAST
ran–tan *n syn* see BINGE 1
rantankerous *adj syn* see CANTANKEROUS
rap *n* **1 syn** see HIT 1
2 syn see REBUKE
rap *vb* **1 syn** see TAP 1
2 syn see CRITICIZE
rap *n* **1 syn** see CHAT 2
2 syn see CONFERENCE 1
rapacious *adj* **1** subsisting on prey *< the rapacious* wolf seized the lamb >
syn predacious, predative, predatorial, predatory, raptorial, vulturine, vulturish, vulturous
2 syn see VORACIOUS
rel ferocious, fierce
rapacity *n syn* see CUPIDITY
rel claim, demand, exaction
rape *vb* to have sexual intercourse with a woman without her consent and chiefly by force or deception *< rape* a young girl >
syn defile, deflorate, deflower, force, outrage, ravish, spoil, violate
rel debauch, devirginate, dishonor, ruin; betray, deceive, mislead; entice, lure, seduce, tempt; compromise, shame, wrong
rapid *adj syn* see FAST 3
rel agile, brisk, nimble; hurried, quickened
ant deliberate; leisurely
rapidity *n syn* see SPEED 2

---

syn synonym(s)
ant antonym(s)
idiom idiomatic equivalent(s)
‖ use limited; if in doubt, see a dictionary

rel related word(s)
con contrasted word(s)

rapidly *adv syn* see FAST 2

rapidness *n syn* see SPEED 2

‖**rapper** *n syn* see LIE

rapport *n syn* see HARMONY 3

rapprochement *n syn* see RECONCILIATION

rapscallion *n syn* see SCAMP

rap session *n syn* see CONFERENCE 2

rapt *adj syn* see INTENT

raptorial *adj syn* see RAPACIOUS 1

rapture *n syn* see ECSTASY

rare *adj* **1** *syn* see THIN 2

   2 *syn* see CHOICE

   rel excellent, fine, unique

   3 *syn* see INFREQUENT

   con accustomed, customary, habitual, usual, wonted; abounding, profuse

   4 *syn* see EXCEPTIONAL 1

rarefied *adj syn* see THIN 2

rarefy *vb syn* see THIN 2

rarely *adv* **1** *syn* see SELDOM

   2 *syn* see EXTRA

raring *adj syn* see EAGER

rascal *n* **1** *syn* see VILLAIN 1

   2 *syn* see SCAMP

rash *adj* **1** acting, done, or expressed with undue haste or disregard for consequences < don't do anything *rash* > < that was a very *rash* statement >

   syn brash, hasty, hotheaded, ill-advised, incautious, incogitant, inconsiderate, mad-brained, madcap, reckless, thoughtless, unadvised, unconsidered, unwary; *compare* CARELESS 1

   rel abrupt, headlong, impetuous, precipitate, precipitous, sudden; foolhardy, foolish, impulsive, silly; careless, heedless, imprudent, indiscreet, injudicious, unthinking, unwise

   con careful, cautious, chary, circumspect, wary; advised, considered, deliberate, designed, premeditated, studied; calm, cool, level-headed

   ant calculating

   2 *syn* see ADVENTUROUS

rash *n syn* see EPIDEMIC

rasp *vb syn* see SCRAPE 1

raspberry *n* a sound of disapproval, contempt, or derision < the crowd gave the umpire a *raspberry* >

   syn bazoo, bird, boo, ‖Bronx cheer, catcall, hiss, hoot, pooh, pooh-pooh, ‖razz

rasping *adj syn* see HARSH 3

raspish *adj syn* see IRRITABLE

raspy *adj syn* see IRRITABLE

rat *n* **1** *syn* see RENEGADE

   2 *syn* see SNOT 1

rat *vb* **1** *syn* see DEFECT

   2 *syn* see INFORM 3

rate *vb syn* see SCOLD 1

rate *n* **1** *syn* see PRICE 1

   2 *syn* see DEGREE 2

rate *vb* **1** *syn* see ESTIMATE 1

   2 *syn* see CLASS 2

   3 *syn* see EARN 2

rather *adv* **1** *syn* see ENOUGH 2

   2 *syn* see INSTEAD

   3 *syn* see SOMEWHAT 2

   4 *syn* see WELL 8

ratherish *adv syn* see SOMEWHAT 2

ratify *vb* to make something legally valid or operative usually by formal approval or sanctioning < agreed to *ratify* the treaty >

   syn confirm

   rel accredit, authorize, commission, license; approve, endorse, sanction; authenticate, validate

   con disown, reject, repudiate

ratio *n syn* see DEGREE 2

ratiocination *n* **1** *syn* see INFERENCE 1

   ant intuition

   2 *syn* see INFERENCE 2

ratiocinative *adj syn* see LOGICAL 2

ration *n* an amount allotted or made available especially from a limited supply < saved up their gasoline *ration* for a vacation trip >

   syn allotment, allowance, apportionment, measure, meed, part, portion, quantum, quota, share; *compare* SHARE 1

   rel assignment, consignment, distribution, division

ration *vb syn* see APPORTION 2

   rel allocate, allot, assign, mete (out)

rational *adj* agreeable to reason < offered a *rational* explanation >

   syn consequent, intelligent, logical, reasonable, sensible, sound

   rel calm, cool, level-headed, sober, stable; circumspect, judicious, prudent; lucid, normal, sane

   con rash, reckless, wild; groundless, illogical, unreasonable, unreasoning, unsound; crazy, demented, deranged

   ant animal, irrational; absurd

rationale *n syn* see EXPLANATION 2

rationalization *n syn* see EXPLANATION 2

rationalize *vb syn* see EXPLAIN 3

rattle *vb* **1** to make a rapid succession of short sharp noises < the window *rattled* in the wind >

   syn bicker, clack, clatter, clitter, ‖ruttle, shatter

   2 *syn* see CHAT 1

   3 *syn* see EMBARRASS

   rel addle, muddle; disturb, upset; bewilder, distract, perplex

rattlebrain *n syn* see SCATTERBRAIN

rattlebrained *adj syn* see GIDDY 1

rattlehead *n syn* see SCATTERBRAIN

rattletrap *n, usu* **rattletraps** *pl syn* see KNICKKNACK

rattletrap *adj syn* see RICKETY

rattling *adv syn* see VERY 1

ratty *adj syn* see IRASCIBLE

raucous *adj* **1** *syn* see HARSH 3

   rel brusque, gruff

   2 *syn* see TURBULENT 1

raunchy *adj* **1** *syn* see SLOVENLY 1

   2 *syn* see OBSCENE 2

ravage *vb* to lay waste (as by plundering or destroying) < the countryside was *ravaged* by the invading soldiers >

   syn deflower, depredate, desecrate, desolate, despoil, devast, devastate, devour, harry, havoc, pillage, sack, scourge, spoil, spoliate, strip, waste

   rel demolish, destroy, raze; loot, plunder, ransack, rob; ruin, wreck; encroach, invade, trespass; crush, overpower, overrun, overthrow, overwhelm

   idiom lay in ruins, lay waste

   con build, improve, rehabilitate

ravager *n syn* see MARAUDER

rave *vb* **1** *syn* see ORATE

   2 *syn* see ENTHUSE 2

ravel *vb syn* see COMPLICATE

raven *adj syn* see BLACK 1

ravening *adj syn* see VORACIOUS

ravenous *adj* **1** *syn* see VORACIOUS

   2 *syn* see HUNGRY

ravine *n* a small narrow steep-sided valley < followed the *ravine* high up into the hills >

   syn arroyo, chasm, cleft, clough, clove, gap, gorge, gulch

   rel cut, notch; defile, pass; abyss, gulf; crevasse, crevice, fissure; ‖dry wash, gully, gutter, ‖wash; canyon

raving *adj syn* see DELIRIOUS 1

ravish *vb* **1** *syn* see TRANSPORT 2

   2 *syn* see RAPE

ravisher *n syn* see MARAUDER

raw *adj* **1** not cooked < a *raw* egg >

   syn uncooked

   2 *syn* see UNREFINED 3

   3 *syn* see RUDE 1

   4 *syn* see NUDE 2

   5 *syn* see INEXPERIENCED

   rel untaught, untutored; unmatured, unripe

   con drilled, exercised; hardened; adult, grown-up, mature, matured, ripe

   6 *syn* see COARSE 3

   ‖**7** *syn* see OBSCENE 2

rawboned *adj syn* see LEAN

rawhider *n syn* see SLAVE DRIVER

rawness *n syn* see INEXPERIENCE

ray *n* **1** one of the lines of light that appear to radiate from a bright or luminous object < the *rays* of the sun >

   syn beam, shaft, shoot

   rel raylet; pencil, streak, stream; moonbeam, sunbeam

   con gleam, glow, incandescence, shine

   2 *syn* see PARTICLE

raze *vb syn* see DESTROY 1
razor–sharp *adj syn* see SHARP 1
‖**razz** *n syn* see RASPBERRY
razz *vb* **1** *syn* see BANTER
  2 *syn* see RIDICULE
re *prep syn* see APROPOS
reach *vb* **1** *syn* see COME 1
  2 *syn* see GAIN 1
  3 to get into contact with especially intellectually or emotionally <there was no common ground on which she could *reach* him>
  syn approach
  rel affect, influence, sway; get, move, touch
  idiom establish contact with, find a common denominator, get through to, get to, have a meeting of minds, make advances to, make overtures to, make up to, reach (*or* share) common ground
  4 to communicate with <you can *reach* me at this number>
  syn contact, get
  idiom get in touch (*or* contact) with, get through to, get to, keep in touch (*or* contact) with, maintain connections with
  5 *syn* see PASS 9
  6 *syn* see RUN 8
reach *n* **1** *syn* see RANGE 2
  2 *syn* see KEN
react *vb* **1** *syn* see ACT 5
  2 *syn* see RETURN 1
reactionarist *n syn* see REACTIONARY
reactionary *adj syn* see CONSERVATIVE 1
reactionary *n* one who strongly resists change and often favors a prior condition <he is a staunch political *reactionary*>
  syn blimp, Bourbon, diehard, reactionarist, reactionist, royalist, ultraconservative, white; *compare* DIEHARD 1, RADICAL
  rel bitter-ender, conservative, intransigent, rightist, right-winger, standpatter; fogy, mossback
  con extremist, radical, revolutionary, revolutionist, ultraist; liberal, progressive, reformer
reactionist *n syn* see REACTIONARY
reactivate *vb syn* see REVIVE 3
read *vb syn* see SHOW 5
readily *adv syn* see EASILY 1
readiness *n* **1** *syn* see ALACRITY
  2 *syn* see ADDRESS 1
  3 the power of doing something without evidence of effort <his *readiness* in repartee>
  syn ease, facility
  rel eloquence, fluency, volubility
  con effort, exertions, pains, trouble
reading *n syn* see INTERPRETATION 2
readjust *vb syn* see REORGANIZE
ready *adj* **1** in a state of mental or physical fitness for some experience or action <*ready* to leave at a moment's notice>
  syn prepared, set
  rel adjusted, fit, qualified; primed
  idiom all ready, all set, champing at the bit
  con unprepared, unqualified
  ant unready
  2 *syn* see WILLING 1
  3 *syn* see QUICK 2
  rel adept, expert, masterly, proficient, skilled, skillful; active, dynamic, live
ready *vb* **1** *syn* see PREPARE 1
  2 *syn* see GIRD 3
ready–made *adj* made for general sale or use rather than prepared according to individual specifications <*ready-made* clothing>
  syn bought, ‖boughten, ready-to-wear, store, store-bought, ‖store-boughten
  idiom off the rack
  con custom-built, made-to-order, tailor-made; handmade
  ant custom-made
ready–to–wear *adj syn* see READY-MADE
ready–witted *adj syn* see INTELLIGENT 2
real *adj* **1** *syn* see AUTHENTIC 2
  ant bogus
  2 *syn* see GENUINE 3
  3 corresponding to known facts <discovered the *real* reason for his hasty departure>
  syn actual, indisputable, true, undeniable, unfabled, veridical

rel being, existing, subsisting; certain, inevitable, necessary; sound, valid, well-grounded
  idiom deniable, disputable, doubtful, questionable; improbable, uncertain, unlikely
  ant unreal; apparent; imaginary
realistic *adj* having no illusions and facing reality squarely <he made a *realistic* appraisal of his chances for advancement>
  syn down-to-earth, earthy, hard, hard-boiled, hardheaded, matter-of-fact, practic, practical, pragmatic, pragmatical, sober, unfantastic, unidealistic, unromantic, unsentimental, utilitarian
  rel rational, reasonable, sane, sensible, sound; astute, prudent, shrewd; nonacademic
  con dreamy, fantastic, imaginative; idealistic, impractical, irrational, romantic, visionary; theoretical
  ant unrealistic; fanciful
reality *n* **1** *syn* see FACT 1
  2 *syn* see ACTUALITY 2
realize *vb* **1** *syn* see GAIN 1
  2 *syn* see THINK 1
really *adv* **1** *syn* see VERY 2
  2 *syn* see WELL 7
realm *n syn* see RANGE 2
ream *n, usu* **reams** *pl syn* see SCAD
ream *vb syn* see CHEAT
‖**ream out** *vb syn* see SCOLD 1
reanimation *n syn* see REVIVAL
reap *vb* to do the work of collecting ripened crops <storms hampered his *reaping*>
  syn garner, gather, harvest, ingather
  rel glean
reaping *n syn* see HARVEST 1
reappearance *n syn* see RECURRENCE
rear *vb* **1** *syn* see BUILD 1
  2 *syn* see ERECT 3
  3 *syn* see LIFT 1
  4 *syn* see BRING UP 1
  rel foster, nurse, nurture; breed, propagate
rear *n* **1** *syn* see BACK 1
  ant front
  2 *syn* see BUTTOCKS
rear *adj syn* see POSTERIOR 2
  ant front
rear end *n syn* see BUTTOCKS
rearmost *adj syn* see LAST
rearrange *vb syn* see REORGANIZE
rearward *n syn* see BACK 1
reason *n* **1** *syn* see EXPLANATION 2
  2 *syn* see MOTIVE 1
  3 a point or points that support something open to question <he soon gave sensible *reasons* for the proposed change>
  syn argument, ground, proof, wherefore, why, whyfor
  rel explanation, justification, rationalization
  4 *syn* see CAUSE 1
  5 the power of the mind by which man attains truth or knowledge <we all must use *reason* to solve this problem>
  syn intellect, understanding
  rel inference, ratiocination
  6 *syn* see WIT 2
reason *vb syn* see THINK 5
reasonable *adj* **1** *syn* see CONSERVATIVE 2
  2 *syn* see MODERATE 2
  3 *syn* see CHEAP 1
  ant extravagant
  4 *syn* see RATIONAL
  ant unreasonable
reasoned *adj syn* see DEDUCTIVE
reasonless *adj* **1** *syn* see INSANE 1
  2 *syn* see ILLOGICAL
reassume *vb syn* see RESUME 1
rebate *vb syn* see DECREASE
rebate *n syn* see DEDUCTION 1
rebel *n* one who breaks with or opposes constituted authority or the established order <he is a *rebel* among educators>

---

syn synonym(s)   *rel* related word(s)
ant antonym(s)   *con* contrasted word(s)
idiom idiomatic equivalent(s)
‖ use limited; if in doubt, see a dictionary

syn anarch, anarchist, frondeur, insurgent, insurrectionist, malcontent, mutineer, revolter
rel adversary, antagonist, opponent; assailant, attacker; extremist, radical, revolutionary, revolutionist, ultraist; debunker, iconoclast
con authoritarian, intransigent, traditionalist; conservative, reactionary, white
rebel *vb syn* see REVOLT 1
rebellious *adj syn* see INSUBORDINATE
rel alienated, disaffected, estranged
con acquiescent, resigned; submissive
rebirth *n* 1 *syn* see CONVERSION 1
2 *syn* see REVIVAL
rebound *vb syn* see RECOVER 3
rebuff *vb syn* see FEND (off)
idiom give the cold shoulder
rebuild *vb syn* see MEND 2
rebuke *vb syn* see REPROVE
rebuke *n* an expression of strong disapproval <his bad behavior earned him a sharp *rebuke* >
syn admonishment, admonition, chiding, rap, reprimand, reproach, reproof, wig
rel dressing down, earful, lecture, lesson, scolding, talking-to, tongue-lashing
idiom a flea in one's ear, slap on the wrist
con applause, compliment, praise
rebut *vb* 1 *syn* see FEND (off)
2 *syn* see DISPROVE 1
recalcitrance *n syn* see DEFIANCE 2
recalcitrant *adj syn* see UNRULY 1
rel obstinate, stubborn; opposing, resisting, withstanding
ant amenable
recall *vb* 1 *syn* see REMEMBER
rel educe, elicit, evoke, extract; arouse, awaken, rouse, stir, waken
2 *syn* see ABJURE
3 *syn* see REVOKE 2
4 *syn* see RESTORE 1
recall *n syn* see MEMORY 2
recant *vb syn* see ABJURE
recapitulation *n syn* see SUMMARY
recede *vb* 1 to move backward <they will return after the floodwaters *recede* >
syn back, fall back, retract, retreat, retrocede, retrograde
rel regress, retrogress; depart, retire, withdraw
ant proceed; advance
2 *syn* see DECREASE
receipts *n pl syn* see REVENUE
receive *vb syn* see TAKE 10
received *adj syn* see ORTHODOX 1
recension *n syn* see REVISION 1
recent *adj* 1 *syn* see NEW 1
2 *syn* see MODERN 1
recently *adv syn* see NEW
receptive *adj* 1 open to ideas, impressions, or suggestions <he has a most *receptive* mind >
syn acceptant, acceptive, influenceable, persuadable, persuasible, responsive, suasible, swayable
rel open, open-minded; accessible, amenable, suggestible
con closed, closed-minded, inhospitable
ant unreceptive
2 *syn* see SYMPATHETIC 2
recess *vb syn* see ADJOURN 2
recession *n syn* see DEPRESSION 3
recherché *adj syn* see CHOICE
rel fresh, new, novel, original; exotic, uncommon, unusual
ant commonplace
recidivate *vb syn* see LAPSE
reciprocal *n syn* see MATE 5
reciprocate *vb* to give back, usually in kind or quantity <they were glad of the chance to *reciprocate* her kindness >
syn recompense, requite, retaliate, return
rel exchange, interchange; compensate, repay; retort, serve out
con accept, acquire, pocket, take
recital *n syn* see DESCRIPTION 2
rel discourse, story; enumeration
recite *vb syn* see RELATE 1
rel count, enumerate, number, tell

reckless *adj* 1 *syn* see ADVENTUROUS
rel desperate, hopeless
2 *syn* see RASH 1
ant calculating
3 *syn* see IRRESPONSIBLE
reckon *vb* 1 *syn* see CALCULATE
rel count, enumerate, number; add, cast, foot, sum, total
2 *syn* see CONSIDER 3
rel conjecture, guess, surmise
3 *syn* see ESTIMATE 3
‖4 *syn* see UNDERSTAND 3
reckon (on) *vb syn* see RELY (on *or* upon)
reckoning *n* 1 *syn* see BILL 1
2 *syn* see COMPUTATION
reclaim *vb syn* see RESTORE 3
recline *vb* 1 *syn* see SLANT 1
2 *syn* see REST 1
reclining *adj syn* see PRONE 4
recluse *adj syn* see SECLUDED
recluse *n* a person who leads a secluded or solitary life <a man who led the life of a *recluse* although living in a busy city>
syn hermit, solitary
rel anchorite, cenobite, eremite
reclusion *n syn* see SECLUSION
reclusive *adj syn* see ANTISOCIAL
recognition *n* 1 a learning process that relates a perception of something new to knowledge already possessed <*recognition* of a genuine diamond>
syn apperception, assimilation, identification
rel cognizance, realization; awareness, consciousness, sensibility
ant irrecognition
2 *syn* see CREDIT 4
ant unrecognition
recognize *vb* 1 to make out as or perceive to be something previously known <said they would *recognize* that face anywhere>
syn know
rel recall, recollect, remember
2 *syn* see IDENTIFY
3 *syn* see ACKNOWLEDGE 2
rel note, notice, observe, remark
recoil *vb* to draw back usually through fear or disgust <*recoiled* from the snake>
syn blanch, blench, flinch, quail, shrink, squinch, start, wince
rel falter, hesitate, waver; balk, shy, stick, stickle; dodge, duck, swerve; quake, shake, shudder, tremble; reel (back)
con advance, approach, near
ant confront; defy
re‑collect *vb syn* see COMPOSE 4
recollect *vb syn* see REMEMBER
rel arouse, awaken, rally, rouse, stir, waken
recollection *n* 1 *syn* see MEMORY 2
2 *syn* see MEMORY 1
recommence *vb syn* see RESUME 2
recommend *vb* 1 *syn* see COMMEND 2
ant discommend
2 *syn* see COUNSEL
recommendation *n syn* see CREDENTIALS
rel approval, endorsement; commendation
recompense *vb* 1 *syn* see COMPENSATE 3
rel accord, award, grant, vouchsafe; balance, offset
2 *syn* see RECIPROCATE
recompense *n syn* see REPARATION
reconcile *vb* 1 *syn* see HARMONIZE 3
idiom bury the hatchet, make peace
ant estrange
2 *syn* see ADAPT
reconcilement *n syn* see RECONCILIATION
reconciliate *vb syn* see HARMONIZE 3
reconciliation *n* establishment of harmony <a *reconciliation* between the two countries was effected after ten years>
syn harmonizing, rapprochement, reconcilement
rel appeasement, conciliation, mollification, propitiation, satisfying
ant disagreement
recondite *adj* beyond the reach of the average intelligence <a *recondite* subject>
syn abstruse, acroamatic, deep, esoteric, heavy, hermetic, occult, orphic, profound, secret

rel erudite, learned, scholarly; academic, pedantic; difficult, hard; dark, enigmatic, obscure; anagogic, cabalistic, mystic, mystical; cryptic, runic, sibylline
con easy, facile, simple, straightforward

recondition *vb* **1** *syn* see RESTORE 3
  2 *syn* see MEND 2

reconnoiter *vb* *syn* see SCOUT

reconsider *vb* to consider again with a view to changing or reversing < was asked to *reconsider* his decision >
syn reevaluate, reexamine, rethink, re-treat, review, reweigh, think (over)
rel draw off; sleep (on); amend, correct, revise
idiom revise one's thoughts, think better of, view in a new light

reconsideration *n* *syn* see REVIEW 5

reconstitute *vb* *syn* see REORGANIZE

reconstruct *vb* **1** *syn* see MEND 2
  2 *syn* see REORGANIZE
  3 *syn* see RESTORE 3

record *vb* *syn* see SHOW 5

record *n* *syn* see DOCUMENT 2

recount *vb* *syn* see RELATE 1

recountal *n* *syn* see DESCRIPTION 2

recounting *n* *syn* see DESCRIPTION 2

recoup *vb* *syn* see RECOVER 1

recourse *n* *syn* see RESOURCE 3

recover *vb* **1** to obtain again < *recover* a lost watch >
syn get back, recoup, recruit, regain, repossess, retrieve
rel reclaim, redeem; reacquire, recapture, retake, rewin; reoccupy, resume; rediscover; balance, compensate, offset
con lose, mislay, misplace; forfeit, sacrifice
  2 to regain health < *recovering* from a bout of pneumonia >
syn come round, rally
rel convalesce, improve, mend, recuperate; perk (up), revive; heal; refresh, rejuvenate, renew, restore
idiom get back in shape, get better, sit up and take nourishment, take a turn for the better
con decline, fail, weaken, worsen; die, expire, perish
  3 to regain a former or normal state < the textile industry was *recovering* quickly from the depression >
syn bounce (back), rebound, snap back
rel rally, revive
con decline, fail
ant worsen
  4 *syn* see RESTORE 3

recreancy *n* *syn* see DEFECTION

recreant *adj* *syn* see FAITHLESS

recreant *n* *syn* see RENEGADE

recreate *vb* **1** *syn* see AMUSE
rel refresh, rejuvenate, renew, restore
  2 *syn* see PLAY 1

recreation *n* **1** *syn* see ENTERTAINMENT
rel ease, relaxation, repose; frolic, rollick; hilarity, jollity, mirth
  2 *syn* see PLAY 1

recrementitious *adj* *syn* see SUPERFLUOUS

recrudesce *vb* *syn* see RETURN 1
rel refurbish, renew, renovate
con repress, suppress; cease, discontinue, stop

recruit *n* *syn* see NOVICE

recruit *vb* *syn* see RECOVER 1
rel refresh, renew, renovate, restore; mend, rebuild, repair

rectify *vb* *syn* see CORRECT 1
rel rebuild, repair

rectitude *n* *syn* see GOODNESS
rel conscientiousness, justness, scrupulousness

recumbent *adj* *syn* see PRONE 4
ant erect, upright

recuperate *vb* *syn* see IMPROVE 3

recur *vb* **1** *syn* see RETURN 1
rel iterate, reiterate, repeat
  2 *syn* see RESORT 2

recurrence *n* a periodic or frequent returning < the *recurrence* of the nightmare upset him >
syn reappearance, reoccurrence, return
rel repetition, reproduction; crebrity, frequency

recurrent *adj* *syn* see INTERMITTENT

recurring *adj* *syn* see INTERMITTENT

Red *n* *syn* see COMMUNIST

red-blooded *adj* *syn* see VIGOROUS

redden *vb* **1** to make red < blood soon *reddened* the bandage >
syn incarnadine, rubify, rubric, ruby, rud, ruddle, ruddy
  2 *syn* see BLUSH

redeem *vb* **1** *syn* see RANSOM
  2 *syn* see FREE
  3 *syn* see COMPENSATE 1

red-handed *adv* in the act of committing a misdeed < caught *red-handed* >
syn dead to rights, flagrante delicto
rel blatantly, openly

red-hot *adj* **1** *syn* see HOT 1
  2 *syn* see IMPASSIONED
  3 *syn* see UP-TO-DATE

red-letter *adj* *syn* see NOTEWORTHY

red-light district *n* a district characterized by brothels < sailors frequented the *red-light district* >
syn levee, stew(s), tenderloin
idiom street of fallen women

red-neck *n* *syn* see RUSTIC

redolence *n* *syn* see FRAGRANCE

redolent *adj* **1** *syn* see SWEET 2
  2 *syn* see REMINISCENT

redouble *vb* *syn* see INTENSIFY

redoubt *n* *syn* see FORT

redoubtable *adj* **1** *syn* see FEARFUL 3
  2 *syn* see FAMOUS 2

redound *vb* *syn* see CONTRIBUTE 2

redraft *n* *syn* see REVISION 1

redraft *vb* *syn* see REVISE

redraw *vb* *syn* see REVISE

redress *vb* **1** *syn* see AVENGE
  2 *syn* see NEUTRALIZE

redress *n* *syn* see REPARATION
rel balancing, offsetting; retaliation, vengeance

reduce *vb* **1** *syn* see DECREASE
  2 to decrease in amount < they decided to *reduce* prices to stimulate sales >
syn clip, cut, cut back, cut down, lower, mark down, pare, shave, slash
rel curtail, decrease, diminish, lessen; deflate, depreciate; scale (down), step down; roll back
con boost, hike, jack (up), jump, put up, raise, up
ant increase
  3 *syn* see CONQUER 1
rel cripple, disable, enfeeble, undermine, weaken; debase, degrade, humble, humiliate
  4 *syn* see DEGRADE 1
ant advance
  5 to lose body weight especially by dieting < ate no cake while *reducing* >
syn slenderize, slim (down)
rel bant, diet
idiom lose flesh, take off weight
ant fatten

reduction *n* **1** *syn* see DEDUCTION 1
  2 *syn* see DEMOTION

redundancy *n* *syn* see VERBIAGE 1
rel flatulence, inflatedness, inflation, tumidity, turgidity

redundant *adj* *syn* see WORDY
rel extra, spare, superfluous, supernumerary, surplus; iterating, reiterating, repetitious
ant concise

reduplicate *vb* *syn* see COPY

reduplication *n* *syn* see REPRODUCTION

reedy *adj* *syn* see THIN 1

reek *vb* *syn* see SMELL 3

reeking *adj* *syn* see MALODOROUS 1

reeky *adj* *syn* see MALODOROUS 1

reel *vb* **1** *syn* see SPIN 2
  2 to move uncertainly or uncontrollably (as in intoxication) < *reeled* down the street >
syn stagger, titubate, totter, wheel

---

rel careen, lurch, ||swaver, sway, swing, weave, wobble; falter, ||stammer, stumble, teeter, topple; bob, waver

reestablish *vb syn* see RESTORE 1

reevaluate *vb syn* see RECONSIDER

reexamination *n syn* see REVIEW 5

reexamine *vb syn* see RECONSIDER

refashion *vb syn* see CHANGE 1

refection *n syn* see MEAL

refer *vb* **1** *syn* see ASCRIBE

2 *syn* see SUBMIT 2

3 to call or direct attention to something < no one *referred* to his recent divorce >
syn advert, allude, bring up, point (out)
rel insert, interpolate, introduce; cite, quote; instance, mention, name, specify; glance, touch
idiom make an allusion to

4 *syn* see RESORT 2
rel advise, commune, confer, consult

referee *n syn* see JUDGE 1

referee *vb syn* see JUDGE 1

reference *n syn* see CREDENTIALS

refine *vb syn* see POLISH 2

refined *adj* **1** *syn* see GENTEEL 1
ant earthy

2 *syn* see FINE 1

refinement *n syn* see CULTURE
rel finish, suavity, urbanity; civility, courtesy, politeness; dignity, elegance, grace
ant vulgarity

reflect *vb* **1** to reproduce or show as a mirror does < the trees on the shore were *reflected* in the water >
syn glass, image, mirror
rel repeat, reproduce

2 *syn* see THINK 5
rel study, weigh

reflecting *adj syn* see THOUGHTFUL 1

reflection *n* **1** *syn* see ANIMADVERSION
rel assault, attack, onset, onslaught; depreciation, derogation, disparagement

2 *syn* see THOUGHT 1

reflective *adj syn* see THOUGHTFUL 1

reformatory *n syn* see JAIL

refractory *adj syn* see OBSTINATE
ant malleable

refrain *vb* **1** to hold oneself back from doing or indulging in something < *refrained* from speaking out of turn >
syn abstain, forbear, keep, withhold
rel arrest, check, halt, interrupt, stop; curb, inhibit, restrain

2 *syn* see DENY 3

refresh *vb syn* see RENEW 1
rel animate, enliven, quicken, vivify; recover, recruit, regain; amuse, divert, recreate
con exhaust, tire
ant addle; jade

refreshed *adj* made or become fresh < awoke a *refreshed* man >
syn new, regenerated, reinvigorated, renewed, revived
rel recreated, renovated; animated, exhilarated, invigorated, stimulated
con exhausted, fagged, fatigued, jaded, tired, tuckered, wearied, worn-down, worn-out

refuge *n* **1** the state of being covered or protected < exiles seeking *refuge* in neutral countries >
syn asylum, harborage, sanctuary, shelter; *compare* SHELTER 1
rel protection, shield; immunity
con exposure, liability, openness; vulnerability

2 *syn* see SHELTER 1

3 *syn* see RESOURCE 3

refugee *n* one who flees for safety < the villagers fed and housed the *refugees* from the bombed city >
syn displaced person, DP, émigré, evacuee, fugitive
rel exile; emigrant, expatriate
idiom stateless person

refulgent *adj syn* see BRIGHT 1

refurbish *vb syn* see RENEW 1

refusal *n syn* see DENIAL 1

refuse *vb* **1** *syn* see DECLINE 4

2 *syn* see DENY 2

refuse *n* matter that is regarded as worthless and fit only for throwing away < heaps of *refuse* left by the former tenant >

syn ||collateral, debris, dreck, ||dust, garbage, junk, kelter, litter, ||muck, ||mullock, offal, outsweepings, ||pelf, riffraff, rubbish, ||sculch, spilth, sweepings, swill, trash, waste
rel dump, dustheap; rejectamenta, scraps; lumber; offscouring(s)

refute *vb syn* see DISPROVE 1

regain *vb syn* see RECOVER 1
rel achieve, attain, compass, gain, reach; reclaim, redeem, save; renew, restore

regal *adj syn* see KINGLY
rel august, imposing, magnificent, stately; glorious, resplendent, splendid, sublime

regale *n syn* see DINNER

regalia *n pl syn* see FINERY

regard *n* **1** *syn* see NOTICE 1

2 *syn* see CONSIDERATION 3
ant disregard

3 *syn* see INTEREST 3

4 a feeling of deferential approval and liking < held in high *regard* by his neighbors >
syn account, admiration, consideration, esteem, estimation, favor, respect
rel deference, homage, honor, reverence; appreciation, cherishing, prizing, valuing; approbation, approval, satisfaction
con deprecation, disapproval; disfavor, disgust, dislike, distaste; contempt, disdain, scorn; detestation, hate, hatred
ant despite

5 *syn* see CARE 4

regard *vb* **1** *syn* see ADMIRE 2
con reject, repudiate, scorn
ant despise

2 *syn* see CONSIDER 3
rel assay, assess, estimate, rate, value

regardful *adj* **1** *syn* see ATTENTIVE 1

2 *syn* see MINDFUL 2

3 *syn* see RESPECTFUL

regarding *prep syn* see APROPOS

regardless *adj syn* see NEGLIGENT

regardless of *prep syn* see AGAINST 4

regenerated *adj syn* see REFRESHED

region *n* **1** *syn* see AREA 1
rel neighborhood, vicinity; division, part, section, sector

2 *syn* see FIELD

register *n syn* see LIST

register *vb* **1** *syn* see ENROLL 1

2 *syn* see SHOW 5

regnant *adj* **1** *syn* see DOMINANT 1

2 *syn* see PREVAILING

regress *vb syn* see REVERT 2

regret *vb* to be very sorry for < *regrets* his mistakes > < *regret* the problems facing minorities >
syn deplore, repent, rue
rel bemoan, bewail, lament; grieve, mourn, sorrow; deprecate, disapprove

regret *n* **1** *syn* see SORROW
rel compunction, contrition, penitence, remorse, repentance; demur, qualm, scruple

2 *regrets pl syn* see APOLOGY 2

regretful *adj syn* see REMORSEFUL

regretless *adj syn* see REMORSELESS

regrettable *adj syn* see DEPLORABLE

regular *adj* **1** *syn* see GENERAL 1
rel customary, ordinary
ant irregular

2 *syn* see ORDERLY 1
rel fixed, set, settled; constant, equable, even, steady, uniform
ant irregular; sporadic

3 *syn* see UTTER

regulate *vb syn* see ADJUST 2
rel arrange, methodize, order, organize, systematize; moderate, temper

regulation *n syn* see LAW 1

rehabilitate *vb syn* see RESTORE 3

rehearse *vb* **1** *syn* see RELATE 1
rel iterate, reiterate, repeat

2 *syn* see EXERCISE 3
rel run through

reify *vb syn* see MATERIALIZE 2

reign *vb* **1** *syn* see GOVERN 1

idiom sit on the throne
  2 syn see RULE 2
reimburse *vb syn* see COMPENSATE 3
  rel recover; balance, compensate, offset
  con default, dishonor, repudiate, welsh
rein *vb syn* see COMPOSE 4
reinforce *vb syn* see STRENGTHEN 2
  rel augment, enlarge, increase, multiply; bolster, buttress, pillar, prop, sustain
  ant undermine
reinstate *vb* **1 syn** see RESTORE 5
  2 syn see RESTORE 1
reintroduce *vb syn* see RESTORE 1
reinvigorated *adj syn* see REFRESHED
reissue *n syn* see EDITION
reiterate *vb syn* see REPEAT
reject *vb* **1 syn** see DECLINE 4
  rel debar, eliminate, exclude, shut out
  ant accept; choose, select
  2 syn see DISCARD
rejection *n syn* see DENIAL 1
rejoin *vb syn* see ANSWER 1
rejoinder *n syn* see ANSWER 1
rejuvenate *vb* **1 syn** see RENEW 1
  2 syn see RESTORE 3
rekindle *vb syn* see REVIVE 3
relapse *n syn* see LAPSE 2
relapse *vb syn* see LAPSE
relate *vb* **1** to tell orally or in writing the details or circumstances of a situation <*related* the story of his life>
  syn describe, narrate, recite, recount, rehearse, report, state
  rel disclose, divulge, reveal, tell; detail, itemize, particularize; depict, express, render; pronounce
  idiom make public
  2 syn see JOIN 1
  rel ascribe, assign, credit, impute, refer
  3 syn see BEAR (on *or* upon)
related *adj* connected by or as if by family ties <persons *related* in the first degree> <physics and mathematics are closely *related*>
  syn affiliated, agnate, akin, allied, cognate, connate, connatural, consanguine, incident, kindred
  rel associated, connected; complementary, convertible, correlative, corresponding, reciprocal; alike, analogous, identical; germane, pertinent, relevant
  con different, dissimilar, divergent, unconnected, unlike
  ant unrelated
relation *n syn* see RELATIVE
relative *n* a person connected with another by blood <all of his *relatives* live out of state>
  syn kin, kinsman, kinswoman, relation
  rel brother, half brother, half sister, sib, sibling, sister; father, mother, parent; child, daughter, son; grandfather, grandmother, grandparent; grandchild, granddaughter, grandson; aunt, half aunt, half uncle, uncle; half nephew, half niece, nephew, niece; cousin, cross-cousin, half cousin, ortho-cousin; agnate, cognate
relative *adj* **1 syn** see DEPENDENT 1
  2 syn see COMPARATIVE
relax *vb* **1 syn** see LOOSE 5
  2 to become less tense or reserved <couldn't *relax* in crowds>
  syn ease off, loosen up, unbend, unlax, unwind
  rel calm (down), collect (oneself), compose (oneself), cool (off), simmer down
  idiom be at ease, breathe easily, feel at home, make oneself at home
  con rack (oneself), tense (up)
  3 syn see REST 2
relaxation *n syn* see REST 1
  rel amusement, diversion, recreation; alleviation, assuagement, mitigation, relief
  ant tension
relaxed *adj* **1 syn** see LOOSE 1
  rel flexuous, sinuous; gentle, lenient, mild, soft
  ant stiff
  2 syn see EASYGOING 3
  con ascetic, austere, severe, stern
  ant tense
release *vb* **1 syn** see FREE

  rel acquit, exculpate, exonerate; relinquish, resign, surrender, yield
  idiom cast loose, set at large
  ant detain
  2 syn see EMIT 2
  3 syn see TAKE OUT (on)
  ant check
relegate *vb* **1 syn** see BANISH
  2 syn see COMMIT 1
  rel accredit, charge, credit, refer
relegation *n* **1 syn** see EXILE 1
  2 syn see DISPOSAL 2
relent *vb syn* see ABATE 4
relentless *adj* **1 syn** see GRIM 3
  rel rigorous, strict, stringent; cruel, ferocious, fierce, inhuman
  con submissive, yielding
  2 syn see INFLEXIBLE 2
relevance *n syn* see USE 3
relevant *adj* relating to or bearing upon the matter in hand <*relevant* testimony>
  syn ad rem, applicable, applicative, applicatory, apposite, apropos, germane, material, pertinent, pointful
  rel allied, cognate, related; appropriate, apt, fit, fitting, proper, suitable; important, significant, weighty; admissible, allowable
  idiom in point, in question, to the point
  con impertinent, inadmissible, inapplicable, inapposite, inappropriate; unallied, unassociated, unconnected, unrelated; alien, extrinsic, foreign
  ant irrelevant; extraneous
reliable *adj* **1** having qualities that merit confidence or trust <a *reliable* friend>
  syn dependable, secure, tried, tried and true, trustworthy, trusty
  rel safe; inerrable, inerrant, infallible, unerring; apposite, cogent, compelling, convincing, meaningful, significant, sound, telling, valid; attested, authenticated, circumstantiated, confirmed, proven, validated, verified; unimpeachable, unquestionable
  con doubtful, dubious, problematic, questionable, suspect; independable, undependable, untried, untrustworthy; unattested, unauthenticated, unconfirmed, unvalidated
  ant unreliable
  2 syn see CERTAIN 3
reliance *n syn* see TRUST 1
reliant *adj syn* see DEPENDENT 1
relic *n* **1 syn** see REMEMBRANCE 3
  2 syn see VESTIGE 1
relief *n* **1 syn** see EASE 3
  rel lightening, softening; allayment, appeasement, assuagement, mollification
  ant anguish
  2 syn see HELP 1
relieve *vb* **1** to make less grievous or more tolerable <drugs that *relieve* pain>
  syn allay, alleviate, assuage, ease, lighten, mitigate, mollify
  rel comfort, console, solace; appease, palliate, relieve, soften; quiet, soothe, subdue; moderate, qualify, temper; decrease, diminish, lessen, reduce; aid, benefit, help
  con aggravate, enhance, heighten, sharpen; reinforce
  ant intensify
  2 syn see ROB 1
  3 to take the place of for a time <sent to *relieve* the sentry>
  syn spell, take over
  rel fill in, sub, substitute; replace, supply
  4 syn see EXEMPT
religion *n* **1** a system of religious belief <tolerant of all *religions*>
  syn creed, cult, faith, persuasion
  rel belief, doctrine
  2 the body of persons who accept a system of religious belief <all the members of my *religion* strive for tolerance>
  syn church, communion, connection, creed, cult, denomination, faith, persuasion, sect

---

syn synonym(s)   **rel** related word(s)
ant antonym(s)   **con** contrasted word(s)
idiom idiomatic equivalent(s)
‖ use limited; if in doubt, see a dictionary

religious *adj syn* see DEVOUT
  rel faithful, staunch, steadfast, true; ethical, moral, noble, righteous, virtuous; honest, honorable, just, upright
  con godless, ungodly
  ant irreligious
relinquish *vb* to let out of one's possession or control completely <few leaders willingly *relinquish* power>
  syn abandon, cede, give up, hand over, lay down, leave, resign, surrender, ‖turn up, waive, yield; *compare* ABDICATE 1
  rel lay aside; quit, throw up; abdicate, renounce; desert, forsake; abnegate, forbear, forgo, sacrifice; cast, discard, shed
  ant keep
relish *n* **1** *syn* see TASTE 3
  2 *syn* see TASTE 4
  rel enjoying, liking, loving; bias, prejudice; flair, leaning, penchant, propensity
  3 *syn* see ENJOYMENT 1
relish *vb* **1** *syn* see ENJOY 1
  2 to eat or drink with pleasure <so hungry that he will *relish* plain food>
  syn savor
  3 *syn* see ADMIRE 1
relishing *adj syn* see PALATABLE
  rel delighting, gratifying, pleasing, regaling, rejoicing, tickling
  con banal, flat, inane, insipid, jejune
reluct *vb syn* see DISGUST
reluctant *adj syn* see DISINCLINED
  rel calculating, cautious, chary, circumspect, wary
rely (on *or* upon) *vb* to place full confidence <*relied* on the doctor for an accurate diagnosis>
  syn bank (on *or* upon), build (on), calculate (on *or* upon), count (on), depend (on *or* upon), ‖lot (on *or* upon), reckon (on), trust (in *or* to)
  rel commit, confide, entrust; await, expect, hope, look
  idiom put faith in, swear by
  con distrust, mistrust
remain *vb syn* see STAY 2
  ant depart
remainder *n* a remaining group, part, or trace <he spent the *remainder* of his life in prison>
  syn balance, heel, leavings, remains, remanet, remnant, residual, residue, residuum, rest
  rel excess, surplus; hangover, leftover
remains *n pl* **1** *syn* see REMAINDER
  2 *syn* see CORPSE
remanet *n syn* see REMAINDER
remark *vb* **1** *syn* see SEE 1
  2 to make observations and pass on one's judgment <he *remarked* on the lack of modern paintings at the gallery>
  syn animadvert, comment, commentate, observe
  rel mention, note
remark *n* **1** *syn* see NOTICE 1
  2 an expression of opinion or judgment <a *remark* that led to a vehement argument>
  syn comment, commentary, note, obiter dictum, observation
  rel assertion, reflection, saying, statement, utterance; clarification, elucidation, explanation, explication, exposition, interpretation; annotation, exegesis, gloss, postil, scholium
remarkable *adj* **1** *syn* see NOTICEABLE
  rel exceptional; important, momentous, significant, weighty; peculiar, singular, strange, unique
  2 *syn* see EXCEPTIONAL 1
remarkably *adv syn* see VERY 1
remedial *adj syn* see CURATIVE
remedy *n* **1** something used for the treatment of disease <a cold *remedy*>
  syn cure, medicament, medicant, medication, medicine, pharmacon, physic
  rel biologic, drug, medicinal, pharmaceutical
  2 something that corrects or counteracts <no easy *remedy* for discontent>
  syn antidote, corrective, counteractant, counteractive, counteragent, countermeasure, counterstep, cure
  rel cure-all, elixir, panacea; nostrum
remedy *vb syn* see CURE
remedying *adj syn* see CURATIVE
remember *vb* to bring an image or idea from the past into the mind <*remembers* the old days>

syn bethink, cite, ‖mind, recall, recollect, remind, reminisce, retain, retrospect, revive, revoke
  rel look back (on *or* upon), think (of), treasure; relive; educe, elicit, evoke, extract
  con disregard, ignore, neglect, overlook; disremember, lose
  ant forget
remembrance *n* **1** *syn* see MEMORY 1
  2 *syn* see MEMORY 2
  3 something that serves to keep a person or thing in mind <wanted to give her a small *remembrance*>
  syn keepsake, memento, memorial, relic, remembrancer, reminder, souvenir, token, trophy
  rel favor, gift, present
remembrancer *n syn* see REMEMBRANCE 3
remind *vb syn* see REMEMBER
  rel hint, imply, intimate, suggest; admonish, advise, warn; jog, prompt
  idiom put in mind
reminder *n* **1** *syn* see EXPRESSION 3
  2 *syn* see REMEMBRANCE 3
  rel memo, memorandum, note, notice; hint, intimation, suggestion; admonition, warning
remindful *adj syn* see REMINISCENT
reminisce *vb syn* see REMEMBER
reminiscence *n* **1** *syn* see MEMORY 1
  2 *syn* see MEMORY 2
reminiscent *adj* tending to remind <shoes *reminiscent* of those worn fifty years ago>
  syn redolent, remindful
  rel evocative, suggestive
  idiom bringing to mind
remise *vb syn* see TRANSFER 4
remiss *adj syn* see NEGLIGENT
  rel faineant, indolent, lazy, slothful
  ant scrupulous
remit *vb* **1** *syn* see EXCUSE 1
  2 *syn* see DEFER
  3 *syn* see SEND 1
remittable *adj syn* see VENIAL
remnant *n syn* see REMAINDER
remonstrance *n syn* see DEMUR 2
remonstrate *vb syn* see OBJECT 1
  rel combat, fight, oppose, resist, withstand
remonstration *n syn* see DEMUR 2
remorse *n syn* see PENITENCE
remorseful *adj* motivated or marked by remorse <a *remorseful* confession>
  syn apologetic, attritional, compunctious, contrite, penitent, penitential, regretful, repentant, sorry
  rel mournful, rueful, sorrowful
  con impenitent, regretless, unregretful; hard, obdurate
  ant remorseless
remorsefulness *n syn* see PENITENCE
remorseless *adj* having no remorse <a *remorseless* villain>
  syn impenitent, regretless, uncontrite, unregretful, unremorseful, unrepentant, unsorry
  rel compassionless, merciless, pitiless, ruthless, uncompassionate, unmerciful
  con penitent, regretful, sorry
  ant remorseful
remote *adj* **1** *syn* see DISTANT 1
  ant close; adjacent
  2 *syn* see BACK 1
  3 *syn* see OBSCURE 2
  4 small in degree <a *remote* possibility>
  syn ‖fat, negligible, off, outside, slender, slight, slim, small
  con great, large; important, significant, weighty
  5 *syn* see INDIFFERENT 2
remotest *adj syn* see EXTREME 5
remove *vb* **1** *syn* see MOVE 4
  2 to take something from a place or position <*removed* the book from the shelf>
  syn take away, take off, take out, withdraw
  rel move, shift, transfer; extract
  3 to take (as a hat) from one's person <*removed* her coat when she entered the house>
  syn doff, douse, put off, take off
  rel cast off, throw off

idiom off with
con don, put on, replace
4 to get rid of <*remove* the causes of poverty>
syn clear away, eliminate, take out
rel dispose (of), eradicate, exterminate, extirpate; blot out, efface, erase, expunge, obliterate
idiom do away with
5 *syn* see PURGE 3
removed *adj* **1** *syn* see DISTANT 1
ant adjoining
2 *syn* see OBSCURE 2
3 *syn* see ALONE 1
remunerate *vb* **1** *syn* see PAY 1
rel accord, award, grant, vouchsafe
2 *syn* see COMPENSATE 3
remunerative *adj syn* see ADVANTAGEOUS 1
renaissance *n syn* see REVIVAL
renascence *n syn* see REVIVAL
rencontre *n syn* see CONTEST 2
rend *vb syn* see TEAR 1
rel divide, separate
render *vb* **1** *syn* see RETURN 3
2 *syn* see REPRESENT 1
3 *syn* see TRANSLATE 1
4 *syn* see ADMINISTER 1
rendering *n* **1** *syn* see INTERPRETATION 2
2 *syn* see VERSION 1
rendezvous *n* **1** *syn* see ENGAGEMENT 3
2 *syn* see RESORT 2
rendezvous *vb syn* see GATHER 6
rendition *n syn* see INTERPRETATION 2
renegade *n* a person who forsakes his faith, party, cause, or allegiance and aligns himself with another <the *renegade* derided his former beliefs>
syn apostate, defector, rat, recreant, runagate, tergiversator, turnabout, turncoat
rel iconoclast, insurgent, rebel; abandoner, deserter, forsaker; heretic, schismatic
con liege man; disciple, follower
ant adherent
renege *vb syn* see BACK DOWN
renew *vb* **1** to make like new <rested to *renew* their strength>
syn modernize, refresh, refurbish, rejuvenate, renovate, restore, update
rel make over, remodel; mend, rebuild, repair; correct, rectify, reform, revise
con bankrupt, deplete, drain, exhaust, impoverish; consume
ant wear out
2 *syn* see RESTORE 1
3 *syn* see REVIVE 3
4 *syn* see REPEAT
5 *syn* see RESUME 2
renewed *adj syn* see REFRESHED
renounce *vb* **1** *syn* see ABDICATE 1
ant arrogate
2 *syn* see ABANDON 1
idiom wash one's hands of
3 *syn* see DEFECT
renouncement *n syn* see RENUNCIATION
renovate *vb* **1** *syn* see REVIVE 3
2 *syn* see RENEW 1
rel clean, cleanse
renown *n* **1** *syn* see FAME 2
2 *syn* see EMINENCE 1
renowned *adj syn* see FAMOUS 2
rel acclaimed, extolled, lauded, praised; outstanding, signal
rent *vb syn* see HIRE 1
rent *adj syn* see LACERATED
rent *n syn* see BREACH 3
rental *n syn* see APARTMENT 1
renunciation *n* voluntary surrender or putting aside of something desired or desirable <led a life of total *renunciation* as a monk>
syn abnegation, denial, renouncement, self-abnegation, self-denial, self-renunciation
rel abjurement, eschewing, forbearing, forgoing, forswearing, sacrifice, self-sacrifice; rejection, repudiation, surrender, yielding
con gripping, holding, keeping

ant retention
reoccupy *vb syn* see RESUME 1
reoccurrence *n syn* see RECURRENCE
reopen *vb syn* see RESUME 2
reorder *vb syn* see REORGANIZE
reorganization *n syn* see SHAKE-UP
reorganize *vb* to arrange in a different way <*reorganize* a bankrupt company>
syn readjust, rearrange, reconstitute, reconstruct, reorder, reorient, reorientate, reshuffle, retool
rel reestablish, refound, resettle; rebuild, regenerate, renovate
con disarrange, disorder, disorganize
reorient *vb syn* see REORGANIZE
reorientate *vb syn* see REORGANIZE
‖**rep** *n* **1** *syn* see FAME 2
2 *syn* see REPUTATION 2
repair *vb* **1** *syn* see GO 1
2 *syn* see RESORT 2
repair *vb syn* see MEND 2
repair *n* **1** *syn* see ORDER 9
2 *syn* see ORDER 10
reparation *n* a return for something lost or suffered, usually through the fault of another <war *reparations*>
syn amends, compensation, indemnification, indemnity, quittance, recompense, redress, reprisal, restitution
rel atonement, expiation; remuneration, requital, retribution, reward; adjustment, settlement
repartee *n* **1** *syn* see RETORT 2
2 *syn* see BANTER
rel humor, irony, sarcasm, satire, wit; rejoinder, response, retort
repast *n syn* see MEAL
repay *vb syn* see COMPENSATE 3
rel balance, offset; accord, award
repeal *vb syn* see REVOKE 2
ant establish; enact
repeat *vb* to say or do again <*repeat* a command>
syn ingeminate, iterate, reiterate, renew, reprise, resay
rel recite, recount, rehearse, relate; hash over, recapitulate, rehash, restate, retell; chime, din, echo, harp, ring; duplicate, reproduce; copy, ditto, imitate; recrudesce, recur, return, revert
repeatedly *adv syn* see OFTEN
idiom day after day, day by day, day in and day out
repel *vb* **1** *syn* see FEND (off)
2 *syn* see RESIST
3 *syn* see DISGUST
ant allure; attract
repellent *adj* **1** *syn* see REPUGNANT 1
con alluring, bewitching, captivating, charming; enticing, luring, seductive, tempting
ant attractive; pleasing
2 *syn* see OFFENSIVE
3 *syn* see ANTIPATHETIC 2
repent *vb syn* see REGRET
repentance *n syn* see PENITENCE
con complacency, self-complacency, self-satisfaction
repentant *adj syn* see REMORSEFUL
rephrase *vb syn* see PARAPHRASE
repine *vb syn* see COMPLAIN
replace *vb* **1** *syn* see RETURN 4
2 *syn* see RESTORE 5
3 to put out of a usual or proper place or into the place of another <the old bridge was *replaced* by a new one last year>
syn outplace, supersede, supplant
rel renew, restore; alter, change; recoup, recover, regain, retrieve
4 *syn* see CHANGE 5
replacement *n syn* see SUBSTITUTE
replete *adj* **1** *syn* see ALIVE 5
2 *syn* see FULL 1
replica *n syn* see REPRODUCTION
replicate *vb syn* see COPY
replication *n syn* see REPRODUCTION

---

syn synonym(s)   *rel* related word(s)
ant antonym(s)   *con* contrasted word(s)
idiom idiomatic equivalent(s)
‖ use limited; if in doubt, see a dictionary

reply *vb syn* see ANSWER 1
   con accuse, charge, impeach, indict; address, greet, salute
reply *n syn* see ANSWER 1
   con argument, dispute; greeting, salute
report *n* 1 common talk or an instance of it that spreads rapidly < spread a false *report* >
   syn buzz, cry, gossip, grapevine, hearsay, murmur, on-dit, rumble, rumor, scuttlebutt, talk, tattle, tittle-tattle, whispering, word
   rel conversation, speech; chat, chatter, chitchat, prating, small talk; canard, dirt, scandal; advice, intelligence, news, tidings
   2 *syn* see REPUTATION 2
   3 *syn* see ACCOUNT 7
   rel declaration, statement; comment, notice, review; brief, bulletin
report *vb syn* see RELATE 1
   rel communicate, impart
repose *vb syn* see REST 1
repose *n syn* see REST 1
   rel refreshment, renewal, restoration
   con strain, stress; agitation, discomposure, perturbation
repository *n syn* see DEPOT 2
repossess *vb* 1 *syn* see RECOVER 1
   2 *syn* see RESUME 1
   3 to resume possession of (an item purchased on installment) in default of payments due < *repossessed* the car >
   syn take back
   rel get back, reclaim, recover, retrieve
reprehend *vb syn* see CRITICIZE
   rel admonish, chide, rebuke, reprimand, reproach, reprove; berate, rate, scold, upbraid
reprehensible *adj syn* see BLAMEWORTHY
represent *vb* 1 to present an image or lifelike imitation of (as in art) < the painting *represents* a spring scene >
   syn delineate, depict, describe, image, interpret, limn, picture, portray, render
   rel express, realize, show; display, exhibit; hint, suggest; draft, outline, sketch; narrate, relate
   con color, distort, falsify, garble, misinterpret, pervert, twist, warp
   2 to serve as the counterpart or image of < a movie hero who *represents* the ideals of the culture >
   syn body (forth), emblematize, embody, epitomize, exemplify, illustrate, mirror, personalize, personate, personify, symbolize, typify; *compare* EMBODY 1
   rel denote, mean, signify; impersonate, substitute; copy, imitate, reproduce
   con belie, distort, garble, twist, warp
   ant misrepresent
representant *n syn* see DELEGATE
representation *n* the act of delineating < an exponent of *representation* in art >
   syn delineation, depiction, description, picture, portraiture, portrayal, presentment
   rel demonstration, exemplification, illustration
representative *adj syn* see TYPICAL 1
   ant atypical
representative *n* 1 *syn* see INSTANCE
   2 *syn* see DELEGATE
repress *vb* 1 *syn* see SUPPRESS 2
   2 *syn* see COMPOSE 4
repression *n* 1 the action or process of putting down by authority or force < *repression* of unpopular opinions >
   syn choking, extinguishment, quashing, quenching, smothering, squashing, squelching, stifling, strangling, suppression, throttling
   rel check, control, curb, restraint; crushing, quelling, subdual
   con emboldening, encouragement, support
   2 an instance of putting down by authority or force < racial *repressions* >
   syn clampdown, crackdown, suppression
   rel crushing, extinction, smothering; limitation, repression, restriction
reprieve *n syn* see RESPITE 1
reprimand *n syn* see REBUKE
reprimand *vb syn* see REPROVE
reprinting *n syn* see EDITION
reprisal *n* 1 *syn* see REPARATION
   2 *syn* see RETALIATION
reprise *vb syn* see REPEAT

reproach *n syn* see REBUKE
   rel blame, censure, discredit
reproach *vb syn* see REPROVE
reprobate *vb* 1 *syn* see CRITICIZE
   2 *syn* see DECLINE 4
reprobate *adj* 1 *syn* see ABANDONED 2
   2 *syn* see WRONG 1
reprobate *n syn* see VILLAIN 1
reproduce *vb* 1 *syn* see PROCREATE 1
   2 *syn* see COPY
reproduction *n* one thing which closely or essentially resembles another that has already been made, produced, or written < printed *reproductions* of the great masters >
   syn carbon, carbon copy, copy, ditto, duplicate, facsimile, reduplication, replica, replication
   ant original
reproof *n syn* see REBUKE
reprove *vb* to criticize adversely, especially in order to warn of or to correct a fault < *reproved* him for talking in class >
   syn admonish, call down, chide, lesson, monish, ‖rack back, rebuke, reprimand, reproach, ‖sneap, tick off; *compare* CRITICIZE, LAMBASTE 3, SCOLD 1
   rel counsel, warn; blame, censure, criticize, reprehend, reprobate; chasten, correct, discipline, punish
   idiom haul over the coals, slap one's wrist, take to task
reptile *n syn* see SYCOPHANT
repudiate *vb* 1 *syn* see DECLINE 4
   con acknowledge, admit, avow, confess, own
   ant adopt
   2 *syn* see DEFECT
   3 *syn* see DISCLAIM
   rel abandon, desert, forsake; cast, discard
   con allow, concede, grant
   ant own
repugnance *n syn* see ABOMINATION 2
repugnancy *n syn* see ABOMINATION 2
repugnant *adj* 1 so alien or unlikable as to arouse antagonism and aversion < the idea of moving again became *repugnant* to her >
   syn abhorrent, invidious, obnoxious, repellent, revulsive
   rel alien, extraneous, extrinsic, foreign; incompatible, incongruous, inconsonant, uncongenial
   con acceptable, bearable, tolerable; agreeable, gratifying, pleasant, pleasing, pleasurable
   ant congenial
   2 *syn* see OFFENSIVE
   3 *syn* see ANTIPATHETIC 2
repulse *vb* 1 *syn* see FEND (off)
   2 *syn* see DISGUST
   ant captivate
repulsion *n syn* see ABOMINATION 2
repulsive *adj syn* see OFFENSIVE
   ant alluring
reputable *adj syn* see RESPECTABLE 1
reputation *n* 1 *syn* see FAME 2
   rel authority, credit, influence, prestige, weight
   2 the estimation in which one is generally held < a good *reputation* >
   syn character, fame, name, ‖rep, report, repute
repute *n* 1 *syn* see FAME 2
   ant disrepute
   2 *syn* see REPUTATION 2
reputed *adj* 1 *syn* see RESPECTABLE 1
   2 *syn* see SUPPOSED 1
request *vb syn* see ASK 2
   rel appeal, petition, pray, sue
requiescence *n syn* see REST 1
require *vb* 1 *syn* see DEMAND 1
   2 *syn* see DEMAND 2
   3 *syn* see LACK
required *adj* 1 *syn* see NEEDFUL
   2 *syn* see MANDATORY
   ant optional
requirement *n* 1 something wanted or needed < production was not sufficient to satisfy *requirements* for cars >
   syn demand, need, want
   2 *syn* see ESSENTIAL 2
requisite *adj* 1 *syn* see NEEDFUL
   2 *syn* see JUST 3

requisite *n syn* see ESSENTIAL 2
requisition *vb syn* see DEMAND 1
requital *n syn* see RETALIATION
requite *vb* **1** *syn* see RECIPROCATE
   rel content, satisfy; revenge
   2 *syn* see COMPENSATE 3
resay *vb syn* see REPEAT
rescind *vb syn* see REVOKE 2
rescript *n syn* see REVISION 1
rescue *vb* to set free (as from confinement or risk) <*rescue* a drowning child>
   syn deliver, save
   rel emancipate, free, liberate, manumit, release; conserve, preserve; disembarrass, disentangle, extricate; recover, regain, retrieve; buy, ransom, redeem
research *n syn* see INQUIRY 1
resect *vb syn* see EXCISE
resemblance *n syn* see LIKENESS
   rel parallel
   ant dissemblance
resemble *vb* to be like or similar to <he *resembles* his father>
   syn favor, ‖feature, simulate
   idiom be a dead ringer for, bear a resemblance to, be the spit and image of, be the very image of, bring to mind, have all the earmarks of, look like, put one in mind of, remind one of, take after
   con differ, vary
resentfully *adv syn* see HARD 6
resentment *n syn* see OFFENSE 2
   rel animosity, animus, antagonism, antipathy, rancor; ill will, malice, malignancy, malignity, spite
reservation *n syn* see CONDITION 1
   rel circumscription
reserve *vb* **1** *syn* see KEEP 5
   2 to set or have set aside or apart <*reserve* a hotel room>
   syn bespeak, book, preengage
   rel contract, engage, retain
reserve *n* something stored or kept available for future use or need <keep a *reserve* of canned foods on hand>
   syn backlog, hoard, inventory, nest egg, reservoir, stock, stockpile, store
   rel fund, supply
   idiom something for a rainy day, something in the sock
reserved *adj* **1** inclined to cautious restraint in the expression of knowledge or opinions <too *reserved* to offer a spontaneous criticism>
   syn constrained, incommunicable, noncommittal, restrained
   rel bashful, diffident, modest, shy; ceremonious, conventional, formal
   con demonstrative, expansive, unconstrained, unrestrained; boisterous, loud, ostentatious; extroverted, open, outgoing
   ant unreserved
   2 *syn* see SILENT 3
   ant effusive
   3 *syn* see UNSOCIABLE
   ant affable
   4 *syn* see ANTISOCIAL
   5 *syn* see QUALIFIED 2
reservoir *n syn* see RESERVE
reshuffle *vb syn* see REORGANIZE
reside *vb* **1** to have as one's habitation or domicile <he *resides* in Boston>
   syn abide, bide, ‖dig, dwell, hang out, live
   rel inhabit, occupy, people, tenant; continue, endure
   2 *syn* see CONSIST 1
residence *n* **1** *syn* see HABITATION 1
   2 *syn* see HABITATION 2
residency *n syn* see HABITATION 2
resident *n syn* see INHABITANT
‖residenter *n syn* see INHABITANT
resider *n syn* see INHABITANT
residual *n syn* see REMAINDER
residue *n syn* see REMAINDER
residuum *n syn* see REMAINDER
resign *vb* **1** *syn* see RELINQUISH
   2 *syn* see ABDICATE 1
   3 *syn* see QUIT 6
resignation *n* **1** *syn* see ACQUIESCENCE

rel humbleness, lowliness, meekness, modesty
   2 *syn* see PATIENCE
resigned *adj syn* see PASSIVE 2
   ant rebellious
resile *vb syn* see BACK DOWN
resilient *adj* **1** *syn* see ELASTIC 1
   2 *syn* see ELASTIC 2
   ant flaccid
resist *vb* to stand firm against a person or influence <the criminal *resisted* the police> <we must learn to *resist* temptation>
   syn buck, combat, contest, dispute, duel, fight, oppose, repel, traverse, withstand
   rel assail, assault, attack; contradict, contravene, gainsay, impugn; baffle, balk, foil, frustrate, thwart; check, counter, hinder, obstruct, stem
   con bow, capitulate, surrender
   ant submit, yield
resolute *adj* **1** *syn* see DECIDED 2
   rel obstinate, pertinacious, stubborn
   2 *syn* see FAITHFUL 1
resoluteness *n syn* see DECISION 2
resolution *n* **1** *syn* see ANALYSIS 1
   2 *syn* see DECISION 1
   3 *syn* see DECISION 2
   4 *syn* see COURAGE
resolve *vb* **1** *syn* see ANALYZE
   ant blend
   2 *syn* see SOLVE 1
   3 *syn* see SOLVE 2
   rel dispel, disperse, dissipate; clear, disabuse, purge, rid
   4 *syn* see DECIDE
resolve *n syn* see DECISION 2
resolved *adj syn* see DECIDED 2
resonant *adj* marked by conspicuously full and rich sounds or tones (as of speech or music) <a deep *resonant* voice rang out>
   syn consonant, fat, orotund, plangent, resounding, ringing, rotund, round, sonorant, sonorous, vibrant
   rel full, mellow, rich; deep, profound; enhanced, heightened, intensified; earsplitting, loud, powerful, stentorian, strident; beating, pulsating, pulsing, throbbing; booming, clangorous, noisy, reverberant, reverberating, sounding, thundering, thunderous; electrifying, thrilling
   con faint, low, murmurous, muted, smothered, soft, weak; flat, toneless, unmusical; cacophonous, discordant, inharmonious, off-key
resort *n* **1** *syn* see RESOURCE 3
   2 a place that is habitually frequented <a favorite *resort* of teenagers>
   syn hangout, haunt, purlieu, rendezvous, stamping ground, watering hole
   rel harbor, haven, refuge, retreat; den, nest
   3 a place providing recreation and entertainment especially to vacationers <returned to the same *resort* every year>
   syn pleasure dome, spa, watering place
   rel hotel, inn, lodge; bath(s), hot spring(s), mineral spring(s), spring(s), thermal spring(s)
resort *vb* **1** *syn* see FREQUENT
   ant avoid
   2 to betake oneself or to have recourse when in need of help or relief <they were unwilling to *resort* to her parents for aid>
   syn apply, go, recur, refer, repair run, turn
   rel address, devote, direct, employ, use, utilize
   idiom avail oneself of, fall back on (or upon)
resound *vb syn* see PRAISE 2
resounding *adj* **1** *syn* see RESONANT
   2 *syn* see EMPHATIC
resource *n* **1** resources *pl syn* see MEAN 3
   2 resources *pl syn* see WEALTH 2
   3 something to which one turns for assistance in difficulty or need in the absence of a usual means or source of supply <has exhausted every *resource* he can think of>

---

syn synonym(s)   *rel* related word(s)
ant antonym(s)   *con* contrasted word(s)
idiom idiomatic equivalent(s)
‖ use limited; if in doubt, see a dictionary

syn dernier ressort, expediency, expedient, makeshift, recourse, refuge, resort, shift, stopgap, string, substitute, surrogate
rel contraption, contrivance, device, lash-up; creation, invention; fashion, manner, method, mode, system, way; means, measure, step; artifice, dodge, stratagem, subterfuge; hope, opportunity, possibility, relief

respect *n syn* see REGARD 4
rel awe, fear, reverence; adoration, veneration, worship
ant scorn

respect *vb syn* see ADMIRE 2
rel revere, reverence, venerate
ant abuse; misuse; scorn

respectable *adj* **1** worthy of esteem or deference < a *respectable* scientist >
syn creditable, estimable, reputable, reputed, well-thought-of
rel honorable, worthy
ant disreputable, unrespectable
2 *syn* see DECOROUS 1
3 *syn* see DECENT 4
4 *syn* see CONSIDERABLE 2
5 acceptable in appearance or standing < wore old but *respectable* clothes >
syn decent, presentable, tolerable; *compare* DECENT 4
rel adequate, satisfactory; acceptable, appropriate, proper, suitable
ant disreputable

respectful *adj* marked by or showing respect or deference < a *respectful* glance >
syn deferential, duteous, dutiful, regardful
rel reverent, reverential, venerating; attentive, civil, courteous, gracious, polite
con abusive, insolent, insulting, offensive; contemptuous, impudent, irreverent, rude
ant disrespectful

respecting *prep syn* see APROPOS
respective *adj syn* see SEVERAL 1
respire *vb syn* see BREATHE 3
respite *n* **1** a temporary suspension of the execution of a capital offender < the murderer won a *respite* >
syn reprieve
2 *syn* see BREAK 4
rel intermission, lull, pause, recess; ease, leisure, rest

resplendent *adj syn* see SPLENDID 2
rel blazing, flaming, glowing

respond *n syn* see ANSWER 1

respond *vb syn* see ANSWER 1
rel act, behave, react

response *n syn* see ANSWER 1

responsible *adj* subject to an authority which may exact redress in case of default < he is *responsible* for the safe delivery of the goods >
syn accountable, amenable, answerable, liable
rel exposed, open, subject
con clear, exempt, immune; irresponsible, unaccountable, unanswerable, unliable
ant irresponsible

responsive *adj* **1** *syn* see RECEPTIVE 1
ant unresponsive
2 *syn* see SENTIENT 3
rel answering, replying, responding
3 *syn* see TENDER
con cold, cool, indifferent

rest *n* **1** freedom from toil or strain < enjoyed his well-deserved *rest* >
syn ease, leisure, relaxation, repose, requiescence
rel deferring, intermission, suspension; quiet, silence, stillness; calm, peace, peacefulness, placidity, restfulness, serenity, tranquillity
con action, work; restlessness, strain
2 *syn* see BASE 1

rest *vb* **1** to dispose oneself at ease in order to relieve or avoid fatigue < she is *resting* in the bedroom after a hard day's work >
syn lie, lie down, recline, repose, stretch (out)
rel doze, nap, nod, sleep, slumber, snooze
2 to refrain from labor or exertion < planned to do nothing but *rest* during his vacation >
syn relax, rest up, unbend, unlax

rel loaf, loll, lounge; ease off, ease up, let down, let up, slacken, slack off
idiom take it easy, take life easy
con labor, toil, work; drudge, grind, slave
3 to allow an interval of rest from exertion < they *rested* for ten minutes before going back to work >
syn breathe, lay off, lie by, spell
idiom lie (*or* rest) on one's oars, stop for breath, take a break (*or* rest), take five (*or* ten), take time out
4 *syn* see BASE
rel depend, hang, hinge; count, rely

rest *n syn* see REMAINDER
rel excess, overplus, superfluity, surplus, surplusage

restart *vb syn* see RESUME 2

restate *vb syn* see PARAPHRASE

restatement *n syn* see VERSION 1

restitute *vb* **1** *syn* see RESTORE 3
2 *syn* see RETURN 4

restitution *n syn* see REPARATION

restive *adj* **1** *syn* see CONTRARY 3
2 *syn* see TENSE 2

restiveness *n syn* see UNREST

restless *adj* lacking rest or giving no rest < the patient was *restless* from pain > < *restless* sleep >
syn uneasy, unpeaceful, unquiet, unrestful, unsettled, untranquil
rel agitated, disturbed, perturbed, troubled; fidgety, jittery, jumpy, nervous, restive; fitful, intermittent, spasmodic
con easy, peaceful, quiet, tranquil
ant restful

restlessness *n syn* see UNREST

restorative *adj* **1** *syn* see CURATIVE
2 *syn* see TONIC 1

restore *vb* **1** to put or bring back (as into existence or use) < *restore* peace in the world >
syn recall, reestablish, reinstate, reintroduce, renew, revive
rel get back, recover, regain, retrieve, win (back)
2 *syn* see RENEW 1
3 to put into a previous good state < made plans to *restore* slum areas >
syn reclaim, recondition, reconstruct, recover, rehabilitate, rejuvenate, restitute
rel redeem, rescue, save; amend, reform, revise; recoup, recruit, regain, retrieve; better, improve; correct, rectify, remedy, right; return
ant deteriorate
4 to help or cause to regain signs of life and vigor < *restore* him to health >
syn resuscitate, revive, revivify
rel cure, heal, remedy; arouse, rally, rouse, stir
5 to put again in possession of something < *restore* the king to his throne >
syn give back, put (back), reinstate, replace, return
6 *syn* see RETURN 4

restrain *vb* **1** to prevent from or control in doing something < *restrained* the child from picking all the flowers >
syn bit, bridle, check, coarct, constrain, crimp, curb, hold back, hold down, hold in, inhibit, keep, pull in, withhold; *compare* HAMPER
rel arrest, interrupt, stop; prevent; forbear, refrain; block, hinder, impede, obstruct; gag, muzzle
idiom keep in line, put (*or* lay) under restraint
con countenance, encourage; incline, induce, move, prompt; persuade; allow, permit
ant impel; incite
2 *syn* see COMPOSE 4
ant abandon
3 *syn* see MODERATE 1

restrained *adj* **1** *syn* see QUIET 4
ant unrestrained
2 *syn* see UNDEMONSTRATIVE
3 *syn* see RESERVED 1
4 *syn* see CONSERVATIVE 2
ant extravagant

restraint *n syn* see RESTRICTION 2

restrict *vb syn* see LIMIT 2
rel bind, tie; shrink

restricted *adj syn* see DEFINITE 1

restriction *n* **1** something that restricts or restrains < they both wanted to be free of the *restriction* of the school >

syn ‖ball and chain, circumscription, cramp, limitation, stint, stricture

rel brake, check, control, curb

2 an act of restricting or the condition of being restricted < undue *restriction* of children >

syn circumscription, confinement, constrainment, constraint, cramp, restraint

rest up *vb syn* see REST 2

restyle *vb syn* see REVISE

result *n* **1** *syn* see EFFECT 1

rel close, conclusion, end, finish, termination; product, production

con origin, root, source

2 *syn* see ANSWER 2

resume *vb* **1** to assume or take again < *resumed* her place in society >

syn reassume, reoccupy, repossess, retake

rel reclaim, recoup, recover, regain, retrieve

2 to return to or begin again after interruption < *resumed* her work >

syn continue, pick up, recommence, renew, reopen, restart, take up

rel carry on, go on, keep up

con cease, discontinue, end, halt, postpone, quit, stop; check, intermit, interrupt

résumé *n syn* see SUMMARY

resurgence *n syn* see REVIVAL

resurrect *vb* **1** to restore to life < believed that his body would be literally *resurrected* >

syn raise

idiom raise from the dead

2 *syn* see REVIVE 3

resurrection *n syn* see REVIVAL

resuscitate *vb* **1** *syn* see RESTORE 4

2 *syn* see REVIVE 3

resuscitation *n syn* see REVIVAL

retail *vb syn* see SELL 3

retain *vb* **1** *syn* see HAVE 1

2 *syn* see KEEP 5

con abdicate, resign; abjure, forswear, recant, renounce, retract

3 *syn* see REMEMBER

retake *vb syn* see RESUME 1

retaliate *vb syn* see RECIPROCATE

rel avenge, revenge

idiom even the score, get back at, get even with, give in kind, give one a dose of his own medicine, give one tit for tat, pay one in his own coin, settle (*or* square) accounts, turn the tables on

retaliation *n* the act of inflicting or the intent to inflict injury in return for injury < they had no opportunity for *retaliation* >

syn avengement, avenging, counterblow, reprisal, requital, retribution, revanche, revenge, vengeance

rel correction, discipline, punishment; indemnification, recompense, repayment; amends, indemnity, redress, reparation, restitution

idiom an eye for an eye, blow for blow, measure for measure, tit for tat

con clemency, grace, lenity, mercy; forgiveness, pardon, remission

retard *vb syn* see DELAY 1

rel decrease, lessen, reduce; clog, fetter, hamper; baffle, balk

ant accelerate; advance

retarded *adj* limited in intellectual or emotional development < a *retarded* child >

syn backward, dim-witted, dull, feebleminded, half-witted, imbecile, moronic, quarter-witted, simple, simpleminded, slow, slow-witted; *compare* SIMPLE 3, STUPID 1

rel dim, ‖dough-baked, ‖dunny, opaque; exceptional, underachieving; touched

idiom not all there, soft in the head

con bright, capable, intelligent

retch *vb* to make an effort to vomit < started to *retch* after drinking it >

syn gag, heave, keck

rethink *vb syn* see RECONSIDER

reticent *adj syn* see SILENT 3

con candid, open, plain

ant frank, unreticent

retinue *n syn* see ENTOURAGE

retire *vb* **1** *syn* see RETREAT 2

2 *syn* see GO 2

rel recede, retreat; abandon, relinquish, surrender, yield

ant advance

3 to cause to withdraw from one's position or occupation < all employees are automatically *retired* at age sixty-five >

syn pension (off), superannuate

rel discharge, dismiss; drop, leave, quit, resign, terminate, vacate

4 to go to bed < youngsters should always *retire* before midnight >

syn bed, ‖flop, pile (in), roll in, turn in

idiom go beddie-bye, go night-night, hit the hay (*or* sack)

con arise, get out, get up, pile (out), roll out, turn out, uprise

ant rise

retired *adj syn* see OBSCURE 2

retirement *n syn* see SECLUSION

retiring *adj* **1** *syn* see SHY 1

ant assertive

2 *syn* see UNDEMONSTRATIVE

ant forward

retool *vb syn* see REORGANIZE

retort *vb syn* see ANSWER 1

retort *n* **1** *syn* see ANSWER 1

2 a quick, witty, or cutting reply < he made a very clever *retort* >

syn back answer, comeback, repartee, riposte

rel reprisal, retaliation, revenge; crack, gag, jape, jest, joke, quip, sally, wisecrack, witticism

retouch *vb syn* see TOUCH UP

retract *vb* **1** *syn* see RECEDE 1

ant protract

2 *syn* see ABJURE

rel eliminate, exclude, rule out, suspend

retral *adj* **1** *syn* see POSTERIOR 2

2 *syn* see BACKWARD 1

retreat *n syn* see SHELTER 1

retreat *vb* **1** *syn* see RECEDE 1

rel quail, recoil, shrink

ant advance

2 to draw back from action or danger < the army *retreated* in disarray >

syn fall back, give back, retire, withdraw

rel abandon, depart, evacuate, go, leave, pull out, quit, vacate; decamp, escape, flee, fly; back down, back out, bow out, climb down

idiom beat a retreat, drop back, give ground, give way, sound a retreat

con advance, move, proceed, progress

ant attack

re–treat *vb syn* see RECONSIDER

retrench *vb syn* see SHORTEN

retribution *n syn* see RETALIATION

rel affliction, trial, tribulation, visitation

retrieve *vb* **1** *syn* see RECOVER 1

2 *syn* see REVIVE 3

retrocede *vb syn* see RECEDE 1

retrograde *adj syn* see BACKWARD 1

retrograde *vb* **1** *syn* see RECEDE 1

rel return, revert; invert, reverse; backslide, lapse, relapse

2 *syn* see DETERIORATE 1

retrogress *vb syn* see REVERT 2

retrospect *n syn* see REVIEW 5

retrospect *vb syn* see REMEMBER

retrospection *n syn* see REVIEW 5

return *vb* **1** to go or come back (as to a person, place, or condition) < the converted sinner soon *returned* to his old ways >

syn react, recrudesce, recur, revert, turn back

rel advert; revolve, rotate, turn; renew, restore; recover, regain; rebound, reflect, repercuss, reverberate

con abandon, depart, leave, quit

ant forsake

---

syn synonym(s)	*rel* related word(s)
ant antonym(s)	*con* contrasted word(s)
idiom idiomatic equivalent(s)	
‖ use limited; if in doubt, see a dictionary	

2 syn see ANSWER 1

3 to bring back (as a writ or verdict) to an office or tribunal < *return* a verdict of not guilty >
syn render

4 to bring, send, or put back to a former or proper place < *return* the gun to its holster >
syn replace, restitute, restore, take back
ant remove

5 syn see RESTORE 5
6 syn see YIELD 5
7 syn see RECIPROCATE
rel bestow, give

return *n* **1 syn** see RECURRENCE
2 syn see ANSWER 1
3 syn see PROFIT
ant outlay

returnless *adj* **syn** see INEVITABLE

revamp *vb* **1 syn** see MEND 2
2 syn see REVISE

revanche *n* **syn** see RETALIATION

reveal *vb* **1** to make known what has been or should be concealed < he solemnly promised he would not *reveal* the truth >
syn betray, blab (out), disclose, discover, divulge, give away, let on, ‖let out, mouth, spill, tell, unbosom, unclose, uncover, uncurtain, unveil
rel break, communicate, impart; announce, blow (about *or* abroad), broadcast, declare, give out, publish, vent; breathe, whisper; leak; acknowledge, admit, avow, confess, let on; peach, rat, ‖split, squeak, squeal (on), ‖stool, talk
idiom let slip, let the cat out of the bag, spill the beans
con cover (up), hide, obscure, veil
ant conceal

2 syn see OPEN 2

revel *vb* **1** to be festive in a noisy or riotous manner < they *reveled* all night long >
syn carouse, frolic, hell, riot, roister, spree, wassail
idiom blow off steam, cut loose, kick up one's heels, let go, let loose, paint the town red, whoop it up

2 syn see WALLOW 3

revel *n* **1 syn** see MERRYMAKING
2 syn see REVELRY 2

revelation *n* disclosure or something disclosed by or as if by divine or preternatural means < a *revelation* closely guarded by members of the sect >
syn apocalypse, oracle, prophecy, vision
ant adumbration

reveling *n* **syn** see MERRYMAKING

revelment *n* **1 syn** see MERRYMAKING
2 syn see REVELRY 2

revelry *n* **1 syn** see MERRYMAKING
2 boisterous partying < they were exhausted after the night of *revelry* >
syn high jinks, revel, revelment, skylarking, wassail, whoop-dedo, whoopee, whoopla, whoop-up

revenant *n* **syn** see APPARITION

revenge *vb* **syn** see AVENGE
rel defend, justify
idiom get one's own back, have one's revenge, take an eye for an eye

revenge *n* **syn** see RETALIATION

revengeful *adj* **syn** see VINDICTIVE
rel adamant, inexorable, inflexible, obdurate

revenue *n* amount received or gained usually measured in money < still holds property that yields a good *revenue* >
syn coming(s) in, income, receipts
rel earnings, gains, salary, wages; proceeds, profit, returns, yield
con expenditure, expense(s); outgoings, outlay

reverberant *adj* **syn** see HOLLOW 1

revere *vb* to honor and admire profoundly and respectfully < he is *revered* for his wisdom >
syn adore, reverence, venerate, worship
rel admire, esteem, regard, respect; appreciate, cherish, prize, treasure, value; exalt, magnify; enjoy, love
con contemn, despise, disdain, scorn, scout; insult, mock, scoff
ant flout

revered *adj* **syn** see VENERABLE 1

reverence *n* **1 syn** see HONOR 1
rel devotion, fealty, loyalty, piety

2 the emotion inspired by what arouses one's deep respect or veneration < a deep *reverence* for honesty >
syn awe, fear
con contempt, despite, disdain, hatred, scorn; insult, mockery

reverence *vb* **syn** see REVERE
idiom hold in reverence

reverend *adj* **syn** see VENERABLE 1

reverend *n* **syn** see CLERGYMAN

reverential *adj* **syn** see VENERABLE 1

reverie *n* the condition of being lost in thought < spent the day in *reverie* before the fire >
syn brown study, muse, study, trance
rel absorption, abstraction, preoccupation; contemplation, meditation, thought; castle-building, daydreaming, dreaming

reversal *n* **1** a causing to move or face in an opposite direction or to appear in an inverted position < a *reversal* in policy > < the *reversal* of objects seen through a simple lens >
syn about-face, changeabout, inversion, reverse, reversement, reversion, right-about, right-about-face, turn, turnabout, turning, volte-face
rel bouleversement, overturning

2 syn see SETBACK

reverse *adj* **syn** see OPPOSITE

reverse *vb* **1** to change to the contrary or opposite side or position < the chairman *reversed* the order in which they would speak >
syn change, inverse, invert, revert, transplace, transpose, turn
rel capsize, overturn, upset; exchange, interchange; shift, transfer

2 syn see REVOKE 2

reverse *n* **1 syn** see OPPOSITE
2 syn see REVERSAL 1
3 syn see SETBACK

reversement *n* **syn** see REVERSAL 1

reversion *n* **1** a return to an ancestral type or condition or an instance of such a return < the law was a shocking *reversion* to earlier times >
syn atavism, throwback
rel backsliding, lapse, relapse
con advance, amendment, bettering, betterment, improvement; reform

2 syn see REVERSAL 1

revert *vb* **1 syn** see RETURN 1
2 to come or go back to a lower or worse condition < *reverted* to savagery >
syn regress, retrogress, throw back
rel backslide, lapse, relapse; decline, degenerate, deteriorate, retrograde
con advance, progress

3 syn see REVERSE 1

review *n* **1 syn** see REVISION 1
2 syn see EXAMINATION
3 syn see CRITICISM
4 syn see JOURNAL
5 a retrospective view of or meditation on past events < an occurrence that in *review* did not surprise him >
syn afterlight, reconsideration, reexamination, retrospect, retrospection, revision
rel reflection, study; second thought
con anticipation, contemplation, foreseeing

review *vb* **syn** see RECONSIDER

reviewal *n* **syn** see CRITICISM

revile *vb* **syn** see SCOLD 1
rel asperse, calumniate, defame, libel, malign, slander, traduce, vilify
con acclaim, eulogize, extol, praise
ant laud

revisal *n* **syn** see REVISION 1

revise *vb* to make a new, amended, improved, or up-to-date version of < the many problems involved in *revising* a dictionary >
syn redraft, redraw, restyle, revamp, rework, rewrite, work over
rel overhaul, reorganize; perfect, polish, upgrade
con discard, disregard

revise *n* **syn** see REVISION 1

revision *n* **1** an act of revising < the *revision* of a manuscript >
syn recension, redraft, rescript, review, revisal, revise
rel amendment, correction, emendation, rectification

2 syn see REVIEW 5

revitalize *vb* **syn** see REVIVE 3

revival n a renewal of life, activity, or prominence <a *revival* of weaving>
syn reanimation, rebirth, renaissance, renascence, resurgence, resurrection, resuscitation, revivification, reviviscence, risorgimento
rel regeneration, rejuvenation, renewal, restoration

revive vb 1 syn see RESTORE 4
rel gain, improve, recuperate
2 syn see RESTORE 1
3 to restore from a depressed, inactive, or unused state <*revived* his hope of escape>
syn reactivate, rekindle, renew, renovate, resurrect, resuscitate, retrieve, revitalize, revivify
rel reanimate, regenerate, reinvigorate, rejuvenate; arouse, galvanize, quicken, stimulate; activate, energize, vitalize
con extinguish, put down, put out, quell, quench, suppress; inhibit
4 syn see REMEMBER

revived adj syn see REFRESHED
revivification n syn see REVIVAL
revivify vb 1 syn see REVIVE 3
2 syn see RESTORE 4
reviviscence n syn see REVIVAL
revoke vb 1 syn see REMEMBER
2 to annul by recalling or taking back <*revoke* a privilege>
syn dismantle, lift, recall, repeal, rescind, reverse
rel abrogate, annul, void; cancel, erase, expunge; invalidate, nullify; countermand, counterorder; abjure, forswear, recant, retract
ant confirm

revolt vb 1 to renounce allegiance or subjection <*revolted* against the king>
syn insurrect, mutiny, rebel, rise (against)
rel defy, oppose, resist; break, renounce, turn (against); boycott, strike; overthrow, overturn, riot
idiom kick over the traces, take up arms against
con obey, submit; aid, assist, help, succor, support; bolster, prop (up), sustain, uphold
2 syn see DISGUST

revolter n syn see REBEL
revolting adj syn see OFFENSIVE
revolute vb syn see REVOLUTIONIZE
revolution n 1 the action or an act of moving around an orbit or circular course <the *revolution* of the earth around the sun>
syn circuit, circulation, circumvolution, gyration, gyre, revolve, rotation, round, turn, wheel, whirl
rel cycle, pirouette, reel, roll, spin, twirl
2 syn see SHAKE-UP

revolution vb syn see REVOLUTIONIZE
revolutional adj syn see EXTREME 3
revolutionary adj syn see EXTREME 3
revolutionary n syn see RADICAL
revolutionist n syn see RADICAL
revolutionist adj syn see EXTREME 3
revolutionize vb to change fundamentally or completely <he *revolutionized* manufacturing processes>
syn revolute, revolution
rel alter, change, modify; recast, refashion, reform, remodel; redraw, restyle, revamp, revise; metamorphose, transfigure, transform, transmogrify; overthrow, overturn
idiom break with the past, make a clean sweep, make a radical change

revolve vb 1 syn see PONDER 2
2 syn see TURN 1
revolve n syn see REVOLUTION 1
revulsion n syn see ABOMINATION 2
revulsive adj syn see REPUGNANT 1
reward n something that is offered or given for some service or attainment <the miner received a *reward* for his hard work>
syn carrot, dividend, guerdon, meed, plum, premium, prize
rel compensation, recompense, remuneration, requital

reweigh vb syn see RECONSIDER
reword vb syn see PARAPHRASE
rework vb syn see REVISE
rewrite vb syn see REVISE
rhadamanthine adj syn see JUST 3
rhapsodize vb syn see ENTHUSE 2
rel acclaim, extol, praise

con blame, condemn, denounce; decry, derogate, detract, minimize
rhapsody n 1 syn see BOMBAST
2 syn see ECSTASY
rhapsody vb syn see ENTHUSE 2
rhetoric n 1 syn see ORATORY
2 syn see BOMBAST
rhetorical adj emphasizing style often at the expense of thought <the candidate was given to windy *rhetorical* speeches>
syn aureate, bombastic, declamatory, euphuistic, florid, flowery, grandiloquent, highfalutin, high-flown, magniloquent, ‖mouthy, oratorical, orotund, overblown, pompous, purple, sonorous, stilted, swelling, swollen, tumescent, tumid, turgid
rel chichi, orchidaceous, ostentatious, pretentious, showy; gassy, inflated, windy; exaggerated, overdone, overwrought; grand, grandiose, high-sounding, imposing; flamboyant, ornate; embellished; articulate, eloquent, fluent, glib, vocal, voluble
con homely, literal, plain, simple, unpretentious; unadorned, undecorated, unembellished, ungarnished, unornamented
ant unrhetorical

rhino n syn see MONEY
rhubarb n syn see QUARREL
rhyme n 1 syn see POETRY 1
2 syn see POEM
3 syn see RHYTHM
rhyme vb syn see AGREE 4
rhymer n syn see POETASTER
rhymester n syn see POETASTER
rhythm n the regular rise and fall in intensity of sounds that is associated chiefly with poetry and music <the *rhythm* of the music made it easy to dance to>
syn beat, cadence, cadency, measure, meter, rhyme, rhythmus, swing
rel lilt; accent
rhythmus n syn see RHYTHM
riant adj syn see MERRY
‖**rib** n syn see WIFE
rib vb syn see BANTER 1
ribald n syn see SCAMP
ribbon n syn see STRIP 1
rich adj 1 having goods, property, and money in abundance <he was a *rich* man, having accumulated his wealth in business>
syn affluent, moneyed, ‖oofy, opulent, wealthy
rel comfortable, easy, independent, prosperous, well-fixed, well-heeled, well-off, well-to-do; fat, flush
idiom flush with money, having money to burn, in the money, rich as Croesus, rolling in money
con destitute, indigent, penurious, poverty-stricken
ant poor
2 syn see ORNATE
3 highly seasoned and fatty, oily, or sweet <ate *rich* desserts every day>
syn heavy
rel cloying, oversweet; filling, satiating, sating; fat
con natural, simple, unseasoned
ant plain
4 syn see FERTILE
5 syn see EXPRESSIVE
richen vb syn see ENRICH
riches n pl syn see WEALTH 2
rick n syn see PILE 1
‖**rick** vb syn see SPRAIN
rickety adj likely to give way or break down <a *rickety* old chair>
syn rachitic, rackety, rattletrap, shaky, wobbly; *compare* WEAK 2
rel unsound, unsteady
con firm, rugged, solid, sturdy, substantial, well-made
ant stable
‖**rickle** n syn see PILE 1
ricochet vb syn see GLANCE 1
rel bound, rebound, recoil
rid vb to set a person or thing free of something that encumbers <*rid* himself of his troubles>

---

syn synonym(s)   *rel* related word(s)
ant antonym(s)   *con* contrasted word(s)
idiom idiomatic equivalent(s)
‖ use limited; if in doubt, see a dictionary

syn clear, lose, shake (off), throw off, unburden
rel free, liberate, release; disembosom, unbosom; eradicate, exterminate, extirpate, remove, uproot; abolish, extinguish
con burden, charge, clog, cumber, encumber, lade, load, lumber, saddle, task, tax, weigh, weight
ant weigh down

riddance *n syn* see DISPOSAL 2

riddle *n syn* see MYSTERY

ride *vb* **1** to travel by automobile < often *rode* out to the countryside>
syn auto, motor
idiom go for a spin
2 *syn* see DRIFT 1
3 *syn* see BAIT 2
rel oppress, persecute; torment, torture
4 *syn* see OVERLAP

ride (out) *vb syn* see SURVIVE 2

ride *n syn* see DRIVE 1
rel excursion, expedition, journey, tour, trip

rider *n syn* see APPENDIX 1

ridge *n* **1** a top or upper part especially when long and narrow < topped the mountain *ridge* >
syn chine, crest, hogback
2 *syn* see WRINKLE

‖**ridge runner** *n syn* see RUSTIC

ridicule *vb* to make an object of laughter < *ridiculed* him for his inability to perform the feat>
syn deride, lout, mock, quiz, rally, razz, scout, taunt, twit
rel ‖barrack, flout, gibe, jape, jeer, scoff, sneer; burlesque, caricature, mimic, travesty; haze, ride, roast
idiom laugh out of court, make fun (or game or sport) of, poke fun at

ridiculous *adj* **1** *syn* see LAUGHABLE
rel absurd, foolish, preposterous, silly; antic, bizarre, fantastic, grotesque
2 *syn* see INDECOROUS

riding *n* **1** *syn* see SHIVAREE
2 *syn* see HARBOR 3

rife *adj* **1** *syn* see PREVAILING
2 *syn* see ALIVE 5

riff (through) *vb syn* see BROWSE

riffle *vb syn* see RIPPLE

riffle (through) *vb syn* see BROWSE

riffraff *n* **1** *syn* see RABBLE 2
2 *syn* see REFUSE

rifle *vb syn* see ROB 1

rift *n* **1** *syn* see CRACK 3
2 *syn* see BREACH 3
rel gap, hiatus, interruption, interval

rig *vb syn* see FURNISH 1

rig *n syn* see COSTUME

‖**rig** *n* **1** *syn* see IMPOSTURE
2 *syn* see PRANK

‖**rig** *vb syn* see DUPE

rigamajig *n syn* DOODAD, business, dingus, dofunny, doohickey, gadget, gizmo, thingum, thingumajig, thingumbob

rigging *n syn* see CLOTHES

‖**riggish** *adj syn* see FAST 7

right *adj* **1** *syn* see UPRIGHT 2
2 *syn* see DECOROUS 1
3 *syn* see JUST 3
4 *syn* see TRUE 3
con specious, unsound; misguided, mistaken
ant unright, wrong
5 *syn* see CORRECT 2
6 *syn* see FIT 1
7 *syn* see AUTHENTIC 2
8 *syn* see SANE 2
9 *syn* see HEALTHY 1
10 *syn* see CONSERVATIVE 1
11 *syn* see DECENT 4

right *n* **1** qualities (as adherence to duty or obedience to lawful authority) that together constitute the ideal of moral propriety or merit moral approval < the *right* is not all on one side>
syn good, straight
rel correctitude, correctness, properness, propriety, rightness
con debt, sin, wickedness; improperness, impropriety, incorrectness, unrightness

ant unright, wrong
2 something to which one has a just claim < the *right* to life, liberty, and the pursuit of happiness>
syn appanage, birthright, perquisite, prerogative, privilege
rel claim, interest, title; freedom, liberty, license
3 *usu* **rights** *pl syn* see DUE 1
4 *syn* see DIEHARD 1
‖**5** *syn* see OBLIGATION 2
‖**6** *syn* see EXCUSE 1

right *adv* **1** *syn* see JUST 1
2 *syn* see WELL 4
ant wrong, wrongly
3 *syn* see DIRECTLY 1
4 *syn* see WELL 3
5 *syn* see AWAY 3
6 *syn* see VERY 1

right *vb* **1** *syn* see CORRECT 1
‖**2** *syn* see MEND 2

right–about *n syn* see REVERSAL 1

right–about–face *n syn* see REVERSAL 1

right away *adv syn* see AWAY 3

righteous *adj* **1** *syn* see MORAL 1
con corrupt, flagitious, nefarious; bad, evil, immoral, reprobate, sinful, vicious, wicked, wrong
ant iniquitous, unrighteous
2 *syn* see GOOD 11
ant unrighteous

righteousness *n syn* see GOODNESS
ant unrighteousness

rightful *adj* **1** *syn* see JUST 3
rel equitable, fair, impartial
ant unrightful
2 *syn* see TRUE 8
ant unrightful
3 *syn* see FIT 1

right hand *n syn* see RIGHT-HAND MAN

right–handed *adj* having the same direction or course as the movement of the hands of a watch viewed from in front < a *right= handed* propeller>
syn clockwise, dextrorotatory, positive

right–hand man *n* a reliable or indispensable person < the boss viewed his efficient assistant as his *right-hand man* >
syn girl Friday, man Friday, right hand

rightist *n syn* see DIEHARD 1
ant leftist

‖**rightle** *vb syn* see MEND 2

rightly *adv syn* see WELL 1

right–minded *adj syn* see MORAL 1

rightness *n* **1** *syn* see GOODNESS
2 *syn* see ORDER 11

right off *adv syn* see AWAY 3

‖**right smart** *adj syn* see CONSIDERABLE 2

‖**right smart** *adv syn* see VERY 1

right wing *n syn* see DIEHARD 1

right–winger *n syn* see DIEHARD 1
ant left-winger

rigid *adj* **1** *syn* see STIFF 1
rel firm, hard, solid
ant elastic
2 *syn* see INFLEXIBLE 2
3 extremely severe or stern < was regarded as a *rigid* disciplinarian>
syn draconian, ironhanded, rigorist, rigorous, strict, stringent, unpermissive
rel austere, severe, stern; hard-line, inflexible, tough, uncompromising, unyielding; adamant, adamantine, inexorable, obdurate
con humoring, indulgent, pampering; loose, relaxed; easy, gentle, mild
ant lax

rigor *n syn* see DIFFICULTY 1
rel austerity, severity, sternness; harshness, roughness; affliction, trial, tribulation, visitation
ant amenity

rigorist *adj syn* see RIGID 3

rigorous *adj* **1** *syn* see RIGID 3
rel inflexible, stiff; ascetic; burdensome, exacting, onerous, oppressive
con easy, effortless, facile, light, smooth

ant mild
2 *syn* see SEVERE 3
rel drastic
con bland, faint, lenient, smooth
3 *syn* see CORRECT 2
rigorously *adv syn* see HARD 5
rile *vb* **1** *syn* see ROIL 1
2 *syn* see IRRITATE
riley *adj syn* see TURBID
rim *n syn* see BORDER 1
rim *vb syn* see BORDER 1
rima *n syn* see CRACK 3
rimation *n syn* see CRACK 3
rime *n syn* see CRACK 3
rime *vb syn* see CAKE 1
rimple *n syn* see WRINKLE
rimple *vb syn* see CRUMPLE 1
‖**rimption** *n, usu* **rimptions** *pl syn* see SCAD
‖**rindle** *n syn* see CREEK 2
ring *n* **1** *syn* see LOOP 2
2 *syn* see LOOP 1
3 *syn* see BOXING
4 *syn* see CLIQUE
5 *syn* see COMBINATION 2
ring *vb syn* see SURROUND 1
ring *vb* to sound clearly and resonantly < the church bells were *ringing* >
syn bell, bong, chime, knell, peal, toll
rel resound, reverberate, sound
‖**ring** (up) *vb syn* see TELEPHONE
ringer *n syn* see IMAGE 1
ringing *adj syn* see RESONANT
‖**ring off** *vb syn* see SHUT UP 2
riot *n* **1** *syn* see DISORDER 2
2 something or someone wildly amusing < the new comedy is a *riot* >
syn howl, ‖panic, scream, sidesplitter
rel sensation, smash, wow
riot *vb syn* see REVEL 1
riot (away) *vb syn* see WASTE 2
riotous *adj syn* see PROFUSE
rip *vb syn* see TEAR 1
rip (out) *vb syn* see SPUTTER 1
ripe *adj* **1** *syn* see MATURE 1
rel seasonable, timely, well-timed; overdue
con callow, crude, raw, rude; immature, unmatured, unmellow
ant unripe; green
2 *syn* see CONSUMMATE 1
3 brought by aging to full flavor or the best state < *ripe* cheese >
syn aged, matured, mellow, ripened
rel ready
ant unripe
‖**ripe** *vb syn* see MATURE
ripen *vb syn* see MATURE
rel better, improve; enhance, heighten, intensify, season
ripened *adj* **1** *syn* see MATURE 1
ant unripened
2 *syn* see RIPE 3
riposte *n syn* see RETORT 2
ripper *n syn* ‖DILLY, ‖corker, crackerjack, dandy, ‖dinger, humdinger, jim-dandy, ‖lulu, nifty, peach
ripping *adj syn* see MARVELOUS 2
ripple *vb* to become fretted or lightly ruffled on the surface (as water) < the pond was *rippled* by rain >
syn cockle, dimple, fret, riffle
ripsnorter *n syn* ‖DILLY, ‖corker, crackerjack, ‖daisy, dandy, ‖dinger, ‖doozer, humdinger, jim-dandy, ‖lulu
rise *vb* **1** to assume an upright or standing position < he *rose* from his chair >
syn get up, stand up, uprise, upspring
rel sit up; straighten up
idiom come to one's feet
con lie, lounge, recline, sit; loll, sprawl
2 *syn* see ROLL OUT
ant retire
3 *syn* see ADJOURN 2
ant sit

4 to move or come up from a lower to a higher level < smoke *rose* from the chimneys >
syn arise, ascend, aspire, lift, mount, soar, up, uprear
rel surge, tower; climb, scale; elevate, raise, rear
con descend, drop, lower; dip, plummet, sink
ant fall; decline
5 *syn* see INTENSIFY
6 *syn* see SURFACE
7 *syn* see INCREASE 2
ant abate; fall
8 *syn* see HAPPEN 1
9 *syn* see SPRING 1
rise (against) *vb syn* see REVOLT 1
rise (to) *vb syn* see APPLAUD 2
rise *n* **1** *syn* see ASCENT
ant fall
2 *syn* see ADDITION
3 an increment in amount, number, or volume < crime is on the *rise* >
syn boost, breakthrough, hike, increase, upgrade, wax
con declension, decline, lessening, letup, reduction, slump; decrement, loss
ant drop
rise and shine *vb syn* see ROLL OUT
risible *adj syn* see LAUGHABLE
ant lachrymose, larmoyant
rising *n syn* see ASCENT
ant falling
risk *n syn* see DANGER
rel accident, chance, fortune, luck; exposedness, exposure, liability, liableness, openness
risk *vb* **1** *syn* see ENDANGER
rel beard, brave, dare, defy, face; confront, encounter, meet
idiom go out of one's depth
2 *syn* see VENTURE 1
3 *syn* see GAMBLE 2
riskless *adj syn* see SAFE 2
risky *adj* **1** *syn* see DANGEROUS 1
rel delicate, precarious, sensitive, ticklish, touchy; speculative
idiom on thin ice
2 *syn* see RISQUÉ
risorgimento *n syn* see REVIVAL
risqué *adj* verging on impropriety or indecency < blushed at his *risqué* stories >
syn blue, broad, off-color, purple, racy, risky, salty, sexy, shady, spicy, suggestive, wicked; *compare* OBSCENE 2
rel naughty, warm; coarse, crude, earthy, gross, lewd, obscene, raunchy, raw, ribald, vulgar; dirty, foul; indecent, indecorous, indelicate, inelegant, unrefined
con clean, decent, proper; restrained; euphemistic
‖**rissom** *n syn* see PARTICLE
rite *n* **1** *syn* see FORM 2
2 forms (as religious rites) appropriate to a particular event < the marriage *rites* >
syn ceremonial, ceremony, formality, liturgy, observance, ritual, service
rel celebration, occasion, solemnity; sacrament, sacramental; form
‖**rithe** *n syn* see CREEK 2
ritual *n* **1** *syn* see RITE 2
2 *syn* see FORM 2
rival *n* one of two or more striving for what only one can possess < political *rivals* for the nomination >
syn competition, competitor, corrival
rel contender, contestant, entrant; adversary, antagonist, opponent
rival *vb* **1** *syn* see COMPETE 1
2 to strive to equal or surpass < *rivaling* each other for the most work done >
syn compete, emulate, rivalize
rel attempt, strive, struggle, try; contend, fight
3 *syn* see EQUAL 3
4 *syn* see AMOUNT 2

---

syn synonym(s)	*rel* related word(s)
ant antonym(s)	*con* contrasted word(s)
idiom idiomatic equivalent(s)	
‖ use limited; if in doubt, see a dictionary	

rivalize *vb syn* see RIVAL 2
rivalry *n syn* see CONTEST 1
rive *vb* **1** *syn* see TEAR 1
  rel divide, separate; chop, hew
  2 *syn* see SHATTER 1
rivel *n syn* see WRINKLE
rivet *vb* **1** *syn* see FASTEN 1
  2 *syn* see FASTEN 3
rivulet *n syn* see CREEK 2
road *n* **1** *often* **roads** *pl syn* see HARBOR 3
  2 *syn* see WAY 1
  3 *syn* see WAY 2
roadblock *n syn* see BAR 2
roadhouse *n syn* see HOTEL
roadman *n syn* see PEDDLER
roadstead *n syn* see HARBOR 3
roadster *n syn* see VAGABOND
roam *vb syn* see WANDER 1
roamer *n syn* see ROVER
roar *vb* to make a very loud and often a continuous or protracted
  noise <the crowd *roared* their disapproval of the speech>
  syn bawl, bellow, bluster, clamor, rout; *compare* BAWL 2
  rel rebound, repercuss, reverberate; shout, vociferate, yell; din
  con breathe, murmur, mutter, whisper
roaring *adj* **1** *syn* see LOUD 1
  2 *syn* see FLOURISHING
roast *vb* **1** *syn* see BURN 3
  2 *syn* see LAMBASTE 3
rob *vb* **1** to take possessions unlawfully <*rob* a bank> <he was
  mugged and *robbed*>
  syn ‖knock off, knock over, loot, plunder, ransack, relieve, rifle,
  stick up; *compare* BURGLARIZE, HOUSEBREAK
  rel ‖heist, hold up; jackroll, roll; strong-arm; filch, hijack, lift,
  pilfer, purloin, steal, thieve; cheat, defraud, hustle, swindle; despoil, pillage, ravage, sack
  2 *syn* see DEPRIVE 2
robber *n* one who commits the crime of robbery <only one *rob-*
  ber was involved in the holdup>
  syn yegg; *compare* THIEF
  rel hijacker; sandbagger; crook, swindler; cat burglar, cat man,
  housebreaker, raffles, second-story man; rifler; holdup man,
  stickup man; ‖bushranger, highwayman, ‖sticker-up
roborant *adj syn* see TONIC 1
robot *n* **1** a machine that looks like a human being and performs
  various complex acts (as walking or talking) of a human being
  <a *robot* that performed household chores>
  syn android, automaton
  rel golem
  2 an efficient, insensitive, often brutalized person <working on
  an assembly line can often turn a man into a *robot*>
  syn automaton, golem, machine
robust *adj* **1** *syn* see FLOURISHING
  2 *syn* see STRONG 3
robustious *adj syn* see BOORISH
rock *vb* **1** *syn* see SHAKE 4
  rel oscillate, sway, swing, undulate; quake, totter, tremble
  2 *syn* see TOSS 2
  3 *syn* see HURRY 2
rock *n* **1** *syn* see ERROR 2
  2 *syn* see DOLLAR
  3 **rocks** *pl syn* see MONEY
rock bottom *n syn* see ESSENCE 2
rock–bottom *adj syn* see BOTTOMMOST
rockbound *adj* **1** *syn* see ROCKY 1
  2 *syn* see INFLEXIBLE 2
rocket *vb* **1** *syn* see SKYROCKET
  rel arise, ascend, levitate, mount, surge, tower
  2 *syn* see HURRY 2
rock pile *n syn* see JAIL
rock–ribbed *adj* **1** *syn* see ROCKY 1
  2 *syn* see INFLEXIBLE 2
rocky *adj* **1** abounding in or consisting of rocks <a *rocky* shore>
  syn rockbound, rock-ribbed
  rel bebouldered, bouldery; stony
  2 *syn* see INSENSIBLE 5
rocky *adj* **1** *syn* see UNSTABLE 2
  2 *syn* see OBSCENE 2
‖Rocky Mountain canary *n syn* see DONKEY 1

rococo *adj* **1** *syn* see OLD-FASHIONED
  2 *syn* see ORNATE
rod *n* **1** *syn* see BAR 1
  2 *syn* see PUNISHMENT
  idiom rod in pickle
rodomont *n syn* see BRAGGART
rodomontade *n* **1** *syn* see BOMBAST
  rel boasting, bragging, vaunting; pride, vainglory, vanity
  2 *syn* see BRAGGART
rodomontade *vb syn* see BOAST
rodomontade *adj syn* see BOASTFUL
rogue *n* **1** *syn* see VILLAIN 1
  rel culprit, delinquent
  2 *syn* see SWINDLER
  3 *syn* see SCAMP
roguery *n syn* see MISCHIEVOUSNESS
roguish *adj* **1** *syn* see DISHONEST
  2 *syn* see PLAYFUL 1
  3 *syn* see COY 2
roguishness *n syn* see MISCHIEVOUSNESS
roil *vb* **1** to make turbid <*roiled* the brook with his splashings>
  syn mud, muddle, muddy, rile
  rel befoul, contaminate, dirty, pollute
  con clear, purify, settle
  2 *syn* see IRRITATE
roily *adj syn* see TURBID
roister *vb syn* see REVEL 1
role *n* **1** characteristic exterior properties and aspects, style, and
  atmosphere in which something intangible is discerned <the
  moral *role* of the legislature>
  syn character, clothing
  rel appearance, face, guise, seeming, semblance, show; aspect,
  look
  2 *syn* see FUNCTION 1
roll *n* **1** *syn* see LIST
  2 *syn* see ROSTER 1
  ‖**3** *syn* see FORTUNE 4
roll *vb* **1** *syn* see PONDER 2
  2 *syn* see SWATHE
  3 to wrap around on itself or something else <this cloth *rolls*
  unevenly>
  syn furl
  4 *syn* see WALLOW 3
  5 *syn* see TURN 1
  6 *syn* see WANDER 1
  7 *syn* see POUR 2
  8 *syn* see RUMBLE
  9 *syn* see TOSS 2
roll call *n syn* see LIST
rollick *vb* **1** *syn* see GAMBOL
  2 *syn* see WALLOW 3
rollick *n syn* see ESCAPADE
rollicking *adj syn* see ANTIC 2
  rel cheerful, glad, happy, joyful, joyous, lighthearted
roll in *vb syn* see RETIRE 4
  ant roll out
rolling stone *n syn* see ROVER
roll out *vb* to leave one's bed <*rolled out* at dawn>
  syn arise, get up, pile (out), rise, rise and shine, turn out, uprise
  ant roll in
roll up *vb syn* see ACCUMULATE
roly–poly *adj syn* see ROTUND 2
romance *n syn* see LOVE AFFAIR
romanesque *adj syn* see EXOTIC 2
romantic *adj syn* see EXOTIC 2
  2 *syn* see SENTIMENTAL
  rel fanciful, fantastic, imaginary, quixotic, visionary; created,
  invented
  ant unromantic; matter-of-fact
Romeo *n syn* see GALLANT 2
romp *n syn* see RUNAWAY
romp *vb syn* see GAMBOL
  idiom cut capers, horse around
rondure *n syn* see BALL
roof *n syn* see TOP 1
roof *vb syn* see HARBOR 1
rook *vb syn* see FLEECE 1
rookie *n syn* see NOVICE

room *n* **1** space in a building enclosed or set apart by a partition <the house had seven *rooms*>
  syn apartment, chamber
  2 rooms *pl syn* see APARTMENT 1
  3 enough space or range for free movement <no *room* for hope>
  syn elbowroom, latitude, leeway, margin, play, scope
  rel clearance; license, range, rein, sway; rope
room *vb syn* see HARBOR 2
room and board *n syn* see ACCOMMODATIONS
roomy *adj syn* see SPACIOUS
  ant cramped
‖**roose** *vb syn* see COMMEND 2
roost *vb* **1** *syn* see ALIGHT
  2 *syn* see HARBOR 2
root *n* **1** *syn* see SOURCE
  rel basis, foundation, ground
  2 *syn* see BASIS 1
  3 *syn* see CENTER 3
  4 *syn* see ESSENCE 2
root *vb syn* see ENTRENCH 1
  ant uproot
root *vb syn* see APPLAUD 2
rootage *n syn* see SOURCE
rootless *adj syn* see WEAK 2
root out *vb syn* see ANNIHILATE 2
  rel demolish, destroy, raze
  ant enroot
rootstock *n syn* see SOURCE
roperipe *n syn* see VILLAIN 1
ropes *n pl syn* see INS AND OUTS
ropy *adj syn* see MUSCULAR 1
rose *vb syn* see BLUSH
roseate *adj syn* see HOPEFUL 2
rose–colored *adj syn* see HOPEFUL 2
rose–colored spectacles *n pl syn* see OPTIMISM
roster *n* **1** a list of officers or enlisted men <an army *roster*>
  syn muster, muster roll, roll
  2 *syn* see LIST
rosy *adj syn* see HOPEFUL 2
rot *vb* **1** *syn* see DECAY
  rel corrupt, debase, vitiate
  2 *syn* see DETERIORATE 1
  3 *syn* see DEBASE 1
rot *n syn* see NONSENSE 2
rotate *vb* **1** *syn* see TURN 1
  2 to succeed or cause to succeed each other in turn <the drivers in the car pool *rotated* each week>
  syn alternate
  rel bandy, exchange, interchange; ensue, follow, succeed; relieve, spell
rotation *n syn* see REVOLUTION 1
rote *n syn* see ROUTINE
rotten *adj* **1** *syn* see BAD 5
  rel foul; tainted, touched; sour
  2 *syn* see VICIOUS 2
  3 *syn* see BAD 8
  4 *syn* see BAD 1
rotter *n syn* see CAD
rotund *adj* **1** *syn* see RESONANT
  2 rounded or swollen with fat <a wheezing *rotund* man lumbered by>
  syn chubby, plump, plumpish, plumpy, podgy, puddy, pudgy, roly-poly, round, roundabout, spuddy, tubby; *compare* FAT 2
  rel beefy, chunky, dumpy, heavyset, squat, stocky, stubby, thick, thickset; paunchy, potbellied; buxom, ‖crummy
  idiom on the plump side
  con angular, gaunt, lank, lanky, lean, rawboned, scrawny, skinny, spare; slender, slight, slim, thin
roturier *n syn* see UPSTART
rouge *vb syn* see BLUSH
rough *adj* **1** not smooth or even <a *rough* undressed block of stone>
  syn asperous, cragged, craggy, hairy, harsh, ironbound, jagged, rugged, scabrous, scraggy, uneven, unlevel, unsmooth
  rel bumpy, choppy; burred; firm, hard, solid; coarse, gross
  con flat, flush, level, plain, plane
  ant smooth

  2 *syn* see WILD 6
  con calm, halcyon, peaceful, placid, serene, tranquil
  3 *syn* see TOUGH 8
  4 *syn* see TIGHT 4
  5 *syn* see INDECOROUS
  6 *syn* see RUDE 1
  idiom in the rough
  7 *syn* see RUDE 3
  8 *syn* see HARSH 3
  9 *syn* see COARSE 3
  rel discourteous, impolite, uncivil, ungracious
  10 *syn* see BLUFF
  11 *syn* see HARD 6
rough *n syn* see TOUGH
rough (out) *vb syn* see SKETCH
rough (up) *vb syn* see MANHANDLE
rough–and–ready *adj syn* see MAKESHIFT
rough–and–tumble *n syn* see BRAWL 2
rough–and–tumble *adj syn* see MAKESHIFT
roughhewn *adj syn* see RUDE 1
roughhouse *n syn* see HORSEPLAY
roughhouse *vb syn* see MANHANDLE
roughhousing *n syn* see HORSEPLAY
roughly *adv* **1** *syn* see HARD 5
  ant smoothly
  2 *syn* see NEARLY
roughneck *n syn* see TOUGH
roughness *n syn* see INEQUALITY 1
  ant smoothness
roughscuff *n syn* see RABBLE 2
round *adj* **1** having every part of the circumference equally distant from a center within <flowers crowded in stiff *round* beds>
  syn circular
  rel annular, globular, orbed, orbicular, rounded, spherical, spiral
  2 *syn* see CURVED
  3 *syn* see ROTUND 2
  4 *syn* see OUTSPOKEN
  5 *syn* see RESONANT
round *adv* **1** *syn* see ABOUT 1
  2 *syn* see NEARLY
  3 *syn* see THROUGH 1
  4 *syn* see ABOUT 6
round *prep* **1** *syn* see NEAR 2
  2 *syn* see ABOUT 4
round *n* **1** *syn* see BALL
  2 *syn* see REVOLUTION 1
  3 *syn* see TOUR 2
  4 *syn* see CYCLE 1
  5 *syn* see CURVE
round *vb* **1** *syn* see BALL
  2 *syn* see SURROUND 1
  3 *syn* see POLISH 2
  4 *syn* see CURVE
round about *adv* **1** *syn* see ABOUT 1
  2 *syn* see ABOUT 6
  3 *syn* see ABOUT 2
roundabout *n* **1** *syn* see DETOUR
  2 *syn* see VERBIAGE 1
  3 *syn* see TOUR 2
  4 *syn* see EXCURSION 1
roundabout *adj* **1** *syn* see INDIRECT 1
  2 *syn* see ROTUND 2
rounded *adj* **1** *syn* see CURVED
  2 *syn* see CURVACEOUS
rounder *n syn* see WASTREL 1
roundly *adv* **1** *syn* see WELL 3
  2 *syn* see NEARLY
round off *vb syn* see CLIMAX
round trip *n syn* see TOUR 2
round up *vb syn* see GROUP 1
rouse *vb* **1** *syn* see WAKE 1

---

syn synonym(s)   *rel* related word(s)
ant antonym(s)   *con* contrasted word(s)
idiom idiomatic equivalent(s)
‖ use limited; if in doubt, see a dictionary

rel animate, enliven, quicken, vivify; excite, provoke, stimulate; foment, incite, instigate
con calm, compose, lull, quiet, quieten, settle, soothe, still, tranquilize
　2 *syn* see INTENSIFY
　3 *syn* see PROVOKE 4
　4 *syn* see STIR 1
rouser *n syn* see ‖DILLY
rousing *adj* **1** *syn* see EXCITING
　2 *syn* see LIVELY 1
‖**roust** *vb syn* see PROVOKE 4
roustabout *n syn* see WORKER
rout *n* **1** *syn* see MOB 2
　2 *syn* see RABBLE 2
　3 *syn* see MULTITUDE 1
rout *vb syn* see ROAR
rout *vb syn* see RUMMAGE 3
rout *n* **1** *syn* see DEFEAT 1
　2 *syn* see RUNAWAY
rout *vb* **1** to put to precipitate flight < the army regrouped and *routed* the enemy >
　syn derout, stampede
　rel chase, dispel, drive, expel
　idiom put to flight
　2 *syn* see WHIP 2
route *n syn* see WAY 2
route *vb* **1** *syn* see SEND 1
　2 *syn* see GUIDE
routine *n* habitual or mechanical and sometimes monotonous performance of an established procedure < settled into the *routine* of factory work >
　syn grind, groove, pace, rote, rut, treadmill
　rel squirrel cage; ‖drill
　idiom the beaten path, the drab monotony of habit
routine *adj* **1** *syn* see ORDINARY 1
　2 *syn* see USUAL 1
rove *vb syn* see WANDER 1
rover *n syn* see PIRATE
rover *n* one who roams habitually < he spent most of his life as a *rover* always on the move >
　syn drifter, meanderer, rambler, roamer, rolling stone, wanderer
　rel gad, gadabout, gadder, runabout; itinerant, peripatetic; floater
　idiom bird of passage
　con homebody
　ant stay-at-home
roving *adj syn* see ITINERANT
row *vb* to propel a boat by means of oars < *rowed* across the lake >
　syn oar, paddle, pull
　rel scull; punt; sail, scud
row *n* **1** *syn* see LINE 5
　2 *syn* see SUCCESSION 2
row *n* **1** *syn* see BRAWL 2
　2 *syn* see QUARREL
　3 *syn* see MOUTH 1
row *vb* ‖**1** *syn* see SCOLD 1
　2 *syn* see QUARREL
rowdiness *n syn* see HORSEPLAY
rowdy *adj syn* see TURBULENT 1
rowdy *n syn* see TOUGH
rowdydow *n* **1** *syn* see COMMOTION 4
　2 *syn* see BRAWL 2
　3 *syn* see BINGE 1
rowdydowdy *adj syn* see TURBULENT 1
rowdyish *adj syn* see TURBULENT 1
royal *adj* **1** *syn* see KINGLY
　rel glorious, resplendent, splendid, superb; august, imposing, stately
　2 *syn* see EASY 1
　3 *syn* see GRAND 1
　4 *syn* see EXCELLENT
royalist *n syn* see REACTIONARY
‖**rozzer** *n syn* see POLICEMAN
rub *vb* **1** *syn* see ABRADE 1
　2 *syn* see CHAFE 3
　rel aggravate, exasperate, nettle, peeve, provoke, rile; annoy, bother, irk, vex

　3 *syn* see POLISH 1
rub *n syn* see OBSTACLE
rubber *n syn* see BUSYBODY
rubberneck *n* **1** *syn* see BUSYBODY
　2 *syn* see TOURIST
rubberneck *vb syn* see LOOK 7
rubber stamp *n syn* see COMMONPLACE
rubbish *n* **1** *syn* see REFUSE
　2 *syn* see NONSENSE 2
　3 *syn* see PAP 2
rubbishing *adj syn* see CHEAP 2
rubbishly *adj syn* see CHEAP 2
rubbishy *adj syn* see CHEAP 2
rube *n syn* see RUSTIC
rubicund *adj syn* see RUDDY
rubify *vb syn* see REDDEN 1
rub out *vb* **1** *syn* see DESTROY 1
　2 *syn* see MURDER 1
rubric *n syn* see NAME 1
rubric *adj syn* see NOTEWORTHY
rubric *vb syn* see REDDEN 1
ruby *vb syn* see REDDEN 1
ruck *n* ‖**1** *syn* see PILE 1
　2 *syn* see GATHERING 2
ruck *n syn* see WRINKLE
ruck (up) *vb syn* see CRUMPLE 1
‖**ruckle** *vb syn* see CRUMPLE 1
rucksack *n syn* see BACKPACK
ruckus *n* **1** *syn* see COMMOTION 3
　rel brawl, broil, melee, scrap
　2 *syn* see QUARREL
ruction *n* **1** *syn* see BRAWL 2
　2 *syn* see COMMOTION 4
‖**ructious** *adj syn* see BELLIGERENT
rud *vb syn* see REDDEN 1
ruddle *vb syn* see REDDEN 1
ruddy *adj* having a healthy reddish color < has a *ruddy* complexion after being out in the cold >
　syn florid, flush, flushed, full-blooded, glowing, rubicund, sanguine
　rel bronzed; blooming; blowsy
　con ashen, ashy, livid, pale, pallid, wan, waxy; anemic, bloodless
ruddy *vb syn* see REDDEN 1
rude *adj* **1** lacking in craftsmanship or artistic finish < a *rude* sketch >
　syn angular, crude, lumpy, raw, rough, roughhewn, undressed, unfashioned, unfinished, unformed, unhewn, unpolished, unworked, unwrought
　rel unlicked; unprocessed; primitive, rudimental, rudimentary
　con dressed, fashioned, finished, formed, hewn, polished, worked, wrought
　2 *syn* see DISSONANT 1
　3 hastily executed and admittedly imperfect or imprecise < *rude* estimates for the cost of building the house >
　syn approximate, proximate, rough
　rel crude, imperfect, imprecise, inexact
　idiom ‖in the ball park
　con accurate, correct; faultless, perfect; exact, precise; meticulous, scrupulous
　4 *syn* see COARSE 3
　5 *syn* see IGNORANT 1
　6 lacking in social refinement < gave a *rude* reply to a polite question >
　syn discourteous, disgracious, disrespectful, ill, ill-bred, ill-mannered, impertinent, impolite, incivil, incondite, inurbane, mannerless, ‖mismannered, uncalled-for, uncivil, uncourteous, uncouth, ungracious, unhandsome, unmannered, unmannerly, unpolished
　rel brusque, crusty, curt, gruff; harsh; intrusive, meddlesome; crabbed, surly; boorish, churlish, clownish, loutish
　con courteous, genteel, mannerly, polite, well-mannered; bland, diplomatic, politic, smooth, suave; affable, considerate, gracious
　ant civil; urbane
　7 *syn* see BARBARIAN 1
　8 *syn* see INEXPERIENCED
rudely *adv syn* see NEARLY
rudiment *n* **1** *syn* see ESSENTIAL 1

2 rudiments *pl* *syn* see ALPHABET 2
rudimental *adj* *syn* see ELEMENTARY 1
rudimentary *adj* *syn* see ELEMENTARY 1
rue *vb* *syn* see REGRET
rue *n* **1** *syn* see SORROW
   2 *syn* see PENITENCE
   3 *syn* see PITY
rueful *adj* **1** *syn* see PITIFUL 1
   2 *syn* see WOEFUL 1
   3 *syn* see MELANCHOLY 2
   rel depressed, oppressed, weighed down; piteous, pitiful; despairing, despondent, hopeless
ruffian *n* **1** *syn* see TOUGH
   2 *syn* see THUG 1
ruffle *vb* **1** *syn* see BLOW 1
   2 *syn* see ABRADE 1
   3 *syn* see ANNOY 1
   ‖**4** *syn* see INTIMIDATE
rugged *adj* **1** *syn* see ROUGH 1
   2 *syn* see SEVERE 3
   rel arduous, difficult
   3 *syn* see HARSH 3
   4 *syn* see BOORISH
   5 *syn* see TOUGH 4
   rel brawny, burly, husky, muscular
   ant fragile
   6 *syn* see HARD 6
ruin *n* **1** *syn* see DETERIORATION 1
   2 *syn* see DOWNFALL 2
   3 the bringing about of or the results of disaster < met *ruin* at the hands of the enemy >
   syn confusion, destruction, devastation, havoc, loss, ruination
   rel crumbling, disintegration; break up, dissolution; disrepair; wreck
   con rebuilding, reconstruction, re-creation
   4 *syn* see INJURY 1
ruin *vb* **1** *syn* see DESTROY 1
   rel deface, disfigure; maim, mangle, mutilate; depredate, desecrate, desolate, despoil, devastate, devour, pillage, sack, spoliate, waste
   ant restore
   2 to subject to forces that are destructive of soundness, worth, or usefulness < in danger of being *ruined* by prosperity >
   syn bankrupt, dilapidate, do in, shipwreck, wreck
   rel corrupt, debase, degenerate, vitiate
   idiom play hob (*or* the devil) with
   con rebuild, renew, restore; reclaim, redeem, retrieve, salvage
   3 to overthrow the fortunes of < was *ruined* during the great crash >
   syn bankrupt, break, bust, fold up, impoverish, pauper, pauperize
   rel beggar, clean out, deplete, drain, draw, draw down, exhaust, use up; wipe (out); reduce
   idiom go under, lose one's shirt (*or* pants), take to the cleaners
   4 *syn* see FRUSTRATE 1
‖**ruinate** *vb* *syn* see DESTROY 1
ruination *n* **1** *syn* see RUIN 3
   2 *syn* see DOWNFALL 2
ruinator *n* *syn* see VANDAL
ruiner *n* *syn* see VANDAL
ruinous *adj* **1** *syn* see DESTRUCTIVE
   2 *syn* see FATAL 2
rule *n* **1** *syn* see LAW 1
   rel order; axiom, fundamental, principle; decorum, etiquette, propriety
   2 *syn* see MAXIM
   rel fundamental, principle
rule *vb* **1** *syn* see GOVERN 1
   rel guide, lead
   2 to hold preeminence in (as by ability, strength, or position) < an actor who rightfully *rules* the Shakespearian stage >
   syn dominate, domineer, predominate, preponderate, prevail, reign
   rel guide, lead; preside
   idiom be number one, take first place (in *or* on)
   3 *syn* see DECIDE
   rel deduce, gather, infer, judge
rule out *vb* **1** *syn* see EXCLUDE

   2 *syn* see PREVENT 2
ruling *n* *syn* see EDICT 1
ruling *adj* **1** *syn* see CENTRAL 1
   con peripheral
   2 *syn* see PREVAILING
‖**rum** *adj* *syn* see STRANGE 4
rumble *vb* to make a low heavy rolling sound < thunder *rumbling* in the distance >
   syn growl, grumble, roll
   rel boom, roar, thunder; peal, resound; blast, burst, clap, crack, crash
rumble *n* *syn* see REPORT 1
rumble–bumble *n* *syn* see MISCELLANY 1
rumbustious *adj* *syn* see TURBULENT 1
rum–dum *adj* *syn* see INTOXICATED 1
rumdum *n* *syn* see DRUNKARD
‖**rum–hole** *n* *syn* see BAR 5
ruminate *vb* **1** *syn* see PONDER 2
   rel consider, excogitate, weigh
   2 *syn* see CHEW 1
ruminative *adj* *syn* see THOUGHTFUL 1
rummage *n* *syn* see CLUTTER 2
   rel conglomeration, hash, hotchpotch, miscellany, patchwork, potpourri
rummage *vb* **1** *syn* see DISORDER 1
   2 *syn* see SCOUR 2
   3 to produce by searching < *rummaged* an old dress out of the attic >
   syn dig out, hunt (down *or* out *or* up), rout
   rel ferret (out), find; fish, search (out), spy (out); poke
rummery *n* *syn* see BAR 5
‖**rum–mill** *n* *syn* see BAR 5
rummy *adj* *syn* see STRANGE 4
rummy *n* *syn* see DRUNKARD
rumor *n* **1** *syn* see REPORT 1
   2 *syn* see MURMUR 1
rumor *vb* *syn* see GOSSIP
rumorer *n* *syn* see GOSSIP 1
rumormonger *n* *syn* see GOSSIP 1
rump *n* *syn* see BUTTOCKS
rumple *vb* *syn* see CRUMPLE 1
‖**rumpot** *n* *syn* see DRUNKARD
rumpus *n* **1** *syn* see COMMOTION 3
   2 *syn* see ARGUMENT 2
rumshop *n* *syn* see BAR 5
run *vb* **1** to move at a fast springing gait in which both feet are momentarily off the ground in the course of each pace < the boy *ran* down the walk >
   syn dash, scamper, scoot, scurry, shin, sprint; *compare* SCUTTLE
   rel career, course, race; bustle, hurry, hustle, rush, speed; scorch
   con crawl, creep, drag, inch, mosey, poke, saunter, stroll, toddle
   2 to hasten away from something that frightens or perturbs < afraid to fight but ashamed to *run* >
   syn bolt, flee, fly, make off, scamper, scoot, ‖screw, skedaddle, skip, skirr
   idiom ‖dog it, make a break, run for it, show a clean pair of heels, take flight, take French leave, take to one's heels
   3 *syn* see HURRY 2
   idiom go all out, go like (greased) lightning
   4 *syn* see RESORT 2
   5 *syn* see FUNCTION 3
   6 *syn* see BECOME 1
   7 *syn* see LIQUEFY
   8 to lie in or take a certain course < the path *runs* along the crest of the hill >
   syn extend, go, make, reach, stretch
   9 *syn* see RANGE 3
   10 *syn* see HUNT 1
   11 *syn* see DRIVE 3
   12 *syn* see THRUST 2
   13 *syn* see SMUGGLE

---

syn synonym(s)   *rel* related word(s)
ant antonym(s)   *con* contrasted word(s)
idiom idiomatic equivalent(s)
‖ use limited; if in doubt, see a dictionary

14 *syn* see OPERATE 3
15 *syn* see CONDUCT 3
run (through *or* over) *vb syn* see BROWSE
run (to *or* into) *vb syn* see AMOUNT 1
run *n* **1** ‖*syn* see CREEK 2
    2 an uninterrupted course of occurrence or repetition especially of like things or events <the play had a long *run* >
    syn continuance, continuation, duration, persistence
    rel continuity, endurance, prolongation
    3 *syn* see TENDENCY 1
    rel course, set; bearing, direction, line, swing
    4 *syn* see TRIP 1
    ‖**5 runs** *pl but sing or pl in constr syn* see DIARRHEA
runagate *n* **1** *syn* see RENEGADE
    2 *syn* see VAGABOND
run along *vb syn* see GO 2
runaround *n* **1** *syn* see DETOUR
    2 *syn* see ESCAPE 2
run away *vb syn* see ELOPE
runaway *n* a one-sided or overwhelming victory <the game was a *runaway*, the home team winning by 30 points>
    syn cakewalk, romp, rout, walkaway, walkover
    rel breather, cinch, duck soup, pushover; setup; shutout; conquest, triumph, victory, win
    con photo finish, tossup
run down *vb syn* see DECRY 2
run–down *adj* **1** *syn* see SHABBY 1
    2 *syn* see NEGLECTED
    rel abandoned, derelict, deserted, desolate, forsaken, lorn
rune *n* **1** *syn* see SPELL
    2 *syn* see POEM
rung *n syn* see DEGREE 1
run in *vb* **1** *syn* see ARREST 2
    2 *syn* see VISIT 2
run–in *n* **1** *syn* see ENCOUNTER
    2 *syn* see QUARREL
runnel *n syn* see CREEK 2
running *n syn* see OVERSIGHT 1
running *adj* **1** *syn* see ACTIVE 1
    2 *syn* see EASY 9
running *adv syn* see TOGETHER 2
running mate *n syn* see ASSOCIATE 3
run–of–mine *adj* **1** *syn* see UNREFINED 3
    2 *syn* see MEDIUM
run–of–the–mill *adj* **1** *syn* see MEDIUM
    rel uncommon, unexceptional
    2 *syn* see GENERAL 1
run on *vb syn* see CHAT 1
run out *vb* **1** *syn* see FAIL 2
    2 *syn* see BANISH
run over *vb syn* see OVERFLOW 2
runt *n syn* see DWARF
runted *adj syn* see STUNTED
run through *vb syn* see GO 4
runtish *adj syn* see STUNTED
runty *adj syn* see STUNTED
run up *vb* **1** *syn* see INCREASE 2

    2 *syn* see THROW UP 1
rupture *n* **1** *syn* see BREACH 3
    rel division, divorce, parting
    2 *syn* see SEPARATION 1
rupture *vb* **1** *syn* see OPEN 3
    rel divide, divorce, part, separate, sunder; cleave, rend, rive, split
    2 *syn* see SEPARATE 1
rural *adj* relating to or characteristic of the country <a peaceful *rural* scene>
    syn agrestic, bucolic, campestral, countrified, country, out-country, outland, pastoral, provincial, rustic
    rel arcadian, idyllic; natural, simple, unsophisticated
    con metropolitan, municipal, oppidan; crammed, crowded, packed, populous; bustling, busy, hustling; artificial, mundane, sophisticated, worldly
    ant urban; citified
ruse *n syn* see TRICK 1
rush *vb* **1** to move or cause to move quickly, impetuously, and often heedlessly <*rushed* around madly trying to get things done>
    syn boil, bolt, charge, chase, dash, fling, lash, race, shoot, ‖swither, tear; *compare* COURSE, HURRY 2, PLUNGE 2, STAMPEDE 2
    rel hasten, hurry, speed; dart, fly, scud; break
    idiom go off half-cocked, not look before one leaps
    2 *syn* see HURRY 2
    3 *syn* see COURSE
rush *n* **1** *syn* see HASTE 2
    2 *syn* see FLOW
rushing *adj syn* see PRECIPITATE 1
rushlight *n syn* see NONENTITY
rustic *adj syn* see RURAL
rustic *n* an inhabitant of a rural or remote area who is usually characterized by an utter lack of sophistication and cultivation <an unbelieving *rustic* gawking at the skyscrapers>
    syn ‖apple knocker, ‖backwoodser, backwoodsman, bucolic, bumpkin, chawbacon, clodhopper, clown, country jake, countryman, greenhorn, hayseed, hick, hillbilly, hillman, ‖hodge, hoosier, jake, jay, joskin, mossback, mountaineer, peasant, provincial, redneck, ‖ridge runner, rube, ‖wayback, woodsy, yap, ‖yob, yokel
    rel rural; exurbanite, suburbanite; agriculturalist, farmer, granger, husbandman
    con burgher, oppidan, townsman; cityite, urbanite; cosmopolitan, cosmopolite
    ant city slicker
rustle *n syn* see HASTE 1
rustler *n syn* see HUSTLER 1
rusty *adj syn* see HARSH 3
‖rusty *adj syn* see ILL-TEMPERED
rut *n syn* see ROUTINE
ruth *n* **1** *syn* see PITY
    2 *syn* see PENITENCE
ruthful *adj syn* see WOEFUL 1
ruthless *adj syn* see GRIM 3
ruttish *adj syn* see LUSTFUL 2
‖ruttle *vb syn* see RATTLE 1
rutty *adj syn* see LUSTFUL 2

sable *adj syn* see BLACK 1
  rel dark, dusky, murky; gloomy, somber
sabotage *n* willful effort by indirect means to hinder, prevent, undo, or discredit (as a plan or activity) <*sabotage* of the project by disgruntled officials>
  syn subversion, undermining, wreckage, wrecking
  rel subversiveness, subversivism; damage, impairment, injury
sabotage *vb* to practice sabotage on <*sabotaged* his opponent's campaign with rumors and smears>
  syn subvert, undermine, wreck
  rel frustrate, hamper, hinder; block, obstruct; damage; break up, destroy
  idiom throw a monkey wrench into
  con assist, back, support
saccharine *adj syn* see INGRATIATING
  rel candied, cloying, honeyed, oversweet, sugar-candy, sugar-coated, sugared, sugary, sweet, syrupy
sacerdotal *adj* of, relating to, or belonging to priests or priesthood <*sacerdotal* vestments>
  syn hieratic, priestal, priestish, priestlike, priestly, sacerdotical
  rel churchly, ecclesiastical, religious; clerical, ministerial; apostolic, papal
sacerdotical *adj syn* see SACERDOTAL
sack *n syn* see BAG 1
  rel container; pocket
sack *vb syn* see DISMISS 3
  rel expel, ship; ‖bump, ‖chuck
  idiom give one the sack, send packing
sack *vb syn* see RAVAGE
  rel forage, raid; strip
sacker *n syn* see MARAUDER
sacred *adj* **1** *syn* see HOLY 1
  rel sacramental; angelic, godly, saintly; cherished
  con lay, secular, temporal; earthly; unhallowed
  ant profane
  2 dedicated to or hallowed by association with a deity <*sacred* songs>
  syn numinous, spiritual; *compare* HOLY 1
  rel hallowed, sanctified
  3 protected (as by law, custom, or human respect) against abuse <a fund *sacred* to charity>
  syn inviolable, inviolate, sacrosanct
  rel defended, guarded, protected, shielded; immune, untouchable
Sacred Writ *n syn* see BIBLE
  idiom Good Book
sacrifice *n syn* see VICTIM 1
  rel burnt offering, oblation; sacrification; hecatomb; sin offering
sacrifice *vb* **1** to offer as a victim in sacrifice <Abraham about to *sacrifice* Isaac>
  syn immolate, victimize
  rel offer (up); consecrate, dedicate, devote; donate, give, yield
  2 *syn* see LOSE 1
  idiom kiss good-bye
  3 *syn* see FORGO
  rel cede, yield
  idiom part with
sacrilege *n syn* see PROFANATION
  rel irreverence; heresy; crime, impiety, offense, sin
sacrilegious *adj* involving or marked by debasement or defilement of what is sacred <*sacrilegious* despoilers of ancient churches>
  syn blasphemous, profane
  rel impious, irreverent, ungodly; evil, sinful, wicked; irreligious
  con godly, pious, reverent; religious
sacrosanct *adj syn* see SACRED 3
  rel esteemed, regarded, respected
sad *adj* **1** affected with or expressing sadness <was *sad* to see him go>
  syn heavyhearted, melancholy, mournful, saddened, sorry, unhappy; *compare* DOWNCAST, MELANCHOLY 2

  rel blue, dejected, dispirited, down, downbeat, downcast, drear, dumpish, dumpy; grieving, unenjoying; depressed, morose; depressing, dismal, joyless, mirthless, saddening, triste; desolate
  con happy, joyful, joyous; blithe, gay, lighthearted; exalted, fired, inspired, uplifted
  ant glad
  2 causing sadness <felt miserable after listening to that *sad* song>
  syn depressing, joyless, melancholic, melancholy, mournful, saddening, triste; *compare* MELANCHOLY 2
  rel dismal, gloomy; afflicting, doleful, dreary, lamentable, sorrowful; pathetic, tear-jerking
  con bright, gay, lively; exhilarating, heartwarming, stimulating, stirring
  ant happy
sadden *vb syn* see DEPRESS 2
  idiom make blue, ‖put into a funk
  ant gladden
saddened *adj syn* see SAD 1
saddening *adj syn* see SAD 2
saddle *vb syn* see BURDEN
  rel hamper, impede, restrict; impose, inflict
  idiom hang like a millstone around one's neck
sadness *n* the quality, state, or an instance of being sad <her feelings of *sadness* and longing persisted long after he left>
  syn blues, dejection, depression, dinge, (the) dismals, (the) dolefuls, dumps, dysphoria, gloom, heavyheartedness, melancholy, mopes, mournfulness, suds, unhappiness
  rel dispiritedness, doldrums, downcastness, downheartedness, downs, ‖funk, listlessness, moodiness; anguish, grief, sorrow, sorrowfulness, woe; desolation, disconsolateness, disconsolation, forlornness, misery, mourning; blue devils, despondency, hopelessness, megrims, melancholia
  idiom slough of despond
  con happiness, joy, joyfulness, joyousness; cheerfulness, cheeriness, gayness, lightheartedness, liveliness; exhilaration, ups
  ant gladness
safe *adj* **1** having been freed from risk, danger, harm, or injury <refugees who found themselves *safe* at last in a neutral country>
  syn scatheless, unharmed, unscathed
  rel unhurt, uninjured; intact
  idiom in (or with) a whole skin, out of harm's way, safe and sound
  con damaged, harmed, hurt, injured
  ant unsafe
  2 affording security from threat of harm, injury, risk, or loss <found a *safe* place to hide>
  syn riskless, secure
  rel guarding, protecting, safeguarding, sheltering, shielding; defended, guarded, protected, sheltered, shielded; unthreatened; impregnable, inviolable, invulnerable, unassailable
  idiom safe as a bank vault
  con insecure, undefended, unguarded, unprotected, vulnerable; threatened; hazardous, risky
  ant dangerous, unsafe
  3 not threatening danger <it's *safe* to go there only in the daytime>
  syn healthy, uninjurious, wholesome; *compare* HARMLESS
  rel innocent, innocuous, inoffensive
  con hazardous, perilous, precarious, risky; harmful, injurious, unhealthy
  ant dangerous, unsafe
  4 *syn* see CAUTIOUS
safeguard *n syn* see DEFENSE 1
  rel palladium; buffer, screen

---

syn synonym(s)   *rel* related word(s)
ant antonym(s)   *con* contrasted word(s)
idiom idiomatic equivalent(s)
‖ use limited; if in doubt, see a dictionary

safeguard *vb syn* see DEFEND 1
 rel conserve, preserve, save; assure, ensure, insure
safekeeping *n* **1** *syn* see CUSTODY
 2 *syn* see PRESERVATION 1
safeness *n syn* see SAFETY
safety *n* the quality, state, or condition of being safe <there's *safety* in numbers>
 syn assurance, safeness, security
 rel cover, protection, shelter; defense; impregnability, inviolability, invulnerability
 con hazard, jeopardy, peril, risk, threat; instability, vulnerability
 ant danger
sag *vb* **1** *syn* see SLIP 6
 2 *syn* see DROOP 3
 rel bend, decline; dangle, flap, flop
 idiom ‖have a case of the sags
 ant tauten
sag *n* **1** *syn* see DEPRESSION 2
 rel settling, sinking
 2 *syn* see DECLINE 3
sagacious *adj* **1** *syn* see WISE 1
 rel clever, intelligent, smart; far-seeing; judicious, prudent, sapient
 idiom wise as an owl
 con dumb, stupid, unintelligent; ignorant, unlearned, untaught; unperceptive, unwise
 2 *syn* see SHREWD
 rel critical, discerning, discriminating
 idiom wise in the ways of the world
sagaciousness *n syn* see SAGACITY
 rel judgment, wiseness
sagacity *n* intelligent application of knowledge <*sagacity* acquired from years of learning and experience>
 syn insight, sagaciousness, sageness, sapience, wisdom
 rel discernment, penetration, perception, perceptiveness, sensitivity; understanding; judiciousness, prudence; comprehension, grasp
sage *adj* **1** *syn* see WISE 1
 rel philosophic; learned; profound
 2 *syn* see WISE 2
 rel acute, penetrating, probing
sage *n* one distinguished for his breadth of knowledge, experience, wisdom, and sound judgment <was one of the renowned *sages* of constitutional law>
 syn savant, scholar, wise man
 rel expert, master
sageness *n syn* see SAGACITY
said *adj syn* see SUCH 1
sail *vb* **1** *syn* see FLY 1
 2 *syn* see FLY 4
sailor *n syn* see MARINER
sailorman *n syn* see MARINER
saintliness *n syn* see HOLINESS
 rel righteousness, worthiness
saintly *adj* being of deeply religious and wholly upright character <a *saintly* old couple>
 syn angelic, godly, holy
 rel righteous, upright, upstanding, virtuous, worthy; devout, God-fearing, pious; sainted; seraph, seraphic, seraphlike
 idiom pure in mind and heart
salable *adj syn* see MARKETABLE
 ant unsalable
salacious *adj syn* see LICENTIOUS 2
salad *n syn* see MISCELLANY 1
salary *n syn* see WAGE
salient *adj syn* see NOTICEABLE
 rel important, pertinent, significant, weighty; impressive, moving; obvious, pronounced; intrusive, obtrusive
saliferous *adj syn* see SALTY 1
saline *adj syn* see SALTY 1
saliva *n* a liquid secreted into the mouth and helpful to digestion <*saliva* drooled down the baby's chin>
 syn slaver, spit, spittle, water
 rel sputum
salivate *vb syn* see DROOL 2
sally *n* **1** *syn* see OUTBURST 1
 2 *syn* see JOKE 1
 3 *syn* see EXCURSION 1

salmagundi *n syn* see MISCELLANY 1
salon *n* **1** a spacious elegant apartment or living room (as in a fashionable house) <her *salon* was decorated à la Louis XV>
 syn drawing room, saloon
 rel parlor; suite
 2 a fashionable assemblage of notables held by custom at the home of a prominent person <was famous for her literary *salons*>
 syn saloon
 rel at home; reception; levee; evening, soiree
saloon *n* **1** *syn* see SALON 1
 rel gallery; hall
 2 *syn* see SALON 2
 rel gathering, party
 3 *syn* see BAR 5
saloonist *n syn* see SALOONKEEPER
saloonkeeper *n* one who owns or manages a bar <the traditional image of the fat cigar-smoking *saloonkeeper*>
 syn barkeeper, boniface, innholder, innkeeper, ‖publican, saloonist, taverner; *compare* BARTENDER
 rel victualler
salt *n* **1** *syn* see LIVING
 2 *syn* see MARINER
salt *adj syn* see SALTY 1
saltate *vb syn* see JUMP 1
salt away *vb syn* see SAVE 4
saltimbanque *n syn* see CHARLATAN
 rel impostor, pretender; cheat, fraud
salty *adj* **1** of, relating to, or containing salt <*salty* deposits>
 syn saliferous, saline, salt
 rel brackish, briny, saltish; salted
 ant saltless
 2 *syn* see RISQUÉ
 3 *syn* see CAUSTIC 1
salubrious *adj syn* see HEALTHFUL
 rel bracing, invigorating, stimulating
 ant insalubrious
salutary *adj syn* see HEALTHFUL
 rel restorative, sanative, sanatory, tonic
 con debilitating, enfeebling, weakening; bad, evil
 ant deleterious; unsalutary
salutation *n* **1** *syn* see GREETING
 2 *syn* see ENCOMIUM
salute *vb syn* see ADDRESS 7
salute *n syn* see GREETING
salutiferous *adj syn* see HEALTHFUL
salvage *vb* to rescue and save from wreckage, destruction, or loss <*salvaged* the torpedoed vessel>
 syn salve
 rel deliver, redeem, rescue, save; reclaim, recover, regain, retrieve; ransom
 con dump, jettison
salvation *n* **1** *syn* see PRESERVATION 1
 2 *syn* see CONSERVATION 1
salve *n syn* see OINTMENT
 rel emollient, lubricant; counterirritant; aid, remedy
salve *vb syn* see SALVAGE
salvo *n* **1** *syn* see BARRAGE
 rel discharge; spray
 2 *syn* see TESTIMONIAL 3
same *adj* **1** being one rather than another or more <went to the *same* hotel each summer>
 syn exact, identical, selfsame, very
 rel comparable, like, similar
 ant different
 2 agreeing fundamentally or absolutely <all the family have the *same* dark eyes>
 syn duplicate, equal, equivalent, identic, identical, indistinguishable, tantamount; *compare* LIKE
 rel comparable, like, similar; coequal
 ant different
 3 not changing or fluctuating <treated everyone with the *same* courtesy>
 syn consistent, constant, invariable, unchanging, unfailing, unvarying
 con changeable, fluctuant, inconsistent, inconstant, irregular, variable, varying
sameness *n* **1** *syn* see IDENTITY 1

rel alikeness; uniformity, uniformness, unity
2 syn see EQUIVALENCE
rel analogy; resemblance, similarity
sample *n syn* see INSTANCE
rel indication, sign; fragment, part, piece, portion, segment; constituent, element; individual, unit
sampling *n syn* see INSTANCE
sanative *adj syn* see CURATIVE
rel healthful, hygienic, salutary, sanitary
sanatory *adj syn* see CURATIVE
sanctified *adj syn* see HOLY 1
rel canonized, deified, sainted
ant unsanctified
sanctify *vb syn* see BLESS 1
sanctimonious *adj syn* see HYPOCRITICAL
rel deceiving, false; snuffling
ant unsanctimonious
sanctimoniousness *n syn* see HYPOCRISY
idiom odor of sanctity
ant unsanctimoniousness
sanctimony *n syn* see HYPOCRISY
sanction *n* **1** explicit authoritative permission or recognition that gives validity to acts of a subordinate <a colonial governor acting under the *sanction* of the king>
syn endorsement, fiat
rel approval, authorization, consent, permission; approbation, confirmation, encouragement, ratification, recommendation, support
con restraint; debarment; interdict, prohibition; disapprobation, disapproval, objection
ant interdiction
2 syn see PERMISSION
sanction *vb syn* see APPROVE 2
rel authorize, commission, license
con ban, disallow, forbid, prohibit
ant interdict
sanctioned *adj syn* see ORTHODOX 1
ant unsanctioned
sanctity *n syn* see HOLINESS
rel godliness; righteousness, uprightness
sanctorium *n syn* see SHRINE
sanctuary *n* **1 syn** see SHRINE
2 syn see SHELTER 1
rel bamah; oasis
3 syn see REFUGE 1
sanctum *n syn* see SHRINE
sand *n syn* see FORTITUDE
rel chutzpah, gall
idiom true (or clear) grit
sandwich shop *n syn* see EATING HOUSE
sane *adj* **1 syn** see HEALTHY 1
2 free from mental disorder <a thoroughly *sane* and well-balanced man>
syn all there, compos mentis, lucid, normal, right
rel balanced, oriented; levelheaded, rational, sensible, sober, sound
idiom of sound mind
con abnormal, unbalanced; neurotic, paranoid, psychopathic, psychotic, schizophrenic; balmy, crazy, ‖cuckoo, non compos, non compos mentis, nuts, screwy; deranged, lunatic, mad, wild
ant insane
3 syn see WISE 2
rel logical, rational, reasonable; good, right; cogent, compelling, convincing, sound
con imprudent, injudicious, unwise
saneness *n syn* see WIT 2
rel clear-mindedness, perception; comprehension, ‖smarts, understanding
sangfroid *n syn* see EQUANIMITY
rel self-containment, self-control; aloofness, coolheadedness, indifference, unconcern
sanguinary *adj* **1 syn** see MURDEROUS
2 syn see BLOODY 1
ant unsanguinary
sanguine *adj* **1 syn** see BLOODY 1
2 syn see MURDEROUS
3 syn see RUDDY
4 syn see CONFIDENT 1

rel expectant; hopeful, undespairing
idiom full of hope
ant hopeless
5 syn see OPTIMISTIC
ant unsanguine
sanguineness *n syn* see OPTIMISM
sanguineous *adj* **1 syn** see BLOODY 1
2 syn see MURDEROUS
sanguinity *n syn* see OPTIMISM
sanity *n syn* see WIT 2
rel intelligence; comprehension
idiom sound mind
ant insanity
sans *prep syn* see WITHOUT 2
sap *n syn* see FOOL 3
sap *vb syn* see WEAKEN 1
rel deplete, drain, exhaust, knock out; ruin, wreck; destroy
saphead *n syn* see FOOL 3
rel ‖boob, jerk
sapid *adj syn* see PALATABLE
idiom fit for a king
con bland, tasteless; repulsive, unpalatable
ant insipid
sapidity *n syn* see TASTE 3
ant insipidity
sapience *n syn* see SAGACITY
sapient *adj syn* see WISE 2
rel erudite, learned, scholarly; thinking; discriminating, sapiential
sapless *adj syn* see INSIPID 3
sapor *n syn* see TASTE 3
saporous *adj syn* see PALATABLE
sappy *adj syn* ‖**1 syn** SUCCULENT, juicy
2 syn see SENTIMENTAL
3 syn see FOOLISH 2
sarcasm *n* a savage bitter form of humor usually intended to hurt or wound <a speech full of personal jabs and *sarcasm*>
syn acerbity, causticity, corrosiveness, sarcasticness
rel humor, irony, raillery, satire, wit; jest, repartee; gibe, lampooning; mockery, ridicule, scorn, sneering; acrimony, invective; rancor, sharpness
con playfulness, waggishness, whimsicality
sarcastic *adj* marked by, expressive of, or given to sarcasm <a critic noted for his *sarcastic* comments on actors' performances>
syn acerb, acerbic, archilochian, caustic, corrosive, ‖sarky; compare CAUSTIC 1
rel dry; cynical, ironic, sardonic, satiric; jeering, mocking, scornful; biting, cutting, incisive; mordant, scathing, sharp, stinging; pungent, tart, trenchant
con droll, playful, sportive, waggish, whimsical
sarcasticness *n syn* see SARCASM
rel bitingness, cuttingness, incisiveness, trenchancy; derision, mocking, taunting
sardonic *adj* characterized by or expressing disdainful, skeptical humor <had a *sardonic* smile that mirrored his fixed expectation of the worst from everyone>
syn cynical, ironic, wry
rel contemptuous, disdainful, scornful; derisive, jeering, mocking, saturnine, sneering; caustic, corrosive, sarcastic, satiric
‖**sarky** *adj syn* see SARCASTIC
sash *n syn* see BELT 1
sashay *vb* to move about often self-consciously and usually in a conspicuous manner <*sashaying* around, trying to walk like a model>
syn flounce, mince, prance, ‖prink, strut
rel swagger
sass *n syn* see BACK TALK
rel impertinence, insolence, sassiness
sassy *adj* **1 syn** see WISE 5
rel brazen, unabashed; audacious
2 syn see DAPPER
Satan *n* **1 syn** see DEVIL 1

---

syn synonym(s)   *rel* related word(s)
ant antonym(s)   *con* contrasted word(s)
idiom idiomatic equivalent(s)
‖ use limited; if in doubt, see a dictionary

rel deuce; Mephistopheles; devil-god
idiom fallen angel, lord of the underworld, prince of darkness
2 syn see DEVIL 2
rel renegade, villain; beast, viper

satanic *adj* **1** of, relating to, or characteristic of Satan < *Satanic* rites >
syn devilish, diabolic, Mephistophelian
rel saturnine
2 syn see FIENDISH
rel evil, wicked

satanism *n* the worship of Satan usually marked by the travesty of Christian rites < interpreted *satanism* as an offshoot of the belief in two coequal and coeternal principles of good and evil >
syn diabolism
rel Black Mass

sate *vb syn* see SATIATE
rel overfill, overstuff, stuff
idiom have (*or* give) a bellyful of, have (*or* give) an overdose of

sated *adj syn* see SATIATED
ant unsated

satellite *n syn* see FOLLOWER
rel favorite, minion

satellite *adj syn* see CONCOMITANT

satiate *adj syn* see SATIATED
idiom stuffed to the gills
con insatiable, unsatiable
ant insatiate, unsatiate

satiate *vb* to satisfy fully or to repletion < tried to titillate rather than *satiate* his readers' interest >
syn cloy, fill, glut, gorge, jade, pall, sate, ‖stall, stodge, surfeit; *compare* SATISFY 3
rel content, fulfill, gratify, indulge, satisfy; overdose, stuff
con coax, court, invite, pique, tantalize, tempt, titillate

satiated *adj* filled to repletion < the mob, *satiated* with violence, finally dispersed >
syn full, glutted, gorged, jaded, sated, satiate, surfeited
rel fulfilled, gratified, indulged, satisfied
con avid, greedy, ravening; craving, hungering, hungry, lusting, thirsting, thirsty
ant unsatiated

satiny *adj syn* see SOFT 3

satire *n* humorous ridicule often used to convey rebuke or criticism or to expose folly or vice < a brilliant writer noted for his *satire* >
syn lampoonery, raillery, satiricalness
rel banter, chaffing; causticity, irony; mockery, ridicule; pasquinade, persiflage, squib; parody, spoof, spoofery, takeoff

satiric *adj* of, relating to, characterized by, or based on satire < witty, eloquent, and *satiric* sermons >
syn lampooning, satirizing
rel bantering, chaffing; caustic, ironic; mocking, ridiculing; parodying, spoofing; farcical; Rabelaisian

satiricalness *n syn* see SATIRE

satirizing *adj syn* see SATIRIC

satisfactorily *adv syn* see WELL 4
rel competently, sufficiently
ant unsatisfactorily

satisfactory *adj* **1 syn** see SUFFICIENT 1
ant unsatisfactory
2 syn see VALID
ant unsatisfactory
3 syn see DECENT 4
rel fair, goodish, passable
ant unsatisfactory

satisfy *vb* **1 syn** see CLEAR 5
2 syn see SUIT 6
3 to satiate desires or longings < strove to *satisfy* his lust for money and power >
syn appease, content, gratify; *compare* SATIATE
rel gladden, humor, indulge, please; sate, satiate; pacify, placate
con tantalize, tease; excite, pique, provoke, stimulate; arouse
4 syn see ASSURE 2
rel induce, inveigle, win (over)
5 measure up to a set of criteria or requirements < courses taken to *satisfy* requirements for graduation >
syn answer, fill, fulfill, meet
rel comply (with), conform (to); serve; do, suffice
idiom fill the bill, make good

satisfying *adj syn* see VALID
ant unsatisfying

satisfyingly *adv syn* see WELL 5
rel gratifyingly, pleasingly
ant unsatisfyingly

saturate *vb* **1 syn** see SOAK 1
rel bathe, douche, wash; imbue, infuse, suffuse
2 syn see PERMEATE
rel pierce, probe; inoculate, instill

saturate *adj syn* see WET 1

saturated *adj syn* see WET 1

saturnalia *n syn* see ORGY 2

saturnine *adj syn* see SULLEN
rel grave, serious, solemn, somber, staid; moping; dark, funereal; reserved, silent, taciturn, uncommunicative
con cheerful, cheery, happy; cordial, polite
ant genial

satyric *adj* **1 syn** see LICENTIOUS 2
2 syn see LUSTFUL 2

sauce *n* **1 syn** see BACK TALK
rel pertness, sauciness
‖**2 syn** see LIQUOR 2

saucebox *n syn* see MINX

saucy *adj* **1** flippant and bold in manner or attitude < a *saucy* little flirt >
syn arch, bantam, ‖cocket, malapert, pert
rel flippant, frivolous, light-minded, volatile; bold, brash, combative; impertinent, impudent, insolent; intrusive, meddlesome, obtrusive; smart, smart-alecky, wise
con gentle, meek, mild, quiet, subdued
ant deferential
2 syn see INSOLENT 2

sault *n syn* see WATERFALL

saunter *vb* to walk slowly in an idle or leisurely manner < *sauntered* about the streets, stopping in at various shops >
syn amble, bummel, drift, linger, mope, mosey, ‖muck, stroll; *compare* WANDER 1
rel meander, ramble, roam, rove, spatiate, ‖stravage, wander; loiter, tarry
con bustle, chase, hustle, scurry, tear

saunter *n syn* see WALK 1

savage *adj* **1** being undomesticated and often destructive or ferocious through lack of restraints or human control < *savage* dogs >
syn feral, vicious, wild; *compare* WILD 1
rel uncivilized, undomesticated, unsocialized; unbroken, unsubdued, untamed; bestial, brutal, brute; ferocious, fierce
con civilized, domesticated, socialized; broken, subdued, tamed; domestic, tame
2 syn see FIERCE 1
rel coldhearted, heartless, implacable, relentless, unrelenting; rapacious, ravenous, voracious; bloodthirsty, bloody, butcherly, murderous, rabid
3 syn see BARBARIAN 1
rel primeval, primitive; uncontrolled, unharnessed; harsh, rough, rugged

savant *n syn* see SAGE

save *vb* **1 syn** see RESCUE
rel unchain, unshackle
idiom snatch from the jaws of death
con desert, leave; condemn, damn
2 syn see MAINTAIN 1
3 to keep secure or maintain intact from injury, decay, or loss < regular painting helps *save* the wood >
syn conserve, preserve; *compare* MAINTAIN 1
rel defend, guard, protect, safeguard, shield
con draw (out), withdraw; consume, spend, use up
4 to accumulate and store up (a supply) for future use < *saved* his money for college >
syn lay aside, lay away, lay by, lay in, lay up, put by, salt away, ‖spare; *compare* HOARD
rel accumulate, cache, collect, stockpile, store (up); hoard, squirrel, stash (away); conserve, husband, manage; keep, reserve, set by; deposit, stow
idiom feather one's nest, keep as a nest egg, save for a rainy day, save to fall back on
con lose, squander, use up, waste
ant consume, spend

5 *syn* see ECONOMIZE

save *prep syn* see EXCEPT

save *conj* **1** *syn* see ONLY

2 *syn* see EXCEPT 1

save–all *adj syn* see STINGY

saving *n* **1** *syn* see PRESERVATION 1

2 *syn* see CONSERVATION 1

saving *prep syn* see EXCEPT

saving *conj syn* see EXCEPT 1

saving *adj syn* see SPARING

savoir faire *n syn* see TACT
rel manners; dignity, elegance, grace; refinement, savoir vivre, taste; aplomb, confidence, self-assurance, self-possession; experience, blaséness, sophistication
con awkwardness, clumsiness, gaucherie, ineptness, maladroitness

savor *n* **1** *syn* see TASTE 3
rel scent, tinge
2 *syn* see QUALITY 1

savor *vb* **1** *syn* see SMACK
2 *syn* see FEEL 2
3 *syn* see RELISH 2

savorless *adj syn* see UNPALATABLE 1
rel bland; thin, watery, weak; unpleasing
con appetizing, pleasing, tempting; piquant, spicy
ant savory

savorous *adj syn* see PALATABLE

savorsome *adj syn* see PALATABLE

savory *adj* **1** *syn* see PALATABLE
rel pleasing, tempting; gustful
con acrid, sharp, strong
ant unsavory
2 *syn* see SWEET 2

║savvy *adj syn* see SHREWD

saw *n syn* see SAYING

║sawbones *n syn* see PHYSICIAN

sawbuck *n syn* see SAWHORSE

saw–edged *adj syn* see SERRATE

sawhorse *n* a rack on which something (as a board) is laid for sawing <*sawhorses* in the carpentry shop>
syn buck, horse, sawbuck, trestle, workhorse

sawtooth *adj syn* see SERRATE

saw–toothed *adj syn* see SERRATE

say *vb* **1** to express in words <learn to *say* what you mean>
syn bring out, chime in, come out (with), declare, deliver, state, tell, throw out, utter; *compare* EXPRESS 2
rel breathe; articulate, enunciate, pronounce; announce, proclaim; animadvert, comment, give, remark; cite, quote, recite, repeat; affirm, assert, aver, avow, protest
idiom out with, put in (*or* into) words, put it
2 *syn* see ARTICULATE 2
rel speak, talk
3 *syn* see SHOW 5

say *n syn* see VOICE 2
rel authority; decision

say *adv syn* see NEARLY

saying *n* an oft-repeated statement usually involving common experience or observation <the old *saying* that ignorance is bliss>
syn adage, byword, proverb, saw, word
rel dictum, maxim; truism

say–so *n syn* see VOICE 2

scabrous *adj syn* see ROUGH 1
rel scabby, scaly, scurfy; downy; knobby, knotty; bristly, prickly, thorny
con bald, glabrescent
ant glabrous, smooth

scad *n, usu* **scads** *pl* a great number or abundance <*scads* of opportunities>
syn gob(s), heap, jillion, load(s), million, oodles, quantities, ream(s), ║rimption(s), slather(s), slew, thousand, trillion, wad(s); *compare* MUCH, MULTITUDE 1
rel great deal, lot
con few, handful, scattering, sprinkle, sprinkling

scalawag *n syn* see SCAMP

scalding *adj syn* see HOT 1
ant freezing

scale *vb* **1** *syn* see SKIN 2

2 to shed scales or fragmentary surface matter <*scaling* skin>
syn desquamate, exfoliate, flake (off), peel
rel chip (off), spall (off)

scale *n syn* see DEGREE 2

scale *vb* **1** *syn* see ASCEND 1
2 *syn* see MEASURE 2

║scamble *vb syn* see SPRAWL 1

scamp *n* a pleasantly mischievous person <what have those little *scamps* done now>
syn devil, enfant terrible, limb, mischief, pixie, rapscallion, rascal, ribald, rogue, scalawag, skeezicks, slyboots, villain
rel bird, chap, dog, ║duck; ║bleeder; joker, prankster
con sobersides

scamper *vb* **1** *syn* see RUN 2
rel hasten (off), hurry (away *or* off), light out, speed (away); dash (off), rush (off), shoot, tear (off), whip (off), whiz (off)
2 *syn* see RUN 1
rel scud, scuddle, scuttle

scan *vb syn* see BROWSE
idiom pass one's eye over

scan *n syn* see EXAMINATION
rel perusal; observation, reconnaissance

scandal *n syn* see DETRACTION
rel aspersion; reproach; discredit, disrepute

║scandal *vb syn* see MALIGN

scandalize *vb* **1** *syn* see MALIGN
2 *syn* see SHOCK 1

scandalizer *n syn* see GOSSIP 1
rel blabber, blabbermouth, talker

scandalmonger *n syn* see GOSSIP 1
rel meddler, snoop; backbiter; muckraker

scandalous *adj* **1** *syn* see LIBELOUS
2 *syn* see OUTRAGEOUS 2

║scant *n syn* see SCARCITY

scant *adj* **║1** *syn* see STINGY
2 *syn* see SHORT 3
3 *syn* see MEAGER 2
ant ample

scant *vb syn* see SPARE 3

scantiness *n syn* see FAILURE 3
rel scarceness, scarcity; sparseness, sparsity
con excess, overage, surplus

scanty *adj* **1** *syn* see MEAGER 2
rel scarce, wanting
con ample, enough; profuse
ant plentiful
2 *syn* see SHORT 3

scape *vb syn* see ESCAPE 1

║scape *n syn* see ESCAPE 1

scape *n syn* see VISTA

scapegoat *n* one that bears the blame for another or others <was made the *scapegoat* for his boss's errors>
syn fall guy, goat, patsy, whipping boy
rel mark, target; victim

scapegrace *n syn* see WASTREL 1

scar *n* a mark left by the healing of injured tissue <still had *scars* from the operation>
syn cicatrix, scarification
rel blemish, defect, flaw; blister, pockmark, scab; disfigurement

scar *vb* to mark with a scar <burns that had *scarred* his face>
syn cicatrize, scarify
rel cut, score, scratch; blemish, disfigure, flaw, mar; damage, deface

scarce *adj* **1** *syn* see SHORT 3
rel curtailed, shortened, truncated
con adequate, sufficient, unwanting
ant abundant
2 *syn* see INFREQUENT
idiom scarce as ice water in hell, scarcer than hen's teeth, seldom met with

scarce *adv syn* see JUST 2

scarcely *adv syn* see JUST 2
idiom just barely, only just

---

syn synonym(s)   *rel* related word(s)
ant antonym(s)   *con* contrasted word(s)
idiom idiomatic equivalent(s)
║ use limited; if in doubt, see a dictionary

scarceness *n syn* see SCARCITY

scarcity *n* smallness of supply, quantity, or number in proportion to demand <a serious *scarcity* of grain>
syn insufficience, insufficiency, paucity, poverty, ‖scant, scarceness; *compare* FAILURE 3
rel deficiency, shortage, underage; meagerness; rareness, uncommonness; absence, dearth, lack
con sufficiency; great deal, much; overabundance, overage, oversupply, surplus
ant abundance

scare *vb syn* see FRIGHTEN
rel panic, shake up; freeze, paralyze, petrify
idiom give a scare to, strike terror into the heart of, throw a scare into

scarecrow *n syn* see RAGAMUFFIN

scared *adj syn* see AFRAID 1
rel startled; panicked, panicky, terror-stricken
con emboldened, heartened, reassured; aggressive, bold
ant unafraid, unscared

scarification *n syn* see SCAR

scarify *vb* 1 *syn* see SCAR
rel deform, disfigure, maim, mar
2 *syn* see LAMBASTE 3

scary *adj syn* see AFRAID 1

scathe *vb syn* see LAMBASTE 3
idiom ‖give holy hell, give the business, rip (someone) up one side and down the other

scatheless *n syn* see SAFE 1

scathing *adj syn* see CAUSTIC 1
rel brutal; burning, scorching, searing, sulphurous

scatological *adj syn* see OBSCENE 2

scatter *vb* 1 to cause to separate or break up <the rain *scattered* the crowd>
syn dispel, disperse, dissipate
rel break up, shatter; disband; diverge, divide, part, separate, sever
con assemble, congregate, convene; accumulate, amass, collect, concentrate, crowd
ant gather
2 *syn* see STREW 1
rel dispense, distribute; cast, discard, shed; besprinkle, sprinkle
con accumulate, amass, concentrate
ant collect

scatterbrain *n* a flighty thoughtless person <his wife is a *scatterbrain*>
syn birdbrain, featherbrain, featherhead, flibbertigibbet, harebrain, rattlebrain, rattlehead, shatterbrain
rel fool, goose, silly, simpleton

scatterbrained *adj syn* see GIDDY 1

scattergood *n syn* see SPENDTHRIFT

scattering *n syn* see FEW

scene *n* 1 the total arrangement of the objects that form the scenic environment in which a drama is enacted <spectacle plays that attempt a realistic, three-dimensional *scene*>
syn mise-en-scène, scenery, set, setting, stage set, stage setting
rel hangings, scene cloth; ‖back cloth, backdrop, background; tableau
2 *syn* see VIEW 4
3 the place of an occurrence or action <the *scene* of the crime>
syn locale, mise-en-scène, site
rel locality, location, place, spot
4 a sphere of activity, interest, or controversy <the drug *scene*>
syn arena
rel compass, field, setting, sphere; culture, environment, milieu

scenery *n syn* see SCENE 1
rel decor; furnishings, furniture; properties, props

scent *vb* 1 *syn* see SMELL 1
2 to imbue or fill with an odor <air *scented* with herbs>
syn aromatize, odorize, perfume

scent *n* 1 *syn* see SMELL 1
rel essence, whiff
2 *syn* see FRAGRANCE

scented *adj* 1 *syn* see SWEET 2
2 *syn* see ODOROUS
ant scentless, unscented

scentless *adj syn* see ODORLESS

schedule *n* 1 *syn* see LIST
rel chart, table
2 *syn* see PROGRAM 1

schedule *vb* 1 to place in a schedule <*schedule* a new train>
syn card, sked
rel list, record, slate
2 *syn* see TIME 1

scheme *n* 1 *syn* see PLAN 1
rel presentation, proposal, proposition, suggestion; arrangement, order, ordering; contrivance, device, expedient
2 *syn* see PLOT 2

scheme (out) *vb syn* see PLOT

schism *n* 1 *syn* see BREACH 3
2 *syn* see HERESY
3 a division of a group into two discordant groups <a *schism* within a political party>
syn chasm, cleavage, cleft, split; *compare* BREACH 3
rel divergence, division, separation; breach, break, rupture; estrangement
con unification, unity; reconciliation

schismatic *n syn* see HERETIC
rel protester; skeptic; radical, Young Turk

schismatic *adj syn* see HERETICAL
rel rebellious; unconventional

schismatist *n syn* see HERETIC

‖**schlemiel** *n syn* see FOOL 3

‖**schmo** *n syn* see FOOL 1

‖**schmuck** *n syn* see FOOL 1

‖**schnook** *n syn* see DUNCE

‖**schnorrer** *n syn* see BEGGAR 1

‖**schnozzle** *n syn* see NOSE 1

scholar *n syn* see SAGE
rel pupil, student; bookman; polymath

scholarliness *n syn* see ERUDITION 2
ant unscholarliness

scholarly *adj syn* see LEARNED
rel studious; intellectual, long-hair; educated, taught, trained
con untaught, untrained
ant unscholarly

scholarship *n* 1 *syn* see EDUCATION 2
2 *syn* see ERUDITION 2

scholastic *adj* 1 *syn* see PEDANTIC
rel lettered, literary; scholarly; formal
2 *syn* see LEARNED
rel conversant, versed
con unconversant, unscholarly

school *vb syn* see TEACH
rel inform; guide, lead, show; advance, cultivate; control, direct, manage

schooling *n syn* see EDUCATION 1
rel knowledge; book learning, booklore

schoolmasterish *adj syn* see DIDACTIC

science *n* 1 *syn* see KNOWLEDGE 2
2 *syn* see EDUCATION 2

scilicet *adv syn* see NAMELY

scintillate *vb syn* see FLASH 1

scintillating *adj syn* see CLEVER 5

scintillation *n syn* see FLASH 1

scions *n pl syn* see OFFSPRING

scoff *vb* to show contempt by derision or mockery <heard his tale and *scoffed* at it>
syn fleer, flout, gibe, gird, jeer, jest, quip (at), scout (at), sneer
rel pooh-pooh; deride, mock, rally, ridicule, taunt, twit; contemn, despise, disdain, scorn; boo
con accept, approve, commend; compliment; acclaim, laud, praise

scoff *n syn* see FOOD 1

scold *n syn* see VIRAGO

scold *vb* 1 to reproach angrily and abusively <loudly *scolded* him for staying out late>
syn baste, bawl out, berate, ‖bless out, ‖cample, ‖carpet, ‖chew, ‖chew out, dress down, jaw, lash, ‖mob, rag, rail, rant, rate, ‖ream out, revile, ‖row, tell off, tongue, tongue-lash, ‖tongue-walk, upbraid, vituperate, wig; *compare* CRITICIZE, LAMBASTE 3, REPROVE
rel blame, censure, criticize, denounce, reprehend, reprobate; admonish, chide, rebuke, reprimand, reproach, reprove; execrate, objurgate; brace, grill, harass, hound; blister, excoriate

idiom jump down one's throat, rake over the coals, read one the riot act, walk into
2 *syn* see GRUMBLE 1
sconce *n syn* see HEAD 1
scoop *n* a news story first obtained and reported by only one source (as a newspaper) <the story was a *scoop* by just a few hours>
syn beat, exclusive
scoop *vb* 1 *syn* see DIP 2
rel gather; lift, pick up
2 *syn* see DIG 2
rel gouge, grub
3 to report a news item in advance of competitors <CBS *scooped* NBC on that story>
syn beat
scoot *vb* 1 *syn* see HURRY 2
2 *syn* see RUN 1
3 *syn* see RUN 2
scope *n* 1 *syn* see ROOM 3
2 *syn* see RANGE 2
3 *syn* see BREADTH 2
scopic *adj syn* see EXTENSIVE 1
scopious *adj syn* see EXTENSIVE 1
scorch *vb* 1 *syn* see LAMBASTE 3
2 *syn* see BURN 3
rel seethe, simmer, stew; ‖plot
scorching *adj syn* see HOT 1
idiom scorching hot, sizzling hot
score *n* 1 scores *pl syn* see MULTITUDE 1
2 a slight cut or line made with or as if with a sharp instrument <cut *scores* on the ham before baking it>
syn scotch, scratch
rel line, mark; nick, notch, serration; cut, slit; cleft, furrow, groove, indentation; gash
3 *syn* see BILL 1
4 an obligation or injury kept in mind for future reckoning <had a *score* to settle with him>
syn account
rel grudge
5 the number of points gained by contestants in a game or contest <a record *score* of 263 for 72 holes>
syn tally
rel account, record; summary, total
idiom the final count
score *vb* 1 *syn* see LAMBASTE 3
rel ream out
idiom tear to pieces
2 *syn* see GAIN 1
3 *syn* see SUCCEED 3
scorn *n syn* see DESPITE 1
rel flouting, gibing, jeering, scoffing; derision, mockery, ridicule, taunt, taunting
con consideration, respectfulness
ant respect
scorn *vb syn* see DESPISE
rel flout, gibe, jeer, scoff; mock, ridicule, taunt
idiom hold in utter contempt
con accept, acknowledge, welcome
ant respect
scotch *n syn* see SCORE 2
Scotch *adj syn* see SPARING
scoundrel *n syn* see VILLAIN 1
scour *vb* 1 *syn* see HURRY 2
2 to make a thorough search or examination of <*scoured* the neighborhood for the lost child>
syn beat, comb, finecomb, fine-tooth-comb, forage, grub, rake, ransack, rummage, search
rel rout; look (for), seek; fan, range; rifle; ferret (out), find
idiom beat the bushes, leave no stone unturned, look high and low, look up and down, turn inside out, turn upside down
scour *vb* 1 *syn* see SCRUB 1
2 *syn* see EAT 3
scour *n, usu* scours *pl syn* see DIARRHEA
scourge *n syn* see PLAGUE 1
scourge *vb* 1 *syn* see WHIP 1
rel hit; knout; frail, whop
idiom whip to ribbons
2 *syn* see RAVAGE

3 *syn* see LAMBASTE 3
scout *vb* to explore in order to obtain information <forward observers *scouted* the terrain before the attack>
syn probe, reconnoiter
rel look (over), survey; observe; check out, examine; ‖case, inspect
idiom run reconnaissance
scout *vb* 1 *syn* see RIDICULE
2 *syn* see DESPISE
rel mock, ridicule
scout (at) *vb syn* see SCOFF
scowl *vb syn* see FROWN 1
idiom look black as thunder, pull a face (*or* scowl)
scrabble *vb* 1 *syn* see SCRIBBLE
2 *syn* see SCRAMBLE 1
scrag *vb* 1 *syn* see HANG 2
2 *syn* see KILL 1
3 *syn* see MURDER 1
scraggy *adj* 1 *syn* see ROUGH 1
2 *syn* see LEAN
rel gangling, spindling, spindly; skeletal; dwarfed, scrubby, stunted, undersize
scram *vb syn* see GET OUT 1
idiom ‖beat it, ‖cheese it, ‖get the hell out
scramble *vb* 1 to move or climb hastily on all fours <*scrambled* across the rocks>
syn clamber, scrabble, ‖spartle, ‖sprauchle
rel scurry, scuttle
2 *syn* see SPRAWL 2
scramble *n syn* see CLUTTER 2
rel conglomeration
scrap *n* 1 *syn* see END 4
rel chip, cutting; scrappage, waste
2 *syn* see PARTICLE
scrap *vb syn* see DISCARD
idiom consign to the scrap heap
scrap *n syn* see BRAWL 2
scrap *vb syn* see QUARREL
scrape *vb* 1 to rub or slide against something that is often harsh, rough, or sharp <chalk *scraping* on the blackboard>
syn grate, rasp, scratch
rel graze, rub, scuff; abrade, chafe, grind
2 *syn* see SCRIMP
3 to make one's way with great difficulty or succeed by a narrow margin <the student barely *scraped* through the exam>
syn shave
rel struggle; get along, get by
idiom cut it (*or* the corner) pretty close, have a close shave
scrape *n syn* see PREDICAMENT
rel trouble; discomfiture, embarrassment
scrapping *n syn* see DISPOSAL 2
scrappy *adj* 1 *syn* see QUARRELSOME 2
2 *syn* see BELLIGERENT
scratch *vb* 1 *syn* see SCRAPE 1
rel squeak, squeal
2 *syn* see SCRIBBLE
scratch *n* 1 *syn* see SCORE 2
‖2 *syn* see MONEY
scrawl *vb syn* see SCRIBBLE
rel inscribe; doodle
scrawny *adj syn* see LEAN
idiom just (*or* nothing but) skin and bones
ant brawny
screak *vb syn* see SQUEAL 2
scream *vb* 1 to voice a sudden piercing loud cry often in shock, terror, or pain <*screamed* at the sight of the accident and then fainted>
syn screech, shriek, shrill, squeal; *compare* SHOUT 1
rel screak, squeak; cry, yell; bellow, roar; caterwaul, howl, wail, ‖yawp
idiom let out a scream (*or* shriek *or* screech)
2 *syn* see SQUEAL 2
3 *syn* see YELL 2

---

syn synonym(s)
ant antonym(s)
idiom idiomatic equivalent(s)
‖ use limited; if in doubt, see a dictionary
rel related word(s)
con contrasted word(s)

rel complain, grumble, protest; blare
idiom raise a howl
4 to produce a vivid, blatant, or startling effect <clothes and furnishings that *screamed* nouveau riche>
syn blare, shout, shriek
scream *n syn* see RIOT 2
screech *vb* **1** *syn* see SCREAM 1
rel penetrate, pierce; vent, voice
2 *syn* see SQUEAL 2
screen *vb* **1** *syn* see DEFEND 1
2 *syn* see SHADE
3 to cut off from view by interposing something resembling a screen <*screen* a view with a tall hedge>
syn block out, close, obstruct, shroud, shut off, shut out
rel conceal, hide; separate, wall off; protect, seclude; embosk
idiom throw up a screen
con bare, disclose, expose, open, reveal
4 *syn* see HIDE
rel defend, guard, protect, safeguard, shield; camouflage, cloak, cover up, disguise
5 to examine carefully and methodically in order to separate, select, or eliminate <the personnel department *screened* seventy candidates for ten jobs>
syn sieve, sift; *compare* SORT 2
rel choose, pick out, select; extract, filter (out), riddle, sort (out), winnow (out)
6 *syn* see CENSOR
‖**screeve** *vb syn* see EXUDE
screw *vb* **1** *syn* see CRUMPLE 1
2 *syn* see EXTORT 1
‖**3** *syn* see CHEAT
4 *syn* see SCRIMP
‖**5** *syn* see RUN 2
‖**screw** (up) *vb syn* see BOTCH
rel confuse, muddle, snafu; spoil
screwball *n syn* see CRACKPOT
screwy *adj* ‖**1** *syn* see INTOXICATED 1
2 *syn* see INSANE 1
idiom having a screw loose
scribble *vb* to write or draw hastily or roughly <*scribbled* a quick note to her on his way out>
syn scrabble, scratch, scrawl, squiggle
rel jot (down); scribe, write
scribe *vb syn* see WRITE
scrimmage *n* **1** *syn* see CLASH 2
rel scuffle; fight; free-for-all
2 *syn* see BRAWL 2
scrimp *adj syn* see MEAGER 2
scrimp *vb* to be extremely frugal and parsimonious in an effort to economize <*scrimped* all year to buy that fur coat>
syn pinch, scrape, screw, skimp, ‖skinch, spare, stint; *compare* SPARE 3
rel scamp; scratch; save (up)
idiom pinch pennies
‖**scrimption** *n syn* see PITTANCE
scrimpy *adj* **1** *syn* see MEAGER 2
2 *syn* see SHORT 3
3 *syn* see STINGY
scrimy *adj syn* see STINGY
script *n syn* see HANDWRITING
Scripture *n syn* see BIBLE
scrooch (down) *vb syn* see CROUCH
scrooge *n syn* see MISER
scrub *n syn* see INFERIOR
scrub *vb* **1** to clean by abrasive action <*scrubbed* the pots and pans>
syn scour
rel brush; rub; cleanse, wash; buff, polish
2 *syn* see CANCEL 2
scrubby *adj syn* see SHABBY 1
scruffy *adj syn* see SHABBY 1
scrumptious *adj syn* see DELIGHTFUL
scrunch *vb* **1** *syn* see CHEW 1
2 *syn* see CRUMPLE 1
‖**scrunty** *adj syn* see STUNTED
scruple *n syn* see PARTICLE
scruple *n syn* see QUALM
rel faltering, hesitancy, hesitation, pause; reconsideration, second thought

scruple *vb syn* see DEMUR
rel question; fret, worry
scrupulous *adj* **1** *syn* see UPRIGHT 2
rel fair-minded; strict; upstanding
con questionable; shifty, slippery; dishonorable, unprincipled; dishonest
ant unscrupulous
2 *syn* see CAREFUL 2
rel critical, fastidious
con careless; undiscriminating, unparticular
ant remiss
scrutinize *vb* **1** to look at or over critically and searchingly <the jeweler *scrutinized* the diamonds to see if they were fakes>
syn canvass, ‖case, check over, check up, con, examine, inspect, perlustrate, study, survey, vet, view
rel look over, overlook, peruse, pore (over), scan; consider, contemplate, weigh; penetrate, pierce, probe; analyze, dig (into), dissect; comb
idiom turn a careful (*or* heedful) eye to (*or* on)
2 *syn* see EYE 2
scrutiny *n* **1** *syn* see EXAMINATION
rel look-in, lookover, look-see
2 *syn* see EYE 3
scud *vb syn* see FLY 1
scuddle *vb syn* see SCUTTLE
scuff *vb syn* see SHUFFLE 3
scuffle *vb* **1** *syn* see WRESTLE
rel cuff, scuff
2 *syn* see SHUFFLE 3
scuffle *n syn* see BRAWL 2
‖**sculch** *n syn* see REFUSE
sculp *vb syn* see SCULPTURE
sculpt *vb syn* see SCULPTURE
sculpture *vb* to form an image or representation from solid material (as wood or stone) <*sculptured* a colossal statue of a horse>
syn carve, chisel, sculp, sculpt
rel cast, form; model, mold, shape
scum *n* **1** *syn* see RABBLE 2
idiom scum of the earth
2 *syn* see SNOT 1
scummy *adj syn* see CONTEMPTIBLE
scurf *n syn* see RABBLE 2
scurrile *adj syn* see ABUSIVE
scurrility *n syn* see ABUSE
rel scurrilousness; maligning, traducing, vilification
scurrilous *adj* **1** *syn* see ABUSIVE
rel coarse, gross; filthy, foul; insulting, offending, offensive, outrageous, outraging
2 *syn* see OBSCENE 2
scurry *vb* **1** *syn* see SCUTTLE
2 *syn* see RUN 1
rel shoot, tear; dart, fly; scuffle, skelter
scurvy *adj syn* see CONTEMPTIBLE
rel base, low, vile
scutter *vb syn* see SCUTTLE
rel hasten, hurry, run, speed
scuttle *vb* to move with or as if with short rapidly alternating steps <armies of fiddler crabs *scuttled* across the road>
syn scuddle, scurry, scutter; *compare* RUN 1
rel scoot; scramble; scud
scuttlebutt *n syn* see REPORT 1
sea *n syn* see OCEAN
sea dog *n syn* see PIRATE
seal *n* an adhesive-backed device bearing a symbolic, pictorial, or official design <the *seal* on a diploma>
syn stamp, sticker
seam *n syn* see JOINT 1
rel bond
seaman *n syn* see MARINER
sear *vb* **1** *syn* see DRY 1
2 to burn or scorch with a sudden application of intense heat <*seared* the steaks in the broiler>
syn sizzle
rel scorch, shrivel, parch; burn (up)
search *vb* **1** *syn* see SCOUR 2
rel run down, scout (around), scrimmage, skirmish
idiom search high and low

2 to subject (a person) to a thorough check for concealed or contraband articles < police *searching* the suspects for weapons >
  syn ‖fan, frisk, shake down
  rel check, examine; inspect, look over, scan, scrutinize, study
search (for *or* out) *vb syn* see SEEK 1
  rel pry (out), scout (out)
search *n syn* see PURSUIT 2
searchingly *adv syn* see HARD 4
sea robber *n syn* see PIRATE
sea rover *n syn* see PIRATE
season *n* a particular period of the year < the Christmas *season* >
  syn time
  rel period, term
season *vb syn* see HARDEN 2
  rel discipline, school, train; fit, prepare; case harden, steel
seasonable *adj syn* see TIMELY 1
  rel apropos, pertinent, relevant; appropriate, apt; convenient
  con irrelevant; inappropriate, inapt; ill-timed, inconvenient, inopportune
  ant unseasonable
seasonably *adv syn* see EARLY 1
  ant unseasonably
seasoned *adj syn* see EXPERIENCED
  rel acclimated, acclimatized, hardened, toughened; case-hardened, steeled
  con inexperienced, unpracticed, unskilled, unversed; unacclimated, unacclimatized, unsteeled, untempered, untried
  ant unseasoned
seat *n* **1** *syn* see BUTTOCKS
  2 *syn* see CENTER 2
  rel fulcrum
  3 *syn* see BASE 1
seat *vb* to cause to be seated < an usher *seated* her in the third row >
  syn sit
  rel establish, place, put
seating *n syn* see BASE 1
sea wolf *n syn* see PIRATE
seclude *vb* to remove or separate (oneself or another) from external influences < in the convent she was *secluded* from secular life >
  syn cloister, sequester
  rel retire, separate, withdraw; closet, confine, enclose, immure, isolate; screen, shut off
secluded *adj* disposed to, living in, or characterized by seclusion < *secluded* monks > < they enjoyed *secluded* country living >
  syn cloistered, hermetic, recluse, secluse, seclusive, sequestered
  rel retired, withdrawn; close, hidden, private, screened, shy; alone, isolated, solitary
  con communal, public
secluse *adj syn* see SECLUDED
seclusion *n* the act or condition of secluding or of being secluded < the queen went into *seclusion* when her husband died >
  syn reclusion, retirement, sequestration; *compare* SOLITUDE
  rel detachment, separation, withdrawal; reclusiveness, seclusiveness; privacy, privateness; aloneness, isolation, separateness, solitude
seclusive *adj syn* see SECLUDED
second *n syn* see INSTANT 1
  idiom the flash of an eyelid
secondary *adj* **1** *syn* see SUBORDINATE
  rel accessory, subservient
  con major, prime; first, first-ranking, first-string
  ant primary
  2 formed from something original, primary, or basic < a *secondary* historical analysis based on original archives >
  syn derivate, derivational, derivative, derived
  rel borrowed, secondhand; consequent, resultant, subsequent
  con basic, principle; first, firsthand, original, uncopied, underived
  ant primary
  3 *syn* see MINOR 2
secondary *n syn* see INFERIOR
  rel second fiddle, second-in-command
second childhood *n syn* see DOTAGE
second-class *adj syn* see INFERIOR 2
second-drawer *adj syn* see INFERIOR 2

second-rate *adj syn* see INFERIOR 2
  ant first-rate
secours *n syn* see HELP 1
secrecy *n* the practice or policy of keeping secrets or maintaining concealment < *secrecy* is an inherent feature of intelligence operations >
  syn hugger-mugger, hugger-muggery, hush, hush-hush, secretiveness, secretness, silence
  rel clandestineness, covertness, furtiveness; concealment, stealth, subterfuge; censorship, suppression
  ant openness
secret *adj* **1** existing or done in such a way as to maintain concealment < was involved in *secret* negotiations with the enemy >
  syn clandestine, covert, furtive, hole-and-corner, hugger-mugger, hush-hush, mystical, sneak, stealthy, sub-rosa, undercover, ‖underneath, under-the-table; *compare* STEALTHY 2, UNDERHAND
  rel underhand, underhanded; unacknowledged, unavowed, undeclared; concealed, hidden, screened; classified, confidential, ‖eyes-only, restricted, top secret
  con acknowledged, avowed, declared, revealed; aboveboard, straightforward, unconcealed; declassified, unclassified, unrestricted; clear, evident, manifest, obvious, patent, plain
  ant open, public
  2 *syn* see OBSCURE 2
  3 *syn* see RECONDITE
secret *n* secrets *pl syn* see GENITALIA
secretaire *n syn* see DESK
secretary *n syn* see DESK
secrete *vb syn* see HIDE
  rel deposit; withhold
secretiveness *n syn* see SECRECY
secretly *adv* in a secret manner < negotiated *secretly* with both sides >
  syn by stealth, clandestinely, covertly, furtively, hugger-mugger, in camera, privately, stealthily, sub rosa, surreptitiously
  rel confidentially; privatim, privily
  idiom behind closed doors, on the qt, on the quiet, under the rose, under the table
  con forthrightly, plainly, publicly; manifestly, overtly
  ant openly
secretness *n syn* see SECRECY
sect *n syn* see RELIGION 2
sectarian *adj* **1** *syn* see HERETICAL
  rel splinter
  con unified, united
  ant nonsectarian
  2 *syn* see INSULAR
sectary *n* **1** *syn* see HERETIC
  rel beatnik, Bohemian, hippie; maverick; liberal, radical, Young Turk; rebel, revolutionary
  con advocate, conformist, follower
  2 *syn* see FOLLOWER
  rel bigot
sectator *n syn* see FOLLOWER
section *n* **1** *syn* see PART 1
  rel district, locality, subdivision, vicinity; area, belt, zone; region, tract; field, sphere, territory
  2 *syn* see QUARTER 2
section *vb* to divide into sections < *sectioned* the class on the basis of ability >
  syn sectionalize, sectionize; *compare* SEGMENT
  rel break up, divide, separate, slice, split; sector, segment
sectionalize *vb syn* see SECTION
sectionize *vb syn* see SECTION
sector *n syn* see QUARTER 2
secular *adj syn* see PROFANE 1
  rel nonclerical, nonreligious
  con clerical, ecclesiastical, ministerial, priestly, regular; eternal
  ant religious
securable *adj syn* see AVAILABLE 1
  rel convenient, handy, reachable, ready
  idiom at one's disposal

---

syn synonym(s) *rel* related word(s)
ant antonym(s) *con* contrasted word(s)
idiom idiomatic equivalent(s)
‖ use limited; if in doubt, see a dictionary

con unavailable, unreachable

secure *adj* 1 *syn* see CONFIDENT 1
2 *syn* see SAFE 2
rel firm, stable, strong
con open, wide-open; assailable, weak; dangerous, precarious
ant insecure
3 *syn* see RELIABLE 1
4 *syn* see FAST 4
rel strong; iron
5 *syn* see STABLE 4
6 *syn* see SURE 1
rel established, settled; balanced
con precarious; unbalanced; unstable, wobbly
ant insecure

secure *vb* 1 *syn* see DEFEND 1
2 *syn* see ENSURE
rel underwrite
3 *syn* see CATCH 1
4 *syn* see FASTEN 2
rel batten (down), clamp, clinch, pinion, rivet, tie down; cement
con unfasten, untie
5 *syn* see GET 1
6 *syn* see EFFECT 1

security *n* 1 *syn* see SAFETY
ant insecurity
2 *syn* see STABILITY
3 *syn* see PLEDGE 1
4 *syn* see GUARANTEE 1
rel assurance; certification; pledge
5 *syn* see DEFENSE 1

sedate *adj* *syn* see SERIOUS 1
rel calm, placid, serene, tranquil; collected, composed, dispassionate, imperturbable, unruffled; decorous, dignified, proper, seemly
con indecorous, undignified, unseemly; airy, flippant, light flighty
ant flighty

sedative *n* an agent or drug that relieves irritability, nervousness, or excitement < took a *sedative* to help her sleep >
syn calmant, calmative, quietive
rel balm; pacifier, tranquilizer; sleeping pill, sleeping tablet; depressant, ‖downer
con energizer; stimulant; ‖upper

sediment *n* matter which settles to the bottom of a liquid < rocks hidden by *sediment* spoiled the cove for diving >
syn deposit, dreg(s), grounds, lees, precipitate, precipitation, settlings
rel bottoms, dross, recrement, scoria, slag; draff, heeltap

sedition *n* an offense against official ruling authority (as a government or sovereign) to which one owes allegiance < considered the defense industry strike to be overt *sedition* >
syn seditiousness, treason
rel alienation, disaffection, estrangement; action, protest, strike; coup, coup d'etat, putsch; insurrection, mutiny, rebellion, revolt, revolution, uprising; quislingism
con allegiance, fealty, fidelity, loyalty; duty, respect, responsibility

seditious *adj* *syn* see INSUBORDINATE
rel alienated, disaffected, dissident; faithless, disloyal, perfidious, traitorous, treacherous; lawless, violent
con faithful, loyal, patriotic

seditiousness *n* *syn* see SEDITION

seduce *vb* 1 *syn* see LURE
rel coax, tease; betray, deceive, delude, mislead; enslave, entrance; overpower, overwhelm
2 to persuade or entice into sexual partnership < lechers who *seduce* silly young girls >
syn debauch, undo
rel deflower; rape, ravish, violate; corrupt, degrade, pervert, ruin

seducement *n* 1 *syn* see SEDUCTION 1
rel undoing
2 *syn* see LURE 2

seduction *n* 1 the act or an instance of seducing or being seduced into a sexual relationship < helping young victims of *seduction* >
syn seducement
rel deflowering; rape, ravishment, violation; corruption, degradation, perversion, ruin

2 *syn* see ATTRACTION 1
rel lorelei, siren song, temptation

seductive *adj* *syn* see ATTRACTIVE 1
rel desirable, mouth-watering, provocative

seductress *n* *syn* see SIREN

sedulous *adj* *syn* see ASSIDUOUS
rel active; busy; hustling, persevering, persistent, unremitting

see *vb* 1 to take cognizance of by physical or mental vision < *saw* that the boat was being driven ashore > < the only one who *saw* the truth >
syn behold, descry, discern, distinguish, espy, mark, mind, note, notice, observe, perceive, remark, twig, view
rel sight; make out; examine, inspect, scan, scrutinize; penetrate, pierce, probe; consider, study; appraise, ponder, weigh
idiom fix one's eyes (*or* mind *or* thoughts) on, occupy oneself with, pay heed (*or* attention) to, take notice of
2 to perceive something by means of the eyes < she *sees* clearly with her new glasses >
syn ‖dekko, look, watch
rel gape, gaze, glare, peek, peep, peer, stare
idiom give the eye, hold in view, keep one's eye on, lay eyes on, turn one's eyes to
3 *syn* see EXPERIENCE 1
4 *syn* see DISCOVER 3
5 *syn* see THINK 1
6 *syn* see APPREHEND 1
rel discern, discriminate, recognize
7 *syn* see FORESEE
idiom see the day when
8 *syn* see LOOK 1
rel look out, watch out
idiom see to it that
9 *syn* see VISIT 2
10 *syn* see DATE
11 *syn* see GUIDE
rel accompany, go (with); attend

seeable *adj* *syn* see VISUAL 2
ant unseeable

seed *n* 1 *syn* see OFFSPRING
2 a beginning or source from which something (as a conception) may later develop < the growing *seeds* of suspicion in her mind >
syn bud, embryo, germ, nucleus, spark
rel rudiment; core, kernel; conceit, concept, conception, image, impression, notion

seed *vb* *syn* see PLANT 1

seedy *adj* *syn* see SHABBY 1
rel drooping, droopy, flagging, sagging, wilted, wilting; messy, slovenly, unkempt, untidy; neglected, overgrown
idiom gone to seed
con manicured, polished, shined

seeing *n* *syn* see EYE 2

seeing *conj* *syn* see BECAUSE
idiom ‖being as how, in that

‖seeing glass *n* *syn* see MIRROR 1

seek *vb* 1 to look for < has gone to *seek* a doctor >
syn cast about, ferret out, hunt, quest, search (for *or* out)
rel bird-dog, delve, dig, fish, mouse, nose, root, smell out, sniff
idiom go in quest (*or* search) of
2 *syn* see TRY 5

seeker *n* *syn* see CANDIDATE
rel bidder; petitioner; solicitant; claimant

seeking *n* *syn* see PURSUIT 2

seem *vb* to give the impression of being without necessarily being so in fact < things are not always the way they *seem* >
syn appear, look, sound
rel resemble, suggest; hint, imply, insinuate, intimate
idiom have (*or* show) every sign of, have the earmarks of

seeming *n* 1 *syn* see APPEARANCE 2
rel feigning, pretense, sham; facade; illusion
idiom false face (*or* front), outward show
2 *syn* see APPEARANCE 1
rel bearing, demeanor, posture; image, style; effect, impression

seeming *adj* *syn* see APPARENT 2

seemingly *adv* *syn* see OSTENSIBLY

seemliness *n* 1 *syn* see ORDER 7
2 *syn* see DECORUM 1
ant unseemliness

seemly *adj syn* see DECOROUS 1
  rel compatible, congenial, congruous, consistent, consonant; pleasing
  con inappropriate, unfit, unseasonable, unsuitable, untimely; incompatible, uncongenial; displeasing, unpleasing
  ant unseemly

seep *vb syn* see EXUDE
  rel drip; leak; flow

seer *n syn* see PROPHET

seesaw *vb* to move backward and forward or up and down from a central axis usually in a swaying often unsteady way < planes landing on the *seesawing* flight deck >
  syn lurch, pitch, swag, tilt, tilter, yaw; *compare* TEETER, TOSS 2
  rel cant, incline, lean, list; rock, roll, sway

seethe *vb* **1** *syn* see BOIL 2
  2 *syn* see SOAK 1
  3 *syn* see ANGER 2
  idiom ‖do a slow burn
  con calm (down), simmer (down)
  ant cool (down)
  4 to be in a state of internal and especially mental agitation, excitement, or turmoil < his brain *seethed* with unanswered questions >
  syn boil, bubble, churn, ferment, ‖moil, simmer, smolder, stir
  rel abound, swarm, teem; fret, fume, sizzle, steam; bubble over, erupt, overflow

see-through *adj syn* see TRANSPARENT 1

segment *n syn* see PART 1

segment *vb* to separate into segments < tried to *segment* the poem into understandable units >
  syn segmentalize, segmentize; *compare* SECTION
  rel categorize, compartmentalize; divide, separate; isolate, seclude, set off

segmentalize *vb syn* see SEGMENT

segmentize *vb syn* see SEGMENT

segregate *vb syn* see ISOLATE
  rel disconnect; choose, select, single
  con mix
  ant desegregate

segregation *n* the quality, state, or condition of being socially or racially excluded or separated < fought against racial *segregation* in the schools >
  syn apartheid, separateness, separation, separatism
  rel discrimination, jim crowism; ghettoization; isolation, seclusion
  ant desegregation

seity *n syn* see INDIVIDUALITY 4

seize *vb* **1** *syn* see APPROPRIATE 1
  rel occupy; usurp
  2 to take possession or control of usually suddenly and forcibly < the cat *seized* the fish and made off > < *seized* the rope and dragged the boat ashore >
  syn catch, clutch, ‖cotch, grab, grapple, nab, ‖nail, snatch, take; *compare* CATCH 1
  rel fasten (onto), grasp, latch (onto), snap (at); apprehend, arrest; capture, secure, take over; abduct, carry off, kidnap, spirit (away *or* off)
  idiom get into one's clutches, get one's hands (*or* paws) on, lay hold (on *or* of)
  con free, loose, release
  3 to affect especially as if by laying hold of < was *seized* with a coughing fit >
  syn catch, strike, take
  rel overtake; afflict

seizure *n syn* see ATTACK 3
  rel convulsion; breakdown

seldom *adv* in few instances < she *seldom* writes home anymore >
  syn hardly ever, infrequently, little, rarely, unfrequently, unoften
  rel occasionally; semioccasionally; irregularly, sporadically; hardly, scarcely
  idiom once in a blue moon
  con regularly; frequently; usually
  ant often

seldom *adj syn* see INFREQUENT

select *adj* **1** singled out from a number or group by fitness or preference < this hotel caters to a *select* clientele >
  syn chosen, elect, exclusive, pick, picked, selected
  rel culled, screened, weeded (out), winnowed (out); favored, preferred; best, elite
  con random; indiscriminate; average, commonplace, mediocre, run-of-the-mill
  2 *syn* see CHOICE
  rel blue-chip, fine, best; top
  3 *syn* see ECLECTIC 1

select *vb syn* see CHOOSE 1
  idiom make a choice (*or* selection)
  con ignore, pass (over); drop
  ant reject

selected *adj syn* see SELECT 1
  rel singled (out); appointed, tagged, tapped

selection *n syn* see CHOICE 1
  rel choosing, culling, draft, drafting, picking; acumen, discernment, discrimination, insight
  ant rejection

selective *adj syn* see ECLECTIC 1
  rel particular, scrupulous

self-abandoned *adj syn* see ABANDONED 2

self-abnegating *adj syn* see SELF-SACRIFICING

self-abnegation *n syn* see RENUNCIATION
  rel abandonment, relinquishment, resignation

self-absorbed *adj syn* see EGOCENTRIC 2
  rel arrogant, cocky, self-important

self-abuse *n syn* see SELF-REPROACH

self-accusation *n syn* see SELF-REPROACH

self-admiration *n syn* see CONCEIT 2

self-asserting *adj syn* see PRESUMPTUOUS
  rel aggressive, militant
  con meek, modest, unassuming; docile, passive
  ant self-effacing

self-assertive *adj* **1** *syn* see AGGRESSIVE
  rel impertinent, intrusive, meddlesome, obtrusive, officious; audacious, bold; cocksure, sure
  2 *syn* see PRESUMPTUOUS

self-assurance *n syn* see CONFIDENCE 2
  rel collectedness, coolness, imperturbability; composure, equanimity, sangfroid
  con insecurity, uncertainness

self-assured *adj syn* see CONFIDENT 1
  rel self-satisfied, smug

self-assuredness *n syn* see CONFIDENCE 2

self-centered *adj* **1** *syn* see SELF-SUFFICIENT
  2 *syn* see EGOCENTRIC 2
  idiom wrapped up in oneself

self-centeredness *n syn* see SELFISHNESS

self-command *n syn* see WILL 3
  rel self-containment, uncommunicativeness

self-complacency *n syn* see CONCEIT 2

self-complacent *adj syn* see COMPLACENT

self-composed *adj syn* see CALM 2

self-conceit *n syn* see CONCEIT 2

self-conceited *adj syn* see VAIN 3

self-concern *n syn* see SELFISHNESS

self-concerned *adj syn* see EGOCENTRIC 2

self-confidence *n syn* see CONFIDENCE 2
  rel sanguineness, sureness; cockiness, overconfidence
  con diffidence, shyness; self-distrust; doubt, uneasiness
  ant self-doubt

self-confident *adj syn* see CONFIDENT 1

self-conscious *adj* aware of the scrutiny of others to the point of not appearing natural or spontaneous < felt *self-conscious* about wearing platform shoes >
  syn affected, conscious, mannered
  rel self-aware; anxious, ill at ease, uncomfortable, uneasy; formal, stiff, stilted; artificial; ‖mim, prim; exhibitionist, flaunty, ostentatious
  con unaware, unconcerned; blithe, easy; natural, spontaneous, unaffected

self-consequence *n syn* see CONCEIT 2

self-contained *adj syn* see SELF-SUFFICIENT

self-contemplation *n syn* see INTROSPECTION

---

syn synonym(s)   *rel* related word(s)
ant antonym(s)   *con* contrasted word(s)
idiom idiomatic equivalent(s)
‖ use limited; if in doubt, see a dictionary

self–contented *adj syn* see COMPLACENT

self–control *n syn* see WILL 3
rel constraint, reserve, self-containedness; balance, stability; dignity
idiom presence of mind
ant self-abandonment

self–criticism *n syn* see SELF-REPROACH

self–deceit *n syn* see SELF-DECEPTION

self–deception *n* the act or an instance of deceiving oneself or of being so deceived < to presume agreement where none exists is a dangerous form of *self-deception* >
syn self-deceit, self-delusion
rel misconception, misinterpretation, misunderstanding; deception, delusion, illusion
idiom kidding oneself

self–defense *n* an act, instance, or means of defending oneself, one's property, or a close relative < sought some measure of *self-defense* against society's lawless elements >
syn self-protection
rel self-preservation

self–delusion *n syn* see SELF-DECEPTION

self–denial *n syn* see RENUNCIATION
rel abstaining, abstemiousness, abstinence; asceticism, selflessness, self-sacrifice, self-sacrificing; self-forgetful, self-forgetting
ant self-indulgence

self–denying *adj syn* see SELF-SACRIFICING

self–dependence *n syn* see SELF-RELIANCE

self–destruction *n syn* see SUICIDE

self–discipline *n syn* see WILL 3

selfdom *n syn* see INDIVIDUALITY 4

self–educated *adj syn* see SELF-TAUGHT

self–effacing *adj syn* see SHY 1

self–esteem *n* 1 *syn* see PRIDE 2
rel self-content, self-contentment; self-satisfaction
con self-distrust, self-doubt; self-contempt
ant self-hate
2 *syn* see CONCEIT 2
rel self-flattery, self-glorification
con self-distrust, self-doubt; self-hate
ant self-contempt

self–evidencing *adj syn* see SELF-EVIDENT

self–evident *adj* evident in itself without need of argument or proof < *self-evident* truths >
syn prima facie, self-evidencing
rel clear, manifest, obvious, plain; unmistakable, unquestionable
con enigmatic, hidden, mysterious, obscure; doubtable, doubtful, questionable, uncertain

self–exaltation *n syn* see CONCEIT 2

self–examination *n syn* see INTROSPECTION

self–existent *adj* existing of or by itself and having no antecedent cause < argues backward to a first great cause, which is itself *self-existent* >
syn increate, self-existing, unbegotten, uncaused, uncreated, unoriginated
rel self-generated, self-originated, self-produced
con consequent, resultant, sequential
ant derivative

self–existing *adj syn* see SELF-EXISTENT

self–explaining *adj syn* see SELF-EXPLANATORY

self–explanatory *adj* capable of being understood without explanation < his actions are *self-explanatory:* he wants to resign >
syn self-explaining; compare CLEAR 5
rel clear, evident, obvious, manifest, plain, self-evident; comprehensible, understandable
con equivocal, obscure, uncertain, unclear, vague; complex; incomprehensible, mysterious; inexplicable, unexplainable

self–forgetful *adj syn* see SELFLESS

self–forgetting *adj syn* see SELFLESS

self–giving *adj syn* see SELF-SACRIFICING

self–glorifying *adj syn* see BOASTFUL

self–glory *n syn* see CONCEIT 2
rel self-aggrandizement, self-glorification

self–governing *adj syn* see DEMOCRATIC

self–government *n syn* see WILL 3

self–gratification *n* the act of pleasing oneself or of satisfying one's desires < human beings driven by unconscious forces toward *self-gratification* >
syn onanism, self-indulgence

rel self-abandonment; self-pleasing, self-satisfaction; autotheism, narcissism, self-worship

selfhood *n* 1 *syn* see INDIVIDUALITY 4
2 *syn* see SELFISHNESS

self–importance *n* 1 *syn* see CONCEIT 2
2 *syn* see EGOTISM 1
rel arrogance, pomposity

self–important *adj syn* see POMPOUS 1

self–imposed *adj* imposed by oneself or itself < insists on working under *self-imposed* handicaps >
syn self-inflicted
rel self-generated, self-produced

self–indulgence *n syn* see SELF-GRATIFICATION
rel indulgence; excess, intemperance, overindulgence
ant abstinence

self–indulgent *adj syn* see SYBARITIC

self–inflicted *adj syn* see SELF-IMPOSED
rel self-determined; accepted; voluntary

self–instructed *adj syn* see SELF-TAUGHT

self–interest *n syn* see SELFISHNESS

self–interested *adj syn* see EGOCENTRIC 2

self–involved *adj syn* see EGOCENTRIC 2

selfish *adj syn* see EGOCENTRIC 2
idiom ‖looking out for number one
con self-denying, selfless, self-sacrificing; altruistic, benevolent, charitable, generous, magnanimous
ant unselfish

selfishness *n* a concern for one's own welfare at the expense of or in disregard of others < his *selfishness* was consummate: he cared for no one but himself >
syn self-centeredness, self-concern, self-hood, self-interest, self-regard, self-seeking
rel egoism, egotism, self-absorption; self, selfism, selfness; autotheism, self-worship
con self-denial, selflessness, self-sacrificing; benevolence, charity, generosity
ant unselfishness

self–knowledge *n* knowledge or understanding of one's own character, motivations, and capabilities < a poet whose verse reflected deep *self-knowledge* and honesty >
syn autognosis, self-understanding
rel self-awareness; introspection, self-examination, self-observation

selfless *adj* having no concern for oneself < *selfless* service to community, state, and nation >
syn self-forgetful, self-forgetting, unselfish
rel self-giving, self-sacrificing; self-renouncing; elevated, generous, high-minded, magnanimous
con self-devoted, self-loving, self-serving
ant self-centered, selfish

self–love *n syn* see CONCEIT 2
idiom the sixth insatiable sense
con self-abuse, self-accusation, self-reproach; self-forgetfulness, selflessness
ant self-hate

self–mastery *n syn* see WILL 3

self–murder *n syn* see SUICIDE

selfness *n syn* see INDIVIDUALITY 4

self–observation *n syn* see INTROSPECTION

self–opinion *n syn* see CONCEIT 2

self–pleased *adj syn* see COMPLACENT

self–possessed *adj syn* see CALM 2
rel aloof, reserved; self-contained, self-controlled; self-assured

self–possession *n syn* see EQUANIMITY

self–pride *n syn* see CONCEIT 2

self–proclaimed *adj syn* see SELF-STYLED

self–protection *n syn* see SELF-DEFENSE

self–questioning *n syn* see INTROSPECTION

self–recrimination *n syn* see SELF-REPROACH

self–reflection *n syn* see INTROSPECTION

self–regard *n* 1 *syn* see SELFISHNESS
2 *syn* see PRIDE 2

self–reliance *n* reliance on one's own resources, efforts, and ability < a strong people characterized by bravery and *self-reliance* >
syn self-dependence
rel confidence, self-assurance, self-confidence; self-sufficiency, self-support

self–renouncing *adj syn* see SELF-SACRIFICING

self–renunciation *n syn* see RENUNCIATION

self–reproach *n* an act or instance of reproaching oneself < experienced both guilt and *self-reproach* after the quarrel >
  syn self-abuse, self-accusation, self-criticism, self-recrimination, self-reproof
  rel contrition, regret, remorse; self-castigation, self-condemnation, self-flagellation, self-punishment; self-contempt
  con self-contentment, self-satisfaction; self-applause
  ant self-approbation

self–reproof *n syn* see SELF-REPROACH

self–respect *n syn* see PRIDE 2

self–restraining *adj syn* see ABSTEMIOUS

self–restraint *n syn* see WILL 3
  ant abandon

self–righteous *adj syn* see HYPOCRITICAL

self–ruling *adj syn* see DEMOCRATIC

self–sacrificing *adj* sacrificing or denying oneself for others < a *self-sacrificing* love >
  syn self-abnegating, self-denying, self-giving, self-renouncing
  rel selfless, unselfish; charitable, generous, kindly, philanthropic
  con self-centered, selfish, self-seeking

selfsame *adj syn* see SAME 1
  rel alike, like
  idiom (the) very same
  con different, unalike
  ant diverse

selfsameness *n syn* see IDENTITY
  ant diverseness

self–satisfied *adj syn* see COMPLACENT

self–scrutiny *n syn* see INTROSPECTION

self–searching *n syn* see INTROSPECTION

self–seeking *n syn* see SELFISHNESS

self–seeking *adj syn* see EGOCENTRIC 2

self–serving *adj syn* see EGOCENTRIC 2

self–slaughter *n syn* see SUICIDE

self–starter *n syn* see HUSTLER 1

self–styled *adj* given a specified designation or title by oneself often without justification < a department cluttered with *self= styled* experts >
  syn self-proclaimed, soi-disant
  rel self-appointed, self-created, self-given; so-called; quasi; would-be

self–sufficient *adj* maintaining or able to maintain oneself without outside aid < organisms are not *self-sufficient*, closed systems >
  syn closed, independent, self-centered, self-contained, self-sufficing, self-supported, self-supporting, self-sustained, self-sustaining
  rel self-dependent, self-reliant; self-subsistent, self-subsisting; individual, one-man, unit
  idiom one's own man, sufficient unto oneself (*or* itself)
  con dependent

self–sufficing *adj syn* see SELF-SUFFICIENT

self–supported *adj syn* see SELF-SUFFICIENT

self–supporting *adj syn* see SELF-SUFFICIENT

self–sustained *adj syn* see SELF-SUFFICIENT

self–sustaining *adj syn* see SELF-SUFFICIENT

self–taught *adj* having knowledge or skills acquired by one's own efforts without formal instruction < a *self-taught* painter >
  syn autodidactic, self-educated, self-instructed

self–trust *n syn* see CONFIDENCE 2

self–understanding *n syn* see SELF-KNOWLEDGE

self–violence *n syn* see SUICIDE

self–willed *adj syn* see OBSTINATE
  con weak, weak-willed, wishy-washy; spineless

sell *vb* 1 *syn* see BETRAY 2
  2 to give up (property) to another for money or other valuable consideration < can *sell* you the house now >
  syn give, market, vend
  ant buy, purchase
  3 to deal in or offer (articles) for sale on a regular basis < he *sells* small appliances >
  syn market, merchandise, retail
  rel barter, deal (in), exchange, trade, traffic; hawk, peddle; vend
  ant buy
  4 to command a specified price < that coat *sells* for $300 >
  syn bring, bring in, fetch
  rel command, draw; realize, return, yield; gross, net

sell *n syn* see IMPOSTURE

sellable *adj syn* see MARKETABLE

sell off *vb syn* see SELL OUT 1

sell out *vb* 1 to dispose of entirely by selling < *sold out* his share of the business >
  syn close out, sell off, ‖sell up
  rel dump, move, unload; sacrifice
  2 *syn* see DECEIVE
  3 *syn* see BETRAY 2

‖sell up *vb syn* see SELL OUT 1

selvage *n syn* see BORDER 1

semblance *n* 1 *syn* see AIR 3
  rel aspect, look
  2 *syn* see LIKENESS
  3 *syn* see APPEARANCE 2
  rel air, pose
  4 *syn* see MASK 2

semblant *adj syn* see APPARENT 2

seminar *n syn* see CONFERENCE 2

semioccasional *adj syn* see INFREQUENT

sempiternal *adj syn* see INFINITE 1

sempiternity *n syn* see ETERNITY 1

send *vb* 1 to cause to go or be taken from one place, person, or condition to another < *send* a messenger to the bank > < his cold *sent* him to bed >
  syn address, consign, dispatch, forward, remit, route, ship, transmit
  rel allocate, assign, commit, delegate; advance, launch; expedite, rush
  ant receive
  2 *syn* see THRILL

senectitude *n syn* see OLD AGE

senescence *n syn* see OLD AGE

senile *adj* exhibiting the weakness and loss of mental faculties often associated with old age < a *senile* professor now unable to lecture coherently >
  syn doddering, doddery, ‖doted, doting
  rel aging, senescent; aged, ancient, old; enfeebled, feeble, weak; decrepit, doddered, shattered
  idiom in one's second childhood

senility *n syn* see DOTAGE
  rel decline; senescence

senior *n* 1 *syn* see OLDSTER
  2 one older than another < he was her *senior* by eight years >
  syn elder
  ant junior
  3 *syn* see SUPERIOR
  con inferior, subordinate, underling

senior citizen *n syn* see OLDSTER

sensation *n* 1 the power to respond or an act of responding to stimuli < the stage of *sensation* precedes that of rational comprehension >
  syn feeling, sense, sensibility, sensitivity
  rel susceptibility; consciousness; sensitiveness, sensitivity; impression, perception, response
  2 *syn* see WONDER 1
  rel bomb, bombshell

sensational *adj* 1 *syn* see SENSORY
  2 arousing or designed to arouse a quick, intense, and usually superficial emotional response < *sensational* crime reporting >
  syn livid, lurid, sensationalistic, sensationist, sultry, tabloid
  rel juicy, piquant, pungent; colored, extravagant; coarse, vulgar
  con exact, factual; dignified, formal, proper, restrained
  3 *syn* see NOTICEABLE
  rel impressive, stunning
  4 *syn* see MARVELOUS 2
  rel boffo, crashing, rousing, slambang, smash, smashing, superfine

sensationalistic *adj syn* see SENSATIONAL 2

sensationist *adj syn* see SENSATIONAL 2

sensatory *adj syn* see SENSORY

sense *n* 1 *syn* see MEANING 1
  rel gist, pith, substance; center, core, focus, nucleus
  2 *syn* see SUBSTANCE 2
  3 *syn* see SENSATION 1

---

syn synonym(s)	*rel* related word(s)
ant antonym(s)	*con* contrasted word(s)
idiom idiomatic equivalent(s)	
‖ use limited; if in doubt, see a dictionary	

rel awareness, cognizance; discernment, discrimination, penetration; appreciation; recognition
4 *usu* **senses** *pl syn* see WIT 2
rel consciousness
5 *syn* see INTELLIGENCE 1
6 ability to make intelligent choices and to reach intelligent conclusions or decisions <had enough *sense* to study something practical>
syn common sense, good sense, gumption, horse sense, judgment, wisdom
rel discretion, foresight, prudence; appreciation, comprehension, understanding; brains, intelligence, ‖smarts, wit
ant folly
sense *vb syn* see FEEL 3
rel anticipate; know, realize
senseless *adj* **1** *syn* see NUMB 1
rel oblivious, unaware; inanimate, wooden
2 *syn* see INSENSATE 1
3 *syn* see INSENSIBLE 2
4 *syn* see SIMPLE 3
rel irrational, surd
5 having no meaning <an ancient custom, now outdated and *senseless*>
syn insignificant, meaningless, pointless, purportless, unmeaning
rel purposeless; trivial, unimportant
idiom without rhyme or reason
con purposeful; important, meaning, meaningful, significant
senselessness *n syn* see FOOLISHNESS
rel illogicality, stupidity
sensibility *n syn* see SENSATION 1
rel discernment, discrimination, insight, keenness, penetration, responsiveness; affection, emotion, heart
con apathy, indifference, insensibleness, insentience, unfeelingness, unresponsiveness
ant insensibility
sensibilize *vb syn* see SENSITIZE
sensible *adj* **1** *syn* see MATERIAL 1
rel concrete, solid
con immaterial, insubstantial; unreal
2 *syn* see PERCEPTIBLE
rel imaginal, perceptual, sensational; weighable; evident, manifest, obvious, patent
con imperceptible; cloudy, unclear
ant insensible
3 *syn* see CONSIDERABLE 2
4 *syn* see SENTIENT 3
5 *syn* see AWARE
rel sensitive, susceptible; noting, observing, perceiving, remarking, seeing; appreciating, comprehending, understanding; intelligent, knowing
con anesthetic, insensate, insensitive
ant insensible
6 *syn* see RATIONAL
rel sensemaking
7 *syn* see WISE 2
rel rational, reasonable; down-to-earth, matter-of-fact
con unreasonable, unsound, unwise; asinine, fatuous
ant absurd, foolish
sensile *adj syn* see SENTIENT 3
sensitive *adj* **1** *syn* see SENTIENT 3
rel hypersensitive, supersensitive
con impervious, insensible, unfeeling, unimpressionable, unresponsive; wooden
ant insensitive, unsensitive
2 *syn* see EMOTIONAL 1
rel high-strung, irritable, nervous, tense; insultable, oversensitive, umbrageous; unstable
con impervious, insensate, insensible, unaffected, unemotional
ant insensitive, unsensitive
3 *syn* see ACUTE 3
rel perceiving, seeing; aware, cognizant, conscious; knowing, understanding
4 *syn* see LIABLE 2
rel affected, impressed, influenced; disposed, inclined, predisposed
ant insensitive
5 *syn* see DELICATE 7
6 *syn* see SENSORY

sensitivity *n syn* see SENSATION 1
sensitize *vb* to cause to become sensitive or more sensitive <*sensitizing* corporate officers to social and environmental problems>
syn sensibilize
rel animate, excite, quicken, sharpen, stimulate, whet
ant desensitize
sensorial *adj syn* see SENSORY
sensory *adj* of or relating to sensation or the senses <*sensory* perception>
syn sensational, sensatory, sensitive, sensorial, sensual
rel sensate; receptive
sensual *adj* **1** *syn* see SENSORY
2 *syn* see CARNAL 2
rel irreligious, unspiritual
3 *syn* see SENSUOUS
4 *syn* see MATERIALISTIC
sensualistic *adj syn* see SENSUOUS
sensuous *adj* producing or characterized by gratification of the senses <*sensuous* pleasures>
syn epicurean, luscious, lush, luxurious, sensual, sensualistic, voluptuous; *compare* CARNAL 2, SYBARITIC
rel bacchic, dionysiac, Dionysian, hedonistic, pleasure-loving, pleasure-seeking; self-indulgent, sybaritic; carnal, fleshly, fleshy
con ascetic, disciplined, restrained
sentence *vb* to decree the fate or punishment of one adjudged guilty, unworthy, or unfit <was *sentenced* to exile>
syn condemn, damn, doom, proscribe
rel adjudge, adjudicate, judge; ordain, rule; blame, denounce; penalize, punish; devote
idiom pass sentence on
con absolve, acquit, exculpate, exonerate, vindicate; discharge, free, liberate, release
sententious *adj syn* see EXPRESSIVE
rel aphoristic, concise, crisp, epigrammatic, piquant, pithy, terse
sentient *adj* **1** *syn* see AWARE
2 *syn* see EMOTIONAL 1
3 capable of receiving and of being readily affected by external stimuli <deeply disturbed in the most *sentient* reaches of his mind>
syn impressible, impressionable, responsive, sensible, sensile, sensitive, susceptible, susceptive
rel sensate; open, receptive, susceptive; reactive
con insensate; closed, unreceptive; unreactive
sentiment *n* **1** *syn* see LEANING 2
2 *syn* see OPINION
rel leaning, predilection, propensity; position, posture
idiom way of thinking
3 *syn* see FEELING 3
rel conception; sensation; emotionalism, sentimentality
sentimental *adj* unduly or affectedly emotional <*sentimental* love stories>
syn bathetic, drippy, gooey, lovey-dovey, maudlin, mawkish, moist, mushy, romantic, sappy, slushy, sobby, sobful, soft≈ boiled, ‖soppy, soupy, sticky, syrupy, tear-jerking
rel dreamy, misty-eyed, moonstruck, nostalgic, oversentimental; inane, insipid, jejune, namby-pamby, schoolgirlish, vapid; rosewater, saccharine, soft, sugar-candy, sugary, sweet; loving, tender; affectionate, demonstrative, effusive; gushing, gushy; passionate
con unaffectionate, undemonstrative; dispassionate, emotionless, unemotional, unresponsive; unfeeling, unloving; dry
ant unsentimental
sentinel *n syn* see GUARD 2
sentry *n syn* see GUARD 2
separate *vb* **1** to become or cause to become disunited or disjoined <forces that *separate* families>
syn break up, dichotomize, disjoin, disjoint, dissect, dissever, disunite, divide, divorce, part, rupture, sever, split (up), sunder, uncombine
rel alienate, discontinue, disunify, estrange; dislink, uncouple, unjoin, unlink; disaggregate, disassemble, disgregate, dispel, disperse, dissolve, scatter; detach, disengage, disrelate, dissociate; halve, quarter
con assemble, associate, blend, mingle, mix; connect, couple, join, link; unify, unite; agglutinate, bind, cement, fuse, weld
ant combine
2 *syn* see KNOW 4

3 *syn* see SORT 2
rel compartment, compartmentalize
4 *syn* see DISCHARGE 7
5 *syn* see ISOLATE

separate *adj* **1** *syn* see SINGLE 2
rel distinctive, peculiar; detached, disconnected, disengaged
2 *syn* see FREE 1
3 *syn* see DISTINCT 1
rel free, independent

separately *adv* *syn* see APART 1
rel distinctly; solely
con conjointly, jointly
ant together

separateness *n* *syn* see SEGREGATION
ant togetherness

separation *n* **1** the act, process, or an instance of separating or of being separated <*separation* of church and state> <their *separation* was a sad occasion>
syn detachment, dissolution, disunion, division, divorce, divorcement, partition, rupture, split-up
rel disrelation, dissociation, disunity, parting, shedding; disconnection, disjointedness, disjointure; breakup, disjunction, dissection, sequestration; diffluence, dispersal; dichotomy, diremption, trichotomy
con combination; unification
ant union
2 *syn* see SEGREGATION

separatism *n* *syn* see SEGREGATION
separatist *n* *syn* see HERETIC
sepulcher *n* *syn* see GRAVE
sepulcher *vb* **1** *syn* see ENTOMB 1
2 *syn* see BURY 1
sepulchral *adj* **1** of, relating to, or serving as a sepulcher or a memorial to the dead <*sepulchral* inscriptions>
syn mortuary, tumulary
rel exequial, funebrial, funeral, funerary, funereal
2 *syn* see HOLLOW 1
sepulture *n* **1** *syn* see BURIAL 2
2 *syn* see GRAVE
sepulture *vb* **1** *syn* see ENTOMB 1
2 *syn* see BURY 1
sequel *n* **1** *syn* see SUCCESSION 2
2 *syn* see EFFECT 1
rel end, ending, termination; close, closing, finish, finishing
3 *syn* see EPILOGUE 2
rel continuation, development; aftermath, outcome, result
sequence *n* **1** *syn* see SUCCESSION 2
rel arrangement, disposition, ordering; procession
2 *syn* see ORDER 3
rel classification, grouping; placement
3 *syn* see EFFECT 1
4 *syn* see ORDER 5
sequent *adj* *syn* see CONSECUTIVE
sequential *adj* *syn* see CONSECUTIVE
sequester *vb* **1** *syn* see ISOLATE
2 *syn* see SECLUDE
rel hide, secrete
3 *syn* see APPROPRIATE 1
rel attach; impound; dispossess
sequestered *adj* *syn* see SECLUDED
rel sheltered; closeted
sequestration *n* *syn* see SECLUSION
rel retreat
sequitur *n* *syn* see INFERENCE 2
seraglio *n* *syn* see BROTHEL
sere *adj* *syn* see DRY 1
serene *adj* *syn* see CALM 2
rel noiseless, quiet, still; quiescent, resting; undisturbed
con agitated, disquieted, upset
serfage *n* *syn* see BONDAGE
serfdom *n* *syn* see BONDAGE
serial *adj* *syn* see CONSECUTIVE
series *n* *syn* see SUCCESSION 2
rel continuance, continuation, run; category, group, set; column, tier; gradation, scale
serious *adj* **1** not light or frivolous (as in disposition, appearance, or manner) <he was disturbed by her stern, *serious* look>
syn earnest, grave, no-nonsense, poker-faced, sedate, sober, sobersided, solemn, somber, staid, weighty

rel businesslike, ‖dern, determined, steady, steady-going; intent, serious-minded; contemplative, meditative, pensive, reflective, thoughtful; austere, severe, stern; humorless, unhumorous; grim
idiom serious as a judge
con flighty, ‖flip, flippant, frivolous, volatile; casual, easy, relaxed
ant light, unserious
2 expressing, involving, or characterized by seriousness or gravity (as of consequence) <a *serious* economic situation>
syn grave, heavy, severe, weighty
rel important, significant; sobering; unamusing, unfunny, unhumorous; grim
idiom no joke, no laughing matter
con inconsequential, insignificant, unimportant, unserious
ant trifling, trivial
3 *syn* see HARD 6
4 *syn* see GRAVE 3
rel menacing, threatening

seriously *adv* **1** in a serious manner <at last settled *seriously* to work>
syn actively, down, earnestly, for real
rel gravely, soberly, solemnly; intently; vigorously, zealously; determinedly, purposefully, resolutely; fervently, passionately
idiom all joking aside, in all seriousness, in earnest
con airily, casually, flippantly, lightly, unconcernedly; carelessly, haphazardly
2 to a serious extent <the cities are *seriously* overcrowded>
syn gravely, intensely, severely
rel decidedly, quite, very; dangerously; critically, deplorably, regrettably

serious–mindedness *n* *syn* see EARNESTNESS
rel thoughtfulness; sober-mindedness

seriousness *n* *syn* see EARNESTNESS
rel sedateness, sobriety, solemnity, staidness
con gaiety, jollity; lightness
ant flippancy, frivolity

sermon *n* a religious discourse delivered in public by a clergyman as part of a worship service <preached his first *sermon* on Sunday>
syn preach, preaching, preachment, sermonizing
rel preachification; sermonary, sermonology; sermonette; exhortation, harangue, lecture, tirade

sermonic *adj* *syn* see DIDACTIC
sermonize *vb* **1** *syn* see PREACH 1
2 *syn* see DISCOURSE 1
3 *syn* see MORALIZE
sermonizer *n* *syn* see CLERGYMAN
sermonizing *n* *syn* see SERMON
sermonizing *adj* *syn* see DIDACTIC
serpent *n* *syn* see DEVIL 1
serpentine *adj* **1** *syn* see FIENDISH
2 *syn* see WINDING
rel serpentiform, serpentile, serpentlike, snakelike; crooked, devious
serrate *adj* notched or toothed on the edge <jagged peaks and *serrate* ridges>
syn denticulate, saw-edged, sawtooth, saw-toothed, serrated, serried
rel indented, notched, scored, toothed; serrulate
serrated *adj* *syn* see SERRATE
serried *adj* *syn* see SERRATE
serve *vb* **1** *syn* see BENEFIT
2 *syn* see ACT 4
3 to prove adequate or sufficient <will not *serve* as a true translation>
syn do, suffice, suit
rel service; function, work; fit; satisfy; make
idiom fill the bill
4 *syn* see MINISTER (to)
5 to put in (a term of imprisonment) <*served* ten years for armed robbery>
syn do
rel put in, spend; undergo

---

syn synonym(s)   *rel* related word(s)
ant antonym(s)   *con* contrasted word(s)
idiom idiomatic equivalent(s)
‖ use limited; if in doubt, see a dictionary

    idiom do a hitch (*or* stretch), serve (out) a sentence, serve time, ‖take a vacation
    6 *syn* see ADVANCE 1
    7 *syn* see TREAT 2
service *n* **1** the performance of military duty in wartime and especially in a combat zone < saw a year's *service* in Vietnam >
    syn action, combat
    rel active duty, duty; fighting
    2 *syn* see FAVOR 4
    3 *syn* see RITE 2
    4 *syn* see USE 3
serviceability *n syn* see USE 3
    rel serviceableness; durability
serviceable *adj* **1 *syn*** see HELPFUL 1
    ant unserviceable
    2 *syn* see PRACTICAL 2
    ant unserviceable
serviceman *n* **1 *syn*** see SOLDIER
    2 servicemen *pl syn* see TROOP 2
servile *adj* **1 *syn*** see SUBSERVIENT 2
    rel obedient, submissive; passive, unresisting; bootlicking, groveling, toadish
    con aggressive
    ant authoritative
    2 *syn* see BASE 3
servility *n syn* see BONDAGE
servitude *n syn* see BONDAGE
    con freedom, independence
set *vb* **1** to position (something) in a specified place < *set* the lamp on the table >
    syn establish, fix, lay, place, put, settle, stick
    rel bestow, deposit, park; emplace, ensconce, install; affix, anchor, wedge
    con displace, replace, supplant; remove, take (away); uproot
    2 *syn* see DIRECT 2
    idiom set one's sights on
    3 *syn* see STATION
    4 *syn* see DICTATE
    rel designate, direct, instruct, specify, stipulate; establish; make, name
    5 to put in order for a meal < she quickly *set* the table for dinner >
    syn lay, spread
    rel fix, prepare, ready; arrange
    ant clear
    6 *syn* see GAMBLE 1
    7 *syn* see INCITE
    ‖**8 *syn*** see SIT 1
    9 *syn* see BELONG 1
    10 *syn* see COAGULATE
    11 *of a fowl* to incubate eggs by crouching upon them < a chicken house filled with hens *setting* on eggs >
    syn brood, ‖clock, cover, sit
    rel hatch, incubate; hover
    12 *of a celestial body* to pass below the horizon < the sun *set* at seven o'clock >
    syn decline, dip, go down, sink
    rel descend, drop
    con ascend, climb, come up
    ant rise
    13 *syn* see HARDEN 1
    rel crystallize, granulate; fix
set (at) *vb syn* see ESTIMATE 1
set *adj* **1 *syn*** see SITUATED
    2 *syn* see DECIDED 2
    3 *syn* see FIRM 4
    rel confirmed, entrenched, established, inveterate, rooted, well-set, well-settled; prescribed, specified
    4 *syn* see LITTLE 2
    rel diehard, inflexible, obstinate, pigheaded, rigid, unbending, unyielding
    5 *syn* see FAST 4
    rel fastened; close; sound
    6 *syn* see EXPRESS 2
    7 *syn* see READY 1
set *n* **1 *syn*** see GIFT 2
    2 *syn* see BEARING 1
    3 *syn* see SCENE 1

    4 *syn* see GROUP 3
    rel assortment, gaggle; kit, pack
    5 a number of people having something (as habit, interest, occupation, or age) in common < the horsey *set* was gathered at the bar >
    syn bunch, circle, crowd, group, lot, push; *compare* CLIQUE
    rel clan, clique, crew, gang, mob; cénacle; camp, faction; company
set back *vb syn* see DELAY 1
setback *n* a checking of progress < loss of his fellowship was a serious *setback* to his education >
    syn backset, check, reversal, reverse; *compare* COMEDOWN
    rel delay, retardation, slowdown; hindrance, impediment, obstacle, stumbling block; disappointment; rebuff; defeat; regress, regression
    idiom reverse of fortune
    con advancement, forwarding, progressing
set down *vb syn* see ALIGHT
set off *vb* **1 *syn*** see COMPENSATE 1
    2 *syn* see MOBILIZE 1
set on *vb syn* see INCITE
set out *vb* **1 *syn*** see DESIGN 3
    2 *syn* see HEAD 3
    idiom set one's course for
setout *n* **1 *syn*** see COSTUME
    2 *syn* see BEGINNING
setting *n syn* see SCENE 1
setting–out *n syn* see DEPARTURE 1
settle *vb* **1 *syn*** see ENSCONCE 2
    2 *syn* see CALM
    rel assure, reassure
    ant unsettle
    3 *syn* see SET 1
    rel found, ground, lodge, seat
    con dislodge, uproot, unseat
    ant unsettle
    4 *syn* see DECIDE
    rel fix, seal
    idiom come to a decision (*or* conclusion), form a judgment, make a decision
    5 *syn* see NEGOTIATE 1
    rel mediate, reconcile, straighten (out)
    idiom bring to terms (*or* agreement)
    6 *syn* see CLEAR 5
    idiom settle the score, settle up (*or* square) accounts
    7 to put in order for final disposal < waiting to *settle* an estate >
    syn clean up, wind up
    8 *syn* see ALIGHT
    rel flop (down), plop (down)
settled *adj* **1 *syn*** see FIRM 4
    rel decided, determined
    con uncertain, undecided
    ant unsettled
    2 *syn* see INVETERATE 1
    3 *syn* see DECIDED 2
    rel certain, fixed
    con irresolute, undecided, undetermined, unresolved, vacillating, wavering
    ant unsettled
settlement *n* **1 *syn*** see HABITATION 1
    2 *syn* see DECISION 1
    rel showdown; quietus
settlings *n pl syn* see SEDIMENT
set to *vb* **1 *syn*** see BEGIN 1
    2 *syn* see PITCH IN 1
set–to *n* **1 *syn*** see BRAWL 2
    2 *syn* see QUARREL
    3 *syn* see ENCOUNTER
set up *vb* **1 *syn*** see ERECT 5
    ant tear down
    2 *syn* see ELATE
    3 *syn* see ERECT 3
    con disassemble, take down
    4 *syn* see FOUND 2
    rel generate, originate; start up; open
    5 *syn* see INTRODUCE 3
    6 *syn* see TREAT 3

setup *n syn* see SNAP 1
seventh heaven *n syn* see ECSTASY
  rel exhilaration; bliss, paradise
  con sadness, unhappiness; blues, doldrums, dumps
sever *vb* **1** *syn* see SEPARATE 1
  2 *syn* see KNOW 4
  3 *syn* see CUT 5
several *adj* **1** possessed by or attributed to a specific individual < the debaters expressed their *several* opinions >
  syn individual, particular, respective, singular
  rel independent; personal, special, specific
  2 *syn* see DISTINCT 1
  3 consisting of an indefinite number more than two and less than many < *several* days passed >
  syn divers, some, sundry, various
  rel particular, separate, single; few; considerable; many, numerous
  idiom not a few
  ‖**4** *syn* see MANY
‖**several** *pron syn* see SUNDRY
severalize *vb syn* see KNOW 4
severally *adv syn* see APART 1
  rel discretely; exclusively
  idiom one at a time
severe *adj* **1** given to or characterized by strict discipline and firm restraint < treated all the students with *severe* impartiality >
  syn ascetic, astringent, austere, mortified, stern
  rel exacting, heavy-handed, onerous, oppressive; disciplined, iron-willed, self-disciplined; inflexible, restrictive, rigid, rigorous, strict, stringent, uncompromising, unyielding
  con easy, easygoing, gentle, mild, soft; clement, forbearing, indulgent, lax, lenient, merciful
  ant tender, tolerant
  2 *syn* see GRIM 2
  rel serious, sober, stern
  3 of a kind to cause discomfort or hardship < a *severe* winter storm >
  syn bitter, brutal, hard, harsh, inclement, intemperate, rigorous, rugged
  rel crimpy, unpleasant; forbidding, hostile, inhospitable; bleak, disagreeable, grim; painful, raw, sharp, smart; blistering, extreme, intense, savage; blustering, blustery, stormy, wintry
  con balmy, calm, equable, gentle, moderate, soft, temperate
  ant mild
  4 *syn* see HARD 6
  5 *syn* see SERIOUS 2
  rel consequential; dear, sore
severely *adv* **1** *syn* see HARD 5
  2 *syn* see SERIOUSLY 2
  rel markedly
‖**sew** *vb syn* see EXUDE
sew up *vb* ‖**1** *syn* see EXHAUST 4
  2 *syn* see MONOPOLIZE
sexy *adj syn* see RISQUÉ
shabby *adj* **1** being ill-kept and showing signs of wear and tear < a *shabby* neighborhood full of depressing tenements >
  syn bedraggled, broken-down, decrepit, dilapidated, dingy, disreputable, down-at-heel, faded, mangy, moth-eaten, run-down, scrubby, scruffy, seedy, shoddy, sleazy, slipshod, squalid, tacky, tagrag, tattered, threadbare, tired
  rel disfigured, dog-eared; decaying, deteriorated, deteriorating; ramshackle, ratty, rickety; bare, miserable, neglected, poor, poverty-stricken; sordid; worm-eaten, outworn, worn-out; abandoned, desolate, ruined, ruinous, wrecked
  idiom gone to seed
  con neat, spick-and-span, tidy, trig, trim, well-kept; brand-new, fresh, new; unused
  ant spruce
  2 *syn* see CONTEMPTIBLE
  3 *syn* see DISREPUTABLE 1
‖**shack** *n syn* see VAGABOND
shack *n syn* see HUT
shackle *n, usu* **shackles** *pl* something that confines the legs or arms so as to prevent free movement < slaves in *shackles* >
  syn bond(s), chains, fetter(s), gyve(s), iron(s)
  rel anklet, bilbo, leg-iron, trammel; bracelet, handcuff, manacle; straitjacket; collar, garrote
shackle *vb syn* see HAMPER

  rel lash, rope, strap; chain, enchain, manacle; handcuff; pinion, secure
  con unchain, unfetter, untie
  ant unshackle
shade *n* **1** comparative darkness or obscurity due to interception of light rays < trees providing *shade* from the sunlight >
  syn adumbration, penumbra, shadow, umbra, umbrage
  rel blackness, darkness, dimness, obscuration, obscurity; cover, shelter
  con brightness, brilliancy, effulgence, radiance; blaze, glare, glow
  2 *syn* see APPARITION
  3 *syn* see COLOR 1
  rel intensity, saturation
  4 *syn* see GRADATION
  rel difference, distinction, variation
  5 *syn* see HINT 2
shade *vb* to cast into shadow by intercepting light rays < avenues *shaded* by large trees >
  syn inumbrate, screen, shadow, umbrage
  rel shelter; cover
  con roast, scorch, swelter; expose
shaded *adj syn* see SHADY 1
  ant unshaded
shadow *n* **1** *syn* see SHADE 1
  2 *syn* see APPARITION
  3 *syn* see VESTIGE 1
  4 *syn* see HINT 2
shadow *vb* **1** *syn* see SHADE
  2 *syn* see OBSCURE
  3 *syn* see TAIL
shadow (forth) *vb* **1** *syn* see SUGGEST 5
  2 *syn* see ADUMBRATE 1
  rel forecast, foretell, predict
shadow *adj syn* see SHADY 1
shadowed *adj syn* see SHADY 1
  ant unshadowed
shadowy *adj* **1** *syn* see IMAGINARY 1
  2 *syn* see GHASTLY 2
  3 *syn* see FAINT 2
  rel amorphous; foggy
  4 *syn* see SHADY 1
  ant bright
shady *adj* **1** producing, affording, or abounding in shade < a *shady* day > < cool, *shady* streets >
  syn shaded, shadow, shadowed, shadowy, umbrageous, umbrous
  rel bosky, screened, sheltered; dusky; dark
  con exposed, unshaded, unshadowed; unsheltered; bright, light
  ant sunny
  2 *syn* see DOUBTFUL 1
  3 *syn* see DISREPUTABLE 1
  rel subreputable
  4 *syn* see RISQUÉ
  rel disreputable, shameful
shaft *n* **1** *syn* see RAY 1
  2 a scornful, cutting, or pithily critical remark < the target of his latest *shaft* is the president himself >
  syn barb, dart
  rel cut, jab, thrust; potshot
shake *vb* **1** to move irregularly to and fro or up and down often in a wavering or oscillating manner < was so frightened that her hands *shook* >
  syn ‖didder, dither, quake, quaver, quiver, shiver, shudder, tremble, tremor, twitter
  rel palpitate, quail, waver; flicker, flit, flitter, flutter; fluctuate, oscillate; chatter, shimmy, vibrate
  idiom shake like an aspen leaf
  2 to undergo strong vibration especially as the result of a physical blow or shock < the platform *shook* as the train passed >
  syn jar, quake, tremble, tremor, vibrate
  rel bounce, jounce; chatter, quiver, shimmy; rock, stagger

---

syn synonym(s)	*rel* related word(s)
ant antonym(s)	*con* contrasted word(s)
idiom idiomatic equivalent(s)	
‖ use limited; if in doubt, see a dictionary	

3 to cause to move in a quick, jerky manner <rattling and *shaking* the latch>
syn jiggle, joggle
rel bounce, ‖chounse, jounce; jostle; rattle; jerk
4 to cause to move to and fro or up and down violently <an earthquake that *shook* the whole coast>
syn agitate, concuss, convulse, rock
rel jog, jostle, rattle, ‖shog; commove, discompose, disorder, jar, jolt, unsettle; disquiet, disturb, perturb, upset; churn, roil, ruffle, stir up, whip
5 to get or keep away from (a pursuer) <tried unsuccessfully to *shake* the man tailing him>
syn lose, slip, throw off; *compare* ESCAPE 2
rel avoid, elude; outwit
idiom get rid of, give (someone) the shake (*or* slip), slip from under the eye of
6 syn see DISMAY 1
rel disturb, jar, rattle, unsettle, upset; bother, worry; unnerve, unstring
shake (off) *vb syn* see RID
shake *n* **1 syn** see EARTHQUAKE
2 shakes *pl syn* see JITTERS
3 syn see INSTANT 1
4 syn see DEAL 2
shake down *vb* **1 syn** see EXTORT 1
2 syn see SEARCH 2
shake up *vb syn* see SPEED 3
shake–up *n* an extensive and often drastic rearrangement <a personnel *shake-up* effected by new management>
syn overturn, reorganization, revolution, turnover
rel liquidation, purge; cleanout, cleanup, clearing out, clear-up; removal, riddance
idiom break with the past, clean sweep
shakiness *n syn* see INSTABILITY
shaking *adj syn* see TREMULOUS
rel unsettled, unstable, unsteady; tottering
con unshakable, unshaken
shaky *adj* **1 syn** see WEAK 2
rel unsettled; infirm, unsound, unsteady; precarious, tottering, tottery
2 syn see DOUBTFUL 1
3 syn see TREMULOUS
4 syn see RICKETY
shallow *adj* **1** lacking physical depth <buried in a *shallow* grave>
syn shoal, superficial
rel shallowish; surface
idiom as deep as a mud puddle, no deeper than a heavy dew, not deep enough to float a match
con bottomless, unfathomable
ant deep
2 syn see SUPERFICIAL 2
rel paltry, petty, trifling, trivial; empty, hollow, idle, vain; bird=witted, featherbrained, flighty
con heavy, profound; discerning, penetrating
ant deep
shallow *n syn* see SHOAL
ant deep
sham *n* **1 syn** see IMPOSTURE
rel facade, fakery, false front, Potemkin village
2 syn see HYPOCRISY
3 syn see MOCKERY 2
sham *vb syn* see ASSUME 4
rel ape, copy, imitate, mock; create, invent; lie, mislead
sham *adj* **1 syn** see FICTITIOUS 2
rel affected, assumed, feigned; pseudo, so-called; make-believe, pretend
2 syn see COUNTERFEIT
3 syn see ARTIFICIAL 2
rel plaster, synthetic; adulterated; bogus
shamble *vb syn* see SHUFFLE 3
shambles *n pl but usu sing in constr syn* see MESS 3
shame *n syn* see DISGRACE
rel chagrin, embarrassment; guilt, mortification, self-reproach, self-reproof
con pride, self-admiration, self-love, self-respect
ant glory
shamed *adj syn* see ASHAMED
rel crestfallen; shamefaced, shamefast; crushed, disgraced

idiom loaded (*or* bowed down) with shame
ant proud
shameful *adj syn* see DISREPUTABLE 1
shameless *adj* characterized by or exhibiting boldness and a lack of shame <a *shameless* hussy>
syn arrant, barefaced, blatant, brassy, brazen, brazenfaced, impudent, overbold, unabashed, unblushing
rel audacious, bold, cheeky, presumptuous; baldfaced, high=handed; abandoned, dissolute, profligate; immodest, lewd; disgraceful, outrageous
idiom bold as brass, dead (*or* lost) to shame
con bashful, diffident, mousy, shy; chaste, decent, modest, pure
‖shamus *n syn* see PRIVATE DETECTIVE
Shangri–la *n syn* see UTOPIA
shanty *n syn* see HUT
shape *vb syn* see MAKE 3
rel devise, plan, work up; tailor
shape *n* **1 syn** see FORM 1
rel appearance, aspect, look, semblance
2 syn see ORDER 9
3 syn see ORDER 10
rel state, whack
shapeful *adj syn* see SHAPELY
ant shapeless
shapeless *adj syn* see FORMLESS
rel unshapely; deformed, misshapen
con proportional, proportionate, proportioned, shapeful, symmetrical
ant shapeful, shapely
shapely *adj* having a regular or pleasing shape <a *shapely* girl>
syn clean-limbed, shapeful, statuesque, trim, well-proportioned, well-turned; *compare* CURVACEOUS
rel balanced, clean-cut, proportioned, regular, symmetrical; comely, pleasing; ‖built, full-figured, rounded, ‖stacked; buxom
con dumpy, squat, stumpy; angular, lank, lean; ill-favored, ill=looking
ant shapeless, unshapely
share *n* **1** something belonging to, assumed by, or falling to one (as in division or apportionment) <wanted his *share* of the prize money>
syn allotment, allowance, bite, cut, lot, part, partage, portion, quota, slice; *compare* RATION
rel proportion, quotient, quotum; commission, percentage; divide, ‖divvy; rake-off
idiom piece of the action, slice of the melon
2 syn see RATION
3 syn see INTEREST 1
share *vb* **1 syn** see APPORTION 2
rel assign, deal (out), dispense, dole (out), give out, mete (out)
idiom ‖go snucks, share and share alike
con retain, withhold; combine, unite
2 to have, get, or use in common with another or others <she *shared* her husband's fate>
syn partake, participate
rel experience
idiom have a share (*or* part) in, have (*or* take) a hand in
shared *adj syn* see COMMON 1
ant unshared
share out *vb syn* see ADMINISTER 2
sharer *n syn* see PARTICIPANT
sharp *adj* **1** having a fine edge <a *sharp* knife makes a clean cut>
syn honed, keen, razor-sharp, unblunted, whetted
rel acute
idiom sharp as a razor blade
con blunted, dulled; unsharpened
ant blunt, dull
2 syn see POINTED 1
3 syn see INTELLIGENT 2
4 possessing or indicative of alert competence and clear understanding <people of *sharp* judgment and refined sensibilities>
syn acute, keen, penetrating, penetrative, quick-sighted, quick=witted, sharp-sighted, sharp-witted; *compare* SHREWD
rel alert, bright; clever, cute, ingenious, original, resourceful; fast, quick
idiom sharp as a knife (*or* tack)
con dull-witted; unintelligent; foolish, simple, slow, stupid
ant dull

5 syn see ACUTE 3
6 syn see WISE 4
rel adroit, nimble; clever, cute; sly, unethical
idiom nobody's fool
7 syn see SHORT 5
rel acrimonious, biting, double-edged, incisive, penetrating, piercing, stabbing, stinging; caustic, virulent, vitriolic
8 causing intense mental or physical distress < a *sharp* pain >
syn acute, knifelike, piercing, shooting, stabbing
rel intense, severe, smart; biting, drilling, stinging; penetrating; agonizing, excruciating; paralyzing
9 syn see ACRID
rel odorous; strong-scented, strong-smelling; suffocating
10 syn see ACUTE 4
11 syn see STYLISH
||**sharp** *vb syn* see SHARPEN
sharp *adv syn* see JUST 1
sharpen *vb* to give a keen edge to < *sharpen* an ax >
syn edge, hone, ||sharp, whet
rel dress, file, grind, stroke
idiom hone to a razor edge, hone to razor sharpness
ant blunt, dull
sharper *n syn* see SWINDLER
sharp-eyed *adj* having keen vision < the *sharp-eyed* child found all the Easter eggs >
syn eagle-eyed, hawk-eyed, lyncean, lynx-eyed, sharp-sighted
rel alert, attentive, aware, keen, lynxlike, observant, sharp, vigilant, watchful
con myopic, nearsighted, shortsighted; dim-sighted, purblind; blind
sharpie *n syn* see SWINDLER
sharply *adv syn* see HARD 4
rel intensely, penetratingly, piercingly
sharpness *n syn* see EDGE 2
ant bluntness, dullness
sharp practice *n syn* see DECEPTION 1
sharp-sighted *adj* **1 syn** see SHARP-EYED
2 syn see SHARP 4
sharp-witted *adj* **1 syn** see SHARP 4
2 syn see WISE 4
shatter *vb* **1** to break into small pieces by or as if by a blow < *shatter* a windowpane with a rock >
syn burst, fragment, ||pash, rive, shiver, smash, ||smatter, splinter, splinterize, splitter; *compare* PULVERIZE 1
rel break, crack, rend, snap, ||spalt, split; crunch, crush; crash, dash; fragmentalize, fragmentize, pulverize; demolish, destroy, disintegrate, ruin, ||total, wreck
idiom smash to smithereens (*or* bits)
2 syn see DESTROY 1
3 syn see RATTLE 1
shatterable *adj syn* see FRAGILE 1
ant shatterproof
shatterbrain *n syn* see SCATTERBRAIN
shattering *adj syn* see DESTRUCTIVE
shattery *adj syn* see FRAGILE 1
idiom as delicate as an eggshell
shave *vb* **1 syn** see SLIVER
2 syn see CUT 6
rel shingle
3 syn see REDUCE 2
4 syn see BRUSH
idiom cut (*or* shave) it close
5 syn see SCRAPE 3
shaveling *n syn* see BOY 1
shear *vb syn* see CUT 6
rel mow; barb, barber; manicure, snip
sheath *n syn* see SKIN 3
sheathe *vb* to cover (a surface) with something that protects < a house *sheathed* with aluminum siding >
syn clad, face, side, skin
rel envelop, surround, wrap; case, cover, encase, jacket; panel
con bare, expose, strip
sheathing *n syn* see SKIN 3
shed *vb* **1 syn** see DISCARD
rel drop; divest
2 to cast off (a body covering) in a periodic process of growth or renewal < a snake *shedding* its skin >
syn exuviate, molt, slip, slough

rel cast off, discard; doff, take off
sheen *n syn* see LUSTER
rel finish; shininess
sheeny *adj syn* see LUSTROUS 1
sheepheaded *adj syn* see SIMPLE 3
sheer *adj* **1 syn** see FILMY
rel airy, chiffon, thin; see-through
2 syn see UTTER
3 syn see PURE 2
rel arrant, bald-faced, complete, outright
4 syn see STEEP 1
sheer *vb* **1 syn** see TURN 6
2 syn see SWERVE 1
||**shekels** *n pl syn* see MONEY
shell *n syn* see HULL
shell *vb* **1 syn** see SHUCK
2 syn see BOMBARD
rel pepper; rake
idiom open fire on
shellac *vb syn* see WHIP 2
shellacking *n syn* see DEFEAT 1
rel ||clobbering, whipping
shell out *vb syn* see SPEND 1
shelter *n* **1** something (as a structure or place) that covers or affords protection < a bomb *shelter* >
syn asylum, cover, covert, harbor, harborage, haven, port, refuge, retreat, sanctuary; *compare* REFUGE 1
rel buen retiro, den, hermitage, hide, hideaway, hideout, hidey=hole, retirement, tower
2 dwellings provided for numbers of people or for a community < *shelter* for the aged >
syn housing, quarterage
rel dwellings, lodging; roof
3 syn see REFUGE 1
shelter *vb syn* see HARBOR 1
shelve *vb syn* see DEFER
rel dish, drop, give up
idiom put on the shelf
shenanigan *n* **1 syn** see TRICK 1
rel fast one, game, legerdemain
2 syn see PRANK
rel frolic; goings-on, mischievousness; stunt
Sheol *n syn* see HELL
shepherd *vb syn* see GUIDE
Sherlock *n syn* see DETECTIVE
Sherlock Holmes *n syn* see DETECTIVE
shibboleth *n* **1 syn** see CATCHWORD
rel platitude, truism
2 syn see COMMONPLACE
||**shick** *adj syn* see INTOXICATED 1
||**shicker** *adj syn* see INTOXICATED 1
||**shicker** *n syn* see DRUNKARD
shield *n syn* see DEFENSE 1
rel buffer, bumper, screen
shield *vb* **1 syn** see HARBOR 1
idiom give cover (*or* shelter) to; take (*or* shield) under one's wing
ant expose
2 syn see DEFEND 1
shift *vb* ||**1 syn** see APPORTION 2
2 syn see CHANGE 5
3 syn see MOVE 4
rel alter, change, vary; budge, stir; shuffle; relocate
idiom shift place
4 syn see CONSUME 5
5 to carry on one's affairs independently and self-sufficiently often under difficult circumstances < had to *shift* for his own maintenance on very meager pay >
syn do, fare, get along, get by, get on, ||make out, manage, muddle through, stagger (on *or* along)
rel contrive, survive; freelance; progress, succeed
idiom fend for oneself, make do, make it alone, make shift, paddle one's own canoe, stand on one's own two feet

---

syn synonym(s)   *rel* related word(s)
ant antonym(s)   *con* contrasted word(s)
idiom idiomatic equivalent(s)
|| use limited; if in doubt, see a dictionary

shift *n* **1** *syn* see CONVERSION 2
  2 *syn* see RESOURCE 3
    rel gambit, maneuver, ploy, strategy
  3 *syn* see SPELL 1
  4 *syn* see TRANSITION
  5 *syn* see TURN 2
shifty *adj* **1** *syn* see EVASIVE 1
  rel dodging, elusive; cagey, collusive, conniving, crafty, cunning; furtive, shifty-eyed, sneaky, tricky; insidious, shady; deceitful, dishonest, fraudulent; treacherous
  idiom shifty as the sand
  2 *syn* see DISHONEST
  3 *syn* see UNDERHAND
  4 *syn* see MUTABLE 2
shill *n* *syn* see DECOY 2
shillaber *n* *syn* see DECOY 2
‖**shillelagh** *n* *syn* see CUDGEL
shilling shocker *n* *syn* see DIME NOVEL
shilly–shally *adj* *syn* see VACILLATING 2
shilly–shally *n* *syn* see HESITATION
shilly–shally *vb* *syn* see HESITATE
shilly–shallying *adj* *syn* see VACILLATING 2
  rel halfhearted, lukewarm
shimmer *vb* *syn* see FLASH 1
shimmer *n* *syn* see FLASH 1
  rel blinking; spangle, spark, sparking
shin *vb* *syn* see RUN 1
shindig *n* **1** a large, festive, and often overly lavish party <threw the *shindig* of the year for the debs>
  syn bash, ‖blowout, shindy
  rel fête, gala; ball, dance; party; affair, shebang; ‖shivoo
  2 *syn* see COMMOTION 3
shindy *n* **1** *syn* see SHINDIG 1
  2 *syn* see COMMOTION 3
shine *vb* **1** to emit rays of light <the storm is over and the sun is *shining*>
  syn beam, burn, gleam, radiate
  rel glimmer, glow; incandesce, luminesce; flash, sparkle, twinkle; flare; glare
  2 *syn* see POLISH 1
shine *n* **1** *syn* see DISPLAY 2
  2 *syn* see LUSTER
    rel finish
  3 *usu* **shines** *pl* *syn* see PRANK
shiner *n* *syn* see BLACK EYE 1
shingle *vb* *syn* see OVERLAP
shining *adj* *syn* see LUSTROUS 1
shiny *adj* *syn* see LUSTROUS 1
ship *vb* **1** *syn* see SEND 1
  rel direct; freight; export
  ant receive
  2 *syn* see MOVE 4
shipshape *adj* *syn* see NEAT 2
shipwreck *vb* **1** to destroy, disable, or seriously damage a ship (as by running aground or causing to founder) <the typhoon *shipwrecked* the entire fishing fleet>
  syn beach, cast away, pile up, strand, wreck
  rel break up; scuttle; founder; capsize; go down, sink
  idiom go aground, go to the bottom (*or* Davy Jones's locker), run on the rocks
  2 *syn* see RUIN 2
shirk *vb* **1** *syn* see SNEAK
  2 *syn* see DODGE 1
  rel bilk, burke; bypass, double, eschew, get around; shuffle off, shun
shirker *n* *syn* see SLACKER
shirty *adj* *syn* see ANGRY
shivaree *n* a noisy mock serenade to a newly married couple <*shivarees* and other such disappearing rural customs>
  syn ‖belling, ‖bull band, ‖callithump, charivari, ‖horning, ‖riding, ‖skimmelton
  rel entertainment, reception, welcome
shiver *vb* *syn* see SHATTER 1
shiver *vb* *syn* see SHAKE 1
‖**shivereens** *n pl* *syn* see SMITHEREENS
shivering *adj* *syn* see TREMULOUS
shivers *n pl* *syn* see JITTERS
shivery *adj* **1** *syn* see TREMULOUS

  2 *syn* see COLD 1
shoal *adj* *syn* see SHALLOW 1
shoal *n* a place where a body of water (as a sea or river) is not deep <dangerous *shoals* in uncharted waters>
  syn shallow
  rel barrier, barrier reef, coral reef, fringing reef, reef, sand reef; bank, bar, sandbank, sandbar, tombolo; hook, spit; seamount
  con abyss, deep, depth
shock *n* *syn* see PILE 1
shock *n* **1** *syn* see IMPACT
  2 *syn* see EARTHQUAKE
  3 *syn* see TRAUMA
  rel prostration, stupefaction
shock *vb* **1** to offend the moral sense of <were *shocked* by pornography>
  syn scandalize
  rel astonish, astound, startle, surprise; jar, jolt, shake up; insult, offend, outrage; appall, horrify; floor, knock out; disgust, nauseate, sicken
  idiom stink in one's nostrils, turn one's stomach
  2 to cause to undergo a physical or psychological shock <his slap *shocked* her out of hysterics>
  syn jolt, startle
  rel shake; jar; electrify
shocked *adj* *syn* see AGHAST 2
  rel jarred, jolted, shaken up, ‖shook up; offended, outraged; appalled, horrified
shocker *n* **1** *syn* see THRILLER
  2 *syn* see DIME NOVEL
shocking *adj* **1** *syn* see FEARFUL 3
  rel heinous, monstrous
  2 *syn* see OUTRAGEOUS 2
  rel burning, glaring; disgraceful, shameful; unspeakable
shoddy *adj* **1** *syn* see CHEAP 2
  rel makeshift, scambling
  2 *syn* see SHABBY 1
  3 *syn* see DISREPUTABLE 1
shoeless *adj* *syn* see BAREFOOT 1
  ant shod
shoestring *adj* *syn* see LITTLE 3
‖**shog** *vb* *syn* see PUSH 2
shoo–in *n* *syn* see SURE THING
‖**shool** *vb* *syn* see SHUFFLE
shoot *vb* **1** to cause (a weapon) to drive a projectile forward <*shoot* an arrow at a target>
  syn discharge, fire, loose
  rel trigger; launch, project; expel; blast; poop
  idiom let fly
  2 *syn* see DESTROY 1
  3 *syn* see DISCREDIT 2
  ‖**4** *syn* see DISCARD
  5 *syn* see VOMIT
  ‖**6** *syn* see PASS 9
  7 *syn* see SHOOT UP 2
  8 *syn* see FLY 1
  9 *syn* see RUSH 1
  rel gallop, highball, hotfoot; spurt
  10 *syn* see PHOTOGRAPH
shoot *n* *syn* see RAY 1
shooting *adj* *syn* see SHARP 8
  ant stationary
shooting match *n* *syn* see AFFAIR 1
shoot up *vb* **1** *syn* see SKYROCKET
  2 to take (a drug) by hypodermic needle <had been *shooting up* heroin for weeks>
  syn ‖mainline, shoot
shop *n* *syn* see STORE 4
  rel boutique
shoplift *vb* to steal displayed goods from a store <the manager caught them *shoplifting* records>
  syn ‖boost
  rel bag, cop, ‖nick, palm, pilfer, pinch, rip off, snitch, swipe
shopworn *adj* *syn* see TRITE
  rel overused, overworked, overworn
shore *n* the land bordering a usually large body of water <watched the ships while walking along the *shore*>
  syn bank, beach, coast, strand

rel coastline, shoreline, waterfront, waterside; coastland, seacoast, seashore; foreshore, littoral, shoreface, shoreside; brink, embankment, riverbank, riverside

shore (up) *vb syn* see SUPPORT 4

shore *n syn* see SUPPORT 3

short *adj* **1** having little length in space or time < a *short* visit >
syn brief
rel abbreviate, abbreviated, abridged, curtailed, decreased, diminished, lessened, shortened; curtate, decurtate
con extensive, lengthy; drawn-out, overlong; extended, prolonged, protracted
ant long
2 having small physical stature < he was the *shortest* boy present >
syn ‖low, low-set, low-statured
rel chunky, dumpy, squat, squatty, stubby, thick, thickset
con gangling, gangly, lanky, rangy; elevated, high, lofty, spiring, towering
ant tall
3 not coming up to a measure or need < fuel was very *short* that year >
syn deficient, failing, inadequate, insufficient, scant, scanty, scarce, scrimpy, shy, skimpy, slender, unsufficient, wanting; *compare* MEAGER 2
rel lacking, needing; exiguous, meager, sparse
con abounding, overflowing, teeming; abundant, ample, copious, plenteous, plentiful
ant long
4 *syn* see BLUFF
ant expansive
5 lacking in graciousness or consideration < his manner was *short* and abrupt >
syn inconsiderate, sharp, thoughtless, unceremonious, ungracious
rel bluff, blunt, brusque, crusty, curt; short-spoken; gruff, irascible
con considerate, gracious, kindly; bland, smooth; ceremonious
6 readily breaking or crumbling < a rich *short* pastry >
syn brittle, crisp, crumbly, ‖crump, crunchy, friable
rel delicate, fragile
con soggy, tough
7 *syn* see CONCISE
rel compact; pointed
idiom to the point
con extended, protracted, spun-out
ant lengthy, long-drawn-out

short *adv* **1** without hesitation or delay < stopped *short* >
syn abruptly, asudden, forthwith, sudden, suddenly
con hesitantly; gradually, slowly
2 *syn* see UNAWARES

short *n syn* see SUBSTANCE 2

short *vb syn* see SPARE 3

shortage *n syn* see FAILURE 3
rel curtailment, pinch, tightness; shortfall
con overage

short and sweet *adj syn* see CONCISE

shortcoming *n syn* see IMPERFECTION
idiom weak point
con forte, long suit

shortcut *n* a route shorter or more direct than the one ordinarily taken < they took a *shortcut* down the back roads >
syn cutoff
rel bypass
ant detour

shorten *vb* to reduce in extent (as of length or duration) < decided to *shorten* their visit > < *shorten* a skirt for summer wear >
syn abbreviate, abridge, curtail, cut, cut back, retrench, slash
rel decrease, diminish, elide, excerpt, lessen, reduce; compress, condense, contract, shrink; bobtail, clip, dock; minimize
idiom cut short
con draw out, protract
ant elongate, lengthen; extend, prolong

shorthanded *adj* short of the necessary number of people < the office was critically *shorthanded* >
syn underhanded, undermanned, understaffed
rel short, wanting
con overmanned, overstaffed

short–lived *adj syn* see TRANSIENT

rel short-haul, short-run, short-term
con long-run, long-term
ant agelong; long-lived

shortly *adv* **1** *syn* see BRIEFLY
2 *syn* see PRESENTLY 1
rel pronto, quickly

short–range *adj syn* see TACTICAL 1
ant long-range

shortsighted *adj syn* see MYOPIC
ant farsighted, longsighted

short–spoken *adj syn* see BLUFF
ant windy

shot *n* **1** *syn* see FLING 1
2 *syn* see OPPORTUNITY
3 *syn* see DRAM

‖**shot** *adj syn* see INTOXICATED 1

shotgun *vb syn* see FORCE 2

should *vb syn* see WANT 3

shoulder *vb syn* see PUSH 2

shout *vb* **1** to utter a sudden loud cry (as to express joy or triumph or to attract attention) < the mob *shouted* for a speech >
syn cry, whoop, yell; *compare* CALL 1, SCREAM 1
rel exclaim; howl, scream, shriek; bawl, bellow, clamor, roar, vociferate
con murmur, whisper
2 *syn* see SCREAM 4
3 *syn* see CALL 1
rel bark; bray
4 *syn* see TREAT 3

shove *vb* **1** *syn* see PUSH 1
rel cram, jam; dig, jab, poke, prod
idiom push and shove
2 *syn* see PUSH 2
3 *syn* see PUSH 6

shove (off) *vb syn* see GO 2
ant pull in

shovel *vb* **1** *syn* see DIG 1
2 *syn* see DIG 2

shovel *vb syn* see SHUFFLE

show *vb* **1** to set out or place on view for customers < we're *showing* lots of long dresses this fall >
syn display, offer
rel afford, supply; exhibit; present, proffer, submit; deal (in), sell
2 to reveal outwardly or make apparent < asked a question or two to *show* his intelligence >
syn demonstrate, evidence, evince, exhibit, illustrate, manifest, mark, ostend, proclaim; *compare* LOOK 4
rel disclose, discover, divulge, lay out, reveal, unveil; present, project
con camouflage, conceal, dissemble, hide, obscure
ant disguise
3 *syn* see STAGE
4 to present in such a way as to invite notice, attention, and admiration < she loved to *show* her jewels to everyone >
syn brandish, display, disport, exhibit, expose, flash, flaunt, parade, show off, trot out
rel air, lay out, set out, spread; blazon, flourish, sport, vaunt
con belittle, deprecate, depreciate, minimize
5 to give an exact and usually automatic reading or indication of < the speedometer *shows* 70 MPH >
syn indicate, mark, read, record, register, say
rel point (to); ring up
6 *syn* see LOOK 4
rel lay out, reveal, unveil
7 *syn* see GUIDE
8 *syn* see ESTABLISH 6
rel present; plead; allege
9 *syn* see APPEAR 1
rel come, show up; materialize
10 *syn* see COME 1
idiom ‖make the scene, put in an appearance, show one's face
11 *syn* see TURN UP 3

---

show *n syn* see APPEARANCE 2
  rel likeness; effect, impression
  idiom outward show
  2 *syn* see MASK 2
  3 *syn* see DISPLAY 2
  4 *syn* see OPPORTUNITY
  5 *syn* see EXHIBITION 1
  6 *syn* see EXHIBITION 2
  7 *syn* see MOVIE
  8 *syn* see SHOWING 1
shower *n syn* see BARRAGE
  rel shatter, spatter, spray
shower *vb syn* see BATHE 1
showing *n* **1** performance in a test of skill, power, or effectiveness < he made a good *showing* in the race >
  syn out, show
  rel record
  2 *syn* see APPEARANCE 2
show–me *adj syn* see INCREDULOUS
show off *vb syn* see SHOW 4
  rel boast, brag, swagger
showpiece *n* a prime or outstanding example used or suitable for exhibition < a Fabergé Easter egg was the *showpiece* of the collection >
  syn chef d'oeuvre, masterpiece, pièce de résistance
  rel gem, jewel; prize
  con claptrap, rubbish, trash, trivia, truck
showroom *n syn* see STORE 4
show up *vb syn* see EXPOSE 4
  rel discredit; invalidate
  2 *syn* see TURN UP 3
  3 *syn* see COME 1
showy *adj* given to or marked by excessive outward display < *showy* decorations >
  syn chichi, flamboyant, orchidaceous, ostentatious, peacockish, peacocky, pretentious, splashy, swank
  rel sporty; flashy, garish, gaudy, jazzy, meretricious, tawdry; gorgeous, resplendent; luxurious, opulent, ornate, sumptuous; overdone, overwrought; sensational
  con muted, quiet, restrained, subdued; elegant, graceful, restrained; appropriate, seemly
  ant unshowy
shred *n syn* see PARTICLE
shred *vb syn* see SLIVER
shreddy *adj syn* see RAGGED
shrew *n syn* see VIRAGO
  rel she-devil, spitfire
shrewd *adj* marked by clever discerning awareness and hard-headed acumen < the captain was a *shrewd* judge of character >
  syn argute, astucious, astute, cagey, heady, perspicacious, sagacious, ‖savvy; *compare* SHARP 4, WISE 2, 4
  rel canny, crafty, foxy, ingenious, ‖pawky, slick, ‖sly, tidy; clever, intelligent, knowing, quick-witted, smart; polite, smooth; judicious, prudent, sensible, wise; penetrating, piercing, probing; acute, keen, sharp; farsighted, foresighted
  con green, naive, simple, soft; foolable, gullible, slow
shrewdness *n syn* see WIT 3
  rel canniness, foxiness
shriek *vb* **1** *syn* see SCREAM 1
  rel squawk, ‖yarm
  2 *syn* see SQUEAL 2
  3 *syn* see SCREAM 4
shrill *vb syn* see SCREAM 1
shrill *adj syn* see ACUTE 4
shrine *n* a structure or place considered sacred by a religious group < pilgrims going to the *shrine* at Lourdes hoping to be healed >
  syn holy place, sanctorium, sanctuary, sanctum
  rel reliquary; enshrinement
shrink *vb* **1** *syn* see CONTRACT 3
  rel shrivel (up), wither
  con amplify, expand
  ant swell
  2 *syn* see FAIL 3
  idiom shrink (or dwindle) down to nothing
  3 *syn* see RECOIL
  rel cower, cringe, crouch, huddle, slink; draw (back), recede, retire, retreat, withdraw; boggle, demur, scruple

shrinking *adj syn* see UNDEMONSTRATIVE
shrivel *vb syn* see WITHER
  rel parch; fossilize
shroud *vb* **1** *syn* see ENFOLD 1
  2 *syn* see SCREEN 3
shrouded *adj syn* see ULTERIOR
shuck *n syn* see HULL
shuck *vb* to strip, break off, or remove the enclosing case or cover of < *shuck* corn >
  syn hull, husk, shell; *compare* SKIN 2
  rel decorticate, peel, skin, strip
shuck (off) *vb syn* see DISCARD
shudder *vb syn* see SHAKE 1
  rel gyrate, shimmy
shuffle *vb* **1** *syn* see DISORDER 1
  2 *syn* see EQUIVOCATE 2
  3 to walk awkwardly in a sliding, dragging way without lifting the feet < an old drunk *shuffling* along in filthy bedroom slippers >
  syn scuff, scuffle, shamble, ‖shool, shovel
  rel drag, pad, scrape, slipper, slip-slop, slur; draggle, straggle, trail (along)
  4 *syn* see STUMBLE 6
shuffle *n syn* see CLUTTER 2
shuffling *adj syn* see EVASIVE 1
shun *vb syn* see ESCAPE 2
  rel decline, refuse, reject; snub; despise, disdain, scorn
  idiom have nothing to do with, keep away from, stand aloof from, steer clear of, turn away from, turn one's back upon
  con accept, adopt, welcome
shunning *n syn* see ESCAPE 2
shunt *vb* **1** to push or turn off to one side < *shunt* a railroad car onto a siding >
  syn sidetrack, switch; *compare* TURN 6
  rel change, move, shift, transfer; avert, deflect, divert, head off
  idiom push aside (or to the side)
  2 *syn* see SHUTTLE
shush *vb* **1** *syn* see SILENCE
  2 *syn* see SUPPRESS 2
shut *vb syn* see CLOSE 1
  rel lock, seal; batten (down)
  ant open
‖**shut–eye** *n syn* see SLEEP 1
shut in *vb syn* see ENCLOSE 1
  ant shut out
shut–in *adj syn* see UNSOCIABLE
shut–mouthed *adj syn* see SILENT 3
  ant openmouthed
shut off *vb syn* see SCREEN 3
shut out *vb syn* see SCREEN 3
shuttle *vb* to travel back and forth frequently < *shuttled* between New York and Washington every week >
  syn shunt
  rel shuttlecock; alternate
shut up *vb* **1** *syn* see SILENCE
  2 to cease speaking < told the boy to sit down and *shut up* >
  syn dry up, dumb (up), ‖dummy (up), pipe down, ‖ring off
  rel hush, quiet (down), shush, soft-pedal
  idiom button (or seal) one's lips, keep quiet
shy *adj* **1** disinclined to obtrude oneself < *shy* in the presence of strangers >
  syn backward, bashful, coy, demure, diffident, modest, rabbity, retiring, self-effacing, timid, unassertive, unassured
  rel backhanded, hesitant, reluctant; conscious, self-conscious, self-distrustful, shamefaced, sheepish; introversive, introvert, introverted, inturned; circumspect, reserved; cautious, chary, suspicious, wary; apprehensive, fearful, nervous, skittish, timorous
  con brash, forward; aggressive, audacious, intrusive, obtruding, pushing, pushy; blunt, crass
  ant bold, obtrusive
  2 *syn* see DISINCLINED
  3 *syn* see SHORT 3
  con excess, over, surplus
shy *vb* **1** *syn* see DEMUR
  rel blench, quail, recoil, shrink
  2 *syn* see ESCAPE 2
shy *n syn* see POTSHOT
Shylock *n syn* see LOAN SHARK

shyster *n syn* see PETTIFOGGER

‖**sib** *adj syn* see SYMPATHETIC 2

sibilate *vb syn* see HISS

sibylline *adj* **1** *syn* see PROPHETIC

  2 *syn* see OBSCURE 3

sic *vb syn* see URGE

  rel agitate, catalyze, inspirit, instigate; abet, aid, countenance, favor

sick *adj* **1** affected with illness or disease <was *sick* with pneumonia>

  syn down, ill; *compare* UNWELL

  rel diseased, disordered, fevered; ailing, ‖cronk, ‖crook, funny, indisposed, unwell; debilitated, sickly, unhealthy; rocky, tottering, wobbly; confined, laid up; lousy, mean, rotten

  idiom ‖on the sick list, sick as a dog

  con healthy, strong

  ant well

  2 *syn* see MORBID

  3 *syn* see FED UP

  idiom ‖up to here with

  4 *syn* see FAULTY

  5 *syn* see SICKLY 2

sick (up) *vb syn* see VOMIT

sicken *vb* **1** *syn* see UPSET 5

  2 *syn* see DISGUST

sicken (with *or* of) *vb syn* see CONTRACT 1

sickening *adj syn* see OFFENSIVE

‖**sicker** *vb syn* see EXUDE

sickliness *n syn* see INFIRMITY 1

sickly *adj* **1** *syn* see UNWELL

  rel ‖cranky, down

  con hale, hearty; healthy, well

  ant robust

  2 accompanying, indicating, or suggesting sickness <a *sickly* complexion>

  syn peaked, ‖peaking, peaky, sick

  rel ‖pimping, puny, sickish, weak; diseased; unhealthy

  con healthy, hearty

  3 *syn* see UNWHOLESOME 1

  4 *syn* see MORBID

sickness *n* **1** the condition of being ill <finally recovered from her *sickness*>

  syn affliction, diseasedness, disorder, illness, indisposition, infirmity, unhealth; *compare* DISEASE 1, INFIRMITY 1

  rel indisposedness, unhealthfulness, unhealthiness, unwellness; affection, ailment, ill

  idiom ill health

  con haleness, healthiness, heartiness

  ant health

  2 *syn* see DISEASE 1

side *n* **1** a place, space, or direction with respect to a center or a line of division <lived on the north *side* of the street> <the morning *side* of the hill> <turned to one *side*>

  syn hand

  rel direction, flank, sector

  2 *syn* see PHASE

  3 *syn* see VIEWPOINT 2

  4 the attitude, position, or action of one person or group as opposed to another <could understand her *side* as well as his in the quarrel>

  syn part; *compare* POSITION 1

  rel attitude, disposition; posture, stance, stand; position, standpoint, viewpoint

side *vb syn* see SHEATHE

side (with) *vb syn* see SUPPORT 2

side action *n syn* see SIDE EFFECT

sideboards *n pl syn* see SIDE-WHISKERS

sideburns *n pl syn* see SIDE-WHISKERS

side effect *n* a secondary and usually adverse effect (as of a drug) <drowsiness is a common *side effect* of antihistimines>

  syn side action, side reaction

  rel effect; reaction, response

side–glance *n* a look or glance directed to one side <she shot an impatient *side-glance* at him>

  syn side-look

  rel glance; stare

sideling *adv syn* see SIDEWAYS 1

sideling *adj syn* see STEEP 1

‖**sidelings** *adv syn* see SIDEWAYS 1

sidelong *adv syn* see SIDEWAYS 1

side–look *n syn* see SIDE-GLANCE

side reaction *n syn* see SIDE EFFECT

sidereal *adj syn* see STELLAR 1

sidesplitter *n syn* see RIOT 2

sidestep *vb* **1** *syn* see EQUIVOCATE 2

  2 *syn* see SKIRT 3

  3 *syn* see DODGE 1

sideswipe *n syn* see POTSHOT

sidetrack *vb syn* see SHUNT 1

sideward *adv syn* see SIDEWAYS 1

sideways *adv* **1** to, toward, or at one side <slipped *sideways* on the ice>

  syn crabwise, laterally, sideling, ‖sidelings, sidelong, sideward, sidewise; *compare* ASIDE 1

  rel obliquely; indirectly

  con straight; directly

  2 *syn* see ASIDE 1

side–whiskers *n pl* the usually shaped growth of whiskers on both sides of a man's face <grew *side-whiskers* and a moustache in order to look older>

  syn burnsides, dundrearies, muttonchops, sideboards, sideburns

sidewise *adv* **1** *syn* see SIDEWAYS 1

  2 *syn* see ASIDE 1

sidle *vb* to move sideways or obliquely especially in an unobtrusive or furtive manner <a suspicious-looking man *sidled* up to her>

  syn edge, ‖slive

  rel ease, slip

siege *n* a sometimes prolonged period of disorder or stress (as of body or mind) <endured a three-week *siege* of flu>

  syn bout, go; *compare* ATTACK 3

  rel attack, onslaught, seizure, spell

siesta *n syn* see NAP

siesta *vb syn* see NAP

sieve *n syn* see GOSSIP 1

sieve *vb syn* see SCREEN 5

sift *vb* **1** *syn* see SCREEN 5

  2 *syn* see SORT 2

  3 *syn* see EXPLORE

sigh *vb* **1** to take in and let out a deep audible breath (as in weariness, grief, or relief) <flopped down in the chair and *sighed* deeply>

  syn ‖sock, sough, suspire

  rel breathe, respire; exhale; gasp, pant, wheeze; groan, moan; sob

  idiom heave a sigh

  2 to make a sound like sighing <the wind *sighed* in the branches>

  syn sough

  rel blow; murmur, whisper; moan; whine; whistle; howl, roar

  3 *syn* see LONG

sighful *adj syn* see MELANCHOLY 2

sight *n* **1** *syn* see EYESORE

  ‖**2** *syn* see MUCH

  3 *syn* see EYE 2

  4 *syn* see LOOK 1

  5 *syn* see VIEW 4

  6 *syn* see VIEW 5

sightless *adj syn* see BLIND 1

  ant sighted

sightseer *n syn* see TOURIST

sign *n* **1** a motion, action, gesture, or word by which a command, thought, or wish is expressed <put a finger to her lips as a *sign* to keep quiet>

  syn high sign, signal

  rel gesticulation, gesture, motion; hint, indication, suggestion, warning

  2 *syn* see CHARACTER 1

  3 *syn* see EXPRESSION 3

  rel symbolization; attestation, evidence, proof

  4 *syn* see INDICATION 3

---

syn synonym(s)   *rel* related word(s)

ant antonym(s)   *con* contrasted word(s)

idiom idiomatic equivalent(s)

‖ use limited; if in doubt, see a dictionary

rel earmark, exponent, indicator; exhibit, show

sign *vb* **1** to affix a signature to <he refused to *sign* a confession>
syn autograph, ink, signature, subscribe
idiom put one's John Hancock on, put one's John Henry down (*or* on)
2 *syn* see SIGNAL

sign (over) *vb syn* see TRANSFER 4

signal *n syn* see SIGN 1
rel alarm, alert, tocsin; movement

signal *vb* to notify by or as if by a signal <*signaled* his wife to keep quiet>
syn flag, gesture, motion, sign, signalize
idiom give the high sign (to)

signal *adj syn* see NOTICEABLE
rel characteristic, distinctive, individual, peculiar, significative; eminent, famous, illustrious, renowned

signalize *vb* **1 *syn*** see CHARACTERIZE 2
2 *syn* see SIGNAL

signature *vb syn* see SIGN 1

significance *n* **1 *syn*** see MEANING 1
2 *syn* see IMPORTANCE
rel authority, credit, influence, merit, prestige; excellence, perfection, virtue
con indifference; triviality, unimportance, worthlessness; irrelevance
ant insignificance

significancy *n syn* see MEANING 1

significant *adj* **1 *syn*** see EXPRESSIVE
rel cogent, compelling, convincing, sound, telling, valid; forceful, powerful; important, momentous, weighty
con meaningless, unexpressive; unimportant
ant insignificant
2 *syn* see IMPORTANT 1
con inconsequential, meaningless, unimportant
ant insignificant

significant *n syn* see INDICATION 3

significantly *adv syn* see WELL 8
ant insignificantly

signification *n* **1 *syn*** see MEANING 1
rel implying, signifying; construction, implication; essence, gist, substance
‖**2 *syn*** see IMPORTANCE

significative *adj syn* see INDICATIVE

signify *vb* **1 *syn*** see MEAN 2
rel bear, carry, convey; bespeak, purport
2 *syn* see MATTER

sign on *vb syn* see ENTER 3

sign up *vb syn* see ENTER 3

silence *n* **1** absence of sound or noise <the heavy *silence* of the night>
syn noiselessness, quiet, quietness, quietude, soundlessness, still, stillness
rel calm, hush, lull
con din, uproar
ant noise
2 *syn* see SECRECY
3 *syn* see DEATH 1

silence *vb* to compel or reduce to silence <*silenced* the courtroom chatter by pounding his gavel>
syn choke (off), hush, quiet, ‖quieten, shush, shut up, still
rel dampen, deaden, dumb, lull, muffle, mute; quash, quell, squash, squelch, suppress; gag, muzzle

silent *adj* **1 *syn*** see DUMB 1
2 characterized by absence of speech <was *silent* as he faced the altar>
syn dumb, mum, ‖mumchance, mute, speechless, wordless; *compare* DUMB 1
rel inarticulate, muted, tongue-tied, voiceless
con speaking, talking
3 showing marked restraint in speaking <a stern, *silent* man>
syn close, close-lipped, closemouthed, close-tongued, dumb, inconversable, reserved, reticent, shut-mouthed, silentious, speechless, taciturn, tight-lipped, tight-mouthed, uncommunicative, wordless
rel checked, curbed, inhibited, restrained; unconversational, unsociable; inarticulate, incoherent; mute, voiceless; mum, secretive
con articulate, fluent, glib, vocal, voluble; babblative, garrulous, loquacious, windy; blabbering, blabbery, chattering

ant talkative
4 *syn* see STILL 3
idiom silent as a post (*or* stone), silent as the grave (*or* tomb)
ant noisy
5 *syn* see UNSPOKEN 1

silentious *adj syn* see SILENT 3

silhouette *n syn* see OUTLINE
rel ‖shade, shadow

silken *adj* **1 *syn*** see SOFT 3
2 *syn* see INGRATIATING

silky *adj* **1 *syn*** see SOFT 3
2 *syn* see INGRATIATING

silliness *n syn* see FOOLISHNESS
rel illogicality
con logic, logicality, logicalness, sanity, sensibleness; wisdom

silly *adj* **1 *syn*** see SIMPLE 3
rel empty, empty-headed, vacuous; irrational, unreasonable; ignorant, unintelligent, unwise
ant sensible
2 *syn* see GIDDY 1
rel ‖balmy, crazy, ‖dippy, irrational, off, ‖wacked-out
idiom silly as a goose
con level-headed, practical, rational, serious
ant sensible
3 *syn* see FOOLISH 2
rel funny, senseless

silvern *adj syn* see SILVERY

silver-tongued *adj syn* see GLIB

silvery *adj* relating to, containing, or resembling silver <repeated polishings gave the wood a *silvery* sheen>
syn argent, argentate, argenteous, argentine, silvern
rel silver; brilliant, glittering, shimmering, shining

similar *adj syn* see LIKE
rel complementary, correlative; reciprocal
idiom much of a muchness, much the same
con antithetical, antonymous, contradictory, contrary, opposite
ant dissimilar

similarity *n syn* see LIKENESS
rel approximation; collation, correlation; association, interrelation; parallel; closeness; coincidence, synonymity
con unlikeness, variance
ant dissimilarity

similarly *adv syn* see ALSO 1
idiom by the same token

simile *n* **1 *syn*** see ANALOGY 2
2 *syn* see LIKENESS

similitude *n* **1 *syn*** see LIKENESS
rel copy, image, replica
ant dissimilitude
2 *syn* see ANALOGY 2

simmer *vb* **1 *syn*** see BOIL 2
2 *syn* see SEETHE 4

simmer down *vb syn* see COMPOSE 4
rel quiet (down), subside
idiom ‖cool it, take it easy
con boil, seethe; explode, fulminate
ant boil over

Simon Legree *n syn* see SLAVE DRIVER

simon-pure *adj syn* see AUTHENTIC 2

simp *n syn* see DUNCE

simper *vb syn* see SMIRK

simple *adj* **1 *syn*** see NATURAL 5
rel childish, childlike; amateur, green, unexperienced; trusting; ‖square
2 *syn* see PLAIN 1
ant elaborate
3 actually or apparently deficient in intelligence <a poor *simple* woman easily duped>
syn asinine, brainless, ‖buffle-headed, fatuous, foolish, insensate, mindless, nitwitted, senseless, sheepheaded, silly, soft, spoony, unintelligent, unwitty, weak-headed, weak-minded, witless; *compare* RETARDED, STUPID 1
rel amateur, green, inexperienced, inexpert; credulous, gullible; childish, childlike, naive; ignorant, illiterate, uneducated, unschooled, untaught; crass, dense, dopey, dull, dumb, slow, stupid; doting, feebleminded, idiotic, retarded, simpleminded
con able, competent; alert, clever, keen; bright, intelligent, understanding

ant wise
4 *syn* see RETARDED
5 *syn* see PURE 2
rel inelaborate, stark; bald, bare, mere; fundamental, uncompounded
6 *syn* see EASY 1
rel incomplex, incomplicate
idiom simple as ABC
ant complex, complicated
simple *n syn* see FOOL 3
simplehearted *adj syn* see NATURAL 5
simpleminded *adj syn* see RETARDED
simplest *adj syn* see ELEMENTARY 1
simpleton *n* **1** *syn* see FOOL 4
2 *syn* see DUNCE
rel bungler, ‖clot
simplify *vb* to make simple or simpler <*simplify* a manufacturing process>
syn boil down, streamline
rel clarify, clean up, disentangle, disinvolve, straighten (out), unscramble; abridge, cut down, reduce, shorten; oversimplify
ant complicate
simply *adv syn* see JUST 3
simulacrum *n* **1** *syn* see IMAGE 1
2 *syn* see IMITATION
3 *syn* see APPEARANCE 2
simulate *vb* **1** *syn* see ASSUME 4
rel ape, copy, imitate, mimic; play-act, pose
idiom ‖make out like (*or* as if)
2 *syn* see RESEMBLE
simulated *adj* **1** *syn* see FICTITIOUS 2
ant genuine
2 *syn* see ARTIFICIAL 2
ant genuine
simultaneous *adj syn* see CONTEMPORARY 1
rel agreeing, concurring, coinciding
simultaneously *adv syn* see TOGETHER 1
idiom in one breath
sin *n* **1** *syn* see EVIL 3
2 *syn* see EVIL 2
3 *syn* see IMPERFECTION
sin *vb syn* see TRESPASS 1
since *prep syn* see AFTER 2
ant before
since *conj syn* see BECAUSE
sincere *adj* **1** genuine in feeling or expression <had a *sincere* dislike for politics>
syn heartfelt, hearty, unfeigned, wholehearted, whole-souled; *compare* GENUINE 3
rel candid, frank, frankhearted, open, plain; faithful, honest, truthful; aboveboard, forthright, pretensionless, straightforward, unpretentious; dear, devout, heartful; meant, unaffected
con affected, artificial, feigned, put-on, unmeant
ant insincere
2 *syn* see GENUINE 3
rel authentic, bona fide; serious; actual
idiom honest to God
ant insincere
sincereness *n syn* see GOOD FAITH
sincerity *n syn* see GOOD FAITH
rel heart; goodwill; singleness, straightforwardness
con cunning, deceit, guile; ill will
ant insincerity
sine qua non *n syn* see ESSENTIAL 2
sinew *n* **1** *syn* see POWER 4
2 *usu* **sinews** *pl syn* see MAINSTAY
sinewy *adj syn* see MUSCULAR 1
rel strong, sturdy, tenacious, tough
ant flabby
2 *syn* see MUSCULAR 2
sinful *adj* **1** *syn* see WRONG 1
rel base, low, vile; disgraceful, shameful; culpable, damnable
2 *syn* see BLAMEWORTHY
ant sinless
sing *vb* **1** to utter words in musical tones and with musical inflections and modulations <children often can *sing* before they converse>
syn chant, tune, vocalize

rel descant; carol, serenade, troll; croon, hum, lull, lullaby; cantillate, hymn, intone; singsong; roar
2 *syn* see TALK 6
‖**3** *syn* see INFORM 3
single *adj* **1** being without a spouse <enjoying life as a *single* girl>
syn sole, spouseless, unmarried, unwed
rel free, unattached, unfettered; celibate; maiden, virgin
idiom footloose and fancy-free
con attached; united; wed
ant married
2 one as distinguished from two or more or all others <a *single* instance of dishonesty has been cited>
syn lone, one, only, particular, separate, sole, solitary, unique
rel individual, singular; especial, special, specific; distinguished, singled-out; distinct
con several; manifold, many, numerous
ant multiple
3 *syn* see FRANK
4 *syn* see SOLE 4
single (out) *vb syn* see CHOOSE 1
rel screen, winnow (out); accept, admit, receive
single–eyed *adj syn* see FRANK
single–hearted *adj syn* see FRANK
single–minded *adj* **1** *syn* see FRANK
2 *syn* see INFLEXIBLE 2
rel diehard; bigoted
singleness *n* **1** *syn* see UNIQUENESS
2 *syn* see UNITY 1
ant multifariousness
singly *adv syn* see APART 1
ant together
singular *adj* **1** *syn* see SEVERAL 1
rel discrete; certain, definite; exclusive
2 *syn* see EXCEPTIONAL 1
ant usual
3 *syn* see ONLY 2
idiom first and last, one and only, one only
4 *syn* see STRANGE 4
idiom passing strange
singularity *n* **1** *syn* see INDIVIDUALITY 4
2 *syn* see INDIVIDUALITY 3
3 *syn* see UNITY 1
ant multiplicity
singularize *vb syn* see CHARACTERIZE 2
singularness *n syn* see UNITY 1
ant multifariousness
sinister *adj* seriously threatening disaster <a *sinister* plot>
syn baleful, malefic, maleficent, malign; *compare* OMINOUS
rel fateful, ill-omened, inauspicious, ominous, portentous, unpropitious; apocalyptic, dire, doomful, ill-boding, threatening; lowering, menacing; evil, malicious
con harmless, innocent, innocuous
sink *vb* **1** to become submerged <the overloaded raft *sank* below the surface>
syn founder, go down, go under, submerge, submerse
rel capsize, overturn, tip (over); dive, plunge; scuttle; shipwreck, wreck
idiom go to Davy Jones's locker, go to the bottom, sink like a rock
con come up, rise
ant float
2 *syn* see SET 12
3 *syn* see DETERIORATE 1
ant rise
4 *syn* see STOOP 2
5 *syn* see LOWER 3
6 *syn* see THRUST 2
7 *syn* see HUMBLE
ant uplift
sink *n* **1** a place marked by a staggering amount of corruption and filth <that area of the city was a *sink* of vice and crime>

---

syn synonym(s)
ant antonym(s)
idiom idiomatic equivalent(s)
‖ use limited; if in doubt, see a dictionary
rel related word(s)
con contrasted word(s)

syn Augean stable, cesspit, cesspool, den, pandemonium, Sodom, sty

rel hellhole; fleshpot

idiom Alsatian den, den of iniquity, sink of corruption

2 *syn* see DEPRESSION 2

sinkage *n syn* see DEPRESSION 2

sinkhole *n syn* see DEPRESSION 2

sinuous *adj syn* see WINDING

rel twisted; snake-shaped

idiom twisting and turning

sip *vb syn* see DRINK 1

siphon *vb* **1** *syn* see CONDUCT 4

2 *syn* see DRAIN 1

sire *n syn* see FATHER 2

sire *vb* **1** *syn* see FATHER 1

2 *syn* see GENERATE 1

siren *n* an enticingly attractive woman who lures men into dangerous or compromising situations <a slinky *siren* of the silent screen era>

syn femme fatale, Lorelei, seductress, temptress

rel charmer, vamp

siren *adj syn* see ATTRACTIVE 1

rel sirenic

siren song *n syn* see LURE 2

sissified *adj syn* see EFFEMINATE

sissy *n syn* see WEAKLING

sissy *adj syn* see EFFEMINATE

sissy–pants (*or* **sissy–britches**) *n pl but sing or pl in constr syn* see WEAKLING

sit *vb* **1** to rest on the buttocks or haunches <she was *sitting* in a chair>

syn ‖set

rel perch, rest; ‖plop (down), seat, sit down; squat

con arise, get up, rise, stand, stand up

2 *syn* see CONVENE 1

3 *syn* see POSE 3

4 *syn* see SET 11

5 *syn* see SEAT

rel ensconce, install, settle

sit down *vb syn* see ALIGHT

site *n* **1** *syn* see PLACE 1

2 *syn* see SCENE 3

3 a place where an archaeological excavation is made <a burial *site*>

syn dig

4 *syn* see HABITAT

sited *adj syn* see SITUATED

‖**sitfast** *adj syn* see IMMOVABLE 1

sitting duck *n syn* see TARGET 1

rel sitter

situate *adj syn* see SITUATED

situated *adj* having a site, situation, or location <a town *situated* on a hill>

syn located, placed, positioned, set, sited, situate

situation *n* **1** *syn* see PLACE 1

2 *syn* see PREGNANCY

3 *syn* see JOB 2

4 *syn* see STATUS 1

5 *syn* see STATE 1

rel bargain

sizable *adj* **1** *syn* see CONSIDERABLE 2

2 *syn* see BIG 1

rel man-sized; giant-sized

sizableness *n syn* see SIZE 2

size *n* **1** the amount of measurable space or area occupied by or comprising a thing <the *size* of the card is 3″x 5″>

syn admeasurement, dimension(s), dimensionality, extent, magnitude, measure, proportion

rel area; body, bulk, mass, volume; height; extension, length; amplitude, breadth, expanse, spread, stretch, width; measurement

2 considerable amount, proportion, volume, character, or importance <left an estate of some *size*>

syn amplitude, bigness, greatness, largeness, magnitude, sizableness

rel dimension, extent

con littleness, smallness; minuteness, tininess

sizz *vb syn* see HISS

sizzle *vb* **1** *syn* see SEAR 2

2 *syn* see HISS

sizzling *adj syn* see HOT 1

‖**skag** *n syn* see CIGARETTE

skate *n syn* see MAN 3

sked *n syn* see PROGRAM 1

sked *vb syn* see SCHEDULE 1

skedaddle *vb* **1** *syn* see RUN 2

rel ‖split; cut out

2 *syn* see GET OUT 1

idiom lift them up and set them down, ‖take off like a bat out of hell

‖**skeet** *vb syn* see HURRY 2

skeezicks *n syn* see SCAMP

skein *n syn* see MAZE 1

skeletal *adj syn* see EMACIATED

skeleton *vb syn* see SKETCH

skeletonize *vb syn* see SKETCH

‖**sken** *vb syn* see SQUINT

skeptic *n* a doubting or incredulous person <men of long experience are often *skeptics*>

syn doubter, doubting Thomas, headshaker, Pyrrhonian, Pyrrhonist, unbeliever, zetetic

rel questioner; agnostic; pessimist; scoffer; cynic, misanthrope; disbeliever

con accepter; apostle, disciple, follower; devotee, diehard

ant believer

skeptical *adj syn* see INCREDULOUS

rel freethinking; dissenting; suspicious; cynical

idiom ‖from Missouri

ant believing

skeptically *adv syn* see ASKANCE 2

idiom with a grain of salt, with a note of skepticism, with a skeptical eye

con trustingly

ant gullibly

skepticism *n syn* see UNCERTAINTY

rel qualm, qualmishness

idiom question in one's mind, shadow of doubt

con belief, trust

ant gullibility

sketch *n syn* see COMPENDIUM 1

sketch *vb* to present succinctly <let's *sketch* our plan of action>

syn adumbrate, block (out), chalk (out), characterize, draft, outline, rough (out), skeleton, skeletonize

rel depict; diagram, diagrammatize; blueprint, delineate, line; draw, plot, trace; design, develop; detail, lay out, map (out)

sketchy *adj syn* see SUPERFICIAL 2

skew *vb* **1** *syn* see SLANT 3

2 *syn* see SWERVE 1

rel skid, slide, slip

skewer *vb syn* see IMPALE

skid *vb* **1** *syn* see SLIDE 3

rel sheer, skew, slue, veer

idiom go into a skid

2 *syn* see PLUMMET

skiddoo *vb syn* see GET OUT 1

idiom go (*or* take) off like a shot

skid road *n syn* see SKID ROW

skid row *n* a city street or district notorious for cheap bars, flophouses, and homeless derelicts <boozy old men wandering the *skid row*>

syn bowery, skid road

skill *n* **1** *syn* see ABILITY 2

2 *syn* see ART 1

3 *syn* see ADDRESS 1

rel ease, skillfulness

skilled *adj* **1** *syn* see PROFICIENT

con skill-less, unproficient

ant unskilled, unskillful

2 *syn* see EXPERIENCED

rel prepared, primed, trained

con unfit, unqualified, untrained

ant unskilled

skillet *n syn* see FRYING PAN

skillful *adj* **1** *syn* see PROFICIENT

rel learned, versant, well-versed

ant unskillful

2 accomplished or done with proficiency or skill < his answer was a very *skillful* evasion >
  syn adroit, clever, good, pretty, ‖skilly, wicked, workmanlike, workmanly; *compare* CLEVER 4, PROFICIENT
  rel expert, masterful
  con clumsy; unskilled
  ant inept, unskillful
‖**skilly** *adj syn* see SKILLFUL 2
skim *vb* **1** *syn* see BRUSH
  2 *syn* see GLANCE 1
  3 *syn* see FLY 1
skim (through) *vb syn* see BROWSE
  con examine, inspect, scrutinize
skimble–skamble *n syn* see GIBBERISH 1
‖**skimmelton** *n syn* see SHIVAREE
skimp *adj syn* see MEAGER 2
skimp *vb* **1** *syn* see SCRIMP
  2 *syn* see SPARE 3
skimpy *adj* **1** *syn* see MEAGER 2
  2 *syn* see SHORT 3
skin *n* **1** *syn* see HIDE
  2 *syn* see HULL
  3 a usually thin casing forming the outside surface of a structure or thing < aircraft *skins* made of aluminum alloys >
  syn sheath, sheathing
  rel facing, siding; case, casing, cover, jacket; shell
  4 *syn* see MISER
  5 *syn* see SWINDLER
  ‖**6** *syn* see DOLLAR
skin *vb* **1** *syn* see SHEATHE
  2 to remove the surface, skin, or thin outer covering of < *skin* a Bermuda onion >
  syn decorticate, excorticate, peel, scale, strip; *compare* SHUCK
  rel cut off, pull off; pare, shave (off), trim; hull, husk, shuck; bark, rind; excoriate, flay, gall
  3 *syn* see OVERCHARGE 1
  4 *syn* see CRITICIZE
  5 *syn* see HURRY 2
‖**skinch** *vb* **1** *syn* see SCRIMP
  2 *syn* see SPARE 3
skinflint *n syn* see MISER
‖**skinhead** *n syn* see BALDHEAD
skinny *adj syn* see LEAN
  rel twiggy, weedy; emaciated; skeletal
  idiom mere skin and bones, skinny as a rail
  ant fleshy
skip *vb* **1** to move or proceed with a light bounding step < children *skipping* home from school >
  syn hop, lope, skitter, spring, trip
  rel caper, cavort, curvet, frisk, gambol; bounce, hippety-hop; jump; leap; bound
  con hobble, shamble, shuffle; hitch, limp, stagger, totter
  2 *syn* see GLANCE 1
  3 *syn* see RUN 2
  idiom ‖split the scene
skip *n syn* see OMISSION
skirmish *n* **1** *syn* see CLASH 2
  rel assault, attack; ambush
  con pitched battle
  2 *syn* see ENCOUNTER
skirr *vb* **1** *syn* see RUN 2
  2 *syn* see FLY 1
skirt *n syn* see BORDER 1
  rel skirting
skirt *vb* **1** *syn* see BORDER 1
  2 to make a detour or circuit (as around a congested area) < *skirted* the city to avoid traffic >
  syn bypass, circumnavigate, circumvent, detour
  idiom go around
  3 to avoid (as a topic or question) because of difficulty, complexity, controversy, or danger < *skirted* all touchy issues >
  syn burke, bypass, circumvent, ‖polly-fox, sidestep; *compare* EQUIVOCATE 2, ESCAPE 2
  rel avoid, dodge, duck, evade, hedge; elude, escape; ignore, skip
  idiom get around
  con confront, face, meet, take on
‖**skite** *n syn* see PRANK
skitter *vb syn* see SKIP 1

skittery *adj syn* see EXCITABLE
skittish *adj* **1** *syn* see GIDDY 1
  rel irresponsible, undependable, unreliable
  2 *syn* see EXCITABLE
  rel restive; nervous
skive *vb syn* see CUT 6
skiver *vb syn* see IMPALE
skookum *adj syn* see EXCELLENT
skookum–house *n syn* see JAIL
skulk *vb syn* see SNEAK
skunk *n syn* see SNOT 1
skunk *vb syn* see WHIP 2
sky *n* the expanse of space surrounding the earth < blue *sky* criss-crossed with jet trails >
  syn empyrean, firmament, heaven(s), welkin
  rel azure; celestial sphere
  idiom the wild blue yonder
sky–high *adv syn* see APART 3
sky–high *adj syn* see EXCESSIVE 1
skylarking *n* **1** *syn* see HORSEPLAY
  idiom ‖making whoopee
  2 *syn* see REVELRY 2
sky pilot *n syn* see CLERGYMAN
  rel chaplain; padre
skyrocket *vb* to rise abruptly and rapidly (as to an unprecedented level or amount) < when the election was over taxes and prices *skyrocketed* >
  syn rocket, shoot up, soar
  rel climb, rise; upsoar, upspring
  con slide; fall; drop
  ant crash, plummet
skyscraping *adj syn* see LOFTY 6
slab *n syn* see BAR 1
  rel chunk, lump
‖**slab** *n syn* see SLIME
slabber *vb syn* see DROOL 2
slack *adj* **1** *syn* see NEGLIGENT
  rel dilatory, lackadaisical, lethargic, sluggish; faineant, indolent, lazy, slothful; inert, stagnant
  con assiduous, busy, diligent, industrious, sedulous
  2 *syn* see LOOSE 1
  rel feeble, infirm, soft, unsteady, weak; inactive, inert, passive, supine; laggard, leisurely, slow
  con tensed, tightened; constant, equable, even, steady, uniform; firm, hard
  ant taut, tight
  3 *syn* see SLOW 3
slack *vb syn* see LOOSE 5
  idiom ‖cut some slack, make slack
  ant tighten
slack *n syn* see SLOWDOWN 1
slacken *vb* **1** *syn* see DELAY 1
  idiom keep back
  ant quicken
  2 *syn* see ABATE 4
  3 *syn* see LOOSE 5
  ant tighten
slackening *n syn* see SLOWDOWN 1
slacker *n* one who shirks work, responsibility, or an obligation < didn't want any *slackers* in his office >
  syn goldbrick, shirker, slinker, ‖spiv
  rel idler, loafer; slugabed, sluggard
slack–spined *adj syn* see WEAK 4
slake *vb syn* see QUENCH 4
slam *n* **1** *syn* see BLOW 1
  2 *syn* see BANG 2
  3 *syn* see ANIMADVERSION
  rel fling, swipe; crack, potshot; rap, slap; dig, jab
slam *vb* **1** to strike with extreme force or violence < *slammed* the ball out of the park > < the car *slammed* into the fence >
  syn belt, blast, clobber, slug, smash, wallop; *compare* STRIKE 2
  rel bang, bat, hit, knock, slap, swat, thwack; cudgel, hammer, mace; batter, beat, pound

---

syn synonym(s)   *rel* related word(s)
ant antonym(s)   *con* contrasted word(s)
idiom idiomatic equivalent(s)
‖ use limited; if in doubt, see a dictionary

2 *syn* see LAMBASTE 3

‖**slam** *adv syn* see WELL 3

slammer *n syn* see JAIL

slander *n syn* see DETRACTION
  rel black wash, muckraking, mud-slinging, roorback, scandal=
mongering

slander *vb syn* see MALIGN
  rel assail, attack; damage, hurt, injure; blackwash, muckrake;
belie, strumpet
  idiom dish the dirt, run a smear campaign, sling the mud
  ant panegyrize

slanderous *adj syn* see LIBELOUS
  rel blackwashing, muckraking, scandal-mongering
  ant panegyrical

slang *n syn* see DIALECT 2
  rel slanginess, slanguage

slangism *n syn* see BARBARISM

slant *adv syn* see ASIDE 1

slant *vb* **1** to set or be set at an angle < *slanted* the ladder against
the wall >
  syn cant, heel, incline, lean, list, recline, slope, tilt, tip
  rel bank, decline, descend; bend, deviate, diverge, splay, swerve,
veer
  2 to direct (written or spoken material) to the interests of a particular audience or group < a magazine *slanted* to farm fami-
lies >
  syn aim, angle
  rel direct, orient, point, train; concentrate, focus; spoon-feed;
bias, skew, warp
  3 to orient (material) from objective presentation so as to favor
a particular bias < accused the media of *slanting* the news
against the president >
  syn angle, bias, skew; *compare* PREJUDICE 2
  rel influence, prejudice; color, distort, twist, warp
  ant objectify, objectivize

slant *n* **1** *syn* see SLOPE
  2 *syn* see VIEWPOINT 2
  rel predilection, predisposition, prejudice

slanted *adj syn* see DIAGONAL

slanting *adj syn* see DIAGONAL

slantingly *adv syn* see ASIDE 1

slantingways *adv* **1** *syn* see ASIDE 1
  2 *syn* see DIAGONALLY

slantly *adv syn* see ASIDE 1

slantways *adv* **1** *syn* see ASIDE 1
  2 *syn* see DIAGONALLY

slantwise *adv* **1** *syn* see ASIDE 1
  2 *syn* see DIAGONALLY

slap *n* **1** *syn* see CUFF
  2 *syn* see AFFRONT
  3 *syn* see FLING 1

slap *vb* **1** to strike quickly and sharply with the hand < *slapped*
the hysterical girl >
  syn blip, box, buffet, cuff, smack, spank, ‖wherret; *compare*
STRIKE 2
  rel ‖biff, ding, hit, sock, swat, whack; ‖wap, wham; bash
  2 *syn* see LAMBASTE 3

‖**slap** *adv syn* see WELL 3

slap around *vb syn* see MANHANDLE

slapdash *adj* **1** *syn* see RANDOM
  2 *syn* see SLIPSHOD 3

‖**slap–up** *adj syn* see EXCELLENT

slash *vb* **1** *syn* see CUT 1
  2 *syn* see HACK
  3 *syn* see LAMBASTE 3
  idiom ‖light into
  4 *syn* see REDUCE 2
  5 *syn* see SHORTEN

slate *n syn* see TICKET 3

‖**slate** *vb syn* see LAMBASTE 3

slather *n, often* **slathers** *pl syn* see SCAD

slattern *n* **1** an untidy slovenly woman < two blowsy *slatterns*
gossiping at the bar >
  syn dowd, dowdy, drab, draggle-tail, ‖malkin, slut, ‖streel,
traipse
  rel frump; slob, ‖slommack, sloven; crone, gammer, hag, witch
  2 *syn* see WANTON
  rel prostitute, whore

slattern *adj syn* see SLATTERNLY

slatternly *adj* being habitually untidy and very dirty especially in
dress or appearance < a filthy, *slatternly* old woman >
  syn blowsy, dowdy, draggletailed, frowsy, slattern, sordid; *compare* SLOVENLY 1
  rel careless, disordered, neglected, poky; bedraggled, disheveled,
draggled, draggly, messy, mussy, slipshod, sloppy, slovenly, unkempt, untidy; dirty, filthy, foul, grimy, squalid
  con clean, fresh, neat, tidy, trim; smart; immaculate, spotless
  ant bandbox

slaughter *n syn* see MASSACRE
  rel slaughtery; annihilation, destruction

slaughter *vb* **1** to kill (animals) for food < *slaughtered* a beef for
the winter >
  syn butcher, slay
  rel stick
  2 to kill (a person) in an especially bloody or barbarous manner
< Jack the Ripper *slaughtered* his victims with a knife >
  syn butcher, slay
  rel kill, murder, ‖total, ‖waste; maim, mangle, mutilate, torture
  3 to kill (people) in large numbers < millions *slaughtered* in
death camps >
  syn annihilate, decimate, exterminate, massacre, wipe (out)

‖**slaunchways** *adv* **1** *syn* see DIAGONALLY
  2 *syn* see ASIDE 1

slave *n* **1** a person held in servitude or bondage < plantations
worked by *slaves* >
  syn bondman, bondslave, bondsman, chattel, mancipium
  rel help, menial, retainer, servant; helot, serf, thrall, vassal
  con freedman, freedwoman; ‖deditician
  ant freeman
  2 one who works at a hard, monotonous, usually menial task
< *slaves* working all night on a senator's speech >
  syn dray horse, drudge, galley slave, peon, slavey, toiler, workhorse
  rel ‖coolie

slave *vb syn* see DRUDGE
  idiom work like a slave

slave driver *n* a person in authority who exacts extreme effort
from his subordinates < the chief proofreader was a real *slave
driver* >
  syn rawhider, Simon Legree, taskmaster
  rel martinet
  idiom a hard taskmaster

slaver *vb* **1** *syn* see DROOL 2
  2 *syn* see FAWN

slaver *n syn* see SALIVA

slavery *n* **1** *syn* see WORK 2
  2 *syn* see BONDAGE
  idiom involuntary servitude, the yoke (*or* chains) of slavery

slavey *n* **1** *syn* see SLAVE 2
  2 *syn* see HACK 2

slavish *adj* **1** *syn* see HARD 6
  2 *syn* see SUBSERVIENT 2
  rel spineless, subdued, tame; miserable, wretched
  ant independent
  3 copying obsequiously something superior < the painting was a
slavish copy of an old master >
  syn apish, emulative, imitative
  rel uninspired; unoriginal
  con fresh, new, novel, original; fanciful, imaginative, ingenious,
inspired; extravagant, high-flown

slay *vb* **1** *syn* see KILL 1
  2 *syn* see MURDER 1
  3 *syn* see SLAUGHTER 2
  4 *syn* see SLAUGHTER 2

slayer *n syn* see MURDERER

sleazy *adj* **1** *syn* see LIMP 1
  rel slight, tenuous, thin; gossamery
  2 *syn* see CHEAP 2
  3 *syn* see SHABBY 1

sleek *vb syn* see POLISH 2

sleek *adj* having a very smooth or lustrous surface or texture
< the car's *sleek* new paint job >
  syn glassy, glossy, polished, ‖sleekit, sleeky, smarmy
  rel smooth; glistening, lustrous

‖**sleekit** *adj syn* see SLEEK

sleeky *adj syn* see SLEEK

sleep *n* **1** the natural periodic suspension of consciousness during which the powers of the body are restored <needed eight hours of *sleep* to function efficiently>
  syn ‖doss, ‖shut-eye, slumber; *compare* DOZE, NAP
  rel repose, rest; slumberland
  idiom land of Nod, the arms of Morpheus
  con wakefulness
  2 *syn* see LETHARGY 1
  3 *syn* see DEATH 1
sleep *vb* to rest in a state of sleep <*slept* for over eight hours>
  syn ‖doss, slumber; *compare* DOZE, NAP
  rel relax, repose, rest; oversleep, sleep in
  idiom be in the land of Nod, be sunk in sleep, pound one's ear, rest in the arms of Morpheus, sleep like a top (*or* log)
  con arouse, awaken, wake (up)
sleeplessness *n* *syn* see INSOMNIA
sleepy *adj* **1** having an inclination for or affected by sleep <was *sleepy* after the long day>
  syn dozy, drowsy, nodding, ‖peepy, ‖sloomy, slumberous, slumbery, snoozy, somnolent, soporific
  rel heavy, heavy-eyed, lethargic, sluggish, torpid; dazed, dopey, listless, oscitant, yawning; asleep, sleeping, slumbering; nepenthean, poppied; comatose, ‖out
  con awake, conscious; restless, sleepless, unsleeping; alert, wide-awake
  ant wakeful
  2 *syn* see INACTIVE
  3 *syn* see SOPORIFIC 1
‖**sleer** *vb* *syn* see SNEER 1
sleight *n* **1** *syn* see ADDRESS 1
  2 *syn* see TRICK 1
‖**sleighty** *adj* *syn* see CLEVER 4
slender *adj* **1** *syn* see THIN 1
  rel slenderish, slimmish; lithe, svelte, trim
  idiom slender as a reed
  2 *syn* see SHORT 3
  3 *syn* see REMOTE 4
slenderize *vb* *syn* see REDUCE 5
sleuth *n* *syn* see DETECTIVE
slew *n* *syn* see SCAD
slewed *adj* *syn* see INTOXICATED 1
slice *n* *syn* see SHARE 1
  rel segment
  idiom a slice of the pie (*or* melon)
slice *vb* **1** *syn* see CUT 1
  2 *syn* see CUT 5
slick *vb* **1** *syn* see POLISH 2
  2 *syn* see DRESS UP 1
  3 *syn* see SLIDE 1
slick *adj* **1** having a glassy surface that often offers insecure footing <a floor *slick* with wax>
  syn greasy, lubricious, ‖sliddery, ‖slipper, slippery, slippy, slithery
  rel oily; ‖slape, smooth; soapy
  idiom slick as a greased pig
  con coarse, gritty, rough, uneven
  2 *syn* see FULSOME
  rel glossy; slippery
  3 *syn* see WISE 4
slicker *n* *syn* see SWINDLER
‖**slidder** *vb* **1** *syn* see SLIDE 3
  2 *syn* see SLITHER 2
‖**sliddery** *adj* *syn* see SLICK 1
slide *vb* **1** to go or progress with a smooth continuous motion <goldfish *slid* across the pool>
  syn glide, glissade, slick, slip, slither
  rel flow, stream
  2 *syn* see SLIP 6
  3 to fall or nearly fall because of loss of balance or footing <stumbled and *slid* on the ice>
  syn skid, ‖slidder, slip, ‖slur
  idiom take a slide (*or* a skid)
  4 to shift or be shifted out of place or away from one's grasp <the packages *slid* from her arms>
  syn slip
  rel shift; move; fall, spill, tumble
  5 *syn* see CREEP 1
  6 to take a natural course <preferred to let the matter *slide* for a while>

  syn coast, drift
  rel glide
  idiom run its course
  7 *syn* see STEAL 3
  8 *syn* see SNEAK
slide *n* *syn* see DECLINE 3
slight *adj* **1** *syn* see THIN 1
  rel slightish, ‖slighty; smallish; pint-sized
  2 *syn* see DELICATE 5
  rel gossamery, sleazy
  3 *syn* see REMOTE 4
slight *vb* *syn* see NEGLECT
  rel skip; contemn, despise; flout, scoff
slightest *adj* *syn* see FIRST 4
  rel ‖fat, negligible
slighting *adj* *syn* see DEROGATORY
slim *adj* **1** *syn* see THIN 1
  rel lissome, lithe, lithesome, svelte
  ant chubby
  2 *syn* see CLEVER 4
  3 *syn* see REMOTE 4
slim (down) *vb* *syn* see REDUCE 5
slime *n* a viscous and usually dirty or offensive substance <a layer of *slime* formed in the bottom of the pool>
  syn muck, ‖slab, slum
  rel ooze, ‖sleech, sludge; scum
sling *vb* **1** *syn* see THROW 1
  rel catapult; sock
  2 *syn* see STRIDE 1
sling *vb* *syn* see HANG 1
slink *vb* *syn* see SNEAK
slink *n* *syn* see SNEAK
slinker *n* *syn* see SLACKER
slip *vb* **1** *syn* see SLIDE 1
  2 *syn* see SNEAK
  3 *syn* see STEAL 3
  4 *syn* see SLIDE 4
  5 *syn* see SLIDE 3
  6 to decline gradually from a standard or accustomed level <sales in some lines *slipped*>
  syn drop (off), fall (off *or* away), sag, slide, slump
  rel erode, soften; decline, go down, sink; dip, drop; nose-dive, plummet, topple; crash
  con better, gain, improve, rally, rebound; ascend, climb, rise; skyrocket, soar
  7 *syn* see SHAKE 5
  8 *syn* see SHED 2
slip (on) *vb* *syn* see DON 1
  ant slip (off)
slip *n* **1** *syn* see WHARF
  2 *syn* see ESCAPE 1
  3 *syn* see ERROR 2
  4 *syn* see DECLINE 3
‖**slipper** *adj* *syn* see SLICK 1
slippery *adj* **1** *syn* see SLICK 1
  2 *syn* see MUTABLE 2
slippy *adj* *syn* see SLICK 1
slipshod *adj* **1** *syn* see SHABBY 1
  2 *syn* see SLOVENLY 1
  3 marked by indifference to exactness, precision, and accuracy <a *slipshod* piece of research>
  syn botchy, careless, messy, slapdash, sloppy, slovenly, unthorough, untidy
  rel neglected, negligent; haphazard, slaphappy, unmeticulous; botched-up, fouled-up, messed-up, ‖screwed-up; faulty, imperfect, inaccurate, inexact
  con fastidious, meticulous, neat; accurate, exact, precise; methodical, orderly, systematic; thorough
slipslop *n* *syn* see NONSENSE 2
slipup *n* *syn* see ERROR 2
slit *vb* *syn* see CUT 1
slither *vb* **1** *syn* see SLIDE 1
  rel ‖sluther

---

syn synonym(s)   *rel* related word(s)
ant antonym(s)   *con* contrasted word(s)
idiom idiomatic equivalent(s)
‖ use limited; if in doubt, see a dictionary

2 to walk or move in a sinuous way < a slinky blonde *slithered* over from the bar >
syn ‖slidder, snake, undulate
rel creep, glide, sidle, steal; lurk, prowl, slink, sneak
slithery *adj syn* see SLICK 1
‖**slive** *vb syn* see SIDLE
sliver *vb* to cut into very thin slices < *slivered* cheese >
syn shave, shred
rel carve, haggle, slice
con chop, dice, mince; comminute, powder, pulverize; crush, mash
slobber *vb syn* see DROOL 2
slobbering *adj syn* see EFFUSIVE
slobbery *adj* **1** *syn* see EFFUSIVE
　2 *syn* see SLOVENLY 1
slog *vb* **1** *syn* see STRIKE 2
　2 *syn* see PLOD 1
　3 *syn* see DRUDGE
slogan *n syn* see CATCHWORD
rel expression, idiom, locution
slogging *n syn* see WORK 2
‖**slommacky** *adj syn* see SLOVENLY 1
‖**sloom** *n syn* see DOZE
‖**sloom** *vb syn* see DOZE
‖**sloomy** *adj syn* see SLEEPY 1
slop *n syn* see PAP 2
slop *vb* **1** *syn* see SPILL 1
　2 *syn* see SPLASH
　3 *syn* see GULP
　4 *syn* see PLOD 1
slope *vb syn* see SLANT 1
slope *n* a natural or artificial inclined surface < the steep *slope* of the hill >
syn grade, gradient, inclination, incline, lean, leaning, slant, tilt
rel acclivity, ascent, rise; declivity, descent; deflection, deviation, obliqueness, obliquity; pitch, swag, sway, tip; bend, skew
con champaign, flat, flatland, mesa, plain(s), plateau, tableland
ant level
sloped *adj syn* see INCLINED 3
slopeways *adv syn* see ASIDE 1
sloping *adj syn* see INCLINED 3
slopped *adj syn* see INTOXICATED 1
sloppy *adj* **1** *syn* see SLIPSHOD 3
rel amateurish; mediocre; awkward, clumsy; poor
ant exact, precise
　2 *syn* see SLOVENLY 1
　3 *syn* see EFFUSIVE
rel soft; oversentimental
　4 *syn* see INTOXICATED 1
slosh *n syn* see BLOW 1
slosh *vb* **1** *of a liquid* to move with a gentle lapping motion or sound < heard water *sloshing* in the bottom of the boat >
syn bubble, burble, gurgle, lap, swash, wash
rel babble; ripple; dash, plash, splash, tumble; bespatter, spatter; churn, whirl; gush, rush; roar
　2 *syn* see SPLASH
　3 *syn* see GULP
‖　**4** *syn* see STRIKE 2
sloth *n* **1** disinclination to action or labor < a bland *sloth-provoking summer day* >
syn idleness, indolence, laze, laziness, slothfulness, slouch, sluggishness
rel ergophobia, faineancy, idling, lazing, loafing; apathy, heaviness, languidness, languor, lassitude, lethargy, listlessness, torpidity; shiftlessness
con assiduity, assiduousness, busyness, diligence, sedulity, sedulousness
ant industriousness, industry
　2 sluggishness and apathy in the practice of virtue < the deadly sin of *sloth* >
syn acedia
rel heedlessness, inattention, inattentiveness
con assiduity
slothful *adj syn* see LAZY
con assiduous, busy, diligent, sedulous
ant industrious
slothfulness *n syn* see SLOTH 1
slouch *n* **1** *syn* see OAF 2

　2 *syn* see SLUGGARD
　3 *syn* see SLOTH 1
slouch *vb* to assume, have, or move with an awkward drooping posture, carriage, or gait < three drunks *slouched* across the room >
syn droop, loll, ‖lollop, lop, slump, trollop
rel loaf, lounge, saunter, shamble, shuffle; bend, lean, stoop; sag, wilt
con erect, straighten (up); sit up, stand up
slough *n* **1** *syn* see SWAMP
　2 *syn* see INLET
‖**slough** *n syn* see HULL
slough *vb* **1** *syn* see SHED 2
　2 *syn* see DISCARD
idiom ‖get shut (*or* shed) of
slough over *vb syn* see NEGLECT
sloven *adj syn* see SLOVENLY 1
slovenly *adj* **1** negligent of or marked by lack of neatness and order especially in appearance or dress < *slovenly* attire >
syn careless, disheveled, ill-kempt, messy, mussy, raunchy, slipshod, slobbery, ‖slommacky, sloppy, sloven, uncombed, unfastidious, unkempt, unneat, untidy; *compare* SLATTERNLY
rel down-at-heel, shabby, sleazy, sluttish, slutty; blowsy, dowdy, frowsy, frumpish
con fastidious, neat, tidy, trim; combed, groomed, well-groomed; immaculate
ant neat
　2 *syn* see SLIPSHOD 3
slow *adj* **1** *syn* see RETARDED
rel limited; ‖dunch
　2 moving, flowing, or proceeding at less than the usual, desirable, or required speed < a *slow* advance toward mutual understanding >
syn deliberate, dilatory, laggard, leisurely, unhasty, unhurried
rel measured, slowish, steady; unhasting, unhurrying; slow-footed, slow-going, slow-paced; plodding, poky, rusty; dragging, flagging, halting, lagging, straggling; dawdling, delaying, postponing, procrastinating; leaden, sluggish; crawling, snaillike, snail-paced, ultra-slow
idiom as slow as a swamp turtle, as slow rapid-paced molasses in January
con blitz, lightning, quick, rapid, swift; fast-going, fast-moving, fast-paced, rapid-paced
ant fast
　3 marked by reduced economic activity (as in sales or patronage) < trading was *slow* on the commodity exchange today >
syn down, off, slack, sluggish
rel moderate; reduced; low; inactive, stagnant
con active; up; heavy
slow (up *or* down) *vb syn* see DELAY 1
rel moderate, qualify, temper; abate, decrease, lessen, reduce
ant speed
slow coach *n syn* see LAGGARD
slowdown *n* **1** a slowing or gradual decrease in activity < a *slowdown* in car sales this quarter >
syn slack, slackening, slow-up
rel decline, downtrend, downturn; drop, drop-off, falloff; inactivity, stagnation; freeze
con increase, rise, upswing, upturn; acceleration, quickening
ant speedup
　2 a deliberate slowing down by workers in the rate and quantity of production < air traffic snarled by a controllers' *slowdown* >
syn ‖ca' canny
rel action; protest; slow-up; sit-down; strike, walkout; stoppage
ant speedup
slowgoing *adj syn* see LAZY
slowpoke *n syn* see LAGGARD
slow-up *n syn* see SLOWDOWN 1
slow-witted *adj syn* see RETARDED
ant quick-witted
‖**slubberdegullion** *n syn* see VILLAIN 1
slue *vb syn* see SWERVE 1
slug *n syn* see SLUGGARD
rel slacker, sloven
slug *n syn* see DRAM
slug *vb syn* see SLAM 1
slugabed *n syn* see SLUGGARD
sluggard *n* an habitually lazy, shiftless, and inactive person < a *sluggard* who wanted to sleep all day >

syn bum, dolittle, do-nothing, faineant, idler, lazybones, loafer, slouch, slug, slugabed
　　rel lie-abed, sleepyhead; dawdler, laggard, slow coach, slowpoke; goldbrick, shirker
　　idiom ‖his idleship, ‖Weary Willie
　　con go-getter, hustler, live wire
　　ant dynamo

sluggish *adj* **1 syn** see LETHARGIC
　　rel dragging, draggy, leaden, lumpish; costive, stiff; apathetic, stupefied
　　con go-getting, hustling, vigorous; expeditious
　　ant brisk
　　2 syn see SLOW 3

sluggishness *n syn* see SLOTH 1

sluice *vb syn* see POUR 2
　　rel flush, wash; douse, drench, soak

slum *n* a densely populated usually urban area marked by run-down housing, poverty, and social disorganization < a *slum* full of vagrants, junkies, pimps, and pushers >
　　syn stew
　　rel slumdom, slumland; tobacco road; tenderloin; skid row; ghetto; hive, kennel, rookery, warren
　　idiom desolation row, the wrong side of the tracks

slum *n syn* see SLIME

slumber *vb* **1 syn** see DOZE
　　2 syn see SLEEP

slumber *n* **1 syn** see SLEEP 1
　　2 syn see DOZE
　　3 syn see LETHARGY 1

slumberous *adj* **1 syn** see SLEEPY 1
　　2 syn see SOPORIFIC 1
　　3 syn see LETHARGIC

slumbery *adj syn* see SLEEPY 1

slump *vb* **1 syn** see FALL 2
　　rel droop, flag, sag
　　idiom come down like a rock (*or* a ton of bricks)
　　2 syn see SLOUCH
　　rel cave in, collapse
　　3 syn see SLIP 6

slump *n* **1 syn** see DECLINE 3
　　2 syn see DEPRESSION 3

slup *vb syn* see SLURP

‖**slur** *vb syn* see SLIDE 3

slur *vb syn* see MALIGN

slur (over) *vb syn* see NEGLECT

slur *n* **1 syn** see ANIMADVERSION
　　2 syn see STIGMA

slurp *vb* to eat or drink noisily < *slurping* soup with a large spoon >
　　syn slup
　　rel guzzle, lap (up), slosh, swill; suck; wolf (down); smack
　　con nibble, pick (at); sip

slushy *adj syn* see SENTIMENTAL

slut *n* **1 syn** see SLATTERN 1
　　2 syn see WANTON
　　3 syn see MINX

sly *adj* **1 syn** see CLEVER 4
　　rel smart; cagey; masterful
　　2 attaining or seeking to attain one's ends by devious means < a *sly* way of upping sales >
　　syn artful, astute, crafty, cunning, deep, ‖downy, foxy, guileful, insidious, subdolous, subtle, tricky, vulpine, wily; *compare* UNDERHAND
　　rel disingenuous, unfrank; calculating, designing, Machiavellian, scheming; cagey, devious, shady, shifty, ‖slanter, slick, slippery, smooth; clandestine, covert, furtive, stealthy; underhand, underhanded, unscrupulous; predatory; crooked, dishonest
　　idiom crazy like a fox, cunning as a fox (*or* serpent), sly as a fox
　　con candid, forthright, frank, honest, open, sincere, straightforward

sly *vb syn* see SNEAK

slyboots *n pl but sing in constr syn* see SCAMP

slyness *n syn* see CUNNING 2

smack *n* **1 syn** see TASTE 3
　　2 syn see HINT 2

smack *vb* to have a trace, vestige, or suggestion of something < that plan *smacks* of radicalism >

syn savor, smell
　　rel resemble, suggest; reek, stink

smack *vb* **1 syn** see KISS 1
　　idiom ‖plant a juicy kiss on
　　2 syn see SLAP 1

smack *n* **1 syn** see CUFF
　　2 syn see BLOW 1

‖**smack–dab** *adv syn* see JUST 1

‖**smacker** *n syn* see DOLLAR

‖**smackeroo** *n syn* see DOLLAR

small *adj* **1** being the opposite of large < a *small* white house >
　　syn bantam, little, monkey, petite, smallish; *compare* TINY
　　rel cramped, limited, narrow, two-by-four; puny, undersized; paltry, petty, piddling, trivial
　　con big, great; considerable, sizable; enormous, huge, immense, vast
　　ant large
　　2 syn see MINOR 2
　　3 syn see LITTLE 2
　　4 syn see LITTLE 3
　　5 syn see PETTY 2
　　6 syn see REMOTE 4

small beer *n syn* see TRIVIA

small–beer *adj syn* see LITTLE 3

small change *n syn* see TRIVIA

smallest *adj syn* see FIRST 4

small–fry *adj syn* see MINOR 2

smallish *adj syn* see SMALL 1
　　ant largish

small–minded *adj syn* see ILLIBERAL
　　ant large-minded

small potato *n, usu* **small potatoes** *pl but sing or pl in constr syn* see TRIVIA

small talk *n* light or casual conversation < had to make *small talk* at the cocktail party >
　　syn bavardage, by-talk, chitchat, chitter-chatter, trifling
　　rel badinage, banter, repartee; babble, babbling, bibble-babble, chatter, prattle, prattling, prittle-prattle

small–time *adj syn* see MINOR 2
　　ant big-time

small–town *adj syn* see INSULAR

‖**smarm** *vb syn* see SMEAR 1

smarmy *adj* **1 syn** see SLEEK
　　2 syn see FULSOME

smart *vb syn* see HURT 4

smart *vb* to cause or produce a sharp stinging and usually localized pain < gave him a slap that was hard enough to *smart* >
　　syn bite, burn, ‖stang, sting; *compare* HURT 4
　　rel prick; tingle; hurt

smart *adj* **1 syn** see INTELLIGENT 2
　　ant stupid
　　2 syn see WISE 4
　　idiom knowing the score, on the ball
　　ant dull, dumb
　　3 syn see CLEVER 5
　　rel pert, saucy
　　4 syn see WISE 5
　　5 syn see STYLISH
　　rel dapper, ‖dinky, spruce
　　ant dowdy
　‖**6 syn** see CONSIDERABLE 2

smart aleck *n* an obnoxiously conceited and self-assertive person with pretensions to smartness or cleverness < was heckled by a *smart aleck* in the back row >
　　syn know-it-all, smarty, smarty-pants, wiseacre, wisecracker, wise guy, wisehead, wisenheimer
　　rel blowhard, boaster, braggadocio, braggart, gasbag, windbag; exhibitionist, grandstander, show-off
　　idiom hot-air artist

smart–alecky *adj syn* see WISE 5

smarten (up) *vb syn* see DRESS UP 1

smart set *n* ultrafashionable often international society < the *smart set* that suns in Cannes and skis in St. Moritz >

---

syn synonym(s)　　　　　　　　　**rel** related word(s)
ant antonym(s)　　　　　　　　　**con** contrasted word(s)
idiom idiomatic equivalent(s)
‖ use limited; if in doubt, see a dictionary

syn beautiful people, jet set, ton

rel aristocracy, aristoi, blue bloods, bon ton, elite, Four Hundred, society, upper crust, who's who

smarty *n syn* see SMART ALECK

smarty–pants *n pl but sing in constr syn* see SMART ALECK

smash *vb* **1** *syn* see SHATTER 1

  2 *syn* see SLAM 1

  3 *syn* see DESTROY 1

smash *n* **1** *syn* see BLOW 1

  2 *syn* see BANG 2

  3 *syn* see IMPACT

  4 *syn* see CRASH 3

  5 *syn* see COLLAPSE 2

  6 a striking success <the new musical was a box-office *smash*>

syn bang, bell ringer, hit, succès fou, ten-strike, wow

rel sensation; knockout

idiom howling (*or* roaring) success, smash hit

con disaster, dud, failure

ant flop

‖**smash** *n syn* see MONEY

‖**smashed** *adj syn* see INTOXICATED 1

smashup *n* **1** *syn* see COLLAPSE 2

  2 *syn* see CRASH 3

smatch *n* **1** *syn* see HINT 2

  2 *syn* see FEW

smatter *vb* ‖**1** *syn* see SHATTER 1

  2 *syn* see CHAT 1

smatter *n syn* see FEW

smatterer *n syn* see AMATEUR 2

smattering *n syn* see FEW

smaze *n syn* see HAZE 1

smear *vb* **1** to overspread with something unctuous, viscous, or adhesive <*smeared* the crack with wet concrete>

syn bedaub, besmear, dab, daub, plaster, ‖smarm, smudge

rel rub; coat, cover, overlay, overspread, spread; smirch, soil

  2 *syn* see TAINT 1

  3 *syn* see MALIGN

idiom use smear tactics (on *or* against)

  4 *syn* see WHIP 2

rel foil, frustrate; repulse

idiom mop up the floor (*or* earth) with

smell *vb* **1** to perceive by means of the olfactory organs <*smelled* a dead skunk>

syn nose, scent, sniff, ‖snift, snuff

rel detect, perceive, sense; whiff; ‖snaffle, snuffle

idiom get a whiff of

  2 *syn* see SMACK

  3 to have or emit an offensive odor <the canal *smells* today>

syn funk, reek, stench, stink

idiom offend the nostrils, smell (*or* stink) to high heaven

smell *n* **1** a quality that makes a thing perceptible to the olfactory sense <the *smell* of a ham cooking>

syn aroma, odor, scent

rel bouquet, fragrance, incense, perfume, redolence, spice; flavor, savor, stench, stink

  2 *syn* see HINT 2

smeller *n syn* see NOSE 1

‖**smellful** *adj syn* see MALODOROUS 1

ant odorless, smell-less

smellfungus *n syn* see CRITIC

smell–less *adj syn* see ODORLESS

ant ‖smellful, smelly

smelly *adj syn* see MALODOROUS 1

con odorless, scentless, smell-less; fragrant, fresh, sweet

smidgen *n syn* see PARTICLE

smile *vb* to express amusement, satisfaction, or pleasure by brightening one's eyes and curving the corners of one's mouth upward <*smiled* as she greeted him>

syn beam, grin

rel simper, smirk

idiom break into a smile, crack a smile

con grimace; glare, glower, lower, scowl

ant frown

smirch *vb syn* see SOIL 2

rel discolor; smear

smirk *vb* to smile in an affected manner <*smirking* children imitating their teacher>

syn simper, ‖smirkle; *compare* SNEER 1

rel grin, smile; fleer, leer, sneer

‖**smirkle** *vb syn* see SMIRK

smitch *n syn* see PARTICLE

smite *vb* **1** *syn* see STRIKE 2

rel bat, belt, clobber; dash

idiom smite a blow

  2 *syn* see AFFLICT

smithereens *n pl* very small particles or fragments <a house blown to *smithereens* by a bomb>

syn ‖shivereens, smithers

rel fragments, particles, pieces

smithers *n pl syn* see SMITHEREENS

smitten *adj syn* see ENAMORED 1

idiom bitten by the love bug

smoke *n syn* see CIGARETTE

smoke *vb syn* see HURRY 2

smolder *vb syn* see SEETHE 4

rel burst, erupt, explode; fulminate

smooch *vb syn* see SOIL 2

smooch *vb syn* see KISS 1

idiom ‖plant a smooch on

‖**smoodge** *vb syn* see KISS 1

smooth *adj* **1** *syn* see LEVEL

rel glossy, sleek, slick; rippleless, unbroken, unwrinkled

con harsh, rugged, scabrous, uneven

ant rough

  2 *syn* see HAIRLESS

  3 *syn* see EASY 9

  4 *syn* see EASY 1

rel smooth-running

idiom smooth and easy

ant labored

  5 *syn* see SUAVE

rel courteous, courtly, polite; smooth-faced, smooth-tongued

con bluff, blunt, brusque, crusty, curt, gruff, harsh

  6 *syn* see GENTLE 1

rel agreeable, soothing

smooth *vb* **1** *syn* see EVEN 1

con corrugate; roughen; wrinkle

ant unsmooth

  2 *syn* see POLISH 2

smooth *adv syn* see EVENLY 3

smoothen *vb syn* see EVEN 1

smoothly *adv* **1** *syn* see EVENLY 3

con unevenly, ununiformly

ant roughly

  2 *syn* see EASILY 1

ant unsmoothly

smooth–spoken *adj syn* see VOCAL 3

ant rough-spoken

smorgasbord *n syn* see MISCELLANY 1

smother *vb* **1** *syn* see SUFFOCATE

  2 *syn* see COMPOSE 4

rel hush up, muffle; cork; quash, quell, squelch; quench

  3 *syn* see WHIP 2

smothering *adj syn* see STIFLING 1

smothering *n syn* see REPRESSION 1

smothery *adj syn* see STIFLING 1

‖**smouch** *vb syn* see KISS 1

smouch *vb syn* see STEAL 1

smudge *vb* **1** *syn* see SOIL 2

rel smear; blotch, splotch

  2 *syn* see SMEAR 1

  3 *syn* see TAINT 1

‖**smudgy** *adj syn* see STIFLING 1

smug *adj syn* see COMPLACENT

idiom pleased with oneself

smug *vb syn* see DRESS UP 1

smuggle *vb* to import or export secretly and in violation of the law <*smuggling* weapons into the country>

syn bootleg, contraband, run

idiom run contraband

smut *vb* **1** *syn* see STAIN 1

  2 *syn* see TAINT 1

smutch *vb* **1** *syn* see SOIL 2

  2 *syn* see TAINT 1

smutty *adj syn* see OBSCENE 2

snack *n* food served or taken informally and usually in small amounts and typically under other circumstances than a regular meal <a milk-and-cookie *snack* after school>
  syn ‖bait, ‖bever, bite, ‖chack, morsel, mug-up, ‖piece, tapa
  rel collation, refreshment, tea
  idiom bite to eat

snack bar (*or* **counter**) *n syn* see EATING HOUSE
‖**snaffle** *vb syn* see STEAL 1
‖**snafu** *vb syn* see CONFUSE 5
snag *n syn* see OBSTACLE
  rel brake, clog, curb, drag; hold-up
  idiom ‖snags and sawyers
snake *n syn* see SNOT 1
snake *vb* ‖1 *syn* see STEAL 1
  2 *syn* see CREEP 1
  3 *syn* see SLITHER 2
  ‖**4** *syn* see SNEAK
snaky *adj syn* see WINDING
snap *vb* **1** to speak in a curt, biting tone <*snapped* at his subordinates for inefficiency>
  syn bark, snarl
  rel growl, grumble, grunt, snort; roar, yell
  idiom bite one's head off, snap off one's head (*or* nose)
  2 *syn* see JERK
  rel clutch, grab, grasp, seize, snaffle, snatch
snap *n* **1** something easily managed or accomplished <that exam was a *snap*>
  syn breeze, child's play, cinch, duck soup, kid stuff, picnic, pie, ‖pipe, pushover, setup, ‖snip, soft touch
  rel sinecure
  idiom a simple twist of the wrist, simplicity itself, soft snap
  con difficulty, headache, problem, trouble; bother, inconvenience, pain
  ant chore
  2 *syn* see PARTICLE
  3 *syn* see MAN 3
  4 *syn* see VIGOR 2
snap back *vb syn* see RECOVER 3
‖**snapper** *vb syn* see STUMBLE 3
snapping *adv syn* see VERY 1
snappish *adj syn* see IRRITABLE
  rel curt, short, ungracious; crabbed, morose, surly
snappy *adj* **1** *syn* see IRRITABLE
  2 *syn* see FAST 3
  3 *syn* see PUNGENT
  rel animated, lively, vivacious; prompt, quick, ready
  4 *syn* see STYLISH
snare *n syn* see LURE 2
  rel chicane, chicanery, deception; ensnarement, entrapment
snare *vb syn* see CATCH 3
  rel seduce, tempt; involve; embrangle, enmesh, ensnarl, trammel
‖**snark** *vb syn* see SNORE
snarl *n* **1** *syn* see CONFUSION 3
  rel entanglement, tangle; complexity, complication, intricacy, intricateness; labyrinth, maze; mishmash, swarm; jam
  idiom tangled skein, wheels within wheels
  2 *syn* see MAZE 1
snarl *vb* **1** *syn* see ENTANGLE 1
  2 *syn* see COMPLICATE
snarl *vb syn* see SNAP 1
snarl up *vb syn* see CONFUSE 5
snatch *vb* **1** *syn* see SEIZE 2
  rel jerk, wrench, yank; nip (up), whip (up)
  ‖**2** *syn* see KIDNAP
sneak *vb* to move or go stealthily and furtively <*sneaked* into the garage and stole the car>
  syn creep, glide, gumshoe, lurk, ‖meech, pussyfoot, shirk, skulk, slide, slink, slip, sly, ‖snake, ‖snook, steal; *compare* STEAL 3
  rel crawl, slither, worm, prowl
  idiom go on (little) cat's feet, move under cover
  con barge, strut, swagger; clump, stamp, stump; stride; march, parade
sneak *n* a person who behaves in a stealthy, furtive, or shifty manner <found out that he was a liar, a cheat, and a *sneak*>
  syn slink, sneaker, sneaksby, weasel
  rel blackguard, knave, scoundrel; cur, heel, louse, reptile, skunk, snake; toad
  idiom Jerry Sneak

sneak *adj syn* see SECRET 1
sneaker *n syn* see SNEAK
sneaking *adj syn* see UNDERHAND
  ant forthright
sneaksby *n syn* see SNEAK
sneaky *adj syn* see UNDERHAND
‖**sneap** *vb syn* see REPROVE
sneer *vb* **1** to smile with attendant facial contortions expressing scorn or contempt <*sneered* haughtily at the beggar>
  syn fleer, leer, ‖sleer; *compare* SMIRK
  rel grin, smile
  idiom curl one's lip, make a scornful (*or* mocking) face
  2 *syn* see SCOFF
  rel belittle, detract, disparage, underrate
  idiom cock a snook at, give the Bronx cheer to, give the raspberry, sneeze at, thumb one's nose at
‖**sneezer** *n syn* see NOSE 1
snicker *vb syn* see LAUGH
  idiom have a case of the snickers
snide *adj* **1** *syn* see COUNTERFEIT
  2 *syn* see CROOKED 2
sniff *vb syn* see SMELL 1
‖**snift** *vb syn* see SMELL 1
  rel ‖snifter
snifter *n syn* see DRAM
‖**sniggle** *vb syn* see LAUGH
snip *n* **1** *syn* see MINX
  ‖**2** *syn* see SNAP 1
snippety *adj syn* see BLUFF
  rel impolite, insolent, rude
snippy *adj syn* see BLUFF
snip–snap *n syn* see BANTER
snit *n* a state of agitation or excited irritation especially over a trivial matter <was in a *snit* because his secretary was one minute late>
  syn fume, stew, sweat, swivet, tizzy
  rel huff, pique; conniption, fit, frenzy, seizure, taking; dither, flap, panic, ‖swither
snitch *vb* **1** *syn* see INFORM 3
  2 *syn* see STEAL 1
snitch *n* ‖**1** *syn* see NOSE 1
  2 *syn* see INFORMER
snob *n* one inclined to rebuff or ignore people or things that he regards as inferior (as in culture or social status) <appeals to real lovers of music rather than musical *snobs*>
  syn high-hat, snoot, snot
  rel name-dropper, snobling; bootlicker, hanger-on, lickspittle, sycophant, toady
snob *vb syn* see CUT 7
snobbish *adj* of, relating to, or characteristic of a snob <a *snobbish* group of jet-set sophisticates>
  syn ‖dicty, high-hat, potty, snobby, snooty
  rel aloof, remote; high-flown, pretentious, snotty, supercilious; haughty, hoity-toity, pompous, ritzy; condescending, patronizing; insecure, uncertain, unconfident, unselfconfident, unsure
  con certain, confident, secure, self-confident
snobby *adj syn* see SNOBBISH
  rel snubbing, snubby
‖**snook** *vb* **1** *syn* see SNOOP
  2 *syn* see SNEAK
snoop *vb* to look, inquire, or search impertinently or intrusively <he knew he had no right to *snoop* into her private life>
  syn busybody, mouse, nose, ‖piroot, poke, pry, ‖snook
  rel peek, peep, peer, stare; interfere, intrude, meddle, mess
  idiom stick (*or* poke) one's nose into
snoop *n syn* see BUSYBODY
snoopy *adj syn* see CURIOUS 2
snoot *n* **1** *syn* see NOSE 1
  2 *syn* see SNOB
snooty *adj syn* see SNOBBISH
snooze *vb syn* see NAP
snooze *n syn* see NAP
‖**snoozle** *vb syn* see DOZE

---

syn synonym(s)   *rel* related word(s)
ant antonym(s)   *con* contrasted word(s)
idiom idiomatic equivalent(s)
‖ use limited; if in doubt, see a dictionary

snoozy *adj syn* see SLEEPY 1

snore *vb* to breathe during sleep with a rough hoarse noise due to vibration of the soft palate <driven to distraction by her sister's *snoring* >
   syn ‖snark
   rel wheeze; snuffle; snort, ‖snotter
   idiom ‖drive pigs to market, ‖saw logs (*or* wood)

snort *n syn* see DRAM

snorter *n syn* see DRAM

snot *n* **1** an utterly contemptible person <a despicable *snot* whom everyone shunned >
   syn ‖bugger, cur, dog, louse, puke, rat, scum, skunk, snake, sod, stinkard, stinkaroo, stinker, toad, wretch; *compare* VILLAIN 1
   rel ‖creep, ‖crumb, lowlife; knave, rogue, scoundrel, ‖skite; pig, reptile
   2 *syn* see SNOB

snout *n syn* see NOSE 1

snowball *vb syn* see INCREASE 2

snub *vb syn* see CUT 7
   rel high-hat, ‖ritz, swank; put down
   idiom look coldly upon, turn a cold shoulder (on *or* upon)

‖**snudge** *vb syn* see SNUGGLE

‖**snuff** *n syn* see OFFENSE 2

snuff *vb syn* see SMELL 1

‖**snuff** (out) *vb syn* see DIE 1

snug *adj* **1** *syn* see NEAT 2
   2 *syn* see COMFORTABLE 2
   idiom snug as a bug in a rug
   ‖**3** *syn* see PROSPEROUS 3

snug *vb syn* see SNUGGLE

snuggle *vb* to assume or be in a warm comfortable position usually near another person or thing <a baby *snuggling* close to his mother>
   syn burrow, ‖croodle, cuddle, nestle, nuzzle, ‖snudge, snug, ‖snuzzle
   rel curl up; huddle; spoon
   idiom snuggle up like a bug in a rug
   con flinch, recoil, shrink

‖**snuzzle** *vb syn* see SNUGGLE

‖**sny** *vb syn* see TEEM

so *adv* **1** *syn* see ALSO 1
   2 *syn* see THUS 1
   3 *syn* see VERY 1
   4 *syn* see THEREFORE

so *conj* with the purpose that <repeated it aloud *so* there'd be no mistake>
   syn so as, so that
   idiom in order that, to the end that, with the intent that

soak *vb* **1** to permeate or be permeated with or as if with water <*soak* a sponge with water> <rain *soaked* her to the skin>
   syn drench, ‖drouk, impregnate, insteep, saturate, seethe, sodden, ‖sog, sop, souse, steep, waterlog; *compare* WET
   rel dip, immerse, submerge; draw, infuse; infiltrate, penetrate, permeate, pervade; water-soak; drown
   2 *syn* see WET
   3 *syn* see ENGAGE 4
   4 *syn* see OVERCHARGE 1
   5 *syn* see DRINK 3
   idiom ‖soak it up like a sponge

soak *n* **1** *syn* see DRUNKARD
   2 *syn* see BINGE 1

soaked *adj syn* see WET 1

soaker *n syn* see DRUNKARD

soaking *adj syn* see WET 1
   idiom soaking wet

so-and-so *adj syn* see DAMNED 2

soapbox *vb syn* see ORATE

soapy *adj syn* see FULSOME

soar *vb* **1** *syn* see RISE 4
   rel climb; shoot
   2 *syn* see SKYROCKET
   ant plummet

soaring *adj syn* see LOFTY 6
   idiom high as the sky

so as *conj syn* see SO

sob *vb syn* see CRY 2

sobby *adj syn* see SENTIMENTAL

sober *adj* **1** *syn* see ABSTEMIOUS

rel controlled, restrained; self-possessed
   con indulgent, overindulgent; uncontrolled, unrestrained; immoderate, intemperate; excessive; profligate
   2 *syn* see SERIOUS 1
   rel decorous, proper; calm, placid, serene, tranquil
   con flippant, light, light-minded; unstable, volatile
   ant
   3 having or exhibiting self-control and avoiding extremes of behavior <his bearing was *sober*, his comments judicious >
   syn moderate, temperate, unimpassioned; *compare* ABSTEMIOUS
   rel rational, reasonable; calm, collected, composed, cool, imperturbable; constrained, disciplined, inhibited, reserved, restrained, self-controlled, self-disciplined; abstaining, forbearing, refraining; abnegating, eschewing, forgoing
   con irrational, unreasonable; emotional, hotheaded, impassioned, overemotional, passionate; intemperate, uncontained, uncontrolled; excited; drunk, intoxicated; abandoned
   ant unsober
   4 *syn* see SUBDUED 2
   5 *syn* see REALISTIC
   rel sober-eyed, sober-minded

sobersided *adj syn* see SERIOUS 1

sobful *adj syn* see SENTIMENTAL

sobriety *n syn* see TEMPERANCE 2
   rel gravity, sedateness, seriousness, soberness
   con excitement; drunkenness, intoxication; abandonment
   ant insobriety

sobriquet *n syn* see NICKNAME

so-called *adj* **1** *syn* see NOMINAL
   2 *syn* see ALLEGED

sociable *adj* **1** *syn* see SOCIAL 2
   ant nonsocial
   2 *syn* see GRACIOUS 1
   rel companionable, convivial; gregarious; close, familiar, intimate; good-natured
   ant unsociable
   3 *syn* see SOCIAL 1
   ant unsociable, unsocial

social *adj* **1** conducive to, marked by, or passed in pleasant companionship with one's friends or associates <a relaxed, *social* evening>
   syn companionable, convivial, sociable
   rel amusing, entertaining, pleasant, pleasurable; cordial, friendly, genial, gracious, hospitable
   con unfriendly, unhospitable; eremitic, solitary
   ant unsociable, unsocial
   2 inclined by nature to association or community life with others of the same species <man is a *social* animal >
   syn gregarious, sociable
   rel social-minded; intersocial
   con eremitic, solitary, unsociable; antisocial, asocial, unsocial; remote, withdrawn
   ant nonsocial

social evil *n, used with* the *syn* see PROSTITUTION

socialize *vb* to participate actively in a social group <*socializes* with his colleagues>
   syn mingle
   rel associate, mix

society *n* **1** *syn* see COMPANY 1
   2 *syn* see ASSOCIATION 2
   3 an organized aggregate of persons who are responsible for a prevailing social order <rules made in the interests of *society* rather than for the chosen few>
   syn community, people, public
   rel masses, populace
   idiom people in general, society at large, the general public
   4 *syn* see ARISTOCRACY
   idiom high society (*or* life)

sock *vb syn* see STRIKE 2

sock *n* **1** *syn* see BLOW 1
   2 *syn* see CUFF

‖**sock** *vb syn* see SIGH 1

sod *n syn* see SNOT 1

sodality *n syn* see ASSOCIATION 2

sodden *adj syn* see WET 1

sodden *vb syn* see SOAK 1

Sodom *n syn* see SINK 1
   rel Babylon

so far *adv syn* see HITHERTO 1
   idiom up till now
soft *adj* **1** *syn* see GENTLE 1
   rel moderate, temperate
   2 *syn* see SUBDUED 2
   ant loud
   3 smooth or delicate in texture, grain, or fiber <the dog's fur was *soft* >
   syn cottony, satiny, silken, silky, velvety
   rel smooth; sleek
   con coarse, rough
   ant harsh
   4 *syn* see COMFORTABLE 2
   ant rough
   5 *syn* see SIMPLE 3
   idiom ||soft in the head
   6 giving way easily to physical touch or pressure <a *soft* cheese>
   syn mushy, pappy, pulpous, pulpy, quaggy, spongy, squashy, squelchy, squishy, squushy, yielding
   rel softish; compressible, malleable, pliable, pliant, workable; doughy, formless; flabby, fleshy
   idiom soft as butter
   con firm, solid; resistant, rigid, tough, unyielding; nail-hard, rock-hard
   ant hard
soft (on) *adj syn* see ENAMORED 1
soft–boiled *adj syn* see SENTIMENTAL
   ant hard-boiled
soften *vb syn* see DEPRECIATE 1
softened *adj syn* see SUBDUED 2
softhead *n syn* see FOOL 4
softhearted *adj syn* see TENDER
   ant hardhearted
soft–pedal *vb* to reduce the emphasis, importance, or effect of something (as an issue) <tried to *soft-pedal* military spending>
   syn de-emphasize, play (down)
   rel tone (down), tune (down); cushion, dampen, muffle, subdue; hush (up), silence, suppress; conceal, disguise
   con emphasize, play (up); focus (on), spotlight
soft–shell *adj syn* see MODERATE 4
soft soap *n syn* see FLATTERY
   rel ||snow job
soft–soap *vb syn* see COAX
soft spot *n* **1** *syn* see APPETITE 3
   2 a vulnerable point <the major *soft spot* in the West's armor>
   syn Achilles' heel
   rel vulnerability, vulnerableness, weakness; chink, loophole
   idiom heel of Achilles, weak link (*or* point), weak link in the chain
   con impregnability, invulnerability; invincibility
soft touch *n* **1** someone who can be easily talked into giving help (as a loan) <recognized him as a *soft touch* when she was broke>
   syn easy mark
   rel softy; dupe, fool, pushover; sucker; mark, sitting duck, target
   con cynic, doubting Thomas, hard case, skeptic
   2 *syn* see SNAP 1
||**sog** *vb syn* see SOAK 1
||**sog** *vb syn* see DOZE
soggy *adj syn* see HUMID
soi–disant *adj syn* see SELF-STYLED
soil *vb* **1** *syn* see CONTAMINATE 1
   ant purify
   2 to make or become unclean <a shirt *soiled* with grease and grime>
   syn begrime, besoil, dirty, foul, grime, muck, ||mucky, muddy, murk, smirch, smooch, smudge, smutch, tarnish; *compare* STAIN 1
   rel ||becoom, ||benasty, ||nasty; bedaub, daub, smear; drabble, draggle; mess, spoil
   con brighten, cleanse, freshen, renew; purify
   ant clean
   3 *syn* see TAINT 1
soil *n* **1** *syn* see EARTH 2
   2 *syn* see COUNTRY

soily *adj syn* see DIRTY 1
soiree *n syn* see EVENING 3
sojourn *n* a temporary but sometimes extended stay <a summer *sojourn* in Nice>
   syn stopover, tarriance, visit
   rel stay, stop; layover
sojourn *vb syn* see VISIT 3
   rel linger; abide
Sol *n syn* see SUN 1
solace *vb syn* see COMFORT
   idiom offer (*or* give) solace to, wipe one's tears away
soldier *n* a person engaged in military service <*soldiers* fighting and dying in futile wars>
   syn fighter, fighting man, GI, man-at-arms, serviceman, swad, ||swaddy, ||sweat, warrior
   rel dogface, doughboy, ||doughfoot, infantryman; trooper; guerrilla, partisan; condottiere, free companion, free lance, mercenary, soldier of fortune
soldierly *adj syn* see BRAVE 1
   rel martial; aggressive, combative, militant, pugnacious, warlike
   con unsoldierly
sole *n syn* see BOTTOM 1
sole *adj* **1** *syn* see SINGLE 1
   2 *syn* see SINGLE 2
   3 *syn* see ONLY 2
   idiom one and only
   4 belonging, granted, or attributed to the one person or group <*sole* rights of publication>
   syn exclusive, single, unshared
   con multiple; shared
solecism *n* **1** *syn* see ANACHRONISM 2
   2 *syn* see BARBARISM
   3 *syn* see FAUX PAS
solely *adv syn* see ONLY 1
solemn *adj* **1** *syn* see CEREMONIAL
   rel full, plenary; august, grand, impressive, magnificent, majestic, overwhelming; ostentatious
   2 *syn* see SERIOUS 1
   idiom as solemn as an owl, grave as an undertaker
solemnize *vb syn* see KEEP 2
   rel dignify, honor, solemnify, venerate
solicit *vb* **1** to seek (as advertising, orders, or votes) especially on a large scale <*solicited* contributions all over the district>
   syn canvass, drum, drum up
   rel ask, request; beg, beseech, implore; claim, demand, exact
   2 *syn* see ASK 2
   rel apply, go, refer, resort, turn
   3 *syn* see DEMAND 1
solicitous *adj syn* see EAGER
solicitude *n* **1** *syn* see CARE 2
   rel attention, heed, watchfulness; presentiment; compunction, qualm, scruple
   con carelessness, heedlessness, indifference, neglect, negligence
   ant unmindfulness
   2 *syn* see CONSIDERATION 3
solid *adj* **1** *syn* see FIRM 2
   rel compacted, concentrated, consolidated
   con spongy; disintegrated; fluid, liquid
   2 *syn* see STABLE 4
   3 *syn* see VALID
   rel firm, hard
   ant insubstantial
   4 *syn* see UNANIMOUS
solid *adv syn* see HARD 9
solidarism *n syn* see SOLIDARITY
solidarity *n* a feeling of unity (as in interests, standards, and responsibilities) that binds members of a group together <*solidarity* among union members is essential in negotiations>
   syn cohesion, solidarism, togetherness
   rel cohesiveness; oneness, singleness, undividedness; integrity, solidity, union, unity; esprit, esprit de corps; firmness, fixity
   con separation; discord, dissension, schism; confusion, disorder, disorganization

---

syn synonym(s)   *rel* related word(s)
ant antonym(s)   *con* contrasted word(s)
idiom idiomatic equivalent(s)
|| use limited; if in doubt, see a dictionary

ant division

solidify *vb syn* see HARDEN 1
  rel compress, contract
  idiom make (*or* become) hard as a rock
  con soften; disintegrate, dissolve
  ant liquefy

solidly *adv* **1** *syn* see HARD 9
  2 *syn* see HARD 7

solitariness *n syn* see SOLITUDE

solitary *adj* **1** *syn* see ANTISOCIAL
  ant gregarious
  2 *syn* see UNSOCIABLE
  3 *syn* see DERELICT 1
  4 *syn* see LONE 1
  rel companionless, unaccompanied, unattended
  ant accompanied
  5 *syn* see SINGLE 2
  6 *syn* see ONLY 2

solitary *n syn* see RECLUSE

solitude *n* the state of one who is alone <a very social person who could not bear *solitude* >
  syn aloneness, isolation, loneness, solitariness; *compare* SECLUSION
  rel detachment, separateness; retirement, withdrawal; confinement, quarantine; loneliness, lonesomeness
  con companionship, company

solo *adj syn* see ONLY 2

so long *interj syn* see GOOD-BYE

solution *n syn* see ANSWER 2

solve *vb* **1** to find an answer or solution for (a problem or difficulty) <mass transit partially *solved* the traffic problem >
  syn fix, resolve, work, work out
  rel decide, determine, settle
  idiom hit upon a solution
  2 to find an explanation or solution for something obscure, mysterious, or incomprehensible <the mystery of the missing cookies has been *solved* >
  syn break, ‖cipher, clear up, decipher, dissolve, ‖dope out, figure out, puzzle out, resolve, unfold, unravel, unriddle
  rel enlighten, illuminate; construe, elucidate, explain, interpret
  idiom get to the bottom of, have it, put two and two together

somatic *adj syn* see BODILY

somber *adj* **1** *syn* see DARK 1
  2 *syn* see GLOOMY 3
  3 *syn* see SERIOUS 1
  idiom as somber as an undertaker

some *adj* **1** *syn* see CERTAIN 2
  2 *syn* see SEVERAL 3

some *adv* **1** *syn* see NEARLY
  2 *syn* see SOMEWHAT 2

somebody *pron* one or some individual of no certain or known identity <*somebody* should be home >
  syn someone
  rel anybody, one
  con none
  ant nobody, no one

somebody *n* **1** *syn* see NOTABLE 1
  ant nobody
  2 *syn* see CELEBRITY 2

someday *adv syn* see YET 2

‖somegate *adv syn* see SOMEHOW

somehow *adv* in some way not yet known or specified <this thing must be done *somehow* >
  syn ‖somegate, someway, somewise
  rel anyhow, anyway, anywise
  idiom by hook or by crook, in one way or another, in some such way, somehow or other (*or* another)
  con nohow, noway, nowise

someone *pron syn* see SOMEBODY

someplace *adv syn* see SOMEWHERE 1
  ant no place

something *adv syn* see SOMEWHAT 2

something *n syn* see ENTITY 1

sometime *adv syn* see YET 2
  idiom one of these days

sometime *adj syn* see FORMER 2

sometimes *adv* at intervals <illustrated by beautiful and *sometimes* outstanding photographs >

syn at times, ‖betimes, ever and again, ever and anon, here and there, now and again, now and then, once and again, ‖otherwhile; *compare* OCCASIONALLY
  rel intermittently, periodically, recurrently; frequently; consistently, constantly
  idiom every now and then (*or* again), every once in a while, every so often, from time to time
  con continually, continuously, unceasingly, uninterruptedly; endlessly, ever, interminably

someway *adv syn* see SOMEHOW

somewhat *adv* **1** *syn* see WELL 8
  2 to some extent or in some degree <felt *somewhat* better but not fine >
  syn fairly, kind of, moderately, more or less, pretty, rather, ratherish, some, something, sort of
  rel adequately, bearably, tolerably; insignificantly, slightly
  idiom rather more than less

somewhen *adv syn* see YET 2

somewhere *adv* **1** to, at, or in some unknown or unspecified location <lived on a farm *somewhere* in the Midwest >
  syn someplace, ‖somewheres
  rel somewhither; elsewhere, otherwhere
  idiom someplace or other
  con anyplace, anywhere, ‖anywheres; no place, ‖nowheres
  ant nowhere
  2 *syn* see NEARLY

‖somewheres *adv syn* see SOMEWHERE 1
  ant ‖nowheres

somewise *adv syn* see SOMEHOW

somnifacient *adj syn* see SOPORIFIC 1

somniferous *adj syn* see SOPORIFIC 1

somnific *adj syn* see SOPORIFIC 1

somnolent *adj* **1** *syn* see SOPORIFIC 1
  2 *syn* see SLEEPY 1
  rel inactive, passive, supine

somnorific *adj syn* see SOPORIFIC 1

so much as *adv syn* see EVEN 4

son *n syn* see BOY 1
  rel sonny; junior

sonance *n syn* see SOUND 1

sonant *adj syn* see VOCAL 1

song *n* **1** *syn* see POETRY 1
  2 music or a piece of music intended for vocal expression <played and sang a *song* >
  syn aria, descant, ditty, hymn, lay, lied; *compare* MELODY
  rel lyric; piece
  3 *syn* see CALL 1

song and dance *n syn* see SPIEL

songful *adj syn* see MELODIOUS 2

sonorant *adj syn* see RESONANT

sonorous *adj* **1** *syn* see RESONANT
  2 *syn* see RHETORICAL
  3 *syn* see NOISY

‖sonsy *adj* **1** *syn* see LUCKY
  2 *syn* see GRACIOUS 1
  3 *syn* see EASYGOING 3

soon *adv* **1** *syn* see PRESENTLY 1
  rel forthwith, instantly, pronto, quickly
  idiom in the near future
  2 *syn* see FAST 2
  3 *syn* see EARLY 1

‖soon *adj syn* see EARLY 2

sooner *adv syn* see BEFORE 3

sooner or later *adv syn* see YET 2

soothe *vb syn* see CALM
  rel comfort, console; hush, subdue
  con annoy, irritate, vex
  ant excite

‖soother *n syn* see CALM

soothsay *vb syn* see FORETELL

soothsayer *n syn* see PROPHET

sop *n* **1** *syn* see WEAKLING
  2 a conciliatory or propitiatory gift or advance <provided the $400 raise as a *sop* > <the new office was a *sop* to his wounded feelings >
  syn sugarplum
  rel douceur, gratuity; ‖baksheesh, ‖boodle, bribe, ‖palm oil
  idiom sop in the pan, sop to Cerberus

sop *vb* **1** *syn* see WET
  2 *syn* see SOAK 1
  3 *syn* see BRIBE
sophic *adj* *syn* see WISE 1
sophism *n* *syn* see FALLACY 2
  rel illogicality, irrationality; invalidity, unsoundness; claptrap
sophistic *adj* *syn* see ILLOGICAL
sophisticate *adj* *syn* see SOPHISTICATED 2
sophisticate *vb* *syn* see ADULTERATE
sophisticated *adj* **1** *syn* see COMPLEX 2
  ant unsophisticated
  2 being experienced in the ways of the world <a *sophisticated*, well-traveled man>
  syn blasé, disenchanted, disentranced, disillusioned, knowing, mondaine, sophistic, worldly, worldly-wise, world-wise; *compare* COSMOPOLITAN 1
  rel adult, mature; experienced, practiced, schooled, seasoned; salty, uncelestial; couth, well-bred; smooth, suave, svelte, urbane; bored, jaded, world-weary; brittle; cynical, skeptical
  con artless, gee-whiz, ingenuous, natural; green, inexperienced, unseasoned, virginal; unworldly
  ant naive, unsophisticated
sophistry *n* *syn* see FALLACY 2
  rel ambiguity, tergiversation
soporiferous *adj* *syn* see SOPORIFIC 1
soporific *adj* **1** tending to induce sleep <a *soporific* drug> <*soporific* prose>
  syn hypnotic, narcotic, opiate, sleepy, slumberous, somnifacient, somniferous, somnific, somnolent, somnorific, soporiferous, soporifical
  rel calming, quietening, sedative, tranquilizing; anesthetic, deadening, numbing
  con arousing, waking; invigorating, stimulating
  2 *syn* see SLEEPY 1
soporifical *adj* *syn* see SOPORIFIC 1
sopping *adj* *syn* see WET 1
soppy *adj* **1** *syn* see WET 1
  ‖**2** *syn* see SENTIMENTAL
sorcerer *n* *syn* see MAGICIAN 1
sorceress *n* *syn* see WITCH 1
sorcerous *adj* *syn* see MAGIC
sorcery *n* *syn* see MAGIC 1
sordid *adj* **1** *syn* see DIRTY 1
  2 *syn* see SLATTERNLY
  3 *syn* see BASE 3
  rel foul, nasty, seamy, sodden
sore *adj* *syn* see PAINFUL 1
sorehead *n* *syn* see GROUCH
sorely *adv* *syn* see HARD 6
sorrow *n* distress of mind <felt great *sorrow* at the loss of her friend>
  syn affliction, anguish, care, ‖dole, grief, heartache, heartbreak, regret, rue, woe
  rel mournfulness, sadness, sorrowfulness, unhappiness; grieving, lamentation, mourning, sorrowing; dejection, depression, melancholy; agony, distress, dolor, misery, suffering, wretchedness
  con cheerfulness, gaiety, gladness, happiness, joyfulness; ecstasy
  ant joy
sorrow *vb* *syn* see GRIEVE 2
  rel groan, moan, sob
  idiom break one's heart over, eat one's heart out
  ant rejoice
sorrowful *adj* **1** *syn* see WOEFUL 1
  rel sorrow-laden, sorrow-stricken, sorrow-struck
  idiom full of (or filled with) sorrow
  con sorrowless
  ant joyful
  2 *syn* see MELANCHOLY 2
  ant gay
sorry *adj* **1** *syn* see SAD 1
  rel bad, regretful, remorseful; miserable, wretched
  ant glad
  2 *syn* see REMORSEFUL
  3 *syn* see CONTEMPTIBLE
  rel inadequate, paltry, poor, trifling; cheesy, scruffy, shoddy; disgraceful
sort *n* **1** *syn* see TYPE
  2 *syn* see GROUP 3

sort *vb* **1** *syn* see ASSORT
  2 to analyze and assort (as individuals or things) to obtain those desired or required <he knew he must *sort* out facts from fancy>
  syn comb, separate, sift, winnow; *compare* SCREEN 5
  rel riddle, screen; choose, cull, pick, select
  con consolidate, join, lump, merge; aggregate, amalgamate, blend, fuse, mix; unify
sort of *adv* *syn* see SOMEWHAT 2
SOS *n* *syn* see ALARM 1
soshed *adj* *syn* see INTOXICATED 1
so–so *adv* *syn* see ENOUGH 2
so–so *adj* *syn* see MEDIUM
sot *n* *syn* see DRUNKARD
‖**sot** *adj* *syn* see OBSTINATE
so that *conj* *syn* see SO
sotto voce *adv* in an inaudible or barely audible voice <made a snide remark to her *sotto voce*>
  syn faintly, mutedly, weakly
  rel low, quietly, softly; muffledly; mutteringly; aside, privately
  idiom below one's breath, between one's teeth, in an aside, in an undertone, in a whisper, out of earshot, under one's breath
  con aloud, out, out loud
sough *vb* **1** *syn* see SIGH 2
  2 *syn* see SIGH 1
soul *n* **1** an animating essence or principle held to be inseparably associated with life or living beings <philosophers who teach that life is a manifestation of *soul*>
  syn anima, animus, élan vital, pneuma, psyche, spirit, vital force
  rel life, vitality
  idiom breath of life
  2 the immortal part of man believed to have permanent individual existence <into God's hands I commit my *soul*>
  syn spirit
  rel life; noumenon
  idiom one's immortal soul
  con flesh
  ant body
  3 *syn* see HEART 1
  rel character, personality, psyche; conscience; spirit
  idiom heart of hearts, heart's core, one's inmost soul (or mind), one's secret (or inner) self, (the) secret recesses of the heart
  4 *syn* see ESSENCE 2
  5 *syn* see HUMAN
soul–searching *n* *syn* see INTROSPECTION
soul–sick *adj* *syn* see DOWNCAST
sound *adj* **1** *syn* see HEALTHY 1
  rel intact, unimpaired; perfect
  idiom sound as a bell (or whistle), sound of mind and body
  con impaired; unfit
  ant unsound
  2 *syn* see WHOLE 1
  3 *syn* see STABLE 4
  ant unsound
  4 *syn* see VALID
  rel errorless, faultless, flawless, impeccable; accurate, correct, exact, precise; rational, reasonable; well-founded, well-grounded
  con questionable, shaky; invalid
  ant unsound
  5 *syn* see ORTHODOX 1
  6 *syn* see RATIONAL
  rel right-minded, sober, sober-minded, sound-minded
  ant unsound
sound *n* **1** a sensation or effect resulting from stimulation of the auditory receptors <the *sound* of thunder>
  syn noise, sonance
  rel vibration; resonance; sonancy; reverberation
  con quiet, soundlessness
  ant silence
  2 *syn* see EARSHOT
sound *vb* **1** *syn* see SEEM
  2 *syn* see DECLARE 1

---

syn synonym(s)   *rel* related word(s)
ant antonym(s)   *con* contrasted word(s)
idiom idiomatic equivalent(s)
‖ use limited; if in doubt, see a dictionary

sound *vb* to measure the depth of (as a body of water) typically with a weighted line < *sounding* the distance to the bottom >
   syn fathom, plumb, plumb-line
   idiom ‖cast (*or* sling) the lead, make a sounding, take soundings
sound (out) *vb syn* see PROBE 2
soundless *adj syn* see BOTTOMLESS 2
   ant soundable
soundless *adj syn* see STILL 3
soundlessness *n syn* see SILENCE 1
soundness *n* **1** *syn* see HEALTH
   ant unsoundness
   2 *syn* see STABILITY
   3 *syn* see WIT 2
   rel level-headedness, sensibleness
   idiom sound mind, soundness of mind
   ant unsoundness
sound off *vb syn* see SPEAK UP
soup *n syn* see PREDICAMENT
soupçon *n syn* see HINT 2
soupy *adj syn* see SENTIMENTAL
sour *adj* **1** causing or characterized by the one of the basic taste sensations produced chiefly by acids < *sour* pickles >
   syn acerb, acerbic, acetose, acid, acidulous, dry, tart
   rel keen, sharp, tangy; ‖blinky, sourish; fermented, soured, turned; acrid, bitter, vinegary
   ant sweet
   2 *syn* see BAD 8
source *n* the point at which something begins its course or existence < the *source* of his wisdom was long practical experience >
   syn derivation, fount, fountain, fountainhead, inception, mother, origin, provenance, provenience, root, rootage, rootstock, spring, well, wellhead, wellspring, whence
   rel birthplace; beginning, commencement, dawn, dawning, onset, opening, start, starting; authorship, origination, rise, rising; antecedent, cause, determinant; parent, paternity
   con end, ending, terminus
   ant termination; outcome
sourpuss *n syn* see GROUCH
   rel killjoy
souse *vb* **1** *syn* see DIP 1
   2 *syn* see WET
   3 *syn* see SOAK 1
souse *n syn* see BINGE 1
soused *adj syn* see WET 1
souvenir *n syn* see REMEMBRANCE 3
   idiom token of remembrance
sovereign *adj* **1** *syn* see FREE 1
   rel self-determined, self-governed
   2 *syn* see DOMINANT 1
   rel commanding, directing, guiding; highest, loftiest
   3 *syn* see EXCELLENT
   4 *syn* see KINGLY
sovereignty *n syn* see SUPREMACY
sow *vb* **1** *syn* see PLANT 1
   2 *syn* see STREW 1
   rel fling, toss; drill
‖**sowf** *vb syn* see HUM
sozzled *adj syn* see INTOXICATED 1
spa *n* **1** a locality featuring mineral springs or water cures < hoped a week at a *spa* would help his arthritis >
   syn baths, ‖hydro, springs, watering place, wells
   rel waters
   idiom health spa
   2 *syn* see RESORT 3
space *n* **1** *syn* see WHILE 1
   rel lapse; interval, term; duration
   2 *syn* see EXPANSE
   rel room, roomage; spaciousness
spaced–out *adj syn* see DRUGGED
spacious *adj* larger in extent or capacity than the average < a mansion with *spacious* rooms and gardens >
   syn ample, capacious, commodious, roomy, wide
   rel big, generous, great, large, spacy; enormous, immense, vast; expansive, extended, extensive; boundless, spaceless
   con circumscribed, confined, cramped, limited, narrow, restricted; small, tiny
   ant strait

spade *vb* **1** *syn* see DIG 2
   2 *syn* see DIG 1
span *n syn* see TERM 2
   rel interval; space
spang *adv syn* see JUST 1
spangle *vb* **1** to adorn with small brilliant objects < a tutu *spangled* with sequins >
   syn bespangle, glitter
   rel adorn, decorate, ornament, trim
   2 *syn* see FLASH 1
spang–new *adj syn* see BRAND-NEW
spaniel *n syn* see SYCOPHANT
spank *vb syn* see SLAP 1
spank *n syn* see CUFF
   idiom a sound spank
spanking *adv syn* see VERY 1
spanking–new *adj syn* see BRAND-NEW
span–new *adj syn* see BRAND-NEW
spare *vb* **1** *syn* see EXEMPT
   2 *syn* see SAVE 4
   3 to refrain from the free use or consumption of < don't *spare* the syrup on my pancakes >
   syn scant, short, skimp, ‖skinch, stint; *compare* SCRIMP
   rel pinch
   4 *syn* see SCRIMP
spare *adj* **1** *syn* see SUPERFLUOUS
   idiom enough and to spare, more than enough
   2 *syn* see LEAN
   ant corpulent
   3 *syn* see MEAGER 2
   ant profuse
sparing *adj* careful in the use of money, goods, or resources < was *sparing* in his expenditures >
   syn canny, chary, economical, frugal, provident, saving, Scotch, stewardly, thrifty, unwasteful, wary; *compare* STINGY
   rel parsimonious, ‖scant, tight, tightfisted, ungiving
   con exuberant, liberal, prodigal, profuse
   ant lavish, unsparing
spark *n syn* see SEED 2
spark *n syn* see SUITOR 2
spark *vb syn* see ADDRESS 8
sparker *n syn* see SUITOR 2
sparkish *adj syn* see DAPPER
sparkle *vb syn* see FLASH 1
sparkle *n syn* see FLASH 1
sparse *adj syn* see MEAGER 2
   rel dispersed, scattered; infrequent, occasional, sporadic; rare, scarce, uncommon
   con close, compact, thick
‖**spartle** *vb syn* see SCRAMBLE 1
spasmodic *adj syn* see FITFUL
   rel spurtive
   con continual, continuous, uninterrupted
spat *n* **1** *syn* see QUARREL
   ‖**2** *syn* see CUFF
spat *vb syn* see QUARREL
spate *n* **1** *syn* see FLOOD 2
   rel progression, series, succession; rain, river, spurt
   2 *syn* see FLOW
spatter *vb* **1** *syn* see SPLASH
   rel sparge
   2 *syn* see SPOT 1
   3 *syn* see MALIGN
   4 *syn* see SPUTTER 2
spatter *n syn* see FEW
spattering *n syn* see FEW
spawn *vb syn* see GENERATE 1
spawning *adj syn* see FERTILE
speak *vb* **1** to articulate words in order to express thoughts < always *speak* clearly >
   syn talk, utter, verbalize, vocalize, voice
   rel drawl, gasp, mouth, mumble, murmur, mutter, shout, splutter, spout, whisper; descant, dilate (on *or* upon), expatiate, perorate; converse, discourse; allege, assert, aver, convey, declare, tell
   idiom break silence, give voice (*or* tongue *or* utterance) to, let fall, make public (*or* known), open one's mouth (*or* lips), put in (*or* into) words, say one's say, speak one's piece

con gabble, gibber, jabber; maunder, mumble, mutter; mispronounce, misspeak

2 syn see TALK 7

3 to have oral command of (a language) <he *speaks* fluent German>

syn converse (in), parley, talk, use

idiom be at ease in

con falter, hesitate, stumble

speaker *n syn* see SPOKESMAN

speaking *n syn* see SPEECH 1

speak out *vb syn* see SPEAK UP

speak up *vb* to speak strongly, boldly, or vigorously <we'll never know how you feel if you don't *speak up*>

syn sound off, speak out

idiom come out with it, have one's say, let one's voice be heard, make oneself heard, speak one's mind, stand up and be counted

spear *vb syn* see IMPALE

rel stick; bore, drill, penetrate, pierce; gouge, ream

special *adj* **1** of or relating to one thing or class <*special* soap for infants>

syn especial, individual, particular, specific

rel characteristic, distinctive, peculiar; exceptional, occasional, rare, uncommon; unique

con common, familiar, ordinary; customary, habitual, usual

2 syn see EXPRESS 2

rel defined, determinate; designated, earmarked

special *adv syn* see ESPECIALLY 1

specialize *vb syn* see ITEMIZE 1

specially *adv* **1 syn** see ESPECIALLY 1

2 syn see EXPRESSLY 2

species *n syn* see TYPE

specific *adj* **1 syn** see SPECIAL 1

rel limited, reserved, restricted, specialized

con general, generic

ant nonspecific, unspecific

2 syn see EXPLICIT

con ambiguous, cloudy, indefinite, uncertain, unexplicit, unspecified, vague

ant nonspecific, unspecific

3 syn see EXPRESS 2

ant nonspecific, unspecific

specifically *adv* **1 syn** see EXPRESSLY 2

2 syn see ESPECIALLY 1

3 syn see EXPRESSLY 1

specificate *vb syn* see SPECIFY 3

specificize *vb syn* see SPECIFY 3

specify *vb* **1 syn** see MENTION

2 syn see ITEMIZE 1

3 to make something (as a condition or requirement) specific <his will *specified* how the money would be divided>

syn detail, particularize, specificate, specificize, stipulate; *compare* ITEMIZE 1

rel determine, establish, fix, settle; condition, limit, set; pin (down); enumerate, list; precise

specimen *n syn* see INSTANCE

rel sort, species, type, variety

specious *adj syn* see FALSE 1

rel apparent, seeming; colorable, plausible; beguiling; illogical, spurious; empty, hollow, idle, nugatory, vain

ant valid

speciousness *n syn* see FALLACY 2

rel speciosity

ant validity

speck *n* **1 syn** see POINT 11

rel pinpoint; tick

2 syn see PARTICLE

speck *vb syn* see SPECKLE 1

speckle *vb* **1** to produce on or mark with small spots, speckles, or blemishes <a *speckled* egg>

syn bespeckle, dot, freckle, pepper, speck, sprinkle, stipple; *compare* SPOT 1

rel dapple, flake, fleck

2 syn see SPOT 2

spectacle *n syn* see EXHIBITION 1

spectacled *adj syn* see BESPECTACLED

spectacular *adj syn* see MARVELOUS 1

rel eye-popping, sensational, striking, thrilling; dramatic, histrionic, stagy, theatrical

ant unspectacular

spectator *n* one who sees or looks upon something <sports *spectators*>

syn beholder, by-sitter, bystander, eyewitness, looker-on, observer, onlooker, stander-by, viewer, watcher, witness

rel gazer; perceiver; seer

specter *n syn* see APPARITION

spectral *adj syn* see GHASTLY 2

rel phantom, phantomlike, shadowlike; disembodied, unearthly; spooky

spectrum *n syn* see APPARITION

speculate *vb syn* see THINK 5

rel excogitate, review, study, weigh

idiom ‖beat one's brains, turn over in one's mind, ‖use the gray matter

speculation *n* **1 syn** see THOUGHT 1

rel excogitation, review, studying, weighing

2 syn see THEORY 2

speculative *adj* **1 syn** see THEORETICAL 1

2 syn see THOUGHTFUL 1

rel musing, ruminating; curious, inquiring, questioning

ant unspeculative

speech *n* **1** communication, expression, or interchange of thoughts in spoken words <considered *speech* as a means of reproducing for one's listeners the images in one's mind>

syn discourse, speaking, talk, utterance, verbalization; *compare* VOCALIZATION

rel articulation, uttering, vocalization, vocalizing, voice, voicing; expressing, expression; language

idiom oral communication, vocal expression

2 a usually formal discourse delivered to an audience <a televised *speech* to the nation>

syn address, allocution, lecture, talk

rel debate, parlance, parley; declamation, harangue, oration, speechification

3 syn see LANGUAGE 1

speechcraft *n syn* see ORATORY

speechless *adj* **1 syn** see DUMB 1

rel aphonic

2 syn see SILENT 2

3 syn see SILENT 3

speed *n* **1 syn** see HASTE 1

rel alacrity, legerity; headway

con dilatoriness, tardiness

2 rate of movement, performance, or occurrence <ran through the exercise at a high *speed*>

syn ‖bat, celerity, gait, pace, quickness, rapidity, rapidness, swiftness, velocity; *compare* TEMPO

rel fastness, fleetness; clip, hickory

speed *vb* **1 syn** see HURRY 2

idiom make haste

ant slow (up *or* down)

2 syn see COURSE

3 to cause to move fast or faster <*sped* our craft forward>

syn accelerate, hasten, hurry, quicken, shake up, step up, swiften

rel advance, aid, ease, encourage, expedite, facilitate, forward, further, help (along), smooth; cheer (on), drive (on), goad (on), spur (on); burn (up)

idiom ‖get the lead out

con hamper, restrain, retard; check, stay; delay, postpone, put off

ant slow (up *or* down)

speedily *adv syn* see FAST 2

idiom against the clock, hell-bent for leather, like a bat out of hell, like all forty, ‖like all get-out, on the double, to beat the band

con deliberately, languidly, leisurely; lazily, lethargically, sluggishly; crawlingly, creepingly

ant slow, slowly

speediness *n syn* see HASTE 1

ant slowness

speedy *adj syn* see FAST 3

---

syn synonym(s)	**rel** related word(s)
ant antonym(s)	**con** contrasted word(s)
idiom idiomatic equivalent(s)	
‖ use limited; if in doubt, see a dictionary	

rel agile, brisk, nimble; prompt, ready
idiom fast as greased lightning, speedy as an arrow
ant dilatory; slow
speerings *n pl syn* see NEWS
‖**spelder** *vb syn* see SPRAWL 1
spell *n* a spoken word or set of words believed to have magic power <cause death by muttering *spells* over her>
    syn charm, conjuration, ‖devil-devil, incantation, rune
    rel bewitching, enchanting, hexing
spell *vb syn* see BEWITCH 1
spell *vb syn* see MEAN 2
spell *vb* 1 *syn* see RELIEVE 3
    2 *syn* see REST 3
spell *n* 1 a limited period or amount of activity <each *spell* of work was followed by a brief rest>
    syn bout, go, shift, stint, time, tour, trick, turn
    rel streak; ‖patch, period; stretch; relay
    2 *syn* see WHILE 1
    3 *syn* see ATTACK 3
spellbind *vb syn* see ENTHRALL 2
spell out *vb syn* see EXPLAIN 1
spend *vb* 1 to distribute or consume in payment or expenditure <*spent* fifty dollars for that dress>
    syn disburse, expend, fork (out), give, lay out, outlay, pay, shell out
    rel blow, drop, hand out; contribute; consume, dissipate, lavish, squander, throw away, waste
    ant save
    2 *syn* see GO 4
    3 to cause or permit to elapse <*spent* the summer at the beach>
    syn pass, while (away)
spender *n syn* see SPENDTHRIFT
    ant saver
spending money *n syn* see POCKET MONEY
spendthrift *n* one who dissipates his resources foolishly and wastefully <a *spendthrift* who lost his estate through gambling>
    syn high roller, prodigal, profligate, scattergood, spender, squanderer, unthrift, waster, wastethrift, wastrel
    con hoarder, miser, saver
spent *adj syn* see EFFETE 2
spew *vb* 1 *syn* see VOMIT
    2 *syn* see ERUPT 1
    rel flood, gush
sphere *n* 1 *syn* see BALL
    2 *syn* see FIELD
    rel circle, jurisdiction, realm
sphere *vb syn* see BALL
spice *n* 1 *syn* see HINT 2
    2 *syn* see FRAGRANCE
spick-and-span *adj* 1 *syn* see BRAND-NEW
    2 *syn* see NEAT 2
spicy *adj* 1 *syn* see SWEET 2
    2 *syn* see PUNGENT
    rel fiery, gingery, high-spirited, spirited, zestful
    3 *syn* see RISQUÉ
    rel sophisticated; piquant
spider *n syn* see FRYING PAN
spiel *n* voluble, glib, or extravagant talk often intended to impress, persuade, or deceive <gave her a long sales *spiel*>
    syn ‖line, pitch, song and dance
    rel demagoguery; dramatics, pyrotechnics, sensationalism
‖**spieler** *n syn* see SWINDLER
spiff *vb syn* see DRESS UP 1
spiffy *adj syn* see DAPPER
‖**spiflicated** *adj syn* see INTOXICATED 1
spigot *n syn* see FAUCET
spike *vb syn* see IMPALE
spill *vb* 1 to cause or allow (something) to fall, flow, or run out and be lost or wasted <accidentally dropped the cup and *spilled* his tea>
    syn slop, squab
    rel dribble, drip, drop; spatter, splash, spray
    2 *syn* see OVERFLOW 2
    3 *syn* see REVEAL 1
spilth *n syn* see REFUSE
spin *vb* 1 to turn or cause to turn rapidly <pinwheels *spinning* in the wind>

syn gyrate, gyre, ‖pirl, pirouette, ‖purl, twirl, whirl, whirligig; *compare* TURN 1
    rel revolve, rotate, wheel; swirl; oscillate, pendulate, vibrate
    idiom spin like a top
    2 to feel as if revolving <her head was *spinning* with figures>
    syn reel, swim, turn, whirl
    rel dizzy, giddy; fluster, mix up, muddle
    idiom be in a whirl
spin (out) *vb syn* see EXTEND 3
spin *n syn* see DRIVE 1
spinal column *n syn* see SPINE
spindling *adj syn* see GANGLING
spindly *adj syn* see GANGLING
spine *n* the articulated column of bones that is the central and axial feature of a vertebrate skeleton <fractured his *spine*>
    syn back, backbone, rachis, spinal column, vertebrae, vertebral column
    rel spinal cord
spineless *adj syn* see WEAK 4
    rel weak-kneed, weak-willed
    idiom as spineless as an amoeba
    con self-willed, strong-willed
spin-off *n syn* see OUTGROWTH 2
spinster *n* a woman who is past the common age for marrying or who seems unlikely ever to marry <a gentle *spinster*, happy in her solitary life>
    syn maiden lady, old maid, spinstress, ‖tabby
spinstress *n syn* see SPINSTER
spiny *adj syn* see THORNY
spiral *vb syn* see WIND 2
spiring *adj syn* see LOFTY 6
spirit *n* 1 *syn* see SOUL 1
    2 *syn* see APPARITION
    3 *syn* see SOUL 2
    4 *syn* see TEMPER 1
    5 a lively or brisk quality in a person or his actions <a man of great *spirit* and courage>
    syn animation, brio, dash, élan, esprit, gimp, life, oomph, verve, vim, zing; *compare* VIGOR 2
    rel ardor, briskness, enthusiasm, liveliness; drive, get-up-and-go, ginger, go, pep, snap, starch, vigor, vitality, zip; character, force, substance
    6 *syn* see COURAGE
    rel ardor, fervor, passion, zeal; energy, force, might, power, strength
    7 *often* **spirits** *pl syn* see LIQUOR
spirit (away) *vb syn* see KIDNAP
spirit (up) *vb syn* see ELATE
spirited *adj* 1 *syn* see LIVELY 1
    rel sharp; fiery, gingery, peppery
    idiom full of life (*or* go)
    ant spiritless
    2 having or manifesting a high degree of vitality, spirit, and daring <the lawyer gave a *spirited* defense of his client>
    syn beany, fiery, gingery, high-hearted, high-spirited, mettlesome, peppery, spunky
    rel game, gritty, resolute; audacious, bold, brave, courageous, dauntless, fearless, intrepid, nervy, plucky, valiant; avid, eager, hot, keen; ardent, enthusiastic, fervent, hot, passionate, peppy, zealous
    con unenthusiastic; flabby, languid, limp; boneless, spineless
    ant spiritless
spiritless *adj* 1 *syn* see DEAD 1
    2 *syn* see DOWNCAST
    idiom down in the dumps
    3 *syn* see LANGUID
    rel tame; broken, subdued, submissive
    ant spirited
spiritual *adj* 1 *syn* see IMMATERIAL 1
    rel supernatural, supramundane
    ant physical
    2 *syn* see SACRED 2
    3 *syn* see ECCLESIASTICAL
    4 appealing to, coming from, or related to the higher emotions or to the aesthetic senses <man's *spiritual* and intellectual life as opposed to his animal instincts>
    syn numinous
    rel cerebral, intellectual, mental; elevated, high, high-minded, lofty; saintly

con low, lower; base
ant animal
spirituous *adj* containing a considerable amount of alcohol < *spirituous* liquors >
syn alcoholic, ardent, hard, strong
rel spiked; inebriating, intoxicating, intoxicative; heady
con nonalcoholic, nonintoxicating, soft
‖**spirity** *adj syn* see LIVELY 1
spit *vb syn* see IMPALE
spit *n* 1 *syn* see SALIVA
2 *syn* see IMAGE 1
rel counterpart; look-alike; twin
spit *vb* 1 *syn* see SPUTTER 1
2 *syn* see SPUTTER 2
spite *n syn* see MALICE
rel rancor; revenge, revengefulness, vengeance, vengefulness, vindictiveness
con sympathy; affection, love, tenderness
spiteful *adj syn* see MALICIOUS
rel antagonistic, hostile; revengeful, vengeful, vindictive
con charitable; sympathetic; affectionate, loving
ant spiteless
spitefulness *n syn* see MALICE
spitish *adj syn* see MALICIOUS
spitting image *n syn* see IMAGE 1
rel mirror image
spittle *n syn* see SALIVA
spit up *vb syn* see VOMIT
‖**spiv** *n* 1 *syn* see PARASITE
2 *syn* see SLACKER
splash *vb* to dash a liquid or semiliquid substance upon or against < *splashed* water onto her face >
syn douse, plash, slop, slosh, spatter, splatter, splosh, splurge, spurtle, swash
rel dash, throw; spray; sprinkle; ‖sprent, squirt; drench, drown, soak, sop, wet
splashy *adj syn* see SHOWY
splathering *adj syn* see CLUMSY 1
splatter *vb syn* see SPLASH
splay *adj syn* see CLUMSY 1
spleen *n syn* see MALICE
rel revenge, revengefulness, vindictiveness; wrath
splendid *adj* 1 *syn* see GRAND 2
rel baroque, flamboyant
2 extraordinarily or transcendently impressive < a *splendid* new city >
syn glorious, gorgeous, magnificent, proud, resplendent, splendiferous, splendorous, sublime, superb
rel eminent, illustrious; grand, impressive, lavish, luxurious, royal, sumptuous; divine, exquisite, lovely; incomparable, matchless, peerless, superlative, supreme, unparalleled, unsurpassed; surpassing, transcendent
con common, ordinary, run-of-the-mill
ant unimpressive
splendiferous *adj syn* see SPLENDID 2
rel dazzling, marvelous; smashing, walloping; rattling, ripping, screaming, terrific
splendorous *adj syn* see SPLENDID 2
splice *vb syn* see MARRY 2
splinter *vb syn* see SHATTER 1
splinterize *vb syn* see SHATTER 1
split *vb* 1 *syn* see CUT 5
rel crack, rive
2 *syn* see TEAR 1
‖3 *syn* see BETRAY 2
split (up) *vb syn* see SEPARATE 1
split *n* 1 *syn* see CRACK 3
2 *syn* see SCHISM 3
3 *syn* see BREACH 3
rel alienating, estranging
split second *n syn* see INSTANT 1
splitter *vb syn* see SHATTER 1
split–up *n syn* see SEPARATION 1
‖**splodge** *vb syn* see SPLOTCH
splosh *vb syn* see SPLASH
splotch *vb* to mark or spot with irregular patches especially of contrasting color < a pallid face *splotched* with red >
syn blotch, mottle, ‖splodge

rel blot, stain; dapple, fleck, marble, motley, variegate; bespot, spot; harlequin
‖**splunge** *vb syn* see PLUNGE 2
splurge *n syn* see SPREE 1
rel extravagance; splash
splurge *vb syn* see SPLASH
splurt *vb syn* see SQUIRT
splutter *vb* 1 *syn* see SPUTTER 2
2 *syn* see SPUTTER 1
spoil *n* something taken from another by force or craft < gold, jewels, and paintings are often *spoils* of war >
syn boodle, booty, loot, plunder, plunderage, prize, ‖spreaghery, ‖spulzie, swag
rel acquisition, grab, haul, take; pickings, stealings; pillage, spoliation
spoil *vb* 1 *syn* see RAVAGE
2 *syn* see INJURE 1
rel ‖snafu; ruin, wreck; demolish, destroy
3 *syn* see RAPE
4 *syn* see BABY
rel accommodate, favor, oblige
idiom spoil (one) rotten, spoil to death
5 *syn* see DECAY
spoiled *adj* 1 *syn* see DAMAGED
ant unspoiled
2 *syn* see BAD 5
rel off, tainted; putrefying, rotting
ant unspoiled
spoiler *n syn* see MARAUDER
spoken *adj* 1 *syn* see ORAL 2
ant written
2 *syn* see VOCAL 1
ant unspoken
spokesman *n* one who speaks as a representative of another < selected as *spokesman* for the party's views >
syn mouth, mouthpiece, speaker, spokesperson, spokeswoman
rel delegate, deputy, representative; champion, protagonist; prophet
spokesperson *n syn* see SPOKESMAN
spokeswoman *n syn* see SPOKESMAN
spoliate *vb syn* see RAVAGE
rel raid; maraud; gut, ravish, sweep
spoliator *n syn* see MARAUDER
sponge *n* 1 *syn* see DRUNKARD
2 *syn* see PARASITE
sponger *n syn* see PARASITE
spongy *adj syn* see SOFT 6
idiom as soft as a sponge
sponsor *n* one that accepts responsibility for another person or thing < the major *sponsor* of this project is the government >
syn angel, backer, backer-up, guarantor, patron, surety
rel advocate, champion, mainstay, supporter, upholder; preferrer, promoter; benefactor, Maecenas
sponsorship *n syn* see BACKING
spontaneity *n syn* see UNCONSTRAINT
rel extemporaneousness, offhandedness, unpremeditatedness
spontaneous *adj* acting or activated without apparent thought or deliberation < a *spontaneous* burst of applause >
syn automatic, impulsive, instinctive, involuntary, unmediated, unpremeditated, unprompted, will-less
rel unconstrained, unforced; unreasoned, unstudied; extemporaneous, extempore, impromptu, improvised, offhand; natural, simple, unsophisticated
con deliberate, intended, intentional, planned, predetermined, preplanned, studied, thought-out, voluntary, willed, willful; forced, prompted; conventional, formal, stylized
ant premeditated
spontoon *n syn* see CUDGEL
spoof *vb syn* see DUPE
spoof *n syn* see IMPOSTURE
spook *n* ‖1 *syn* see APPARITION
‖2 *syn* see ECCENTRIC
3 *syn* see SPY

‖**spook** *vb* **1** *syn* see FRIGHTEN
 2 *syn* see GHOSTWRITE
spooky *adj* **1** *syn* see WEIRD 1
 rel spookish; ominous
 2 *syn* see NERVOUS
‖**spoon** *n* *syn* see DUNCE
spoony *adj* *syn* see SIMPLE 3
spoony (over *or* on) *adj* *syn* see ENAMORED 1
spoor *n* *syn* see FOOTPRINT
sporadic *adj* **1** *syn* see FITFUL
 ant regular
 2 *syn* see INFREQUENT
 rel separate, single
 ant frequent
sporadically *adv* *syn* see OCCASIONALLY
 ant regularly
sport *vb* *syn* see PLAY 1
sport *n* **1** *syn* see PLAY 1
 2 sports *pl* *syn* see ATHLETICS
 3 *syn* see FUN 1
 rel jollification; antics, high jinks, horseplay
 4 *syn* see LAUGHINGSTOCK
 5 *syn* see CHANGE 2
sporting girl *n* *syn* see PROSTITUTE
sporting house *n* *syn* see BROTHEL
sportive *adj* *syn* see PLAYFUL 1
sportiveness *n* *syn* see MISCHIEVOUSNESS
sportsmanlike *adj* *syn* see FAIR 5
 ant unsporting, unsportsmanlike
sportsmanly *adj* *syn* see FAIR 5
 ant unsporting, unsportsmanlike
sporty *adj* *syn* see WILD 7
spot *n* **1** *syn* see STIGMA
 2 *syn* see DRAM
 3 *syn* see PARTICLE
 4 *syn* see PLACE 1
 rel scene; section, sector
 5 *syn* see JOB 2
 idiom job slot
 6 *syn* see PREDICAMENT
spot *vb* **1** to mark or stain (something) with spots <a white dress *spotted* with red mud>
 syn bespatter, bespot, spatter; *compare* SPECKLE 1
 rel blot, blotch, mottle; fleck, marble, streak, stripe; dot, pepper, speck, speckle, sprinkle, stipple; splash; dirty, soil, stain
 2 to form or appear as spots on <a bleak landscape *spotted* with cottages>
 syn dot, pimple, speckle, sprinkle, stud
 rel intersperse
 3 *syn* see IDENTIFY
 rel ascertain; see
 4 *syn* see FIND 1
spot *adj* *syn* see RANDOM
spotless *adj* **1** *syn* see CLEAN 1
 rel hygienic, sanitary
 2 *syn* see CHASTE
 ant spotted
spotty *adj* **1** lacking uniformity <*spotty* illumination>
 syn irregular, patchy, uneven
 rel unequal; flickering, fluctuating
 con equal, even, regular, uniform
 2 *syn* see FITFUL
spousal *n* *syn* see WEDDING
spousal *adj* *syn* see MATRIMONIAL
spouse *n* a marriage partner <consulted with her *spouse* before buying the dress>
 syn consort, mate
spouseless *adj* *syn* see SINGLE 1
 con espoused
‖**spout** *vb* *syn* see PAWN
spout *n* *syn* see WATERFALL
spraddle *vb* *syn* see SPRAWL 1
sprain *vb* to injure (a joint) by a sudden twisting motion that stretches and lacerates the ligaments <*sprained* her ankle>
 syn ‖rick, turn, twist, wrench
 rel pull, strain, stretch; tear; dislocate, throw; break, fracture
sprangle *vb* *syn* see SPRAWL 2
sprat *n* *syn* see TWERP

‖**sprauchle** *vb* *syn* see SCRAMBLE 1
sprawl *vb* **1** to lie or sit with arms and legs stretched out carelessly and awkwardly <the dog lay *sprawled* out on the sofa>
 syn drape, ‖scamble, ‖spelder, spraddle, spread-eagle
 rel loll, lounge; slouch, slump
 2 to grow, develop, or spread irregularly and without apparent design or plan <the city *sprawls* down the whole coast>
 syn ramble, scramble, sprangle, spread-eagle, straddle, straggle
 rel extend, stretch; spread
spread *vb* **1** to extend or cause to extend over a considerable area or space <they *spread* the news far and wide> <clouds *spread* over the sky>
 syn circulate, diffuse, disperse, disseminate, distribute, propagate, radiate, strew; *compare* STREW 1
 rel deal, dispense; broadcast, communicate, pass (on), transmit; dissipate, scatter, sow; peddle, push, retail
 idiom spread abroad (*or* far and wide)
 con hold (in); contain; compress
 2 *syn* see OPEN 4
 con fold; close
 3 *syn* see SET 5
spread *n* **1** *syn* see EXPANSION 2
 rel diffusion; profusion; stretch, sweep
 2 *syn* see EXPANSE
 3 *syn* see DINNER
 4 *syn* see BEDSPREAD
spread–eagle *vb* **1** *syn* see SPRAWL 1
 2 *syn* see SPRAWL 2
‖**spreaghery** *n* *syn* see SPOIL
spree *n* **1** an unrestrained indulgence in or outburst of an activity <a shopping *spree*>
 syn binge, fling, orgy, rampage, splurge
 2 *syn* see BINGE 1
spree *vb* *syn* see REVEL 1
sprightful *adj* *syn* see LIVELY 1
sprightly *adj* **1** *syn* see LIVELY 1
 rel perky; breezy
 2 *syn* see ANTIC 2
 rel sportive; coltish, frisky
 3 *syn* see AGILE
 4 *syn* see CLEVER 5
 rel pungent, sharp; keen-witted, quick-witted
spring *vb* **1** to have something as a source <the primitive cultures from which civilization *springs*>
 syn arise, birth, come (from), derive (from), emanate, flow, head, issue, originate, proceed, rise, stem, upspring; *compare* BEGIN 2
 rel appear, emerge, come out, loom; arrive, come; begin, commence, hatch, start
 2 *syn* see SKIP 1
 3 *syn* see JUMP 1
 4 *syn* see START 1
 ‖**5** *syn* see FREE
spring *n* **1** *usu* **springs** *pl* *syn* see SPA 1
 2 *syn* see SOURCE
 3 *syn* see YOUTH 1
 ant autumn
 4 *syn* see MOTIVE 1
 rel excitant, impetus, incitement, stimulant, stimulus
 5 the season between winter and summer <planting flowers in the *spring*>
 syn budtime, springtide, springtime
 rel ‖blackberry winter
 idiom prime of the year
 con autumn, fall
spring *adj* *syn* see VERNAL
springe *n* *syn* see PITFALL
springlike *adj* *syn* see VERNAL
springtide *n* **1** *syn* see SPRING 5
 2 *syn* see YOUTH 1
 ant autumn
springtime *n* **1** *syn* see SPRING 5
 2 *syn* see YOUTH 1
 ant autumn
springy *adj* *syn* see ELASTIC 1
 rel rebounding, recoiling
 ant rigid; springless
sprinkle *vb* **1** to scatter (something) in small drops or particles <*sprinkle* chocolate shot on whipped cream>

syn besprinkle, dust, powder, ‖strinkle; *compare* STREW 1
rel shake; scatter; pepper; sparge
2 *syn* see SPECKLE 1
3 *syn* see SPOT 2
4 *syn* see BAPTIZE
5 to rain lightly <it's only *sprinkling,* so we can still take our walk>
syn drizzle, ‖mizzle
rel mist; shower; spit
con pour, stream
sprinkling *n* **1 *syn*** see HINT 2
2 *syn* see DUSTING
3 *syn* see FEW
sprint *vb syn* see RUN 1
sprit *vb syn* see SQUIRT
sprite *n syn* see FAIRY
‖spritz *vb syn* see SQUIRT
spruce *adj syn* see DAPPER
ant slouchy
spruce (up) *vb syn* see DRESS UP 1
sprucy *adj syn* see DAPPER
spry *adj syn* see AGILE
rel prompt, quick, ready; energetic, vigorous; healthy, robust, sound
ant doddering
spuddy *adj syn* see ROTUND 2
‖spulzie *n syn* see SPOIL
spume *n syn* see FOAM
spunk *n* **1 *syn*** see FORTITUDE
rel bulldoggedness, doggedness
idiom clear (*or* true) grit
ant funk
2 *syn* see COURAGE
spunkless *adj syn* see COWARDLY
ant spunky
spunky *adj* **1 *syn*** see BRAVE 1
idiom full of spunk
ant spunkless; funky
2 *syn* see SPIRITED 2
ant funky
spur *n syn* see STIMULUS
rel excitant; activation, actuation
ant checkrein, curb
spur *vb syn* see URGE
rel rowel; arouse, awaken, rally, rouse, stir; instigate; countenance, favor
ant curb
spurious *adj* **1 *syn*** see ILLEGITIMATE 1
2 *syn* see ARTIFICIAL 2
3 of doubtful authenticity <claimed they had bought a *spurious* painting>
syn apocryphal, bastard, unauthentic, ungenuine; *compare* ARTIFICIAL 2, COUNTERFEIT
rel bogus, counterfeit, fake, phony, pseudo, sham; false, unreal
idiom not what (*or* all) it's cracked up to be
con actual, real, true; bona fide, genuine, veritable
ant authentic
4 *syn* see ARTIFICIAL 3
rel make-believe, pretend, pretended, pseudo
5 *syn* see COUNTERFEIT
spuriousness *n syn* see FALLACY 2
spurn *vb syn* see DECLINE 4
rel conspue, contemn, despise, disdain, scorn, scout; flout, scoff, sneer
con crave, desire, want
ant embrace
spur–of–the–moment *adj syn* see EXTEMPORANEOUS
spurt *vb syn* see SQUIRT
spurtle *vb syn* see SPLASH
sputter *vb* **1** to utter (words or ejaculations) hastily, explosively, and sometimes indistinctly <pompously *sputtering* his objections>
syn rip (out), spit, splutter
rel ejaculate, eject, throw (out); gibber, jabber; bluster, heckle, hector, rage, rant, rave, storm
2 to make a series of sudden short crackling or popping sounds <bacon *sputtering* in the pan>
syn spatter, spit, splutter

rel crackle, pop; hiss
spy (on *or* upon) *vb* to make furtive, stealthy, or secret observations of <had private detectives *spying* on his wife>
syn ‖stag
rel stake out; watch
spy *n* one who keeps secret watch to obtain information <was convicted on evidence produced by a *spy*>
syn agent, spook, undercover man; *compare* INFORMER
rel detective, investigator, sleuth; scout; beagle
idiom inside man, secret agent
spying *n syn* see ESPIONAGE
squab *adj syn* see STOCKY
‖squab *vb syn* see PRESS 1
squab *vb syn* see SPILL 1
squabble *n syn* see QUARREL
squabble *vb* **1 *syn*** see QUARREL
rel clash, encounter
idiom have a squabble over
2 *syn* see ARGUE 2
idiom get into (*or* have) a hassle, have a verbal wrestling match
squalid *adj* **1 *syn*** see DIRTY 1
rel disheveled, slipshod, sloppy, slovenly, unkempt; frowzy, slatternly; dingy, shoddy, sleazy
2 *syn* see SHABBY 1
3 *syn* see BASE 3
squall *vb* **1** to make a raucous noise <angry street urchins fighting and *squalling* at each other>
syn caw, ‖quawk, squark, squawk, yawp (*or* yaup)
rel bellow, howl, roar, shout, yell; bark, yap, yip; croak
2 *syn* see BAWL 2
rel squeal; screech, shriek; yelp
squall *n syn* see QUARREL
squander *vb syn* see WASTE 2
idiom make ducks and drakes of, play ducks and drakes with
squander *n syn* see EXTRAVAGANCE 2
squanderer *n syn* see SPENDTHRIFT
square *n* **1 *syn*** see COMMON 2
2 *syn* see FOGY
square *adj* **1** having four equal sides and four right angles <a large *square* Georgian mansion>
syn foursquare, quadrate, quadratic, quadratical
rel boxlike, boxy, squarish
2 *syn* see EVEN 5
3 *syn* see FAIR 4
4 *syn* see CONVENTIONAL 1
square *vb* **1 *syn*** see ADAPT
2 *syn* see CLEAR 5
3 *syn* see BRIBE
4 *syn* see AGREE 4
rel balance; coincide
square *adv syn* see JUST 1
squarehead *n syn* see DUNCE
squarely *adv* **1 *syn*** see EVENLY 1
2 *syn* see JUST 1
squark *vb syn* see SQUALL 1
squash *vb* **1 *syn*** see PRESS 1
2 *syn* see CRUSH 2
3 *syn* see CRUSH 5
4 *syn* see PRESS 7
squash *n* **1 *syn*** see SQUELCH
2 *syn* see CROWD 1
squashing *n syn* see REPRESSION 1
squashy *adj syn* see SOFT 6
ant firm
squat *vb* to sit on one's haunches <they were *squatting* around the fire>
syn hunker (down), ‖quat, ‖swat; *compare* CROUCH
rel crouch; hunch; stoop
squat *adj syn* see STOCKY
rel squattish, squatty
con long, tall; twiggy
ant lanky
‖squaw *n syn* see WIFE

---

syn synonym(s) | *rel* related word(s)
ant antonym(s) | *con* contrasted word(s)
idiom idiomatic equivalent(s)
‖ use limited; if in doubt, see a dictionary

squawk *vb* **1** *syn* see SQUALL 1
  2 *syn* see GRIPE
  rel yap, yip
squawker *n syn* see INFORMER
squawky *adj syn* see HARSH 3
  con liquid, mellow, smooth
squdgy *adj syn* see STOCKY
squeak *vb* **1** to utter or make a short shrill cry or noise <mice *squeaking* in the barn>
  syn ‖queak; *compare* SQUEAL 2
  rel creak, grate, screak, screech, squeal; pipe; scream
  2 *syn* see TALK 6
  3 *syn* see INFORM 3
squeak *n syn* see OPPORTUNITY
‖**squeaker** *n syn* see INFORMER
squeal *vb* **1** *syn* see SCREAM 1
  idiom squeal like a stuck pig
  2 to make a harsh piercing sometimes rasping noise <tires *squealing* on wet pavement>
  syn screak, scream, screech, shriek; *compare* SQUEAK 1
  rel creak, grate, rasp
  3 *syn* see INFORM 3
  4 *syn* see TALK 6
  5 *syn* see YELL 2
  rel bitch, bleat, complain, gripe, squawk
  idiom raise a howl, scream bloody murder
squealer *n syn* see INFORMER
squeam *n syn* see QUALM
squeamish *adj* **1** inclined to become nauseated <felt *squeamish* after the heavy meal on the ship>
  syn ‖pensy, qualmish, qualmy, queasy, queer, ‖wambly; *compare* NAUSEATED
  rel unsettled, upset; dizzy, shaky, vertiginous
  2 *syn* see NAUSEATED
  idiom sick at (*or* to) one's stomach
  3 *syn* see NICE 1
squeamishness *n syn* see NAUSEA
squeamy *adj syn* see NICE 1
squeeze *vb* **1** *syn* see PRESS 1
  rel contract, ‖scruze
  2 *syn* see EMBRACE 1
  3 *syn* see EXTORT 1
  4 *syn* see EKE OUT 2
  5 *syn* see PRESS 8
  6 *syn* see PRESS 7
squeezy *adj syn* see CRAMPED
squelch *n* a sound of or as if of semiliquid matter under suction <the *squelch* of his feet in the mud>
  syn squash, squidge, squish
squelch *vb syn* see SUPPRESS 2
squelching *n syn* see REPRESSION 1
squelchy *adj syn* see SOFT 6
‖**squench** *vb* **1** *syn* see EXTINGUISH 1
  2 *syn* see QUENCH 4
squidge *n syn* see SQUELCH
squiffed *adj syn* see INTOXICATED 1
squiggle *vb* **1** *syn* see WRIGGLE
  2 *syn* see SCRIBBLE
squinch *vb* **1** *syn* see RECOIL
  2 *syn* see SQUINT
squinny *vb syn* see SQUINT
squinny *adj syn* see THIN 1
squint *vb* to look or peer with the eyes partly closed <*squinted* in the bright sunlight>
  syn ‖sken, squinch, squinny
  idiom look asquint, screw up one's eyes
  ant goggle
squirm *vb* **1** *syn* see WRIGGLE
  2 *syn* see WRITHE 1
squirrel *vb syn* see HOARD
squirt *vb* to come forth in a sudden rapid usually narrow stream <water *squirting* from the hose>
  syn jet, splurt, sprit, ‖spritz, spurt, ‖squitter
  rel pour, stream, surge; spatter; spray
  con dribble, drip, trickle
squirt *n* ‖**1 squirts** *pl syn* see DIARRHEA
  2 *syn* see TWERP
squish *n* **1** *syn* see PRESS 1

  2 *syn* see SQUELCH
squishy *adj syn* see SOFT 6
‖**squit** *n syn* see TWERP
‖**squitter** *vb syn* see SQUIRT
squush *vb syn* see PRESS 1
squushy *adj syn* see SOFT 6
stab *n* **1** *syn* see PRICK
  2 *syn* see POKE 1
  3 *syn* see FLING 1
stab *vb syn* see THRUST 2
  rel dagger, dirk, poniard, prong
stabbing *adj syn* see SHARP 8
stabile *adj syn* see STEADY 2
stabilify *vb syn* see STABILIZE
stabilitate *vb syn* see STABILIZE
stability *n* the ability to withstand force or stress without alteration of position and without material change <the structural *stability* of the bridge>
  syn firmness, security, soundness, stableness, steadiness, strength
  rel dependability, durability, reliability; solidity, solidness, sturdiness; cohesion, toughness
  con insecurity, undependability, unreliability, unsoundness, unsteadiness; weakness
  ant instability, unstability
stabilize *vb* to make or keep stable, steadfast, or firm <a policy that *stabilized* the economy>
  syn ballast, poise, stabilify, stabilitate, steady
  rel balance, counterbalance, counterpoise, equalize, equipoise; prop, support, sustain; fix, secure, set, settle
  ant unstabilize
stable *adj* **1** *syn* see SURE 1
  rel balanced, poised; fixed, set, solid, sound, steadfast
  con wobbling, wobbly
  ant instable, unstable
  2 *syn* see STEADY 2
  3 *syn* see LASTING
  rel constant, steady; safe, secure, sound; staunch, steadfast, resolute
  4 marked by solidity, firmness, and stability especially in design or construction <a *stable* foundation for the building>
  syn firm, secure, solid, sound; *compare* FAST 4, SURE 1
  rel strong, sturdy; unassailable, unshakable
  idiom as firm as (the rock of) Gibraltar, solid as a rock
  con insecure, shaky, unsound, weak, wobbling, wobbly
  ant instable, unstable
stableness *n syn* see STABILITY
  ant unstableness
stack *n syn* see PILE 1
stack *vb syn* see HEAP 1
‖**stacked** *adj syn* see CURVACEOUS
stade *n syn* see STADIUM
stadium *n* a large usually unroofed structure with tiered seats enclosing a field used especially for sports <a football *stadium*>
  syn bowl, coliseum, stade
  rel arena, garden, gymnasium
‖**stag** *vb syn* see SPY (on *or* upon)
stage *n* **1** *used with the syn* see DRAMA
  2 *syn* see DEGREE 1
  rel level; phase; period
stage *vb* to present on the stage <*staged* a play>
  syn mount, produce, put on, show
  rel bring out, open; give, present; do, execute, perform, play
stage set *n syn* see SCENE 1
stage setting *n syn* see SCENE 1
stagger *vb* **1** *syn* see REEL 2
  2 *syn* see LURCH 2
  idiom pitch and plunge
  3 *syn* see TEETER
  rel ‖stiver, ‖stoit, ‖stoiter, ‖stot
  4 *syn* see HESITATE
  5 to affect with great wonder or bewilderment <a plot so bizarre as to *stagger* the imagination>
  syn boggle, dumbfound, nonplus
  rel perplex, puzzle, stump; amaze, astonish, astound, flabbergast; bowl (over), floor, knock over; devastate, overpower, overwhelm, shatter; paralyze
  idiom take (one) aback

stagger (on *or* along) *vb syn* see SHIFT 5
‖**stagger** *n syn* see FLING 1
staggering *adj syn* see MARVELOUS 1
stagnant *adj syn* see STATIC
stagnate *vb* 1 *syn* see VEGETATE
   2 *syn* see STULTIFY
stagnation *n syn* see DEPRESSION 3
staid *adj syn* see SERIOUS 1
   rel decorous, formal; collected, composed, cool; priggish, smug; starchy, stuffy
   con breezy, devil-may-care, easy, frivolous; debonair, jaunty; playful, sportive; hoydenish, rakish; fresh, irreverent; uncontrolled, unrestrained
   ant unstaid
stain *vb* 1 to soil often permanently with foreign matter < a shirt *stained* with grease >
   syn bestain, blot, discolor, smut; *compare* SOIL 2
   rel tinge; bedaub, daub, smear; besmirch, smirch, smudge, smutch
   2 *syn* see TAINT 1
   3 *syn* see DEBASE 1
stain *n* 1 *syn* see STIGMA
   rel blemish, defect, flaw
   idiom blot on the escutcheon
   2 *syn* see COLOR 6
stainless *adj syn* see CHASTE
   con tainted, tarnished
   ant stained
stake *n* 1 *syn* see BET
   2 *syn* see INTEREST 1
stake *vb* 1 *syn* see GAMBLE 1
   rel stake down
   2 *syn* see CAPITALIZE
stale *adj* 1 *syn* see MALODOROUS 1
   2 *syn* see TRITE
   rel dusty, fusty; dead
   ant fresh
‖**stale** *n syn* see LURE 2
stalemate *n syn* see DRAW 4
stalk *vb* 1 to pursue (game) stealthily or under cover < *stalk* deer >
   syn still-hunt
   rel follow, track; drive, chase, pursue; walk up; flush (out); ambush
   2 *syn* see STRIDE 1
stalky *adj syn* see THIN 1
stall *vb* ‖1 *syn* see SATIATE
   2 *syn* see ARREST 1
   rel brake, slow (down); hold off, put off, stand off; suspend; shut down
   idiom pull the checkstring
   con spur
stalwart *adj* 1 *syn* see STRONG 2
   rel athletic, brawny, husky, muscular, sinewy
   2 *syn* see BRAVE 1
stamina *n syn* see TOLERANCE 1
stammer *vb* 1 to make involuntary stops and repetitions in uttering syllables and words < the frightened child *stammered* and fell silent >
   syn ‖hammer, ‖stut, stutter
   rel falter, hesitate; stumble; splutter, sputter; gibber, jabber
   ‖2 *syn* see TEETER
stamp *vb* 1 *syn* see TRAMPLE 2
   rel clomp, clump, stump
   2 *syn* see IMPRESS 3
   rel etch, imprint, infix, inscribe, print
   idiom impress on the mind
stamp *n* 1 *syn* see IMPRESSION 1
   2 *syn* see TYPE
   3 *syn* see SEAL
stampede *vb* 1 *syn* see ROUT 1
   2 to take to sudden headlong flight in panic < cattle *stampeding* across the plain >
   syn pell-mell; *compare* RUSH 1
   rel bolt, charge, chase, crash, dash, fling, hurry, rush, shoot, tear
   idiom run like a pack of scalded dogs
stamping ground *n* 1 *syn* see HABITAT

   2 *syn* see RESORT 2
stance *n* 1 *syn* see POSTURE 1
   2 *syn* see POSITION 1
stanch *vb syn* see STEM
stand *vb* 1 *syn* see BEAR 10
   idiom ‖hack it, take lying down
   2 *syn* see TREAT 3
stand (on *or* upon) *vb syn* see DEPEND (on *or* upon) 1
   idiom be contingent on
stand *n syn* see POSITION 1
standard *n* 1 *syn* see FLAG
   2 *syn* see MODEL 2
   3 a means of determining what a thing should be < each generation has its own *standards* of morality >
   syn benchmark, criterion, gauge, measure, touchstone, yardstick
   rel average, mean, median, norm, par; axiom, belief, fundamental, principle; law, rule; exemplar, model, pattern
   idiom rule of thumb
   4 a fixed, customary, or official measure (as of quantity, quality, or price) < governmental *standards* of weights and measures >
   syn assize
   rel ‖dick
stander-by *n syn* see SPECTATOR
stand-in *n syn* see SUBSTITUTE
   rel second; assistant
standing *n* 1 *syn* see TERM 5
   2 *syn* see STATUS 1
   3 *syn* see STATUS 2
standoff *adj syn* see UNSOCIABLE
standoff *n syn* see DRAW 4
standoffish *adj* 1 *syn* see UNSOCIABLE
   2 *syn* see ANTISOCIAL
stand out *vb* 1 *syn* see BULGE
   2 *syn* see LOOM 3
standout *adj syn* see SUPERB 3
stand over *vb syn* see DEFER
standpat *n syn* see DIEHARD 1
standpatter *n syn* see DIEHARD 1
standpoint *n syn* see VIEWPOINT 2
standstill *n* cessation of movement < the car came to a *standstill* in the mud >
   syn stay, stillstand, stop
   rel arrest, check; pause; cessation, halt
   con start; movement
   ant start-up
stand up *vb syn* see RISE 1
stand-up *adj syn* see ERECT
   con lowered; flat, horizontal
‖**stang** *vb syn* see SMART
staple *n syn* see LOOP 2
staple *n syn* see BODY 3
star *n syn* see CHIEF 2
starch *n syn* see VIGOR 2
star-crossed *adj syn* see UNLUCKY
stare *vb* 1 *syn* see LOOK 7
   idiom ‖take a gander at
   2 *syn* see GAZE 1
   idiom fix (*or* rivet) one's eyes on
stare down *vb* to overcome (someone) by or as if by staring < the teacher could not *stare* the boy *down* >
   syn look down, outstare
   rel glare; master, quell, subdue, suppress; overcome, overwhelm
stark *adj* 1 *syn* see UTTER
   2 *syn* see NUDE 2
   3 *syn* see EMPTY 1
stark-naked *adj syn* see NUDE 2
   idiom bare (*or* naked) as a newborn babe, ‖naked as a jaybird, naked as the day one was born
‖**starny** *adj syn* see STELLAR 1
starry *adj syn* see STELLAR 1
start *vb* 1 to move suddenly and violently from a state of stillness or rest < *started* from his bed at the sound of shots >
   syn bolt, jump, spring, startle

---

syn synonym(s)   *rel* related word(s)
ant antonym(s)   *con* contrasted word(s)
idiom idiomatic equivalent(s)
‖ use limited; if in doubt, see a dictionary

rel dart; bounce; bound, leap; draw (back), flinch, recoil
idiom jump out of one's skin, start aside
ant stay
2 syn see RECOIL
3 syn see BEGIN 2
rel proceed, spring
ant end
4 syn see FOUND 2
5 syn see BEGIN 1
ant stop
start *n* **1 syn** see BEGINNING
ant finish
2 syn see ADVANTAGE 3
startle *vb* **1 syn** see START 1
2 syn see SHOCK 2
3 syn see FRIGHTEN
rel astonish, surprise
idiom make one jump out of one's skin, ‖scare the pants off
startlish *adj syn* see EXCITABLE
starved *adj syn* see HUNGRY
rel underfed, undernourished; weakened; half-famished, half-starved
con fed, nourished; overfed
ant well-fed
starving *adj syn* see HUNGRY
rel craving, famishing, hungering; dying, perishing
idiom crazy for food
stash *vb* **1 syn** see HOARD
2 syn see HIDE
rel hoard, squirrel
stasis *n syn* see BALANCE 1
state *n* **1** the way in which one manifests existence or the circumstances under which one exists or by which one is given distinctive character < remained in a weakened *state* for weeks >
syn condition, mode, posture, situation, status
rel circumstances; attitude, position, stand
idiom state of being
2 syn see STATUS 1
3 syn see STATUS 2
state *vb* **1 syn** see RELATE 1
rel elucidate, explain, expound, interpret; set forth
2 syn see ENUNCIATE 1
3 syn see SAY 1
4 syn see EXPRESS 2
ant imply
stated *adj syn* see FIRM 4
stately *adj* **1 syn** see CEREMONIAL
rel dignified, grand, noble; imperial, kingly, princely, regal, royal
2 syn see COURTLY
3 syn see GRAND 1
con lowly, poor; shabby; cheap
statement *n* **1 syn** see EXPRESSION 1
rel outgiving; articulation, presentation, presentment, verbalization, vocalization
2 syn see WORD 1
rel description, narrative, recital
3 syn see BILL 1
static *adj* characterized by relatively little or no movement, progression, or change (as in conditions) < a *static* economy >
syn immobile, stagnant, stationary, unmoving; *compare* STEADY 2
rel constant, stabile, stable, unchanging, unfluctuating; fixed, immovable, rigid, sticky; inactive, inert; stalled, stopped, stuck
idiom at a standstill, standing still
con active, changing, mobile, moving, progressing; erratic, fluctuating, inconstant, unstable
ant dynamic
station *n* **1 syn** see PLACE 1
2 syn see RAILROAD STATION
3 syn see STATUS 1
station *vb* to appoint or assign to an office or duty < *stationed* guards around the camp >
syn post, set
rel appoint, assign; place, position
stationary *adj syn* see STATIC
rel motionless, stock-still
ant moving

station house *n syn* see RAILROAD STATION
statuesque *adj syn* see SHAPELY
stature *n* **1 syn** see QUALITY 2
rel prestige, standing, status; ability, capacity; competence, qualification
2 syn see STATUS 2
status *n* **1** rating or positioning in relation to others (as in a social order, community, class, or profession) < his *status* as a slave >
syn capacity, character, footing, place, position, quality, rank, situation, standing, state, station
rel rating
2 social or professional importance or distinction < a lawyer of international *status* >
syn cachet, consequence, dignity, position, prestige, rank, standing, state, stature
rel caliber, merit, worth; distinction, renown; eminence, prominence
con inconsequence, insignificance, unimportance
3 syn see STATE 1
rel status quo
idiom state of affairs
statute *n syn* see LAW 1
rel act, enactment
staunch *adj* **1 syn** see SURE 1
2 syn see FAITHFUL 1
rel firm, strong
idiom as staunch as an oak, tried and true
con mercurial; shaky, unsteady
stave *vb syn* see HURRY 2
stave off *vb* **1 syn** see FEND (off)
rel beat off, drive (off), fight (off); block, parry
2 syn see PREVENT 2
staving *adv syn* see VERY 1
ant barely
stay *vb* **1 syn** see ARREST 1
rel postpone, prorogue, put off
2 to continue to be in one place for a noticeable time < *stayed* late at the office >
syn abide, bide, linger, remain, stick around, tarry, wait
rel dally, delay, dillydally, lag, procrastinate; hang around, loiter; outstay, stay out
ant go
3 syn see VISIT 3
rel bide, dwell, live
4 syn see DEFER
stay *n syn* see STANDSTILL
stay *n syn* see SUPPORT 3
stay *vb syn* see BASE
stead *vb syn* see HELP 1
steadfast *adj* **1 syn** see IMMOVABLE 1
2 syn see INFLEXIBLE 2
ant unsteadfast, vacillating
3 syn see SURE 2
ant capricious
4 syn see FAITHFUL 1
rel unfaltering, unflinching, unquestioning, unwavering
steadfastly *adv syn* see HARD 7
rel staunchly, strongly
steadiness *n syn* see STABILITY
ant unsteadiness
steady *adj* **1 syn** see SURE 2
rel unswerving; eternal, never-ending
2 being neither markedly varying nor variable in course or extent < a *steady* rain > < *steady* prices >
syn constant, equable, even, stabile, stable, unchanging, unfluctuating, uniform, unvarying; *compare* STATIC
rel steady-going; certain, changeless, fixed, set, sure, unchangeable; unflickering, unwavering; durable, reliable
con inconstant, uneven, unstable; changeable; changing, fluctuating, uncertain, undependable, undulating, unsure, varying, wavering
ant unsteady
3 syn see FAITHFUL 1
steady *vb syn* see STABILIZE
steady *n* **1 syn** see BOYFRIEND 2
2 syn see GIRL FRIEND 2
steal *vb* **1** to take another's possession illegally and without his knowledge < *stole* a car >

syn abstract, annex, appropriate, cabbage, ‖clout, ‖cly, collar, ‖coon, ‖cop, ‖crook, filch, ‖heist, hook, lift, nab, ‖nail, ‖nick, nim, nip, pilfer, pillage, pinch, pocket, ‖prig, purloin, smouch, ‖snaffle, ‖snake, snitch, swipe, thieve, vulture
rel mooch; fleece, frisk; grab, grasp, seize, snatch, take; hijack, shanghai; poach, rustle; burglarize, rob; loot, plunder, rifle
idiom make off (*or* away) with, run away (*or* off) with
2 *syn* see SNEAK
3 to move or go quietly so as not to disturb <*stole* out of the sickroom on tiptoe>
syn creep, glide, mouse, slide, slip; *compare* SNEAK
rel tiptoe
con clump, stamp, stomp, stump
steal *n* **1** *syn* see THEFT
2 *syn* see BARGAIN 1
stealage *n* *syn* see THEFT
stealer *n* *syn* see THIEF
stealing *n* *syn* see THEFT
stealthily *adv* *syn* see SECRETLY
ant openly
stealthy *adj* **1** *syn* see SECRET 1
rel crafty, cunning, sly, wily; skulking, slinking, sneaking; cat-like
con direct, straight, straightforward
ant open
2 being so quiet, slow, and deliberate in movement as to escape observation <the *stealthy* movements of the cat burglar>
syn catlike, catty, feline, furtive; *compare* SECRET 1
rel noiseless, pantherine, pantherish, quiet, silent; shifty, skulking, sly, sneak, sneaking, sneaky
steam *n* *syn* see POWER 4
steamroller *vb* *syn* see WHIP 2
steam up *vb* *syn* see ANGER 1
steel *vb* **1** *syn* see GIRD 3
rel rally; nerve; buck up; reinforce
idiom grit one's teeth, set one's jaw, take the bit in one's teeth
ant unsteel
2 *syn* see ENCOURAGE 1
steep *adj* **1** having an incline approaching the perpendicular <a *steep* trail up the mountain>
syn abrupt, arduous, precipitate, precipitous, sheer, sideling, steepdown, steep-to, steep-up, ‖stickle
rel elevated, lifted, raised; steepish; high, lofty; prerupt; perpendicular, straight-up; breakneck
con easy, gentle, gradual, moderate; shelfy, shelving, shelvy
2 *syn* see EXCESSIVE 1
steep *vb* **1** *syn* see SOAK 1
2 *syn* see INFUSE 1
steepdown *adj* *syn* see STEEP 1
steep–to *adj* *syn* see STEEP 1
steep–up *adj* *syn* see STEEP 1
steer *vb* *syn* see GUIDE
idiom steer one's course
steer *n* *syn* see TIP
stellar *adj* **1** of, relating to, or suggestive of a star or group of stars <*stellar* light>
syn astral, sidereal, ‖starny, starry, stellular
rel gleaming, luminous, lustrous, shining, starlike, twinkling; star-spangled
con starless
2 *syn* see CHIEF 2
stellify *vb* *syn* see EXALT 1
stellular *adj* *syn* STELLAR 1, astral, sidereal, ‖starny, starry
stem *vb* *syn* see SPRING 1
stem *vb* to hinder or prevent by or as if by damming <*stem* the flow of blood>
syn stanch, stop
rel arrest, check, control
stemma *n* *syn* see GENEALOGY
stench *vb* *syn* see SMELL 3
stenchful *adj* *syn* see MALODOROUS 1
stenchy *adj* *syn* see MALODOROUS 1
stentorian *adj* *syn* see LOUD 1
rel orotund; clamorous, vociferous; gravelly, rough; clarion‐voiced, loudmouthed, loud-voiced, trumpet-tongued
stentorious *adj* *syn* see LOUD 1
rel orotund; clamorous, vociferous; gravelly, rough; clarion‐voiced, loudmouthed, loud-voiced, trumpet-tongued

stentorophonic *adj* *syn* see LOUD 1
step *n* **1** *syn* see FOOTPRINT
2 *syn* see DEGREE 1
3 *syn* see MEASURE 7
rel act, action; motion
step *vb* **1** *syn* see WALK 1
2 *syn* see DANCE 1
step–by–step *adj* *syn* see GRADUAL
step in *vb* **1** *syn* see VISIT 2
2 *syn* see INTERPOSE 2
step up *vb* *syn* see SPEED 3
ant step down
stereotyped *adj* *syn* see TRITE
idiom worn thin
stereotypical *adj* *syn* see TRITE
ant original
sterile *adj* **1** lacking the power to bear offspring or produce fruit <a hybrid that is completely *sterile*>
syn barren, effete, impotent, infecund, infertile, unfruitful
rel sterilized; fallow, fruitless, unproductive; unprolific; arid, bare, dry; dead, desolate
con potent, productive, rich; bearing, fruiting, fruitive, producing, turning out, yielding; fecund, fruitful, prolific, teeming
ant fertile
2 *syn* see UNORIGINAL
rel flat, insipid, jejune, vapid; stale; effete, worn-out; impotent
con fertile, fruitful, potent, producing, productive, prolific
ant fecund
sterlize *vb* to make incapable of producing offspring <*sterilizing* animals in medical experiments>
syn alter, castrate, change, desexualize, fix, geld, mutilate, neuter, unsex
rel emasculate; caponize, poulardize; spay
sterling *adj* *syn* see HONORABLE 1
rel pure, true
stern *adj* *syn* see SEVERE 1
rel grim, implacable, unrelenting; inexorable, inflexible
ant lenient, soft
‖**stern** *n* *syn* see BUTTOCKS
stew *n* **1** *syn* see BROTHEL
2 *usu* stews *pl* *syn* see RED-LIGHT DISTRICT
3 *syn* see SLUM
4 *syn* see MISCELLANY 1
5 *syn* see SNIT
rel boil
6 *syn* see COMMOTION 2
stew *vb* **1** *syn* see BOIL 2
2 *syn* see WORRY 3
idiom be in a stew
stewardly *adj* *syn* see SPARING
‖**stewed** *adj* *syn* see INTOXICATED 1
stick *n* **1** *syn* see BAR 1
2 *syn* see DECOY 2
3 sticks *pl,* used with the *syn* see FRONTIER 2
idiom the middle of nowhere
stick *adv* *syn* see ALL 1
stick *vb* **1** *syn* see THRUST 2
2 to become or cause to become closely and firmly attached <papers all *stuck* together>
syn adhere, cleave, cling, cohere
rel affix, attach, fasten, fix; glue; cement; fuse, weld; braze, solder
idiom stick close, stick like a wet shirt, stick like the paper on the wall, stick like wax, stick to like a barnacle (*or* leech)
con loosen; detach, disengage
ant unstick
3 *syn* see SET 1
4 *syn* see NONPLUS 1
5 *syn* see FLEECE 1
6 *syn* see OVERCHARGE 1
‖**7** *syn* see BEAR 10
8 *syn* see DEMUR
stickage *n* *syn* see ADHERENCE 1

---

syn synonym(s)   *rel* related word(s)
ant antonym(s)   *con* contrasted word(s)
idiom idiomatic equivalent(s)
‖ use limited; if in doubt, see a dictionary

stick around *vb syn* see STAY 2
stick–at–nothing *adj syn* see UNSCRUPULOUS
sticker *n syn* see SEAL
sticking *n syn* see ADHERENCE 1
stick–in–the–mud *n syn* see FOGY
‖**stickle** *adj syn* see STEEP 1
stickle *vb syn* see DEMUR
  rel hold out, stall; contend, kick, object, protest
stick out *vb* **1** *syn* see BULGE
  rel outstretch, outthrust, protend, push
  2 *syn* see STRIKE 1
  3 *syn* see BEAR 10
stick up *vb syn* see ROB 1
sticky *adj* **1** having the quality of sticking by or as if by adhesion
  < *sticky* syrup >
  syn adhesive, ‖claggy, ‖clarty, cloggy, gluey, gooey, gummy,
  stodgy
  rel tacky; viscid, viscous
  2 *syn* see HUMID
  3 *syn* see HARD 6
  4 *syn* see SENTIMENTAL
‖**stickybeak** *n syn* see BUSYBODY
sticky–fingered *adj syn* see LARCENOUS
stiff *adj* **1** incapable of or highly resistant to bending or flexing
  < a *stiff* cardboard packing box >
  syn immalleable, impliable, incompliant, inelastic, inflexible,
  rigid, unbending, unflexible, unyielding; *compare* INFLEXIBLE 2
  rel stiffish; hard, resistant; hardened; petrified; stark
  idiom stiff as a board (*or* poker)
  con soft, softened; yielding; bendable, pliable, pliant; limber,
  supple, willowy
  ant flexible, flexile
  2 *syn* see INTOXICATED 1
  3 *syn* see OBSTINATE
  4 characterized by a lack of ease, grace, or spontaneity especially in style < a play whose dialogue and characters were *stiff*
  and perfunctory >
  syn buckram, cardboard, muscle-bound, stilted, wooden
  rel rigid, set, studied; machine-made, mechanical, stereotyped,
  stock; arid, dry, dull
  con expressive, graphic, vivid; easy, fluent, graceful, smooth
  5 *syn* see EXCESSIVE 1
stiff *n* **1** *syn* see CORPSE
  2 *syn* see DRUNKARD
  3 *syn* see MISER
stiff–necked *adj syn* see OBSTINATE
stifle *vb* **1** *syn* see SUFFOCATE
  2 *syn* see MUFFLE 2
  3 *syn* see SUPPRESS 3
  4 *syn* see STULTIFY
stifling *adj* **1** producing or seeming to produce suffocation < *sti-*
  fling heat >
  syn smothering, smothery, ‖smudgy, suffocating, suffocative;
  compare HUMID, STUFFY 1
  rel oppressive, overpowering; unbearable, unendurable
  2 *syn* see STUFFY 1
stifling *n syn* see REPRESSION 1
stigma *n* a mark of shame or discredit < the *stigma* of personal
  cowardice >
  syn bar sinister, black eye, blot, blur, brand, odium, onus, slur,
  spot, stain
  rel besmirchment, disfigurement, smudge, smutch, taint, taint-
  ing; disgrace, dishonor, shame
  con credit, distinction, glory, honor; bay(s), crown, laurel(s)
still *adj* **1** *syn* see MOTIONLESS
  2 *syn* see CALM 1
  rel peaceful, unperturbed
  con roiled, roily, turbid
  3 devoid of or making no stir, sound, or noise < the streets
  were *still* at 3:00 A.M. >
  syn hush, hushful, noiseless, quiet, silent, soundless, stilly,
  whist
  rel calm, hushed, peaceful, placid, serene, tranquil; deathlike,
  deathly
  idiom deathly still, still as death
  ant noisy
still *vb* **1** *syn* see CALM
  ant agitate

  2 *syn* see SILENCE
still *adv* **1** *syn* see HOWEVER
  2 *syn* see YET 1
  idiom still (*or* even) more
  3 *syn* see ALSO 2
still *n syn* see SILENCE 1
still and all *adv syn* see HOWEVER
still–hunt *vb syn* see STALK 1
stillness *n syn* see SILENCE 1
stillstand *n syn* see STANDSTILL
stilly *adj* **1** *syn* see STILL 3
  con agitated, disturbed, noisy
  ant noiseful
  2 *syn* see CALM 1
stilted *adj* **1** *syn* see RHETORICAL
  2 *syn* see STIFF 4
  3 *syn* see GENTEEL 3
  rel conventional, formal; decorous; prim
stimulant *n syn* see STIMULUS
stimulate *vb* **1** *syn* see PROVOKE 4
  rel enliven, vivify; activate, dynamize, energize, vitalize
  idiom build a fire under, get one started (*or* moving)
  con unnerve; deaden
  2 *syn* see ELATE
stimulating *adj* **1** *syn* see EXCITING
  rel enlivening, lively; provocative, seminal, suggestive; incitory,
  stimulative, stimulatory
  2 *syn* see INVIGORATING
stimulative *adj syn* see INVIGORATING
stimulus *n* something that rouses the mind or spirits or incites to
  activity < the war proved a *stimulus* to the economy > < sought
  a *stimulus* to take her mind off her own troubles >
  syn catalyst, goad, impetus, impulse, incentive, incitation, incitement, instigation, motivation, propellant, provocative, push,
  spur, stimulant; *compare* MOTIVE 1
  rel boost, encouragement, inducement, invitation, urging; cause,
  motive; excitement, piquing, provocation, stimulation
sting *vb syn* see SMART
stingy *adj* being unwilling or showing unwillingness to share with
  others < too *stingy* to tip the waiter >
  syn cheeseparing, ‖chinchy, close, closefisted, costive, hardfisted, hardhanded, ironfisted, mean, mingy, miserly, ‖narrow,
  narrow-fisted, narrowhearted, niggard, niggardly, parsimonious,
  penny-pinching, penny-wise, penurious, pinching, pinchpenny,
  save-all, ‖scant, scrimpy, scrimy, tight, tightfisted, ungenerous,
  ungiving; *compare* SPARING
  rel economical, frugal, Scotch, sparing, thrifty; scaly, screwy
  idiom as close as a vise, as close (*or* tight) as paper on a wall,
  as tightfisted as a kulak, near (*or* close *or* tight) as the bark on
  a tree
  con bountiful, giving, liberal, munificent, open-handed, philanthropic, unsparing, unstinting; prodigal
  ant generous
stink *vb syn* see SMELL 3
stinkard *n syn* see SNOT 1
stinkaroo *n syn* see SNOT 1
stinker *n syn* see SNOT 1
stinking *adj* **1** *syn* see MALODOROUS 1
  idiom stinking to high heaven
  ‖**2** *syn* see INTOXICATED 1
‖**stinko** *adj syn* see INTOXICATED 1
stinky *adj syn* see MALODOROUS 1
stint *vb* **1** *syn* see SCRIMP
  2 *syn* see SPARE 3
stint *n* **1** *syn* see RESTRICTION 1
  2 *syn* see TASK 1
  rel amount, quantity; allotment, apportionment; participation,
  share
  3 *syn* see SPELL 1
stipend *n syn* see WAGE
  rel award, consideration, payment
stipple *vb syn* see SPECKLE 1
stipulate *vb syn* see SPECIFY 3
  rel designate; state; provide
stipulated *adj syn* see FIRM 3
  rel designated, pinned down
  con implied, unstated, unwritten
stipulation *n syn* see CONDITION 1

rel specification; circumscription, limit

stir *vb* **1** to cause to shift from quiescence or torpor into activity <a teacher who *stirred* the minds of his most sluggish students>
  syn arouse, awaken, bestir, challenge, kindle, rally, rouse, wake, waken, whet; *compare* PROVOKE 4
  rel excite, galvanize, inspire, provoke, quicken, stimulate; agitate, foment, incite, instigate; activate, energize, vitalize; actuate, drive, move, impel; ||roust, rout
  idiom make (*or* have) an impact on, set astir, set on fire
  2 *syn* see WAKE 1
  3 *syn* see SEETHE 4

stir (up) *vb syn* see INCITE
  idiom add fuel to the flame, apply the torch, feed the fire, pour oil on the fire, stir the embers

stir *n* **1** signs of excited activity, hurry, or commotion <noticed a *stir* within the crowd>
  syn ado, bustle, flurry, furore, fuss, pother, whirl, whirlpool, whirlwind; *compare* COMMOTION 4
  rel agitation, disquiet, stir-up; commotion, disturbance; din, hubbub, pandemonium, stirabout, tumult
  con calm, peace, placidity; inaction, inactivity
  ant tranquillity
  2 *syn* see MOTION 1

||**stir** *n syn* see JAIL

||**stirra** *n syn* see MAN 3

stirring *n syn* see MOTION 1

stirring *adj syn* see EXCITING
  rel heart-stirring, soul-stirring

stitch *n syn* see PAIN 1

stivy *adj syn* see STUFFY 1

stock *n* **1** *syn* see FAMILY 1
  2 *syn* see ESTIMATION 1
  3 *syn* see TRUST 1
  4 *syn* see SUPPLY
  5 *syn* see RESERVE

stock *vb* to equip, furnish, supply, or have material requisites (as for sale) <a bar that *stocks* all the best brands of liquor>
  syn carry, keep
  rel have; furnish, supply
  idiom have (*or* keep) in stock, keep on hand

stockade *n syn* see JAIL

stockpile *n* **1** *syn* see PILE 1
  2 *syn* see RESERVE

stockpile *vb syn* see ACCUMULATE

stock–still *adj syn* see MOTIONLESS

stocky *adj* being compact and broad in build and often short in stature <a *stocky* but quick and hard-hitting catcher>
  syn ||chuffy, ||chumpy, chunky, dumpy, heavyset, squab, squat, squdgy, stubby, ||stuggy, stumpy, thick, thick-bodied, thickset
  rel plump, stout; bunty, low-set, short; lumpish, lumpy, pudgy; corpulent, fat
  con lean, skinny, thin, wiry

stodge *vb* **1** *syn* see SATIATE
  2 *syn* see PLOD 1

stodgy *adj* **1** *syn* see STICKY 1
  2 *syn* see DULL 9
  rel unexciting; pedantic; heavy, ponderous, weighty
  3 *syn* see TACKY 2

stoic *adj syn* see IMPASSIVE 1
  rel aloof, detached, indifferent, unconcerned; self-controlled, Spartan; indomitable, unassailable; long-suffering, patient, resigned

stoicism *n syn* see APATHY 1
  rel backbone, fortitude, grit, guts, pluck, sand

||**stoit** *vb syn* see LURCH 2

||**stoiter** *vb syn* see LURCH 2

stolid *adj syn* see IMPASSIVE 1
  rel blunt, dull, obtuse; dense, dull, dumb, slow, stupid; inactive, inert, passive, supine
  ant sensitive

stolidity *n syn* see APATHY 1
  rel dullness, dumbness, slowness, stupidity; inactiveness, inactivity, inertia, passivity
  con aptness, quickness, readiness; animation, enlivening, quickening; ardor, enthusiasm, fervor, passion, zeal; fire
  ant sensitivity

stomach *n* **1** *syn* see ABDOMEN

2 *syn* see APPETITE 1

stomach *vb syn* see BEAR 10

stomachache *n* abdominal pain <she has a terrible *stomach-ache*>
  syn bellyache, colic, collywobbles, gripe(s)
  rel distress, misery

||**stomachy** *adj syn* see IRASCIBLE

stomp *vb syn* see TRAMPLE 2

stone–blind *adj syn* see BLIND 1

stone–broke *adj syn* see POOR 1

stoned *adj* **1** *syn* see INTOXICATED 1
  2 *syn* see DRUGGED

stone–still *adj syn* see MOTIONLESS

stony *adj* **1** *syn* see UNFEELING 2
  ant soft
  2 *syn* see POOR 1

stonyhearted *adj syn* see UNFEELING 2
  rel flinty, hard, stonelike
  idiom as cold as marble
  ant softhearted

stooge *n* **1** one who plays a subordinate or compliant role to a principal <an executive who was only a *stooge* with no real power>
  syn Charlie McCarthy, dummy, yes-man
  2 *syn* see TOOL 2

stool *n syn* see INFORMER

||**stool** *vb syn* see INFORM 3

stoolie *n syn* see INFORMER

stool pigeon *n syn* see INFORMER

stoop *vb* **1** to descend from one's level (as of rank or dignity) usually to do something <a king who would not *stoop* to consider the common people>
  syn condescend, deign
  rel relax, thaw, unbend; accord, concede; accommodate, favor, oblige
  idiom be so good as to, come (*or* get) down from one's high horse, lower oneself
  2 to drop in status or dignity by indulgence in pettiness or unworthy behavior <a man who would not *stoop* to tell a lie>
  syn descend, sink
  idiom act beneath oneself, debase (*or* demean) oneself, lower oneself
  3 *syn* see DUCK 2

stop *vb* **1** *syn* see STEM
  2 *syn* see FILL 1
  rel disrupt, hinder, interrupt; cut off, shut off, turn off
  ant unstop
  3 to suspend or cause to suspend activity <the conversation *stopped*>
  syn cease, desist, ||deval, discontinue, give over, halt, knock off, leave off, quit, surcease; *compare* ARREST 1
  rel ||can, refrain (from); arrest, check, cut off, interrupt; stay, suspend; ||cheese, lay off; break off, break up, end, terminate
  con continue, go on, keep (on), keep up, persist
  ant start
  4 to come to a standstill <the car *stopped* at the intersection>
  syn bring up, draw up, fetch up, halt, haul up, pull up
  con start; move; pull out
  ant go

stop (in *or* by) *vb syn* see VISIT 2

stop (over) *vb syn* see VISIT 3
  idiom make a stopover

stop *n* **1** *syn* see END 2
  ant start
  2 *syn* see BAR 2
  3 *syn* see STANDSTILL

stopcock *n syn* see FAUCET

stopgap *adj syn* see MAKESHIFT

stopgap *n syn* see RESOURCE 3

stopover *n syn* see SOJOURN

stopper *vb syn* see FILL 1
  ant unstopper

store *vb syn* see STOW

---

syn synonym(s)   *rel* related word(s)
ant antonym(s)   *con* contrasted word(s)
idiom idiomatic equivalent(s)
|| use limited; if in doubt, see a dictionary

store (up) *vb syn* see ACCUMULATE
  rel deposit; cache
store *n* **1** *syn* see RESERVE
  2 *syn* see SUPPLY
  3 *syn* see DEPOT 2
  4 a business establishment where goods are shown for sale < a food *store* >
  syn market, outlet, shop, showroom
  rel discounter, discount house, discount store, emporium
store *adj syn* see READY-MADE
store–bought *adj syn* see READY-MADE
‖**store–boughten** *adj syn* see READY-MADE
storehouse *n syn* see DEPOT 2
storm *n* **1** *syn* see COMMOTION 4
  2 *syn* see BARRAGE
storm *vb syn* see ATTACK 1
storm and stress *n syn* see UNREST
stormful *adj syn* see WILD 6
  rel threatening; dusty, murky; foul; howling, riproaring, roaring
  ant calm
stormily *adv syn* see HARD 2
stormy *adj syn* see WILD 6
  rel threatening; dusty, murky; foul; howling, riproaring, roaring
  ant calm
story *n* **1** *syn* see ACCOUNT 7
  2 a recital of real or imaginary happenings that is less elaborate than a novel < told the *story* of his escape > < a simple *story* of heartwarming devotion >
  syn anecdote, narration, narrative, tale, yarn; *compare* ACCOUNT 7
  rel conte; description; fable; folktale, legend, märchen; Canterbury tale, cock-and-bull story, fabrication, fairy tale, fiction
  3 *syn* see LIE
storyteller *n syn* see LIAR
‖**stot** *vb syn* see LURCH 2
stout *adj* **1** *syn* see BRAVE 1
  idiom bold as a lion
  con irresolute; fainthearted
  2 *syn* see STRONG 2
  rel resolute, steadfast; hard; indomitable, invincible
  idiom as strong (*or* stalwart) as an English oak
  3 *syn* see FAT 2
  rel thick-bodied; ‖plenitudinous
  ant spare
stouthearted *adj syn* see BRAVE 1
stow *vb* to put (articles) into a storage space < *stowed* his gear belowdecks >
  syn bestow, pack, store, warehouse
  ant unstow
straddle *vb* **1** *syn* see BESTRIDE 2
  2 *syn* see SPRAWL 2
straggle *vb* **1** *syn* see WANDER 1
  2 *syn* see SPRAWL 2
straggler *n syn* see LAGGARD
straight *adv* **1** *syn* see AWAY 3
  2 *syn* see DIRECTLY 1
straight *adj* **1** *syn* see DIRECT 2
  idiom as straight as an arrow
  ant circuitous
  2 *syn* see STRAIGHTFORWARD 2
  3 free from admixture or extraneous matter < a shot of *straight* liquor >
  syn neat, plain, pure, unadulterated, undiluted, unmixed
  rel unmodified; concentrated; strong
  con adulterated, blended, mixed; watered-down; weak
  4 *syn* see CONVENTIONAL 1
straight *n syn* see RIGHT 1
straightaway *adv syn* see AWAY 3
straightforward *adj* **1** *syn* see DIRECT 2
  2 free from all that is dishonest or secretive < a *straightforward* answer >
  syn aboveboard, forthright, plain dealing, straight; *compare* FRANK
  rel pretenseless; honest, honorable, just, upright, upstanding; candid, frank, open, plain, unequivocal; direct, outspoken
  con equivocal, evasive, shuffling; indirect; prevaricative; dishonest, untruthful
  ant devious

  3 *syn* see FRANK
  rel barefaced, straight-from-the-shoulder
  4 *syn* see CLEAR 5
straightly *adv syn* see DIRECTLY 1
straight off *adv syn* see AWAY 3
straight–out *adj syn* see UTTER
straight–up *adj* **1** *syn* see ERECT
  2 *syn* see VERTICAL
straightway *adv syn* see AWAY 3
strain *n* **1** *syn* see HINT 2
  2 *syn* see MELODY
  3 *syn* see MOOD 1
strain *vb* **1** *syn* see TRY 2
  rel stretch
  idiom put a strain on
  2 to injure (as a body part) by overuse or misuse < *strained* a muscle while lifting weights >
  syn pull
  3 *syn* see LABOR 1
  4 *syn* see EXUDE
  5 *syn* see DEMUR
strain *n syn* see STRESS 1
strained *adj syn* see FORCED
  rel taut, tense, tight
  con unforced, unlabored; unconstrained
  ant unstrained
strait *n syn* see JUNCTURE 2
  rel bind, squeeze; difficulty, hardship, rigor, vicissitude; bewilderment, mystification, perplexity
straitlaced *adj syn* see PRIM 1
  rel hidebound, intolerant, narrow, narrow-minded; rigorous, strict
  idiom prim and proper
  con easygoing, relaxed; broadminded, liberal, liberal-minded; libertine
strake *vb syn* see STREAK
‖**stramash** *n syn* see CRASH 3
strand *n syn* see SHORE
strand *vb syn* see SHIPWRECK 1
stranded *adj syn* see AGROUND
  idiom high and dry, run aground
strange *adj* **1** *syn* see EXOTIC 2
  2 *syn* see UNFAMILIAR 1
  rel unknown; alien
  3 *syn* see MARVELOUS 1
  4 deviating from what is ordinary, usual, or to be expected < a *strange*, unpredictable man >
  syn bizarre, curious, eccentric, erratic, idiosyncratic, odd, oddball, outlandish, peculiar, quaint, queer, ‖rum, rummy, singular, uncouth, unusual, weird; *compare* EXCEPTIONAL 1, MYSTERIOUS
  rel aberrant, abnormal, atypical, off, off-the-wall; fishy, funny; far-out, freaky, ‖kinky, kooky, offbeat, outré, ‖scatty; crazy, nutty; fantastic, grotesque
  idiom as strange as they come
  con common, ordinary, unexceptional, usual; expected, predictable
  ant familiar
stranger *n* a nonresident or an unknown person in a community < he felt he had become a *stranger* in a foreign land >
  syn alien, auslander, foreigner, inconnu, outcomer, outlander, outsider
  rel out-of-stater, outstater; transient; visitor; immigrant; wanderer
  idiom stranger within the gates
  con inhabitant, resident; aboriginal, aborigine, autochthon, indigene, native
strangle *vb* **1** *syn* see CHOKE 1
  2 *syn* see SUPPRESS 2
strangling *n syn* see REPRESSION 1
strapped *adj syn* see POOR 1
stratagem *n syn* see TRICK 1
  rel conspiracy, intrigue, machination, plot
strategy *n syn* see PLAN 1
stratospheric *adj syn* see EXCESSIVE 1
straw *adj syn* see BLOND 1
  rel strawish, strawy
straw *vb syn* see STREW 1
stray *vb* **1** *syn* see WANDER 1

2 syn see ERR
idiom stray from the straight and narrow
3 syn see DIGRESS 2
idiom get off the track, get sidetracked
stray *adj syn* see ERRATIC 1
   rel random, sporadic
streak *n syn* see HINT 2
streak *vb* to make irregular lines or stripes of contrasting colors on or in <hair *streaked* with gray>
   syn strake, striate, stripe
   rel dapple, fleck, spot; marble, variegate, vein
stream *n* **1 syn** see CREEK 2
   2 syn see FLOW
stream *vb syn* see POUR 2
streamer *n syn* see FLAG
streamline *vb syn* see SIMPLIFY
||**streel** *n syn* see SLATTERN 1
street *n syn* see WAY 1
   rel ruelle, streetlet; drive
street arab *n syn* see VAGABOND
street girl *n syn* see PROSTITUTE
streetwalker *n syn* see PROSTITUTE
streetwalking *n syn* see PROSTITUTION
strength *n* **1 syn** see POWER 4
   rel brawn; sturdiness, toughness; healthiness, soundness
   con feebleness
   ant weakness
   2 syn see STABILITY
   3 syn see SUBSTANCE 2
strengthen *vb* **1 syn** see ENCOURAGE 1
   2 to make strong or stronger <exercise is needed to *strengthen* the body>
   syn energize, fortify, invigorate, reinforce
   rel brace, support, undergird; anneal, ruggedize, sinew, tone (up), toughen; cheer, embolden, encourage, enhearten, ensteel, hearten, inspirit, nerve, steel
   con cripple, debilitate, disable, enfeeble, tear down, undermine; deject, discourage, dishearten, dispirit; emasculate, enervate, unman, unnerve
   ant weaken
   3 syn see GIRD 3
   idiom gather one's resources, recruit one's strength
||**strengthy** *adj syn* see STRONG 1
strenuous *adj* **1 syn** see VIGOROUS
   2 syn see HARD 6
   rel breathless, energy-consuming; mean, wicked; Herculean
   idiom a long hard pull, an uphill climb, tough going
   con comfortable, cushy, light, unburdensome
   ant effortless
stress *n* the action or effect of force exerted within or upon a thing <the bridge trusses slowly yielded to *stress* and buckled under the weight of the deck>
   syn pressure, strain, tension
   rel pinch; burden, weight
   2 syn see EMPHASIS
   rel import, importance
stress *vb* **1 syn** see TRY 2
   2 syn see EMPHASIZE
stretch *vb* **1 syn** see RUN 8
   rel range, roll
   2 syn see EXTEND 3
   con abbreviate, shorten; condense, curtail, cut, trim
   3 syn see EMBROIDER
stretch (out) *vb syn* see REST 1
stretch *n* **1 syn** see RANGE 2
   2 syn see DISTANCE 1
   3 syn see EXPANSE
   rel area, region, tract
   4 syn see WHILE 1
stretch *adj syn* see ELASTIC 1
stretchy *adj syn* see ELASTIC 1
strew *vb* **1** to spread (something) loosely or at intervals usually over a substantial area <*strew* seed for birds>
   syn bestrew, broadcast, disject, disseminate, scatter, sow, straw; *compare* SPREAD 1, SPRINKLE 1
   rel dust, pepper; dissipate; cover
   2 syn see SPREAD 1
striate *vb syn* see STREAK

strict *adj* **1 syn** see RIGID 3
   rel exacting, oppressive, unsparing; dour, forbidding, grim, hard-boiled, harsh, tough
   idiom not to be trifled (*or* messed) with
   con easy, easygoing; lax, loose; permissive
   ant lenient
   2 syn see TRUE 3
stricture *n* **1 syn** see RESTRICTION 1
   2 syn see ANIMADVERSION
||**striddle** *vb* **1 syn** see BESTRIDE 2
   2 syn see STRIDE 1
stride *vb* **1** to move or walk with long often purposeful steps <*strode* to the door and slammed it>
   syn march, sling, stalk, ||striddle
   rel clump, stamp, stomp, tramp, tromp
   2 syn see BESTRIDE
strident *adj* **1 syn** see HARSH 3
   rel loud, stentorian, stertorous
   2 syn see VOCIFEROUS
stridulent *adj syn* see HARSH 3
stridulous *adj syn* see HARSH 3
strife *n* **1 syn** see DISCORD
   rel argument, controversy, dispute; altercation, quarrel, squabble, wrangle; brawl, broil, fracas; affray, combat, fight, fray
   ant accord
   2 syn see CONTEST 1
strike *vb* **1** to engage in a temporary work stoppage to effect compliance with demands made on an employer <they *struck* for higher wages>
   syn stick out, walk out
   idiom go (*or* be) on strike
   2 to deliver (a blow) in a strong, vigorous manner <angrily *struck* the boy>
   syn ||biff, catch, clout, ||devel, ding, hit, ||nail, pop, slog, ||slosh, smite, sock, swat, whack; *compare* SLAM 1, SLAP 1
   rel beat, pummel, ||slat, ||swap, ||wap, whop; cudgel, hammer, mace; ||plug, poke, ||puck, punch; bang, bash, crash, ||pandy, slam; ||stoush, thrash
   idiom hang one on, let one fly
   3 syn see GIVE 10
   4 syn see AFFLICT
   5 syn see SEIZE 3
   6 syn see ATTACK 1
   7 syn see OCCUR 2
   8 syn see AFFECT
   9 syn see DON 2
strike *n syn* see DISCOVERY
strike out *vb syn* see HEAD 3
striker *n syn* see HELPER
striking *adj syn* see NOTICEABLE
   rel showy; forceful, powerful; cogent, compelling, telling
strikingly *adv syn* see VERY 1
string *n* **1 syn** see LINE 5
   2 syn see RESOURCE 3
   3 syn see SUCCESSION 2
   4 strings *pl syn* see POWER 1
string (up) *vb syn* see HANG 2
string along *vb syn* see TRIFLE 1
   idiom keep (someone) dangling
stringent *adj* **1 syn** see RIGID 3
   rel binding, confining, drawing
   2 syn see GRIM 2
strings *n pl syn* see CONDITION 1
stringy *adj syn* see MUSCULAR 1
||**strinkle** *vb syn* see SPRINKLE 1
strip *vb* **1** to remove the clothing of <guards *stripped* and searched the prisoners>
   syn denude, disrobe, unclothe, undress
   rel doff, peel, take off; bare, denudate, expose, uncover; disfrock, unfrock
   idiom strip to the buff
   con clothe, dress, robe; cover

---

syn synonym(s)   **rel** related word(s)
ant antonym(s)   **con** contrasted word(s)
idiom idiomatic equivalent(s)
|| use limited; if in doubt, see a dictionary

2 to take something (as honors, privileges, functions, or trappings) away from <an exiled king now *stripped* of his power>
syn bankrupt, bare, denudate, denude, deprive, dismantle, disrobe, divest; *compare* DEPRIVE 2
rel bereave; deplenish, disfurnish, ‖displenish, dispossess; despoil, rob
con clothe, endow, furnish, grant, vest; install
ant invest
3 *syn* see RAVAGE
4 *syn* see SKIN 2
strip *n syn* see STRIPTEASE
strip *n* **1** a relatively long and narrow piece or section <tear old linen into *strips* for bandages>
syn band, bandeau, banding, fillet, ribbon, stripe
rel piece; section; segment; shred
2 *syn* see BAR 1
stripe *vb syn* see WHIP 1
stripe *n* **1** *syn* see STRIP 1
2 *syn* see TYPE
stripe *vb syn* see STREAK
stripling *n syn* see BOY 1
stripped *adj* **1** *syn* see NUDE 2
con attired; covered
ant clothed, dressed
2 *syn* see OPEN 2
con covered, unexposed; protected
stripper *n syn* see STRIPTEASER
stripping *n syn* see STRIPTEASE
striptease *n* entertainment in which a female performer removes her clothing piece by piece in view of an audience <a nightclub featuring *striptease*>
syn strip, stripping
idiom exotic dancing
stripteaser *n* one who performs a striptease <worked part-time as a model and *stripteaser*>
syn ecdysiast, peeler, stripper, stripteuse, teaser
idiom exotic dancer, ‖pantie peeler, ‖strip-and-shake artist, strip artist
stripteuse *n syn* see STRIPTEASER
strive *vb* **1** *syn* see LABOR 1
2 *syn* see TRY 5
rel labor, toil, travail, work; drive, strain
striving *n* **1** *syn* see CONTEST 1
rel contending; combat, fight
2 *syn* see ATTEMPT
rel labor, toil, travail, work
stroll *vb syn* see SAUNTER
stroll *n syn* see WALK 1
strong *adj* **1** having great physical strength <had the *strong* hands and arms of a wrestler>
syn mighty, powerful, ‖strengthy, wieldy; *compare* MUSCULAR 2
rel firm, robust, stark, strapping, sturdy, two-handed; able-bodied, tough; brawny, muscular, sinewy; lusty, vigorous
idiom strong as a bull (*or* ox)
con feeble, frail; puny, weak-bodied; forceless, impotent, powerless, strengthless
ant weak
2 having or manifesting great force or power (as in acting or resisting) <a *strong* constitution>
syn stalwart, stout, sturdy, tenacious, tough
rel hardy, robust, rugged, strapping; firm, solid, staunch; durable, enduring; forceful, potent, powerful; lusty, vigorous
con frail; forceless, impotent, powerless, strengthless; depleted, failing
ant weak
3 being rich in a characteristic ingredient <*strong* coffee>
syn concentrated, full-bodied, lusty, potent, robust
rel strong-flavored, strong-tasting; straight, undiluted, unmixed; rich; heroic, large, powerful
con diluted, mixed, watered-down
ant weak
4 *syn* see SPIRITUOUS
5 *syn* see SURE 1
rel solid, substantial, unmoving, unyielding
6 *syn* see MALODOROUS 1
strong arm *n* **1** *syn* see POWER 4
2 *syn* see THUG 1
strong-arm *vb syn* see INTIMIDATE

stronghold *n syn* see FORT
strongly *adv syn* see HARD 1
ant weakly
strong man *n syn* see TYRANT
strong suit *n syn* see FORTE
structure *n* **1** *syn* see BUILDING
rel construction, erection, pile
2 *syn* see EDIFICE
3 something made up of more or less interdependent elements and having a definite organizational pattern <the complex bureaucratic *structure* of modern government>
syn framework
rel anatomy, skeleton; build, construction, frame; arrangement, composition, form, format, makeup, morphology; complex, network, system
struggle *vb syn* see TRY 5
rel compete, vie
idiom make a valiant attempt (*or* try)
ant give up
struggle *n syn* see ATTEMPT
strum *vb syn* see HUM
strumpet *n syn* see WANTON
‖**strunt** *vb syn* see STRUT 2
‖**strunt** *n syn* see LIQUOR 2
strut *vb* **1** *syn* see SASHAY
2 to walk with an air of pomposity or affected dignity <a pompous general *strutting* off the parade ground>
syn ‖strunt, swagger
rel flaunt, parade
con cower, cringe; slink
stubborn *adj* **1** *syn* see OBSTINATE
rel contumacious, insubordinate, rebellious; cantankerous, ornery; ‖stunkard, ‖stunt
idiom set in one's ways, stubborn as a mule
con adaptable, pliable, pliant; amenable, tractable
ant docile
2 *syn* see INFLEXIBLE 2
stubbornness *n syn* see DEFIANCE 2
rel cantankerousness, orneriness
stubby *adj syn* see STOCKY
stube *n syn* see ALEHOUSE
stuck-up *adj syn* see VAIN 3
idiom too big for one's breeches, wise in one's own conceit
stud *vb syn* see SPOT 2
studied *adj syn* see DELIBERATE 1
rel thoughtful; intentional, voluntary, willful, willing
con natural, offhand
ant unstudied
studio *n* the working place of an artist (as a painter) <moved to a larger *studio*>
syn atelier, bottega
rel shop, workroom, workshop
studious *adj syn* see DELIBERATE 1
ant impromptu
study *n* **1** *syn* see REVERIE
2 *syn* see ATTENTION 1
rel contemplation, weighing; abstraction, meditation, musing, pondering, rumination
3 *syn* see EXERCISE 4
study *vb* **1** *syn* see CONSIDER 1
idiom give careful study to
2 *syn* see SCRUTINIZE 1
stuff *n* **1** *syn* see PERSONAL EFFECTS
2 *syn* see MONEY
3 *syn* see THING 4
4 *syn* see ESSENCE 2
stuff *vb syn* see CRAM 1
rel overfill, overstuff
idiom fill to overflowing, fill to the brim
stuffed *adj syn* see FULL 1
stuffed shirt *n* a smug usually pompous person with an inflexibly conservative or reactionary outlook <a *stuffed shirt* with a starched mind>
syn Blimp, Colonel Blimp, fuddy-duddy
rel diehard; prig, prude, smug
con freethinker, latitudinarian, liberal, libertarian, libertine; avant garde
stuffing *n syn* see ENTRAILS

rel ‖tar

stuffy *adj* **1** marked by a heavy oppressive quality of air < a *stuffy* room that needed airing >
syn airless, breathless, close, stifling, stivy, suffocating, sultry; *compare* HUMID, STIFLING 1
rel heavy, oppressive, thick; stagnant; shut-up, unventilated
con airy, breezy; open, ventilated; bracing, invigorating, refreshing, stimulating
2 *syn* see PRIM 1
rel dull, humdrum, stodgy; hidebound, illiberal, narrow, narrow-minded
3 *syn* see POMPOUS 1

‖**stuggy** *adj syn* see STOCKY

stultify *vb* to deprive of vitality and render futile especially by enfeebling or repressive influences < artistic creativity *stultified* by the intrusion of propaganda >
syn constipate, stagnate, stifle, trammel
rel discourage, inhibit, restrain; check, stunt; enfeeble, impair, weaken; deaden, dull; repress, smother, suffocate, suppress; invalidate, nullify
con encourage, foster, nourish; pique, provoke, stimulate

stultiloquence *n syn* see CHATTER

stumble *vb* **1** *syn* see WALLOW 2
rel falter, waver; trip; fall
2 *syn* see DEMUR
3 to move so clumsily and awkwardly as to lose one's balance or trip and fall < *stumbled* across the darkened room and fell >
syn blunder, bumble, lurch, ‖snapper; *compare* WALLOW 2
rel reel, stagger, totter; trip; pitch, topple
4 *syn* see LUMBER
5 *syn* see TEETER
rel careen, swing
6 to act, proceed, or execute in a hesitant and clumsily faltering manner < *stumbled* through his Latin translation >
syn limp, muddle, shuffle
rel falter, hesitate, wobble; blunder, bumble; botch, bungle, ‖muck
ant breeze
7 *syn* see HAPPEN 2
idiom come (*or* run) up against, fall upon, stub one's toe upon (*or* on)
8 *syn* see PUZZLE

stumblebum *n* a clumsy inept or blundering person < a staff consisting of third-raters and *stumblebums* >
syn blunderbuss, blunderer, bungler
rel incompetent
con crackerjack, ‖dab, ‖darb, expert, topnotcher, whiz; natural; professional

stumbling block *n syn* see OBSTACLE

stump *vb* **1** *syn* see NONPLUS 1
2 *syn* see LUMBER

stump *n syn* see DEFIANCE 1

stumpy *adj syn* see STOCKY

‖**stumpy** *n syn* see MONEY

stun *vb syn* see DAZE 2
rel nonplus; amaze, astound, flabbergast; knock out
idiom strike dumb (*or* dead)

stunner *n* **1** *syn* see WONDER 1
2 *syn* see BEAUTY

stunning *adj* **1** *syn* see EXCELLENT
2 *syn* see BEAUTIFUL

‖**stunpoll** *n syn* see DUNCE

‖**stunt** *adj syn* see STUNTED

stunt *vb* to hinder the normal growth and development of < the inhospitable climate had *stunted* all vegetation >
syn dwarf, suppress
rel check, curb, hold back; impair

stunt *n syn* see TRICK 3

stunted *adj* having had one's growth and development hindered or arrested < the children were *stunted* from malnutrition >
syn runted, runtish, runty, ‖scrunty, ‖stunt
rel undersized; dwarf
con able-bodied, robust well-set, well-set-up; giant, oversize; healthy, strong, sturdy, vigorous

‖**stupe** *n syn* see DUNCE

stupefy *vb* **1** *syn* see DULL 5
2 *syn* see DAZE 2
rel addle, faze, rattle; nonplus

stupendous *adj* **1** *syn* see MARVELOUS 1
2 *syn* see MONSTROUS 1

stupid *adj* **1** lacking in or exhibiting a lack of power to absorb ideas or impressions < a willing boy but too *stupid* to succeed in school >
syn beefheaded, beef-witted, beetleheaded, blear-eyed, blear-witted, blockheaded, blockish, chuckleheaded, dense, doltish, dull, dumb, duncical, fatheaded, goosey, hammerheaded, numskulled, pinhead, pinheaded, thick, thickheaded, thick-witted; *compare* RETARDED, SIMPLE 3
rel asinine, fatuous, foolish, silly, simple; brute, brutish, dummel, lumbering, oafish, slow, slow-witted, sluggish; crass; backward, half-witted, retarded; idiotic, imbecilic
idiom ‖dead above (*or* between) the ears, ‖dead from the neck up, having a block for a head, having cotton between the ears, ‖muscle-bound between the ears
con acute, alert, bright, clever, keen, knowing, quick, quick-witted, sharp, smart; sage, wise; brilliant; able, competent
ant intelligent
2 *syn* see LETHARGIC

stupid *n syn* see DUNCE

stupor *n syn* see LETHARGY 1
rel sopor; anesthesia, insensibility

sturdy *adj syn* see STRONG 2
rel sound, substantial
ant decrepit

Sturm und Drang *n syn* see UNREST

‖**stut** *vb syn* see STAMMER 1

stutter *vb syn* see STAMMER 1

sty *n* **1** an extremely unkempt or filthy place < the basement was a rat-infested *sty* >
syn dump, pigpen, pigsty
2 *syn* see SINK 1

stygian *adj syn* see INFERNAL 2

style *n* **1** *syn* see VEIN 1
2 *syn* see NAME 1
3 *syn* see FASHION 3
4 an individual's characteristic attitudes and taste as expressed or indicated in his way of life < she liked the man's sophisticated *style* >
syn manner, way
rel behavior; bearing, carriage; characteristic, trait; idiosyncrasy, peculiarity

style *vb syn* see NAME 1

stylish *adj* being in accordance with or conforming to current fashion < she was a *stylish* dresser >
syn a la mode, chic, ‖classy, dashing, exclusive, fashionable, in, modish, posh, sharp, smart, snappy, swank, swish, tonish, tony, ‖trendy, trig, ultrafashionable, with-it; *compare* DAPPER
rel new, new-day, newfangled, new-fashioned; modern, modernistic, up-to-date; chichi, doggish, doggy, natty, rakish, sassy, swagger; ostentatious, pretentious, ritzy, showy, swell; sleek, slick
idiom in fashion, in the mode
con styleless; old-fashioned, outmoded, out-of-date; drab, tasteless
ant dowdy, unstylish

suasible *adj syn* see RECEPTIVE 1

suave *adj* being conspicuously and ingratiatingly tactful and well-mannered < a man of *suave*, well-bred equanimity >
syn bland, civilized, smooth, urbane; *compare* TACTFUL
rel affable, cordial, genial, gracious, sociable; courteous, courtly, polite; diplomatic, politic; cultivated, cultured, distingué, polished, refined, well-bred; sophisticated, worldly; ingratiating, soft, soft-spoken; fulsome, slick, unctuous
con clumsy, unpolished, unskilled; tactless, undiplomatic, untactful
ant bluff

sub *adj syn* see SUBORDINATE

sub *n syn* see SUBSTITUTE

subaltern *n syn* see INFERIOR

subaquatic *adj syn* see SUBMARINE

subaqueous *adj syn* see SUBMARINE

---

syn synonym(s)
ant antonym(s)
idiom idiomatic equivalent(s)
‖ use limited; if in doubt, see a dictionary
rel related word(s)
con contrasted word(s)

subaverage *adj syn* see LOW 9

subconscious *n* mental activities that occur just below the threshold of consciousness <a motive probably rooted in his *subconscious*>
syn underconsciousness, undersense
rel subliminal; subconsciousness; subliminal self
idiom subconscious (*or* submerged) mind
con consciousness; awareness

subdolous *adj syn* see SLY 2

subdue *vb syn* see CONQUER 1
rel extinguish, put down, quash, quell, quench, squelch, suppress

subdued *adj* 1 *syn* see QUIET 4
2 reduced or lacking in force, intensity, or vividness <*subdued* colors> <she answered his questions in a timid *subdued* voice>
syn low-key, low-keyed, sober, soft, softened, toned down
rel moderated, tempered; controlled, restrained; mellow; neutral; quiet
con enlivened, intensified; bright, intense, strong; brilliant, vivid; saturated; blaring, glaring, harsh, screaming
3 *syn* see TAME
ant unsubdued

subduer *n syn* see VICTOR 1

subfusc *adj syn* see DULL 8

subitaneous *adj syn* see PRECIPITATE 1

subjacent *adj syn* see INFERIOR 1
ant superjacent

subject *n* 1 *syn* see CITIZEN 2
2 the basic idea or the principal object of attention in a discourse or artistic composition <the Puritans as soldiers of Christ was the *subject* of her paper>
syn argument, head, matter, motif, motive, point, subject matter, text, theme, topic
rel material, substance; problem, question; leitmotiv; core, meat
con elaboration, enlargement, enlarging, expatiation; development, explication

subject *adj* 1 *syn* see SUBORDINATE
rel servile, slavish, subservient
ant dominant, sovereign
2 *syn* see LIABLE 2
rel apt, likely

subject *vb syn* see EXPOSE 1

subjective *adj* peculiar to a particular individual as modified by individual bias and limitations <*subjective* judgments>
syn unobjective
rel biased, prejudiced; abstract, nonobjective, nonrepresentational, nonrepresentative
ant objective

subject matter *n syn* see SUBJECT 2

subjoin *vb syn* see ADD 1
rel combine, conjoin, unite
con part, separate, sever

subjugate *vb* 1 *syn* see CONQUER 1
rel compel, coerce, force
2 *syn* see ENSLAVE
ant liberate

subjugator *n syn* see VICTOR 1

sublease *vb syn* see SUBLET

sublet *vb* to turn over to another one's right of occupancy of (rented or leased housing) <*sublet* her apartment to a friend>
syn sublease, underlease, underlet

sublime *vb syn* see EXALT 1

sublime *adj* 1 *syn* see GRAND 3
2 *syn* see SPLENDID 2
rel abstract, ideal, transcendent, transcendental; divine, holy, sacred, spiritual; august, majestic, noble, stately

sublimity *n syn* see APEX 2

sublunary *adj syn* see EARTHLY 1

submarine *adj* being, acting, growing, or used under water <a *submarine* camera>
syn subaquatic, subaqueous, underwater

submerge *vb* 1 *syn* see DIP 1
rel drench, impregnate, saturate, soak
2 *syn* see DELUGE 1
3 *syn* see SINK 1

submerse *vb* 1 *syn* see DIP 1
2 *syn* see SINK 1

submission *n syn* see SURRENDER
rel bowing, submitting; acquiescence, compliance, resignation; cringing, servility; prostration
ant resistance

submissive *adj* 1 *syn* see TAME
rel complying, conformable, obeying; bowing down, unerect; menial, servile, slavish, subservient
ant rebellious
2 *syn* see PASSIVE 2

submit *vb* 1 *syn* see YIELD 2
ant resist, withstand
2 to offer or commit (something) for consideration, study, or decision <*submitted* his report directly to the general>
syn hand in, refer
rel bring, deliver, present; offer, proffer, tender; send in; provide
3 *syn* see SUGGEST 4
4 *syn* see FALL 3
ant hold out, resist

subnormal *adj syn* see LOW 9
rel subpar

subordinate *adj* placed in or occupying a lower class, rank, or status <making the executive *subordinate* to the legislative branch>
syn collateral, dependent, secondary, sub, subject, tributary, under
rel adjuvant, auxiliary, contributory, subsidiary; satellite; inferior, subaltern, subalternate; accessory, parergal, supplementary
con chief, first, leading, main; dominant, master, superior

subordinate *n syn* see INFERIOR

sub rosa *adv syn* see SECRETLY
ant aboveboard

sub-rosa *adj syn* see SECRET 1
ant aboveboard

subscribe *vb* 1 *syn* see SIGN 1
2 *syn* see CONTRIBUTE 1
3 *syn* see ASSENT
rel approve, endorse, favor, sanction

subsequent *adj* 1 being, occurring, or carried out at a time after something else <*subsequent* events disproved his predictions>
syn after, ensuing, later, posterior, postliminary, subsequential
rel following, next, succeeding; consequential, resultant, resulting
con exordial, introductory, prefatory, preliminary, preludial; anterior, precedent, preceding, prior
ant antecedent
2 *syn* see CONSECUTIVE
ant antecedent

subsequential *adj* 1 *syn* see SUBSEQUENT 1
2 *syn* see CONSECUTIVE
ant antecedent

subsequently *adv syn* see AFTER
ant antecedently, priorly

subsequent to *prep syn* see AFTER 2

subservient *adj* 1 *syn* see AUXILIARY
2 showing extreme compliance or abject obedience <a *subservient* minor bureaucrat>
syn menial, obeisant, obsequious, servile, slavish
rel acquiescent, compliant, resigned, submissive; cowering, cringing, fawning, truckling; abject, ignoble, mean
idiom as obedient as a dog
con aggressive; arrogant, haughty; rebellious; independent, irrepressible, uncontainable
ant domineering, overbearing

subside *vb syn* see ABATE 4
idiom dwindle down

subsidiary *adj syn* see AUXILIARY
rel back-up; minor, tributary

subsidize *vb syn* see ENDOW 2
rel back; promote; help

subsidy *n syn* see APPROPRIATION
rel subsidization; gift, reward

subsist *vb syn* see BE

subsistence *n syn* see LIVING

substance *n* 1 *syn* see TENOR 1
rel import, meaning
idiom the general drift
2 the inner significance or central meaning of something written or said <just give me the *substance* of his speech>

syn amount, body, burden, core, crux, gist, kernel, matter, meat, nub, nubbin, pith, purport, sense, short, strength, sum and substance, sum total, thrust, upshot; *compare* BODY 3, ESSENCE 2, MEANING 1, TENOR 1
rel center, focus, heart, nucleus; point; import, meaningfulness
3 syn see BODY 3
rel drift, tenor
4 syn see ESSENCE 2
5 syn see THING 4
6 syn see WEALTH 2
substantial *adj* **1 syn** see MATERIAL 1
con airy, ethereal
ant unsubstantial
2 syn see IMPORTANT 1
rel key, principal; strong; serious
3 syn see PROSPEROUS 3
rel solid, solvent
substantiate *vb* **1 syn** see EMBODY 1
rel substantialize, substantify
2 syn see CONFIRM 2
rel demonstrate, prove, test, try
substitutable *adj syn* see INTERCHANGEABLE
substitute *n* **1** a person who takes the place of or acts instead of another < found a *substitute* for the sick teacher >
syn alternate, fill-in, locum tenens, pinch hitter, replacement, stand-in, sub, succedaneum, surrogate
rel relay, relief; deputy, procurator, proxy; supply; double, understudy
2 syn see RESOURCE 3
substitute *vb syn* see EXCHANGE 2
substitute *adj* **1** serving or fitted for use as a substitute < a *substitute* driver was needed for the long trip >
syn alternate, alternative, surrogate
rel additional, another; other, second; back-up, reserve; supplemental, supplementary, suppletory
2 syn see ARTIFICIAL 2
substract *vb syn* see DEDUCT 1
substratal *adj syn* see ELEMENTAL 1
substratum *n* **1 syn** see BASIS 1
rel core, meat, stuff, substance
2 syn see BASE 1
substruction *n syn* see BASE 1
substructure *n syn* see BASE 1
ant superstructure
subsume *vb syn* see INCLUDE
subterfuge *n syn* see DECEPTION 1
subterrane *n syn* see CAVE
subterranean *adj* being, lying, functioning, or operating under the surface of the earth < *subterranean* hot springs that emerge as geysers >
syn subterrestrial, underearth, underfoot, underground
con aboveground, surface, surficial
subterranean *n syn* see CAVE
subterrestrial *adj syn* see SUBTERRANEAN
subtile *adj syn* see THIN 2
subtle *adj* **1 syn** see THIN 2
2 syn see FINE 1
ant unsubtle
3 syn see LOGICAL 2
rel dexterous, skillful
con blunt; dense
4 syn see SLY 2
ant unsubtle
subtract *vb syn* see DEDUCT 1
ant add
subtraction *n syn* see DEDUCTION 1
ant addition
suburbs *n pl syn* see ENVIRONS 2
rel fringes; suburbia
subvention *n syn* see APPROPRIATION
subversion *n syn* see SABOTAGE
rel demolishing, destroying, destruction
subvert *vb syn* see SABOTAGE
rel overthrow, overturn, upset; demolish, destroy, ruin; corrupt, debase, deprave, pervert
con sustain, uphold
succedaneum *n syn* see SUBSTITUTE
succedent *adj syn* see CONSECUTIVE

succeed *vb* **1 syn** see FOLLOW 1
ant precede
2 to result favorably according to plans and desires < that advertising campaign really *succeeded* >
syn click, come off, go, go over, pan out, prove out
rel catch on; prevail
idiom go over big, go over with a bang, hit the mark, make a hit, turn out well
ant fail, flop
3 to attain or be attaining a desired end < how to *succeed* in big business >
syn arrive, flourish, go, make out, prosper, score, thrive
rel ‖dow; get ahead; boom; achieve, attain, gain, reach; accomplish, effect, fulfill; conquer, prevail, triumph, win (out)
idiom do all right by oneself, do well, gain one's end, get places, get somewhere, get to the top of the ladder, make a success, make it (big), make one's mark, ‖make the big time, make the grade
con dwindle, languish; fall down, flounder, founder; lose (out); bust
ant fail
succeeding *adj syn* see CONSECUTIVE
succès fou *n syn* see SMASH 6
success *n* a succeeding fully or in accordance with one's desires < attributed his business *success* to hard work and attention to detail >
syn arrival, ‖do, flying colors, go, prosperity, successfulness
rel accomplishment, achievement, attainment; triumph, victory
ant failure; nonsuccess, unsuccessfulness
successful *adj* resulting in or having gained success < a *successful* business venture >
syn prosperous, thriving; *compare* FLOURISHING
rel extraordinary, notable, noteworthy, outstanding, smash, smashing
idiom crowned (or blessed or flushed) with success, ‖out front
con failing, thriveless, unprosperous; defeated, disappointed, failed, frustrated; bankrupt, broken, destroyed, ruined
ant successless, unsuccessful
successfully *adv syn* see WELL 5
ant unsuccessfully
successfulness *n syn* see SUCCESS
ant nonsuccess, unsuccessfulness
succession *n* **1 syn** see ORDER 5
2 a number of things that follow each other in some order < another *succession* of price hikes >
syn alternation, chain, consecution, course, order, progression, row, sequel, sequence, series, string, suite, train; *compare* CYCLE 1
rel successiveness; round, round robin
successional *adj syn* see CONSECUTIVE
successive *adj syn* see CONSECUTIVE
rel alternating, rotating
successively *adv syn* see TOGETHER 2
succinct *adj syn* see CONCISE
rel blunt, brusque
idiom right to the point
ant discursive
succinctly *adv syn* see BRIEFLY
ant discursively
succor *n syn* see HELP 1
rel ministration, ministry; maintenance, nourishment, sustenance
succubus *n syn* see DEVIL 2
succulent *adj* full of juice < a *succulent* roast >
syn juicy, ‖sappy
succumb *vb* **1 syn** see YIELD 2
rel abandon, relinquish, resign
2 syn see FALL 3
idiom hand over one's sword, meet one's Waterloo, show (or wave) the white flag, strike (or haul down) one's colors
3 syn see COLLAPSE 2
idiom bite the dust, ‖take the count
4 syn see DIE 1

syn synonym(s)   rel related word(s)
ant antonym(s)   con contrasted word(s)
idiom idiomatic equivalent(s)
‖ use limited; if in doubt, see a dictionary

idiom yield one's breath

such *adj* **1** being previously characterized or specified < authorized to seize illegally parked cars and impound *such* vehicles >
syn aforementioned, aforesaid, said
2 being of so extreme a degree or quality < *such* nonsense as I had never heard before >
syn that
3 *syn* see LIKE

such *pron* **1** *syn* see SUCH A ONE
2 *syn* see SUCHLIKE
idiom the like

such a one *pron* someone or something that has been, is being, or will be stated, implied, or exemplified < the area is full of caverns; *such a one* may be found here >
syn such

suchlike *adj syn* see LIKE

suchlike *pron* a person or thing of the same or similar kind < airplanes, missiles, rockets, and *suchlike* >
syn such

sucker *n* **1** *syn* see PARASITE
2 *syn* see FOOL 3
idiom easy pickings

sucker *vb syn* see CHEAT

suck in *vb syn* see DECEIVE

||**suck–in** *n syn* see DECEPTION 1

suckle *vb syn* see NURSE 1

sudden *adj syn* see PRECIPITATE 1
rel accelerated, quickened, speeded; expeditious, fast, fleet, rapid, swift

sudden *adv* **1** *syn* see UNAWARES
2 *syn* see SHORT 1

suddenly *adv* **1** *syn* see SHORT 1
2 *syn* see UNAWARES
idiom of (*or* on) a sudden, on the sudden

suds *n pl but sing or pl in constr* **1** *syn* see SADNESS
2 *syn* see FOAM

sue *vb syn* see ADDRESS 8
idiom make (*or* pay) suit to, press one's suit

sue (for *or* to) *vb syn* see PETITION

suffer *vb* **1** *syn* see BEAR 10
rel accept, admit, receive
idiom grin and abide
2 *syn* see EXPERIENCE 1
3 *syn* see LET 2
rel countenance; accept, admit, receive; acquiesce, bow, submit, yield
||**4** *syn* see HURT 4

sufferable *adj syn* see BEARABLE
ant insufferable

sufferance *n syn* see PERMISSION

suffering *n syn* see DISTRESS
rel adversity, misfortune

suffice *vb syn* see SERVE 3

sufficiency *n syn* see ENOUGH
ant insufficiency

sufficient *adj* **1** being what is requisite or needed especially without superfluity < there is *sufficient* bread left for breakfast >
syn adequate, comfortable, competent, decent, enough, satisfactory, sufficing; *compare* DECENT 4
rel ample, plenteous, plentiful, plenty; commensurable, commensurate, due, proportionate; acceptable, agreeable, pleasing
con inadequate, unsufficing; deficient; failing, lacking, missing, wanting
ant insufficient
2 *syn* see DECENT 4
idiom fair to middling

sufficient *n syn* see ENOUGH

sufficiently *adv syn* see ENOUGH 1
ant insufficiently

sufficing *adj syn* see SUFFICIENT 1

suffocate *vb* to stop the respiration of (as by asphyxiation) < the child was *suffocated* in an old refrigerator >
syn asphyxiate, choke, ||quackle, smother, stifle; *compare* CHOKE 1
rel stive; strangle

suffocating *adj* **1** *syn* see STIFLING 1
2 *syn* see STUFFY 1

suffocative *adj syn* see STIFLING 1

suffrage *n* the right, privilege, or power of expressing one's choice or wish (as in an election or in the determination of policy) < universal *suffrage* >
syn ballot, franchise, vote
rel voice

suffuse *vb syn* see INFUSE 1
rel interject, interpose, introduce

||**sugar** *n syn* see MONEY

sugar (over) *vb syn* see SUGARCOAT 1

sugarcoat *vb* **1** to make (something difficult or unpleasant) superficially easy or attractive < *sugarcoated* the reproach with a smile >
syn candy, honey, sugar (over), sweeten
rel edulcorate
2 *syn* see PALLIATE

sugarplum *n syn* see SOP 2

suggest *vb* **1** to convey an idea indirectly < designing attractive books with jackets that truly *suggest* their contents >
syn connote, hint, imply, insinuate, intimate; *compare* POINT 2
rel advert, allude, refer; denote
idiom bring to mind
con demonstrate, display, exhibit, manifest, set out, show
ant express
2 *syn* see POINT 2
rel promise
idiom be the sign of, point in the direction of
3 *syn* see PROPOSE 1
4 to offer (as an idea or theory) for consideration < this, I *suggest*, is what really happened >
syn submit, theorize
rel conjecture; imagine
5 to represent another thing indirectly, figuratively, and sometimes obscurely by evoking a thought, image, or conception of it < the meaning of a poem is often *suggested* in its title >
syn adumbrate, shadow (forth); *compare* ADUMBRATE 1
rel outline, sketch; betoken, symbolize; typify
con display, flaunt, parade
ant manifest

suggestion *n* **1** *syn* see PROPOSAL
2 *syn* see HINT 1
rel implication, innuendo
3 *syn* see ASSOCIATION 4
rel allusion; reminder
con demonstration, display, exhibition, manifestation, show
ant expression
4 *syn* see HINT 2

suggestive *adj* **1** *syn* see EVOCATIVE
rel significative
2 *syn* see RISQUÉ
rel erotic, sexy

suicide *n* the act or an instance of taking one's own life voluntarily and intentionally < committed *suicide* by shooting herself >
syn felo-de-se, hara-kiri, self-destruction, self-murder, self=slaughter, self-violence

suit *n* **1** a legal proceeding instituted for the sake of demanding justice or enforcing a right < filed a *suit* to recover her property >
syn action, case, cause, lawsuit
2 *syn* see PRAYER
rel asking, request, requesting, solicitation, soliciting

suit *vb* **1** *syn* see AGREE 4
idiom be in accord with, check out to the letter
2 *syn* see SERVE 3
3 *syn* see ADAPT
4 to be suitable for or to < the right word is the one that *suits* the occasion >
syn agree (with), become, befit, fit, go (together *or* with); *compare* SUIT 6
rel harmonize (with); benefit; please, satisfy
idiom answer a need (*or* the purpose), hit the spot
con clash, conflict, disaccord, disagree
5 *syn* see FLATTER
6 to meet the needs or desires of < this arrangement *suits* me fine >
syn please, satisfy; *compare* SUIT 4
con discontent, displease, dissatisfy; disappoint, fail, let down

suitability *n syn* see ORDER 11

ant unsuitability

suitable *adj* **1 syn** see GOOD 2
 ant unsuitable
 2 syn see JUST 3
 rel reasonable; advisable, expedient, politic
 ant unsuitable
 3 syn see FIT 1
 rel nice, presentable, seemly
 ant unbecoming, unsuitable
 4 syn see ELIGIBLE
 ant unsuitable
suitableness *n* *syn* see ORDER 11
 ant unsuitableness
suitably *adv* *syn* see WELL 4
 ant unsuitably
suite *n* **1 syn** see ENTOURAGE
 2 syn see GROUP 3
 3 syn see APARTMENT 1
 4 syn see SUCCESSION 2
suited *adj* *syn* see ASSORTED 2
 ant unsuited
suitor *n* **1 syn** see SUPPLIANT
 2 one who courts a woman or seeks to marry her < a *suitor* for the king's daughter >
 syn spark, sparker, swain, wooer
 rel beau, boyfriend; cavalier, gallant; lover, man, paramour
sulk *vb* to be sullen or morose in mood usually because of a grievance < *sulked* all day when he didn't call >
 syn ‖dort, grump, ‖mump, pet, pout, ‖sull
 rel frown, glower, lower, scowl; brood, gloom, mope, take on
 idiom be in a sulk, have the sulks, ‖take the dods
sulk *n*, *often* **sulks** *pl* the state, condition, or mood of one sulking < sat in a *sulk* all day after being reprimanded >
 syn ‖dods, ‖dorts, grumps, mulligrubs, mumps, pouts, sullens
 rel sourness, sulkiness, surliness; glumness, grouchiness
 idiom a case of the sulks
sulky *adj* *syn* see SULLEN
 rel cranky, testy, touchy; cantankerous, irritable, querulous
 idiom having the sulks
‖**sull** *vb* *syn* see SULK
sullen *adj* showing a forbidding or disagreeable mood < stalked out in *sullen* silence >
 syn ‖chuff, ‖chuffy, crabbed, crabby, ‖dorty, dour, gloomy, glum, morose, mumpish, saturnine, sulky, surly, ugly
 rel moody; tenebrific, tenebrose, tenebrous; frowning, glowering, lowering, scowling; cross, fretful, grumpy, ill-humored, peevish, petulant, pouting, pouty, sour, sourpussed; black, hostile, malevolent, malicious, malign, mean, ‖runty; cynical, pessimistic
 con easy, gay, high-spirited, insouciant, lighthearted, smiling
sullens *n* *pl* *syn* see SULK
sully *vb* *syn* see TAINT 1
 rel disgrace, shame
sulphurous *adj* *syn* see INFERNAL 1
sultry *adj* **1 syn** see HUMID
 rel smothering, smothery, ‖smudgy, stifling, suffocating
 2 syn see STUFFY 1
 3 syn see HOT 1
 idiom hot as Hades, ‖hot as old Billy Hell
 4 syn see SENSATIONAL 2
sum *n* **1 syn** see WHOLE 1
 2 syn see WHOLE 2
 rel body, bulk, mass; structure
 3 syn see SUMMARY
sum *vb* **1 syn** see ADD 2
 2 syn see EPITOMIZE 1
sum (*to or into*) *vb* *syn* see AMOUNT 1
sum and substance *n* **1 syn** see SUBSTANCE 2
 2 syn see MEANING 1
summarize *vb* *syn* see EPITOMIZE 1
 rel recapitulate, résumé, retrograde
summary *adj* **1 syn** see CONCISE
 rel compact, compacted
 ant circumstantial
 2 done or executed on the spot and without formality < a *summary* trial and speedy execution >
 syn drumhead
summary *n* a short restatement of the main points < a *summary* of the news >

syn epitome, recapitulation, résumé, sum, summation, summing-up, sum-up
 rel outline; run-through; roundup; inventory
 con amplification, elaboration, enlargement, expansion
summate *vb* **1 syn** see ADD 2
 2 syn see EPITOMIZE 1
summation *n* *syn* see SUMMARY
summative *adj* *syn* see CUMULATIVE
summer *n* the season between spring and autumn < liked to swim during the *summer* >
 syn summertide, summertime
 rel midsummer
summerhouse *n* a covered structure in a garden or park designed to provide a shady resting place < watched the sea from the *summerhouse* >
 syn alcove, belvedere, garden house, gazebo, pagoda
summertide *n* *syn* see SUMMER
summertime *n* *syn* see SUMMER
summing-up *n* *syn* see SUMMARY
summit *n* **1 syn** see TOP 1
 2 syn see APEX 2
summon *vb* **1 syn** see CONVOKE
 2 to demand or request the presence or service of < were *summoned* to the principal's office >
 syn call, call in, convene, summons; *compare* CONVOKE
 rel bid, command, enjoin, order; cite, subpoena
 idiom bid come
summons *vb* *syn* see SUMMON 2
‖**sump** *n* *syn* see SWAMP
sumptuous *adj* **1 syn** see LUXURIOUS 3
 rel gorgeous, resplendent, splendid, superb; lavish, rich
 2 syn see GRAND 2
 rel awe-inspiring, grandiose, imposing
sum total *n* **1 syn** see WHOLE 1
 2 syn see SUBSTANCE 2
sum up *vb* *syn* see EPITOMIZE 1
sum-up *n* *syn* see SUMMARY
sun *n* **1** the heavenly body about which the earth rotates < up in time to see the *sun* rise >
 syn daystar, phoebus, Sol
 rel celestial body, luminary, orb, star
 idiom old Sol
 2 the radiation of the sun < enjoying the warm spring *sun* >
 syn sunlight, sunshine
 rel daylight; radiance, radiation
sun *vb* to expose to sunshine < *sunned* himself too long and got badly burned >
 syn bask, insolate
 rel sunbathe; sunburn, sun-cure, sun-dry, tan
sunbeamy *adj* *syn* see CHEERFUL 1
Sunday best *n* *syn* see FINERY
 idiom Sunday-go-to-meeting clothes
sunder *vb* **1 syn** see SEPARATE 1
 rel cleave, rend, rive
 2 syn see CUT 5
‖**sundowner** *n* *syn* see VAGABOND
sundries *n* *pl* miscellaneous small articles, details, or items < supplied such *sundries* as needles, pins, and thread >
 syn etceteras, oddments, odds and ends, this and that(s)
 rel notions
sundry *adj* **1 syn** MANY, legion, multifarious, multitudinal, multitudinous, numerous, populous, ‖several, various, voluminous
 idiom all and sundry
 2 syn see SEVERAL 3
 idiom all sorts of
sundry *pron*, *pl in constr* an indeterminate number of more than one or two < *sundry* were interviewed; a few were selected >
 syn divers, many, ‖several, various
 idiom all and sundry, quite a few
sunk *adj* *syn* see DOWNCAST
sunlight *n* *syn* see SUN 2
sunny *adj* **1 syn** see FAIR 2
 rel bright, brilliant

---

syn synonym(s)	*rel* related word(s)
ant antonym(s)	*con* contrasted word(s)

idiom idiomatic equivalent(s)
‖ use limited; if in doubt, see a dictionary

idiom bright and sunny
2 syn see CHEERFUL 1
sunrise *n syn* see DAWN 1
sunset *n syn* see EVENING 2
sunshine *n syn* see SUN 2
sunshine *adj syn* see FAIR 2
sunshining *adj syn* see FAIR 2
sunshiny *adj syn* see FAIR 2
sunup *n syn* see DAWN 1
sup (off *or* up) *vb syn* see DRINK 1
super *adj syn* see MARVELOUS 2
idiom out of this world
super *adv* **1 syn** see VERY 1
2 syn see EVER 6
superabundant *adj* abounding to a great, abnormal, or excessive degree < *superabundant* harvests had brought down prices >
syn overabounding, overabundant, overflowing
rel abounding, abundant, cornucopian, plenteous, plentiful; excess, excessive, overmuch, surplus; crawling, teeming; overspilling; epidemic, rampant
superadd *vb syn* see ADD 1
superannuate *vb* **1 syn** see OUTDATE
2 syn see RETIRE 2
superb *adj* **1 syn** see GRAND 3
rel noble; majestic
2 syn see SPLENDID 2
rel imposing, stately; opulent
3 consummately impressive and supremely excellent of its kind < the writer's style is brilliant and his command of words and imagery, *superb* >
syn magnificent, outstanding, standout, superexcellent, superlative; *compare* SUPREME
rel gorgeous, glorious, marvelous, resplendent; crashing, rousing, sensational, slambang, super, superfine, wonderful; best, optimal, optimum, prime; sublime
idiom very best
con inferior, mediocre, poor, substandard; atrocious, awful, dreadful, shocking; deplorable, dismal, lamentable, pitiful, woeful; abominable, execrable, outrageous, shameful
ant wretched
superbity *n syn* see PRIDE 3
supercilious *adj syn* see PROUD 1
rel sniffish, sniffy, snifty, snippy, snuffy; sneering
superciliousness *n syn* see PRIDE 3
supererogant *adj syn* see SUPEREROGATORY
supererogative *adj syn* see SUPEREROGATORY
supererogatory *adj* given or done without compulsion, need, or warrant < people who offer *supererogatory* advice >
syn gratuitous, supererogant, supererogative, unasked, uncalled-for, wanton
rel nonessential, superfluous, supernumerary, unnecessary, unneeded
con essential, indispensible, vital; compulsory, obligatory; called-for, needful, required, requisite, sought, wanted
superexcellent *adj syn* see SUPERB 3
rel incomparable, matchless, unparalleled, unsurpassed
superficial *adj* **1 syn** see SHALLOW 1
2 lacking in depth, solidity, and comprehensiveness < wrote only a *superficial* report on the situation >
syn cursory, depthless, shallow, sketchy, uncritical
rel bird's-eye, general; one-dimensional, skin-deep; smattery
con comprehensive, full, inclusive; deep, detailed, in-depth, thorough; critical
ant exhaustive
superficies *n syn* see TOP 2
superfluent *adj syn* see SUPERFLUOUS
superfluity *n* **1 syn** see EXCESS 1
rel overflowing, swarming, teeming
2 syn see LUXURY
superfluous *adj* exceeding what is needed or indispensable < omitted all *superfluous* information >
syn de trop, excess, extra, recrementitious, spare, superfluent, supernumerary, surplus
rel unnecessary, unneeded, unwanted; needless, useless; dispensable, nonessential; gratuitous, supererogatory, unasked, uncalled-for
con critical, crucial, imperative; essential, fundamental, vital; consequential, important, momentous, notable, noteworthy; defective, inadequate

ant deficient
superhuman *adj* **1 syn** see SUPERNATURAL 1
2 syn see SUPERNATURAL 2
superhuman *n syn* see SUPERMAN
superincumbent *adj* **1 syn** see SUPERIOR 1
2 syn see ONEROUS
superintend *vb syn* see SUPERVISE
superintendence *n syn* see OVERSIGHT 1
rel direction, presidence
superintendency *n syn* see OVERSIGHT 1
rel direction, presidence
superior *adj* **1** being or regarded as being above the level of another < the new assistant received a *superior* rating for his work >
syn greater, higher, over, overlying, superincumbent, superjacent
rel major, primary, senior
con lesser, lower, nether, under
ant inferior
2 syn see SUPERNATURAL 1
3 syn see BETTER 2
ant inferior
4 being of higher quality, accomplishment, or merit < a class of *superior* students >
syn exceptional, premium; *compare* MARVELOUS 2
rel noteworthy, remarkable, unusual
con commonplace, ordinary, unexceptional, unremarkable
ant average
5 syn see CHOICE
6 syn see EXCELLENT
ant inferior
7 syn see PROUD 1
superior *n* one standing above another in a hierarchy of rank < was always respectful to his *superiors* in the department >
syn better, brass hat, elder, higher-up, senior
rel heavyweight
ant inferior
superiority *n syn* see BETTER 2
rel ascendancy, dominance, supremacy
ant inferiority
superjacent *adj syn* see SUPERIOR 1
ant subjacent
superlative *adj syn* see SUPERB 3
rel accomplished, consummate, finished
superman *n* a person of extraordinary power or achievement < a space program run by scientific *supermen* >
syn demigod, superhuman
idiom Triton among the minnows
con also-ran, loser, underdog
ant subhuman
supermundane *adj syn* see SUPERNATURAL 1
supernatural *adj* **1** of, relating to, or proceeding from an order of existence beyond the visible observable universe < many then believed in a *supernatural* force that directs history >
syn metaphysical, miraculous, numinous, preternatural, superhuman, superior, supermundane, suprahuman, supramundane, supranatural, unearthly
rel paranormal, rare, unusual; spiritual; celestial, heavenly; divine
2 being much more than is natural or normal < had a *supernatural* ability to win money >
syn superhuman, supernormal, superordinary, supranormal, uncanny, unnatural
rel extraordinary, outstanding, phenomenal, remarkable; paranormal
3 syn see EXCESSIVE 1
supernormal *adj syn* see SUPERNATURAL 2
ant subnormal
supernumerary *adj syn* see SUPERFLUOUS
superordinary *adj syn* see SUPERNATURAL 2
ant ordinary
superpatriot *n syn* see PATRIOTEER
superscribe *vb syn* see ADDRESS 6
supersede *vb syn* see REPLACE 3
rel reject, repudiate; abandon, desert, forsake; discard
superseded *adj syn* see OBSOLETE
supersensible *adj syn* see PSYCHIC 1
supersensory *adj syn* see PSYCHIC 1

supertemporal *adj syn* see INFINITE 1

supervene *vb syn* see FOLLOW 1

supervenient *adj syn* see ADVENTITIOUS

supervise *vb* to have or exercise the charge, direction, and oversight of < *supervised* the construction of the new stadium >
syn boss, chaperon, overlook, oversee, quarterback, superintend, survey
rel guide, steer; administer, conduct, direct; manage, run; control; monitor, proctor

supervision *n syn* see OVERSIGHT 1

supper club *n syn* see NIGHTCLUB

supplant *vb* 1 to supersede (another) by or as if by force, trickery, or treachery < a wife who found herself *supplanted* by another woman >
syn cut out, displace, usurp
rel crowd (out), force (out); bounce, cast (out), eject, expel, oust
idiom give the bum's rush, give the old heave-ho, step into the shoes of
2 *syn* see REPLACE 3

supple *adj* 1 *syn* see ELASTIC 1
ant stiff
2 *syn* see PLASTIC
3 showing freedom and ease of bodily movement (as in bending or twisting) < the light *supple* spring of a cat >
syn limber, lissome, lithe, lithesome
rel agile, graceful, willowy, wiry, withy
con awkward, clumsy, gawky, maladroit, unhandy; ungraceful; arthritic, creaky, decrepit
ant stiff

supplement *n* 1 *syn* see COMPLEMENT 1
2 *syn* see APPENDIX 1

suppliant *n* one who asks (as for a favor or gift) humbly < a room full of *suppliants* waiting to see the king >
syn asker, beggar, petitioner, prayer, suitor, supplicant, supplicator
rel solicitant, solicitor

supplicant *n syn* see SUPPLIANT

supplicate *vb syn* see BEG
idiom ask on bended knee, ‖come down on one's marrowbones

supplication *n syn* see PRAYER

supplicator *n syn* see SUPPLIANT

supply *vb syn* see GIVE 3
rel fulfill, outfit, provision

supply *n* an accumulation of something that is a source from which things may be drawn < an unending *supply* of new talent >
syn armamentarium, fund, inventory, stock, store
rel accumulation; reserve, reservoir, stockpile, surplus; hoard

supply *adj syn* see TEMPORARY

support *vb* 1 *syn* see BEAR 10
2 to favor actively in the face of opposition < *support* an unpopular economic policy >
syn advocate, back, backstop, champion, side (with), uphold
rel applaud, approve, endorse, favor, plunk (for), pull (for), root; adopt, embrace, espouse; defend, maintain, sustain
idiom align oneself with, be on (someone's) side, take (someone's) side
con battle, combat, counter, fight, oppose; withstand
ant buck
3 to supply what is needed for sustenance < *support* his family >
syn maintain, provide (for)
idiom boil the pot, bring home the bacon, make a living for, take care of
4 to hold up in position by serving as a foundation or base for < pillars *supporting* an arch >
syn bear up, bolster, brace, buttress, carry, prop, shore (up), sustain, upbear, uphold
rel stand
5 to keep from yielding, sinking, or losing courage or stability < her friends *supported* her during the crisis >
syn bolster, buoy (up), prop, sustain, underprop, uphold; *compare* ENCOURAGE 1
rel encourage; fortify, stiffen, strengthen

support *n* 1 *syn* see HELP 1
2 *syn* see HELP 2

3 a supporting means, agency, medium, or device < girders as structural *supports* > < strong economic *support* for the government >
syn brace, buttress, column, prop, shore, stay, underpinner, underpinning, underpropping
rel base, foundation; sustentation
4 *syn* see LIVING

supportable *adj syn* see BEARABLE
ant insupportable, unsupportable

supporter *n* 1 *syn* see FOLLOWER
2 *syn* see EXPONENT
ant antagonist

supposable *adj syn* see THINKABLE 2
ant insupposable

supposal *n syn* see THEORY 1

suppose *vb* 1 *syn* see UNDERSTAND 3
rel presuppose
2 *syn* see CONJECTURE

suppose *n syn* see THEORY 2

supposed *adj* 1 accepted or advanced as true or real on the basis of less than conclusive evidence < the *supposed* efficiency of the new machine >
syn conjectural, hypothetical, putative, reputed, suppositional, suppositious, supposititious, suppositive, suppository; *compare* ALLEGED
rel assumed, postulated, postulatory, presumed, presupposed; provisional, tentative; academic, speculative, theoretical; alleged
con sure; known, proved, proven; ascertained, demonstrated, observed, recognized
ant certain
2 *syn* see ALLEGED
ant proved, proven

supposition *n* 1 *syn* see ASSUMPTION 2
2 *syn* see THEORY 2

suppositional *adj syn* see SUPPOSED 1

suppositious *adj* 1 *syn* see FICTITIOUS 1
2 *syn* see SUPPOSED 1
rel doubtful, dubious, questionable; pretended, simulated

supposititious *adj* 1 *syn* see ILLEGITIMATE 1
2 *syn* see FICTITIOUS 1
3 *syn* see SUPPOSED 1

supposititiousness *n syn* see ILLEGITIMACY 1

suppositive *adj syn* see SUPPOSED 1

suppository *adj syn* see SUPPOSED 1

suppress *vb* 1 *syn* see CRUSH 5
idiom ride roughshod over
2 to hold back more or less forcefully someone or something that seeks an outlet < management tried to *suppress* the workers' discontent > < there was no way to *suppress* her short of murder >
syn muffle, ‖quelch, repress, shush, squelch, strangle; *compare* CRUSH 5
rel curb, restrain; arrest, check, interrupt; put down, slap down; quash, quell, squash; cut off, spike; abolish, annihilate, extinguish
idiom bring to naught, crack (*or* clamp) down on, put the kibosh on
3 to keep from public knowledge < *suppress* all news from the front >
syn burke, hush (up), stifle
rel repress; censor; silence
idiom put the lid on
con disclose, divulge, leak, ‖let out, reveal; broadcast, circulate, diffuse, publish, spread
4 *syn* see COMPOSE 4
rel drown; swallow
5 *syn* see STUNT

suppression *n* 1 *syn* see REPRESSION 1
2 *syn* see REPRESSION 2

supra *adv syn* see ABOVE 2
ant infra

suprahuman *adj syn* see SUPERNATURAL 1

supramundane *adj syn* see SUPERNATURAL 1

---

syn synonym(s)   *rel* related word(s)
ant antonym(s)   *con* contrasted word(s)
idiom idiomatic equivalent(s)
‖ use limited; if in doubt, see a dictionary

supranatural *adj syn* see SUPERNATURAL 1

supranormal *adj syn* see SUPERNATURAL 2

supremacy *n* the position of being first (as in rank, power, or influence) < Britain once enjoyed *supremacy* on the seas >
syn ascendancy, ascendant, dominance, domination, dominion, masterdom, preeminence, preponderance, preponderancy, preponderation, prepotence, prepotency, sovereignty
rel authority, control, driver's seat, power, sway; mastership, mastery, principality, superiority; transcendence

supreme *adj* developed to the utmost and not exceeded by any other in degree, quality, or intensity < dying for one's principles is an example of *supreme* sacrifice >
syn incomparable, preeminent, surpassing, towering, transcendent, ultimate, unequalable, unmatchable, unsurpassable; *compare* ALONE 3, EXCELLENT, MARVELOUS 2, MAXIMUM, SUPERB 3
rel crowning, master, sovereign; unequaled, unmatched, unparalleled, unrivaled, unsurpassed; final, last; absolute, perfect

surcease *vb syn* see STOP 3

sure *adj* **1** firmly settled or established < trying to find a *sure* footing on the rugged slope >
syn fast, firm, secure, stable, staunch, strong; *compare* FAST 4, STABLE 4
2 free from doubt, hesitation, or fear < upheld a *sure* faith >
syn abiding, enduring, firm, fixed, never-failing, steadfast, steady, unfaltering, unqualified, unquestioning, unshakable, unshaken, unwavering, wholehearted
rel assured, changeless, constant, unchangeable, unchanging, uncompromising, unfailing, unvarying; certain, fixed, set
con insecure, uncertain, unreliable; feeble, infirm, shaky, unsound; doubtful, dubious, hesitant
ant unsure
3 *syn* see INFALLIBLE 1
4 *syn* see INFALLIBLE 2
5 marked by unwavering assurance especially as to the rightness of one's views or actions < was *sure* he knew the answer >
syn certain, cocksure, confident, positive
rel assured, self-assured, self-possessed, self-satisfied; arrogant, cocky, pert; decided, decisive
con doubtful, hesitant, uncertain
ant unsure
6 *syn* see POSITIVE 3
rel convincing, telling; absolute, definite; genuine, real, valid

sure–enough *adj* **1** *syn* see ACTUAL 2
2 *syn* see AUTHENTIC 2

surefire *adj syn* see INFALLIBLE 2

sureness *n syn* see CERTAINTY
ant unsureness

sure thing *n* one that is bound to be successful < was deemed a *sure thing* in the race >
syn shoo-in
rel certainty; winner

surety *n* **1** *syn* see CERTAINTY
2 *syn* see GUARANTEE 1
3 *syn* see SPONSOR

surface *n syn* see TOP 2
rel exterior, outside; cover, covering
con body, mass; inside, interior; lining

surface *vb* to come to the surface (as of water) < a submarine *surfaced* outside the harbor >
syn rise
rel come up
con go down, go under; submerge; dive

surfeit *n syn* see EXCESS 1

surfeit *vb syn* see SATIATE
rel overfill, overindulge
idiom have all one can take (*or* stand)
ant whet

surfeited *adj syn* see SATIATED
ant unsatisfied

surge *vb syn* see POUR 2

surly *adj syn* see SULLEN
rel discourteous, ill-mannered, rude, ungracious; bearish, boorish, churlish; fractious, irritable, snappish, waspish
idiom as surly as a bear
con affable, cordial, genial, gracious
ant amiable

surmise *vb syn* see CONJECTURE
rel consider, regard; hypothesize, theorize

idiom risk assuming, venture a guess

surmount *vb* **1** *syn* see OVERCOME 1
rel best, better, outdo, outstrip, outtop, outtower, surpass
idiom rise superior to
2 *syn* see CLEAR 8
3 to stand or lie at the top of < a cross *surmounts* the cupola >
syn cap, crest, crown, top
rel finish; terminate
4 *syn* see TOP

surpass *vb* **1** to be or become greater than or superior to < *surpassed* all his fellows in scholarship >
syn ‖bang, beat, best, better, cap, cob, ding, exceed, excel, outdo, outgo, outmatch, outshine, outstrip, pass, top, transcend, trump
rel distance, outdistance, outpace, outperform, outpoint, outrange, outrival, outrun, outvie; eclipse, outrank, outtop, outtower, outweigh, overshadow, overtop, rank
idiom have it all over, put to shame
2 *syn* see EXCEED 1

surpassing *adj syn* see SUPREME

surpassingly *adv syn* see VERY 1

surplus *n* **1** *syn* see EXCESS 1
ant deficiency
2 *syn* see EXCESS 2
ant shortage

surplus *adj syn* see SUPERFLUOUS

surplusage *n* **1** *syn* see EXCESS 2
ant shortage, underage
2 *syn* see EXCESS 1
ant shortage

surprise *vb* **1** to attack unawares < hijackers *surprised* the truck driver and took his cargo >
syn ambush, lay (for), waylay
rel bushwhack, dry-gulch; capture, catch; grab, grasp, seize, take
2 to impress forcibly through unexpectedness, startlingness, or unusualness < was *surprised* by his violent jealousy >
syn amaze, astonish, astound, dumbfound, flabbergast
rel startle; bewilder, confound, discomfit, disconcert, dismay, nonplus, ‖swan; faze, rattle, rock; bowl (over), floor, stagger; stun, stupefy
idiom leave open-mouthed (*or* aghast), take aback (*or* by surprise)

surprising *adj syn* see MARVELOUS 1
rel unexpected, unforeseen, unlooked-for; eye-opening, eye-popping

surrender *vb* **1** *syn* see RELINQUISH
rel commit, consign, entrust
2 *syn* see FALL 3
rel give in, give up
idiom haul down one's colors, strike the (*or* one's) flag

surrender *n* the yielding of one's person, forces, or possessions to another < the victors demanded unconditional *surrender* >
syn capitulation, dedition, submission
rel appeasement, Munich; relenting, succumbing, yielding; white flag

surreptitious *adj syn* see SECRET 1
rel skulking, slinking, slinky, sneaking, sneaky
con obvious, open, overt
ant brazen

surreptitiously *adv syn* see SECRETLY
con openly, overtly, plainly
ant brazenly

surrogate *n* **1** *syn* see SUBSTITUTE
2 *syn* see RESOURCE 3

surrogate *adj syn* see SUBSTITUTE 1

surround *vb* **1** to close in or as if in a ring about something < a crowd *surrounded* the accident victim >
syn begird, beset, circle, compass, encircle, encompass, environ, gird, girdle, hem, loop, ring, round
rel embosom, enclave, enclose, envelop; circumscribe, circumvent, confine, limit
2 *syn* see BORDER 1

surroundings *n pl syn* see ENVIRONMENT

surveillance *n* **1** *syn* see EYE 3
idiom peeled eye
2 *syn* see LOOKOUT 3
rel surveyance

idiom watchful (*or* weather) eye

survey *vb* **1 syn** see ESTIMATE 1
  rel measure, size, size up
  2 syn see SUPERVISE
  3 to view from or as if from a high place or position <*surveyed* the view from his penthouse window>
  syn overlook, oversee
  4 syn see SCRUTINIZE 1
survey *n* **1 syn** see EXAMINATION
  2 syn see COMPENDIUM 1
‖**survigrous** *adj syn* see VIGOROUS
survive *vb* **1 syn** see OUTLIVE
  2 to continue to exist or function in spite of a usually adverse condition or development <a company that managed to *survive* the recession>
  syn come through, pull through, ride (out)
  rel carry on, carry through, continue, endure, last, persist; live down, outlast, outlive; recover, revive
  idiom come out of it, live to fight again, make it through, ride out (*or* weather) the storm
  con collapse, crash, fold, fold up, go down, go under; founder, sink; close (down), close up; bankrupt, bust
  ant perish
susceptible *adj* **1 syn** see LIABLE 2
  rel disposed, inclined, predisposed
  ant immune, unsusceptible
  2 syn see EASY 3
  rel nonresistant, soft; movable, persuadable
  ant unsusceptible
  3 syn see SENTIENT 3
  rel affected, impressed, influenced, swayed, touched; aroused, roused, stirred
  ant unsusceptible
susceptive *adj syn* see SENTIENT 3
suscitate *vb syn* see PROVOKE 4
suspect *adj syn* see DOUBTFUL 1
  idiom ‖a bit thin (*or* thick), open to suspicion
suspect *vb* **1 syn** see DISTRUST
  idiom have doubts about
  2 syn see UNDERSTAND 3
  idiom be inclined to think
suspend *vb* **1 syn** see EXCLUDE
  2 syn see DEFER
  rel arrest, check, interrupt; cease, discontinue, stop
  idiom lay on the table, put on the shelf
  3 syn see HANG 1
suspended *adj* hung or seeming as if hung from a support <bunches of grapes *suspended* from the vines>
  syn hanging, pendent, pendulant, pendulous, pensile
  rel dangling, swinging
suspenders *n pl* a pair of supporting bands worn across the shoulders to support trousers, skirt, or belt <*suspenders* are out of style>
  syn braces, ‖gallows, ‖galluses
suspense *n syn* see SUSPENSION 2
suspension *n* **1 syn** see ABEYANCE
  2 a temporary withholding of action or cessation of activity <asked for *suspension* of judgment until all the evidence was in>
  syn moratorium, suspense
  rel cessation, concluding, conclusion, end, ending, finish, period, termination
  con resumption; continuance
suspicion *n* **1 syn** see UNCERTAINTY
  rel apprehension, foreboding, misgiving, presentiment; distrust
  2 syn see HINT 2
‖**suspicion** *vb syn* see DISTRUST
suspicious *adj* **1 syn** see DOUBTFUL 1
  rel questionable; queer
  2 given or prone to suspicion <was *suspicious* of everyone's motives>
  syn distrustful, jealous, mistrustful
  rel careful, cautious; leery, wary, watchful; skeptical, unbelieving
  con trustful, trusting, unsuspecting; naive, dupable, easy, exploitable, gullible
  ant unsuspicious
suspiciously *adv syn* see ASKANCE 2

  rel distrustingly, mistrustingly
  ant unsuspiciously
suspire *vb* **1 syn** see SIGH 1
  idiom draw a long breath
  2 syn see LONG
sustain *vb* **1 syn** see MAINTAIN 1
  rel nourish, support; prolong
  2 syn see SUPPORT 4
  rel lug, pack, tote
  3 syn see SUPPORT 5
  rel befriend, favor
  idiom stand by
  con abandon, forsake; ignore
  4 syn see BEAR 10
  5 syn see EXPERIENCE 1
  rel bear, endure
sustainable *adj syn* see BEARABLE
  ant unsustainable
sustenance *n* **1 syn** see FOOD 2
  idiom bodily sustenance
  2 syn see LIVING
sustentation *n syn* see PRESERVATION 1
susurration *n syn* see MURMUR 1
‖**swack** *n syn* see CUFF
‖**swacked** *adj syn* see INTOXICATED 1
swad *n syn* see SOLDIER
swaddle *vb syn* see SWATHE
  rel ‖sweel
  ant unswaddle
‖**swaddy** *n syn* see SOLDIER
swag *vb* **1 syn** see SEESAW
  2 syn see DROOP 3
swag *n* **1 syn** see SPOIL
  2 syn see MONEY
swagger *vb* **1 syn** see LORD
  rel swash, swashbuckle
  2 syn see STRUT 2
  rel bluster, brandish, flourish
  con blench, quail; shrink, wince; truckle
‖**swagger** *n syn* see VAGABOND
‖**swagman** *n syn* see VAGABOND
swain *n* **1 syn** see BOYFRIEND 1
  2 syn see SUITOR 2
swainish *adj syn* see BOORISH
swallow *vb* **1** to receive through the esophagus into the stomach <*swallowed* the pills easily with a sip of water>
  syn down, take
  rel drop, gulp, ‖quilt, toss; ingest, ingurgitate
  2 syn see DRINK 1
  3 syn see BELIEVE 1
  idiom swallow (something) hook, line, and sinker
  4 syn see BEAR 10
  5 syn see ACCEPT 2
  6 syn see MUMBLE
swamp *n* wet spongy land saturated and sometimes partially covered with water <hunted alligators in the Florida *swamps*>
  syn baygall, bog, fen, marsh, marshland, mire, morass, ‖moss, muskeg, ‖purgatory, ‖puxy, quag, quagmire, slough, ‖sump, swampland, ‖swang, ‖vlei
  rel bottoms, ‖holm; ‖glade; jheel; quake ooze; shaking prairie, trembling prairie
swamp *vb* **1 syn** see DELUGE 1
  2 syn see DELUGE 3
swampland *n syn* see SWAMP
‖**swang** *n syn* see SWAMP
swank *vb syn* see LORD
swank *adj* **1 syn** see SHOWY
  2 syn see STYLISH
swap *vb* **1 syn** see EXCHANGE 2
  2 syn see TRADE 1
  idiom ‖swap horses, swap out of
‖**swap** *n syn* see BLOW 1
‖**swapping** *adj syn* see HUGE

---

syn synonym(s)   *rel* related word(s)
ant antonym(s)   *con* contrasted word(s)
idiom idiomatic equivalent(s)
‖ use limited; if in doubt, see a dictionary

||**swarf** *vb syn* see FAINT

swarm *vb syn* see TEEM
 idiom gather (*or* swarm) like bees

swarming *adj syn* see ALIVE 5

swart *adj syn* see DARK 3

swarth *adj syn* see DARK 3

swarthy *adj syn* see DARK 3

swash *vb* **1** *syn* see SLOSH 1
 2 *syn* see SPLASH

swashy *adj syn* see INSIPID 3

swat *vb* ||**1** *syn* see SQUAT
 2 *syn* see STRIKE 2
 rel blip, box, buffet, cuff, smack; belt, clobber, slug, smash, wallop

swat *n syn* see HIT 1

swathe *vb* to cover or bind completely with clothing or material <legs *swathed* in bandages> <the baby was *swathed* in a warm shawl>
 syn drape, enswathe, envelop, enwrap, roll, swaddle, wrap (up); *compare* ENFOLD 1
 rel enfold; encase; cover
 con bare, denude, expose, strip, uncover, unswaddle, unwrap
 ant unswathe

sway *vb* **1** *syn* see SWING 2
 2 *syn* see LURCH 2
 3 *syn* see GOVERN 1
 4 *syn* see AFFECT
 rel bias, dispose, incline, predispose; conduct, control, direct, manage; govern, rule

sway *n syn* see POWER 1
 rel range, reach, scope, sweep; amplitude, expanse, spread, stretch

swayable *adj syn* see RECEPTIVE 1

swear *vb* **1** *syn* see VOW
 idiom swear on a stack of Bibles, swear to God, swear up and down
 2 *syn* see TESTIFY 2
 3 to use profane, blasphemous, or obscene language <*swore* when the horse threw him>
 syn bedamn, curse, cuss, damn, execrate, imprecate
 rel blaspheme; rail, rant; abuse, revile, vilify, vituperate
 idiom ||chew the dirty rag, curse and swear, fall a-cursing, ||let out religion, make the air blue, rip (*or* rap) out an oath, swear like a sailor (*or* trooper), use language

swear *n syn* see SWEARWORD

swearing *n syn* see BLASPHEMY 1

swearword *n* a profane, blasphemous, or obscene word <let loose with a string of *swearwords*>
 syn curse, cuss, cussword, expletive, oath, swear
 rel four-letter word, obscenity, scurrility
 idiom blue word, one-horse oath, raw one, ripe (*or* juicy) word, sailor's blessing, six-cornered oath, strong word

sweat *vb* **1** *syn* see EXUDE
 2 *syn* see FLEECE 1

sweat *n* **1** *syn* see WORK 2
 2 *syn* see SNIT
 ||**3** *syn* see SOLDIER

sweatful *adj syn* see SWEATY

sweating *adj syn* see SWEATY

sweat out *vb syn* see BEAR 10

sweaty *adj* producing, accompanied by, or characterized by sweat <he still held the racket tight in *sweaty* hands>
 syn asweat, perspiring, perspiry, ||puggy, sweatful, sweating
 rel clammy; sticky; wet
 idiom bathed in sweat, covered with sweat, drenched with (*or* in) sweat, in a muck of a sweat, wet with sweat (*or* perspiration)

sweep *vb syn* see FLY 4

sweep *n syn* see RANGE 2

sweeping *n* sweepings *pl syn* see REFUSE

sweeping *adj* **1** *syn* see ALL-AROUND 2
 rel all-embracing, all-encompassing
 2 *syn* see INDISCRIMINATE 1
 rel all-out, out-and-out, whole-hog; across-the-board, blanket

sweet *adj* **1** distinctly pleasing or charming <a *sweet* smile>
 syn dulcet, engaging, winning, winsome
 rel agreeable, pleasant, pleasing; beautiful, fair, lovely; delectable, delicious, delightful, luscious; angelic, heavenly
 con disagreeable, unpleasant; displeasing, obnoxious, repulsive

 ant bitter
 2 having a pleasant smell <the *sweet* odor of flowers and incense>
 syn ambrosial, aromal, aromatic, balmy, fragrant, perfumed, perfumy, redolent, savory, scented, spicy; *compare* ODOROUS
 rel clean, fresh; sweetish
 con funky, fusty, musty, noisome, putrid, rancid, rotten, stale, stinking, strong, whiffy; fetid, foul, olid, rank, smelly
 ant malodorous
 3 *syn* see MELODIOUS 1

sweet *n syn* see SWEETHEART 1

sweeten *vb* **1** *syn* see PACIFY
 2 *syn* see SUGARCOAT 1

sweetheart *n* **1** one who is dearly beloved — often used as a term of endearment <was her childhood *sweetheart*> <*sweetheart*, you know I'll wait>
 syn beloved, darling, dear, flame, heartthrob, honey, honeybunch, love, loveling, sweet, sweetling, turtledove
 rel ||cutie pie, deary, pigsney; pet, puggy
 2 *syn* see GIRL FRIEND 2
 rel doll baby, lovey-dovey, ||tootsie
 3 *syn* see BOYFRIEND 2
 rel paramour; ||dreamboat

sweetheart *vb syn* see ADDRESS 8

sweetie *n syn* see GIRL FRIEND 2
 rel sweetie pie

sweetling *n syn* see SWEETHEART 1

sweetness and light *n syn* see AMENITY 1

sweet-talk *vb syn* see COAX

swell *vb* **1** *syn* see EXPAND 3
 rel balloon, belly, bloat, blow up, bosom; pouch, pout; overblow
 con compress, condense, constrict, contract
 ant shrink
 2 *syn* see LORD
 rel puff
 idiom act the grand seigneur, swell it

swell *n syn* see EXPERT

swell *adj syn* see MARVELOUS 2

swelled head *n syn* see CONCEIT 2

swellheadedness *n syn* see CONCEIT 2

swelling *adj syn* see RHETORICAL

||**swelt** *vb* **1** *syn* see DIE 1
 2 *syn* see FAINT

swelter *vb syn* see BURN 3

sweltering *adj syn* see HOT 1
 idiom ||hot as the hinges of hell
 ant frigid

sweltry *adj syn* see HOT 1

swerve *vb* **1** to turn or be turned away abruptly from a straight line or course <*swerved* the car to avoid collision>
 syn dip, sheer, skew, slue, train off, veer
 2 to be deflected from a fixed or right course of action or conduct <never *swerved* from the concept of duty, honor, country>
 syn depart, deviate, digress, diverge
 rel shift; waver; err, stray, wander
 idiom deviate from the straight and narrow, get off the proper course (*or* path)

swift *adj syn* see FAST 3
 rel headlong, precipitate, sudden; double-quick; supersonic
 ant sluggish

swift *adv syn* see FAST 2
 ant sluggishly

swiften *vb syn* see SPEED 3

swiftly *adv syn* see FAST 2
 con slowly
 ant sluggishly

swiftness *n* **1** *syn* see SPEED 2
 ant sluggishness
 2 *syn* see HASTE 1
 ant slowness

swig *n syn* see DRINK 3

swig *vb syn* see DRINK 3

swill *vb* **1** *syn* see DRINK 3
 2 *syn* see CONSUME 5

swill *n* **1** *syn* see REFUSE
 2 *syn* see DRINK 3

swillbowl *n syn* see DRUNKARD

swiller *n syn* see DRUNKARD

swim *vb syn* see SPIN 2

  idiom have one's head swim

swimming *adj syn* see DIZZY 2

  rel fluctuating, swaying, wavering

swimmingly *adv syn* see WELL 5

swimmy *adj syn* see DIZZY 2

swindle *vb syn* see CHEAT

  rel rogue; victimize

  idiom sell one a bill of goods, take for a ride, take for a sucker

swindle *n syn* see IMPOSTURE

swindler *n* one who defrauds usually of money and especially by imposture or by gaining the victim's confidence <lost their savings to *swindlers* in a get-rich-quick scheme>

  syn bunco steerer, cheat, cheater, chiaus, come-on, confidence man, con man, defrauder, diddler, double-dealer, flimflammer, ‖grifter, gyp, gypper, ‖mace, mountebank, Peter Funk, rogue, sharper, sharpie, skin, slicker, ‖spieler, trickster

  rel bilk, bilker, blackleg, charlatan, chiseler, crook, deceiver, dodger, fraud, gouger, harpy, highbinder, hoaxer, operator, rook, shark, sharp, sharpster, tricker; scoundrel

swing *vb* 1 *syn* see HANDLE 2

  2 to move rhythmically to and fro, up and down, or back and forth <the clock's pendulum *swung* slowly>

  syn oscillate, pendulate, sway

  rel undulate, wave; rock, roll; revolve, rotate, switch, wheel; jiggle, wag, waggle, wiggle, wigwag

  3 *syn* see TURN 6

  4 *syn* see LURCH 2

swing *n* 1 *syn* see RHYTHM

  2 *syn* see HANG

‖swingeing *adj syn* see EXCELLENT

swinish *adj syn* see BRUTISH

swipe *n syn* see HIT 1

swipe *vb syn* see STEAL 1

swirl *vb* to move swiftly in circles, eddies, or undulations <water *swirled* into the storm drains>

  syn eddy, gurge, purl, swoosh, whirl, whirlpool, whorl

  rel boil, roil; gush, surge

swish *vb syn* see HISS

swish *adj syn* see STYLISH

switch *vb* 1 *syn* see WAG

  2 *syn* see EXCHANGE 2

  3 *syn* see SHUNT 1

‖swither *vb syn* see RUSH 1

swivet *n syn* see SNIT

swizzle *vb syn* see DRINK 3

swollen *adj syn* see RHETORICAL

swoon *vb syn* see FAINT

  rel die away, drown

swoon *n syn* see FAINT

swoosh *vb syn* see SWIRL

sworn *adj syn* see INVETERATE 1

sybarite *n syn* see HEDONIST

sybaritic *adj* marked by or given to luxury or voluptuous living <the *sybaritic* grandeur of a sultan's harem> <a man of *sybaritic* and self-indulgent habits>

  syn hedonistic, onanistic, self-indulgent, sybaritical, sybaritish; *compare* SENSUOUS

  rel apolaustic, pleasure-loving; epicurean, luxurious; carnal, sensual, voluptuous

sybaritical *adj syn* see SYBARITIC

sybaritish *adj syn* see SYBARITIC

sycophancy *n syn* see DETRACTION

sycophant *n* a base or servilely attentive flatterer and self-seeker <*sycophants* who slavishly curried favor with the king>

  syn apple-polisher, bootlick, bootlicker, ‖brownnose, ‖brownnoser, ‖clawback, creature, ‖easy rider, footlicker, groveler, lickspit, lickspittle, minion, reptile, spaniel, toad, toadeater, toadier, toady, truckler, yes-man; *compare* PARASITE

  rel flunky, gopher, lackey, slave, stooge; flatterer, self-seeker; snob, tuft-hunter

sycophant *adj syn* see FAWNING

sycophantic *adj syn* see FAWNING

sycophantical *adj syn* see FAWNING

sycophantish *adj syn* see FAWNING

syllable *n syn* see PARTICLE

syllabus *n syn* see COMPENDIUM 1

sylloge *n syn* see COMPENDIUM 1

symbol *n* 1 something that stands for something else by reason of relationship, association, convention, or accidental resemblance <the lion is often used as a *symbol* of courage>

  syn attribute, emblem; *compare* INDICATION 3

  rel indication, token, type; badge, mark, note, sign, stamp; character, design, device, figure, motif, pattern; representation

  2 *syn* see CHARACTER 1

symbolism *n syn* see ALLEGORY 1

symbolization *n syn* see ALLEGORY 1

symbolize *vb syn* see REPRESENT 2

symmetrical *adj syn* see PROPORTIONAL

symmetry *n* beauty of form or arrangement arising from balanced proportions <the superb *symmetry* of the design>

  syn balance, harmony, proportion

  rel arrangement, order; agreement, conformity; equality, evenness, regularity; rhythm; finish

  con asymmetry, dissymmetry; disproportion, imbalance, irregularity, unbalance

sympathetic *adj* 1 *syn* see CONSONANT 1

  ant unsympathetic

  2 favorably inclined <found his hearers *sympathetic* to his proposal>

  syn friendly, receptive, ‖sib, well-disposed

  rel agreeable, congenial, favorable; amenable, open, openminded, receptive, responsive

  con ill-disposed, unfriendly, unreceptive; cool, indifferent, lukewarm; neutral

  ant unsympathetic

  3 *syn* see TENDER

  rel benign, benignant, kind, kindly; appreciating, comprehending, understanding

  ant unsympathetic

sympathize (with) *vb syn* see COMPASSIONATE

  rel appreciate, comprehend, understand

sympathy *n* 1 *syn* see ATTRACTION 2

  ant antipathy

  2 a feeling for or a capacity for sharing in the interests of another <he was in *sympathy* with her desire to succeed>

  syn compassion, empathy, fellow feeling

  rel responsiveness, sensitivity; feelings, heart; tenderness, warmheartedness, warmth; benignancy, benignness, kindliness, kindness

  con disinterest, unconcern

  3 *syn* see PITY

symphonic *adj syn* see HARMONIOUS 1

symphonious *adj syn* see HARMONIOUS 1

symphonize *vb syn* see HARMONIZE 4

symphony *n syn* see ORCHESTRA

  rel concert band, symphony band; symphony orchestra

symptom *n syn* see INDICATION 3

synchronal *adj syn* see CONTEMPORARY 1

synchronic *adj syn* see CONTEMPORARY 1

synchronous *adj syn* see CONTEMPORARY 1

syncope *n syn* see FAINT

syndicate *n* a combination of interlocked companies or enterprises <a large newspaper *syndicate*>

  syn cartel, chain, combine, conglomerate, group, pool, trust

  rel association, organization; partnership, union

syndrome *n syn* see DISEASE 1

synergetic *adj syn* see COOPERATIVE

  ant counteractive

synergic *adj syn* see COOPERATIVE

  ant counteractive

synopsis *n syn* see ABRIDGMENT

synopsize *vb syn* see EPITOMIZE 1

  idiom hit the high spots, put it in a nutshell

synthesize *vb syn* see HARMONIZE 4

synthetic *adj* formed or developed by human art, skill, or effort and not by natural processes <*synthetic* plastics>

  syn artificial, factitious, man-made; *compare* ARTIFICIAL 2

  rel manufactured; constructed, fabricated, made

---

syn synonym(s)   *rel* related word(s)

ant antonym(s)   *con* contrasted word(s)

idiom idiomatic equivalent(s)

‖ use limited; if in doubt, see a dictionary

con natural

syrupy *adj syn* see SENTIMENTAL

system *n* **1** an organized integrated whole made up of diverse but interrelated and interdependent parts < the capitalist *system* >
syn complex; *compare* WHOLE 2
rel aggregation, array; mesh, network; arrangement, disposition, scheme, setup; order, pattern
con disorganization; chaos
2 *syn* see WHOLE 2
3 *syn* see ORDER 8

rel proceeding, procedure, process
4 *syn* see METHOD 1

systematic *adj syn* see ORDERLY 1
rel arranged, ordered, organized, systematized; analytical, logical
con disorganized; chaotic
ant unsystematic

systematize *vb syn* see ORDER 1
rel contrive, frame
con confuse, disorder, jumble

tab *n* **1** *syn* see EYE 3
2 *syn* see BILL 1
3 *syn* see CHECK 2
4 *syn* see PRICE 1

tabby *n* **1** *syn* see GOSSIP 1
‖**2** *syn* see SPINSTER

tabernacle *n syn* see HOUSE OF WORSHIP

table *n* **1** a piece of furniture on which food is customarily served < a feast on the *table* >
syn board, dining table, dinner table, mahogany, ‖table-board
rel bar, buffet, counter, sideboard
2 a condensed ordered enumeration of items usually arranged in columns < a *table* of weights and measures >
syn chart, tabulation
rel list; diagram
3 *syn* see PLATEAU

‖**table–board** *n syn* see TABLE 1

tableland *n syn* see PLATEAU

tabloid *adj syn* see SENSATIONAL 2

taboo *n* a restraint imposed by social usage or as a protective measure < a society rife with antiquated moral *taboos* >
syn ban, forbiddance, interdiction, prohibition, proscription
rel inhibition, limitation, reservation, restraint, restriction; regulation, sanction; don't
con acceptance, toleration; approval, authorization, permission, permit, permittance

taboo *vb syn* see FORBID

tabulation *n syn* see TABLE 2

tacit *adj* **1** expressed or conveyed without words, speech, or forthright reference < they made a *tacit* agreement to work together >
syn implicit, implied, inarticulate, inferred, undeclared, understood, unexpressed, unsaid, unspoken, unuttered, wordless
rel alluded (to), hinted (at), intimated, suggested; assumed
con expressed, spoken, verbal; categorical, explicit, express, unequivocal
2 *syn* see UNSPOKEN 1

taciturn *adj syn* see SILENT 3
rel laconic, unexpressive; brooding, dour
con chatty, communicative, loquacious, talkative; convivial, uninhibited, unreserved, unrestrained
ant garrulous

tack *n syn* see TURN 2
rel alteration; digression, tangent; swerve, zigzag

tackle *n syn* see EQUIPMENT

tackle *vb syn* see ATTACK 2
rel take on, undertake; plunge into, set about
idiom get on the job, put one's shoulder to the wheel, start the ball rolling
con avoid, delay, hesitate, put off

tackling *n syn* see EQUIPMENT

tacky *adj* **1** *syn* see SHABBY 1
rel dowdy, outmoded, unstylish; messy, sloppy, slovenly, unkempt, untidy; blowsy, frowzy, frumpish
idiom gone to seed
2 marked by a lack of style or good taste < an old *tacky* scarf spoiled her outfit >

syn dowdy, frumpish, frumpy, outmoded, out-of-date, stodgy, unstylish
rel unbecoming; crude, inelegant, tasteless; incorrect, unsuitable; cheap, gaudy
con ‖mod, modern, modish, smart, stylish, tasteful; elegant

tact *n* skill and grace in dealing with others < handled the embarrassing situation with great *tact* >
syn address, delicatesse, diplomacy, poise, savoir faire, tactfulness; *compare* ADDRESS 1
rel control, head, presence, repose; amenity, courtesy, gallantry; policy, politicness, smoothness, suavity, urbanity; adroitness, deftness, skill; acumen, finesse, perception, sensitivity
con abruptness, bluntness, coarseness, discourtesy, rudeness
ant tactlessness

tactful *adj* marked by or exhibiting tact < his *tactful* skill in handling negotiations >
syn delicate, diplomatic, politic, tactical; *compare* SUAVE
rel polished, suave, urbane; adroit, deft, skilled, skillful; perceptive, sensitive
con clumsy, unpolished, unskilled; discourteous, impolite, rude; undiplomatic
ant blunt, tactless, untactful

tactfulness *n syn* see TACT
rel civility, civilness, politeness; polish
ant tactlessness

tactic *adj syn* see TACTILE 2

tactical *adj* **1** made or carried out with only a limited or immediate end in view < had time only for *tactical* decisions and not strategic planning >
syn short-range
con long-range
ant strategic
2 *syn* see EXPEDIENT
3 *syn* see TACTFUL

tactile *adj* **1** *syn* see TANGIBLE 1
2 of or relating to the sense of touch < *tactile* responses >
syn tactic, tactual

tactility *n syn* see TOUCH 3

taction *n syn* see TOUCH 2

tactless *adj* marked by a lack of tact < his *tactless* remark hurt her >
syn brash, impolitic, maladroit, undiplomatic, unpolitic, untactful
rel impolite, inconsiderate, indelicate, rude; bungling, inept
con diplomatic, polite, tactical
ant tactful

tactual *adj syn* see TACTILE 2

tad *n syn* see BOY 1

tag *n* **1** *syn* see COMMONPLACE
2 *syn* see TICKET 1

tag *vb syn* see TAIL

tag and rag *n syn* see RABBLE 2

tag end *n syn* see TAIL END 2

tagrag *adj syn* see SHABBY 1

tagrag and bobtail *n syn* see RABBLE 2

tail *n syn* see BUTTOCKS

tail *vb* to follow (someone) for purposes of surveillance < detectives *tailing* the suspects >
syn bedog, dog, shadow, tag, trail; *compare* EYE 2, FOLLOW 2

rel hound, pursue

tail end *n* **1** *syn* see BUTTOCKS

2 the hindmost end of something <watched the *tail end* of the parade march off>

syn tag end

tailor *vb syn* see ADAPT

rel style; dovetail; shape up

tailor–made *adj syn* see CUSTOM-MADE

tailor–make *vb syn* see ADAPT

taint *vb* **1** to touch or affect with something bad or undesirable <his good reputation was *tainted* by the scandal>

syn besmear, besmirch, blur, cloud, defile, dirty, discolor, smear, smudge, smut, smutch, soil, stain, sully, tar, tarnish; *compare* CONTAMINATE 1

rel discredit; brand, stigmatize; blacken; damage, harm, hurt

idiom cast a slur upon; give a bad name to, give a black mark to

con brighten, cleanse, clear

2 *syn* see DECAY

rel befoul, contaminate, foul

3 *syn* see CONTAMINATE 1

taintless *adj syn* see CLEAN 1

ant tainted

take *vb* **1** *syn* see CATCH 1

2 *syn* see SEIZE 2

idiom make off with

con drop, dump, give up, relinquish, surrender

3 *syn* see APPROPRIATE 1

con relinquish, yield

4 to lay hold of (as with the hands or an instrument) <took the ax by the handle>

syn clasp, grasp, grip

rel hold; handle

idiom take hold of

con drop, release

5 *syn* see SEIZE 3

rel contract, get; harrow, reach, torment

6 *syn* see CATCH 7

7 *syn* see ATTRACT 1

8 *syn* see SWALLOW 1

9 *syn* see EAT 1

10 to bring into and accept in a particular capacity or relationship <took his son as a member of the firm>

syn admit, receive, take in

rel bring; accept; have, include

11 *syn* see BUY 1

12 *syn* see CHOOSE 1

13 *syn* see DEMAND 2

14 to obtain from another source by means of derivation <takes his name from his father's>

syn derive, draw

rel get, obtain; borrow

15 *syn* see BEAR 10

rel withstand; undergo; ‖hack

idiom take it lying down, take it on the chin

16 *syn* see CONTRACT 1

idiom take sick with

17 *syn* see APPREHEND 1

18 *syn* see UNDERSTAND 3

19 *syn* see DEDUCT 1

20 *syn* see TREAT 2

21 *syn* see CHEAT

rel bamboozle, hoodwink

idiom take for a ride

22 *syn* see ACT 5

take (from) *vb syn* see DECRY 2

take (to) *vb syn* see HABITUATE 2

rel enjoy, fancy, favor, like

idiom get used to

take away *vb* **1** *syn* see REMOVE 2

rel separate

2 *syn* see DEDUCT 1

3 *syn* see DECRY 2

take back *vb* **1** *syn* see RETURN 4

2 *syn* see REPOSSESS 3

3 *syn* see ABJURE

take down *vb syn* see DISMOUNT

take in *vb* **1** *syn* see TAKE 10

2 *syn* see INCLUDE

3 *syn* see APPREHEND 1

rel perceive; ‖savvy; absorb, assimilate, digest

4 *syn* see DECEIVE

rel flimflam, take; trick

take off *vb* **1** *syn* see REMOVE 2

2 *syn* see REMOVE 3

3 *syn* see DEDUCT 1

4 *syn* see KILL 1

5 *syn* see MIMIC

idiom do a takeoff on

6 *syn* see GET OUT 1

7 *syn* see HEAD 3

idiom hit the road (or trail)

8 *syn* see GO 2

takeoff *n syn* see CARICATURE 2

take on *vb* **1** *syn* see DON 2

2 *syn* see ADD 1

3 to proceed to deal with <took on a new job with more responsibility>

syn take up, undertake

rel begin, commence, enter (upon); attempt, endeavor, try; launch, venture

idiom set about, take upon oneself

con abandon, drop, forsake

ant give up

4 *syn* see ENGAGE 5

5 *syn* see EMPLOY 2

6 *syn* see ADOPT

ant give up

take out *vb* **1** *syn* see REMOVE 2

2 *syn* see REMOVE 4

3 *syn* see DEDUCT 1

4 *syn* see DATE

take out (on) *vb* to find release for (as emotions) <took out his anger on the dog>

syn loose, release, unleash, vent

idiom give vent to, let loose (or fly)

con control, govern, restrain; bottle (up), check, keep down, quell, smother; repress, suppress

take over *vb syn* see RELIEVE 3

take up *vb* **1** *syn* see LIFT 1

2 *syn* see BEGIN 1

3 *syn* see TAKE ON 3

rel assume; tackle

idiom address oneself to

4 *syn* see ADOPT

rel support; affiliate

5 *syn* see RESUME 2

taking *adj syn* see INFECTIOUS 3

tale *n* **1** *syn* see STORY 2

rel myth, saga

2 *syn* see DETRACTION

3 *syn* see LIE

rel fiction; yarn

4 *syn* see WHOLE 1

tale *vb syn* see COUNT 1

talebearer *n* **1** *syn* see INFORMER

2 *syn* see GOSSIP 1

talent *n syn* see GIFT 2

rel art, craft, skill; endowment; expertise, forte

talisman *n syn* see CHARM 2

idiom good-luck piece, lucky piece (or charm)

talk *vb* **1** *syn* see SPEAK 3

2 *syn* see SPEAK 1

3 *syn* see CONVERSE

4 *syn* see CHAT 1

rel palaver, spout off

idiom talk one's arm (or ear or leg) off, flap (or wag) the (or one's) tongue

5 *syn* see GOSSIP

6 to reveal secret or confidential information usually concerning illegal acts <at last the suspect *talked* to the police>

---

syn synonym(s)   *rel* related word(s)

ant antonym(s)   *con* contrasted word(s)

idiom idiomatic equivalent(s)

‖ use limited; if in doubt, see a dictionary

syn sing, squeak, squeal; *compare* INFORM 3
rel inform (on); divulge, reveal; confess
idiom spill one's guts, spill the beans, tell all
7 to give a talk < he *talks* to community groups on ecology >
syn address, lecture, prelect, speak
rel declaim, harangue, hold forth, perorate, speechify, spout
talk (into) *vb syn* see INDUCE 1
talk *n* **1** *syn* see SPEECH 1
2 *syn* see CONVERSATION 2
3 *syn* see CHAT 2
4 a formal or prearranged discussion, exchange, or negotiation usually of a political nature < summit *talks* on nuclear arms >
syn conference, meeting, parley, powwow
rel dialogue, discussion, exchange; negotiation; deliberation
5 *syn* see REPORT 1
6 *syn* see SPEECH 2
rel spiel; conference, discussion
talkative *adj* given to talk or talking < a *talkative*, sociable man >
syn babblative, chatty, gabby, garrulous, loose-lipped, loose-tongued, loquacious, mouthy, multiloquent, multiloquous, talky, tonguey; *compare* GLIB
rel articulate, eloquent, fluent; vocal, voluble; buzzy, gossipy
con closemouthed, laconic, reserved, reticent, uncommunicative; speechless
ant silent
talkee–talkee *n syn* see CHATTER
talky *adj syn* see TALKATIVE
tall *adj syn* see HIGH 1
rel high-reaching, sky-high, skyscraping
idiom higher than a cat's back
con abbreviated, truncated; low
ant short
tally *n syn* see SCORE 5
tally *vb* **1** *syn* see INVENTORY
2 *syn* see COUNT 1
3 *syn* see AGREE 4
rel equal, match; balance, complement
con conflict (with), differ (from), disagree (with)
tame *adj* docilely tractable < a *tame* lion >
syn domestic, domesticated, domitae naturae, subdued, submissive
rel broken (in), ‖busted, housebroken, trained; amenable, biddable, docile, obedient, tractable; pliable, pliant; meek, mild
idiom gentle as a lamb
con fierce, savage, tameless; undomesticated, untrained; unbridled, unbroken
ant untamed, wild
tame *vb syn* see DOMESTICATE
tamp *vb syn* see CRAM 1
rel fill up (*or* in), plug up; concentrate
tamper (with) *vb* **1** *syn* see BRIBE
2 *syn* see MEDDLE
rel interpose, intervene; doctor, manipulate
tang *n syn* see TASTE 3
rel bite, nip, piquancy, twang; aroma, pungency; spiciness, tanginess
tangible *adj* **1** capable of being perceived especially by the sense of touch < primitives who find *tangible* expression of divinity in idols >
syn palpable, tactile, touchable; *compare* PERCEPTIBLE
rel corporeal, physical; embodied, material, real, substantial
con ethereal, spiritual, unreal
ant intangible
2 *syn* see MATERIAL 1
3 *syn* see PERCEPTIBLE
rel distinct, evident, manifest, obvious, patent, plain
con clouded, cloudy, imperceptible, indistinct, unclear
ant intangible
tangle *vb* **1** *syn* see INVOLVE 1
idiom make a party to
ant untangle
2 *syn* see CATCH 3
ant untangle
3 *syn* see ENTANGLE 1
rel foul up, mix up
4 *syn* see COMPLICATE
ant untangle
tangle *n syn* see MAZE 1

tanked *adj syn* see INTOXICATED 1
tank town *n syn* see BURG
tank up *vb syn* see DRINK 3
tantalize *vb syn* see WORRY 1
rel badger, bait; frustrate
tantamount *adj syn* see SAME 2
rel alike, like, uniform; selfsame, very
idiom as much as to say
tap *n* **1** *syn* see FAUCET
2 *syn* see BAR 5
tap *vb syn* see DRAIN 1
tap *vb* **1** to strike or hit audibly and usually lightly < *tapped* her pencil on the desk >
syn bob, knock, rap, tunk
rel bang, beat, hammer, hit, pound, smite, strike, thud, thump
2 *syn* see DESIGNATE 2
tapa *n syn* see SNACK
taper *vb syn* see DECREASE
taper off *vb syn* see DECREASE
taproom *n syn* see BAR 5
tapster *n syn* see BARTENDER
tar *n syn* see MARINER
tar *vb syn* see TAINT 1
taradiddle *n syn* see LIE
tardy *adj* not arriving, occurring, or done at the set, due, or expected time < be *tardy* for school >
syn behindhand, belated, late, lated, overdue, unpunctual
rel delayed, detained; dilatory, laggard, slow; delinquent
con beforehand, early; convenient, opportune, seasonable, timely; precise, punctilious
ant prompt, punctual
target *n* **1** an object of ridicule, attack, or abuse < made him the chief *target* of political satire >
syn butt, mark, sitting duck
rel victim; fall guy, scapegoat, whipping boy
2 *syn* see AMBITION 2
3 *syn* see USE 4
tariff *n* **1** *syn* see TAX 1
2 *syn* see PRICE 1
‖**tarnation** *adj syn* see UTTER
tarnish *vb* **1** *syn* see DULL 1
2 *syn* see SOIL 2
rel contaminate, defile, pollute, stain, taint
con clean, cleanse; shine (up)
ant polish
3 *syn* see INJURE 1
4 *syn* see TAINT 1
rel defame, disgrace, embarrass; slander
tarpaulin *n syn* see MARINER
tarriance *n syn* see SOJOURN
tarry *vb* **1** *syn* see DELAY 2
rel falter, flag
2 *syn* see STAY 2
rel dawdle; sojourn
3 *syn* see VISIT 3
tart *adj syn* see SOUR 1
rel piquant, pungent
ant flat
tart *n syn* see DOXY 1
Tartarean *adj syn* see INFERNAL 1
Tartuffe *n syn* see HYPOCRITE
Tartuffery *n syn* see HYPOCRISY
Tartuffism *n syn* see HYPOCRISY
task *n* **1** a piece of work assigned or to be done < laboratory *tasks* assigned to chemistry students >
syn assignment, chare, chore, devoir, duty, job, stint
rel enterprise, project, undertaking; errand, labor, toil, work; charge, function, mission, office, province; business, calling, employment, occupation, vocation
2 a necessary undertaking that is usually difficult, dull, disagreeable, or problematic < deciphering his handwriting is a real *task* >
syn chore, effort, job, taskwork
rel burden, onus, strain, tax; bother, headache, nuisance, pain, trouble
idiom a hard (*or* long) row to hoe
con child's play, cinch, duck soup, picnic, ‖pipe, sinecure, snap
3 *syn* see LOAD 3

task *vb syn* see BURDEN
taskmaster *n syn* see SLAVE DRIVER
taskwork *n syn* see TASK 2
taste *vb syn* see FEEL 2
  idiom be exposed to, run up against
taste *n* **1** *syn* see HINT 2
  rel bit, sample, sampling
  2 *syn* see APPETITE 1
  3 the property of a substance which makes it perceptible to the gustatory sense <children often dislike the *taste* of olives>
  syn flavor, relish, sapidity, sapor, savor, smack, tang
  4 a liking for or enjoyment of something because of the pleasure it gives <had a *taste* for fast cars>
  syn gusto, heart, palate, relish, zest
  rel appreciation, comprehension, understanding; partiality, predilection, prepossession; disposition, inclination, predisposition
  con dislike, disrelish; allergy, aversion, repugnance, repulsion
  ant antipathy; distaste
  5 *syn* see APPETITE 3
  ant distaste
  6 the power or practice of discerning and enjoying whatever constitutes excellence (as in the fine arts) <a room whose decoration reflected her exquisite *taste* >
  syn tastefulness
  rel correctness; finesse, polish, refinement; elegance, grace
  con gracelessness, inelegance, unrefinement; incorrectness, vulgarity
  ant tastelessness
tasteful *adj* **1** *syn* see PALATABLE
  rel rich
  ant savorless, tasteless
  2 *syn* see QUIET 4
  ant tasteless
tastefulness *n syn* see TASTE 6
  ant tastelessness
tasteless *adj* **1** *syn* see UNPALATABLE 1
  rel bland, dull, stale, vapid; unflavored; uninteresting
  con flavorful, pleasing
  ant tasteful, tasty
  2 *syn* see BARBARIC 1
  rel inelegant, unpolished, unrefined
  idiom in bad taste
  ant tasteful, tasty
tasty *adj* **1** *syn* see PALATABLE
  idiom fit for a king
  con unsavory; bland, flavorless, unpalatable
  ant savorless, tasteless
  2 *syn* see QUIET 4
  ant tasteless
‖**tats** *n pl* *syn* see DICE
‖**tatter** *vb syn* see HURRY 2
tatterdemalion *n syn* see RAGAMUFFIN
tattered *adj* **1** *syn* see RAGGED
  2 *syn* see SHABBY 1
tatters *n pl* *syn* see RAGS 1
tattle *vb syn* see GOSSIP
  idiom tell tales out of school
tattle *n syn* see REPORT 1
tattler *n syn* see INFORMER
tattletale *n syn* see INFORMER
tatty *adj syn* see CHEAP 2
taunt *vb syn* see RIDICULE
  rel banter, chaff; provoke; upbraid; disdain, scorn; affront, insult, offend, outrage
taut *adj syn* see TIGHT 3
  rel firm, trim; stretched
  con flabby; relaxed
  ant slack
tautology *adj syn* see VERBIAGE 1
  rel reiteration, repetition, repetitiousness; padding
tavern *n* **1** *syn* see BAR 5
  2 *syn* see HOTEL
tavern car *n syn* see PARLOR CAR
taverner *n syn* see SALOONKEEPER
tawdry *adj syn* see GAUDY
  rel common, sleazy; flaring, screaming
tax *vb* **1** *syn* see BURDEN
  rel overtax

  idiom press hard upon, tax the strength of, weigh heavy on (or upon)
  2 *syn* see ACCUSE
tax *n* **1** a charge usually of money imposed by authority upon persons or property for public purposes <federal, state, and local *taxes* bear heavily on the thrifty >
  syn assessment, ‖cess, duty, impost, levy, tariff
  rel tithe, tribute; boodle, boondoggle, giveaway, pork barrel
  2 *syn* see LOAD 3
  rel difficulty, strain; demand, imposition
taxi *n syn* see TAXICAB
taxicab *n* an automobile that carries passengers for a fare <took a *taxicab* from the airport to his hotel >
  syn cab, hack, taxi
  rel ‖crawler, nighthawk
taxing *adj syn* see ONEROUS
  rel wearing; tedious, troublesome
TB *n syn* see TUBERCULOSIS
‖**tea** *n syn* see MARIJUANA
teach *vb* to cause to acquire knowledge or skill <*teach* a child to read >
  syn discipline, educate, instruct, school, train
  rel communicate, impart; implant, inculcate, instill; edify, enlighten, indoctrinate; fit, ground, prepare, rear; drill, exercise, practice; coach, tutor; lesson
  idiom give instruction
teaching *n syn* see EDUCATION 1
teachy *adj syn* see DIDACTIC
tear *vb* **1** to separate (one part of a substance or object from another) forcibly <*tore* a chunk from the loaf on the table>
  syn cleave, rend, rip, rive, split
  rel cut, gash, incise, slash, slit; devil, pull (apart), rift, sever, sunder; ribbon, shred; break, crack, rupture; damage, impair, injure
  2 *syn* see EXTRACT 1
  3 *syn* see RUSH 1
  4 *syn* see COURSE
tear *n syn* see BINGE 1
tear down *vb* **1** *syn* see DESTROY 1
  ant build up
  2 *syn* see MALIGN
  ant build up
teardrops *n pl* *syn* see TEARS
tearful *adj* flowing with or accompanied by tears <*tearful* entreaties >
  syn lachrymose, teary, weeping, weepy
  rel lamenting, mournful; sniveling; bawling, blubbering, crying, sobbing
  con dry-eyed
  ant tearless
tearing *adj syn* see EXCRUCIATING
tear–jerking *adj syn* see SENTIMENTAL
tears *n pl* a profuse secretion of saline fluid that overflows the eyelids and dampens the face <a blow that brought *tears* to his eyes >
  syn teardrops, water
teary *adj syn* see TEARFUL
  ant tearless
tease *vb syn* see WORRY 1
  rel disturb, importune
  idiom give a bad time
teaser *n syn* see STRIPTEASER
tease up *vb syn* see TOUCH UP
‖**tec** *n syn* see DETECTIVE
teched *adj syn* see INSANE 1
technique *n syn* see METHOD 1
tedious *adj* **1** *syn* see IRKSOME
  2 *syn* see ARID 2
  rel dragging, mortal, slow, tiresome
tedium *n* a state of dissatisfaction and weariness <incessant routine without variety breeds *tedium* >
  syn boredom, doldrums, ennui, yawn

---

rel irksomeness, tediousness, tiresomeness, wearisomeness; dullness, monotony
con enlivenment, interest, invigoration, refreshment
teem *vb* to be abundantly stocked or provided < rivers *teeming* with fish >
syn abound, crawl, flow, pullulate, ‖sny, swarm
rel bristle, bustle; cram, crowd, jam, pack; overbrim, overflow, overrun
con lack, want
teem *vb syn* see POUR 3
teeming *adj syn* see ALIVE 5
rel multitudinous, populous, pregnant; bristling
con rare, sparse, uncommon; empty, lacking, void, wanting
teensy *adj syn* see TINY
teensy–weensy *adj syn* see TINY
teenty *adj syn* see TINY
teeny *adj syn* see TINY
teeny–weeny *adj syn* see TINY
tee off *vb syn* see BEGIN 1
teeter *vb* to progress (as by walking) unsteadily < *teetered* along on 4-inch heels >
syn falter, lurch, stagger, ‖stammer, stumble, topple, totter, wobble; *compare* LURCH 2, SEESAW
rel sway, weave
teethy *adj syn* see TOOTHY 1
teetotal *adj syn* see DRY 3
tehee *vb syn* see LAUGH
telephone *vb* to communicate with (a person) by telephone < *telephoned* him yesterday >
syn ‖buzz, call, phone, ‖ring (up)
idiom ‖get (one) on the horn, give (one) a buzz (*or* ring)
telestic *adj syn* see MYSTICAL 1
tell *vb* **1** *syn* see COUNT 1
2 *syn* see SAY 1
rel communicate, convey, impart
3 *syn* see REVEAL 1
rel recite, recount, rehearse, relate; acquaint, apprise, inform
4 *syn* see INFORM 2
5 *syn* see COMMAND
6 *syn* see WEIGH 3
telling *adj syn* see VALID
rel power-packed; influential, weighty; significant, striking
tell off *vb syn* see SCOLD 1
rel call down; denounce
idiom give (one) a piece of one's mind, tell (one) a thing or two, tell (one) where to get off
telltale *n* **1** *syn* see GOSSIP 1
2 *syn* see HINT 1
tellurian *adj syn* see EARTHLY 1
telluric *adj syn* see EARTHLY 1
temblor (*or* **tremblor**) *n syn* see EARTHQUAKE
temerarious *adj syn* see ADVENTUROUS
rel heedless, imprudent, incautious, injudicious
temerity *n* conspicuous or flagrant boldness (as in speech, behavior, or action) < had the *temerity* to order an attack when hopelessly outnumbered >
syn assurance, audacity, brashness, hardihood, hardiness, nerve
rel daring, foolhardiness, heedlessness, rashness, recklessness, venturesomeness; impetuosity, precipitateness; impertinence, intrusiveness
con deliberation, judgment, judiciousness, prudence; heed, heedfulness
ant caution
temper *vb syn* see MODERATE 1
rel dilute, season; ease, pacify, soften; adjust, modify; curb, tune down
idiom take the edge off
temper *n* **1** a general or prevailing quality or characteristic (as of moral or social attitudes and behavior) < riots reflected the *temper* of the times >
syn mood, spirit, timbre, tone
rel atmosphere, aura, climate; orientation, outlook; disposition, drift, leaning, tendency, trend; character, nature, peculiarity
2 *syn* see DISPOSITION 3
rel condition, posture, state; attribute, property, quality; style, type, way
idiom turn of mind
3 *syn* see MOOD 1

idiom frame (*or* state) of mind
4 an outbreak or display of anger < a childish fit of *temper* >
syn passion
rel anger, fury, ire, rage; conniption, fit, outburst, tantrum
temperament *n syn* see DISPOSITION 3
rel mentality, mind; kind, type, way
idiom inner nature
temperamental *adj* **1** *syn* see MOODY
2 *syn* see INCONSTANT 1
ant steady
temperance *n* **1** an avoidance of extremes (as in action, thought, or feeling) < a man who knew no *temperance* in his opinions >
syn measure, moderateness, moderation
rel reasonableness; constraint, restraint
idiom happy medium
con extremeness, radicalness; excess, excessiveness; immoderateness, immoderation, unconstraint, unreasonableness, unrestraint
ant intemperance, intemperateness
2 strict habitual and usually complete self-denial in the gratification of appetites or passions < an ascetic who practiced complete *temperance* >
syn abstinence, continence, sobriety
rel abnegation, eschewal, forbearance, forgoing, refrainment, sacrifice, self-denial, self-deprivation; control, restraint, self-control, self-discipline; asceticism, austerity, mortification
con intemperance, intemperancy, intemperateness, prodigality
ant excess
temperate *adj* **1** *syn* see MODERATE 2
rel constant, equable, even, steady; checked, curbed, regulated, restrained
ant intemperate
2 *syn* see ABSTEMIOUS
rel indulgent; self-indulgent
con intemperate; dissipated, prodigal, profligate
ant excessive
3 *syn* see CONSERVATIVE 2
4 *syn* see SOBER 3
temperish *adj syn* see IRASCIBLE
tempersome *adj syn* see ILL-TEMPERED
tempestuous *adj syn* see WILD 6
rel tumultuous, unbridled, unrestrained, violent
ant calm, quiet
temple *n syn* see HOUSE OF WORSHIP
tempo *n* rate of performance or delivery < increased sales and production *tempo* >
syn pace, time; *compare* SPEED 2
rel speed; momentum
temporal *adj* **1** *syn* see MATERIALISTIC
ant nontemporal
2 *syn* see PROFANE 1
rel material, physical; nonsacred, nonspiritual, unhallowed, unsanctified, unspiritual
con celestial, heavenly
ant spiritual
temporary *adj* lasting, continuing, or serving for a limited time < was *temporary* president of the company for nine months >
syn acting, ad interim, interim, pro tem, pro tempore, supply; *compare* TRANSIENT
rel alternate, substitute; interimistic, provisional, provisory; jackleg, make-do, makeshift, stopgap
ant permanent
tempt *vb syn* see LURE
rel provoke, rouse; court, invite, solicit, vamp, woo
idiom whet the appetite
con discourage; dissuade; repel, repulse, revolt
temptation *n syn* see LURE 2
tempting *adj syn* see ENTICING
rel appetizing, mouth-watering; provoking, rousing, tantalizing
con repellent, repulsive
ant untempting
temptress *n syn* see SIREN
ten *n syn* see BREAK 4
tenable *adj* **1** capable of being defended against attack < the platoon's position was no longer *tenable* >
syn defendable, defensible
rel impregnable, secure
con insecure, vulnerable; defenseless, helpless, unprotected; dangerous, precarious, risky

ant untenable
2 syn see JUSTIFIABLE
rel believable, credible, maintainable, plausible
con indefensible, inexcusable, unbelievable, unjustifiable
ant untenable

tenacious *adj* **1 syn** see STRONG 2
rel bulldogged, bulldoggish, bulldoggy, dogged, obstinate, pertinacious, stubborn; resolute, steadfast, true; persevering, persisting
2 syn see VISCOUS
rel cohesive; tacky; sticky
3 syn see FAST 4
con lax, slack

tenant *vb syn* see INHABIT

tenantable *adj syn* see LIVABLE 1
idiom fit to live in
con uninhabitable

tend *vb* **1 syn** see TILL
2 to supervise or take charge of < employed a girl to *tend* the children each day >
syn attend, care (for), mind, watch
rel cherish, cultivate, foster, minister, nurse, nurture, serve; defend, guard, protect, safeguard, shield; supervise
idiom look after, see after, see to, take care of, take under one's wing
con disregard, ignore, neglect

tend *vb* **1** to have or exhibit an inclination or tendency < he *tends* to praise people too highly >
syn incline, lean, look; *compare* INCLINE 3
idiom be disposed
2 syn see CONTRIBUTE 2

tendency *n* **1** a movement or course having a particular direction and character < a growing *tendency* to underestimate the potential strength of that nation >
syn current, drift, run, tenor, trend
rel curve, inclination, leaning, propensity; turn; shift; custom, habit, usage, way
2 syn see LEANING 2

tendentious *adj syn* see BIASED 2

tender *adj* showing or expressing affectionate interest in another < his mother was very *tender* with her wayward son >
syn compassionate, kindhearted, responsive, softhearted, sympathetic, warm, warmhearted
rel gentle, lenient, mild, soft, yielding; considerate, solicitous, thoughtful; affectionate, fond, loving; benevolent, charitable, humane, mild; commiserative; forgiving, merciful, tolerant
con callous, hard, harsh; inhumane, uncharitable, unfeeling
ant rough, severe

tender *vb syn* see OFFER 1
rel propose, purpose, submit, suggest

tenderfoot *n syn* see NOVICE

tenderloin *n syn* see RED-LIGHT DISTRICT

tenebrific *adj syn* see GLOOMY 3

tenebrous *adj* **1 syn** see DARK 1
2 syn see OBSCURE 3

tenement *n syn* see APARTMENT 1

tenet *n syn* see DOCTRINE
rel belief, conviction, persuasion, view

tenor *n* **1** the course of thought that is retained through something spoken or written < the *tenor* of the book is first expressed in the introduction >
syn drift, purport, substance; *compare* BODY 3, MEANING 1, SUBSTANCE 2
rel intent; inclination, trend; mood, tone; core, gist, meat, stuff
2 syn see TENDENCY 1

tense *adj* **1 syn** see TIGHT 3
rel strained, stretched
ant relaxed
2 feeling or showing nervous tension < the soldiers were *tense* as they waited for the order to advance >
syn edgy, nervy, restive, uneasy, uptight
rel queasy; jittery, rusty, unquiet; anxious, concerned, overanxious
con easy; calm, cool, ‖loose, placid, unconcerned; firm, nerveless, unshaken
ant relaxed

tension *n* **1 syn** see STRESS 1
rel tautness, tenseness, tightness

idiom stress and strain
ant relaxation
2 emotional strain < was suffering from nervous *tension* >
syn unease, uptightness
rel strain, stress; anxiety, nerves, nervousness, uneasiness; agitation, discomfort, disquiet, misease

ten–strike *n syn* see SMASH 6

tent *vb syn* see CAMP

tentative *adj* **1 syn** see CONDITIONAL 1
rel acting, ad interim, makeshift, temporary; probationary; experimental, test, trial
con conclusive, decisive, definitive
ant final
2 syn see VACILLATING 2
rel disinclined, reluctant

tenue *n syn* see BEHAVIOR

tenuous *adj* **1 syn** see THIN 2
2 syn see THIN 1
rel aerial, airy, ethereal, fine
con abundant
ant dense
3 having little substance or strength and usually not firmly based < only a *tenuous* link in the chain of evidence >
syn feeble, insubstantial, unsubstantial; *compare* IMPLAUSIBLE
rel flimsy, weak; insignificant
con significant, sound, strong
ant substantial

tenure *n syn* see HOLD

tepid *adj* **1** moderately warm < a *tepid* bath >
syn lukewarm, milk-warm, warmish
rel mild, temperate, warm
con cold, cool, freezing, frozen; heated, hot, steaming
2 lacking in animation, force, passion, conviction, or commitment < gave only a *tepid* endorsement to the candidate >
syn halfhearted, lukewarm, unenthusiastic; *compare* ARID 2
rel indifferent; colorless, dull, lifeless, unlively; feeble, marrowless, pithless, sapless, spiritless; dim, faint, forceless, weak
con animated, forceful; fiery, impassioned, passionate, spirited

tergiversate *vb* **1 syn** see DEFECT
idiom fall away from
2 syn see EQUIVOCATE 2
idiom beg the question

tergiversation *n* **1 syn** see DEFECTION
rel about-face, reversal, reverse; denial, disavowal, forswearing, renunciation, repudiation
2 syn see AMBIGUITY

tergiversator *n syn* see RENEGADE

tergiverse *vb* **1 syn** see DEFECT
2 syn see EQUIVOCATE 2

term *n* **1 syn** see LIMIT 1
rel terminus
2 a limited, definite, or measurable extent of time during which something exists, lasts, or is in progress < the office has a *term* of four years >
syn duration, span, time
rel phase; go, period, spell, stretch; hitch, tour, turn; standing
3 syn see WORD 2
4 terms *pl syn* see CONDITION 1
rel detail, item, particular, point; limit
5 terms *pl* mutual social relationship or relative position < fight on equal *terms* > < the two were on *terms* of great intimacy >
syn footing, standing
rel coequality, equipollence, status; equality, equivalence, par, parity; balance

term *vb syn* see NAME 1

termagant *n syn* see VIRAGO

termagant *adj syn* see TURBULENT 1

terminable *adj* liable to be terminated or subject to termination < marriage is a *terminable* institution >
syn determinable, endable
rel finite, limited; limitable

terminal *adj syn* see LAST
con beginning, starting

---

syn synonym(s)   *rel* related word(s)
ant antonym(s)   *con* contrasted word(s)
idiom idiomatic equivalent(s)
‖ use limited; if in doubt, see a dictionary

ant initial

terminate *vb* **1** *syn* see CLOSE 3
rel abolish, extinguish; discontinue, wind down
idiom put the lid on
ant initiate
2 *syn* see ADJOURN 2
3 *syn* see DISMISS 3
4 *syn* see QUIT 6

terminated *adj syn* see COMPLETE 4

terminating *adj syn* see LAST
ant initial

termination *n syn* see END 2
rel issue, outcome, ‖pay-off, result
con source; beginning, start
ant initiation

terminology *n* the specialized or technical terms and expressions peculiar to a field, subject, or trade < the *terminology* of the plastics industry >
syn cant, dictionary, jargon, language, lexicon, palaver, vocabulary; *compare* DIALECT 2
rel shoptalk; gibberish, gobbledygook

terminus *n syn* see END 2

terra firma *n syn* see EARTH 2

terrain *n* **1** the physical configuration and features of a tract of land < made an analysis of the *terrain* via aerial photos >
syn topography
rel contour, form, profile, shape
2 an area devoted to a specified activity < the whole county had become breeding and racing *terrain* >
syn territory, turf
3 *syn* see FIELD

terrene *adj* **1** *syn* see EARTHLY 1
2 *syn* see EARTHY 1

terrestrial *adj* **1** *syn* see EARTHLY 1
rel earthbound, prosaic; profane, secular, unspiritual
ant empyreal
2 *syn* see EARTHY 1

terrible *adj* **1** *syn* see FEARFUL 3
2 *syn* see HARD 6
3 *syn* see INTENSE 1
4 *syn* see GHASTLY 1

terribly *adv syn* see VERY 1

terrific *adj* **1** *syn* see FEARFUL 3
rel terrorizing; agitating, disquieting, upsetting
2 *syn* see MARVELOUS 2
rel magnificent, superb; rattling, screaming

terrified *adj syn* see AFRAID 1
rel horrified, shocked; terrorized; frozen, paralyzed
con unfearful, unfearing, unfrightened
ant unafraid

terrify *vb syn* see FRIGHTEN
rel freeze, paralyze, petrify, stun, stupefy
idiom put the fear of God into, strike fear into the heart of

terrifying *adj syn* see GHASTLY 1
ant unterrifying

territory *n* **1** *syn* see AREA 1
2 *syn* see FIELD
3 *syn* see TERRAIN 2

terror *n syn* see FEAR 1
rel awe, fearfulness

terroristic *adj* characterized by or practicing terror as a means of coercion < used torture and other *terroristic* tactics to extract confessions >
syn gestapo
rel coercive, strong-arm; brutal, cruel, merciless; immoral, improper, unsanctioned

terrorize *vb* **1** *syn* see FRIGHTEN
idiom scare to death
2 *syn* see INTIMIDATE
idiom use gestapo tactics on

terse *adj syn* see CONCISE
rel close, compact; lean, precise; clear-cut, crisp, incisive; taut
con circuituous; pleonastic, redundant, repetitious

tersely *adv syn* see BRIEFLY
rel closely, compactly; crisply, incisively, precisely; abruptly, curtly
idiom in as few words as possible
ant prolixly

test *n syn* see EXPERIMENT
rel inspection, scrutiny; confirmation, corroboration, substantiation, verification

test *vb* **1** *syn* see TRY 1
rel assay, essay; confirm, substantiate, verify
idiom bring to test
2 *syn* see PROVE 1

test (out) *vb syn* see EXPERIMENT

test *adj syn* see EXPERIMENTAL 2
rel proving, testing, trying; probationary, speculative

testament *n syn* see TESTIMONY

testify *vb* **1** to serve as evidence of < present conditions *testify* to the accuracy of his predictions >
syn attest, point (to)
rel affirm; demonstrate, show; prove
con discredit, disprove, invalidate; confute, refute
2 to make a solemn declaration under oath for the purpose of establishing a fact (as in court) < *testified* against the defendant >
syn depone, depose, ‖mount, swear
idiom give testimony
3 *syn* see INDICATE 2

testimonial *n* **1** *syn* see TESTIMONY
rel indication, manifestation, show, sign, symbol, token
2 *syn* see CREDENTIALS
3 an expression of great approval and high esteem < a dinner was planned as a *testimonial* in his honor >
syn appreciation, salvo, tribute
rel salute; triumph; jubilee; commemoration, memorialization, remembrance
4 *syn* see MONUMENT 2

testimony *n* something that serves as tangible verification < the results are remarkable *testimony* to the accuracy of his predictions >
syn attestation, confirmation, evidence, proof, testament, testimonial, witness; *compare* INDICATION 3
rel demonstration, illustration; affirmation, corroboration, documentation, substantiation, verification

testy *adj syn* see IRASCIBLE
rel annoyed, exasperated, grouchy, irritable

tetchy *adj syn* see IRASCIBLE
rel ill-humored; cantankerous

tête-à-tête *n* a private conversation between two people < had a *tête-à-tête* with her in a quiet corner >
syn vis-à-vis
rel causerie, chat, coze; conversation, talk; argument, discussion

tetrad *n syn* see QUARTET

‖**tew** *vb syn* see WORRY 3

text *n syn* see SUBJECT 2
rel consideration, issue; fundamentals; idea

texture *n* **1** *syn* see ESSENCE 1
2 a basic often highly complex underlying scheme, structure, or pattern < war destroys the very *texture* of a society >
syn fabric, fiber, web
rel framework, structure; composition, constitution, makeup; pattern, scheme

thalassic *adj syn* see MARINE 1

thankful *adj syn* see GRATEFUL 1
con unappreciative, ungrateful
ant thankless, unthankful

thankless *adj* **1** not inclined to give thanks < a *thankless* guest >
syn unappreciative, ungrateful, unthankful
rel self-centered; careless, heedless, thoughtless; unappreciative, ungrateful, unmindful
con appreciative, grateful, mindful; careful, heedful, thoughtful
ant thankful
2 not likely to obtain thanks < a *thankless* job >
syn unappreciated, ungrateful, unthankful
rel disagreeable, distasteful, unpleasant; miserable, wretched
con thankworthy

thanks *n pl syn* see GRACE 1

thanksgiving *n syn* see GRACE 1

thankworthy *adj syn* see WORTHY 1

thank-you-ma'am *n syn* see BUMP 3

that *adj* **1** being the other < we argued it this way and we argued it *that* way >
syn another
ant this

2 *syn* see SUCH 2

thaumaturgic *adj syn* see MAGIC

thaumaturgy *n syn* see MAGIC 1

thaw *vb syn* see LIQUEFY

theater *n syn* see DRAMA

theatral *adj syn* see DRAMATIC 1

theatric *adj syn* see DRAMATIC 1

theatrical *adj* 1 *syn* see DRAMATIC 1
2 having qualities resembling a stage play or an actor's performance < he slowly made an exaggerated *theatrical* bow >
syn dramatic
rel histrionic, melodramatic, staged; affected, artificial, exaggerated, mannered, unnatural

theft *n* the unlawful taking and carrying away of property without the consent of its owner < was found guilty of auto *theft* >
syn larceny, lift, pinch, purloining, steal, stealage, stealing, thievery, thieving, ‖touch
rel filching, pilferage, pilfering, swiping; robbery, robbing, ‖stouth, ‖stouthrief; ‖score

theme *n* 1 *syn* see SUBJECT 2
2 *syn* see ESSAY 2

then *adv* 1 at another time < science as it was taught *then* >
syn again, anon, when; *compare* BEFORE 2
rel before, formerly
2 *syn* see AGAIN 4
3 *syn* see THEREFORE

thence *adv* 1 *syn* see AWAY 1
2 *syn* see THEREFROM

thenceforth *adv* from that time forward < the island which was *thenceforth* to be their home >
syn thenceforward, thereafter; *compare* HENCEFORTH
idiom from then on

thenceforward *adv syn* see THENCEFORTH

theorem *n syn* see PRINCIPLE 1

theoretical *adj* 1 concerned principally with abstractions and theories < *theoretical* versus applied physics >
syn academic, closet, speculative
rel conjectural, hypothetical, notional, suppositional, unproved; analytical, problematical
con practical; factual; proved
ant applied
2 *syn* see ABSTRACT 1
rel idealized, ivory-tower
ant concrete

theorize *vb syn* see SUGGEST 4

theory *n* 1 a belief, policy, or procedure proposed or followed as the basis of action < an educational system that was based on the *theory* that men learn best by experience >
syn hypothesis, supposal; *compare* ASSUMPTION 2
rel base, basis, grounds, position, premise, understanding
ant practice
2 something taken for granted especially on trivial or inadequate grounds < her *theory* that the house was haunted >
syn conjecture, perhaps, speculation, suppose, supposition
rel guess, guesswork, surmise; feeling, hunch, impression, presentiment, suspicion
con assurance, certainty, knowledge

there *adv* to or into that place < they seldom go *there* anymore >
syn thither, thitherward, yon
rel yonder
ant here

thereafter *adv syn* see THENCEFORTH

thereby *adv* in consequence of that < lied to the jury, *thereby* negating his testimony >
syn therethrough; *compare* THEREFROM

therefore *adv* for this or that reason < I think, *therefore* I am >
syn accordingly, consequently, ergo, hence, so, then, thereupon, thus
rel thence, therefrom

therefrom *adv* from that thing, fact, or circumstance < public opinion and a policy deriving *therefrom* >
syn thence, thereof; *compare* THEREBY

thereof *adv syn* see THEREFROM

thereon *adv* on or upon that < knew both the text and commentary *thereon* >
syn thereupon
rel therein, thereof, thereto

therethrough *adv syn* see THEREBY

theretofore *adv* up to that time < *theretofore* obscure communities >
syn thereuntil
rel ‖afore, before, previously
idiom before then

thereuntil *adv syn* see THERETOFORE
idiom until then

thereupon *adv* 1 *syn* see THEREON
2 *syn* see THEREFORE

thesis *n* 1 a position assumed or a point made especially in controversy < his *thesis* about the assassination was arguable >
syn contention, contestation
rel point, position; argument; belief, opinion, sentiment(s), view(s)
2 *syn* see ASSUMPTION 2
3 *syn* see DISCOURSE 2
rel exposition; argument, argumentation

thespian *adj syn* see DRAMATIC 1

thespian *n syn* see ACTOR 1

thew *n syn* see MUSCLE 1

thick *adj* 1 *syn* see STOCKY
rel broad, wide; bulky, burly, husky; blubber, blubbery, massive, obese
con slender, slight, slim; lanky, spare; skeletal
2 *syn* see CLOSE 4
rel concentrated, crammed; localized
con dispersed, scattered
ant diffuse
3 *syn* see STUPID 1
4 *syn* see FAMILIAR 1
idiom hand in glove, thick as thieves
5 *syn* see IMPLAUSIBLE
idiom a little too thick

thick–bodied *adj syn* see STOCKY

thickhead *n syn* see DUNCE
rel ‖clot

thickheaded *adj syn* see STUPID 1

thickset *adj syn* see STOCKY
rel fleshy, portly

thickskull *n syn* see DUNCE
rel lout

thick–witted *adj syn* see STUPID 1

thief *n* one who steals < a *thief* took her money >
syn filcher, larcener, larcenist, nimmer, pilferer, prig, purloiner, stealer; *compare* ROBBER
rel burglar, cat burglar, cat man, housebreaker; hijacker, robber; ‖booster, ‖dip, lifter, shoplifter; nip, pickpocket

thieve *vb syn* see STEAL 1

thievery *n syn* see THEFT

thieving *adj syn* see LARCENOUS

thieving *n syn* see THEFT

thievish *adj syn* see LARCENOUS

thin *adj* 1 not thick, heavy, or broad (as in configuration or physique) < a *thin* body >
syn attenuate, reedy, slender, slight, slim, squinny, stalky, tenuous, twiggy; *compare* LEAN
rel lank, lanky, lathy, lean, macilent, spare; cadaverous, gaunt, pinched, skeletal, wasted; meager, puny, small, twiglike
con broad, wide; compact, dense, solid; heavy, massive; corpulent, fat, obese
ant thick
2 characterized by wide separation of component particles < *thin* air at high altitudes >
syn attenuate, attenuated, rare, rarefied, subtile, subtle, tenuous
rel diffuse, diluted, dispersed; fine, refined
con heavy, thick
ant dense
3 *syn* see DILUTE
4 *syn* see ACUTE 4
rel high-pitched
con low, low-pitched; guttural; deep
5 *syn* see IMPLAUSIBLE
rel vapid; transparent; questionable; untenable

---

syn synonym(s)   *rel* related word(s)
ant antonym(s)   *con* contrasted word(s)
idiom idiomatic equivalent(s)
‖ use limited; if in doubt, see a dictionary

idiom a bit thin
con believable, convincing, sound, substantial
thin *vb* **1** to make thin or thinner <a once powerful frame *thinned* by privation>
syn attenuate, extenuate, wiredraw
rel diminish, reduce; weaken
con broaden, enlarge; strengthen
ant thicken
2 to make or become less dense <the air *thinned* at high altitudes>
syn attenuate, rarefy
ant densify
3 *syn* see DILUTE
thing *n* **1** *syn* see AFFAIR 1
2 *syn* see OCCURRENCE
3 *syn* see ACTION 1
rel exploit, feat, stunt
4 whatever is apprehended as having actual, distinct, and demonstrable existence <there is a place for each *thing* in the lab>
syn article, object
rel entity, item
5 that which can be known as having existence in space or time <virtue is not a *thing*, but an attribute of a *thing*>
syn being, entity, individual, material, matter, object, stuff, substance
rel item, particular
con attribute, characteristic, property, quality
6 *syn* see ENTITY 1
ant nonentity, nonexistence
7 things *pl syn* see POSSESSION 2
8 things *pl syn* see PERSONAL EFFECTS
9 things *pl syn* see CLOTHES
10 *syn* see POINT 1
11 *syn* see FASHION 3
12 *syn* see FETISH 2
thingum *n syn* see DOODAD
thingumajig *n syn* see DOODAD
thingumbob *n syn* see DOODAD
thingummy *n syn* see DOODAD
think *vb* **1** to form an idea of something in the mind <try to *think* exactly how the accident happened>
syn conceive, envisage, envision, fancy, feature, image, imagine, project, realize, see, vision, visualize
rel consider, contemplate, study, weigh; appreciate, comprehend, understand; cerebrate, ideate; conjecture, guess, surmise
2 *syn* see UNDERSTAND 3
3 *syn* see CONJECTURE
4 *syn* see FEEL 3
rel estimate; regard
5 to use one's powers of conception, judgment, or inference <the power to *think* sets humans apart from other animals>
syn cerebrate, cogitate, deliberate, reason, reflect, speculate
rel consider, contemplate; brood, meditate, mull, muse, ponder, ruminate; intellectualize, logicalize, logicize, rationalize; conclude, deduce, infer, judge
idiom put on one's thinking cap, set one's brain to work, use one's head, use the old bean
think (out *or* over) *vb syn* see CONSIDER 1
think (over) *vb syn* see RECONSIDER
thinkable *adj* **1** capable of being thought about <concepts that are easy enough to be *thinkable*>
syn cogitable
rel imaginable, presumable, supposable; comprehendible, comprehensible
con unimaginable; incomprehensible, uncomprehensible
ant unthinkable
2 capable of being made actual <nationalism at this time would be scarcely *thinkable*>
syn conceivable, imaginable, supposable
rel likely, possible; convincing, plausible; feasible, practicable, practical
con inconceivable, unimaginable; impossible, unlikely; implausible; impractical, unfeasible
ant unthinkable
thinking *adj syn* see THOUGHTFUL 1
ant unthinking
third degree *n syn* see CROSS-EXAMINATION

third estate *n syn* see COMMONALTY
thirst *vb syn* see LONG
rel covet; desire, wish
thirsting *adj syn* see THIRSTY 1
thirsty *adj* **1** experiencing a desire for drink <the long hot walk had made him *thirsty*>
syn athirst, dry, thirsting
rel juiceless, parched, sapless
2 *syn* see DRY 1
3 *syn* see EAGER
idiom hungry for, itching for, wild for
ant sated, satiated
this and that *n, often* **this and thats** *pl syn* see SUNDRIES
thither *adv syn* see THERE
ant hither
thitherward *adv syn* see THERE
ant hitherward
thorny *adj* bristling with perplexities, points of controversy, or other conflicting elements <the *thorny* question of states' rights>
syn nettlesome, prickly, spiny
rel troublesome, vexatious; difficult; tricky
thorough *adj* **1** *syn* see EXHAUSTIVE
rel absolute
2 *syn* see CIRCUMSTANTIAL
thoroughbred *adj syn* see PUREBRED
con mixed, mongrel
thoroughfare *n syn* see WAY 1
thoroughgoing *adj* **1** *syn* see EXHAUSTIVE
2 *syn* see UTTER
thoroughly *adv* **1** *syn* see WELL 3
2 in a detailed and complete manner <*thoroughly* investigated the accusations>
syn completely, detailedly, exhaustively, in and out, inside out, up and down
idiom item by item, to the last detail
con casually, offhandedly, sketchily, superficially
ant cursorily
3 *syn* see VERY 1
4 *syn* see HARD 3
though *adv syn* see HOWEVER
though *conj* in spite of the fact that <*though* they know the war is lost, they continue to fight>
syn albeit, although, howbeit, much as, when, whereas, while
thought *n* **1** the act or process of thinking <sat immersed in deep *thought*>
syn brainwork, cerebration, cogitation, deliberation, reflection, speculation
rel contemplation; meditation, musing, pondering, rumination
2 *syn* see IDEA
thoughtful *adj* **1** characterized by or exhibiting the power to think <the doctor had a shrewd rather than a *thoughtful* face>
syn cogitative, contemplative, meditative, pensive, ‖pensy, pondering, reflecting, reflective, ruminative, speculative, thinking
rel analytical, calculating, logical, rational; earnest, grave, melancholy, serious, sober, studious; brainy, intellectual; deep, in-seeing, introspective
con irrational; dull, slow, stupid, unthinking; empty-headed, shallow, vacuous
ant thoughtless
2 *syn* see MINDFUL 2
3 mindful of others <the thank-you note was a *thoughtful* gesture>
syn attentive, considerate
rel anxious, careful, concerned, heedful, mindful, solicitous; chivalrous, civil, courteous, gallant, gracious, polite, well-bred
con careless, heedless, inattentive, negligent, remiss, unconcerned, unmindful, unthinking; inconsiderate; discourteous, impolite
ant thoughtless, unthoughtful
thoughtfully *adv syn* see WELL 2
rel courteously, politely, solicitously
con discourteously, impolitely; inconsiderately, heedlessly, unkindly
ant thoughtlessly, unthoughtfully
thoughtless *adj* **1** *syn* see RASH 1
2 *syn* see CARELESS 1
con mindful

ant thoughtful
3 syn see SHORT 5
rel discourteous, impolite, rude; selfish
ant thoughtful

thought–out *adj syn* see DELIBERATE 1
rel investigated; analyzed
idiom thought over (*or* through)

thousand *n syn* see SCAD

thrall *n syn* see BONDAGE

thralldom *n syn* see BONDAGE

thrash *vb* **1 syn** see BEAT 1
2 syn see WHIP 2
3 syn see WHIP 1
rel strike; paddywhack, ‖pail

thrashing *n syn* see DEFEAT 1

thrash out *vb syn* see DISCUSS 1

threadbare *adj* **1 syn** see SHABBY 1
rel damaged, impaired, injured; frayed, ragged; shopworn, time-worn, worn
idiom the worse for wear, worn to rags (*or* threads)
2 syn see TRITE
rel common, familiar; imitative, uncreative; set, stock; banal, corny
con fresh, new; different, novel, original, unconventional, unusual; memorable

threaten *vb* to announce or forecast impending danger or evil < bullies *threatening* the child with a beating >
syn menace
rel browbeat, bulldoze, cow, intimidate; augur, forebode, portend, presage; caution, forewarn, warn
idiom make (*or* utter) threats against

threatening *adj* **1 syn** see IMMINENT 2
rel impending; forthcoming, upcoming; close, near
2 syn see OMINOUS

threesome *n syn* see TRIAD

threshold *n syn* see VERGE 2

thrift *n syn* see ECONOMY
rel austerity, economizing; saving; parsimony
ant waste

thriftiness *n syn* see ECONOMY
ant thriftlessness

thriftless *adj syn* see IMPROVIDENT
ant thrifty

thrifty *adj* **1 syn** see FLOURISHING
rel blooming, burgeoning; growing
2 syn see SPARING
rel foresighted, prudent; conserving, preserving
con extravagant, improvident
ant wasteful

thrill *vb* to fill with emotions that stir or excite or to be so excited < an audience *thrilled* by the brilliant spectacle >
syn electrify, enthuse, send
rel animate, excite, galvanize, move, quicken, stimulate; arouse, inspire, rally, rouse, stir
idiom thrill to pieces (*or* to bits)
con bore, ennui, weary

thrill *n* sudden emotional stimulation, excitement, or enjoyment < they both got a *thrill* out of small-boat racing >
syn bang, boot, kick, wallop
rel excitement, lift, stimulation, titillation

thriller *n* a work of fiction or drama designed to hold the interest by use of a high degree of intrigue, adventure, or suspense < wrote cheap detective *thrillers* >
syn chiller, shocker, thriller-diller
rel gothic, mystery; dime novel, penny dreadful, shilling shocker

thriller–diller *n syn* see THRILLER

thrive *vb* **1 syn** see BOOM
rel come on, develop, grow; increase; prosper
con stagnate; fail; bust
2 syn see SUCCEED 3
rel advance, progress
idiom make a go, turn out well

thriving *adj* **1 syn** see FLOURISHING
rel blooming, growing; advancing, progressing
idiom going strong
con shriveling; dying
2 syn see SUCCESSFUL

thriving *n syn* see PROSPERITY 2

throb *vb syn* see PULSATE
rel thump; resonate

throe *n* **1 syn** see ATTACK 3
rel convulsion
2 syn see PAIN 1
rel stab

throne *n syn* see TOILET

throng *n syn* see CROWD 1
rel assemblage, assembly, collection, congregation, gathering; bunch, flock, group, pack

thronged *adj syn* see ALIVE 5
rel crawling

throttle *vb syn* see CHOKE 1
rel garrote

throttling *n syn* see REPRESSION 1

through *prep* **1 syn** see VIA 1
2 syn see VIA 2
3 syn see OVER 6
4 syn see ABOUT 4
idiom clear through

through *adv* **1** from beginning to end < the region has a mild climate the whole year *through* >
syn around, over, round, throughout
2 syn see OVER 5

through *adj* **1 syn** see DIRECT 2
con obstructed; interrupted
2 syn see COMPLETE 4
3 having no further value, strength, or resources < when he lost his voice, his singing career was *through* >
syn done for, finished, washed-up
rel ended; over
4 being at the very end of a course, concern, or relationship < was *through* with his wife >
syn done, washed-up
rel finished

through–and–through *adv syn* see DOWN 2

throughout *adv* **1 syn** see EVERYWHERE 1
2 syn see THROUGH 1

throughout *prep* **1 syn** see ABOUT 4
2 syn see DURING

throw *vb* **1** to cause to move swiftly through space by a propulsive movement or a propelling force < *throw* a ball to first base >
syn ‖bung, cast, fire, fling, heave, hurl, launch, pitch, sling, toss
rel ding, drive, impel, precipitate, shoot; project, propel, push, shove, thrust; flick, flip; ‖chuck, shy, tumble; lift, lob
2 to dislodge from one's seat especially in horseback riding < was *thrown* while taking a hurdle >
syn buck (off), pitch, unhorse, unseat
rel ding (off), fling (off)
3 syn see OVERCOME 1
4 syn see DON 1
5 syn see EXERT
6 syn see ADDRESS 3

throw away *vb* **1 syn** see DISCARD
ant salvage
2 syn see WASTE 2
con lay away, lay by, lay up

throw back *vb syn* see REVERT 2

throwback *n syn* see REVERSION 1

throw down *vb syn* see FELL 1
rel cast down

throw in *vb syn* see INTRODUCE 6
rel contribute

throwing away *n syn* see DISPOSAL 2
ant salvaging

throw off *vb* **1 syn** see RID
2 syn see SHAKE 5
3 syn see EMIT 2
rel disgorge, eject, exhaust, expel
4 syn see CONFUSE 2

throw out *vb* **1 syn** see EJECT 1

---

syn synonym(s) *rel* related word(s)
ant antonym(s) *con* contrasted word(s)
idiom idiomatic equivalent(s)
‖ use limited; if in doubt, see a dictionary

2 syn see DISCARD

3 syn see SAY 1

4 syn see CONFUSE 2

throw over *vb syn* see ABANDON 1

throw up *vb* **1** to construct or erect hastily and often carelessly <makeshift buildings *thrown up* almost overnight>

   syn jerry-build, run up

   rel roughcast, roughhew

   idiom slap together, throw together

   2 syn see VOMIT

thrum *vb syn* see HUM

   rel birr, purr

thrust *vb* **1 syn** see PUSH 1

   rel crowd, jam; bump, elbow, jostle, nudge, prod, shoulder

   2 to cause (as a pointed instrument) to penetrate forcibly <*thrust* the dagger through her heart>

   syn dig, drive, plunge, ram, run, sink, stab, stick

   rel jab, shove; impale; pierce; embed; put

thrust *n syn* see SUBSTANCE 2

thud *vb* to make a dull sound by or as if by striking a surface with something thick and heavy <heard footsteps *thudding* down the hall>

   syn clonk, clunk, thump

   rel tunk; hit, smite, strike; beat, pound

thug *n* **1** a person inclined or hired to treat another roughly, brutally, or murderously <was beaten and robbed by *thugs*>

   syn ‖gorilla, ‖hood, hoodlum, hooligan, ruffian, strong arm; *compare* TOUGH

   rel bully, ‖larrikan, plug-ugly, roughneck, rowdy, tough; punk; cutthroat, gangster, gunman, mobster; goon, hatchet man

   2 syn see TOUGH

thumb *vb syn* see HITCHHIKE

   idiom thumb a ride

thumb (through) *vb syn* see BROWSE

thump *vb syn* see THUD

   rel hammer, knock

thunder *n* the sound that follows a flash of lightning and is caused by sudden expansion of the air in the path of the electrical discharge <he was more afraid of *thunder* than of lightning>

   syn thunderclap, thundercrack, thundering

   rel fulmination

thunderbolt *n* a single discharge of lightning with the accompanying thunder <he was startled by the *thunderbolt*>

   syn bolt, thunderstroke

thunderclap *n syn* see THUNDER

thundercrack *n syn* see THUNDER

thundering *n syn* see THUNDER

thunderstroke *n syn* see THUNDERBOLT

thunderstruck *adj syn* see AGHAST 2

   rel bewildered, staggered; breathless, stunned

   idiom struck dumb

thus *adv* **1** in this or that manner <summoned his counselors and spoke *thus* to them>

   syn so, thus and so, thus and thus, thusly

   2 syn see THEREFORE

thus and so *adv syn* see THUS 1

thus and thus *adv syn* see THUS 1

thus far *adv syn* see HITHERTO 1

thusly *adv syn* see THUS 1

thwack *n syn* see BLOW 1

thwart *adj syn* see TRANSVERSE

thwart *vb syn* see FRUSTRATE 1

   rel curb, restrain, scotch; cross; foul up, gum up, queer; stymie

   con aid, assist, help, support; abet, encourage

‖tick *n syn* see INSTANT 1

ticket *n* **1** a slip giving information (as of ownership, identity, or price) <the price of the iron is on the *ticket*>

   syn label, tag

   rel card; slip; sticker

   2 a card of admission <theater *tickets*>

   syn carte d'entrée

   rel pass

   3 a list of candidates for appointment, nomination, or election <vote the party *ticket*>

   syn slate

   rel choice; lineup; list

   4 syn see BALLOT 1

5 syn see PASSPORT

ticklish *adj* **1 syn** see UNSTABLE 2

   2 syn see DELICATE 7

   rel critical

   3 syn see INCONSTANT 1

tick off *vb* **1 syn** see ENUMERATE 2

   2 syn see REPROVE

tidbit (or **titbit**) *n syn* see DELICACY

‖tiddly *adj syn* see INTOXICATED 1

tide *n syn* see FLOW

tidings *n pl syn* see NEWS

tidy *adj syn* see NEAT 2

   rel sleek, spruce

   ant untidy

tie *n* **1 syn** see BOND 3

   rel fastener, fastening; attachment

   2 syn see DRAW 4

tie *vb* **1** to make fast and secure <*tie* a bundle with strong cord>

   syn bind, tie up

   rel attach, fasten; connect, join, link; anchor, moor, rivet, secure; lash, truss (up); band, cinch, gird, rope

   con loose, loosen; disconnect

   ant untie

   2 syn see MARRY 2

   3 syn see HAMPER

   idiom tie hand and foot, tie one's hands

   ant untie

   4 syn see EQUAL 3

tier *n* **1 syn** see LINE 5

   rel layer

   2 syn see CLASS 1

tie up *vb* **1 syn** see TIE 1

   2 syn see HAMPER

tie–up *n syn* see ASSOCIATION 1

   rel linkup

tiff *n syn* see QUARREL

tiff *vb syn* see QUARREL

tiffany *adj syn* see FILMY

tight *adj* **1 syn** see FAST 4

   rel clasped; solid, steadfast

   con lax, limp; shaky

   ant loose

   2 syn see CLOSE 4

   ant loose

   3 fitting, drawn, or stretched so that there is no slackness or looseness <a *tight* drumhead>

   syn close, taut, tense

   rel skintight; constricted, contracted, drawn, tightened; inflexible, rigid, stiff

   con loosened, slack, unconstricted

   ant loose

   4 difficult to cope with, get through, or circumvent <a very *tight* diplomatic situation>

   syn arduous, rough, tricksy, trying

   rel difficult; exacting; tense; critical; punishing; distressing, disturbing, upsetting

   5 syn see STINGY

   6 syn see INTOXICATED 1

   idiom tight as a tick

tight *adv syn* see HARD 7

tightfisted *adj syn* see STINGY

   rel grudging, mean, shabby

tight–laced *adj syn* see PRIM 1

tight–lipped *adj syn* see SILENT 3

   idiom with one's lips sealed

tightly *adv syn* see HARD 7

tight–mouthed *adj syn* see SILENT 3

tightwad *n syn* see MISER

till *prep syn* see UNTIL

till *conj* up to the time when <be sure to wait *till* I come>

   syn until

till *vb* to prepare (soil) for the raising of crops <*till* the soil>

   syn cultivate, dress, ‖labor, tend, work

   rel harrow, hoe, mulch, plow, turn; plant, sow

tillable *adj syn* see ARABLE

   ant untillable

tilt *vb* **1 syn** see SLANT 1

   2 syn see SEESAW

tilt *n syn* see SLOPE
tilted *adj syn* see INCLINED 3
tilter *vb syn* see SEESAW
tilting *adj syn* see INCLINED 3
timber *n* **1** *syn* see FOREST
   2 a large squared or dressed piece of wood < roof *timbers* >
   syn balk, beam
   rel girder, rafter
timberland *n syn* see FOREST
timbre *n syn* see TEMPER 1
time *n* **1** *syn* see WHILE 1
   rel season
   2 *syn* see OCCASION 5
   3 *syn* see OPPORTUNITY
   idiom the proper moment
   4 *syn* see PERIOD 2
   5 *syn* see TERM 2
   6 *syn* see SEASON
   7 *syn* see TEMPO
   8 *syn* see SPELL 1
   ‖**9** *syn* see BINGE 1
time *vb* **1** to arrange or set the time of < *timed* his visits to coincide with her vacations >
   syn book, schedule
   rel plan, program, set up
   2 to ascertain or record the time, duration, or rate of < *timed* the car at 100 mph >
   syn clock
   idiom hold the clock on
time and again *adv syn* see OFTEN
timeless *adj* **1** *syn* see CONTINUAL
   2 *syn* see ETERNAL 4
timely *adv syn* see EARLY 1
timely *adj* **1** done or occurring at a suitable time < await a more *timely* moment >
   syn auspicious, favorable, opportune, propitious, prosperous, seasonable, timeous, well-timed
   rel appropriate, fit, fitting, meet, proper, suitable; likely, promising
   con improper, inappropriate, unfitting; inauspicious, inopportune, unfavorable, unpropitious, unsuitable; ill-timed
   ant untimely
   2 *syn* see PUNCTUAL 2
timeous *adj syn* see TIMELY 1
timetable *n syn* see PROGRAM 1
   rel table; plan
timeworn *adj* **1** *syn* see ANCIENT 1
   2 *syn* see TRITE
timid *adj* **1** *syn* see SHY 1
   rel humble; shrinking
   ant bold
   2 marked by or exhibiting a lack of boldness, courage, or determination < was too *timid* to ski >
   syn timorous, ‖timorsome, undaring
   rel gentle, mild, milk-toast, milky; cautious, chary, wary; jumpy, nervous, skittish; afraid, apprehensive, fainthearted, fearful; chicken, chickenhearted, henhearted, mouselike, mousy, pigeonhearted; cowardly, yellow; funky, panicky
   con audacious, brave, courageous, daring, doughty, fearless, intrepid, lionhearted, unafraid, valiant, valorous
   ant bold
   3 *syn* see VACILLATING 2
timorous *adj syn* see TIMID 2
   rel quailing, recoiling, shrinking; quivering, shivering, shuddering, trembling
   ant assured
‖**timorsome** *adj syn* see TIMID 2
tincture *n* **1** *syn* see COLOR 6
   2 *syn* see HINT 2
   rel smattering
tincture *vb syn* see TINT
   rel pigment; stain
ting *vb syn* see TINKLE 1
tinge *vb syn* see TINT
   rel streak
tinge *n* **1** *syn* see COLOR 1
   rel coloration, coloring, tincture; stain
   2 *syn* see HINT 2

tingle *vb* **1** *syn* see TINKLE 1
   rel chime
   2 *syn* see JINGLE
tinker *vb syn* see FIDDLE 2
   idiom play around
tinkle *vb* **1** to make a repeated light high-pitched ringing sound < wind-bells *tinkling* in the breeze >
   syn plink, ting, tingle
   rel clink, jangle, jingle
   2 *syn* see JINGLE
   3 *syn* see CHAT 1
tinsel *adj syn* see GAUDY
tint *n syn* see COLOR 1
   rel tincture, touch; coloration, pigmentation; dye, stain, wash
tint *vb* to color with a slight shade or stain < white blossoms *tinted* with pale pink >
   syn complexion, tincture, tinge
   rel color, dye; shade, touch (up); stain, wash
tintamarre *n syn* see DIN
tiny *adj* exceptionally or remarkably small < the first *tiny* buds of spring flowers >
   syn ‖bitsy, diminutive, dwarf, dwarfish, itsy-bitsy, itty-bitty, lilliputian, midget, miniature, minikin, minute, peewee, pint-size, pocket, pocket-size, pygmy, teensy, teensy-weensy, teenty, teeny, teeny-weeny, wee, weensy, weeny; *compare* SMALL 1
   rel minuscular, minuscule; infinitesimal, microscopic, minim
   con colossal, enormous, gigantic, immense, mammoth, vast
   ant huge
tip *n syn* see POINT 9
tip *vb syn* see SLANT 1
tip *vb syn* see TIPTOE
   rel creep, mince, pussyfoot, steal
tip (over) *vb syn* see OVERTURN 1
   idiom turn upside down
tip *n syn* see GRATUITY
tip *n* a piece of advice or confidential information given by one thought to have access to special or inside sources < gave him a *tip* on which horse would win >
   syn point, pointer, steer, tip-off
   rel advice; information; clue, cue, hint; forecast, prediction
   idiom a bit of inside advice, a bug in the ear, a word to the wise
tip–off *n syn* see TIP
tipped *adj syn* see INCLINED 3
tipple *vb syn* see DRINK 3
   idiom drown one's cares (*or* sorrows)
tipple *n syn* see LIQUOR 2
tippler *n syn* see DRUNKARD
tipster *n syn* see INFORMER
tipsy *adj syn* see INTOXICATED 1
   rel dazed, unsteady
tiptoe *vb* to walk or proceed quietly on or as if on the ends of the toes < *tiptoed* through the dark house >
   syn tip, toe
   rel creep, gumshoe, pussyfoot, steal
   con clomp, clump, stamp, stomp, stump
tirade *n* a violent, often protracted, and usually denunciatory speech or writing < lashed out with a vicious *tirade* of angry protest >
   syn diatribe, harangue, jeremiad, philippic
   rel rant, rodomontade, screed; abuse, invective, revilement, vituperation; censure, condemnation, denunciation; berating, tongue=lashing; lecture, sermon
tire *vb* **1** to deplete the strength and energy of < the plane trip *tired* him >
   syn drain, fatigue, jade, wear, wear down, weary; *compare* EXHAUST 4
   rel debilitate, enervate, enfeeble, sap, weaken; exhaust, wear out
   con brace (up), invigorate, strengthen; animate, energize, enliven, pep (up), quicken, stimulate, vitalize
   2 *syn* see BORE
   rel jade, wear; irk; disgust, nauseate, sicken
   idiom make one tired, put one to sleep

---

syn synonym(s)   *rel* related word(s)
ant antonym(s)   *con* contrasted word(s)
idiom idiomatic equivalent(s)
‖ use limited; if in doubt, see a dictionary

tired *adj* **1** being depleted of strength and energy <was too *tired* to go on>
  syn fatigued, jaded, wearied, weary, worn, worn down
  rel overtaxed, overworked; drained, run-down; ‖beat, ‖bushed, dog-tired, exhausted, fagged, frazzled, overworn, ‖pooped, ‖tucked up, tuckered, worn-out; collapsing, consumed, knocked out, prostrate, spent
  idiom worn to a frazzle
  con active, energetic, lively, strong, tireless
  ant rested; fresh, untired
  2 *syn* see SHABBY 1
  3 *syn* see FED UP
  rel annoyed, bothered, displeased, irked
  idiom having a bellyful of, having about enough of
  4 *syn* see TRITE
tiredness *n syn* see FATIGUE
  rel collapse, prostration
tireless *adj syn* see INDEFATIGABLE
  rel active, enthusiastic
  con inactive, listless, tired, unenergetic, unenthusiastic, weak
tiresome *adj syn* see IRKSOME
  rel dull; jading; burdensome, onerous, oppressive; difficult, hard
tiring *adj syn* see IRKSOME
Titan *adj syn* see HUGE
titanic *adj syn* see HUGE
title *n* **1** *syn* see CLAIM 1
  rel argument, ground, justification, proof, reason; desert, due, merit
  2 *syn* see NAME 1
title *vb syn* see NAME 1
titter *vb syn* see LAUGH
  rel twitter
  idiom laugh behind (*or* in) one's hand, laugh in one's beard
tittle *n syn* see PARTICLE
  rel fleck, flyspeck, speck; crumb, grain, scrap, snippet
tittle–tattle *n* **1** *syn* see CHATTER
  2 *syn* see REPORT 1
titubate *vb syn* see REEL 2
titular *adj syn* see NOMINAL
tizzy *n syn* see SNIT
to *prep* **1** in the direction of and as far as <was driving *to* the city>
  syn into
  rel toward
  ant from
  2 *syn* see AGAINST 2
  rel on, over, upon
  3 *syn* see BEFORE 1
  4 *syn* see UNTIL
  5 for the particular purpose of <a market study tailored *to* your needs>
  syn for
  idiom in contemplation (*or* consideration) of, with an eye to, with a view to
  6 in complement to <played Romeo *to* her Juliet>
  syn opposite
toad *n syn* see SNOT 1
toad *n syn* see SYCOPHANT
toadeater *n syn* see SYCOPHANT
toadier *n syn* see SYCOPHANT
toady *n syn* see SYCOPHANT
toady *vb syn* see FAWN
  rel follow, tag, tail, trail
toadying *adj syn* see FAWNING
toadyish *adj syn* see FAWNING
to–and–fro *n* **1** *syn* see HESITATION
  2 *syn* see QUARREL
toast *n syn* see DRINK 2
to–be *n syn* see FUTURE
tocsin *n syn* see ALARM 1
  rel sign, signal
today *adv* at the present time <youth *today* do not know what poverty is>
  syn now, nowadays, presently
  idiom in this day and age, these days
  con then, yesteryear
today *n syn* see PRESENT
todayish *adj syn* see PRESENT

to–do *n* **1** *syn* see COMMOTION 4
  2 *syn* see COMMOTION 3
toe *vb syn* see TIPTOE
tog (out *or* up) *vb syn* see DRESS UP 1
together *adv* **1** at one and the same time <events that occurred *together*>
  syn at once, coincidentally, coincidently, coinstantaneously, concurrently, simultaneously
  idiom all at once, all together
  ant separately
  2 in succession usually without intermission <was moody for days *together*>
  syn consecutively, continually, continuously, hand running, night and day, running, successively, unintermittedly, uninterruptedly
  idiom on end
  3 in or by combined action or effort <students and faculty protested *together*>
  syn conjointly, jointly, mutually
  rel collectively, concertedly, unanimously
  idiom in one breath, in the same breath, with one accord, with one voice
  ant separately
togetherness *n* **1** *syn* see ASSOCIATION 1
  2 *syn* see SOLIDARITY
‖toggle *vb syn* see DRESS UP 1
togs *n pl syn* see CLOTHES
toil *n syn* see WORK 2
  idiom sweat of one's brow, toil and trouble
toil *vb* **1** *syn* see LABOR 1
  2 *syn* see DRUDGE
  3 *syn* see PLOD 1
toil *n, usu* **toils** *pl syn* see WEB 2
toiler *n syn* see SLAVE 2
toilet *n* a fixture for defecation and urination
  syn ‖can, convenience, ‖donicker, head, john, johnny, latrine, lavatory, ‖loo, ‖pot, ‖potty, privy, ‖throne, water closet
  rel hopper
toilful *adj syn* see HARD 6
toilsome *adj syn* see HARD 6
toilsomely *adv syn* see HARD 8
token *n* **1** *syn* see INDICATION 3
  rel harbinger, omen, portent; characteristic, earmark; indicator, smack
  2 *syn* see REMEMBRANCE 3
  3 *syn* see EXPRESSION 3
  4 *syn* see PLEDGE 1
‖tokus *n syn* see BUTTOCKS
tolerable *adj* **1** *syn* see BEARABLE
  ant intolerable
  2 *syn* see RESPECTABLE 5
  3 *syn* see DECENT 4
  rel fair, goodish, OK, tidy
  idiom better than nothing, good enough
  ant intolerable
tolerably *adv syn* see ENOUGH 2
tolerance *n* **1** the capacity to bear something unpleasant, painful, or difficult <had always had a high *tolerance* to pain>
  syn endurance, stamina, toleration
  rel fortitude, grit, guts; strength, vigor; long-suffering, patience, sufferance; steadfastness, steadiness; opposition, resistance
  ant intolerance
  2 *syn* see FORBEARANCE 2
  rel liberality, liberalness, open-mindedness, permissiveness
  con narrow-mindedness; prejudice; dogmatism; bigotry
  ant intolerance
tolerant *adj* **1** *syn* see LIBERAL 3
  rel open-minded; permissive
  con narrow, narrow-minded; prejudiced; dogmatic; bigoted
  ant intolerant
  2 *syn* see FORBEARING
  rel benevolent, humane; condoning, excusing, forgiving, sympathetic, understanding
  con severe, stern; uncompromising, unforgiving, unsympathetic
  ant intolerant
tolerate *vb* **1** *syn* see ACCEPT 2
  rel condone, countenance; allow, consent (to), permit; have, hear (to)

2 *syn* see BEAR 10
  rel sustain
toleration *n* **1** *syn* see FORBEARANCE 2
  2 *syn* see TOLERANCE 1
toll *n* *syn* see EXPENSE 2
toll *vb* *syn* see LURE
toll *vb* *syn* see RING
‖**tomato** *n* *syn* see PROSTITUTE
tomb *n* *syn* see GRAVE
  rel box, coffin, ‖trough
tomb *vb* **1** *syn* see BURY 1
  ant untomb
  2 *syn* see ENTOMB 1
  ant disentomb, untomb
tomboy *n* a girl exhibiting boyish behavior <a *tomboy* who still rode, fished, and fought with her brothers>
  syn gamine, hoyden
  rel romp
tombstone *n* an inscribed memorial stone set at a place of interment <read the epitaph on the *tombstone* of her ancestor>
  syn footstone, grave marker, gravestone, headstone, ledger, monument
  rel memorial; cenotaph
tome *n* *syn* see BOOK 1
tomfool *n* *syn* see FOOL 1
tomfool *adj* *syn* see FOOLISH 2
tomfoolery *n* **1** *syn* see NONSENSE 2
  2 *syn* see PRANK
tommyrot *n* *syn* see NONSENSE 2
Tom o' Bedlam *n* *syn* see LUNATIC 1
Tom Thumb *n* *syn* see DWARF
ton *n* **1** *syn* see FASHION 3
  2 *syn* see SMART SET
tone *n* **1** *syn* see INFLECTION
  2 *syn* see VEIN 1
  3 *syn* see COLOR 1
  rel blend
  4 the state of a living body or any of its organs or parts in which the functions are healthy and performed with due vigor <diet and exercise contributed to his good muscle *tone*>
  syn tonicity, tonus
  rel health, healthiness; elasticity, resiliency; strength, vigor
  5 *syn* see TEMPER 1
  rel current, movement
  idiom (the) state of things
  6 *syn* see MOOD 1
toned down *adj* *syn* see SUBDUED 2
tongue *n* *syn* see LANGUAGE 1
tongue *vb* *syn* see SCOLD 1
tongue–lash *vb* *syn* see SCOLD 1
  idiom give one the rough side of one's tongue
tongue–tied *adj* *syn* see INARTICULATE 3
  con loose-lipped, loose-tongued
‖**tongue–walk** *vb* *syn* see SCOLD 1
  idiom give one the rough side of one's tongue
tonguey *adj* *syn* see TALKATIVE
tonic *adj* **1** increasing or restoring physical or mental tone <the *tonic* effect of a vacation>
  syn astringent, restorative, roborant
  rel invigorating, refreshing, renewing, strengthening; bracing, sharp
  con debilitating, enfeebling, weakening; enervating; exhausting, grueling, sapping
  2 *syn* see INVIGORATING
tonicity *n* *syn* see TONE 4
tonish *adj* *syn* see STYLISH
tonus *n* *syn* see TONE 4
tony *adj* *syn* see STYLISH
too *adv* **1** *syn* see ALSO 2
  2 *syn* see EVER 6
  rel exorbitantly, immoderately, unconscionably, unmeasurably
  3 *syn* see VERY 1
‖**toodle–oo** *interj* *syn* see GOOD-BYE
tool *n* **1** *syn* see IMPLEMENT
  rel machine, mechanism
  2 one used or manipulated by another to accomplish his purposes <had no intention of being used as a *tool* by either faction>

  syn cat's-paw, pawn, puppet, stooge
  rel agent, hireling, vehicle; chump, sucker
tool *vb* *syn* see DRIVE 5
toot *vb* *syn* see DECLARE 1
toot *n* *syn* see BINGE 1
toothful *n* *syn* see DRAM
toothsome *adj* *syn* see PALATABLE
  rel agreeable, pleasant, pleasing
toothy *adj* **1** having or showing prominent teeth <a wide *toothy* grin>
  syn teethy
  2 *syn* see PALATABLE
too–too *adj* *syn* see GENTEEL 3
  rel chichi
‖**tootsie** *n* *syn* see DOXY 1
top *n* **1** the highest point <hiked to the *top* of the mountain>
  syn apex, crest, crown, fastigium, peak, roof, summit, vertex
  rel acme, climax, culmination, height, pinnacle; cusp, head, point, tip
  con base, foot, sole; nadir
  ant bottom
  2 the outer or upper part <the *top* of the table>
  syn face, superficies, surface
  3 *syn* see BEST
  ant bottom
top *vb* **1** to remove or cut back the top of <*top* a tree>
  syn crop, detruncate, pollard, truncate
  rel clip, dock, prune, trim; curtail, shorten
  2 *syn* see SURPASS 1
  3 *syn* see SURMOUNT 3
top *adj* **1** of, relating to, or being at the top <the *top* floor of the house>
  syn apical, highest, loftiest, topmost, uppermost
  con bottommost, lowest
  ant bottom
  2 *syn* see EXCELLENT
  3 *syn* see MAXIMUM
top–drawer *adj* *syn* see EXALTED 1
tope *vb* *syn* see DRINK 3
toper *n* *syn* see DRUNKARD
Tophet *n* *syn* see HELL
topic *n* *syn* see SUBJECT 2
  rel proposition; issue
topless *adj* *syn* see LOFTY 6
toploftical *adj* *syn* see PROUD 1
toplofty *adj* *syn* see PROUD 1
  rel inflated, puffed; egotistic
  con crestfallen
topmost *adj* **1** *syn* see TOP 1
  ant bottommost
  2 *syn* see MAXIMUM
top–notch *adj* *syn* see EXCELLENT
top off *vb* *syn* see CLIMAX
topography *n* *syn* see TERRAIN 1
topple *vb* **1** *syn* see FALL 2
  2 *syn* see TEETER
  3 *syn* see OVERTURN 1
  4 *syn* see OVERTHROW 2
top–ranking *adj* *syn* see EXALTED 1
topsy–turviness *n* *syn* see CONFUSION 3
topsy–turvy *adj* **1** *syn* see UPSIDE-DOWN 1
  2 *syn* see UPSIDE-DOWN 2
  rel cockeyed, disarranged, disjointed, disordered, unhinged
torch *n* *syn* see INCENDIARY
toreador *n* *syn* see BULLFIGHTER
torero *n* *syn* see BULLFIGHTER
torment *vb* **1** *syn* see AFFLICT
  rel distress, trouble; hurt, pain, punish
  2 *syn* see MOLEST
tormented *adj* *syn* see DISTRAUGHT
tormenting *adj* *syn* see EXCRUCIATING
torn *adj* *syn* see LACERATED

---

syn synonym(s)   *rel* related word(s)
ant antonym(s)   *con* contrasted word(s)
idiom idiomatic equivalent(s)
‖ use limited; if in doubt, see a dictionary

tornado *n* a violent destructive whirling wind accompanied by a funnel-shaped cloud extending downward from a cumulonimbus cloud < the *tornado* caused extensive destruction >
   syn cyclone, twister; *compare* HURRICANE, WHIRLWIND 1

torpedo *n syn* see ASSASSIN

torpid *adj syn* see LETHARGIC
   rel dull, leaden, sodden; motionless, static; numb
   con lively; frisky, sprightly, vigorous; fast
   ant active

torpidity *n syn* see LETHARGY 1
   rel listlessness, passivity, stagnation

torpidness *n syn* see LETHARGY 1
   ant activeness

torpor *n syn* see LETHARGY 1
   rel stolidity; passivity
   ant activity; animation

torrent *n syn* see FLOOD 2
   rel flux, rush

torrid *adj* **1** *syn* see HOT 1
   idiom burning hot, hot enough to roast an ox
   ant arctic
   2 *syn* see IMPASSIONED
   rel sultry
   ant frigid

tort *n syn* see EVIL 3

tortuous *adj syn* see WINDING
   rel involute, vermiculate; cranky; involved

torture *vb* **1** *syn* see AFFLICT
   rel oppress, persecute, wrong; hurt, wound; maim, mangle, mutilate
   idiom put on the rack, put to torture
   2 *syn* see DEFORM

torturing *adj syn* see EXCRUCIATING

torturous *adj syn* see EXCRUCIATING

tory *n syn* see DIEHARD 1
   rel loyalist, traditionalist

tory *adj syn* see CONSERVATIVE 1

tosh *n syn* see NONSENSE 2

toss *vb* **1** *syn* see THROW 1
   2 to rise and fall often rhythmically or with alternate motions < a small boat *tossing* in heavy seas >
   syn heave, pitch, rock, roll; *compare* SEESAW
   rel bob; sway
   3 *syn* see DRINK 1
   4 *syn* see WRITHE 1
   idiom toss and turn

toss (around) *vb syn* see DISCUSS 1
   rel bandy (about)

tosspot *n syn* see DRUNKARD

tot *n syn* see DRAM

tot *vb syn* see ADD 2

total *adj* **1** *syn* see WHOLE 4
   rel overall; comprehensive, full, inclusive, plenary; teetotal
   ant partial
   2 *syn* see UTTER
   3 *syn* see TOTALITARIAN 1
   rel authoritative; absolute, arbitrary, despotic; omnipotent
   4 *syn* see TOTALITARIAN 2
   rel monopolistic
   5 concentrating and employing all resources on a single objective < a *total* offensive >
   syn all-out, full-blown, full-out, full-scale, totalitarian, unlimited
   rel out-and-out, unreserved, unrestricted
   con hampered, impeded, trammeled; restrained, restricted; stinted
   ant limited

total *n* **1** *syn* see WHOLE 1
   2 *syn* see BODY 5

total *vb* **1** *syn* see ADD 2
   2 *syn* see AMOUNT 1
   rel comprise, consist (of); stack up; equal, result (in), yield
   idiom mount up to, pile up to
   3 to make a total wreck of < *totaled* his car when he hit the wall >
   syn demolish, wreck; *compare* DESTROY 1
   rel crack up, smash

totalistic *adj syn* see TOTALITARIAN 1
   con democratic; individualistic

totalitarian *adj* **1** of or relating to centralized control by one autocratic leader or party considered to be infallible < Nazi Germany was a *totalitarian* state >
   syn authoritarian, total, totalistic; *compare* ABSOLUTE 4, DICTATORIAL
   con democratic, popular; constitutional
   2 having or exercising dictatorial powers often tending toward monopoly < antitrust legislation reversing the trend toward the *totalitarian* collectivism of big business >
   syn total
   3 *syn* see TOTAL 5

totalitarianism *n syn* see TYRANNY

totality *n* **1** *syn* see WHOLE 1
   2 *syn* see ENTIRETY 1
   3 *syn* see WHOLE 2
   rel configuration, form

totalize *vb syn* see ADD 2

totally *adv syn* see ALL 1

tote *vb syn* see CARRY 1
   rel cart, haul; shoulder

‖**tote** *n syn* see WHOLE 1

tote *vb syn* see ADD 2

totter *vb* **1** *syn* see TEETER
   rel shimmy
   2 *syn* see REEL 2
   rel blunder, stumble, trip; dodder, ‖dotter; flounder

touch *vb* **1** to probe with a sensitive part of the body (as a finger) so as to get or produce a sensation often in the course of examining or exploring < *touch* an iron to test its temperature >
   syn feel, finger, handle, palpate, paw
   rel brush, graze; caress, fondle, rub, stroke, toy (with); palm, thumb; examine, inspect, probe, scrutinize; investigate
   2 *syn* see ADJOIN
   3 *syn* see EQUAL 3
   4 *syn* see AFFECT
   rel arouse, stir; excite, quicken, stimulate
   idiom touch a chord
   5 *syn* see AMOUNT 2
   rel come (to), verge (on)

touch *n* **1** *syn* see CONTACT 1
   rel junction; communication
   2 an act of touching or feeling < woke her with a light *touch* on her hand >
   syn palpation, taction
   rel brush, pat, stroke; contact
   3 tactile sensitivity < a blanket soft to the *touch* >
   syn feel, tactility
   rel feeling
   4 a specified sensation conveyed through the tactile receptors < the velvety *touch* of a fabric >
   syn feel, feeling
   5 *syn* see HINT 2
   6 distinctive manner or method < this house needs a woman's *touch* >
   syn hand
   rel manner, style, way
   ‖**7** *syn* see THEFT

touchable *adj syn* see TANGIBLE 1
   ant untouchable

touch down *vb syn* see ALIGHT

touching *prep* **1** *syn* see AGAINST 2
   idiom up against
   2 *syn* see APROPOS

touching *adj* **1** *syn* see ADJACENT 3
   rel meeting; impinging; overlapping
   2 *syn* see MOVING 2
   rel compassionate, responsive, sympathetic, tender; piteous, pitiable, pitiful, tear-jerking

touch–me–not–ish *adj syn* see UNSOCIABLE

touchstone *n syn* see STANDARD 3
   rel check, test, trial; barometer, scale; demonstration, proof

touch up *vb* to improve or perfect by small additional strokes or alterations < *touch up* a picture >
   syn brush up, retouch, touch up
   rel improve, perfect, polish; do (up), fix (up)
   idiom put finishing touches on

touchy *adj* **1** *syn* see IRASCIBLE
   rel hypersensitive, oversensitive, sensitive, thin-skinned; temperamental, volatile; miffy

ant imperturbable
2 syn see DELICATE 7
rel dicey, risky, unpredictable; harmful, hazardous, unsafe
tough *adj* **1 syn** see STRONG 2
rel flinty, hard, unyielding; resistant, unbreakable, withstanding
idiom tough as leather (*or* nails)
con breakable; brittle; yielding
ant fragile
2 syn see VISCOUS
3 advocating a persistently firm course of action < a *tough* foreign policy >
syn hard-line, inflexible, uncompromising, unyielding
rel stiff, taut; fixed, confirmed, hard-shell, narrow, rigid; arbitrary, immutable, unalterable; hard-boiled, hardened, obdurate; harsh, procrustean, rigorous, severe, strict; drastic
con liberal, relaxed; compromising, flexible, laissez-faire, yielding
ant soft
4 having or exhibiting great physical endurance (as to strain, hardship, or labor) < the rigorous climate created a *tough* people >
syn hardy, rugged
rel conditioned, hard-bitten, hardened, seasoned, steeled; fit, healthy, lusty, robust, vigorous; stalwart, strong, sturdy
con delicate, fragile, frail, tender; half-hardy, puny; weakened
ant weak
5 syn see OBSTINATE
rel hardfisted, hardhanded, hardheaded, tough-minded
6 syn see HARD 6
ant soft
7 syn see ONEROUS
ant soft
8 frequented by rowdy or criminal elements < lived in a *tough* neighborhood >
syn bad, rough
rel disorderly, rowdy; dangerous, unsafe; ghetto, inner-city, underprivileged
con orderly, quiet, safe
tough (out) *vb* **syn** see ACCEPT 2
tough *n* a rough or unruly person often taking part in bullying or violent behavior < attacked by a gang of *toughs* >
syn ‖b'hoy, bullyboy, mucker, mug, plug-ugly, punk, rough, roughneck, rowdy, ruffian, thug, toughie, yahoo; *compare* BULLY 1, THUG 1
rel goon, hood, hoodlum, hooligan
toughen *vb* **syn** see HARDEN 2
rel develop, strengthen
ant weaken
toughie *n* **syn** see TOUGH
rel ‖heavy
tour *n* **1 syn** see SPELL
2 a journey in which one eventually returns to the starting point < made a quick *tour* of all the bars >
syn circuit, round, roundabout, round trip; *compare* TRIP 1
rel turn; circle tour
tour de force *n* **1 syn** see FEAT 2
2 syn see MASTERPIECE 1
tourist *n* one who makes a tour for pleasure or culture < *tourists* going through the castle >
syn rubberneck, sightseer, ‖tripper
rel day-tripper, excursionist; traveler; visitor
tout *n* **syn** see LOOKOUT 3
tout *vb* to overly publicize < was *touted* as the world's most modern shopping center >
syn ballyhoo, herald, trumpet
rel proclaim, publicize; plug, promote; acclaim, laud, praise
idiom praise to the skies
tow *vb* **syn** see PULL 2
rel propel; push
idiom take in tow
toward *adj* **syn** see GOOD 1
ant untoward
toward *prep* **1 syn** see APROPOS
2 syn see AGAINST 1
tower (above *or* over) *vb* **syn** see OVERLOOK 2
towering *adj* **1 syn** see LOFTY 6
rel altitudinous, high, tall; stratospheric
2 syn see SUPREME

3 syn see MONSTROUS 1
4 reaching a high point of greatness, intensity, or violence < a *towering* rage >
syn monumental, overwhelming
rel ‖crashing; overpowering; mind-blowing
con minor, petty, piddling, puny, trivial
5 syn see EXCESSIVE 1
towery *adj* **syn** see LOFTY 6
to wit *adv* **syn** see NAMELY
towner *n* **syn** see TOWNSMAN
townish *adj* of, relating to, or characteristic of a town or of urban life < enjoyed a fast-paced, competitive, *townish* life-style >
syn towny
rel city, metropolitan, urban
con bucolic, rural; isolated, lonely, solitary
townman *n* **syn** see TOWNSMAN
townsman *n* a town dweller < population composed mostly of *townsmen* and a few countrymen >
syn burgher, cit, citizen, towner, townman, towny
towny *n* **syn** see TOWNSMAN
towny *adj* **syn** see TOWNISH
tow–row *n* **syn** see COMMOTION 4
toxic *adj* **syn** see POISONOUS
ant nontoxic
toxicant *adj* **syn** see POISONOUS
toy *n* **1 syn** see KNICKKNACK
2 something for a child to play with < games, dolls, and other *toys* >
syn ‖die, ‖play-pretty, plaything, ‖pretty
toy *vb* **syn** see TRIFLE 1
rel disport, frolic, play, sport; fiddle (with), tease; caress, cosset, cuddle, dandle, pet
idiom fool (*or* mess) around with
trace *n* **1 syn** see TRACK 1
rel evidence, proof
2 syn see VESTIGE 1
rel mark, token
3 syn see HINT 2
trace *vb* **syn** see TRACK 1
track *n* **1** detectable evidence that something has passed < the *track* of a sleigh in the snow >
syn trace, tread
rel impress, imprint, mark, print; sign, vestige
2 syn see TRAIL
rel footpath, footway, walk
idiom beaten path
3 syn see WAY 1
rel roadway, trackway
4 syn see FOOTPRINT
rel scent, slot
track *vb* **1** to follow the tracks or traces of < *track* a wounded deer >
syn trace, trail
rel follow; dog, shadow, tail; chase, pursue; find, hunt (down), smell (out)
idiom be hot on the trail of
2 syn see TRAVEL 2
tract *n* **1 syn** see AREA 1
rel amplitude, spread, stretch; part, portion, section, sector
2 syn see LOT 3
3 syn see FOOTPRINT
tractable *adj* **syn** see OBEDIENT
rel flexible, pliable, pliant; manageable; subdued
con headstrong, unmanageable, willful; obstinate, refractory, stubborn
ant intractable, unruly
tractate *n* **syn** see DISCOURSE 2
trade *n* **1** a pursuit followed as an occupation or means of livelihood and requiring technical knowledge and skill < the *trade* of a carpenter >
syn art, calling, craft, handicraft, métier, profession, vocation
rel employment, occupation, pursuit, work
con avocation, hobby

---

syn synonym(s)   *rel* related word(s)
ant antonym(s)   *con* contrasted word(s)
idiom idiomatic equivalent(s)
‖ use limited; if in doubt, see a dictionary

2 syn see BUSINESS 4
rel market
3 syn see PATRONAGE 2
trade vb **1** to give one thing in return for another with an expectation of gain <*traded* furs for tobacco and rum>
syn bargain, barter, exchange, swap, traffic, truck; *compare* EXCHANGE 2
rel market, merchandise, sell; deal; argue, chaffer, dicker, haggle, wrangle
idiom make (*or* strike) a bargain, make a deal
2 syn see EXCHANGE 2
trademark n **syn** see MARK 7
trader n **syn** see MERCHANT
tradesman n **syn** see MERCHANT
tradition n **1** an inherited or established way of thinking, feeling, or doing <America's Puritan *tradition* is still very much alive>
syn heritage
rel culture; convention, custom, ethic, form; birthright, inheritance, legacy
2 syn see LORE 2
traditional adj **1** of or relating to tradition <a *traditional* interpretation of the Bible>
syn conventional, tralatitious; *compare* CONVENTIONAL 1
rel ancestral, immemorial, old; customary, habitual, usual; acknowledged, established, establishmentarian, fixed; common, popular
con new; unconventional, unusual; individualistic, original, personal
2 syn see ORAL 2
traditionalist n **syn** see PURIST
traditionalistic adj **syn** see CONSERVATIVE 1
traduce vb **syn** see MALIGN
rel mock; disgrace; betray; violate
traducing adj **syn** see LIBELOUS
traffic n **1 syn** see BUSINESS 4
2 syn see COMMERCE 2
rel relations, relationship; closeness, connection, familiarity, intimacy
3 syn see PATRONAGE 2
4 the number or volume of vehicles or pedestrians moving along a route <freeway *traffic* is heavy during the rush hour>
syn travel
traffic vb **1 syn** see TRADE 1
2 to engage in illegal or disreputable business or activity <*trafficked* in drugs>
syn truck
rel deal (in), push, shove; black-market; bootleg, moonshine; fence
idiom handle (*or* deal in) under the counter
trafficable adj **syn** see MARKETABLE
trafficker n **syn** see MERCHANT
tragedy n **1 syn** see DISASTER
rel blow, shock
2 syn see MISFORTUNE
rel unluckiness; curse, lot; woe(s)
con prosperity, success
ant triumph
trail vb **1 syn** see DRAG 3
2 syn see DELAY 2
rel plod, trudge; falter, flag; halt
3 syn see TRACK 1
rel nose (out), sniff (out)
idiom follow a scent
4 syn see TAIL
5 syn see FOLLOW 2
trail n a rough course or way formed by or as if by repeated chance footsteps <an old Indian *trail*>
syn path, pathway, track, ‖trod
rel footpath, footwalk, footway
train vb **syn** see LURE
train n **1 syn** see ENTOURAGE
2 syn see SUCCESSION 2
rel course, run; line, thread; gradation, scale, tier
train vb **1 syn** see TEACH
rel cultivate, develop, shape; accustom, habituate; harden, season
2 syn see DIRECT 2
training n **syn** see EDUCATION 1

train off vb **syn** see SWERVE 1
traipse vb **1 syn** see WANDER 1
2 syn see WALK 1
3 syn see DRAG 3
traipse n **syn** see SLATTERN 1
trait n **1 syn** see QUALITY 1
2 syn see CHARACTERISTIC 1
rel denominator; attribute, quality
traitorous adj **syn** see FAITHLESS
rel apostate, renegade; mutinous, rebellious, seditious; alienated, disaffected, estranged; unpatriotic
con faithful; patriotic
traject vb **syn** see CONDUCT 4
tralatitious adj **syn** see TRADITIONAL 1
idiom handed down from time immemorial
tralucent adj **syn** see TRANSLUCENT 3
trammel vb **1 syn** see ENTANGLE 3
2 syn see HAMPER
rel circumscribe, confine, limit; bind, enchain, handcuff, manacle
3 syn see STULTIFY
tramp vb **1** to walk, tread, or step especially heavily <heard hobnailed boots *tramping* across the square>
syn trample, tromp; *compare* PLOD 1
rel march; thud; footslog, stodge, trudge; stamp, stomp
2 syn see HIKE 2
3 syn see TRAMPLE 2
tramp n **1 syn** see VAGABOND
2 syn see WANTON
3 a journey on foot or a walking trip <took a long *tramp* through the woods>
syn hike, walkabout
rel ramble, saunter, stroll, walk; traipse
tramper n **syn** see VAGABOND
trample vb **1 syn** see TRAMP 1
2 to tread on forcibly and repeatedly so as to crush or injure <was *trampled* to death by his horse>
syn stamp, stomp, tramp, tromp
rel ‖stoach, ‖stramp, ‖stunt; pound; tread (on); override
trance vb **syn** see TRANSPORT 2
trance n **syn** see REVERIE
tranquil adj **syn** see CALM 2
rel irenic, pacific, peaceful; quiet, still; stable, steady
con stirred up, troubled
ant agitated
tranquilize vb **syn** see CALM
rel hush; sedate; subdue
idiom pour oil on troubled waters
ant agitate
transaction n **syn** see CONTRACT
transcend vb **syn** see SURPASS 1
idiom go beyond, rise above
transcendent adj **1 syn** see SUPREME
rel accomplished, consummate, finished; entire, intact, perfect, whole
2 syn see ABSTRACT 1
rel absolute, ultimate; boundless, eternal, infinite
transcendental adj **1 syn** see OTHERWORLDLY 1
2 syn see ABSTRACT 1
rel supernatural, supranatural, ultimate
transfer vb **1 syn** see MOVE 4
rel carry, convey; relocate
2 syn see GIVE 3
rel convey, transmit
3 syn see TRANSFORM
4 to shift the title of (property) from one owner to another <to preserve the farm intact he *transfers* it to a single heir>
syn abalienate, alien, alienate, assign, cede, convey, deed, make over, remise, sign (over)
transfigure vb **syn** see TRANSFORM
transfix vb **syn** see IMPALE
transform vb to make over to a radically different form, composition, state, or disposition <the interaction of social forces *transforms* custom and produces a new tradition>
syn change, commute, convert, metamorphize, metamorphose, mutate, transfer, transfigure, translate, transmogrify, transmute, transpose, transubstantiate; *compare* CHANGE 1
rel alter; denature

transformation *n* *syn* see CONVERSION 2

transfuse *vb* *syn* see PERMEATE

transgress *vb* **1** *syn* see VIOLATE 1
  2 *syn* see TRESPASS 1

transgression *n* *syn* see BREACH 1
  rel erring, error, lapse, slip; overstepping; misbehavior, misstepping

transient *adj* lasting or staying only a short time < features of a *transient* culture now extinct >
  syn ephemeral, evanescent, fleeting, fugacious, fugitive, impermanent, momentaneous, momentary, passing, short-lived, transitory, volatile; *compare* TEMPORARY
  rel deciduous, flitting, unstable; temporal, temporary; insubstantial
  idiom as transient as the clouds, here today and gone tomorrow
  con lasting, perdurable, permanent, substantial; durable, stable
  ant perpetual

transit *n* **1** *syn* see PASSAGE 1
  2 *syn* see TRANSITION
  3 *syn* see TRANSPORTATION 1
  4 public conveyance of passengers or goods as a commercial enterprise < mass *transit* >
  syn transport, transportation

transition *n* passage from one state or condition to another < the *transition* from boyhood to manhood >
  syn alteration, passage, shift, transit
  rel change, conversion, metamorphosis, transformation; development, evolution; growth, progress

transitional *adj* involving or characterized by passage from one stage, condition, or state to another < a *transitional* phase of social development >
  syn transitive, transitory
  rel developing, evolving; altering, changing, shifting
  idiom being in a state of flux

transitive *adj* *syn* see TRANSITIONAL

transitory *adj* **1** *syn* see TRANSIENT
  rel changeable; nonpermanent, unenduring; brief, short-term
  2 *syn* see TRANSITIONAL

translate *vb* **1** to make a version of in another language < *translated* many secret documents from French to English >
  syn put, render, transpose, turn
  rel transliterate; transcribe; interpret; metaphrase, paraphrase
  2 *syn* see TRANSFORM

translate (into) *vb* *syn* see PARAPHRASE

translation *n* *syn* see VERSION 1

translucent *adj* **1** *syn* see TRANSPARENT 1
  2 *syn* see CLEAR 4
  rel apparent, obvious, unmistakable
  3 admitting and diffusing light so that objects beyond cannot be clearly distinguished < *translucent* amber >
  syn clear, tralucent, translucid, transparent; *compare* TRANSPARENT 1
  rel lucent, lucid

translucid *adj* *syn* see TRANSLUCENT 3

transmarine *adj* *syn* see OVERSEAS

transmigrate *vb* *syn* see MIGRATE

transmigratory *adj* *syn* see MIGRATORY

transmit *vb* **1** *syn* see SEND 1
  rel convey, transport
  2 *syn* see COMMUNICATE 1
  3 *syn* see HAND DOWN
  rel instill; transfuse, translate
  4 *syn* see CONDUCT 4

transmogrify *vb* *syn* see TRANSFORM

transmundane *adj* *syn* see OTHERWORLDLY 1

transmute *vb* *syn* see TRANSFORM

transparent *adj* **1** admitting light without appreciable diffusion or distortion so that objects beyond are entirely visible < a sheet of *transparent* plastic >
  syn clear, limpid, pellucid, see-through, translucent; *compare* TRANSLUCENT 3
  rel crystal, crystalline, glassy; diaphanous
  idiom clear as glass (*or* crystal)
  con dark, smoky; cloudy, foggy hazy, misty, nubilous
  ant opaque
  2 *syn* see FILMY
  3 *syn* see TRANSLUCENT 3

4 *syn* see CLEAR 4
  rel distinguishable, recognizable; articulate, distinct, plain; unambiguous, unequivocal
  con muddy, turbid

transpicuous *adj* *syn* see CLEAR 4

transpierce *vb* *syn* see IMPALE

transpire *vb* **1** *syn* see GET OUT 2
  2 *syn* see HAPPEN 1
  rel eventuate, result

transplace *vb* *syn* see REVERSE 1
  rel remove; rearrange

transport *vb* **1** *syn* see CARRY 1
  2 to carry away by strong and usually pleasant emotion < *transported* with ecstasy >
  syn enrapture, enravish, entrance, ravish, trance
  rel excite, move, provoke, quicken, stimulate; agitate, inflame, stir (up); elevate, uplift; carry away, delight, imparadise, ‖send, slay, thrill, ‖wow
  3 *syn* see BANISH

transport *n* **1** *syn* see TRANSPORTATION 1
  2 *syn* see ECSTASY
  rel ardor, enthusiasm, fervor, passion; happiness
  3 *syn* see VEHICLE 3
  4 *syn* see TRANSIT 4

transportable *adj* *syn* see PORTABLE

transportation *n* **1** an act, process, or instance of transporting or being transported < arranged for the *transportation* of his luggage >
  syn carriage, carrying, conveyance, transit, transport, transporting
  rel hauling, moving
  2 *syn* see VEHICLE 3
  3 *syn* see TRANSIT 4

transporting *n* *syn* see TRANSPORTATION 1

transpose *vb* **1** *syn* see TRANSFORM
  2 *syn* see TRANSLATE 1
  3 *syn* see REVERSE 1

transubstantiate *vb* *syn* see TRANSFORM

transude *vb* *syn* see EXUDE

transversal *adj* *syn* see TRANSVERSE
  rel bent; intersecting

transverse *vb* *syn* see TRAVERSE 4

transverse *adj* extended or lying in a direction across something else < the *transverse* arches of the cathedral ceiling >
  syn crossing, crosswise, thwart, transversal, traverse
  rel diagonal, oblique; across, crossed
  con perpendicular
  ant longitudinal

transversely *adv* *syn* see OVER 1

transversely *adv* *syn* see OVER 1

trap *n* **1** *syn* see LURE 2
  rel artifice, feint, gambit, maneuver, ploy, ruse, stratagem, wile; birdlime, net; ambuscade, ambush; conspiracy, intrigue, machination, plot
  ‖**2** *syn* see POLICEMAN
  ‖**3** *syn* see MOUTH 1

trap *vb* *syn* see CATCH 3
  rel mousetrap, snag

trapfall *n* *syn* see PITFALL

traps *n pl* *syn* see PERSONAL EFFECTS

trash *n* **1** *syn* see REFUSE
  rel leavings
  2 *syn* see NONSENSE 2
  3 *syn* see RABBLE 2

‖**trash** *vb* *syn* see VANDALIZE

trash *vb* *syn* see PLOD 1

trashy *adj* *syn* see CHEAP 2
  rel third-rate

trauma *n* intense mental, emotional, or physical disturbance resulting from stress < a broken home may produce persistent *trauma* in children >
  syn shock, traumatism

---

syn synonym(s)   *rel* related word(s)
ant antonym(s)   *con* contrasted word(s)
idiom idiomatic equivalent(s)
‖ use limited; if in doubt, see a dictionary

rel blow, stress; traumatization; derangement, disturbance, upset; collapse

traumatism *n syn* see TRAUMA

travail *n* **1** *syn* see WORK 2
rel task; struggle
idiom toil and trouble
con relaxation, rest
2 *syn* see LABOR 2
rel contractions, pains
idiom birth throe

travel *vb* **1** *syn* see GO 1
rel move (on); voyage; roam, trek; explore
2 to journey over (as by conveyance) < certain roads can be *traveled* only on horseback >
syn cover, do, pass (over), track, traverse
rel cross

travel *n* **1** *syn* see PASSAGE 1
2 *often* **travels** *pl syn* see JOURNEY
3 *syn* see TRAFFIC 4

travelable *adj syn* see PASSABLE

‖**traveler** *n syn* see VAGABOND

traverse *n syn* see OBSTACLE

traverse *vb* **1** *syn* see RESIST
2 *syn* see DENY 4
rel oppose; dismiss; squash, squelch
3 *syn* see TRAVEL 2
4 to extend or lie across (something) < a highway *traversing* the entire state >
syn cross, transverse
rel crisscross, intersect, quarter
idiom cut across
5 to pass over, along, or to and fro especially on foot < deep in thought he *traversed* the terrace again and again >
syn perambulate, walk
rel peregrinate; track, tread; pace

traverse *adj syn* see TRANSVERSE

travesty *n* **1** *syn* see CARICATURE 2
rel mimicry; distortion, exaggeration; ridicule
2 *syn* see MOCKERY 2

travesty *vb syn* see MIMIC

treacherous *adj* **1** *syn* see FAITHLESS
rel undependable, unreliable, untrustworthy; betraying, deceptive, double-crossing, falsehearted, misleading, Punic
ant dependable; trustworthy
2 *syn* see DANGEROUS 1
rel deceptive, ticklish, tricky; precarious

treacherousness *n syn* see TREACHERY
ant dependability; trustworthiness

treachery *n* betrayal of a trust or confidence < corruption in public office is little short of *treachery* >
syn disloyalty, faithlessness, perfidiousness, perfidy, treacherousness, treason; *compare* INFIDELITY
rel falseheartedness, falseness; double cross, double-dealing; sell-out
idiom dirty pool, dirty work at the crossroads
con incorruptibility, reliability; probity, rectitude, uprightness; constancy, fidelity, loyalty, staunchness
ant dependability; trustworthiness

tread *vb* **1** *syn* see DANCE 1
2 *syn* see WALK 1
rel march, stride; tromp

tread *n syn* see TRACK 1

treadmill *n syn* see ROUTINE

treason *n* **1** *syn* see TREACHERY
rel deceit, deceitfulness; duplicity; Machiavellianism
idiom breach of trust (*or* faith)
con allegiance, loyalty
ant staunchness
2 *syn* see SEDITION
rel disloyalty, treacherousness, treachery; high treason; misprision
ant allegiance

treasure *n syn* see FIND 1
rel catch, plum, prize; pearl

treasure *vb syn* see APPRECIATE 1
rel conserve, guard, preserve, save; idolize, revere, reverence, venerate, worship
idiom hold dear

treasure–house *n* **1** *syn* see TREASURY 1
2 *syn* see BONANZA

treasure trove *n* **1** *syn* see FIND 1
2 *syn* see BONANZA

treasury *n* **1** a place (as a room or building) where valuables are kept < priceless gold candlesticks kept in the *treasury* of the cathedral >
syn treasure-house
rel archive(s), gallery, museum; depository, repository, storehouse
idiom treasure room
2 the place of deposit, retention, and disbursement of collected funds < the union *treasury* held emergency strike funds >
syn chest, coffer, exchequer, war chest
rel depositary, depository
3 *syn* see BONANZA

treat *vb* **1** *syn* see CONFER 2
rel consider, study, weigh; deliberate, reason, think
2 to have to do with or behave toward (a person or thing) in a specified manner < *treat* all employees fairly and impartially >
syn deal (with), handle, play, serve, take, use
rel conduct, do with, manage, ‖wield; regard, respect; account, consider, hold; appraise, estimate, evaluate, rate, value
idiom act with regard to, conduct oneself toward, do by
3 to pay for another's entertainment < *treated* her to a few drinks >
syn blow, set up, ‖shout, stand
rel stake
idiom go treat, pick up the tab for, stand treat
4 to give medical treatment to < was *treated* by an eye specialist >
syn doctor
rel attend, care (for), minister (to), nurse

treat *n syn* see DELICACY

treatise *n syn* see DISCOURSE 2
rel writing; book; argument, discussion, exposition

treaty *n* a formal, usually written, arrangement made by negotiation between two or more political authorities < the two nations finally signed an arms-limitation *treaty* >
syn agreement, concord, convention, pact; *compare* CONTRACT
rel arrangement, entente, understanding; bargain, contract; charter, compact, concordat, covenant; alliance, cartel, league; accord, reconciliation, settlement

treble *adj syn* see ACUTE 4
ant bass

tree *vb syn* see CORNER

trek *n syn* see JOURNEY

tremble *vb* **1** *syn* see SHAKE 1
rel shrink, wince
idiom tremble like a leaf
2 *syn* see SHAKE 2

trembling *adj syn* see TREMULOUS
ant steady

tremendous *adj* **1** *syn* see FEARFUL 3
2 *syn* see MONSTROUS 1
3 *syn* see HUGE
rel amazing, astounding, flabbergasting; terrific
idiom great big
ant minute

tremendousness *n syn* see ENORMITY 2
rel bigness, largeness

tremor *n syn* see EARTHQUAKE

tremor *vb* **1** *syn* see SHAKE 1
2 *syn* see SHAKE 2

tremorous *adj syn* see TREMULOUS

tremulant *adj syn* see TREMULOUS

tremulous *adj* characterized by or affected with trembling or tremors < her *tremulous* hands could scarcely hold the book >
syn aquake, aquiver, ashake, ashiver, quaking, quaky, quivering, quivery, shaking, shaky, shivering, shivery, trembling, tremorous, tremulant
rel aguish; aspen; palpitating; vibrating
idiom having the shakes
con firm, settled, stable, steady, unmoving

trench *n* a long narrow furrow in the ground < dig a *trench* for a sewer pipe >
syn cut, ditch
rel gully; drill, furrow; fosse; trough; drain, sink

trench *vb syn* see BORDER 3

trenchant *adj* **1** *syn* see INCISIVE
  rel piercing, probing, razor-sharp; sarcastic, sardonic, satiric; acrid; piquant, poignant, pungent
  2 *syn* see CAUSTIC 1
  rel scalding, scorching

trend *n* **1** *syn* see TENDENCY 1
  rel movement; flow; direction, orientation; swing, wind; progression
  2 *syn* see FASHION 3

‖**trendy** *adj syn* see STYLISH
  rel ultramodern
  con dated, outmoded

trepidation *n syn* see FEAR 1
  ant unapprehensiveness

trepidity *n syn* see FEAR 1
  ant intrepidity, intrepidness

trespass *n syn* see BREACH 1
  rel encroachment, entrenchment, invasion; intrusion, obtrusion

trespass *vb* **1** to commit an offense <exhibited scrupulous fairness even to those who *trespassed* against him>
  syn offend, sin, transgress
  rel deviate, err, lapse
  idiom do wrong by
  2 to make inroads on the property, territory, or rights of another <warned the hunters not to *trespass* on his land>
  syn encroach, entrench, infringe, invade
  rel enter, penetrate, pierce, probe; interlope, intermeddle, intrude; transgress
  idiom crash the gate

trestle *n syn* see SAWHORSE

triad *n* a union or group of three often closely related individuals or things <a *triad* of deities>
  syn threesome, trine, trinity, trio, triple, triumvirate, triune, troika; *compare* TRIUMVIRATE 1

trial *n* **1** the state or fact of being tested (as by suffering) <the Vietnam war period was a time of great national *trial*>
  syn affliction, calvary, cross, crucible, ordeal, tribulation, visitation
  rel agony, distress, misery, suffering; anguish, grief, heartbreak, sorrow, woe; adversity, misfortune; difficulty, hardship, rigor, vicissitude
  idiom crown of thorns, fiery ordeal, trial and tribulation
  2 a source of vexation or annoyance <living in a crowded hotel is a real *trial*>
  syn care, trouble, worry
  rel complication, difficulty; annoyance, distress, misfortune; ordeal
  3 *syn* see EXPERIMENT
  4 *syn* see ATTEMPT

trial *adj syn* see EXPERIMENTAL 2

trial and error *n syn* see EXPERIMENT

trial balloon *n syn* see FEELER
  rel trial

trial run *n syn* see EXPERIMENT

tribe *n syn* see FAMILY 1

tribulation *n syn* see TRIAL 1
  rel oppression, persecution, wronging

tribunal *n syn* see COURT 2

tributary *adj syn* see SUBORDINATE
  rel conquered, subdued, subjugated, vanquished; accessory, minor; satellite

tribute *n* **1** *syn* see TESTIMONIAL 3
  rel recognition; monument
  2 *syn* see ENCOMIUM

trice *n syn* see INSTANT 1

trick *n* **1** an indirect, ingenious, and often cunning means to gain an end <used every *trick* in the bag to cover up the scandal>
  syn artifice, chouse, device, feint, gambit, gimmick, jig, maneuver, play, ploy, ‖prat, ruse, shenanigan, sleight, stratagem, whizzer, wile; *compare* PRANK
  rel contrivance, craft, expediency; blind, bluff, diversion, dodge, dodgery, red herring; curve, deception, sham, stall; fraud, ‖rort, scheme, shift, skin game
  2 *syn* see PRANK
  rel boutade; escapade; practical joke
  3 an ingenious or dexterous act or procedure designed to puzzle or amuse <a juggler's *trick*>

  syn feat, stunt
  rel accomplishment
  4 tricks *pl syn* see PERSONAL EFFECTS
  5 *syn* see HANG
  6 *syn* see HABIT 1
  7 *syn* see SPELL

trick *adj* somewhat defective and inclined to function abnormally on occasion <a *trick* lock that doesn't always catch>
  syn tricky, undependable
  rel catchy, touchy; unreliable, untrustworthy; insecure, shaky, unstable; defective, dysfunctioning, malfunctioning

trick *vb syn* see DUPE
  rel outtrick, outtrump, outwit; have
  idiom take (someone) for a ride

trick (off, out, *or* up) *vb syn* see DRESS UP 1

trickery *n syn* see DECEPTION 1
  rel double-cross; underhandedness
  idiom underhand dealing

trickle *vb syn* see DRIP
  ant gush

trickster *n* **1** *syn* see SWINDLER
  idiom gyp artist
  2 *syn* see MAGICIAN 2

tricksy *adj syn* see TIGHT 4

tricky *adj* **1** *syn* see SLY 2
  rel deceptive, delusive; delusory, misleading; deceitful, dishonest
  2 *syn* see UNSTABLE 1
  rel catchy, difficult, trappy; quirky
  3 *syn* see DELICATE 7
  4 *syn* see TRICK

tried *adj syn* see RELIABLE 1
  rel constant, faithful, staunch, steadfast; demonstrated, proved, tested; approved, certified
  ant untried

tried and true *adj syn* see RELIABLE 1

trifle *n* **1** *syn* see KNICKKNACK
  rel rope yarn
  2 *syn* see HINT 2

trifle *vb* **1** to behave amorously without serious intent <was interested only in *trifling* with her, not marrying her>
  syn coquet, dally, flirt, fool, lead on, string along, toy, wanton
  rel play (with); mess around, ‖muck, mucker; philander; mash
  2 *syn* see FIDDLE 1

trifle (away) *vb syn* see WASTE 2
  rel misuse; burn (up), use up
  con retain, save

trifling *n syn* see SMALL TALK

trifling *adj syn* see PETTY 2
  rel banal, inane, insipid, jejune, vapid; empty, frivolous, hollow, idle, nugatory, otiose, vain; insignificant, unimportant

trig *adj* **1** *syn* see NEAT 2
  2 *syn* see STYLISH
  ‖**3** *syn* see FULL 1

triggerman *n syn* see ASSASSIN

trill *vb syn* see DRIP

trillion *n syn* see SCAD

trim *vb* **1** *syn* see ADORN
  2 *syn* see WHIP 2
  rel ‖skin
  3 *syn* see CUT 6

trim *adj* **1** *syn* see NEAT 2
  rel clean, clean-cut, fit, spruce; shapely, streamlined, symmetrical
  con disordered, shapeless, straggly
  ant frowsy
  2 *syn* see SHAPELY

trim *n syn* see ORDER 10
  rel commission; whack

trine *n syn* see TRIAD

trinity *n syn* see TRIAD

trinket *n syn* see KNICKKNACK
  rel plaything; frippery, showpiece, tinsel; trinketry, trinkums

trio *n syn* see TRIAD

---

syn synonym(s)   *rel* related word(s)
ant antonym(s)   *con* contrasted word(s)
idiom idiomatic equivalent(s)
‖ use limited; if in doubt, see a dictionary

trip *vb syn* see SKIP 1

trip *n* **1** a single passage of a vehicle between two points or to a point and return < a regular bus *trip* to and from the city >
syn run; *compare* DRIVE 1, JOURNEY, TOUR 2
rel drive; progress
2 *syn* see JOURNEY
rel run
3 *syn* see ERROR 2

tripes *n pl syn* see ENTRAILS

triple *n syn* see TRIAD

tripped out *adj syn* see DRUGGED

‖**tripper** *n syn* see TOURIST

triste *adj syn* see SAD 2

trite *adj* used or occurring so often as to have lost interest, freshness, or force < unrequited love has become a *trite* theme >
syn bathetic, chain, cliché, clichéd, commonplace, corny, hack, hackneyed, musty, old hat, shopworn, stale, stereotyped, stereotypical, threadbare, timeworn, tired, twice-told, warmed-over, well-worn, worn-out
rel common, ordinary; banal, dull, flat, jejune, mildewed, vapid; bedridden, drained, exhausted, used-up; bromidic, platitudinous, prosaic, ready-made, set, stock
con first, new, seminal; novel, unique; creative, imaginative; uncopied; memorable; distinctive
ant fresh, original

triturate *vb syn* see PULVERIZE 1

triumph *n* **1** *syn* see VICTORY 1
rel ascendancy, gain; surmounting, vanquishing, vanquishment
ant defeat
2 *syn* see EXULTATION
rel joy; festivity, merriment, reveling

triumph *vb* **1** *syn* see EXULT
rel gloat
2 *syn* see WIN 1
rel prosper, succeed; conquer, surmount
idiom get the best (*or* better) of
con lose
ant fail
3 *syn* see CONQUER 2

triumphal *adj syn* see EXULTANT

triumphant *adj syn* see EXULTANT
rel rejoicing, triumphing

triumvirate *n* **1** an administrative or ruling body of three < a monarchy replaced by a *triumvirate* of generals >
syn troika; *compare* TRIAD
rel junta
2 *syn* see TRIAD

triune *n syn* see TRIAD

trivia *n pl but sometimes sing in constr* unimportant matters < they became bored with the *trivia* of everyday life >
syn minutia(e), small beer, small change, small potato(es), triviality

trivial *adj* **1** *syn* see LITTLE 3
rel slight; negligible
idiom no great shakes
con considerable
ant momentous, weighty
2 *syn* see PETTY 2
rel captious, fribbling, frivolous; shallow, superficial

triviality *n syn* see TRIVIA
rel shallowness, superficiality, unimportance
con basic(s), essential(s), fundamental(s)

‖**trod** *n syn* see TRAIL

troika *n* **1** *syn* see TRIUMVIRATE 1
2 *syn* see TRIAD

trollop *n syn* see WANTON
idiom (a) fast number

trollop *vb syn* see SLOUCH

tromp *vb* **1** *syn* see TRAMP 1
2 *syn* see HIKE 2
rel slog, trudge
3 *syn* see TRAMPLE 2
4 *syn* see BEAT 1

troop *n* **1** *syn* see COMPANY 4
rel assemblage, assembly, collection, gathering; army, host, legion, multitude
2 troops *pl* members of a nation's military units < Marines, GI's, and Seabees were among the *troops* sent to war >

syn armed forces, forces, military, servicemen
rel combatants; soldiers, troopers
idiom fighting men

troop *vb syn* see WALK 1

trophy *n syn* see REMEMBRANCE 3

tropic *adj syn* see TROPICAL
rel baking, broiling, scorching, sweltering
con arctic

tropical *adj* of, relating to, or occurring in the tropics < *tropical* fruits >
syn tropic
rel equatorial, semitropical, subtropical; warm; hot, sultry, torrid
con temperate

tropical cyclone *n syn* see HURRICANE

tropical storm *n syn* see HURRICANE

trot *n* **1** *syn* see HAG 2
2 *syn* see PONY

troth *n syn* see ENGAGEMENT 2

trot out *vb syn* see SHOW 4

troubadour *n syn* see BARD 1
rel balladist; rhymer, rhymester

trouble *vb* **1** to cause to be uneasy or upset < sorrows that *trouble* the strongest of men >
syn ail, cark, distress, upset, worry
rel agitate, concern, discompose, disquiet, disturb, perturb, rowel, ‖worrit; annoy, bother, fret, irk, vex; ‖destroy, haunt
2 *syn* see TRY 2
rel upset, worry; discompose, disconcert, disturb; harry, irritate; afflict, torment
3 *syn* see INCONVENIENCE
rel annoy, pester, plague, worry; impose (on *or* upon), intrude

trouble *n* **1** *syn* see TRIAL 2
2 *syn* see EFFORT 1
rel ado, bustle, flurry, fuss, pother; bother, inconvenience; difficulty, hardship, rigor; strain, stress
3 a condition of annoyance, disturbance, or distress < got him into *trouble* by repeating gossip >
syn Dutch, hot water
rel bind, difficulty, predicament

troubled *adj syn* see DISTRAUGHT

troublemaker *n* a person who consciously or unconsciously causes trouble < a *troublemaker* who set father against daughter >
syn bad actor, mischief-maker
rel agitator, inciter, inflamer, instigator

troublesome *adj* giving trouble or anxiety < a *troublesome* infection >
syn mean, pesky, troublous, ugly, vexatious, wicked
rel annoying, bothersome, vexing; alarming, disquieting, disturbing, upsetting; infestive; painful
con untroublesome
ant innocuous

troublesomeness *n syn* see INCONVENIENCE
rel difficulty; irritation, vexation

troublous *adj syn* see TROUBLESOME
rel troubling

trounce *vb syn* see WHIP 2
idiom walk all over

trouncing *n syn* see DEFEAT 1

troupe *n syn* see COMPANY 4

trouper *n syn* see ACTOR 1
rel entertainer; artiste

trove *n syn* see ACCUMULATION

truce *n* a suspension of or an agreement for suspending hostilities < the high command ordered a *truce* for the holidays >
syn armistice, cease-fire
rel break, ‖breather, letup, lull, pause, respite; de-escalation, ‖wind-down; accord, reconciliation; peace

truck *vb* **1** *syn* see TRADE 1
rel handle; peddle, retail
2 *syn* see TRAFFIC 2
idiom have truck with

truck *n syn* see COMMERCE 2

truckle *vb syn* see FAWN
rel knuckle down, knuckle under, succumb; follow, tag, tail, trail
idiom kiss (*or* lick) one's boots, lick the feet of, make a doormat of oneself

truckler *n syn* see SYCOPHANT
truckling *adj syn* see FAWNING
truculent *adj* **1** *syn* see FIERCE 1
  rel browbeating, bullying, cowing, intimidating; frightening, terrifying, terrorizing
  2 *syn* see ABUSIVE
  rel caustic, mordacious, mordant, scathing, sharp, trenchant; harsh, rough, severe; vitriolic
  3 *syn* see BELLIGERENT
trudge *vb syn* see PLOD 1
true *adj* **1** *syn* see FAITHFUL 1
  rel sincere, unfeigned, whole-hearted, whole-souled
  ant false, fickle
  2 *syn* see UPRIGHT 2
  rel creditable, estimable, worthy; high-principled, right-minded, truehearted
  3 conformable to fact or to a standard, rule, or model < gave a *true* account of the accident >
  syn faithful, just, right, strict, undistorted, veracious, veridical
  rel careful, conscientious, meticulous, punctilious, scrupulous; finicky, fussy, overnice; accurate, precise; absolute, mathematical
  idiom true to the letter
  con imprecise, inaccurate, incorrect, inexact; erroneous, false
  ant untrue
  4 *syn* see GENUINE 3
  con deceitful
  5 *syn* see AUTHENTIC 2
  rel genuine, kosher; sincere, unfaked, unfeigned
  con artificial, fake, faked, feigned; insincere
  ant false
  6 *syn* see REAL 3
  rel natural, normal, regular, typical
  ant false
  7 being such as it should be < meanings presented in their *true* relationship >
  syn appropriate, desired, fitting, proper
  rel acceptable; applicable, befitting, likely, suitable
  con inappropriate, unfitting
  8 being such by right < the *true* heir >
  syn legitimate, rightful
  rel lawful, legal, proper
  con illegitimate, spurious, supposititious
  ant false
  9 that can be relied on < polls can provide a *true* projection of public sentiment >
  syn authoritative, dependable, trustable, trustworthy
  rel meaningful, significant; expressive, indicative, suggestive
  con independable, undependable, untrustworthy; doubtful, questionable
truelove *n* **1** *syn* see GIRL FRIEND 2
  2 *syn* see BOYFRIEND 2
  idiom one and only
true–tongued *adj syn* see TRUTHFUL
truism *n* **1** *syn* see VERACITY 2
  2 *syn* see MAXIM
  3 *syn* see COMMONPLACE
trull *n syn* see WANTON
truly *adv* **1** *syn* see VERY 2
  rel absolutely, positively
  2 *syn* see EVEN 3
  rel confidently, really
  3 *syn* see WELL 7
  rel probably; surely
trump *n syn* see TRUMP CARD
trump *vb syn* see SURPASS 1
trump card *n* something decisive or telling often held in reserve < kept a political *trump card* up his sleeve till election eve >
  syn clincher, trump
  rel ace; coup, coup de grace, coup de main
  idiom ace in the hole
trumpery *n syn* see NONSENSE 2
trumpery *adj syn* see CHEAP 2
trumpet *vb syn* see TOUT
truncate *vb syn* see TOP 1
  rel abbreviate, abridge; cut off, lop; shear
truncheon *n syn* see CUDGEL
trust *n* **1** complete assurance and certitude regarding the character, ability, strength, or truth of someone or something < they continue to have *trust* in his judgment >

  syn confidence, dependence, faith, hope, reliance, stock
  rel assurance, certainty, certitude, conviction; belief, credence, credit; positiveness, sureness; entrustment; overconfidence, oversureness
  con doubt, dubiety, dubiosity, skepticism, suspicion, uncertainty
  ant mistrust
  2 *syn* see SYNDICATE
  3 *syn* see CUSTODY
trust *vb syn* see ENTRUST 1
  rel commit, consign, hand over
trust (in *or* to) *vb syn* see RELY (on *or* upon)
  rel assume, imagine, presume
  idiom have no reservations
trustable *adj syn* see TRUE 9
  ant trustless
trustless *adj syn* see UNRELIABLE 1
  rel unworthy; unfaithful; suspect, suspicious; dishonest; deceitful; treacherous
  ant trustable, trustworthy
trustworthy *adj* **1** *syn* see RELIABLE 1
  rel veracious, truthful; honest, scrupulous, upright
  con deceitful; dishonest
  ant untrustworthy
  2 *syn* see TRUE 9
  rel accurate, exact; valid; realistic
  con inaccurate, inexact; invalid; unrealistic; suspect
  ant untrustworthy
  3 *syn* see AUTHENTIC 1
trusty *adj* **1** *syn* see RELIABLE 1
  rel predictable, stable; firm, sound; responsible, ‖straight
  con capricious
  ant untrusty
  2 *syn* see AUTHENTIC 1
  ant untrusty
truth *n* **1** *syn* see VERACITY 1
  rel precision, rightness, trueness; authenticity, genuineness, veritableness; candor
  idiom unvarnished truth (or truthfulness)
  con equivocation, evasion, hedging; deception, deceptiveness, falseness
  ant falsity, untruth
  2 *syn* see VERACITY 2
  rel reality
  idiom (the) gospel truth, (the) truth of the matter
  ant lie, untruth
truthful *adj* observant of or telling the truth < a *truthful* witness >
  syn true-tongued, truth-speaking, truth-telling, veracious, veridical
  rel candid, frank, honest, sincere; accurate, factual; real, realistic
  con false, insincere, truthless, uncandid; inaccurate; unrealistic
  ant untruthful
truthfulness *n syn* see VERACITY 1
  ant untruthfulness
truthlessness *n syn* see MENDACITY
truth–speaking *adj syn* see TRUTHFUL
truth–telling *adj syn* see TRUTHFUL
try *vb* **1** to subject to testing < *try* the door to be sure it's locked >
  syn check, examine, prove, test
  rel inspect, scrutinize; appraise, judge, weigh
  idiom make trial of, put to proof, put to the test
  2 to subject to stress < the fine print *tried* her eyes >
  syn distress, harass, irk, pain, strain, stress, trouble
  rel annoy, bother, vex
  3 *syn* see AFFLICT
  4 *syn* see PROVE 1
  5 to make an effort to do or accomplish something < the baby is *trying* to walk >
  syn assay, attempt, endeavor, essay, offer, seek, strive, struggle, undertake
  rel aim, aspire, hope, strike

---

syn synonym(s)   *rel* related word(s)
ant antonym(s)   *con* contrasted word(s)
idiom idiomatic equivalent(s)
‖ use limited; if in doubt, see a dictionary

idiom do one's best (*or* utmost) to, have a go at

try (out) *vb syn* see EXPERIMENT
  rel examine, inspect, scrutinize; demonstrate, prove
  idiom cut and try, put to trial, try for size

try *n* **1** *syn* see ATTEMPT
  2 *syn* see FLING 1
  rel dab, jab

trying *adj* **1** *syn* see TIGHT 4
  rel annoying, bothersome, irksome, irritating, troublesome, vexing; strenuous; sticky, tricky
  2 *syn* see ONEROUS

try on *vb syn* see EXPERIMENT

tryst *n syn* see ENGAGEMENT 3

‖**tub** *n syn* see FATTY

tub *vb syn* see BATHE 1

tubby *adj syn* see ROTUND 2
  idiom plump as a dumpling (*or* partridge)

tuberculosis *n* a communicable bacterial disease typically marked by wasting, fever, and formation of cheesy tubercles often in the lungs < Victorian heroines fading away with *tuberculosis* >
  syn consumption, phthisis, TB, white plague

tuck (in) *vb syn* see BED
  rel snug (down *or* up), snuggle

‖**tuck** *n syn* see FOOD 1

tuck *n syn* see ENERGY 2

‖**tucked up** *adj syn* see CRAMPED

tucker *vb syn* see EXHAUST 3
  rel gruel; wilt; drop
  idiom take the tuck out of

tug *vb* **1** *syn* see CONTEND 1
  2 *syn* see LABOR 1
  3 *syn* see PULL 2

tug–of–war *n syn* see CONTEST 1

tuition *n syn* see EDUCATION 1

tumble *vb* **1** *syn* see FALL 2
  rel trip; come (down), descend
  2 *syn* see PLUMMET
  rel depreciate; sag, slump
  idiom take a downward spiral, take a nosedive
  3 *syn* see HAPPEN 2
  4 *syn* see DISCOVER 3
  5 *syn* see OVERTHROW 2
  6 *syn* see FELL 1
  7 *syn* see CONFUSE 5
  8 *syn* see DISORDER 1

tumble (to) *vb syn* see APPREHEND 1

tumble *n syn* see CLUTTER 2

tumescent *adj* **1** *syn* see INFLATED
  rel bloated; bulging
  2 *syn* see RHETORICAL

tumid *adj* **1** *syn* see INFLATED
  rel dilated, distended, expanded, swollen
  2 *syn* see RHETORICAL

tummy *n syn* see ABDOMEN

tumulary *adj syn* see SEPULCHRAL 1

tumult *n* **1** *syn* see COMMOTION 1
  rel disturbance, turmoil, uproar
  2 *syn* see COMMOTION 4
  rel babel, din, hullabaloo, pandemonium, racket
  con calm, hush, lull, quietude
  3 *syn* see COMMOTION 2
  rel seething; disorder, unsettlement; ferment, maelstrom, paroxysm
  4 *syn* see DIN
  rel noise; ‖corroboree
  idiom ‖all hell broken loose

tumultuous *adj syn* see TURBULENT 1

tumultuously *adv syn* see HARD 2

tun *n syn* see CASK
  rel vat

tune *n* **1** *syn* see MELODY
  rel carol; composition, number, piece
  2 *syn* see HARMONY 1
  3 *syn* see HARMONY 2
  4 *syn* see ORDER 4

tune *vb* **1** *syn* see SING 1
  2 *syn* see HARMONIZE 3
  rel fix, regulate

3 to adjust with respect to resonance < *tune* a TV set to a local station >
  syn dial

tune (up) *vb syn* see ADJUST 2

tuned *adj syn* see MELODIOUS 2

tuneful *adj* **1** *syn* see MELODIOUS 2
  2 *syn* see MELODIOUS 1
  ant tuneless

tunk *vb syn* see TAP 1

turbid *adj* clouded with or as if with roiled sediment < a *turbid* stream >
  syn muddy, riley, roily
  rel dark, dense, obscure; mucky, thick; clouded, cloudy, murky, opaque, smoky; dull
  con translucent; lucid, pellucid, transparent; crystal, crystalline; clean, pure, undefiled
  ant clear, limpid

turbulence *n syn* see COMMOTION 2
  rel babel, din, pandemonium, uproar; unruliness; fracas, fight
  con calmness, composure, placidity, quiet

turbulent *adj* **1** given to insubordination and disorder < a *turbulent* and irresponsible group >
  syn boisterous, disorderly, rambunctious, raucous, rowdy, rowdydowdy, rowdyish, rumbustious, termagant, tumultuous, unruly; *compare* UNRULY 1
  rel mutinous; fast, roisterous, uncontrollable, uninhibited, wild; clamorous, loudmouthed; brawling, quarrelsome, rough, roughhouse; hell-for-leather, rip-roaring, tempestuous
  con calm, placid, quiet, tranquil; controlled, orderly, peaceful, restrained
  2 *syn* see WILD 6
  rel agitated, convulsed, moiling, stirred up; boiling, roily, ruffled, swirling; howling, riotous, roaring; tempest-tossed

turbulently *adv syn* see HARD 2
  rel blusteringly

turf *n syn* see TERRAIN 2
  rel area, region, sphere

turgid *adj* **1** *syn* see INFLATED
  rel swelling, turgescent
  2 *syn* see RHETORICAL

turmoil *n* **1** *syn* see COMMOTION 2
  rel jitteriness, nervousness, restlessness, unease, uneasiness; disorder, disruption; moil; riot, strife, uproar
  2 *syn* see UNREST
  rel distress; anxiety, anxiousness
  ant tranquillity
  3 *syn* see COMMOTION 4

turn *vb* **1** to move or cause to move in a curved or circular path on or as if on an axis < *turned* the wheel sharply to avoid a collision >
  syn circle, circumduct, gyrate, gyre, revolve, roll, rotate; *compare* SPIN 1
  rel orbit; pirouette, spin, twirl, whirl; twist, weave, wind; circulate, eddy, swirl; oscillate, sway, swing, vibrate
  2 *syn* see SPRAIN
  3 *syn* see REVERSE 1
  4 *syn* see PLOW
  5 *syn* see UPSET 5
  rel discompose, undo; unbalance
  6 to change or cause to change course or direction < *turned* his car down a side road >
  syn avert, deflect, divert, pivot, sheer, swing, veer, volte-face, wheel, whip, whirl; *compare* SHUNT 1
  rel depart, detract, deviate, digress, diverge; move, shift; switch, swivel, twist, zigzag; call off, double (back), reverse; shunt, sidetrack; bend, curve, sway; detour, rechannel, turn away
  7 *syn* see DIRECT 2
  con call off, detract (from), distract, divert (from), draw (away)
  8 *syn* see ADDRESS 3
  rel employ, use; plunge (into), undertake
  idiom turn one's hand (*or* energies) to
  con avoid, dodge, shy (away)
  9 *syn* see CURDLE
  10 *syn* see DECAY
  11 *syn* see CHANGE 1
  12 *syn* see TRANSLATE 1
  13 *syn* see DULL 3
  14 *syn* see SPIN 2

15 *syn* see DEFECT
16 *syn* see RESORT 2
17 *syn* see BECOME 1
rel change (into), pass (into)
turn (on *or* upon) *vb syn* see DEPEND (on *or* upon) 1
turn *n* **1** *syn* see REVOLUTION 1
2 an often sudden change in course or trend <his health took a *turn* for the better>
syn bend, deflection, deviation, double, shift, tack, yaw
rel course, drift, trend
3 *syn* see REVERSAL 1
4 a point at which a change of course takes place <hidden by a *turn* in the road>
syn angle, bend, bow, flection, flexure, turning
rel curve, twist; corner
5 *syn* see WALK 1
6 *syn* see DRIVE 1
7 *syn* see SPELL 1
8 *syn* see CHANGE 1
9 *syn* see GIFT 2
rel bias, disposition, predisposition
10 an unusual, unexpected, or special interpretation or construction <gave a new *turn* to the old joke>
syn twist
rel construction, interpretation; device, gimmick, trick
11 *syn* see ATTACK 3
turnabout *n* **1** *syn* see REVERSAL 1
2 *syn* see RENEGADE
rel backslider, coward, quitter, turnback
turn back *vb syn* see RETURN 1
turncoat *n syn* see RENEGADE
rel deserter, straggler; betrayer, quisler, quisling, traitor; spy
turn down *vb syn* see DECLINE 4
turned on *adj syn* see DRUGGED
turn in *vb syn* see RETIRE 4
ant turn out
turning *n* **1** *syn* see TURN 4
2 *syn* see DEVIATION 1
rel detour
3 *syn* see REVERSAL 1
turning point *n syn* see JUNCTURE 2
rel climax, culmination, peak
idiom moment of truth
turnip *n syn* see DUNCE
turn off *vb* **1** *syn* see DISMISS 3
2 *syn* see HANG 2
turn out *vb* **1** *syn* see FURNISH 1
rel deck, dress (out)
2 *syn* see BEAR 9
3 *syn* see ROLL OUT
turnout *n* **1** *syn* see COSTUME
2 *syn* see OUTPUT
turn over *vb* **1** *syn* see OVERTURN 1
2 *syn* see PLOW
3 *syn* see PONDER 2
idiom turn over in one's mind
4 *syn* see GIVE 3
rel assign, confer, consign, convey, delegate, relegate; give up, relinquish, ‖turn up
idiom come across with, put into the hands of
con get back, reclaim, recover, regain, retrieve, take back
5 *syn* see COMMIT 1
turnover *n syn* see SHAKE-UP
turn up *vb* **1** *syn* see FIND 1
rel see; uncover, unearth; track (down)
idiom come across
‖**2** *syn* see RELINQUISH
3 to arrive when or where expected <*turned up* for dinner promptly at seven o'clock>
syn show, show up
rel appear, arrive, come, materialize; blow in, pop (in), punch in, roll (in), weigh in
idiom make one's appearance, put in an appearance
4 *syn* see COME 1
turtledove *n syn* see SWEETHEART 1
tussle *vb syn* see WRESTLE
rel scrap, skirmish, spar; hassle
idiom get into a tussle

tutelage *n syn* see EDUCATION 1
twaddle *n syn* see NONSENSE 2
rel gabble; wish-wash
twaddle *vb* **1** *syn* see BABBLE 2
2 *syn* see CHAT 1
twang *n syn* see HINT 2
tweedle *vb syn* see CHIRP
tween *prep syn* see BETWEEN 2
tweet *vb syn* see CHIRP
twerp *n* a usually young or insignificant upstart who meddles beyond his competence or concern <ignored the protests of that insolent *twerp*>
syn pup, puppy, sprat, squirt, ‖squit
rel upstart; ‖squib; fool, jerk, ‖twit; brat
idiom small-time big shot
twice-told *adj syn* see TRITE
twiddle *vb syn* see FIDDLE 1
rel finger, manipulate, palpate; monkey (with), toy (with)
idiom twiddle around with
twiddle *vb syn* see CHAT 1
twig *vb* **1** *syn* see SEE 1
2 *syn* see APPREHEND 1
‖**twig** *n syn* see FASHION 3
twiggy *adj syn* see THIN 1
twilight *n* **1** *syn* see EVENING 1
rel afterglow, afterlight
2 *syn* see EVENING 2
rel decline; end
twin *adj* made up of two very closely matched or identical aspects, elements, individuals, or parts <the *twin* threats of inflation and recession>
syn double, dual, paired
rel bifold, binary, twofold; identical, matched, matching; like, similar
con independent, separate; dissimilar, unlike
twin *n syn* see MATE 5
twine *vb syn* see WIND 2
rel interweave; undulate; enmesh, entangle, tangle
twinge *n syn* see PAIN 1
twinkle *vb* **1** *syn* see BLINK 2
rel illuminate, light, light up; shine
2 *syn* see FLASH 1
3 *syn* see WINK
twinkle *n* **1** *syn* see INSTANT 1
2 *syn* see FLASH 1
twinkling *n syn* see INSTANT 1
idiom the twinkling of an eye
twirl *vb syn* see SPIN 1
twist *vb* **1** *syn* see SPRAIN
2 *syn* see MISREPRESENT
3 *syn* see WIND 2
ant untwist
twist *n syn* see TURN 10
twister *n syn* see TORNADO
twisting *adj syn* see CROOKED 1
twit *vb syn* see RIDICULE
rel jive, josh, tease; chide, reproach, reprove; blame, censure, reprehend
twitch *vb syn* see JERK
rel clutch, grasp, pluck, snatch; nip, pinch
twitter *vb* **1** *syn* see CHIRP
2 *syn* see CHAT 1
3 *syn* see SHAKE 1
twittery *adj syn* see NERVOUS
rel flustered; twittering
idiom all atwitter, all fluttery, all of a twitter
twitty *adj syn* see IRRITABLE
twixt *prep syn* see BETWEEN 2
twofold *adj* **1** having two parts, elements, or aspects <the problem is *twofold*: to find gasoline and to be able to pay for it>
syn bifold, binary, double, double-barreled, dual, dualistic, duple, duplex
rel dyadic; paired, twin

---

syn synonym(s)	*rel* related word(s)
ant antonym(s)	*con* contrasted word(s)
idiom idiomatic equivalent(s)	
‖ use limited; if in doubt, see a dictionary	

con distinct, separate
2 being twice as large, as great, or as many < a *twofold* increase in enrollment >
   syn double, double-barreled
   idiom twice over
two–handed *adj* **1** designed for or requiring the use of both hands < a *two-handed* sword >
   syn bimanual
2 having or being efficient with two hands < *two-handed* tennis players are rare >
   syn ambidextrous, bimanual
twosome *n syn* see COUPLE
two–time *vb syn* see DECEIVE
two–wheeler *n syn* see BICYCLE
tycoon *n syn* see MAGNATE
tyke *n syn* see DOG 1
type *n* a number of individuals thought of as a group because of a common quality or qualities < political radicals of whatever *type* >
   syn breed, cast, character, class, cut, description, feather, ilk, kidney, kind, lot, mold, nature, order, persuasion, sort, species, stamp, stripe, variety, way
   rel blazon, brand, form; sample, specimen; category, group, rubric
typhoon *n syn* see HURRICANE
typic *adj syn* see GENERAL 1
   rel average, ordinary
typical *adj* **1** constituting or having the nature of a type < a *typical* instance of guilt by association >
   syn archetypal, classic, classical, exemplary, ideal, model, paradigmatic, prototypal, prototypical, quintessential, representative
   rel characteristic; emblematic, symbolic; absolute, consummate, perfect
   con uncharacteristic; unusual
   ant atypical, untypical

2 *syn* see GENERAL 1
   rel old hat, unexceptional; collective, quintessential, representative; characteristic, specific
   idiom being the rule and not the exception
   con distinctive; exceptional, extraordinary, unusual; abnormal
   ant atypical, untypical
typification *n syn* see ALLEGORY 1
typify *vb* **1** *syn* see REPRESENT 2
2 *syn* see EPITOMIZE 2
   rel model
tyrannical *adj syn* see ABSOLUTE 4
   rel brutal, harsh, oppressive; roughshod
tyrannize *vb* to exercise arbitrary power over often with unjust and oppressive severity < a country *tyrannized* by a dictator and his secret police >
   syn despotize
   rel dictate, dominate, domineer, overlord; crush, oppress, trample; shackle; terrorize
tyrannous *adj syn* see ABSOLUTE 4
   rel lordly; fascistic, totalitarian
tyranny *n* absolute government in which unlimited power is vested in a single usually severe and oppressive ruler < the *tyranny* of Hitler >
   syn autocracy, despotism, dictatorship, totalitarianism
   rel monocracy; absolutism, authoritarianism, fascism; domination, oppression, totality; terrorism
   idiom iron heel (*or* boot)
   con democracy; freedom; anarchy
tyrant *n* a ruler who exercises absolute power oppressively and brutally < Hitler and Stalin as twentieth-century *tyrants* >
   syn despot, dictator, duce, oppressor, strong man
   rel autocrat, totalitarian
   idiom man on horseback
tyro *n* **1** *syn* see AMATEUR 2
2 *syn* see NOVICE

uberrima fides *n syn* see GOOD FAITH
ubiquitous *adj syn* see OMNIPRESENT
ugly *adj* **1** *syn* see GRAVE 3
2 unpleasing to the sight < an *ugly* decaying neighborhood >
   syn hideous, ill-favored, ill-looking, unbeautiful, uncomely, unsightly
   rel homely, plain; bizarre, grotesque; repelling, repugnant, repulsive; unattractive, uninviting, unpleasing, unprepossessing
   idiom homely as a mud (*or* hedge) fence, not much to look at, short on looks
   con comely, fair, good-looking, handsome, lovely, pretty; attractive, prepossessing
   ant beautiful
3 *syn* see BASE 3
4 *syn* see TROUBLESOME
5 *syn* see SULLEN
ukase *n syn* see EDICT 1
ulterior *adj* lying behind what is manifest or avowed < an *ulterior* motive >
   syn buried, concealed, covert, guarded, hidden, obscured, privy, shrouded
   rel ambiguous, cryptic, dark, enigmatic, equivocal, obscure
   idiom hidden under the rug, kept behind a screen, under cover, under wraps
   con clear, open, overt, plain, straightforward; explicit, expressed
ultimate *adj* **1** *syn* see LAST
2 *syn* see SUPREME
3 being so fundamental as to stand at the extreme limit of the actually or conceivably knowable < *ultimate* realities >
   syn absolute, categorical
   rel empyreal, empyrean, sublime, transcendental; exalted, grand, lofty
ultimate *n syn* see APOTHEOSIS 1
ultimate *vb syn* see CLOSE 3

ultimately *adv syn* see YET 2
ultra *adj* **1** *syn* see EXTREME 3
2 *syn* see OUTLANDISH 3
ultraconservative *n syn* see REACTIONARY
ultrafashionable *adj syn* see STYLISH
ultraist *n syn* see RADICAL
ultraist *adj syn* see EXTREME 3
ultramarine *adj syn* see OVERSEAS
ululate *vb syn* see HOWL 1
   rel bewail, lament
umbra *n* **1** *syn* see APPARITION
2 *syn* see SHADE 1
umbrage *n* **1** *syn* see SHADE 1
2 *syn* see FOLIAGE
3 *syn* see OFFENSE 2
   rel annoyance, irking, vexation; exasperation, irritation, nettling, provoking; fury, ire, rage, wrath
umbrage *vb* **1** *syn* see SHADE
2 *syn* see ANGER 1
umbrageous *adj syn* see SHADY 1
umbrous *adj syn* see SHADY 1
umpire *n syn* see JUDGE 1
umpire *vb syn* see JUDGE 1
unabashed *adj syn* see SHAMELESS
   ant abashed
unabbreviated *adj syn* see UNABRIDGED
   ant abbreviated
unabridged *adj* not shortened by omission of parts (as words) < published an *unabridged* edition of Shakespeare's plays >
   syn complete, unabbreviated, uncondensed, uncut, undocked, whole-length
   rel entire, intact, whole
   con condensed, cropped, curtailed, cut, incompleted, shortened, trimmed

ant abridged

unacceptable *adj syn* see OBJECTIONABLE
  ant acceptable
unaccompanied *adj syn* see ALONE 1
  ant accompanied, companioned
unaccomplished *adj syn* see AMATEURISH
  ant accomplished, skilled
unaccountable *adj* 1 *syn* see INEXPLICABLE
  ant accountable
  2 *syn* see MYSTERIOUS
unaccustomed *adj syn* see UNFAMILIAR 1
  ant accustomed, familiar
unacquaintance *n syn* see IGNORANCE 2
  ant acquaintance
unacquainted *adj syn* see IGNORANT 2
  ant acquainted
unacquaintedness *n syn* see IGNORANCE 2
  ant acquaintance
unacquired *adj syn* see INNATE 1
  ant acquired
unadorned *adj syn* see PLAIN 1
  ant adorned
unadulterated *adj* 1 *syn* see PURE 2
  2 *syn* see STRAIGHT 3
  ant adulterated
unadvisable *adj syn* see INADVISABLE
  ant advisable
unadvised *adj syn* see RASH 1
  ant advised, thought-out
unaffable *adj syn* see UNDEMONSTRATIVE
  ant affable
unaffected *adj syn* see NATURAL 5
  ant affected, artificial
unafraid *adj syn* see BRAVE 1
  rel composed, cool, imperturbable; assured, confident, sure
  con apprehensive, fearful
  ant afraid
unaimed *adj syn* see RANDOM
unalert *adj syn* see INCAUTIOUS 1
  ant alert
unalike *adj syn* see DIFFERENT 1
  ant alike
unalloyed *adj syn* see PURE 2
unalluring *adj syn* see PLAIN 5
  ant alluring, attractive
unalterable *adj syn* see INFLEXIBLE 3
  ant alterable
unambiguous *adj* 1 *syn* see CLEAR 4
  ant ambiguous, obscure
  2 *syn* see EXPLICIT
  ant ambiguous
  3 *syn* see CLEAR 5
unanimated *adj syn* see DEAD 1
unanimous *adj* being of one mind < they were *unanimous* in their determination to win >
  syn consentaneous, consentient, solid
  rel agreed, agreeing, concordant, concurrent, harmonious
  idiom of one accord, of one (*or* the same) mind, with one voice
  con differing, disagreed, disagreeing, discordant, inharmonious
unanticipatedly *adv syn* see UNAWARES
unapparent *adj syn* see IMPERCEPTIBLE
  ant apparent, detectable
unappeasable *adj* 1 *syn* see INSATIABLE
  ant appeasable
  2 *syn* see GRIM 3
  ant appeasable, placable
unappetizing *adj syn* see UNPALATABLE 1
  ant appetizing
unappreciable *adj syn* see IMPERCEPTIBLE
  ant appreciable
unappreciated *adj syn* see THANKLESS 2
  ant appreciated
unappreciative *adj syn* see THANKLESS 1
  ant appreciative
unapproachable *adj* 1 *syn* see INACCESSIBLE
  ant approachable, attainable
  2 *syn* see UNSOCIABLE
  ant accessible, approachable

unapt *adj* 1 *syn* see IMPROPER 1
  2 *syn* see UNSKILLFUL 1
  ant apt
unarm *vb syn* see DISARM 2
unartful *adj syn* see NATURAL 5
  ant artful
unarticulate *adj syn* see DUMB 1
  ant articulate
unartificial *adj syn* see NATURAL 5
  ant affected, artificial
unasked *adj* 1 not asked or invited < annoyed by his *unasked* advice >
  syn unbidden, uninvited, unrequested, unsought
  rel arrogant, impudent, overbearing, presumptuous; spontaneous, voluntary; unacceptable, unwanted, unwelcome
  con desired, invited, sought, wanted; acceptable, welcome
  ant asked
  2 *syn* see SUPEREROGATORY
unassailable *adj syn* see INVINCIBLE 1
  rel stalwart, stout, strong, sturdy, tenacious, tough
  ant assailable
unassertive *adj syn* see SHY 1
  ant aggressive, assertive
unassorted *adj syn* see MISCELLANEOUS
unassuming *adj syn* see HUMBLE 1
  ant assuming, presumptuous
unassured *adj* 1 *syn* see UNSAFE
  2 *syn* see SHY 1
  ant assured
  3 *syn* see INSECURE 1
unattainable *adj* 1 *syn* see INACCESSIBLE
  ant attainable
  2 *syn* see IMPOSSIBLE 1
unattractive *adj syn* see PLAIN 5
  ant alluring, attractive
unauthentic *adj syn* see SPURIOUS 3
  ant authentic, genuine
unavailable *adj syn* see FUTILE
unavailing *adj syn* see FUTILE
unavoidable *adj syn* see INEVITABLE
  ant avoidable
unavoidably *adv syn* see WILLY-NILLY
unaware *adv syn* see UNAWARES
unaware *adj syn* see IGNORANT 2
  ant aware, conscious
unawaredly *adv syn* see UNAWARES
unawareness *n syn* see IGNORANCE 2
  ant awareness, consciousness
unawares *adv* without warning < caught *unawares* by company >
  syn aback, short, sudden, suddenly, unanticipatedly, unaware, unawaredly, unexpectedly
  rel unprepared, unready
  idiom like a bolt from the blue, off base, out of a clear sky, out of the blue
unbalance *vb syn* see MADDEN 1
unbalance *n syn* see INSANITY 1
  rel disorientation, instability
unbalanced *adj* 1 *syn* see LOPSIDED
  ant balanced
  2 *syn* see INSANE 1
unbearable *adj syn* see INSUFFERABLE
  ant bearable, supportable
unbearing *adj syn* see BARREN 2
unbeatable *adj syn* see INVINCIBLE 1
  ant beatable, defeatable
unbeauteous *adj syn* see PLAIN 5
  ant beauteous
unbeautified *adj syn* see PLAIN 1
  ant beautified, embellished
unbeautiful *adj* 1 *syn* see PLAIN 5
  ant beautiful
  2 *syn* see UGLY 2
  ant beautiful

---

syn synonym(s)   *rel* related word(s)
ant antonym(s)   *con* contrasted word(s)
idiom idiomatic equivalent(s)
|| use limited; if in doubt, see a dictionary

unbecoming *adj* **1** *syn* see INDECOROUS
   rel awkward, clumsy, gauche, inept, maladroit
   ant becoming, seemly
   2 *syn* see IMPROPER 1
unbecomingness *n syn* see IMPROPRIETY 1
   ant becomingness, seemliness
unbefitting *adj syn* see IMPROPER 1
   ant apropos, befitting
unbegotten *adj syn* see SELF-EXISTENT
unbelief *n* the attitude or state of mind of one who does not believe <after so much deception, so many lies, she could offer
   nothing but *unbelief* to his words>
   syn disbelief, incredulity, unbelievingness, unfaith
   rel doubt, dubiety, dubiosity, skepticism, uncertainty; distrust,
   mistrust, suspicion; apprehension, misgiving, qualm
   con assurance, certitude, security, trust; dependence, reliance,
   stock, store
   ant belief
unbelievable *adj* **1** *syn* see INCREDIBLE 1
   ant believable, credible
   2 *syn* see IMPLAUSIBLE
   ant believable, credible
unbelieve *vb syn* see DISBELIEVE
   ant believe, credit
unbeliever *n syn* see SKEPTIC
   ant believer
unbelieving *adj syn* see INCREDULOUS
   ant believing
unbelievingness *n syn* see UNBELIEF
unbend *vb* **1** *syn* see RELAX 2
   2 *syn* see REST 2
unbendable *adj syn* see INFLEXIBLE 2
   ant bendable
unbending *adj* **1** *syn* see STIFF 1
   ant bendable
   2 *syn* see INFLEXIBLE 2
   3 *syn* see UNSOCIABLE
unbiased *adj syn* see FAIR 4
   rel aloof, uninterested
   ant biased
unbidden *adj syn* see UNASKED
unbind *vb* **1** *syn* see LOOSE 3
   ant bind
   2 *syn* see FREE
   ant bind
unblamable *adj syn* see GOOD 11
   ant blamable, blameworthy
unblemished *adj* **1** *syn* see WHOLE 1
   ant blemished, flawed
   2 *syn* see CHASTE
unblenched *adj syn* see BRAVE 1
unblenching *adj syn* see BRAVE 1
unblock *vb syn* see OPEN 1
   ant block
unblunted *adj syn* see SHARP 1
   ant blunt, blunted
unblurred *adj syn* see CLEAR 4
   ant blurred
unblushing *adj syn* see SHAMELESS
unbodied *adj syn* see IMMATERIAL 1
   ant bodied, incarnate
unbookish *adj syn* see UNSCHOLARLY
   ant bookish
unbosom *vb syn* see REVEAL 1
unbounded *adj syn* see LIMITLESS
   ant bounded, limited
unbrace *vb syn* see WEAKEN 1
   ant brace, reinforce
unbroken *adj syn* see WHOLE 1
   ant broken
unbrookable *adj syn* see INSUFFERABLE
unbuild *vb syn* see DESTROY 1
   ant build
unburden *vb syn* see RID
   rel discharge, disencumber, unload
   con encumber, lade, load, saddle, tax, weight
   ant burden
unbury *vb syn* see EXHUME

   ant bury
uncalled–for *adj* **1** *syn* see UNNECESSARY
   ant required
   2 *syn* see SUPEREROGATORY
   3 *syn* see BASELESS
   rel absurd, foolish, preposterous, silly; impertinent, intrusive,
   officious
   ant well-founded
   4 *syn* see RUDE 6
uncandid *adj syn* see DISINGENUOUS
   ant candid
uncanny *adj* **1** *syn* see WEIRD 1
   2 *syn* see SUPERNATURAL 2
uncared–for *adj syn* see NEGLECTED
   ant cared-for
uncareful *adj syn* see IRRESPONSIBLE
   ant careful
uncaring *adj syn* see CARELESS 1
   ant careful
uncaused *adj syn* see SELF-EXISTENT
unceasing *adj syn* see CONTINUAL
uncelebrated *adj syn* see OBSCURE 5
   ant celebrated, noted
uncelestial *adj syn* see EARTHLY 1
   ant celestial
unceremonious *adj* **1** *syn* see INFORMAL 1
   ant ceremonious
   2 *syn* see SHORT 5
uncertain *adj* **1** not stable, consistent, or predictable <was in very
   uncertain health>
   syn capricious, chancy, erratic, fluctuant, iffy, incalculable, unpredictable, whimsical; *compare* INCONSTANT 1
   rel questionable, undependable, unsettled; fickle, inconstant,
   insecure, unstable, unsure; changeable, mutable, protean, variable; unexpectable, unforeseeable
   idiom in a state of uncertainty, in suspense
   2 *syn* see INCONSTANT 1
   3 *syn* see MUTABLE 2
   4 *syn* see DOUBTFUL 1
   ant certain
   5 *syn* see MOOT
   ant certain
   6 *syn* see OBSCURE 3
   7 *syn* see VACILLATING 2
   idiom at a loss
   ant certain, set
uncertainty *n* a feeling of unsureness about someone or something
   <troubled by a growing *uncertainty* about the future>
   syn concern, doubt, doubtfulness, dubiety, dubiosity, dubitancy,
   incertitude, mistrust, query, skepticism, suspicion, uncertitude,
   wonder
   rel anxiety, bother, disquiet, trouble, worry; agitation, distress,
   perturbation, uneasiness; disfaith, distrust; hesitation, reserve,
   salt
   con assurance, certitude, confidence, conviction; complacency,
   content, satisfaction
   ant certainty
uncertitude *n syn* see UNCERTAINTY
   ant certitude
unchain *vb syn* see FREE
   ant chain
unchangeable *adj syn* see INFLEXIBLE 3
   ant changeable
unchanging *adj* **1** *syn* see STEADY 2
   2 *syn* see SAME 3
   ant changeable, changing
uncharnel *vb syn* see EXHUME
unchaste *adj* **1** *syn* see IMPURE 1
   ant chaste
   2 *syn* see FAST 7
   ant chaste
unchristian *adj syn* see OUTRAGEOUS 1
   ant ‖Christian
uncivil *adj* **1** *syn* see BARBARIAN 1
   2 *syn* see RUDE 6
   rel coarse, crass, crude
   con polished, smooth, urbane
   ant civil

uncivilized *adj* **1** *syn* see BARBARIAN 1
 ant civilized
 2 *syn* see BOORISH
 ant civilized
 3 *syn* see OUTRAGEOUS 1
unclad *adj* *syn* see NUDE 2
unclean *adj* **1** *syn* see IMPURE 1
 ant clean, pure
 2 *syn* see DIRTY 1
 ant clean, cleanly
 3 *syn* see IMPURE 3
 ant clean; purified
uncleanly *adj* **1** *syn* see IMPURE 1
 ant cleanly
 2 *syn* see DIRTY 1
 ant clean, cleanly
unclear *adj* **1** *syn* see OBSCURE 3
 ant clear
 2 *syn* see FAINT 2
 ant clear, distinct
 3 *syn* see DOUBTFUL 1
 ant clear
uncloak *vb* *syn* see EXPOSE 4
 ant cloak
unclose *vb* **1** *syn* see OPEN 1
 ant close
 2 *syn* see REVEAL 1
unclosed *adj* *syn* see OPEN 1
 ant closed
unclothe *vb* **1** *syn* see STRIP 1
 ant clothe, dress
 2 *syn* see OPEN 2
unclothed *adj* *syn* see NUDE 2
 ant clothed, dressed
unclouded *adj* *syn* see FAIR 2
 ant clouded, cloudy
uncluttered *adj* *syn* see NEAT 2
 ant cluttered
uncolored *adj* *syn* see FAIR 4
 ant colored, partial
uncombed *adj* *syn* see SLOVENLY 1
uncombine *vb* *syn* see SEPARATE 1
 ant combine
un–come–at–able *adj* *syn* see INACCESSIBLE
 ant come-at-able
uncomely *adj* **1** *syn* see IMPROPER 1
 2 *syn* see PLAIN 5
 ant comely
 3 *syn* see UGLY 2
 ant comely
uncomfortable *adj* causing or likely to cause discomfort <kept an *uncomfortable* chair for uninvited callers>
 syn comfortless, discomforting, harsh, uncomforting, uncomfy
 rel distressing, easeless, uneasy
 con comforting, easy, soothing
 ant comfortable
uncomforting *adj* *syn* see UNCOMFORTABLE
 ant comforting
uncomfy *adj* *syn* see UNCOMFORTABLE
 ant comfy
uncommon *adj* **1** *syn* see INFREQUENT
 con commonplace, everyday, ordinary
 ant common
 2 *syn* see EXCEPTIONAL 1
 ant common, commonplace
‖**uncommon** *adv* *syn* see EXTRA
uncommonly *adv* **1** *syn* see OCCASIONALLY
 ant commonly
 2 *syn* see EXTRA
uncommunicative *adj* **1** *syn* see SILENT 3
 ant communicative
 2 *syn* see UNSOCIABLE
uncompanionable *adj* *syn* see UNSOCIABLE
 ant companionable
uncompassionate *adj* *syn* see UNFEELING 2
 ant compassionate
uncompensated *adj* *syn* see UNPAID 1
 ant compensated

uncomplainingness *n* *syn* see PATIENCE
 ant complainingness, discontent
uncomplete *adj* *syn* see DEFICIENT 1
 ant complete
uncompliant *adj* *syn* see INFLEXIBLE 2
 ant compliant
uncomplimentary *adj* *syn* see DEROGATORY
 ant complimentary
uncomprehensible *adj* *syn* see INCOMPREHENSIBLE 1
 ant comprehensible, graspable
uncompromising *adj* **1** *syn* see INFLEXIBLE 2
 2 *syn* see TOUGH 3
unconcealed *adj* *syn* see FRANK
unconceivable *adj* *syn* see IMPLAUSIBLE
 ant conceivable
unconcern *n* *syn* see APATHY 2
 ant concern
unconcerned *adj* *syn* see INDIFFERENT 2
 rel collected, composed, cool, nonchalant
 con anxious, careful, solicitous, worried
 ant concerned
uncondensed *adj* *syn* see UNABRIDGED
 ant condensed
unconfident *adj* *syn* see INSECURE 1
 ant confident
unconfined *adj* *syn* see FREE 2
 ant confined
uncongenial *adj* **1** *syn* see ANTIPATHETIC 2
 rel displeasing, unattractive, unlikable, unpleasing
 ant congenial
 2 *syn* see INHARMONIOUS 2
unconnected *adj* *syn* see INCOHERENT 2
 ant connected, ordered
unconquerable *adj* **1** *syn* see INVINCIBLE 1
 rel insuperable, unsurmountable; proof, resistant, secure, tight
 idiom more than a match for
 con beatable, vincible; expugnable, pregnable, vulnerable; insecure, open, unprotected
 ant conquerable
 2 *syn* see INSUPERABLE
 ant conquerable
unconscionable *adj* **1** *syn* see UNSCRUPULOUS
 ant conscientious, conscionable
 2 *syn* see EXCESSIVE 1
 3 *syn* see UNREASONABLE 2
 4 *syn* see OUTRAGEOUS 1
unconscious *adj* *syn* see INSENSIBLE 2
 ant conscious
unconsequential *adj* *syn* see PETTY 2
 ant consequential
unconsidered *adj* **1** *syn* see PETTY 2
 2 *syn* see RANDOM
 ant considered, planned
 3 *syn* see RASH 1
 ant considered
unconsolable *adj* *syn* see INCONSOLABLE
 ant consolable
unconspicuous *adj* *syn* see INCONSPICUOUS
 ant conspicuous
unconstrained *adj* **1** *syn* see EASYGOING 3
 2 *syn* see DEMONSTRATIVE
 ant constrained
unconstraint *n* freedom from constraint or pressure <had always been used to the *unconstraint* of a happy affectionate family>
 syn abandon, ease, naturalness, spontaneity, unrestraint; *compare* ABANDON 2
 rel impulsiveness, instinctiveness; ingenuousness, naiveté, simplicity, unsophistication
 con pressure, strain, stress, tension; formality, rigidity; sophistication
 ant constraint
uncontainable *adj* *syn* see IRREPRESSIBLE
uncontent *adj* *syn* see DISCONTENTED

---

syn synonym(s)   *rel* related word(s)
ant antonym(s)   *con* contrasted word(s)
idiom idiomatic equivalent(s)
‖ use limited; if in doubt, see a dictionary

ant content, contented

uncontented *adj syn* see DISCONTENTED
ant content, contented

uncontestable *adj syn* see POSITIVE 3
ant contestable

uncontinuous *adj syn* see INCOHERENT 2

uncontrite *adj syn* see REMORSELESS
ant contrite

uncontrollable *adj* **1** *syn* see UNRULY 1
ant controllable
2 *syn* see IRREPRESSIBLE
ant controllable

uncontrovertible *adj syn* see POSITIVE 3
ant controvertible, disputable

unconversant *adj syn* see INEXPERIENCED
ant conversant, versed

unconvincing *adj syn* see IMPLAUSIBLE
ant convincing

uncooked *adj syn* see RAW 1
ant cooked

‖**uncorporal** *adj syn* see IMMATERIAL 1

uncorrectable *adj syn* see HOPELESS 2
ant correctable

uncostly *adj syn* see CHEAP 1
ant costly

uncountable *adj* **1** *syn* see INNUMERABLE
ant countable
2 *syn* see INCALCULABLE 1

uncounted *adj syn* see INNUMERABLE

uncouple *vb syn* see DETACH
ant couple

uncourteous *adj syn* see RUDE 6
ant courteous

uncouth *adj* **1** *syn* see STRANGE 4
2 *syn* see DERELICT 1
3 *syn* see COARSE 3
ant couth
4 *syn* see RUDE 6

uncover *vb* **1** *syn* see REVEAL 1
2 *syn* see EXPOSE 1
3 *syn* see OPEN 2
ant cover

uncovered *adj syn* see OPEN 2

uncreate *vb syn* see ANNIHILATE 2

uncreated *adj syn* see SELF-EXISTENT
ant created

uncreative *adj syn* see UNORIGINAL
ant creative

uncritical *adj syn* see SUPERFICIAL 2
rel imprecise, inaccurate, inexact; careless, casual, offhand, perfunctory, slipshod
con accurate, exact, precise; careful; discerning, discriminating, penetrating
ant critical

uncrown *vb syn* see DEPOSE 1
ant coronate, crown

unction *n syn* see OINTMENT

unctious *adj syn* see FULSOME

unctuous *adj* **1** *syn* see FATTY 2
2 *syn* see FULSOME

uncultivated *adj* **1** *syn* see COARSE 3
ant cultivated
2 *syn* see BARBARIAN 1
ant cultivated
3 *syn* see WILD 1
ant cultivated

uncultured *adj* **1** *syn* see BOORISH
ant cultured
2 *syn* see COARSE 3

uncurable *adj syn* see HOPELESS 2
ant curable

uncurbed *adj syn* see AUDACIOUS 4
ant curbed

uncurious *adj syn* see INDIFFERENT 2
ant curious

uncurtain *vb syn* see REVEAL 1

uncustomary *adj syn* see EXCEPTIONAL 1
ant customary

uncut *adj syn* see UNABRIDGED
ant cut

undamaged *adj syn* see WHOLE 1
ant damaged

undaring *adj syn* see TIMID 2
ant daring

undarkened *adj syn* see FAIR 2

undauntable *adj syn* see BRAVE 1

undaunted *adj syn* see BRAVE 1
ant daunted

undear *adj syn* see CHEAP 1
ant dear

undeceive *vb syn* see DISABUSE
ant deceive

undecided *adj* **1** *syn* see PENDING
ant decided
2 *syn* see DOUBTFUL 1

undecipherable *adj syn* see ILLEGIBLE
ant decipherable

undecisive *adj syn* see VACILLATING 2
ant decisive

undeclared *adj syn* see TACIT 1

undecorated *adj syn* see PLAIN 1
ant decorated

undecorous *adj syn* see INDECOROUS
ant decorous

undefeatable *adj syn* see INVINCIBLE 1
ant defeatable

undefiled *adj syn* see CHASTE

undefined *adj syn* see FAINT 2
ant defined

undeflowered *adj syn* see VIRGIN 1
ant deflowered

undelude *vb syn* see DISABUSE
ant delude

undemonstrated *adj syn* see UNTRIED 1
ant demonstrated

undemonstrative *adj* not socially outgoing < a shy *undemonstrative* person yet capable of deep feeling >
syn aseptic, restrained, retiring, shrinking, unaffable, unexpansive, withdrawn; *compare* UNSOCIABLE
rel chill, cold, frigid, glacial, icy; emotionless, indifferent, unemotional, uninterested; aloof, distant, reserved, standoffish
con free and easy, hail-fellow-well-met, outgiving, outgoing, palsy-walsy; sociable
ant demonstrative

undeniable *adj* **1** *syn* see POSITIVE 3
ant deniable
2 *syn* see REAL 3

undenominational *adj syn* see NONSECTARIAN
ant denominational

undependable *adj* **1** *syn* see UNRELIABLE 1
ant dependable
2 *syn* see UNSAFE
ant dependable
3 *syn* see TRICK
ant dependable

under *adv syn* see BELOW 1
ant above, over

under *prep syn* see BELOW 1
ant over

under *adj* **1** *syn* see INFERIOR 1
2 *syn* see SUBORDINATE

underage *n syn* see FAILURE 3
ant overage

underconsciousness *n syn* see SUBCONSCIOUS

undercover *adj syn* see SECRET 1

undercover man *n syn* see SPY

undercroft *n syn* see CRYPT

underdeveloped *adj syn* see BACKWARD 6

underdog *n syn* see VICTIM 2
ant overdog, top dog

underearth *adj syn* see SUBTERRANEAN

underfoot *adj* **1** *syn* see SUBTERRANEAN
2 *syn* see DOWNTRODDEN

undergo *vb syn* see EXPERIENCE 1
rel abide, bear, endure, tolerate; bow, defer, submit, yield

underground *adj syn* see SUBTERRANEAN

underhand *adj* characterized by sly unobtrusive craft or deceit < ready to use the most *underhand* methods to gain his ends >
syn devious, duplicitous, guileful, indirect, shifty, sneaking, sneaky, underhanded; *compare* SECRET 1, SLY 2
rel deceitful, dishonest; crooked, oblique; crafty, cunning, insidious, sly, tricky, wily; furtive, hangdog
con candid, frank, open, plain; forthright, straight-forward
ant aboveboard

underhanded *adj* **1** *syn* see UNDERHAND
ant aboveboard
2 *syn* see SHORTHANDED

underivative *adj* *syn* see PRIMARY 5
ant derivative

underived *adj* *syn* see PRIMARY 5
ant derived

underlease *vb* *syn* see SUBLET

underlet *vb* *syn* see SUBLET

underline *vb* *syn* see EMPHASIZE

underline *n* *syn* see CAPTION

underling *n* *syn* see INFERIOR

underly *adj* *syn* see UNWELL

underlying *adj* **1** *syn* see FUNDAMENTAL 1
rel cardinal, essential, vital; critical, crucial; indispensable, necessary, needful
2 *syn* see ELEMENTAL 1

undermanned *adj* *syn* see SHORTHANDED
ant overmanned

undermine *vb* **1** *syn* see WEAKEN 1
rel ruin, wreck; foil, frustrate, thwart
idiom bore from within
ant reinforce
2 *syn* see SABOTAGE

undermining *n* *syn* see SABOTAGE

undermost *adj* *syn* see BOTTOMMOST
ant uppermost

underneath *prep* *syn* see BELOW 1

underneath *adv* *syn* see BELOW 1

‖**underneath** *adj* *syn* see SECRET 1

underneath *n* *syn* see BOTTOM 1

underpinner *n* *syn* see SUPPORT 3

underpinning *n* **1** *syn* see BASIS 1
2 *syn* see BASE 1
3 *syn* see SUPPORT 3

underprivileged *adj* deficient in basic economic and social resources < the role of the school in bettering the lot of *underprivileged* children >
syn depressed, deprived, disadvantaged
rel handicapped; hapless, ill-fated, ill-starred, unfortunate, unlucky; impoverished, needy, poor
idiom badly off, in adverse circumstances, out of luck
con advantaged, fortunate, privileged; coddled, indulged, spoiled

underprize *vb* *syn* see DEPRECIATE 1
ant overprize

underprop *vb* *syn* see SUPPORT 5

underpropping *n* *syn* see SUPPORT 3

underrate *vb* *syn* see DEPRECIATE 1
ant overrate

underscore *vb* *syn* see EMPHASIZE

undersense *n* *syn* see SUBCONSCIOUS

undersexed *adj* *syn* see FRIGID 3
ant oversexed

underside *n* *syn* see BOTTOM 1

understaffed *adj* *syn* see SHORTHANDED
ant overstaffed

understand *vb* **1** *syn* see APPREHEND 1
idiom get the drift
ant misunderstand
2 *syn* see KNOW 1
idiom get the hang of
3 to view as plausible or likely < I *understand* he is expected home soon >
syn assume, believe, ‖conceit, conceive, expect, gather, imagine, ‖reckon, suppose, suspect, take, think, ‖wit; *compare* CONJECTURE
rel conclude, deduce, infer; conjecture, guess, presume, surmise; fancy; consider
con know; challenge, doubt, question

understandable *adj* of a kind to be readily understood < her style was smooth and easy, her language *understandable* >

syn apprehensible, comprehendible, comprehensible, fathomable, graspable, intelligible, knowable, lucid, luminous; *compare* CLEAR 4, 5
rel clear-cut, unambiguous, unblurred; plain, simple, straightforward; exoteric, lay, popular
con mysterious, obscure, strange, vague; cryptic, esoteric, hidden

understanding *n* **1** *syn* see REASON 5
rel discernment, discrimination, insight, penetration; awareness, intuition; apprehension, comprehension, grasp
2 *syn* see AGREEMENT 2
3 *syn* see MEANING 1

understood *adj* *syn* see TACIT 1

understrapper *n* *syn* see INFERIOR

understructure *n* *syn* see BASE 1
ant superstructure

undersurface *n* *syn* see BOTTOM 1

undertake *vb* **1** *syn* see TRY 5
rel begin, commence, start
idiom put (*or* set) one's hand to
2 *syn* see TAKE ON 3
3 *syn* see PROMISE 1
rel certify, warrant
idiom stand back of (*or* behind)

undertaker *n* **1** *syn* see ENTREPRENEUR 1
2 *syn* see MORTICIAN

undertaking *n* **1** *syn* see ATTEMPT
2 *syn* see PROJECT 2

under–the–table *adj* *syn* see SECRET 1
ant aboveboard

undertone *n* **1** *syn* see MURMUR 1
2 *syn* see ASSOCIATION 4

undervalue *vb* *syn* see DEPRECIATE 1
ant overvalue

underwater *adj* *syn* see SUBMARINE

underwit *n* *syn* see FOOL 4

underworld *n* *syn* see HELL

undescribable *adj* *syn* see UNUTTERABLE
ant describable

undesignated *adj* *syn* see ANONYMOUS

undesigned *adj* *syn* see UNINTENTIONAL
ant designed

undesigning *adj* *syn* see GENUINE 3
ant designing

undesirable *adj* *syn* see OBJECTIONABLE
ant desirable

undesired *adj* *syn* see UNWELCOME 1
ant desired

undestroyable *adj* *syn* see INDESTRUCTIBLE
ant destroyable, destructible

undeterminable *adj* *syn* see INDEFINITE 1
ant determinable

undetermined *adj* **1** *syn* see PENDING
ant determined
2 *syn* see FAINT 2

undeveloped *adj* **1** *syn* see BACKWARD 6
ant developed
2 *syn* see PRIMITIVE 3
ant advanced

undeviatingly *adv* *syn* see DIRECTLY 1

undevised *adj* *syn* see UNINTENTIONAL
ant devised

undexterous *adj* *syn* see UNSKILLFUL 1
ant dexterous

undifferenced *adj* *syn* see LIKE

undifferentiated *adj* *syn* see LIKE
ant differentiated

undiluted *adj* **1** *syn* see STRAIGHT 3
ant diluted
2 *syn* see PURE 2

undiplomatic *adj* *syn* see TACTLESS
ant diplomatic

undiscernible *adj* *syn* see IMPERCEPTIBLE

---

ant discernible
undisciplinable *adj syn* see UNRULY 1
undisciplined *adj syn* see UNRULY 1
  ant disciplined
undiscriminated *adj syn* see INDISCRIMINATE 1
  ant discriminate, discriminated
undiscriminating *adj syn* see INDISCRIMINATE 1
undisguised *adj syn* see FRANK
undisputable *adj syn* see POSITIVE 3
  ant controvertible, disputable
undissembled *adj* **1** *syn* see GENUINE 3
  ant dissembled, feigned
  2 *syn* see FRANK
undissembling *adj syn* see FRANK
  ant dissembling
undistinct *adj syn* see FAINT 2
  ant clear, distinct
undistinctive *adj syn* see FAIR 4
undistinguishing *adj syn* see INDISCRIMINATE 1
undistorted *adj syn* see TRUE 3
  ant distorted
undistracted *adj syn* see WHOLE 5
undivided *adj syn* see WHOLE 5
  ant divided
undo *vb* **1** *syn* see LOOSE 3
  2 *syn* see OPEN 1
  rel loose, untie
  3 *syn* see ABOLISH 1
  4 *syn* see DESTROY 1
  5 *syn* see OUTWIT
  idiom bring down (*or* low), bring to naught
  6 *syn* see SEDUCE 2
undocked *adj syn* see UNABRIDGED
  ant docked
undoing *n syn* see DOWNFALL 2
undomesticated *adj syn* see WILD 1
  ant domesticated
undoubtable *adj syn* see POSITIVE 3
  ant doubtable, questionable
undoubted *adj syn* see AUTHENTIC 2
  ant doubtful, questionable
undoubtedly *adv syn* see WELL 7
undoubtful *adj syn* see CONFIDENT 1
  ant doubtful
undress *vb* **1** *syn* see STRIP 1
  ant dress
  2 *syn* see EXPOSE 4
  ant dress up
undressed *adj* **1** *syn* see NUDE 2
  ant dressed
  2 *syn* see RUDE 1
  ant dressed, finished
undubitable *adj syn* see AUTHENTIC 2
  ant dubitable
undue *adj* **1** *syn* see IMPROPER 1
  2 *syn* see EXCESSIVE 1
  3 *syn* see UNREASONABLE 2
undulate *vb syn* see SLITHER 2
unduly *adv syn* see EVER 6
  ant duly
unduteous *adj syn* see IMPIOUS 2
  ant duteous
undutiful *adj syn* see IMPIOUS 2
  ant dutiful
undying *adj syn* see IMMORTAL 1
  rel continuing, persistent; interminable, unceasing; inextinguishable, unquenchable
  ant mortal
uneager *adj syn* see DISINCLINED
  ant eager
unearth *vb syn* see DISCOVER 3
  rel exhibit, expose, show; disclose, reveal; delve, dig
unearthing *n syn* see DISCOVERY
unearthly *adj* **1** *syn* see SUPERNATURAL 1
  2 *syn* see WEIRD 1
  3 *syn* see FOOLISH 2
unease *n* **1** *syn* see CARE 2
  2 *syn* see TENSION 2

  3 *syn* see EMBARRASSMENT
  ant ease, easiness
uneasiness *n* **1** *syn* see CARE 2
  2 *syn* see EMBARRASSMENT
  ant ease, easiness
uneasy *adj* **1** *syn* see TENSE 2
  rel anxious, careful, concerned, solicitous, worried; agitated,
  disquieted, disturbed, perturbed
  idiom on pins and needles
  ant easy
  2 *syn* see RESTLESS
  3 *syn* see DOUBTFUL 1
uneatable *adj syn* see INEDIBLE
  ant eatable
uneducated *adj syn* see IGNORANT 1
  ant educated, lettered
unelaborate *adj syn* see PLAIN 1
  ant elaborate
unembellished *adj syn* see PLAIN 1
  ant embellished
unembodied *adj syn* see IMMATERIAL 1
unembroidered *adj syn* see PLAIN 1
unemotional *adj* **1** *syn* see COLD 2
  rel dispassionate; unfeeling; impassive
  con affective, feeling; affectionate, demonstrative
  ant emotional
  2 *syn* see UNFEELING 2
unemphatic *adj syn* see INCONSPICUOUS
unemployed *adj* lacking a gainful occupation <the problems of
  unemployed workers>
  syn jobless, workless
  rel free, unengaged, unoccupied; underemployed; fired, laid off
  idiom at liberty, let go, on layoff, out of work
  ant employed
unending *adj* **1** *syn* see EVERLASTING 1
  2 *syn* see CONTINUAL
unendurable *adj syn* see INSUFFERABLE
  ant endurable
unenlarged *adj syn* see ILLIBERAL
unenlightened *adj syn* see BACKWARD 5
  ant enlightened
unennobled *adj syn* see IGNOBLE 1
  ant ennobled, noble
unentangle *vb syn* see EXTRICATE 2
  ant entangle
unenthusiastic *adj syn* see TEPID 2
  ant enthusiastic
unequal *adj* **1** *syn* see DIFFERENT 1
  2 *syn* see LOPSIDED
unequalable *adj syn* see SUPREME
unequaled *adj syn* see ALONE 3
  ant equaled
unequipped *adj syn* see UNFIT 2
unequitable *adj syn* see INEQUITABLE
  ant equitable
unequivocal *adj* **1** *syn* see CLEAR 5
  ant equivocal
  2 *syn* see POSITIVE 1
  ant equivocal
  3 *syn* see POSITIVE 3
unequivocally *adv syn* see EASILY 2
uneradicable *adj syn* see INDELIBLE
  ant eradicable
unerasable *adj syn* see INDELIBLE
  ant erasable
unerring *adj syn* see INFALLIBLE 1
unescapable *adj syn* see INEVITABLE
  ant escapable
unessential *adj* **1** *syn* see UNNECESSARY
  ant essential
  2 *syn* see DISPENSABLE
  ant essential
unethical *adj syn* see CORRUPT 2
  ant ethical
unevadable *adj syn* see INEVITABLE
  ant evadable
uneven *adj* **1** *syn* see ROUGH 1
  ant even

2 *syn* see LOPSIDED
   ant even
3 *syn* see SPOTTY 1
   rel differing, disparate, unequal; discrepant, inconsistent
   con consistent, equal, regular
unevenness *n* **1** *syn* see DISPARITY
   2 *syn* see INEQUALITY 1
uneventful *adj syn* see COMMON 6
   ant eventful
unevolved *adj syn* see PRIMITIVE 3
   ant advanced, evolved
unexaminable *adj syn* see MYSTERIOUS
unexampled *adj syn* see ONLY 2
unexceptionable *adj syn* see DECENT 4
   ant exceptionable
unexceptional *adj* **1** *syn* see DECENT 4
   2 *syn* see COMMON 6
   ant exceptional
unexcessive *adj syn* see CONSERVATIVE 2
   ant excessive
unexpansive *adj syn* see UNDEMONSTRATIVE
   ant expansive
unexpectedly *adv syn* see UNAWARES
unexpedient *adj syn* see INADVISABLE
   ant expedient
unexperienced *adj syn* see INEXPERIENCED
   ant experienced
unexpert *adj syn* see INEFFICIENT 2
   ant expert
unexplainable *adj syn* see INEXPLICABLE
   ant explainable, explicable
unexplicit *adj syn* see OBSCURE 3
   ant explicit
unexpressed *adj* **1** *syn* see UNSPOKEN 1
   ant expressed
   2 *syn* see TACIT 1
   ant expressed
unexpressible *adj syn* see UNUTTERABLE
   ant expressible
unexpressive *adj syn* see EXPRESSIONLESS
   ant expressive
unextreme *adj syn* see CONSERVATIVE 2
unfabled *adj syn* see REAL 3
   ant fabled
unfacile *adj syn* see UNSKILLFUL 1
unfailing *adj* **1** *syn* see SAME 3
   2 *syn* see INFALLIBLE 2
   ant fallible
unfair *adj syn* see INEQUITABLE
   ant fair
unfairness *n syn* see INJUSTICE 1
   ant fairness
unfaith *n syn* see UNBELIEF
   ant faith
unfaithful *adj syn* see FAITHLESS
   ant faithful
unfaithfulness *n syn* see INFIDELITY
   ant faithfulness
unfaltering *adj syn* see SURE 2
unfamed *adj syn* see OBSCURE 5
   ant famed
unfamiliar *adj* **1** not well known < trying to find her way about the *unfamiliar* room in the dark >
   syn new, strange, unaccustomed
   rel exotic, foreign; curious, peculiar, remarkable; unknown
   con accustomed, commonplace, customary, ordinary, usual, wonted
   ant familiar
   2 *syn* see IGNORANT 2
   ant familiar
unfamiliarity *n syn* see IGNORANCE 2
unfantastic *adj syn* see REALISTIC
   ant fantastic
unfashioned *adj syn* see RUDE 1
unfasten *vb syn* see LOOSE 3
   ant fasten
unfastidious *adj syn* see SLOVENLY 1
   ant fastidious

unfathered *adj syn* see ILLEGITIMATE 1
unfathomable *adj* **1** *syn* see BOTTOMLESS 2
   ant fathomable
   2 *syn* see INCOMPREHENSIBLE 1
   ant fathomable
unfathomed *adj syn* see HUGE
unfavorable *adj* **1** *syn* see ADVERSE 2
   ant favorable
   2 *syn* see EVIL 5
unfavorably *adv syn* see AMISS 2
unfearful *adj syn* see BRAVE 1
   ant fearful
unfearing *adj syn* see BRAVE 1
   ant fearing
unfeasible *adj syn* see IMPOSSIBLE 1
   ant feasible, practicable
unfeeling *adj* **1** *syn* see INSENSATE 1
   ant feeling
   2 lacking in normal human sympathy < an *unfeeling* response to a plea for help >
   syn callous, cold-blooded, coldhearted, compassionless, hard≠boiled, hardened, hardhearted, heartless, ironhearted, marble-hearted, obdurate, stony, stonyhearted, uncompassionate, unemotional, unsympathetic; *compare* PITILESS
   rel brutal, cruel, indurated, merciless, roughhearted, ruthless, tough; exacting, severe; unamiable, uncordial, unkind; cantankerous, churlish, crotchety, curmudgeonly, surly
   idiom hard of heart
   con considerate, gentle, thoughtful; kind, merciful; compassionate, sympathetic, warmhearted
   ant feeling
   3 *syn* see NUMB 1
unfeigned *adj* **1** *syn* see SINCERE 1
   ant feigned
   2 *syn* see GENUINE 3
   ant dissembled, feigned
unfertile *adj syn* see BARREN 2
   ant fertile
unfinished *adj* **1** *syn* see RUDE 1
   ant dressed, finished
   2 *syn* see AMATEURISH
   ant finished
unfit *adj* **1** not adapted or appropriate to a particular end < land *unfit* for farming >
   syn ill-adapted, ill-suited, inappropriate, inapt, unfitted, unmeet, unsuitable, unsuited
   rel discordant, inharmonious; improper, infelicitous, unbecoming; incompatible, incongruous, uncongenial
   idiom out of drawing, out of one's element, out of place
   con adapted, appropriate, apt, suitable, suited; congruous, harmonious
   ant fit
   2 lacking essential qualifications < politicians *unfit* to govern >
   syn disqualified, incapable, incompetent, ineligible, unequipped, unfitted, unqualified
   rel awkward, blundering, bungling; butterfingered, heavy-handed, maladjusted, maladroit, unhandy; inefficient, inexpert, unproficient, unskillful
   con capable, competent, qualified; adroit, dexterous, handy; expert, skilled
unfitted *adj* **1** *syn* see UNFIT 1
   2 *syn* see UNFIT 2
   ant fitted
unfitting *adj syn* see IMPROPER 1
   ant fitting
unfix *vb* **1** *syn* see LOOSE 3
   ant fix
   2 *syn* see DETACH
unfixedness *n syn* see INSTABILITY
unflagging *adj syn* see INDEFATIGABLE
   rel constant, steady
   ant flagging
unflappable *adj syn* see COOL 2

---

syn synonym(s)   *rel* related word(s)
ant antonym(s)   *con* contrasted word(s)
idiom idiomatic equivalent(s)
|| use limited; if in doubt, see a dictionary

rel easy, relaxed

unflawed *adj syn* see PERFECT 2
  ant flawed

unfledged *adj syn* see YOUNG 1
  ant fledged

unfleshed *adj syn* see INEXPERIENCED

unfleshly *adj syn* see IMMATERIAL 1
  ant fleshly

unflexible *adj syn* see STIFF 1
  ant flexible

unflinching *adj syn* see GRIM 3

unfluctuating *adj syn* see STEADY 2
  ant fluctuant, fluctuating

unfold *vb* **1** *syn* see OPEN 4
  ant fold
  2 *syn* see SOLVE 2
  3 to disclose by degrees to the sight or understanding < shyly she *unfolded* her hopes for the future >
  syn develop, elaborate, evolve
  rel demonstrate, evidence, evince, manifest, show; disclose, display, exhibit, expose, reveal

unfolding *n syn* see DEVELOPMENT

unforbearing *adj syn* see INTOLERANT 1
  ant forbearing

unforced *adj syn* see VOLUNTARY
  ant forced

unforgivable *adj syn* see INEXCUSABLE
  ant forgivable

unformed *adj* **1** *syn* see FORMLESS
  rel unfinished
  ant formed
  2 *syn* see RUDE 1

unfortunate *adj* **1** *syn* see UNLUCKY
  rel infelicitous; deplorable, miserable, sad, wretched; malefic
  con auspicious, favorable, propitious
  ant fortunate
  2 *syn* see INFELICITOUS
  3 *syn* see DEPLORABLE

unfounded *adj syn* see BASELESS
  rel deceptive, misleading; dishonest, mendacious, untruthful
  ant well-founded

unframe *vb syn* see DESTROY 1

unfrank *adj syn* see DISINGENUOUS
  ant frank

unfrequent *adj syn* see INFREQUENT
  ant frequent

unfrequently *adv syn* see SELDOM
  ant frequently

unfriendly *adj syn* see HOSTILE 1
  ant friendly

unfruitful *adj syn* see STERILE 1
  con fecund, fertile
  ant fruitful, prolific

unfunctional *adj syn* see IMPRACTICABLE 2
  ant functional

unfussy *adj syn* see EASYGOING 3
  ant fussy

ungainly *adj syn* see CLUMSY 1
  rel blundering, lubberly, maladroit
  con graceful, supple, willowy; gainly

ungarnished *adj syn* see PLAIN 1
  ant garnished

ungenerous *adj* **1** *syn* see PETTY 2
  ant generous
  2 *syn* see STINGY
  ant generous

ungenial *adj syn* see ANTIPATHETIC 2
  ant genial

ungenuine *adj syn* see SPURIOUS 3
  ant genuine

ungetatable *adj syn* see INACCESSIBLE
  ant getatable

ungifted *adj syn* see AMATEURISH
  ant gifted

ungiving *adj syn* see STINGY

ungodly *adj* **1** *syn* see IMPIOUS 1
  ant godly
  2 *syn* see INDECOROUS

3 *syn* see OUTRAGEOUS 1

ungovernable *adj syn* see UNRULY 1
  ant governable

ungoverned *adj syn* see AUDACIOUS 4

ungracious *adj* **1** *syn* see RUDE 6
  ant gracious
  2 *syn* see SHORT 5
  ant gracious

ungraded *adj syn* see UNREFINED 3

ungraspable *adj syn* see INCOMPREHENSIBLE 1
  ant comprehensible, graspable

ungrateful *adj* **1** *syn* see THANKLESS 1
  ant grateful
  2 *syn* see THANKLESS 2
  3 *syn* see OFFENSIVE

ungratified *adj syn* see DISCONTENTED
  ant gratified

ungrounded *adj syn* see BASELESS

unguarded *adj syn* see INCAUTIOUS 1
  ant guarded

unguent *n syn* see OINTMENT

unguessed *adj syn* see MYSTERIOUS

unguilty *adj syn* see INNOCENT 2
  ant guilty

unhallowed *adj* **1** *syn* see IMPIOUS 1
  2 *syn* see FIENDISH

unhampered *adj syn* see AUDACIOUS 4
  ant hampered

unhandsome *adj* **1** *syn* see PLAIN 5
  ant handsome
  2 *syn* see RUDE 6

unhandy *adj* **1** *syn* see UNWIELDY
  2 *syn* see UNSKILLFUL 1
  ant handy
  3 *syn* see AWKWARD 2
  ant handy

unhappiness *n* **1** *syn* see MISERY 1
  ant happiness
  2 *syn* see SADNESS
  ant happiness

unhappy *adj* **1** *syn* see UNLUCKY
  ant happy
  2 *syn* see INFELICITOUS
  ant happy
  3 *syn* see AWKWARD 2
  4 *syn* see SAD 1
  ant happy
  5 *syn* see BAD 8
  6 *syn* see GLOOMY 3

unharmed *adj syn* see SAFE 1

unharmonious *adj* **1** *syn* see DISSONANT 1
  ant harmonious
  2 *syn* see INHARMONIOUS 2
  ant harmonious

unhasty *adj syn* see SLOW 2
  ant hasty

unhealth *n syn* see SICKNESS 1
  ant health

unhealthful *adj syn* see UNWHOLESOME 1
  ant healthful

unhealthiness *n syn* see INFIRMITY 1
  ant healthiness

unhealthy *adj* **1** *syn* see UNWHOLESOME 1
  ant healthy
  2 *syn* see DANGEROUS 1
  3 *syn* see VICIOUS 2

unheard-of *adj syn* see OBSCURE 5

unheavy *adj syn* see LIGHT 1
  ant heavy

unheeding *adj* **1** *syn* see INATTENTIVE
  ant heedful, heeding
  2 *syn* see CARELESS 1
  ant heedful, heeding

unhewn *adj syn* see RUDE 1

unhinge *vb* **1** *syn* see UPSET 5
  2 *syn* see MADDEN 1
  3 *syn* see DISCOMPOSE 1

unholy *adj* **1** *syn* see IMPIOUS 1

ant holy
2 syn see BLAMEWORTHY
3 syn see OUTRAGEOUS 1
unhonest *adj syn* see DISHONEST
ant honest
unhorse *vb* **1 syn** see THROW 2
2 syn see OVERTHROW 2
unhurried *adj syn* see SLOW 2
ant hurried
unhurt *adj syn* see WHOLE 1
unicity *n syn* see UNIQUENESS
unidealistic *adj syn* see REALISTIC
ant idealistic
unification *n* a bringing together or being brought together into an integrated whole < *unification* of mass transit facilities is increasingly needed >
syn coadunation, coalition, combination consolidation, melding, mergence, merger, merging, union; *compare* ALLIANCE 2
rel affiliation, connection, interlocking, joining, linkage; coupling, hookup
con dissociation, disunion, division, parting, partition, separation
ant disunification
uniform *adj* **1 syn** see LIKE
ant various
2 syn see STEADY 2
rel compatible, consistent, consonant; ordered, orderly, regular
ant multiform
uniformly *adv syn* see EVENLY 3
ant variably
unify *vb* **1** to gather or combine parts or elements into a close mass or a coherent whole < minorities that are *unified* by persecution >
syn compact, concentrate, consolidate, integrate; *compare* UNITE 2
rel articulate, concatenate; order, organize, systematize; bind, tie
idiom make one
con divide, part, scatter; disorder, disorganize; disunite, divide, separate
ant break up, disunify
2 syn see HARMONIZE 4
ant disunify
unifying *adj syn* see INTEGRATIVE
ant disunifying
unilluminated *adj syn* see DARK 1
ant illuminated
unimaginable *adj* **1 syn** see INCONCEIVABLE 1
ant imaginable
2 syn see EXCEPTIONAL 1
3 syn see INCREDIBLE 1
unimpaired *adj syn* see WHOLE 1
ant impaired
unimpassioned *adj* **1 syn** see MATTER-OF-FACT 3
ant impassioned
2 syn see SOBER 3
rel impassive, phlegmatic, stoic, stolid; calm, placid, tranquil
con ardent, fervent, fervid, heated, keen
ant impassioned, passionate
unimpeachable *adj syn* see DECENT 4
unimportant *adj syn* see LITTLE 3
ant important
unimpressible *adj syn* see INSUSCEPTIBLE
ant impressible
unimpressionable *adj syn* see INSUSCEPTIBLE
ant impressionable
unindifferent *adj syn* see BIASED 2
ant indifferent
unindulgent *adj syn* see INTOLERANT 1
ant indulgent
uninflammable *adj syn* see NONCOMBUSTIBLE
ant flammable, inflammable
uninformed *adj syn* see IGNORANT 2
ant informed
uninhibited *adj syn* see AUDACIOUS 4
ant inhibited
uninhibitedness *n syn* see ABANDON 2
uninitiate *n syn* see AMATEUR 2

uninjured *adj syn* see WHOLE 1
ant injured
uninjurious *adj syn* see SAFE 3
uninspired *adj* **1 syn** see UNORIGINAL
ant inspired
2 syn see PONDEROUS 2
ant inspired
uninstructed *adj* **1 syn** see IGNORANT 2
2 syn see IGNORANT 1
unintelligent *adj syn* see SIMPLE 3
ant intelligent
unintelligible *adj* **1 syn** see INCOMPREHENSIBLE 1
ant intelligible
2 syn see OBSCURE 3
ant intelligible
unintended *adj syn* see UNINTENTIONAL
ant intended
unintentional *adj* not the result of intent or design < her slight of the newcomer was quite *unintentional* >
syn inadvertent, undesigned, undevised, unintended, unplanned, unpremeditated, unpurposed, unthought; *compare* ACCIDENTAL, EXTEMPORANEOUS
rel causeless, chance, haphazard, purposeless, random; unanticipated, unexpected, unforeseen, unlooked-for; unthinking, unwitting
con deliberate, designed, devised, intended, planned, premeditated, purposed
ant intentional
uninterested *adj syn* see INDIFFERENT 2
ant interested
uninteresting *adj syn* see ARID 2
ant interesting
uninterrupted *adj syn* see CONTINUAL
ant intermitted, intermittent
unintermittedly *adv syn* see TOGETHER 2
unintermittent *adj syn* see CONTINUAL
ant intermitted, intermittent
uninterrupted *adj* **1 syn** see CONTINUAL
ant interrupted
2 syn see DIRECT 2
uninterruptedly *adv syn* see TOGETHER 2
ant interruptedly
uninventive *adj syn* see UNORIGINAL
ant inventive
uninvited *adj syn* see UNASKED
ant invited
union *n* **1 syn** see UNIFICATION
ant disunion
2 syn see ASSOCIATION 2
3 syn see JOINT 1
4 syn see ALLIANCE 2
unique *adj* **1 syn** see ONLY 2
2 syn see SINGLE 2
3 syn see ALONE 3
4 syn see EXCEPTIONAL 1
uniqueness *n* the quality or state of standing alone and without a peer < the time she rode in an old-time sleigh — never would she forget the *uniqueness* of that experience >
syn oneness, singleness, unicity, uniquity
rel curiousness, oddity, peculiarity, quaintness, singularity, strangeness; import, mark, moment, note, significance; memorability, notability, remarkableness, unusualness
con commonness, commonplaceness, ordinariness, routineness; monotony, sameness, tediousness
uniquity *n syn* see UNIQUENESS
unite *vb* **1 syn** see JOIN 1
rel amalgamate, blend, merge, mix
ant alienate; disunite, divide
2 to join forces especially in order to act more effectively < citizen groups *uniting* to further the fight against crime >
syn band, coadjute, combine, concur, conjoin, cooperate, league; *compare* UNIFY 1

---

syn synonym(s)   *rel* related word(s)
ant antonym(s)   *con* contrasted word(s)
idiom idiomatic equivalent(s)
‖ use limited; if in doubt, see a dictionary

rel affiliate, ally, associate, confederate; coalesce, commingle, fuse, mingle, weld
  idiom draw together, hook up with, join forces (with), make common cause (with), throw in with
  con break up, disband, separate, split (up)
  ant disunite, part

unity *n* **1** the condition of being or consisting of one < *unity* — the idea conveyed by whatever we visualize as one thing >
  syn individuality, oneness, singleness, singularity, singularness
  rel identity, selfsameness, soleness, uniqueness, uniquity
  ant multiplicity
  2 *syn* see HARMONY 3
  rel agreement, identity, oneness, union; solidarity; conformance, congruity
  ant disunity

universal *adj* **1** *syn* see OMNIPRESENT
  2 present or significant throughout the world < *universal* aspirations for a better world >
  syn catholic, cosmic, cosmopolitan, ecumenical, global, planetary, worldwide
  rel all-embracing, all-inclusive; broad, extensive, sweeping; all, entire, total, whole
  con narrow, petty, provincial
  ant parochial
  3 *syn* see GENERAL 2
  ant particular

universe *n* the totality of physical entities < theories of the expanding *universe* >
  syn cosmos (*or* kosmos), creation, macrocosm, macrocosmos, megacosm, nature, world

univocal *adj* *syn* see CLEAR 5
  ant ambiguous

unjust *adj* *syn* see INEQUITABLE
  ant just

unjustifiable *adj* **1** *syn* see UNREASONABLE 2
  ant justifiable
  2 *syn* see INEXCUSABLE
  ant justifiable

unjustness *n* *syn* see INJUSTICE 1
  ant justice, justness

unkempt *adj* *syn* see SLOVENLY 1
  ant kempt

unknow *vb* *syn* see FORGET 1

unknowable *adj* **1** *syn* see INCOMPREHENSIBLE 1
  ant knowable
  2 *syn* see INCONCEIVABLE 1
  ant knowable
  3 *syn* see MYSTERIOUS

unknowing *adj* *syn* see IGNORANT 2
  ant knowing

unknowingness *n* *syn* see IGNORANCE 2
  ant knowingness

unknown *adj* *syn* see OBSCURE 5
  ant well-known

unlade *vb* *syn* see UNLOAD
  ant lade, load

unlawful *adj* contrary to or prohibited by law < the spread of *unlawful* wiretapping >
  syn criminal, illegal, illegitimate, illicit, lawless, wrongful
  rel flagitious, iniquitous, nefarious; black-market, bootleg, under-the-counter; exceptionable, improper, intolerable, objectionable
  idiom against the law
  con condign, due, rightful; allowable, justifiable, permissible
  ant lawful

unlawfulness *n* *syn* see ILLEGALITY
  ant lawfulness

unlax *vb* **1** *syn* see RELAX 2
  2 *syn* see REST 2

unlearned *adj* *syn* see UNSCHOLARLY
  ant erudite, learned

unleash *vb* *syn* see TAKE OUT (on)

unless *conj* *syn* see EXCEPT 1

unlettered *adj* *syn* see IGNORANT 1
  ant educated, lettered

unlevel *adj* *syn* see ROUGH 1
  ant level

unlike *adj* *syn* see DIFFERENT 1

  ant like

unlikely *adj* *syn* see IMPROBABLE 1
  ant likely

unlikeness *n* *syn* see DISSIMILARITY
  rel incompatibility, incongruousness, inconsistence
  ant likeness

unlimited *adj* **1** *syn* see LIMITLESS
  ant limited, measured
  2 *syn* see TOTAL 5
  ant limited

unload *vb* to remove cargo or the cargo of < *unload* cattle from a truck >
  syn disburden, discharge, off-load, unlade, unship, unstow
  rel disencumber, dump, jettison, lighten; stevedore; debark, disembark, land
  idiom break bulk
  ant lade, load

unloose *vb* *syn* see LOOSE 3

unloosen *vb* *syn* see LOOSE 3

unloyal *adj* *syn* see FAITHLESS
  ant loyal

‖**unluck** *n* *syn* see MISFORTUNE
  ant luck

unlucky *adj* **1** *syn* see OMINOUS
  2 involving or suffering misfortune that results from chance < in spite of careful planning the expedition was *unlucky* from the start >
  syn hapless, ill-fated, ill-starred, luckless, misfortunate, star-crossed, unfortunate, unhappy, untoward
  rel calamitous, cataclysmic, catastrophic, dire, disastrous, tragical
  idiom down on one's luck, out of luck
  con fortunate, happy, providential; prosperous, successful; coming, made
  ant lucky

unmake *vb* **1** *syn* see DESTROY 1
  2 *syn* see DEPOSE 1
  ant make

unman *vb* *syn* see UNNERVE
  rel deplete, drain, exhaust, impoverish; abase, degrade; disqualify, paralyze, prostrate, unfit
  idiom knock the bottom (*or* stuffing) out of
  con brace, fortify
  ant man

unmanageable *adj* *syn* see UNRULY 1
  ant manageable

unmanly *adj* **1** *syn* see COWARDLY
  ant manly
  2 *syn* see EFFEMINATE
  ant manly

unmannered *adj* **1** *syn* see RUDE 6
  2 *syn* see FRANK

unmannerly *adj* *syn* see RUDE 6
  ant mannerly

unmarred *adj* *syn* see WHOLE 1
  ant marred

unmarried *adj* *syn* see SINGLE 1
  ant married, wed

unmarry *vb* *syn* see DIVORCE 2

unmask *vb* *syn* see EXPOSE 4

unmatchable *adj* *syn* see SUPREME

unmatched *adj* **1** *syn* see ALONE 3
  2 *syn* see ODD 1
  ant matched

unmaterial *adj* *syn* see IMMATERIAL 1
  ant material

unmeaning *adj* *syn* see SENSELESS 5
  ant meaningful

unmeasurable *adj* **1** *syn* see INCALCULABLE 1
  ant measurable
  2 *syn* see EXCESSIVE 1

unmeasured *adj* **1** *syn* see INCALCULABLE 1
  ant measurable
  2 *syn* see LIMITLESS
  ant limited, measured

unmeditated *adj* *syn* see SPONTANEOUS
  ant meditated

unmeet *adj* *syn* see UNFIT 1

ant meet

unmeetness *n syn* see IMPROPRIETY 1

unmellowed *adj syn* see YOUNG 1
  con developed, matured, ripened
  ant mellow, mellowed

unmerciful *adj syn* see PITILESS
  ant merciful

unmindful *adj syn* see FORGETFUL
  con anxious, careful, concerned
  ant mindful; solicitous

unmindfulness *n syn* see APATHY 2
  ant mindfulness

unmistakable *adj syn* see CLEAR 5
  ant mistakable

unmitigated *adj* 1 *syn* see PURE 2
  2 *syn* see UTTER

unmixable *adj syn* see INCONSONANT 1

unmixed *adj* 1 *syn* see STRAIGHT 3
  ant blended, mixed
  2 *syn* see PURE 2

unmodern *adj syn* see OLD-FASHIONED
  ant modern

unmodifiable *adj syn* see INFLEXIBLE 3
  ant modifiable

unmovable *adj* 1 *syn* see IMMOVABLE 1
  ant mobile, movable
  2 *syn* see INFLEXIBLE 3

unmoving *adj syn* see STATIC
  ant mobile

unmusical *adj syn* see DISSONANT 1
  ant musical

unnamed *adj syn* see ANONYMOUS

unnatural *adj* 1 *syn* see IRREGULAR 1
  2 *syn* see SUPERNATURAL 2
  ant natural

unneat *adj syn* see SLOVENLY 1
  ant neat

unnecessary *adj* not needed or unavoidable <*unnecessary* loss of life>
  syn inessential, needless, uncalled-for, unessential, unneeded, unneedful, unrequired
  rel excess, redundant, superfluous, surplus; lavish, prodigal, profuse; gratuitous, supererogatory
  con essential, needed, required, vital; inevitable, unescapable
  ant necessary; unavoidable

unneeded *adj syn* see UNNECESSARY
  ant needed; unavoidable

unneedful *adj syn* see UNNECESSARY
  ant needful; unavoidable

unnerve *vb* to deprive of strength, spirit, and vigor <a man so *unnerved* as to be bereft of sense and judgment>
  syn castrate, emasculate, enervate, unman, unstring
  rel enfeeble, sap, undermine, weaken; bewilder, confound, distract; agitate, perturb, upset
  con brace (up), inspirit, invigorate, reinforce, strengthen; encourage, hearten, steel
  ant nerve

unneutral *adj syn* see BIASED 2
  ant neutral

unnoted *adj syn* see OBSCURE 5
  rel unconsidered, unobserved, unremarked
  ant noted

unnoteworthy *adj syn* see COMMON 6
  ant noteworthy

unnoticeable *adj syn* see INCONSPICUOUS
  ant noticeable

unnoticing *adj syn* see INATTENTIVE
  ant noticing

unnumberable *adj syn* see INNUMERABLE

unnumbered *adj syn* see INNUMERABLE
  ant numbered

unobjectionable *adj syn* see DECENT 4
  ant objectionable

unobjective *adj syn* see SUBJECTIVE
  ant objective

unobservable *adj syn* see IMPERCEPTIBLE

unobservant *adj syn* see INATTENTIVE
  ant observant, observing

unobserving *adj syn* see INATTENTIVE
  ant observant, observing

unobstructed *adj syn* see OPEN 1
  con clogged, plugged
  ant obstructed

unobtainable *adj syn* see INACCESSIBLE

unobtrusive *adj syn* see QUIET 4
  ant obtrusive

unoffending *adj syn* see HARMLESS
  ant offending

unoffensive *adj syn* see HARMLESS
  ant offensive

unofficial *adj syn* see INFORMAL 1

unoften *adv syn* see SELDOM
  ant often

unordinary *adj syn* see EXCEPTIONAL 1
  ant ordinary

unorganized *adj syn* see INCOHERENT 2
  ant organized

unoriginal *adj* lacking or manifesting a lack of capacity for originality <a good man but with a mind stolid and *unoriginal*>
  syn noncreative, sterile, uncreative, uninspired, uninventive, unoriginative; *compare* ARID 2
  rel arid, barren, dry; dull, prosaic, staid, stodgy, stuffy, unfired
  con creative, inspired, inventive, originative; alert, aware, keen; constructive, productive
  ant original

unoriginated *adj syn* see SELF-EXISTENT

unoriginative *adj syn* see UNORIGINAL
  ant originative

unornamented *adj syn* see PLAIN 1

unorthodox *adj syn* see HERETICAL
  ant orthodox

unorthodoxy *n syn* see HERESY
  ant orthodoxy

unostentatious *adj syn* see PLAIN 1
  ant ostentatious

unpaid *adj* 1 serving without pay <a charity manned by *unpaid* assistants>
  syn uncompensated, unrecompensed, unremunerated
  rel freewill, gratuitous, voluntary, volunteer
  con compensated, recompensed, remunerated
  ant paid
  2 not cleared by payment <an *unpaid* bill>
  syn due, mature, outstanding, overdue, owing, payable, unsettled
  idiom in arrears
  con cleared, discharged, liquidated, settled
  ant paid

unpaired *adj syn* see ODD 1
  ant paired

unpalatable *adj* 1 lacking appeal to the sense of taste <threw together a greasy *unpalatable* meal>
  syn distasteful, flat, flavorless, ill-flavored, insipid, savorless, tasteless, unappetizing, unsavory
  rel loathsome, nauseous, sickening; thin, washy, watery, weak
  con appetizing, delectable, delicious, flavorsome, sapid, savory, tasty
  ant palatable
  2 *syn* see BITTER 2

unparagoned *adj syn* see ALONE 3
  ant paragoned

unparalleled *adj syn* see ALONE 3
  ant paralleled

unpardonable *adj syn* see INEXCUSABLE
  ant pardonable

unparented *adj syn* see ORPHAN

unpassioned *adj syn* see NEUTRAL
  ant impassioned, passionate

unpatient *adj syn* see IMPATIENT 1
  ant patient

unpeace *n syn* see DISCORD
  ant peace

---

syn synonym(s)   *rel* related word(s)
ant antonym(s)   *con* contrasted word(s)
idiom idiomatic equivalent(s)
‖ use limited; if in doubt, see a dictionary

unpeaceful *adj syn* see RESTLESS
  ant peaceful
unpedantic *adj syn* see LIVELY 1
  ant pedantic
unperceivable *adj syn* see IMPERCEPTIBLE
unperceiving *adj* 1 *syn* see IMPERCEPTIVE
  ant perceiving, perceptive, percipient
  2 *syn* see INATTENTIVE
unperceptive *adj syn* see IMPERCEPTIVE
  ant perceiving, perceptive, percipient
unperishable *adj syn* see INDESTRUCTIBLE
  ant perishable
unpermissive *adj syn* see RIGID 3
  ant permissive
unphysical *adj syn* see IMMATERIAL 1
  ant physical
unpierceable *adj syn* see IMPASSABLE 1
  ant pierceable
unpitying *adj syn* see PITILESS
  ant pitying
unplanned *adj* 1 *syn* see RANDOM
  ant planned
  2 *syn* see UNINTENTIONAL
  ant planned
unpleasant *adj syn* see BAD 8
unpliable *adj syn* see OBSTINATE
  ant pliable, pliant
unpliant *adj syn* see OBSTINATE
  ant pliable, pliant
unpolished *adj* 1 *syn* see RUDE 1
  idiom in the rough
  ant polished
  2 *syn* see RUDE 6
  3 *syn* see BOORISH
  ant polished
unpolitic *adj syn* see TACTLESS
  ant politic
unpractical *adj syn* see IMPRACTICAL 1
  ant practical
unpracticed *adj* 1 *syn* see UNTRIED 1
  2 *syn* see INEXPERIENCED
  ant practiced
unpredictable *adj syn* see UNCERTAIN 1
  ant predictable
unprejudiced *adj syn* see FAIR 4
  ant prejudiced
unpremeditated *adj* 1 *syn* see SPONTANEOUS
  2 *syn* see UNINTENTIONAL
  ant premeditated
unprepossessed *adj syn* see FAIR 4
  ant prepossessed
unprescribed *adj syn* see VOLUNTARY
  ant prescribed
unpretentious *adj syn* see PLAIN 1
  ant pretentious
unpretty *adj syn* see PLAIN 5
  ant pretty
unprevailing *adj syn* see FUTILE
unprincipled *adj* 1 *syn* see UNSCRUPULOUS
  ant principled
  2 *syn* see ABANDONED 2
  rel corrupt, crooked, unscrupulous; dishonest, unconscientious, unethical
  3 *syn* see CORRUPT 2
  ant principled
unproductive *adj* 1 *syn* see BARREN 2
  rel impotent, infecund, unprolific
  ant productive
  2 *syn* see FUTILE
  ant productive
unprofane *adj syn* see HOLY 1
  ant profane
unproficient *adj syn* see UNSKILLFUL 1
  ant proficient, skilled
unprogressive *adj* 1 *syn* see BACKWARD 6
  ant progressive
  2 *syn* see BACKWARD 5
  ant progressive

unprompted *adj syn* see SPONTANEOUS
unpropitious *adj syn* see OMINOUS
  rel adverse, antagonistic, counter
  con cheering, encouraging, reassuring
  ant propitious
unproportionate *adj syn* see LOPSIDED
  ant proportionate
unprosperous *adj syn* see POOR 1
  ant prosperous
unprosperousness *n syn* see POVERTY 1
  ant prosperousness
unprotected *adj syn* see HELPLESS 1
  rel undefended, unguarded, unsheltered, unshielded; insecure, unsafe
  ant protected
unproved *adj syn* see UNTRIED 1
  ant proved
unpunctual *adj syn* see TARDY
  ant punctual
unpurposed *adj* 1 *syn* see UNINTENTIONAL
  2 *syn* see FECKLESS 1
unqualified *adj* 1 *syn* see UNFIT 2
  rel unskilled; unsuitable
  ant qualified
  2 *syn* see SURE 2
  rel unconditional, unlimited, unreserved; clear, explicit, express; entire, perfect, utter
  ant qualified
  3 *syn* see UTTER
  4 *syn* see PURE 2
unquenchable *adj syn* see INSATIABLE
  ant quenchable
unquestionable *adj* 1 *syn* see AUTHENTIC 2
  ant doubtable, questionable
  2 *syn* see POSITIVE 3
  rel dependable, reliable; established, well-founded, well=grounded
  ant doubtable, questionable
  3 *syn* see DOWNRIGHT 2
unquestionably *adv syn* see EASILY 2
  ant questionably
unquestioning *adj syn* see SURE 2
  ant questioning
unquiet *adj syn* see RESTLESS
  ant quiet
unravel *vb syn* see SOLVE 2
  rel disentangle, extricate, untangle
unreachable *adj syn* see INACCESSIBLE
  ant reachable
unreadable *adj syn* see ILLEGIBLE
  ant legible, readable
unreal *adj syn* see FICTITIOUS 1
  ant real
unrealistic *adj syn* see IMPRACTICAL 1
  ant realistic
unrealizable *adj syn* see IMPOSSIBLE 1
  ant realizable
unreasonable *adj* 1 *syn* see ILLOGICAL
  rel incongruous, loose, self-contradictory
  ant reasonable
  2 exceeding the bounds of reason or right < the constitutional guarantees against *unreasonable* searches and seizures >
  syn unconscionable, undue, unjustifiable, unwarrantable, unwarranted
  rel arbitrary, peremptory; excessive, immoderate, inordinate, overmuch; improper, unlawful, unrightful, wrongful
  con lawful, licit; proper, right, tolerable
  ant reasonable
unreasoned *adj syn* see ILLOGICAL
  ant reasoned
unrecking *adj syn* see CARELESS 1
unreckonable *adj syn* see INCALCULABLE 1
unrecompensed *adj syn* see UNPAID 1
  ant recompensed
unrecoverable *adj syn* see HOPELESS 2
unrefined *adj* 1 *syn* see BOORISH
  ant refined
  2 *syn* see COARSE 3

ant refined

3 not freed from unwanted material <shipped the *unrefined* ore>

syn crude, impure, native, raw, run-of-mine, ungraded, unsorted

rel rough, roughcast, roughhewn; coarse, natural, undressed, unprocessed

idiom in the rough

con dressed, processed

ant refined

unreflective *adj syn* see CARELESS 1

unregretful *adj syn* see REMORSELESS

ant regretful

unregular *adj syn* see IRREGULAR 1

ant regular

unrehearsed *adj syn* see EXTEMPORANEOUS

ant rehearsed

unrelenting *adj syn* see GRIM 3

ant relenting

unreliable *adj* **1** not to be counted on <it is certain that much of the testimony was *unreliable*>

syn dubious, fly-by-night, questionable, trustless, undependable, unsure, untrustworthy, untrusty

rel fickle, inconstant, unstable, vacillating; faithless, false, untrue; falsehearted, perfidious; shifty, slick, slippery, tricky; inaccurate, inexact, unfaithful

idiom not to be depended (or relied) on

con dependable, trustworthy, trusty; constant; faithful, true

ant reliable

2 *syn* see UNSAFE

ant reliable

unreligious *adj syn* see IRRELIGIOUS

ant religious

unremarkable *adj syn* see ORDINARY 1

unremitting *adj syn* see CONTINUAL

unremittingly *adv syn* see HARD 3

unremorseful *adj syn* see REMORSELESS

ant remorseful

unremunerated *adj syn* see UNPAID 1

ant remunerated

unrenowned *adj syn* see OBSCURE 5

ant renowned

unrepealable *adj syn* see IRREVOCABLE

ant repealable

unrepeatable *adj syn* see ONLY 2

unrepentant *adj syn* see REMORSELESS

ant repentant

unrepresentative *adj syn* see ABNORMAL 1

unrequested *adj syn* see UNASKED

unrequired *adj* **1** *syn* see UNNECESSARY

ant required

2 *syn* see DISPENSABLE

ant required

unreserved *adj* **1** *syn* see FRANK 1

ant reserved

2 *syn* see DEMONSTRATIVE

ant reserved

3 *syn* see EASYGOING 3

unresistant *adj syn* see PASSIVE 2

ant resistant, resisting

unresisting *adj syn* see PASSIVE 2

ant resistant, resisting

unresolved *adj syn* see VACILLATING 2

ant resolved

unrespectable *adj syn* see DISREPUTABLE 1

ant respectable

unresponsive *adj* **1** *syn* see INSUSCEPTIBLE

ant responsive

2 *syn* see FRIGID 3

unresponsiveness *n syn* see APATHY 1

ant responsiveness

unrest *n* a disturbed uneasy state <that popular *unrest* that, unchecked, can lead to insurrection and anarchy>

syn ailment, disquiet, disquietude, ferment, inquietude, restiveness, restlessness, storm and stress, Sturm und Drang, turmoil

rel agitation, commotion, confusion, convulsion, tumult, turbulence, upheaval; anarchy, chaos, disorder

con calm, easiness, peace, quiet

unrestful *adj* **1** *syn* see RESTLESS

ant restful

2 *syn* see NERVOUS

unrestrainable *adj syn* see IRREPRESSIBLE

ant restrainable

unrestrained *adj* **1** *syn* see EXCESSIVE 2

2 *syn* see FREE 2

ant restrained

3 *syn* see AUDACIOUS 4

rel candid, frank, open; forthright, plainspoken, straightforward; bluff, blunt, brusque

ant restrained

4 *syn* see DEMONSTRATIVE

ant restrained

unrestraint *n* **1** *syn* see UNCONSTRAINT

ant restraint

2 *syn* see ABANDON 2

unrestricted *adj syn* see OPEN 4

unriddle *vb syn* see SOLVE 2

unrighteous *adj syn* see INEQUITABLE

ant righteous

unripe *adj syn* see YOUNG 1

unrivaled *adj syn* see ALONE 3

unromantic *adj syn* see REALISTIC

ant romantic

unruffled *adj syn* see COOL 2

ant discomposed, ruffled

unruly *adj* **1** resistant to discipline or control <a stubborn *unruly* boy>

syn fractious, indocile, indomitable, intractable, recalcitrant, uncontrollable, undisciplinable, undisciplined, ungovernable, unmanageable, untoward, wild; *compare* OBSTINATE, TURBULENT 1

rel contumacious, incorrigible, insubordinate, rebellious; contrary, froward, perverse, wayward; boisterous, obstreperous, rampageous; disorderly, raffish, rambunctious, rowdy, turbulent

idiom out of hand

con controlled, easy, mild, restrained; disciplined, governable, manageable; amenable, biddable, obedient; correct, proper

ant docile, tractable

2 *syn* see TURBULENT 1

rel hard, ruffianly, tough

3 *syn* see DISOBEDIENT

unsacred *adj syn* see PROFANE 1

ant sacred

unsafe *adj* not to be depended on or trusted <an *unsafe* investment>

syn unassured, undependable, unreliable, untrustworthy

rel insecure, shaky, tottery, unsound, unstable; chancy, hazardous, risky; dangerous, jeopardous, perilous; erratic, uncertain

con dependable, trustworthy; secure, sound, stable, substantial

ant safe

unsaid *adj syn* see TACIT 1

unsalutary *adj syn* see UNWHOLESOME 1

ant salutary

unsandaled *adj syn* see BAREFOOT 1

ant sandaled

unsane *adj syn* see INSANE 1

ant sane

unsatiate *adj syn* see INSATIABLE

ant satiate, satiated

unsatisfactory *adj syn* see BAD 1

ant satisfactory

unsatisfiable *adj syn* see INSATIABLE

ant satisfiable

unsavory *adj syn* see UNPALATABLE 1

ant savory

unsay *vb syn* see ABJURE

unscathed *adj syn* see SAFE 1

unscholarly *adj* not devoted to scholarly pursuits <*unscholarly* concerns>

syn inerudite, unbookish, unlearned, unstudious

rel unenlightened, uninformed, uninitiated; callow, green, unripe; inexperienced, naive

---

syn synonym(s)   *rel* related word(s)

ant antonym(s)   *con* contrasted word(s)

idiom idiomatic equivalent(s)

‖ use limited; if in doubt, see a dictionary

con bookish, erudite, learned; enlightened, informed; experienced
ant scholarly

unschooled *adj* **1** *syn* see IGNORANT 1
2 *syn* see NATURAL 5

unscramble *vb syn* see EXTRICATE 2

unscrupulous *adj* **1** lacking in moral scruples < *unscrupulous* conduct of political leaders >
syn conscienceless, stick-at-nothing, unconscionable, unprincipled
rel crafty, deceitful, scheming; improper, unseemly, wrongful; corrupt, crooked, dishonest; questionable, shady, sinister, underhand
con conscientious, dutiful, proper, upright; dependable, reliable, responsible
ant scrupulous
2 *syn* see CORRUPT 2
con meticulous, particular, punctilious, strict
ant scrupulous

unseasonable *adj* **1** involving or occurring at an inappropriate or unexpected time < his wife's sudden return proved most *unseasonable* >
syn ill-seasoned, ill-timed, inopportune, malapropos, mistimed, untimely
rel deplorable, inappropriate, inconvenient, unsuitable; inauspicious, infelicitous, undesirable, unfavorable, unfortunate
con apropos, opportune, timely, well-timed
ant seasonable
2 *syn* see IMPROPER 1

unseasoned *adj syn* see INEXPERIENCED
ant seasoned

unseat *vb syn* see THROW 2

unsectarian *adj syn* see NONSECTARIAN
ant sectarian

unseemliness *n syn* see IMPROPRIETY 1
ant propriety, seemliness

unseemly *adj* **1** *syn* see INDECOROUS
rel coarse, crude, inelegant, unrefined; raffish, rowdy, ruffianly
con prim, restrained, starchy, stiff, stilted; elegant, gracious, polished, refined
ant seemly
2 *syn* see IMPROPER 1
ant seemly

unselfish *adj syn* see SELFLESS
ant selfish

unsentimental *adj syn* see REALISTIC
ant sentimental

unserviceable *adj syn* see IMPRACTICABLE 2
ant serviceable

unsettle *vb* **1** *syn* see DISORDER 1
rel agitate, disquiet, perturb; discommode, incommode, trouble
con calm, ease, quiet, stabilize, steady
ant settle
2 *syn* see UPSET 5
ant settle
3 *syn* see DISCOMPOSE 1

unsettled *adj* **1** *syn* see RESTLESS
2 *syn* see CHANGEABLE 1
ant settled
3 *syn* see DOUBTFUL 1
4 *syn* see PENDING
ant settled
5 *syn* see BACK 1
6 *syn* see UNPAID 2
ant settled

unsettledness *n syn* see INSTABILITY

unsex *vb syn* see STERILIZE

unshackle *vb syn* see FREE
ant shackle

unshakable *adj syn* see SURE 2
ant shakable

unshaken *adj syn* see SURE 2
ant shaken

unshaped *adj syn* see FORMLESS
ant shaped

unshared *adj syn* see SOLE 4
ant shared

unship *vb syn* see UNLOAD

unshod *adj syn* see BAREFOOT 1
ant shod

unshroud *vb syn* see EXPOSE 4
ant shroud

unshut *vb syn* see OPEN 1
ant shut

unsightly *adj syn* see UGLY 2
rel ill-shaped, unshapely; unesthetic; drab, dull, lackluster
ant sightly

unsimilar *adj syn* see DIFFERENT 1
ant similar

unskilled *adj* **1** *syn* see AMATEURISH
ant skilled
2 *syn* see INEFFICIENT 2
ant skilled

unskillful *adj* **1** lacking in skill or proficiency < an ardent but *unskillful* home mechanic >
syn inadept, inapt, inept, inexpert, unapt, undexterous, unfacile, unhandy, unproficient
rel incapable, incompetent; unfitted, unqualifed, unready
con adept, apt, dexterous, expert, handy, proficient
ant skillful
2 *syn* see INEFFICIENT 2

unsleeping *adj syn* see WATCHFUL
ant sleeping

unsmooth *adj syn* see ROUGH 1
ant smooth

unsober *adj syn* see INTOXICATED 1
ant sober

unsociable *adj* disinclined to active social intercourse < tried to hide his basically shy *unsociable* nature under a professional heartiness of manner >
syn aloof, cool, distant, insociable, offish, reserved, shut-in, solitary, standoff, standoffish, touch-me-not-ish, unapproachable, unbending, uncommunicative, uncompanionable, withdrawn; *compare* INDIFFERENT 2, UNDEMONSTRATIVE
rel self-contained, self-sufficient; exclusive, inaccessible, remote; prickly, sensitive; brooding, secretive; diffident, shy, timid
con cordial, genial, hearty, outgoing; companionable, friendly, gregarious
ant sociable, social

unsoiled *adj syn* see CLEAN 1
ant soiled, sullied

unsoluble *adj syn* see INSOLUBLE
ant soluble, solvable

unsolvable *adj syn* see INSOLUBLE
ant soluble, solvable

unsophisticated *adj syn* see NATURAL 5
rel authentic, bona fide, genuine; callow, crude, green, uncouth
con finished, polished, smooth, suave
ant sophisticated

unsorry *adj syn* see REMORSELESS
ant sorry

unsorted *adj* **1** *syn* see MISCELLANEOUS
2 *syn* see UNREFINED 3
ant sorted

unsought *adj* **1** *syn* see UNASKED
2 *syn* see UNWELCOME 1

unsound *adj* **1** *syn* see INSANE 1
ant sound
2 *syn* see WEAK 1
rel damaged, faulty, flawed, imperfect
con solid, strong, substantial
ant sound
3 *syn* see FALSE 1
ant sound
4 *syn* see DANGEROUS 1

unsparing *adj syn* see LIBERAL 1
ant close, sparing

unspeakable *adj syn* see UNUTTERABLE
rel loathsome, offensive, repulsive, revolting; abominable, detestable, hateful, odious; distasteful, obnoxious, repellent, repugnant; atrocious, disgusting, outrageous

unspoiled *adj syn* see VIRGIN 2

unspoken *adj* **1** not put into words < met regularly by a sort of *unspoken* agreement >
syn silent, tacit, unexpressed, unuttered, unvoiced, wordless
rel implicit, implied, understood; hinted, intimated, suggested; mute, unsaid, unstated

con mentioned, said, stated, told, voiced
ant spoken
2 *syn* see TACIT 1
ant spoken
unstability *n syn* see INSTABILITY
ant stability
unstable *adj* **1** *syn* see MOVABLE
ant stable
2 difficult to manage because of lack of physical steadiness
<the canoe is an inherently *unstable* craft>
syn rocky, ticklish, tricky
rel insecure, uncertain, unsteady
con secure, steady
ant stable
3 *syn* see WEAK 2
ant stable
4 *syn* see INCONSTANT 1
rel buoyant, effervescent, elastic, resilient; freakish
ant stable
5 *syn* see CHANGEABLE 1
ant stable
6 *syn* see MUTABLE 2
ant stable
7 *syn* see DOUBTFUL 1
unstableness *n syn* see INSTABILITY
ant stability, stableness
unsteadfast *adj syn* see MOVABLE
ant steadfast
unsteadfastness *n syn* see INSTABILITY
ant steadfastness
unsteadiness *n syn* see INSTABILITY
ant steadiness
unsteady *adj* **1** *syn* see MOVABLE
2 *syn* see CHANGEABLE 1
ant steady
3 *syn* see MUTABLE 2
ant steady
unsteel *vb syn* see DISARM 2
unstop *vb syn* see OPEN 1
ant stop
unstow *vb syn* see UNLOAD
unstrengthen *vb syn* see WEAKEN 1
ant strengthen
unstring *vb syn* see UNNERVE
unstudied *adj* **1** *syn* see NATURAL 5
ant studied
2 *syn* see EXTEMPORANEOUS
unstudious *adj syn* see UNSCHOLARLY
ant studious
unstylish *adj syn* see TACKY 2
ant stylish
unsubstantial *adj* **1** *syn* see TENUOUS 3
ant substantial
2 *syn* see IMPLAUSIBLE
3 *syn* see IMMATERIAL 1
ant substantial
4 *syn* see WEAK 1
rel insecure, shaky, undependable
ant substantial
unsuccess *n syn* see FAILURE 2
ant success, successfulness
unsuccessfulness *n syn* see FAILURE 2
ant success, successfulness
unsufferable *adj syn* see INSUFFERABLE
ant sufferable
unsufficient *adj syn* see SHORT 3
ant sufficient
unsuitable *adj* **1** *syn* see UNFIT 1
rel undesirable, unhappy
ant suitable
2 *syn* see IMPROPER 1
ant suitable
unsuited *adj syn* see UNFIT 1
rel inadmissible, objectionable, unacceptable; disappointing, inadequate
ant suited
unsullied *adj* **1** *syn* see CHASTE
ant sullied

2 *syn* see CLEAN 1
ant soiled, sullied
unsupportable *adj syn* see INSUFFERABLE
ant bearable, supportable
unsure *adj* **1** *syn* see INSECURE 1
ant sure
2 *syn* see WEAK 2
3 *syn* see DOUBTFUL 1
ant sure
4 *syn* see UNRELIABLE 1
unsurmountable *adj syn* see INSUPERABLE
ant surmountable
unsurpassable *adj syn* see SUPREME
ant surpassable
unsusceptible *adj syn* see INSUSCEPTIBLE
ant susceptible
unsuspecting *adj syn* see CREDULOUS
ant suspecting, suspicious
unsuspicious *adj syn* see CREDULOUS
ant suspecting, suspicious
unswayable *adj syn* see INFLEXIBLE 2
ant suasible
unswerving *adj syn* see WHOLE 5
rel constant, steadfast, steady, unremitting; firm, unfaltering, unwavering
unsymmetrical *adj syn* see LOPSIDED
ant symmetrical
unsympathetic *adj* **1** *syn* see ANTIPATHETIC 2
rel dislikable, unlikable; displeasing, unpleasant, unpleasing
con appealing, congenial, likable; pleasant, pleasing
ant sympathetic
2 *syn* see UNFEELING 2
rel cold, cool, frigid; disinterested, halfhearted, indifferent, lukewarm
ant sympathetic
untactful *adj syn* see TACTLESS
ant tactful
untangle *vb syn* see EXTRICATE 2
ant entangle, tangle
untapped *adj syn* see VIRGIN 2
untaught *adj syn* see IGNORANT 1
untellable *adj syn* see UNUTTERABLE
ant expressible
untempered *adj syn* see EXCESSIVE 2
ant temperate, tempered
untenable *adj syn* see INEXCUSABLE
untended *adj syn* see NEGLECTED
untested *adj syn* see UNTRIED 1
ant tested, tried
unthankful *adj* **1** *syn* see THANKLESS 2
2 *syn* see THANKLESS 1
ant thankful
unthinkable *adj* **1** *syn* see EXCEPTIONAL 1
2 *syn* see INCREDIBLE 1
ant thinkable
unthinking *adj syn* see CARELESS 1
unthorough *adj syn* see SLIPSHOD 3
ant thorough
unthought *adj syn* see UNINTENTIONAL
ant aforethought
unthrift *n* **1** *syn* see EXTRAVAGANCE 2
ant thrift
2 *syn* see SPENDTHRIFT
unthrift *adj syn* see IMPROVIDENT
unthrifty *adj syn* see IMPROVIDENT
ant thrifty
untidy *adj* **1** *syn* see SLOVENLY 1
ant tidy
2 *syn* see SLIPSHOD 3
untie *vb syn* see EXTRICATE 2
untighten *vb syn* see LOOSE 5
ant tighten

---

syn synonym(s)   *rel* related word(s)
ant antonym(s)   *con* contrasted word(s)
idiom idiomatic equivalent(s)
‖ use limited; if in doubt, see a dictionary

until *prep* up to a stipulated time <we never met him *until* last night>
syn before, in advance of, prior to, till, to, up till, up to; *compare* BEFORE 1
until *conj* **syn** see TILL
untimely *adj* **1 syn** see EARLY 2
  ant timely
  2 syn see UNSEASONABLE 1
  con opportune, pat, seasonable, well-timed
  ant timely
  3 syn see IMPROPER 1
  ant timely
untiring *adj* **syn** see INDEFATIGABLE
  con casual, disinterested, intermittent
untold *adj* **1 syn** see HUGE
  2 syn see INNUMERABLE
untouchable *n* **syn** see OUTCAST
  rel déclassé, outcaste, outsider
untouched *adj* **1 syn** see WHOLE 1
  2 syn see VIRGIN 2
untoward *adj* **1 syn** see UNRULY 1
  2 syn see UNLUCKY
  3 syn see INDECOROUS
untowardness *n* **syn** see IMPROPRIETY 1
untrammeled *adj* **syn** see AUDACIOUS 4
untranquil *adj* **syn** see RESTLESS
untried *adj* **1** not subjected to test or proof (as by experience or use) <the fledgling's *untried* wings>
  syn undemonstrated, unpracticed, unproved, untested
  rel inexperienced, unseasoned; callow, green, immature; fresh, half-baked, unripe
  con practiced, proven, tested; accomplished, finished, skilled; initiated
  ant tested, tried
  2 syn see INEXPERIENCED
untroubled *adj* **syn** see CALM 1
  ant troubled
untroublesome *adj* **syn** see EASY 1
untrue *adj* **1 syn** see FAITHLESS
  ant true
  2 syn see FALSE 1
  rel imprecise, inexact, unprecise; forsworn, perjured
  con exact, precise
  ant true
untruism *n* **syn** see LIE
  ant truism
untrustworthy *adj* **1 syn** see UNRELIABLE 1
  ant trustworthy
  2 syn see UNSAFE
  ant trustworthy
untrusty *adj* **syn** see UNRELIABLE 1
  ant trusty
untruth *n* **1 syn** see FALLACY 1
  ant truth
  2 syn see LIE
  ant truth
untruthful *adj* **syn** see DISHONEST
  rel deceptive, delusive, delusory, misleading; false, wrong; inaccurate, incorrect
  ant truthful
untruthfulness *n* **syn** see MENDACITY
  ant truthfulness
untune *vb* **syn** see DISCOMPOSE 1
untutored *adj* **1 syn** see IGNORANT 1
  2 syn see NATURAL 5
untwine *vb* **syn** see EXTRICATE 2
untypical *adj* **syn** see ABNORMAL 1
  ant typical
ununderstandable *adj* **syn** see INCONCEIVABLE 1
  ant understandable
unusable *adj* **syn** see IMPRACTICABLE 2
  ant usable
unused *adj* **syn** see VACANT 4
unusual *adj* **1 syn** see EXCEPTIONAL 1
  idiom the exception rather than the rule
  ant usual
  2 syn see STRANGE 4
  ant usual

unusually *adv* **syn** see EXTRA
unutterable *adj* being beyond human power to tell or describe <*unutterable* spiritual bliss>
  syn incommunicable, indefinable, indescribable, ineffable, inenarrable, inexpressible, undescribable, unexpressible, unspeakable, untellable
  rel inconceivable, incredible, unbelievable, unimaginable; awesome, awful, marvelous, prodigious, wonderful, wondrous
  idiom beyond expression
  con commonplace, humdrum, ordinary; monotonous, samely, unvarying
unuttered *adj* **1 syn** see UNSPOKEN 1
  ant uttered
  2 syn see TACIT 1
  ant uttered
unvarnished *adj* **syn** see FRANK
unvarying *adj* **1 syn** see STEADY 2
  ant varying
  2 syn see SAME 3
  ant variable, varying
unveil *vb* **1 syn** see OPEN 2
  ant veil
  2 syn see REVEAL 1
  ant veil
unveracity *n* **syn** see MENDACITY
  ant veracity
unversed *adj* **syn** see INEXPERIENCED
  ant versed
unvigilant *adj* **syn** see INCAUTIOUS 1
  ant vigilant
unvital *adj* **syn** see PETTY 2
  ant vital
unvocal *adj* **syn** see INARTICULATE 3
  ant vocal
unvoiced *adj* **syn** see UNSPOKEN 1
  ant voiced
unwanted *adj* **1 syn** see UNWELCOME 1
  ant wanted
  2 syn see OBJECTIONABLE
unwarrantable *adj* **syn** see UNREASONABLE 2
  ant warrantable
unwarranted *adj* **1 syn** see BASELESS
  2 syn see UNREASONABLE 2
unwary *adj* **1 syn** see INCAUTIOUS 1
  ant wary
  2 syn see CREDULOUS
  3 syn see RASH 1
  ant wary
unwashed *adj* **syn** see IGNOBLE 1
unwashed *n* **syn** see RABBLE 2
unwasteful *adj* **syn** see SPARING
  ant wasteful
unwatchful *adj* **1 syn** see INATTENTIVE
  ant watchful
  2 syn see INCAUTIOUS 1
  ant watchful
unwatered *adj* **syn** see DRY 1
  ant watered
unwavering *adj* **syn** see SURE 2
  ant wavering
unweariable *adj* **syn** see INDEFATIGABLE
  ant weariable
unwearying *adj* **syn** see INDEFATIGABLE
  rel constant, steady; interminable, unceasing
unwed *adj* **syn** see SINGLE 1
  ant married, wed
unwelcome *adj* **1** not of a kind to be welcome <an *unwelcome* interruption that scattered his train of thought>
  syn undesired, unsought, unwanted, unwished
  rel distasteful, obnoxious, repellent; unasked; undesirable, unpleasant, unpleasing
  con desired, sought, wanted; agreeable, desirable, pleasant, pleasing
  ant welcome
  2 syn see OBJECTIONABLE
  ant welcome
unwell *adj* somewhat disordered in health <had felt *unwell* from the moment she got up>

syn ailing, ‖donsie, indisposed, low, mean, off-color, offish, poorly, sickly, underly; *compare* SICK 1
rel rocky, shaky, wobbly; feeble, frail, infirm, weakly; ill, sick; qualmish, queasy, squeamish
idiom out of sorts, under the weather
ant well

unwholesome *adj* **1** likely to be detrimental to physical, mental, or moral health <an *unwholesome* crime-ridden neighborhood>
syn insalubrious, insalutary, noisome, noxious, sickly, unhealthful, unhealthy, unsalutary
rel baneful, deleterious, detrimental, pernicious; harmful, hurtful, injurious, mischievous
con healthful, hygienic, salubrious, salutary
ant wholesome
2 syn see OFFENSIVE
ant wholesome

unwieldy *adj* clumsy and difficult to handle usually because of excessive weight and awkward form <a massive *unwieldy* sledgehammer>
syn cumbersome, cumbrous, ponderous, unhandy; *compare* HEAVY 1
rel awkward, inconvenient; uncontrollable, unmanageable; bulky, clumsy, lumbering, massive; burdensome, encumbering, onerous
con compact, neat, trig, trim; adaptable, convenient, handy; easy, facile, light
ant wieldy

unwilling *adj* **syn** see DISINCLINED
ant willing

unwind *vb* **syn** see RELAX 2

unwise *adj* not marked by or according with good sense or sound judgment <his decision to quit school was most *unwise*>
syn ill-advised, ill-judged, impolitic, imprudent, indiscreet, injudicious
rel senseless, thoughtless, witless; impractical, unsound; fatuous, inane, inept; inappropriate, undesirable, unfortunate; foolish, misguided, unintelligent; childish, immature, naive
idiom penny-wise and pound-foolish
con discreet, judicious, prudent; sane, sensible, sound; appropriate, apt, desirable
ant wise

unwished *adj* **syn** see UNWELCOME 1

unwishful *adj* **syn** see DISINCLINED
ant wishful

unwitting *adj* **1** **syn** see FORGETFUL
ant witting
2 syn see IGNORANT 2
ant witting

unwitty *adj* **syn** see SIMPLE 3
ant ‖witty

unwonted *adj* **syn** see EXCEPTIONAL 1
ant wonted

unworkable *adj* **1** **syn** see IMPOSSIBLE 1
2 syn see IMPRACTICABLE 2
ant workable

unworked *adj* **syn** see RUDE 1
ant worked, wrought

unworkmanlike *adj* **syn** see INEFFICIENT 2
ant workmanlike, workmanly

unworldly *adj* **1** **syn** see DREAMY 1
2 syn see NATURAL 5
ant worldly

unworthy *adj* **syn** see WORTHLESS 1
ant worthy

unwritten *adj* **syn** see ORAL 2
ant written

unwrought *adj* **syn** see RUDE 1
ant worked, wrought

unyielding *adj* **1** **syn** see STIFF 1
ant yielding
2 syn see OBSTINATE
rel firm, fixed, rigid
ant yielding
3 syn see GRIM 3
4 syn see TOUGH 3
ant yielding
5 syn see INFLEXIBLE 2

up *adj* **1** **syn** see BAD 1

2 syn see FAMILIAR 3
3 syn see UP-TO-DATE

up *vb* **1** **syn** see RISE 4
2 syn see RAISE 9

up-and-coming *adj* **syn** see ENTERPRISING 2
rel alert, eager, keen, ready

up and down *adv* **syn** see THOROUGHLY 2

up-and-down *adj* **syn** see DOWNRIGHT 2

upbear *vb* **syn** see SUPPORT 4

upbeat *adj* **syn** see OPTIMISTIC

upbraid *vb* **syn** see SCOLD 1

upchuck *vb* **syn** see VOMIT

upclimb *vb* **syn** see ASCEND 1

upcoming *adj* **syn** see FORTHCOMING
rel foreseen, prospective
idiom in prospect, on the horizon

up-country *n* **syn** see FRONTIER 2

update *vb* **syn** see RENEW 1

upend *vb* **syn** see WHIP 2

upgo *vb* **syn** see ASCEND 1

upgrade *vb* **syn** see ADVANCE 2
ant downgrade

upgrade *n* **syn** see RISE 3

upgrading *n* **syn** see ADVANCEMENT 1
ant downgrading

upgrowth *n* **syn** see DEVELOPMENT

upheaval *n* **syn** see COMMOTION 1
rel cataclysm, catastrophe, disaster; alteration, change; churning, heaving, stirring

upheaved *adj* **syn** see ELEVATED 1
ant downthrown

uphill *adj* **syn** see HARD 6

uphold *vb* **1** **syn** see SUPPORT 5
rel defend, justify, maintain, vindicate; aid, assist, help
ant contravene; subvert
2 syn see SUPPORT 2
3 syn see SUPPORT 4
4 syn see LIFT 1

upholstered *adj* **1** **syn** see LUXURIOUS 3
2 syn see FAT 2

upland *n* **syn** see PLATEAU

uplay *vb* **syn** see ACCUMULATE

uplift *vb* **1** **syn** see LIFT 1
2 syn see ILLUMINATE 2
ant degrade

uplifted *adj* **syn** see ELEVATED 1

upon *prep* **1** **syn** see OVER 3
2 syn see OVER 4

upper class *n* **syn** see ARISTOCRACY

upper crust *n* **syn** see ARISTOCRACY
rel (the) Four Hundred

upper hand *n* **syn** see BETTER 2

uppermost *adj* **syn** see TOP 1
ant lowermost

‖upper story *n* **syn** see MIND 1

‖upperworks *n pl* **syn** see MIND 1

uppish *adj* **syn** see PRESUMPTUOUS

uppity *adj* **syn** see PRESUMPTUOUS

upraise *vb* **1** **syn** see LIFT 1
2 syn see COMFORT
ant depress

upraised *adj* **syn** see ELEVATED 1

uprear *vb* **1** **syn** see LIFT 1
2 syn see BUILD 1
3 syn see EXALT 1
con bust, demote, downgrade
ant degrade
4 syn see RISE 4

upright *adj* **1** **syn** see ERECT
2 having or manifesting a strict regard for what is morally right <an *upright* man ready to give even the devil his due>
syn conscientious, honest, honorable, just, right, scrupulous, true

---

syn synonym(s)   **rel** related word(s)
ant antonym(s)   **con** contrasted word(s)
idiom idiomatic equivalent(s)
‖ use limited; if in doubt, see a dictionary

rel ethical, moral, principled, righteous, virtuous; equitable, fair, impartial; elevated, high-minded, noble; blameless, exemplary, good, pure
con crooked, devious, oblique; depraved; base, low, vile; ignoble, mean
ant corrupt

uprightness *n syn* see GOODNESS
rel nobility, reputability, worthiness; honesty, integrity
ant corruption

uprise *vb* **1** *syn* see RISE 1
2 *syn* see ROLL OUT

uprisen *adj syn* see ELEVATED 1

uproar *n* **1** *syn* see DIN
rel chaos, confusion, disorder; brawl, broil, fracas, melee; commotion, confusion, turbulence, turmoil
con calm, peace, quiet
2 *syn* see COMMOTION 4
3 *syn* see COMMOTION 3

uproarious *adj syn* see NOISY

uproot *vb syn* see ANNIHILATE 2
rel demolish, destroy; overthrow, overturn, subvert; displace, replace, supersede, supplant; move, shift, transplant
ant establish; inseminate

upset *vb* **1** *syn* see OVERTURN 1
rel invert, reverse; bend, curve, turn
2 *syn* see DISCOMPOSE 1
rel bewilder, confound, distract; unman, unnerve
idiom rock the boat
3 *syn* see TROUBLE 1
4 *syn* see DISORDER 1
5 to disturb the normal functioning especially of body or mind < her stomach was badly *upset* by too many sweets >
syn derange, disorder, sicken, turn, unhinge, unsettle
rel afflict, indispose, lay up; ail, suffer; debilitate, incapacitate, invalid

upshot *n* **1** *syn* see EFFECT 1
rel ending, termination; climax, culmination; completion, conclusion, finish
2 *syn* see SUBSTANCE 2

upside–down *adj* **1** having the upper and lower parts reversed in position < *upside-down* letters >
syn inverted, topsy-turvy
rel reversed
2 confused utterly even to the point of inversion of the normal or reasonable < *upside-down* logic that confused cause with effect >
syn arsy-varsy, downside-up, topsy-turvy
rel inverted, reversed; chaotic, confused, helter-skelter, jumbled, mixed-up; fouled-up, haywire, ‖snafu
con orderly, well-ordered; logical, reasonable, sensible, sound; legitimate, plausible

upspring *vb* **1** *syn* see SPRING 1
2 *syn* see RISE 1

upstanding *adj syn* see ERECT

upstart *n* a usually crude and pushing person who has recently reached a position of prominence, power, or wealth < declared the new executive an *upstart* lacking all breeding and culture >
syn arriviste, nouveau riche, parvenu, roturier
rel bounder, cad, outsider; guttersnipe, mucker, slob, vulgarian; boor, lout, roughneck, rowdy; comer; social climber

upsurge *vb syn* see INCREASE 2

uptight *adj syn* see TENSE 2

uptightness *n syn* see TENSION 2

up till *prep syn* see UNTIL

up to *prep syn* see UNTIL

up–to–date *adj* completely modern (as in style or outlook) < using *up-to-date* methods of study >
syn abreast, au courant, contemporary, down-to-date, red-hot, up, up-to-the-minute
rel convenient, opportune, timely; expedient, fitting, suitable; advanced, modern, stylish; a la mode, dashing, modish
idiom abreast of the times
con dusty, rusty, stale, timeworn; antiquated, outmoded, superannuated
ant out-of-date; archaic

up–to–the–minute *adj syn* see UP-TO-DATE

upturn *n syn* see COMMOTION 1

uranian *adj syn* see HOMOSEXUAL

uranian *n syn* see HOMOSEXUAL

uranist *n syn* see HOMOSEXUAL

urban *adj* of, relating to, or characteristic of a city < *urban* disorders >
syn burghal, city, municipal
rel inner city; metropolitan; civic, popular, public; oppidan, town, village
ant rural

urbane *adj* **1** *syn* see COSMOPOLITAN 1
2 *syn* see SUAVE
rel balanced, poised
ant bucolic, clownish
3 *syn* see GENTEEL 1
rel affable, civil, courteous, gracious, obliging
ant rude

urchin *n* a pert or roguish youngster < *urchins* pilfering apples on their way from school >
syn gamin, imp, monkey
rel brat, bratling, cub, dickens, pup, whelp, whippersnapper; guttersnipe, mudlark, ragamuffin, street arab; hobbledehoy

urge *vb* to press or impel to action, effort, or speed < his conscience *urged* him to tell the truth >
syn egg (on), exhort, goad, prick, prod, prompt, propel, sic, spur
rel hurry, hustle, push, rush, shove; blandish, cajole, coax, encourage, incite, needle, solicit, wheedle; constrain, drive, high-pressure, press, pressure; provoke, set (on), tar (on)
idiom bring pressure to bear on, twist one's arm
con brake, check, constrain, curb, hold back, inhibit, restrain

urge *n syn* see DESIRE 1
rel goad, incentive, motive, spring, spur

urgent *adj syn* see PRESSING
rel driving, impelling; demanding

usable *adj syn* see OPEN 5
ant unusable

usage *n* **1** *syn* see HABIT 1
rel choice, preference; procedure, proceeding, process; guidance, guiding, lead
2 *syn* see FORM 3
rel ceremony, formality

usance *n syn* see USE 1

use *n* **1** the act or practice of using something or the state of being used < all tools must be kept ready for instant *use* >
syn appliance, application, employment, operation, play, usance; *compare* EXERCISE 1
con desuetude, disuse
ant nonuse
2 *syn* see EXERCISE 1
3 the quality of being appropriate or valuable to some end < even the scraps had some *use* >
syn account, advantage, applicability, appropriateness, avail, fitness, relevance, service, serviceability, usefulness, utility
rel adaptability, availability, benefit, efficacy; profit, value, worth
con inadequacy, inapplicability, inappropriateness, insufficiency, unfitness, unserviceability, uselessness, worthlessness
4 a particular service or end < industrial *uses* of atomic energy >
syn duty, function, goal, mark, object, objective, purpose, target
5 *syn* see HABIT 1
rel ceremony, formality
6 *syn* see NEED 3

use *vb* **1** *syn* see ACCUSTOM
2 to put into action or service < it is necessary to *use* resources wisely >
syn apply, bestow, employ, exercise, exploit, handle, utilize
rel manipulate, operate, ply, wield; control, govern, manage, regulate
idiom avail oneself of, bring into play, fall back (on *or* upon), make use of, press into service, put into action, put to use
con dissipate, exhaust, use up; waste
3 *syn* see OPERATE 3
4 *syn* see SPEAK 3
5 *syn* see EXPLOIT 2
idiom make the most of, make use of
6 *syn* see TREAT 2

used up *adj syn* see EFFETE 2

useful *adj* **1** *syn* see PRACTICAL 2
  2 *syn* see GOOD 1
  ant useless
  3 *syn* see GOOD 2
  ant useless
usefulness *n* *syn* see USE 3
  ant uselessness
useless *adj* **1** *syn* see FUTILE
  ant useful
  2 *syn* see IMPRACTICABLE 2
  ant useful
  3 *syn* see FECKLESS 1
use up *vb* **1** *syn* see CONSUME 1
  2 *syn* see GO 4
  3 *syn* see DEPLETE
usher *vb* *syn* see PRECEDE 3
usher in *vb* *syn* see INTRODUCE 3
usual *adj* **1** familiar through frequent or regular repetition < the sort that would perform her *usual* chores while waiting for the end of the world >
  syn accepted, accustomed, chronic, customary, habitual, routine, wonted
  rel natural, normal, regular, typical; common, familiar, ordinary; current, prevailing, prevalent, rife
  idiom that make up one's daily round
  con exceptional, rare, unaccustomed; remarkable, strange, unexpected
  ant unusual
  2 *syn* see GENERAL 1
  3 *syn* see ORDINARY 1
usually *adv* **1** by or in accord with habit or custom < establishments of a kind *usually* restricted to back streets >
  syn as usual, consistently, customarily, habitually, wontedly
  2 more often than not < he is *usually* late for work >
  syn as a rule, by ordinary, commonly, frequently, generally, ordinarily
  rel now and again (*or* now and then), occasionally, once and again, sometimes
  idiom for the most part, in the main
  con infrequently, seldom, uncommonly
  ant rarely
usurer *n* *syn* see LOAN SHARK
usurp *vb* **1** *syn* see ARROGATE 1
  ant abdicate
  2 *syn* see SUPPLANT 1
utensil *n* *syn* see IMPLEMENT

utile *adj* *syn* see PRACTICAL 2
  ant inutile
utilitarian *adj* *syn* see REALISTIC
utility *n* *syn* see USE 3
  ant inutility
utilize *vb* *syn* see USE 2
  rel advance, forward, further, promote
utmost *adj* **1** *syn* see EXTREME 5
  2 *syn* see MAXIMUM
  3 *syn* see EXTREME 1
utopia *n* an often imaginary place or situation of perfection and delight < able to make an enduring *utopia* of the humblest house >
  syn arcadia, Cockaigne, fairyland, heaven, lubberland, paradise, promised land, Shangri-la, wonderland, Zion
  rel dreamland, dreamworld, never-never
utopian *adj* **1** *syn* see IDEALISTIC
  rel abstract, ideal, transcendental
  2 *syn* see AMBITIOUS 2
  rel impossible, impracticable, unfeasible; arcadian, edenic, millennial, otherworldly
utopian *n* *syn* see DREAMER
utter *adj* being such without qualification — used especially to intensify the noun modified < acted like an *utter* idiot >
  syn absolute, all-fired, arrant, black, blamed, blank, blankety-blank, blasted, bleeding, blessed, blighted, blinding, ‖blinking, blithering, ‖blooming, blue, complete, confounded, ‖consarned, consummate, crashing, dad-blamed, dad-blasted, dad-burned, damned, dang, darn (*or* durn), dashed, deuced, doggone, double-distilled, double-dyed, downright, flat-out, goldarn, gross, hell-fired, infernal, out-and-out, outright, perfect, positive, ‖proper, pure, ‖puredee (*or* pure-D), rank, regular, sheer, stark, straight-out, ‖tarnation, thoroughgoing, total, unmitigated, unqualified; *compare* PURE 2
utter *vb* **1** *syn* see SPEAK 1
  idiom give utterance to
  2 *syn* see SAY 1
utterance *n* **1** *syn* see WORD 1
  2 *syn* see VOCALIZATION
  3 *syn* see EXPRESSION 1
  4 *syn* see SPEECH 1
uttering *n* *syn* see VOCALIZATION
utterly *adv* **1** *syn* see WELL 3
  2 *syn* see ALL 1
uttermost *adj* **1** *syn* see EXTREME 5
  2 *syn* see EXTREME 1

vacancy *n* *syn* see VACUITY 2
  rel desertedness
  ant occupancy
vacant *adj* **1** *syn* see EMPTY 1
  rel tenantless, unfilled, unoccupied, untaken
  con inhabited, tenanted
  ant occupied
  2 *syn* see VACUOUS 2
  3 *syn* see EXPRESSIONLESS
  rel empty-headed, inane, thoughtless, witless
  4 not being put to normal or appropriate use < *vacant* land >
  syn idle, unused
  rel bare, empty; unfilled, unoccupied
  con filled; used
  ant occupied
vacate *vb* **1** *syn* see ANNUL 4
  rel repeal, rescind, retract, reverse, revoke
  idiom declare null and void
  2 to make something (as an office, post, or dwelling) vacant or empty < *vacate* a house >
  syn clear, empty, void
  rel abandon, give up, part (with *or* from), relinquish; leave, quit

vacation *n* a period spent away from one's usual activity or work often in travel or recreation < took a two-week *vacation* to Florida >
  syn holiday, leave
  rel break, breathing space (*or* breathing spell), intermission, recess; time off; respite, rest; furlough
vacillant *adj* *syn* see VACILLATING 2
vacillate *vb* *syn* see HESITATE
  rel swag, sway, ‖swither; alternate, seesaw, teeter, teeter-totter, wag, waggle, wigwag, wobble; dally, dawdle, fiddle-faddle
  idiom blow hot and cold, hem and haw, swing from one thing to another
  con decide, resolve, settle
vacillating *adj* **1** *syn* see WEAK 2
  rel unfixed; unsettled, unsteady; changeable, fickle, inconstant; eccentric, erratic, mercurial, volatile
  con constant, steady, unchanging; strong

syn synonym(s)	*rel* related word(s)
ant antonym(s)	*con* contrasted word(s)
idiom idiomatic equivalent(s)	
‖ use limited; if in doubt, see a dictionary	

2 given to or manifesting hesitation or vacillation <a *vacillating* witness>
syn double-minded, faltering, halting, hesitant, hesitating, indecisive, irresolute, pendulous, shilly-shally, shilly-shallying, tentative, timid, uncertain, undecisive, unresolved, vacillant, vacillatory, wavering, weak-kneed, whiffling, wiggle-waggle, wobbly
rel doubtful, doubting, unsure; fluctuating, oscillating, shifting; dallying, dawdling, demurring, dillydallying, stalling
con certain, decisive, resolute, resolved, sure; definite, positive
vacillation *n syn* see HESITATION
rel dallying, demurral, dillydallying, stalling
vacillatory *adj syn* see VACILLATING 2
rel alternating, seesawing, varying; indecisive, irresolute, uncertain
vacuity *n* **1** *syn* see HOLE 3
2 the condition, fact, or quality of being vacuous <the utter *vacuity* of his expression>
syn blankness, emptiness, vacancy, vacuousness, voidness
rel bareness, barrenness, bleakness, desolateness, hollowness; dullness, inaneness, inanity, stupidity
3 *syn* see NOTHINGNESS
vacuous *adj* **1** *syn* see EMPTY 1
2 characterized by a lack of substance, thought, or intellectual content <a *vacuous* mind>
syn empty-headed, vacant; *compare* STUPID 1
rel shallow, superficial; blank, empty; dull, foolish, inane, silly
vacuousness *n syn* see VACUITY 2
vade mecum *n syn* see HANDBOOK
vag *n syn* see VAGABOND
vagabond *adj syn* see ITINERANT
rel vagabondish
vagabond *n* a person who wanders at will or as a habit <a park full of *vagabonds* sleeping on benches>
syn arab, ||bindle stiff, bum, canter, clochard, derelict, drifter, floater, ||gangrel, hobo, piker, roadster, runagate, ||shack, street arab, ||sundowner, ||swagger, ||swagman, tramp, tramper, ||traveler, vag, vagrant, Weary Willie
rel roamer, rover, wanderer; boomer, migrant, runabout, straggler, stray, transient; bohemian, gypsy, picaro, picaroon; ||casual; stiff; beggar, rogue
idiom knight of the road
vagabond *vb syn* see WANDER 1
vagabondage *n syn* see VAGRANCY
vagabondia *n syn* see VAGRANCY
vagabondism *n syn* see VAGRANCY
vagabondize *vb syn* see WANDER 1
vagarious *adj syn* see ARBITRARY 1
rel unreasonable; kinky
vagary *n syn* see CAPRICE
rel daydream, dream, fantasy; kink, quirk
idiom passing fancy
vagrancy *n* the act or state of wandering from place to place usually with no means of support <dropped out of society and lived a life of *vagrancy*>
syn hoboism, vagabondage, vagabondia, vagabondism
rel itineracy, itinerancy, nomadism; rambling, roaming, roving, wandering
vagrant *n syn* see VAGABOND
vagrant *adj syn* see ITINERANT
rel aimless, errant, erratic; straying; sauntering, strolling
vague *adj* **1** *syn* see OBSCURE 3
rel indeterminate, indistinct, unplain; cloudy, dim, hazy, nebulous; muddy
con clear, distinct
ant express
2 *syn* see FAINT 2
rel nebulous, unsubstantial; indefinite, unplain; uncertain, unrecognizable; dreamlike, dreamy
3 *syn* see HAZY
rel bleared, bleary, blurry
vain *adj* **1** devoid of worth or significance <the *vain* pursuits of a luxurious life>
syn empty, hollow, idle, nugatory, otiose
rel profitless, unprofitable, useless, valueless, void, worthless; ineffective, ineffectual, inefficacious; bootless, fruitless; abortive, futile
con useful, valuable, worthy; effective, effectual, efficacious
2 *syn* see FUTILE

rel paltry, petty, puny, trifling, trivial; delusive, delusory, misleading
3 having or exhibiting undue or excessive pride especially in one's appearance or achievements <was *vain* about his clothes>
syn conceited, ||conceity, narcissistic, self-conceited, stuck-up, vainglorious; *compare* PROUD 1
rel arrogant, egocentric, egoistic, haughty, ||pensy, proud, self-important, swollen-headed; boastful, self-exalting; coxcombical, dandyish, foppish
idiom stuck on oneself
con humble, meek, modest; bashful, diffident, retiring, shy
vainglorious *adj syn* see VAIN 3
rel boastful, bragging, vaunting; disdainful, insolent, supercilious
vainglory *n syn* see CONCEIT 2
rel arrogance, haughtiness; boastfulness, bombast; exhibition, flaunting, parading
con lowliness, meekness; bashfulness, diffidence, self-effacement, shyness; modesty
ant humility
vainness *n syn* see CONCEIT 2
vale *n syn* see VALLEY
valedictory *adj syn* see PARTING
valiance *n syn* see HEROISM
con feebleness, ineffectiveness; fear
valiancy *n syn* see HEROISM
con feebleness, ineffectiveness; fear
valiant *adj syn* see BRAVE 1
ant pusillanimous
valid *adj* having the power to impress others as right and well-founded <a *valid* conclusion>
syn cogent, convincing, satisfactory, satisfying, solid, sound, telling
rel persuasive, potent, strong; attested, confirmed, corroborated, demonstrated, determined, established, substantiated, validated, verified; lawful, legal, licit; effective, effectual; conclusive, decisive, definitive, determinative; acceptable
con groundless, shaky, unconvincing, unfounded, unsound; fallacious, false, misleading, sophistical; counterfeit, fictitious
ant invalid
validate *vb syn* see CONFIRM 2
rel approve, endorse, legalize, ratify, rubber-stamp, sanction
con abolish, abrogate, annul, cancel, repeal; void
ant invalidate
validity *n syn* see POINT 3
rel efficacy, gravity, soundness; persuasiveness, potency
con inconsistency; unsoundness; fallacy, falsity
ant invalidity, invalidness
validness *n syn* see POINT 3
ant invalidity, invalidness
valley *n* an elongate depression of the earth's surface commonly situated between ranges of hills or mountains <small farms dotted the floor of the *valley*>
syn ||combe, dale, glen, vale
rel dell, dingle, hollow; ||rincon; canyon
valor *n syn* see HEROISM
rel mettle, resolution, spirit, tenacity; indomitableness, invincibility, unconquerableness; backbone, fortitude, guts, sand
con cowardliness, fear
ant pusillanimity, pusillanimousness
valorous *adj syn* see BRAVE 1
ant pusillanimous
valorousness *n syn* see HEROISM
rel chivalrousness, chivalry; manliness
con cowardliness
ant pusillanimity, pusillanimousness
valuable *adj syn* see PRECIOUS 1
rel dear, expensive; appreciated, prized, treasured, valued; admired, esteemed, respected
idiom of great value
con cheap, inexpensive, trashy; unmarketable, unsalable; unworthy
ant valueless, worthless
valuate *vb syn* see ESTIMATE 1
valuation *n* **1** *syn* see ESTIMATE 1
rel judgment, opinion, rating
2 *syn* see WORTH 1

rel charge, cost, price
value *n* **1** *syn* see WORTH 1
  rel appraisal, assessment; charge, cost, expense, price
  2 *syn* see QUALITY 2
value *vb* **1** *syn* see ESTIMATE 1
  rel compute, figure, gauge, reckon
  idiom place a value (*or* price) on
  2 *syn* see APPRECIATE 1
  rel care (for); revere, reverence, venerate
  idiom set much by
valueless *adj* *syn* see WORTHLESS 1
  ant valuable
valve *n* *syn* see FAUCET
  rel shutoff
‖**vamoose** *vb* *syn* see GET OUT 1
vamp *vb* *syn* see MEND 2
  rel brush up, fix up, touch up; furbish, refurbish
vamp (up) *vb* *syn* see CONTRIVE 2
vamp *n* *syn* see FLIRT
  rel charmer, enchantress, enticer, femme fatale, gold digger, inveigler, seductress, siren, temptress
vandal *n* one who willfully destroys or mars something valuable < *vandals* had knocked off the head of the statue >
  syn defacer, despoiler, destroyer, ruinator, ruiner, wrecker
  rel hoodlum, hooligan, lout, ruffian; devastator, ravager, spoiler, spoliator; looter, pillager, plunderer; iconoclast
vandalize *vb* to destroy or deface (as public or private property) willfully or maliciously < youths *vandalized* the shop >
  syn ‖trash, wreck
  rel ‖rip off; destroy, tear up
vanish *vb* to pass from view or out of existence < the moon *vanished* behind a cloud >
  syn clear, disappear, evanesce, evanish, evaporate, fade
  rel dematerialize, dissolve, melt (away); die
  idiom do the vanishing act, vanish from sight, vanish into thin air, vanish like a dream
  con arise, break out (*or* through), come (forth *or* out), emerge, issue, loom (up), materialize, show (up)
  ant appear
vanished *adj* *syn* see EXTINCT 2
  rel expired, passed away; annihilated, no more, perished
vanity *n* *syn* see CONCEIT 2
  rel autotheism, self-worship
vanquish *vb* *syn* see CONQUER 1
  rel surmount; overturn, subvert; humble, trample
vanquisher *n* *syn* see VICTOR 1
  rel champ, champion
  con loser
vanquishment *n* *syn* see DEFEAT 1
  rel mastery, subdual, subjugation
vantage *n* *syn* see ADVANTAGE 3
  ant disadvantage
vapid *adj* *syn* see INSIPID 3
  rel flavorless, milk-toast, tasteless, weak; dull, unimaginative, uninteresting
  idiom neither hot nor cold, neither one thing nor the other
  con brisk, lively, tangy, zesty; crisp, forceful, incisive, trenchant; expressive, meaningful, pregnant, significant, telling
vaporous *adj* **1** *syn* see HAZY
  2 *syn* see AIRY 3
  rel unsubstantial, wispy; illusory, unreal
vapory *adj* **1** *syn* see HAZY
  2 *syn* see AIRY 3
  rel gaseous
variable *adj* **1** *syn* see CHANGEABLE 1
  rel fitful, spasmodic; irregular, unequable, unequal, ununiform
  con unchanging, unvarying; immobile, stable, unmoving; equable, equal, uniform
  ant constant, invariable
  2 *syn* see MUTABLE 2
  3 *syn* see INCONSTANT 1
variance *n* **1** the quality, state, or fact of being variable < a daily *variance* of 1°F. >
  syn difference, variation
  rel change, deviation, fluctuation
  ant invariance
  2 *syn* see DISCORD
  rel division, separation, severing, sundering

variation *n* **1** *syn* see CHANGE 1
  rel difference, dissimilarity; deflection, discrepancy
  con stability, unchangeableness
  2 *syn* see VARIANCE 1
  rel shift; divergence; discrepancy, disparity
  con uniformity
varicolored *adj* *syn* see VARIEGATED
  ant solid
varied *adj* *syn* see MISCELLANEOUS
variegated *adj* having a pattern involving different colors or shades of color < *variegated* leaves >
  syn dappled, discolor, motley, multicolor, multicolored, multi-hued, parti-color, parti-colored, polychromatic, polychrome, varicolored, versicolor, versicolored
  rel checked, checkered; piebald, pied, skewbald; freaked, streaked; flecked; stippled; marbled; mottle, mottled, spattered, speckled, spotted; calico; pinto
  ant solid
variety *n* **1** the quality or state of being composed of different parts, elements, or individuals < the *variety* of the city's cultural life >
  syn diverseness, diversity, multeity, multifariousness, multiformity, multiplicity, variousness
  rel diversification, heterogeneity, variation
  2 a collection of different things, forms, or qualities especially of a particular class < had a great *variety* of jobs in his lifetime >
  syn assortment
  rel conglomeration, medley, miscellany
  3 *syn* see TYPE
  rel classification; grade, rank
various *adj* **1** *syn* see MANY
  rel assorted, heterogeneous, miscellaneous, omnifarious, omnigenous
  2 *syn* see DIFFERENT 1
  rel changing, variant, varied, varying; distinct, separate; distinctive, individual, peculiar
  ant uniform
  3 *syn* see SEVERAL 3
  ant many, numerous
  4 *syn* see DISTINCT 1
  5 *syn* see CERTAIN 2
various *pron, pl in constr* *syn* see SUNDRY
variously *adv* *syn* see OTHERWISE 1
variousness *n* *syn* see VARIETY 1
varnish *vb* *syn* see PALLIATE
vary *vb* **1** *syn* see CHANGE 1
  rel modulate, qualify
  2 *syn* see DIFFER 1
  3 *syn* see DIFFER 2
  rel depart, deviate, digress, diverge; divide, part, separate
  ant agree
  4 *syn* see RANGE 3
vast *adj* *syn* see HUGE
  rel big, large; ample, capacious, spacious; broad, expansive, far-flung, wide, widespread; astronomical, cosmic
  con confined, limited, narrow, restricted
vastness *n* *syn* see ENORMITY 2
vatic *adj* *syn* see PROPHETIC
vaticinal *adj* *syn* see PROPHETIC
vaticinate *vb* *syn* see FORETELL
vault *n* *syn* see CRYPT
vault *vb* **1** *syn* see JUMP 1
  rel upleap, upspring; overjump, overleap; clear; rise, soar; ascend, mount; surmount
  2 *syn* see CLEAR 8
vaulting *adj* *syn* see AMBITIOUS 1
  rel enthusiastic; opportunistic
vaunt *vb* *syn* see BOAST
  rel brandish, display, exhibit, expose, flaunt, parade, show off
  idiom puff oneself
vaunter *n* *syn* see BRAGGART
vaunting *adj* *syn* see BOASTFUL

---

syn synonym(s)   *rel* related word(s)
ant antonym(s)   *con* contrasted word(s)
idiom idiomatic equivalent(s)
‖ use limited; if in doubt, see a dictionary

vector *n* an agent capable of transmitting a pathogen from one organism to another <fleas are *vectors* of bubonic plague>
syn carrier, vehicle

veer *vb* **1** *syn* see TURN 6
2 *syn* see SWERVE 1
rel depart, deviate, digress, diverge; angle off, bear off; twist; pivot, turn, wheel

vegetate *vb* to lead a passive existence without exertion of body or mind <he never really lived his life—he merely *vegetated* >
syn stagnate
rel idle; languish; hibernate
idiom idle life away, live the life of a clam, pass the time

vehement *adj syn* see INTENSE 1
rel emphatic, pronounced; energetic, hearty, lively, zealous; forceful, potent, powerful; ardent, fervent, fervid, heated, impassioned, passionate, perfervid; delirious, frantic, furious, rabid, wild

vehicle *n* **1** *syn* see VECTOR
rel agent
2 *syn* see MEAN 2
rel implement, tool
3 a means of transporting goods or passengers <his *vehicle* was an old battered coupe>
syn conveyance, transport, transportation

veil *n* *syn* see MASK 2

veil *vb* *syn* see ENFOLD 1
rel mantle, overspread, spread (over); blanket, curtain; camouflage, cloak, cover (up), disguise, mask; conceal, hide, screen, secrete
con exhibit, lay (open), open up, reveal, uncover, unmask; bare, expose, show
ant unveil

vein *n* **1** a distinctive method of expression <wrote his speech in the proper *vein* for a very sophisticated audience>
syn fashion, manner, mode, style, tone
rel way; line; mood, tenor
2 *syn* see HINT 2
3 *syn* see MOOD 1
rel complexion, disposition, fettle, temperament; character, nature, spirit

velitation *n* *syn* see ENCOUNTER

velleity *n* *syn* see WILL 1
rel volition; wish

vellicate *vb* *syn* see JERK
rel nip, pinch; fidget, jig, jiggle

velocipede *n* *syn* see BICYCLE

velocity *n* *syn* see SPEED 2
rel headway, impetus, momentum; dispatch, expedition, haste, hurry

velutinous *adj syn* see VELVETY

velvetlike *adj syn* see VELVETY
idiom soft as velvet

velvety *adj* **1** having the extreme softness associated with the surface or appearance of velvet <wore a *velvety* red flower in her hair>
syn velutinous, velvetlike
rel plush, plushy, smooth, soft; glossy, sleek, slick; satiny, silken, silky
2 *syn* see SOFT 3

venal *adj* **1** open to corrupt influence and especially bribery <a *venal* legislator>
syn bribable, buyable, corruptible, purchasable; *compare* CORRUPT 2, CROOKED 2
rel corrupt, flagitious, infamous, iniquitous, nefarious, vicious; hack, hireling, mercenary, paid; ignoble, sordid; unethical, unprincipled, unscrupulous
2 *syn* see CORRUPT 2

vend *vb* **1** *syn* see SELL 2
2 *syn* see PEDDLE 2
3 *syn* see DECLARE 1

vendee *n* *syn* see PURCHASER

vendetta *n* a prolonged mutual enmity marked by bitter hostility and conflict <a long-standing *vendetta* between two rival gangs>
syn feud
rel dispute, quarrel; rhubarb, row, wrangle; conflict, fight, set-to; blood feud, blood vengeance

vendible *adj syn* see MARKETABLE

ant unvendible

vendible *n, usu* **vendibles** *pl syn* see MERCHANDISE

vendor *n syn* see PEDDLER

veneer *n syn* see MASK 2

veneer *vb syn* see PALLIATE

venerable *adj* **1** deserving to be venerated usually by reason of prolonged testing (as of character) <a *venerable* judge with an impressive knowledge of the law>
syn patriarchal, revered, reverend, reverential; *compare* HONORABLE 1
rel dignified, imposing, stately; admirable, estimable; honored, reverenced; worshipful; sacred
ant unvenerable
2 *syn* see ANCIENT 1
rel elderly; patriarchal, reverenced, reverend, venerated
con contemporary, current; fresh, inexperienced, new, untried, unused

venerate *vb syn* see REVERE
rel honor; idolize
idiom put on a pedestal

venery *n syn* see HUNTING

venge *vb syn* see AVENGE
idiom even (up) the score, repay in kind, settle accounts (*or* an account)

vengeance *n syn* see RETALIATION
rel return; repayment; revengefulness, vengefulness

vengeful *adj syn* see VINDICTIVE
rel antagonistic, hostile, inimical, rancorous
con charitable, forgiving, kind; benevolent, benign, inoffensive

venial *adj* of a kind that can be remitted and that does not warrant punishment or penalty <the *venial* indiscretions of youth>
syn excusable, forgivable, pardonable, remittable
rel allowable, unobjectionable; insignificant, minor, trifling, trivial; harmless, tolerable
con criminal, damning, deadly, mortal; grievous, outrageous, serious; inexcusable, unforgivable, unpardonable, unremittable
ant heinous

venom *n syn* see POISON
rel ill will, malignity, rancor, venomousness, virulence, vitriol
con antidote, remedy

venomous *adj syn* see POISONOUS
rel malevolent, malign, malignant; baleful, malefic, maleficent; viperish, viperlike, viperous

vent *vb* **1** *syn* see EMIT 2
rel cast out, discharge, exhaust
2 *syn* see EXPRESS 2
rel utter, voice; assert, declare
idiom come out with, give vent to
con check, curb, inhibit, restrain; repress, suppress
3 *syn* see TAKE OUT (on)

vent *n* **1** *syn* see APERTURE
2 *syn* see EXPRESSION 1
rel articulation, verbalization, vocalization

venter *n syn* see ABDOMEN

ventilate *vb* **1** *syn* see BROACH
2 *syn* see EXPRESS 2
rel go into, take up; debate, deliberate, discourse (about), discuss, ‖rap (about), talk over (*or* of *or* about), thresh out; advertise, broadcast, publish
idiom chew the fat (*or* the rag)

ventilation *n syn* see CONFERENCE 1

venture *vb* **1** to expose to risk or loss <*ventured* their capital in foreign trade>
syn adventure, chance, hazard, risk, wager; *compare* GAMBLE 2
rel endanger, imperil, jeopard, jeopardize, jeopardy, peril; expose, lay (open)
idiom take chances (*or* risks) on (*or* with)
2 *syn* see GAMBLE 2
rel bet, operate, play (for), speculate, stake; jeopard, jeopardize, jeopardy
idiom luck it
3 *syn* see FACE 3

venture *n syn* see ADVENTURE
rel attempt, undertaking; crack, fling; dare, gamble, risk, speculation
idiom leap in the dark

venturesome *adj syn* see ADVENTUROUS
rel stalwart, stout, sturdy; brave; overbold

con timid, timorous; afraid, apprehensive, fearful
venturous *adj syn* see ADVENTUROUS
   rel aggressive, enterprising, hustling
veracious *adj* **1** *syn* see TRUTHFUL
   rel direct; undeceitful, undeceptive
   con equivocal; deceitful, dishonest, insincere; false, untruthful
   ant unveracious
   2 *syn* see TRUE 3
   rel unquestionable, valid
   con illusory, invalid, wrong
   ant unveracious
veraciousness *n syn* see VERACITY 1
   rel artlessness, openness; trustworthiness
   con falseness, insincerity
veracity *n* **1** the quality or state of keeping close to fact and avoiding distortion or misrepresentation <questions the *veracity* of that witness>
   syn truth, truthfulness, veraciousness, veridicality, verity
   rel accuracy, correctness, exactness, factualness; frankness, honesty
   con inaccuracy, incorrectness; deception, dishonesty, untruth, untruthfulness
   ant unveracity
   2 something that is true <can make lies sound like *veracities*>
   syn gospel, truism, truth, verity
   rel verisimilitude; actuality; fact
   con lie, untruth
   ant unveracity
verbal *adj* **1** *syn* see ORAL 2
   2 *syn* see VERBATIM
verbalism *n* **1** *syn* see WORDING
   rel styling
   2 *syn* see VERBOSITY
verbality *n syn* see VERBIAGE 1
   rel verbalism, verboseness, verbosity, wordiness
verbalization *n syn* see SPEECH 1
verbalize *vb syn* see SPEAK 1
   rel air, express, give, say, state, vent, ventilate, word
   idiom couch in terms, find words to express
verbatim *adv* in the same words <repeated their earlier conversation *verbatim*>
   syn direct, directly, literally, literatim, word for word
   rel accurately, exactly, precisely
   idiom to the letter
   con basically, essentially, in essence; carelessly, imprecisely, inaccurately, inexactly
verbatim *adj* using the same words <court stenographers took down the *verbatim* testimony>
   syn literal, verbal, word-for-word
   rel close, faithful, strict; exact, precise
   idiom following the letter, true to the letter
   con careless, imprecise, inaccurate, inexact
verbiage *n* **1** a stylistic fault involving excessive wordiness that obscures or unduly complicates expression <the florid *verbiage* of the dissertation>
   syn circumambages, circumbendibus, circumlocution, periphrase, periphrasis, pleonasm, redundancy, roundabout, tautology, verbality; *compare* VERBOSITY
   rel nimiety; repetition; expansiveness, floridity, floridness; longiloquence, long-windedness
   idiom purple prose
   con breviloquence, brevity, briefness, terseness
   ant concision
   2 *syn* see WORDING
verbose *adj syn* see WORDY
   rel flowery, grandiloquent, magniloquent; circumlocutory, periphrastic, pleonastic, tautologous
   con precise; close, compact, lean, tight
   ant concise; laconic
verboseness *n syn* see VERBOSITY
   ant conciseness
verbosity *n* the quality or state or an instance of being wordy <his two-hour lecture was the epitome of *verbosity*> <flowery *verbosities* weakened his speech>
   syn prolixity, prolixness, verbalism, verboseness, windiness, wordiness; *compare* VERBIAGE 1
   rel bombast, grandiloquence; long-windedness; redundancy
   con conciseness, preciseness, succinctness, terseness; leanness, tightness

verboten *adj syn* see FORBIDDEN
   rel disallowed, disapproved; unauthorized, unlicensed, unsanctioned; outlawed, taboo
   con allowed, permitted; authorized, licensed; approved, endorsed, sanctioned
verdure *n syn* see FOLIAGE
verge *n* **1** *syn* see BORDER 1
   2 a time interval or set of circumstances marking the imminent beginning of a new state, condition, or action <on the *verge* of war>
   syn brink, edge, point, threshold
   rel border line
verge *vb* **1** *syn* see BORDER 1
   rel approach; incline, lean, tend (to *or* toward); touch (on *or* upon)
   2 *syn* see ADJOIN
   3 *syn* see BORDER 3
veridical *adj* **1** *syn* see TRUTHFUL
   2 *syn* see REAL 3
   3 *syn* see TRUE 3
   rel uncolored, undistorted, unvarnished; actual, real
   con invalid; illusory, unreal
veridicality *n syn* see VERACITY 1
   rel genuineness
verificatory *adj syn* see CORROBORATIVE
verify *vb syn* see CONFIRM 2
   rel demonstrate, prove, test, try; document, establish, settle
verily *adv syn* see EVEN 3
verisimilitude *n* the quality of a representation that causes it to appear true <his characters are too stilted for *verisimilitude*>
   syn color, plausibility, verisimility
   rel authenticity, genuineness, veritableness; likeness, resemblance, similarity
verisimility *n syn* see VERISIMILITUDE
veritable *adj syn* see AUTHENTIC 2
   rel undenied, unrefuted; actual, factual
   con doubtful, questionable; imaginary, unreal, untrue; artificial, factitious; counterfeit, false, spurious
veritably *adv syn* see VERY 2
verity *n* **1** *syn* see VERACITY 2
   ant falsity
   2 *syn* see VERACITY 1
vernacular *adj* of or relating to everyday speech <*vernacular* Welsh differs greatly from literary Welsh>
   syn colloquial, vulgar, vulgate
vernacular *n* **1** *syn* see LANGUAGE 1
   rel mother tongue
   idiom native tongue
   2 *syn* see DIALECT 2
   3 a commonly spoken as opposed to a prestige variety of a language <literary Chinese and the various *vernaculars*>
   syn colloquial, patois, vulgate; *compare* DIALECT 2
   rel dialect, lingo, slang
vernacularism *n syn* see BARBARISM
vernacularity *n syn* see BARBARISM
vernal *adj* of, relating to, or resembling the spring of the year <*vernal* sunshine>
   syn spring, springlike
versant *adj syn* see FAMILIAR 3
   ant unversed
versatile *adj* having a wide range of skills, aptitudes, or interests <a *versatile* artist, who is at home in any medium>
   syn adaptable, all-around, ambidextrous, many-sided, mobile, myriad-minded
   rel elastic, flexible, plastic, pliable; adroit, dexterous, facile; able, skilled, skillful; accomplished, conversant; gifted, talented; well-rounded
   con inadequate, limited
verse *n* **1** *syn* see POETRY 1
   2 *syn* see POEM
   rel jingle; ballad, lay; sonnet; lyric; ode; epic
versed *adj* **1** *syn* see EXPERIENCED
   rel competent

---

syn synonym(s)   *rel* related word(s)
ant antonym(s)   *con* contrasted word(s)
idiom idiomatic equivalent(s)
‖ use limited; if in doubt, see a dictionary

con incompetent
ant unversed
2 *syn* see FAMILIAR 3
ant unversed
verseman *n syn* see POETASTER
versemonger *n syn* see POETASTER
verser *n syn* see POETASTER
versesmith *n syn* see POETASTER
versicolor *adj syn* see VARIEGATED
versicolored *adj syn* see VARIEGATED
versificator *n syn* see POETASTER
versifier *n syn* see POETASTER
version *n* **1** a restating often in simpler language of something previously stated or written < a simple *version* of Beowulf for the use of children >
syn paraphrase, rendering, restatement, translation
rel rendition; clarification, interpretation; condensation, simplification; rewording; restipulation
2 *syn* see ACCOUNT 7
rel tale
3 *syn* see INTERPRETATION 2
versus *prep* **1** in conflict with < the case of John Doe *versus* Richard Roe >
syn against
rel con, contra
idiom at cross-purposes with (*or* to), at odds with, at outs with, at variance with, on the outs with
2 in contrast with < the age-old argument about free trade *versus* protection >
syn over against, vis-à-vis
idiom as opposed to
vertebrae *n syn* see SPINE
vertebral column *n syn* see SPINE
vertex *n syn* see TOP 1
rel cap; tip-top; apogee, zenith
idiom upper extremity
vertical *adj* situated at right angles to the plane of the horizon or extending from that plane at such an angle < *vertical* walls >
syn perpendicular, plumb, straight-up
rel erect, upright; steep, up-and-down
con flat, plane
ant horizontal
verticalism *n syn* see VERTICALITY
verticality *n* the quality or state of being vertical < the soaring *verticality* of the spires >
syn perpendicularity, plumbness, verticalism, verticalness
rel erectness, uprightness
con flatness, lowness
ant horizontality
verticalness *n syn* see VERTICALITY
vertiginous *adj syn* see DIZZY 2
verve *n syn* see SPIRIT 5
rel liveliness, vivacity; bounce, buoyancy, elasticity, resiliency, spring; fire, gusto, zest
very *adj* **1** *syn* see AUTHENTIC 2
rel hundred-percent, perfect; correct, exact, right
con fake, fraudulent, mock, sham
2 *syn* see PRECISE 4
rel especial, express, special
3 *syn* see PERFECT 3
4 being as stated without addition or superfluity < the *very* thought of it makes me ill >
syn bare, mere
5 *syn* see SAME 1
idiom (the) very same
very *adv* **1** to a high or exceptional degree < a *very* successful meeting >
syn ‖awful, awfully, ‖big, ‖crazy, damned, ‖dreadful, dreadfully, eminently, exceedingly, exceptionally, extremely, greatly, highly, hugely, insatiably, ‖larruping, ‖main, mightily, mighty, ‖monstrous, ‖mortacious, mortally, most, much, notably, parlous, pesky, ‖pure, rattling, remarkably, right, ‖right smart, snapping, so, spanking, staving, strikingly, super, surpassingly, terribly, thoroughly, too, vitally, whacking, whopping
rel passing, quite, somewhat; perfectly, seriously, significantly, tellingly
idiom nothing if not
con inconsiderably, little, scarcely, slightly

2 in actual fact < told the *very* same story >
syn actually, de facto, genuinely, really, truly, veritably
rel exactly, precisely; almost, nearly, practically, well-nigh
idiom in point of fact, in truth
con apparently, ostensibly, outwardly, seemingly
vest *vb* **1** *syn* see INVEST 2
2 *syn* see BELONG 2
vestibule *n* an entrance chamber between the outer door and the interior of a building < the *vestibule* of a theater >
syn foyer, lobby
rel entrance hall, entry, entryway; portal, portico; antechamber, anteroom; narthex
vestige *n* **1** something (as a mark or visible sign) left by a material thing formerly present but now lost or unknown < digging for the *vestiges* of past civilizations >
syn memento, relic, shadow, trace
rel remainder, remains; rag, remnant, scrap, tag
2 *syn* see FOOTPRINT
rel path; trail
vet *vb syn* see SCRUTINIZE 1
idiom go over with a fine-tooth comb
vet *adj syn* see EXPERIENCED
vet *n syn* see VETERAN
veteran *n* one having knowledge or ability gained through long experience < was a political campaign *veteran* of long standing >
syn longtimer, old hand, old-timer, vet
rel expert, master, past master
con amateur, freshman, youngster
ant novice
veteran *adj syn* see EXPERIENCED
rel wise; sophisticated, worldly
idiom dry behind the ears, not born yesterday, wise in the ways of the world
con inexperienced, unpracticed, unversed; unqualified, unskilled, untrained
veto *vb* to refuse to admit or approve < the President *vetoed* the bill >
syn kill, negative, ‖nix, non-placet
rel decline, deny, disallow, forbid, prohibit, refuse, reject; defeat
idiom put one's veto on
con admit, approve, assent (to); pass
vex *vb syn* see ANNOY 1
rel ‖chaw, embarrass; plague; anger, infuriate
con appease, mollify, pacify, propitiate, smooth (over); please, regale
ant soothe
vexation *n syn* see ANNOYANCE 1
rel aggravation, irritation
vexatious *adj syn* see TROUBLESOME
vexing *n syn* see ANNOYANCE 1
via *prep* **1** over a route that passes through < shipped to New York *via* the Panama Canal >
syn by, by way of, through
rel along; over
2 using as a means of approach or action < reached the voters *via* mass-media advertising >
syn by, by dint of, by means of, by virtue of, by way of, per, through, with
idiom through the medium of
viable *adj syn* see POSSIBLE 1
viands *n pl syn* see FOOD 1
rel fare
vibrant *adj syn* see RESONANT
vibrate *vb syn* see SHAKE 2
vice *n* **1** degrading or immoral habits and practices < an exposé of *vice* and crime in the city >
syn corruption, depravity, immorality, wickedness
rel decay, rot, squalor; evil, ill, sin, wrong; indecency, unchastity; debasement, debauchery, licentiousness, perversion
con morality; respectability; uprightness
ant virtue
2 *syn* see FAULT 2
rel shortcoming
idiom weak point
3 *syn* see BLEMISH
vice versa *adv syn* see AGAIN 5
vicinage *n syn* see LOCALITY 1

vicinity *n* **1** *syn* see LOCALITY 1
2 *syn* see ORDER 4
vicious *adj* **1** *syn* see WRONG 1
2 highly offensive or reprehensible in character, nature, or conduct < *vicious* parents who were a bad influence on their children >
syn corrupt, degenerate, depraved, flagitious, infamous, miscreant, nefarious, perverse, putrid, rotten, unhealthy, villainous
rel bad, faulty, poor, unsound; opprobrious, reprehensible; contaminated, obnoxious, septic
con good, moral, righteous, right-minded
ant virtuous
3 *syn* see SAVAGE 1
rel brutish; bloodthirsty
4 *syn* see MALICIOUS
5 *syn* see INTENSE 1
rel severe
vicissitude *n* **1** *syn* see CHANGE 2
rel alternation; reversal; transposition; progression; diversity, variety
2 *syn* see DIFFICULTY 1
rel chop and change, ups and downs; adversity, mischance, misfortune; affliction, trial, tribulation
victim *n* **1** a living being sacrificed (as in a religious rite) < offered up human *victims* to appease their bloodthirsty gods >
syn offering, sacrifice
2 one subjected to oppression, loss, or suffering < *victims* of social injustice >
syn bottom dog, casualty, prey, underdog
rel quarry
3 *syn* see FOOL 3
idiom easy mark, easy pickings
victimize *vb* **1** *syn* see SACRIFICE 1
2 *syn* see DUPE
victor *n* **1** one that defeats an enemy < the Allies were the *victors* of World War II >
syn conqueror, defeater, master, subduer, subjugator, vanquisher
rel winner
con conquered, defeated, subjugated; loser
ant vanquished
2 a successful contender < emerged as *victor* in the swimming meet >
syn winner
rel champ, champion; first, top
idiom conquering hero
ant loser
Victorian *adj* *syn* see PRIM 1
rel old-fashioned, old-maidish; hidebound; starchy
con easy going; trendy, with-it
victory *n* **1** the overcoming of an opponent < won a knockout *victory* in the first round >
syn conquest, triumph, win
rel command, control, dominion, mastery, subjugation; superiority, supremacy; walkaway, walkover
idiom a feather in one's cap
con loss; bust, failure, fizzle, flop, ‖floperoo, washout; comedown, cropper
ant defeat
2 *syn* see BETTER 2
victuals *n pl* *syn* see FOOD 1
videlicet *adv* *syn* see NAMELY
vie *vb* **1** *syn* see COMPETE 1
rel challenge; match; outvie
2 *syn* see OPPOSE 1
view *n* **1** *syn* see LOOK 1
rel examination, inspection, scan, scrutiny
2 *syn* see EXAMINATION
3 *syn* see EYE 4
4 what is revealed to the vision or can be seen < the *view* from the window >
syn outlook, scene, sight
rel panorama, picture, prospect, vista
5 extent or range of vision < there were still no ships in *view* >
syn sight
rel look; apprehension, scan
6 something (as an aim, end, or motive) to or by which the mind is directed < kept this *view* in mind while negotiating >

syn object
rel intent, intention, purpose; aim, ambition, goal, objective; design, plan, project; consideration, notion; expectation
7 *syn* see OPINION
rel concept, conception; deduction, inference
view *vb* **1** *syn* see SCRUTINIZE 1
2 *syn* see EYE 1
rel observe
3 *syn* see SEE 1
4 *syn* see CONSIDER 3
viewable *adj* *syn* see VISUAL 2
viewer *n* *syn* see SPECTATOR
viewpoint *n* **1** *syn* see EYE 4
2 the position or attitude that determines how something is seen, presented, or evaluated < from this *viewpoint* the picture looks askew > < consider totalitarianism from the German *viewpoint* >
syn angle, direction, outlook, side, slant, standpoint; *compare* EYE 4
rel estimation; attitude, position, posture, stand; long view, perspective
idiom frame of reference, point of view, vantage point
viewy *adj* *syn* see IMPRACTICAL 1
vigil *n* *syn* see LOOKOUT 3
vigilance *n* *syn* see LOOKOUT 3
vigilant *adj* *syn* see WATCHFUL
rel agog, anxious, avid, eager, keen; acute, sharp, sharp-eyed; attentive
idiom on one's guard, with a weather eye open
con lax, neglectful, negligent, remiss, slack; forgetful, oblivious, unmindful
vigor *n* **1** *syn* see POWER 4
2 a quality of physical or mental force or forcefulness < the *vigor* of youth >
syn bang, drive, getup, get-up-and-go, go, pep, punch, push, snap, starch, vitality; *compare* ENERGY 2, ENTERPRISE 4, SPIRIT 5
rel bounce, energy, force, might, muscularity, power, strength; healthiness, soundness; lustiness, manliness, virility
con slowness, sluggishness
ant weakness
3 *syn* see ENERGY 2
rel dash, drive, dynamism, fire, punch, starch, steam, vim, zing, zip; ability, capability, capacity
con ineffectiveness; impotence; incompetence, uselessness, worthlessness
vigorous *adj* having or manifesting great vitality and force < seemed as *vigorous* as a youth half his age >
syn dynamic, energetic, lusty, red-blooded, strenuous, ‖survigrous, vital
rel brisk, dashing, lively, slashing; exuberant, mettlesome, proud, spirited; driving, hard-driving, hard-hitting, robust, rough-and-ready, zealous; bouncing, hardy, healthy, hearty, masterful, potent, powerful, strong, tough; rude, stout, sturdy; athletic, husky, muscular, sinewy
con languorous, unenergetic; decrepit, feeble, infirm, weak; impotent
ant lethargic
vigorously *adv* *syn* see HARD 1
rel alertly, eagerly; boldly, firmly, purposefully, resolutely, unfalteringly, zealously; lustily, robustly
con aimlessly, languorously; falteringly, indecisively; impotently
vile *adj* **1** *syn* see BASE 3
rel corrupted, debased, debauched, depraved, perverted; coarse, gross, obscene, vulgar; disgusting, foul, nasty; abhorrent, contemptible, loathsome, offensive, repulsive, revolting
2 *syn* see OFFENSIVE
vilify *vb* *syn* see MALIGN
rel abuse, mistreat, misuse, outrage; assail, attack, berate; denounce
con commend, compliment; acclaim, exalt; celebrate, glorify, honor; adore, worship
ant eulogize
vilifying *adj* *syn* see LIBELOUS

---

syn synonym(s)   *rel* related word(s)
ant antonym(s)   *con* contrasted word(s)
idiom idiomatic equivalent(s)
‖ use limited; if in doubt, see a dictionary

villa *n syn* see MANSION

villain *n* **1** a low, mean, reprehensible person utterly lacking in principle <was an insufferable bully, a tyrant, and a *villain* in general>
  syn blackguard, heel, knave, lowlife, miscreant, rascal, reprobate, rogue, roperipe, scoundrel, ‖slubberdegullion; *compare* SNOT 1, DEVIL 2
  rel meanie; evildoer, offender, sinner; criminal, malefactor
  2 *syn* see SCAMP

villainize *vb syn* see MALIGN
  ant eulogize

villainous *adj syn* see VICIOUS 2
  rel contrary, detestable, objectionable, offensive; debased, perverted; atrocious, heinous, outrageous; abandoned, dissolute, profligate

villenage *n syn* see BONDAGE

vim *n syn* see SPIRIT 5
  rel pepper; kick, push

vinculum *n syn* see BOND 3

vindicable *adj syn* see JUSTIFIABLE
  rel inoffensive, unobjectionable, venial
  con indefensible, unjustifiable; inexcusable, unforgivable; heinous, mortal

vindicate *vb* **1** *syn* see AVENGE
  2 *syn* see MAINTAIN 2
  rel advocate, plead (for), second, support, uphold; rationalize; bear out, prove
  3 *syn* see EXCULPATE
  rel confute, disprove, refute; defend, guard, protect, shield
  con accuse, attack, calumniate
  ant convict

vindictive *adj* showing or motivated by a desire for vengeance <*vindictive* hatred for his brother>
  syn revengeful, vengeful, wreakful
  rel grim, implacable, merciless, relentless, unrelenting; malicious, malign, malignant, spiteful
  con charitable, forgiving, merciful, relenting
  ant unvindictive

vinegarish *adj syn* see CANTANKEROUS

vinegary *adj syn* see CANTANKEROUS

vintage *adj* **1** being of old, recognized, and enduring interest, importance, or quality <a *vintage* comedy from the silent movie era>
  syn classic, classical
  2 *syn* see OLD-FASHIONED

violate *vb* **1** to fail to keep <people who thoughtlessly *violate* the law>
  syn breach, break, contravene, infract, infringe, offend, transgress
  rel disregard, trample (on *or* upon); err, sin; overpass, trespass
  con abide by, carry out, fulfill, submit (to); heed, keep, mind
  ant observe; obey
  2 *syn* see RAPE

violation *n* **1** *syn* see BREACH 1
  rel break; encroachment; illegality, misdemeanor, offense, wrong
  ant observance
  2 *syn* see PROFANATION
  rel defacement, defacing

violence *n syn* see FORCE 4
  rel frenzy, fury, savagery; assault, attack, clash, foul play, onslaught, rampage, struggle, tumult, uproar
  con passiveness, passivity; peace, peacefulness
  ant nonviolence

violent *adj syn* see INTENSE 1
  rel forceful, forcible, mighty, potent, powerful, strong; extreme, immoderate, inordinate; acute, cutting, piercing, splitting
  con calm, moderate, peaceful
  ant nonviolent

violently *adv syn* see HARD 2
  rel combatively; destructively, ruinously
  idiom like fury, with a vengeance

VIP *n syn* see NOTABLE 1

virago *n* a woman of extremely pugnacious temperament <an overbearing *virago* who screamed at her children and squabbled with her neighbors>
  syn amazon, fishwife, harpy, ogress, scold, shrew, termagant, vixen, Xanthippe

  rel cat; dragon; fury

virgin *adj* **1** never having had sexual relations <*virgin* girls were sacrificed>
  syn intact, maiden, undeflowered, virginal
  rel innocent, untouched; single, spouseless, unmarried, unwed; abstinent, celibate
  2 not marred or altered from a natural or original state <a *virgin* forest>
  syn unspoiled, untapped, untouched, virginal
  rel primeval, pristine; fresh, new; unmarred, unsullied

virginal *adj* **1** *syn* see VIRGIN 1
  2 *syn* see VIRGIN 2

virginity *n* the quality or state of being a virgin <lost her *virginity*>
  syn maidenhead, maidenhood
  rel chasteness, chastity, purity

virile *adj* characterized by the energy and drive considered typical of a man or of men <developed a strong *virile* prose style>
  syn male, manlike, manly, masculine
  rel manful, mannish; decisive, driving, forceful; energetic, potent, robust; ultramasculine
  con effeminate, womanish; emasculated, weak, weakened; impotent

virtual *adj syn* see IMPLICIT 2
  rel basic, essential, fundamental
  ant actual

virtuality *n syn* see ESSENCE 2

virtually *adv* not absolutely or actually, yet so nearly so that the difference is negligible <that request is *virtually* an order>
  syn in essence, morally, practically; *compare* ALMOST 2
  rel basically, essentially, fundamentally; absolutely, actually
  idiom for all practical purposes, in effect, in substance, to all intents and purposes

virtue *n* **1** *syn* see GOODNESS
  rel fealty, fidelity, loyalty, piety; virtuousness
  con dishonesty; disloyalty, infidelity; evil; immorality; depravity
  ant vice
  2 *syn* see EXCELLENCE
  rel attribute, characteristic, feature, property; effectiveness, effectualness, efficacy; force, might, power, strength
  3 *syn* see QUALITY 1
  4 *syn* see QUALITY 2
  5 *syn* see POWER 4

virtuosic *adj syn* see CONSUMMATE 1

virtuoso *n* **1** *syn* see EXPERT
  2 *syn* see MUSICIAN

virtuous *adj* **1** *syn* see EFFECTIVE
  ant virtueless
  2 *syn* see MORAL 1
  rel spotless, unsullied, untainted, untarnished; worthy
  con dishonest; unjust; unworthy; impure, tainted; immodest, immoral, indecent; vicious, wicked
  ant unvirtuous, virtueless
  3 *syn* see GOOD 11
  rel faultless, sinless
  idiom innocent as a lamb, in the clear, without reproach
  con bad, impure, unrighteous
  ant unvirtuous, virtueless; vicious

virulent *adj* **1** *syn* see POISONOUS
  rel malign, malignant
  2 *syn* see BITTER 3
  rel biting, cutting, scathing, sharp, stabbing; hateful, spiteful, unfriendly

virus *n syn* see POISON
  rel corruption, taint

visage *n* **1** *syn* see FACE 1
  2 *syn* see LOOK 2

vis–à–vis *n* **1** *syn* see OPPOSITE NUMBER
  2 *syn* see TÊTE-À-TÊTE

vis–à–vis *prep* **1** *syn* see AGAINST 1
  rel opposite
  2 *syn* see VERSUS 2

viscera *n pl syn* see ENTRAILS

visceral *adj* **1** *syn* see INNER 2
  2 *syn* see INSTINCTIVE 1

viscerous *adj syn* see INNER 2

viscid *adj syn* see VISCOUS
  rel jellylike, slabby

viscose *adj syn* see VISCOUS
  rel smeary

viscous *adj* having a glutinous adhesive consistency or quality < a *viscous* scum covered the surface of the platter >
  syn tenacious, tough, viscid, viscose
  rel ‖slab, slimy, thick; glutinous, gummy, ropy, sticky; semifluid; stiff

visibility *n* the quality or state of being visible < very poor *visibility* due to fog >
  syn visuality

visible *adj syn* see VISUAL 2
  rel seen

vision *n* **1** *syn* see REVELATION
  rel apparition, phenomenon, presence
  2 *syn* see FANCY 4
  rel muse
  idiom phantom of the mind
  3 *syn* see EYE 2

vision *vb syn* see THINK 1

visional *adj syn* see VISUAL 1

visionary *adj* **1** *syn* see DREAMY 1
  rel abstracted, introspective, musing; impractical
  idiom out of this world, up in the clouds
  2 *syn* see IDEALISTIC
  rel exalted, grandiose, lofty, noble, pretentious
  ant pragmatic, pragmatical
  3 *syn* see AMBITIOUS 2
  rel radical

visionary *n syn* see DREAMER
  ant pragmatist

visionless *adj syn* see BLIND 1

visit *vb* **1** *syn* see INFLICT 2
  rel afflict, bother, pain, trouble; avenge, punish
  idiom bring down upon
  2 to make a social call upon < *visited* friends briefly in the evening >
  syn call, come by, come over, drop (in *or* by), look in, look up, pop (in), run in, see, step in, stop (in *or* by)
  3 to reside with temporarily as a guest < *visited* with friends in the country for a few weeks >
  syn sojourn, stay, stop (over), tarry
  rel frequent; reside
  4 *syn* see CONVERSE

visit *n* **1** a coming to stay with another temporarily and usually briefly < pay a *visit* to friends >
  syn call, visitation
  2 *syn* see SOJOURN

visitant *n syn* see VISITOR 1

visitation *n* **1** *syn* see VISIT 1
  2 *syn* see TRIAL 1
  rel mischance; calamity, catastrophe, disaster

visitor *n* **1** one who visits another < there are *visitors* in the living room >
  syn caller, guest, visitant; *compare* COMPANY 2
  rel invitee
  2 **visitors** *pl syn* see COMPANY 2

visor *n* **1** a projecting front brim on a cap or hat for shading the eyes < the *visor* kept out the sun >
  syn bill, peak
  rel eyeshade
  2 *syn* see MASK 1

vista *n* an extensive or distant view < a long flat tree-lined *vista* >
  syn lookout, outlook, perspective, prospect, scape
  rel panorama, scene, sight, view; range, scope, survey
  idiom long view

visual *adj* **1** of or relating to or used in vision < the *visual* sense >
  syn ocular, optic, optical, visional
  2 capable of being seen < *visual* objects >
  syn ocular, seeable, viewable, visible
  rel discernible, perceivable, perceptible

visuality *n syn* see VISIBILITY

visualize *vb* **1** *syn* see THINK 1
  rel picture, view; objectify; call up, conjure (up)
  idiom bring (*or* call) to mind, conjure up a mental image (*or* picture) of, see in the mind's eye
  2 *syn* see FORESEE

vital *adj* **1** *syn* see LIVING 1
  rel breathing

2 *syn* see VIGOROUS
3 *syn* see ESSENTIAL 2
  rel indispensable, needed, needful, required, requisite; integral, prerequisite

vital force *n syn* see SOUL 1

vitality *n syn* see VIGOR 2
  rel animation, life, liveliness, pulse; endurance, energy, spirit, vim

vitalize *vb* to arouse to activity, animation, or life < atomic energy is a force that can *vitalize* or destroy human civilization >
  syn actify, activate, activize, energize
  rel animate, enliven, invigorate, quicken, vivify; dynamize, excite, galvanize, provoke, stimulate; pep up, strengthen
  idiom put life into
  con eviscerate, weaken
  ant atrophy; devitalize

vitalizing *adj syn* see INVIGORATING
  ant devitalizing

vitally *adv syn* see VERY 1

vitiate *adj syn* see DEBASED
  ant purified

vitiate *vb* **1** *syn* see INJURE 1
  rel twist, warp
  2 *syn* see DEBASE 1
  rel defile, soil, sully, taint; prostitute; contaminate
  idiom drive to the dogs
  ant purify
  3 *syn* see ABOLISH 1

vitiated *adj syn* see DEBASED
  rel contaminated, defiled, polluted, tainted; impaired, injured, spoiled
  ant purified

vitriolic *adj syn* see BITTER 3

vituperate *vb syn* see SCOLD 1
  rel condemn, lambaste; asperse, calumniate, malign, traduce; bark (at), growl (at), yell (at); abuse, curse
  idiom rip into
  con applaud, commend, compliment; eulogize, extol, praise
  ant acclaim

vituperation *n syn* see ABUSE
  rel blame, censure, revilement, scolding, tongue-lashing
  con eulogy, extolment
  ant acclaim, praise

vituperative *adj syn* see ABUSIVE
  rel censorious, critical; severe; railing, scolding

vituperatory *adj syn* see ABUSIVE
  rel censorious, critical; severe; railing, scolding

vituperous *adj syn* see ABUSIVE
  rel censorious, critical; severe; railing, scolding

vivacious *adj* **1** *syn* see LIVELY 1
  rel breezy, vibrant, zesty; frolicsome, playful, sportive
  idiom gay as a lark
  ant languid
  2 *syn* see EXUBERANT 1

viva voce *adj syn* see VOCAL 1

vivid *adj* **1** *syn* see COLORFUL
  2 *syn* see GRAPHIC 1
  rel acute, intense, keen, sharp; dramatic, dramaturgic, theatrical; eloquent, expressive, meaningful, rich; animated, lively, spirited, vigorous

vivificate *vb syn* see QUICKEN 1
  rel revive

vivify *vb syn* see QUICKEN 1
  rel refresh, renew, restore; excite, galvanize
  idiom give life to, imbue with life, put new life into

vivres *n pl syn* see FOOD 1

vixen *n syn* see VIRAGO

vizard *n syn* see MASK 1

‖vlei *n syn* see SWAMP

vocable *n syn* see WORD 2
  rel verbalism

---

syn synonym(s)   *rel* related word(s)
ant antonym(s)   *con* contrasted word(s)
idiom idiomatic equivalent(s)
‖ use limited; if in doubt, see a dictionary

vocabulary *n* **1** the sum or set of words employed by a language, group, individual, or work or in relation to a subject < Latin contributes heavily to the *vocabulary* of English >
syn lexicon, word-hoard, word-stock
idiom stock of words
2 *syn* see TERMINOLOGY
rel phraseology

vocal *adj* **1** uttered by the voice or having to do with such utterance < the infant's primitive *vocal* sounds from which language develops >
syn articulate, oral, sonant, spoken, viva voce, voiced
rel intonated; expressed, uttered
con unexpressed, unuttered, unvoiced
ant nonvocal
2 *syn* see VOCALIC
ant consonantal
3 being able to express oneself clearly or easily < he was hardly *vocal:* he could scarcely express the simplest concepts >
syn articulate, eloquent, fluent, smooth-spoken
rel expressing, voicing; expressive; outspoken, stentorian, venting
con faltering, halting, hesitant, stumbling
4 *syn* see OUTSPOKEN

vocalic *adj* marked by, consisting of, or functioning as a vowel or vowels < *vocalic* and consonantal sounds >
syn vocal, vowel, vowely
rel vowellike

vocalism *n syn* see VOCALIZATION

vocalization *n* the exercise of the vocal organs in song or speech < his *vocalization* of a previously unstated thought >
syn articulation, utterance, uttering, vocalism; *compare* SPEECH 1
rel mouth, mouthing; sounding, voice, voicing; diction, enunciation, verbalization; speaking, speech

vocalize *vb* **1** *syn* see SPEAK 1
rel emit, let out; express; enunciate, pronounce; communicate, convey, impart
idiom execute vocally
2 *syn* see SING 1

vocation *n* **1** *syn* see TRADE 1
2 *syn* see MISSION

vocative *adj syn* see GLIB
rel chatty, garrulous, loquacious, talkative, windy; slick, smooth

vociferant *adj syn* see VOCIFEROUS

vociferate *vb syn* see CALL 1

vociferous *adj* so loud, noisy, and insistent as to compel attention < the crowd made *vociferous* protests against the speaker's statement >
syn blatant, boisterous, clamorous, ‖dinsome, loudmouthed, multivocal, obstreperous, openmouthed, strident, vociferant
rel distracting; loud, noisy, shrill
con close-lipped, reserved, silent, uncommunicative; noiseless, quiet, still

vogue *n syn* see FASHION 2
rel bon ton, fashionableness, stylishness

voice *n* **1** *syn* see EXPRESSION 1
rel speech
2 the right to express a wish, choice, or opinion or to influence a situation < even the youngest had a *voice* in planning the party >
syn say, say-so

voice *vb syn* see SPEAK 1
rel sound; articulate, enunciate, pronounce; formulate, phrase, present, put; recount, tell

voiced *adj syn* see VOCAL 1

voiceless *adj syn* see DUMB 1

void *adj* **1** *syn* see EMPTY 1
ant full
2 *syn* see DEVOID
rel scant, short, shy; bare, bereft, denuded, deprived
3 *syn* see NULL
rel negated

void *n syn* see HOLE 3

void *vb* **1** *syn* see VACATE 2
rel evacuate; deplete, drain, eliminate; eject, remove, throw out
2 *syn* see DISCHARGE 5

void *vb syn* see ANNUL 4
idiom declare (*or* make) null and void

voidness *n syn* see VACUITY 2
ant fullness

volage *adj syn* see GIDDY 1

volant *adj syn* see AGILE

volatile *adj* **1** *syn* see ELASTIC 2
rel capricious, fickle, inconstant, mercurial, unstable; flighty, flippant, frivolous, light-minded; changeable, protean, variable
2 *syn* see EXCITABLE
rel explosive
3 *syn* see INCONSTANT 1
4 *syn* see TRANSIENT

volatility *n syn* see LIGHTNESS
rel animation, sprightliness; inconstancy, instability, mercurialness; changeability, variability

volition *n syn* see WILL 2
rel choice, election, option, selection; desire, preference
con coercion, compulsion, duress, force

volley *n syn* see BARRAGE

volte-face *n syn* see REVERSAL 1

volte-face *vb syn* see TURN 6
rel about-face, face (about), right-about-face

voluble *adj syn* see GLIB

volume *n* **1** *syn* see BOOK 1
2 *syn* see BULK 1
rel amount, content, quantity
3 *syn* see BODY 4

voluminous *adj syn* see MANY

voluntary *adj* consisting of or proceeding from an exercise of free will < the law requires that a confession be *voluntary* >
syn deliberate, intentional, unforced, unprescribed, willful, willing, witting
rel chosen, elected, opted, volitional; autonomous, free, independent
con coerced, compelled, forced; unintentional, unplanned, unwilling, unwitting
ant involuntary

voluptuous *adj syn* see SENSUOUS
rel indulgent, self-gratifying; abandoned, dissipated, dissolute, excessive, wanton
con self-contained, self-denying
ant ascetic

vomit *vb* to discharge the contents of the stomach through the mouth < the churning seas made several passengers *vomit* >
syn barf, bring up, ‖cack, ‖cascade, ‖cast, ‖cat, disgorge, ‖heave, shoot, sick (up), spew, spit up, throw up, upchuck
rel gag, regurgitate, retch; keck; eject, expel
idiom ‖blow one's lunch, holler New York, lose one's cookies

voodoo *n* **1** *syn* see MAGICIAN 1
2 *syn* see JINX

voodoo *vb syn* see BEWITCH 1

voodooist *n syn* see MAGICIAN 1

voracious *adj* excessively greedy (as in appetite, reactions, or behavior) < the wolverine is an extremely *voracious* eater >
syn edacious, gluttonous, rapacious, ravening, ravenous
rel acquisitive, covetous, grasping, greedy; devouring, gorging, satiating, sating, surfeiting; avid, insatiable

vortex *n syn* see EDDY
rel spiral, spout

votary *n* **1** *syn* see ADDICT
rel disciple; freak
2 *syn* see AMATEUR 1
rel hound

vote *n* **1** *syn* see BALLOT 1
2 *syn* see SUFFRAGE

vote (in) *vb syn* see ELECT 2
rel choose, decide
idiom cast one's vote for

vouch *vb syn* see CERTIFY 1
rel support, uphold; confirm, corroborate, prove, substantiate, verify; assure, guarantee

vouchsafe *vb syn* see GRANT 1
rel condescend, deign, stoop; accommodate, favor, oblige

vow *vb* to promise solemnly < *vowed* never to leave each other >
syn covenant, pledge, plight, swear; *compare* PROMISE 1
rel assert, declare, ‖swan; promise
idiom give (*or* make) a solemn promise, give one's word of honor

vowel *adj syn* see VOCALIC

vowely *adj syn* see VOCALIC

voyage *n* a journey by water <took the new ship on a long *voyage* >
syn cruise
rel journey, tour, trip

voyeur *n syn* see PEEPING TOM

vulgar *adj* **1** *syn* see VERNACULAR
rel conversational, spoken; idiomatic
2 *syn* see PUBLIC 4
3 *syn* see COARSE 3
4 *syn* see OBSCENE 2
rel base, low, vile; loathsome, offensive, repulsive, revolting; indecorous, indelicate, uncouth
con decent, delicate, refined; high-minded, lofty, noble
5 *syn* see BARBARIC 1
rel inelegant, ungraceful; improper, incorrect, unseemly; uncouth, unpolished, unrefined

idiom in very poor taste
con elegant, graceful; correct, proper, seemly

vulgarism *n syn* see BARBARISM

vulgate *adj syn* see VERNACULAR

vulgate *n syn* see VERNACULAR 3

vulnerability *n syn* see EXPOSURE
rel vincibility

vulnerableness *n syn* see EXPOSURE
rel weakness

vulnerary *adj syn* see CURATIVE

vulpine *adj syn* see SLY 2

vulture *vb syn* see STEAL 1

vulturine *adj syn* see RAPACIOUS 1

vulturish *adj syn* see RAPACIOUS 1

vulturous *adj syn* see RAPACIOUS 1

‖**wack** *n syn* see ECCENTRIC

wacky *adj* **1** *syn* see FOOLISH 2
2 *syn* see INSANE 1

wad *n* **1** *syn* see LUMP 1
2 *often* **wads** *pl syn* see SCAD
3 *syn* see FORTUNE 4

wade (in *or* into) *vb syn* see PITCH IN 1

‖**waffle** *vb syn* see BABBLE 2

wag *vb* to move to and fro <the dog *wagged* his tail briskly>
syn beat, lash, switch, waggle, wave, woggle
rel shake, twitch, wiggle; oscillate; wigwag

wag *n* **1** a person full of sportive humor <a gay young *wag*, always full of fun>
syn card, comedian, humorist, joker, zany
rel clown, cutup, madcap, prankster, show-off; jester, kidder, quipster, wisecracker, wit
idiom life of the party
2 *syn* see ZANY 2
3 *syn* see HUMORIST 2

wage *n, often* **wages** *pl* the price paid a person for his labor or services <high *wages* are often seen as a factor in inflation>
syn emolument, fee, hire, pay, pay envelope, salary, stipend
rel compensation, recompense, remuneration, reward; earnings, income, receipts, return(s), take

wager *n syn* see BET

wager *vb* **1** *syn* see VENTURE 1
2 *syn* see GAMBLE 1
idiom lay a wager

waggery *n* **1** *syn* see MISCHIEVOUSNESS
2 *syn* see JOKE 1

waggish *adj syn* see PLAYFUL 1
rel facetious, humorous, jocose, jocular, witty; comic, comical, droll, funny, laughable, ludicrous; arch, pert, saucy
con earnest, grave, sedate, serious, sober, staid

waggishness *n syn* see MISCHIEVOUSNESS

waggle *vb syn* see WAG
rel sway, waddle, wobble

wail *vb* **1** *syn* see CRY 2
idiom make an outcry
2 *syn* see HOWL 1
3 *syn* see BAWL 2
4 *syn* see COMPLAIN

wailful *adj syn* see MELANCHOLY 2

waistband *n syn* see BELT 1

wait *vb syn* see STAY 2
rel anticipate, foresee; await, expect
idiom bide one's time, cool one's heels, look forward to, mark time
con depart, go, leave

wait (on) *vb syn* see MINISTER (to)

waive *vb* **1** *syn* see RELINQUISH
rel allow, concede, grant

con claim, demand, exact, require; assert, defend, maintain
2 *syn* see DEFER

wake *vb* **1** to stop sleeping <she usually *woke* before dawn>
syn awake, awaken, rouse, stir, waken
rel arise, get up, roll out
con catnap, doze, drowse, nap, nod, snooze; sleep, slumber
2 *syn* see STIR 1
rel freshen, renew
con calm, ease, mollify, relax

waken *vb* **1** *syn* see STIR 1
rel freshen, renew
con calm, ease, mollify, relax
2 *syn* see WAKE 1

wale *n syn* see WHEAL

walk *vb* **1** to advance on foot step by step <often *walked* to work on pleasant mornings>
syn ambulate, foot (it), hoof, pace, step, traipse, tread, troop
rel circumambulate, perambulate, promenade, ramble, stroll; hike, tramp; lumber, plod, slog, stride, stump, trudge; leg, race, run
idiom beat one's feet, heel and toe it, ride shanks' mare
con drive, ride
2 *syn* see TRAVERSE 5

walk *n* **1** a usually brief journey on foot for pleasure or exercise <always took a *walk* before breakfast>
syn constitutional, ramble, saunter, stroll, turn
rel hike, march, tramp; deambulation, parade, promenade; airing, stretch
2 *syn* see FIELD

walkabout *n syn* see TRAMP 3

walkaway *n syn* see RUNAWAY

walk out *vb syn* see STRIKE 1

walkover *n syn* see RUNAWAY

wall *n syn* see BAR 2

wall *vb syn* see ENCLOSE 1

wallop *n* **1** *syn* see BLOW 1
2 *syn* see IMPACT
3 *syn* see THRILL

wallop *vb* **1** *syn* see BEAT 1
2 *syn* see WHIP 2
3 *syn* see SLAM 1

walloping *adj syn* see HUGE

wallow *vb* **1** to roll or move in an indolent and ungainly yet comfortable fashion <hogs *wallowing* in a cool mudhole>
syn welter
rel flounder, roll, tumble; cuddle, nestle, snuggle

---

2 to move or progress unsteadily and clumsily as if beset by obstacles <*wallowed* through the mire for miles trying to get help>

    syn blunder, flounder, lurch, stumble; *compare* STUMBLE 3

    rel reel, stagger, sway, totter, wamble, welter

    idiom make heavy weather (of)

3 to become deeply or excessively involved in or with something subjectively felt as pleasant <*wallowing* in luxury>

    syn bask, indulge, luxuriate, revel, roll, rollick, welter

    rel baby, humor, pamper, spoil; appreciate, delight (in), enjoy, relish

    con abstain, refrain; avoid, eschew, shun

waltz *vb syn* see BREEZE

‖**wambly** *adj syn* see SQUEAMISH 1

‖**wampum** *n syn* see MONEY

wan *adj* **1** *syn* see PALE 1

    rel cadaverous, haggard, worn; blanched, bleached, washed-out; anemic, bloodless

  2 *syn* see WEAK 4

wander *vb* **1** to move about from place to place more or less aimlessly and without obvious plan <*wandering* through the forest>

    syn bat, circumambulate, drift, gad, gallivant, maunder, meander, mooch, ‖project, ramble, range, roam, roll, rove, straggle, stray, traipse, vagabond, vagabondize; *compare* SAUNTER

    rel amble, saunter, stroll; divagate, diverge, trail; boom, bum, tramp

  2 *syn* see DIGRESS 2

  3 *syn* see ERR

wanderer *n syn* see ROVER

wandering *adj* **1** *syn* see ITINERANT

  2 *syn* see ERRATIC 1

  3 *syn* see DELIRIOUS 1

wane *vb* **1** *syn* see ABATE 4

    ant wax

  2 *syn* see FAIL 3

    ant wax

wangle *vb syn* see ENGINEER

    rel outflank, outgeneral, outmaneuver, overreach

waning *n syn* see FAILURE 4

    ant waxing

‖**wanky** *adj syn* see WEAK 1

want *vb* **1** *syn* see LACK

    idiom be found wanting, fall short, feel the want of

  2 *syn* see DESIRE 1

    rel choose, prefer

    idiom could do with, have a mind (*or* an eye) to

  3 to have as a duty or responsibility <you *want* to behave yourself>

    syn must, ought, should

    rel become, befit, behoove; need (to)

    idiom be wise to, had better (*or* best)

want *n* **1** *syn* see ABSENCE

    rel exigency, necessity, need

    con sufficiency

  2 *syn* see POVERTY 1

    rel exiguousness, meagerness, scantiness, skimpiness; inadequacy, insufficiency

    con riches

  3 *syn* see REQUIREMENT 1

wanting *adj syn* see ABSENT 1

  2 *syn* see SHORT 3

  3 *syn* see DEFICIENT 1

wanting *prep syn* see WITHOUT 2

wanton *adj* **1** *syn* see FAST 7

    rel lax, slack, wayward

    idiom of easy virtue, of loose morals

    con austere, puritanical, restrained, self-restrained

    ant chaste

  2 *syn* see SUPEREROGATORY

    rel malevolent, malicious, spiteful; contrary, perverse, wayward

wanton *n* a woman who engages in lewd unseemly conduct <giddy *wantons* flaunting themselves in bars>

    syn baggage, ‖bim, ‖bimbo, cyprian, hussy, jade, jezebel, ‖pig, slattern, slut, strumpet, tramp, trollop, trull, wench

    idiom loose woman

wanton *vb syn* see TRIFLE 1

wantwit *n syn* see DUNCE

war *vb syn* see CONTEND 1

    rel attempt, endeavor, essay, strive, struggle; challenge, engage, take on

    idiom draw the sword against, lift one's hand against, take up the cudgels

warble *n syn* see MELODY

war chest *n syn* see TREASURY 2

war club *n syn* see CUDGEL

war cry *n syn* see BATTLE CRY

ward *n* **1** *syn* see GUARD 2

  2 *syn* see DEFENSE 1

  3 *syn* see CUSTODY

ward *vb* **1** to cause to miss an objective by or as if by turning aside <*warded* the stroke of his enemy's sword with his shield>

    syn deflect, fend, parry

    rel block, check, halt, stay, stymie; avert, divert, turn

    idiom keep at arm's length, turn aside

  2 *syn* see PREVENT 2

    rel balk, foil, frustrate, thwart; check, interrupt

    ant conduce (to)

ward (off) *vb syn* see FEND (off)

    ant bring on

warden *n syn* see CUSTODIAN

ware *adj syn* see AWARE

warehouse *vb syn* see STOW

    rel accommodate; guard, protect, shelter

wares *n pl syn* see MERCHANDISE

warfare *n syn* see CONTEST 1

warhorse *n syn* see COURSER

warlike *adj* **1** *syn* see BELLIGERENT

    ant peaceable

  2 *syn* see MARTIAL

    rel battling, contending, fighting, warring

    ant unwarlike

warlock *n syn* see MAGICIAN 1

warm *adj* **1** *syn* see ENTHUSIASTIC

  2 *syn* see TENDER

    rel ardent, fervent, passionate; affable, cordial, gracious; heartfelt, hearty, sincere, wholehearted

    ant cool; austere

warmed–over *adj syn* see TRITE

warmhearted *adj syn* see TENDER

    rel benign, benignant, kind, kindly, outgoing

    con austere, cold, cool, frigid, frosty, severe, stern

    ant coldhearted

warming *n syn* see DEFEAT 1

warmish *adj syn* see TEPID 1

warn *vb* **1** to let one know of approaching danger or risk <police and the weather service join to *warn* travelers of hazardous road conditions>

    syn caution, forewarn

    rel advise, alert, apprise, inform, notify, tip; counsel, direct, guide

    idiom address a warning to, give warning, put a flea in one's ear, put one on guard

  2 *syn* see INFORM 2

  3 *syn* see COMMAND

warning *n* something and especially a statement that warns or is intended to warn <gave them *warning* that disobedience would lead to punishment>

    syn admonition, caution, caveat, commonition, forewarning, monition

    rel advice, counsel, guidance, recommendation; hint, suggestion, tip

    idiom flea (*or* word) in the ear, word to the wise

warning *adj syn* see MONITORY

warp *vb* **1** *syn* see DEBASE 1

    rel contort, crook, distort, twist

    con disentangle, rectify, straighten, unkink

  2 *syn* see DEFORM

    rel bend, crook, kink, twist

  3 *syn* see MISREPRESENT

war paint *n* **1** *syn* see FINERY

  2 *syn* see MAKEUP 3

warped *adj syn* see BIASED 2

    ant unwarped

warrant *n* **1** *syn* see PLEDGE 1

2 syn see BASIS 3

3 syn see WORD 8

warrant *vb* **1 syn** see MAINTAIN 2

rel state; assure, ensure, insure

2 to give assurance of the worth of something especially in respect to quality, quantity, or condition < *warranted* the merchandise to be exactly as described in the catalog >

syn certify, guarantee, guaranty

rel assure, insure, secure; back, sponsor, stipulate; affirm, claim, state

idiom stand behind

3 syn see JUSTIFY 4

rel endorse; call (for), need, require

warrantable *adj syn* see JUSTIFIABLE

ant unwarrantable

warranty *n syn* see GUARANTEE 1

warrior *n syn* see SOLDIER

wary *adj* **1 syn** see CAUTIOUS

rel distrustful, doubting, leery, suspicious; vigilant, watchful

idiom on one's guard

con careless, heedless, thoughtless; devil-may-care, reckless, venturesome

ant foolhardy; unwary

2 syn see SPARING

wash *vb* **1 syn** see BATHE 1

2 syn see BATHE 2

3 syn see DRIFT 1

4 syn see SLOSH 1

washed–out *adj syn* see EFFETE 2

washed–up *adj* **1 syn** see THROUGH 3

2 syn see THROUGH 4

wash out *vb* **1 syn** see FAIL 4

2 syn see DISCARD

wash up *vb syn* see GO 4

washy *adj syn* see DILUTE

waspish *adj* **1 syn** see IRRITABLE

rel contrary, impatient, perverse; malicious, sharp, spiteful; crabbed, cross-grained

2 syn see CANTANKEROUS

waspy *adj* **1 syn** see IRRITABLE

rel contrary, impatient, perverse; malicious, sharp, spiteful; crabbed, cross-grained

2 syn see CANTANKEROUS

wassail *n* **1 syn** see BINGE 1

2 syn see REVELRY 2

wassail *vb syn* see REVEL 1

waste *n* **1** an area of the earth unsuitable for cultivation or general habitation < the scattered dwellers of southern Africa's dry *wastes* >

syn badland, barren, desert, wasteland, wild, wilderness, wild land, wildness

rel brush, brushland, bush; jungle

2 syn see EXTRAVAGANCE 2

3 syn see REFUSE

rel rubble, rummage

waste *vb* **1 syn** see RAVAGE

idiom reduce to a shambles

ant conserve

2 to spend or expend freely and usually foolishly or futilely < *wasted* his inheritance on women and gambling > < *waste* one's time on trifles >

syn blow, blunder (away), cast away, consume, dissipate, dribble (away), drivel, fool (away), fritter, frivol away, muddle (away), potter (away), prodigalize, riot (away), squander, throw away, trifle (away)

rel disburse, expend, spend; dispense, distribute; deplete, drain, exhaust, impoverish; dispel, disperse, scatter; misspend

idiom let slip through one's fingers, pour down the drain, throw good money after bad

ant save; conserve

waste (away) *vb syn* see FAIL 3

wasted *adj syn* see EMACIATED

rel meager; shriveled, withered, wizened

con healthy, robust; stalwart, stout, strong, sturdy

wastefulness *n syn* see EXTRAVAGANCE 2

ant frugality

wasteland *n syn* see WASTE 1

waster *n* **1 syn** see SPENDTHRIFT

rel dissipater, fritterer; idler, loafer, lounger

2 syn see WASTREL 1

wastethrift *n syn* see SPENDTHRIFT

wastrel *n* **1** a worthless, self-indulgent, and reprehensible person < loafers and other *wastrels* lounging on the corner >

syn ||bad lot, good-for-nothing, ne'er-do-well, no-good, profligate, rounder, scapegrace, waster

rel lecher, libertine, rake, rip, roué; blackguard, black sheep, knave, rascal, rogue, scoundrel; rapscallion, scalawag, scamp

idiom sad case

2 syn see SPENDTHRIFT

rel dissipater, fritterer; idler, loafer, lounger

watch *vb* **1 syn** see SEE 2

rel examine, follow, inspect, scan, scrutinize

idiom keep an eye on, keep tabs on

2 syn see EYE 2

3 syn see TEND 2

idiom keep watch over

4 syn see LOOK 1

watch *n* **1 syn** see LOOKOUT 3

2 syn see GUARD 2

3 syn see EYE 3

watch and ward *n syn* see LOOKOUT 3

watchdog *n syn* see CUSTODIAN

watcher *n syn* see SPECTATOR

watchfire *n syn* see BEACON 1

watchful *adj* paying close attention usually with a view to anticipating approaching danger or opportunity < adopted a policy of *watchful* waiting >

syn alert, open-eyed, unsleeping, vigilant, wakeful, wide-awake

rel cautious, chary, circumspect, wary; prompt, quick, ready

idiom keeping one's eyes peeled (or open), on the watch (or lookout)

con careless, heedless, thoughtless; inadvertent; absentminded, abstracted, faraway

ant unwatchful

watchman *n syn* see GUARD 2

watch out *vb syn* see BEWARE

watchword *n* **1 syn** see PASSWORD 1

2 syn see PASSWORD 3

3 syn see CATCHWORD

water *n* **1 syn** see TEARS

2 syn see SALIVA

water *vb syn* see DROOL 1

water closet *n syn* see TOILET

watercourse *n syn* see CHANNEL 1

watered–down *adj syn* see DILUTE

waterfall *n* a precipitous descent of water or the site of this < heard the roar of the *waterfall* >

syn cascade, cataract, chute, fall(s), ||force, sault, spout

rel rapid(s), riffle, shoot; eddy, surge, vortex, whirlpool

watering hole *n* **1 syn** see RESORT 2

2 syn see BAR 5

3 syn see NIGHTCLUB

watering place *n* **1 syn** see SPA 1

2 syn see RESORT 3

3 syn see BAR 5

4 syn see NIGHTCLUB

waterish *adj* **1 syn** see DILUTE

2 syn see PALE 2

3 syn see INSIPID 3

waterless *adj syn* see DRY 1

ant watered

waterlog *vb syn* see SOAK 1

watery *adj* **1 syn** see DILUTE

2 syn see PALE 2

3 syn see INSIPID 3

wave *vb syn* see WAG

waver *vb syn* see HESITATE

rel palter, shift, trim; seesaw, teeter

idiom back and fill, hem and haw

wavering *n syn* see HESITATION

wavering *adj* **1 syn** see VACILLATING 2

---

syn synonym(s)　　　　　**rel** related word(s)

ant antonym(s)　　　　　**con** contrasted word(s)

idiom idiomatic equivalent(s)

|| use limited; if in doubt, see a dictionary

ant unwavering
2 syn see WEAK 2
wax *vb* **1 syn** see INCREASE 2
ant wane
2 syn see BECOME 1
wax *n syn* see RISE 3
ant wane
waxen *adj syn* see PALE 1
waxy *adj syn* see ANGRY
way *n* **1** a public and unobstructed passage leading from one place to another <tracing the remains of an old lumberman's *way* >
syn artery, avenue, boulevard, ‖drag, highway, path, road, street, thoroughfare, track
rel course, line, passage, route; alley, byway, lane, ride, row
2 that along which one passes in going from one place to another <his *way* led through wooded hills >
syn course, line, passage, path, road, route
3 syn see DOOR 2
4 syn see METHOD 1
rel custom, habit, habitude, practice, usage, use, wont
5 syn see STYLE 4
6 syn see HABIT 1
7 syn see DISTANCE 2
8 syn see TYPE
‖**wayback** *n syn* see RUSTIC
wayfaring *adj syn* see ITINERANT
waylay *vb syn* see SURPRISE 1
rel lurk, prowl, skulk, slink
idiom lay wait for, lie in wait for
ways *n pl but sing in constr syn* see DISTANCE 2
wayward *adj* **1 syn** see CONTRARY 3
rel capricious, fickle, inconstant, unstable, variable
con complaisant, good-natured
2 syn see ARBITRARY 1
weak *adj* **1** lacking physical, mental, or moral strength <a *weak* spirit in a *weak* body >
syn decrepit, feeble, flimsy, fragile, frail, infirm, insubstantial, puny, unsound, ‖wanky, weakly
rel debilitated, enfeebled, sickly, spindly, weakened; forceless, impotent, impuissant, powerless
con stalwart, stout, sturdy, tenacious, tough; dynamic, energetic, forceful, vigorous
ant strong
2 deficient in stability <a love too *weak* to bear the trials of daily life >
syn dickey, fluctuant, insecure, rootless, shaky, unstable, unsure, vacillating, wavering, wobbly; *compare* RICKETY
rel hesitant, irresolute, trimming, uncertain; insubstantial, undependable, unreliable
con certain, secure, solid, stable, sure; dependable, reliable, substantial
ant strong
3 syn see IMPLAUSIBLE
4 not equal to the requirements and demands of a situation <a *weak* executive >
syn boneless, emasculate, forceless, impotent, inadequate, ineffective, ineffectual, invertebrate, slack-spined, spineless, wan
rel unfit, unqualified, unsuitable; bungling, incompetent, inept
con able, competent, effective, efficient; adequate, fit, qualified, satisfactory, sufficient, suitable; manly, masculine, virile
ant strong
5 syn see DILUTE
ant strong
weaken *vb* **1** to lose or cause to lose strength, vigor, or energy <his hesitation *weakened* the force of his argument >
syn attenuate, blunt, cripple, debilitate, disable, enfeeble, sap, unbrace, undermine, unstrengthen; *compare* PARALYZE 1
rel emasculate, enervate, incapacitate, unman, unnerve; damage, impair, injure; lessen, minimize, reduce; dilute, thin
con better, improve; activate, energize, invigorate, vitalize
ant strengthen
2 syn see FAIL 1
3 syn see FAIL 3
4 syn see DILUTE
weak-headed *adj syn* see SIMPLE 3
weak-kneed *adj syn* see VACILLATING 2
weakling *n* a person lacking in stamina and character <his speech deplored the characterless *weaklings* in critical positions >

syn baby, doormat, invertebrate, jellyfish, milksop, Milquetoast, ‖molly, mollycoddle, namby-pamby, pantywaist, sissy, sissy≠pants (*or* sissy-britches), sop
rel butt, mark, pushover, sucker; drip, mama's boy, misfit, mother's boy, sad sack, weak sister
idiom shrinking violet
weakly *adv syn* see SOTTO VOCE
ant strongly
weakly *adj syn* see WEAK 1
weak-minded *adj syn* see SIMPLE 3
weakness *n syn* see APPETITE 3
weal *n syn* see WHEAL
weald *n syn* see FOREST
wealth *n* **1 syn** see MEAN 3
2 one's worldly possessions <at that point his *wealth* consisted of the clothes he stood in and a solitary quarter >
syn fortune, property, resources, riches, substance, worth
rel assets, estate, goods, holdings, possessions
wealthy *adj syn* see RICH 1
con impoverished, penniless, poor
ant indigent
wean *vb syn* see ESTRANGE
ant addict
wear *vb* **1 syn** see ABRADE 1
2 syn see TIRE 1
wear (away) *vb syn* see EAT 3
wear down *vb syn* see TIRE 1
wearied *adj syn* see TIRED 1
ant refreshed; unwearied, unweary
weariful *adj syn* see ARID 2
weariless *adj syn* see INDEFATIGABLE
weariness *n syn* see FATIGUE
2 syn see ARID 2
wear out *vb* **1 syn** see EXHAUST 4
‖**2 syn** see WHIP 1
weary *vb* **1 syn** see TIRE 1
rel debilitate, enfeeble, weaken; depress, oppress, weigh
con animate, energize, vitalize; enliven, quicken, vivify
ant refresh
2 syn see BORE
weary *adj* **1 syn** see TIRED 1
ant refreshed, unwearied, unweary
2 syn see FED UP
Weary Willie *n syn* see VAGABOND
weasel *n syn* see SNEAK
weasel *vb syn* see EQUIVOCATE 2
weathery *adj syn* see CHANGEABLE 1
weave *vb syn* see LURCH 2
web *n* **1 syn** see TEXTURE 2
2 something by which one is ensnared, held fast, or inextricably involved <diplomacy caught in its own *web* of double-dealing >
syn cobweb, entanglement, mesh(es), toil(s); *compare* ENTANGLEMENT 1
rel complexity, complication; labyrinth, maze, morass, skein, snarl, tangle; embroilment, enmeshment, ensnarement, entrapment, involvement
idiom a tangled web
3 syn see MAZE 1
wed *vb* **1 syn** see MARRY 1
2 syn see MARRY 2
3 syn see JOIN 1
wedded *adj syn* see MATRIMONIAL
con unwed, unwedded
wedding *n* the marriage ceremony usually with its accompanying festivities <one of the most elaborate *weddings* of the social season >
syn bridal, espousal(s), marriage, nuptial(s), spousal
wedlock *n syn* see MARRIAGE 1
wee *adj syn* see TINY
weed *n syn* see MARIJUANA
weensy *adj syn* see TINY
weeny *adj syn* see TINY
weep *vb* **1 syn** see DEPLORE 1
2 syn see EXUDE
3 syn see CRY 2
4 syn see DRIP
weeping *adj syn* see TEARFUL

weepy *adj syn* see TEARFUL

weigh *vb* **1** *syn* see CONSIDER 1
rel appraise, evaluate, rate
2 *syn* see BURDEN
3 to carry intellectual weight <this evidence *weighed* heavily against him>
syn count, militate, tell
rel import, matter, register, signify
idiom amount to some shucks, be something, carry weight, cut (some) ice
4 *syn* see MATTER

weigh down *vb syn* see DEPRESS 2
ant raise (*one's spirits*)

weight *n* **1** *syn* see LOAD 2
2 *syn* see IMPORTANCE
3 *syn* see INFLUENCE 1
rel effectiveness, efficacy; forcefulness, forcibleness, potency, powerfulness
4 *syn* see LOAD 3

weight *vb* **1** *syn* see ADULTERATE
rel burden, cumber, encumber; contaminate, corrupt, foul up, spoil
2 *syn* see BURDEN

weightiness *n syn* see IMPORTANCE

weightless *adj syn* see LIGHT 1
ant weighty

weighty *adj* **1** *syn* see IMPORTANT 1
2 *syn* see SERIOUS 1
3 *syn* see SERIOUS 2
4 *syn* see HEAVY 1
ant weightless
5 *syn* see FAT 2
6 *syn* see ONEROUS

weird *n* **1** *syn* see FATE
2 *syn* see PREDICTION

weird *adj* **1** fearfully and mysteriously strange or fantastic <shuddered at the *weird* unearthly glow that swept across the sky>
syn eerie, spooky, uncanny, unearthly
rel creepy, haunting, unnatural; preternatural, supernatural; supernal; curious, odd, peculiar, queer, strange; inscrutable, mysterious; awe-inspiring, awful, dreadful, fearful, horrific
con common, commonplace, everyday, quotidian; natural, normal, ordinary
2 *syn* see STRANGE 4

welcome *adj syn* see PLEASANT 1
rel congenial, cordial, genial, sympathetic; contenting, satisfying
ant unwelcome

welfare *n* a state of thriving and progress <parents who seek their children's *welfare*>
syn advantage, benefit, good, interest, prosperity, well-being
rel fortune, luck, success; contentment, felicity, happiness, satisfaction
ant illfare

welkin *n syn* see SKY

well *n* **1** **wells** *pl syn* see SPA 1
2 *syn* see SOURCE

well *adv* **1** in a good, proper, or acceptable manner <the children behaved very *well* at the party>
syn aright, befittingly, correctly, decently, decorously, fitly, fittingly, justly, nicely, properly, rightly
rel bearably, passably, tolerably, unobjectionably; considerately, pleasantly, thoughtfully, white; appropriately
con badly, improperly, objectionably, obnoxiously, outrageously
ant ill
2 in a pleasant, cooperative, or thoughtful manner <he speaks *well* of your new proposal>
syn considerately, generously, heedfully, kindly, thoughtfully
rel concernedly, interestedly; approvingly
con contemptuously, disdainfully, scornfully
3 to a full extent or degree <you are *well* aware of the problems we face>
syn à fond, altogether, clear, ‖cleverly, completely, entirely, fully, perfectly, ‖plumb, quite, right, roundly, ‖slam, ‖slap, thoroughly, utterly, wholly
rel certainly, obviously, surely, undoubtedly, unquestionably; sublimely
idiom all the way
con barely, hardly, scarcely

4 in an adequate or appropriate manner <any large box will answer our need very *well*>
syn acceptably, adequately, amply, appropriately, becomingly, fittingly, properly, right, satisfactorily, suitably
5 in a desirable or pleasing manner <everything went *well* on the trip>
syn favorably, fortunately, happily, prosperously, satisfyingly, successfully, swimmingly
rel comfortably, easily, smoothly
con amiss, wrong
ant badly
6 *syn* see EASILY 1
7 in all likelihood <the fighting may *well* continue for years>
syn doubtlessly, easily, indeed, really, truly, undoubtedly
rel conceivably, perhaps, possibly; likely, probably
8 to a considerable extent or degree <they landed *well* beyond the wharf>
syn considerably, far, quite, rather, significantly, somewhat
idiom by a long way, by a wide margin

well *adj* **1** *syn* see PROSPEROUS 3
2 *syn* see HEALTHY 1
ant ill, unwell
3 *syn* see LUCKY

well–behaved *adj syn* see GOOD 13

well–being *n* **1** *syn* see PROSPERITY 2
ant ill-being
2 *syn* see WELFARE
ant ill-being

well–bred *adj syn* see GENTEEL 1
ant ill-bred

well–conditioned *adj syn* see HEALTHY 1

well–developed *adj syn* see CURVACEOUS

well–disposed *adj syn* see SYMPATHETIC 2
ant ill-disposed

well–favored *adj syn* see BEAUTIFUL
ant ill-favored

well–fixed *adj syn* see PROSPEROUS 3
ant badly off

well–founded *adj* having a firm foundation in fact or logic <offered *well-founded* arguments to support his position>
syn cogent, good, just, justified, well-grounded
rel sound, substantial, telling, valid; rational, reasonable, reasoned; fundamental, meaty, pithy
con unjustified; insubstantial, invalid, unsound; irrational, unreasonable

well–groomed *adj* **1** *syn* see NEAT 2
2 *syn* see DAPPER

well–grounded *adj syn* see WELL-FOUNDED

wellhead *n syn* see SOURCE

well–heeled *adj syn* see PROSPEROUS 3
ant badly off

well–hung *adj syn* see GLIB

well–known *adj* much talked about <a *well-known* hospital>
syn famous, leading, noted, notorious, popular, prominent; *compare* FAMOUS 2
rel conspicuous, important, outstanding
idiom on everyone's tongue
con inconspicuous, obscure, unheard-of, unimportant, unnoted, unpopular
ant unknown

well–liked *adj syn* see FAVORITE 2

well–liking *adj syn* see HEALTHY 1

well–mannered *adj syn* see CIVIL 2
ant ill-mannered

well–nigh *adv* **1** *syn* see NEARLY
2 *syn* see ALMOST 2

well–off *adj syn* see PROSPEROUS 3
ant badly off

well over *vb syn* see OVERFLOW 2

well–paying *adj syn* see ADVANTAGEOUS 1

well–proportioned *adj syn* see SHAPELY

wellspring *n syn* see SOURCE

well–thought–of *adj syn* see RESPECTABLE 1

---

syn synonym(s)   *rel* related word(s)
ant antonym(s)   *con* contrasted word(s)
idiom idiomatic equivalent(s)
‖ use limited; if in doubt, see a dictionary

well–timed *adj syn* see TIMELY 1
  con premature, untimely; behindhand, late, tardy
  ant ill-timed
well–to–do *adj syn* see PROSPEROUS 3
  ant badly off
well–turned *adj syn* see SHAPELY
well–worn *adj syn* see TRITE
welsh *vb syn* see BACK DOWN
welt *n* **1** *syn* see WHEAL
  ‖**2** *syn* see BLOW 1
weltanschauung *n syn* see IDEOLOGY
welter *vb* **1** *syn* see WALLOW 1
  rel strive, struggle; toss, tumble, writhe; grovel
  2 *syn* see WALLOW 3
welter *vb syn* see WITHER
wench *n* **1** *syn* see GIRL 1
  2 *syn* see WANTON
wend *vb syn* see GO 1
western *n* a motion picture or radio or television play with its scene laid in the western U.S. and having cowboys as its main characters < young boys delighting in Saturday morning *westerns* >
  syn horse opera, oater
  rel shoot-'em-up
wet *vb* to make wet by or as if by saturating with water < they were *wet* thoroughly by the pouring rain >
  syn deluge, douse, drench, drown, soak, sop, souse; *compare* SOAK 1
  rel damp, dampen, moisten; humidify, humify; fill, impregnate, saturate; irrigate; lave, rinse, wash
  ant desiccate, dry
wet *adj* **1** containing or impregnated with liquid < change *wet* clothing for dry >
  syn drenched, dripping, madid, saturate, saturated, soaked, soaking, sodden, sopping, soppy, soused, wringing-wet
  rel soggy, water-logged; damp, dank, moist, wettish
  idiom dripping (*or* soaking *or* sopping) wet
  con bone-dry, dehydrated, desiccated, parched, sere, waterless
  ant dry
  2 *syn* see INTOXICATED 1
  ‖**wet** *n syn* see DRAM
wettish *adj syn* see DAMP
whack *vb syn* see STRIKE 2
whack *n* **1** *syn* see BLOW 1
  2 *syn* see FLING 1
whacking *adj syn* see HUGE
whacking *adv syn* see VERY 1
whale *n syn* see GIANT
whale *vb syn* see WHIP 1
whaling *adj syn* see HUGE
wham *n syn* see BANG 2
whammy *n syn* see JINX
whangdoodle *n syn* see NONSENSE 2
wharf *n* a structure used by boats and ships for taking on or landing cargo and passengers < brought the boat alongside the *wharf* and moored her >
  syn berth, dock, jetty, levee, pier, quay, slip
what–do–you–call–it *n* a thing or person that the speaker cannot (as from not knowing or from forgetting) name < hand me one of those little *what-do-you-call-its* > < went to *what-do-you-call-her's* house last week >
  syn what-is-it, whatsis, what's its name, what-you-call-it, what-you-may-call-it, whatyoumayjigger; *compare* DOODAD, GADGET 1
what–is–it *n syn* see WHAT-DO-YOU-CALL-IT
whatnot *n syn* see KNICKKNACK
whatsis *n syn* see WHAT-DO-YOU-CALL-IT
what's its name *n syn* see WHAT-DO-YOU-CALL-IT
what–you–call–it *n syn* see WHAT-DO-YOU-CALL-IT
what–you–may–call–it *n syn* see WHAT-DO-YOU-CALL-IT
whatyoumayjigger *n syn* see WHAT-DO-YOU-CALL-IT
wheal *n* a ridge raised on the skin by or as if by a stroke of a lash < the convict's back was covered with *wheals* and old scars >
  syn wale, weal, welt, whelk, ‖whelp
  rel strake, streak, stripe
wheedle *vb syn* see COAX
wheel *n* **1** *syn* see CYCLE 1
  2 *syn* see REVOLUTION 1

  3 *syn* see LEAGUE 4
wheel *vb* **1** *syn* see REEL 2
  2 *syn* see DRIVE 5
  3 *syn* see TURN 6
wheeze *vb syn* see HISS
wheeze *n syn* see PRANK
whelk *n syn* see WHEAL
whelm *vb* **1** *syn* see DELUGE 1
  2 *syn* see DELUGE 3
  3 *syn* see OVERWHELM 4
‖**whelp** *n syn* see WHEAL
when *adv syn* see THEN 1
when *conj syn* see THOUGH
whence *n syn* see SOURCE
where *adv* **1** *syn* see WHEREVER
  2 *syn* see WHITHER 1
where *n syn* see PLACE 1
whereabouts *adv syn* see WHITHER 1
  con hereabouts, thereabouts
whereas *conj* **1** *syn* see BECAUSE
  2 *syn* see THOUGH
‖**whereaway** *adv syn* see WHITHER 1
wherefore *n syn* see REASON 3
whereto *adv syn* see WHITHER 2
whereunto *adv syn* see WHITHER 2
wherever *adv* at, in, or to any or every place in or to which < he goes *wherever* he is needed >
  syn everywhere, where
  con here, there
‖**wherret** *vb syn* see SLAP 1
‖**wherret** *vb syn* see WORRY 1
whet *vb* **1** *syn* see SHARPEN
  2 *syn* see STIR 1
whet *n* ‖**1** *syn* see WHILE 1
  2 *syn* see APPETIZER
whether or no *adv syn* see WILLY-NILLY
whetted *adj syn* see SHARP 1
whicker *vb syn* see NEIGH
whiff *n syn* see HINT 2
whiffet *n syn* see NONENTITY
whiffle *vb syn* see HESITATE
whiffling *adj syn* see VACILLATING 2
whiffy *adj syn* see MALODOROUS 1
whigmaleerie *n* **1** *syn* see CAPRICE
  2 *syn* see KNICKKNACK
while *n* **1** a somewhat indefinite period of time < sat down to rest for a *while* >
  syn bit, space, spell, stretch, time, ‖whet
  2 *syn* see OCCASION 5
  3 *syn* see EFFORT 1
while *conj syn* see THOUGH
while *vb* to pass time and especially leisure time without boredom or in pleasant ways < *whiled* odd hours away in dreaming >
  syn beguile, fleet, wile
  rel amuse, divert, entertain; brighten, enliven, lighten
while (away) *vb syn* see SPEND 3
whilom *adj syn* see FORMER 2
whim *n syn* see CAPRICE
  rel idea; disposition, inclination, thought; dream, fantasy, vision
whimper *vb* to cry feebly and often plaintively or peevishly < a baby *whimpering* in its sleep >
  syn pule, whine; *compare* CRY 2
whimsical *adj* **1** *syn* see ARBITRARY 1
  2 *syn* see UNCERTAIN 1
whimsied *adj syn* see ARBITRARY 1
whimsy *n syn* see CAPRICE
  rel idea; disposition, inclination, thought; dream, fantasy, vision
whim–whams *n pl syn* see JITTERS
whine *vb* **1** *syn* see WHIMPER
  2 *syn* see COMPLAIN
‖**whinner** *vb syn* see NEIGH
whinny *vb syn* see NEIGH
whiny *adj syn* see IRRITABLE
whip *vb* **1** to strike repeatedly with or as if with a lash or rod < *whip* a dog for stealing from the table >
  syn flagellate, flog, hide, ‖larrup, lash, lather, scourge, stripe, thrash, ‖wear out, whale, ‖yerk
  rel beat, belabor, drub, wallop; bastinado, birch, bludgeon, cane, cudgel, quirt, switch

2 to defeat utterly < *whipped* their traditional rival by a score of 40 to 7>
syn beat, blast, ‖bowl (down *or* out), ‖clean up (on), ‖clobber, ‖cream, curry, drub, dust, lambaste, ‖larrup, lick, mop (up), overrun, overwhelm, rout, shellac, skunk, smear, smother, steamroller, thrash, trim, trounce, upend, wallop, whomp; *compare* CONQUER 1, DEFEAT 2
rel conquer, defeat, overcome, subdue, vanquish
idiom cook one's goose, deal a crushing defeat, settle one's hash, snow one under
3 to agitate with an instrument so as to stiffen and increase the bulk of by incorporation of air < *whip* cream for a shortcake>
syn beat, whisk
4 *syn* see TURN 6

whip (up) *vb syn* see INCITE
ant calm (down)
whip hand *n syn* see BETTER 2
whippersnapper *n syn* see NONENTITY
whipping boy *n syn* see SCAPEGOAT
whippy *adj syn* see ELASTIC 1
whipster *n syn* see NONENTITY
whirl *vb* **1** *syn* see SPIN 1
  2 *syn* see SWIRL
  3 *syn* see TURN 6
  4 *syn* see HURRY 2
  5 *syn* see SPIN 2
whirl *n* **1** *syn* see REVOLUTION 1
  2 *syn* see EDDY
  3 *syn* see COMMOTION 4
  4 *syn* see STIR 1
  5 *syn* see FLING 1
whirlblast *n syn* see WHIRLWIND 1
whirligig *vb syn* see SPIN 1
whirlpool *n* **1** *syn* see EDDY
  2 *syn* see STIR 1
whirlpool *vb syn* see SWIRL
‖**whirlpuff** *n syn* see WHIRLWIND 1
whirlwind *n* **1** a rotating windstorm of limited extent that is often accompanied by a column of dust or vapor < *whirlwinds* moved across the plowed land>
  syn whirlblast, ‖whirlpuff, whirly; *compare* HURRICANE, TORNADO
  rel dust devil, rainspout, sand column, sand spout, waterspout
  2 *syn* see STIR 1
whirly *n syn* see WHIRLWIND 1
whish *vb* **1** *syn* see HISS
  2 *syn* see HURRY 2
whisk *vb* **1** *syn* see HURRY 2
  2 *syn* see WHIP 3
whisker *n syn* see HAIR
whiskered *adj* **1** *syn* see BEARDED
  2 *syn* see HAIRY 1
whiskers *n pl syn* see BEARD
whisper *vb* **1** *syn* see HISS
  2 *syn* see CONFIDE 1
whisper *n* **1** *syn* see MURMUR 1
  2 *syn* see HINT 2
whispering *n syn* see REPORT 1
whist *adj syn* see STILL 3
whistle–stop *n syn* see BURG
whit *n syn* see PARTICLE
white *adj syn* see FAVORABLE 5
  ant black
white *n syn* see REACTIONARY
  ant red
white *vb* **1** *syn* see WHITEN 1
  2 *syn* see PALLIATE
whited sepulcher *n syn* see HYPOCRITE
white–haired *adj syn* see FAVORITE 1
white–headed *adj syn* see FAVORITE 1
white–hot *adj* **1** *syn* see HOT 1
  2 *syn* see IMPASSIONED
white lightning *n syn* see MOONSHINE 2
white–livered *adj syn* see COWARDLY
whiten *vb* **1** to free from color and make white or whiter < *whiten* linen in the sun>
  syn blanch, bleach, blench, decolor, decolorize, white
  rel dim, dull, fade, lighten, pale; etiolate; frost, grizzle, silver
  con color, darken

ant blacken
  2 *syn* see PALLIATE
white plague *n syn* see TUBERCULOSIS
whitewash *vb syn* see PALLIATE
whither *adv* **1** to what place < *whither* did they go?>
  syn where, whereabouts, ‖whereaway
  2 to what point, conclusion, or end < *whither* is our nation drifting?>
  syn whereto, whereunto
whiz *vb* **1** *syn* see HISS
  2 *syn* see HURRY 2
whiz *n syn* see EXPERT
  ant dub, dud, duffer
whiz–bang *adj syn* see EXCELLENT
whizzer *n syn* see TRICK 1
whole *adj* **1** free from damage, defect, or flaw < feared the eggs were broken but found them *whole* >
  syn entire, flawless, good, intact, perfect, sound, unblemished, unbroken, undamaged, unhurt, unimpaired, uninjured, unmarred, untouched
  rel complete, plenary; healthy, well
  con broken, damaged, defective, impaired, injured, marred
  2 *syn* see HEALTHY 1
  3 lacking nothing that properly belongs to it < the effect of the *whole* mural>
  syn choate, complete, entire, full, integral, perfect
  rel orbicular, rounded, well-rounded
  ant partial
  4 including every constituent element or individual < the *whole* community rose to his defense>
  syn all, complete, entire, gross, outright, total
  ant partial
  5 not scattered or dispersed < gave the matter his *whole* attention>
  syn concentrated, exclusive, fixed, undistracted, undivided, unswerving
whole *n* **1** the total supply or amount < the *whole* of our creative literature>
  syn aggregate, all, be-all and end-all, entirety, gross, sum, sum total, tale, total, totality, ‖tote
  rel amount, supply; result, resultant, summation; bulk, mass, quantity, quantum
  con detail, division, fraction, fragment, portion, section, segment, share
  ant part
  2 an organized array of parts or elements forming or functioning as a unit < stars, planets, galaxies — all but parts of one stupendous *whole*, the universe>
  syn entity, integral, integrate, sum, system, totality; *compare* SYSTEM 1
  rel being, organism, organization; coherence, cohesion, linkage; unity
  con accumulation, aggregation, heap, pile, mass; section, segment; selection
  ant part; agglomeration
wholehearted *adj* **1** *syn* see SURE 2
  2 *syn* see SINCERE 1
  rel ardent, fervent, impassioned, passionate; earnest, serious; authentic, bona fide, genuine
whole–hog *adj syn* see EXHAUSTIVE
whole–length *adj syn* see UNABRIDGED
wholeness *n* **1** *syn* see HEALTH
  rel integrity; heartiness, robustness, vigor
  2 *syn* see ENTIRETY 1
  3 *syn* see INTEGRITY 2
whole number *n syn* see NUMBER
wholesale *adj syn* see INDISCRIMINATE 1
wholesome *adj* **1** *syn* see HEALTHFUL
  ant noxious; unwholesome
  2 *syn* see CURATIVE
  3 *syn* see HEALTHY 1
  4 *syn* see SAFE 3
  ant noxious

---

syn synonym(s)   *rel* related word(s)
ant antonym(s)   *con* contrasted word(s)
idiom idiomatic equivalent(s)
‖ use limited; if in doubt, see a dictionary

whole–souled *adj syn* see SINCERE 1
  rel ardent, fervent, impassioned; earnest, intense, serious
wholly *adv* **1** *syn* see WELL 3
  2 *syn* see ALL 1
whomp *vb syn* see WHIP 2
whoop *vb syn* see SHOUT 1
whoop *n syn* see PARTICLE
whoop–de–do *n syn* see REVELRY 2
whoopee *n* **1** *syn* see REVELRY 2
  2 *syn* see MERRYMAKING
whoopla *n* **1** *syn* see COMMOTION 4
  2 *syn* see REVELRY 2
whoop–up *n syn* see REVELRY 2
whoosh *vb syn* see HISS
whop *vb syn* see BEAT 1
whop *n syn* see BLOW 1
whopping *adj syn* see HUGE
whopping *adv syn* see VERY 1
whore *n* **1** *syn* see HARLOT 1
  2 *syn* see PROSTITUTE
whoredom *n syn* see PROSTITUTION
whorehouse *n syn* see BROTHEL
whoreson *n syn* see BASTARD 1
whorish *adj syn* see FAST 7
whorl *vb syn* see SWIRL
who's who *n syn* see ARISTOCRACY
why *n* **1** *syn* see REASON 3
  2 *syn* see MYSTERY
whyfor *n syn* see REASON 3
wicked *adj* **1** *syn* see WRONG 1
  ant upright
  2 *syn* see PLAYFUL 1
  3 *syn* see RISQUÉ
  4 *syn* see MALICIOUS
  5 *syn* see DANGEROUS 1
  6 *syn* see TROUBLESOME
  7 *syn* see OUTRAGEOUS 1
  8 *syn* see SKILLFUL 2
  9 *syn* see ABLE
wickedness *n* **1** *syn* see EVIL 2
  2 *syn* see VICE 1
wide *adj* **1** *syn* see SPACIOUS
  2 *syn* see EXTENSIVE 1
  3 *syn* see LIBERAL 3
wide–awake *adj syn* see WATCHFUL
  rel alive, awake, aware, conscious, sensible
widen *vb syn* see BROADEN
wideness *n syn* see BREADTH 2
widespread *adj syn* see PREVAILING
widget *n syn* see GADGET 1
width *n syn* see RANGE 2
wield *vb* **1** *syn* see HANDLE 2
  rel conduct, control
  2 *syn* see EXERT
wieldy *adj syn* see STRONG 1
wiener *n syn* see FRANKFURTER
wienerwurst *n syn* see FRANKFURTER
‖**wienie** *n syn* see FRANKFURTER
wife *n* the female partner in a marriage < *wives* unwilling to share responsibility>
  syn ‖ball and chain, lady, ‖little woman, ‖missus, Mrs., ‖old lady, ‖old woman, ‖rib, ‖squaw, woman
  rel consort, helpmate, helpmeet, mate, other half, spouse; bride, dowager, matron; concubine
  idiom better half
  con maid, maiden; widow
wig *n syn* see REBUKE
wig *vb syn* see SCOLD 1
wiggle *vb syn* see WRIGGLE
wiggle–waggle *adj syn* see VACILLATING 2
wiggle–waggle *vb syn* see HESITATE
wiggy *adj syn* see POMPOUS 1
wight *n syn* see HUMAN
wild *adj* **1** living and growing in a state of nature and without human intervention <lived on *wild* plants and game animals>
  syn agrarian, agrestal, native, natural, uncultivated, undomesticated; *compare* SAVAGE 1
  rel escaped, feral; unsubdued, untamed

  ant cultivated, domesticated
  2 *syn* see SAVAGE 1
  ant tame, tamed
  3 *syn* see IRRESPONSIBLE
  rel adventurous, audacious, daring, dashing; brash, cocksure, rash
  4 *syn* see FURIOUS 2
  rel bewildered, distracted, perplexed; agitated, perturbed, upset; addled, confused, muddled; crazy, demented, deranged, mad
  con easy, relaxed
  5 *syn* see UNRULY 1
  6 marked by turmoil and fury especially of natural elements <a *wild* night of howling winds and driving snow>
  syn blustering, blustery, ‖coarse, furious, raging, rough, stormful, stormy, tempestuous, turbulent
  rel blatant, boisterous, clamorous, ungovernable, unruly; brutal, harsh, severe
  con calm, peaceful, placid, quiet, stormless; halcyon, irenic, serene
  7 given to unrestrained self-indulgence and pursuit of pleasure <her son got in with a *wild* bunch and took to drink>
  syn devil-may-care, fast, gay, raffish, rakehell, rakish, sporty
  rel boisterous, roisterous, rollicking, swaggering; careless, heedless, irresponsible, thoughtless; lewd, loose, unchaste, wanton
  con moderate, restrained, sober, sparing, temperate; bridled, controlled, curbed; self-controlled
  8 *syn* see EXTRAVAGANT 1
  9 *syn* see BARBARIAN 1
  ant cultivated, cultured
  10 *syn* see BARBARIC 1
wild *n syn* see WASTE 1
wilderness *n syn* see WASTE 1
  rel backcountry, backland(s), hinterland
  idiom back of beyond
wild land *n syn* see WASTE 1
wildly *adv syn* see HARD 2
wildness *n syn* see WASTE 1
wile *n syn* see TRICK 1
  rel chicane, chicanery, trickery; cunning, deceit, dissimulation, guile
  con candor, frankness, openness, plain dealing, straightforwardness, unconstraint; artlessness, naturalness, sincerity
wile *vb* **1** *syn* see ATTRACT 1
  2 *syn* see WHILE
wiliness *n syn* see CUNNING 2
will *vb* to be inclined <you may decide whichever way you *will*>
  syn choose, elect, like, please, wish
  rel crave, desire, want
  idiom have a mind to, see (*or* think) fit
will *n* **1** a desire to act in a particular way or have a particular thing <I've no *will* to be sociable tonight>
  syn fancy, inclination, liking, mind, pleasure, velleity
  rel appetite, desire, passion, urge; hankering, longing, pining, yearning
  idiom heart's desire
  con aversion, dislike, distaste, repugnance, repulsion, revulsion
  2 the aspect of mind involved in choosing or deciding <problems arise when one's *will* and judgment come in conflict>
  syn volition
  rel design, intent, purpose, wishes; character, disposition, temper
  3 power of controlling one's actions, impulses, or emotions <a self-indulgent man of feeble character and little *will*>
  syn discipline, self-command, self-control, self-discipline, self-government, self-mastery, self-restraint, willpower
  rel aplomb, assurance, confidence, poise, self-possession; control, discretion, restraint
  con gratification, indulgence, self-indulgence
will *vb* to give to another by will <*will* family treasures to a relative>
  syn bequeath, devise, leave, legate
willful *adj* **1** *syn* see OBSTINATE
  rel contumacious, factious
  idiom having the bit in one's teeth, not yielding an inch
  con amenable, docile, obedient, tractable
  ant biddable
  2 *syn* see VOLUNTARY

rel intentional, purposive; decided, determined, resolved; dogged, obstinate, pertinacious, stubborn

con accidental, chance, involuntary, unintentional, unplanned

willies *n pl syn* see JITTERS

willing *adj* **1** prepared in mind or by disposition <*willing* to help>

syn disposed, fair, inclined, minded, predisposed, prone, ready

rel agreeable, compliant, favorable; forward, game, prompt

idiom in the mood

con averse, disinclined, indisposed, loath, reluctant, unminded

ant unwilling

2 *syn* see VOLUNTARY

rel disposed, inclined, predisposed; open, prone

will–less *adj syn* see SPONTANEOUS

willpower *n syn* see WILL 3

willy–nilly *adv* surely and without regard to plans or inclination <it seems that we must drift *willy-nilly* toward disaster>

syn helplessly, inescapably, inevitably, perforce, unavoidably, whether or no

idiom as a matter of course, come what may, of necessity, without let or choice

‖**willy–willy** *n syn* see HURRICANE

wilt *vb* **1** *syn* see WITHER

2 *syn* see COLLAPSE 2

3 *syn* see DROOP 3

wily *adj syn* see SLY 2

rel sagacious, shrewd; clever, knowing

con aboveboard, forthright, straightforward; guileless, open, trusting

win *vb* **1** to gain the victory <the home team *won* by a wide margin>

syn beat, overcome, prevail, triumph; *compare* CONQUER 1

idiom bear off the palm (*or* prize), bring home the bacon, carry the day, come out first (*or* ahead), finish in front

ant lose

2 *syn* see GAIN 1

3 *syn* see EARN 1

rel produce, yield

4 *syn* see GET 1

ant lose

win (over) *vb* **1** *syn* see DISARM 2

2 *syn* see INDUCE 1

win *n syn* see VICTORY 1

wince *vb syn* see RECOIL

rel dodge, duck, jib, sheer, swerve, turn; cower, cringe

wind *n* **1** *syn* see NOTHING 1

2 *syn* see HINT 1

wind *vb syn* see BLOW 1

wind *vb* **1** *syn* see DEFORM

2 to follow a circular, spiral, or writhing course <the vine *wound* its way up the pillar>

syn coil, corkscrew, curl, entwine, spiral, twine, twist, wreathe; *compare* CURVE

rel bend, curve, meander, weave; circle, encircle, enlace, gird, girdle, surround; enclose, envelop

windbaggery *n syn* see NONSENSE 2

windiness *n syn* see VERBOSITY

winding *adj* curving repeatedly first one way then another <a *winding* country road>

syn anfractuous, convoluted, flexuous, meandering, meandrous, serpentine, sinuous, snaky, tortuous; *compare* CROOKED 1

rel bending, curving, twisting; crooked, devious; circuitous, indirect, roundabout

con direct, straight

window dressing *n syn* see MASK 2

windrow *n syn* see PILE 1

wind up *vb* **1** *syn* see CLOSE 3

2 *syn* see SETTLE 7

windup *n syn* see FINALE

windy *adj* **1** marked by more wind than usual <a *windy* March day>

syn airy, blowy, breezy, gusty

rel brisk, fresh; drafty

con breathless, motionless, still

ant windless

2 *syn* see INFLATED

3 *syn* see WORDY

wing *n syn* see ANNEX

rel expansion, prolongation; bulge, projection, protrusion, protuberance

wing *vb syn* see FLY 4

wink *vb* to close and open the eyelids quickly <*winking* involuntarily as the light struck his eyes>

syn bat, blink, nictate, nictitate, twinkle

rel squinch, squinny, squint; flutter

wink (at) *vb syn* see CONNIVE 1

wink *n* **1** *syn* see INSTANT 1

2 *syn* see HINT 2

winker *n syn* see EYE 1

winner *n syn* see VICTOR 2

ant loser

winning *adj syn* see SWEET 1

winnow *vb* **1** *syn* see BLOW 1

2 *syn* see SORT 2

winsome *adj syn* see SWEET 1

rel adorable, lovable, lovesome

wipe (out) *vb* **1** *syn* see ERASE

2 *syn* see ANNIHILATE 2

3 *syn* see SLAUGHTER 3

wipe *n* **1** *syn* see HIT 1

‖**2** *syn* see HANDKERCHIEF

‖**wiped out** *adj syn* see DRUGGED

‖**wiper** *n syn* see HANDKERCHIEF

‖**wire** *n syn* see PICKPOCKET

wiredraw *vb syn* see THIN 1

wiry *adj syn* see MUSCULAR 1

wisdom *n* **1** *syn* see KNOWLEDGE 2

2 *syn* see SAGACITY

3 *syn* see SENSE 6

rel judiciousness, sageness, saneness, sapience; perspicacity, sagacity, shrewdness

ant folly

wise *n syn* see METHOD 1

wise *adj* **1** having or exhibiting a capacity for discernment and the intelligent application of knowledge <to be *wise* is to use knowledge well>

syn discerning, gnostic, insighted, insightful, knowing, knowledgeable, perceptive, sagacious, sage, sophic, wisehearted

rel aware, grasping, intuitive, sensing; acute, keen, perspicacious; cogitative, contemplative, reflective, thoughtful; astute, sharp, shrewd

con dull, obtuse, slow, slow-witted; insensitive, unaware, unknowing

ant unwise

2 exercising or involving sound judgment <*wise* management of scarce resources>

syn judgmatic, judicious, prudent, sage, sane, sapient, sensible; *compare* SHREWD

rel canny, discreet, foresighted, provident; astute, perspicacious, sagacious, shrewd; alert, bright, intelligent, keen, smart

con careless, heedless, injudicious; improvident, imprudent, indiscreet, short-sighted

ant foolish, unwise

3 *syn* see EXPEDIENT

4 shrewdly aware and subtly resourceful <a *wise* operator with his eye always on the main chance>

syn canny, hep, knowing, nimble-witted, quick, quick-witted, sharp, sharp-witted, slick, smart; *compare* INTELLIGENT 2, SHREWD

rel cagey, foresighted, shrewd; artful, crafty, cunning, slippery, smooth, tricky, wily; steel-trap

idiom in the groove, not born yesterday, on the beam

con narrow, prim, puritanical, straitlaced; conservative, plodding, ‖square

5 presumptuously confident and self-assured <a bunch of *wise* kids tearing up the neighborhood>

syn ‖biggety, bold, bold-faced, cheeky, forward, fresh, impudent, nervy, pert, procacious, sassy, smart, smart-alecky

rel arrogant, brash, cocky, insolent; flip, flippant, impertinent, lippy, saucy

con demure, mannerly, modest, proper; dull, priggish, stuffy

wise (up) *vb syn* see INFORM 2

---

syn synonym(s)	*rel* related word(s)
ant antonym(s)	*con* contrasted word(s)
idiom idiomatic equivalent(s)	
‖ use limited; if in doubt, see a dictionary	

wiseacre *n syn* see SMART ALECK
wisecrack *n syn* see JOKE 1
wisecracker *n syn* see SMART ALECK
wise guy *n syn* see SMART ALECK
wisehead *n syn* see SMART ALECK
wisehearted *adj syn* see WISE 1
wise man *n syn* see SAGE
wisenheimer *n syn* see SMART ALECK
wish *vb* **1** *syn* see DESIRE 1
  rel expect, hope; fancy
  2 *syn* see WILL
  3 *syn* see IMPOSE 4
wishy–washy *adj* **1** *syn* see INSIPID 3
  rel enervated, languid, listless, spiritless; flavorless, savorless
  idiom neither flesh, fowl, nor good red herring, neither one thing nor the other
  2 *syn* see CHARACTERLESS
wistful *adj syn* see PENSIVE 2
‖**wit** *vb syn* see UNDERSTAND 3
wit *n* **1** *syn* see MIND 1
  rel perspicacity, sagacity; apprehension, awareness, comprehension
  2 *often* **wits** *pl* mental soundness and health <frightened nearly out of her *wits*>
  syn lucidity, ‖marbles, mind, reason, saneness, sanity, sense(s), soundness
  rel balance, rationality
  con aberration; craziness, derangement, insanity, lunacy, madness, mania
  ant witlessness
  3 acuteness of perception or judgment <had the *wit* to know that he was out of his depth in such a discussion>
  syn acumen, astucity, astuteness, clear-sightedness, discernment, discrimination, keenness, penetration, percipience, perspicacity, shrewdness; *compare* PRUDENCE 1
  rel awareness, comprehension, grasp, insight, perception, understanding; prudence, sagaciousness, sagacity, sageness, sapience, wisdom; clairvoyance, divination, ESP, sensing
  con aridity, dullness, prosaicness, unimaginativeness; fatuity, foolishness, inanity, silliness, stupidity
  4 *syn* see INTELLIGENCE 1
  5 a talent for banter or persiflage <a jolly man, noted for his kindly *wit*>
  syn esprit, humor
  rel alertness, keenness, quick-wittedness; brilliance, cleverness, intelligence, smartness
  6 *syn* see HUMOR 5
  7 *syn* see HUMORIST 2
witch *n* **1** a woman who practices the black arts <ancient laws against *witches*>
  syn bruja, enchantress, hag, hex, lamia, sorceress, witchwoman; *compare* MAGICIAN 1
  2 *syn* see HAG 2
witch *vb syn* see BEWITCH 1
witchcraft *n* **1** *syn* see MAGIC 1
  2 *syn* see CHARM 3
witchery *n* **1** *syn* see MAGIC 1
  2 *syn* see CHARM 3
witching *n syn* see MAGIC 1
witchwoman *n syn* see WITCH 1
witchy *adj syn* see MAGIC
with *prep* **1** *syn* see OVER 3
  2 *syn* see FOR 2
  3 *syn* see VIA 2
withal *adv* **1** *syn* see ALSO 2
  2 *syn* see HOWEVER
withdraw *vb* **1** *syn* see REMOVE 2
  ant deposit
  2 *syn* see ABJURE
  3 *syn* see GO 2
  rel quail, recoil, retreat, shrink; recede
  idiom give ground, give way
  con advance, progress; arrive, come
  4 *syn* see RETREAT 2
  ant advance
withdrawal *n syn* see DEPARTURE 1
  ant approach
withdrawn *adj* **1** *syn* see UNDEMONSTRATIVE

  ant outgiving
  2 *syn* see INDIFFERENT 2
  3 *syn* see UNSOCIABLE
  ant outgoing
wither *vb* to lose substance and freshness by or as if by loss of natural moisture <projects that *wither* and die from lack of popular interest>
  syn dry up, mummify, mummy, shrivel, welter, wilt, wizen
  rel cave in, collapse, deflate, fold; constrict, contract, shrink; decline, wane
  con freshen, revive, revivify; develop, grow, increase, wax
  ant flourish
withhold *vb* **1** *syn* see RESTRAIN 1
  2 *syn* see KEEP 5
  con award, concede, grant, vouchsafe
  ant accord
  3 *syn* see DENY 2
  4 *syn* see REFRAIN 1
within *adv syn* see INDOORS
  ant without
within *n syn* see INTERIOR
  ant without
withindoors *adv syn* see INDOORS
  ant withoutdoors
withinside *adv syn* see INDOORS
  ant withoutside
with–it *adj syn* see STYLISH
without *prep* **1** *syn* see BEYOND 1
  2 not having <living *without* decent housing or adequate food>
  syn awanting, lacking, minus, sans, wanting
without *adv syn* see OUTDOORS
  ant within
without *n syn* see OUTDOORS
‖**without** *conj syn* see EXCEPT 1
withoutdoors *adv syn* see OUTDOORS
  ant indoors, withindoors
with respect to *prep syn* see APROPOS
withstand *vb syn* see RESIST
  rel bear, endure, stand, suffer, tolerate
  con capitulate, submit, yield
witless *adj* **1** *syn* see SIMPLE 3
  2 *syn* see INSANE 1
witlessness *n syn* see FOOLISHNESS
witness *n* **1** *syn* see TESTIMONY
  2 *syn* see SPECTATOR
witness *vb* **1** *syn* see CERTIFY 1
  rel affirm; endorse, subscribe
  2 *syn* see INDICATE 2
witticism *n syn* see JOKE 1
wittiness *n syn* see HUMOR 4
witting *adj* **1** *syn* see AWARE
  ant unwitting
  2 *syn* see VOLUNTARY
  ant unwitting
witty *adj* provoking or intended to provoke mirth <a whimsical *witty* discussion on the foreignness of honesty to politics>
  syn facetious, humorous, jocose, jocular
  rel amusing, diverting, entertaining; scintillating, sparkling; penetrating, piercing, probing; funny, ridiculous, risible
  con foolish, senseless, silly; brash, cheeky, fresh; earnest, serious, sober, solemn
  ant unwitty
wiz *n syn* see EXPERT
  ant dub, dud, duffer
wizard *n* **1** *syn* see MAGICIAN 1
  2 *syn* see EXPERT
  ant dub, dud, duffer
wizardly *adj syn* see MAGIC
wizardry *n syn* see MAGIC 1
wizen *vb syn* see WITHER
  rel decrease, diminish, dwindle, reduce
wobble *vb* **1** *syn* see LURCH 2
  2 *syn* see TEETER
  3 *syn* see SHAKE
wobbly *adj* **1** *syn* see RICKETY
  2 *syn* see WEAK 2
  3 *syn* see VACILLATING 2

woe *n* **1** *syn* see SORROW
  rel bemoaning, bewailing, deploring, lamentation
  con bliss, felicity, happiness
  2 *syn* see MISERY 1
  3 *usu* **woes** *pl syn* see DISASTER
woebegone *adj* **1** *syn* see DOWNCAST
  rel lugubrious, melancholy
  con alert, concerned, interested, spirited; lively, vigorous; avid, eager, keen
  2 *syn* see GLOOMY 3
  rel dilapidated, outworn, shabby, worn
  con bright, crisp, fresh, gay
woeful *adj* **1** full of or expressive of woe < a *woeful* countenance>
  syn afflicted, doleful, dolent, dolorous, miserable, rueful, ruthful, sorrowful, wretched
  rel harrowed, racked, tortured, wrung; crushed, overcome, stricken; disconsolate, heartsick, inconsolable; dejected, depressed, dispirited, downcast, downhearted, low-spirited
  idiom cut to the heart, cut up, in the dumps (*or* depths *or* doldrums), on the rack
  con content, satisfied; easy, peaceful, quiet; cheerful, gay, lighthearted
  ant joyful
  2 *syn* see MELANCHOLY 2
  3 *syn* see DEPLORABLE
  rel dismal, grave, sad; unprecedented
woggle *vb syn* see WAG
wolf *n* a man forward, direct, and zealous in amorous pursuit of women < known far and wide as a lecherous old *wolf* >
  syn Casanova, chaser, Don Juan, ladies' man, lady-killer, masher, philander, philanderer, womanizer
  rel amorist; lecher, libertine, Lothario, profligate, rip, roué, rounder
  idiom man on the make, skirt chaser
wolf *vb* **1** *syn* see GULP
  2 *syn* see PHILANDER
wolfish *adj syn* see FIERCE 1
woman *n* **1** *syn* see WIFE
  2 *syn* see MISTRESS
womanize *vb syn* see PHILANDER
womanizer *n syn* see WOLF
wonder *n* **1** something that causes fascinated astonishment or admiration < the seven *wonders* of the ancient world >
  syn marvel, miracle, phenomenon, portent, prodigy, sensation, stunner
  rel curiosity, cynosure, gazingstock, spectacle
  idiom one for the book(s), something to shout (*or* write home) about
  2 the complex emotion aroused by the strange and incomprehensible and especially the awe-inspiring < stood gazing in wide-eyed *wonder* at the scene unveiled before her >
  syn admiration, amaze, amazement, marveling, wonderment
  rel awe, fear, reverence; bewilderment, perplexity, puzzlement; astonishment, marvel, shock
  con disinterest, incuriosity, indifference, unconcern; dispassion, impassivity; casualness, offhandedness; boredom, ennui
  3 *syn* see UNCERTAINTY
  rel assailability, vulnerability
  con unconcern
wonderful *adj* **1** *syn* see MARVELOUS 1
  2 *syn* see MARVELOUS 2
  ant lousy
wonderland *n syn* see UTOPIA
wonderment *n syn* see WONDER 2
wondrous *adj syn* see MARVELOUS 1
wont *n syn* see HABIT 1
wont *vb syn* see ACCUSTOM
wonted *adj syn* see USUAL 1
  ant unwonted
wontedly *adv syn* see USUALLY 1
  ant unwontedly
woo *vb syn* see ADDRESS 8
  idiom bill and coo, pitch woo
wood *n, often* **woods** *pl but sing or pl in constr syn* see FOREST
wooden *adj* **1** *syn* see STIFF 4
  rel awkward, clumsy; heavy, ponderous, weighty
  con limber, supple; plastic, pliable, pliant

  2 *syn* see AWKWARD 2
woodenhead *n syn* see DUNCE
woodland *n syn* see FOREST
woods colt *n syn* see BASTARD 1
woodsy *n syn* see RUSTIC
wooer *n syn* see SUITOR 2
woolly *adj syn* see HAIRY 1
word *vb* to convey (as an impression, a thought, or a need) in words < seemed scarcely to know how to *word* her appeal >
  syn couch, express, formulate, phrase, put; *compare* EXPRESS 2
  rel convey, offer, submit; say, state, tell
word *n* **1** something that is said < didn't tell a *word* about his plans >
  syn statement, utterance
  rel announcement, declaration, pronouncement
  2 a pronounceable sound or combination of sounds that expresses and symbolizes an idea < be sure you learn the meaning of each *word* >
  syn term, vocable
  rel expression, idiom, locution, phrase
  3 *syn* see COMMAND 1
  4 *syn* see NEWS
  5 *syn* see REPORT 1
  6 *syn* see MESSAGE 1
  7 *syn* see SAYING
  8 a statement whose weight or worth depends on the truthfulness or authority of its maker < had the doctor's *word* that no operation would be needed >
  syn assurance, guarantee, pledge, warrant; *compare* PROMISE
  rel commitment, engagement, undertaking; oath, vow; promise
  9 *syn* see PROMISE
  10 *usu* **words** *pl syn* see QUARREL
  11 *syn* see PASSWORD 3
  12 *syn* see PASSWORD 1
wordage *n syn* see WORDING
word for word *adv syn* see VERBATIM
word-for-word *adj syn* see VERBATIM
word-hoard *n syn* see VOCABULARY 1
wordiness *n syn* see VERBOSITY
  con crispness, pithiness, trenchancy
  ant laconicism, laconism
wording *n* manner or style of verbal expression < take care with the *wording* of a formal invitation >
  syn diction, parlance, phrase, phraseology, phrasing, verbalism, verbiage, wordage
  rel language, mode, style
wordless *adj* **1** *syn* see TACIT 1
  2 *syn* see SILENT 2
  3 *syn* see SILENT 3
  4 *syn* see UNSPOKEN 1
  ant wordy
word-of-mouth *adj syn* see ORAL 2
word-stock *n syn* see VOCABULARY 1
wordy *adj* using or marked by the use of more words than are needed to express an idea < tired of dull *wordy* editorials >
  syn diffuse, long-winded, palaverous, prolix, redundant, verbose, windy
  rel flatulent, inflated, tumid, turgid; garrulous, glib, loquacious, talkative, voluble; bombastic, highfalutin, rhetorical
  con compendious, concise, pithy, succinct, summary, terse; lean, taut
  ant laconic
work *n* **1** the activity that affords one his livelihood < laborers hurrying to *work* at dawn >
  syn business, calling, employment, job, line, occupation, pursuit, ‖racket; *compare* JOB 2
  rel art, craft, handicraft, métier, profession, trade, vocation, walk
  2 strenuous activity that involves difficulty and effort and usually affords no pleasure < had done much hard *work* during his life >
  syn bullwork, donkeywork, drudge, drudgery, grind, labor, moil, plugging, slavery, slogging, sweat, toil, travail

---

syn synonym(s)   *rel* related word(s)
ant antonym(s)   *con* contrasted word(s)
idiom idiomatic equivalent(s)
‖ use limited; if in doubt, see a dictionary

rel effort, exertion, pains, trouble; chore, duty, job; elucubration; striving; spadework
ant play
3 works *pl syn* see FACTORY
work *vb* **1** *syn* see OPERATE 3
 2 *syn* see TILL
 3 *syn* see SOLVE 1
 4 *syn* see LABOR 1
 5 *syn* see FUNCTION 3
 6 *syn* see ACT 5
work (for) *vb syn* see BENEFIT
workable *adj syn* see POSSIBLE 1
 rel applicable, exploitable, usable
 ant unworkable
workaday *adj* **1** *syn* see PROSAIC 3
 2 *syn* see ORDINARY 1
workday *adj syn* see PROSAIC 3
worker *n* one who earns a living by labor and especially by manual labor <weary *workers* straggling home each night>
 syn hand, laborer, ‖mozo, operative, roustabout, workhand, workingman, workman
 rel artisan, craftsman, handicraftsman, mechanic; employee
 ant idler
workhand *n syn* see WORKER
workhorse *n* **1** *syn* see SLAVE 2
 2 *syn* see SAWHORSE
work in *vb syn* see INSINUATE 3
working *adj* **1** *syn* see ACTIVE 1
 2 *syn* see BUSY 1
workingman *n syn* see WORKER
workless *adj syn* see UNEMPLOYED
workman *n syn* see WORKER
workmanlike *adj syn* see SKILLFUL 2
 ant unworkmanlike
workmanly *adj syn* see SKILLFUL 2
work off *vb syn* see FOIST 3
work out *vb syn* see SOLVE 1
work over *vb syn* see REVISE
work–shy *adj syn* see LAZY
work up *vb syn* see GENERATE 3
world *n* **1** *syn* see EARTH 1
 2 *syn* see UNIVERSE
worldly *adj* **1** *syn* see EARTHLY 1
 ant otherworldly
 2 *syn* see MATERIALISTIC
 ant otherworldly, unworldly
 3 *syn* see SOPHISTICATED 2
 ant unworldly
worldly–wise *adj syn* see SOPHISTICATED 2
 rel callous, hard-boiled, hardened
 con naive, unsophisticated, unworldly
worldwide *adj syn* see UNIVERSAL 2
 con parochial
world–wise *adj syn* see SOPHISTICATED 2
world–without–end *adj syn* see EVERLASTING 1
world–without–end *n syn* see ETERNITY 2
worm *n syn* see WRETCH 1
worm *vb* **1** *syn* see INSINUATE 3
 2 *syn* see WRIGGLE
wormling *n syn* see WRETCH 1
worn *adj* **1** *syn* see TIRED 1
 2 *syn* see HAGGARD
worn down *adj syn* see TIRED 1
worn–out *adj* **1** *syn* see EFFETE 2
 2 *syn* see TRITE
worried *adj syn* see DISTRAUGHT
 ant unworried
worry *vb* **1** to disturb one or destroy one's peace of mind by repeated or persistent tormenting attacks <vain regrets that *worry* his spirit>
 syn annoy, bedevil, beleaguer, dun, gnaw, hagride, harass, harry, needle, pester, plague, tantalize, tease, ‖wherret
 rel beset, bother, fret, pelt, trouble, vex; goad, test, try; afflict, torment, torture; aggrieve, oppress, persecute, wrong
 idiom give one gyp
 con comfort, console, solace; alleviate, assuage, ease, relieve
 2 *syn* see TROUBLE 1
 3 to experience concern, disquietude, or anxiety <*worrying* over her children's health>

syn cark, fret, fuss, pother, stew, ‖tew
 rel carry on, take on; despair, give up; bother, concern (oneself); agitate, disquiet, disturb, trouble
 idiom be upset, bite one's nails
 con accept, submit; abide, bear, endure, stand, support; disregard, ignore, overlook, pass over
worry *n* **1** *syn* see CARE 2
 rel presentiment; doubt, mistrust, uncertainty; anguish, heartache, woe
 con composure, equanimity, sangfroid; assurance, certainty, certitude, confidence, security
 2 *syn* see TRIAL 2
worrywart *n syn* see PESSIMIST
worsen *vb syn* see DETERIORATE 1
 rel blast, blight, debase, degrade, humble, lower; corrupt, foul, taint
 idiom get worse, grow worse
 ant better
worship *n syn* see ADORATION
worship *vb* **1** *syn* see REVERE
 con contemn, despise, disdain, flout, scorn; curse, execrate, vilify
 2 *syn* see ADORE 3
 ant abominate; scorn
 3 *syn* see LOVE 2
worst *vb syn* see DEFEAT 2
worth *n* **1** equivalence in good qualities (as utility, importance, or desirability) express or implied <impossible to estimate the *worth* of such a man to the community>
 syn account, valuation, value
 rel class, excellence, merit, perfection, quality, virtue; rate; use, usefulness, utility; consequence, importance, mark, moment, note, significance, weight
 con baseness, meanness, paltriness, poorness
 ant worthlessness
 2 *syn* see QUALITY 2
 3 *syn* see WEALTH 2
worthless *adj* **1** lacking all excellence or value <gave me a *worthless* check>
 syn draffy, drossy, good-for-nothing, inutile, ‖no-account, no-good, nothing, unworthy, valueless
 rel inferior, mediocre, poor, second-rate; defective, flawed, imperfect; bootless, ineffectual, unavailing, useless; contemptible, dusty, mean, sad, sorry
 idiom dear at any price, of no earthly value (*or* worth)
 con esteemed, precious; useful, valuable, worthwhile; invaluable, priceless
 ant worthful
 2 *syn* see FECKLESS 1
 rel incapable, incompetent, unqualified
worthwhile *adj syn* see ADVANTAGEOUS 1
worthy *adj* **1** having worth or merit <a *worthy* custom handed down from our ancestors>
 syn admirable, commendable, deserving, estimable, laudable, meritable, meritorious, praisable, praiseworthy, thankworthy
 rel invaluable, precious, priceless; desirable, pleasing, satisfying; divine
 con good-for-nothing, ‖no-account, no-good, valueless; contemptible, sad, sorry
 ant worthless
 2 *syn* see HONORABLE 1
 ant unworthy
wound *vb syn* see INJURE 3
wow *n syn* see SMASH 6
‖wowser *n syn* see PRUDE
wrack *vb syn* see DESTROY 1
wrackful *adj syn* see DESTRUCTIVE
wraith *n syn* see APPARITION
wrangle *vb* **1** *syn* see QUARREL
 2 *syn* see ARGUE 2
wrangle *n syn* see QUARREL
wrap *vb syn* see ENFOLD 1
 rel camouflage, cloak, mask
 ant unwrap
wrap (up) *vb* **1** *syn* see BUNDLE UP
 2 *syn* see SWATHE
wrapped *adj syn* see INTENT
wrapped up *adj syn* see INTENT

wrap up *vb syn* see CLOSE 3

wrath *n syn* see ANGER

  rel acerbity, acrimony, asperity; offense, resentment

wrathful *adj syn* see ANGRY

wrathy *adj syn* see ANGRY

‖**wraxle** *vb syn* see WRESTLE

wreak *vb syn* see INFLICT 2

wreakful *adj syn* see VINDICTIVE

wreath *n* a circlet of intertwined leaves or flowers worn upon the head as an ornament or as a mark of honor or esteem <received the laurel *wreath* of victory from the emperor's own hand>

  syn anadem, chaplet, coronal, coronet, crown, garland

  rel bay(s), laurel

wreathe *vb syn* see WIND 2

wreck *n* **1** *syn* see CRASH 3

  2 *syn* see COLLAPSE 2

  3 *syn* see JALOPY

wreck *vb* **1** *syn* see VANDALIZE

  2 *syn* see DESTROY 1

  rel despoil, loot, plunder, ravage; cripple, disable

  3 *syn* see TOTAL 3

  4 *syn* see SABOTAGE

  5 *syn* see SHIPWRECK 1

  6 *syn* see RUIN 2

  7 *syn* see INFLICT 2

wreckage *n* **1** *syn* see SABOTAGE

  2 *syn* see DRIFTWOOD

wrecker *n syn* see VANDAL

wreckful *adj syn* see DESTRUCTIVE

wrecking *n syn* see SABOTAGE

wrench *vb* **1** to shift the position of or move by or as if by vigorous twisting <suddenly *wrenched* her around to face him>

  syn wrest, wring, wry

  rel bend, twist; coerce, compel, constrain, force; drag, rend, tear; contort, distort

  2 *syn* see SPRAIN

  3 *syn* see MISREPRESENT

  4 *syn* see EXTORT 1

wrest *vb* **1** *syn* see WRENCH 1

  rel arrogate, confiscate, usurp; elicit, extort, extract

  2 *syn* see EXTORT 1

  3 *syn* see MISREPRESENT

wrestle *vb* to struggle with an opponent at close quarters <determined to solve the problem if he had to *wrestle* with it all night>

  syn grapple, scuffle, tussle, ‖wraxle

  rel contend, fight, struggle; endeavor, essay; labor, moil, toil, travail, work; exert, strain, stretch, strive

wretch *n* **1** a worthless and often vicious or contemptible person <a treacherous drink-sodden *wretch*>

  syn ‖blighter, lowlife, mucker, no-good, worm, wormling

  rel good-for-naught, good-for-nothing, ne'er-do-well; blackguard, caitiff, devil, knave, rapscallion, rascal, rogue, rotter, scalawag, scoundrel, villain

  idiom sad case

  2 *syn* see SNOT 1

wretched *adj* **1** *syn* see WOEFUL 1

  rel melancholy; abject, mean, sordid; piteous, pitiable, pitiful; despairing, despondent, forlorn, hopeless

  con animated, gay, lively; content, contented, satisfied; gratified, pleased

  2 *syn* see BASE

wretchedness *n syn* see MISERY 1

wriggle *vb* to move or advance with wormlike motions <the attackers *wriggled* stealthily through the underbrush>

  syn squiggle, squirm, wiggle, worm, writhe

  rel flow, glide, ooze, slide, slip

wring *vb* **1** *syn* see EXTORT 1

  2 *syn* see WRENCH 1

  rel press, squeeze

  3 *syn* see AFFLICT

wringing–wet *adj syn* see WET 1

wrinkle *n* a small linear prominence or depression on a surface <a benign old face netted with *wrinkles*>

  syn corrugation, crease, crinkle, fold, furrow, plica, ridge, rimple, rivel, ruck

  rel crow's foot; pleat, pucker

wrinkle *vb syn* see CRUMPLE 1

write *vb* to form characters or words on a surface (as of paper) usually with pen or pencil <learned to *write* at an early age>

  syn engross, indite, inscribe, scribe

  rel dot (down), jot, note; chalk, pen, pencil; scratch, scrawl, scribble; draft, draw, make out; write down, write up

  idiom push one's pen, put in writing, take down

write down *vb syn* see DEPRECIATE 1

  ant write up

write off *vb* **1** *syn* see DEPRECIATE 1

  2 *syn* see DECRY 2

write–up *n syn* see PUFF 3

writhe *vb* **1** to twist and turn in physical or mental distress <*writhing* in anguish with a throbbing toothache>

  syn agonize, squirm, toss

  rel blench, flinch, recoil, shrink, wince; contort, distort; bend, twist; thrash, tumble

  2 *syn* see WRIGGLE

writing *n syn* see PRINT 2

writing desk *n syn* see DESK

wrong *n* **1** *syn* see INJUSTICE 2

  2 *syn* see EVIL 2

  3 *syn* see EVIL 3

  4 *syn* see INJUSTICE 1

wrong *adj* **1** rejecting or deviating from the dictates of moral or divine law <had a *wrong* outlook on life> <*wrong* principles of conduct>

  syn bad, evil, immoral, iniquitous, reprobate, sinful, vicious, wicked

  rel blamable, blameworthy, censurable, reprehensible; corrupt, debauched, depraved; abandoned, dissolute, infamous, villainous; blasphemous, unholy, unrighteous; accursed, unblessed

  con ethical, high-principled, moral, righteous, upright; chaste, innocent, pure, virtuous

  ant right

  2 *syn* see FALSE 1

  idiom at fault, barking up the wrong tree, in error, on the wrong track

  con exact, precise

  ant right

  3 *syn* see BAD 1

  rel improper, inappropriate, inapt, infelicitous, unfit, unfitting, unhappy, unsuitable

  con appropriate, fit, fitting, proper, suitable

  4 *syn* see MISTAKEN

  ant right

  5 *syn* see INSANE 1

wrong *adv syn* see AMISS 2

  ant right

wrong *vb* to inflict injury on another without justification <these men who have *wronged* the public trust deserve no consideration>

  syn aggrieve, oppress, outrage, persecute

  rel abuse, ill-treat, maltreat, mistreat; harm, hurt, injure; offend

  idiom do wrong to (or by)

  con guard, protect, safeguard; care (for), cherish; honor, love, respect

wrongdoing *n* **1** *syn* see EVIL 3

  2 *syn* see MISCONDUCT

wrongful *adj syn* see UNLAWFUL

  ant rightful

wrongheaded *adj* **1** *syn* see OBSTINATE

  2 *syn* see CONTRARY 3

wrongly *adv syn* see AMISS 1

  ant rightly

wroth *adj syn* see ANGRY

wrothful *adj syn* see ANGRY

wrothy *adj syn* see ANGRY

wry *vb syn* see WRENCH 1

wry *adj syn* see SARDONIC

---

syn synonym(s)   *rel* related word(s)

ant antonym(s)   *con* contrasted word(s)

idiom idiomatic equivalent(s)

‖ use limited; if in doubt, see a dictionary

XYZ

x *n syn* see ERROR 1
x (out) *vb syn* see ERASE
Xanthippe *n syn* see VIRAGO
Xmas *n syn* see CHRISTMAS
yahoo *n syn* see TOUGH
yak *n syn* see CHATTER
yak *vb syn* see CHAT 1
‖yak *n syn* see JOKE 1
yakety–yak *n syn* see CHATTER
yakety–yak *vb syn* see CHAT 1
yak–yak *n syn* see CHATTER
yak–yak *vb syn* see CHAT
yammer *vb* 1 *syn* see GRIPE
    2 *syn* see CHAT 1
yank *vb* 1 *syn* see JERK
    rel tug; clutch, grab, snatch
    2 *syn* see EXTRACT 1
yap *n* 1 *syn* see RUSTIC
    ‖2 *syn* see MOUTH 1
yard *n syn* see COURT 1
yardstick *n syn* see STANDARD 3
yare *adj syn* see AGILE
yarn *n* 1 *syn* see STORY 2
    2 *syn* see CHAT 2
yarn *vb syn* see CONVERSE
yatter *n syn* see CHATTER
yatter *vb syn* see CHAT 1
yaw *n syn* see TURN 2
yaw *vb syn* see SEESAW
yaw *vb syn* see YAWN
yawn *vb* to breathe deeply with jaws widespread usually in reaction to fatigue or boredom <*yawned* again and again in the stuffy room>
    syn gape, yaw
    rel doze, drowse, nap, snooze
yawn *n syn* see TEDIUM
yawning *adj syn* see CAVERNOUS 1
yawp (*or* yaup) *vb* 1 *syn* see SQUALL 1
    2 *syn* see GRIPE
yea *adv* 1 *syn* see ALSO 2
    2 *syn* see YES 1
    3 *syn* see EVEN 3
yearbook *n* a book issued yearly to chronicle a particular part of the preceding year's activities <sports editor of his school *yearbook*>
    syn annual, annuary
yearn *vb syn* see LONG
    rel covet, desire, wish; pant
    ant dread
years *n pl syn* see OLD AGE
yeast *n syn* see FOAM
yeasty *adj syn* see GIDDY 1
yegg *n syn* see ROBBER
yell *vb* 1 *syn* see SHOUT 1
    2 to complain vigorously or vociferously <let the opposition *yell*; we got the vote>
    syn howl, scream, squeal, yip, yowl
    rel cry, lament, squall, wail, weep; bemoan, bewail, deplore
    idiom beat one's breast, make an outcry, tear one's hair, yell to high heaven
    con acclaim, applaud, cheer, hail
    3 *syn* see CALL 1
yellow *adj syn* see COWARDLY
yellowback *n syn* see DIME NOVEL
yellowbelly *n syn* see COWARD
    rel fink, rat, stinker
yellow dog *n syn* see CAD
yen *vb syn* see LONG
‖yep *adv syn* see YES 1
    ant ‖nope
‖yerk *vb syn* see WHIP 1

yes *adv* 1 —used as a function word to express assent, agreement, understanding, or acceptance <*yes*, I can do that>
    syn agreed, all right, aye, OK (*or* okay), ‖okeydoke, yea, ‖yep
    rel assuredly, certainly, gladly, willingly; undoubtedly, unquestionably
    idiom beyond a doubt, beyond any shade (*or* shadow) of doubt, with all my heart, without the least doubt
    2 *syn* see EXACTLY 3
yes *vb syn* see ASSENT
yes–man *n* 1 *syn* see STOOGE 1
    2 *syn* see SYCOPHANT
yesterday *n syn* see PAST
    ant tomorrow
yesteryear *n syn* see PAST
yet *adv* 1 beyond this — used as an intensive to stress the comparative degree <in spite of her protest he went *yet* faster>
    syn even, still
    2 at some future time <just wait, we'll get there *yet*>
    syn eventually, finally, someday, sometime, somewhen, sooner or later, ultimately
    idiom after a while, in due course, in the course of time
    3 *syn* see ALSO 2
    4 *syn* see HITHERTO 1
    5 *syn* see HOWEVER
yet *conj syn* see ONLY
yield *vb* 1 *syn* see RELINQUISH
    con appropriate, arrogate, confiscate
    2 to give way before a force that one cannot longer resist <*yielded* to temptation>
    syn bow, buckle (under), capitulate, cave, defer, knuckle, knuckle under, submit, succumb
    rel accord, award, concede, grant; cede, surrender, waive; break, fail
    idiom give ground, give place, give way
    con bear up, hold out, resist
    ant withstand
    3 *syn* see BEAR 9
    4 *syn* see GIVE 7
    rel discharge, eject, emit, vent
    5 to produce as return or revenue <an investment that *yields* 10 percent>
    syn bring in, pay, return
    rel afford, furnish, provide, supply; hold out, offer, proffer, tender
    idiom afford (*or* give *or* provide) a return of, put at one's disposal
    6 *syn* see GIVE 12
yield *n syn* see OUTPUT
yielding *adj* 1 *syn* see SOFT 6
    ant unyielding
    2 *syn* see PASSIVE 2
yip *vb syn* see YELL 2
‖yob *n syn* see RUSTIC
yoke *n* 1 *syn* see BONDAGE
    2 *syn* see BOND 3
yoke *vb* 1 *syn* see HITCH 2
    2 *syn* see JOIN 1
yokel *n syn* see RUSTIC
yon *adv* 1 *syn* see BEYOND 1
    2 *syn* see THERE
yonder *adv syn* see BEYOND 1
yore *n syn* see PAST
young *adj* 1 being in an early stage of life, growth, or development <*young* shoots of new grass>
    syn callow, green, immature, infant, juvenile, unfledged, unripe, youthful
    rel fresh, new; crude, raw, unfinished, unformed
    con full-grown, grown-up, mature, ripe; aged, elderly, superannuated
    ant old; adult
    2 *syn* see INEXPERIENCED
youngling *n syn* see CHILD 1

young man *n syn* see BOYFRIEND 1
young one *n syn* see CHILD 1
youngster *n syn* see CHILD 1
youth *n* **1** the period of life in which one passes from childhood to maturity <the thought of regaining one's *youth*>
syn adolescence, greenness, juvenility, prime, puberty, pubescence, spring, springtide, springtime, youthfulness, youthhood
rel callowness, immaturity, inexperience, unripeness; dewiness
idiom awkward age, flower (*or* springtime *or* May) of life, salad days
ant age
2 *syn* see CHILD 1
youthful *adj syn* see YOUNG 1
rel beardless, boyish, puerile; maiden, virgin, virginal
con adult, matured
ant aged, elderly
youthfulness *n syn* see YOUTH 1
youthhood *n syn* see YOUTH
yowl *vb* **1** *syn* see YELL 2
2 *syn* see BAWL 2
yule *n syn* see CHRISTMAS
yuletide *n syn* see CHRISTMAS
yummy *adj syn* see DELIGHTFUL
zakuska *n syn* see APPETIZER
zany *n* **1** *syn* see CLOWN 3
rel comic, farceur, funnyman
2 one who makes an exhibition of himself for the amusement of others <tired of having her parties spoiled by drunken *zanies*>
syn clown, cutup, farceur, joker, jokester, wag
rel practical joker, pranker, prankster, trickster; exhibitionist, show-off
3 *syn* see WAG 1
4 *syn* see FOOL 4
zeal *n syn* see PASSION 6
rel energy, gusto, spirit, zest; fierceness, intensity, vehemence; avidity, keenness, readiness, urgency; earnestness, seriousness, sincerity
con coolness, halfheartedness, indifference, lukewarmness; carelessness, heedlessness, insouciance, negligence, unmindfulness; disinterest, lackadaisy, unconcern
ant apathy
zealot *n syn* see ENTHUSIAST
rel adherent, disciple, follower, partisan, sectary

zealous *adj syn* see ENTHUSIASTIC
rel afire, ardent, fervent, fervid, fired; avid, eager; dedicated, fanatic, frenetic, rabid, wild-eyed; infatuated, obsessed, possessed
con cool, halfhearted, indifferent, lukewarm; careless, heedless, insouciant, negligent, unmindful; disinterested, lackadaisical, uninterested
ant apathetic
zemi *n syn* see CHARM 2
zenith *n syn* see APEX 2
ant nadir
zero *n* **1** a numerical symbol 0 denoting the absence of all magnitude or quantity <wrote a row of *zeros* after the decimal point>
syn aught (*or* ought), cipher, goose egg, naught (*or* nought), nothing, zilch
rel blank, nil, void
2 *syn* see NONENTITY
zero (in) *vb syn* see DIRECT 2
zero hour *n syn* see JUNCTURE 2
zest *n syn* see TASTE 4
rel ardor, eagerness, enthusiasm, fervor, passion, zeal; delectation, delight, enjoyment, pleasure, satisfaction; bliss, ecstasy, elation
zesty *adj syn* see PUNGENT
zetetic *n syn* see SKEPTIC
zilch *n* **1** *syn* see ZERO 1
2 *syn* see NONENTITY
zing *n* **1** *syn* see EAGERNESS
2 *syn* see SPIRIT 5
Zion *n* **1** *syn* see HEAVEN 2
2 *syn* see UTOPIA
zip *vb* **1** *syn* see BREEZE
2 *syn* see HURRY 2
zippy *adj syn* see AGILE
rel alert, keen, ready; dynamic, forceful, intense
zoetic *adj syn* see LIVING 1
Zoilus *n syn* see CRITIC
zombie *n* **1** *syn* see DUNCE
2 *syn* see ECCENTRIC
zone *n syn* see AREA 1
rel section, sector, segment
zonked *adj* **1** *syn* see INTOXICATED 1
2 *syn* see DRUGGED

syn synonym(s)   *rel* related word(s)
ant antonym(s)   *con* contrasted word(s)
idiom idiomatic equivalent(s)
‖ use limited; if in doubt, see a dictionary